Flat Horses

of 2004

Flat Horses

of 2004

Edited by Graham Dench
and Nick Pulford

Cover photographs: North Light moves to the front at Tattenham Corner, by Tony Marshall/EMPICS.
Ouija Board in Texas by Reuters.

Other photographs: Edward Whitaker, Getty, APRH, Scoop/Dyga, Caroline Norris, Associated Press, Frank Sorge, Stefano Grasso, Martin Lynch, Reuters, Bill Selwyn, Racingfotos.com, George Shelton, Gerry Cranham, PA, NTRA, Inpho.

Programming and data by Brett Campbell.

Special thanks for their invaluable assistance to Mark Bowers, James Crispe, Rosy Gahan, John Kettle, Nigel Jones, Victor Jones and Andy Smith.

Published in 2004 by Raceform Ltd,
Compton, Newbury, Berkshire RG20 6NL.
Raceform Ltd is a wholly-owned subsidiary of Trinity Mirror plc.

A catalogue record for this book is available from the British Library.

ISBN 1-904317-60-X

Designed by Robin Gibson and Tracey Scarlett.
Printed by William Clowes, Suffolk.

Flat Horses

of 2004

Contents

Foreword

by Simon Crisford

A GENERATION ago, this book would have been a very different publication. In that era, horses trained in Europe raced generally only on their own continent. Some trainers would have made forays further afield, but most would have looked no further than their domestic programme book.

The idea of horses proving themselves on the international stage was still one that was being nurtured by only a few far-sighted pioneers. And the idea of horses coming from Dubai and elsewhere to challenge for the British Classics would have been seen by most as unthinkable.

It has been greatly to the benefit of the sport in Britain and around the globe that the racing world looks a very different place today than it did 20 or 30 years ago. Our sport is now about the best taking on the best all over the world. Reputations are made – and often lost – in the international arena.

The horses whose exploits are so memorably chronicled in this book have proved themselves not only at Newmarket, Ascot and York but at Nad Al Sheba, Lone Star Park, Churchill Downs, Woodbine, Flemington, Sha Tin, Leopardstown and Longchamp.

We at Godolphin are proud to have been at the forefront of stretching racing's boundaries. From the outset, Sheikh Mohammed has insisted that our stable should have a global focus and we have been happy to take our horses around the world to compete at the highest level.

It was therefore a particular pleasure for us to see the process reversed to a significant degree during 2004 when owners and trainers from around the world took up Sheikh Mohammed's challenge and brought their horses to Nad Al Sheba to take part in the inaugural Dubai International Racing Carnival.

Next year's Carnival looks certain to play host to the most sustained period of international competition yet seen.

Everyone at Godolphin relishes the prospect of taking on all-comers on our home course and we will also be travelling far and wide next season in search of more major prizes.

We were very pleased to win Group 1 races in five countries in 2004 with Dubawi winning in Ireland, Sulamani in Canada, Crimson Palace in the United States and Ancient World in Italy to complement the British Group 1 successes of Doyen, Papineau, Refuse To Bend, Rule Of Law and Sulamani. In addition, we won Group 2 prizes in Dubai, Australia and Britain.

It is always a pleasure to be reminded of those successes in the pages of this book.

We were delighted, too, to end the 2004 season as champion owner in Britain with Saeed Bin Suroor also reclaiming the trainers' title and Frankie Dettori lifting the jockeys' championship again after a memorable duel with Kieren Fallon.

But reading about the brilliant performances of other people's horses during the past year also serves to remind us that we all start the new season on zero and it is going to be tougher than ever to win the top prizes around the world.

Dubai, November 2004

Introduction

by Graham Dench

WELCOME to the second volume in the Racing Post's Flat Horses series. Flat Horses of 2004 follows a similar format to its predecessor, combining in-depth features on the season's top 100 horses with an extended introduction to more than 70 juveniles who are likely to be challenging for a place in that section in 2005. Once again, there is also an A to Z directory of every horse who ran in Britain, along with their definitive Racing Post Ratings.

The top 100 will inevitably be the section that attracts most attention, and for 2004 we have bolstered the writing line-up with the addition of Racing Post heavyweights David Ashforth and Howard Wright. They join an impressive team that includes Paul Haigh, Tom O'Ryan, Brough Scott and James Willoughby – writers who are all driven by the same passion for racing but express that passion in different styles.

In addition, Robert Carter of the International Racing Bureau has unearthed some fascinating tales about some of the more obscure French and Italian Group 1 winners and the people connected to them.

Flat Horses also provides an opportunity to showcase new talent. Since contributing extensively to Flat Horses of 2003, Lee Mottershead has gone on to pen the authorised biography of Persian Punch. A name of which you will see more, following his first contributions to this volume, is that of Steve Dennis.

Each feature is complemented by a detailed race record, plus full breeding details and tabulated pedigrees. The breeding copy is provided once again by Tony Morris and Janet Hickman, whose forthright opinions and insights will be familiar to readers of the Racing Post's bloodstock pages.

In choosing the top 100 we again used as our starting point the winners of Group 1 races in Britain, France and Ireland, of which there were more than 50 individual horses. We then included the Triple Crown winners from the United States, Smarty Jones and Birdstone, plus others of particular interest from the other side of the Atlantic, including the Dubai World Cup winner Pleasantly Perfect, the record-breaking mare Azeri and the brilliant Breeders' Cup Classic winner Ghostzapper.

The absence of Hong Kong-based sprinter Silent Witness may disappoint some, but his most important win of 2003 came in December's Hong Kong Sprint, after we had gone to press, and his proposed clash with Var in the 2004 renewal of the corresponding race also falls outside the parameters of this book.

His relevance to the European scene is questionable, with connections adamant that he will not be raced away from home, but his standing as the world's number one sprinter has been alluded to in the feature on his compatriot Cape Of Good Hope, a truly international competitor who was third in Japan's big sprint after finishing in the frame three times in similar company in Britain in the summer.

The 100 horses are completed by our idea of the 'best of the rest', combining the highest-rated horses who failed to succeed at Group 1 level with some of the season's fastest improvers.

In assembling the young pretenders' section we included the highest-rated juveniles who did not make the top 100, plus horses of real potential who have caught the eye of Racing Post racereaders and analysts. For back-up, we consulted the ante-post lists for the Classics, which so often highlight future stars before they have properly announced themselves on the racecourse.

The Racing Post Ratings are the work of award-winning team Paul Curtis and Simon Turner. Their assessments of the top horses from around the world are included in an international classification that takes account of the best races in Europe, North America, Australia, Hong Kong, Japan and the UAE.

Once again, our records cover all racing up to the end of the British turf season (November 6).

The top 100 horses

of 2004

Figure in bold by each horse's name is its definitive Racing Post Rating

Pedigree assessments by Tony Morris (TM) and Janet Hickman (JH)

Acropolis (Ire)

3yo bay colt **123**

Sadler's Wells (USA) - Dedicated Lady (Ire) (Pennine Walk)

Owner Michael Tabor

Trainer A P O'Brien

Breeder Quay Bloodstock & Samac Ltd

Career: **6 starts**   won **2**   second **0**   third **1**   **£118,841** win and place

By Alan Sweetman

THE absence of Acropolis for most of the 2004 season deprived Aidan O'Brien of a significant talent. That much is clear from the performance of the Sadler's Wells colt in staying on for a highly creditable fourth place behind Bago in the Prix de l'Arc de Triomphe on his second and final outing of the campaign.

Acropolis was not among the first rank of O'Brien's juveniles in 2003. Only a moderate seventh in a Tipperary maiden in August, he showed sufficient improvement to beat an undistinguished field at Galway's September meeting, scoring by one length from Pretty Tricky, at that stage a 77-rated nursery horse who was still a maiden more than 12 months later. A press-room wit was heard to remark that the name of the runner-up could equally refer to the winner, whose high head-carriage in the closing stages provided grounds for suspecting a difficult attitude.

Multiple representation in Group 1 events has become a hallmark of Ballydoyle policy, an approach that has sometimes yielded spectacular dividends, perhaps most memorably when High Chaparral, Sholokhov and Ballingarry brought off a clean sweep in the 2002 Irish Derby. Successive runnings of the Irish 2,000 Guineas in 2001 and 2002 also produced a one-two-three for the stable, while Ballingarry, Castle Gandolfo and Black Sam Bellamy accomplished the same feat in the Criterium de Saint-Cloud in 2001.

Thus it was not untypical when Acropolis formed part of a three-pronged challenge for O'Brien in the Prix Jean-Luc Lagardere at Longchamp, taking on three French-trained rivals in the seven-furlong event. The trio of Newton, Tycoon and Acropolis formed a one-two-three of a rather different sort, filling the last three places in the field of six, though only after Newton and Tycoon were demoted a place. For Acropolis, the indignity of finishing last was compounded by his

Acropolis, right, had just two runs in 2004, but managed to take fourth in the Arc after this Listed win at Leopardstown

tendency to hang in the straight, rekindling the doubt that had been sparked at Galway.

With opportunities running out closer to home, O'Brien looked again to France in order to give Acropolis further experience before putting him away for the winter. At the beginning of November, he sent him for the Criterium International at Saint-Cloud where the opposition was headed by the unbeaten Bago, one of the stars of the French season. The son of Nashwan was in a different league, surging to a six-length win from the Mick Channon-trained Top Seed, with Acropolis another four lengths away, third of the seven runners. It was not a particularly auspicious ending to the campaign.

During the spring and summer of 2004, many of Ballydoyle's main hopes for the season's top races fell by the wayside. High-ranking horses such as One Cool Cat and Antonius Pius failed to deliver, and after the Gallinule winner Meath had finished last in the Vodafone Derby only Tycoon provided some solace by finishing third at extravagant odds in the Irish Derby. By the first week of September, One Cool Cat's second coming as a sprinter had been extinguished by his defeat in the Haydock Sprint Cup, and the following Saturday

2004   Race record

4th Prix de l'Arc de Triomphe Lucien Barriere (Group 1) (Longchamp, October 3) 3yo+ 12f Good **123** (TS 123) 19 ran. *In rear, 15th straight, ran on towards inside under pressure from over 1½f out to take 4th on line (J P Spencer), beaten 3½l by Bago*

1st O2 Kilternan Stakes (Listed) (Leopardstown, September 11) 3yo+ 10f Good to firm **107** (TS 100) 6 ran. *Held up in rear, 5th approaching straight, headway into 3rd 1f out, edged left close home, led near finish (J P Spencer), beat Lord Admiral by ½l*

2003

3rd Criterium International (Group 1) (Saint-Cloud, November 1) 2yo 1m Very soft **98** 7 ran ● **6th** Prix Jean-Luc Lagardere (Grand Criterium) (Group 1) (Longchamp, October 5) 2yo 7f Holding **97** 6 ran ● **1st** Irish Stallion Farms EBF Maiden (Galway, September 9) 2yo 1m½f Good to yielding **77** 9 ran ● **7th** Irish Stallion Farms EBF Maiden (Tipperary, August 21) 2yo 7½f Good **57** 15 ran

Tycoon could finish only third in the St Leger, O'Brien's final throw of the Classic dice.

On the same afternoon at Leopardstown, Acropolis, thus far kept on the sidelines by a series of minor problems, finally made his seasonal debut as one of six runners in the ten-furlong Kilternan Stakes. Backed from 5-2 to 2-1 favourite, he was patiently ridden by Jamie Spencer, who delayed his challenge to the front-running Lord Admiral until well inside the final furlong. Spencer pulled his stick to take evasive action as his mount edged slightly to the left near the finish, a manoeuvre that played its part in ensuring that a stewards' inquiry was needed to uphold the outcome.

O'Brien was sufficiently encouraged by the performance to run Acropolis in the Arc just over three weeks later. In a 19-runner field at Longchamp, Spencer held up Acropolis at the back, and as the race began to unfold from under three furlongs down he still had only one behind, with his passage blocked along the inside. It took a while for the gap to appear, but once it did he found plenty under pressure and stayed on to such effect that he got up to snatch fourth place by a short head from the Epsom hero North Light. Two lengths in front of him in third was the dual Oaks winner Ouija Board, who went on to Breeders' Cup success, and he was beaten only three and a half lengths in total by Bago, who had left him ten adrift at Saint-Cloud 11 months earlier.

Accustomed to winning Group 1 races with remarkable regularity, O'Brien may regard a fourth place in the Arc as fairly small beer, but it was quite a feat of training to bring a horse with a quirky nature to this level of form on the back of an abridged campaign. He remains in training at four and there will be good opportunities for him in Pattern company if his physical and temperamental wellbeing can be sustained through 2005.

Acropolis   *bay colt, 26-2-2001*

			Nearctic	Nearco
				Lady Angela
		Northern Dancer		
			Natalma	Native Dancer
	Sadler's Wells			Almahmoud
	b 1981			
			Bold Reason	Hail To Reason
				Lalun
		Fairy Bridge		
			Special	Forli
				Thong
			Persian Bold	Bold Lad (Ire)
				Relkarunner
		Pennine Walk		
			Tifrums	Thatch
	Dedicated Lady			Pesian Apple
	b 1989			
			Sallust	Pall Mall
				Bandarilla
		Salabella		
			Supreme Lady	Grey Sovereign
				Ulupi's Sister

Bred by Quay Bloodstock and Samac Ltd in Ireland. 550,000gns Tattersalls Houghton yearling

Sire **Sadler's Wells**

Won 6 of 11 races, inc. Beresford S.-Gr3, Irish Derby Trial-Gr2, Irish 2,000 Guineas-Gr1, Eclipse S.-Gr1, Phoenix Champion S.-Gr1. Also 2nd in Prix du Jockey-Club-Gr1, King George VI & Queen Elizabeth S.-Gr1. Impeccably bred top-class performer from 8-12f, handsome, tough and consistent. Sire of Gr1 winners: Braashee, French Glory, In The Wings (x3), Old Vic (x2), Prince Of Dance, Scenic, Salsabil (x5), Opera House (x3), Runyon, Saddlers' Hall, El Prado, Johann Quatz, Masad, Barathea (x2), Fatherland, Fort Wood, Intrepidity (x3), Carnegie (x2), King's Theatre (x2), Northern Spur (x2), Moonshell, Muncie, Poliglote, Chief Contender, Dance Design, Darazari, Luna Wells, Cloudings, Ebadiyla (x2), Entrepreneur, In Command, Kayf Tara (x4), Dream Well (x2), Greek Dance, King Of Kings (x2), Leggera, Commander Collins, Daliapour, Montjeu (x6), Saffron Walden, Aristotle, Beat Hollow (x4), Subtle Power, Galileo (x3), Imagine (x2), Milan, Perfect Soul, Sequoyah, Sligo Bay, Ballingarry, Black Sam Bellamy (x2), Gossamer (x2), High Chaparral (x6), Islington (x4), Quarter Moon, Sholokov, Alberto Giacometti, Brian Boru (x2), Doyen, Powerscourt, Refuse to Bend (4), Yesterday, Quiff, Playful Act.

Dam **Dedicated Lady**

Won 3 of 14 starts at 2 and 3. At 2, won 3 (5-6f) of 7 starts, including Goffs Fillies' Challenge, also 3rd Marble Hill S-Listed. At 3, placed once over 7f from 7 starts. By high-class miler but overall modest sire, out of placed half-sister to Irish St Leger winner M-Lolshan. Dam of: Shewillifshewants (1994 f by Alzao; unraced), Fairy Queen (1996 f by Fairy King; Gr2 winner), Speedfit Free (1997 c by Night Shift; winner), Lady Emmaline (1998 f by Charnwood Forest; unraced), Tashawak (1999 f by Night Shift; Gr2 winner), Taipo Prince (2000 c by Entrepreneur; placed), Acropolis (2001 c by Sadler's Wells; Listed winner, Gr1 placed), De Laurentiis (2002 c by Sadler's Wells; unraced), 2003 f by Sadler's Wells.

Pedigree assessment

Acropolis gave notice with his Arc fourth that he could be a high-class middle-distance performer in 2005. That is in keeping with his dam's record, despite her own speedy and precocious racing career. To Sadler's Wells's brother Fairy King she foaled Fairy Queen, winner of the Group 2 Ribblesdale Stakes and Prix de Royallieu over 12f. She has also produced Group 2 Falmouth Stakes winner Tashawak to another son of Northern Dancer in the speed influence Night Shift. Dedicated Lady's foals have tended to be at their best after their 2yo season, while Sadler's Wells has an excellent record with his older performers, so on pedigree Acropolis should do well in 2005. *JH*

Ad Valorem (USA)

2yo bay colt   **121**

Danzig (USA) - Classy Women (USA) (Relaunch (USA))
Owner Mrs John Magnier
Trainer A P O'Brien
Breeder Calumet Farm

Career: **3** starts   won **3**   **£145,066** win and place

By Alan Sweetman

ONE of the most striking statistics of the 2004 two-year-old campaign was that Aidan O'Brien had failed to win a juvenile race in Britain by the end of September. At that stage the three Group 1 events on the domestic calendar had already eluded him, and a healthy strike-rate in Irish maidens provided scant compensation for an apparent paucity of top-class ammunition for the 2005 Classic campaign.

Then in the first days of October a healthier sheen was applied to the season, thanks to a couple of Group 1 wins outside Ireland, and several encouraging performances on the domestic scene later in the month further remedied the situation. The charge was led by Ad Valorem, who became the stable's third winner of the Middle Park Stakes from the last five renewals, following Minardi in 2000 and Johannesburg in 2001.

For Johannesburg, the six-furlong Newmarket event marked the penultimate win in an unbeaten seven-race sequence that culminated in a Breeders' Cup Juvenile triumph. Like Johannesburg, Ad Valorem carries an unblemished record into winter quarters, and while his achievements paled in comparison to a horse who won at the top level in four countries, he showed notable progress during the course of a campaign that was squeezed into a four-week period. Besides, there is every reason to believe that he will prove a smart three-year-old. He needs only to remain healthy and sound in order to avoid the anti-climactic nightmare of Johannesburg's second season.

It was not until the first weekend of September that Ad Valorem made his first appearance in a six-furlong maiden at The Curragh. Among the horses with previous form, the leading fancy was Lightwood Lady, a filly who had finished second to O'Brien's Chinese Dragon in a weak maiden at the same venue the previous month, so it was no surprise that the Danzig colt was sent off the 6-4 favourite in a field of 23. Jamie Spencer jumped him off smartly and, though Lightwood Lady moved up to dispute

Ad Valorem, left, wins the Middle Park from Rebuttal, completing a hat-trick from his three juvenile starts

the lead two furlongs out, he soon asserted to win by three and a half lengths.

A fortnight later, on the day that Dubawi overpowered the local opposition in the National Stakes, O'Brien brought Ad Valorem back to The Curragh to contest the St Bernard Blenheim Stakes. He faced just five opponents in the six-furlong Listed event, but the quintet had acquired plenty of experience. Indesatchel was having his sixth outing and had been placed in two Group 3 events following a course maiden win, while Belle Artiste was running for the ninth time, two weeks after finishing a respectable fifth to Chelsea Rose in the Moyglare Stud Stakes. In addition, the British challenger Cupid's Glory had progressed to win twice more since a maiden success on the all-weather.

In the interval since his first appearance the ground at The Curragh had changed from good to firm to yielding, but Ad Valorem had little difficulty in adapting and again quickened up well after getting to the front over a furlong out. He beat Indesatchel by one length, with Cupid's

2004   Race record

1st Shadwell Stud Middle Park Stakes (Group 1) (Newmarket, October 1) 2yo 6f Good **121** (TS 105) 9 ran. *Tracked leaders, led over 1f out, driven out (J P Spencer), beat Rebuttal by ³/₄l*

1st St Bernard Blenheim Stakes (Listed) (Curragh, September 19) 2yo 6f Yielding **108** (TS 84) 6 ran. *Settled 3rd, close 2nd and challenged under 2f out, led over 1f out, ran on well (J P Spencer), beat Indesatchel by 1l*

1st Bloodstock Underwriting EBF Maiden (Curragh, September 5) 2yo 6f Good to firm **98** (TS 98) 23 ran. *Led, joined briefly 2f out, quickened clear over 1f out, impressive (J P Spencer), beat Lightwood Lady by 3¹/₂l*

Glory only half a length farther back in third, though well clear of fourth-placed Belle Artiste.

O'Brien is inclined to be somewhat vague in immediate post-race discussions about targets for his winning two-year-olds. His stock repertoire typically includes phrases such as "he's in all the big races", "you could go anywhere with him", and "we'll just have to see where he slots in", but on this occasion he was specific in hinting that Ad Valorem was bound for the Middle Park. The colt's brother, Designer, had finished third to Hayil in the race when still a maiden in 1997, and O'Brien was satisfied that he was progressing quickly enough to have a fighting chance.

Sent off joint second favourite at Newmarket, behind the Coventry Stakes winner Iceman, Ad Valorem was ridden close to the pace by Spencer as the field of nine split into two groups in the early part of the race. He got to the head of affairs over a furlong down and responded well to pressure to score by three-quarters of a length from the Mill Reef third Rebuttal, who hung left towards him in the closing stages. There was another two and a half lengths to Iceman, a solid yardstick who was beaten a similar margin in fourth behind Shamardal in the Dewhurst on his final outing.

The manner of Ad Valorem's three wins suggests that he should get a mile next year, and it is unthinkable that he will not be afforded the opportunity to do so. Such was the fate of his brother Designer, a maiden winner over six furlongs at Newmarket on a belated first appearance as a three-year-old. He lost form thereafter and ended his career as a thoroughly unsatisfactory sprint handicapper in the Emirates, his final efforts marked by a tendency to rear up in the stalls.

As a morale boost for Ballydoyle, Ad Valorem's Middle Park victory was badly needed and it set in train a sequence of promising displays from the stable's juveniles in the closing weeks of the season. Oratorio won the Prix Jean-Luc Lagardere two days later and went on to finish second in the Dewhurst, while Footstepsinthesand emerged as a substantial talent with two wins on home territory. The likelihood is that this trio will be at the heart of O'Brien's plans for the 2,000 Guineas.

Ad Valorem

bay colt, 27-4-2002

			Nearctic	Nearco
				Lady Angela
		Northern Dancer		
			Natalma	Native Dancer
	Danzig			Almahmoud
	b 1977			
			Admiral's Voyage	Crafty Admiral
				Olympia Lou
		Pas de Nom		
			Petitioner	Petition
				Steady Aim
			In Reality	Intentionally
				My Dear Girl
		Relaunch		
			Foggy Note	The Axe
	Classy Women			Silver Song
	b 1988			
			Proud Clarion	Hail To Reason
				Breath o' Morn
		Aironlass		
			Classic Perfection	Never Bend
				Mira Femme

Bred by Calumet Farm in US. $450,000 Fasig-Tipton Saratoga yearling

Sire: Danzig

Unbeaten in 3 starts (Belmont maiden at 2 years, allowance races at Aqueduct and Belmont at 3 years). Stocky, 15.3hh, with incorrect foreleg conformation. Off the track for 11 months between first 2 starts following bone chips, retired with slab fracture of knee. Had high reputation, but never competed with top-class horses. By an exceptional sire out of a tough stakes-winning mare (ran 42 times) whose grand-dam won the Oaks. In retirement at Claiborne Farm, Kentucky. Champion sire in North America 1991 and 1992. Sire of 21 crops of racing age, including Gr1 winners: Chief's Crown (x 8), Contredance, Stephan's Odyssey (x 2), Danzig Connection (x 2), Green Desert, Lotka, Polish Navy (x 3), Polonia, Qualify, Danehill, One Of A Klein, Polish Precedent (x 2), Shaadi (x 2), Adjudicating (x 2), Dayjur (x 3), Dance Smartly, Polish Patriot, Versailles Treaty (x 4), Easy Now, Furiously, Hamas, Lure (x 3), Petit Loup, Pine Bluff, Dispute (x 4), Maroof, Strolling Along, Tribulation, Zieten, Anabaa (x 2), Langfuhr (x 3), Yamanin Paradise [in Japan], Blue Duster, Elnadim, Military, Pas de Reponse, Yashmak, Agnes World (x 2), Golden Snake (x 4), Mujahid, Brahms, War Chant.

Dam Classy Women

Won 4 of her 10 starts in US from 2 to 4. All wins at 3, notably Hillsborough H-Gr3, also 3rd Test S-Gr1. Effective dirt and turf, best form at up to 1m. By high-class US performer at around 1m, good sire and also broodmare sire of Ghostzapper, out of stakes-winning half-sister to useful French 2yo Premium Win (dam of Grade 1 winners Tight Spot, Valiant Nature). Dam of: Petite Princess (1994 f by Dayjur; winner, Gr3 placed, dam of CanGr3 winner Raylene), Designer (1995 c by Danzig; winner, Gr1 placed), Polish Pianist (1996 c by Forty Niner; winner), Arbitrator (1997 c by Unbridled; unplaced), Loner (1998 c by Pleasant Colony; unraced), Squadron (1999 c by Danzig; unraced), Ode To Richard (2000 c by Deputy Minister; unraced), Fleeting Glance (2001 f by Charismatic; winner), Ad Valorem (2002 c by Danzig; Middle Park S-Gr1), 2003 c by Lemon Drop Kid.

Pedigree assessment

There is plenty of speed in this pedigree and Ad Valorem is far from certain to stay the mile of the Guineas. In fact, there is a fair chance he will be one of Danzig's many sprinters. He is a full-brother to Designer, who was a close third behind Hayil in the 1997 Middle Park but failed to live up to that subsequently, and several of the dam's other foals either have been unraced or had light careers. In the light of this, although Ad Valorem's record to date is without blemish, he is not the most obvious candidate to make good progress from 2 to 3. *JH*

Albanova

5yo grey mare   **112**

Alzao (USA) - Alouette (Darshaan)

Owner Miss K Rausing

Trainer Sir Mark Prescott

Breeder Miss K Rausing

Career: **11** starts   won **7**   second **1**   third **0**   **£283,954** win and place

By Paul Haigh

NOBODY has ever accused Sir Mark Prescott of over-facing even his best horses early on. So it was no surprise when he gave Albanova, a full-sister to the dual Champion Stakes winner Alborada, whom he had also trained for Kirsten Rausing, a couple of confidence-boosting wins against modest opposition in her first two outings as a three-year-old before asking her to take on anything decent.

It wasn't until her third outing at three therefore – she had won only a Class D maiden at two – that she showed she might have something like her sister's ability. In a Listed race at Chepstow George Duffield, perhaps riding with uncharacteristic over-confidence, set her quite a difficult task in asking her to run down Salim Toto after that useful mare, quickening off a pace she'd set herself on firm ground that she favoured, had gone three lengths clear. Albanova took a second or two to find her gear, then flew, cutting down Salim Toto, who was certainly not stopping, in about half a furlong. It was such an impressive effort that the daughter of Alzao and the Darshaan mare Alouette was next asked to make the huge step up in class to the Prix Vermeille, in which she ran respectably without ever looking likely to get into the finish after racing wide throughout.

In 2003 she still seemed a filly most at home at Listed or Group 3 level. Every time she stepped up in class she found a few too good. Her second to Mamool in the 12-furlong Group 1 Preis von Europa at Cologne in September suggested, however, that she might be improving as she matured, even though she disappointed when stepped up to just shy of two miles in the Prix Royal-Oak a month later, when on what she had already shown was her favourite soft ground she gave the impression that the trip may have been too far.

It wasn't until 2004, as a fully grown five-year-old, that she really began to fulfil her potential. Prescott, perhaps in the belief that she might like to run where she'd run well before, but almost certainly having made the

Albanova lands the Preis von Europa at Cologne to complete a summer hat-trick in German Group 1 races

judgement that Group 1s in Germany still take a bit less winning than those in Britain, sent her back to Germany for her seasonal reappearance in the West LB Deutschlandpreis at Dusseldorf in July. To nearly everyone's mild surprise – the fact that she was ridden by local jockey Terry Hellier suggests even Sir Mark was no more than hopeful – she hit the front under hard driving inside the final furlong to win by a neck at 11-1. The horse she beat, Dayano, was nothing special, but she did have the 2003 St Leger winner Brian Boru six lengths behind her in fifth.

Hellier kept the ride when she returned to Germany the following month for what may, to English ears anyway, be the least elegantly named Group 1 in Europe, the Rheinland-Pokal der Stadtsparkasse Koln, again over what was becoming her specialist trip of 12 furlongs. Albanova delivered again, this time at just under 6-1, even after suffering minor interference when failing to get a run up the rail. Once pulled out, she still had time to catch High Accolade and beat him three-quarters of a length.

Her trainer must have been even more impressed by that, as, for her third trip to Germany, this time for the Preis von Europa, again at Cologne, he sent Seb Sanders with her. Although she had to fight to beat the local

2004 Race record

1st IVG - Preis von Europa (Group 1) (Cologne, September 26) 3yo+ 12f Soft **111** 9 ran. *Broke well and settled in touch, headway well over 2f out, went 2nd 2f out, driven and challenged over 1f out, led close home, driven out (S Sanders), beat Saldentigerin by ½l*

1st Rheinland-Pokal der Stadtsparkasse Koln (Group 1) (Cologne, August 15) 3yo+ 12f Good **111** 7 ran. *Close 3rd to straight, looking for gap 2f out, switched to rails and squeezed 1½f out, switched out distance, quickened to lead 100yds out, ran on well (T Hellier), beat High Accolade by ¾l*

1st West LB Deutschlandpreis (Group 1) (Dusseldorf, July 25) 3yo+ 12f Soft **111** 7 ran. *Always in touch, 3rd on inside straight, soon went 2nd, hard ridden over 1f out, driven to lead well inside final furlong, ran on (T Hellier), beat Dayano by nk*

2003

6th Prix Royal-Oak (Group 1) (Longchamp, October 26) 3yo+ 15½f Holding **105** 14 ran ● **2nd** Preis von Europa (Group 1) (Cologne, September 28) 3yo+ 12f Soft **111** 6 ran ● **7th** Vodafone Coronation Cup (Group 1) (Epsom, June 6) 4yo+ 12f Good **106** 9 ran ● **1st** EBF Pinnacle Stakes (Listed) (Haydock, May 24) 4yo+ 12f Heavy **112** 6 ran

Other runs

2002 **5th** Prix Vermeille Hermitage Barriere de la Baule (Group 1) (Longchamp, September 15) 3yo 12f Good to firm **111** 11 ran ● **1st** Oakgrove Stud Golden Daffodil Stakes (Listed) (Chepstow, July 26) 3yo+ 10f Good to firm **107** 9 ran ● **1st** Saffie Joseph & Sons Classified Stakes (Pontefract, July 9) 3yo (0-75) 10f Good to soft **87** 3 ran ● **2001** **1st** EBF Stanley Racing Maiden Stakes (Div II) (Haydock, September 29) 2yo 7f Heavy **71** 9 ran

three-year-old Saldentigerin she still did so, by half a length, to complete a Group 1 hat-trick.

The question has to be: how good were those performances? Or maybe: how cunning was her trainer in finding her Group 1 races she could win? But there are a couple of reasons for thinking she's a very worthy Group 1 performer who could, had she stayed in training, have become a force even when the language of Goethe wasn't ringing in her ears. In the Rheinland-Pokal she beat the subsequent Canadian International runner-up, Simonas, further than Warrsan did in winning Germany's greatest race, the Grosser Preis von Baden, three weeks later; and in the Preis von Europa she had Egerton, beaten only a neck by Warrsan at Baden-Baden, a length and three-quarters away in fourth. One line of form could be misleading. Two lines suggest she just might be in the same league as Clive Brittain's durable dual Coronation Cup winner, who was much too good for her when she took him on in the Epsom race as a four-year-old.

Albanova retires to stud with a record even Alborada can't quite match statistically. Albanova boasts seven wins from 11 starts, three of them Group 1; Alborada managed six from ten, of which her two in the Champion Stakes were the only ones at that level.

Albanova *grey mare, 16-2-1999*

			Nearctic
		Northern Dancer	Natalma
	Lyphard		
		Goofed	Court Martial
Alzao			Barra
b 1980			
		Sir Ivor	Sir Gaylord
			Attica
	Lady Rebecca		
		Pocahontas	Roman
			How
		Shirley Heights	Mill Reef
			Hardiemma
	Darshaan		
		Delsy	Abdos
Alouette			Kelty
gr 1990			
		Crystal Palace	Caro
			Hermieres
	Alruccaba		
		Allara	Zeddaan
			Nucciolina

Bred by Miss K. Rausing in England.

Sire Alzao

Won 4 of 12 races, inc. Premio Ellington-Gr3. Also 2nd in La Coupe de Maisons-Laffitte and respectable 8th of 19 in Champion S. (only Gr1 start) at 3. Strong, compact sort, effective on any going, scored only Pattern win in only race at 12f. Extremely well-bred, by a champion sire on both sides of the Atlantic, out of a daughter of a brilliant Derby winner who was herself half-sister to US Classic winner and successful sire Tom Rolfe. Stands at Coolmore, 2004 fee €8,000 (Oct 1). Sire of 17 crops of racing age, inc. Gr1 winners: Alcando (Beverly Hills H.), Pass The Peace (Cheveley Park S.), Capricciosa (Moyglare Stud S., Cheveley Park S.), Second Set (Sussex S.), Alpride (Beverly Hills H., Yellow Ribbon Invitational S.), Wind In Her Hair (Aral Pokal), Matiya (Irish 1,000 Guineas), Waky Nao (Premio Vittorio di Capua), Alborada (Champion S. [twice]), Shahtoush (Oaks S.), Winona (Irish Oaks), Timi (Oaks d'Italia), Albanova (Deutschland Preis, Aral Pokal, Preis von Europa).

Dam Alouette

Won 3 of 11 races. Also placed 6 times, inc. 3rd in Moyglare Stud S.-Gr1. Leggy, lengthy individual, seemingly effective on any ground, stayed 12f well. A tough and genuine performer. Sister to Classic-placed Listed winner Arrikala, half-sister to dual Gr2 winner Last Second and Gr3 winner Alleluia, and to the dam of Gr1 winners Quarter Moon and Yesterday. Dam 2-y-o winner, half-sister to 3 other winners. Grand-dam a winner and closely related to major winners Aliysa (dam of Desert Story), Aliya, Nishapour, Nassipour, etc. From a celebrated Aga Khan family. Dam of: Alborada (1995 f by Alzao; dual Gr1 winner), Dapper (1997 c by Hernando; unraced), Alakananda (1998 f by Hernando; winner), Albanova (1999 f by Alzao; triple Gr1 winner), Alba Stella (2000 f by Nashwan; winner), Albinus (2001 c by Selkirk; Listed-placed winner). She has a yearling filly and a colt foal, both by Sadler's Wells, and is due in 2005 to Green Desert.

Pedigree assessment

Alborada's Group 3 win as a two-year-old, and her grand-dam's earlier successful tryst with Alzao, which resulted in Last Second, provided ample justification for the return of Alouette to the son of Lyphard in 1998. The wisdom of that decision was proved when Alborada won the Champion Stakes as both three- and four-year-old, but it did leave younger sister Albanova with a hard act to follow. Another wise decision – to keep her in training as a five-year-old – paid splendid dividends. Kirsten Rausing has done a marvellous job in developing this family, and now has two champion sisters of virtually equal ability to extend it further. *TM*

Alexander Goldrun (Ire)

3yo bay filly **118**

Gold Away (Ire) - Renashaan (Fr) (Darshaan)
Owner Mrs N O'Callaghan
Trainer J S Bolger
Breeder Dermot Cantillon

Career: **14** starts won **6** second **4** third **1** **£351,101** win and place

By Alan Sweetman

LEXANDER GOLDRUN provided a telling illustration of Jim Bolger's enduring skill as a trainer of fillies with her victory in the Prix de l'Opera at Longchamp on Arc day. Bolger's emergence as a big-race trainer was achieved with a band of talented fillies in the early 1980s. The likes of Condessa, Flame Of Tara, Give Thanks and Park Appeal won major races outside Ireland, and in the latter half of the decade Park Express, Polonia and rags-to-riches mare Noora Abu further enhanced his reputation. Jet Ski Lady contributed a stunning Oaks victory in 1991, Ivyanna and Treasure Hope won major races in Italy in 1992, and midway through the 1990s Priory Belle and Eva Luna were Group 1 winners on an increasingly competitive Irish scene. In 2002, ten years after his best-ever colt St Jovite had won the Irish Derby, it was Margarula who put him back on the Classic map with a 33-1 victory in the Irish Oaks.

Though possessed of a pedigree that suggested she would stay considerably further than five furlongs, Alexander Goldrun was sent straight into battle as a two-year-old, finishing a satisfactory fifth to Colossus at The Curragh in the first juvenile race of 2003. The benefit of the run was evident when she returned to the same venue to win a maiden in April, and once the nursery campaign started in July, she was again in the vanguard. Third at Tipperary in her first handicap, she was then the victim of an unfortunate mishap at Galway, where her stall failed to open and she forced her way out after her rivals had jumped off.

The experience could easily have had a detrimental effect on a relatively immature filly, but Alexander Goldrun was made of sterner stuff. She showed no ill-effects in battling her way to a narrow victory over Castledale in a nursery at Leopardstown, getting just 3lb from the runner-up who won the Grade 1 Santa Anita Derby the following spring. She then finished second in nurseries at Listowel and Gowran before confirming her ability and resolution by winning the Listed Silken Glider Stakes at The Curragh. She had been

**Alexander Goldrun crowns her long and consistent season
with Group 1 victory in the Prix de l'Opera at Longchamp**

on the go for seven months and had shown a sustained level of improvement
that provided a healthy omen for her three-year-old campaign.

In 2004 Bolger again wasted no time in getting her season under way.
She proved that she had trained on satisfactorily when capturing the
opening-day Listed race at The Curragh honouring former stable star
Park Express, and provided further evidence of a determined attitude
in the Derrinstown Stud 1,000 Guineas Trial at Leopardstown. Having
been checked after almost clipping heels in the early stages, she failed
to get a clear run until late in the day but never gave up, delivering a
last-gasp challenge between horses to beat Misty Heights by a short head.

From now on she would be campaigned exclusively in Group 1 races.
She harried the brilliant Attraction as best she could in finishing second
in the Irish 1,000 Guineas, the only home-trained filly to get into the
first five, and showed no lack of stamina when fourth to Latice in the
Prix de Diane at Chantilly before returning to The Curragh for the Pretty
Polly Stakes. There was an initial sense of disappointment when she failed
to overhaul the front-running Chorist, but in hindsight it was no disgrace

2004   Race record

1st Prix de l'Opera Casino Barriere d'Enghien (Group 1) (Longchamp, October 3) 3yo+ 10f Good **118** (TS 87) 10 ran. *Held up, 7th on inside straight, progress from over 2f out, pushed along to chase leaders 1½f out, ran on to lead 100yds out, pushed out (K J Manning), beat Grey Lilas by 1l*

2nd Audi Pretty Polly Stakes (Group 1) (Curragh, June 26) 3yo+ 10f Good **118** (TS 109) 6 ran. *Tracked leaders in 4th, improved into 2nd and challenged under 2f out, every chance, no extra close home (K J Manning), beaten ½l by Chorist*

4th Prix de Diane Hermes (Group 1) (Chantilly, June 13) 3yo 10½f Good to soft **113** (TS 103) 17 ran. *Mid-division, headway towards inside over 2f out, squeezed through to dispute 3rd well over 1f out, one pace final furlong (K J Manning), beaten 2l by Latice*

2nd Boylesports Irish 1,000 Guineas (Group 1) (Curragh, May 23) 3yo 1m Good to firm **114** (TS 90) 15 ran. *Always prominent, 2nd from 3f out, ridden to challenge under 2f out, no impression inside final furlong, kept on well (K J Manning), beaten 1l by Attraction*

1st Derrinstown Stud 1,000 Guineas Trial (Group 3) (Leopardstown, May 9) 3yo 7f Good to yielding **99** (TS 40) 9 ran. *Slowly into stride, checked after 1½f, 7th and ridden early straight, 3rd 1f out, ran on well between horses to lead near finish (K J Manning), beat Misty Heights by shd*

1st Irish Stallion Farms EBF Park Express Stakes (Listed) (Curragh, March 21) 3yo+ 1m Heavy **102** (TS 52) 10 ran. *Tracked leaders on stands' side, headway 3f out, led and quickened clear under 2f out, kept on under pressure final furlong (K J Manning), beat Blue Reema by 1l*

2003

1st Gerrardstown House Stud Silken Glider Stakes (Listed) (Curragh, October 25) 2yo 1m Good **97** 12 ran ● **2nd** Irish Stallion Farms EBF Premier Nursery (Gowran Park, October 11) 2yo 1m Good to firm **97** 16 ran ● **2nd** Irish Stallion Farms EBF Premier Nursery (Listowel, September 15) 2yo 1m Good **93** 8 ran ● **1st** Irish Stallion Farms EBF Premier Nursery Handicap (Leopardstown, September 6) 2yo 7f Good to firm **94** 11 ran ● **9th** Irish Stallion Farms EBF Premier Nursery Handicap (Galway, August 2) 2yo 7f Yielding **63** 11 ran ● **3rd** Premier County Nursery (Handicap) (Tipperary, July 20) 2yo 5f Heavy **88** 8 ran ● **1st** Michael Murphy & Co Ltd Newbridge EBF Median Auction Fillies Maiden (Curragh, April 6) 2yo 5f Good to yielding **83** 9 ran ● **5th** Tally Ho Stud EBF Maiden (Curragh, March 23) 2yo 5f Yielding to soft **63** 14 ran

to lose out to the five-year-old mare, who crowned her career with her second to Haafhd in the Champion Stakes.

With Chorist missing from the Prix de l'Opera, the task facing Alexander Goldrun was undeniably eased. Her victory over the Prix du Moulin winner Grey Lilas nonetheless represented genuine Group 1 form, and it was achieved despite a difficult passage. Slowly away, she was still at the rear three furlongs out before making up ground on the rail and finding another gear inside the last furlong. She already had the upper hand when giving Grey Lilas a slight nudge by edging right near the line.

A tough mare who could be even better at four, she has been a great credit to her trainer and to her rider throughout her career, Kevin Manning, a consistently reliable stable jockey to his father-in-law.

Alexander Goldrun   *bay filly, 9-2-2001*

		Nureyev	**Northern Dancer** Special
	Goldneyev		
		Gold River	Riverman Glaneuse
Gold Away ch 1995			
		Blushing Groom	Red God Runaway Bride
	Blushing Away		
		Sweet Revenge	Raja Baba Away
		Shirley Heights	Mill Reef Hardiemma
	Darshaan		
		Delsy	Abdos Kelty
Renashaan b 1989			
		Lyphard	**Northern Dancer** Goofed
	Gerbera		
		Greenway	Targowice Gracious

Bred by Dermot Cantillon in Ireland. €40,000 Goffs November foal.

Sire **Gold Away**

Won 5 (5-9f) of 16 starts over 3 seasons. Smart 2yo, won 1m Prix Thomas Bryon-Gr3, later won Prix de Guiche-Gr3, Prix Edmond Blanc-Gr3, Prix du Muguet-Gr2 and multiple Gr1 placed over 7-9f. By high-class 2yo/miler, half-brother to Gr3 winners Blushing Gleam, Danzigaway. Stands at Haras du Quesnay, France, 2004 fee €4,000. Oldest progeny 3, sire of: Alexander Goldrun (Prix de l'Opera-Gr1), Clifden (Gr3).

Dam **Renashaan**

Very useful 8-9f peformer in France. Won 2 races at 2 and 3, also 3rd Prix Vanteaux-Gr3. Granddaughter of smart 2yo/sprinter Greenway (ancestress of Gr1 winners Guadalupe, Royal Rebel). Dam of: Highshaan (1994 f by Pistolet Bleu; winner), Renazig (1995 c by Polish Precedent; winner), Renaleon (1996 c by Generous; winner), Kalliopino (1998 c by Machiavellian; unraced), Medecis (1999 c by Machiavellian; Gr3 winner, Gr1 placed), Alexander Goldrun (2001 f by Gold Away; Prix de l'Opera-Gr1), Rio (2002 c by Namid; unraced), 2004 c by Machiavellian. In foal to Pivotal for 2005.

Pedigree assessment

The main flagbearer for a young French sire who has gained a higher profile thanks to this filly's admirable efforts. Alexander Goldrun's stamina is predictable from her pedigree; both parents, plus high-class half-brother Medecis, generally excelled in the 7-10f bracket. An admirable filly who will make an exciting broodmare in time. *JH*

American Post

3yo brown colt **117**

Bering - Wells Fargo (Sadler's Wells (USA))
Owner K Abdullah
Trainer Mme C Head-Maarek
Breeder Juddmonte Farms

Career: **9** starts won **6** second **1** third **0** **£495,759** win and place

By Lee Mottershead

YOU wanted to cheer her up. Standing in the Longchamp unsaddling enclosure, Criquette Head-Maarek was a seriously downcast figure. Her face told a story of dejection and disappointment as she reflected on her horse's performance, a performance that had been some way short of what she had expected. This was one unhappy lady. So much so that, if you hadn't just seen it happen, you would never have guessed that Head-Maarek had trained American Post to win the French 2,000 Guineas.

Her reaction said as much about what she had expected to happen as about what actually had transpired. She had expected American Post to dazzle the Longchamp cognoscenti and storm away from his rivals to win the Poule d'Essai des Poulains by clear daylight. But the 4-11 favourite had not done that. Indeed, American Post should not even have won at all. It was only thanks to Antonius Pius that he had a Classic in the bag.

Classic success had always seemed likely for American Post. Khalid Abdullah's home-bred colt, a son of Prix du Jockey-Club hero Bering, had stamped himself a tremendously talented two-year-old, twice successful at Group 1 level. At Longchamp, in the Prix Jean-Luc Lagardere, he was sensational, displaying the rare ability to quicken in a swamp. Then, at Doncaster, he captured the Racing Post Trophy on ground that seemed quicker than he appreciated, running below the level he had posted in Paris but still doing more than enough to win readily. Quoted as short as 6-1 favourite for the Vodafone Derby in the immediate aftermath of his Doncaster triumph, American Post went into winter quarters with plenty of good stuff behind him and the promise of a lot more to come.

One snag had, though, raised its ugly head during American Post's first year on the track. He had a temperament problem. Reluctant to even set foot on the racecourse before his Longchamp Group 1 romp, he had then proceeded to cause all sorts of problems at the start before eventually

American Post lands a fortuitous win in the French 2,000 Guineas, following Antonius Pius's dramatic late swerve

deigning to enter the stalls. Head-Maarek had to try to find a solution to American Post's waywardness. She did. It was a root vegetable.

Not many ace three-year-olds find their salvation in a carrot, but American Post did. Out surprisingly early for his three-year-old debut, and with Abdullah's retained rider Richard Hughes on board, he was persuaded into the stalls for a Saint-Cloud Listed race on the last day of March by the lure of a juicy carrot. The carrot did the trick and American Post ran out an impressive victor of the Prix Omnium.

Keen to give American Post more racecourse experience before the Poulains, Head-Maarek then sent him to race over the course and distance of the Longchamp Classic, her star performer making all under Christophe Soumillon – Hughes was suspended – to notch a two-length win in the Prix de Fontainebleau. Two trials completed and two trials won easily, it was no surprise that many viewed the French 2,000 Guineas as nothing less than a penalty kick.

That was not, however, how it turned out. American Post never looked happy during the Poulains. Neither as fluent nor as smooth as he had been on his previous outings, he seemed uneasy on the good to firm ground, struggling ahead over a furlong out while at no point stamping his authority on proceedings. When Antonius Pius surged through the gears

2004   Race record

10th Netjets Prix du Moulin de Longchamp (Group 1) (Longchamp, September 5) 3yo+ 1m Good to soft **113** (TS 79) 11 ran. *Slowly into stride, soon close up, 3rd straight, disputed 2nd 1 1/2f out, weakening when not much room just inside final furlong, not recover (R Hughes), beaten 4 1/2l by Grey Lilas*

6th Vodafone Derby Stakes (Group 1) (Epsom, June 5) 3yo 12f Good **113** (TS 109) 14 ran. *Took keen hold, prominent, 4th straight, smooth progress to press winner 3f out, ridden and not quicken 2f out, weakened entering final furlong (R Hughes), beaten 6 1/2l by North Light*

1st Gainsborough Poule d'Essai des Poulains (Group 1) (Longchamp, May 16) 3yo 1m Good to firm **113** (TS 101) 7 ran. *Raced in 3rd to straight, ridden and every chance inside final furlong, left in front 50yds out, driven out (R Hughes), beat Diamond Green by 1/2l*

1st Prix de Fontainebleau (Group 3) (Longchamp, April 25) 3yo 1m Good to soft **111** (TS 96) 4 ran. *Made all, quickened over 1f out, ran on well (C Soumillon), beat subsequently disqualified Antonius Pius by 1l*

1st Prix Omnium (Saint-Cloud, March 31) 3yo 1m Good **106** 5 ran. *Raced in 2nd on outside, led after 3f, pushed along and headed over 1 1/2f out, quickened readily to lead again 150yds out, soon clear, pushed out (R Hughes), beat Joursanvault by 4l*

2003

1st Racing Post Trophy (Group 1) (Doncaster, October 25) 2yo 1m Good to firm **115** 4 ran ● **1st** Prix Jean-Luc Lagardere (Grand Criterium) (Group 1) (Longchamp, October 5) 2yo 7f Holding **117** 6 ran ● **1st** Prix du Casino Barriere de Royan (Longchamp, September 14) 2yo 7f Good to soft **99** (TS 98) 9 ran ● **2nd** Prix du Pre d'Auge (Unraced Colts & Geldings) (Deauville, July 31) 2yo 6f Soft **102** 6 ran

to lead inside the final furlong, the favourite faced certain defeat. And defeat is what he would have suffered had Antonius Pius not crashed inexplicably into the rail 75 yards from the line, allowing American Post to steal an unlikely and undeserved victory.

"I'm disappointed because he would have been second and he was beat," said Head-Maarek, agreeing with Hughes that American Post had hated the fast conditions. But, although miserable, they now wanted to prove to the world just how good American Post was. There would be no better stage to do that than at Epsom in the Derby. Head-Maarek once said that she had long dreamed of running American Post in the Blue Riband, describing him as "the perfect type" for the race. He wasn't. He failed to stay, travelling better than anything for the first mile, but gradually dropping away up the straight to finish sixth.

Stamina was the problem at Epsom. Quite what the problem was when American Post returned three months later in the Prix du Moulin is hard to say, but what is clear is that the former star was now a pale shadow of himself. He beat just one of his ten rivals and never raced again.

The great horse American Post once looked like becoming never materialised. He won the Poulains only because another horse conspired to lose it. It seems bizarre to call a Classic-winning season disappointing, but for American Post it was.

American Post   *brown colt 3-2-2001*

		Sea-Bird	Dan Cupid
	Arctic Tern		Sicalade
Bering		Bubbling Beauty	Hasty Road
ch 1983			Almahmoud
	Beaune	Lyphard	**Northern Dancer**
			Goofed
		Barbra	Le Fabuleux
			Biobelle
	Sadler's Wells	**Northern Dancer**	Nearctic
			Natalma
Wells Fargo		Fairy Bridge	Bold Reason
b 1996			Special
	Cruising Height	Shirley Heights	Mill Reef
			Hardiemma
		Nomadic Pleasure	Habitat
			Petite Marmite

Bred by Juddmonte Farms in England.

Sire Bering

Won 5 of 7 races, inc. Prix Noailles-Gr2, Prix Hocquart-Gr2, Prix du Jockey-Club-Gr1, Prix Niel-Gr3. Also 2nd (to Dancing Brave) in Prix de l'Arc de Triomphe. Handsome, striking individual. Top-notch middle-distance performer, effective on any ground, with an outstanding turn of foot. Chipped a bone in a knee in final start. Sire of: Beau Sultan (Gr3), Peter Davies (Racing Post Trophy-Gr1), Serrant (Gr2), Steamer Duck (Gran Criterium-Gr1), Break Bread (Gr3), Special Price (Gr2), Signe Divin (Gr2), Matiara (Poule d'Essai des Pouliches-Gr1, Ramona H.-Gr1), Pennekamp (Prix de la Salamandre-Gr1, Dewhurst S.-Gr1, 2,000 Guineas-Gr1), Salmon Ladder (Gr3), Vertical Speed (Gr2), Glorosia (Fillies' Mile-Gr1), Miss Berbere (Gr2), Moiava (Gr2), Neptune's Bride (Gr3), Stella Berine (Gr3), Urban Ocean (Gr3), Three Points (Gr3), Art Contemporain (Gr3), Ing Ing (Gr3), Lady Catherine (Gr3), American Post (Prix Jean-Luc Lagardere-Gr1, Racing Post Trophy-Gr1, Poule d'Essai des Poulains).

Dam Wells Fargo

Did not race. Half-sister to Yorkshire Oaks and St Leger runner-up, High And Low. Dam of American Post (2001 c by Bering; triple Gr1 winner), her only foal.

Pedigree assessment

We remarked here last year that American Post's best shot at Classic glory would come in the Poule d'Essai des Poulains, and that judgement proved sound, but he was an extremely lucky winner at Longchamp, scoring only by dint of Antonius Pius's "own goal". Connections persisted in their belief that he would last 12 furlongs, and he was well supported for the Derby, but the trip – and his reluctance to settle – found him out. While he has numerous antecedents who were suited by a mile and a half, including his sire, it is also a fact that in his long stud career Bering has not got a Group 1 winner beyond nine furlongs. American Post might be said to have run true to his sire's production, rather than to his performance. He will stand at the Haras d'Etreham. *TM*

Ancient World (USA)

4yo bay gelding **120**

Spinning World (USA) - Headline (Machiavellian (USA))

Owner Godolphin

Trainer Saeed Bin Suroor

Breeder Darley Stud Management

Career: **10** starts won **5** second **2** third **0** **£243,502** win and place

By Graham Dench

FRANKIE DETTORI needs little prompting these days in order to perform a flying dismount. Witnessed at one time just a handful of times a year, usually in the rarefied atmosphere that follows a Classic or Group 1 success, they can now be seen the length and breadth of the country, seemingly whenever there is the merest hint of occasion. There was even one at Bath one evening.

Traditionalists abhor such showmanship, and some racecourse regulars found it impossible to suppress a snigger when at Ascot one day Dettori for once failed to execute the manoeuvre with his usual grace and elegance and landed on his backside.

However, the value of Dettori's dismounts should not be underestimated. The public still flock to the winner's enclosure in the hope of catching one, and they are invariably greeted with a roar of approval.

Those that rushed down from the stands after Ancient World's superb weight-carrying performance in the William Hill Mile at Goodwood in July were in for a disappointment, however. For the highly strung Ancient World was a horse upon whom Dettori was not prepared to take any chances.

One might have expected Ancient World to be exhausted after humping 9st 10lb to a resounding length-and-a-quarter defeat of Impeller and 19 others in one of the hottest handicaps of the year, but he was still full of himself – very much on edge and unable to stand still for a moment.

It was a case of safety first, yet this was the 'new, improved' Ancient World, back on the racecourse for the first time since being subjected to what is euphemistically referred to as 'the unkindest cut'.

It's a contradiction in more than one sense, of course, to say that the gelding operation can make a man of a horse, but it certainly transformed Ancient World. For Goodwood represented a turning point

Ancient World confirms his improvement as a gelding by landing the Group 1 Premio Vittorio di Capua in Milan

in the career of a horse whose temperament threatened to overwhelm his considerable natural talent.

Recruited along with Doyen from Andre Fabre at the end of 2003 after two impressive, though relatively low-key, Longchamp wins in Sheikh Mohammed's colours, Ancient World reportedly worked like a champion for Godolphin in Dubai in the spring yet was beaten at cramped odds at both Windsor and Nottingham when first carrying the blue silks. His mind was not on the job, and gelding was the only option.

He may still have been living on his nerves to some extent at Goodwood, but his attitude in the race itself could not be faulted. There were few classier performances in that sort of company all year, and for once the overused 'Group horse in a handicap' cliche had the ring of truth about it.

While Ancient World's Group-race debut resulted in ignominious defeat behind Norse Dancer at Salisbury, he could be excused as connections argued that he hated the sticky ground. Later in August he looked a different horse when a length-and-a-quarter winner from that hardened battler

2004   Race record

1st Premio Vittorio di Capua (Group 1) (San Siro, October 10) 3yo+ 1m Good **120** 7 ran. *Soon led, pushed out, ran on well (L Dettori), beat Majestic Desert by 1¼l*

1st Stan James Winter Hill Stakes (Group 3) (Windsor, August 28) 3yo+ 10f Good to soft **116** (TS 116) 8 ran. *Held up in touch, led over 2f out, ridden out (K McEvoy), beat Gateman by 1¼l*

8th totesport Sovereign Stakes (Group 3) (Salisbury, August 12) 3yo+ 1m Good to soft **105** (TS 86) 12 ran. *Held up in rear, headway on outside from 3f out, effort over 2f out, never going pace to leaders and weakened approaching final furlong (L Dettori), beaten 5½l by Norse Dancer*

1st William Hill Mile (Heritage Handicap) (Goodwood, July 30) 3yo+ 1m Good to firm **117** (TS 110) 21 ran. *Always well placed, eased off rail and quickened to lead 1f out, ridden out (L Dettori), beat Impeller by 1¼l*

2nd Illuma - The Dawn of A New Era Conditions Stakes (Nottingham, June 2) 3yo+ 1m Good to firm **109** (TS 78) 6 ran. *Chased winner, ridden and every chance 2f out, not quicken inside final furlong (L Dettori), beaten 1½l by Shot To Fame*

2nd totesport.com Royal Windsor Stakes (Listed) (Windsor, May 10) 3yo+ 1m½f Soft **104** (TS 60) 4 ran. *Led until ran wide and headed after 2f, stayed tracking winner, challenged inside final 2f, edged right under pressure inside final furlong, weakened close home (L Dettori), beaten 2½l by Putra Pekan*

2003

1st Prix d'Orsay (Longchamp, October 9) 3yo 1m Holding 8 ran ● **1st** Prix de Villeneuve L'Etang (Longchamp, September 7) 3yo 1m½f Good to soft 10 ran ● **4th** Prix Banstar (Maisons-Laffitte, July 27) 3yo 1m Very soft 8 ran ● **4th** Prix de Chaumieres (Deauville, July 9) 3yo 1m Good to soft **94** 9 ran

Gateman in Windsor's Group 3 Winter Hill Stakes. With Kerrin McEvoy substituting for the suspended Dettori, he travelled well all the way and won impressively. However, the best was yet to come.

Upped to Group 1 company for the Premio Vittorio di Capua at the San Siro in October, he led home a British 1-2-3 as he made virtually all the running and held on readily by a length and a quarter from Majestic Desert, with the previous weekend's good Longchamp second Hurricane Alan in third. It was a fourth success in the race in six years for both Godolphin and Dettori following their wins with Muhtathir in 1999, and with Slickly in both 2001 and 2002. They were also second with Blatant in 2003.

Godolphin can look back proudly upon a job well done with Ancient World, but it might prove a hard act to follow in 2005, when he will be burdened with a Group 1 penalty in all but the best races. The Vittorio di Capua represents solid form, however, stronger than that of many continental Group 1 races, and it is possible that Ancient World is capable of better still, since he is relatively unexposed and connections insist that he improved mentally with every race once he was gelded. What's more, he seems similarly effective at a mile and ten furlongs. The Dubai Duty Free Stakes, a Group 1 over an extended mile on Dubai World Cup night, would make an attractive starting point.

Ancient World | *bay gelding 19-3-2000*

			Nearctic
		Northern Dancer	Natalma
	Nureyev		
		Special	Forli
Spinning World			Thong
ch 1993			Never Bend
		Riverman	River Lady
	Imperfect Circle		
		Aviance	Northfields
			Minnie Hauk
		Mr Prospector	Raise A Native
			Gold Digger
	Machiavellian		
		Coup de Folie	Halo
Headline			Raise The Standard
b 1993			Bold Ruler
		Irish Castle	Castle Forbes
	Priceless Fame		
		Comely Nell	Commodore M.
			Nellie L.

Bred by Darley Stud Management in Kentucky.

Sire **Spinning World**

Won 8 of 14 races, inc. Prix Saint-Roman-Gr3, Irish 2,000 Guineas-Gr1, Prix Jacques le Marois-Gr1 [twice], Prix du Muguet-Gr2, Prix du Moulin de Longchamp-Gr1, Breeders' Cup Mile-Gr1. Also 2nd in Poule d'Essai des Poulains, Prix du Moulin de Longchamp, and Breeders' Cup Mile at 3. Attractive, well-made sort, rather leggy in training. Top-class miler, won only start at 9f, would probably have stayed 10f. Effective on any ground, showed excellent turn of foot. Sire of: King Of Happiness (Gr3), Quad's Melody (Gr3), Ancient World (Premio Vittorio di Capua-Gr1), Echoes In Eternity (Gr2), Spinola (Gr2).

Dam **Headline**

Did not race. Well-bred half-sister to Gr1 winners Dunbeath (by Grey Dawn) and Saratoga Six (by Alydar). Dam of: Dubai Moon (1998 c by Seattle Slew; placed), Jilbab (1999 f by A.P. Indy; Gr1 winner), Ancient World (2000 g by Spinning World; Gr1 winner), Bandeau (2001 f by Quiet American; unraced), World Music (2002 f by Dixieland Band; placed). She has a yearling colt by Old Trieste.

Pedigree assessment

Lightly raced, and seemingly on the upgrade, when he joined Godolphin, Ancient World did not make the expected progress straight away, but after his defeat at odds-on in a Nottingham Listed event an effective remedy was found. Following castration he won three out of four, reaching a new peak in his final start, when successful in a Group 1 mile in Milan. Nobody aware of what an unpleasant character his sire has become at stud would be surprised at the need to correct Ancient World's attitude, but the evident success of the surgery raises hopes that the gelding will be competitive in Pattern company between a mile and ten furlongs for a few seasons to come. He is the best in these parts by Spinning World, whose reputation is somewhat higher in Australia. *TM*

Antonius Pius (USA)

3yo bay colt **121**

Danzig (USA) - Catchascatchcan (Pursuit Of Love)

Owner M Tabor & Mrs John Magnier

Trainer A P O'Brien

Breeder Dr T Ryan

Career: **11** starts won **2** second **1** third **2** **£316,896** win and place

By Daniel Hill

HORSES as naturally talented as Antonius Pius are few and far between. What a shame that he should squander his gift so wilfully. Take his Breeders' Cup Mile second for example. It was typical of him. Although many would have conceded that he probably had it in him to win the race if only he would consent to put his best foot forward, he had by then suffered such an exasperating run of defeats that few would stand for him any longer. He was 31-1 on the Pari-Mutuel.

Yet for a moment or two it looked as if he might just pull it off. Having been held up by Jamie Spencer, the horse weaved his way through the field and went after Singletary in the short Lone Star Park straight. His challenge gathered the momentum to win, but as he got to the leader's quarters well inside the final furlong he jinked and threw his chance away. Spencer had given him one crack too many, and the colt wasn't having it. Spencer admitted afterwards: "I should have won. I gave him two cracks to get him running, but if I rode the race again I wouldn't have given him a third because he jinked. He has so much ability – as much as any horse I've ridden. You have to get into his head. It's a mental problem."

There had been a hint of what was to come on his seasonal reappearance, when Antonius Pius finished a length second behind American Post in Longchamp's one-mile Prix de Fontainebleau, but was demoted to last of four for hanging right under pressure and hampering Blackdoun and Diamond Green. Spencer was given a four-day suspension.

Then, three weeks later in the Poule d'Essai des Poulains, the French 2,000 Guineas, things went from bad to worse. Although a 9-1 chance in a seven-runner field dominated by American Post at 4-11, Antonius Pius found room in the straight and quickened impressively to lead inside the final furlong. Then, just 60 yards from the post, he veered violently to the right and hit the running rail, interfering with Byron and, again, Diamond

Antonius Pius almost puts Jamie Spencer over the rail as he throws away the French Guineas in dramatic style

Green. He couldn't recover, and finished fifth. To add salt into the wound, Spencer was stood down for six days for not keeping straight, although it's hard to know what he might have done to prevent such a sudden deviation. The race went to American Post.

Next stop was the St James's Palace Stakes. Aidan O'Brien was having a trying time on more than one front, but things, surely, could only get better. With a tongue strap fitted for the first time Antonius Pius was preferred only by Haafhd, Azamour and Bachelor Duke in a field of 11, and for much of the way justified O'Brien's assertion that he travels like Nijinsky. Then, having cruised up to the leaders full of running, he found nothing when asked to go and win his race, eventually finishing a neck and three-quarters of a length behind Azamour and Diamond Green in third.

O'Brien defended Antonius Pius in defeat and voiced the opinion that a drop in trip would be beneficial, so it was on to the July Cup, a race he had already won with milers reverting to sprinting in 1999 with Stravinsky and two years later with Mozart. Although he was not disgraced, Antonius Pius never looked like winning and was beaten just over three lengths into seventh behind Frizzante.

With sprinting obviously not the way forward, Antonius Pius reverted to the top mile events. A visor was fitted for the Sussex Stakes, but he

2004   Race record

2nd NetJets Breeders' Cup Mile (Grade 1) (Turf) (Lone Star Park, October 30) 3yo+ 1m Yielding **121** 14 ran. *Towards rear, driven and headway approaching straight, disputing 4th straight, ridden to challenge 1f out, every chance 100yds out, no extra (J P Spencer), beaten ¹/₂l by Singletary*

9th Queen Elizabeth II Stakes (Sponsored By NetJets) (Group 1) (Ascot, September 25) 3yo+ 1m Good to firm **88** (TS 76) 11 ran. *Took keen hold, well placed, ridden 2f out, found nil and soon weakened (K Fallon), beaten 17¹/₂l by Rakti*

3rd Netjets Prix du Moulin de Longchamp (Group 1) (Longchamp, September 5) 3yo+ 1m Good to soft **120** (TS 93) 11 ran. *Held up in midfield, 6th straight, disputed 2nd inside final furlong, ran on (J P Murtagh), beaten 1l by Grey Lilas*

5th Cantor Odds Sussex Stakes (Group 1) (Goodwood, July 28) 3yo+ 1m Good **116** (TS 109) 11 ran. *Tracked leaders going well, not clear run over 2f out to just over 1f out, found nothing when in the clear final furlong (J P Spencer), beaten 4¹/₂l by Soviet Song*

7th Darley July Cup (Group 1) (Newmarket (July), July 8) 3yo+ 6f Good to soft **112** (TS 93) 20 ran. *Chased leaders, pushed along halfway, kept on (J P Spencer), beaten 3¹/₂l by Frizzante*

3rd St James's Palace Stakes (Group 1) (Ascot, June 15) 3yo 1m Good to firm **119** (TS 120) 11 ran. *Held up in last trio, progress on inner 2f out, switched left over 1f out, cruised up to leaders, ridden entering final furlong, found nil (J P Spencer), beaten 1l by Azamour*

5th Gainsborough Poule d'Essai des Poulains (Group 1) (Longchamp, May 16) 3yo 1m Good to firm **119** (TS 95) 7 ran. *5th straight, 6th and looking for room from 2f out, found gap distance, led inside final furlong, went sharply right and hit rails 75yds out, not recover (J P Spencer), beaten 1¹/₂l by American Post*

4th Prix de Fontainebleau (Group 3) (Longchamp, April 25) 3yo 1m Good to soft **109** (TS 93) 4 ran. *Raced in last, headway over 1f out, driven to go 2nd final furlong, hung right, ran on but no impression, finished 2nd, disqualified and placed last (J P Spencer), beaten 2l by American Post*

2003

11th Darley Dewhurst Stakes (Group 1) (Newmarket, October 18) 2yo 7f Good to firm **102** 12 ran ● **1st** Anheuser Busch Railway Stakes (Group 2) (Curragh, June 29) 2yo 6f Good **102** 7 ran ● **1st** May EBF Maiden (Gowran Park, May 14) 2yo 7f Yielding to soft **90** 3 ran

---

suffered traffic problems and again found little when it mattered, finishing around four and a half lengths fifth of 11 behind Soviet Song.

The visor was dispensed with for the remainder of the season. His third to Grey Lilas and Diamond Green, with Johnny Murtagh on board, in the Prix du Moulin wasn't a bad effort, but in the Queen Elizabeth II Stakes even Kieren Fallon's persuasive powers had no effect and he beat just two home after racing too keenly. Then there was Lone Star Park.

Antonius Pius is likely to stay in training, and Spencer has not given up on him. Speaking on At The Races a day after the Breeders' Cup he conceded that Antonius Pius is "a challenge" to ride and added: "Some day I hope I'll get no daylight until the last 100 yards and produce him on the line." Some day, perhaps, he will, but we shouldn't hold our breath.

Antonius Pius

bay colt, 23-4-2001

		Nearctic	Nearco
			Lady Angela
	Northern Dancer		
		Natalma	Native Dancer
	Danzig		Almahmoud
	b 1977		
		Admiral's Voyage	Crafty Admiral
			Olympia Lou
	Pas de Nom		
		Petitioner	Petition
			Steady Aim
		Groom Dancer	Blushing Groom
			Featherhill
	Pursuit Of Love		
		Dance Quest	Green Dancer
	Catchascatchcan		Polyponder
	b 1995		
		Mill Reef	Never Bend
			Milan Mill
	Catawba		
		Catalpa	Reform
			Ostrya

Bred by Dr Tony Ryan in Kentucky. $1.5 million Keeneland September yearling

Sire **Danzig**

Unbeaten in 3 starts (Belmont maiden at 2 years, allowance races at Aqueduct and Belmont at 3 years). Stocky, 15.3hh, with incorrect foreleg conformation. Off the track for 11 months between first 2 starts following bone chips, retired with slab fracture of knee. Had high reputation, but never competed with top-class horses. By an exceptional sire out of a tough stakes-winning mare (ran 42 times) whose grand-dam won the Oaks. In retirement at Claiborne Farm, Kentucky. Champion sire in North America 1991 and 1992. Sire of 21 crops of racing age, including Gr1 winners: Chief's Crown (x 8), Contredance, Stephan's Odyssey (x 2), Danzig Connection (x 2), Green Desert, Lotka, Polish Navy (x 3), Polonia, Qualify, Danehill, One Of A Klein, Polish Precedent (x 2), Shaadi (x 2), Adjudicating (x 2), Dayjur (x 3), Dance Smartly, Polish Patriot, Versailles Treaty (x 4), Easy Now, Furiously, Hamas, Lure (x 3), Petit Loup, Pine Bluff, Dispute (x 4), Maroof, Strolling Along, Tribulation, Zieten, Anabaa (x 2), Langfuhr (x 3), Yamanin Paradise [in Japan], Blue Duster, Elnadim, Military, Pas de Reponse, Yashmak, Agnes World (x 2), Golden Snake (x 4), Mujahid, Brahms, War Chant.

Dam **Catchascatchcan**

Ran only at 3 years, won all 4 of her races, each at around 12f, inc. Lancashire Oaks-Gr3, Yorkshire Oaks-Gr1. Tall, leggy, angular individual. Late-developing, high-class performer who progressed from maiden company to Gr1 winner in a nine-week career. Won on firm and soft ground, still improving when stopped by injury (hairline knee fracture). Well-bred. Sister and half-sister to 6 other winners, inc. Listed-placed Licorne by Sadler's Wells. By a high-class sprinter-miler out of a Listed-placed winning half-sister to 6 other winners. Excellent Plantation Stud family, responsible for Oncidium (Coronation Cup) and three consecutive generations of Ribblesdale winners. Dam of: Antonius Pius (2001 c by Danzig; Gr2 winner), Princess Zara (2002 f by A.P. Indy; unraced to date). She has a yearling filly by Storm Cat.

Pedigree assessment

We never knew what to expect from Antonius Pius during 2004, except, perhaps, some kind of disaster. Once he had thrown away the Poulains, it seemed inevitable that he would go through the season without a win, and so it proved. Only in the Prix du Moulin could he be said to have nearly done himself justice. Who can know the source of his quirkiness? His parents were both unbeaten, model racehorses. But breeding thoroughbreds was never meant to be easy. *TM*

Ask For The Moon (Fr)

3yo bay filly **110**

Dr Fong (USA) - Lune Rouge (Ire) (Unfuwain (USA))
Owner J-P Dubois
Trainer J-C Rouget
Breeder Mme Gilles Forien & Jean Francois Gribomont

Career: **8** starts   won **5**   second **2**   third **0**   **£131,257** win and place

By Robert Carter

PROVINCIAL trainers have become an ever more influential part of French racing in the last 20 years. Motorways have released them from a narrow regional base and that freedom has helped them to attract better horses.

Guy Henrot broke the Chantilly domination when training most winners three times between 1986 and 1989. No Chantilly trainer has topped that category since Andre Fabre produced 146 winners in 1988. Since 1990 there has been only one trainer at the top, Jean-Claude Rouget, who has sent out more than 2,800 winners in that period. The 2004 season was his fifth season with more than 200 wins and his best for ten years. It also lifted Ioritz Mendizabal to what appears certain to be his first jockeys' championship.

Ask For The Moon, the star of a team that also included other Group winners like Lord du Sud, Mister Sacha, Silverskaya and Star Valley, has an owner with a record quite as remarkable as that of his trainer. Jean-Pierre-Joseph Dubois is still driving trotters at the age of 64.

Dubois has been a professional since he was 15 and started training at 18. He has been champion owner, breeder, trainer and driver of trotters in France and has also trained and bred in Italy, Canada and the USA. He drove the 85-1 High Echelon to win French trotting's greatest race, the Prix d'Amerique, in 1979 and owned, trained and drove Hymour to win the race three years later.

Dubois was always willing to experiment but his opportunities expanded when he teamed up with Daniel Wildenstein, owner of the 1996 Prix d'Amerique winner, Coktail Jet. He was joint-owner with Wildenstein of the 2000 Grand Steeple-Chase de Paris winner, Kotkijet, and with Wildenstein's heirs when the horse won the race again in 2004. He also bred Super Celebre, runner-up to Dalakhani in both the Prix Lupin and Prix du Jockey-Club in the Wildenstein colours. And he also trains his own horses over jumps.

Ask For The Moon, right, wins the Group 1 Prix Saint-Alary for her provincial connections, by a neck from Asti

Jean-Philippe and Jean-Etienne, his two sons, are successful trotting trainers themselves and Jean-Etienne bred, trained and drove Coktail Jet. Jean-Philippe also owns Maia Eria, one of this season's best four-year-old hurdlers. All three have stud farms in the department of Orne, south of Deauville. Jean-Pierre-Joseph is at the Haras de la Brosse, Jean-Philippe at Haras de la Cour de Fresneaux and Jean-Etienne at Haras de la Perriere. Between them, they stand 18 trotting stallions.

All three breed thoroughbreds but Ask For The Moon cost €110,000 (then about £64,270) at Deauville. She was brought along steadily as a two-year-old, running four times before her first try on the Paris courses. She made her debut with a second at La Teste, on the coast west of Bordeaux, in August 2003 and was second again in another maiden there in September, before gaining her first success in a minor mile race at Lyon-Parilly in November.

Ask For The Moon started odds-on that day, as she did on her reappearance in another little race, over a mile and a quarter at Salon-de-Provence in early February. Southern horses hold a definite early-season advantage over their Parisian rivals and Ask For The Moon was the second leg of a Rouget

2004   Race record

7th Prix de Diane Hermes (Group 1) (Chantilly, June 13) 3yo 10½f Good to soft **104** (TS 94) 17 ran. *Held up towards rear, effort 2f out, kept on same pace from over 1f out (I Mendizabal), beaten 7½l by Latice*

1st Prix Saint-Alary (Group 1) (Longchamp, May 23) 3yo 10f Good **110** (TS 67) 7 ran. *Disputed 3rd, 4th straight, pushed along 2f out, headway to challenge 1½f out, led 150yds out, driven out (I Mendizabal), beat Asti by nk*

1st Prix Penelope (Group 3) (Saint-Cloud, April 9) 3yo 10½f Good **95** (TS 46) 6 ran. *Held up in 3rd, 2nd straight, smooth headway to lead 1½f out, shaken up to go clear 1f out, pushed out, easily (I Mendizabal), beat Super Lina by 2l*

1st Prix Gazala (Saint-Cloud, March 6) 3yo 10½f Good to soft **102** 5 ran. *(I Mendizabal), beat Agata by 3l*

1st Prix Jules Morgan (Salon-de-Provence, February 5) 3yo 10f Good 9 ran. *(I Mendizabal), beat Big Emotion by ½l*

2003

1st Prix des Orchidees (Lyon-Parilly, November 9) 2yo 1m Holding 13 ran ● **2nd** Prix des Fleurs (La Teste De Buch, September 14) 2yo 1m Good 16 ran ● **2nd** Prix des Sirenes (La Teste De Buch, August 13) 2yo 1m Good to firm 12 ran

treble when she beat Agata by an easy three lengths in the Prix Gazala, over one mile, two and a half furlongs at Saint-Cloud a month later.

Mendizabal, who had ridden her to both those victories, was again in the saddle in the Group 3 Prix Penelope, over the same course and distance in April, while Christophe Soumillon was on Super Lina, another filly in the same colours but trained by Yves de Nicolay. Ask For The Moon moved up to second before halfway and remained there until strolling to the front one furlong out. She scored by a comfortable two lengths, while Super Lina stayed on late to complete the forecast.

Ask For The Moon was favourite for the Group 1 Prix Saint-Alary at Longchamp in May. Mendizabal held her up in third but she was unsettled when the hard-pulling Australie went by and started to pull herself. She was fourth into the straight but soon switched out from behind Asti. She caught the front-running Super Lina halfway through the final furlong and was driven out to hold Asti and Agata by a neck and half a length. It was Mendizabal's first Group 1 victory.

By that time, Ask For The Moon had already been sold to the California-based agent Emmanuel de Seroux. But she ran once more for Dubois, finishing seventh, seven and a half lengths behind Latice, in the Prix de Diane. Agata finished well for fifth while Asti was ninth. Ask For The Moon and Latice were in rear as far as the straight but, whereas Latice was able to sustain her run all the way to the line, Ask For The Moon reached fifth at the furlong marker and then faded.

The plan was to send her to be trained by Laura de Seroux and to bring her back in the Del Mar Oaks on August 21. But she never made it. Instead that Grade 1 race was won by the 19-1 Amorama, an ex-French filly bred by Jean-Etienne Dubois.

Ask For The Moon — bay filly, 26-1-2001

	Dr Fong ch 1995	Kris S	Roberto	Hail To Reason
				Bramalea
			Sharp Queen	Princequillo
				Bridgework
		Spring Flight	Miswaki	Mr Prospector
				Hopespringseternal
			Coco La Investment	Coco La Terreur
				Great Investment
	Lune Rouge b 1996	Unfuwain	Northern Dancer	Nearctic
				Natalma
			Height of Fashion	Bustino
				Highclere
		Luvia	Cure The Blues	Stop The Music
				Quick Cure
			Lucaya	Mill Reef
				La Mirande

Bred by Mme Aliette Forien & Jean-Francois Gribomont in France. €110,000 Deauville August yearling

Sire Dr Fong

Won 5 (7-10f) of 15 races, inc. St James's Palace S.-Gr1, Prix Eugene Adam-Gr2. Also placed 2nd, 3rd and 4th in Gr1 races in England, France and USA. Consistent high-class performer, effective at 8-10f on grass and dirt, but best efforts at a mile on grass. Well-made, attractive sort, 16.0hh, with excellent temperament. Well-bred. Brother to top-class 2004 3-y-o Lucky Story. By a leading sire of major winners on both sides of the Atlantic, inc. Kris Kin, Brocco, Prized, Soaring Softly, etc. Dam Listed-placed winner of 8 races, half-sister to 5 other winners, inc. 2 at Listed level in Florida. Grand-dam winner, only foal of an unraced half-sister to 11 winners. Family of high-class US performers Summer Scandal, Esops Foibles and Mr Nickerson. Will stand in 2005 at Highclere Stud, Berkshire, fee £10,000 (Oct. 1). Sire of 2 crops of racing age, inc: Ask For The Moon (Prix Saint-Alary-Gr1).

Dam Lune Rouge

Ran only at 3 years, won 1 of 5 races. Also 4th in Listed race at Maisons-Laffitte, 5th in Gr3 Prix Penelope. Never realised promise shown in easy debut victory on heavy ground. Quite well-bred. Half-sister to several winners, inc. 2 Listed-placed and dams of Listed winners in France and USA, and of a Gr2 winner in Peru. By a top-class middle-distance performer who became a good sire out of a winning sister to Lucratif (Premio Parioli-Gr1). Grand-dam winner in England, half-sister to Le Glorieux (Gr1 winner in Germany, Japan and USA) and to Gr3 winner La Tritona (dam of Gr1 winner Le Triton). Third dam winner, placed in Prix de Royallieu. Same family as Tambourine (Irish Derby) and Nasram (King George VI & Queen Elizabeth Stakes). Dam of: Ask For The Moon (2001 f by Dr Fong; Gr1 winner), A Sinda (2002 f by Sinndar; unraced to date). She has a yearling colt by Mark Of Esteem.

Pedigree assessment

It was a shame that we did not see more of Ask For The Moon, who notched her fifth win in a row in the Prix-Saint-Alary, then ran close to that form when three other Group 1 winners finished in front of her in the Prix de Diane. She was the first top-level winner for her first-crop sire Dr Fong, whose repatriation from the States gave British breeders a chance to use a high-class miler with nothing of Northern Dancer in his background. The son of Kris S has made a good start, and it is no surprise that many of his early winners, including Ask For The Moon, have Northern Dancer in their background. In this case he seems to have pepped up a family that had not delivered a lot of class in recent years. *TM*

Attraction

3yo bay filly   **123**

Efisio - Flirtation (Pursuit Of Love)
Owner Duke Of Roxburghe
Trainer M Johnston
Breeder Floors Farming

Career: **12** starts   won **9**   second **2**   third **0**   **£781,848** win and place

By Tom O'Ryan

IT IS, as they say, an inexact science. And, for that, we should be truly thankful. If, for instance, picking and purchasing potential winners – and superstars – as yearlings merely consisted of relying on the best pedigrees, coupled with near-perfect conformation, then this game would quickly become very predictable, and would, as a result, be governed by those with the most money, in the privileged position to acquire 'guaranteed' success.

The fact is, it isn't like that at all. And, even more pertinently, because nobody knows – really knows for sure – just how talented an untried horse will become, the genuine fascination of racing, fuelled by dreams, will never fade.

Horses like Attraction merely serve to reinforce and vividly illustrate those dreams, and provide everyone involved in breeding, owning and training with true, genuine and undiluted inspiration.

Corny as it may sound, in many ways she is the British version of Seabiscuit, whose remarkable rags-to-riches exploits in the US back in the 1930s took America by storm; a wonderful story that has been resurrected in recent years by a best-selling book and a blockbuster film.

In authentic Seabiscuit-style, Attraction is hardly bred in the purple and, also like him, she possesses far-from-perfect forelegs and also has a peculiar and ungainly galloping gait. That she also returned in 2004 from a serious injury is another thing she has in common with Seabiscuit, whose future had been similarly threatened. And that's not all. The current star is a trailblazer, just as the American hero of yesteryear often was. And, it seems, both were blessed with lion-sized hearts.

Few will need reminding of Attraction's juvenile campaign. In a nutshell, she was invincible among her age and gender, gaining five straight wins, which included impressive successes in the Queen Mary Stakes and the Cherry Hinton. Alas, after the latter, x-rays on her knees revealed what

Attraction, legs splayed, makes a Classic comeback from injury with an all-the-way win in the 1,000 Guineas

her owner-breeder, the Duke of Roxburghe, has since described as "some quite significant bone changes," which, he added, resulted in one leading Newmarket vet advising that she be retired. A second opinion was sought, and the decision was made to carry on and get her sound, which was duly achieved, only for her to suffer a fracture to the outside of a hind pedal-bone a week before her planned return in the Cheveley Park Stakes, an injury that necessitated two months' box-rest.

That a question mark consequently hung, at least for a while, over her 2004 prospects, is obvious. But such is her remarkable story that she not only resumed her career as she had prematurely ended it as a juvenile, but went on to make history, as the first filly to complete the English-Irish 1,000 Guineas double. Add to that a further brace of Group 1 wins and it's easy to see why this extraordinary filly became the season's main Attraction.

She was first seen in public at three on a raceday at Ripon in April, in a six-furlong gallop with a stablemate that told us little more than that she was alive and kicking and, seemingly, bang on course for the 1,000

2004 Race record

1st Kingdom of Bahrain Sun Chariot Stakes (Group 1) (Newmarket, October 2) 3yo+ 1m Good **123** (TS 117) 5 ran. *Made all, ridden over 1f out, ran on gamely, edged left towards finish (K Darley), beat Chic by nk*

2nd Coolmore Fusaichi Pegasus Matron Stakes (Group 1) (Leopardstown, September 11) 3yo+ 1m Good to firm **123** (TS 104) 6 ran. *Attempted to make all, clear entering straight, strongly pressed final furlong, headed 100yds from finish, no extra (K Darley), beaten ½l by Soviet Song*

10th Prix Fresnay-le-Buffard-Jacques Le Marois (Group 1) (Deauville, August 15) 3yo+ 1m Soft **75** (TS 45) 10 ran. *Raced in 2nd, pushed along halfway, lost place over 2f out, weakened (K Darley), beaten 23l by Whipper*

2nd UAE Equestrian And Racing Federation Falmouth Stakes (Group 1) (Newmarket (July), July 6) 3yo+ 1m Good to firm **116** (TS 103) 7 ran. *Led, ridden and headed over 1f out, unable to quicken inside final furlong (K Darley), beaten 2½l by Soviet Song*

1st Coronation Stakes (Group 1) (Ascot, June 18) 3yo 1m Firm **121** (TS 121) 11 ran. *Made all, quickened clear 2f out, in no danger after, ridden out, impressive (K Darley), beat Majestic Desert by 2½l*

1st Boylesports Irish 1,000 Guineas (Group 1) (Curragh, May 23) 3yo 1m Good to firm **116** (TS 93) 15 ran. *Made virtually all, ridden and strongly pressed over 1f out, kept on well, comfortably (K Darley), beat Alexander Goldrun by 1l*

1st UltimateBet.com 1,000 Guineas Stakes (Group 1) (Newmarket, May 2) 3yo 1m Good **115** (TS 105) 16 ran. *Made all towards far side, ridden and edged right over 1f out, stayed on gamely (K Darley), beat Sundrop by ½l*

2003

1st Chippenham Lodge Stud Cherry Hinton Stakes (Group 2) (Newmarket (July), July 8) 2yo 6f Good **117** 8 ran ● **1st** Queen Mary Stakes (Group 3) (Ascot, June 18) 2yo 5f Good to firm **116** 14 ran ● **1st** Hilary Needler Trophy (Listed) (Beverley, June 4) 2yo 5f Good to firm **104** 9 ran ● **1st** EBF Carlton Miniott Novice Fillies' Stakes (Thirsk, May 17) 2yo 5f Good **91** 6 ran ● **1st** Harby Novice Median Auction Stakes (Nottingham, April 29) 2yo 5f Good **86** 9 ran

---

Guineas a week later. That trainer Mark Johnston was pleased with her preparation spoke volumes, and so did the fact that many of his staff at Kingsley House in Middleham had taken fancy prices about her clinching the first fillies' Classic.

Come the day, Attraction looked in superb order and took everything in her stride beforehand. She was opposed by 15 rivals, including Red Bloom, winner of the Group 1 Fillies' Mile as a juvenile, and Cheveley Park Stakes winner Carry On Katie, plus Majestic Desert and Silca's Gift, respective winners of the two key trials, the Fred Darling Stakes and the Nell Gwyn Stakes.

For all of Johnston's colossal success as a trainer, one of the traits that sets him apart from most others is his healthy insistence in allowing horses to run at an even gallop, usually up with the pace, and to interfere with them as little as possible. These trademark tactics were again boldly employed with Attraction, even though she had never raced beyond six furlongs and her juvenile style had consistently smacked of brilliant speed. While her

Attraction, right, wins at The Curragh to become the first filly to complete the English/Irish 1,000 Guineas double

pedigree suggested a mile would probably be within her scope, one wonders how many of Johnston's training colleagues would in similar circumstances have urged restraint, in an attempt to conserve unproven stamina?

As it was, Attraction, who was sent off the 11-2 second favourite behind Red Bloom, never saw another horse. Bowling along, but beautifully relaxed, at the head of affairs from the start under Kevin Darley, she did not need to be asked a question until inside the final two furlongs. Edging slightly to her right, she responded magnificently and, although her lead was being eroded towards the finish, she crossed the line with half a length and the same to spare over Sundrop and Hathrah, with Red Bloom a length and a quarter back in fourth. It was the North's first success in the race since Mick Easterby's Mrs McArdy in 1977 and Johnston's second domestic Classic, following Mister Baileys, who won the 1994 2,000 Guineas.

The victory confirmed Attraction's enormous prowess. And class. It was her sixth win in a row. Three weeks later, she made it a magnificent seven. And wrote her name into the record books.

In the 82-year history of the Irish 1,000 Guineas, eight winners of the English equivalent had tried and failed to achieve a famous encore. Attraction, though, proved the exception to that rule by becoming the ninth to try and the first to post this particular Classic double at Newmarket and The Curragh.

Once again, Darley elected to do his own thing. Soon in front, he allowed his mount, the 2-1 favourite, to use herself and, once again, when he asked her to pick up, she proved admirably willing, repelling the challenge of Alexander Goldrun more than a furlong out to win by a length. Illustrious Miss was two lengths away in third, while Secret Charm, fifth to Attraction at Newmarket, occupied the same position again, though beaten a little further this time.

The fairytale that was happening in front of our eyes was set to continue. Next up was the Coronation Stakes at Royal Ascot and a different challenge for Attraction, who was racing on a round course for the first time.

Johnston pooh-poohed any suggestion that a turning track would hinder her, his only concern being that a bout of coughing in his yard, which had affected some 45 of his horses, might also claim his stable star. It didn't, and, as predicted, nor did galloping right-handed lower Attraction's resistance to opposition.

Again adopting her habitual position at the front, she ran her rivals ragged, fractionally missing out on the course record, set by Russian Rhythm in the same race the previous year, in beating Majestic Desert by two and a half lengths. A head further back in third was Red Bloom.

The superlatives flowed about the winner, as well they might. Eight runs, eight wins, her latest three at Group 1 level. Most good things, though, come to an end, and Attraction's unblemished record was no exception.

In the first week of July, she lined up against older rivals for the first time in the seven-runner Falmouth Stakes and, in a nutshell, came up short. Not that there was any disgrace in being gunned down inside the final furlong by the year-older Soviet Song, also a proven Group 1 filly, who put two and a half lengths between herself and Attraction at the line in one of the fastest races run over the mile of the July course.

Johnston's gut feeling immediately afterwards was to wonder whether Darley had gone quickly enough through the first half of the race, while Darley, sure that he had, pondered on the possibility that Attraction may have been "a bit below par" and stated that she "just wasn't flowing". It was also later reported that Attraction, according to Johnston's wife Deirdre, had been "very heavily in season for a few days following the Falmouth" and that "while we are certainly not using that as an excuse, it is quite unusual for her."

There was, though, a valid excuse for Attraction's next defeat, in the Prix Jacques le Marois at Deauville. While many, if not most, of Efisio's stock appear to relish soft ground, Attraction, perhaps because of her conformation and unusual action, is plainly unsuited by such conditions. The ground caught her out big-time and she finished last of ten to Whipper.

Underfoot conditions were much more favourable the following month at Leopardstown for the Matron Stakes, and a rematch with Soviet Song, who had since added the Sussex Stakes to her Falmouth triumph.

On her first attempt on a round course, Attraction romps home in the Coronation from Majestic Desert, right

Once more, Attraction was forced to concede to her superior older opponent, but not without a fight. There was only half a length in it at the line after Soviet Song had made up a four-length deficit from a furlong-and-a-half down in what proved to be a rousing battle.

The pair were on a collision course to meet again at Ascot a couple of weeks later in the Queen Elizabeth II Stakes. But round three failed to materialise after Johnston, understandably fearful of asking Attraction to tackle unsuitable conditions again after her Deauville flop, was "horrified" to discover that Ascot intended to water on top of ground that was "only marginally faster than good".

He duly pulled Attraction out of the QE II, in favour of ending her season in the Sun Chariot Stakes at Newmarket on October 2. Again, he was frustrated by watering of the ground, which, following a further soaking by natural means, was less than ideal; officially good, good to soft in places for the five-runner affair.

Fears surrounding Attraction's ability to cope with the ground saw Chic, winner of Goodwood's Celebration Mile, sent off a surprise favourite at 9-4, with French challenger Nebraska Tornado, winner of the 2003 Prix

Back at Newmarket for the Sun Chariot, Attraction holds off Chic to land her fourth Group 1 of a brilliant season

de Diane and Prix du Moulin, a 5-2 shot and Attraction only third choice at 11-4.

Showing all her customary early pace against the far rail from the outset, Attraction soon had her rivals trailing. Entering the final furlong, however, Chic threw down a major challenge and looked, for a moment, as if she might succeed. However, Attraction is nothing if not a fighter and she battled home in typically resolute fashion to claim the prize by a neck, with a further one and a half lengths back to Nebraska Tornado.

It was a fitting climax to a truly magnificent campaign for this extraordinary filly, now the winner of nine of her 12 races; four Group 1s, including two Classics; and prize-money of more than £780,000.

In true Seabiscuit style, what Attraction has achieved reflects colossal credit on herself and her connections. And, like Seabiscuit, who also had to overcome adversity and injury, her huge talent is superseded only by her gigantic popularity.

What Attraction did for the 2004 season is, in many ways, impossible to evaluate. Even more exciting is the fact that she will be back for more in 2005. Something else for which we should all be truly thankful.

Attraction   *bay filly, 19-2-2001*

		Forli	Aristophanes
			Trevisa
	Formidable		
		Native Partner	Raise a Native
Efisio			Dinner Partner
b 1982		High Top	Derring-Do
			Camenae
	Eldoret		
		Bamburi	Ragusa
			Kilifi
		Groom Dancer	Blushing Groom
			Featherhill
	Pursuit Of Love		
		Dance Quest	Green Dancer
Flirtation			Polyponder
b 1994		Sun Prince	Princely Gift
			Costa Sola
	Eastern Shore		
		Land Ho	Primera
			Lucasland

Bred by Floors Farming in England

Sire **Efisio**

Won 8 of 26 races, inc. Horris Hill S.-Gr3, Challenge S.-Gr3, Premio Emilio Turati-Gr1, Premio Chiusura-Gr2. Also 3rd in Prix Jacques le Marois at 4. Smallish (15.3hh), lengthy, strong-quartered type. Best at 7-8f. Round-actioned, but effective on any ground. Inclined to get worked up in preliminaries, but always raced genuinely. The only Gr1 winner by his sire (high-class sprinting 2yo who did not quite fulfil expectations. Half-brother to Mountain Bear (G1 winner in US) and to 3 other winners, and to dam of Timboroa (G1 winner in Italy & US). Dam won 2 races, half-sister to 2 other winners. Family of Princely Gift. Sire of 14 crops of racing age, inc: Casteddu (Gr3), Pips Pride (Phoenix S.-Gr1), Young Ern (Gr3), Hever Golf Rose (Prix de l'Abbaye de Longchamp-Gr1), Tomba (Prix de la Foret-Gr1), Uruk (Gr3), Heads Will Roll (Gr3), Frizzante (July Cup-Gr1), Guys and Dolls (Gr3), Pearly Shells (Prix Vermeille-Gr1), Le Vie dei Colori (Premio Vittorio di Capua-Gr1), Attraction (1,000 Guineas-Gr1, Irish 1,000 Guineas-Gr1, Coronation S.-Gr1, Sun Chariot S.-Gr1).

Dam **Flirtation**

Ran only once, 5th in 7f maiden at Haydock as a 3yo. Tall, leggy type in training. Showed some promise on debut, though clearly backward and green. Failed to reappear. Quite well-bred. Half-sister to several winners, inc. Gr2-placed, Listed-winning stayer Carmita (by Caerleon). By a high-class 6-7f performer out of a placed half-sister to Listed winners Easy Landing and Lifting, and to the dam of Gr1 winner Lord Of Men and Gr1-placed Her Ladyship. Noted family of top-class miler Sonic Lady, descending from July Cup winner Lucasland. Dam of: Aunty Mary (1999 f by Common Grounds; winner), Attraction (2001 f by Efisio; Gr2 winner), Infantryman (2002 c by Inchinor; unraced to date).

Pedigree assessment

Attraction made fools of the conformation critics who said she could never make a racehorse, then did much the same with pedigree pundits who felt she would not carry her speed as far as a mile. She famously did that, to the extent of winning four Group 1 races at a mile, while taking on the late Persian Punch's mantle as the public's favourite horse in training. Her pedigree led us astray once, but we are inclined to trust it on the score of her prospects of training on as a four-year-old. Her sire Efisio was still effective at five, and he has had many representatives who have kept their soundness and appetite for racing over long periods, including notable mares in Hever Golf Rose and Frizzante. We look forward to her proving just as difficult to peg back in 2005. *TM*

Azamour (Ire)

3yo bay colt **126**

Night Shift (USA) - Asmara (USA) (Lear Fan (USA))
Owner H H Aga Khan
Trainer John M Oxx
Breeder H H Aga Khan

Career: **7** starts | won **4** second **1** third **2** £739,108 win and place

---

By Brough Scott

ALL THOSE years of selective breeding had definitely not been in vain. Azamour walked round John Oxx's collecting barn the morning of the Irish Champion Stakes in September the very epitome of a classy thoroughbred. That afternoon he would prove it.

He had looked the part from the moment he had come to Oxx's stables on the western edge of the Curragh Plain a good 18 months before. He had presence then, now his swagger suggested little short of majesty. Standing 16.3 hands at the shoulder, almost 500 kilos of gleaming, dark bay muscle, it was no wonder the guys in the yard were making him their banker that afternoon. But this would be only his fourth race of the season, after just two as a juvenile. Azamour is an example of the demands the Classic schedule makes on a young colt's mind as well as his muscles.

Azamour was lucky enough to be brought up in the Aga Khan's horse academies at Ballymany and Sheshoon, not five miles from his later racing quarters. At Oxx's they knew his family and were struck by his composure. "I have quite a few nice two-year-olds," said his trainer after Azamour kept his unbeaten record in the Beresford Stakes in October 2003, and then added prophetically, "but this might be the best of them." That meant that his colt was on the Classic journey.

But not this time what Oxx calls the 'Sinndar route' towards the Epsom Derby, as trod in 2003 by Alamshar. Azamour, being by Night Shift out of a Lear Fan mare, was likely to have stamina doubts. The Guineas would have to be his Classic. But with heavy ground conditions prevailing in Ireland he had to arrive at Newmarket without a trial race and started at 25-1. Nonetheless he was the John Oxx Guineas runner – when did they ever come over as forlorn hopes?

The first quarter-mile, as watchers will remember, was one of the most bizarre spectacles ever to masquerade as a Classic: the 14 runners spread right across the track in seemingly unconnected little groups, like novices

Azamour, centre, after two good Guineas efforts, scores his first Group 1 victory in the St James's Palace Stakes

in a point-to-point. Setting the stalls in the middle of the track was part of the problem but so too were the separate pacemakers for Godolphin and Ballydoyle, neither of whom were followed by their respective first strings. "It was a mad race," remembered Mick Kinane. "He missed the start, nobody seemed to know where they were going and then he took time to get going when the whole thing quickened up."

From a seemingly impossible position Azamour finished so strongly that he snatched third place, just under three lengths behind Haafhd, in a decent final time of 1min 36.64sec (0.56sec faster than the Racing Post's standard). This run inspired speculation that he might be Epsom bound, but Oxx was quietly resolute on the miler's route for the time being. "He didn't have the experience to cope with Newmarket," said Oxx, "but he buckled down really well so we were very hopeful that he would be spot on for the Irish Guineas."

So too were the punters who made him 6-4 favourite, and it looked as if they were about to collect when Azamour came to the front a furlong out in his expected duel with the Newmarket fourth Grey Swallow. There

2004   Race record

3rd Emirates Airline Champion Stakes (Group 1) (Newmarket, October 16) 3yo+ 10f Soft **122** (TS 87) 11 ran. *Held up in rear, headway 3f out, stayed on same pace final 2f (M J Kinane), beaten 3½l by Haafhd*

1st Baileys Irish Champion Stakes (Group 1) (Leopardstown, September 11) 3yo+ 10f Good to firm **126** (TS 126) 8 ran. *Held up in rear, 7th and ridden entering straight, 4th 1f out, ran on strongly to lead near finish (M J Kinane), beat Norse Dancer by ½l*

1st St James's Palace Stakes (Group 1) (Ascot, June 15) 3yo 1m Good to firm **122** (TS 123) 11 ran. *Tracked leaders, effort over 2f out, hard ridden over 1f out, ran on to lead last 150yds, driven out (M J Kinane), beat Diamond Green by nk*

2nd Boylesports Irish 2,000 Guineas (Group 1) (Curragh, May 22) 3yo 1m Good to firm **118** (TS 83) 8 ran. *Tracked leaders on far rail, 3rd halfway, 4th under 2f out, improved to lead under 1f out, headed 100yds from finish (M J Kinane), beaten 1l by Bachelor Duke*

3rd UltimateBet.com 2,000 Guineas Stakes (Group 1) (Newmarket, May 1) 3yo 1m Good **120** (TS 111) 14 ran. *Held up centre, headway over 1f out, ran on (M J Kinane), beaten 2¾l by Haafhd*

2003

1st Juddmonte Beresford Stakes (Group 2) (Curragh, October 12) 2yo 1m Good to yielding **109** 6 ran ● **1st** Pizza Stop EBF Maiden (Curragh, September 14) 2yo 7f Good to firm **97** 9 ran

had been no great early pace and for a moment Azamour was blocked when Kinane first challenged up the far rail.

But once he was switched to the centre he took Grey Swallow's measure, only for a flash of yellow to come up on the outside as Bachelor Duke snatched a poignant posthumous Classic for the recently deceased Duke of Devonshire. "He mugged us," said Kinane. "Azamour did everything to win and loved the fast ground, only for the winner to rush past us at the finish."

No disgrace then, but plenty of value when Azamour lined up at 9-2 for his next race, the St James's Palace Stakes at Royal Ascot. By now his trainer was "pretty hopeful that this might be his day", which in Oxx speak would make you rush for your wallet, even though the field included Bachelor Duke, Haafhd, the French Guineas second Diamond Green and the erratically brilliant Antonius Pius.

Early in the straight Haafhd took over from the pacemaking Castleton with Azamour, Diamond Green and the apparently cruising Antonius Pius coming at him. Kinane got a really gutsy response from his colt to take over and hold off the attack of Diamond Green, while Antonius Pius blatantly threw in the towel. At the line he had it by a neck and three-quarters of a length, with Haafhd only a neck away fourth.

Azamour had added another laurel to the Aga Khan's racing and breeding records and assured him of a new addition to the stud roster. Better still if he could add a Group 1 over further. "He's a lovely, big colt," said Kinane, very obviously overjoyed by this endorsement of his move from Ballydoyle. "He has the scope and physique to improve with racing as

Azamour, left, cuts down the luckless Norse Dancer in the closing stages of the Group 1 Irish Champion Stakes

His Highness's horses always do. A mile and a quarter would have to be a very serious consideration."

So York's Juddmonte International was targeted and Azamour duly flew in for battle. But so too did Yorkshire's August rains and a reminder of why the racecourse is known as the Knavesmire. Quite literally it was the "mire" where "knaves" were hung outside the city walls.

August 2004 did not have any hangings, but Azamour had struggled at home on the soft and Oxx was anxious not to flatten him just three weeks ahead of the Irish Champion. Azamour had his racecourse visit without the effort, but the run-up to that September morning was not without incident. "He got cast in his box," recalled Oxx, "and had another niggly problem with his back. We were still quite hopeful and in the event everything turned out fine."

Doyen had looked the best in Europe over a mile and a half in Ascot's King George and, with Godolphin pacemaker Millstreet to stretch the gallop and Ballydoyle's Powerscourt ready to attack, Azamour's stamina would be tested. After a good break and a fast opening section, Kinane took a decision. He dropped back last. He would keep his powder dry.

Up front the pace was hectic enough to ensure an ultra-rapid final clocking of 2min 1.9sec for the Leopardstown mile and a quarter. But as Millstreet gave way Doyen was already in trouble and it was the talented but exasperating Norse Dancer who swept through to duel with Powerscourt.

As Doyen folded, Irish Derby winner Grey Swallow began to fly up the outside. Azamour was behind him, and surely too far away. Into the final furlong and Norse Dancer was getting the better of Powerscourt with Azamour in pursuit. With 70 yards to go Norse Dancer had it, but Azamour was a hungry greyhound at his side and Norse Dancer didn't know where the winning post was. Hard though John Egan tried, Norse Dancer's ears flicked up in achievement. Beside him Kinane and Azamour bit hard into the turf and surged by to score by half a length.

Norse Dancer and Egan had covered themselves in glory but this was Azamour and Kinane's day. "I was thinking of his speed," said the jockey as he was led back afterwards. "I had planned to be handy but he has great speed. He has improved so much mentally and physically. I felt sure he would get there."

Azamour was now a Group 1 winner at both eight and ten furlongs. He would be such a perfect foil at stud to the Aga Khan's recent Arc winners Sinndar and Dalakhani that one wondered if his campaign would end there and then at Leopardstown. Happily it did not, and after a tilt at the Emirates Champion Stakes at Newmarket it was confirmed that he would return in 2005.

An autumn monsoon rendered the ground for Champions Day so soft that the apparently fast-run Champion Stakes took 2min 6.90sec (a full 5.64 seconds slower than standard). But with no further targets for the season Azamour was allowed to take his chance and, after struggling early on, he ran on admirably to finish third behind the resurgent Haafhd and pace-setting Chorist, beaten three and a half lengths.

"We found out a lot there," Oxx concluded. "Obviously he does not want it heavy, but next year we would not be frightened of softish ground. He is mentally very strong, so tough and reliable, he never let us down.

"He looked a Group 1 horse all along," he added in tribute. "He was outstanding, a terrific eater and had a tremendous all-round constitution, a real king of the herd. He improved all season. His Highness could see it in the paddock at Newmarket and we feel he has more improvement to come. He has such speed that we would probably stay at a mile and a quarter, but we would have a shot at a mile and a half towards the end of the season."

A fast-ground Arc or a Breeders' Cup Turf would seem the best options, and Kinane is looking forward to the prospect. "He's a great athlete, so full of life," he said. "He progressed very well through the season and if he was to improve another five or six pounds he would be a very serious horse."

For perfectly understandable stud reasons it is extremely rare for the Aga Khan to campaign a top colt at four. The change of policy with Azamour will not have been taken lightly. But it could prove as wise as it is welcome.

Azamour

bay colt, 8-3-2001

		Nearctic	Nearco
			Lady Angela
	Northern Dancer		
		Natalma	Native Dancer
Night Shift			Almahmoud
b 1980			
		Chop Chop	Flares
	Ciboulette		Sceptical
		Windy Answer	Windfields
			Reply
		Roberto	Hail to Reason
			Bramalea
	Lear Fan		
		Wac	Lt Stevens
Asmara			Belthazar
b 1993			
		Darshaan	Shirley Heights
	Anaza		Delsy
		Azaarika	Ribero
			Arcana

Bred by H H Aga Khan's Studs in Ireland.

Sire Night Shift

Won 1 (6f maiden) of 7 starts. Small (15.2 hh), quite well-made individual. A poor racehorse, evidently not very sound, or injury-prone in training. Brother to Fanfreluche (champion filly in Canada, winner of Gr1-calibre events in USA, dam of major US winners L'Enjoleur and D'Accord, and of Canadian champions La Voyageuse and Medaille d'Or). Also brother to passable sire Barachois and half-brother to the dam of Russian Bond (Gr2). Stands at Coolmore Stud, Ireland, 2004 fee €20,000 (Oct 1). Sire of 16 crops of racing age, inc G1 winners: In The Groove (Irish 1,000 Guineas, York International S., Champion S., Coronation Cup), Nicolotte (Premio Vittorio di Capua), Listening (Hollywood Oaks, Milady H.), Lochangel (Nunthorpe S.), Daryaba (Prix de Diane, Prix Vermeille), Night Style (Gran Criterium), Azamour (St James's Palace S., Irish Champion S.).

Dam Asmara

Won 2 of 10 races, inc. Trigo S.-Listed. Also 2nd 3 times (2 Listed), 3rd once (Listed), 4th once (Gr3). Leggy sort. Smart performer, successful on fast and soft ground. Showed progressive form at 3, stayed 10.5f well, but poorest effort only attempt at 12f. Quite well bred. Half-sister to Prix Ganay winner Astarabad (by Alleged) and to 6 other winners. By a leading miler and successful sire out of a Listed winner who is grand-dam of Gr3-placed Listed winner Anzari (by Nicolotte). Dam of: Arameen (1998 f by Halling; winner), Ahsanabad (1999 c by Muhtarram; Gr3-placed winner), Arawan (2000 c by Entrepreneur; winner), Azamour (2001 c by Night Shift; dual Gr1 winner), Arafan (2002 c by Barathea; unraced to date). She has a yearling colt by Sinndar and a colt foal by Selkirk.

Pedigree assessment:

Veteran sire Night Shift has made his name chiefly with sprinters and milers, but even as a two-year-old Azamour gave hints that he might prove one of the rare exceptions to the rule. Note that the best of those exceptions, In The Groove and Daryaba, who were his only multiple Group 1 winners until 2004, were proficient at a mile and a half, and it is easy to recognise why John Oxx has come around to thinking that Azamour is one of the exceptional, rather than typical, Night Shifts. The colt claimed some notable scalps in the Leopardstown Champion Stakes and again acquitted himself well, on unsuitable ground, in the Newmarket Champion. Don't rule him out if he lines up for a top 12-furlong event in 2005. *TM*

Azeri (USA)

6yo chestnut mare   **125**

Jade Hunter (USA) - Zodiac Miss (Aus) (Ahonoora)
Owner Allen E Paulson Living Trust
Trainer D Wayne Lukas
Breeder Allen E Paulson

Career: **24** starts won **17** second **4** third **0**   **£2,611,800** win and place

By James Willoughby

GAINST a backdrop of conflicting emotions, Azeri ran as hard as ever through her final campaign. She put serious injury behind her, but her return caused other deep wounds that will take much longer to heal.

In 2002, Azeri romped through a joyous season that culminated with victory in the Breeders' Cup Distaff at Arlington. Such was her dominance of the division that she was named US Horse of the Year, becoming only the fourth filly or mare to receive the award. Her every step embellished the reputation of Laura de Seroux, who herself became the first female trainer of a horse receiving this honour.

The tenor of Azeri's triumphant career was soon to become more troubled. It was announced that she would be sold as part of the remaining dispersal of the late Allen Paulson's bloodstock interests. His death, aged 78, in 2000 had endowed his son Michael with the responsibility of co-directing his trust fund, but there was much discord over the direction that this new concern should take.

Michael Paulson used the Horse of the Year acceptance speech to describe the acrimony that existed between trustees. He vowed to buy Azeri when she came under the hammer in March and to put her back into training.

The dispute over Azeri centred on Paulson's widow Madeleine and his three sons from a previous marriage, Michael, Richard and Jim. Fortunately, the parties reached a settlement and Azeri's sale was circumvented, with Michael becoming the sole trustee of his father's bloodstock interests.

And so Azeri's career got back on track in 2003. She returned in April to defend her title in the Apple Blossom Handicap at Oaklawn in the gamest possible fashion, trapped wide on the home turn and having to dig very deep to better the talented Take Charge Lady. She went on to add a third renewal of this prestigious Grade 1.

Azeri lands her third consecutive Apple Blossom Handicap at Oaklawn, on her controversial return to action in 2004

Azeri was clearly as good as ever in the 2003 season, and she underlined the point by reeling off three more victories, including her 11th consecutive Graded stakes win at Del Mar in August. In truth, she was barely tested by outclassed rivals, but the Grade 2 Lady's Secret Handicap at Santa Anita in late September would be a different matter.

Conceding 10lb to a talented field, Azeri suffered only her second loss in 16 at the hands of Got Koko, succumbing to her rival's powerful finishing kick close home. At the weights, it was a thoroughly creditable effort, particularly as she had missed the break, but De Seroux felt there was more at play. And the trainer knew best. Azeri had bled heavily into her lungs, despite the usual addition of lasix. She was found to have contracted a virus.

Azeri recovered in time to be trained for the Breeders' Cup Distaff at Santa Anita. A week before the race, she was surprisingly scratched, however, with her trainer initially refusing to comment.

2004 Race record

5th Breeders' Cup Classic - Powered by Dodge (Grade 1) (Dirt) (Lone Star Park, October 30) 3yo+ 10f Fast **113** 13 ran. *Tracked leader, 3rd on inside straight, one pace (P Day), beaten 9¾l by Ghostzapper*

1st Overbrook Spinster Stakes (Grade 1) (Dirt) (Keeneland, October 10) 3yo+ 9f Fast **116** 7 ran. *Tracked leader to straight, led 1½f out, pushed out to go clear final furlong (P Day), beat Tamweel by 3l*

2nd Personal Ensign Handicap (Grade 1) (Dirt) (Saratoga, August 27) 3yo+ 10f Fast **118** 5 ran. *Tracked leaders, led 3f out to distance, unable to quicken inside final furlong (P Day), beaten 1¼l by Storm Flag Flying*

1st Go For Wand Handicap (Grade 1) (Saratoga, August 1) 3yo+ 9f Fast **124** 5 ran. *Made all, driven out (P Day), beat Sightseek by 1¾l*

4th Ogden Phipps Handicap (Grade 1) (Dirt) (Belmont Park, June 19) 3yo+ 1m½f Fast **103** 4 ran. *(P Day), beaten 12l by Sightseek*

8th Metropolitan Handicap (Grade 1) (Dirt) (Belmont Park, May 31) 3yo+ 1m Fast **106** 9 ran. *(P Day), beaten 7l by Pico Central*

2nd Humana Distaff Handicap (Grade 1) (Dirt) (Churchill Downs, May 1) 4yo+ 7f Fast **120** 4 ran. *(M E Smith), beaten hd by Mayo On The Side*

1st Apple Blossom Handicap (Grade 1) (Oaklawn Park, April 3) 4yo+ 1m½f Fast **124** 6 ran. *Made most, ridden out, ran on well (M E Smith), beat Wild Spirit by 1½l*

2003

2nd Lady's Secret Breeders' Cup Handicap (Grade 2) (Santa Anita, September 28) 3yo+ 1m½f Fast **125** 6 ran ● **1st** Clement L Hirsch Handicap (Grade 2) (Del Mar, August 10) 3yo+ 1m½f Fast **125** 5 ran ● **1st** Vanity Handicap (Grade 1) (Dirt) (Hollywood Park, June 21) 3yo+ 9f Fast **125** 7 ran ● **1st** Milady Breeders' Cup Handicap (Grade 1) (Dirt) (Hollywood Park, May 24) 3yo+ 1m½f Fast **125** 6 ran ● **1st** Apple Blossom Handicap (Grade 1) (Oaklawn Park, April 5) 4yo+ 1m½f Fast **123** 7 ran

Other runs

2002 **1st** Breeders' Cup Distaff (Grade 1) (Arlington, October 26) 3yo+ 9f Fast **127** 8 ran ● **1st** Lady's Secret Breeders' Cup Handicap (Grade 2) (Santa Anita, October 2) 3yo+ 1m½f Fast **129** 7 ran ● **1st** Clement L Hirsch Handicap (Grade 2) (Del Mar, August 11) 3yo+ 1m½f Fast5 ran ● **1st** Vanity Handicap (Grade 1) (Dirt) (Hollywood Park, June 22) 3yo+ 9f Fast **128** 5 ran ● **1st** Milady Breeders' Cup Handicap (Grade 1) (Hollywood Park, May 25) 3yo+ 1m½f Fast **127** 6 ran ● **1st** Apple Blossom Handicap (Grade 1) (Dirt) (Oaklawn Park, April 6) 4yo+ 1m½f Fast **119** 5 ran ● **1st** Santa Margarita Invitational Handicap (Grade 1) (Dirt) (Santa Anita, March 10) 4yo+ 9f Fast **114** 7 ran ● **2nd** LacCanada Stakes (Grade 2) (Santa Anita, February 9) 4yo 9f Fast 6 ran ● **1st** Claimer (Santa Anita, January 12) 4yo+ 1m Fast 6 ran **2001** **1st** Allowance Race (Hollywood Park, December 17) 3yo+ 6½f Fast 7 ran ● **1st** Maiden (Santa Anita, November 1) 3yo+ 6f Fast 9 ran

Paulson displayed much more candour. "I was very concerned to see two very fast works over the last two weeks, and her response to such has not made me feel confident that she is ready to compete," he said.

De Seroux broke her silence the same day to reveal that Azeri had been diagnosed with acute tendonitis in her left-fore. Suspicion that she might be ailing had been aroused when Azeri refused to go out for exercise, displaying completely untypical recalcitrance.

"Thank God we did not continue to run her," said De Seroux, her deep affection for Azeri once again apparent. "She now goes on to the next phase of her life."

In hastily alluding to a stud career as the only option for Azeri, De Seroux had painted herself into a corner. She could have little notion of the mixed feelings she would experience over the next 12 months.

When a trainer and owner display such public enmity, it is a pretty safe bet that they will go their separate ways. Paulson soon transferred all eight horses he had with De Seroux to barns on the East coast. Even more painfully, he announced in due course that Azeri had made a miraculous recovery and would race on – against the wishes of her previous trainer.

Enter D Wayne Lukas, undoubtedly one of the greatest trainers of all time, but a man certainly not unaware of his position within the milieu. In this case, his swaggering gait and cowboy apparel equipped him neatly for the role of the bad sheriff, though in taking on the training of Azeri he was doing nothing more sinister than his job.

The next phase of Azeri's life turned out to be the most controversial. Race on she did, through seven straight Grade 1s on the road to the latest Breeders' Cup. As well as the Apple Blossom, she picked up the Go For Wand at Saratoga and the Spinster at Keeneland, inflicting an inspired defeat on her biggest rival Sightseek in the former.

In the first half of the season, Lukas attracted consternation with his idiosyncratic placing of the champion mare. Three consecutive defeats, including one over seven furlongs and another against males, led critics to suggest that Azeri's reputation was being cast to the wind.

Though arguably not the same athletic force as in her prime, Azeri was still just as strong in spirit. Victory in the Spinster – her 11th in Grade 1 company – invoked such a positive reaction that even some of those staunchly opposed to her return began to wonder if it was such an unfeeling decision after all.

But, if Paulson and Lukas had begun to divest themselves of their villainous mantle in the eyes of their opponents, their next decision was to cloak them with permanent antipathy: rather than the Breeders' Cup Distaff, Azeri was to contest the Classic at Lone Star Park.

No matter how this move was portrayed as a sporting gesture, it did not convince the majority that it was not a betrayal of Azeri's cause. The Distaff was perceived to be a fitting coronation for Azeri, ranging opponents at her that should make easy meat. Instead, it was contended, Azeri had effectively been thrown to the wolves.

De Seroux featured in a television interview during the preamble to the Breeders' Cup in which she discussed her feelings about Azeri. While outwardly philosophical, it was not difficult to discern that she had experienced a good deal of anguish over the fate of her star pupil being in other people's hands.

Azeri's only previous try at the Classic distance of a mile and a quarter had strongly suggested that she did not stay, but her connections took the view that she had been ridden with too much aggression. Consequently, her jockey Pat Day elected to keep her away from the lead in the early stages of the Classic, but the decision backfired.

It is extremely doubtful that Azeri could have troubled either Ghostzapper or the runner-up Roses In May, but the early pace was tepid for such a high-class contest and Azeri might have done better if allowed to stride on. In the event, she never got near to making a significant challenge, and it was all that she could do to hang on to a respectable fifth.

They say it is not over until the fat lady sings, or, in this case, the tycoon's son relents. At the time of writing, Azeri was due to have two more outings before retiring to the paddocks in March, which should swell her owner's coffers even further beyond the $4 million mark. She is already the record holder for earnings by a US female racehorse.

This achievement brought about a posthumous double for Allen Paulson, for he also raced the money leader among males – Cigar, the Horse of the Year in 1995 and '96 and winner of $9.9 million. The familiar stars-and-stripes colours were also carried by many other equine luminaries, among them Breeders' Cup winners Ajina, Arazi, Eliza, Escena, Fraise, Opening Verse and Theatrical. Perhaps the most famous among these in Europe is Arazi, whose sensational victory in the 1991 Juvenile at Churchill Downs cut one of the abiding images of Breeders' Cup history.

The combined efforts of this roster of champions have resulted in Paulson being the leading owner/breeder in the 21-year history of the event. He did not live to see Azeri race, but she represents a typical product of the disparate threads brought together in many of his pedigrees.

Azeri's sire Jade Hunter was purchased from Sheikh Mohammed and developed into a top-class dirt horse, while her dam Zodiac Miss was bred in Australia and had limited racing ability. To add to the mix, Zodiac Miss is by Ahonoora, a high-class sprinter in Britain at the end of the 1970s.

Azeri was named after a checkpoint and commemorates her late breeder's passion for aviation. Paulson founded the Gulfstream Aeronautical Corporation, which constructed planes in which he himself set 35 world records.

It is to be hoped that the hurt caused by Azeri's prolonged career can be salved when she retires, so that everyone involved with her is untroubled by their memory. After all, great racehorses like her are supposed to bring people together.

Azeri   *chestnut mare, 6-5-1998*

		Raise A Native	Native Dancer / Raise You
	Mr Prospector		
		Gold Digger	Nashua / Sequence
Jade Hunter ch 1984			
		Pharly	Lyphard / Comely
	Jadana		
		Janina	Match / Jennifer
		Lorenzaccio	Klairon / Phoenissa
	Ahonoora		
		Helen Nichols	Martial / Quaker Girl
Zodiac Miss ch 1989			
		Try My Best	Northern Dancer / Sex Appeal
	Capriconia		
		Franconia	Rheingold / Miss Glasso

Bred by Allen Paulson in US. $110,000 (retained) Keeneland September yearling

Sire Jade Hunter

Won 6 of 14 starts from 2 to 4. At 2, unplaced in 3 starts in Britain. At 3 in North America, won 4 (6-7f) of 9 starts, also 2nd Widener H-Gr1, Seminole H-Gr2. At 4, won both starts (Gulfstream Park H-Gr1, Donn H-Gr1). By outstanding sire out of US stakes-winning half-sister to Dewhurst Stakes winner Monteverdi. Stands at Hill 'n' Dale Farm in Kentucky, 2004 fee $10,000. Oldest progeny 14, sire of (northern hemisphere foals): AP Grand Prix (JapGr3), Diazo (Strub S-Gr1, Pegasus H-Gr1), Stuka (Santa Anita H-Gr1), Jade Flush (Gr2), Yagli (Manhattan H-Gr1, United Nations H-Gr1), Halory Hunter (Gr2), Jadada (Gr3), Pratella (Gr3), Azeri (Breeders' Cup Distaff-G1, Apple Blossom H-G1 [three times], Santa Margarita Invitational-G1, Vanity H-G1 [twice], Milady BCH-G1 [twice], Go For Wand H-G1, Spinster S-G1), Foufa's Warrior (Gr3), Midway Road (Gr3).

Dam Zodiac Miss

Won 3 of 9 starts in Australia and North America. In Australia, won 2 stakes (5-6f), inc. Gr3 event at 2. In US, 2nd once from 2 starts at 4. By top-class British sprinter and very good sire of 2yos, sprinters and milers who formerly shuttled to Australia. Dam unraced, very closely related to dam of Breeders' Cup Mile winner Silic. Dam of: Simon Bray (1997 c by Blushing John; unraced), Azeri (1998 f by Jade Hunter; Breeders' Cup Distaff-G1, Apple Blossom H-G1 three times, Santa Margarita Invitational-G1, Vanity H-G1 twice, Milady BCH-G1 twice, Go For Wand H-G1, Spinster S-G1). Died 1999 (along with Theatrical filly foal, both struck by lightning).

Pedigree asssessment

The highest distaff earner in North American history. Her sire, who was unplaced for Henry Cecil at two in 1986, was very progressive and Azeri has taken after him. She excelled on dirt, but on pedigree she had a fair chance of acting on turf. Hopefully when she eventually goes to stud she will have better fortune than her dam and grand-dam, both of whom had few surviving foals. Her sire Jade Hunter is maternal grandsire of the 2004 Arlington Million winner Kicken Kris. *JH*

Bachelor Duke (USA)

3yo bay colt   **120**

Miswaki (USA) - Gossamer (USA) (Seattle Slew (USA))

Owner Exors of the late Duke of Devonshire

Trainer J A R Toller

Breeder Airlie Stud

Career: **6** starts   won **1** | second **0** | third **2** **£183,194** win and place

By Nicholas Godfrey

RUMOURS of the decline of the British aristocracy have been greatly exaggerated if evidence from the Turf in 2004 is anything to go by. A notable feature of the Flat season was the re-emergence at the top level of members of the nobility, mainly thanks to the exploits of those admirable fillies Attraction and Ouija Board, owned respectively by the Duke of Roxburghe and Lord Derby.

Bachelor Duke also did his bit. The Irish 2,000 Guineas winner carried the famous straw silks of the Duke of Devonshire, best known in racing circles as the owner of Park Top. (And for flicking the French crowds a V-sign when they booed his illustrious mare after she was beaten at Longchamp.)

Bachelor Duke's victory at The Curragh – where he became the first maiden to win a major European Classic since Sun Princess in the 1983 Oaks – was also a first Classic win for both trainer James Toller, in his 24th year with a licence, and rider Seb Sanders, signalling his arrival in the big time early in his first season as Sir Mark Prescott's stable jockey.

It would also have been the Duke of Devonshire's first Classic win, and his first Group 1 win of any kind since Compton Place's July Cup in 1997. However, Bachelor Duke's courteous, sporting owner was not there to witness it, Andrew Devonshire having died at the age of 84 less than three weeks earlier, after his colt had finished seventh in the Newmarket Guineas on his seasonal debut. The title passed to his son and heir Lord Hartington, former BHB chairman and the Queen's representative at Ascot; the official winning owner of the Irish Classic went down in the record books as the "Exors of the late Duke of Devonshire". Little wonder, then, that there were tears in the unsaddling enclosure, where the Duke's daughter Sophie said: "I hope he was watching on celestial TV – he would have been absolutely thrilled!"

Bachelor Duke makes the sole win of his career a big one by swooping fast and late in the Irish 2,000 Guineas

A son of Miswaki bought at Goffs by the late Joss Collins, the much-respected bloodstock agent who died in February 2004, Bachelor Duke's career had a somewhat bizarre shape to it. By the end of his three-year-old career he had only six races altogether, three during a promising juvenile campaign that lasted barely a month, and three more the following season when his active service was extended to a month and a half, the gap between the Guineas meeting and Royal Ascot.

Despite a generally progressive profile overall before his disappointing final outing, Bachelor Duke's reputation must rest on the Irish Guineas, his sole victory.

His seasonal debut in the Newmarket version augured well enough when, after chasing the pace for a long way, he finished around six lengths behind the winner, Haafhd. A maiden race looked a formality, but just before his owner's death a crack at the Irish Guineas was discussed and, with Haafhd an absentee, Bachelor Duke was pitched in against seven rivals at The Curragh.

He was sent off 12-1 fourth choice in a contest largely billed as a two-horse race between Azamour and Grey Swallow, who had finished third and fourth at Newmarket. But if the pair were to become Ireland's flagbearers later in the year, events conspired to make this Bachelor Duke's day. Firstly, he benefited from ground appreciably faster than

2004   Race record

7th St James's Palace Stakes (Group 1) (Ascot, June 15) 3yo 1m Good to firm **112** (TS 109) 11 ran. *Took keen hold, held up in midfield, ridden and not quicken 3f out, no danger after, kept on inside final furlong (S Sanders), beaten 4¼l by Azamour*

1st Boylesports Irish 2,000 Guineas (Group 1) (Curragh, May 22) 3yo 1m Good to firm **120** (TS 86) 8 ran. *Held up in 6th, 5th and switched to outer 2f out, challenged 1f out, led 100yds from finish, stayed on well (S Sanders), beat Azamour by 1l*

7th UltimateBet.com 2,000 Guineas Stakes (Group 1) (Newmarket, May 1) 3yo 1m Good **113** (TS 100) 14 ran. *Chased leaders centre, ridden over 2f out, no extra final furlong (S Sanders), beaten 6l by Haafhd*

2003

4th Darley Dewhurst Stakes (Group 1) (Newmarket, October 18) 2yo 7f Good to firm **115** 12 ran ● **3rd** Somerville Tattersall Stakes (Group 3) (Newmarket, October 2) 2yo 7f Good to firm **111** 8 ran ● **3rd** EBF Maiden Stakes (Yarmouth, September 17) 2yo 7f Good to firm **77** 15 ran

at Newmarket, and then had the race run to suit him, unlike the pair of horses who were later to collect Ireland's most prestigious Group 1 events over further.

The race began at a crawl with Bachelor Duke settled no worse than fifth before coming fast, late and wide with a powerful finish that caught out the market leaders, who were engaged in a private battle for supremacy eventually won by Azamour by half a length. Azamour, though, was only second, a length behind Bachelor Duke.

The victory seemed to leave its mark on what proved to be Bachelor Duke's only subsequent outing, when he finished down the field behind his old rival Azamour in the St James's Palace Stakes. Despite talk of both a move up to a mile and a quarter and down to seven furlongs, Bachelor Duke did not appear again. Much of Toller's string went down with an infection after Royal Ascot and his stable star was a late withdrawal from the Queen Elizabeth II Stakes, when he was said to be "slightly lame behind". He was put away for the season – later to be retired to stud – and so frustrated attempts to quantify his achievements with complete confidence.

Undeniably a talented colt, did he look so good at The Curragh in beating two top performers simply because he got slightly lucky? On the limited evidence available, it is tempting to suggest that perhaps he did. Taken literally, his defeat of Azamour and Grey Swallow would make him a legitimate contender for the season's top miler, which would surely be fanciful. Still, he achieved his career-best Racing Post Rating at The Curragh with a provisional mark of 121, which was later downgraded to 120.

That figure puts The Curragh form around 6lb below that of Haafhd's Newmarket success, but it is doubtful that anyone even remotely connected with the Duke of Devonshire will quibble. And who could blame them?

Bachelor Duke

bay colt, 11-3-2001

		Raise A Native	Native Dancer
			Raise You
	Mr Prospector		
		Gold Digger	Nashua
Miswaki			Sequence
ch 1978			
		Buckpasser	Tom Fool
			Busanda
	Hopespringseternal		
		Rose Bower	Princequillo
			Lea Lane
		Bold Reasoning	Boldnesian
			Reason To Earn
	Seattle Slew		
		My Charmer	Poker
Gossamer			Fair Charmer
b 1991			
		Northern Dancer	Nearctic
			Natalma
	Lisaleen		
		Lisadell	Forli
			Thong

Bred by Airlie Stud in Kentucky. €125,000 Goffs Orby yearling

Sire Miswaki

Won 6 of 13 races, inc. Prix de la Salamandre-Gr1, US Listed race. Also 2nd in Prix Morny, 3rd in Dewhurst S. at 2, 2nd in Fall Highweight H. at 3. High-class 2yo in France, smart performer on dirt and grass, just below top level, at 3. Small (15.3hh), but well-made sort, strong behind the saddle. Made little physical improvement from 2 to 3, but competed honestly in open-age company. Quite well bred. From the third crop of a horse who developed into a major stud influence, out of an unraced mare from a family of noted performers. 2nd and 3rd dams both major stakes winners. Half-brother to Northern Eternity (Gr2-placed, dam of Gr1 winner Eternity Star), Lone Secretariat (Gr3-placed), and Hope For All (dam of Gr1 winner Lacovia, grand-dam of Gr1 winner Tobougg). Stands at Walmac Farm, Kentucky; no advertised fee. Sire of 20 crops of racing age, inc. G1 winners: Papal Power (Hopeful S.), Waki River (Criterium de Saint-Cloud), Black Tie Affair (Philip H. Iselin H.), Breeders' Cup Classic), Misil (Premio Parioli, Gran Premio del Jockey Club), Umatilla (Karrakatta Plate [Aus]), Urban Sea (Prix de l'Arc de Triomphe), Marvelous Crown (Japan Cup), Kistena (Prix de l'Abbaye de Longchamp), Etoile Montante (Prix de la Foret), Bachelor Duke (Irish 2,000 Guineas).

Dam Gossamer

Won 2 of 15 races, both at 4 years. Also placed 2nd 4 times and 3rd twice. Unplaced only race on dirt, just a useful miler on grass. Well-bred. Half-sister to German Gr3 winner Miss Tobacco and to Japanese stakes-placed Road Ahead (both by Forty Niner), to minor winners by Mr Prospector, Woodman and Red Ransom, and to unraced dam of Listed winners White Gulch and Bodyguard. Exceptional international family. Dam of: Translucid (1998 c by Woodman; Listed winner on dirt in Germany), Allover (1999 c by Spinning World; winner), Kincob (2000 f by Kingmambo; placed), Bachelor Duke (2001 c by Miswaki; Classic winner); Trylko (2002 f by Diesis). She has a yearling filly by War Chant.

Pedigree assessment

Few colts with only one victory are awarded a place at stud, but Bachelor Duke might be truly said to have earned his opportunity, having broke his maiden in the Irish 2,000 Guineas, without any semblance of a fluke. He will stand at Ballylinch Stud, Kilkenny, and Irish breeders will surely give him chances; he is by one of the best Mr Prospector horses for racing in Europe, and comes from the family of Sadler's Wells. *TM*

Bago (Fr)

3yo bay colt **129**

Nashwan (USA) - Moonlight's Box (USA) (Nureyev (USA))

Owner Niarchos Family

Trainer J E Pease

Breeder Niarchos Family

Career: **9** starts won **7** second **0** third **2** **£1,113,364** win and place

By James Willoughby

LET us rewind to the opening few scenes of Bago's dramatic season and hastily spool through them, cutting them together starkly and with no conjunction. Everybody knows the denouement, but there is much else to explore.

It is Chantilly in June: the Group 1 Prix Jean Prat. Bago, unbeaten in four starts at two, faces seven rivals over nine furlongs. They go a good gallop with Bago settled in fourth. Soon after straightening up, the result is explosive. Bago powers into the lead and stretches clear, winning by three lengths.

Next is Longchamp: another Group 1 race – the Grand Prix de Paris over a mile and a quarter. This time, Bago turns for home adrift off a slow pace. Cacique, the horse that followed him home at Chantilly, is making a bold strike for home. It looks as though Bago will never catch him. Time is running out. Then the long-striding colt lengthens again and is well on top passing the post, despite the narrow margin of half a length.

Consider what was reported about Bago after this workmanlike success. "We went much faster in the Prat," jockey Thierry Gillet says. "The pace was not fast enough," trainer Jonathan Pease says.

Six out of six. The scene is now different, however, shifting countries and taking on an unfamiliar backdrop for Bago. Gone is the magnificent chateau, the thick woods, the windmill. It is York in August, the International Stakes, and the clouds are gathering for Bago – in more ways than one.

The rains come and the turf is left sticky. The early tempo is again slow, as in the Grand Prix de Paris. Then the field sprint for home, and Bago is caught out of his ground. Nothing has prepared him for racing in England. He just cannot cope, though he keeps on trying. He is only third at the line, a length and a half behind the winner, Sulamani.

The next race is the Prix Niel at Longchamp in September. Prospect Park strikes for home and Valixir follows, Bago is still getting into gear. He reaches full stride too late and is again third, a length and a quarter behind the latter.

**Bago justifies trainer Jonathan Pease's exalted opinion of
him as he bounces back from two defeats to land the Arc**

Now, the action can slow down. It is time to reflect, to put the above
in context. We have reached the Prix de l'Arc de Triomphe.

A horse of this profile does not appear remarkable; no more than a
respectable candidate for the Arc, you might conclude. But no proper
understanding of Bago – either his history or prospects – is possible without
reference to the human element.

Specifically, to Pease, an Old Etonian of capacious frame but diffident manner.
If one aspect of his personality has become clear to those that know him
only by reputation, it is his distaste for hype. Good horses have come Pease's
way and he has made full use of them. Spinning World and Tikkanen were
both successful at the Breeders' Cup; Act One won two Group 1 races and
was runner-up in the Jockey-Club before injury halted his career. You may
not have worked out they were special from listening to Pease, however.

Then this: "Bago is the best horse I have trained, by some way." It is
usually sensible to discard such talk. Given the source of this particular
recommendation, however, there was always a general sense of
expectation around Bago.

2004	**Race record**

1st Prix de l'Arc de Triomphe Lucien Barriere (Group 1) (Longchamp, October 3) 3yo+ 12f Good **129** (TS 130) 19 ran. *Held up, 9th straight on inside, switched left and headway 2f out, went 2nd 1f out, led final 50yds, ran on well (T Gillet), beat Cherry Mix by ¹/₂l*

3rd Prix Niel Casino Barriere d'Enghien (Group 2) (Longchamp, September 12) 3yo 12f Soft **117** (TS 116) 8 ran. *Held up in 5th, pushed along 2f out and headway to chase leaders, kept on final furlong but not reach leading pair (T Gillet), beaten 1l by Valixir*

3rd Juddmonte International Stakes (Group 1) (York, August 17) 3yo+ 10¹/₂f Good **123** (TS 96) 9 ran. *Tracked leaders, driven along over 4f out, kept on same pace inside final furlong (T Gillet), beaten 1¹/₂l by Sulamani*

1st Juddmonte Grand Prix de Paris (Group 1) (Longchamp, June 27) 3yo 10f Good to soft **113** (TS 71) 4 ran. *Last after 1f, 3rd straight and shaken up in centre 2f out, driven to challenge 1f out, led close home, pushed out (T Gillet), beat Cacique by ¹/₂l*

1st Prix Jean Prat (Group 1) (Chantilly, June 6) 3yo 9f Good to soft **118** (TS 102) 8 ran. *Raced in 4th, smooth headway from 2f out, pushed along to lead 1¹/₂f out, quickened clear over 1f out, ran on strongly, impressive (T Gillet), beat Cacique by 3l*

2003

1st Criterium International (Group 1) (Saint-Cloud, November 1) 2yo 1m Very soft **118** 7 ran ● **1st** Prix des Chenes (Group 3) (Longchamp, September 20) 2yo 1m Good **113** 7 ran ● **1st** Prix des Aigles (Longchamp, September 2) 2yo 1m Soft **98** 7 ran ● **1st** Prix de Bourguebus (Unraced Colts & Geldings) (Deauville, August 5) 2yo 1m Good to soft **94** 11 ran

After Bago was defeated at York, he occupied a position in the pantheon of racehorses nowhere near so exalted as the one his trainer had foretold. In defeat, he had run his best-ever race, meriting a Racing Post Rating of 123 which, although very smart, is not particularly heady.

Now, factor in the Niel: a similar performance visually but one of lesser merit. Where was this story going? It was now becoming a melodrama entitled "Bago: horse or superhorse?" and veering markedly from the ordained narrative.

In this context, Bago became one of those divisive horses that tends to be assessed by the racing public according to their faith in the experience of a horse's trainer. There are, after all, two ways to look at it: either a trainer knows precisely how good his good horses are, or else in making such an assessment he lacks the objectivity of a neutral.

In this case, the cynics – as some would refer to them – were left to pay the ultimate price, pari-mutuelly speaking. Here was a horse with good form on the board who had not yet been seen at his best. The common theme of Bago's defeats at York and Longchamp was pace. Or, to be more precise, lack of it. Gillet had already warned that the colt's energetic finish needed the oxygen of a strong gallop.

So now, having seen our hero at his lowest ebb, the stage is set for the payoff: the Prix de l'Arc de Triomphe, and deliverance day for Bago.

Bago needed a strong pace and he got it, from the Derby winner North Light, no less. And, if he alone could not be relied on to describe a tempo of mutual benefit to all, then why not add in the hoofbeats of the Japanese front-runner Tap Dance City?

Bago lengthens well off a slow pace to overhaul Cacique in the Group 1 Grand Prix de Paris at Longchamp in June

They went fast, very fast, and it told. While North Light clung on for fifth, the ones that beat Sir Michael Stoute's gallant colt were all at various removes from the front early on. In short, it set up beautifully for Bago, though he had to be a good horse to take advantage.

Gillet really excelled. He saved ground on the bends and turned for home about ninth on the inside. Without his mount changing gear, he was sucked closer to the front as the leaders started to tire. With a furlong to go, only Cherry Mix was in front of him. After the ravages of kicking for home off such a strong pace, however, the hapless leader had no semblance of a rally in him.

As Bago passed the line half a length ahead of Cherry Mix, he did so with a great deal of momentum – both literally and metaphorically. It seemed a moment when all the chaotic elements that influence the outcome of a horserace had aligned themselves in his favour. He got a strongly run race, a clean run round – so important in the Arc – and a well-judged ride.

Granted the stage to display his talent, Bago delivered his most effective performance. The field finished relatively compact – the first seven were separated by only around four lengths – and the winner achieved a Racing Post Rating of 129.

For the record, only those of Sagamix (126) and Marienbard (127) have rated lower among Prix de l'Arc de Triomphe winning performances within the last decade. Montjeu and Peintre Celebre share top billing on 137 within this period, while there are four others judged to have achieved more on the day than Bago and one, Helissio, much the same.

As ever when making these comparisons, it must be remembered that we are talking only about a single performance. Bago could go on to show himself the greatest horse to have won the Arc since Sea-Bird, for all that anybody knows now. Similarly, he may disappear into ignominy. Neither scenario should colour the assessment of what he achieved on the day, nor where it ranks historically according to Racing Post Ratings.

The fact that Bago recorded the second-fastest time in the race's history of 2min 25.0sec – 0.4sec slower than Peintre Celebre in 1997 – is neither here nor there when evaluating his merit. It does indicate that the ground was very fast, however, and under such conditions it is harder to express full superiority than on soft going. Mind you, that did not stop the brilliant Peintre Celebre winning by five lengths.

For most horses, victory in the Prix de l'Arc de Triomphe would be a suitable climax to their career. For their owners, the onset of riches associated with a lucrative stallion career might very well follow. For Bago, the Arc is not enough. As with so many of his top-class contemporaries, he stays in training in 2005 and promises to be one of the star turns.

While there ought to be more great victories, more opportunities to celebrate his talent, we have also learned something about his vulnerabilities. Specifically, he seems beholden to a strong gallop if he is to show form on a par with the Arc. It is likely that only when Bago gets into championship events, with their corresponding contentious pace, that the full extent of his capabilities will be apparent.

In the aftermath of victory at Longchamp, Pease was quick to absolve Bago of his two defeats. "Nashwans like good ground and it was soft at York. Then for the Niel, I possibly hadn't given him enough work," he said. While these factors were undoubtedly influential, together they suggest at a rather revisionist view of Bago's career; that his defeats were beyond his control. They also came about because he needs the race run to suit him. He is not unbeaten and not unbeatable.

One of the most intriguing questions for next season is whether he will be allowed to take his chance in the Breeders' Cup Classic on dirt at Belmont Park. Until his victory in the Arc, the same race at Lone Star had been his season-long objective, according to the pronouncements of his connections.

When Bago proved he stays a mile and a half – contrary to the balance of his pedigree – it rather moved the goalposts. Had he been sent to Texas, it might have been for the Breeders' Cup Turf. So do his connections still harbour the ambition to take on the best US horses on dirt? Or has the focus now shifted towards a second Arc? Anything is still possible for Bago.

Bago

bay colt, 3-2-2001

		Red God	Nasrullah Spring Run
	Blushing Groom		
		Runaway Bride	Wild Risk Aimee
Nashwan ch 1986			
		Bustino	Busted Ship Yard
	Height Of Fashion		
		Highclere	Queen's Hussar Highlight
		Northern Dancer	Nearctic Natalma
	Nureyev		
		Special	Forli Thong
Moonlight's Box b 1996			
		Mr Prospector	Raise A Native Gold Digger
	Coup de Genie		
		Coup de Folie	Halo Raise The Standard

Bred by Niarchos Family in France

Sire **Nashwan**

Won 6 of 7 races, inc. 2,000 Guineas-Gr1, Derby-Gr1, Eclipse Stakes-Gr1, King George VI & Queen Elizabeth Stakes-Gr1. Big, rangy individual and a superb mover. A tip-top performer from 8-12f, much the most impressive of his generation. Died in July 2002. Sire of: Wandesta (Santa Ana H.-Gr1, Santa Barbara H.-Gr1, Matriarch S.-Gr1), Aqaarid (Fillies' Mile-Gr1), Didina (Gr2), Myself (Gr3), Silent Warrior (Gr3), Swain (Coronation Cup-Gr1, King George VI & Queen Elizabeth S.-Gr1 [twice]), Bint Salsabil (Gr3), Bint Shadayid (Gr3), One So Wonderful (York International S.-Gr1), Elhayq (Gr2), Haami (Gr3), Rabah (Gr3), Special Nash (Gr2), Mistle Song (Gr3), Nadia (Prix Saint-Alary-Gr1), Najah (Gr2), With Reason (Gr3), Miss Nashwan (Gr3), Bago (Criterium International-Gr1, Prix Jean Prat-Gr1, Grand Prix de Paris-Gr1, Prix de l'Arc de Triomphe-Gr1).

Dam **Moonlight's Box**

Unraced, but is half-sister to Gr1 winner Denebola and Gr3 winners Snake Mountain and Loving Kindness, her dam's only other racing-age produce. Dam of Bago (2001 c by Nashwan; 4-time Gr1 winner), Million Wishes (2002 f by Darshaan; winner). She has a yearling colt, Wulimaster, by Hernando, and a filly foal by Selkirk.

Pedigree assessment

If we were to indulge in some self-congratulation over last year's prediction that the long wait for a second Nashwan superstar (after Swain) was over, we must confess that our forecast of stardom for Bago did not extend to a belief in his merit over a mile and a half. In fact, the stamina question was pretty much a toss-of-the-coin thing, for Nashwan held out promise of staying power, while the family of Moonlight's Box indicated a preponderance of speed. Our assessment did not seem far wrong when Bago failed his first 12-furlong test in the Prix Niel, but his smashing display in the Arc left no doubt that the trip was well within his compass. The season to come promises to be particularly competitive at middle distances, but Bago would seem a sound bet to add to his already impressive score of four Group 1 wins. *TM*

Bahamian Pirate (USA)

9yo chestnut gelding **118**

Housebuster (USA) - Shining Through (USA) (Deputy Minister (Can))

Owner Lucayan Stud

Trainer D Nicholls

Breeder Trackside Farm & Liberation Farm & G A Seelbinder

Career: **70** starts won **11** second **12** third **6** **£430,026** win and place

By Richard Austen

LACKING in cut-throat tendencies, Bahamian Pirate had built up the sort of strike rate that would have seen his namesakes forced to walk the plank. While 2000 had been a year of rich spoils – the Ayr Gold Cup and a Listed race among them – in 30 Group-race forays from May 2001, Bahamian Pirate sailed off with first prize only once, at Leopardstown in August 2001.

That year and the next, Bahamian Pirate was regularly involved in tight skirmishes and, with going on the soft side, he went close once in the July Cup and twice in the Abbaye. Sometimes fortune was simply not on Bahamian Pirate's side. In 2003, however, he finished at more respectful distances and was beaten favourite (once at 4-11) when dropped to two conditions stakes. David Nicholls, his trainer, later confirmed that Bahamian Pirate sometimes lost his confidence.

Jockeys come and go on Bahamian Pirate and a dozen tried their luck during a 26-race losing sequence. At the first time of asking in 2004, however, he won again. Less taxing opposition in that Class D at Nottingham in March had a lot to do with it and he took further conditions stakes at Beverley in May and Newmarket in July.

In a quiet way, Bahamian Pirate had regained the knack of winning. He was also probably back to his best form, on his day, because at Newmarket he beat July Cup third Balmont on good to firm. He was still making no inroads in Group races, however, including when the ground looked in his favour, and the final straw for many punters was long gone before the rain also arrived for the Nunthorpe at York.

In a 12-runner field, One Cool Cat threatened to be a class above the established sprinters, who were an exposed bunch with little between them. There was prolonged soul-searching before One Cool Cat was allowed to take his chance on the ground. The others had little to lose.

Bahamian Pirate, at the grand old age of nine, lands his first Group 1 success in the Nunthorpe Stakes at York

Those up with the pace included Avonbridge, Fayr Jag and Airwave; The Tatling, travelling well, and 16-1 shot Bahamian Pirate, pushed along but unimpeded, were in mid-division; second favourite Orientor was labouring a few lengths further back and favourite One Cool Cat, held up, had even more to do.

When One Cool Cat found his stride, it was too late, Aidan O'Brien blaming "the shock of coming back to five furlongs in that bad ground". The shock for many of those watching was that the winner was Bahamian Pirate. Having led about 150 yards out, Bahamian Pirate, in the words of his jockey Seb Sanders, "finished very slowly" but he had a neck in hand over The Tatling.

That Bahamian Pirate was easily the oldest Nunthorpe winner and The Tatling a seven-year-old gives a big clue that this was far from the strongest renewal. It was reflected too when Bahamian Pirate started 40-1 and 20-1 when mid-division in the Haydock Sprint Cup and Abbaye on his two subsequent starts.

He's no Long John Silver but Bahamian Pirate has reportedly had four operations on his joints and knees, helping to explain why he goes particularly well on a soft surface. He deserves lots of credit, as does Nicholls, for his still being on the scene when everything fell into place.

2004   Race record

9th Prix de l'Abbaye de Longchamp Majestic Barriere (Group 1) (Longchamp, October 3) 2yo+ 5f Good **103** (TS 100) 15 ran. *Always midfield (S Sanders), beaten 5l by Var*

12th Stanleybet Sprint Cup (Group 1) (Haydock, September 4) 3yo+ 6f Good **106** (TS 97) 19 ran. *Behind, not clear run over 1f out, soon ridden, stayed on, never troubled leaders (D Holland), beaten 6l by Tante Rose*

1st Victor Chandler Nunthorpe Stakes (Group 1) (York, August 19) 2yo+ 5f Soft **118** (TS 108) 12 ran. *Chased leaders, pushed along halfway, ridden over 1f out, stayed on well to lead inside final furlong, driven out (S Sanders), beat The Tatling by nk*

6th King George Stakes (Group 3) (Goodwood, July 29) 3yo+ 5f Good to firm **105** (TS 97) 13 ran. *Raced in midfield, ridden halfway, struggling after, stayed on inside final furlong (E Ahern), beaten 2³⁄₄l by Ringmoor Down*

1st Vibe FM Conditions Stakes (Newmarket (July), July 23) 3yo+ 5f Good to firm **116** (TS 108) 7 ran. *Scratchy to post, pushed along in rear, ridden and effort over 1f out, kept on gamely to lead final 50yds (K Fallon), beat Balmont by nk*

17th Darley July Cup (Group 1) (Newmarket (July), July 8) 3yo+ 6f Good to soft **100** (TS 82) 20 ran. *Slowly into stride, held up, never dangerous (K Darley), beaten 7¹⁄₄l by Frizzante*

10th Foster's Lager Chipchase Stakes (Group 3) (Newcastle, June 26) 3yo+ 6f Soft **59** (TS 56) 11 ran. *Chased stands' side leaders, never on terms (E Ahern), beaten 18¹⁄₂l by Royal Millennium*

8th Golden Jubilee Stakes (Group 1) (Ascot, June 19) 3yo+ 6f Firm **104** (TS 100) 14 ran. *Held up, switched right 1f out, never near to challenge (Gary Stevens), beaten 4³⁄₄l by Fayr Jag*

7th King's Stand Stakes (Group 2) (Ascot, June 15) 3yo+ 5f Good to firm **109** (TS 97) 19 ran. *Slowly into stride, headway over 1f out, not much room inside final furlong, ran on (Gary Stevens), beaten 3l by The Tatling*

10th Duke of York Hearthstead Homes Stakes (Group 2) (York, May 11) 3yo+ 6f Good to soft **83** (TS 66) 15 ran. *Held up in rear, effort 2f out, never near leaders (S W Kelly), beaten 12l by Monsieur Bond*

1st Coachman Caravans Conditions Stakes (Beverley, May 8) 3yo+ 5f Heavy **110** (TS 90) 8 ran. *Tracked leaders, effort approaching final furlong, ran on to lead last strides (K Darley), beat Bishops Court by hd*

2nd Freephone Stanleybet Conditions Stakes (Haydock, May 1) 3yo+ 6f Good **103** (TS 88) 7 ran. *Held up, headway over 3f out, led over 2f out, ridden and headed over 1f out, not pace of winner inside final furlong (S W Kelly), beaten 3¹⁄₂l by Steenberg*

4th totesport Leicestershire Stakes (Listed) (Leicester, April 24) 4yo+ 7f Good to soft **102** (TS 62) 11 ran. *Tracked leaders, ridden over 1f out, stayed on same pace (L Dettori), beaten 2³⁄₄l by Tout Seul*

4th NGK Spark Plugs Abernant Stakes (Listed) (Newmarket, April 15) 3yo+ 6f Good **97** (TS 62) 8 ran. *Chased leaders, ridden over 1f out, hampered inside final furlong, soon weakened (J P Murtagh), beaten 6l by Arakan*

1st April Conditions Stakes (Nottingham, March 31) 3yo+ 5f Good **101** (TS 86) 7 ran. *Tracked leaders, ridden to lead inside final furlong, ran on (J P Murtagh), beat Fromsong by 1¹⁄₄l*

Other major wins

2001 1st Phoenix Sprint Stakes (Group 3) (Leopardstown, August 12) 3yo+ 6f Yielding **113** 9 ran ● **2000** 1st Ladbroke (Ayr) Gold Cup Showcase Handicap (Ayr, September 16) 3yo+ 6f Soft **100** 28 ran

Bahamian Pirate — *bay gelding, 3-3-1995*

	Mt Livermore	Blushing Groom	Red God
			Runaway Bride
Housebuster br 1987		Flama Ardiente	Crimson Satan
			Royal Rafale
	Big Dreams	Great Above	Minnesota Mac
			Ta Wee
		Dolphins Dream	New Prospect
			Green Dolphin
	Deputy Minister	Vice Regent	Northern Dancer
			Victoria Regina
Shining Through ch 1989		Mint Copy	Bunty's Flight
			Shakney
	Solar	Halo	Hail To Reason
			Cosmah
		Sex Appeal	Buckpasser
			Best In Show

Bred by Trackside Farm, Liberation Farm and G Seelbinder in US. unsold $42,000 Keeneland September yearling

Sire Housebuster

Outstanding US sprinter, twice North American champion. Won 15 (14 of them stakes) of 22 starts from 2 to 4, notably Jerome H-Gr1, Vosburgh S-Gr1, Carter H-Gr1, Withers S-Gr2, Forego H-Gr2, Sheridan S-Gr3, Hutcheson S-Gr3, Lafayette S-Gr3, Derby Trial S-Gr3, King's Bishop S-Gr3, Swale S-Gr3. By Grade 2 winner and very good US sire, half-brother to Grade 2 winner Quero Quero. Originally stood in US, sent to Japan in 1999, repatriated in 2002, stood 2004 at Blue Ridge Farm in Virginia, fee $7,500. Oldest progeny 11. Sire of: Swing And Miss (Gr3), Midnight Bet (JapGr2), Bahamian Pirate (Nunthorpe S-Gr1), Compassionate (Gr3), Electronic Unicorn (Stewards' Cup-HKGr1), Morluc (Gr3), Reserve Your Heart (JapGr3), Secret Liaison (Gr3), Buster's Daydream (Gr2).

Dam Shining Through

Unraced. Very well bred, by outstanding North American dirt sire who died in 2004, out of a smart Irish 2yo who is a half-sister to El Gran Senor and Try My Best. Family of Domedriver, Castle Gandolfo. Dam of: unnamed (1994 f by Ogygian), Bahamian Pirate (1995 g by Housebuster; Nunthorpe S-Gr1), Alpine Mickey (1996 c by Crafty Prospector; winner), unnamed (1997 c by Crafty Prospector), Litigasion (1998 c by Miesque's Son; winner), Strong Hope (2000 c by Grand Slam; Gr2 winner, Gr1 placed), Houndstooth (2001 c by Grand Slam), Venetian Sunset (2002 c by Old Triste).

Pedigree assessment

Has emulated his sire in terms of toughness and predilection for sprints. Housebuster is generally regarded as a dirt sire, and Bahamian Pirate's half-brother Strong Hope is a high-class 7f+ dirt performer who has a $30,000 fee for his stud debut at Claiborne in 2005. But most of the top performers from this family in recent generations have turf records. *JH*

Bandari (Ire)

5yo bay horse **123**

Alhaarth (Ire) - Miss Audimar (USA) (Mr Leader (USA))
Owner Hamdan Al Maktoum
Trainer M Johnston
Breeder Rathasker Stud

Career: **23** starts | won **10** second **1** | third **3** | **£407,170** win and place

By Seb Vance

MARK JOHNSTON reflected at the end of 2004 that Bandari had completed a "very good" season, and four wins from ten starts, one of them at Group 2 level, is a reflection of that. Yet the one-time Derby hope still left many feeling he could have done more.

A talented individual but a real character, he promised to deliver a career-first Group 1 win on a couple of occasions, but never quite got there. A game defeat of Sulamani in Newmarket's Princess of Wales's Stakes showed what he was capable of. Yet while Sulamani went on to win the Juddmonte International and the Canadian International, all Bandari managed afterwards was two thirds at Group 3 level.

Sulamani admittedly had a 5lb Group 1 penalty to carry at Newmarket, but it was still some effort from Bandari, who was stepping back up to 12 furlongs, once thought to be his best trip, after regaining the winning habit with three wins in a month at ten furlongs. Perhaps the slow pace, which made the race more like a mile-and-a-quarter contest, was the key, for Bandari quickened impressively to win a duel with Sulamani by half a length and post an effort to rival the best of his career.

That win earned him a crack at the King George VI and Queen Elizabeth Diamond Stakes and, while it didn't happen for him there, the fact that he was sent off at only 12-1 showed how far he had come since his reappearance in the John Porter, when his 11th of 17 forced Johnston and owner Sheikh Hamdan into a rethink that saw the former St Leger third dropped back to ten furlongs.

It was a big step for a horse who many regarded as a relentless galloper without an apparent turn of foot but it resulted in a hat-trick of wins. Starting out in a conditions race at Newmarket in May, a weak race in which Bandari was the only Group winner, he won so readily that he was ready to roll again just five days later at Chester in the Listed Huxley Stakes. A tactical change was made here, with regular partner Richard

Bandari, left, wins a duel with Sulamani to take the Group 2 Princess of Wales's Stakes at Newmarket in July

Hills deciding to bide his time after a slow start rather than adopt the usual front-running tactics. Bandari swooped late to beat decent enough opposition with a surprising burst of acceleration.

Bandari stepped back into Group company for the Brigadier Gerard Stakes at Sandown, but Hills switched to Ikhtyar, also owned by Sheikh Hamdan. Willie Supple, the Sheikh's long-standing number two, took over on Bandari, and the pair prevailed by a neck after a terrific duel that saw them pull fully seven lengths clear of a decent field.

Three successive wins at ten furlongs encouraged connections to aim high in the Prince of Wales's Stakes at Royal Ascot. The lightning-fast ground was an obvious excuse for Bandari, who trailed in ninth of ten, but it was frustrating nevertheless, for Ikhtyar's third place confirmed that the Sandown form had been well above average for a Group 3.

Bandari did not run over ten furlongs again. Following his Newmarket defeat of Sulamani he ran a respectable seventh in the King George and then took third in both the September and Cumberland Lodge Stakes, far from disgraced in either, although beaten in the Cumberland Lodge

2004   Race record

9th Gran Premio del Jockey Club (Group 1) (San Siro, October 17) 3yo+ 12f Soft **95** 9 ran. *Soon tracking winner, 2nd straight, weakened well over 2f out (W Supple), beaten 15l by Shirocco*

3rd Barnardo's Cumberland Lodge Stakes (Group 3) (Ascot, September 26) 3yo+ 12f Good to firm **117** (TS 91) 9 ran. *Raced in 5th, shaken up 3f out, progress to chase leading pair over 1f out, hanging right final furlong, closing near finish (R Hills), beaten 1l by High Accolade*

3rd Pentax UK September Stakes (Group 3) (Kempton, September 4) 3yo+ 12f Good to firm **121** (TS 84) 4 ran. *Led until just over 2f out, not quicken inside final furlong (R Hills), beaten 1¾l by Mamool*

7th King George VI And Queen Elizabeth Diamond Stakes (Group 1) (Ascot, July 24) 3yo+ 12f Good to firm **117** (TS 86) 11 ran. *Settled in 9th place, ridden and effort on outer over 2f out, kept on one pace from over 1f out, never able to threaten leaders (R Hills), beaten 7l by Doyen*

1st Princess of Wales's cantorodds.com Stakes (Group 2) (Newmarket (July), July 7) 3yo+ 12f Good to firm **123** (TS 69) 8 ran. *Held up, switched right and headway over 1f out, soon led, ridden out (R Hills), beat Sulamani by ½l*

9th Prince of Wales's Stakes (Group 1) (Ascot, June 16) 4yo+ 10f Good to firm **101** (TS 93) 10 ran. *Pressed leaders, ridden over 3f out, weakened over 2f out (W Supple), beaten 13l by Rakti*

1st betfair.com Brigadier Gerard Stakes (Group 3) (Sandown, June 1) 4yo+ 10f Good to soft **123** (TS 77) 9 ran. *Tracked leader, led halfway, driven and joined 2f out, battled on well to gain upper hand close home (W Supple), beat Ikhtyar by nk*

1st Breitling Watches & Waltons of Chester Huxley Stakes (for the Tradesman's Cup) (Listed) (Chester, May 6) 4yo+ 10½f Good to soft **117** (TS 90) 10 ran. *Sweating, chased leaders, lost place after 2f, not clear run over 4f out, ridden and headway over 3f out, ran on to lead well inside final furlong (R Hills), beat Parasol by 1¾l*

1st Ruinart Champagne Conditions Stakes (Newmarket, May 1) 4yo+ 10f Good **111** (TS 62) 10 ran. *Made all, ridden over 1f out, ran on gamely (J Fanning), beat Private Charter by 1l*

11th Dubai Irish Village Stakes (Registered As The John Porter Stakes) (Group 3) (Newbury, April 17) 4yo+ 12f Good **90** (TS 78) 17 ran. *Soon led, headed inside final 3f, weakened 2f out (R Hills), beaten 17l by Dubai Success*

Other wins

2002 **1st** Great Voltigeur Stakes (Group 2) (York, August 20) 3yo 12f Good **118** 6 ran ● **1st** Peugeot Gordon Stakes (Group 3) (Goodwood, July 30) 3yo 12f Good to firm **123** 4 ran ● **1st** attheraces Sky Channel 418 Derby Trial Stakes (Group 3) (Lingfield, May 11) 3yo 11½f Good **118** 6 ran 2001 **1st** Tote Bookmakers Silver Tankard Stakes (Listed Race) (Pontefract, October 22) 2yo 1m Soft **113** 12 ran ● **1st** Carrick Architects EBF Novice Stakes (Ayr, September 22) 2yo 1m Good to firm **91** 5 ran ● **1st** EBF Journal Maiden Stakes (Beverley, August 15) 2yo 7½f Good **90** 11 ran

by the Princess of Wales's third High Accolade. At the end of a long season he was given one last chance in the Group 1 Gran Premio del Jockey Club but trailed in last of nine. Johnston had no excuse.

A career record of 10 wins from 23 starts is an admirable one by almost any standards, but that elusive Group 1 win looks as far away as ever. Perhaps another return to ten furlongs would help.

Bandari

bay horse, 29-4-1999

			Northern Dancer	Nearctic
				Natalma
		Unfuwain		
			Height Of Fashion	Bustino
	Alhaarth			Highclere
	b 1993			
			Irish River	Riverman
				Irish Star
		Irish Valley		
			Green Valley	Val de Loir
				Sly Pola
			Hail To Reason	Turn-to
				Nothirdchance
		Mr Leader		
			Jolie Deja	Djeddah
	Miss Audimar			Bellesoeur
	b 1981			
			Viceregal	Northern Dancer
				Victoria Regina
		Quick Selection		
			Lachine	Grey Sovereign
				Loved One

Bred by Rathasker Stud in Ireland. Ir£40,000 Goffs Orby yearling

Sire Alhaarth

Won 8 of 17 races, inc. Vintage S.-Gr3, Solario S.-Gr3, Champagne Stakes-Gr2, Dewhurst S.-Gr1, Prix du Rond-Point-Gr2, Curragh International S.-Gr2, Prix Dollar-Gr2. Also 3rd in Sussex S. and Champion S. Strong, well-proportioned, handsome individual, 16.0hh. Excellent mover, fluent and powerful in action. Champion European 2yo who did not rise to predicted heights, but acquitted himself well in high-class company. Wore blinkers 3 times at 3. Visored and heavily bandaged last (winning) start at 4. Appeared to stay 12f, but best form over shorter distances. By a top-class 12f performer, a half-brother to Nashwan who did well at stud and died in January 2002. Half-brother to Gr3 winner Green Pola (by Nijinsky) and 2 lesser winners. Dam unplaced half-sister to Green Dancer (by Nijinsky). Stands at Derrinstown Stud, Ireland, at a 2004 fee of €25,000 (Oct 1).

Dam Miss Audimar

Won 4 of 20 starts at 2 and 3 in US, including 2 stakes events at 3, also 3rd Boiling Springs H-Gr3. By high-class US performer and fair sire who is also broodmare sire in 2004 of top-class US 3yo Lion Heart, out of US stakes winner from family of Group 1 winners Park Express, Waky Nao. Half-sister to US stakes winner Charge My Account (by Majestic Prince). Dam of: Belle Of Kentuck (1986 f by Key To Content; winner), Express Account (1987 f by Carr de Naskra; winner), Noora Park (1988 f by Ahonoora; winner), Rosy Sunset (1989 f by Red Sunset; unplaced, dam of Grade 3 winner Evening Promise), Orry Main (1991 c by Don't Forget Me; winner), Diaghilef (1992 c by Royal Academy; winner), Gaily Eagle (1993 c by Mujtahid; stakes winner in Japan), Kilcora (1995 f by Mujadil; winner), Admire Missile (1996 c by Mujtahid; placed), Keltech Night (1997 f by Night Shift; unraced), Gold Standard (1998 c by Goldmark; winner), Bandari (1999 c by Alhaarth; Gr2 winner, Gr1 placed), Given A Choice (2002 c by Trans Island; unplaced), 2003 f by Fruits Of Love.

Pedigree assessment

Well established as a high-class 10-12f performer, and no reason he should not continue to do well. Alhaarth is relentlessly improving his standing as a stallion, with Haafhd his latest celebrity. That will do Bandari's future stud prospects no harm. *JH*

Birdstone (USA)

3yo bay colt **125**

Grindstone (USA) - Dear Birdie (USA) (Storm Bird (Can))
Owner Marylou Whitney Stables
Trainer N Zito
Breeder Marylou Whitney Stables

Career: **9** starts | won **5** | second **0** | third **0** | £902,713 win and place

By James Willoughby

YOU can take the horse out of New York, but you can't take New York out of the horse. Belmont and Travers Stakes winner Birdstone was a colt after his owner Marylou Whitney's heart.

Whitney is the matriarch of New York racing. The colt she bred landed the city's two most important races for three-year-olds. That he did not show his form on big occasions elsewhere was of little account to his owner.

Birdstone added his name to the list of Triple Crown spoilers when staying on dourly to defeat Smarty Jones in the 136th Belmont Stakes. It was rare stamina for an American horse that won him the mile-and-a-half Classic, and a fitting exhibition considering the bloodlines from which he descends.

In a nine-runner field for the Belmont, in which the market was dominated by the Kentucky Derby and Preakness winner at around 1-3, Birdstone was sent off at 36-1. His starting price sounds incredible in retrospect, but it was hardly surprising in the light of his inconsistent record.

Birdstone was a smart juvenile, putting a poor run behind him to land the Grade 1 Champagne Stakes at Belmont on the last of three starts. He was lightly campaigned in his first season by his trainer Nick Zito owing to his lack of size and power. As is usually his wont, Zito bypassed the Breeders' Cup Juvenile with Birdstone. The trainer, who has now won all three US Classics, including the Kentucky Derby twice, believes a hard race is to the detriment of an unfurnished youngster, and the statistics certainly seem to back him up.

Following a four-month break, it was a supposedly much stronger Birdstone who reappeared at Gulfstream in February. His abbreviated two-year-old campaign immediately bore fruit, for he was eligible for an allowance race confined to winners of no more than two races. This made for a soft spot in which to reappear, and Birdstone won with the minimum of fuss.

The Grade 2 Lane's End Stakes at Turfway Park was his chosen Kentucky Derby trial, but the storm clouds which gathered shortly before

Birdstone stays on strongly in the Belmont to overhaul Smarty Jones and foil his rival's Triple Crown bid

the meeting on March 20 were to prove an inauspicious metaphor. The track had to be 'sealed', or packed down tightly, and the resulting firm surface was not to the liking of the round-actioned Birdstone.

The Lane's End proved to be an apt dress rehearsal for Churchill Downs, though not in the manner that Zito intended. On another wet track, Birdstone again seemed to lack zest, keeping on steadily from midfield to finish eighth, more than 15 lengths behind Smarty Jones.

With his Derby dreams shattered, Zito now went to the textbook in search of Classic success. Missing out the Preakness and taking a colt into the Belmont fresh has proved a savvy move for trainers, and it was just the right decision for the delicate Birdstone. In beating Smarty Jones by a length with such obvious determination, he added another link to the chain binding the Whitneys and New York racing together.

Whitney's late husband Sonny bred and owned two Belmont winners, Phalanx in 1948 and Counterpoint three years later. The latter is the sire of Birdstone's fourth dam Honey Dear, while his third dam You All and second dam Hush Dear were also raced by the family. Hush Dear was sold at the end of her racing days, but Marylou acquired one of her

2004	Race record

7th Breeders' Cup Classic - Powered by Dodge (Grade 1) (Dirt) (Lone Star Park, October 30) 3yo+ 10f Fast **111** 13 ran. *Never a factor (E Prado), beaten 12½l by Ghostzapper*

1st Travers Stakes (Grade 1) (Dirt) (Saratoga, August 28) 3yo 10f Fast **125** 7 ran. *Held up in 5th or 6th, headway to lead just under 2f out, ran on strongly (E Prado), beat The Cliff's Edge by 2½l*

1st Belmont Stakes (Grade 1) (Dirt) (Belmont Park, June 5) 3yo 12f Fast **125** 9 ran. *Always in touch on outside, went 2nd 3f out, hung right distance, driven to lead 70yds out, ran on (E Prado), beat Smarty Jones by 1l*

8th Kentucky Derby (Grade 1) (Dirt) (Churchill Downs, May 1) 3yo 10f Sloppy **98** 18 ran. *Midfield, 9th 2f out, soon ridden and unable to quicken (E Prado), beaten 15½l by Smarty Jones*

5th Lane's End Stakes (Grade 2) (Turfway Park, March 20) 9f Fast 11 ran. *(J D Bailey), beaten 11l by Sinister G*

1st Allowance race (Gulfstream Park, February 14) 1m½f Fast 6 ran. *(J D Bailey), beat Sinister G by 11l*

2003

1st Champagne Stakes (Grade 1) (Belmont Park, October 4) 2yo 1m½f Fast **117** 7 ran ● **4th** Hopeful Stakes (Grade 1) (Dirt) (Saratoga, August 30) 2yo 7f Fast **104** 7 ran ● **1st** Maiden Special Weight (Saratoga, August 2) 6f Muddy 9 ran

offspring, Dear Birdie, the dam of Birdstone and 2003 Kentucky Oaks winner Bird Town.

Having already assured himself of a place within these annals, Birdstone gilded the lily by winning the Grade 1 Travers Stakes at Saratoga in August. If his Classic win had characterised him as a grinder in the eyes of many, this was a much more fluid performance. Tracking the pace in midfield and moving comfortably throughout under Edgar Prado, Birdstone stormed round the outside on the turn and drew away with tremendous power. He is listed as having beaten The Cliff's Edge by two and a half lengths, but only yards after the wire the gap between them was growing fast.

Zito confirmed that there were two keys to Birdstone's uneven form. Primarily, he had to be fresh, but it was also important that he could see daylight in his races and wasn't intimidated. Both factors were related to his lack of size.

With the first point in mind, Birdstone was prepared for the Breeders' Cup Classic two months later with no further outings. He first appeared at Lone Star with a bad skin rash, but this had no effect on the way he trained. Unfortunately, he was caught in heavy traffic in a tight race and once again ran well below form away from the New York circuit.

Less than a week later, Birdstone was found to have a bone chip floating in his left-front ankle. It would have required surgery to return to the racecourse, so Whitney made the decision to retire him.

"I would have to rank him right up there with the best horses I have trained," Zito said. "The heart he had was beyond belief."

Birdstone   *bay colt, 16-5-2001*

		Fappiano	Mr Prospector
	Unbridled		Killaloe
Grindstone		Gana Facil	Le Fabuleux
br 1993			Charedi
		Drone	Sir Gaylord
	Buzz My Bell		Cap And Bells
		Chateaupavia	Chateaugay
			Glenpavia
		Northern Dancer	Nearctic
	Storm Bird		Natalma
Dear Birdie		South Ocean	New Providence
ch 1987			Shining Sun
		Silent Screen	Prince John
	Hush Dear		Prayer Bell
		You All	Nashua
			Honey Dear

Bred by Marylou Whitney Stables in US

Sire **Grindstone**

Won 3 of 6 starts at 2 and 3. At 2, won 1 (5f) of 2 starts. At 3, won 2 (Louisiana Derby-Gr3, Kentucky Derby-Gr1) of 4 starts, also 2nd Arkansas Derby-Gr3. By Kentucky Derby and Breeders' Cup Classic winner who was very good sire, mainly of 1m+ performers, out of 2yo Grade 1 winner. Half-brother to 2 minor US stakes winners. Stands at Overbrook Farm in Kentucky, 2005 fee $10,000. Oldest progeny 6, sire of: Ommadon (Gr3), Ekolu Place (JapGr3), Smooth Maneuvers (Gr3), Birdstone (Champagne S-Gr1, Belmont S-Gr1, Travers S-Gr1), Organ Grinder (CanGr3).

Dam **Dear Birdie**

Won 2 of 20 starts, stakes placed in US. Sire top-class 2yo in Europe, sire of Storm Cat. Dam won 5 Grade 2 races and excelled on turf, also dam of US stakes winner Noactor (Theatrical). Dam of: Dear Proper (1992 c by Proper Reality; winner), Honey Bird (1993 f by Proper Reality; winner), Bird Cage (1994 f by Kris S; winner), Brave All The Way (1995 g by Cryptoclearance; winner), Dearest Gulch (1996 f b Gulch; winner), Cviano (1997 c by Rubiano; winner), Mountain Bird (1998 f by Mt Livermore; winner, Gr2 placed), Bird Town (2000 f by Cape Town; Kentucky Oaks-Gr1, Acorn S-Gr1), Birdstone (2001 c by Grindstone; Champagne S-Gr1, Belmont S-Gr1, Travers S-Gr1), So Long Birdie (2002 c by Pioneering; unplaced on debut), 2003 c by Silver Charm.

Pedigree assessment

An interesting stallion newcomer for 2005, when he stands at Gainesway Farm in Kentucky for $10,000. That fee looks modest compared to other stallion newcomers, in the light of his racing record and pedigree. His half-sister Bird Town was one of the leading three-year-old fillies of 2003, and his well-bred, top-class sire Grindstone has done fairly well at stud. Birdstone is well endowed with stamina and is likely to get mostly two-turn performers. *JH*

Blue Canari (Fr)

3yo chestnut colt **118**

Acatenango (Ger) - Delicieuse Lady (Trempolino (USA))
Owner Ecurie Jean-Louis Bouchard
Trainer P Bary
Breeder Meridian Stud

Career: **8** starts   won **2**   second **0**   third **3**   **£471,100** win and place

By Robert Carter

NOT for the first time Jean-Louis Bouchard and Pascal Bary won the Prix du Jockey-Club. Not for the first time, either, it was with a horse who did not progress.

But it would be wrong to damn Bary's great record in the race because of that. Blue Canari was his fifth Jockey-Club winner in 11 years. The colt had the stamina to outrun his rivals in the Classic and that's all that matters. Bouchard had already won with Celtic Arms (1994) and Ragmar (1996), neither of whom scored again that season, and he also owned a half-share in Dream Well, who carried the Niarchos colours to victory in 1998. Bary also won with Sulamani in 2002.

Bouchard is chairman of Groupe Econocom, which specialises in advising big companies on managing their IT equipment and claims that it can cut their costs by as much as 30 per cent. The chairman lives in Chantilly and likes to visit his horses several times a week.

It was his wife, Celine, who spotted Blue Canari at the Deauville sales and Bouchard bought the chestnut for €135,000 (then about £86,000). Blue Canari did not make his debut until late October 2003, when a close third behind Fast And Furious at Deauville. He then won the Prix Mieuxce, over nine furlongs at Maisons-Laffitte the following month, by a head from Reefscape. That was his only success in five races before the Jockey-Club.

Returning in the Prix de Courcelles, at Longchamp, Blue Canari shared last place with Millemix to the straight, where Millemix went to the outside while he followed the favourite, Prospect Park. He could never match the leading pair but ran on to finish third, a head and one and a half lengths behind Prospect Park and Millemix.

Millemix was giving 4lb all round that day and started favourite when Blue Canari took him on again in the Group 2 Prix Greffulhe, a race that Bary had won with Ragmar. Blue Canari again settled at

Blue Canari gets it right on the big day at Chantilly as he lands another Prix du Jockey-Club for trainer Pascal Bary

the back, racing in seventh as far as the straight and then switching towards the outside. He was running on when slightly hampered by Esperanto inside the last furlong, but kept on for fifth, about three lengths behind Millemix. He moved up to fourth on the disqualification of Esperanto.

It was a never-dangerous and clearly below-par third behind Reefscape in the Prix de l'Avre at Longchamp which saw him sent him off at 33.2-1 in the Jockey-Club but it later emerged that he had been coughing after the Greffulhe. His odds would have been longer still but for two disasters – Millemix shattering his pastern in five places while cantering at Chantilly 12 days ahead of the race and then Voix du Nord injuring himself on the morning before the race. The Prix du Jockey-Club had lost the first two in the Lupin and was left wide open.

Thierry Thulliez, who had ridden him in all his races, kept Blue Canari at the back, in company with Ange Gardien and Reefscape. He was last of the 15 at halfway and remained on the inside round the turn. This is usually a recipe for trouble, when the pacemakers drop back through the field, and pulling towards the outside early in the straight had not worked particularly well at Longchamp. This time, however,

2004	Race record

12th Prix de l'Arc de Triomphe Lucien Barriere (Group 1) (Longchamp, October 3) 3yo+ 12f Good **118** (TS 110) 19 ran. *Held up, 13th straight, stayed on at same pace final 2f (C-P Lemaire), beaten 8¼l by Bago*

5th Prix Niel Casino Barriere d'Enghien (Group 2) (Longchamp, September 12) 3yo 12f Soft **108** (TS 103) 8 ran. *Held up, 7th straight, some late headway but never a threat (T Thulliez), beaten 7¼l by Valixir*

1st Prix du Jockey-Club (Group 1) (Chantilly, June 6) 3yo 12f Good to soft **118** (TS 112) 15 ran. *Held up in rear, 11th on inside straight, pushed along and headway 2f out, ridden 1f out and quickened to challenge 100yds out, led final stride (T Thulliez), beat Prospect Park by hd*

3rd Prix de l'Avre (Listed) (Longchamp, May 19) 3yo 12f Good **97** (TS 73) 7 ran. *Held up, went 3rd 1½f out but outpaced by first two (T Thulliez), beaten 3¼l by Reefscape*

4th Prix Greffulhe (Group 2) (Longchamp, April 25) 3yo 10½f Good to soft **103** (TS 86) 8 ran. *Raced in 7th, stayed on from over 1f out on outside, crossed briefly by Esperanto inside final furlong, nearest at finish, finished 5th, promoted to 4th (T Thulliez), beaten 3l by Millemix*

3rd Prix de Courcelles (Listed) (Longchamp, April 4) 3yo (C & G) 10½f Good to soft **101** (TS 39) 6 ran. *Held up in rear, stayed on well final 150yds to take 3rd closing stages (T Thulliez), beaten 1¾l by Prospect Park*

2003	

1st Prix Mieuxce (Round Course) (Maisons-Laffitte, November 7) 2yo 9f Holding 6 ran ● **3rd** Prix de Saint Desir (Unraced Colts & Geldings) (Round Course) (Deauville, October 21) 2yo 1m Good 13 ran

everything went smoothly. Thulliez edged left from over two furlongs out to reach the outside behind Prospect Park with more than a furlong to run. He was still eighth at that point and fourth behind Prospect Park, Day Flight and Valixir halfway through the final furlong. But he produced a strong run to lead two strides from the line and beat Prospect Park a head.

Like most winners of the Jockey-Club these days, Blue Canari did not reappear until September's Prix Niel, in which he was entirely devoid of a turn of foot and came home fifth, around seven lengths behind the tightly grouped first four, Valixir, Prospect Park, Bago and Lord du Sud. It was much the same story in the Arc, in which he finished a one-paced 12th, although only about eight lengths behind the victorious Bago. After five defeats at the course, perhaps Longchamp is just not his track.

His owner went back to Deauville in 2003 to buy another son of Acatenango, Musketier, for €52,000 (about £35,000). Musketier won on his second outing, then ran second in the Group 3 Prix des Chenes before winning the Group 3 Prix de Conde. Bouchard and Bary would already be dreaming of Chantilly on the first Sunday in June, were it not for the reduction in the distance of the Jockey-Club to ten and a half furlongs. But perhaps Musketier will be their first winner of the Grand Prix de Paris, the new one-and-a-half-mile summer classic.

Blue Canari

chestnut colt, 2-2-2001

		Literat	Birkhahn
	Surumu		Lis
		Surama	Reliance
Acatenango			Suncourt
ch 1982		Aggressor	Combat
	Aggravate		Phaetonia
		Raven Locks	Mr Jinks
			Gentlemen's Relish
		Sharpen Up	Atan
	Trempolino		Rocchetta
		Trephine	Viceregal
Delicieuse Lady			Quiriquina
ch 1995		Caerleon	Nijinsky
	Savoureuse Lady		Foreseer
		Amazer	Mincio
			Alzara

Bred by Meridian Stud in France. Sold €135,000 at Deauville August Yearling Sale

Sire **Acatenango**

Won 16 of 24 starts, inc. Grosser Hertie Preis-Gr2, Union Rennen-Gr2, Deutsches Derby-Gr1, Aral Pokal-Gr1 [twice], Gerling Preis-Gr3 [twice], Grosser Preis der Badischen Wirtschaft-Gr2, Grand Prix de Saint-Cloud-Gr1, Grosser Preis von Berlin-Gr1, Grosser Preis von Baden-Gr1 [twice], Grosser Hansa Preis-Gr2. Also 3rd in Coronation Cup and 6th in King George VI & Queen Elizabeth Stakes at 5 years. Big, rangy, quite attractive, with a round action. Not at all precocious, but developed into a top-class international performer over 12f and would have stayed further. Honest, consistent, effective on any surface. Three times German Racehorse of the Year. By a Deutsches Derby winner and multiple champion sire, half-brother to the dam of dual Gr1 winner Abary. In retirement at Gestüt Fährhof. Sire of 14 crops of racing age, inc. G1 winners: Lando (Deutsches Derby, Grosser Preis von Baden [twice], Gran Premio del Jockey Club, Gran Premio di Milano, Deutschland Preis, Japan Cup), Borgia (Deutsches Derby, Grosser Preis von Baden), Sabiango (Aral Pokal, Deutschland Preis, Charles Whittingham Memorial H.), Blue Canari (Prix du Jockey-Club).

Dam **Delicieuse Lady**

Won 4 (6-9f) of 25 races in Scandinavia, viz. 2 out of 5 at 2 years, 0 out of 8 at 3 years, 2 out of 12 at 4 years. Also 2nd 4 times, 3rd 3 times, inc. Swedish 1,000 Guineas. Earned Kr165,680. Useful performer, trained in Norway, best at around a mile. Unplaced in 12f Scandinavian Classics. Well-bred. Half-sister to Gr3-placed Listed winner Quest For Ladies (dam of Gr3-placed winner Westcliffe). By a winner of the Arc de Triomphe out of a Gr3-winning half-sister to multiple Gr1 winner Mtoto, and to the dams of Mutamam (Gr2), Ruffle (Gr3) and Lugana Beach (Gr3). Dam of: Blue Canari (2001 c by Acatenango; Classic winner), Crabapple (2002 c by Unfuwain; unraced to date). She has a yearling colt by Anabaa.

Pedigree assessment

If the plan to reduce the distance of the Prix du Jockey-Club succeeds, Blue Canari will presumably be identified as the one who drove the final nail into the old Classic's coffin. He was a surprise runner at Chantilly, having previously finished behind several of the contenders, and a shock winner; he later did nothing to advertise the form. Nevertheless, he has an intriguing cosmopolitan pedigree, and is more worthy of a place at stud than many who are afforded chances. It will be interesting to see whether he is given any sort of opportunity. *TM*

Cacique (Ire)

3yo bay colt   **117**

Danehill (USA) - Hasili (Ire) (Kahyasi)
Owner K Abdullah
Trainer A Fabre
Breeder Juddmonte Farms

Career: **7** starts won **4** second **2** third **0** **£220,795** win and place

By Graham Dench

IT'S a pity Cacique didn't join the party at Lone Star Park, for his credentials bore close inspection. The Breeders' Cup Mile had been nominated as his next likely target after his Prix Daniel Wildenstein defeat of Hurricane Alan at Longchamp on the Saturday of Arc weekend, and two earlier second placings behind Bago looked very much better after the Arc itself.

That sort of form put Cacique only just behind Antonius Pius and Six Perfections, both of whom were placed in Texas, and there were grounds for thinking he might do even better under American conditions.

After all, his trainer Andre Fabre is the joint most successful European trainer at the Breeders' Cup, with three winners, and Cacique is a full-brother to one of them, the runaway 2001 Filly & Mare Turf winner Banks Hill, who sandwiched that success between European Group 1 wins in the Coronation Stakes and the Prix Jacques le Marois and returned for the 2002 Breeders' Cup and was second in the Filly & Mare Turf.

What's more, Cacique's other three older siblings have also done well in the States, two of them at the Breeders' Cup. Hasili's first foal, the Danehill colt Dansili, was third in the 2000 Breeders' Cup Mile after finishing second in the French 2,000 Guineas and Prix de la Foret; Heat Haze, an exception in that she was by Green Desert, not Danehill, finished fourth in the Filly & Mare Turf in 2003 as a four-year-old, when she enjoyed Grade 1 wins in the Beverly D and Matriarch Stakes; and while Intercontinental, third to Russian Rhythm in the 1,000 Guineas, missed the Breeders' Cup itself, she won the Grade 2 Just A Game Breeders' Cup Handicap at Belmont in June.

While all this may seem largely academic now, Cacique stays in training and should get his own Breeders' Cup chance in 2005 when the fixture returns to Belmont, the scene of Banks Hill's stunning victory.

Cacique could not overcome Bago but showed plenty of promise with Group wins at Chantilly and Longchamp

Cacique clearly had a lot to live up to when he belatedly set foot on a racecourse for the first time in a newcomers race at Saint-Cloud in April. Odds of 7-10 suggested he was expected to win rather more easily than by the eventual short head, but a win is a win, and another at Longchamp five weeks later earned him immediate elevation to Group 1 company.

It was Cacique's misfortune to run into Bago when he moved up in grade. And not just the once, either. Stepping up to nine furlongs for the Prix Jean Prat at Chantilly on Prix du Jockey-Club day, he was beaten comprehensively, running on from the back of the field to finish a three-length second without having any chance with the impressive winner. Three weeks later, however, regular partner Gary Stevens rode Cacique more prominently in a muddling Grand Prix de Paris, over ten furlongs at Longchamp, and he got much closer. While Bago perhaps did not have to pull out all the stops, he certainly had to work a good bit harder. Indeed Stevens for a moment thought he would land the first Group 1 win of what turned out to be a short-lived association with Fabre.

Using a curious turn of phrase before going on to pay Bago a major compliment, the jockey said: "For a moment my head blew up and then the air came out very slowly. Cacique ran a very, very good race and there was no disgrace in losing to Bago. He's as good as I've seen in my career and I've seen a few good horses."

2004	Race record

1st Prix Daniel Wildenstein Casino Barriere La Rochelle (Group 2) (Longchamp, October 2) 3yo+ 1m Good **117** (TS 97) 11 ran. *Held up, 8th straight, headway on outside 2f out, led final furlong, ran on well (C Soumillon), beat Hurricane Alan by ½l*

4th Juddmonte International Stakes (Group 1) (York, August 17) 3yo+ 10½f Good **114** (TS 87) 9 ran. *Held up, effort 4f out, edged left 2f out, never reached leaders (Gary Stevens), beaten 6½l by Sulamani*

1st Prix Daphnis (Group 3) (Chantilly, July 29) 3yo 9f Good **113** (TS 48) 6 ran. *Made all, shaken up 2f out, pushed clear over 1f out, eased close home, easily (Gary Stevens), beat Ershaad by 1½l*

2nd Juddmonte Grand Prix de Paris (Group 1) (Longchamp, June 27) 3yo 10f Good to soft **112** (TS 70) 4 ran. *Restrained in 2nd, led approaching straight, shaken up and ran on from 1½f out until headed and no extra close home (Gary Stevens), beaten ½l by Bago*

2nd Prix Jean Prat (Group 1) (Chantilly, June 6) 3yo 9f Good to soft **112** (TS 93) 8 ran. *Held up in rear, disputing 6th and pushed along on inside straight, ran on to take 2nd 1f out, no chance with winner (Gary Stevens), beaten 3l by Bago*

1st Prix du Vert Galant (Longchamp, May 19) 3yo 1m Good **105** (TS 62) 8 ran. *Always close up, joined leaders halfway, led over 1f out, ran on well (Gary Stevens), beat Svedov by 1½l*

1st Prix Sica Boy (Unraced Colts & Geldings) (Saint-Cloud, April 14) 3yo 7f Good to soft (TS 62) 6 ran. *Always close up, going well, led over 1f out, became unbalanced, headed 150yds out, ran on to lead again last strides (Gary Stevens), beat Estihdaaf by shd*

Dropping two grades for a confidence booster in the Prix Daphnis back at Chantilly, Cacique made short work of Group 3 opposition, making all and winning easily by a length and a half without turning a hair, but then it was straight back up to Group 1 again at York for a third clash with Bago in the Juddmonte International.

Bago easily got the best of this one, Cacique trailing in five lengths behind him, but Sulamani and Norse Dancer beat them both. Judged on the figures, Cacique had shown marginally improved form, but Fabre clearly felt it was not the colt's true running. With so many options open to the colt in the remainder of the season, it looked significant that he was dropped back to a mile for the Prix Daniel Wildenstein.

With Christophe Soumillon taking over from Stevens, who had by now returned home, Cacique came from off the pace on the outside to lead a furlong out and beat the consistent, though hardly top-drawer, British challenger Hurricane Alan by half a length.

Speaking afterwards, Fabre's thoughts went back to York, and his comments suggested he felt that with so much experience of Cacique's family he really should have known better. He said: "I probably made a mistake trying to go further with him. Although he's laid-back, he's probably a miler like the rest of his family."

It's not a mistake Fabre is likely to make again in 2005, when Cacique should be a major player in the top races at around a mile as he builds up towards Belmont, where he will have a strong family tradition to uphold.

Cacique

bay colt, 2-5-2001

		Northern Dancer	Nearctic
			Natalma
	Danzig		
		Pas de Nom	Admiral's Voyage
Danehill			Petitioner
b 1986			
		His Majesty	Ribot
			Flower Bowl
	Razyana		
		Spring Adieu	Buckpasser
			Natalma
		Ile de Bourbon	Nijinsky
			Roseliere
	Kahyasi		
		Kadissya	Blushing Groom
Hasili			Kalkeen
b 1991			
		High Line	High Hat
			Time Call
	Kerali		
		Sookera	Roberto
			Irule

Bred by Juddmonte Farms in Ireland

Sire Danehill

Won 4 of 9 races, inc. Cork and Orrery Stakes-Gr3, Haydock Park Sprint Cup-Gr1. Also 3rd in 2,000 Guineas. Medium-sized, strong, good-bodied individual, markedly back at the knee. Showed quick, fluent action, effective on any ground from dead to firm, never ran on really soft surface. Died May 2003. Sire of Gr1 winners: Danish (Queen Elizabeth II Challenge Cup), Kissing Cousin (Coronation S.), Danehill Dancer (Phoenix S., National S.), Tsukuba Symphony (NHK Mile Cup), Desert King (National S., Irish 2,000 Guineas, Irish Derby), Fairy King Prawn (Yasuda Kinen), Tiger Hill (Grosser Preis von Baden [twice], Bayerisches Zuchtrennen), Indian Danehill (Prix Ganay), Wannabe Grand (Cheveley Park S.), Aquarelliste (Prix de Diane, Prix Vermeille, Prix Ganay), Banks Hill (Coronation S., Breeders' Cup Filly & Mare Turf, Prix Jacques le Marois), Mozart (July Cup, Nunthorpe S.), Regal Rose (Cheveley Park S.), Dress To Thrill (Matriarch S.), Landseer (Poule d'Essai des Poulains), Rock Of Gibraltar (Grand Criterium, Dewhurst S., 2,000 Guineas, Irish 2,000 Guineas, St James's Palace S., Sussex S., Prix du Moulin), Westerner (Prix du Cadran, twice, Prix Royal-Oak, twice), Clodovil (Poule d'Essai des Poulains), Light Jig (Yellow Ribbon S.), Spartacus (Phoenix S., Gran Criterium), Grey Lilas (Prix du Moulin de Longchamp), North Light (Derby S.), Oratorio (Prix Jean-Luc Lagardere).

Dam Hasili

Won 4 (5-8f) of 17 races at 2 and 3. At 2, won 4 of 8 races inc. 8f Listed event. At 3, non-winner but Listed placed over 7-8f. By top-class 12f performer and decent French-based sire. Sister to 15f Listed winner Arrive and half-sister to Listed-placed Skiable (dam of top-class 2yo Three Valleys) out of half-sister to top-class sprinter So Factual. Grand-dam Sookera won Cheveley Park S-Gr1. Dam of: Dansili (1996 c by Danehill; Gr2 winner, Gr1 placed), Banks Hill (1998 f by Danehill; Coronation S-Gr1, Breeders' Cup Filly & Mare Turf-Gr1, Prix Jacques le Marois-Gr1), Heat Haze (1999 f by Green Desert; Beverly D S-Gr1, Matriarch S-Gr1), Intercontinental (2000 f by Danehill; Gr2 winner, Gr1 placed), Cacique (2001 c by Danehill; Gr2 winner, Gr1 placed), unnamed (2003 c by Danehill). In foal to Sadler's Wells for 2005.

Pedigree assessment

The combination of Danehill and Hasili was tested before Cacique was conceived, and subsequent events suggest it has been one of the most potent in worldwide breeding over the last couple of decades. Cacique will make a popular stallion whatever he achieves in the future on the racetrack, especially as brother Dansili has shown good promise with his first runners in 2004. *JH*

Cape Of Good Hope

6yo chestnut gelding **121**

Inchinor - Cape Merino (Clantime)
Owner Exors of the late R Carstairs
Trainer D Oughton
Breeder Mrs D Ellis

Career: **31** starts   won **5**   second **6**   third **5**   **£1,033,256** win and place

By Nick Pulford

CAPE Of Good Hope may have represented Hong Kong in the big summer sprints, but he is as British as they come. Right down to the bit about being a gallant loser.

The six-year-old is trained by an Englishman, David Oughton, and runs in the colours of the late Ronald Carstairs, a Scottish, Hong Kong-based banker. He was also bred in Britain by Diana Ellis, a former owner with Oughton when he trained at Findon in the early 1980s. And he began his career in Britain – three starts for David Elsworth, all as a three-year-old, with a seven-furlong Newmarket win to his credit.

"It's all for the prestige – Royal Ascot is something special," said Oughton on his homecoming. It certainly wasn't for money. Cape Of Good Hope arrived with earnings of almost £900,000 from 24 starts in Hong Kong – that works out at around £37,000 per run, even though he had been unplaced in half of them and had won only four times. In Royal Ascot's King's Stand Stakes, his first intended target, he would be racing for a first prize of £81,200 – the bare minimum for a horse of his standard in Hong Kong.

Oughton, who has won many of Hong Kong's big prizes since moving there in 1987, had also brought over Bowman's Crossing, who was to finish seventh in the Queen Anne Stakes and sixth in the Group 3 Silver Trophy, also at Ascot. Cape Of Good Hope was his main chance, however. He had already been Group 1-placed when third in the Hong Kong Sprint the previous December (with solid British sprinters Acclamation, The Trader and The Tatling all behind him) and he would relish Ascot's stiff five furlongs and likely fast ground.

The imponderable was whether he could reproduce his form, given that he had raced nine times during the ten-month Hong Kong season that was just about to end.

He was not quite Choisir, who had taken Royal Ascot by storm in 2003, but he was not too shabby either. Drawn on the stands rail in the King's

Cape Of Good Hope was in the thick of the action all year in top sprints in Britain, Japan and Hong Kong

Stand, he held every chance inside the final furlong but could not repel The Tatling's fast finish and was beaten one and a half lengths into second. It was a familiar tale for a horse who had finished second or third eight times from 17 starts since his last win, and the frustration was summed up in Oughton's comment: "Before the race The Tatling was one horse I felt sure we would beat."

Having come so far, Oughton decided to try again in the Group 1 Golden Jubilee Stakes four days later. This time, despite being hampered slightly a furlong out, Cape Of Good Hope went even closer, beaten a head and the same into third behind Fayr Jag. Frustration upon frustration.

Third time lucky might have been the thought when Oughton gave Cape Of Good Hope another chance in the July Cup. The gelding ran his heart out again but was beaten around two and a half lengths into fourth. There was more frustration in the fact that he had beaten the first two, Frizzante and Ashdown Express, at Royal Ascot.

Before re-entering the fray in the 2004-05 Hong Kong season, which began in September, Oughton sent Cape Of Good Hope abroad again,

2004   Race record

3rd Sprinters Stakes (Grade 1) (Nakayama, October 3) 3yo+ 6f Heavy **115** 16 ran. *(B Prebble), beaten 4 ¼ l by Calstone Light O*

4th Darley July Cup (Group 1) (Newmarket (July), July 8) 3yo+ 6f Good to soft **114** (TS 97) 20 ran. *Raced centre, held up, joined main group 4f out, headway under pressure over 1f out, ran on (M J Kinane), beaten 2 ½ l by Frizzante*

3rd Golden Jubilee Stakes (Group 1) (Ascot, June 19) 3yo+ 6f Firm **116** (TS 117) 14 ran. *Held up, headway and not much room over 1f out, hard ridden and ran on inside final furlong (M J Kinane), beaten ½ l by Fayr Jag*

2nd King's Stand Stakes (Group 2) (Ascot, June 15) 3yo+ 5f Good to firm **114** (TS 102) 19 ran. *Held up, ridden and headway 2f out, every chance inside final furlong, not quicken (M J Kinane), beaten 1 ½ l by The Tatling*

2nd Chairman's Sprint Prize (HK Group 1) (Sha Tin, April 25) 3yo+ 6f Good to firm **118** 13 ran. *In rear early, niggled along until being pressured 2 ½ f out, quickened well on straightening, closest finish (G Mosse), beaten 2 ½ l by Silent Witness*

2nd Centenary Sprint Cup (HK Group 1) (Sha Tin, March 13) 3yo+ 5f Good to firm **118** 10 ran. *Niggled to keep racing within 2l of lead early stages, improved to get within a length of lead 2f out and ridden hard to challenge leader, unable to draw any closer final stages (M J Kinane), beaten 2 ½ l by Silent Witness*

3rd Bauhinia Sprint Trophy (HK Group 1) (Sha Tin, February 1) 3yo+ 5f Good to firm **118** 7 ran. *Within 5l of lead in rear, headway over 1f out, just missed 2nd; iron slipped and rider unbalanced halfway (D Whyte), beaten 3l by Silent Witness*

6th Chinese Club Challenge Cup (HK Group 3) (Handicap) (Sha Tin, January 1) 3yo+ 7f Good to firm **113** 12 ran. *Always three wide mostly with cover in midfield through to home straight, always looked held thereafter (D Whyte), beaten 5 ½ l by Hidden Dragon*

Other notable runs

2003 3rd Hong Kong Sprint (Group 1) (Sha Tin, December 14) 3yo+ 5f Good to firm **121** 14 ran **2001 1st** Chippenham Maiden Stakes (Newmarket, May 18) 3yo 7f Good to soft **82** 19 ran

this time to Japan for the Grade 1 Sprinters Stakes in October. Events conspired against him, with an unfavourable high draw, steady early pace and heavy going, but again he ran into the placings with a creditable third of 16 behind clear-cut winner Calstone Light O. With Ashdown Express and Fayr Jag well beaten it meant that at some stage he has beaten four of the six horses who finished in front of him in his British runs. It was just that his turn never came.

Oughton is not deterred ("He'll win a big one, there's no doubt about that") and plans to run him in Japan again in March followed by a return to Britain. Royal Ascot's switch to York in 2005 is not in Cape Of Good Hope's favour, so the big target is likely to be the July Cup.

The most telling point of all is that Oughton is prepared to go almost anywhere to avoid Silent Witness, Hong Kong's super sprinter. Cape Of Good Hope faced him six times during the 2003-04 season and never got closer than one and three-quarter lengths – "we won't beat him, not when he's on his game," Oughton admits. Yet in Britain Cape Of Good Hope was right in amongst our best sprinters.

Cape Of Good Hope   *chestnut gelding, 21-1-1998*

Inchinor ch 1990	Ahonoora	Lorenzaccio	Klairon Phoenissa
		Helen Nichols	Martial Quaker Girl
	Inchmurrin	Lomond	Northern Dancer My Charmer
		On Show	Welsh Pageant African Dancer
Cape Merino ch 1991	Clantime	Music Boy	Jukebox Veronique
		Penny Pincher	Constable Midnight Dollar
	Laena	Roman Warrior	Porto Bello Colliers
		Poshteen	Royal Smoke Camlet

Bred by Mrs D Ellis in Britain. 25,000gns Doncaster St Leger yearling

Sire Inchinor

Won 5 of 10 starts, inc. Greenham S.-Gr3, Criterion S.-Gr3, Hungerford S.-Gr3. Also 2nd in Dewhurst S., 3rd in Sussex S. Small (15.1 1/2 hh), well-made, attractive sort, and a grand mover. Very game, consistent performer, effective in most conditions (not raced on extremes). Speedy, owned a sharp turn of foot, stayed a mile well. Well-bred. Half-brother to 1 Listed and 4 other winners, inc. dams of Listed winners. By a leading sprinter and successful sire out of a small but very game and talented racemare (Gr2 winner, Gr1-placed). Grand-dam bred 8 winners in all, inc. Welney (Gr2) and Guest Artiste (Gr1-placed), and the dam of Balisada (Gr1). 3rd dam won Park Hill S., placed in Oaks, Yorkshire Oaks. Died in 2003. Stood at Woodland Stud, last fee £10,000 (Oct 1). Sire of 8 crops of racing age, inc. notable winners: Golden Silca (Gr2), Palanca (Gr3), Summoner (Queen Elizabeth II S.-Gr1), Umistim (Gr3), Bannister (Gr2), Orientor (Gr3), Felicity (Gr3), Latice (Prix de Diane-Gr1), Secret Melody (Gr3), Satchem (Gr3).

Dam Cape Merino

Won 4 of 9 starts from 2 to 5. At 2, won 2 (5-6f, inc. Redcar Tote Two-Year-Old Trophy) from 4 starts. At 3, won 1 (5f Bovis Hcap) of 4 starts. Unraced at 4, won sole start (5f) at 5. By smart and very tough sprinter who tended to get tough progeny, out of placed 2yo. Dam of: Cape Of Good Hope (1998 c by Inchinor; winner, Gr1 placed), Cape Vincent (2000 c by Paris House; winner), Cape Columbine (2002 f by Diktat; winner), 2003 f by Cape Cross (230,000gns yearling).

Pedigree assessment

The speedily bred Cape Merino surpassed the racecourse achievements of her closest relatives, and she has carried on the work at stud with Cape Of Good Hope and the potentially smart Tattersalls Autumn Auction Stakes winner Cape Columbine. The gelded Cape Of Good Hope will continue his quest for a stakes win in 2005. *JH*

Chelsea Rose (Ire)

2yo chestnut filly   **106**

Desert King (Ire) - Cinnamon Rose (USA) (Trempolino (USA))
Owner Mrs A J Donnelly
Trainer C Collins
Breeder Airlie Stud

Career: **3** starts   won **2**   second **0**   third **1**   **£136,140** win and place

By Steve Dennis

ACK in the days when a man named Vincent was the O'Brien who answered the phone at Ballydoyle, Con Collins sent out Princess Pati, in the famous Mullion tartan silks, to win the Irish Oaks under a young Pat Shanahan.

Now, 20 years on, Collins finds himself with another Irish Oaks contender in the shape of Chelsea Rose, whose victory, under a slightly older Shanahan, in the Moyglare Stud Stakes propelled her 80-year-old trainer – who, when asked his age in the post-race debrief, said simply: "I'm getting on a bit" – back into the big-race limelight.

Collins and Shanahan are the Irish equivalent of Sir Mark Prescott and George Duffield in that they have been inseparable on the racecard for decades and now, in Chelsea Rose, a daughter of dual Classic winner Desert King, they may have unearthed the perfect way to write a final glorious chapter in their partnership.

In her three runs Chelsea Rose has shown herself to be an above-average filly with stamina as her long suit, a characteristic evidently no secret to her connections, who started her off over seven furlongs in a Leopardstown maiden in June.

She was fourth choice in the market against 12 rivals, the favourite being the well-regarded Silk And Scarlet, from Aidan O'Brien's yard. That rival made the running but had no answer to the sustained run of Chelsea Rose, who hit the front inside the final furlong and won going away by two lengths.

After the race, Collins told the press: "There should be a lot of improvement in this filly. The Moyglare Stud Stakes is a long way off, but she is entered for it."

That comment indicated that Collins was not entertaining an angel unawares, and after a two-month break Chelsea Rose was back in action at The Curragh, again at seven furlongs but this time in Group 2 company for the Robert H Griffin Debutante Stakes. Silk And Scarlet, who had

**Pat Shanahan celebrates on Chelsea Rose after winning
the Moyglare Stud Stakes for his old partner Con Collins**

won a Listed race since their Leopardstown meeting, was again in opposition and this time both fillies were ridden differently, Chelsea Rose disputing the lead from the outset and Silk And Scarlet hidden away at the rear of the eight-strong field.

Admittedly Chelsea Rose showed grit and determination when headed by Luas Line inside the final quarter-mile, but this time the boot was firmly on the other foot as Silk And Scarlet strolled through to win with consummate ease. Chelsea Rose also lost her battle with Luas Line and was beaten a total of two and a half lengths into third place.

Whether the ground – officially good to firm, but pretty quick nonetheless – was a contributing factor to her defeat, or whether the change of tactics had a part to play was unclear. In any case, she was now Group-placed and that represented a considerable step up on her debut performance.

Collins still had his plan to stick to, though, and the following month Chelsea Rose was stepped up once more in class for the Group 1 Moyglare Stud Stakes back at The Curragh. Once again, Silk And Scarlet led the opposition, which also included Cherry Hinton Stakes winner Jewel In The Sand and the promising Jim Bolger-trained filly Pictavia.

1st Moyglare Stud Stakes (Group 1) (Curragh, September 5) 2yo 7f Good to firm **106** (TS 103) 12 ran. *Tracked leaders on outer, improved to lead 2½f out, strongly pressed 1f out, kept on well under pressure (P Shanahan), beat Pictavia by ¾l*

3rd Robert H Griffin Debutante Stakes (Group 2) (Curragh, August 8) 2yo 7f Good to firm **91** (TS 90) 8 ran. *Disputed lead, headed under 2f out, kept on under pressure (P Shanahan), beaten 2½l by Silk And Scarlet*

1st Irish Stallion Farms EBF Fillies Maiden (Leopardstown, June 9) 2yo 7f Good to firm **82** (TS 35) 13 ran. *Tracked leaders in 5th, progress approaching straight, 2nd 1½f out, led inside final furlong, stayed on well, comfortably (P Shanahan), beat Silk And Scarlet by 2l*

Since the Moyglare was extended from six furlongs to seven in the early 1990s it has been won by several high-class fillies, notably Sayyedati, Tarascon, Quarter Moon and Necklace, and Silk And Scarlet was an 11-8 chance to add her name to that list, with Jewel In The Sand second choice and Chelsea Rose fifth in the market at 9-1. However, this time Chelsea Rose was ridden just off the pace by Shanahan and turned the tables on Silk And Scarlet in emphatic style.

Shanahan sent his filly to the front with two and a half furlongs to run, knowing her stamina to be sure, and she repelled all boarders inside the final furlong with a very gutsy display, passing the post three-quarters of a length ahead of Pictavia in a finish that saw just three lengths covering the first seven home.

That fact, in itself, might militate against the value of the form, especially as Silk And Scarlet and Jewel In The Sand both ran poor races, but there was certainly no fluke about Chelsea Rose's win.

Shanahan said: "My filly travelled really well and, as I knew she would stay, I decided to kick on almost three down. The ground wasn't ideal for her – she likes a bit of an ease – but it wasn't as fast as it was when she ran here last month, and that helped her."

Connections have set out their stall for 2005, with the trainer's daughter Tracey saying: "We deliberately didn't enter her for the 1,000 Guineas and she will be trained with the Irish Oaks in mind."

The Irish Oaks is never the most fiercely contested of Classics, usually attracting a small field dominated by the Epsom Oaks winner, and it seems a sensible target at this stage for Chelsea Rose. A mile is unlikely to see her at her best – it will come as a surprise if she possesses the wherewithal to match the likes of Damson at that sort of trip – but a mile and a quarter looks a formality and there seem no reasons why a mile and a half will not be within her compass. Her dam, the Trempolino mare Cinnamon Rose, won over ten furlongs and Trempolino himself won the 1987 Prix de l'Arc de Triomphe – add that evidence to her own demeanour and her Irish Derby-winning sire and connections have every right to be confident about her stamina.

Collins may be "getting on a bit", but he'll feel a lot younger if Chelsea Rose wins him another Classic. About 20 years younger.

Chelsea Rose *chestnut filly, 11-2-2002*

Desert King b 1994	Danehill	Danzig	Northern Dancer Pas de Nom
		Razyana	His Majesty Spring Adieu
	Sabaah	Nureyev	Northern Dancer Special
		Dish Dash	Bustino Loose Cover
Cinnamon Rose ch 1994	Trempolino	Sharpen Up	Atan Rocchetta
		Trephine	Viceregal Quiriquina
	Sweet Simone	Green Dancer	Nijinsky Green Valley
		Servilia	Aureole Senones

Bred by Airlie Stud in Ireland. 38,000gns Tattersalls October yearling

Sire Desert King

Won 5 of 12 starts at 2 and 3. At 2, won 2 (inc. National S-Gr1) of 5 starts. At 3, won 3 (Tetrarch S-Gr3, Irish 2,000 Guineas-Gr1, Irish Derby-Gr1) of 7 starts, also 2nd Juddmonte International S-Gr1, Irish Champion S-Gr1. By top-class sprinter-miler and outstanding sire of 2yos and performers across the distance range. Brother to very useful 2yo/10f performer Chianti, half-brother to 2004 Listed winner Cairdeas. Dam placed half-sister to Gr1-winning miler Maroof out of Ribblesdale Stakes winner Dish Dash. Originally stood at Coolmore Stud in Ireland, exported to Japan after 2001 season. Oldest progeny 5, sire of (northern hemisphere foals): Makybe Diva (Melbourne Cup-Gr1 x 2, Sydney Cup-Gr1), Maranilla (Gr3), Mr Dinos (Gold Cup-Gr1), Place Rouge (Gr2), Urban King (Gr2), Darsalam (Gr2), Chelsea Rose (Moyglare Stud S-Gr1).

Dam Cinnamon Rose

Won 1 of 9 starts from 2 to 4. At 2, 4th both starts. At 3, won 1 (10f) of 3 starts. At 4, 4th 9f Listed event from 4 starts. By Arc winner and fair sire, mostly of 1m+ performers. Half-sister to 10f Gr2 winner River Warden and 2yo Gr3 winner Sweettuc. Dam of: Ruente (1999 c by Persian Bold; winner), European (2000 c by Great Commotion; Listed winner), Chelsea Rose (2002 f by Desert King; Moyglare Stud S-Gr1), 2004 c by Fasliyev.

Pedigree assessment

This is the pedigree of a filly who can be expected to make good progress from two to three and stay 10f, with 12f a strong possibility. Chelsea Rose has already done more than her pedigree suggested she might, by winning a Group 1 event at two – after which she was unraced – and connections clearly have her 3yo career in mind. Desert King's progeny tend to make good progress with age and most of the talented ones stay at least 10f. Cinnamon Rose stayed 10f, in keeping with her pedigree. All this paves the way for a middle-distance campaign for Chelsea Rose in 2005. *JH*

Cherry Mix (Fr)

3yo grey colt   **128**

Linamix (Fr) - Cherry Moon (USA) (Quiet American (USA))

Owner Lagardere Family

Trainer A Fabre

Breeder Snc Lagardere Elevage

Career: **8** starts   won **2**   second **4**   third **2**   **£361,713** win and place

By Richard Austen

TWO furlongs out in the Prix de l'Arc de Triomphe, Cherry Mix moved smoothly into the lead. He'd moved well throughout the race and was pushed two lengths clear. Europe's most important prize was almost in his grasp.

Like Mubtaker 12 months previously, Cherry Mix was running in his first Group 1 race. When asked to set out a case for the Prix du Jockey-Club in the spring, he had failed to make it persuasive, placed but beaten about three lengths in a Listed race, the Prix Noailles and the Prix Hocquart. A total of five different horses had finished in front of him at level weights.

In midsummer, instead of in the Jockey-Club, Cherry Mix appeared at Saint-Cloud on their Grand Prix day, and not in the Grand Prix; he was on the undercard, out of Group and Listed company, and he lost that ordinary prize as well, in a bunched finish back over ten and a half furlongs.

Judged on those four races, it's not hard to see why Cherry Mix's starting price for the Arc with the British bookmakers was as long as 33-1, but two starts away from Paris later in the summer may have gone unnoticed or unheeded.

First a Listed event at Vichy saw Cherry Mix give weight and win comfortably. The ground was holding that day and it was heavy five weeks later in the Grand Prix de Deauville. Only one of the six other runners at Deauville started at a longer price. Andre Fabre, Cherry Mix's trainer, had two of the rest and, with Gary Stevens on Martaline and Christophe Soumillon on Bailador, it looked very much as if Cherry Mix with Thierry Gillet was his third string. That did not stop Cherry Mix from winning the Group 2 by four lengths, coming from the back to lead one furlong out and quickly take the prize out of reach from his two stablemates.

Roland de Longevialle, racing manager to the Lagardere family, owners of Cherry Mix, said after the Deauville victory that "we have no option

**Cherry Mix joined Godolphin after a season that brought
Group 2 success at Deauville and second place in the Arc**

now but to go for the Arc." Gillet reported: "He's a real swimmer. If the
going is the same at Longchamp in October he would have a chance of
making his presence felt."

The going on Arc day, however, turned out to be good officially and
actually much more like good to firm. It's not surprising that British punters
overlooked the dual soft-ground winner, but perhaps the French crowd
had more regard for him, for it wasn't just Prix Niel winner Valixir who
explained the coupled Lagardere runners going off at 73-10 on the Pari-
Mutuel.

They would certainly have had regard for his trainer and jockey. Bidding
to give Fabre his sixth Arc triumph and Soumillon his second in a row,
Cherry Mix was drawn next to the rails and gave Soumillon a dream
ride. With North Light stretching the field on the final turn and fifth-
placed Cherry Mix travelling strongly, Soumillon needed only a slight
manoeuvre to take his mount off the rails and improve between Prospect
Park and Mamool before going for home. Cherry Mix had daylight between
himself and his pursuers for most of the last two furlongs, but Bago had

2004   Race record

2nd Prix de l'Arc de Triomphe Lucien Barriere (Group 1) (Longchamp, October 3) 3yo+ 12f Good **128** (TS 129) 19 ran. *Close up, 4th straight, quickened to lead just over 1½f out, 2 lengths clear approaching final furlong, headed and no extra 50yds out (C Soumillon), beaten ½l by Bago*

1st Grand Prix de Deauville Lucien Barriere (Group 2) (Deauville, August 29) 3yo+ 12½f Heavy **118** (TS 33) 7 ran. *Held up in rear, 6th straight, good headway 2f out, led 1f out, pushed clear, ran on strongly (T Gillet), beat Martaline by 4l*

1st Prix Frederic de Lagrange (Listed) (Vichy, July 24) 3yo 12f Holding **109** 9 ran. *Tracked leaders pulling hard, switched outside to lead 2f out, ran on well (T Gillet), beat Anabaa Republic by 3l*

2nd Prix Auriban (Saint-Cloud, July 4) 3yo 10½f Good to soft **105** (TS 41) 7 ran. *Dropped out racing keenly behind slow pace, headway on outside to lead over 2f out, headed and no extra close home (Gary Stevens), beaten nk by Staramix*

3rd Prix Hocquart (Group 2) (Longchamp, May 13) 3yo 12f Very soft **105** (TS 88) 6 ran. *Raced in 4th to straight, stayed on at one pace final 2f, took 3rd 100yds out (Gary Stevens), beaten 3¾l by Lord du Sud*

2nd Prix Noailles (Group 2) (3yo Colts & Fillies) (Longchamp, April 11) 3yo 11f Good to soft **107** (TS 98) 9 ran. *Raced in 7th, disputing 6th on inside straight, pushed along 1½f out, stayed on under pressure from over 1f out to take 2nd close home (Gary Stevens), beaten 3l by Voix du Nord*

3rd Prix Maurice Caillault (Listed) (Saint-Cloud, March 18) 3yo c & g 10½f Good to soft **93** (TS 45) 8 ran. *Held up pulling hard, plenty to do 2f out, stayed on strongly from over 1f out to take 3rd close home (C Soumillon), beaten 3½l by Kurm*

2003

2nd Prix de la Sorbonne (Longchamp, October 12) 2yo 1m½f Very soft 10 ran

squeezed through behind him and was running on the stronger in the last 100 yards. Cherry Mix was caught 50 yards out and beaten half a length.

Like plenty of other top races in the latest season, the Arc was a triumph for the owner-breeder. Sporting famous colours, Bago, Cherry Mix, third-placed Ouija Board, fifth home North Light and Vallee Enchantee in sixth were all owner bred. Four of those were from families that had been at the same studs for generations.

Previously owned by the Dupre family, the grey and pink colours carried by Cherry Mix were well known for decades before Jean-Luc Lagardere bought them, along with the Dupre stud. Cherry Mix's dam does not come from that stock but – no surprises – he is by Lagardere's flagbearing stallion Linamix. Following Lagardere's death in March 2003, his string have been running for the Lagardere family, but there have been reports that their bloodstock will be sold off to pay death duties.

Whatever happens, the Lagardere silks will not now be carried by Cherry Mix. Lagardere's 1999 Arc winner Sagamix eventually went on to run for Godolphin, the Maktoum team snapped up 2002 Arc runner-up Sulamani, and shortly after the latest Arc came the not entirely surprising news that they had also bought Cherry Mix.

Cherry Mix

grey colt, 15-2-2001

Linamix gr 1987	Mendez	Bellypha	Lyphard / Belga
		Miss Carina	Caro / Miss Pia
	Lunadix	Breton	Relko / La Melba
		Lutine	Alcide / Mona
Cherry Moon b 1995	Quiet American	Fappiano	Mr Prospector / Killaloe
		Demure	Dr Fager / Quiet Charm
	Datsdawayitis	Known Fact	In Reality / Tamerett
		Baton Twirler	Reverse / Dixie B

Bred by Lagardere Elevage in France

Sire Linamix

Won 4 (all 1m) of 10 starts from 2 to 3. At 2, won Prix la Rochette-Gr3 and 2nd Grand Criterium-Gr1 from 3 starts. At 3, won Prix de Fontainebleau-Gr3 and Poule d'Essai des Poulains-Gr1, 2nd Prix Jacques le Marois-Gr1, Prix du Moulin-Gr1, Champion S-Gr1. By top-class miler who had just 2 seasons at stud in France before export to Japan. Half-brother to Luna Wells (Prix Saint-Alary-Gr1) and Gr2 winner Long Mick. Stands at Haras du Val Henry in France, 2004 fee €40,000. Oldest progeny 12, sire of: Diamond Mix (Gr2), Housamix (Gr2), Miss Satamixa (Prix Jacques le Marois-Gr1), Walk On Mix (Gr2), Manninamix (Gr3), Clodora (Gr2), Fragrant Mix (Grand Prix de Saint-Cloud-Gr1), Oa Baldixe (Gr3), Diamonixa (Gr3), Pinmix (Gr3), Sagamix (Prix de l'Arc de Triomphe-Gr1), Amilynx (Prix Royal-Oak-Gr1 x 2), Artistique (Gr3), Sage et Jolie (Gr2), Slickly (Grand Prix de Paris-Gr1, Prix du Moulin-Gr1, Premio Vittorio di Capua-Gr1 x 2), Goldamix (Criterium de Saint-Cloud-Gr1), Miraculous (Gr3), Diamilina (Gr2), Fair Mix (Prix Ganay-Gr1), Vahorimix (Poule d'Essai des Poulains-Gr1, Prix Jacques le Marois-Gr1), Bernimixa (Gr2), Martaline (Gr2), Diasilixa (Gr3), Walkamia (Gr3), Visorama (Gr3), Cherry Mix (Gr2), Linda Regina (Gr3), Lord du Sud (Gr2), Millemix (Gr2), Reefscape (Gr2).

Dam Cherry Moon

Won 4 of 21 starts in North America from 2 to 4, including minor stakes event at 3. Most wins at up to 1m. By top-class 9-10f dirt performer who has had just sporadic success as a sire. Half-sister to 2yo stakes winner Dawaytogold (f Candi's Gold) out of minor winner, from workmanlike family. Dam of: Cherry Mix (2001 c by Linamix; Gr2 winner, Gr1 placed), Moon Mix (2003 c by Linamix).

Pedigree assessment

The late Jean-Luc Lagardere mated his stallion Linamix with many US-bred mares, with spectacular results, and Cherry Mix is an example. His dam's family is modest and reasonably speedy, yet it has linked with Linamix to produce a top-class 12f performer. Godolphin purchased another Lagardere-bred son of Linamix who had performed prominently in the Arc – 1998 winner Sagamix, who was disappointing subsequently – and they should have better fortune with Cherry Mix. He should prove a leading older 10-12f performer in 2005. *JH*

Chic

4yo chestnut filly   **123**

Machiavellian (USA) - Exclusive (Polar Falcon (USA))
Owner Cheveley Park Stud
Trainer Sir Michael Stoute
Breeder Cheveley Park Stud

Career: **14** starts   won **5**   second **2**   third **2**   **£184,162** win and place

By Graham Dench

THE niggling problems that kept Russian Rhythm off the course after her successful reappearance in the Lockinge must have been frustrating for all concerned, but the Guineas winner's absence meant more opportunities for two of Cheveley Park Stud's other good fillies, and they made the most of them. Chorist hit the jackpot, with a Group 1 success in the Audi Pretty Polly Stakes at The Curragh in June. And following a sticky start to the season, Chic did almost as well.

Chic's Celebration Mile defeat of Nayyir represented high-class form, according to Racing Post Ratings the equal of anything Russian Rhythm ever achieved, and while she was beaten in the Sun Chariot Stakes on her only appearance in a Group 1, she made the remarkable Attraction pull out all the stops.

Chic's hopes of graduating to Group level in 2004 got off to an inauspicious start when she could do no better than sixth behind Gonfilia in a Listed race at Goodwood, but in the Group 2 Windsor Forest Stakes at Royal Ascot next time she was still tanking along when she clipped Beneventa's heels and was nearly brought down. On that basis she was a popular choice to gain compensation in the Group 3 Oak Tree Stakes at Goodwood, and her strong-finishing third behind Phantom Wind after being given plenty to do was a step in the right direction.

If the first half of the season brought nothing but frustration, the second half more than made up for it. For Chic improved out of all recognition. An impressive defeat of Suggestive in Newbury's Hungerford Stakes – a race, incidentally, in which she went into the fray officially rated the second worst of 13 runners – would in itself have justified the decision to keep her in training, but the best was yet to come.

A crack at the Celebration Mile meant returning to the scene of her unlucky Oak Tree defeat and moving back up a level to Group 2 on the softest ground she had ever encountered. It also pitched her in against

Chic, winner of Goodwood's Celebration Mile and later runner-up to Attraction at Newmarket, stays in training

a genuine Group 1 contender in Nayyir, the recent Sussex Stakes second. One way and another, Chic had plenty to prove, and when she was still at the back of the field with only two furlongs to go, having been pushed along from before the straight, she was reportedly laid at 100-1 on Betfair. However, Naahy and Passing Glance had taken each other on at a suicidal pace, and the picture was about to change dramatically.

Chic began to close, and having passed a weakening rival or two she suddenly took off. With Nayyir in front a bit too soon and beginning to flag, Chic hit the front with around 75 yards to go and came away to win by a length and a quarter, the pair pulling five lengths clear. If the Oak Tree had not been Kieren Fallon's finest ride, this was one he could look back upon with considerable satisfaction.

A minor knock while out at exercise denied Chic the opportunity to stand in for Russian Rhythm in the Queen Elizabeth II Stakes, but the Sun Chariot Stakes, granted Group 1 status for the first time and run just a week later, was a perfect alternative. There was an unspecified scare on the eve of the race, but she was allowed to take her chance in

2004   Race record

2nd Kingdom of Bahrain Sun Chariot Stakes (Group 1) (Newmarket, October 2) 3yo+ 1m Good **122** (TS 117) 5 ran. *Behind, headway halfway, ridden to chase winner final furlong, soon every chance, edged left towards finish, ran on (K Fallon), beaten nk by Attraction*

1st totesport Celebration Mile (Group 2) (Goodwood, August 28) 3yo+ 1m Good to soft **123** (TS 76) 7 ran. *Raced in last, pushed along from 5f out, progress well over 1f out, weaved through to chase leader inside final furlong, driven to lead last 75yds (K Fallon), beat Nayyir by 1¼l*

·**1st** Stan James Online Hungerford Stakes (Group 3) (Newbury, August 14) 3yo+ 7f Good **117** (TS 90) 13 ran. *Tracked leaders, driven to lead inside final 2f, edged left inside final furlong but kept on strongly (K Fallon), beat Suggestive by 1¾l*

3rd Oak Tree Stakes (Group 3) (Goodwood, July 30) 3yo+ 7f Good to firm **104** (TS 94) 12 ran. *Raced in rear, effort 2f out, squeezed through 1f out, ridden and ran on to take 3rd near finish, too much to do (K Fallon), beaten 1¾l by Phantom Wind*

7th Windsor Forest Stakes (Group 2) (Ascot, June 16) 4yo+ 1m Good to firm **107** (TS 75) 10 ran. *Held up towards rear, effort when badly hampered and nearly fell approaching final 2f, not recover (Gary Stevens), beaten 11l by Favourable Terms*

6th Excel Schroders London Boat Show EBF Conqueror Stakes (Listed Race) (Goodwood, May 20) 3yo+ 1m Good to firm **85** (TS 66) 8 ran. *Tracked leaders, ridden to challenge over 2f out, weakened over 1f out (K Fallon), beaten 8½l by Gonfilia*

2003

1st Miles And Morrison October Stakes (Listed) (Ascot, October 11) 3yo+ 7f Good to firm **94** 12 ran ● **2nd** JRA London Office's Kyoto Sceptre Stakes (Listed) (Doncaster, September 11) 3yo+ 7f Good **96** 17 ran ● **6th** City of York Stakes (Listed) (York, August 21) 3yo+ 7f Good to firm **95** 8 ran ● **3rd** Sandringham Rated Stakes (0-110 handicap) (Listed Race) (Ascot, June 21) 3yo 1m Firm **96** 11 ran ● **1st** Pemberton Greenish Redfern Handicap (0-95) (Kempton, June 4) 3yo+ 1m Good to firm **104** 7 ran ● **1st** Norfolk Hotel Birmingham Maiden Fillies' Stakes (Chester, May 7) 3yo 7f Good to firm **88** 9 ran

Other runs

2002 **4th** EBF Hare Maiden Fillies' Stakes (Div I) (Leicester, October 14) 2yo 7f Good to firm **74** 17 ran ● **4th** EBF Meddler Stud Maiden Stakes (Newmarket (July), August 24) 2yo 6f Good to firm **70** 10 ran

a small, but select, line-up, taking on not only the dual 1,000 Guineas winner Attraction, but also Nebraska Tornado, who was twice a Group 1 winner in 2003, and two more fillies with form at the highest level in Majestic Desert and Miss Mambo.

Reservations about the Guineas winner's effectiveness on the watered ground contributed to Chic being sent off a surprise favourite, and when she came through to press Attraction approaching the furlong marker she looked the likelier winner. However, Attraction is devilishly hard to pass, and she held on gamely by a neck.

Chic is likely to stay in training at five. To begin with it would be no surprise to see her bidding to follow in the footsteps of Russian Rhythm in the Lockinge, but she looks worth trying at a mile and a quarter too.

Chic

chestnut filly, 27-2-2000

		Raise A Native	Native Dancer
			Raise You
	Mr Prospector		
		Gold Digger	Nashua
			Sequence
Machiavellian			
b 1987		Halo	Hail to Reason
			Cosmah
	Coup de Folie		
		Raise The Standard	Hoist The Flag
			Natalma
		Nureyev	Northern Dancer
			Special
	Polar Falcon		
		Marie d'Argonne	Jefferson
			Mohair
Exclusive			
ch 1995		Exclusive Native	**Raise A Native**
			Exclusive
	Exclusive Order		
		Bonavista	Dead Ahead
			Ribotina

Bred by Cheveley Park Stud Ltd in England

Sire **Machiavellian**

Won 4 of 7 races, inc. Prix Morny-Gr1, Prix de la Salamandre-Gr1. Also 2nd in 2,000 Guineas. Medium-sized (16.0hh), quick-actioned, with a useful turn of foot. Not raced in very soft conditions, barely lasted a mile. Presumed best of an ordinary crop at 2, did not really progress at 3. Died in June 2004, having sired: Kokuto Julian (Japan Gr3), Phantom Gold (Gr2), Sinyar (Gr3), Vettori (Poule d'Essai des Poulains-Gr1), Susu (Gr2), Titus Livius (Gr2), Whitewater Affair (Gr2), Invermark (Prix du Cadran-Gr1), Kahal (Gr2), Majorien (Gr2), Rebecca Sharp (Coronation S.-Gr1), Almutawakel (Prix Jean Prat-Gr1, Dubai World Cup-UAE Gr1), Fictitious (Gr3), Horatia (Gr3), Best Of The Bests (Prix d'Ispahan-Gr1), Medicean (Lockinge S.-Gr1, Eclipse S.-Gr1), Morning Pride (Gr3), Magic Mission (Gr3), No Excuse Needed (Gr2), Patavellian (Prix de l'Abbaye de Longchamp-Gr1), Storming Home (Champion S.-Gr1, Charles Whittingham Memorial H.-Gr1, Clement L. Hirsch Memorial Championship S.-Gr1), St Paul House (Gr3), Street Cry (Dubai World Cup-UAE Gr1), Medecis (Gr3), Right Approach (Dubai Duty Free [dead-heat]-UAE Gr1), Chic (Gr2), Evolving Tactics (Gr2), Birthstone (Gr3).

Dam **Exclusive**

Won 2 of 6 races, inc. Coronation S.-Gr1. Also placed 3rd in Fillies' Mile and 1,000 Guineas. Big, lengthy, well-made sort. Lightly raced high-class performer, best efforts at a mile, but appeared to stay 10f. Acted well on firm and good to soft ground. Dam of: Chic (2000 f by Machiavellian; Gr2 winner), Echoes (2001 f by Rainbow Quest; unraced), Echelon (2002 f by Danehill; winner). Her yearling is a filly by Grand Lodge.

Pedigree assessment

A Pattern winner in France as a three-year-old, Exclusive Order has founded a thriving family at Cheveley Park since her purchase at Keeneland in 1987. There are now so many of her descendants on the stud that her grand-daughter Chic is to be allowed another season in training before beginning her career as a broodmare. That decision seems likely to pay off, as the filly made significant progress through her 2004 campaign, finally giving Attraction a tremendous run for her money in the Group 1 Sun Chariot Stakes. Like her sire, her dam and her dam's half-brother Entrepreneur, she seems ideally suited by a mile and it will be surprising if she does not take an opportunity to secure a Group 1 bracket over that distance in 2005. *TM*

Chorist

5yo chestnut mare **121**

Pivotal - Choir Mistress (Chief Singer)

Owner Cheveley Park Stud
Trainer W J Haggas
Breeder Cheveley Park Stud

Career: **21** starts won **9** second **5** third **3** **£423,246** win and place

---

By Paul Haigh

THE worst thing that happened to Chorist in her 2004 season was injuring herself slightly as she was being loaded on to the plane for Paris just before the Arc meeting. Or perhaps it was just the worst thing that happened to her connections.

William Haggas had thought a plane journey would be less stressful than boxes and a sea crossing. Well, that's the way it goes sometimes. It was surely quite inevitable, after that inadvertent knock, that the Group 1 Prix de l'Opera, which was to have been her target that weekend, should go to a filly Chorist had already beaten.

How was Haggas to console himself? Maybe with the thought that perhaps the admirable Alexander Goldrun had improved past Chorist in any case. As it turned out he found a better way by running her in the Champion Stakes instead. Even if her run there did suggest quite frustratingly that Chorist probably was still better than Jim Bolger's three-year-old, the satisfaction that her trainer would have derived from her, to most of us, quite startling second place to Haafhd must have been considerable.

Chorist began the season as a five-year-old who had already come quite some way from the days when she was winning handicaps at three, but you wouldn't necessarily have guessed the progress she was going to make by what she achieved in her first outing. In fact you might have guessed that the choice of the Weatherbys Bank Pipalong Stakes over a mile at Pontefract was a recognition of the fact that Listed was just about her level. Chorist duly made most – she's always preferred either to front-run or to sit just off the pace – but the style of her victory wasn't particularly spectacular, nor was the form itself. The run clearly did her good though, psychologically as well as physically, and provided an ideal prep for her next, much more difficult, assignment, the Pretty Polly Stakes at The Curragh, upgraded for the first time to Group 1.

**Chorist's Group 1 win in the Pretty Polly at The Curragh
looked strong form by the end of the season**

It was in the Pretty Polly that she met, and beat, Alexander Goldrun, making the running again and never really looking likely to get caught, even though the runner-up made some ground on her in the final furlong. At the time the reasonable assumption might have been that this was a weak race for a Group 1, even though her principal victim had previously got to within a length of Attraction in the Irish 1,000 Guineas. The Prix de l'Opera, in which Alexander Goldrun showed herself superior to the best French miling filly Grey Lilas, as well as Chorist's subsequent exploit at Newmarket, now suggests it was anything but.

Chorist then moved on to the Nassau Stakes at Goodwood, but here, perhaps with not quite enough use being made of her by Darryll Holland, she just got run out of it, finishing a short head and a neck behind an old rival, Favourable Terms (whom she'd beaten at Chepstow in 2003), and Silence Is Golden. Three weeks later she arrived at Deauville for the Prix Jean Romanet and her performance there in third behind Whortleberry, on ground much softer than ideal, should have alerted us all to the fact that she was a mare on the upgrade.

2004	Race record

2nd Emirates Airline Champion Stakes (Group 1) (Newmarket, October 16) 3yo+ 10f Soft **121** (TS 85) 11 ran. *Led 2f, led over 3f out until over 1f out, not quicken (K Fallon), beaten 2½l by Haafhd*

3rd Prix Jean Romanet (Group 2) (Deauville, August 22) 4yo+ 10f Very soft **116** (TS 69) 13 ran. *Led to 3f out, 2nd straight, soon led again, headed well over 1f out, kept on same pace (D Holland), beaten 2¼l by Whortleberry*

3rd Vodafone Nassau Stakes (Group 1) (Goodwood, July 31) 3yo+ 10f Good to firm **114** (TS 80) 6 ran. *Tracked leader, led 3f out, hard ridden and headed over 1f out, pressed winner after, held when not much room and lost 2nd near finish (D Holland), beaten ½l by Favourable Terms*

1st Audi Pretty Polly Stakes (Group 1) (Curragh, June 26) 3yo+ 10f Good **119** (TS 110) 6 ran. *Made all, ridden and strongly pressed from under 2f out, stayed on well close home (D Holland), beat Alexander Goldrun by ½l*

1st Weatherbys Bank Pipalong Stakes (Listed) (Pontefract, June 7) 4yo+ 1m Good to firm **105** (TS 75) 7 ran. *Led after 1f, quickened 3f out, 3 lengths clear inside final furlong, eased closing stages (K Fallon), beat Ice Palace by 1¼l*

2003	

3rd Princess Royal Willmott Dixon Stakes (Group 3) (Ascot, October 11) 3yo+ 12f Good to firm **101** 9 ran ● **1st** Irish National Stud Blandford Stakes (Group 3) (Curragh, September 14) 3yo+ 10f Good to firm **114** 6 ran ● **8th** Aston Upthorpe Yorkshire Oaks (Group 1) (York, August 20) 3yo+ 12f Good to firm **90** 8 ran ● **1st** Oakgrove Stud Golden Daffodil Stakes (Group 3) (Chepstow, July 25) 3yo+ 10f Good **112** 4 ran ● **1st** EBF Hoppings Stakes (Listed) (Newcastle, June 28) 3yo+ 10f Good to soft **107** 7 ran ● **2nd** tote.co.uk Middleton Stakes (Listed) (York, May 14) 4yo+ 10½f Good to firm **111** 6 ran

Other wins

2002 1st EBF Upavon Fillies' Stakes (Listed) (Salisbury, August 14) 3yo+ 10f Good to firm **106** 8 ran ● **1st** Waitrose Rated Stakes Showcase Handicap (0-100) (Newmarket (July), July 19) 3yo 10f Good to firm **101** 8 ran ● **1st** TFM Cyntergy Classified Stakes (Newbury, June 6) 3yo (0-80) 1m Soft **86** 10 ran ● **1st** Fulford Maiden Stakes (Beverley, April 25) 3yo+ 1m½f Good to firm **75** 12 ran

Even so, when she turned up at Newmarket in the middle of that month for a championship event against colts, it looked a rather quixotic tilt. Someone must have fancied her, though, because she shortened from 33-1 to 20-1 and, ridden forcefully by Kieren Fallon, she turned in what was undoubtedly the performance of her career. She beat all except the resurgent 2,000 Guineas winner, Haafhd, in a field that included Group 1 winners Doyen, Azamour and Refuse To Bend (at least a couple of whom may, admittedly, have gone over the top). With a furlong to go, in fact, it actually looked as if Chorist might pull off an upset, but, although she kept on, she was unable to resist the powerful finish of Haafhd.

Clearly the still improving Chorist was a Listed/Group 3 filly no more. Connections were sorely tempted by the idea of racing her again at six, but she has been retired to Cheveley Park Stud, where she is due to be covered by King's Best.

Chorist
chestnut mare, 11-2-1999

Pivotal ch 1993	Polar Falcon	Nureyev	Northern Dancer Special
		Marie d'Argonne	Jefferson Mohair
	Fearless Revival	Cozzene	Caro Ride The Trails
		Stufida	Bustino Zerbinetta
Choir Mistress b 1990	Chief Singer	Ballad Rock	Bold Lad True Rocket
		Principia	Le Fabuleux Pia
	Blessed Event	Kings Lake	Nijinsky Fish-Bar
		Friedrichsruh	Dschingis Khan Friedensbotschaft

Bred by Cheveley Park Stud Ltd in England

Sire Pivotal

Won 4 of 6 races, inc. King's Stand S.-Gr2, Nunthorpe S.-Gr1. Powerfully built, attractive sort, high-class sprinter on preferred fast ground, seemingly best at 5f. Stands at Cheveley Park Stud, 2005 fee £65,000. Sire of: Golden Apples (Del Mar Oaks-Gr1, Beverly D S.-Gr1, Yellow Ribbon S.-Gr1), Kyllachy (Nunthorpe S.-Gr1), Low Pivot (Gr3), Needwood Blade (Gr3), Ratio (Gr3), Silvester Lady (Preis der Diana-Gr1), Captain Rio (Gr2), Chorist (Pretty Polly S.-Gr1), Megahertz (John C. Mabee H.-Gr1), Ringmoor Down (Gr3), Stolzing (Gr3), Humouresque (Gr3), Pivotal Point (Gr2), Somnus (Haydock Sprint Cup-Gr1, Prix Maurice de Gheest-Gr1, Prix de la Foret-Gr1), Windsor Knot (Gr3).

Dam Choir Mistress

Unraced. Quite well-bred. By a top-class sprinter-miler who became an indifferent sire, but got excellent broodmare Alidiva. Dam a high-class middle-distance performer (Listed winner, 2nd and 4th in Gr1) who produced 5 winners, inc. Sacrament (by Shirley Heights; Gr2, also Gr1-placed) and the dam of Icicle (Gr3). Grand-dam won Preis der Diana, 2nd in Schwarzgold Rennen, produced 5 winners, plus the dam of Faberger (Gr1 in Italy, Gr3 in France). Family of Derby winners Blue Peter, Blakeney and Morston. Dam of: Operatic (1995 f by Goofalik; winner), Choirgirl (1996 f by Unfuwain; winner, Gr3-placed), Cuneythan (1997 c by Slip Anchor; Gr2 winner in Turkey), Choir School (1998 c by Unfuwain; unraced), Chorist (1999 f by Pivotal; Gr 1 winner), Cantoris (2000 g by Unfuwain; placed), Choir Leader (2001 f by Sadler's Wells; winner), Choralist (2002 f by Danehill; unraced to date). Her yearling is a colt by King's Best, Valiant, she has a filly foal by Pivotal, and is due to Singspiel in 2005.

Pedigree assessment

Cynics reckoned that the promotion of the Pretty Polly Stakes to Group 1 status in 2004 had just enabled Chorist to gain a slice of cheap top-level prestige. That judgement ignored the fact that the five-year-old had put up a career-best effort, and by the end of the season it could be dismissed as mere hogwash; her runner-up, Alexander Goldrun, had herself gone on to a Group 1 triumph in the well-established Prix de l'Opera, and Chorist had attained even greater heights as second-best to Haafhd in the Champion Stakes, with a host of celebrities behind her. The plan to keep her in training at six sadly had to be abandoned, but Chorist will prove a tremendous asset to Cheveley Park Stud, whose flagship sire she has done so much to promote. *TM*

Damson (Ire)

2yo bay filly **110**

Entrepreneur - Tadkiyra (Ire) (Darshaan)
Owner Mrs John Magnier & M Tabor
Trainer David Wachman
Breeder Epona Bloodstock Ltd

Career: **5** starts | won **4** | second **0** | third **1** | **£234,605** win and place

By Alan Sweetman

A GENERATION ago the marriage of Vincent O'Brien's daughter Susan to John Magnier cemented an alliance that has profoundly influenced the history of racing and breeding in Ireland. The legendary trainer and his visionary son-in-law inaugurated a bloodstock empire that has dwarfed its domestic competitors and has exerted a worldwide impact. With the marriage in 2002 of his daughter Katie to David Wachman, Magnier, in his turn, became a father-in-law to a talented young trainer who started out with jumpers and cheaply-bought two-year-olds.

Wachman's marriage raised his profile and brought some better-bred horses into his yard to run in the colours of his mother-in-law, and of Coolmore associate Michael Tabor. Among the 2004 juveniles was an Entrepreneur filly who cost €160,000 as a yearling. Named Damson, she made her debut in a five-runner fillies' maiden at Cork in April.

With Ballydoyle unrepresented in the race, Jamie Spencer was free to take the mount, but punters failed to draw any positive conclusion from the riding arrangement and the filly drifted from 9-4 to 5-1 in the face of support for Cookie Cutter, a Mick Kinane-partnered newcomer. The race provided an ideal introduction for Damson, who quickened up well to score by a comfortable two lengths from The Quiet Woman, who had finished third in an above-average renewal of the opening two-year-old race of the season at The Curragh.

Next stop for Damson was the Listed Swordlestown Stud Sprint for fillies over six furlongs at Naas in early June. Only six lined up, but five were previous winners, including the British challenger Umniya, and it proved an informative contest. Spencer was again available, and Damson picked up in stylish fashion from two furlongs out to beat Pictavia, a Leopardstown maiden winner over seven furlongs who would later boost the form by finishing second to Chelsea Rose in the Moyglare Stud Stakes. Umniya was third and fourth place went to Slip Dance, whose maiden

Damson announces her arrival with victory at Royal Ascot before going on to Group 1 success in the Phoenix Stakes

win at humble Ballinrobe was the prelude to a season that brought further victories at Newmarket and The Curragh.

Wachman's initial reaction was to dismiss the possibility of a challenge for the Queen Mary at Royal Ascot, but a rethink was prompted in the week before the race when the trainer alerted his father-in-law to Racing Post Ratings that put her 5lb clear of the remainder. Duly despatched as the sole Irish challenger for the five-furlong Group 2 event, she was sent off the 11-2 joint favourite with Soar. After settling for Spencer off the pace, she began her move through the field a quarter of a mile out and was switched to the right to take the lead from the pace-setting outsider Bunditten just inside the last furlong. At the finish she had three lengths to spare over Soar.

By the time of her next outing in the Group 1 Independent Waterford Wedgwood Phoenix Stakes at The Curragh in August, Soar had franked the form by winning the Princess Margaret Stakes at Ascot, while the domestic programme had yet to unveil a juvenile colt of star quality. Rather surprisingly, British stables ignored the race, and in a six-runner field

2004   Race record

3rd Sky Bet Cheveley Park Stakes (Group 1) (Newmarket, September 30) 2yo 6f Good **106** (TS 95) 7 ran. *Chased leaders, ridden and every chance from over 1f out, ran on (K Fallon), beaten ¹/₂l by Magical Romance*

1st Independent Waterford Wedgwood Phoenix Stakes (Group 1) (Curragh, August 8) 2yo 6f Good to firm **110** (TS 86) 6 ran. *Always in touch, 3rd and ridden over 2f out, improved to challenge 1¹/₂f out, led under 1f out, stayed on well (K Fallon), beat Oratorio by ³/₄l*

1st Queen Mary Stakes (Group 2) (Ascot, June 16) 2yo 5f Good to firm **110** (TS 97) 17 ran. *Settled in rear and well off the pace, rapid progress 2f out, switched right over 1f out, led just inside final furlong, driven clear, impressive (J P Spencer), beat Soar by 3l*

1st Swordlestown Stud Sprint Stakes (Listed) (Fillies) (Naas, June 7) 2yo 6f Good to firm **104** (TS 82) 6 ran. *Tracked leaders, improved to lead travelling well under 2f out, ridden clear 1f out, eased close home, comfortably (J P Spencer), beat Pictavia by 2l*

1st Irish Stallion Farms EBF Fillies Maiden (Cork, April 12) 2yo 5f Yielding **84** 5 ran. *Tracked leaders in 4th, 3rd halfway, ridden to lead over 1f out, stayed on well to go clear inside final furlong (J P Spencer), beat The Quiet Woman by 2l*

Aidan O'Brien supplied the only meaningful opposition with Russian Blue, winner of his first three races before finishing second in the Railway Stakes, and the Anglesey Stakes winner Oratorio. With Spencer on Russian Blue, Kieren Fallon took over on Damson, and there was a brief moment of anxiety for her supporters when he had to rouse her over two furlongs out. The response was not as visually striking as at Royal Ascot, but she picked up effectively enough to lead a furlong out, staying on to beat Oratorio by three-quarters of a length with Russian Blue half a length back in third.

Wachman now prepared Damson for the Cheveley Park Stakes in which she would clash again with Soar, who had added further lustre to the Queen Mary form by beating the consistent Salsa Brava in the Lowther Stakes at York. Soar became upset in the stalls and was slowly away, but everything seemed to be going to script for Damson when she began to wind up a challenge from two furlongs out. However, on this occasion the acceleration was absent, and in a bunch finish she was beaten a neck and the same behind nursery graduate Magical Romance and Suez.

The proximity of Golden Legacy in fourth, and of compatriot Slip Dance, unlucky not to finish closer than fifth, cast a shadow over the form, and for the first time Damson's credentials as a 1,000 Guineas aspirant began to look less certain. Perhaps she was feeling the effects of a season that began back in April, but her overall form has proved a great credit to Wachman in his first exposure to the demands of Group 1 competition. Doubtless his remarkably shrewd father-in-law has his own ideas about whether the filly will avoid the eventual fate of her close relative Geminiani, a King Of Kings filly who won both starts at two and finished second in the Musidora only to lose form thereafter, but he will have derived particular pleasure from Damson's emergence as Ireland's best juvenile filly of 2004.

Damson

bay filly, 21-4-2002

		Northern Dancer	Nearctic
			Lady Angela
	Sadler's Wells		
		Fairy Bridge	Bold Reason
Entrepreneur			Special
b 1994			
		Exclusive Native	Raise A Native
			Exclusive
	Exclusive Order		
		Bonavista	Dead Ahead
			Ribotina
		Shirley Heights	Mill Reef
			Hardiemma
	Darshaan		
		Delsy	Abdos
Tadkiyra			Kelty
b 1989			
		Silver Shark	Buisson Ardent
			Palsaka
	Tremogia		
		Tonnera	Wild Risk
			Texana

Bred by Epona Bloodstock in Ireland. €160,000 Goffs Orby yearling

Sire Entrepreneur

Won 3 of 6 races at 2 and 3. At 2, won 2 (7-8f) of 3 starts. At 3 won 1 (2,000 Guineas-Gr1) of 3 starts, also 4th Derby-Gr1. By outstanding stamina-orientated sire out of high-class 6-7f filly. Brother to Oaks 2nd Dance A Dream and 12-13f Listed winner Sadler's Image, half-brother to Coronation Stakes winner Exclusive (dam of high-class miler Chic). Retired to Coolmore Stud in Ireland, exported to Japan after 2001 season. Oldest progeny 5, sire of (northern hemisphere foals): Princely Venture (Gr2), Vintage Tipple (Irish Oaks-Gr1), Damson (Phoenix S-Gr1).

Dam Tadkiyra

Unraced at 2, won 1 (10f) of 5 starts at 3 in France. By top-class 12f performer, very good sire and outstanding broodmare sire, out of unraced daughter of Prix Saint-Alary winner and Pouliches 2nd Tonnera. Half-sister to Group 3 winners Tashkourgan, Tashtiya and Tassmoun, plus Listed winners Tarikhana (dam of Gr1 winner Tiraaz) and Talaja (dam of Gr3 winner Tiangar). Family of 2yo Group winners Blue Dakota, Tarwiya. Dam of: Takipy (1995 f by Persian Bold; unraced), Sir Legend (1996 c by El Gran Senor; placed), Cuts Both Ways (1998 c by Diesis; unplaced), Geminiani (2000 f by King Of Kings; Gr3 winner), Motorway (2001 c by Night Shift; winner), Damson (2002 f by Entrepreneur; Gr1 winner), 2003 c by King Charlemagne (200,000gns yearling).

Pedigree assessment

This family traces to the fast Texana, but Damson has shown more speed than most of her closest relatives, and a little more than might be anticipated from her pedigree. She should stay a mile but probably no further, even though very close relative Geminiani was placed in the Musidora Stakes over an extended 10f. Entrepreneur's record at stud is patchy, but in general his progeny have progressed from 2 to 3. Damson – along with National Stakes runner-up Berenson – is precocious for an Entrepreneur, but on pedigree there is every reason to believe she will train on. *JH*

Darasim (Ire)

6yo bay gelding **116**

Kahyasi - Dararita (Ire) (Halo (USA))

Owner Markus Graff

Trainer M Johnston

Breeder His Highness The Aga Khan's Studs

Career: **34** starts | won **10** | second **2** | third **6** | **£341,973** win and place

---

By Mark Blackman

ONCE in a while, a horse comes along whose preferences are so pronounced, it's nigh-on impossible to miss them. In these days of electronic form books, a racehorse's entire career can be viewed on a single screen, and his good days and bad days on the track stand out like sore thumbs.

Darasim practically represents a case study in this phenomenon. By the end of his 2004 campaign, he had raced 34 times, in four countries. It's clear he hates soft or heavy ground, so strip those out of his record. He doesn't really show his best at distances short of a mile and three-quarters, either, so ignore anything he has done over shorter. And he doesn't really stay distances beyond two miles – although he has often tried them – so forget them too.

What's left are 11 starts, producing form figures of 11232711111. The only real blot on his copybook came at a time when trainer Mark Johnston insisted he "wasn't firing" and his most recent run of five straight successes under his optimum conditions included two defeats of Westerner, admittedly before connections of the outstanding French stayer had found the key to him, and an impressive victory in the 2004 Goodwood Cup.

Darasim in so many ways embodies the type of horse with which Johnston excels – a point-and-go front-runner who will run his heart out for as long as his stamina will allow. Like his trainer, he's always trying.

His first two starts in 2004 amply illustrated his going preferences. Beaten miles in a forgettable Sagaro Stakes run in a bog at Ascot in April, he encountered a much better surface in a Group 3 contest at Baden-Baden less than four weeks later, and ran out a ready all-the-way winner.

He returned to Ascot for the Gold Cup at the Royal meeting in June. The ground was riding fast, but the two-and-a-half-mile distance was beyond his best and he was up in class. He never got to the front, but after holding every chance at the quarter-mile mark, stayed on at one pace to finish

Darasim, with conditions to suit in the Goodwood Cup, takes full advantage to complete an all-the-way success

third behind the highly progressive Papineau and Westerner, beaten four lengths. It was a performance that ranked not far off his best, and he had stretched his stamina and class out longer than many had anticipated.

Not surprisingly, Darasim's next port of call was Glorious Goodwood, a fixture that had proved a happy hunting ground for him in both 2002 and 2003, when he had gained a handicap win and a good placing on each occasion. This time, connections focused all their attention on just the one contest — the Group 2 Goodwood Cup.

The distance of two miles and the good to firm going were ideal for him. On recent form he held a significant edge over his eight rivals and he looked assured of the uncontested lead that played to his strengths. Tom Segal, Pricewise of the Racing Post, highlighted the great value to be had in odds of 5-2 and by post time Darasim was trading at 11-8.

Everything went to script. Bounced straight into the lead by regular partner Joe Fanning, Darasim was soon controlling matters at the head of affairs. A mile passed with no challenge to his lead and a kick in the belly at the three-furlong marker was all the encouragement Darasim

2004   Race record

6th Prix du Cadran Casino Les Princes Barriere de Cannes (Group 1) (Longchamp, October 3) 4yo+ 2m4f Good **106** (TS 64) 8 ran. *Pushed along to race in close 2nd, led over 3f out to over 2f out, no extra once headed (K Darley), beaten 11½l by Westerner*

5th GNER Doncaster Cup (Group 2) (Doncaster, September 9) 3yo+ 2m2f Good **111** (TS 36) 8 ran. *Led, quickened 4f out, headed over 2f out, faded approaching final furlong (J Fanning), beaten 8½l by Kasthari and Millenary*

1st Lady O Goodwood Cup (Group 2) (Goodwood, July 29) 3yo+ 2m Good to firm **113** (TS 85) 9 ran. *Made all, set steady pace until kicked on over 3f out, urged along and drew clear from 2f out, unchallenged (J Fanning), beat Royal Rebel by 2½l*

3rd Gold Cup (Group 1) (Ascot, June 17) 4yo+ 2m4f Good to firm **116** (TS 98) 13 ran. *Chased leaders, ridden and every chance 2f out, stayed on same pace (J Fanning), beaten 4l by Papineau*

1st Betty Barclay-Rennen (Group 3) (Baden- Baden, May 22) 4yo+ 2m Good **110** 8 ran. *Made all, ridden out (J Fanning), beat Bailamos by 1½l*

6th Bovis Homes Sagaro Stakes (Group 3) (Ascot, April 28) 4yo+ 2m Soft 13 ran. *Chased leaders until weakened 7f out, tailed off (J Fanning), beaten 87+l by Risk Seeker*

Other wins

2003 1st Prix Gladiateur Royal Thalasso Barriere (Group 3) (Longchamp, September 14) 4yo+ 1m7½f Good to soft **119** 9 ran ● **1st** Prix Kergorlay (Group 2) (Deauville, August 24) 3yo+ 1m7f Good to soft **116** 9 ran ● **1st** ladbrokes.com Prestige Handicap (0-105) (Goodwood, July 29) 3yo+ 1m6f Good **119** 15 ran **2002 1st** Lady O Memorial Glorious Rated Stakes (0-110 handicap) (Listed Race) (Goodwood, August 2) 4yo+ 12f Good to firm **110** 5 ran ● **1st** NetBetSports TeleBet 0808 100 1121 Conditions Stakes (Ripon, April 27) 4yo+ 12½f Good to firm **108** 5 ran **2001 1st** Tote Exacta Mallard Stakes Showcase Handicap (0-105) (Doncaster, September 14) 3yo+ 1m6½f Good to soft **108** 12 ran ● **1st** Esso Three Rivers Oil McEnery Cup Handicap (0-95) (Gowran Park, June 24) 3yo+ 1m6f Good to firm **92** 10 ran ● **1st** Kilmore Quay Maiden (Wexford, May 5) 3yo 1m5f Yielding to soft **78** 6 ran

needed to take advantage of the head start he had been gifted. He had only to be pushed out inside the final furlong to beat his stablemate Royal Rebel by two and a half lengths.

Given a short break until the autumn, Darasim returned for two more cracks at the top stayers but, while he got his ground on each occasion, he once again demonstrated that extreme distances stretch his stamina. In the two-and-a-quarter-mile Doncaster Cup, he led to the two-furlong pole before fading into fifth behind the dead-heaters Millenary and Kasthari. Up to two and a half miles for the Prix du Cadran at Longchamp in October, he was again at the head of affairs with two furlongs to run before being swamped by Westerner and others. He stays, but he doesn't stay forever.

Tough and consistent, Darasim managed to raise his profile in 2004 without ever matching the Racing Post Rating of 119 he had achieved at Longchamp in September 2003.

"He'll try again next year," said Deirdre Johnston after he had bowed out for the campaign. You can count on that.

Darasim
bay gelding, 7-5-1998

	Kahyasi b 1985	Ile de Bourbon	Nijinsky	Northern Dancer
				Flaming Page
			Roseliere	Misti
				Peace Rose
		Kadissya	Blushing Groom	Red God
				Runaway Bride
			Kalkeen	Sheshoon
				Gioia
	Dararita b 1991	Halo	Hail To Reason	Turn-to
				Nothirdchance
			Cosmah	Cosmic Bomb
				Almahmoud
		Darara	Top Ville	High Top
				Sega Ville
			Delsy	Abdos
				Kelty

Bred by the Aga Khan in Ireland

Sire Kahyasi

Won sole start at 2. At 3, won 4 (inc. Lingfield Derby Trial-Gr3, Derby-Gr1, Irish Derby-Gr1) of 6 starts, also 2nd Prix Niel-Gr2. By top-class 12f performer who had just reasonable success before his export to Japan. Half-brother to Group 3 winner Kaliana from family of Gr1 winners Key Change and Milan. Stands at Haras de Bonneval in France, 2005 fee €6,000. Oldest progeny 14, sire of: Massyar (Gr2), Shaiybara (Gr3), Bayrika (Gr3), Shemaran (Gr2), Shamadara (Gr2), Vereva (Prix de Diane-Gr1), Enzeli (Gold Cup-Gr1), Zainta (Prix Saint-Alary-Gr1, Prix de Diane-Gr1), Mouramara (Gr2), Nazirali (Gr2), Choc Ice (E P Taylor S-Gr1), Darasim (Gr2), Sharbayan (Gr3), Khalkevi (Grand Prix de Paris-Gr1), Kalabar (Gr2).

Dam Dararita

Winner of only start, over 12f at 3 in France. By top-class US performer and excellent sire, out of top-class 12f filly. Half-sister to Diaghilev (HKGr1), Darazarai (AusGr1), Rhagaas (3rd Prix du Jockey-Club-Gr1), Kilimanjaro (Gr2 placed) and Dariyoun (Gr3 placed). Family of Darshaan. Dam of: Darak (1996 c by Doyoun; jumps winner), Darariyna (1997 f by Shirley Heights; winner), Darasim (1998 c by Kahyasi; Gr2 winner, Gr1 placed), Darabela (2000 f by Desert King; winner), Darabanka (2001 f by In The Wings; winner), 2003 f by Barathea.

Pedigree assessment

The Aga Khan is peerless at breeding high-class stayers, and the massive size of his operation means that he inevitably culls not only future successful broodmares but also future smart performers. Darasim is an example. His third dam Delsy has a marvellous record for the Aga Khan's studs, not least as dam of Darshaan. And his homebred sire Kahyasi has had virtually all of his major success at stud for the Aga, though his daughter Hasili has produced a string of top performers for Khalid Abdullah. The gelded Darasim should continue to be a major force in European staying events in 2005. *JH*

Diamond Green (Fr)

3yo bay colt   **121**

Green Desert (USA) - Diamonaka (Fr) (Akarad (Fr))

Owner Lagardere Family

Trainer A Fabre

Breeder Lagardere Elevage Snc

Career: **10** starts | won **3** | second **4** | third **1** | **£212,062** win and place

By Steve Dennis

DEVOTEES of the Tour de France, particularly French ones, have a deep-seated affection for Raymond Poulidor, who never won a Tour but who will forever be remembered as 'the eternal second' after his long career encompassed five-time winners Jacques Anquetil and Eddy Merckx.

Poulidor was runner-up in three Tours and third in five more; the unfortunate Diamond Green endured a three-year-old campaign that brought him an equivalent lack of glory. France has found itself a new Poulidor.

One of the most promising juveniles of 2003, he was expected to cross the Channel for the Newmarket 2,000 Guineas, but was diverted towards his home equivalent as connections did not wish to try him in the heat of Classic competition without a prep outing. Stepped up to a mile for the first time in the Prix de Fontainebleau on his reappearance, Diamond Green finished last of the four runners behind Racing Post Trophy winner American Post, but was promoted a place following the disqualification of the wayward Antonius Pius, who had hampered him.

Diamond Green was then sent back to Longchamp for the Poule d'Essai des Poulains and a rematch with both American Post and Antonius Pius. Ridden by Gary Stevens and sent off the 6-1 second choice, Diamond Green enhanced his reputation considerably despite his half-length defeat by American Post in a notorious race – thanks to our old friend Antonius Pius, who earned his rider Jamie Spencer a six-day ban when lurching across to the far rail well inside the final furlong and seriously impeded Diamond Green, who held every chance at the time.

While Diamond Green could not be said to have been robbed of Classic victory, there was a possibility that his run would have carried him to success. Stevens was more certain, saying that his mount would have been "a sure winner if the incident hadn't happened". The view from the saddle is often skewed, but Diamond Green was most definitely unlucky.

**Diamond Green had a consistent but frustrating season,
going closest when second to Azamour at Royal Ascot**

The St James's Palace Stakes at Royal Ascot is the magnet for Guineas
winners and placed horses alike, and Diamond Green had his first race
outside France when lining up – once again alongside his nemesis Antonius
Pius – in a field that also included Guineas winners Haafhd, Bachelor
Duke and Brunel and the crack Irish miler Azamour, placed at both
Newmarket and The Curragh.

At least this time Diamond Green managed to steer clear of, and finish
ahead of, Antonius Pius, though he again missed out on Group 1 glory
– this time by a neck – when Azamour proved just the stronger in the
dying strides. It was another Poulidor moment for the French colt, who
went on to finish runner-up for the third consecutive time in the Group
3 Prix Messidor at Deauville, on good to soft ground, before returning
to Group 1 level in the Prix du Moulin, the traditional French mile
championship, at Longchamp in early September.

Ranged against him were several of the usual suspects, notably American
Post and Antonius Pius – Diamond Green must have been sick of the
sight of him. Fate had another trap in store for Diamond Green, however,
as he was drawn on the wide outside in the 11-runner field and was always
likely to find such an exposed position compromising his chance.

2004   Race record

8th NetJets Breeders' Cup Mile (Grade 1) (Turf) (Lone Star Park, October 30) 3yo+ 1m
Yielding **113** 14 ran. *Held up in 13th, 10th straight, never dangerous (L Dettori), beaten 4l by Singletary*

8th Queen Elizabeth II Stakes (Sponsored By NetJets) (Group 1) (Ascot, September 25) 3yo+ 1m Good to firm **94** (TS 83) 11 ran. *Settled in rear, going well enough over 2f out, ridden well over 1f out, weakened (C Soumillon), beaten 15l by Rakti*

2nd Netjets Prix du Moulin de Longchamp (Group 1) (Longchamp, September 5) 3yo+ 1m Good to soft **120** (TS 94) 11 ran. *Held up, 9th straight, good headway approaching final furlong to dispute 2nd 100yds out, kept on same pace to just hold 2nd (T Gillet), beaten 1l by Grey Lilas*

2nd Prix Messidor (Group 3) (Deauville, July 11) 3yo+ 1m Good to soft **113** (TS 99) 6 ran. *Pressed leader on outside until led narrowly just under 2f out, headed over 1f out, no extra (Gary Stevens), beaten 2¹/₂l by Ryono*

2nd St James's Palace Stakes (Group 1) (Ascot, June 15) 3yo 1m Good to firm **121** (TS 122) 11 ran. *Held up in midfield, effort over 2f out, ridden and progress over 1f out, challenged entering final furlong, ran on but just held (Gary Stevens), beaten nk by Azamour*

2nd Gainsborough Poule d'Essai des Poulains (Group 1) (Longchamp, May 16) 3yo 1m Good to firm **112** (TS 99) 7 ran. *Held up in 6th to straight, got through on rail 1¹/₂f out, every chance when slightly hampered inside final furlong, rallied close home (Gary Stevens), beaten ¹/₂l by American Post*

3rd Prix de Fontainebleau (Group 3) (Longchamp, April 25) 3yo 1m Good to soft **103** (TS 85) 4 ran. *Tracked winner to straight, pressed him briefly over 1¹/₂f out, one pace when crossed and snatched up inside final furlong, finished 4th, promoted to 3rd (Gary Stevens), beaten 3³/₄l by American Post*

2003

1st Prix la Rochette (Group 3) (Longchamp, September 11) 2yo 7f Soft **111** 7 ran ● 1st Prix des Roches Noires (Deauville, August 19) 2yo 7f Good to soft **98** 5 ran ● 1st Prix de Marolles (Unraced Colts & Geldings) (Deauville, July 6) 2yo 7f Good to soft 10 ran

In what was, unusually, a top French race run at a decent clip throughout, Diamond Green again ran an honest, high-class race but found himself playing second fiddle yet again, a lament made more ironic by the fact that it was his stablemate Grey Lilas who beat him by a length. Antonius Pius was at his bridle, a nose back in third.

Roland de Longevialle, racing manager to the Lagardere family, said afterwards: "Diamond Green has been involved in the finishes of the Poulains, the St James's Palace and the Moulin, and is one of the best milers in Europe in a vintage year." Few could argue with him, but to the connections of a potential stallion the most fortunate Group 1 success is worth far more than any number of worthy what-might-have-beens.

Unfortunately, Diamond Green's season then drifted into obscurity. He could never get into the race when eighth in the Queen Elizabeth II Stakes at Ascot and occupied the same position in the Breeders' Cup Mile, when he missed the break and found it impossible to make his presence felt. It was a shabby end to a season that had promised so much.

Diamond Green

brown colt, 7-4-2001

		Northern Dancer	Nearctic / Natalma
	Danzig		
Green Desert b 1983		Pas de Nom	Admiral's Voyage / Petitioner
	Foreign Courier	Sir Ivor	Sir Gaylord / Attica
		Courtly Dee	Never Bend / Tulle
	Akarad	Labus	Busted / Cordovilla
Diamonaka gr 1990		Licata	Abdos / Gaia
	Diamond Seal	Persian Bold	Bold Lad (Ire) / Relkarunner
		Panserina	Sovereign Path / Pampalina

Bred by Lagardere Elevage Snc in France

Sire Green Desert

Won 5 of 14 races at 2 and 3, inc. July S-Gr3, Flying Childers S-Gr2, July Cup-Gr1, Haydock Sprint Cup-Gr2. Also 2nd 2,000 Guineas. Small, strong, good mover. Tough, consistent, effective 6-8f. Stands at Nunnery Stud, 2005 fee £85,000. Oldest progeny 16, sire of G1 winners: Sheikh Albadou (Nunthorpe S, Breeders' Cup Sprint, Haydock Sprint Cup), Owington (July Cup), Oriental Express (Queen Elizabeth II Cup-HK), Cape Cross (Lockinge S), Desert Prince (Irish 2,000 Guineas, Prix du Moulin, Queen Elizabeth II S), Tamarisk (Haydock Sprint Cup), White Heart (Charles Whittingham H, Churchill Downs Turf Classic), Invincible Spirit (Haydock Sprint Cup), Rose Gypsy (Poule d'Essai des Pouliches), Heat Haze (Beverly D S, Matriarch S), Oasis Dream (Middle Park S, July Cup, Nunthorpe S).

Dam Diamonaka

Smart 12f 3yo in France, won 1 of 5 starts, also 2nd Prix de Malleret-Gr2, 2nd Prix de Royaumont-Gr3. By top-class French 12f performer and fair sire out of useful 10f Irish filly. Half-sister to Gr3 winner Diamond Dance (by Dancehall), Gr2 winner Diamond Mix (Linamix) and Gr3 winner Diasilixa (Linamix). Diamond Seal grand-daughter of Irish Oaks winner Pampalina. Dam of: Diamonixa (1995 f by Linamix; Gr3 winner), Dalis Grey (1996 f by Linamix: winner), Diamond Gift (1997 c by Cadeaux Genereux; winner), Diamilina (1998 f by Linamix; Gr2 winner, Gr1 placed), Diable Mix (1999 c by Linamix; winner), Dimonix (2000 c by Linamix; winner), Diamond Green (2001 c by Green Desert; Gr3 winner, Gr1 placed), Diaxmona (2002 f by Linamix; unraced), 2003 c by Grand Lodge.

Pedigree assessment

This family has done extremely well for the late Jean-Luc Lagardere over the last decade, thanks in great measure to use of the owner-breeder's stallion Linamix. Green Desert is a very different sort of stallion, and he is responsible for Diamond Green's miling speed. However, there is a fair chance Diamond Green will stay 10f on pedigree. Green Desert has had poor fortune with his stallion sons, with Sheikh Albadou, Owington and Tamarisk having had their stud careers truncated for various reasons. But the emergence of Ouija Board's sire Cape Cross and continued success of Desert Prince in 2004 has reinforced Green Desert's popularity as a sire of sires, and if Diamond Green can gain a top-level win he should make a popular sire. *JH*

Divine Proportions (USA)

2yo bay filly **117**

Kingmambo (USA) - Myth To Reality (Fr) (Sadler's Wells (USA))
Owner Niarchos Family
Trainer P Bary
Breeder Flaxman Holdings Ltd

Career: **5** starts | won **5** second **0** third **0** **£275,388** win and place

By James Willoughby

IT WAS like deja vu, all over again. The Niarchos family and trainer Pascal Bary captured the Group 1 Prix Marcel Boussac for a third successive year, this time with Divine Proportions.

Divine Proportions proved herself the champion juvenile filly of Europe with her Longchamp success. In assessing her prospects of achieving a similar status at three, we must refer to her name. For a two-year-old, she did indeed have ideal dimensions. But has she the size and scope to train on?

Of course, plenty of horses have defied gloomy prognostications surrounding their physique. Just as there is no guarantee that a big two-year-old will still enjoy the same physical advantage in its second season, there is equally no reason why a smallish horse should not bulk up. So enough of the hypothesis, let us concentrate on what Divine Proportions has actually achieved.

Divine Proportions has already put the record straight on the matter of her stamina. Starting at 8-11, she won the Prix Marcel Boussac on the Arc undercard by two lengths from Titian Time. A steadily run race did not really provide her with the ideal set-up to display the extent of her superiority. Nonetheless, she remained unbeaten after five starts with complete authority. "Each time she wins, she wins more easily," said Bary. It was hard to disagree.

Bary and Divine Proportions' jockey Christophe Lemaire had never doubted their filly's ability to stay a mile. When a two-year-old shows as much precocity as the daughter of Kingmambo, there is always a doubt, however small. Back in May, Divine Proportions was forward enough to win a newcomers' event at Maisons-Laffitte over five furlongs, and spanning a distance range of three furlongs is a rare enough achievement for a juvenile.

That initial success gave Bary his cue to launch Divine Proportions into Group company. A month later at Chantilly, she came up against the much-vaunted Great Blood in the Group 3 Prix du Bois, still over

Divine Proportions lands the Group 1 Prix Marcel Boussac to confirm her position as favourite for the 1,000 Guineas

the minimum trip. Conceding experience and first run, she stormed past the odds-on favourite after taking a little while to gather stride, finally extending the margin to four lengths. This was a very serious performance and signalled the depth of her talent.

It would be trite to say that Divine Proportions went on to prove herself against colts in the Group 2 Prix Robert Papin in July. Only three of the eight-strong field were of that sex, and none started at shorter than 14-1. The betting suggested Andre Fabre's Portrayal posed the biggest threat, and she had been successful in only a minor event at Chantilly.

That Divine Proportions seemed to make hard work of winning by a length tells us more about her racing character than her limitations. She is inclined to race lazily when first picked up and asked to quicken, and for a stride or two during all four of her Pattern-race wins it looked as if she might even be struggling. This is a deceptive impression, however, and being something of an introvert is no bad thing in a racehorse.

The Papin is over five and a half furlongs, so Divine Proportions only had another 110 yards to travel in the Group 1 Prix Morny. It was a bigger step up in terms of class, however.

Fabre was intent on another crack at her with the wildly impressive Prix de Cabourg winner Layman and there was international competition,

2004

1st Prix Marcel Boussac Royal Barriere Deauville (Group 1) (Longchamp, October 3) 2yo 1m Good **114** (TS 111) 10 ran. *Tracked leaders, disputing 2nd straight, pushed along over 1½f out, driven to challenge approaching final f, led 1f out, ridden clear (C-P Lemaire), beat Titian Time by 2l*

1st Prix Morny Casinos Barriere (Group 1) (Deauville, August 22) 2yo 6f Very soft **117** (TS 117) 9 ran. *Always in touch, led inside final furlong, ridden out (C-P Lemaire), beat Layman by 1½l*

1st Prix Robert Papin (Group 2) (Maisons-Laffitte, July 25) 2yo 5½f Good **103** (TS 76) 8 ran. *Close 3rd on outside, driven to lead just inside final furlong, pushed out (C-P Lemaire), beat Shifting Place by 1l*

1st Prix du Bois (Group 3) (Chantilly, June 28) 2yo 5f Good **111** (TS 100) 7 ran. *Tracked leaders, 3rd halfway, ridden 1½f out, quickened to lead approaching final furlong, went clear inside final furlong, easily (C-P Lemaire), beat Great Blood by 4l*

1st Prix Chateau Bouscat (Unraced) (Maisons-Laffitte, May 26) 2yo 5f Good to soft **80** 9 ran. *(C-P Lemaire), beat Pivock by ¾l*

too. From Ireland came Russian Blue, who carried important juvenile form lines on his shoulders; from England, the July Stakes winner Captain Hurricane, Mystical Land, Tournedos and Doctor's Cave; from Italy, even, the Papin runner-up Shifting Place, beaten once by Divine Proportions but not yet vanquished to the satisfaction of her connections.

They may as well have stayed at home. Divine Proportions showed her own brand of everyday brilliance, sustaining a powerful run from the back to wear down Layman and win by a length and a half, with Russian Blue the same distance back in third and a three-length gap to Captain Hurricane. Very strong form, by any handicapper's standards.

An interesting point came out of this race. On deep ground at Deauville, and off a strong pace, several of her rivals came off a true line as they progressed to the end of their ability. Not so Divine Proportions. Many took this as the stamp of her professionalism, but there was another explanation: Divine Proportions was not going to lose balance because, despite appearances, she really wasn't fully extended.

To Paris, then, for her coronation. She had no trouble at all. After all, it was hardly the strongest field assembled for the Boussac, though the ground was the fastest she had encountered by a fair margin.

So, what will happen next year? For those of a statistical bent, since 1991 no Boussac winner has gone on to win a Classic, though Six Perfections should have done so. True, the race has produced subsequent Group 1 winners, such as Gold Splash, Sierra Madre and Ryafan, not to mention Six Perfections, but all have missed their Classic cue.

Conventional wisdom suggests caution about Divine Proportions' future development, but Bary thinks differently. "She is a handy filly and very well balanced. She is improving all the time," he said.

When it comes to Divine Proportions, beauty is in the eye of the beholder.

Divine Proportions   *bay filly, 13-3-2002*

Kingmambo b 1990	Mr Prospector	Raise A Native	Native Dancer / Raise You
		Gold Digger	Nashua / Sequence
	Miesque	Nureyev	**Northern Dancer** / **Special**
		Pasadoble	Prove Out / Santa Quilla
Myth To Reality b 1986	Sadler's Wells	**Northern Dancer**	Nearctic / Natalma
		Fairy Bridge	Bold Reason / **Special**
	Millieme	Mill Reef	Never Bend / Milan Mill
		Hardiemma	Hardicanute / Grand Cross

Bred by Flaxman Holdings Ltd in Kentucky

Sire Kingmambo

Won 5 of 13 races, inc. Poule d'Essai des Poulains-Gr1, St James's Palace S.-Gr1, Prix du Moulin de Longchamp-Gr1. Medium-sized, attractive individual. Among the best milers of his generation, game, consistent, with a good turn of foot. Sire of G1 winners: El Condor Pasa (NHK Mile Cup, Japan Cup, Grand Prix de Saint-Cloud), Lemon Drop Kid (Futurity S., Belmont S., Travers S., Whitney S., Woodward H.), Bluemamba (Poule d'Essai des Pouliches), King's Best (2,000 Guineas), Malhub (Golden Jubilee S.), Okawango (Grand Criterium), Voodoo Dancer (Garden City H.), Dubai Destination (Queen Anne S.), Russian Rhythm (1,000 Guineas, Coronation S., Nassau S., Lockinge S.), Rule Of Law (St Leger S.), Divine Proportions (Prix Morny, Prix Marcel Boussac).

Dam Myth To Reality

Won 4 of 14 races, inc. 3 Listed. Good consistent mostly provincial performer, well suited by 12f, respectable 5th in Gr2 Prix de Royallieu, runner-up in Gr3 Prix Minerve. Effective on any ground. Did not progress at four. Very well bred. Dam of: Sonofogy (1992 g by Ogygian; winner), Magic Spin (1993 f by Lord Avie; winner), Assos (1994 g by Alleged; Listed winner), Mambo Jambo (1995 f by Kingmambo; winner, dam of Gr1-placed Ocean Silk), Fireinthewind (1996 c by Alleged; winner), Indigo Myth (1997 g by Kingmambo; Listed-placed winner), Meteorite Sun (1998 g by Miesque's Son; winner), Whipper (2001 c by Miesque's Son; dual Gr1 winner), Divine Proportions (2002 f by Kingmambo; dual Gr1 winner). Her yearling is a filly by Mt Livermore and she has a colt foal by Lemon Drop Kid.

Pedigree assessment

Divine Proportions is ostensibly very closely related to Whipper, the pair being by full-brothers out of the same mare. The "ostensibly" is a necessary qualification, because the relationship does not allow us to assert that they have most of the genes important to a racehorse in common, and it is fascinating to note that each has a full-sibling who was not so distinguished in competition. That said, Divine Proportions did emulate Whipper in the Prix Morny, putting up a better performance, and she later went on to a smooth Group 1 win at a mile, as Whipper did, albeit after a longer interval. The filly was perhaps named ironically, because she is small and no oil painting, but she has bags of class and an admirable racing attitude. If she trains on, she will prove hard to beat at a mile next spring. *TM*

Doyen (Ire)

4yo bay colt **131**

Sadler's Wells (USA) - Moon Cactus (Kris)

Owner Godolphin

Trainer Saeed Bin Suroor

Breeder Sheikh Mohammed

Career: **11** starts | won **5** | second **2** | third **0** | **£687,670** win and place

By Nicholas Godfrey

JUST imagine if Ron Manager, the cliche-prone caricature TV football pundit, ever got hold of Doyen. "It's a game of two halves, Saeed," he might suggest. "Star signing from abroad . . . hmm? . . . superb with the sun on his back . . . marvellous! . . . but the weather turns and the pitch gets cut up . . . doesn't it? . . . he just goes into hiding, doesn't like it up him . . . ho ho! . . . it's not like the old days . . . small boys on the park . . . jumpers for goalposts . . . hmm?"

Looking at Doyen's record in 2004, the type of reasoning lampooned in the xenophobic blue-blazered buffoon might not, in this instance, have been laughed out of court. Not entirely, anyway.

Consider the evidence. Transferred to Godolphin from Andre Fabre's yard following a very promising three-year-old campaign in 2003, expectations could not have been higher that Doyen would become one of their galacticos, just like Swain, who came from the same French source.

A pair of stunning victories on fast ground, including an emphatic effort in the King George, suggested he was more than up to such exalted billing, and unquestionably Doyen was the major player in the Godolphin squad in a pivotal year for the Dubai team. This was a brilliant racehorse, one who could be judged Europe's best on the basis of those outings. If the season had stopped at the end of July, there would have been few arguments about Doyen's superstar status.

But the season *did not* stop there, and Doyen's two subsequent outings were as deflating as the previous two had been energising. Connections suggested they would have to go back to square one. It was hard to quibble.

Yet it had all started so well, with Doyen looking set to become the poster boy of a fine season for Godolphin, remodelled in 2004 to focus more on Europe after a relatively lacklustre 2003.

**Doyen eases to an impressive win in the King George, the
high point of a season that fizzled out in the autumn**

The Sheikh demanded his team went outside what he described as
their "safety zone". Put bluntly, they had to get their act together in
2004. Substantial changes were made, the most obvious development
being Saeed Bin Suroor's handling their vast array of two-year-old talent,
a move that followed David Loder's decision (later reversed) to retire.
Godolphin's early-season approach was also modified, with the top horses
mainly sidestepping the Dubai World Cup meeting in favour of later
targets.

Frankie Dettori was resurgent, which may or may not have had something
to do with the presence of potential heir Kerrin McEvoy, employed to
help with the increased workload. Either way, Dettori's tussle with Kieren
Fallon for the jockeys' championship was one of the highlights of the season.
He rode the 2,000th winner of his career on King George day itself –
on Doyen himself according to the sport's leading historian John Randall,
although this was the subject of some debate on the day in question and
the landmark appears to have become the subject of a case of premature
celebration on behalf of the rider.

2004   Race record

7th Emirates Airline Champion Stakes (Group 1) (Newmarket, October 16) 3yo+ 10f Soft **108** (TS 70) 11 ran. *Held up in rear, ridden and some headway 3f out, no impression final 2f (L Dettori), beaten 12l by Haafhd*

7th Baileys Irish Champion Stakes (Group 1) (Leopardstown, September 11) 3yo+ 10f Good to firm **117** (TS 117) 8 ran. *Settled 3rd, 2nd and effort entering straight, no impression from 2f out, weakened and eased inside final furlong (L Dettori), beaten 4³⁄₄l by Azamour*

1st King George VI And Queen Elizabeth Diamond Stakes (Group 1) (Ascot, July 24) 3yo+ 12f Good to firm **131** (TS 97) 11 ran. *Raced in 5th place, eased out over 2f out, effort to lead well over 1f out, drew clear entering final furlong, impressive (L Dettori), beat Hard Buck by 3l*

1st Hardwicke Stakes (Group 2) (Ascot, June 19) 4yo+ 12f Firm **129** (TS 123) 6 ran. *Held up in 5th, smooth progress 3f out, led well over 1f out, soon clear, pushed out, impressive (L Dettori), beat High Accolade by 6l*

2nd Vodafone Coronation Cup (Group 1) (Epsom, June 4) 4yo+ 12f Good **121** (TS 96) 11 ran. *Settled in midfield, 6th straight, effort when not clear run over 2f out and well over 1f out, ridden to chase winner last 100yds, no impression (L Dettori), beaten 1³⁄₄l by Warrsan*

Other runs

2003 **4th** Prix de l'Arc de Triomphe Lucien Barriere (Group 1) (Longchamp, October 5) 3yo+ 12f Holding **121** 13 ran ● **2nd** Prix Niel Casino Barriere d'Enghien (Group 2) (Longchamp, September 14) 3yo 12f Good to soft **117** 7 ran ● **1st** Prix du Lys (Group 3) (Longchamp, June 22) 3yo 12f Good to soft **115** 4 ran ● **1st** Coupe des Trois Ans (Listed) (Lyon-Parilly, May 28) 3yo 12f Soft 7 ran ● **1st** Prix Cadet Roussel (Saint-Cloud, March 29) 3yo 12f Good 9 ran 2002 **5th** Prix Hunyade (Unraced) (Maisons-Laffitte, October 2) 2yo 9f Good 17 ran

Not everything in the Godolphin garden was rosy straight away, mind you. Despite some near-misses, the Classic drought was not alleviated until the St Leger, and at the start of the season the team surely would not have envisaged being without runners at the Breeders' Cup from their Newmarket base.

Nevertheless, a third jockeys' title for Dettori and a fourth trainers' championship for Bin Suroor – with 115 winners in Britain and nearly 50 individual two-year-old scorers – provided a tangible reward.

The 2003 tally of Group 1s was finally surpassed in late October, with older horses yet again the long suit. Doyen was a major contributor. Even after his later flops, the son of Sadler's Wells – a full-brother to early Godolphin star Moonshell – remained Godolphin's No.1 earner in terms of win prize-money, although Rule Of Law collected more overall, mainly by virtue of finishing runner-up in the Derby.

Royal Ascot provided the turning point for Godolphin's season and it was here that Doyen signalled his arrival as a potential dominant force at the highest level.

The colt's seasonal reappearance in the Coronation Cup had augured extremely well. Reported to have needed the race, he really took the eye in second, beaten under two lengths by the gallant Warrsan after being short of daylight at a crucial stage.

However, such a promising performance did not entirely prepare us for the sensational nature of Doyen's victory in the Hardwicke Stakes. Sent off the 6-5 favourite, he flattened the opposition in the Group 2 event, in the process smashing the long-standing track record, held since 1983 by Stanerra, by the equivalent of about two lengths.

Displaying a high cruising speed and, despite his breeding, obviously having no issue whatsoever with the rock-hard ground, Doyen was always travelling easily off a scorching pace. He never looked for a moment like being beaten, leading on the bridle a furlong and a half out and stretching clean away from the useful High Accolade, who was six lengths back in second. "He reminds me of the good old days with Swain and Daylami," said Dettori.

With the superlatives flying around, Doyen was made a short-priced favourite for the King George, his next target. Godolphin have an enviable record in Ascot's midsummer all-aged championship, having won it four years out of five between 1995 and 1999 with Lammtarra, Swain (twice) and Daylami, and taken second with Classic Cliche, Nedawi, Fantastic Light (twice) and Sulamani. Doyen was joined by a pair of stablemates in the 2004 version, a talented second string in Sulamani and the pacemaker Lunar Sovereign, a top-level winner in his own right in the States in 2003.

While 'Team Godolphin' faced eight rivals, the Ascot showpiece did not feature the strongest line-up in living memory, with just one representative of the Classic generation in shock Irish Derby third Tycoon.

Nevertheless, Doyen was one of just four of the 11 who had never triumphed in the top grade. Second favourite behind him was the French-trained Hong Kong Vase winner Vallee Enchantee, while a more exotic international flavour was added by an imaginative raid from the USA in the shape of Hard Buck. Doyen's old rival Warrsan, Grand Prix de Saint-Cloud victor Gamut and Phoenix Reach, who won the 2003 Canadian International, were the others with top-flight victories to their name.

All eyes were on Doyen, though, as reflected in his starting price of 11-10. He duly delivered in a style that suggested he could rank among the very best, proving his versatility by adapting to a race run in an entirely different fashion to the Hardwicke.

Unexpectedly, Lunar Sovereign slowed things down approaching Swinley Bottom before a sharp burst at halfway. Hard Buck kept close tabs, pulling hard until the steady early pace was increased, before taking over when the pacemaker folded two out. Doyen's was a murderously intimidating presence at this stage, however, and he swamped the US hope in a matter of strides, going on to win by three lengths in the manner of a real top-notcher. Hard Buck stayed on well to keep second from Sulamani, who, despite not liking the fast ground, came from well off the pace with one of his trademark late flourishes.

Godolphin were exultant. Dettori described Doyen as a "great horse", while Sheikh Mohammed said: "The sky is the limit." The latter made a change – the Sheikh doesn't usually like to impose parameters of any sort on his vaulting ambition.

Doyen was clearly on the threshold of superstar status, but a Racing Post Rating of 131 – 2lb above the Hardwicke – was lower than that achieved by four of the five previous winners of the race. However, even if it was a relatively ordinary renewal of the King George, he was undeniably impressive and, what's more, had now demonstrated a potent array of weapons, being equally adept at both crushing rivals off a blistering gallop or delivering a decisive burst off a moderate pace.

With him already installed as short-priced favourite for the Arc, it was impossible to envisage a middle-distance performer to beat Doyen. And then it went wrong.

With the drop back to ten furlongs "not a concern at all", according to Simon Crisford, Godolphin's racing manager, the Irish Champion Stakes was supposed to be a coronation, despite the race looking much stronger on paper than the King George. But as the three-year-old Azamour scored a memorable success, the odds-on Doyen flopped, weakening after a half-hearted effort two furlongs out to finish seventh of the eight runners, beating only his own pacemaker.

So out of character did it seem that the Racing Post handicapper declined to offer a rating immediately afterwards. No explanation has ever come to light for such a lifeless show: Doyen should have liked the good to firm ground, and when his baffled and bewildered connections said he may not have liked going left-handed, there was a slight hint of desperation about it. "I think we left the engine in Newmarket," said Dettori. "The run was too bad to be true. Maybe he had one too many drinks the night before! He didn't pick up like he usually does."

Perhaps two fine efforts on fast ground had simply left their mark, but with the Arc ruled out almost immediately, it was surprising to see Doyen running again just over a month later in the Champion Stakes. Never a great worker at home, he was reportedly giving the right signals ahead of the Newmarket contest. That's as maybe, because he didn't give them out in the race, once again failing to pick up behind Haafhd.

Doyen was not given a hard time in those dreadful conditions and he will be back at five after a winter in Dubai, no doubt with all the big middle-distance races on his agenda. Take away those last two shocking runs and you would be confident of predicting great things. With them, and the excuses about the 'bounce' factor and the ground that need to be invoked on Doyen's behalf, you wouldn't know what to expect.

The question, set to be resolved in 2005, is straightforward enough. Will the real Doyen please stand up?

Doyen   *bay colt, 22-4-2000*

		Nearctic	Nearco
			Lady Angela
	Northern Dancer		
		Natalma	Native Dancer
			Almahmoud
Sadler's Wells			
b 1981			
		Bold Reason	Hail To Reason
			Lalun
	Fairy Bridge		
		Special	Forli
			Thong
		Sharpen Up	Atan
			Rocchetta
	Kris		
		Doubly Sure	Reliance
			Soft Angels
Moon Cactus			
b 1987			
		Mill Reef	Never Bend
			Milan Mill
	Lady Moon		
		Moonlight Night	Levmoss
			Lovely Light

Bred by Sheikh Mohammed in Ireland

Sire **Sadler's Wells**

Won 6 of 11 races, inc. Beresford S.-Gr3, Irish Derby Trial-Gr2, Irish 2,000 Guineas-Gr1, Eclipse S.-Gr1, Phoenix Champion S.-Gr1. Also 2nd in Prix du Jockey-Club-Gr1, King George VI & Queen Elizabeth S.-Gr1. Impeccably bred top-class performer from 8-12f, handsome, tough and consistent. Sire of Gr1 winners: Braashee, French Glory, In The Wings (x3), Old Vic (x2), Prince Of Dance, Scenic, Salsabil (x5), Opera House (x3), Runyon, Saddlers' Hall, El Prado, Johann Quatz, Masad, Barathea (x2), Fatherland, Fort Wood, Intrepidity (x3), Carnegie (x2), King's Theatre (x2), Northern Spur (x2), Moonshell, Muncie, Poliglote, Chief Contender, Dance Design, Darazari, Luna Wells, Cloudings, Ebadiyla (x2), Entrepreneur, In Command, Kayf Tara (x4), Dream Well (x2), Greek Dance, King Of Kings (x2), Leggera, Commander Collins, Daliapour, Montjeu (x6), Saffron Walden, Aristotle, Beat Hollow (x4), Subtle Power, Galileo (x3), Imagine (x2), Milan, Perfect Soul, Sequoyah, Sligo Bay, Ballingarry, Black Sam Bellamy (x2), Gossamer (x2), High Chaparral (x6), Islington (x4), Quarter Moon, Sholokov, Alberto Giacometti, Brian Boru (x2), Doyen, Powerscourt, Refuse to Bend (4), Yesterday, Quiff, Playful Act.

Dam **Moon Cactus**

Won 3 of 7 races, inc. Prestige S.-Gr3, Lupe S.-Listed. Also 2nd in Fillies' Mile, Prix de Diane, 3rd in Nassau S. Leggy, plain sort, with a rather round action. A hard puller. Had restricted vision in left eye. High-class performer up to 10.5f (unraced beyond). Well-bred. Dam of: Moonshell (1992 f by Sadler's Wells; Classic winner), Moonfire (1993 f by Sadler's Wells; placed), Ocean Of Storms (1995 c by Arazi; Listed winner, Gr2-placed), Hatha Anna (1997 c by Sadler's Wells; Gr2 winner in Australia), Shamaat Hayaaty (1998 f by Sadler's Wells; Listed-placed winner), Avionic (1999 g by In The Wings; winner), Doyen (2000 c by Sadler's Wells; Gr1 winner), Hawksmoor (2002 c by In The Wings; unraced to date). She has a yearling filly and a colt foal, both by In The Wings.

Pedigree assessment

After his impressive fourth behind more seasoned rivals in the 2003 Arc, Doyen was every pundit's nap selection to improve and make his mark at Group 1 level in 2004. As it turned out, two wins from five starts was something short of sensational, though he was profoundly impressive in both his Ascot races and at that time looked certain to maintain his dominance. He appeared to have been severely over-trained before his flop at Leopardstown, and he again looked lean, and seemed edgy, in the paddock before a dire effort in the Champion Stakes. He is a superbly bred individual, and an extremely talented one; he will be a force again at five if trained right. *TM*

Dubawi (Ire)

2yo bay colt   **122**

Dubai Millennium - Zomaradah (Deploy)

Owner Godolphin

Trainer Saeed Bin Suroor

Breeder Darley

Career: **3** starts   won **3**   **£152,962** win and place

---

By Tony Smurthwaite

AN unbeaten, decisive, Group 1 winner, son of Dubai Millennium and winter favourite for the Vodafone Derby. What more could one ask for?

Historically, however, the path of winter favourites rarely runs smooth. Just ask those who included Yeats in Ten To Follow lists or invested in him for a Derby win after his two-year-old campaign. Yeats' season was over by the end of May as he simply became the latest to live down to a billing as winter favourite for the Derby. Commander Collins, Beat Hollow, Nayef, Hawk Wing and Brian Boru all held the chalice now passed to Dubawi, and not one won the Derby.

Whether the best of Dubawi is to come or has already gone is the same question that has vexed turf followers for centuries. His prowess as a two-year-old presents a powerful case in the affirmative for those clutching Derby vouchers bearing the 33-1 available after Dubawi beat 11 others in the Group 3 Superlative Stakes at Newmarket in July; each and every one of them a previous winner.

Come the close of the season, the Derby book had a very different look. Bookmakers were willing only to offer a top price of 10-1 and skinniest of 6-1 that Dubawi would put the seal on a spree of compelling storylines by winning at Epsom. The cause of his odds contracting was his Group 1 triumph, by a clear margin, over a fair if not outstanding field for the National Stakes at The Curragh.

The seven-furlong race bears an honourable roll call; the names of Santa Claus, Sir Ivor, Roberto and El Gran Senor figure thereon. More recently Sinndar won both the National and the Derby and there is a convincing case for arguing that Dubawi's ante-post odds for both the Derby and the 2,000 Guineas subconsciously take account of the impressive cast of former winners.

There are other external issues to put to one side when considering Dubawi. What is needed is an examination of the compact bay colt as a racehorse.

The unbeaten Dubawi stamps his authority in the Group 1 National Stakes to go into the winter as Derby favourite

Not, as was his turn during the year, as a well-touted representative of the only crop of Dubai Millennium, as the first of that exclusive club to run, as the first to win, and as the first to bring a Group 1 success for an ill-fated sire whose romantic hold over Sheikh Mohammed seems as sure as ever. Nor of Dubawi's distinction as Frankie Dettori's possible partner at Epsom in June in a race he is still waiting to win.

Dubawi owes his eminence to victory in Ireland. With just two opponents rated in single-figure odds, the 8-13 favourite was expected to furnish racegoers with a spectacle. This he did, beating the once-raced maiden winner Berenson by three lengths with Railway Stakes one-two Democratic Deficit and Russian Blue filling the next two places in the reverse order to their earlier meeting.

Victory was a ready accomplishment. Dettori was able to coast along throughout and then cruise to the front-running Russian Blue with two furlongs to go. When asked for a winning effort Dubawi quickly asserted, went past that rival and rushed clear in exciting fashion, in a fast time considering the yielding ground.

1st Dunnes Stores National Stakes (Group 1) (Curragh, September 19) 2yo 7f Yielding **122** (TS 119) 7 ran. *Settled 2nd, led travelling best under 2f out, ridden and quickened clear from over 1f out, impressive (L Dettori), beat Berenson by 3l*

1st Weatherbys Superlative Stakes (Group 3) (Newmarket (July), July 8) 2yo 7f Good to soft **104** (TS 85) 12 ran. *Held up, headway over 1f out, ran on to lead towards finish (L Dettori), beat Henrik by ½l*

1st Green & Black's Organic Chocolate EBF Maiden Stakes (Goodwood, June 4) 2yo 6f Good to firm **89** (TS 79) 5 ran. *Slowly into stride, switched right and good headway to challenge 2f out, ran green but led over 1f out, ran on well final furlong (L Dettori), beat Fox by 1¼l*

The early pace had been generous enough, Russian Blue dropping away quickly when headed, giving the winner's turn of foot a further seal of approval. Berenson, an Entrepreneur colt with stamina elements in his pedigree, was staying on well on only his second career run but did not appear again during the campaign to test a two-stone improvement in form. Democratic Deficit, a force in the Railway, looked outgunned off the decent fractions and went on to disappoint again, over the same trip, but on firmer ground, in the Prix Jean-Luc Lagardere.

The aspect of Dubawi's performance that stood out almost as much as his dominance was a late jink to the left, then another to the right, requiring corrective action by Dettori.

Dettori had already resorted to colourful language in ascribing a character to Dubawi, calling him "a little bastard" after he required some firm handling on his maiden win at Goodwood in June, then suggesting "he loves a fight, he wants to kill people" after the Superlative.

At The Curragh Dettori, when asked about the deviation off a line, gave an answer worthy of Silvio Berlusconi at his most cunning. "It was a good sign," he said. "When a horse does something like that it usually means that he is not fully extended and has more to give. That was the case here and he is a great prospect for next year when he might give me my first Derby win."

Simon Crisford, Godolphin's racing manager, exclaimed that Dubawi would stay the 12 furlongs of the Derby "standing on his head".

Certainly Dubawi looked to have matured physically and mentally for a ten-week break, and had been working well in Newmarket. For all that, there was the whiff of over-indulgence in the team's comments, a genuflection to 'the Boss', Sheikh Mohammed, whose zeal in collecting as many offspring of Dubai Millennium as possible in order to race them is well chronicled.

Of 56 foals, 27 went into training in 2004 with Saeed Bin Suroor. Dubawi was the figurehead but once-raced winners Belenus and Descartes, and Oude, third in the Champagne Stakes, also offered promise.

Ladbrokes started the season going 12-1 that the 2005 Derby winner would be sired by Dubai Millennium. They ended it going only 6-1 Dubawi.

Dubawi

bay colt, 7-2-2002

Dubai Millennium b 1996	Seeking The Gold	Mr Prospector	Raise A Native Gold Digger
		Con Game	Buckpasser Broadway
	Colorado Dancer	Shareef Dancer	Northern Dancer Sweet Alliance
		Fall Aspen	Pretense Change Water
Zomaradah b 1995	Deploy	Shirley Heights	Mill Reef Hardiemma
		Slightly Dangerous	Roberto Where You Lead
	Jawaher	Dancing Brave	Lyphard Navajo Princess
		High Tern	High Line Sunbittern

Bred by Darley in England

Sire **Dubai Millennium**

Won 9 of 10 races, inc. Prix Eugene Adam-Gr3, Prix Jacques le Marois-Gr1, Queen Elizabeth II S.-Gr1, Dubai World Cup-Gr1, Prince of Wales's S.-Gr1. Big (16.2hh), strong, handsome individual, not the best of movers in his slower paces, but a powerful galloper, effective on any turf surface and on dirt. Very well-bred, by a dual Grade 1 winner, out of a high-class racemare Grade 2 winner, whose own dam was the outstanding broodmare of modern times. Deceased. Stood one season at Dalham Hall Stud, Newmarket, at a fee of £100,000. Sire of one crop of racing age, inc. notable winner: Dubawi (National S.-Gr1).

Dam **Zomaradah**

Won 6 of 12 races, inc. Oaks d'Italia-Gr1, E.P. Taylor S.-Can Gr1, Royal Whip S.-Gr2, Premio Lydia Tesio-Gr2. Also 3rd in Breeders' Cup Filly & Mare Turf S. High-class, round-actioned, consistent performer, acted on any going. Well suited by 11f, should have stayed further, but disappointed in only race at 12f. Very well bred. The best daughter of her sire, out of a non-winning half-sister to Derby winner High-Rise. Dam of: Dubawi (2002 c by Dubai Millennium; Gr1 winner). She was barren to Sadler's Wells in 2001, and to both Singspiel and Halling in 2004. She has a yearling filly by Barathea, and visited Alhaarth in 2004.

Pedigree assessment

The first and only crop by Dubai Millennium was keenly awaited, and it did not disappoint. Ten of his 18 runners were winners, headed by the unbeaten Dubawi, who was put away after an authoritative victory in what seemed to be an uncompetitive renewal of the National Stakes. Judged on his pedigree, the colt is already well ahead of schedule, because he is bred to be much more effective as a three-year-old, and to improve for longer distances. The Derby was the only race in which his sire was defeated, but the bottom half of his son's pedigree is all about class and form at a mile and a half. While he is speedy enough to make his presence felt in the Guineas, expect Dubawi to be better over longer trips. *TM*

Execute (Fr)

7yo chestnut horse **117**

Suave Dancer (USA) - She's My Lovely (Sharpo)
Owner Ecurie Chalhoub
Trainer J E Hammond
Breeder Ecurie Kura

Career: **28** starts   won **9**   second **6**   third **3**   **£269,354** win and place

By Robert Carter

EXECUTE has raced every year since 1999 and 14 of his last 15 runs have been in either Group 1 or Group 2 company. No Group 1 victory was more deserved than his in the Prix Ganay. It looks like a case of 'if at first you don't succeed', for Execute had run in the Group 2 Prix d'Harcourt for the past three years, finishing first, sixth and second, as a prelude to the Ganay. He was runner-up in the Group 1 race to Aquarelliste in 2002 and to Fair Mix 12 months later, so it was obvious that he would try for third time lucky.

In fact, only an accident made him run there. He was being trained for the Audemars Piguet Queen Elizabeth II Cup, at Sha Tin in April, but injured a foot days before he was due to travel. Execute soon recovered and was redirected to the Ganay, the race that ended the career of his sire, Suave Dancer, when he suffered a leg injury after finishing third to Subotica in 1992.

John Hammond did not hurry Execute, whose juvenile career consisted of two thirds in November, but the colt improved steadily at three, winning all five of his races and ending with a Listed victory. Even as a four-year-old, only one of his five races was in Group company. He did not develop into a Group horse until after winning at Compiegne in early March 2002 but he has not dropped below that level ever since.

Execute, who was sent off at around 12-1 for his reappearance in the Prix d'Harcourt, was drawn on the rails in a field of eight. He settled behind the leaders, Weightless and Nysaean, remaining there until well in the straight and only edging out when Nysaean took over. He was under strong pressure and had every chance one furlong from home but Vangelis was too quick for him and beat him three-quarters of a length. Execute likes to be covered up and Thierry Jarnet, who rode him, said that he had been hoping that the leaders would hang on a bit longer.

Backers assumed that he would have little chance against Vangelis when they met again in the Ganay and he started at 21-1 in another field of

Execute, after many years of trying, lands his first Group 1 success, taking the Prix Ganay at the age of seven

eight, five of whom were Group 1 winners. Polish Summer, Vespone, Fair Mix and Vallee Enchantee, all members of that quintet, led the market. Execute was held up, sharing fourth place with Fair Mix behind a strong pace set by Vespone, and remained in that spot to the straight. Thierry Gillet was soon looking for room on the inside and got through approaching the final furlong, when Chancellor weakened and Touch Of Land edged out to try to challenge. Execute quickened through the gap, soon caught Vespone and was given a couple of slaps to go clear. He ran on to beat the Godolphin raider by one and a half lengths, with Fair Mix third. Vangelis was over six lengths back in seventh this time.

Execute missed the summer but his trainer had dreams of success elsewhere. Hammond has always been willing to travel, and his 2004 adventure was with Gruntled, owned like Execute and Suave Dancer by the Lebanese insurance man, Henri Chalhoub. After finishing ninth in both the Singapore Airlines Gold Cup at Kranji and the Prix du Chemin de Fer du Nord at Chantilly, Gruntled was leased by Nursultan Nazarbayev, President of Kazakhstan, for the Prize of the President of the Russian

2004 Race record

6th Premio Roma SIS (Group 1) (Capannelle, November 7) 3yo+ 10f Soft 10 ran. *Held up and behind, last straight, headway on inside to chase leaders 2f out, kept on steadily but never a threat (T Gillet), beaten 2¾l by Soldier Hollow*

11th Prix de l'Arc de Triomphe Lucien Barriere (Group 1) (Longchamp, October 3) 3yo+ 12f Good **117** (TS 111) 19 ran. *Close up, 6th straight, tracking leader on inside over 1½f out, 4th 1f out, weakened (D Boeuf), beaten 7¾l by Bago*

1st Prix Ganay (Group 1) (Longchamp, May 2) 4yo+ 10½f Very soft **117** (TS 109) 8 ran. *Raced in 5th to straight, headway on rail over 1f out, led 150yds out, ran on well (T Gillet), beat Vespone by 1½l*

2nd Prix d'Harcourt (Group 2) (Longchamp, April 4) 4yo+ 10f Good to soft **117** (TS 96) 8 ran. *Settled in 3rd to straight, not clear run on rail 1½f out, switched left hard ridden and led for a few strides over 150yds out, ran on same pace (T Jarnet), beaten ¾l by Vangelis*

2003

6th Premio Roma - SIS (Group 1) (Capannelle, November 16) 3yo+ 10f Good to soft **109** 10 ran ● **2nd** Prix Perth (Group 3) (Saint-Cloud, November 1) 3yo+ 1m Very soft **111** 7 ran ● **3rd** Prix Dollar - Fouquet's Barriere (Group 2) (Longchamp, October 4) 3yo+ 9½f Holding **115** 14 ran ● **5th** Prix d'Ispahan (Group 1) (Longchamp, May 18) 4yo+ 9f Soft **112** 8 ran ● **2nd** Prix Ganay (Group 1) (Longchamp, April 27) 4yo+ 10½f Very soft **117** 9 ran ● **6th** Prix d'Harcourt (Group 2) (Longchamp, March 30) 4yo+ 10f Good **115** 11 ran

Other wins

2002 **1st** Prix d'Harcourt (Group 2) (Longchamp, March 31) 4yo+ 10f Soft **115** 10 ran ● **1st** Prix Touchstone (Compiegne, March 8) 10f Very soft 7 ran **2001** **1st** Prix de Gaillon (Longchamp, October 11) 4yo+ 12f Very soft 8 ran **2000** **1st** Grand Prix du Nord (Listed) (Le Croise-Laroche, November 16) 10½f Soft 8 ran ● **1st** Prix de Maurepas (Maisons-Laffitte, October 27) 3yo 10f Very soft 7 ran ● **1st** Prix Horse Expo (Deauville, October 17) 3yo 10f Heavy 7 ran ● **1st** Prix du Mail (Longchamp, May 18) 3yo 12f Good 9 ran ● **1st** Prix France Galop (Argentan, March 5) 3yo 9½f Good 11 ran

Federation at the Moscow Hippodrome on July 3. However, Gruntled was no match for the 2003 Russian Derby winner, Akbash (by the once Henry Cecil-trained Balliol Boy), who beat him 14 lengths. Vladimir Putin presented the trophy and gave lunch to the presidents of eight Russian republics at what became an informal summit. Akbash is the best horse seen in Russia for many years but cannot run elsewhere because his female family is not recognised by the Stud Book.

Execute returned in the Arc. He was covered up in ninth, being just in front of Bago at halfway, and stayed on up the inside to reach third over one furlong from home. That was his limit, however, and he faded to finish 11th. He went on to run sixth in the Group 1 Premio Roma for the second year. Gillet held him up in last place until over two furlongs from home and then tried to challenge on the rails. Execute was soon under pressure but he kept on gamely and finished less than three lengths behind the winner, Soldier Hollow.

Execute   *bay horse, 15-4-1997*

			Northern Dancer
		Nijinsky	Flaming Page
	Green Dancer		
		Green Valley	Val de Loir
Suave Dancer			Sly Pola
b 1988			
		Alleged	Hoist The Flag
			Princess Pout
	Suavite		
		Guinevere's Folly	Round Table
			Lodge

			Atan
		Sharpen Up	Rocchetta
	Sharpo		
		Moiety Bird	Falcon
She's My Lovely			Gaska
b 1984			
		Birdbrook	Mossborough
			Game Bird
	Girl Friend		
		View Mistress	King's Troop
			My Margaret

Bred by Ecurie Chalhoub in France

Sire **Suave Dancer**

Outstanding 10-12f 3yo. Won 5 of 9 starts from 2 to 4, notably Prix du Jockey-Club-Gr1, Irish Champion S-Gr1, Prix de l'Arc de Triomphe-Gr1. Also 2nd Irish Derby-Gr1, Prix Lupin-Gr1, 3rd Prix Ganay-Gr1. By top-class 2yo and very good turf sire. Half-brother to Gr2-placed Ultra Finesse out of a Grade 3-placed mare. Retired to stud in France, later stood at National Stud, also shuttled to Australia, died late 1998. Oldest progeny 10, sire of: Craigsteel (Gr2), Bernardon (Gr2), Compton Admiral (Eclipse S-Gr1), Execute (Prix Ganay-Gr1), Volvoreta (Prix Vermeille-Gr1), Dust Dancer (Gr3).

Dam **She's My Lovely**

Unraced. By top-class sprinter and decent sire, out of tough and very high-class sprinter who was also 2nd in 1,000 Guineas. Half-sister to very smart 6-7f performer Comrade In Arms (Brigadier Gerard). Dam of: Little Brosna (1988 f by R B Chesne; unplaced), Achilleus (1989 c by Formidable; winner), Tot Ou Tard (1990 c by Robellino; Gr2 winner), Domniga (1991 f by Be My Guest; winner), Glorious Linda (1994 f by Le Glorieux; stakes-placed winner), Hasene (1995 f by Akarad; Listed-placed winner), Carmel (1996 f by Highest Honor; unraced), Execute (1997 c by Suave Dancer; Prix Ganay-Gr1), Ing Ing (1998 f by Bering; Gr3 winner), She Is Zen (1999 f by Zieten; placed), Syssiss (2001 f by River Bay; unraced), unnamed (2002 f by Tel Quel), My Pearly (2003 f by Sagamix).

Pedigree assessment

She's My Lovely had very talented sprinters as parents, but that is not how she has behaved at stud. Her son Tot Ou Tard won two Group events over 12f, Execute stays that distance, her other Group winner Ing Ing struck over 1m, and French stakes performer Hasene was best over 8-10f. But Execute probably owes his stamina to Suave Dancer, who tended to get late-maturing middle-distance performers. Execute is likely to operate in time as a dual-purpose sire. *JH*

Favourable Terms

4yo bay filly **116**

Selkirk (USA) - Fatefully (USA) (Private Account (USA))

Owner Maktoum Al Maktoum

Trainer Sir Michael Stoute

Breeder Gainsborough Stud Management Ltd

Career: **8** starts | won **5** second **1** third **0** **£292,692** win and place

By John Hopkins

NIGGLING problems limited Favourable Terms to a three-race, 46-day campaign in 2004, but it was no write-off. Successful in Group 1 company, she also scored at Royal Ascot and was described as "the most fluent mover I've ever ridden" by a smitten Kieren Fallon. And the good news is that we'll get to see her in action once again in 2005.

Favourable Terms was precisely the type that the European race planners had in mind when they expanded the programme for older fillies and mares, in the process upgrading races like the Falmouth and Sun Chariot to Group 1 status. Unraced at two for Sir Michael Stoute, she had won a mile Listed event at Sandown and an uncompetitive renewal of the Group 2 Matron Stakes at Leopardstown during a five-race three-year-old career, the sort of credible, black-type campaign that in the old days would have seen her packed off to the paddocks without comment, but with questions unanswered, particularly after a dismal finale in the Sun Chariot. Now the opportunity was there for her to fulfil the promise of her first four races.

Favourable Terms returned to racecourse action with a bang. Lining up in the inaugural running of the Windsor Forest Stakes, a Group 2 mile race for fillies at Royal Ascot, she was sent off at 13-2 (the first time she hadn't been favourite in a race) behind the Godolphin hotpot Crimson Palace, the former South African-based mare who had confirmed the big impression she made in Dubai by landing York's Middleton Stakes. While the favourite struggled on the fast ground, Favourable Terms, held up, responded to Fallon's trademark driving and produced a withering run to settle matters swiftly in the penultimate furlong. She was driven out to score by two lengths from Monturani.

It was a faultless comeback, although some suggested that this new race was weak for its status, particularly as the favourite was obviously

Favourable Terms just manages to keep her head in front as she records her first Group 1 win in the Nassau Stakes

below par. The proximity of 20-1 Monturani in second and 25-1 Soldera in third added substance to the view, although the fifth, Marbye, would go on to land the Group 1 Prix d'Astarte. Favourable Terms was awarded a Racing Post Rating of 116, 8lb up on her previous best and only 2lb behind that given to stablemate Russian Rhythm after her Lockinge win.

Favourable Terms flopped unaccountably on her next start, when pitched into the Group 1 Falmouth Stakes at Newmarket, for she was never sighted behind Soviet Song and Attraction and trailed in sixth of seven. It was too bad to be true. She was beaten more than 14 lengths and even finished well behind Monturani.

But whatever was amiss didn't trouble her for long. Kept to her own sex for the ten-furlong Nassau Stakes, a race Stoute had won six times, including in the last two seasons with Islington and Russian Rhythm, Favourable Terms faced five rivals, notably Chorist, winner of her last two starts. Fallon had endured a troubled meeting, with controversial defeats on the Stoute pair Chic and Peeress, but here he was brilliant.

2004	**Race record**

1st Vodafone Nassau Stakes (Group 1) (Goodwood, July 31) 3yo+ 10f Good to firm **115** (TS 81) 6 ran. *Held up in touch, pulled out and effort over 2f out, shaken up to lead over 1f out, hard ridden and edged right inside final furlong, just held on (K Fallon), beat Silence Is Golden by shd*

6th UAE Equestrian And Racing Federation Falmouth Stakes (Group 1) (Newmarket (July), July 6) 3yo+ 1m Good to firm **89** (TS 70) 7 ran. *Held up, pushed along over 4f out, headway 3f out, ridden and weakened over 1f out (K Fallon), beaten 14½l by Soviet Song*

1st Windsor Forest Stakes (Group 2) (Ascot, June 16) 4yo+ 1m Good to firm **116** (TS 103) 10 ran. *Held up in touch, effort over 2f out, led over 1f out, ridden clear (K Fallon), beat Monturani by 2l*

2003

5th Peugeot Sun Chariot Stakes (Group 2) (Newmarket, October 4) 3yo+ 1m Good to firm **103** 10 ran ● **1st** betfair.com Matron Stakes (Group 2) (Leopardstown, September 6) 3yo+ 1m Good to firm **108** 9 ran ● **2nd** Oakgrove Stud Golden Daffodil Stakes (Group 3) (Chepstow, July 25) 3yo+ 10f Good **108** (TS 90) 4 ran ● **1st** Distaff Stakes (Listed) (Sandown, July 5) 3yo 1m Good to firm **103** 9 ran ● **1st** Chichester Festival Theatre Maiden Fillies' Stakes (Goodwood, May 21) 3yo 7f Good to firm **82** 15 ran

Favourable Terms travelled well, but she made heavy weather of mastering Chorist and Fallon had to resort to corrective measures to prevent her lugging in on her rival, before resuming his drive. Chorist kept pressing, and then Silence Is Golden arrived on the scene. The three fillies passed the post separated by just a short head and a neck, but Favourable Terms just had the call.

The form was nothing special by Group 1 standards, notwithstanding Chorist's subsequent Champion Stakes second, and it earned Favourable Terms a Racing Post Rating of 115, 8lb and 6lb respectively lower than that achieved by Islington and Russian Rhythm in the same race. But here was an unexposed filly back in the winning groove, for whom anything once again appeared possible. The usually reticent Stoute was talking freely about a Breeders' Cup tilt.

Instead, nothing. Stoute revealed at Goodwood that Favourable Terms was troubled by a back problem, which may have explained her Newmarket flop, and which meant that "even after she gallops, she has to have physio treatment". A recurrence meant that a tilt at a repeat victory in the Matron Stakes, upgraded to Group 1, was shelved at the 11th hour, before the news finally emerged that Favourable Terms would not be travelling to Texas after all.

Connections consider that the lightly raced Favourable Terms has more to offer; she will have a range of options at a mile to a mile and a quarter and Stoute has no peers when it comes to maintaining the progress of older horses. Let's hope the sporting decision to keep her in training is rewarded with a more substantial campaign in 2005.

Favourable Terms

bay filly, 4-2-2000

		Atan	Native Dancer Mixed Marriage
	Sharpen Up		
		Rocchetta	Rockefella Chambiges
Selkirk ch 1988			
		Nebbiolo	Yellow God Novara
	Annie Edge		
		Friendly Court	Be Friendly No Court
		Damascus	Sword Dancer Kerala
	Private Account		
		Numbered Account	Buckpasser Intriguing
Fatefully b 1993			
		Topsider	Northern Dancer Drumtop
	Fateful		
		Fate's Reward	Key To The Mint Cast The Die

Bred by Gainsborough Stud Management in Britain

Sire Selkirk

Won 6 of 15 starts from 2 to 4. At 2, won 1m Listed event from 2 starts. At 3, won 2 (inc. Queen Elizabeth II S-Gr1) of 6 starts. At 4, won 3 (Lockinge S-Gr2, Goodwood Mile-Gr2, Challenge S-Gr2) of 7 starts. By high-class 2yo/sprinter and very good sire whose stock often stayed better than he did, out of high-class 7-10f filly who also foaled stakes winners Rimrod, Rory Creek, Seebe, Skillington, Syncline. Stands at Lanwades Stud in Britain, 2004 fee £30,000. Oldest progeny 10, sire of: Hidden Meadow (Gr3), Kirkwall (Gr2), Orford Ness (Gr3), Squeak (Beverly Hills H-Gr1, Matriarch H-Gr1), Country Garden (Gr2), Field Of Hope (Prix de la Foret-Gr1), Trans Island (Gr2), Sign Of Hope (Gr2), Valley Chapel (Gr3), Wince (1,000 Guineas-Gr1), Harbour Island (Gr3), Altieri (Premio Presidente della Repubblica-Gr1), The Trader (Gr3), Highdown (Gr2), Highest (Gr3), Leadership (Gran Premio di Milano-Gr1), Sulk (Prix Marcel Boussac-Gr1), Welsh Diva (Gr3), Favourable Terms (Nassau S-Gr1), Felicity (Gr3), Prince Kirk (Prix d'Ispahan-Gr1), Etendard Indien (Gr3), Red Bloom (Fillies' Mile-Gr1), Etlaala (Gr2).

Dam Fatefully

Won 4 (7-8f) of 13 starts, inc. Rosemary Rated Stakes-Listed, October Stakes-Listed. Useful, best over 1m. Half-sister to several winners, including fair 5-7f British performer Inter Vision, out of a 6-7f winner. Her third dam, US stakes winner Cast The Die, foaled 1990s Graded stakes winners Devils Orchid (Gr1) and Double Sixes (Gr3). Dam of: Opportunist (1999 c by Machiavellian; winner), Favourable Terms (2000 f by Selkirk; Nassau S-Gr1), Have Faith (2001 f by Machiavellian; winner), 2002 unnamed (c by Grand Lodge). In foal to Selkirk for 2005.

Pedigree assessment

There is a fair amount of speed on the dam's side of Favourable Terms' pedigree, but top-class miler Selkirk has a number of talented fillies who stay at least 10f. His influence might have helped Favourable Terms step up from a mile successfully in the Nassau, although the filly's half-brother Opportunist (by another miler) won over 10f in Dubai last year. The family is a decent one, though largely unspectacular in recent generations. JH

Fayr Jag (Ire)

5yo bay gelding **118**

Fayruz - Lominda (Ire) (Lomond (USA))

Owner Jonathan Gill

Trainer T D Easterby

Breeder Canice M Farrell Jnr

Career: **30** starts   won **9**   second **5**   third **2**   **£310,643** win and place

By Graham Dench

IT SEEMED a good idea at the time. A first prize of approaching £500,000 and place money down to eighth, plus a virtual guarantee of fast ground, made Fayr Jag's expenses-paid invitation to Japan's prestigious Sprinters Stakes over six furlongs at Nakayama hard to resist, even though the race took place on the same weekend as Longchamp's Prix de l'Abbaye.

After all, the Abbaye is worth a fraction of that sum to the winner and is run over five furlongs, a distance over which Fayr Jag had not been successful since his maiden win at Thirsk as a juvenile. Even more to the point, it is nearly always run on softish ground and that is no use whatsoever to Fayr Jag, as he had lately confirmed in the clearest possible terms in both the Nunthorpe and Baden-Baden's Goldene Peitsche.

The decision made, the Golden Jubilee winner set off for Japan a fortnight before the race, accompanied by the July Cup runner-up Ashdown Express, another with a preference for fast ground, on a trip that would pit the pair against some of the best sprinters in the Far East. It was going to be tough, but with any sort of luck one or both of them would surely return with a share of the purse.

Then it rained. And rained. A typhoon that hit the region days before the race was followed by torrential rain. The going was changed to heavy and both Fayr Jag and Ashdown Express literally might as well have stayed at home. Fayr Jag finished last of 16. Ashdown Express fared only a little better in 13th. It was a frustrating end to an ambitious venture that deserved better. What made it all the more frustrating was the proximity at the finish of the Hong Kong challenger Cape Of Good Hope in third. For Fayr Jag had beaten Cape Of Good Hope two heads into third in the Golden Jubilee, and Ashdown Express had him back in fourth place in the July Cup.

**Fayr Jag narrowly holds on in the Group 1 Golden Jubilee
Stakes from Crystal Castle, right, and Cape Of Good Hope**

The Golden Jubilee was easily the highlight of Fayr Jag's season, and
indeed of his career so far. Incredibly, it was the only occasion all season
when he got his ground.

Returning to the scene of his dead-heat with Ratio in a high-class finish
to the previous year's Wokingham Handicap and a 12-1 chance in a field
of 14, he was among the few that really relished the lightning-fast ground
and travelled so well that he found himself in front with two furlongs still
to run – sooner than ever before. Having then edged right in front, despite
the application of a ring bit, he held on by just the skin of his teeth from
Ratio's stablemate Crystal Castle and Cape Of Good Hope.

While it was a good effort, it would be impossible to rate the form
anything special by Group 1 standards. Indeed it was a result that
appeared to confirm the widely held conviction that in the sprint division
there is precious little between the leading handicappers and even the
top performers. Racing Post Ratings have Fayr Jag running to just 118
in victory, a mere 2lb higher than the figure he achieved in the
Wokingham, when the first six finishers all went on to win Group races
before the end of the year.

2004   Race record

16th Sprinters Stakes (Grade 1) (Nakayama, October 3) 3yo+ 6f Heavy **74** 16 ran. *Mid-division until weakened well over 1f out (N Yokoyama), beaten 21l by Calstone Light O*

9th Fahrhof Goldene Peitsche (Group 2) (Baden- Baden, September 1) 3yo+ 6f Soft **90** 16 ran. *Behind and soon pushed along, never in contention (A Culhane), beaten 7¼l by Raffelberger*

10th Victor Chandler Nunthorpe Stakes (Group 1) (York, August 19) 2yo+ 5f Soft **99** (TS 87) 12 ran. *Close up, ridden and every chance well over 1f out, soon driven, weakened and eased inside final furlong (W Supple), beaten 5¾l by Bahamian Pirate*

13th Darley July Cup (Group 1) (Newmarket (July), July 8) 3yo+ 6f Good to soft **105** (TS 88) 20 ran. *Held up, not clear run over 1f out, never troubled leaders (W Supple), beaten 5½l by Frizzante*

1st Golden Jubilee Stakes (Group 1) (Ascot, June 19) 3yo+ 6f Firm **118** (TS 119) 14 ran. *Held up mid-division, headway to lead 2f out, edged right inside final furlong, driven out (W Supple), beat Crystal Castle by hd*

13th Duke of York Hearthstead Homes Stakes (Group 2) (York, May 11) 3yo+ 6f Good to soft **57** (TS 31) 15 ran. *Chased leaders, fading when hampered over 1f out (W Supple), beaten 21l by Monsieur Bond*

Other wins

2003 **1st** Ridgewood Pearl Stakes (Group 3) (Curragh, September 13) 3yo+ 6f Good **115** 12 ran ● **1st** Hopeful Stakes (Listed) (Newmarket (July), August 22) 3yo+ 6f Good to firm **95** 6 ran ● **1st Dead-heat** Wokingham Stakes Showcase Handicap (0-110) (Ascot, June 21) 3yo+ 6f Firm **116** 29 ran ● **1st** SportingOptions.co.uk Rated Stakes (0-100 Handicap) (York, June 13) 4yo+ 6f Good to firm **111** 11 ran ● **1st** William Hill Rated Stakes (0-95 handicap) (Pontefract, June 1) 3yo+ 6f Good to firm **106** 16 ran **2002** **1st** Moulton Rated Stakes (0-95 handicap) (Newmarket (July), June 29) 3yo 6f Good to firm **97** 12 ran ● **1st** NetBetSports.com Handicap (0-95) (Ripon, April 27) 3yo 6f Good to firm **86** 15 ran **2001** **1st** EBF Thomas Lord Maiden Stakes (Thirsk, August 4) 2yo 5f Firm **68** 6 ran

While the form was by no means outstanding, it was a moment to savour for connections, not least of them owner Jonathan Gill, who is in the haulage business (fair jag is evidently jargon for a good load, and it is 'Fayr' because of sire Fayruz), and regular rider Willie Supple.

Gill has had tremendous value out of the 8,000-guinea yearling and Supple has seldom had a dull moment with him. Besides their six wins together there has been no shortage of incident for Fayr Jag and Supple, who recalled: "We've had a few scrapes. As a three-year-old he went mad in the stalls and banged his head so hard he broke a bone in his face. Then last year, he clipped another horse's heels, came down and left me battered and bruised. But we seem to hit it off."

Fayr Jag returned from Japan safe and sound and will be in action once again in 2005. His main targets will be the obvious ones, although this time of course the Golden Jubilee will be run at York and Tim Easterby might not be in quite such a hurry to take up another invitation to Japan. The ground will be crucial again, but he surely cannot be so unlucky on that score.

Fayr Jag

bay gelding, 17-3-1999

Fayruz b 1983	Song	Sing Sing	Tudor Minstrel
			Agin The Law
		Intent	Vilmorin
			Under Canvas
	Friendly Jester	Be Friendly	Skymaster
			Lady Sliptic
		Lady Jester	Bleep-Bleep
			Witcracker
Lominda b 1988	Lomond	Northern Dancer	Nearctic
			Natalma
		My Charmer	Poker
			Fair Charmer
	Olinda	Sassafras	Sheshoon
			Ruta
		Jodee Zee	Jim J
			Shawl

Bred by Canice Farrell in Ireland. 8,000gns Doncaster St Leger yearling

Sire **Fayruz**

Won 7 of his 19 races at 2 and 3, all over 5f. Smart 2yo, won 6 races and 2nd Cornwallis S-Gr3, later useful sprinter, 2nd Bentinck S-L. Bred for speed, by influential sprint sire out of 5f winner from fast family of Averti, Jester, Reesh and Tadwin. Stands at Rossenara Stud in Ireland, 2004 fee €3,500. Oldest progeny 16, sire of: Fayr Jag (Golden Jubilee S-Gr1), Listed winners Don Fayruz, Farhana, Fay Breeze, Festive Cheer, Gaelic Symphony, Good Chocolate, Innocenti Evasioni, Master Fay, Monkston Point, Whittingham.

Dam **Lominda**

Won 6f maiden from 3 2yo starts, unplaced at 3 over 7-10f. Sire won 2,000 Guineas and has produced handful of high-class horses in modest stud career. Dam quite useful 7f 2yo winner who produced 9 winners, including an Italian Listed scorer. Dam of: Come On In (1993 g by Most Welcome; placed over hurdles), Barr Beacon (1996 g by Puissance; placed), Hellofafella (1998 c by Reprimand; unplaced), Fayr Jag (1999 g by Fayruz; Golden Jubilee S-Gr1), Skehana (2000 f by Mukaddamah; winner), 2002 f by Fayruz.

Pedigree assessment

The outstanding son of his sire, who is known primarily as a source of speedy and precocious 2yos, and the outstanding performer from his family in recent generations. Fayr Jag is still young, compared to some of the most prominent sprinters of this season, and should continue to be a force in stakes company. *JH*

Firebreak

5yo bay horse   123

Charnwood Forest (Ire) - Breakaway (Song)

Owner Godolphin

Trainer Saeed Bin Suroor

Breeder R P Williams

Career: **21** starts   won **8**   second **5**   third **0**   **£990,532** win and place

By John Hopkins

"**H**E'S KIND, he's honest, he's tough, with the ability to match." "He's worth his weight in gold." Firebreak may not belong to the Godolphin premier league, but Sheikh Mohammed's team were at pains to emphasise his importance to the stable after this somewhat unsung hero had reached his career zenith with a commanding performance in Newmarket's Challenge Stakes.

The Group 2 seven-furlong contest, part of Champions Day in October, confirmed that the generally consistent Firebreak had, in common with much of the Godolphin team, raised his game for 2004. Racing over his ideal trip, he dominated his rivals. With Frankie Dettori at his tactical best, he made all, cranking up the pace every time a new challenger emerged. Firebreak battled on strongly in the closing stages to defeat the former Lockinge winner Keltos by a length, improving on his 2002 showing in the same race, when second to Nayyir.

Firebreak arguably enjoyed the run of the race on a day when it paid to be close to the pace. In addition, some runners were below form on the testing ground, while others, such as Joel Stakes winner Polar Ben, who finished ninth, shaped as if this was a race too many. Nonetheless, it would be churlish in the extreme to crab such a positive performance, particularly as Firebreak was the only runner burdened by a 4lb penalty. On the day, he was simply in a different class.

There were clues on his final start in 2003 that a re-energised Firebreak might emerge. He had barely registered on the British scene in the summer, but there was plenty to like about his performance in the Group 1 Hong Kong Mile at Sha Tin in December. Staying on promisingly in the final two furlongs, he was beaten only around a length and a half into fifth behind local star Lucky Owners.

Firebreak confirmed his resurgence in spectacular fashion on his next start. Bidding for a second successive victory in the Group 2 Godolphin

Firebreak, having started the year with a Group 2 dirt win, scores at the same level on turf in the Challenge Stakes

Mile on dirt at Nad Al Sheba on Dubai World Cup night, he annihilated a field that included the American Grade 2 winner During, producing a visually most taking performance to score by four and a half lengths. "When I pressed the button, he took off," said Dettori.

The jockey may have been impressed, but he opted for a new recruit over the stable stalwart when Firebreak returned to British action in the Lockinge Stakes at Newbury in May. With Dettori on Refuse To Bend, Kerrin McEvoy partnered Firebreak, who was sent off a generous 16-1 chance. He ran well and looked a possible winner a furlong out. But, and not for the first time, he shaped as if a truly run mile on turf was beyond him, fading to finish fourth, beaten under two lengths by Russian Rhythm. Refuse To Bend, out of form on this occasion, was eighth.

Ruled out of a tilt at the Queen Anne Stakes at Royal Ascot on the day, Firebreak was to have one more run before his Challenge triumph. Dropped back to seven furlongs in a competitive renewal of the Park Stakes at Doncaster in September, Firebreak, the 5-2 favourite, was in the firing line until swamped for pace by Pastoral Pursuits and beaten a length and a quarter. It was another brave effort – he was conceding the highly progressive winner 4lb more than weight-for-age.

2004   Race record

1st Victor Chandler Challenge Stakes (Group 2) (Newmarket, October 16) 3yo+ 7f Soft **123** (TS 110) 12 ran. *Made all, driven along over 1f out, ridden out final 50 yds (L Dettori), beat Keltos by 1l*

2nd GNER Park Stakes (Group 2) (Doncaster, September 9) 3yo+ 7f Good to firm **119** (TS 98) 8 ran. *Raced wide tracked leader centre, edged right and every chance over 2f out, not quicken inside final furlong (L Dettori), beaten 1¼l by Pastoral Pursuits*

4th Juddmonte Lockinge Stakes (Group 1) (Newbury, May 15) 4yo+ 1m Good **117** (TS 94) 15 ran. *Tracled leaders, led inside final 3f, headed inside final furlong, stayed on same pace (K McEvoy), beaten 1¾l by Russian Rhythm*

1st Godolphin Mile (Group 2) (Dirt) (Nad Al Sheba, March 27) 3yo+ 1m Fast **120** (TS 102) 9 ran. *In touch in mid-division, steady headway 4f out, ridden to lead 2f out, soon clear, pushed out (L Dettori), beat Tropical Star by 4½l*

2003

5th Hong Kong Mile (Group 1) (Sha Tin, December 14) 3yo+ 1m Good to firm **116** 14 ran ● **10th** Lennox Stakes (Group 2) (Goodwood, July 29) 3yo+ 7f Good **97** 13 ran ● **11th** Golden Jubilee Stakes (Group 1) (Ascot, June 21) 3yo+ 6f Firm **97** 17 ran ● **1st** Godolphin Mile (Group 2) (Nad Al Sheba, March 29) 3yo+ 1m Fast **117** 16 ran ● **2nd** Al Shindagha Sprint (Nad Al Sheba, January 30) 3-4yo 6f Fast **114** 9 ran

Other runs

2002 **2nd** Victor Chandler Challenge Stakes (Group 2) (Newmarket, October 19) 3yo+ 7f Good **116** 17 ran ● **1st** Charlton Hunt Supreme Stakes (Group 3) (Goodwood, September 26) 3yo+ 7f Good to firm **113** 10 ran ● **4th Dead-heat** Celebration Mile (Group 2) (Goodwood, August 24) 3yo+ 1m Good to firm **114** 7 ran ● **6th** Gainsborough Poule d'Essai des Poulains (Group 1) (Longchamp, May 12) 3yo 1m Soft **114** 13 ran ● **10th** UAE Derby (Group 2) (Dirt) (Nad Al Sheba, March 23) 3yo 10f Fast **76** 14 ran ● **2nd** UAE 2,000 Guineas (Group 3) Nad Al Sheba, February 28) 3yo 1m Fast 8 ran **2001** **1st** Dubai Duty Free Mill Reef Stakes (Group 2) (Newbury, September 21) 2yo 6f Good to firm **109** 10 ran ● **4th** Prix Morny Casinos Barriere (Group 1) (Straight) (Deauville, August 26) 2yo 6f Good to soft **107** 11 ran ● **1st** Prix de Cabourg (Group 3) (Deauville, August 4) 2yo 6f Soft **110** 7 ran ● **2nd** Coventry Stakes (Group 3) (Ascot, June 19) 2yo 6f Good to firm **110** 20 ran ● **1st** Brian Yeardley Continental Two Year Old Trophy (Conditions Stakes) (Beverley, June 6) 2yo 5f Good to firm **103** 6 ran ● **1st** Anne Frances Stevens Memorial Maiden Stakes (Goodwood, May 22) 2yo 5f Good to firm **87** 7 ran

Firebreak was better than ever in 2004, in line with the renaissance enjoyed by his yard. It would be simplistic, however, to attribute his improvement to that factor. Saeed Bin Suroor described him as "a much stronger horse" at the start of the year, and a tongue tie, which was fitted for the first time in the Godolphin Mile, became a regular part of his equipment. In addition, Godolphin seem to understand him better now. He is a horse who is at his very best at seven furlongs on turf, and he needs time between races. A second tilt at the Hong Kong Mile was on the cards after the Challenge Stakes, and 2005 is likely to kick off in a third Godolphin Mile. On the fast Nad Al Sheba dirt track, that trip evidently poses no problems.

Firebreak

bay horse, 6-3-1999

		Known Fact	In Reality
			Tamerett
	Warning		
		Slightly Dangerous	Roberto
Charnwood Forest			Where You Lead
br 1992			
		Sadler's Wells	Northern Dancer
			Fairy Bridge
	Dance Of Leaves		
		Fall Aspen	Pretense
			Change Water
		Sing Sing	Tudor Minstrel
			Agin The Law
	Song		
		Intent	Vilmorin
Breakaway			Under Canvas
b 1985			
		Tower Walk	High Treason
			Lorrikeet
	Catherine Howard		
		Righteous Girl	Right Boy
			Chamossura

Bred by R P Williams in Britain. 27,000gns Tattersalls October yearling, 525,000gns Tattersalls Horses-in-Training 2yo

Sire **Charnwood Forest**

Won 4 of his 11 starts. At 2, 2nd over 6f on only start. At 3, won 2 (7-8f) of 3 starts, also 2nd St James's Palace S-Gr1, At 4, won 2 (Queen Anne S-Gr2, Challenge S-Gr2), of 7 starts, also 2nd Lockinge S-Gr1, Sussex S-Gr1. Developed into top-class 7-8f performer. By top-class 2yo/miler and very good sire, mainly of speedy performers. Half-brother to 2yo Gr1 winner Medaaly. Dam unraced sister to Group 1 winner Fort Wood and half-sister to Gr1 winners Hamas, Northern Aspen, Timber Country, plus Gr2 winners Bianconi, Colorado Dancer (dam of Dubai Millennium), Elle Seule (dam of Elnadim, Mehthaaf). Stood at Rathbarry Stud in Ireland, died June 2001. Oldest progeny 6, sire of (northern hemisphere foals): Astrocharm (Gr3), Firebreak (Gr2), Autumn Glory (Gr3), T E Lawrence (Gr3), Carrizo Creek (Gr2).

Dam **Breakaway**

Won 3 of 14 starts at 2 and 3. At 2, won 2 (both 5f) of 6 starts, also 2nd 6f Listed event. At 3, won 1 (5f) of 8 starts. Quite useful 2yo, later fair sprint handicapper. By top-class sprinter and influential speed sire. Sister to quite useful sprint 2yo Chantaco. Dam of: Kingsdown Cavalier (1990 c by Superlative; winner), Bye-Bye (1992 f by Superlative; unplaced), Hippy (1993 f by Damister; winner), Roma Caveau (1994 c by Damister; winner), Stop Out (1995 f by Rudimentary; winner, Listed placed), Sirene (1997 f by Mystiko; winner), Firebreak (1999 c by Charnwood Forest; Gr2 winner), Sharplaw Venture (2000 f by Polar Falcon; winner, Listed placed), South Africa (2001 f by Cape Cross; winner), 2003 f by Fantastic Light (retained 25,000gns yearling).

Pedigree assessment

An admirable and high-class performer over 7-8f, much like his sire. Firebreak is precociously bred on his dam's side (his half-sister Sharplaw Venture won the valuable Watership Down Stud Fillies' Stakes at two in 2002) and was high class as a juvenile, but he has maintained his form subsequently, in common with many other talented performers by Charnwood Forest. Expect more of the same in 2005 from Firebreak, who deserves his chance at stud in time, even if it does not happen for him at Dalham. *JH*

Frizzante

5 yo bay mare **119**

Efisio - Juliet Bravo (Glow (USA))
Owner Mrs Jan Hopper & Mrs Elizabeth Grundy
Trainer J R Fanshawe
Breeder Mrs Jan Hopper & Mrs Elizabeth Grundy

Career: **15** starts won **7** second **1** third **1** **£243,660** win and place

By Richard Austen

FRIZZANTE'S achievement in passing almost the entire field in little more than half a furlong to win the 2004 July Cup was impressive enough in itself. It looks even more so from a historical perspective because she was the first filly or mare to win the race since the legendary Habibti in 1983.

Habibti's success came just two years after that of the equally brilliant Marwell, and in the 1970s it was won by Parsimony (1972) and Lianga (1975). Since 1983, however, there had been only near misses. Sonoma, Soba, Committed (twice), Dafayna, Gwydion, Gayane and Golden Opinion finished either second or third in the 1980s. In the 1990s Hoh Magic and Hever Golf Rose were the only ones even placed. In the new millennium, Pipalong, Cassandra Go, Danehurst and Airwave played second or third fiddle before the latest renewal.

Even without the metaphorical weight of history on her shoulders, Frizzante had her work cut out in a highly competitive and cosmopolitan line-up. She was improving, but she was no Marwell or Habibti and started at 14-1, with eight others at the same price or shorter. Following a gamble on the day, the 4-1 favourite was the Australian challenger Exceed And Excel. Japan had Seeking The Dia, while Cape Of Good Hope from Hong Kong had gone close in the King's Stand and Golden Jubilee and the race was packed with established European sprinters, including Group 1 winners Somnus, Patavellian, Porlezza and Fayr Jag; Continent and Bahamian Pirate had been first and second when the 2002 July Cup was run on similar rain-softened ground. High-class older horse Nayyir was stepping back in distance, as were, from the Classic crop, Jersey Stakes winner Kheleyf and French Guineas miscreant Antonius Pius.

"She loves to pass horses, that's her style," James Fanshawe observed of Frizzante, and she had a maximum field of 20 to cope with here, the

Frizzante, nearside, swoops from the rear to beat rank outsider Ashdown Express a neck in a thrilling July Cup

most ever assembled for a race first run in 1876. Using official ratings as the arbiter, Dorubako from Japan and Lydgate from the United States were among five horses eliminated.

With Continent very slow starting, Frizzante was last of the remaining 19 for most of what followed, while Exceed And Excel led the way with Patavellian. The front-runners were still there approaching the final furlong but not for much longer. Seeking The Dia and Balmont threw down challenges on either side, with Antonius Pius on the premises under the whip, but it was 100-1 shot Ashdown Express who burst through between horses and Frizzante who arrived latest, widest and strongest of all.

Frizzante, who approaching the furlong marker had been only about a length and a half in front of the last horse and four and a half behind the leader, hit the front 100 yards out and kept her nose in front of Ashdown Express. She was a second Group 1 winner at the meeting for both Fanshawe and jockey Johnny Murtagh, successful earlier with Soviet Song.

Frizzante's effectiveness with a late challenge made itself apparent early in her career because she was usually slowly away. First raced in May as a three-year-old, she required two maidens to get off the mark, jarred her knees in the process, and had only one more run in 2002. Resuming the following May, there was no looking back and Frizzante arrived late on the scene to the same telling effect in increasingly hot company, moving through handicaps to Listed and Group races.

2004 Race record

17th Stanleybet Sprint Cup (Group 1) (Haydock, September 4) 3yo+ 6f Good **95** (TS 84) 19 ran. *Held up, pushed along 2f out, never on terms (J P Murtagh), beaten 8½l by Tante Rose*

10th Prix Maurice de Gheest (Group 1) (Deauville, August 8) 3yo+ 6½f Good to soft **103** 18 ran. *Held up in rear on outside, effort and unable to quicken over 1f out (J P Murtagh), beaten 5¼l by Somnus*

1st Darley July Cup (Group 1) (Newmarket (July), July 8) 3yo+ 6f Good to soft **119** (TS 101) 20 ran. *Slowly into stride, held up, hung left over 1f out, ran on to lead well inside final furlong (J P Murtagh), beat Ashdown Express by nk*

3rd King's Stand Stakes (Group 2) (Ascot, June 15) 3yo+ 5f Good to firm **110** (TS 98) 19 ran. *Behind, ridden and headway when not clear run over 1f out, switched left inside final furlong, finished well (J P Murtagh), beaten 1¾l by The Tatling*

1st Victor Chandler Palace House Stakes (Group 3) (Newmarket, May 1) 3yo+ 5f Good **116** (TS 74) 13 ran. *Outpaced, headway over 1f out, ran on under pressure to lead post (J P Murtagh), beat Avonbridge by shd*

2nd NGK Spark Plugs Abernant Stakes (Listed) (Newmarket, April 15) 3yo+ 6f Good **113** (TS 82) 8 ran. *Held up, switched right and headway over 1f out, edged left and chased winner inside final furlong, ran on (L Dettori), beaten ½l by Arakan*

Other runs

2003 **1st** EBF Christo Philipson Boadicea Fillies' Stakes (Listed) (Newmarket, October 16) 3yo+ 6f Good to firm **100** 13 ran ● **1st** Lone Star Park Fillies' Rated Stakes (0-105 handicap) (Newmarket, October 2) 3yo+6f Good to firm **107** 11 ran ● **6th** Tote Ayr Gold Cup Showcase Handicap (Ayr, September 20) 3yo+ 6f Good **100** 26 ran ● **4th** Vodafone Stewards' Cup Showcase Handicap (Goodwood, August 2) 3yo+ 6f Good **107** 29 ran ● **1st** Tattenham Corner Fillies' Handicap (0-80) (Doncaster, June 7) 4yo+ 6f Good **95** 15 ran ● **1st** Graham Mack Attack Handicap (0-75) (Leicester, May 26) 3yo+ 6f Good **92** 20 ran **2002** **10th** East Anglian Daily Times Showcase Handicap (0-80) (Newmarket (July), August 16) 3yo+ 6f Good **64** 18 ran ● **1st** Askew Design & Print 80th Anniversary Median Auction Maiden Stakes (Doncaster, June 1) 3yo 5f Good to firm **72** 11 ran ● **5th** 0808 100 1121 NetBetSports Telebet Maiden Stakes (Beverley, May 11) 3yo 5f Good **76** 11 ran

Coming from the back requires plenty of luck (look at the recent career of Airwave) and Frizzante did look unfortunate in two of the calendar's most prestigious handicaps in 2003, appearing best in her group in both the Stewards' Cup and Ayr Gold Cup but on the "wrong side". While she won four times, it could easily have been six.

Building up to the July Cup in 2004, Frizzante was a close second in the Abernant, short-headed Avonbridge in the five-furlong Palace House and ran on strongest of all for a close third in the King's Stand at Royal Ascot. After the July Cup, she disappointed in a troubled trip to France for the Prix Maurice de Gheest and was again well below form in the Haydock Sprint Cup, but that was not enough to prevent her latest and final season from being a resounding success. Retired, her last entry in 2004 was for the Newmarket sales.

Frizzante

bay mare, 21-3-1999

		Forli	Aristophanes
			Trevisa
	Formidable		
		Native Partner	Raise A Native
			Dinner Partner
Efisio			
b 1982		High Top	Derring-Do
			Camenae
	Eldoret		
		Bamburi	Ragusa
			Kilifi
		Northern Dancer	Nearctic
			Natalma
	Glow		
		Glisk	Buckpasser
			Regal Gleam
Juliet Bravo			
b 1990		Prince Tenderfoot	Blue Prince
			La Tendresse
	Countess Olivia		
		Coralivia	Le Levanstell
			Hot Coral

Bred by Mrs Jan Hopper and Mrs Elizabeth Grundy in England

Sire Efisio

Won 8 of 26 races, inc. Horris Hill S.-Gr3, Challenge S.-Gr3, Premio Emilio Turati-Gr1, Premio Chiusura-Gr2. Also 3rd in Prix Jacques le Marois at 4. Smallish (15.3hh), lengthy, strong-quartered type. Best at 7-8f. Round-actioned, but effective on any ground. Inclined to get worked up in preliminaries, but always raced genuinely. The only Gr1 winner by his sire (high-class sprinting 2yo who did not quite fulfil expectations. Half-brother to Mountain Bear (G1 winner in US) and to 3 other winners, and to dam of Timboroa (G1 winner in Italy & US). Dam won 2 races, half-sister to 2 other winners. Family of Princely Gift. Stands at Highclere Stud, 200 fee £10,000 (Oct 1). Sire of 14 crops of racing age, inc: Casteddu (Gr3), Pips Pride (Phoenix S.-Gr1), Young Ern (Gr3), Hever Golf Rose (Prix de l'Abbaye de Longchamp-Gr1), Tomba (Prix de la Foret-Gr1), Uruk (Gr3), Heads Will Roll (Gr3), Frizzante (July Cup-Gr1), Guys And Dolls (Gr3), Pearly Shells (Prix Vermeille-Gr1), Le Vie dei Colori (Premio Vittorio di Capua-Gr1), Attraction (1,000 Guineas-Gr1, Irish 1,000 Guineas-Gr1, Coronation S.-Gr1, Sun Chariot S.-Gr1).

Dam Juliet Bravo

Won 1 of 24 races. Also placed 2nd 4 times, 3rd 4 times. Strong, lengthy, dipped-backed type, but a good mover. Modest sprint handicapper, who usually raced up with the pace, most effective on top of the ground or on fibresand. Half-sister to Donna Viola (Gr2 winner in France, dual Gr1 winner in US) and 3 lesser winners, also to dams of 2 Listed-placed winners. By a well-bred horse who won a Gr2 race on grass in US, but proved a bad sire. Dam a game, useful performer won 2 (7-10f) of her 9 races, out of a half-sister to Gr3 12f winner Ballyhot. 3rd dam sister to very speedy filly Ballisland. Died in 2002. Dam of: Glowing (1995 f by Chilibang; winner), Colonel Mustard (1996 g by Keen; winner), Miss Marple (1997 f by Puissance; placed), Frizzante (1999 f by Efisio; Gr1 winner), Firenze (2001 f by Efisio; winner), Zidane (2002 c by Danzero; unraced to date).

Pedigree assessment

A major contributor to a wonderful year for her sire, Frizzante won Pattern events on both Newmarket courses, following her Group 3 victory in the Palace House Stakes with a stirring effort that brought her Group 1 honours in the July Cup. The latter success provided an unforgettable occasion for her owner-breeders while serving to inspire other enthusiasts with meagre resources. The big battalions can be beaten, even with a cheaply bred product of a mare who was herself of plating class. In fact Frizzante comes from a family which was held in high regard 30 years ago, but only Donna Viola brought it any kind of prominence until Efisio provided the spark to ignite it again. *TM*

Gamut (Ire)

5yo bay horse   **121**

Spectrum (Ire) - Greektown (Ela-Mana-Mou)

Owner Mrs G Smith

Trainer Sir Michael Stoute

Breeder Ballymacoll Stud Farm Ltd

Career: **14** starts   won **5**   second **4**   third **2**   **£343,411** win and place

By Mark Blackman

IN winning the Grand Prix de Saint-Cloud in July, Gamut became the latest in a long line of Sir Michael Stoute-trained horses to make the breakthrough at Group 1 level well beyond their Classic season – in his case at the age of five. He is unlikely ever to go down as one of the trainer's all-time greats, but it was a triumph nevertheless.

In his youth, Gamut was touted as a Derby prospect for his then owner Lord Weinstock, but setbacks meant that he was restricted to just four starts by the end of his three-year-old campaign. Fourth place in a Listed contest was the best he could manage.

At four he elevated himself to Listed winner, but ran his best race when beaten a length into second by Vinnie Roe in the Irish St Leger. Many predicted 2004 could be his year in the staying ranks, but his trainer had other ideas and mapped out a course taking in some of the most valuable mile-and-a-half events in Europe, in which Gamut's liking for cut in the ground was expected to prove a major asset.

Racing now for Gay Smith, who bought him prior to a disappointing final start at four, he reappeared in the Group 3 Dubai Irish Village Stakes, better known as the John Porter. Sent off 7-2 favourite in a field of 17, he was kicked into the lead three furlongs out – just as he had been when winning at the track on his 2003 reappearance – but on this occasion surrendered the advantage to the Barry Hills-trained Dubai Success 125 yards from the post. Rallying gamely, he was beaten only on the nod and showed his appetite for a scrap was as keen as ever.

Just over a fortnight later, he lined up against six rivals in the Group 2 Jockey Club Stakes at Newmarket and again was sent off favourite at 7-4. Always travelling well on the officially good ground, he ran into some traffic problems at the quarter-mile pole, but once in the clear he needed only to be shaken up to assert inside the final furlong and beat Systematic and subsequent dual Group 1 winner Warrsan.

Gamut takes the Group 2 Jockey Club Stakes before going on to land the Group 1 Grand Prix de Saint-Cloud

Two months later came the Grand Prix de Saint-Cloud and his first Group 1 opportunity since the Irish St Leger. It was not the strongest of fields, although Phoenix Reach, Westerner and Polish Summer were already winners at a similar level, and the good to soft ground was ideal. Everything went right this time. Always handy under regular partner Kieren Fallon, he was kicked on two furlongs out and this time they were unable to get back at him. He extended inside the final furlong and by the line had three lengths to spare over the subsequent Prix Foy winner Policy Maker. It was a performance that earned Gamut a Racing Post Rating of 121, jointly the best of his career.

Gamut had emerged as an unlikely candidate for the King George VI and Queen Elizabeth Diamond Stakes at Ascot in late July, but a doubt persisted that his two good wins had merely created an illusion of progress, for his Racing Post Ratings suggested he was not actually getting any better. Even on the Saint-Cloud form he needed to find around 10lb improvement to win a typical King George.

The race could have gone better, for having been a bit slowly away he found himself carried further back on the rail by Warrsan, and then did not enjoy the strong pace that would have brought his stamina into play. However, in finishing fourth behind the impressive Doyen he ran about as well as his form entitled him to.

2004 — Race record

5th Grosser Volkswagen Preis Von Baden (Group 1) (Baden-Baden, September 5) 3yo+ 12f Soft **116** 11 ran. *Tracked leader after 2f, led briefly approaching straight, 2nd straight, hard ridden and every chance over 1f out, one pace (K Fallon), beaten 5l by Warrsan*

4th King George VI And Queen Elizabeth Diamond Stakes (Group 1) (Ascot, July 24) 3yo+ 12f Good to firm **120** (TS 89) 11 ran. *Snatched up after 1f, raced on inner in 6th place, driven and effort over 2f out, chased leading pair over 1f out, no impression, lost 3rd final 150yds (K Fallon), beaten 5l by Doyen*

1st Grand Prix de Saint-Cloud (Group 1) (Saint-Cloud, July 4) 3yo+ 12f Good to soft **121** (TS 105) 10 ran. *Always close up, went 2nd after 3f, led well over 2f out (entering straight), ridden clear approaching final furlong, ran on well (K Fallon), beat Policy Maker by 3l*

1st UltimateBet.com Jockey Club Stakes (Group 2) (Newmarket, May 2) 4yo+ 12f Good **120** (TS 83) 7 ran. *Tracked leaders, not clear run over 2f out, shaken up to lead well inside final furlong, ran on (K Fallon), beat Systematic by 1¼l*

2nd Dubai Irish Village Stakes (Registered As The John Porter Stakes) (Group 3) (Newbury, April 17) 4yo+ 12f Good **117** (TS 105) 17 ran. *Tracked leaders, led inside final 3f, ridden and stayed on from over 1f out, headed final 125yds, rallied gamely, just failed (K Fallon), beaten shd by Dubai Success*

2003

3rd CIU Serlby Stakes (Listed) (Doncaster, November 8) 3yo+ 12f Good **115** 7 ran ● **2nd** Irish Field St Leger (Group 1) (Curragh, September 13) 3yo+ 1m6f Good to firm **121** 6 ran ● **1st** '2004 Royal Windsor Three Day Racing Festival' Conditions Stakes (Windsor, August 23) 3yo+ 11½f Good to firm **118** 5 ran ● **3rd** Princess of Wales's UAE Equestrian And Racing Federation Stakes (Group 2) (Newmarket (July), July 8) 3yo+ 12f Good **117** 6 ran ● **1st** skybet.com Stakes (Registered As The Aston Park Stakes) (Listed) (Newbury, May 17) 4yo+ 1m5½f Good **114** 10 ran

Other wins

2002 **1st** Peter Smith Memorial Maiden Stakes (Newbury, April 19) 3yo 11f Good to firm **96** (TS 105) 9 ran

There was just one more sighting of Gamut after the King George, some six weeks later in the Grosser Preis von Baden, Germany's premier all-aged mile-and-a-half contest. Here he encountered officially soft ground for the first time in his life.

Always prominent with front-running compatriot Mubtaker, the pair were both travelling well as they turned into the straight, but they had possibly been going a shade faster than was ideal for either of them through the early fractions. Gamut kept going longer than Mubtaker, but faded inside the final furlong to finish fifth behind Warrsan. It was his worst run of the season.

Gamut will be in training again as a six-year-old. He ended 2004 rated 121, just as he had ended 2003, and the challenge for connections will be to find another Group 1 he can win without needing to improve significantly on that mark.

Gamut
bay horse, 19-3-1999

Spectrum b 1992	Rainbow Quest	Blushing Groom
		Red God
		Runaway Bride
		I Will Follow
		Herbager
		Where You Lead
	River Dancer	Irish River
		Riverman
		Irish Star
		Dancing Shadow
		Dancer's Image
		Sunny Valley
Greektown ch 1985	Ela-Mana-Mou	Pitcairn
		Petingo
		Border Bounty
		Rose Bertin
		High Hat
		Wide Awake
	Edinburgh	Charlottown
		Charlottesville
		Meld
		Queen's Castle
		Sovereign Path
		Country House

Bred by Ballymacoll Stud Farm in Ireland

Sire Spectrum

Won 4 of 9 races, inc. Irish 2,000 Guineas-Gr1, Champion S-Gr1. Rangy, good-looking, fine mover with good turn of foot. By top-class 8-12f performer and excellent middle-distance sire out of high-class French 2yo and miler. Half-brother to dam of top-class 12f filly Petrushka from family of Let The Lion Roar and Millenary. Stood until 2004 at Coolmore Stud, 2004 fee €15,000, subsequently sold to South Africa. Oldest progeny 6, sire of (northern hemisphere): Gamut (Grand Prix de Saint-Cloud-Gr1), Golan (2,000 Guineas-Gr1, King George VI & Queen Elizabeth S-Gr1), Dancing (Gr2), Just James (Gr2), Hamairi (Gr3), Marionnaud (Gr3), Rum Charger (Gr3).

Dam Greektown

Won 2 of 9 starts at 2 and 3 in France. Placed at 2, 10-12f winner at 3 including Listed Prix de Tourelles. Half-sister to top-class stayer Sought Out (by Rainbow Quest, dam of 2004 Derby winner North Light and 2004 Listed winner Researched), smart 10-12f filly Queen Helen (by Troy) and minor winner Scots Lass (by Shirley Heights; grand-dam of Golan) out of smart 2yo and middle-distance filly Edinburgh. Dam of: Athens Belle (1990 f by Groom Dancer; Listed winner), Grecian Knight (1991 c by Groom Dancer; unraced), Multicoloured (1993 c by Rainbow Quest; Gr2 winner), Grecian Bride (1994 f by Groom Dancer; unraced), Greek Myth (1996 f by Sadler's Wells; unplaced), Town Girl (1997 f by Lammtarra; unplaced), Danse Grecque (1998 f by Sadler's Wells; unraced), Gamut (1999 c by Spectrum; Grand Prix de Saint-Cloud-Gr1), Rainbow City (2000 f by Rainbow Quest; winner), Wedding Cake (2001 f by Groom Dancer; winner).

Pedigree assessment

Another distinguished member of a family much in vogue, for it is also source of Derby winner North Light and smart stayer Researched. Gamut is bred on similar lines to that pair's dam Sought Out, whose sire Rainbow Quest is responsible for Spectrum. He is also closely related to Golan, another top-class son of Spectrum. Gamut has continued to progress with age, like many members of his family, and has the pedigree to excel over further than 12f if given the chance in 2005. *JH*

Ghostzapper (USA)

4yo bay colt   **133**

Awesome Again (Can) - Baby Zip (USA) (Relaunch (USA))

Owner Stronach Stables

Trainer R J Frankel

Breeder Adena Springs

Career: **10** starts   won **8**   second **0**   third **1**   **£1,702,773** win and place

By James Willoughby

THE BAR has been set high for Ghostzapper. He is no Secretariat, Man O'War or Spectacular Bid, no Dr Fager, Forego or Citation, no Native Dancer, Swaps or Affirmed. Not yet, anyway.

The facts of Ghostzapper's decisive victory in the Breeders' Cup Classic at Lone Star Park make impressive reading: the winning distance of three lengths was the third-largest, and the winning time of 1min 59.02sec the fastest, in the 21-year history of the event.

Neither wide margins nor fast times are proof alone that a horse is one of the all-time greats. Volponi won the Classic by six and a half lengths in 2002, while Cat Thief recorded 1min 59.52sec in 1999; neither was even US Horse of the Year.

It is not until factoring in the strength of opposition that Ghostzapper faced, and the speed of the surface on which he competed, that these two facets of his performance can be put into proper context.

The 13-strong Classic field comprised eight runners successful in Grade 1 company, including the Japanese runner Personal Rush and the top-class mare Azeri. The Kentucky Derby and Preakness winner Smarty Jones had long since been retired, but present were winners of the latest renewals of the Belmont, Travers, Whitney, Woodward, Pacific Classic and Jockey Club Gold Cup. In short, it was a line-up of representative standard for the race – and strictly no better.

Ghostzapper beat them comprehensively, and the fact that runner-up Roses In May pulled four lengths clear of the previous year's winner Pleasantly Perfect set the seal on a top-class performance. According to Racing Post Ratings, it was probably the best in Classic history.

That Ghostzapper's winning time was faster than Secretariat's Kentucky Derby record is not a meaningful comparison, considering the respective maturity of the two horses at the time. Neither is it valid to refer to it as unique in US racing history. Swaps dipped under 1min

Ghostzapper streaks home in the Breeders' Cup Classic, inviting comparison with some of the American greats

59sec in 1956, Affirmed achieved the same feat twice in 1979, while Greinton in 1985 and In Excess in 1991 are among others to have recorded faster times than Ghostzapper. The record holder is Spectacular Bid, who eclipsed the 1min 58sec barrier at Santa Anita in 1980.

All those marks were, however, achieved on dirt surfaces regarded as harder than those of today. Safety considerations have encouraged track superintendents to include a higher sand content, making it highly unlikely that Spectacular Bid's achievement will be matched. For the record, Ghostzapper's time is the fastest achieved in the last three years, eclipsing Candy Ride's 1min 59.11sec in the 2003 Pacific Classic at Del Mar.

Ghostzapper was awarded a Beyer speed figure of 124 for his victory at Lone Star Park, equal-best with Sunday Silence in 1989 among winners of the Classic. These ratings are the established measure of racehorse performance in the US and take the speed of the surface into account. The best recorded is the 138 of 31-length Belmont winner Secretariat in 1973.

Ghostzapper did, in fact, get closer to this mark on his second start of the season at Monmouth Park. On a sloppy, tiring track that caused horses to run much slower times than usual, the four-year-old won the Grade 3 Philip H Iselin Handicap by more than 10 lengths. His Beyer figure of

2004   Race record

1st Breeders' Cup Classic - Powered by Dodge (Grade 1) (Dirt) (Lone Star Park, October 30) 3yo+ 10f Fast **133** 13 ran. *Made all, driven clear over 1f out, ran on well (J Castellano), beat Roses In May by 3l*

1st Woodward Stakes (Grade 1) (Dirt) (Belmont Park, September 11) 3yo+ 9f Fast **121** 7 ran. *Pressed leader, carried wide entering straight, hard ridden to dispute lead and bumped rival 1f out, led final 100yds, all out (J Castellano), beat Saint Liam by nk*

1st Philip H Iselin Breeders' Cup Handicap (Grade 3) (Monmouth Park, August 21) 3yo+ 9f Sloppy 6 ran. *Raced in 2nd until led well over 2f out, drew clear 1f out, very easily (J Castellano), beat Presidentialaffair by 10³⁄₄l*

1st Tom Fool Handicap (Grade 2) (Belmont Park, July 4) 3yo+ 7f Fast **122** 4 ran. *Close up until led over 2½f out, quickened clear, easily (J Castellano), beat Aggadan by 4¹⁄₄l*

2003

1st Vosburgh Stakes (Grade 1) (Belmont Park, September 27) 3yo+ 6½f Fast **125** 10 ran ● **3rd** Kings Bishop Stakes (Grade 1) (Dirt) (Saratoga, August 23) 3yo 7f Fast **119** 13 ran ● **1st** Allowance race (Saratoga, July 26) 3yo+ 7f Fast 6 ran ● **1st** Allowance race (Belmont Park, June 20) 3yo+ 6f Muddy 6 ran

Other runs

2002 **4th** Allowance race (Santa Anita, December 26) 2yo 6f Fast 8 ran ● **1st** Maiden Special weight (Hollywood Park, November 16) 2yo 6½f Fast 10 ran

128 is the best since the Daily Racing Form began carrying them in 1992.

These stellar performances did not come out of left field. From the moment Ghostzapper stepped on a racecourse as a two-year-old he looked something very special, and his latest achievements merely represent the result of steady progression.

A rangy colt who took time to develop, Ghostzapper made his debut at Hollywood Park in November 2002. He had been working well, but those who had observed his impressive paces had equally noted that he was something of a gawky individual, likely to need racing experience. Moreover, he was encountering a strong and well-regarded group.

When the opening split times appeared for the six-and-a-half-furlong maiden, Ghostzapper immediately made a big impression. He was travelling strongly just behind the lead, and by the end of the back straight he hit the front. Nothing could live with him, and by the time the six-furlong split of 1min 9sec had flashed on the board, Ghostzapper was home and dry. He won by nine lengths in stakes-calibre time for a juvenile.

Nobody who had witnessed Ghostzapper's debut could forget him, despite what happened next. Perhaps influenced by his impressive sectional time, trainer Bobby Frankel chose to drop him to six furlongs for an allowance race at Santa Anita on Boxing Day. This time, his inexperience showed, for after a bump at the start he never got into the race and could finish only fourth. To be fair, it was a very useful contest run in just over 1min 8sec, and the form worked out well.

Ghostzapper was put away to mature, and it wasn't until the following June that he had another crack at the same level of competition. Frankel switched his training to the East coast and equipped him with blinkers for another six-furlong race at Belmont run on a muddy track.

Even in the headgear, Ghostzapper ran lazily through the early stages. He was fully 12 lengths behind after the field had gone a quarter of a mile. He was still five lengths behind passing the furlong marker, but now he was absolutely flying. He won by better than three, making up nearly ten lengths within a furlong on a horse who was to win his next race impressively.

This was unmistakably star quality, and Ghostzapper confirmed it in a similar event at Saratoga the following month. The chance to race over seven furlongs seemed to suit him, as he kept much closer tabs on the lead, but he had to work hard to haul in Clock Stopper. With the benefit of hindsight this was hardly surprising, as the runner-up went on to give subsequent Breeders' Cup Sprint winner Cajun Beat a real test at Turfway Park and has since been Grade 1-placed.

The next move that Frankel made with Ghostzapper is typical of the master conditioner's methods. A proponent of the bounce theory, Frankel believes it is better to aim high with an improving horse, rather than waste peak efforts in less valuable events moving up the ladder. This is at variance with the methods of the traditional US trainer, such as those exemplified by Shug McGaughey with horses owned and bred by the Phipps family.

Sent straight into Grade 1 company in the Kings Bishop Stakes at Saratoga, Ghostzapper nearly justified his trainer's move. He reverted to his indolent ways during the early stages, with the result that he was 11 lengths behind with three furlongs left to race. The after-burner soon kicked in, however, and he made up all but half a length of it. Indeed, such was the vigour with which he finished that he was well clear of the winner, Valid Video, soon after the line.

Perhaps Frankel had erred a little in his belief that Ghostzapper had sufficient seasoning for this assignment, but it did not matter. He destroyed the opposition in the Grade 1 Vosburgh Stakes next time out. His trademark wide sweep was less interrupted by the easier bends of Belmont and the slightly deeper surface enabled him to get better purchase for the latent power of his finishing kick.

The Vosburgh naturally encouraged the perception that here was a strong candidate for the Breeders' Cup Sprint. Frankel ran into trouble with him, however, as the cumulative effects of training and racing caused Ghostzapper sore feet. This might have been a blessing in disguise, as it spared the colt a hard race at Santa Anita and allowed him precious time for development.

Again, there were a few physical problems to overcome, and it was not until July that he made his 2004 reappearance in the Grade 2 Tom Fool Handicap over seven furlongs. The rest had clearly done him good. Showing much sharper tactical speed through slick fractions for the distance, Ghostzapper paralysed three opponents while barely expending energy. His four-and-a-quarter-length victory was worth a Beyer speed figure of 120, which was the best over sprint distances all year.

The Iselin in August was just the spot to step Ghostzapper up in trip and send him around two turns. Despite his impressive victory, there were some who still doubted his stamina when stiffer competition came his way.

The Grade 1 Woodward Stakes back at Belmont over nine furlongs was the acid test. It was to prove not just his distance credentials, but also his stomach for a fight. The fractions were murderous and smashed up the seven-strong field. They ran the first six furlongs in under 1min 9sec, the equivalent of July Cup pace. It was no surprise that Ghostzapper was hard on the bridle, but he wasn't the only one.

Saint Liam, a rapidly improving horse, was still nosing up the inside by the home turn and even shaded the lead with the benefit of saving ground. When he began to hang right exiting the turn, Ghostzapper was muscled into the middle of the track, and the two fought a close battle all the way to the line.

Here it became obvious for the first time that Ghostzapper's regular rider, Javier Castellano, is not in the premier league. He looked overmatched against Edgar Prado on Saint Liam, but finally managed to elicit a significant response from Ghostzapper inside the final 100 yards. Really beginning to surge in the last few jumps, Ghostzapper won by a neck.

The truth about the subsequent Breeders' Cup Classic is that it really did not test Ghostzapper anything like so much. He was able to dominate while going through much slower fractions than in the Woodward and he also skimmed the rail all the way from his inside draw. His victory might have looked extremely comfortable, but the fact that he enjoyed the run of the race must be taken into account.

So where will Ghostzapper rank by the end of next season? He has already been beaten twice – once more than Native Dancer; he has won just eight races – 24 less than Citation, 26 less than Forego and 31 less than Kelso; he has broken just one track record – four less than Man O'War and Secretariat and eight less than Swaps; he has won just three Grade 1 races – 10 less than Spectacular Bid and 11 less than Affirmed; and he has carried just 9st to victory in a top-class handicap – 13lb less than Dr Fager.

Ghostzapper may well be the best horse in this world, but he must now prove himself on another plane entirely. There are a few ghosts left for him to zap.

Ghostzapper

bay colt, 6-4-2000

		Vice Regent	Northern Dancer
	Deputy Minister		Victoria Regina
Awesome Again		Mint Copy	Bunty's Flight
b 1994			Shakney
	Primal Force	Blushing Groom	Red God
			Runaway Bride
		Prime Prospect	Mr Prospector
			Square Generation
	Relaunch	In Reality	Intentionally
			My Dear Girl
Baby Zip		Foggy Note	The Axe
b 1991			Silver Song
	Thirty Zip	Tri Jet	Jester
			Haze
		Sailaway	Hawaii
			Quick Wit

Bred by Adena Springs in Kentucky

Sire Awesome Again

Won 9 of 12 races, inc. Jim Dandy S.-Gr2, Stephen Foster H.-Gr2, Whitney H.-Gr1, Saratoga Cup H.-Gr2, Hawthorne Gold Cup H.-Gr3, Breeders' Cup Classic S.-Gr1. Also 3rd in Travers S. at 3. Medium-sized (16.0hh), well-made sort. Good at 3, made striking progress to become very good at 4. Usually stalked pace and produced sharp turn of foot. Stayed 10f well. Well-bred. Half-brother to champion 2yo Macho Uno (by Holy Bull). By a champion 2yo and champion sire. Dam won 4 races (6-7f), half-sister to dam of Miss Ra He Ha (Gr3). Grand-dam smart stakes winner at 5 years, from family of 1987 champion older mare North Sider. Stands at Adena Springs Kentucky, 2005 fee $125,000. Sire of 3 racing crops, inc: Awesome Time (Gr3), Ghostzapper (Vosburgh S.-Gr3), Woodward S.-Gr1, Breeders' Cup Classic S.-Gr1), Snorter (Gr3), Toccet (Champagne S.-Gr1, Hollywood Futurity-Gr1), Wilko (Breeders' Cup Juvenile S.-Gr1), Personal Legend (Gr3).

Dam Baby Zip

Won 4 of 16 races, inc. one minor stakes race. Just a useful sprinter. Unplaced only 2 efforts on grass. Sister to one and half-sister to nine other winners, inc. Win River Win (by Virginia Rapids, champion imported horse in Turkey), and minor stakes winner Lucette (by Dayjur). Dam tough, smart performer on dirt and grass, Gr1-placed, stakes winner (5 Listed) in each of 4 racing seasons. Half-sister to hardy sprinter Cutter Sam and to dam of Kentucky Derby winner Lil E. Tee. Dam of: Catch The Ghost (1996 f by Silver Ghost; winner), Getaway Girl (1997 f by Silver Deputy; winner), City Zip (1998 c by Carson City; Gr1 winner), Zip To The Wire (1999 f by Birdonthewire; placed), Ghostzapper (2000 c by Awesome Again; multiple Gr1 winner), Aristocrat (2002 c by Awesome Again; placed 4th on debut). She has a yearling filly by Golden Missile and a colt foal by Mr Greeley. She is due to Sligo Bay in March 2005.

Pedigree assessment

In the week before the Breeders' Cup, Frank Stronach's Adena Springs Kentucky announced an unchanged fee of $75,000 for Awesome Again for the 2005 season. After Wilko had won the Juvenile and Ghostzapper had emulated his sire in the Classic, the charge was swiftly amended to $125,000. Awesome Again won his Classic over what was surely the best field ever assembled for that race, but he was certainly no more impressive in doing so than his son was. Ghostzapper sprinted the ten furlongs, yet found another gear in the last of them. He was unquestionably the best horse in the world in 2004, and it is great news that he will be back in action in 2005. So long as he remains sound, another flawless season seems a certainty. *TM*

Grey Lilas (Ire)

3yo grey filly   **118**

Danehill (USA) - Kenmist (Kenmare (Fr))

Owner Gestut Ammerland

Trainer A Fabre

Breeder Azienda Agricola Il Tiglio Di Amelia Prevedello

Career: **9** starts   won **4**   second **3**   third **1**   £326,214 win and place

---

By Richard Austen

THE American jockey and sometime actor Gary Stevens has had problems over the years knowing when it was time to make his exit stage left. Or stage right. In the twilight years of his illustrious racing career, this member of the United States Racing Hall of Fame has had retirements and short-lived spells based in Europe as stable jockey for Sir Michael Stoute and now Andre Fabre. There must be something about life stateside in late August, because Stevens called time on his 1999 British visit on August 21 and did the same on this season's French stay on August 24.

Stevens had 45 British wins when with Stoute and 50 in France in 2004. In 2003 he appeared on cinema screens, playing the part of a jockey, in the Oscar-nominated film Seabiscuit and one of several reasons he gave for quitting the post with Fabre was that he'd been offered a job as the host of a reality TV show. He must have been having a very bad time indeed.

A second reason for Stevens leaving France appeared to be disappointment with results, including for the Fabre team at Deauville in August, and it was therefore with impeccable theatrical timing, 12 days after Stevens' bidding adieu, that Fabre gained his first Group 1 success of the season in one of Europe's top mile races, the Prix du Moulin.

The Moulin winner was Grey Lilas and it would be very hard to give her the blame for Stevens' waning enthusiasm for life in France. She provided Stevens with three of his French wins, the last one however not enough to dissuade him from resigning from the Fabre job on the same day. She was as reliable as they come, and good enough to take advantage if the luck went her way.

Commencing the season a maiden after two starts, Grey Lilas wasted no time in shedding that tag over a mile at Longchamp and then returned

**Grey Lilas gains a deserved reward at the highest level
with victory in the Group 1 Prix du Moulin at Longchamp**

to the same course and distance three weeks later in April to put herself
into Classic contention by adding the Prix de la Grotte.

In the Poule d'Essai des Pouliches, Torrestrella was the only one to
beat her, while over two and a half furlongs further in the Prix de Diane
at Chantilly, it was Latice, Millionaia and arguably lack of stamina as
Grey Lilas had the lead over two furlongs out until just inside the last.
Subsequent events, though, showed that she stayed at least a mile and
a quarter and was not yet at her peak at Chantilly.

The Prix de la Nonette at Deauville helped to demonstrate the
former point but didn't go the whole way, given that it was such a
bizarre renewal. In the late absence of Latice because of testing ground,
Grey Lilas was the one to beat and had only five rivals. In a false-
start fiasco, three of the jockeys either didn't see or ignored a recall
flag and completed the course, headed by the German Guineas winner
Shapira, with only one of those runners returning when the event
was restaged two days later. Finally settling the issue, Grey Lilas
set a very slow pace and easily saw off the three opponents that
remained.

2004 — Race record

2nd Prix de l'Opera Casino Barriere d'Enghien (Group 1) (Longchamp, October 3) 3yo+ 10f Good **116** (TS 85) 10 ran. *Prominent, 2nd straight, pushed along to lead 2f out, driven over 1f out, headed 100yds out, no extra (E Legrix), beaten 1l by Alexander Goldrun*

1st Netjets Prix du Moulin de Longchamp (Group 1) (Longchamp, September 5) 3yo+ 1m Good to soft **118** (TS 93) 11 ran. *Tracked leader, led entering straight 2½f out, ridden out, ran on well (E Legrix), beat Diamond Green by 1l*

1st Prix de La Nonette (Group 3) (Deauville, August 24) 3yo 10f Very soft **113** 4 ran. *Set very slow pace, quickened 3f out, pushed clear 1½f out, very easily (Gary Stevens), beat Trinity Joy by 5l*

3rd Prix de Diane Hermes (Group 1) (Chantilly, June 13) 3yo 10½f Good to soft **114** (TS 105) 17 ran. *Soon tracking leader, led well over 2f out to 150yds out, one pace (Gary Stevens), beaten 1¼l by Latice*

2nd Gainsborough Poule d'Essai des Pouliches (Group 1) (Longchamp, May 16) 3yo 1m Good to firm **111** (TS 105) 13 ran. *Raced in 3rd place to straight, ridden and every chance 1½f out, no extra inside final furlong (Gary Stevens), beaten 1½l by Torrestrella*

1st Prix de la Grotte (Group 3) (Longchamp, April 25) 3yo 1m Good to soft **106** (TS 98) 8 ran. *Raced in close 2nd, disputing 2nd straight, smooth headway to lead 150yds out, pushed out (Gary Stevens), beat Petit Calva by 1½l*

1st Prix du Louvre (Longchamp, April 4) 3yo 1m Good to soft **91** 6 ran. *(Gary Stevens), beat Divine Story by 1½l*

2003

2nd Prix Coaraze (Fontainebleau, September 3) 2yo 6f Soft 5 ran ● **6th** Prix du Haras de Bernesq (Deauville, August 12) 2yo 6f Good to soft 6 ran **63**

With nothing taken out of her, Grey Lilas was supplemented for the much sterner challenge of the Netjets Prix du Moulin de Longchamp, coupled at 10-1 in an 11-runner race. Stevens having departed, it was Eric Legrix who got the leg up and he excelled in seizing the initiative when the pacesetting Lucky Story capitulated early in the straight. On previous evidence, Jacques le Marois winner Whipper, Poule d'Essai des Poulains principals American Post, Diamond Green and Antonius Pius and the Sussex Stakes third Le Vie dei Colori might all have been well fancied to chase Grey Lilas down, but they had plenty of ground to make up. None did so, and none looked like doing so. Diamond Green and Antonius Pius did best, but Grey Lilas held on by a length.

The Moulin was another improved show from Grey Lilas, travelling well, quickening and running on with great zest, but when Legrix tried to repeat the feat with her at odds-on in the Prix de l'Opera over a mile and a quarter on fast ground, she never established the same advantage and was collared late on by Alexander Goldrun. Before leaving France, Stevens had stated that he would be riding Grey Lilas in America, but when the Breeders' Cup came round neither of them was present.

Grey Lilas

grey filly, 28-1-2001

			Northern Dancer	Nearctic
		Danzig		**Natalma**
	Danehill		Pas de Nom	Admiral's Voyage
	b 1986			Petitioner
			His Majesty	Ribot
		Razyana		Flower Bowl
			Spring Adieu	Buckpasser
				Natalma
			Kalamoun	Zeddaan
		Kenmare		Khairunissa
	Kenmist		Belle Of Ireland	Milesian
	gr 1994			Belle Of The Ball
			Simply Great	Mill Reef
		Mistral's Collette		Seneca
			Kitty's Sister	Bustino
				Sky Fever

Bred by Azienda Agricola il Tiglia di Amelia Prevedello in Ireland. Sold privately €150,000 as Deauville August yearling

Sire Danehill

Won 4 of 9 races, inc. Cork and Orrery Stakes-Gr3, Haydock Park Sprint Cup-Gr1. Also 3rd in 2,000 Guineas. Medium-sized, strong, good-bodied individual, markedly back at the knee. Showed quick, fluent action, effective on any ground from dead to firm, never ran on really soft surface. Died May 2003. Sire of Gr1 winners: Danish (Queen Elizabeth II Challenge Cup), Kissing Cousin (Coronation S.), Danehill Dancer (Phoenix S., National S.), Tsukuba Symphony (NHK Mile Cup), Desert King (National S., Irish 2,000 Guineas, Irish Derby), Fairy King Prawn (Yasuda Kinen), Tiger Hill (Grosser Preis von Baden [twice], Bayerisches Zuchtrennen), Indian Danehill (Prix Ganay), Wannabe Grand (Cheveley Park S.), Aquarelliste (Prix de Diane, Prix Vermeille, Prix Ganay), Banks Hill (Coronation S., Breeders' Cup Filly & Mare Turf, Prix Jacques le Marois), Mozart (July Cup, Nunthorpe S.), Regal Rose (Cheveley Park S.), Dress To Thrill (Matriarch S.), Landseer (Poule d'Essai des Poulains), Rock Of Gibraltar (Grand Criterium, Dewhurst S., 2,000 Guineas, Irish 2,000 Guineas, St James's Palace S., Sussex S., Prix du Moulin), Westerner (Prix du Cadran, twice, Prix Royal-Oak, twice), Clodovil (Poule d'Essai des Poulains), Light Jig (Yellow Ribbon S.), Spartacus (Phoenix S., Gran Criterium), Grey Lilas (Prix du Moulin de Longchamp), North Light (Derby S.), Oratorio (Prix Jean-Luc Lagardere).

Dam Kenmist

Won 2 of 8 races, inc. Listed handicap at Ascot. Also 3rd in Italian Gr3 at 1m. Leggy, angular individual. Showed useful form at 3, best at a mile. Seemed to act on any going. Failed to train on at 4. Quite well-bred. Half-sister to 4 winners in Italy, inc. Jar (c by Niniski; multiple Listed winner, twice Gr3-placed). Dam Gr3-placed Listed winner, full-sister to Listed winner General Cloney. Grand-dam poor performer, but sister to Gr3 winner and Gr2-placed Kittyhawk, half-sister to Gr2-placed Thorndown. Dam of: Stendhal (2000 c by Polish Precedent; winner), Grey Lilas (2001 f by Danehill; Gr1 winner), Night Dhu (2002 f by Montjeu; unraced to date). Her yearling is a colt by Green Desert (unsold 290,000gns, Tattersalls' October Sale, Part 1).

Pedigree assessment

There can be little doubt that Danehill was the key factor in Grey Lilas's pedigree, as the family had lingered a long while in the doldrums before a brief renaissance in the late Lord Carnarvon's stud, and another slump into mediocrity. Grey Lilas is very smart over 10 and 11 furlongs, but a mile suits her best. *TM*

Grey Swallow (Ire)

3yo grey colt **126**

Daylami (Ire) - Style Of Life (USA) (The Minstrel (Can))

Owner Mrs Rochelle Quinn

Trainer D K Weld

Breeder Mrs C L Weld

Career: **8** starts   won **4** second **0** third **1** **£641,557** win and place

---

By Tony Smurthwaite

RATHER like his own name, a mix of the opaque and the beautiful, Grey Swallow proved a racehorse of contradictions in 2004. Ireland's best youngster of 2003 turned into a performer who lost when looking best primed to win, and won when others looked to have his measure. For all that, connections will look back on the year and savour especially a win in the Irish Derby and not be diverted by four other defeats in Group 1 races, always when fancied.

His trainer Dermot Weld will surely settle for the 12-month bragging rights imbued by a triumph in his domestic Derby, run yards from his front door. So what if he dearly wanted to add victory in the Prix de l'Arc de Triomphe, the other major objective for Grey Swallow in 2004?

Victory in the Irish Derby afforded Grey Swallow his halo, all just a short walk from his box at Weld's Rosewell House Stables on The Curragh. Those same stables were the base for Charlie Weld to issue the winners of more than 1,000 races and from where his son has crafted a niche for himself that is perhaps unparalleled in racing.

Weld trades in a currency alien to 99 per cent of trainers. He remains the only European trainer to have won a leg of the US Triple Crown and the Melbourne Cup in Australia. He has also won the American Derby three times in five years, an achievement to make any US trainer proud.

In Grey Swallow, Weld began the year with a colt who had won his two races by an aggregate of 18 lengths. A very smart juvenile at seven furlongs, by Daylami from a family with stamina depths, it would not be hard to imagine that Weld envisaged Grey Swallow's future over further than a mile. Though he would in all probability decline to admit it, Weld identified two races that he wanted Grey Swallow to win: the Irish Derby and the Arc.

Still, the season began with eyes fixed firmly on the 2,000 Guineas. Weld even delivered Grey Swallow for the Leopardstown 2,000 Guineas

**Grey Swallow bounces back from two Classic defeats at a
mile to beat Epsom hero North Light in the Irish Derby**

Trial, despite worrying at only a two-week gap before Newmarket rather
than the usual three.

Grey Swallow maintained his 100 per cent win record with a head
verdict at Leopardstown over the well-respected Ballydoyle runner Meath.
A decent pace in testing ground left Grey Swallow blowing hard afterwards,
and saddled with the qualified eulogy from his trainer that he was "brave,
honest and genuine".

Afterwards, Weld told everyone willing to listen that the 2,000 Guineas
might come too early. Two weeks on, he was right. It was a race spoiled
by the field splitting chaotically into three. Quite why the stalls were
placed in the middle of the Rowley Mile course was not explained properly
beforehand. After the field fanned out like yachts on the Solent the query
became more pressing.

Grey Swallow would not have won whatever the run of the race. In the
circumstances Pat Smullen steered his mount after a slow start into fourth
behind Haafhd, Snow Ridge and Azamour. Smullen would talk later of how
deflated he was after this race. Certainly it marked the end of Grey Swallow's
unbeaten record but he lost little in defeat. Few could have handled Haafhd
that afternoon and initial comments from the Weld camp suggested fast
ground that inspired a time well inside standard may not have suited.

2004

18th Prix de l'Arc de Triomphe Lucien Barriere (Group 1) (Longchamp, October 3) 3yo+ 12f Good **98** (TS 90) 19 ran. *Midfield on outside, 8th straight, effort and edged left just over 2f out, soon weakened (P J Smullen), beaten 19l by Bago*

4th Baileys Irish Champion Stakes (Group 1) (Leopardstown, September 11) 3yo+ 10f Good to firm **123** (TS 123) 8 ran. *Settled 5th, progress early straight, 3rd 1½f out, no impression inside final furlong, kept on (P J Smullen), beaten 1½l by Azamour*

1st Budweiser Irish Derby (Group 1) (Curragh, June 27) 3yo 12f Good to firm **126** (TS 125) 10 ran. *Tracked leaders, 5th halfway, smooth headway into 3rd 2f out, soon challenged, led under 1f out, stayed on well (P J Smullen), beat North Light by ½l*

3rd Boylesports Irish 2,000 Guineas (Group 1) (Curragh, May 22) 3yo 1m Good to firm **116** (TS 81) 8 ran. *Tracked leaders in 4th, 3rd and ridden over 1½f out, challenged 1f out, kept on under pressure (P J Smullen), beaten 1½l by Bachelor Duke*

4th UltimateBet.com 2000 Guineas Stakes (Group 1) (Newmarket, May 1) 3yo 1m Good **118** (TS 108) 14 ran. *Slowly into stride, held up centre, headway over 1f out, ran on (P J Smullen), beaten 3¾l by Haafhd*

1st Leopardstown 2,000 Guineas Trial Stakes (Listed) (Leopardstown, April 18) 3yo 1m Soft **110** (TS 69) 5 ran. *Close up in 4th, 3rd and challenged early straight, led inside final furlong, kept on well when pressed close home (P J Smullen), beat Meath by hd*

2003

1st Killavullan Stakes (Group 3) (Leopardstown, October 27) 2yo 7f Good **117** 4 ran ● **1st** GPT Access Equipment EBF Maiden (Galway, July 28) 2yo 7f Soft **105** 9 ran

With Haafhd and Snow Ridge absentees from the Irish 2,000 Guineas at The Curragh, Grey Swallow was thrust higher up the scale of expectations. His odds of 10-1 at Newmarket were replaced by 2-1 for The Curragh, with Azamour the 6-4 favourite.

After a smart early pace, the field settled. Smullen was poised, then launched a challenge with a furlong to run. A strong finish looked assured a furlong out until the maiden Bachelor Duke, unconsidered back in seventh at Newmarket, came galloping by to win. Third place was reserved for Grey Swallow, and more irritation for Smullen, who again felt the ground was a bit fast.

All of a sudden the season had the appearance of a letdown after the fireworks of the autumn and a winter of expectation. More grey than swallow. Weld, time would prove, was not unduly worried. Five weeks passed, in which time North Light won the Derby. The Guineas form, as is the way post-Epsom, looked jaded by comparison.

North Light and his three closest rivals from the Derby – Rule Of Law, Let The Lion Roar and Percussionist – all ventured across to The Curragh for the Irish Derby on June 27. It was the first time in the 139 years of the race that the first four from Epsom had renewed acquaintances and they dominated the build-up. Dry weather cursed the track and prompted the late withdrawal of Day Flight, a stablemate of Percussionist, amid comments from their trainer, John Gosden, that the going was, in large parts, firm.

This, on all known form, would detract from the chance of Grey Swallow. Yet other factors were at play that were difficult to gauge. Weld felt his horses were not at their peak in early season after some changeable weather, so come mid-summer those irritations ought to have abated. More convincingly, two factors pointed in favour of Grey Swallow's chance over a trip half as long again as any he had tried.

Firstly, physically and mentally he was a different specimen for gaining racing experience and time to mature. Secondly, his sire and broodmare sire (The Minstrel) had both won over a mile and a half; the latter, by happenstance, in the 1977 Irish Derby.

As the runners left the stalls it was noticeable that the pace was far from breakneck. Smullen on Grey Swallow tracked Kieren Fallon on North Light. It was to become apparent that Fallon was much less at ease than at Epsom just 22 days earlier. With fully half a mile to go, Fallon pressed the button on North Light. It was an audacious manoeuvre and one that looked all the more daring when his three Epsom foes failed to rise to the brutal challenge.

However, a second glance revealed Smullen to be still in control of a partner yet to yield. Grey Swallow, with his new-found maturity, his family background and his preparation in the tough streets of two Classics, was able to gallop well enough within himself to keep abreast of developments. Those final furlongs, reacting to North Light's lung-bursting effort, then finding the will to go past and win, are those that separate the good from the special.

A charged Smullen was close to tears afterwards. He explained that he had been mentally wired to win two Guineas and only now found relief from the torment brought on by two defeats.

For Weld, in his 32nd year as a trainer, victory was multi-layered. His mother Gita had bred the winner, and owned a stake in him as well. Equally, it was not lost on the trainer that Smullen had ridden a race of great composure. Ultimately, though, Weld was ready, willing and more than able to remould the story of Grey Swallow's season.

He pointed out that The Minstrel was also beaten in two Guineas before finding fame and fortune. A neat rejoinder if ever there was one, excusing two defeats and comparing Grey Swallow to a master racehorse in the turn of a phrase. More interesting was Weld's remark that "today was the day". Usually the domain of trainers following a handicap coup, Weld commandeered the comment to illustrate his conviction to train horses as he sees fit. Use two Classics as prep races for a third? Why not?

Weld had won his 12th Irish Classic, so the strategy turned to widening Grey Swallow's circle of influence, dropping to ten furlongs for the Irish Champion Stakes and then stepping back to a mile and a half for the Prix de l'Arc de Triomphe.

That meant an 11-week layoff, with all the attendant concerns as to whether Grey Swallow would be at absolute fever pitch. Weld removed any such doubts, bluntly issuing the comment that the Leopardstown outing was a 'prep race' for the Arc.

Come raceday, with good to firm ground prevailing, Grey Swallow found a pleasing cadence in response to a decent but not onerous pace, quickened well when asked, but flattened out when it mattered most as Norse Dancer went clear only to be pegged back by the express train that was Azamour, rattling up the outside under Mick Kinane. Fourth of eight was Grey Swallow's fate, one that translated well if considering his chances in the Arc some three weeks down the road.

Unfortunately, potholes emerged. Grey Swallow was reported to have picked up a low-grade infection and was off his food for a number of days after the Irish Champion. As one of the few qualified veterinary surgeons among the ranks of trainers, Weld has gone on record as saying that one of his areas of fascination is how the racehorse handles stress. A man-made breed that is highly strung at the best of times, when pressured to the extremities of their ability in the cauldron of competition they are liable to wilt. Weld must surely have realised the game was up in terms of winning an Arc.

Was it the lack of readiness for Leopardstown that backfired on the trainer and made the horse sick? There is no strong evidence either way. Given Grey Swallow's lifeless display in the Arc there are questions to be answered when he emerges as a four-year-old. Mental stresses can leave mental scars and, as "tough, honest and genuine" as Grey Swallow was dubbed, some racehorses, like the livestock familiar to any veterinary surgeon, can turn into stubborn recalcitrants on a whim.

Paris was not a rewarding venture. It was a late decision to pay the supplementary entry fee required, and the air of prevarication, though failing to permeate the betting market, looked more telling in hindsight.

Memorably, the need for a supplementary entry offered one of the season's most hilarious examples of the notion that a little information is a dangerous thing. Earlier in Arc week a list of acceptors was published and, clearly, Grey Swallow was not among them; he had, however, never been among the original entries, and supplements were not to be made until later that week. Undaunted, one punter on Betfair took this as a sign that Weld's runner was out of the race and offered to lay it – at odds of 219-1.

There must have been some sweaty palms when Grey Swallow burst from his stall for the Arc as 5-1 second favourite. Weld later cited "a combination of factors" for a dismal defeat in 18th place of 19.

Fast ground and an interrupted build-up were two of those factors, but surely Grey Swallow was capable of a less inconspicuous finishing position.

It looked too hard a verdict to read. Opaque rather than beautiful.

Grey Swallow

grey colt, 19-2-2001

Daylami gr 1994	Doyoun	Mill Reef	Never Bend / Milan Mill
		Dumka	Kashmir / Faizebad
	Daltawa	Miswaki	Mr Prospector / Hopespringseternal
		Damana	Crystal Palace / Denia
Style Of Life b 1985	The Minstrel	Northern Dancer	Nearctic / Natalma
		Fleur	Victoria Park / Flaming Page
	Bubinka	Nashua	Nasrullah / Segula
		Stolen Date	Sadair / Stolen Hour

Bred by Mrs C.L. Weld in Ireland. 150,000gns Newmarket Houghton yearling

Sire Daylami

Won 11 of 21 races, inc. Prix de Fontainebleau-Gr3, Poule d'Essai des Poulains-Gr1, Tattersalls Gold Cup-Gr2, Eclipse S.-Gr1, Man o' War S.-Gr1, Coronation Cup-Gr1, King George VI & Queen Elizabeth S.-Gr1, Irish Champion S.-Gr1, Breeders' Cup Turf-Gr1. High-class performer in all 4 seasons, noted for toughness, honesty, consistency and a rare zest for racing. Effective on any surface, and endowed with superior powers of acceleration. Well-made individual, just over 16.0hh, and very well-bred. Half-brother to Dalakhani (4 Gr1 wins) and Daymarti (Gr1-placed Listed winner). Sire won 2,000 Guineas, 3rd in Derby, also sire of Kalanisi; dam Listed winner, also Gr3-placed). Stands at Gilltown Stud, Ireland, at a 2004 fee of €20,000. Sire of 2 crops of racing age, inc: Grey Swallow (Irish Derby-Gr1).

Dam Style Of Life

Won 2 of 10 races. Useful, consistent performer up to a mile, indifferent to ground conditions. Wore blinkers in both wins (Phoenix Park and Naas), but always raced gamely enough. Sister to Seasonal Pickup (won 4 Listed, Gr3-placed), half-sister to 2 other winners. By a dual Derby winner and successful sire out of a Gr3 winner who was sister to Listed winner Stoshka and half-sister to Gr2-placed Taufan (useful sire). Dam of: Style For Life (1990 f by Law Society; Listed-placed winner; dam of Gr1 winner in Italy), The Breadman (1991 g by Thatching; unplaced), Stylish Ways (1992 g by Thatching; Gr3-placed winner), Yudrik (1994 g by Lahib; winner), Central Lobby (1995 c by Kenmare; Gr3-placed winner), Rustic (1996 f by Grand Lodge; Gr3-placed winner), unnamed (1997 c by Caerleon; unraced), Irish Style (1999 f by Mujadil; winner), Grey Swallow (2001 c by Daylami; Classic winner), Moonlight Dance (2002 f by Sinndar; modest form in 3 runs to date).

Pedigree assessment

Grey Swallow had shown enough in his first season to suggest that he would be the one to establish Daylami as a front-rank sire in 2004. Sure enough, the colt reached a lofty peak when a worthy winner of the Irish Derby, propelling his sire to prominence, but that was Grey Swallow's one big moment in an in-and-out campaign, and there was a measure of disappointment in the fact that Daylami's back-up team, while registering a good wins-to-runs ratio, contained no other real stars. Grey Swallow, in new colours, is expected to be his sire's principal standard-bearer again in 2005. He is certainly a far better colt than his Arc de Triomphe placing might suggest, having had a less than ideal preparation for the race, then no luck in running. *TM*

Haafhd

3yo chestnut colt   **129**

Alhaarth (Ire) - Al Bahathri (USA) (Blushing Groom (Fr))

Owner Hamdan Al Maktoum

Trainer B W Hills

Breeder Shadwell Estate Company Limited

Career: **9** starts   won **5**   second **0**   third **2**   £492,288 win and place

By Lee Mottershead

2,000 GUINEAS winner should not have been forgotten so quickly. And not just any old 2,000 Guineas winner, either. At Newmarket in May, Haafhd was ruthless in charging to Classic glory, completely dominant, outstanding on the day that mattered. Yet little more than five months later and back at the scene of his greatest triumph, he seemed to have been dismissed as a soon-to-be also-ran, a horse whose participation in the Champion Stakes was welcome, but not especially significant. As he embarked on what would turn out to be his final competitive journey, this was a horse with a point to prove. He was on the same mission at the same place back in April.

Haafhd had been an exciting juvenile, but also one who didn't quite deliver what had once seemed likely. Winner of a six-furlong maiden on Newmarket's July course on his racecourse debut in August 2003, the Barry Hills-trained colt had made a massive impression when following up two weeks later in the Listed Washington Singer Stakes at Newbury, thumping his opponents by upwards of five lengths. Immediately he was viewed as one of the principal players for the Guineas. But in finishing third in both the Champagne and Dewhurst Stakes, there was a feeling that, while Haafhd had confirmed himself an extremely talented individual, he had perhaps deceived us with those first impressions.

He set about proving his doubters wrong as soon as he could. The Craven Stakes was identified by Hills as the stage for Haafhd's return to action, the place where the bonny chestnut would seek to earn the right to a shot at the Guineas just over a fortnight later. As he walked around the Newmarket parade ring, it was apparent that this was a horse who had made excellent physical strides from two to three. Haafhd had always had the breeding to support lofty ambitions. A son of Alhaarth out of

Haafhd, centre, follows his impressive Craven win with a convincing defeat of Snow Ridge in the 2,000 Guineas

Irish 1,000 Guineas winner Al Bahathri, he already held a special place in his owner-breeder Sheikh Hamdan Al Maktoum's heart, just as his sire and dam had. Now, though, he also possessed the physique. The boy had become a man.

As would be the case through much of Haafhd's career, the pre-race talk was not predominantly about him, but another. On this occasion, the other was Three Valleys, the horse who had finished one place ahead of him in the Dewhurst and who had held a much more vaunted reputation than Haafhd since his impressive Coventry Stakes victory early the previous summer.

Rarely, though, has a horse been upstaged to a greater degree. For while Three Valleys pulled fiercely for most of the race before tiring through the rest of it, Haafhd was exemplary. Sent straight to the lead, he at no point looked like being beaten, accelerating into the Dip under a canny Richard Hills ride before powering five lengths clear. Visually at least, this was nothing less than dazzling, one of the most taking displays witnessed in recent Craven history. It was also a performance that got Barry Hills waxing more lyrically than he had in years.

Hills has been training top horses for more than 30 years. Many of those good horses have been milers, horses like Tap On Wood, 2,000

2004 — Race record

1st Emirates Airline Champion Stakes (Group 1) (Newmarket, October 16) 3yo+ 10f Soft **129** (TS 93) 11 ran. *Chased leaders, went 2nd 3f out, led over 1f out, ridden out (R Hills), beat Chorist by 2½l*

9th Cantor Odds Sussex Stakes (Group 1) (Goodwood, July 28) 3yo+ 1m Good **105** (TS 97) 11 ran. *Prominent, every chance just over 2f out, weakened over 1f out, no chance when hampered just inside final furlong (R Hills), beaten 9½l by Soviet Song*

4th St James's Palace Stakes (Group 1) (Ascot, June 15) 3yo 1m Good to firm **119** (TS 119) 11 ran. *Tracked leader, led 2f out, hard pressed from over 1f out, headed and one pace last 150yds (R Hills), beaten 1¼l by Azamour*

1st UltimateBet.com 2,000 Guineas Stakes (Group 1) (Newmarket, May 1) 3yo 1m Good **127** (TS 119) 14 ran. *Tracked leaders centre, led over 2f out, ridden and edged right over 1f out, ran on (R Hills), beat Snow Ridge by 1¾l*

1st bet365 Craven Stakes (Group 3) (Newmarket, April 15) 3yo 1m Good **121** (TS 90) 5 ran. *Made all, quickened 2f out, soon clear, ran on well (R Hills), beat Three Valleys by 5l*

2003

3rd Darley Dewhurst Stakes (Group 1) (Newmarket, October 18) 2yo 7f Good to firm **114** 12 ran ● **3rd** Champagne Stakes (Group 2) (Doncaster, September 12) 2yo 7f Good **107** 6 ran ● **1st** Stan James Online Stakes (Registered As The Washington Singer Stakes) (Listed) (Newbury, August 15) 2yo 7f Good to firm **114** 8 ran ● **1st** Hugo And The Huguenotes EBF Maiden Stakes (Newmarket (July), August 1) 2yo 6f Good to soft **87** 10 ran

Guineas victor in 1979. Despite that, Hills found himself making a statement that made everyone who heard it take notice. "I've trained horses like Tap On Wood, Distant Relative and Distant Music," he said, "but I think this horse is as good as I've had over a mile." They were words that Hills soon wished he had not uttered, not because he didn't believe in them, but because they placed extra pressure on both Haafhd and himself. Now the expectation was enormous. Surely only a 2,000 Guineas triumph could save Hills from looking stupid.

The problem was that this looked a solid running of the first colts' Classic. Salford City had been almost as impressive as Haafhd in winning the Greenham Stakes, and Godolphin had high hopes for Snow Ridge. France had a serious threat in Whipper, while the Irish were shouting for Grey Swallow, Azamour and, in particular, the heavily touted Aidan O'Brien-trained 15-8 favourite One Cool Cat.

However, One Cool Cat, soon to be diagnosed with a dicky ticker, would beat just one home. Haafhd beat them all, and in style. But assessing the 2004 Guineas was tricky at the time, and remains tricky now. After setting off from stalls placed in the middle of the track, the 14 runners proceeded to spread out across the far half of the racecourse, making for a somewhat perplexing sight. Happy to race prominently, Haafhd received a positive ride from Richard

Haafhd roars back to form on the final start of his career with victory over a star-studded field in the Champion

Hills, the rider – one of the best judges of pace in the weighing room – tracking a Godolphin pacemaker up the middle of the track before sending Haafhd into a race-winning lead passing the Bushes. Always in command thereafter, they passed the post a length and three-quarters in front of Snow Ridge. While some of his opponents had clearly not run their races, the time was excellent and the handicappers seemed impressed, Haafhd's 2,000 Guineas Racing Post Rating of 127 ranking him below only King's Best among the race's five most recent winners.

With four Derby seconds behind him, it was inevitable that Hills senior would be asked whether Haafhd would go to Epsom. He would not. Neither Alhaarth nor Al Bahathri had stayed beyond ten furlongs, so Haafhd would, for the time being at least, stay at a mile. He would not, however, tackle the Irish Guineas, his connections instead preferring to wait for the St James's Palace Stakes.

At Royal Ascot, Haafhd was not the horse he had been at Newmarket. Racing around a bend for the first time in his life, he led early in the straight but could not retain control and dropped away for fourth. It was disappointing, but not disastrous. Goodwood was disastrous. Buoyed by a pleasing racecourse gallop at Newbury, the Haafhd team sent the colt for the Sussex Stakes, only to witness a thoroughly laboured display. Edgy at the start, where he needed to be re-shod, Haafhd could manage only ninth of 11 on his first outing against his elders. The memory of Newmarket in May was becoming increasingly distant.

Fast ground at both Ascot and Goodwood was offered by the Haafhd entourage as one possible explanation for the two reverses. It was also the reason why Haafhd missed the Queen Elizabeth II Stakes, his planned comeback contest after a two-month spell on the sidelines. With Ascot swerved just hours before the off, it was decided that he should return to Newmarket for the Champion Stakes. There, he would tackle a mile and a quarter for the first time, with Barry Hills adamant that Haafhd, like the rest of his string, was now back to his best after being below par through the summer. Reported to have been "bucking and kicking" at home, as he had in the spring, Haafhd went into the Champion with his closest supporters expecting a big run. Nobody else was, punters sending him off a weak 12-1 shot in the 11-runner field.

Quite whether Haafhd's Champion Stakes demolition job can be taken at face value is highly debatable. On heavy ground, many in what was a high-class line-up simply failed to run their races. Doyen, Refuse To Bend, Norse Dancer and Lucky Story all performed way below their best in a contest in which, like the Guineas, the runners spread out, making for a frustratingly messy heat.

That, in itself, though, should not detract from what Haafhd achieved. Back racing over a straight track, he travelled better than anything else, staying on the bridle longer and coming home better than the rest to thump the admirable – but surely not outstanding – Chorist by two and a half lengths, with Azamour – clearly unhappy on the ground – a game, but weary, third.

Given a Racing Post Rating of 129, up 2lb on his Guineas effort and on a par with that recorded by fellow three-year-old Bago in the Arc, Haafhd returned to a fanfare and to new dreams. We – and that includes Barry Hills – assumed that Haafhd would race on at four. Hills had already drawn up a programme for the first half of the horse's 2005 campaign. He soon had to tear it up.

In announcing Haafhd's retirement, Sheikh Hamdan's racing manager Angus Gold said that his boss "felt the horse was more important to him at stud". The decision swam against the tide of keeping top three-year-olds in training at four and was all the more disappointing since we were waving goodbye to Haafhd just as we had savoured him posting a personal best. And at his best Haafhd was very good indeed; a horse who does not deserve to be forgotten.

Haafhd

chestnut colt, 18-2-2001

	Unfuwain	Northern Dancer	Nearctic
Alhaarth b 1993			Natalma
		Height Of Fashion	Bustino
			Highclere
	Irish Valley	Irish River	Riverman
			Irish Star
		Green Valley	Val de Loir
			Sly Pola
Al Bahathri ch 1982	Blushing Groom	Red God	Nasrullah
			Spring Run
		Runaway Bride	Wild Risk
			Aimee
	Chain Store	Nodouble	Noholme
			Abla-Jay
		General Store	To Market
			Generals Sister

Bred by Shadwell Estate Co. Ltd in England

Sire Alhaarth

Won 8 of 17 races, inc. Vintage S.-Gr3, Solario S.-Gr3, Champagne Stakes-Gr2, Dewhurst S.-Gr1, Prix du Rond-Point-Gr2, Curragh International S.-Gr2, Prix Dollar-Gr2. Also 3rd in Sussex S. and Champion S. Strong, well-proportioned, handsome individual, 16.0hh. Champion European 2-y-o who did not rise to predicted heights, but acquitted himself well in high-class company. By a top-class 12f performer, a half-brother to Nashwan who did well at stud and died in January 2002. Half-brother to Gr3 winner Green Pola (by Nijinsky) and 2 lesser winners. Dam unplaced half-sister to Green Dancer (by Nijinsky). Stands at Derrinstown Stud, Ireland, at a 2004 fee of €25,000 (Oct 1). Sire of 4 crops of racing age, inc: Bandari (Gr2), Dominica (Gr2), Misterah (Gr3), Maharib (Gr3), Phoenix Reach (Canadian Gr1), Haafhd (2,000 Guineas-Gr1, Champion S.-Gr1).

Dam Al Bahathri

Won 6 of 12 races, inc. Lowther S.-Gr2, Irish 1,000 Guineas-Gr1, Coronation S.-Gr2, Falmouth S.-Gr3. Also 2nd in Cheveley Park S. and 1,000 Guineas. Attractive, somewhat lightly made sort, and a grand mover with a long stride. A natural front-runner, but owned a change of pace. Probably got 10f, but easily best form at a mile. Very well bred. Dam of: Hasbah (1987 f by Kris; Listed winner, Gr1-placed; died at 5), Almaaseh (1988 f by Dancing Brave; placed; dam of Gr3 winner Almaty), Gmaasha (1989 f by Kris; unraced), Alyakkh (1990 f by Sadler's Wells; winner; dam of Listed winners Nafisah and Mutakarrim), Goalwah (1992 f by Sadler's Wells; winner, Listed-placed; died at 5), Mithali (1993 c by Unfuwain; winner), Za-Im (1994 c by Green Desert; winner, Gr3-placed), Almurooj (1995 f by Zafonic; unplaced; dam of Listed winner Judhoor), Munir (1998 c by Indian Ridge; Gr2 winner), Munib (2000 c by Mark Of Esteem; unraced, died at 3 yrs), Haafhd (2001 c by Alhaarth; dual Gr1 winner). She has a yearling colt by King's Best, and is due to Alhaarth in 2005.

Pedigree assessment

It was not all plain sailing for Haafhd in 2004, but when he was right he was as good as any of his age over a mile, and he signed off by dominating a star-studded Champion Stakes field, registering his career-best effort at ten furlongs. He might well have gone on to further glories at four, but Sheikh Hamdan has opted to take him home to Derrinstown, where he will stand alongside his sire. He is certainly the best of Alhaarth's stock to date, the only one to have won in Group 1 company in Europe, and also ranks as the best product of his illustrious dam, Al Bahathri. *TM*

Hard Buck (Brz)

5yo brown horse **123**

Spend A Buck (USA) - Social Secret (Secreto (USA))

Owner Team Victory

Trainer K McPeek

Breeder Haras Old Friends

Career: **19** starts won **9** second **5** third **0** **£616,287** win and place

---

By James Willoughby

CHOISIR was always going to be a hard act to follow. A year after the visit of the Australian sprinter, it was an American middle-distance runner who infused a showpiece event at Ascot with international intrigue.

Hard Buck could not match Choisir's Royal meeting double, but his second to Doyen in the King George VI and Queen Elizabeth Diamond Stakes in July was still a terrific performance and his trainer Kenny McPeek has vowed to have another crack at the race.

Sadly, it won't be with Hard Buck. In October, it was reported that he had met with a career-ending setback during his preparation for the Canadian International. His potential thus remained unfulfilled, for he was just coming to the peak of his powers.

Hard Buck's life began in Brazil, where McPeek first laid eyes on him as a four-year-old, two and a half hours out of Rio de Janeiro. He was hardly an unknown quantity, however, having already won a Grade 1 race in a nation that has supplied top-class stock to the US before.

"He was a beautiful horse," McPeek said. "You had to say, if he can't run, something's wrong. I had to put my money where my mouth was."

McPeek's boldness was rewarded. Hard Buck won his first three races in the States in 2003, two minor stakes and the Grade 3 River City Handicap at Churchill Downs in November. When opportunities in Kentucky became sparse following the onset of winter, McPeek shipped Hard Buck down to Gulfstream Park in Florida, where the Grade 3 Canadian Turf Handicap at the end of January looked a perfect spot to run him.

Heavy rain forced the executive to switch the race to the dirt track, but only five others took their chance, so McPeek decided not to scratch his runner. Unfortunately, Hard Buck never got the chance to show the full extent of his capabilities on the surface, owing to the way the race was run, and he faded into a remote fourth behind the ex-Aidan O'Brien-trained Newfoundland.

Hard Buck goes to post at Ascot, before performing with great credit in second behind Doyen in the King George

This first race for 11 weeks was not lost on Hard Buck, however. It served as a sharpener for the Grade 1 Gulfstream Park Handicap over 11 furlongs. Faced by a decent field, including the redoubtable Balto Star and Kicken Kris, he had to come wide into the straight but got up to win by a head. There could be little doubt that he was better than the bare form.

A disappointing effort in the previous season's UAE Derby, on dirt, did not discourage McPeek from returning Hard Buck to Dubai for his next start, the Group 1 Sheema Classic over a mile and a half. Though it was perhaps not the deepest field assembled for the race, Hard Buck proved he could run with smart European horses by finishing a fine second to Polish Summer.

It was probably this positive experience that fixed the plan to bring Hard Buck to Ascot in his trainer's mind. Upon his return from Dubai – a journey regarded as particularly draining – McPeek used a minor

2004
Race record

2nd King George VI And Queen Elizabeth Diamond Stakes (Group 1) (Ascot, July 24) 3yo+
12f Good to firm **123** (TS 92) 11 ran. *Took keen hold, tracked leader, led briefly 2f out,
chased winner after, no chance final furlong but kept on well to hold on to 2nd
near finish (Gary Stevens), beaten 3l by Doyen*

5th United Nations Stakes (Grade 1) (Monmouth Park, July 3) 3yo+ 11f Firm **117** 11 ran.
*Held up towards rear, 8th 3f out, stayed on at same pace final 2f to take 5th on
line (B Blanc), beaten 4½l by Request For Parole*

2nd Opening Verse Handicap (Churchill Downs, June 12) 3yo+ 1m½f Yielding **117** 3 ran.
*Raced in 3rd, 4th straight, staying on when not much room 110yds out, took 2nd
closing stages (B Blanc), beaten 1¼l by Senor Swinger*

2nd Dubai Sheema Classic (Group 1) (Turf) (Nad Al Sheba, March 27) 4yo+ 12f Good to firm
117 (TS 99) 13 ran. *Tracked leader, 2nd straight, stayed on well to lead 1f out,
headed well inside final furlong (J R Velazquez), beaten ½l by Polish Summer*

1st Gulfstream Park Breeders' Cup Handicap (Grade 1) (Gulfstream Park, February 22) 3yo+
11f Firm **117** 8 ran. *Tracked pace in 4th or 5th, three wide final turn, stayed on
under pressure to lead closing stages, driven out (E Prado), beat Balto Star by hd*

4th Canadian Turf Handicap (Grade 3) (Gulfstream Park, January 31) 3yo+ 1m½f Sloppy
6 ran. *Prominent on inside 4f, gradually weakened (E Prado), beaten 14l by
Newfoundland*

Other wins

2003 **1st** River City Handicap (Grade 3) (Churchill Downs, November 16) 3yo+ 9f Yielding
10 ran ● **1st** Kentucky Cup Mile Stakes (Kentucky Downs, September 20) 3yo+ 1m Firm 8
ran ● **1st** TriState Handicap (Ellis Park, September 1) 9f Good 3 ran **2002** **1st** Clasico Emani
de Freitas (Listed) (Gavea, December 1) 3yo 1m Firm 9 ran ● **1st** Grande Premio Linneo de
Paula Machado (Group 1) (Gavea, October 13) 3yo+ 10f Firm 11 ran ● **1st** Clasico Justica do
Trabalho (Listed) (Gavea, September 15) 10f Soft 10 ran ● **1st** Premio Haras Jahu (Gavea,
August 17) 3yo 7f Good 8 ran ● **1st** Maiden (Gavea, May 30) 2yo 7f Soft 12 ran

contest back at Churchill Downs to hone his charge for another tilt at
Grade 1 company, in the United Nations Handicap at Monmouth.

The timing of this race was perfect for the trip to Ascot, coming 21
days before the King George. It was less than ideal that Hard Buck had
a rough experience and finished a disappointing fifth, after starting slowly
and getting boxed in. Nonetheless, McPeek kept his nerve.

"If he finishes fourth or better, I'll be happy," the 41-year-old said before
the King George. "If we win, great, that's gravy."

Ridden by Gary Stevens, Hard Buck took a keen hold behind the steady
early gallop. He cornered adeptly, having practised the skill of turning
right-handed at Newmarket, and he hit the front two furlongs out. Doyen
was absolutely cantering in behind him, however, and it looked as if Hard
Buck's bid for glory would be short-lived.

The Godolphin star duly eclipsed him, but Hard Buck kept on really
strongly to hold off another, Sulamani, on the climb to the line; he also
had the likes of Gamut, Vallee Enchantee, Tycoon, Bandari, High Accolade
and Warrsan behind him. Considering the rigours of the journey and the
unfamiliar topography of the course, it was a first-rate performance.

Hard Buck

bay horse, 1999

		Buckpasser	Tom Fool
	Buckaroo		Busanda
		Stepping High	No Robbery
Spend A Buck			Bebop
br 1982		Speak John	Prince John
	Belle de Jour		Nuit de Folies
		Battle Dress	Jaipur
			Armorial
		Northern Dancer	Nearctic
	Secreto		Natalma
		Betty's Secret	Secretariat
Social Secret			Betty Loraine
b 1986		Vaguely Noble	Vienna
	Expediency		Noble Lassie
		Gazala	Dark Star
			Belle Angevine

Bred by Haras Old Friends in Brazil

Sire Spend A Buck

Won 10 of 15 starts at 2 and 3, notably Arlington-Washington Futurity-Gr1, Kentucky Derby-Gr1, Monmouth H-Gr1. Also 2nd Young America S-Gr1, 3rd Breeders' Cup Juvenile-Gr1, 2nd Haskell Invitational-Gr1. North American Horse of the Year and champion 3yo colt in 1985. Half-brother to Jode (dam of Irish 1,000 Guineas winner Hula Angel) and useful British/Scandinavian performer Raheen. Retired to stud in Kentucky, later stood in Louisiana, also shuttled to Brazil, sold to Brazil after 2001 breeding season, died November 2002. Oldest progeny 17, sire of (northern hemisphere): Cheerful Spree (Gr3), Table Limit (Gr3), Worth Avenue (Gr3), Pie In Your Eye (Gr3), Adhocracy (Gr2), Dust Bucket (Gr3), No Spend No Glow (Gr3), Antespend (Del Mar Oaks-Gr1, Santa Anita Oaks-Gr1, Las Virgenes S-Gr1), Hard Buck (Gulfstream Park BCH-Gr1), Pico Central (Carter H-Gr1, Metropolitan H-Gr1, Vosburgh S-Gr1).

Dam Social Secret

Unplaced in 5 British starts at 2 and 3 over 7-12f. Half-sister to Gr3 winners Bin Shaddad (Riverman) and Oh So Risky (Kris) out of full-sister to Gonzales (Irish St Leger-Gr1) and Mississipian (Grand Criterium-Gr1) and half-sister to Youth (Prix du Jockey-Club-Gr1). Next dam Gazala won Poule d'Essai des Pouliches-Gr1, Prix de Diane-Gr1. Dam of: Lord Secret (1991 c by Formidable; winner), Nordic Secret (1992 c by Bowling; placed), Old Secret (1993 f by Bowling, stakes-placed winner), Private Secret (1994 f by Roi Normand; stakes winner, Gr1 placed), Secret Miss (1996 f by Roi Normand; winner), Frank's Friend (1997 c by Roi Normand; winner), Grand Champion (1998 f by Spend A Buck; unraced), Hard Buck (1999 c by Spend A Buck; Grande Premio Linneo de Paula Machado-BrzGr1, Gulfstream Park H-Gr1), Jubaga (2001 c by Irish Fighter), Lets Try Again (2003 f by Spend A Buck).

Pedigree assessment

Hard Buck is Brazilian by nationality, but his pedigree is largely North American and is familiar in Europe. His dam was bred in Britain by Pat Eddery, and though she was a poorer performer lots of her relatives were at least smart over middle distances. Given that Spend A Buck stayed well, it is no surprise that Hard Buck lasts 12 furlongs. He has been retired to Bracklyn Stud in Ireland, where his 2005 fee is €3,500. *JH*

Helios Quercus (Fr)

2yo brown colt   **112**

Diableneyev (USA) - Criss Cross (Fr) (Crystal Palace (Fr))

Owner T Maudet

Trainer C Diard

Breeder D Chassagneux

Career: **8** starts   won **6**   second **0**   third **0**   **£177,569** win and place

---

By Robert Carter

THIERRY MAUDET, a UN peacekeeper, returned to the town of his birth, La Fleche, near Le Mans, early in 2004 and visited one of the local trainers in search of a horse. Cyriaque Diard offered him a choice from five possibles and Maudet, who had never owned a racehorse before, picked Helios Quercus. He was in Kosovo when the colt won first time out but did not miss any of his subsequent races.

Maudet and Diard began with a precocious youngster – sharp enough to win his first race 47 days before his second birthday – and ended the year with a Classic hope. Nobody could have predicted more, but the pressures will be very different in 2005.

Diard supplemented Helios Quercus for the Prix du Debut, which in the old days opened the French two-year-old season proper (other than the odd claimer) on May 1 but had to be run on March 26 to hold that place in 2004. He knew he had a smart youngster because he had tried Helios Quercus with Jabal Safi, his winner of the very first race of the season for two-year-olds, a claimer at Bordeaux-Le Bouscat on March 7.

Parisian backers favoured Molto Bello, ridden by Christophe Soumillon, and allowed the provincial visitor with the little-known provincial jockey, Alexandre Roussel, to start at 88-10. Helios Quercus came up the stands rail to catch Molto Bello inside the final furlong and ran on to beat him a short neck. He was a first winner for his sire, Diableneyev, who was a smart performer but ended with just three wins from 21 outings.

Helios Quercus followed up with a comfortable success at Fontainebleau and was an unlucky fourth, after being hampered at halfway, behind the speedy Grey Palm filly Great Blood at Chantilly in mid-May. He then stepped up to six furlongs at Maisons-Laffitte. He found a gap

Helios Quercus, nearside, holds on in the Group 3 Prix des Chenes, before going on to Group 1 success at Saint-Cloud

over one furlong from home, soon took command and scored by four lengths from Molto Bello.

Diard and Roussel, who rode him every time, agreed that Helios Quercus was good enough to win a Listed race, but the one they picked was over five furlongs at Vichy. There with every chance a furlong out, he could not quicken and wound up fourth of five, though beaten only three lengths. It was the only false step in the whole of his career.

He returned to action in the valuable Prix des Yearlings, over seven furlongs on his trainer's birthday, August 10, giving 8lb and a one-and-a-half-length beating to Nanabanana, who made her remaining two juvenile starts in England and was second in Goodwood's Prestige Stakes.

Diard worked Helios Quercus on nearby Cholet racecourse in preparation for his next step up the ladder, the Group 3 Prix des Chenes at Longchamp, in which Roussel always had him close up and sent him past the Mick Channon-trained Capable Guest just inside the final furlong. He was driven out to hold the efforts of Musketier and Vatori by a short neck and a neck. By the time that Helios Quercus lined up for the Criterium International, six weeks later, the second had won the Group 3 Prix de Conde and the third had won the Group 3 Prix Thomas Bryon.

1st Criterium International (Group 1) (Saint-Cloud, October 31) 2yo 1m Very soft **112** (TS 105) 8 ran. *Led 1f, 3rd straight, led over 1f out, driven out (A Roussel), beat Dubai Surprise by 1½l*

1st Prix des Chenes (Group 3) (Longchamp, September 18) 2yo 1m Good to soft **107** (TS 92) 7 ran. *In touch disputing 4th straight, pushed along and headway to challenge 1½f out, led just inside final furlong, ran on (A Roussel), beat Musketier by short nk*

1st Prix des Yearlings (Deauville, August 10) 2yo 7f Very soft **104** (TS 76) 6 ran. *(A Roussel), beat Nanabanana by 1½l*

4th Prix des Reves d'Or (Listed) (Vichy, July 24) 2yo 5f Holding 5 ran. *(A Roussel), beaten 3l by Beautifix*

1st Prix Pot au Feu (Maisons-Laffitte, June 1) 2yo 6f Soft **102** (TS 69) 6 ran. *(A Roussel), beat Molto Bello by 4l*

4th Prix du Mont de Po (Chantilly, May 17) 2yo 5f Good 7 ran. *(A Roussel), beaten 3l by Great Blood*

1st Prix des Perce-Neige (Fontainebleau, April 19) 2yo 5f Heavy 8 ran. *(A Roussel), beat Sabelio by 2l*

1st Prix du Debut (Unraced) (Maisons-Laffitte, March 26) 2yo 4½f Holding 11 ran. *(A Roussel), beat Molto Bello by short nk*

Helios Quercus deserved his Group 1 success but was fortunate to claim it. The first to show in front, he was settled in a share of third behind the favourite, Early March, and one of the four British raiders, Merchant. Roussel made sure of a definite third on the inside entering the straight but then he was caught on the rails. If Early March had kept on as expected, Helios Quercus would have had nowhere to go. But the favourite hung off the rail at the vital moment and Roussel drove his colt through the gap. He had to ride vigorously to repel the challenge of the English raider, Cupid's Glory, then ran on to hold the late efforts of Dubai Surprise (conqueror of Nanabanana at Goodwood) and Walk In The Park by one and a half lengths and a short neck. Connections immediately named him a candidate for the first running of the rebranded Prix du Jockey-Club and are confident that he will stay the one and a quarter miles.

Diard has proved quite successful on the Flat, with a career-best 58 wins from 91 starters in 2001, but most of his horses have been half-breds and jumping types, rather than quality two-year-olds. His biggest previous win on the Flat was with Jabal Safi's sire, Pinmix, in a Listed event at Longchamp in May 2000. That was also his best year over jumps, when he landed a Grade 3 double with Darastan and Ilians de Juilley at Auteuil in the spring and won the Grade 2 Grand Steeplechase d'Enghien with Darastan that October. He was confident enough to try his luck with Idole des Fontaines and Havre de Thaix at Cheltenham in 2002 but neither ran with much distinction. Roussel, 29, has worked for Diard through most of his career and rode Pinmix to that Longchamp victory.

Helios Quercus

brown colt, 12-5-2002

Diableneyev b 1995	Nureyev	**Northern Dancer**	Nearctic Natalma
		Special	Forli Thong
	La Pitie	Devil's Bag	Halo Ballade
		Empiracle	Forli Queen Empress
Criss Cross b 1982	Crystal Palace	Caro	Fortino Chambord
		Hermieres	Sicambre Vieille Pierre
	Zelide	Lyphard	**Northern Dancer** Goofed
		Zelinda	Le Haar Toledane

Bred by D Chassagneux in France

Sire Diableneyev

Won 3 of 21 starts in France from 2 to 5. At 2, won 1 (7f) of 2 starts, also 2nd Criterium de Maisons-Laffitte-Gr2. At 3, won 1 (6f) of 7 starts, twice Listed-placed over 5-6f. At 4, won 1 (Prix Cor de Chasse-Listed) of 8 starts. At 5, placed once in 4 starts. Effective 5-7f. By top-class miler and outstanding sire with several good stallion sons. Brother to Listed-placed Empireneyev and half-brother to Listed-placed Tender Morn out of winning grand-daughter of top-class US racemare Queen Empress (ancestress of several top-class performers including Jewel Princess, Silver Fling). Stands at Haras de la Rousseliere in France, 2004 fee reported as €965. Oldest progeny 2, sire of: Helios Quercus (Criterium International-Gr1).

Dam Criss Cross

Won 1 of 11 starts in France over 2 seasons, also placed 4 times. By 1977 Prix du Jockey-Club winner Crystal Palace, a fair sire in relatively short French stint before his export to Japan. Half-sister to French Listed winner Gay Warrior out of a French Listed-placed winner. Next dam Zelinda won Prix d'Astarte. Dam of: Cross Bar (1988 f by Jupiter Island; unplaced), Monster (1989 c by Lashkari; winner), Eria Allegro (1991 f by Diamond Prospect; winner), Eria Litta (1992 f by Shining Steel; winner), Re Quercus (1993 c by Tagel; placed), Venus Eria (1995 f by Sarhoob; placed), Ares Quercus (1997 c by Hero's Honor; Listed-placed winner), Fidius Quercus (1998 c by Midyan; winner), Helios Quercus (2002 c by Diableneyev; Criterium International-Gr1).

Pedigree assessment

This family has not produced anything that has demonstrated the class of Helios Quercus for several generations. It is, however, a prolific source of winners over 1m+ in France. That stamina is not matched by the speedy Diableneyev, from whose first (small and cheaply conceived) crop he comes. Helios Quercus, therefore, is not certain to last much beyond the mile of the Criterium International, although his prospects in the Prix du Jockey-Club have been boosted considerably by the forthcoming reduction in distance. *JH*

Latice (Ire)

3yo chestnut filly **121**

Inchinor - Laramie (USA) (Gulch (USA))
Owner E Ciampi
Trainer J-M Beguigne
Breeder Petra Bloodstock Agency Ltd

Career: **6** starts   won **4**   second **0**   third **0**   **£253,849** win and place

By Robert Carter

EVERYTHING went right for Latice in the first half of her career. Then everything went wrong. A convincing victory in fast time on her debut at Fontainebleau, and two Group 3 wins at Longchamp, brought her to a peak for her triumph in the Prix de Diane. She then missed her intended return at Deauville and followed that misfortune with two failed attempts to stay one and a half miles. That was the owner's decision, however. It was Enrico Ciampi's ambition to win the Arc and his trainer, Jean-Marie Beguigne, accepted it. A final verdict on her season depended on bidders at Tattersalls on December 1. If unsold, there was the possibility of a return to action in the Hong Kong Vase.

Latice arrived at Chantilly unbeaten in three races, two of them as a juvenile. She had started the outsider of six for the Prix de Conde at Longchamp but proved too sharp for her all-male opposition, coming with a strong run to lead 50 yards from home. She scored by half a length from Voix du Nord, with Prospect Park, Day Or Night and Ange Gardien next. All four earned a place in the field for the Prix du Jockey-Club six months later.

Ioritz Mendizabal rode Latice at Fontainebleau while Christophe Lemaire took over in the Conde. But Christophe Soumillon had finished behind her on each occasion and he begged the mount during the winter.

Latice reappeared in the Prix Vanteaux on the first Sunday of May. Trinity Joy set a steady pace while Latice relaxed in fourth. She closed up soon after halfway and tracked the new leader, Polyfirst, into the straight, then quickened to lead at the distance and had no trouble holding Asti by one length.

Latice was odds-on for the Vanteaux and favourite again for the Diane, with only two of her 16 opponents, Ask For The Moon and Torrestrella, shorter than 12-1. She was drawn on the wide outside and Soumillon

**Christophe Soumillon celebrates aboard Latice after his
patient ride had brought victory in the Prix de Diane**

did not hurry her, so that she had only three or four behind her as far
as the straight where she moved to the outside. Her white face was soon
evident as she progressed from over two furlongs out to lead 150 yards
from home. She beat Millionaia by three-quarters of a length with Grey
Lilas half a length further back.

Beguigne was winning the Classic at the fourth attempt. He entered
racing as an apprentice with the legendary Etienne Pollet at the age
of 13, in 1968, the year that Pollet won the Arc with Vaguely Noble.
After military service, he had four years as assistant to Francois Mathet
before starting on his own in 1981. His best year was 1988, when Saint
Andrews, Indian Rose and Oczy Czarnie were all Group 1 winners.
He had two more Group 1 victories in 1989 but his stable was hit by
a virus the following year and went into decline. Beguigne was forced
out of business in 1995 and did not return until 1999. Latice is the
first Group 1 winner of his comeback.

Owner Ciampi is a Monte Carlo-based Italian, who did not want to
pay more than €60,000 (£37,880) for Latice at the Deauville yearling

2004	Race record

7th Prix de l'Arc de Triomphe Lucien Barriere (Group 1) (Longchamp, October 3) 3yo+ 12f Good **121** (TS 116) 19 ran. *Midfield, 7th straight on inside, switched off rail 2f out, headway in 5th or 6th when not much room 1½f out, switched left, stayed on final furlong (M J Kinane), beaten 4¼l by Bago*

8th Prix Vermeille Fouquet's Barriere (Group 1) (Longchamp, September 12) 3-4yo 12f Soft **109** (TS 101) 13 ran. *Tracked leaders in 4th on rail, led entering straight, ridden and ran on 1½f out until headed 100yds out, no extra (C Soumillon), beaten 1¾l by Sweet Stream*

1st Prix de Diane Hermes (Group 1) (Chantilly, June 13) 3yo 10½f Good to soft **116** (TS 107) 17 ran. *Drawn on outside, held up in rear, 15th straight and moved to outside, headway over 2f out, hung right distance, led 150yds out, driven out (C Soumillon), beat Millionaia by ¾l*

1st Prix Vanteaux (Group 3) (Longchamp, May 2) 3yo 9f Very soft **111** (TS 64) 6 ran. *Always close up, 3rd straight, led approaching final furlong, shaken up, ran on well (C Soumillon), beat Asti by 1l*

2003

1st Prix de Conde (Group 3) (Longchamp, October 19) 2yo 9f Good to soft **105** 6 ran ● **1st** Prix de l'Abbaye du Lys (Unraced Fillies) (Fontainebleau, September 8) 2yo 1m Good to soft 15 ran

sales. She soon passed that limit but Paul Nataf, Ciampi's agent and partner in the filly, continued to bid to €75,000, at which point she was led out unsold. However, Nataf was able to do a private deal at €60,000. Latice has carried the stable. The other seven horses that Ciampi had run by the end of October managed only three places between them.

Latice had to miss her intended Arc prep in the Prix de la Nonette, over one and a quarter miles at Deauville, because of the very soft ground. Instead the Prix Vermeille became her comeback race. A close sixth in the false straight, she could easily have been boxed in, but Soumillon slipped her through on the rails and she led straightening up. However, she was headed with 100 yards to run and, though beaten two lengths at most, was passed by seven horses in the last half-furlong.

She had not seen out the one and a half miles and Beguigne said her next race would be the Prix de l'Opera, over a two furlongs shorter trip. She would surely have won it, for the first two, Alexander Goldrun and Grey Lilas, had finished fourth and third respectively behind her in the Diane. But her owner held to his dream and Latice contested the Arc.

Mick Kinane was booked, as Soumillon was claimed for Cherry Mix, and he had Latice inside Bago in midfield entering the straight, where she again made several places by slipping up the inside. Short of room when looking for a gap two furlongs out, and again half a furlong later, Latice finished seventh, beaten little more than four lengths. Courage rather than stamina had carried her through, and it would be a treat to see her back over a more suitable distance.

Latice   *chestnut filly, 9-3-2001*

		Lorenzaccio	Klairon
			Phoenissa
	Ahonoora		
		Helen Nichols	Martial
Inchinor			Quaker Girl
ch 1990			
		Lomond	Northern Dancer
			My Charmer
	Inchmurrin		
		On Show	Welsh Pageant
			African Dancer
		Mr Prospector	Raise A Native
			Gold Digger
	Gulch		
		Jameela	Rambunctious
Laramie			Asbury Mary
b 1994			
		Shirley Heights	Mill Reef
			Hardiemma
	Light The Lights		
		Lighted Glory	Nijinsky
			Lighted Lamp

Bred by Petra Bloodstock Agency Ltd in Ireland. €60,000 Deauville August yearling

Sire Inchinor

Won 5 of 10 starts, inc. Greenham S.-Gr3, Criterion S.-Gr3, Hungerford S.-Gr3. Also 2nd in Dewhurst S., 3rd in Sussex S. Small (15.1 1/2 hh), well-made, attractive sort, and a grand mover. Very game, consistent performer, effective in most conditions (not raced on extremes). Speedy, owned a sharp turn of foot, stayed a mile well. Well-bred. Half-brother to 1 Listed and 4 other winners, inc. dams of Listed winners. By a leading sprinter and successful sire out of a small but very game and talented racemare (Gr2 winner, Gr1-placed). Grand-dam bred 8 winners in all, inc. Welney (Gr2) and Guest Artiste (Gr1-placed), and the dam of Balisada (Gr1). 3rd dam won Park Hill S., placed in Oaks, Yorkshire Oaks. Died in 2003. Stood at Woodland Stud, last fee £10,000 (Oct. 1). Sire of 8 crops of racing age, inc. notable winners: Golden Silca (Gr2), Palanca (Gr3), Summoner (Queen Elizabeth II S.-Gr1), Umistim (Gr3), Bannister (Gr2), Orientor (Gr3), Felicity (Gr3), Latice (Prix de Diane-Gr1), Secret Melody (Gr3), Satchem (Gr3).

Dam Laramie

Ran twice, unplaced in 1 start at 2 years, 4th in 1 start at 3 years. Modest performer, on limited evidence. Showed mild promise on reappearance at 3. Ran only at 7f. Well-bred. By a top-class dirt runner in US, effective sire on grass (Nayef, Harayir, etc). Out of French Gr2 winner at 13f, half-sister to Gr3 winners Liastra and Last Light. Grand-dam Gr3 winner, 2nd in Gr1. 3rd dam half-sister to 2yo champion Crocket. Excellent branch of family responsible for Royal Palace, Fairy Footsteps, etc. Dam of: Lariat (1999 g by Dolphin Street; placed), Latice (2001 f by Inchinor; unbeaten Classic winner), Satri (2002 c by Mujadil; unraced to date). She has a yearling filly, Larme, by Soviet Star, and a colt foal by Invincible Spirit.

Pedigree assessment

The phenomenon is so common that we could have predicted a banner year for Inchinor to follow immediately on his death. Sure enough, the late Woodland Stud stallion was represented by no fewer than five individual Pattern winners in Europe, his team being led by an admirable daughter in Latice. Having come out of the Prix de Diane still unbeaten, she seemed to find the Vermeille distance beyond her and it was widely assumed that she would not try 12 furlongs again. In fact, she acquitted herself really well in the Arc de Triomphe and on that evidence she could hardly be termed a non-stayer; perhaps Shirley Heights and Nijinsky helped her in that regard. Let's hope she stays in training; she remains lightly raced and may well improve. *TM*

Let The Lion Roar

3yo bay colt **121**

Sadler's Wells (USA) - Ballerina (Ire) (Dancing Brave (USA))

Owner L Neil Jones

Trainer J L Dunlop

Breeder Abergwaun Farm

Career: **8** starts | won **2** | second **2** | third **2** | **£233,434** win and place

By David Dew

THERE'S no doubt that he was bred to win a Classic, and John Dunlop trained him accordingly as a two-year-old. But even after Let The Lion Roar had extended his record to two wins from three starts with a good win on his seasonal return at Newbury in April, bookmakers were still unconvinced.

Let The Lion Roar landed a conditions contest by half a length from the Group 1-placed Top Seed, with a yawning 17 lengths back to the third, but the layers barely batted an eyelid and left his odds at around 50-1 for the Derby.

There was talk after Newbury of a crack at the Chester Vase or the Lingfield Derby Trial, but the half-brother to 2000 St Leger winner Millenary was instead sent to York for the Group 2 Dante Stakes. And it was there that he had his first encounter with a horse who was to dominate his season.

Dunlop trained subsequent Derby winner Erhaab to win the Dante in 1994 and was also responsible for Sakhee, who landed the York contest before finishing second at Epsom. But Let The Lion Roar was not going to live up to that formidable standard.

He ran an odd race at York, languishing at the rear for much of the contest before coming with a late rattle and having to settle for third place, three lengths behind North Light. And it was to be a similar story in the Derby at Epsom the following month, although some deemed him an unlucky loser.

Let The Lion Roar had been beaten by North Light and Rule Of Law at York, and all three lined up for an intriguing rematch on the first Saturday of June. Sporting a first-time visor, Let The Lion Roar was sent off a 14-1 shot but, as Mick Kinane highlighted in his post-race analysis, there was a crucial moment that sealed the fate of Dunlop's charge: "I had a good position in the race, but on the downhill run into Tattenham Corner we got behind Percussionist, who was going nowhere, and he didn't come down the hill very well. He fell down it really, but when he got on the level he fairly flew."

Let The Lion Roar goes to post for the Dante, where he was third before going on to fill the same position in the Derby

The result was a virtual repeat of the Dante Stakes, although Let The Lion Roar actually showed the most improvement of the trio and was beaten only around a length and three-quarters. For Dunlop, though, it was all too familiar, as his Silver Patriarch had looked all at sea coming down the hill in 1997, only to finish like a train but still get beaten.

Dunlop laid his cards on the table and expressed a keen interest in re-opposing the two principals in the Irish Derby three weeks later, arguing that his colt might turn around the form on a flatter track such as The Curragh. But it was not to be. Perhaps Epsom had left its mark. Perhaps the quicker ground was not to his liking, but he could only plug on at one pace to finish around five lengths back in fifth place as Grey Swallow swooped to beat North Light. And who finished one place in front of him once again? You guessed it – Rule Of Law.

Connections must have been thoroughly brassed off to find the Godolphin colt in opposition again when Let The Lion Roar turned up at York in August for the Great Voltigeur, and even more so when he stayed on too strongly in the closing stages and prevailed by two and a half lengths.

2004   Race record

8th betfair.com St Leger Stakes (Group 1) (Doncaster, September 11) 3yo 1m6½f Good to firm **105** (TS 88) 9 ran. *Took keen hold in rear, headway over 3f out, ridden and hung right, lost place over 2f out (T Quinn), beaten 13½l by Rule Of Law*

2nd Daily Telegraph Great Voltigeur Stakes (Group 2) (York, August 17) 3yo 12f Good **117** (TS 51) 7 ran. *Tracked leaders, headway over 2f out, effort to chase winner well over 1f out, soon ridden and one pace (M J Kinane), beaten 2½l by Rule Of Law*

5th Budweiser Irish Derby (Group 1) (Curragh, June 27) 3yo 12f Good to firm **118** (TS 116) 10 ran. *Tracked leaders in 4th, close up entering straight, no impression from over 2f out, kept on same pace (M J Kinane), beaten 4¾l by Grey Swallow*

3rd Vodafone Derby Stakes (Group 1) (Epsom, June 5) 3yo 12f Good **121** (TS 119) 14 ran. *Dwelt, raced in midfield, lost place downhill and 11th straight, pulled out and effort 2f out, ran on well final furlong, took 3rd on post (M J Kinane), beaten 1¾l by North Light*

3rd totesport Dante Stakes (Group 2) (York, May 12) 3yo 10½f Good to soft **114** (TS 86) 10 ran. *Pushed along in rear 1f, niggled along halfway, headway on outer 4f out, ridden to chase leaders 2f out, soon driven and kept on same pace (M J Kinane), beaten 3l by North Light*

1st Arabian International Raceday Conditions Stakes (Newbury, April 16) 3yo 10f Good **113** (TS 86) 5 ran. *Tracked leaders in 3rd, good headway to lead inside final 3f, idled and ridden over 1f out, kept on under pressure when challenged final furlong (M J Kinane), beat Top Seed by ½l*

2003

2nd Haynes, Hanson And Clark Conditions Stakes (Newbury, September 19) 2yo 1m Good to firm **95** 5 ran ● **1st** Skybet Vegas Maiden Stakes (Newmarket (July), August 15) 2yo 1m Good to firm **78** 8 ran

Not for the first time, there was a hint here that Let The Lion Roar might be saving a little for himself, for he found little for pressure when really up against it. That questionable attitude was to prove his downfall on his final outing.

When North Light was ruled out of the St Leger, bookmakers made Let The Lion Roar their ante-post favourite, and Dunlop's secretary Marcus Hosgood was not backward in coming forward regarding the colt's chance at Doncaster. Asked if he could finally reverse form with Rule Of Law, he answered with an emphatic "of course". Once again, however, it was not to be.

While Rule Of Law was given a fine front-running ride and held on to score by the skin of his teeth, the lion was hardly roaring. In fact, he could muster barely a squeak, as he pulled hard in the early stages, refused to settle and then hung when it really mattered. He eventually trailed home a thoroughly disappointing eighth of nine.

It was a frustrating end to a frustrating campaign. Here was a horse bred to be a champion, but one who lost his best chance when the run of the race conspired against him at Epsom and then seemed to have lost his zest for the game when offered a good opportunity for compensation three months later.

Let The Lion Roar

bay colt, 27-2-2001

		Nearctic	Nearco
			Lady Angela
	Northern Dancer		
		Natalma	Native Dancer
			Almahmoud
Sadler's Wells			
b 1981			
		Bold Reason	Hail To Reason
			Lalun
	Fairy Bridge		
		Special	Forli
			Thong
		Lyphard	Northern Dancer
			Goofed
	Dancing Brave		
		Navajo Princess	Drone
			Olmec
Ballerina			
b 1991			
		Dancer's Image	Native Dancer
			Noors Image
	Dancing Shadow		
		Sunny Valley	Val de Loir
			Sunland

Bred by Abergwaun Farm in Britain

Sire Sadler's Wells

Won 6 of 11 races, inc. Beresford S.-Gr3, Irish Derby Trial-Gr2, Irish 2,000 Guineas-Gr1, Eclipse S.-Gr1, Phoenix Champion S.-Gr1. Also 2nd in Prix du Jockey-Club-Gr1, King George VI & Queen Elizabeth S.-Gr1. Impeccably bred top-class performer from 8-12f, handsome, tough and consistent. Sire of Gr1 winners: Braashee, French Glory, In The Wings (x3), Old Vic (x2), Prince Of Dance, Scenic, Salsabil (x5), Opera House (x3), Runyon, Saddlers' Hall, El Prado, Johann Quatz, Masad, Barathea (x2), Fatherland, Fort Wood, Intrepidity (x3), Carnegie (x2), King's Theatre (x2), Northern Spur (x2), Moonshell, Muncie, Poliglote, Chief Contender, Dance Design, Darazari, Luna Wells, Cloudings, Ebadiyla (x2), Entrepreneur, In Command, Kayf Tara (x4), Dream Well (x2), Greek Dance, King Of Kings (x2), Leggera, Commander Collins, Daliapour, Montjeu (x6), Saffron Walden, Aristotle, Beat Hollow (x4), Subtle Power, Galileo (x3), Imagine (x2), Milan, Perfect Soul, Sequoyah, Sligo Bay, Ballingarry, Black Sam Bellamy (x2), Gossamer (x2), High Chaparral (x6), Islington (x4), Quarter Moon, Sholokov, Alberto Giacometti, Brian Boru (x2), Doyen, Powerscourt, Refuse to Bend (4), Yesterday, Quiff, Playful Act.

Dam Ballerina

Won 1 of 5 races. Lengthy, quite attractive type, good mover. Seemed to stay 10f. Lightly raced, and only on good or faster surface. Very well-bred, by a top-class runner and good sire. Half-sister to Gr3 winner Dancing Bloom (by Sadler's Wells) and Gr1-placed River Dancer (by Irish River, dam of Classic winner Spectrum, grand-dam of Classic winner Petrushka). Dam winner, Gr2-placed, half-sister to Sun Princess (Oaks, St Leger) and Saddlers' Hall (Coronation Cup). Dam of: Little Giant (1996 c by Caerleon; placed at 2 in Ireland), Millenary (1997 c by Rainbow Quest; Classic winner), Head In The Clouds (1998 f by Rainbow Quest; Gr3 winner), Angel Of The Gwaun (1999 f by Sadler's Wells; unraced), Let The Lion Roar (2001 c by Sadler's Wells; Classic-placed winner), Dancingintheclouds (2002 f by Rainbow Quest; unplaced in only start to date), 2003 King In Waiting (c by Sadler's Wells).

Pedigree assessment

This family has been a superb source of very talented 12f performers in recent years, and Let The Lion Roar is an example. He is bred on similar lines to Dancing Bloom and Saddlers' Hall, both by Sadler's Wells. There is every encouragement from his pedigree that Let The Lion Roar will make good progress from three to four, and if he does so he could yet prove himself in the same league as half-brother Millenary. In common with that horse, Let The Lion Roar will find 12f his minimum and should stay 14f or even further. *JH*

Le Vie dei Colori

4yo bay colt **121**

Efisio - Mystic Tempo (USA) (El Gran Senor (USA))
Owner Scuderia Archi Romani
Trainer L M Cumani
Breeder Scuderia Archi Romani

Career: **18** starts   won **12**   second **2**   third **2**   **£487,381** win and place

By Mark Blackman

TAKE one Italian trainer, well seasoned. Add one high-quality Italian racehorse, hardened and tough. Bring to the boil quickly and simmer for several months, until displaying a solid consistency. The result – Falbrav, a race sensation that will linger long in the memory.

Who can blame other Italian-based owners for eyeing this recipe for success and wanting their own taste of the action? Salselon and Sunstrach were switched to the Newmarket yard of Luca Cumani early in 2004, and in June they were joined by an even classier compatriot in Le Vie dei Colori. A Group 1 winner in his home country for Roberto Brogi, he was sent to Britain by owners Scuderia Archi Romani because it was feared he would not be able to cope with the blisteringly hot summer that was forecast in Italy. A dish best served cool, it would seem.

Le Vie dei Colori arrived at Cumani's yard with a Racing Post Rating of 118 – some 5lb behind the level Falbrav had achieved before his own switch. He had been pipped by Hold That Tiger in the Grand Criterium at Longchamp as a two-year-old, and at three, in a light campaign played out in Italy, had won the Premio Parioli (Italian 2,000 Guineas) and Group 1 Premio Vittorio di Capua at the expense of Godolphin's Blatant.

His 2004 season had begun with a couple of minor successes in Italy before an ineffectual attempt at ten furlongs in May. That seemed to confirm that he was at his best at distances up to a mile.

Le Vie dei Colori arrived in Newmarket with an interesting-looking entry for the Queen Anne Stakes at Royal Ascot, but that was sidestepped, giving the four-year-old more time to settle into his new surroundings.

It was not until late July that he set foot on the racecourse for his new trainer, in the Group 1 arena of the Sussex Stakes at Glorious Goodwood. He had attracted some each-way support at long odds in the ante-post market and by post time was a 12-1 shot in a field of 11 that included

Le Vie dei Colori makes his British debut at Glorious Goodwood, where he finished third in the Sussex Stakes

three other Group 1 winners – the rejuvenated Soviet Song, and the 2,000 Guineas heroes Refuse To Bend and Haafhd.

Well drawn in seven, Le Vie dei Colori broke well to track the confirmed front-runner Passing Glance and the two Guineas winners, who pressed the leader. With a quarter of a mile to run, as Passing Glance hit his class barrier and beat a retreat, Darryll Holland took the Cumani colt to the front with a shake or two of the reins and immediately had Refuse To Bend and Haafhd off the bridle. But as that pair made their excuses and bowed out, Queen Anne runner-up Soviet Song ranged up stylishly, followed a moment or two later by Goodwood specialist Nayyir after he had managed to extricate himself from a pockct.

Le Vie dei Colori surrendered his advantage approaching the final furlong and, try as he might, he could not muster a further challenge to two horses who had conserved their energy at the rear of the field. He finished third, around two lengths behind the duelling leaders, and the same distance in front of Group 1 stalwart Norse Dancer. Given the likely improvement to come, this was a most satisfying debut for his new yard.

Everything pointed to the colt having another Group 1 mile contest in his locker, and the race chosen for him was the Prix du Moulin at Longchamp in early September. However, while he started fourth favourite

3rd Prix de la Foret (Group 1) (Longchamp, October 9) 3yo+ 7f Soft **119** (TS 70) 7 ran. *Raced in 3rd, 5th and pushed along straight, stayed on steadily under pressure to retake 3rd from over 1f out (C Soumillon), beaten 1¾l by Somnus*

8th Netjets Prix du Moulin de Longchamp (Group 1) (Longchamp, September 5) 3yo+ 1m Good to soft **116** 11 ran. *Disputing 3rd and pulling early, 5th straight, ran on one pace final furlong (L Dettori), beaten 2½l by Grey Lilas*

3rd Cantor Odds Sussex Stakes (Group 1) (Goodwood, July 28) 3yo+ 1m Good **121** (TS 116) 11 ran. *Tracked leaders, shaken up to lead 2f out, headed just over 1f out, outpaced final furlong (D Holland), beaten 2¼l by Soviet Song*

4th Premio Presidente della Repubblica SIS (Group 1) (Capannelle, May 16) 4yo+ 10f Good to soft **108** 7 ran. *Held up in 4th, kept on but never able to challenge (D Vargiu), beaten 5¼l by Altieri*

1st Premio Natale di Roma (Listed) (Capannelle, April 25) 4yo+ 1m Heavy **111** 6 ran. *Tracked leader, led well over 1f out, ran on well (D Vargiu), beat Duca d'Atri by 1l*

1st Premio Dane Friendly (4yo+) (Capannelle, April 4) 4yo+ 1m½f Good 6 ran. *Close up, led 2f out, ran on well (G Temperini), beat Giovane Imperatore by 1½l*

Other wins

2003 **1st** Premio Vittorio di Capua (Group 1) (San Siro, October 12) 3yo+ 1m Good to firm **118** 11 ran ● **1st** Premio Campidoglio (Capannelle, September 2) 3yo+ 1m Good 5 ran ● **1st** Premio Parioli (Group 2) (Capannelle, April 27) 3yo 1m Good **114** 10 ran ● **1st** Premio Daumier (Capannelle, April 13) 1m Good 2002 **1st** Prix la Rochette Royal Thalasso Barriere (Group 3) (Longchamp, September 15) 2yo 7f Good to firm **108** (TS 97) 6 ran ● **1st** Criterium Nazionale Memorial Enrico Arcari (San Siro, September 1) 2yo 6f Good 5 ran ● **1st** Premio Primi Passi (Group 3) (San Siro, June 16) 2yo 6f Firm **103** 7 ran ● **1st** Premio Alberto Giublio (Listed) (Capannelle, May 26) 2yo 5½f Good to firm ● **1st** Premio Bella Speranzo (Capannelle, May 12) 2yo 6f Good ● **1st** (Capannelle, April 28) 2yo 5f Good

in a field of 11, the good to soft ground was a worry. Despite having a heavy-ground victory on his CV, it was at long odds-on in Listed company, and his preference was for a sound surface.

In the event, he pulled too hard for his own good. Third early on and fifth turning into the straight, he lost three more places but not all that much ground up the stretch. He finished eighth behind the Andre Fabre-trained pair Grey Lilas and Diamond Green, yet was beaten less than three lengths.

For his final start, he returned to Longchamp for another Group 1 contest – the Prix de la Foret over seven furlongs in October. This time the ground was soft, but he handled the conditions well and, according to Racing Post Ratings, was close to his Sussex Stakes form with a staying-on third behind high-class sprinter Somnus and a back-to-form Denebola. There were plenty of reasons to crab the form of those behind him, but it was a performance that confirmed Le Vie dei Colori as a worthy candidate for European Group 1 events at distances around a mile.

Connections plan to campaign him again at five and, with shrewd placing, he could score again at the highest level. Whether he will ever match the achievements of Falbrav is a very different matter.

Le Vie dei Colori

bay colt, 25-2-2000

		Forli	Aristophanes
			Trevisa
	Formidable		
		Native Partner	Raise A Native
			Dinner Partner
Efisio			
b 1982			
		High Top	Derring-Do
			Camenae
	Eldoret		
		Bamburi	Ragusa
			Kilifi
		Northern Dancer	Nearctic
			Natalma
	El Gran Senor		
		Sex Appeal	Buckpasser
			Best In Show
Mystic Tempo			
ch 1993			
		Timeless Moment	Damascus
			Hour Of Parting
	Doubling Time		
		Lodeve	Shoemaker
			Locust Time

Bred by Scuderia Archi Romani in England

Sire Efisio

Won 8 of 26 races, inc. Horris Hill S.-Gr3, Challenge S.-Gr3, Premio Emilio Turati-Gr1, Premio Chiusura-Gr2. Also 3rd in Prix Jacques le Marois at 4. Smallish (15.3hh), lengthy, strong-quartered type. Best at 7-8f. Round-actioned, but effective on any ground. Inclined to get worked up in preliminaries, but always raced genuinely. The only Gr1 winner by his sire (high-class sprinting 2yo who did not quite fulfil expectations. Dam won 2 races, half-sister to 2 other winners. Family of Princely Gift. Stands at Highclere Stud, 2004 fee £10,000 (Oct 1). Sire of 14 crops of racing age, inc G1 winners: Pips Pride (Phoenix S.), Hever Golf Rose (Prix de l'Abbaye de Longchamp), Tomba (Prix de la Foret), Frizzante (July Cup), Pearly Shells (Prix Vermeille), Le Vie dei Colori (Premio Vittorio di Capua), Attraction (1,000 Guineas, Irish 1,000 Guineas, Coronation S., Sun Chariot S.).

Dam Mystic Tempo

Won 3 of 11 races (Pontefract maiden and 2 Wolverhampton sellers). Small, modest sprint performer, more effective at 6f than 5f, but not tried over further. Effective on fibresand, poorest effort on fast turf. By an outstanding miler who was also a Classic winner at 12f, and who has compiled a fine stud record in difficult circumstances. Half-sister to smart Timely (by Kings Lake; Gr1-placed at 2 years; dam of Gr3 winner Shining Hour and Gr3-placed Axford), and to modest winners in USA and Yugoslavia. Dam a Longchamp winner, placed 2nd in Gr3 and Listed company, half-sister to multiple Gr1 winner and useful sire Baillamont and to Gr1-placed Listed winner Lazaz. Grand-dam unraced half-sister to Faraway Son and Liloy, and to the dam of Fair Salinia. Dam of: Bel Tempo (1998 f by Petong; unplaced), Cuore di Aliante (1999 f by Alhijaz; winner in Italy), Le Vie dei Colori (2000 c by Efisio; Gr2 winner, Gr1-placed), Stai Su (2001 f by Dr Fong; winner), Drumroll (2002 c by Diktat; unraced to date). She has a yearling colt, Mail Express, by Cape Cross.

Pedigree assessment

A Group 1 winner in Italy in 2003, Le Vie dei Colori switched to England and failed to win for Luca Cumani, but his Sussex Stakes third behind Soviet Song and Nayyir was arguably the best performance of his career. Another grand advertisement for Efisio, whose stud record is exceptional when the generally low quality of his mares is taken into account. Similarly, broodmare sire El Gran Senor, never very fertile, got a creditable quota of high-class runners. Mystic Tempo was not one of them, being a runner of little account, but she came from quite a distinguished family, which thrived in the Wildenstein stud in the 1970s. *TM*

Lucky Story (USA)

3yo bay colt   **127**

Kris S (USA) - Spring Flight (USA) (Miswaki (USA))

Owner Gainsborough Stud

Trainer M Johnston

Breeder WinStar Farm

Career: **9** starts   won **4**   second **2**   third **0**   **£200,793** win and place

---

By Richard Austen

STRANGE as it may seem, the second highest-rated three-year-old trained in Britain never actually won a race at three. The considerable mitigating circumstance was that Lucky Story was denied most of his second season.

He had not been starved of success as a juvenile, winning the last four of his five starts, including the Vintage Stakes and Champagne Stakes, but injury prevented him from completing a Classic preparation. While Haafhd – the only British three-year-old to head him on Racing Post Ratings – picked off the Craven and 2,000 Guineas, it was August before Lucky Story returned to racecourse action.

Lucky Story had beaten Haafhd just over two lengths in the Champagne and was as short as 9-1 for the Guineas when he twice went lame in early April, the problem being diagnosed in his right tibia. He was ready to canter again at the end of May and had his next "true gallop" six days before lining up in the Group 3 Sovereign Stakes at Salisbury.

"Whatever he does, he's going to come on for it," said trainer Mark Johnston. "If he can put this under his belt, or even go close, he'll move on straight to Group 1 company." Lucky Story did not win but go close he certainly did. The 9-2 third favourite, he went on over a furlong out and took the measure of a host of Group-race winners and top handicappers, but was beaten a short head by a horse who hadn't won for two years. Losing out to Norse Dancer might not read too well given that horse's win tally but he was the proven class act in the field. Lucky Story's career was back on track.

Lucky Story's three subsequent starts were all Group 1 but although, just as Johnston predicted, he stepped up significantly on the Salisbury form, he failed to do so at the first time of asking. The Prix du Moulin de Longchamp saw Lucky Story make the running but finish seventh.

Lucky Story and Darryll Holland before their second place behind Rakti in the Queen Elizabeth II Stakes at Ascot

He was not beaten far but it took only another three weeks before Lucky Story showed he was capable of a lot better.

After the Moulin, Johnston reflected: "We set the pace but he couldn't go quickly enough. Next time we could run a pacemaker or he could go over a longer trip." In the Queen Elizabeth II Stakes, Godolphin had a pacemaker and 16-1 chance Lucky Story raced in second early on, then third behind the pacemaker and Rakti. Rounding the turn, it looked as though Lucky Story had no chance of keeping tabs on Rakti and was highly likely to be passed by several of the others. Antonius Pius did indeed head him for a stride or two and Refuse To Bend got to his withers, but Lucky Story stuck on in fantastically tenacious fashion. In doing his best to chase Rakti down, Lucky Story emulated his brother Dr Fong, beaten an identical half-length in the 1998 Queen Elizabeth, and drew two and a half lengths clear of third-placed Refuse To Bend.

2004   Race record

9th Emirates Airline Champion Stakes (Group 1) (Newmarket, October 16) 3yo+ 10f Soft 11 ran. *Mid-division, ridden halfway, soon weakened (D Holland), beaten 48+l by Haafhd*

2nd Queen Elizabeth II Stakes (Sponsored By NetJets) (Group 1) (Ascot, September 25) 3yo+ 1m Good to firm **127** (TS 120) 11 ran. *Prominent, ridden well over 2f out, chased winner well over 1f out, gradually closed final furlong, always held (D Holland), beaten ½l by Rakti*

7th Netjets Prix du Moulin de Longchamp (Group 1) (Longchamp, September 5) 3yo+ 1m Good to soft **117** (TS 88) 11 ran. *Led to straight (2½f out), 4th and weakening 1½f out, kept on final furlong (D Holland), beaten 2½l by Grey Lilas*

2nd totesport Sovereign Stakes (Group 3) (Salisbury, August 12) 3yo+ 1m Good to soft **116** (TS 98) 12 ran. *In touch, nudged along 4f out, headway over 2f out, driven to lead 1f out, edged left under pressure inside final furlong, edged right and headed last strides (D Holland), beaten shd by Norse Dancer*

2003

1st Champagne Stakes (Group 2) (Doncaster, September 12) 2yo 7f Good **117** 6 ran ● **1st** Veuve Clicquot Vintage Stakes (Group 2) (Goodwood, July 30) 2yo 7f Good to soft **111** 9 ran ● **1st** Spindrifter Conditions Stakes (Pontefract, June 30) 2yo 6f Good to soft **103** 7 ran ● **1st** Lisa Mobs 30th Birthday Maiden Stakes (Ayr, June 20) 2yo 6f Good to firm **87** 4 ran ● **4th** EBF Ayr May Novice Stakes (Ayr, May 29) 2yo 6f Good to soft **67** 7 ran

On the strength of this performance, as good as any all season by a three-year-old over a mile, Lucky Story was 9-2 second favourite in the Champion Stakes. The showdown with Haafhd was finally on, but as the Guineas winner added another top prize his better-fancied contemporary was floundering a long way out and ended tailed off.

Lucky Story looked well worth a try at a mile and a quarter going into the Champion and was not beaten by the trip that day. He had never raced on ground that soft before but that may not be the explanation either for such a poor run.

Following a none-too-lucky story of gambling losses in a West End casino, Lucky Story's lease from Gainsborough Stud to Abdulla Buhaleeba was cancelled before the Champion, and he was subsequently among a host of big names switched to Godolphin. With the benefit of a winter in Dubai he ought to have significantly more opportunities to show his true form in 2005.

Lucky Story can sweat up, like several other notable offspring of Kris S, and he wore earplugs at Newmarket. He also tends to prick his ears and wander off a straight line under pressure, but there's no doubt that he's a game racehorse, as well as a top-class one. In the mountain of superlatives heaped on Rakti after the Queen Elizabeth, it would have been easy to miss that Lucky Story finished just half a length behind him. And the margin was shrinking.

Lucky Story

bay colt, 1-2-2001

		Hail To Reason	Turn-to
	Roberto		Nothirdchance
Kris S		Bramalea	Nashua
br 1977			Rarelea
	Sharp Queen	Princequillo	Prince Rose
			Cosquilla
		Bridgework	Occupy
			Feale Bridge
	Miswaki	Mr Prospector	Raise A Native
			Gold Digger
Spring Flight		Hopespringseternal	Buckpasser
b 1987			Rose Bower
	Coco La Investment	Coco La Terreur	Nearctic
			Ciboulette
		Great Investment	Saidam
			Modern

Bred by WinStar Farm in US. $95,000 Keeneland September yearling

Sire **Kris S**

Won 3 of 5 starts, including minor 9f stakes event at 3. By Derby winner and excellent sire whose other stallion sons include Dynaformer, Lear Fan, Red Ransom, Robellino, Silver Hawk. Stood in Kentucky, died in May 2002. Sire of: Evening Kris (Jerome H-Gr1), Prized (Breeders' Cup Turf-Gr1, San Luis Rey S-Gr1), Stocks Up (Hollywood Starlet S-Gr1), Cheval Volant (Hollywood Starlet S-Gr1, Las Virgenes S-Gr1), Lyin To The Moon (Gr2), Hollywood Wildcat (Hollywood Oaks-Gr1, Breeders' Cup Distaff-Gr1, Gamely H-Gr1), Kissin Kris (Haskell Invitational S-Gr1), Brocco (Breeders' Cup Juvenile-Gr1), Santa Anita Derby-Gr1), You And I (Metropolitan H-Gr1), Class Kris (Gr2), Arch (Super Derby-Gr1), Diamond On The Run (Gr2), Dr Fong (St James's Palace S-Gr1), Midnight Line (Gr2), Soaring Softly (Flower Bowl Invitational H-Gr1, Breeders' Cup Filly & Mare Turf-Gr1), Adonis (Gr2), Apple Of Kent (Gr2), Krisada (Gr2), Peshtigo (Gr3), Bowman Mill (Gr2), Kiss The Devil (Gr3), Kudos (Oaklawn H-Gr1), Kumari Continent (Gr2), Julie Jalouse (Gr2), Symboli Kris S (Arima Kinen-JapGr1, Tenno Sho-JapGr1), Whitmore's Conn (Sword Dancer Invitational S-Gr1), Adreamisborn (Gr3), Epicentre (Gr3), Kicken Kris (Secretariat S-Gr1, Arlington Million-Gr1), Kris Kin (Derby-Gr1), Sabre d'Argent (Gr3), Action This Day (Breeders' Cup Juvenile-Gr1), Lucky Story (Gr2), Rock Hard Ten (Gr2).

Dam **Spring Flight**

Won 8 of 34 starts, 2 out of 6 at 2, 2 (inc. minor 1m stakes) out of 10 at 3, 3 out of 16 at 4, 1 out of 2 at 5. Effective at up to 1m, mainly ran on dirt, did win on turf. By top-class French performer and very good sire. Half-sister to 2 minor US stakes winners. Dam of: Stylized (1994 f by Sovereign Dancer; winner), Dr Fong (1995 c by Kris S; St James's Palace S-Gr1), Crown Of Spring (1996 f by Chief's Crown; winner), Holy Belle (1997 f by Holy Bull; winner), Northward Bound (1998 c by Kris S; unraced), Lucky Story (2001 c by Kris S; Gr2 winner), Lemoncello (2002 c by Lemon Drop Kid; unraced), 2003 c by Tiznow.

Pedigree assessment

Despite an enigmatic year, Lucky Story confirmed himself a top-class miler, just like his full-brother Dr Fong. The difference between the two is that Lucky Story is yet to win at Group 1 level. However, Kris S generally gets progressive offspring, and Lucky Story is an obvious candidate to improve his record in 2005. A Group 1 win would seal his stud prospects, especially as Dr Fong has done well with his first crop, who were three-year-olds in 2004. *JH*

Magical Romance (Ire)

2yo bay filly **107**

Barathea (Ire) - Shouk (Shirley Heights)

Owner F C T Wilson

Trainer B J Meehan

Breeder Quay Bloodstock and Samac Ltd

Career: **5** starts | won **3** | second **0** | third **0** | **£121,586** win and place

By Seb Vance

MAGICAL ROMANCE'S shock 40-1 success in the Cheveley Park Stakes was recognised at the time more for having provided the talented Robert Winston with a first Group 1 win than for the emergence of a serious contender for Classic or sprint honours in 2005.

It was a gutsy performance by both horse and rider to see off Suez by a neck, but it was one that many found easy to crab. Magical Romance's winning odds, the longest since 1945, suggested the race was not run to form and that view was backed by a bunch finish – often perceived as an unreliable form guide – with little more than a length covering the first five home.

A major contributory factor to the outcome was the ground, changed during the day from good to firm, to good, good to firm in places and then good, good to soft in places. Such were conditions that the stalls were moved to the middle of the track for the next two days. Furthermore, Magical Romance's main rivals all had valid excuses.

It is also worth pointing out that no Cheveley Park winner since Sayyedati in 1992 has gone on to Guineas success. On that basis, the 25-1 offered about Magical Romance for next year's 1,000 Guineas was arguably about right.

However, having rubbed a bit of the gloss off a remarkable training performance by Brian Meehan, let's not forget that the daughter of Barathea is bred for a mile, which makes her win over six furlongs all the more commendable, and, more importantly, she beat what were perceived to be three of the season's leading juvenile fillies.

The line-up included hitherto unbeaten duo Suez and Damson, already a Group 1 scorer, plus the Lowther and Cherry Hinton Stakes winners Soar and Jewel In The Sand. Yet their reputations took a battering from Magical Romance under a strong ride from Winston, who remained patient when his filly was outpaced going down the hill, before picking her up on the rising ground and wearing down Suez in a driving finish.

Magical Romance, right, scores a 40-1 upset in the Group 1 Cheveley Park Stakes at Newmarket, ahead of Suez

Winston had not partnered his first Pattern winner until scoring on Golden Nun in Ireland in June. His next one was most unexpected and came about when he was contacted only the night before and asked to deputise for Jimmy Fortune, who had been sidelined by a kick in the Salisbury paddock.

While Fortune's luck was out, Winston had earned his call-up, having ridden Magical Romance ten days before the Cheveley Park when she made all in a Leicester nursery off a mark of 83, a confidence-boosting victory that followed a two-month layoff. While she did it impressively enough that day, Newmarket represented a massive step up in class.

The odds-on Damson loomed dangerously two furlongs from home on the outside, but then subsided surprisingly tamely and was beaten two necks into third, trainer David Wachman arguing afterwards that it may have been a race too many. Soar was desperately disappointing, managing only sixth, but she had been a doubtful contender through illness and James Fanshawe felt that antibiotics may have taken their toll.

2004	Race record

1st Sky Bet Cheveley Park Stakes (Group 1) (Newmarket, September 30) 2yo 6f Good **107** (TS 97) 7 ran. *Chased leader, ridden and every chance from over 1f out, ran on to lead near finish (R Winston), beat Suez by nk*

1st iBetX.com - The Punter's Choice Fillies' Nursery (Leicester, September 20) 2yo (0-85 handicap) 6f Good to soft **94** (TS 95) 13 ran. *Made all, ridden clear over 1f out, eased near finish (R Winston), beat Aberdeen Park by 3l*

6th Princess Margaret Stakes (Group 3) (Ascot, July 24) 2yo 6f Good to firm **66** (TS 40) 6 ran. *Went right start, led to over 4f out, prominent until weakened 2f out (J Fortune), beaten 13l by Soar*

1st City & Suburban EBF Median Auction Maiden Fillies' Stakes (Kempton, July 14) 2yo 6f Good to firm **84** (TS 84) 13 ran. *Raced stands' side, soon chasing leaders and led that group after 2f, driven to take overall lead approaching final furlong, ridden out (J Fortune), beat Miss Malone*

4th Royal Marbella Group Quality Homes Abroad Fillies' Median Auction Maiden Stakes (Windsor, June 28) 2yo 5f Good **67** (TS 58) 9 ran. *Dwelt, recovered to chase leaders after 2f, disputed 3rd but outpaced 2f out, one pace after (J Fortune), beaten 5 ¼l by Roodeye*

Runner-up Suez was stepping up in class, having won a Listed contest at Salisbury, but her attempts to trailblaze from start to end were only just foiled. Connections had cited easy ground as a worry before the race. As for Jewel In The Sand, she barely showed.

The excuse book may have been well thumbed, but Meehan was not listening and believes he has a serious Classic prospect. "I've always thought a lot of her, that's why we ran her in the Princess Margaret, but she came back a bit jarred up from that," he said after the Newmarket win. "We thought we'd get her confidence up at Leicester for this. I feel she is a Guineas filly. She wobbled at the top of the hill, but that was through inexperience. She'll definitely stay, and Robert agrees with me."

Meehan insists the Princess Margaret, in which Magical Romance trailed home last of six behind Soar, should be discarded because of the ground. In addition, it came only ten days after her maiden win at Kempton, in the immediate aftermath of which Meehan said the Princess Margaret would come too soon.

The Kempton win, in a race whose two most recent runnings had been won by Soviet Song and Ruby Rocket, had hinted that the 125,000-guinea yearling might have what it takes, for she showed the benefit of a promising debut at Windsor by dominating the main bunch from a long way out and winning well from Miss Malone.

Take away her Ascot run and she has done everything right. Yet going into the winter, she was on offer at a bigger price than some of those whose reputations she shredded in the Cheveley Park. It does not quite add up, even allowing for the extenuating circumstances at Newmarket.

Magical Romance could skip the trials and head straight for the Guineas and, if the ground turned up on the easy side and French star Divine Proportions stayed at home, then we might have another upset on the cards. It's a big 'might', though.

Magical Romance

bay filly, 5-2-2002

		Northern Dancer	Nearctic / Natalma
	Sadler's Wells		
Barathea		Fairy Bridge	Bold Reason / Special
b 1990		Habitat	Sir Gaylord / Little Hut
	Brocade		
		Canton Silk	Runnymede / Clouded Lamp
		Mill Reef	Never Bend / Milan Mill
	Shirley Heights		
Shouk		Hardiemma	Hardicanute / Grand Cross
b 1994		Ahonoora	Lorenzaccio / Helen Nichols
	Souk		
		Soumana	Pharly / Faizebad

Bred by Quay Bloodstock and Samac Ltd in Ireland. 125,000gns Tattersalls October yearling

Sire **Barathea**

Won 5 of 16 starts from 2 to 4. At 2, won both starts over 7f. At 3, won Irish 2,000 Guineas-Gr1, also 2nd 2,000 Guineas-Gr1, Queen Elizabeth II S-Gr1. At 4, won Queen Anne S-Gr2, Breeders' Cup Mile-Gr1, 2nd Sussex S-Gr1, Queen Elizabeth II S-Gr1. Top-class miler, though showed very smart form in Gr1 events over 6f and 12f. Full-brother to Gossamer (Fillies' Mile-Gr1, Irish 1,000 Guineas-Gr1), half-brother to high-class 1m+ filly Free At Last (dam of Gr2 winner Coretta) and high-class 7-8f gelding Zabar. Dam very high-class 7f performer. Stands at Rathbarry Stud in Ireland, 2005 fee €25,000. Oldest progeny 8, sire of (northern hemisphere): Barafamy (Gr3), Enrique (Gr3), La Sylphide (Gr3), Red Sea (Gr3), Barathea Guest (Gr3), Cornelius (Gr2), Hidalguia (Gr3), Blue Steller (Gr3), Siringas (Gr2), Tobougg (Prix de la Salamandre-Gr1, Dewhurst S-Gr1), Kardthea (Gr3), Pongee (Gr2), Rag Top (Gr3), Shield (Gr3), Tante Rose (Haydock Sprint Cup-Gr1), Apsis (Gr3), Hazarista (Gr3), Magical Romance (Cheveley Park S-Gr1).

Dam **Shouk**

Won 1 of 8 starts. Placed over 7f from 2 starts at 2, 10.5f winner from 2 starts at 3, fair form over 10-12f at 4. Very closely related to very useful 12-14f filly Puce (dam to Barathea of Lancashire Oaks winner and 2004 Yorkshire Oaks 2nd Pongee, and dam to Sadler's Wells of very useful 10-12f colt Pukka). Dam useful 7f 2yo/3yo winner. Family of Pouliches winner Dumka and her 2,000 Guineas-winning son Doyoun. Dam of: Grand Wizard (2000 c by Grand Lodge; winner), Saree (2001 f by Barathea; winner), Magical Romance (2002 f by Barathea; Cheveley Park S-Gr1), 2003 f by Sadler's Wells, 420,000gns yearling.

Pedigree assessment

On pedigree, Magical Romance should progress well from two to three and should stay 10f, with 12f a real possibility. But she has not really obeyed her pedigree so far. Barathea does get high-class autumn 2yos, but Magical Romance comes from an unprecocious family; you have to go back to the descendants of fourth dam Faizebad to find a high achiever at two. In addition, she is very closely related to late-developing, very smart 12f filly Pongee, whose breeder-owner-trainer Luca Cumani bred Shouk. It therefore has to be open to doubt whether Magical Romance will be the sort of 3yo her pedigree indicates she should be. *JH*

Magistretti (USA)

4yo bay colt   **125**

Diesis - Ms Strike Zone (USA) (Deputy Minister (Can))

Owner M Tabor

Trainer P L Biancone

Breeder Tri-County Farms

Career: **16** starts   won **4**   second **6**   third **0**   **£730,224** win and place

By Paul Haigh

WHEN Magistretti began his 2004 season, his reputation rested mainly on the fact that in the Juddmonte International of 2003 he'd managed to get within two lengths of the mighty Falbrav. By the time he finished the season, that reputation had probably been enhanced, although it certainly didn't look as though it was going to be after his first few efforts – or perhaps that should read absence thereof.

There was only a little encouragement for Neville Callaghan and Michael Tabor in his first two runs in Britain, behind Warrsan in the Coronation Cup and behind Bandari in the Princess of Wales's Stakes at Newmarket in July, and there was none at all in his next outing when, dropped to Listed class and what seemed a more favourable ten furlongs, he struggled home over eight lengths behind Muqbil at Newbury. In this last race he ran as though there was either something wrong with him, or as if he had lost interest in competing, and it was unsurprising that his connections tried a completely different tack with him straight afterwards.

The transformation came when he was sent to race in America, where the addition of blinkers, and perhaps more significantly Lasix, enabled him to return to something very close to the form he'd shown at York a year earlier. Still in Callaghan's care, he went to Chicago in August for the Arlington Million, in which he produced a strong finish off a fast pace and easily his best performance of the season thus far to snatch third. He was beaten two and a half lengths and was later promoted to second behind the very fortunate Kicken Kris, following the disqualification of the winner-on-merit, Powerscourt.

It now seemed obvious that America was where Magistretti's future lay, and after Patrick Biancone took over his training the improvement continued. Edgar Prado, who had partnered him in the Million, kept

Magistretti comes home fourth in the Breeders' Cup Turf, having acquitted himself well since his switch to the US

the ride for the Grade 1 Man O'War Stakes at Belmont and once again got the best out of the son of Diesis, bringing him fast and late to confirm his Arlington superiority over the German-trained winner of the Singapore International Cup, Epalo. He collared Epalo well inside the last of the 11 furlongs to win going away by a length and a quarter. Back in fourth, and unable to make any impression on Magistretti on the fast ground, was the subsequent Breeders' Cup Turf winner Better Talk Now.

Magistretti stayed at Belmont for his next race, the Joe Hirsch Turf Classic Invitational, and once again ran with distinction. This time, though, the combination of 12 furlongs and the finishing kick of Kitten's Joy, the best turf three-year-old America has produced for some time, proved too much for him. He found himself overwhelmed in the final furlong, in much the same way as he'd overwhelmed Epalo three weeks earlier. If there were consolations, apart from the substantial second prize-money, they could be found in the facts that he had decent Europeans Tycoon and Polish Summer behind him and that he had managed to turn the tables on Kicken Kris, who this time finished down the field. He had also confirmed his new position as one of the best middle-distance turf horses, and probably the best older turf horse in America.

Daily Racing Form editor, Steven Crist, who isn't a bad judge, thought Magistretti had run a rather stop-start race in the Turf Classic and didn't think it impossible that, if racing more willingly throughout,

4th John Deere Breeders' Cup Turf (Grade 1) (Lone Star Park, October 30) 3yo+ 12f Yielding **118** 8 ran. *Disputed 4th early, 4th halfway, driven entering straight, crossed by winner over 1f out, no extra final furlong (E Prado), beaten 5l by Better Talk Now*

2nd Joe Hirsch Turf Classic Invitational (Grade 1) (Belmont Park, October 2) 3yo+ 12f Yielding **122** 7 ran. *Raced in 2nd until led just under 4f out, headed approaching final furlong, one pace (E Prado), beaten 2½l by Kitten's Joy*

1st Man O'War Stakes (Grade 1) (Turf) (Belmont Park, September 11) 3yo+ 11f Yielding **122** 8 ran. *Held up in 7th, switched wide and headway over 2f out, strong run to lead well inside final furlong (E Prado), beat Epalo by 1¼l*

2nd Arlington Million XXII (Grade 1) (Arlington, August 14) 3yo+ 10f Firm **119** 13 ran. *Raced in 9th, headway 3f out, 7th straight, stayed on well final furlong to take 3rd close home, finished 3rd, placed 2nd (E Prado), beaten 2½l by subsequently disqualified Powerscourt, race awarded to Kicken Kris*

4th cantorodds.com Steventon Stakes (Listed) (Newbury, July 17) 3yo+ 10f Good **103** (TS 91) 7 ran. *Chased leaders, ridden to chase leader inside final 3f but soon no impression, weakened from 2f out (D Holland), beaten 8¼l by Muqbil*

4th Princess of Wales's cantorodds.com Stakes (Group 2) (Newmarket (July), July 7) 3yo+ 12f Good to firm **113** (TS 58) 8 ran. *Held up, headway 3f out, soon every chance, ridden and weakened over 1f out (D Holland), beaten 6½l by Bandari*

6th Vodafone Coronation Cup (Group 1) (Epsom, June 4) 4yo+ 12f Good **117** (TS 87) 11 ran. *Soon tracked leaders, 4th straight, ridden and outpaced over 2f out, no danger after, kept on near finish (J P Murtagh), beaten 4½l by Warrsan*

2003

2nd Juddmonte International Stakes (Group 1) (York, August 19) 3yo+ 10½f Good to firm **125** 8 ran ● **2nd** Juddmonte Grand Prix de Paris (Group 1) (Longchamp, June 22) 3yo 10f Good to soft **117** 11 ran ● **9th** Vodafone Derby Stakes (Group 1) (Epsom, June 7) 3yo 12f Good **104** 20 ran ● **1st** Tote Dante Stakes (Group 2) (York, May 14) 3yo 10½f Good to firm **112** 10 ran ● **1st** bet365 Feilden Stakes (Listed) (Newmarket, April 17) 3yo 9f Good to firm **109** 6 ran

Other wins

2002 **1st** Palletline Tenth Anniversary Maiden Stakes (Sandown, June 15) 2yo 7f Good **83** 4 ran

he might have some hope against Kitten's Joy in the Breeders' Cup Turf. As it turned out neither of them could cope with Better Talk Now, who was undoubtedly helped by the softening of the ground at Lone Star Park by heavy rain earlier in the week and – no point in looking for any more complicated explanations – simply outstayed them both.

Once again, however, Magistretti had run well, and in American conditions he seems to have found a consistency that was missing on this side of the Atlantic. Perhaps 12 furlongs will always be just beyond his limit, but at ten or eleven he remains formidable, particularly in the slightly less competitive American turf environment. He'll no doubt continue to win good races over there, perhaps even at shorter trips, for as long as Tabor decides to keep him in training.

Magistretti

bay colt, 5-3-2000

Diesis ch 1980	Sharpen Up	Atan	Native Dancer Mixed Marriage
		Rocchetta	Rockefella Chambiges
	Doubly Sure	Reliance	Tantieme Relance
		Soft Angels	Crepello Sweet Angel
Ms Strike Zone b 1994	Deputy Minister	Vice Regent	Northern Dancer Victoria Regina
		Mint Copy	Bunty's Flight Shakney
	Bat Prospector	Mr Prospector	Raise A Native Gold Digger
		Batucada	Roman Line Whistle A Tune

Bred by Tri-County Farms in US. $150,000 Keeneland November foal, Ir£170,000 Goffs Orby yearling

Sire Diesis

Won 3 of 6 starts, notably Middle Park S-Gr1, Dewhurst S-Gr1. By top-class 2yo and excellent sire. Brother to top-class miler and very good sire Kris plus smart miler Keen, half-brother to smart Presidium and Rudimentary. Stands at Mill Ridge Farm in Kentucky, 2004 fee $30,000. Oldest progeny 19, sire of Gr1 winners: Diminuendo (Oaks, Irish Oaks, Yorkshire Oaks), Elmaamul (Eclipse S, Irish Champion S), Keen Hunter (Prix de l'Abbaye), Rootentootenwooten (Demoiselle S), Knifebox (Premio Roma), Husband (Canadian International), Halling (Eclipse S x 2, York International x 2, Prix d'Ispahan), Storm Trooper (Hollywood Turf H), Ramruma (Oaks, Irish Oaks, Yorkshire Oaks), Love Divine (Oaks), Continuously (Hollywood Turf Cup), Magistretti (Man o' War S).

Dam Ms Strike Zone

Won 1 of 6 starts in US at 2 and 3. Placed at 2 from 2 starts, winner at 3. By excellent North American sire out of winning sister to high-class 10-12f colt Damister. Dam of: Zonaki (1999 c by Miswaki; unplaced), Magistretti (2000 c by Diesis; Man o' War S-Gr1), Dream Out Loud (2001 f by Stravinsky; unplaced), 2003 f by King Of Kings, 2004 f by Orientate. In foal to Empire Maker.

Pedigree assessment

Has achieved the top-level success in the US that just eluded him in Europe, and he promises to build on his record. However, he has every chance of returning to Europe for his stud career in time. Diesis, though based in the US for his entire stud career, has had virtually all his influence in Europe, where Daggers Drawn, Elmaamul and Halling are among sons to have sired smart Flat offspring. *JH*

Majestic Desert

3yo bay filly   **113**

Fraam - Calcutta Queen (Night Shift (USA))

Owner Jaber Abdullah

Trainer M R Channon

Breeder Bloodhorse International Limited

Career: **14** starts   won **3**   second **6**   third **1**   **£369,284** win and place

By Graham Dench

T'S a splendid record – indeed a remarkable one for a filly that changed hands for just €15,000 as a yearling. But there's something missing from it still, and so Majestic Desert will be in training once again as a four-year-old.

The filly that Mick Channon described at the start of 2004 as "bombproof" and "not only a trainer's dream but a jockey's dream too" more than paid her way and was seldom out of the frame. Yet despite a string of good efforts at the highest level, she could never again get as agonisingly close as she had done at two, when she failed by just a short head to end Carry On Katie's unbeaten run in the Cheveley Park Stakes. Her only win of the year came at Group 3 level and, welcome though it was at the time, three further Group 1 seconds must have left connections frustrated.

Majestic Desert's much-improved Cheveley Park form had thrust her firmly into the 1,000 Guineas reckoning, and after wintering well she consolidated her place in the betting by taking Newbury's Fred Darling Stakes, when her success completed a double in the main fillies' trials for trainer Mick Channon, successful with Silca's Gift in the Nell Gwyn three days earlier.

The Fred Darling, or rather the Dubai Duty Free Stakes as it was called in 2004, was run in a slow time, and the form was nothing special. However, Majestic Desert showed a very good attitude in beating Nyramba by a length and Channon was thrilled.

Desperate luck had twice robbed Channon of excellent chances in the 1,000 Guineas, when Bint Allayl had to be put down after a gallops accident and when Queen's Logic went lame the day before the race, but while Majestic Desert had not been quite as good as either of those outstanding fillies at two he was fully entitled to be optimistic. He said: "She wasn't as good a two-year-old as Queen's Logic, but this spring she has felt as good a three-year-old. I feel she could be the one."

Majestic Desert starts on a winning note at Newbury but failed to add to her tally despite several good efforts

Channon's past experience should have prepared him for what was to come at Newmarket, but he must have been bitterly disappointed within. Sent off 7-1 co-fourth favourite in an open market, Majestic Desert failed to run her race and came home in ninth, beaten a place behind her longer-priced stablemate Silca's Gift, who had been supplemented for the race.

It was a similar story for Majestic Desert at The Curragh, when connections sought compensation in the Irish 1,000 Guineas. She finished a couple of places closer to Attraction this time in seventh, but she was beaten a little further.

The Coronation Stakes has often provided consolation for fillies who have not done themselves justice in the Classics, and it was the obvious mid-summer target for Majestic Desert. She was a 25-1 chance, but no forlorn hope in Channon's eyes, as she had started to please in her work again. Channon's faith was not misplaced, but she was still nowhere near good enough to trouble Attraction, who beat her two and a half lengths into second.

Again and again Majestic Desert ran to a similar level, but she couldn't get her head in front. In five subsequent races she was three times second, to the rapidly improving Tropical Lady in a Group 3 at Leopardstown on the only occasion she had her sights lowered, to the relatively

2004   Race record

2nd Premio Vittorio di Capua (Group 1) (San Siro, October 10) 3yo+ 1m Good **113** 7 ran. *Held up, 6th straight, headway on outside over 2f out, quickened to chase winner from over 1f out, hard ridden and no impression last 150yds (D Holland), beaten 1¼l by Ancient World*

4th Kingdom of Bahrain Sun Chariot Stakes (Group 1) (Newmarket, October 2) 3yo+ 1m Good **107** (TS 102) 5 ran. *Chased leaders, ridden over 2f out, edged right and weakened inside final furlong (D Holland), beaten 6¾l by Attraction*

4th Prix Fresnay-le-Buffard-Jacques Le Marois (Group 1) (Deauville, August 15) 3yo+ 1m Soft **113** (TS 90) 10 ran. *In touch, disputing 3rd halfway, effort and led 1½f out, ridden and ran on until headed 1f out, kept on one pace (T E Durcan), beaten 4l by Whipper*

2nd Prix d'Astarte (Group 1) (Straight Course) (Deauville, August 1) 3yo+ 1m Good **111** (TS 77) 8 ran. *Held up behind leaders on rails, switched towards outside well over 1f out, driven to go 2nd well inside final furlong, ran on (T E Durcan), beaten ½l by Marbye*

2nd Irish Stallion Farms EBF Brownstown Stakes (Group 3) (Leopardstown, July 3) 3yo+ 7f Good to yielding **110** (TS 92) 8 ran. *Tracked leaders, challenged in 2nd from under 2f out, led 1f out, kept on well final furlong, headed close home (T E Durcan), beaten nk by Tropical Lady*

2nd Coronation Stakes (Group 1) (Ascot, June 18) 3yo 1m Firm **113** (TS 113) 11 ran. *Held up in rear, progress from 2f out, stayed on well to take 2nd final 100yds, no chance with winner (T E Durcan), beaten 2½l by Attraction*

7th Boylesports Irish 1,000 Guineas (Group 1) (Curragh, May 23) 3yo 1m Good to firm **99** 15 ran. *Chased leaders, 6th 1½f out, kept on same pace (T E Durcan), beaten 7½l by Attraction*

9th UltimateBet.com 1,000 Guineas Stakes (Group 1) (Newmarket, May 2) 3yo 1m Good **104** (TS 88) 16 ran. *Raced towards far side, prominent, ridden over 2f out, weakened final furlong (D Holland), beaten 4¾l by Attraction*

1st Dubai Duty Free Stakes (Registered As The Fred Darling Stakes) (Group 3) (Newbury, April 17) 3yo 7f Good **110** (TS 53) 8 ran. *Prominent, quickened to lead 1f out, pushed out (K Fallon), beat Nyramba by 1l*

2003

2nd Sky Bet Cheveley Park Stakes (Group 1) (Newmarket, October 2) 2yo 6f Good to firm **109** 10 ran ● **1st** Tattersalls Breeders Stakes (Curragh, August 23) 2yo 6f Good to firm **84** 24 ran ● **3rd** Queen Mary Stakes (Group 3) (Ascot, June 18) 2yo 5f Good to firm **84** 14 ran ● **2nd** EBF Novice Fillies' Stakes (York, May 13) 2yo 6f Good to firm **86** 8 ran ● **1st** Sunrise Median Auction Maiden Fillies' Stakes (Warwick, April 21) 2yo 5f Good to firm **59** 8 ran

unconsidered Marbye in the Prix d'Astarte at Deauville, and finally to reformed character Ancient World in the Premio Vittorio di Capua at the San Siro.

That last race, after which she was put away for the season, was her second in open company. She had also run well to finish fourth behind Whipper and Six Perfections in the Prix Jacques le Marois at Deauville.

The decision to postpone Majestic Desert's broodmare career is understandable, as there is more to gain than to lose. There is no reason to think she might be another Soviet Song, but her value will increase significantly if she can improve on her solitary Group 3 win.

Majestic Desert
bay filly, 24-3-2001

Fraam b 1989	Lead On Time	Nureyev	Northern Dancer Special
		Alathea	Lorenzaccio Vive La Reine
	Majestic Kahala	Majestic Prince	Raise A Native Gay Hostess
		Charvak	Alcibiades Exclusive
Calcutta Queen ch 1989	Night Shift	Northern Dancer	Nearctic Natalma
		Ciboulette	Chop Chop Windy Answer
	Happy Snap	Jalmood	Blushing Groom Fast Ride
		Photo	Blakeney Photo Flash

Bred by Bloodhorse International in Britain. €15,000 Tattersalls (Ireland) September yearling

Sire Fraam

Unraced at 2, won 5 of 23 starts from 3 to 6. At 3, won 1 of 2 starts. At 4, won 2 of 7 starts, also 2nd Ben Marshall S-Listed. At 5, won 2 (Schweppes Golden Mile H, Joel S-Listed) of 7 starts, also 2nd City of York S-Listed, Strensall S-Listed. At 6, won 0 of 7 starts, also 2nd Doncaster Mile-Listed, Premio Natale di Roma-Gr3, Prix du Chemin de Fer du Nord-Gr3. Best over 7-8f. By high-class 2yo and 6-8f performer who had fair results from sparse chances at stud. Half-brother to smart Canadian 2yo Crowning Honors and very useful British-raced 12f performers Malaak and Majestic Endeavour. Stands at Tweenhills Stud in Britain, 2004 fee £5,000. Oldest progeny 7, sire of: Lady Lahar (Gr3), Majestic Desert (Gr3).

Dam Calcutta Queen

Unraced at 2, placed both 3yo starts over 1m, unplaced only start at 4. By minor winner but very good sire, particularly of 2yos, sprinters and milers, out of unraced half-sister to dams of high-class 2yos Atlantis Prince and Hello and to dam of high-class and durable Scandinavian performer Dano-Mast. Third dam Photo Flash finished 2nd in 1968 1,000 Guineas. Dam of: Calcutta King (1996 c by Democratic; unplaced), Gremlin One (1997 c by Democratic; unplaced), Majestic Desert (2001 f by Fraam; Gr3 winner, Gr1 placed), Gold Majesty (2002 f by Josr Algarhoud; unplaced). Mare dead.

Pedigree assessment

Majestic Desert, unfortunate not to have landed a Group 1 contest, has outrun her pedigree in class terms. Fraam has a fair record from hitherto limited chances, while the first two dams achieved very little else either on the racecourse or at stud. Go back further, however, and this is the excellent Joel family of Welsh Pageant and some even greater names earlier on in the 20th century. It is tempting to believe Majestic Desert has inherited this family ability, and it will be interesting to see what she achieves at stud in time. *JH*

Marbye (Ire)

4yo bay filly **112**

Marju (Ire) - Hambye (Distant Relative)

Owner Teruya Yoshida

Trainer B Grizzetti

Breeder Curtasse Snc

Career: **24** starts   won **11**   second **4**   third **2**   **£354,893** win and place

By Robert Carter

TERUYA YOSHIDA, one of the world's leading breeders, follows Italian racing closely. Perhaps he was inspired by his father, whose colours were carried to victory by Sortingo in the 1978 Gran Premio di Milano. Zenya Yoshida also bought another Italian star, the 1988 Arc winner, Tony Bin, just before he made his final start in the Japan Cup. And Teruya Yoshida owned a half-share in the ex-Italian Falbrav in his final season, having bought into the horse when he crowned his period under the care of Luciano d'Auria with victory in the 2002 Japan Cup.

Teruya Yoshida also bought three recent winners of the Premio Regina Elena (Italian 1,000 Guineas) – Shenck (1999), Xua (2000) and Rumba Loca (2004). One of his best purchases has been Marbye, a filly trained by Bruno Grizzetti, like the other three. She won three of her first four races for a syndicate, Scuderia Cocktail, and changed hands shortly before the Group 3 Prix de Cabourg, on the first weekend of August 2002. Marbye was a moderate sixth on that first visit but returned to Deauville on the same weekend in the next two years. She finished third to Bright Sky and Six Perfections in the Prix d'Astarte in 2003 but showed that the flat and straight Deauville mile was her ideal course when winning that race, newly promoted from Group 2 to Group 1, in 2004.

Marbye returned to Italy after the Cabourg and took the Premio Eupili, a Listed event that her dam had won in 1996. She needed three runs early in her second season, 2003, before she started winning again. Success in a one-mile conditions event and a nine-furlong Listed race took her to Deauville. She then added a further win in a Listed race before beating Monturani by three-quarters of a length in the Group 3 Premio Sergio Cumani, over one mile.

She gained her ninth success, and her first away from her home track, San Siro, when beating Crodam di San Jore and Miss Nashwan at the

Italian jockey Mirco Demuro celebrates on Marbye as they pass the post in the Group 1 Prix d'Astarte at Deauville

Capannelle on her reappearance in 2004. But the heavy going did for her when she returned to Rome for another newly promoted contest, the Group 3 Premio Carlo Chiesa, and she was only fourth of seven behind Miss Nashwan. Back at San Siro, and racing on firmish ground, she proved a very different filly in the Group 2 Premio Emilio Turati, making virtually all to beat Honey Bunny by an easy three and a half lengths.

Marbye then took her chance in the Group 2 Windsor Forest Stakes at Royal Ascot. She was held up towards the rear and could not find a clear passage early in the straight, before staying on to finish fifth, more than eight lengths behind the winner, Favourable Terms. Grizzetti blamed the undulating course for her moderate run.

When Marbye made her second attempt at the Prix d'Astarte, stablemate Rumba Loca was set to pacemaking while Mirco Demuro held up Marbye joint-sixth of the eight runners. Rumba Loca lasted until two furlongs out, by which time Marbye had closed up. Demuro had been looking for a gap behind Monturani and Rumba Loca, and inside the ex-Italian Martha Stewart, but was obliged to switch to the outside 350 yards from home. His mount took time to pick up but responded well entering the final furlong to lead about 120 yards from home. She was not hard ridden once in front and held off Majestic Desert by half a length while the favourite Nebraska Tornado got the best of a tight finish for third.

13th Premio Lydia Tesio Darley (Group 1) (3yo+ Fillies & Mares) (Capannelle, October 24) 3yo+ 10f Good to soft **69** 14 ran. *Held up in rear until headway on inside entering straight, close up and hard ridden over 2f out, soon beaten and eased (M Demuro), beaten 23l by Lune d'Or*

6th Premio Vittorio di Capua (Group 1) (San Siro, October 10) 3yo+ 1m Good **101** 7 ran. *Raced in 3rd to straight, weakened 1f out (M Demuro), beaten 8l by Ancient World*

1st Prix d'Astarte (Group 1) (Straight Course) (Deauville, August 1) 3yo+ 1m Good **112** (TS 79) 8 ran. *Held up in 6th, edged to outside and headway 2f out, ridden over 1f out, led 120yds out, driven out (M Demuro), beat Majestic Desert by ¹/₂l*

5th Windsor Forest Stakes (Group 2) (Ascot, June 16) 4yo+ 1m Good to firm **97** (TS 84) 10 ran. *Held up in rear, effort over 2f out, stayed on approaching final furlong, not pace to challenge (M Demuro), beaten 8¹/₄l by Favourable Terms*

1st Premio Emilio Turati (Group 2) (San Siro, June 2) 3yo+ 1m Good to firm **112** 7 ran. *Soon led, quickened approaching final furlong, ran on well (M Demuro), beat Honey Bunny by 3¹/₂l*

4th Premio Carlo Chiesa (Group 3) (Capannelle, May 1) 4yo+ 1m Heavy **100** 7 ran. *Raced in 6th, effort in centre 2f out, soon ridden and unable to quicken (S Mulas), beaten 2³/₄l by Miss Nashwan*

1st Premio Zafonic (Capannelle, March 21) 4yo+ 9f Good **110** 3 ran. *Held up but always well in touch, quickened to lead inside final furlong, cleverly (M Demuro), beat Crodam di San Jore by ³/₄l*

2003

3rd Premio Ribot (Group 2) (Capannelle, November 16) 3yo+ 1m Good to soft **107** 14 ran ● **1st** Premio Sergio Cumani (Group 3) (San Siro, October 19) 3yo+ 1m Good **107** 18 ran ● **4th** Premio Vittorio di Capua (Group 1) (San Siro, October 12) 3yo+ 1m Good to firm **107** 11 ran ● **1st** Premio Pietro Bessero - Rathbarry Stud (Listed) (San Siro, September 28) 3yo+ (Fillies & Mares) 1m Good 6 ran ● **3rd** Prix d'Astarte (Group 2) (Straight Course) (Deauville, August 3) 3yo+ (Fillies & Mares) 1m Good to soft **109** (TS 104) 12 ran ● **1st** Premio FIA EBF (Listed) (San Siro, July 6) 3yo+ 9f Good to firm 9 ran ● **1st** Premio Dyreen (San Siro, June 8) 3yo 1m Good 5 ran ● **2nd** Premio Carlo Chiesa (San Siro, May 25) 1m Good ● **2nd** Premio Chiumbi (San Siro, May 2) 6f Good ● **2nd** Premio Vespucci (Florence, April 10) 6f Good

Other wins

2002 1st Premio Eupili-Trofeo Tattersalls (Listed) (San Siro, September 15) 2yo 6f Good to soft 5 ran ● Premio Vittori Crespi (Listed) (San Siro, June 23) 2yo Fillies 6f Firm 7 ran ● **1st** Premio BBS Italia (San Siro, May 18) 2yo 5f Good 4 ran ● **1st** Premio Poncia (Unraced Fillies) (San Siro, May 1) 2yo 5f Good to soft 5 ran

She did not reproduce her Deauville form in two October outings and, when sixth to Ancient World in the Group 1 Premio Vittorio di Capua, she came home six and three-quarter lengths behind the runner-up, Majestic Desert. Marbye did not stay one and a quarter miles in the Group 1 Premio Lydia Tesio and dropped out to beat only one home. There were options for her in Hong Kong, in either the Hong Kong Cup or Mile, but her future lies with the 550 or so mares owned by the three Yoshida brothers.

Marbye

bay filly, 10-2-2000

		Try My Best	Northern Dancer Sex Appeal
	Last Tycoon		
		Mill Princess	Mill Reef Irish Lass
Marju br 1988			
		Artaius	Round Table Stylish Pattern
	Flame Of Tara		
		Welsh Flame	Welsh Pageant Electric Flash
		Habitat	Sir Gaylord Little Hut
	Distant Relative		
		Royal Sister	Claude Ribasha
Hambye b 1994			
		Final Straw	Thatch Last Call
	Paglietta Gener		
		Miss Puddleduck	Mummy's Pet Goosie-gantlet

Bred by Curtasse Snc di Michele Solbiati in Ireland. 95 million lire ANAC yearling

Sire Marju

Won 3 of 7 races, inc. Craven Stakes-Gr3, St James's Palace Stakes-Gr1. Also 2nd in the Derby (to Generous). Had an abbreviated first season owing to a slight setback, in-and-out at 3 because of a persistent stifle problem, and eventually lost his action completely. Good-bodied, lengthy, short-legged, showing quality. Among the best sons of his sire (also got Ezzoud, Bigstone, Taipan and Mahogany). Half-brother to 10 other winners, inc. Salsabil, Danse Royale, Song Of Tara and Flame Of Athens. Out of a top-class 8-12f runner, from an extremely successful family. Stands at Derrinstown Stud, Co. Kildare, (2004) fee €16,000 (Oct 1). Sire of 10 crops of racing age, inc. notable winners: My Emma (Prix Vermeille-Gr1), Sil Sila (Prix de Diane-Gr1, Yorkshire Oaks-Gr1), Della Scala (Gr3), Mahboob (Gr3), Oriental Fashion (Gr2), Miletrian (Gr2), Naheef (Gr3), Marbye (Prix d'Astarte-Gr1), Soviet Song (Fillies' Mile-Gr1, Falmouth S.-Gr1, Sussex S.-Gr1, Matron S.-Gr1), Stormont (Gr2), Brunel (Gr2), Red Feather (Gr2).

Dam Hambye

Very useful Italian-trained sprinter, won 5 races at 2 and 3 over 5-6f including Listed event at two. By top-class miler and fair sire, especially of fillies. Half-sister to a useful 2yo in Italy. Dam of: Halzal (1999 f by Zilzal; winner), Marbye (2000 f by Marju; Prix d'Astarte-Gr1), Halham (2001 c by Alhaarth; placed), 2002 c by Desert Prince.

Pedigree assessment

Has the Group 1 success that makes her a valuable broodmare prospect, even though the family has been unremarkable in recent generations. She has excelled over a mile, like her paternal half-sister Soviet Song, and that is the limit of her stamina on pedigree. *JH*

Millenary

7yo bay horse   **121**

Rainbow Quest (USA) - Ballerina (Ire) (Dancing Brave (USA))

Owner L Neil Jones

Trainer J L Dunlop

Breeder Abergwaun Farms

Career: **29** starts | won **10** | second **6** | third **6** | **£806,931** win and place

By John Hopkins

THE sight of Millenary travelling with conspicuous ease became a familiar one to fans of long-distance Flat races in 2004. Happily, on three of his five starts he was able to deliver on that promise, and a charitable view can be taken of the two occasions when he found less than might have been expected.

Connections opted to break from the old routine this time around. Millenary, winner of the 2000 St Leger, had been found wanting in the highest class over a mile and a half and, at the age of seven, that was unlikely to change. However, his final run of 2003, when a short-head second to Persian Punch in a classic finish to the Jockey Club Cup, seemed to allay any doubts over his stamina.

Those doubts were to resurface on his return in the Sagaro Stakes at Ascot, where, in a gruelling contest overshadowed by the death of Persian Punch, he emptied completely and trailed in third, 29 lengths behind the impressive Risk Seeker. In all probability, however, it was simply too big an 'ask' first time out in such testing conditions.

There was nothing wrong with Millenary on his next start. Back to a mile and six furlongs on good to soft ground in the Yorkshire Cup, he ran out an emphatic winner. Under a waiting ride from Richard Quinn, who had ridden him at Ascot for the first time since the St Leger, he unleashed a decisive turn of foot to lead at the furlong marker and score by three lengths from Alcazar. The blinkers Millenary wore in his later races in 2003 were back on, and they stayed on.

The York race is usually a stepping-stone to the Ascot Gold Cup, but it left John Dunlop in a quandary. For not only did Millenary have stamina to prove, he had been beaten in all his four races at Ascot. In the event Millenary didn't run at Ascot, the issue being taken out of Dunlop's hands by a throat bug that affected Millenary among others in the stable.

**Millenary, left, and Kasthari dead-heat in the Doncaster
Cup in one of the most memorable finishes of the season**

When Millenary did reappear, it was in the Lonsdale Cup at York in August. Although the ground was not as taxing as in the Sagaro, it was softer than the official good and that, combined with a fast-run race over two miles on what was his first start for three months, caught him out. Sent off 11-8 favourite, he again travelled fluently but found little under pressure, finishing just over three lengths third behind First Charter.

If it had been a mixed campaign so far, Millenary finished it in style with wins in both the Doncaster Cup and the Jockey Club Cup. Doncaster's two-mile-two-furlong trip looked certain to be beyond Millenary judged on previous evidence, and he was sent off at 7-1 in a market dominated by the Goodwood Cup winner Darasim. However, the pace was not strong and he travelled with customary ease before cruising into a narrow lead inside the last. If his battle with Persian Punch at Newmarket had been the finish of 2003, then his nail-biting final-furlong tussle with the unheralded Kasthari at Doncaster has claims to being regarded the best of 2004. This time, however, he at least enjoyed a share of the spoils, the pair crossing the line together before what must have been the quickest-ever announcement of a dead-heat.

2004   Race record

1st Persian Punch Jockey Club Cup (Group 3) (Newmarket, October 16) 3yo+ 2m Soft **121** (TS 96) 11 ran. *Took keen hold towards rear, patiently ridden, headway on bit 2f out, led inside final furlong, ridden out (T Quinn), beat Franklins Gardens by 1¼l*

1st Dead-heat GNER Doncaster Cup (Group 2) (Doncaster, September 9) 3yo+ 2m2f Good **120** (TS 46) 8 ran. *Held up, smooth headway 4f out, stayed on to take narrow lead inside final furlong, joined post (T Quinn), dead-heated with Kasthari*

3rd Weatherbys Insurance Lonsdale Cup (Group 2) (York, August 17) 3yo+ 2m Good **117** (TS 111) 10 ran. *Held up, smooth headway on outer 3f out, challenged over 1f out and every chance until ridden and one pace inside final furlong (M J Kinane), beaten 3¼l by First Charter*

1st Emirates Airline Yorkshire Cup (Group 2) (York, May 13) 4yo+ 1m6f Good to soft **121** (TS 74) 10 ran. *Held up in touch, smooth headway 4f out, close up over 2f out, effort and quickened to lead entering final furlong, soon clear (T Quinn), beat Alcazar by 3l*

3rd Bovis Homes Sagaro Stakes (Group 3) (Ascot, April 28) 4yo+ 2m Soft **94** (TS 13) 13 ran. *Headway 10f out, tracked leaders 6f out, went 2nd travelling well approaching final 2f, soon ridden and weakened (T Quinn), beaten 29l by Risk Seeker*

2003

2nd Jockey Club Cup (Group 3) (Newmarket, October 18) 3yo+ 2m Good to firm **119** 6 ran ● **4th** Grand Prix de Deauville Lucien Barriere (Group 2) (Deauville, August 31) 3yo+ 12½f Soft **112** 7 ran ● **8th** King George VI And Queen Elizabeth Diamond Stakes (Group 1) (Ascot, July 26) 3yo+ 12f Good **114** 12 ran ● **1st** Princess of Wales's UAE Equestrian And Racing Federation Stakes (Group 2) (Newmarket (July), July 8) 3yo+ 12f Good **121** 6 ran ● **2nd** Prix Jean de Chaudenay (Group 2) (Saint-Cloud, May 21) 4yo+ 12f Good to soft **121** 6 ran ● **2nd** Sagitta Jockey Club Stakes (Group 2) (Newmarket, May 2) 4yo+ 12f Good to soft **121** 6 ran

Other wins

2002 1st Princess of Wales's UAE Equestrian And Racing Federation Stakes (Group 2) (Newmarket (July), July 9) 3yo+ 12f Good to soft **118** 7 ran **2001 1st** Sagitta Jockey Club Stakes (Group 2) (Newmarket, May 4) 4yo+ 12f Good **121** (TS 91) 7 ran **2000 1st** Rothmans Royals St Leger Stakes (Group 1) (Doncaster, September 9) 3yo 1m6½f Good to firm **119** 11 ran ● **1st** Peugeot Gordon Stakes (Group 3) (Goodwood, August 1) 3yo 12f Good to firm **118** 10 ran ● **1st** Victor Chandler Chester Vase (Group 3) (Chester, May 9) 3yo 12½f Good **104** 8 ran ● **1st** Peter Smith Memorial Maiden Stakes (Newbury, April 14) 3yo 11f Soft **85** 6 ran

It was rather easier for Millenary at Newmarket, where he was a fitting winner of a Jockey Club Cup run in memory of Persian Punch. The value of the form is debatable, given that the previously out-of-form Franklins Gardens was second and the former Scandinavian-trained outsider True Lover third, but Millenary was in a different league. He was cruising throughout and won easily by a length and a quarter.

Millenary was just about as good as ever in 2004, when he twice achieved a Racing Post Rating of 121, and in all probability he will be back again at eight to play a leading role in the Cup races. A winner of ten of his 29 lifetime starts, including nine Group races, he's a real credit to Dunlop and owner Neil Jones.

Millenary   *bay horse, 21-4-1997*

Rainbow Quest b 1981	Blushing Groom	Red God	Nasrullah
			Spring Run
		Runaway Bride	Wild Risk
			Aimee
	I Will Follow	Herbager	Vandale
			Flagette
		Where You Lead	Raise A Native
			Noblesse
Ballerina b 1991	Dancing Brave	Lyphard	Northern Dancer
			Goofed
		Navajo Princess	Drone
			Olmec
	Dancing Shadow	Dancer's Image	Native Dancer
			Noors Image
		Sunny Valley	Val de Loir
			Sunland

Bred by Abergwaun Farms

Sire Rainbow Quest

Won 6 of 14 starts, inc. Great Voltigeur Stakes-Gr2, Coronation Cup-Gr1, Prix de l'Arc de Triomphe-Gr1. Also 2nd in Dewhurst Stakes, Irish Derby, Eclipse Stakes, 3rd in Prix du Jockey-Club, King George VI & Queen Elizabeth Stakes, 4th in 2,000 Guineas. Medium-sized (16.0hh), attractive, good mover, somewhat light and leggy in training. Top-class performer in each of 3 seasons, only once out of the frame, effective on any ground except heavy. Stands at Banstead Manor Stud, Cheveley, Newmarket, at a fee of £35,000 (Oct 1). Sire of 16 crops of racing age, inc. G1 winners: Knight's Baroness (Irish Oaks), Quest For Fame (Derby S., Hollywood Turf H.), Saumarez (Grand Prix de Paris, Prix de l'Arc de Triomphe), Sought Out (Prix du Cadran), Armiger (Racing Post Trophy), Bright Generation (Oaks d'Italia), Raintrap (Prix Royal Oak, Canadian International Championship S., San Juan Capistrano H.), Urgent Request (Santa Anita H.), Rainbow Dancer (Hollywood Turf H., Oak Tree Turf Championship S.), Sakura Laurel (Spring Tenno Sho, Arima Kinen), Sunshack (Critérium de Saint-Cloud, Coronation Cup, Prix Royal Oak), Spectrum (Irish 2,000 Guineas, Champion S.), Fiji (Gamely H., Yellow Ribbon S.), Croco Rouge (Prix Lupin, Prix d'Ispahan), Nedawi (St Leger S.), Special Quest (Criterium de Saint-Cloud), Edabiya (Moyglare Stud S.), Millenary (St Leger S.).

Dam Ballerina

Won 1 of 5 races. Lengthy, quite attractive type, good mover. Seemed to stay 10f. Lightly raced, and only on good or faster surface. Very well-bred, by a top-class runner and good sire. Dam of: Little Giant (1996 c by Caerleon; placed at 2 in Ireland), Millenary (1997 c by Rainbow Quest; Classic winner), Head In The Clouds (1998 f by Rainbow Quest; Gr3 winner), Angel Of The Gwaun (1999 f by Sadler's Wells; Let The Lion Roar (2001 c by Sadler's Wells; Classic-placed winner), Dancingintheclouds (2002 f by Rainbow Quest; unplaced in only start to date). She has a yearling colt, King In Waiting, by Sadler's Wells.

Pedigree assessment

Four years after his St Leger victory Millenary continued to show high-class form in 2004, adding three more Pattern victories to bring his total up to nine. We are no longer in doubt about whether he truly gets two miles, after his battling performance in the Doncaster Cup and his classy display in the Jockey Club Cup. The stigma of having won the St Leger has meant that there has never been any demand for Millenary's services at stud, but while breeders sneer, racegoers cheer. He is a great public favourite who will surely delight and distinguish himself again in 2005. *TM*

Mister Monet (Ire)

3yo bay colt **124**

Peintre Celebre (USA) - Breyani (Commanche Run)

Owner Syndicate 2002

Trainer M Johnston

Breeder Barronstown Stud, Orpendale and Mrs T Stack

Career: **8** starts | won **5** | second **1** | third **1** | **£118,735** win and place

---

By Tom O'Ryan

IT'S a brutal truth. What should have been a celebration of talent, a glowing account of a deeply progressive horse, has, in fact, taken the depressing form of an obituary.

Mister Monet, a hugely exciting performer who had fairly bounded up the merit ladder through the summer, lost his life on Champions Day at Newmarket in October, casting a jet-black cloud over a meeting that had otherwise proved gloriously memorable for his trainer Mark Johnston, triumphant as he was in the Dewhurst Stakes with Shamardal and the Cesarewitch with Contact Dancer.

Sandwiched between the two, the Emirates Airlines Champion Stakes, however, produced only misery. Mister Monet, sent off the 5-1 third favourite, suddenly went wrong after four furlongs and was pulled up after sickeningly suffering a multiple fracture to his near-hind leg. Although every effort was made to save him, it was, sadly, to no avail and he had to be put down.

The premature end to Mister Monet's life robbed a good, and potentially very good, horse of a bright future and denied his admirers the chance to further acknowledge and celebrate this burgeoning star.

That Mister Monet had worked his way firmly into the reckoning for a Group 1 race like the Champion Stakes bears testimony to his remarkable rise during a season that had seen him make a belated start to his three-year-old campaign after a juvenile term restricted to only two outings – and one win – before he sustained a fractured tibia.

When he reappeared at Newmarket's July meeting it was virtually 12 months to the day since he'd last been seen in victory at Sandown. He was denied by only a short head on his comeback outing, Kehaar outpointing him on the nod of heads in a 0-100 handicap over a mile.

A week later, in a conditions race at Hamilton, he comfortably went one better, justifying odds-on favouritism at the main expense of Always First by a convincing four lengths.

Mister Monet wins at Ascot, the second leg in a four-timer, but the season ended with his sad death at Newmarket

Another week on and Mister Monet duly doubled up, beating Courageous Duke by a cosy two lengths in a ten-furlong handicap at Ascot, showing a most willing attitude, which was becoming his hallmark, and which was again in evidence a fortnight later at Haydock.

Sent off the evens favourite for the Petros Rose of Lancaster Stakes, Mister Monet successfully bridged the gap between handicaps and Group 3 company, trouncing Muqbil by a length and a half, the pair finishing no less than five lengths clear of third-placed Checkit. Anyone not yet convinced that Mister Monet was a horse very much on the upgrade was either blind, indifferent or in hibernation.

Further evidence that this half-brother to Irish 1,000 Guineas winner Tarascon was flying high came in France in the third week of August. Tackling eight rivals in the ten-furlong Group 2 Prix Guillaume d'Ornano at Deauville, Mister Monet again responded to a positive ride. In front from the outset under Joe Fanning, who was fast developing a formidable association with the colt, he never looked like being reeled in. Driven clear inside the final quarter-mile, he never needed to be touched with the whip to post a four-length victory over Delfos, with fellow British

Pulled Up Emirates Airline Champion Stakes (Group 1) (Newmarket, October 16) 3yo+ 10f Soft 11 ran. *Chased leaders until broke down and pulled up over 6f out (K Darley)*

1st Prix Guillaume d'Ornano (Group 2) (Deauville, August 21) 3yo 10f Heavy **121** (TS 121) 9 ran. *Made all, pushed clear well over 1f out, pushed out and ran on strongly (J Fanning), beat Delfos by 4l*

1st Petros Rose of Lancaster Stakes (Group 3) (Haydock, August 7) 3yo+ 10½f Good **124** (TS 118) 6 ran. *Led early, chased leader, led over 3f out, ridden over 2f out, clear and edged left over 1f out, kept on (J Fanning), beat Muqbil by 1½l*

1st Solitare Diamond Rated Stakes (0-105 handicap) (Ascot, July 24) 3yo+ 10f Good to firm **114** (TS 95) 9 ran. *Tracked leading pair, not clear run over 2f out, switched right well over 1f out, ridden to lead 1f out, ran on strongly (J Fanning), beat Courageous Duke by 2l*

1st Daily Record Conditions Stakes (Hamilton, July 15) 3yo 9f Good to firm **98** (TS 60) 4 ran. *Made all, quickened over 2f out, kept on strongly (K Dalgleish), beat Always First by 4l*

2nd Venture Lifestyle Photography Handicap (0-100) (Newmarket (July), July 8) 3yo 1m Good to soft **105** (TS 94) 16 ran. *Overall leader on far side, ridden over 2f out, 3 lengths clear inside final furlong, just caught (K Dalgleish), beaten shd by Kehaar*

1st EBF Maiden Stakes (Sandown, July 4) 2yo 7f Good **84** 7 ran ● **3rd** Leonard Sainer EBF Maiden Stakes (York, June 14) 2yo 6f Good to firm **82** 6 ran

challengers Gatwick and Lord Mayor finishing fifth and sixth respectively on the officially heavy ground.

He was described that day as a "proper horse" by Johnston, who, perhaps ruefully, also recalled that but for "a problem with his right fetlock" he would have been prepared for a tilt at the 2,000 Guineas in the spring.

What goes around often comes around and, come the Champion Stakes, Mister Monet was pitted against Guineas winner Haafhd. What's more, he was priced at less than half the odds of the Classic hero. Doyen and Lucky Story – the latter also trained by Johnston – were the only runners in the 11-strong line-up to be priced shorter than Mister Monet.

With Azamour, Refuse To Bend and Chorist, all Group 1 winners, also facing the starter, a cracking contest was assured, even allowing for the very soft ground. Alas, while Haafhd, after two summer defeats, bounced back to his best to beat Chorist and Azamour, the thoughts of many were on the stricken Mister Monet, some six furlongs from the stands.

How good he really was and how good he might have become is anyone's guess. Heartbreakingly, particularly for his connections, we shall never know the answers for sure.

What we do know is that Mister Monet helped light up the summer by rattling up a four-win sequence in double-quick time in the unmistakable style of a horse at the top of his game. That he was then lost was one of the deepest troughs to go alongside the various peaks of the 2004 season.

Mister Monet

bay colt, 20-3-2001

Peintre Celebre ch 1994	Nureyev	Northern Dancer	Nearctic Natalma
		Special	Forli Thong
	Peinture Bleue	Alydar	Raise A Native Sweet Tooth
		Petroleuse	Habitat Plencia
Breyani b 1987	Commanche Run	Run The Gantlet	Tom Rolfe First Feather
		Volley	Ratification Mitrailleuse
	Molokai	Prince Tenderfoot	Blue Prince La Tendresse
		Cake	Never Say Day La Marseillaise

Bred by Barronstown Stud, Orpendale and Liz Stack in Ireland. 62,000gns Tattersalls Houghton yearling

Sire Peintre Celebre

Won 5 of 7 races, inc. Prix Greffulhe-Gr2, Prix du Jockey-Club-Gr1, Grand Prix de Paris-Gr1, Prix de l'Arc de Triomphe-Gr1. Not an outstanding physical specimen, but quite well-made, medium-sized individual. Tip-top performer at 10-12f, with exceptional powers of acceleration. Effective on any ground. The best son of his outstanding sire, with more stamina than most. Dam Listed winner in France and Gr2 winner (12f on grass) in US, impeccably bred, by top-class runner and leading sire out of a Gr3 winner in England who was half-sister to outstanding racemare Pawneese (Oaks, Prix de Diane, King George VI & Queen Elizabeth Stakes, etc). Stands at Coolmore Stud, Ireland, at a 2004 fee of €30,000. Sire of 3 crops of racing age, including: Dai Jin (Deutsches Derby-Gr1, Aral Pokal-Gr1), Pride (Gr2), Super Celebre (Gr2), Vallee Enchantee (Hong Kong Vase-Gr1), Castledale (Gr3), Mister Monet (Gr2), Pearl Of Love (Gran Criterium-Gr1).

Dam Breyani

Won 4 of 14 starts. Unraced at 2, placed over 10-14f at 3 in 4 starts, won 4 (11-16f) of 10 starts at 4, also twice 4th in Listed events. Sire top-class 10-14f performer who disappointed as Flat stallion but has sired top-class jumpers. Dam Molokai winning full-sister to high-class 2yo Icing (dam of top-class 2yo Al Hareb and Gr3 winner Dr Somerville). Dam of: Fairy Highlands (f 1993 by Fairy King; placed), Tarascon (1995 f by Tirol; Moyglare Stud S-Gr1, Irish 1,000 Guineas-Gr1), Delphini (1996 f by Seattle Dancer; winner), Mala Mala (1998 f by Brief Truce; winner, Gr1 placed), Gaily Raffle (1999 c by Danehill; non-winner), Mister Monet (2001 c by Peintre Celebre; Gr2 winner), Biriyani (2002 f by Danehill; unplaced on debut).

Pedigree assessment

Mister Monet excelled over 10f in his short career but should have stayed 12f on pedigree. Although there are several very talented 2yos in this family, both Mister Monet's sire and dam progressed well with age and there is every chance their son would have continued to do the same. He already was close to being the best son of good young stallion Peintre Celebre, who stood the 2001 northern hemisphere season in Japan so has no Irish-conceived 2yos in 2004. Consequently, expect him to have a much quieter 2005. *JH*

Motivator

2yo bay colt   **118**

Montjeu (Ire) - Out West (USA) (Gone West (USA))

Owner The Royal Ascot Racing Club

Trainer M L W Bell

Breeder Deerfield Farm

Career: **2** starts   won **2**   **£124,803** win and place

By Seb Vance

KIEREN FALLON'S big-race haul for the 2004 season makes for impressive reading. A third Derby and a third Oaks, an Irish Oaks, a Breeders' Cup Filly & Mare Turf, and four more domestic Group 1 triumphs, culminating with Motivator's stirring performance in the Racing Post Trophy, was a remarkable harvest.

Most, though, including Fallon, will remember the year principally for the dramatic events of one late-summer morning, the ramifications of which cast a long shadow over one of the most colourful careers of recent times.

The way the six-time champion jockey leads his life, both on and off the track, has made him a persistent target for tabloids and authorities alike. Having earlier in the season apparently overcome alcoholism and a Sunday newspaper expose that followed hot on the heels of, and was related to, the infamous Ballinger Ridge affair, when he dropped his hands and snatched defeat from certain victory, Fallon found himself up against a new challenge on September 1.

That was the day Fallon and 15 others were arrested for conspiracy to defraud, a scandal that rocked racing, and especially Fallon, to the core. His confidence was visibly shot to bits and his challenge for a seventh title started to stumble, just as his only real rival, Frankie Dettori, found fresh momentum.

An agonising second in the St Leger on Quiff did not help Fallon's confidence, and nor did his fifth in the Arc on Derby winner North Light, on whom he had tried to make almost all of the running.

The title eventually had to be conceded, but Fallon was still determined to sign off his domestic season with a triumph to remember. Enter Motivator, the colt who ended the season dominating the Derby betting alongside Dubawi.

Motivator's victory in the Racing Post Trophy, the final top-level showdown of the domestic season, was timely for Fallon. It proved to

Motivator storms into the Classic picture with a decisive success in the Group 1 Racing Post Trophy at Doncaster

racegoers that he was still made of the right stuff and put him in a positive frame of mind for the following weekend's Breeders' Cup. And his renewed confidence was there for all to see in a brilliant victory on his dual Oaks heroine Ouija Board, on racing's biggest stage of all.

While the victory at Doncaster was an important part of Fallon's resurgence, it was also a landmark for Michael Bell, whose 16-year wait for a domestic Group 1 success was finally ended.

And it wasn't only the Newmarket trainer who partied well that night. For Motivator was carrying the support of the Royal Ascot Racing Club, whose 230 members own the colt, plus a weight of money that forced him down to 6-4 favouritism.

As the plunge indicated, the vibes were buzzing hard for the son of Montjeu. Newmarket gossip had it that Motivator had been ripping up the gallops and that Fallon was so impressed with a piece of work three days prior to the contest that he had described it as one of the best he had ever been involved with.

Punters had only one public appearance to go on – a one-mile Newmarket maiden in August – but that was enough for most. The 75,000 guineas

1st Racing Post Trophy (Group 1) (Doncaster, October 23) 2yo 1m Soft **118** (TS 118) 8 ran. *Tracked leaders, smooth headway to lead 2½f out, ridden and edged right over 1f out, stayed on strongly (K Fallon), beat Albert Hall by 2½l*

1st Learndirect Maiden Stakes (Newmarket (July), August 13) 2yo 1m Soft **89** (TS 76) 11 ran. *Held up in touch, led over 1f out, soon clear (K Fallon), beat Sunday Symphony by 6l*

he had cost as a yearling looked money very well spent when he sluiced up in the soft ground, scoring by six lengths from Godolphin's Sunday Symphony, who went on to win his next two races.

The Royal Lodge Stakes was bypassed because of fast ground, leaving the Racing Post Trophy, run at a time when conditions are almost guaranteed to be on the easy side, as the obvious target.

The field included Beresford Stakes winner Albert Hall, hailing from the Aidan O'Brien camp that had captured four of the last seven renewals, Henrik, who had got to within half a length of Dubawi at Newmarket in July, and the Royal Lodge fourth Elliots World.

It was asking a lot of Motivator on only his second racecourse appearance to win a race that in the previous three years had gone to future Classic winners American Post, Brian Boru and High Chaparral, but Bell's confidence was infectious.

The day before the race he said: "On what he shows at home I think he's got an outstanding chance. All his work has been on the bridle – he's a very exciting horse – but he's got to transfer that to the course."

Bell's optimism was well founded as Motivator comfortably assumed a position behind the leaders before easing to the front two furlongs from home. Albert Hall, his main market rival, tracked him through but couldn't go with him and had to settle for second, two and a half lengths adrift.

While the result itself was expected, Fallon's post-race comments took most by surprise. "He's a lot better than that and he was a bit flat to be honest," he said. "I thought it would be a lot easier."

Not that the 230 winning owners, including celebrities Simon Cowell, Mel Smith, Ken Bates and Lord Lloyd Webber, who pay upwards of £5,000 for their membership card, cared one jot.

Spokesman Harry Herbert said: "When we started the aim was to own a winner, then have one at Royal Ascot, which we achieved a couple of years ago, but now to have a Group 1 winner is simply amazing."

For Bell, it was also a moment to treasure. "He's got plenty of speed, but I have him as a Derby prospect, although I wouldn't rule out the Guineas," he said.

A Racing Post Rating of 118 gives Motivator every chance of making the Classic grade, as it is marginally superior to the figures achieved by the three previous Racing Post Trophy winners at the same stage.

Fallon will be desperate to maintain this successful partnership.

Motivator

bay colt, 22-2-2002

			Nearctic
		Northern Dancer	Natalma
	Sadler's Wells		
		Fairy Bridge	Bold Reason
Montjeu			Special
b 1996			High Top
		Top Ville	Sega Ville
	Floripedes		
		Toute Cy	Tennyson
			Adele Toumignon
		Mr Prospector	Raise A Native
			Gold Digger
	Gone West		
		Secrettame	Secretariat
Out West			Tamerett
br 1994			Atan
		Sharpen Up	Rocchetta
	Chellingoua		
		Uncommitted	Buckpasser
			Lady Be Good

Bred by Deerfield Farm in England. 75,000gns Tattersalls October, Part 1 yearling

Sire Montjeu

Won 11 of 16 races, inc. Prix Greffulhe-Gr2, Prix du Jockey-Club-Gr1, Irish Derby-Gr1, Prix Niel-Gr2, Prix de l'Arc de Triomphe-Gr1, Tattersalls Gold Cup-Gr1, Grand Prix de Saint-Cloud-Gr1, King George VI & Queen Elizabeth S.-Gr1, Prix Foy-Gr2. Also 2nd in Prix Lupin at 3, and in Champion S. at 4. Tallish, well-made, but not strikingly handsome individual. Not a good mover in his slower paces, seemed unsuited by firm ground, but acted on any other, and possessed a tremendous turn of foot. One of the best 12f horses of recent times. Well-bred. The best son of his outstanding sire. Out of a lightly raced high-class stayer (won Prix de Lutece-Gr3, 2nd in Prix Royal Oak-Gr1), who was among the best daughters of her sire. Family of multiple Pattern-winning stayer Dadarissime, Gr3 winner Le Mamamouchi and Dear Doctor (Arlington Million). Stands at Coolmore Stud at a 2004 fee of €30,000. Sire of 1 racing crop, inc: Motivator (Racing Post Trophy-Gr1).

Dam Out West

Won 2 (1 Listed) of 5 races. Also 3rd once and 4th twice. Leggy individual, who showed useful form in good company until poor effort in fifth start. Did not run beyond 9f, but gave impression she would stay further. By one of Mr Prospector's best sons at stud. Half-sister to US Gr3-placed multiple turf winner Auggies Here (c by Hilal) and to lesser winners by Northern Baby and Miswaki. Dam placed in France and US, half-sister to US Gr1 winner and sire Wavering Monarch. Dam of: Warsaw Girl (2000 f by Polish Precedent; winner), Gabana (2001 f by Polish Precedent; placed 5 times), Motivator (2002 c by Montjeu; Gr1 winner). She has a yearling colt by Fantastic Light (sold to John Ferguson, 220,000gns, Tattersalls October Sale, Part 1) and a colt foal by Montjeu.

Pedigree assessment

Having created a notable impression on his debut, Motivator confirmed his promise with a smooth and emphatic win on soft ground in the Racing Post Trophy. Few had expected the first crop of Montjeu to shine as two-year-olds, and the flurry of winners in the second half of the season bodes well for the future of a stallion whose pedigree, in modern terms, is loaded with stamina. The prospect of Motivator's proving himself a chip off the old block in 2005 is exciting, given that his sire showed such outstanding form at a mile and a half. The colt's dam provides no such assurance of staying power, although Out West, in a brief career, did seem to own a little more stamina than most of Gone West's progeny. If he truly takes after his sire, he must be considered a first-rate Derby candidate. *TM*

Mubtaker (USA)

7yo chestnut horse **132**

Silver Hawk (USA) - Gazayil (USA) (Irish River (Fr))

Owner Hamdan Al Maktoum

Trainer M P Tregoning

Breeder Warren W Rosenthal

Career: **20** starts   won **9**   second **6**   third **3**   **£586,796** win and place

By Richard Austen

A SEASON in the company of Mubtaker has seldom been that demanding in terms of racecourse attendances but the latest season was the first time that we really felt the loss. Prior to 2003, Mubtaker was a consistent, honest racehorse, an admirable and classy sort but one performing to a level that dozens of others could manage. Entering 2004, he was the highest-rated horse trained in Britain. Second place in the Arc had added a top-class performance to all those admiring adjectives and Mubtaker was a horse to look forward to with greed. But patience with him has always been the main requirement.

Mubtaker has had more than his fair share of physical problems. Winter training in Dubai was tried twice to damaging effect, and when the 2003 European turf season came to a close it was decided to send him to Pisa in Italy instead. Mubtaker was the city's second well-known resident with questionable supports and he again ended up on the easy list, this time with tendonitis. Connections have tried hard, but he seems destined never to appear in the Sheema Classic.

"The Italian experience worked really, really well – up to a point," said Marcus Tregoning, Mubtaker's trainer. "We were able to work him on grass the whole time, but a deluge of rain the last fortnight he was there spoiled the plan. He still had a couple of bits of work to do and the other horses stood it – Alkaadhem and Bustan, horses like that, they stood the treatment – but unfortunately he succumbed to his injury. He's had one or two of these things in the past but this was a brand new one."

Considering his record of absenteeism, other trainers targeting the Geoffrey Freer Stakes at Newbury in August might count themselves highly unlucky that Mubtaker keeps turning up. With a great deal more fanfare in the latest season, his presence had a discouraging effect on would-be rivals and only four took part. Mubtaker was sent off 30-100

Mubtaker, right, makes a successful reappearance in the Group 2 Geoffrey Freer Stakes but he could not win again

and gained his third successive victory in the race readily from Dubai Success. As in 2003, Mubtaker wore a crossed noseband for this reappearance in anticipation of his racing freely.

With Mubtaker looking a bit backward, this seemed an encouraging return. His two subsequent races, however, are the only ones in a 20-race career in which Mubtaker has failed to finish in the first three. He was sent off at evens in a strong field for the Grosser Preis von Baden but, after racing freely again and making the running, he ran out of steam and finished seventh. After that, it was a losing battle to get him ready for the Arc, Tregoning reporting that the race "arrived two weeks early for him".

Three weeks later, however, Mubtaker was again below form in the Canadian International at Woodbine. At the time, the ground was blamed for the German performance (the trainer said it was "very rough", the jockey that it was "too sticky") and a slow start for what transpired in Canada.

With further reflection, Tregoning added: "He was a long time out of training, a bit ring-rusty in the Geoffrey Freer and the race took a bit

2004 Race record

4th Pattison Canadian International (Grade 1) (Woodbine, October 24) 3yo+ 12f Good **118** 10 ran. *Missed break, soon recovered to race in 6th on outside, 4th straight, went 3rd over 1f out, lost 3rd close home (R Hills), beaten 4¼l by Sulamani*

7th Grosser Volkswagen Preis Von Baden (Group 1) (Baden- Baden, September 5) 3yo+ 12f Soft **113** 11 ran. *Pulled his way to the lead after 1f, headed briefly on final turn, led straight to over 1f out, soon weakened (R Hills), beaten 7¼l by Warrsan*

1st Stan James Geoffrey Freer Stakes (Group 2) (Newbury, August 14) 3yo+ 1m5½f Good **121** (TS 82) 4 ran. *Tracked leader after 2f, improved from 4f out to take slight lead inside final 3f, driven and edged left over 1f out, forged clear, readily (R Hills), beat Dubai Success by 2½l*

2003

2nd Prix de l'Arc de Triomphe Lucien Barriere (Group 1) (Longchamp, October 5) 3yo+ 12f Holding **132** 13 ran ● **1st** Coral September Stakes (Group 3) (Kempton, September 6) 3yo+ 12f Good **129** 5 ran ● **1st** Stan James Geoffrey Freer Stakes (Group 2) (Newbury, August 16) 3yo+ 1m5½f Good to firm **123** 5 ran ● **1st** cantorindex.co.uk 'Instant Account Opening' Steventon Stakes (Listed) (Newbury, July 19) 3yo+ 10f Good to firm **119** 7 ran

Other notable runs

2002 **1st** Stan James Geoffrey Freer Stakes (Group 2) (Newbury, August 17) 3yo+ 1m5½f Good to firm **123** 7 ran ● **2nd** Princess of Wales's UAE Equestrian And Racing Federation Stakes (Group 2) (Newmarket (July), July 9) 3yo+ 12f Good to soft **118** 7 ran **2001** **3rd** Levy Board St Simon Stakes (Group 3) (Newmarket, November 2) 3yo+ 12f Good to soft **110** 5 ran ● **1st** Fishpools Furnishings Godolphin Stakes (Listed) (Newmarket, October 5) 3yo+ 12f Good **121** 9 ran ● **1st** Ladbrokes Fred Archer Stakes (Listed) (Newmarket (July), June 30) 4yo+ 12f Good to firm **117** 7 ran ● **1st** Badger Brewery Festival Stakes (Listed) (Goodwood, May 24) 4yo+ 10f Good to firm **111** 5 ran **2000** **1st** Vineyard At Stockcross Maiden Stakes (Newbury, October 21) 3yo 10f Heavy **101** 12 ran

more out of him than we first thought. The German race was too big a step up, it's quite obvious now. It came a bit too soon and we never really got him back."

It's a touch ironic, therefore, but connections will be more mindful than ever to give Mubtaker time between races when he returns as an eight-year-old. A first victory in a Group 1 (he's run in only three) is not the overriding priority, seeing as his merit was so well advertised in the 2003 Arc. Top prizes over a mile and a quarter were mentioned in 2004 as well as his more usual assignments at around a mile and a half. Baden-Baden in 2004 may not have been to his liking but he otherwise seems to act on any going.

"I've never trained a horse as consistent as him. With all the things that have gone wrong with him he gives you 100% every time," asserted Tregoning. Mubtaker's problem has not been his heart and this winter he will probably be giving the likes of Dubai and Pisa a miss and seeing more of his box at Kingwood House Stables.

Mubtaker   *chestnut horse, 31-2-1997*

			Hail To Reason	Turn-to
				Nothirdchance
		Roberto		
	Silver Hawk		Bramalea	Nashua
	b 1979			Rarelea
			Amerigo	Nearco
		Gris Vitesse		Sanlinea
			Matchiche	Mat de Cocagne
				Chimere Fabuleuse
			Riverman	Never Bend
				River Lady
		Irish River		
			Irish Star	Klairon
	Gazayil			Botany Bay
	ch 1985		Far North	Northern Dancer
				Fleur
		Close Comfort		
			Caterina	Princely Gift
				Radiopye

Bred by Warren W. Rosenthal in Kentucky

Sire **Silver Hawk**

Won 3 of 8 races, inc. Craven Stakes. Also 2nd in Irish Derby, 3rd in Derby. Cracked a cannon-bone in July at 3 and retired. Smallish, strong, well-made sort, high-class from a mile up, well suited by 12f. Sire of: Silver Lane (Gr3), Dansil (Gr2), Hawkster (Norfolk S.-Gr1, Secretariat S.-Gr1, Oak Tree Invitational S.-Gr1), Lady In Silver (Prix de Diane-Gr1), Silver Medallion (Gr3), Silver Ending (Pegasus H.-Gr1), Magnificent Star (Yorkshire Oaks-Gr1), Red Bishop (San Juan Capistrano H.-Gr1), Silver Ray (Gr3), Silver Wisp (Gr2), Silver Wizard (Gr2), Zoonaqua (Oak Leaf S.-Gr1), Rory Creek (Gr3), Silver Wedge (Gr3), Devil River Peek (Premio Vittorio di Capua-Gr1), Fahal (Gr3), Hawk Attack (Secretariat S.-Gr1), Magnificient Style (Gr3), Memories Of Silver (Queen Elizabeth II Invitational Challenge Cup S.-Gr1, Beverly D S.-Gr1), Benny The Dip (Derby S.-Gr1), Albarahin (Gr2), Grass Wonder (Asahi Hai Sansai S.-Gr1, Takarazuka Kinen-Gr1, Arima Kinen-Gr1), Miracle Time (Gr3), Silver Rhapsody (Gr3), Mutafaweq (St Leger S.-Gr1, Deutschland Preis-Gr1), Silver Comic (Gr3), Aiglonne (Gr3), Mubtaker (Gr2), Narooma (Gr3), Wonder Again (Garden City H.-Gr1), Almushahar (Gr2), Silverskaya (Gr3).

Dam **Gazayil**

Won 2 of 11 races, a Chepstow maiden at 2 and a minor race at Morphettville (Australia) at 4. Lengthy, sparely made type who showed early promise, but made little physical progress, and showed only modest form. Dam of: Inspirasi (1991 f by Jackson Square; winner in Australia); Prime Ville (1993 f by Polish Patriot; winner in Australia), Cinnamon Sky (1994 g by Damister; winner in Australia), Crystal Downs (1996 f by Alleged; winner, Gr1-placed), Mubtaker (1997 c by Silver Hawk; dual Gr2 winner), El Giza (1998 c by Cozzene; unplaced), unnamed (1999 f by Thunder Gulch; unraced), Spirit Of Gold (2000 c by Silver Hawk; unplaced), Tree Chopper (2001 c by Woodman; winner). She has a yearling colt by King Of Kings.

Pedigree assessment

Even the most consistent horses have an off-day once in a while, and the admirable Mubtaker finally contrived to finish out of the first three on his venture to Germany for the Grosser Preis von Baden in September. It was a most uncharacteristic display that might have been taken as a hint that he was at last tired of racing, but when he missed out again, in Canada, his fourth place there showed him in his familiar honest guise. In his brief 2004 campaign he did not reach the peak he attained in the previous year's Arc de Triomphe. At that peak, however, he was a cut above his under-valued sire's Classic winners, Benny The Dip and Mutafaweq. *TM*

Nayyir

6yo chestnut gelding **126**

Indian Ridge - Pearl Kite (USA) (Silver Hawk (USA))

Owner Abdulla Al Khalifa

Trainer G A Butler

Breeder Saeed Manana

Career: **20** starts | won **6** second **3** third **2** **£446,526** win and place

---

By Bill Barber

TRAINER Gerard Butler walked across the parade ring at York's Dante meeting, yet to send out a winner on turf in 2004. Stooping down he picked up a coin, flicked it into the air, caught it and put it in his pocket. A passer-by commented on his good luck, to which he replied ruefully: "I could do with some." Butler's luck did eventually change but none of it rubbed off on his stable star Nayyir.

A first Group 1 was the aim for 2004 and the quest began on Dubai World Cup night at Nad Al Sheba in March. Butler had assembled a useful team for the new, richly endowed Spring Carnival, but had failed to score, despite coming close on several occasions. Unfortunately, Nayyir followed the same pattern. In a fashion that was to be repeated later in the year, Nayyir had victory in the Dubai Duty Free snatched away from him at the death, caught in the shadow of the post by both Paolini and Right Approach after being delivered to lead just half a furlong out. He was beaten a neck by the dead-heaters.

Given a long break to recuperate from his travels, Nayyir returned to action in the July Cup at Newmarket, by which time his trainer, though not exactly firing in winners left, right and centre, had started to enjoy some success again. However, the chestnut's previous attempts over sprint distances had failed to cause much of a stir and this time he was beaten just over six lengths behind Frizzante, having been hampered.

The Sussex Stakes was next and there was plenty of encouragement from the fact that Nayyir's two previous runs at Goodwood had both yielded victories. The third almost brought up the hat-trick and was, despite defeat, probably the finest performance of his career. While the betting concentrated on Queen Anne Stakes winner Refuse To Bend – well beaten by Nayyir in Dubai – Attraction's nemesis Soviet Song and 2,000 Guineas hero Haafhd, Nayyir was quietly fancied and sent off a 12-1 chance.

Mick Kinane held up his mount as Passing Glance, Refuse To Bend

Nayyir, far side, is just touched off in the Dubai Duty Free, starting a frustrating campaign in a series of top races

and Haafhd set too strong a pace for their own good but, as so often happens at Goodwood, Nayyir met trouble in running over a furlong out. Soviet Song, short of room earlier in the race, challenged for the lead just as Nayyir was momentarily stopped and she grabbed a decisive advantage. Once free Nayyir stayed on strongly, but he was still a neck down as they passed the post.

The Celebration Mile, although only a Group 2, would at least have given Nayyir a much-deserved success but again circumstances conspired against him. After a sleepless night Butler waited until the last minute before allowing the gelding to run on the rain-softened ground. However, it was not the ground but the way the race played out that cost Nayyir his chance. As pace-setters Naahy and Passing Glance fell in a heap two furlongs out, Kinane found himself in front far earlier than he wanted on Nayyir. He soon had what looked a commanding advantage but, almost inevitably and to the horror of Butler and those betting exchange players who had backed him at long odds-on, he faltered and was caught by Chic under a power-packed ride from Kieren Fallon.

2004	Race record

6th Prix de la Foret (Group 1) (Longchamp, October 9) 3yo+ 7f Soft **108** (TS 57) 7 ran. *Held up, last and shaken up straight, never dangerous (J Fortune), beaten 6l by Somnus*

4th Queen Elizabeth II Stakes (Sponsored By NetJets) (Group 1) (Ascot, September 25) 3yo+ 1m Good to firm **118** (TS 108) 11 ran. *Dwelt, held up in last, progress on outer 2f out, stayed on final furlong, nearest finish (J Fortune), beaten 4¼l by Rakti*

2nd totesport Celebration Mile (Group 2) (Goodwood, August 28) 3yo+ 1m Good to soft **124** (TS 76) 7 ran. *Held up, closed on leaders over 2f out, pulled out and led well over 1f out, hanging but soon ridden clear, headed last 75yds (M J Kinane), beaten 1¼l by Chic*

2nd Cantor Odds Sussex Stakes (Group 1) (Goodwood, July 28) 3yo+ 1m Good **126** (TS 121) 11 ran. *Held up towards rear, not clear run briefly well over 1f out, angled out to chase winner entering final furlong, strong challenge last 100yds, just held (M J Kinane), beaten nk by Soviet Song*

16th Darley July Cup (Group 1) (Newmarket (July), July 8) 3yo+ 6f Good to soft **103** (TS 86) 20 ran. *Slowly into stride, held up, headway over 2f out, ridden when hampered over 1f out, soon weakened (R Hughes), beaten 6¼l by Frizzante*

3rd Dubai Duty Free Stakes (Group 1) (Turf) (Nad Al Sheba, March 27) 3yo+ 9f Good to firm **119** (TS 94) 11 ran. *Mid-division, 5th straight, ridden and headway over 1f out, led 110yds out until headed near finish (M J Kinane), beaten nk by Right Approach and Paolini*

2003	

2nd Victor Chandler Challenge Stakes (Group 2) (Newmarket, October 18) 3yo+ 7f Good to firm **123** 11 ran ● **8th** Prix Maurice de Gheest (Group 1) (Deauville, August 10) 3yo+ 6½f Good to soft **103** 12 ran ● **1st** Lennox Stakes (Group 2) (Goodwood, July 29) 3yo+ 7f Good **119** 13 ran ● **6th** Kronenbourg 1664 Chipchase Stakes (Group 3) (Newcastle, June 28) 3yo+ 6f Good to soft **103** 12 ran

Other wins

2002 1st Victor Chandler Challenge Stakes (Group 2) (Newmarket, October 19) 3yo+ 7f Good **123** 17 ran ● **1st** Theo Fennell Lennox Stakes (Group 3) (Goodwood, August 2) 3yo+ 7f Good to firm **118** 9 ran ● **1st** Vodafone Diomed Stakes (Group 3) (Epsom, June 8) 3yo+ 1m½f Good to soft **116** 9 ran ● **1st** John Johnson 'Lifetime In Racing' Rated Stakes (0-95 handicap) (Beverley, May 21) 3yo+ 1m½f Good **103** 9 ran ● **1st** Call Bet Direct Free On 0800 329393 Maiden Stakes (Div II) (Lingfield (A.W), March 6) 3yo+ 7f Standard **88** 11 ran

Whether Kinane was blamed for that defeat was never made clear but Jimmy Fortune replaced him when Nayyir ran in the Queen Elizabeth II Stakes at Ascot the following month. He again stayed on strongly to finish in the money, but he could not be described as unlucky, as he was only fourth, beaten four and a quarter lengths by the impressive Rakti.

Returned to seven furlongs for his final run of the season in the Prix de la Foret at Longchamp, Nayyir turned in a lifeless performance and beat just one of the seven runners home.

Nayyir will be back again in 2005 but might miss Dubai this time in favour of possibly starting out in the Lockinge. He is not getting any younger and that elusive Group 1 victory may prove beyond him, but there should be another good race in him – given some luck.

Nayyir

chestnut gelding, 7-4-1998

Indian Ridge ch 1985	Ahonoora	Lorenzaccio	Klairon Phoenissa
		Helen Nichols	Martial Quaker Girl
	Hillbrow	Swing Easy	Delta Judge Free Flowing
		Golden City	Skymaster West Shaw
Pearl Kite b 1991	Silver Hawk	Roberto	Hail To Reason Bramalea
		Gris Vitesse	Amerigo Matchiche
	Spur Wing	Storm Bird	Northern Dancer South Ocean
		Equal Change	Arts And Letters Fairness

Bred by Saeed Manana in Britain. 15,000gns Tattersalls October yearling, 57,000gns Tattersalls Breeze-up 2yo

Sire Indian Ridge

Won 5 of 11 starts from 2 to 4. At 2, won 2 of his 4 starts. At 3, won Jersey S-Gr3 from 4 starts. At 4, won Duke of York S-Gr3 and King's Stand S-Gr2 from 3 starts. By top-class sprinter and excellent sire who got top-class horses across the distance spectrum. Stands at Irish National Stud, 2004 fee €85,000. Oldest progeny 13, sire of: Fumo di Londra (Gr3), Island Magic (Gr3), Ridgewood Ben (Gr3), Blomberg (Gr3), Definite Article (National S-Gr1), Ridgewood Pearl (Irish 1,000 Guineas-Gr1, Coronation S-Gr1, Prix du Moulin-Gr1, Breeders' Cup Mile-Gr1), Tumbleweed Ridge (Gr3), Compton Place (July Cup-Gr1), Handsome Ridge (Gr2), Indian Rocket (Gr2), Bardonecchia (Gr3), Cassandra Go (Gr2), Namid (Prix de l'Abbaye-Gr1), St Clair Ridge (Gr3), Indian Mary (Gr3), Nicobar (Gr2), Domedriver (Breeders' Cup Mile-Gr1), High Pitched (Gr3), Indian Creek (Gr2), Monturani (Gr2), Munir (Gr3), Nayyir (Gr2), Sights On Gold (Gr3), Campsie Fells (Gr3), Indian Haven (Irish 2,000 Guineas-Gr1), Snow Ridge (Gr2), Tahreeb (Gr3)

Dam Pearl Kite

Won only start at 2 over 1m. At three, placed in 4 of her 6 starts, notably 3rd Ribblesdale S-Gr2, 2nd March S-L, 3rd Doonside Cup-L. Effective 12-14f. By top-class miler and very good sire of middle-distance horses. Very closely related to useful stayer Jaseur (by Lear Fan) out of a US Grade 3 winner. Dam of: Pearl Barley (1996 f by Polish Precedent; winner), Shamaiel (f by Lycius; Listed winner), Nayyir (1998 c by Indian Ridge; Gr2 winner, Gr1 placed), Highest (1999 c by Selkirk; Dubai Gr3 winner, Gr1 placed), College Fund Girl (2000 f by Kahyasi; winner), 2002 Desert King c.

Pedigree assessment

Long established as a tough and very high-class 7-8f performer and should continue in like mould in 2005, especially as he will have no Pattern penalty from 2004. He is far speedier than most of his siblings, who include the ill-fated Highest, and Indian Ridge undoubtedly is responsible for that. *JH*

Norse Dancer (Ire)

4yo bay colt **125**

Halling (USA) - River Patrol (Rousillon (USA))

Owner J C Smith

Trainer D R C Elsworth

Breeder Ralph Ergnist and Bruno Faust

Career: **21** starts | won **3** | second **2** | third **3** | **£516,117** win and place

By Lee Mottershead

ERHAPS David Elsworth summed it up best before the Eclipse. Speaking then, ahead of Norse Dancer's latest attempt to break the most infamous Group 1 duck in Flat racing, the colt's unfailingly loyal trainer sought to find a reason why his immensely talented charge continued to frustrate at the top level. "I don't think he takes racing as seriously as we do," was his considered observation. He might just have hit the nail on the head.

Some have questioned Norse Dancer's resolution, his readiness to dig deep when it hurts most. None have questioned his ability. For Norse Dancer is quite simply one of the most gifted horses around. That he has yet to taste Group 1 glory does not alter the fact that, in terms of pure ability, Norse Dancer is up there with the very best.

Watching Elsworth admiring Norse Dancer in his box at the start of the 2004 campaign was to see a man positively brimming over with anticipation. Rarely does a horse make the physical improvement that the son of Halling enjoyed from three to four. Already big and butch, he had become bigger and butcher, handsome with it, and with as strong a neck as a thoroughbred could wish for. The raw material was there. All he had to do now was win a few races.

Winning races, though, had always been Norse Dancer's problem. Without a victory since landing his first two races, his second campaign featured narrow defeats in the 2,000 Guineas, Derby and Sussex Stakes.

The first outing of 2004 for Jeff Smith's horse was typical of many that had gone before and were to follow, in that it contained one overriding ingredient – frustration. Richard Quinn's mount had gone into the Group 2 Sandown Mile off a slightly interrupted preparation, yet he still looked likely to win beginning the climb up the Esher slope, only for his effort to peter out when it needed to be at its strongest. A whack across the face mid-straight had hardly helped, but this was still a performance that

**Norse Dancer, second left, lands the Sovereign Stakes at
Salisbury, his only win of a frustrating 2004 campaign**

left one thinking of what might have been. We were left with similar thoughts
again and again.

All but one of Norse Dancer's next nine outings were at Group 1 level.
He did not win any of the big ones, his only success coming when dropped
to Group 3 class in August at Salisbury, where he edged out subsequent
Queen Elizabeth II Stakes runner-up Lucky Story in a bobbing finish.
In winning there, Norse Dancer showed that he could indeed deliver when
the going got tough. Both before and after, he came close to doing the
same when it really mattered.

At Newbury in May, he made up an enormous amount of ground to
grab the lead in the Lockinge Stakes only then to be headed by Russian
Rhythm and Salselon with the line within touching distance. Fourth in
both the Eclipse and Sussex, he went even closer in the Juddmonte
International. Only five days after his Salisbury win and with that day's
rider John Egan back on board, Norse Dancer hit the front well over a
furlong out. It seemed that in front was where he would stay, only for a
charging rival to deny him in the final cruel yards. Sulamani was the
burglar at York. At Leopardstown it was Azamour who nailed Norse Dancer
on the line, the British raider forging to the front of a top-class Irish

4th Emirates Airline Champion Stakes (Group 1) (Newmarket, October 16) 3yo+ 10f Soft **112** (TS 75) 11 ran. *Held up in rear, effort 4f out, stayed on final furlong, never reached leaders (J F Egan), beaten 9½l by Haafhd*

10th Queen Elizabeth II Stakes (Sponsored By NetJets) (Group 1) (Ascot, September 25) 3yo+ 1m Good to firm **79** (TS 68) 11 ran. *Never going well and pushed along in rear after 2f, no chance (J F Egan), beaten 21l by Rakti*

2nd Baileys Irish Champion Stakes (Group 1) (Leopardstown, September 11) 3yo+ 10f Good to firm **125** (TS 125) 8 ran. *Tracked leaders in 4th, improved into 2nd 1½f out, led under 1f out, kept on well, headed near finish (J F Egan), beaten ½l by Azamour*

2nd Juddmonte International Stakes (Group 1) (York, August 17) 3yo+ 10½f Good **125** (TS 98) 9 ran. *Tracked leaders, led 2f out, headed and no extra towards finish (J F Egan), beaten ¾l by Sulamani*

1st totesport Sovereign Stakes (Group 3) (Salisbury, August 12) 3yo+ 1m Good to soft **116** (TS 100) 12 ran. *Behind, pushed along 4f out, headway on outside from 3f out, chased leaders 1f out, strong run inside final furlong, carried right and led last strides, all out (J F Egan), beat Lucky Story by shd*

4th Cantor Odds Sussex Stakes (Group 1) (Goodwood, July 28) 3yo+ 1m Good **117** (TS 111) 11 ran. *Held up in last pair, effort on outer over 2f out, ridden and progress over 1f out, found nil inside final furlong (T Quinn), beaten 4¼l by Soviet Song*

4th Coral-Eclipse Stakes (Group 1) (Sandown, July 3) 3yo+ 10f Good to soft **118** (TS 107) 12 ran. *Held up in last, not clear run briefly 2f out, progress well over 1f out, stayed on inside final furlong, no danger (T Quinn), beaten 4¾l by Refuse To Bend*

14th Queen Anne Stakes (Group 1) (Ascot, June 15) 4yo+ 1m Good to firm **56** (TS 41) 16 ran. *Mid-division, pushed along over 4f out, ridden over 3f out, weakened well over 1f out (T Quinn), beaten 29l by Refuse To Bend*

3rd Juddmonte Lockinge Stakes (Group 1) (Newbury, May 15) 4yo+ 1m Good **119** (TS 96) 15 ran. *Held up in rear, rapid headway from 2f out to lead inside final furlong, headed and found no extra final 100yds (T Quinn), beaten ¾l by Russian Rhythm*

4th BETFRED.com Mile (Group 2) (Sandown, April 24) 4yo+ 1m Good to soft **113** (TS 106) 10 ran. *Took keen hold, held up in midfield, progress 2f out, ridden to challenge entering final furlong, soon not quicken (T Quinn), beaten 1½l by Hurricane Alan*

7th Queen Elizabeth II Stakes (Group 1) (Ascot, September 27) 3yo+ 1m Good to firm **110** 8 ran ● **6th** Juddmonte International (Group 1) (York, August 19) 3yo+ 10½f Good to firm **115** 8 ran ● **3rd** Sussex Stakes (Group 1) (Goodwood, July 30) 3yo+ 1m Good to soft **117** 9 ran ● **12th** Coral-Eclipse (Group 1) (Sandown, July 5) 3yo+ 10f Good to firm **95** 15 ran ● **4th** Vodafone Derby (Group 1) (Epsom, June 7) 3yo 12f Good **119** 20 ran ● **3rd** Sagitta 2,000 Guineas (Group 1) (Newmarket, May 3) 3yo 1m Good **115** 20 ran

Other wins

2002 1st Alfred Franks & Bartlett Novice Stakes (Ascot, July 13) 2yo 7f Good **101** 9 ran ● **1st** Herbert And Gwen Blagrave Maiden Stakes (Salisbury, June 27) 2yo 7f Firm **86** 9 ran

Champion Stakes field only then to prick his ears, appear to idle and fall to a half-length defeat.

Fourth in Newmarket's Champion Stakes on his last start of 2004, Norse Dancer has now finished fourth or better in nine Group 1 contests. Described

Norse Dancer

bay colt, 03-4-2000

		Sharpen Up	Atan / Rocchetta
	Diesis		
Halling		Doubly Sure	Reliance / Soft Angels
ch 1991		Green Dancer	Nijinsky / Green Valley
	Dance Machine		
		Never A Lady	Pontifex / Camogie
		Riverman	Never Bend / River Lady
	Rousillon		
River Patrol		Belle Dorine	Marshua's Dancer / Palsy Walsy
b 1988		Habitat	Sir Gaylord / Little Hut
	Boathouse		
		Ripeck	Ribot / Kyak

Bred by Ralph Ergnist and Bruno Faust in Ireland. 26,000gns Tattersalls December foal

Sire Halling

Won 12 (8-10f) of 18 races from 3 to 5. Won 4 (inc. Cambridgeshire) at 3, won 4 (inc. Eclipse S-Gr1, York International-Gr1) at 4, won 4 (inc. Prix d'Ispahan-Gr1, Eclipse S-Gr1, York International-Gr1) at 5. Originally based at Dalham Hall Stud, stood 2004 at Emirates Stud Farm in Dubai for £30,000. Oldest progeny 6, sire of: Chancellor (Gr2), Dandoun (Gr2), Giovane Imperatore (Gr2), Fisich (Gr2), Mkuzi (Gr3), Franklins Gardens (Gr3), Norse Dancer (Gr3).

Dam River Patrol

Won 1 of 8 starts in Britain. Placed over 7f at 2, won over 10f at 3, when also Listed placed over 10f. Later placed in US. Half-sister to St Leger third Dry Dock, to smart 7-8f colt Showboat and to dam of Gr1-winning 2yo Mail The Desert. Sold 17,000gns carrying Norse Dancer at 1999 Tattersalls December Sale. Dam of: Regal Patrol (1994 c by Red Ransom; winner), Russillo (1995 c by Belmez; winner), Rouanne (1996 f by Unfuwain; winner), Riviera Ligure (1997 f by Hernando; non-winner), Norse Dancer (2000 c by Halling; Gr3 winner, Gr1 placed), Blue River (2001 f by Ashkalani; placed), Rosewater (2002 f by Winged Love), Rhapsody In Blue (2003 f by Winged Love). In foal to Samum for 2005.

Pedigree assessment

One Group 3 success does no justice to Norse Dancer, the best son of Halling. In common with his sire, Norse Dancer has progressed with age. It would be no surprise if he emulated him by having his most successful season at the age of five. *JH*

by Smith as "slightly kinky, but only slightly", he will be back again to pursue that first Group 1 coronation in 2005. "We'll win the bloody lot next year," declared Smith in the Leopardstown unsaddling enclosure. Maybe not the lot. But surely he deserves at least one.

North Light (Ire)

3yo bay colt **125**

Danehill (USA) - Sought Out (Ire) (Rainbow Quest (USA))
Owner Ballymacoll Stud
Trainer Sir Michael Stoute
Breeder Ballymacoll Stud

Career: **6** starts | won **3** | second **2** | third **0** | **£1,086,275** win and place

By Lee Mottershead

ORGET the similarities, it's the differences that matter. Like Kris Kin one year earlier, North Light triumphed in the Vodafone Derby for Sir Michael Stoute and Kieren Fallon. Like Kris Kin, North Light failed to notch another three-year-old success and, like Kris Kin, North Light ended his second season with defeat in the Prix de l'Arc de Triomphe.

These, though, are not two peas from the same pod. Kris Kin has gone down in history as one of the most forgettable victors of the Blue Riband's modern era, a distinctly ordinary Derby winner, quickly consigned to turf history and life as a near bargain-basement stallion. Not so North Light. A better horse, who even in defeat has achieved more, his racing career is far from over. For what we could be about to receive, may we all be truly excited.

The ironic thing about "North Light: The Story so Far" is that perhaps his most persuasive performance came in his most comprehensive loss. Previously never worse than second, the Weinstock family's latest star went into winter quarters with a fifth-place finish to his name, a first unplaced effort, posted in both a confusing and revealing running of Europe's middle-distance championship. On that glorious autumn day in Paris, North Light took plaudits but no prize. Four months earlier, on a glorious summer day at Epsom, he took both.

The road to immortality had begun at Sandown the previous August. A fast-finishing short-head second under a considerate hands-and-heels Fallon drive, North Light went one better at 1-5 in a weak Goodwood maiden. A merely workmanlike winner, the son of Danehill nevertheless marked himself down as an obvious big-race prospect for his master trainer. That Stoute was aiming at the biggest race of all came as no surprise.

The first public appraisal of North Light in 2004 was supposed to come in the Lingfield Derby Trial. His preparation went well, he was declared, but he did not run. Instead, as Percussionist ploughed through the mud for a runaway romp, North Light stood in his Newmarket box, having

North Light holds a decisive advantage in the closing stages of the Derby, despite the late efforts of his rivals

been withdrawn on the morning of the race due to Stoute's anxiety over what he considered unsuitably soft conditions. Luckily for Stoute, whose early ground concerns would turn full circle come the autumn, he had confirmed North Light's entry the previous day for the Dante Stakes, held four afternoons after Lingfield. North Light was rerouted north.

He may have been relatively unfancied in the ring at 6-1, but in the race North Light was dominant. Contesting the trial used as a springboard to Derby glory by Stoute's second Epsom conqueror Shahrastani, North Light showed himself to be enthusiastic, wonderfully uncomplicated and, crucially, extremely useful. Ridden prominently by Fallon, who expressed fears that prevailing conditions on the soft side might be unsuitable for a colt he considered a top-of-the-ground horse, North Light was sent for home early in the straight and kicked clear over three furlongs out, from where he was always in charge. Cheekily eased down about 50 yards from the line, he had stamped himself a serious Derby challenger, beating the fast-finishing Rule Of Law by half a length, with Let The Lion Roar thumped in a distant third. Hugely impressed, Fallon described his new ally as an individual boasting "everything you need with which to go into a Derby". Stoute was typically more cautious. "He has an each-way chance," he said. The way he said it, you fancied that Stoute knew his only possible Derby runner had a fair bit more of a chance than that.

5th Prix de l'Arc de Triomphe Lucien Barriere (Group 1) (Longchamp, October 3) 3yo+ 12f Good **123** (TS 122) 19 ran. *Led, joined 6f out until led again 3f out, headed just over 1½f out, lost 4th on line (K Fallon), beaten 3½l by Bago*

2nd Budweiser Irish Derby (Group 1) (Curragh, June 27) 3yo 12f Good to firm **125** (TS 124) 10 ran. *Settled 3rd, driven along 4f out, challenged entering straight, led under 2f out, headed under 1f out, kept on under pressure (K Fallon), beaten ½l by Grey Swallow*

1st Vodafone Derby Stakes (Group 1) (Epsom, June 5) 3yo 12f Good **124** (TS 123) 14 ran. *Tracked leader, led entering straight and kicked on, driven 2l clear over 2f out, never going to be caught after (K Fallon), beat Rule Of Law by 1½l*

1st totesport Dante Stakes (Group 2) (York, May 12) 3yo 10½f Good to soft **120** (TS 92) 10 ran. *Took keen hold, held up in touch, headway to lead over 4f out, quickened 3f out, ridden 2f out, kept on well (K Fallon), beat Rule Of Law by ½l*

1st Uniq Foodservice Gold Cup EBF Maiden Stakes (Goodwood, September 24) 2yo 1m Good to firm **87** 5 ran ● **2nd** Pacemaker EBF Maiden Stakes (Sandown, August 29) 2yo 7f Soft **88** 14 ran

The nerve-racking countdown to Epsom passed smoothly and, as Derby Day came closer, North Light's odds became shorter. So much shorter, in fact, that when the 14 participants in the 225th running of the world's most famous Flat race headed on their way opposite the packed grandstands, North Light was joint-favourite, backed in from his biggest post-Dante quote of 12-1 to 7-2, a price he shared with a horse whose history closely matched his own. The paths of North Light and Snow Ridge had crossed before.

They both came from the same place. Like the incomparable Arkle 44 years earlier, North Light and Snow Ridge entered the world in box two at the late Lord Weinstock's Ballymacoll Stud in Ireland's County Meath. Born on March 1, 2001, North Light was Snow Ridge's elder by some five weeks. He came first then and, in the eyes of Ballymacoll supremo Peter Reynolds, he always would. For North Light, the colt Reynolds described as "always the king", would bid for the Derby in the Ballymacoll Stud colours. Snow Ridge would not. Despite winning the Group 2 Royal Lodge Stakes for his breeders at two, the ill-fated subsequent 2,000 Guineas second was sold to Godolphin. North Light was retained. He would be the one they would cheer at Epsom.

Not that this was a two-horse Derby. The Dante second and third, Rule Of Law and Let The Lion Roar, were back for more, while Percussionist and French 2,000 Guineas hero American Post added extra spice. On paper, this was not a vintage Derby, but nor was it a bad one either.

Watched by Arnold Weinstock's widow Lady Netta, North Light was ruthless, Fallon immaculate. Like Lester Piggott and Walter Swinburn before him, Fallon has become the master of Epsom. He rides the Derby's mile and a half to perfection. It had been a troubled year for the rider,

**North Light wins the Dante at York from Rule Of Law and
Let The Lion Roar – the order later repeated at Epsom**

his name making headlines for the wrong reasons, but never did a jockey
show more unflappable composure in the saddle than Fallon did on that
first Saturday in June.

Twenty-four hours after partnering Ouija Board to a famous Oaks
triumph, the Irishman had North Light perfectly positioned throughout.
Settled on the heels of pace-setter Meath, Fallon satisfied himself with
second until grabbing the lead almost as soon as he bade farewell to
Tattenham Corner. The Derby was won there and then. The more you
review the race, the more impressed by North Light you become. Two
lengths clear a quarter of a mile out, at no point thereafter did he look
in the slightest danger of being headed. Old rivals Rule Of Law and Let
The Lion Roar came from nowhere to follow him home, but they were
effectively in a different race, a race in which Snow Ridge finished only
seventh. A literal interpretation of the form meant that North Light earned
an unexceptional Racing Post Rating of 124, but no matter. Here was a
Derby winner – Stoute's fourth – to revel in.

He was beaten in Ireland. He should not have been. That, at least,
was Fallon's view, and one not too difficult to support. "No disrespect to
Grey Swallow," he said, "but if the ground hadn't been so fast my horse
would have won the Irish Derby as well."

Given that he returned from County Kildare an injured horse, you could
see what Fallon meant. Although once again superior to Rule Of Law
and Let The Lion Roar, North Light – this time in front just under two

furlongs out – was unable to shrug off the sneaky late challenge of Grey Swallow, who was up in trip after highly creditable runs in the Newmarket and Irish 2,000 Guineas. Visibly unhappy on the good to firm ground, the 8-11 favourite went down by half a length, yet inside the final 50 yards he came back at Grey Swallow, reacting too late to being passed in battle for the first time in his life.

The race took its toll. North Light returned home lame on his right hind and with very sore quarters. Intensive physiotherapy followed. The King George did not. Ascot was bypassed, and so were both the Juddmonte International and Prix Niel, races that had been identified by Stoute as possible targets for the Derby winner. We didn't see him again until the Arc.

The will he, won't he saga of North Light's French participation was a long one. Finally confirmed just over a week before the race, North Light was described by Fallon as "my best-ever chance of winning the Arc", a race in which Ballymacoll had been placed on six occasions.

The Prix de l'Arc de Triomphe is almost never run on such fast ground, yet the 2004 edition was. Just like his dam, Sought Out, who had herself secured Group 1 honours on Arc weekend 12 years earlier when lifting the Prix du Cadran, North Light was now unquestionably a horse who appreciated juice in the turf beneath him. Cruelly for the horse and his connections, he set out in the 2004 Arc on a Longchamp racecourse thirstier than it had been for years.

He tried to win it from the front. At York and Epsom he had showed himself to be a horse who flowed happily when allowed to put pace to a race. At Longchamp, he put into the race plenty of pace, but probably too much. Booted quickly into the lead by Fallon, he dictated a strong gallop, which became stronger when Tap Dance City ranged alongside six furlongs out. The Japanese raider's harassment was costly. It meant that for a crucial section of the contest North Light was over-extending himself, going too fast for his own good. First into the straight and, for a few fleeting moments, seemingly in command, North Light boxed on doggedly, even after being headed a furlong out. Tap Dance City, Mamool and Prospect Park, the horses who had followed him most closely through the Arc's first three-quarters, were beaten out of sight. North Light was beaten less than four lengths. It had been a mighty effort.

"Just think what he would have done if he'd been able to put his head down and race," rued Fallon, bemoaning the fast ground on which the evidently uncomfortable North Light had constantly changed his legs.

The past cannot be changed. The future is there to be shaped. A supremely handsome, imposing and – when conditions are right – free-flowing thoroughbred, North Light will in 2005 become the first Stoute-trained Epsom hero to stay in training at four. We should not lose faith. Whatever the ratings or handicappers might say, North Light has already shown himself to be a fine Derby winner. He could yet prove to be a prodigious one.

North Light

bay colt 1-3-2001

	Danzig	Northern Dancer	Nearctic
			Natalma
Danehill		Pas de Nom	Admiral's Voyage
b 1986			Petitioner
	Razyana	His Majesty	Ribot
			Flower Bowl
		Spring Adieu	Buckpasser
			Natalma
	Rainbow Quest	Blushing Groom	Red God
			Runaway Bride
Sought Out		I Will Follow	Herbager
b 1988			Where You Lead
	Edinburgh	Charlottown	Charlottesville
			Meld
		Queen's Castle	Sovereign Path
			Country House

Bred by Ballymacoll Stud Farm Ltd in Ireland

Sire Danehill

Won 4 of 9 races, inc. Cork and Orrery Stakes-Gr3, Haydock Park Sprint Cup-Gr1. Also 3rd in 2,000 Guineas. Sire of Gr1 winners: Danish (Queen Elizabeth II Challenge Cup), Kissing Cousin (Coronation S.), Danehill Dancer (Phoenix S., National S.), Tsukuba Symphony (NHK Mile Cup), Desert King (National S., Irish 2,000 Guineas, Irish Derby), Fairy King Prawn (Yasuda Kinen), Tiger Hill (Grosser Preis von Baden [twice], Bayerisches Zuchtrennen), Indian Danehill (Prix Ganay), Wannabe Grand (Cheveley Park S.), Aquarelliste (Prix de Diane, Prix Vermeille, Prix Ganay), Banks Hill (Coronation S., Breeders' Cup Filly & Mare Turf, Prix Jacques le Marois), Mozart (July Cup, Nunthorpe S.), Regal Rose (Cheveley Park S.), Dress To Thrill (Matriarch S.), Landseer (Poule d'Essai des Poulains), Rock Of Gibraltar (Grand Criterium, Dewhurst S., 2,000 Guineas, Irish 2,000 Guineas, St James's Palace S., Sussex S., Prix du Moulin), Westerner (Prix du Cadran, twice, Prix Royal-Oak, twice), Clodovil (Poule d'Essai des Poulains), Light Jig (Yellow Ribbon S.), Spartacus (Phoenix S., Gran Criterium), Grey Lilas (Prix du Moulin de Longchamp), North Light (Derby S.), Oratorio (Prix Jean-Luc Lagardere).

Dam Sought Out

Won 5 of 21 races, inc. Prix de Lutece-Gr3, Oleander Rennen-Gr3, Prix Kergorlay-Gr2, Prix du Cadran-Gr1. Front-running, high-class stayer, a tail-swisher, but utterly genuine. Dam of: Treasure Chest (1995 g by Last Tycoon; winner), Hidden Bounty (1996 c by Generous; unplaced), Cover Up (1997 g by Machiavellian; Gr3-placed winner), Search Me (1998 c by Suave Dancer; unraced), Researched (1999 g by Danehill; Listed winner), North Light (2001 c by Danehill; Derby winner), Paper Hunt (2002 c by Indian Danehill; died as a yearling). Her yearling is a filly by Kalanisi, and she is due in 2005 to Danehill Dancer. Barren to Pennekamp in 2000, and to Sinndar in 2004.

Pedigree assessment

In the – blessed – days when every breeder wanted to produce a Derby winner, the old horseman's lore advocated "speed in the mare". While nobody with such an aim would dream of using a stallion who did not stay 12 furlongs, a mare who had shown speed was more than acceptable; she was advisable. Ballymacoll Stud won its second Derby in 2004, and each was gained by the reverse process. After Troy (by miler Petingo out of La Milo, whose minimum distance was 12 furlongs) in 1979 came North Light, whose sire was a sprinter and whose dam scored her biggest win at 2m4f. Troy dominated his crop at three, which North Light was unable to achieve, but don't be surprised if he enhances his reputation in 2005. *TM*

One Cool Cat (USA)

3yo bay colt **121**

Storm Cat (USA) - Tacha (USA) (Mr Prospector (USA))

Owner Mrs John Magnier & M Tabor

Trainer A P O'Brien

Breeder WinStar Farm

Career: **10** starts won **5** second **0** third **1** **£325,492** win and place

By James Willoughby

ONE COOL CAT'S status as wonder-horse-in-waiting vanished in a heartbeat. The image of him trailing behind in the 2,000 Guineas was the most arresting of the season.

Depending on your point of view, One Cool Cat was either a serious talent compromised by infirmity or a vehicle for hype that went off the road. The majority will be inclined fairly towards the former assessment, but there is a rising tide of cynicism about the endorsements given to potential stallions these days.

One Cool Cat's two Group 1 wins as a juvenile were very much for real. He ended that season as one of the best of his age, so it is churlish to describe him as a horse who fell short of his home work on the track. Nevertheless, his every step was followed by lavish praise from his trainer Aidan O'Brien, and in the end this worked to the detriment of his reputation. Ironic, isn't it?

When the rangy son of Storm Cat stepped out into the paddock at Newmarket in May, there cannot have been anybody who was not impressed. A big, black colt – were such a colouration truly associated with the thoroughbred – he appeared to have staved off any thoughts that he might not train on merely by his appearance. But, as it turned out, the trouble was more than skin deep.

For the first four furlongs of the Guineas, One Cool Cat appeared to travel well. He had a raking stride at his cruising speed, and it was not hard to believe that he impressed on the gallops. When he was asked to go through the gears, however, nothing happened.

Or, rather, something must have. His legs appeared to continue at the same beat, but there was a total absence of power and impulsion. One Cool Cat was beaten in strides and Jamie Spencer allowed him to coast home; he finished, a bedraggled sight, more than 50 lengths behind the winner, Haafhd.

One Cool Cat returns to sprinting, and apparently to top form, at The Curragh, but the revival proved short-lived

One Cool Cat was diagnosed with a fibrillating heart. There is no telling the extent of his internal distress that day, for that particular malaise is a symptom as well as a condition.

This must have been a difficult time for O'Brien. Despite his magnificent record, the pressure is constantly on. True, he is guaranteed a regular supply of some of the world's best-bred young stock. But even this is not enough to ensure him the champions by which he seems to be measured.

Despite his Guineas flop, One Cool Cat did make it back to the track. The Group 3 International Stakes at The Curragh in July was chosen as a suitable target to relaunch his career, but he was less the dangerous wounded tiger than simply a timorous pussycat. Again, he showed little zest off the bridle and finished down the field behind Red Feather. His trainer blamed the slow pace; the rest of us noted his comments. Sceptically.

A rare statement made in public by One Cool Cat's owner John Magnier, the Coolmore supremo, seemed to suggest that this was the end of the road for the much-vaunted colt. But O'Brien hasn't got where he is today without being able to pull rabbits out of hats.

Dropped back to six furlongs in the 'Last Chance Saloon' Stakes – better known as the Group 3 Phoenix Sprint at The Curragh – One Cool Cat

2004

6th Stanleybet Sprint Cup (Group 1) (Haydock, September 4) 3yo+ 6f Good **113** (TS 108) 19 ran. *Midfield, ridden and headway over 1f out, not pace to challenge (J P Spencer), beaten 3½l by Tante Rose*

3rd Victor Chandler Nunthorpe Stakes (Group 1) (York, August 19) 2yo+ 5f Soft **114** (TS 103) 12 ran. *Held up and behind, switched left and headway 2f out, switched right and ridden when not much room entering final furlong, driven and finished well (J P Spencer), beaten 1¼l by Bahamian Pirate*

1st Patrick P. O'Leary Memorial Phoenix Sprint Stakes (Group 3) (Curragh, August 8) 3yo+ 6f Good to firm **121** (TS 89) 10 ran. *Held up in rear, in touch travelling easily over 1f out, quickened to lead 150yds from finish, driven clear, easily (J P Spencer), beat The Kiddykid by 1l*

5th ladbrokes.com International Stakes (Group 3) (Curragh, July 17) 3yo 1m Good **105** (TS 52) 7 ran. *In rear, improved into 4th and ridden 1½f out, soon no impression, hampered close home (J P Spencer), beaten 6¼l by Red Feather*

13th UltimateBet.com 2,000 Guineas Stakes (Group 1) (Newmarket, May 1) 3yo 1m Good 14 ran. *Held up centre, ridden 3f out, soon weakened and eased (J P Spencer), beaten a distance by Haafhd*

2003

1st Dunnes Stores National Stakes (Group 1) (Curragh, September 14) 2yo 7f Good to firm **119** 8 ran ● **1st** Independent Waterford Wedgwood Phoenix Stakes (Group 1) (Curragh, August 10) 2yo 6f Good **117** 7 ran ● **1st** Dubai Duty Free Anglesey Stakes (Group 3) (Curragh, July 13) 2yo 6½f Good **115** 6 ran ● **1st** Leonard Sainer EBF Maiden Stakes (York, June 14) 2yo 6f Good to firm **99** 6 ran ● **4th** Mull Of Kintyre EBF Maiden (Curragh, April 27) 2yo 5f Good to yielding **78** 10 ran

affected the miracle comeback, sailing through on the bridle to defy a Group 1 penalty in the manner of a Group 1 horse.

The lofty Racing Post Rating that One Cool Cat earned for this victory did not hold up when he tackled stiffer competition. At York in August, he did not look a five-furlong horse in the Nunthorpe Stakes, running on belatedly to finish just over a length third to Bahamian Pirate.

O'Brien said that soft going was not to One Cool Cat's advantage, which is fair enough, but, even so, the form was muddling and a long way below his apparent achievement at The Curragh. More worryingly, One Cool Cat once again looked uncomfortable under pressure.

A return to six furlongs in the Stanleybet Sprint Cup at Haydock should have suited him, but he did not benefit. It was once again obvious that he could not – or would not – go through the gears.

At the end of September, One Cool Cat broke down on the gallops and was found to have a condylar fracture of his near-hind leg. A successful operation means he will serve as a stallion, either at Coolmore or Ashford, its sister stud in Kentucky.

Few can doubt that One Cool Cat had serious natural talent, but he wasn't tough enough to continue his Group 1 exploits beyond the age of two. He proved neither his trainer nor Oscar Wilde correct: it is not always better to be talked about.

One Cool Cat   *bay colt 26-3-2001*

		Northern Dancer	Nearctic Natalma
	Storm Bird		
		South Ocean	New Providence Shining Sun
Storm Cat br 1983			
		Secretariat	Bold Ruler Somethingroyal
	Terlingua		
		Crimson Saint	Crimson Satan Bolero Rose
		Raise A Native	Native Dancer Raise You
	Mr Prospector		
		Gold Digger	Nashua Sequence
Tacha b/br 1992			
		Northern Dancer	**Nearctic Natalma**
	Savannah Dancer		
		Valoris	Tiziano Vali

Bred by Winstar Farm LLC in Kentucky. $3.1 million Keeneland July yearling

Sire Storm Cat

Won 4 of 8 races, inc. Young America S.-Gr1 at 2 years. Also 2nd (beaten a nose) in Breeders' Cup Juvenile S. Medium-sized, strongly made sort, who took more after his dam than his sire. Top-class, extremely game 2yo who had surgery for bone chips in off knee at end of season; never wholly sound thereafter. Sire of: Gr1 winners Harlan (Vosburgh S.), November Snow (Test S., Alabama S.), Desert Stormer (Breeders' Cup Sprint), Missed The Storm (Test S.), Mistle Cat (Premio Vittorio di Capua), Sardula (Hollywood Starlet S., Kentucky Oaks), Tabasco Cat (Preakness S., Belmont S.), Hennessy (Hopeful S.), Aldiza (Go For Wand H.), Sharp Cat (Matron S., Hollywood Starlet S., Las Virgenes S., Santa Anita Oaks, Acorn S., Ruffian H.), Catinca (Ruffian H.), Aljabr (Prix de la Salamandre, Sussex S., Lockinge S.), Cat Thief (Swaps S., Breeders' Cup Classic), Forestry (King's Bishop S.), Tactical Cat (Hollywood Futurity), Finder's Fee (Matron S., Acorn S.), Giant's Causeway (Prix de la Salamandre, St James's Palace S., Sussex S., York International S., Irish Champion S.), High Yield (Hopeful S., Fountain of Youth S., Blue Grass S.), Black Minnaloushe (Irish 2,000 Guineas, St James's Palace S.), Raging Fever (Matron S., Frizette S., Ogden Phipps H.), Sophisticat (Coronation S.), Dessert (Del Mar Oaks), Hold That Tiger (Grand Criterium), Nebraska Tornado (Prix de Diane, Prix du Moulin de Longchamp), Storm Flag Flying (Matron S., Frizette S., Breeders' Cup Juvenile Fillies' S., Personal Ensign H.), Denebola (Prix Marcel Boussac), One Cool Cat (Phoenix S., National S.), Sweet Catomine (Del Mar Debutante S.).

Dam Tacha

Won 1 of 9 races. Just a useful miler, placed 2nd once from 2 outings on grass. Sister to Gr2 winner Sha Tha (dam of Gr2 winner State Shinto). Dam of: Dominique's Show (1999 f by Theatrical; unraced), Seattle Tac (2000 f by Seattle Slew; winner), One Cool Cat (2001 c by Storm Cat; Gr1 winner), Don't Tacha Me (2002 f by A.P. Indy; unraced). Her yearling and foal are colts by Storm Cat.

Pedigree assessment

As mentioned here last year, many Storm Cats who excel at two do less well at three, and One Cool Cat came into that category. He proved a decided disappointment in his second season, giving only one display – in a Gr3 event at six furlongs – that so much as hinted at merit of a high order. At two he had looked as though a mile would suit him, and there was enough in his background – his grand-dam was out of an Oaks winner – to suggest that he might stay further, but his two runs at a mile were his worst of the year. His days as an enigmatic racehorse are over, and it is now up to breeders to decide what to make of him. His pedigree, at least, will stand him in good stead. *TM*

Oratorio (Ire)

2yo bay colt   **119**

Danehill (USA) - Mahrah (USA) (Vaguely Noble)

Owner Mrs John Magnier & M Tabor

Trainer A P O'Brien

Breeder Barronstown Stud & Orpendale

Career: **7** starts   won **4**   second **2**   third **0**   **£339,662** win and place

By Lee Mottershead

IN a season when much went wrong for Aidan O'Brien and Jamie Spencer, they deserved a little slice of luck. At Longchamp on Arc day, in a dramatic running of the Prix Jean-Luc Lagardere, they got it.

It had been at the Paris track in mid-May that the two men had suffered their cruellest blow of the whole year. With the French 2,000 Guineas there for the taking and with only a handful of strides left to cover, Ballydoyle raider Antonius Pius veered sharply into the running rail, throwing away what would have been certain Classic triumph. Spencer, just months into his new job as O'Brien's stable jockey, was left to walk back to the Longchamp weighing room shaking his head at the barely credible events that had just occurred.

Yet if Spencer thought that Longchamp had it in for him, he was wrong. For if he lost a Group 1 on Antonius Pius that should rightfully have been his, he arguably won a Group 1 on Oratorio that should have gone elsewhere. Not that Oratorio was not a wholly admirable victor of the Grand Criterium-that-was, France's premier juvenile prize. The shock surrounding his victory was merely that Lady Luck chose to bestow her favours upon him.

Early in the straight, Oratorio's chance appeared to be fading. With Early March dictating the pace up front, the son of Danehill appeared to be struggling, forfeiting what had been a decent position off the home turn and seemingly going backwards. Even entering the final furlong, there did not appear to be much chance of an Oratorio win. By now, the Olivier Peslier-ridden Early March was engaged in a furious battle with Christophe Soumillon on Layman, the pair two lengths clear of the Irish challenger with the race surely to themselves. Then, though, something beautiful happened; at least beautiful if you were part of the Oratorio entourage.

Early March shifted off the rail, in the process both interfering with Layman and creating a monstrous gap for Oratorio to aim at. Oratorio

Oratorio squeezes home in the Group 1 Prix Jean-Luc Lagardere, but he was later beaten by Shamardal

surged. Accelerating against the fence, Spencer's mount quickly moved up through the gears, eating into the deficit until, inches from the post, he had forced his nose in front. As O'Brien remarked on greeting his winner, "it's a funny old game".

In many ways, it was fitting that Oratorio should net Ballydoyle an unusually rare top-flight success in 2004 because, in a season when many of the operation's leading lights failed to come up to scratch, he was Mr Dependable. First or second in six of his seven appearances, he also seemed to get better each time he raced.

The first time we saw him was at The Curragh on Irish Guineas weekend. Having created a serious impression when landing his maiden there, Oratorio became the stable's obvious hope for the Coventry Stakes, but the occasion proved too much and he could finish only seventh, greenness rather than the opposition getting the better of him. That defeat knocked Oratorio down the pecking order at home, or at least in the eyes of Spencer, as he was downgraded to stable second string for his next two starts. If

2nd Darley Dewhurst Stakes (Group 1) (Newmarket, October 16) 2yo 7f Soft **119** (TS 119) 9 ran. *Prominent, ridden over 2f out, not quicken approaching final furlong (J P Spencer), beaten 2¹/₂l by Shamardal*

1st Prix Jean-Luc Lagardere (Group 1) (Longchamp, October 3) 2yo 7f Good **118** (TS 98) 6 ran. *Prominent, 3rd on rail straight, dropped back but then driven and ran on from 2f out, ridden and challenged strongly 1f out, led final strides (J P Spencer), beat Early March by short nk*

1st Galileo EBF Futurity Stakes (Group 2) (Curragh, August 21) 2yo 7f Good to firm **114** (TS 94) 5 ran. *Close up in 2nd, slightly hampered halfway, led travelling easily 2¹/₂f out, quickened clear under 2f out, eased close home, impressive (J P Spencer), beat Democratic Deficit by 2l*

2nd Independent Waterford Wedgwood Phoenix Stakes (Group 1) (Curragh, August 8) 2yo 6f Good to firm **111** (TS 86) 6 ran. *Prominent, 2nd before halfway, 3rd under pressure 1¹/₂f out, kept on inside final furlong (J A Heffernan), beaten ³/₄l by Damson*

1st Dubai Duty Free Anglesey Stakes (Group 3) (Curragh, July 18) 2yo 6¹/₂f Good **109** (TS 97) 8 ran. *Close up in 2nd, led 2f out, ridden clear from over 1f out, kept on well (J A Heffernan), beat Cougar Cat by 1l*

7th Coventry Stakes (Group 2) (Ascot, June 15) 2yo 6f Good to firm **91** (TS 77) 13 ran. *With leaders, every chance well over 1f out, weakened just over 1f out (J P Spencer), beaten 6l by Iceman*

1st Boylesports Everyday Specials EBF Maiden (Curragh, May 23) 2yo 6f Good to firm **87** (TS 59) 7 ran. *Led, joined over 2f out, ridden to regain lead over 1f out, kept on well, easily (J P Spencer), beat Shamoan*

put out by the snub, he did not let it show. Partnered by Seamus Heffernan, the likeable bay colt beat the Spencer selected in both the Group 3 Anglesey and Group 1 Phoenix Stakes, winning the former from Cougar Cat and getting to within three-parts of a length of Damson in the latter.

Not surprisingly, Spencer did not get off Oratorio again. Back on board for the horse's crack at the Group 2 Futurity Stakes, Spencer was able to enjoy an armchair ride, Oratorio tanking throughout the contest before quickening smartly inside the final quarter-mile to put the race in safe keeping within an instant. It was an effort that earned him his place at Longchamp, and it was at Longchamp that he earned his place at Newmarket, where he took on Britain's top juveniles in the Dewhurst Stakes. Only one of them proved too good for him.

While it could be argued that Oratorio was not helped by racing deep on the track, wide of the rail-running all-the-way winner Shamardal, in truth he was beaten by a much better horse on the day. That, in itself, however, was no disgrace. Although two and a half lengths down on Shamardal at the line, he still earned a better Racing Post Rating of 119 than he had achieved when giving O'Brien his fourth victory in the Grand Criterium. While he will not go down as the finest two-year-old ever to race for Ballydoyle, and while there is a strong chance that there will be a few better than him at three, he delivered a big prize when a big prize was needed. As he proved at Longchamp, Oratorio had perfect timing.

Oratorio   *bay colt, 29-4-2002*

			Northern Dancer	Nearctic Natalma
		Danzig		
			Pas de Nom	Admiral's Voyage Petitioner
	Danehill b 1986			
			His Majesty	Ribot Flower Bowl
		Razyana		
			Spring Adieu	Buckpasser Natalma
			Vienna	Aureole Turkish Blood
		Vaguely Noble		
			Noble Lassie	Nearco Belle Sauvage
	Mahrah b 1987			
			Alydar	Raise A Native Sweet Tooth
		Montage		
			Katonka	Minnesota Mac Minnetonka

Bred by Barronstown Stud & Orpendale in Ireland

Sire Danehill

Won 4 of 9 races, inc. Cork and Orrery Stakes-Gr3, Haydock Park Sprint Cup-Gr1. Also 3rd in 2,000 Guineas. Medium-sized, strong, good-bodied individual, markedly back at the knee. Showed quick, fluent action, effective on any ground from dead to firm, never ran on really soft surface. Died May 2003. Sire of Gr1 winners: Danish (Queen Elizabeth II Challenge Cup), Kissing Cousin (Coronation S.), Danehill Dancer (Phoenix S., National S.), Tsukuba Symphony (NHK Mile Cup), Desert King (National S., Irish 2,000 Guineas, Irish Derby), Fairy King Prawn (Yasuda Kinen), Tiger Hill (Grosser Preis von Baden [twice], Bayerisches Zuchtrennen), Indian Danehill (Prix Ganay), Wannabe Grand (Cheveley Park S.), Aquarelliste (Prix de Diane, Prix Vermeille, Prix Ganay), Banks Hill (Coronation S., Breeders' Cup Filly & Mare Turf, Prix Jacques le Marois), Mozart (July Cup, Nunthorpe S.), Regal Rose (Cheveley Park S.), Dress To Thrill (Matriarch S.), Landseer (Poule d'Essai des Poulains), Rock Of Gibraltar (Grand Criterium, Dewhurst S., 2,000 Guineas, Irish 2,000 Guineas, St James's Palace S., Sussex S., Prix du Moulin), Westerner (Prix du Cadran, twice, Prix Royal-Oak, twice), Clodovil (Poule d'Essai des Poulains), Light Jig (Yellow Ribbon S.), Spartacus (Phoenix S., Gran Criterium), Grey Lilas (Prix du Moulin de Longchamp), North Light (Derby S.), Oratorio (Prix Jean-Luc Lagardere).

Dam Mahrah

Won 1 of 6 starts at 2 and 3. At 2, placed over 7f from 2 starts. At 3, won 1 (1m) of 4 starts, also placed over 9-11f. Half-sister to 12f Group 2 winner Andros Bay (by Alleged) and to useful 2yo/sprinter Juniper (by Danzig) out of winning half-sister to Grade 2 winners Give Me Strength and Talakeno (Vaguely Noble). Dam of: Kanun (1992 f by Dancing Brave; unraced), Fahim (1993 c by Green Desert; US stakes winner, Gr1 placed), Hawzah (1994 f by Green Desert; unraced), Khafaya (1995 f by Unfuwain; placed), Hadeb (1996 f by Unfuwain; winner), Elauyun (1997 f by Muhtarram; unraced), Mowaadah (1998 f by Alzao; Listed winner), Miss Mirage (2000 f by Alhaarth; winner), Glimmering (2001 f by Sadler's Wells; winner), Oratorio (2002 c by Danehill; Prix Jean-Luc Lagardere-Gr1).

Pedigree assessment

Bred along very similar lines to former Ballydoyle inmate Juniper – who was a sprinter – and also Fahim, who was Grade 1-placed over 12f. Oratorio already has shown more stamina than Juniper, and he should have no problem with a mile. However, he is unlikely to stay as far as Fahim. Danehill needs a big dose of stamina on the dam's side to get a middle-distance horse, and Mahrah does not provide it. *JH*

Ouija Board

3yo bay filly **124**

Cape Cross (Ire) - Selection Board (Welsh Pageant)
Owner Lord Derby
Trainer E A L Dunlop
Breeder Stanley Estate and Stud Co

Career: **8** starts | won **5** | second **0** | third **3** | **£932,879** win and place

---

By Lee Mottershead

THERE is something rather wonderful about Ouija Board. It is because of her and because of the people around her. It is because of what she has done and because of the way she has done it. It is because of all the glorious little subplots that, combined, made her rise to stardom arguably the defining story of the 2004 British Flat season. It is because she made the year so much more enjoyable than it would have been without her – and because we have it all to look forward to again in 2005.

Such an amazing tale. Such an unlikely tale. The only racehorse to carry the colours of a distinguished English aristo, one of whose forebears gave his name to the sport's most famous race, she was victorious in the Classic first won by the same forebear 225 years earlier. A filly nobody outside her stable truly considered likely to be one of the season's leading lights at the start of the campaign, she went on to complete a famous Classic double before proving herself the best filly in Europe and then, on a spectacular day in Texas, the best turf filly in the world.

And in doing all this she triggered within her team scenes of such sincere, spontaneous and uncontrollable joy that even the most hardened observer was softened. It is not just Lord Derby, Ed Dunlop and Kieren Fallon who owe a debt of gratitude to Ouija Board. We all do.

Yet at the start of the year it had all seemed so unlikely. Not seen on a racecourse until early October 2003, she completed three starts within the space of four weeks, showing herself to be a smart performer, but in no way an embryonic wonder woman.

Placed in a maiden race at Newmarket before an impressive win in a minor conditions event at Yarmouth, she was then a beaten favourite in an unheralded November Listed race at Newmarket that had come into existence only a few years earlier. Her four-length third behind Spotlight suggested she had limitations, and on that basis an official mark of 93

**Ouija Board stretches out in fine style at Epsom to land
the Oaks by seven lengths under Kieren Fallon**

seemed fair enough. It would have been no great surprise had she started
her three-year-old season in a handicap. Instead she started it in a Classic
trial.

What Ouija Board did in the Pretty Polly Stakes at Newmarket had
something of the wow factor about it. That she was sent off a warm
2-1 favourite for the mile-and-a-quarter Listed race was surprising in
itself, but, given what had come before, what she then proceeded to achieve
at her local racecourse was positively astonishing. For while the Pretty
Polly is not traditionally one of the leading Oaks trials, Ouija Board showed
that she was a serious Epsom prospect by routing her eight rivals with
a six-length win.

Partnered by Fallon for the first time, her acceleration running
into the Dip instantly sealed victory. Within a few strides of taking the
lead just inside the final quarter-mile, Ouija Board had surged clear, so
much so that the prize was already in safe keeping as the final furlong
marker was passed. Crossing the line a street length clear of Sahool, Ouija
Board had immediately thrust herself into the Oaks equation, Ladbrokes'
20-1 Classic quote seeming uncharacteristically generous.

Perhaps because the Pretty Polly had not been shown live on terrestrial
television, or perhaps because Newmarket was still agog with Attraction's
earlier 1,000 Guineas triumph, Ouija Board's procession earned a strangely
muted response. No matter. The hype machine would soon start rolling

2004   Race record

1st Alberto VO5 Breeders' Cup Filly & Mare Turf (Grade 1) (Lone Star Park, October 30) 3yo+ 11f Yielding **121** 12 ran. *Raced in touch, 4th halfway, headway 3f out, 3rd and going well straight, ran on strongly to lead over 1f out, pushed out (K Fallon), beat Film Maker by 1½l*

3rd Prix de l'Arc de Triomphe Lucien Barriere (Group 1) (Longchamp, October 3) 3yo+ 12f Good **123** (TS 124) 19 ran. *Held up, 14th straight, not much room 2f out, strong run down outside from 1½f out to go 3rd 100yds out, stayed on (J P Murtagh), beaten 1½l by Bago*

1st Darley Irish Oaks (Group 1) (Curragh, July 18) 3yo 12f Good to firm **117** (TS 117) 7 ran. *Dwelt, settled in 5th, 4th and headway entering straight, ridden to lead over 1½f out, stayed on well, eased near finish (K Fallon), beat Punctilious by 1l*

1st Vodafone Oaks (Group 1) (Epsom, June 4) 3yo 12f Good **124** (TS 120) 7 ran. *Dwelt, raced in 6th until 4th and progress straight, led over 2f out, shaken up and surged clear from over 1f out (K Fallon), beat All Too Beautiful by 7l*

1st RL Davison Pretty Polly Stakes (Listed) (Newmarket, May 2) 3yo 10f Good **111** (TS 81) 9 ran. *Held up, headway over 2f out, led over 1f out, ridden clear (K Fallon), beat Sahool by 6l*

2003

3rd EBF Montrose Fillies' Stakes (Listed) (Newmarket, November 1) 2yo 1m Good to soft **92** 12 ran ● **1st** EBF Novice Stakes (Yarmouth, October 21) 2yo 7f Good to firm **91** 6 ran ● **3rd** Beech House Stud EBF Maiden Stakes (Newmarket, October 3) 2yo 7f Good to firm **76** 23 ran

and the question would soon start being asked. Would Ouija Board take her place in the Oaks?

There would be no decision for a while, yet there was no hiding Dunlop's affection for his new star filly. He had already proved himself particularly adept with fillies. Ta Rib had given him a career-launching Poule d'Essai des Pouliches victory, while he had masterminded Lailani's march from the handicap ranks to glory in the Irish Oaks. But speaking in a Racing Post interview shortly after the Pretty Polly, it was evident in everything that Dunlop said that nobody knew better than he that his Maktoum Al Maktoum-owned yard needed another star to keep it in the premier league. It was also evident that he knew he had only one horse capable of taking on that role.

Asked about Ouija Board, Dunlop's response of "aahh . . ." made it plain that not only was Ouija Board admired, but she was also looked on with no little affection. She would be looked on with even more affection if she could win the Oaks. Dunlop, though, was clear in his own mind that the decision to go or not to go to Epsom was not down to him. It was down to Lord Derby. And Dunlop had no intention of trying to sway his Lordship one way or the other.

To some it might have seemed a no-brainer. The 19th Earl of Derby – known to his friends as Teddy – and his family had the closest of ties with Epsom. The 12th Earl of Derby had founded the Oaks in 1779

It's harder work this time, but Ouija Board completes an Oaks double that was last achieved by Ramruma in 1999

and won the first renewal with his filly Bridget. At dinner on the night of that first Oaks, the idea of a similar Classic for colts was proposed. Lord Derby and Sir Charles Bunbury tossed a coin to decide whose name the new race should carry. Bunbury would have to settle for a seven-furlong handicap at Newmarket's July meeting.

It was not, though, an easy decision. For the first time in years, Lord Derby had only the one horse in training, and the horse in question could not be guaranteed to stay a mile and a half. A daughter of Cape Cross out of a sister to the family's outstanding gelding Teleprompter, Ouija Board was deemed by many breeding commentators to have more chance of showing her best over the French Oaks' ten and a half furlongs. It would be either Epsom or Chantilly. Lord Derby's wife Cassie, who came up with Ouija Board's name during an M6 traffic jam near Sandbach services, thought Epsom. "She said you cannot buy dreams and we had the chance of a very special dream," revealed Lord Derby. After many sleepless nights, he sided with his good lady.

Ouija Board went to Epsom. Lady D deserved the kiss she got after the race.

True, it didn't look a great Oaks on paper, but within the seven-horse field was some serious talent. Godolphin's Sundrop had come close to robbing Attraction in the Guineas, while her stablemate Punctilious had won the Musidora Stakes by a jumping distance. Add in Ballydoyle's heavily touted All Too Beautiful, and it was obvious that the Oaks would not be won easily. Yet Ouija Board won the Oaks easily. More than that, she pulverised them.

Positioned perfectly by Fallon, Ouija Board may not have been particularly happy negotiating Tattenham Corner, but she was ecstatic for the remaining three and a half furlongs. In front just over two furlongs out, she positively surged clear. Rarely is a Classic won as far out as Ouija Board won the 2004 Oaks. Seven lengths ahead of All Too Beautiful at the line, she left her trainer in tears and her owner, his family and friends on the highest of highs. "I felt as if I was being lifted off the ground," was how Lord Derby summed it up at the time. He would have good reason to be happier still in the days and weeks that followed.

Judged by the Racing Post handicapper to be the finest Oaks winner of the last decade with a Racing Post Rating of 124, Ouija Board seemed only to have to turn up at The Curragh – once she had been supplemented – to complete a Classic double. As at Epsom, there was no denying Ouija Board's superiority. Although this time only a length in front of Punctilious, hers was a margin of victory that underplayed the performance.

In the rear as the race developed and still only fourth as heads were turned for home, Ouija Board was always the one on whom eyes were fixed. When Fallon asked the filly beneath him to win her race, she did so with the minimum of fuss, taking over a furlong and a half out before passing the judge a workmanlike but authoritative winner. She recorded the fastest time ever by a filly over The Curragh's mile and a half as she justified 4-7 favouritism without ever looking likely to be denied.

The Curragh came in mid-July. Longchamp came in early October. York was supposed to come somewhere in between, except it never did. The Yorkshire Oaks was the obvious place to go next. In another Group 1 restricted to fillies and mares, Ouija Board had a massive chance on paper, even if she wouldn't have Fallon, Sir Michael Stoute having claimed his number one rider for Quiff. But it rained, then rained some more, and, having walked the track with Lord Derby, Dunlop scratched Ouija Board less than an hour before the race. In doing so, he executed the finest decision made by a trainer all year. By swerving what had looked like a possible penalty kick, Dunlop – supported by his owner – had opened new possibilities for Ouija Board.

With a gruelling race on heavy ground in her legs, could Ouija Board have done what she did in the Prix de l'Arc de Triomphe? Probably not.

**A superb climax to a magnificent season as Ouija Board
adds the Breeders' Cup Filly & Mare Turf to her Oaks wins**

Kept under wraps until the Arc, having also passed up on the Prix Vermeille, Ouija Board returned for Europe's premier Flat race with Johnny Murtagh replacing Fallon – claimed for his Derby hero North Light – and with a whole host of British support behind her. It was agonising and exhilarating at the same time, for Ouija Board could – and in truth, should – have won it.

Not that her defeat was Murtagh's fault. Only running in the Arc after connections once again swerved easy pickings by declining the same day's Prix de l'Opera, Ouija Board experienced the troubled Longchamp passage that so many past Arc losers have suffered. Shuffled back through a huge field, she found herself with precious few behind her at the top of the short straight, but only two in front of her at the line. Interfered with two furlongs out and forced wide, Ouija Board finished better than anything else inside the final furlong and a half, passing horses one by one, mowing down the principals, only for the line to come too soon. Third, and just a length and a half off Bago where it mattered most, Ouija Board had covered herself with glory.

At Epsom and The Curragh, Dunlop and Lord Derby had been magnificent in victory. At Longchamp they were both magnificent in defeat. Hardly able to talk as he fought back the lump in his throat, Dunlop hailed Ouija Board "the best filly in Europe". Lord Derby could barely stop smiling. This was defeat, but not as we know it.

There would be one further chance for Dunlop to cry and for Lord Derby to smile. Sending Ouija Board to the Breeders' Cup was yet another brave move that could so easily have backfired. All concerned with the horse admitted that the Lone Star Park track was worryingly tight, while the rain that fell in the days before the Breeders' Cup eased the ground and placed her participation in jeopardy even after she had arrived.

Looked after superbly in America by Dunlop's head groom Chris Hinson, and with a $90,000 supplementary fee paid, Ouija Board was given the go-ahead to tackle the Filly & Mare Turf – that race chosen in preference to the Turf – after much agonising in the days before the contest. One of only two British horses to run at the 'World Thoroughbred Championships', she would be cheered on by the whole of British racing. And how we would revel in her triumph.

It was easy. Looking superbly well for a filly who had been on the go through spring, summer and now well into the autumn, Ouija Board was a perfect partner to Fallon, who gave her the perfect ride, just as he had aboard Islington to win the same contest 12 months earlier. Placed in the box seat by Fallon and brought three wide around the final bend before being sent for home a furlong out, Ouija Board needed only minimal encouragement from the man on board to crush the Americans.

Under a largely hands-and-heels drive, she simply oozed class as she sauntered past the line a length and a half clear of Film Maker, a four-year-old who had beaten the 2003 Oaks winner Casual Look into third in a Grade 1 at Keeneland just over 12 months previously. Ouija Board's owner, trainer and their families were ecstatic. "She is a world champion," declared Lord Derby. Indeed my Lord, she is.

Based on simple handicapping assessment, Ouija Board is no superstar. But while she falls behind even some of her fellow three-year-olds in terms of official ratings, she has earned her place high on the list of Britain's finest ever fillies. Blessed with a tremendous turn of foot and searing acceleration, she is a dual Oaks winner who went on to fly the flag in the Breeders' Cup. As such, she deserves to be talked of in the same breath as the likes of Pebbles and Oh So Sharp, if only because of the impact she has made on, and pleasure she has given to, British racing fans.

A filly representing special people, she has become the people's filly, and the people's filly will be back again at four. The days of doffing caps to the aristocracy may be gone, but doff your proverbial cap to Ouija Board. She deserves that respect. She has done her country proud.

Ouija Board

bay filly, 6-3-2001

		Danzig	Northern Dancer
			Pas de Nom
	Green Desert	Foreign Courier	Sir Ivor
Cape Cross			Courtly Dee
b 1994		Ahonoora	Lorenzaccio
			Helen Nichols
	Park Appeal	Balidaress	Balidar
			Innocence
		Tudor Melody	Tudor Minstrel
			Matelda
	Welsh Pageant	Picture Light	Court Martial
Selection Board			Queen Of Light
b 1982		Silly Season	Tom Fool
			Double Deal
	Ouija	Samanda	Alycidon
			Gradisca

Bred by Stanley Estate & Stud Co. in England

Sire Cape Cross

Won 5 of 19 races, inc. Lockinge S.-Gr1, Queen Anne S.-Gr2, Goodwood Mile-Gr2. Also 2nd 3 times, 3rd 3 times and 4th 3 times. Big, strong, well-made type. High-class miler, notably game and consistent. Effective on firm, good and good to soft ground. Well-bred. Half-brother to 4 winners, inc. Lord Of Appeal (Listed) and the dams of Kareymah (Gr3) and Diktat (Gr1). By a top-class sprinter-miler out of a champion 2yo filly. Stands at Kildangan Stud, Co. Kildare, Ireland, at a (2004) fee of €20,000. Sire of 2 crops of racing age, inc: Mac Love (Gr3), Mazuna (Gr3), Mokabra (Gr3), Ouija Board (Oaks S.-Gr1, Irish Oaks-Gr1, Breeders' Cup Filly & Mare Turf-Gr1).

Dam Selection Board

Ran only twice, placed 2nd in Ayr maiden at 2, unplaced at 3. Plain, leggy, evidently less than sound. Well-bred. Sister to top-class miler Teleprompter, half-sister to Chatoyant (c by Rainbow Quest; Gr3), Message Pad (c by Rousillon; Gr3-placed), and Rosia Bay (f by Blakeney; winner, dam of Gr1 winners Ibn Bey and Roseate Tern, grand-dam of Gr1-placed Red Camellia, 3rd dam of Gr1 winner Red Bloom). Same family as Owington and Kingston Town. Dam of: Officer Cadet (1987 c by Shernazar; winner), Draft Board (1989 f by Rainbow Quest; winner), Star Selection (1991 g by Rainbow Quest; Listed-placed winner), Pass Mark (1992 f by Never So Bold; placed), Cruinn A Bhord (1995 f by Inchinor; winner), Victor Ludorum (1996 f by Rainbow Quest; unraced), Spectrometer (1997 c by Rainbow Quest; winner), unnamed (1998 g by Rainbow Quest; unraced), Coalition (1999 g by Polish Precedent; winner), Ouija Board (2001 f by Cape Cross; Oaks winner), Illuminati (2002 g by Inchinor; unraced). Died in 2002.

Pedigree assessment

Green Desert's career at stud has been all about the generation of speed and, in keeping with his own racing exploits, his tendency has been to get rather more sprinters than milers. Cape Cross was slightly different, in that he excelled over a mile and appeared to get a shade further, but the best bet about the outcome of his mating with a full-sister to Teleprompter was surely a miler. It is clear now that other factors came into play. The great stayer Alycidon is four generations back, but a closer possible source of stamina is Ouija Board's broodmare sire, Welsh Pageant, who got many who stayed better than he did himself, including the Gold Cup victor, Longboat. What is certain is that Ouija Board derived stamina from somewhere that enables her to stay a mile and a half admirably in top company. It is splendid news that we shall see her again in 2005. *TM*

Paita

2yo bay filly   **109**

Intikhab (USA) - Prada (Ger) (Lagunas)

Owner M Hofer & Stall Steigenberger

Trainer Mario Hofer

Breeder Gestut Fahrhof

Career: **2** starts | won **2** | **£86,465** win and place

By Robert Carter

JOCKEY-turned-pinhooker Emma O'Gorman found a real bargain when she paid 10,000gns for an Intikhab filly, already named Patia, at the Tattersalls October Yearling Sales. One would have thought that this German-bred half-sister to a Preis der Diana (German Oaks) winner would have attracted plenty of German interest. But that did not emerge until O'Gorman sent her back to the same ring for the April Breeze-Up Sale. This time, she was bought by another former jockey, Manfred Hofer, who was German champion three times in the 1980s.

Hofer has become a very successful agent, among other things organising a number of syndicates, including Turf Syndikat 97, which owned the 1999 Deutsches Derby winner Belenus, and Turf Syndikat 2001, which had the 2004 Canadian International runner-up Simonas. He celebrated Belenus' Derby triumph in uproarious fashion, smoking a cigar while riding the colt into the winner's enclosure behind his jockey Kevin Darley. And he later accompanied the colt's trainer, his brother-in-law Andreas Wohler, for a swim, fully clothed, in the lake in the middle of the course.

Hofer paid 32,000gns at Newmarket, a price that looks a real bargain now. He sent her to be trained by yet another ex-jockey, his brother Mario, who, as the British turf season was ending, led all rivals in Germany on number of winners, a category in which he has just missed being top on more than one occasion.

Paita did not contribute to his domestic success. Like so many German horses these days, she made her debut in Italy in order that she was qualified to contest the many valuable conditions events, as well as the Group and Listed stakes that are open to all. Hofer sent two beginners on the long journey from his Krefeld stables to San Siro for a pair of nine-furlong races against fellow newcomers on October 13.

Paita scores a notable Group 1 victory for Germany in the Criterium de Saint-Cloud, ahead of Aidan O'Brien's Yehudi

Laredo Sound, a gelding by Singspiel, bred and owned by Gestut Olympia, contested the first of them, the Premio Casteletto Ticino. Starting 6-4 favourite in a field of eight, he followed the leader until going on more than a furlong from home and ran on to hold the Bruno Grizzetti-trained Blu Roman by three-quarters of a length.

Grizzetti had a much more strongly fancied candidate for the fillies' division, the Premio Alla Novella, in Colleen Mix. Paita was favourite but only fractionally, starting at 1.43-1 with Colleen Mix at 1.54-1. But Hofer let slip later that, if Laredo Sound could win, then Paita must have been a certainty, for she was much better than him at home. Colleen Mix set off in front, but Paita was covering her all the way and took over with a quarter of a mile to run, forging steadily clear to beat her market rival by six lengths.

Most German trainers use one of the best local jockeys for their raiders but Hofer brought down the Austrian-born Andreas Suborics, who was champion jockey in 2002 and held a long lead over his nearest rivals, Jean-Pierre Carvalho and the reigning champion Andrasch Starke, as British turf racing was ending. He followed up his October 13 double with a big-race treble four days later, including the Group 1 Gran Premio del Jockey Club Italiano on Shirocco (on whom he had also won the Deutsches Derby) and the Group 3 Premio Omenoni on the Mario Hofer-trained Raffelberger.

2004 Race record

1st Criterium de Saint-Cloud (Group 1) (Saint-Cloud, November 6) 2yo 10f Very soft **109** (TS 48) 7 ran. *Held up, close 6th straight, switched right 2f out, ridden 1f out, ran on to lead 100yds out, well in command close home (A Suborics), beat Yehudi by ¾l*

1st Premio Alla Novella (San Siro, October 13) 2yo 9f Soft. *Tracked leader, led 2f out, soon clear (A Suborics), beat Colleen Mix by 6l*

Paita runs in the name of Manfred Hofer but carries the red and white colours of his partner, Stall Steigenberger. Albert Steigenberger was once one of Germany's leading owners and had the homebred Platini, German Horse of the Year in 1992. That was also the year that he caused a bit of a stir in England, when his 1990 Deutsches St Leger winner Elsurimo finished sixth in the Goodwood Cup. Mark Rimmer appeared in the paddock with the legend 'Steigenberger Hotels' emblazoned across his back, the first time that a jockey's silks had ever carried advertising in Britain. A scandalised Jockey Club investigated and it was a few more years before the new BHB actually encouraged advertising. In the meantime Steigenberger had greatly reduced his involvement. He was the breeder of 22 foals in 1992 and of just six in 2002.

The Hofers knew they had a useful filly after Paita's easy debut score, but they were not expecting more than a place in the Criterium de Saint-Cloud, even after one of the leading candidates, the Group 3 Prix Thomas Bryon winner Vatori, had been scratched, leaving seven runners. Paita, who was drawn two, lightly bumped the Aidan O'Brien-trained Yehudi leaving the stalls and pushed him onto Laverock. The incident was not important, however, as first Eligibilis, then Yehudi, then Eligibilis again, set such a moderate pace.

Paita was at or near the back but never more than five lengths behind and settled without problem. Suborics had her sixth into the straight and switched her to the outside two furlongs from home. She responded well to a couple of slaps a furlong out and headed Yehudi with 100 yards to run. Paita was in command from that point and won by three-quarters of a length from the hard-ridden Yehudi, with Laverock one length back in third.

This was Germany's fourth Group-race success of the season in France. Martillo had won the Group 2 Prix du Muguet, Ryono the Group 3 Prix Messidor and Quilanga the Group 3 Prix de Psyche. It was also a first Group 1 success in France for Mario Hofer and a second for Suborics, victorious on A Magicman in the Prix de la Foret back in 1996. After her debut, the trainer said that Paita would be aimed for the Diana. Following the Criterium de Saint-Cloud, he substituted a final 'e' in place of the 'a'. Patia will be trained for the Prix de Diane, France's Oaks.

Paita

bay filly, 16-2-2002

			Hail To Reason
		Roberto	Bramalea
	Red Ransom		
		Arabia	Damascus
Intikhab			Christmas Wind
b 1994			
		Crafty Prospector	Mr Prospector
			Real Crafty Lad
	Crafty Example		
		Zienelle	Danzig
			Past Example
		Ile de Bourbon	Nijinsky
			Roseliere
	Lagunas		
		Liranga	Literat
Prada			Love In
br 1992			
		Abary	Roi Dagobert
			Antioquia
	Pradera		
		Pedra	Carcol
			Palmares

Bred by Gestut Fahrhof. 10,000gns Tattersalls October yearling, 32,000gns Tattersalls Breeze-up 2yo

Sire **Intikhab**

Won 8 of 14 starts from 2 to 5. At 2, won 2 (6f) of 3 starts. At 3, won 3 (1m, inc. 2 Listed races) of 6 starts. At 4, won 3 (8-9f) of 4 starts inc. Diomed S-Gr3, Queen Anne S-Gr2. At 5, unplaced sole start. By lightly raced, top-class US performer and very good sire. Dam unplaced, from family of top-class milers Culture Vulture and Polish Precedent. Stands at Derrinstown Stud in Ireland, 2004 fee €8,000. Oldest progeny 3, sire of: Paita (Criterium de Saint-Cloud-Gr1), Toupie (Gr3)

Dam **Prada**

Unraced at 2, won 3 of 8 starts at 3 in Germany inc. 10f Listed event. By Deutsches Derby winner out of 2yo/3yo winner. Dam of: Puntilla (1997 f by Acatenango; Preis der Diana-Gr2), Palanda (1998 f by Lando; unraced), Pailita (1999 f by Monsun; unraced), Palmeira (2000 f by Lomitas; winner), Paita (2002 f by Intikhab; Criterium de Saint-Cloud-Gr1), 2003 c by Xaar.

Pedigree assessment

Intikhab has injected some precocity into Paita, enabling her to excel at 2, but her ability to last 10f surely is down to her dam's family. There is every chance she will train on well from 2 to 3, and despite her sire she should stay 12f. *JH*

Papineau

4yo chestnut colt   **121**

Singspiel (Ire) - Early Rising (USA) (Grey Dawn)
Owner Godolphin
Trainer Saeed Bin Suroor
Breeder Exors of the late Peter Winfield

Career: **7** starts | won **5**   second **1**   third **0**   **£259,921** win and place

---

By Graham Dench

"**H**E'S the new Kayf Tara – maybe better," enthused Sheikh Mohammed, recalling his dual Ascot Gold Cup winner, who won eight Group races in all, including two Irish St Legers. "This horse has the class to win a Group 1 at a mile and a half," insisted Frankie Dettori.

Bold claims, both, but few who saw Papineau outspeed the outstanding French stayer Westerner in the Gold Cup would have argued. Unfortunately, while the King George and the Prix de l'Arc de Triomphe were among a series of Group 1 mile-and-a-half races that came under consideration for the four-year-old, we will have to wait until 2005 for those claims to be tested, for Papineau was not seen out again in public.

Papineau had less than a month in the limelight, but what a month it was. One of Godolphin's best-kept secrets at the start of the season, he made a big impression at Goodwood in May on his debut for the team, when he quickened up smartly once pulled towards the centre of the track by fellow Godolphin new boy Kerrin McEvoy and beat stablemate Songlark in style in a conditions event that was a Group race in all but name. What made his performance all the more impressive was that it was Papineau's first outing since his fifth to Dalakhani for Andre Fabre in the previous year's Prix du Jockey-Club, when he was the first beaten and returned with a chipped bone in a knee.

There was no mention of the Gold Cup in Goodwood's post-race debriefing, but a supplementary entry for Sandown's Henry II Stakes signalled his connections' intentions, and a length-and-a-half defeat of the 2003 Gold Cup hero Mr Dinos gave them all the encouragement they needed, even though Mr Dinos was conceding 7lb and was at a distinct disadvantage in what developed into something of a sprint finish. His stamina might not have been tested to everyone's satisfaction, but one could hardly have asked for more from him.

Papineau comes home clear of Westerner in the Gold Cup at Royal Ascot, but was not seen out again in 2004

If the Gold Cup field of 2004 did not quite match up to its immediate predecessor, it was not a bad one, for it featured two previous winners of the race in Mr Dinos and Royal Rebel, plus two St Leger winners in Brian Boru, who had won at Doncaster, and Westerner, who the previous autumn had been a runaway winner of the Prix du Cadran before confirming himself a stayer with a change of gear with another hugely impressive success in the Prix Royal-Oak, the French St Leger. What it lacked of course, was Persian Punch, who year in, year out, had ensured that the race was the gruelling test it was always intended to be.

Royal Ascot punters made Mr Dinos a warm order to reverse Sandown placings and repeat his 2003 success, but the pace was not strong enough for him and, after struggling to get past the Japanese front-runner Ingrandire three out, he was beaten straightening for home. Westerner looked the winner when the pacesetters folded, but he was in front plenty soon enough and in any case Dettori, who had begun his move on Papineau halfway down the back straight, always felt he could take him. Papineau was in front a furlong or so out and once there showed no sign of stopping. He passed the post a length and a half clear of Westerner, with Darasim third and Mr Dinos back in sixth.

It used to be common practice for Gold Cup winners to drop back to a mile and a half for the King George, and a similar move by Godolphin

2004   Race record

1st Gold Cup (Group 1) (Ascot, June 17) 4yo+ 2m4f Good to firm **121** (TS 103) 13 ran. *Dwelt, held up towards rear, headway 4f out, led 1f out, ridden out (L Dettori), beat Westerner by 1½l*

1st bonusprint.com Henry II Stakes (Group 2) (Sandown, May 31) 4yo+ 2m½f Good to firm **116** (TS 103) 9 ran. *Prominent, tracked leader over 2f out, pushed into lead well over 1f out, edged right final furlong, kept on (L Dettori), beat Mr Dinos by 1½l*

1st M-Real Conditions Stakes (Goodwood, May 19) 4yo+ 12f Good to firm **111** (TS 97) 14 ran. *Held up, headway over 2f out, short of room and switched over 1f out, strong run to lead inside final furlong and went clear (K McEvoy), beat Songlark by 2½l*

2003

5th Prix du Jockey-Club (Group 1) (Chantilly, June 1) 3yo 12f Good **102** 7 ran ● **1st** Prix de l'Avre (Listed) Longchamp, May 15) 3yo 12f Good 5 ran ● **1st** Prix d'Ellon (Saint-Cloud, April 28) 3yo Colts & Geldings 12f Soft 6 ran ● **2nd** Prix Aveu (Saint-Cloud, April 2) 3yo Colts & Geldings 12f Good to soft 7 ran

with their 1996 Gold Cup winner Classic Cliche was rewarded with second place behind Pentire. Papineau certainly looked better equipped for the task than other recent Gold Cup winners, and bookmakers took the idea seriously, Paddy Power quoting him at just 12-1, despite the stable having two far more obvious candidates in Doyen and Sulamani.

However he missed the race, having reportedly suffered from a bruised foot, and the Grosser Preis von Baden, which was mooted as a possible next target, also passed without him. Although he still figured prominently in lists for the Prix de l'Arc de Triomphe it was announced at the beginning of September that he had suffered another setback and was out for the remainder of the season.

Papineau is a big, strong, heavy-topped colt, and therein lies the problem. He is clearly not easy to keep sound, and when he resumes action as a five-year-old he will have just seven races to his name. There is every chance we have yet to see the best of him, but connections will want to choose his targets carefully. The Gold Cup, in which he would be bidding to emulate Kayf Tara, would represent the easier option, but it would prove little and easy options have seldom appealed to Sheikh Mohammed.

Provided he returns fit and well Papineau will surely be given the chance to confirm his class and versatility by landing one of the top mile-and-a-half races. His half-brother Silver Patriarch, the 1997 St Leger winner, won two Group 1 races at the trip, on the first occasion beating Swain no less in the Coronation Cup. Epsom might not suit Papineau ideally, but there are plenty of attractive alternatives, and he may yet get his chance in the King George. He remains a horse to look forward to.

Papineau

chestnut colt 6-4-2000

		Sadler's Wells	Northern Dancer / Fairy Bridge
Singspiel b 1992	In The Wings	High Hawk	Shirley Heights / Sunbittern
	Glorious Song	Halo	Hail To Reason / Cosmah
		Ballade	**Herbager** / Miss Swapsco
Early Rising gr 1980	Grey Dawn	**Herbager**	Vandale / Flagette
		Polamia	Mahmoud / Ampola
	Gliding By	Tom Rolfe	Ribot / Pocahontas
		Key Bridge	Princequillo / Blue Banner

Bred by Executors of the late Peter Winfield. 85,000gns Tattersalls December foal

Sire Singspiel

Won 9 of 20 races, inc. Gordon Richards S.-Gr3, Select S.-Gr3, Canadian International S.-Gr1, Japan Cup-Gr1, Coronation Cup-Gr1, Eclipse S.-Gr1, York International S.-Gr1. Also 2nd in Coronation Cup and Breeders' Cup Turf at 4. Strong, medium-sized (15.3 1/2hh), quite attractive, lengthy type. Tough, game and consistent performer, effective on any ground, top-class from 10-12f. Retired after having fractured off-fore cannon shortly before 1997 Breeders' Cup Turf. Sire of: Moon Ballad (Dubai World Cup-Gr1), Papineau (Gold Cup-Gr1), Puppeteer (Gr3), Songlark (Gr3), Sweet Folly (Gr3), Via Milano (Gr3), Nouvelle Noblesse (Gr3).

Dam Early Rising

Won 1 of 9 races. Very big (17.0 hh), but well-made and a good mover, with excellent temperament. Dam of: Fort Riley (1985 g by Timeless Moment; won 11 races), Mississippi Music (1986 g by The Minstrel; unraced), Silver Singing (1987 f by Topsider; won 5 races), Count Of Nine (1988 c by Spectacular Bid; won 3 races), Spectacular Dawn (1989 f by Spectacular Bid; won 4 races), My Patriarch (1990 c by Be My Guest; Gr3 winner), Brave Patriarch (1991 g by Alzao; winner), unnamed (1992 c by Royal Academy; suffered paddock accident, destroyed), Silver Patriarch (1994 c by Saddlers' Hall; Classic winner), Regal Patriarch (1995 c by Marju; unplaced), Silver Grey Lady (1998 f by Saddlers' Hall; Listed-placed winner), Papineau (2000 c by Singspiel; Gr1 winner), unnamed (2001 c by Unfuwain; died as a foal). She has a yearling filly by Singspiel, and was covered by him again in 2003. She was not covered in 1995, was barren to In The Wings in 1997, to Sadler's Wells in 1999, and to Polish Precedent in 2002.

Pedigree assessment

Papineau's rise to Gold Cup glory was one of the most welcome developments in the first half of the season, his complete absence from the second half a wretched disappointment. Here was a colt who had started third favourite for the 2003 Prix du Jockey-Club and, because of a knee injury incurred in that race, had become sidelined for nearly a year. Another long layoff, as soon as he had established himself as a colt of rare proven versatility, came as a cruel blow. If he returns once more, fit and well, he will be a serious candidate at the top level over a variety of distances. As the son of a horse who improved with age, and half-brother to others who distinguished themselves as older horses, chances are that he still has improvement to make. *TM*

Percussionist (Ire)

3yo bay colt   **121**

Sadler's Wells (USA) - Magnificient Style (USA) (Silver Hawk (USA))

Owner Sangster Family

Trainer J H M Gosden

Breeder Swettenham Stud

Career: **10** starts   won **2**   second **2**   third **2**   **£133,394** win and place

By Mark Blackman

NYONE who has ever stood near the winner's circle at the Cheltenham Festival will know jump racing can bring raw emotion to the surface in a way that Flat racing rarely does. The summer game, with its heavy preoccupation with future stallion fees and black type, is protected by such a crust of commercialism that sentimentality scarcely gets a look-in at the highest level.

For a few weeks in the late spring of 2004, though, the largely unheralded Percussionist threatened to write one of the most poignant chapters in Turf history. When he lined up as the 7-1 fourth favourite for the Epsom Derby, the beautifully bred colt wasn't running for his future in the breeding sheds. He was running for Robert.

Robert Sangster – co-founder of the Coolmore empire, pioneer of stallion shuttling and the most influential owner-breeder of his generation – had lost his long battle against pancreatic cancer on April 7. Six days later, Percussionist, who had shown promise when placed in a couple of maidens at two, got off the mark over 12 furlongs at Newmarket in Sangster's famous blue, green and white colours.

Those colours had been carried to victory in the Derby by The Minstrel and Golden Fleece, but he had never bred the winner. Glacial Storm, Blue Stag and City Honours had all gone close in second. Could Percussionist, a product of his wonder-sire Sadler's Wells, finally be the one to end the hoodoo in the first running of the Classic after Sangster's death?

Percussionist's next test was the Lingfield Derby Trial, and he lined up as the 11-4 third-favourite in a field of four. Handling the soft conditions admirably, he led three furlongs out and simply stretched further and further clear, despite veering from the inside of the track to the wide outside. By the line, he had ten lengths to spare over the progressive Listed winner Hazyview.

Gosden put Percussionist's erratic course down to an aversion to the mobile Channel 4 camera on the inside of the track. The colt had also

Percussionist starts with a victory at Newmarket, before going on to a trial win at Lingfield and fourth in the Derby

been edgy in the preliminaries, and perhaps it was the doubts about his readiness for the Derby Day razzmatazz that caused him to be offered at 40-1 for the Derby immediately afterwards. Certainly on bare form, he deserved to be a good bit shorter.

That Percussionist's odds should have tumbled so much by post time, without him setting foot on the track, owed much to the dearth of serious contenders. Trials had been won by geldings and handicap graduates, and several starters had stamina doubts. Percussionist was regarded as a potential St Leger candidate if he fell short at Epsom – he would stay all day.

Percussionist became a little uneasy in the saddling enclosure when his earplugs were removed, but the explosion of temperament that some feared failed to materialise. As the stalls opened, Kevin Darley was able to get a good position in the opening furlong, but maintaining it soon became hard work. He turned into the straight in about eighth, his cause seemingly lost, but as others came to the end of their tether he kept up his gallop. North Light had flown straightening for home, but in behind Percussionist

2004   Race record

5th Prix Royal-Oak (Group 1) (Longchamp, October 24) 3yo+ 1m7½f Heavy **110** (TS 73) 8 ran. *Led until headed 4f out, 2nd straight, soon weakened (J Fortune), beaten 10l by Westerner*

6th Gran Premio del Jockey Club (Group 1) (San Siro, October 17) 3yo+ 12f Soft **109** 9 ran. *Slowly into stride, soon prominent, 5th and pushed along straight, headway under pressure well over 1f out, nearest at finish (J Fortune), beaten 7l by Shirocco*

3rd Prix Chaudenay Casino Barriere de Menton (Group 2) (Longchamp, October 2) 3yo 1m7f Good **110** (TS 109) 7 ran. *First to show, settled in 4th, close 5th straight on outside, stayed on at one pace final 2f (L Dettori), beaten 7l by Reefscape*

2nd Weatherbys Bank Stakes (Registered As The Doonside Cup) (Listed) (Ayr, September 18) 3yo+ 11f Soft **119** (TS 95) 6 ran. *In touch, driven along over 4f out, disputed 2nd over 3f out, outpaced over 2f out, stayed on under pressure to regain 2nd inside final furlong (K Darley), beaten 5l by Into The Dark*

10th Budweiser Irish Derby (Group 1) (Curragh, June 27) 3yo 12f Good to firm 10 ran. *Never travelling, dropped to rear halfway, soon weakened, completely tailed off (K Darley), beaten 69+l by Grey Swallow*

4th Vodafone Derby Stakes (Group 1) (Epsom, June 5) 3yo 12f Good **121** (TS 118) 14 ran. *Prominent but soon pushed along, lost place downhill and 8th straight, progress to chase winner 200yds out, kept on gamely, lost 2 places on post (K Darley), beaten 2l by North Light*

1st Gallagher Group Ltd Derby Trial Stakes (Group 3) (Lingfield, May 8) 3yo 11½f Soft **116** (TS 74) 4 ran. *Tracked leaders, went 2nd over 7f out, pressed leader 5f out, led inside final 3f, ridden, hung badly right and came clear throughout final furlong (L Dettori), beat Hazyview by 10l*

1st Warren Hill Maiden Stakes (Newmarket, April 13) 3yo 12f Good to soft **93** (TS 63) 8 ran. *Chased leaders, ridden over 4f out, stayed on under pressure to lead inside final furlong (K Darley), beat Chaplin by 1½l*

2003

2nd betfair.com Maiden Stakes (Yarmouth, October 29) 2yo 1m Soft **75** 19 ran ● **3rd** Ford Magic EBF Maiden Stakes (Sandown, September 17) 2yo 1m Good **69** 11 ran

was making ground and places. Passing the furlong pole, he surged into second place, for just a stride or two looking as though he might mount a serious challenge. Equally quickly, though, his exertions took their toll and he flattened out. The fast-finishing Rule Of Law and Let The Lion Roar relegated him to fourth in the dying strides.

Derby Day was as good as it got for Percussionist. He ran abysmally on fast ground in the Irish equivalent, missed the St Leger and ran well below his Epsom form in four starts in Britain, France and Italy in the autumn, including when tackling staying distances.

On the balance of his form, he had been flattered in the Derby, but perhaps that simply illustrates how narrow the margin can be between the great and the good in Flat racing. If he'd just found another another two lengths, he'd have been heading for his place in immortality. Instead, his future lies over jumps following his sale for 340,000 Guineas to Graham Wylie at Doncaster Sales in November.

Percussionist

bay colt, 06-4-2001

			Nearco
		Nearctic	Lady Angela
	Northern Dancer		Native Dancer
		Natalma	Almahmoud
Sadler's Wells			
b 1981			**Hail To Reason**
		Bold Reason	Lalun
	Fairy Bridge		Forli
		Special	Thong
			Hail To Reason
		Roberto	Bramalea
	Silver Hawk		Amerigo
		Gris Vitesse	Matchiche
Magnificent Style			
b 1993			**Nearctic**
		Icecapade	Shenanigans
	Mia Karina		Tom Rolfe
		Basin	Delta

Bred by Swettenham Stud in Ireland

Sire Sadler's Wells

Won 6 of 11 races, inc. Beresford S.-Gr3, Irish Derby Trial-Gr2, Irish 2,000 Guineas-Gr1, Eclipse S.-Gr1, Phoenix Champion S.-Gr1. Also 2nd in Prix du Jockey-Club-Gr1, King George VI & Queen Elizabeth S.-Gr1. Impeccably bred top-class performer from 8-12f, handsome, tough and consistent. Sire of Gr1 winners: Braashee, French Glory, In The Wings (x3), Old Vic (x2), Prince Of Dance, Scenic, Salsabil (x5), Opera House (x3), Runyon, Saddlers' Hall, El Prado, Johann Quatz, Masad, Barathea (x2), Fatherland, Fort Wood, Intrepidity (x3), Carnegie (x2), King's Theatre (x2), Northern Spur (x2), Moonshell, Muncie, Poliglote, Chief Contender, Dance Design, Darazari, Luna Wells, Cloudings, Ebadiyla (x2), Entrepreneur, In Command, Kayf Tara (x4), Dream Well (x2), Greek Dance, King Of Kings (x2), Leggera, Commander Collins, Daliapour, Montjeu (x6), Saffron Walden, Aristotle, Beat Hollow (x4), Subtle Power, Galileo (x3), Imagine (x2), Milan, Perfect Soul, Sequoyah, Sligo Bay, Ballingarry, Black Sam Bellamy (x2), Gossamer (x2), High Chaparral (x6), Islington (x4), Quarter Moon, Sholokov, Alberto Giacometti, Brian Boru (x2), Doyen, Powerscourt, Refuse to Bend (4), Yesterday, Quiff, Playful Act.

Dam Magnificent Style

Won 2 of 11 races, inc. Musidora S.-Gr3. Briefly showed smart form in England, placed 4 times without success in US. Half-sister to US Gr1 winner Siberian Summer. Remotely connected with European Gr1 winners Taipan, Ali-Royal and Sleepytime. Dam of: Styleistick (1999 f by Storm Cat; Listed winner, Gr3-placed in US), Echoes In Eternity (2000 f by Spinning World; Gr2 winner), Percussionist (2001 c by Sadler's Wells; Gr3 winner), Playful Act (2002 f by Sadler's Wells; Gr1 winner). She has a yearling filly by Danehill and a colt foal by Peintre Celebre, and is currently in foal again to Sadler's Wells.

Pedigree assessment

A brother to Playful Act and half-brother to Echoes In Eternity, Percussionist promised much when he followed his rout of Hazyview in the Lingfield Derby Trial with a bold effort at Epsom, robbed of a place in the shadow of the post. After several more tries, his potential remains unfulfilled. The fast ground on the Curragh's Derby day undoubtedly troubled him, and that experience came at the wrong time for a colt who had previously shown himself to be a nervous sort who had not grown up mentally. It will be interesting to see how he takes to his new role. Horses with his level of Flat form are seldom given a chance over jumps and he has the physique for it. *TM*

Persian Punch (Ire)

11 yo chestnut gelding **120**

Persian Heights - Rum Cay (USA) (Our Native (USA))

Owner J C Smith

Trainer D R C Elsworth

Breeder Adstock Manor Stud

Career: **63** starts | won **20** | second **8** | third **11** | **£1,008,785** win and place

By Lee Mottershead

H E IS the one horse who should not feature in this book, yet this book would be sorely incomplete without him. For despite not completing a single race in 2004, Persian Punch generated more emotion than any other horse did or could for the rest of the year.

The death of Persian Punch, or more accurately the manner in which it came, represented modern Flat racing's darkest day. On a grey, dank and drizzly April afternoon at Ascot, one of the most popular horses ever to grace the sport lost his life in the most dramatic and heartbreaking circumstances. Only a heart of stone could have failed to be moved.

There had been such anticipation that morning. Ever since the mighty horse brought his magnificent 2003 campaign to such a glorious conclusion at Newmarket, his return had been eagerly awaited. When the afternoon of the Sagaro Stakes finally came, there came with it the sense of once again being united with the dearest of friends. Something that had been missing had returned. And we were glad.

Yet only minutes after we had first caught sight of him strolling proudly around the Ascot pre-parade ring he was gone again, and this time he was gone for good. The memory of that race will live long and painfully in the memory. For much of the contest, everything seemed to be going just as we would have liked it to have gone. Appearing to shrug off the atrociously soft conditions, the old warrior was in front as the Sagaro field swung right to race down the far side. Bold and attacking in the pole position he had adopted so many times before, in front he stayed until just before the home turn. Even then, there was much to be pleased about in his seasonal reappearance. But from satisfaction to dejection – how quickly things changed.

There is no need here to go into the precise details of what happened, except to remark upon the sad irony in the manner in which Persian Punch died, the horse having taken himself to the point of exhaustion

Persian Punch at Ascot before his final, tragic appearance in the Sagaro. His death cast a pall over the early season

until, for the first time in his life, he went beyond that point, so far indeed that he reached the point of no return. If there had been a pre-ordained way for Persian Punch to say the last goodbye, it was surely like this.

The following five races passed in an almost eerie quiet. While Martin Dwyer fulfilled his riding duties for the rest of the card, trainer David Elsworth and owner Jeff Smith – both with Persian Punch for the final moments – left Ascot as soon as possible. With the Sagaro meeting having been dropped from terrestrial schedules for the first time, news of what had happened crept out gradually but, once it had, it dominated sports bulletins.

Writing in The Independent the following day, Richard Edmondson noted that "a horse and a little bit of racing died at Ascot yesterday". He was right. Since winning his first race, a Windsor maiden, at odds of 20-1 in May 1996, a large, lumbering, yet somehow graceful, horse had increasingly captivated an entire sport. And not just in Britain. Twice sent to the other side of the world, he became a hero in Australia with two third-place finishes in the Melbourne Cup. They were both honourable defeats, right up there with his many outstanding successes;

2004   Race record

Pulled Up Bovis Homes Sagaro Stakes (Group 3) (Ascot, April 28) 4yo+ 2m Soft 13 ran. *Led after 3f, headed 4f out, soon ridden, weakened over 2f out, collapsed and died final furlong (Martin Dwyer)*

Career wins

2003 1st Jockey Club Cup (Group 3) (Newmarket, October 18) 3yo+ 2m Good to firm **119** 6 ran ● 1st GNER Doncaster Cup (Group 2) (Doncaster, September 11) 3yo+ 2m2f Good **120** 6 ran ● 1st Lady O Goodwood Cup (Group 2) (Goodwood, July 31) 3yo+ 2m Good **119** 9 ran ● 1st Addleshaw Goddard Stakes (Registered As The Esher Stakes) (Listed) (Sandown, July 5) 4yo+ 2m½f Good to firm **113** 5 ran **2002** 1st Jockey Club Cup (Group 3) (Newmarket, October 19) 3yo+ 2m Good **117** 8 ran ● 1st Catisfield Hinton And Stud Conditions Stakes (Salisbury, September 5) 3yo+ 1m6f Good to firm **110** 5 ran **2001** 1st Weatherbys Insurance Lonsdale Stakes (Group 3) (York, August 21) 3yo+ 2m Good **122** 10 ran ● 1st JPMorgan Private Bank Goodwood Cup (Group 2) (Goodwood, August 2) 3yo+ 2m Good **123** 12 ran **2000** 1st Jockey Club Cup (Group 3) (Newmarket, October 14) 3yo+ 2m Good to soft **124** 9 ran ● 1st Prix Kergorlay Groupe Lucien Barriere (Group 2) (Deauville, August 20) 3yo+ 1m7f Good to soft **116** 7 ran ● 1st Bonusprint Stakes (Registered As The Henry II Stakes) (Group 3) (Sandown, May 29) 4yo+ 2m½f Heavy **113** 7 ran **1999** 1st Dransfield Novelty Company Conditions Stakes (Doncaster, November 5) 3yo+ 1m6½f Soft **104** 5 ran **1998** 1st Weatherbys Insurance Lonsdale Stakes (Group 3) (York, August 18) 3yo+ 2m Good to firm **115** 5 ran ● 1st Bonusprint Henry II Stakes (Group 3) (Sandown, May 25) 4yo+ 2m½f Good **116** 11 ran ● 1st Sagaro Stakes Group 3 (Newmarket, May 1) 4yo+ 2m Good to soft **118** 10 ran **1997** 1st Bonusprint Henry II Stakes (Sandown, May 26) 4yo+ 2m½f Good to firm **106** 7 ran ● 1st Quantel Aston Park Stakes (Newbury, May 17) 4yo+ 1m5½f Soft **114** 6 ran **1996** 1st Bahrain Trophy (Listed) (Newmarket (July), July 11) 3yo 1m7f Good to firm **100** 6 ran ● 1st Bishopstone Conditions Stakes (Salisbury, June 11) 3yo 1m6f Good **88** 5 ran ● 1st Bowring Group Median Auction Maiden Stakes (Windsor, May 13) 3yo 10f Good to firm **76** 18 ran

three Jockey Club Cups, three Henry II Stakes, two Goodwood Cups, two Lonsdale Stakes, a Doncaster Cup, a Sagaro Stakes, a Prix Kergorlay, an Esher Stakes and a Bahrain Trophy.

Ridden by 14 different jockeys at 13 different racecourses in four different countries in two different hemispheres, he had deservedly attained iconic status. That status, though, was earned as much because of how he achieved what he did as because of the achievements themselves. As Elsworth said, "if ever a horse did take on human qualities, particularly of response and affection, then he did." No wonder then, that on the first anniversary of his final victory in the 2003 Jockey Club Cup, Newmarket announced plans to build a life-size sculpture of the horse.

Understandably, the passing of Persian Punch moved many to tears. Yet in life, his heroism, spirit and desire to please had done the same. When his legion of fans think of him, they may still shed a tear, but they will do so for the right reasons. And they will smile. And so they should.

Persian Punch · *chestnut gelding, 13-4-1993*

		Bold Lad	Bold Ruler
	Persian Bold		Barn Pride
Persian Heights		Relkarunner	Relko
ch 1985			Running Blue
	Ready and Willing	Reliance	Tantieme
			Relance
		No Saint	Narrator
			Vellada
	Our Native	Exclusive Native	Raise a Native
			Exclusive
Rum Cay		Our Jackie	Crafty Admiral
ch 1985			Rakahanga
	Oraston	Morston	Ragusa
			Windmill Girl
		Orange Cap	Red God
			Hymette

Bred by Adstock Manor Stud in Ireland. 14,000gns Tattersalls October yearling

Sire Persian Heights

Won 4 of 10 races, inc. St James's Palace S.-Gr1. Also disqualified 'winner' of York International-al, 2nd in Champion S. Quite well-bred, rangy, handsome horse, and a game, consistent per-former with a sharp turn of foot. Died in March 1993. Sire of: Persian Brave (Gr3), Persian Punch (Gr2 x 4, Gr3 x 9).

Dam Rum Cay

Ran only 3 times at 4 years, winning a 2m bumper and a 14.6f maiden. Leggy, angular type. Dam of: Visual (1990 c by Rousillon; winner), Island Magic (1991 c by Indian Ridge; Gr3 winner), Persian Punch (1993 g by Persian Heights; multiple Pattern winner), Rum Baba (1994 g by Tirol; winner), Cobra Lady (1995 f by Indian Ridge; unplaced), Bahamas (1997 g by Barathea; winner), Red Bartsia (1998 f by Barathea; winner), Wadmaan (1999 c by Singspiel; placed), Bourbonella (2000 f by Rainbow Quest; unraced), Grand Bahama (2002 c by Singspiel; unraced to date). She has a yearling colt by Mozart.

Pedigree assessment

The most exciting moments on the racecourse in 2003 were provided by Persian Punch. How indescribably cruel that he should also provide the saddest moment on the racecourse in 2004. He was a huge public favourite, the like of which probably had not been seen since the retirement of Brown Jack 70 years ago, and there were many similarities between the pair, although one could never win at Ascot, whereas the other always did. Both were geldings who kept winning until ten years old, excelling over long distances, and each owned a pedigree that provided no hint of an outstanding career. Persian Heights got only one other Pattern winner during his brief innings at stud, and Rum Cay's only other runner of much consequence was a Group 3 winner at two. Punch was a one-off, a marvel who defied explanation. *TM*

Pivotal Point

4yo bay gelding   **119**

Pivotal - True Precision (Presidium)

Owner R A Bernard

Trainer P J Makin

Breeder T R Lock

Career: **13** starts   won **5**   second **3**   third **1**   **£179,915** win and place

By Bill Barber

ROM problem pupil to potential head boy – that might be the school report for Pivotal Point, who ended 2004 a prime candidate for championship honours in the sprint division in 2005.

Originally with Linda Perratt, Pivotal Point's initial attitude towards racing was very much like that of many boys when first sent to school. He hated it, twice had to be withdrawn at the start, and remained unraced until he was three. By that time, in order to be close to 'horse whisperer' Gary Witherford, he had been moved south to join Peter Makin, who described him on arrival as "a great big bruiser" and had him gelded.

Pivotal Point made steady progress in 2003, ending the term with decent efforts in a classy handicap at Ascot and a conditions race at Newmarket, yet there was no sign that he would reach the heights he has.

Neither were the portents that encouraging on his first two starts of 2004, although he did have excuses both times. He pulled too hard on his seasonal debut at York in May, finishing tenth behind Quito in a rated stakes, and filled the same slot from a poor draw in a valuable handicap at Windsor the following month.

Both those runs had been over six furlongs but he was dropped to the minimum trip for his next run in a Class C handicap at Ascot in July where, ridden by Frankie Dettori, he ran out a one-length winner.

Makin was now in a quandary. The Ascot win incurred just a 3lb penalty for the Stewards' Cup but the trainer still felt Pivotal Point was a typical Pivotal and might find the ground too quick at Goodwood. The alternative was the Hong Kong Jockey Club Sprint, run over the course and distance he had just won over on potentially better ground six days beforehand, but in that race the penalty was a stiff 8lb. In the end he ran in both. He nearly won both, too.

Pivotal Point continues his rise with victory in the Group 2 Diadem Stakes, having earlier won the Stewards' Cup

In a field of 24 at Ascot, where he was ridden by Johnny Murtagh, Pivotal Point showed terrific speed and failed by just a neck to hold Baltic King. On to Goodwood where, as ever, the draw was the big talking point before the race, with high stalls traditionally favoured. At the 'draw for the draw' there was a headlong rush for the far side. When Makin eventually had his turn he had little choice but to plump for stall one, where Pivotal Point would at least have a rail to run against.

Ignoring past results, punters latched on to Pivotal Point, ridden on this occasion by the in-form Seb Sanders, and backed him down to 7-1 co-favourite. Although he did not break as well as usual, he was clearly cruising with two furlongs to run and quickened up impressively to score by a length and a quarter from Fantasy Believer, who had come from a mile back to 'win' what was almost a separate race on the far side.

Stepped up to Group 3 class and back to five furlongs in the Prix du Petit Couvert at Longchamp in September, Pivotal Point saw off none other than The Tatling by a length, although he did receive 6lb from the runner-up. Dettori, reunited with the four-year-old, noticed the improvement he had made in just a couple of months and said: "I rode him earlier in the season and he is certainly a different horse now."

1st GNER Diadem Stakes (Group 2) (Ascot, September 25) 3yo+ 6f Good to firm **119** 12 ran. *Took keen hold, tracked leader, led over 1f out, soon ridden clear (S Sanders), beat Airwave by 3l*

5th Dubai International Airport World Trophy (Group 3) (Newbury, September 18) 3yo+ 5f Good **106** (TS 107) 11 ran. *Chased leaders, ridden halfway, outpaced inside final furlong (L Dettori), beaten 3l by The Tatling*

1st Prix du Petit Couvert (Group 3) (Longchamp, September 5) 3yo+ 5f Good to soft **117** (TS 83) 9 ran. *Always close up on rails, led well over 1f out, driven out (L Dettori), beat The Tatling by 1l*

1st Vodafone Stewards' Cup (Heritage Handicap) (Goodwood, July 31) 3yo+ 6f Good to firm **106** (TS 93) 28 ran. *Slowly into stride, soon tracked near side leaders, going easily 2f out, ridden to lead over 1f out, edged right but in command final furlong (S Sanders), beat Fantasy Believer by 1 1/4l*

2nd Hong Kong Jockey Club Sprint (Heritage Handicap) (Ascot, July 25) 3yo+ 5f Good to firm **106** (TS 77) 24 ran. *Disputed lead far side, definite advantage 1f out, worn down final 50yds (J P Murtagh), beaten nk by Baltic King*

1st Millennium & Copthorne Hotels Handicap (0-100) (Ascot, July 10) 3yo+ 5f Good **104** (TS 99) 8 ran. *Made virtually all, shaken up 1f out, stayed on well (L Dettori), beat Jimmy Ryan by 1l*

10th Royal Marbella Group Quality Homes Abroad Stakes (Heritage Handicap) (0-105) (Windsor, June 26) 3yo+ 6f Good to firm **66** (TS 50) 16 ran. *Behind, headway halfway, soon ridden, weakened 2f out (D Sweeney), beaten 12l by Zilch*

10th Langleys Solicitors Rated Stakes (0-105 handicap) (York, May 13) 4yo+ 6f Good to soft **50** (TS 9) 14 ran. *Pulled hard, close up until weakened quickly over 2f out (S Sanders), beaten 18l by Quito*

2nd Newmarket Thanks The Red Cross Conditions Stakes (Newmarket, October 31) 2-3yo 6f Good **98** 9 ran ● **5th** ladbrokes.com Handicap (0-110) (Ascot, October 11) 3yo+ 5f Good to firm **78** 20 ran ● **3rd** Letheby And Christopher Rated Stakes (0-95 handicap) (Newmarket (July), June 28) 3yo 6f Good to firm **93** 9 ran ● **1st** Bet attheraces Maiden Stakes (Windsor, June 1) 3yo 6f Good to firm **82** 18 ran ● **2nd** Butler & Co Equine Tax Planning Maiden Stakes (Div I) (Salisbury, May 4) 3yo+ 6f Good to soft **74** 17 ran

A blip occurred when Pivotal Point could finish only fifth behind The Tatling at Newbury 13 days later, but Makin was inclined to blame the loose ground, for by now it was clear that Pivotal Point is very well suited by fast going, and it had been much quicker than the official good to soft at Longchamp. Brought back quickly for the Group 2 Diadem Stakes at Ascot, run around a bend due to the redevelopment of the course, he romped home by three lengths from Airwave. While the unusual circumstances raised a legitimate question mark over the form, it was still the performance of his life.

Those three quick runs ruled out a crack at the Prix de l'Abbaye, but he looks sure to be a major force in top-level sprints in 2005, both at five furlongs and six. There is every chance that this once errant pupil will end up top of his class.

Pivotal Point
bay gelding, 2-3-2000

		Nureyev	Northern Dancer
	Polar Falcon		Special
		Marie d'Argonne	Jefferson
Pivotal			Mohair
ch 1993		Cozzene	Caro
	Fearless Revival		Ride The Trails
		Stufida	Bustino
			Zerbinetta
		General Assembly	Secretariat
	Presidium		Exclusive Dancer
		Doubly Sure	Reliance
True Precision			Soft Angels
b 1990		Sparkler	Hard Tack
	Madam Muffin		Diamond Spur
		Northern Lady	The Brianstan
			Lady From Aske

Bred by T R Lock in Britain. 9,000gns Doncaster St Leger yearling

Sire **Pivotal**

Won 4 of 6 races, inc. King's Stand S.-Gr2, Nunthorpe S.-Gr1. Powerfully built, attractive sort, high-class sprinter on preferred fast ground, seemingly best at 5f. Stands at Cheveley Park Stud, 2005 fee £65,000. Sire of: Golden Apples (Del Mar Oaks-Gr1, Beverly D S.-Gr1, Yellow Ribbon S.-Gr1), Kyllachy (Nunthorpe S.-Gr1), Low Pivot (Gr3), Needwood Blade (Gr3), Ratio (Gr3), Silvester Lady (Preis der Diana-Gr1), Captain Rio (Gr2), Chorist (Pretty Polly S.-Gr1), Megahertz (John C. Mabee H.-Gr1), Ringmoor Down (Gr3), Stolzing (Gr3), Humouresque (Gr3), Pivotal Point (Gr2), Somnus (Haydock Sprint Cup-Gr1, Prix Maurice de Gheest-Gr1, Prix de la Foret-Gr1), Windsor Knot (Gr3).

Dam **True Precision**

Placed over 5f at 2, later won 3 races over 5-7f at 3 and 4, from total of 26 runs. Fair sprint handicapper, won 0-105 Coral Handicap at Newmarket in 1993. By very smart 2yo half-brother to Kris/Diesis who has modest stud record but is also maternal grandsire of 2004 Grade 2 winner Mr O'Brien. Dam placed daughter of triple 2yo winner, no stakes winners in family until Pivotal Point's sixth dam Puff Adder (foaled 1941), ancestress of Gr1 Irish St Leger winners M-Lolshan and Vinnie Roe. Dam of: Foreign Editor (1996 c by Magic Ring; winner), Uncle Exact (1997 c by Distant Relative; winner), Hot Pants (1998 f by Rudimentary; winner), Pivotal Point (2000 c by Pivotal; Gr2 winner), True Magic (2001 f by Magic Ring; winner), 2003 f by Lujain.

Pedigree assessment

It is no surprise Pivotal Point should be a sprinter. Talented sons of his sire Pivotal tend to be fast, while the dam was speedy and has pace in excess of stamina in her pedigree. Pivotal Point, however, has shown far more talent than any other descendant of his fifth dam. It is easy to give the credit to Pivotal, who has come up with a number of good runners from modest backgrounds. But it is also worth crediting True Precision, who won the 0-105, 6f Coral Sprint Handicap at Newmarket off a mark of 73 and put in several decent efforts off marks in the 80s. She has a 100 per cent win record from her foals, all of whom have struck at sprint trips and all of whom were sold as yearlings for less than 10,000gns. Pivotal Point is still youthful compared to a number of other top current sprinters, and expect him to be a major force again in 2005. *JH*

Playful Act (Ire)

2yo bay filly   **113**

Sadler's Wells (USA) - Magnificient Style (USA) (Silver Hawk (USA))

Owner Sangster Family

Trainer J H M Gosden

Breeder Swettenham Stud

Career: **4** starts | won **3** | second **1** | **£65,255** win and place

By Lee Mottershead

AFTER Doncaster John Gosden was convinced. He had just watched Playful Act carry the late Robert Sangster's colours to victory in the May Hill Stakes. He knew exactly what her long-term target was, and what her long-term target wasn't. "We won't even mess around with a Guineas preparation," he declared in the Town Moor winner's enclosure. "Stamina looks to be her strong suit and we see her as an Oaks filly." Playful Act would bid for Classic glory at Epsom. Newmarket wasn't even on the agenda.

Then came Ascot. Ascot changed his mind. Going into the Meon Valley Stud Fillies' Mile, Playful Act was already ante-post favourite for the Vodafone Oaks. After Ascot, and a resounding 'go to whoa' triumph, the enthusiastic daughter of Sadler's Wells was as short as 12-1 for Newmarket, and her trainer had altered his opinion. "She'll head straight to Newmarket," said the master of Manton, standing on the soon-to-be-dug-up Ascot turf. "If she's training great we'll be having a real good go at the Guineas." Suddenly Playful Act was a dual Classic contender.

Her pedigree entitles her to be just that. One of the principal contributors to her incomparable father's 14th coronation as Britain's champion sire, Playful Act is hardly let down on her distaff side either. A daughter of the Musidora Stakes winner Magnificient Style, she played out her juvenile season in the same year that her half-sister Echoes In Eternity posted a second Group victory in the Park Hill Stakes and her full-brother Percussionist dotted up in the Lingfield Derby Trial en route to a fourth-place finish in the big race at Epsom. Three extremely talented horses, they have not only their mother in common. They also have Sangster.

Robert Sangster's submission to pancreatic cancer at the premature age of 67 in April 2004 robbed the racing and bloodstock industry of a truly towering figure. One of the sport's leading owners and breeders for

Playful Act, left, lands the Fillies' Mile at Ascot, to put herself in the reckoning for both the Guineas and Oaks

over 30 years, his famous blue, green and white silks were carried to victory in most of the world's major contests, including the Derby, King George, Prix de l'Arc de Triomphe, Melbourne Cup and Breeders' Cup Mile. A pioneer of the most audacious variety, Sangster was instrumental in changing the face of international bloodstock in the mid-1970s, joining forces with the legendary Vincent O'Brien and John Magnier in a concentrated effort to buy leading stallion prospects from the Keeneland sales ring. Bolstered by the Vernon pools family fortune, he bought them, and they excelled, winning a plethora of top-flight contests for a man whose name will forever be linked with the likes of Alleged, El Gran Senor, The Minstrel, Golden Fleece and Assert, as well as the mighty Sadler's Wells himself. Many of his equine ambassadors were also bred by him, horses like Echoes In Eternity and Percussionist. Horses like Playful Act.

Sangster died before Playful Act even set foot on a racecourse, but in just four races she has already ensured that his legacy has become even richer. Not seen out until August, she made her debut in a seven-furlong

1st Meon Valley Stud Fillies' Mile (Group 1) (Ascot, September 25) 2yo 1m Good to firm **113** (TS 108) 9 ran. *Made all, driven 2l clear well over 1f out, stayed on under pressure (J Fortune), beat Maids Causeway by 1l*

1st betfair.com May Hill Stakes (Group 2) (Doncaster, September 9) 2yo 1m Good **110** (TS 105) 8 ran. *Tracked 1st two, quickened to lead over 1f out, held on well (J Fortune), beat Queen Of Poland by ³⁄₄l*

1st Beaches Resorts EBF Maiden Fillies' Stakes (Div II) (Newmarket (July), August 27) 2yo 7f Soft **82** (TS 44) 9 ran. *Made all, pushed out (J Fortune), beat Naivety by 1³⁄₄l*

2nd Hoofbeats Tours Maiden Fillies' Stakes (Newmarket (July), August 14) 2yo 7f Good to soft **82** (TS 54) 14 ran. *Slowly in to stride, held up, headway over 2f out, ran on, no chance with winner (R Havlin), beaten 2¹⁄₂l by Cassydora*

maiden on Newmarket's July course. That she had ability was immediately apparent. Slowly away – something that she wouldn't repeat in any of her three subsequent races – and soon with plenty to do, she came from an uncompromising mid-race position, making up ground hand over first inside the final quarter-mile to take an eye-catching second. This was a run that augured well for the future, an impression underlined when a return trip to the same course and distance two weeks later yielded an easy all-the-way success.

With her pedigree and potential, there was never much doubt that Playful Act would soon dip her hooves into Group-race waters. When she did, in the May Hill, she did everything her connections could have wanted, and more. Comprehensively reversing form with her first-time-out conqueror, Cassydora, Playful Act sat in the slipstream of a strong pace, quickening to lead over a furlong out before showing a willing attitude to repel Queen Of Poland and Maids Causeway.

That willing attitude would be in evidence once again at Ascot, where Playful Act was upped from Group 2 to Group 1 company for Britain's premier staying prize for juvenile females.

The 2004 edition of the Fillies' Mile was arguably a less than vintage one. It was indisputably a rough one, though not for Playful Act. While further back, the hot and heavily touted favourite Echelon got into all sorts of trouble, Playful Act and Jimmy Fortune enjoyed a hassle-free trip. Sending his mount to the front from the start, Fortune maximised his horse's guaranteed stamina, setting a painful pace that none of her rivals could ever better. At least two lengths clear entering the final furlong, Playful Act's lead was eaten into by Maids Causeway and Dash To The Top close home, but never did she look like being beaten, and she wasn't.

"I'm not surprised she's favourite for Epsom," said Gosden. "She has the form to go with her stamina-filled pedigree."

Such a statement from someone like Gosden makes you sit up and take notice. In Playful Act, he has a genuine Oaks candidate, who might even land a blow in the Guineas. The Sangster torch continues to burn bright.

Playful Act   *bay filly 12-4-2002*

Sadler's Wells b 1981	Northern Dancer	**Nearctic**	Nearco
			Lady Angela
		Natalma	Native Dancer
			Almahmoud
	Fairy Bridge	Bold Reason	**Hail To Reason**
			Lalun
		Special	Forli
			Thong
Magnificient Style b 1993	Silver Hawk	Roberto	**Hail To Reason**
			Bramalea
		Gris Vitesse	Amerigo
			Matchiche
	Mia Karina	Icecapade	**Nearctic**
			Shenanigans
		Basin	Tom Rolfe
			Delta

Bred by Swettenham Stud in Ireland

Sire Sadler's Wells

Won 6 of 11 races, inc. Beresford S.-Gr3, Irish Derby Trial-Gr2, Irish 2,000 Guineas-Gr1, Eclipse S.-Gr1, Phoenix Champion S.-Gr1. Also 2nd in Prix du Jockey-Club-Gr1, King George VI & Queen Elizabeth S.-Gr1. Impeccably bred top-class performer from 8-12f, handsome, tough and consistent. Sire of Gr1 winners: Braashee, French Glory, In The Wings (x3), Old Vic (x2), Prince Of Dance, Scenic, Salsabil (x5), Opera House (x3), Runyon, Saddlers' Hall, El Prado, Johann Quatz, Masad, Barathea (x2), Fatherland, Fort Wood, Intrepidity (x3), Carnegie (x2), King's Theatre (x2), Northern Spur (x2), Moonshell, Muncie, Poliglote, Chief Contender, Dance Design, Darazari, Luna Wells, Cloudings, Ebadiyla (x2), Entrepreneur, In Command, Kayf Tara (x4), Dream Well (x2), Greek Dance, King Of Kings (x2), Leggera, Commander Collins, Daliapour, Montjeu (x6), Saffron Walden, Aristotle, Beat Hollow (x4), Subtle Power, Galileo (x3), Imagine (x2), Milan, Perfect Soul, Sequoyah, Sligo Bay, Ballingarry, Black Sam Bellamy (x2), Gossamer (x2), High Chaparral (x6), Islington (x4), Quarter Moon, Sholokov, Alberto Giacometti, Brian Boru (x2), Doyen, Powerscourt, Refuse to Bend (4), Yesterday, Quiff, Playful Act.

Dam Magnificient Style

Won 2 of 11 races, inc. Musidora S.-Gr3. Briefly showed smart form in England, placed 4 times without success in US. Half-sister to US Gr1 winner Siberian Summer. Dam of: Stylestick (1999 f by Storm Cat; Listed winner, Gr3-placed in US), Echoes In Eternity (2000 f by Spinning World; Gr2 winner), Percussionist (2001 c by Sadler's Wells; Gr3 winner), Playful Act (2002 f by Sadler's Wells; Gr1 winner). She has a yearling filly by Danehill and a colt foal by Peintre Celebre, and is currently in foal again to Sadler's Wells.

Pedigree assessment

Until 2004 only one broodmare had been represented by three individual Pattern winners in the same season. That record was set by Alidiva, whose successful trio in 1997 were Taipan, Ali-Royal and Sleepytime, all at Group 1 level. Magnificent Style, who has the same third dam (Delta) as Alidiva, notched a hat-trick of her own with Percussionist in the Group 3 Lingfield Derby Trial, Echoes In Eternity in the Group 2 Park Hill Stakes and Playful Act in the Group 1 Fillies' Mile. The youngest of the group has the potential to be the best, and in view of her full-brother's fine effort in the Derby, it was understandable that she should figure as a leading winter favourite for the Oaks. She looks a more straightforward individual than her brother, and at Doncaster and Ascot displayed a thoroughly admirable attitude. *TM*

Pleasantly Perfect (USA)

6yo bay horse **128**

Pleasant Colony (USA) - Regal State (USA) (Affirmed (USA))

Owner Diamond A Racing Corporation

Trainer Richard E Mandella

Breeder Clovelly Farms

Career: **18** starts   won **9**   second **3**   third **2**   £4,576,346 win and place

By James Willoughby

THERE is no denying that top-class dirt racing takes horses to the edge. The competition is fierce and attritional in nature; horses effectively trade punches from the bell and the last one standing wins. This environment requires a horse who wants to run hard. Sheer force of will is a much larger part of racing merit than on turf.

When the irresistible force meets the immovable object, the result can be epic confrontation: Ferdinand and Alysheba; Sunday Silence and Easy Goer; Affirmed and Alydar, to name just three.

Pleasantly Perfect and Medaglia d'Oro can be added to this list. Their rivalry was resolved in favour of the former in the latest Dubai World Cup, but its context was provided by the 2003 Breeders' Cup Classic.

That Santa Anita contest was to provide two pitched battles in one. The common element was Medaglia d'Oro, the Bobby Frankel-trained colt whose world-class ability was undermined by only the merest chink in his resolution. This foible was never seriously exposed until he looked one of similar talent in the eye.

Medaglia d'Oro was involved in a fierce struggle with Congaree from the moment the stalls opened. By the home straight, Medaglia d'Oro had won the battle, but he had nothing left to win the war. The late-running Pleasantly Perfect felled him with a single blow and won by a length and a half. It was a decisive result, but was it an entirely fair fight?

When it was announced four months later that Pleasantly Perfect and Medaglia d'Oro would spearhead a four-strong US challenge for the Dubai World Cup, a great race was instantly in the offing. This time, there would be no Congaree to provide Pleasantly Perfect with indemnity from Medaglia d'Oro's speed.

Sure enough, the pace was honest but not breakneck, and the tactical situation that ensued was nowhere near so detrimental to Medaglia d'Oro. The Frankel runner was comfortable on the shoulder of the leader,

Pleasantly Perfect beats his old rival Medaglia d'Oro after an enthralling battle in the Dubai World Cup

Fleetstreet Dancer, with Pleasantly Perfect closer behind than was usual for him. The pace began to increase halfway down the back straight, but Jerry Bailey, on board Medaglia d'Oro, chose to bide his time; Alex Solis on Pleasantly Perfect was forced to bide his.

Mindful not to give his rival a target, Bailey waited until the straight to send Medaglia d'Oro for home. Instantly, Solis eased Pleasantly Perfect into a striking position and uncorked his finishing burst. The trailer had conceded a two-length advantage, and this time there was more life in his rival's legs.

A terrific struggle followed. Pleasantly Perfect reached the throat latch of the leader sooner than expected. Rather than this being the trigger for Medaglia d'Oro to raise the white flag, he seemed to redouble his efforts. The two eyeballed each other and synchronised strides only briefly, however, as Pleasantly Perfect's momentum and desire proved irresistible to his foe. He triumphed, with such authority as if to subdue his rival forever, by three-quarters of a length. Fair and square.

According to some in the US, a trip to the desert is supposed to leave its mark on a horse, and Medaglia d'Oro never raced again. Pleasantly Perfect, however, continued his run of success at the highest level in the Pacific Classic at Del Mar in August, using the traditional prep of

2004

3rd Breeders' Cup Classic - Powered by Dodge (Grade 1) (Dirt) (Lone Star Park, October 30) 3yo+ 10f Fast **121** 13 ran. *Held up towards rear, good headway on outside from 3f out, ridden when carried wide and 6th straight, stayed on same pace (J D Bailey), beaten 7l by Ghostzapper*

1st Pacific Classic (Grade 1) (Del Mar, August 22) 3yo+ 10f Fast **126** 8 ran. *Raced keenly in 6th early, headway over 2f out, bumped by Total Impact 1½f out, led approaching final furlong, driven out (J D Bailey), beat Perfect Drift by 1l*

2nd San Diego Handicap (Grade 2) (Del Mar, August 1) 3yo+ 1m½f Fast **123** 7 ran. *Close up when tightened up first turn, pulled way into lead halfway, soon headed, led again 2f out, went 1½l clear, headed and no extra final 100yds (M E Smith), beaten ¾l by Choctaw Nation*

1st Dubai World Cup (Group 1) (Dirt) (Nad Al Sheba, March 27) 3yo+ 10f Fast **128** (TS 114) 12 ran. *Tracked leaders, 3rd straight, headway over 2f out, led over 1f out, stayed on well under pressure (A Solis), beat Medaglia d'Oro by ¾l*

1st San Antonio Handicap (Grade 2) (Santa Anita, January 31) 4yo+ 9f Fast 4 ran. *Pulled hard early, tracked leaders, effort 2f out to lead entering final furlong, drifted into rail, pushed out, easily (A Solis), beat Star Cross by 4l*

2003

1st Breeders' Cup Classic - Powered by Dodge (Grade 1) (Santa Anita, October 25) 3yo+ 10f Fast **128** 10 ran ● **1st** Goodwood Breeders' Cup Handicap (Grade 2) (Santa Anita, October 4) 3yo+ 9f Fast **118** 8 ran ● **4th** Santa Anita Handicap (Grade 1) (Santa Anita, March 1) 4yo+ 10f Fast **108** 6 ran ● **3rd** San Antonio Handicap (Grade 2) (Santa Anita, February 2) 4yo+ 9f Fast **117** 6 ran

Other runs

2002 1st Goodwood Breeders' Cup H'cap (Grade 2) (Santa Anita, October 6) 3yo+ 9f Fast 9 ran ● **4th** Pacific Classic (Grade 1) (Dirt) (Del Mar, August 25) 3yo+ 10f Fast 14 ran ● **1st** Claimer (Del Mar, August 4) 1m½f Fast 7 ran ● **1st** Allowance Race (Hollywood Park, June 20) 1m½f Fast 6 ran ● **2nd** Claimer (Santa Anita, April 6) 1m½f Fast 9 ran ● **1st** Maiden (Santa Anita, February 27) 1m Fast 5 ran ● **4th** Maiden (Santa Anita, February 13) 9f Firm 9 ran ● **2nd** Maiden (Santa Anita, January 27) 1m½f Fast 7 ran **2001 Pulled Up** Maiden (Hollywood Park, May 31) 1m½f Firm 10 ran

the Grade 2 San Diego Handicap there three weeks earlier. In the latter contest, he was defeated at odds-on by a talented runner named Choctaw Nation, though it was not totally surprising given that he needed the race.

The last two bouts of Pleasantly Perfect's career were due to be the Breeders' Cup Classic and the Japan Cup. He never got as far as the Orient, however, as the disappointment of his seven-length third at Lone Star Park was followed by the diagnosis of a near-hind ankle injury.

Pleasantly Perfect retired to William Farish's Lane's End Farm in Kentucky at a fee of $40,000, after the former US ambassador to Britain bought an interest in him from the Diamond A Racing Corporation. The son of 1981 Kentucky Derby winner Pleasant Colony won 19 races and ranks as the fourth-leading money earner in his country's racing history with $7,789,880. He fought hard for every cent.

Pleasantly Perfect

bay horse, 2-4-2001

Pleasant Colony b 1978	His Majesty	Ribot	Tenerani / Romanella
		Flower Bowl	Alibhai / Flower Bed
	Sun Colony	Sunrise Flight	Double Jay / Misty Morn
		Colonia	Cockrullah / Nalga
Regal State ch 1983	Affirmed	Exclusive Native	Raise A Native / Exclusive
		Won't Tell You	Crafty Admiral / Scarlet Ribbon
	La Trinite	Lyphard	Northern Dancer / Goofed
		Promessa	Darius / Peseta

Bred by Clovelly Farms in Kentucky. $725,000 Keeneland September yearling

Sire Pleasant Colony

Won 6 of 14 races, inc. Remsen S.-Gr2, Wood Memorial S.-Gr1, Kentucky Derby-G1, Preakness S.-Gr1, Woodward S.-Gr1. Champion 3yo colt. Big (16.3hh), strong individual. Not precocious, but developed top-class form under new trainer in spring at 3, effective from 9f up, stayed 12f. Retired from stud after 1999 season, died December 2002. Sire of 18 crops of racing age, inc Gr1 winners: Pleasant Variety (San Luis Rey S.), Cherokee Colony (Flamingo S.), Colonial Waters (John A. Morris H.), Pleasant Tap (Suburban H., Jockey Club Gold Cup, Roanoke (Californian S.), Sir Beaufort (Santa Anita H.), Shared Interest (Ruffian H.), Pleasant Stage (Breeders' Cup Juvenile Fillies S.), St Jovite (Irish Derby, King George VI & Queen Elizabeth S.), Colonial Affair (Belmont S., Whitney H., Jockey Club Gold Cup), Behrens (Gulfstream Park H. [twice], Oaklawn H.), Forbidden Apple (Manhattan H.), Denon (Hollywood Derby, Charles Whittingham Memorial H., Turf Classic Invitational, Manhattan H.), Colonial Colony (Stephen Foster H.), Pleasantly Perfect (Breeders' Cup Classic, Dubai World Cup, Pacific Classic).

Dam Regal State

Won 2 of 12 starts, inc. Prix Morny-Gr1. High-class, effective from 6-8f and on any going. By a US Triple Crown winner who did quite well at stud out of a Gr3-placed winner whose dam was a sister to Oaks winner Pia (grand-dam of Gr1 sprinter-miler Chief Singer). Dam of: Royal Tern (1989 c by Arctic Tern; placed twice in France), Law's Delay (1990 c by Alleged; unraced), Etoile Ascendante (1991 f by Arctic Tern; unplaced in 9 starts in France), Eben Naas (1993 g by Dayjur; winner in England), Hurricane State (Gr3 winner in France), Nuts In May (1997 f by A.P. Indy; unplaced in 4 starts in England), Pleasantly Perfect (1998 c by Pleasant Colony; triple Gr1 winner), Highclere Memory (2000 f by Cryptoclearance; unplaced in 8 starts in England), Swagger Stick (2001 c by Cozzene; winner in England), Cavalry Charge (2002 c by Honour And Glory).

Pedigree assessment

If we were not entirely convinced of Pleasantly Perfect's merit in 2003, when his Breeders' Cup Classic win seemed to represent much better form than he had ever shown before, after his 2004 efforts we have to concede: yes, he really was that good. In Dubai and at Del Mar he gave displays of similar calibre to his BC performance at Santa Anita. He may well have been the best of his sire's numerous notable US-raced stock, and he was certainly the best out of his dam, whose speed and precocity he did not inherit. *TM*

Powerscourt

4yo bay colt **124**

Sadler's Wells (USA) - Rainbow Lake (Rainbow Quest (USA))

Owner Mrs John Magnier

Trainer A P O'Brien

Breeder Juddmonte Farms

Career: **15** starts | won **4** | second **5** | third **3** | **£623,981** win and place

---

By James Willoughby

"**B**EING young is greatly overestimated. Any failure seems so total. Later on, you realise you can have another go." Mary Quant's philosophical response to early misadventure should be of only so much comfort to Jamie Spencer. Like fashion designers, retained jockeys can be in one day and out the next.

Butterfly collars and kipper ties will be back in vogue before Spencer forgets his association with Powerscourt. The 24-year-old endured severe criticism after two of America's biggest races. In the first, he could have avoided disqualification. In the second, he took a sizeable gamble and it did not come off.

Powerscourt thereby ended his season in deep frustration. He could so easily have been anointed as a triple Group/Grade 1 winner. But, while his jockey will get a shot at redemption, the colt's own best chance of elevated status has probably gone.

It all started so well. In May, Spencer took up the reins for the first time on Powerscourt in the Group 1 Tattersalls Gold Cup at The Curragh. If not an open goal, the race certainly had the appearance of a soft target after Sulamani was scratched. And, on this occasion, Powerscourt's aim was true.

Allowed to bowl along in front, Powerscourt was able to use his energy smoothly and efficiently. He picked up strongly from two furlongs out and strode home six lengths clear of Livadiya with a good deal of authority.

Powerscourt gave his stallion prospects a significant upgrade with this mile-and-a-quarter success. His three-year-old season had been spent competing mainly over longer distances, culminating in a fine third to Vinnie Roe and Gamut in the Irish St Leger over a mile and six furlongs.

A stud career is that much more lucrative if a horse can display a measure of pace, however. Powerscourt's reappearance seemed to prove his

Powerscourt comes first at Arlington, but rival rider Kent Desormeaux's whip-waving is the prelude to demotion

versatility, but there remained a doubt over whether his acceleration would remain deadly against more hostile opponents.

His next three starts seemed to suggest not. While he ran a fine race to finish second to Rakti in the Prince of Wales's Stakes at Royal Ascot, his fifth to Refuse To Bend in the Eclipse and, worse still, odds-on defeat in Germany, seemed to suggest that he needed a return to longer distances.

With this in mind, Powerscourt looked a lamb to the slaughter when connections went ahead with their plan to run in the Arlington Million. The firm ground and tight bends would surely place the accent on pace to an untenable degree.

Powerscourt confounded this suggestion in the most dramatic fashion. Settled back from a wide draw, he travelled strongly behind an honest pace. Making ground as the field compacted towards the end of the back straight, he looked sure to take a hand.

2004

3rd John Deere Breeders' Cup Turf (Grade 1) (Lone Star Park, October 30) 3yo+ 12f Yielding **119** 8 ran. *Missed break, raced in 6th, good headway to lead over 3f out, driven over 1½f out, ran on until headed just inside final furlong, no extra close home (J P Spencer), beaten 2¾l by Better Talk Now*

3rd Baileys Irish Champion Stakes (Group 1) (Leopardstown, September 11) 3yo+ 10f Good to firm **124** (TS 125) 8 ran. *Close up in 2nd, led entering straight, soon quickened clear, strongly pressed over 1f out, headed under 1f out, kept on (J P Spencer), beaten ¾l by Azamour*

4th Arlington Million XXII (Grade 1) (Arlington, August 14) 3yo+ 10f Firm **118** 13 ran. *Held up in 10th, headway around outside from over 2f out, led and hung left 1f out (J P Spencer), finished 1st, beat Kicken Kris by 1½l, disqualified and placed 4th*

2nd Grosser Dallmayr-Preis Bayerisches Zuchtrennen (Group 1) (Munich, August 1) 3yo+ 10f Good **115** 9 ran. *Set strong pace, headed 100yds out, one pace (J P Spencer), beaten 1½l by Intendant*

5th Coral-Eclipse Stakes (Group 1) (Sandown, July 3) 3yo+ 10f Good to soft **118** (TS 106) 12 ran. *Prominent, led 4f out to 3f out, stayed with leader, every chance over 1f out, faded inside final furlong (J P Spencer), beaten 5l by Refuse To Bend*

2nd Prince of Wales's Stakes (Group 1) (Ascot, June 16) 4yo+ 10f Good to firm **122** (TS 114) 10 ran. *Tracked leaders, effort 2f out, ridden to chase winner just over 1f out, stayed on but never able to challenge (J P Spencer), beaten 2l by Rakti*

1st Tattersalls Gold Cup (Group 1) (Curragh, May 23) 4yo+ 10½f Good to firm **122** (TS 101) 6 ran. *Made all, quickened clear 2f out, stayed on well, easily (J P Spencer), beat Livadiya by 6l*

2003

3rd Irish Field St Leger (Group 1) (Curragh, September 13) 3yo+ 1m6f Good to firm **121** 6 ran ● **1st** Daily Telegraph Great Voltigeur Stakes (Group 2) (York, August 19) 3yo 12f Good to firm **121** 9 ran ● **1st** Seapoint Race (Leopardstown, July 16) 3yo+ 10f Good **112** 5 ran ● **6th** Budweiser Irish Derby (Group 1) (Curragh, June 29) 3yo 12f Good **110** 9 ran

Other runs

2002 **2nd** Racing Post Trophy (Group 1) (Doncaster, October 26) 2yo 1m Soft **111** 9 ran ● **1st** www.punchestown.com EBF Maiden (Punchestown, October 17) 2yo 7½f Soft **92** 17 ran ● **2nd** JRA London Office's 10th Anniversary Maiden Stakes (Newmarket, October 2) 2yo 1m Good to firm **102** 6 ran ● **2nd** Orpen EBF Maiden (Naas, August 5) 2yo 7f Yielding to soft **85** 16 ran

Spencer's first decision was a good one. Rather than burrow up the inside – as is often his wont – he elected to take a no-nonsense path around the outside. This is the preferred tactic on US turf courses, whose short straights allow precious little time for waiting in traffic.

Powerscourt's response was total. He looped the field with profound acceleration, leaving talented rivals behind on his inner, despite covering more ground. By the time the stagger unwound entering the home straight, it seemed as if he had built up sufficient momentum to roll home unopposed.

But the observer guilty of preoccupation with Powerscourt was oblivious to the charge of Kicken Kris. His jockey Kent Desormeaux had taken the contrasting route to Spencer, with the consequent lack of room causing delay.

Kicken Kris could not shake loose while Powerscourt struck for home. Finally, a hole appeared for him on the inside, but the door was slammed shut again almost instantaneously when the tiring Epalo edged left. Contiguous to the German runner was Powerscourt, and the subsequent head-on review revealed that it was he who had initiated a knock-on effect by hanging left.

A second look at the race immediately cast Spencer as the villain of the piece. His mount's fleet of foot had required his rider's sleight of hand. Rather than using his whip as a magician would a magic wand, however, he had wielded it as a castigator would a cudgel. The correction Powerscourt required was of a defter manner: merely for Spencer to switch his whip hand and straighten his course.

Once Kicken Kris had recovered his poise, he went after the leader with a venom. Ground was running out, however, and Powerscourt had a decisive advantage. He passed the post a length and a half clear, in his wake Desormeaux gesticulating wildly that he had been wronged.

While it required a leap of faith to believe that Kicken Kris would have bridged the eventual margin of a length and a half with a clear run, it was inevitable that the winner's number would be taken down. Under local rules, the significant detail is that Powerscourt was the cause of interference to both runner-up Kicken Kris and fourth-placed Epalo, and that he may have improved his placing as a result. He was therefore placed behind the latter.

So Powerscourt returned to Ballydoyle the equivalent of roughly £100,000 light. He had four weeks to get over his trip to Chicago before the Irish Champion Stakes at Leopardstown in September. It was clearly enough to restore his energy levels.

Powerscourt ran another huge race, following the tearaway Godolphin pacemaker Millstreet until quickening clear off the home turn. He had done too much, too soon, however, and tired inside the final furlong. Norse Dancer was the first to get to him, but he, in turn, was collared by the patiently ridden Azamour.

As Powerscourt prepared for his next assignment, the Breeders' Cup Turf at Lone Star Park, one wondered whether his sequence of excellent efforts and mounting total of air-miles would finally catch up with him. In the event, there was no change to his performance level – and nor to his luck.

For all his undoubted toughness and talent, Powerscourt had also revealed a wayward streak during the campaign. He had more than once meandered in front, though to assume from this proclivity a lack of commitment on his part would be going a little too far. The most obvious facet of his racing character was that he did not like bullying, particularly if it resulted in premature exposure to the front.

That, however, is exactly how Spencer treated him once again. On rain-soaked ground, which was somewhere between good-to-soft and good by British standards, the quarter-mile splits for the mile-and-a-half Turf were as follows: 24.90, 24.26, 24.80, 26.18, 24.01, 25.55. In other words, the fastest part of the race came between four and two furlongs out – exactly where Powerscourt was forced to go clear.

The video corroborates the official chart recording that Powerscourt went from half a length down on the leader Star Over The Bay to two lengths clear, an individual split of 23.61sec. This was an ill-timed move. A thoroughbred can maintain top speed for only two furlongs, and Powerscourt duly came home in 26.1sec, which is not going to win many Breeders' Cup Turfs.

Anyone can make a mistake, and the sectionals also throw significant light on the reason why Spencer made his move. The pace had slowed dramatically just before this juncture and Powerscourt had been able to get into striking position without doing extra work. Perhaps sensing this lull, and mindful that the hot favourite Kitten's Joy was armed with an incredible burst of speed, Spencer tried to steal a march.

It was the right thing to do, but the wrong horse to do it on. While there is always a degree of exoneration for every tactical error a jockey makes, the objective assessment of races allows no room for intention nor motive.

Racing generally allows far too much sentiment to enter the equation in this regard. On the day, Spencer had a split-second decision to make and erred. It is impossible to know for sure whether he would have beaten the winner Better Talk Now, rather than finishing two and three-quarter lengths third. Equally, nobody – least of all Spencer himself – should fail to recognise that races on flat tracks are rarely won with such uneven distribution of energy.

Following the Breeders' Cup, Spencer was roundly condemned in the US, not just for his ride on Powerscourt, but also his earlier effort on Antonius Pius in the Mile. The most scathing came from the Daily Racing Form's Mike Watchmaker: "Jamie Spencer's rides in this country make more than a few wonder what such an astute trainer as Aidan O'Brien sees in him."

Most journalists are especially fond of criticising foreign riders, and it must be remembered that Kieren Fallon received similar reviews for his early Breeders' Cup forays on Borgia and Islington. Now, Fallon has many in the US eating out of his hand, with the result that he was invited to ride at Churchill Downs in November.

At the time of writing, it was planned that Powerscourt will return to training as a five-year-old and take in the same programme of races.

The chance for sweet revenge in the US could therefore be waiting for Spencer. And, given his level of talent, who would bet against him taking it? After all, it even took the Spice Girls a while to catch on over there.

Powerscourt

bay colt, 1-4-2000

Sadler's Wells b 1981	Northern Dancer	Nearctic	Nearco / Lady Angela
		Natalma	Native Dancer / Almahmoud
	Fairy Bridge	Bold Reason	Hail To Reason / Lalun
		Special	Forli / Thong
Rainbow Lake b 1990	Rainbow Quest	Blushing Groom	Red God / Runaway Bride
		I Will Follow	Herbager / Where You Lead
	Rockfest	Stage Door Johnny	Prince John / Peroxide Blonde
		Rock Garden	Roan Rocket / Nasira

Bred by Juddmonte Farms in England

Sire Sadler's Wells

Won 6 of 11 races, inc. Beresford S.-Gr3, Irish Derby Trial-Gr2, Irish 2,000 Guineas-Gr1, Eclipse S.-Gr1, Phoenix Champion S.-Gr1. Also 2nd in Prix du Jockey-Club-Gr1, King George VI & Queen Elizabeth S.-Gr1. Impeccably bred top-class performer from 8-12f, handsome, tough and consistent. Sire of Gr1 winners: Braashee, French Glory, In The Wings (x3), Old Vic (x2), Prince Of Dance, Scenic, Salsabil (x5), Opera House (x3), Runyon, Saddlers' Hall, El Prado, Johann Quatz, Masad, Barathea (x2), Fatherland, Fort Wood, Intrepidity (x3), Carnegie (x2), King's Theatre (x2), Northern Spur (x2), Moonshell, Muncie, Poliglote, Chief Contender, Dance Design, Darazari, Luna Wells, Cloudings, Ebadiyla (x2), Entrepreneur, In Command, Kayf Tara (x4), Dream Well (x2), Greek Dance, King Of Kings (x2), Leggera, Commander Collins, Daliapour, Montjeu (x6), Saffron Walden, Aristotle, Beat Hollow (x4), Subtle Power, Galileo (x3), Imagine (x2), Milan, Perfect Soul, Sequoyah, Sligo Bay, Ballingarry, Black Sam Bellamy (x2), Gossamer (x2), High Chaparral (x6), Islington (x4), Quarter Moon, Sholokov, Alberto Giacometti, Brian Boru (x2), Doyen, Powerscourt, Refuse To Bend (4), Yesterday, Quiff, Playful Act.

Dam Rainbow Lake

Won 3 of 6 races, inc. Lancashire Oaks-Gr3. Lean, leggy type in training. High-class performer at best, successful on firm, good and soft ground. Sister and half-sister to 5 other winners, inc. Vertex (c by Shirley Heights; Listed in Italy). By a top-class runner and sire, out of a Gr3-placed winner. Dam of: Brimming (1995 c by Generous; winner), Barbican (1996 c by Caerleon; unplaced), Unaware (1997 g by Unfuwain; winner), Polish Lake (1998 f by Polish Precedent; unraced), Lake Of Dreams (1999 g by Polish Precedent; unplaced), Powerscourt (2000 c by Sadler's Wells; Gr1 winner), Kind (2001 f by Danehill; winner), Marella (2002 f by Desert Prince; unraced to date). She has a yearling colt by Zafonic and a colt foal by Sadler's Wells.

Pedigree assessment

One of several high-class performers by Sadler's Wells bred on a foal-sharing arrangement by Juddmonte Farms, Powerscourt enjoyed a splendid season as a four-year-old – and not as the kind of horse many might have supposed him to be after his close third in the 2003 Irish St Leger. He was clearly one of the best around at ten furlongs, displaying his talents in four different countries. Surprisingly, he is the only Pattern winner to date sired by Sadler's Wells from a daughter of his old racecourse rival Rainbow Quest; the link would have seemed a natural to produce an honest, classy performer, but it may be that breeders have worried about a possible excess of stamina. Powerscourt may have dispelled some fears. *TM*

Prince Kirk (Fr)

4yo bay colt   **121**

Selkirk (USA) - Princess Manila (Can) (Manila (USA))

Owner Scuderia Pieffegi

Trainer E Borromeo

Breeder Srl So Li Ca

Career: **16** starts   won **6**   second **5**   third **3**   **£311,419** win and place

---

By Robert Carter

IRST-TIME blinkers helped to produce an early-season surprise, when Prince Kirk beat Six Perfections by half a length in the Group 1 Prix d'Ispahan. Looking from one direction, it could be represented as a total surprise, for Prince Kirk had run 13 times in Italy and only two of those races had been in Group company. He had run two and a half lengths second to Le Vie dei Colori in the Group 2 Premio Parioli but only tenth of 11, behind the same horse, in the Group 1 Premio Vittorio di Capua.

On the other hand, he had made two previous journeys to France, also in 2003, running second to Vespone in the Group 1 Prix Jean Prat and third to Kalabar and Saturn in the Group 2 Prix Guillaume d'Ornano. Prince Kirk's record may reveal more about his trainer Emilio Borromeo's careful planning than about his own ability.

The d'Ispahan might have looked like a match between Six Perfections and Nebraska Tornado, but Prince Kirk was supported at 66-10, much shorter than his remaining two rivals, his former stablemate Sunstrach, now trained by Luca Cumani and third in a Group 3 on his English debut four weeks earlier, and the Mick Channon-trained Checkit.

Prince Kirk broke with the others but was snatched back to race fourth with only Six Perfections behind him. Checkit appeared to be setting a true pace but by halfway, at which point Prince Kirk was last, the pursuers were all keen to go faster. Prince Kirk remained last until two furlongs from home, where he tried to edge to the outside. But Six Perfections blocked his way and so jockey Marco Monteriso sent him through a gap between Sunstrach and Nebraska Tornado. Six Perfections reached the front one furlong out but Prince Kirk was already under a strong drive on the rails and headed her more than 100 yards from home. He jumped five or six strides from home and brushed the rail, much as Antonius

Prince Kirk, left, upsets Six Perfections to land the Group 1 Prix d'Ispahan in May, but was not seen again in 2004

Pius had done in the Poule d'Essai des Poulains seven days earlier, but it did not stop him.

Just as Ioritz Mendizabal had done with Ask For The Moon in the Prix Saint-Alary half an hour earlier, Monteriso was winning his first Group 1. The son of a trainer, he had made a bright start to his riding career and won the Group 2 Premio Guido Berardelli on Shibuni's Falcon in November 1999, when a 19-year-old apprentice. He had his best season with 86 winners in 2000 and accepted a contract to ride for Andreas Lowe in Germany in 2002, but this was not a success and it took time to re-establish himself at home.

There were other hands involved, quite literally, in this triumph. Borromeo was quick to pay tribute to Dr Dominique Giniaux, who had made a special journey to his Pisa stables to treat the horse. Giniaux qualified as a vet at Toulouse but was not interested in ordinary practice. After studying osteopathy at Bobigny, outside Paris, he became a pioneer

2004   Race record

1st Prix d'Ispahan (Group 1) (Longchamp, May 23) 4yo+ 9f Good **121** (TS 81) 5 ran. *Held up, last straight, ridden and headway over 1½f out, ran on up inner to lead 100yds out, jinked right close home but kept on to line (M Monteriso), beat Six Perfections by ½l*

3rd Premio Ambrosiano (Listed) (San Siro, May 2) 4yo+ 10f Heavy 6 ran. *(M Monteriso), beaten 4¼l by Altieri*

1st Premio Andred (Listed) (Pisa, March 28) 4yo+ 10f Good 9 ran. *(M Monteriso), beat Syrakus by 2¾l*

2003

2nd Conditions race (Capannelle, November 1) 3yo+ 10f Heavy 12 ran ● **10th** Premio Vittorio di Capua (Group 1) (San Siro, October 12) 3yo+ 1m Good to firm **90** 11 ran ● **3rd** Premio del Piazzale (Listed) (San Siro, September 21) 3yo+ 1m Good 6 ran ● **3rd** Prix Guillaume d'Ornano (Group 2) (Deauville, August 15) 3yo 10f Good to soft **104** 5 ran ● **2nd** Prix Jean Prat (Group 1) (Chantilly, June 1) 3yo 9f Good **113** 8 ran ● **2nd** Premio Parioli (Group 2) (Capannelle, April 27) 3yo 1m Good **109** 10 ran ● **1st** Premio Gardone (Listed race) (San Siro, March 30) 3yo+ 1m Good 5 ran ● **1st** Premio Calvarate (Conditions race) (San Siro, March 16) 3yo+ 1m Good 6 ran

Other wins

2002 **1st** Premio Valtellina (Conditions Race) (San Siro, October 27) 2yo+ 7½f Heavy 4 ran ● **1st** Premio Chisola (Maiden) (San Siro, October 2) 2yo+ 7½f Soft 11 ran

of equine osteopathy and treated many good horses, both trotters and thoroughbreds. He suffered a heart attack in mid-April and died on May 4, 2004. Many people at Longchamp were still sharply aware of his early death when the Italian trainer revealed how much the success of Prince Kirk owed to him.

Prince Kirk had reappeared in the first Listed event of 2004, the Premio Andred, at his home course of Pisa. Monteriso held him up behind the front-running German raider, Syrakus, before bringing him with a steady run to beat him two and three-quarter lengths.

His next outing was in another Listed race, the Premio Ambrosiano at San Siro. He could do no better than third behind Altieri. The heavy going may have been too much for him but the form looked a lot better after Altieri beat Vespone, Nonno Carlo and Le Vie dei Colori in the Group 1 Premio Presidente della Repubblica on the Sunday before the Prix d'Ispahan.

After Prince Kirk's Group 1 success, Borromeo said he had immediate possibilities but preferred to wait for targets later in the season. His return was already in doubt by September, however, and the trainer's alternative plan was to take him to Dubai in March. If he makes it back for a second crack at the d'Ispahan, he will find that the distance has been reduced to one mile, as part of the revised Group 1 programme announced in October.

Prince Kirk

bay colt 31-1-2000

		Atan	Native Dancer
			Mixed Marriage
	Sharpen Up		
		Rocchetta	Rockefella
Selkirk			Chambiges
ch 1988		Nebbiolo	Yellow God
			Novara
	Annie Edge		
		Friendly Court	Be Friendly
			No Court
		Lyphard	Northern Dancer
			Goofed
	Manila		
		Dona Ysidra	Le Fabuleux
Princess Manila			Matriarch
b 1990		Halo	Hail To Reason
			Cosmah
	Halo's Princess		
		Taberet	Viceregal
			Tabola

Bred by Srl So li Ca in France

Sire Selkirk

Won 6 of 15 starts from 2 to 4. At 2, won 1m Listed event from 2 starts. At 3, won 2 (inc. Queen Elizabeth II S-Gr1) of 6 starts. At 4, won 3 (Lockinge S-Gr2, Goodwood Mile-Gr2, Challenge S-Gr2) of 7 starts. By high-class 2yo/sprinter and very good sire whose stock often stayed better than he did, out of high-class 7-10f filly who also foaled stakes winners Rimrod, Rory Creek, Seebe, Skillington, Syncline. Stands at Lanwades Stud in Britain, 2004 fee £30,000. Oldest progeny 10, sire of: Hidden Meadow (Gr3), Kirkwall (Gr2), Orford Ness (Gr3), Squeak (Beverly Hills H-Gr1, Matriarch H-Gr1), Country Garden (Gr2), Field Of Hope (Prix de la Foret-Gr1), Trans Island (Gr2), Sign Of Hope (Gr2), Valley Chapel (Gr3), Wince (1,000 Guineas-Gr1), Harbour Island (Gr3), Altieri (Premio Presidente della Repubblica-Gr1), The Trader (Gr3), Highdown (Gr2), Highest (Gr3), Leadership (Gran Premio di Milano-Gr1), Sulk (Prix Marcel Boussac-Gr1), Welsh Diva (Gr3), Favourable Terms (Nassau S-Gr1), Felicity (Gr3), Prince Kirk (Prix d'Ispahan-Gr1), Etendard Indien (Gr3), Red Bloom (Fillies' Mile-Gr1), Etlaala (Gr2).

Dam Princess Manila

Unplaced in sole start in US. Half-sister to 1991 Derby Italiano winner Hailsham (by Riverman) and Grade 3-placed Royal Minister (by Deputy Minister) out of smart Canadian 2yo+ filly Halo's Princess. Dam of: Princer (1995 c by Irish River; winner), Platel (1996 f by Alysheba; winner), Prince Honor (1997 c by Highest Honor; winner), Petrova (1998 f by Kendor; placed), Paranui (1999 c by Exit To Nowhere; non-winner), Prince Kirk (2000 c by Selkirk; Prix d'Ispahan-Gr1), Pankova (2002 f by Sendawar; unraced), Prince Esteem (2003 c by Mark Of Esteem).

Pedigree assessment

One of the stars of a strong year in Europe for his sire. Prince Kirk appreciates 8-10f, in keeping with his pedigree, and his French Group 1 win ensures he has a future as a stallion. It is too early to judge Selkirk as a source of sire sons, but the Sharpen Up male line continues to have a major influence in Europe. *JH*

Prospect Park

3yo bay colt **118**

Sadler's Wells (USA) - Brooklyn's Dance (Fr) (Shirley Heights)

Owner Wertheimer Et Frere

Trainer C Laffon-Parias

Breeder Wertheimer Et Frere

Career: **9** starts | won **3** | second **3** | third **2** | £269,297 win and place

By Bill Barber

ADLER'S WELLS ended 2004 with his reputation as the leading stallion in Europe intact, yet his crop of three-year-olds failed to yield a Classic success. Quiff went close in the St Leger, but Prospect Park went even closer when caught on the line in the Prix du Jockey-Club at Chantilly in June.

His precise standing among the best three-year-olds in France is difficult to assess, as the main contenders tended to take turns to beat each other as the year progressed, but at different points in the season Prospect Park finished ahead of the Jockey-Club winner Blue Canari, as well as Bago and Cherry Mix, the first and second in the Prix de l'Arc de Triomphe.

Prospect Park had mixed it with the best as a juvenile, finishing a respectful third behind Bago on his debut at Longchamp and then filling the same position behind Latice in the Prix de Conde at the same track.

While the Cheltenham Festival was occupying people's thoughts in Britain, Prospect Park made his seasonal debut at Saint-Cloud, winning a minor contest over ten and a half furlongs.

Stepped up in class for his next run, the colt was sent off the 11-10 favourite for the Prix de Courcelles over the same distance at Longchamp in April and won again, beating the ill-fated Millemix, from whom he was receiving 4lb, a head with Blue Canari a length and a half back in third.

With the Prix du Jockey-Club firmly in their sights, connections then sent Prospect Park for one of the main trials, the Prix Hocquart over 12 furlongs in May. Sent off the 6-4 favourite but unsuited by a pedestrian early pace, Olivier Peslier's mount suffered his first defeat of the campaign, going down by three-quarters of a length to Lord du Sud, with Cherry Mix three lengths further adrift in third. Trainer Carlos Laffon-Parias was not too disheartened by the reverse and said: "He was caught for

Prospect Park, left, is unable to hold off Valixir in the Prix Niel, and the form was overturned by Bago in the Arc

speed early in the straight. We're not going to change plans and he's still going for the Jockey-Club."

Prospect Park came agonisingly close to bringing those plans to glorious fruition. Fifth turning for home, Peslier's mount challenged for the lead a furlong and a half out and was in front with 100 yards to go until the last stride, at which point Blue Canari, whom he had beaten in April, swooped to snatch the prize from his grasp. "The colt did everything right and we were just caught at the bitter end," said his rider after the race.

Prospect Park had proved himself to be one of the best three-year-olds in France but had yet to land a Group race, an omission that connections chose to deal with three weeks later in the Prix du Lys at Longchamp.

He was sent off the odds-on favourite for the Group 3 contest, but it did not go by without incident. With his mount keen and pulling hard following a typically French slow early pace, Peslier survived a scare two furlongs out when Prospect Park stumbled, but he quickly recovered to record an easy length-and-a-half victory over Lord Darnley.

Laffon-Parias decided to give Prospect Park a mid-season break, with the Prix de l'Arc de Triomphe his autumn target. His options for a warm-up race were the Grosser Preis von Baden-Baden or the Prix

2004   Race record

16th Prix de l'Arc de Triomphe Lucien Barriere (Group 1) (Longchamp, October 3) 3yo+ 12f Good **113** (TS 107) 19 ran. *Prominent, 3rd straight, went 2nd briefly 2f out, weakened (O Peslier), beaten 9½l by Bago*

2nd Prix Niel Casino Barriere d'Enghien (Group 2) (Longchamp, September 12) 3yo 12f Soft **118** (TS 118) 8 ran. *Raced in 3rd, led entering straight, pushed along 2f out, joined approaching final furlong, ran on and led again inside final furlong, headed close home (O Peslier), beaten nose by Valixir*

1st Prix du Lys (Group 3) (Longchamp, June 27) 3yo 12f Good to soft **108** (TS 108) 6 ran. *Held up in 5th, disputed 3rd from over 5f out, 4th straight, not clear run when stumbled over 2f out, pulled out, led inside final furlong, pushed out (O Peslier), beat Lord Darnley by 1½l*

2nd Prix du Jockey Club (Group 1) (Chantilly, June 6) 3yo 12f Good to soft **118** (TS 111) 15 ran. *Mid-division, disputing 5th straight, pushed along and ran on 2f out, ridden to challenge 1½f out, led 100yds out, ran on until headed final stride (O Peslier), beaten hd by Blue Canari*

2nd Prix Hocquart (Group 2) (Longchamp, May 13) 3yo 12f Very soft **110** (TS 94) 6 ran. *Restrained in rear, last straight, headway on outside from 2f out, chased winner final furlong, nearest at finish (O Peslier), beaten ¾l by Lord du Sud*

1st Prix de Courcelles (Listed) (Longchamp, April 4) 3yo 10½f Good to soft **104** (TS 42) 6 ran. *Raced in 4th pulling hard, quickened to lead over 1f out, held on well under pressure closing stages (O Peslier), beat Millemix by hd*

1st Prix Belfonds (Saint-Cloud, March 11) 3yo 10½f Good to soft (TS 63) 6 ran. *Raced in 4th behind slow pace, quickened to lead over 1f out, canter (O Peslier), beat Vaillant Prince by 3l*

2003

3rd Prix de Conde (Group 3) (Longchamp, October 19) 2yo 9f Good to soft **103** 6 ran ● **3rd** Prix des Aigles (Longchamp, September 2) 2yo 1m Soft **83** 7 ran

Niel, and the trainer decided on the traditional route, even though it meant taking on Bago at Longchamp.

Prospect Park managed to finish ahead of Bago in the Niel but, once again, a horse he had beaten earlier in the season proved his undoing.

Provided with a pacemaker in the shape of Primaxis, Prospect Park took over from his stablemate early in the straight but was caught inside the final furlong by Valixir, who had finished a place behind him in the French Derby. He battled back gamely as the winner idled but was still a nose down at the line.

While the result of the Niel failed to give that much encouragement for the Arc, his performance at Longchamp the following month was still a disappointment as he beat only three home in the field of 19. It was, however, the first time he had run when the word "soft" was not in the going description.

Prospect Park stays in training in 2005, with the King George VI and Queen Elizabeth Diamond Stakes a possible target according to Laffon-Parias. With just a Group 3 to his name so far, he will enjoy the advantage of not being overburdened with penalties in his prep races.

Prospect Park

bay colt, 31-3-2001

Sadler's Wells b 1981	**Northern Dancer**	Nearctic	Nearco / Lady Angela
		Natalma	Native Dancer / Almahmoud
	Fairy Bridge	Bold Reason	Hail To Reason / Lalun
		Special	Forli / Thong
Brooklyn's Dance b 1988	Shirley Heights	Mill Reef	Never Bend / Milan Mill
		Hardiemma	Hardicanute / Grand Cross
	Vallee Dansante	Lyphard	**Northern Dancer** / Goofed
		Green Valley	Val de Loir / Sly Pola

Bred by Wertheimer et Frere in Britain

Sire Sadler's Wells

Won 6 of 11 races, inc. Beresford S.-Gr3, Irish Derby Trial-Gr2, Irish 2,000 Guineas-Gr1, Eclipse S.-Gr1, Phoenix Champion S.-Gr1. Also 2nd in Prix du Jockey-Club-Gr1, King George VI & Queen Elizabeth S.-Gr1. Impeccably bred top-class performer from 8-12f, handsome, tough and consistent. Sire of Gr1 winners: Braashee, French Glory, In The Wings (x3), Old Vic (x2), Prince Of Dance, Scenic, Salsabil (x5), Opera House (x3), Runyon, Saddlers' Hall, El Prado, Johann Quatz, Masad, Barathea (x2), Fatherland, Fort Wood, Intrepidity (x3), Carnegie (x2), King's Theatre (x2), Northern Spur (x2), Moonshell, Muncie, Poliglote, Chief Contender, Dance Design, Darazari, Luna Wells, Cloudings, Ebadiyla (x2), Entrepreneur, In Command, Kayf Tara (x4), Dream Well (x2), Greek Dance, King Of Kings (x2), Leggera, Commander Collins, Daliapour, Montjeu (x6), Saffron Walden, Aristotle, Beat Hollow (x4), Subtle Power, Galileo (x3), Imagine (x2), Milan, Perfect Soul, Sequoyah, Sligo Bay, Ballingarry, Black Sam Bellamy (x2), Gossamer (x2), High Chaparral (x6), Islington (x4), Quarter Moon, Sholokov, Alberto Giacometti, Brian Boru (x2), Doyen, Powerscourt, Refuse To Bend (4), Yesterday, Quiff, Playful Act.

Dam Brooklyn's Dance

Won 3 of 8 starts in France. At 3, won Prix Cleopatre-Gr3 (10.5f), also 2nd Prix de Royallieu-Gr2. By top-class 12f performer and very good sire, including of broodmares. Half-sister to Listed-placed Krissante (dam of Gr1 winner Okawango) out of winning very close relative of Green Dancer. Family of Alhaarth. Dam of: West Brooklyn (1993 f by Gone West; winner), Gold Dodger (1994 f by Slew o' Gold; Listed winner), Brooklyn's Gold (1995 c by Seeking The Gold; Listed winner), Brooklyn's Storm (1996 f by Storm Cat; winner), Out Of Control (1997 c by Gulch; Listed-placed winner), Brooklyn Gleam (1998 f by Caerleon; winner), unnamed (2000 f by Sadler's Wells; unraced), Prospect Park (2001 c by Sadler's Wells; Gr3 winner, Gr1 placed), Le Reveur (2002 c by Machiavellian; winner).

Pedigree assessment

Yet another top-class example of the cross between Sadler's Wells and Shirley Heights or his son Darshaan. Prospect Park has already proven himself over 12f and that will be his trip in 2005. Many sons of Sadler's Wells have progressed with age, and Prospect Park has the pedigree to reach the top. *JH*

Punctilious

3yo bay filly **114**

Danehill (USA) - Robertet (USA) (Roberto (USA))

Owner Godolphin

Trainer Saeed Bin Suroor

Breeder Bjorn E Nielsen

Career: **9** starts | won **4** | second **2** | third **2** | **£309,344** win and place

By Richard Austen

BEST of the rest. Of the 32 different fillies or mares that tried to beat Ouija Board in 2004, Punctilious was one of 32 that failed. But she did finish the closest. The Irish Oaks was Ouija Board's worst form in a Group race and Punctilious's best, but the Godolphin filly was still a length behind.

That was the second time that the two of them had gone head to head. The first was in the Oaks at Epsom and, at 100-30 compared to 7-2, Punctilious shaded Ouija Board in the betting. Both were just behind All Too Beautiful and Sundrop. In the race, however, there was a seven-length gulf between Ouija Board and the rest, and Punctilious underperformed in going down by ten and a half lengths in third.

Punctilious had a good crack at the lead in both Classics, sent on seven furlongs out at Epsom and two furlongs out at The Curragh, before Ouija Board put her in her place. She also had her moments of triumph, though. At 8-11, she was fully expected to win the Musidora Stakes at York on her debut for Godolphin and she earned a prominent place in Oaks calculations when she scored by six lengths.

Subsequent events showed that the ease of that win had a lot to do with some tame opposition, but Punctilious looked good on the day, setting a steady pace and pushed steadily clear from the two-furlong marker.

"I've absolutely no idea who I'll ride. It's a very, very tough choice. One day I'm thinking Sundrop, the next I'm thinking Punctilious," revealed Frankie Dettori of his dilemma in the build-up to the Oaks. "Punctilious is like a lion," observed Shiekh Mohammed.

Dettori eventually decided to take the ride on Punctilious but this was a lion that didn't act on the track. With her high head carriage in the sheepskin noseband and her sometimes flashing tail, Punctilious does

Punctilious, having failed to handle the track at Epsom, bounces back to win the Ribblesdale at Royal Ascot

not look the most elegant of gallopers at the best of times and, on the Epsom camber, the Oaks was far from being her best. Three furlongs out Punctilious was rapidly left behind. "Her legs were going everywhere," said Dettori. "She hated the track but she's very clever, apart from being tough, and pulled herself up."

Just 13 days after Epsom, Punctilious was back on her game to gain compensation in the Ribblesdale Stakes at Royal Ascot. Starting 9-2 second favourite in a field of nine, and with Dettori's confidence in her stamina undented, she was always close up, led a furlong out and put the issue beyond doubt in the last 100 yards to come home in front by one and a half lengths and the same from an honest rival in Sahool and a very promising one in Quiff.

After the second crack at Ouija Board in Ireland – a far more creditable one but with Punctilious readily outpointed in the end – the Godolphin filly was due to have a third go in the Yorkshire Oaks at the Knavesmire in August. Ouija Board's late absence because of soft ground deprived her of that opportunity and Punctilious wouldn't have won whether the dual Oaks winner had run or not. Three other fillies beat her and, headed

2004   Race record

2nd E P Taylor Stakes (Grade 1) (Woodbine, October 24) 3yo+ 10f Good **114** 8 ran. *Raced in 5th, led briefly just inside final furlong, soon headed and one pace (L Dettori), beaten ½l by Commercante*

4th Aston Upthorpe Yorkshire Oaks (Group 1) (York, August 18) 3yo+ 12f Soft **92** (TS 56) 8 ran. *Led until 6f out, chased winner until weakened over 2f out, eased inside final furlong (L Dettori), beaten 22l by Quiff*

2nd Darley Irish Oaks (Group 1) (Curragh, July 18) 3yo 12f Good to firm **114** (TS 115) 7 ran. *Chased leaders in 4th, 3rd into straight, led 2f out, headed over 1½f out, kept on under pressure (L Dettori), beaten 1l by Ouija Board*

1st Ribblesdale Stakes (Group 2) (Ascot, June 17) 3yo 12f Good to firm **111** (TS 112) 9 ran. *Tracked leader, ridden to challenge 2f out, led narrowly 1f out, drew clear last 100yds (L Dettori), beat Sahool by 1½l*

3rd Vodafone Oaks (Group 1) (Epsom, June 4) 3yo 12f Good **108** (TS 99) 7 ran. *Raced in 3rd until led 7f out, ridden and headed 3f out, soon beaten, finished tired (L Dettori), beaten 10½l by Ouija Board*

1st Tattersalls Musidora Stakes (Group 3) (York, May 11) 3yo 10½f Good to soft **111** (TS 41) 6 ran. *Led, quickened over 5f out, shaken up over 1f out, went left, stayed on (L Dettori), beat Glen Innes by 6l*

2003

3rd Meon Valley Stud Fillies' Mile (Group 1) (Ascot, September 27) 2yo 1m Good to firm **110** (TS 130) 7 ran ● **1st** Butler & Co Equine Tax Planning EBF Novice Stakes (Salisbury, September 4) 2yo 1m Good to firm **94** 7 ran ● **1st** EBF Maiden Fillies' Stakes (Yarmouth, July 3) 2yo 7f Good **79** 6 ran

by Quiff, they beat her by a long way. Perhaps the going accounted for that disappointment, though Punctilious also failed to impress in appearance beforehand.

One further attempt at Group 1 glory saw Punctilious in a much better light but she could not win that race either. The E.P. Taylor Stakes over a mile and a quarter at Woodbine in October saw her sent off at 11-10 and she got her head in front in the final furlong, but second favourite Commercante could not be shaken off and Punctilious was beaten half a length.

Punctilious's attitude attracted a fair amount of comment in her second season, with Godolphin racing manager Simon Crisford observing after the Musidora that "she is a strong-minded individual and certainly hard enough mentally to win a Classic. The streak she possesses is not down to inexperience but probably ingrained."

Punctilious has looked game enough in action and, as the Oaks should be forgiven, the Yorkshire Oaks on soft ground was her only blemish. If there was a problem with her it was that Godolphin's top middle-distance filly of the year wasn't all that good in a wider context. "You can work her with a claimer or a Group 1 horse and she will only do enough," remarked Dettori. But Punctilious could not do enough to win a Group 1 race.

Punctilious

bay filly, 7-5-2001

		Northern Dancer	Nearctic
	Danzig		Natalma
Danehill		Pas de Nom	Admiral's Voyage
b 1986			Petitioner
		His Majesty	Ribot
	Razyana		Flower Bowl
		Spring Adieu	Buckpasser
			Natalma
		Hail To Reason	Turn-to
	Roberto		Nothirdchance
		Bramalea	Nashua
Robertet			Rarelea
b 1986		Nijinsky	Northern Dancer
	Ethics		Flaming Page
		Fairness	Cavan
			Equal Venture

Bred by Bjorn Nielsen in England

Sire Danehill

Won 4 of 9 races, inc. Cork and Orrery Stakes-Gr3, Haydock Park Sprint Cup-Gr1. Also 3rd in 2,000 Guineas. Died May 2003. Sire of Gr1 winners: Danish (Queen Elizabeth II Challenge Cup), Kissing Cousin (Coronation S.), Danehill Dancer (Phoenix S., National S.), Tsukuba Symphony (NHK Mile Cup), Desert King (National S., Irish 2,000 Guineas, Irish Derby), Fairy King Prawn (Yasuda Kinen), Tiger Hill (Grosser Preis von Baden [twice], Bayerisches Zuchtrennen), Indian Danehill (Prix Ganay), Wannabe Grand (Cheveley Park S.), Aquarelliste (Prix de Diane, Prix Vermeille, Prix Ganay), Banks Hill (Coronation S., Breeders' Cup Filly & Mare Turf, Prix Jacques le Marois), Mozart (July Cup, Nunthorpe S.), Regal Rose (Cheveley Park S.), Dress To Thrill (Matriarch S.), Landseer (Poule d'Essai des Poulains), Rock Of Gibraltar (Grand Criterium, Dewhurst S., 2,000 Guineas, Irish 2,000 Guineas, St James's Palace S., Sussex S., Prix du Moulin), Westerner (Prix du Cadran, twice, Prix Royal-Oak, twice), Clodovil (Poule d'Essai des Poulains), Light Jig (Yellow Ribbon S.), Spartacus (Phoenix S., Gran Criterium), Grey Lilas (Prix du Moulin de Longchamp), North Light (Derby S.), Oratorio (Prix Jean-Luc Lagardere).

Dam Robertet

Won 2 of 15 races, inc. Grand Prix de Deauville-Gr2. Burly staying type, admirably consistent, best effort at 15.5f. By a Derby winner and successful sire. Dam unraced sister to Eclipse S. winner Solford. Grand-dam unraced sister to US Triple Crown winner Assault. Died in 2001, having produced: Redwood Falls (1992 f by Dancing Brave; Listed winner), Requin (1993 c by Thatching; winner, died at 3 years), Ruwenzori (1994 f by Alzao; placed), Rubis Royal (1995 c by Bluebird, winner over jumps), Red Valley (1997 f by Wolfhound; unplaced), Red Star (1998 f by Lure; winner), Risk Seeker (2000 c by Elmaamul; triple Gr3 winner), Punctilious (2001 f by Danehill; Gr3 winner).

Pedigree assessment

After the Musidora, Punctilious appeared certain to improve for longer distances. A third in the Oaks, a win in the Ribblesdale and a second in the Irish Oaks provided sufficient proof that she stayed a mile and a half, but at that trip on a gluey Knavesmire she was left way behind as favourite for the Yorkshire Oaks. It seemed significant that when she finally managed to step up appreciably on her Musidora form it was as close runner-up in Woodbine's E.P. Taylor Stakes, back at ten furlongs. Racecourse evidence suggests that if she stays in training to seek a Group 1 victory in Europe, she might find a better opportunity at ten furlongs than at a mile and a half. *TM*

Quiff

3yo bay filly **122**

Sadler's Wells (USA) - Wince (Selkirk (USA))

Owner K Abdullah

Trainer Sir Michael Stoute

Breeder Juddmonte Farms

Career: **5** starts   won **2**   second **1**   third **1**   **£256,851** win and place

By Lee Mottershead

E DOESN'T do words. At least not in public. Listen to Sir Michael Stoute in a television interview or read his thoughts in print, and you won't learn a lot. That's intentional, how he likes it to be. What Stoute truly thinks, he prefers to keep to himself and his closest entourage.

Sometimes, though, words are not required. It was like that following the St Leger, the Classic that still eludes him. After Quiff had gone down by just a head to Rule Of Law, with stablemate Maraahel fourth, Stoute's response to journalists was simply: "I'm delighted with them both – thrilled!" He almost certainly was, but delight wasn't his overpowering emotion. His face told the true story.

The Leger is the one British Classic missing from Stoute's curriculum vitae. Ever since the unbeatable Shergar was beaten in 1981, the great man has tried to secure Doncaster's showpiece event and failed. Going into the 2004 renewal, he had already saddled four seconds. He didn't need another.

Quiff boasted the right credentials. An awesome 11-length winner of the Yorkshire Oaks, the magnificently bred Sadler's Wells daughter of 1,000 Guineas winner Wince was heading to Doncaster as very much the horse to beat. True, she had the Vodafone Derby second and third, Rule Of Law and Let The Lion Roar, to overcome, but a reproduction of her Knavesmire procession would surely be enough. The only snag was that the Yorkshire Oaks had been run in a soft-ground swamp that Quiff adored. The Leger would be run on an altogether different surface.

Doncaster in September can be a soggy stage, but not this time. With the connections of Khalid Abdullah's filly adamant that fast ground was not her cup of tea, the lack of rain over Yorkshire concerned them more as each day passed. As the going became ever faster, Quiff's Leger

**Quiff revels in the soft conditions and the absence of
Ouija Board to take the Yorkshire Oaks by 11 lengths**

participation was cast in doubt, the following afternoon's Prix Vermeille
becoming an alternative. Even when Paris was shunned and her Leger
entry confirmed at the 48-hour declaration stage, nothing was certain.
Only two hours before the race, after Stoute had set foot on the track
and satisfied himself that the officially good to firm going was suitable,
were we sure that Quiff would take her chance. She was a runner. All
she had to do now was win.

And she might have done, had Lady Luck smiled more kindly upon
her. Instead, Quiff and Kieren Fallon found themselves trapped on the
rail as they progressed up the long Doncaster straight, the front-running
Rule Of Law making a canny bid for glory ahead of them. With just
two furlongs to go, and still with plenty of horse beneath him but nowhere
to go, Fallon decided that enough was enough. Prepared to halt Quiff's
momentum, he pulled her around the field, taking her four horses wide

2004 Race record

2nd betfair.com St Leger Stakes (Group 1) (Doncaster, September 11) 3yo 14½f Good to firm **119** (TS 102) 9 ran. *Tracked leaders, not clear run on inside and switched outside over 2f out, stayed on to challenge last 100yds, no extra near line (K Fallon), beaten hd by Rule Of Law*

1st Aston Upthorpe Yorkshire Oaks (Group 1) (York, August 18) 3yo+ 12f Soft **122** (TS 93) 8 ran. *Held up, headway 7f out, led over 3f out, edged right and stayed on strongly to forge clear final furlong (K Fallon), beat Pongee by 11l*

3rd Ribblesdale Stakes (Group 2) (Ascot, June 17) 3yo 12f Good to firm **107** (TS 106) 9 ran. *Held up in last trio, pushed along 5f out, not clear run well over 2f out, driven and stayed on final 2f to take 3rd near finish (K Fallon), beaten 3l by Punctilious*

1st Wise Catering Maiden Fillies' Stakes (Div I) (Salisbury, May 13) 3yo+ 10f Good **83** (TS 72) 10 ran. *Tracked leaders, went 2nd well over 1f out, quickened to lead inside final furlong, comfortably (B Doyle), beat Dawn Surprise by 1l*

2003

5th Stan James EBF Maiden Fillies' Stakes (Newmarket (July), August 22) 2yo 7f Good to firm **67** 8 ran

and propelling her forward as only Fallon can. For the next furlong and a half she slashed Rule Of Law's advantage, edging left, but closing in on a memorable triumph. She seemed sure to win. Then, with 100 yards left, her effort flattened out. Try as she might, she could not get past, and she did not. She had been beaten a head.

A Channel 4 camera, which had been monitoring Stoute throughout the race, caught his reaction as Quiff flashed past the post in second. It was one of complete frustration. A few weeks earlier and a few miles north, it had been one of complete delight. Nobody could have envisaged quite how easily Quiff would land the Yorkshire Oaks. A Salisbury maiden winner on her seasonal bow before finishing a staying-on third in a Ribblesdale Stakes run on a firm surface that visibly discomforted her, Quiff led over three furlongs out at York before powering further and further clear up the centre of the track, imperious and alone, revelling in the glorious mud to thrash Lancashire Oaks winner Pongee by a street length. Before the race, there had been surprise in some quarters that Stoute had insisted Fallon ride Quiff, rather than release him to partner his (subsequently withdrawn) dual Oaks heroine Ouija Board. After York, it became obvious why Stoute felt his number one rider should be on board.

The Leger done and dusted, Quiff's team considered supplementing her for the Arc, only to decide against it when it seemed certain that Longchamp would ride much faster than ideal. She will, however, be one of many top-class middle-distance three-year-olds to race on at four. A rangy filly, who should improve further for filling out her frame, her chance to end Stoute's Leger hoodoo has passed. She could, though, still give him plenty to talk about.

Quiff

bay filly, 2-3-2001

		Nearctic	Nearco
			Lady Angela
	Northern Dancer		
		Natalma	Native Dancer
Sadler's Wells			Almahmoud
b 1981			
		Bold Reason	Hail To Reason
			Lalun
	Fairy Bridge		
		Special	Forli
			Thong
		Sharpen Up	Atan
			Rocchetta
	Selkirk		
		Annie Edge	Nebbiolo
			Friendly Court
Wince			
b 1996			
		Lyphard	**Northern Dancer**
			Goofed
	Flit		
		Nimble Folly	Cyane
			Instant Sin

Bred by Juddmonte Farms in England

Sire Sadler's Wells

Won 6 of 11 races, inc. Beresford S.-Gr3, Irish Derby Trial-Gr2, Irish 2,000 Guineas-Gr1, Eclipse S.-Gr1, Phoenix Champion S.-Gr1. Also 2nd in Prix du Jockey-Club-Gr1, King George VI & Queen Elizabeth S.-Gr1. Impeccably bred top-class performer from 8-12f, handsome, tough and consistent. Sire of Gr1 winners: Braashee, French Glory, In The Wings (x3), Old Vic (x2), Prince Of Dance, Scenic, Salsabil (x5), Opera House (x3), Runyon, Saddlers' Hall, El Prado, Johann Quatz, Masad, Barathea (x2), Fatherland, Fort Wood, Intrepidity (x3), Carnegie (x2), King's Theatre (x2), Northern Spur (x2), Moonshell, Muncie, Poliglote, Chief Contender, Dance Design, Darazari, Luna Wells, Cloudings, Ebadiyla (x2), Entrepreneur, In Command, Kayf Tara (x4), Dream Well (x2), Greek Dance, King Of Kings (x2), Leggera, Commander Collins, Daliapour, Montjeu (x6), Saffron Walden, Aristotle, Beat Hollow (x4), Subtle Power, Galileo (x3), Imagine (x2), Milan, Perfect Soul, Sequoyah, Sligo Bay, Ballingarry, Black Sam Bellamy (x2), Gossamer (x2), High Chaparral (x6), Islington (x4), Quarter Moon, Sholokov, Alberto Giacometti, Brian Boru (x2), Doyen, Powerscourt, Refuse To Bend (4), Yesterday, Quiff, Playful Act.

Dam Wince

Won 4 of 9 races, inc. Fred Darling S.-Gr3, 1,000 Guineas-Gr1. Tall, lengthy, attractive individual, and a good mover. One of the best of her sex over a mile at three, though only an average Guineas winner. Half-sister to Gr1 runner-up Fleeting Glimpse (herself dam of Gr3 winner Half Glance and Classic-placed Tycoon) and Listed winner Ulundi, both by Rainbow Quest. By a top-class miler and successful sire out of a minor winner who is full-sister to Skimble (5 Graded wins, dam of Gr1 winner Skimming) and Nimble Mind (Gr3-placed). Dam of: Quiff (2001 f by Sadler's Wells; Gr1 winner). She has a colt foal by Sadler's Wells.

Pedigree assessment

Putting the best to the best is still not a bad formula, and occasionally it delivers the hoped-for result. In the case of Wince's mating, in her first season at stud, with the perennial leading sire, there were grounds for optimism about the result, but the distance over which the produce might excel was really anybody's guess. Wince took after her sire, relishing distances up to a mile, but that seemed to be her limit. However, Quiff shaped like a potential stayer on her only start at two, and at three she was trained for longer trips and kept improving. She dominated in the Yorkshire Oaks, gave Rule Of Law a run for his money in the St Leger, and was a legitimate fancy for the Arc until the ground turned against her. Lightly raced, she is entitled to improve again next year. *TM*

Rakti

5yo bay horse **129**

Polish Precedent (USA) - Ragera (Ire) (Rainbow Quest (USA))

Owner Gary A Tanaka

Trainer M A Jarvis

Breeder Azienda Agricola Rosati Colarieti

Career: **19** starts   won **10**   second **3**   third **1**   **£1,658,550** win and place

By Paul Haigh

RAKTI may well be the most talented racehorse in the world. What's certain, however, is that he is one of the most exasperating and, at least by the criteria we humans choose to apply to equine psychology, one of the most infuriatingly deranged.

When he runs to his best, as he did (probably) in the Champion Stakes at Newmarket in 2003, he seems to be on the brink of becoming an all-time great. When he decides he's damned if he's going to do just what these humans want him to do, he seems determined to disqualify himself as a competitor. Only his immense ability can have saved him from the gelding knife and the joys of jumping.

As a three-year-old he developed a tendency to plant himself on the way to the start and then another tendency, when – or if – he'd got there, to refuse to enter the stalls. He'd already demonstrated his willingness to throw in the occasional apparently inexplicable 'stinker' after he'd shown in winning the Derby Italiano just what a good horse he could be.

Whether his idiosyncrasies are genetic or something had happened to traumatise him during his early career in Italy for Bruno Grizzetti is hard to say. But his hugely respected and patient current trainer Michael Jarvis, to whom Gary Tanaka had sent him at the end of his three-year-old season, finally called in the legendary British 'horse whisperer', Steve 'Yarmie' Dyble, and asked him to put Rakti on his psychiatrist's couch.

For a while at the end of 2003 it looked as though the therapy had done the trick. Well-documented stories told how the horse could recognise Dyble's voice at a range of 50 yards, and of the calming effect the sound would have on him at once. By going down to the start with him for the Champion Stakes at Newmarket, Dyble was able to persuade Rakti not only to enter the stalls without fuss but also to perform to a level that required form students to assume that nearly all his opponents had "gone over the top". When 'Yarmie' accompanied him to Hong Kong in December

**Philip Robinson is able to check for any danger as Rakti
starts his season with an impressive win at Royal Ascot**

2003, Rakti again seemed on his best behaviour, this time chasing home
Falbrav in the Hong Kong Cup, and, significantly after that great horse
had got first run, actually gaining ground on him in the final furlong.

After these two displays there was a widespread assumption that in
2004 Rakti would assume his former compatriot's mantle as the best
older horse trained in Britain, and very probably the best ten-furlong
horse trained anywhere; and when he made his seasonal reappearance
in the Prince of Wales's Stakes at Royal Ascot this assumption was only
strengthened. Despite pulling quite hard early on Rakti had far too much
pace two furlongs out for a field that included Powerscourt and
Sulamani. If this was what Rakti could do on his first run of the season,
when he was clearly too fresh and eager early on, what, people wondered,
would he be able to achieve when he was even fitter and willing to accept
early restraint?

Sadly we never quite got the chance to find out. Next time he ran was
three weeks later in the Eclipse, for which he was made a red-hot favourite,
but far from having been encouraged to settle by the Ascot experience

2004	Race record

1st Queen Elizabeth II Stakes (Sponsored By NetJets) (Group 1) (Ascot, September 25) 3yo+ 1m Good to firm **128** (TS 122) 11 ran. *Soon tracked leader, led over 2f out, drew 3l clear well over 1f out, driven and held on final furlong (P Robinson), beat Lucky Story by ½l*

5th Baileys Irish Champion Stakes (Group 1) (Leopardstown, September 11) 3yo+ 10f Good to firm **122** (TS 122) 8 ran. *Slowly into stride, held up in 6th, kept on under pressure straight (P Robinson), beaten 2l by Azamour*

8th Coral-Eclipse Stakes (Group 1) (Sandown, July 3) 3yo+ 10f Good to soft **111** (TS 98) 12 ran. *Dwelt, pulled hard and rapid progress to go prominent after 1f, led 3f out to well over 1f out, weakened (P Robinson), beaten 9l by Refuse To Bend*

1st Prince of Wales's Stakes (Group 1) (Ascot, June 16) 4yo+ 10f Good to firm **129** (TS 118) 10 ran. *Pulled hard, raced in 3rd until tracked leader 3f out, led well over 1f out, soon clear, driven out (P Robinson), beat Powerscourt by 2l*

2003

2nd Hong Kong Cup (Group 1) (Sha Tin, December 14) 3yo+ 10f Good to firm **125** 14 ran ● **1st** Emirates Airline Champion Stakes (Group 1) (Newmarket, October 18) 3yo+ 10f Good to firm **125** 12 ran ● **2nd** Prince of Wales's Stakes (Group 1) (Ascot, June 18) 4yo+ 10f Good to firm **123** 10 ran ● **1st** Premio Presidente della Repubblica (Group 1) (Capannelle, May 11) 4yo+ 10f Good **114** 8 ran

Other wins

2002 **1st** Premio Villa Borghese (Listed) (Capannelle, September 8) 3yo 10f Good to soft 7 ran ● **1st** Derby Italiano (Group 1) (Capannelle, May 26) 3yo 12f Good to firm **116** 16 ran ● **1st** Premio Botticelli (Listed) (Capannelle, May 1) 3yo 10½f Good 10 ran ● **1st** Premio Barba Toni (Conditions Race) (Capannelle, March 10) 3yo 11f Heavy 8 ran **2001** **1st** Premio Furigolo (Conditions Race) (Capannelle, November 25) 2yo 10f Soft 9 ran ● **1st** Premio Teatro Gozzoli (Maiden) (Pisa, November 2) 2yo 10f Good 7 ran

he seemed to have taken it as another invitation to resume his attempts to dislocate Philip Robinson's shoulders. Even if he hadn't pulled like a pit bull for the whole of the first three furlongs he probably couldn't have won in any case as Robinson was sure that Rakti's sullen mood had started on the way to post, as soon as he tested the rain-softened ground.

After another period of head scratching Jarvis came to the conclusion that the Eclipse had come too soon after Ascot and that what Rakti needed to show his true ability was plenty of time between his races and the firm ground on which he had put up most of his best performances (although just to confuse matters, it should be noted that Rakti had appeared to have no objection to rain-affected ground when he won on heavy going by eight lengths in his first outing at three). The Juddmonte International, almost seven weeks after the Sandown debacle, seemed the ideal opportunity.

In the week before York, though, the rain started to come down. Looking out over the sun-baked Arlington track in Chicago, where he had come to watch his German-trained Singapore Airlines Cup winner, Epalo, on the eve of the Million and three days before the Juddmonte, Tanaka was

Dropped back to a mile in the Queen Elizabeth II Stakes, Rakti, left, finds his form again to defeat Lucky Story

as close as he gets to being cheesed off. "We sent him to York because we thought he'd get his ground," he said, "but he would have loved this."

His mood could not have been improved by the fact that Powerscourt, whom Rakti had defeated with ease in spite of having pulled at Ascot, passed the post clear of his field in the Million while Rakti had to be pulled out of his race at York as the ground turned against him. The fall-back plan was the Irish Champion Stakes.

At Leopardstown, however, Rakti again failed to do himself justice. This time Robinson put his poor mood and therefore poor effort down to the fact that, after being slightly fractious at the start, Rakti banged his head on leaving the stalls and never much felt like it afterwards, although he did put in a token bit of refusing to settle again. The fact that Powerscourt, a close-up third to Azamour, finished in front of him suggested that either Powerscourt had improved or that Rakti just wasn't himself.

Now connections reverted to Plan B – or maybe that should be Plan C, or even D. After the 2003 Champion Stakes Robinson had been so impressed by the horse's speed that he'd said on dismounting that "this might be the best miler in the world". Later in a TV interview he expressed his astonishment that a horse with that much pace had ever been able to win a Classic at a mile and a half. In his pre-Arlington conversation Tanaka had already begun to muse about the Breeders' Cup Mile and said that at one point after the Eclipse there had been thoughts of the Sussex Stakes, which had been dismissed mainly on the grounds that Goodwood's undulations would probably not have been suitable.

The target now was to be the Queen Elizabeth II Stakes at the Ascot Festival, a race that's just about superseded the Sussex as the British season's major mile race. Although there could be only a reasonable chance that the ground would be suitable for him at the end of such an infuriatingly wet summer, there had to be every likelihood that the faster pace of a top-class mile would persuade Rakti not to fight Robinson early on.

This time the calculations proved correct. The ground stayed good. Godolphin ran Blatant as a pacemaker for their Eclipse winner Refuse To Bend. Rakti, fitted with a cross noseband to give Robinson better control, still tossed his head about early on, but as Blatant set a Maroof/Summoner style gallop Rakti had no difficulty in following it. Even before the home turn it was quite evident that the Godolphin tactic had played into their opponents' hands as nothing in the field was going anywhere near as well as the horse who was following Blatant in second place.

Robinson kicked Rakti on early in the straight. The horse quickly opened up a two or three-length gap, and even though Mark Johnston's also enigmatic Lucky Story ran on strongly to close to within half a length at the line, there was never a point at which he looked likely to get in a blow at the winner. Refuse To Bend was two and a half lengths away in third.

That one race established Rakti as Britain's champion miler and once again talk began about the Breeders' Cup Mile. Tanaka thought about Texas, considered the fact that Rakti would have to be supplemented and that the Lone Star track might not suit him, and decided to miss the meeting in favour of another crack at Hong Kong instead.

Whatever his fate there, the parallels between his career and that of the Hong Kong Cup's infinitely more tractable 2003 winner Falbrav are obvious. Both started in Italy. Both were brilliant at a mile and a quarter, slightly less so at further. Both were able to drop back in trip for the QE II to prove themselves champions at a mile, too.

One really big difference is in their respective temperaments, of course. Falbrav was one of the best organised and most willing competitors who has ever raced. To say that Rakti has his quirks is comic understatement. But there might be one other difference, too. Rakti has so much pace that he might just have made a champion sprinter if asked to go that route. It's not going to happen, obviously, but how interesting would it have been to have seen the "deranged" hard puller with the tremendous turn of foot just given his head over five furlongs in an attempt to take on "the world's fastest horse on grass", Silent Witness, in the Hong Kong Sprint?

Rakti

bay horse 10-2-1999

		Northern Dancer	Nearctic / Natalma
	Danzig		
		Pas de Nom	Admiral's Voyage / Petitioner
Polish Precedent b 1986			
		Buckpasser	Tom Fool / Busanda
	Past Example		
		Bold Example	Bold Lad / Lady Be Good
		Blushing Groom	Red God / Runaway Bride
	Rainbow Quest		
		I Will Follow	Herbager / Where You Lead
Ragera b 1992			
		High Top	Derring-Do / Camenae
	Smageta		
		Christine	Crocket / Denning Report

Bred by Azienda Agricola Rosati Colarieti in England

Sire **Polish Precedent**

Won 7 of 9 races, inc. Prix du Palais Royal-Gr3, Prix de la Jonchere-Gr3, Prix Messidor-Gr3, Prix Jacques le Marois-Gr1, Prix du Moulin de Longchamp-Gr1). Big, lengthy sort, top-class miler, inferior only to Zilzal at 3. Sire of: Red Route (Gr2), Pilsudski (Grosser Preis von Baden-Gr1, Breeders' Cup Turf-Gr1, Eclipse S.-Gr1, Irish Champion S.-Gr1, Champion S.-Gr1, Japan Cup-Gr1), Pure Grain (Irish Oaks-Gr1, Yorkshire Oaks-Gr1), Riyadian (Gr2), Predappio (Gr2), Social Harmony (Gr3), Noushkey (Gr3), Polish Summer (Gr2), Sobieski (Gr2), First Charter (Gr3), Rakti (Derby Italiano-Gr1, Premio Presidente della Repubblica-Gr1, Champion S.-Gr1, Prince of Wales's S-Gr1, Queen Elizabeth II S.-Gr1).

Dam **Ragera**

Placed twice from 3 starts at 3 in Italy, modest performer on limited evidence available. Dam of: Riksha (1997 f by Zilzal; won 12 races in Italy), Rasana (1998 f by Royal Academy; unplaced in Italy and Ireland), Rakti (1999 c by Polish Precedent; triple Gr1 winner), Radha (2000 f by Bishop Of Cashel; unraced).

Pedigree assessment

Our comments on Rakti here last year included the view that he had the speed to figure at the top level over a mile, and the suggestion that, like Falbrav, he could easily make his mark over a variety of distances in 2004. As it turned out, he was kept to ten furlongs until the autumn, adding a fourth Group 1 win in the Prince of Wales's Stakes at Royal Ascot, but number five came at a mile on the same course in the Queen Elizabeth II Stakes, and it was as good a performance as any miler gave during the year. Rakti is the best son of Polish Precedent since Pilsudski, and he is the first of his stock to show top-class form over a mile, which suited the sire so well. He is a rare individual, having notched his first Group 1 success over 12 furlongs in the Derby Italiano. *TM*

Refuse To Bend (Ire)

4yo bay colt   **126**

Sadler's Wells (USA) - Market Slide (USA) (Gulch (USA))

Owner Godolphin

Trainer Saeed Bin Suroor

Breeder Moyglare Stud Farm Ltd

Career: **15** starts   won **7**   second **0**   third **1**   **£780,895** win and place

By David Ashforth

RACING is like a yo-yo, full of ups and downs. So was Refuse To Bend. When he was good, to misquote Longfellow, he was very, very good, but when he was bad he was horrid. At least, not nearly as good as when he was good.

He first became horrid in the 2003 Derby, the first defeat of his career, having previously won the 2,000 Guineas. At Epsom, Refuse To Bend had an excuse for finishing 13th, having failed to stay the trip, an achievement made easier by his determination to arrive at the start first, despite having set off for it virtually last.

Throughout his career, Refuse To Bend's breeding remained a source of fascination. By Sadler's Wells, and a half-brother to Melbourne Cup winner Media Puzzle, there were respectable grounds for expecting Refuse To Bend to prove best at beyond a mile, with a good chance of him favouring a mile and a half.

After the Derby, Dermot Weld confined Refuse To Bend to one mile, a decision resoundingly justified when, after a break, he easily defied his Group 1 penalty to win the Group 3 Desmond Stakes at Leopardstown impressively. It was therefore a nasty surprise when, three weeks later, Refuse To Bend ran a stinker in the Prix du Moulin at Longchamp.

Good or bad, Refuse To Bend remained a well-bred Classic winner with stallion potential, and Sheikh Mohammed had happy memories of buying a Classic winner who had subsequently disappointed, then been revived. In 1997, he had bought Daylami, the winner of that year's Poule d'Essai des Poulains, who, confined to races over a mile, had failed to win again.

So, after the Prix du Moulin, Sheikh Mohammed bought Refuse To Bend and was philosophical when, leased back to his previous owner for a run in the Breeders' Cup Mile at Santa Anita, his new recruit flopped again. Jockey Pat Smullen reported that Refuse To Bend had disliked the firm ground.

Refuse To Bend, third left, rediscovers his best mile form to defeat Soviet Song, right, in the Group 1 Queen Anne

In the Godolphin camp, the established theory was that, given time and a winter of Dubaian sunshine, Refuse To Bend might be restored to success, as Daylami had been. If Refuse To Bend appreciated Al Quoz and the sunshine, he didn't immediately show it on the racecourse. Forming part of Godolphin's small team at the World Cup meeting in March, Refuse To Bend was relaunched in the nine-furlong Dubai Duty Free Stakes but, ominously, Frankie Dettori opted to ride the South African star, Crimson Palace, and Refuse To Bend was well beaten.

He was well beaten again in the Juddmonte Lockinge Stakes over a mile at Newbury in May, and it may have taken only one more poor run for Refuse To Bend to have been sent scuttling off to stud. "He has been a big disappointment," trainer Saeed Bin Suroor admitted. "The problem is that he looks good. There is nothing wrong with him at all, but he just hasn't been running as well as we thought he would."

That was the trouble. He looked well, he worked well. Everything was well except where and when it mattered, on the racecourse.

Bin Suroor didn't immediately try Refuse To Bend over ten furlongs. Instead, at Sheikh Mohammed's insistence, he was wheeled out for a potentially embarrassing assault on the Group 1 Queen Anne Stakes at

5th Emirates Airline Champion Stakes (Group 1) (Newmarket, October 16) 3yo+ 10f Soft **111** (TS 74) 11 ran. *Mid-division, ridden over 2f out, no impression (K McEvoy), beaten 10l by Haafhd*

3rd Queen Elizabeth II Stakes (Sponsored By NetJets) (Group 1) (Ascot, September 25) 3yo+ 1m Good to firm **121** (TS 112) 11 ran. *Settled towards rear, progress over 2f out, chased leading pair over 1f out, kept on same pace final furlong (L Dettori), beaten 3l by Rakti*

11th Cantor Odds Sussex Stakes (Group 1) (Goodwood, July 28) 3yo+ 1m Good **87** (TS 80) 11 ran. *Tracked leader, led over 3f out, ridden and headed 2f out, weakening when badly hampered just inside final furlong (L Dettori), beaten 17¹/₂l by Soviet Song*

1st Coral-Eclipse Stakes (Group 1) (Sandown, July 3) 3yo+ 10f Good to soft **126** (TS 117) 12 ran. *Took keen hold early, close up, effort over 2f out, led well over 1f out, driven out, just held on (L Dettori), beat Warrsan by hd*

1st Queen Anne Stakes (Group 1) (Ascot, June 15) 4yo+ 1m Good to firm **123** (TS 111) 16 ran. *Tracked leaders, ridden over 2f out, switched right over 1f out, ran on to lead near finish (L Dettori), beat Soviet Song by nk*

8th Juddmonte Lockinge Stakes (Group 1) (Newbury, May 15) 4yo+ 1m Good **108** (TS 85) 15 ran. *Chased leaders, ridden over 2f out, soon one pace (L Dettori), beaten 5¹/₂l by Russian Rhythm*

8th Dubai Duty Free Stakes (Group 1) (Turf) (Nad Al Sheba, March 27) 3yo+ 9f Good to firm **110** (TS 84) 11 ran. *Led until headed 1f out, soon weakened (K McEvoy), beaten 4³/₄l by Right Approach*

11th NetJets Breeders' Cup Mile (Grade 1) (Santa Anita, October 25) 3yo+ 1m Firm **103** 13 ran ● **11th** Netjets Prix du Moulin de Longchamp (Group 1) (Longchamp, September 7) 3yo+ 1m Good to soft **107** 14 ran ● **1st** Desmond Stakes (Group 3) (Leopardstown, August 17) 3yo+ 1m Good to firm **123** 7 ran ● **13th** Vodafone Derby Stakes (Group 1) (Epsom, June 7) 3yo 12f Good **99** 20 ran ● **1st** Sagitta 2,000 Guineas Stakes (Group 1) (Newmarket, May 3) 3yo 1m Good **118** 20 ran ● **1st** Leopardstown 2,000 Guineas Trial Stakes (Listed) (Leopardstown, April 13) 3yo 1m Good to firm **111** 8 ran

1st Aga Khan Studs National Stakes (Group 1) (Curragh, September 15) 2yo 7f Good to firm **113** 7 ran ● **1st** Bagenalstown EBF Maiden (Div I) (Gowran Park, August 14) 2yo 7f Good **87** 13 ran

Royal Ascot, where Six Perfections, Soviet Song and Nebraska Tornado lay in wait among an unusually large, 16-runner field.

With the runners towed along by stablemate Lateen Sails, Dettori had Refuse To Bend, travelling well, close to the pace throughout and caught Soviet Song on the final thrust to the post, an effort that earned Dettori a one-day suspension for excessive use of the whip. It was Godolphin's first Group 1 success of the year, the opening salvo of an exceptional Royal Ascot for Bin Suroor and the team.

A pleasantly surprised Simon Crisford, Godolphin's manager, said, "The explanation for Refuse To Bend's form this year is that there is no

A second Group 1 success for Refuse To Bend, this time over ten furlongs, as he holds off Warrsan in the Eclipse

explanation." A similarly puzzled but equally delighted Dettori echoed, "I've been worried because there was no answer for his poor runs."

"It must be remembered," said Sheikh Mohammed, "that Daylami was disappointing but we managed to get him back. It has been the same with Refuse To Bend. Horses lose their form, and the key is to be patient with them. If you press too hard, they go down and down."

On the up, at least for the time being, Refuse To Bend, having pleased Bin Suroor in his work, was supplemented for the ten-furlong Coral-Eclipse Stakes, a race Godolphin had last won with Daylami in 1998. With Rakti, the impressive winner of the Prince of Wales's Stakes at Royal Ascot, disliking the softer ground and declining to settle, it was left to Refuse To Bend to demonstrate his versatility as regards ground conditions as well as distance. Driven on inside the final furlong, Refuse To Bend just held off the staying-on Warrsan, with the rest well adrift.

"I knew Warrsan had the edge on stamina," said Dettori. "The line came just quickly enough. I've loved this horse since I first rode him. I don't know why he ran so badly twice. Perhaps he lost his confidence."

Who knows? If Refuse To Bend knew the answer, he wasn't saying. Whether or not his confidence had been fully restored, that of punters had, sufficiently at least for them to make Refuse To Bend favourite for his next outing, the Sussex Stakes at Goodwood. It was an opportunity for Refuse To Bend to stake his claim to being Britain's best miler. Perhaps the sultry conditions affected him, perhaps the race came too soon, perhaps there were other reasons. There were 11 runners. Soviet Song finished first, and Refuse To Bend last.

"I tried to get a good position," Dettori reported. "I couldn't get him to switch off and he ran out of gas. I think the combination of Ascot and then the Eclipse was probably a bit too much for him and the race at Goodwood just didn't go right. We were in front way too early. He was pulling. We went flat out and then he died. It was a disaster."

After a healthy two-month break, Dr Jekyll, or Mr Hyde, returned to Ascot's mile course and faster ground for the Group 1 Queen Elizabeth II Stakes. Both trainer and jockey approached the test, featuring Rakti and Soviet Song, in contented mood.

Once again, there was nothing wrong with Refuse To Bend at home, and little wrong, on this occasion, at the racecourse. The faster conditions were in Rakti's favour and, having been drawn wide and carried wider, it was no disgrace, if no celebration either, for Refuse To Bend to finish three lengths third, with the improving Lucky Story between them.

"The draw didn't make that much difference," was Crisford's opinion. "We are delighted with the way he's run. That has laid the ghost of the Sussex Stakes. He is right back to form."

Unfortunately, it didn't last. The Champion Stakes promised to be an intriguing and revealing contest, with several high-class horses, including Haafhd and Doyen, seeking to recapture their best form. Azamour, winner of the St James's Palace Stakes and Irish Champion Stakes, and Norse Dancer, knocking on the door at the highest level, added further quality, with Lucky Story and the improving Mister Monet lively challengers.

As a balanced contest, the race went wrong before it started, with testing conditions proving no obstacle to Haafhd, but a considerable hindrance to several of his rivals. Refuse To Bend finished in anonymous midfield, albeit ahead of Doyen, Dettori's choice. Kerrin McEvoy said: "He travelled well during the early and middle stages of the race but then found it hard work on the wet ground. He tried his best."

And that was that. Refuse To Bend was retired and will stand at Darley's Kildangan Stud in 2005. His erratic season ended on a flat note, yet the low spots seemed so disappointing only because we knew what high notes he was capable of hitting when on song. Very few horses win Group 1 races as two, three and four-year-olds, as Refuse To Bend did, so it was all the more frustrating that he was unable to maintain the level of consistency that might have positioned him at the very top of the tree, instead of floating on and off the highest branch.

Despite that shortcoming, at his best Refuse To Bend was a match for any of his generation.

Refuse To Bend

bay colt, 17-3-2000

			Nearctic	Nearco
				Lady Angela
		Northern Dancer		
			Natalma	Native Dancer
	Sadler's Wells			Almahmoud
	b 1981			
			Bold Reason	Hail To Reason
				Lalun
		Fairy Bridge		
			Special	Forli
				Thong
			Mr Prospector	Raise A Native
				Gold Digger
		Gulch		
			Jameela	Rambunctious
	Market Slide			Asbury Mary
	ch 1991			
			Grenfall	Graustark
				Primonetta
		Grenzen		
			My Poly	Cyclotron
				Polywich

Bred by Moyglare Stud Farm Ltd in Ireland

Sire **Sadler's Wells**

Won 6 of 11 races, inc. Beresford S.-Gr3, Irish Derby Trial-Gr2, Irish 2,000 Guineas-Gr1, Eclipse S.-Gr1, Phoenix Champion S.-Gr1. Also 2nd in Prix du Jockey-Club-Gr1, King George VI & Queen Elizabeth S.-Gr1. Impeccably bred top-class performer from 8-12f, handsome, tough and consistent. Sire of Gr1 winners: Braashee, French Glory, In The Wings (x3), Old Vic (x2), Prince Of Dance, Scenic, Salsabil (x5), Opera House (x3), Runyon, Saddlers' Hall, El Prado, Johann Quatz, Masad, Barathea (x2), Fatherland, Fort Wood, Intrepidity (x3), Carnegie (x2), King's Theatre (x2), Northern Spur (x2), Moonshell, Muncie, Poliglote, Chief Contender, Dance Design, Darazari, Luna Wells, Cloudings, Ebadiyla (x2), Entrepreneur, In Command, Kayf Tara (x4), Dream Well (x2), Greek Dance, King Of Kings (x2), Leggera, Commander Collins, Daliapour, Montjeu (x6), Saffron Walden, Aristotle, Beat Hollow (x4), Subtle Power, Galileo (x3), Imagine (x2), Milan, Perfect Soul, Sequoyah, Sligo Bay, Ballingarry, Black Sam Bellamy (x2), Gossamer (x2), High Chaparral (x6), Islington (x4), Quarter Moon, Sholokov, Alberto Giacometti, Brian Boru (x2), Doyen, Powerscourt, Refuse To Bend (4), Yesterday, Quiff, Playful Act.

Dam **Market Slide**

Won 5 of 19 races in Ireland and US. Lengthy sort, useful sprinter on turf and dirt, half-sister to Twilight Agenda. Dam of: Media Puzzle (1997 g by Theatrical; Gr1 winner), Ripple of Pride (1999 f by Sadler's Wells; winner), Refuse To Bend (2000 c by Sadler's Wells; Classic winner), Genuine Charm (2001 f by Sadler's Wells; placed) She has a yearling colt by Danehill.

Pedigree assessment

After disappointing early efforts for Godolphin, Refuse To Bend got agreeably back on track with several fine performances in 2004 and retires to Kildangan with the commendable – and rather rare – distinction of having won in Group 1 company in each of his three seasons in training. We learnt at three that he was not one of those Sadler's Wellses for whom 12 furlongs comes naturally, and he did not try that distance again, but the Eclipse surely proved that he was just as adept at a mile and a quarter as at a mile. He was no superstar at either distance, but he is sure to be granted plenty of chances at stud. Breeders would do well to recognise that he was more a product of his family than of his sire. *TM*

Royal Millennium (Ire)

6yo bay gelding   **121**

Royal Academy (USA) - Galatrix (Be My Guest (USA))

Owner Jackie & George Smith

Trainer M R Channon

Breeder Mrs G Smith

Career: **44** starts   won **6**   second **9**   third **8**   **£262,895** win and place

By Mark Blackman

EVERYTHING comes to he who waits. Riders of talented hold-up sprinter Royal Millennium have lived by that maxim throughout his career, and it proved pertinent for his trainer and owners in 2004 as the consistent gelding finally made his Group-race breakthrough at the age of six.

As a three- and four-year-old, the son of Royal Academy established something of a reputation for flashing home from the rear to grab a minor berth in valuable handicaps – usually in desperately unlucky circumstances. It was a trait he displayed in the biggest arenas and the biggest races – Glorious Goodwood, the Tote International, the Ayr Gold Cup, Ascot's Festival of Racing.

By 2003, at the age of five, he was showing similar tendencies, but had rather upgraded himself. Now he was finishing strongly to collect prize-money in Group races – second in the Group 1 Prix de la Foret, second in the Group 3 Bentinck Stakes at Newmarket, fourth in another Group 3 at Maisons-Laffitte.

Then in 2004 he finally delivered what he had promised for so long. Three Group wins over six furlongs (all by narrow margins) and a strong-finishing third behind the emerging force Var in the Group 1 Prix de l'Abbaye at Longchamp in October turned a career tally of three wins from 38 starts into a far more respectable six from 44.

That he made it to the track at all at six was another test of the patience of his connections. Reportedly "not an easy horse to train" at home, and hindered by a setback in the first half of the campaign, it was not until late June that he reappeared in the Group 3 Chipchase Stakes at Newcastle. The very soft ground was also a concern to trainer Mick Channon, but he needn't have worried. The field split into two, but the far-side group in which Royal Millennium found himself always held sway and, after travelling well throughout, he needed only to be shaken up to collar the high-class

Royal Millennium takes the Renaissance at The Curragh, one of three Group 3 wins for the consistent sprinter

and race-fit Somnus to prevail by a neck. Granted, he was getting 8lb from the Group 1-winning runner-up, but Tim Easterby's star is a tough nut to crack when the mud is flying, and this went down as a fine performance. Royal Millennium had made the breakthrough, and there was surely more to come.

Defeats followed in two Group 1s, though he was far from disgraced in the Haydock Sprint Cup, where he finished with his customary gusto to get within around two lengths of Tante Rose.

By the autumn, Royal Millennium was in the form of his life. He didn't need to run up to his Haydock form to beat Moss Vale and Grand Reward in the Group 3 Ballygallon Stud Renaissance Stakes at The Curragh, before his storming effort in the Abbaye at Longchamp. "We'd have won in another 100 yards," was the view of regular partner Ted Durcan after he had flashed home to get within a length and a half of Var, over a five-furlong distance that unquestionably played far more to the strengths of Clive Brittain's speedster.

Royal Millennium's campaign in Europe closed with another Group 3 success, this time in the Bentinck Stakes at Newmarket. Sent off the 7-2 favourite in a field of 14, he again found himself travelling in the favoured of the two groups into which the field split. After all those fine

2004   Race record

1st Igloos Bentinck Stakes (Group 3) (Newmarket, October 15) 3yo+ 6f Soft **121** (TS 89) 14 ran. *Raced towards stands' side, chased leader, ridden over 2f out, led well inside final furlong, ran on (T E Durcan), beat Moss Vale by shd*

3rd Prix de l'Abbaye de Longchamp Majestic Barriere (Group 1) (Longchamp, October 3) 2yo+ 5f Good **115** (TS 112) 15 ran. *Towards rear early, headway on inside before halfway, switched right 1½f out, ran on well final furlong to take 3rd last strides (T E Durcan), beaten 1½l by Var*

1st Ballygallon Stud Renaissance Stakes (Group 3) (Curragh, September 18) 3yo+ 6f Yielding **115** (TS 98) 12 ran. *Held up in touch, headway 2f out, 3rd over 1f out, led inside final furlong, kept on well (T E Durcan), beat Moss Vale by ½l*

4th Stanleybet Sprint Cup (Group 1) (Haydock, September 4) 3yo+ 6f Good **118** (TS 112) 19 ran. *Behind, headway when not clear run and switched left over 1f out, ran on inside final furlong (T E Durcan), beaten 2¼l by Tante Rose*

12th Prix Maurice de Gheest (Group 1) (Deauville, August 8) 3yo+ 6½f Good to soft **105** 18 ran. *In touch, ridden and hung right 1½f out, soon beaten (T E Durcan), beaten 5¾l by Somnus*

1st Foster's Lager Chipchase Stakes (Group 3) (Newcastle, June 26) 3yo+ 6f Soft **115** (TS 115) 11 ran. *Prominent far side, smooth headway over 1f out, shaken up to lead close home (T Quinn), beat Somnus by nk*

Other wins

2003 **1st** Q Associates Rated Stakes Showcase Handicap (0-110) (Newbury, October 24) 3yo+ 6f Good to firm **115** 16 ran **2002** **1st** EBF Racegoers Club Classified Stakes (Goodwood, August 3) 3yo+ (0-95) 7f Good to firm **104** 5 ran **2001** **1st** BKL Tenon Maiden Stakes (Div II) (Salisbury, June 12) 3yo 7f Good to firm **82** 13 ran

efforts on the 'wrong' side in handicaps in his younger days, it seems the gods were prepared to give him a break at last.

Delivered to grab the initiative inside the final furlong, Royal Millennium held on gamely by a short head from old rival Moss Vale under a 4lb penalty. Given a mark of 121 by Racing Post Ratings, it represented the best performance of his career on his 44th racecourse appearance.

Royal Millennium, who did not race at two, was rated 100 at the end of his three-year-old season; he climbed to 111 at four; 116 at five; and 121 at six. His has been a career of relentless improvement, year on year. With no career at stud to look forward to, he is certain to be back in action again at the age of seven, and if he can improve again by as much as he has with every passing season so far, a first Group 1 success looks far from a forlorn hope.

A winner over seven furlongs in his younger days, he now seems most at home over a strongly run six with some give in the ground, conditions that have prevailed for each of his three biggest successes. And, as ever, he still needs to be delivered as late as possible. "He pulls himself up in front," says Channon. "Has done all his life."

At least now he's getting to the front.

Royal Millennium

bay gelding, 16-4-1998

		Northern Dancer	Nearctic
	Nijinsky		Natalma
Royal Academy		Flaming Page	Bull Page
b 1987			Flaring Top
		Crimson Satan	Spy Song
	Crimson Saint		Papila
		Bolero Rose	Bolero
			First Rose
		Northern Dancer	Nearctic
	Be My Guest		Natalma
Galatrix		What A Treat	Tudor Minstrel
b 1986			Rare Treat
		Alleged	Hoist The Flag
	Alligatrix		Princess Pout
		Shore	Round Table
			Delta

Bred by Jackie Smith in Ireland

Sire Royal Academy

Won 4 of 7 starts. At 2, won 1 (6f) of 2 starts. At 3, won 3 (Tetrarch S-Gr3, July Cup-Gr1, Breeders' Cup Mile-Gr1) of 5 starts, also 2nd Irish 2,000 Guineas, Haydock Sprint Cup. By Triple Crown winner and outstanding sire, though with patchy record as a sire of sires, out of US stakes winner. Brother to Gr2-placed Encino, half-brother to Gr2 winner Pancho Villa, stakes winner Alydariel (dam of Gr2 winner Jeune Homme), Gr2 winner Terlingua (dam of Storm Cat). Stands at Ashford in US, 2005 fee $17,500. Oldest progeny 12, sire of (northern hemisphere foals): Bolshoi (Gr2), Centaine (Gr2), Oscar Schindler (Irish St Leger-Gr1 x 2), Painter's Row (Gr3), Ali-Royal (Sussex S-Gr1), Flame Of Athens (Gr3), Truth Or Dare (Gr3), Carmine Lake (Prix de l'Abbaye-Gr1), Equal Rights (Gr3), Key Royal (Gr3), Sleepytime (1,000 Guineas-Gr1), Dernier Croise (Gr3), El Maimoun (Gr2), Impressionist (Gr3), Zalaiyka (Poule d'Essai des Pouliches-Gr1), Circle Of Gold (Gr3), Lavery (Phoenix S-Gr1), Lucido (Gr3), Tiger Royal (Gr3), Val Royal (Breeders' Cup Mile-Gr1), Il Bacio (JapGr3), Avorado (Gr3), CD Europe (Gr3), Miss Gazon (Gr3), Royal Millennium (Gr3), Academic Angel (Gr3), Bullish Luck (HK Gold Cup-Gr1), Mananan McLir (Gr2), Royal Experiment (Gr3), Acago (Gr3), Quero Quero (Gr2), Art Master (Gr3).

Dam Galatrix

Unraced at 2, won 1 (1m) of 9 starts at 3, also placed over 6-8f. By top-class 2yo/miler and very good sire, out of smart 2yo Alligatrix. Half-sister to Gr1 winner Croco Rouge and Listed winners Alidiva (dam of Gr1 winners Ali-Royal, Sleepytime, Taipan) and Persianalli. Dam of: Jonty Rhodes (1991 c by Petorius; placed), Dramatic Entry (1993 f by Persian Bold; winner), Trixmare (1994 f by Kenmare; unraced), Millitrix (1995 f by Doyoun; placed), Royal Millennium (1998 c by Royal Academy; Gr3 winner, Gr1 placed), Berkeleysquare Boy (1999 c by Spectrum; unplaced), 2003 c by Mark Of Esteem (67,000gns yearling).

Pedigree assessment

The exploits of Ali-Royal and Sleepytime doubtless led to the mating that produced Royal Millennium. Whereas his close relatives were milers, Royal Millennium is best over 6-7f. One of several geldings who made a big impact on the European sprinting scene in 2004, the very tough Royal Millennium is likely to be prominent again in 2005. *JH*

Rule Of Law (USA)

3yo bay colt **122**

Kingmambo (USA) - Crystal Crossing (Ire) (Royal Academy (USA))

Owner Godolphin

Trainer Saeed Bin Suroor

Breeder Robert Sangster and Ben Sangster

Career: **9** starts | won **4** | second **2** | third **2** | **£721,261** win and place

By James Willoughby

THE argument for reducing the distance of the St Leger met with its ultimate rebuttal in Rule Of Law. The race's 228th winner exemplified the characteristics that the great race distils best in the Classic thoroughbred: courage, doggedness, durability.

Rule Of Law led for every step of the one mile, six furlongs and one hundred and thirty-two yards. And the drama was in the detail, for it took until the dying strides for him to subdue the opposition.

Three months earlier, there were plenty who doubted Rule Of Law's ability to last even a mile and a half in the Derby. A smart staying two-year-old when trained by David Loder, he had returned with a promising second to North Light in the Dante Stakes, on his first start for Godolphin. The vigour with which he finished, after being checked in his run, suggested that longer distances would suit. But his pedigree did not give the corresponding guarantee, at least the way that many of us read it at the time.

Frankie Dettori had ridden Rule Of Law at York, but preferred the chances of the 2,000 Guineas runner-up Snow Ridge at Epsom. That left the ride to Kerrin McEvoy, an Australian recruited as second rider to Godolphin after creating a good impression both in his native country and in Dubai. It was McEvoy's first ride in the Derby and many thought it showed.

Rule Of Law was last of the 14 runners for the first seven furlongs. Watching the race again, it seemed as if this was a deliberate ploy. While it later became clear that positive tactics suited the colt, the doubts about his stamina might have influenced his connections in this regard.

Turning for home, he had only a couple behind him, but when McEvoy became urgent Rule Of Law made very good ground. He was inclined to hang left and took time to gain his balance, even stumbling over a furlong out. Though he never looked a serious threat to win once North

Rule Of Law, under a fine front-running ride from Kerrin McEvoy, holds off Quiff to take the spoils in the St Leger

Light had asserted, he continued to run on strongly and took second from Let The Lion Roar in the final few yards.

It was suggested that Rule Of Law might have got even closer to North Light than a length and a half had his partner had more experience of the course. The Derby was a strongly run race, however, and it is likely that no particular advantage accrued to those who were forwardly placed. It might even have been an advantage to hang back during the frenetic opening uphill stages.

If Rule Of Law was unlucky at Epsom, it did not show in the Irish Derby, for which a supplementary fee of €95,000 had to be paid. Reunited with Dettori and ridden more prominently, he led for a few strides around two furlongs out before being outgunned by Grey Swallow, North Light and, last of all, Tycoon. Despite the change in tactics, he was beaten marginally further by the winner and performed to a similar level. "He ran a good, solid race. He just couldn't quicken when he needed to," said Dettori.

At this stage, Rule Of Law was given a rest. He had suffered a low-grade respiratory infection after Epsom that had ruled him out of Royal

2004   Race record

1st betfair.com St Leger Stakes (Group 1) (Doncaster, September 11) 3yo 1m6½f Good to firm **122** (TS 106) 9 ran. *Set moderate pace, shaken up and lengthened over 2f out, found extra inside final furlong, gamely (K McEvoy), beat Quiff by hd*

1st Daily Telegraph Great Voltigeur Stakes (Group 2) (York, August 17) 3yo 12f Good **121** (TS 56) 7 ran. *Set steady pace, quickened 4f out, pushed along and quickened again 2f out, ridden over 1f out and stayed on well (L Dettori), beat Let The Lion Roar by 2½l*

4th Budweiser Irish Derby (Group 1) (Curragh, June 27) 3yo 12f Good to firm **122** (TS 121) 10 ran. *Close up in 2nd, challenged entering straight, led over 2f out, headed under 2f out, no extra inside final furlong (L Dettori), beaten 2¼l by Grey Swallow*

2nd Vodafone Derby Stakes (Group 1) (Epsom, June 5) 3yo 12f Good **121** (TS 120) 14 ran. *Held up, last to 5f out, 12th straight, hanging left but progress from 3f out, stayed on well final furlong to snatch 2nd on post (K McEvoy), beaten 1½l by North Light*

2nd totesport Dante Stakes (Group 2) (York, May 12) 3yo 10½f Good to soft **118** (TS 91) 10 ran. *In touch, pushed along and outpaced 3f out, headway 2f out, switched left over 1f out, soon ridden and kept on well (L Dettori), beaten ½l by North Light*

2003

3rd Hackney Empire Royal Lodge Stakes (Group 2) (Ascot, September 27) 2yo 1m Good to firm **109** 10 ran ● **1st** Acomb Stakes (Listed) (York, August 19) 2yo 7f Good to firm **104** 7 ran ● **1st** Ramesys Maiden Stakes (York, July 11) 2yo 7f Good to firm **98** 11 ran ● **3rd** Palletline Maiden Stakes (Sandown, June 14) 2yo 7f Good to firm **66** 8 ran

Ascot and forced the hand of his connections in sending him to The Curragh one week later. This could not have been the ideal preparation for a Classic, and the race might have taken even more out of him than normal.

Rule Of Law was back in strong work by the beginning of August, and ten days before his next intended outing in the Great Voltigeur Stakes he impressed in a piece of work with Millstreet on Racecourse Side at Newmarket. It was all systems go for a St Leger campaign.

Six horses opposed him at York, chief among them being Let The Lion Roar and the Aidan O'Brien-trained Go For Gold. Rule Of Law looked superb in the paddock and went off a solid favourite. The small field enabled Dettori to dictate the pace and the Italian took full advantage, increasing the tempo early in the straight and again two furlongs out. Rule Of Law came home two and a half lengths clear of his old rival – the same distance as at The Curragh.

With Dettori required to ride Doyen in Ireland, it was clear more than two weeks before the St Leger that McEvoy would take over the reins on Rule Of Law. To this point, the 23-year-old had ridden more than 30 winners in his first season with Godolphin, including the Group 2 Betfair Cup on Byron. There had been a bump or two along the road, however.

"The variety is great and it took me a while to get the hang of it," he later admitted. "I soon found out that you need to be a horseman as well as a jockey over here."

The Leger was to be the acid test for the man from Streaky Bay, near Adelaide. He had risen to prominence back home when winning the 2000 Melbourne Cup on Brew, but moving to a different country requires a jockey to prove himself anew.

In the run-up to the St Leger, McEvoy received a timely boost to his confidence. He took over as Godolphin's number one jockey for 24 hours at the final night meeting of the season at Windsor, after Dettori received a suspension, and two good rides yielded two winners for his employer, on Naheef in a Listed race and Ancient World in the Group 3 Winter Hill Stakes. Then, the weekend before the St Leger, McEvoy scored his first Group 1 win in Europe when the Clive Brittain-trained Warrsan took the Grosser Preis von Baden.

Godolphin's fortunes were clearly on a high, but the St Leger was no easy task for McEvoy and Rule Of Law. Sir Michael Stoute confirmed that impressive Yorkshire Oaks winner Quiff would join her stable companion Maraahel, successful in the Group 3 Gordon Stakes at Goodwood. O'Brien was sending Go For Gold, Mikado and Tycoon from Ballydoyle and the field of nine was completed by Let The Lion Roar, progressive handicapper Frank Sonata and Czech St Leger winner Darsalam.

In Rule Of Law's favour was the going. Quiff had appeared to be well suited by a soft surface at York, and freakishly fast times during the first few days of the Doncaster meeting underscored the fact that the ground was unseasonably firm. Quiff even had her participation put in doubt briefly, but Rule Of Law would be in his element.

When the stalls opened, nothing was keen to go on. Reacting to the situation, McEvoy allowed Rule Of Law to slide into the lead, which was not the rider's original intention. Windy conditions made judging the pace even more difficult and McEvoy could not afford to err much from the ideal, especially given the poor record of front runners on Town Moor.

It was most surprising that Rule Of Law was allowed to have things his own way. Had O'Brien been allowed to interpose at this point, he might have instructed Jimmy Fortune on Mikado or Seb Sanders on Go For Gold to pressurise the Godolphin colt. This would have helped his third contender Tycoon, a horse who is always held up. As it was, the other jockeys allowed McEvoy to ride a good race – and he did not miss his chance.

Tracked into the final three furlongs by Kieren Fallon on Quiff, McEvoy asked his mount for more energy. When Quiff was forced to switch shortly after, the distance that Rule Of Law stole was in excess of the winning margin. Nevertheless, the filly was now finding her full stride down the outside and Fallon had not yet gone for everything.

Had McEvoy gone a stride faster through the early stages, Rule Of Law might have been a sitting duck. Inside the final furlong, Fallon was becoming more urgent on Quiff and time was running out. Rule Of Law responded to his partner's urgings to find one extra burst about 100 yards out, and the extra momentum killed off Quiff's challenge. The winning margin was a head, but it seemed as decisive as a length.

It was one of those moments of synergy between horse and rider that makes it obvious from where horseracing draws some of its appeal. Jockeys tend to get too much praise when they win and too much criticism when they lose. But if their influence is generally overstated, it really seemed for that moment as if Rule Of Law and McEvoy had actually taken part in a team game. The determination of one had inspired the other in a positive feedback loop.

The St Leger is often one of the most exciting races of the season. By sending Classic three-year-olds further than they necessarily want to go, the race has the capacity to take them somewhere else entirely: somewhere they can display the virtues that are just as important for a potential stallion as speed and class.

Shortly after the St Leger, plans to reduce the distance of the Prix du Jockey-Club to ten and a half furlongs were announced by French racing supremo Louis Romanet. Given its proximity to the Derby, this move does seem to make sense. It induced former BHB chairman Peter Savill to suggest a parallel reshaping to the Classic programme in Britain.

"Maybe all Derbys should go to a mile and a quarter and the Leger should be the race over a mile and a half," he said. "It's sad when you win the Leger and it's regarded as the kiss of death. It's not even considered for most decent mile-and-a-half horses. To them, it's a diminution of their breeding value."

Would it not be the tail wagging the dog if modifications to the Pattern took place because of the type of horse that breeders want to produce? Winning the Leger proves that a horse has stamina, not a lack of speed. If a tough, genuine and consistent horse like Rule Of Law is not valued as the type of animal to strengthen the breed, then the acumen that breeders are displaying has a very short-term aspect.

Winning the St Leger will certainly not help Rule Of Law when he returns to training in 2005. He will have to carry a Group 1 penalty in lesser Pattern events and it could be that Godolphin send him to the continent in search of further success at the top level. That is not to say that he cannot make improvement, however, and he certainly seemed a more tactically versatile horse by the season's end.

There may be better horses in training next season, but few will be as dependable. Make no mistake: he will punish any shortcomings.

Rule Of Law

bay colt 6-3-2001

Kingmambo b 1990	Mr Prospector	Raise A Native	Native Dancer Raise You
		Gold Digger	Nashua Sequence
	Miesque	Nureyev	**Northern Dancer** Special
		Pasadoble	Prove Out Santa Quilla
Crystal Crossing b 1994	Royal Academy	Nijinsky	**Northern Dancer** Flaming Page
		Crimson Saint	Crimson Satan Bolero Rose
	Never So Fair	Never So Bold	Bold Lad Never Never Land
		Favoletta	Baldric Violetta

Bred by Robert & Ben Sangster in Kentucky

Sire Kingmambo

Won 5 of 13 races, inc. Poule d'Essai des Poulains-Gr1, St James's Palace S.-Gr1, Prix du Moulin de Longchamp-Gr1). Medium-sized, attractive individual. Among the best milers of his generation, game, consistent, with a good turn of foot. Sire of: American Boss (Gr2), El Condor Pasa (NHK Mile Cup-Gr1, Japan Cup-Gr1, Grand Prix de Saint-Cloud-Gr1), Mambo Twist (Gr3), Parade Ground (Gr2), Admire Mambo (Gr2), Lemon Drop Kid (Futurity S.-Gr1, Belmont S.-Gr1, Travers S.-Gr1, Whitney S.-Gr1, Woodward H.-Gr1), Monarch's Maze (Gr2), Bluemamba (Poule d'Essai des Pouliches-Gr1), King Cugat (Gr2), Kingsalsa (Gr3), King's Best (2,000 Guineas-Gr1), Parade Leader (Gr2), Penny's Gold (Gr3), King Fidelia (Gr3), Malhub (Golden Jubilee S.-Gr1), Okawango (Grand Criterium-Gr1), Voodoo Dancer (Garden City H.-Gr1), Dubai Destination (Queen Anne S.-Gr1), Walzerkonigin (Gr2), Governor Brown (Gr3), Russian Rhythm (1,000 Guineas-Gr1, Coronation S.-Gr1, Nassau S.-Gr1, Lockinge S.-Gr1), Illustrious Miss (Gr3), Mambo Slew (Gr3), Rule Of Law (St Leger S-Gr1), Divine Proportions (Prix Morny-Gr1, Prix Marcel Boussac-Gr1).

Dam Crystal Crossing

Won 1 of 7 races. Showed useful form at 2 in England and Ireland, and at 3 in US. Sister to Gr3 winner Circle Of Gold, from family of speedy and precocious Amaranda and Derby winner Teenoso. Dam of: Crossbreeze (1999 f by Red Ransom; placed), Crystal Class (2000 c by Mr Prospector; placed), Rule Of Law (2001 c by Kingmambo; Gr1 winner). She has a yearling colt by Rahy and a filly foal by Elusive Quality.

Pedigree assessment

A brief glance at Rule Of Law's pedigree background might have suggested that if he were to earn distinction on the racecourse, it would be as a miler. That was the distance favoured by his sire, while his maternal grandsire was probably equally adept at six furlongs and eight. His dam's only win came in a juvenile sprint, and her dam was the daughter of a champion sprinter. In fact Rule Of Law never ran at less than ten furlongs as a three-year-old, got better as the distances lengthened, and wound up making all the running in the St Leger. Here was a reminder that, where stamina is concerned, pedigree may offer clues, but does not provide definitive answers. The most reliable guide is the horse himself, and the way he travels through his races. After the Derby, it was always a fair bet that Rule Of Law would cope with the Leger distance. *TM*

Russian Rhythm (USA)

4yo chestnut filly   **123**

Kingmambo (USA) - Balistroika (USA) (Nijinsky (Can))

Owner Cheveley Park Stud

Trainer Sir Michael Stoute

Breeder Brushwood Stable

Career: **10** starts   won **7** | second **2** | third **0** | **£770,120** win and place

By Graham Dench

RUSSIAN RHYTHM or Soviet Song? It must have been a pretty straightforward choice for most Ten To Follow entrants debating which filly was likely to profit most from the considerably enhanced opportunities provided in 2004 for high-class older fillies.

After all, Russian Rhythm had carried all before her against her own sex as a three-year-old, winning the 1,000 Guineas and the Coronation Stakes and adding a third Group 1 prize in Goodwood's Nassau Stakes before being beaten twice by the colts in the autumn. Soviet Song, on the other hand, had remained winless since landing the Fillies' Mile at Ascot and had finished behind Russian Rhythm on all three occasions that they met.

Russian Rhythm featured in no fewer than 16,082 of the competition's 48,574 entries, whereas Soviet Song attracted a mere 1,211 votes, a good proportion of them probably submitted by members of the Elite Racing Club, who own her.

Nobody could have guessed it at the time, but Russian Rhythm's season was over almost before it had started. Newbury's Juddmonte Lockinge Stakes, in which she accounted for a classy field of 14 rivals, including Norse Dancer, Refuse To Bend and Indian Haven, turned out to be her only race. Although there were suggestions that she would be back later on and entries were made for her in both the Sun Chariot Stakes and the Champion Stakes at Newmarket in October, she was never seen again in public.

Soviet Song, however, staged a dramatic comeback after being beaten on her first two starts of the season, including at odds of 4-11 in a weak race at Kempton, and recorded a Group 2 win at The Curragh, second place in the Queen Anne Stakes and three successive Group 1 wins, the first two of them in precisely the races that Russian Rhythm was kept in training for.

The Lockinge was Russian Rhythm's only win in open company and looked top-class form at the time. The half-length second Salselon went

Russian Rhythm, right, wins the Lockinge on her only run of 2004. Norse Dancer, left, is third, with Salselon second

off a 66-1 chance but was a multiple Group winner in Italy and there was every chance that he had improved significantly for new trainer Luca Cumani. With Norse Dancer third and two Classic winners down the field it seemed reasonable to take a positive view, but Salselon turned out to be an underachiever and the race did not work out anything like as well as one would have hoped.

It nevertheless looked a perfect launching pad for another highly successful season for Russian Rhythm. She was installed favourite for Royal Ascot's Queen Anne Stakes when the first ante-post list was issued but missed that race, having returned from Newbury "under the weather" and with "a bit of a temperature".

Before long rumours circulated that she was to be retired, but while Chris Richardson, the managing director of Cheveley Park Stud, admitted that she had suffered a strain to her off-fore suspensory, he insisted it was not as serious as it might have been. The vet, he said, had given her the all-clear to resume trotting towards the end of June, with a view to an autumn return.

2004 Race record

1st Juddmonte Lockinge Stakes (Group 1) (Newbury, May 15) 4yo+ 1m Good **118** (TS 95) 15 ran. *Held up mid-division, headway 2f out, strong run from over 1f out, led final 100yds, gamely (K Fallon), beat Salselon by ½l*

2003

5th Emirates Airline Champion Stakes (Group 1) (Newmarket, October 18) 3yo+ 10f Good to firm **110** 12 ran ● **2nd** Queen Elizabeth II Stakes (Sponsored By NetJets) (Group 1) (Ascot, September 27) 3yo+ 1m Good to firm **121** 8 ran ● **1st** Vodafone Nassau Stakes (Group 1) (Goodwood, August 2) 3yo+ 10f Good **121** 8 ran ● **1st** Coronation Stakes (Group 1) (Ascot, June 20) 3yo 1m Good to firm **123** 9 ran ● **1st** Sagitta 1,000 Guineas Stakes (Group 1) (Newmarket, May 4) 3yo 1m Good to firm **118** 19 ran

2002

2nd Betfair Cheveley Park Stakes (Group 1) (Newmarket, October 4) 2yo 6f Firm **109** 6 ran ● **1st** Peugeot Lowther Stakes (Group 2) (York, August 22) 2yo 6f Good to firm **114** 5 ran ● **1st** Princess Margaret Stakes (Group 3) (Ascot, July 27) 2yo 6f Good to firm **111** 6 ran ● **1st** Villas At Stonehaven Tobago EBF Maiden Fillies' Stakes (Newmarket (July), June 28) 2yo 6f Good to firm **90** 6 ran

It was suggested that Russian Rhythm might return in the Queen Elizabeth II Stakes, in which she was second to Falbrav in 2003, or the Sun Chariot, which was among those races upgraded to Group 1 status for the first time, but her retirement was announced just days before the former race following a further setback. She was reportedly suffering from muscle stiffness, and as she had been off for such a long time Sir Michael Stoute was finding it difficult to get her back to fitness.

Stoute described Russian Rhythm as "a wonderful specimen" and added that he would miss her. So too will Kieren Fallon, who was on board the filly for all her ten runs and said: "She has to be one of the best fillies I have ridden. She had bags of class – just look what she did to Soviet Song every time they met."

If the brave decision to keep Russian Rhythm in training for a third season back-fired somewhat, she retired with a magnificent record. She won seven of her ten races, four of them at Group 1 level, and according to Racing Post Ratings, her 1,000 Guineas defeat of Six Perfections following a troubled preparation was the best in the race since Cape Verdi in 1998. She finished worse than second only once, when past her best following a long season in the 2003 Champion Stakes.

The 440,000 guineas that Cheveley Park Stud paid for her as a yearling proved a snip, and with her younger half-brother Perfectperformance emerging as another Classic possible following his win in Ascot's Royal Lodge Stakes one simply could not put a price on her now. She will be covered in 2005 by Pivotal, one of Cheveley Park Stud's own stallions.

Russian Rhythm   *chestnut filly 12-2-2000*

		Raise A Native	Native Dancer
	Mr Prospector		Raise You
Kingmambo		Gold Digger	Nashua
b 1990			Sequence
		Nureyev	Northern Dancer
	Miesque		Special
		Pasadoble	Prove Out
			Santa Quilla
		Northern Dancer	Nearctic
	Nijinsky		Natalma
Balistroika		Flaming Page	Bull Page
ch 1988			Flaring Top
		Balidar	Will Somers
	Balidaress		Violet Bank
		Innocence	Sea Hawk
			Novitiate

Bred by Brushwood Stable in Kentucky. $370,000 Keeneland November foal, 440,000gns
Tattersalls Houghton yearling

Sire **Kingmambo**

Won 5 of 13 races, inc. Poule d'Essai des Poulains-Gr1, St James's Palace S.-Gr1, Prix du Moulin-Gr1). Medium-sized, attractive individual. Among the best milers of his generation. Sire of: American Boss (Gr2), El Condor Pasa (NHK Mile Cup-Gr1, Japan Cup-Gr1, Grand Prix de Saint-Cloud-Gr1), Mambo Twist (Gr3), Parade Ground (Gr2), Admire Mambo (Gr2), Lemon Drop Kid (Futurity S.-Gr1, Belmont S.-Gr1, Travers S.-Gr1, Whitney S.-Gr1, Woodward H.-Gr1), Monarch's Maze (Gr2), Bluemamba (Poule d'Essai des Pouliches-Gr1), King Cugat (Gr2), Kingsalsa (Gr3), King's Best (2,000 Guineas-Gr1), Parade Leader (Gr2), Penny's Gold (Gr3), King Fidelia (Gr3), Malhub (Golden Jubilee S.-Gr1), Okawango (Grand Criterium-Gr1), Voodoo Dancer (Garden City H.-Gr1), Dubai Destination (Queen Anne S.-Gr1), Walzerkonigin (Gr2), Governor Brown (Gr3), Russian Rhythm (1,000 Guineas-Gr1, Coronation S.-Gr1, Nassau S.-Gr1, Lockinge S.-Gr1), Illustrious Miss (Gr3), Mambo Slew (Gr3), Rule Of Law (St Leger S-Gr1), Divine Proportions (Prix Morny-Gr1, Prix Marcel Boussac-Gr1).

Dam **Balistroika**

Unraced half-sister to Gr1 winners Desirable (also dam of Gr1 winner Shadayid), Park Appeal (also dam of Gr1 winner Cape Cross and grand-dam of Gr1 winner Diktat) and Alydaress. Dam of Lanseria (1993 f by Diesis; unraced), unnamed (1994 f by Diesis; died young), Alawal (1995 c by Miswaki; winner), Zenno Keima (1996 c by Gone West; winner), Ive Gota Bad Liver (1997 f by Mt Livermore; winner, Gr3-placed), Balade Russe (1999 f by Gone West; winner), Russian Rhythm (2000 f by Kingmambo; Gr1 winner), Marisa (2001 f by Swain; unraced), Perfectperformance (2002 c by Rahy; Gr2 winner). Her yearling is a colt by Rahy and her foal a filly by Kingmambo.

Pedigree assessment

It was a shame that Russian Rhythm, one of the most consistent and gifted fillies of recent years, could manage only one start as a four-year-old. Her form in the Lockinge showed her to be as good as ever, and there were sound reasons to suppose that she would improve from that outing. Niggling problems decreed that we should see her no more, and her future lies as a broodmare for Cheveley Park Stud. She promises to be a tremendous asset in that role, with an impeccable pedigree that is regularly updated with new star performers in the family, the latest being her juvenile half-brother, Group 2 winner Perfectperformance. *TM*

Salselon

5yo bay horse   **120**

Salse (USA) - Heady (Rousillon (USA))

Owner Scuderia Briantea SRL

Trainer L M Cumani

Breeder Whitsbury Manor Stud

Career: **30** starts   won **8**   second **7**   third **5**   **£421,390** win and place

By Lee Mottershead

LIKE Brussels sprouts and bagpipes, Salselon is something of an acquired taste. If you've ever backed him – particularly on one infamous day at Newmarket – there's a good chance you may loathe him as you have never loathed a racehorse before. Yet if you haven't backed him, Salselon is a gloriously rich source of entertainment. You'll enjoy him more if you stay in the latter camp.

We knew of his wayward tendencies before his Joel Stakes display but, even by his own high standards, this was something else. Formerly trained in Italy, Salselon was transferred to an Italian in Britain for the 2004 season, seeking to improve on a worthy record of four Group 3 victories with the help of Luca Cumani. By the time he went after a fifth Group 3 triumph at Newmarket in October, Salselon had already showed himself capable of better form than he had ever achieved in his native country, with two Group 1 placings secured earlier in the campaign. There could be little doubt that Salselon was more than capable of winning the Joel Stakes if Salselon wanted to win the Joel Stakes.

The early signs were not good. While the other 12 runners raced as one through the first half of the contest, Salselon raced alone, sitting many lengths off the pack, his dummy well and truly spat out. Then, as the one-mile contest entered its final quarter-mile, Salselon suddenly decided to take an interest. Racing towards the stands side, some way apart from those fighting for the spoils up the centre of the track, the blinkered five-year-old rushed through the gears. Unleashing a tremendous turn of foot, the sort that very few horses possess, Salselon swept to the front and to certain victory.

Except that with Salselon victory is never certain. It was about 50 yards from the line when he seemed to take in what was happening. As the realisation dawned on him that he had propelled himself into a clear lead,

Salselon frustrates connections and punters alike as he stops in front and throws away victory in the Joel Stakes

Salselon immediately, and decisively, took corrective action. Rarely has a horse stopped so quickly. With ears pricked, and leaving skid marks in the turf, our hero applied the brakes. That was that. With Frankie Dettori's frantic urgings having no effect whatsoever, Salselon slowed right down and Polar Ben snatched the most unlikely of wins.

Dettori showed an impressive command of English swear words, while Cumani looked to the clouds and drew hard on his filter tip. "What to do with him?" he asked. There was no shortage of suggestions.

This was Salselon at his worst, but it wasn't the first time he had misbehaved. At Newbury in May, he came to win the Lockinge Stakes only to flick his ears inside the final furlong, lose concentration and wave Russian Rhythm by. At Royal Ascot he left his supporters frustrated, coming from miles behind to take third in the Queen Anne Stakes, just as he would on his seasonal swansong in Italy. Back at Ascot as 7-4 favourite for a distinctly winnable Group 3 in July, he found nothing off the bridle and trailed in seventh. At Goodwood in September, he refused to respond to Kieren Fallon's urgings and lost a race he should have won. In the Champion Stakes, he veered so badly right that The Form Book recorded, "he almost ended up on the July Course". Not

2004 — Race record

3rd Premio Ribot (Group 2) (Capannelle, November 7) 3yo+ 1m Soft 13 ran. *Dropped out in rear, last straight, stayed on strongly down outside from over 1f out, nearest finish (A Parravani), beaten ¹/₂l by Eagle Rise*

6th Emirates Airline Champion Stakes (Group 1) (Newmarket, October 16) 3yo+ 10f Soft **111** (TS 73) 11 ran. *Steadied start, held up and behind, effort and veered badly right 2f out, never near to challenge (J P Murtagh), beaten 10¹/₂l by Haafhd*

2nd Shadwell Stud Joel Stakes (Group 3) (Newmarket, October 1) 3yo+ 1m Good **118** (TS 105) 13 ran. *Slowly into stride, behind, headway to lead over 1f out, not run on and headed towards finish (L Dettori), beaten ³/₄l by Polar Ben*

3rd Select Racing UK On Sky 432 Stakes (Group 3) (Goodwood, September 12) 3yo+ 10f Good to firm **109** (TS 100) 7 ran. *Held up in touch, pushed along and no response 3f out, effort to chase winner 1f out, found little and no impression (K Fallon), beaten 2¹/₂l by Alkaadhem*

2nd sportingoptions.co.uk Betting Exchange Strensall Stakes (Group 3) (York, September 1) 3yo+ 9f Good **117** (TS 38) 4 ran. *Held up in rear, outpaced briefly over 3f out, headway 2f out, ridden and chance just inside final furlong, no impression on winner (L Dettori), beaten ¹/₂l by Red Bloom*

5th Prix Fresnay-le-Buffard-Jacques Le Marois (Group 1) (Deauville, August 15) 3yo+ 1m Soft **115** (TS 93) 10 ran. *Held up, took closer order over 3f out, ridden and stayed on at one pace from 2f out (J P Murtagh), beaten 4¹/₂l by Whipper*

7th Michael Page International Silver Trophy Stakes (Group 3) (Ascot, July 10) 4yo+ 1m Good **108** (TS 96) 10 ran. *Tracked leaders, shaken up well over 1f out, found nil and beaten after (J P Murtagh), beaten 3³/₄l by Shot To Fame*

3rd Queen Anne Stakes (Group 1) (Ascot, June 15) 4yo+ 1m Good to firm **120** (TS 109) 16 ran. *Held up and behind, pulled out over 1f out, headway final furlong, ran on (D Holland), beaten 1l by Refuse To Bend*

2nd Juddmonte Lockinge Stakes (Group 1) (Newbury, May 15) 4yo+ 1m Good **120** (TS 97) 15 ran. *Held up in rear, rapid headway on far side from 2f out, strong challenge inside final furlong, no extra final 100yds (J P Murtagh), beaten ¹/₂l by Russian Rhythm*

9th BETFRED.com Mile (Group 2) (Sandown, April 24) 4yo+ 1m Good to soft **93** (TS 83) 10 ran. *Always well in rear, last and ridden over 4f out, never on terms (Martin Dwyer), beaten 11l by Hurricane Alan*

Other wins

2003 1st Premio Chiusura (Group 3) (San Siro, November 2) 2yo+ 7f Heavy 14 ran ● 1st Prix Edmond Blanc (Group 3) (Saint-Cloud, March 29) 4yo+ 1m Good **114** 12 ran **2002** 1st Premio Chiusura (Group 3) (San Siro, November 2) 2yo+ 7f Very soft **115** 13 ran ● 1st Premio Casaletto (San Siro, October 26) 3yo 7f Holding 7 ran ● 1st Premio Pisa SIS (Listed) (Pisa, March 24) 3yo 7¹/₂f Good 9 ran **2001** 1st Premio Chiusura (Group 3) (San Siro, November 3) 2yo+ 7f Soft 13 ran ● 1st Premio del Dado (Listed) (San Siro, September 23) 2yo Colts & Geldings 1m Heavy **98** 12 ran ● 1st Premio Toceno (Maiden) (San Siro, September 9) 2yo 7f Good 7 ran

content with disgracing himself during his races, he once also made an unfortunate impression on a stalls handler by kicking him where no stalls handler wants to be kicked.

This is a rare beast indeed. He is a loser par excellence. We should hail him as such.

Salselon

bay horse, 8-2-1999

Salse b 1985	Topsider	Northern Dancer	Nearctic Natalma
		Drumtop	Round Table Zonah
	Carnival Princess	Prince John	Princequillo Not Afraid
		Carnival Queen	Amerigo Circus Ring
Heady b 1991	Rousillon	Riverman	Never Bend River Lady
		Belle Dorine	Marshua's Dancer Palsy Walsy
	Ghislaine	Icecapade	Nearctic Shenanigans
		Cambretta	Roberto Cambrienne

Bred by Whitsbury Manor Stud in Britain. 33,000gns Tattersalls October yearling

Sire Salse

Won 8 of 13 starts at 2 and 3. At 2, won 3 (6-7f) of 4 starts, including Somerville Tattersall S-Listed, also 3rd Futurity S-Gr1. At 3, won 5 (Beeswing S-Gr3, Hungerford S-Gr3, Park S-Gr3, Challenge S-Gr2, Prix de la Foret-Gr1) of 9 starts, also 2nd Jersey S-Gr3, Criterion S-Gr3, Queen Elizabeth II S-Gr1. Top class over 7-8f. By top-class US sprinter and very good sire, out of half-sister to Oaks d'Italia winner Carnauba. Stood at Side Hill Stud in Britain, died in 2001. Oldest progeny 14, sire of: Lemon Souffle (Moyglare Stud S-Gr1), Classic Cliche (St Leger-Gr1, Gold Cup-Gr1), Luso (Derby Italiano-Gr1, Aral-Pokal-Gr1, Deutschland-Preis-Gr1, Erdgas-Preis-Gr1), Spout (Gr3), Air Express (Queen Elizabeth II S-Gr1), Bianca Nera (Moyglare Stud S-Gr1), Timboroa (Premio Presidente Della Repubblica-Gr1, Turf Classic-Gr1), Lunasalt (Gr3), Salselon (Gr3).

Dam Heady

Unraced. By top-class 8-10f performer who had only sporadic success at stud in Britain before his export to Japan. Half-sister to top-class miler Markofdistinction and useful fillies Ahead and Criquette, both the dams of stakes performers. Dam of: Tipsy (1996 f by Kris; winner, Gr3 placed), Tipsy Topsy (1998 f by Ashkalani; winner), Salselon (1999 c by Salse; Gr3 winner, Gr1 placed), Sumingasedit (2000 f by Peintre Celebre; unraced), Osiris Way (2002 c by Indian Ridge; unraced), 2003 c by Fantastic Light (75,000gns yearling).

Pedigree assessment

Salse – who had his last, tiny crop in 2001 – has produced a number of tough and high-class males over a variety of trips, and despite his enigmatic behaviour Salselon is another example. He comes from a family that did well over 8-12f during the last two decades for the late Gerald Leigh. Salselon will help his cause at stud if he can gain a Group 1 success, and he certainly has the ability to do so. From limited Flat chances, Salse's sons have done well at stud. *JH*

Shamardal (USA)

2yo bay colt   **125**

Giant's Causeway (USA) - Helsinki (Machiavellian (USA))

Owner Gainsborough Stud

Trainer M Johnston

Breeder Brilliant Stable

Career: **3** starts | won **3** | **£198,819** win and place

By Richard Austen

MARK JOHNSTON'S second two-year-old champion came hot on the heels of his first. Twelve months after Attraction headed the fillies' ratings, Shamardal was the champion colt. In three races, Shamardal was never headed. The third of them was the Dewhurst.

Don't expect, though, to see Johnston celebrating his second winner of the 2,000 Guineas in 2005. At this stage, Shamardal looks clearly the race's most likely winner, but Johnston had only eight days to savour Shamardal's Dewhurst triumph before the colt was whisked off to join Godolphin. In April Johnston will probably be just an interested bystander.

Trainers are constantly being asked to compare their top horses, and almost as often they state that they don't like to make comparisons or that it's impossible to do so. "This horse reminds me so much of Attraction," said Johnston, however.

"I've said all along that he's one of the best two-year-olds I've ever trained, if not the best, because he has always been exceptionally sharp and speedy. I've made the comparison before but he's so much like Attraction in that he goes from a long way out and puts pressure on the others with his natural speed."

Making the running is nothing new for a Johnston-trained horse, but doing it in such a purposeful and, above all, very fast way, as Attraction and Shamardal have, is a rarity for horses from any stable.

One difference between the two as juveniles is that Attraction didn't have a chance to race after July 8, whereas Shamardal wasn't seen until July 12. On that debut in a seven-runner maiden over six furlongs at Ayr, Shamardal was the 11-10 favourite and had no trouble scoring by eight lengths.

Everyone, it seemed, had a high opinion of Shamardal after that and his trainer's view was clear enough when Shamardal appeared 16 days

Shamardal puts up the season's best performance by a juvenile with a decisive success in the Dewhurst Stakes

later in the Group 2 Vintage Stakes at Goodwood, a race he'd won in 1993 with subsequent Guineas winner Mister Baileys and in 2003 with Lucky Story.

Several among the opposition had form in Listed or Group races, notably Wilko and Fox, who had not been beaten far when third and fourth to Dubawi in the Superlative Stakes at Newmarket.

In 2003, Lucky Story was sent off at 6-5 after two previous wins. Shamardal started at 8-13 and there were no particular nuances to what followed: Shamardal set off in front under Joe Fanning, had a couple of his rivals in close attendance three furlongs out but had forced them all off the bridle soon afterwards, completing the last two furlongs pretty much in splendid isolation.

Two and a half lengths back, Wilko was second. Wilko competed honourably in a host of Group races before his shock success in the Breeders' Cup Juvenile and is as good a yardstick as any among the latest crop of leading two-year-olds, but after Goodwood Shamardal was set to do his own talking in a Group 1.

1st Darley Dewhurst Stakes (Group 1) (Newmarket, October 16) 2yo 7f Soft **125** (TS 127) 9 ran. *Made all, ridden and ran on well final 2f (K Darley), beat Oratorio by 2½l*

1st Veuve Clicquot Vintage Stakes (Group 2) (Goodwood, July 28) 2yo 7f Good **114** (TS 99) 10 ran. *Made all, pushed along and drew clear from 2f out, in no danger after, impressive (J Fanning), beat Wilko by 2½l*

1st EBF Maiden Stakes (Ayr, July 12) 2yo 6f Good **97** (TS 97) 7 ran. *Made all, shaken up and quickened clear from over 1f out, readily (J Fanning), beat No Commission by 8l*

The first one pencilled in was the National Stakes at The Curragh in September, which he missed because of a slight setback. Other colts, therefore, had the opportunity to put their credentials on view before Shamardal reappeared in the Dewhurst Stakes at Newmarket. Those who took him on were Champagne Stakes first and second Etlaala and Iceman, Royal Lodge winner Perfectperformance, the Prix Jean-Luc Lagardere first and fourth Oratorio and Montgomery's Arch, and three last-time-out winners in Librettist, Home Affairs and Tremar.

Etlaala, so impressive at Doncaster, was 9-4 while Shamardal was a drifting second favourite at 9-2. The pair disputed ante-post favouritism for the Guineas, with Kevin Darley on board the Middleham challenger as Fanning was only just returning from injury. "Shamardal is our best two-year-old," said Johnston, "and I think he's exceptional. He is ready to show how good he is." For those eight opponents, the combination of Shamardal and heavy going were to provide far too stern a test.

Racing next to the rails, for most of the race Shamardal led by about a length. Etlaala failed to settle in rear. Two and a half furlongs out, the whole field was fanned out and off the bridle. Having carried his head to the left for a long way, Shamardal straightened up and added another two and a half lengths to his lead running into the Dip. Perfectperformance and Etlaala were well adrift in seventh and eighth, leaving Oratorio and Montgomery's Arch to stick on best of the pursuers, but never with any hope of reeling in Shamardal, who went on to win by two and a half lengths.

"It is difficult with a horse like him to know what to expect," Johnston said beforehand. "He has not seen another horse in his two races. We don't know how he will react when he does." It was a nice difficulty to face and, although Shamardal will not have seen much, if anything, of his Dewhurst rivals either, there's no doubt about the way he reacts to pressure after this performance, one backed up by a very good time.

Twelve months before, Johnston fretted because Attraction, although clearly the best filly of her age, had no Group 1 win. Shamardal had his. "Now he is a Group 1 winner, which is always elusive in terms of a stallion career, and that represents a slight change of stable policy," said the trainer. "I have missed Group 1s with some of my best horses and I was determined not to let that happen this year."

Shamardal is quick to make the grade in Pattern class as he wins the Group 2 Vintage Stakes on only his second run

Shamardal is top of the ratings in his division – not only that, but also the best two-year-old on Racing Post Ratings since Xaar won the Dewhurst by seven lengths in 1997. He is currently rated 3lb and 4lb clear, respectively, of possible Guineas rivals Dubawi and Ad Valorem.

Shamardal's figure of 125 has also been good enough to win maybe eight of the last ten runnings of the 2,000 Guineas, so if he makes the usual improvement from two to three Shamardal will probably be the one to beat on the Rowley Mile on the last Saturday in April. He also has the size and scope usually associated with a horse who can make more than average progress. At Goodwood, Johnston described Shamardal as "a big, soft horse who can only improve".

There was a time when the future for Shamardal looked a lot less rosy. An intriguing story emerged that, within a few months of being bought back by his breeders for $485,000 as a foal in November 2002, Shamardal was diagnosed as a grade three wobbler.

Being a 'wobbler' is far more serious than the folksy label might suggest. The symptoms are an unsteady, uncoordinated gait, which in its most severe form would see a horse falling over and unable to get up. The causes are unclear but may well be injury to the spinal cord. One British insurer told Racing Post bloodstock correspondent Rachel Pagones that, "in the eyes of underwriters, being a grade three [wobbler] or worse is as good as being dead. 99 out of 100 of them would be put down."

Shamardal's breeders made a mortality claim and were paid out. The colt was then bought from the underwriters, received treatment and made such a dramatic recovery that he was accepted for the Houghton yearling sale. Some points of conformation may have been partly to blame, but his eventual price of 50,000 guineas was one of the lowest of the sale, and there wasn't much wrong with his pedigree.

Johnston was one of only two bidders and he dropped out when the other, Michael Goodbody of Gainsborough Stud, agreed to let him train the colt. The trainer later commented that "if we'd known his history we wouldn't have bought him".

The case brought back memories of the Criquette Head-trained Anabaa, a wobbler as a two-year-old and given away by his owner to the trainer's father, who hoped the colt might be able to act as a teaser. Two years later, and in Head's colours, Anabaa was the champion sprinter. Anabaa's generous former owner, who was offered the colt back when he returned to training, was Maktoum Al Maktoum, who owns Gainsborough Stud and had its colours carried by Shamardal in the Dewhurst. A case of karma on the turf.

A less happy tale of chance and fate associated with Shamardal's ownership is that he was leased to Maktoum associate Abdulla Buhaleeba for his first two starts but had his ownership transferred back shortly before Champions Day. According to newspaper reports, this was in the aftermath of Buhaleeba's brother having lost millions of pounds playing roulette on three tables at the same time at a West End casino. Lucky Story was among five other horses who made the same change of ownership.

If Ahmed Buhaleeba wanted to mount a retrieving mission by backing Shamardal for the Guineas, the colt was a worthy 5-1 favourite at the end of the turf season. Johnston now has a struggle on his hands to unearth another plausible Guineas candidate.

At the same stage in 2003, despite Duke Of Venice making the transfer to Godolphin and both Lucky Story and Pearl Of Love suffering injuries, the trainer still had the already-injured Attraction, who made a goodish recovery. Johnston lacks that strength in depth this time, but while the loss of Shamardal looks a massive blow to a trainer with championship ambitions, his chances of training future Maktoum horses cannot have been done any harm – for their two-year-old careers at least. For the integrity of the sport's big races, however, it would be a significant blow if Shamardal and Dubawi didn't take each other on in the first Classic.

Shamardal is bred to stay a mile and a quarter and has raced only on good or heavy going. Others in the Dewhurst field, with Etlaala probably top of the list, might have given him a fight on firmer ground, but they will have to prove it.

Shamardal

bay colt, 27-3-2002

		Storm Bird	Northern Dancer
			South Ocean
	Storm Cat		
		Terlingua	Secretariat
Giant's Causeway			Crimson Saint
ch 1997			
		Rahy	Blushing Groom
			Glorious Song
	Mariah's Storm		
		Immense	Roberto
			Imsodear
		Mr Prospector	Raise A Native
			Gold Digger
	Machiavellian		
		Coup de Folie	Halo
Helsinki			Raise The Standard
b 1993			
		Troy	Petingo
			La Milo
	Helen Street		
		Waterway	Riverman
			Boulevard

Bred by Brilliant Stable in USA. Unsold $485,000 as Keeneland November foal; 50,000gns Tattersalls Houghton yearling

Sire Giant's Causeway

Won 9 of 13 starts, inc. Curragh Futurity S.-Gr3, Prix de la Salamandre-Gr1, Gladness S.-Gr3, St James's Palace S.-Gr1, Eclipse S.-Gr1, Sussex S.-Gr1, York International S.-Gr1, Irish Champion S.-Gr1. Also 2nd in 2,000 Guineas, Irish 2,000 Guineas, Queen Elizabeth II S. and Breeders' Cup Classic. A striking individual, and a tough, top-class performer from 8-10.5f. Big, strong, consistent, effective on fast and soft turf and on dirt. By a champion North American sire out of a winner of 6 Graded races. Stands at Ashford Stud, Kentucky, fee $75,000. Sire of one crop of racing age, inc: Footstepsinthesand (Gr3), Maids Causeway (Gr2), Shamardal (Dewhurst S.-Gr1).

Dam Helsinki

Ran only at 3 years, won 1 (10f newcomers' race at Deauville) out of 3 starts. Placed 3rd in Listed, 6th in Gr3. Late May foal who was slow to come to hand, seemingly frail. Appeared to stay 12f. Sister to Street Cry (earned $5 million, Gr1 winner in Dubai and US), half-sister to Listed winner Historian (f by Pennekamp), Listed-placed winner Sovetsky (c by Soviet Star) and to 3 lesser winners, inc. Grecian Slipper (dam of 2 Gr3 winners). By the leading European-based son of Mr Prospector out of a winner of the Irish Oaks. From a notable Ballymacoll Stud family. Dam of: Lushs Lad (1998 c by Wolfhound; winner), Helsinka (2000 f by Pennekamp; placed), Shamardal (2002 c by Giant's Causeway; Gr1 winner). She has a yearling colt by Maria's Mon and a filly foal by Unbridled's Song.

Pedigree assessment

Once apparently under sentence of death as a sufferer from wobbler syndrome, Shamardal was granted a reprieve and proceeded to become the season's top two-year-old; his story would have seemed all too far-fetched as fiction. The most successful to date of his sire's first-crop runners, he was understandably named favourite for the 2,000 Guineas after his Dewhurst victory. One more furlong of the Rowley Mile is certainly not going to bother him, and there are elements in his pedigree - notably maternal grandam Helen Street and her sire Troy - which might suggest stamina for longer trips. But it is all too soon to make a judgement regarding the Derby. Giant's Causeway undoubtedly will get some who prosper beyond his own preferred distance, and we await Shamardal's Guineas performance for more evidence in his case. *TM*

Six Perfections (Fr)

4yo bay filly **123**

Celtic Swing - Yogya (USA) (Riverman (USA))

Owner Flaxman Holdings Ltd

Trainer P Bary

Breeder Niarchos Family

Career: **14** starts | won **6** | second **6** | third **1** | **£1,171,421** win and place

By Steve Dennis

THERE is an art in knowing when to quit. Do you pick up the roses and head for the dressing room basking in the warmth of a job well done, or do you ask a stagehand to raise the curtain one more time and risk the sight of an abandoned auditorium?

Such was the dilemma facing the Niarchos family, owner of Six Perfections, who had completed her three-year-old campaign with a show-stopping display in the Breeders' Cup Mile. Should they risk an encore after a year spent at concert pitch?

The decision to keep her in training was a bold one – there was little left to prove after two seasons of almost unalloyed success, two narrow 1,000 Guineas defeats aside. Even though the Group-race programme had been expanded and upgraded in an attempt to encourage the campaigning of fillies after their Classic season, it would have been seen as something of a comedown if Six Perfections had trod the Pretty Polly/Falmouth route. There were only a few races prestigious enough to concern her connections and Six Perfections would again be required to mix it with the best around, including colts.

Her first test was the nine-furlong Group 1 Prix d'Ispahan at Longchamp in late May, and though the extra furlong was unknown territory it was still a disappointment when the 'niece' of the phenomenal Miesque could play only a supporting role, half a length behind the relatively unconsidered Italian raider Prince Kirk.

The reaction after the race was that the ninth furlong had found her out, as she had eased into the lead at the furlong pole before losing her advantage in the final 100 yards. Her jockey, Thierry Thulliez, explained: "We were going to win easily and then she cracked. She didn't quite get home." The great performer had simply been practising her scales; at a mile next time out she would surely be restored to perfect pitch.

**A frustrating year for Six Perfections (rail), who is beaten
by Whipper when bidding for a second Jacques Le Marois**

That next engagement was the Group 1 Queen Anne Stakes at Royal
Ascot, in which she was made 5-2 favourite to see off 15 rivals who couldn't
match her best form. However, Six Perfections ran the worst race of her
life, trailing in sixth behind the revitalised Refuse To Bend. It was the
first time she had finished outside the first two; it was the first time she
had looked as if she didn't belong in the top class.

When Thulliez asked her to quicken, she hung right on the fast ground
and offered little response, eventually finishing four lengths adrift of the
winner. Connections laid the blame squarely on the ground – officially
good to firm. However, at sunbaked Santa Anita eight months earlier
she had seen off a quality field on firm going, and in the 1,000 Guineas
the previous May had been an unlucky runner-up behind Russian Rhythm
on good to firm ground. Were straws being clutched?

Deauville's Prix Jacques le Marois was the next stop. Twelve months
earlier she had won the Group 1 contest with a game short-neck defeat
of stablemate Domedriver, but there was to be no repeat of that virtuoso
display as Whipper, hitherto considered more of a sprinter, got first
run on the filly and had a length to spare at the line. This time the
soft ground was regarded as her downfall. Alan Cooper, the Niarchos
family's racing manager, said: "She didn't quite get home on the sticky
ground." Thulliez concurred: "We didn't handle the ground as well
as Whipper."

3rd NetJets Breeders' Cup Mile (Grade 1) (Turf) (Lone Star Park, October 30) 3yo+ 1m Yielding **116** 14 ran. *Mid-division, disputing 8th straight, ridden and ran on 1f out in centre to take 3rd on line (J D Bailey), beaten 2l by Singletary*

2nd Prix Fresnay-le-Buffard-Jacques Le Marois (Group 1) (Deauville, August 15) 3yo+ 1m Soft **119** (TS 98) 10 ran. *Mid-division, disputing 6th halfway, effort and ran on 1 1/2f out, went 2nd 100yds out, not catch winner (T Thulliez), beaten 1l by Whipper*

6th Queen Anne Stakes (Group 1) (Ascot, June 15) 4yo+ 1m Good to firm **110** (TS 99) 16 ran. *Held up, switched right and headway when hung right over 1f out, one pace final furlong (T Thulliez), beaten 4l by Refuse To Bend*

2nd Prx d'Ispahan (Group 1) (Longchamp, May 23) 4yo+ 9f Good **117** (TS 77) 5 ran. *Held up, 4th straight, headway 1 1/2f out to lead 1f out, headed 100yds out, kept on (T Thulliez), beaten 1/2l by Prince Kirk*

2003

1st NetJets Breeders' Cup Mile (Grade 1) (Santa Anita, October 25) 3yo+ 1m Firm **121** 13 ran ● **1st** Prix du Haras de Fresnay-Le Buffard-Jacques le Marois (Group 1) (Deauville, August 17) 3yo+ 1m Good to soft **123** 12 ran ● **2nd** Prix d'Astarte (Group 2) (Straight Course) (Deauville, August 3) 3yo+ 1m Good to soft **112** 12 ran ● **2nd** Entenmann's Irish 1,000 Guineas (Group 1) (Curragh, May 25) 3yo 1m Soft **117** 8 ran ● **2nd** Sagitta 1,000 Guineas Stakes (Group 1) (Newmarket, May 4) 3yo 1m Good to firm **115** 19 ran ● **1st** Prix Imprudence (Maisons-Laffitte, April 7) 3yo 7f Good **106** 7 ran

Other wins

2002 **1st** Prix Marcel Boussac Criterium Pouliches-Royal Barriere de Deauville (Group 1) (Longchamp, October 6) 2yo 1m Good **118** 10 ran ● **1st** Prix du Calvados (Group 3) (Deauville, August 23) 2yo 7f Good **109** 8 ran ● **1st** Prix Roland de Chambure (Listed) (Deauville, July 11) 2yo 7f Very soft **105** 7 ran

This was a little confusing. However, what could comfortably be discerned was that Six Perfections was not a spent force. She still had it in her, and the biggest stage of all was beckoning for a second time. She had had America in the palm of her hand before, she would do it again. Back-to-back victories in the Breeders' Cup Mile was the assignment – just like her 'auntie' Miesque – and her faithful following bought tickets once again, making her joint-favourite to go out with a bang.

She wasn't the horse she was. Six Perfections plugged on late in the day to take third place, her class and courage shining through even though her brilliance had dulled. While the bottom-of-the-bill upstart Singletary and the incorrigible Antonius Pius hogged the spotlight for different reasons, Six Perfections stepped back into the shadows stage left, ready for a quieter life, ready to start a family.

She is booked to visit Storm Cat first. However, while her losing season will not affect her stud value in the slightest, it will undermine her status in the memory. People remember the last acts of a superstar; it might have been better to leave us wanting more.

Six Perfections

brown filly, 24-2-2000

Celtic Swing br 1992	Damister	Mr Prospector	Raise A Native Gold Digger
		Batucada	Roman Line Whistle A Tune
	Celtic Ring	Welsh Pageant	Tudor Melody Picture Light
		Pencuik Jewel	Petingo Fotheringay
Yogya ch 1993	Riverman	Never Bend	Nasrullah Lalun
		River Lady	Prince John Nile Lily
	Pasadoble	Prove Out	Graustark Equal Venture
		Santa Quilla	Sanctus Neriad

Bred by Niarchos family in France

Sire Celtic Swing

Won 5 of 7 races. At 2, won all 3 starts, inc. Racing Post Trophy-Gr1. At 3, won 2 (Greenham S-Gr3, Prix du Jockey-Club-Gr1) of 4 starts, also 2nd 2,000 Guineas-Gr1. Outstanding 2yo, then top class over 8-12f. By high-class 10-12f performer whose sire record overall was modest, out of winning mare from stout family of Moon Madness, Ragstone and Sheriff's Star. Stands at Irish National Stud in Ireland, 2005 fee €9,000. Oldest progeny 6, sire of (northern hemisphere): Six Perfections (Prix Marcel Boussac-Gr1, Prix Jacques le Marois-Gr1, Breeders' Cup Mile-Gr1), Listed winners Celtic Silence, Sangreal, Celtic Mill, Torrigiana, Slip Dance.

Dam Yogya

Unraced. By top-class French miler and excellent sire, particularly of broodmares. Half-sister to outstanding miler Miesque (dam of Gr1 winners East Of The Moon, Kingmambo). Dam of: Six Perfections (2000 f by Celtic Swing; Prix Marcel Boussac-Gr1, Prix Jacques le Marois-Gr1, Breeders' Cup Mile-Gr1).

Pedigree assessment

There may not have been any wins in 2004, but Six Perfections once again showed top-class form at a mile. She is a priceless broodmare prospect, not least because her dam's outstanding half-sister Miesque has compiled a phenomenal record at stud. The fact that Six Perfections has a pedigree free of Northern Dancer means that there are endless mating options for her. *JH*

Smarty Jones (USA)

3yo chestnut colt   **131**

Elusive Quality (USA) - I'll Get Along (USA) (Smile (USA))

Owner Someday Farm

Trainer John C Servis

Breeder Someday Farm

Career: **9** starts   won **8**   second **1**   **£1,479,913** win and place

By Nicholas Godfrey

CAN you imagine a top American horserace without Tom Durkin's voice describing the action? Durkin is revered for his matchless ability to find the right form of words to reflect the sense of occasion, to embellish the drama as it reaches its denouement.

Occasions in US racing don't come much bigger than an equine phenomenon attempting to become the first horse to win the Triple Crown for more than a quarter of a century, and Durkin was not going to miss his opportunity as Smarty Jones – a celebrity from New York to LA and beyond – turned into the stretch three lengths clear in the Belmont Stakes.

In front of a record-breaking crowd of 120,139, the elusive Holy Grail of American racing must have seemed within touching distance. "It's been 26 years and it's just a furlong away," called Durkin amid deafening roars from the crowd.

But the final furlong of the race known as the 'Test of a Champion' is one of the longest furlongs in racing. It was too long for Smarty Jones, whose stride faltered as a 36-1 outsider shattered the dream. The race-caller's voice faltered just as much. "Birdstone wins the Belmont Stakes," he moaned. Gripped by a palpable sense of anticlimax, the only time the track had been quieter in the previous few hours was during a minute's silence for Ronald Reagan, whose death was announced midway through a marathon 13-race card.

Instead of joining the likes of Citation, Secretariat and Affirmed in the equine pantheon, Smarty Jones did what Silver Charm, Real Quiet, Charismatic, War Emblem and Funny Cide had all done since 1997. He failed at the Belmont, much to the chagrin of the vast majority of US racing enthusiasts, whose feelings surely echoed those of Smarty Jones's little-known trainer, John Servis. "We're starving for a Triple Crown winner and everyone thought this was the one, including myself," he said. "It hurt."

Smarty Jones wins the Kentucky Derby, starting a fairytale run that was shattered by defeat in the Belmont

It was impossible to avoid a sense of deja vu. Twelve months previously, in the year horseracing unearthed its own celluloid hero thanks to the hit movie Seabiscuit, the American branch of the sport was captivated by the feelgood fairytale of Funny Cide, the unfashionable gelding who came from next to nowhere to win the Kentucky Derby.

You can't have a hit movie without a sequel, so in 2004 came the story of Smarty Jones, another that could have come straight from the pen of a Hollywood screenwriter. Smarty Jones became a national icon in the two short weeks it took him to win the Kentucky Derby and the Preakness, earning front-page status in Sports Illustrated.

Apart from a happy ending, his story had nearly everything. First, there were owners Roy and Pat Chapman. The former suffers from emphysema and takes a supply of oxygen everywhere, sometimes creating a worrying impression as he struggles for breath at the track. They named their stud Someday Farm to reflect their dreams of someday winning a big prize – okay, it's a bit twee, but they like to ladle on the schmaltz over there – yet had all but disbanded their equine interests when their original

2004   Race record

2nd Belmont Stakes (Grade 1) (Dirt) (Belmont Park, June 5) 3yo 12f Fast **124** 9 ran. *Soon pressing leaders on outside, narrow lead 1m out, clear leader 3f out, hung right under pressure well over 1f out, headed 70yds out, one pace (Shane Elliott), beaten 1l by Birdstone*

1st Preakness Stakes (Grade 1) (Pimlico, May 15) 3yo 9½f Fast **131** 10 ran. *Raced in 2nd until led over 2f out, ridden clear, impressive (Shane Elliott), beat Rock Hard Ten by 11½l*

1st Kentucky Derby (Grade 1) (Dirt) (Churchill Downs, May 1) 3yo 10f Sloppy **125** 18 ran. *Raced in 4th, went 2nd over 4f out, pressing leader over 2f out, led approaching final furlong, ridden out (Shane Elliott), beat Lion Heart by 2¾l*

1st Arkansas Derby (Grade 2) (Oaklawn Park, April 10) 3yo 9f Muddy 11 ran. *(Shane Elliott), beat Borrego by 1½l*

1st Rebel Stakes (Oaklawn Park, March 20) 3yo 1m½f Fast 9 ran. *(Shane Elliott), beat Purge by 3¼l*

1st Southwest Stakes (Oaklawn Park, February 28) 3yo 1m Fast 9 ran. *(Shane Elliott), beat Two Down Automatic by ¾l*

1st Count Fleet Stakes (Aqueduct, January 3) 1m½f Fast 7 ran. *(Shane Elliott), beat Risky Trick by 5l*

2003

1st Pennsylvania Nursery Stakes (Philadelphia Park, November 22) 2yo 7f Fast 11 ran ● **1st** Maiden Special Weight (Philadelphia Park, November 9) 6f Fast 10 ran

trainer Bobby Camac and his wife Maryann were shot dead by the former's stepson. That's *all but* disbanded – they kept only one horse, who was born on February 28, the birthday of Pat's mother, Mildred Jones, and named after her childhood nickname, 'Smarty'.

The idea of relatively humble roots was lent added credence by the blue-collar trainer-jockey team of Servis and Stewart Elliott, neither of them exactly household names. They were both based on the lower rungs of the US scene at Philadelphia Park and had never before been anywhere near such a national spotlight. Elliott, for good measure, had his share of problems in the past, mainly drink-related.

Smarty Jones, for his part, was lucky to be racing at all after severely injuring himself as a two-year-old in a stalls injury that resulted in multiple fractures and the nickname 'Quasimodo'. Three weeks in a veterinary hospital and a month on the farm passed before Smarty Jones was put back in training – and thereafter he thrived, going unbeaten from a lowly start at his local track through to his victory in the Arkansas Derby three weeks before the Kentucky Derby.

The 'Run for the Roses' is by far the most popular event in US horseracing, the only time the public at large takes any real notice of the sport, rather like the Grand National in Britain. Much of the focus of the lengthy preamble to the race billed as "the greatest two minutes in sports" focused on Smarty Jones, whose colourful tale – backstory, to use the Hollywood vernacular – caught the attention of the media.

Despite the experts' severe doubts about his stamina, Smarty Jones was made 4-1 favourite to win the 130th Kentucky Derby. If the 18-runner event looked a really open race on paper, a pre-race deluge that turned the track sloppy didn't help to clarify matters. In the event, though, only two horses ever looked like winning, Smarty Jones, and Michael Tabor's Lion Heart, the Patrick Biancone-trained second favourite.

In front of a crowd of more than 140,000 who braved the torrential rain at Churchill Downs, Lion Heart made most of the running only to be brushed aside two furlongs out by Smarty Jones, whose rider said he had been carrying a "loaded gun". He mercilessly mowed down the leader to record an emphatic two-and-three-quarter-length verdict – albeit in a slow time – and thereby become the first unbeaten horse since Seattle Slew in 1977 to win the Derby.

The winner's purse of $854,800 (£482,000) was boosted by a $5 million bonus for the colt's wins in both the Rebel Stakes and Arkansas Derby at Oaklawn Park. Racecourse owner Charles Cella, who had offered the bonus to mark his track's centennial, laid off his liability with an insurance company just before the Derby. "I couldn't be happier," he said. "These are great people, this is a great horse, and this story could be a movie. By the time this is over, this story is going to pale Seabiscuit."

The immediate aftermath to one of the most romantic chapters in Derby history suggested he was not exaggerating. America, a country desperate for heroes, went Smarty Jones-crazy ahead of the Preakness Stakes. He soon had the lot, including a fully fledged hype machine proffering baseball caps, T-shirts and a website.

Few were quibbling after the Preakness, mind you. Smarty Jones put up a truly devastating performance to win the second leg of the Triple Crown by a record 11 and a half lengths from the useful Rock Hard Ten. It was the best performance of his career, and such was Smarty Jones' appeal that the race garnered its best televised ratings since 1990 with a 110-minute NBC broadcast watched by an estimated 15 million, 25 per cent more than had watched Funny Cide win the same race.

With eight wins in eight starts, Smarty Jones was now being dubbed 'America's horse'. All eyes were turned towards the nation's oldest Classic three weeks away in the expectation of seeing the first Triple Crown winner since Affirmed in 1978.

It was almost as if the Belmont was not meant to be a coronation, but a royal procession, the US three-year-old crop long since reduced to supporting roles at the court of Smarty Jones. The one-time hunchback was sent off a 1-3 chance, a price that reflected hundreds of $2 win tickets bought for souvenir purposes that would never have been cashed, while leading trainer Bob Baffert, who did not have a runner in the race, said anyone who did not want Smarty Jones to win was a "sick individual".

Nevertheless, according to Servis, his representative entered the 136th Belmont with "a bullseye on his back". So it seemed as his three main rivals on the book – first Purge, then Rock Hard Ten (twice!) and Eddington – served it up to him up front. The chestnut with the distinctive white bridle put them away one by one, being sent to the front after only half a mile to a massive roar from the stands. The early fractions had not been startling and Elliott speeded matters up after taking over. But although he was still in front halfway down the home stretch, he had done too much, too soon, and Smarty Jones was outstayed by Birdstone.

Yet again, for the sixth time in eight years, the Belmont had proved a step too far for a horse chasing the Triple Crown. This one hurt more than most, though, because Smarty Jones came from the top bracket of recent Kentucky Derby winners, an impression only accentuated by his Preakness romp. Remarkably, Birdstone's connections even felt moved to apologise for spoiling the party!

Still, if the Belmont was a massive disappointment, at least Smarty Jones' multitude of fans could look forward to seeing him again.

Or so they thought, because the closing scenes left a bitter taste when 'America's horse' was retired to stud after a relatively minor injury reported as chronic bruising of the bottom of the cannonbone in all four of the colt's fetlock joints.

Servis admitted that three months' rest would probably have provided a full recovery. "But this is Smarty Jones," he added. "I don't see any way he can earn on the racetrack in a year what he can earn next spring in the breeding shed."

That was true enough. After turning away the blandishments of Sheikh Mohammed, the Chapmans had already agreed a deal with Three Chimneys in Kentucky that valued Smarty Jones at $39 million.

Smarty Jones's connections were certainly not flavour of the month. Writing in New York's Newsday, Paul Moran explained: "Were he more seriously injured, retirement would have been easier for most to understand. But Smarty Jones has sore ankles, a condition found in any horse who has been in training for a long time. The retirement of Smarty Jones has nothing to do with his ability to carry on."

It was later reported that the Chapmans had considered taking Smarty Jones out of retirement for a comeback. However, it was then discovered that there was some lack of cartilage in an ankle, which meant that any such plans had to be shelved. To stud it was.

As the season progressed without Smarty Jones, however, a certain irony became apparent. As the gelded Funny Cide was back winning in Grade 1 company, the crown of his successor as public champion – considered a markedly superior racehorse – had become tarnished, albeit through no fault of his own.

It was a far from fitting finale to the Smarty Jones story. Hollywood would have demanded a rewrite.

Smarty Jones

chestnut colt 28-2-2001

			Raise A Native
		Mr Prospector	Gold Digger
	Gone West		Secretariat
	Elusive Quality	Secrettame	Tamerett
	b 1993		Northern Dancer
		Hero's Honor	Glowing Tribute
	Touch Of Greatness		Sir Ivor
		Ivory Wand	Natashka
			Intentionally
		In Reality	My Dear Girl
	Smile		Boldnesian
	I'll Get Along	Sunny Smile	Sunny Sal
	b 1992		What A Pleasure
		Foolish Pleasure	Fool-Me-Not
	Don't Worry Bout Me		Herbager
		Stolen Base	Bases Full

Bred by Someday Farm in Pennsylvania

Sire Elusive Quality

Won 9 of 20 races, inc. Jaipur H.-Gr3, Poker H.-Gr3. Also Gr2-placed at 3 and 4 years. Tall (16.2hh), strongly made, attractive individual. Smart sprinter-miler on dirt and grass, best at 5, when rated 112 on International Classifications (19lb below champion Skip Away). Sire of: Chimichurri (Gr3), Elusive City (Prix Morny-Gr1), Omega Code (Gr3), Elusive Diva (Gr3), Smarty Jones (Kentucky Derby-Gr1, Preakness S.-Gr1).

Dam I'll Get Along

Won 12 of 39 races, inc. 2 minor stakes. Placed once at Listed level. Successful in each of 5 consecutive seasons. Half-sister to a Gr3-winning sprinter. From a branch of the celebrated La Troienne family. Dam of: Be Happy My Love (2000 f by Formal Gold; winner), Smarty Jones (2001 c by Elusive Quality; dual Classic winner), unnamed (2002 f by Doneraile Court; died as a foal). She has a yearling colt by Hennessy and a colt foal by Orientate.

Pedigree assessment

The mantle of greatness was thrust on Smarty Jones rather too readily by media hype. He probably was the best of his crop, but they were an unconvincing group, and it was only on Preakness day that he really stood out from the crowd. As a physical specimen he never stood out from the crowd, and his early departure to stud at a huge fee was widely regarded as a cynical move. The injury that stopped him would have mended in a few months, and as the son of a sire who improved with age and a dam who kept going until six, he surely had plenty of racing mileage left on the clock. Who knows? He might have truly earned the mantle of greatness in inter-age competition in 2005. *TM*

Snow Ridge (Ire)

3yo bay colt   **123**

Indian Ridge - Snow Princess (Ire) (Ela-Mana-Mou)

Owner Godolphin

Trainer Saeed Bin Suroor

Breeder Ballymacoll Stud Co

Career: **5** starts | won **2** | second **1** | third **0** | **£129,930** win and place

---

By Richard Austen

JUST nine months after his racecourse debut, Snow Ridge's racing career was over. His life lasted little longer. Sold by the Weinstock family to Godolphin after his two-year-old season, he had only two runs for his new stable and did enough for his loss to be felt particularly keenly. He was the only credible challenger the Godolphin millions could muster for the 2,000 Guineas and he started joint-favourite for the Derby.

Guineas or Derby? Which Classic would see Snow Ridge to best advantage was a discussion point throughout the close season, but there was little or no debate over whether he was good enough to be worth his place in at least one of them. He was much better than his ninth of 12 in the Dewhurst suggested and Marcus Tregoning, his trainer in 2003, had described him as the best two-year-old he'd ever trained.

Although greenness played a big part, the way Snow Ridge had found his stride late in the day to gain victory in the Royal Lodge Stakes over a mile at Ascot might have suggested that longer distances would suit him. His sire Indian Ridge is a speed influence and his dam Snow Princess stayed all day, so looking at the pedigree did not make the issue an awful lot clearer.

Snow Ridge's place in the Guineas line-up under Frankie Dettori, along with a prominent place in the betting, was sealed by a performance at Nad Al Sheba in mid-April. Formerly billed as the Godolphin Guineas trials but now described as a private racecourse gallop, in whatever guise this workout took place there was no mistaking that Snow Ridge tuned up in most impressive style when he breezed home well clear of stablemates that included Duke Of Venice, Bayeux and Byron.

Dettori appeared to have no doubts about Snow Ridge's speed for a mile when they took the field as 8-1 shots in the 2,000 Guineas at Newmarket two and a half weeks later, for he held him up well off the

Snow Ridge makes his first appearance for Godolphin in the 2,000 Guineas, where he finished second to Haafhd

strong pace set by stable companion Golden Sahara. As the race developed in unusual fashion, with runners scattering across the Rowley Mile, Snow Ridge may have been left at a disadvantage.

Haafhd, who had been tracking the leaders far more closely, went on under Richard Hills two furlongs out and when he did so Snow Ridge was racing well away from him and had about three lengths to make up in eighth place. He made good inroads on the rest to dispute second at the furlong marker and won that battle, but although Snow Ridge kept up the effort, Haafhd was going on strongly as well and there was still a length and three-quarters between them at the line. Sectional times revealed that Haafhd, Snow Ridge and third-placed Azamour covered the final furlong in almost exactly the same time.

In the aftermath, Snow Ridge's jockey stated that "we've always said he was a stayer" and his trainer that "a mile and two furlongs or a mile and a half will be best for him".

Snow Ridge had earned his crack at the Derby, and Dettori reckoned that, after 11 previous rides in the race and placings thanks to Tamure

7th Vodafone Derby Stakes (Group 1) (Epsom, June 5) 3yo 12f Good **111** (TS 105) 14 ran. *Held up in rear, progress and 7th straight, ridden to chase leaders 2f out, no impression, weakened over 1f out (L Dettori), beaten 8¼l by North Light*

2nd UltimateBet.com 2,000 Guineas Stakes (Group 1) (Newmarket, May 1) 3yo 1m Good **123** (TS 114) 14 ran. *Held up centre, headway over 2f out, ridden over 1f out, ran on (L Dettori), beaten 1¾l by Haafhd*

2003

9th Darley Dewhurst Stakes (Group 1) (Newmarket, October 18) 2yo 7f Good to firm **108** 12 ran ● **1st** Hackney Empire Royal Lodge Stakes (Group 2) (Ascot, September 27) 2yo 1m Good to firm **113** 10 ran ● **1st** Coral Fantasy 4-4-2 Conditions Stakes (Kempton, September 6) 2yo 7f Good **95** 7 ran

in 1995, Shantou in 1996 and Tobougg in 2001, this was the best chance he'd had so far to win it. On Derby Day, in the late absence of Ballydoyle first string Yeats, Snow Ridge headed the betting at 7-2 along with North Light.

Despite the visual impression of what he'd done at a mile, however, Snow Ridge was far less likely than the Dante winner to stay the Derby distance. Both were bred by Ballymacoll Stud with class and stamina on the dam's side, but Snow Ridge's sire has very few runners who stay a mile and a half.

Snow Ridge wasn't one of them. Held up in rear early on, he was disputing seventh on the outside entering the straight as North Light, contrastingly, was sent for home, Kieren Fallon entirely confident in his stamina. Carrying his head a bit high, as normal, Snow Ridge responded to hold a place chance (along with at least six others) one and a half furlongs out before his effort petered out and Dettori gave up on him, the pair finishing just over eight lengths down in seventh.

An uncontroversial initial reaction was that Snow Ridge still had a good future if put back to shorter distances. After all, there are plenty of attractive options at around ten furlongs, including the Juddmonte International, the Irish Champion Stakes and the Champion Stakes itself. In late July, however, Godolphin racing manager Simon Crisford had worrying news. "He has not been in good form since the Derby," he reported. "He has not done any fast work since then and there are no imminent plans to bring him back."

The last bulletin on Snow Ridge came on September 9. "He had a respiratory problem following the Derby," said Crisford, "and we decided to give him time off but keep him in training next year. But sadly he developed laminitis. We did everything we could to save him but we didn't want him to suffer any further and the decision was taken to humanely destroy him."

It was a sad end for a real talent.

Snow Ridge

bay colt, 9-4-2001

Indian Ridge ch 1985	Ahonoora	Lorenzaccio	Klairon
			Phoenissa
		Helen Nichols	Martial
			Quaker Girl
	Hillbrow	Swing Easy	Delta Judge
			Free Flowing
		Golden City	Skymaster
			West Shaw
Snow Princess b 1992	Ela-Mana-Mou	Pitcairn	Petingo
			Border Bounty
		Rose Bertin	High Hat
			Wide Awake
	Karelia	Sir Ivor	Sir Gaylord
			Attica
		Karelina	Sea-Bird
			Running Juliet

Bred by Ballymacoll Stud Co in Ireland

Sire Indian Ridge

Won 5 of 11 starts from 2 to 4. At 2, won 2 of his 4 starts. At 3, won Jersey S-Gr3 from 4 starts. At 4, won Duke of York S-Gr3 and King's Stand S-Gr2 from 3 starts. By top-class sprinter and excellent sire who got top-class horses across the distance spectrum. Stands at Irish National Stud, 2004 fee €85,000. Oldest progeny 13, sire of: Fumo di Londra (Gr3), Island Magic (Gr3), Ridgewood Ben (Gr3), Blomberg (Gr3), Definite Article (National S-Gr1), Ridgewood Pearl (Irish 1,000 Guineas-Gr1, Coronation S-Gr1, Prix du Moulin-Gr1, Breeders' Cup Mile-Gr1), Tumbleweed Ridge (Gr3), Compton Place (July Cup-Gr1), Handsome Ridge (Gr2), Indian Rocket (Gr2), Bardonecchia (Gr3), Cassandra Go (Gr2), Namid (Prix de l'Abbaye-Gr1), St Clair Ridge (Gr3), Indian Mary (Gr3), Nicobar (Gr2), Domedriver (Breeders' Cup Mile-Gr1), High Pitched (Gr3), Indian Creek (Gr2), Monturani (Gr2), Munir (Gr3), Nayyir (Gr2), Sights On Gold (Gr3), Campsie Fells (Gr3), Indian Haven (Irish 2,000 Guineas-Gr1), Snow Ridge (Gr2), Tahreeb (Gr3)

Dam Snow Princess

Won 6 of 19 starts from 2 to 5. At 2, unplaced only start. At 3, won 4 of 6 starts including 12f November Handicap. At 4, won 2 of 6 starts including 15f Listed event in Italy, also 2nd Northumberland Plate. At 5, 2nd Prix Royal-Oak-Gr1 and Princess Royal S-Gr3 from 6 starts. By top-class 12f performer and decent sire. Half-sister to smart Australian performer Gopak, out of a useful French 12f performer. Dam of: White Queen (1999 f by Spectrum; winner), White King (2000 c by Spectrum; placed), Snow Ridge (2001 c by Indian Ridge; Gr2 winner, Gr1 placed), Snow Plough (2002 c by Indian Ridge; unraced), 2003 f by Green Desert (120,000gns yearling). In foal to Indian Ridge.

Pedigree assessment

A top-class miler who never had the chance to prove himself conclusively over slightly further, with a seventh in the Derby the only evidence. On pedigree, given his dam's stamina and his sire's record with stoutly bred mares, Snow Ridge had a good chance of staying at least 10f. *JH*

Somnus

4yo bay gelding   **124**

Pivotal - Midnight's Reward (Night Shift (USA))
Owner Legard Sidebottom & Sykes
Trainer T D Easterby
Breeder Lady Legard

Career: **19** starts | won **9** | second **3** | third **0** | **£652,648** win and place

---

By Howard Wright

THE leading sprinter of the European season was trained in Yorkshire, yet he was beaten on all four outings in his home country. Somnus confirmed the title in France, on the second of two wins there. When he did match his peak performance in Britain, attempting a second successive victory in the Sprint Cup at Haydock, he was beaten a short head by the filly Tante Rose.

Connections of Somnus are getting used to their gutsy gelding attaching himself to racing oddities. As a two-year-old he soared to an official rating of 118 without running in a Pattern race. Trainer Tim Easterby aimed him at the two valuable sales races at Redcar and Doncaster, and won both. The opposition was of sufficiently high standard to push Somnus towards the top of a ranking list headed by horses who had run in the more traditional juvenile markers.

Somnus was sent to the Doncaster sales as a yearling but did not change hands. He was able to run in races with an auction qualification only by virtue of having been bought in for 13,500gns by his breeder, Lady Caroline Legard. Had anyone pressed a little harder they would have taken away the winner of nine races from 19 starts, and over £650,000 in prize-money.

Instead, Lady Legard called up Roger Sidebottom and Sir Tatton Sykes to form a partnership. Though money usually talks at some stage, they would almost certainly need to see an array of noughts on a cheque even to contemplate cashing in, even though all stallion value was removed from Somnus before he ran.

The early gelding operation has ensured that, all things being equal, Somnus will be around for some considerable time. All things rarely are equal, but if Somnus retains his form and the standard of top-class European sprinters continues at a relatively undistinguished level, he will be a force.

Connections had to wait a while for Somnus to demonstrate that he was as good at four years as he had been at three. In an early-season

Somnus holds on in the Maurice de Gheest, giving Gary Stevens the only Group 1 win of his brief stay in France

interview, Easterby reported that Somnus had "done extremely well" over the winter. However, that observation might have been treated in two ways, especially since he went on to point out that Somnus had spent the winter at Lady Legard's stud, where presumably he was treated with all the attention that a proud owner could muster.

When Somnus did reappear in the 15-runner, Group 2 Duke of York Stakes at York's May meeting, the betting suggested that a number of his rivals were expected to do rather better than him, and that proved the case. On suitably softish going, he faded and finished seventh to Monsieur Bond. Though carrying a Group 1 penalty, the bare form was still about 10lb below his best.

However, it took only six weeks for Somnus to prove he really was as good as in 2003. He missed the Royal meeting at Ascot, a track at which he has been beaten on all three visits, and was instead sent to Newcastle for the Group 3 Chipchase Stakes, where heavy rain in the week of the Northumberland Plate meeting made the going testing.

Again, a Group 1 penalty did for Somnus, who chased the leaders on the far side, where a strip of better ground had been opened for the feature

1st Prix de la Foret (Group 1) (Longchamp, October 9) 3yo+ 7f Soft **123** (TS 75) **7** ran. *Held up, 6th straight, pushed along and headway in centre from 2f out, driven to challenge over 1f out, led close home, pushed out (M J Kinane), beat Denebola by ¾l*

2nd Stanleybet Sprint Cup (Group 1) (Haydock, September 4) 3yo+ 6f Good **124** (TS 119) 19 ran. *Always prominent, ridden to lead over 1f out, headed post (M J Kinane), beaten shd by Tante Rose*

1st Prix Maurice de Gheest (Group 1) (Deauville, August 8) 3yo+ 6½f Good to soft **120** 18 ran. *Tracked leader on stands' rail until joined main group halfway, pushed along to lead 3f out, ridden 2f out, held on gamely under pressure (Gary Stevens), beat Whipper by nk*

5th Darley July Cup (Group 1) (Newmarket (July), July 8) 3yo+ 6f Good to soft **114** (TS 96) 20 ran. *Raced centre, joined main group over 4f out, mid-division, headway halfway, soon ridden, staying on when edged left inside final furlong (T E Durcan), beaten 2¾l by Frizzante*

2nd Foster's Lager Chipchase Stakes (Group 3) (Newcastle, June 26) 3yo+ 6f Soft **122** (TS 122) 11 ran. *Chased far side leaders, led approaching final furlong, kept on, headed close home (P Robinson), beaten nk by Royal Millennium*

7th Duke of York Hearthstead Homes Stakes (Group 2) (York, May 11) 3yo+ 6f Good to soft **108** (TS 97) 15 ran. *Chased leaders, kept on same pace final 2f (T E Durcan), beaten 5¾l by Monsieur Bond*

2003

7th Prix de l'Abbaye de Longchamp - Majestic Barriere (Group 1) (Longchamp, October 5) 2yo+ 5f Holding **108** 19 ran ● **1st** Stanley Leisure Sprint Cup (Group 1) (Haydock, September 6) 3yo+ 6f Good to soft **123** 10 ran ● **2nd** Hopeful Stakes (Listed) (Newmarket (July), August 22) 3yo+ 6f Good to firm **98** 6 ran ● **4th** Dubai Duty Free Shergar Cup Sprint (Ascot, August 9) 3yo 6f Good to firm **102** 9 ran ● **1st** David Wilson Homes Stakes (Registered As The Hackwood Stakes) (Listed) (Newbury, July 19) 3yo+ 6f Good to firm **113** 14 ran ● **1st** Thwaites Smooth Beer Conditions Stakes (Haydock, July 5) 3yo+ 6f Good **118** 11 ran ● **8th** Jersey Stakes (Group 3) (Ascot, June 18) 3yo 7f Good to firm **87** 14 ran ● **5th** Sodexho Pavilion Stakes (Listed) (Ascot, April 30) 3yo 6f Good **93** 9 ran

Other runs

2002 **1st** betabet Two-Year-Old Trophy (Redcar, October 5) 2yo 6f Firm **114** 18 ran ● **1st** £200000 St Leger Yearling Stakes (Doncaster, September 11) 2yo 6f Good **104** 21 ran ● **1st** Steve Nesbitt Challenge Trophy Nursery (Ripon, August 27) 2yo 6f Good **94** 13 ran ● **1st** John O'Brien Median Auction Maiden Stakes (York, July 13) 2yo 6f Good **77** 19 ran ● **5th** EBF Hoopers For Fashion Maiden Stakes (Ripon, June 20) 2yo 6f Good to firm **53** 6 ran

day of the fixture. He led approaching the final furlong, but when Royal Millennium ranged alongside in the final 100 yards, and push came to shove, Somnus had to give best. He was beaten a neck, conceding 8lb to Royal Millennium.

Somnus was ridden for the first time by Philip Robinson at Newcastle, as Ted Durcan, who had become the gelding's regular rider, had a tie-up with trainer Mick Channon that took him to Newmarket that day.

Somnus, this time ridden by Mick Kinane, wins his second Group 1 of the season to take top spot in the sprint ranks

Durcan, who had won four times on Somnus, was back in the saddle for the Darley July Cup, but that was the last time he rode him in 2004. Ironically, the Channon connection put Durcan on to Royal Millennium – the mount of Richard Quinn at Newcastle – in two of the last three races for which Easterby prepared Somnus.

Durcan did nothing wrong in the July Cup. Nor did Somnus, other than running a few pounds below his absolute best. Giving a clear indication that there is no outstanding European-trained sprinter, there was a maximum field of 20, and Somnus initially raced in the middle of the course from stall 17 before joining the main group on the far side after two furlongs. He soon made headway but was ridden along and, though he was staying on in the final furlong, he tended to edge left.

Somnus finished fifth behind Frizzante, beaten under three lengths. The next five finishers were within a length of Somnus, who might have been better suited by softer ground than the official 'good to soft'.

Going conditions are important for Somnus. Taking on appreciably lesser opposition, a firm surface would not necessarily be against him. However, his three best performances, judged on Racing Post Ratings, have been on 'good', 'good to soft' and 'soft'. Two of those were achieved after the July Cup, in the Haydock Sprint Cup and the Prix de la Foret.

In the meantime, Somnus made his first excursion of the season to France, for Deauville's Prix Maurice de Gheest, where he had another new jockey, his sixth, in Gary Stevens.

One of America's best international riders of recent years, Stevens has had a rollercoaster career that would make an ideal subject for a limited-audience film. And after his Oscar-nominated debut in Seabiscuit, there would be no need to look elsewhere for an actor to play the leading role.

Stevens' latest incarnation was as Andre Fabre's stable jockey – as much a shock to Stevens on being approached at the start of the season as it was to race fans when the news was announced. The job lasted until August when, almost as swiftly as he had arrived, Stevens handed in his notice to quit and headed back to the States.

He rode just one Group 1 winner in that time – on Somnus. "I needed an English-speaking horse," Stevens joked after the race. Yes, but one with a Yorkshire accent?

As at Newmarket, the Maurice de Gheest drew a big field, 18 on this occasion, and there was early doubt in several jockeys' minds about where to find the best position. Stevens kept Somnus to the stands rails, but he moved across to join the main pack in the centre after two furlongs.

Somnus smoothly went to the front with a furlong to run and held off the challenges of the three-year-olds Whipper and Dolma by a neck and the same, with Ashdown Express (100-1 runner-up in the July Cup) a head away fourth. Newmarket winner Frizzante disappointed in tenth.

A tilt at the Haydock Sprint double had been Easterby's main 2004 target for Somnus, but with Stevens back in the States and Durcan claimed for Royal Millennium, he was forced again to seek out a jockey. This time he turned to Ireland and a choice out of the top drawer, Mick Kinane.

Replaced by Jamie Spencer at Ballydoyle for the 2004 season, Kinane had lost none of his skill, though he had not been as active in England as some had anticipated. While Spencer and the Aidan O'Brien-trained favourite One Cool Cat continued to disappoint, Kinane and Somnus did everything right without quite winning. They were worn down by Tante Rose only in the final strides and beaten just a short head.

Conceding the 3lb fillies' allowance to Tante Rose meant that Somnus could be counted the best horse at the weights. He repeated the feat when reunited with Kinane for the Group 1 Prix de la Foret at Longchamp, but this time he received full reward for his efforts, tackling the leader Denebola inside the final furlong and winning by three-parts of a length.

The soft ground was in Somnus's favour, but this was his first win on only his second attempt at seven furlongs, and he recorded a Racing Post Rating to equal his best. Suddenly a whole new set of options for 2005 have opened up – provided Europe gets some rain.

Somnus   *bay gelding, 27-4-2000*

		Nureyev	**Northern Dancer** Special
	Polar Falcon		
		Marie d'Argonne	Jefferson Mohair
Pivotal ch 1993			
		Cozzene	Caro Ride The Trails
	Fearless Revival		
		Stufida	Bustino Zerbinetta
		Northern Dancer	Nearctic Natalma
	Night Shift		
		Ciboulette	Chop Chop Windy Answer
Midnight's Reward b 1986			
		Tesco Boy	Princely Gift Suncourt
	Margaret's Ruby		
		Pixie Jet	Polly's Jet Sailanna

Bred by Lady Legard in England. Bought in 13,500gns Doncaster St Leger Yearling Sales

Sire **Pivotal**

Won 4 of 6 races, inc. King's Stand S.-Gr2, Nunthorpe S.-Gr1. Powerfully built, attractive sort, high-class sprinter on preferred fast ground, seemingly best at 5f. Stands at Cheveley Park Stud, fee (2005) £65,000. Sire of: Golden Apples (Del Mar Oaks-Gr1, Beverly D S.-Gr1, Yellow Ribbon S.-Gr1), Kyllachy (Nunthorpe S.-Gr1), Low Pivot (Gr3), Needwood Blade (Gr3), Ratio (Gr3), Silvester Lady (Preis der Diana-Gr1), Captain Rio (Gr2), Chorist (Pretty Polly S.-Gr1), Megahertz (John C. Mabee H.-Gr1), Ringmoor Down (Gr3), Stolzing (Gr3), Humouresque (Gr3), Pivotal Point (Gr2), Somnus (Haydock Sprint Cup-Gr1, Prix Maurice de Gheest-Gr1, Prix de la Foret-Gr1), Windsor Knot (Gr3).

Dam **Midnight's Reward**

Won 1 of 8 races. Useful sprinter in modest company at 2, cracked bone and retired after two indifferent runs at 3. Died in 2001. Dam of: Lettermore (1990 f by Elegant Air; winner in Belgium), Soca King (1992 c by Midyan; winner), Midnight Cookie (1993 c by Midyan; placed), Damaya (1994 f by Formidable; winner in France), Dayo (1996 g by Robellino; unplaced), Midnight's Dream (1997 c by Elmaamul; winner, stakes-placed in Poland), Pasithea (1998 f by Celtic Swing; winner), Forest Prize (1999 f by Charnwood Forest; winner), Somnus (2000 g by Pivotal; triple Gr1 winner).

Pedigree assessment

Somnus kept us waiting in 2004 for a display of the sort of form he had shown when winning the Haydock Park Sprint the previous year, but eventually turned it on in style, sandwiching a close second in the same Haydock event between Group 1 triumphs at Deauville and Longchamp. It is evident now that he is just as proficient at seven furlongs as he is at six, and he seems certain to figure among the best around at those distances again in 2005. Somnus has played a significant part in the promotion of his sire, Pivotal, who got him when he stood at only £5,000. The stallion's proven facility to upgrade his mares has resulted in progressive increases in the charge for his services, and he will cover a distinguished book at £65,000 next time around. *TM*

Soviet Song (Ire)

4yo bay filly   **124**

Marju (Ire) - Kalinka (Ire) (Soviet Star (USA))

Owner Elite Racing Club

Trainer J R Fanshawe

Breeder Elite Racing Club

Career: **15** starts   won **7**   second **3**   third **1**   **£770,813** win and place

By Brough Scott

NO filly has ever given so much pleasure to so many owners as Soviet Song. In her third season she returned to the brilliance of her unbeaten two-year-old days, capturing three consecutive Group 1 races and beating the colts in the Sussex Stakes. For the 15,000 members of the Elite Racing Club, whose operation both owned and bred her, this has to be the ultimate racing dream.

Yet it has not all been easy. Soviet Song was beaten at 4-11 in her comeback race at Kempton, and when she again failed to justify favouritism next time at Sandown she had gone 19 months without victory. The Racing Post noted gloomily that "her record does not inspire confidence these days."

Victory, a ruthless six-length defeat of Livadiya in the Ridgewood Pearl Stakes at The Curragh, put the season back on track and returned confidence to her trainer. "Things did not quite work out for her as a three-year-old," he said. "Getting her ready for the 1,000 Guineas took a bit out of her. She ran a decent second to Russian Rhythm in the Coronation Stakes at Ascot but had a break until the autumn and didn't click then either. But at the beginning of this year she had done some really brilliant bits of work. In hindsight she was not quite ready for Kempton but I was keen to get a run into her and the soft ground found her out."

Defeat at Sandown might have extended Soviet Song's "failure" record but connections were now more frustrated than concerned. "I didn't ride her that well," said jockey Johnny Murtagh. "She had just died on me a little bit at Kempton but Sandown is a difficult place and it didn't really happen for me. I pulled her out and then had to switch to the inner and never got a proper run."

Beaten only a length and a neck by Hurricane Alan and Gateman, Soviet Song had not actually done that badly on softish ground. The winning time of 1min 43.67sec for the Sandown Mile was 2.67 seconds slower than the Racing Post's standard, and subsequent events suggested that

Soviet Song hits top form at Newmarket's July meeting as she scores a decisive win over Attraction in the Falmouth

while Soviet Song may have won on the soft as a two-year-old and been jarred up a little against Russian Rhythm in the Coronation Stakes on "good to firm", it is fast ground that brings the best out of her.

It was officially good to firm when she cruised up at The Curragh, and the same conditions prevailed when she took on the colts in the Queen Anne Stakes at Royal Ascot. By now Murtagh was appreciating both the class and the difficulties of his talented partner. "She has terrific acceleration," he said, "but once you move on her she takes you there. At Ascot I picked off the leader [the French filly Nebraska Tornado] almost too quickly and just could not hold off Refuse To Bend at the line."

A neck defeat by the previous year's 2,000 Guineas winner, who ran the mile in 1min 39.14sec, a time 1.26 seconds fast, was a career best on Racing Post Ratings and in her next race, the Falmouth Stakes, only understandable awe at Attraction's eight-race unbeaten record saw Soviet Song start at 11-4. In truth the race was made for the older filly. As ever Attraction had to set the pace and so gave Murtagh a perfect target on Soviet Song, just as the final climb sapped the strength of the leader.

At 1min 36.11sec (1.69 seconds quicker than standard) this was the

6th Queen Elizabeth II Stakes (Sponsored By NetJets) (Group 1) (Ascot, September 25) 3yo+ 1m Good to firm **103** (TS 93) 11 ran. *Raced midfield, eased out and ridden 2f out, no response and beaten after (J P Murtagh), beaten 9½l by Rakti*

1st Coolmore Fusaichi Pegasus Matron Stakes (Group 1) (Leopardstown, September 11) 3yo+ 1m Good to firm **124** (TS 106) 6 ran. *Held up in 5th, headway approaching straight, 2nd 1½f out, ridden to challenge inside final furlong, led 100yds from finish, comfortably (J P Murtagh), beat Attraction by ½l*

1st Cantor Odds Sussex Stakes (Group 1) (Goodwood, July 28) 3yo+ 1m Good **124** (TS 118) 11 ran. *Settled in midfield, not much room over 2f out, progress soon after, led and quickened just over 1f out, ridden out, held on well (J P Murtagh), beat Nayyir by nk*

1st UAE Equestrian And Racing Federation Falmouth Stakes (Group 1) (Newmarket (July), July 6) 3yo+ 1m Good to firm **122** (TS 111) 7 ran. *Held up, headway over 2f out, ridden to lead over 1f out, ran on (J P Murtagh), beat Attraction*

2nd Queen Anne Stakes (Group 1) (Ascot, June 15) 4yo+ 1m Good to firm **119** (TS 108) 16 ran. *Always prominent, ridden to lead 1f out, headed near finish (J P Murtagh), beaten nk by Refuse To Bend*

1st Ridgewood Pearl Stakes (Group 2) (Curragh, May 22) 4yo+ 1m Good to firm **118** (TS 81) 5 ran. *Tracked leaders in 3rd, smooth headway over 2f out, quickened into lead 1½f out, clear final furlong, easily (J P Murtagh), beat Livadiya by 6l*

3rd BETFRED.com Mile (Group 2) (Sandown, April 24) 4yo+ 1m Good to soft **111** (TS 104) 10 ran. *Held up in last trio, effort over 2f out, switched right over 1f out, ran on final furlong, nearest finish (J P Murtagh), beaten 1¼l by Hurricane Alan*

2nd Surrey Herald Snowdrop Fillies' Stakes (Listed Race) (Kempton, April 10) 4yo+ 1m Good to soft **106** (TS 69) 8 ran. *Held up in rear, steady headway from 2f out, led just inside final furlong, soon ridden, no extra and headed last strides (J P Murtagh), beaten hd by Beneventa*

5th Queen Elizabeth II Stakes (Sponsored By NetJets) (Group 1) (Ascot, September 27) 3yo+ 1m Good to firm **111** 8 ran ● **4th** Netjets Prix du Moulin de Longchamp (Group 1) (Longchamp, September 7) 3yo+ 1m Good to soft **114** 14 ran ● **2nd** Coronation Stakes (Group 1) (Ascot, June 20) 3yo 1m Good to firm **118** 9 ran ● **4th** Sagitta 1000 Guineas Stakes (Group 1) (Newmarket, May 4) 3yo 1m Good to firm **108** 19 ran

2002 **1st** Meon Valley Stud Fillies' Mile (Group 1) (Ascot, September 28) 2yo 1m Good to firm **112** 10 ran ● **1st** Milcars Sweet Solera Stakes (Listed Race) (Newmarket (July), August 10) 2yo 7f Soft **111** 8 ran ● **1st** EBF Median Auction Maiden Fillies' Stakes (Kempton, July 17) 2yo 6f Good to firm **83** 15 ran

fastest mile Soviet Song ever ran, and seeing her coursing down the leader as Murtagh slipped her up the outside was to witness something pretty close to perfection in filly form. It says much for racing's wish for instant headlines rather than on-track reality that the first public reaction was one of disappointment, even dismay, at Attraction's defeat, rather than celebration of the shining fulfilment of what had been such an outstanding prospect two seasons before.

Soviet Song is now a big, slightly masculine filly, standing over 16 hands

Now it's the turn of the colts to suffer as Soviet Song lands the Sussex Stakes, her second Group 1 success of July

and pulling 464 kilos on the weighbridge when fully fit. "She's a good tough mare," said Murtagh admiringly, "good long ears on her but a bit of a tomboy." Her assertiveness forces her trainer to saddle her in the open but apart from getting stewed up a little before the Queen Elizabeth II Stakes, when her long season was probably catching up with her, the aggression has been channelled into the race.

This was certainly true in her consecutive Group 1 victories in the Sussex Stakes at Goodwood and the Matron Stakes at Leopardstown, both of which earned her career-best ratings of 124. The Sussex was made a particular ordeal when Haafhd lost a plate, causing a long delay on just about the hottest afternoon of the summer. And while the final clocking of 1min 36.98sec for the mile was 0.32 seconds quicker than standard, the gallop set by Passing Glance was not fast enough to avoid quite a bit of scrimmaging as the pack closed up for their efforts with a quarter of a mile to run.

Refuse To Bend led briefly before getting bumped back to last place as he weakened, and then the former Italian star Le Vie dei Colori took over before Murtagh got Soviet Song some space and let the arrow fly. Once again, her acceleration was almost too rapid, taking her a good length clear with the possibility that she might be in front too soon.

But it had been the right move at the right time. For although Nayyir got out of the pack to run her to a neck at the line, her speed had given her the winning kick. And while the delayed start and the bunching could be offered as possible excuses for others, this was still a good Group 1 event, and on the day Soviet Song was the clear ruler of the pack.

She and Murtagh then took their winning run to Leopardstown, and to watch them close up that September day was as good a memory as any season gives – especially as there was a passage of the race when it seemed as if the jockey had this time misread the rhythm and settled his partner too far away from the front-running Attraction.

The final turn at Leopardstown dips down and up before hitting the final straight. Into this Kevin Darley sent Attraction as if the hounds of hell were on her heels. Murtagh had settled Soviet Song behind Yesterday, whom he had thought would have towed him close to the pace, only to find her fourth and himself fifth as Red Feather and Phantom Wind followed Attraction in Indian file.

Swinging into line for home Phantom Wind ran past Red Feather, but as Soviet Song was finally loosed up the outside Attraction must have had a good four lengths advantage and did not seem to be stopping. For a few desperate seconds (for Soviet Song's supporters, that is!) it seemed as if Murtagh had allowed too big a gap to develop, as if this time even his partner's extraordinary acceleration would not be enough.

But in the manner of class performers in any sporting discipline, the jockey did not panic. With smooth compulsion he and Soviet Song began to eat into the gap. A furlong out he reached back for one quick back-crack of the whip before putting both hands back on the reins to stretch his filly ever closer to her younger rival.

It had not looked possible but now it was. We were into the final 100 yards, Attraction was not weakening but Soviet Song had got to her quarters. The Murtagh whip flourished briefly. The older filly stretched on and clinched it. There was a half-length between them at the line.

A winning time of 1min 36.80sec was 1.60 seconds quicker than standard. Once again the clock had confirmed what the eye had seen. These were two tremendous fillies. Attraction is as fine a front runner as we have seen of her sex, but her style is made for Soviet Song's arrow-like finish. A rematch would be worth going a long way to see, though the prospect of one was in some doubt after it was reported in November that Soviet Song had been "intermittently lame" since the QE II due to a "minor" fetlock injury.

Fanshawe, who remains hopeful that the filly will return to action in 2005, gives special credit for her success to work rider Mark Denaro, whose "from-the-saddle judgements" proved spot-on all season. The trainer can take full pride himself as, most of all, can the members of the Elite Racing Club who have stayed loyal to their filly when cashing a big cheque could have been an easier option.

In an age when Group 1 races have become a millionaire's preserve, there has been something magical in seeing the rejoicing among Elite members whose organisers have pulled off the greatest David and Goliath Flat racing story of our age. They have shown that even the mountain tops of the game can be scaled by all of us. Their subscriptions must have been one of the racing bargains of all time.

Soviet Song

bay filly, 18-2-2000

		Try My Best	**Northern Dancer**
			Sex Appeal
	Last Tycoon		
		Mill Princess	Mill Reef
Marju			Irish Lass
b 1988			
		Artaius	Round Table
			Stylish Pattern
	Flame Of Tara		
		Welsh Flame	Welsh Pageant
			Electric Flash
		Nureyev	**Northern Dancer**
			Special
	Soviet Star		
		Veruschka	Venture
Kalinka			Marie d'Anjou
b 1994			
		Tromos	Busted
			Stilvi
	Tralthee		
		Swalthee	Sword Dancer
			Amalthee

Bred by Elite Racing Club

Sire Marju

Won 3 of 7 races, inc. Craven Stakes-Gr3, St James's Palace Stakes-Gr1. Also 2nd in the Derby (to Generous). Had an abbreviated first season owing to a slight setback, in-and-out at 3 because of a persistent stifle problem, and eventually lost his action completely. Good-bodied, lengthy, short-legged, showing quality. Among the best sons of his sire (also got Ezzoud, Bigstone, Taipan and Mahogany). Half-brother to 10 other winners, inc. Salsabil, Danse Royale, Song Of Tara and Flame Of Athens. Out of a top-class 8-12f runner, from an extremely successful family. Stands at Derrinstown Stud, Co. Kildare, (2004) fee €16,000 (Oct 1). Sire of 10 crops of racing age, inc. notable winners: My Emma (Prix Vermeille-Gr1), Sil Sila (Prix de Diane-Gr1, Yorkshire Oaks-Gr1), Della Scala (Gr3), Mahboob (Gr3), Oriental Fashion (Gr2), Miletrian (Gr2), Naheef (Gr3), Marbye (Prix d'Astarte-Gr1), Soviet Song (Fillies' Mile-Gr1, Falmouth S.-Gr1, Sussex S.-Gr1, Matron S.-Gr1), Stormont (Gr2), Brunel (Gr2), Red Feather (Gr2).

Dam Kalinka

Won 1 of 10 races. Also 2nd once, 3rd once, 4th 4 times, and placed 4th and 6th (poor form) in 2 outings over hurdles. Big, leggy sort. Fairly useful, showed quite consistent form at 3. Stayed 10f, indifferent to ground conditions on grass, ran poorly when tried on all-weather (blinkered) final start. Quite well-bred. Half-sister to 12f winner Dancing Tralthee (by Dancing Brave). By a high-class miler and successful sire, out of smart racemare (won Rockfel and Lupe S, both Listed) who was sister to 6 lesser winners, inc. dam of US Gr3 winners Club Champ and Ask Anita. Grand-dam winner in France, half-sister to the dams of Galant Vert (Gr3 winner, Gr1-placed), Irish Noir (Gr3 winner, Gr2-placed), Bleu de France (Gr3 winner), Nain Bleu (Listed winner, Gr2-placed), and Rutheford (Gr3 winner). Dam of: Baralinka (1999 f by Barathea; winner), Soviet Song (2000 f by Marju; dual Gr1 winner), Penzance (2001 c by Pennekamp; winner), Kazatzka (2002 f by Groom Dancer; unraced to date).

Pedigree assessment

Villainess turned heroine, that was Soviet Song, who dealt a great public favourite in Attraction her first defeat in the Falmouth Stakes, then gathered a fan club for herself by collecting two more Group 1 victories, including one against all-male opposition in the Sussex Stakes. When she beat Attraction a second time, at Leopardstown, she got full credit from an appreciative crowd. We knew Soviet Song was good at two, but things just never went her way at three, and she needed to bounce back as a four-year-old. She did that to such effect that she must now rank as the best product of her sire, Marju, who has never had a colt to win above Group 2 level, but has four daughters who have achieved that distinction. *TM*

Sulamani (Ire)

5yo bay horse **128**

Hernando (Fr) - Soul Dream (USA) (Alleged (USA))

Owner Godolphin

Trainer Saeed Bin Suroor

Breeder Niarchos Family

Career: **17** starts | won **9** | second **3** | third **1** | **£3,072,326** win and place

---

By David Ashforth

FOR Saeed Bin Suroor, Sulamani had always been a joy; a joy, and a worry. Sulamani had the right number of ribs. You knew that, because you could often see them. Lean and athletic, the stoutly bred but sparely built five-year-old often looked like a horse teetering on the brink of an eating disorder. The flying toast-rack.

So Bin Suroor was delighted when his favourite horse, and one of Sheikh Mohammed's favourites, emerged from his second winter in Dubai bigger and promising to be better than ever before. "Last year, he was skinny and light," said Bin Suroor, at the start of the season. "There wasn't much there; no condition, and he wasn't moving great. This year you will see a different horse. He is a different shape; he has more condition and he is moving much better. He looks happier and more athletic."

A bigger and better Sulamani promised to be an international champion to savour for, in 2003, the former winner of the Prix du Jockey-Club had won the Group 1 Dubai Sheema Classic, finished runner-up to Alamshar in the Group 1 King George VI and Queen Elizabeth Diamond Stakes, then won two Grade 1 races in the USA, the Arlington Million (on a disqualification) and the Turf Classic Invitational. He was officially one of the best ten turf horses in the world.

It was a fine record but, like a star pupil who does well in his exams without excelling as his teachers believe he is capable of doing, Sulamani, who boasted acceleration as well as athleticism, rarely quite stretched to his full height. Now, perhaps, we would see what Sulamani was truly capable of.

The horse who had given Godolphin their 100th Group 1 winner seemed ready to become the latest in a distinguished line of international jetsetters. Not another Dubai Millennium but maybe a Swain or a Daylami, whose early careers were also forged in France.

Sulamani finally gets some ease in the ground and takes advantage to land the Juddmonte International at York

Early-season rigours at the Dubai World Cup meeting were eschewed in favour of the Tattersalls Gold Cup at The Curragh late in May, a relatively gentle introduction to a year full of Godolphin ambition.

Sulamani had been working well and, on the Monday before his intended reappearance, Frankie Dettori rode him in a piece of work with Naheef, a Listed-race winner the previous year. "It was the best work I have seen him do," a satisfied Bin Suroor reported. "That was special."

A suspension for a whip offence at York ruled Dettori out of the saddle and offered Kerrin McEvoy, Godolphin's new recruit from Australia, an early chance of glory, but it wasn't to be. The day before the race, Sulamani nicked his leg and developed a slight infection. It was trivial, but enough to prompt a change of plan.

Plan B was put into effect the following month, at Royal Ascot. Godolphin, enjoying a season as satisfying as the previous year's had been frustrating, could not have been in better form. Sheikh Mohammed's blue-blooded and blue-silked team accounted for a remarkable six winners at the meeting, including, courtesy of Papineau and Refuse To Bend, two Group 1 successes, topped by Doyen's superlative victory in the

1st Pattison Canadian International (Grade 1) (Woodbine, October 24) 3yo+ 12f Good **124** 10 ran. *Held up towards rear on inside, angled out 3f out, 6th straight, headway on outside to lead just inside final furlong, ran on strongly (L Dettori), beat Simonas by 1½l*

1st Juddmonte International Stakes (Group 1) (York, August 17) 3yo+ 10½f Good **126** (TS 99) 9 ran. *Held up, steady headway 4f out, stayed on final 2f, led final 50yds (L Dettori), beat Norse Dancer by ¾l*

3rd King George VI And Queen Elizabeth Diamond Stakes (Group 1) (Ascot, July 24) 3yo+ 12f Good to firm **123** (TS 92) 11 ran. *Held up in 8th, plenty to do over 2f out, steady progress from well over 1f out, ran on final furlong, just failed to snatch 2nd place (K McEvoy), beaten 3¼l by Doyen*

2nd Princess of Wales's cantorodds.com Stakes (Group 2) (Newmarket (July), July 7) 3yo+ 12f Good to firm **127** (TS 73) 8 ran. *Held up, headway and switched left over 2f out, hung right and every chance from over 1f out, ran on (L Dettori), beaten ½l by Bandari*

4th Prince of Wales's Stakes (Group 1) (Ascot, June 16) 4yo+ 10f Good to firm **118** (TS 110) 10 ran. *Held up towards rear, effort over 2f out, ridden and unable to quicken well over 1f out, hanging right and no impression leaders final furlong (L Dettori), beaten 4l by Rakti*

5th John Deere Breeders' Cup Turf (Grade 1) (Santa Anita, October 25) 3yo+ 12f Firm **118** 9 ran ● **1st** Turf Classic Invitational Stakes (Grade 1) (Belmont Park, September 27) 3yo+ 12f Firm **123** 7 ran ● **1st** Arlington Million XXI (Grade 1) (Arlington, August 16) 3yo+ 10f Good **120** 13 ran ● **2nd** King George VI And Queen Elizabeth Diamond Stakes (Group 1) (Ascot, July 26) 3yo+ 12f Good **128** 12 ran ● **4th** Grand Prix de Saint-Cloud (Group 1) (Saint-Cloud, June 29) 3yo+ 12f Good **113** 10 ran ● **1st** Dubai Sheema Classic (Group 1) (Nad Al Sheba, March 29) 4yo+ 12f Good **126** 16 ran

2002 **2nd** Prix de l'Arc de Triomphe - Lucien Barriere (Group 1) (Longchamp, October 6) 3yo+ 12f Good **126** 16 ran ● **1st** Prix Niel Casino Barriere-d'Enghien les Bains (Group 2) (Longchamp, September 15) 3yo 12f Good to firm **110** 3 ran ● **1st** Prix du Jockey-Club (Group 1) (Chantilly, June 2) 3yo 12f Good **124** 15 ran ● **1st** Prix de L'Avre (Chantilly, May 15) 3yo 12f Good to soft **107** 8 ran ● **1st** Prix Sanctus (Maisons-Laffitte, April 30) 3yo 12f Soft 7 ran ● **7th** Prix de Champerret (French-Bred Colts & Geldings) (Longchamp, April 7) 3yo 10f Good to firm 13 ran

Hardwicke Stakes. Sulamani, earmarked for the head of the table, ended up sitting in mild disgrace on a stool in the corner.

Again reported to have been working well, and sent off favourite for the Prince of Wales's Stakes, Sulamani ran below expectations to finish a well-beaten fourth to Rakti. Rakti put up a fine performance and ten furlongs was a bare minimum for Sulamani but, hanging quite badly, he looked uncomfortable on the fast ground. It was clear confirmation that, to be seen at his best, Sulamani had to be seen on forgiving going.

Yet fast ground was what Sulamani would continue to encounter, for he was a horse for whom things rarely went right for long; a horse seemingly forever on the brink of something better, on the edge of greatness.

It would have required a convincing act of restoration in the King George VI and Queen Elizabeth Diamond Stakes, by which time Doyen had supplanted Sulamani in race fans' affections. If an older horse was to take a firm grip on the 2004 season, Doyen now seemed much the more likely candidate.

Sulamani's performance in the Group 2 Princess of Wales's Stakes at Newmarket, early in July, did nothing to alter the pecking order. Reasons could be unearthed for his narrow defeat by Bandari, a doughty battler receiving 5lb from Sulamani, and better suited by the untaxing pace in the mile-and-a-half contest, but Sulamani again looked awkward under pressure. This time, was he resenting the whip as well as the fast conditions?

There may not have been a complex key to unlock but there certainly seemed to be a need for Godolphin's potential flagship to have conditions and the shape of each race to suit.

Less than three weeks later, back at Ascot, when Sulamani paraded with Doyen for the King George, his jockey was McEvoy, not Dettori, and the cap McEvoy was wearing was white, not blue. Sulamani was the second string. Dettori had opted to ride Doyen, the 11-10 favourite.

It was not a difficult choice and Sulamani was confirmed as a runner only after Dettori advised Godolphin that the ground was not firm enough to be a serious problem. His choice of mount was spectacularly justified. While Doyen won with unarguable ease, Sulamani stayed on to challenge, but not pass, Hard Buck for the privilege of being runner-up. It was a creditable effort, on ground again too fast for comfort, but it was not the effort of a champion.

When ground conditions finally relented, at York the following month, Sulamani was seen in a predictably better light. At ten and a half furlongs, the Juddmonte International was short of Sulamani's ideal trip. Indeed, on breeding, being by Hernando out of an Alleged mare who won over 11 furlongs, it would have been interesting to see Sulamani, despite his noted turn of foot, raced over trips well beyond a mile and a half.

At York, stablemate Millstreet performed the role of pacemaker and his strong pace gave Sulamani the test he needed to gain his first success of the year. Norse Dancer, however, made Sulamani fight for victory, and when Dettori asked Sulamani to take on the leader, he briefly hung fire. Dettori was serious enough with the whip to be given a one-day suspension.

"There was no concern about him dropping back in trip," said Simon Crisford, Godolphin's racing manager. "He has plenty of speed as long as the pace is genuine, as well as terrific acceleration."

Rather bizarrely, Sulamani's first success of the year won him the BHB's Middle Distance Championship and £100,000 – further evidence of the difficulty of creating convincing horseracing awards. Now, he seemed set to end the season with a flourish.

Just behind Norse Dancer was the favourite, the previously unbeaten, triple Group 1-winning three-year-old Bago. Bago's target was the Prix de l'Arc de Triomphe, and that was the natural destination for Sulamani, too. As a three-year-old, in his final race for Pascal Bary before being acquired by Godolphin, Sulamani had come from an unhelpfully long way back to finish second to Godolphin's Marienbard. He had hung on that occasion, too.

Unlike the Breeders' Cup and Japan Cup, other possible autumn targets, the Arc is rarely run on fast ground. Sulamani was promoted to 8-1 in the ante-post market and subsequently cut to 3-1 favourite after Doyen had ruled himself out by disappointing badly in the Irish Champion Stakes and Bago had been beaten in the Prix Niel.

No sooner were things looking rosy, however, than they began to look worse. A few days after the Arc trials at Longchamp, it was reported that Sulamani had been unusually quiet since York and had missed some work. At the end of September, it was announced that time had run out.

After toying with a possible run in the Champion Stakes at Newmarket, Godolphin opted for the $1.5 million Canadian International at Woodbine, Toronto, a race regularly won by European horses, including Godolphin's Mutafaweq four years earlier.

The race looked as competitive as the $2 million Breeders' Cup Turf, due to be run at Lone Star Park in Texas six days later, although neither Brian Boru, the 2003 St Leger winner, nor Mubtaker, runner-up to Dalakhani in the 2003 Arc, had maintained that level of form.

The local challenge was not strong. North America's best turf horse, Kitten's Joy, was on his way to the Breeders' Cup, leaving Senor Swinger, the recent winner of a Grade 2 event at Belmont, and King's Drama, third to Magistretti in the Grade 1 Man O'War, to fly the Stars and Stripes.

Woodbine offered a better chance of good ground than Lone Star Park. Ironically, in the run-up to the race, the going seemed likely to be fast, while unexpectedly heavy rainfall threatened soft conditions at the Breeders' Cup. In the event, it rained at Woodbine and dried out, although still spongy, at Lone Star Park.

Sulamani was simply too good for his opponents. Settled in the rear, looking for room and forced to come wide to make his challenge, he accelerated into the lead in the final furlong and won easily from the German-trained Simonas and Brian Boru. If he had run in the Breeders' Cup Turf instead, Sulamani would probably have won that.

Godolphin immediately announced Sulamani's retirement to stud. The Canadian International was his sixth Group 1 win in 17 starts. In a now familiar pattern with Godolphin's older stars, Sulamani's top-level successes were gained on three continents, in five countries – France, Dubai, USA, England and Canada.

His record at the top level over three seasons marked him out as an exceptional racehorse and one with a turn of foot that was stirring to anticipate and enjoy. Yet there lingered the feeling that, without the niggling physical problems, Sulamani might have climbed still higher.

Sulamani

bay colt, 9-4-1999

Hernando b 1990	Niniski	Nijinsky	**Northern Dancer** Flaming Page
		Virginia Hills	**Tom Rolfe** Ridin' Easy
	Whakilyric	Miswaki	Mr Prospector Hopespringseternal
		Lyrism	Lyphard Pass A Glance
Soul Dream br 1990	Alleged	Hoist The Flag	**Tom Rolfe** Wavy Navy
		Princess Pout	Prince John Determined Lady
	Normia	Northfields	**Northern Dancer** Little Hut
		Mia Pola	Relko Polamia

Bred by the Niarchos Family in Ireland

Sire Hernando

Won 7 of 20 races, inc. Prix Lupin-Gr1, Prix du Jockey Club-Gr1, Prix Niel-Gr2, Prix Gontaut-Biron-Gr3 (twice). Also 2nd in Irish Derby, Prix de l'Arc de Triomphe, Turf Classic, 3rd and 4th in Japan Cup. Strong, attractive, fluent mover, with an excellent turn of foot. Acted on any ground, equally effective at 10f and 12f. Tough, very genuine performer, competitive at the top level on 3 continents. Stands at Lanwades Stud, fee (2004) £14,000. Sire of: Holding Court (Prix du Jockey-Club-Gr1), Asian Heights (Gr3), Mr Combustible (Gr2), Sulamani (Prix du Jockey-Club-Gr1, Arlington Million-Gr1, Turf Classic Invitational S.-Gr1, York International S-Gr1, Canadian International S. Gr1), Tau Ceti (Gr3), Hanami (Gr2), Just Wonder (Gr3), Samando (Gr2), Songerie (Gr3).

Dam Soul Dream

Won 1 of 6 races. Leggy, plain, modest performer, apparently acted on any ground and stayed 12f. Dam of Dream Well (1995 c by Sadler's Wells; dual Derby winner), Archipelago (1996 c by Caerleon; winner), Conundrum (1998 c by Caerleon; unraced), Sulamani (1999 c by Hernando; multiple Gr1 winner), Awakened (2000 c by Sadler's Wells; unraced), Kyatikyo (2001 c by Machiavellian; unraced to date), unnamed (2002 c by Machiavellian; unraced). She has a filly foal by Storm Cat.

Pedigree assessment

Sulamani continued to distinguish himself at the top level in 2004, and when he had conditions exactly to his liking, he won. He concluded his globe-trotting career at Woodbine with an easy victory over an international field, and retires to stud in Newmarket at a fee of £7,000. His racing record will commend him to breeders, who should also recognise an impressive pedigree background, accented towards stamina, but not without strong elements of speed, notably in his female line. Among the best in training for three consecutive seasons, he may be cited as proof of the old adage that handsome is as handsome does. *TM*

Sundrop (Jpn)

3yo bay filly   **114**

Sunday Silence (USA) - Oenothera (Ire) (Night Shift (USA))
Owner Godolphin
Trainer Saeed Bin Suroor
Breeder Y Hosakawa

Career: **5** starts | won **2** | second **2** | third **0** | **£141,061** win and place

By Seb Vance

THE Godolphin way was so nearly the right way for the first two Classics of 2004. The Dubai operation don't bother with the conventional trials any more; their Guineas contenders lined up having wintered in Dubai, with only the private Godolphin trials resembling any sort of prep outing.

While Snow Ridge's second in the 2,000 Guineas was a commendable effort in itself, it was not unexpected. That wasn't the case with Sundrop, according to the bookmakers, who made the daughter of Sunday Silence a 16-1 chance. They underestimated Godolphin's faith in her ability, as she nearly beat one of 2004's star performers, Attraction, getting to within half a length of the flying filly in finishing second.

While Frankie Dettori wore the first colours on Carry On Katie, Sundrop was in no way neglected by trainer Saeed Bin Suroor, who also saddled third-string Cairns.

On the bare form of her 2003 public outings, she deserved to take a hand in the season's second Classic. Having won her maiden on the all-weather at Lingfield, the Japanese-bred bay bridged the chasm to Group 1 company by finishing one and a quarter lengths second to Red Bloom in the Fillies' Mile at Ascot.

Dettori rode Sundrop in Godolphin's fillies' trial in mid-April to finish just behind the John Carroll-partnered Cairns. Yet when asked for his verdict on the Guineas contenders, which also included Carry On Katie, who sidestepped the trial, it was Sundrop that Bin Suroor picked out first. "I really like her," he said.

The 1,000 Guineas was also notable as Kerrin McEvoy's British Classic debut. The leading Australian jockey had been recruited as Godolphin's second rider and this was the first chance to showcase his talent on the big stage. He didn't disappoint on Sundrop, who had clearly benefited from the winter sun and looked outstanding in the paddock.

Sundrop, after four months off following her two Classic runs, scores a narrow win in the Listed Severals Stakes

McEvoy chose to bide his time from a low draw, which meant Sundrop was stuck out wide, with the field spreading from the middle of the track to the far rail. Attraction scorched away up front on the far side and, two furlongs out, McEvoy thought he had the whole field covered apart from the leader, who, he felt, could not sustain such a mighty pace.

Unfortunately for connections, they had come up against one of a kind in Attraction and, while Sundrop ran on well, there was not enough track left to wear down Mark Johnston's most successful star. She failed by half a length.

While Godolphin could console themselves in the knowledge that they housed the 3-1 Oaks favourite, the Guineas turned out to be the high point of Sundrop's season. Indeed it was Epsom that almost finished her. The Oaks build-up was dominated by discussion about whether Dettori would partner Sundrop or impressive Musidora Stakes winner Punctilious. In the end, the riders stuck to the mounts they had previously partnered and Sheikh Mohammed's team went to post with every chance of not just landing the Oaks, but bringing home a one-two.

2004 {#race-record}

1st Lanwades Stud Severals Stakes (Listed) (Newmarket, October 14) 3yo+ 10f Soft **97** (TS 45) 10 ran. *Held up in rear, not clear run 2f out, switched outside and good headway over 1f out, ridden and ducked left inside final furlong, kept on to lead close home (L Dettori), beat I Had A Dream by ½l*

6th Vodafone Oaks (Group 1) (Epsom, June 4) 3yo 12f Good **70** (TS 52) 7 ran. *Raced freely early, tracked leader to 7f out, 5th and losing place straight, ridden and hung badly right 3f out, tailed off (K McEvoy), beaten 34l by Ouija Board*

2nd UltimateBet.com 1,000 Guineas Stakes (Group 1) (Newmarket, May 2) 3yo 1m Good **114** (TS 103) 16 ran. *Raced centre, held up, headway over 1f out, ran on well (K McEvoy), beaten ½l by Attraction*

2003

2nd Meon Valley Stud Fillies' Mile (Group 1) (Ascot, September 27) 2yo 1m Good to firm **110** 7 ran ● **1st** EBF Maiden Fillies' Stakes (Div II) (Lingfield (AW), September 9) 2yo 7f Standard **82** 10 ran

Despite Dettori's decision, Bin Suroor reiterated his faith in Sundrop, saying: "She looks better now than she did [in the Guineas]. I hope she handles the ups and downs of Epsom but we think she will."

For once, Bin Suroor's hopes proved way off the mark. Sundrop was sent off second favourite but, like many before her, detested Epsom's idiosyncrasies. She raced keenly and by Tattenham Corner was a spent force, coming in a tailed-off sixth. It was a horrible experience and it left its mark.

While Ouija Board annihilated her field, Godolphin were also left to muse over Punctilious's distant third, though she was able to bounce back quickly in the Ribblesdale at Royal Ascot. Sundrop would have to wait a lot longer.

It emerged that Sundrop had suffered a soft-tissue injury. Given plenty of time to recover, she returned more than four months later, bidding for her first win on turf in the mile-and-a-quarter Listed Severals Stakes at Newmarket. On her Guineas form she had more than a stone in hand of her rivals and was fully entitled to 11-8 favouritism. Yet question marks remained over whether she was back to her best and also if she could cope with the soft ground.

In the end, her ability won through in the desperate conditions. With Dettori at the helm this time, Sundrop was waited with as usual, but when a clear pathway failed to emerge, Dettori switched to the outside to mount what looked like a decisive challenge. However, whether she was feeling an injury, hated the ground or was simply ring-rusty, Sundrop certainly thought twice about the whole thing. She wandered about under pressure, but Dettori persuaded her to finish the job off and she scored by half a length from I Had A Dream.

As for 2005, another winter in the sun, from which she clearly benefited the previous year, will surely help. The Dubai Carnival should give an even clearer indication of what she might still have to offer.

Sundrop

bay filly, 16-3-2001

		Hail To Reason	Turn-to
			Nothirdchance
	Halo		
		Cosmah	Cosmic Bomb
Sunday Silence			Almahmoud
br 1986			
		Understanding	Promised Land
			Pretty Ways
	Wishing Well		
		Mountain Flower	Montparnasse
			Edelweiss
		Northern Dancer	Nearctic
			Natalma
	Night Shift		
		Ciboulette	Chop Chop
Oenothera			Windy Answer
ch 1990			
		Rheingold	Faberge
			Athene
	Fruition		
		Welsh Flame	Welsh Pageant
			Electric Flash

Bred by Y Hosakawa in Japan. Y50 million Japan Racing Horse Association Select foal

Sire Sunday Silence

Won 9 (6-10f) of 14 races. At 2, won 1 of 3 starts. At 3, won 7 (inc. San Felipe H-Gr2, Santa Anita Derby-Gr1, Kentucky Derby-Gr1, Preakness S-Gr1, Super Derby-Gr1, Breeders' Cup Classic-Gr1) of 9 starts, also 2nd Belmont S-Gr1. At 4, won 1 (Californian S-Gr1) of 2 starts. By smart turf performer and very good US sire, out of a US stakes winner. Retired to Shadai Stallion Station in Japan, died August 2002. Oldest progeny 12, sire of Gr1 winners (northern hemisphere foals): Dance Partner, Fuji Kiseki, Genuine, Marvelous Sunday, Tayasu Tsuyoshi, Bubble Gum Fellow, Dance In The Dark, Ishino Sunday, Silence Suzuka, Stay Gold, Special Week, Admire Vega, Stinger, To The Victory, Agnes Flight, Air Shakur, Cheers Grace, Believe, Manhattan Cafe, Mejiro Bailey, Durandal, Gold Allure, Admire Groove, Neo Universe, Peace Of World, Still In Love, Zenno Rob Roy, Dance In The Mood, Daiwa El Cielo, Daiwa Major. Also sire of European Group winners Sunday Picnic (Gr3), Silent Honor (Gr3), Layman (Gr3).

Dam Oenothera

Won 3 of 16 starts at 3 and 4. At 3, won 2 (10-11f) of 12 starts. At 4, won 1 (10f Listed event in Germany) of 4 starts, also 2nd 10f Gr3 event. Half-sister to Northern Spur (Breeders' Cup Turf-Gr1, Oak Tree Invitational-Gr1), Great Marquess and Kneller (both Doncaster Cup-Gr3, Jockey Club Cup-Gr3). Dam Fruition Listed-placed half-sister to Group 2 winner Flame Of Tara (dam of Gr1 winners Marju, Salsabil) and Listed-placed Welsh Love (dam of Gr1 winner Second Empire). Dam of: Machikanetsukigata (1997 c by Machiavellian; winner), Juno Browny (1998 f by Brian's Time; winner), Sundrop (2001 f by Sunday Silence; Listed winner, Gr1 placed), unnamed (2002 f by Sunday Silence; unraced).

Pedigree assessment

Bred to appreciate 10f and finally achieved her stakes win over that trip, having excelled over 1m. Sundrop reportedly remains in training in 2005, when a Group win should be well within her compass, and despite her Oaks failure she has fair prospects of staying 12f. She is by a phenomenal, late sire and is from a superb family, which makes her an exciting broodmare prospect. *JH*

Sweet Stream (Ity)

4yo bay filly **112**

Shantou (USA) - Snug Dinner (Ire) (Jareer (USA))

Owner Team Valor

Trainer J E Hammond

Breeder Paolo Torrente

Career: **14** starts   won **5**   second **1**   third **4**   **£211,264** win and place

---

By Bill Barber

WEET STREAM may not have scaled the same heights as Falbrav and Rakti, but hers is another name to add to the list of those who enjoyed top-level success elsewhere after starting their careers in Italy.

Her Group 1 victory came in the Prix Vermeille at Longchamp in September, a win dismissed as a fluke at the time but one that vindicated her American owners' decision to persevere with her in Europe.

Sweet Stream was sent off a 16-1 chance for the race, having finished third in the Prix de Pomone at Deauville on her previous run. Several of the principals from that contest were in opposition again, among them the winner Lune d'Or, who was 2lb better off with Team Valor's four-year-old filly, having beaten her just under a length at Deauville, and the fifth and sixth, Royal Fantasy and Whortleberry.

In the absence of Ouija Board, the Vermeille was expected to be merely a convenient stepping-stone for Prix de Diane winner Latice on her way to the Arc. Those expectations looked set to be realised when Latice was kicked into a clear lead in the straight, but fears that the 12-furlong trip would find out the 11-10 favourite proved well founded when her stride faltered and a host of challengers emerged from the pack. One of those challengers was Sweet Stream.

Sweet Stream had been under pressure from jockey Thierry Gillet from early in the race but enjoyed a charmed run up the rail to challenge over a furlong out. She hung on for a half-length victory over Royal Fantasy, with Pride, behind whom Sweet Stream had finished 11th and last in the Prix Allez France at Chantilly in May, a further half-length back in third. There were barely two lengths between Sweet Stream and eighth-placed Latice.

While many British visitors to Longchamp that day will have viewed the result with disbelief, trainer John Hammond was far from shocked.

Sweet Stream, having been denied the chance to race in the US, lands a European Group 1 in the Prix Vermeille

He said: "This victory wasn't exactly a surprise. Sweet Stream has been working very well and always finds her form in the autumn."

It had only been by chance that the daughter of Shantou had arrived at the Englishman's stable, for she was set to be exported to the United States until trouble obtaining an import licence led her to stay in France. "She came for a short time but stayed on in France – rather like me," said Hammond.

Sweet Stream was bred by a farrier, Paolo Torrente, who bought the dam cheaply on the recommendation of Palla Colombo and put her to the St Leger winner Shantou, who stood locally at Varese, north of Milan. She did well for him in Italy as a two-year-old, winning twice and finishing fifth in the Group 3 Premio Dormello, and while the level of her form was unexceptional, she must have had something about her to attract the interest of American owners Team Valor, whose shrewd purchases include The Deputy, My Memoirs, Ipi Tombe and Crimson Palace. Team Valor bought her and sent her to Hammond after the plan to ship her across the Atlantic was aborted. In all probability, she is better suited to

2004

Race record

3rd Gran Premio del Jockey Club (Group 1) (San Siro, October 17) 3yo+ 12f Soft **112** 9 ran. *Broke well, soon held up in rear, last straight, headway on inside 3f out, ridden 2f out, kept on at one pace, finished 4th, placed 3rd (T Gillet), beaten 1¼l by Shirocco*

1st Prix Vermeille Fouquet's Barriere (Group 1) (Longchamp, September 12) 3-4yo 12f Soft **112** (TS 109) 13 ran. *Mid-division, pushed along 4f out, took closer order on rail entering straight, effort and ran on to challenge over 1f out, ridden out (T Gillet), beat Royal Fantasy by ½l*

3rd Prix de Pomone (Group 2) (Deauville, August 7) 3yo+ 12½f Good to soft **106** (TS 101) 12 ran. *Held up in rear, 10th on inside straight, headway to go 3rd over 1f out, kept on under pressure (T Gillet), beaten ¾l by Lune d'Or*

11th Prix Allez France (Group 3) (Chantilly, May 7) 4yo+ 10f Soft **95** (TS 70) 11 ran. *Raced in 5th, 8th and weakening straight, tailed off final 2f (T Gillet), beaten 6½l by Pride*

Other wins

2003 **1st** Prix Belle du Nuit (Listed) (Maisons-Laffitte, November 19) 3yo+ 12f Heavy **108** 18 ran ● **1st** Prix du Manoir (Handicap) (Saint-Cloud, October 30) 3yo 12f Soft 18 ran **2002** **1st** Premio Maremma (San Siro, September 25) 2yo 1m½f Heavy 6 ran ● **1st** Premio Forcora (Maiden) (San Siro, September 17) 2yo 1m Good 9 ran

racing in Europe, for ideally she prefers both 12 furlongs and a soft surface, two things she would seldom have got in the States.

As a three-year-old she came into her own in the autumn, winning a handicap on soft ground at Saint-Cloud over a mile and a half before landing a Listed contest over the same trip on heavy ground at Maisons-Laffitte. The Prix Allez France and the Prix de Pomone were her only two starts in 2004 prior to the Vermeille.

A supplementary entry for the Arc was considered. Barry Irwin, president of Team Valor, said: "Our feeling is that everyone thought her win was something of a fluke, but we think we know her a bit better than they do. She's a filly who comes to herself at this time of year and she likes the turf a lot softer than she had that day. She's come out of the race well and if she is training well before the entry deadline and the ground looks like being suitable, we'll go for it."

In the event, Sweet Stream did not figure among the supplementaries. Instead she was returned to Italy two weeks after the Arc for an alternative Group 1, the Gran Premio del Jockey Club at San Siro.

Far from disgraced, she finished fourth past the post, behind German star Shirocco and Electrocutionist, who was meeting his first defeat and subsequently joined Angel Penna jnr in New York. Sweet Stream was then promoted a place following the controversial demotion of original third Imperial Dancer.

Connections were planning to extend Sweet Stream's season for the Hong Kong Vase at the Sha Tin International meeting in December and she will stay in training as a five-year-old in 2005.

Sweet Stream

bay filly, 22-4-2000

		Hoist The Flag	Tom Rolfe
			Wavy Navy
	Alleged	Princess Pout	Prince John
Shantou			Determined Lady
b 1993		Shareef Dancer	**Northern Dancer**
			Sweet Alliance
	Shaima	Oh So Sharp	Kris
			Oh So Fair
		Northern Dancer	Nearctic
			Natalma
	Jareer	Fabuleux Jane	Le Fabuleux
Snug Dinner			Native Partner
b 1991		Home Guard	Forli
			Stay At Home
	Stand By Me	St John's Wood	Saint Crespin
			Maryland Wood

Bred by Paolo Torrente in Italy

Sire Shantou

Unraced at 2, won 6 of 14 starts at 3 and 4. Won 4 of 10 races at 3, notably St Leger-Gr1, Gran Premio del Jockey Club-Gr1, also 3rd Derby-Gr1, 4th Breeders' Cup Turf-Gr1. At 4, won Gran Premio di Milano-Gr1, Princess of Wales's S-Gr2. By dual Arc winner and very good stamina-orientated sire, out of Grade 2-winning daughter of outstanding filly Oh So Sharp. Stands at Allevamento di Besnate in Italy, 2004 fee €6,000. Oldest progeny 4, sire of: Sweet Stream (Prix Vermeille-Gr1), Listed winner Bening.

Dam Snug Dinner

Won 3 (9-10f) of 21 starts in 2 seasons in Italy. By a $7.1million yearling and useful middle-distance performer who was a modest sire. Moderate family in recent generations, though further back this is the source of Coigach, Craigsteel, Invermark, Saros and The Whistling Teal. Dam of: Sfiziosa (1998 f by College Chapel; winner), El Cimbro (1999 c by Petardia; winner), Sweet Stream (2000 f by Shantou; Prix Vermeille-Gr1), Spark Of Stream (2001 f by Shantou), Sofia's Dream (2002 f by Shantou).

Pedigree assessment

The most prominent European winner to carry the (ITY) suffix in recent years. She is also the most prominent runner by Shantou, who is one of the best performers to retire to stud directly to Italy in recent times and has done reasonably well with several stakes performers. Shantou was quite late developing, and there is every chance Sweet Stream can build on her record in 2005. *JH*

Tante Rose (Ire)

4yo bay filly **121**

Barathea (Ire) - My Branch (Distant Relative)

Owner B E Nielsen

Trainer R Charlton

Breeder Addison Racing Ltd

Career: **13** starts   won **5**   second **0**   third **2**   **£225,546** win and place

By Richard Austen

WHEN Wafic Said sold his bloodstock interests in 2003, Classic winners Bosra Sham and Lady Carla were his best-known entries in the December Sales. The catalogue didn't say so, but there was at least one other winner of a Group 1 in his consignment. Tante Rose had not won hers yet.

A strapping filly, the three-year-old Tante Rose won the Fred Darling and went close in the Lennox Stakes for Barry Hills, but she fell well short when tried in Group 1 company, where her record was 16th in the 1,000 Guineas, eighth in the July Cup and seventh in the Prix Maurice de Gheest.

While the ten-year-old Lady Carla went through the sales ring for 1,050,000 guineas (Bosra Sham was sold privately in the run-up) and Tante Rose's two-year-old half-sister Bay Tree fetched 450,000 guineas, Tante Rose made 350,000 guineas to reappear in 2004 in the care of Roger Charlton and the colours of Bjorn Nielsen.

For them, Tante Rose never tasted defeat. Her only race over six furlongs as a three-year-old had seen her outpaced from the word go in the July Cup, but all her starts in 2004 were over six and she was a revelation.

First, Charlton tested Tante Rose in relatively quiet waters, sending her out in a Listed race at Haydock at the start of June for which she had clearly the best chance on form. Starting 7-4 favourite, she came late to collar Ruby Rocket and win by a neck. A satisfactory start.

The competition was tougher in the Group 3 Summer Stakes at York five weeks later, but Ruby Rocket again proved the chief danger and this time Tante Rose beat her by two and a half lengths, and easily at that, despite meeting trouble in running after halfway. A new career-best.

After that second win of the year against her own sex, Charlton observed: "I was slightly worried about her number one draw, given that she prefers

**Tante Rose, right, scores a narrow success in the Group 1
Haydock Sprint Cup, ahead of 2003 winner Somnus**

to drop in, get a lead and challenge between horses, but it didn't matter.
I thought she was pretty impressive. That's two Group 3 races she's won
now, so the aim will be to win a Group 2 race or get her placed in a
Group 1."

The Sprint Cup at Haydock showed that those ambitions were on the
modest side. The race's 2003 winner Somnus was back (along with third-
placed Airwave) and had registered another Group 1 success the previous
month in the Maurice de Gheest; Frizzante and Ashdown Express had
been first and second in the July Cup; Bahamian Pirate and One Cool
Cat first and third in the Nunthorpe; Royal Millennium, The Trader,
Monsieur Bond and Orientor had all won Group sprints in 2004; and
Patavellian was the previous year's Abbaye winner. In short, the field
was well up to scratch.

Tante Rose, however, entered the race under something of a cloud,
along with stablemate Patavellian, because Charlton's string had been
sick and he had not sent out a winner for three weeks. Tante Rose, a

2004 Race record

1st Stanleybet Sprint Cup (Group 1) (Haydock, September 4) 3yo+ 6f Good **121** (TS 116) 19 ran. *Midfield, ridden and headway over 1f out, ran on strongly inside final furlong to lead post (R Hughes), beat Somnus by shd*

1st Cuisine De France Summer Stakes (Group 3) (York, July 9) 3yo+ 6f Good to soft **116** (TS 114) 9 ran. *Steadied and switched right start, held up, not clear run over 2f out, smooth headway over 1f out, quickened to lead 150yds out, impressive (M Hills), beat Ruby Rocket by 2½l*

1st Joseph Heler Cheese Cecil Frail Stakes (Listed) (Haydock, June 5) 3yo+ 6f Good **101** (TS 99) 11 ran. *Held up, headway over 1f out, ran on to lead well inside final furlong (S Drowne), beat Ruby Rocket by nk*

2003

7th Victor Chandler Challenge Stakes (Group 2) (Newmarket, October 18) 3yo+ 7f Good to firm **109** 11 ran ● **4th** GNER Park Stakes (Group 3) (Doncaster, September 11) 3yo+ 7f Good **106** 9 ran ● **7th** Prix Maurice de Gheest (Group 1) (Deauville, August 10) 3yo+ 6½f Good to soft **104** 12 ran ● **3rd** Lennox Stakes (Group 2) (Goodwood, July 29) 3yo+ 7f Good **111** 13 ran ● **8th** Darley July Cup (Group 1) (Newmarket (July), July 10) 3yo+ 6f Good to firm **104** 16 ran ● **6th** Jersey Stakes (Group 3) (Ascot, June 18) 3yo 7f Good to firm **105** 14 ran ● **16th** Sagitta 1,000 Guineas Stakes (Group 1) (Newmarket, May 4) 3yo 1m Good to firm **67** 19 ran ● **1st** Dubai Duty Free Stakes (Registered As The Fred Darling Stakes) (Group 3) (Newbury, April 12) 3yo 7f Good to firm **106** 12 ran

Other runs

2002 **1st** EBF George Colling Maiden Stakes (Newmarket, November 1) 2yo 6f Good to soft **89** 17 ran ● **3rd** EBF Hare Maiden Fillies' Stakes (Div II) (Leicester, October 14) 2yo 7f Good **79** 6 ran

late withdrawal from the Maurice de Gheest, had been kept in isolation, with Charlton reporting "each day has been a nightmare, wondering if she was going to be the next one to cough."

Tante Rose gave easily the best performance of her career. One Cool Cat was favourite, not for the first time, and disappointed, not for the first time, and while he put up a flat display it was Tante Rose who emerged from the pack to cut down Somnus and Patavellian, leading on the post to win by a short head and three-quarters of a length.

Richard Hughes, her jockey, said: "Most top-class sprinters go flat out from start to finish, full speed ahead. But this filly has a serious turn of foot off a good gallop, and that's against the best of them. She does have amazing acceleration."

There was no outstanding sprinter in the latest season and Tante Rose is not the top-rated, as Somnus conceded a 3lb sex allowance at Haydock. Retired to the paddocks on a high note, Tante Rose came into her own as a four-year-old and over six furlongs with some give in the ground, but also won the Fred Darling over seven furlongs on good to firm.

Tante Rose   *bay filly, 10-4-2000*

			Nearctic
		Northern Dancer	Natalma
	Sadler's Wells		
		Fairy Bridge	Bold Reason
			Special
Barathea			
b 1990			Sir Gaylord
		Habitat	Little Hut
	Brocade		
		Canton Silk	Runnymede
			Clouded Lamp
			Sir Gaylord
		Habitat	Little Hut
	Distant Relative		
		Royal Sister	Claude
			Ribasha
My Branch			
b 1993			Derring-do
		High Top	Camenae
	Pay The Bank		
		Zebra Grass	Run The Gantlet
			Ash Lawn

Bred by Addison Racing in Ireland. 350,000gns Tattersalls December 3yo

Sire **Barathea**

Won 5 of 16 starts from 2 to 4. At 2, won both starts over 7f. At 3, won Irish 2,000 Guineas-Gr1, also 2nd 2,000 Guineas-Gr1, Queen Elizabeth II S-Gr1. At 4, won Queen Anne S-Gr2, Breeders' Cup Mile-Gr1, 2nd Sussex S-Gr1, Queen Elizabeth II S-Gr1. Top-class miler, though showed very smart form in Gr1 events over 6f and 12f. Full-brother to Gossamer (Fillies' Mile-Gr1, Irish 1,000 Guineas-Gr1), half-brother to high-class 1m+ filly Free At Last (dam of Gr2 winner Coretta) and high-class 7-8f gelding Zabar. Dam very high-class 7f performer. Stands at Rathbarry Stud in Ireland, 2005 fee €25,000. Oldest progeny 8, sire of (northern hemisphere): Barafamy (Gr3), Enrique (Gr3), La Sylphide (Gr3), Red Sea (Gr3), Barathea Guest (Gr3), Cornelius (Gr2), Hidalguia (Gr3), Blue Steller (Gr3), Siringas (Gr2), Tobougg (Prix de la Salamandre-Gr1, Dewhurst S-Gr1), Kardthea (Gr3), Pongee (Gr2), Rag Top (Gr3), Shield (Gr3), Tante Rose (Haydock Sprint Cup-Gr1), Apsis (Gr3), Hazarista (Gr3), Magical Romance (Cheveley Park S-Gr1).

Dam **My Branch**

Won 4 of 21 starts. High-class 2yo, won Firth of Clyde S-Listed, 2nd Cheveley Park S-Gr1. Later high-class 7-8f filly, won Sceptre S-Listed, 3rd Irish 1,000 Guineas, 4th 1,000 Guineas. Bred along similar lines to smart 7f performer Atavus. Dam of: Future Flight (1998 f by Polar Falcon; winner), Rosie's Posy (1999 f by Suave Dancer; winner), Tante Rose (2000 f by Barathea; Haydock Sprint Cup-Gr1), Bay Tree (2001 f by Daylami; Listed winner, Gr3 placed), 2003 f by Grand Lodge.

Pedigree assessment

Bjorn Nielsen picked up a relative bargain when he paid 350,000gns for Tante Rose in 2003. He now has a valuable Group 1-winning broodmare prospect with several smart female relatives, not least her high-class dam My Branch, who also was bought by Nielsen for 420,000gns in 2002. Tante Rose's first mate is scheduled to be Daylami and the produce will be closely related to 2004 Group 3 Musidora Stakes third Bay Tree. *JH*

The Tatling (Ire)

7yo brown gelding   **119**

Perugino (USA) - Aunty Eileen (Ahonoora)
Owner Dab Hand Racing
Trainer J M Bradley
Breeder Patrick J Power

Career: **58** starts   won **9**   second **14**   third **9**   **£494,949** win and place

By Daniel Hill

THE TATLING has taken Milton Bradley places he would scarely even have dreamed of just a few years ago. Most of Bradley's 30-odd years as a trainer have been spent around the west country gaff tracks, but in 2003 The Tatling gave him a first Group win and then took him not just on his first trip abroad, to Paris for the Prix de l'Abbaye, but also on to Hong Kong.

The latest season brought another first for the 69-year-old crop farmer, for the one-time claiming horse took him to the Royal Ascot winner's spot after The Tatling had landed the King's Stand Stakes. Bradley was bewildered, even though the seven-year-old had finished third in the race the previous year, and said: "I never imagined I would be here – that's why I didn't dress up in a morning suit!"

If the BHB were ever to create an award for the most consistent horse in training, they could do worse than hand it to The Tatling. For in his 11 races in 2004 prior to an intended return to Hong Kong (including a further four trips to France) he only once finished out of the first four, and his placings included seconds in the Nunthorpe, in which he was also runner-up in 2003, and the Prix de l'Abbaye.

The Tatling started 8-1 in a field of 19 in the King's Stand, which included the previous season's Cornwallis and Molecomb Stakes winner Majestic Missile, the Palace House winner Frizzante (who started the 9-2 favourite) and Hong Kong challenger Cape Of Good Hope. The Tatling got the fast pace he excels behind and led inside the final furlong to beat Cape Of Good Hope by one and a half lengths. Frizzante, who had met trouble in running, was a neck away in third.

Four defeats followed before he next entered the winner's enclosure at Newbury in September, in the Dubai International Airport World Trophy, but it was a performance worth waiting for. The Tatling took what turned out to be a most notable scalp in the shape of former American-trained

The Tatling, one of the most consistent sprinters around, scores his biggest win in the Group 2 King's Stand Stakes

sprinter Var, whom he pipped in the last strides and beat a head, with Airwave one and a quarter lengths away in third.

A return to Longchamp for another crack at the Prix de l'Abbaye had long been The Tatling's aim and that race was only a fortnight away, yet the gelding's owners were keen to run him first in the Diadem Stakes at Ascot, even though that meant stepping up to six furlongs, a distance over which he had won only a York handicap, and racing around a bend, owing to the redevelopment work that was going on at Ascot. Bradley himself was less enthusiastic, and one can see why, for The Tatling had just about everything against him and there was a danger that the race would take the edge off him before Longchamp.

The Tatling was well below form in third behind Pivotal Point but cannot have taken too much out of himself, for he was back in the form of his life again at Longchamp. He improved upon his 2003 third but this time could never quite get to grips with Var, who showed blinding speed up the middle of the track and held him by half a length. It was a terrific effort, especially as The Tatling was in the stalls longer than he should have been – a request to have him put in last having seemingly been ignored – and he saw more daylight than ideal.

2004 Race record

2nd Prix de l'Abbaye de Longchamp Majestic Barriere (Group 1) (Longchamp, October 3) 2yo+ 5f Good **119** (TS 116) 15 ran. *Raced in 7th, headway on outside to go 2nd inside final f, ran on but not reach winner (R L Moore), beaten ½l by Var*

3rd GNER Diadem Stakes (Group 2) (Ascot, September 25) 3yo+ 6f Good to firm **110** 12 ran. *Tracked leaders, going well 2f out, ridden and one pace over 1f out (R L Moore), beaten 4¼l by Pivotal Point*

1st Dubai International Airport World Trophy (Group 3) (Newbury, September 18) 3yo+ 5f Good **119** (TS 119) 11 ran. *In touch, ridden and headway to chase leader 1f out, stayed on strongly under pressure to lead last strides (R L Moore), beat Var by hd*

2nd Prix du Petit Couvert (Group 3) (Longchamp, September 5) 3yo+ 5f Good to soft **119** (TS 85) 9 ran. *Always in touch, headway to go 2nd 1f out, ran on but never able to challenge (R L Moore), beaten 1l by Pivotal Point*

2nd Victor Chandler Nunthorpe Stakes (Group 1) (York, August 19) 2yo+ 5f Soft **117** (TS 107) 12 ran. *Tracked leaders going well, headway 2f out, effort over 1f out, soon ridden and kept on well final furlong (R L Moore), beaten nk by Bahamian Pirate*

3rd King George Stakes (Group 3) (Goodwood, July 29) 3yo+ 5f Good to firm **119** (TS 111) 13 ran. *Held up in rear, progress over 1f out, ran on to chase leading pair inside final furlong, just unable to challenge (R L Moore), beaten 1l by Ringmoor Down*

9th Champagne Laurent-Perrier Sprint Stakes (Group 3) (Sandown, July 3) 3yo+ 5f Good to soft **91** (TS 71) 12 ran. *Steadied start, raced on inner and held up towards rear, effort when not clear run 2f out, no progress after (D Holland), beaten 9½l by Orientor*

1st King's Stand Stakes (Group 2) (Ascot, June 15) 3yo+ 5f Good to firm **119** (TS 108) 19 ran. *Held up, headway over 2f out, ridden over 1f out, led inside final furlong, ran on well (D Holland), beat Cape Of Good Hope by 1½l*

4th Prix du Gros-Chene (Group 2) (Chantilly, June 6) 3yo+ 5f Good to soft **108** (TS 92) 8 ran. *Raced in 5th, pushed along 2f out towards outside, stayed on final furlong to take 4th on line (D Holland), beaten 2¼l by Avonbridge*

3rd Favourites Racing Achilles Stakes (Listed) (Kempton, May 29) 3yo+ 5f Good to firm **113** (TS 77) 10 ran. *Held up in touch, not much much room inside final 2f, ridden and headway to chase leaders final furlong, going on close home (D Holland), beaten 1½l by Boogie Street*

2nd Prix de Saint-Georges (Group 3) (Longchamp, May 16) 3yo+ 5f Good to firm **116** (TS 100) 12 ran. *Soon close up on rails, led well over 1f out to inside final f, ran on one pace (L Dettori), beaten 2l by The Trader*

Other wins

2003 **1st** King George Stakes (Group 3) (Goodwood, July 31) 3yo+ 5f Good **111** 9 ran ● **1st** Porcelanosa Sprint Stakes (Listed) (Sandown, July 5) 3yo+ 5f Good **116** 13 ran 2002 **1st** Coral Eurobet Sprint Trophy (0-105 handicap) (York, October 12) 3yo+ 6f Good to firm **107** 19 ran ● **1st** Sunshine Coach Rated Stakes (0-100 handicap) (Sandown, August 31) 3yo+ 5f Good to firm **96** 15 ran ● **1st** Leyburn Claiming Stakes (Catterick, July 24) 3yo+ 5f Good to firm **90** 16 ran 1999 **1st** EBF/Laurent-Perrier Novice Median Auction Stakes (Brighton, August 18) 2yo 5½f Soft **83** 4 ran ● **1st** Joe Pasquale Summer Season Maiden Stakes (Yarmouth, July 14) 2yo 5f Good to firm **92** 7 ran

Clearly as good as ever in 2004, The Tatling will be back for more. He has already earned more than £150,000 in win money alone in Bradley's hands. Not bad for a horse who was picked up from David Nicholls in July 2002 for just £15,000 after winning a lowly Catterick claimer.

The Tatling
brown gelding, 23-4-1997

Perugino br 1991	Danzig	Northern Dancer	Nearctic / Natalma
		Pas de Nom	Admiral's Voyage / Petitioner
	Fairy Bridge	Bold Reason	Hail To Reason / Lalun
		Special	Forli / Thong
Aunty Eileen b 1983	Ahonoora	Lorenzaccio	Klairon / Phoenissa
		Helen Nichols	Martial / Quaker Girl
	Safe Haven	Blakeney	Hethersett / Windmill Girl
		Amazer	Mincio / Alzara

Bred by Patrick Power in Ireland. Ir54,000gns Tattersalls (Ireland) September yearling, 11,000gns Tattersalls July 4yo

Sire Perugino

Won only race, over 6f at 2. Extremely well bred, by outstanding speed sire out of dam of Fairy King/Sadler's Wells/Tate Gallery (all by Danzig's sire Northern Dancer). Originally stood at Coolmore Stud, based in Germany (Gestut Rheinberg) in 2002, now at Collingrove Stud in Australia, 2004 fee A$9,900. Oldest progeny 8, sire of (northern hemisphere foals): Banyumanik (Gr3), Gino's Spirits (Gr3), The Tatling (Gr2), Next Gina (Preis der Diana-Gr1).

Dam Aunty Eileen

Unraced. By top-class sprinter and excellent sire, half-sister to high-class sprinter Lugana Beach (by Tumble Wind). Dam half-sister to outstanding 10-12f performer Mtoto, Gr3 winner Savoureuse Lady (grand-dam of Blue Canari) and Listed-placed Petal Girl (dam of Mutamam). Dam of: unnamed (1988 c by Soughaan; unraced), Ambitious Venture (1989 c by Gorytus; winner), Moving Image (1990 f by Nordico; winner), Just Do It Joey (1991 f by Glenstal; stakes winner in South Africa), Astuti (1993 f by Waajib; winner), Daintree (1994 f by Tirol; winner), Amazing Dream (1996 f by Thatching; Listed winner, Gr3 placed), The Tatling (1997 c by Perugino; Gr2 winner, Gr1 placed), unnamed (1998 c by Dolphin Street; unraced), Moritat (2000 c by Night Shift; placed), Garibaldi (2002 c by Fasliyev; unraced, died), unnamed (2003 c by King Charlemagne; 14,000gns yearling), 2004 c by Montjeu.

Pedigree assessment

An admirable sprinter, much like his 'uncle' Lugana Beach. The Tatling's sire Perugino, a son of Danzig, helped contribute to his speed, while the toughness appears to come from the dam's line. This family is best known in recent times for middle-distance quartet Blue Canari, Circus Plume, Mtoto and Mutamam – all by stout stallion influences – but it goes back to 1951 Cheveley Park Stakes and 1952 1,000 Guineas winner Zabara. As a gelding, it will be another season of Group sprints at the age of eight for The Tatling in 2005. *JH*

Torrestrella (Ire)

3yo bay filly   115

Orpen (USA) - Sea Ring (Fr) (Bering)

Owner M Rankowitz

Trainer Christophe Clement

Breeder Francis Montauban

Career: **8** starts   won **3**   second **2**   third **0**   **£172,426** win and place

By Robert Carter

IT WAS the year of the Deauville yearling – at least in the French Classics. Blue Canari cost €135,000 (then about £85,240) and won the Prix du Jockey-Club. Latice was bought privately, after failing to meet her reserve, for €60,000 (£37,880) and won the Prix de Diane. And the Poule d'Essai des Pouliches winner, Torrestrella, was the cheapest of all, at €30,000 (£18,940).

Grey Lilas and Via Milano, second and fourth to her at Longchamp, also went through the ring at Deauville. Only American Post, the fortunate winner of the Poule d'Essai des Poulains, who was homebred by Khalid Abdullah's Juddmonte Farms, was not a Deauville yearling.

Torrestrella was foaled in Ireland, where her dam was visiting Bahhare, but she was raised in France and qualified for both the breeders' and owners' premiums. Francis Montauban, her breeder, lives near Bordeaux and brought the filly home to spend her infancy at the nearby Haras des Granges, owned by Mathieu Daguzan-Garros. Another close neighbour, Bernard Bargues, who lives little more than a mile from the stud, was to become her owner. He was represented at Deauville by Francois Rohaut, one of the increasingly formidable band of provincial trainers, with a 90-strong stable.

Rohaut, like Pascal Bary a former assistant to Sir Mark Prescott, is based at Sers, a training centre on the outskirts of Pau. So the whole combination, of breeder, studmaster, owner and trainer, contributed to an all-round triumph for the south-west. It was there, too, that Torrestrella began her career. She was second at Tarbes, the next big town east of Pau, when making her two-year-old debut in October, and second again when travelling still further east for a more competitive event at Toulouse the following month.

She ran creditably each time without looking capable of catching either winner. But she was ready early for her Classic season, and ready also

Torrestrella makes a successful raid from the south-west of France by landing the Poule d'Essai des Pouliches

to take on Parisian rivals. She reappeared at Maisons-Laffitte on March 2, only the second meeting of the year on the capital's courses, and, with Christophe Soumillon up, started favourite for the Prix Dorina, a conditions event over one mile. Torrestrella, who pulled early, was always well in touch, took over inside the final two furlongs and had no trouble holding the efforts of the debutante Silent Flight by two lengths.

Rohaut already had his eye on Torrestrella's next target, the Listed Prix Finlande, run over nine furlongs at Longchamp the following month. It was an easy enough choice, for he had won the race with Turtle Bow and Baie in the previous two years.

Again ridden by Soumillon, and again favourite, Torrestrella raced keenly, pressing Autumn Forest for the lead from the start. She led halfway up the straight and ran on to hold another raider from Pau, Miss Me, by half a length. Rohaut had made only one Classic entry, in the Prix de Diane, but Soumillon advised him to bid for the Pouliches and she was supplemented for €21,000, or 10.5 per cent of her eventual prize.

Soumillon, though, was claimed for Miss Mambo, another filly he had ridden to two recent successes. The mount on Torrestrella went to Olivier Peslier, who soon placed her second behind Frankie Dettori and the

2004   Race record

5th Allowance race (Aqueduct, October 28) 3yo+ Fillies & Mares 1m Firm 7 ran. *(J Bravo), beaten 7l by Humoristic*

6th Garden City Breeders' Cup Handicap (Grade 1) (Belmont Park, September 12) 3yo 9f Good **96** 7 ran. *(C Nakatani), beaten 12l by Lucifer's Stone*

11th Prix de Diane Hermes (Group 1) (Chantilly, June 13) 3yo 10½f Good to soft **98** (TS 88) 17 ran. *Prominent, 4th straight, ridden 2f out, soon beaten (G Mosse), beaten 11l by Latice*

1st Gainsborough Poule d'Essai des Pouliches (Group 1) (Longchamp, May 16) 3yo 1m Good to firm **115** (TS 110) 13 ran. *Tracked leader until led just over 2f out, driven out (O Peslier), beat Grey Lilas by 1½l*

1st Prix Finlande (Listed) (Longchamp, April 11) 3yo 9f Good to soft **101** (TS 62) 10 ran. *(C Soumillon), beat Miss Me by ½l*

1st Prix Dorina (Round Course) (Maisons-Laffitte, March 2) 3yo Fillies 1m Soft 10 ran. *(C Soumillon), beat Silent Flight by 2l*

2003

2nd Prix Sud Radio (Toulouse, November 11) 2yo 1m Good to soft 6 ran ● **2nd** Prix des Pyrenees (Tarbes, October 19) 2yo 7½f Good 14 ran

Godolphin filly Carry On Katie. Torrestrella took over with two furlongs to run but she was quickly challenged by the favourite Grey Lilas, and had to be driven out to hold that filly by one and a half lengths, with Miss Mambo two lengths back in third.

It was Peslier's third success in the first four races that day, and also a third Group 1 success for Rohaut, who had won the 1986 Prix Robert Papin with Balbonella at the very start of his training career and the 2002 Prix Vermeille with Pearly Shells.

Rohaut's first thoughts were of the Coronation Stakes and the Prix d'Astarte, but Torrestrella's exploits had attracted attention. She was sold to Peter Karches and Mike Rankowitz early in June and was redirected to the Prix de Diane, in which she carried the colours of Karches, a former president and chief executive officer of Morgan Stanley Institutional Securities and Investment Banking.

She raced in fourth behind Prairie Flower (a Wildenstein pacemaker), Grey Lilas and Menhoubah as far as the straight, but when she tried to challenge Grey Lilas for the lead two furlongs from home, she was soon under pressure and finding nothing.

When she reappeared in September, it was at Belmont and she was now trained by Christophe Clement. She was narrowly favoured over Aidan O'Brien's raider, Necklace, in the Garden City Handicap but fought her jockey in the early stages and finished sixth of seven. The following month she was soundly beaten in an allowance race at Aqueduct.

Her new trainer has a notable record with former European horses on American turf, but Torrestrella will have to settle if she is to add to her wins.

Torrestrella

bay filly, 6-5-2001

		Danzig	Northern Dancer
			Pas de Nom
	Lure		
		Endear	Alydar
Orpen			Chappaquiddick
b 1996			
		Devil's Bag	Halo
			Ballade
	Bonita Francita		
		Raise The Standard	Hoist The Flag
			Natalma
		Arctic Tern	Sea-Bird
			Bubbling Beauty
	Bering		
		Beaune	Lyphard
Sea Ring			Barbra
b 1990			
		Riverman	Never Bend
			River Lady
	Blue River		
		Azurella	High Hat
			Azorelle

Bred by Francis Montauban in Ireland. €30,000 Agence Francaise Deauville August yearling

Sire Orpen

Won both starts at 2 over 6f, notably Prix du Moulin-Gr1. At 3, placed once (3rd Irish 2,000 Guineas-Gr1) from 4 starts over 6-8f. By outstanding US turf miler but sub-fertile (now retired) sire. Half-brother to useful stayer Etterby Park (Silver Hawk), Grade 3 winner Jules (Forty Niner) and Black Penny (dam of Poule d'Essai des Pouliches winner Bluemamba). Outstanding family of Bago, Coup de Genie, Denebola, Exit To Nowhere, Machiavellian. Stands at Coolmore (Castle Hyde) Stud, 2004 fee €7,000. Sire of (northern hemisphere foals): Gracefully (Gr3), Torrestrella (Poule d'Essai des Pouliches-Gr1), Listed winner Kaypen.

Dam Sea Ring

Won 2 of 10 starts in France, over 8-10f at 3 and 4. By top-class 10-12f performer and good French sire, out of useful French 2yo Blue River. Half-sister to 6f Listed winner Rayon Bleu (Last Tycoon) and 12f Listed-placed Stani River (Shahrastani). Grand-dam, smart 12f filly Azurella, also 3rd dam of Gr1 winner Goldamix and promising 2004 2yo Descartes. Dam of: Torrealta (1996 f by In The Wings; winner, Listed placed), Comandante (1998 c by Apple Tree; jumps winner), Lingo (1999 c by Poliglote; winner, Gr1 hurdle winner), Campo Charro (2000 c by Alhaarth; winner), Torrestrella (2001 f by Orpen; Poule d'Essai des Pouliches-Gr1), Summer Sea (2002 f by Bahhare; unraced), unnamed (2003 c by Lomitas; €180,000 yearling).

Pedigree assessment

Has provided her very well-bred sire with a Classic winner in his first large crop. She is the speediest offspring of her dam, who has done well from a varied collection of stallions. Nine or perhaps ten furlongs might be within her compass, which gives her plenty of options if she continues her career in the US. *JH*

Tycoon

3yo bay colt **123**

Sadler's Wells (USA) - Fleeting Glimpse (Rainbow Quest (USA))

Owner Mrs John Magnier

Trainer A P O'Brien

Breeder Juddmonte Farms

Career: **9** starts | won **1** | second **1** | third **4** | **£212,155** win and place

By Richard Austen

IDAN O'BRIEN'S best middle-distance three-year-olds of 2004 were probably not that high in the pecking order at the start of the year. When Yeats, O'Brien's main hope, went missing with injury, it was left to Tycoon and Acropolis to put up the season's best performances at a mile and a half by a Ballydoyle three-year-old.

Tycoon and Acropolis did good work in top races over a mile and a half and more, but neither of them actually won one. They showed their hands relatively late, with Tycoon making his three-year-old debut on June 27 and Acropolis on September 11. What's more, when Tycoon emerged as a high-class colt in the Irish Derby he was a 150-1 shot, and when Acropolis did so in the Arc it was at an industry price of 100-1.

The Irish Derby followed a two-year-old campaign in which Tycoon had been runner-up in the Chesham on his second start and won a maiden on his third but been put well in his place (along with Acropolis) in the Prix Jean-Luc Lagardere.

None of O'Brien's five runners in the Irish Derby was given more than the slimmest of chances, but while Cobra was 25-1, Five Dynasties 33-1, Moscow Ballet 50-1 and Book Of Kings 66-1, Tycoon started at well over twice the price of any other horse in the field. This quintet finished in the opposite order and Tycoon did easily the best.

Colm O'Donoghue guided Roosevelt, another O'Brien-trained 150-1 shot, into third behind Alamshar in 2003 and he repeated the trick on Tycoon. Held up and a detached last at halfway, Tycoon had moved into sixth two furlongs out and stayed on stoutly to be beaten two lengths, just passing Rule Of Law but with Grey Swallow and North Light out of reach.

In truth, Tycoon never got to grips with the first two in any of his races in 2004 but three of his four starts after the Irish Derby backed up that

Tycoon, who failed to win in 2004 but was placed in two Classics and in a Grade 1 race in the United States

result and left no question of his merit. Finishing six and three-quarter lengths behind Doyen when the Godolphin star was in his pomp in the King George was full of credit and the result could have been better still because, travelling well two furlongs out, 16-1 shot Tycoon lost any chance of making the frame when hampered on the rails. Who would have dreamed one month earlier that Tycoon would be the only three-year-old in the King George?

The 2004 race in which Tycoon had his best chance was the St Leger, though the matter wasn't so clear on the day. He'd beaten Rule Of Law at The Curragh, but while Rule Of Law enhanced his St Leger claims at York in the Great Voltigeur, Tycoon's appearance at the Ebor meeting in the International saw the worst race of his life. The shorter trip, soft ground, his high-strung pre-race demeanour and difficulty in getting him settled in the race could all help explain why, when Jamie Spencer asked Tycoon to improve his position, the opposite happened and Tycoon was allowed to coast home tailed off.

The 6-1 fourth favourite at Doncaster, the shortest-priced of three O'Brien runners, Tycoon was seen to vastly better effect. With Spencer at

2004   Race record

3rd Joe Hirsch Turf Classic Invitational (Grade 1) (Belmont Park, October 2) 3yo+ 12f Yielding **123** 7 ran. *Raced in 6th, went 3rd 2f out, stayed on (J P Spencer), beaten 3¼l by Kitten's Joy*

3rd betfair.com St Leger Stakes (Group 1) (Doncaster, September 11) 3yo 1m6½f Good to firm **120** (TS 103) 9 ran. *Dwelt, held up in last place, steady headway over 2f out, shaken up over 1f out, stayed on inside final furlong (D Holland), beaten 1¾l by Rule Of Law*

9th Juddmonte International Stakes (Group 1) (York, August 17) 3yo+ 10½f Good (TS 13) 9 ran. *Dwelt, always behind, driven along over 4f out, no response, eased and tailed off (J P Spencer), beaten 44+l by Sulamani*

6th King George VI And Queen Elizabeth Diamond Stakes (Group 1) (Ascot, July 24) 3yo+ 12f Good to firm **122** (TS 86) 11 ran. *Held up in last, plenty to do 3f out, rapid progress on inner when ran into back of weakening pacemaker 2f out, switched and kept on, not recover (J P Spencer), beaten 6¾l by Doyen*

3rd Budweiser Irish Derby (Group 1) (Curragh, June 27) 3yo 12f Good to firm **122** (TS 122) 10 ran. *Held up in rear, 9th into straight, 6th 2f out, stayed on well to go 3rd close home (C O'Donoghue), beaten 2l by Grey Swallow*

2003

5th Prix Jean-Luc Lagardere (Group 1) (Longchamp, October 5) 2yo 1m Holding **98** 6 ran ● **1st** Irish Stallion Farms EBF Maiden (Leopardstown, September 6) 2yo 7f Good to firm **91** 17 ran ● **2nd** Chesham Stakes (Listed) (Ascot, June 18) 2yo 7f Good to firm **96** 13 ran ● **3rd** EBF Maiden (Gowran Park, June 1) 2yo 7f Good to yielding **81** 12 ran

Leopardstown for Powerscourt in the Irish Champion Stakes, the ride was taken by Darryll Holland, who stuck to the template established successfully by Mick Kinane on Milan in 2001 and Spencer on Brian Boru in 2003, waiting well off the pace and biding his time as the battle raged ahead up the long straight. The canny pace set by Rule Of Law played against the tactic, however. Although Tycoon travelled well to get within four lengths of the leader one and a half furlongs out, he took a while to find his stride and was never going to manage better than third, closing at the line but still a length and a half behind Rule Of Law and Quiff.

A tactical contest also looked against him when Tycoon was a creditable third, again, over a mile and a half on yielding ground in the Joe Hirsch Turf Classic Invitational at Belmont Park, the last race before his sale to Sheikh Mohammed's son Rashid and a winter in Dubai.

When Tycoon reappears in 2005, he will be in with a shout of Group 1 success somewhere but needs to improve if he's to trouble the best mile-and-a-half horses. There's an issue with his temperament, too, as he has sometimes threatened to boil over in the preliminaries, and that might help to explain why he was always held up towards the rear in 2004. The evidence is inconclusive, but soft ground may well be against him.

Tycoon

bay colt, 21-3-2001

		Nearctic	Nearco
			Lady Angela
	Northern Dancer		
		Natalma	Native Dancer
			Almahmoud
Sadler's Wells			
b 1981			
		Bold Reason	Hail To Reason
			Lalun
	Fairy Bridge		
		Special	Forli
			Thong
		Blushing Groom	Red God
			Runaway Bride
	Rainbow Quest		
		I Will Follow	Herbager
			Where You Lead
Fleeting Glimpse			
b 1994			
		Lyphard	Northern Dancer
			Goofed
	Flit		
		Nimble Folly	Cyane
			Instant Sin

Bred by Juddmonte Farms in Britain

Sire **Sadler's Wells**

Won 6 of 11 races, inc. Beresford S.-Gr3, Irish Derby Trial-Gr2, Irish 2,000 Guineas-Gr1, Eclipse S.-Gr1, Phoenix Champion S.-Gr1. Also 2nd in Prix du Jockey-Club-Gr1, King George VI & Queen Elizabeth S.-Gr1. Impeccably bred top-class performer from 8-12f, handsome, tough and consistent. Sire of Gr1 winners: Braashee, French Glory, In The Wings (x3), Old Vic (x2), Prince Of Dance, Scenic, Salsabil (x5), Opera House (x3), Runyon, Saddlers' Hall, El Prado, Johann Quatz, Masad, Barathea (x2), Fatherland, Fort Wood, Intrepidity (x3), Carnegie (x2), King's Theatre (x2), Northern Spur (x2), Moonshell, Muncie, Poliglote, Chief Contender, Dance Design, Darazari, Luna Wells, Cloudings, Ebadiyla (x2), Entrepreneur, In Command, Kayf Tara (x4), Dream Well (x2), Greek Dance, King Of Kings (x2), Leggera, Commander Collins, Daliapour, Montjeu (x6), Saffron Walden, Aristotle, Beat Hollow (x4), Subtle Power, Galileo (x3), Imagine (x2), Milan, Perfect Soul, Sequoyah, Sligo Bay, Ballingarry, Black Sam Bellamy (x2), Gossamer (x2), High Chaparral (x6), Islington (x4), Quarter Moon, Sholokov, Alberto Giacometti, Brian Boru (x2), Doyen, Powerscourt, Refuse To Bend (4), Yesterday, Quiff, Playful Act.

Dam **Fleeting Glimpse**

Unraced at 2, won 10f maiden at 3 and 2nd Prix Saint-Alary-Gr1. By top-class 8-12f performer and excellent sire/broodmare sire, sister to smart 10f performer and hurdler Ulundi and half-sister to 1,000 Guineas winner Wince (dam to Sadler's Wells of Yorkshire Oaks-Gr1 winner Quiff). Dam sister to Grade 2 winner Skimble (dam of Grade 1 winner Skimming) and half-sister to Grade 1 winner Contredance and to dam of high-class 2yo Eltish. Dam of: Half Glance (1999 f by Danehill: Gr3 winner), unnamed (2000 c by Sadler's Wells; unraced), Tycoon (2001 c by Sadler's Wells: winner, Gr1 placed). Mare died in 2002.

Pedigree assessment

Tycoon's pedigree says top-class 10f+ performer, and that is what he is. His pedigree bears much similarity to two prominent 2004 performers in Quiff, a very close relative he finished a place behind in the St Leger, and Powerscourt. Sadler's Wells frequently gets top-level winners aged four and above, and the aim in 2005 will be to ensure Tycoon is another of them. *JH*

Valixir (Ire)

3yo bay colt **118**

Trempolino (USA) - Vadlamixa (Fr) (Linamix (Fr))

Owner Lagardere Family

Trainer A Fabre

Breeder S N C Lagardere Elevage

Career: **9** starts | won **5** | second **1** | third **2** | £**230,294** win and place

By Richard Austen

THE ARC was a triumph for the three-year-olds, who provided the first five home and seven of the first eight, but three of their best hopes finished well held. Prospect Park, Grey Swallow and Valixir were all sent off at between 5-1 and 15-2 on the Pari-Mutuel and finished 16th, 18th and tenth respectively.

"He got very nervous in the starting stalls and I think the colt still lacks a certain amount of maturity," said jockey Eric Legrix of Valixir. "He didn't have his normal energy on this occasion."

Concerns about the horse's maturity, or lack of it, were a regular feature of Valixir's season as he notched up wins in a Listed race and two Group 2s during five races before the Arc and was edged out in the Prix du Jockey-Club. If he ever wises up, Valixir will be some horse.

The winner of his first two starts as a two-year-old, over six furlongs, Valixir ran into a horse called Bago on his third and was a beaten favourite. Having returned to action with a smooth Listed success, aspirations for him seemed to be dented when he was only third in the Prix Lupin, but he was a far more potent force when filling the same position in the Jockey-Club three weeks later.

Trying a mile and a half for the first time, Valixir went down by a head and half a length to Blue Canari and Prospect Park, which was impressive given that he had not shown that much conviction with his finishing effort when defeated over shorter distances. Legrix, though, saw room for improvement, stating that "he's still rather green" and that "he quickened well but then took it a little easy".

In the following month's Prix Eugene Adam over a mile and a quarter at Maisons-Laffitte, Valixir easily made all for his first Group victory. Dictating the pace, a steady one, had not been the plan. Neville Callaghan, who booked Ioritz Mendizabal for his Hazyview and reportedly told him to make the running, later complained that "nothing suited us, including

**Valixir, nearside, wins the Prix Niel from Prospect Park
but Bago, defeated here, beat them easily in the Arc**

Mendizabal," but they were up against it at level weights against odds-
on Valixir.

As befits a serious French challenger for the Arc, Valixir rested for the
remainder of the summer before warming up in the Prix Niel over the
Arc course and distance. Blue Canari and Prospect Park did the same,
while Bago was the 4-5 favourite.

As a trial, the latest Prix Niel was tricky to read. Two pacemakers set
off quickly initially but the eventual first four finished in a heap. Valixir
was top of the heap. Prospect Park led entering the straight but Valixir
came at him in the final furlong and had a nose to spare after Prospect
Park's rally, with Bago and Lord du Sud never quite in the mix but finishing
on their heels.

Of the winner, Legrix said: "Every time I've ridden him he has shown
mental and physical improvement. He used to be a little tense and keen."

Andre Fabre's considered view about Valixir's chances of giving him
a sixth Arc was: "There's a question mark over his stamina. With the

2004 — Race record

10th Prix de l'Arc de Triomphe Lucien Barriere (Group 1) (Longchamp, October 3) 3yo+ 12f
Good **117** (TS 112) 19 ran. *Midfield, 12th straight, effort on outside 2f out, kept on at
same pace (E Legrix), beaten 7¼l by Bago*

1st Prix Niel Casino Barriere d'Enghien (Group 2) (Longchamp, September 12) 3yo 12f Soft
118 (TS 119) 8 ran. *Raced in 4th, 2nd and pushed along 2f out, ridden to challenge
approaching final furlong, ran on to lead close home, driven out (E Legrix), beat
Prospect Park by nose*

1st Prix Eugene Adam (Group 2) (Maisons-Laffitte, July 14) 3yo 10f Soft **117** 6 ran. *Made
all, set steady pace, pushed clear over 1½f out, easily (E Legrix), beat Delfos by 3l*

3rd Prix du Jockey-Club (Group 1) (Chantilly, June 6) 3yo 12f Good to soft **117** (TS 110)
15 ran. *Mid-division, pushed along and closed up 2f out, ridden and ran on 1½f
out, stayed on strongly to line, nearest at finish (E Legrix), beaten ¾l by Blue
Canari*

3rd Prix Lupin (Group 1) (3yo Colts & Fillies) (Longchamp, May 16) 3yo 10½f Good to firm
112 (TS 95) 5 ran. *Tracked leader from 6f out, led 2f out to just over 1½f out, no
extra from distance (Gary Stevens), beaten 2l by Voix du Nord*

1st Prix Matchem (Listed) (Maisons-Laffitte, April 20) 3yo Colts & Geldings 9f Holding **97**
(TS 77) 5 ran. *Pressed leader at slow pace until quickened to lead 1½f out, easily
(Gary Stevens), beat Red Tune by 4l*

2003

2nd Prix des Chenes (Group 3) (Longchamp, September 20) 2yo 1m Good **105** 7 ran ● **1st**
Prix Irish River (Deauville, August 12) 2yo 6f Good to soft **98** 6 ran ● **1st** Prix Hunyade
(Unraced Colts & Geldings) (Maisons-Laffitte, July 15) 2yo 6f Good 10 ran

speed he has, he could win a nice race over a mile and he should have
won more easily in the Prix Niel – the jockey said he stopped in front
but I'm not convinced. He'll have come on a little but we're not talking
10lb."

Most importantly, though, the nervousness about the stalls that Legrix
later detected in Valixir was one shared by his connections. Valixir was
drawn widest of all in the Arc in stall 20. "I think with that draw I've
lost most of my hopes," said Fabre. "It will be very difficult to survive
that."

Fabre and the Lagardere family had not had all their hopes dashed
and their grey and pink colours surged into the lead two furlongs out,
but they were carried by Cherry Mix. Valixir had pulled hard despite
Legrix managing fairly quickly to find him some cover, and although he
made some progress from mid-division in the straight, he was hanging
badly to his right all the while and ran out of steam approaching the final
furlong.

Perhaps fast ground had something to do with Valixir's unsatisfactory
demeanour – his Lupin showing on good to firm also attracted negative
comment. It could also be that he will prove as good over a mile and a
quarter as at a mile and a half. Whatever his ground and trip, settling
Valixir down clearly remains a prime requirement for his trainer. If he
succeeds, it could unlock a major talent.

Valixir

bay colt, 31-3-2001

		Atan	Native Dancer
			Mixed Marriage
	Sharpen up		
		Rocchetta	Rockefella
Trempolino			Chambiges
ch 1984			
		Viceregal	Northern Dancer
			Victoria Regina
	Trephine		
		Quiriquina	Molvedo
			La Chaussee
		Mendez	Bellypha
			Miss Carina
	Linamix		
		Lunadix	Breton
Vadlamixa			Lutine
gr 1992			
		Bikala	Kalamoun
			Irish Bird
	Vadlava		
		Vadsa	Halo
			Rainbows Edge

Bred by Societe Lagardere in Ireland

Sire **Trempolino**

Won 4 of his 11 starts at 2 and 3. At 2, won 1 (1m) of 3 starts, also 3rd Criterium de Maisons-Laffitte-Gr2. At 3, won 3 (inc. Prix Niel-Gr2, Prix de l'Arc de Triomphe-Gr1) of 8 starts, also 2nd Prix Lupin-Gr1, Prix du Jockey-Club-Gr1, Breeders' Cup Turf-Gr1, 3rd Grand Prix de Paris-Gr1, Prix Guillaume d'Ornano-Gr2. By high-class 2yo and very good sire who also produced good stallions Diesis, Kris, Selkirk and Sharpo, out of Group-placed half-sister to top-class 10-12f performer Trepan. Originally stood in Kentucky, switched to France after 1999 covering season. Stands at Haras du Mezeray, 2004 fee €6,000. Oldest progeny 15, sire of: Summer Ensign (Gr3), Trampoli (Gr2), Cox Orange (Gr3), Dernier Empereur (Champion S-Gr1), Hidden Trick (Gr2), Kindergarten (Gr3), Talloires (Gr2), Triarius (Gr3), Germany (Bayerisches Zuchtrennen-Gr1, Grosser Preis Von Baden-Gr1), For Valour (Gr3), Neuilly (Gr3), Saugerties (Gr3), Arkadian Hero (Gr2), Snow Polina (Beverly D S-Gr1), Juvenia (Prix Marcel Boussac-Gr1), Valixir (Gr2).

Dam **Vadlamixa**

Won 2 of 11 starts at 2 and 3 in France. Won over 1m at 2, then won 1m Listed event at 3. By top-class miler and excellent French sire, mainly of 8-12f performers. Half-sister to Breeders' Cup Mile winner Val Royal (Royal Academy) and Group 2 winner Vadlawys (Always Fair). Dam Listed-placed sister to Listed winner Vagrancy and half-sister to Listed winner Vadsa Honor (dam of Gr1 winner Vahorimix, by Linamix). Dam of: Vadaza (1997 f by Zafonic; Listed-placed winner), Vadlaviria (1998 f by Bering; winner), Vallahilla (1999 f by Danehill), Vadagreen (2000 c by Green Desert; unraced), Valixir (2001 c by Trempolino; G2 winner, Gr1 placed), Vadasin (2002 c by Sinndar; unraced).

Pedigree assessment

The late Jean-Luc Lagardere did particularly well with this branch of a strong US family, aided as ever by use of his stallion Linamix. Most family members have tended to be best in the 8-10f bracket, and it is possible Valixir will turn out to be better suited to 10f than 12f. He provides a boost to 1987 Arc winner Trempolino, now in France after a long stint in Kentucky and enjoying an excellent recent spell as a broodmare sire, not least with Action This Day, Blue Canari and Chelsea Rose. *JH*

Vallee Enchantee (Ire)

4yo bay filly **121**

Peintre Celebre (USA) - Verveine (USA) (Lear Fan (USA))

Owner Ecurie Wildenstein

Trainer E Lellouche

Breeder Dayton Investments Ltd

Career: **14** starts won **5** second **0** third **3** **£803,351** win and place

By Seb Vance

THE late Daniel Wildenstein appeared to delight in sacking and humiliating high-profile jockeys and trainers, and the family trait continues through his son Alec.

Dominique Boeuf, one of the most respected French jockeys of the last decade, had barely dismounted following Vallee Enchantee's luckless third in Epsom's Coronation Cup when the wealthy art trader launched an astonishing attack on him, branding him an "asshole" within full earshot of both racegoers and media.

Boeuf had needed to find only a length with a furlong of the mile-and-a-half contest remaining but, having opted to take the shortest route up the rail, he ran into a dead end. Godolphin's big hope, Doyen, also suffered traffic problems, whereas Warrsan enjoyed a free run to flash home on the outside and win the race for the second successive year.

Although Boeuf kept his own counsel, he might admit that he hadn't given the Elie Lellouche-trained hold-up filly the very best of rides, but then Frankie Dettori's effort on Doyen wasn't too special either.

Godolphin, however, can take defeat as well as they can victory. Not so Ecurie Wildenstein. So far as Wildenstein was concerned, it was the final straw in a disintegrating relationship, and the unfortunate Boeuf lost one of the most prized jobs in French racing.

The owner, insisting Boeuf had disobeyed orders by not making his challenge on the outside, said: "We weren't unlucky, she was ridden by an asshole who didn't follow instructions. He has lost two Group 1s on this horse this year and that's enough. Look at the ride he gave her in the Ganay. I could have strung him up by the neck then."

Boeuf, who took a retainer with Wildenstein in May 2001 and enjoyed much success with Classic-winning filly Aquarelliste, among others, conducted himself with rather more grace and dignity. "Apparently we don't understand each other any more, so we thought it best to bring

**Vallee Enchantee goes to post for the Coronation Cup,
but it was the run back that sported so much controversy**

things to an end," he said. "It makes me feel a little queasy, as we've
had so many good years together."

It had all been so different six months earlier, when Boeuf partnered
the daughter of Peintre Celebre to a career-best performance in the Hong
Kong Vase. Boeuf, who was based in Hong Kong at the time, settled her
towards the back. She had no fewer than ten of her 13 opponents ahead
of her entering the Sha Tin straight, but under strong persuasion closed
relentlessly and hit the front yards from the line to beat Polish Summer
by three-quarters of a length.

The £640,000 first prize represented a fabulous reward for a filly who
had appeared to have shortcomings when tried at Group 1 level previously
in France, but it was forgotten when she made her seasonal debut in the
Prix Ganay.

Vallee Enchantee and Boeuf endured another dreadful passage in the
extended ten-furlong contest, when the filly again made her effort from
the back of the field and looked the likely winner with a furlong and a
half to go – provided she got a gap. She did, but it was too late and she
finished only fourth behind Execute.

| **2004** | | | **Race record** |

6th Prix de l'Arc de Triomphe Lucien Barriere (Group 1) (Longchamp, October 3) 3yo+ 12f Good **120** (TS 119) 19 ran. *Held up on outside, 16th straight, stayed on down outside final 1½f, nearest finish (S Pasquier), beaten 4l by Bago*

5th King George VI And Queen Elizabeth Diamond Stakes (Group 1) (Ascot, July 24) 3yo+ 12f Good to firm **115** (TS 84) 11 ran. *Raced on outer in 7th, driven and effort over 2f out, one pace and no impression on leaders over 1f out (O Peslier), beaten 6l by Doyen*

3rd Vodafone Coronation Cup (Group 1) (Epsom, June 4) 4yo+ 12f Good **121** (TS 90) 11 ran. *Settled in rear, 8th straight, effort over 2f out, hampered well over 1f out, ran on final furlong, nearest finish (D Boeuf), beaten 2l by Warrsan*

4th Prix Ganay (Group 1) (Longchamp, May 2) 4yo+ 10½f Very soft **109** (TS 101) 8 ran. *Held up, 7th straight, headway well over 1f out, looking for gap from distance to 100yds out, ran on (D Boeuf), beaten 2½l by Execute*

2003

1st Hong Kong Vase (Group 1) (Sha Tin, December 14) 3yo+ 12f Good to firm **115** 14 ran ● **1st** Prix du Conseil de Paris (Group 2) (Longchamp, October 19) 3yo+ 12f Good to soft **113** 9 ran ● **4th** Prix Vermeille Fouquet's Barriere (Group 1) (Longchamp, September 14) 3yo 12f Good to soft **113** 11 ran ● **1st** Prix de Pomone (Group 2) (Deauville, August 10) 3yo+ 13½f Good to soft **114** 5 ran ● **7th** Prix de Diane Hermes (Group 1) (Chantilly, June 8) 3yo 10½f Good **107** 10 ran ● **3rd** Prix Cleopatre (Group 3) (Saint-Cloud, May 12) 3yo 10½f Good **102** 8 ran ● **6th** Prix Penelope (Group 3) (Saint-Cloud, April 8) 3yo 10½f Good **98** 9 ran

Other runs

2002 **1st** Prix Isonomy (Listed) (Saint-Cloud, November 22) 2yo 1m Heavy **93** 7 ran ● **1st** Prix de Vulaines (Round Course) (Maisons-Laffitte, October 18) 2yo 9f Soft 9 ran ● **3rd** Prix Discrete (Unraced Fillies) (Saint-Cloud, September 9) 2yo 1m Good 19 ran

Following the Epsom fiasco, Vallee Enchantee was aimed at the King George VI and Queen Elizabeth Diamond Stakes at Ascot, a race Daniel Wildenstein won with Pawneese in 1976.

Olivier Peslier, Boeuf's replacement, took no chances and kept her out of trouble on the outside, but when he asked her for her effort the response was limited and she merely stayed on at one pace into fifth behind Doyen. While the pair were separated by just a short head at Epsom, there was nearly six lengths between them this time.

Her ill fortune continued when she was forced to miss the Prix Vermeille in September because of coughing, and so she had to go directly for the Prix de l'Arc de Triomphe.

With Peslier claimed to ride Prospect Park, Stephane Pasquier became Vallee Enchantee's third jockey in as many races. However, an outside draw in stall 16 spelt disaster for her and she had just three of the 19-strong field behind her into the straight. She flew down the outside to do best of the older runners in sixth, but she had been too far back to take a hand.

Few would begrudge her some better luck, although not everyone would be as pleased for her owner.

Vallee Enchantee

bay filly, 27-3-2000

			Northern Dancer	Nearctic
				Natalma
		Nureyev		
			Special	Forli
	Peintre Celebre			Thong
	ch 1994			
			Alydar	Raise a Native
				Sweet Tooth
		Peinture Bleue		
			Petroleuse	Habitat
				Plencia
			Roberto	Hail to Reason
				Bramalea
		Lear Fan		
			Wac	Lt Stevens
	Verveine			Belthazar
	b 1989			
			Nureyev	**Northern Dancer**
				Special
		Venise		
			Virunga	Sodium
				Vale

Bred by Dayton Investements Ltd in Ireland

Sire Peintre Celebre

Won 5 of 7 races, inc. Prix Greffulhe-Gr2, Prix du Jockey-Club-Gr1, Grand Prix de Paris-Gr1, Prix de l'Arc de Triomphe-Gr1. Not an outstanding physical specimen, but quite well-made, medium-sized individual. Tip-top performer at 10-12f. The best son of his outstanding sire, with more stamina than most. Dam Listed winner in France and Gr2 winner (12f on grass) in US, impeccably bred, by top-class runner and leading sire out of a Gr3 winner in England who was half-sister to outstanding racemare Pawneese (Oaks, Prix de Diane, King George VI & Queen Elizabeth Stakes, etc). Stands at Coolmore Stud, Ireland, at a (2004) fee of €30,000. Sire of 3 crops of racing age, including: Dai Jin (Deutsches Derby-Gr1, Aral Pokal-Gr1), Pride (Gr2), Super Celebre (Gr2), Vallee Enchantee (Hong Kong Vase-Gr1), Castledale (Gr3), Mister Monet (Gr2), Pearl Of Love (Gran Criterium-Gr1).

Dam Verveine

Won 3 of 13 races, inc. Prix du Calvados-Gr3, Prix de l'Opera-Gr2. Also placed 2nd in Prix Gontaut-Biron and Hong Kong International, 3rd in Prix Marcel Boussac, Prix de la Grotte, Prix Saint-Alary and Prix de Diane, 4th in Prix Vermeille and Yellow Ribbon S. Smallish, quite attractive sort. High-class, consistent performer. Stayed 12f, but considered better over shorter trips. One of the best daughters of a top-class miler and underrated sire. Half-sister to Gr2 winner Vetheuil (by Riverman) and to the dam of Gr3 winner La Sylphide. Dam (half-sister to Gr1 winner Vin de France, Gr2 winner Vacarme, and Gr1-placed Vosges) unraced daughter of a top-class miler and sire out of a Gr3 winner, also 3 times Gr1-placed. Dam of: Vagabond (1995 g by Alzao; winner), Victory Cry (1996 f by Caerleon; Gr3 winner), Virginian (1997 g by In The Wings; winner), Volga (1998 f by Caerleon; Gr3 winner), Visionnaire (1999 f by Sadler's Wells; winner), Vallee Enchantee (2000 f by Peintre Celebre; Gr1 winner), Vassilievsky (2001 c by Peintre Celebre; placed), Voltmeter (2002 c by Giant's Causeway; unraced to date). She has a colt foal, Vortex Generator, by Rock Of Gibraltar.

Pedigree assessment

It would not have been every breeder's idea to inbreed closely to Nureyev, but the Wildensteins have never been conformists in breeding, and they have achieved phenomenal success. She had no wins to show for bold efforts against the best colts in 2004 but earned kudos a-plenty, not least as first home of the senior runners in the Arc de Triomphe. That was probably as good a performance as she has ever delivered, and there is nothing about her pedigree to suggest that another season in training would not be worthwhile. *TM*

Var (USA)

5yo brown horse **121**

Forest Wildcat (USA) - Loma Preata (USA) (Zilzal (USA))

Owner Mohammed Rashid

Trainer C E Brittain

Breeder Dr John Eaton

Career: **18** starts | won **7** | second **2** | third **1** | **£188,201** win and place

By Nicholas Godfrey

VAR'S Prix de l'Abbaye win had many interesting facets. There was the human angle, for example, with the five-year-old's ever-popular veteran trainer Clive Brittain, a man christened 'Monsieur l'Optimiste' by French equine daily Paris-Turf. Then there was the more sober, reflective route of examining the apparent state of decline among European sprinters, as seemingly epitomised by the victory of an ex-American-trained claimer.

The abiding memory, however, is the explosive impression created by Var on that sunny day in Paris as he blasted away from 14 rivals in the continent's premier five-furlong event. Virtually unheard of a month prior to the race, Var produced a startling display of power sprinting under Frankie Dettori in one of the most memorable performances of the entire season. For once, even 'Monsieur l'Optimiste' must have been a little taken aback by such a thunderous effort.

Var had joined Brittain's string in March, having been transferred from Bill Mott's barn in America, where he carried the colours of Sheikh Mohammed's Darley operation. A multiple winner on turf across the Atlantic, he was nevertheless considered well below the top grade over there and his most recent US victory, in January, had been achieved in a minor event at Calder in Florida worth just £9,000.

Var was not seen on a British racecourse until September – by now carrying the colours of Maktoum associate Mohammed Rashid – when he blew away a fair field in Listed company over six furlongs at Goodwood. At the time, it was difficult to know what to make of the run. True, Var showed plenty of pace, but there were suggestions that he may have been flattered since he was able to dictate matters racing on his own next to the rail. On the other hand, Brittain revealed that he had been able to give the horse only two proper gallops since his arrival thanks to two accidents at home.

A week later over the minimum trip at Newbury, Var showed he could

Trainer Clive Brittain and jockey Frankie Dettori cannot contain their delight after Var's impressive Abbaye win

hold his own in better company when he was just touched off by The Tatling, having had the worst of the draw this time and racing on his own up the centre of the track until past halfway. Var did much the best of those who had raced with the pace and his trainer, typically, wasted little time in stating his intention to supplement his horse to the Abbaye.

While it lacked a truly outstanding sprinter – none existed in Europe in 2004 – the race featured a competitive-looking field, headed by the previous year's winner Patavellian, the ante-post favourite. Var was sent off an 8-1 chance according to the betting industry's own starting price in Britain, but on course he was the subject of remarkable support. With the 'Frankie factor' probably playing a part thanks to the usual hordes of cross-Channel punters, Var ended up 2.9-1 Pari-Mutuel market leader, an unexpected development given that he was meeting The Tatling on 5lb worse terms than at Newbury and had a poor draw in a race usually heavily influenced by the boxes.

2004 Race record

1st Prix de l'Abbaye de Longchamp Majestic Barriere (Group 1) (Longchamp, October 3) 2yo+ 5f Good **121** (TS 117) 15 ran. *Made all, ridden over 1½f out, driven out (L Dettori), beat The Tatling by ½l*

2nd Dubai International Airport World Trophy (Group 3) (Newbury, September 18) 3yo+ 5f Good **113** (TS 114) 11 ran. *Raced wide until joined leaders 3f out, led over 1f out, stayed on well under pressure final furlong, caught last strides (R Hills), beaten hd by The Tatling*

1st Starlit Stakes (Listed) (Goodwood, September 11) 3yo+ 6f Good to firm **112** (TS 97) 7 ran. *Went right start, made all, ridden over 1f out, stayed on well final furlong (J Quinn), beat Ruby Rocket by 1½l*

1st Allowance Optional Claiming Race (Calder, January 2) 4yo+ 5f Firm 3 ran. *Close up on inside until led over 2f out, ran on well (R Douglas), beat Tacirring by 1½l*

Other wins

2003 1st Allowance Optional Claiming Race (Churchill Downs, November 6) 3yo+ 5f Good ● **1st** Allowance (Churchill Downs, June 28) 3yo+ 5f Firm ● **1st** Claimer (Churchill Downs, April 27) 3yo+ 6f Fast ● **1st** Maiden (Aqueduct, March 12) 4yo+ 6f Fast

Having said that, the Abbaye was run on much faster ground than usual, and that clearly played to Var's strengths. He left the stalls like a cannonball and went on to show blinding speed up the centre of the track. He was at least three lengths up after a furlong, by which time Patavellian was already beaten, and a second burst midway through the race crushed what little resistance remained elsewhere, as Dettori explained afterwards. "He's American and he's very fast," said the rider. "I told all the others, 'Goodbye, see you later!' I asked him for a burst at halfway and that's what won him the race."

Though the final margin was only a diminishing half-length from The Tatling, Var had never looked like being caught as he led home a British-trained 1-2-3, with Royal Millennium in third. His time of 55 seconds flat was just 0.7sec outside Habibti's 1983 track record.

The victory was awarded a Racing Post Rating of 121, the same as Haydock Sprint Cup winner Tante Rose but 3lb below that of the division's leader Somnus in the same race. Here, though, the bare figures are inadequate, for there was no more devastating performance of sprinting pure and simple in Europe in 2004.

It was inevitably construed as yet another example of the apparent lack of star quality among Europe's sprinters, seemingly in decline since the era of Dayjur. Not that any of this mattered to the thousands of Brits at Longchamp who backed Var, nor indeed to the ebullient Brittain, who was relishing the task of taking on the likes of Silent Witness at the Hong Kong International meeting in December 2004. "I just don't know how he escaped from America," the trainer reflected.

Maybe not, but anyone who witnessed Var's performance in the Abbaye will be glad that he did. And given the perception of the relative lack of talent in the European sprint division, he is unlikely to be the last.

Var

brown horse, 6-5-1999

		Storm Bird	**Northern Dancer**
			South Ocean
	Storm Cat		
Forest Wildcat		Terlingua	Secretariat
b 1991			Crimson Saint
		Bold Native	Raise A Native
			Spring Beauty
	Victoria Beauty		
		Abifaith	Seaneen
			Sherry Jen
		Nureyev	**Northern Dancer**
			Special
	Zilzal		
Loma Preata		French Charmer	Le Fabuleux
b 1994			Bold Example
		Key To The Kingdom	Bold Ruler
			Key Bridge
	Halley's Comeback		
		Promised Princess	Promised Land
			Crafty Princess

Bred by John Eaton in US. $120,000 Keeneland September yearling

Sire Forest Wildcat

Very smart sprinter in US. Won 9 of 20 starts from 2 to 5, notably Maryland Breeders' Cup H-Gr3, Finger Lakes Breeders' Cup S-Gr3. By top-class 2yo/3yo and outstanding dirt sire. Half-brother to Grade 2 winner Queen Alexandra (by Determined King) and US stakes winner Medieval Victory (by Medieval Man). Oldest progeny 6. Stands at Brookdale Farm, Kentucky, 2004 fee $40,000. Sire of (northern hemisphere): Forest Secrets (Acorn S-Gr1), D'Wildcat (Frank J DeFrancis Memorial Dash-Gr1), Snow Dance (Gr2), Var (Prix de l'Abbaye-Gr1), Forest Heiress (Gr3), Wild Snitch (Gr3).

Dam Loma Preata

Won 2 of 11 starts. Dual winner and Listed-placed from 5 starts in France at 2, later unplaced in 6 North American starts on turf and dirt. By outstanding turf miler and reasonable sire. Half-sister to North American 2yo stakes winner Dixie Band (by Dixieland Band) out of half-sister to grand-dam of 2003 dual Grade 1 winner Wild Spirit. Dam of: Var (1999 f by Forest Wildcat; Prix de l'Abbaye-Gr1). Died in 2001.

Pedigree assessment

The fact that Var is a sprinter is predictable from his pedigree. His sire was fast, his dam generally was campaigned at short of a mile, his grand-dam was a (modest) winning sprinter, and there are plenty of speedy horses in the family. Var's turf preference is harder to pinpoint. Forest Wildcat is not a recognised turf sire – though Storm Cat does get some top-class turf runners – and his only other British stakes winner is Rosencrans, a dirt winner in the States and Dubai before his Polytrack win in the Listed ladbrokes.com Spring Cup. Loma Preata, however, recorded her best form on turf, and her sire Zilzal achieved little with his dirt runners during his early years at stud in the US. In common with his sire, Var won his first stakes race at the age of five. *JH*

Vinnie Roe (Ire)

6yo brown horse   **126**

Definite Article - Kayu (Tap On Wood)

Owner Seamus Sheridan

Trainer D K Weld

Breeder Mrs Virginia Moeran

Career: **24** starts | won **12** | second **4** | third **2** | £**1,147,781** win and place

By Alan Sweetman

THERE is a sense in which the outcome of the 2004 Melbourne Cup can be considered the perfect result. The record-breaking Australian mare Makybe Diva recorded a historic victory, while the best of the European horses Vinnie Roe finished second, supplying a continuing international context to an occasion that only a decade ago was of essentially local significance. For the sake of Australian racing, it is important that the visitors keep coming, but it would be a sorry day if it ever came to look like easy pickings. That is hardly the case now. Only one man has found the knack of cracking it.

Even the most insular Australian race fan can appreciate the role played by Dermot Weld in giving the event an enhanced international profile, and the achievement of Vinnie Roe in finishing second to a mare of the calibre of Makybe Diva has further underlined Weld's remarkable feat of targeting. The race remains firmly on the wish-list for Godolphin – and one of these years they will probably win it – but its sustained mystique in this part of the world is founded on the victories of Vintage Crop and Media Puzzle, and now Vinnie Roe's gallant second.

Vinnie Roe had won the Irish St Leger for a record-breaking third successive time in 2003, but it had been an abridged campaign, with his reappearance delayed until August in the wake of his exertions the previous November when fourth to Media Puzzle in Melbourne. In 2004, by contrast, Weld was able to get him to the track before the end of May to contest the Saval Beg Stakes over a mile-and-six at Leopardstown.

Sent off 1-2 favourite to repeat his 2002 win, Vinnie Roe was held up by Pat Smullen in a six-runner field as Johnny Murtagh established an early advantage on Ted Walsh's Windermere. By halfway Windermere's lead was huge and, even though he began to tire in the straight, Vinnie Roe was still four and a half lengths adrift at the finish, having stayed on well over the last furlong and a half. Smullen and the other defeated

Vinnie Roe makes history with a fourth win in the Irish St Leger, before his gallant effort in the Melbourne Cup

riders were summoned before the stewards to explain themselves, and Smullen argued that his mount had been carrying 10st 2lb on his first outing of the season and that he was not prepared to commit him early in a race in which the leader had gone off at a sprint pace.

After missing his intended mid-season target, the Ascot Gold Cup, in which he had finished second in 2002, it was not until the middle of August that Vinnie Roe returned to Leopardstown to attempt to win the Ballyroan Stakes for the third year in succession. Once again he was thwarted by a front-runner, the British-trained Foreign Affairs. Weld observed that at the age of six Vinnie Roe's speed over a mile and a half showed signs of having been blunted, but stressed that he regarded the performance as a satisfactory trial for another Irish St Leger bid.

His rivals at The Curragh in September included the 2003 St Leger winner Brian Boru, providing an echo of his first triumph in the race three years earlier, when the runner-up was Millenary, who had won at Doncaster the previous season. For the first time since he has come to make the race his own, the opposition reached double figures, including

2004   Race record

2nd Emirates Melbourne Cup (Group 1) (Handicap) (Flemington, November 2) 3yo+ 2m Good to soft **126** 24 ran. *Raced in 12th, 10th straight on outside, ridden to lead briefly approaching final furlong, ran on under pressure but not pace of winner (P J Smullen), beaten 1¼l by Makybe Diva*

1st Irish Field St Leger (Group 1) (Curragh, September 18) 3yo+ 1m6f Good **124** (TS 86) 13 ran. *Settled 4th, 3rd from over 5f out, improved to challenge travelling easily entering straight, led over 2f out, clear over 1f out, easily (P J Smullen), beat Brian Boru*

2nd Ballyroan Stakes (Listed) (Leopardstown, August 15) 3yo+ 12f Good to firm **114** (TS 60) 7 ran. *Held up in touch, 6th and driven along 3f out, headway on inner straight, 2nd inside final furlong, ran on well close home (P J Smullen), beaten nk by Foreign Affairs*

2nd Saval Beg Stakes (Listed) (Leopardstown, May 26) 3yo+ 1m6f Good to firm **114** (TS 71) 6 ran. *Held up, remote 4th halfway, remote 2nd early straight, kept on well, no chance with winner (P J Smullen), beaten 4½l by Windermere*

Other wins

2003 1st Irish Field St Leger (Group 1) (Curragh, September 13) 3yo+ 1m6f Good to firm **122** (TS 38) 6 ran ● **1st** Ballyroan Stakes (Listed) (Leopardstown, August 17) 3yo+ 12f Good to firm **107** 6 ran **2002 1st** Jefferson Smurfit Memorial Irish St Leger (Group 1) (Curragh, September 14) 3yo+ 1m6f Good to firm **121** 8 ran ● **1st** Ballyroan Stakes (Listed) (Leopardstown, August 18) 3yo+ 12f Good **118** 8 ran ● **1st** Saval Beg Stakes (Listed) (Leopardstown, May 30) 3yo+ 1m6f Soft **116** 7 ran **2001 1st** Prix Royal-Oak (Group 1) (Longchamp, October 28) 3yo+ 1m7½f Heavy **116** 13 ran ● **1st** Jefferson Smurfit Memorial Irish St Leger (Group 1) (Curragh, September 15) 3yo+ 1m6f Good to firm **124** 8 ran ● **1st** Ballycullen Stakes (Listed) (Curragh, August 25) 3yo+ 1m6f Good **113** 8 ran ● **1st** www.ppg.ie Challenge Stakes (Listed) (Leopardstown, July 21) 3yo+ 1m6f Good **107** 6 ran **2000 1st** EBF Eyrefield Stakes (Listed) (Leopardstown, November 12) 2yo 9f Soft **106** 19 ran ● **1st** Goffs Median Auction Maiden (Leopardstown, June 28) 2yo 7f Good to firm **86** 9 ran

a five-strong British challenge headed by the Lonsdale Cup winner First Charter and the progressive-looking March Stakes winner Orange Touch. In spite of his record in the event it looked a demanding task, but he proved more than equal to it. In a race run in driving rain that had eased the ground in his favour, Vinnie Roe travelled powerfully into the straight, and once Smullen asked him to stretch clear from two furlongs down it was all over. Brian Boru and First Charter provided solidity to the form in taking the place-money, and the style of the performance was at least as impressive as his previous three wins in the race.

From there it was on to Melbourne, where Weld produced Vinnie Roe in superb shape. When Smullen delivered his challenge wide on the track in the straight, it looked for an instant that he might have stolen it, but Glen Boss got a perfect run on the inside on Makybe Diva, and there were no excuses. A history-maker on the home stage, Vinnie Roe had played no small part in a splendid renewal of this faraway race that has been brought closer to us over the years by Weld's pioneering efforts. He may well return in 2005.

Vinnie Roe
brown horse, 6-4-1998

		Ahonoora	Lorenzaccio
			Helen Nichols
	Indian Ridge		
		Hillbrow	Swing Easy
Definite Article			Golden City
b 1992			
		Moorestyle	Manacle
			Guiding Star
	Summer Fashion		
		My Candy	Lorenzaccio
			Candy Gift
		Sallust	Pall Mall
			Bandarilla
	Tap On Wood		
		Cat o'Mountaine	Ragusa
Kayu			Marie Elizabeth
ch 1985			
		English Prince	Petingo
			English Miss
	Ladytown		
		Supreme Lady	Grey Sovereign
			Ulupis Sister

Bred by Virginia Moeran in Ireland. Ir48,000gns Goffs November foal, Ir£50,000 Goffs Orby yearling

Sire Definite Article

Won 5 of 11 starts, viz. won both starts at 2 including National S-Gr1, won 1 (Silver S-Listed) of 4 starts at 3, also 2nd Irish Derby-Gr1, won 2 (Mooresbridge S-Listed, Tattersalls Gold Cup-Gr2) of 5 starts at 4. Effective 10-12f, stayed better than pedigree indicates. By top-class sprinter and excellent sire. Half-brother to Salford Express (Dante S-Gr2) and Salford City (Greenham S-Gr3). Stands at Morristown Lattin Stud in Ireland, 2004 fee €8,000. Oldest progeny 6, sire of: Vinnie Roe (Irish St Leger-Gr1 (x4), Prix Royal-Oak-Gr1), Grammarian (Gr2), Supreme Rabbit (HKGr2).

Dam Kayu

Unraced. By top-class miler who is also broodmare sire of Ridgewood Pearl (by Indian Ridge), out of half-sister to Irish St Leger winner M-Lolshan, from family of Arc fourth Acropolis, Fairy Queen, Right Wing and Tashawak. Dam of: Rich Victim (1992 c by Lapierre; HK stakes winner), Vincitore (1993 c by Petorius; winner), Acquaiura (1994 f by Astronef; winner), Khartoum (1996 c by Common Grounds; winner), Divine Prospect (1997 f by Namaqualand; winner), Vinnie Roe (1998 c by Definite Article; Irish St Leger-Gr1 x 4). Mare died 2003.

Pedigree assessment

As a son of an Indian Ridge stallion and a Tap On Wood mare, he is bred along similar lines to Breeders' Cup Mile winner Ridgewood Pearl and Native Roots, the dam of Breeders' Cup Juvenile winner Wilko, yet he has long been established as a top-class stayer, and in stamina terms he outlasts his pedigree. The decision to persevere with him on the racecourse once again in 2004 was vindicated in glorious fashion, but he will surely make a popular dual-purpose sire in time. *JH*

Voix du Nord (Fr)

3yo bay colt **115**

Valanour (Ire) - Dame Edith (Fr) (Top Ville)

Owner Baron Thierry Van Zuylen De Nyevelt

Trainer D Smaga

Breeder Baron Thierry Van Zuylen De Nyevelt

Career: **8** starts   won **4**   second **3**   third **0**   **£217,634** win and place

By Robert Carter

BARON Thierry van Zuylen van Nyevelt van de Haar inherited racehorses and broodmares in 1960 on the death of his father, Baron Egmont, but it was a year or two before he was convinced that racing should become an important part of his life.

His brother-in-law, Baron Guy de Rothschild, took him on a tour of the Chantilly stables occupied by his own trainer, Geoffrey Watson, and shortly afterwards Baron Thierry became an owner there as well. One of the first horses to carry his colours was Duc de Gueldre, winner of the Prix Lupin but beaten half a length and three-quarters of a length by Sanctus II and Nyrcos in the 1963 Prix du Jockey-Club. Duc de Gueldre was bred by his father. Ever since, Baron Thierry has been trying to breed one good enough to achieve what that colt just failed to do.

He had the right horse at last in 2004, but Voix du Nord pulled up lame after a canter on the day before the big race. He had sustained a hairline fracture to his off-fore pastern and it seemed probable that his career was at an end. The previous September Baron Thierry had seen his recent Prix de la Nonette winner State Of Art break down when a leading fancy for the Prix Vermeille. State Of Art failed to survive, but Voix du Nord was well enough to return to David Smaga's stable in the autumn and will be back on the racecourse at four. With luck, he will be as good as ever.

Voix du Nord was no certainty for the Jockey-Club but he would have started favourite. His connections probably have no doubt that he should have won, for Valixir finished a nose and two lengths behind him in the Prix Lupin and went on to finish only a head and half a length behind Blue Canari and Prospect Park at Chantilly.

Voix du Nord's first serious work took place on a foggy morning at Chantilly in June 2003. All that Smaga saw was the colt coming past

Voix du Nord, centre, beats Millemix by a nose in the Prix Lupin – but injury, in one case fatal, awaited both colts

him still behind a hard-held leader. But Dominique Boeuf told him when dismounting that this was next year's Prix du Jockey-Club winner. Smaga said: "I don't know what made him say that but he told me that I wouldn't sleep all winter because the horse would be odds-on for the Jockey-Club."

For a future Classic winner, he was a lot busier as a juvenile than most similar prospects. He won a minor race from three starts at Deauville, then moved on to Paris to become the link between the best juveniles of both sexes, running fourth to Bago in the Prix des Chenes and second to Latice in the Prix de Conde, before claiming Group 1 glory for himself in the Criterium de Saint-Cloud.

It was a creditable record in the old-fashioned way, in which future Classic winners were expected to progress with increasing distances as juveniles before reaching a peak in the early months of their second season. Smaga told Emmanuel Roussel of Paris-Turf: "Voix du Nord ran six times at two. It's a lot, but I have seen many colleagues stop with their good two-year-olds and then be unable to bring them back."

2004 Race record

1st Prix Lupin (Group 1) (3yo Colts & Fillies) (Longchamp, May 16) 3yo 10½f Good to firm **115** (TS 100) 5 ran. *Held up last to straight but always close up, driven to challenge distance, narrow lead 150yds to 100yds out, led line, all out (D Boeuf), beat Millemix by nose*

1st Prix Noailles (Group 2) (3yo Colts & Fillies) (Longchamp, April 11) 3yo 11f Good to soft **112** (TS 103) 9 ran. *Disputed 3rd, 3rd straight, pushed along to lead over 1½f out, driven clear over 1f out, readily (C Soumillon), beat Cherry Mix by 3l*

2003

1st Criterium de Saint-Cloud (Group 1) (Saint-Cloud, November 8) 2yo 10f Good to soft **114** 10 ran ● **2nd** Prix de Conde (Group 3) (Longchamp, October 19) 2yo 9f Good to soft **107** 6 ran ● **4th** Prix des Chenes (Group 3) (Longchamp, September 20) 2yo 1m Good **100** 7 ran ● **2nd** Criterium du Fonds Europeen de l'Elevage (Listed) (Deauville, August 23) 2yo 1m Good to soft **100** 8 ran ● **1st** Prix d'Etreham (Round Course) (Deauville, August 9) 2yo 7½f Good to soft **95** 9 ran ● **2nd** Prix de Marolles (Unraced Colts & Geldings) (Deauville, July 6) 2yo 7f Good to soft 10 ran

With Boeuf claimed for the Wildenstein colt Malevitch, Christophe Soumillon rode Voix du Nord for the first time when he reappeared in the Group 2 Prix Noailles at Longchamp. Smaga provided a pacemaker, Alcinos, but he was not needed, for Eric Legrix soon blasted five lengths clear on the 57-1 chance Kensington. When the chasing Alcinos was taken wide approaching the straight Soumillon sent the favourite up to join Kensington before taking over just inside the final quarter-mile. Soon in command, Voix du Nord scored by three lengths from the future Grand Prix de Deauville winner and Arc second Cherry Mix, who got the best of a four-way photo for second.

While Voix du Nord was a ready winner of the Noailles, he was all out to gain his second Group 1 success in the Prix Lupin. This time, Alcinos did have to do the donkey work, taking over from Esperanto behind the *petit bois* and leading as far as the straight. Voix du Nord went past well over one furlong from home but he was soon joined and headed by Millemix. The pair were locked together throughout the final furlong. Voix du Nord had a head advantage until 100 yards out, but Millemix appeared to have his nose in front in the last 50 yards. Equidia, the local racing TV service, certainly thought that the race was his, but a strong drive from Boeuf had forced his mount back up on the line.

It was a hard race but one that made the colt a worthy favourite for the Jockey-Club. Then disaster struck. But at least Voix du Nord will be back next year. To the horror of trainer Criquette Head-Maarek and all connected with him, Millemix suffered a fatal injury 12 days before the big race. He had to be put down after shattering his off-hind pastern in five places in a freak accident moments after setting off in a gallop at Chantilly racecourse.

Voix du Nord

bay colt, 27-2-2001

		Northern Dancer	Nearctic / Natalma
	Lomond	My Charmer	Poker / Fair Charmer
Valanour b 1992		Mill Reef	Never Bend / Milan Mill
	Vearia	Val Divine	Val de Loir / Pola Bella
		High Top	Derring-Do / Camenae
	Top Ville	Sega Ville	Charlottesville / La Sega
Dame Edith b 1995		Legend Of France	Lyphard / Lupe
	Girl Of France	Water Girl	Faraway Son / Warsaw

Bred by Baron Thierry van Zuylen de Nyevelt in France

Sire Valanour

Won 5 of 9 races, inc. Prix de Guiche-Gr3, Grand Prix de Paris-Gr1, Prix d'Harcourt-Gr2, Prix Ganay-Gr1. Medium-sized, strong, well-made sort. Never tested at 12f or on soft ground in public. Won 5 of his 6 races in France, beaten in every race abroad. Capable of a telling burst of acceleration. The best son of his sire, an impeccably bred 2,000 Guineas winner who began well at stud in Ireland, but subsequently lost favour and was sent to the US, then to Italy. Dam, Listed winner, also produced Prix de Diane winner Vereva (by Kahyasi). Grand-dam, winner and Listed-placed, also dam of Vayrann (Gr1), Yashgan (Gr1 in US) and Valiyar (Gr3), and the dam of Prix du Jockey-Club winner Natroun. Third dam top-class miler, daughter of 1,000 Guineas, Oaks and Champion Stakes winner Bella Paola. Stands at Haras National du Houga, France, at a (2004) fee of €1,700. Sire of 5 crops of racing age, inc: Valentino (Gr3), Voix du Nord (Criterium de Saint-Cloud-Gr1, Prix Lupin-Gr1).

Dam Dame Edith

Ran only 3 times, always unplaced. Showed no worthwhile form up to 10f, evidently not very sound, unraced after June of 3yo season. Respectably bred. Half-sister to Gr3 winner Varxi (by Kaldoun), to Listed winner and Gr2 fourth Snow Cap (by Bering), and to Kadence (by Kaldoun (winner, Gr3-placed). By a winner of the Prix du Diane (by Kahyasi, also an effective sire and broodmare sire. Out of a Listed winner in France and US, also placed in Gr3 in France and in Gr2 in US. Grand-dam (also bred Listed winner Bonus Award) half-sister to Walensee (Prix Vermeille, dam of multiple Gr1 winner Westerner and Gr2 winner War Game), and to the dam of Walk On Mix (Gr2) and Walkamia (Gr3). Dam of: Clear Run (2000 f by Exit to Nowhere; placed), Voix du Nord (2001 c by Valanour; dual Gr1 winner), Captivante (2002 f by Kendor; unraced to date). She has a yearling colt, Elvard, by Highest Honor.

Pedigree assessment

Strongly progressive, and with two Group 1 victories already to his credit, Voix du Nord was unfortunate to pick up an injury before the Prix du Jockey-Club, for which he would probably have started favourite. It was a cruel blow for owner-breeder Thierry van Zuylen, who had been out of luck in big races for many years, and who seemed to have found another champion at last. Voix du Nord is an intriguingly bred colt; his sire's dam and his dam's sire sprang from families developed first by Francois Dupre and later by the Aga Khan, while the female line is an offshoot of the Wildenstein family which produced another major 2004 winner in Westerner. *TM*

Warrsan (Ire)

6yo bay horse   **126**

Caerleon (USA) - Lucayan Princess (High Line)

Owner Saeed Manana

Trainer C E Brittain

Breeder Saeed Manana

Career: **33** starts | won **8** | second **9** | third **4** | **£1,274,674** win and place

By Paul Haigh

WARRSAN, so his trainer's few critics would say, is a typical Clive Brittain horse. You never quite know where you are with him, you never quite know when he's going to pop up. Warrsan, so his trainer's many fans would say, is a typical Clive Brittain horse all right: hard-working, tough as old boots, always being campaigned at the outer limit of his ability, always with the capacity to surprise.

The latest season was the six-year-old's best – the one in which he finally proved himself a Group 1 performer worthy of the name. He proved that when, under a sensible, uncomplicated ride from Darryll Holland, he beat the apparently unlucky pair Doyen and Vallee Enchantee to win his second successive Coronation Cup. Vallee Enchantee was a Group 1 winner herself, six months earlier in the Hong Kong Vase, in which Warrsan had been one of her victims. Doyen may have been disappointing at the end of the season, but after his subsequent victories in the Hardwicke and the King George he was being hailed as one of the greats.

Warrsan proved it again in the Eclipse a month later, when it was only by a head that he failed to get the better of Refuse To Bend. Then he proved it a third time in the Grosser Preis von Baden in September, when, under another fine ride, this time from Kerrin McEvoy, he beat a field that included the previous year's Arc runner-up Mubtaker and the 2004 Grand Prix de Saint-Cloud winner Gamut, as well as the Germans Egerton, Shirocco (later to win the Gran Premio del Jockey Club) and Simonas (later second to Sulamani in the Canadian International). In between these runs it had sometimes seemed that maybe Warrsan was flying just a bit too high – and maybe just a bit too often.

As with all his trainer's good horses, distance is no object when it comes to making entries, and after the Hong Kong race in December he had been sent to Dubai, where, this time asked to make all in the Sheema Classic, he battled bravely but eventually faded into fifth behind Polish

Warrsan makes it back-to-back victories in the Coronation Cup, the first of two Group 1 wins in another fine season

Summer, who, just to confuse the form students, had been only a short-head in front of him at Sha Tin. Five weeks later, back home at Newmarket in the Group 2 Jockey Club Stakes, he failed to concede to Gamut and Systematic the 5lb penalty he'd incurred in the race a year earlier.

After these two efforts his Coronation Cup victory was something of a revelation as well as a reminder that you could never write him off. Many put the performance down to the ride, his liking for the track and the possibility that rivals had run below their best. But besides Doyen and Vallee Enchantee he had High Accolade, Brian Boru, Magistretti and Scott's View behind him – far too many good horses for it to have possibly been a fluke. Now people began to think they'd got a grip on him. What he needed was 12 furlongs, firm ground and a left-handed track (preferably Epsom).

Quite possibly, but how then were they going to explain his strong-finishing second on good to soft ground in the ten-furlong Eclipse? One thing Warrsan did prove to everybody's satisfaction a month later was that he has a genuine aversion to Ascot, even though Holland was inclined to blame his stinker in the King George on the fact that Warrsan didn't get the end-to-end gallop he's thought to need.

2004 Race record

9th Prix de l'Arc de Triomphe Lucien Barriere (Group 1) (Longchamp, October 3) 3yo+ 12f Good **118** (TS 113) 19 ran. *Held up in rear, 18th straight, stayed on steadily down outside final 1½f (K McEvoy), beaten 7¼l by Bago*

1st Grosser Volkswagen Preis Von Baden (Group 1) (Baden-Baden, September 5) 3yo+ 12f Soft **124** 11 ran. *Midfield, good headway on outside 4f out, 4th straight, ridden well over 1f out, driven to lead just inside final furlong, hung left last 100yds, ran on (K McEvoy), beat Egerton by nk*

9th King George VI And Queen Elizabeth Diamond Stakes (Group 1) (Ascot, July 24) 3yo+ 12f Good to firm **112** (TS 80) 11 ran. *Tracked leading pair, ridden 3f out, weakened well over 1f out (D Holland), beaten 10½l by Doyen*

2nd Coral-Eclipse Stakes (Group 1) (Sandown, July 3) 3yo+ 10f Good to soft **126** (TS 116) 12 ran. *Chased leaders, effort over 2f out, driven to press winner over 1f out, stayed on well near finish, just failed (D Holland), beaten hd by Refuse To Bend*

1st Vodafone Coronation Cup (Group 1) (Epsom, June 4) 4yo+ 12f Good **124** (TS 100) 11 ran. *Prominent, lost place halfway and pushed along, 7th straight, pulled wide and driven over 2f out, progress to lead just over 1f out, stayed on well (D Holland), beat Doyen by 1¾l*

3rd UltimateBet.com Jockey Club Stakes (Group 2) (Newmarket, May 2) 4yo+ 12f Good **121** (TS 84) 7 ran. *Led, ridden 3f out, headed over 1f out, no extra towards finish (D Holland), beaten 2¾l by Gamut*

5th Dubai Sheema Classic (Group 1) (Turf) (Nad Al Sheba, March 27) 4yo+ 12f Good to firm **114** (TS 94) 13 ran. *Led, ridden straight, headed 1f out, weakened near finish (M J Kinane), beaten 2½l by Polish Summer*

Other wins

2003 **1st** Vodafone Coronation Cup (Group 1) (Epsom, June 6) 4yo+ 12f Good **121** 9 ran ● **1st** Sagitta Jockey Club Stakes (Group 2) (Newmarket, May 2) 4yo+ 12f Good to soft **120** 6 ran ● **1st** Dubai Irish Village Stakes (Registered As The John Porter Stakes) (Group 3) (Newbury, April 12) 4yo+ 12f Good to firm **116** 9 ran **2002** **1st** Qualitair Holdings Conditions Stakes (Newmarket (July), July 19) 3yo+ 12f Good to firm **109** 4 ran ● **1st** Bonusprint Rated Stakes Showcase Handicap (0-100) (Goodwood, May 23) 4yo+ 1m6f Good **104** 11 ran **2001** **1st** Jim Macdonald-Buchanan Handicap (0-85) (Sandown, July 26) 3yo 1m6f Good to firm **85** 10 ran

After that flop, by no means his first at Ascot, he was only mildly fancied at Baden-Baden against Mubtaker and Gamut, but once again Warrsan made mugs of the analysts. Brittain had walked the track and knew the official going of soft was wrong after five days of baking sun. "I also knew," he said, "that Warrsan would be one of the few to act on the ground and told Kerrin that if he brought him with a late run, he'd win."

He turned out again for the Arc, in which he ran respectably in ninth, and was then being considered for the Japan Cup or the Hong Kong Vase again. The 2004 campaign was probably his last, and he will retire to stud as a something of an enigma. Brittain would say there was nothing particularly complicated about him. He's just a good horse who keeps delivering whenever the circumstances are right. "Funny, isn't it," he remarked mischievously after the Grosser Preis, "that whenever he wins, it's always supposed to be because all the others haven't run their race."

Warrsan   *bay horse, 28-2-1998*

		Northern Dancer	Nearctic
			Natalma
	Nijinsky		
		Flaming Page	Bull Page
Caerleon			Flaring Top
b 1980		Round Table	Princequillo
			Knight's Daughter
	Foreseer		
		Regal Gleam	Hail To Reason
			Miz Carol
		High Hat	Hyperion
			Madonna
	High Line		
		Time Call	Chanteur
Lucayan Princess			Aleria
b 1983		Sir Gaylord	Turn-to
			Somethingroyal
	Gay France		
		Sweet And Lovely	Tanerko
			Lilya

Bred by Saeed Manana in Ireland

Sire Caerleon

Won 4 of 8 races, inc. Anglesey S.-Gr3, Prix du Jockey-Club-Gr1, Benson & Hedges Gold Cup-Gr1. Also 2nd in Irish Derby. Good-looking, compact, top-class middle-distance performer. Died in February 1998. Sire of Gr1 winners: Caerwent (National S.), Welsh Guide (Gran Premio d'Italia, Premio Roma), Kostroma (Yellow Ribbon S., Santa Barbara Handicap, Beverly D S.), Atoll (Oaks d'Italia), Caerlina (Prix de Diane), Generous (Dewhurst S., Derby S., Irish Derby, King George VI & Queen Elizabeth S.), In A Tiff (Derby Italiano), Only Royale (Yorkshire Oaks x 2), Tenby (Grand Criterium), Moonax (St Leger S., Prix Royal Oak), Auriette (Gamely Handicap), Fusaichi Concorde (Tokyo Yuushun), Grape Tree Road (Grand Prix de Paris), Lady Carla (Oaks S.), Shake The Yoke (Coronation S.), Cape Verdi (1,000 Guineas S.), Mukhalif (Derby Italiano), Sunspangled (Fillies' Mile), Marienbard (Deutschlandpreis, Grosser Preis von Baden, Prix de l'Arc de Triomphe), Preseli (Moyglare Stud Stakes), Warrsan (Coronation Cup [twice], Grosser Preis von Baden).

Dam Lucayan Princess

Won 2 of 4 races. inc. Sweet Solera S.-Listed. Leggy, light-framed, attractive sort, effective on any ground, stayed 12f well. Same family as Kris Kin. Dam of: Celia Brady (1988 f by Last Tycoon; winner), Lucca (1989 f by Sure Blade; unplaced), Needle Gun (1990 c by Sure Blade; Gr2 winner, Gr1-placed), Luana (1991 f by Shaadi; winner, Listed-placed), Luso (1992 c by Salse; multiple Gr1 winner), Lunda (1993 f by Soviet Star; unplaced) Cloud Castle (1995 f by In The Wings; Gr3 winner), Maskunah (1997 f by Sadler's Wells; unraced) Warrsan (1998 c by Caerleon; Gr1 winner), Mreef (1999 c by Sadler's Wells; unraced), Mantesera (2000 f by In The Wings; unraced).

Pedigree assessment

Warrsan is as fiercely competitive as his trainer, always ready to have a go in the best of company, and the pair are two of a kind again in showing no deterioration with advancing years. The six-year-old arguably gave the two best displays of his career in the Eclipse and at Baden-Baden, and he had excuses for below-par runs in both the King George and the Arc. This fellow is still no back number, and a third win in the Coronation Cup is by no means out of the question. A thoroughly admirable racehorse, he is just what his pedigree said he should be, a late-maturing, tough, honest competitor with more than a dash of class. Would that there were more like him! *TM*

Westerner

5yo bay horse **121**

Danehill (USA) - Walensee (Troy)
Owner Ecurie Wildenstein
Trainer E Lellouche
Breeder Dayton Investments Ltd

Career: **22** starts won **8** second **8** third **1** **£491,795** win and place

By Howard Wright

WESTERNER confirmed his status as France's leading stayer, and established himself in the top two in Europe, in 2004. Yet the Danehill horse's crowning season will be remembered just as much for owner Alec Wildenstein's unwelcome knack of dragging headlines of the wrong kind into the five-year-old's success.

The art-dealing Wildenstein family has rarely been far removed from controversy, for all that it has consistently featured among the leading European-based racehorse owners over the last 30 years, and Alec has readily taken over the mantle worn by his late father Daniel, who famously sacked two scions of British racing, Pat Eddery and Henry Cecil.

In 2004, stable jockey Dominique Boeuf found himself on the wrong end of the Wildenstein wrath and was given the heave-ho, just 48 hours after Alec was reported to have publicly described the rider in language that owed more to Anglo-Saxon than Gallic origins.

Boeuf was blamed for the defeat of Vallee Enchantee in the Coronation Cup, though he had probably set himself on the slippery slope with Wildenstein a fortnight earlier, when Westerner was beaten at long odds-on in the Prix Vicomtesse Vigier at Longchamp.

Westerner was returning to Longchamp exactly one month after completing a successful reappearance in the Prix de Barbeville, on going officially interpreted from the penetrometer reading as 'good to soft'.

Ground conditions that day were ideal, judged on Westerner's late-improving runs over a distance in 2003, when he became the first horse to complete the Prix du Cadran-Prix Royal-Oak double since the Cadran was moved to the Arc de Triomphe weekend in 1991.

In a six-runner field, where Swing Wing, trained by Paul Cole, provided the sole British-based opposition, Westerner's apparently generous even-money starting price could probably be attributed to it being his first outing of the season, and to his 7lb Group 1 penalty.

Westerner, who was at the centre of so much controversy, completes a second Prix du Cadran-Prix Royal-Oak double

Westerner comfortably achieved his third victory in a row, winning by two lengths from a group that passed the post in the order Forestier, Idaho Quest, Le Carre and Swing Wing but were separated by little more than whiskers.

In the Vicomtesse Vigier, Westerner confirmed the placings with Le Carre and Idaho Quest on 5lb better terms, but not with Forestier, who struck for home on the final turn and held him off by a neck. Clear Thinking stayed on to be beaten three-quarters of a length into third place.

Trainer Elie Lellouche blamed Boeuf for making his effort too early in a slowly run race. With Vallee Enchantee on the horizon, that proved to be the 17th and last time Boeuf rode Westerner – ironic in one sense, because he was credited with having made Westerner the horse he became.

In the late summer of 2003, Boeuf apparently suggested Westerner should be fitted with ear plugs, which could be taken out in the course of a race, as French rules allow, in order that he could better settle the colt in the early stages. The initial objective achieved, removing the

| 2004 | Race record |

1st Prix Royal-Oak (Group 1) (Longchamp, October 24) 3yo+ 1m7½f Heavy **119** (TS 85) 8 ran. *Held up, 5th straight, led just under 2f out, ran on well, easily (S Pasquier), beat Behkara by 2½l*

1st Prix du Cadran Casino Les Princes Barriere de Cannes (Group 1) (Longchamp, October 3) 4yo+ 2m4f Good **117** (TS 75) 8 ran. *Prominent, 3rd halfway, 2nd and challenged straight, led over 2f out, pushed clear over 1½f out, easily (O Peslier), beat Cut Quartz by 3l*

1st Prix Gladiateur Royal Thalasso Barriere (Group 3) (Longchamp, September 12) 4yo+ 1m7½f Soft **121** (TS 38) 8 ran. *Held up, disputing 5th straight, headway over 2f out, challenged 1½f out, ridden to lead 1f out, ran on well to hold challenge of 2nd close home (O Peslier), beat Cut Quartz by short nk*

9th Grand Prix de Saint-Cloud (Group 1) (Saint-Cloud, July 4) 3yo+ 12f Good to soft **110** (TS 93) 10 ran. *Held up in rear, last straight, hard ridden 1½f out, no headway (O Peslier), beaten 7½l by Gamut*

2nd Gold Cup (Group 1) (Ascot, June 17) 4yo+ 2m4f Good to firm **119** (TS 100) 13 ran. *Held up in midfield, smooth headway 4f out, led 2f out until 1f out, kept on (G Mosse), beaten 1½l by Papineau*

2nd Prix Vicomtesse Vigier (Group 2) (Longchamp, May 23) 4yo+ 1m7½f Good **113** 6 ran. *Raced in 5th, 1½ lengths off leader entering straight, pushed along to challenge 2f out, every chance 1½f out until ridden and no extra inside final furlong (D Boeuf), beaten nk by Forestier*

1st Prix de Barbeville (Group 3) (Longchamp, April 22) 4yo+ 1m7½f Good to soft **120** 6 ran. *Held up in last, headway on outside over 1½f out, edged right, led inside final furlong, pushed out, ran on strongly (D Boeuf), beat Forestier by 2l*

2003

1st Prix Royal-Oak (Group 1) (Longchamp, October 26) 3yo+ 1m7½f Holding **120** 14 ran ● **1st** Prix du Cadran - Casinos Barriere (Group 1) (Longchamp, October 5) 4yo+ 2m4f Holding **122** 10 ran ● **2nd** Prix Gladiateur Royal Thalasso Barriere (Group 3) (Longchamp, September 14) 4yo+ 1m7½f Good to soft **113** 9 ran ● **2nd** Prix Kergorlay (Group 2) (Deauville, August 24) 3yo+ 1m7f Good to soft **112** 9 ran ● **2nd** Prix Maurice de Nieuil (Group 2) (Maisons-Laffitte, July 19) 4yo+ 1m6f Good to soft **110** 7 ran ● **5th** Grand Prix de Chantilly (Group 2) (Chantilly, June 8) 4yo+ 12f Good **105** 7 ran ● **1st** Prix de la Porte de Madrid (Listed) (Longchamp, May 8) 4yo+ 12f Soft **100** 8 ran ● **11th** Prix Altipan (Listed) (Saint-Cloud, March 15) 4yo+ 1m Good to soft 13 ran

Other notable runs

2002 **3rd** Prix Tantieme (Listed) (Saint-Cloud, November 19) 3yo+ 1m Heavy **95** 11 ran ● **2nd** Prix de Tourgeville (Listed) (Deauville, August 6) 3yo 1m Very soft **100** 8 ran ● **2nd** Prix de Pontarme (Listed) (Chantilly, May 29) 3yo 1m Soft 5 ran ● **1st** Prix du Coeur Volant (Maisons-Laffitte, May 7) 3yo 1m Soft 8 ran

cotton-wool appliance about two furlongs from the finish would produce a sudden increased awareness in Westerner and trigger the horse's natural flight mechanism.

That, and the opportunity to race over an extended distance, certainly contributed to galvanising Westerner at the back-end of 2003, and the plugs remained part of his racing equipment, to be taken out by his jockey at the appropriate moment.

However, they were to be the cause of the controversy that enveloped Wildenstein, who was well aware that removal during a race in Britain is specifically outlawed under Jockey Club Instruction H3.

Despite the Vicomtesse Vigier blip, the Gold Cup at Royal Ascot became Westerner's midsummer target, and his first race outside France. Gerald Mosse was called up to replace Boeuf and given the assurance that Wildenstein would pay the inevitable fine imposed by the stewards for removing the offending ear plugs.

Wildenstein knew the score. He had paid fines of £250 and £500 – charged to Boeuf, no less – after playing the same trick with Risk Seeker at Ascot and Sandown earlier in the season, and though the Jockey Club had thought about making a change, they declared they would stick by the letter of the Instruction.

Mosse carried out his brief, removing the plugs as Papineau challenged inside the final two furlongs, and the Royal Ascot stewards relieved him of £1,000.

It was another doubled fine that would represent nothing more than loose change to Wildenstein, who promptly topped up his lack of grace by suggesting to anyone who would listen that Papineau's performance meant "the dope-testing machine must be broken".

This time it was the Jockey Club's turn to resort to ear plugs, for they decided to take no action over the potentially slanderous observation, which might have been construed as bringing racing – if not the Godolphin stable – into disrepute.

A spokesman said: "The remarks portray him [Wildenstein] in a poorer light than they do the sport." A Jockey Club executive further warned that a future willingness to break the Rules could prompt the authorities to refuse the owner's entries.

All this left Westerner struggling for the recognition his performance merited. He had run close to his best and on firmer going than he had previously encountered, the 'good to firm' going for his debut at Longchamp, in April 2002, hardly being comparable with the same description at Ascot on Gold Cup day 2004, especially when the official return was altered to 'firm' after the next race.

Held up in midfield as usual, travelling strongly, he made smooth headway from the half-mile marker but was left in front two furlongs out, probably sooner than intended, when first Ingrandire and then Mr Dinos dropped off the lead.

Westerner looked a likelier winner than Papineau when he struck the front, but the year-younger horse, tackling the distance for the first time, proved the stronger and won by a length and a half. Westerner was two and a half lengths ahead of Darasim, reversing the order in two races immediately before the French-trained colt's massive autumn progress in 2003.

In the post-race euphoria of the Gold Cup, Papineau's connections and Wildenstein talked – separately – of returning to Ascot the following month for the King George VI and Queen Elizabeth Diamond Stakes. Neither eventuality came about.

Papineau had a setback and did not run again; Westerner ran in the mile-and-a-half Grand Prix de Saint-Cloud just 17 days after the Gold Cup, and beat only a pace-making stablemate in a ten-horse field.

The race almost certainly came too soon after Ascot for him to perform at his best, but there is a lesson to be learned from the experience regardless. Westerner has a turn of foot, but he is not a middle-distance horse, and any attempt to turn him into one at the highest class at this stage of his career is doomed to fail.

Proof was soon to be revealed, for having been given a two-month break, Westerner returned for an autumn campaign that realised three wins from as many runs over two miles or more.

Ridden by Boeuf's longer-term replacement Olivier Peslier, he held off Cut Quartz, who was receiving 7lb, by a short neck in the Prix Gladiateur. Three weeks later he turned the advantage into three lengths at level weights in the Prix du Cadran, where he travelled strongly behind Anak Pekan and Darasim, and settled the issue in a matter of strides a furlong out.

Completing a second double in the Cadran and Prix Royal-Oak proved the formality it had seemed on paper. The Anglo-Irish team of Alcazar, Percussionist, Franklins Gardens and Holy Orders made up half the field, but none could counter Westerner's superiority once he cruised to the front a furlong and a half out. Behkara claimed second place, two and a half lengths adrift of the unchallenged winner. Alcazar did much the best of the visitors in third.

One of the oddities of the race was that Stephane Pasquier, riding his first Group 1 winner after Peslier was claimed for another runner, presumably forgot the latest orders about ear plugs in his understandable excitement.

After all the midsummer madness, connections of Westerner executed a curious twist, and he was plugged throughout the Gladiateur and the Cadran. "We're teaching our horses to run with them, in case we go to England again," was Lellouche's quirky explanation.

Maybe Pasquier has done form followers a favour. It seems that as well as acting on almost any type of going, Westerner is now capable of running at, or near, peak performance, whether the ear plugs are removed during the race or not.

Armed with that information, there is every reason to hope that if Westerner manages to retain his form at the age of six and travels to York for the transferred Gold Cup in 2005, the best stayer to come out of France for a number of years will attract attention on his own account. He deserves to.

Westerner

bay horse, 17-5-1999

			Nearctic
		Northern Dancer	Natalma
	Danzig		
		Pas de Nom	Admiral's Voyage
Danehill			Petitioner
b 1986			
		His Majesty	Ribot
			Flower Bowl
	Razyana		
		Spring Adieu	Buckpasser
			Natalma
			Petition
		Petingo	Alcazar
	Troy		
		La Milo	Hornbeam
Walensee			Pin Prick
b 1982			
		Bon Mot	Worden
			Djebel Idra
	Warsaw		
		War Path	Blue Prince
			Alyxia

Bred by Dayton Investments in Britain

Sire Danehill

Won 4 of 9 races, inc. Cork and Orrery Stakes-Gr3, Haydock Park Sprint Cup-Gr1. Also 3rd in 2,000 Guineas. Medium-sized, strong, good-bodied individual, markedly back at the knee. Showed quick, fluent action, effective on any ground from dead to firm, never ran on really soft surface. Died May 2003. Sire of Gr1 winners: Danish (Queen Elizabeth II Challenge Cup), Kissing Cousin (Coronation S.), Danehill Dancer (Phoenix S., National S.), Tsukuba Symphony (NHK Mile Cup), Desert King (National S., Irish 2,000 Guineas, Irish Derby), Fairy King Prawn (Yasuda Kinen), Tiger Hill (Grosser Preis von Baden [twice], Bayerisches Zuchtrennen), Indian Danehill (Prix Ganay), Wannabe Grand (Cheveley Park S.), Aquarelliste (Prix de Diane, Prix Vermeille, Prix Ganay), Banks Hill (Coronation S., Breeders' Cup Filly & Mare Turf, Prix Jacques le Marois), Mozart (July Cup, Nunthorpe S.), Regal Rose (Cheveley Park S.), Dress To Thrill (Matriarch S.), Landseer (Poule d'Essai des Poulains), Rock Of Gibraltar (Grand Criterium, Dewhurst S., 2,000 Guineas, Irish 2,000 Guineas, St James's Palace S., Sussex S., Prix du Moulin de Longchamp), Westerner (Prix du Cadran, twice, Prix Royal-Oak, twice), Clodovil (Poule d'Essai des Poulains), Light Jig (Yellow Ribbon S.), Spartacus (Phoenix S., Gran Criterium), Grey Lilas (Prix du Moulin de Longchamp), North Light (Derby S.), Oratorio (Prix Jean-Luc Lagardere).

Dam Walensee

Won 3 of her 5 starts at 3, notably Prix Vermeille-Gr1. At 4, unplaced in 4 starts. By Derby winner who had decent results in very short stud career. Half-sister to Walk On Air (dam of Group winners Walk On Mix, Walkamia) and Water Girl (3rd dam of Voix du Nord) out of Listed-winning half-sister to top-class US filly Waya. Dam of: 1988 Waldensian (c by Shareef Dancer; winner), 1990 War Arrow (c by Top Ville; jumps winner), 1991 Wild Ride (f by Niniski; placed), 1993 Wild Life (f by Nashwan; unraced), 1994 World Cup (c by Epervier Bleu; unraced), 1995 Wagram (f by Nashwan; unraced), 1996 War Game (f by Caerleon; Gr2 winner), 1998 Watteau (c by Loup Solitaire; winner), 1999 Westerner (c by Danehill; Prix du Cadran-Gr1, twice, Prix Royal-Oak-Gr1, twice) 2001 Wildest Hope (c by Wolfhound; placed).

Pedigree assessment

Undisputed king of the French stayers, and he has every chance of retaining his crown in 2005. His stamina counts against him when it comes to a future Flat stallion career, even though he is by one of the most fashionable sires of stallions in the world and out of a Group 1-winning mare from a family that continues to turn out smart performers every year. *JH*

Whipper (USA)

3yo bay colt   **124**

Miesque's Son (USA) - Myth To Reality (Fr) (Sadler's Wells (USA))

Owner R C Strauss

Trainer Robert Collet

Breeder Flaxman Holdings Ltd

Career: **13** starts   won **5**   second **1**   third **1**   **£471,775** win and place

By James Willoughby

"**I**T IS the resort for magic rendezvous, long walks along the beach, fireside chats, pink geraniums and brown shrimps. Take in the breeze and get a breath of fresh air, encounter happiness Deauville style."

This atmosphere of romance, as described by the local tourist office, clearly did not permeate the town's bloodstock sales when Whipper was in the ring. He was led out without a bid as a yearling.

When Whipper returned for another dose of "elegance, prestige and sophistication" in the Prix Jacques le Marois, he left both brown shrimps and high-class opponents in his wake. His victory perhaps even rubbed one or two noses in the pink geraniums, imbued the odd fireside chat with a sense of regret and caused at least one long walk along the beach to be undertaken in an uncommonly reflective manner.

Neither was this Whipper's only magic rendezvous with the seaside splendour. Once he takes in the breeze and gets a breath of fresh air, happiness Deauville-style truly is his. His five ventures to Deauville's elegant racecourse have yielded two Group 1 wins, plus a fine second to Somnus in the Prix Maurice de Gheest at the same level.

Whipper started his second campaign with a win in the more urban surroundings of Maisons-Laffitte. His trainer Robert Collet was eager for a tilt at the 2,000 Guineas at Newmarket and used the traditional French prep of the Prix Djebel to bring his charge into peak condition.

The Rowley Mile was not an unfamiliar destination for Whipper. He had been a fast-closing fourth in the Group 1 Middle Park Stakes as a two-year-old, encouraging his connections that there was nothing to fear over an extra two furlongs the following spring.

And for the larger part of the Guineas, it looked as if this view would be justified. Whipper travelled extremely well up with the strong pace and was bang there two furlongs out. As Haafhd began to stretch away,

Whipper shows his liking for the Deauville straight track by landing the Group 1 Prix Jacques le Marois in August

however, Whipper began to weaken, and he was beaten around four lengths into fifth. It appeared as though Whipper was found out by lack of stamina on his first try at a mile. Interestingly, his final start of the season in the Breeders' Cup Mile created a similar impression, though he got the trip well enough in the Marois.

For his next outing he dropped back in trip for the Maurice de Gheest, in which he showed improved form while seeming to find the six and a half furlongs too sharp. No matter. The race was intended mainly as a prep for the Marois, also at Deauville, and just seven days later.

In a well-run race, Whipper raced towards the middle of the track while in mid-division. The favourite Six Perfections was located much nearer the stands rail and, when the race reached its hottest part, their relative locations were to prove important.

Lacking the same push-button speed as her rival, Six Perfections was quite seriously compromised by having to wait for room for a stride or two. When she had cleared the trouble, Whipper was in full flight and nearly two lengths clear. The filly only found top gear and started to cut into this margin 100 yards out, by which point Whipper was home for all money.

10th NetJets Breeders' Cup Mile (Grade 1) (Turf) (Lone Star Park, October 30) 3yo+ 1m Yielding **111** 14 ran. *Prominent in 4th on rail, driven and disputing 2nd entering straight, hard ridden final furlong, no extra (C Soumillon), beaten 5l by Singletary*

5th NetJets Prix du Moulin de Longchamp (Group 1) (Longchamp, September 5) 3yo+ 1m Good to soft **118** (TS 90) 11 ran. *Held up, last straight, headway on outside over 1f out, never nearer (C Soumillon), beaten 2l by Grey Lilas*

1st Prix Fresnay-le-Buffard-Jacques Le Marois (Group 1) (Deauville, August 15) 3yo+ 1m Soft **124** (TS 103) 10 ran. *Mid-division, disputing 6th halfway, pushed along to chase leaders over 1½f out, ridden to lead 1f out, ran on well, driven out (C Soumillon), beat Six Perfections by 1l*

2nd Prix Maurice de Gheest (Group 1) (Deauville, August 8) 3yo+ 6½f Good to soft **121** 18 ran. *Held up, headway 2f out, ridden 1f out, ran on but not reach winner (C Soumillon), beaten nk by Somnus*

5th UltimateBet.com 2,000 Guineas Stakes (Group 1) (Newmarket, May 1) 3yo 1m Good **118** (TS 107) 14 ran. *Tracked leaders centre, every chance 2f out, weakened inside final furlong (C Soumillon), beaten 4l by Haafhd*

1st Prix Djebel (Listed) (Maisons-Laffitte, April 6) 3yo Colts & Geldings 7f Holding **115** (TS 107) 6 ran. *Close up until led over 1½f out, pushed clear, very easily, (C Soumillon), beat Red Mo by 8l*

2003

1st Criterium de Maisons-Laffitte (Group 2) (Maisons-Laffitte, October 31) 2yo 6f Holding **116** 10 ran ● **4th** Shadwell Stud Middle Park Stakes (Group 1) (Newmarket, October 3) 2yo 6f Good to firm **110** 12 ran ● **1st** Prix Morny Casinos Barriere (Group 1) (Deauville, August 31) 2yo 6f Soft **117** 8 ran ● **1st** Prix de Longchamp (Chateaubriant, August 18) 2yo 5½f Soft 7 ran ● **4th** Prix de Cabourg (Group 3) (Deauville, August 2) 2yo 6f Good to soft **93** 8 ran ● **3rd** Prix des Reves d'Or (Vichy, July 20) 2yo 5f Good 12 ran ● **5th** Prix du Bois (Group 3) (Deauville, July 5) 2yo 5f Soft **85** 8 ran

Excluding the runner-up and Attraction, who failed to handle the soft going and returned a distant last, the vanquished remainder collectively did not represent the same threat as even a single top-class opponent. So it is not surprising that Whipper's Racing Post Rating of 124 is unexceptional by the standards of this traditionally strong Group 1 test. Nonetheless, it represented further evidence that he was improving.

If Whipper's form seemed on an upward curve, it pretty soon took a downward turn, first gradually and then with much greater severity. The dip came in the Moulin, possibly as a direct result of an unsuitably slow pace and wide trip. Equally, there has to be a strong chance that a straight course suits him best.

Whipper has developed into a high-class sprinter/miler and should win more races when there is give in the ground. Indeed, it would come as no surprise if, "after the springtime apple blossom has come" and "before the autumn skies become studded with film stars" and "the winter stores up charm and poetry", "Deauville the enchantress" once again witnesses Whipper in his pomp.

Whipper

bay colt, 13-3-2001

			Native Dancer
		Raise A Native	Raise You
	Mr Prospector		
		Gold Digger	Nashua
Miesque's Son			Sequence
b 1992			**Northern Dancer**
		Nureyev	**Special**
	Miesque		
		Pasadoble	Prove Out
			Santa Quilla
		Northern Dancer	Nearctic
			Natalma
	Sadler's Wells		
		Fairy Bridge	Bold Reason
Myth To Reality			**Special**
b 1986			Never Bend
		Mill Reef	Milan Mill
	Millieme		
		Hardiemma	Hardicanute
			Grand Cross

Bred by Flaxman Holdings Ltd in Kentucky. $4,000 Keeneland November foal; €30,000 Deauville yearling (private sale)

Sire Miesque's Son

Won 1 (Prix de Ris-Orangis-Gr3) of 9 races. Also 2nd in Prix Maurice de Gheest and Prix de la Foret. Quite well-made, close-coupled individual. Had training problems at 2 and 3, smart 6-7f performer at 4, best with some give in the ground. Impeccably bred. Brother to Classic winner and successful sire Kingmambo, half-brother to dual Classic winner East Of The Moon (f by Private Account), Gr3 winner Mingun (c by A.P. Indy), and to Gr3- placed winner Moon Is Up (f by Woodman). Out of an outstanding racemare, one of the best milers of her sex in recent times. Stands at Haras des Chartreux, France, 2004 fee €5,000. Sire of 5 crops of racing age, inc: Miesque's Approval (Gr3), Whipper (Prix Morny-Gr1, Prix Jacques le Marois-Gr1).

Dam Myth To Reality

Won 4 of 14 races, inc. 3 Listed. Good, consistent, mostly provincial performer, well suited by 12f, respectable 5th in Gr2 Prix de Royallieu, runner-up in Gr3 Prix Minerve. Effective on any ground. Did not progress at four. Very well bred. By the outstanding sire of the age out of a placed full sister to Derby winner Shirley Heights, and three-parts sister to Gull Nook (Ribblesdale S.; dam of King George VI & Queen Elizabeth S. winner Pentire, and Gr3 winner Spring). Family of Miletrian, Mr Combustible, Mr Pintips, Banket, etc. Dam of: Sonofogy (1992 g by Ogygian; winner), Magic Spin (1993 f by Lord Avie; winner), Assos (1994 g by Alleged; Listed winner), Mambo Jambo (1995 f by Kingmambo; winner, dam of Gr1-placed Ocean Silk), Fireinthewind (1996 c by Alleged; winner), Indigo Myth (1997 g by Kingmambo; Listed-placed winner), Meteorite Sun (1998 g by Miesque's Son; winner), Whipper (2001 c by Miesque's Son; dual Gr1 winner), Divine Proportions (2002 f by Kingmambo; dual Gr1 winner). Her yearling is a filly by Mt Livermore and she has a colt foal by Lemon Drop Kid.

Pedigree assessment

Sold by the Niarchos family for the pittance of $4,000 as a foal, Whipper made a telling response to the insult, depriving his breeders of a Group 1 victory by defying their Breeders' Cup heroine Six Perfections in the Prix Jacques le Marois. As a markedly inferior brother to Kingmambo, Whipper's sire Miesque's Son was afforded few real chances as a stallion in America, but he made the most of his second opportunity with Myth To Reality, as Kingmambo did by getting Divine Proportions from the same mare. Transferred now to France, Miesque's Son should enjoy better patronage.*TM*

Wilko (USA)

2yo chestnut colt **120**

Awesome Again (Can) - Native Roots (Ire) (Indian Ridge)
Owner J Paul Reddam & Susan Roy
Trainer J Noseda
Breeder Ro Parra

Career: **11** starts won **3** second **2** third **4** **£490,901** win and place

By Richard Austen

"DID you have him? You're going to collect big," said the NBC anchorman before he went to a commercial. Wilko was a shock winner of the Breeders' Cup Juvenile and the long odds were not down just to a parochial approach by the Americans. He was almost as big an outsider with his audience on this side of the Atlantic, where Wilko had been eclipsed on every occasion – and there were plenty of them – that he ventured into Group company.

Wilko was also beaten in the two maidens that kicked off his career with Jeremy Noseda in unspectacular fashion in May. Soft ground probably had something to do with it. With firmer conditions Wilko won a novice stakes at Yarmouth and then began his series of commendable efforts in Listed and Group events, commendable but never in a leading role. He did win a second Yarmouth novice, but he was workmanlike to say the least, and his reputation in Britain was established in defeat.

Whazzat, Brecon Beacon, Dubawi, Henrik, Shamardal, Kings Quay, Etlaala, Iceman, Oude, Perfectperformance and Scandinavia all finished in front of him after his early-season soft-ground defeats and, on those results, they were better horses at the weights. Wilko had run twice a month for five months without ever setting the handicapper's pulse racing but there were some reasons for optimism behind the form, and he was always running on at the finish. In the Royal Lodge he did so after being hampered twice and that effort, his best form, came on his first venture at a mile. He was indisputably tough and game, and he had also improved with his greatest test of stamina.

These qualities would serve Wilko well at the Breeders' Cup. Whether he would be good enough to play a significant role under Frankie Dettori (displacing Eddie Ahern) was another matter, but his sire Awesome Again was a top-class dirt performer – Swain's conqueror in the 1998 Breeders' Cup Classic – and Wilko had not yet raced on dirt.

**Wilko scores a sensational win on dirt at the Breeders'
Cup, having failed to win a Group race in Britain on turf**

The Breeders' Cup Juvenile at Lone Star Park was considered a strong
renewal. Afleet Alex, Proud Accolade and Consolidator were Grade 1
winners and Roman Ruler had won two Grade 2s by an aggregate of
eleven and a half lengths.

Wilko could boast of the EBF Holiday Park Novice Stakes, the Customs
Kitchens Novice Stakes and win earnings of £8,119, but once under way
at the Breeders' Cup he never looked out of place. Unlike so many
European challengers, he was swiftly out of the stalls and took a prominent
position, despite emerging from the widest berth. On the final turn, Afleet
Alex came round him and Wilko seemed to be back-pedalling, but entering
the straight he started coming back at the three leaders and just inside
the final furlong the three horses battling line abreast became four. On
the outside, Wilko was going the fastest now and passed the best that
America had to offer.

At the post, Wilko was three-quarters of a length to the good over Afleet
Alex and another neck ahead of Sun King. "I love America," shouted
Dettori. Wilko's odds were 28-1 on course and 20-1 in Britain.

1st Bessemer Trust Breeders' Cup Juvenile (Grade 1) (Dirt) (Lone Star Park, October 30) 2yo 1m½f Fast **120** 8 ran. *Close up on outside, dropped back to 4th and pushed along over 2½f out, ridden 2f out, stayed on dourly down outside to lead 100yds out, driven out (L Dettori), beat Afleet Alex by ¾l*

3rd Hackney Empire Royal Lodge Stakes (Group 2) (Ascot, September 25) 2yo 1m Good to firm **112** (TS 105) 8 ran. *Tracked leaders, effort to challenge 2f out, unable to quicken and held when not much room twice over 1f out, stayed on inside final furlong (E Ahern), beaten 2¾l by Perfectperformance*

4th SGB Champagne Stakes (Group 2) (Doncaster, September 10) 2yo 7f Good to firm **103** (TS 82) 10 ran. *Chased leaders, driven along and slightly outpaced over 2f out, switched right approaching final furlong, stayed on (E Ahern), beaten 4¼l by Etlaala*

2nd Stan James Stakes (Registered As The Washington Singer Stakes) (Listed) (Newbury, August 13) 2yo 7f Good to soft **100** (TS 68) 5 ran. *Disputed close 2nd, ridden over 2f out, chased winner final furlong, kept on but no impression close home (E Ahern), beaten ½l by Kings Quay*

1st Custom Kitchens Novice Stakes (Yarmouth, August 4) 2yo 7f Good to firm **81** (TS 34) 4 ran. *Led 1f, tracked leader, shaken up to lead over 1f out, ran on (E Ahern), beat Shrine Mountain by ½l*

2nd Veuve Clicquot Vintage Stakes (Group 2) (Goodwood, July 28) 2yo 7f Good **103** (TS 91) 10 ran. *Chased leaders, ridden and effort over 2f out, chased winner over 1f out, kept on well but no impression (E Ahern), beaten 2½l by Shamardal*

3rd Weatherbys Superlative Stakes (Group 3) (Newmarket (July), July 8) 2yo 7f Good to soft **102** (TS 82) 12 ran. *Held up, headway over 1f out, ran on (E Ahern), beaten ¾l by Dubawi*

3rd Chesham Stakes (Listed) (Ascot, June 19) 2yo 7f Firm **101** (TS 87) 11 ran. *Pulled hard on outside, switched left to stands' rail over 5f out, ridden over 3f out, switched right and headway over 1f out, ran on (E Ahern), beaten 3¾l by Whazzat*

1st EBF/Vauxhall Holiday Park Novice Stakes (Yarmouth, June 2) 2yo 6f Firm **85** (TS 51) 7 ran. *Broke well, pulled hard, steadied soon after start, headway over 1f out, led inside final furlong, ran on well (E Ahern), beat Dance Anthem by 1l*

7th EBF Maiden Stakes (York, May 12) 2yo 6f Good to soft **71** (TS 56) 11 ran. *Close up, ridden along 2f out, weakened over 1f out (E Ahern), beaten 4¼l by Pivotal Flame*

3rd EBF Sharp Minds Betfair Maiden Stakes (Kempton, May 3) 2yo 5f Heavy **65** (TS 34) 8 ran. *Tracked leaders, pushed along over 2f out, outpaced over 1f out (E Ahern), beaten 11½l by Turnkey*

Before the Breeders' Cup 75 per cent of Wilko was sold to American Paul Reddam and Wilko's became a one-way ticket, to be trained by Craig Dollase in California, whatever happened at Lone Star Park. Spotting Wilko's potential for dirt racing was shrewd indeed, but asked at the trophy presentation "what made you think he could do this?" Reddam's comment was "well, I didn't know that he could actually."

"There is everything to gain and absolutely nothing to lose," said Noseda before the Juvenile. Given the horse's impending transfer, it is impossible to argue with that, but even without the sale Wilko would still have run in Texas. British trainers seem to be getting the hang of things with their Breeders' Cup challenges and Noseda's marvellous achievement on dirt with Wilko should embolden them further.

Wilko

chestnut colt, 13-1-2002

		Vice Regent	Northern Dancer / Victoria Regina
	Deputy Minister		
		Mint Copy	Bunty's Flight / Shakney
Awesome Again b 1994			
		Blushing Groom	Red God / Runaway Bride
	Primal Force		
		Prime Prospect	Mr Prospector / Square Generation
		Ahonoora	Lorenzaccio / Helen Nichols
	Indian Ridge		
		Hillbrow	Swing Easy / Golden City
Native Roots ch 1997			
		Tap On Wood	Sallust / Cat o'Mountaine
	Phazania		
		Contrail	Roan Rocket / Azurine

Bred by Ro Parra in US. $35,000 Keeneland November foal, $75,000 Keeneland September yearling

Sire **Awesome Again**

Won 9 of 12 races, inc. Jim Dandy S.-Gr2, Stephen Foster H.-Gr2, Whitney H,-Gr1, Saratoga Cup H.-Gr2, Hawthorne Gold Cup H.-Gr3, Breeders' Cup Classic S.-Gr1. Also 3rd in Travers S. at 3. Medium-sized (16.0hh), well-made sort. Good at 3, made striking progress to become very good at 4. Usually stalked pace and produced sharp turn of foot. Stayed 10f well. Well-bred. Half-brother to champion 2yo Macho Uno (by Holy Bull). By a champion 2yo and champion sire. Dam won 4 races (6-7f), half-sister to dam of Miss Ra He Ha (Gr3). Grand-dam smart stakes winner at 5 years, from family of 1987 champion older mare North Sider. Stands at Adena Springs Kentucky, 2005 fee $125,000. Sire of 3 racing crops, inc: Awesome Time (Gr3), Ghostzapper (Vosburgh S.-Gr1, Woodward S.-Gr1, Breeders' Cup Classic S.-Gr1), Snorter (Gr3), Toccet (Champagne S.-Gr1, Hollywood Futurity-Gr1), Wilko (Breeders' Cup Juvenile S.-Gr1), Personal Legend (Gr3).

Dam **Native Roots**

Won 1 of 11 starts at 2 and 3 in North America. At 2, unplaced in 3 starts. At 3, won 1 of 8 starts. By top-class sprinter and very good sire of 2yos, sprinters and milers, out of Listed-placed 6-8f 2yo winner whose half-sister Muffitys is grand-dam of useful 2004 2yo Valentin, 2002 Japanese champion 2yo filly Peace Of World and 1998 Japanese horse of the year Taiki Shuttle. Dam of: Wilko (2002 c by Awesome Again; Breeders' Cup Juvenile-Gr1), 2004 f by Talk Is Money.

Pedigree assessment

Awesome Again's fantastic Breeders' Cup featured Ghostzapper and Wilko, who stepped up on his English turf form at Lone Star Park. Top-class US performer Awesome Again almost certainly is responsible for Wilko's affinity for dirt, for Native Roots is from a solidly European family. Most performers close up in this family have been best at up to a mile, and it is far from certain that Wilko will excel over the 10f of the Kentucky Derby. However, there are no such worries for the top spring North American Classic trials over 8-9f. *JH*

Yeats (Ire)

3yo bay colt   **117**

Sadler's Wells (USA) - Lyndonville (Ire) (Top Ville)

Owner Mrs John Magnier & Mrs David Nagle

Trainer A P O'Brien

Breeder Barronstown Stud & Orpendale

Career: **3** starts | won **3** | **£103,068** win and place

---

By Nicholas Godfrey

IF THE disappointments associated with One Cool Cat provided the nadir of a mainly troubled season for Aidan O'Brien's Ballydoyle yard, then Yeats being forced to miss the Vodafone Derby through injury cannot have been too far behind.

Apologists may point to the stable's customary hatful of winners in Ireland, including a softish Group 1 success for Powerscourt, but in reality it seemed as if little went right for O'Brien and his new stable jockey Jamie Spencer, at least not until the autumn. And, even then, problems seemed to follow them everywhere.

This seemed especially the case during the early weeks of the 2004 turf season. Then, after One Cool Cat's Guineas debacle, Yeats carried a burden of expectation on his rangy shoulders. But while the big, long-striding son of Sadler's Wells was to remain unbeaten at the end of his three-year-old campaign, his season lasted only two runs in which he beat a total of five horses, albeit in a pair of Group races.

This was not the level of return O'Brien had been hoping for when he described Yeats as "a beauty" and "a proper horse all the way at home" following his victory in a fairly ordinary maiden at The Curragh on his only start as a two-year-old in 2003, after which he was installed as favourite for the Derby.

O'Brien immediately pledged to send him down the tried-and-tested 'Galileo route' to Epsom, and he proved as good as his word. Yeats's status as Ballydoyle's anointed one was confirmed when the colt duly ran in the Ballysax Stakes and the Derrinstown Stud Derby Trial, the races won by both Galileo and High Chaparral, the stable's two Derby winners, en route to their Epsom successes in 2001 and 2002 respectively.

By the time Yeats lined up for the ten-furlong Ballysax in April, he was only 6-1 for the Derby. Sent off a 1-3 shot in the Group 3 event at Leopardstown, his dismissal of two vastly inferior opponents proved little

**Yeats wins the Derrinstown Stud Derby Trial, but he never
made it to the big race and was not seen again in 2004**

in terms of form – in hindsight, the race's Racing Post Rating of 117 seems
a trifle generous – but the manner in which he won was very taking to
the eye, as was the colt's impressive physical presence. Setting off at a
good pace considering the soft ground, Yeats showed himself a relentless
galloper, putting his rivals in trouble fully half a mile out before winning
with absolute authority, by ten lengths from recent Listed-race second
Dabiroun, who was not seen out again. It looked just a "good canter around",
as Spencer suggested; bookmakers took the opportunity to shave a couple
of points off his Derby price.

Three weeks later, Yeats was an even hotter favourite to win his next
race, the Group 2 Derrinstown Stud Derby Trial. He did so, but this
time his performance did not satisfy everyone. While Yeats again made
all and looked for a few strides after turning for home as if he was going
to stretch away from his three rivals, he ultimately had only a length
and a half to spare over Relaxed Gesture. Yeats had to be ridden, albeit
not strongly, to maintain the advantage; the whip was waved at him.

1st Derrinstown Stud Derby Trial Stakes (Group 2) (Leopardstown, May 9) 3yo 10f Good to yielding **111** (TS 77) 4 ran. *Made all, edged clear 3f out, ridden and kept on well straight, comfortably (J P Spencer), beat Relaxed Gesture by 1½l*

1st P.W.McGrath Memorial Ballysax Stakes (Group 3) (Leopardstown, April 18) 3yo 10f Soft **117** (TS 56) 3 ran. *Made all, quickened clear 1½f out, eased final furlong, impressive (J P Spencer), beat Dabiroun by 10l*

2003

1st Korean Racing Association EBF Maiden (Curragh, September 21) 2yo 1m Good to firm **94** 15 ran

---

After the race O'Brien stressed that, "trials are trials and everyone has their own opinion." That they did: some bookmakers took the opportunity to lengthen Yeats's odds a fraction for Epsom, although he remained favourite all round, with Ladbrokes as short as 9-4.

O'Brien also pointed out that Galileo had not pleased everybody in the same race before making massive improvement in the Derby itself. Unfortunately, we will never know if Yeats would have done the same, for he was the subject of an injury scare a fortnight before the Classic when he was reported a "shade stiff" after exercise.

O'Brien suggested the colt may have "tweaked a muscle" and played down its seriousness. While he can take credit for informing the public of the setback, his prognosis proved wide of the mark. With bookmaking sources suggesting Yeats was no better than 50-50 to make the Derby line-up, Ballydoyle called in renowned equine physiotherapist Liz Kent to work her magic on Yeats.

The problem – described as muscle stiffness between his hip and backbone on the near-hind side – would not go away and the colt was finally withdrawn three days before the Derby. While bookmakers are sometimes accused of plucking figures from thin air, it is probably worth mentioning here their claim that his non-appearance had cost punters around £500,000 in ante-post stakes.

We did not see Yeats again, a lengthy period of rest being prescribed to cure his ailment, but he reportedly stays in training as a four-year-old, when he will finally have the chance to make good O'Brien's suggestion that he has "always worked like a champion".

Whether Yeats will ever be a champion on the racetrack is another matter. He's got the breeding, he's had the hype, and he hasn't really done too much wrong on the racecourse. The problem is that he has never had the chance to do that much right, either, and he was perhaps merely considered the best of what turned out to be an average three-year-old bunch by Ballydoyle standards.

Even if Yeats is able to overcome the muscle problems that curtailed his Classic season, he still has a lot to prove. Let's just hope he has the chance to do so.

Yeats

bay colt 23-4-2001

			Nearco
		Nearctic	Lady Angela
	Northern Dancer		
		Natalma	Native Dancer
Sadler's Wells			Almahmoud
b 1981			Hail To Reason
		Bold Reason	Lalun
	Fairy Bridge		
		Special	Forli
			Thong
			Derring-Do
		High Top	Camenae
	Top Ville		
		Sega Ville	Charlottesville
Lyndonville			La Sega
b 1988			Hard Tack
		Sparkler	Diamond Spur
	Diamond Land		
		Canaan	Santa Claus
			Rustic Bridge

Bred by Barronstown Stud & Orpendale in Ireland

Sire **Sadler's Wells**

Won 6 of 11 races, inc. Beresford S.-Gr3, Irish Derby Trial-Gr2, Irish 2,000 Guineas-Gr1, Eclipse S.-Gr1, Phoenix Champion S.-Gr1. Also 2nd in Prix du Jockey-Club-Gr1, King George VI & Queen Elizabeth S.-Gr1. Impeccably bred top-class performer from 8-12f, handsome, tough and consistent. Sire of Gr1 winners: Braashee, French Glory, In The Wings (3), Old Vic (2), Prince Of Dance, Scenic, Salsabil (5), Opera House (3), Runyon, Saddlers' Hall, El Prado, Johann Quatz, Masad, Barathea (2), Fatherland, Fort Wood, Intrepidity (3), Carnegie (2), King's Theatre (2), Northern Spur (2), Moonshell, Muncie, Poliglote, Chief Contender, Dance Design, Darazari, Luna Wells, Cloudings, Ebadiyla (2), Entrepreneur, In Command, Kayf Tara (4), Dream Well (2), Greek Dance, King Of Kings (2), Leggera, Commander Collins, Daliapour, Montjeu (6), Saffron Walden, Aristotle, Beat Hollow (4), Subtle Power, Galileo (3), Imagine (2), Milan, Perfect Soul, Sequoyah, Sligo Bay, Ballingarry, Black Sam Bellamy (2), Gossamer (2), High Chaparral (6), Islington (4), Quarter Moon, Sholokov, Alberto Giacometti, Brian Boru (2), Doyen, Powerscourt, Refuse To Bend (4), Yesterday, Quiff, Playful Act.

Dam **Lyndonville**

Won 1 of 3 starts. Showed progressive form in brief career, stayed 14f well. Dam of: Tsukuba Symphony (1993 c by Danehill; Gr3 winner in Japan), Anchored In Love (1994 f by Alzao; unplaced), Lady Fairy (1996 f by Fairy King; unplaced), Lion Of Judah (1997 c by Caerleon; unplaced), Chalice Wells (1998 f by Sadler's Wells; unraced), Solskjaer (2000 c by Danehill; Gr2 winner), Yeats (2001 c by Sadler's Wells; Gr2 winner), Magnolia Lane (2002 f by Sadler's Wells; unraced to date).

Pedigree assessment

Montjeu advertised the Sadler's Wells/Top Ville cross so well that some breeders fancied they had recognised a "nick" and acted accordingly. At the head of the Derby market for months, Yeats was hailed by some pundits as the next Montjeu, but in truth, while remaining unbeaten, he has shown nothing approaching the class or brilliance of the dual Derby, King George and Arc hero. His prolonged absence from the racecourse is to be regretted and we must hope that he is able to return to action; even as a "second division" son of Sadler's Wells he warrants respect, and it is possible that he may gain promotion. He seems tailor-made for 12 furlongs. *TM*

The young pretenders

of 2004

Figure in bold by each horse's name is its definitive Racing Post Rating

Comments by Richard Austen (RA), Graham Dench (GD) and
Simon Turner (ST)

Pedigree assessments by Janet Hickman

Ad Valorem
121

See entry in the top 100 horses, page 16

Albert Hall
111

b c Danehill (USA) - Al Theraab (USA) (Roberto (USA)) April 18
Owner Mrs John Magnier & M Tabor **Trainer** A P O'Brien **Breeder** Bjorn E Nielsen
3 starts: won **1**, second **2**, **£108,197** win & place prize-money

THE task of extending Aidan O'Brien's excellent record – four wins in the previous seven years – in the Racing Post Trophy was entrusted principally to Albert Hall. As short as 11-8 on the morning of the Group 1 race, he drifted to a starting price of 5-2 in the face of heavy support for Motivator and, just as 12 months earlier, the market moves were well founded.

Holding Albert Hall up last of the eight runners, Jamie Spencer tracked Motivator through as the favourite moved into contention but could not keep tabs on him from the two-furlong marker, Albert Hall struggling to race on an even keel off the bridle but keeping on well enough to pass all except the two-and-a-half-length winner. "He's been a bit slow to learn but the penny is dropping, although he would have hated the ground," O'Brien reported afterwards.

Albert Hall had two races to prepare him for this slog over a mile through heavy ground, as did the third-placed Henrik, and Motivator only one. Motivator is the more striking example but the placed colts are promising as well. The downside with Albert Hall is that he has had three starts and looked awkward under pressure in all three. But then much the same observation was made about High Chaparral on heavy ground in the 2001 Racing Post Trophy.

Albert Hall's first two races were tight finishes earlier in the autumn at The Curragh, losing out in a maiden over seven furlongs but getting home in front over the same trip after setting the pace in the five-runner Group 2 Juddmonte Beresford Stakes. He was odds-on in both, and the ground was very much on the soft side in both, as it was in the Racing Post Trophy.

With such a stern test at Doncaster, however, there is a strong suspicion that O'Brien would have preferred his main hopes to be vested in a son of Sadler's Wells, who gave him three of his four Racing Post Trophy winners and was responsible for the 2004 second string, Hills Of Aran.

Albert Hall is a Group 2 winner and Group 1 runner-up

The Danehill colt Albert Hall is out of a dam who showed her best form at a mile and a half, but it is no cast-iron certainty that this son will prove a middle-distance performer judged on that pedigree. Albert Hall's sister Barsine, for instance, a useful performer in France, was seen last winning a six-furlong handicap as a three-year-old. *RA*

Race record

2nd Racing Post Trophy (Group 1) (Doncaster, October 23) 2yo 1m Soft **111** (TS 110) 8 ran.
1st Juddmonte Beresford Stakes (Group 2) (Curragh, October 10) 2yo 1m Yielding to soft **106** (TS 95) 5 ran.
2nd Tinnakill House EBF Maiden (Curragh, September 19) 2yo 7f Yielding **90** (TS 85) 18 ran.

Pedigree assessment

Sire Danehill (Danzig) Useful 6f 2yo winner, improved at 3 into top-class sprinter, won Haydock Sprint Cup-Gr1 but also smart over 1m. Excellent sire, has done well with 2yos and older progeny, mainly at up to 1m but capable of getting top-class 10f+ performers from stoutly bred dams. Best progeny include Aquarelliste, Banks Hill, Cacique, Desert King, Landseer, Mozart, North Light, Oratorio, Rock Of Gibraltar, Westerner. **Dam Al Theraab** 1m 3yo winner, placed in decent handicap over 12f. Bred along similar lines to Brian's Time (Gr1), Darby Creek Road (Gr2), Dynaformer (Gr2), Memories Of Silver (Gr1), Ryafan (Gr1), Sunshine Forever (Gr1), all of whom were best over 9f+. Her 8 earlier foals include 6f 2yo Listed winner Barsine (by Danehill) and several other winners at up to 1m.
Conclusion Has won a Group 2 over 1m and thus stays better than full-sister Barsine and most of his other half-siblings. Has fair chance of staying 10f but 12f probably beyond him.

Allexina   100

ch f Barathea (Ire) - Grecian Bride (Ire) (Groom Dancer (USA)) March 19
Owner J Higgins **Trainer** John M Oxx **Breeder** Gerrardstown House Stud
3 starts: won **2**, second **0**, third **0**, £33,487 win & place prize-money

THE bare form of Allexina's Tipperary maiden win over an extended seven furlongs in September was only modest, an impression backed up by assistant trainer Slim O'Neill's post-race remarks. "She looked as if she handled this [soft] ground. She will run again towards the back-end but there are no real plans," he said.

It was something of a surprise, then, to see the daughter of Barathea upped to Listed company at Fairyhouse next time when, dropped back to seven furlongs, she struggled to make any impression behind Gaff in the El Gran Senor Stakes, nevertheless showing much-improved form in defeat.

Connections persisted with her in Listed company, this time stepping her up in trip over a mile at The Curragh in the Silken Glider Stakes,

Race record
1st Gerrardstown House Stud Silken Glider Stakes (Listed) (Curragh, October 23) 2yo 1m Soft **100** (TS 97) 13 ran.
6th El Gran Senor Stakes (Listed) (Fairyhouse, September 29) 2yo 7f Good to yielding **84** 7 ran.
1st Irish Stallion Farms EBF Maiden (Tipperary, September 16) 2yo 7½f Soft **68** 16 ran.

Pedigree assessment
Sire Barathea (Sadler's Wells) Useful 7f winner at 2, progressed into top-class miler, won Irish 2,000 Guineas and Breeders' Cup Mile. Also showed smart form over 6f and 12f. Good record as a sire, including with 2yos (Barathea Guest, Charming Prince, Magical Romance, Tobougg) and older performers mainly over 1m+ (Enrique, Pongee), also gets occasional good sprinter (Tante Rose). **Dam Grecian Bride** Unraced sister to 10f Listed winner Athens Belle and very closely related to 12f Group 1 winner Gamut and high-class 12f+ performer Multicoloured. Family of Golan, North Light. Her two earlier foals include modest 9f 3yo winner Champain Sands (by Green Desert). **Conclusion** Allexina comes from a stout female family whose members generally stay at least 10f. Allexina is certain to stay that trip and has every chance of being effective over 12f. The family is not precocious, with members making good improvement from 2 to 3, so if Allexina follows suit she could be very smart.

and she didn't disappoint. Bounced out in front by Mick Kinane, Allexina travelled notably well, having all her field bar runner-up Adaala in trouble turning into the straight. Her stamina then came into play and she held off her challenger in pleasing style. Sure to stay middle distances, Allexina is likely to improve further and her astute trainer can place her to advantage at Pattern level. *ST*

Ayam Zaman (Ire)   98

b f Montjeu (Ire) - Kardashina (Fr) (Darshaan) February 8
Owner Saif Ali **Trainer** M A Jarvis **Breeder** Dr T A Ryan
3 starts: won **2**, second **0**, third **0**, **£20,090** win & place prize-money

THERE were several smart prospects on show on Newmarket's all-juvenile card in mid-September, and there were some eye-catching performances, not least from Ayam Zaman.

Held up on a day when the fast ground and tailwind made racing close to the pace a distinct advantage, the Michael Jarvis-trained filly stayed on in taking fashion from the rear over the straight mile, making up considerable late ground.

The promise of that debut made her a popular selection next time at Pontefract where, stepped up to ten furlongs, she justified short odds in impressive fashion, handing out a comprehensive beating to her rivals.

That success suggested she was better than a handicapper and she proved it on her final start of the season in the Listed Zetland Stakes at Newmarket, staying on strongly to take the step up in class in her stride. The bare form of the Zetland was not quite up to scratch for an average Listed race but Ayam Zaman won with authority and can be expected to improve again at three given her middle-distance pedigree.

She should be competitive at Group level in 2005 and will not be out of place in one of the traditional Oaks trials. *ST*

Race record

1st William Claridge Memorial Zetland Stakes (Listed) (Newmarket, October 30) 2yo 10f Good to soft **98** (TS 81) 9 ran.
1st EBF Claxton Bay Maiden Stakes (Pontefract, October 4) 2yo 10f Good to firm **85** (TS 70) 15 ran.
5th Robinsons Mercedes-Benz EBF Maiden Fillies' Stakes (Newmarket, September 21) 2yo 1m Good to firm **75** (TS 73) 15 ran.

Pedigree assessment

Sire Montjeu (Sadler's Wells) Useful dual 8-9f 2yo winner, progressed into outstanding 12f performer at 3 and 4, won Prix du Jockey-Club, Irish Derby, Arc, King George, also dual Gr1 winner over 10f. Stoutly bred, out of very smart stayer by Top Ville. First 2yos in 2004 include Racing Post Trophy winner Motivator and Gr1-placed Dash To The Top and Walk In The Park. **Dam Kardashina** Triple 11-12f 3yo winner in France. Half-sister to 1999 Pouliches runner-up Karmifira (by Always Fair) and two very useful 1m+ French performers out of a 10f Gr3 winner. Her 2 earlier foals are 10f winner Rudood (by Theatrical) and 12f winner Russian Tsar (by King Of Kings). **Conclusion** Ample stamina here. Montjeu's results with his first 2yos indicate, predictably, that his progeny will like middle distances. The dam stayed 12f and is by an outstanding stamina-orientated broodmare sire who links particularly well with Montjeu's sire Sadler's Wells. No problems at 12f in 2005 with Ayam Zaman, who has the pedigree to make good progress from 2 to 3.

Ballinteni 85

b c Machiavellian (USA) - Silabteni (USA) (Nureyev (USA)) March 21
Owner Godolphin **Trainer** Saeed Bin Suroor **Breeder** Gainsborough Stud
Management Ltd
1 start: won **1, £3,542** win & place prize-money

HOW to sort the wheat from the chaff – that's the problem outsiders face when trying to establish any sort of pecking order among the many lightly raced two-year-old winners sent out by Godolphin under their new regime in 2004. Much will depend upon how they winter in Dubai and shape up in the private trials, but in the meantime a great many of them merit respect.

Race record

1st Dransfield Novelty Company EBF October Maiden Stakes (Div I) (Doncaster, October 22) 2yo 7f Soft **85** (TS 59) 13 ran.

Pedigree assessment

Sire Machiavellian (Mr Prospector) Top-class 2yo over 6-7f, won Prix Morny-Gr1, Prix de la Salamandre-Gr1. High-class miler at 3, 2nd 2,000 Guineas-Gr1. By outstanding sire out of outstanding broodmare, most family members best around 1m. Very good sire, fair record with 2yos (Best Of The Bests, Titus Livius) but better one with older horses, mainly over 6-10f (Almutawakel, Medicean, Rebecca Sharp, Storming Home, Street Cry). Sires occasional high-class 12f+ performer (Invermark, Phantom Gold, Whitewater Affair) out of stout dam. **Dam Silabteni** Unraced. Half-sister to outstanding 10f filly Indian Skimmer. Her 4 surviving earlier foals are led by top-class US miler Touch Of The Blues (Cadeaux Genereux), who also was a 7f Gr2 winner at 2 in France. She has also produced a 6f 3yo winner by Warning and a 10f 3yo winner by Nashwan. **Conclusion** Likely to be a miler. Machiavellian's progeny generally make decent progress from 2 to 3. Bred on a successful cross – Machiavellian's 2004 fillies include 2yo Gr3 winner Birthstone (out of a Nureyev mare) and high-class miler Chic (out of a mare by Nureyev's son Polar Falcon).

Ballinteni might not even be in their top ten, but there was certainly plenty to admire in his winning debut in a soft-ground seven-furlong Doncaster maiden towards the end of the season. In a race that featured so many backward and unfancied youngsters that a 68-rated colt having his fifth start was the 4-1 favourite, Ballinteni went off second best at 5-1. His inexperience showed and he needed his mind making up for him, but he responded once given a couple of smacks and picked up well in the final furlong to win by two and a half lengths from fellow newcomer Full Of Zest.

Ballinteni's half-brother Touch Of The Blues was a smart juvenile in France in 1999 and went on to do well in the States, eventually winning a Grade 1 race. Ballinteni looks sure to train on too, but quite what heights he will scale is anyone's guess at this stage. *GD*

Ballinteni, left, wins at Doncaster on his only start

Belenus (Ire)   86

ch c Dubai Millennium - Ajhiba (Ire) (Barathea (Ire)) March 22
Owner Godolphin **Trainer** Saeed Bin Suroor **Breeder** Gainsborough Stud
Management Ltd
1 start: won **1**, **£8,443** win & place prize-money

A MAJOR change to the Godolphin operation in 2004 saw main trainer
Saeed Bin Suroor take responsibility for not only the older horses but
the mountain of juvenile talent the operation boasts as well. The early
signs from the change are highly encouraging, with Dubawi ranking
second in the Racing Post Ratings juvenile classification and many others
showing stacks of promise in what was a very busy year.

One of the most interesting unbeaten colts in Bin Suroor's care is
Belenus, who appeared at Newmarket's July meeting to win the
Strutt & Parker Maiden, traditionally a hot race and the starting point
for the likes of Alhaarth, Colonel Collins and Mark Of Esteem in the
past.

After his success Bin Suroor said: "He's one of the best and has always
pleased us in his work. He's still a baby and will be better at three.
We won't overface him this year and will look for a little conditions
race next."

Belenus was certainly given the kid-glove treatment afterwards, being put away with a three-year-old campaign in mind. His reappearance is awaited with great interest. *ST*

Race record

1st Strutt & Parker Maiden Stakes (Newmarket (July), July 6) 2yo 7f Good to firm **86** (TS 80) 15 ran.

Pedigree assessment

Sire **Dubai Millennium** (Seeking The Gold) Won sole start over 1m at 2, later outstanding 8-10f performer, won Prix Jacques le Marois-Gr1, Queen Elizabeth II S-Gr1, Dubai World Cup-Gr1, Princess of Wales's S-Gr1. By top-class 6f+ US dirt performer out of 12-14f Group winner from outstanding family. Sole crop of 2yos includes Gr1 winner Dubawi. **Dam Ajhiba** Unraced at 2, 10f Listed winner from 3 starts at 3. Half-sister to several talented runners, notably high-class 2yo/miler Second Empire (by Fairy King) from family of Salsabil. Her one earlier foal is unraced. **Conclusion** Reasonable amount of stamina on the dam's side, which suggests Belenus should be effective over 1m and has a decent chance of staying 10f. Unlikely to have the stamina for 12f, however. On pedigree, there is every prospect he will do well from 2 to 3.

Berenson (Ire) 114

b c Entrepreneur - On Air (Fr) (Chief Singer) March 17
Owner Mrs T Stack **Trainer** T Stack **Breeder** Jerry O'Brien
2 starts: won **1**, second **1**, £49,591 win & place prize-money

---

THE Ballydoyle inmates Oratorio and Ad Valorem topped the pecking order among the Irish two-year-old colts in 2004, but Berenson wasn't too far behind them and who's to say he won't make a better three-year-old than either of them.

Although bred to benefit from more time, Berenson had clearly given out all the right signals before his debut in a seven-furlong maiden at The Curragh, for he already boasted some classy entries and was sent off favourite at 7-2 in a field of 18. He won well and, while nobody could argue it was a strong maiden by the track's usual high standards (Email From Josh, who finished 11th, was the sole winner to emerge from it), it was a promising start.

A variety of options were nominated for Berenson, but connections aimed high and ran him next in the Group 1 National Stakes, over the same course and distance a month later but on softer ground, even though it meant taking on the might not only of Ballydoyle, but also of Godolphin.

Seven furlongs proved too sharp for Berenson in that grade, but he stayed on stoutly to finish a fine second behind Dubawi, whose third win in three starts saw him elevated to favouritism for the Derby. Although beaten three lengths by Dubawi, Berenson was clear of Russian Blue

Race record

2nd Dunnes Stores National Stakes (Group 1) (Curragh, September 19) 2yo 7f Yielding **114** (TS 110)
7 ran.
1st Mongey Communications EBF Maiden (Curragh, August 21) 2yo 7f Good to firm **85** (TS 79)
18 ran.

Pedigree assessment

Sire Entrepreneur (Sadler's Wells) Dual 7-8f winner at 2, won 2,000 Guineas and 4th Derby at
3. Brother to Oaks 2nd Dance A Dream and half-brother to 1m Gr1 winner Exclusive. Patchy record as
sire, though responsible for top-class 2yo Damson and Irish Oaks winner Vintage Tipple. Most progeny
quite late-developing. **Dam On Air** Dual 10f winner at 6, also won over hurdles. Half-sister to 12f
Gr2 winner Another Dancer out of daughter of 10f Sun Chariot Stakes winner Ranimer. Her 2 earlier
foals include Berenson's full-sister Swiss Roll, a fair 12-14f winner. **Conclusion** Far from certain to
stay as far as his sister, but likely to last 10f in time. Judged on sire's record and dam's family, should
make good progress from 2 to 3.

and Democratic Deficit, both of whom had already shown smart form
in Group company, so there is little reason to knock the form. Indeed a
Racing Post Rating of 114 may even underestimate him.

Berenson is presumably earmarked for the Irish Derby, and if all goes
well with him in the meantime he ought to be right in the reckoning.
There is plenty of stamina on the dam's side. *GD*

Birthstone 104

ch f Machiavellian (USA) - Baya (USA) (Nureyev (USA)) March 24
Owner Sheikh Mohammed **Trainer** H-A Pantall **Breeder** Darley
2 starts: won **2**, **£36,619** win & place prize-money

HER two-year-old campaign comprised just two races and she was not
tested at the highest level. Nevertheless, the Sheikh Mohammed-owned
Birthstone made a big impression and her background suggests she is
sure to figure in the French Classics.

Birthstone made her debut in very soft ground over a mile at Deauville
at the end of August and won by half a length and three from Torte and
Tivadare, both of whom were previous winners. Stepped up to Group
3 company for the Prix d'Aumale on much faster ground at Chantilly
17 days later it was more of the same, and in a field of six she took it
up a furlong and a half out and needed merely pushing out to win
comfortably, by a length and a half from Portrayal, who was in the same
ownership.

There was talk of supplementing Birthstone for the Prix Marcel
Boussac, but Sheikh Mohammed relied on Portrayal there. Portrayal
was only just run out of the places behind two-length winner Divine

Proportions, and it is a fair bet that Birthstone would have made her presence felt.

Birthstone's dam Baya did not race at two, but she was smartly off the blocks at three and went close in both the Poule d'Essai des Pouliches and the Prix de Diane, in the latter race beaten only a nose by Shemaka in a controversial finish. Expect Birthstone to make a bold bid to make amends. *GD*

Race record

1st Prix d'Aumale (Group 3) (Chantilly, September 13) 2yo 1m Good **104** (TS 90) 6 ran.
1st Prix de Tanit (Round Course) (Deauville, August 27) 2yo 1m Very soft **79** 7 ran.

Pedigree assessment

Sire Machiavellian (Mr Prospector) Top-class 2yo over 6-7f, won Prix Morny and Prix de la Salamandre. High-class miler at 3, 2nd in 2,000 Guineas. By outstanding sire out of outstanding broodmare, most family members best around 1m. Very good sire, fair record with 2yos (Best Of The Bests, Titus Livius) but better record with older horses, mainly over 6-10f (Almutawakel, Medicean, Storming Home, Rebecca Sharp, Street Cry). Does get occasional high-class 12f+ performer. **Dam Baya** (Nureyev) High-class 10-11f 3yo in France, won Prix de la Grotte-Gr3 and 2nd Prix de Diane-Gr1. Very closely related to high-class 10f+ performer Narrative out of Gr3-winning sister to Triptych. Baya's 5 earlier foals include quite useful miler Bayberry. **Conclusion** Should be effective over the French distaff Classic distances of 1m and 10f. Superbly bred, and family members generally progressive, so not hard to see this one proving top class.

Blue Dakota (Ire) 106

b c Namid - Touraya (Tap On Wood) April 7
Owner A F Nolan, Mrs J M Ryan, Mrs P Duffin **Trainer** J Noseda **Breeder** Michael O'Donnell
5 starts: won **4**, second **0**, third **0**, **£56,880** win & place prize-money

NAMID hardly saw the racecourse as a two- or three-year-old, showing he was a top-flight sprinter only on his final start at four, so with Blue Dakota, the star of his first crop, it has not so far been a case of "like father, like son".

Blue Dakota was the most precocious horse of his generation, the speediest two-year-old around – but only from April until June. Well below form on his only start in July, at Glorious Goodwood, he did not get a chance to put the emerging two-year-olds through their paces in the second half of the season.

"There's no reason to say he won't train on, he has the physical scope," observed Jeremy Noseda, Blue Dakota's trainer, in June, "but he is very well developed already so we will campaign him hard this year and worry about next year at the end of the season."

Blue Dakota, right, wins the Norfolk Stakes at Royal Ascot

Blue Dakota had certainly been busy until that point, stamping his authority on the two-year-old sprint scene as early as April 15 when he made his debut in a Newmarket maiden. Everyone seemed to know that Noseda had a talented youngster to go to war with, as he was heavily backed down to 10-11. There was no mistaking it when Blue Dakota scorched home by five lengths. The starting prices were 1-8 and 2-9 when Blue Dakota added, from the front, a novice stakes and a conditions stakes at Windsor in the space of one week in May, on the second occasion beating a useful sort in Beaver Patrol, and he looked one of the bankers of the meeting when he turned up next at Royal Ascot.

The Norfolk Stakes was his for the taking, despite the presence of two runners in Maktoum colours and representatives of Aidan O'Brien and Richard Hannon. At 5-4, Blue Dakota duly obliged but this time he had a fight on his hands after disputing a very strong early pace with the Godolphin colt Skywards. Blue Dakota looked to be travelling much the better in that duel but from one and a half furlongs out he had to dig deep as Skywards kept on and, posing the bigger threat, Mystical Land closed him down to get within a neck.

Given six weeks off, Blue Dakota tried six furlongs for the first time in the Richmond Stakes at Goodwood and it didn't work out. Trying to put him under a firm grip early on might have been counterproductive, as he failed to settle, and jockey Eddie Ahern later speculated that his mount might well have pulled a muscle in his hind quarters. For whatever reason, Blue Dakota failed to respond when switched to make his challenge.

Race record

6th Richmond Stakes (Group 2) (Goodwood, July 30) 2yo 6f Good to firm **89** (TS 57) 8 ran.
1st Norfolk Stakes (Group 3) (Ascot, June 17) 2yo 5f Good to firm **106** (TS 97) 9 ran.
1st Court House Clinics Conditions Stakes (Windsor, May 17) 2yo 5f Good to firm **100** (TS 74) 6 ran.
1st Sandhurst Marquees Novice Stakes (Windsor, May 10) 2yo 5f Soft **96** (TS 76) 5 ran.
1st Creature Comforts EBF Maiden Stakes (Newmarket, April 15) 2yo 5f Good **98** (TS 71) 8 ran.

Pedigree assessment

Sire Namid (Indian Ridge) Smart 6f 2yo winner, later top-class sprinter, won Prix de l'Abbaye. By high-class sprinter and very good sire. First 2yos in 2004, good haul of early 5-6f winners led by Blue Dakota. **Dam Touraya** Winner over 1m at 3 in France. By top-class miler from family of Damson. Her 10 earlier foals include very smart 2yo Tarwiya and 2 winners (over 6f and 7f) by Indian Ridge. **Conclusion** Bred to be fast, and no pretensions to being other than a sprinter. Namid is an unknown quantity with his progeny aged 3+, but there has to be a fair chance Blue Dakota will not match the progress from 2 to 3 of some of his contemporaries.

Caesar Beware (Ire)   112

b g Daggers Drawn (USA) - Red Shareef (Marju (Ire)) February 8
Owner H E Sheikh Rashid Bin Mohammed **Trainer** H Candy **Breeder** Glending Bloodstock
4 starts: won **3**, second **1**, **£232,725** win & place prize-money

AS A gelding, Caesar Beware has no pretensions to Classic glory. However, he might still emerge as a contender for major honours at six or seven furlongs, possibly even a mile. His impressive win in the St Leger Yearling Stakes was one of the juvenile performances of the season, and there was an excuse on the occasion of his only defeat in a four-race campaign.

Chepstow seldom plays host to a top-class two-year-old, but it was the chosen venue for Caesar Beware's introduction and his reputation preceded him. A gambled-on favourite in a field of 18, he won in style from Don Pele, who went on to win his next two races, including a Listed race at Newbury. Two months later Caesar Beware was even more impressive in a conditions race at Windsor, settling the issue in strides and storming home six lengths clear of Al Qudra.

A red-hot favourite for the St Leger Yearling Stakes at Doncaster despite an interrupted preparation and a moderate draw, he came from a fair way back on the outside of the stands-side group and forged to the front 100 yards out before coming away to win by two lengths from Distinctly Game in course-record time.

The opportunity to go for another big pot at Redcar three weeks later proved impossible to resist and Caesar Beware was sent off a 4-7 chance in a field of 24 for the betfair.com Two-Year-Old Trophy, in which he was running for the first time in the colours of Sheikh Rashid. However,

Doncaster may have taken more out of him than was apparent at the time, especially after the difficulties in preparing him for that race, and he was a long way below form in finishing second to Obe Gold, only just in front of two 33-1 chances.

With the benefit of a winter in Dubai, Caesar Beware should be a force to reckon with at three. A reproduction of the Doncaster form would be more than enough to win many Group 2 or Group 3 races, and if he improves a few pounds so much the better. *GD*

Race record

2nd betfair.com Two-Year-Old Trophy (Listed) (Redcar, October 2) 2yo 6f Good to firm **101** (TS 99) 24 ran.
1st £200,000 St Leger Yearling Stakes (Doncaster, September 8) 2yo 6f Good **112** (TS 106) 22 ran.
1st Ian Hutchinson Memorial Conditions Stakes (Windsor, August 8) 2yo 6f Good to firm **107** (TS 95) 6 ran.
1st Wendy Fair Markets Maiden Auction Stakes (Chepstow, June 3) 2yo 6f Good **97** (TS 70) 18 ran.

Pedigree assessment

Sire Daggers Drawn (Diesis) High-class 6-7f 2yo, won Richmond S-Gr2 and Champagne S-Gr2. Very disappointing in 2 starts at 3 over 1m. By top-class 2yo and very good sire, out of fair 6-8f filly from good middle-distance family. Oldest progeny 3, has sired several very useful performers in northern hemisphere, mainly around 8-10f, but no stand-outs. **Dam Red Shareef** Won 3 races in Italy over 8-11f. By top-class miler out of 7f 2yo Listed winner. This is her first foal. **Conclusion** Should be effective over further than 6f and has every chance of staying 1m, but others may have more scope for improvement from 2 to 3.

Cape Columbine 98

b f Diktat - Cape Merino (Clantime) January 31
Owner Mrs R F Lowe **Trainer** D R C Elsworth **Breeder** Templeton Stud
2 starts: won **1**, second **1**, **£71,300** win & place prize-money

DAVID ELSWORTH can look back upon Newmarket's big autumn meetings with considerable satisfaction. Spanish Don's 100-1 win in the big race made for a memorable Cambridgeshire meeting. A fortnight later it was the turn of the fillies, Cape Columbine netting a massive prize in the Tattersalls Autumn Auction Stakes and Something Exciting winning the Houghton Conditions Stakes.

In pure form terms, Something Exciting's impressive defeat of colts shades it. But the Houghton was Something Exciting's sixth race. What Cape Columbine lacks so far in achievement is more than made up for in potential, for the filly's two-length defeat of Redcar's Two-Year-Old Trophy winner Obe Gold in a field of 29 came just two weeks after she had been beaten at Goodwood on her racecourse debut.

Cape Columbine is massive by juvenile filly standards and dwarfed her opponents at Goodwood, where she was beaten only by lack of experience on a track that one would not have expected to suit her. She looked a certain future winner in going down by just a short head to odds-on favourite Love Thirty, but at the time few can have expected her to get off the mark quite so soon, or in such a competitive affair. Not that there was any shortage of confidence behind her at Newmarket, for she started 5-1 joint favourite. She looked to have an impossible task when detached in last in the middle of three groups but made up ground hand over fist to lead well inside the final furlong and win by two lengths, going away.

It remains to be seen if Cape Columbine stays well enough to be a genuine Guineas contender, but she will be given her chance in one of the trials. A half-sister to the good Hong Kong-based sprinter Cape Of Good Hope, who also started his career with Elsworth, she probably has speed in excess of stamina but is undoubtedly very promising. *GD*

Race record

1st £100,000 Tattersalls Autumn Auction Stakes (Newmarket, October 14) 2yo 6f Soft **98** (TS 80) 29 ran.
2nd EBF Paddy Power Median Auction Maiden Fillies' Stakes (Goodwood, September 30) 2yo 6f Good **78** (TS 79) 10 ran.

Pedigree assessment

Sire Diktat (Warning) Unplaced sole start at 2, later top-class 6-8f performer, won Prix Maurice de Gheest-Gr1, Haydock Sprint Cup-Gr1, also won 2 7f Gr3 races and Gr1 placed over 1m. By top-class miler, from excellent family of 2yos and milers. Oldest progeny 2, sire of 7f Gr3 winner Diktatorial. **Dam Cape Merino** Very useful sprint 2yo, won 6f Redcar 2yo Trophy, later quite useful sprinter. Speedily but modestly bred. Her 2 earlier foals feature high-class sprinter Cape Of Good Hope (by Inchinor). **Conclusion** Winner over 6f, and that may be her trip at 3. May last 7f but no further. Both sire and half-brother progressed well with age, suggesting this one may do better still in 2005.

Captain Hurricane 107

b c Desert Style (Ire) - Ravine (Indian Ridge) February 11
Owner The Comic Strip Heroes **Trainer** P W Chapple-Hyam **Breeder** Highclere Stud Ltd
5 starts: won **1**, second **2**, third **0**, **£56,456** win & place prize-money

AFTER defeats, albeit narrow ones, at Yarmouth and Salisbury, Captain Hurricane got it right in the Group 2 TNT July Stakes at Newmarket. If those first two performances had needed a little fine-tuning, Captain Hurricane's run in the July Stakes could not have been tuned any finer. For he was the only maiden against six previous winners who had already acquitted themselves well in Group or Listed events.

Coventry Stakes runner-up Council Member set a steady pace in the face of a stiff headwind, with Captain Hurricane and Norfolk Stakes runner-up Mystical Land asked at the furlong marker to pull out all the stops

Captain Hurricane, nearside, gets up in the July Stakes

in their pursuit of the favourite, both making inroads and Captain Hurricane nailing Council Member on the line. Mystical Land ran out of room in the last 100 yards but would not have won.

Captain Hurricane did not win again and did not look like winning. The Prix Morny pitched him against some very classy rivals on soft ground and he was not disgraced in finishing six lengths fourth of nine, but he reportedly finished sore in the valuable sales race won by Caesar Beware at Doncaster and was not seen again.

With some free-going tendencies to curb, Captain Hurricane looked very much a sprinter as a two-year-old and might well struggle to get a mile at three. It's too early to state his ground preferences. *RA*

Race record

16th £200000 St Leger Yearling Stakes (Doncaster, September 8) 2yo 6f Good **93** (TS 73) 22 ran.

4th Prix Morny Casinos Barriere (Group 1) (Deauville, August 22) 2yo 6f Very soft **105** (TS 96) 9 ran.

1st TNT July Stakes (Group 2) (Newmarket (July), July 7) 2yo 6f Good to firm **107** (TS 75) 7 ran.

2nd Piper Heidsieck Champagne Auction Stakes (Conditions Race) (Salisbury, June 24) 2yo 6f Good **92** (TS 78) 10 ran.

2nd EBF Novice Median Auction Stakes (Yarmouth, June 10) 2yo 6f Firm **78** (TS 76) 5 ran.

Pedigree assessment

Sire Desert Style (Green Desert) Very smart 6-7f performer at 2 and 3. By top-class 6-8f performer and very good sire, from family of Barathea. Fair record as stallion, sire of dual Classic-winning miler Bachir and Deutsches Derby winner Next Desert. **Dam Ravine** Unplaced sole start at 2, dual 6-7f winner at 3. Half-sister to high-class 2yo/miler Niche from family of varied performers, including Little Wolf, Sheikh Albadou and Smuggler. This is her first foal. **Conclusion** Likely to prove best at 6-7f.

Centaurus   96

gr c Daylami (Ire) - Dandanna (Ire) (Linamix (Fr)) January 26
Owner Godolphin **Trainer** Saeed Bin Suroor **Breeder** Newgate Stud Co
1 start: won **1**, **£4,998** win & place prize-money

THE Godolphin team have stacks of juvenile talent to work with to produce a smart three-year-old squad and Centaurus could be an important member of it.

Fairly strong in the market on his debut in an end-of-season seven-furlong maiden at Newmarket, Centaurus showed plenty of natural speed before defeating another smart prospect, Master Of The Race, by a length and a quarter.

The form looks very strong – good enough to suggest that Centaurus should win Listed races at least – and, with the likelihood of significantly better to come as he steps up in trip, Centaurus looks highly likely to win at Pattern level in 2005. *ST*

Race record
1st EBF Maiden Stakes (Newmarket, October 30) 2yo 7f Good to soft **96** (TS 98) 19 ran.

Pedigree assessment
Sire Daylami (Doyoun) Very smart 1m winner at 2, top-class miler at 3 (won Poulains), later top-class and very tough 10-12f performer, won Eclipse S, King George and Breeders' Cup Turf. Oldest progeny 3, sire of Irish Derby winner Grey Swallow, most progeny make good progress from 2 to 3 and stay beyond 1m. **Dam Dandanna** Winner over 6f at 2 on only start. Likely to have stayed at least 10f on pedigree, by very good French sire of 1m+ performers, half-sister to very smart 10f+ colt Courteous out of sister to Darshaan from excellent middle-distance family. This is her first foal. **Conclusion** Judged on both sides of his pedigree, he is likely to make good progress from 2 to 3 and stay at least 10f, with 12f a strong possibility. Has the pedigree to be at least very smart.

Centifolia (Fr)   114

gr f Kendor (Fr) - Djayapura (Fr) (Fabulous Dancer (USA)) March 15
Owner S Berland **Trainer** Robert Collet **Breeder** Sca De La Perrigne
5 starts: won **4**, second **0**, third **0**, **£109,366** win & place prize-money

THERE'S a chance that Centifolia will turn out to be a sprinter, but if she gets a mile she will merit plenty of respect in the 1,000 Guineas or its French equivalent, the Poule d'Essai des Pouliches. While the Pouliches tends to be the softer option, trainer Robert Collet is not one to duck a challenge and had a crack at the 2,000 Guineas in May 2004 with Whipper, another whose stamina was unproven at the time.

The filly staked her claim when making all of the running to win the six-furlong Criterium de Maisons-Laffitte by two lengths from Salut Thomas and Campo Bueno, two colts who already had solid Group-race form to their names. It was her fourth win, and with British challengers Prince Charming and Obe Gold, both of them solid yardsticks with Racing Post Ratings in the low 100s, behind in fourth and fifth, the form is hard to fault.

Collet, who was in Texas supervising Whipper's Breeders' Cup preparation, said: "She is a classy filly with plenty of speed. Centifolia will reappear in the Prix Imprudence and will be entered in the 1,000 Guineas and the Poule d'Essai des Pouliches."

The one note of caution was sounded by jockey Ioritz Mendizabal, France's new champion jockey, who said: "She is very fast and she may not stay much further than six furlongs."

One can understand Mendizabal's stamina worries, for just a fortnight earlier Centifolia had been impressive over five furlongs in a Listed race on the same course, when a four-length winner from Salut Thomas. But there is nothing to lose by trying her over a mile, and if she can sustain her speed over the extra distance she could be top class. If she doesn't stay, there are good opportunities over sprint distances. *GD*

Race record

1st Criterium de Maisons-Laffitte (Group 2) (Maisons-Laffitte, October 29) 2yo 6f Very soft **114** (TS 116) 9 ran.
1st Criterium de Vitesse (Listed Race) (Maisons-Laffitte, October 15) 2yo 5f Holding **111** (TS 78) 7 ran.
1st Prix de Pontpoint (Chantilly, September 28) 2yo 6f Good **102** (TS 56) 8 ran.
10th Criterium du Bequet (Listed) (La Teste De Buch, August 8) 2yo 6f Good **54** 10 ran.
1st Prix La Belle II (Unraced Fillies) (Maisons-Laffitte, July 17) 2yo 6f Good (TS 63) 12 ran.

Pedigree assessment

Sire **Kendor** (Kenmare) Top-class 2yo and miler in France, won Grand Criterium-Gr1, Poule d'Essai des Poulains-Gr1. Good sire in France, has sired top-class 2yos (Charge d'Affaires) and milers (Keltos), capable of siring smart middle-distance horses. Dam **Djayapura** Middle-distance winner at 3 in France. Half-sister to smart 10f filly Green Oasis, from family with smart performers ranging from sprinters to stayers. Her one previous foal was placed on the Flat in France. **Conclusion** Shows a lot of speed and has so far won only over 5-6f, but pedigree gives her a good chance of staying 1m.

Chateau Istana 109

ch c **Grand Lodge** (USA) - **Miss Queen** (USA) (**Miswaki** (USA)) April 26
Owner Ivan Allan **Trainer** N P Littmoden **Breeder** High Bramley Grange Stud Ltd
6 starts: won **3**, second **0**, third **0**, £70,699 win & place prize-money

IF Chateau Istana wins good races in 2005, he will be flying in the face of an ugly trend. Since 1990, 12 Flying Childers winners have appeared in Europe as three-year-olds, running a total of 69 times for just three wins: Paris House won a Listed race in 1992, Cayman Kai the Free Handicap in 1996 and Land Of Dreams the King George Stakes in 1998. Expectations for the Group-winning sprinters so often have to be lowered when they turn three, particularly when they have to shoulder a Group 2 penalty.

Chateau Istana's Flying Childers success came in undeniably good style, working his way to the front one and a half furlongs out and stretching his advantage over Molecomb Stakes winner Tournedos to two lengths at the line, with the first five strung out. He was an above-average winner of the race.

That was the high point of Chateau Istana's first season, but there were obvious low points as well, the Flying Childers result being easily the biggest reminder, if not the only one, of the day he'd emerged as a classy sprinter three months earlier. Chateau Istana first, Tournedos second, had also been the result of the Windsor Castle Stakes at Royal Ascot, in which Leicester maiden winner Chateau Istana had gradually emerged from mid-division, despite being hit over the head with a whip, and led 100 yards out to beat Tournedos by half a length.

Race record

9th Shadwell Stud Middle Park Stakes (Group 1) (Newmarket, October 1) 2yo 6f Good **102** (TS 79) 9 ran.
1st Polypipe Flying Childers Stakes (Group 2) (Doncaster, September 11) 2yo 5f Firm **109** (TS 70) 11 ran.
7th TNT July Stakes (Group 2) (Newmarket (July), July 7) 2yo 6f Good to firm **71** (TS 37) 7 ran.
1st Windsor Castle Stakes (Listed) (Ascot, June 15) 2yo 5f Good to firm **100** (TS 98) 15 ran.
1st BBC Radio Leicester Maiden Stakes (Leicester, May 18) 2yo 5f Good to firm **95** (TS 77) 10 ran.
6th windsor-racecourse.co.uk Maiden Stakes (Windsor, April 19) 2yo 5f Good to soft **63** (TS 48) 9 ran.

Pedigree assessment

Sire **Grand Lodge** (Chief's Crown) Top-class 2yo, won Dewhurst S-Gr1, later top-class 8-10f colt, won St James's Palace S-Gr1. Very good sire, has good record with 2yos (Chateau Istana, Queen's Logic, Raise A Grand) but better one with 3yos over 1m+ (Grandera, Indian Lodge, Sinndar). **Dam Miss Queen** Sprint winner at 3 on dirt in US. By sire who has good record wth 2yos, sprinters and milers with occasional good 10f+ horse. Half-sister to smart 6f 2yo winner Tajannub. Her 2 earlier foals are Chateau Istana's very modest sister Miss You, placed over 7f, and useful 7-8f winner Mandobi (Mark Of Esteem). **Conclusion** Has won 2 stakes events over 5f, but pedigree entitles him to get further, although 1m probably beyond him in good company.

It looks significant that all three of Chateau Istana's victories were on fast ground. It was good to soft on his unsuccessful debut and there was some give in the ground when he finished last of nine in the Middle Park on his final outing, though he also faced his toughest task in the latter and did not settle too well on his step up to six furlongs. He had one previous attempt over that trip when also trailing the entire field in the July Stakes, a far worse effort but one seemingly explained when he went down with an infection soon afterwards.

Chateau Istana was a first Royal Ascot winner for his jockey Tom Queally, trainer Nick Littmoden and owner Ivan Allan. Queally went on to be champion apprentice. Allan, who ended his training career in Hong

Chateau Istana, no.2, takes the Windsor Castle Stakes

Kong in June, also owned, among others, Commanche Run, who took the main event at Doncaster 20 years before the St Leger day success of Chateau Istana. Littmoden's record with enduring sprinters such as Cretan Gift, Peruvian Chief and Smokin Beau offers hope that Chateau Istana will not sink without trace, like some of his Flying Childers-winning predecessors. *RA*

Chelsea Rose   106

See entry in the top 100 horses, page 98

Clear Impression (Ire) 84

b f Danehill (USA) - Shining Hour (USA) (Red Ransom (USA)) January 7
Owner Exors of the late R E Sangster **Trainer** P W Chapple-Hyam
Breeder Swettenham Stud **1** start: second **1, £3,210** win & place prize-money

DURING his days at Manton, Peter Chapple-Hyam had to sit and suffer when the late Robert Sangster sold subsequent Classic winners

Balanchine and Cape Verdi to Godolphin. Chapple-Hyam enjoys considerably more independence these days at his new base in Newmarket, but one wonders if past experience was in the back of his mind when he kept under wraps the highly promising Clear Impression, another Sangster filly, following her eye-catching maiden second at Glorious Goodwood in July.

Clear Impression, the first foal of Chapple-Hyam's Queen Mary winner Shining Hour, arrived at Goodwood with a big reputation and was sent off 7-4 favourite in a field of eight. She recovered from a slowish start to travel well and look a big danger two out, where there were five in a line, but despite forging four lengths and more clear of the pack she had run up against a smart rival in Suez, who knew her job and beat her by two and a half lengths.

Both fillies shaped as if they might have Classic potential, and Suez confirmed it by winning a Listed race at Salisbury and going down by just a neck to Magical Romance in the Cheveley Park Stakes, after which she joined Godolphin. Clear Impression wasn't seen again, but Chapple-Hyam confirmed at the end of the season that all was well with her, and that she remains as highly regarded as ever. Although still a maiden, it would be no surprise if she started 2005 in one of the trials. *GD*

Race record

2nd Findon Maiden Fillies' Stakes (Goodwood, July 28) 2yo 6f Good **84** (TS 83) 8 ran.

Pedigree assessment

Sire **Danehill** (Danzig) Useful 6f 2yo winner, improved at 3 into top-class sprinter, won Haydock Sprint Cup but also smart over 1m. Excellent sire, has done well with 2yos and older progeny, mainly at up to 1m but capable of getting top-class 10f+ performers from stout female families. Best progeny include Aquarelliste, Banks Hill, Cacique, Desert King, Landseer, Mozart, North Light, Oratorio, Rock Of Gibraltar, Westerner. Dam **Shining Hour** Smart 2yo, won Queen Mary S-Gr2, not seen again. Sister to Titian Time (2nd 2004 Prix Marcel Boussac-Gr1). By top-class US performer and very good sire with talented horses across the distance spectrum, out of useful 7-10f 3yo. This is her first foal. Conclusion Had the pedigree to make a very smart 6f 2yo but not seen out after debut. At 3, her distance ceiling will be a mile, and she may well prove best at slightly shorter.

Cupid's Glory 108

b c Pursuit Of Love - Doctor's Glory (USA) (Elmaamul (USA)) April 9
Owner Hesmonds Stud **Trainer** Sir Mark Prescott **Breeder** Cheveley Park Stud
7 starts: won **4**, second **0**, third **1**, **£53,287** win & place prize-money

---

"I'VE no idea what happens in March, April and May. It's a completely new kingdom for me!" So said Sir Mark Prescott after Cupid's Glory had stamped himself a live 2,000 Guineas outsider with an impressive soft-ground win in the Horris Hill Stakes at Newbury.

Cupid's Glory was a strong favourite that afternoon, and in conditions that blunted the speed of most horses he managed to pick up impressively when switched and asked to go and win his race, coming home four lengths clear of Johnny Jumpup. He had won three of his five previous races, including a nursery on the Polytrack at Lingfield off a mark of 93, and he had also been third to the subsequent Middle Park winner Ad Valorem in what turned out to be a very warm Listed affair at The Curragh.

A little of the gloss was taken off a campaign that had seen Cupid's Glory improve relentlessly when he was only fourth to Helios Quercus in the Group 1 Criterium International at Saint-Cloud, for Prescott had supplemented him for the race and clearly hoped for better. However, while that two-and-a-half-length defeat arguably exposed Cupid's Glory's limitations, it may have been too stiff a test of stamina at that stage of his career.

Soft ground clearly suits Cupid's Glory extremely well, and for that reason it would be no surprise if he sidesteps Newmarket in favour of a crack at the French Guineas, which is usually a weaker race. But whichever race he goes for, you can expect to see him out months ahead of most of his stablemates in order to make the most of any ease in the ground. *GD*

Race record

4th Criterium International (Group 1) (Saint-Cloud, October 31) 2yo 1m Very soft **108** (TS 97) 8 ran.

1st Stan James Horris Hill Stakes (Group 3) (Newbury, October 22) 2yo 7f Soft **108** (TS 107) 13 ran.

3rd St Bernard Blenheim Stakes (Listed) (Curragh, September 19) 2yo 6f Yielding **104** (TS 78) 6 ran.

1st Castlemaine XXXX Nursery (Lingfield (AW), August 26) 2yo 7f Standard **103** (TS 98) 14 ran.

1st Blue Square Pays Double Results Conditions Stakes (Chester, August 21) 2yo 6f Soft **97** (TS 96) 5 ran.

1st lingfield-racecourse.co.uk EBF Median Auction Maiden Stakes (Div I) (Lingfield (AW), August 9) 2yo 6f Standard **87** (TS 82) 10 ran.

6th Jap Kitchen Contracts Median Auction Maiden Stakes (Div I) (Lingfield (AW), July 21) 2yo 7f Standard **68** (TS 44) 13 ran.

Pedigree assessment

Sire **Pursuit Of Love** (Groom Dancer) Very useful 7f 2yo winner, later high-class 6-8f performer, won Prix Maurice de Gheest-Gr1, 2nd July Cup, 3rd 2,000 Guineas. By top-class 10f performer from high-class speed-orientated family. Fair sire, has good record with 2yos at up to 7f, older performers often speedy but some (Catchascatchcan, Love Everlasting) have stayed at least 10f Dam **Doctor's Glory** Fair winner of 2 races over 5-6f at 2 and 3, also placed over 7f. Half-sister to very useful stayer On Call (by Alleged) from speedy family of Cassandra Go and Verglas. Her 3 earlier foals include Cupid's Glory's full-sister Courting, a useful 7f 2yo and 8-10f 3yo winner, and 1m winner Instructor (by Groom Dancer). **Conclusion** Lots of speed on both sides of family but has already outstayed his pedigree.

Damson 110

See entry in the top 100 horses, page 114

Dark Cheetah (USA) 108

b c Storm Cat (USA) - Layounne (USA) (Mt. Livermore (USA)) April 18
Owner Mrs John Magnier **Trainer** A P O'Brien **Breeder** Brushwood Stable
3 starts: won **2**, second **0**, third **0**, £39,877 win & place prize-money

WHEN a horse wins a nursery impressively off a rating in the high 90s
it usually indicates a Pattern-class performer. Dark Cheetah is a case in
point.

Off the mark on his debut in a four-runner maiden over five furlongs
at Cork on fast ground, the son of Storm Cat then stepped up in class
at Royal Ascot, apparently running a slightly disappointing race in the
Windsor Castle Stakes, finishing seventh behind Chateau Istana.

On the strength of those efforts an official handicap mark of 99 looked
rather harsh but Dark Cheetah had clearly improved plenty by the
autumn when he had his third and final start in a six-furlong nursery on
easy ground at Naas, where he ran out an impressive two-and-a-half-
length winner in a fast time.

Following the race Aidan O'Brien said: "We thought a lot of him but
he jarred a joint at Ascot and he's not that long back. It's possible he
could go for the Kilavullan Stakes at Leopardstown."

Dark Cheetah did not appear again in 2004 but the form of his
nursery win marks him down as a horse well capable of winning Pattern

Race record
1st Derrinstown Stud EBF Birdcatcher Premier Nursery (Naas, October 17) 2yo 6f Yielding to soft **108**
(TS 105) 13 ran.
7th Windsor Castle Stakes (Listed) (Ascot, June 15) 2yo 5f Good to firm **88** (TS 85) 15 ran.
1st Fermoy Maiden (Cork, May 28) 2yo 5f Firm **88** 4 ran.

Pedigree assessment
Sire **Storm Cat** (Storm Bird) Top-class US dirt 2yo, very lightly raced at 3. By top-class European
2yo from strong, speedy family of Royal Academy. Excellent sire, particularly of dirt performers, good
record with European 2yos (One Cool Cat, Denebola, Hold That Tiger) and older 7-10f performers
(Aljabr, Black Minnaloushe, Giant's Causeway, Nebraska Tornado, Sophisticat). Dam **Layounne**
Placed on turf in US. Half-sister to smart sprint 2yo Bernstein and Grade 3 winners Caress and
Country Cat (all by Storm Cat), and also to very smart 7-10f performer Della Francesca (by Danzig).
Her one earlier foal won at 2 in US. **Conclusion** Lots of speed in this pedigree, so though he
could last 1m he has a good chance of proving best over 6-7f.

Dark Cheetah wins a Naas nursery but is set to go higher

races. Likely to be at his best over a mile or shorter, Dark Cheetah is another potentially smart three-year-old in the making for Team Ballydoyle. *ST*

Dash To The Top 110

b f Montjeu (Ire) - Millennium Dash (Nashwan (USA)) February 20
Owner Helena Springfield Ltd **Trainer** L M Cumani **Breeder** Meon Valley Stud
3 starts: won **1**, second **1**, third **1**, **£29,245** win & place prize-money

MOTIVATOR is not the only Classic prospect by first-season sire Montjeu. The filly Dash To The Top was very green in her three starts and looks sure to relish middle distances at three, but nevertheless she was good enough to finish third in the Group 1 Fillies' Mile at Ascot.

Dash To The Top looked very inexperienced in a pair of mile maidens, when taking second at Nottingham (at 14-1) and when getting up late on at Leicester, so she went to Ascot as a filly of obviously untapped potential. She had still not got the message.

A 16-1 chance, she looked unsettled in the early stages and entered the straight four horses wide, before proceeding to run all over the place. She carried her head high and edged right, brushed Mona Lisa two furlongs out and then swerved left under the whip just before the furlong marker. It was only in the last 100 yards that she seemed to knuckle down a bit better and she was running on well at the post, where she was one and three-quarter lengths behind the winner, Playful Act.

Greenness can sometimes turn into something more worrying, but Dash To The Top must be given the chance to show what she can do with more time and distance. Firm ground could be another mitigating factor at Ascot and remember that Montjeu too was known for carrying his head high and sometimes going off a straight line.

Dash To The Top is from a fine family and has the physique of a filly who is highly likely to improve as a three-year-old. The final word goes to Luca Cumani, who said: "She should do very well over a mile and a half next year and she's an Oaks filly through and through." *RA*

Race record

3rd Meon Valley Stud Fillies' Mile (Group 1) (Ascot, September 25) 2yo 1m Good to firm **110** (TS 105) 9 ran.
1st EBF Filbert Maiden Fillies' Stakes (Leicester, September 7) 2yo 1m Good to firm **79** (TS 85) 13 ran.
2nd BBAG Baden-Badener Yearling Sales Maiden Fillies' Stakes (Nottingham, August 18) 2yo 1m Good to soft **77** (TS 94) 18 ran.

Pedigree assessment

Sire **Montjeu** (Sadler's Wells) Useful dual 8-9f 2yo winner, progressed into outstanding 12f performer at 3 and 4, won Prix du Jockey-Club, Irish Derby, Arc, King George, also dual Gr1 winner over 10f. Stoutly bred, out of very smart stayer by Top Ville. First 2yos in 2004 include Racing Post Trophy winner Motivator, Gr1-placed Walk In The Park and Listed winners Ayam Zaman and Kings Quay. **Dam Millennium Dash** Unraced at 2, very lightly raced 10f winner at 3. By top-class 8-12f performer out of top-class miler Milligram. This is her first foal. **Conclusion** Bred to make considerable progress from 2 to 3 (little precocity on either side of her pedigree) and should appreciate at least 10f, with 12f likely to be within her capabilities. That should make her a serious Oaks candidate.

Democratic Deficit (Ire) 110

b c Soviet Star (USA) - Grandiose Idea (Ire) (Danehill (USA)) January 31
Owner D H W Dobson **Trainer** J S Bolger **Breeder** J S Bolger
5 starts: won **2**, second **1**, third **0**, **£95,161** win & place prize-money

"HOW can 59,017,382 people be so DUMB" – Daily Mirror front page, November 4. With the US presidential election going on, the Jim Bolger-trained racehorse was never going to be the Democratic Deficit that occupied minds most in the autumn of 2004. This €50,000 buy earned a place on the ballot paper against the big-money battalions' top campaigners but, in the event, his candidacy proved as futile as that of a Democrat trying to beat George W Bush in Florida.

Democratic Deficit's two Group 1 assignments were the National Stakes at The Curragh and the Prix Jean-Luc Lagardere at Longchamp and no stewards' inquiry was required afterwards to try to ascertain whether he was robbed of victory. In the National Stakes, Democratic Deficit underperformed when trailing Godolphin's Dubawi by seven and a half lengths in fourth, and at Longchamp, although there was plenty of negative campaigning in a rough race up the straight, he was clearly beaten on merit.

The outsider of the field at Longchamp, back on fast ground, Democratic Deficit was held up in rear but well within striking distance, and he threw down a challenge two furlongs out. On the outside, he was disputing the lead at one point but Kevin Manning was having problems keeping him straight. A whip in front of his face did not help as Democratic Deficit's challenge crumbled and Manning gave up on him early in the final furlong, leaving the colours of Mrs Magnier, Khalid Abdullah and Sheikh Mohammed to battle it out for supremacy.

Democratic Deficit had lost out once already to the Lagardere winner Oratorio, in a low turnout for the Futurity Stakes at The Curragh in August, when he was beaten two lengths, giving Oratorio 4lb. Democratic Deficit was putting an unbeaten record on the line that day, after taking an auction maiden at Leopardstown in May and upsetting the O'Brien-trained 1-2 shot Russian Blue by three-quarters of a length in the Railway Stakes at The Curragh.

Democratic Deficit is bred to stay a mile but was not crying out for it as a juvenile. Bred by his trainer, he changed hands at the yearling sales for those €50,000. Democratic Deficit struggling in vain against the established order was the theme in the autumn. Whether anything better can be hoped for in 2005 remains to be seen. *RA*

Race record

5th Prix Jean-Luc Lagardere (Group 1) (Longchamp, October 3) 2yo 7f Good **108** (TS 85) 6 ran.
4th Dunnes Stores National Stakes (Group 1) (Curragh, September 19) 2yo 7f Yielding **103** (TS 96) 7 ran.
2nd Galileo EBF Futurity Stakes (Group 2) (Curragh, August 21) 2yo 7f Good to firm **110** (TS 92) 5 ran.
1st Anheuser Busch Railway Stakes (Group 2) (Curragh, June 27) 2yo 6f Good to firm **107** (TS 88) 7 ran.
1st Irish Stallion Farms EBF Auction Maiden (Leopardstown, May 9) 2yo 6f Good to yielding **94** (TS 81) 9 ran.

Pedigree assessment

Sire **Soviet Star** (Nureyev) Smart 2yo winner, later tough and top-class 6-8f performer. Decent sire, can get smart 2yos but most of his talented progeny best at 7-10f (Ashkalani, Sensation, Soviet Line, Starborough, Volochine among them). Gets occasional good sprinter and 12f+ horse. **Dam Grandiose Idea** Winner over 1m at 2 from 2 starts. By excellent sire of 2yos, sprinters and milers with occasional top-class middle-distance horse, out of daughter of a high-class US racemare. This is her first foal. **Conclusion** Should stay 1m but no further. No reason on pedigree why he should not train on.

Descartes

86

b c Dubai Millennium - Gold's Dance (Fr) (Goldneyev (USA)) February 5
Owner Godolphin **Trainer** Saeed Bin Suroor **Breeder** Darley
1 start: won **1, £6,734** win & place prize-money

SHEIKH MOHAMMED must have been scouring his massed ranks of Dubai Millennium two-year-olds for any reminders of that late, lamented star. Dubawi did best on the racecourse with his Group 1 win in Ireland, but the less heralded Descartes is another for whom the Sheikh must have high hopes.

Descartes had only one opportunity to impress away from home and that was in the quagmire at Newbury's final Flat meeting in October. There were 15 runners for that mile maiden but very little form going into the race and Descartes was virtually the only contender in whom punters showed any interest, an even-money favourite while the next shortest-priced horse was Peter Chapple-Hyam's Los Organos at 9-1.

After a slow start, Descartes made an unhurried way to the front on the stands rail over two furlongs out and went on to win by a very comfortable length and a quarter from High Card. The runner-up had not shown much in two previous starts and there was not time left in the turf season to put the Newbury result to much of a collateral form test. Los Organos, who finished third, went on to be last of eight in a Newmarket Listed race, so the form probably isn't that special. But there was something striking about the way that Descartes strode through the race, something that prompted memories of Dubai Millennium. *RA*

Race record

1st cantorodds.com EBF Maiden Stakes (Div II) (Newbury, October 23) 2yo 1m Heavy **86** (TS 77) 15 ran.

Pedigree assessment

Sire Dubai Millennium (Seeking The Gold) Won sole start over 1m at 2, later outstanding 8-10f performer, won Prix Jacques le Marois-Gr1, Queen Elizabeth II S-Gr1, Dubai World Cup-Gr1, Princess of Wales's S-Gr1. By top-class 6f+ US dirt performer out of 12-14f Group winner from outstanding family. Sole crop of 2yos includes Gr1 winner Dubawi.
Dam Gold's Dance Dual middle-distance winner in France. Half-sister to 11f Gr3 winner Solveig out of smart middle-distance filly, family of Torrestrella. Her 4 earlier foals feature 2yo 10f Group 1 winner Goldamix (by Linamix), later 3rd in Prix de Diane.
Conclusion Fair amount of stamina on dam's side, which suggests Descartes may well stay 10f. However, 12f more problematical, although sire is an unknown quantity with his 3yos.

Discuss is a promising maiden for Sir Michael Stoute

Discuss (USA) 81

b f Danzig (USA) - Private Line (USA) (Private Account (USA)) May 26
Owner K Abdullah **Trainer** Sir Michael Stoute **Breeder** Juddmonte Farms Inc
1 start: second **1**, £2,525 win & place prize-money

HAVING been foaled on May 26, Discuss was the youngest member of the 13-strong six-furlong fillies' maiden field that contested a high-quality contest at Newmarket in October. Sir Michael Stoute's filly was becoming the first of Private Line's four foals to race as a juvenile and, despite a

Race record
2nd Suffolk Insulation And Renovation Services EBF Maiden Fillies' Stakes (Newmarket, October 2) 2yo 6f Good **81** (TS 84) 13 ran.

Pedigree assessment
Sire Danzig (Northern Dancer) Unbeaten winner of 3 races at 2 and 3 in US at up to 7f. Outstanding sire, excels with 2yos, sprinters and milers, very rarely gets high-class horses over 10f+. **Dam Private Line** Winner over 7f on only 2yo start, later very useful miler. Half-sister to high-class 2yo Most Precious (dam of high-class 8-10f performers Marathon, Matiara), family of Sanglamore. Her 3 earlier foals comprise 10f Group 3 winner Dance Dress (by Nureyev) and 2 other 10f winners. **Conclusion** Likely to be one of her sire's milers.

pedigree that suggested she would need time, had already been the subject of interest for the 1,000 Guineas.

In the race Discuss showed her inexperience, falling out of the stalls before recovering well to hold every chance a furlong out. She showed a smart change of gear from there, powering clear of her rivals in her group but being unable to peg back Loyal Love, who effectively raced alone on the far side of the track.

That highly promising debut augurs extremely well for Discuss, who is likely to stay ten furlongs but may prove best at around a mile. She is one of many exciting two-year-old fillies the Stoute team has to look forward to next year. *ST*

Divine Proportions 117

See entry in the top 100 horses, page 126

Dubai Surprise (Ire) 107

b f King's Best (USA) - Toujours Irish (USA) (Irish River (Fr)) March 21
Owner Dr Ali Ridha **Trainer** D R Loder **Breeder** James F Hanly
5 starts: won **2**, second **1**, third **1**, **£68,953** win & place prize-money

---

WE didn't see the best of Dubai Surprise in the Fillies' Mile at Ascot. That much is evident from her subsequent fine second to the good French colt Helios Quercus in the Criterium International at Saint-Cloud.

Dubai Surprise beat only one home in the Fillies' Mile, but that was the only blot in a five-race campaign. She probably would not have made the frame even on her best form, but she would have been a good bit closer, and it's a fair bet that the fast ground that prevailed at Ascot was as big a factor in her comprehensive defeat as the slight interference she met when already starting to struggle.

She had been a different proposition when coming from off the pace in a fast-run race to beat French challenger Nanabanana in the Prestige Stakes at Goodwood, a fast-run race in which the ground was so soft that they all came across to race towards the stands side. And she was a different proposition on even more testing ground at Saint-Cloud, when she stayed on to take second late on, with the easy Horris Hill winner Cupid's Glory giving the form a solid look in fourth.

It is difficult to know where Dubai Surprise will be seen to best advantage at three, for a mile is likely to be on the sharp side for her and she is not guaranteed to stay a mile and a half. Perhaps a return to France for the Prix de Diane, over an intermediate distance, will be the answer. *GD*

Race record

2nd Criterium International (Group 1) (Saint-Cloud, October 31) 2yo 1m Very soft **107** (TS 97) 8 ran.
8th Meon Valley Stud Fillies' Mile (Group 1) (Ascot, September 25) 2yo 1m Good to firm **94** (TS 81) 9 ran.
1st Citroen C5 Prestige Stakes (Group 3) (Goodwood, August 29) 2yo 7f Good to soft **103** (TS 74) 12 ran.
1st EBF Maiden Fillies' Stakes (Redcar, August 7) 2yo 7f Good to firm **78** (TS 69) 7 ran.
3rd Mountgrange Stud Maiden Fillies' Stakes (Newbury, July 16) 2yo 7f Good **76** (TS 61) 13 ran.

Pedigree assessment

Sire King's Best (Kingmambo) Smart dual 7f 2yo winner, won 2,000 Guineas in 2 completed 3yo outings. By top-class 2yo/miler and excellent sire. Half-brother to several good performers, notably Arc winner Urban Sea (dam of Galileo), from very strong middle-distance family. Oldest progeny 2, also sire of 7f Listed winner Elliots World. **Dam Toujours Irish** Unraced. By top-class 2yo/miler and very good sire, including of broodmares. Half-sister to high-class 9-12f filly Athyka (dam of top-class 8-10f colt Atticus). Her 2 earlier foals (Celtic Note, Liffey) have won at up to 1m. **Conclusion** Sire an unknown quantity with his 3yos but it will be no surprise if he gets good horses beyond a mile, and Dubai Surprise could be one of them. Likely to be effective over 8-10f, but unlikely to last 12f. Every chance she will progress well from 2 to 3.

Dubawi 122

See entry in the top 100 horses, page 136

Early March 117

br c Dansili - Emplane (USA) (Irish River (Fr)) January 28
Owner K Abdullah **Trainer** Mme C Head-Maarek **Breeder** Juddmonte Farms
4 starts: won **2**, second **1**, third **0**, **£88,387** win & place prize-money

EARLY MARCH gave a battling display in the Prix Jean-Luc Lagardere but in hanging off the rails he handed away the victory. He caught Layman close home, but Oratorio caught him even closer to the line. The final margins between the three were a short neck and a nose.

Having gone freely to post, an obstreperous Early March looked for a few moments as if he would not enter the stalls, but there was no hanging around once they opened. However, after making most of the running under Olivier Peslier, he had three of his five rivals appear alongside him one and a half furlongs out.

Carrying his head rather high, Early March had already started to shy away from the rails and, as the tendency became pronounced, a fourth opponent, Oratorio, was switched inside to take advantage. Layman was a neck ahead and looked the likely winner, but Early March straightened up and fought back strongly in the final furlong, edging in front of Layman a second before Oratorio did the same to him.

Early March lined up in the Lagardere unbeaten after two races, a newcomers event at Clairefontaine and the Group 3 Prix la Rochette at Longchamp, both also over seven furlongs. In the Rochette, he made all for a one-and-a-half-length win over the Andre Fabre-trained favourite Stop Making Sense.

After the Lagardere, Early March had another attempt at Group 1 glory in the Criterium International at Saint-Cloud and was a disappointing favourite. The hard race four weeks earlier may have had its effect. The ground at Saint-Cloud was much softer than at Longchamp but he won on similar going on his debut. There is little doubt after his Lagardere performance that he should stay at least a mile. A big, well-bred colt, and a striking individual, Early March should be a major force again in Group 1 events in 2005. *RA*

Race record

6th Criterium International (Group 1) (Saint-Cloud, October 31) 2yo 1m Very soft **99** (TS 81) 8 ran.
2nd Prix Jean-Luc Lagardere (Group 1) (Longchamp, October 3) 2yo 7f Good **117** (TS 97) 6 ran.
1st Prix la Rochette (Group 3) (Longchamp, September 9) 2yo 7f Good **105** (TS 87) 6 ran.
1st Prix des Pommiers (Unraced Colts & Geldings) (Clairefontaine, August 26) 2yo 7f Very soft **79** 3 ran.

Pedigree assessment

Sire **Dansili** (Danehill) Won sole 2yo start over 1m, later top-class 7-8f colt, triple Group winner and placed in 6 Gr1 events. Brother to Banks Hill, Cacique, Intercontinental. Oldest progeny 2. **Dam Emplane** Unraced at 2, fair 1m winner at 3. Sister to smart 10f performer Boatman out of 11f Listed-winning half-sister to top-class miler Al Bahathri (dam of Haafhd). Her 2 earlier foals include French 3yo winner Coach Lane. **Conclusion** Dansili is yet to have 3yos, but the chances are he will get talented middle-distance performers only from stoutly bred dams. Emplane does not quite come into that category. Early March should continue to excel at around 1m and might last 10f in time but no further.

Echelon   104

---

b f Danehill (USA) - Exclusive (Polar Falcon (USA)) April 15
Owner Cheveley Park Stud **Trainer** Sir Michael Stoute **Breeder** Cheveley Park Stud
2 starts: won **1**, second **0**, third **0**, **£4,891** win & place prize-money

---

ECHELON'S Classic aspirations may have taken a knock in the Fillies' Mile, but so did Echelon. Slowly away and going a little in snatches under Kieren Fallon, Echelon tried to make her ground towards the outside

Echelon makes a winning debut at Newmarket in August

but was slightly checked early in the straight and, after regaining some momentum, Fallon was forced to snatch up on her at the furlong marker by the errant Dash To The Top. Without the latter interference, she looked to be in a battle for only minor honours.

Echelon started 15-8 favourite at Ascot, after one previous run. That was four weeks earlier in contrasting conditions – six furlongs on good to soft ground – for a maiden at Newmarket, the form of which has stood up well. Her rider that day was Nicky Mackay, who, after finding himself a bit tight for room over two furlongs out, reported: "I was worried they might get away from us, but then she came back on the bridle and she quickened away well from them."

Race record

7th Meon Valley Stud Fillies' Mile (Group 1) (Ascot, September 25) 2yo 1m Good to firm **104** (TS 90) 9 ran.
1st McKeever St Lawrence EBF Maiden Stakes (Newmarket (July), August 28) 2yo 6f Good to soft **93** (TS 87) 13 ran.

Pedigree assessment

Sire **Danehill** (Danzig) Useful 6f 2yo winner, improved at 3 into top-class sprinter, won Haydock Sprint Cup but also smart over 1m. Excellent sire, has done well with 2yos and older progeny, mainly at up to 1m but capable of getting top-class 10f+ performers from stout female families. Best progeny include Aquarelliste, Banks Hill, Cacique, Desert King, Landseer, Mozart, North Light, Oratorio, Rock Of Gibraltar, Westerner. Dam **Exclusive** Winner over 7f and Gr1-placed from 2 2yo outings, won Coronation S-Gr1 at 3. Half-sister to 2,000 Guineas winner Entrepreneur and Oaks 2nd Dance A Dream (both by Sadler's Wells), out of smart 6-7f filly. Her one previous foal is high-class miler Chic (by Machiavellian) **Conclusion** Bred to be top class over 7-8f, and has every chance on pedigree of making good progress from 2 to 3.

Things obviously did not go her way in smart company at Ascot and it's much too early to be inferring that Echelon will continue to fall short at that level. The family tend to progress over time, a prime example being Chic, Echelon's four-year-old half-sister, who found her feet in fine style in Group races in the 2004 season.

Exclusive, Echelon's dam, also ran in the Fillies' Mile after a successful debut, finishing third of eight. She won the Coronation Stakes at three (and was beaten about three and a half lengths in the Juddmonte International, her only start at around a mile and a quarter) and the family is full of good winners, so it is hardly going out on a limb to suggest that Echelon is likely to be another one. *RA*

Echo Of Light 74

b c Dubai Millennium - **Spirit Of Tara (Ire)** (Sadler's Wells (USA)) March 7
Owner Godolphin **Trainer** Saeed Bin Suroor **Breeder** Kilcarn Stud
1 start: won **0**, second **0**, third **0**, **£551** win & place prize-money

---

ECHO OF LIGHT had quite a reputation by the time he made his racecourse debut over a mile at Newmarket in mid-October but proved rather disappointing in finishing an eight-length fourth to Proclamation. However, he showed notable promise under a considerate Frankie Dettori and is likely to repay the kindness at three.

Prior to his debut Godolphin racing manager Simon Crisford spoke

---

Race record
4th Federation of Bloodstock Agents Maiden Stakes (Newmarket, October 15) 2yo 1m Soft **74** (TS 65) 21 ran.

Pedigree assessment
Sire Dubai Millennium (Seeking The Gold) Won sole start over 1m at 2, later outstanding 8-10f performer, won Prix Jacques le Marois-Gr1, Queen Elizabeth II S-Gr1, Dubai World Cup-Gr1, Princess of Wales's S-Gr1. By top-class 6f+ US dirt performer out of 12-14f Group winner from outstanding family. Sole crop of 2yos includes Gr1 winner Dubawi. **Dam Spirit Of Tara** Unraced at 2, useful 10-12f filly at 3. Sister to outstanding 8-12f filly Salsabil, half-sister to Marju, from excellent family. Her 3 earlier foals feature useful 8-10f colt Multazem and quite useful 9-12f winner Akarem (both by Kingmambo). **Conclusion** A sales-topping yearling buy with the pedigree to match. Certainly bred to be better at 3 than 2, and should be effective over 8-10f. However, 12f looks doubtful for him.

---

encouragingly about the son of Dubai Millennium: "We think a lot of him. We're keen to get a run into him and didn't want to wait until Doncaster next week. While we know he'll improve a lot, he's ready to go. He's been working nicely but he still needs to develop and strengthen.

"We're not expecting too many fireworks today because he hasn't been asked many questions at home, but we very much hope he'll develop into a really nice colt for next season."

His reappearance is awaited with interest. *ST*

Etlaala   117

ch c Selkirk (USA) - **Portelet (Night Shift (USA))** February 23
Owner Hamdan Al Maktoum **Trainer** B W Hills **Breeder** Matthews Breeding and Racing Ltd
3 starts: won **2**, second **0**, third **0**, **£66,422** win & place prize-money

---

FOR all the overwhelming superiority of Shamardal, Dubawi and Motivator in their moments of Group 1 victory, the most memorable two-year-old performance of 2004 could still be Etlaala's in the Champagne Stakes at Doncaster.

"Last time he jumped out in front and didn't learn anything," jockey Richard Hills reported of Etlaala's previous race, a winning debut in a Newbury maiden. On that basis, the slow-starting Etlaala will have learned enough in the Champagne to go on Mastermind.

Three furlongs out, Etlaala was tanking along but still at the back and requiring a few breaks – Hills had to take a pull. Two furlongs out, Etlaala was switched towards the outside and full of running – Hills had to take a pull. One and a half furlongs out, Hills had to move out again and Etlaala was finally in the clear.

Coventry Stakes winner Iceman, ridden along towards the rear from a long way out but unimpeded, had built up some momentum of his own and was challenging the Godolphin colt Oude for the lead, but Etlaala was only just behind him. There were about one and a half lengths for Etlaala to make up and, in a dash for the line that took the pair of them three lengths clear, he put his head in front of Iceman half a furlong out and went on to beat him by half a length.

Oude hung on for third, with subsequent Breeders' Cup Juvenile winner Wilko in fourth. The winner's form was smart and the impression he made rather better. With his white face and double shift across the track, it was inevitable that Etlaala would catch the eye, but there's no doubt that this was the performance of a colt who was capable of better.

"He's out of the top drawer," was the view of Barry Hills, Etlaala's trainer. Punters took that view as well, sending him off favourite in preference to Shamardal in the Dewhurst, but Etlaala floundered and eventually had to come home in his own time.

The heavy ground at Newmarket (it had been good to firm at Doncaster) means that this is a result that needs no other excuse. His impressive physique gives every encouragement that Etlaala will emerge as a high-class performer in his second season. However, there is one other issue to be resolved before Etlaala is marked down as a top-flight Guineas prospect, and that is stamina. The Doncaster run over seven furlongs showed that he has bags of speed, but he can also race freely (as in the Dewhurst) and his dam gained her wins front-running over five. Etlaala's brother Selective was very useful in 2003 at seven furlongs as well as at a mile. Etlaala is probably a Group 1 winner in the making, but it is not certain that he will be best over the Guineas distance. *RA*

Race record

8th Darley Dewhurst Stakes (Group 1) (Newmarket, October 16) 2yo 7f Soft **79** (TS 66) 9 ran.
1st SGB Champagne Stakes (Group 2) (Doncaster, September 10) 2yo 7f Good to firm **117** (TS 93) 10 ran.
1st Stan James Supporting Wessex Heartbeat EBF Maiden Stakes (Div I) (Newbury, August 14) 2yo 7f Good **89** (TS 67) 10 ran.

Pedigree assessment

Sire **Selkirk** (Sharpen Up) Very useful 1m 2yo winner, later top-class 7-8f colt, won Queen Elizabeth II S-Gr1 and 3 Gr2 events. By sire of Diesis, Kris, Sharpo and Trempolino out of high-class miler and excellent broodmare. Very good sire, decent source of 2yos (Red Bloom, Sulk) but better record with 3yos, mainly over 1m+ (Favourable Terms, Field Of Hope, Prince Kirk, Wince), sires occasional talented sprinter (The Trader). **Dam Portelet** Unplaced at 2, later won 4 races over 5f. By speed influence out of unraced half-sister to smart 7-8f filly Ghariba and stayer Braashee. Her 3 earlier foals feature quite useful 7-8f performer Selective (by Selkirk). **Conclusion** Lots of pace on the dam's side, and Etlaala is not guaranteed to stay a mile. He may prove best around 7f.

Flag Lieutenant 81

b c Machiavellian (USA) - Fairy Godmother (Fairy King (USA)) February 26
Owner The Queen **Trainer** Sir Michael Stoute **Breeder** The Queen
1 start: second **1, £1,840** win & place prize-money

NOISY in the paddock, bred to be better at three and seemingly unfancied, Flag Lieutenant's prospects did not look bright on his debut at Leicester.

However, the Machiavellian colt, who is out of the Earl of Sefton Stakes runner-up Fairy Godmother, belied his inexperience by running a race full of promise in finishing runner-up in a strong-looking maiden. Showing plenty of pace to track the leaders, he stayed on to some purpose inside the final furlong, running the experienced Eqdaam to half a length.

Highly likely to leave that form behind at three, Flag Lieutenant should stay middle distances and looks an exciting prospect for Her Majesty the Queen. *ST*

Footstepsinthesand, right, wins from Gaff at Leopardstown

Race record

2nd EBF ladbrokes.com Reference Point Maiden Stakes (Leicester, October 12) 2yo 7f Good **81** (TS 80) 19 ran.

Pedigree assessment

Sire **Machiavellian** (Mr Prospector) Top-class 2yo over 6-7f, won Prix Morny-Gr1, Prix de la Salamandre-Gr1. High-class miler at 3, 2nd 2,000 Guineas-Gr1. By outstanding sire out of outstanding broodmare, most family members best around 1m. Very good sire, fair record with 2yos (Best Of The Bests, Titus Livius) but better one with older horses, mainly over 6-10f (Almutawakel, Medicean, Rebecca Sharp, Storming Home, Street Cry). Sires occasional high-class 12f+ performer. **Dam Fairy Godmother** Unraced at 2, later lightly raced but smart 9-10f filly. By very good sire of variety of performers, half-sister to high-class 12f colt Blueprint out of smart 12f filly Highbrow, who is a half-sister to Height Of Fashion. This is her first foal. **Conclusion** Bred to make very good progress from 2 to 3, when he should stay 10f and might last 12f. Family is a prolific source of highly talented runners, and no surprise if Flag Lieutenant is another.

Footstepsinthesand   112

b c Giant's Causeway (USA) - Glatisant (Rainbow Quest (USA)) February 15
Owner Michael Tabor **Trainer** A P O'Brien **Breeder** Hascombe and Valiant Studs
2 starts: won **2**, **£40,850** win & place prize-money

BOOKMAKERS at Naas on October 17 have good cause to remember Footstepsinthesand. A wider audience is now advised to do the same. Footstepsinthesand landed a gamble on that Naas debut, won in good style again when she moved up to Group 3 company only eight days later, and is now likely to be prominent in Aidan O'Brien's plans for the 2,000 Guineas.

Those betting shops that reportedly had Footstepsinthesand available at 20-1 for his maiden were caught out, as were the on-course bookmakers who offered 10-1 and 8-1. Footstepsinthesand went off the 3-1 favourite, usurping Olympic who drifted from 2-1 to 7-2, an eye-catching aspect of the gamble being that they were unraced stablemates, with Olympic ridden by O'Brien's top jockey Jamie Spencer and Footstepsinthesand by Colm O'Donoghue.

"Colm rides the winner every day at home so he rode him in the race," explained O'Brien after Footstepsinthesand had easily beaten Olympic by four and a half lengths.

It was Spencer, however, who was able to report back in glowing terms after Footstepsinthesand won the six-runner Kilavullan Stakes at Leopardstown. "He has an enormous amount of ability and when I gave him a kick rounding the final turn he shot four lengths clear," said the jockey. "Yet he was doing so little that he spent the whole of the final furlong with his ears pricked."

A 170,000-guinea yearling, Footstepsinthesand is bred to stay a mile and a quarter. Although he has raced only on a soft surface so far, O'Brien reckons that fast ground will suit him much better. He is one to look out for. *RA*

Race record
1st Kilavullan Stakes (Group 3) (Leopardstown, October 25) 2yo 7f Soft **112** (TS 114) 6 ran.
1st Tifrums EBF Maiden (Naas, October 17) 2yo C & G 6f Yielding to soft **97** (TS 94) 20 ran.

Pedigree assessment
Sire Giant's Causeway (Storm Cat) Top-class 2yo, won all 3 races over 6-7f inc. Prix de la Salamandre-Gr1, then tough and top-class 8-10f 3yo, won 5 more Gr1 events. By outstanding US sire out of high-class US 8-9f filly. Oldest progeny 2, sire of Footstepsinthesand (Gr3), Maids Causeway (Gr2), Shamardal (Dewhurst S-Gr1). **Dam Glatisant** Smart winner of both 2yo races over 6-7f, disappointing at 3, though Listed placed over 1m. Half-sister to several useful fillies over 1m+ and to dam of Superstar Leo, out of smart 8-10f filly. Her 4 earlier foals include 6f 2yo winner Frappe (by Inchinor) and 12-18f winner Theme Song (Singspiel). **Conclusion** Glatisant has had a patchy racing and stud career but has the credentials to produce smart 1m+ performers. Footstepsinthesand will stay 1m and has a good chance of lasting 10f, although sire is an unknown quantity with his 3yos.

Fraloga (Ire) 107

b f Grand Lodge (USA) - Fragrant Hill (Shirley Heights) March 20
Owner Lagardere Family **Trainer** A Fabre **Breeder** Snc Lagardere Elevage
3 starts: won **1**, second **0**, third **1**, **£31,954** win & place prize-money

FRALOGA is a filly to take seriously for top prizes as a three-year-old. Divine Proportions earned the headlines when extending her unbeaten record in the Prix Marcel Boussac, but Fraloga provided an interesting subtext after finishing a game third despite things going against her at two different stages.

Fraloga's first problem came when the draw was made and she was allotted the widest berth. In a ten-runner field, that might not have proved insuperable but things looked grim when Portrayal (a stablemate!) swerved left from the stall next to her and Fraloga, knocked sideways, took a major diversion.

Doubly unfortunately, the plan seemed to be to make plenty of use of her. The redirected Fraloga was quickly up into second place behind Titian Time but when asked to quicken entering the straight, it didn't really happen, not in comparison with Divine Proportions anyway, and the favourite gave her a slight bump for good measure when going past one and a half furlongs out. Knocked out of her stride for the second time in the race, Fraloga stuck to her guns in admirable style and only narrowly failed to regain second place.

It cannot be argued that Fraloga was a better filly than two-length winner Divine Proportions as a two-year-old, but she is a bit better than the Marcel Boussac result suggests and looks the type to train on well. The dam's four winners by Linamix all scored over at least a mile and a half and she is likely to excel over middle distances next year. *RA*

Race record

3rd Prix Marcel Boussac Royal Barriere Deauville (Group 1) (Longchamp, October 3) 2yo 1m Good **107** (TS 104) 10 ran.
1st Prix de la Forterelle (Chantilly, September 8) 2yo 1m Good **90** (TS 55) 10 ran.
4th Prix du Mezeray (Deauville, July 31) 2yo 7½f Good to soft **84** 10 ran.

Pedigree assessment

Sire Grand Lodge (Chief's Crown) Top-class 2yo, won Dewhurst S-Gr1, later top-class 8-10f colt, won St James's Palace S-Gr1. Very good sire, has good record with 2yos (Chateau Istana, Queen's Logic, Raise A Grand) but better one with 3yos over 1m+ (Grandera, Indian Lodge, Sinndar). **Dam Fragrant Hill** Winner over 7f at 2, later useful 10-11f winner. By Derby winner and very good stamina sire. Half-sister to high-class 10f filly Spring Oak (Mark Of Esteem) out of high-class 10f filly English Spring. Her 8 previous foals include high-class 12f performer Fragrant Mix and useful 2004 10-13f 3yo winner Fracassant (both by Linamix). **Conclusion** Bred to appreciate at least 10f and has fairly good chance of lasting 12f. Family members generally very progressive, so could be a major force in 2005.

Gaff (USA) 107

b c Maria's Mon (USA) - lonlyhaveeyesforu (USA) (Tunerup (USA)) March 28
Owner L W Heiligbrodt **Trainer** D K Weld **Breeder** Earlie Irving Mack
3 starts: won 1, second 1, third 0, £32,338 win & place prize-money

KEENELAND'S four-and-a-half-furlong track under fast conditions differs markedly from Leopardstown's seven furlongs on soft ground and few horses can have experienced both. Gaff, who finished down the field at Keeneland in April, is surely the only horse to do so in the same year.

The fact that Dermot Weld started Gaff off in the Listed El Gran Senor Stakes at Fairyhouse in September demonstrated his regard for the colt, who let nobody down, battling on well to take a slightly substandard renewal and give Maria's Mon, sire of Kentucky Derby winner Monarchos, a rare winner on Irish soil.

Gaff only raced once more for his new trainer and showed much-improved form in finishing runner-up to Footstepsinthesand in the Group 3 Kilavullan Stakes, the pair pulling fully seven lengths clear of the remainder.

Likely to stay beyond a mile and be suited by quicker ground than he has encountered so far in Ireland, Gaff looks a fascinating prospect for his talented trainer and could improve considerably on his current level of form at three. *RA*

Race record

2nd Kilavullan Stakes (Group 3) (Leopardstown, October 25) 2yo 7f Soft **107** (TS 108) 6 ran.
1st El Gran Senor Stakes (Listed) (Fairyhouse, September 29) 2yo 7f Good to yielding **96** 7 ran.
7th Maiden Special Weight (Keeneland, April 15) 2yo 4½f Fast 10 ran.

Pedigree assessment

Sire **Maria's Mon** (Wavering Monarch) Champion North American 2yo, effective over 7-8f, very lightly raced thereafter. By top-class 8-10f US dirt performer. Sire of Kentucky Derby winner Monarchos, very few runners in Europe to date. **Dam Ionlyhaveeyesforu** Unraced at 2, won 4 races in US at up to 1m on turf and dirt from 3 to 5. Sister to very smart dirt sprinter Ifyoucouldseemenow. Her 3 earlier foals have won in US. **Conclusion** Has the pedigree of a dirt miler, so interesting to see this $7,000 foal doing well on turf in Europe after making his debut in US. Related to several smart and tough 3yo+ performers, so should train on.

Galeota (Ire) 111

b c Mujadil (USA) - Refined (Ire) (Statoblest) April 5
Owner J A Lazzari **Trainer** R Hannon **Breeder** W Maxwell Ervine
6 starts: won **3**, second **0**, third **0**, **£53,949** win & place prize-money

A SWITCH to more forcing tactics seemed to make the difference with Galeota after cheekpieces had failed to bring any significant improvement in Kempton's Sirenia Stakes. Galeota was only fifth in the Sirenia, having occupied the same position and run to a similar level in the Gimcrack at York on his previous start. Both were sound efforts, but probably not of quite the level connections had hoped for when he began his career as an odds-on (and beaten) favourite at Salisbury in May.

Just a week after Kempton, Galeota was in action again, in a Doncaster conditions race won 12 months previously by Kheleyf. In a field of four jockey Ryan Moore wasted no time in grabbing the rail on Galeota. The favourite, Rajwa, kept him in his sights and looked a big threat, but Galeota saw him off in the final furlong and beat him two lengths, with good yardstick Obe Gold back in third.

Galeota wins at Doncaster, later adding a Group 2 victory

Race record

1st Dubai Duty Free Mill Reef Stakes (Group 2) (Newbury, September 18) 2yo 6f Good to soft **111** (TS 94) 9 ran.

1st GNER Conditions Stakes (Doncaster, September 11) 2yo 6f Firm **104** (TS 104) 4 ran.

5th Pentax Sirenia Stakes (Group 3) (Kempton, September 4) 2yo 6f Good to firm **100** (TS 75) 8 ran.

5th Scottish Equitable Gimcrack Stakes (Group 2) (York, August 18) 2yo 6f Soft **100** (TS 86) 11 ran.

1st Choisir Maiden Stakes (Windsor, July 12) 2yo 6f Good to soft **87** (TS 80) 15 ran.

4th "Jamaica Inn At Salisbury Playhouse" Maiden Stakes (Div I) (Salisbury, May 13) 2yo 5f Good **68** (TS 41) 10 ran.

Pedigree assessment

Sire Mujadil (Storm Bird) Very smart 5f 2yo, disappointing at 3 over 5-6f. By top-class 2yo best known as sire of Bluebird and Storm Cat, half-brother to high-class 10-12f performer Fruits Of Love. Useful sire of 2yos, mostly sprinters and many precocious. **Dam Refined** Dual 5f 2yo winner, disappointing in 2 sprint starts at 3. By high-class sprinter, half-sister to smart 7-8f performer Pipe Major. Her one previous foal is Galeota's full-sister, dual 5f 2yo winner Vermilliann, who disappointed in sprints at 3 in 2004. **Conclusion** Sire known for imparting precocity, and there is little encouragement from full-sister or from dam that Galeota will match his juvenile form at 3. Likely to be a sprinter.

The Doncaster win earned Galeota a crack at Newbury's Dubai Duty Free Mill Reef Stakes, and although the opposition looked much tougher he followed up, making all again and holding on by a length from Mystical Land and the subsequent Middle Park second Rebuttal.

Galeota was one of the season's leading sprinting juveniles, but he might not be easy to place with his Group 2 penalty at three. The Mill Reef result might flatter him, in that he was allowed an easy lead and both he and Mystical Land got first run on the strong-finishing Rebuttal, and he is hardly one of those two-year-olds who are likely to improve with time and longer distances, since he was relatively precocious and is not sure to stay a great deal further than six furlongs. *GD*

Grand Central (Ire)   91

b c Sadler's Wells (USA) - Rebecca Sharp (Machiavellian (USA)) April 7
Owner Mrs John Magnier **Trainer** A P O'Brien **Breeder** Hascombe & Valiant Studs
1 start: won **1**, **£9,169** win & place prize-money

GRAND CENTRAL comes under the 'could be anything' heading at this early stage of his career.

By Sadler's Wells out of Coronation Stakes winner Rebecca Sharp, he is certainly bred to be smart and he made the perfect start to his career when a comfortable winner of a seven-furlong, soft-ground maiden at Leopardstown in October. He was just nudged out when going on and looked value for more than the official four-length winning margin.

The bare form of that performance, coupled with the style in which it was recorded, suggests Grand Central could take high rank among his trainer's powerful three-year-old team in 2005. *ST*

Race record
1st Irish Stallion Farms EBF Maiden (Leopardstown, October 25) 2yo 7f Soft **91** (TS 80) 7 ran.

Pedigree assessment
Sire Sadler's Wells (Northern Dancer) Smart 7-8f winner at 2, improved into top-class 8-12f colt at 3, won Irish 2,000 Guineas-Gr1, Eclipse S-Gr1, Irish Champion S-Gr1. Outstanding sire, particularly of 3yo+ over 8-12f, also has good record with autumn 2yos. **Dam Rebecca Sharp** Placed only start at 2, top-class 7-8f filly at 3, won Coronation S-Gr1, 2nd Queen Elizabeth II S-Gr1, Challenge S-Gr2. Half-sister to useful 10f+ performers Hidden Hope, Mystic Knight. Her 3 earlier foals feature useful miler Miss Pinkerton (Danehill). **Conclusion** Every encouragement on pedigree that he will make good progress from 2 to 3. Should be effective over 1m and has decent chance of staying 10f, but unlikely to stay 12f.

Gypsy King (Ire)   84

b c Sadler's Wells (USA) - Love For Ever (Ire) (Darshaan) February 11
Owner Mrs John Magnier **Trainer** A P O'Brien **Breeder** Premier Bloodstock
1 start: won **1**, **£9,169** win & place prize-money

GYPSY KING made the perfect start to his racing career when landing odds of 4-9 in a seven-furlong, heavy-ground Leopardstown maiden on the last day of the Irish Flat season.

The son of Sadler's Wells initiated a double for Jamie Spencer, who was crowned champion jockey in Ireland for the first time just hours after arriving back from a difficult night at the Breeders' Cup.

The racecourse gossip suggested it was just a case of going down and coming back for Gypsy King but a flag start complicated matters, especially when he lost considerable ground at the start. However, he had little difficulty in overcoming that handicap, leading just inside the final furlong before going on to record an easy success.

Bred to do much better over middle distances at three, Gypsy King is one of many smart prospects for Ballydoyle. *ST*

Race record

1st Irish Stallion Farms EBF Maiden (Leopardstown, October 31) 2yo 7f Soft to heavy **84** (TS 84) 18 ran.

Pedigree assessment

Sire Sadler's Wells (Northern Dancer) Smart 7-8f winner at 2, improved into top-class 8-12f colt at 3, won Irish 2,000 Guineas-Gr1, Eclipse S-Gr1, Irish Champion S-Gr1. Outstanding sire, particularly of 3yo+ over 8-12f, also has good record with autumn 2yos. **Dam Love For Ever** Unraced at 2, dual 1m winner at 3 in France. Half-sister to smart 8-10f filly Wedding Ring (by Never So Bold) out of a smart middle-distance filly. Her 2 earlier foals, also by Sadler's Wells, are fair 12f+ performer Albanov and 10f winner Napoleon. **Conclusion** Certain to stay at least 10f, and likely to last 12f. Also bred to make good progress from 2 to 3, and no surprise if he surpasses the achievements of his brothers. The Sadler's Wells-Darshaan cross has been phenomenally successful.

Helios Quercus   112

See entry in the top 100 horses, page 190

Henrik   109

b c Primo Dominie - Clincher Club (Polish Patriot (USA)) March 21
Owner Sheikh Hamdan Bin Mohammed Al Maktoum **Trainer** M R Channon
Breeder Jeremy Green and Sons
3 starts: won **1**, second **1**, third **1**, **£36,571** win & place prize-money

WE didn't see much of Henrik in his first season, but from the limited evidence available we can safely conclude that he was a pretty classy youngster. A winning debut in a Goodwood maiden was the perfect start, even if he did get home by only a short head, but it was his second in the Group 3 Superlative Stakes at Newmarket's July meeting that provided much more tangible evidence of his talent.

The Superlative looked a hot race at the time – all 12 runners were already successful, and five of them, including Henrik, were the promising winners of their only start so far – but the true merit of Henrik's performance emerged only later in the season. For in a close finish that saw the first three put daylight between themselves and the rest, Henrik managed to split two subsequent Group 1 winners in Dubawi, who went on to an easy win in the National Stakes, and Wilko, who much later was the shock winner of the Breeders' Cup Juvenile.

Bought privately after the Superlative by one of Sheikh Mohammed's sons, Sheikh Hamdan, Henrik was given a break and aimed for the Dewhurst Stakes, but unusually testing ground at Newmarket prompted his late withdrawal. Instead he was given his chance in the Racing Post Trophy at Doncaster, but that was also run on softish ground and meant stepping up to a mile. One couldn't say that Henrik failed to stay at Doncaster, because his third behind Motivator and Albert Hall, beaten three and a half lengths by the winner, represented improved form once again. But while he finished a long way clear of the rest, he is not short of speed and nobody could argue he got the final furlong as well as the first two.

Dropping back to seven furlongs might suit Henrik ideally, although a mile should not be a problem on better ground at three. It will be interesting to see what the future holds for him under new ownership. *GD*

Race record

3rd Racing Post Trophy (Group 1) (Doncaster, October 23) 2yo 1m Soft **109** (TS 107) 8 ran.
2nd Weatherbys Superlative Stakes (Group 3) (Newmarket (July), July 8) 2yo 7f Good to soft **103** (TS 83) 12 ran.
1st Delta International EBF Maiden Stakes (Goodwood, May 19) 2yo 6f Good to firm **84** (TS 80) 7 ran.

Pedigree assessment

Sire Primo Dominie (Dominion) Top-class 5-6f 2yo, won Coventry S-Gr3, July S-Gr3, Richmond S-Gr2, later smart sprinter, won King George S-Gr3. Influence for speed and precocity as sire, does well with 2yos (inc. Middle Park winners First Trump, Primo Valentino) and sprinters, very rarely gets smart 9f+ performers (Imperial Dancer is one). **Dam Clincher Club** Won over 5f at 2 and 7f at 3. Speedily bred, by July Cup winner out of winning half-sister to Tina's Pet. Her 3 earlier foals feature fair 6f 2yo winner Bishop's Lake (Lake Coniston) and 6-8f winner Spritzeria (by Bigstone). **Conclusion** Bred to be a sprinter, so has already outstayed his pedigree by recording smart form at up to 1m. However, likely to be best at short of a mile at 3, and his pedigree suggests he may not have the same scope for improvement as some others.

Home Affairs 83

b c Dansili - Orford Ness (Selkirk (USA)) March 2
Owner K Abdullah **Trainer** Sir Michael Stoute **Breeder** Juddmonte Farms
3 starts: won **1**, second **0**, third **0**, **£5,255** win & place prize-money

HOME AFFAIRS had shown significant promise prior to tackling the Dewhurst Stakes in October, running well in a decent seven-furlong maiden behind Librettist before landing his maiden at Yarmouth in good style.

Home Affairs wins his maiden in good style at Yarmouth

Race record

9th Darley Dewhurst Stakes (Group 1) (Newmarket, October 16) 2yo 7f Soft **76** (TS 62) 9 ran.
1st EBF/Norton Peskett Legal Services Maiden Stakes (Yarmouth, September 15) 2yo 7f Good **83** (TS 77) 14 ran.
5th Vibe FM Production Kings Maiden Stakes (Newmarket (July), July 16) 2yo 7f Good **78** (TS 57) 11 ran.

Pedigree assessment

Sire **Dansili** (Danehill) Won sole 2yo start over 1m, later top-class 7-8f colt, triple Group winner and placed in 6 Gr1 events. Brother to Banks Hill, Cacique, Intercontinental. Oldest progeny 2.
Dam **Orford Ness** Winner over 1m at 2, smart dual 1m winner (inc. Prix de Sandringham-Gr3) at 3. By top-class miler out of useful 10-12f filly. Her 2 earlier foals are dual 10f Group winner Weightless (by In The Wings) and 11f winner Castle Rising (by Indian Ridge). **Conclusion** Likely to be a miler. Family members generally do better at 3 than 2.

Whilst those efforts were highly promising it was something of a surprise to see him upped to the highest level at Newmarket, where he was well beaten behind the classy Shamardal. Nevertheless, it is an indication of the regard in which he was held at the time, and he can be forgiven for being beaten so far because Kieren Fallon eased him when his chance had gone and later reported that he had failed to handle the very testing conditions.

Almost certain to be at his best between a mile and ten furlongs at three, Home Affairs remains a bright prospect and it will be interesting to see how his powerful stable campaigns him. *ST*

Iceman

117

b c Polar Falcon (USA) - Virtuous (Exit To Nowhere (USA)) March 27
Owner Cheveley Park Stud **Trainer** J H M Gosden **Breeder** Cheveley Park Stud
6 starts: won **2**, second **2**, third **1**, £104,322 win & place prize-money

HE'S called Iceman but there's something of the lazy bones in there as well. Perseverance on the part of his jockeys got a good response, however, and ensured a successful first season. With precocity in the mix as well, this was Iceman the Coventry Stakes winner. He had to make do with minor honours after Royal Ascot but was always running on at the death and does not look the sort of Coventry-winning talent that is going to fizzle out as a three-year-old.

Kieren Fallon was the perfect man to have on board when Iceman found himself out the back after a furlong at Royal Ascot. The situation was never desperate but Iceman needed plenty of assistance from the saddle,

Race record

4th Darley Dewhurst Stakes (Group 1) (Newmarket, October 16) 2yo 7f Soft **117** (TS 116) 9 ran.
3rd Shadwell Stud Middle Park Stakes (Group 1) (Newmarket, October 1) 2yo 6f Good **111** (TS 92) 9 ran.
2nd SGB Champagne Stakes (Group 2) (Doncaster, September 10) 2yo 7f Good to firm **117** (TS 97) 10 ran.
1st Coventry Stakes (Group 2) (Ascot, June 15) 2yo 6f Good to firm **109** (TS 101) 13 ran.
1st David Wilson Homes Maiden Stakes (Newbury, May 15) 2yo 6f Good **93** (TS 86) 13 ran.
2nd EBF Maiden Stakes (Bath, May 4) 2yo 5f Soft **76** (TS 66) 14 ran.

Pedigree assessment

Sire **Polar Falcon** (Nureyev) Top-class 6-8f colt, won Haydock Sprint Cup-Gr1, Lockinge S-Gr2, Prix Edmond Blanc-Gr3. Good sire, capable of siring smart 2yos (Icicle, Red Camellia) but better record with 3yo+ sprinters (Pivotal) and milers (Exclusive, Frenchmans Bay, Passing Glance, Polar Ben), gets occasional smart 12f+ performer (Pole Star). **Dam Virtuous** Quite useful 1m 2yo winner, Listed placed over 11f at 3. By top-class miler out of winning half-sister to Entrepreneur (by Sadler's Wells) and Exclusive. Her 2 earlier foals are 6f 2yo winner Liberty (by Singspiel) and 10f 3yo winner Peace (by Sadler's Wells). **Conclusion** Bred on similar lines to Exclusive. Has every chance of staying 1m at 3, and should prove effective at slightly shorter too. Has shown fair amount of precocity but plenty of encouragement on pedigree that he can continue to show at least smart form at 3.

not least with the route-finding skills needed to negotiate a safe passage through the pack, and he emerged in pursuit of Godolphin's Council Member just in time.

That was Iceman's third start and his second success following a maiden at Newbury. The race he went closest to winning after Royal Ascot was the Champagne Stakes at Doncaster. He nearly took advantage of all the travails suffered by Etlaala and, while his come-from-behind act was a lot less spectacular, he lost out by only half a length as the pair dashed clear in the final furlong. Giving the winner 5lb, he came out the best horse at the weights on the bare result.

After clearly suffering for the step back to six furlongs in the Middle Park, but still capturing third, Iceman had Etlaala well behind him in the Dewhurst. So too did most of the other runners, but Iceman put up a commendably tenacious effort, looking as if he was going to be badly found out at the two-furlong marker but back in a battle for the place money behind Shamardal as he passed the post.

Iceman acts on good to firm ground and soft, but the evidence of his first season is that he will probably be outpointed on both when he takes on the top performers again as a three-year-old. The step up to a mile, however, will suit him well. *RA*

Intrigued   106

gr f Darshaan - Last Second (Ire) (Alzao (USA)) February 2
Owner Faisal Salman **Trainer** Sir Mark Prescott **Breeder** Belgrave Bloodstock Ltd
3 starts: won **1**, second **0**, third **1**, **£16,352** win & place prize-money

---

THE mere fact that Sir Mark Prescott took Intrigued to France for the Prix Marcel Boussac was significant enough, and in finishing fourth to Divine Proportions she acquitted herself well. Yet we didn't see the best of her there because of the way the race panned out, and that makes her all the more interesting as a middle-distance prospect for 2005.

Race record

4th Prix Marcel Boussac Royal Barriere Deauville (Group 1) (Longchamp, October 3) 2yo 1m Good **106** (TS 102) 10 ran.
1st PKF EBF Maiden Stakes (Epsom, September 8) 2yo 1m½f Good **91** (TS 93) 5 ran.
3rd EBF BP Saltend Maiden Fillies' Stakes (Beverley, August 28) 2yo 7½f Good to soft **72** (TS 37) 12 ran.

Pedigree assessment

Sire Darshaan (Shirley Heights) Won Gr2 event over 1m at 2, top-class 10-12f performer at 3, won Prix du Jockey-Club. Very good sire, excels with 10f+ performers (Dalakhani, Hellenic, Key Change, Kotashaan, Mutamam, Mezzo Soprano), also gets occasional top miler (Mark Of Esteem, Olden Times) and 2yo (Dilshaan, Necklace). **Dam Last Second** (Alzao) Smart dual 7f winner at 2, progressed into top-class 8-10f filly, won Nassau S-Gr2, Sun Chariot S-Gr2, 2nd Coronation S-Gr1. Half-sister to several talented fillies, including Alouette (by Darshaan; dam of Albanova, Alborada), and also to Jude (dam of Quarter Moon, Yesterday). Her 2 earlier foals include smart 10f filly Approach (by Darshaan). **Conclusion** On pedigree, it would be difficult to come up with a better prospect for the top fillies' races over 10-12f. Highly likely to make good progress over the winter, and on pedigree has every chance of making a major Oaks candidate.

In a race that favoured runners who were kept close to the front, Intrigued was out the back for much of the way and still only disputing sixth when the pace was hotting up turning into the straight. She got a bit outpaced, but then stayed on well in the final furlong to be beaten little more than half a length by Titian Time in a good battle for second, just over two and a half lengths behind the impressive 1,000 Guineas favourite Divine Proportions.

The Marcel Boussac was Intrigued's third run, following an unlucky debut defeat at Beverley – Prescott was to joke later that he managed to get the filly's close relative Alborada, subsequently a dual Champion Stakes winner, beaten twice before she won her maiden – and a convincing five-length win at Epsom, after which the trainer laid his cards on the table and spoke openly about his Group-race hopes.

That Epsom experience will stand Intrigued in good stead should she return to the track, as connections presumably hope, for the Oaks. She will need to improve again to win there, but there is every likelihood that she will, for she is from a highly talented family that get better and better. The dam Last Second won the Nassau and Sun Chariot Stakes for the stable at three, having shown juvenile form no better than Intrigued's, and Albanova, another close relative, worked her way up from modest enough beginnings to win three continental Group 1s in 2004. Intrigued looks one to follow. *GD*

Intriguing (Ire) 84

b f Fasliyev (USA) - Sea Mistress (Habitat) March 11
Owner Michael Tabor **Trainer** David Wachman **Breeder** Tony Coyle
1 start: won **1**, **£9,169** win & place prize-money

THE David Wachman-trained Intriguing will have a lot to live up to when she returns to the racecourse after Jamie Spencer unwittingly saw to it that her reputation far outweighs her achievement. For Spencer was evidently referring to Intriguing when, in the heat of the moment after stablemate Damson's win in the Queen Mary Stakes, he claimed: "He's got one better and she's already won!"

Whereas Damson went on to win the Phoenix Stakes and to finish third in the Cheveley Park, Intriguing missed a couple of tentative engagements in decent company, including York's Lowther Stakes, and was not seen again. The only racecourse evidence on which we can judge her, therefore, is her win in a six-furlong maiden race at Cork in May, when she made all. That bare form amounts to little – after all, by the end of the season the next five home had mustered wins in only a modest

Intriguing, a highly regarded filly after her win at Cork

Race record
1st Irish Stallion Farms EBF Fillies Maiden (Cork, May 14) 2yo 6f Good to firm **84** 12 ran.

Pedigree assessment
Sire **Fasliyev** (Nureyev) Top-class 2yo over 5-6f, won Phoenix S-Gr1, Prix Morny-Gr1, then suffered career-ending injury. Oldest progeny 3, excellent start with first 2yos, many of whom were precocious, speedy and smart (Carry On Katie, Much Faster, King's Point, Russian Valour), not so successful in 2004 both with 2yos and 3yos though still sire of several useful 2yos. **Dam Sea Mistress** Unraced. By influential speed sire out of 2yo-winning half-sister to Irish Oaks winner Pampalina. Her 11 earlier foals include smart 6-7f performer Nautical Pet (by Petorius) and several winners over variety of trips. **Conclusion** Lots of speed here, and likely to appreciate distances below a mile.

Fairyhouse nursery and a Roscommon maiden between them. However, Intriguing won with the minimum of fuss, and while Wachman would not be drawn on the relative merits of his two fillies, he did not dismiss Spencer's claim either.

Wachman insists Intriguing's absence was not a consequence of any serious problem – he had her ready to run in the autumn, he said, but the ground had gone against her – and she remains a bright prospect. Only time will tell if she is as good as Damson, let alone better, but it would be risky to underestimate her. *GD*

Jazz Princess (Ire) 109

b/br f Bahhare (USA) - Jazz Up (Cadeaux Genereux) March 4
Owner T Curran **Trainer** Mrs John Harrington **Breeder** Kill Na Moragh Stud
3 starts: won **3**, **£56,409** win & place prize-money

TRAINER Jessica Harrington has enjoyed big success with her runners under the winter code and now seems intent on cracking the Flat game too. In 2004 Moscow Flyer had a seriously talented stablemate in the shape of unbeaten two-year-old filly Jazz Princess.

Making her debut in mid-August, Jazz Princess stayed on strongly to make the perfect start to her racing career in a soft-ground fillies' auction race over Sligo's extended six furlongs.

That success marked the daughter of Bahhare down as an astute purchase at just €9,200 but there was much better to come for connections as she went on to success in stronger company at Galway, proving admirably suited by an extra two furlongs.

Race record

1st C L Weld Park Stakes (Group 3) (Curragh, October 2) 2yo 7f Yielding to soft **109** (TS **109**) 9 ran.
1st www.galwayraces.com Auction Race (Galway, September 6) 2yo 1m½f Good **85** 15 ran.
1st Tattersalls Ireland Fillies Auction Race (Sligo, August 18) 2yo 6½f Soft **80** 14 ran.

Pedigree assessment

Sire **Bahhare** (Woodman) Unbeaten triple 7f winner at 2, inc. Champagne S-Gr2, later showed smart form over 8-10f. Half-brother to top-class miler Bahri. Fair stud record, has sired several very smart fillies over 1m+ (inc. Gr2 winners Baqah, Katdogawn), most progeny better at 3+ than at 2. **Dam Jazz Up** Unraced. By top-class sprinter and speed influence, half-sister to useful Italian 2yo/sprinter-miler Mister Cavern out of 1m 3yo Listed winner Slow Jazz, who is very closely related to top-class 5-6f 2yos Blue Duster and Zieten. This is her first foal. **Conclusion** Has won over 1m, and that could well be her trip at 3, with plenty of speed on the distaff side.

A drop back to seven furlongs and step up in grade to the Group 3 C L Weld Park Stakes looked a stiff test but Jazz Princess showed much-improved form, making all the running on the soft underfoot conditions to record an impressive three-length success from Moyglare third Saoire.

After saddling her first Group-race winner on the Flat, Harrington remarked rather conservatively: "We knew she'd handle the ground. She's an improving filly to win the way she did."

The story of Jazz Princess is already something of a fairytale and could get better in 2005. She could have more improvement in the locker and, rated around four lengths behind top filly Divine Proportions, deserves to be taken seriously at the top level at three. *ST*

Kitty O'Shea 85

b f Sadler's Wells (USA) - Eva Luna (USA) (Alleged (USA)) April 23
Owner Mrs John Magnier **Trainer** A P O'Brien **Breeder** Juddmonte Farms
1 start: won **1**, **£8,759** win & place prize-money

THIS full-sister to the 2003 St Leger winner Brian Boru takes her moniker from the lover and eventual wife of Charles Stuart Parnell, the Irish MP who brought Home Rule to Ireland. She could prove well named.

Parnell's affair with Kitty O'Shea was one of the great romantic epics. O'Shea's equine namesake looked quite feisty herself when making a winning debut in a decent end-of-season maiden at Navan over a mile.

Propelled along by her swishing tail through the final furlong, she just got the better of Kevin Prendergast's Maria Luisa and another rival in a narrow finish, the trio pulling fully six lengths clear of the remainder

On that evidence it appears Kitty O'Shea possesses a good measure of her brother's ability. She will be very well suited by middle distances and has the potential to make up into a famous filly in her own right in 2005 providing the signs of temperament she showed at Navan do not get the better of her. ST

Race record

1st Kilcarn Stud EBF Fillies Maiden (Navan, October 13) 2yo 1m Soft **85** 18 ran.

Pedigree assessment

Sire **Sadler's Wells** (Northern Dancer) Smart 7-8f winner at 2, improved into top-class 8-12f colt at 3, won Irish 2,000 Guineas-Gr1, Eclipse S-Gr1, Irish Champion S-Gr1. Outstanding sire, particularly of 3yo+ over 8-12f, also has good record with autumn 2yos. **Dam Eva Luna** Unraced at 2 and 3, later smart 12-16f performer, won Park Hill S-Gr3. Stoutly bred, by dual Arc winner and stamina influence out of Oaks 2nd Media Luna. Her 3 earlier foals include Racing Post Trophy and St Leger winner Brian Boru (Sadler's Wells) and smart 10-13f winner Moon Search (Rainbow Quest). **Conclusion** Guaranteed to stay 12f, highly likely to make good progress from 2 to 3, and could easily make a serious Oaks candidate.

Layman (USA) 117

ch c Sunday Silence (USA) - Laiyl (Ire) (Nureyev (USA)) April 7
Owner Sheikh Mohammed **Trainer** A Fabre **Breeder** Darley
4 starts: won **2**, second **1**, third **1**, **£100,461** win & place prize-money

"A SNEEZING cat is a sign of future wealth." There must have been a lot of sneezing cats in Dubai a few years back, but perhaps Sheikh Mohammed is not a man for old wives' tales. There's an old saying in the horse business that ends something like "three white feet, look well about him; four white feet, do without him," or, more graphically, "three white feet, see how he goes; four white feet, feed him to the crows." It will be intriguing to see whether the case for or against that maxim is bolstered by the three-year-old season of Layman, who has four white socks and has joined Godolphin.

Layman was the joint top-rated two-year-old in France in 2004, but he lost the two top races he contested. Trained by Andre Fabre and carrying Sheikh Mohammed's maroon and white, he emerged quickly as a smart colt in the summer, when adding a five-length front-running success in the Group 3 Prix de Cabourg at Deauville to his debut victory in a newcomers race at the same course.

Three weeks after the Cabourg, Layman was back at the Normandy track for his first Group 1, the Prix Morny. Repeating the forcing tactics, Gary Stevens and Layman got home in front of well-known Group-race principals such as Russian Blue, Captain Hurricane and Mystical Land but had no answer to the filly Divine Proportions.

Layman's second appearance in the top flight came over an extra furlong in the Prix Jean-Luc Lagardere at Longchamp, a race of zigzagging paths up the straight and rapidly changing fortunes in the final furlong in which Layman was always in a leading role.

With Christophe Soumillon on board, Layman joined the front-running Early March one and a half furlongs out, but so did Montgomery's Arch and Democratic Deficit. Despite being carried left, Layman had a narrow lead for most of the final furlong and he got a bit of his own back on Early March by drifting right under the whip just before the line. However, he also lost the lead and then lost second as well as the Irish challenger Oratorio became the third horse to hold a narrow advantage in the last 70 yards. Layman was beaten a short neck and a nose.

An imposing colt, he looks the sort who will be back for more in top races as a three-year-old. Which races remains to be seen, because while Layman seemed less stout a stayer than the two colts who ultimately had his measure in the Lagardere, he looks bred to stay a mile at the very least. *RA*

Race record

3rd Prix Jean-Luc Lagardere (Group 1) (Longchamp, October 3) 2yo 7f Good **117** (TS 96) 6 ran.
2nd Prix Morny Casinos Barriere (Group 1) (Deauville, August 22) 2yo 6f Very soft **116** (TS 114) 9 ran.
1st Prix de Cabourg (Group 3) (Deauville, August 1) 2yo 6f Good **115** (TS 83) 7 ran.
1st Prix de Marolles (Unraced Colts & Geldings) (Straight Course) (Deauville, July 10) 2yo 7f Soft 7 ran.

Pedigree assessment

Sire **Sunday Silence** (Halo) Won at 2, then outstanding US dirt 3yo over 9-10f, won Kentucky Derby-Gr1, Breeders' Cup Classic-Gr1. Outstanding Japanese-based sire, does sire top-class 2yos but excels with older progeny over 8-12f. Dam **Laiyl** Unraced at 2, 10f winner at 3 from 2 starts. By top-class miler and excellent sire out of Irish Oaks winner Alydaress from outstanding family. Very closely related to 11f Gr3 winner Allurement. Her one previous foal is Layman's full-sister Silent, a useful 7-10f filly at 2 and 3 in France. **Conclusion** From outstanding family. Certain to stay 1m and likely to last 10f at 3 on pedigree. There is a chance he will stay 12f, but worth bearing in mind he showed lots of speed at 2.

Layman chases home Divine Proportions in the Morny

Librettist (USA) 115

b c Danzig (USA) - Mysterial (USA) (Alleged (USA)) April 17
Owner Godolphin **Trainer** Saeed Bin Suroor **Breeder** Calumet Farm
3 starts: won 2, second 0, third 0, £18,047 win & place prize-money

"THE ground was the problem again for our horses," said Saeed Bin Suroor after the Dewhurst Stakes. A much bigger problem presumably for Perfectperformance, who finished 12 lengths behind Librettist, while the latter showed easily his best form to date.

With the field splitting into two groups, Librettist led the outer one under Kerrin McEvoy and was still there one and a half furlongs out when hopes for most of the other runners had already been sunk in the testing ground. Librettist was never going to beat the near-side leader Shamardal, however, and in the scrap for second he tired in the final furlong and ended up in fifth.

The Dewhurst was over seven furlongs, as were a maiden at Newmarket in July and a conditions stakes at Doncaster in September, both of which were on good ground and saw Librettist win without Frankie Dettori having to get too exercised.

Bin Suroor said at Doncaster that "if he learns to relax during the winter I think he could be a Guineas horse. He could be my number one come next May but at this stage I would have to say Dubawi has the edge."

The likes of Shamardal and Layman have already been drafted in as well, however, and who is to say there won't be more?

Librettist is a Danzig half-brother to the sometimes high-class miler Dubai Destination. He's also a close relation to the July Cup winner Agnes World, another colt by Danzig. It's hard to see for sure which way Librettist will lean regarding his best trip – six furlongs, seven and a mile are all plausible. He looked a bit revved up initially as a two-year-old and his mental development is reportedly something to be worked on over the winter. Physically, however, Librettist looks the type to develop into an imposing colt; one who will be well worth further appearances in high-class company. *RA*

Race record
5th Darley Dewhurst Stakes (Group 1) (Newmarket, October 16) 2yo 7f Soft **115** (TS 114) 9 ran.
1st McKeever St Lawrence Conditions Stakes (Doncaster, September 8) 2yo 7f Good **108** (TS 90) 5 ran.
1st Vibe FM Production Kings Maiden Stakes (Newmarket (July), July 16) 2yo 7f Good **93** (TS 70) 11 ran.

Pedigree assessment
Sire **Danzig** (Northern Dancer) Unbeaten winner of 3 races at 2 and 3 in US at up to 7f. Outstanding sire, excels with 2yos, sprinters and milers, very rarely gets high-class horses over 10f+. **Dam Mysterial** Unplaced in 2 starts in US. By dual Arc winner and stamina influence, half-sister to top-class sprinter Agnes World (by Danzig) and high-class Japanese sprinter-miler Hishi Akebono (by Woodman) out of useful 8-11f filly Mysteries. Her 3 earlier foals feature high-class 2yo/miler Dubai Destination and fair 10-11f winner Destination Dubai (both by Kingmambo). **Conclusion** Very closely related to Agnes World. May not be quite so speedy as that one, but unlikely to stay beyond 1m.

Magical Romance   107

See entry in the top 100 horses, page 210

Maids Causeway (Ire)   111

ch f Giant's Causeway (USA) - Vallee des Reves (USA) (Kingmambo (USA))
March 11
Owner Martin S Schwartz **Trainer** B W Hills **Breeder** The Vallee des Reves Syndicate
7 starts: won 3, second 3, third 1, £129,225 win & place prize-money

GIANT'S CAUSEWAY'S son Shamardal may have been the outstanding two-year-old on view at Newmarket on Champions Day, but it was Maids Causeway who proved most reminiscent of the sire. Giant's Causeway made a habit of staring defeat in the face but winning, and that was exactly what transpired with Maids Causeway in the Owen Brown Rockfel Stakes.

Penkenna Princess appeared to be going the stronger entering the last 100 yards and her jockey Seb Sanders looked confident, while Michael Hills on Maids Causeway was pulling out all the stops. Penkenna Princess took a narrow lead but on the line, to the surprise of the jockeys and connections of both fillies, it was Maids Causeway who had the fractional advantage.

That tenacious performance at Newmarket was not a one-off for her but Maids Causeway was by no means indomitable. Playful Act got the better of her not once but twice, in the May Hill at Doncaster and the Fillies' Mile at Ascot. A gritty Maids Causeway finished within a length of the winner in both and showed form that made her very much the one to beat in the Rockfel.

Maids Causeway went down narrowly in two of her four starts before Doncaster and won the others, a maiden at Kempton and the Sweet Solera Stakes at Newmarket. She was bought by an American owner after the latter but Barry Hills, her trainer, has reported that he will have charge of her until the Guineas at least.

After her final win, 33-1 was available about Maids Causeway for the Classic. But while Hills's 1998 Rockfel winner Hula Angel won the Irish Guineas after finishing sixth at Newmarket, Maids Causeway will surely have to add markedly better form to her game attitude if she is to win at that level. A mile will suit her better than seven furlongs and she might get a bit further. Sometimes warm in the preliminaries but thoroughly reliable in her races so far, she has already shown that she acts on any going. *RA*

Race record

1st Owen Brown Rockfel Stakes (Group 2) (Newmarket, October 16) 2yo 7f Soft **109** (TS 96) 8 ran.

2nd Meon Valley Stud Fillies' Mile (Group 1) (Ascot, September 25) 2yo 1m Good to firm **111** (TS 105) 9 ran.

3rd betfair.com May Hill Stakes (Group 2) (Doncaster, September 9) 2yo 1m Good **111** (TS 105) 8 ran.

1st Swynford Paddocks Hotel Sweet Solera Stakes (Group 3) (Newmarket (July), August 7) 2yo 7f Good to firm **100** (TS 71) 11 ran.

2nd Star Stakes (Listed) (Sandown, July 22) 2yo 7f Good to firm **100** (TS 93) 9 ran.

1st EBF Maiden Fillies' Stakes (Kempton, June 23) 2yo 7f Good **83** (TS 22) 8 ran.

2nd Wedgewood Estates Maiden Auction Fillies' Stakes (Newbury, June 9) 2yo 6f Good to firm **86** (TS 76) 19 ran.

Pedigree assessment

Sire Giant's Causeway (Storm Cat) Top-class 2yo, won all 3 races over 6-7f inc. Prix de la Salamandre-Gr1, then tough and top-class 8-10f 3yo, won 5 more Gr1 events. By outstanding US sire out of high-class US 8-9f filly. Oldest progeny 2, very encouraging start, sire of Footstepsinthesand (Gr3), Maids Causeway (Gr2), Shamardal (Dewhurst S-Gr1). **Dam Vallee des Reves** Unraced. By top-class 2yo/miler and excellent sire, half-sister to smart miler Vetheuil and high-class 10f filly Verveine (dam of Vallee Enchantee) plus Vanishing Prairie (dam of Vespone). Her 2 earlier foals include unplaced Dream Valley (by Sadler's Wells). **Conclusion** From a very strong 1m+ French family, with most members doing better at 3+ than at 2. Given sire's race record, Maids Causeway should continue to do well at 3, when she should be effective over 8-10f and has an outside chance of staying 12f.

Master Of The Race 93

ch c Selkirk (USA) - Dust Dancer (Suave Dancer (USA)) April 29
Owner Saeed Suhail **Trainer** Sir Michael Stoute **Breeder** Hesmonds Stud Ltd
1 start: second 1, £1,538 win & place prize-money

AS the fourth foal of high-class broodmare Dust Dancer, who has already produced Grade 2 winner Spotlight, Master Of The Race is bred to go a bit and has every chance of being Dust Dancer's best yet.

Sir Michael Stoute's son of Selkirk created quite an impression when finishing runner-up to Centaurus in a warm seven-furlong Newmarket maiden in late October, going on strongly at the finish after racing notably green during the race. That form marks him down as a horse who can win at Listed level at least and a maiden success, should connections bother, will surely be just a formality.

Likely to be at his best over middle distances at three, Master Of The Race is a horse to follow and could prove one of his trainer's best in 2005. *ST*

Race record
2nd EBF Maiden Stakes (Newmarket, October 30) 2yo 7f Good to soft **93** (TS 94) 19 ran.

Pedigree assessment
Sire **Selkirk** (Sharpen Up) Very useful 1m 2yo winner, later top-class 7-8f colt, won Queen Elizabeth II S-Gr1 and 3 Gr2 events. By sire of Diesis, Kris, Sharpo and Trempolino out of high-class miler and excellent broodmare. Very good sire, decent source of 2yos (Red Bloom, Sulk) but better record with 3yos, mainly over 1m+ (Favourable Terms, Field Of Hope, Prince Kirk, Wince), sires occasional talented sprinter (The Trader). Dam **Dust Dancer** Placed over 6f at 2, smart 7-12f winner at 3 (inc. 10f Prix de la Nonette-Gr3). By top-class 12f performer, half-sister to smart 10f filly Bulaxie. Her 3 earlier foals are 9f Grade 2 winner Spotlight (by Dr Fong), quite useful 7-8f filly Dusty Answer (Zafonic) and fair 7f 3yo winner Tyranny (Machiavellian). Conclusion Certain to stay 1m and has good chance of staying 10f. Every encouragement on both sides of his pedigree that he can progress well from 2 to 3.

Merger (USA) 105

gr c Mr Greeley (USA) - Toledo Queen (Ire) (El Gran Senor (USA)) March 16
Owner Michael W J Smurfit **Trainer** D K Weld **Breeder** Hinkel Farms
2 starts: won 1, second 1, £22,260 win & place prize-money

MERGER didn't see a racecourse until late September but certainly made an impression when he did, thrashing a fair field of maidens over a mile at Thurles by upwards of five lengths.

Merger goes down before his promising Beresford second

That highly promising debut helped persuade Dermot Weld to pitch him into the Group 2 Beresford Stakes next time and the son of Mr Greeley performed admirably, only narrowly losing out to subsequent Racing Post Trophy runner-up Albert Hall in a sustained battle to the line, the pair drawing four and a half lengths clear of British raider Sant Jordi.

The bare facts of the result didn't tell the whole story, as Albert Hall's tendency to lug left under pressure, coupled with Merger running green, meant that Pat Smullen was unable to draw his whip at a crucial stage.

Whether that made the difference between victory and defeat is debatable, but the fact that Merger is a high-class prospect is not. He could hardly be in better hands. *ST*

Race record

2nd Juddmonte Beresford Stakes (Group 2) (Curragh, October 10) 2yo 1m Yielding to soft **105** (TS 93) 5 ran.
1st Killinan Maiden (Thurles, September 30) 2yo 1m Good to yielding **85** 10 ran.

Pedigree assessment

Sire **Mr Greeley** (Gone West) High-class 6-8f performer on dirt in US. By sire of Zafonic out of daughter of top-class sprinter Lianga. Decent US sire, best known in Europe for high-class 6-8f colt Reel Buddy. Dam **Toledo Queen** Won 3 races over 7-8f at 2 and 3 in Britain, later won in US. By outstanding miler out of high-class sprint 2yo Grey Dream. Her 5 earlier foals include 2 winners in US. **Conclusion** Already effective over 1m, but that should be the limit of his stamina on pedigree.

Mona Lisa

112

ch f Giant's Causeway (USA) - **Colorsnap (Shirley Heights)** March 6
Owner Michael Tabor **Trainer** A P O'Brien **Breeder** Meon Valley Stud
4 starts: won **0**, second **1**, third **0**, £13,126 win & place prize-money

AT THE end of Mona Lisa's first season, any smile would have to be at its most enigmatic. This was a smart filly but, beyond that knowledge, four starts gave connections and supporters scant reward, as she was twice beaten at odds-on, interference cost her any chance of winning a big prize on her third outing and she rounded off the campaign by looking thoroughly rattled.

The odds were 8-15 and then 1-2 when Mona Lisa got turned over in maidens at The Curragh and Leopardstown in the summer, in the latter leading over a furlong out before being short-headed as Saoire finished strongly.

Saoire went on to be placed in the Moyglare Stud Stakes and the C L Weld Park Stakes. Mona Lisa made her own Group appearances

Race record

11th Breeders' Cup Juvenile Fillies (Grade 1) (Dirt) (Lone Star Park, October 30) 2yo 1m½f Fast **81** 12 ran.

4th Meon Valley Stud Fillies' Mile (Group 1) (Ascot, September 25) 2yo 1m Good to firm **112** (TS 102) 9 ran.

2nd Irish Stallion Farms EBF Fillies Maiden (Leopardstown, August 15) 2yo 7f Good to firm **81** (TS 31) 18 ran.

4th ladbrokes.com EBF Fillies Maiden (Curragh, July 17) 2yo 7f Good **70** (TS 64) 10 ran.

Pedigree assessment

Sire **Giant's Causeway** (Storm Cat) Top-class 2yo, won all 3 races over 6-7f inc. Prix de la Salamandre-Gr1, then tough and top-class 8-10f 3yo, won 5 more Gr1 events. By outstanding US sire out of high-class 8-9f filly. Oldest progeny 2, very encouraging start, sire of Footstepsinthesand (Gr3), Maids Causeway (Gr2), Shamardal (Dewhurst S-Gr1). Dam **Colorsnap** Unraced half-sister to Irish Oaks winner Colorspin (dam of Kayf Tara, Opera House, Zee Zee Top), high-class 8-9f filly Bella Colora and high-class 10f colt Cezanne out of high-class 12f filly Reprocolor. Her 8 earlier foals include 7f 2yo Listed winners Croeso Cariad and Photogenic. **Conclusion** Two half-sisters did well at 2, but pedigree indicates Mona Lisa will be better at 3, when she should stay 10f. Greater question mark over her stamina for 12f, with sire largely an unknown quantity stamina wise.

in much stronger races, starting with the Fillies' Mile at Ascot, in which she performed a great deal better than odds of 14-1 suggested she might but captured only a slither of the prize-money. Disputing the early lead, she was then hemmed in just behind the leaders until the straight. After getting comprehensively squeezed out just before the two-furlong marker, Mona Lisa was always fighting a losing battle, but she stayed on steadily and was about two lengths behind winner Playful Act at the line, in fourth.

On her final start, in total contrast to the Fillies' Mile, Mona Lisa looked hopelessly out of place. Her performance in the Breeders' Cup Juvenile Fillies' on dirt at Lone Star Park was the sort of worst-case scenario that gives European trainers nightmares. Mona Lisa started out the back, after falling out of the stalls, and she remained there, a desperate move to the wide outside on the final turn seeing her labour even further in arrears rather than sparking any improvement in her position.

All is not lost, of course. Mona Lisa shapes as though she will relish middle distances and there is plenty of stamina in her excellent family to support that view. Her purchase price as a yearling of 1,250,000 guineas would seem appropriate for either an illustriously bred filly or a great art work (though it would not buy the Mona Lisa). Her merit purely as a racehorse has not yet been established. *RA*

Montgomery's Arch (USA) 118

b/br c Arch (USA) - Inny River (USA) (Seattle Slew (USA)) January 30
Owner Franconson Partners **Trainer** P W Chapple-Hyam **Breeder** Sycamore Hall Farm Llc
4 starts: won **2**, second **0**, third **1**, **£86,749** win & place prize-money

PETER CHAPPLE-HYAM'S first and second winners of the Richmond Stakes were separated by nine years and a lot of miles. The first was Polaris Flight in 1995 – when Chapple-Hyam was the top trainer at Glorious Goodwood – in the colours of Robert Sangster, whose decision to install John Gosden instead at Manton in 2000 led to Chapple-Hyam's exit to Hong Kong. The second was Montgomery's Arch, in Chapple-Hyam's first campaign since making the switch from Hong Kong to Newmarket.

A fine season it was too, considering he did not have anything like the numerical strength of old. Claiming the three-year-old African Dream in February proved a smart move, as he'd won four more races before June, including the Sandown Classic Trial and the Dee Stakes, and July was a good month too, with further Group victories from Captain Hurricane and Montgomery's Arch.

The Richmond at Glorious Goodwood was a big step up in class for Montgomery's Arch after a successful debut, well backed and impressive, three weeks earlier in a maiden event at Folkestone. Norfolk Stakes winner Blue Dakota bombed out, but there was still the Norfolk runner-up Mystical Land to consider and that rival led briefly in the final furlong before front-running Montgomery's Arch battled back for a neck victory.

It was his two efforts in defeat after the Richmond, however, that earned Montgomery's Arch his eventual high position in the juvenile rankings. Three lengths fourth to Oratorio in the Prix Jean-Luc Lagardere at Longchamp might have been better still with easier ground, and Montgomery's Arch very nearly turned the tables when they met again on heavy going in the Dewhurst at Newmarket, Shamardal however much too good for them both.

Montgomery's Arch looks the type to train on well and, for all that he won a good prize over Goodwood's sharp six furlongs, he will probably prove better at a mile than the shorter trips he encountered as a two-year-old. *RA*

Race record

3rd Darley Dewhurst Stakes (Group 1) (Newmarket, October 16) 2yo 7f Soft **118** (TS 118) 9 ran.
4th Prix Jean-Luc Lagardere (Group 1) (Longchamp, October 3) 2yo 7f Good **111** (TS 88) 6 ran.
1st Richmond Stakes (Group 2) (Goodwood, July 30) 2yo 6f Good to firm **109** (TS 84) 8 ran.
1st EBF Median Auction Maiden Stakes (Div I) (Folkestone, July 8) 2yo 7f Good to soft **89** (TS 60) 10 ran.

Pedigree assessment

Sire Arch (Kris S) Won sole 2yo start, later high-class US dirt performer at around 8-9f. By very good sire of dirt/turf performers, most over 1m+, from strong family of Green Desert. Fair US sire, has sired several Graded winners. **Dam Inny River** Sprint-placed on dirt in US. By outstanding 1m+ dirt performer and sire, half-sister to smart 8-10f performer Lotus Pool and to dam of high-class 8-10f colt Lear Spear. Her 2 earlier foals include a 2yo winner in US. **Conclusion** Plenty of turf indicators in his pedigree despite race record of parents. Likely to excel at around 8-9f.

Motivator   118

See entry in the top 100 horses, page 234

Oratorio   119

See entry in the top 100 horses, page 260

Oude battles hard for second place in the Acomb at York

Oude (USA) 106

b/br c Dubai Millennium - Chosen Lady (USA) (Secretariat (USA)) March 16
Owner Godolphin **Trainer** Saeed Bin Suroor **Breeder** Darley and Stonerside Stable
3 starts: won **1**, second **1**, third **1**, £21,388 win & place prize-money

OUDE showed stacks of ability in three runs as a juvenile and has the potential to be rated significantly higher still – providing he proves amenable to restraint as he gains further experience.

The son of Dubai Millennium made an impressive debut when scoring at Newmarket in late July, showing a nice turn of foot to claim his seven-furlong maiden cosily. Stepped up in class on his next start in York's Acomb Stakes, Oude travelled supremely well but was left short of room for a few strides at a vital stage, and despite quickening up well in pursuit of Elliots World, was never quite able to close the gap.

That effort suggested Oude could show a lot more when given the chance and he proved it in a strong renewal of Doncaster's Champagne Stakes, where once again he failed to settle effectively.

There was no disgrace in finishing third behind the exciting Etlaala and Coventry Stakes winner Iceman and he will do better again in time, providing he learns to conserve his energy more efficiently. *ST*

Race record

3rd SGB Champagne Stakes (Group 2) (Doncaster, September 10) 2yo 7f Good to firm **106** (TS 85) 10 ran.
2nd National Stud Never Say Die Club Acomb Stakes (Listed) (York, August 17) 2yo 7f Good **100** (TS 84) 7 ran.
1st NSPCC EBF Maiden Stakes (Newmarket (July), July 25) 2yo 7f Good **91** (TS 62) 12 ran.

Pedigree assessment

Sire Dubai Millennium (Seeking The Gold) Won sole start over 1m at 2, later outstanding 8-10f performer, won Prix Jacques le Marois-Gr1, Queen Elizabeth II S-Gr1, Dubai World Cup-Gr1, Princess of Wales's S-Gr1. By top-class 6f+ US dirt performer out of 12-14f Group winner from outstanding family. Sole crop of 2yos includes Gr1 winner Dubawi. **Dam Chosen Lady** Placed in dirt sprint in US. By outstanding dirt performer, sister to high-class turf performer Academy Award and very closely related to the dam of high-class 2yo Tomahawk. Her 9 earlier foals feature 3yo 8.5f dirt Grade 1 winner Well Chosen (by Deputy Minister) and smart dirt 7-9f performer In Contention (by Devil's Bag). **Conclusion** Likely to prove best at around 1m.

Paita   109

See entry in the top 100 horses, page 272

Penkenna Princess (Ire)   106

b f Pivotal - Tiriana (Common Grounds) May 2
Owner Mrs H M Chamberlain **Trainer** R M Beckett **Breeder** Mill House Stud
5 starts: won 2, second 1, third 1, £35,997 win & place prize-money

---

FOR A young trainer looking to make a name for himself, a win in the Group 2 Rockfel Stakes on Champions Day at Newmarket would be very welcome. It would have been for Ralph Beckett in the latest season and his Penkenna Princess looked highly likely to do the job for most of the final furlong. But Maids Causeway and the photo finish decreed otherwise.

Beckett should have time on his side and the same might be said for Penkenna Princess. She will probably be appearing in some hot events as a three-year-old, initially at least, but very much looks the type to make further progress. She's done nothing but improve so far, and in pretty spectacular style. A mile is likely to be her limit judged on pedigree.

The underbidder when Penkenna Princess made 16,000 guineas as a yearling, Beckett got her a few months later for 60,000 guineas at the breeze-up sales. It wasn't until mid-August that Penkenna Princess got a chance to repay that renewed faith, and her eighth of nine in a Goodwood maiden wasn't obviously auspicious, but early in September she went in at 16-1 in a similar event at Kempton.

Third in a Newmarket nursery, Penkenna Princess was entered in another one there the following week on a mark of 84 but, despite the trainer being told that he was mad, she turned up instead in a Listed race on the same card and won it at 25-1. Giving Beckett his first success at that level, Penkenna Princess showed class by travelling strongly to challenge and then held off Favourita, who also finished close behind her in the Rockfel.

Reflecting on her nursery defeat, Beckett had said: "I couldn't believe my eyes when she got beaten, I thought she was the best thing ever." He might have had the same reaction, but for different reasons, after the Rockfel. *RA*

Race record

2nd Owen Brown Rockfel Stakes (Group 2) (Newmarket, October 16) 2yo 7f Soft **106** (TS 92) 8 ran.

1st Finnforest Oh So Sharp Stakes (Listed) (Newmarket, October 2) 2yo 7f Good **103** (TS 91) 14 ran.

3rd Robinsons Mercedes-Benz Nursery (Newmarket, September 21) 2yo (0-85 handicap) 6f Good to firm **91** (TS 84) 10 ran.

1st Rukba Cantor Sport EBF Maiden Fillies' Stakes (Div II) (Kempton, September 3) 2yo 6f Good **83** (TS 77) 13 ran.

8th EBF Chichester City Median Auction Maiden Stakes (Goodwood, August 14) 2yo 6f Good **48** (TS 39) 9 ran.

Pedigree assessment

Sire Pivotal (Polar Falcon) Won 2 races over 5-6f at 2, high-class sprinter at 3, won King's Stand S-Gr2 and Nunthorpe S-Gr1. By top-class sprinter-miler. Very good sire, strong record with 2yos and also with 3yo+ over variety of trips. Particularly strong record with fillies (Chorist, Golden Apples, Megahertz, Silvester Lady), who tend to stay better than colts. **Dam Tiriana** Placed at 2, 11f winner at 3 in France. By top-class 2yo, half-sister to useful sprint 2yo Head Over Heels. Her 2 earlier foals are 1m 3yo+ winner Madamoiselle Jones (by Emperor Jones) and 10-16f winner Salut Saint Cloud (by Primo Domine). **Conclusion** Every chance she will stay 1m at 3, but probably no further.

Perfectperformance (USA)

112

ch c Rahy (USA) - Balistroika (USA) (Nijinsky (Can)) February 24
Owner Godolphin **Trainer** Saeed Bin Suroor **Breeder** Brushwood Stable
5 starts: won **3**, second **1**, third **0**, £86,390 win & place prize-money

WITH his $1,100,000 purchase price, Russian Rhythm as a big sister and a name like his, Perfectperformance did not have much to live up to, did he? Connections of an earlier half-sister played it a bit more cagily when they called their charge Ive Gota Bad Liver.

Another moniker for Perfectperformance, judged on his two-year-old campaign, might be Progressiveperformanceuntilthegroundwassoft. The Godolphin colt was not expected to live up to his name on his debut in late June judged on the betting – there was a 1-2 shot in opposition – but he won that maiden at Salisbury by a neck. "The further he went the better he looked," was a comment that summed up that effort and kept recurring.

Perfectperformance found the more experienced Brecon Beacon too good at Newmarket in July but returned to Salisbury to land a three-runner Listed race in clear-cut fashion, as expected at 4-5, from another useful performer in Grand Marque.

The runner-up's solid show in the Champagne Stakes was another encouraging sign for Perfectperformance's Group-race debut in the Royal

Race record

7th Darley Dewhurst Stakes (Group 1) (Newmarket, October 16) 2yo 7f Soft **88** (TS 78) 9 ran.

1st Hackney Empire Royal Lodge Stakes (Group 2) (Ascot, September 25) 2yo 1m Good to firm **112** (TS 114) 8 ran.

1st Weatherbys Stonehenge Stakes (Listed) (Salisbury, August 11) 2yo 1m Good to firm **104** (TS 84) 3 ran.

2nd turftours.com For Sporting Hospitality Conditions Stakes (Newmarket (July), July 30) 2yo 7f Good to firm **99** (TS 96) 8 ran.

1st Herbert And Gwen Blagrave EBF Maiden Stakes (Div I) (Salisbury, June 24) 2yo 7f Good **90** (TS 20) 8 ran.

Pedigree assessment

Sire Rahy (Blushing Groom) High-class 6f 2yo, 2nd Middle Park S-Gr1. Useful miler in Britain at 3, later smart on dirt at around 1m in US. By top-class miler and excellent sire, half-brother to Singspiel from outstanding family. Very good sire, does get high-class 2yos (Noverre) but most progeny best as 3yo+ over 1m+ (Fantastic Light, Serena's Song). **Dam Balistroika** Unraced. By Triple Crown winner and outstanding sire, half-sister to Gr1 winners Alydaress, Desirable, Park Appeal, from outstanding family. Her 7 previous foals feature top-class 2yo/8-10f filly Russian Rhythm (by Kingmambo) and US stakes-placed Ive Gota Bad Liver (by Mt Livermore, by Blushing Groom). **Conclusion** Should excel over 8f at 3 but doubtful whether he will stay much further. Every chance he will train on well.

Lodge Stakes at Ascot and he was heavily backed at 4-6. More importantly, the mile on a stiff track looked certain to suit Frankie Dettori's mount, and so it proved. He tracked the leaders on the outside and grabbed the lead one and a half furlongs out, but put clear water between himself and the Ballydoyle colt Scandinavia only in the last 100 yards. As further evidence of his improvement, Perfectperformance increased his superiority over Grand Marque.

Given the way he did the job at Ascot, it was a bit of a surprise that Perfectperformance ran next in the seven-furlong Dewhurst, but in the event it was testing ground that almost certainly goes furthest to explaining his modest show at 8-1.

Perfectperformance looked the part in the paddock before the Dewhurst and should make a very good three-year-old. He's not so far exhibited the star quality of some of his contemporaries but looks sure to improve

Perfectperformance lands the Group 2 Royal Lodge Stakes

and will be helped by at least a mile and a quarter. He shapes as if he will stay further than that and Saeed Bin Suroor stated after the Royal Lodge: "I think a mile is the best trip for him this year, but next year it is likely that he'll race at a mile and a half." *RA*

Playful Act   113

See entry in the top 100 horses, page 292

Plea Bargain   90

b c Machiavellian (USA) - Time Saved (Green Desert (USA)) February 24
Owner Sheikh Mohammed **Trainer** J H M Gosden **Breeder** W and R Barnett Ltd
2 starts: won 1, third 1, £5,085 win & place prize-money

AT 425,000 guineas one would hope Plea Bargain would be able to run quite fast and thankfully he can. John Gosden's son of Machiavellian is out of a half-sister to top-class performers Zinaad and Time Allowed

Race record

1st EBF/Potters Leisure Resort Maiden Stakes (Div II) (Yarmouth, October 27) 2yo 7f Soft **90** (TS 91) 14 ran.
3rd EBF/Subscribe To Racing UK On 08700 860432 Maiden Stakes (Div I) (Salisbury, September 29) 2yo 1m Good to soft **78** (TS 77) 15 ran.

Pedigree assessment

Sire Machiavellian (Mr Prospector) Top-class 2yo over 6-7f, won Prix Morny-Gr1, Prix de la Salamandre-Gr1. High-class miler at 3, 2nd 2,000 Guineas-Gr1. By outstanding sire out of outstanding broodmare, most family members best around 1m. Very good sire, fair record with 2yos (Best Of The Bests, Titus Livius) but better one with older horses, mainly over 6-10f (Almutawakel, Medicean, Rebecca Sharp, Storming Home, Street Cry). Sires occasional high-class 12f+ performer (Invermark, Phantom Gold, Whitewater Affair) out of stout dam. **Dam Time Saved** Unraced at 2, 10f winner at 3. By very good sire of 2yos, sprinters and milers, out of outstanding 10-12f racemare Time Charter. Half-sister to 12f Group 2 winners Time Allowed and Zinaad to dam of 2m Group 2 winner First Charter. This is her first foal. **Conclusion** Should make good progress from 2 to 3. Likely to prove most effective over 10f, has outside chance of staying 12f.

and looks a smart prospect in his own right judged on the way he annihilated a big field of maidens over seven furlongs at Yarmouth in late October.

He had shown stacks of promise under a sympathetic ride when finishing third in a decent Salisbury mile maiden and duly left that level of form behind when scooting home at Yarmouth by five lengths, value for further on the day.

Plea Bargain promises to be suited by a much stiffer test of stamina at three and could well turn out to be Gosden's best middle-distance colt. *ST*

Proclamation (Ire) 90

gr c King's Best (USA) - Shamarra (Fr) (Zayyani) May 1
Owner Abdullah Saeed Belhab **Trainer** J Noseda **Breeder** Cathal M Ryan
1 start: won **1, £7,163** win & place prize-money

JEREMY NOSEDA no longer has charge of his Breeders' Cup Juvenile winner Wilko and the gap will be a difficult one to fill. Nevertheless, he still has some bright young prospects to look forward to in 2005.

Proclamation heads the list after winning a soft-ground mile maiden at Newmarket in taking style in October, pulling three and a half lengths clear of Unfurled, with another 19 rivals well strung out. He was the subject of persistent support from longish odds, and those who played were rewarded with a performance that suggests he will be contesting Pattern races in time.

A half-brother to No Refuge, Proclamation is bred to stay well. It will be interesting to see how far up the class ladder he can progress. *ST*

Race record
1st Federation of Bloodstock Agents Maiden Stakes (Newmarket, October 15) 2yo 1m Soft **90** (TS 90) 21 ran.

Pedigree assessment
Sire King's Best (Kingmambo) Smart dual 7f 2yo winner, won 2,000 Guineas in 2 completed 3yo outings. By top-class 2yo/miler and excellent sire. Half-brother to several good performers, notably Arc winner Urban Sea (dam of Galileo), from very strong middle-distance family. Oldest progeny 2, sire of Dubai Surprise (Gr3), Elliots World (Listed). **Dam Shamarra** Unraced. By smart miler, half-sister to very useful 12f performer Shantaroun and to dam of smart stayer Shaiybara. Her 4 earlier foals include useful 12-15f winner No Refuge (by Hernando) and 6f 2yo winner Denmark (by Danehill). **Conclusion** Has won over 1m, and that should be his minimum in 2005. Should stay 10f, but question mark over his stamina for 12f.

Public Forum 76

b c Rainbow Quest (USA) - Valentine Girl (Alzao (USA)) January 10
Owner K Abdullah **Trainer** Sir Michael Stoute **Breeder** Juddmonte Farms
1 start: won **1**, **£4,595** win & place prize-money

PUBLIC FORUM followed the example of his illustrious parents by winning at the first time of asking in the October mud.

By Rainbow Quest out of Cheshire Oaks winner Valentine Girl, he is bred to be smart and did all that he could in defeating Miss L'Augeval

---

Race record
1st Eversheds Royal Standard Novice Stakes (Nottingham, October 20) 2yo 1m Heavy **76** (TS 68) 5 ran.

Pedigree assessment
Sire Rainbow Quest (Blushing Groom) High-class 2yo, later top class over 10-12f, won Coronation Cup-Gr1, Arc-Gr1. Very good sire, occasionally sires smart 2yos (Armiger) but most progeny better as 3yos+. Sires occasional top-class miler (Spectrum), most progeny excel over 10f+ (Knight's Baroness, Millenary, Quest For Fame, Saumarez). **Dam Valentine Girl** Useful 7f 2yo winner, later showed useful form over 11-15f. Dam middle-distance winner, sister to smart 10f+ performers Jalaajel and Non Partisan and half-sister to Suntrap (dam of top-class 12f+ performers Raintrap and Sunshack, both by Rainbow Quest, and grand-dam of 2004 10f+ Gr1 winners Meteor Storm and Polish Summer). **Conclusion** Bred to a successful, stout formula. Virtually guaranteed to progress well from 2 to 3, when he should excel over 12f.

with something to spare in a mile novice event at Nottingham under an educational ride from Kieren Fallon.

There were eight lengths back to the remainder and Sir Michael Stoute's colt could hardly have made a more pleasing start to his career.

He sits in the 'could be anything' file ahead of his three-year-old campaign. *ST*

Queen Of Poland 108

b f Halling (USA) - Polska (USA) (Danzig (USA)) February 28
Owner Sheikh Mohammed **Trainer** D R Loder **Breeder** Darley
4 starts: won **2**, second **1**, third **0**, **£38,293** win & place prize-money

QUEEN OF POLAND had two memorable head-to-head battles with
Maids Causeway, winning both by a narrow margin but with both fillies
deserving high praise for their dedication to the cause.

Their first meeting was in a Listed race over seven furlongs at Sandown
in July, when both were graduating from wins in maiden races. Queen
Of Poland's had been her debut at Yarmouth when looking the stable
second choice on jockey bookings but making her first experience of
tight finishes a winning one at 16-1. Maids Causeway headed three
fillies that were preferred to Queen Of Poland in the betting at Sandown
and, for most of the closing stages, looked likely to get the better of this
first duel, but it was Queen Of Poland who did so to win by a head.

The rematch came in the May Hill at Doncaster, where it was Queen
Of Poland's turn to start favourite, in receipt of 3lb from what was no doubt

Race record
6th Prix Marcel Boussac Royal Barriere Deauville (Group 1) (Longchamp, October 3) 2yo 1m Good **105**
(TS 100) 10 ran.
2nd betfair.com May Hill Stakes (Group 2) (Doncaster, September 9) 2yo 1m Good **108** (TS 103) 8 ran.
1st Star Stakes (Listed) (Sandown, July 22) 2yo 7f Good to firm **101** (TS 94) 9 ran.
1st EBF Maiden Fillies' Stakes (Yarmouth, July 1) 2yo 7f Firm **80** (TS 77) 10 ran.

Pedigree assessment
Sire Halling (Diesis) Unraced at 2, later progressed into top-class 9-10f performer. Good sire, can
get smart 2yos but most talented progeny excel as 3yos+ over 8-10f. **Dam Polska** Won only start
at 2 over 6f, later showed fair form over 7-8f. By outstanding speed influence out of smart US 1m
dirt/turf filly Aquaba. Very closely related to smart 2yo/sprinter Millstream (by Dayjur), dam to Halling of
useful 2yo/miler Baaridd. Her 4 earlier foals include 2yo winners White Hawk (7f) and Grizel (5-6f) and a
7f 3yo winner in US by Machiavellian. **Conclusion** Already has shown smart form over 1m, and
that is likely to be the limit of her stamina on pedigree.

labelled her "old rival". The two of them were locked together from a long
way out and this time Queen Of Poland prevailed by only a short head.
Both, however, were three-quarters of a length behind Playful Act.

Admirable though Queen Of Poland was as a two-year-old, plenty of
other fillies have to be rated higher. Five finished in front of her on her
final start in the Marcel Boussac at Longchamp, though in Queen Of
Poland's defence it should be pointed out that a draw next to the rails
was always going to spell trouble for her and she was duly in a modest
position when asked to quicken with the others in the straight.

Queen Of Poland, right, beats Maids Causeway at Sandown

As she is owned by Sheikh Mohammed, Queen Of Poland could be appearing for Saeed Bin Suroor instead of David Loder as a three-year-old. Presumably she will be if the owner thinks she is good enough. On what was seen of her in 2004, and unless it turns out that she is well suited by more give in the ground, Queen Of Poland will not be winning at the top level over a mile. Her racing style suggests that she will get a bit further than that, but she does not look bred for a mile and a half. *RA*

Rebuttal (USA)   119

b c Mr Greeley (USA) - Reboot (USA) (Rubiano (USA)) March 12
Owner P Minikes **Trainer** B J Meehan **Breeder** Cho Llc & J P R Stables Llc
4 starts: won **1**, second **2**, third **1**, **£56,257** win & place prize-money

REBUTTAL was touted as a possible for the Breeders' Cup Juvenile at Lone Star Park until 12 days before the race, and he would have been an interesting runner there. He had earned a second crack at a top-level juvenile race with his much-improved three-quarter length second to Ad Valorem in the Middle Park Stakes, and his American pedigree – by the 1995 Breeders' Cup Sprint second Mr Greeley out of a mare who was a multiple sprint winner in the States –

suggested he would adapt well to racing on dirt. However, while Wilko bucked the trend, it can be particularly tough for British two-year-olds over there, and Rebuttal had a big question to answer stamina-wise. For the Breeders' Cup Juvenile was run over an extended mile, and Rebuttal has a speed pedigree and has raced exclusively at six furlongs so far.

According to Brian Meehan it was not the stamina worry that dissuaded him from sending Rebuttal to Texas, for he was encouraged by the opinions of Jimmy Fortune and Pat Smullen and is confident the colt will stay a mile. It was more a matter of the long-term interests of the colt being given priority, for Meehan regards Rebuttal as a "hugely talented" colt and a serious challenger for the 2,000 Guineas, which could be his first race of 2005. He was anxious not to overtax him at two and also pulled him out of the Horris Hill Stakes.

The Middle Park was Rebuttal's fourth race in a campaign that saw

Race record

2nd Shadwell Stud Middle Park Stakes (Group 1) (Newmarket, October 1) 2yo 6f Good **119** (TS 102) 9 ran.

3rd Dubai Duty Free Mill Reef Stakes (Group 2) (Newbury, September 18) 2yo 6f Good to soft **108** (TS 90) 9 ran.

1st Evening Standard Maiden Stakes (Kempton, August 18) 2yo 6f Soft **92** (TS 58) 8 ran.

2nd Guinness Maiden Stakes (Windsor, August 9) 2yo 6f Good to soft **87** (TS 84) 18 ran.

Pedigree assessment

Sire **Mr Greeley** (Gone West) High-class 6-8f performer on dirt in US. By sire of Zafonic out of daughter of top-class sprinter Lianga. Decent US sire, best known in Europe for high-class 6-8f colt Reel Buddy. **Dam Reboot** Unraced at 2, won 4 dirt sprints in US at 3 and 4. By top-class 6-9f dirt performer out of US sprint stakes winner on dirt. Her 1 earlier foal won at 3 in US. **Conclusion** Has been campaigned exclusively over 6f so far, and on pedigree is not certain to stay a great deal further.

him improve with every run. A promising second at Windsor on his debut, he went on to make all at odds-on in a maiden at Kempton, despite worries about the soft ground, and then stepped up to Group company for his last two starts. He was unlucky not to finish second at least in the Mill Reef Stakes at Newbury, where the waiting tactics were overdone and Galeota and Mystical Land both got first run on him. However, he had his chance in the Middle Park and simply ran into one that was a bit too good for him in the unbeaten Ad Valorem, who just outstayed him, the pair pulling clear.

Connections have nothing to lose by trying to stretch Rebuttal to a mile in the spring, as there are few alternatives over shorter distances. However, the chances are that he's a sprinter, and a pretty smart one too. *GD*

Rob Roy (USA)   86

b/br c Lear Fan (USA) - Camanoe (USA) (Gone West (USA)) March 27
Owner Philip Newton **Trainer** Sir Michael Stoute **Breeder** Millsec Ltd
1 start: won **1**, **£8,628** win & place prize-money

RUN on the same day at Newmarket in October, the Group 1 Middle Park Stakes was won by Ad Valorem and the Beech House Stud EBF Maiden Stakes (Division 2) by Rob Roy. Neither ran again, yet within a month they could both be backed at the same price for the 2,000 Guineas.

The bookmakers are happy to populate their Classic lists with once-raced wonders and in 2004 Rob Roy was the one that seemingly impressed backers and layers the most. Few of the 23 runners in Rob Roy's maiden had run before and none had accomplished anything of note. The initial results of those that ran again did not make attractive reading either. Little was expected of the second and third, if starting prices of 66-1 are anything to go by.

Those are some of the negatives, but there's no denying that Rob Roy

Race record
1st Beech House Stud EBF Maiden Stakes (Newmarket, October 1) 2yo 7f Good **86** (TS 96)
23 ran.

Pedigree assessment
Sire Lear Fan (Roberto) High-class 2yo, then top-class miler. By Derby-winning sire of good sires Dynaformer, Kris S, Robellino, Silver Hawk, out of smart US 2yo. Very good sire, mainly of 3yo+ over 8-10f (Lear Spear, Loup Solitaire, Ryafan, Sarafan, Windsharp). **Dam Camanoe** Unraced at 2, unplaced in 2 1m starts at 3. Half-sister to very high-class 9f+ performers Public Purse (by Private Account) and Super Staff (by Secretariat). This is her first foal. **Conclusion** Should be effective over 8-10f at 3, and encouragement on both sides of his pedigree that he will make good progress over the winter.

is a horse of major promise. In the paddock, he left a very strong impression with his scopey physique, and in the race he won with complete authority after being sent off 4-1 favourite and held up in the early stages. He will surely leave the form of that two-and-a-half-length success well behind as a three-year-old.

Rob Roy won over seven furlongs and should stay a mile. His dam appeared in two maidens over that trip as a three-year-old but suffered an irregular heartbeat on the second occasion and was not seen again. At $300,000, he was the highest-priced offspring at auction from the last three crops by Lear Fan. *RA*

Russian Blue (Ire)   113

b c Danehill (USA) - **Soviet Artic (Fr)** (Bering) March 15
Owner Sangster Family **Trainer** A P O'Brien **Breeder** Swettenham Stud
8 starts: won **3**, second **1**, third **3**, **£130,529** win & place prize-money

RUSSIAN BLUE ultimately fell several lengths short of the best of his generation but ran with great credit at the highest level on a number of occasions, being a little unlucky not to collect a Group prize along the way.

The son of Danehill started early, giving Aidan O'Brien his fifth win in six years in Ireland's first juvenile race of the season before completing a quick-fire Curragh hat-trick with two further wins before the end of May, including in the Marble Hill Stakes. Long odds-on for that Listed-

Race record

5th Shadwell Stud Middle Park Stakes (Group 1) (Newmarket, October 1) 2yo 6f Good **109** (TS 89) 9 ran.

3rd Dunnes Stores National Stakes (Group 1) (Curragh, September 19) 2yo 7f Yielding **111** (TS 105) 7 ran.

3rd Prix Morny Casinos Barriere (Group 1) (Deauville, August 22) 2yo 6f Very soft **113** (TS 108) 9 ran.

3rd Independent Waterford Wedgwood Phoenix Stakes (Group 1) (Curragh, August 8) 2yo 6f Good to firm **110** (TS 84) 6 ran.

2nd Anheuser Busch Railway Stakes (Group 2) (Curragh, June 27) 2yo 6f Good to firm **105** (TS 85) 7 ran.

1st Isabel Morris Marble Hill Stakes (Listed) (Curragh, May 22) 2yo 5f Good to firm **98** (TS 76) 4 ran.

1st Choisir EBF Race (Curragh, May 3) 2yo 5f Good **92** (TS 84) 5 ran.

1st Tally Ho Stud EBF Maiden (Curragh, March 21) 2yo 5f Heavy **88** (TS 77) 8 ran.

Pedigree assessment

Sire Danehill (Danzig) Useful 6f 2yo winner, improved at 3 into top-class sprinter, won Haydock Sprint Cup-Gr1 but also smart over 1m. Excellent sire, has done well with 2yos and older progeny, mainly at up to 1m but capable of getting top-class 10f+ performers from stoutly bred dams. Best progeny include Aquarelliste, Banks Hill, Cacique, Desert King, Landseer, Mozart, North Light, Oratorio, Rock Of Gibraltar, Westerner. **Dam Soviet Artic** Unraced at 2, middle-distance winner at 3 in France, showed fair form at up to 14f. Half-sister to several fair performers in France, most at 1m+, from good family of 8-12f performers. This is her second foal; her first is unplaced Mr Loverman. **Conclusion** Likely to be effective over 1m at 3. Already very experienced, and may not have as much scope for improvement as some of his contemporaries.

race success, he scored comfortably enough, making all the running to see off his three rivals.

Aidan O'Brien's recent domination of the Railway Stakes came to an end along with Russian Blue's unbeaten record, as he failed to overhaul Democratic Deficit after an uncharacteristic tardy start.

After that it was Group 1 all the way for Russian Blue as he showed improved form by finishing third in the Phoenix Stakes before going on to fill the same berth in the Prix Morny and the National Stakes.

Russian Blue lands the Listed Marble Hill Stakes

He held his form admirably well considering the early start, still being able to run within a length or so of his best when finishing fifth on his final start of the year behind stablemate Ad Valorem in the Middle Park.

Russian Blue will need to improve to be successful at the top level as a three-year-old, though if he is able to reproduce his juvenile form he should have little trouble gaining a well-deserved first Group-race victory. *ST*

Satchem (Ire)   110

br c Inchinor - Mohican Princess (Shirley Heights) February 11
Owner Sheikh Hamdan Bin Mohammed Al Maktoum **Trainer** C E Brittain
Breeder K Molloy
5 starts: won **3**, second **1**, third **0**, **£48,028** win & place prize-money

---

SOME of their father's love of the turf seems to have rubbed off on Sheikh Mohammed's sons, Sheikh Rashid and Sheikh Hamdan. Sheikh Rashid, who rode in two amateur riders' races (finishing third once) in Britain in 2000, was the champion owner in Dubai in the winter of 2003-04 and is a growing force as an owner in British racing and the sales rings.

Now Sheikh Hamdan Bin Mohammed Al Maktoum is joining in and purchased the smart two-year-olds Satchem and Henrik during the latest season. A powerful trend could be under way, as these two are by no means the last of Sheikh Mohammed's children, and he got married again in 2004.

Satchem had three runs and two wins under his belt when Sheikh Hamdan snapped him up, along with another Lucayan Stud winner in Stetchworth Prince. The first of Satchem's wins had been in a novice stakes at Yarmouth and a nursery at Newmarket, favourite for the latter and understandably so as it came one day after his Yarmouth victim Captain Hurricane had won the July Stakes.

The sale was concluded at the end of July and Satchem was transferred to Clive Brittain from David Loder, making his next start in the Sirenia

Race record

4th Shadwell Stud Middle Park Stakes (Group 1) (Newmarket, October 1) 2yo 6f Good **110** (TS 91) 9 ran.

1st Pentax Sirenia Stakes (Group 3) (Kempton, September 4) 2yo 6f Good to firm **110** (TS 85) 8 ran.

1st newmarketracecourses.co.uk Nursery (Newmarket (July), July 8) 2yo 7f Good to soft **94** (TS 96) 13 ran.

1st EBF Novice Median Auction Stakes (Yarmouth, June 10) 2yo 6f Firm **79** (TS 78) 5 ran.

2nd Pytchley Hunt Maiden Stakes (Leicester, May 24) 2yo 6f Good to firm **79** (TS 74) 7 ran.

Pedigree assessment

Sire Inchinor (Ahonoora) High-class 2yo and 3yo over 6-8f. By top-class sprinter out of high-class 2yo/miler. Decent sire, has reasonable record with 2yos (Bannister, Golden Silca), also does well with older sprinters (Cape Of Good Hope, Orientor), milers (Summoner) and occasional 10f performer (Latice). **Dam Mohican Princess** Unplaced over 10f at 3 on only start. Had good chance of staying 12f on pedigree, by stamina influence out of very useful 10-11f filly Mohican Girl, whose half-sisters include high-class 12f fillies Sally Brown and Untold. This is her first foal. **Conclusion** Stamina on dam's side, but looks to have inherited some speed from sire. Likely to be effective over 1m at 3, and may stay a little further.

Stakes at Kempton and winning it from Godolphin's established Group-race performer Council Member.

"You know me, the sky's the limit now," said Brittain, adding: "This is all down to David Loder. He trained the horse and it was up to me to lift him up in class."

There is no better man for that, but a further step up, when Satchem was supplemented into the Middle Park line-up, did not work out quite so well, with Satchem's connections having to settle for a creditable fourth in the six-furlong Group 1. His nursery win was over seven furlongs and his pedigree suggests that trip, at least, may suit him better at three. Satchem is not a substantial colt at all, but Brittain has observed that "he has so much heart and ability, we won't worry about the scope." *RA*

Saywaan (USA)   83

ch f Fusaichi Pegasus (USA) - Sharp Cat (USA) (Storm Cat (USA)) April 5
Owner Godolphin **Trainer** Saeed Bin Suroor **Breeder** The Thoroughbred Corporation
1 start: won **1**, **£5,694** win & place prize-money

SAYWAAN may not have beaten a great deal when scoring easily on her debut over seven furlongs at Leicester in October, but she could hardly have completed her task with greater aplomb and looks a bright prospect.

The $1.5m purchase, a daughter of exciting first-season sire Fusaichi Pegasus out of top American racemare Sharp Cat, was always going well

Race record
1st EBF Hare Maiden Fillies' Stakes (Div II) (Leicester, October 11) 2yo 7f Good **83** (TS 74 19 ran.

Pedigree assessment
Sire Fusaichi Pegasus (Mr Prospector) Placed only start at 2, top-class 8-10f dirt performer at 3, won Kentucky Derby-Gr1. By outstanding sire out of stakes-placed sister to Preakness Stakes winner Pine Bluff. Oldest progeny 2, sire in US of Roman Ruler (Gr2) and in Europe of Listed winner Witten and Gr2-placed Scandinavia. **Dam Sharp Cat** Outstanding US dirt filly from 2 to 4, winner of 13 Graded races, 7 of them Grade 1. By top-class 2yo and outstanding sire, half-sister to top-class 10-12f colt Royal Anthem (Theatrical). This is her second foal. **Conclusion** Has outstanding pedigree, one that suggests she can make good progress from 2 to 3. Likely to be effective over 1m, and may stay 10f, but that looks the likely limit of her stamina.

and, once asked to put her stamp on the race, quickly went clear to record a comprehensive three-and-a-half length success.

After the race Godolphin representative Diana Cooper said: "We hope she has the makings of a good filly. This will be her only start this year but we are looking forward to seeing her back next year."

Likely to stay middle distances at three, she is a filly we are likely to hear a great deal more of. *ST*

Scandinavia (USA)   109

b c Fusaichi Pegasus (USA) - Party Cited (USA) (Alleged (USA)) May 8
Owner Mrs John Magnier **Trainer** A P O'Brien **Breeder** Rancho San Peasea Sa
5 starts: won **1**, second **3**, third **0**, **£36,932** win & place prize-money

THE Breeders' Cup Juvenile had an invigorating effect on Wilko and a debilitating one on his fellow long-distance traveller Scandinavia. On their previous outing there was just one and a quarter lengths between them and Scandinavia came out on top.

That much happier experience for Scandinavia came in the Royal Lodge Stakes at Ascot, for which Wilko arrived with a creditable Group-race record whereas Scandinavia's CV boasted two odds-on defeats and one odds-on victory, all in maidens and the win coming when 1-3 at Galway in July. Sent off at 8-1 at Ascot and held up towards the rear early on, Scandinavia followed Perfectperformance through and, despite hanging right, posed the only threat to him in the last furlong

---

Race record
8th Bessemer Trust Breeders' Cup Juvenile (Grade 1) (Dirt) (Lone Star Park, October 30) 2yo 1m½f Fast **87** 8 ran.
2nd Hackney Empire Royal Lodge Stakes (Group 2) (Ascot, September 25) 2yo 1m Good to firm **109** (TS 109) 8 ran.
1st Dawn Hi And Lo EBF Maiden (Galway, July 31) 2yo 1m½f Good to firm **92** 7 ran.
2nd Curragh Equine Groundcare EBF Maiden (Curragh, June 25) 2yo 7f Good **86** (TS 80) 13 ran.
2nd Irish Stallion Farms EBF Maiden (Tipperary, June 10) 2yo 7½f Firm **86** 8 ran.

Pedigree assessment
Sire Fusaichi Pegasus (Mr Prospector) Placed only start at 2, top-class 8-10f dirt performer at 3, won Kentucky Derby-Gr1. By outstanding sire out of stakes-placed sister to Preakness Stakes winner Pine Bluff. Oldest progeny 2, sire in US of Roman Ruler (Gr2) and in Europe of Listed winner Witten. **Dam Party Cited** Useful placed form over 1m at 2, useful 8-10f performer at 3, then progressed into high-class 8-10f turf filly in US. By dual Arc winner and stamina influence, half-sister to useful milers Amid Albadu and Dehoush. Her 6 earlier foals feature top-class US dirt 2yo/3yo Composure (by Touch Gold). **Conclusion** Already suited by 1m, and should be effective at up to 10f.

---

and a half; at his withers at the furlong marker, however, Scandinavia lost ground in the last 100 yards to go down by one and a half lengths. Wilko was third, having been checked as Scandinavia began his challenge.

Then for the Breeders' Cup. "He loves the dirt at home, is naturally quick to break, and is very much on the upgrade," Aidan O'Brien reported beforehand, none of which was apparent in Texas as slow-starting Scandinavia ran a bit wide towards the rear and capitulated totally entering the straight, finishing last of eight.

How Scandinavia is going to fit in as a three-year-old in Europe is not clear. He is bred to stay a mile and a quarter and has raced chiefly on fast ground when on turf. *RA*

Shamardal   125

See entry in the top 100 horses, page 352

Shanghai Lily scores the first of her two wins at Newbury

Shanghai Lily (Ire)   100

b f King's Best (USA) - Marlene-D (Selkirk (USA)) March 2
Owner Cheveley Park Stud **Trainer** Sir Michael Stoute **Breeder** Mrs Monica Hackett
2 starts: won **2**, **£17,028** win & place prize-money

THE Sir Michael Stoute-trained Shanghai Lily would probably have started favourite for the Rockfel Stakes had she not been withdrawn because of the rain-sodden going. "Michael didn't want to risk pulling

Race record

1st Dubai Duty Free Full of Surprises EBF Fillies' Conditions Stakes (Newbury, September 17) 2yo 7f Good **100** (TS 86) 4 ran.
1st stanjamesuk.com EBF Maiden Fillies' Stakes (Div I) (Newbury, August 13) 2yo 6f Good to soft **85** (TS 82) 11 ran.

Pedigree assessment

Sire King's Best (Kingmambo) Smart dual 7f 2yo winner, won 2,000 Guineas in 2 completed 3yo outings. By top-class 2yo/miler and excellent sire. Half-brother to several good performers, notably Arc winner Urban Sea (dam of Galileo), from very strong middle-distance family. Oldest progeny 2, sire of Dubai Surprise (Gr3), Elliots World (Listed). **Dam Marlene-D** Unplaced sole 2yo start, 9f winner at 3. By top-class miler and very good sire, half-sister to very useful stayer Arden (by Ardross) and useful sprinter Kerulen (by Cadeaux Genereux). Her one earlier foal is 7f 2yo winner Eden Rock (by Danehill). **Conclusion** Has the pedigree of a miler. Every likelihood on pedigree she that she will make good progress from 2 to 3.

her about on that ground, so she's been put away for the winter," said Chris Richardson of Cheveley Park Stud, which owns her. "I imagine she'll probably go straight to the Guineas."

At the end of the season Shanghai Lily was around a 20-1 chance for that Classic. She was not that much longer after making a winning debut at Newbury in August. The form of that maiden race is nothing special, she lacked big-race entries and, although starting favourite, she was hardly all the rage beforehand, but Shanghai Lily looked in a class of her own in the last quarter-mile. "She's a proper horse," said Kieren Fallon in highly admiring tones.

The Dubai Duty Free Full of Surprises EBF Fillies' Conditions Stakes at the same track five weeks later brought no surprises as Shanghai Lily prevailed in much the same style as in her maiden.

Those races were over six and seven furlongs and Shanghai Lily is bred to stay at least a mile. Richardson has reported that she needs time between her races. Those fillies put against her in 2003 did not provide a serious test. Cheveley Park Stud has a few cards to shuffle before it decides on its hand for the Guineas, but Shanghai Lily looks a Group winner in waiting. *RA*

Silk And Scarlet 102

b f Sadler's Wells (USA) - Danilova (Lyphard) March 20
Owner Mrs John Magnier **Trainer** A P O'Brien **Breeder** Juddmonte Farms
4 starts: won **2**, second **1**, third **0**, £85,542 win & place prize-money

SILK AND SCARLET finished only seventh behind Chelsea Rose when a hot favourite for the Moyglare Stud Stakes, but at the end of the year she was still among the market leaders for the Oaks.

It can pay to forgive her that one blip in an otherwise progressive profile.

Race record
7th Moyglare Stud Stakes (Group 1) (Curragh, September 5) 2yo 7f Good to firm **99** (TS 96) 12 ran.
1st Robert H Griffin Debutante Stakes (Group 2) (Curragh, August 8) 2yo 7f Good to firm **102** (TS 99) 8 ran.
1st Silver Flash Stakes (Listed) (Leopardstown, July 14) 2yo 6f Good to yielding **102** (TS 93) 12 ran.
2nd Irish Stallion Farms Maiden (Leopardstown, June 9) 2yo 7f Good to firm **77** (TS 30) 13 ran.

Pedigree assessment
Sire Sadler's Wells (Northern Dancer) Smart 7-8f winner at 2, improved into top-class 8-12f colt at 3, won Irish 2,000 Guineas-Gr1, Eclipse S-Gr1, Irish Champion S-Gr1. Outstanding sire, particularly of 3yo+ over 8-12f, also has good record with autumn 2yos. **Dam Danilova** A daughter of the Ribblesdale winner Ballinderry, and a half-sister to the Prix du Jockey-Club winner Sanglamore. Her previous foals include the smart 5-7f winner Danger Over (by Warning), but he is an exception in a predominantly middle-distance family. **Conclusion** Showed pace at two but bred to improve with time and longer distances, so it would be surprising if we have seen the best of her. Has obvious Oaks potential.

For while she was never properly competitive and was beaten around two and a half lengths, Aidan O'Brien was adamant she had not given her running and Jamie Spencer offered an excuse when he revealed that she got a bit of a bump when towards the rear at around halfway and was never happy afterwards, possibly having had a fright.

Silk And Scarlet had the Moyglare winner Chelsea Rose back in third when a ready winner of a Group 2 at The Curragh four weeks previously, and there is little question she is a talented filly. What's more, she is entitled to improve significantly when stepped up to ten or 12 furlongs at three, since she is by Sadler's Wells and from the family of the Prix du Jockey-Club winner Sanglamore and a host of other classy middle-distance performers. *GD*

Soar   110

b f Danzero (Aus) - **Splice (Sharpo)** February 4
Owner Cheveley Park Stud **Trainer** J R Fanshawe **Breeder** Cheveley Park Stud
5 starts: won **3**, second **1**, third **0**, £98,815 win & place prize-money

---

THE blanket finish to the Cheveley Park Stakes involved five of the seven runners but not the co-second favourite Soar. She wasn't that far behind but never posed a threat and it was not anything like her true form. Soar's participation had been in major doubt when she had a dirty scope the previous Saturday and was given antibiotics.

"I think the antibiotics may have taken the edge off her and she got a bit upset in the stalls," reflected James Fanshawe, Soar's trainer, afterwards. The latter observation was beyond dispute and Soar also sweated up in the preliminaries. Hopefully, it will just be a one-off. Soar's dam, Splice, sometimes looked a pretty highly strung individual but stood a lot of racing and showed her best form in her fourth and final season.

Everything prior to the Cheveley Park had progressed smoothly for Soar. She found Damson too smart in the Queen Mary at Royal Ascot but had won her other three outings, looking good in a Kempton maiden at the start of June and adding further clear-cut victories in the Princess Margaret Stakes at Ascot and the Lowther Stakes at York.

Salsa Brava had gone close in the Cherry Hinton on her previous start, but Soar brushed her aside at York. Conceding 3lb to the rest and with Johnny Murtagh intent on finding cover for as long as he could, Soar was switched to challenge at the furlong marker and went on in good style.

Soar naturally appeared in the Guineas markets after that but there's a very good chance that she will be kept to sprinting. That looks her game on the current evidence and she comes from a notably speedy family. Having already shown her effectiveness on very fast ground at Royal Ascot, Soar won the Lowther on soft.

"She has always been a bit special – and had to be for me to have a two-year-old out so early," Fanshawe observed. In fact, he had not had a juvenile run as early as June 2, as Soar did, since 1999. His first two-year-old runner was a winner that year, and also in 1998 and 1997; in the new millennium, they had failed to win (placed three times, last once) before Soar came along. *RA*

Race record

6th Sky Bet Cheveley Park Stakes (Group 1) (Newmarket, September 30) 2yo 6f Good **93** (TS 78) 7 ran.
1st Jaguar Lowther Stakes (Group 2) (York, August 19) 2yo 6f Soft **110** (TS 68) 8 ran.
1st Princess Margaret Stakes (Group 3) (Ascot, July 24) 2yo 6f Good to firm **104** (TS 91) 6 ran.
2nd Queen Mary Stakes (Group 2) (Ascot, June 16) 2yo 5f Good to firm **100** (TS 85) 17 ran.
1st HH Associates EBF Median Auction Maiden Stakes (Kempton, June 2) 2yo 5f Good **89** (TS 80) 8 ran.

Pedigree assessment

Sire Danzero (Danehill) Top-class 2yo in Australia, won 3 stakes events over 5-6f inc. Golden Slipper S-Gr1, smart sprint winner at 3. By outstanding shuttle sire out of minor stakes winner. Very good Australasian sire, does particularly well with 2yos (inc. 6-8f Gr1 winner Dance Hero), most of his progeny best at up to 1m but has sired top-class Australasian 1m+ 3yo Fairway. Oldest European progeny 3. **Dam Splice** Fair triple 5f winner at 2, later tough and very useful quadruple 6f winner, showed form over 5-7f. By top-class sprinter out of 7f Group 3 winner. Her 5 earlier foals feature smart sprinter Feet So Fast (by Pivotal), fair 5f 2yo winner Entwine (by Primo Domine) and 6-7f 2yo+ winner Rise (by Polar Falcon). **Conclusion** There is a major doubt over her stamina for 1m. Likely to continue to prove best at around 6f. Fair amount of precocity in pedigree – although dam was durable – and not certain to prove equally effective at 3.

Something Exciting 106

ch f Halling (USA) - Faraway Waters (Pharly (Fr)) March 7
Owner Setsquare Recruitment **Trainer** D R C Elsworth **Breeder** R E Crutchley
7 starts: won **3**, second **1**, third **0**, £25,372 win & place prize-money

TIME CHARTER was a notable exception, but Oaks winners seldom emerge from the nursery arena. It's still a long shot, but Something Exciting might just be another.

David Elsworth's filly made dramatic progress when granted a test of stamina and just 12 days after completing her nursery qualification she began a roll that barely a month later saw her installed near the top of the tree among the season's best staying fillies. Making her nursery debut at Salisbury off a mark of 71, she came from the back with a surging late run to win. It was a similar story at Goodwood a fortnight later when,

Something Exciting beats the colts in the Houghton Stakes

off a 7lb higher mark and on ground the jockeys insisted rode easier than the official 'good, good to firm in places', she powered down the outside to win going away. But the best was yet to come.

Raised in class for the Houghton Conditions Stakes at Newmarket, a race that has been won by some pretty smart operators, she was up against seven winning colts in a field of nine, among them the Solario second Embossed. In a race run on unusually soft ground for Newmarket, Embossed trounced the other colts in a stamina-sapping affair, yet Something Exciting trounced Embossed, sweeping to the front approaching

Race record

2nd Best Bet John 0800 587 7086 EBF Montrose Fillies' Stakes (Listed) (Newmarket, October 30) 2yo 1m Good to soft **98** (TS 60) 8 ran.

1st Heathavon Stud Houghton Conditions Stakes (Newmarket, October 15) 2yo 1m Soft **106** (TS 90) 9 ran.

1st 3663 Nursery Stakes (Goodwood, September 30) 2yo (0-85 handicap) 1m Good **87** (TS 80) 17 ran.

1st Axminster Carpets Nursery (Salisbury, September 14) 2yo (0-85 handicap) 1m Soft **78** (TS 55) 12 ran.

13th EBF Quidhampton Maiden Fillies' Stakes (Div I) (Salisbury, September 2) 2yo 7f Good **58** (TS 25) 15 ran.

10th EBF New Ham Maiden Fillies' Stakes (Goodwood, July 29) 2yo 7f Good to firm **67** (TS 33) 13 ran.

4th Mountgrange Stud Maiden Fillies' Stakes (Newbury, July 16) 2yo 7f Good **76** (TS 61) 13 ran.

Pedigree assessment

Sire Halling (Diesis) Unraced at 2, later progressed into top-class 9-10f performer. Good sire, can get smart 2yos but most talented progeny excel as 3yos+ over 8-10f. **Dam Faraway Waters** Won over 6f at 2, later showed useful form over 10f. By top-class miler who tended to do best with middle-distance horses, half-sister to useful 8-10f performer Prince Of Denial, from decent middle-distance family. Her 3 earlier foals have achieved little. **Conclusion** Should make good progress from 2 to 3, when her ideal trip may be around 10f.

the furlong marker after being pushed along in rear and scoring by three lengths. It was an impressive performance, and what made it all the more remarkable is that she carried a whopping 10lb penalty.

A Listed prize for fillies, back over the same course and distance a fortnight later, proved impossible to resist, but Something Exciting was beaten by the 16-1 chance Squaw Dance. It was not a disaster, though, as the steady pace was against her, and she still might have won but for tending to drift both left and right. Remember, Ouija Board was beaten in the same race 12 months previously.

Something Exciting has the pedigree of a filly who is not destined to reach her full powers until tackling middle distances at three, and she does not need to improve much now to be a real force in the top fillies' races. However, the evidence strongly suggests that she appreciates plenty of give underfoot. *GD*

Storm Silk (Can)   97

b/br c Stormin Fever (USA) - Carpenter's Lace (USA) (Woodman (USA))
February 28
Owner Godolphin **Trainer** Saeed Bin Suroor **Breeder** J Everatt and Janeane Everatt
2 starts: won **1**, second **0**, third **0**, £7,606 win & place prize-money

---

WHEN Storm Silk finished a promising fourth on his debut at Goodwood in August he appeared nothing more than a bit-part player in the mighty operation that is Godolphin.

However, that race proved to be stronger than it appeared at the time with both the winner Moth Ball, a subsequent Listed winner, and runner-up Yajbill, who won his next three starts, doing plenty for the form.

Storm Silk was upped in class to a seven-furlong conditions event at Kempton on his next and only other outing as a juvenile. After strong

---

Race record
1st Pentax "Light & Image" Conditions Stakes (Kempton, September 4) 2yo 7f Good to firm **97** (TS 53) 8 ran.
4th EBF Chichester City Median Auction Maiden Stakes (Goodwood, August 14) 2yo 6f Good **79** (TS 79) 9 ran.

Pedigree assessment
Sire Stormin Fever (Storm Cat) Minor 2yo winner, later high-class dirt performer at up to 1m. By top-class 2yo and outstanding sire, brother to top-class 2yo+ US dirt filly Pennant Fever. Oldest progeny 3, sire in Europe of Howick Falls (Gr2). **Dam Carpenter's Lace** Unplaced in 4 2yo starts on dirt, only season to race. By top-class 2yo out of dirt sprint winner. Her 7 earlier foals include 4 winners, one of them a Graded-placed stakes winner over 1m+ on turf. **Conclusion** Fair amount of speed in his background, so on pedigree Storm Silk looks unlikely to stay beyond 1m.

market support, he was bounced out of the stalls before making all to outpoint a promising field in the style of a smart prospect.

Although much less impressive on pedigree than many similar types in the care of Godolphin, Storm Silk boasts form just as strong and will warrant respect however he is campaigned at three. *ST*

Suez   106

b f Green Desert (USA) - Repeat Warning (Warning) February 21
Owner Sheikh Mohammed **Trainer** M A Jarvis **Breeder** Meon Valley Stud
3 starts: won **2**, second **1**, **£71,236** win & place prize-money

---

SUEZ joined Godolphin at the end of the season, following the route trodden 12 months earlier by the subsequent Oaks third and Ribblesdale winner Punctilious, another filly who showed smart form for Michael Jarvis in the Sheikh Mohammed colours. However, the 1,000 Guineas, rather than the Oaks, will be the target for Suez, who has no pretensions to staying any further than a mile and shows such speed that she is not guaranteed to get even that far.

Suez had all her juvenile races over six furlongs. Her most significant performance came on the occasion of her only defeat, when she was sent off in front and saw off her most obvious rivals Damson and Soar in the Cheveley Park Stakes, only to succumb near the finish to 40-1 chance Magical Romance and go down by a neck.

She had beaten another well-regarded filly, Clear Impression, on her maiden debut at Goodwood and had gone on to beat the subsequent Cornwallis winner Castelletto decisively in a Listed race at Salisbury

Race record

2nd Sky Bet Cheveley Park Stakes (Group 1) (Newmarket, September 30) 2yo 6f Good **106** (TS 96) 7 ran.
1st EBF/Irish Thoroughbred Marketing Dick Poole Fillies' Stakes (Listed) (Salisbury, September 2) 2yo 6f Good **105** (TS 85) 11 ran.
1st Findon Maiden Fillies' Stakes (Goodwood, July 28) 2yo 6f Good **91** (TS 93) 8 ran.

Pedigree assessment

Sire Green Desert (Danzig) High-class sprint 2yo, top-class sprinter-miler at 3, won July Cup-Gr1, 2nd 2,000 Guineas-Gr1. Excellent sire, excels with 2yos (Bint Allayl, Oasis Dream) and older horses at up to 1m (Cape Cross, Desert Prince, Diamond Green, Heat Haze, Owington, Sheikh Albadou, Tamarisk). **Dam Repeat Warning** Unraced at 2, placed over 1m at 3 from 2 starts. By top-class 2yo/miler out of smart 12f filly Reprocolor. Half-sister to top-class trio Bella Colora (1m), Cezanne (Irish Champion S-Gr1) and Colorspin (Irish Oaks-Gr1, dam of 3 Gr1 winners), from outstanding 1m+ family. **Conclusion** A mile looks her trip at 3. From a family whose members tend to progress well from 2 to 3.

that has been won by some smart fillies over the years. In both races it was her speed that was particularly impressive.

Suez does not need to improve too much in order to figure prominently in the 1,000 Guineas, and a winter in Dubai may help. Her stamina may well be tested in one of the Godolphin trials, and it will be interesting to see how she fares. A sound surface is considered essential, as she has a fast-ground action and missed York's Lowther Stakes when the ground went against her. *GD*

Teeba (USA) 84

ch f Seeking The Gold (USA) - Shadayid (USA) (Shadeed (USA)) April 27
Owner Hamdan Al Maktoum **Trainer** J L Dunlop **Breeder** Shadwell Farm
1 start: won **0**, second **0**, third **0**, **£544** win & place prize-money

AS a daughter of the 1,000 Guineas winner Shadayid and a half-sister to the likes of Bint Shadayid and Imtiyaz, Teeba has a lot to live up to, but she showed enough on her sole start as a juvenile to suggest she can win some decent races herself.

John Dunlop's filly made her debut in a high-quality end-of-season Newmarket maiden over six furlongs and looked in need of the experience, starting slowly and taking a while to grasp what was required. She

Race record
4th Robert Sangster Memorial EBF Maiden Stakes (Newmarket, October 14) 2yo 6f Soft **84** (TS 80) 23 ran.

Pedigree assessment
Sire Seeking The Gold (Mr Prospector) Won sole 2yo start, later top-class dirt performer at up to 10f. Very good stallion, in Europe has sired top-class 2yos (Enthused, Lujain), sprinters and milers (Dubai Millennium, Mutakddim, Seeking The Pearl, Spain Lane). **Dam Shadayid** Top-class 2yo, won all 3 races inc. Prix Marcel Boussac-Gr1. Won 1,000 Guineas at 3, also showed smart form over 6f (3rd Haydock Sprint Cup-Gr1) and 12f (3rd Oaks-Gr1). By top-class miler out of top-class 6f 2yo from excellent family. Her 8 previous foals include smart 2yo/miler Bint Shadayid (Nashwan), useful 2yo/sprinter Alshadiyah (Danzig), and smart 2yo/8-10f horse Imtiyaz (Woodman). **Conclusion** The dam's good performers have tended to have fair amount of speed, and the sire transmits pace, so Teeba is unlikely to stay beyond 1m and might prove best at slightly shorter.

gradually got the hang of things and stayed on in taking fashion under a kind ride from Richard Hills when the race was all but over, finishing fourth behind Tomoohat.

Teeba is the sort to do considerably better with that experience under her belt, and she could well make up into a really smart three-year-old. *ST*

Tiger Dance, Giant's Causeway's brother, wins his only start

Tiger Dance (USA)   90

b c Storm Cat (USA) - Mariah's Storm (USA) (Rahy (USA)) May 16
Owner Mrs John Magnier **Trainer** A P O'Brien **Breeder** Pacelco S A
1 start: won **1**, **£11,461** win & place prize-money

"THIS is a lovely, scopey colt. He's a great mover and has plenty of class."
The same could have been said, and probably has been, about scores of
two-year-olds from Aidan O'Brien's over the years. In this instance,
O'Brien was talking about Tiger Dance.

On paper, there is not much to mark Tiger Dance out from the rest –
with the notable exception that, in a season in which the offspring of Giant's

Race record
1st Irish Stallion Farms EBF Maiden (Leopardstown, September 11) 2yo 7f Good to firm **90** (TS 12) 7 ran.

Pedigree assessment
Sire **Storm Cat** (Storm Bird) Top-class US dirt 2yo, very lightly raced at 3. By top-class European 2yo
from strong, speedy family of Royal Academy. Excellent sire, particularly of dirt performers, good record
with European 2yos (Denebola, Hold That Tiger, One Cool Cat) and older 7-10f performers (Aljabr, Black
Minnaloushe, Giant's Causeway, Nebraska Tornado, Sophisticat). **Dam Mariah's Storm** Grade 2
winner at 2 in US, later high-class dirt performer at around 8-9f, also won on turf. By high-class European
2yo and very good sire of both dirt and turf performers. Very closely related to high-class 10-12f colt
Panoramic. Her 5 earlier foals feature Tiger Dance's full-brothers Giant's Causeway, Freud (useful 6-8f),
Roar Of The Tiger (fair 6-8f) and Tumblebrutus (useful 6-7f). **Conclusion** His brother Giant's Causeway
was effective over 1m and stayed 10f, but balance of pedigree indicates Tiger Dance may prove a miler.
Dam's progeny have tended to train on, suggesting Tiger Dance can make an impact in stakes company.

Causeway were thick on the ground and causing such a stir, Tiger Dance is a brother to Giant's Causeway.

When Tiger Dance made his debut in a seven-runner maiden at Leopardstown in September, he did so at 4-5 and won easily. Quickening on in the penultimate furlong, he scored by four and a half lengths under restraint. The opposition could have been very weak but he had no difficulty disposing of what there was.

"We'll step him up to Group company next time but we'll wait on him to tell us when he's ready," said his pleased trainer. Tiger Dance did not lack for big-race entries but he evidently failed to pipe up and therefore embarks on his three-year-old campaign after one race and one victory at two.

The powerful Tiger Dance looks the part, although it was a little disconcerting to see him with a tongue strap first time out. His maiden was over seven furlongs on good to firm and if the career of Giant's Causeway proves any precedent, he will go on to prove effective at a mile and a mile and a quarter. He's in the higher reaches of the Guineas betting. *RA*

Titian Time (USA)   107

b f Red Ransom (USA) - **Timely** (King's Lake (USA)) February 5
Owner Lady Bamford & The Sangster Family **Trainer** J H M Gosden
Breeder Swettenham Stud
4 starts: won 1, second 2, third 1, £49,138 win & place prize-money

---

JOHN GOSDEN is under no illusions. Titian Time was beaten fair and square by Divine Proportions in Longchamp's Prix Marcel Boussac and will not be taking her on again in the immediate future. "She will go for whichever Guineas Divine Proportions doesn't run in," he said.

That is not to say Gosden was in any way disappointed with the filly. On the contrary, Titian Time did him proud, and her two-length second after attempting to make all was a massive step up on her maiden form, which had seen her beat Hallowed Dream by a length and a quarter at Newmarket following solid placings at both Newbury and Kempton.

Titian Time would not be good enough to win the 1,000 Guineas, but one could see her going well if she is returned to Longchamp for the French equivalent, the Poule d'Essai des Pouliches, where another astute front-running ride would see her in the thick of the action in the straight in a race that is unlikely to be run at anything like such a strong pace.

However she fares at either Newmarket or Longchamp – and remember the stable has an even brighter Classic prospect in the Fillies' Mile winner Playful Act – she can surely be placed to win in Group company at around a mile. *GD*

Race record

2nd Prix Marcel Boussac Royal Barriere Deauville (Group 1) (Longchamp, October 3) 2yo 1m Good **107** (TS 105) 10 ran.
1st Robinsons Mercedes-Benz EBF Maiden Fillies' Stakes (Newmarket, September 21) 2yo 1m Good to firm **84** (TS 85) 15 ran.
3rd Rukba PAFS EBF Fillies' Conditions Stakes (Kempton, September 3) 2yo 7f Good **81** (TS 50) 7 ran.
2nd Stan James Supporting Wessex Heartbeat EBF Maiden Stakes (Div II) (Newbury, August 14) 2yo 7f Good **75** (TS 50) 11 ran.

Pedigree assessment

Sire Red Ransom (Roberto) Impressive winner of both 2yo starts in sprints, placed at 3 on only other start. Very good sire, had strong European record before switch to stand in Britain, has sired high-class 2yos (Shining Hour, Sri Pekan), milers (China Visit, Intikhab) and 10f+ performers (Casual Look, Ekraar, Ransom O'War). **Dam Timely** Very useful 2yo and 3yo over 7-10f. By top-class miler out of Group-placed half-sister to top-class 9f+ colt Baillamont. Her 7 earlier foals feature Titian Time's sister Shining Hour (Queen Mary S-Gr2) and 7f 3yo winner Modern Era (Diesis). **Conclusion** Already has smart form over 1m, and that is likely to be the limit of her stamina at 3.

Tomoohat (USA) 89

b f Danzig (USA) - Crystal Downs (USA) (Alleged (USA)) February 17
Owner Hamdan Al Maktoum **Trainer** Sir Michael Stoute **Breeder** Monticule Llc
1 start: won **1**, **£7,072** win & place prize-money

SIR MICHAEL STOUTE has almost an embarrassment of riches in the two-year-old filly department and Tomoohat could prove to be one of his best.

The daughter of Danzig and Crystal Downs – who ran with plenty of credit at the highest level, including when fourth in the Irish 1,000

Race record

1st Robert Sangster Memorial EBF Maiden Stakes (Newmarket, October 14) 2yo 6f Soft **89** (TS 110) 23 ran.

Pedigree assessment

Sire Danzig (Northern Dancer) Unbeaten winner of 3 races at 2 and 3 in US at up to 7f. Outstanding sire, excels with 2yos, sprinters and milers, very rarely gets high-class horses over 10f+. **Dam Crystal Downs** Smart 2yo and 3yo over 7-8f. By dual Arc winner and stamina influence, half-sister to top-class 12f performer Mubtaker (by Silver Hawk) and closely related to smart 10f colt Husyan (by Alleged), speedy family further back. This is her 2nd foal. **Conclusion** Enough stamina on dam's side for her to last 1m.

Guineas – made the perfect start to her racing career when taking a strong six-furlong maiden at Newmarket in October, tracking the pace before showing a nice change of gear to put her seal on the race.

The bare form of that performance suggests Tomoohat is not far off Listed level, and with the promise of much better to come there is every chance that she will be winning Group races in 2005. A mile should suit on pedigree and she could yet prove a strong contender for the 1,000 Guineas. *ST*

Tremar   108

b c Royal Applause - Sabina (Prince Sabo) March 14
Owner T Jacobs **Trainer** T G Mills **Breeder** Mrs Mary Taylor
7 starts: won **2**, second **1**, third **1**, £37,618 win & place prize-money

THE 2004 season was a tough one for Terry Mills but the ebullient trainer bounced back from adversity to land a Group 3 win with Tremar, who, on figures at least, can be considered one of the best two-year-olds the Epsom trainer has handled.

Tremar failed to run to expectations in two outings during the spring, at a time when his stable was suffering from the effects of a virus. However, like many of his stablemates, he showed much-improved form when

Race record
6th Darley Dewhurst Stakes (Group 1) (Newmarket, October 16) 2yo 7f Soft **97** (TS 90) 9 ran.
1st Prix Eclipse (Group 3) (Chantilly, October 1) 2yo 6f Good **108** (TS 91) 7 ran.
4th Pentax Sirenia Stakes (Group 3) (Kempton, September 4) 2yo 6f Good to firm **100** (TS 75) 8 ran.
1st Castlemaine XXXX Median Auction Maiden Stakes (Div II) (Lingfield (AW), August 26) 2yo 6f Standard **85** (TS 85) 12 ran.
2nd Evening Standard Maiden Stakes (Kempton, August 18) 2yo 6f Soft **91** (TS 57) 8 ran.
3rd French Brothers Median Auction Maiden Stakes (Windsor, April 5) 2yo 5f Good to soft **72** (TS 57) 8 ran.
4th EBF Freephone Stanleybet 0808 100 1221 Maiden Stakes (Kempton, March 27) 2yo 5f Soft **65** (TS 43) 7 ran.

Pedigree assessment
Sire Royal Applause (Waajib) Top-class 2yo and sprinter, won 6 Group races inc. Middle Park S-Gr1, Haydock Sprint Cup-Gr1. Good sprint sire, excels with 2yos (Auditorium, Majestic Missile, Mister Cosmi, Nevisian Lad, Peak To Creek), can get high-class sprinters (Acclamation) and occasional smart 1m+ performer (Ticker Tape). **Dam Sabina** Won over 6f at 2, placed over 5f at 3. By top-class 2yo and influence for speed/precocity, half-sister to high-class 10f filly Lady In Waiting (by Kylian) and smart stayer Savannah Bay (In The Wings) out of half-sister to useful sprint 2yos Maid For The Hills (by Indian Ridge) and Maid For Walking (by Prince Sabo). Her one previous foal is 5f 2yo winner Zafine (by Zafonic). **Conclusion** A sprinter on pedigree. Precociously bred, and may not step up on juvenile form at 3.

Tremar, pictured at Kempton, is already a Group 3 winner

reappearing later on in the summer, finishing runner-up to Rebuttal, who went on to finish second in the Middle Park, in a warm Kempton maiden.

Tremar collected his maiden on the all-weather at Lingfield before finishing fourth in a red-hot renewal of the Sirenia Stakes at Kempton. That effort suggested he had a future at Pattern level and he proved it when taking the Group 3 Prix Eclipse at Chantilly with some solid performers from the home team well held.

The Dewhurst proved a step too far for Tremar as he finished a well-beaten sixth behind the champion two-year-old elect Shamardal, quite possibly finding the combination of seven furlongs on testing ground and the effects of a long season catching up with him.

Tremar has yet to prove his stamina beyond six furlongs and could prove difficult to place at three if failing to get a longer trip. However, if he does stay further he could give his trainer, who knows how to handle a good horse, more Group-level success. *ST*

Wilko   120

See entry in the top 100 horses, page 448

Windsor Knot (Ire)   108

ch c Pivotal - Triple Tie (USA) (The Minstrel (Can)) March 3
Owner Sheikh Mohammed **Trainer** J H M Gosden **Breeder** Tally-Ho Stud
3 starts: won **2**, second **0**, third **0**, **£31,350** win & place prize-money

WINDSOR KNOT carried Sheikh Mohammed's colours as a two-year-old and John Gosden, his trainer, must have had the feeling at an early stage that he would lose the colt to Godolphin. However, Gosden had time to pick up a Group race with him, the Solario Stakes at Sandown in August.

Windsor Knot's racecourse career with Gosden in fact lasted just one month. His never-nearer fourth at 14-1 in the Sandown maiden won by Embossed was full of promise and he made all in two starts afterwards.

Beating rivals already with Godolphin is not the best policy for those hoping to dodge their advances and 4-5 shot Windsor Knot beat their Monsoon Rain with plenty of authority when he registered his maiden success on good to firm at Newmarket. And then it was the Solario.

"John told me he had the experience, would stay and, as he is a big horse, I should let him stride on and not turn the race into a sprint," said Frankie Dettori after the Group 3. "Everything worked out really well." Two furlongs out, the other seven runners were fanned out in pursuit of Windsor Knot but they dropped away one by one and Windsor Knot stretched clear.

This time Windsor Knot, at 9-2, beat 14-1 shot Embossed two and a half lengths into second. The three other shortest-priced horses were the last three home, which suggested that the form for this soft-ground contest might not be that good, but the winner was improving markedly with every start and looked certain to be very well suited by a mile.

Race record

1st Iveco Daily Solario Stakes (Group 3) (Sandown, August 21) 2yo 7f Soft **108** (TS 105) 8 ran.
1st Mykal Industries Maiden Stakes (Newmarket (July), August 6) 2yo 7f Good to firm **91** (TS 76) 14 ran.
4th Panmure Gordon Investment Trust EBF Maiden Stakes (Sandown, July 21) 2yo 7f Good to firm **80** (TS 69) 15 ran.

Pedigree assessment

Sire Pivotal (Polar Falcon) Won 2 races over 5-6f at 2, high-class sprinter at 3, won King's Stand S-Gr2 and Nunthorpe S-Gr1. By top-class sprinter-miler. Very good sire, strong record with 2yos and also with 3yo+ over variety of trips. Particularly strong record with fillies (Chorist, Golden Apples, Megahertz, Silvester Lady), who tend to stay better than colts. **Dam Triple Tie** Placed over 7f at 2, 14f winner at 3. By Derby winner and decent sire out of a stakes-placed half-sister to high-class sprinter Faliraki. Her 3 earlier foals include a 5-6f 3yo winner in Hungary by Bin Ajwaad. **Conclusion** Effective over 7f and looks likely to stay 1m, but pedigree gives little encouragement that he will stay much further.

Windsor Knot never got a chance to prove it, which was a shame, but is the rangy sort likely to flourish as a three-year-old. Middle distances may be his brief, for all that his sire is the sprinter Pivotal. *RA*

Yehudi (Ire)   111

b c Sadler's Wells (USA) - Bella Vitessa (Ire) (Thatching) May 7
Owner Mrs John Magnier **Trainer** A P O'Brien **Breeder** Barronstown Stud
& Orpendale
3 starts: won 2, second 1, £63,392 win & place prize-money

AFTER the storm, the calm. Jamie Spencer had his presentations as Irish champion jockey to look forward to on the day after the Breeders' Cup, along with the rides at Leopardstown on two promising Aidan O'Brien-trained two-year-olds in Gypsy King and Yehudi. Both won in good style.

Yehudi's assignment was a nine-furlong Listed event on heavy going. Only two of the nine runners, Yehudi and Imperial Brief, seemed seriously fancied in the betting and they started 7-4 joint favourites. Imperial Brief had had four runs to prepare him for this slog, with wins in the last two, and Yehudi only the one. That was a soft-ground maiden at Navan earlier in October in which he was 8-1, led over two furlongs out

Race record
2nd Criterium de Saint-Cloud (Group 1) (Saint-Cloud, November 6) 2yo 10f Very soft **111** (TS 50) 7 ran.
1st Eyrefield Stakes (Listed) (Leopardstown, October 31) 2yo 9f Soft to heavy **101** (TS 105) 9 ran.
1st Irish Stallion Farms EBF Maiden (Navan, October 13) 2yo C & G 1m Soft **84** 16 ran.

Pedigree assessment
Sire **Sadler's Wells** (Northern Dancer) Smart 7-8f winner at 2, improved into top-class 8-12f colt at 3, won Irish 2,000 Guineas-Gr1, Eclipse S-Gr1, Irish Champion S-Gr1. Outstanding sire, particularly of 3yo+ over 8-12f, also has good record with autumn 2yos. **Dam Bella Vitessa** Unraced at 2, unplaced at 3 over 10-14f. By high-class sprinter and speed influence, half-sister to very high-class 12f filly Wind In Her Hair and very smart 10f filly Capo di Monte out of useful very close relative of Height Of Fashion. Her 5 earlier foals include Yehudi's full-brother Broomers Hill (placed in bumper) and 2 winners at up to a mile by Danehill and Alzao. **Conclusion** Yehudi appears to have inherited the family stamina, and he is likely to have no problem with 12f. Family members tend to progress well with age.

and held on by a short head from a Spencer-ridden stablemate, the 8-11 shot Down Mexico Way.

At Leopardstown, there was no just holding on. Yehudi disputed the lead on the rails and then was pushed a length clear rounding the home turn, while the held-up Imperial Brief came round the outside. That gave Yehudi an advantage but it was impossible to question his superiority as, despite looking rather green, he galloped further and further clear until being eased close home and scoring by three lengths.

Six days later, Yehudi was staying on relentlessly again and bidding for a Group 1 triumph, in the mile-and-a-quarter Criterium de Saint-Cloud. This time, though, as the German-trained filly Paita arrived late on the scene, it was not quite good enough for him to win.

Yehudi looks an honest, strong-galloping colt and a good prospect for races over a mile and a half. Of course, his stable will have others, including by his sire Sadler's Wells, but Yehudi's name is firmly on the list. He has raced only on testing ground. *RA*

Zalongo 86

ch c Zafonic (USA) - Tamassos (Dance In Time (Can)) February 7
Owner Athos Christodoulou **Trainer** Sir Michael Stoute **Breeder** A Christodoulou
1 start: won 1, £4,192 win & place prize-money

SIR MICHAEL STOUTE invariably has a strong team of three-year-old talent at his disposal and certainly has a colt of some potential in the shape of Zalongo, who became the fourth foal (from 12) of high-class mare Tamassos to win as a juvenile when scoring impressively over seven furlongs at Yarmouth at the first time of asking in October.

A half-brother to top-class middle-distance performer Posidonas, Zalongo looked a long-term prospect in winning at Yarmouth, running

Race record
1st EBF/Potters Leisure Resort Maiden Stakes (Div I) (Yarmouth, October 27) 2yo 7f Soft **86** (TS 83) 14 ran.

Pedigree assessment
Sire **Zafonic** (Gone West) Outstanding 2yo, won all 4 races over 6-7f inc. Prix Morny-Gr1, Prix de la Salamandre-Gr1, Dewhurst S-Gr1. Won 2,000 Guineas in short 3yo campaign. Decent sire, particularly of 2yos (Count Dubois, Endless Summer, Xaar, Zipping) and 8-9f performers (Dupont, Pacino, Zafeen, Zee Zee Top) Dam **Tamassos** Placed over 5f at 2, 11f winner at 3. Half-sister to very high-class 10-12f performer Ile de Chypre. Her 11 earlier foals feature top-class 12f performer Posidonas (by Slip Anchor) and very useful 10-12f colt Carry The Flag (Tenby). **Conclusion** If taking after his dam's best progeny he should make good progress from 2 to 3. Dam's stamina should enable him to stay 10f, but his pedigree raises doubts about him getting 12f.

green before staying on late in the style of a colt who will relish further at three.

The bare form of that contest suggests Zalongo should prove better than a handicapper and, as he is bred to improve at three and is in the best of hands, he ought to develop into a Group performer. *ST*

Racing Post Classification

The Racing Post Classification lists the Racing Post Ratings for the world's leading racehorses. The classification takes into account performances in Group 1 and Grade 1 races worldwide, Group racing as a whole throughout Europe and all racing in Britain and Ireland. They provide a fascinating insight into the relative merits of the best horses that represented each of the major racing nations in 2004. Racing Post Ratings are compiled by our team of independent handicappers who rely primarily on collateral form as the basis of the figures. The ratings incorporate weight-for-age allowances to facilitate direct comparison of the merit of horses of different ages. The 'distance(s)' column in the table indicates the distance, or distances, at which the horse achieved the rating

Note that the classification for dirt horses includes three-year-olds and upwards

European two-year-olds

Rating	Name & sex	Trainer	Country	Distance(s)
125	Shamardal (USA) C	M Johnston	UK	7f
122	Dubawi (Ire) C	Saeed Bin Suroor	UK	7f
121	Ad Valorem (USA) C	A P O'Brien	Ireland	6f
119	Oratorio (Ire) C	A P O'Brien	Ireland	7f
	Rebuttal (USA) C	B J Meehan	UK	6f
118	Montgomery's Arch (USA) C	P W Chapple-Hyam	UK	7f
	Motivator C	M L W Bell	UK	8f
117	Divine Proportions (USA) F	P Bary	France	6f
	Early March C	Mme C Head-Maarek	France	7f
	Etlaala C	B W Hills	UK	7f
	Iceman C	J H M Gosden	UK	7f
	Layman (USA) C	A Fabre	France	7f
115	Librettist (USA) C	Saeed Bin Suroor	UK	7f
114	Berenson (Ire) C	T Stack	Ireland	7f
	Centifolia (Fr) F	Robert Collet	France	6f
113	Playful Act (Ire) F	J H M Gosden	UK	8f
	Russian Blue (Ire) C	A P O'Brien	Ireland	6f
112	Caesar Beware (Ire) G	H Candy	UK	6f
	Footstepsinthesand C	A P O'Brien	Ireland	7f
	Helios Quercus (Fr) C	C Diard	France	8f
	Mona Lisa F	A P O'Brien	Ireland	8f
	Perfectperformance (USA) C	Saeed Bin Suroor	UK	8f
	Salut Thomas (Fr) C	Robert Collet	France	6f
	Wilko (USA) C	J Noseda	UK	8f
111	Albert Hall C	A P O'Brien	Ireland	8f
	Campo Bueno (Fr) C	X Nakkachdji	France	6f
	Galeota (Ire) C	R Hannon	UK	6f
	Maids Causeway (Ire) F	B W Hills	UK	8f
	Moth Ball C	J A Osborne	UK	6f
	Yehudi (Ire) C	A P O'Brien	Ireland	10f
110	Damson (Ire) F	David Wachman	Ireland	5f, 6f
	Dash To The Top F	L M Cumani	UK	8f
	Democratic Deficit (Ire) C	J S Bolger	Ireland	7f
	Satchem (Ire) C	C E Brittain	UK	6f
	Soar F	J R Fanshawe	UK	6f

Three-year-olds

Rating	Name & sex	Trainer	Country	Distance(s)
129	Bago (Fr) C	J E Pease	France	12f
	Haafhd C	B W Hills	UK	10f
128	Cherry Mix (Fr) C	A Fabre	France	12f
127	Lucky Story (USA) C	M Johnston	UK	8f
126	Azamour (Ire) C	John M Oxx	Ireland	10f
	Grey Swallow (Ire) C	D K Weld	Ireland	12f
	Kitten's Joy (USA) C	Dale Romans	USA	12f
125	North Light (Ire) C	Sir Michael Stoute	UK	12f
124	Mister Monet (Ire) C	M Johnston	UK	11f
	Ouija Board F	E A L Dunlop	UK	12f
	Whipper (USA) C	Robert Collet	France	8f
123	Acropolis (Ire) C	A P O'Brien	Ireland	12f
	Attraction F	M Johnston	UK	8f
	Egerton (Ger) C	P Rau	Germany	12f
	Snow Ridge (Ire) C	Saeed Bin Suroor	UK	8f
122	Quiff F	Sir Michael Stoute	UK	12f
	Rule Of Law (USA) C	Saeed Bin Suroor	UK	12f, 15f
	Shirocco (Ger) C	A Schutz	Germany	12f
	Tycoon C	A P O'Brien	Ireland	12f
121	Antonius Pius (USA) C	A P O'Brien	Ireland	8f
	Diamond Green (Fr) C	A Fabre	France	8f
	Latice (Ire) F	J-M Beguigne	France	12f
	Let The Lion Roar C	J L Dunlop	UK	12f
	Mustanfar (USA) C	K McLaughlin	USA	12f
	One Cool Cat (USA) C	A P O'Brien	Ireland	6f
	Percussionist (Ire) C	J H M Gosden	UK	12f
	Reset (Aus) C	G Rogerson	Australia	7f
	Stay Young (Ire) C	J Moore	Hong Kong	8f
120	Alinghi (Aus) F	Lee Freedman	Australia	6f, 7f, 8f
	Bachelor Duke (USA) C	J A R Toller	UK	8f
	Electrocutionist (USA) C	A Penna	USA	12f
	Grand Zulu (Aus) G	Gwenda Markwell	Australia	12f
	Plastered (Aus) G	L Smith	Australia	13f
	Savabeel (Aus) C	G Rogerson	Australia	10f

Three-year-olds continued

Rating	Name & sex	Trainer	Country	Distance(s)
	Spark Of Life (Aus) G	A Denham	Australia	6f
119	Denebola (USA) F	P Bary	France	7f
	King Kamehameha (Jpn) C	K Matsuda	Japan	8f, 12f
	Maraahel (Ire) C	Sir Michael Stoute	UK	15f
	Sweep Tosho (Jpn) F	A Tsurudome	Japan	10f
118	Able Prince (Aus) C	J Moore	Hong Kong	6f
	Ace (Ire) C	A P O'Brien	Ireland	8f
	Alexander Goldrun (Ire) F	J S Bolger	Ireland	10f
	Blue Canari (Fr) C	P Bary	France	12f
	Count Ricardo (Aus) G	S Theodore	Australia	13f
	Grey Lilas (Ire) F	A Fabre	France	8f
	Mikado C	A P O'Brien	Ireland	15f
	Niello (Aus) C	J Hawkes	Australia	10f
	Pastoral Pursuits C	H Morrison	UK	7f
	Prospect Park C	C Laffon-Parias	France	12f
	Red Bloom F	Sir Michael Stoute	UK	9f
	Reefscape C	A Fabre	France	15f
	Salford City (Ire) C	D R C Elsworth	UK	7f
	Valixir (Ire) C	A Fabre	France	12f
	Yamanin Sucre (Jpn) F	Hidekazu Asami	Japan	10f
117	Byron C	Saeed Bin Suroor	UK	7f
	Cacique (Ire) C	A Fabre	France	8f
	Daiwa Major (Jpn) C	Hiroyuki Uehara	Japan	10f
	Dance In The Mood (Jpn) F	Kazuo Fujisawa	Japan	8f
	Econsul (NZ) C	G Rogerson	Australia	8f
	Heart's Cry (Jpn) C	K Hashiguchi	Japan	12f
	Into The Dark C	Saeed Bin Suroor	UK	11f
	Lord Du Sud (Fr) C	J-C Rouget	France	15f
	Mac Love G	J Akehurst	UK	7f
	Malinas (Ger) C	P Schiergen	Germany	11f, 12f
	Moss Vale (Ire) C	B W Hills	UK	6f
	Yeats (Ire) C	A P O'Brien	Ireland	10f
116	Barely A Moment (Aus) C	T McEvoy	Australia	8f
	Book Of Kings (USA) C	A P O'Brien	Ireland	12f

Rating	Name & sex	Trainer	Country	Distance(s)
	Daiwa El Cielo (Jpn) F	K Matsuda	Japan	12f
	Darsalam (Ire) C	A Shavuyev	Czech Republic	15f
	Day Flight C	J H M Gosden	UK	12f
	Delta Blues (Jpn) C	Katsuhiko Sumii	Japan	15f
	Dolma (Fr) F	N Clement	France	7f
	Groom Tesse C	L Camici	Italy	12f
	Hollow Bullet (Aus) F	J McArdle	Australia	8f
	Intendant (Ger) C	A Bertram	Germany	10f
	Mister Sacha (Fr) C	J-C Rouget	France	8f
	Peak To Creek C	J Noseda	UK	7f
	Zosima (USA) F	Saeed Bin Suroor	UK	8f
115	African Dream G	P W Chapple-Hyam	UK	10f
	Ambulance (Aus) G	J Hawkes	Australia	6f, 10f
	Balmont (USA) C	J Noseda	UK	6f
	Boogie Street C	R Hannon	UK	5f
	Brunel (Ire) C	W J Haggas	UK	7f, 8f
	Bull Run (Ire) C	Saeed Bin Suroor	UK	10f
	Castleton C	H J Cyzer	UK	8f
	Cosmo Bulk (Jpn) C	K Tabe	Japan	10f
	Gatwick (Ire) C	M R Channon	UK	9f
	Go For Gold (Ire) C	A P O'Brien	Ireland	12f
	Greek Sun (USA) C	R J Frankel	USA	9f
	Kylikwong (Aus) F	Mick Price	Australia	13f
	Lucifer's Stone (USA) F	Linda Rice	USA	9f
	Master William (Can) C	M Dickinson	USA	9f
	Millemix (Fr) C	C Head-Maarek	France	11f
	Millionaia (Ire) F	E Lellouche	France	11f
	Necklace F	A P O'Brien	Ireland	10f
	Pepperstorm (Ger) C	U Ostmann	Germany	8f
	Silverskaya (USA) F	J-C Rouget	France	12f
	Soi Cowboy (Aus) C	Mick Price	Australia	13f
	Storm Alert (Aus) F	D Freedman	Australia	13f
	Tahreeb (Fr) C	M P Tregoning	UK	8f
	Taikun (Aus) G	J B Cummings	Australia	6f

Three-year-olds continued

Rating	Name & sex	Trainer	Country	Distance(s)
	Torrestrella (Ire) F	Christophe Clement	USA	8f
	Voix Du Nord (Fr) C	D Smaga	France	11f

Four-year-olds-plus

Rating	Name & sex	Trainer	Country	Distance(s)
131	Doyen (Ire) C	Saeed Bin Suroor	UK	12f
129	Rakti H	M A Jarvis	UK	10f
128	Silent Witness (Aus) G	A Cruz	Hong Kong	5f
127	Sulamani (Ire) H	Saeed Bin Suroor	UK	12f
126	Calstone Light O (Jpn) H	H Oneda	Japan	6f
	Nayyir G	G A Butler	UK	8f
	Refuse To Bend (Ire) C	Saeed Bin Suroor	UK	10f
	Vinnie Roe (Ire) H	D K Weld	Ireland	16f
	Warrsan (Ire) H	C E Brittain	UK	10f, 12f
125	Norse Dancer (Ire) C	D R C Elsworth	UK	10f
124	Better Talk Now (USA) G	H G Motion	USA	12f
	Powerscourt C	A P O'Brien	Ireland	10f
	Somnus G	T D Easterby	UK	6f
	Soviet Song (Ire) F	J R Fanshawe	UK	8f
123	Bandari (Ire) H	M Johnston	UK	10f, 12f
	Chic F	Sir Michael Stoute	UK	8f
	Firebreak H	Saeed Bin Suroor	UK	7f
	Hard Buck (Brz) H	K McPeek	USA	12f
	Kalaman (Ire) C	Sir Michael Stoute	UK	10f
	Kicken Kris (USA) C	M Matz	USA	10f
	Makybe Diva M	Lee Freedman	Australia	16f
	Nothing To Lose (USA) C	R J Frankel	USA	8f
	Singletary (USA) C	D Chatlos Jr	USA	8f
122	Ikhtyar (Ire) C	J H M Gosden	UK	10f
	Lonhro (Aus) H	J Hawkes	Australia	8f
	Simonas (Ire) H	A Wohler	Germany	12f
	Star Over The Bay (USA) G	M Mitchell	USA	10f
	Telegnosis (Jpn) H	H Sugiura	Japan	8f

Rating	Name & sex	Trainer	Country	Distance(s)
	Tiber (Ire) C	J Moore	Hong Kong	8f
	Touch Of Land (Fr) C	H-A Pantall	France	10f
	Tsurumaru Boy (Jpn) H	K Hashiguchi	Japan	8f
	Zenno Rob Roy (Jpn) C	Kazuo Fujisawa	Japan	10f
121	Ashdown Express (Ire) G	C F Wall	UK	6f
	Chorist M	W J Haggas	UK	10f
	Electronic Unicorn (USA) G	J Size	Hong Kong	8f
	Figures (NZ) G	D Oughton	Hong Kong	8f
	Gamut (Ire) H	Sir Michael Stoute	UK	12f
	Grand Armee (Aus) G	Gai Waterhouse	Australia	10f
	High Accolade C	M P Tregoning	UK	12f
	Le Vie Dei Colori C	L M Cumani	UK	8f
	Lucky Owners (NZ) G	A Cruz	Hong Kong	10f
	Millenary H	J L Dunlop	UK	14f, 16f
	Mr O'Brien (Ire) G	Robin L Graham	USA	11f
	Mubtaker (USA) H	M P Tregoning	UK	13f
	Papineau C	Saeed Bin Suroor	UK	20f
	Patavellian (Ire) G	R Charlton	UK	6f
	Polar Way G	A J Perrett	UK	7f
	Policy Maker (Ire) C	E Lellouche	France	12f
	Prince Kirk (Fr) C	E Borromeo	Italy	9f
	Risk Seeker C	E Lellouche	France	16f
	Royal Millennium (Ire) G	M R Channon	UK	6f
	Super Kid (Nz) H	J Size	Hong Kong	8f
	Tante Rose (Ire) F	R Charlton	UK	6f
	Tap Dance City (USA) H	S Sasaki	Japan	11f
	Vallee Enchantee (Ire) F	E Lellouche	France	12f
	Var (USA) H	C E Brittain	UK	5f
	Westerner H	E Lellouche	France	16f
120	Ancient World (USA) G	Saeed Bin Suroor	UK	8f
	Balto Star (USA) G	T Pletcher	USA	11f
	Epalo (Ger) H	A Schutz	Germany	10f
	Gin And Sin (USA) G	Darrin Miller	USA	9f
	Ingrandire (Jpn) H	Y Shimizu	Japan	16f

Four-year-olds-plus continued

Rating	Name & sex	Trainer	Country	Distance(s)
	Magistretti (USA) C	P L Biancone	USA	11f, 12f
	Paolini (Ger) H	A Wohler	Germany	9f
	Passing Glance H	A M Balding	UK	9f
	Perfect Soul (Ire) H	R L Attfield	Canada	8f
	Request For Parole (USA) H	S Hough	USA	11f, 12f
	Right Approach H	M F De Kock	South Africa	9f
	Salselon H	L M Cumani	UK	8f
	Sarafan (USA) G	N Drysdale	USA	10f, 11f
	Scintillation (Aus) G	C S Shum	Hong Kong	5f
	Soaring Free (Can) G	M Frostad	Canada	8f
119	Avonbridge C	R Charlton	UK	5f
	Balance Of Game (Jpn) H	Y Munakata	Japan	8f
	Brian Boru C	A P O'Brien	Ireland	12f, 14f
	Elvstroem (Aus) C	T Vasil	Australia	9f, 12f
	Fair Mix (Ire) H	M Rolland	France	10f
	Fields Of Omagh (Aus) G	T McEvoy	Australia	10f
	Frizzante M	J R Fanshawe	UK	6f
	Imperial Dancer H	M R Channon	UK	12f
	Mamool (Ire) H	Saeed Bin Suroor	UK	12f
	Monsieur Bond (Ire) C	B Smart	UK	6f, 7f
	Mr Dinos (Ire) H	P F I Cole	UK	16f
	Muqbil (USA) C	J L Dunlop	UK	10f, 11f
	My Risk (Fr) H	J-M Beguigne	France	8f
	Nebraska Tornado (USA) F	A Fabre	France	8f
	Osterhase (Ire) G	J E Mulhern	Ireland	5f
	Pivotal Point G	P J Makin	UK	6f
	Senex (Ger) C	H Blume	Germany	12f
	Six Perfections (Fr) F	P Bary	France	8f
	Soldier Hollow C	P Schiergen	Germany	10f
	Starcraft (NZ) C	G Newham	Australia	10f
	Super Elegant (Aus) G	T Vasil	Australia	6f
	Surveyor (SAF) G	M F De Kock	South Africa	9f
	The Tatling (Ire) G	J M Bradley	UK	5f
	Utopia (Jpn) C	K Hashiguchi	Japan	8f

Rating	Name & sex	Trainer	Country	Distance(s)
	Vangelis (USA) H	R J Frankel	USA	10f
	Vespone (Ire) C	Saeed Bin Suroor	UK	9f
118	Alkaadhem C	M P Tregoning	UK	10f
	Alkaased (USA) C	L M Cumani	UK	12f
	Bahamian Pirate (USA) G	D Nicholls	UK	5f
	Barolo G	P W Harris	UK	14f
	Big Bad Bob (Ire) C	J L Dunlop	UK	10f
	Blue Stitch G	A T Millard	Hong Kong	8f
	Bullish Luck (USA) G	A S Cruz	Hong Kong	10f
	Cape Of Good Hope G	D Oughton	Hong Kong	5f, 6f
	Dancing Bay G	N J Henderson	UK	16f
	Defier (Aus) G	G Walter	Australia	11f
	Fayr Jag (Ire) G	T D Easterby	UK	6f
	Firebolt (Ire) G	D Ferraris	Hong Kong	5f
	First Charter H	Sir Michael Stoute	UK	14f, 16f
	Hidden Dragon (Aus) G	A S Cruz	Hong Kong	8f
	Hurricane Alan (Ire) C	R Hannon	UK	8f
	Maktub (Ity) H	M A Jarvis	UK	12f
	Martillo (Ger) C	R Suerland	Germany	8f, 9f
	Mummify (Aus) G	Lee Freedman	Australia	10f, 12f, 16f
	Orientor H	J S Goldie	UK	5f
	Palette Natural (NZ) G	J Size	Hong Kong	8f
	Polish Summer H	A Fabre	France	12f
	Quantum Merit (USA) G	Del W Carroll	USA	8f
	Red Fort (Ire) G	M A Jarvis	UK	10f
	Regal Roller (Aus) G	C McDonald	Australia	8f
	River Dancer (Ire) G	J Size	Hong Kong	12f
	Russian Rhythm (USA) F	Sir Michael Stoute	UK	8f
	Ryono (USA) H	P Lautner	Germany	8f
	Scooter Roach (USA) G	D Kassen	USA	8f
	Scott's View G	M Johnston	UK	10f
	Sights On Gold (Ire) H	Saeed Bin Suroor	UK	11f
	Silk Famous (Jpn) H	I Sameshima	Japan	11f
	Silver Tree (USA) C	W Mott	USA	9f

Four-year-olds-plus continued

Rating	Name & sex	Trainer	Country	Distance(s)
	Systematic H	M Johnston	UK	12f, 13f
	The Tin Man (USA) H	Richard E Mandella	USA	10f
	The Trader (Ire) G	M Blanshard	UK	5f, 6f
117	Alcazar (Ire) G	H Morrison	UK	14f
	Altieri H	V Caruso	Italy	10f
	Autumn Glory (Ire) C	G Wragg	UK	9f
	Checkit (Ire) C	M R Channon	UK	9f
	Cloudy's Knight (USA) G	Frank J Kirby	USA	8f, 9f
	Court Masterpiece C	E A L Dunlop	UK	7f
	Crystal Castle (USA) G	J E Hammond	France	6f
	Distinction (Ire) G	Sir Michael Stoute	UK	12f
	Dubai Success C	B W Hills	UK	12f, 13f, 14f
	Eagle Cafe (USA) H	F Kojima	Japan	8f
	Execute (Fr) H	J E Hammond	France	10f, 11f, 12f
	Film Maker (USA) F	H G Motion	U.S.A	11f
	Gateman G	M Johnston	UK	8f, 9f, 10f
	Kasthari (Ire) G	J Howard Johnson	UK	18f
	Keltos (Fr) H	C Laffon-Parias	France	7f
	Lohengrin (Jpn) H	M Ito	Japan	8f
	Megahertz M	R J Frankel	USA	10f
	Megantic (USA) H	Norman R Pointer	USA	11f
	Nysaean (Ire) H	R Hannon	UK	10f
	Orange Touch (Ger) C	A J Perrett	UK	12f
	Perfect Partner (Aus) G	C Fownes	Hong Kong	8f
	Porlezza (Fr) M	Y De Nicolay	France	5f
	Quito (Ire) R	D W Chapman	UK	6f
	Royal Regalia (USA) G	Justin J Nixon	USA	8f
	Self Flit (NZ) G	C S Shum	Hong Kong	8f
	Steenberg (Ire) G	M H Tompkins	UK	6f
	Stroll (USA) C	W Mott	USA	9f
	Sunningdale (Jpn) H	T Setoguchi	Japan	6f
	Wonder Again (USA) M	James J Toner	USA	11f
116	Ain't Here (Aus) G	D Hayes	Hong Kong	10f
	Aubonne (Ger) F	E Libaud	France	10f

Rating	Name & sex	Trainer	Country	Distance(s)
	Babodana C	M H Tompkins	UK	8f, 9f
	Baltic King C	H Morrison	UK	5f
	Bayamo (Ire) G	J Canani	USA	9f, 10f
	Bishops Court G	J R Ramsden	UK	5f
	Bowman's Crossing (Ire) G	D Oughton	Hong Kong	8f, 10f
	Compton Bolter (Ire) G	G A Butler	UK	10f
	Dantsu Judge (Jpn) H	K Yamauchi	Japan	8f
	Darasim (Ire) G	M Johnston	UK	20f
	Durandal (Jpn) H	M Sakaguchi	Japan	6f
	Exceed And Excel (Aus) C	T Martin	Australia	6f
	Favourable Terms F	Sir Michael Stoute	UK	8f
	Gem Of India (NZ) G	J Size	Hong Kong	8f
	Leporello (Ire) C	P W Harris	UK	10f
	Lincoln (Jpn) C	H Otonashi	Japan	11f
	Look Honey (Ire) C	C Lerner	France	10f
	Meiner Morgen (Jpn) C	M Horii	Japan	8f
	Meteor Storm H	W Dollase	USA	10f
	Mine (Ire) H	J D Bethell	UK	8f
	Pentastic (Aus) G	C Alderson	Australia	11f
	Persian Majesty (Ire) C	P W Harris	UK	12f
	Phoenix Reach (Ire) C	A M Balding	UK	10f
	Polar Bear G	W J Haggas	UK	7f
	Polar Ben G	J R Fanshawe	UK	7f
	Precision (Fr) G	D Oughton	Hong Kong	10f
	Short Pause H	A Fabre	France	12f
	Smokin Beau G	N P Littmoden	UK	5f, 6f
	Special Ring (USA) G	J Canani	USA	9f
	The Whistling Teal G	G Wragg	UK	13f
	Tillerman H	A J Perrett	UK	8f
	Trade Fair C	R Charlton	UK	7f
	Whortleberry (Fr) F	F Rohaut	France	10f
115	Arakan (USA) C	Sir Michael Stoute	UK	6f
	Balmuse (NZ) G	K Myers	New Zealand	10f
	Beethoven (NZ) G	D Hayes	Hong Kong	10f

Four-year-olds-plus continued

Rating	Name & sex	Trainer	Country	Distance(s)
	Chancellor (Ire) H	G A Butler	UK	10f
	Commercante (Fr) F	R J Frankel	USA	10f
	Delzao (Aus) C	G Kavanagh	Australia	10f
	Dimitrova (USA) F	N Drysdale	USA	9f
	Dr More (Aus) G	J Size	Hong Kong	10f
	Elegant Fashion (Aus) M	D Hayes	Hong Kong	8f
	Franklins Gardens C	M H Tompkins	UK	16f
	Kalabar C	P Bary	France	12f
	King's Chapel (Aus) C	Mark Walker	New Zealand	10f
	King's Drama (Ire) G	R J Frankel	USA	11f
	Marshall (Fr) C	C Laffon-Parias	France	10f
	Martaline H	A Fabre	France	12f
	Meridian Star (Aus) G	D Hayes	Hong Kong	8f
	Musical Chimes (USA) F	N Drysdale	USA	9f
	Nonno Carlo (Ire) C	M Grassi	Italy	10f
	Olaso (Ger) G	P Vovcenko	Germany	11f, 12f
	Planet Ruler (USA) G	D Hayes	Hong Kong	5f
	Putra Pekan H	M A Jarvis	UK	8f
	Razkalla (USA) G	Saeed Bin Suroor	UK	12f
	Rotteck (Ger) C	H Steguweit	Germany	11f
	Sabiango (Ger) H	Tim Yakteen	USA	12f
	Scenic Peak (Aus) G	D Bougoure	Australia	7f
	Shane (HK) C	J Moore	Hong Kong	10f
	Silence Is Golden M	B J Meehan	UK	10f
	Special Kaldoun (Ire) H	D Smaga	France	10f
	Striking Ambition C	R Charlton	UK	6f
	Sublimity (Fr) G	Sir Michael Stoute	UK	8f
	Suggestive G	W J Haggas	UK	7f
	Supreme Rabbit (Ire) G	K W Lui	Hong Kong	12f
	Swing Wing G	P F I Cole	UK	16f
	Takeover Target (Aus) G	J Janiak	Australia	6f
	Tropical Lady (Ire) F	J S Bolger	Ireland	8f
	Yell (Aus) G	J Hawkes	Australia	6f, 7f

Dirt

Rating	Name & sex	Trainer	Country	Distance(s)
133	Ghostzapper (USA) C	R J Frankel	USA	10f
131	Smarty Jones (USA) C	John C Servis	USA	10f
128	Pico Central (Brz) H	P Lobo	USA	6f
	Pleasantly Perfect (USA) H	Richard E Mandella	USA	10f
	Roses In May (USA) C	Dale Romans	USA	10f
127	Medaglia D'Oro (USA) H	R J Frankel	USA	10f
126	Speightstown (USA) H	T Pletcher	USA	6f
125	Birdstone (USA) C	N Zito	USA	10f, 12f
124	Azeri (USA) M	D Wayne Lukas	USA	9f
	Champali (USA) C	Gregory D Foley	USA	6f
	Perfect Drift (USA) G	Murray W Johnson	USA	9f, 10f
123	Cajun Beat (USA) G	R J Frankel	USA	7f
	Lion Heart (USA) C	P L Biancone	USA	9f
	Sightseek (USA) M	R J Frankel	USA	9f
	Total Impact (Chi) H	Laura De Seroux	USA	10f
122	During (USA) C	B Baffert	USA	9f
	Funny Cide (USA) G	B Tagg	USA	10f
	Kela (USA) H	M Mitchell	USA	6f
	Southern Image (USA) C	M Machowsky	USA	10f
121	Bluesthestandard (USA) G	Ted H West	USA	6f
	Newfoundland (USA) C	T Pletcher	USA	9f, 10f
	Our New Recruit (USA) H	J W Sadler	USA	6f
	Saint Liam (USA) C	R Dutrow	USA	9f
	The Cliff's Edge (USA) C	N Zito	USA	9f, 10f
120	Fire Slam (USA) C	David M Carroll	USA	6f, 7f
	Firebreak H	Saeed Bin Suroor	UK	8f
	My Cousin Matt (USA) G	Jeff Mullins	USA	6f
	Peace Rules (USA) C	R J Frankel	USA	10f
	Pohave (USA) G	D O'Neill	Australia	6f, 7f
	Purge (USA) C	T Pletch	USA	9f
	Victory Moon (SAF) H	A M Balding	UK	9f, 10f

The directory

The directory lists every horse who ran in Britain to the end of the 2004 turf season, plus top overseas performers. Each entry includes the horse's full form figures, with distance and going (in raised figures) for each run, seasonal wins-places-runs statistics and seasonal total prize-money. Each horse is given a definitive Racing Post Rating, and an all-weather rating (a) where appropriate

A Beetoo (Ire) *J R Best* a33
4 b f Bahhare (USA) - Sonya's Pearl (Ire)
9^10sd 0-0-1

A Bid In Time (Ire) *D Shaw* 50 a28
3 b f Danetime (Ire) - Bidni (Ire)
8^5sd 8^5sd 2^5s 9^5g 6^5gs 6^5g 6^6s 8^6gf 0-1-8
£830

A Bit Of Fun *J J Quinn* 34 a47
3 ch g Unfuwain (USA) - Horseshoe Reef
5^8ss 2^9sw 7^8sd 1^9sd 8^8gf 11^8gs 1-1-6
£1,821

A Double Ewe Bee *W G M Turner* 32
3 b f Kingsinger (Ire) - Some Dream
12^9sd 9^8s 0-0-2

A Little Bit Yarie *K R Burke* 78
3 b g Paris House - Slipperose
3^5s 7^5s 4^5g 7^6gs 11^5g 12^5s 0-1-6
£2,259

A Monk Swimming (Ire) *John Berry* 38
3 br g Among Men (USA) - Sea Magic (Ire)
4^8gf 3^12gf 7^11gf 0-1-3 £440

A One (Ire) *H J Manners* 89 a49
5 b g Alzao (USA) - Anita's Contessa (Ire)
4^7sd 3^7gf 1^7gf 1^8gf 1^10gf 8^7g 1^10gf 1^10gf
5^8gf 10^12gf 7^10gs 17^10g 11^5gf 5-1-13
£27,205

A Qui Le Tour *M R Hoad* 40
2 b g Pyramus (USA) - Dolphin Beech (Ire)
10^5gs 8^5sd 8^7gs 0-0-3

A Teen *P Howling* 60 a58
6 ch h Presidium - Very Good
5^6sd 2^6sd 7^6sd 1^6sd 6^6sd 6^6gs 13^6gf 16^6g
6^6g 10^6gf 10^6gf 10^6g 5^6gs 6^5s 7^6g 18^6g 8^6s
6^7sd 1-1-18 £3,842

A Woman In Love *Miss B Sanders* 84 a58
5 gr m Muhtarram (USA) - Ma Lumiere (Fr)
6^7sd 1^7gf 1^7f 1^8f 1^8gf 4^7g 7^8gf 15^8f
4-0-8 £17,305

Aahgowangowan (Ire) *M Dods* 71
5 b m Tagula (Ire) - Cabcharge Princess (Ire)
12^5g 7^5hy 5^5gf 2^5g 1^5gs 5^5g 9^5g 5^5gs
2^5gs 11^5gs 15^5gs 1-2-11 £11,873

Aastral Magic *R Hannon* 83
2 b f Magic Ring (Ire) - Robanna
1^6gf 1^6gf 4^6gf 6^6gs 2-0-4 £7,684

Abbajabba *C W Fairhurst* 78 a46
8 b g Barrys Gamble - Bo' Babbity
10^6ss 10^6g 11^6gs 13^6s 2^6s 8^6s 5^7gf 9^7s
6^6s 12^7sd 0-1-10 £1,644

Abbeygate *T Keddy* 51 a58
3 b g Unfuwain (USA) - Ayunli
10^10g 11^10gs 10^12sd 11^12g 10^14sd 0-0-5

Abbiejo (Ire) *G Fierro* 28 a37
7 b m Blues Traveller (Ire) - Chesham Lady (Ire)
6^5ss 5^7ss 6^8sd 6^7sd 7^6g 14^10s 0-0-6

Abelard (Ire) *R A Fahey* 64 a61
3 b g Fasliyev (USA) - Half-Hitch (USA)
6^5gs 5^5gf 10^6s 5^6f 15^5gf 2^5gf 9^6sd 3^5sd
0-2-8 £2,297

Aberdeen (Ire) *P Mitchell* 82 a68
2 b c Xaar - Olivia Jane (Ire)
6^7sd 2^6gf 4^9g 0-1-3 £2,490

Aberdeen Park *Mrs H Sweeting* 70
2 gr f Environment Friend - Michelee
5^5s 10^6g 8^5g 4^6f 5^7gs 2^6gs 2^7gf 8^7gs

3^6hy 0-3-9 £4,335

Aberdovey *M L W Bell* 76
2 b f Mister Baileys - Annapurna (Ire)
5^6gf 1^6f 3^6gf 5^7g 10^7g 1-0-5 £4,623

Abide (Fr) *R Hannon* 74
2 ch f Pivotal - Ariadne (Ger)
6^7g 2^7gf 6^7g 0-1-3 £1,620

Abigail Adams *P W Harris* 42
3 ch f Kris - Rose Vibert
8^8s 10^10gf 0-0-2

Abington Angel *B J Meehan* 59 a62
3 ch f Machiavellian (USA) - Band (USA)
15^7g 13^8gf 8^9s 1^12sd 14^12gs 1-0-5
£3,779

Ablaj (Ire) *E A L Dunlop* 52 a50
3 ch g Horse Chestnut (SAF) - Passe Passe (USA)
8^8gs 4^7gf 4^7f 5^12sd 0-0-4 £271

Able Baker Charlie (Ire) *J R Fanshawe* 102
5 b g Sri Pekan (USA) - Lavezzola (Ire)
4^8g 2^8gf 8^8g 16^9g 0-2-4 £22,770

Able Charlie (Ger) *Mrs J R Ramsden* 75
2 ch g Lomitas - Alula (Ger)
2^6gs 5^7gs 7^6g 0-1-3 £1,138

Able Mind *A C Whillans* 62
4 b g Mind Games - Chlo-Jo
12^6gf 10^10s 6^7gs 3^8g 3^7gs 0-2-5 £1,374

Aboustar *M Brittain* 39 a39
4 b g Abou Zouz (USA) - Three Star Rated (Ire)
5^8sd 8^7sw 5^6sd 5^5g 0-0-4

Above Board *R F Marvin* 14 a53
9 b g Night Shift (USA) - Bundled Up (USA)
5^6sd 8^6sd 8^6sd 3^6ss 14^6sw 1^6sd 14^5sd
6^6sd 14^6s 11^6s 1-2-11 £2,507

Abracadabjar *Miss Z C Davison* a26
6 b g Royal Abjar (USA) - Celt Song (Ire)
8^11sd 0-0-1

Abraxas *J Akehurst* 45 a57
6 b g Emperor Jones (USA) - Snipe Hall
5^5sd 9^5sd 7^5ss 7^5s 9^5hy 0-0-6

Abraxas Antelope (Ire) *J Howard Johnson* 102
2 b c Imperial Ballet (Ire) - Lypharden (Ire)
1^6gf 1^6gs 3^6s 2^6gs 2-2-4 £30,792

Abrogate (Ire) *P C Haslam* 36 a51
3 b g Revoque (Ire) - Czarina's Sister
12^8sd 2^8sd 4^8sd 5^8gf 9^8gf 0-1-5 £726

Absent Friends *J Balding* 95
7 b g Rock City - Green Supreme
8^5hy 6^5gf 13^5gf 6^5gs 10^5gs 10^5gs 8^5g
9^5gf 4^5g 7^5gf 11^5s 0-0-11 £804

Absinther *M R Bosley* 56
7 b g Presidium - Heavenly Queen
8^12gf 2^12gf 1^12f 4^12gf 3^12f 3^12gs 12^10s
8^12gf 1-3-8 £7,164

Absolut Edge *J A Pickering*
2 ch g Atraf - Sparkling Edge
11^5gf 6^5sd 0-0-2

Absolute Utopia (USA) *J L Spearing* 63 a70
11 b g Mr Prospector (USA) - Magic Gleam (USA)
7^10sd 2^10sd 2^10sd 3^10sd 4^10sd 1^10sd 1^10g
PU^10f 2-3-8 £6,008

Absolutely Fab (Ire) *Mrs C A Dunnett* 14 a9
3 ch f Entrepreneur - Hamama (USA)
14^7f 14^12sd 10^8sd 0-0-3

Absolutely Soaked (Ire) *Dr J D Scargill* 58
3 b f Alhaarth (Ire) - Vasilopoula (Ire)

5^{10gs} 6^{10hy} 8^{12s} 9^{10gf} 10^{10gf} 2^{7gs} 11^{6s}
0-1-7 £1,119

Absolutelythebest (Ire) *E A L Dunlop*   87 a75
3 b c Anabaa (USA) - Recherchee
1^{10sd} 2^{12g} 2^{12gs} 6^{12gf} 4^{14f} 5^{12gs} 8^{14gs}
9^{11g} **1-2-8 £8,582**

Abstract Folly (Ire) *J D Bethell*   65
2 b g Rossini (USA) - Cochiti
4^{7f} 4^{7gf} **0-0-2 £269**

Abuelos *D W Thompson*   45 a47
5 b g Sabrehill (USA) - Miss Oasis
3^{7sd} 4^{8sd} 10^{6sd} 12^{7sd} 5^{16gf} 10^{8gs} 6^{9gs}
6^{8f} 5^{9f} **0-1-9 £240**

Academy (Ire) *Andrew Turnell*   63
9 ch g Archway (Ire) - Dream Academy
2^{16gf} 11^{17gf} 9^{16f} 2^{16gf} PU^{16f} **0-2-5**
£2,168

Acca Larentia (Ire) *R M Whitaker*   51 a29
3 gr f Titus Livius (Fr) - Daisy Grey
14^{10gf} 10^{8f} 3^{7s} 10^{7gs} 9^{8gf} 6^{7gf} 5^{10f}
6^{10gf} 9^{9sd} **0-1-9 £562**

Acceleration (Ire) *R Allan*   69
4 b g Groom Dancer (USA) - Overdrive
1^{16s} 6^{16gf} 13^{12g} 11^{16gs} **1-0-4 £3,614**

Accendere *R M Beckett*   60 a34
3 b g Machiavellian (USA) - Littlewick (Ire)
12^{7sd} 14^{7sd} 5^{7gs} 7^{8s} 1^{7gf} 7^{7gf} 3^{7gf} **1-1-7**
£4,190

Accepting *J Mackie*   61
7 b g Mtoto - D'Azy
5^{18s} 13^{22s} 2^{19gf} 4^{16g} 10^{17gf} **0-1-5**
£1,534

Ace (Ire) *A P O'Brien*   118
3 b c Danehill (USA) - Tea House
1^{8g} 1^{8gf} 1^{8gf} 5^{8gf} **3-0-4 £56,079**

Ace Club *J Hetherton*   72 a65
3 ch g Indian Rocket - Presently
5^{6s} 9^{6gf} 7^{6sd} 4^{6f} 2^{5hy} 11^{6gf} 12^{6gf} 16^{6s}
0-1-8 £1,352

Ace Coming *D Eddy*   71
3 b g First Trump - Tarry
12^{10g} 3^{8s} 1^{8s} 1^{9gs} 13^{8gs} 8^{9gf} 10^{8g}
16^{9gs} 14^{8gf} 14^{10s} **2-1-10 £7,792**

Ace In The Hole *F Jordan*   11
4 br f So Factual (USA) - Timely Raise (USA)
20^{11gs} 17^{8gf} **0-0-2**

Ace Of Hearts *C F Wall*   98
5 b g Magic Ring (Ire) - Lonely Heart
14^{8g} 5^{8gs} 15^{8gs} 2^{8gf} 1^{8gf} 1^{8f} 1^{8gf} 9^{8gs}
13^{8gs} 3^{8g} 16^{8s} 9^{8gs} **3-2-12 £30,069**

Ace-Ma-Vahra *S R Bowring*   46 a51
6 b m Savahra Sound - Asmarina
6^{8sd} 7^{8ss} 6^{7sd} 1^{8sd} 6^{11ss} 13^{8sd} 12^{6s}
10^{5gf} 5^{7sd} 9^{5g} 36^{gf} 14^{5g} 6^{6sd} 3^{6sd} 3^{8sd} 5^{6f}
14^{8gs} 5^{6sw} **1-4-21 £4,837**

Achilles Rainbow *K R Burke*   a45
5 ch g Deploy - Naughty Pistol (USA)
4^{10sd} 12^{8sd} 6^{10sd} F^{10sd} **0-0-4**

Acola (Fr) *R M H Cowell*   58 a41
4 ch f Acatenango (Ger) - Wardara
8^{8g} 8^{10gs} 10^{10sd} 13^{10f} 10^{8g} **0-0-5**

Acomb *M W Easterby*   85
4 b g Shaamit (Ire) - Aurora Bay (Ire)
12^{7g} 6^{7gs} 9^{8g} 1^{8f} 3^{8gs} 7^{8gf} 8^{10g} 6^{8g}
9^{7gf} **2-0-9 £9,343**

Acorazado (Ire) *G L Moore*   50 a69
5 b g Petorius - Jaldi (Ire)
7^{7sd} 2^{7sd} 7^{7sd} 1^{8sd} 6^{8sd} 2^{8sd} 7^{7gf} 4^{7sd}
6^{8hy} **1-2-9 £5,056**

Acropolis (Ire) *A P O'Brien*   123
3 b c Sadler's Wells (USA) - Dedicated Lady (Ire)
1^{10gf} 4^{12g} **1-0-2 £91,845**

Act Of The Pace (Ire) *M Johnston*   86
4 b f King's Theatre (Ire) - Lady In Pace
4^{11g} 1^{12gf} 2^{12g} 6^{13gf} 3^{15s} **1-2-5 £8,555**

Action Fighter (Ger) *N P Littmoden*   a91
4 ch g Big Shuffle (USA) - Action Art (Ire)
3^{8sd} 14^{7sd} **0-1-2 £1,362**

Active Account (USA) *Mrs H Dalton*   66 a74
7 b/br g Unaccounted For (USA) - Ameritop (USA)
2^{8sw} 2^{8ss} 5^{8sd} 6^{8g} 6^{8f} 3^{10gs} 9^{11gs} 8^{10g}
14^{10gf} 6^{10f} **0-3-10 £2,773**

Active Asset (Ire) *M R Channon*   87
2 ch c Sinndar (Ire) - Sacristy
2^{6gf} 1^{7gf} 2^{7gf} 8^{10gs} **1-1-4 £6,595**

Actrice (Ire) *E Lellouche*   109
4 b f Danehill (USA) - Ange Bleu (USA)
1^{10gs} 6^{10s} 1^{11gs} 4^{8gf} 11^{8gs} 5^{10g} **2-0-6**
£70,028

Acuzio *W M Brisbourne*   59
3 b c Mon Tresor - Veni Vici (Ire)
6^{11g} 6^{8gf} 8^{8gs} 4^{7g} 8^{8gs} 8^{7gf} 5^{8hy} 8^{10hy}
0-0-8

Ad Valorem (USA) *A P O'Brien*   121
2 b c Danzig (USA) - Classy Women (USA)
1^{6gf} 1^{6g} 1^{6g} **3-0-3 £145,066**

Adaikali (Ire) *Sir Michael Stoute*   96
3 b c Green Desert (USA) - Adaiyka (Ire)
7^{7g} 2^{8gf} 1^{10gf} 2^{10gf} 9^{10gf} 4^{10f} 2^{8g} **1-3-7**
£18,130

Adalar (Ire) *P D Evans*   68 a78
4 br g Grand Lodge (USA) - Adalya (Ire)
9^{12sd} 9^{10sd} 11^{10sd} 11^{12sd} 6^{10sd} 10^{10g}
7^{10gf} 10^{12gf} 4^{10f} 7^{8g} 2^{8gf} 2^{8gf} 9^{8g} **0-2-13**
£2,333

Adalpour (Ire) *C W Moore*   a26
6 b g Kahyasi - Adalya (Ire)
7^{16sd} 8^{12sd} **0-0-2**

Adantino *B R Millman*   64 a64
5 b g Glory Of Dancer - Sweet Whisper
6^{6sd} 3^{7gs} 1^{7sd} 3^{7sd} 3^{7sd} 6^{7gf} 3^{6f}
1^{6g} 6^{6gf} 8^{6gf} 6^{7sd} **2-4-12 £6,623**

Adaptable *H Candy*   54
3 b f Groom Dancer (USA) - Adeptation (USA)
8^{8gf} 9^{10g} **0-0-2**

Adeeba (Ire) *E A L Dunlop*   a40
3 b f Alhaarth (Ire) - Nedaarah
6^{9sd} 13^{10sd} **0-0-2**

Adees Dancer *B Smart*   50
3 b f Danehill Dancer (Ire) - Note (Ger)
10^{8gs} 11^{10gf} 5^{10gf} 8^{16gs} 16^{12gf} **0-0-5**

Adjawar (Ire) *J J Quinn*   49
6 b g Ashkalani (Ire) - Adjriyna
8^{10gs} 18^{11hy} 8^{12gs} **0-0-3**

Adjiram (Ire) *A W Carroll*   38 a39
8 b g Be My Guest (USA) - Adjriyna
3^{10sd} 5^{12sd} 4^{9sw} 1^{8g} 2^{12sd} 12^{12gf} **1-2-6**
£1,847

Admiral (Ire) *Sir Michael Stoute*   94
3 b c Alhaarth (Ire) - Coast Is Clear (Ire)

9^{8g} 1^{12gf} 3^{12g} 1^{12gf} 11^{12g} **2-1-5**
£40,836

Admiral Compton *J R Boyle* 76 a72
3 ch c Compton Place - Sunfleet
2^{8g} 2^{7gf} 3^{8gf} 1^{8sd} **1-3-4 £7,716**

Admittance (USA) *Mrs J R Ramsden* 51
2 b/br f Red Ransom (USA) - Quittance (USA)
8^{6gs} 8^{6g} 11^{6s} 11^{7gs} 10^{7gf} **0-0-5**

Adobe *W M Brisbourne* 74 a59
9 b g Green Desert (USA) - Shamshir
15^{8s} 7^{8gf} 3^{8gf} 4^{8f} 2^{8g} 9^{8gf} 7^{8gf} 4^{8f}
8^{8gf} 5^{8gf} 10^{8gf} 7^{8g} 11^{8gs} 13^{8gf} 1^{9sd} 5^{9sd}
1-2-17 £5,039

Adorata (Ger) *J Jay* 74 a66
3 b f Tannenkonig (Ire) - Adora (Ger)
10^{6ss} 11^{6sd} 7^{6s} 3^{6gf} 2^{7f} 12^{7gf} 2^{7g} 3^{6sd}
9^{9g} 2^{8gs} 1^{8sd} 12^{8gs} 7^{10g} 11^{8hy} 6^{8s} **1-5-15**
£8,406

Adoration *M Johnston* 75
2 b c Royal Applause - Unconditional Love (Ire)
3^{5gs} 2^{6gf} 5^{6g} 12^{7gs} 8^{8g} 10^{6hy} **0-2-6**
£3,096

Adriatic Adventure (Ire) *J L Spearing* a15
3 ch f Foxhound (USA) - Theda
10^{6sd} 12^{8sd} **0-0-2**

Aegean Mist *M Mullineaux* 42
4 ch f Prince Sabo - Dizzydaisy
4^{6gf} **0-0-1 £313**

Aesculus (USA) *L M Cumani* 78
3 b f Horse Chestnut (SAF) - Crafty Buzz (USA)
12^{8gs} 5^{7gf} 3^{6f} 20^{7gf} 3^{10gf} 2^{8g} 1^{8f} **1-3-7**
£21,404

Aetheling (USA) *Mrs A J Perrett*
3 b f Swain (Ire) - Etheldreda (USA)
9^{12sd} **0-0-1**

Afrashad (USA) *Saeed Bin Suroor* a98
2 ch c Smoke Glacken (USA) - Flo White (USA)
1^{6sd} **1-0-1 £4,303**

African Breeze *R M Whitaker* 80
2 b f Atraf - Luanshya
7^{5gf} 4^{5gf} 1^{5g} 4^{6g} 5^{5f} 11^{7g} 8^{6s} **1-0-7**
£5,040

African Dawn *L G Cottrell* 57 a40
6 b g Spectrum (Ire) - Lamu Lady (Ire)
6^{12gf} 14^{12gf} 9^{13g} 4^{16sd} **0-0-4**

African Dream *P W Chapple-Hyam* 115 a83
3 b g Mark Of Esteem (Ire) - Fleet Hill (USA)
3^{8sd} 1^{8sd} 1^{9s} 1^{8g} 1^{10gs} 1^{10gs} 10^{10gs} 4^{10s}
7^{8gs} **5-1-9 £101,704**

African Emperor (Fr) *W Jarvis* a44
2 gr g Highest Honor (Fr) - Land Of Ivory (USA)
6^{6f} 9^{8sd} 8^{6sd} **0-0-3**

African Gift *J G Given* 64
2 b f Cadeaux Genereux - African Light
3^{6gs} 7^{6g} 6^{7gf} 7^{5gf} 11^{6s} **0-1-5 £901**

African Sahara (USA) *Miss D Mountain* 91 a88
5 br h El Gran Senor (USA) - Able Money (USA)
6^{9ss} 1^{10sd} 11^{10sd} 6^{8sd} 8^{8g} 6^{8gs}
15^{10g} 17^{8gs} 6^{8g} 9^{8g} 3^{8gs} 4^{8gf} 3^{8gf} 1^{8gf} 4^{8gs}
2^{8gs} 2^{8g} **3-4-18 £44,029**

African Spur (Ire) *D Carroll* 54 a70
4 b g Flying Spur (Aus) - African Bloom
9^{6sd} 7^{5sd} 2^{6sd} 2^{5sw} 15^{6gs} 10^{7s} 14^{6hy}
19^{6s} 13^{7g} 16^{6g} 19^{5gf} 6^{6f} 5^{7gf} 10^{6sd} 10^{8g}
11^{10sd} 7^{5gf} 4^{6gf} 6^{6f} 16^{6gf} **0-2-20 £1,565**

African Star *Mrs A J Perrett* 53 a58
3 b c Mtoto - Pass The Rose (Ire)
6^{7sd} 5^{11gf} 6^{11f} 4^{10sd} 11^{10gs} 9^{10f} **0-0-6**

African Storm (Ire) *S Kirk* 82
2 b c Fasliyev (USA) - Out Of Africa (Ire)
5^{5gf} 2^{5g} 2^{5gf} 7^{6gf} 6^{5s} 9^{5s} **0-2-6**
£2,748

African Sunset (Ire) *J Howard Johnson* 52
4 b g Danehill Dancer (Ire) - Nizamiya
3^{10gf} 5^{10gf} **0-0-2 £848**

After All (Ire) *G A Butler* a52
3 gr f Desert Story (Ire) - All Ashore
3^{5sd} 5^{6sd} **0-0-2 £566**

After Lent (Ire) *P A Blockley* 61
3 b g Desert Style (Ire) - Yashville
8^{8gf} 6^{9gf} 9^{7hy} **0-0-3**

After The Show *J R Jenkins* 71
3 b c Royal Applause - Tango Teaser
6^{6gs} 10^{5g} 6^{9g} 7^{5gf} 2^{6g} 8^{5g} 15^{6s} 15^{7s}
0-1-8 £1,204

After The Snow (Ire) *I A Wood* 39
2 b f Danetime (Ire) - State
16^{6gf} 5^{7g} **0-0-2**

Again Jane *J M Jefferson*
4 ch f Then Again - Janie-O
7^{12sd} **0-0-1**

Age Of Kings (USA) *J H M Gosden* 86
2 b c Kingmambo (USA) - Everhope (USA)
3^{5g} 6^{5gf} **0-1-2 £1,315**

Agent Kensington *R Hannon* 68
2 b f Mujahid (USA) - Monawara (USA)
2^{5g} 2^{5s} 5^{6gf} 3^{6g} 2^{5gf} 4^{5gf} 2^{6gf} 9^{5f} 24^{7g}
9^{5gs} **0-5-10 £5,424**

Aggi Mac *Andrew Turnell* 31 a40
3 b f Defacto (USA) - Giffoine
5^{7sd} 17^{6gf} 7^{8sd} 8^{8f} 8^{7g} 9^{8hy} **0-0-6**

Aggravation *Andrew Reid* 46 a52
2 b g Sure Blade (USA) - Confection
9^{7sd} 13^{6sd} 9^{7s} 7^{7sd} **0-0-4**

Agilete *L G Cottrell* 75
2 b g Piccolo - Ingerence (Fr)
9^{5s} 3^{6f} 3^{5gf} 5^{5gs} 13^{6gf} **0-0-5 £1,239**

Agilis (Ire) *Jamie Poulton* 53 a77
4 b g Titus Livius (Fr) - Green Life
11^{8sd} 6^{8sd} 11^{7sd} 9^{8sd} 9^{8sd} 12^{8gf} 10^{8gf}
7^{7gf} 6^{7f} **0-0-9 £310**

Agouti *D W P Arbuthnot* 28
3 b f Pennekamp (USA) - La Dama Bonita (USA)
16^{8gf} 10^{10gf} **0-0-2**

Agreat Dayoutwithu *P T Midgley* 19
2 ch f Defacto (USA) - Lonely Lass
8^{6gf} 11^{5gs} 15^{5gf} **0-0-3**

Aguila Loco (Ire) *Mrs Stef Liddiard* 63 a63
5 ch g Eagle Eyed (USA) - Go Likecrazy
3^{6sd} 2^{6sd} 6^{5gs} 5^{8sd} 3^{5ss} 17^{5sw} 4^{7sd}
7^{7sd} 6^{6sd} 2^{7ss} 10^{6gs} 3^{6sd} 7^{7sd} 3^{7gf} 6^{6gf} 8^{6sd}
8^{7f} 10^{7f} 4^{6sd} **1-6-20 £6,505**

Aguilera *M Dods* 35
3 ch f Wolfhound (USA) - Mockingbird
7^{5s} 8^{6f} 10^{7s} 4^{5g} 13^{6gf} 9^{6f} 12^{5s} 8^{5g}
0-0-8 £291

Ahaz *J F Coupland* 46
2 b g Zaha (Can) - Classic Faster (Ire)
14^{5g} 6^{6gs} 12^{7gf} 5^{6f} 4^{6gf} 6^{7gf} 16^{6gf}
0-0-7

Ahdaaf (USA) *J L Dunlop* 78
2 ch/br f Bahri (USA) - Ashraakat (USA)
3^{6gs} 3^{6gf} 4^{6g} **0-2-3 £2,637**

Aimee's Delight *J G Given* 70
4 b f Robellino (USA) - Lloc
9^{8gs} 6^{8gf} 6^{8g} 8^{8gf} 10^{8gf} 7^{8t} 12^{8gs} 9^{8gf}
0-0-8

Aintnecessarilyso *N E Berry* 61 a68
6 ch g So Factual (USA) - Ovideo
5^{7sd} 5^{7sd} 1^{6ss} 4^{6sd} 3^{6sd} 6^{5ss} 3^{6sd} 3^{6ss}
3^{5gs} 2^{5g} 2^{5gf} 2^{6sd} 3^{6f} 6^{6g} 1^{6g} 1^{6g} 5^{6gf} 3^{6g} **3-8-21**
£16,901

Air Mail *Mrs N Macauley* a83
7 b g Night Shift (USA) - Wizardry
4^{9ss} 8^{7sd} 9^{8ss} 12^{7ss} 4^{7st} 6^{8sd} 8^{8sd} 6^{8sd}
4^{7sf} **0-0-9 £983**

Air Of Esteem *Ian Emmerson* a51
8 b g Forzando - Shadow Bird
5^{8sd} 5^{8sd} 6^{9ss} 7^{8sw} 2^{8sd} 4^{7sd} 5^{7sd} 9^{8sd}
0-1-8 £414

Air Of Supremacy (Ire) *J Noseda* 72 a56
3 gr c Royal Applause - Lap Of Luxury
7^{7sd} 6^{8sd} 7^{8g} **0-0-3**

Aire De Mougins (Ire) *P C Haslam* 75
2 b g Pennekamp (USA) - Colouring (Ire)
8^{6gs} 4^{6gf} 4^{7s} 4^{7gf} 2^{8s} **0-2-5 £2,389**

Airedale Lad (Ire) *J R Norton* a17
3 b g Charnwood Forest (Ire) - Tamarsiya (USA)
6^{8sd} 4^{7sd} 5^{8sd} 13^{8gs} 13^{12g} **0-0-5**

Airgusta (Ire) *C P Morlock* 55 a58
3 b g Danehill Dancer (Ire) - Ministerial Model (Ire)
8^{7sd} 10^{8s} 7^{12s} 10^{10gs} 9^{12sd} **0-0-5**

Airwave *H Candy* 108
4 b f Air Express (Ire) - Kangra Valley
6^{6gs} 6^{6f} 9^{6gs} 1^{5gf} 6^{5s} 11^{6g} 3^{5g} 2^{6gf}
1-2-8 £53,150

Aitana *S C Williams* a32
4 b f Slip Anchor - Tsungani
6^{12sd} 4^{12ss} 9^{9ss} **0-0-3**

Ajeel (Ire) *J L Dunlop* 63
5 b g Green Desert (USA) - Samheh (USA)
8^{7gf} **0-0-1**

Akash (Ire) *M Johnston* 101
4 b g Dr Devious (Ire) - Akilara (Ire)
1^{10s} 2^{12g} 12^{10g} 10^{12g} 11^{10gs} 17^{11hy} **1-1-6**
£13,554

Akimbo (USA) *H R A Cecil* 82
3 b c Kingmambo (USA) - All At Sea (USA)
3^{8g} **0-1-1 £960**

Akiramenai (USA) *Mrs L Stubbs* 54
4 br f Salt Lake (USA) - Bold Wench (USA)
9^{5sd} 4^{6s} 10^{7f} 6^{6g} 7^{5gs} 14^{6g} 10^{6gs}
13^{10sd} **0-0-8 £278**

Akraan *E A L Dunlop* 67
2 ch f Erhaab (USA) - Nafhaat (USA)
9^{7gf} 7^{7g} 5^{8gs} 2^{8s} **0-1-4 £1,274**

Akritas *P F I Cole* 93
3 b c Polish Precedent (USA) - Dazzling Heights
4^{12gs} 4^{12gf} 5^{12g} 3^{16gf} **0-1-4 £3,532**

Akshar (Ire) *D K Weld* 105
5 b g Danehill (USA) - Akilara (Ire)
7^{10y} 3^{10gf} 11^{10f} 10^{12gf} **0-0-4 £5,704**

Al Azhar *M Dods* 44 a30
10 b g Alzao (USA) - Upend
6^{11sd} 3^{12g} 3^{12gf} **0-1-3 £1,055**

Al Beedaa (USA) *J L Dunlop* 78
3 ch f Swain (Ire) - Histoire (Fr)
4^{12s} 3^{15gs} 3^{12gf} 10^{14g} **0-0-4 £1,700**

Al Garhoud Bridge *M R Channon* 87
2 b c Josr Algarhoud (Ire) - Pluck
5^{6g} 7^{6g} 1^{7gf} 4^{7gf} **1-0-4 £5,094**

Al Mabrook (Ire) *N G Richards* a14
9 b g Rainbows For Life (Can) - Sky Lover
7^{14sd} **0-0-1**

Al Qudra (Ire) *B J Meehan* 89 a83
2 b c Cape Cross (Ire) - Alvilda (Ire)
5^{5g} 1^{6sd} 12^{7gs} 5^{6g} 2^{6gf} 10^{7gf} 15^{6g} **1-1-7**
£6,625

Al Shuua *C E Brittain* 74
3 b f Lomitas - Sephala (USA)
2^{9gf} 12^{10gf} 4^{10f} 13^{10g} 10^{10g} **0-1-5**
£1,957

Al Sifaat *Saeed Bin Suroor* 76
3 ch f Unfuwain (USA) - Almurooj
7^{10gf} 4^{8gf} **0-0-2 £757**

Al's Glennmay *M S Saunders* a14
2 b f High Estate - Payvashooz
15^{7s} **0-0-1**

Alaared (USA) *M R Channon* 54
4 b g King Of Kings (Ire) - Celtic Loot (USA)
3^{12gf} **0-0-1 £412**

Alafdal (USA) *R Allan* 29
4 b g Gone West (USA) - Aqaarid (USA)
8^{13f} **0-0-1**

Alafzar (Ire) *P D Evans* 64 a69
6 b g Green Desert (USA) - Alasana (Ire)
4^{7sd} 7^{7sd} 3^{8sd} 1^{7sd} 3^{7gf} 14^{7gf} 4^{7f}
9^{7gf} 4^{8gf} 4^{7sd} 10^{8gs} 1^{8gf} 8^{8sd} 15^{8s} **3-3-15**
£10,835

Alaipour (Ire) *Lindsay Woods* 66
5 b h Kahyasi - Alaiyda (USA)
3^{13gf} 16^{16g} 5^{13gy} 12^{16s} PU^{12sd} **0-1-5**
£500

Alaloof (USA) *J L Dunlop* 68
3 b f Swain (Ire) - Alattrah (USA)
6^{10g} 6^{12g} 8^{11gf} **0-0-3**

Alam (USA) *P Monteith* 71
5 b g Silver Hawk (USA) - Ghashtah (USA)
6^{17s} 7^{13s} 5^{15s} **0-0-3**

Alamiyan (Ire) *Sir Michael Stoute* 57
2 b c King's Best (USA) - Alasana (Ire)
6^{8s} **0-0-1**

Alani (Ire) *Jedd O'Keeffe* 63
2 b f Benny The Dip (USA) - Toi Toi (Ire)
2^{7s} 5^{8s} 9^{8g} **0-1-3 £1,393**

Alastair Smellie *S L Keightley* 52 a46
8 ch g Sabrehill (USA) - Reel Foyle (USA)
10^{5ss} 8^{7ss} 2^{6gs} 2^{6sd} 1^{6sd} 15^{6sd} 12^{6sd}
10^{6sd} 15^{5s} 13^{5sd} **1-2-10 £3,036**

Albadi *C E Brittain* 54
3 b g Green Desert (USA) - Lyrist
11^{7gs} 9^{7gf} 7^{8gf} 1^{7f} 17^{7gf} 12^{7gf} 19^{8g}
1-0-7 £3,532

Albanov (Ire) *M Johnston* 99
4 b g Sadler's Wells (USA) - Love For Ever (Ire)
15^{21g} 8^{16g} 4^{13s} 19^{14g} 8^{12gf} 2^{13s} 22^{12s}
0-1-7 £6,556

Albanova *Sir Mark Prescott* 111
5 gr m Alzao (USA) - Alouette
1^{12s} 1^{12g} 1^{12s} **3-0-3 £197,182**

Albashoosh *D Nicholls* 80
6 b g Cadeaux Genereux - Annona (USA)
6⁶ᵍˢ 5⁷ᶠ 6⁷ᵍᶠ 1⁶ᵍᶠ 8⁶ᶠ 3⁶ᵍˢ 4⁶ᵍᶠ 3⁶ᵍᶠ
2⁶ᵍˢ 15⁷ˢ **1-3-10 £8,519**

Albavilla *P W Harris* 81 a83
4 b f Spectrum (Ire) - Lydia Maria
3¹²ᵍ 2¹²ᵍᶠ 5¹²ᵍ 8¹²ᵍ 3¹²ˢ 1¹⁴ˢᵈ 8¹⁴ˢ **1-3-7**
£7,211

Albee (Ire) *Miss Gay Kelleway* 29 a60
4 b g Grand Lodge (USA) - Wolf Cleugh (Ire)
6⁹ˢˢ 6⁹ˢᵈ 4⁹ˢˢ 7¹²ᵍ 11⁸ʰʸ **0-0-5 £261**

Albert Hall *A P O'Brien* 111
2 b c Danehill (USA) - Al Theraab (USA)
2⁷ʸ 1⁸ʸˢ 2⁸ˢ **1-2-3 £108,197**

Albertine *C A Dwyer* 31 a15
4 b f Bahhare (USA) - Rosa Royale
9⁶ᵍᶠ 8⁸ᶠ 8⁸ˢᵈ **0-0-3**

Albinus *A M Balding* 111
3 gr c Selkirk (USA) - Alouette
10⁸ᵍ 2¹⁰ᵍᶠ 1¹²ᵍᶠ 1¹²ᵍ 3¹²ˢ 5¹¹ᵍ **2-1-6**
£25,286

Albury Heath *T M Jones* a28
4 b g Mistertopogigo (Ire) - Walsham Witch
12⁶ˢᵈ 11⁸ˢᵈ **0-0-2**

Alcaidesa *Miss J A Camacho* 66
3 b g Charnwood Forest (Ire) - Calachuchi
4⁸ʰʸ 11⁷ᵍˢ **0-0-2**

Alcazar (Ire) *H Morrison* 117
9 b g Alzao (USA) - Sahara Breeze
1¹⁴ᵍ 2¹⁴ᵍˢ 13²⁰ᵍᶠ 5¹⁴ᵍ 3¹⁶ʰʸ 1¹⁶ᵍˢ **2-2-6**
£92,146

Alcharinga (Ire) *T J Etherington* 63
2 b g Ashkalani (Ire) - Bird In Blue (Ire)
5⁵ᵍᶠ 9⁵ᵍᶠ 4⁵ᵍᶠ **0-0-3 £423**

Alchemist Master *R M Whitaker* 79 a77
5 b g Machiavellian (USA) - Gussy Marlowe
6⁸ᶠ 2⁷ᵍ 2⁷ᶠ 2⁸ᵍ 1⁷ᵍᶠ 1⁸ᵍ 4⁸ᵍˢ 6⁷ᵍᶠ 3⁸ᶠ
10⁸ᵍˢ 7⁷ˢᵈ 3¹²ᵍᶠ PU⁷ᵍᶠ **2-5-13 £16,362**

Alchera *R F Johnson Houghton* 68
3 b g Mind Games - Kind Of Shy
13⁶ᵍˢ 13⁶ˢ 6⁵ᵍᶠ 4⁵ᵍ 4⁵ᵍ 10⁵ᵍᶠ 4⁷ᵍᶠ 7⁸ᵍˢ
7⁸ᵍᶠ 5⁸ᵍᶠ 8⁸ᵍ **0-0-11 £1,136**

Aldente *Sir Mark Prescott* 72
2 gr f Green Desert (USA) - Alruccaba
2⁷ᵍᶠ PU⁷ˢ **0-1-2 £1,336**

Alderney Race (USA) *R Charlton* 108 a57
3 ch c Seeking The Gold (USA) - Oyster Catcher (Ire)
5⁶ˢᵈ 2⁶ˢ 1⁶ᵍᶠ 4⁶ᵍᶠ 1⁶ᵍ 2⁶ᵍ 1⁶ᵍˢ **3-3-7**
£71,848

Alekhine (Ire) *P W Harris* 88
3 b g Soviet Star (USA) - Alriyaah
2⁸ᵍᶠ 3⁸ᵍᶠ 16¹⁰ᵍ 8⁸ᵍ 6¹⁰ᵍ 9¹⁰ᵍᶠ 5⁸ᵍᶠ 10¹⁰ˢ
0-2-8 £3,585

Alenushka *H Candy* 69
3 b f Soviet Star (USA) - National Portrait (Ire)
9¹⁰ᵍᶠ 6⁸ᵍᶠ 4⁸ᵍᶠ 2⁸ᵍᶠ **0-1-4 £2,024**

Aleron (Ire) *J J Quinn* 80
6 b g Sadler's Wells (USA) - High Hawk
2¹²ᵍˢ 1¹⁰ʰʸ 2¹⁰ᵍᶠ 10¹²ᵍ 4⁹ˢ 3¹⁰ᵍ 5¹²ˢ
2¹²ᵍᶠ 8¹²ᵍˢ **1-4-9 £11,864**

Aleshanee *J R Best*
2 b f Bold Edge - Nesyred (Ire)
10⁵ᵍ 7⁵ˢ 18⁶ᵍˢ 17⁶ᵍᶠ **0-0-4**

Alethea Gee *K G Reveley* 33
6 b m Sure Blade (USA) - Star Flower

11⁸ᵍ 8⁷ᵍᶠ 6¹⁰ᵍᶠ **0-0-3**

Aleutian *D R Loder* 76 a105
4 gr g Zafonic (USA) - Baked Alaska
1⁶ˢᵈ 1⁷ˢᵈ 1⁷ˢˢ 6⁷ˢᵈ 11⁷ᵍˢ 13⁶ᵍˢ **3-0-6**
£15,470

Alexander Ambition (Ire) *S Kirk* a69
3 b f Entrepreneur - Lady Alexander (Ire)
4¹⁰ˢᵈ 3⁸ˢᵈ 4⁷ˢᵈ 2⁸ˢᵈ 1⁷ˢᵈ **1-2-5 £5,595**

Alexander Capetown (Ire) *B W Hills* 71
2 b f Fasliyev (USA) - Hawas
2⁵ˢ 5⁵ᵍˢ 6⁶ᵍ 4⁶ᵍˢ 4⁶ᵍᶠ 8⁶ᵍˢ 11⁶ʰʸ **0-2-7**
£2,964

Alexander Duchess (Ire) *J G Burns* 103
3 b f Desert Prince (Ire) - Lionne
6⁷ˢ 7¹¹ᵍˢ 2⁷ᵍ 6⁸ᵍ 8⁸ᵍᶠ 10⁷ˢ **0-1-6**
£10,760

Alexander Goldrun (Ire) *J S Bolger* 118
3 b f Gold Away (Ire) - Renashaan (Fr)
1⁸ʰʸ 1⁷ᵍʸ 2⁸ᵍᶠ 4¹¹ᵍˢ 2¹⁰ᵍ 1¹⁰ᵍ **3-2-6**
£283,212

Alexei *J R Fanshawe* 26 a65
3 ch g Ashkalani (Ire) - Sherkova (USA)
7⁸ˢ 2¹²ˢᵈ 5¹³ˢᵈ 9¹²ˢ **0-1-4 £826**

Alexia Rose (Ire) *A Berry* 82
2 b f Mujadil (USA) - Meursault (Ire)
6⁶ᵍᶠ 13⁵ᵍ 4⁵ᵍˢ 3⁵ᵍ 2⁵ᶠ 1⁶ʰʸ 2⁵ᵍˢ 7⁶ˢ
1-3-8 £11,044

Aleyah *C F Wall*
2 ch f Bachir (Ire) - Silver Peak (Fr)
13⁶ᵍ **0-0-1**

Alfelma (Ire) *P R Wood* 33
4 gr f Case Law - Billie Grey
9⁶ᵍᶠ 15⁶ᵍᶠ 18⁵ᵍ **0-0-3**

Alfhala (Ire) *M J Gingell* 42
3 b f Acatenango (Ger) - Maid Of Kashmir (Ire)
18⁸ᵍ **0-0-1**

Alfie Lee (Ire) *D A Nolan* 40
7 ch g Case Law - Nordic Living (Ire)
7⁵ᵍᶠ 4⁵ᵍᶠ 13⁵ˢ **0-0-3 £536**

Alfie Noakes *Mrs A J Perrett* 83 a71
2 b c Groom Dancer (USA) - Crimson Rosella
3⁷ᵍ 5⁸ᵍˢ 3⁸ˢᵈ **0-2-3 £1,602**

Alfonso *B W Hills* 91 a81
3 ch g Efisio - Winnebago
1⁷ˢˢ 7⁸ᵍ 12⁸ᵍ 2⁷ᵍˢ 4⁸ˢ 2⁸ˢ 1⁷ᵍˢ **2-2-7**
£17,392

Alfred The Great (Ire) *M Johnston* 36
2 b c King's Best (USA) - Aigue
11⁸ᵍˢ **0-0-1**

Alfridini *D R C Elsworth* 81 a72
3 ch c Selkirk (USA) - Vivre En Paix
11⁸ˢᵈ 8⁷ˢᵈ 2⁷ˢᵈ 2⁷ˢᵈ 1¹⁰ˢᵈ 4⁸ˢᵈ 12¹²ᵍˢ
1⁸ᶠ 3¹⁰ᵍ 5⁸ᵍˢ 5¹⁰ᵍᶠ **2-2-11 £11,489**

Alghaazy (Ire) *L M Cumani* 54
3 b g Mark Of Esteem (Ire) - Kentmere (Fr)
10⁸ʰʸ 11¹⁰ᵍˢ **0-0-2**

Algorithm *T D Easterby* 59
2 b f Danehill Dancer (Ire) - Dominelle
8⁵ˢ 6⁶ᵍᶠ 5⁵ᶠ 6⁷ᵍᶠ 2⁷ᵍᶠ 3⁷ᶠ 4⁸ᵍᶠ 9⁷ᵍ 15⁸ˢ
0-2-9 £3,394

Alhaadh (USA) *J H M Gosden* 62
2 b f Diesis - Wishah (USA)
9⁶ᵍ **0-0-1**

Ali Bruce *G L Moore* 70 a71
4 b g Cadeaux Genereux - Actualite

5^{10gf} 2^{8g} 1^{7sd} 3^{7sd} 4^{8gs} **1-3-5 £4,932**

Ali Deo *W J Haggas* 78 a71
3 ch g Ali-Royal (Ire) - Lady In Colour (Ire)
1^{7gf} 3^{8gf} 11^{8s} 6^{10gf} 12^{7gf} 7^{8g} 7^{9sd} 4^{10sd}
4^{9sd} **1-0-9 £5,662**

Ali Pasha *W M Brisbourne*
5 b g Ali-Royal (Ire) - Edge Of Darkness
6^{9sd} **0-0-1**

Aliabad (Ire) *J G M O'Shea*
9 b/br g Doyoun - Alannya (Fr)
5^{16sd} **0-0-1**

Alianna (Fr) *S Dow* 34 a34
3 b f Anabaa (USA) - Ambassadrice (Fr)
12^{7sd} 11^{8sd} 10^{9gs} 14^{10gs} 11^{12sd} 5^{9sd}
0-0-6

Aliba (Ire) *B Smart* 48 a65
3 ch g Ali-Royal (Ire) - Kiba (Ire)
4^{7sd} 10^{7f} 11^{7sd} 2^{7sw} 13^{8g} 9^{7sd} **0-1-6**
£834

Alibongo (Cze) *P A Blockley* a12
3 ch g Dara Monarch - Alvilde
13^{6ss} 9^{7sd} **0-0-2**

Alice Blackthorn *B Smart* 49 a61
3 b f Forzando - Owdbetts (Ire)
15^{6g} 7^{6g} 5^{7f} 10^{7gf} 8^{7gf} 13^{7gs} 1^{7sd} **1-0-7**
£1,473

Alice King (Ire) *W G M Turner* 26 a49
2 b f Key Of Luck (USA) - Java Jive
4^{5s} 4^{5s} 9^{5gf} 2^{5sd} 5^{6f} 7^{6sd} **0-1-6 £999**

Alimiste (Ire) *I A Wood* a40
4 b f Ali-Royal (Ire) - Miss Senate (Ire)
9^{10sd} 9^{10sd} 9^{10sd} 8^{12sd} 10^{13sd} 8^{10gs} **0-0-6**

Alinda (Ire) *P W Harris* 84
3 b f Revoque (Ire) - Gratclo
1^{7g} 1^{7gf} **2-0-2 £12,194**

Alisa (Ire) *B I Case* 30 a59
4 b f Slip Anchor - Ariadne (Ger)
8^{8sd} 3^{12sd} 5^{12sd} 5^{12sd} 6^{10sd} 11^{12gf} **0-1-6**
£540

Alizar (Ire) *S Dow* 61 a61
3 b f Rahy (USA) - Capua (USA)
9^{7sd} 2^{5sd} 3^{6sd} 1^{6sd} 4^{5sd} 2^{5sd} 3^{6sd} 6^{5gf}
7^{5gf} 6^{6gf} 18^{6gf} 1^{6f} 11^{5f} 9^{5gf} 9^{6gf} 7^{6gs} 19^{6gf}
11^{5g} **2-4-18 £8,140**

Aljaareh (USA) *M P Tregoning* 60
3 b/br c Storm Cat (USA) - Muhbubh (USA)
12^{8g} **0-0-1**

Aljafliyah *L M Cumani* 43
3 ch f Halling (USA) - Arruhan (Ire)
UR^{8gf} 8^{7g} 7^{7g} 9^{7gs} 15^{8gs} **0-0-5**

Aljomar *R E Barr* a30
5 b g College Chapel - Running For You (Fr)
9^{7sd} 6^{11sd} 10^{8ss} 12^{8sw} **0-0-4**

Alkaadhem *M P Tregoning* 118
4 b c Green Desert (USA) - Balalaika
5^{8g} 4^{8g} 1^{10gf} 11^{8gf} 4^{10gs} 3^{12gf} 1^{10gf} 1^{10g}
3-2-8 £70,600

Alkaased (USA) *L M Cumani* 118
4 b c Kingmambo (USA) - Chesa Plana
2^{12gf} 1^{12g} 1^{12gf} 2^{12gf} **2-1-4 £71,832**

All A Dream *Mrs L Williamson* a73
2 b f Desert Story (Ire) - Alioli
6^{5sd} 10^{5sd} 3^{7sd} 7^{6sd} **0-1-4 £800**

All Bleevable *Mrs S Lamyman* 48

7 b g Presidium - Eve's Treasure
6^{12gf} 6^{12gf} 7^{12g} **0-0-3**

All Blue (Ire) *Saeed Bin Suroor* 74
3 b g Green Desert (USA) - Talented
4^{8gs} 4^{10gf} 8^{14gs} 8^{10hy} **0-0-4 £771**

All For Laura *D R Loder* 92
2 ch f Cadeaux Genereux - Lighthouse
4^{6gf} 1^{5gf} 5^{5g} 5^{6g} 8^{7g} 4^{6s} **1-0-6 £8,956**

All Night Dancer (Ire) *David Wachman* 83
2 b f Danehill Dancer (Ire) - Nocturnal (Fr)
1^{5gf} 5^{6gf} 2^{6g} 10^{6gy} 9^{7gf} 7^{7y} 2^{6y} 7^{6ys}
1-2-8 £40,101

All On My Own (USA) *I W McInnes* 41 a38
9 ch g Unbridled (USA) - Someforall (USA)
8^{15sd} 4^{8sd} 4^{10sd} 8^{8sw} 12^{8sd} 5^{8sd} 3^{8g}
4^{10hy} 9^{8gf} **0-2-10 £590**

All Quiet *R Hannon* 78
3 b f Piccolo - War Shanty
3^{6gf} 2^{7gf} 3^{8f} 5^{7gf} 5^{6gs} 5^{7gf} 7^{6gf} **0-3-7**
£3,295

All Too Beautiful (Ire) *A P O'Brien* 113
3 b f Sadler's Wells (USA) - Urban Sea (USA)
1^{10y} 1^{10y} 2^{12g} 4^{12gf} 3^{10g} **2-2-5**
£134,412

Allegretto (Fr) *S Kirk* 69
2 b c Anabaa (USA) - Aimores (Ire)
2^{6hy} **0-1-1 £1,900**

Allerton Boy *Evan Williams* a40
5 ch g Beveled (USA) - Darakah
4^{5sd} 7^{6sd} 6^{5ss} 8^{5sd} **0-0-4**

Allexina *John M Oxx* 100
2 ch f Barathea (Ire) - Grecian Bride (Ire)
1^{7s} 6^{7gy} 1^{8s} **2-0-3 £33,487**

Allez Mousson *A Bailey* 40
6 b g Hernando (Fr) - Rynechra
11^{18g} 13^{18s} 9^{16s} 7^{16gs} 9^{17gs} **0-0-5**

Allied Cause *L M Cumani* 63 a70
2 ch f Giant's Causeway (USA) - Alligram (USA)
8^{7gs} 5^{7g} 1^{7gf} **1-0-3 £5,265**

Allied Victory (USA) *E J Alston* 77 a64
4 b c Red Ransom (USA) - Coral Dance (Fr)
1^{8sd} 3^{8gf} 9^{11sd} 2^{11g} 8^{11gs} 3^{9s} 7^{12s} 4^{12g}
1-1-8 £8,662

Allizam *B A McMahon* 50
2 b c Tragic Role (USA) - Mazilla
12^{6s} 4^{6g} 18^{5gs} 9^{8hy} **0-0-4 £419**

Allodarlin (Ire) *P F I Cole* 34
3 b f Cape Cross (Ire) - Sharp Circle (Ire)
8^{10gf} 12^{11gf} 11^{8gf} **0-0-3**

Allstar Princess *R A Fahey* 47
2 b f Environment Friend - Turf Moor (Ire)
7^{6g} 11^{6g} 7^{7g} 12^{7gs} **0-0-4**

Ally Makbul *Ian Emmerson* a61
4 b f Makbul - Clarice Orsini
1^{8sd} 8^{4sd} 4^{12sd} 8^{8sd} 1^{9gs} **2-0-5 £2,793**

Almah (SAF) *Miss Venetia Williams* 92
6 b m Al Mufti (USA) - Jazz Champion (SAF)
14^{16g} 12^{14g} 6^{16g} 17^{14g} 9^{16gf} **0-0-5**
£1,804

Almanac (Ire) *B P J Baugh* 19 a46
3 b c Desert Style (Ire) - Share The Vision
7^{8sd} 11^{8sd} 10^{8sd} 10^{8gf} **0-0-4**

Almanshood (USA) *J H M Gosden* 71
2 b/br c Bahri (USA) - Lahan
5^{7gs} 3^{8gs} **0-1-2 £935**

Almansoora (USA) *Saeed Bin Suroor* 84
2 b f Bahri (USA) - Bashayer (USA)
2^{6gs} 1^{7g} **1-1-2 £13,182**

Almara *Miss K B Boutflower* a23
4 b f Wolfhound (USA) - Alacrity
15^{7sd} 4^{5sd} 11^{6sd} 5^{6sd} **0-0-4**

Almaty Express *M Todhunter* 65
2 b g Almaty (Ire) - Express Girl
3^{5hy} 8^{6hy} 7^{5f} 3^{5gf} 4^{5gs} 1^{5gf} **1-1-6**
£4,307

Almaviva (Ire) *J Noseda* 67
4 b f Grand Lodge (USA) - Kafayef (USA)
7^{8gs} 15^{10g} **0-0-2**

Almendrados (Ire) *J Noseda* 86
2 b f Desert Prince (Ire) - Sevi's Choice (USA)
3^{6gf} **0-1-1 £728**

Almizan (Ire) *M R Channon* 88
4 b g Darshaan - Bint Albaadiya (USA)
10^{19gs} 9^{14gf} 4^{18g} 8^{20gf} 4^{21g} 3^{16s} 10^{16gf}
17^{18s} 5^{16gs} **0-2-9 £3,524**

Almnadia (Ire) *S Gollings* 49
5 b m Alhaarth (Ire) - Mnaafa (Ire)
9^{16s} 5^{16gf} 6^{14gf} **0-0-3**

Almond Beach *B J Meehan* a30
4 ch g Hector Protector (USA) - Dancing Spirit (Ire)
7^{7sd} 10^{8sd} **0-0-2**

Almond Willow (Ire) *J Noseda* 70 a77
3 b f Alhaarth (Ire) - Miss Willow Bend (USA)
9^{10g} 2^{8gs} 7^{8hy} 6^{8gs} 2^{9sd} 3^{10sd} **0-3-6**
£3,858

Almost Perfect (Ire) *T D Barron* 66 a17
2 ch f Priolo (USA) - Talbiya (Ire)
6^{5ss} 3^{6gf} **0-1-2 £615**

Almost Welcome *S Dow* 51 a50
3 b g First Trump - Choral Sundown
10^{7sd} 9^{8sd} 3^{10sd} 5^{10sd} 7^{11gs} 10^{12f} 10^{10sd}
0-1-7 £581

Almuraad (Ire) *Sir Michael Stoute* 109
3 b c Machiavellian (USA) - Wellspring (Ire)
18^{gf} 10^{9s} **1-0-2 £8,398**

Alnaja (USA) *W J Haggas*
5 b g Woodman (USA) - Cursory Look (USA)
PU^{12hy} 9^{15s} **0-0-2**

Along Came Molly *B J Meehan*
2 ch f Dr Fong - Torrid Tango (USA)
14^{8hy} **0-0-1**

Along The Nile *Mrs J R Ramsden* 73
2 b g Desert Prince (Ire) - Golden Fortune
7^{6gf} 3^{6gf} 6^{6s} 9^{6gs} 10^{7f} 4^{7f} 6^{8gs} 9^{7gs}
0-2-8 £1,444

Alpaga Le Jomage (Ire) *B J Meehan* 88
2 b c Orpen (USA) - Miss Bagatelle
3^{5g} 3^{5s} 2^{5s} 4^{5gf} 5^{5g} 8^{5gf} 5^{5gf} 1^{5gs} 4^{5g}
7^{6gf} **1-2-10 £16,999**

Alph *R Ingram* a73
7 b g Alflora (Ire) - Royal Birthday
4^{12sd} **0-0-1 £280**

Alpha Echo (USA) *M F Harris* a36
5 b/br h Spinning World (USA) - Add (USA)
79^{ss} **0-0-1**

Alpha Juliet (Ire) *G M Moore* 46
3 b f Victory Note (USA) - Zara's Birthday (Ire)
6^{7s} 6^{9f} 6^{12gs} **0-0-3**

Alpha Zeta *C W Thornton* 32
3 b g Primo Dominie - Preening

Alphecca (USA) *Sir Michael Stoute* 103
3 b c Kingmambo (USA) - Limbo (USA)
1^{10gf} 3^{10gf} 6^{10g} **1-0-3 £6,411**

Alpine Gold (Ire) *J L Dunlop* 88
2 b f Montjeu (Ire) - Ski For Gold
12^{7gf} 7^{7gs} 1^{8s} 1^{8s} 7^{8gs} **2-0-5 £14,257**

Alpine Hideaway (Ire) *J S Wainwright* 53
11 b g Tirol - Arbour (USA)
14^{7gf} 6^{7gf} 10^{8gs} 1^{8gs} 7^{8f} 7^{10gf} **1-0-6**
£3,571

Alpine Special (Ire) *P C Haslam* 76 a72
3 gr g Orpen (USA) - Halomix
6^{7g} 10^{12sd} 2^{11hy} 2^{12s} 12^{14gf} 7^{12sd}
0-2-7 £3,196

Alpino Chileno (Arg) *Rune Haugen* 107
5 gr h Alpino Fitz (Arg) - Fairyland (Arg)
1^{12g} 1^{14g} 1^{12g} 5^{11g} 6^{12g} 4^{9s} 4^{12gf} 8^{12gf}
3-0-8 £25,130

Alqaahir (USA) *Saeed Bin Suroor* 75
2 b c Swain (Ire) - Crafty Example (USA)
3^{7g} **0-1-1 £808**

Alqwah (Ire) *Saeed Bin Suroor* 87
3 b f Danehill (USA) - Delage
1^{7g} **1-0-1 £5,687**

Alrafid (Ire) *G L Moore* 93
5 ch g Halling (USA) - Ginger Tree (USA)
14^{10g} 5^{10g} 6^{8g} 2^{9g} 7^{8g} 12^{10g} 6^{9gf} 7^{8gf}
0-1-8 £9,332

Alrafidain (Ire) *M Johnston* 84
2 b c Monsun (Ger) - Demeter (USA)
4^{8g} 2^{7gs} **0-1-2 £2,378**

Alrida (Ire) *R A Fahey* 75
5 b g Ali-Royal (Ire) - Ride Bold (USA)
4^{16s} 1^{21g} **1-0-2 £23,993**

Alright My Son (Ire) *R Hannon* 89
2 b c Pennekamp (USA) - Pink Stone (Fr)
8^{5s} 2^{5s} 4^{6f} 5^{7gf} 2^{7gf} 4^{8s} 7^{8gf} 2^{8gf} 1^{8g}
6^{8s} **1-3-10 £15,138**

Alsharq (Ire) *M P Tregoning* 67
2 b f Machiavellian (USA) - Balaabel (USA)
9^{7g} 8^{7gs} **0-0-2**

Alshawameq (Ire) *J L Dunlop* 92
3 b g Green Desert (USA) - Azdihaar (USA)
3^{8gf} 1^{8gf} 7^{8f} 5^{8gs} 3^{8g} 2^{8gs} **1-1-6**
£15,866

Alsu (Ire) *A M Balding* 71
2 b f Fasliyev (USA) - Pourquoi Pas (Ire)
3^{5g} 1^{6gs} 10^{6g} 6^{6g} 3^{5gf} 3^{5g} 6^{5s} **1-2-7**
£5,582

Alta Petens *M L W Bell* 88
2 b f Mujadil (USA) - Be Exciting (Ire)
4^{5s} 1^{6gf} 10^{6f} 12^{5g} 4^{7gf} 5^{8gf} 6^{7g} 7^{7g}
5^{6s} **1-0-9 £17,349**

Altares *P Howling* a38
3 b c Alhaarth (Ire) - Reach The Wind (USA)
10^{10sd} 8^{gd} 13^{8ss} 9^{11gf} 9^{12gs} **0-0-5**

Altay *R A Fahey* 83
7 b g Erin's Isle - Aliuska (Ire)
11^{10g} 3^{12gs} **0-1-2 £536**

Altitude Dancer (Ire) *P A Blockley* 57 a69
4 b g Sadler's Wells - Height Of Passion
3^{16sd} 2^{16sd} 1^{16sd} 4^{16ss} 8^{18g} 11^{16s} **1-2-6**
£4,811

Alula *R Hannon* 54
2 ch f In The Wings - Aryaf (Can)
10⁶ᵍˢ 9⁸ᵍᶠ 13⁸ᵍᶠ **0-0-3**

Alvarinho Lady *D Haydn Jones* 70
2 b f Royal Applause - Jugendliebe (Ire)
1⁵ᵍ 5⁵ˢ 4⁶ᵍ 4⁶ᵍˢ 13⁶ᵍˢ 19⁷ᵍ **1-0-6**
£5,900

Always Believe (USA) *Mrs P Ford* a14
8 b g Carr De Naskra (USA) - Wonder Mar (USA)
9⁷ˢˢ 9⁹ˢʷ **0-0-2**

Always Daring *C J Teague* 11
5 b m Atraf - Steamy Windows
14⁷ᵍᶠ 11⁷ˢᵈ 9⁶ᶠ **0-0-3**

Always Esteemed (Ire) *G Wragg* 104 a104
4 b g Mark Of Esteem (Ire) - Always Far (USA)
2⁸ᵍˢ 7¹⁰ᵍˢ 14¹⁰ᵍᶠ 4⁸ᵍᶠ 1⁸ˢᵈ 4⁸ᵍᶠ 13⁸ˢ
13⁸ᶠ 15⁷ˢ **1-1-9 £15,988**

Always First *Sir Michael Stoute* 113
3 b c Barathea (Ire) - Pink Cristal
8⁸ᵍᶠ 2⁹ᵍᶠ 3¹²ᵍ 4¹²ᵍ 8¹¹ᵍ **0-1-5 £19,500**

Always Flying (USA) *N Wilson* 70 a67
3 ch g Fly So Free (USA) - Dubiously (USA)
1⁹ˢᵈ 5¹⁰ˢᵈ 2¹⁰ᵍ 6⁹ᵍˢ 6¹⁰ᵍᶠ 8⁹ᵍ 2⁷ᵍ 7⁷ᵍˢ
17⁸ᵍᶠ 8⁸ᵍ 4¹⁰ˢ **1-2-11 £5,954**

Always Mine *Mrs A J Perrett* 88
2 ch f Daylami (Ire) - Mamoura (Ire)
5⁷ᵍ 6⁸ᵍˢ **0-0-2 £375**

Always Rainbows (Ire) *B S Rothwell* 55
6 b g Rainbows For Life (Can) - Maura's Guest (Ire)
16¹⁶ᵍˢ 8¹²ᵍˢ **0-0-2**

Always Waining (Ire) *P L Clinton* 102
3 b c Unfuwain (USA) - Glenarff (USA)
3⁹ᵍ 3¹¹ᵍᶠ 1¹²ᵍᶠ 5¹²ᵍ 3¹²ᵍˢ 1¹²ᵍᶠ 6¹²ᵍ 9¹⁴ˢ
4¹²ᵍ 1¹²ˢ 24¹²ˢ **3-3-11 £27,327**

Alyousufeya (Ire) *J L Dunlop* 45
3 ch f Kingmambo (USA) - Musicale (USA)
4⁸ᵍ **0-0-1 £273**

Alzarma *A Bailey* 62 a44
2 b g Alzao (USA) - Skimra
11⁶ᵍ 3⁶ᵍ 7⁵ᵍˢ 6⁶ᵍᶠ 13⁶ᵍ 6⁷ˢᵈ **0-1-6**
£458

Amalfi Coast *W S Cunningham* 43
5 b g Emperor Jones (USA) - Legend's Daughter (USA)
8¹⁰ᵍˢ 11¹²ᵍ 17¹⁰ᵍᶠ 16¹⁶ᵍ **0-0-4**

Amalgam (Ire) *Mrs P N Dutfield* 45 a19
2 ch f Namid - Carhue Gold (Ire)
14⁵ˢ 16⁶ᵍᶠ 11⁷ᵍ 5⁵ᵍᶠ 7⁷ˢᵈ 10⁶ᵍ **0-0-6**

Amalie (Ire) *C E Brittain* 88
2 b f Fasliyev (USA) - Princess Amalie (USA)
7⁷ᵍ 1⁶ᶠ **1-0-2 £3,926**

Amanda's Lad (Ire) *M C Chapman* 67 a50
4 b g Danetime (Ire) - Art Duo
6⁸ˢᵈ 3⁶ˢᵈ 4⁶ˢᵈ 9⁵ᵈ 6⁶ˢᵈ 4⁸ˢᵈ 5⁵ˢ 6⁶ˢ
3⁶ᵍ 5⁶ᵍˢ 5⁷ᵍˢ 10⁵ᵍᶠ 4⁶ᵍᶠ 2⁷ᵍᶠ 7⁶ᵍᶠ 3⁶ᵍᶠ 5⁵ᵍˢ
4⁵ᵍᶠ **0-7-24**
£4,174

Amanderica (Ire) *M C Chapman* 88
2 b f Indian Lodge (Ire) - Striking Gold (USA)
10⁵ᵍᶠ 10⁷ᵍ 7⁷ᵍˢ 10⁸ᵍᶠ **0-0-4**

Amandus (USA) *D R Loder* 104
4 b g Danehill (USA) - Affection Affirmed (USA)
9¹⁰ˢ 7⁸ˢˢ 2⁸ᵍ 4⁸ᵍᶠ 7⁷ᵍˢ 12⁸ᵍᶠ **0-2-6**
£8,080

Amankila (Ire) *M L W Bell* 71 a46
3 b f Revoque (Ire) - Steel Habit

9¹⁰ᵍˢ 3¹⁰ᵍˢ 1¹⁰ˢ 6¹²ˢᵈ 4⁸ᵍᶠ 13⁸ˢ **1-1-6**
£3,676

Amanpuri (Ger) *P A Blockley* 43 a33
6 b g Fairy King (USA) - Aratika (Fr)
12⁷ˢᵈ 9⁷ˢᵈ 9⁹ˢʷ 9⁹ˢʷ 2¹⁵ᵍ 7¹³ᵍ **0-1-6**
£452

Amar (Cze) *P A Blockley* a11
3 ch g Beccari (USA) - Autumn (Fr)
14⁷ˢᵈ 7¹¹ˢᵈ 11¹⁴ᶠ **0-0-3**

Amaretto Express (Ire) *R E Barr*
5 b g Blues Traveller (Ire) - Cappuchino (Ire)
14¹⁰ᶠ **0-0-1**

Amazin *R Hannon* 96
2 b c Primo Dominie - Aegean Blue
2⁶ᵍᶠ 1⁶ᵍᶠ 2⁵ᵍ 5⁶ᵍᶠ 4⁵ᶠ 16⁶ᵍᶠ 9⁵ˢ **1-2-7**
£15,967

Amazing Grace Mary *S R Bowring* 26
2 b f Dancing Spree (USA) - Frisky Miss (Ire)
12⁵ᵍᶠ 8⁶ᵍᶠ **0-0-2**

Amazing Valour (Ire) *M Johnston* 75
2 b c Sinndar (Ire) - Flabbergasted (Ire)
2⁸ᶠ 8¹⁰ᵍᶠ 7¹⁰ʰʸ **0-1-3 £1,716**

Amazonic *T T Clement*
3 b f First Trump - Mystic Beauty (Ire)
13¹⁰ˢᵈ **0-0-1**

Amber Fox (Ire) *P D Evans* 52 a42
3 b f Foxhound (USA) - Paradable (Ire)
5⁶ᶠ 6⁵ᵍᶠ 5⁶ᵍᶠ 10⁸ᵍᶠ 3⁷ʰʸ 7⁷ᵍᶠ 6⁷ˢᵈ **0-1-7**
£441

Amber Legend *Ms Deborah J Evans* a38
3 b f Fraam - Abstone Queen
9⁵ˢˢ 8⁶ˢᵈ **0-0-2**

Ambersong *A W Carroll* 59 a58
6 ch g Hernando (Fr) - Stygian (USA)
3¹³ˢᵈ 3¹²ˢᵈ 8¹⁶ˢᵈ 6¹⁴ˢᵈ 4¹²ˢᵈ 3¹²ᵍᶠ 3¹⁴ᶠ
11¹²ᵍ 11²ᵍᶠ 4¹⁰ᵍᶠ 3¹¹ᵍ 6¹¹ᵍᶠ 14¹²ᵍ **1-5-13**
£5,662

Ambushed (Ire) *P Monteith* 49
8 b g Indian Ridge - Surprise Move (Ire)
6⁸ᵍ 8¹⁰ᵍ 10⁹ᵍᶠ **0-0-4**

Ameeq (USA) *M P Tregoning* 83
2 b/br c Silver Hawk (USA) - Haniya (Ire)
3⁷ᵍ 3⁸ᵍ 9⁸ᵍᶠ **0-2-3 £1,782**

Amelia (Ire) *W M Brisbourne* 67 a57
6 b m General Monash (USA) - Rose Tint (Ire)
5⁶ˢᵈ 2⁶ˢᵈ 5⁶ˢˢ 5⁶ˢᵈ 5⁵ˢˢ 3⁷ˢᵈ 10⁶ˢᵈ 1⁶ˢ
3⁶ˢ 2⁶ᵍᶠ 5⁶ᵍᶠ 3⁶ᵍ 3⁸ᵍᶠ 8⁵ᵍᶠ **1-6-14 £8,422**

American Cousin *D Nicholls* 65
9 b g Distant Relative - Zelda (USA)
1⁶ᵍˢ 17⁶ᵍˢ 1⁵ᵍᶠ 16⁶ᵍᶠ 2⁵ᵍᶠ 5⁵ᵍᶠ 8⁶ˢ 14⁵ᵍᶠ
6⁵ᵍᶠ 6⁵ᵍᶠ 5⁶ᵍ 7⁵ˢ **2-1-12 £6,878**

American Duke (USA) *B J Meehan* 79
3 b g Cryptoclearance (USA) - Prologue (USA)
14⁷ᵍᶠ 8¹⁰ᵍˢ 2¹⁰ᵍᶠ 7¹⁰ᵍᶠ 5¹¹ᵍ 1¹⁰ᵍˢ 13⁹ˢ
1-1-7 £5,246

American Post *Mme C Head-Maarek* 113
3 br c Bering - Wells Fargo
1⁸ᵍ 1⁸ᵍˢ 1⁸ᵍᶠ 6¹²ᵍ 10⁸ᵍˢ **3-0-5**
£202,772

Amethyst Rock *P L Gilligan* 14 a44
6 b g Rock Hopper - Kind Lady
11¹²ˢᵈ 3⁹ˢᵈ 1⁸ˢᶠ 8⁸ˢᵈ 2⁸ˢᵈ 9¹²ᵍᶠ 16⁸ˢᵈ
1-1-7 £2,060

Ameyrah (Ire) *M R Channon* 30 a54
3 b f In The Wings - Alfaaselah (Ger)

7¹⁰ˢᵈ 7¹²ᵍˢ 11¹⁰ᵍˢ **0-0-3**

Amica *G L Moore* 78
2 b f Averti (Ire) - Friend For Life
2⁶ᵍᶠ 2⁵ᵍˢ 1⁶ᵍ 5⁶ᵍᶠ **1-2-4 £8,000**

Amid The Chaos (Ire) *D K Weld* 91
4 ch c Nashwan (USA) - Celebrity Style (USA)
10¹⁰ᵍᶠ 16²⁰ᵍᶠ 1¹⁴ᵍ 5¹²ᵍᶠ **1-0-4 £7,785**

Amigra (Ire) *Miss Jacqueline S Doyle* 28 a63
2 b f Grand Lodge (USA) - Beaming
16⁶ᵍˢ 12⁶ᵍᶠ 4⁸ˢᵈ **0-0-3 £265**

Amir Zaman *J R Jenkins* a84
6 ch g Salse (USA) - Colorvista
1¹²ˢᵈ 6¹¹ˢˢ 11¹⁷ˢᵈ **1-0-3 £2,884**

Ammenayr (Ire) *T G Mills* 83 a78
4 b g Entrepreneur - Katiyfa
9⁸ˢᵈ 8⁷ˢ 3⁷ᵍˢ 5⁷ᵍˢ 3⁷ᵍᶠ 6⁷ᵍˢ 15⁷ᵍ 5⁷ˢᵈ
6⁶ˢᵈ **0-1-9 £1,698**

Ammirare *C W Thornton* 46
2 b f Diktat - Mathaayl (USA)
8⁵ᵍ 7⁷ᵍˢ **0-0-2**

Amnesty *G L Moore* 68 a61
5 ch g Salse (USA) - Amaranthus
8¹²ˢᵈ 4¹⁰ˢᵈ 5¹³ˢᵈ 8¹⁰ˢᵈ 11¹⁰ˢᵈ 6⁸ˢᵈ 1⁸ᵍˢ
1¹⁰ˢ 5⁸ᵍ 2⁸ˢ 13⁸ᵍᶠ 15⁸ʰʸ 12¹⁰ʰʸ **2-1-13
£7,948**

Among Dreams *A G Newcombe* 36 a37
3 ch f Among Men (USA) - Russell Creek
15⁷ˢᵈ 15⁷ˢ 13⁸ᵍᶠ **0-0-3**

Among Equals *M Meade*
7 b g Sadler's Wells (USA) - Epicure's Garden (USA)
18¹⁰ᵍ **0-0-1**

Among Friends (Ire) *B Palling* 54
4 b g Among Men (USA) - Anita's Contessa (Ire)
6⁷ᵍˢ 9⁶ᵍˢ 8⁵ᵍᶠ 7⁶ᵍᶠ 11⁸ᵍˢ 14¹⁰ᵍ 16⁶ˢ
0-0-7

Ampelio (Ire) *Sir Michael Stoute* 53
2 ch c Grand Lodge (USA) - Bordighera (USA)
13⁸ᵍ 8⁸ᵍ **0-0-2**

Amphitheatre (Ire) *R F Johnson Houghton* 65 a60
2 b g Titus Livius (Fr) - Crimson Ring
5⁵ᵍᶠ 16⁶ᵍ 3⁶ᵍᶠ 11⁷ᵍˢ 3⁶ˢᵈ 3⁷ᵍᶠ 11⁷ˢᵈ
1⁷ᵍᶠ **1-3-8 £4,856**

Amsterdam (Ire) *A P O'Brien* 97
2 b c Danehill (USA) - Dathiyna (Ire)
5⁶ᵍˢ 1⁶ᵍ 3⁷ᵍᶠ **1-0-3 £12,373**

Amusement *D G Bridgwater* a49
8 ch g Mystiko (USA) - Jolies Eaux
4¹⁵ˢᵈ 6¹²ˢᵈ 12¹⁰ˢᵈ 3¹⁶ˢᵈ **0-0-4 £413**

Amwell Brave *J R Jenkins* 59 a71
3 b g Pyramus (USA) - Passage Creeping (Ire)
2¹⁰ˢᵈ 2¹⁰ˢᵈ 3¹⁰ˢᵈ 5¹⁰ˢᵈ 10⁸ᵍ 5¹⁰ᵍˢ
8⁸ˢ 8⁸ˢ 7¹²ˢᵈ 6¹⁰ᵍ 7¹⁰ʰʸ 9⁹ˢᵈ **0-4-13 £5,048**

Anacapri *W S Cunningham* 6 a20
4 b f Barathea (Ire) - Dancerette
8⁸ˢᵈ 5⁷ˢᵈ 11¹¹ˢᵈ 7¹⁰ᵍ **0-0-4**

Anak Pekan *M A Jarvis* 110
4 ch g In The Wings - Trefoil (Fr)
1¹⁶ᵍˢ 1¹⁹ᵍˢ 3¹⁶ˢ 8¹⁶ᵍᶠ 7²⁰ᵍ 7¹⁶ˢ **2-1-6
£99,273**

Analyze (Fr) *B G Powell* 80 a82
6 b g Anabaa (USA) - Bramosia
2⁸ᵍᶠ 3⁸ᵍᶠ 5⁸ᶠ 4¹⁰ᵍ 11¹⁰ᵍ 1⁸ˢᵈ 2⁸ˢᵈ 4⁸ˢᵈ
1-3-8 £6,205

Anani (USA) *E A L Dunlop* 108 a111
4 ch c Miswaki (USA) - Mystery Rays (USA)

7⁹ᶠᵗ 3¹⁰ᵍᶠ 4¹⁰ᶠᵗ 2¹⁰ˢᵈ 13¹²ᵍ 6¹⁰ᵍᶠ 7¹⁰ᶠ
4¹⁰ᵍ 15⁸ˢ **0-2-9 £32,857**

Anatolian Queen (USA) *J M P Eustace* 77
3 b f Woodman (USA) - Imia (USA)
3⁸ʰʸ 4⁸ᵍˢ 1⁷ᵍ **1-1-3 £6,823**

Anatom *P S McEntee* 26 a28
3 ch f Komaite (USA) - Zamarra
7⁵ˢʷ 5⁶ˢᵈ 4⁶ʰʸ 9⁶ˢᵈ **0-0-4**

Anchor Date *B W Hills* 75
2 b c Zafonic (USA) - Fame At Last (USA)
2⁶ˢ 7⁶ˢ **0-1-2 £1,798**

Ancient Egypt *J H M Gosden* 51
2 b c Singspiel (Ire) - Nekhbet
10⁸ᵍˢ **0-0-1**

Ancient World (USA) *Saeed Bin Suroor* 120
4 b/br g Spinning World (USA) - Headline
2⁸ˢ 2⁸ᵍᶠ 1⁸ᵍᶠ 8⁸ᵍˢ 1¹⁰ᵍˢ 1⁸ᵍ **3-1-6
£226,749**

And Toto Too *P D Evans* 88 a77
4 br f Averti (Ire) - Divina Mia
11⁸ˢᵈ 6⁷ˢᵈ 2⁶ˢᵈ 4⁷ˢᵈ 4⁷ˢᵈ 2⁷ᵍ 4⁷ᵍᶠ 8⁸ᵍᶠ
2⁷ᵍᶠ 10⁸ᵍᶠ 4⁷ᶠ 4⁷ᵍ 2⁷ᵍ 1⁷ᵍᶠ 4⁷ᵍᶠ 7⁸ᵍᶠ 6⁶ᵍ
9⁸ˢᵈ 8⁹ˢᵈ **1-6-19 £15,566**

Andaad *D J Daly* a53
4 b f Alzao (USA) - Ghazwat (USA)
5¹⁰ˢᵈ 4¹²ˢˢ 7¹⁰ˢᵈ **0-0-3 £254**

Andaluza (Ire) *P D Cundell* 76 a67
3 b f Mujadil (USA) - Hierarchy
4⁶ˢᵈ 1⁷ˢᵈ 3⁷ᵍ 8⁷ᵍᶠ **1-1-4 £4,152**

Andean *D R Loder* 101
3 b c Singspiel (Ire) - Anna Matrushka
1⁸ᵍᶠ 5¹⁰ᵍˢ **1-0-2 £7,076**

Andreyev (Ire) *J S Goldie* 35
10 ch g Presidium - Missish
6⁶ᵍ 11⁶ᵍˢ 10⁶ˢ 14⁷ᵍᶠ 5⁸ᵍ 11⁸ˢ **0-0-6**

Andronikos *P F I Cole* 104
2 ch c Dr Fong (USA) - Arctic Air
15⁶ᶠ 2⁶ˢ 7⁶ᵍˢ 1⁶ˢ **2-1-4 £50,894**

Anduril *J M P Eustace* 70 a64
3 ch c Kris - Attribute
6⁸ˢᵈ 7⁷ᵍˢ 3⁸ᵍᶠ 6⁸ˢ 4¹⁰ᵍᶠ 10¹⁰ᵍᶠ 8¹⁰ᵍᶠ 4⁸ʰʸ
8¹⁰ᵍ 17¹²ʰʸ **0-0-10 £1,573**

Andy Mal *R A Fahey* 47
2 b f Mark Of Esteem (Ire) - Sunflower Seed
8⁷ᵍˢ 6⁷ᵍˢ 8⁷ᶠ **0-0-3**

Anfield Dream *J R Jenkins* 71
2 b c Lujain (USA) - Fifth Emerald
6⁵ᵍ 3⁵ᵍᶠ 12⁵ᵍᶠ **0-1-3 £582**

Angel Isa (Ire) *R A Fahey* 46
4 b f Fayruz - Isa
14⁶ᶠ 11⁶ᶠ 12⁷ᶠ 7⁷ᵍᶠ 3⁶ᶠ 3⁶ᵍᶠ 9⁶ᵍˢ **0-2-7
£673**

Angel Maid *G B Balding*
3 b f Forzando - Esilam
9⁵ᵍᶠ **0-0-1**

Angel Rays *G A Butler* a66
2 ch f Unfuwain (USA) - Success Story
4⁷ˢᵈ 5⁷ˢᵈ **0-0-2 £327**

Angel River *M J Ryan* 46
2 ch f Bold Edge - Riviere Rouge
14⁷ˢ 10⁶ˢ **0-0-2**

Angel Sprints *L G Cottrell* 85
2 b f Piccolo - Runs In The Family
3⁵ᵍ 3⁵ᶠ 6⁵ᵍ 1⁶ᵍᶠ 1⁶ᵍˢ 4⁶ᵍˢ **2-2-6
£12,522**

Angela's Girl *J M Bradley* 23
2 gr f Baryshnikov (Aus) - Filly Bergere (Ire)
7⁵ᶠ 9⁵ᵍᶠ 10⁶ᵍ **0-0-3**

Angelica Garnett *T E Powell* a53
4 ch f Desert Story (Ire) - Vanessa Bell (Ire)
10⁷ˢᵈ 6⁸ˢᵈ 10⁸ˢᵈ 10⁸ˢᵈ 1¹²ˢᵈ 10¹²ᵍˢ
17¹²ˢ **1-0-7 £1,662**

Angelo's Pride *J A Osborne* a59
3 ch c Young Ern - Considerable Charm
3⁹ˢᵈ 7⁷ˢᵈ 2⁹ˢˢ 3⁸ˢˢ 3⁸ˢˢ 3⁷ˢˢ 1⁹ˢᵈ 5¹²ˢᵈ
1-4-8 £4,108

Angelofthenorth *J D Bethell* 65
2 b f Tomba - Dark Kristal (Ire)
3⁵ᵍˢ 4⁵ᶠ 3⁵ᵍᶠ 3⁶ᵍᶠ 3⁶ˢ 10⁵ᵍ 1⁵ᵍᶠ 22⁶ˢ
1-2-8 £7,422

Angels Venture *J R Jenkins* a20
8 ch g Unfuwain (USA) - City Of Angels
11¹³ˢᵈ **0-0-1**

Angiolini (USA) *A E Jones*
7 ch g Woodman (USA) - Danse Royale (Ire)
11¹²ˢʷ **0-0-1**

Anglo Saxon (USA) *D R Loder* 84
4 b c Seeking The Gold (USA) - Anna Palariva (Ire)
11⁸ᵍˢ 9¹⁰ᵍ 3¹⁰ᵍ 6¹⁰ᵍ **0-1-4 £838**

Angry Bark (USA) *H S Howe* 62 a42
3 ch f Woodman (USA) - Polemic (USA)
4¹¹ᵛˢ 2⁹ˢ 4¹⁰ᵍ 7⁸ˢᵈ 8¹⁰ˢ **0-0-5 £2,526**

Anicaflash *M Dods* 19
3 b f Cayman Kai (Ire) - Sharp Top
14⁷ᵍˢ 8⁸ᵍ **0-0-2**

Anisette *Julian Poulton* 45 a43
3 b f Abou Zouz (USA) - Natural Gold (USA)
3⁶ˢᵈ 7⁷ˢᵈ 6⁶ˢᵈ 16⁶ᵍᶠ 6⁸ˢᵈ 4¹¹ᶠ 9¹⁰ᵍ 8⁸ˢᵈ
6¹⁰ᵍᶠ 3⁸ᵍᶠ 6⁸ᵍˢ 5¹⁰ᵍᶠ 3¹⁰ᵍ 7¹⁰ᵍ **0-2-14 £798**

Anissati *C E Brittain*
2 ch f Machiavellian (USA) - Inchacooley (Ire)
10⁸ˢ **0-0-1**

Anna Gayle *R Rowe* 36 a24
3 ch f Dr Fong (USA) - Urban Dancer (Ire)
12¹⁰ᵍᶠ 14⁸ᵍᶠ 5¹²ᵍᶠ 11¹⁰ᵍᶠ 9¹⁰ˢᵈ **0-0-5**

Anna Pallida *P W Harris* 91
3 b f Sadler's Wells (USA) - Masskana (Ire)
18⁸ᵍ 2¹⁰ᵍ 2¹⁰ᵍᶠ 3¹²ᵍˢ 1¹⁰ᵍᶠ 2¹⁰ᵍ 8¹⁰ˢ 3⁸ᶠ
6⁹ᵍ **1-4-9 £15,628**

Anna Panna *H Candy* 73
3 b f Piccolo - Miss Laetitia (Ire)
6⁷ᵍ 2⁶ᵍᶠ 5⁶ᵍᶠ 5⁸ᵍᶠ 2⁸ˢ 8⁸ᵍˢ **0-2-6
£3,062**

Anna Walhaan (Ire) *Ian Williams* 78
5 b g Green Desert (USA) - Queens Music (USA)
14⁸ˢ 7⁸ᵍᶠ 2⁸ᵍˢ 5¹⁰ᵍᶠ 12⁸ᵍˢ **0-1-5
£1,724**

Annakita *W J Musson* 49 a27
4 b f Unfuwain (USA) - Cuban Reef
9¹²ᵍˢ 7¹⁶ˢᵈ 10¹⁴ᵍᶠ 4¹⁴ᶠ 1¹⁶ᵍᶠ 2¹⁴ˢ 3¹⁴ᵍˢ
1-2-7 £4,929

Annals *H Candy* 80
2 b f Lujain (USA) - Anna Of Brunswick
1⁶ˢ 4⁷ᵍ **1-0-2 £5,897**

Annambo *D R Loder* 77
4 ch g In The Wings - Anna Matrushka
11¹²ᵍ 8¹²ᶠ **0-0-2**

Annatalia *B J Meehan* 85 a69
2 ch f Pivotal - See You Later
4⁵ᵍᶠ 6⁶ᵍ 1⁵ᶠ 2¹⁵ᵍ 8⁵ᵍᶠ 8⁵ᵍᶠ 8⁵ˢᵈ **1-0-7**

£5,730

Annibale Caro *Sir Mark Prescott* a65
2 b c Mtoto - Isabella Gonzaga
11⁶ˢᵈ 5⁷ˢᵈ 8⁷ˢᵈ **0-0-3**

Annie Harvey *B Smart* 63 a75
3 ch f Fleetwood (Ire) - Resemblance
20⁶ᵍ 8⁷ˢ 2⁸ˢᵈ 5⁸ᵍˢ **0-1-4 £1,054**

Annie Miller (Ire) *M J Wallace* 56
3 b f Night Shift (USA) - Lost Dream
9⁶ᵍ 7⁷ᵍᶠ **0-0-2**

Annijaz *J M Bradley* 61
7 b m Alhijaz - Figment
2⁶ˢ 2⁷ˢ 4⁷ᶠ 14⁷ᵍ 4⁷ᵍᶠ 6⁷ᵍ 7⁷ᶠ 7⁷ᵍ
14⁷ᵍᶠ 8⁸ᵍᶠ 14⁸ᵍᶠ 16⁷ᵍˢ **0-3-13 £4,208**

Annishirani *G A Butler* a77
4 b f Shaamit (Ire) - Silent Miracle (Ire)
12⁸ˢᵈ 6⁷ˢᵈ **0-0-2**

Anniversary Guest (Ire) *Mrs Lucinda Featherstone*
44 a42
5 b/br m Desert King (Ire) - Polynesian Goddess (Ire)
8¹⁶ˢᵈ 3¹²ˢᵈ 4¹⁵ᵍ 3¹⁶ˢᵈ 7¹³ˢᵈ 9¹³ᵍᶠ 5¹⁴ᵍᶠ
7¹²ᵍᶠ **0-2-8 £420**

Another Bottle (Ire) *T P Tate* 92
3 b g Cape Cross (Ire) - Aster Aweke (Ire)
8⁷ᵍ 1⁹ᵍᶠ 1⁸ᵍᶠ 3⁸ᵍ 1⁸ᵍˢ **3-0-5 £22,830**

Another Choice (Ire) *N P Littmoden* 89
3 ch c Be My Guest (USA) - Gipsy Rose Lee (Ire)
3⁸ᵍ 1¹⁰ᵍˢ 1¹⁰ᵍ 10¹¹ᵍ 10¹²ᵍˢ 11¹⁰ᵍ 4¹⁰ᵍˢ
1¹⁰ˢ 6¹⁰ᵍ 2¹⁰ˢ 2¹⁰ˢ 7¹²ˢ **3-3-12 £18,376**

Another Con (Ire) *P Howling* 46 a69
3 b f Lake Coniston (Ire) - Sweet Unison (USA)
4¹⁰ˢᵈ 1¹⁰ˢᵈ 4¹⁰ˢᵈ 5¹²ˢᵈ 1¹¹¹ᵍˢ 12¹⁰ᵍ 2¹²ˢᵈ
8¹²ᵍᶠ 5¹²ˢᵈ 8¹⁰ˢᵈ 12¹⁰ᵍᶠ 8¹⁶ˢᵈ 1¹²ˢᵈ **2-1-13
£7,375**

Another Deal (Fr) *R J Hodges* 46
5 ch g Barathea (Ire) - Mill Rainbow (Fr)
9⁷ᵍᶠ 9⁸ᵍˢ 11¹⁰ˢ **0-0-3**

Another Expletive *J White* a22
3 b f Wizard King - French Project (Ire)
8⁷ˢᵈ 6⁸ˢᵈ **0-0-2**

Another Faux Pas (Ire) *R Hannon* 79
3 b f Slip Anchor - Pirie (USA)
1⁷ᵍᶠ 11⁸ᵍˢ **1-0-2 £5,512**

Another Glimpse *Miss B Sanders* 78 a90
6 b g Rudimentary (USA) - Running Glimpse (Ire)
4⁵ˢᵈ 1⁶ˢᵈ 9⁵ˢ 2⁶ˢ 3⁵ˢ 2⁶ˢᵈ 9⁶ᵍᶠ 8⁷ˢᵈ
4⁶ˢᵈ 3⁵ˢᵈ **1-4-11 £9,545**

Another Plan (Ire) *M G Quinlan* 41 a32
2 b g Entrepreneur - Tammany Hall (Ire)
14⁸ᵍ 12⁸ˢᵈ **0-0-2**

Another Secret *G L Moore* a53
6 b m Efisio - Secrets Of Honour
3¹⁰ˢᵈ 5¹⁰ˢᵈ 4¹⁰ˢᵈ **0-1-3 £429**

Another Victim *M R Bosley* 38
10 ch g Beveled (USA) - Ragtime Rose
6⁵ᵍ 15⁵ᵍˢ **0-0-2**

Anousa (Ire) *P Howling* 103
3 b c Intikhab (USA) - Annaletta
12⁹ᵍˢ 1⁹ʰʸ 11¹²ᵍˢ 8¹⁰ᵍˢ 7¹²ᵍᶠ 3¹²ᵍ 1¹⁵ᵍᶠ
7¹²ˢ 4¹⁴ᵍᶠ 17¹⁵ˢ 7¹⁴ᵍ **2-1-11 £26,096**

Ansells Legacy (Ire) *A Berry* 51
2 b g Charnwood Forest (USA) - Hanzala (Fr)
8⁷ᵍᶠ 12⁷ˢ 9⁵ᵍᶠ **0-0-4**

Answer Do *M J Polglase* 10
4 b f Groom Dancer (USA) - Be My Lass (Ire)

6^f 0-0-1

Answered Promise (Fr) *I A Wood*   61 a52
5 ro g Highest Honor (Fr) - Answered Prayer
9^{8sd} 7^{9sd} 6^{10sd} 2^{10sd} 3^{8f} 3^{8f} 8^{8g} 0-2-7
£2,592

Antediluvian *Sir Michael Stoute*   104
3 b f Air Express (Ire) - Divina Mia
1^{8g} 1^{8gs} 2-0-2 £28,072

Anthemion (Ire) *Mrs J C McGregor*   71
7 ch g Night Shift (USA) - New Sensitive
10^{7gf} 2^{8g} 11^{8gs} 9^{8g} 10^{9gs} 5^{8g} 3^{8gf}
1^{9gf} 3^{8gf} 2^{9gf} 15^{9gs} 9^{8gf} 7^{7s} 8^{8gf} 14^{8gf}
1-3-16 £8,935

Anthos (Ger) *J R Fanshawe*   79
3 b f Big Shuffle (USA) - Anemoni (Ger)
5^{6gf} 8^{6g} 0-0-2 £357

Anticipating *A M Balding*   95 a84
4 b g Polish Precedent (USA) - D'Azy
9^{13sd} 4^{12g} 7^{12f} 2^{12gf} 14^{14g} 7^{12s} 8^{12g}
12^{11g} 0-1-8 £4,120

Antigiotto (Ire) *L M Cumani*   74 a41
3 ch g Desert Story (Ire) - Rofool (Ire)
8^{8sd} 11^{7g} 11^{10s} 4^{10gf} 2^{10g} 2^{10gf} 8^{12f}
10^{10g} 3^{9s} 0-3-9 £3,989

Antigua Bay (Ire) *J A R Toller*   74 a46
3 b f Turtle Island (Ire) - Vilanika (Fr)
11^{7g} 8^{8gf} 2^{6gf} 6^{7sw} 3^{6g} 4^{7g} 7^{8sd} 0-1-7
£1,947

Antley Court (Ire) *A Berry*
2 ch g Tagula (Ire) - Changed Around (Ire)
13^{5f} 0-0-1

Antoinette (USA) *Sir Michael Stoute*   75
2 b f Silver Hawk (USA) - Excellentadventure (USA)
6^{7gs} 0-0-1

Antonio Canova *Bob Jones*   86
8 ch g Komaite (USA) - Joan's Venture
9^{6gs} 10^{6s} 1^{6gs} 11^{6g} 7^{6gf} 5^{7gf} 15^{6gs}
11^{6gs} 1-0-8 £3,701

Antonio Stradivari (Ire) *A M Balding*   64 a66
2 b/br c Stravinsky (USA) - Dearest (USA)
7^{6gf} 7^{7sd} 5^{6g} 0-0-3

Antonius Pius (USA) *A P O'Brien*   121
3 b c Danzig (USA) - Catchascatchcan
4^{8gs} 5^{8gf} 3^{8gf} 7^{6gs} 5^{8g} 3^{8gs} 9^{8gf} 2^{8y}
0-3-8 £258,078

Antony Ebeneezer *C R Dore*   33 a47
5 ch h Hurricane Sky (Aus) - Captivating (Ire)
5^{11sd} 3^{12sd} 9^{14sd} 10^{13sd} 1^{12sd} 5^{12sd} 11^{13sd}
12^{10gf} 2^{12sd} 6^{10f} 1-2-10 £4,247

Anuvasteel *N A Callaghan*   79
3 gr g Vettori (Ire) - Mrs Gray
6^{9s} 8^{8g} 9^{7gf} 6^{7g} 12^{7g} 0-0-5

Any News *Miss M E Rowland*
7 ch g Karinga Bay - D'Egliere (Fr)
13^{9sd} 0-0-1

Anyhow (Ire) *Miss K M George*   73 a71
7 b m Distant Relative - Fast Chick
9^{10sd} 11^{12sd} 2^{12sd} 11^{12sd} 4^{10sd} 5^{12sd} 4^{12g}
2^{10sd} 11^{13gf} 5^{12gf} 3^{12f} 11^{13gf} 8^{12sd} 5^{12gf}
5^{12gf} 8^{17g} 13^{12sd} 2^{12sd} 3-5-19 £18,585

Aoninch *Mrs P N Dutfield*   70 a63
4 ch f Inchinor - Willowbank
6^{12sd} 11^{14s} 5^{12gs} 8^{13gf} 6^{10gf} 8^{12gf} 2^{12gs}
6^{12gf} 2^{12gf} 6^{12s} 10^{13gs} 5^{14gs} 9^{12sd} 0-2-13
£3,356

Apache Point (Ire) *N Tinkler*   60
7 ch g Indian Ridge - Ausherra (USA)
10^{8hy} 8^{8s} 5^{10g} 4^{9f} 5^{8g} 5^{8g} 2^{9g} 3^{10gf} 5^{8g}
5^{9gs} 5^{9hy} 5^{7g} 9^{8gf} 5^{8gf} 5^{9gs} 0-2-15 £2,127

Aperitif *W J Haggas*   96
3 ch g Pivotal - Art Deco Lady
7^{8gs} 4^{8gf} 3^{8gs} 3^{7gf} 1^{8hy} 7^{8g} 3^{10s} 1^{8s}
10^{8s} 4^{8s} 2-3-10 £17,794

Apetite *N Bycroft*   64
2 ch g Timeless Times (USA) - Petite Elite
10^{5gf} 9^{6gf} 10^{5gs} 2^{7gs} 1^{6gs} 10^{7gf} 10^{8s}
11^{6gf} 14^{9g} 1-1-9 £4,199

Apex *E A L Dunlop*   93
3 ch g Efisio - Royal Loft
1^{7s} 5^{8gf} 12^{8gf} 3^{8gs} 2^{7gf} 1^{6gs} 11^{6gs}
10^{7gf} 13^{7s} 2-2-9 £16,388

Apollo Gee (Ire) *B J Meehan*   a18
3 b g Spectrum (Ire) - Suspiria (Ire)
13^{8sd} 8^{7sd} 0-0-2

Apologies *B A McMahon*   77 a74
2 b c Robellino (USA) - Mistook (USA)
7^{5g} 1^{5s} 4^{5gs} 13^{7gs} 6^{5s} 10^{5g} 3^{5gs} 6^{5gf}
3^{6gs} 3^{6sd} 1-3-10 £7,230

Appalachian Trail (Ire) *I Semple*   96
3 b g Indian Ridge - Karinski (USA)
3^{8g} 1^{8g} 2^{8gs} 14^{8gs} 4^{8gf} 1^{8gf} 6^{7gs} 6^{8g}
5^{7gf} 5^{8g} 2-3-10 £27,004

Appetina *J G Given*   62
3 b f Perugino (USA) - Tina Heights
5^{9gf} 5^{10gf} 4^{10gs} 14^{12s} 10^{8s} 14^{6g}
0-0-7 £425

Apple Of My Eye *J R Jenkins*   72
2 b f Fraam - Fresh Fruit Daily
10^{5g} 4^{6gf} 1^{6gf} 10^{6gs} 18^{7g} 1-0-5
£5,852

Appolonious *D R C Elsworth*   55 a48
3 b g Case Law - Supreme Thought
7^{8sd} 7^{8sd} 7^{6g} 9^{7gf} 6^{6gf} 11^{6s} 0-0-6

April Ace *R J Baker*   a4
8 ch g First Trump - Champ D'Avril
7^{12sd} 0-0-1

April Shannon *J E Long*   9
2 b f Tipsy Creek (USA) - Westering
16^{6gf} 11^{7gs} 0-0-2

Apron (Ire) *M J Ryan*   58
3 b f Grand Lodge (USA) - Sultana
9^{10g} 9^{10g} 11^{8f} 12^{10hy} 7^{11s} 0-0-5

Apsara *H R A Cecil*   85
3 br f Groom Dancer (USA) - Ayodhya (Ire)
2^{10g} 1^{10gf} 4^{10gf} 1-1-3 £8,104

Aqribaa (Ire) *A J Lockwood*   43
6 b g Pennekamp (USA) - Karayb (Ire)
13^{8gf} 15^{10gf} 0-0-2

Aqua Pura (Ger) *B J Curley*
5 b g Acatenango (Ger) - Actraphane
8^{16sd} 0-0-1

Aqualung *B W Hills*   90
3 b c Desert King (Ire) - Aquarelle
12^{10g} 1^{9g} 8^{10gf} 15^{8f} 1-0-4 £4,804

Arabian Ana (Ire) *B Smart*   74
2 b c Night Shift (USA) - Al Shaqrah (USA)
6^{6gf} 1^{7g} 4^{7s} 4^{8s} 1-0-4 £4,454

Arabian Dancer *M R Channon*   86
2 b f Dansili - Hymne (Fr)
2^{6f} 6^{6f} 5^{6gf} 3^{8gf} 5^{6gs} 1^{5f} 2^{7g} 4^{6s} 1-3-8

£74,105

Arabian Knight (Ire) *R J Hodges*   65 a36
4 ch g Fayruz - Cheerful Knight (Ire)
12^{6sd} 8^{5ss} 7^{6g} 9^{6gs} 8^{6s} 13^{6gf} 20^{7gf}
0-0-7

Arabian Moon (Ire) *R Brotherton*   73 a62
8 ch g Barathea (Ire) - Excellent Alibi (USA)
1^{12gf} 8^{12gs} 7^{16g} 9^{12sd} **1-0-4 £2,884**

Arabie *Ian Williams*   63 a21
6 b g Polish Precedent (USA) - Always Friendly
11^{12gf} 12^{10ft} 12^{10gf} 17^{10gs} 4^{7g} 11^{8sd}
0-0-6 £312

Aragon Dancer *T M Jones*
3 b g Aragon - Jambo
8^{6sd} **0-0-1**

Aragon's Boy *T D Easterby*   74
4 ch g Aragon - Fancier Bit
17^{10g} 11^{7g} 1^{8f} 7^{8g} 4^{8gf} 11^{8f} 7^{7gf} 13^{8gf}
1-0-8 £3,152

Arakan (USA) *Sir Michael Stoute*   115
4 br c Nureyev (USA) - Far Across
1^{6g} 3^{6gs} 2^{6gf} 12^{8gf} 1^{7gf} **2-2-5 £68,104**

Aramat *J R Boyle*   a27
2 b f Cigar - Winze Kible
14^{5gs} 14^{7sd} 10^{7sd} **0-0-3**

Arawan (Ire) *M W Easterby*   54 a8
4 b g Entrepreneur - Asmara (USA)
10^{11s} 20^{10gs} 19^{10g} 14^{9f} 8^{10gf} 10^{8gf}
10^{8gf} 7^{9gs} 13^{11sd} **0-0-9**

Arbella *P W Harris*   95
2 ch f Primo Dominie - Kristal Bridge
2^{7gf} 4^{7gf} 4^{7gf} 3^{7gf} **0-2-4 £4,796**

Arbors Little Girl *B R Millman*   66
2 b f Paris House - Arbor Ealis (Ire)
1^{5gf} 1^{6g} 5^{6gs} 3^{6gf} **2-1-4 £6,588**

Arc El Ciel (Arg) *Mrs Stef Liddiard*   a87
6 b g Fitzcarraldo (Arg) - Ardoise (USA)
1^{7sd} 3^{8sd} 5^{8ss} 9^{8sd} 7^{8ss} 3^{8sw} 11^{8sd} 6^{7ss}
1-1-8 £5,022

Arc En Ciel *G L Moore*   a53
6 b g Rainbow Quest (USA) - Nadia Nerina (Can)
4^{16sd} 8^{13sd} **0-0-2**

Arc Of Light (Ire) *B W Hills*   63
2 b c Spectrum (Ire) - Siwaayib
5^{6gf} 7^{6gs} 11^{7gf} **0-0-3**

Arcalis *J Howard Johnson*   110
4 gr g Lear Fan (USA) - Aristocratique
1^{10gf} 1^{10g} **2-0-2 £99,607**

Arch Folly *J G Portman*   61
2 b g Silver Patriarch (Ire) - Folly Fox
7^{8gf} 8^{8g} 7^{8gs} **0-0-3**

Archduke Ferdinand (Fr) *P F I Cole*   93
6 ch g Dernier Empereur (USA) - Lady Norcliffe (USA)
13^{19gs} 2^{14gf} 14^{16g} **0-1-3 £4,875**

Archenko *A Berry*   41
4 b g Weldnaas (USA) - Silverdale Rose
8^{12gf} 7^{11g} 6^{12g} 5^{10gf} **0-0-4**

Archeology (USA) *Saeed Bin Suroor*   72 a72
2 b/br f Seeking The Gold (USA) - Caress (USA)
5^{6g} 9^{6g} 2^{7sd} **0-1-3 £1,620**

Archerfield (Ire) *J W Hills*   64 a72
3 ch f Docksider (USA) - Willow River (Can)
2^{8sd} 2^{8sd} 3^{8sd} 11^{8g} 17^{7g} 2^{8f} 3^{9gf} 3^{9g}
4^{9gf} 4^{8g} 9^{8f} **0-6-11 £5,549**

Archias (Ger) *J J Quinn*   65

5 b g Darshaan - Arionette
7^{16g} **0-0-1**

Archie Babe (Ire) *J J Quinn*   75
8 ch g Archway (Ire) - Frensham Manor
10^{12g} 1^{12hy} 5^{12gs} 13^{10g} 11^{12g} 15^{12hy} 7^{12g}
9^{14s} **1-0-8 £5,128**

Archie Clarke (Ger) *J Gallagher*
4 b g Taishan (Ger) - Antheia (Ger)
13^{9sd} **0-0-1**

Archie Glenn *M S Saunders*   77
2 b c Lake Coniston (Ire) - La Ballerine
7^{5gf} 15^{6gf} 4^{6gf} 2^{6hy} 8^{6g} **0-1-5 £1,525**

Archie Wright *R Hannon*   48
2 ch c Lake Coniston (Ire) - Roisin Clover
17^{7s} 7^{7gs} 4^{9g} 7^{6g} **0-0-4 £418**

Archirondel *M D Hammond*   63 a59
6 b g Bin Ajwaad (Ire) - Penang Rose (NZ)
6^{10sd} 10^{10sd} UR^{12g} 14^{12hy} 8^{10gs} 2^{8s} 1^{9f}
10^{8gf} 12^{12g} 5^{11gf} 5^{12gf} **2-2-12 £8,308**

Arctic Blue *M J Gingell*   35 a31
4 b g Polar Prince (Ire) - Miss Sarajane
9^{11f} 10^{16sd} **0-0-2**

Arctic Burst (USA) *D Shaw*   53 a37
4 b/br g Royal Academy (USA) - Polar Bird
12^{5gs} 15^{6s} 30^{6g} 12^{6sd} 18^{5gf} 11^{7gf}
14^{5gf} 12^{5gf} 12^{5gs} **0-0-9**

Arctic Cove *J Nicol*
3 b g Vettori (Ire) - Sundae Girl (USA)
17^{8gs} **0-0-1**

Arctic Desert *A M Balding*   85 a86
4 b g Desert Prince (Ire) - Thamud (Ire)
13^{7sd} 18^{7ss} 3^{6f} 14^{6gf} 18^{7g} 11^{7gf} 6^{7sd}
1^{7g} 6^{8gs} 2^{7gf} 9^{7g} 9^{7g} 2^{7gs} **1-2-13 £8,869**

Arctic Silk *Saeed Bin Suroor*   81
3 ch f Selkirk (USA) - Cape Verdi (Ire)
10^{10g} 3^{8g} 2^{8gf} 9^{8gs} **0-2-4 £2,540**

Ardasnails (Ire) *P Burgoyne*   27
2 b g Spectrum (Ire) - Fey Lady (Ire)
12^{7gf} 12^{7gf} **0-0-2**

Ardere (USA) *H R A Cecil*   39
3 ch f El Prado (Ire) - Flaming Torch
7^{10g} **0-0-1**

Ardkeel Lass (Ire) *D Haydn Jones*   62
3 ch f Fumo Di Londra (Ire) - Wot-A-Noise (Ire)
9^{5g} 14^{5gf} 2^{5gf} 4^{5g} 5^{5hy} 12^{6f} 6^{5gf} **0-1-7**
£1,093

Are You There *P S McEntee*   a42
3 b f Presidium - Scoffera
9^{7sd} 6^{6sd} 4^{7sd} 9^{8sd} **0-0-4**

Arfinnit (Ire) *M R Channon*   66
3 b g College Chapel - Tidal Reach (USA)
19^{7g} 3^{6gs} 12^{7s} 16^{7gf} 6^{7gf} 6^{6g}
1^{6g} 6^{6gf} 4^{5g} 8^{5g} 8^{6gf} 7^{6g} 2^{6gf} 4^{5hy} 6^{5s}
16^{6gs} 4^{5s} **2-2-19 £8,734**

Argent *Miss L A Perratt*   50
3 b g Barathea (Ire) - Red Tiara (USA)
PU^{12ss} 8^{12g} 2^{10hy} 7^{8gf} 15^{8g} 8^{8gf} 2^{9gf}
3^{9gs} **0-2-8 £3,428**

Argentum *Lady Herries*   62
3 b g Sillery - Frustration
10^{8gs} 5^{7gs} 1^{10gs} 2^{12gf} 8^{14gs} **1-1-5**
£5,290

Argonaut *Sir Michael Stoute*   96
4 b g Rainbow Quest (USA) - Chief Bee
6^{10s} 3^{12gf} 7^{12gf} 4^{15s} **0-2-4 £3,033**

Arian *C G Cox* 70
2 b f Josr Algarhoud (Ire) - Hope Chest
5⁷ᵍ **0-0-1**

Arian's Lad *B Palling* 52 a21
3 b g Prince Sabo - Arian Da
8⁵ᵍᶠ 12⁵ᵍᶠ 7⁷ˢᵈ 3⁷ᵍˢ **0-1-4 £536**

Ariane Star (Ire) *M A Jarvis* 53
2 b f Marju (Ire) - Northgate Raver
9⁶ᵍᶠ 11⁶ᵍ 5⁵ᵍᶠ 11⁷ᵍᶠ **0-0-4**

Aricia (Ire) *J H M Gosden* 94 a85
3 b f Nashwan (USA) - Rahaam (USA)
8⁷ᵍ 17ᵍᶠ 10⁸ᶠ 11⁸ᵍˢ 6⁸ˢᵈ **1-0-5 £6,027**

Aries (Ger) *M J Wallace* 57 a43
4 ch f Big Shuffle (USA) - Auenlust (Ger)
9⁸ᶠ 14¹⁰ˢᵈ **0-0-2**

Ariesanne (Ire) *R A Fahey* 33
3 ch f Primo Dominie - Living Legend (Ity)
3⁵ˢ 7⁵ᵍˢ 6⁶ᶠ **0-0-3 £729**

Ariodante *J M P Eustace* 77
2 b g Groom Dancer (USA) - Maestrale
3⁶ᵍᶠ 16ᵍᶠ 4⁷ᵍᶠ 12⁷ˢ **1-1-4 £4,654**

Arjay *S B Clark* 52 a48
6 b g Shaamit (Ire) - Jenny's Call
12¹⁰ˢᵈ 15⁸ᵍˢ 3⁹ˢᵈ 5⁹ˢᵈ 3⁹ᶠ 12¹²ˢᵈ 10¹¹ˢ
0-2-7 £970

Ark Admiral *C L Tizzard* 60
5 b g Inchinor - Kelimutu
12⁹ᵍᶠ 10⁶ᵍ 11⁸ᵍᶠ **0-0-3**

Arkholme *P Winkworth* 88
3 b g Robellino (USA) - Free Spirit (Ire)
4¹⁰ˢ 13¹²ᵍ 2⁸ᵍᶠ 1⁸ᵍ 2⁸ᵍᶠ 9¹⁰ᵍᶠ 3⁸ᵍˢ 1⁸ᵍ
4⁸ᵍᶠ 4⁸ᵍ **2-4-10 £23,500**

Armagnac *M A Buckley* 89
6 b g Young Ern - Arianna Aldini
19⁶ᵍ 7⁶ᵍˢ 8⁶ᵍˢ 3⁶ᵍᶠ 6⁶ᵍᶠ 8⁶ᵍᶠ 10⁶ᵍ 2⁷ᵍ
3⁶ᵍ 2⁶ᵍᶠ 3⁷ᵍᶠ 7⁷ᵍ 11⁶ᵍᶠ 1⁷ᵍ 7⁷ᵍ 5⁷ᵍ **1-5-16
£19,273**

Armatore (USA) *E R Oertel* 64
4 b g Gone West (USA) - Awesome Account (USA)
11¹¹ᵍᶠ 13¹⁰ᵍ **0-0-2**

Armentieres *J L Spearing* 59 a21
3 b f Robellino (USA) - Perfect Poppy
6¹⁰ˢᵈ 8¹²ᵍᶠ 7¹⁰ᵍˢ 6¹⁰ᵍˢ 2⁸ʰʸ 3⁷ᵍ 4⁷ᵍᶠ 7⁸ᵍ
1⁷ᵍ 7⁸ʰʸ **1-3-10 £4,282**

Arms Acrossthesea *J Balding* 61 a66
5 b g Namaqualand (USA) - Zolica
2¹²ᵍ 1¹¹ᶠ 1⁹ˢᵈ 4¹⁰ᵍ 10¹³ᶠ 7⁸ˢᵈ 1¹⁰ᵍᶠ 6¹⁰ᵍᶠ
17¹⁰ᵍᶠ 13¹⁰ᵍˢ **3-1-10 £10,001**

Army Of Angels (Ire) *Saeed Bin Suroor* 94
2 ch c King's Best (USA) - Angelic Sounds (Ire)
2⁶ᵍᶠ 1⁶ᵍ 2⁶ᵍ **1-1-3 £10,249**

Arogant Prince *J Pearce* 67 a67
7 ch g Aragon - Versaillesprincess
4⁷ˢᵈ 4⁶ˢᵈ 7⁶ˢᵈ 6⁷ˢˢ 3⁶ˢᵈ 1⁵ˢˢ 10⁶ˢˢ 1⁵ˢʷ
7⁶ˢʷ 8⁵ˢ 7⁵ˢˢ 1⁶ˢ 1¹ˢˢ 17⁵ᵍᶠ 6⁶ᵍᶠ 12⁷ˢᵈ
13⁷ˢᵈ 13⁶ˢᵈ **3-1-18 £9,080**

Arous (Fr) *J L Dunlop* 59
2 br f Desert King (Ire) - Moneefa
7⁶ᵍᶠ **0-0-1**

Arran *V Smith* 59 a70
4 ch g Selkirk (USA) - Humble Pie
9⁷ᶠ 3⁸ᵍᶠ 9⁷ᵍᶠ 2⁸ˢᵈ 1⁸ˢᵈ 9⁷ˢᵈ 5⁸ᵍˢ 13⁷ᵍ
8⁷ᵍ **1-2-9 £4,872**

Arran Scout (Ire) *K A Ryan* 74
3 b g Piccolo - Evie Hone (Ire)

3⁸ᵍ 10⁸ᵍᶠ 11¹⁰ᵍˢ 2⁷ˢ **0-2-4 £2,996**

Arresting *J R Fanshawe* 91
4 b g Hector Protector (USA) - Misbelief
1¹²ᵍˢ 11¹⁴ʰʸ 6¹²ᵍᶠ 5¹⁵ᵍᶠ 10¹²ᵍ **1-0-5
£4,764**

Arrgatt (Ire) *M A Jarvis* 91
3 gr c Intikhab (USA) - Nuit Chaud (USA)
3⁸ᵍᶠ 2¹⁰ᶠ 2¹¹ᵍ 1⁸ᵍᶠ 4¹⁰ᵍᶠ **1-2-5 £10,583**

Arrivato *A M Balding* a65
2 b f Efisio - Beloved Visitor (USA)
9⁷ˢᵈ **0-0-1**

Arrjook *A C Stewart* 69
3 b c Intikhab (USA) - Chief Ornament (USA)
4⁸ᵍᶠ **0-0-1 £425**

Arrow *Mrs L B Normile* a46
5 b g Pivotal - Cremets
9¹⁰ˢᵈ **0-0-1**

Arry Dash *M R Channon* 92 a95
4 b g Fraam - Miletrian Cares (Ire)
4¹⁰ˢᵈ 9⁸ᵍ 2¹¹ˢ 13¹⁰ˢ 7¹⁰ᵍᶠ 3⁸ᵍᶠ 7¹⁰ᵍ 6¹⁰ᵍᶠ
11¹⁰ᵍᶠ 6⁸ᵍᶠ 2⁹ᵍˢ 3⁸ˢ 2¹⁰ᵍˢ 3¹⁰ᵍᶠ 2¹⁰ᵍᶠ 5¹⁰ᵍ 7⁸ᵍᶠ
8¹⁰ᵍ 1¹⁰ˢ **1-6-19 £16,474**

Art Elegant *B W Hills* 71
2 b c Desert Prince (Ire) - Elegant (Ire)
10⁷ᵍᶠ 5⁸ᵍ 7⁸ᵍ **0-0-3**

Art Expert (Fr) *Mrs N Macauley* a24
6 b g Pursuit Of Love - Celtic Wing
7¹²ˢᵈ **0-0-1**

Art Eyes (USA) *D R C Elsworth* 74
2 ch f Halling (USA) - Careyes (Ire)
3⁷ᵍ **0-1-1 £876**

Art Legend *D R C Elsworth* 54
2 b g Indian Ridge - Solo Performance (Ire)
4⁵ᵍˢ 12⁶ᵍ 10⁸ᵍˢ **0-0-3 £403**

Art Royal (USA) *Mrs A J Perrett* 77
2 b c Royal Academy (USA) - Chelsea Green (USA)
5⁷ᵍᶠ 18⁷ᵍ **0-0-2**

Art Trader (USA) *Mrs A J Perrett* 108
3 b c Arch (USA) - Math (USA)
2¹⁰ᵍ 1¹⁰ᵍᶠ **1-1-2 £46,748**

Artadi *P M Phelan* 49 a28
2 b f Bien Bien (USA) - Gibaltarik (Ire)
7⁵ˢ 3⁵ˢ 5⁵ᵍᶠ 6⁷ᵍᶠ 5⁵ˢʷ 46⁹ᶠ 6⁷ᵍᶠ 6⁸ᵍ
0-0-8 £531

Arte Et Labore (Ire) *K A Ryan* a7
4 b f Raphane (USA) - Bouffant
8⁹ˢᵈ **0-0-1**

Arthur Wardle (USA) *M L W Bell* 69
2 b g Stravinsky (USA) - Avanti Sassa (Ger)
2⁶ᵍᶠ 5⁶ᵍ 13⁶ᵍᶠ 6⁶ᵍᶠ 13⁷ᵍᶠ **0-1-5 £1,702**

Arthurs Dream (Ire) *J G M O'Shea* 54
2 b c Desert Prince (Ire) - Blueprint (USA)
13⁶ᵍᶠ 7⁸ˢ **0-0-2**

Artic Fox *T D Easterby* 60
2 b g Robellino (USA) - Lets Be Fair
5⁶ˢ 12⁶ᵍ 13⁶ˢ 9⁸ᵍ 8⁸ᵍᶠ 5⁷ᵍ 5⁷ˢ **0-0-7**

Articulation *H R A Cecil* 88
3 b c Machiavellian (USA) - Stiletta
4¹⁰ᵍᶠ 2¹²ᵍᶠ 1¹¹ᵍ **1-1-3 £8,084**

Artie *T D Easterby* 93
5 b g Whittingham (Ire) - Calamanco
13⁶ᵍ 7⁶ˢ 2⁵ᵍ 1⁵ʰʸ 18⁵ᵍˢ 15⁵ᵍˢ 1⁵ᵍˢ 7⁶ᵍᶠ
16⁵ᵍ 7⁶ˢ 14⁶ᵍ 7⁵ˢ 4⁶ᵍᶠ 5⁵ᵍˢ 5⁶ˢ **2-1-15
£21,125**

Artie's Lad (Ire) *D Nicholls* 59

3 ch g Danehill Dancer (Ire) - Bold Avril (Ire)
5^{6gs} 0-0-1

Artist Rifle (Ire) *J L Dunlop* 21
3 b g Orpen (USA) - Rosy Scintilla (Ire)
12^{8gf} 0-0-1

Artistic Lad *Sir Michael Stoute* 86
4 ch c Peintre Celebre (USA) - Maid For The Hills
5^{10gf} 0-0-1 £500

Artistic Style *B Ellison* 101
4 b c Anabaa (USA) - Fine Detail (Ire)
8^{6hy} 6^{8g} 8^{8g} 7^{8f} 1^{8g} 3^{9gf} 1^{10g} 1^{9hy} 1^{11s}
2^{12hy} 1^{10s} 6^{12s} 5-2-12 £23,426

Artisticimpression (Ire) *E A L Dunlop* a29
3 b c Rainbow Quest (USA) - Entice (Fr)
10^{8sd} 11^{10s} 0-0-2

Artistry *B J Meehan* 63 a69
4 b f Night Shift (USA) - Arriving
1^{7sd} 5^{8gf} 10^{7gs} 10^{7gf} 5^{7g} 2^{7sd} 1-1-6
£4,647

Artists Retreat *B D Leavy*
5 ch m Halling (USA) - Jumairah Sunset
11^{10gf} 10^{10s} 0-0-2

Arturius (Ire) *Sir Michael Stoute* 59
2 b c Anabaa (USA) - Steeple
6^{7s} 0-0-1

Artzola (Ire) *C A Horgan* 43 a43
4 b f Alzao (USA) - Polistatic
9^{8sd} 12^{10sd} 7^{7sd} 7^{10gf} 0-0-4

As Handsome Does *N Tinkler* 66
2 ch g Handsome Ridge - Fast To Light
2^{6g} 13^{6g} 13^{6gs} 7^{7gf} 0-1-4 £916

Asaateel (Ire) *J L Dunlop* 65
2 br c Unfuwain (USA) - Alabaq (USA)
10^{7g} 8^{8gs} 4^{8s} 9^{7gs} 0-0-4 £272

Asadara *N Bycroft* 47
2 ch f Timeless Times (USA) - Julie's Gift
6^{5gf} 0-0-1

Asaleeb *E F Vaughan* 91
3 b f Alhaarth (Ire) - Gharam (USA)
2^{10gf} 1^{11f} 1^{12gf} 15^{12f} 2-1-4 £12,846

Asawer (Ire) *Sir Michael Stoute* 67
2 b f Darshaan - Sassy Bird (USA)
3^{8s} 0-1-1 £673

Asbo *Dr J D Scargill* 64 a63
4 b f Abou Zouz (USA) - Star
5^{6gf} 4^{6gf} 3^{6s} 5^{6gs} 6^{6g} 3^{6sd} 4^{7sd} 0-2-7
£1,699

Ascertain (Ire) *N P Littmoden* a105
3 ch g Intikhab (USA) - Self Assured (Ire)
1^{10sd} 2^{10sd} 1^{8sd} 5^{9ft} 2-1-4 £52,355

Ash Bold (Ire) *B Ellison* 48 a51
7 ch g Persian Bold - Pasadena Lady
4^{8gs} 2^{8s} 9^{9gs} 3^{9sd} 0-2-4 £1,331

Ash Hab (USA) *A B Haynes* 42
6 b g A.P. Indy (USA) - Histoire (Fr)
10^{14gf} 11^{16sd} 14^{16sd} 0-0-3

Ash Laddie (Ire) *J S Wainwright* 43 a28
4 ch g Ashkalani (Ire) - Lady Ellen
20^{7gs} 11^{9f} 12^{8f} 13^{8sd} 16^{8f} 0-0-5

Asharon *C E Brittain* 73
2 b c Efisio - Arriving
7^{8g} 6^{8s} 6^{8g} 13^{8gf} 5^{5s} 17^{7gs} 0-0-6

Ashdown Express (Ire) *C F Wall* 121
5 ch g Ashkalani (Ire) - Indian Express
3^{6g} 12^{6gs} 2^{6gf} 7^{6f} 2^{6gs} 4^{7gs} 9^{6g} 13^{6hy}

11^{6s} 0-3-9 £72,942

Ashes (Ire) *K R Burke* 61
2 b f General Monash (USA) - Wakayi
11^{5g} 5^{6gs} 4^{5gf} 10^{5gf} 5^{6g} 6^{5hy} 0-0-6
£430

Ashkal Way (Ire) *E A L Dunlop* 78
2 ch c Ashkalani (Ire) - Golden Way (Ire)
5^{8gf} 0-0-1

Ashstanza *Mrs L Richards* 39 a64
3 gr g Ashkalani (Ire) - Poetry In Motion (Ire)
4^{8sd} 3^{11sd} 4^{12s} 13^{10gs} 10^{8g} 9^{6f} 14^{7sd}
0-1-7 £730

Ashtaroute (USA) *M C Chapman* 40 a35
4 b f Holy Bull (USA) - Beating The Buzz (USA)
6^{16sd} 9^{12gf} 5^{16gs} 0-0-3

Ashtree Belle *D Haydn Jones* a84
5 b m Up And At 'Em - Paris Babe
2^{7sd} 0-1-1 £1,254

Ashwaaq (USA) *J L Dunlop* 70
3 b f Gone West (USA) - Wasnah (USA)
1^{8g} 15^{7gs} 7^{8gf} 1-0-3 £4,040

Asia Winds (Ire) *B W Hills* 93
3 ch f Machiavellian (USA) - Ascot Cyclone (USA)
5^{10gs} 9^{8gf} 12^{7g} 11^{7g} 0-0-4 £1,375

Asian Heights *G Wragg*
6 b h Hernando (Fr) - Miss Rinjani
7^{12hy} 0-0-1

Asian Tiger (Ire) *R Hannon* 82 a65
2 b c Rossini (USA) - Dry Lightning
2^{5gs} 2^{5g} 5^{5gf} 3^{6g} 5^{7gs} 8^{7sd} 16^{6f} 1-3-7
£8,306

Asiatic *M Johnston* 92
3 ch c Lomitas - Potri Pe (Arg)
2^{12gs} 13^{12gs} 10^{12gf} 4^{12gf} 0-1-4 £3,740

Ask For Rain *B W Hills* 65
2 gr f Green Desert (USA) - Requesting
12^{7g} 3^{6g} 0-1-2 £1,022

Ask For The Moon (Fr) *J-C Rouget* 110
3 b f Dr Fong (USA) - Lune Rouge (Ire)
1^{10g} 1^{11gs} 1^{11g} 1^{10g} 7^{11gs} 4-0-5
£123,788

Ask The Clerk (Ire) *V Smith* 81 a65
3 b g Turtle Island (USA) - Some Fun
12^{7sd} 3^{6sd} 5^{5sd} 11^{5sd} 1^{6gs} 13^{6gs} 2^{6s}
8^{6gs} 3^{6f} 4^{6gf} 6^{7gf} 4^{6g} 3^{7g} 3^{6gf} 7^{6gf} 5^{6gs} 4^{6gf}
2^{7g} 3^{7s} 2-9-23
£18,835

Ask The Driver *D J S Ffrench Davis* 57 a57
3 b g Ashkalani (Ire) - Tithcar
28^{8g} 4^{8s} 3^{10sd} 3^{8g} 7^{10g} 13^{10sd} 5^{8g} 0-3-7
£1,982

Askwith (Ire) *J D Bethell* 66
2 b g Marju (Ire) - Hayward
5^{7g} 3^{7gs} 0-1-3 £562

Aspen Ridge (Ire) *C Tinkler* 58 a53
2 ch f Namid - Longueville Lady (Ire)
9^{5g} 7^{5gf} 7^{6sd} 10^{6gs} 5^{6gs} 0-0-5

Aspired (Ire) *J R Fanshawe* 63
3 b f Mark Of Esteem (Ire) - Dreams
7^{10gf} PU^{10gs} 0-0-2

Assoon *G L Moore* 63
5 b g Ezzoud (Ire) - Handy Dancer
7^{7gf} 3^{18gs} 0-1-2 £643

Assured (Ire) *P W D'Arcy* 42
2 ch f Shinko Forest (Ire) - Errazuriz (Ire)

16^{7gf} 17^{6g} 14^{8gf} 10^{7sd} **0-0-4**

Asteem *R F Johnson Houghton*   53
2 b g Mark Of Esteem (Ire) - Amidst
14^{6gf} 5^{6gs} 8^{6gs} 10^{7gf} 8^{6f} **0-0-5**

Aston Lad *M D Hammond*   63
3 b c Bijou D'Inde - Fishki
4^{10gf} 6^{10gf} 6^{14gf} 2^{9s} 5^{10gs} 8^{14gs} 5^{9s}
10^{10s} **0-1-8 £1,571**

Astrac (Ire) *Mrs A L M King*   56 a47
13 b g Nordico (USA) - Shirleen
5^{5gs} 9^{6sd} 17^{6s} 2^{7gf} 4^{6gf} 9^{7gf} 8^{6gf} 7^{6f}
4^{5f} 9^{6g} **0-1-10 £2,119**

Astral Prince *Mrs K Walton*   45
6 ch g Efisio - Val D'Erica
5^{8hy} 6^{12g} **0-0-2**

Astrocharm (Ire) *M H Tompkins*   102
5 b m Charnwood Forest (Ire) - Charm The Stars
5^{8g} 1^{12gf} 7^{12gf} 5^{10gf} 1^{12g} 2^{12gs} 1^{12gf}
1^{14gf} 7^{15g} 5^{12gf} **4-1-10 £54,979**

Astromancer (USA) *M H Tompkins*   56 a56
4 b/br f Silver Hawk (USA) - Colour Dance
10^{12sd} 4^{16sd} 5^{14g} 8^{16g} 7^{13f} 3^{14gf} 1^{14g}
7^{14f} 3^{16gs} 15^{16g} **1-2-10 £4,563**

Astronomic *J Howard Johnson*   62
4 b g Zafonic (USA) - Sky Love (USA)
13^{12gs} **0-0-1**

Astronomical (Ire) *B W Hills*   75
2 b c Mister Baileys - Charm The Stars
3^{7s} 7^{8g} **0-1-2 £564**

Astyanax (Ire) *Sir Mark Prescott*   87
4 b c Hector Protector (USA) - Craigmill
18^{14g} 5^{16gs} 9^{16gf} 1^{14gf} 8^{16s} 2^{16g} 1^{16gf}
21^{18s} **2-1-8 £13,291**

Aswan (Ire) *S R Bowring*   75
6 ch g Ashkalani (Ire) - Ghariba
5^{10gf} 3^{8gf} 12^{8gf} 9^{7gs} 18^{8gf} 12^{7g} **0-0-6**
£632

At Your Request *Ian Williams*   72
3 gr g Bering - Requesting
3^{10s} 3^{12gs} 3^{12gf} **0-2-3 £1,725**

Atacama Star *B G Powell*   77
2 ch g Desert King (Ire) - Aunty (Fr)
15^{7g} 2^{6gf} 10^{7g} **0-1-3 £1,865**

Atahuelpa *A King*   94 a62
4 b g Hernando (Fr) - Certain Story
9^{10fz} 7^{8s} 10^{8sd} 3^{8gf} 3^{11f} **0-1-5 £1,500**

Atavus *G G Margarson*   98
7 b h Distant Relative - Elysian
12^{8gs} 6^{7gf} 22^{7f} 5^{7gf} 15^{7gs} 18^{7gf} 2^{6gs}
6^{6gf} 11^{7g} **0-1-9 £8,381**

Athboy *M J Wallace*   a71
3 ch c Entrepreneur - Glorious
11^{10sd} 1^{8sd} 1^{7sd} 9^{8sd} 8^{8sd} 13^{8hy} **2-0-6**
£6,810

Athboy Nights (Ire) *M J Wallace*   30
2 b f Night Shift (USA) - Missing Love (Ire)
12^{6g} 14^{6hy} **0-0-2**

Athollbrose (USA) *Mrs C J Kerr*   57
3 b g Mister Baileys - Knightly Cut Up (USA)
4^{10s} 2^{10gs} 4^{13s} 5^{10gf} 4^{8gf} 10^{8g} 12^{8gs}
3^{10f} **0-2-8 £2,983**

Atlantic Ace *B Smart*   71 a70
7 b g First Trump - Risalah
18^{8g} 11^{8g} 7^{8gf} 6^{8gf} 8^{8gf} 9^{8gs} 11^{8g} 12^{8g}
15^{7gf} 8^{8gf} 2^{9sd} 2^{9sd} **0-2-12 £1,764**

Atlantic Breeze *Mrs N Macauley*   42 a44
3 br f Deploy - Atlantic Air
7^{9sd} 7^{11sd} 9^{7ss} 7^{10gs} 7^{10gs} 3^{12sd} 9^{10s}
0-1-7 £411

Atlantic City *Mrs L Richards*   69 a68
3 ch g First Trump - Pleasuring
2^{10gf} 5^{10gf} 11^{12sd} **0-1-3 £1,085**

Atlantic Quest (USA) *K R Burke*   89
5 b g Woodman (USA) - Pleasant Pat (USA)
14^{7g} 5^{7g} 7^{10gs} 12^{7f} 1^{7f} 5^{8f} 16^{8g} BD^{7gf}
10^{8gf} 4^{8gf} **1-1-10 £6,906**

Atlantic Story (USA) *Saeed Bin Suroor*   92
2 b/br c Stormy Atlantic (USA) - Story Book Girl (USA)
8^{7s} 1^{7g} 2^{8s} **1-1-3 £7,836**

Atlantic Tern *N M Babbage*   9 a56
3 b c Atraf - Great Tern
6^{10sd} 11^{10sd} 10^{10g} **0-0-3**

Atlantic Viking (Ire) *D Nicholls*   100
9 b g Danehill (USA) - Hi Bettina
13^{5gf} 10^{5gf} 4^{5gf} 8^{5s} 16^{5gf} 1^{6gf} 4^{6g} 1^{5g}
17^{6g} **2-0-9 £28,545**

Atlantic Waltz *J J Sheehan*
4 b g Singspiel (Ire) - Fascination Waltz
15^{10gs} **0-0-1**

Atriffic Story *Miss Gay Kelleway*   53
2 ch g Atraf - Composition
10^{6gs} **0-0-1**

Atsos (Ire) *R Hannon*   61
2 b g Imperial Ballet (Ire) - Victim Of Love
6^{5hy} 6^{5g} 13^{6gf} 5^{5gf} 6^{6g} 17^{7gf} **0-0-6**

Attacca *J R Weymes*   62
3 b g Piccolo - Jubilee Place (Ire)
6^{8g} 10^{6g} 11^{6gs} 7^{8f} 16^{6gs} 18^{6gf} **0-0-6**
£220

Attack Minded *L R James*   15
3 ch g Timeless Times (USA) - French Ginger
8^{8g} **0-0-1**

Attila The Hun *F Watson*   29 a20
5 b g Piccolo - Katya (Ire)
4^{5sw} 6^{5gf} 11^{5gf} 5^{5gf} **0-0-4**

Attishoe *Miss B Sanders*   48
2 b f Atraf - Royal Shoe
8^{5gs} 11^{6gf} **0-0-2**

Attorney *D Shaw*   60 a61
6 ch g Wolfhound (USA) - Princess Sadie
3^{6sd} 7^{6sd} 1^{6sd} 10^{6sd} 7^{6ss} 4^{6sd} 7^{5ss} 11^{6ss}
6^{5sw} 3^{6sd} 9^{6sd} 7^{6sd} 15^{sd} 1^{6sd} 2^{5gs} 8^{5ss}
3^{6gf} 15^{5sd} **3-4-28 £6,292**

Attraction *M Johnston*   123
3 b f Efisio - Flirtation
1^{8g} 1^{8gf} 1^{8f} 2^{8gf} 10^{8s} 2^{8gf} 1^{8g} **4-2-7**
£680,398

Attune *B J Meehan*   105
3 br f Singspiel (Ire) - Arriving
4^{7g} 10^{8s} 18^{gf} 13^{8gs} 8^{8gf} 1^{7gf} 1^{7g} 1^{7gf}
10^{8g} **4-0-9 £47,576**

Audience *J Akehurst*   106
4 b g Zilzal (USA) - Only Yours
10^{8g} 12^{7gs} 7^{8hy} 7^{7gf} 8^{8gf} 2^{8g} 4^{8g} 6^{8gf}
1^{8s} 3^{8g} 23^{9g} 10^{8gs} **1-3-12 £27,000**

Auditorium *Sir Michael Stoute*   101
3 b c Royal Applause - Degree
4^{7gf} 12^{7gf} 8^{8gf} **0-0-3 £1,500**

Auentraum (Ger) *D Flood*   a24
4 br c Big Shuffle (USA) - Auenglocke (Ger)

3^{6s} 7^{5g} 12^{6sd} **0-0-3 £1,831**

Aunt Doris *Paul Johnson*
7 b m Distant Relative - Nevis
10^{6sd} 11^{8sd} **0-0-2**

Aunt Julia *R Hannon*   72
2 b f In The Wings - Original
3^{7gf} **0-1-1 £810**

Aunty Euro (Ire) *E J O'Neill*   58 a58
2 br f Cape Cross (Ire) - Alexander Goddess (Ire)
4^{5sd} 3^{5s} 3^{6gf} 2^{6sd} 9^{7gf} 6^{7sd} **0-2-6**
£2,676

Aurelia *Sir Mark Prescott*   80
3 b f Rainbow Quest (USA) - Fern
3^{12f} 8^{16gf} **0-0-2 £888**

Auroville *M L W Bell*   67
3 b c Cadeaux Genereux - Silent Tribute (Ire)
8^{7gs} 4^{8s} 7^{8gf} 5^{8gf} 7^{10gf} 7^{10g} 6^{12gf} 2^{10gf}
PU^{10sd} 5^{11g} 6^{10g} **0-2-11 £1,130**

Australian *J H M Gosden*   80
2 b c Danzero (Aus) - Auspicious
1^{8gf} **1-0-1 £5,304**

Authenticate *B A McMahon*   69
2 b f Dansili - Exact Replica
4^{6g} 6^{8s} 10^{7g} 18^{7g} **0-0-4 £464**

Authority (Ire) *Lady Herries*   a59
4 b g Bluebird (USA) - Persian Tapestry
5^{8sd} 8^{7sd} **0-0-2**

Autumn Daze *M J Ryan*   a13
2 b f Danzig Connection (USA) - Autumn Stone (Ire)
10^{6sd} 11^{8sd} 11^{7sd} 17^{6s} **0-0-4**

Autumn Fantasy (USA) *B Ellison*   51
5 b h Lear Fan (USA) - Autumn Glory (USA)
4^{14g} 12^{16g} 7^{16gf} 8^{16gf} **0-0-4 £519**

Autumn Flyer (Ire) *C G Cox*   57
3 ch g Salse (USA) - Autumn Fall (USA)
9^{10gf} 9^{10gf} 8^{10g} 5^{12gf} 10^{12f} **0-0-5**

Autumn Glory (Ire) *G Wragg*   117
4 b c Charnwood Forest (Ire) - Archipova (Ire)
1^{8g} 1^{8gs} 28^{8gf} 16^{7gf} 6^{8gs} 1^{8hy} 5^{7gs} 1^{9s}
4-0-8 £98,794

Autumn Melody (Fr) *Saeed Bin Suroor*   70
2 b f Kingmambo (USA) - Dance Of Leaves
5^{7gf} 6^{7gf} 5^{7gf} **0-0-3**

Autumn Pearl *M A Jarvis*   103
3 b f Orpen (USA) - Cyclone Flyer
1^{6hy} 2^{5g} 3^{5gf} 6^{5gf} 13^{5gf} 2^{5s} 10^{6vs} **1-3-7**
£42,829

Autumn Wealth (Ire) *Mrs A J Perrett*   89
3 ch f Cadeaux Genereux - Prickwillow (USA)
2^{10gf} 2^{10gf} 1^{10s} 11^{12s} 3^{10s} **2-3-5**
£17,103

Auwitesweetheart *B R Millman*   70
2 b f Josr Algarhoud (Ire) - Miss Kirsty (USA)
5^{6g} 5^{5gs} 5^{6s} 3^{5gs} 2^{5s} **0-2-5 £2,062**

Aveiro (Ire) *Miss Gay Kelleway*   42 a70
8 b g Darshaan - Avila
2^{12sd} 11^{11sd} 3^{12ss} 3^{12sd} 3^{16sw} 2^{12sd} 1^{16ss}
2^{12ss} 8^{22s} 10^{14s} 7^{12gf} 5^{15sd} 8^{13gf} **2-4-13**
£8,445

Avening *J E Hammond*   24
4 br g Averti (Ire) - Dependable
1^{5g} 2^{7vs} 0^{7g} 0^{6gs} 1^{6gs} 0^{6g} 4^{5vs} 2^{6g}
17^{6gs} **2-1-9 £31,274**

Aventura (Ire) *S R Bowring*   79 a88
4 b g Sri Pekan (USA) - La Belle Katherine (USA)

14^{10sd} 9^{8sw} 4^{8sd} 19^{8g} 10^{11s} 9^{6g} 7^{7s} 7^{7gf}
15^{7s} 11^{7sd} **0-0-10 £318**

Averami *A M Balding*   40 a55
3 b/br f Averti (Ire) - Friend For Life
9^{7sd} 5^{7sd} 11^{6ss} 13^{7gf} 6^{5sd} 10^{6gf} 11^{6gs}
6^{7sd} **0-0-8**

Averlline *B De Haan*   62
3 b f Averti (Ire) - Spring Sunrise
7^{6f} 8^{6g} 8^{7f} 10^{6gs} **0-0-4**

Aversham *R Charlton*   94 a88
4 b c Averti (Ire) - Vavona
11^{7gf} 9^{6ft} 15^{8ft} 3^{6gf} 5^{6gf} 4^{6sd} **0-1-6**
£2,163

Avertaine *G L Moore*   53 a48
3 b f Averti (Ire) - Roufontaine
9^{7sd} 12^{7sd} 5^{10gs} 2^{10gs} 7^{12gf} 6^{10sd} 5^{8f} 8^{8g}
0-1-8 £846

Avertigo *W R Muir*   75
2 b c Averti (Ire) - Green Run (USA)
5^{6gf} 3^{6gf} 2^{6g} 11^{6gs} 2^{6gf} 4^{6g} 25^{6s} **0-2-7**
£2,584

Averting *R F Johnson Houghton*   63
2 br c Averti (Ire) - Sweet Compliance
5^{5f} 2^{6gf} 7^{6gf} 19^{6gs} 17^{5gf} **0-1-6**
£1,284

Avesomeofthat (Ire) *Mrs P N Dutfield*   58
3 b g Lahib (USA) - Lacinia
6^{10gf} 9^{12g} **0-0-2**

Avessia *G L Moore*   69
3 b f Averti (Ire) - Alessia
4^{6gf} **0-0-1 £439**

Aviation *R Hannon*   76
2 b g Averti (Ire) - Roufontaine
7^{6s} 3^{6g} 5^{6gf} 5^{7gs} 9^{6g} **0-1-5 £880**

Avit (Ire) *P L Gilligan*   42 a48
4 ch f General Monash (USA) - Breakfast Boogie
8^{5sd} 11^{6sd} 2^{5sd} 3^{5sd} 9^{5g} 6^{5sd} 8^{6sd} 1^{5f}
4^{5gf} 5^{5gf} 11^{5gf} 2^{5gf} 15^{5g} 7^{6gf} 6^{6gs} **1-3-15**
£4,897

Avizandum (Ire) *T J Etherington*   27
2 b g Daggers Drawn (USA) - Miss Dilletante
12^{6g} 15^{8g} **0-0-2**

Avonbridge *R Charlton*   119
4 b c Averti (Ire) - Alessia
2^{5g} 1^{5gs} 5^{6f} 4^{5gf} 4^{5s} 5^{5g} **1-1-6**
£75,926

Awaaser (USA) *M P Tregoning*   62
2 ch f Diesis - Forest Storm (USA)
4^{6g} **0-0-1 £511**

Awake *D Nicholls*   93
7 ch g First Trump - Pluvial
12^{5g} 6^{6s} 5^{5s} 11^{5hy} 1^{5gf} 6^{5gs} 2^{5gf} 9^{5gf}
1^{5s} 13^{5g} 15^{5ss} 14^{5g} **2-1-12 £15,692**

Awaken *G A Swinbank*   52
3 b f Zafonic (USA) - Dawna
7^{10g} 7^{12s} **0-0-2**

Awarding *Dr J R J Naylor*   60 a70
4 ch g Mark Of Esteem (Ire) - Monaiya
5^{6sd} 8^{5sd} 14^{6sd} 17^{6gf} 8^{10g} 7^{8gf} 15^{6gs}
0-0-7

Awesome Love (USA) *M Johnston*   80
3 b c Awesome Again (Can) - Circus Toons (USA)
3^{7gf} 2^{8gf} 7^{7g} 2^{8g} 6^{10gf} 12^{8gf} 5^{11s} **0-4-7**
£5,960

Awwal Marra (USA) *E W Tuer*   45

4 ch f King Of Kings (Ire) - Secretariat Lass (USA)
7^{12gf} 3^{8gf} 14^{10gf} 9^{10gs} 16^{12g} **0-1-5**
£1,078

Axford Lord *A C Whillans*   36
4 gr g Petong - Bellyphax
6^{10g} 8^{6s} 15^{7s} 16^{9gs} **0-0-4**

Ayam Zaman (Ire) *M A Jarvis*   98
2 b f Montjeu (Ire) - Kardashina (Fr)
5^{8gf} 1^{10gf} 1^{10gs} **2-0-3 £20,090**

Aylmer Road (Ire) *P F I Cole*   81
2 b c Groom Dancer (USA) - Pekan's Pride
2^{8g} 4^{10hy} **0-1-2 £1,998**

Aynsley *M A Jarvis*   59 a29
2 ch f Tomba - Eggy
4^{5g} 5^{5f} 8^{5sd} **0-0-3 £383**

Aza Wish (Ire) *Ms Deborah J Evans*   58
2 b f Mujadil (USA) - Kilcsem Eile (Ire)
7^{5g} 5^{5s} 16^{6g} 8^{6f} 6^{7gf} 5^{7g} 5^{9gs} 8^{8s} **0-0-8**

Azahara *K G Reveley*   67
2 b f Vettori (Ire) - Branston Express
16^{6gs} 7^{7gs} 1^{7g} 11^{8s} **1-0-4 £3,542**

Azamour (Ire) *John M Oxx*   126
3 b c Night Shift (USA) - Asmara (USA)
3^{8g} 2^{8gf} 1^{8gf} 1^{10gf} 3^{10s} **2-3-5**
£675,796

Azarole (Ire) *J R Fanshawe*   104
3 b g Alzao (USA) - Cashew
5^{7g} 4^{8gf} 4^{7g} **0-0-3 £3,750**

Azeri (USA) *D Wayne Lukas*   a124
6 ch m Jade Hunter (USA) - Zodiac Miss (Aus)
1^{9ft} 2^{7ft} 8^{8ft} 4^{9ft} 1^{9ft} 2^{10ft} 1^{9ft} 5^{10ft}
3-1-8 £576,119

Azizam *P W Chapple-Hyam*   64
2 ch f Singspiel (Ire) - Perdicula (Ire)
7^{8s} **0-0-1**

Azreme *D K Ivory*   84 a59
4 ch c Unfuwain (USA) - Mariette
1^{7hy} 5^{8g} 7^{7gf} 4^{7sd} 5^{6sd} 4^{8g} 3^{7g} 12^{7g} 2^{7s}
7^{7g} 1^{7s} 2^{7s} 12^{7gs} 7^{7s} **2-3-14 £23,527**

Azuree (Ire) *R Hannon*   70
2 b f Almutawakel - Cappella (Ire)
2^{5s} 6^{6gs} 3^{6gf} 8^{5g} 4^{5gf} 7^{7f} 13^{5gs} 5^{7gf}
4^{6gf} 13^{6hy} **0-2-10 £4,831**

B A Highflyer *M R Channon*   67 a42
4 b g Compton Place - Primulette
13^{6sd} 5^{7gs} 9^{8s} 12^{6g} 13^{7f} 5^{6gf} 4^{6gs}
BD^{6gf} **0-0-8 £279**

Ba Clubman (Ire) *S C Williams*   12
4 b g Royal Abjar (USA) - Ah Ya Zein
14^{10gs} 5^{10s} 9^{12gf} **0-0-3**

Baawrah *M Todhunter*   66 a74
3 ch g Cadeaux Genereux - Kronengold (USA)
2^{10sd} 1^{10sd} 4^{10sd} 13^{10g} 6^{10s} 14^{12g} **1-1-6**
£6,019

Baba (Ire) *T P Tate*   48
3 ch g Indian Ridge - Theory Of Law
8^{7gs} 9^{7g} 12^{5s} **0-0-3**

Babe Maccool (Ire) *B W Hills*   63
2 ch c Giant's Causeway (USA) - Kotama (USA)
6^{5s} 6^{6g} **0-0-2**

Babodana *M H Tompkins*   116
4 ch c Bahamian Bounty - Daanat Nawal
1^{8g} 6^{8gs} 3^{7g} 5^{8gf} 5^{8g} 4^{7g} 6^{7s} 4^{9g} 3^{9s}
2^{8s} **1-3-10 £90,125**

Baboosh (Ire) *J R Fanshawe*   74
3 b f Marju (Ire) - Slipper
2^{8gs} 1^{8gf} 11^{10s} **1-1-3 £7,730**

Baboushka (Ire) *Miss J A Camacho*   24
3 b f Soviet Star (USA) - Kabayil
8^{8hy} 12^{10gs} **0-0-2**

Baby Barry *Mrs G S Rees*   56 a34
7 b g Komaite (USA) - Malcesine (Ire)
11^{6gf} 13^{6f} 11^{8sd} 3^{8g} 10^{7gf} 2^{7gf} 8^{7s} 2^{8f}
1^{8g} 8^{9sd} **1-3-10 £5,988**

Bachelor Affair *W Jarvis*   50
2 b c Bachir (Ire) - Profit Alert (Ire)
14^{7g} 10^{7gs} **0-0-2**

Bachelor Duke (USA) *J A R Toller*   120
3 b c Miswaki (USA) - Gossamer (USA)
7^{8g} 1^{8gf} 7^{8gf} **1-0-3 £164,225**

Back At De Front (Ire) *N E Berry*   38 a65
3 b f Cape Cross (Ire) - Bold Fashion (Fr)
1^{6sd} 5^{6sd} 5^{5sd} 4^{6sd} 5^{5ss} 6^{5sd} 13^{7sd} 18^{6g}
11^{6gf} 8^{6sd} 6^{6sd} **1-0-11 £3,290**

Back In Action *M A Magnusson*   67
4 b g Hector Protector (USA) - Lucca
7^{8gf} 14^{12gs} **0-0-2**

Back In Fashion *J Mackie*
3 b f Puissance - Spring Collection
16^{7g} **0-0-1**

Back In Spirit *B A McMahon*   48 a35
4 ch g Primo Dominie - Pusey Street Girl
10^{6sd} 10^{6ss} 10^{5sd} 7^{6sd} 2^{6g} 4^{5sd} 14^{7hy}
0-1-7 £829

Back To Reality *B Palling*   47
2 ch g Magic Ring (Ire) - Arian Da
13^{7gf} 8^{10g} 8^{8hy} **0-0-3**

Backgammon *D R Loder*   81
3 b c Sadler's Wells (USA) - Game Plan
2^{10hy} 3^{9gs} 1^{8g} 4^{8gf} 11^{8s} **1-1-5 £7,036**

Backlash *A W Carroll*   49 a41
3 b f Fraam - Mezza Luna
8^{6sd} 13^{6sd} 7^{6ss} 5^{7s} 5^{8sd} 1^{8gs} **1-0-6**
£1,522

Backstreet Lad *B R Millman*   57 a22
2 b c Fraam - Forest Fantasy
15^{7gs} 9^{7s} 10^{8gs} 9^{9sd} **0-0-4**

Bad Intentions (Ire) *Miss D Mountain*   52
4 b f Victory Note (USA) - Fallacy
6^{6f} 14^{6f} 10^{6g} 6^{7gf} 10^{7s} **0-0-5**

Baddam *J L Dunlop*   67
2 b c Mujahid (USA) - Aude La Belle (Fr)
4^{6gf} 8^{7gf} 6^{7gs} 3^{8s} **0-1-4 £1,044**

Badminton *Saeed Bin Suroor*   104
3 b f Zieten (USA) - Badawi (USA)
1^{7gf} 8^{7s} **1-0-2 £17,400**

Badou *L Montague Hall*   35 a56
4 b g Averti (Ire) - Bint Albadou (Ire)
6^{8sd} 17^{ss} 4^{8sd} 16^{sd} 7^{6sd} 7^{7sd} 12^{7sd} 2^{6sd}
4^{5hy} 9^{7f} 10^{6g} 13^{7gf} 12^{6gf} **2-1-13 £3,568**

Badr (USA) *M Johnston*   63
3 b c Theatrical - Bejat (USA)
6^{9g} 7^{10gf} 5^{11gf} 17^{10g} 7^{9g} **0-0-5**

Baffle *J L Dunlop*   76
3 b f Selkirk (USA) - Elude
1^{8s} 5^{9hy} 7^{8g} 6^{8g} 13^{8g} **1-0-5 £5,902**

Bagan (Fr) *H R A Cecil*   96
5 b/br h Rainbow Quest (USA) - Maid Of Erin (USA)
4^{12g} 4^{12g} 4^{10gs} 18^{12g} 4^{12gf} 15^{12g} **0-2-6**

£3,685

Bago (Fr) *J E Pease*   129
3 b c Nashwan (USA) - Moonlight's Box (USA)
1^{9gs} 1^{10gs} 3^{10g} 3^{12s} 1^{12g} **3-2-5**
£984,241

Bahama Belle *Mrs L C Jewell*   53 a11
3 b f Bahamian Bounty - Barque Bleue (USA)
13^{6g} 4^{7gf} 12^{6g} 7^{5gf} 14^{7sd} 10^{7sd} **0-0-6**
£467

Bahama Reef (Ire) *B Gubby*   59 a59
3 b g Sri Pekan (USA) - Caribbean Dancer
8^{7sd} 9^{8g} 5^{6sd} 2^{7f} 8^{8gf} 3^{7gf} 3^{7gf} 3^{8gf}
11^{7gf} **0-4-9 £2,600**

Bahamian Bay *M Brittain*   36
2 b f Bahamian Bounty - Moly
8^{7gs} 13^{6gf} 8^{5gf} **0-0-3**

Bahamian Belle *P S McEntee*   59 a55
4 b f Bahamian Bounty - Marjorie's Memory (Ire)
6^{6sd} 6^{6sd} 4^{5g} 7^{6s} 15^{5g} 18^{5gf} 13^{5gf} 8^{5f}
9^{5f} 5^{5gs} 7^{6gf} 13^{6gf} 4^{7g} **0-1-13 £321**

Bahamian Breeze *J Noseda*   61
3 b g Piccolo - Norgabie
9^{6g} 12^{5gf} **0-0-2**

Bahamian Magic *D R Loder*   78 a85
2 b c Royal Applause - Out Like Magic
4^{6g} 3^{5sd} 1^{6g} 12^{6g} 2^{6sd} **1-2-5 £6,533**

Bahamian Pirate (USA) *D Nicholls*   118
9 ch g Housebuster (USA) - Shining Through (USA)
1^{5g} 4^{6g} 4^{7gs} 2^{6g} 1^{5hy} 10^{6gs} 7^{5gf} 8^{6f}
10^{6s} 17^{6gs} 15^{gf} 6^{5gf} 1^{5s} 12^{6g} 9^{5g} **4-1-15**
£148,919

Bahamian Spring (Ire) *D R Loder*
2 b g Danehill Dancer (Ire) - Siana Springs (Ire)
12^{7s} **0-0-1**

Bahia Breeze *R Guest*   96
2 b f Mister Baileys - Ring Of Love
4^{6s} 1^{6gf} 8^{6gf} 1^{6s} **2-0-4 £19,153**

Bahiano (Ire) *C E Brittain*   106 a99
3 ch c Barathea (Ire) - Trystero
2^{8sd} 1^{7sd} 2^{8sd} 3^{7sd} 6^{7g} 7^{7gs} 17^{8gf} 4^{7gf}
19^{7gf} 9^{8gf} 12^{7g} 8^{7gf} **1-3-12 £21,903**

Bahja (USA) *J H M Gosden*   82
2 ch f Seeking The Gold (USA) - Valentine Waltz (Ire)
4^{7gs} 3^{7g} **0-1-2 £2,084**

Bailamos (Ger) *P Schiergen*   108
4 b c Lomitas - Bandeira (Ger)
5^{16s} 3^{15s} 2^{16g} 1^{16g} 4^{14g} 8^{16g} 5^{15s} 3^{17s}
1-1-8 £33,979

Bailaora (Ire) *B W Duke*   71
3 b/br c Shinko Forest (Ire) - Tart (Fr)
6^{8hy} 8^{8g} 6^{7gf} 3^{10gs} 7^{10gf} 5^{10g} 12^{12gf} 4^{10g}
0-1-8 £907

Bailey Gate *R Hannon*   82
2 b f Mister Baileys - Floppie (Fr)
7^{6gs} 9^{6g} 1^{6s} **1-0-3 £5,980**

Baileys Applause *C A Dwyer*   67 a45
2 b f Royal Applause - Thicket
5^{5g} 3^{5sd} 6^{6gf} 12^{5g} 12^{6gs} 6^{5gs} 4^{5f} **0-0-7**
£530

Baileys Dancer *M Johnston*   82
3 b g Groom Dancer (USA) - Darshay (Fr)
8^{8gs} 4^{8gs} 9^{10gf} 12^{8gf} 2^{10gf} 10^{12s} 1^{12f}
9^{12s} 8^{12gf} **1-1-9 £8,401**

Baileys Honour *M Johnston*   46 a27
2 b f Mark Of Esteem (Ire) - Kanz (USA)

BD^{6f} 12^{8g} 10^{8sd} **0-0-3**

Bailieborough (Ire) *D Nicholls*   75 a59
5 b g Charnwood Forest (Ire) - Sherannda (USA)
10^{7g} 6^{7s} 7^{8gs} 3^{7g} 4^{8gs} 8^{8f} 1^{8gf} 3^{7g} 8^{8sd}
1^{9g} 6^{10gs} 5^{7g} 1^{8gf} 1^{7gf} 3^{9gs} 2^{9gf} 9^{8gf} **4-4-17**
£17,624

Baker Of Oz *D Burchell*   78 a72
3 b c Pursuit Of Love - Moorish Idol
2^{8sd} 6^{8ss} 4^{7gs} 1^{8gf} 7^{7g} 9^{9gf} 7^{8gs} 9^{7gs}
1-1-8 £5,150

Bakhtyar *R Charlton*   61 a57
3 gr g Daylami (Ire) - Gentilesse
8^{12gs} 12^{12s} 4^{12gs} 5^{16sd} 4^{18gs} 14^{16sd} **0-1-6**
£656

Bakiri (Ire) *Andrew Reid*   68
6 b g Doyoun - Bakiya (USA)
13^{8gs} 4^{15s} 12^{12gs} 5^{14g} 2^{12g} 3^{12gf} 2^{12f}
4^{13f} 7^{11gf} 9^{12gf} 1^{12gs} **1-3-11 £7,054**

Bakke *M P Tregoning*   63
2 b g Danehill (USA) - Valagalore
9^{6g} 14^{7gf} **0-0-2**

Balakiref *M Dods*   81
5 b g Royal Applause - Pluck
1^{6gs} 9^{6s} 2^{7gs} 2^{6g} 2^{7hy} UR^{7gf} 1^{7g} 10^{6s}
9^{7g} 8^{7g} 5^{6hy} 1^{6s} 3^{6gs} 4^{6s} **3-5-14 £24,993**

Balalaika Tune (Ire) *W Storey*   38 a35
5 b m Lure (USA) - Bohemienne (USA)
8^{7sd} 7^{8sd} 9^{11sd} 6^{11ss} 13^{10hy} 4^{13g} 7^{16g}
10^{12gf} 4^{16f} 6^{14g} 13^{17g} 3^{12g} 2^{12gf} 6^{12gf} **0-1-14**
£1,588

Balashova *K R Burke*   38
2 b f Imperial Ballet (Ire) - Almasi (Ire)
5^{5gs} UR^{5s} **0-0-2**

Balavista (USA) *R Charlton*   83
3 br c Distant View (USA) - Balabina (USA)
1^{8g} 9^{8g} **1-0-2 £5,629**

Balearic Star (Ire) *B R Millman*   78
3 b c Night Shift (USA) - La Menorquina (USA)
6^{8g} 7^{9hy} 1^{8gf} 7^{9gf} 14^{10gs} 6^{8gf} 1^{8gs} **2-0-7**
£11,459

Balerno *R Ingram*   71 a56
5 b g Machiavellian (USA) - Balabina (USA)
1^{8sd} 3^{8sd} 11^{8sd} 4^{8sd} 5^{8sd} 8^{7sd} 5^{7sd} 2^{7gf}
3^{7g} 7^{8f} 4^{7gf} 7^{8gf} 1^{7gf} 2^{7gf} 5^{8gf} 11^{7s}
6^{7gf} **2-6-18 £10,021**

Balgarth (USA) *T D Barron*   54
2 b g Zamindar (USA) - Vaguely Regal (Ire)
11^{6gs} **0-0-1**

Bali Royal *M S Saunders*   97
6 b m King's Signet (USA) - Baligay
6^{5gf} 4^{6f} 8^{5gs} 12^{5gs} 9^{5gf} 10^{6g} **0-0-6**
£2,200

Bali-Star *R J Hodges*   56 a41
9 b g Alnasr Alwasheek - Baligay
10^{5sd} 2^{5sd} 4^{5sd} 7^{5sd} 17^{5gs} 4^{5sd} 1^{5gs}
16^{5s} 9^{6gf} **1-1-9 £1,967**

Balimaya (Ire) *E Libaud*   65
3 b f Barathea (Ire) - Banque Privee (USA)
8^{8g} 6^{10gs} 1^{8s} 2^{8sd} 6^{10gs} 10^{8gs} **1-1-6**
£9,929

Balkan Knight *D R Loder*   91
4 b c Selkirk (USA) - Crown Of Light
6^{10g} 1^{12gs} 12^{12g} 3^{15g} **1-0-4 £11,568**

Balkan Leader (USA) *Saeed Bin Suroor*   51 a69
2 b c Stravinsky (USA) - Baydon Belle (USA)
4^{6f} 2^{7sd} **0-1-2 £1,628**

Ball Boy *M R Channon* 73
2 b g Xaar - Tanz (Ire)
7⁷ᵍᶠ 5⁷ᵍ 2⁷ᵍᶠ 5⁸ˢ **0-1-4 £1,520**

Ballare (Ire) *Bob Jones* 55 a56
5 b g Barathea (Ire) - Raindancing (Ire)
9¹⁰ˢᵈ 3⁸ˢᵈ 4⁸ˢᵈ 6⁷ˢᵈ 1⁸ˢᵈ 10⁷ᵍᶠ 4⁷ᵍˢ 14⁸ᶠ
9⁷ᵍᶠ 11¹⁰ᵍᶠ 2⁷ˢᵈ 1⁸ᵍˢ 10⁹ˢᵈ **2-2-13 £4,207**

Ballerina Suprema (Ire) *C R Egerton* 83
4 b f Sadler's Wells (USA) - Gravieres (Fr)
5¹⁰ᵍᶠ 7¹⁴ᵍᶠ **0-0-2**

Ballet Ballon (USA) *M A Jarvis* 45
2 b f Rahy (USA) - Bella Ballerina
11⁷ᵍᶠ **0-0-1**

Ballet Ruse *Sir Mark Prescott* 21
3 ch f Rainbow Quest (USA) - El Opera (Ire)
16⁸ᵍᶠ 11⁸ᵍᶠ 7¹⁶ˢ **0-0-3**

Balletomaine (Ire) *B W Hills* 62 a39
2 b f Sadler's Wells (USA) - Ivy (USA)
8⁷ᵍᶠ 7⁷ᵍˢ 8⁷ˢᵈ **0-0-3**

Balletto *K R Burke* 65
2 b f Robellino (USA) - Denial
3⁶ᵍᶠ 7⁶ᵍᶠ **0-1-2 £836**

Ballin Rouge *T J Fitzgerald* 27
3 ch f Dr Fong (USA) - Bogus John (Can)
10⁷ᵍᶠ 7¹⁰ᵍ 6⁸ᶠ **0-0-3**

Ballinger Express *A M Balding* 68 a64
4 ch f Air Express (Ire) - Branston Ridge
8⁸ˢᵈ 5⁸ˢᵈ 3⁸ˢᵈ 2⁷ᶠ 9⁶ᵍᶠ 15⁶ᵍᶠ 2⁶ᵍᶠ 9⁵ᵍᶠ
10⁵ᵍᶠ 13⁶ᵍˢ 3⁶ᵍᶠ **0-4-11 £4,333**

Ballinger Ridge *T G McCourt* 68 a68
5 b g Sabrehill (USA) - Branston Ridge
2⁸ˢᵈ 3⁷ˢᵈ 2⁸ˢᵈ 2⁸ˢᵈ 1¹⁰ˢᵈ 6⁸ˢᵈ 2⁸ᶠ 8¹⁰ᵍ
11⁸ᵍ 14⁷ᵍᶠ 5⁸ᵍᶠ **1-5-11 £5,379**

Ballinteni *Saeed Bin Suroor* 85
2 b c Machiavellian (USA) - Silabteni (USA)
1⁷ˢ **1-0-1 £3,542**

Bally Hall (Ire) *G A Butler* a69
4 b g Saddlers' Hall (Ire) - Sally Rose
11¹⁰ˢᵈ **0-0-1**

Ballyboro (Ire) *M J Wallace* 46
3 b f Entrepreneur - Tathkara (USA)
6⁷ᵍˢ 11⁷ᶠ 9¹¹ᶠ **0-0-3**

Ballybunion (Ire) *D Nicholls* 65
5 ch g Entrepreneur - Clarentia
10⁶ᵍ 15⁵ᵍᶠ 11⁵ᵍᶠ 11⁶ᵍᶠ 5⁵ᵍᶠ 3⁵ᵍ 9⁵ᵍˢ
10⁶ᵍ 9⁵ᵍˢ 9⁵ᵍˢ 5⁶ᵍᶠ 1⁵ᵍᶠ 7⁶ᵍᶠ 3⁶ᵍᶠ 2⁶ᵍ 13⁵ᵍˢ
4⁵ᶠ 4⁵ᵍᶠ **1-4-18 £6,982**

Ballycroy Girl (Ire) *A Bailey* 72
2 ch f Pennekamp (USA) - Hulm (Ire)
6⁶ᵍᶠ 2⁷ᵍ 5⁷ᵍˢ 1⁷ᵍᶠ 8⁷ᵍᶠ 6⁷ᵍᶠ 7⁸ˢ **1-1-7
£6,812**

Ballygriffin Kid *Miss Gay Kelleway* 31 a43
4 gr g Komaite (USA) - Ballygriffin Belle
8⁷ˢᵈ 3⁶ˢᵈ 4⁵ˢᵈ 1⁷ˢᵈ 10⁸ᵍᶠ **1-1-5 £1,668**

Ballyhurry (USA) *J S Goldie* 76 a58
7 b g Rubiano (USA) - Balakhna (Fr)
11⁷ᵍᶠ 6⁷ᶠ 4⁷ᵍᶠ 6⁷ᵍ 8⁸ᵍᶠ 4⁷ᵍᶠ 4⁷ᵍ 5⁷ˢᵈ
0-1-8 £1,457

Ballyliffin (Ire) *S Kirk* 57
3 b g Daggers Drawn (USA) - Blues Quartet
18¹⁰ᵍ 2¹⁰ˢ **0-1-2 £844**

Ballyrush (Ire) *K R Burke* 34 a64
4 ch g Titus Livius (Fr) - Mandoline (Ire)
8⁹ˢˢ 5⁸ˢʷ 4⁸ˢʷ 5¹¹ˢˢ 6⁸ᵍˢ 5¹⁰ᵍˢ 2⁹ˢᵈ 1⁸ˢᵈ
12⁸ᵍᶠ **1-1-9 £1,862**

Balmacara *Miss K B Boutflower* 46 a46
5 b m Lake Coniston (Ire) - Diabaig
7⁸ˢᵈ 9⁸ˢᵈ 6⁸ᶠ 12⁸ᵍᶠ 5⁸ᵍ 10⁷ᵍᶠ 9⁷ˢᵈ **0-0-7**

Balmont (USA) *J Noseda* 115
3 b c Stravinsky (USA) - Aldebaran Light (USA)
3⁶ᵍˢ 2⁵ᵍᶠ 7⁵ˢ 5⁷ˢ **0-2-4 £33,192**

Balthasar *P A Blockley* 58
2 b c Lujain (USA) - Anatase
15⁵ᵍᶠ 6⁸ˢ 7⁶ᵍˢ 6⁶ᵍˢ **0-0-4**

Baltic Blazer (Ire) *P W Harris* 74
4 b g Polish Precedent (USA) - Pine Needle
5¹¹ᵍˢ 9¹⁰ᵍ 17¹⁰ᵍ **0-0-3**

Baltic Dip (Ire) *R Hannon* 96
2 b f Benny The Dip (USA) - Drei (USA)
1⁶ᵍᶠ 4⁶ᵍᶠ 8⁷ᵍ 4⁷ᵍ **1-0-4 £14,604**

Baltic King *H Morrison* 116
4 b c Danetime (Ire) - Lindfield Belle (Ire)
6⁵ᵍ 8⁶ᵍᶠ 15⁶ᶠ 3⁵ᵍˢ 6⁵ᵍᶠ 1⁵ᵍᶠ 3⁵ᵍ 5⁶ˢ
2-2-8 £57,946

Baltic Wave *T D Barron* 89
3 b g Polish Precedent (USA) - Flourish
6⁷ᶠ 4⁷ᵍ 11⁶ᵍ **0-0-3 £728**

Balwearie (Ire) *Miss L A Perratt* 47
3 b g Sesaro - Eight Mile Rock
6⁵ᵍ 9⁸ᵍᶠ 6⁶ᵍᶠ **0-0-3 £231**

Bamboozled *P D Evans* 9 a41
2 b f Mujadil (USA) - Tintinara
6⁵ˢᵈ 9⁵ʰʸ 7⁵ˢᵈ 5⁵ᵍᶠ **0-0-4 £315**

Bamford Castle (Ire) *R Ford* a16
9 b g Scenic - Allorette
9¹⁶ˢᵈ **0-0-1**

Bamzooki *J R Fanshawe* 60
2 b f Zilzal (USA) - Cavernista
4⁶ᵍᶠ 5⁶ᵍˢ **0-0-2 £264**

Banana Grove (Ire) *A Berry* 68
3 b g Sesaro - Megan's Dream (Ire)
3⁹ᵍᶠ 7⁸ᵍᶠ PU⁸ᵍ 1⁹ᶠ 4⁹ᵍˢ 7⁸ᵍˢ 6⁹ˢ 3⁸ˢ
1-0-8 £6,784

Banchieri *Saeed Bin Suroor* 82
2 b c Dubai Millennium - Belle Et Deluree (USA)
3⁷ᵍᶠ 3⁷ᵍ 2⁸ᵍˢ **0-3-3 £3,636**

Band *B A McMahon* 62 a35
4 b g Band On The Run - Little Tich
12⁸ˢ 12⁸ᵍᶠ 12⁸ˢᵈ 10¹⁰ᵍ 4¹¹ᵍˢ 8¹¹ˢ 5¹¹ᵍ
1⁸ᶠ 7⁸ᵍ 6⁸ʰʸ 4¹⁰ʰʸ **1-1-11 £4,211**

Bandari (Ire) *M Johnston* 123
5 b h Alhaarth (Ire) - Miss Audimar (USA)
11¹²ᵍ 1¹⁰ᵍ 1¹⁰ᵍˢ 1¹⁰ᵍˢ 9¹⁰ᵍᶠ 1¹²ᵍᶠ 7¹²ᵍᶠ
3¹²ᵍᶠ 3¹²ᵍᶠ 9¹²ˢ **4-1-10 £130,567**

Bandbox *M Salaman* 29 a27
9 ch g Imperial Frontier - Dublah (USA)
8⁷ˢᵈ 5⁷ˢᵈ 7⁷ˢᵈ 3⁶ᶠ **0-0-4 £417**

Bandit Queen *W Jarvis* 94
4 b f Desert Prince (Ire) - Wildwood Flower
3⁶ᵍ 4⁶ᵍᶠ 2⁷ᵍᶠ 9⁷ᵍ **0-2-4 £5,922**

Bandos *I Semple* 79
4 ch g Cayman Kai (Ire) - Lekuti
3⁷ᶠ 13⁷ᵍ 18⁷ˢ 4⁷ˢ 5⁷ᵍᶠ **0-1-5 £1,607**

Banjo Bay (Ire) *D Nicholls* 85
6 b g Common Grounds - Thirlmere
8⁸ᵍˢ 14⁶ᵍᶠ 3⁶ᵍᶠ 11⁶ᵍ 18⁷ᶠ 6⁵ᵍˢ 8⁶ᵍᶠ 8⁷ᶠ
10⁵ᵍ 7⁷ᵍᶠ 5⁶ᶠ 14⁶ᵍᶠ **0-1-12 £847**

Banjo Patterson *G A Huffer* 41
2 b c Green Desert (USA) - Rumpipumpy

15⁶ˢ **0-0-1**

Bank Games *M W Easterby* 34 a45
3 b g Mind Games - Piggy Bank
8⁶ᵍᶠ 8⁶ˢᵈ 6⁶ˢᵈ 5⁵ᵍᶠ 11⁷ᵍˢ 14⁶ᵍˢ **0-0-6**

Bank On Him *G L Moore* 58 a69
9 b g Elmaamul (USA) - Feather Flower
1¹⁰ˢᵈ 6¹⁰ˢᵈ 1¹⁰ˢᵈ 2⁸ˢᵈ 2¹⁰ˢᵈ 2¹⁰ˢᵈ
5⁸ˢᵈ 1¹⁰ᵍᶠ 3¹²ˢᵈ 4⁹ᵍᶠ 3¹⁰ˢᵈ **3-7-12 £13,914**

Banknote *A M Balding* 75
2 b c Zafonic (USA) - Brand
4⁶ᵍᶠ 4⁶ᵍ 1⁷ᵍᶠ 13⁸ᵍᶠ **1-0-4 £6,012**

Banners Flying (Ire) *D W Chapman* 32 a46
4 ch g Zafonic (USA) - Banafsajee (USA)
8⁷ˢᵈ 13⁸ˢᵈ 4¹²ˢᵈ 11⁸ᵍ 4¹²ˢᵈ 13¹²ˢᵈ 9¹⁶ᵍˢ
12¹⁴ᵍᶠ 10¹⁰ᶠ 9¹²ˢᵈ **0-0-10**

Banningham Blaze *A W Carroll* 56 a58
4 b f Averti (Ire) - Ma Pavlova (USA)
11¹¹ˢᵈ 9¹⁴ᵍ 4¹²ᵍᶠ 1¹²ᵍᶠ 2¹²ᵍᶠ 2¹²ᶠ 3¹³ᶠ
6¹²ᶠ 5¹²ᵍᶠ 3¹²ᵍᶠ 1¹⁴ᵍᶠ 3¹²ᶠ 2¹²ᶠ 2¹²ᵍᶠ 2¹²ᵍ
3¹⁶ᵍᶠ 2¹³ᵍˢ 5¹²ᵍ **3-11-21 £14,510**

Bannister *Mrs Stef Liddiard* 66 a63
6 ch g Inchinor - Shall We Run
3⁶ˢᵈ 9⁶ˢʷ 3⁷ᵍˢ 14⁸ᵍ **0-2-4 £1,058**

Bansha Bru (Ire) *Miss E C Lavelle* a58
4 b g Fumo Di Londra (Ire) - Pride Of Duneane (Ire)
3⁸ˢᵈ 5ᵁ¹⁰ˢ **0-1-2 £526**

Baqah (Ire) *F Head* 111
3 ch f Bahhare (USA) - Filfilah
3⁶ʰᵒ 1⁶ˢ 2⁶ᵛˢ 1⁷ᵍ 1⁸ᵍˢ 3⁸ᵍᶠ 7⁸ˢ 9⁸ᵍ **3-2-8 £100,521**

Bar Of Silver (Ire) *R Brotherton* a42
4 ch g Bahhare (USA) - Shaping Up (USA)
9⁹ˢᵈ 5⁸ˢᵈ 11⁶ˢʷ 5⁷ˢᵈ **0-0-4**

Barabella (Ire) *B A Pearce* 58
3 gr f Barathea (Ire) - Thatchabella (Ire)
12⁸ᵍ 5⁵ᵍ 14⁶ˢ 4⁶ᶠ 5⁶ᵍ 13⁵ᵍ 4⁷ᵍᶠ 5⁶ᶠ
12⁶ᵍˢ 15⁶ᵍ 11⁷ʰʸ **0-0-11 £330**

Baradore (Ire) *M G Quinlan* 87
2 ch f Barathea (Ire) - High Flying Adored (Ire)
2⁷ᵍ 1⁸ᵍᶠ **1-1-2 £4,954**

Baraka (Ire) *A P O'Brien* 107
3 b f Danehill (USA) - Cocotte
1¹¹ˢ 9¹⁰ᵍ **1-0-2 £29,750**

Barakana (Ire) *C Tinkler* a25
6 b g Barathea (Ire) - Safkana (Ire)
10¹⁰ˢᵈ **0-0-1**

Baranook (Ire) *P W Harris* 66 a74
3 b c Barathea (Ire) - Gull Nook
13¹⁰ᵍᶠ 7¹⁰ᵍᶠ 5¹¹ᵍ 3¹²ˢᵈ **0-1-4 £566**

Barathea Blue *P W Harris* 78 a70
3 ch c Barathea (Ire) - Empty Purse
5¹⁰ᵍᶠ 2¹⁰ᵍ 1¹⁰ᵍᶠ 7¹²ˢᵈ **1-1-4 £6,775**

Barathea Dreams (Ire) *J S Moore* 91 a68
3 b c Barathea (Ire) - Deyaajeer (USA)
1¹⁰ˢᵈ 1¹⁰ˢᵈ 4¹²ˢᵈ 1⁸ᵍˢ 3⁸ᵍˢ 10¹⁰ᶠ 7⁸ᵍᶠ 5⁸ᵍ
14⁸ᵍᶠ 5⁷ᵍˢ **3-1-10 £24,868**

Barati (Ire) *John M Oxx* 103
3 b g Sadler's Wells (USA) - Oriane
1⁸ˢ 4¹⁰ᵍʸ 3¹⁰ᵍᶠ 3¹²ᶠ 5¹⁰ᵍʸ **1-0-5 £31,066**

Barbajuan (Ire) *N A Callaghan* 98
3 b c Danehill Dancer (Ire) - Courtier
5⁸ᵍˢ 12⁸ᵍ 8¹⁰ᵍˢ 7⁸ᵍᶠ 13⁶ᵍ 10⁸ᵍ 13⁷ᵍᶠ
5¹⁰ᵍ 11⁸ˢ **0-0-9 £1,273**

Barbary Coast (Fr) *W R Muir* 81
2 b c Anabaa (USA) - Viking's Cove (USA)
6⁷ᵍ 8⁷ᵍ 2⁸ᵍ 11⁸ˢ **0-1-4 £1,744**

Barbilyrifle (Ire) *H H G Owen* 58 a41
3 b g Indian Rocket - Age Of Elegance
9⁵ˢᵈ 11⁶ˢᵈ 3⁶ᵍˢ 9⁶ˢ **0-1-4 £374**

Barbirolli *J H M Gosden* 39
2 b c Machiavellian (USA) - Blushing Barada (USA)
12⁸ᵍˢ **0-0-1**

Barcardero (USA) *M Johnston* 65
2 b c Danzig (USA) - Very Confidential (USA)
8⁷ˢ **0-0-1**

Barcelona *G L Moore* 42
7 b g Barathea (Ire) - Pipitina
9¹²ᵍ **0-0-1**

Bargain Hunt (Ire) *W Storey* 46
3 b g Foxhound (USA) - Atisayin (USA)
10¹⁰ˢ 2⁹ᵍ 7¹²ᵍ 7¹⁰ᶠ 3⁸ᵍ 6⁹ᵍ 10⁶ᵍᶠ 11⁷ᵍᶠ
4⁸ᵍᶠ 3⁸ᶠ **0-4-10 £2,074**

Barholm Charlie *M A Buckley* 11
3 b g Atraf - Lady-H
19⁶ᵍᶠ 14⁵ᵍᶠ 8¹¹ᵍ **0-0-3**

Barking Mad (USA) *M L W Bell* 89
6 b/br g Dayjur (USA) - Avian Assembly (USA)
6¹⁰ᵍ 4¹⁰ᵍᶠ 3¹⁰ᵍᶠ 2¹⁰ᵍ 1¹⁰ᵍ 6¹⁰ᵍ 2¹⁰ᵍᶠ 6¹⁰ᵍˢ
1¹⁰ᵍˢ 2⁹ᵍᶠ 7¹⁰ᵍᶠ 7¹⁰ˢ **2-2-12 £18,546**

Barman (USA) *P F I Cole* 89
5 ch g Atticus (USA) - Blue Tip (Fr)
10¹²ᵍ 7¹²ᵍᶠ 1¹⁴ᵍᶠ **1-0-3 £13,183**

Barnbrook Empire (Ire) *I A Wood* 60
2 b f Second Empire (Ire) - Home Comforts
14⁶ᵍ 5⁷ᵍ 3⁶ᵍᶠ 7⁶ᵍᶠ **0-1-4 £551**

Barolo *P W Harris* 118
5 b g Danehill (USA) - Lydia Maria
12¹²ᵍ 1¹⁴ᵍᶠ 17¹⁶ˢ 1¹⁴ᵍʸ 1¹⁴ᵍ **3-0-5 £45,026**

Baron Rhodes *J S Wainwright* 86
3 b f Presidium - Superstream
2⁵ˢ 2⁵ᵍ 2⁵ᶠ 3⁵ᵍˢ 1⁵ᵍᶠ 3⁵ᵍ 7⁶ᵍᶠ 5⁵ᵍˢ 1⁵ᵍᶠ
3⁵ᵍˢ 13⁵ˢ 8⁵ᵍˢ 7⁵ˢ 10⁵ᵍˢ 3⁵ᵍ 8⁵ˢ 9⁵ᵍˢ **2-8-17 £23,939**

Baron's Pit *R Hannon* 109
4 b c Night Shift (USA) - Incendio
1⁶ᵍˢ **1-0-1 £8,343**

Barons Spy (Ire) *A W Carroll* 72
3 b c Danzero (Aus) - Princess Accord (USA)
4⁷ᵍᶠ 2⁷ᶠ 10⁸ᵍᶠ 3⁸ᵍ 2⁷ᵍ **0-2-5 £3,806**

Baroque *C Smith* 2
3 b c Merdon Melody - Dubitable
10⁸ˢˢ 8¹²ᵍˢ 13¹⁰ᵍ 6¹⁰ʰʸ 14¹⁴ᶠ 10¹²ᵍᶠ **0-0-6**

Barrantes *Miss Sheena West* 74
7 b m Distant Relative - Try The Duchess
9⁶ᵍᶠ 7⁸ᵍᶠ 9⁶ᵍ 1⁴¹²ᵍᶠ **0-0-5**

Barras (Ire) *Miss Gay Kelleway* 50 a57
3 b g Raphane (USA) - Lady Fleetsin (Ire)
8⁶ˢᵈ 8⁵ˢᵈ 3⁶ˢˢ 5⁶ˢˢ 4⁵ˢˢ 5⁷ˢᵈ 11⁷ᵍᶠ 3⁵ᵍᶠ **0-2-8 £880**

Barrissimo (Ire) *W J Musson* 64
4 b g Night Shift (USA) - Belle De Cadix (Ire)
18¹⁰ᵍ 11¹⁰ᵍˢ **0-0-2**

Barry Island *D R C Elsworth* 85 a85
5 b g Turtle Island (Ire) - Pine Ridge
1¹⁰ˢᵈ 5¹²ˢᵈ 2¹²ˢᵈ 4¹⁰ˢᵈ 4¹⁰ˢᵈ 3¹⁰ᵍ 10¹⁰ᵍ
9¹⁰ᵍ 3¹²ᵍᶠ 8¹⁰ᵍᶠ 6¹²ᵍ 4¹⁰ᵍᶠ 1¹⁰ᵍᶠ 14¹⁰ˢ **2-3-14**

£25,857

Barton Flower *M W Easterby* 36
3 br f Danzero (Aus) - Iota
7^{8hy} 8^{8hy} 9^{10gf} 11^{12gf} 14^{16gs} 7^{14gs} **0-0-6**

Barton Sands (Ire) *Andrew Reid* 73
7 b g Tenby - Hetty Green
11^{1g} 1^{10gf} 2^{11g} 4^{9gf} 4^{10gf} **2-1-5 £6,296**

Barzak (Ire) *S R Bowring* 56 a74
4 b g Barathea (Ire) - Zakuska
8^{7sd} 5^{8sd} 3^{6sd} 10^{7gs} 8^{8gs} 8^{7gf} 15^{7g} **0-1-7 £469**

Basic System (USA) *Sir Michael Stoute* 70
2 b c Belong To Me (USA) - Foible (USA)
8^{6g} 5^{7gf} **0-0-2**

Basinet *J J Quinn* 59
6 b g Alzao (USA) - Valiancy
12^{8gs} 12^{8gs} 8^{9f} 4^{8s} 8^{8gf} 6^{9gf} 4^{8gs} 8^{10gf} 8^{8gf} **0-1-9 £633**

Basserah (Ire) *B W Hills* 73
2 b f Unfuwain (USA) - Blueberry Walk
7^{8gf} 9^{8s} **0-0-2**

Batchworth Beau *E A Wheeler* 44
3 ch g Bluegrass Prince (Ire) - Batchworth Belle
11^{6s} 16^{8g} 9^{6gf} 10^{5gf} **0-0-4**

Batchworth Breeze *E A Wheeler* a13
6 ch m Beveled (USA) - Batchworth Dancer
9^{6sd} **0-0-1**

Bathwick Bill (USA) *B R Millman* 85
3 ch g Stravinsky (USA) - Special Park (USA)
9^{6gs} 6^{6s} 2^{5f} 3^{6g} 8^{6gf} 11^{6gf} 11^{6gs} 8^{5g}
0-2-8 £3,524

Bathwick Bruce (Ire) *B R Millman* 58
6 b g College Chapel - Naivity (Ire)
7^{8s} 7^{8gs} **0-0-2**

Bathwick Dream *B R Millman* a19
7 b m Tragic Role (USA) - Trina
12^{13sd} **0-0-1**

Bathwick Finesse (Ire) *B R Millman* 80
2 b f Namid - Lace Flower
7^{6gs} 1^{8g} 4^{8s} 14^{8s} **1-0-4 £3,864**

Batik (Ire) *L M Cumani* 81
3 gr f Peintre Celebre (USA) - Dali's Grey
3^{8gf} 1^{10g} 5^{12s} **1-1-3 £4,745**

Battle Back (Bel) *S C Williams* a27
3 b f Pursuit Of Love - Batalya (Bel)
12^{7sd} 9^{9sd} **0-0-2**

Battle Chant (USA) *Mrs A J Perrett* 111
4 b g Coronado's Quest (USA) - Appointed One (USA)
3^{8g} 18^{8gf} 2^{10g} 2^{10gf} 3^{10g} 5^{9s} **0-4-6 £24,498**

Battledress (Ire) *M P Tregoning* 77
2 b g In The Wings - Chaturanga
8^{7s} 3^{8g} 4^{10g} **0-1-3 £912**

Bay Hawk *A M Balding* 74
2 b c Alhaarth (Ire) - Fleeting Vision (Ire)
3^{7gs} **0-1-1 £935**

Bay Solitaire *T D Easterby* 39
3 b g Charnwood Forest (Ire) - Golden Wings (USA)
6^{10f} 8^{12gf} 9^{14gs} **0-0-3**

Bay Tree (Ire) *D R Loder* 98
3 b f Daylami (Ire) - My Branch
6^{7g} 3^{10gs} 11^{8gf} 8^{10gs} **0-0-4 £6,800**

Bayadere (Ger) *V Smith* 59
4 br f Lavirco (Ger) - Brangane (Ire)

8^{10g} 8^{10s} 20^{12s} **0-0-3**

Bayard (USA) *D R C Elsworth* 69
2 gr c Lord Avie (USA) - Mersey
4^{8hy} 8^{8gs} **0-0-2 £518**

Bayberry (UAE) *H R A Cecil* 109
4 ch f Bering - Baya (USA)
5^{10gf} 2^{8s} 3^{10gf} **0-1-3 £9,925**

Baychevelle (Ire) *Mrs H Dalton*
3 ch f Bahamian Bounty - Phantom Ring
12^{6s} **0-0-1**

Bayeux (USA) *Saeed Bin Suroor* 101
3 b c Red Ransom (USA) - Elizabeth Bay (USA)
5^{10g} 3^{8gf} 7^{10g} 10^{8f} 3^{7s} **0-1-5 £4,710**

Bayeux De Moi (Ire) *Mrs A J Perrett* 88
2 b c Barathea (Ire) - Rivana
4^{7gf} 1^{8gs} 2^{10g} **1-1-3 £8,810**

Bayhirr *M A Jarvis* 95
3 b c Selkirk (USA) - Pass The Peace
3^{10gs} 5^{10gs} 2^{8gf} 11^{8g} **1-2-5 £10,576**

Baylaw Star *K A Ryan* 74
3 b g Case Law - Caisson
6^{5s} 3^{5g} 7^{6g} 4^{5gs} 9^{5gf} 10^{5g} 6^{5gs} 15^{6gs}
11^{5gf} 6^{6s} **0-0-10 £1,990**

Baymist *M W Easterby* 67
2 b f Mind Games - Milliscent
5^{9g} 5^{9gs} 1^{5gs} 4^{6gf} 1^{5g} 6^{5gs} 7^{5gf} **2-0-7 £7,310**

Bayonet *Jane Southcombe* 38
8 b m Then Again - Lambay
8^{7gf} 8^{6gs} **0-0-2**

Bayou Princess *S T Lewis* 54
3 ch f Bluegrass Prince (Ire) - Josifina
7^{10s} 7^{12gf} 5^{10gf} 3^{12gs} 6^{16gs} **0-0-5 £415**

Bayreuth *J G Given* 41
2 ch f Halling - South Shore
13^{8gs} **0-0-1**

Baytown Flyer *P S McEntee* 57 a58
4 ch f Whittingham (Ire) - The Fernhill Flyer (Ire)
2^{7sd} 2^{8sd} 10^{6sd} 1^{7sd} 1^{6sd} 1^{7sd} 2^{7sd} 1^{6g}
1^{7sd} 2^{6sd} 14^{6sd} 15^{6g} 7^{6sd} 5^{7sd} 7^{7sd} **5-4-15 £8,767**

Bazelle *P W D'Arcy* 78
2 ch f Ashkalani (Ire) - Dona Royale (Ire)
16^{6gf} 4^{7gs} 2^{8gf} 6^{8gf} **0-1-4 £1,748**

Be Bop *N Tinkler* 49
2 ch g Groom Dancer (USA) - Norpella
11^{8f} 9^{9f} 9^{8gs} **0-0-3**

Be Bop Aloha *I A Wood* 51 a43
2 b f Most Welcome - Just Julia
15^{5g} 6^{6gf} 3^{7sd} 5^{7gf} 11^{7gf} 8^{8gf} 18^{7gf}
14^{7gf} **0-1-8 £420**

Be My Alibi (Ire) *W M Brisbourne* 27 a31
3 ch f Daggers Drawn - Join The Party
7^{7s} 5^{6sd} 10^{5gf} 11^{7g} 7^{6s} **0-0-5**

Be Wise Girl *J G Given* 56 a49
3 ch f Fleetwood (Ire) - Zabelina (USA)
3^{8sd} 1^{10g} 14^{11gs} 8^{9sd} **1-1-4 £3,335**

Beach Party (Ire) *M L W Bell* a58
3 b f Danzero (Aus) - Shore Lark (USA)
3^{8sd} 9^{8sd} **0-1-2 £415**

Beacon Blue (Ire) *M Johnston* 57
3 ch f Peintre Celebre (USA) - Catch The Blues (Ire)
6^{12g} 7^{8gf} 13^{12gs} **0-0-3**

Beacon Star (USA) *M Johnston* 10

2 ch c Stravinsky (USA) - Careless Kitten (USA)
8⁵ʰʸ 12⁷ˢ **0-0-2**

Beady (Ire) *B Smart* 50
5 b g Eagle Eyed (USA) - Tales Of Wisdom
6¹⁰ᵍˢ **0-0-1**

Beamish Prince *G M Moore* 60
5 ch g Bijou D'Inde - Unconditional Love (Ire)
7¹⁰ᵍˢ 7⁸ᵍᶠ **0-0-2**

Beamsley Beacon *Ian Emmerson* 48 a42
3 ch g Wolfhound (USA) - Petindia
12¹⁰ˢ 9⁸ˢ 4⁶ᶠ 11⁷ᵍᶠ 6⁶ˢᵈ 4⁶ˢᵈ 4⁸ˢᵈ 8⁷ᵍˢ
5⁷ᶠ **0-0-9 £258**

Beat The Heat (Ire) *Jedd O'Keeffe* 86
6 b g Salse (USA) - Summer Trysting (USA)
2¹⁰ᵍ **0-1-1 £3,399**

Beau Jazz *W De Best-Turner* 37 a67
3 br c Merdon Melody - Ichor
5⁵ˢᵈ 3⁵ˢᵈ 7⁵ˢᵈ 6⁶ᵍˢ 13⁶ᵍ 14⁵ᵍ 14⁵ᵍᶠ
12⁵ˢᵈ **0-1-8 £466**

Beau Marche *I A Wood* 69
2 b g My Best Valentine - Beau Dada (Ire)
5⁶ᵍ 8⁵ᵍᶠ 13⁶ᵍˢ 2⁶ᵍᶠ 11⁸ᵍᶠ 1⁶ᵍ 7⁶ʰʸ **1-1-7**
£2,298

Beauchamp Pilot *G A Butler* 107
6 ch g Inchinor - Beauchamp Image
6⁹ᵍ 16⁸ᵍᶠ 4⁸ᵍᶠ **0-0-3 £2,625**

Beauchamp Ribbon *A J Chamberlain* 14
4 b f Vettori (Ire) - Beauchamp Kate
7¹²ᵍ 19¹²ᵍᶠ 9¹⁰ᵍᶠ **0-0-3**

Beauchamp Star *G A Butler* 74
3 ch f Pharly (Fr) - Beauchamp Cactus
9⁷ᵍˢ 3⁷ᵍˢ 2⁸ˢ 8⁹ᵍᶠ 4¹⁰ᶠ 2¹¹ᶠ **0-3-6**
£3,288

Beauchamp Trump *G A Butler* 64 a63
2 b g Pharly (Fr) - Beauchamp Kate
7⁶ˢᵈ 10⁷ᵍ 4⁷ᵍᶠ **0-0-3 £428**

Beauchamp Turbo *G A Butler* 60 a65
2 ch g Pharly (Fr) - Compton Astoria (USA)
5⁶ˢᵈ 5⁶ᵍᶠ 6⁷ˢ 13⁷ᵍˢ **0-0-4**

Beauchamp Twist *G A Butler* 56 a31
2 b f Pharly (Fr) - Beauchamp Cactus
8⁵ᵍᶠ 10⁵ᵍᶠ 12⁷ˢᵈ 6⁸ᵍᶠ 4⁷ˢ **0-0-5 £532**

Beaumont Girl (Ire) *G A Swinbank* 53
2 ch f Trans Island - Persian Danser (Ire)
7⁵ʰʸ 1⁷ᵍˢ 15⁸ᵍ 16⁷ᶠ **1-0-4 £3,255**

Beaune *W J Haggas* 75 a51
2 b c Desert Prince (Ire) - Tipsy
3⁵ᵍ 6⁶ᵍˢ 10⁶ˢᵈ **0-1-3 £766**

Beauteous (Ire) *M J Polglase* 71 a69
5 ch g Tagula (Ire) - Beauty Appeal (USA)
8⁷ˢᵈ 9⁹ˢˢ 6⁷ˢʷ 4⁷ᵍᶠ 1⁶ˢᵈ 18ˢᵈ 18ˢᵈ
1⁷ˢᵈ 4⁸ᵍ **4-0-10 £6,430**

Beautiful Maria (Ire) *P F I Cole* 33
2 b f Sri Pekan (USA) - Puteri Wentworth
7⁵ᵍ **0-0-1**

Beautiful Mover (USA) *J W Hills* 73 a72
2 ch f Spinning World (USA) - Dancer's Glamour (USA)
2⁶ᵍᶠ 3⁶ᶠ 8⁵ᵍ 4⁶ˢᵈ 18⁵ᵍᶠ **0-2-5 £2,292**

Beautiful Noise *D Morris* 67
3 b f Piccolo - Mrs Moonlight
14⁸ˢ 6⁷ᵍᶠ 5⁷ᵍᶠ 5⁷ᵍᶠ 5⁶ᵍᶠ 5⁸ᵍˢ 2⁸ᶠ
9⁸ᵍᶠ **0-1-9 £1,069**

Beauty Of Dreams *M R Channon* 63 a51
3 b f Russian Revival (USA) - Giggleswick Girl
9⁸ᵍ 10⁶ˢ 7⁷ᵍᶠ 5⁷ᵍᶠ 3⁸ᵍᶠ 12⁷ˢ 6⁷ᵍˢ 8⁸ᵍ

4⁸ᶠ 3⁸ˢ 8⁹ˢᵈ 8⁸ˢᵈ 4⁹ˢᵈ **0-2-13 £1,554**

Beauvrai *G C H Chung* 85 a47
4 b g Bahamian Bounty - Lets Be Fair
12⁶ˢᵈ 9⁵ˢᵈ 8⁶ᵍ 11⁵ᵍᶠ 5⁵ᵍᶠ 3⁶ᵍᶠ 13⁵ᵍᶠ
12⁵ᵍ 2⁶ᵍᶠ 3⁵ᶠ 1⁶ʰʸ 1⁶ᵍ 3⁵ᵍ 13⁵ˢ **2-3-14**
£14,498

Beaver Diva *W M Brisbourne* 51
3 b f Bishop Of Cashel - Beaver Skin Hunter
4¹⁰ʰʸ 7⁹ᵍ 7⁷ˢᵈ 2⁶ᵍ 2⁵ᵍ 16⁶ˢ 9⁷ᶠ 17⁶ᵍᶠ
0-2-8 £2,131

Beaver Patrol (Ire) *R F Johnson Houghton* 105
2 ch c Tagula (Ire) - Erne Project (Ire)
1⁵ᵍˢ 3⁵ᵍˢ 2⁵ᵍᶠ 1⁶ᵍᶠ 11⁶ᵍᶠ 6⁶ᵍ 2⁷ᵍ 1⁶ᵍᶠ
5⁶ᵍᶠ 5⁸ˢ **3-3-10 £134,986**

Bebopskiddly *B G Powell* 33 a36
3 b c Robellino (USA) - Adarama (Ire)
10⁸ˢᵈ 6¹¹ˢ **0-0-2**

Beckermet (Ire) *R F Fisher* 102
2 b g Second Empire (Ire) - Razida (Ire)
3⁵ᵍ 1⁵ᵍᶠ 1⁵ᵍ 2⁵ᵍᶠ 1⁵ᵍ 1⁵ᵍ 9⁵ᵍ 4⁵ˢ 11⁵ᶠ
5⁵ˢ **4-1-10 £26,782**

Bedtime Blues *J A Glover* 48
2 b f Cyrano De Bergerac - Boomerang Blade
9⁵ᵍ 8⁵ᵍˢ **0-0-2**

Bee Dees Legacy *G L Moore* 32 a52
3 b g Atraf - Bee Dee Dancer
8¹⁰ˢᵈ 10¹²ˢᵈ 9⁸ᵍᶠ 9¹²ᵍˢ **0-0-4**

Bee Minor *Ms Deborah J Evans* 75
3 b f Barathea (Ire) - Bee Off (Ire)
8⁷ᵍᶠ 2⁶ᵍᶠ 8⁷ᵍᶠ 16⁶ˢ 2⁶ᵍᶠ 4⁶ᵍˢ 7⁶ᵍˢ **0-2-7**
£3,950

Bee Stinger *I A Wood* 73
2 b c Almaty (Ire) - Nest Egg
10⁶ᵍᶠ 3⁷ᵍᶠ 2⁶ᵍᶠ 2⁷ᵍ 4⁶ᵍ **0-3-5 £2,815**

Beeches Theatre (Ire) *R Brotherton* 14
2 b f King's Theatre (Ire) - Sandpiper
11⁵ᵍᶠ 11⁵ᵍ **0-0-2**

Beechy Bank (Ire) *Mrs Mary Hambro* 72 a65
6 b m Shareef Dancer (USA) - Neptunalia
8¹³ˢᵈ 7¹³ᵍᶠ 5¹³ᵍᶠ 3¹⁶ᵍ 5¹⁶ᵍᶠ 9¹⁶ᵍ **0-0-6**
£669

Beejay *P F I Cole* 77 a56
3 b f Piccolo - Lettuce
1⁶ᵍ 20⁷ᵍ 12⁶ᵍᶠ 8⁶ᵍˢ 6⁵ᵍ 7⁶ˢᵈ 11⁶ˢᵈ **1-0-7**
£3,629

Beekeeper *D R Loder* 95
6 b h Rainbow Quest (USA) - Chief Bee
8¹⁰ᵍ **0-0-1**

Beenaboutabit *Mrs L C Jewell* 28 a3
6 b m Komaite (USA) - Tassagh Bridge (Ire)
9⁶ˢᵈ 15⁷ˢᵈ 5⁵ᶠ 16⁵ᵍ **0-0-4**

Befitting *J A Osborne* 51
2 b g Inchinor - Ellebanna
8⁵ˢ **0-0-1**

Before The Dawn *A G Newcombe* 50
2 b f Lugana Beach - Chayanee's Arena (Ire)
7⁶ᵍ 8⁶ᵍᶠ 12⁶ᵍˢ 9⁶ᵍᶠ 11⁵ᵍˢ **0-0-5**

Behan *A Crook* a34
5 ch g Rainbows For Life (Can) - With Finesse
9¹²ˢᵈ 5¹²ˢᵈ 7¹⁶ˢᵈ **0-0-3**

Belenus (Ire) *Saeed Bin Suroor* 86
2 ch c Dubai Millennium - Ajhiba (Ire)
1⁷ᵍᶠ **1-0-1 £8,443**

Belisco (USA) *C A Dwyer* 66 a67
3 b g Royal Academy (USA) - A Mean Fit (USA)

7^{10g} 7^{10g} 6^{8g} 1^{10sd} 13^{10gf} 8^{10sd} 14^{10sd}
1-0-7 £4,225

Bella Beguine *A Bailey*   54 a52
5 b m Komaite (USA) - On The Record
5^{6sd} 14^{6sd} 2^{7sd} 14^{7gf} 4^{7g} 4^{5gs} 5^{5gf} 12^{7s}
11^{5gs} **0-1-9 £1,233**

Bella Boy Zee (Ire) *P A Blockley*   63 a53
3 b f Anita's Prince - Waikiki (Ger)
3^{5sd} 2^{6ss} 5^{5sw} 1^{5gf} 8^{6f} 14^{5gs} **1-2-6**
£5,627

Bella Miranda *D R Loder*   a32
2 ch f Sinndar (Ire) - Bella Lambada
11^{7sd} **0-0-1**

Bella Pavlina *W M Brisbourne*   11 a79
6 ch m Sure Blade (USA) - Pab's Choice
1^{9sd} 2^{12sd} 1^{12sd} 1^{12sd} 4^{12ss} 1^{12sd} 5^{12sw}
1^{12ss} 17^{12g} 3^{12sd} **5-1-10 £16,575**

Bella Plunkett (Ire) *W M Brisbourne*   55 a32
2 ch f Daggers Drawn (USA) - Amazona (Ire)
12^{6g} 7^{6g} 7^{7gs} 6^{8gf} 2^{7g} 10^{6sd} **0-1-6**
£1,016

Bella Tutrice (Ire) *I A Wood*   72 a74
3 b f Woodborough (USA) - Institutrice (Ire)
15^{5gf} 36^{gf} 4^{5g} 10^{6sd} 3^{6sd} 9^{6gf} 12^{6g}
17^{6gf} 10^{6sd} 10^{6gs} **0-2-10 £1,794**

Bellalou *N A Callaghan*   48 a38
2 b f Vettori (Ire) - Spinning Mouse
8^{6gf} 7^{7gf} 3^{6gf} 11^{7sd} **0-1-4 £364**

Belle Chanson *J R Boyle*   52 a44
2 b f Kingsinger (Ire) - Tallulah Belle
7^{6s} 8^{6g} 11^{7sd} **0-0-3**

Belle Largesse *C B B Booth*   23 a23
2 b f Largesse - Palmstead Belle (Ire)
5^{5s} 13^{5gf} 12^{6sd} **0-0-3**

Belle Rouge *C A Horgan*   87 a70
6 b m Celtic Swing - Gunner's Belle
2^{12sd} 2^{14s} 1^{12gs} 2^{16g} 1^{16sd} 2^{16gf} 1^{13gs}
2^{16g} 1^{12g} 1^{12s} 3^{15s} **5-6-11 £30,009**

Bells Beach (Ire) *P Howling*   53 a59
6 b m General Monash (USA) - Clifton Beach
6^{6sd} 2^{6sd} 8^{6ss} 1^{6sd} 9^{6sd} 1^{6sd} 5^{6sd} 6^{6sd}
1^{6sd} 9^{6s} 4^{6sd} 4^{6gf} 1^{6sd} 5^{5gf} 10^{6g} 8^{7sd} 7^{6sd}
9^{6gs} **4-1-18 £10,134**

Bells Boy's *K A Ryan*   38 a43
5 b g Mind Games - Millie's Lady (Ire)
3^{5sd} 3^{6sd} 5^{6sw} 15^{6sw} 4^{6sd} 12^{6sd} 3^{5sd} 3^{6gf}
14^{6f} 14^{6gf} 15^{6f} **0-4-11 £843**

Belly Dancer (Ire) *P F I Cole*   76 a82
2 gr f Danehill Dancer (Ire) - Persian Mistress (Ire)
6^{5gf} 4^{5sd} 2^{7gs} 6^{7g} 2^{7sd} 3^{6sd} **0-3-6**
£3,580

Belshazzar (USA) *T P Tate*   69
3 b c King Of Kings (Ire) - Bayou Bidder (USA)
9^{9g} 4^{10gf} 7^{8g} 5^{8gs} 13^{11g} **0-0-5 £374**

Beltane *W De Best-Turner*   53 a51
6 b g Magic Ring (Ire) - Sally's Trust (Ire)
10^{10sd} 11^{10sd} 1^{8sd} 2^{8sd} 12^{7gf} 13^{8g} 15^{8gf}
5^{8f} 7^{8g} 9^{8g} 19^{8gs} **1-1-11 £2,303**

Belton *Ronald Thompson*   56
2 b c Lujain (USA) - Efficacious (Ire)
13^{6gf} 8^{6gf} 7^{7s} 8^{8hy} 17^{7gf} 17^{gf} **1-0-6**
£3,146

Ben Bacchus (Ire) *M H Tompkins*   36
2 b c Bahhare (USA) - Bodfaridistinction (Ire)
15^{7gs} **0-0-1**

Ben Casey *B Smart*   65
2 b c Whittingham (Ire) - Hot Ice (Ire)
18^{5gf} 6^{5g} 3^{5gf} 5^{5g} **0-2-5 £1,072**

Ben Hur *W M Brisbourne*   82
5 b g Zafonic (USA) - Gayane
18^{10gs} 1^{8gf} 13^{7g} 2^{8f} 1^{8g} 1^{10g} 5^{9gf} 4^{10g}
5^{12gf} 6^{9gs} 3^{10gs} 9^{9gs} 14^{9gs} **3-2-13 £14,403**

Ben Kenobi *Mrs P Ford*   45 a39
6 ch g Accondy (Ire) - Nour El Sahar (USA)
5^{7sd} 2^{7sd} 2^{9sd} 7^{11f} 2^{13gf} 8^{12g} 7^{12sd} **0-3-7**
£1,720

Ben Lomand *B W Duke*   59 a53
4 ch g Inchinor - Benjarong
12^{6gs} 13^{6g} 3^{6gs} 9^{7s} 9^{6gs} 10^{7s} 6^{6sd} **0-1-7**
£852

Ben's Revenge *M Wellings*   41
4 b g Emperor Jones (USA) - Bumble Boogie (Ire)
6^{12gf} 11^{11g} 5^{12gs} 6^{12sd} **0-0-4**

Benbaun (Ire) *M J Wallace*   111
3 b g Stravinsky (USA) - Escape To Victory
1^{6g} 8^{6s} 1^{5gf} 2^{5gf} 1^{5gf} 3^{5gf} 2^{5gf} **3-3-7**
£50,278

Benbyas *D Carroll*   86
7 b g Rambo Dancer (Can) - Light The Way
6^{12g} 1^{12gs} 1^{14s} 5^{10s} **2-0-4 £9,974**

Bendarshaan *M Johnston*   92
4 b c Darshaan - Calypso Run
14^{10ft} 10^{9ft} 13^{11g} 4^{12gf} 1^{12gf} 1^{15g} 2^{12gf}
9^{14g} 5^{13gs} 18^{14g} 5^{14s} 8^{12s} 3^{12s} 3^{12s} **2-3-14**
£21,327

Benedict *Sir Michael Stoute*   57
2 b c Benny The Dip (USA) - Abbey Strand (USA)
7^{6g} 8^{7g} **0-0-2**

Benedict Bay *G B Balding*   65
2 b c In The Wings - Persia (Ire)
6^{7g} 10^{7gs} 7^{7gf} 12^{8s} 12^{7gs} **0-0-5**

Beneking *R Hollinshead*   59
4 b/br g Wizard King - Gagajulu
9^{8hy} 3^{7gf} 8^{7gf} 6^{6gf} 13^{8g} 5^{10gf} 10^{10gs}
8^{10gf} 14^{10gf} 14^{12gf} **0-1-10 £552**

Beneventa *J L Dunlop*   114
4 b f Most Welcome - Dara Dee
18^{gs} 1^{9g} 2^{10gs} 8^{8gf} 1^{12g} 10^{13gs} 7^{12gf}
3-1-7 £74,800

Benjamin (Ire) *Jane Southcombe*   29 a42
6 b g Night Shift (USA) - Best Academy (USA)
2^{8sd} 2^{9sd} 11^{8gf} 14^{8gf} 15^{12g} 5^{7f}
0-2-7 £776

Bennanabaa *S C Burrough*   54 a58
5 b g Anabaa (USA) - Arc Empress Jane (Ire)
13^{10sd} 5^{8sd} 7^{7sd} 9^{8g} 12^{8sd} 11^{7gf} 8^{5f}
5^{5gf} 13^{6gf} 8^{6gs} 8^{6hy} 13^{5g} **0-0-12**

Benny Bathwick (Ire) *B R Millman*   50
3 b g Midyan (USA) - Sweet Pavlova (USA)
7^{7gf} 12^{8gs} **0-0-2**

Benny The Ball (USA) *N P Littmoden*   74 a57
3 b/br g Benny The Dip (USA) - Heloise (USA)
15^{7g} 11^{8gf} 9^{6g} 10^{7sd} 11^{9sd} **0-0-5**

Benny The Bus *Mrs G S Rees*   63
2 b g Komaite (USA) - Amy Leigh (Ire)
11^{7gf} 10^{5g} 11^{6gs} 2^{5g} **0-1-4 £1,051**

Bentley's Ball (USA) *R Hannon*   93
3 b/br g Stravinsky (USA) - Slide By
6^{6gs} 13^{8f} 8^{7gs} 3^{7gf} 4^{6gs} 4^{7gf} **0-1-6**
£4,453

Bentley's Bush (Ire) *R Hannon* 91
2 ch f Barathea (Ire) - Veiled Threat (Ire)
5⁵ᵍ 2⁶ᵍᶠ 1⁶ᵍ 3⁶ᵍ 3⁷ᵍᶠ **1-3-5 £10,652**

Benvolio *I W McInnes*
7 br g Cidrax (Fr) - Miss Capulet
11¹²ᵍᶠ **0-0-1**

Berenson (Ire) *T Stack* 114
2 b c Entrepreneur - On Air (Fr)
1⁷ᵍᶠ 2⁷ʸ **1-1-2 £49,591**

Beresford Boy *D K Ivory* 15 a59
3 b g Easycall - Devils Dirge
PU⁶ᶠ 10⁶ᵍᶠ 2⁶ˢᵈ **0-1-3 £832**

Bergamo *B Ellison* a30
8 b g Robellino (USA) - Pretty Thing
7¹⁶ˢᵈ 7¹⁴ˢˢ **0-0-2**

Berham Maldu (Ire) *M J Wallace* 24
2 b f Fraam - Corniche Quest (Ire)
15⁵ᵍ 10⁵ᵍ 11⁸ᵍ **0-0-3**

Berkeley Heights *Mrs J Candlish* 39 a46
4 b f Hector Protector (USA) - Dancing Heights (Ire)
4¹²ˢᵈ 10¹¹ˢᵈ 6¹⁴ˢˢ 2¹⁶ˢᵈ 3¹⁶ˢᵈ 4¹⁴ˢᶠ 1¹⁴ˢᵈ
9¹⁹ᵍᶠ 12¹⁶ᵍ **1-1-9 £2,059**

Berkhamsted (Ire) *J A Osborne* 99
2 b c Desert Sun - Accounting
1⁵ᵍˢ 6⁶ᵍᶠ 2⁷ᵍ 5⁷ᵍ 1⁸ʰʸ 8⁸ᵍᶠ 5⁸ˢ 6⁸ˢ **2-1-8**
£50,767

Berry Racer (Ire) *N P Littmoden* 29
3 ch f Titus Livius (Fr) - Opening Day
11⁶ᶠ **0-0-1**

Berrywhite (Ire) *C Grant* 44 a28
6 ch g Barathea (Ire) - Berryville (USA)
7¹²ˢᵈ 8¹⁰ʰʸ 3¹⁴ˢ 3¹⁶ᵍᶠ 5¹ᶠ **0-2-5 £1,056**

Bertocelli *G G Margarson* 72
3 ch c Vettori (Ire) - Dame Jude
14⁶ᵍ 14⁷ᵍᶠ 3⁷ᵍᶠ 4⁸ᵍᶠ 8⁷ᵍ 7⁸ᵍᶠ 6⁷ᵍᶠ 8⁸ᵍ
7¹⁰ᵍᶠ 10⁸ᵍ 4¹⁰ᵍᶠ 4¹⁰ᵍ **0-0-12 £1,116**

Bertrose *J L Dunlop* 78
2 ch c Machiavellian (USA) - Tularosa
4⁷ᵍ 5⁸ᵍ 3⁸ᵍ 11⁸ᵍ **0-1-4 £1,346**

Beseeka Runnin Fox *Mrs L Williamson*
3 b f Hi Nod - Windsor Fox (Ire)
7¹²ᵍᶠ **0-0-1**

Bespoke *Sir Mark Prescott* 47
2 ch g Pivotal - Immaculate
5⁶ᵍᶠ 6⁶ᵍ 9⁶ᵍᶠ 8⁸ˢ **0-0-4**

Bessemer (Jpn) *I Semple* 92
3 b g Carnegie (Ire) - Chalna (Ire)
5⁷ᵍ 3⁸ᵍᶠ 6⁷ᵍ 1¹⁰ᵍᶠ 4¹⁰ˢ 19¹⁰ˢ 3⁸ˢ 19¹²ˢ
1-0-8 £9,490

Best About *D R Loder* 57
2 ch f King's Best (USA) - Up And About
7⁷ᵍᶠ **0-0-1**

Best Be Going (Ire) *P W Harris* 85
4 b g Danehill - Bye Bold Aileen (Ire)
17¹⁰ᵍ 7¹⁰ᵍᶠ 5⁹ᵍᶠ 4¹²ᵍᶠ 14¹²ᵍ 16¹⁰ᵍᶠ 1¹⁰ᵍ
1-0-7 £7,750

Best Before (Ire) *P D Evans* 87 a66
4 b g Mujadil (USA) - Miss Margate (Ire)
7⁶ˢᵈ 7⁸ˢᵈ 1⁸ˢᵈ 2⁸ᵍ 2⁸ˢ 16⁸ᵍᶠ 2⁹ᵍᶠ 1⁸ᵍᶠ
3⁸ᵍᶠ 3⁸ᵍᶠ 3⁹ᵍᶠ 1⁸ᵍ 8⁸ᵍᶠ 9⁸ˢ 13⁹ᵍ 12⁸ʰʸ 17⁷ᵍˢ
3-6-17 £16,558

Best Desert (Ire) *J R Best* 68 a63
3 b g Desert Style (Ire) - La Alla Wa Asa (Ire)
4⁷ᵍᶠ 2⁷ᵍᶠ 14⁷ᵍᶠ 8⁸ᵍˢ 5⁷ᵍᶠ 1⁷ᶠ 5⁸ᵍˢ 12⁸ˢ
7⁶ˢ 6⁸ᵍᶠ 3⁷ˢᵈ 4⁸ˢᵈ 8⁹ˢᵈ **1-2-13 £5,214**

Best Flight *B W Hills* 69
4 gr g Sheikh Albadou - Bustling Nelly
11¹⁰ᵍˢ 15¹⁰ᵍ 4¹⁰ᵍᶠ 11¹⁶ᵍᶠ 9¹²ᵍ 9¹³ᵍˢ **0-0-6**
£425

Best Force *G A Butler* 53
3 b f Compton Place - Bestemor
4⁵ᵍ 7⁶ˢ **0-0-2 £288**

Best Game *G A Butler* 58
2 b g Mister Baileys - Bestemor
12⁸ᵍ 7⁷ˢ 6⁸ˢ 14⁸ˢ **0-0-4**

Best Lead *Ian Emmerson* 61 a71
5 b g Distant Relative - Bestemor
1⁵ˢᵈ 9⁵ˢᵈ 4⁶ˢᵈ 4⁵ˢˢ 3⁵ˢᵈ 4⁵ᵍ 3⁵ᵍᶠ 3⁵ᵍ
3⁵ᵍᶠ 3⁶ˢ 8⁶ᵍ **1-5-11 £5,190**

Best Port (Ire) *J Parkes* 71 a57
8 b g Be My Guest (USA) - Portree
10¹⁴ᵍ 1¹⁴ᵍ 11¹⁶ˢᵈ 1¹⁴ᵍᶠ 6¹⁶ˢ 1¹⁶ᶠ 9¹⁴ᵍᶠ
4¹⁴ᶠ 3¹⁴ᵍᶠ 5¹⁸ᵍ 2¹⁷ˢᵈ **3-2-11 £12,838**

Bestbyfar (Ire) *J G Given* 56
2 b c King's Best (USA) - Pippas Song
7⁷ˢ **0-0-1**

Bestseller *J G M O'Shea* a51
4 ch f Selkirk (USA) - Top Shop
4¹²ˢᵈ 3¹²ˢᵈ 5¹²ˢʷ **0-0-3 £775**

Betfred *A Berry*
3 b g Pursuit Of Love - Shamaka
8⁹ᵍᶠ **0-0-1**

Bethanys Boy (Ire) *B Ellison* 43
3 ch g Docksider (USA) - Daymoon (USA)
14¹⁰ᵍ 10⁸ᵍ 8⁸ᵍ **0-0-3**

Bettalatethannever (Ire) *S Dow* 103 a98
3 ch g Titus Livius (Fr) - Shambodia (Ire)
1⁷ˢᵈ 4⁷ˢᵈ 20⁷ʸ 12⁷ᵍ 2⁸ᵍ 8⁸ˢᵈ 7⁷ᵍᶠ 8⁷ᵍᶠ
1⁷ᵍ **2-0-9 £26,383**

Better Off *Mrs N Macauley* a47
6 ch g Bettergeton - Miami Pride
5⁷ˢᵈ 8⁷ˢᵈ 6⁷ˢˢ 13⁹ˢᵈ 5⁸ˢᵈ **0-0-5**

Better Pal *P R Wood*
5 ch g Prince Sabo - Rattle Along
14⁸ˢᵈ **0-0-1**

Betterthedeviluno *D McCain*
5 b g Hector Protector (USA) - Aquaglow
12⁸ˢᵈ **0-0-1**

Betterware Boy *P M Phelan* 51 a59
4 ch g Barathea (Ire) - Crystal Drop
7¹⁶ˢᵈ 11¹²ᵍᶠ **0-0-2**

Betty Stogs (Ire) *C G Cox* 75
3 b f Perugino (USA) - Marabela (Ire)
9⁸ˢ 5⁸ˢ 14⁷ᵍ 16⁷ᵍ **0-0-4**

Bettys Pride *M Dods* 62
5 b m Lion Cavern (USA) - Final Verdict (Ire)
9⁵ᵍᶠ 4⁵ᶠ 12⁵ᵍᶠ 6⁵ᶠ 6⁶ᵍ 13⁵ᵍᶠ 1⁵ᵍᶠ 7⁵ᵍᶠ
6⁵ᵍᶠ 1⁵ᵍᶠ 12⁵ᵍᶠ **2-0-11 £6,889**

Bettys Valentine *D W Barker* 30
4 b f My Best Valentine - Fairy Ballerina
4¹¹ˢʷ 10⁸ʰʸ 8⁸ᵍ 12⁷ᵍᶠ 9⁵ᵍᶠ 13⁶ˢ **0-0-6**

Beverley Beau *Mrs L Stubbs* 66 a54
2 b g Inchinor - Oriel Girl
5⁵ᵍᶠ 5⁵ᵍ 4⁵ᵍᶠ 4⁶ᵍᶠ 4⁵ᵍᶠ 5⁵ᵍᶠ 6⁵ˢᵈ **0-0-7**
£583

Bevier *T Wall* 15 a52
10 b g Nashwan (USA) - Bevel (USA)
5⁹ˢᵈ 3¹²ˢʷ 4⁹ˢʷ 8¹²ᵍˢ 4¹²ˢᵈ 7⁹ˢᵈ
12¹⁰ˢ 15⁹ᶠ **0-2-9 £654**

Beyond Calculation (USA) *J M Bradley* 61

10 ch g Geiger Counter (USA) - Placer Queen
18⁵ᵍ 16⁵ᵍ 7⁵ᵍᶠ 10⁵ᶠ 4⁶ᵍ 7⁶ˢ 4⁶ᵍ 4⁶ᵍ
5⁵ᵍᶠ 11⁶ᶠ 8⁶ᵍ **0-1-11 £270**

Beyond The Clouds (Ire) *J S Wainwright*   83
8 b g Midhish - Tongabezi (Ire)
12⁵ᵍᶠ 12⁵ᵍ 12⁵ᵍᶠ 2⁵ᵍˢ 9⁵ᵍˢ 9⁵ᵍˢ 3⁵ᵍ 7⁵ᵍˢ
15⁵ᵍᶠ 6⁵ᵍˢ 2⁵ᵍᶠ 7⁵ᵍˢ 10⁵ᵍᶠ 17⁵ᵍ **0-3-14**
£5,603

Beyond The Pole (USA) *B R Johnson*   a64
6 b g Ghazi (USA) - North Of Sunset (USA)
1¹³ˢᵈ 12¹²ˢᵈ 1¹²ˢᵈ **2-0-3 £5,929**

Bhutan (Ire) *G B Balding*   51
9 b g Polish Patriot (USA) - Bustinetta
10¹²ᵍᶠ 2¹⁰ᵍᶠ 8¹²ᵍᶠ **0-1-3 £870**

Bi Polar *D R C Elsworth*   81
4 b g Polar Falcon (USA) - Doctor Bid (USA)
23⁶ᵍ 19⁷ᵍ 2⁷ᵍᶠ 2⁷ᵍᶠ 13⁷ᵍ 3⁷ˢ 6⁷ᵍᶠ 3⁷ᵍ
0-4-8 £4,459

Bibi Helen *N A Callaghan*   57
2 b f Robellino (USA) - Tarry
6⁶ᵍᶠ 11⁷ᵍᶠ 11⁸ˢ **0-0-3 £188**

Bibury Flyer *J Noseda*   96
2 br f Zafonic (USA) - Affair Of State (Ire)
2⁵ˢ 2⁵ʰʸ 3⁵ᵍᶠ 3⁵ᶠ 5⁵ᵍ 2⁵ᵍᶠ 2⁵ᵍˢ 6⁵ᵍ 1⁵ᵍᶠ
2⁶ᵍᶠ 9⁶ᶠ 7⁶ᵍˢ 3⁵ˢ 3⁵ˢ 3⁷ᵍ 2⁷ᵍᶠ 4⁷ᵍ 5⁷ᵍʸ 8⁶ˢ **3-6-22**
£90,865

Bid For Fame (USA) *C G Cox*   59 a82
7 b/br g Quest For Fame - Shroud (USA)
15¹⁶ᵍˢ 13¹⁶ᵍ 14¹⁴ᵍˢ 10¹⁴ᶠ 8¹⁶ˢ 7¹⁷ˢᵈ
0-0-6

Bid Spotter (Ire) *Mrs Lucinda Featherstone*   a35
5 b g Eagle Eyed (USA) - Bebe Auction (Ire)
4¹²ˢˢ 13¹⁴ˢᵈ 13¹¹ᶠ **0-0-3**

Bien Good *K G Reveley*   43
3 b f Bien Bien (USA) - Southern Sky
3¹⁴ᵍᶠ 5⁹ˢ 20¹⁶ᵍ 8¹⁰ˢ **0-0-4 £413**

Bienheureux *Miss Gay Kelleway*   51 a41
3 b g Bien Bien (USA) - Rochea
9⁸ˢᵈ 8⁸ˢᵈ 13⁷ˢᵈ 11⁸ᶠ 2¹²ᵍᶠ 1¹²ᵍᶠ 5¹⁶ᵍᶠ
1-1-7 £4,144

Bienvenue *M P Tregoning*   78
3 ch f Bien Bien (USA) - Mossy Rose
4¹⁰ᵍᶠ 1¹²ᵍᶠ 2¹²ᵍˢ 6¹⁴ᵍᶠ 8¹²ᵍᶠ 6¹²ᵍ **1-1-6**
£5,488

Big Bad Bob (Ire) *J L Dunlop*   118
4 br c Bob Back (USA) - Fantasy Girl (Ire)
3¹⁰ᵍᶠ 4¹⁰ᵍˢ 5¹⁰ᵍᶠ 1¹⁰ᵍᶠ **1-1-4 £20,041**

Big Bad Burt *G C H Chung*   69 a68
3 ch g Efisio - Mountain Bluebird (USA)
4⁸ˢᵈ 2⁷ˢᵈ 2⁶ˢᵈ 3⁷ˢᵈ 7⁸ʰʸ 3⁸ᵍ 4⁷ᵍᶠ 6⁸ᵍᶠ
9⁸ˢᵈ 9¹⁰ᵍ 4¹⁰ᵍᶠ 7¹²ˢ 4¹⁰ᵍˢ **0-4-13 £3,072**

Big Bambo (Ire) *Mrs P N Dutfield*   21
2 ch c Monashee Mountain (USA) - Bamboo (Ire)
8⁵ᵍˢ 17⁶ᵍᶠ **0-0-2**

Big Bertha *John Berry*   74 a73
6 ch m Dancing Spree (USA) - Bertrade
4¹³ˢᵈ 2¹³ˢᵈ 8¹²ˢᵈ 15¹⁰ᵍᶠ 4¹²ˢ **0-1-5**
£1,648

Big Bradford *P G Murphy*   93 a82
3 b g Tamure (Ire) - Heather Honey
2⁶ᵍᶠ 12⁶ᵍᶠ 16⁶ᵍ 12⁷ᵍˢ 6⁷ˢᵈ 14⁶ᵍᶠ 18⁶ᵍˢ
0-1-7 £8,000

Big Hassle (Ire) *T D Easterby*   87
2 b c Namid - Night After Night
5⁵ᵍ 2⁵ᵍ 1⁵ᵍˢ 9⁶ˢ **1-1-4 £5,243**

Big Hoo Hah *C A Cyzer*   65
2 ch f Halling (USA) - Gentilesse
16⁷ᵍᶠ 8⁷ᵍ 8⁷ˢᵈ 7⁸ᵍ **0-0-4 £274**

Big Hurry (USA) *R Charlton*   47
3 b f Red Ransom (USA) - Call Me Fleet (USA)
11⁹ᵍᶠ **0-0-1**

Big Moment *Mrs A J Perrett*   104
6 ch g Be My Guest (USA) - Petralona (USA)
3¹⁹ᵍˢ 5²²ᶠ 6¹⁴ᵍ 2¹⁴ˢ 2¹²ˢ 1¹²ˢ **1-3-6**
£44,805

Big Mystery (Ire) *J R Best*   a23
3 b f Grand Lodge (USA) - Mysterious Plans (Ire)
9⁵ˢᵈ **0-0-1**

Big Smoke (Ire) *J Howard Johnson*   53 a60
4 gr g Perugino (USA) - Lightning Bug
11⁸ᵍᶠ 4¹¹ˢᵈ 5¹²ˢᵈ 3¹²ᵍᶠ **0-0-4 £436**

Big Tom (Ire) *D Carroll*   62 a6
3 ch c Cadeaux Genereux - Zilayah (USA)
5⁸ʸˢ 9⁶ʸ 16⁶ʸ 9⁸ᵍ 11⁵ˢᶠ 10⁵ᵍˢ 19⁶ᵍ
16⁸ᵍˢ **0-0-8**

Bigalos Bandit *J J Quinn*   95
2 ch c Compton Place - Move Darling
1⁵ˢ 2⁵ᵍˢ 4⁵ᵍᶠ 4⁵ᵍ 3⁵ˢ 3⁵ᵍˢ 15⁶ᵍ 1⁵ᵍˢ
2-2-9 £23,459

Bijan (Ire) *R Hollinshead*   a42
6 b m Mukaddamah (USA) - Alkariyh (USA)
8⁶ˢᵈ 4⁷ˢᵈ 9⁷ˢᵈ **0-0-3**

Bijou Dan *I Semple*   56
3 ch g Bijou D'Inde - Cal Norma's Lady (Ire)
4⁸ᵍᶠ 6¹⁰ᵍᶠ 7⁹ˢ 5¹⁰ˢ 9¹²ˢ **0-0-5 £539**

Bijou Dancer *M R Bosley*   52 a35
4 ch g Bijou D'Inde - Dancing Diana
12⁸ᵍ 7⁸ᵍᶠ 6⁷ˢᵈ 17¹⁰ᵍˢ **0-0-4**

Bill Bennett (Fr) *J Jay*   86 a61
3 b g Bishop Of Cashel - Concert
6¹⁰ˢᵈ 9⁹ˢᵈ 6¹²ˢᵈ 5¹²ᵍ 1¹¹ᵍˢ 1¹³ˢ 2¹⁴ˢ 5¹²ᵍᶠ
7¹⁴ᵍˢ 1¹²ᵍˢ 4¹²ᵍˢ 8¹⁴ᵍ 3¹⁶ˢ 7¹⁶ˢ **3-2-14**
£15,520

Billy Bathwick (Ire) *J M Bradley*   63 a48
7 ch g Fayruz - Cut It Fine (USA)
9¹⁰ᵍᶠ 8¹⁰ᶠ 3¹⁰ᵍᶠ 3¹⁰ᵍᶠ 1¹⁰ᶠ 7¹⁰ᵍ 5¹⁰ᵍ 8⁹ᵍᶠ
12¹¹ᵍ 7¹⁰ᵍˢ 14¹²ˢᵈ 17¹²ᵍˢ **1-2-12 £5,083**

Billy One Punch *P W Chapple-Hyam*   68
2 b c Mark Of Esteem (Ire) - Polytess (Ire)
7⁷ˢ **0-0-1**

Billy Two Rivers (Ire) *D R MacLeod*   19
5 ch g Woodborough (USA) - Good Visibility (Ire)
5¹⁶ᵍ **0-0-1**

Billy Whistler *J Balding*
3 ch c Dancing Spree (USA) - Polar Refrain
12⁸ˢ **0-0-1**

Binanti *P R Chamings*   91 a83
4 b g Bin Ajwaad (Ire) - Princess Rosananti (Ire)
13⁸ᵍᶠ 6⁷ᵍᶠ 6⁷ᵍᶠ 9⁸ˢᵈ 17⁷ᵍᶠ 5⁷ᵍˢ 5⁷ˢᵈ 3⁷ᵍ
7⁸ᵍ **0-1-9 £1,919**

Binary Vision (USA) *J H M Gosden*   105
3 ch c Distant View (USA) - Binary
1⁸ᵍᶠ 6⁸ᵍᶠ **1-0-2 £6,943**

Binnion Bay (Ire) *R Hannon*   61
3 b g Fasliyev (USA) - Literary
8⁶ᵍ 11⁸ᵍ 9⁸ᵍ 6⁷ᵍᶠ 7⁸ᵍᶠ **0-0-5**

Bint Il Sultan (Ire) *E A L Dunlop*   60 a50
2 b f Xaar - Knight's Place (Ire)
3⁶ᵍ 7⁷ᵍᶠ 12⁶ᵍᶠ 8⁷ˢᵈ **0-0-4 £718**

Bint Royal (Ire) *Miss V Haigh*   67 a71

6 ch m Royal Abjar (USA) - Living Legend (USA)
5^{6sd} 5^{6gf} 12^{7gf} 3^{6gf} 4^{7f} 7^{6gf} 4^{6gf} 3^{7gf}
8^{6gf} 9^{7f} 5^{7gs} 8^{8g} 8^{8g} 19^{7gf} 2^{7gf} 1^{7f} 13^{7gf}
1^{7f} 5^{6gf} 5^{6g} **2-2-20 £10,996**

Binty *J L Spearing* 44
2 b f Prince Sabo - Mistral's Dancer
10^{6s} 11^{6s} **0-0-2**

Birchall (Ire) *Ian Williams* 58
5 b g Priolo (USA) - Ballycuirke
7^{12hy} 14^{12y} 2^{8hy} 7^{10gf} 14^{10g} **0-1-5**
£1,020

Bird Key *R Guest* 25
3 b f Cadeaux Genereux - Portelet
8^{6gf} **0-0-1**

Bird Over *R M Beckett* a58
2 b f Bold Edge - High Bird (Ire)
4^{7sd} 1^{7sd} **1-0-2 £1,477**

Birdstone (USA) *N Zito* a125
3 b c Grindstone - Dear Birdie (USA)
1^{8ft} 5^{9ft} 8^{10sy} 1^{12ft} 1^{10ft} 7^{10ft} **3-0-6**
£690,838

Birikina *A Berry* a22
3 b f Atraf - Fizzy Fiona
6^{6sd} 7^{6sd} **0-0-2**

Biriyani (Ire) *P W Harris* 74
2 b f Danehill (USA) - Breyani
4^{6g} **0-0-1 £403**

Birth Of The Blues *A Charlton* 45 a45
8 ch g Efisio - Great Steps
8^{10sd} 8^{13sd} 6^{12sw} 3^{12sd} 1^{13sd} 4^{12sd} 6^{12gf}
6^{12gf} **1-1-8 £1,658**

Birthday Star (Ire) *W J Musson* 49
2 b c Desert King (Ire) - White Paper (Ire)
14^{6gf} **0-0-1**

Birthday Suit (Ire) *T D Easterby* 90
3 ch f Daylami (Ire) - Wanton
3^{6g} 3^{8gs} **0-0-2 £4,923**

Birthstone *H-A Pantall* 104
2 ch f Machiavellian (USA) - Baya (USA)
1^{8vs} 1^{8g} **2-0-2 £36,619**

Biscar Two (Ire) *B J Llewellyn* 58 a40
3 b g Daggers Drawn (USA) - Thoughtful Kate
4^{8sd} 6^{11sd} 2^{8s} 2^{8gs} 8^{10gf} 1^{10g} 9^{10gs}
1-3-8 £5,986

Bish Bash Bosh (Ire) *M F Harris* a27
3 b f Bien Bien (USA) - Eurolink Virago
9^{6sd} 8^{7sd} **0-0-2**

Bishop To Actress *M J Polglase*
3 ch f Paris House - Chess Mistress (USA)
13^{6sd} 15^{5ss} **0-0-2**

Bishopric *H Candy* 100
4 b g Bishop Of Cashel - Nisha
19^{10gs} 1^{8g} 14^{8g} 10^{10s} **1-0-4 £10,010**

Bishops Bounce *T A K Cuthbert* 28
3 b g Bishop Of Cashel - Heights Of Love
14^{8g} 8^{6f} **0-0-2**

Bishops Court *Mrs J R Ramsden* 116
10 ch g Clantime - Indigo
1^{5g} 2^{5hy} 7^{5gs} 3^{5g} 3^{5gs} 7^{5g} 10^{5gf} 2^{5g}
5^{5s} 6^{5g} 5^{5gf} 8^{5s} 7^{5s} 6^{5s} **1-4-14 £38,486**

Bishopstone Man *H Candy* 73
7 b g Piccolo - Auntie Gladys
18^{8gs} 7^{8gs} 4^{8gf} 8^{8f} 6^{8g} 2^{7gf} **0-1-6**
£1,743

Bla Shak (Ire) *M P Tregoning*

2 b c Alhaarth (Ire) - Really Gifted (Ire)
PU^{6g} **0-0-1**

Black Combe Lady (Ire) *A Berry* 2
2 br f Indian Danehill (Ire) - Florinda (Can)
12^{5f} 7^{6gf} 7^{7g} 13^{7gf} 11^{7sd} **0-0-5**

Black Draft *Jean-Rene Auvray* 63
2 b/br g Josr Algarhoud (Ire) - Tilia
9^{5g} 8^{5gf} **0-0-2**

Black Falcon (Ire) *Ian Williams* a71
4 ch g In The Wings - Muwasim (USA)
10^{17sd} **0-0-1**

Black Legend (Ire) *R Lee* 42 a43
5 b g Marju (Ire) - Lamping
2^{10gs} 4^{14sd} 9^{10s} 5^{12g} 6^{13gs-} **0-2-5 £774**

Black Oval *S Dow* 56 a60
3 b f Royal Applause - Corniche Quest (Ire)
4^{7sd} 4^{5g} 5^{5g} 11^{6g} 3^{5s} 8^{6gf} 12^{7g} 5^{5f} 8^{6g}
8^{6gf} 11^{6gf} 9^{5g} **0-1-12 £683**

Black Sabbeth *Miss A Stokell* 68 a17
3 br g Desert Story (Ire) - Black Orchid (Ire)
11^{8hy} 11^{7gf} 10^{7gf} 6^{6f} 4^{5gf} 18^{6gf} 13^{6gs}
11^{7sd} **0-0-8 £257**

Black Swan (Ire) *G A Ham* 43
4 b g Nashwan (USA) - Sea Spray (Ire)
13^{12gf} 5^{14f} 8^{18gs} 13^{16gf} **0-0-4**

Black Velvet *M P Tregoning* 100
2 br g Inchinor - Three Owls (Ire)
1^{5g} 2^{6g} 8^{7g} **1-1-3 £10,147**

Blackburn Meadows *P R Wood*
7 b m Flying Tyke - Hatshepsut
12^{7s} **0-0-1**

Blackchurch Mist (Ire) *B W Duke* 38
7 b m Erin's Isle - Diandra
11^{22f} **0-0-1**

Blackcomb Mountain (USA) *M F Harris* 61 a67
2 b/br f Royal Anthem (USA) - Ski Racer (Fr)
5^{7g} 3^{7gs} 4^{7sd} 9^{7s} 3^{8gf} 6^{8f} 6^{9gs}
0-1-8 £1,843

Blackheath (Ire) *D Nicholls* 96
8 ch g Common Grounds - Queen Caroline (USA)
14^{6g} 4^{5gs} 4^{6g} 13^{6gf} 6^{6g} 2^{6gf} 2^{6g} 6^{5gs}
4^{5gs} 5^{6gf} 5^{5g} 23^{6gf} 12^{5g} 13^{5g} 26^{6s}
1-2-16 £29,949

Blackmail (USA) *Miss B Sanders* 23 a72
6 b g Twining (USA) - Black Penny (USA)
13^{7sd} 14^{12g} 10^{8sd} 5^{12sd} **0-0-4**

Blacknyello Bonnet (USA) *M Johnston* 43
2 b/br f Seeking The Gold (USA) - Salt It (USA)
9^{6gs} 8^{7gf} 8^{7s} **0-0-3**

Blackpool Jack *F P Murtagh*
3 b g Mtoto - Endearing Val
11^{7f} 11^{9gs} 11^{7s} **0-0-3**

Blackthorn *Mrs J R Ramsden* 67
5 ch g Deploy - Balliasta (USA)
4^{12g} 12^{14s} 3^{12gf} 3^{12g} 6^{16f} **0-3-5 £1,410**

Blade Of Gold (Ire) *J A Osborne* 48
2 ch f Daggers Drawn (USA) - Be Prepared (Ire)
10^{6gf} **0-0-1**

Blade Runner (Ire) *D Haydn Jones* 19
2 ch f Daggers Drawn (USA) - Leitrim Lodge (Ire)
10^{5gs} 14^{6gs} 13^{6g} **0-0-3**

Blade's Daughter *K A Ryan* 25 a19
3 gr f Paris House - Banningham Blade
6^{6s} 11^{6sd} 7^{5g} **0-0-4**

Blade's Edge *A Bailey* 64 a51

3 b c Daggers Drawn (USA) - Hayhurst
12⁷ˢᵈ 5⁶ˢᵈ 3⁶ᵍ 9⁵ᵍ 8⁷ᵍ 18⁶ᵍ 12⁸ᵍ 12⁷ᵍᶠ
18⁶ᶠ 10⁷ᶠ 3⁷ˢ **0-2-11 £1,048**

Blades Boy K A Ryan 61
2 ch g Paris House - Banningham Blade
8⁶ᵍˢ 9⁶ᵍᶠ 1⁵ᵍᶠ **1-0-3 £3,386**

Blaeberry P L Gilligan 69
3 b f Kirkwall - Top Berry
11⁸ᵍ 7¹⁰ᵍ 5⁸ᶠ 5⁸ᶠ 4¹⁰ᵍᶠ 1⁷ᵍᶠ 5⁷ᵍᶠ 1⁷ᵍᶠ
2⁸ᶠ 10⁷ᵍᶠ 12⁸ᵍᶠ **2-1-11 £8,876**

Blaina D R C Elsworth 76
4 ch f Compton Place - Miss Silca Key
5⁸ᵍᶠ 8⁷ᵍᶠ **0-0-2**

Blaise Castle (USA) G A Butler 95
4 b f Irish River (Fr) - Castellina (USA)
4⁷ˢ 2⁷ᵍᶠ 11⁶ᵍ 3⁸ˢ 12⁷ˢ **0-2-5 £9,188**

Blaise Hollow (USA) R Charlton 83
2 b g Woodman (USA) - Castellina (USA)
8⁶ᵍ 5⁷ᵍ 18ᵍᶠ 5⁸ᵍ **1-0-4 £3,484**

Blaise Wood (USA) G L Moore 61 a16
3 b g Woodman (USA) - Castellina (USA)
10⁸ᵍ 6¹⁰ᵍ 8⁷ᶠ 2⁸ᶠ 11⁶ᵍᶠ 7⁷ᶠ 11¹⁰ˢᵈ **0-1-7
£732**

Blake Hall Lad (Ire) Miss J Feilden 61 a52
3 b g Cape Cross (Ire) - Queen Of Art (Ire)
9⁷ᵍˢ 14⁷ˢ 5⁷ˢ 1⁸ᵍ 6⁸ˢᵈ 13⁸ˢ **1-0-6
£2,679**

Blakeset T D Barron a84
9 ch g Midyan (USA) - Penset
1⁷ˢᵈ 16⁷ˢᵈ 16ˢᵈ 1⁷ˢˢ 2⁶ˢᵈ 37ˢᵈ 11⁷ˢˢ 5⁶ˢˢ
36ˢᵈ 2⁶ˢᵈ **3-4-10 £12,305**

Blakeseven W J Musson 47 a56
4 b g Forzando - Up And Going (Fr)
3⁸ˢᵈ 2⁷ˢᵈ 2⁸ˢᵈ 3⁷ˢᵈ 7⁷ᵍ 7⁷ᵍ 6⁸ᵍˢ
0-4-8 £2,626

Blakeshall Girl J L Spearing a9
4 ch f Piccolo - Giggleswick Girl
12⁶ˢᵈ 8⁸ˢˢ **0-0-2**

Blakeshall Hope P D Evans 57 a38
2 ch g Piccolo - Elite Hope (USA)
3⁶ᵍᶠ 8⁶ˢᵈ 7⁵ᵍᶠ 4⁵ᵍᶠ **0-0-4 £815**

Blakeshall Quest R Brotherton 56 a77
4 b f Piccolo - Corniche Quest (Ire)
9⁶ˢʷ 4⁶ˢᵈ 4⁶ˢᵈ 4⁶ˢᵈ 5⁷ˢʷ 1⁵ˢˢ 9⁵ᵍˢ 1⁶ˢᵈ
14⁶ˢ 8⁶ˢᵈ 18⁶ᵍ 10⁶ˢᵈ 7⁶ˢᵈ **2-0-13 £7,448**

Blatant Saeed Bin Suroor 72 a96
5 ch h Machiavellian (USA) - Negligent
8⁸ᶠ 5⁹ᶠ 6¹⁰ᶠ 11⁸ᵍᶠ **0-0-4**

Blau Grau (Ger) N E Berry 14
7 gr g Neshad (USA) - Belle Orfana (Ger)
15¹⁷ᵍ 10¹⁰ᵍ **0-0-2**

Blaze Of Colour Sir Michael Stoute 83
3 ch f Rainbow Quest (USA) - Hawait Al Barr
3¹⁰ʰʸ 4¹²ᵍᶠ 2¹²ᵍˢ 3¹²ᵍ 1¹²ᵍᶠ 4¹²ᶠ 2¹²ᵍ
4¹²ᵍˢ **1-3-8 £12,453**

Blaze The Trail Jean-Rene Auvray 21
3 b f Classic Cliche (Ire) - Explorer
11⁸ᵍˢ 6¹²ᵍᶠ 14¹⁰ᵍᶠ 10¹⁰ˢ **0-0-4**

Blazing Saddles (Ire) Mrs J Candlish a25
5 b g Sadler's Wells (USA) - Dalawara (Ire)
6¹⁴ˢᵈ **0-0-1**

Blazing The Trail (Ire) J W Hills 74 a68
4 ch g Indian Ridge - Divine Pursuit
4¹⁰ˢᵈ 8¹⁰ˢᵈ 2¹⁰ˢᵈ 5¹⁰ˢᵈ 11⁰ˢᵈ 3¹⁰ᵍˢ 2¹⁰ˢ
3¹⁰ᵍᶠ 10¹⁰ᵍᶠ 6¹⁰ᵍᶠ 6¹¹ᵍ 11¹⁰ᵍˢ 4¹⁰ᵍ **1-5-13**

£7,657

Blazing View (USA) E A L Dunlop 63
2 b f Bahri (USA) - Dixie Eyes Blazing (USA)
5⁶ᵍᶠ 9⁶ᵍᶠ 13⁶ᵍ **0-0-3**

Blessed Place D J S Ffrench Davis 59 a40
4 ch g Compton Place - Cathedra
8⁵ˢᵈ 11⁵ˢˢ 13⁶ˢᵈ 12⁵ˢ 8⁵ˢᵈ 16⁸ᶠ 3⁵ᶠ
3⁶ᵍᶠ 5⁵ᵍ 4⁵ᶠ 1⁵ᵍˢ 5⁵ᵍᶠ 12⁵ᵍ 7⁵ᵍᶠ 6⁶ᵍᶠ 9⁵ˢᵈ
1-3-16 £4,663

Blessingindisguise M W Easterby 39
11 b g Kala Shikari - Blowing Bubbles
9⁶ᵍᶠ 8⁵ᵍ 17⁵ᵍ **0-0-3**

Blissphilly R A Fahey 31
2 b f Primo Dominie - Majalis
9⁵ᵍᶠ 6⁶ᵍᶠ 11⁷ᵍᶠ **0-0-3**

Blofeld W Jarvis a75
3 b g Royal Applause - Bliss (Ire)
1⁶ˢᵈ 6⁶ˢᵈ **1-0-2 £8,027**

Blonde En Blonde (Ire) N P Littmoden 57 a74
4 ch f Hamas (Ire) - Hulm (Ire)
6⁷ˢᵈ 6⁷ˢᵈ 8⁷ˢᵈ 1⁷ˢᵈ 2⁷ˢᵈ 13⁷ˢᵈ 36ˢᵈ 3⁷ˢᵈ
10⁸ˢᵈ 12⁶ᵍᶠ 3⁷ᵍ 9⁶ᵍ 5⁷ᶠ 6⁷ᶠ 7⁷ˢᵈ 12⁸ˢᵈ 3⁷ˢᵈ
1-5-17 £6,003

Blonde Streak (USA) T D Barron 86 a79
4 ch f Dumaani (USA) - Katiba (USA)
4⁸ᵍᶠ 4⁸ᵍᶠ 7⁸ᵍ 1⁸ᵍˢ 6⁸ˢ 8⁹ᵍ 6⁹ˢᵈ **1-0-7
£7,284**

Blood Money N A Callaghan 13
2 b g Dracula (Aus) - Guinea
17⁷ᵍˢ **0-0-1**

Bloom Of Tara (Ire) S J Mahon 48 a10
6 ch m Midhish - No Diplomacy (Ire)
10¹⁶ʸ 5¹⁰ᵍᶠ 7⁸ʸˢ 5⁷ᶠ 9⁸ʸ 11¹⁰ᵍ 1⁶ˢᵈ
10⁷ˢᵈ **1-0-8 £4,622**

Blue Azure (USA) G A Butler a69
2 b/br f American Chance (USA) - Kibitzing (USA)
5⁷ˢᵈ **0-0-1**

Blue Bajan (Ire) Andrew Turnell 66
2 b g Montjeu (Ire) - Gentle Thoughts
6⁸ᵍᶠ 7⁷ᵍˢ **0-0-2**

Blue Bijou T T Clement
4 b g Bijou D'Inde - Jucea
12⁷ˢˢ 5¹¹ˢʷ 10⁸ᵍ **0-0-3**

Blue Canari (Fr) P Bary 118
3 ch c Acatenango (Ger) - Delicieuse Lady
3¹¹ᵍˢ 4¹¹ᵍˢ 3¹²ᵍ 1¹²ᵍˢ 5¹²ˢ 12¹²ᵍ **1-0-6
£460,029**

Blue Circle M Mullineaux
4 b c Whittingham (Ire) - Reshift
11⁶ˢᵈ 9⁶ˢᵈ **0-0-2**

Blue Crush (Ire) K R Burke 90
3 ch f Entrepreneur - Prosaic Star (Ire)
7⁵ʸ 9⁶ᵍᶠ 13⁵ᵍᶠ 10⁵ᵍᶠ 10⁵ˢ 10⁵ᵍᶠ 6⁵ᵍᶠ
7⁵ᵍ **0-0-8 £226**

Blue Dakota (Ire) J Noseda 106
2 b c Namid - Touraya
1⁵ᵍ 1⁵ˢ 1⁵ᵍᶠ 1⁵ᵍᶠ 6⁶ᵍᶠ **4-0-5 £56,880**

Blue Daze Edward Lynam 70
3 b f Danzero (Aus) - Sparkling
14⁷ᵍ 12⁷ᵍᶠ 5⁸ᵍᶠ 5⁸ᵍ 5⁸ᵍ 11⁷ᵍᶠ 7⁹ˢ 7⁷ˢ
6⁷ᵍˢ **0-0-9**

Blue Dream (Ire) T Hogan 100
4 b f Cadeaux Genereux - Hawait Al Barr
10⁷ᵍᶠ 2⁶ᵍᶠ 5⁸ᵍᶠ 4⁷ˢ 2⁶ᵍ 8⁷ᵍᶠ 13⁶ʸˢ
0-3-8 £15,317

Blue Emperor (Ire) *P T Midgley* 39 a15
3 b g Groom Dancer (USA) - Bague Bleue (Ire)
14⁶ss 7⁶gs 5⁷sd 7⁷sd 11⁶f 11⁸g 12⁸g
0-0-7

Blue Empire (Ire) *P A Blockley* 60 a79
3 b g Second Empire (Ire) - Paleria (USA)
4⁸sd 5⁷sd 7⁷sd 4¹⁰sd 2⁸sd 6⁷ss 15⁹g 8⁸gf
1-1-8 £5,052

Blue Hedges *H J Collingridge* 62 a68
2 b c Polish Precedent (USA) - Palagene
13⁷sd 10⁸s 4⁸sd **0-0-3 £321**

Blue Hills *P W Hiatt* 56
3 b g Vettori (Ire) - Slow Jazz (USA)
11¹²gs 5¹²g 11¹⁴gs 11¹¹⁶gs 16¹⁴gs **0-0-5**

Blue Java *H Morrison* 63 a64
3 ch g Bluegrass Prince (Ire) - Java Bay
9⁷gf 8⁷gf 12⁹g 2⁷g 5⁸sd 2⁸sd 8⁹sd **0-2-7**
£2,162

Blue Kandora (Ire) *M A Jarvis* 70
2 b c Cape Cross (Ire) - Party Dress
4⁵gs 7⁷gf **0-0-2 £373**

Blue Knight (Ire) *P Howling* 80 a81
5 ch g Bluebird (USA) - Fer De Lance (Ire)
2⁵sd 4⁶sw 7⁶sd 6⁵s 2⁵gf 11⁶g 4⁶gf 12⁶sd
8⁷sd 10⁷sd **0-2-10 £3,484**

Blue Leader (Ire) *G Brown* a
5 b g Cadeaux Genereux - Blue Duster (USA)
15¹²sd **0-0-1**

Blue Line *M Madgwick* 59
2 gr f Bluegrass Prince (Ire) - Out Line
17⁵gf 5⁵f 8⁷f **0-0-3**

Blue Maeve *J Hetherton* 73 a34
4 b g Blue Ocean (USA) - Louisville Belle (Ire)
4⁷sd 11⁸ss 4⁷ss 13⁸ss 8⁵gf 4⁵gf 2⁵s 4⁵gs
2⁵gf 1⁵gf 5⁵gs 12⁵s 15⁶gf 1⁵f 3⁵gf 11⁵g
2-3-16 £12,471

Blue Marble *C E Brittain* 73
2 b g Fraam - Fizzy Fiona
4⁵g 6⁶g 16⁶gf 1⁵g 7⁵g 9⁶gf **1-0-6**
£4,198

Blue Mariner *W R Swinburn* 74 a69
4 b g Marju (Ire) - Mazarine Blue
9⁸g 3⁷f 2¹⁰gf 2¹⁰g 14⁹gf 9⁸gf 15⁸gf 1⁹sd
1-3-8 £7,723

Blue Moon Hitman (Ire) *R Brotherton* 62
3 ch g Blue Ocean (USA) - Miss Kookaburra (Ire)
3⁵f 7⁶gf 3⁵gf 3⁵gf 8⁵gf 13⁶gs 12⁵sd **0-1-7**
£1,410

Blue Nun *Mrs A Duffield* 34
3 b f Bishop Of Cashel - Matisse
5¹⁰hy 8⁹g 10⁸gf 5¹⁰gf 8⁹gs 9⁷gs 14⁸f
0-0-7

Blue Oasis (Ire) *R Guest* 95
3 b f Sadler's Wells (USA) - Humble Eight (USA)
1⁸g 5⁹g 2¹⁰s 13⁹gs 9¹⁰g 5¹⁰s 10¹⁰s **1-1-7**
£14,398

Blue Opal *Miss S E Hall* 63
2 b f Bold Edge - Second Affair (Ire)
3⁷s **0-1-1 £727**

Blue Otis (Ire) *Mrs H Sweeting* a
2 ch f Docksider (USA) - Minstrel's Gift
12⁷sd **0-0-1**

Blue Patrick *K A Ryan* 84 a68
4 gr g Wizard King - Great Intent
10¹²sd 11¹⁰gs 14⁸gf 2⁶gf 11⁶gf 6⁷gf 5⁷s

12⁸g 5⁸s 8⁷g **0-1-10 £1,320**

Blue Power (Ire) *K R Burke* 69 a69
3 b c Zieten (USA) - La Miserable (USA)
10⁵sd 9⁵sd 3⁵sd 5⁵s 3⁵f 1⁵sd 8⁵g 2⁵s
16⁵s 2⁵sf 12⁵gs 13⁵s **1-3-12 £7,196**

Blue Prince (USA) *R Charlton* 69
2 ch c Dixieland Band (USA) - Tussle (USA)
2⁷gs **0-1-1 £1,524**

Blue Quiver (Ire) *C A Horgan* 50 a61
4 b g Bluebird (USA) - Paradise Forum
6¹⁰sd 2⁸sd 9⁷g 15¹⁰s 11⁸g **0-1-5 £866**

Blue Rondo (Ire) *Ian Williams* a10
4 b g Hernando (Fr) - Blueberry Walk
7¹³sd **0-0-1**

Blue Savanna *J G Portman* 49 a51
4 ch g Bluegrass Prince (Ire) - Dusk In Daytona
6¹⁶sd 4⁸ss 2¹⁰sd 1¹²sd 12¹²gs 5¹²gf 6¹²sd
4¹²gs 4¹²gf 2¹²f 6¹²sd **1-2-11 £4,502**

Blue Sky Thinking (Ire) *K R Burke* 100 a108
5 b g Danehill Dancer (Ire) - Lauretta Blue (Ire)
1¹⁰sd 5¹⁰sd 6¹⁰sd 13⁸g 3¹⁰gf 4⁸gs 6⁸s 2⁸gs
7¹⁰gf **1-2-9 £23,138**

Blue Spectrum (Ire) *J S Moore* 52
2 b g Spectrum (Ire) - Storm River (USA)
12⁷g 9⁸gf 10⁷gf 14⁸gf **0-0-4**

Blue Spinnaker (Ire) *M W Easterby* 114
5 b g Bluebird (USA) - Suedoise
7⁸g 1⁸g 4⁸gs 1¹⁰gf 10¹⁰g 4¹⁰s 6⁸f 3¹⁰gs
4⁹g **2-3-9 £65,915**

Blue Streak (Ire) *G L Moore* 44 a24
7 ch g Bluebird (USA) - Fleet Amour (USA)
10¹⁰sd 5¹²f 5¹¹g **0-0-3**

Blue Tomato *P F I Cole* 67
3 b c Orpen (USA) - Ocean Grove (Ire)
9⁷g **0-0-1**

Blue Torpedo (USA) *Mrs A J Perrett* 54 a83
2 ch c Rahy (USA) - Societe Royale
8⁷gs 1⁷sd **1-0-2 £4,251**

Blue Track (Ire) *M J Attwater* 35
3 b c Woodborough (USA) - Aryaah
8¹⁰gf 7¹²gf 8¹⁰sd **0-0-3**

Blue Train (Ire) *Sir Michael Stoute* 69
2 b c Sadler's Wells (USA) - Igreja (Arg)
4⁸g **0-0-1 £416**

Blue Trojan (Ire) *S Kirk* 98 a77
4 b g Inzar (USA) - Roman Heights (Ire)
2¹⁰sd 2¹⁰gf 7⁸s 15⁸gf 18⁸gf 4⁸gf 12⁹g
15⁷f 4⁸g 2⁷g 11⁸g 7⁷gs 8⁸gs 2⁷g 1⁸gf 8⁹g
2-5-16 £32,468

Blue Venture (Ire) *P C Haslam* 49 a35
4 ch g Alhaarth (Ire) - September Tide (Ire)
8⁸ss 9¹⁰hy 9⁸f 4¹²gf 13¹²gf 14¹⁷g 3¹²gf
0-1-7 £430

Blue Viking (Ire) *J R Weymes* 6 a44
3 b g Danetime (Ire) - Jenny Spinner (Ire)
8¹⁰gf 5⁸sd 10¹²sd 11⁹sd **0-0-4**

Blue Water *M Mullineaux* a
4 b f Shaamit (Ire) - November Song
10¹²sw **0-0-1**

Blueberry Jim *T H Caldwell* 35
3 ch g First Trump - Short And Sharp
8¹⁰g 11⁸g **0-0-2**

Blueberry Rhyme *P A Blockley* 64 a71
5 b g Alhijaz - Irenic
2⁵sw 2⁵sd 1⁵ss 8⁵ss 1⁵ss 5⁶gs 8⁵gf 14⁵gf

20⁶ᵍ 1⁵ᵍˢ 10⁶ˢᵈ **3-2-11 £15,165**

Blueberry Tart (Ire) *B J Meehan* 76 a54
2 b f Bluebird (USA) - Tart (Fr)
5⁶ᵍˢ 4⁷ˢ 10⁷ᵍ 7⁷ˢᵈ **0-0-4 £423**

Bluebok *D R Loder* 67 a61
3 ch c Indian Ridge - Blue Sirocco
2⁷ᵍˢ 3⁶ᵍᶠ 7⁷ˢᵈ **0-2-3 £1,945**

Bluefield (Ire) *R F Johnson Houghton* 56
3 b c Second Empire (Ire) - Imco Reverie (Ire)
4⁸ᵍ **0-0-1 £318**

Bluegrass Boy *G B Balding* 70
4 b g Bluegrass Prince (Ire) - Honey Mill
3¹⁰ᵍ 11¹⁰ᵍᶠ 8¹⁰ᵍᶠ 8¹¹ᵍᶠ 3¹⁰ᵍᶠ 1¹⁰ᵍᶠ 7¹⁰ᵍᶠ
5¹⁰ᵍˢ 14¹⁰ᵍ **1-2-9 £5,252**

Blues And Royals (USA) *Saeed Bin Suroor* 96
2 b c Honour And Glory (USA) - Dixieland Blues (USA)
1⁶ᵍᶠ 2⁷ᵍ 4⁷ᵍᶠ **1-1-3 £9,246**

Blues Over (Ire) *W J Musson* a1
3 b f Sri Pekan (USA) - Crystal Blue (Ire)
8¹⁰ˢᵈ **0-0-1**

Blues Princess *R A Fahey* 37
4 b f Bluebird (USA) - Queen Shirley (Ire)
13⁵ᵍᶠ 14⁵ᵍ 12⁵ᵍ 14⁶ᶠ **0-0-4**

Bluetoria *J A Glover* 72
3 b f Vettori (Ire) - Blue Birds Fly
4⁸ᵍᶠ 7⁸ᵍᶠ 5¹⁰ᵍᶠ 13¹⁰ᵍᶠ **0-0-4 £375**

Blunham *M C Chapman* 51 a39
4 b g Danzig Connection (USA) - Relatively Sharp
4⁵ˢᵈ 5⁶ˢᵈ 9⁶ˢᵈ 14⁷ᵍ 6⁷ᵍ 2⁸ᵍ 17⁷ᵍᶠ 16⁸ᵍˢ
16⁷ᵍ **0-1-9 £1,302**

Blushing Prince (Ire) *Mrs L Stubbs* a35
6 b g Priolo (USA) - Eliade (Ire)
5⁹ˢˢ **0-0-1**

Blushing Russian (Ire) *P C Haslam* 58
2 b g Fasliyev (USA) - Ange Rouge
8⁶ᵍᶠ 9⁵ᵍ 3⁷ᶠ 12⁸ᵍˢ **0-1-4 £539**

Blythe Knight (Ire) *E A L Dunlop* 110
4 ch c Selkirk (USA) - Blushing Barada (USA)
4¹⁰ᵍˢ 1¹⁰ˢ 4¹⁰ᵍ 6¹⁰ᵍ 3¹⁰ᶠ 15¹⁰ᵍ 13¹⁰ᵍ
8¹⁰ˢ 6⁹ᵍ 5¹⁰ʰʸ **1-3-10 £27,989**

Blythe Spirit *R A Fahey* 78 a88
5 b g Bahamian Bounty - Lithe Spirit (Ire)
5⁶ᵍᶠ 13⁶ᵍᶠ 9⁶ᵍ 12⁶ᵍᶠ 6⁷ᵍᶠ 6⁷ᵍᶠ 1⁶ᵍᶠ 1⁶ˢᵈ
1⁶ˢᵈ 3⁶ˢᵈ **3-1-10 £13,855**

Bo McGinty (Ire) *R A Fahey* 92
3 ch g Fayruz - Georges Park Lady (Ire)
7⁶ˢ 1⁶ᵍˢ 2⁶ᵍᶠ 7⁶ᵍᶠ 8⁶ᵍᶠ 4⁶ᵍᶠ 5⁵ᵍ 1⁵ᵍ 5⁶ˢ
2-1-9 £22,720

Boanerges (Ire) *J M Bradley* 67
7 br g Caerleon (USA) - Sea Siren
18⁵ᵍˢ 5⁵ʰʸ 6⁵ᵍᶠ 5⁷ᵍᶠ 5⁷ᵍᶠ 12⁵ᵍˢ 5⁵ᵍ
11⁵ᶠ 15⁵ᵍˢ 15⁶ᵍᶠ VOI⁵ᵍᶠ 10⁵ˢ 9⁶ᵍ **0-1-14**
£1,064

Boavista (Ire) *P D Evans* 68 a66
4 b f Fayruz - Florissa (Fr)
9⁶ˢᵈ 3⁷ˢˢ 2⁶ˢᵈ 4⁷ˢᵈ 5⁷ˢᵈ 3⁶ˢᵈ 4⁶ᵍˢ 4⁵ᵍˢ
2⁶ˢᵈ 2⁵ᵍᶠ 1⁶ᶠ 10⁵ᵍᶠ 9⁶ᵍᶠ 8⁶ᵍᶠ 2⁶ᵍ 2⁵ᵍ 8⁵ᵍᶠ
3⁵ᵍᶠ 5⁵ᵍᶠ 6⁵ᵍᶠ **1-9-20 £12,227**

Bob Baileys *P R Chamings* 38 a63
2 b g Mister Baileys - Bob's Princess
4⁶ˢᵈ 10⁷ᵍˢ **0-0-2 £273**

Bob's Buzz *S C Williams* 74 a76
4 ch g Zilzal (USA) - Aethra (USA)
11⁶ᵍˢ 5⁶ᶠ 3⁷ᵍ 5⁷ᵍᶠ 2⁷ˢᵈ 14⁷ᵍᶠ 5⁷ᵍᶠ 2⁶ˢᵈ
6⁶ˢᵈ 2⁷ᵍ 7⁶ˢᵈ **0-4-11 £4,832**

Bob's Flyer *J G M O'Shea* 64 a64
2 br f Lujain (USA) - Gymcrak Flyer
15⁶ᵍˢ 4⁵ᵍˢ 8⁵ᶠ 2⁵ᵍ 4⁵ᵍᶠ 4⁵ᵍᶠ 1⁵ˢᵈ **1-1-7**
£4,746

Bobbie Love *M R Channon* 58
2 ch g Fraam - Enlisted (Ire)
6⁷ᵍᶠ 8⁷ᵍᶠ **0-0-2**

Bobby Charles *Dr J D Scargill* 64
3 ch g Polish Precedent (USA) - Dina Line (USA)
9⁸ᵍˢ **0-0-1**

Bobering *B P J Baugh* 7 a32
4 b g Bob's Return (Ire) - Ring The Rafters
9⁹ᵍ 9⁷ˢᵈ **0-0-2**

Bobsleigh *Mrs A J Perrett* 78
5 b g Robellino (USA) - Do Run Run
6¹⁸ᵍ 13¹⁶ᵍˢ 4¹⁵ᵍ 6²¹ᵍ 3¹⁴ᵍᶠ **0-1-5**
£1,430

Bodden Bay *C A Dwyer* 48 a51
2 b g Cayman Kai (Ire) - Badger Bay (Ire)
9⁸ᶠ 8⁷ᶠ 10⁶ᵍᶠ 13⁶ˢᵈ **0-0-4**

Bodfari Dream *M Mullineaux* 23
3 ch f Environment Friend - Al Reet (Ire)
11⁸ʰʸ 7¹⁰ᵍˢ **0-0-2**

Bodhi Tree (USA) *J H M Gosden* a61
2 b f Southern Halo (USA) - Dharma (USA)
3⁷ˢᵈ **0-1-1 £652**

Bogaz (Ire) *P A Blockley* 60 a59
2 b c Rossini (USA) - Fastnet
2⁵ˢ 8⁵ᵍᶠ 7⁶ˢᵈ 14⁶ᵍᶠ 9⁵ˢᵈ **0-0-5 £1,296**

Bohola Flyer (Ire) *R Hannon* 81 a67
3 b f Barathea (Ire) - Sharp Catch (Ire)
1⁶ˢᵈ 4⁶ᵍˢ 6⁶ˢ 4⁶ˢ 1⁶ᶠ 1⁶ᵍᶠ 4⁶ᵍ 5⁶ᵍ 2⁶ᵍᶠ
11⁶ᵍᶠ 5⁵ᵍ 6⁶ᵍᶠ **3-2-12 £17,736**

Boing Boing (Ire) *Miss S J Wilton* 51
4 b g King's Theatre (Ire) - Limerick Princess (Ire)
15⁷ᵍᶠ 6¹³ᵍ 5¹¹ᵍ **0-0-3**

Boisdale (Ire) *S L Keightley* 51 a54
6 b g Common Grounds - Alstomeria
6⁶ˢᵈ 1⁶ˢᵈ 5⁶ˢᵈ 19⁵ᵍ 1⁶ˢᵈ 3⁶ᵍᶠ 3⁷ˢ
5⁵ˢ 11⁶ˢᵈ **2-1-10 £5,106**

Bojangles (Ire) *R Brotherton* 63 a50
5 b g Danehill (USA) - Itching (Ire)
7¹²ˢʷ 8¹¹ˢ 18ᵍˢ 38ʰʸ 10⁸ᶠ 3⁸ᵍᶠ 4⁸ˢᵈ 5⁹ᵍᶠ
3¹³ᵍ 4¹²ᵍᶠ 1¹⁰ᵍˢ 2¹⁰ˢ 5¹⁶ᵍᶠ 1¹¹ᵍˢ 5¹²ᵍ 10¹⁷ˢᵈ
3-5-16 £11,264

Bold Blade *M J Polglase* 71 a72
3 b g Sure Blade (USA) - Golden Ciel (USA)
2⁹ˢᵈ 5⁸ˢᵈ 16⁷ᵍˢ 14⁸ᵍˢ 1¹²ˢᵈ 8¹²ᵍ 10⁸ˢᵈ
2¹⁶ᵍᶠ 4¹²ˢ 9¹⁴ᵍᶠ 9¹⁶ᵍˢ 7¹⁴ᵍᶠ 6¹⁴ᶠ 18¹⁴ᵍ **1-2-14**
£5,185

Bold Bunny *S C Williams* 56
3 b f Piccolo - Bold And Beautiful
3⁶ᶠ 3⁶ᵍᶠ 7⁶ˢ **0-2-3 £1,099**

Bold Counsel (Ire) *B J Meehan* 66 a61
2 b c Titus Livius (Fr) - Daisy Dobson
5⁷ᶠ 2⁷ᶠ 6⁷ˢᵈ 1⁸ᵍᶠ **1-1-4 £2,600**

Bold Diktator *W R Muir* 53 a63
2 b c Diktat - Madam Bold
10⁷ᵍ 6⁷ᵍᶠ 6⁷ˢᵈ **0-0-3**

Bold Eagle (Ire) *Sir Michael Stoute* 57
2 ch c Rainbow Quest (USA) - Britannia (Ger)
12⁸ˢ **0-0-1**

Bold Effort (Fr) *K O Cunningham-Brown*
12 b g Bold Arrangement - Malham Tarn
9⁷ˢᵈ 10⁶ˢʷ **0-0-2**

Bold Haze *Miss S E Hall*　　60
2 ch g Bold Edge - Melody Park
3^{6s} 16^{6gf} 4^{7s} **0-1-3 £772**

Bold Maggie *G L Moore*　　50
2 ch f Bold Edge - Vera's First (Ire)
6^{5gf} **0-0-1**

Bold Marc (Ire) *K R Burke*　　86 a80
2 b g Bold Fact (USA) - Zara's Birthday (Ire)
4^{5gs} 1^{5gf} 2^{5g} 1^{5gf} 11^{5gf} 6^{6gf} 4^{5gf} 6^{6g}
3^{6sd} 5^{6sd} **2-2-10 £10,078**

Bold Minstrel (Ire) *M Quinn*　　83 a84
2 br c Bold Fact (USA) - Ponda Rosa (Ire)
7^{5gf} 3^{5f} 2^{5gf} 1^{5g} 2^{5gf} 4^{5g} 2^{6gs} 5^{6gf} 5^{5gf}
6^{5g} 2^{5sd} **1-3-11 £9,182**

Bold Phoenix (Ire) *B J Curley*　　65
3 b c Dr Fong (USA) - Subya
10^{8gf} 8^{10gf} 6^{10gf} 8^{8s} 10^{8gs} 16^{10hy} **0-0-6**

Bold Pursuit (Ire) *Mrs A Duffield*　　45
2 br c Bold Fact (USA) - Lyphard Belle
13^{7gs} **0-0-1**

Bold Ridge (Ire) *B G Powell*　　41 a36
4 b g Indian Ridge - Cutting Ground (Ire)
10^{8g} 8^{6gf} 11^{10f} 6^{9sd} **0-0-4**

Bold Trump *Jean-Rene Auvray*　　42 a49
3 b g First Trump - Blue Nile (Ire)
4^{7sd} 12^{6s} 15^{7gs} 10^{6f} **0-0-4**

Bold Wolf *J L Spearing*　　50 a52
3 b g Wolfhound (USA) - Rambold
4^{6sd} 4^{7s} 4^{6sd} 14^{6gf} 18^{6gf} 9^{6gf} 8^{6gf} 4^{6sw}
10^{7sd} 7^{6s} **0-0-10 £287**

Boldini (USA) *Mrs Stef Liddiard*　　a43
3 ch g Atticus (USA) - Bold Bold (Ire)
8^{7vs} 3^{11g} 7^{9sd} **0-1-3 £2,324**

Boleyn Castle (USA) *P S McEntee*　　90
7 ch g River Special (USA) - Dance Skirt (Can)
10^{5gf} 28^{6f} 7^{5gf} 4^{6gf} 9^{6gs} 10^{5gf} 6^{6g}
11^{5g} **0-0-8 £968**

Bollin Annabel *T D Easterby*　　55
3 b f King's Theatre (Ire) - Bollin Magdalene
2^{12gs} 5^{10hy} 10^{12gf} 4^{14f} 9^{14g} 12^{16gs} **0-1-6**
£1,664

Bollin Archie *T D Easterby*　　55
3 b c First Trump - Bollin Joanne
5^{6g} 11^{6gs} 4^{6hy} **0-0-3 £432**

Bollin Edward *T D Easterby*　　71
5 b g Timeless Times (USA) - Bollin Harriet
6^{6gf} 5^{6gf} 3^{7f} 2^{6g} 7^{6gf} 2^{7gf} 7^{7f} 2^{6gs}
11^{7gf} 4^{7s} **0-5-10 £5,082**

Bollin Janet *T D Easterby*　　57
4 b f Sheikh Albadou - Bollin Emily
11^{6s} 15^{6g} 10^{5gf} 12^{6g} 9^{5g} **0-0-5**

Bollin Ruth *T D Easterby*　　38
2 gr f Silver Patriarch (Ire) - Bollin Roberta
8^{7f} **0-0-1**

Bollin Thomas *T D Easterby*
6 b g Alhijaz - Bollin Magdalene
7^{14s} **0-0-1**

Bolodenka (Ire) *W J Musson*　　76 a73
2 b c Soviet Star (USA) - My-Lorraine (Ire)
8^{6gs} 2^{6sd} 3^{6s} **0-2-3 £2,079**

Bolshevik (Ire) *T D Easterby*　　31
3 b g Fasliyev (USA) - Cheviot Amble (Ire)
11^{6hy} 10^{8f} 11^{7gf} **0-0-3**

Bolshoi Ballet *J Mackie*　　45
6 b g Dancing Spree (USA) - Broom Isle
11^{14g} 6^{15g} **0-0-2**

Bolton Hall (Ire) *R A Fahey*　　83
2 b g Imperial Ballet (Ire) - Muneera (USA)
1^{5gf} 6^{7f} 5^{6g} 6^{6gs} 5^{7g} 11^{5gf} 7^{6g} **1-0-7**
£12,269

Bon Nuit (Ire) *G Wragg*　　81
2 b f Night Shift (USA) - Pray (Ire)
1^{6gf} **1-0-1 £4,751**

Bond Babe *B Smart*　　69 a45
2 b f Forzando - Lindfield Belle (Ire)
4^{5gf} 2^{5f} 3^{5gs} 3^{5gs} 5^{5f} 8^{6sd} **0-2-6**
£2,770

Bond Boy *B Smart*　　98 a97
7 b g Piccolo - Arabellajill
4^{6sd} 7^{6sd} 8^{5s} 4^{6ss} 7^{5g} 6^{5gs} 8^{6g} 3^{5gs} 8^{6g}
11^{6s} 10^{6s} 4^{5g} 14^{6s} 8^{5gs} 4^{5s} 4^{5gs} **0-2-16**
£7,117

Bond Cat (Ire) *B Smart*　　53
2 ch f Raise A Grand (Ire) - Merrily
4^{7s} 6^{8gs} **0-0-2**

Bond City (Ire) *B Smart*　　95 a94
2 b g Trans Island - Where's Charlotte
8^{6gf} 1^{5g} 3^{5gf} 3^{5g} 5^{5s} 5^{5gs} 10^{6gf}
1^{5s} 2^{5gs} 1^{5sd} **3-3-11 £34,196**

Bond Domingo *B Smart*　　a36
5 b g Mind Games - Antonia's Folly
11^{6sw} 12^{5ss} 3^{5sd} 6^{6sd} 4^{5sd} **0-1-5 £205**

Bond Finesse (Ire) *B Smart*　　55 a52
2 b f Danehill Dancer (Ire) - Funny Cut (Ire)
4^{5g} 4^{5hy} 7^{6sd} 4^{7g} 3^{6sd} **0-1-5 £552**

Bond May Day *B Smart*　　70
4 b f Among Men (USA) - State Romance
18^{10g} 7^{12f} 4^{13gf} 4^{10gs} 8^{10f} 13^{12f} **0-0-6**
£290

Bond Millennium *B Smart*　　71 a69
6 ch g Piccolo - Farmer's Pet
10^{8sd} 11^{10g} 2^{8gf} 8^{8gf} 15^{10g} 4^{9sd} 7^{9sd}
0-1-7 £1,084

Bond Moonlight *B Smart*　　12 a65
3 ch g Danehill Dancer (Ire) - Interregnum
2^{8sd} 2^{12sw} 3^{8ss} 2^{12ss} 9^{10s} 8^{10s} **0-4-6**
£3,470

Bond Playboy *B Smart*　　74 a91
4 b g Piccolo - Highest Ever (Fr)
5^{6sd} 6^{5sd} 7^{6ss} 6^{6ss} 10^{5s} 16^{6s} 8^{6s} 17^{7f}
14^{7g} 3^{7gs} 1^{6gs} 1^{6gs} 19^{6s} 3^{7s} **2-2-14 £9,095**

Bond Puccini *B Smart*　　63
2 b g Piccolo - Baileys By Name
7^{5gs} 2^{5gs} 7^{5g} 15^{6gf} **0-1-4 £1,252**

Bond Romeo (Ire) *B Smart*　　37 a43
3 ch g Titus Livius (Fr) - At Amal (Ire)
9^{5gs} 5^{5s} 8^{5sd} **0-0-3**

Bond Royale *B Smart*　　a83
4 ch f Piccolo - Passiflora
2^{6sd} 13^{6sd} 8^{6sw} **0-1-3 £1,245**

Bond Shakira *B Smart*　　54 a42
3 ch f Daggers Drawn (USA) - Cinnamon Lady
3^{5s} 14^{6gs} 4^{5g} 8^{5sd} 16^{5g} 4^{5sd} 5^{6sd} 11^{5s}
0-2-8 £826

Bonecrusher *D R Loder*　　114 a105
5 b g Revoque (Ire) - Eurolink Mischief
6^{9gf} 4^{10sd} 8^{8s} 5^{10gs} 2^{10s} 9^{12gs} 5^{10f} 5^{10gs}
3^{10g} 6^{11g} 4^{10gf} 3^{11s} 9^{9s} 3^{10s} **0-2-14**
£25,005

Bonfire *M Johnston*   65
2 b c Machiavellian (USA) - Forest Express (Aus)
4⁷ᵍᶠ 7⁷ᵍˢ **0-0-2 £575**

Bongoali *M R Channon*   67
2 b f Fraam - Stride Home
4⁷ᵍᶠ 5⁷ᶠ 2⁸ʰʸ 5⁸ᶠ 17⁸ᵍ 8¹⁰ᵍᶠ 16⁸ˢ **0-1-7
£1,274**

Bonjour Bond (Ire) *B Smart*   50 a26
3 ro g Portrait Gallery (Ire) - Musical Essence
4⁸ˢᵈ 7¹⁰ᵍˢ 11¹³ˢ 3¹⁰ʰʸ 11¹²ᵍᶠ 3¹⁰ᵍ 10⁸ᵍˢ
5¹²ᵍᶠ 8⁸ᵍˢ 5¹⁴ᶠ **0-0-10 £904**

Bonnabee (Ire) *C F Wall*   52 a42
2 b f Benny The Dip (USA) - Samhat Mtoto
11⁷ᵍ 7⁷ˢᵈ 6⁸ᵍᶠ **0-0-3**

Bonne De Fleur *B Smart*   98
3 b f Whittingham (Ire) - L'Estable Fleurie (Ire)
1⁶ᵍ 10⁶ᵍᶠ 13⁶ᵍ 5⁶ᵍᶠ 7⁵ˢ 9⁶ᵍ **1-0-6
£18,302**

Bonnetts (Ire) *H Candy*   53
3 ch f Night Shift (USA) - Brief Lullaby (Ire)
11⁷ᵍᶠ 17⁸ᵍ 8⁷ᵍˢ 10⁸ᵍˢ **0-0-4**

Bonsai (Ire) *R T Phillips*   65
3 b f Woodman (USA) - Karakia (Ire)
7⁸ᵍᶠ 9¹⁰ᵍˢ 10⁹ᵍᶠ 14⁸ᵍˢ 18⁸ᵍ **0-0-5**

Bontadini *D Morris*   42 a54
5 b g Emarati (USA) - Kintail
5¹⁰ˢᵈ 11¹⁰ˢᵈ 7⁹ˢˢ 3¹⁰ᶠ 7¹⁰ᶠ 17¹⁰ᵍ **0-0-6
£366**

Bonus (Ire) *W J Haggas*   97
4 b g Cadeaux Genereux - Khamseh
6⁶ᵍ 11⁶ᵍˢ 9⁶ᵍᶠ 9⁶ᵍᶠ 5⁵ᵍᶠ 6⁶ᵍ **0-0-6 £827**

Bonus Points (Ire) *B J Meehan*   56 a59
3 b c Ali-Royal (Ire) - Asta Madera (Ire)
9⁸ˢᵈ 6¹⁰ˢᵈ 10¹⁰ˢᵈ 3¹⁰ᵍᶠ **0-1-4 £543**

Boo *K R Burke*   74
2 b g Namaqualand (USA) - Violet (Ire)
4⁶ˢ 6⁶ᵍᶠ 4⁸ˢ 9⁷ᵍˢ **0-0-4 £837**

Boogie Magic *G A Huffer*   58 a37
4 b f Wizard King - Dalby Dancer
10⁷ᶠ 2¹¹ᶠ 3¹²ᵍˢ 13¹⁰ᵍᶠ 4¹²ˢᵈ **0-1-5
£1,580**

Boogie Street *R Hannon*   115
3 b c Compton Place - Tart And A Half
3⁵ᵍ 2⁶ᵍᶠ 1⁵ᵍᶠ 6⁵ᵍᶠ 4⁵ᵍˢ 2⁵ᵍᶠ 10⁵ᵍ **1-3-7
£45,100**

Book Matched *B Smart*   43 a74
3 b g Efisio - Princess Latifa
3⁸ˢˢ 1⁸ˢʷ 4⁸ˢˢ 18⁸ᵍ 6⁸ˢᵈ 10⁹ᵍ 1⁸ˢᵈ 3⁸ˢᵈ
19⁸ᵍˢ 14⁷ᵍ **2-2-10 £7,854**

Bookiesindexdotcom *J R Jenkins*   29 a54
3 b f Great Dane (Ire) - Fifth Emerald
9⁷ˢˢ 3⁷ˢˢ 7⁶ˢᵈ 6⁶ˢˢ 6⁷ˢᵈ 8⁸ˢ 5⁷ˢᵈ 5⁶ˢᵈ
6⁷ᶠ 12⁷ᵍˢ **0-0-10 £519**

Boom Or Bust (Ire) *Miss K M George*   a40
5 ch g Entrepreneur - Classic Affair (USA)
8¹⁰ˢᵈ 7¹²ˢᵈ 13¹⁰ˢᵈ **0-0-3**

Boot 'n Toot *C A Cyzer*   84
3 b f Mtoto - Raspberry Sauce
9¹⁰ᵍˢ 1¹⁰ᵍᶠ 9¹⁰ᵍ 6¹⁰ᵍˢ **1-0-4 £4,701**

Boozy Douz *H S Howe*   23 a12
4 ch f Abou Zouz (USA) - Ackcontent (USA)
8⁹ˢ 6⁷ˢᵈ 8¹⁰ᵍᶠ **0-0-3**

Boppys Babe *R A Fahey*   6
3 ch f Clan Of Roses - Joara (Fr)
11¹⁰ᵍˢ 13⁷ᵍˢ **0-0-2**

Boppys Dream *R A Fahey*   29
2 ch f Clan Of Roses - Laurel Queen (Ire)
6⁵ᵍᶠ 11⁵ᵍᶠ 5⁶ᵍ **0-0-3**

Boppys Princess *R A Fahey*   75 a63
3 b f Wizard King - Laurel Queen (Ire)
1⁸ᵍˢ 2⁸ᵍᶠ 1⁸ʰʸ 1⁸ˢ 5⁸ᵍᶠ 1⁹ˢᵈ 1⁸ʰʸ **5-1-7
£19,940**

Boracay Beauty *J R Weymes*   16
2 b f Tipsy Creek (USA) - Grandads Dream
10⁵ˢ 9⁵ᵍ 11⁶ᶠ 8⁵ᵍᶠ **0-0-4**

Boracay Dream (Ire) *P W Chapple-Hyam*   50
2 ch c Grand Lodge (USA) - Mild Intrigue (USA)
8⁷ᵍˢ **0-0-1**

Border Artist *K G Reveley*   71
5 ch g Selkirk (USA) - Aunt Tate
11⁶ᵍˢ 11⁸ᵍˢ 1⁷ᵍᶠ 7⁸ᶠ 9⁸ᵍᶠ 4⁷ᶠ 3⁷ᵍ 4⁸ᵍ
5⁷ᵍᶠ 5⁶ᵍᶠ **1-1-10 £5,560**

Border Castle *Sir Michael Stoute*   95
3 b c Grand Lodge (USA) - Tempting Prospect
1¹⁰ᵍˢ 7¹⁰ᵍᶠ **1-0-2 £15,428**

Border Edge *J J Bridger*   75 a79
6 b g Beveled (USA) - Seymour Ann
11⁷ˢᵈ 10⁷ˢᵈ 10⁸ᵍˢ 9⁸ᵍ 16⁷ᵍ 8⁷ᵍ 9¹⁰ᵍ
0-0-7

Border Music *A M Balding*   84 a83
3 b g Selkirk (USA) - Mara River
7⁷ˢᵈ 8⁸ᵍ 3⁸ᵍ 2⁸ᵍ 2⁸ᵍ 3¹⁰ᵍ 4⁸ᵍᶠ 8⁸ᵍˢ **0-5-8
£7,322**

Border Saint *M L W Bell*   79 a66
3 b g Selkirk (USA) - Caramba
3¹²ˢᵈ 7¹²ˢᵈ 14¹²ᵍˢ **0-1-4 £1,048**

Border Subject *R Charlton*   95
7 b g Selkirk (USA) - Topicality (USA)
6⁶ᵍ 9⁵ᵍᶠ 15⁶ᵍᶠ **0-0-3 £312**

Border Tale *N A Twiston-Davies*   a88
4 b g Selkirk (USA) - Likely Story (Ire)
8¹²ˢᵈ 1¹²ˢˢ 7¹²ˢʷ **1-0-3 £2,877**

Border Terrier (Ire) *M D Hammond*   43
6 b g Balnibarbi - Ring Side (Ire)
16¹⁰ʰʸ 8¹²ᵍᶠ 9¹¹ᵍˢ 3¹¹ᵍ 12¹²ᵍᶠ 4¹¹ᵍ 4¹⁴ᵍᶠ
12¹²ᵍ **0-1-8 £732**

Borderlescott *R Bastiman*   67
2 b c Compton Place - Jeewan
6⁵ᵍᶠ 10⁵ᵍ 3⁵ᵍˢ 1⁶ᵍᶠ **1-1-4 £5,826**

Boris The Spider *M D Hammond*   50
3 b g Makbul - Try Vickers (USA)
2⁶ʰʸ 9⁶ᵍ 8⁶ᶠ 5⁷ᵍᶠ 5⁸ᵍ 4⁸ᵍˢ 6¹⁰ᵍˢ 1¹³ˢ
1-1-8 £3,194

Born For Dancing (Ire) *B W Hills*   72
2 b f Fasliyev (USA) - Fancy Boots (Ire)
2⁵ᶠ 5⁵ᶠ 2⁵ᵍᶠ 3⁵ᵍˢ **0-2-4 £3,523**

Born For Diamonds *B W Hills*   58
2 b f Night Shift (USA) - Kirri (Ire)
7⁶ᵍᶠ 5⁶ᵍᶠ 11⁷ˢ **0-0-3**

Borodinsky *R E Barr*   48
3 b g Magic Ring (Ire) - Valldemosa
5⁶ᵍᶠ 7⁷ᶠ 4⁶ˢ 7⁷ᵍ 2⁷ᵍᶠ 4⁹ᶠ 8⁷ʰʸ 2⁷ᶠ **0-2-8
£3,066**

Borrego (Ire) *C E Brittain*   84
4 br c Green Desert (USA) - Pripet (USA)
2⁷ᵍᶠ 8⁷ᵍᶠ 6⁸ᶠ 11⁸ᵍ 14⁸ᶠ 4⁷ᵍᶠ 1⁷ᵍᶠ 8⁸ᵍᶠ
8⁷ᵍᶠ **1-1-9 £9,843**

Borthwick Girl (Ire) *B J Meehan*   97
2 b f Cape Cross (Ire) - Shannon Dore (Ire)
1⁶ᵍᶠ 4⁷ᵍᶠ 9⁷ᵍᶠ 3⁷ᵍ 3⁸ᵍˢ **1-2-5 £12,167**

Borzoi Maestro *J L Spearing* 79 a49
3 ch g Wolfhound (USA) - Ashkernazy (Ire)
2^{6s} 3^{5gf} 1^{6f} 9^{5f} 4^{5gf} 3^{6gf} 8^{5gf} 5^{5gf}
12^{6gs} 6^{5g} 7^{6g} 5^{5g} 5^{5g} 5^{6sd} 10^{6sd} **1-3-15**
£6,307

Boschette *J D Bethell* 52
2 b f Dansili - Secret Dance
5^{8g} 11^{7g} **0-0-2**

Bosco (Ire) *P S McEntee* 55
3 br c Petardia - Classic Goddess (Ire)
9^{12gs} 10^{12g} 13^{10gf} 11^{10f} 6^{10g} 8^{12gs} 13^{10g}
1-0-7 £2,562

Bosphorus *D G Bridgwater* a51
5 b g Polish Precedent (USA) - Ancara
3^{12sd} 1^{12sd} **1-0-2 £1,666**

Boston Lodge *G A Butler* 106
4 ch g Grand Lodge (USA) - Ffestiniog (Ire)
3^{8gf} 2^{7gf} 3^{7gf} 2^{7f} 4^{5g} 13^{5gf} 9^{6f} 8^{8gs}
3^{7gf} 2^{7gf} 11^{7gf} **0-6-11 £50,023**

Botanical (USA) *Saeed Bin Suroor* 97
3 b c Seeking The Gold (USA) - Satin Flower (USA)
5^{6g} 15^{7g} 8^{6gs} **0-0-3 £750**

Bottomless Wallet *F Watson* 57
3 ch f Titus Livius (Fr) - Furry Dance (USA)
6^{10g} 4^{10s} **0-0-2 £271**

Bought Direct *R J Smith* 59 a54
5 b h Muhtarram (USA) - Muhybh (USA)
12^{9ss} 11^{8sd} 6^{8ss} 5^{9sd} 4^{8sd} 6^{7g} 8^{9gf} **0-0-7**

Boule D'Or (Ire) *R Ingram* 96
3 b c Croco Rouge (Ire) - Saffron Crocus
4^{7gf} 1^{9gf} 4^{12gf} 2^{10gs} 9^{8g} 1^{10gs} 4^{10g} 4^{10gf}
3^{10g} 2^{8s} **2-4-10 £25,672**

Boumahou (Ire) *A P Jarvis* 57 a82
4 b c Desert Story (Ire) - Kilbride Lass (Ire)
3^{16sd} 3^{13sd} 1^{16sd} 7^{14s} **1-1-4 £5,725**

Bound To Please *Miss A Stokell*
9 b g Warrshan (USA) - Hong Kong Girl
10^{6g} 6^{6sd} 7^{8sd} **0-0-3**

Boundless Prospect (USA) *J W Hills* 83 a74
5 b g Boundary (USA) - Cape (USA)
7^{8sd} 10^{8sd} 11^{8gf} 10^{8gf} 2^{7g} 3^{7gf} 1^{7g} 6^{8gf}
11^{7g} 8^{8g} **1-2-10 £7,979**

Bountiful *M Blanshard* 62
2 gr f Pivotal - Kinsaile
7^{6g} **0-0-1**

Bounty Quest *R Hannon* 78
2 b c Fasliyev (USA) - Just Dreams
3^{5gf} 4^{6g} 3^{7gf} **0-2-3 £2,197**

Bourgainville *A M Balding* 107 a107
6 b g Pivotal - Petonica (Ire)
8^{10sd} 4^{10sd} 5^{10gs} 5^{10gs} 14^{12gf} 13^{10gf}
17^{10g} 7^{10gf} 8^{10hy} **0-0-9 £5,875**

Bourgeois *T D Easterby* 106
7 ch g Sanglamore (USA) - Bourbon Girl
2^{10s} 3^{12gs} 1^{12f} 10^{12g} 12^{14g} 9^{10s} 12^{15gf}
1-2-7 £16,833

Bow Strada *P J Hobbs* 77
7 ch g Rainbow Quest (USA) - La Strada
3^{16g} **0-1-1 £654**

Bow Wave *H Candy* 72
2 b c Danzero (Aus) - Moxby
1^{6gs} **1-0-1 £4,473**

Bowing *P G Murphy* 22 a58
4 b g Desert Prince (Ire) - Introducing

13^{8sd} 5^{12sd} 13^{10sd} 17^{12gs} 12^{10f} 9^{12sd}
0-0-6

Bowland Bride (Ire) *A Berry* 48 a3
2 b f Raise A Grand (Ire) - Red Riding Hood (Fr)
5^{5s} 10^{5g} 4^{6g} 4^{6f} 1^{6f} 7^{6gf} 7^{7sd} 5^{5gf}
10^{7sd} **1-0-9 £3,875**

Bowled Out (Ger) *P J McBride* 65
2 b f Dansili - Braissim
4^{7s} 12^{6gf} 18^{7g} 1^{8s} **1-0-4 £4,563**

Bowlegs Billy *J Balding* 36
4 gr g Raphane (USA) - Swallow Bay
12^{5g} 8^{5gs} 10^{7gf} 16^{8gf} **0-0-4**

Bowling Along *M E Sowersby* 66
3 b f The West (USA) - Bystrouska
5^{6s} 8^{6gf} 8^{6gf} 9^{6gf} 4^{7gf} 3^{6gf} 2^{6f} 14^{6gf}
10^{7gf} 1^{6f} 6^{6gf} 10^{6gf} 7^{8g} **1-2-13 £5,844**

Bowman's Crossing (Ire) *D Oughton* 116
5 b g Dolphin Street (Fr) - Biraya
3^{8gy} 3^{10gf} 5^{8gf} 4^{10gf} 3^{10g} 7^{8gf} 6^{8g} 2^{8gf}
0-4-8 £333,393

Bowsprit *B G Powell*
4 ch g Fleetwood (Ire) - Longwood Lady
9^{12sd} **0-0-1**

Bowstring (Ire) *J H M Gosden* 103
3 b f Sadler's Wells (USA) - Cantanta
1^{10gs} 2^{10s} 2^{11s} 3^{10hy} 3^{15g} 3^{14s} 9^{10s} **1-4-7**
£37,291

Box Builder *H Morrison* a73
7 ch g Fraam - Ena Olley
1^{16sd} 2^{14sd} **1-1-2 £4,164**

Boxgrove (Fr) *J E Pease* a40
3 ro g Trempolino (USA) - Little Emily
7^{8sd} 6^{8sd} 6^{12sd} **0-0-3**

Boxhall (Ire) *P W Harris* 70
2 b c Grand Lodge (USA) - March Hare
6^{7s} 10^{7g} **0-0-2**

Brace Of Doves *T D Barron* 69 a40
2 b g Bahamian Bounty - Overcome
14^{5gs} 5^{6sd} 3^{5gf} 2^{7gf} 3^{7gs} 10^{8g}
7^{7f} 7^{8g} **0-5-10 £5,936**

Brads House (Ire) *J G M O'Shea* 47
2 b c Rossini (USA) - Gold Stamp
11^{7gs} **0-0-1**

Brag (Ire) *R Charlton* 83
2 b f Mujadil (USA) - Boast
2^{5g} 4^{5f} 7^{5g} 1^{5gf} 3^{5f} 9^{5gs} **1-2-6 £7,694**

Bragadino *Lindsay Woods* 82 a49
5 b h Zilzal (USA) - Graecia Magna (USA)
12^{8hy} 8^{7s} 13^{6gf} 16^{7gf} 6^{8g} 14^{7gf} 12^{8y}
6^{7sd} 10^{6sd} 11^{5sd} **0-0-10**

Brahminy Kite (USA) *M Johnston* 92
2 b c Silver Hawk (USA) - Cope's Light (USA)
2^{7gs} 1^{8gs} **1-1-2 £10,117**

Brain Washed *T D Easterby* 66
3 b f Mind Games - Bollin Dorothy
16^{6gf} 4^{6g} 2^{6s} 5^{7gf} 3^{5gs} 3^{6gf} 6^{6g} **0-3-7**
£2,592

Bramantino (Ire) *R A Fahey* 69 a62
4 b g Perugino (USA) - Headrest
5^{8sd} 3^{9ss} 11^{1ss} 12^{12sd} 2^{12hy} 5^{14gf} 7^{12gf}
5^{14gs} 5^{12s} 1^{12s} 1^{12g} 3^{10gf} 5^{12hy} **3-3-13**
£15,745

Brandexe (Ire) *B W Hills* 66
2 b f Xaar - Tintara (Ire)
11^{7g} 5^{7gf} 4^{7s} 10^{7gs} **0-0-4 £424**

Brandy Cove *B Smart* — a67
7 b g Lugana Beach - Tender Moment (Ire)
4^{8sd} 13^{8sd} 5^{8sd} 5^{8sd} 5^{8sd} 0-0-5

Brandywine Bay (Ire) *A P Jones* — 46 a37
4 b f Mujadil (USA) - Ned's Contessa (Ire)
8^{8sd} 4^{8sd} 1^{7f} 5^{6gs} 9^{7gf} 17^{8gs} 1-0-6
£2,975

Branston Lily *Mrs J R Ramsden* — 65
2 ch f Cadeaux Genereux - Indefinite Article (Ire)
3^{6gf} 4^{6f} 9^{6gf} 13^{7g} 0-0-4 £1,142

Branston Nell *C R Dore* — a30
5 b m Classic Cliche (Ire) - Indefinite Article (Ire)
12^{12ss} 5^{13sd} 0-0-2

Branston Penny *P D Evans* — 11 a47
2 ch f Pennekamp (USA) - Branston Jewel (Ire)
13^{6gf} 2^{7sd} 8^{6sd} 0-1-3 £760

Branston Tiger *P D Evans* — 73 a72
5 b g Mark Of Esteem (Ire) - Tuxford Hideaway
5^{7ss} 11^{6g} 14^{6s} 8^{6gs} 6^{6gs} 5^{7f} 15^{7gf} 7^{7gs}
16^{sd} 4^{6gs} 3^{6gs} 8^{7s} 3^{6s} 7^{6g} 9^{6sd} 1-2-15
£4,711

Brantwood (Ire) *B A McMahon* — 64 a64
4 b g Lake Coniston (Ire) - Angelic Sounds (Ire)
14^{6g} 16^{5gs} 9^{5hy} 4^{5g} 3^{6gf} 2^{6sd} 3^{6g} 10^{7gf}
6^{6gf} 18^{6g} 5^{5gs} 8^{5gs} 0-4-12 £2,969

Brave Burt (Ire) *D Nicholls* — 91 a47
7 ch g Pips Pride - Friendly Song
18^{5gf} 10^{5g} 14^{5gf} 2^{5g} 17^{6g} 11^{5s} 11^{5g}
10^{5s} 9^{5g} 9^{5sd} 0-1-10 £1,992

Brave Chief *J A Pickering* — 23 a48
3 ch c Komaite (USA) - Victoria Sioux
7^{6sd} 17^{6gf} 5^{6sd} 6^{6sd} 15^{5sd} 5^{5sd} 0-0-6

Brave Dane (Ire) *A W Carroll* — 79 a82
6 b g Danehill (USA) - Nuriva (USA)
1^{10sd} 1^{10sd} 5^{10sd} 6^{10sd} 1^{10g} 2^{8sd} 10^{10sd}
10^{7gf} 2^{7f} 7^{10g} 3-2-10 £12,124

Brave Knight *N Bycroft* — 43
7 b g Presidium - Agnes Jane
8^{12gs} 0-0-1

Brave Tara (Ire) *T D Easterby* — 11
2 b f Brave Act - Gone With The Wind (Ire)
14^{7gs} 12^{7f} 12^{5gf} 0-0-3

Bravely Does It (USA) *W M Brisbourne* — 62 a53
4 gr g Holy Bull (USA) - Vigors Destiny (USA)
9^{12gs} 10^{10g} 6^{10gf} 2^{14gf} 12^{16s} 17^{12gf} 5^{12sd}
5^{17sd} 0-1-8 £928

Bravemore (USA) *B J Meehan* — 74
2 b c Diesis - Private Indy (USA)
6^{7g} 0-0-1

Bravo Maestro (USA) *D W P Arbuthnot* — 94 a95
3 b c Stravinsky (USA) - Amaranthus (USA)
6^{7sd} 7^{8sd} 5^{7gf} 9^{7gf} 9^{8g} 0-0-5 £1,125

Brazil Nut *Miss K Marks*
3 b g Deploy - Garota De Ipanema (Fr)
15^{16gf} 0-0-1

Brazilian Terrace *M L W Bell* — 82 a82
4 ch f Zilzal (USA) - Elaine's Honor (USA)
3^{8sd} 4^{8sd} 10^{8gf} 1^{8g} 1^{8f} 3^{8f} 9^{8sd} 2^{8gf}
2^{8gf} 9^{8gs} 3^{8g} 2-5-11 £16,504

Bread Of Heaven *Mrs A J Perrett* — 57
3 b f Machiavellian (USA) - Khubza
7^{6hy} 6^{7gf} 0-0-2

Breaking Shadow (Ire) *R A Fahey* — 81
2 br g Danehill Dancer (Ire) - Crimbourne
2^{5gs} 3^{5f} 3^{5g} 1^{6gs} 10^{6gf} 6^{6g} 7^{7gs} 8^{8s}

1^{7gs} 2-2-9 £14,504

Breaking The Rule (Ire) *P R Webber* — 47 a44
3 ch f King Of Kings (Ire) - Thirtysomething (USA)
10^{10sd} 6^{12f} 5^{10gf} 15^{10gs} 10^{10f} 0-0-5

Breamore *Mrs A J Perrett* — 54
2 b c Dansili - Maze Garden (USA)
8^{8s} 0-0-1

Breathing Fire *W J Musson* — 76
2 b c Pivotal - Pearl Venture
5^{6gs} 3^{6hy} 0-1-2 £542

Breathing Sun (Ire) *W J Musson* — 79
3 b g Bahhare (USA) - Zapata (Ire)
14^{10g} 10^{8gs} 9^{10gs} 3^{10gf} 12^{10s} 0-0-5
£1,073

Brecon *D R C Elsworth* — 81
2 ch f Unfuwain (USA) - Welsh Valley (USA)
1^{7s} 4^{7hy} 4^{10gs} 1-0-3 £6,166

Brecon Beacon *P F I Cole* — 101
2 b c Spectrum (Ire) - Ffestiniog (Ire)
1^{5gs} 1^{5gf} 2^{7f} 1^{7gf} 4^{7gs} 4^{7s} 3-1-6
£27,890

Breeder's Folly *T J Fitzgerald* — 30
2 b f Mujahid (USA) - Wynona (Ire)
11^{5gs} 7^{7s} 0-0-2

Breezer *J A Geake* — 42
4 b g Forzando - Lady Lacey
7^{10g} 12^{8gs} 3^{12gs} 0-1-3 £364

Breezit (USA) *S R Bowring* — 55 a55
3 b f Stravinsky (USA) - Sharka
4^{8g} 4^{8gf} 5^{6f} 12^{8gf} 3^{6sd} 5^{9sd} 3^{8sd} 0-2-7
£429

Bregaglia *R M H Cowell* — 24 a29
2 ch f Zaha (Can) - Strath Kitten
14^{7gf} 15^{7gf} 14^{7gs} 3^{5sw} 13^{6gf} 0-1-5
£363

Brego (Ire) *J H M Gosden* — 57
2 b g Monashee Mountain (USA) - White-Wash
14^{8g} 8^{8gf} 11^{7hy} 13^{8s} 0-0-4

Bressbee (USA) *N P Littmoden* — a77
6 ch g Twining (USA) - Bressay (USA)
8^{8sd} 2^{11sd} 4^{11ss} 8^{12sd} 1^{9ss} 12^{8sd} PU^{10gs}
1-1-7 £3,948

Bretton *B A Pearce* — 41 a53
3 b g Polar Prince (Ire) - Understudy
2^{9sw} 6^{9sd} 6^{8s} 4^{12s} 4^{8ss} 4^{10hy} 3^{12sd} 7^{8sd}
2^{10sd} 5^{10sd} 9^{10sd} 13^{10gf} 9^{16sd} 2^{12sd} 0-3-14
£2,581

Brevity *J G M O'Shea*
9 b g Tenby - Rive (USA)
10^{5gf} 16^{8g} 0-0-2

Brian Boru *A P O'Brien* — 119
4 b c Sadler's Wells (USA) - Eva Luna (USA)
1^{10y} 5^{10gf} 5^{12g} 5^{20gf} 5^{12s} 2^{15vs} 2^{14g} 3^{12g}
1-3-8 £166,631

Briannie (Ire) *J R Boyle* — 59
2 b f Xaar - Annieirwin (Ire)
6^{6g} 6^{7gs} 7^{6s} 0-0-3

Briannsta (Ire) *M R Channon* — 75
2 b c Bluebird (USA) - Nacote (Ire)
6^{6gs} 5^{8gf} 2^{7g} 1^{7gs} 10^{8s} 11^{7gs} 1-1-6
£5,103

Briar (Cze) *M Pitman* — a22
5 b h House Rules (USA) - Bright Angel (Aut)
6^{8sd} 0-0-1

Briar Ghyll *I A Wood* — 13

2 ch f Zaha (Can) - Charlotte Penny
12^{8hy} **0-0-1**

Briareus *A M Balding* — 86 a83
4 ch g Halling (USA) - Lower The Tone (Ire)
10^{12sd} 10^{12sd} 10^{10g} 2^{10gs} 7^{10g} 3^{11gs} 6^{12f}
7^{12g} 6^{11g} **0-2-9 £5,445**

Bridegroom *E A L Dunlop* — a59
2 b c Groom Dancer (USA) - La Piaf (Fr)
5^{9sd} **0-0-1**

Bridewell (USA) *F Watson* — 27 a9
5 b g Woodman (USA) - La Alleged (USA)
15^{11ss} 8^{14gf} 6^{10g} 8^{12sd} **0-0-4**

Bridge Pal *P Monteith* — 15
4 ch f First Trump - White Domino
6^{12gf} 9^{14g} **0-0-2**

Bridge Place *B J Meehan* — 72
2 b c Polar Falcon (USA) - Dark Eyed Lady (Ire)
7^{5s} 3^{6gf} 2^{6gf} 1^{7gf} **1-1-4 £5,336**

Bridge T'The Stars *R F Johnson Houghton* — 71 a54
2 b f Josr Algarhoud (Ire) - Petra's Star
1^{6g} 5^{6g} 10^{7sd} **1-0-3 £3,353**

Bridgewater Boys *K A Ryan* — 85 a78
3 b g Atraf - Dunloe (Ire)
4^{6sd} 1^{7ss} 3^{7ss} 1^{6g} 1^{6gf} 2^{6gf} 1^{6gf} 5^{6g}
9^{6gs} 8^{7sd} 6^{6sd} 3^{6sd} 8^{7sd} **4-2-13 £24,667**

Brief Goodbye *John Berry* — 86
4 b g Slip Anchor - Queen Of Silk (Ire)
1^{8gf} 4^{10gs} 8^{8gf} 1^{8gf} 4^{8g} 10^{8g} 6^{7g} 11^{7s}
2-1-8 £12,188

Briery Mec *H J Collingridge* — a30
9 b g Ron's Victory (USA) - Briery Fille
7^{11sd} 6^{12sd} 15^{10gf} **0-0-3**

Brigadier Monty (Ire) *Mrs S Lamyman* — 60
6 b g College Chapel - Miss St Cyr
11^{7gs} 6^{5hy} 7^{5gf} 5^{5gf} 5^{5gs} 5^{5gs} 10^{5gf}
3^{5gs} 10^{5gf} 9^{6g} 10^{5s} **0-2-12 £2,016**

Brigadore *J R Weymes* — 72
5 b g Magic Ring (Ire) - Music Mistress (Ire)
6^{5g} 3^{5gf} 5^{5gf} 12^{5gf} **0-1-4 £884**

Bright Fire (Ire) *W J Musson* — 57 a21
3 b f Daggers Drawn (USA) - Jarmar Moon
5^{6sw} 4^{8gf} 6^{10gf} 2^{10gs} **0-1-4 £1,342**

Bright Mist *B Palling* — a31
5 b m Anita's Prince - Out On Her Own
12^{5gs} 4^{5sd} 7^{7sd} 16^{6sd} **0-0-4**

Bright Moll *M L W Bell* — 87
2 b f Mind Games - Molly Brown
1^{5gs} 2^{5s} 2^{5gf} 5^{5gf} 1^{6g} **2-1-5 £12,431**

Bright Sun (Ire) *N Tinkler* — 81
3 b c Desert Sun - Kealbra Lady
8^{6gs} 10^{8gs} 10^{7gs} 4^{6gf} 3^{6g} 3^{8s} 4^{7gf}
1^{8gs} 8^{7gs} 6^{8s} 8^{9g} 11^{10s} **1-1-13 £6,963**

Brilliant Red *Jamie Poulton* — 53 a85
11 b g Royal Academy (USA) - Red Comes Up (USA)
16^{12sd} 9^{10sd} 6^{16sd} 4^{12sd} 7^{13sd} 5^{10sd} 15^{12g}
0-0-7 £627

Brilliant Waters *D W P Arbuthnot*
4 ch g Mark Of Esteem (Ire) - Faraway Waters
15^{7sd} **0-0-1**

Brilliantrio *M C Chapman* — 63 a48
6 ch m Selkirk (USA) - Loucoum (Fr)
2^{7sd} 4^{7sd} 9^{8sd} 6^{7sd} UR^{7sd} 3^{7ss} 6^{6sd} 2^{8f}
1^{8f} **1-3-9 £5,966**

Brillyant Dancer *Mrs A Duffield* — a5
6 b m Environment Friend - Brillyant Glen (Ire)

6^{7sd} 11^{7sw} **0-0-2**

Brindisi *B W Hills* — 99
3 b f Dr Fong (USA) - Genoa
3^{8g} 4^{10g} 1^{8gf} 4^{8gf} 4^{8gs} 6^{8gf} 1^{8gf} 7^{8gf}
13^{9s} **2-2-9 £29,916**

Brios Boy *K R Burke*
4 ch g My Best Valentine - Rose Elegance
12^{12sd} **0-0-1**

Brioso (Ire) *J M P Eustace* — a30
4 b g Victory Note (USA) - Presently
7^{6ss} **0-0-1**

Broadway Score (USA) *M W Easterby* — 70
6 b g Theatrical - Brocaro (USA)
7^{8s} 9^{11s} 9^{10gs} 13^{10g} 9^{10g} 10^{10g} 11^{8gf}
8^{10s} **0-0-8**

Bronwen (Ire) *J Noseda* — 55
2 b f King's Best (USA) - Tegwen (USA)
6^{7s} **0-0-1**

Bronx Bomber *Dr J D Scargill* — 32 a51
6 ch g Prince Sabo - Super Yankee (Ire)
1^{6sd} 7^{7sd} 7^{7sd} 13^{6sf} **2-0-4 £2,891**

Bronze Dancer (Ire) *G A Swinbank* — 68
2 b g Entrepreneur - Scrimshaw
12^{7gf} 8^{8f} 7^{7g} 1^{7gf} 9^{8gs} **1-0-5 £2,954**

Brooklands Lodge (USA) *M J Attwater* — 64 a59
3 ch f Grand Lodge (USA) - Princess Dixieland (USA)
6^{8gf} 9^{8gs} 9^{10gf} 8^{11ff} 19^{10gf} 10^{11g} 3^{12sd}
2^{12sd} **0-2-8 £1,946**

Brooklands Time (Ire) *I W McInnes* — 9 a37
3 b f Danetime (Ire) - Lute And Lyre (Ire)
7^{6sd} 7^{6sw} 11^{6sd} 12^{7sd} 16^{7g} **0-0-5**

Brooklime (Ire) *J A Osborne* — 80 a61
2 b c Namid - Wildflower
6^{6sd} 4^{6g} 1^{6gs} 10^{6gs} 5^{6gs} 2^{7gs} 6^{7gf} 7^{7gs}
6^{7gs} 16^{6hy} **1-1-10 £5,435**

Brooklyn's Gold (USA) *Ian Williams* — 70 a83
9 b g Seeking The Gold (USA) - Brooklyn's Dance (Fr)
6^{10sd} 8^{11hy} 10^{10g} **0-0-3 £390**

Brother Cadfael *John A Harris* — 39 a46
3 ch g So Factual (USA) - High Habit
3^{8sd} 8^{8sd} 3^{8sd} 2^{7gs} 6^{8g} 6^{7g} 6^{7g} 7^{8gs} 7^{8sd}
7^{8gf} 10^{10gf} 18^{10g} **0-3-12 £1,497**

Brough Supreme *H Morrison* — 69 a62
3 b g Sayaarr (USA) - Loriner's Lady
5^{10g} 4^{14gs} 6^{11gf} 8^{14g} 3^{10sd} **0-1-5 £587**

Broughton Bounty *W J Musson* — 41
3 b f Bahamian Bounty - Sleave Silk (Ire)
12^{8gf} **0-0-1**

Broughton Knows *Miss Gay Kelleway* — 59 a72
7 b g Most Welcome - Broughtons Pet (Ire)
1^{12sd} 1^{12sd} 11^{11ss} 2^{12sd} 9^{14sd} 4^{14s}
4^{12g} 1^{12sd} 12^{12g} **5-3-10 £11,482**

Broughton Melody *W J Musson* — a40
5 ch m Alhijaz - Broughton Singer (Ire)
3^{14sd} 8^{14sd} 4^{16sw} 4^{14sd} 5^{14sd} **0-0-5 £471**

Broughtons Flush *Paul John Gilligan* — 44 a50
6 b g First Trump - Glowing Reference
7^{16sd} 8^{14sd} 5^{14sf} 1^{14sd} 8^{16hy} **1-0-5
£3,474**

Broughtons Mill *J A Supple* — a41
9 gr g Ron's Victory (USA) - Sandra's Desire
5^{10sd} 6^{12sd} 6^{10sd} 8^{8sw} 6^{12sd} **0-0-5**

Brown Dragon *D Haydn Jones* — 40 a65
3 ch g Primo Dominie - Cole Slaw
6^{6sd} 2^{6ss} 2^{6ss} 12^{6gs} 10^{6gf} 6^{6sd} **0-2-6**

£2,064

Brumaire (Ire) *J L Dunlop* 37
2 b c Second Empire (Ire) - Ar Hyd Y Knos
9⁷ᵍˢ 11⁷ˢ **0-0-2**

Brunel (Ire) *W J Haggas* 115
3 b c Marju (Ire) - Castlerahan (Ire)
1⁷ᵍ 1⁸ᵍ 5⁸ᵍᶠ 11⁷ᵍˢ 6⁸ᵍˢ **2-0-5 £95,353**

Brut *D W Barker* 57
2 b g Mind Games - Champenoise
10⁵ᵍ 6⁵ᵍᶠ 2⁵ᵍ 17⁶ˢ 5⁵ˢ 5⁵ᵍᶠ **0-1-6**
£1,030

Brut Force (Ire) *Miss V Haigh* 48
2 b g Desert Style (Ire) - La Foscarina
9⁷ˢ **0-0-1**

Bruzella *A J Lidderdale* a31
5 b m Hernando (Fr) - Hills' Presidium
9¹⁰ˢᵈ 11¹²ˢᵈ **0-0-2**

Bubbling Fun *T Wall* 72
3 b f Marju (Ire) - Blushing Barada (USA)
4¹⁰ᵍˢ 7¹⁰ᵍ 4¹⁰ᶠ 3¹⁰ᵍᶠ 3¹¹ᵍᶠ 2¹²ᵍᶠ 6¹⁰ᵍᶠ 2⁹ˢ
2¹⁰ᵍ **0-5-9 £5,603**

Buchanan Street (Ire) *J G M O'Shea* 49
3 b c Barathea (Ire) - Please Believe Me
16⁸ᶠ 6⁸ᶠ 6⁸ᶠ 2¹⁰ᵍ 5¹⁶ᵍᶠ 7¹²ᵍˢ 15¹⁰ᵍᶠ
0-1-7 £930

Buckenham Stone *J Pearce* 34 a21
5 ch m Wing Park - Walk That Walk
11⁷ˢ 9¹⁰ᵍᶠ 7⁸ˢᵈ 7¹⁰ˢᵈ 8¹⁰ᵍ 9¹²ˢᵈ **0-0-6**

Buckeye Wonder (USA) *M A Jarvis* 90
3 b c Silver Hawk (USA) - Ameriflora (USA)
2¹⁰ᵍˢ 1¹⁰ᵍ 13¹⁰ᶠ **1-1-3 £7,443**

Bucks *D K Ivory* 87 a71
7 b g Slip Anchor - Alligram (USA)
14¹²ˢᵈ 3¹²ᵍˢ 11¹²ˢ 2¹⁴ˢ 1¹⁴ᵍ 1¹²ᵍᶠ 2¹²ᵍ
5¹⁴ᵍᶠ 8¹²ᵍᶠ 2¹⁰ᵍᶠ 2¹²ᵍᶠ 5¹²ˢ 6¹⁴ᵍˢ 8¹²ᵍᶠ **2-5-14**
£28,230

Buddy Brown *J Howard Johnson* 88
2 b c Lujain (USA) - Rose Bay
1⁷ᵍ 2⁶ˢ 17⁸ᵍᶠ 14⁷ˢ **1-1-4 £5,884**

Bugle Call *K O Cunningham-Brown* a46
4 b g Zamindar (USA) - Petillante
10¹²ˢˢ 7⁷ˢᵈ 8⁸ˢʷ 13⁸ˢʷ **0-0-4**

Bukit Fraser (Ire) *P F I Cole* 90
3 b g Sri Pekan (USA) - London Pride (USA)
1¹¹ᵍˢ 4¹¹ᵍ 7¹²ᵍ 9¹²ᵍ 9¹⁴ᵍᶠ 5¹⁴ᵍᶠ 10¹⁵ˢ
12¹²ᵍ **1-0-8 £6,428**

Bulawayo *Andrew Reid* 42 a57
7 b g Prince Sabo - Ra Ra Girl
5⁷ˢᵈ 3⁷ˢᵈ 7⁷ˢˢ 3⁸ˢˢ 8⁸ˢʷ 6⁸ˢᵈ 1⁷ˢˢ 7⁶ˢᵈ
6⁷ᵍᶠ 4⁷ˢᵈ 2⁷ˢᵈ 1⁸ˢᵈ 8⁸ˢᵈ 4⁸ˢᵈ 4⁸ˢᵈ 11⁷ˢᵈ 12⁸ˢᵈ
2-4-17 £6,869

Bulberry Hill *M G Quinlan* 43 a26
3 b g Makbul - Hurtleberry (Ire)
8⁸ˢʷ 5⁸ˢˢ 5⁷ᵍ 8⁷ᵍˢ 10¹⁰ᵍᶠ **0-0-5**

Bulgaria Moon *C Grant* 36
4 ch g Groom Dancer (USA) - Gai Bulga
7¹⁴ˢ 9¹⁴ᵍᶠ 7¹⁶ᶠ 8¹⁷ᵍ **0-0-4**

Bull Run (Ire) *Saeed Bin Suroor* 115
3 gr c Daylami (Ire) - Bulaxie
1¹⁰ᵍˢ 1¹⁰ˢ **2-0-2 £16,852**

Bullseye *P W D'Arcy* 8
2 b c Polish Precedent (USA) - Native Flair
18⁷ᵍˢ **0-0-1**

Bulwark (Ire) *Mrs A J Perrett* 65
2 b c Montjeu (Ire) - Bulaxie

10⁷ᵍ 4⁸ᵍ 5⁸ʰʸ **0-0-3 £436**

Bumptious *M H Tompkins* 91
3 b c Mister Baileys - Gleam Of Light (Ire)
3¹⁰ᵍˢ 3¹²ᵍ 1¹²ᵍ 4¹⁴ᵍˢ 4¹⁶ᶠ 3¹⁵ᵍᶠ 14¹⁵ˢ
1-2-7 £11,910

Bundaberg *P W Hiatt* 4 a53
4 b g Komaite (USA) - Lizzy Cantle
4⁸ˢˢ 2⁷ˢᵈ 2⁷ˢˢ 3⁷ˢᵈ 10⁹ˢᵈ 12⁸ʰʸ **0-2-6**
£1,242

Bunditten (Ire) *Andrew Reid* 92 a73
2 gr f Soviet Star (USA) - Felicita (Ire)
1⁵ˢᵈ 3⁵ᵍᶠ 4⁵ᵍᶠ 4⁵ᵍˢ 8⁵ᶠ 7⁵ˢ 6⁶ˢ **1-1-7**
£20,130

Bundy *M Dods* 73
8 b g Ezzoud (Ire) - Sanctuary Cove
8⁷ᵍˢ 13⁶ˢ 10⁷ʰʸ 2⁶ᵍᶠ 2⁶ᵍᶠ 3⁶ᵍ 2⁶ᵍˢ 8⁶ᵍᶠ
4⁶ᵍ 4⁶ᵍᶠ 11⁷ˢ 7⁶ˢ **0-3-12 £5,500**

Bunino Ven *S C Williams* 50 a31
3 gr g Silver Patriarch (Ire) - Plaything
8¹⁰ˢᵈ 4¹⁰ᵍᶠ 7¹²ˢ 5¹²ᵍ 4¹²ˢᵈ **0-0-5**

Bunkhouse *Mrs N Macauley* 42 a24
4 ch g Wolfhound (USA) - Maid Welcome
8⁶ᵍᶠ 7⁶ᵍᶠ 13⁷ᵍᶠ 8⁸ˢᵈ 8⁷ᶠ 14¹⁰ᵍˢ **0-0-6**

Bunny Rabbit (USA) *B J Meehan* 94 a81
2 b c Cherokee Run (USA) - Jane's The Name (USA)
3⁶ᵍᶠ 5⁷ᵍᶠ 4⁷ˢᵈ 8⁸ᵍᶠ 1⁸ᵍᶠ **1-0-5 £15,844**

Bunyah (Ire) *E A L Dunlop* a37
3 ch f Distant View (USA) - Miss Mistletoes (Ire)
9⁷ˢᵈ **0-0-1**

Bureaucrat *J H M Gosden* 82
2 b c Machiavellian (USA) - Lajna
4⁸ᵍˢ 6⁸ˢ **0-0-2 £445**

Burgundian (USA) *J Noseda* 73
2 b c Red Ransom (USA) - Prospectora (USA)
4⁷ᵍ **0-0-1 £404**

Burgundy *P Mitchell* 72 a70
7 b g Lycius (USA) - Decant
6¹⁰ˢᵈ 3⁸ˢᵈ 4⁸ˢᵈ 2¹⁰ˢᵈ 7¹¹ᵍˢ 9¹⁰ᵍᶠ 8¹⁰ᵍᶠ
3¹⁰ᶠ 6¹⁰ᵍᶠ 1⁹ᵍᶠ 1¹⁰ˢᵈ 1¹⁰ˢᵈ 2¹⁰ᵍᶠ 18ᵍᶠ 2¹⁰ᵍᶠ
5¹⁰ᵍ 4⁸ᵍᶠ 6¹²ᵍ **4-5-18 £19,305**

Burkees Graw (Ire) *Mrs S Lamyman* 49 a29
3 ch g Fayruz - Dancing Willma (Ire)
7⁷ˢᵈ 7⁷ˢˢ 9⁵ˢᵈ 14⁷ᵍᶠ 2⁵ᵍᶠ 17⁵ᵍˢ 2⁵ᵍᶠ
10⁵ˢᶠ **0-2-8 £1,666**

Burley Firebrand *J G Given* 53
4 b g Bahamian Bounty - Vallauris
19¹¹ᵍˢ 8¹⁰ᵍ 15¹¹ᵍ **0-0-3**

Burley Flame *J G Given* 82 a86
3 b g Marju (Ire) - Tarsa
4⁷ᵍˢ 3⁸ᵍᶠ 1⁷ᵍᶠ 22⁸ᶠ 3⁸ᵍ 1⁷ᵍˢ 6⁸ᵍᶠ
7⁷ᵍᶠ 7⁷ᵍˢ 11⁹ᵍ 16⁸ᵍ 8⁶ˢ **3-3-13 £20,527**

Burlington Place *S Kirk* 63 a58
3 b g Compton Place - Wandering Stranger
10⁷ᵍᶠ 7⁷ˢᵈ 2⁸ᵍ 8⁸ᶠ 18⁸ᵍ **0-1-5 £2,246**

Burn *M L W Bell* 60
3 ch f Selkirk (USA) - River Cara (USA)
7¹⁰ᵍᶠ 3⁹ᵍ 11⁸ᵍᶠ 12⁸ᵍᶠ **0-0-4 £860**

Burning Moon *J Noseda* 87
3 b c Bering - Triple Green
5⁸ˢ 1¹⁰ˢ 15¹²ᵍˢ 11¹⁰ᵍˢ 10¹⁰ˢ 3¹⁰ᵍ **1-1-6**
£6,987

Burning Truth (USA) *M Sheppard* 32
10 ch g Known Fact (USA) - Galega
9¹⁴ᵍᶠ **0-0-1**

Burnley Al (Ire) *R A Fahey* 62

2 ch g Desert King (Ire) - Bold Meadows
5^{6s} 10^{6gf} **0-0-2**

Burnt Copper (Ire) *J R Best*   62 a47
4 b g College Chapel - Try My Rosie
10^{12gf} 1^{10gf} 8^{12g} 9^{12gf} 9^{10gf} 10^{9sd} 9^{9sd}
1-0-7 £5,057

Burton Ash *J G Given*   70
2 b/br f Diktat - Incendio
7^{5gs} 4^{6f} 3^{6g} 4^{7gf} 9^{7gf} 9^{8f} **0-1-6**
£1,602

Busaco *J L Dunlop*   62 a69
2 b c Mister Baileys - War Shanty
15^{6gf} 4^{7f} 6^{8sd} **0-0-3 £263**

Buscador (USA) *W M Brisbourne*   45 a52
5 ch g Crafty Prospector (USA) - Fairway Flag (USA)
8^{9sd} 9^{10hy} 13^{10g} 9^{9f} 9^{9g} 8^{10g} **0-0-6**

Bushido (Ire) *Mrs S J Smith*   57
5 br g Brief Truce (USA) - Pheopotstown
6^{14gs} 8^{12s} 2^{16f} 8^{17gf} **0-1-4 £883**

Business Matters (Ire) *H Alexander*   67 a16
4 b f Desert Style (Ire) - Hear Me
11^{12sd} 10^{10hy} 12^{8s} 3^{8s} 5^{9gf} 15^{9gs} **0-1-6**
£500

Business Traveller (Ire) *R J Price*
4 ch g Titus Livius (Fr) - Dancing Venus
15^{16gs} **0-0-1**

Bust (Ire) *T D Easterby*   44
2 b c Fraam - Purse
13^{5gf} 6^{7g} **0-0-2**

Bustan (Ire) *M P Tregoning*   109 a108
5 b h Darshaan - Dazzlingly Radiant
3^{10sd} 2^{10gs} 9^{10gs} 4^{10gs} **0-2-4 £15,620**

Bustling Rio (Ire) *P C Haslam*   a71
8 b g Up And At 'Em - Une Venitienne (Fr)
4^{16sd} 7^{16sd} 1^{16sd} 8^{18s} **1-0-4 £2,884**

Buthaina (Ire) *T H Caldwell*   50
4 b f Bahhare (USA) - Haddeyah (USA)
12^{8g} 9^{7s} 15^{8f} 10^{8g} 9^{10g} 11^{8g} 10^{6g}
0-0-7

Buy On The Red *W R Muir*   91 a75
3 b c Komaite (USA) - Red Rosein
2^{6sd} 2^{5s} 1^{6gf} 1^{6gf} 7^{6gf} 2^{5gf} 12^{5gf} 12^{6g}
2-3-8 £33,688

Buying A Dream (Ire) *Andrew Turnell*   a43
7 ch g Prince Of Birds (USA) - Cartagena Lady (Ire)
5^{12sw} 13^{11ss} 1^{12sd} 3^{11sf} 1^{12sd} **2-0-5**
£2,749

Buz Kiri (USA) *A W Carroll*   50 a53
6 b g Gulch (USA) - Whitecorners (USA)
3^{12sd} 2^{13sd} 1^{12ss} 2^{11sd} 2^{14ss} 1^{12sw} 2^{16sw}
2^{12ss} 6^{12ss} 2^{10gs} 1^{12g} **3-7-11 £7,075**

Buzz Buzz *C E Brittain*   57
3 b f Mtoto - Abuzz
13^{8gf} 8^{10s} 18^{7s} **0-0-3**

Buzz Maite *P Butler*
2 b g Komaite (USA) - Scotland Bay
5^{6gf} **0-0-1**

By Definition (Ire) *J C Tuck*
6 gr m Definite Article - Miss Goodbody
8^{9sd} 15^{8ss} 9^{8sd} **0-0-3**

Bygone Days *W J Haggas*   98
3 ch g Desert King (Ire) - May Light
1^{6s} 3^{7gs} 4^{6gf} 5^{6s} 1^{6gf} 3^{5s} **2-3-6**
£23,448

Byinchka *S L Keightley*   a16

4 br g Inchinor - Bystrouska
9^{8sd} **0-0-1**

Byo (Ire) *M Quinn*   77 a72
6 gr g Paris House - Navan Royal (Ire)
7^{5sd} 6^{5s} 2^{5s} 10^{5s} 1^{5gf} 7^{5f} 6^{6f} 6^{6f} 7^{6f}
12^{6g} 1^{5gf} 3^{5f} 4^{6gf} 8^{5g} 4^{5g} 3^{5g} 2^{25sd} **2-4-17**
£11,845

Byrd Island *D Morris*   14
3 b f Turtle Island (Ire) - Arusha (Ire)
14^{8g} 17^{8gf} 10^{10gf} **0-0-3**

Byron *Saeed Bin Suroor*   117
3 b c Green Desert (USA) - Gay Gallanta (USA)
3^{8gf} 8^{8gf} 1^{7g} 9^{8s} **1-0-4 £86,173**

Byron Bay *J J Bridger*   64
2 b c My Best Valentine - Candarela
9^{6g} 9^{8g} 5^{7s} 12^{7gf} 3^{8s} 14^{7s} **0-1-6 £698**

Ca'D'Oro *J A Geake*   40
11 b g Cadeaux Genereux - Palace Street (USA)
12^{8gs} 5^{8hy} **0-0-2**

Cabin Fever *J C Fox*   59
2 b f Averti (Ire) - Julietta Mia (USA)
8^{6g} 5^{6gf} 7^{6gs} 8^{6gf} 3^{8gf} **0-1-5 £217**

Cabopino Lad (USA) *Mrs L Stubbs*   42
2 b g Comic Strip (USA) - Roxanne (USA)
10^{9f} **0-0-1**

Cacique (Ire) *A Fabre*   117
3 b c Danehill (USA) - Hasili (Ire)
1^{7gs} 1^{8g} 2^{9gs} 2^{10gs} 1^{9g} $£^{10g}$ 1^{8g} **4-1-7**
£220,795

Cadeaux Rouge (Ire) *Mrs P N Dutfield*   57
3 ch f Croco Rouge (Fr) - Gift Of Glory (Fr)
4^{12gs} 7^{14s} 15^{12g} 19^{10gf} **0-0-4 £271**

Cadogen Square *D W Chapman*   43
2 ch f Takhlid (USA) - Mount Park (Ire)
12^{5gf} 9^{5gs} 10^{6gf} 4^{6gf} 8^{5gf} 10^{5f} 7^{7gf}
0-0-7

Cadwallader (USA) *P Burgoyne*   38 a27
4 ch g Kingmambo (USA) - Light On Your Feet (USA)
4^{12ss} 6^{12sd} 5^{12sd} UR^{16sd} 8^{16gf} 13^{14gf} **0-0-6**

Caerphilly Gal *P L Gilligan*   60 a44
4 b f Averti (Ire) - Noble Lustre (USA)
9^{6gf} 13^{7g} 9^{2gf} 8^{7g} 3^{8g} 3^{7gs} 1^{8gs}
7^{9sd} 8^{8hy} **2-2-10 £3,860**

Caesar Beware (Ire) *H Candy*   112
2 b g Daggers Drawn (USA) - Red Shareef
1^{6g} 1^{6gf} 1^{6g} **3-1-4 £232,725**

Cafe Americano *D W P Arbuthnot*   56
4 b g Labeeb - Coffee Ice
7^{7gf} 5^{7gf} 9^{7gf} 2^{6gf} 2^{7gs} 7^{6s} 12^{8g} **0-2-7**
£2,108

Cairns (UAE) *Saeed Bin Suroor*   106
3 b f Cadeaux Genereux - Tanami
10^{8g} 6^{8gf} 19^{8f} **0-0-4 £324**

Caitlin (Ire) *B Smart*   79 a71
2 ch f Intikhab (USA) - Esteraad (Ire)
6^{5hy} 2^{6sd} 4^{6sd} 1^{7sd} 3^{7sd} 1^{7gf} 2^{7f} 3^{8gf}
PU^{7g} **2-4-9 £13,288**

Cake It Easy (Ire) *K G Reveley*
4 ch f Kendor (Fr) - Diese Memory (USA)
9^{13gs} **0-0-1**

Cal Mac *M J Gingell*   53
5 b g Botanic (USA) - Shifting Mist
18^{8g} 11^{8sd} 7^{8f} 2^{10f} 7^{10gs} 10^{10sd} **0-1-6**
£828

Cala Fons (Ire) *N Tinkler*   38
2 b f Alhaarth (Ire) - Lemon Tree (USA)
16⁶ᵍˢ 10⁷ᵍˢ 7⁸ᵍ 11⁷ᵍ **0-0-4**

Calamari (Ire) *Mrs A Duffield*   59
2 ch f Desert King (Ire) - Mrs Fisher (Ire)
10⁶ᵍᶠ 4⁷ᵍˢ 15⁸ᵍᶠ **0-0-3 £432**

Calamintha *M C Pipe*   72
4 b f Mtoto - Calendula
2¹⁴ˢ 6¹³ᵍᶠ 1¹⁸ᵍ 3¹⁶ᵍᶠ 5¹⁶ᵍˢ **1-1-5 £7,398**

Calara Hills *W M Brisbourne*   50
3 ch f Bluegrass Prince (Ire) - Atlantic Line
11¹⁰ᵍ 3¹³ˢ 12¹²ᵍᶠ **0-1-3 £705**

Calatagan (Ire) *J M Jefferson*   71
5 ch g Danzig Connection (USA) - Calachuchi
3¹⁴ᵍ 1¹⁰ᵍˢ 5¹²ᵍ 5¹⁰ᵍ 2¹²ᵍ 18¹¹ˢ 5¹²ᵍ **1-2-7 £6,299**

Calcar (Ire) *Mrs S Lamyman*   23
4 b g Flying Spur (Aus) - Poscimur (Ire)
9¹²ˢᵈ 7¹²ˢ **0-0-2**

Calculaite *Mrs G S Rees*   62 a61
3 b g Komaite (USA) - Miss Calculate
9⁸ᵍᶠ 6⁶ᵍᶠ 6⁶ᵍᶠ 4⁶ᵍ 5⁶ᵍˢ 7⁶ˢʷ 1⁸ᶠ 3⁷ˢᵈ
4⁹ˢᵈ 6⁹ᵍˢ 3⁹ˢᵈ **1-3-11 £2,437**

Calcutta *B W Hills*   107
8 b h Indian Ridge - Echoing
10⁷ᵍˢ 13⁸ᵍˢ 10⁷ᵍᶠ 8⁸ᵍᶠ 2⁸ᵍᶠ 12⁸ᵍˢ
3⁸ᵍᶠ 9⁸ᵍ 1⁹ᵍᶠ 1⁸ᶠ 7⁸ᵍ **2-2-12 £30,646**

Caldy Dancer (Ire) *M R Channon*   83
3 ch f Soviet Star (USA) - Smile Awhile (USA)
11⁹ᵍᶠ 11⁸ᵍᶠ **0-0-2**

Caledonian (Ire) *D R C Elsworth*   68
3 b g Soviet Star (USA) - Supercal
22⁷ᵍ 9⁸ᵍ **0-0-2**

Calendar Girl (Ire) *P J Makin*   a39
4 b f Revoque (Ire) - March Fourteenth (USA)
10⁵ˢᵈ 6⁵ˢᵈ **0-0-2**

Calfraz *M D Hammond*   49
2 b/br g Tamure (Ire) - Pas De Chat
9⁷ᶠ 7⁷ˢ **0-0-2**

Caliban (Ire) *Ian Williams*   55
6 ch g Rainbows For Life (Can) - Amour Toujours (Ire)
7¹⁵ˢᵈ 10¹⁴ᵍᶠ 3¹⁹ᵍᶠ 10¹⁶ᵍˢ 8¹³ᵍˢ **0-1-5 £612**

Calibre (USA) *J H M Gosden*   94
4 b c Lear Fan (USA) - Carya (USA)
6¹²ᵍᶠ 14¹⁴ᵍ **0-0-2 £450**

Call Me Max *E A L Dunlop*   81
2 b g Vettori (Ire) - Always Vigilant (USA)
4⁷ᵍᶠ 3⁸ᵍᶠ 5⁷ᵍ 3⁸ᵍ **0-2-4 £1,090**

Call Me Sunshine *P C Haslam*   67 a60
4 b f Robellino (USA) - Kirana
1⁹ˢᵈ 7¹²ˢˢ 5¹²ˢᵈ 17¹²ᵍˢ 3¹²ᵍᶠ 7¹⁴ᵍᶠ **1-1-6 £4,155**

Call Of The Wild *R A Fahey*   48 a59
4 ch g Wolfhound (USA) - Biba (Ire)
8¹²ˢᵈ 9¹³ˢʷ 3⁸ˢᵈ 3⁹ˢˢ 6¹¹ˢ 4⁹ˢᵈ 4⁸ˢᵈ 2⁹ˢᵈ
12⁸ᶠ 12⁸ˢᵈ **0-3-10 £2,061**

Called Up *H Candy*   67 a6
3 b g Easycall - Clued Up
4⁶ˢ 7⁶ᵍᶠ 9⁷ᵍᶠ 5⁶ᵍᶠ 11⁷ˢᵈ 4⁶ᵍᶠ 3⁶ᵍˢ **0-1-7 £1,046**

Calomeria *D McCain*   65
3 b f Groom Dancer (USA) - Calendula
11¹⁰ᵍˢ 8¹⁰ᵍ 14¹²ᵍ 4¹²ᵍˢ 10¹⁴ᵍ 3¹⁶ˢ 8¹⁶ᵍˢ
7¹⁸ᵍˢ 3¹⁴ᶠ 3¹³ᵍˢ **0-3-10 £1,469**

Calonnog (Ire) *H R A Cecil*   65
4 ch f Peintre Celebre (USA) - Meadow Spirit (USA)
2¹²ᵍ 9¹⁰ᵍᶠ **0-1-2 £1,700**

Caluki *L Camici*   87 a112
7 b h Kris - Chevisaunce
1¹⁰ˢᵈ 4¹⁰ˢᵈ 1¹⁰ˢᵈ 9⁹ᶠᵗ 7⁸ᵍᶠ **2-0-5 £64,979**

Calusa Lady (Ire) *J A Geake*   57
4 ch f Titus Livius (Fr) - Solas Abu (Ire)
5⁶ˢ 9⁷ᵍᶠ 2⁶ᵍ 17⁶ᵍ 3⁷ᵍ 4⁶ˢ **0-3-6 £1,531**

Calvados (USA) *John A Quinn*   53 a50
5 b g Seattle Slew (USA) - A Votre Sante (USA)
2¹²ˢʷ 8¹²ʰʸ 9¹³ᵍᶠ **0-1-3 £1,020**

Caly Dancer (Ire) *D R C Elsworth*   90
2 ch g Entrepreneur - Mountain Dancer (Ire)
9⁵ᵍˢ 5⁵ᵍ 3⁵ᵍ 3⁶ᵍᶠ 3⁷ᵍᶠ 1⁶ᵍˢ 5⁸ˢ **1-3-7 £5,855**

Calypso Dancer (Fr) *T D Barron*   54 a56
4 b f Celtic Swing - Calypso Grant (Ire)
0⁶ᵍˢ 4⁶ 2⁵ᵛˢ 4⁵ᵍ 0⁵ᵛˢ 19⁵ᵍᶠ 14⁵ᶠ 10⁵ᵍ
6⁷ˢᵈ **0-0-9 £4,436**

Camacho *H R A Cecil*   93
2 b c Danehill (USA) - Arabesque
1⁶ᵍ 3⁷ᵍ **1-0-2 £6,077**

Camberley (Ire) *P F I Cole*   98
7 b g Sri Pekan (USA) - Nsx
2⁷ˢ 5⁷ᵍˢ 26⁶ᵍ **0-1-3 £3,553**

Camberwell *T G Mills*   87
3 b g Royal Applause - Into Orbit
1⁷ᵍᶠ 5⁷ᵍˢ 9⁷ᵍᶠ 14⁸ᵍ 13⁷ᵍˢ **1-0-6 £6,721**

Cambo (Fr) *R Ford*   35 a58
3 b/br g Mansonnien (Fr) - Royal Lie (Fr)
12¹¹ᵍ 6¹⁰ᵛˢ F¹²ᵍ 4¹⁶ˢᵈ 5¹⁷ˢ **0-0-5**

Cameron Orchid (Ire) *M A Jarvis*   72
2 b f Sri Pekan (USA) - London Pride (USA)
9⁷ᵍˢ **0-0-1**

Camille Pissarro (USA) *D J Wintle*   56
4 b g Red Ransom (USA) - Serenity
9⁸ʰʸ 29⁹ᵍ 16¹⁰ᵍ 14⁸ʰʸ 14¹⁰ʰʸ **0-0-5**

Cammies Future *P W Chapple-Hyam*   94
2 gr c Efisio - Impulsive Decision (Ire)
3⁵ˢ 1⁶ᵍˢ 2⁵ʰʸ 6⁶ᵍ **1-2-4 £18,494**

Camp Commander (Ire) *C R Dore*   105 a95
5 gr h Pennekamp (USA) - Khalatara (Ire)
9⁷ˢ 4⁷ᵍᶠ 5⁸ᵍᶠ 7⁸ᵍˢ 17⁸ᵍ 8⁸ᵍ 7⁷ᵍˢ 18¹⁰ᵍˢ
1⁷ˢᵈ 8⁹ˢᵈ **1-1-10 £9,721**

Campbell's Tale (Ire) *T J Fitzgerald*   87
5 gr g Lake Coniston (Ire) - Fair Tale (USA)
11⁸ˢᵈ 12⁶ˢᵈ **0-0-2**

Campbells Lad *A Berry*   50 a45
3 b c Mind Games - T O O Mamma'S (Ire)
5⁵ˢᵈ 4⁷ˢᵈ 8⁶ᵍ 12⁸ˢ 3¹²ᵍᶠ 14¹⁰ᵍˢ 2⁹ᶠ
4¹⁰ˢ 3⁹ˢᵈ 2⁸ˢ **0-4-11 £2,010**

Campeon (Ire) *M J Wallace*   73 a51
2 b g Monashee Mountain (USA) - Arcticlead (USA)
12⁵ᵍ 5⁵ᵍˢ 9⁵ᵍ 5⁵ᵍᶠ 2⁷ᵍᶠ 4⁸ᵍᶠ 36ᵍᶠ 5⁵ᵍ
2⁶ᵍᶠ 4⁶ˢʷ 2⁵ᵍˢ **0-4-11 £5,224**

Camrose *J L Dunlop*   98
3 ch c Zafonic (USA) - Tularosa
4¹⁰ᵍˢ 3¹¹ᵍᶠ 2¹⁰ᵍᶠ 5¹²ᵍᶠ 2¹⁰ᵍ 1¹²ᵍᶠ 10¹²ᵍ
1-2-7 £20,856

Can Can Flyer (Ire) *M Johnston*   76
3 ch c In The Wings - Can Can Lady

1^{10gs} 2^{12s} 2^{14gf} 7^{12hy} 7^{12g} **1-2-5 £6,916**

Canadian Danehill (Ire) *R M H Cowell* a25
2 b c Indian Danehill (Ire) - San Jovita (Can)
9^{7sd} 13^{9sd} **0-0-2**

Canadian Storm *Miss Venetia Williams* 64
3 gr c With Approval (Can) - Sheer Gold (USA)
5^{7g} 7^{7gf} 4^{12g} 5^{10f} 1^{10g} **1-0-5 £4,445**

Canary Dancer *P C Haslam* 59
2 b f Groom Dancer (USA) - Bird Of Time (Ire)
11^{6f} 4^{5gf} 2^{6gf} 8^{7gf} 9^{7s} 7^{7gs} **0-1-6**
£1,618

Canatrice (Ire) *T D McCarthy*
4 gr f Brief Truce (USA) - Cantata (Ire)
15^{12s} **0-0-1**

Candleriggs (Ire) *D Nicholls* 61
8 ch g Indian Ridge - Ridge Pool (Ire)
13^{5hy} 13^{5gf} 7^{6f} 13^{5gf} **0-0-4**

Candy Anchor (Fr) *R E Peacock* a44
5 b m Slip Anchor - Kandavu
2^{10sd} 7^{10sd} 7^{8sd} **0-1-3 £415**

Canlis *D W Thompson* 53
5 b g Halling (USA) - Fajjoura (Ire)
7^{7gf} 2^{8gf} 12^{7gf} 7^{12gf} 5^{8gs} 7^{12g} 9^{8f}
8^{10f} 6^{7s} **0-1-10 £1,362**

Canni Thinkaar (Ire) *P Butler* 59 a51
3 b g Alhaarth (Ire) - Cannikin (Ire)
6^{10gf} 15^{12g} 7^{14f} 4^{10g} 10^{10gf} 3^{10sd} 12^{9gf}
0-1-7 £972

Cantarna (Ire) *J Mackie* 75
3 ch f Ashkalani (Ire) - Lancea (Ire)
2^{8gs} 3^{8gf} 5^{10gf} 1^{8gs} 6^{8gf} 7^{8s} **1-2-6**
£7,660

Cantemerle (Ire) *W M Brisbourne* 61
4 b f Bluebird (USA) - Legally Delicious
2^{12hy} 7^{12gf} 7^{12gs} 6^{12g} 7^{16s} 9^{12g} **0-1-6**
£974

Canterloupe (Ire) *C A Dwyer* 84 a67
6 b m Wolfhound (USA) - Missed Again
8^{6sd} 10^{6gf} 7^{6gf} 7^{6g} 1^{6g} 8^{6s} 8^{6g} 5^{5sd}
1-0-8 £6,825

Canton (Ire) *R Hannon* 96 a87
2 b c Desert Style (Ire) - Thirlmere
6^{5s} 1^{5sd} 4^{5gs} 4^{5g} 3^{5sd} 3^{5gs} 3^{6gs}
13^{6g} **1-2-9 £10,834**

Cantoris *C L Popham* 34
4 b g Unfuwain (USA) - Choir Mistress
12^{18f} **0-0-1**

Cantrip *Miss B Sanders* 58 a43
4 b f Celtic Swing - Circe
8^{16sd} 14^{12sd} 7^{12gf} 17^{12gf} 12^{14gf} 9^{14gf}
12^{16sd} 5^{12gf} 11^{16sd} 5^{16g} **1-1-11 £3,896**

Caona (USA) *J Noseda* 58
2 b f Miswaki (USA) - Hawzah
8^{6gf} 5^{6gf} 10^{6gs} **0-0-3**

Capable Guest (Ire) *M R Channon* 106
2 b/br c Cape Cross (Ire) - Alexander Confranc (Ire)
3^{6gs} 3^{6gf} 3^{6gf} 2^{7gf} 1^{7gf} 4^{7g} 3^{8gf} 4^{8gs}
1-4-8 £25,825

Cape Canaveral (Ire) *G L Moore* a38
5 b g Sadler's Wells (USA) - Emmaline (USA)
7^{12sd} **0-0-1**

Cape Columbine *D R C Elsworth* 98
2 b f Diktat - Cape Merino
2^{6g} 1^{6s} **1-1-2 £71,300**

Cape Enterprise (USA) *J W Hills* a61
2 b c Cape Canaveral (USA) - Principessa (USA)
7^{7sd} 3^{7sd} **0-1-2 £556**

Cape Fear *B J Meehan* 101
3 b c Cape Cross (Ire) - Only In Dreams
10^{7s} 7^{8gs} 5^{6gs} **0-0-3**

Cape Greko *A M Balding* 93
2 ro c Loup Sauvage (USA) - Onefortheditch (USA)
2^{7g} 1^{7g} **1-1-2 £7,266**

Cape Of Good Hope *D Oughton* 118
6 ch g Inchinor - Cape Merino
6^{7gf} 3^{5gf} 2^{5gf} 2^{6gf} 2^{5gf} 3^{6f} 4^{6gs} 3^{6hy}
0-5-8 £378,076

Cape Quest *R Hannon* 85
2 b c Piccolo - Belle Vue
10^{7gf} 3^{6gf} 1^{6gf} 8^{7f} **1-1-4 £6,728**

Cape Royal *Mrs J R Ramsden* 97
4 b g Prince Sabo - Indigo
9^{5g} 6^{5gf} 1^{5s} 7^{5gs} 6^{5gs} 11^{5gf} 2^{5g} 8^{5gs}
3^{5g} 2^{5gf} 17^{5g} **1-3-11 £16,601**

Cape St Vincent *H Morrison* 81 a88
4 gr g Paris House - Cape Merino
10^{6gs} 1^{6sd} 2^{6gf} 7^{6gf} 8^{6gf} **1-1-5 £6,219**

Cape Vincent *J H M Gosden* 91
3 b c Cape Cross (Ire) - Samhat Mtoto
1^{7gs} 5^{9gs} **1-0-2 £5,804**

Caper *R Hollinshead* 30
4 b g Salse (USA) - Spinning Mouse
9^{14gf} 15^{14sd} 11^{12g} 14^{16f} 11^{12sd} **0-0-5**

Capestar (Ire) *B G Powell* 78
3 b f Cape Cross (Ire) - Sedulous
6^{7g} 2^{7gs} 18^{8gf} 4^{7g} **1-1-4 £7,670**

Capetown Girl *K R Burke* 79
3 b f Danzero (Aus) - Cavernista
1^{6s} 12^{8s} 8^{7gf} 7^{7g} 10^{7g} 12^{6gf} 13^{7s}
11^{7gs} **1-0-8 £5,473**

Capitole (Ire) *E F Vaughan* 66
3 b g Imperial Ballet (Ire) - Blue Glass
11^{8gf} 4^{10gf} 5^{8gs} 4^{8g} 11^{8gf} 3^{14s} **0-1-6**
£1,260

Capped For Victory (USA) *Sir Michael Stoute* 91
3 b c Red Ransom (USA) - Nazoo (Ire)
2^{8g} 7^{8gf} 12^{7gf} **0-1-3 £1,784**

Capricho *J Akehurst* 105
7 gr g Lake Coniston (Ire) - Star Spectacle
17^{6g} 4^{6g} 11^{7gf} 10^{7gf} 11^{7s} 16^{6g} 9^{6s}
6^{6gf} 12^{6s} **0-0-9 £4,669**

Captain Clipper *D Nicholls* 82
4 b g Royal Applause - Collide
3^{10s} 1^{12s} 17^{12gs} **1-1-3 £4,449**

Captain Cloudy *M Madgwick* 59 a58
4 b g Whittingham (Ire) - Money Supply
5^{7sd} 6^{8sd} 6^{7sd} 14^{5gf} 10^{5gf} 3^{7f} 12^{8gf} 4^{6g}
7^{7gf} 4^{8g} **0-3-10 £697**

Captain Crusoe *P Howling* a65
6 b g Selkirk (USA) - Desert Girl
3^{11ss} 10^{12sd} **0-1-2 £364**

Captain Darling (Ire) *R M H Cowell* 70 a65
4 b g Pennekamp (USA) - Gale Warning (Ire)
6^{7sw} 7^{10sd} 2^{7gs} 9^{8gs} 7^{8gf} 5^{7gf} 7^{6gf} 14^{7sd}
0-1-8 £1,293

Captain Fearless *Mrs C A Dunnett* 1
3 ch g Defacto (USA) - Madam Poppy
13^{8sd} 8^{10sd} 6^{10gf} **0-0-3**

Captain Hurricane *P W Chapple-Hyam* 107
2 b c Desert Style (Ire) - Ravine

2[6f] 2[6g] 1[6gf] 4[6vs] 16[6g] **1-2-5 £56,456**

Captain Johnno (Ire) *D R Loder*　　75 a82
2 b g Tagula (Ire) - Thornby Park
7[7gs] 3[6gs] 3[5gf] 1[6sd] **1-2-4 £4,532**

Captain Margaret *J Pearce*　　63
2 b f Royal Applause - Go For Red (Ire)
10[6gs] 5[7gf] 10[7gs] 12[8g] 3[7gf] 12[8s] **0-1-6 £581**

Captain Marryat *J Akehurst*　　68 a69
3 ch g Inchinor - Finlaggan
2[8g] 11[8hy] 2[8f] 2[8gf] 3[8g] 2[11g] 3[10gf] 2[12sd] **0-7-8 £7,507**

Captain Miller *N J Henderson*　　79
8 b g Batshoof - Miller's Gait
2[14gs] 2[12gf] 15[15s] **0-2-3 £5,562**

Captain Saif *N Wilson*　　85
4 b c Compton Place - Bahawir Pour (USA)
14[8g] 16[7gf] 11[8g] 4[9gf] 3[7g] 14[7gf] 17[10s] **0-1-7 £945**

Cara Bella *D R Loder*　　81
3 ch f Seeking The Gold (USA) - Cherokee Rose (Ire)
7[7g] 5[8s] 3[7gf] 6[7f] **0-1-4 £1,393**

Cara Fantasy (Ire) *J L Dunlop*　　86
4 b f Sadler's Wells (USA) - Gay Fantasy
4[14s] 7[14gf] 2[15g] **0-1-3 £2,102**

Cara Sposa (Ire) *Mrs Stef Liddiard*　　22
2 b c Lend A Hand - Charlton Spring (Ire)
11[6s] **0-0-1**

Caracara (Ire) *M Johnston*
3 ch f Nashwan (USA) - Vividimagination (USA)
13[10gs] **0-0-1**

Caradak (Ire) *John M Oxx*　　112
3 b c Desert Style (Ire) - Caraiyma (Ire)
4[8gy] 1[7gf] 1[8gf] 3[8g] 6[7s] **2-1-5 £42,053**

Cardinal Venture (Ire) *K A Ryan*　　96 a97
6 b g Bishop Of Cashel - Phoenix Venture (Ire)
2[7ss] 11[8g] 7[7g] 15[8gs] 1[6gs] 8[6f] 16[7gs] 15[6s] 15[6g] 4[7gs] **1-2-10 £9,036**

Cargo *B A Pearce*　　53 a56
5 b g Emarati (USA) - Portvasco
11[6sd] 4[6sd] 2[6sd] 11[6sd] 2[7sd] 3[6sd] 2[7gf] 8[8gf] 7[6g] 2[7gf] 2[6f] 9[8gf] 9[6gf] 2[6g] 1[5sd] 1[5sd] **2-7-16 £7,113**

Caribbean Blue *R M Whitaker*　　45
3 b f First Trump - Something Blue
5[6gf] 8[7gf] 9[6s] 19[6gf] 7[6gf] 18[6gs] **0-0-6**

Caribbean Coral *J J Quinn*　　106
5 ch g Brief Truce (USA) - Caribbean Star
8[5g] 2[5gs] 1[5gf] 1[5s] 13[6gf] 11[5gs] 3[5gf] 11[5g] 4[5g] 4[5s] 9[5s] **2-2-11 £68,840**

Caribbean Dancer (USA) *M Johnston*　　71
2 b f Theatrical - Enticed (USA)
10[7gs] 8[8f] 2[9gs] 13[8s] **0-1-4 £1,681**

Caribbean Diamond (Ire) *I A Wood*　　24
2 b f Imperial Ballet (Ire) - Bebe Auction (Ire)
9[8gf] **0-0-1**

Caribe (Fr) *A Berry*　　71 a36
5 b g Octagonal (NZ) - Caring Society
6[8s] 12[7f] 10[6gf] 8[6sd] 10[7sd] **0-0-5 £219**

Carini *H Candy*　　95
3 b f Vettori (Ire) - Secret Waters
3[10gf] 6[12g] 3[10gf] 8[10hy] 5[12gs] **0-0-5 £5,112**

Cark *J Balding*　　20 a56
6 b g Farfelu - Precious Girl

6[5sd] 1[5sd] 2[5sd] 8[5ss] 7[5sw] 13[5sd] 14[5hy] **1-1-7 £2,935**

Carla Moon *C F Wall*　　34
3 b f Desert Prince (Ire) - Khambani (Ire)
11[7gf] 19[6g] 12[10gf] 10[7gf] **0-0-4**

Carlburg (Ire) *C E Brittain*　　56 a41
3 b g Barathea (Ire) - Ichnusa
10[11gf] 11[7g] 12[7gf] 12[8sd] 8[9sd] **0-0-5**

Carlton (Ire) *C R Dore*　　66 a64
10 ch g Thatching - Hooray Lady
8[7sd] 4[6sd] 4[7sw] 10[6sd] 2[6gs] 4[7gf] 5[7sd] 2[6hy] 2[6s] 2[6hy] 7[7s] 8[7sd] 5[7gs] 9[7gs] 9[6gs] 10[7gs] **0-5-16 £4,585**

Carlys Quest *Ferdy Murphy*　　15
10 ch g Primo Dominie - Tuppy (USA)
27[20gf] **0-0-1**

Carmania (Ire) *R P Elliott*　　53
2 b g Desert Sun - Scatter Brain
16[6g] 5[5g] 9[5fy] 13[5gf] 12[5f] **0-0-5**

Carmarthen Belle *Miss L C Siddall*
4 b f Merdon Melody - Woodland Steps
18[6gs] 17[8s] **0-0-2**

Carnivore *T D Barron*　　71
2 ch c Zafonic (USA) - Ermine (Ire)
25[f] **0-1-1 £1,912**

Carnt Spell *Ms Deborah J Evans*　　24
3 b g Wizard King - Forever Shineing
13[8hy] **0-0-1**

Carols Choice *A Sadik*　　a39
7 b m Emarati (USA) - Lucky Song
6[6sd] 5[5sd] 10[5sd] **0-0-3**

Caronte (Ire) *S R Bowring*　　16 a41
4 b g Sesaro (USA) - Go Likecrazy
10[7sd] 12[5sd] 12[6ss] 13[7sd] 10[7sd] 1[5sd] 8[6sd] 8[5f] 7[5gf] 1-0-9 £1,452

Caroubier (Ire) *J Gallagher*　　82 a82
4 ch g Woodborough (USA) - Patsy Grimes
5[9sd] 2[9sd] 1[8sd] 2[8sw] 9[8sd] 1[8gs] 9[10g] 9[8gf] 14[10gf] 15[8g] 6[12sd] 12[13gs] 14[10gf] **2-2-13 £9,342**

Carriacou *P W D'Arcy*　　73 a67
3 b f Mark Of Esteem (Ire) - Cockatoo Island
6[9gs] 4[8sd] 5[7s] 9[8g] 5[7g] 3[10gf] 7[10gf] 4[9s] 7[10g] 3[12gs] 10[12sd] 6[12s] **0-2-12 £2,009**

Carrizo Creek (Ire) *B J Meehan*　　104
3 b c Charnwood Forest (Ire) - Violet Spring (Ire)
7[7g] 7[7g] **0-0-2**

Carrowdore (Ire) *G A Huffer*　　76 a66
4 b c Danehill (USA) - Euromill
2[12sd] 4[12gf] 3[13gf] 4[15gf] 2[10f] 2[11f] 4[10gf] 3[11g] 4[12g] **0-6-9 £6,706**

Carry On Doc *J W Hills*　　87 a68
3 b c Dr Devious (Ire) - Florentynna Bay
3[7sd] 6[8f] 1[8gf] 5[7gf] 3[7f] 1[9g] 11[9g] 7[9g] **2-0-8 £17,058**

Carry On Katie (USA) *Saeed Bin Suroor*　　108
3 br f Fasliyev (USA) - Dinka Raja (USA)
6[8g] 9[8gf] **0-0-2 £4,841**

Carte Diamond (USA) *B Ellison*　　108
3 ch c Theatrical - Liteup My Life (USA)
1[11g] 1[12gs] 2[14g] 3[12g] 1[12s] **3-2-5 £60,590**

Carte Noire *J G Portman*　　63 a37
3 b f Revoque (Ire) - Coffee Cream
5[8g] 1[7gf] 8[7sd] 11[8gf] 11[7gf] 7[8f] **1-0-6 £3,059**

Carte Royale *M Johnston*　　87

2 ch g Loup Sauvage (USA) - Noble One
1⁵ᶠ 2⁵ᶠ 6⁶ᵍ **1-0-3 £5,071**

Carte Sauvage (USA) *M Johnston*   102 a96
3 gr/ro c Kris S (USA) - See You (USA)
6⁸ᶠᵗ 13¹⁰ʰʸ 4¹⁰ˢ **0-0-3 £1,500**

Cartography (Ire) *Saeed Bin Suroor*   111
3 b c Zafonic (USA) - Sans Escale (USA)
3⁷ᵍᶠ 3⁷ᵍᶠ 2⁶ᵍ 18⁶ᵍ 2⁶ˢ **0-4-5 £21,667**

Cartronageeraghlad (Ire) *J A Osborne*   82 a75
3 b g Mujadil (USA) - Night Scent (Ire)
10⁷ᵍ 12⁶ᵍˢ 9⁷ˢ 9⁸ᵍᶠ 2⁹ᵍᶠ 4¹⁰ᵍᶠ 4⁹ᵍᶠ 5¹⁰ᵍˢ
4¹⁰ᵍᶠ 12¹⁰ᵍᶠ 8⁹ᵍˢ 8⁹ᵍˢ 6⁹ˢᵈ **0-2-13 £3,995**

Casalese *M D Hammond*   36
2 ch g Wolfhound (USA) - Little Redwing
13⁷ᶠ 7⁸ˢ 8⁸ˢ **0-0-3**

Casantella *M J Polglase*   a44
3 b f Atraf - Ramajana (USA)
8⁸ˢᵈ 4⁷ˢᵈ 5⁸ˢᵈ 7⁸ˢᵈ 5⁸ˢˢ 10⁸ˢᵈ 8⁷ˢᵈ 9¹⁰ˢᵈ
0-0-8

Cascade Lakes *W M Brisbourne*   24
2 ch f Fraam - Spring Flyer (Ire)
13⁷ˢ **0-0-1**

Casey's House *F Watson*   24
4 gr f Paris House - Case Dismissed (Ire)
12⁷ᵍᶠ 8⁵ʰʸ 10⁶ᵍ 11⁶ˢᵈ **0-0-4**

Cash *Paul Johnson*   65 a69
6 b g Bishop Of Cashel - Ballad Island
7⁶ˢᵈ 1⁵ˢˢ 3⁵ˢʷ 5⁵ˢˢ 18⁵ᵍ 11⁵ʰʸ 14⁶ˢ 1⁵ᵍ
18⁵ᵍᶠ 13⁵ˢ **2-1-10 £6,420**

Cash On (Ire) *M P Tregoning*   56 a61
2 ch c Spectrum (Ire) - Lady Lucre (Ire)
13⁸ˢ 9⁸ˢᵈ **0-0-2**

Cash Time *J O'Reilly*   34
2 ch f Timeless Times (USA) - Cashmirie
6⁶ᵍᶠ 14⁶ᵍ 4⁵ᵍᶠ 12⁷ˢ **0-0-4**

Cashbar *J R Fanshawe*   81 a64
3 b f Bishop Of Cashel - Barford Sovereign
2⁸ˢᵈ 1⁸ᵍᶠ 8⁸ᵍˢ **1-1-3 £4,138**

Cashel House (Ire) *Daniel Mark Loughnane* 67 a68
2 b c Bishop Of Cashel - Forest Treasure (USA)
2⁵ᶠ 3⁵ᶠ 14⁷ʸ 5⁵ᵍ 4⁵ˢᵈ **0-1-5 £3,175**

Cashel Mead *J L Spearing*   71 a84
4 b f Bishop Of Cashel - Island Mead
5⁶ˢᵈ 9⁶ˢᵈ 8⁷ˢᵈ 6⁶ᵍˢ 15⁶ᵍˢ 12⁶ᵍˢ 7⁷ˢᵈ
10⁶ˢᵈ **0-0-8**

Cashema (Ire) *Mrs P N Dutfield*   50
3 b f Cape Cross (Ire) - Miss Shema (USA)
8⁸ᵍˢ 16¹⁰ˢ 8⁸ᵍ 16¹²ᵍˢ **0-0-4**

Cashier *J H M Gosden*   73
2 gr c Alhaarth (Ire) - Cashew
3⁷ˢ **0-1-1 £545**

Cashneem (Ire) *W M Brisbourne*   69
6 b g Case Law - Haanem
4⁷ʰʸ 6⁷ᶠ 1⁷ᶠ 4⁷ᵍᶠ 9⁸ˢ 14⁷ᵍ 24⁸ᵍᶠ
18⁷ᵍ **1-0-9 £4,070**

Caspian Dusk *W G M Turner*   a70
3 b g Up And At 'Em - Caspian Morn
2⁸ˢˢ 3¹⁰ˢᵈ 1⁸ˢᵈ 2⁸ˢˢ 1¹¹ˢᵈ 3¹²ˢᵈ 7¹¹ˢᵈ
2-3-7 £6,506

Caspian Lake (Ire) *Mrs L C Jewell*   23 a50
3 ch g Lake Coniston (Ire) - Hardtimes (Ire)
9⁸ᵍ 8⁹ˢᵈ 7⁷ˢᵈ **0-0-3**

Cassanos (Ire) *Miss Gay Kelleway*   a45
3 b g Ali-Royal (Ire) - I'm Your Girl
3⁹ˢʷ 6⁸ˢᵈ **0-1-2 £470**

Cassydora *J L Dunlop*   97
2 b f Darshaan - Claxon
6⁷ᵍ 17ᵍˢ 48ᵍ **1-0-3 £9,557**

Castagna (USA) *H R A Cecil*   86
3 ch f Horse Chestnut (SAF) - Thrilling Day
4¹⁰ᵍᶠ 1¹⁰ᵍᶠ 7¹²ˢ 8¹²ᵍᶠ **1-0-4 £5,435**

Castaigne (Fr) *B W Duke*   56 a56
5 ch m Pivotal - Storm Warning
7¹⁰ˢᵈ 13¹⁰ˢᵈ 6¹⁰ᵍᶠ 7¹⁰ᶠ 4¹¹ᵍᶠ 4¹⁰ᵍˢ 11¹⁰ᵍᶠ
0-0-7 £269

Castanet *A E Price*   46
5 b m Pennekamp (USA) - Addaya (Ire)
5¹⁶ᵍˢ 9¹²ᵍᶠ **0-0-2**

Castaway Queen (Ire) *W R Muir*   69 a38
5 ch m Selkirk (USA) - Surfing
2¹⁰ᵍ 13¹⁰ˢᵈ 8¹⁰ᵍᶠ 3⁸ᶠ 9¹⁰ᵍ **0-2-5 £1,835**

Castelletto *B A McMahon*   104
2 b f Komaite (USA) - Malcesine (Ire)
3⁵ˢ 5⁵ᵍᶠ 2⁵ᵍ 1⁵ᵍ 2⁵ᵍ 5⁶ˢ 2⁶ᵍ 3⁶ˢ
1⁵ˢ **2-5-10 £41,731**

Casterossa *D Haydn Jones*   70
2 ch f Rossini (USA) - First Musical
6⁶ᵍ 4⁶ᵍᶠ 6⁶ᵍˢ 1⁹⁷ᵍ **0-0-5 £799**

Castleshane (Ire) *S Gollings*   82
7 b g Kris - Ahbab (Ire)
11¹⁰ᵍᶠ **0-0-1**

Castleton *H J Cyzer*   115
3 b c Cape Cross (Ire) - Craigmill
2⁷ˢ 3¹⁰ᵍᶠ 18ᵍᶠ 6⁸ᵍᶠ **1-1-4 £13,852**

Casual Glance *A M Balding*   53
2 b f Sinndar (Ire) - Spurned (USA)
13⁷ᵍᶠ 9⁸ᵍˢ **0-0-2**

Cat's Whiskers *M W Easterby*   86
5 b g Catrail (USA) - Haut Volee
7¹¹ˢ 3⁸ᵍ 4⁸ᵍ 15¹⁰ᵍ 2⁸ᵍˢ 7¹⁰ᵍˢ 5⁹ᵍˢ **0-2-7
£5,869**

Catalini *M R Channon*   73 a76
3 ch g Seeking The Gold (USA) - Calando (USA)
2⁸ˢᵈ 5⁸ˢᵈ 5⁷ᶠ 6⁸ᵍˢ **1-0-4 £946**

Catch A Star *N A Callaghan*   84
2 ch f Giant's Causeway (USA) - Amy Hunter (USA)
3⁶ᵍᶠ 5⁶ᵍᶠ 8⁷ᵍᶠ 3⁶ᵍˢ 1⁸ᵍˢ 3⁷ᵍ 6⁸ᵍ **1-3-7
£12,177**

Catch The Cat (Ire) *J S Wainwright*   79
5 b g Catrail (USA) - Tongabezi (Ire)
3⁵ᵍ 7⁶ˢ 2⁵ʰʸ 8⁵ᵍ 1⁵ᵍᶠ 6⁵ᵍᶠ 5⁶ᵍᶠ 7⁵ᵍˢ 7⁵ᵍˢ
10⁵ᵍᶠ 1⁵ᵍᶠ 8⁵ᵍᶠ 8⁵ᵍˢ 14⁵ᵍᶠ 14⁵ᵍᶠ **2-2-15
£20,617**

Catch The Fox *J J Bridger*   49 a31
4 b g Fraam - Versaillesprincess
12⁷ᵍˢ 3⁷ᵍ 7⁷ʰʸ 10¹⁰ᵍᶠ 4⁹ᵍ 12⁹ᵍᶠ 9⁸ᵍᶠ
10¹⁰ᵍˢ 4⁸ᵍˢ 7⁸ˢᵈ 3⁷ᵍ 3⁸ᵍ 17⁹ˢ **0-3-13 £1,841**

Catch The Wind *I A Wood*   88 a75
3 b f Bahamian Bounty - Tinkerbird
13⁶ˢ 5⁵ˢᵈ 6⁵ᵍˢ 1⁵ᵍᶠ 2⁵ᵍᶠ 2⁵ᵍˢ 12⁵ᵍ
1-2-8 £7,384

Catchthebatch *E A Wheeler*   34 a55
8 b g Beveled (USA) - Batchworth Dancer
4⁵ˢᵈ 3¹¹ˢˢ 11⁵ˢᵈ 11⁵ˢᵈ 16⁵ᵍᶠ 10⁶ᵍ
15⁵ᵍ **0-1-8 £370**

Caterham Common *D W Chapman*   a33
5 b g Common Grounds - Pennine Pink (Ire)
11⁸ˢᵈ 6⁷ˢᵈ 8⁸ˢ 10⁸ˢʷ 5⁷ˢᵈ **0-0-5**

Catherine Howard *M R Channon*   74
3 b f Kingmambo (USA) - Darling Flame (USA)

4^{8g} 9^{8gf} 4^{8gf} 5^{8gf} **0-0-4 £1,196**

Catherine Wheel *J R Fanshawe* 82 a82
3 b f Primo Dominie - Prancing
2^{6gs} 1^{5gf} 1^{6gf} 1^{6sd} **3-1-4 £14,620**

Catstar (USA) *Saeed Bin Suroor* 93 a108
3 b/br f Storm Cat (USA) - Advancing Star (USA)
1^{8ft} 5^{7g} 5^{7gf} **1-0-3 £92,282**

Catwalk Cleric (Ire) *M J Wallace* 88
2 b c Orpen (USA) - Ministerial Model (Ire)
4^{5gs} 1^{5s} 2^{6g} 13^{6gf} 4^{6gs} 4^{8s} 8^{6s} **1-1-7**
£20,764

Cause Celebre (Ire) *B W Hills* 83
3 gr f Peintre Celebre (USA) - Madame Belga (USA)
1^{10gf} 10^{12g} 1^{11gf} 6^{10g} 13^{11g} 8^{10gf} **2-0-6**
£9,431

Causeway Girl (Ire) *D M Simcock* 42
2 br f Giant's Causeway (USA) - Darbela (Ire)
17^{7g} 17^{7gs} **0-0-2**

Caustic Wit (Ire) *M S Saunders* 93 a67
6 b g Cadeaux Genereux - Baldemosa (Fr)
1^{6sd} 13^{6sd} 1^{6s} 1^{6gf} 1^{6gf} 1^{6gf} 2^{6gf} 2^{6gf}
9^{6g} 12^{6gs} 4^{5s} 6^{6g} 6^{6gs} **5-2-13 £42,713**

Cava Bien *J G Given* 68
2 b g Bien Bien (USA) - Bebe De Cham
7^{7f} 3^{7g} 3^{7gf} 7^{8g} 5^{10gf} 1^{8gs} **1-1-6**
£2,535

Cavalarra *B W Hills* 59
2 b c Green Desert (USA) - Ya Tarra
8^{5g} 5^{6gs} **0-0-2**

Cavan Gael (Fr) *P Howling* 65
2 b c Dansili - Time Will Show (Fr)
9^{8g} 6^{7s} 8^{6gs} **0-0-3**

Cavaradossi *B J Meehan*
2 gr c Lake Coniston (Ire) - Floria Tosca
PU^{16f} 15^{6g} **0-0-2**

Cave Of The Giant (Ire) *T D McCarthy* 73
2 b c Giant's Causeway (USA) - Maroussie (Fr)
5^{8g} 9^{8g} **0-0-2**

Caveral *R Hannon* 101
3 ch f Ashkalani (Ire) - Melting Gold (USA)
8^{8s} 7^{7g} 1^{6gf} 10^{6g} 3^{6g} 10^{7g} 6^{7gf} 11^{7gf}
1-1-8 £13,039

Cavorting *D R Loder* 73
2 ch g Polar Falcon (USA) - Prancing
4^{5g} 7^{5g} **0-0-2 £367**

Cayenne (Ger) *D M Simcock* 52
2 ch f Efisio - Carola Rouge
5^{5g} 5^{7f} **0-0-2**

Cayman Breeze *J M Bradley* 60 a57
4 b g Danzig (USA) - Lady Thynn (Fr)
12^{7sd} 5^{7sd} 4^{6sd} 1^{7sd} 8^{7gf} 5^{6gf} 9^{8gf} 10^{6g}
4^{7g} 12^{7sd} **1-1-10 £1,312**

Cayman Calypso (Ire) *J M Jefferson* 63
3 ro g Danehill Dancer (Ire) - Warthill Whispers
9^{8gf} 3^{7gf} 6^{7gf} 7^{6gf} 8^{8gf} 2^{8g} 2^{8gs} 12^{10gs}
12^{8gf} 17^{8gf} 14^{10g} **0-2-11 £1,959**

Cayman King *R Craggs*
2 b g Cayman Kai (Ire) - Distinctly Laura (Ire)
14^{6gf} **0-0-1**

Cayman Mischief *James Moffatt* 31
4 b f Cayman Kai (Ire) - Tribal Mischief
7^{9sd} 14^{6s} 6^{6f} 8^{5s} **0-0-4**

Cayman Sunrise (Ire) *E A L Dunlop* a57
4 gr f Peintre Celebre (USA) - Sum (USA)
8^{9sd} **0-0-1**

Caymans Gift *A C Whillans* 60
4 ch g Cayman Kai (Ire) - Gymcrak Cyrano (Ire)
4^{12g} 5^{9gs} 8^{8gf} 3^{13g} 10^{12g} **0-0-5 £827**

Cayuse *T T Clement* 1
2 b f Double Trigger (Ire) - Suile Mor
18^{7s} 18^{7gs} **0-0-2**

Cazenove *M G Quinlan* 61
3 b g Royal Applause - Celestina (Ire)
10^{9g} 4^{7gs} 6^{7g} 7^{7gf} 13^{7gf} **0-0-5 £268**

Cazisa Star (USA) *P W Harris* 47
3 ch f Mister Baileys - Placer Queen
11^{10gf} 8^{10f} 9^{12gf} **0-0-3**

Cd Europe (Ire) *J J Quinn* 94
6 ch g Royal Academy (USA) - Woodland Orchid (Ire)
8^{6gf} 25^{6f} 17^{6s} 10^{7g} 6^{6gf} 10^{6gf} 10^{6s}
2^{6gf} 2^{6s} **0-2-9 £13,127**

Cd Flyer (Ire) *B Ellison* 95
7 ch g Grand Lodge (USA) - Pretext
5^{6g} 2^{6s} 19^{6g} 7^{6gs} 16^{6g} 13^{6s} 4^{7g}
3^{6gf} 5^{6s} 6^{6s} 18^{6s} 2^{7g} 12^{6s} 14^{7gs} **1-3-15**
£25,790

Ceasar (Ire) *P A Blockley* 56 a52
3 b g Orpen (USA) - Fen Princess (Ire)
2^{8sd} 11^{1sd} 10^{12ss} 1^{12s} 3^{12gf} 9^{14f} **2-2-6**
£7,857

Cedar Master (Ire) *J R Boyle* 65
7 b g Soviet Lad (USA) - Samriah (Ire)
10^{14gf} 7^{16g} **0-0-2**

Cedric Coverwell *D K Ivory* 41 a35
4 ch g Charmer - Marsara
4^{6sd} 17^{7gs} 13^{6s} 11^{5gf} 12^{5f} 16^{6g} 5^{5gf}
9^{6f} **0-0-8**

Cefira (USA) *M H Tompkins* 66
3 b f Distant View (USA) - Bold Jessie
3^{6s} 8^{6g} 1^{6f} 7^{6gs} 17^{6s} **1-1-5 £4,329**

Ceiriog Valley *B W Hills* 83
2 b f In The Wings - Bodfari Quarry
8^{7gf} 1^{7s} 11^{8g} **1-0-3 £7,280**

Celadon (Ire) *N P Littmoden* a56
3 b g Fasliyev (USA) - Dancing Drop
2^{5sd} **0-1-1 £1,244**

Celebre Citation (Ire) *J R Fanshawe* 62
3 ch g Peintre Celebre (USA) - Kotama (USA)
12^{8gf} 5^{10gf} 12^{8gs} 18^{12hy} **0-0-4**

Celestial Arc (USA) *P F I Cole* 71
2 b c Southern Halo (USA) - Perfect Arc (USA)
3^{7g} 11^{7gs} 7^{6gf} 12^{8gf} 7^{10gf} **0-1-5 £848**

Cellarmaster (Ire) *E F Vaughan* 86
3 ch g Alhaarth (Ire) - Cheeky Weeky
3^{12gs} 1^{10g} 4^{10gs} 3^{11g} 8^{10s} **1-2-5 £6,395**

Cellino *Andrew Turnell* 46
3 b f Robellino (USA) - Celandine
12^{5ss} 4^{5gf} 10^{5gf} 7^{6gf} 10^{6gs} 10^{8f} 9^{7gs}
0-0-7

Cello *R Hannon* 88
3 gr c Pivotal - Raffelina (USA)
2^{7gs} 1^{9s} 6^{8gs} 9^{7g} 25^{8f} 4^{9gs} 2^{9gs} 3^{8gf}
1^{8s} **2-3-9 £18,783**

Celtic Blaze (Ire) *B S Rothwell* 62
5 b m Charente River (Ire) - Firdaunt
3^{16gs} 8^{16f} 7^{16gs} 5^{16g} **0-1-4 £859**

Celtic Carisma *K G Reveley* 36
2 b f Celtic Swing - Kathryn's Pet
11^{6g} 10^{7s} **0-0-2**

Celtic Heroine (Ire) *M A Jarvis* 109

3 ch f Hernando (Fr) - Celtic Fling
2[9gs] 1[8gs] 2[8gf] 1[8gf] 2[8g] 5[10gf] 2[8gf] 6[8vs]
2-3-8 £55,660

Celtic Mill *D W Barker*   113   a94
6 b g Celtic Swing - Madam Millie
1[6sd] 4[6ss] 15[6g] 1[6gf] 1[6gf] 9[6s] 5[7gf] 6[6gs]
1[5gf] 8[5g] 4[6gf] **4-0-11 £58,047**

Celtic Promise (Ire) *Mrs A J Perrett*   62   a28
2 b f Celtic Swing - Tainted Halo (USA)
14[7sd] 6[10hy] 5[10s] **0-0-3**

Celtic Romance *Ms Sue Smith*   53
5 b m Celtic Swing - Southern Sky
14[8hy] 8[7s] 8[8s] 5[7s] 8[8f] 6[7g] 7[7gf] 4[12gf]
0-0-8 £268

Celtic Solitude (Ire) *Mrs M Reveley*   10
3 b f Celtic Swing - Smart 'n Noble (USA)
12[9g] 13[14f] **0-0-2**

Celtic Spa (Ire) *Mrs P N Dutfield*   83   a64
2 gr f Celtic Swing - Allegorica (Ire)
7[5g] 1[5s] 7[5gf] 5[5f] 3[5gf] 13[5g] 4[6gf] 7[6hy]
9[6hy] 11[6sd] **1-0-10 £20,499**

Celtic Star (Ire) *J G M O'Shea*   60
6 b g Celtic Swing - Recherchee
11[13f] 6[10f] 15[10gf] **0-0-3**

Celtic Tanner (Ire) *D J Wintle*   a49
5 b g Royal Abjar (USA) - Mills Pride (Ire)
11[9sd] **0-0-1**

Celtic Thatcher *N P Littmoden*   a56
6 b g Celtic Swing - Native Thatch (Ire)
2[8sd] **0-1-1 £746**

Celtic Thunder *T J Etherington*   85
3 b g Mind Games - Lake Mistassiu
2[5g] 9[5gf] 5[5f] 8[5gf] 2[6g] 7[6g] 4[6f] 18[6gf]
5[5g] 16[5g] **0-2-11 £6,025**

Celtic Vision (Ire) *M Appleby*   71   a10
8 b g Be My Native (USA) - Dream Run
6[14g] 6[12hy] 10[7gs] 14[16gs] 4[16g] 6[15sd] 5[11f]
0-0-7 £450

Celtique *Sir Michael Stoute*   81   a69
2 b f Celtic Swing - Heart's Harmony
2[7s] 3[8gf] 2[7sd] **0-3-3 £4,186**

Cemgraft *Miss E C Lavelle*   64   a47
3 b f In The Wings - Soviet Maid (Ire)
5[11gf] 9[12gf] 6[8s] 16[12sd] **0-0-4**

Centaurus *Saeed Bin Suroor*   96
2 gr c Daylami (Ire) - Dandanna (Ire)
1[7gs] **1-0-1 £4,998**

Centifolia (Fr) *Robert Collet*   114
2 gr f Kendor (Fr) - Djayapura (Fr)
1[6g] 10[6g] 1[6g] 5[1ho] 1[6vs] **4-0-5 £109,366**

Cerebus *N P Littmoden*   77
2 b f Wolfhound (USA) - Bring On The Choir
6[6gs] 4[6gf] 2[6g] 3[7gf] 3[7f] 6[6gs] 14[7g] **0-3-7**
£3,563

Certa Cito *D Flood*   61
4 b f Mind Games - Bollin Dorothy
10[6gs] 13[6s] 5[6f] 13[6gf] 10[5g] 4[5gf] 7[7g]
0-1-7

Certain Justice (USA) *P F I Cole*   82   a65
6 gr g Lit De Justice (USA) - Pure Misk
8[8gs] 6[7s] 5[8gf] 10[8sd] 5[7g] 7[8sd] **0-0-6**

Certifiable *Andrew Reid*   74   a77
3 b g Deploy - Gentle Irony
4[9ss] 1[8sd] 1[8sd] 5[8gs] 12[8gs] 5[10f] 11[8sd] 7[7sd]
2-0-8 £8,352

Cerulean Rose *A W Carroll*   78
5 ch m Bluegrass Prince (Ire) - Elegant Rose
4[5s] 9[5gf] 2[5f] 8[6gf] 3[5gf] 15[5g] 2[5gs] 4[5s]
20[6s] 13[5g] **0-3-10 £4,540**

Cesar Manrique (Ire) *B W Hills*   79
2 ch c Vettori (Ire) - Norbella
9[5gs] 5[5g] 4[5f] 1[5s] **1-0-4 £4,555**

Cesare *J R Fanshawe*   73
3 b g Machiavellian (USA) - Tromond
2[8s] 1[8gs] 11[9g] **1-1-3 £5,316**

Ceylon Round (Fr) *M J Wallace*   57   a20
3 b g Royal Applause - Tea Colony (USA)
7[8gf] 7[8gf] 6[10gf] 10[9sd] 12[7sd] **0-0-5**

Cezzaro (Ire) *T A K Cuthbert*   47   a35
6 ch g Ashkalani (Ire) - Sept Roses (USA)
5[8sd] 6[8sf] 11[12gf] 2[10g] 2[12g] 12[8gs] 15[12gf]
9[12sd] 5[12gf] 9[8s] **0-2-10 £1,887**

Chain Of Hope (Ire) *D E Cantillon*   38
3 ch g Shinko Forest (Ire) - Fleeting Smile (Ire)
16[6gs] 10[6g] 7[8g] **0-0-3**

Chairman Bobby *B A McMahon*   77   a47
6 ch g Clantime - Formidable Liz
5[5gf] 7[5g] 19[6g] 3[5gs] 26[6f] 19[6gf] 2[5gf] 5[6gf]
8[5f] 11[6gf] 9[5gf] 17[5gs] 10[6gf] 8[6sd] 11[7sd] **0-3-15**
£3,589

Chairman Rick (Ire) *D Nicholls*   62   a51
2 b c Danehill Dancer (Ire) - Come Together
7[7gs] 6[6sd] 4[5g] 7[6gf] 7[6g] **0-0-5 £258**

Chakra *C J Gray*   36   a17
10 gr g Mystiko (USA) - Maracuja (USA)
6[6sd] 5[10g] 3[8g] 8[7sd] 10[10f] **0-1-5 £206**

Chalison (Ire) *R Hannon*   80
2 b c Anabaa (USA) - Raincloud
2[5gs] 3[6gf] 5[7g] **0-1-3 £1,788**

Chambray (Ire) *A M Balding*   56
3 b f Barathea (Ire) - Spurned (USA)
8[8g] 8[8gf] 5[12g] **0-0-3**

Champagne Brandy (Ire) *P D Evans*   32
2 ch f Spectrum (Ire) - Petite Liqueurelle (Ire)
13[5g] 13[6g] 12[6gf] **0-0-3**

Champagne Cracker *Miss L A Perratt*   65
3 ch f Up And At 'Em - Kiveton Komet
8[6s] 3[6f] 1[5gs] 9[6gf] 9[5gf] 6[6s] 25[5gs]
1-0-8 £4,306

Champagne In Paris *J A Glover*
2 gr f Paris House - Ashleen
11[5gs] **0-0-1**

Champagne Lujain *M W Easterby*   40
2 b g Lujain (USA) - Brief Glimpse (Ire)
12[6gf] 5[7s] 12[7s] **0-0-3**

Champagne Rider *D Shaw*   a46
8 b g Presidium - Petitesse
3[7sd] 5[7sd] 1[6sd] **1-1-3 £1,715**

Champagne Rossini (Ire) *M C Chapman*   53   a51
2 b g Rossini (USA) - Alpencrocus (Ire)
9[5gs] 5[8gf] 6[6sw] 12[8g] 6[6sd] **0-0-5**

Champagne Shadow (Ire) *G L Moore*   60   a76
3 b c Kahyasi - Moet (Ire)
8[8sd] 4[10sd] 12[10sd] 2[12sd] 8[12g] 2[12sd] 3[10sd]
2[12sd] 9[16g] 7[12sd] **0-4-10 £4,211**

Champain Sands (Ire) *W M Brisbourne*   65   a50
5 b g Green Desert (USA) - Grecian Bride (Ire)
3[9sd] 4[10g] 22[9gf] 7[10g] 9[10s] 9[10gf] 6[8gf]
0-2-8 £2,385

Champion Lion (Ire) *M R Channon*   75

5 b g Sadler's Wells (USA) - Honey Bun
15¹²g 10¹⁴s 5¹²s 7¹²g 6¹²gs 3¹⁰g 3¹¹s
5¹⁰gf 8¹²gs **0-2-9 £1,750**

Chance For Romance *W R Muir*   85
3 ch f Entrepreneur - My First Romance
2⁶g 6⁶g 5⁶gf 7⁶f 10⁶g **0-1-5 £1,726**

Chancellor (Ire) *G A Butler*   115
6 ch h Halling (USA) - Isticanna (USA)
9¹⁰gs 1¹⁰gs 8¹¹vs 9¹⁰gs 12¹⁰gs 6¹¹g **1-0-6**
£29,975

Chandelier *M S Saunders*   58 a61
4 ch g Sabrehill (USA) - La Noisette
5⁷sd 3⁸sd 6⁸sd 7⁸sd 3⁷sd 2⁷sd 15⁸f 1⁸g
6⁷g 10⁸gf 8⁸gs 6⁸s RR⁸f 3⁸sd 10⁷g **1-3-15**
£4,531

Chanfron *B R Millman*   60 a28
3 ch g Double Trigger (Ire) - Mhargaidh Nua
7¹²g 5¹²gs 5¹⁶g 9¹²gf 14¹²sd **0-0-5**

Changari (USA) *R Charlton*   62
3 b f Gulch (USA) - Danzari
5⁵gf **0-0-1 £390**

Chantaco (USA) *A M Balding*   74
2 b c Bahri (USA) - Dominant Dancer
5⁷gf 2⁷f 1⁷f **1-1-3 £4,556**

Chantelle (Ire) *S Kirk*   59 a45
4 b f Lake Coniston (Ire) - Kristabelle (Ire)
10⁵y 1⁵y 15⁶gf 8⁵f 5⁵g 8⁶f 7⁵g 12⁵gf
4⁷gs 7⁷sd 3⁷sd **1-1-11 £5,077**

Chantelle's Dream *I A Wood*   5
2 ch f Compton Place - Polar Peak
10⁵sd 6⁵g **0-0-2**

Chanteloup *J R Fanshawe*   95 a53
3 ch f Grand Lodge (USA) - Nibbs Point (Ire)
2⁸gs 4¹⁰gs 4¹⁰gf 3¹¹g 5¹²g 10¹³sd **0-2-6**
£5,347

Chanterelle (Ire) *J L Dunlop*   87
3 ch f Indian Ridge - Chantereine (USA)
6⁶g 6⁷s 17⁷gs **0-0-3 £441**

Chanteuse *D W Chapman*   a8
4 b f Rudimentary (USA) - Enchanting Melody
10⁶sd 6⁶sd 11⁷ss **0-0-3**

Chantilly Beauty (Fr) *R Pritchard-Gordon*   90
2 b f Josr Algarhoud (Ire) - Lysabelle (Fr)
7⁵hy 1⁶g 14⁶f 6⁸gs 3⁶g 4⁶g 2⁶g **1-1-7**
£13,275

Chantilly Gold (USA) *J M Bradley*   a20
5 ch m Mutakddim (USA) - Bouffant (USA)
10⁷sd 5⁶sd 10⁸sd **0-0-3**

Chantilly Sunset (Ire) *J Balding*
3 b f General Monash (USA) - Alpine Sunset
8⁶f 15⁷g **0-0-2**

Chantress *Mrs J R Ramsden*   89
4 b f Peintre Celebre (USA) - Up Anchor (Ire)
8⁹g 3¹²gf 7¹²g **0-0-3 £4,400**

Chantry Falls (Ire) *J G Given*   35 a33
4 br g Mukaddamah (USA) - Woodie Dancer (USA)
8⁷ss 6⁹sd 11⁶f 12⁷g **0-0-4**

Chapel Royale (Ire) *Mrs N S Sharpe*   a27
7 gr g College Chapel - Merci Royale
6⁹sd 5¹²ss **0-0-2**

Chapelco *J L Dunlop*   54
3 b g Robellino (USA) - Lady Kris (Ire)
6¹⁰gf 7¹²gf PU¹²gs **0-0-3**

Chaplin *B W Hills*   90
3 b c Groom Dancer (USA) - Princess Borghese (USA)

2¹²gs 8¹²gs 4¹²s **0-1-3 £2,059**

Chappel Cresent (Ire) *Ms Joanna Morgan*   102 a60
4 ch g College Chapel - Inshad
8⁸ss 12⁶ss 8⁶y 5⁷hy 2⁷gs 5⁸g 1⁸gs 5⁶gs
17⁷s 19⁶g 10⁸s 12⁶sh **1-1-12 £15,650**

Chapter (Ire) *R Hannon*   75
2 ch c Sinndar (Ire) - Web Of Intrigue
2⁷gf 2⁷g 7⁸gs 3⁸f 5⁸g **0-3-5 £4,146**

Chapter House (USA) *M W Easterby*   61 a70
5 b g Pulpit (USA) - Lilian Bayliss (Ire)
6⁸sd 7¹³gf 15¹²s **0-0-4**

Chara *J R Jenkins*   66 a39
3 ch f Deploy - Subtle One (Ire)
3¹⁰gs 1¹²gs 7¹²g 5¹¹s 5¹⁰gf 5¹²gf 9¹⁴gs
12¹²gf 8¹²sd **1-1-9 £5,394**

Charing Cross (Ire) *G L Moore*   38 a40
3 ch c Peintre Celebre (USA) - Charlotte Corday
5¹¹s 13¹²sd 7¹²sd 9¹²s 6¹⁰g 12¹²s **0-0-6**
£634

Chariot (Ire) *M R Bosley*
3 ch g Titus Livius (Fr) - Battle Queen
9⁸ss 18⁸s **0-0-2**

Charlatan (Ire) *Mrs C A Dunnett*
6 b g Charnwood Forest (Ire) - Taajreh (Ire)
16⁶f **0-0-1**

Charleston *R Rowe*   76 a69
3 ch g Pursuit Of Love - Discomatic (USA)
2⁸hy 2¹⁰gf 2¹⁰g 4¹²sd 11¹²gf **0-3-5**
£4,196

Charlie Bear *P Bowen*   70 a71
3 ch c Bahamian Bounty - Abi
10¹¹gs 2⁸gf 8⁸gf 3⁷sd **0-2-4 £1,950**

Charlie George *P Monteith*   51
3 ch g Idris (Ire) - Faithful Beauty (Ire)
9⁸g 6¹¹g 5⁹s **0-0-3**

Charlie Masters *P Howling*   32 a61
3 b g Polar Falcon (USA) - Bowden Rose
13⁷gf 14¹⁰gf 9⁸sd 2⁹sd **0-1-4 £425**

Charlie Parkes *M Mullineaux*   57
6 ch g Pursuit Of Love - Lucky Parkes
12⁵gf 11⁵gf **0-0-2**

Charlie Tango (Ire) *N Tinkler*   72 a75
3 b g Desert Prince (Ire) - Precedence (Ire)
3¹⁰sd 7¹⁰gs 10⁸hy 11¹⁰gf 3⁹gf 9¹⁰gs 4⁸f
1⁹g 3¹⁰f 4¹⁰g 3⁹gf 5¹¹gf 7¹⁰g 9⁸gs 12⁸g 4⁸gf
8⁹sd 2¹⁰s 4⁸s **1-4-19 £8,937**

Charlieismydarling *J A Osborne*   39
3 b g Mind Games - Blessed Lass (Hol)
4⁶gf 8⁷gf 10⁸f **0-0-3**

Charlies Profit *J J Bridger*
3 ch f Deploy - Care And Comfort
13¹⁰sd **0-0-1**

Charlieslastchance *J J Bridger*
2 b f Sure Blade (USA) - Sea Mist (Ire)
19⁸gf 14⁸g **0-0-2**

Charlotte Vale *M D Hammond*   79
3 ch f Pivotal - Drying Grass Moon
6⁸gs 5⁸g 3¹¹s 11²gf 2¹²f 3¹²s
6¹³gs **2-3-9 £15,264**

Charlottebutterfly *T T Clement*   59 a59
4 b f Millkom - Tee Gee Jay
11⁶s 4⁶gf 9⁶f 8⁷gf 3⁶gs 15⁷g 4⁶gf 1⁷sd
1-1-8 £4,132

Charlottine (Ire) *M P Sunderland*   61
3 b f Spectrum (Ire) - Lady Dulcinea (Arg)

5hy 138gf 58f 38f 58g 167gf 310hy **0-2-7**
£1,028

Charmatic (Ire) *J A Glover*   70 a70
3 br f Charnwood Forest (Ire) - Instamatic
58hy 28s 28s 18hy 58gf 410gf 510g 710s
68gf 812g 29sd 29sd **1-4-12 £9,758**

Charmed By Fire (USA) *Mrs A J Perrett*   70
3 br c Silver Charm (USA) - Mama Dean (USA)
1110gf 79gf 510gs 1110gs **0-0-4**

Charming Admiral (Ire) *Mrs A Duffield*   56
11 b g Shareef Dancer (USA) - Lilac Charm
618s 222s **0-1-2 £2,115**

Charnock Bates One (Ire) *T D Easterby*   79
3 b f Desert Sun - Fleetwood Fancy
47gs 68s 88s 18gs 28s 28gf 210s 311s 610s
1210s **1-4-10 £15,515**

Charnwood Pride (Ire) *P W Harris*   42
3 gr g Charnwood Forest (Ire) - Pride Of Pendle
1210gf 1110g 912gf **0-0-3**

Charnwood Street (Ire) *D Shaw*   a33
5 b g Charnwood Forest (Ire) - La Vigie
514sd 514sd **0-0-2**

Chase The Rainbow *Miss K M George*   57 a32
3 gr f Danzig Connection (USA) - Delta Tempo (Ire)
68sd 69g 128sd 67g 117gf 118f **0-0-6**
£220

Chasing The Dream (Ire) *A M Balding*   70 a77
3 b f Desert Sun - Dream Of Jenny
18sd 210sd 610s 109gf 38gf 48g **1-0-6**
£6,466

Chasm *M Johnston*   72
2 b c Gulch (USA) - Subito
37gf 58gf **0-0-2 £856**

Chateau Istana *N P Littmoden*   109
2 ch c Grand Lodge (USA) - Miss Queen (USA)
65gs 15gf 15gf 76gf 15f 96g **3-0-6**
£70,699

Chateau Nicol *B G Powell*   90 a90
5 b g Distant Relative - Glensara
16sd 36sd 137sd 17sd 47sd 17gs 36s 37s
37g 47g 17g 56gf 67g 66g 77gf 17g 47sd 36s
97gs **5-4-19 £38,793**

Chater Flair *B D Leavy*
7 b g Efisio - Native Flair
1212sd **0-0-1**

Chatshow (USA) *A W Carroll*   62 a59
3 br g Distant View (USA) - Galanty Show
106gf 158sd 46f 126f 58sd 86gf 106gf
127hy 36g 75gs 16s 25sd 26s **1-3-13 £4,569**

Checkit (Ire) *M R Channon*   117
4 br c Mukaddamah (USA) - Collected (Ire)
49gf 39gf 38f 69gf 88gs 78g 39g 49g 88gf
38g 410gf 88g 311g 69s 28s 29gs 78g **0-4-17**
£102,948

Cheeky Chi (Ire) *P S McEntee*   61 a60
3 b f Desert Style (Ire) - Grey Patience (Ire)
47sd 47sd 36sd 15s 46s 135s 75gf 115gf
85gf 65hy 126sd 136s **1-1-12 £4,623**

Cheese 'n Biscuits *G L Moore*   79 a65
4 b f Spectrum (Ire) - Bint Shihama (USA)
118gf 206g 28s 88gf 117g 157g 117sd
57s 47g 127sd 117s 256s 77sd 128sd **0-0-14**
£2,432

Chek Oi *W R Muir*   55 a49
2 b c Dr Fong (USA) - Silver Sun
85g 97gf 76sd 66gf PU7sd **0-0-5**

Chelsea Rose (Ire) *C Collins*   106
2 ch f Desert King (Ire) - Cinnamon Rose (USA)
17gf 37gf 17gf **2-1-3 £136,140**

Chelsea's Diamond *J Akehurst*   43
4 b f Man Among Men (Ire) - Sharp Thistle
512f 1311gf 97gf **0-0-3**

Chem's Legacy (Ire) *W R Muir*   48
4 b g Victory Note (USA) - Merlannah (Ire)
126gf 48gf 87gf **0-0-3 £429**

Cherished Number *I Semple*   85
5 b g King's Signet (USA) - Pretty Average
98s 48g 98gf 38gf 310g 108g 48g
48gf 79gf 58gf 39gs 78gs 49gf 39gs 38s 47gs
0-6-17 £8,561

Cherokee (USA) *A P O'Brien*   102
2 b f Storm Cat (USA) - Totemic (USA)
16gf 57s **1-0-2 £38,426**

Cherokee Bay *G L Moore*   a43
4 b f Primo Dominie - Me Cherokee
410sd 38sd 128sd 1210sd **0-1-4 £234**

Cherokee Nation *P W D'Arcy*   74 a79
3 br c Emperor Jones (USA) - Me Cherokee
410g 49sd 16gf 76gf 26gf 16f 16g 106gf
36s 56g 96sd 156gf 26sd 46sd **3-4-14**
£21,234

Cherry Mix (Fr) *A Fabre*   128
3 gr c Linamix (Fr) - Cherry Moon (USA)
311gs 211gs 312vs 211gs 112ho 113hy 212g
2-4-7 £358,336

Chertsey (Ire) *C E Brittain*   60 a35
3 ch f Medaaly - Cerisette (Ire)
37f 38f 56gf 98g 57f 66gf 57sw **0-0-7**
£936

Cherubim (Jpn) *D R Loder*   76 a79
3 ch f Sunday Silence (USA) - Curly Angel (Jpn)
510g 58gf 110f 210sd 1012g 1216g 99sd
1-1-7 £5,129

Chesnut Ripple *D Shaw*   a42
5 ch m Cosmonaut - Shaft Of Sunlight
48sd **0-0-1 £262**

Chestall *R Hollinshead*   60
3 b g Polar Prince (Ire) - Maradata (Ire)
412gf 412gf 512g **0-0-3 £537**

Chestminster Girl *A P Jones*
2 ch f Tomba - Nannie Annie
148gf 117sd 148hy **0-0-3**

Cheverak Forest (Ire) *Don Enrico Incisa*   61
3 ch g Shinko Forest (Ire) - Meranie Girl (Ire)
107gs 1210gf 98s 168gs 138gf 47gs **0-0-6**
£401

Chevin *R A Fahey*   50
5 ch m Danzig Connection (USA) - Starr Danias (USA)
512g 1412gf 114gf 714gf 912g 812g **1-0-6**
£4,251

Chevronne *B Llewellyn*   64
4 b g Compton Place - Maria Isabella (Fr)
1710s 107gf 27gf 169gf 167g **0-1-5 £904**

Chic *Sir Michael Stoute*   123
4 ch f Machiavellian - Exclusive
68gf 78gf 37gf 17g 18gs 28g **2-2-6**
£136,950

Chica (Ire) *J A Osborne*   a22
3 gr f Spectrum (Ire) - Wild Rose Of York
117sd **0-0-1**

Chica Roca (USA) *B J Meehan*   61 a39

3 ch f Woodman (USA) - Amenixa (Fr)
9^{8g} 16^{7g} 6^{6gf} 9^{6gf} 10^{8sd} 0-0-5

Chicago Bond (USA) B Smart   40
3 b f Real Quiet (USA) - Shariyfa (Fr)
7^{7s} 11^{10gf} 6^{9s} 9^{8f} 0-0-4

Chicago Nights (Ire) Ronald Thompson   49 a25
2 ch f Night Shift (USA) - Enclave (USA)
4^{5gs} 7^{5gf} 10^{6gf} 5^{6sd} 2^{6s} 14^{7gf} 11^{6g}
0-1-7 £1,045

Chickado (Ire) D Haydn Jones   59 a67
3 b f Mujadil (USA) - Arcevia (Ire)
3^{6sd} 6^{6gs} 7^{6gf} 6^{6gs} 2^{6sd} 0-2-5 £1,230

Chickasaw Trail R Hollinshead   45 a11
6 ch m Be My Chief (USA) - Maraschino
9^{9sd} 10^{9sw} 6^{9ss} 5^{8g} 1^{8g} 11^{10hy} 5^{8gf}
15^{7gf} 14^{8f} 1-0-10 £1,442

Chicken Soup J A Osborne   67 a73
2 br c Dansili - Radiancy (Ire)
6^{6g} 3^{6sd} 7^{7g} 19^{7gf} 3^{7gs} 0-2-5 £964

Chicks Babe B Palling   a24
2 br f Chickawicka (Ire) - Ballasilla
8^{7sd} 0-0-1

Chico Guapo (Ire) J A Glover   85 a75
4 b g Sesaro (USA) - Summer Queen
8^{5sd} 5^{5sd} 16^{5g} 8^{5s} 1^{5g} 17^{5gs} 5^{5gf} 9^{5gf}
11^{5gf} 17^{5f} 12^{5gf} 13^{5gs} 13^{5gf} 13^{5g} 12^{5f}
1-0-15 £5,707

Chief Dipper P J McBride   31 a66
2 b c Benny The Dip (USA) - Cuban Reef
15^{8gf} 4^{6sd} 4^{6sd} 0-0-3 £432

Chief Exec C A Cyzer   50 a76
2 b g Zafonic (USA) - Shot At Love (Ire)
13^{6s} 2^{7sd} 0-1-2 £1,584

Chief Scout B J Meehan   84
2 br c Tomba - Princess Zara
7^{6s} 4^{7s} 1^{7s} 8^{7g} 1-0-4 £5,845

Chigorin J M P Eustace   71 a68
3 b g Pivotal - Belle Vue
9^{8gf} 6^{8gf} 7^{8s} 8^{8gf} 3^{8gs} 8^{10sd} 0-1-6 £870

Chilali (Ire) A Berry   58 a46
2 b f Monashee Mountain (USA) - Pam Story
5^{5g} 7^{5sd} 3^{5gf} 3^{5g} 9^{5gf} 3^{5g} 6^{5gf} 4^{5f} 9^{5g}
2^{5sw} 0-4-10 £3,274

Chillin Out W Jarvis   8
2 ch c Bahamian Bounty - Steppin Out
16^{6s} 0-0-1

Chilly Cracker R Hollinshead   71 a66
2 ch f Largesse - Polar Storm (Ire)
2^{5gs} 6^{5s} 1^{5sd} 10^{6gf} 8^{5g} 3^{5gf} 1^{5gs} 11^{5hy}
2-2-8 £11,062

Chimali (Ire) J R Boyle   77 a76
3 b g Foxhound (USA) - Mari-Ela (Ire)
1^{5gs} 4^{5gs} 3^{6sd} 1^{6gf} 3^{6gf} 2-2-5 £9,409

Chimes At Midnight (USA) Luke Comer   60
7 b h Danzig (USA) - Surely Georgies (USA)
24^{20gf} 11^{20gf} 12^{12gf} 8^{14gy} 9^{10gf} 22^{16gf}
12^{14g} 19^{10ys} 18^{10s} 0-0-9

Chimes Eight R A Fahey   a32
3 b f Octagonal (NZ) - Bell Toll
8^{9sd} 0-0-1

Chin Dancer B R Millman   23 a23
2 ch f Inchinor - Red Hot Dancer (USA)
17^{7gf} 10^{7g} 6^{7sd} 10^{7gf} 0-0-4

Chinalea (Ire) C G Cox   69
2 b c Danetime (Ire) - Raise-A-Secret (Ire)

5^{6g} 5^{6g} 4^{6gs} 0-0-3 £344

Chinese Puzzle H R A Cecil   74
2 b c Dr Fong (USA) - Verbose (USA)
6^{7gs} 6^{7gf} 9^{7gf} 3^{8f} 3^{9f} 0-2-5 £1,482

Chinkara B J Meehan   98
4 ch g Desert Prince (Ire) - You Make Me Real (USA)
19^{8g} 10^{8gf} 23^{8gf} 4^{9gf} 10^{10g} 3^{9gf} 24^{9g}
0-1-7 £2,870

Chiqitita (Ire) Miss M E Rowland   47 a38
3 b f Saddlers' Hall (Ire) - Funny Cut (Ire)
11^{7sd} 10^{6sd} 13^{6g} 10^{6s} 9^{8sd} 7^{7g} 6^{7gf}
8^{10gf} 5^{8f} 10^{10g} 0-0-10

Chiracahua (Ire) B J Meehan   a35
2 ch g Desert Prince (Ire) - Irish Celebrity (USA)
16^{7g} 7^{6sd} 10^{7sd} 0-0-3

Chisel M Johnston   59
3 ch g Hector Protector (USA) - Not Before Time (Ire)
8^{7gf} 10^{8gf} 6^{7g} 8^{9gs} 10^{10gs} 8^{10gf} 5^{9gs}
11^{8s} 0-0-8

Chiselled (Ire) K R Burke   85
2 b g Rossini (USA) - Con Dancer
4^{5s} 2^{5g} 2^{5gf} 9^{5g} 4^{5gs} 2^{5g} 0-3-6 £4,440

Chivalry J Howard Johnson   90
5 b g Mark Of Esteem (Ire) - Gai Bulga
18^{8g} 0-0-1

Chivite (Ire) P J Hobbs   66
5 b g Alhaarth (Ire) - Laura Margaret
9^{13gf} 9^{12gs} 0-0-2

Chocolate Boy (Ire) G L Moore   66 a62
5 b g Dolphin Street (Fr) - Kawther
5^{8sd} 2^{8sd} 4^{10sd} 4^{12sd} 1^{12sd} 10^{13sd} 2^{12gf}
5^{12f} 6^{10f} 7^{12sd} 1-2-10 £4,065

Chocolate Caramel (USA) Mrs A J Perrett   a75
2 b c Storm Creek (USA) - Sandhill (Brz)
5^{8sd} 0-0-1

Choir Leader W J Haggas   97
3 b g Sadler's Wells (USA) - Choir Mistress
13^{10gs} 1^{8gf} 3^{8gs} 1-1-3 £7,268

Chookie Heiton (Ire) I Semple   109
6 br g Fumo Di Londra (Ire) - Royal Wolff
4^{6g} 5^{6g} 14^{7gs} 11^{6gf} 1^{5gs} 12^{6s} 1-0-6
£19,420

Choreographic (Ire) R A Fahey   60
2 b c Komaite (USA) - Lambast
7^{5gf} 3^{6gf} 10^{6g} 8^{6g} 0-1-4 £592

Chorist W J Haggas   121
5 ch m Pivotal - Choir Mistress
1^{8gf} 1^{10g} 3^{10gf} 3^{10vs} 2^{10s} 2-2-5
£241,499

Choristar W R Muir   60
3 ch g Inchinor - Star Tulip
6^{7gf} 2^{7gf} 5^{6g} 3^{8gf} 0-2-4 £1,303

Chorus B R Millman   38 a61
7 b m Bandmaster (USA) - Name That Tune
9^{7sd} 3^{6sd} 13^{8gs} 20^{6g} 10^{5gs} 26^{sd} 1^{7sd}
1-2-7 £2,274

Chorus Beauty G Wragg   55 a72
3 b f Royal Applause - Happy Lady (Fr)
14^{6g} 10^{8hy} 7^{7gf} 3^{8sd} 1^{7sd} 1-1-5 £3,394

Christina's Dream P W Harris   72 a45
3 b f Spectrum (Ire) - Christine Daae
5^{7gf} 8^{7sd} 0-0-2

Christmas Truce (Ire) Ian Williams   a14
5 b g Brief Truce (USA) - Superflash
10^{11sd} 9^{16sd} 0-0-2

Christom G A Butler — 53 a49
2 b c Groom Dancer (USA) - Throw Away Line (USA)
13⁸ʰʸ 7⁸ˢᵈ 12⁷ᵍˢ 9¹⁰ˢ **0-0-4**

Chubbes B J Llewellyn — 51
3 b g Kris - St Radegund
13⁸ᵍᶠ 10¹⁰ᵍᶠ 4⁷ᵍ 4⁸ᵍ 7⁸ᵍᶠ 1⁷ᶠ 13¹⁰ˢ
10⁸ᶠ **1-0-8 £3,164**

Chutney Mary (Ire) J G Portman — 72 a68
2 b/br f Indian Danehill (Ire) - Grade A Star (Ire)
12⁵ᵍ 6⁵ᵍᶠ 2⁷ᵍ 2⁷ˢᵈ 5⁷ˢᵈ 2⁷ᶠ 5⁶ᵍˢ 11⁷ᵍᶠ
3⁶ᵍ 6⁷ᵍ 5⁷ˢᵈ **0-4-11 £3,779**

Ciacole Mrs B K Thomson — 48 a48
3 b f Primo Dominie - Dance On A Cloud (USA)
13⁷ˢᵈ 4⁸ˢˢ 10¹²ᵍˢ 3¹²ˢ 11¹⁰ʰʸ 13¹²ᵍᶠ 8¹²ᵍᶠ
5¹⁰ᵍ **1-1-8 £3,644**

Ciel Bleu B W Hills — 35
2 ch f Septieme Ciel (USA) - Valthea (Fr)
13⁷ᵍˢ **0-0-1**

Ciendra Girl (Ire) R Brotherton
2 ch f Rossini (USA) - Simply Special (Ire)
12⁷ᵍᶠ 11⁸ᵍ 11⁶ˢ **0-0-3**

Cilla's Smile M A Buckley — 54
2 b f Lake Coniston (Ire) - Tinkerbird
8⁵ᵍ 6⁵ᵍ 18⁶ᵍᶠ 6⁵ᵍˢ **0-0-4**

Cimyla (Ire) C F Wall — 98
3 b c Lomitas - Coyaima (Ger)
3⁹ˢ 12¹⁰ᵍ 18ᵍˢ 10⁸ᵍᶠ 1⁹ᵍᶠ **2-1-5**
£21,346

Cinnamon Ridge (Ire) B J Meehan — 46
3 b g Indian Ridge - Savoury
8⁵ˢ 9⁶ᵍᶠ 7⁵ᶠ **0-0-3**

Circassian (Ire) Sir Mark Prescott — 89 a82
3 b g Groom Dancer (USA) - Daraliya (Ire)
9¹⁰ᵍᶠ 2¹²ᵍˢ 1¹¹ᵍ 12²ᶠ 4¹²ʰʸ 2¹³ᵍˢ 5¹²ˢᵈ
2-3-7 £18,348

Circle Of Wolves H J Manners — 23
6 ch g Wolfhound (USA) - Misty Halo
9¹³ᵍˢ **0-0-1**

Circuit Dancer (Ire) A Berry — 101
4 b g Mujadil (USA) - Trysinger (Ire)
3⁶ˢ 4⁶ᵍ 14⁶ᵍˢ 16⁶ᵍᶠ 16⁶ᶠ 5⁶ᵍ 22⁶ᵍᶠ 4⁷ˢ
7⁶ᵍˢ 13⁶ˢ 4⁶ˢ 11⁶ˢ **1-0-12 £17,251**

Circumspect (Ire) P C Haslam — 70
2 b g Spectrum (Ire) - Newala
2⁶ᶠ **0-1-1 £1,764**

Circus Maximus (USA) Ian Williams — 61 a22
7 b g Pleasant Colony (USA) - Crockadore (USA)
9¹⁴ᵍᶠ 4¹⁴ᵍ 12¹⁶ᵍˢ 2¹⁷ᵍ 3¹⁶ᵍᶠ 9¹⁶ˢᵈ 11¹⁷ᵍ
0-2-7 £1,579

Cirrious B Palling — 60
3 gr f Cloudings (Ire) - Westfield Mist
8⁸ᵍˢ 6⁸ᵍᶠ 5¹⁰ˢ **0-0-3**

Citrine Spirit (Ire) J H M Gosden — 77
3 gr f Soviet Star (USA) - Casessa (USA)
6¹⁰ᵍˢ 1⁸ˢ 3⁸ᵍᶠ 9⁸ᵍᶠ 10⁸ᵍ 7⁷ˢ **1-1-6**
£6,074

Citrus Magic K Bell — a47
7 b g Cosmonaut - Up All Night
1¹⁵ˢᵈ 2¹⁴ˢᵈ 7¹²ˢᵈ **1-1-3 £1,680**

City Affair Mrs L C Jewell — a60
3 b g Inchinor - Aldevonie
10⁵ˢᵈ 9⁶ˢᵈ 4⁷ˢᵈ 14⁷ᵍ **0-0-4**

City General (Ire) J S Moore — 56
3 ch g General Monash (USA) - Astra (Ire)
3⁷ᵍ 3⁷ᵍˢ 4⁷ᵍ 3⁷ᵍᶠ 5⁸ᵍᶠ 7⁷ᵍᶠ 2⁷ᶠ 7⁷ᵍᶠ 5⁸ᵍᶠ

1⁸ᵍᶠ 14⁷ᵍˢ 5¹⁰ᵍᶠ 6⁸ᵍˢ 7⁸ᶠ 7⁸ᵍ 7⁸ᵍˢ **1-3-16**
£4,707

City Lass M E Sowersby
4 b f Rock City - Kilkenny Lass (Ire)
12⁸ᵍˢ **0-0-1**

City Palace B W Hills — 76
3 ch g Grand Lodge (USA) - Ajuga (USA)
1⁸ˢ 9¹⁰ᵍˢ **1-0-2 £3,656**

City Torque (USA) T D Barron — 53
2 ch f Marquetry (USA) - Citiscape (USA)
6⁵ᵍᶠ 8⁵ᵍᶠ **0-0-2**

City Trader C E Brittain — 29
2 ch c Entrepreneur - Kameez (Ire)
15⁷ᵍᶠ 16⁸ʰʸ 16¹⁰ˢ **0-0-3**

Clann A Cougar I A Wood — 60 a41
4 ch g Bahamian Bounty - Move Darling
7⁸ˢˢ 7⁷ˢᵈ 6⁸ˢ 8⁸ᵍˢ 6⁷ᵍᶠ 11⁷ᵍᶠ 7¹²ᵍ **0-0-7**

Claptrap R Brotherton — a57
4 b c Royal Applause - Stardyn
2¹²ˢʷ 5¹²ˢᵈ 6¹⁶ˢᵈ **0-1-3 £834**

Clara Bow (Ire) B W Hills — 67
2 b f Sadler's Wells (USA) - Brigid (USA)
6⁷ᵍᶠ 7⁷ʰʸ **0-0-2**

Claradotnet M R Channon — 70
4 b f Sri Pekan (USA) - Lypharitissima (Fr)
16¹²ᵍˢ 9¹²ᵍ 8¹²ᵍ 6¹⁴ᵍᶠ 3¹¹ᵍᶠ 8¹⁴ᶠ 3¹⁴ᵍᶠ
2¹⁶ᶠ 10¹⁴ᵍᶠ 10¹⁷ᵍ 10¹⁴ᵍ 6¹⁸ᵍ **0-2-12 £2,266**

Claranete Princess (Ire) M J Wallace — 39 a47
3 b f Princely Heir (Ire) - Sheryl Lynn
6⁷ˢᵈ 12⁸ˢ **0-0-2**

Clare Galway S Kirk — 54 a54
3 b f Compton Place - Oublier L'Ennui (Fr)
9⁶ˢᵈ 5⁸ˢᵈ 9¹⁰ˢᵈ 10¹¹ᵍᶠ 4¹⁰ˢᵈ 9¹⁰ˢᵈ 1⁸ˢ
8⁷ˢᵈ **1-0-8 £3,367**

Claret And Amber R A Fahey — 95
2 b g Forzando - Artistic Licence
3⁵ᵍᶠ 5⁶ᵍ 5⁶ᵍᶠ 1⁶ᶠ 1⁷ˢ 5⁶ᵍ 2⁶ᵍˢ 6⁸ᵍ **2-2-8**
£32,569

Clarinch Claymore J M Jefferson — 80
8 b g Sabrehill (USA) - Salu
2¹⁴ᵍ 12¹⁴ᵍᶠ 5¹⁶ᵍ 3¹⁵ᵍ 1¹⁶ᵍˢ 5¹⁶ᵍˢ **1-2-6**
£9,080

Clasp M L W Bell — 83
2 ch c Singspiel (Ire) - Embrace Me
8⁷ᵍ 2⁸ᵍ **0-1-2 £1,569**

Classic Event (Ire) T D Easterby — 62
3 ch g Croco Rouge (Ire) - Delta Town (USA)
7¹²ᵍ 10¹²ᵍ 2¹²ᵍᶠ 3¹²ˢ **0-2-4 £2,252**

Classic Expression B A McMahon — 34 a26
3 ch f Classic Cliche - Breezy Day
6⁶ˢᵈ 7⁶ᵍᶠ 7⁸ˢᵈ 15⁸ʰʸ **0-0-4**

Classic Guest M R Channon — 59
2 b f Xaar - My Lass
4⁶ᵍ 6⁵ᵍᶠ 15⁷ᵍ 12⁶ᵍᶠ **0-0-4 £359**

Classic Lease R Hollinshead — 55
3 b g Cyrano De Bergerac - Vado Via
10⁸ᵍ 5⁷ᵍᶠ 3⁸ʰʸ 10¹¹ᵍ **0-0-4 £870**

Classic Lin (Fr) A Berry
4 gr f Linamix (Fr) - Classic Storm
8¹²ˢʷ **0-0-1**

Classic Millennium W J Musson — 63 a52
6 b m Midyan (USA) - Classic Colleen (Ire)
7¹³ˢᵈ 2¹²ˢᵈ 2¹²ˢᵈ 5¹³ᵍᶠ 7¹³ᵍᶠ 4¹³ᵍᶠ **0-2-6**
£2,011

Classic Role *R Ingram*   86 a84
5 b g Tragic Role (USA) - Clare Island
4^{12sd} 12^{12sd} 3^{12sd} 4^{12sd} 1^{12sd} 2^{12gs} 2^{11gs}
10^{10s} 10^{10g} 8^{10gf} **1-4-10 £8,104**

Classic Style (Ire) *T D Easterby*   60 a37
2 b f Desert Style (Ire) - Classic Ring (Ire)
5^{5sd} 9^{6s} 7^{7sd} 5^{7g} **0-0-4**

Classic Vision *W J Haggas*   59 a56
4 b f Classic Cliche (Ire) - Orient
1^{6sd} 9^{6sd} 10^{6sd} 4^{6sd} 5^{7g} 11^{8f} 1^{8gf} 7^{8gf}
6^{8g} 8^{8g} 11^{8g} 14^{8g} **2-0-12 £8,112**

Classical Dancer *H Candy*   100
3 ch f Dr Fong (USA) - Gorgeous Dancer (Ire)
1^{8gs} 2^{8gf} 3^{10gf} 8^{10g} **1-1-4 £14,190**

Classical Waltz (Ire) *J J Sheehan*   31 a28
6 ch m In The Wings - Fascination Waltz
4^{9sd} 3^{9sd} 9^{10gf} 7^{12gf} **0-0-4 £206**

Classicism (USA) *Saeed Bin Suroor*   79
2 b/br f A.P. Indy (USA) - Colour Chart (USA)
5^{7g} **0-0-1**

Clear Impression (Ire) *P W Chapple-Hyam*   84
2 b f Danehill (USA) - Shining Hour (USA)
2^{6g} **0-1-1 £3,210**

Clearing Sky (Ire) *J R Boyle*   50
3 gr f Exploit (USA) - Litchfield Hills (USA)
6^{6gf} 17^{6s} **0-0-2**

Cleaver *W Jarvis*   54
3 ch g Kris - Much Too Risky
5^{11gs} 9^{11gf} **0-0-2**

Cleo Collins (Ire) *S Kirk*
2 b f General Monash (USA) - Madrina
13^{5s} **0-0-1**

Cleveland Way *J O'Reilly*   35 a51
4 b g Forzando - Fallal (Ire)
1^{6sd} 2^{7sd} 6^{6sd} 5^{6sd} 4^{5sw} 5^{5ss} 11^{6gs}
2^{6sd} 2^{6sf} 6^{7sd} 2^{5sd} 1^{6sd} 14^{6gf} 15^{5gf} 13^{6gf}
2-4-16 £4,781

Cliffie (Ire) *J Hetherton*   17
2 ch g Timeless Times (USA) - Suppression
8^{6f} 10^{8gs} 14^{7s} **0-0-3**

Climate (Ire) *K A Ryan*   84 a79
5 ch g Catrail (USA) - Burishki
5^{8sd} 4^{8gs} 11^{8s} 2^{8gf} 1^{8sd} 6^{8gf} 3^{8gf} 9^{6gf}
9^{7gs} **1-2-9 £6,048**

Climate Change (USA) *J H M Gosden*
2 ch c Langfuhr (Can) - Summer Mist (USA)
12^{8hy} **0-0-1**

Clinet (Ire) *P M Phelan*   68 a50
2 b f Docksider (USA) - Oiche Mhaith
8^{5g} 5^{6gf} 13^{6g} 5^{6g} 10^{7gf} 7^{7sd} 1^{8f}
3^{10gf} **1-2-9 £7,880**

Clipper Hoy *Mrs H Sweeting*   10
2 ch c Bahamian Bounty - Indian Flag (Ire)
6^{5hy} 14^{6s} **0-0-2**

Clipperdown (Ire) *P W Harris*   80
3 b g Green Desert (USA) - Maroussie (Fr)
3^{8g} 7^{8g} 1^{8gf} 6^{10gf} **1-1-4 £6,261**

Cliquey *R H Buckler*   a39
5 b g Muhtarram (USA) - Meet Again
11^{9sd} 11^{12sd} 9^{12sd} **0-0-3**

Cloann (Ire) *R Hannon*   58
2 b f Danetime (Ire) - Rustic Lawn
5^{6gf} 11^{5gf} 1^{6gf} **1-0-3 £2,884**

Cloonavery (Ire) *J A Osborne*   74 a80
2 b g Xaar - Hero's Pride (Fr)

4^{8gf} 1^{9sd} **1-0-2 £3,222**

Cloud Catcher (Ire) *M Appleby*   20 a13
3 br f Charnwood Forest (Ire) - Notley Park
7^{7g} 12^{8sd} 11^{10gf} 7^{12gf} 11^{9sd} **0-0-5**

Cloud Dancer *K A Ryan*   85 a82
5 b/br m Bishop Of Cashel - Summer Pageant
3^{7sd} 8^{7sd} 2^{7ss} 2^{8sw} 1^{6gf} 3^{6gf} 5^{6g} 17^{7gf}
4^{6g} 5^{7gf} 6^{7gf} 3^{9sd} **1-6-12 £13,274**

Cloudingswell *D L Williams*   49 a27
3 b f Cloudings (Ire) - L'Ancressaan
10^{10g} 6^{13s} 6^{8gf} 4^{10g} 4^{11g} 8^{13gs} 7^{9sd} **0-0-7**
£534

Cloudless (USA) *J W Unett*   45 a62
4 b/br f Lord Avie (USA) - Summer Retreat (USA)
11^{6sd} 2^{8ss} 4^{7sd} 10^{7sd} 7^{7ss} 3^{5ss} 6^{8s} 6^{5s}
19^{6gf} 9^{7sd} 18^{5g} 12^{6g} 19^{6s} **0-3-13 £2,026**

Clouds Of Gold (Ire) *J S Wainwright*   43
3 b f Goldmark (USA) - Tongabezi (Ire)
10^{7gf} 3^{6hy} 11^{9g} 18^{6f} 13^{7sd} **0-1-5 £864**

Cloudy Sky (Ire) *Simon Earle*   70
8 b g Sadler's Wells (USA) - Dancing Shadow
14^{14s} **0-0-1**

Clove (USA) *B W Hills*   86
2 b f Distant View (USA) - Nidd (USA)
4^{5g} 1^{5gf} 2^{5f} 9^{5gf} **1-1-4 £6,850**

Clueless *W J Haggas*   86
2 b c Royal Applause - Pure
4^{8g} 3^{8g} **0-1-2 £1,699**

Coalition *H Candy*   85
5 b g Polish Precedent (USA) - Selection Board
9^{12g} 2^{14g} 2^{14gf} 3^{16gf} **0-3-4 £5,922**

Coat Of Honour (USA) *J Howard Johnson*   107
4 gr g Mark Of Esteem (Ire) - Ballymac Girl
16^{10g} 1^{10g} 2^{11g} 1^{13f} **2-1-4 £52,799**

Cobalt Blue (Ire) *W J Haggas*   55 a50
3 b g Bluebird (USA) - Amy Hunter (USA)
8^{8gf} 6^{8g} 1^{8gf} 5^{10g} 5^{10sd} 9^{12gs} 3^{10gf} 11^{8gs}
2^{10f} **1-2-9 £4,140**

Cobalt Runner (Ire) *Miss D A McHale*
3 b c Fayruz - Bui-Doi (Ire)
8^{5sd} 13^{5gf} **0-0-2**

Coco Point Breeze *J G Given*   32 a29
3 b f Great Dane (USA) - Flying Colours (Ire)
7^{8sd} 8^{8gf} 7^{8gf} 10^{10g} 14^{9f} **0-0-5**

Coco Reef *B Palling*   36 a50
3 b f Kingsinger (Ire) - Highland Blue
6^{7g} 12^{6sd} 5^{6sd} 10^{6gf} 14^{5sd} **0-0-5**

Coconut Cookie *R Hannon*   43
3 ch f Bahamian Bounty - Spicy Manner (USA)
18^{7g} 11^{8gf} 7^{8f} **0-0-3**

Coconut Moon *R A Fahey*   46
2 b f Bahamian Bounty - Lunar Ridge
6^{5gs} **0-0-1**

Coconut Penang (Ire) *P W Chapple-Hyam*   103
4 b c Night Shift (USA) - Play With Fire (Fr)
14^{6g} 7^{5gs} 2^{6f} 18^{7gs} 25^{6gf} 6^{5gs} PU^{16s}
0-1-7 £18,350

Coconut Squeak *Mrs Stef Liddiard*   65
2 b f Bahamian Bounty - Creeking
3^{7g} 6^{7s} 7^{7gs} 9^{7gf} 1^{6gf} 9^{6s} **1-1-6**
£7,648

Code Orange *J H M Gosden*   82
2 b f Green Desert (USA) - Warning Belle
2^{6gf} 2^{6g} **0-2-2 £3,340**

Cody *G A Ham*   a46

5 ch g Zilzal (USA) - Ibtihaj (USA)
3^{16sd} 14^{17g} **0-1-2 £213**

Coeur Courageux (Fr) *D Flood* 50
2 b c Xaar - Linoise (Fr)
7^{7gf} **0-0-1**

Cois Na Tine Eile *Ms Deborah J Evans* 52 a4
2 br f Cois Na Tine (Ire) - Water Pixie (Ire)
3^{6g} 10^{7sd} 3^{7gs} 13^{8gf} 10^{10gf} 8^{9gs} **0-2-6**
£1,051

Cold Climate *Bob Jones* 64 a73
9 ch g Pursuit Of Love - Sharpthorne (USA)
9^{7sd} 4^{7sd} 7^{6f} 5^{7gf} 2^{6gf} 2^{6gf} 9^{6gs} 4^{7gf}
0-2-8 £3,328

Cold Encounter (Ire) *R M Stronge* a13
9 ch g Polar Falcon (USA) - Scene Galante (Fr)
13^{16sd} **0-0-1**

Cold Turkey *G L Moore* 98 a98
4 b/br g Polar Falcon (USA) - South Rock
1^{12sd} 1^{12sd} 3^{12sd} 2^{13sd} 4^{16gs} 1^{12s} 2^{12g}
4^{14gf} 10^{10g} 13^{12s} 2^{17sd} **3-5-11 £51,914**

Colemanstown *B Ellison* 67
4 b g Charnwood Forest (Ire) - Arme Fatale (Ire)
11^{7hy} 7^{7gs} 18^{6gf} 12^{6g} 8^{6gf} 16^{7s} 10^{7gf}
14^{7gf} 7^{7gs} 3^{8g} 10^{7g} **0-1-11 £545**

Coleorton Dancer *K A Ryan* 91 a53
2 ch g Danehill Dancer (Ire) - Tayovullin (Ire)
8^{5g} 4^{5g} 4^{5sd} 4^{5gf} 7^{5g} 1^{5gs} 1^{5g} 1^{5g} 1^{6gs}
9^{6g} 13^{6s} **4-0-11 £29,823**

Coleorton Dane *K A Ryan* 78
2 gr g Danehill Dancer (Ire) - Cloudy Nine
6^{6gs} 3^{7gf} 2^{7gf} 1^{7gf} 3^{6gs} 14^{8gf} **1-3-6**
£5,787

Coleorton Prince (Ire) *K A Ryan*
3 b g Paris House - Tayovullin (Ire)
10^{6sd} **0-0-1**

Colisay *E F Vaughan* 108
5 b g Entrepreneur - La Sorrela (Ire)
3^{7gf} 6^{8gs} 4^{8g} 1^{10gf} 4^{10g} 14^{10s} **1-0-6**
£24,381

Collada (Ire) *J H M Gosden* 47
3 b f Desert Prince (Ire) - Bright Spells (USA)
18^{8gs} 12^{9gf} 6^{7gf} 16^{7gs} **0-0-4**

College Delinquent (Ire) *K Bell* a73
5 br g College Chapel - St Cyr Aty (Ire)
3^{8sd} 4^{8sd} 6^{8sd} 7^{8sd} **0-1-4 £913**

College Hippie *J F Coupland* 23
5 b m Cosmonaut - Eccentric Dancer
12^{5g} 16^{5f} 15^{5g} 14^{5gs} **0-0-4**

College Maid (Ire) *J S Goldie* 65
7 b m College Chapel - Maid Of Mourne
4^{5gf} 13^{5g} 6^{5g} 7^{5gf} 7^{5gf} 2^{6gf} 4^{6gf} 1^{7g}
3^{6g} 5^{5g} 6^{7gf} 6^{6gf} 5^{6gf} 5^{6gf} 3^{6s} 13^{6gf}
17^{5gs} 6^{5gf} 15^{6gs} **1-2-20 £7,440**

College Queen *S Gollings* 70
6 b m Lugana Beach - Eccentric Dancer
11^{6g} 6^{5gf} 5^{6gf} 4^{5f} 5^{6gs} 11^{6gf} 7^{5g}
5^{6gf} 3^{5gf} 15^{6gs} 16^{5g} **0-2-12 £2,076**

College Star *J F Coupland* a12
6 b g Lugana Beach - Alis Princess
8^{8sd} 8^{7sd} **0-0-2**

Collier Hill *G A Swinbank* 110
6 ch g Dr Devious (Ire) - Polar Queen
11^{9gs} 11^{2gs} 14^{16s} 3^{14g} 9^{14s} 11^{2gf} 5^{12hy}
2-2-7 £64,906

Colloseum *T J Etherington* 53

3 b g Piccolo - Trig Point
7^{7gf} 4^{8gf} 12^{7f} 16^{10g} 8^{9gf} 6^{8g} **0-0-6**

Colne Valley Amy *Mrs S J Smith* a47
7 b m Mizoram (USA) - Panchellita (USA)
4^{8sd} 2^{10sd} 8^{8sd} 8^{8sd} 12^{8sd} **0-1-5 £429**

Colonel Bilko (Ire) *B R Millman* 67
2 b g General Monash (USA) - Mari-Ela (Ire)
2^{5gs} 10^{5g} 6^{8gf} 10^{6gf} **1-1-5 £6,457**

Colonel Cotton (Ire) *N A Callaghan* 105
5 b g Royal Applause - Cutpurse Moll
6^{5y} 10^{5gs} 6^{5hy} 5^{5gf} 5^{5g} 16^{5gf} 3^{5gs} 10^{6g}
6^{5gf} 5^{6gf} 3^{6g} 4^{5gf} 15^{5g} 10^{6s} **0-2-14**
£12,749

Colonial Girl (Ire) *T D Easterby* 68 a66
2 b f Desert Style (Ire) - Telemania (Ire)
4^{5gf} 3^{5gf} 2^{5sd} 4^{5g} **0-2-4 £2,553**

Colonnade *N Wilson* 14 a50
5 b m Blushing Flame (USA) - White Palace
2^{14sd} 7^{16sd} 3^{14s} 9^{14s} 7^{12f} 9^{14s} **0-2-6**
£644

Colophony (USA) *K A Morgan* 76
4 ch g Distant View (USA) - Private Line (USA)
12^{10g} 4^{10gf} 7^{12g} 6^{10g} **0-0-4 £426**

Colorado Falls (Ire) *P Monteith* 84
6 b g Nashwan (USA) - Ballet Shoes (Ire)
1^{13g} 5^{12gf} 4^{13g} 8^{13gf} 4^{16gs} 3^{13gs} 4^{14s}
1-1-7 £10,228

Colour Blind (Ire) *M L W Bell* 4
2 b c Spectrum (Ire) - Sarooh's Love (USA)
19^{8s} 15^{8hy} **0-0-2**

Colour Code (Ire) *M P Tregoning* 31
3 b g Spectrum (Ire) - Viendra Nur (USA)
14^{7gs} **0-0-1**

Colour Wheel *R Charlton* 95
3 ch c Spectrum (Ire) - Risanda
6^{8gs} 15^{8gf} 2^{7gf} 11^{7g} 7^{7gf} 10^{7g} **0-1-6**
£3,703

Colourful Lady (USA) *P W Harris* a30
4 b f Quest For Fame - Special Park (USA)
5^{12sd} **0-0-1**

Columbian Emerald (Ire) *T J Etherington* 50
3 ch g Among Men (USA) - Sarabi
7^{9g} 4^{10gf} 5^{12gf} 7^{11gf} 10^{16sd} **0-0-5 £424**

Colway Ritz *W Storey* 69
10 b g Rudimentary (USA) - Million Heiress
11^{12s} 2^{10gf} 2^{12f} 5^{14gf} 5^{10g} 3^{10g} **0-3-6**
£4,381

Comanche Woman *K O Cunningham-Brown*
4 b f Distinctly North (USA) - Possibility
9^{15sd} **0-0-1**

Come Away With Me (Ire) *M A Buckley* 62
4 b f Machiavellian (USA) - Vert Val (USA)
2^{6gf} 1^{6g} **1-1-2 £4,957**

Come Good *R Hannon* 69
2 ch g Piccolo - The Frog Lady (Ire)
5^{5s} 5^{6gf} 3^{6gf} 2^{6gs} 7^{6g} **0-3-6**
£4,400

Come On *J Hetherton* 61 a53
5 b g Aragon - All On
5^{6gs} 5^{5sd} **0-0-2**

Come On Jonny (Ire) *R M Beckett* 77
2 b c Desert King (Ire) - Idle Fancy
12^{6gs} 3^{6gs} 4^{6g} 1^{8s} 13^{8g} **1-1-5 £5,126**

Come To Daddy (Ire) *F Jordan* 48
2 ch g Fayruz - Forgren (Ire)

13⁶ᵍᶠ 5⁶ᵍˢ 12⁷ˢ **0-0-3**

Come What July (Ire) *Mrs N Macauley*　　66 a75
3 b g Indian Rocket - Persian Sally (Ire)
1¹⁰ˢᵈ 2⁹ˢʷ 5¹⁰ˢᵈ 6¹²ᵍ 6¹⁰ˢ 11⁸ᵍᶠ 3¹²ˢᵈ
5¹¹ᵍ 1⁸ˢᵈ 7¹⁰ᵍˢ 3¹⁰ᵍᶠ 6¹⁰ᵍˢ 7⁸ˢᵈ 13¹⁰ˢᵈ **2-3-14**
£8,973

Comeraincomeshine (Ire) *T G Mills*　　68 a42
3 ch f Night Shift (USA) - Future Past (USA)
3⁵ˢᵈ 6⁵ᵍ 4⁵ᵍᶠ 2⁶ᵍᶠ 7⁶ᵍ 15⁵ᵍᶠ 1⁶ᶠ **1-1-7**
£5,834

Comfy (USA) *Sir Michael Stoute*　　111
5 b h Lear Fan (USA) - Souplesse (USA)
5¹⁰ᵍˢ 7¹⁰ᵍᶠ **0-0-2 £1,250**

Comic Genius *D Haydn Jones*　　35 a39
3 b f Comic Strip (USA) - Itsy Bitsy Betsy (USA)
3⁸ˢˢ 5⁸ˢˢ 9¹⁰ᵍˢ 6¹²ᵍˢ **0-1-4 £365**

Comic Strip *Sir Mark Prescott*　　104 a84
2 b g Marju (Ire) - Comic (Ire)
1⁶ˢᵈ 4⁷ᵍˢ 1⁷ᵍ 1⁸ˢ 1⁹ᵍ 1⁸ᵍ **5-0-6**
£53,674

Comic Tales *M Mullineaux*　　44
3 b g Mind Games - Glorious Aragon
6⁶ᶠ 6⁷ᵍᶠ 7⁷ᵍˢ 6⁷ᶠ 5⁶ᵍ **0-0-5**

Comic Times *M Mullineaux*
4 b f Puissance - Glorious Aragon
19⁵ᵍ **0-0-1**

Comical Errors (USA) *P C Haslam*　　61
2 b g Distorted Humor (USA) - Fallibility (USA)
11⁶ᵍᶠ 4⁷ᵍˢ 5⁷ᵍˢ 15¹⁰ᵍᶠ **0-0-4 £288**

Coming Again (Ire) *D McCain*　　80
3 b g Rainbow Quest (USA) - Hagwah (USA)
5¹⁰ᵍˢ 2¹⁰ᵍᶠ 12¹²ᵍ **0-1-3 £1,384**

Comintrue (Ire) *E J O'Neill*　　44 a30
2 ch f Namid - Gute (Ire)
7⁵ˢᵈ 7⁵ᵍˢ 11⁶ᵍᶠ 2⁵ᵍ 7⁵ᵍᶠ 14⁶ᵍᶠ **0-1-6**
£1,046

Commander Bond *B Smart*　　55 a74
3 b g Piccolo - Lonesome
8⁶ᵍ 12⁷ᵍᶠ 1⁷ˢᵈ 9⁷ᵍ 8⁶ˢᵈ 8⁶ᵍᶠ 7⁷ˢᶠ 5⁸ᵍˢ
11⁷ᵍˢ 7⁷ˢᵈ **1-0-10 £5,395**

Commander Flip (Ire) *R Hollinshead*　　a47
4 ch g In Command (Ire) - Boldabsa
4¹²ˢʷ 14¹²ᵍˢ **0-0-2 £260**

Commando Scott (Ire) *A Berry*　　93
3 b g Danetime (Ire) - Faye
1⁶ᵍˢ 12⁶ˢ 8⁶ᵍᶠ 2⁶ᵍ 2⁷ˢ 2⁶ᵍ 6⁷ᵍˢ 1⁶ˢ 1⁶ˢ
5⁶ᵍ 8⁶ᵍ 7⁶ˢ **3-3-12 £23,056**

Commemoration Day (Ire) *M E Sowersby*　　59
3 b g Daylami (Ire) - Bequeath (USA)
7⁸ᵍ 6¹²ᵍᶠ 8¹²ˢᵈ 15¹⁰ᵍ **0-0-4**

Commendable Coup (USA) *T D Barron*　　68
2 b/br c Commendable (USA) - Bird Dance (USA)
5⁶ᵍˢ 7⁶ᵍ 6⁸ᵍ **0-0-3**

Commitment Lecture *M Dods*　　64 a53
4 b f Komaite (USA) - Hurtleberry (Ire)
5⁸ʰʸ 1⁸ˢ 4⁸ʰʸ 6⁸ᵍᶠ 5⁹ˢᵈ 3⁸ʰʸ **1-1-6**
£4,605

Compassion (Ire) *Miss L A Perratt*　　48 a13
3 b f Alhaarth (Ire) - Titania
10⁸ˢᵈ 10⁶ᵍᶠ 7⁸ᵍ 4⁸ᵍ 5¹²ᵍˢ 3⁹ᵍ 6⁷ᵍ
8⁷ᶠ 3⁷ᵍᶠ 8⁸ˢ **0-2-11 £1,767**

Competitor *J Akehurst*　　62 a73
3 b c Danzero (Aus) - Ceanothus (Ire)
2¹⁰ˢᵈ 9⁸ᵍᶠ 12¹⁰ᵍ 5¹⁰ᵍˢ 13¹⁰ᵍ 6¹⁰ᵍˢ 15¹²ᵍˢ
5¹⁰ˢᵈ 9¹⁰ˢᵈ **0-1-9 £975**

Complication *J A R Toller*　　78
4 b f Compton Place - Hard Task
7⁶ᵍᶠ 6⁶ᵍᶠ 2⁶ᵍᶠ 4⁶ᵍᶠ 2⁶ᵍᶠ 1⁶ᵍᶠ 7⁶ᶠ **1-3-7**
£21,226

Compton Arrow (Ire) *A W Carroll*　　40
8 b g Petardia - Impressive Lady
10⁶ʰʸ 15⁷ᵍ 14⁷ᵍᶠ 11⁷ᵍᶠ 18⁶ᵍ 15⁷ᵍᶠ **0-0-6**

Compton Aviator *A W Carroll*　　55 a59
8 ch g First Trump - Rifada
6¹⁰ˢᵈ 11¹²ˢ 5¹²ˢᵈ 9¹²ᵍ 6¹¹ᵍ 5¹¹ᵍᶠ 8⁸ᵍ
0-0-7

Compton Banker (Ire) *P D Evans*　　76 a56
7 br g Distinctly North (USA) - Mary Hinge
15⁵ˢᵈ 6⁷ᵍᶠ 5⁶ᶠ 2⁵ᶠ 7⁶ᵍˢ 3⁵ᵍᶠ 15⁶ᵍˢ 15⁶ᶠ
0-1-8 £2,264

Compton Bay *M Brittain*　　a27
4 b g Compton Place - Silver Sun
11⁷ˢᵈ 9⁶ˢʷ 11⁶ˢᵈ 5⁷ˢᵈ **0-0-4**

Compton Bolter (Ire) *G A Butler*　　116 a91
7 b g Red Sunset - Milk And Honey
4¹⁰ᶠᵗ 10¹²ᵍᶠ 5¹²ᶠ 10¹²ᵍᶠ 3¹³ᵍˢ 2¹⁰ᵍᶠ 5¹⁰ᵍ
10¹⁰ᶠ 6¹⁰ᵍˢ 5¹²ᵍᶠ 3¹³ᵍ 3¹²ᵍˢ 2¹²ᵍᶠ 3¹¹ᵍ 4¹²ᵍᶠ
0-4-15 £47,863

Compton Classic *J S Goldie*　　55
2 b c Compton Place - Ayr Classic
7⁶ᵍᶠ 6⁵ᵍᶠ 6⁶ᵍˢ 12⁶ˢ **0-0-4**

Compton Commander *Ian Williams*　　a80
6 ch g Barathea (Ire) - Triode (USA)
11¹⁰ˢᵈ 8¹²ˢʷ **0-0-2**

Compton Dragon (USA) *D Nicholls*　　83 a80
5 ch g Woodman (USA) - Vilikaia (USA)
8⁷ˢᵈ 12⁸ᵍ 5¹⁰ᵍˢ 12¹⁰ᵍ 5¹¹ᵍᶠ 2¹⁰ᵍ 2¹⁰ᵍᶠ
5¹²ᶠ 12¹⁰ᵍ 6⁹ᵍᶠ 10¹⁰ᵍᶠ 4¹⁰ˢ 10¹⁰ᵍˢ
0-3-14 £4,353

Compton Drake *G A Butler*　　81 a87
5 b g Mark Of Esteem (Ire) - Reprocolor
17⁸ᵍ 2¹⁰ᵍᶠ 1⁸ᵍˢ 2⁹ᵍ 4¹¹ᵍ 1¹⁰ˢᵈ 10⁹ᵍ **2-2-7**
£16,615

Compton Eagle *J J Lambe*　　46 a14
4 b g Zafonic (USA) - Gayane
11⁷ᵍˢ 6⁷ˢᵈ **0-0-2**

Compton Eclaire (Ire) *B Ellison*　　66 a61
4 ch f Lycius (USA) - Baylands Sunshine (Ire)
3¹²ˢᵈ 3¹³ᵍ 2¹⁵ˢᵈ 4¹³ᵍᶠ 12¹²ᶠ 11³ᶠ 2¹²ᶠ 4¹²ᵍ
2¹⁶ˢᵈ 4¹⁴ᵍˢ 7¹⁶ˢᵈ **1-4-11 £9,855**

Compton Micky *J Balding*　　57 a59
3 ch c Compton Place - Nunthorpe
8⁷ᵍ 6⁶ᵍᶠ 7⁵ᵍ 9⁶ˢ 5⁸ˢ 12¹⁰ᵍˢ
14⁷ᵍˢ 1⁷ˢᵈ 5⁹ˢᵈ **1-0-11 £1,473**

Compton Plume *W H Tinning*　　71
4 ch g Compton Place - Brockton Flame
7⁶ᵍ 3⁶ᶠ DSQ⁶ᶠ 3⁶ᵍᶠ 2⁶ᵍ 1⁶ᵍᶠ 7⁶ᵍᶠ 13⁵ᵍᶠ
7⁵ᵍˢ 1⁵ᵍᶠ 9⁶ᵍᶠ **2-3-11 £9,328**

Compton Princess *Miss S E Forster*　　43 a5
4 b f Compton Place - Curlew Calling (Ire)
3⁶ᵍˢ 6⁶ˢᶠ 10⁶ᵍˢ 14⁷ᵍᶠ 9⁷ᵍᶠ 8⁶ᵍᶠ **0-1-6**
£593

Compton Quay *A King*　　68 a76
2 ch c Compton Place - Roonah Quay (Ire)
6⁷ᵍᶠ 7⁷ᵍˢ 6⁷ˢᵈ **0-0-3**

Compton Spark *J S Goldie*　　a2
2 ch g Compton Place - Rhinefield Beauty (Ire)
11⁶ˢᵈ **0-0-1**

Compton's Eleven *M R Channon*　　102
3 gr g Compton Place - Princess Tara

8^{gs} 8^{6s} 7^{7gf} 8^{8gs} 5^{7gf} 2^{7gf} 1^{6g} 2^{7gf} 2^{6g}
2^{6g} 2^{7gf} 11^{6g} **1-5-12 £31,008**

Comtesse Lalande (USA) *M L W Bell*   53
2 ch f King Of Kings (Ire) - Beyond The Realm (USA)
6^{5g} **0-0-1**

Concer Eto *S C Williams*   84 a78
5 ch g Sabrehill (USA) - Drudwen
12^{8sd} 10^{7sd} 28^{sd} 38^{sd} 48^{gf} 17^{gf} 28^{gf}
10^{7g} 10^{7gf} 48^g 2^{7g} 38^{sd} **1-5-12 £11,214**

Concert Hall (USA) *Mrs A J Perrett*   40
3 b f Stravinsky (USA) - Proflare (USA)
4^{10gs} 6^{10g} **0-0-2 £284**

Concert Time *C R Dore*   38 a46
2 ch f Timeless Times (USA) - Thalya
7^{5g} 3^{5gf} 6^{6f} 5^{7sd} 3^{5g} 3^{6sd} 10^{5gs} **0-3-7**
£1,358

Conchonita *B Palling*
4 b f Bishop Of Cashel - Cactus Road (Fr)
9^{9sd} **0-0-1**

Concubine (Ire) *J R Boyle*   66
5 b m Danehill (USA) - Bye Bold Aileen (Ire)
3^{7f} 7^{7f} 2^{7gf} 4^{6gf} 7^{7gf} 12^{8gf} 13^{6g} **0-1-7**
£2,996

Confuzed *D Flood*   52 a56
4 b g Pivotal - Times Of Times (Ire)
9^{6sd} 3^{5sd} 6^{7sd} 14^{6sd} 9^{5sd} 11^{6sd} 8^{5sd} 4^{6gf}
11^{6sd} 9^{6gf} 3^{7hy} 3^{8f} 13^{10gs} **0-2-13 £1,154**

Congo Man *D W Whillans*   13
11 b g Rainbow Quest (USA) - African Dance (USA)
10^{13gf} 8^{16s} **0-0-2**

Conjuror *A M Balding*   79
3 b c Efisio - Princess Athena
UR^{6gf} 1^{6gf} 11^{6g} **1-0-3 £5,434**

Connect *M H Tompkins*   98
7 b g Petong - Natchez Trace
2^{5gf} 4^{5gf} 10^{5gf} 4^{5gs} 5^{5gf} 8^{5gf} 11^{5g}
15^{6g} 19^{6s} 4^{6g} 6^{5s} **1-4-12 £22,380**

Connotation *P W D'Arcy*   73 a73
2 b f Mujahid (USA) - Seven Wonders (USA)
2^{5f} 2^{5sd} 3^{6f} 13^{7sd} 1^{5f} 6^{6gf} 3^{5sd} **1-3-7**
£7,265

Conquering Love (Ire) *C Grant*   65
6 b g Pursuit Of Love - Susquehanna Days (USA)
11^{12gs} RR^{12gf} PU^{12f} **0-0-3**

Consensus (Ire) *M Brittain*   83
5 b m Common Grounds - Kilbride Lass (Ire)
4^{6g} 16^{5hy} 13^{6g} 3^{6gf} 20^{6gf} 12^{6gf} 4^{5gf}
6^{5gs} 16^{5gs} 8^{6f} 10^{5gf} **0-2-11 £2,178**

Consider This *W M Brisbourne*   79
2 b f Josr Algarhoud (Ire) - River Of Fortune (Ire)
2^{6gf} 5^{6g} 3^{6gf} 2^{6gs} 7^{7g} 2^{7s} 3^{8s} 4^{7s} 2^{7gs}
0-6-9 £7,782

Considine (USA) *J M P Eustace*   76 a30
3 b c Romanov (Ire) - Libeccio (NZ)
8^{8sd} 1^{12hy} 2^{14gs} 1^{14f} 8^{16s} 2^{14gf} 6^{14gs}
4^{14gf} **2-2-8 £13,460**

Consignia (Ire) *D Haydn Jones*   a39
5 ch m Definite Article - Coppelia (Ire)
11^{9sd} 9^{9sd} 5^{8sd} **0-0-3**

Consonant (Ire) *D G Bridgwater*   100 a100
7 ch g Barathea (Ire) - Dina Lina (Fr)
1^{8sd} 1^{8sd} 1^{8sw} 1^{10sd} 9^{10gs} 6^{8gf} 8^{9gf} 2^{8g}
3^{8g} 14^{10g} 7^{8s} 7^{9gf} **4-2-12 £30,360**

Constable Burton *Mrs A Duffield*   38 a66
3 b g Foxhound (USA) - Actress

9^{7gf} 1^{7sd} 18^{7s} 8^{7sd} 4^{7sd} **1-0-5 £3,153**

Constantine *G L Moore*   42
4 gr g Linamix (Fr) - Speremm (Ire)
14^{12gf} **0-0-1**

Constructor *C A Cyzer*   51 a61
3 b g So Factual (USA) - Love And Kisses
10^{8gf} 7^{12sd} 9^{12sd} 12^{8gf} **0-0-4**

Consular *M A Jarvis*   69
2 br c Singspiel (Ire) - Language Of Love
3^{8hy} **0-1-1 £983**

Contact Dancer (Ire) *M Johnston*   93
5 b g Sadler's Wells (USA) - Rain Queen
6^{16gs} 4^{16s} 1^{18s} 3^{17s} **1-0-4 £78,007**

Contented (Ire) *E A L Dunlop*   a59
2 b c Orpen (USA) - Joyfullness (USA)
5^{7sd} 3^{8sd} **0-1-2 £644**

Continent *D Nicholls*   111
7 ch g Lake Coniston (Ire) - Krisia
3^{6g} 1^{56gs} 1^{5g} 7^{5gs} 5^{5gf} 3^{6s} 10^{5g} **1-2-7**
£23,929

Continental Flyer (Ire) *M Dods*   29
2 b f Piccolo - Sunshine Coast
RR^{7gs} 8^{7gf} **0-0-2**

Convent Girl (Ire) *Mrs P N Dutfield*   95
4 b f Bishop Of Cashel - Right To The Top
23^{8g} 8^{8gs} 12^{8gf} 7^{9g} 30^{8gf} 17^{8gf} 6^{7g}
8^{8gf} 12^{8s} **0-0-9 £394**

Conviction *J R Fanshawe*   54
3 b g Machiavellian (USA) - Beldarian (Ire)
5^{10gf} 14^{10g} **0-0-2**

Convince (USA) *M A Buckley*   82 a52
3 ch g Mt. Livermore (USA) - Conical
9^{6gs} 8^{7gs} 13^{8gf} 5^{7g} 6^{7gf} 5^{7gf} 12^{10g}
11^{10sd} **0-0-8 £313**

Cooden Beach (Ire) *M L W Bell*   50 a47
4 b f Peintre Celebre (USA) - Joyful (Ire)
11^{9sd} 4^{10sd} 4^{8sd} 4^{8g} 20^{8f} **0-1-5**

Cool Bart *B P J Baugh*
4 ch g Cool Jazz - Margaretrose Anna
11^{6sd} **0-0-1**

Cool Bathwick (Ire) *B R Millman*   50 a65
5 b g Entrepreneur - Tarafa
1^{12sd} 2^{12sd} 10^{11gs} 7^{12s} 7^{10g} 7^{12gf}
9^{14gf} 4^{17g} 5^{14gf} **1-2-10 £4,540**

Cool Clear Water (USA) *B J Meehan*   60 a41
3 b f Seeking The Gold (USA) - Miznah (USA)
11^{7sd} 11^{10gs} 8^{9gf} 6^{10g} **0-0-4**

Cool Cristal *M W Easterby*   12
2 ch f Loup Sauvage (USA) - Lyrical Bid (USA)
12^{7gf} 10^{5g} 9^{6g} **0-0-3**

Cool Panic (Ire) *M L W Bell*   84
2 b c Brave Act - Geht Schnell
7^{5gf} 2^{6gf} 5^{6g} 1^{7gs} 6^{7s} **1-1-5 £6,722**

Cool Sands (Ire) *D Shaw*   a51
2 b c Trans Island - Shalerina (USA)
8^{7gs} 14^{6g} 6^{5sd} **0-0-3**

Cool Temper *P F I Cole*   70
8 b g Magic Ring (Ire) - Ovideo
5^{8gf} 3^{9s} 11^{8g} 8^{10gf} 10^{8gf} 2^{8gs} 13^{8s}
0-2-7 £2,862

Coolfore Jade (Ire) *N E Berry*   48 a62
4 ch f Mukaddamah (USA) - Cashel Princess (Ire)
9^{10sd} 1^{12sd} 4^{9sd} 11^{1sd} 4^{12sd} 3^{12ss} 5^{12ss}
8^{12sd} 5^{12sd} 12^{12sd} 7^{12ss} 19^{10gf} 6^{12gf} 3^{12sd} 8^{12sd}
10^{10gs} 9^{10s} 6^{12gf} **2-1-21**

612 The directory

£6,171

Cooling Castle (Fr) *Evan Williams*　　　a16
8 ch g Sanglamore (USA) - Syphaly (USA)
8¹²ˢʷ **0-0-1**

Coombe Centenary *S Dow*　　　48 a43
2 b f Robellino (USA) - Shining Dancer
7⁶ᵍᶠ 10⁶ᵍᶠ 11⁷ᵍ 9⁷ˢᵈ **0-0-4**

Copperfields Lass *W G M Turner*　　　a15
5 b m Millkom - Salvezza (Ire)
9⁷ˢᵈ 7⁷ˢˢ **0-0-2**

Coppice (Ire) *L M Cumani*　　　77
3 ch c Rainbow Quest (USA) - Woodwin (Ire)
6⁸ᵍᶠ 4⁹ᵍᶠ 5¹⁰ᵍ 3⁸ᵍˢ **0-1-4 £1,226**

Coppington Flyer (Ire) *B W Duke*　　　38 a56
4 ch f Eagle Eyed (USA) - Miss Flite (Ire)
4⁷ˢᵈ 8⁸ˢᵈ 8⁸ˢᵈ 10⁸ˢᵈ 4⁸ˢᵈ 12⁸ᵍ 17⁷ᵍᶠ
4⁷ᵍᶠ **0-0-8**

Copplestone (Ire) *W Storey*　　　35
8 b g Second Set (Ire) - Queen Of The Brush
7¹²ˢᵈ 6¹³ᵍ 9¹⁴ᵍ **0-0-3**

Coqueteria (USA) *G Wragg*　　　99 a80
3 b f Cozzene (USA) - Miss Waikiki (USA)
2⁸ᵍˢ 3⁸ˢ 2⁸ᵍ 10⁸ˢᵈ **0-3-4 £25,109**

Coranglais *J M Bradley*　　　74
4 ch g Piccolo - Antonia's Folly
16⁷ᵍ 13⁷ᵍ 8⁶ᵍ 8⁶ᵍᶠ 9⁶ᵍ 4⁵ᶠ 1⁵ᵍ 12⁵ᵍᶠ
7⁶ᵍᶠ 5⁶ᵍˢ 12⁶ᵍᶠ 8⁶ᶠ 5⁵ᵍᶠ 10⁵ᵍᶠ 2⁵ˢ 2⁵ˢ **1-2-16
£5,360**

Corbel (USA) *Miss Gay Kelleway*　　　41
4 b f Diesis - Corsini
11⁸ᵍˢ 16⁷ˢ **0-0-2**

Corcoran (USA) *Mrs A J Perrett*　　　76
2 b f Lear Fan (USA) - Corsini
1⁷ᵍ **1-0-1 £5,707**

Cordage (Ire) *G A Butler*　　　76
2 ch c Dr Fong (USA) - Flagship
5⁶ᵍ 4⁶ᵍ 4⁶ᵍ 4⁸ᵍˢ 2¹⁰ˢ **0-1-5 £2,277**

Cordier *D R Loder*　　　48
2 b c Desert Style (Ire) - Slipper
10⁸ᵍᶠ **0-0-1**

Corker *G A Butler*　　　54
2 ch g Grand Lodge (USA) - Immortelle
6⁶ᶠ 5⁶ᵍ **0-0-2**

Corky (Ire) *R Hannon*　　　83 a38
3 b g Intikhab (USA) - Khamseh
4⁷ᵍᶠ 3⁶ᵍᶠ 1⁷ᵍˢ 11⁷ᵍᶠ 3⁷ᵍˢ 14⁷ᵍ 10⁸ˢᵈ
1-2-7 £5,486

Cormorant Wharf (Ire) *T E Powell*　　　78 a81
4 b g Alzao (USA) - Mercy Bien (Ire)
7⁶ˢᵈ 6⁸ˢᵈ 5⁷ˢᵈ 8⁷ˢᵈ 10⁸ˢᵈ 5⁶ˢᵈ 8⁶ˢᵈ 7⁶ᵍᶠ
6⁶ᵍ 4⁸ᵍᶠ 2⁹ᵍᶠ 2⁹ˢ **0-3-13 £4,508**

Cornelius *P F I Cole*　　　93 a56
7 b g Barathea (Ire) - Rainbow Mountain
12⁸ˢˢ 9⁸ʰʸ 5⁸ᵍ **0-0-3 £397**

Corniche Dancer *M R Channon*　　　68 a68
2 b f Marju (Ire) - Sellette (Ire)
12⁷ᵍ 8⁶ᵍ 10⁸ᵍᶠ 2⁶ˢᵈ 1⁶ᵍᶠ 26⁷ᵍ 5⁶ᶠ 2⁶ˢᵈ
9⁷ˢ 8⁶ʰʸ **1-2-10 £5,753**

Cornish Gold *N J Henderson*　　　67
3 b f Slip Anchor - Sans Diablo (Ire)
12¹⁰ᵍᶠ 2¹⁰ᵍ 7⁹ˢ **0-1-3 £1,130**

Cornus *R Hannon*　　　104
2 ch c Inchinor - Demerger (USA)
1⁵ᵍˢ 1⁵ᵍˢ 2⁵ˢ 2⁵ˢ 7⁶ˢ **2-2-5 £19,968**

Cornwallis *T D Barron*　　　70 a42

---

3 b g Forzando - Up And Going (Fr)
11⁶ˢᵈ 1⁶ˢ 2⁶ᵍ 14⁸ᵍᶠ 7⁶ˢᵈ **1-1-5 £4,068**

Coronado Forest (USA) *M R Hoad*　　　25 a62
5 b g Spinning World (USA) - Desert Jewel (USA)
2¹⁰ˢᵈ 4¹⁰ˢᵈ 1¹⁰ˢᵈ 10¹⁰ˢᵈ 14¹⁰ˢᵈ 9¹⁰ˢ 6¹⁰ᶠ
10¹⁰ˢᵈ **1-1-8 £5,119**

Corps De Ballet (Ire) *J L Dunlop*　　　90 a79
3 b f Fasliyev (USA) - Dwell (USA)
7⁵ᶠ 1⁶ᵍᶠ 19⁶ᵍ 10⁶ᵍᶠ 9⁶ᵍᶠ 5⁵ᵍ 2⁵ᵍ 8⁶ˢᵈ
1-1-8 £8,761

Corran Ard (Ire) *Mrs John Harrington*　　　84
3 b g Imperial Ballet (Ire) - Beeper The Great (USA)
4¹¹ᵍ 1⁹ᵍʸ 6¹⁰ᵍᶠ 3¹⁰ᵍᶠ **1-1-4 £7,812**

Corrib Eclipse *Jamie Poulton*　　　107
5 b g Double Eclipse (Ire) - Last Night's Fun (Ire)
1²²ᶠ 6¹⁶ᵍˢ 6¹⁶ᵍ 6¹⁸ᵍ 1¹⁸ᶠ 4¹⁶ᵍᶠ **2-0-6
£32,960**

Corridor Creeper (Fr) *J M Bradley*　　　106
7 ch g Polish Precedent (USA) - Sonia Rose (USA)
5⁵ᵍˢ 4⁵ᵍˢ 4⁵ᵍᶠ 2⁵ᵍᶠ 6⁵ᵍᶠ 2⁶ᶠ 2⁵ˢ 3⁵ᵍˢ
6⁵ᵍᶠ 18⁶ᵍᶠ 3⁵ᵍ 5⁵ᵍ 7⁶ᵍ 3⁵ˢ 2⁵ᵍ 1⁵ˢ 2⁵ˢ 5⁵ˢ
1-8-18 £54,702

Corrine (Ire) *S-E Lilja*　　　99
5 gr m Spectrum (Ire) - La Luna (USA)
1¹²ᵍ 1¹²ᵍ 12¹¹ᵛˢ 2¹⁰ˢ 1¹²ˢ 2¹¹ᵍᶠ 2¹⁴ˢ
3-1-7 £20,925

Coriolanus (Ger) *P Mitchell*　　　104 a103
4 b c Zamindar (USA) - Caesarea (Ger)
3¹⁰ˢᵈ 11¹⁰ˢᵈ 7¹⁰ˢ 16¹⁰ˢ 6¹²ᵍᶠ 9¹⁰ᶠ 6¹⁰ᵍᶠ
1¹⁰ᵍᶠ 14⁹ˢ 8⁸ᶠ 7¹⁰ᵍ **1-1-11 £11,806**

Corsican Native (USA) *Mrs A J Perrett*　　　100
3 b c Lear Fan (USA) - Corsini
1¹⁰ᵍᶠ 2¹⁰ᵍ 13¹²ᵍ **1-1-3 £11,559**

Corton (Ire) *P F I Cole*　　　88
5 gr g Definite Article - Limpopo
3¹⁶ᵍᶠ 6¹⁶ᵍᶠ 18¹²ˢ 9¹⁶ᵍˢ **0-1-4 £1,067**

Corton Denham *G P Enright*　　　a15
3 ch g Wolfhound (USA) - Wigit
12¹⁰ˢᵈ **0-0-1**

Cosi Fan Tutte *M C Pipe*　　　63 a51
6 b g Inchinor - Bumpkin
2¹²ᵍᶠ 3¹⁰ᵍ 7¹²ᵍᶠ 7¹⁰ᵍᶠ 2¹⁰ᵍᶠ 2¹²ˢᵈ **0-4-6
£2,905**

Cosmic Case *J S Goldie*　　　53
9 b m Casteddu - La Fontainova (Ire)
1¹³ᶠ 7¹³ᵍᶠ 3¹³ᵍᶠ 5¹³ᵍ 2¹²ᵍ 3¹³ᵍ 7¹³ᵍᶠ 3¹⁵ᵍᶠ
1¹³ᵍᶠ 2¹²ᵍᶠ 5¹⁴ᵍᶠ 8¹⁴ᵍ **2-4-12 £9,167**

Cosmic Destiny (Ire) *E F Vaughan*　　　65
2 b f Soviet Star (USA) - Cruelle (USA)
7⁶ᵍᶠ **0-0-1**

Cosmic Ranger *H Alexander*
6 b g Magic Ring (Ire) - Lismore
9¹²ˢᵈ **0-0-1**

Cost Analysis (Ire) *M A Jarvis*　　　63
2 ch g Grand Lodge (USA) - Flower Girl
10⁷ˢ 6⁷ᵍᶠ 5⁸ᵍˢ 13⁷ˢ **0-0-4**

Costa Del Sol (Ire) *J J Bridger*　　　30 a43
3 ch g General Monash (USA) - L'Harmonie (USA)
9⁶ˢᵈ 11⁷ˢᵈ 11⁷ˢᵈ 4⁸ˢᵈ 10⁷ᵍᶠ 16⁹ᵍᶠ 6⁶ᵍᶠ
9⁷ᶠ 8⁶ᵍ 13¹⁰ˢᵈ **0-0-10**

Cote Quest (USA) *S C Williams*　　　97
4 b f Green Desert (USA) - West Brooklyn (USA)
4⁸ᵍˢ 11⁷ˢ 14⁸ᵍˢ 4⁸ᵍᶠ 3¹⁰ˢ 6¹⁰ᵍ
12⁸ᵍᶠ 12⁸ᵍᶠ **0-0-9 £8,800**

Cote Soleil *C R Egerton*　　　24

7 ch g Inchinor - Sunshine Coast
10^{12sd} 8^{10gs} 7^{8gs} **0-0-3**

Cotosol *B A McMahon* 82 a80
3 b g Forzando - Emerald Dream (Ire)
7^{7g} 1^{7gs} 5^{7s} 8^{8gs} 3^{7sd} **1-1-5 £4,580**

Cottam Grange *M W Easterby* a8
4 b c River Falls - Karminski
10^{12sd} **0-0-1**

Cottam Karminski *J S Wainwright* 35
3 b f River Falls - Karminski
11^{7gf} 8^{7gf} 13^{6f} 6^{5gs} 14^{8gs} 14^{8gf} **0-0-6**

Cottingham (Ire) *M C Chapman* 67 a63
3 b c Perugino (USA) - Stately Princess
1^{8sd} 4^{7s} 6^{8gs} 6^{8s} 12^{7gf} 2^{8s} 15^{8gs} 6^{10gf}
6^{7gf} 6^{10gs} 2^{10f} 4^{12s} 11^{8g} **1-3-13 £4,463**

Cotton Easter *Mrs A J Bowlby* 56
3 b f Robellino (USA) - Pluck
12^{7g} 9^{8gf} 6^{8gf} 12^{8gf} 7^{7gf} 7^{10gs} 3^{10s}
1^{10hy} 6^{12s} **1-1-9 £3,849**

Cougar Cat (USA) *A P O'Brien* 106
2 b c Storm Cat (USA) - Excellent Meeting (USA)
1^{5gf} 4^{5gf} 2^{6g} **1-1-3 £21,360**

Could She Be Magic (Ire) *T D Easterby* 28 a59
3 b f Titus Livius (Fr) - Ponteilla (Fr)
2^{8sd} 1^{7ss} 7^{7ss} 2^{7sd} 8^{7hy} 5^{6gf} **1-2-6**
£6,023

Councellor (Fr) *R Hannon* 83
2 b c Gilded Time (USA) - Sudden Storm Bird (USA)
3^{6gf} 4^{7gf} 4^{6g} 2^{7gf} **0-2-4 £3,560**

Council Member (USA) *Saeed Bin Suroor* 107
2 b c Seattle Slew (USA) - Zoe Montana (USA)
1^{5g} 2^{6gf} 2^{6gf} 11^{6s} 2^{6gf} **1-3-5 £43,223**

Counsel's Opinion (Ire) *C F Wall* 111
7 ch g Rudimentary (USA) - Fairy Fortune
3^{10gs} 4^{10g} 11^{12f} 9^{12g} 4^{10gf} 2^{12g} 17^{10gs}
0-2-7 £15,302

Count Boris *G B Balding* 65
3 b g Groom Dancer (USA) - Bu Hagab (Ire)
13^{8g} 7^{8g} 7^{10gs} 9^{8gf} 3^{9s} 2^{10s} **0-2-6**
£1,845

Count Cougar (USA) *S P Griffiths* 45 a67
4 b g Sir Cat (USA) - Gold Script (USA)
3^{5sd} 10^{5sd} 17^{5gf} 6^{5gf} 14^{5gf} 17^{5gf} 11^{5gf}
0-1-7 £621

Count Dracula *Jean-Rene Auvray* 38 a59
3 b g Dracula (Aus) - Chipaya
1^{8sd} 13^{9gs} 6^{8sd} 12^{8gf} **1-0-4 £3,311**

Count Kristo *C G Cox* 83
2 br c Dr Fong (USA) - Aryadne
2^{7g} 12^{7gs} **0-1-2 £1,976**

Count On Us *P Burgoyne* a25
4 ch g Danehill Dancer (Ire) - Capricious Lady (Ire)
13^{10sd} **0-0-1**

Count Walewski *S Dow* 8 a7
4 b g Polish Precedent (USA) - Classic Beauty (Ire)
20^{10g} 12^{8sd} **0-0-2**

Countdown *Sir Mark Prescott* 90 a80
2 ch c Pivotal - Quiz Time
3^{5gf} 2^{5sd} 1^{5g} 1^{5s} 2^{5gs} 8^{6g} 5^{5sd} **2-2-7**
£14,973

Countess Elton (Ire) *R E Barr*
4 ch f Mukaddamah (USA) - Be Prepared (Ire)
12^{8sd} **0-0-1**

Country Rambler (USA) *B W Hills* 93

2 b c Red Ransom (USA) - Country Garden
10^{6gf} 1^{7f} 7^{7gs} 3^{8g} 1^{6gf} **2-0-5 £15,245**

Country Reel (USA) *Saeed Bin Suroor* 114
4 b c Danzig (USA) - Country Belle (USA)
8^{6gs} 4^{6gf} 4^{6f} 11^{6gs} 12^{7g} 2^{6g} 5^{6gf} 4^{6s}
0-1-8 £22,432

Countrywide Dream (Ire) *A Berry* 10
2 ch g Definite Article - Grosvenor Miss (Ire)
11^{5gf} 14^{6f} 8^{7gf} 5^{7gf} **0-0-4**

Countrywide Flyer (Ire) *T D Barron* a96
3 b g Revoque (Ire) - Unbidden Melody (USA)
5^{8sd} 1^{8sd} 2^{8ss} 3^{10sd} **1-1-4 £7,360**

Countrywide Girl (Ire) *A Berry* 4 a46
5 ch m Catrail (USA) - Polish Saga
10^{6sd} 3^{8gf} 11^{8sd} 5^{4sd} 3^{6sd} 3^{7sd}
2^{6sd} 7^{5sd} 5^{7sd} 3^{7sd} 4^{8sd} 10^{7g} 11^{6g} 9^{6sd}
1-6-16 £3,078

Countrywide Luck *N P Littmoden* 91
3 b g Inchinor - Thelma
6^{8g} 2^{11g} 1^{9g} 6^{10g} 7^{12s} **1-1-5 £5,217**

Countrywide Star (Ire) *C N Kellett*
6 ch g Common Grounds - Silver Slipper
12^{9sw} **0-0-1**

Countrywide Sun *N P Littmoden* 53 a57
2 b g Benny The Dip (USA) - Sundae Girl (USA)
8^{5g} 10^{6gs} 7^{7gs} 2^{7gf} 4^{7sd} 18^{8g} 15^{7g} **0-1-7**
£1,426

County Clare *A M Balding* 77
2 ch f Barathea (Ire) - Input
10^{6gf} 2^{6gf} 3^{7gs} 15^{7g} 6^{6g} **0-2-5 £2,782**

Countykat (Ire) *K R Burke* 80 a84
4 b g Woodborough (USA) - Kitty Kildare (USA)
6^{12sd} 13^{12sd} 7^{10hy} 2^{8gf} 1^{7sd} 2^{8g} 7^{8gf} 7^{8gf}
1-2-8 £9,489

Coup D'Etat *J L Dunlop* 85
2 b c Diktat - Megdale (Ire)
4^{6gf} 2^{6g} 6^{7s} 4^{7gs} 3^{7s} **0-3-5 £3,765**

Coup De Chance (Ire) *P A Blockley* 92 a69
4 ch f Ashkalani (USA) - Tout A Coup (USA)
11^{13sd} 12^{12gf} 3^{19gf} 13^{12gf} **0-0-4 £2,248**

Courageous Duke (USA) *J Noseda* 102
5 b g Spinning World (USA) - Araadh (USA)
3^{10gf} 10^{20gf} 2^{10gf} 3^{10gf} 2^{10gf} 2^{10gf}
0-4-7 £25,452

Courageously *P F I Cole* 33
2 b c Aljabr (USA) - Eishin Eleuthera (Ire)
5^{5gf} **0-0-1 £523**

Courant D'Air (Ire) *Mrs Lucinda Featherstone* 42 a34
3 b g Indian Rocket - Red River Rose (Ire)
7^{8sd} 3^{8sd} 6^{11sd} 5^{8sd} 1^{7g} 7^{8f} **1-1-6**
£1,841

Cours De La Reine (Ire) *P W Chapple-Hyam* 105
2 b f Fasliyev (USA) - Society Queen (Ire)
3^{6gf} 13^{6f} 1^{7hy} 10^{8g} 4^{7hy} **1-1-5**
£31,577

Court Chancellor *P Mitchell* 35
3 b g Primo Dominie - Welcome Home
13^{8gf} 12^{8f} 7^{6gf} 17^{7gf} 10^{7g} **0-0-5**

Court Emperor *R J Price* 42
4 b g Mtoto - Fairfields Cone
9^{12gs} 9^{10gs} 9^{14gs} **0-0-3**

Court Masterpiece *E A L Dunlop* 117
4 b c Polish Precedent (USA) - Easy Option (Ire)
3^{7g} 5^{7gf} 4^{7gf} 2^{7gs} 1^{7gf} 4^{8gs} 3^{7gf} 6^{7g}
1-2-8 £122,476

Court Music (Ire) *R E Barr* a34
5 b/br m Revoque (Ire) - Lute And Lyre (Ire)
7⁷ˢᵈ 2⁶ˢᵈ 6⁶ˢᵈ 9⁶ˢʷ **0-1-4 £394**

Court Of Appeal *B Ellison* 98
7 ch g Bering - Hiawatha's Song (USA)
1¹⁴ᵍ 1¹²ᵍˢ 3¹²ᶠ 2¹²ᵍᶠ 10¹²ᵍᶠ 2¹²ᵍ 6¹¹ˢ
2-3-7 £24,843

Court One *R J Price* 50
6 b g Shareef Dancer (USA) - Fairfields Cone
14¹²ˢᵈ 7¹¹ᵍᶠ 1¹⁵ᵍ 1¹⁴ᵍᶠ 1¹¹⁴ᵍᶠ 7¹⁴ᵍᶠ 8¹⁶ᵍˢ
11¹⁶ᵍᶠ **2-0-8 £3,244**

Court Ruler *R J Price*
2 b g Kayf Tara - Fairfields Cone
5⁷ᵍˢ UR⁸ᵍˢ 10¹⁰ʰʸ **0-0-3**

Courtintime *T D Easterby* 6
2 b f Atraf - Royal Girl
9⁵ᵍᶠ 13⁵ᵍᶠ **0-0-2**

Courtledge *Mrs C A Dunnett* a11
9 b g Unfuwain (USA) - Tremellick
7¹⁰ˢᵈ **0-0-1**

Coustou (Ire) *A R Dicken* 65
4 b g In Command (Ire) - Carranza (Ire)
6⁷ᵍᶠ 10⁶ᵍ 8⁶ᵍ 4⁷ᵍᶠ 3⁷ᶠ 3⁹ᵍ 7⁹ᵍᶠ **0-2-7
£1,428**

Coventina (Ire) *J L Dunlop* 95
3 gr f Daylami (Ire) - Lady Of The Lake
7¹⁰ᵍ 8¹²ᵍ 2¹²ᵍᶠ 3¹⁴ᶠ 3¹⁴ᵍᶠ 1¹⁶ᵍᶠ **1-2-6
£18,184**

Coy (Ire) *Sir Michael Stoute* 109
3 b f Danehill (USA) - Demure
5⁸ᵍᶠ 2⁷ᵍ 2⁸ᵍᶠ 1⁸ᵍᶠ **1-2-4 £32,000**

Crackleando *N P Littmoden* 66 a55
3 ch g Forzando - Crackling
3¹⁰ˢᵈ 10¹⁰ˢᵈ 3¹²ʰʸ 1¹⁴ˢ 16¹⁴ᵍ 3¹⁴ᵍᶠ 2¹⁷ᵍˢ
7¹⁷ᵍᶠ 9¹⁵ˢ **1-2-9 £7,179**

Cracow (Ire) *W K Goldsworthy* 51
7 b g Polish Precedent (USA) - Height Of Secrecy
2¹²ᵍᶠ 14¹²ˢᵈ 4¹²ᵍᶠ 5¹⁴ᵍᶠ 8¹²ᶠ 11¹²ᵍ **0-1-6
£1,388**

Crafty Calling (USA) *P F I Cole* 68
4 b c Crafty Prospector (USA) - Glorious Calling (USA)
9⁶ᵍ 17⁷ᵍᶠ 11⁷ᵍᶠ 4⁶ᵍᶠ 8⁷ˢ **0-0-5**

Crafty Fancy (Ire) *D J S Ffrench Davis* 91
3 ch f Intikhab (USA) - Idle Fancy
2⁷ˢ 3⁶ˢ 8⁶ᵍ 10⁸ᵍᶠ 17⁸ᵍ **0-1-5 £9,900**

Crafty Politician (USA) *G L Moore* 43 a51
7 ch h Supremo (USA) - Sauve Qui Peut (Can)
4⁷ˢᵈ 1⁶ˢᵈ 2⁷ˢᵈ 5⁶ᵍᶠ 6⁵ᵍ 13⁵ᵍᶠ **1-1-6
£1,670**

Craic Sa Ceili (Ire) *M S Saunders* 72
4 b f Danehill Dancer (Ire) - Fay's Song (Ire)
10⁸ˢ 17⁷ᵍ 9⁸ᵍᶠ 4⁷ᵍᶠ 8⁶ᵍ 5⁸ᵍ 12⁷ᵍ **0-0-7
£454**

Craigmor *M F Harris* a5
4 br g Polar Falcon (USA) - Western Horizon (USA)
8⁸ˢᵈ 8⁸ˢᵈ **0-0-2**

Crail *C F Wall* 82
4 b g Vettori - Tendency
3⁸ˢ 7⁸ᵍˢ 4⁸ᵍᶠ 1⁸ᵍˢ 10⁸ᵍˢ 10⁷ᵍˢ **1-1-6
£5,041**

Craiova (Ire) *B W Hills* 88
5 b h Turtle Island (Ire) - Velvet Appeal (Ire)
16⁸ᵍ 22⁸ᵍ 7⁷ᵍ 7⁷ᵍ 9⁸ᵍ 9⁷ᵍ 4⁷ᵍ 12⁷ᵍ
0-1-8 £599

Crathes *J G Given* 55 a33

3 ch f Zilzal (USA) - Sweet Dreams
2⁶ˢ 4⁷ᵍ 6⁸ˢᵈ **0-1-3 £1,996**

Crathorne (Ire) *J D Bethell* 88 a69
4 b g Alzao (USA) - Shirley Blue (Ire)
4¹²ᵍˢ 3¹²ᵍᶠ 4¹²ᶠ 13¹²ᵍˢ 11¹²ᵍ 13¹²ᶠ 13⁹ᵍˢ
8¹²ˢᵈ 17¹⁰ᵍ **0-2-9 £2,100**

Crazy Like A Fool (Ire) *B Mactaggart*
5 b g Charnwood Forest (Ire) - Shanghai Girl
13⁸ᵍ **0-0-1**

Cream Of Esteem *N Tinkler* 45
2 b g Mark Of Esteem (Ire) - Chantilly (Fr)
13⁷ˢ 13⁶ᵍˢ **0-0-2**

Creative Character (USA) *P F I Cole* 73
2 b/br c Theatrical - Shannkara (Ire)
4⁷ᵍ 9⁸ᵍˢ 9⁷ᵍᶠ **0-0-3 £343**

Credit (Ire) *R Hannon* 95
3 b c Intikhab (USA) - Tycooness (Ire)
3⁸ᵍ 3⁸ᵍ 1⁸ᵍ 10⁸ᶠ 7⁸ᵍˢ 4¹⁰ᵍ 1¹⁰ᵍᶠ 3¹⁰ᵍ
3¹²ᵍ 3¹²ᵍᶠ 12¹²ˢ **2-5-11 £21,245**

Cree *W R Muir* 69
2 b c Indian Ridge - Nightitude
8⁵ᵍ 13⁵ᵍ 5⁵ᶠ 2⁵ᵍ 5⁵ᵍˢ 2⁵ˢ 36⁶ᶠ 1⁵ʰʸ 4⁵ᵍ
5⁶ʰʸ 2⁵ʰʸ **1-4-11 £9,406**

Creek Dancer *R Guest* 37
2 b f Josr Algarhoud (Ire) - Dance Land (Ire)
17⁷ᵍ **0-0-1**

Creme De La Creme (Ire) *D R Loder* 63 a50
2 b f Montjeu (Ire) - Pride Of Place (Ire)
8⁸ᵍˢ 13⁷ˢᵈ **0-0-2**

Creskeld (Ire) *B Smart* 74 a89
5 b g Sri Pekan (USA) - Pizzazz
3⁸ˢ 12⁸ʰʸ 14⁸ᵍˢ 14⁸ᵍˢ 9⁸ᵍ 8⁷ᵍˢ 1⁹ᵍˢ
4⁸ᵍˢ 14⁸ˢ 5¹⁰ˢ 13⁹ˢᵈ **1-1-11 £14,874**

Cressex Katie *J R Best* a25
5 b m Komaite (USA) - Kakisa
13⁷ˢᵈ **0-0-1**

Cretan Gift *N P Littmoden* a65
13 ch g Cadeaux Genereux - Caro's Niece (USA)
5⁷ˢᵈ 4⁶ˢᵈ **0-0-2**

Crete (Ire) *W J Haggas* 68
2 b c Montjeu (Ire) - Paesanella
4⁸ʰʸ **0-0-1 £491**

Crewes Miss Isle *A G Newcombe* 62 a71
3 b f Makbul - Riviere Rouge
4⁶ˢᵈ 6⁶ˢ 1⁵ˢᵈ 5⁶ˢ 8⁵ᵍᶠ 9⁶ᵍᶠ 7⁶ˢᵈ 5⁶ᵍᶠ 8⁵ˢ
11⁶ˢᵈ 7⁷ˢᵈ **1-0-11 £3,337**

Crimson Bow (Ger) *J G Given* 51
2 ch f Night Shift (USA) - Carma (Ire)
9⁶ᵍ **0-0-1**

Crimson Palace (SAF) *Saeed Bin Suroor* 113
5 b m Elliodor (Fr) - Perfect Guest (SAF)
1⁹ᵍᶠ 4¹⁰ᵍᶠ 1¹⁰ᵍˢ 6⁸ᵍᶠ 1¹⁰ᶠ **3-0-5
£356,519**

Crimson Silk *D Haydn Jones* 99
4 ch g Forzando - Sylhall
8⁶ᵍ 8⁶ᵍ 10⁷ᵍˢ 12⁷ˢ 9⁷ᵍᶠ 36⁶ᶠ 11⁶ᵍ 3⁶ᵍˢ
0-2-8 £7,871

Crimson Star (Ire) *C Tinkler* 52 a47
3 b/br f Soviet Star (USA) - Crimson Shower
7⁸ˢ 11¹⁰ˢᵈ 12⁷ᵍᶠ 15⁸ᵍᶠ 3⁶ᵍ 2⁷ᵍᶠ 2⁸ˢᵈ
2⁶ᵍᶠ **0-4-8 £1,665**

Crimson Sun (USA) *Saeed Bin Suroor* 103
2 b c Danzig (USA) - Crimplene (Ire)
2⁶ᵍˢ 1⁶ᵍᶠ 1⁶ᵍᶠ 8⁶ˢ 2⁷ᵍ **2-2-5 £24,163**

Cripsey Brook *Don Enrico Incisa* 92

6 ch g Lycius (USA) - Duwon (Ire)
6⁸ᵍ 6¹⁰ᵍˢ 7¹⁰ᵍᶠ 7⁹ᵍᶠ 2¹⁰ᵍ 5⁸ᵍ 6⁸ᵍᶠ 12¹¹ᵍ
7¹⁰ᵍˢ 12¹²ᶠ 5¹⁰ᵍ **0-1-11 £4,834**

Crispin House *R J Price*
4 b f Inchinor - Ayr Classic
12¹⁴ᵍᶠ **0-0-1**

Cristoforo (Ire) *B J Curley*   87
7 b g Perugino (USA) - Red Barons Lady (Ire)
11¹¹ˢ 10¹⁰ᵍˢ 1¹²ᵍᶠ 1¹²ᵍᶠ 1¹⁰ᵍᶠ 1¹²ᵍᶠ **5-0-6**
£19,591

Critical Stage (Ire) *J D Frost*   68 a71
5 b g King's Theatre (Ire) - Zandaka (Fr)
3⁹ˢᵈ 1¹¹ˢˢ 3¹²ˢᵈ 10¹²ᵍᶠ 6⁸ᵍᶠ 4¹⁰ᵍˢ 4¹²ᵍˢ
1-3-7 £6,104

Crociera (Ire) *M H Tompkins*   53
3 b g Croco Rouge (Ire) - Ombry Girl (Ire)
4¹⁰ˢ 9¹³ˢ 17¹²ᵍ 8¹²ᵍ **0-0-4 £313**

Crocodile Dundee (Ire) *Jamie Poulton*   113 a96
3 b c Croco Rouge (Ire) - Miss Salsa Dancer
7⁷ˢᵈ 6⁸ˢᵈ 3¹⁰ᵍ 2¹¹ᵍ 2¹⁰ᶠ 1¹⁰ᵍˢ 1¹²ᵍ **2-2-7**
£64,600

Crocodile Kiss (Ire) *J A Osborne*   70
2 b f Rossini (USA) - Pipe Opener
5⁶ᵍᶠ 5⁶ᶠ 10⁶ᵍˢ 6⁶ʰʸ **0-0-4**

Crocolat *Mrs Stef Liddiard*   74 a79
3 ch f Croco Rouge (Ire) - Lamanka Lass (USA)
20⁸ᵍ 9¹⁰ˢ 5⁷ᶠ 2¹²ᶠ 4¹²ˢᵈ 1¹²ˢᵈ 1¹²ˢʷ 3¹⁶ᵍ
2¹⁷ᵍᶠ **2-3-9 £9,419**

Croix De Guerre (Ire) *P J Hobbs*   56
4 gr g Highest Honor (Fr) - Esclava (USA)
3¹³ᵍˢ **0-1-1 £443**

Croix Rouge (USA) *Mrs A J Perrett*   73
2 b c Chester House (USA) - Rougeur (USA)
3⁷ᵍᶠ 12⁸ᵍᶠ 9⁷ᵍ **0-1-3 £984**

Cromarty Bay *A P James*
3 b f Victory Note (USA) - Cromarty
11¹⁰ᵍᶠ **0-0-1**

Cronkyvoddy *Miss Gay Kelleway*   61
3 b g Groom Dancer (USA) - Miss Pout
6⁷ᶠ 11⁸ˢᵈ 6⁸ᵍ 4¹⁰ˢ **0-0-4 £280**

Croon *L M Cumani*   a59
2 b c Sinndar (Ire) - Shy Minstrel (USA)
6⁷ˢᵈ **0-0-1**

Cross Ash (Ire) *R Hollinshead*   52 a53
4 ch g Ashkalani (USA) - Priorite (Ire)
7⁶ˢ 10⁷ᵍ 14⁸ˢᵈ 17⁷ᵍᶠ 11⁶ᵍ 6⁷ᵍ 3⁹ˢᵈ
10⁸ˢᵈ **0-1-8 £211**

Cross My Shadow (Ire) *M F Harris*   53
2 b g Cape Cross (Ire) - Shadowglow
7⁸ᵍᶠ 5⁷ʰʸ 9⁷ᵍˢ 7⁶ᵍ 12⁶ʰʸ 7⁷ᵍˢ **0-0-6**

Cross The Line (Ire) *A P Jarvis*   a63
2 b c Cape Cross (Ire) - Baalbek
4⁸ˢᵈ **0-0-1 £322**

Cross Time (USA) *M R Channon*   55
2 b c Cape Cross (Ire) - Reine Maid (USA)
6⁸ʰʸ **0-0-1**

Crosspeace (Ire) *M Johnston*   91
2 b c Cape Cross (Ire) - Announcing Peace
2⁶ᵍ 1⁶ᵍᶠ 1⁷ˢ **2-1-3 £20,480**

Crossways *P D Evans*   76 a70
6 b g Mister Baileys - Miami Dancer (USA)
4¹⁰ˢᵈ 11³ˢᵈ 9¹²ˢᵈ 4¹⁴ᵍ 2¹⁴ᵍᶠ 2¹³ᵍᶠ **1-3-6**
£6,303

Crow Wood *J G Given*   103
5 b g Halling (USA) - Play With Me (Ire)

8¹⁰ˢ 3¹⁰ᵍˢ 3¹⁰ᵍᶠ 5¹⁰ᵍᶠ 2¹²ᵍ 13¹⁴ˢ 6¹⁴ᵍ
6¹⁴ˢ **0-3-8 £23,442**

Crown Agent (Ire) *A M Balding*   74 a66
4 b g Mukaddamah (USA) - Supreme Crown (USA)
10¹²ˢᵈ 5¹²ᵍ 8¹²ᵍˢ 9¹⁴ˢ 7¹²ˢᵈ **0-0-5**

Crown City (USA) *B P J Baugh*   5 a34
4 b f Coronado's Quest (USA) - Trisha Brown (USA)
7⁸ˢᵈ 8¹⁰ˢᵈ 9⁸ˢᵈ 10⁸ᵍ **0-0-4**

Crown Of Medina *P W Harris*   49 a62
2 ch c Fraam - Medina De Rioseco
15⁷ᵍ 6⁷ˢᵈ **0-0-2**

Cruise Director *W J Musson*   93 a93
4 b g Zilzal (USA) - Briggsmaid
3¹²ˢᵈ 13¹²ˢᵈ 3¹²ˢˢ 7¹²ˢˢ 1¹²ᵍˢ 13¹²ᵍ 11¹²ᵍ
2¹²ᵍˢ 4¹¹ʰʸ 5¹²ˢ 5¹²ˢ **1-3-11 £12,515**

Crunchy (Ire) *B Ellison*   38
6 ch g Common Grounds - Credit Crunch (Ire)
13¹⁰ᵍ **0-0-1**

Crusoe (Ire) *A Sadik*   a63
7 b g Turtle Island (Ire) - Self Reliance
3⁸ˢʷ 11⁹ˢʷ 4⁸ˢᵈ 18¹⁰ᵍ 8⁸ˢᵈ 4⁹ˢᵈ 2⁸ˢᵈ
7⁹ˢᵈ 11¹¹ᵍˢ 2⁸ˢᵈ 9⁸ˢᵈ 10⁸ˢᵈ **0-3-13 £2,377**

Crusty Lily *R M H Cowell*   19 a23
8 gr m Whittingham (Ire) - Miss Crusty
3⁶ˢᵈ 13⁶ᵍᶠ 7⁶ᶠ 12⁸ᵍ **0-0-4 £205**

Crux *C W Thornton*   37
2 b g Pivotal - Penny Dip
14⁵ᵍᶠ **0-0-1**

Cry Of The Wolf *N P Littmoden*   48
2 ch c Loup Sauvage (USA) - Hopesay
9⁶ᵍᶠ 8⁶ᵍᶠ **0-0-2**

Cryfield *N Tinkler*   68 a58
7 b g Efisio - Ciboure
15¹⁰ᵍ 8⁸ᵍˢ 6⁸ᵍˢ 2⁷ᵍᶠ 4⁸ᶠ 7⁷ᵍ 8⁷ᵍ 1⁸ᵍᶠ
6⁸ᵍˢ 4⁸ᵍᶠ 3⁹ᵍᶠ 4⁸ˢʷ 9⁸ᵍ 11¹⁰ᵍˢ 6⁷ᵍᶠ 6⁹ˢᵈ 8⁹ˢᵈ
1-3-17 £9,134

Cryptogam *M E Sowersby*   44
4 b f Zamindar (USA) - Moss
8¹²ˢᵈ 8¹⁶ˢᵈ 9⁸ˢᵈ 10⁹ᶠ 11⁸ᶠ 5¹²ᵍᶠ 11¹²ᵍᶠ
16¹²ᵍᶠ **0-0-8**

Crystal (Ire) *B J Meehan*   89
3 b f Danehill (USA) - Solar Crystal (Ire)
2¹⁰ᵍ 1¹⁰ᵍ 5¹²ᵍ 11¹⁰ʰʸ 8¹⁰ᵍ 5¹²ˢ **1-1-6**
£14,781

Crystal Castle (USA) *J E Hammond*   117
6 b g Gilded Time (USA) - Wayage (USA)
3⁷ˢ 3⁷ᵍˢ 5⁷ᵍ 17⁷ᵍˢ **0-3-5 £69,965**

Crystal Choir *N J Henderson*   60
4 b f Singspiel (Ire) - Crystal Ring (Ire)
15¹⁰ᵍˢ 6¹⁰ᵍ 13⁹ᵍ **0-0-3**

Crystal Curling (Ire) *B W Hills*   99
3 ch f Peintre Celebre (USA) - State Crystal (Ire)
3¹¹ᵍˢ 3¹⁰ᵍ 7¹²ᵍᶠ 5¹⁰ˢ 5¹⁰ᵍ 13⁸ᵍᶠ **0-1-6**
£10,072

Crystal Mystic (Ire) *B Palling*   58 a28
2 b c Anita's Prince - Out On Her Own
11⁷ᵍᶠ 4⁷ʰʸ 10⁶ˢᵈ 11⁶ʰʸ **0-0-4**

Crystalline *D R Loder*   72
2 b f Green Desert (USA) - Crown Of Light
3⁷ᵍᶠ 11⁷ᵍ **0-0-2 £740**

Ctesiphon (USA) *J G Given*   35 a6
3 b f Arch (USA) - Beautiful Bedouin (USA)
8¹⁰ᵍˢ 10⁸ˢᵈ 10⁸ˢᵈ **0-0-3**

Cubic Confessions (Ire) *J A Osborne*   a47
2 b f Cape Cross (Ire) - Debinnair (Fr)

4^{5sd} 4^{5sd} 4^{5gf} **0-0-3 £1,309**

Cuddles (Fr) *K O Cunningham-Brown*   66 a77
5 b m Anabaa (USA) - Palomelle (Fr)
7^{10sd} 5^{10gs} 9^{12gs} 4^{8gf} 5^{9g} 3^{10g} 8^{8gf}
10^{10gf} 7^{8gs} 6^{10g} 11^{11gs} 7^{8sd} 12^{9sd} **0-1-13 £867**

Cugina Nicola *G B Balding*   55
3 b f Nicolotte - Cugina
10^{10gf} 10^{11g} 9^{10gf} **0-0-3**

Culcabock (Ire) *P Monteith*   38
4 b g Unfuwain (USA) - Evidently (Ire)
7^{14g} **0-0-1**

Culminate *J E Long*
7 ch g Afzal - Straw Blade
11^{7ss} **0-0-1**

Cultured *Mrs A J Bowlby*   58
3 b f Danzero (Aus) - Seek The Pearl
5^{10s} 6^{9gf} **0-0-2**

Cumbria *M Johnston*   69
3 b f Singspiel (Ire) - Whitehaven
3^{12s} 4^{12gf} **0-0-2 £1,267**

Cumbrian Knight (Ire) *J M Jefferson*   49
6 b g Presenting - Crashrun
8^{10gf} **0-0-1**

Cumbrian Princess *M Blanshard*   34 a48
7 gr m Mtoto - Cumbrian Melody
4^{12sd} 10^{8sd} 8^{8ss} 1^{8sd} 1^{8sd} 3^{8sd} 6^{8sd} 3^{10sd}
6^{10sd} 6^{9gs} 10^{8gs} **2-1-11 £3,517**

Cummiskey (Ire) *J A Osborne*   82
2 b c Orpen (USA) - Ansariya (USA)
5^{5gs} 3^{6gf} 4^{5gf} 2^{6gf} 2^{6gf} **0-3-5 £4,485**

Cumwhitton *R A Fahey*   a51
5 b m Jumbo Hirt (USA) - Dominance
5^{11sd} 9^{11ss} 1^{11sd} 6^{11sd} **1-0-4 £1,449**

Cunning Pursuit *M L W Bell*   49 a32
3 b g Pursuit Of Love - Mistitled (USA)
10^{8gf} 6^{8sd} 5^{6s} 6^{8gf} 2^{11f} 10^{14g} 9^{16gf}
1^{10gf} 4^{10gf} **1-1-9 £2,466**

Cup Of Love (USA) *R Guest*   54
2 ch f Behrens (USA) - Cup Of Kindness (USA)
8^{6g} 12^{8gf} 9^{6s} **0-0-3**

Cupid's Glory *Sir Mark Prescott*   108 a103
2 b c Pursuit Of Love - Doctor's Glory (USA)
6^{7sd} 1^{6sd} 1^{6s} 1^{7sd} 3^{6y} 1^{7s} 4^{8vs} **4-0-7
£53,287**

Curate (USA) *A Dickman*
5 ch g Unfuwain (USA) - Carniola
6^{10gf} **0-0-1**

Curfew *J R Fanshawe*   95
5 b m Marju (Ire) - Twilight Patrol
4^{5g} 5^{5g} 8^{5gf} 13^{5gs} **0-0-4 £2,250**

Curragh Gold (Ire) *Mrs P N Dutfield*   20 a17
4 b f Flying Spur (Aus) - Go Indigo (Ire)
9^{10gf} 11^{10g} 12^{16sd} **0-0-3**

Currency *J M Bradley*   86 a80
7 b g Sri Pekan (USA) - On Tiptoes
12^{6sd} 3^{5sd} 2^{6sd} 4^{5sd} 7^{7sd} 12^{7sd} 14^{6g}
4^{5gf} 9^{6gf} 6^{6gf} 3^{5gf} 9^{5gf} 11^{6gf} 5^{6gf} 2^{6gs} 1^{6gf}
4^{5gf} 5^{6g} **1-5-21 £9,405**

Curzon Lodge (Ire) *C Tinkler*   38 a42
4 ch g Grand Lodge (Ire) - Curzon Street
9^{10sd} 10^{7gf} PU^{8gf} **0-0-3**

Cusco (Ire) *R Hannon*   96
3 ch f Titus Livius (Fr) - John's Ballad (Ire)
2^{6hy} 6^{8gs} 9^{8gf} 2^{6gf} 9^{7gf} 2^{7s} 9^{7g} 9^{6g}
0-3-8 £9,583

Cusoon *G L Moore*   82
2 b c Dansili - Charming Life
3^{5gf} 1^{6f} 4^{6gs} 4^{6gf} 12^{7gf} 14^{7gs} **1-1-6
£4,932**

Cusp *C W Thornton*   54
4 b f Pivotal - Bambolona
2^{14s} **0-1-1 £850**

Cut And Dried *D M Simcock*   66 a69
3 ch g Daggers Drawn (USA) - Apple Sauce
1^{5sd} 1^{5sd} 6^{5sd} 9^{5sd} 5^{5gf} 4^{5f} 6^{5gf} 4^{5gf}
5^{6sd} 11^{6sd} 7^{6gf} 10^{5gf} **2-0-12 £7,621**

Cut Ridge (Ire) *J S Wainwright*   59
5 b m Indian Ridge - Cutting Ground (Ire)
18^{6gf} 9^{5gf} 17^{5g} 11^{8gf} 3^{7gf} 2^{7f} 1^{8gf} 2^{6gs}
5^{6gs} 7^{7g} 13^{7f} **1-3-11 £6,214**

Cut Short (USA) *J H M Gosden*   86
3 b/br f Diesis - Sun And Shade
5^{7gf} 1^{8gf} 3^{8gs} **1-0-3 £6,422**

Cut To The Chase *N Tinkler*   17
2 b g Fraam - Chasetown Cailin
14^{6gs} **0-0-1**

Cute Cait *Mrs G S Rees*   13 a8
3 b f Atraf - Clunk Click
13^{7sd} 6^{8g} **0-0-2**

Cutlass Gaudy *R Hollinshead*   82
2 br c Nomination - Cutlass Princess (USA)
4^{5gf} 7^{6gf} 2^{5gf} 5^{5g} **0-1-4 £2,107**

Cutthroat *P J Hobbs*   21
4 ch g Kris - Could Have Been
7^{10gf} **0-0-1**

Cutting Crew (USA) *P W Harris*   105
3 ch c Diesis - Poppy Carew (Ire)
3^{10gs} 1^{12gs} 6^{11gf} 2^{12g} 1^{12g} **2-2-5
£60,570**

Cyber Santa *J Hetherton*   53
6 b g Celtic Swing - Qualitair Ridge
6^{12gf} 8^{12gf} 2^{12s} 8^{12s} **0-1-4 £1,075**

Cyclical *G A Butler*   95 a87
2 b c Pivotal - Entwine
1^{5gs} 1^{6gf} 3^{6g} 2^{5sd} **2-2-4 £14,430**

Cyclonic Storm *R A Fahey*   64
5 b m Catrail (USA) - Wheeler's Wonder (Ire)
3^{9gf} 4^{9g} 10^{8gf} **0-1-3 £1,130**

Cyfrwys (Ire) *B Palling*   66 a58
3 b f Foxhound (USA) - Divine Elegance (Ire)
16^{7g} 2^{6gf} 2^{6sd} 6^{7gf} 10^{6gs} 6^{6gf} 1^{6g} 13^{6g}
1-2-8 £3,771

Czar Wars *J Balding*   a34
9 b g Warrshan (USA) - Dutch Czarina
8^{6sd} 6^{6sd} 7^{6sd} **0-0-3**

Czarina Waltz *Miss Gay Kelleway*   90 a76
5 b m Emperor Jones (USA) - Ballerina Bay
2^{10gf} 10^{10gf} 6^{10sd} 6^{8gs} 19^{10g} **0-1-5
£1,740**

Czech Summer (Ire) *R M Flower*   —
3 b g Desert Sun - Prague Spring
8^{12sd} 12^{13sd} 10^{8g} **0-0-3**

Dabbers Ridge (Ire) *B W Hills*   58
2 b c Indian Ridge - Much Commended
7^{6gs} **0-0-1**

Dabus *M C Chapman*   35
9 b g Kris - Licorne
8^{12gf} **0-0-1**

Dafa *B J Curley*   a49
8 b g Deploy - Linpac North Moor

1⁷ˢᵈ 1¹⁰ˢᵈ 6¹²ˢˢ 8¹⁰ˢᵈ 6¹³ˢᵈ 4⁸ˢᵈ **2-0-6**
£2,887

Dafina (Ire) *H Morrison* 56 a57
4 b f Mtoto - Dafayna
4¹¹ᶠ 3⁸ˢᵈ **0-1-2 £710**

Dafore *R Hannon* 83
3 b c Dr Fong (USA) - Aquaglow
1⁶ˢ 7⁸ᵍᶠ 9⁸ˢ 10⁸ᵍˢ **1-0-4 £5,843**

Daggers Canyon *Julian Poulton* 66
3 ch g Daggers Drawn (USA) - Chipewyas (Fr)
2¹⁰ᵍˢ 9⁸ᵍ 1¹⁰ᵍᶠ **1-1-3 £5,151**

Dagola (Ire) *C A Dwyer* 70
3 b g Daggers Drawn (USA) - Diabola (USA)
1⁸ᵍ 7⁸ᵍ 10¹⁰ᵍ 3⁸ᵍᶠ 4⁸ᵍᶠ 2⁸ᵍᶠ 4⁸ᵍᶠ 11⁸ᵍᶠ
1-2-8 £5,655

Dahjee (USA) *Saeed Bin Suroor* 74
3 b c Seeking The Gold (USA) - Colorado Dancer
4¹²ᵍᶠ **0-0-1 £428**

Dahliyev (Ire) *P W Harris* 72
2 b g Fasliyev (USA) - Thaidah (Can)
9⁶ᵍ 3⁷ᵍ 9⁷ᵍˢ **0-1-3 £686**

Dahman *Saeed Bin Suroor* 79
2 b c Darshaan - Nuriva (USA)
4⁷ᵍ 11⁸ᵍˢ **0-0-2 £376**

Dahteer (Ire) *M R Channon* 91
2 b g Bachir (Ire) - Reematna
4⁶ᵍ 1⁶ᶠ 1⁶ᵍᶠ 6⁷ᵍˢ 10⁷ᵍ 2⁶ˢ 3⁷ᵍ 3⁶ʰʸ 9⁶ᵍ
2-2-9 £13,705

Daimajin (Ire) *Mrs Lucinda Featherstone* 56 a65
5 b g Dr Devious (Ire) - Arrow Field (USA)
1⁸ˢᵈ 9⁸ˢᵈ 5⁸ˢ 4¹²ˢʷ 11⁷ˢ 12¹⁰ᵍˢ 9¹⁰ˢ
11⁸ʰʸ 8⁹ˢᵈ 7⁸ᵍᶠ 9¹⁰ᶠ 10⁸ᵍ 17⁸ᵍᶠ 7¹¹ᵍ 6¹³ᵍᶠ
10¹⁰ᵍᶠ 13⁸ᵍᶠ 12⁹ᶠ 12¹⁰ˢᵈ 15⁶ᵍᶠ **1-0-20 £2,947**

Daintree Affair (Ire) *Mrs H Sweeting* a46
4 b g Charnwood Forest (Ire) - Madam Loving
9⁵ˢᵈ **0-0-1**

Daisy Bucket *D M Simcock* 64
2 b f Lujain (USA) - Masrora (USA)
9⁷ᵍᶠ 3⁷ᵍᶠ 1⁷ʰʸ 16⁷ᵍ 14⁸ˢ **1-1-5 £3,852**

Daisy Pooter (Ire) *T D Barron* 50
2 b f Charnwood Forest (Ire) - Idrak
12⁶ᵍˢ **0-0-1**

Daisys Girl *B Hanbury* 50
2 b f Inchinor - Andbell
10⁶ᵍ 6⁵ᵍᶠ 6⁵ᵍᶠ 3⁶ᵍ **0-1-4 £530**

Daldini *J A Osborne* 86
2 b c Josr Algarhoud (USA) - Arianna Aldini
4⁶ᵍᶠ 1⁶ʰʸ 2⁶ᵍ 9⁷ˢ **1-1-4 £6,555**

Dalida *P C Haslam* 48
3 ch f Pursuit Of Love - Debutante Days
UR⁸ˢˢ 5⁷ᵍ 5⁸ˢ 13⁷ᵍᶠ 10⁸ᵍᶠ **0-0-5**

Dalisay (Ire) *Sir Michael Stoute* 72 a74
3 b f Sadler's Wells (USA) - Dabiliya
3¹⁰ᵍᶠ 3¹⁰ᵍᶠ 2¹²ˢᵈ 6¹³ˢᵈ **0-2-4 £2,842**

Daliya (Ire) *Sir Michael Stoute* 69
2 b f Giant's Causeway (USA) - Dalara (Ire)
6⁷ᵍᶠ 2⁶ˢ **0-1-2 £1,604**

Dalkeys Lass *Mrs L B Normile* 20
3 gr f Wolfhound (USA) - Dalkey Sound
8⁸ᵍᶠ 9⁴ᵍᶠ 9⁹ᵍˢ **0-0-3 £475**

Dallaah *M A Jarvis* 42
3 b f Green Desert (USA) - Saeedah
6⁵ᵍᶠ **0-0-1 £234**

Dallington Brook *Dr J R J Naylor*
5 b g Bluegrass Prince (Ire) - Valetta

7⁶ᵍᶠ **0-0-1**

Dallool *M A Jarvis* 92
3 b c Unfuwain (USA) - Sardonic
5¹²ᵍˢ 1¹²ˢ 4¹²ᵍˢ 4¹²ᵍ 1¹²ᵍ 8¹²ˢ **2-0-6**
£12,717

Dalmarnock (Ire) *B Smart* 58
3 ch g Grand Lodge (USA) - Lochbelle
10⁹ᵍ 9⁸ᵍ 5⁸ᵍᶠ **0-0-3**

Dalon (Pol) *D B Feek* 41 a49
5 b g Winds Of Light (USA) - Dikte (Pol)
7¹⁰ˢ 6¹²ˢᵈ 11¹⁶ᵍˢ **0-0-3**

Dalriath *M C Chapman* 42 a44
5 b m Fraam - Alsiba
10⁷ˢᵈ 6¹¹ˢᵈ 6⁷ˢᵈ 4⁸ˢˢ 2⁸ᶠ 1⁸ˢᵈ 2⁸ˢᵈ 5⁸ᶠ
9⁸ᶠ 3¹²ᵍˢ 5⁸ˢᵈ 2¹²ᵍᶠ 10¹²ᵍᶠ 8¹²ᵍᶠ 4¹²ˢʷ **1-4-15**
£3,937

Dalyan (Ire) *A J Lockwood* 10
7 b g Turtle Island (Ire) - Salette
10⁸ᵍᶠ **0-0-1**

Damask Dancer (Ire) *J A Supple* a32
5 b g Barathea (Ire) - Polish Rhythm (Ire)
7¹⁰ˢᵈ 11¹²ˢᵈ **0-0-2**

Damburger Xpress *D M Simcock* 53
2 b c Josr Algarhoud (Ire) - Upping The Tempo
6⁷ᵍ **0-0-1**

Dame De Noche *J G Given* 96 a93
4 b f Lion Cavern (USA) - Goodnight Kiss
6⁸ᵍˢ 13⁸ᵍˢ 3⁷ᵍᶠ 10⁶ᶠ 11⁶ᵍᶠ 5⁵ᵍᶠ
3⁶ᶠ 9⁶ᵍᶠ 7⁵ᵍᶠ 1⁵ᵍ 4⁶ᵍ 4⁷ˢᵈ **1-1-13 £14,799**

Dame Margaret *J A B Old*
4 ch f Elmaamul (USA) - Pomorie (Ire)
5¹²ˢˢ 14¹²ˢᵈ **0-0-2**

Dame Nova (Ire) *P C Haslam* 46
3 b f Definite Article - Red Note
13⁶ᵍˢ 9⁶ᶠ 15¹²ˢᵈ 9¹²ᵍᶠ 12¹⁰ᶠ **0-0-5**

Dami (USA) *C E Brittain* 84
3 b f Dynaformer (USA) - Trampoli (USA)
5⁸ᵍᶠ 5¹¹ᶠ 2⁸ᶠ 2⁸ᵍᶠ 1¹⁰ᶠ 1⁹ᵍᶠ 5¹⁰ᵍ 5¹⁰ᵍ
7¹⁰ᵍ **2-2-9 £14,567**

Damson (Ire) *David Wachman* 110
2 b f Entrepreneur - Tadkiyra
1⁵ʸ 1⁶ᵍᶠ 1⁵ᵍᶠ 1⁶ᵍᶠ 3⁶ᵍ **4-0-5 £234,605**

Dan Di Canio (Ire) *P W Harris* 64
3 b g Bahri (USA) - Khudud
5⁸ᵍᶠ 9⁸ᵍˢ 5⁸ᵍ 5⁸ᵍᶠ 12¹⁰ᵍᶠ 8⁸ᵍ **0-0-6**

Dan's Heir *P C Haslam* 55 a37
2 b g Dansili - Million Heiress
8⁵ᵍᶠ 2⁷ᶠ 7⁷ᵍᶠ 2⁷ᵍᶠ 9⁷ˢᵈ 7⁷ᵍᶠ **0-2-6**
£2,362

Danaatt (USA) *M P Tregoning* 16
2 b f Gulch (USA) - Agama (USA)
15⁵ᵍ **0-0-1**

Danakil *S Dow* 81 a79
9 b g Warning - Danilova (USA)
12¹⁰ˢᵈ 14¹²ˢᵈ 9¹²ᵍ 9¹²ˢ 2¹²ᵍᶠ 4¹²ᵍᶠ 1¹²ˢᵈ
2¹²ᵍᶠ 12¹²ᵍ 4¹²ᵍᶠ 6¹²ˢ 11¹²ᵍ 13¹²ᵍᶠ **1-3-13**
£8,363

Danakim *J R Weymes* 54 a38
7 b g Emarati (USA) - Kangra Valley
6⁵ˢˢ 1⁵ˢᵈ 7⁶ˢᵈ 8⁵ˢˢ 4⁵ˢᵈ 7⁵ˢᶠ 1⁶ᵍᶠ
5⁶ᵍᶠ 12⁶ᵍ 10⁶ᵍ 13⁶ᵍ 9⁶ᵍᶠ 7⁵ᵍᶠ 4⁵ᵍᶠ 2⁶ᶠ 10⁵ᵍᶠ
8⁶ᵍᶠ **2-2-21 £4,568**

Dance Anthem *M G Quinlan* 86
2 b c Royal Academy (USA) - Statua (Ire)
1⁵ᵍ 2⁶ᶠ 10⁶ᵍᶠ 8⁵ˢ **1-1-4 £4,832**

Dance Away *M L W Bell* — 91
2 ch f Pivotal - Dance On
2^5g 1^5g 12^5g 5^6s **1-1-4 £7,323**

Dance Flower (Ire) *M R Channon* — 78
2 b f Cape Cross (Ire) - Ninth Wonder (USA)
2^6g 3^6gf 5^6gf 4^7g 2^8f 15^7g **0-4-6 £6,258**

Dance In The Sun *Mrs A J Perrett* — a95
4 ch f Halling (USA) - Sunny Davis (USA)
6^10sd 4^12sd 2^10sd 1^10sd **1-2-4 £14,238**

Dance Light (Ire) *T T Clement* — 64 a50
5 b m Lycius (USA) - Embracing
10^16sd 8^16gf 5^19gf 3^16gs 19^21g 10^16g 5^16gf 14^16g **0-0-8 £600**

Dance Night (Ire) *B A McMahon* — 102
2 b c Danehill Dancer (Ire) - Tiger Wings (Ire)
2^5g 1^5g 1^5g 6^5gf 7^6g 6^5g 1^5s 11^6g 3^5s **3-2-9 £39,834**

Dance On The Top *J R Boyle* — 82 a101
6 ch g Caerleon (USA) - Fern
1^8sd 1^8sd 9^7sd 6^8f 5^8sd 7^8f 14^9g 10^8gf **2-0-8 £12,426**

Dance Party (Ire) *M W Easterby* — 70 a69
4 b f Charnwood Forest (Ire) - Society Ball
3^10sd 3^12sd 11^10sd 8^10g 4^12s 7^10gf 7^10sd 7^12gf 12^10gf 9^9sd **0-2-10 £1,210**

Dance To My Tune *M W Easterby* — 74 a44
3 b f Halling (USA) - Stolen Melody
6^8sd 1^8hy 7^8gf 4^9gf 1^10g 2^10gs 4^10gf 2^11s 4^12g **2-3-9 £12,502**

Dance To The Blues (Ire) *B De Haan* — 64
3 br f Danehill Dancer (Ire) - Blue Sioux
9^5gf 3^5gf 1^5gf 8^5g **1-1-4 £3,902**

Dance World *Miss J Feilden* — 79 a69
4 b g Spectrum (Ire) - Dansara
1^12sd 12^12g 3^14hy 7^10g 7^12sd 5^10g 1^12g 13^13gs **2-1-8 £9,161**

Danceinthevalley (Ire) *G A Swinbank* — 39
2 b c Imperial Ballet (Ire) - Dancing Willma (Ire)
10^5g 9^5gf **0-0-2**

Dancer King (USA) *T P Tate* — 55
3 b g King Of Kings (Ire) - Tigresa (USA)
5^7s 9^8g 9^7gf 3^8s 7^10gs 6^13s **0-1-6 £566**

Dancer's Serenade (Ire) *T P Tate* — 66
2 b g Almutawakel - Dance Serenade (Ire)
3^7g 5^7s 9^7g 10^10gf **0-0-4 £643**

Dances In Time *C N Kellett* — a50
4 b f Danetime (Ire) - Yo-Cando (Ire)
8^9sd 5^7sd 12^6sd 10^6sd 12^5ss 3^7sw 9^6sd **0-0-7 £205**

Dances With Angels (Ire) *J W Unett* — 46 a34
4 b f Mukaddamah - Lady Of Leisure (USA)
11^10sd 11^12sd 3^12g 9^12gf 12^14gf PU^11gf 12^10gf 6^8hy 4^10s 5^12s **0-1-10 £487**

Dancing Bay *N J Henderson* — 118
7 b g Suave Dancer (USA) - Kabayil
1^16g 2^22f 2^16g 3^18g 4^20g 4^16s **1-3-6 £66,119**

Dancing Bear *Julian Poulton* — 61 a49
3 b g Groom Dancer (USA) - Sickle Moon
4^10g 9^10g 3^10gf 4^12gf 10^12sd 4^9sd **0-0-6 £1,240**

Dancing Deano (Ire) *R M Whitaker* — 52
2 b g Second Empire (Ire) - Ultimate Beat (USA)
9^6g 6^6gs 12^7g 5^6g **0-0-4**

Dancing Dolphin (Ire) *Julian Poulton* — 27 a4
5 b m Dolphin Street (Fr) - Dance Model
3^10gs 6^12sd 6^10hy 12^10gf **0-1-4 £211**

Dancing Forest (Ire) *D K Ivory* — a59
4 br g Charnwood Forest (Ire) - Fauna (Ire)
9^8sd 5^10sd **0-0-2**

Dancing King (Ire) *P W Hiatt* — 87 a55
8 b g Fairy King - Zariysha (Ire)
5^8sd 11^8sd 4^8sd 11^8sd 5^7sd 2^8sd 1^7ss 3^8ss 1^8sw 5^8ss 4^8sw 8^8sd 8^7ss 6^7ss 2^8ss 6^7gs 2^8hy 5^9sd 6^8hy 6^7sd **2-4-26 £7,801**

Dancing Lyra *J W Hills* — 96 a75
3 b g Alzao (USA) - Badaayer (USA)
6^8sd 1^10sd 1^10s 2^9g 4^10g 11^10gf 6^10gs 10^10g 5^10hy **2-2-9 £34,823**

Dancing Moonlight (Ire) *Mrs N Macauley* — 20 a21
2 b f Danehill Dancer (Ire) - Silver Moon
6^5g 13^7sd 9^6gf 7^5sd 9^6gf **0-0-5**

Dancing Mystery *E A Wheeler* — 90 a101
10 b g Beveled (USA) - Batchworth Dancer
1^5sd 3^5sd 5^5sd 17^5g 12^5s 8^5s 14^5gf 1^5f 4^6gf 5^5g 9^5gf 8^5g 8^5g 2^5s 9^5gs 14^5gf 3^5gs 3^5gs **2-4-18 £23,158**

Dancing Pearl *C J Price* — 55
6 ch m Dancing Spree (USA) - Elegant Rose
12^10gs 5^14s 7^19gf 3^17g **0-1-4 £438**

Dancing Phantom *James Moffatt* — a63
9 b g Darshaan - Dancing Prize (Ire)
3^12sw 2^12sd **0-2-2 £1,247**

Dancing Prince (Ire) *A P Jarvis* — a49
3 b g Imperial Ballet (Ire) - Eastern Aura (Ire)
5^6sd 4^8sd 9^7sd 13^7sd 8^7sd **0-0-5**

Dancing Ridge (Ire) *A Senior* — a23
7 b g Ridgewood Ben - May We Dance (Ire)
9^6sw 15^6gs 5^5sd 6^5sf 7^5sd **0-0-5**

Dancing Rose (Ire) *C G Cox* — 75
2 b f Danehill Dancer (Ire) - Shinkoh Rose (Fr)
2^5gs 3^5gf 1^5gs 5^6gf 11^6hy **1-2-5 £7,121**

Dancing Shirl *C W Fairhurst* — 58
2 b f Dancing Spree (USA) - Shirl
6^7gf 3^7gf 8^8hy 3^8g **0-3-4 £2,062**

Dancing Tilly *R A Fahey* — 49 a49
6 b m Dancing Spree (USA) - L'Ancressaan
4^9sd 2^11sd 4^11sd 6^10sd 4^8f 1^9f 2^10gf 6^10gs 5^9sd 5^11sd **1-2-10 £2,447**

Dancingintheclouds (Ire) *J L Dunlop* — 58
2 b f Rainbow Quest (USA) - Ballerina (Ire)
8^8gf **0-0-1**

Danclare (USA) *J H M Gosden* — 90
3 ch f Stravinsky (USA) - Beyond Temptation (USA)
12^7g 6^7gf 5^8gf 4^8gf **0-0-4 £1,983**

Dandouce *P W Chapple-Hyam* — 73 a48
3 b f Danzero (Aus) - Douce Maison (Ire)
6^7s 3^7gf 4^8gf 9^7g 3^6gs 11^6sd 16^6g **0-1-7 £1,357**

Dandoun *J L Dunlop* — 94
6 b h Halling (USA) - Moneefa
16^9s 3^8hy **0-1-2 £2,292**

Dandy Jim *D W Chapman* — 11 a24
3 b c Dashing Blade - Madam Trilby
8^6ss 5^6sd 9^7sw 9^6ss 5^8sd 6^8hy 7^6sd 8^7sd 13^8gf **0-0-9**

Dandygrey Russett (Ire) *G L Moore* — 61
3 gr f Singspiel (Ire) - Christian Church (Ire)

11^{8g} 4^{8hy} 4^{8s} 9^{10s} 0-0-4 £872

Dane Rhapsody (Ire) *B Palling*   50 a26
3 b/br f Danetime (Ire) - Hil Rhapsody
10^{6sd} 5^{5gf} 13^{6gf} 5^{5gf} 9^{7gs} 5^{6f} 12^{6sd}
0-0-7

Dane's Castle (Ire) *B J Meehan*   79 a73
2 b g Danetime (Ire) - Faypool
3^{6gf} 2^{6sd} 2^{5gf} 3^{6sd} 3^{5g} 1^{5gf} 1-5-6
£8,115

Dane's Rock (Ire) *Mrs H Sweeting*   50 a46
2 b g Indian Danehill (Ire) - Cutting Ground (Ire)
4^{5sd} 7^{6gf} 6^{5gf} 2^{6gf} 7^{6sd} 9^{7s} 4^{8hy} 0-1-7
£888

Danebank (Ire) *J Mackie*   63
4 b g Danehill (USA) - Snow Bank (Ire)
11^{10s} 5^{10g} 1^{13g} 2^{12gf} 3^{13gs} 13^{12hy} 2^{12gf}
3^{14gs} 1-4-8 £7,286

Danecare (Ire) *J G Burns*   95
4 b c Danetime (Ire) - Nordic Flavour (Ire)
18^{6y} 9^{6y} 2^{6gf} 4^{6gs} 5^{5gf} 4^{6gf} SU^{7gf} 0-1-7
£4,715

Danefonique (Ire) *D Carroll*   55 a46
3 b f Danetime (Ire) - Umlaut
8^{10g} 3^{10gs} 2^{10g} 2^{12gf} 5^{12g} 6^{14f} 8^{12sd} 4^{12gf}
12^{10gs} 2^{10gs} 6^{12g} 7^{10s} 0-5-12 £3,368

Danehill Angel *M J Polglase*   45 a10
2 ch f Danehill Dancer (Ire) - Ace Girl
7^{5ss} 12^{6f} 0-0-2

Danehill Dazzler (Ire) *A P Jarvis*   66
2 b f Danehill Dancer (Ire) - Finnegans Dilemma (Ire)
4^{7g} 0-0-1 £408

Danehill Fairy (Ire) *Mrs A Duffield*   41
2 b f Danehill Dancer (Ire) - Turntable (Ire)
7^{5s} 2^{5s} 15^{5gf} 6^{5gf} 3^{5g} 3^{6f} 3^{5gf} 2^{6s}
12^{6gf} 4^{5hy} 8^{6gs} 0-4-11 £3,340

Danehill Lad (Ire) *T Keddy*
4 b g Danehill (USA) - River Missy (USA)
PU^{13sd} 0-0-1

Danehill Stroller (Ire) *R M Beckett*   89
4 b g Danetime (Ire) - Tuft Hill
13^{6gf} 17^{6f} 9^{6gf} 4^{6g} 12^{5gf} 10^{6gf} 18^{7g}
17^{6g} 5^{6gs} 0-1-9 £1,164

Danehill Willy (Ire) *N A Callaghan*   86
2 b c Danehill Dancer (Ire) - Lowtown
2^{5g} 8^{7gf} 9^{7s} 1^{7gs} 1^{8s} 7^{10gs} 2-1-6
£12,699

Danelissima (Ire) *J S Bolger*   107
3 br f Danehill (USA) - Zavaleta (Ire)
5^{7s} 4^{10gf} 4^{9gf} 1^{12gf} 2^{12gf} 3^{12g} 6^{12gf} 6^{12s}
1-2-8 £73,644

Danelor (Ire) *R A Fahey*   93 a89
6 b g Danehill (USA) - Formulate
4^{8ss} 5^{8g} 7^{10g} 8^{12gf} 5^{8gf} 8^{8gs} 1^{9s} 8^{8gs}
5^{10gs} 8^{10gf} 9^{9g} 1-0-11 £15,104

Danescourt (Ire) *J M Bradley*   61 a62
2 b c Danetime (Ire) - Faye
5^{6sd} 8^{6sw} 3^{6gf} 0-1-3 £423

Danesmead (Ire) *T D Easterby*   95
3 b c Danehill Dancer (Ire) - Indian Honey
6^{7gs} 11^{6gf} 0-0-2

Danethorpe Lady (Ire) *D Shaw*   37
2 b f Brave Act - Annie's Travels (Ire)
6^{5gs} 4^{5gf} 8^{6gf} 0-0-3 £323

Danettie (Ire) *W M Brisbourne*   59 a11
3 b f Danzero (Aus) - Petite Heritiere

9^{8s} 5^{9gf} 4^{8gs} 5^{12s} 4^{7f} 17^{8g} 10^{7sd} 0-0-7
£589

Danger Bird (Ire) *R Hollinshead*   a60
4 ch f Eagle Eyed (USA) - Danger Ahead
2^{9sd} 3^{9sd} 8^{9sd} 2^{9ss} 4^{8sw} 4^{9ss} 1^{9sd} 5^{7sd}
8^{8sd} 6^{9sd} 10^{12sd} 9^{9sd} 1-3-12 £5,123

Danger Zone *Mrs A J Perrett*   68 a68
2 b c Danzero (Aus) - Red Tulle (USA)
12^{6gs} 8^{8gf} 5^{7gs} 15^{7gf} 3^{7sd} 0-1-5 £213

Dangerous Dave *Jamie Poulton*   21
5 b g Superpower - Lovely Lilly
9^{7g} 0-0-1

Dangle (Ire) *Edward Lynam*   104
3 b f Desert Style (Ire) - Dawn Chorus (Ire)
2^{7g} 1^{7g} 8^{8gf} 2^{7g} 5^{6y} 4^{7hy} 5^{6ys} 9^{6s}
1-2-9 £16,331

Dani Ridge (Ire) *E J Alston*   88
6 b m Indian Ridge - Daniella Drive (USA)
4^{6g} 7^{5f} 4^{6gf} 9^{6g} 15^{6g} 0-0-5 £2,754

Daniel Thomas (Ire) *Mrs A J Perrett*   86 a82
2 b c Dansili - Last Look
2^{7gf} 2^{6gf} 3^{6s} 2^{7s} 1^{7sd} 1-4-5 £9,930

Daniella *R Guest*   46
2 b f Dansili - Break Point
13^{7g} 0-0-1

Danielle's Lad *B Palling*   76 a79
8 b g Emarati (USA) - Cactus Road (Fr)
4^{7sd} 2^{8sd} 9^{7sd} 4^{7sw} 1^{8sw} 3^{8ss} 7^{7gs} 3^{8sd}
7^{7s} 17^{8gf} 1-2-10 £6,070

Danifah (Ire) *P D Evans*   73 a44
3 b f Perugino (USA) - Afifah
12^{7sd} 7^{5g} 16^{6gf} 8^{6gf} 4^{6f} 10^{6g} 13^{5f} 4^{8gf}
4^{8gf} 6^{8gf} 1^{7gs} 1^{6g} 3^{6gf} 16^{7gf} 1^{8hy} 13^{6gf} 7^{8gs}
17^{7s} 9^{7sd} 3-1-19 £11,258

Danish Monarch *A D W Pinder*   62
3 b g Great Dane - Moly
11^{8gs} 13^{7gf} 3^{6gf} 19^{7gf} 19^{7gf} 6^{6gs} 9^{6gf}
12^{7gf} 0-1-8 £604

Danita Dancer (Ire) *B Palling*   46
2 b f Barathea (Ire) - Carranita (Ire)
12^{8gf} 12^{8g} 0-0-2

Danny Leahy (Fr) *M D Hammond*   62 a41
4 b g Danehill (USA) - Paloma Bay (Ire)
5^{12sd} 10^{16s} 9^{18s} 0-0-3

Dante's Battle (Ire) *Miss K Marks*
12 b/br g Phardante (Fr) - No Battle
11^{12sd} 0-0-1

Dante's Devine (Ire) *A Bailey*   56 a36
3 b g Ashkalani (Ire) - Basilea (Fr)
8^{9sd} 6^{5sw} 8^{8gf} 4^{8sd} 10^{7sd} 9^{6g} 1^{7gf}
2^{8gs} 1-1-9 £1,953

Dante's Diamond (Ire) *F Jordan*   76
2 b c Orpen (USA) - Flower From Heaven
2^{5g} 2^{10gs} 5^{5gf} 11^{6gs} 4^{7gs} 5^{7s} 10^{7gs}
0-2-8 £3,290

Danum *R Hollinshead*   a22
4 b c Perpendicular - Maid Of Essex
4^{11sd} 5^{9ss} 8^{11ss} 0-0-3

Danzare *M P Tregoning*   58 a64
2 b f Dansili - Shot Of Redemption
7^{7gf} 4^{9sd} 0-0-2

Danzatrice *C W Thornton*   67
2 b f Tamure (Ire) - Miss Petronella
9^{5g} 5^{6hy} 5^{8s} 0-0-3

Danze Romance *J L Dunlop*   65

3 b f Danzero (Aus) - By Arrangement (Ire)
8[8g] 14[9gf] 5[8g] 4[10g] 11[12s] 13[10hy] **0-0-6**
£500

Danzig River (Ire) B W Hills   102
3 b g Green Desert (USA) - Sahara Breeze
2[6gs] 16[6gf] 9[6gf] 16[6gf] 13[5gf] 10[6g] 4[6g]
6[6s] 7[6g] 2[6s] **0-2-10 £8,809**

Danzig Star P R Chamings
4 b f Danzig Connection (USA) - Julie's Star (Ire)
6[8ss] **0-0-1**

Danzili Bay R M Beckett   81
2 b c Dansili - Lady Bankes (Ire)
4[5f] 4[5gf] 1[5gf] 11[5gf] **1-0-4 £3,317**

Daphne's Doll (Ire) Dr J R J Naylor   a15
9 m Polish Patriot (USA) - Helietta
10[8sd] **0-0-1**

Dara Girl (Ire) Mrs P N Dutfield   47
2 b f Key Of Luck (USA) - Tavildara (Ire)
13[6gf] 15[7gf] 9[6g] **0-0-3**

Dara Mac N Bycroft   67
5 b g Presidium - Nishara
14[8s] 2[7gf] 6[7f] 3[8g] 1[8gs] 7[8s] 13[8gf] 18[gs]
9[7g] 6[8gs] 14[8gf] 4[8g] 7[7gf] 9[8gf] 19[7g] **2-3-15**
£8,788

Darab (Pol) Mrs S J Smith   52
4 ch g Alywar (USA) - Damara (Pol)
9[10gf] 11[10gf] **0-0-2**

Darasim (Ire) M Johnston   116
6 b g Kahyasi - Dararita (Ire)
6[16s] 1[16g] 3[20gf] 1[16gf] 5[18g] 6[20g] **2-1-6**
£112,043

Darcie Mia J R Weymes
3 ch f Polar Falcon (USA) - Marie La Rose (Fr)
12[9sd] **0-0-1**

Dareneur (Ire) W M Brisbourne   55
4 ch f Entrepreneur - Darayna (Ire)
7[9sd] 8[8s] 5[10gf] **0-0-3**

Darghan (Ire) P D Evans   77
4 b g Air Express (Ire) - Darsannda (Ire)
4[8g] 6[9f] 6[10g] 6[11f] 2[9g] 10[10g] 5[8hy] 13[7gs]
0-0-8 £4,524

Daring Affair K R Burke   65 a70
3 b f Bien Bien (USA) - Daring Destiny
3[6sd] 2[6sd] 1[7sd] 5[7ss] 1[8sd] 4[8hy] 1[8sd] **3-1-7**
£11,112

Daring Aim Sir Michael Stoute   88
3 b f Daylami (Ire) - Phantom Gold
5[10g] 1[12gf] 5[14gf] 8[12gf] **1-0-4 £6,762**

Daring Games B Ellison   40
3 b f Mind Games - Daira
5[12gf] 6[10gf] 15[8g] **0-0-3**

Daring Ransom (USA) J Noseda   83
2 b c Red Ransom (USA) - Young And Daring (USA)
1[8g] **1-0-1 £5,414**

Dario Gee Gee (Ire) K A Ryan   95
2 ch c Bold Fact (USA) - Magical Peace (Ire)
1[5g] 2[5gs] 2[6gf] 8[6gf] 2[6gs] 1[6s] 5[6gs] 19[6g]
3[6gf] **2-4-9 £43,609**

Dark Champion R E Barr   67 a55
4 b g Abou Zouz (USA) - Hazy Kay (Ire)
2[6sd] 9[7sd] 4[6sd] 6[6sd] 5[6sd] 3[6g] 9[6f] 13[5gf]
4[6gf] 5[6gf] 12[5gf] 16[6gf] 14[5gs] 10[6hy] 4[6gs] **0-2-15**
£2,055

Dark Charm (Fr) R A Fahey   97
5 b g Anabaa (USA) - Wardara

3[8g] 12[8s] 8[9gf] 5[9gf] 12[8g] **0-1-5 £10,000**

Dark Cheetah (USA) A P O'Brien   108
2 b c Storm Cat (USA) - Layounne (USA)
1[5f] 7[5gf] 1[6ys] **2-0-3 £39,877**

Dark Cut (Ire) H Alexander   42 a11
4 b g Ali-Royal (Ire) - Prima Nox
13[10sd] 13[12hy] 17[14g] 7[13g] 12[9gs] 9[10gf]
11[8f] 13[8gs] **0-0-8**

Dark Day Blues (Ire) M D Hammond   69
3 ch g Night Shift (USA) - Tavildara (Ire)
8[8g] 14[8hy] 11[8gf] 1[7f] 8[7s] 6[7gf] 5[7gf] 5[8gf]
13[7gf] 10[7gf] 9[8gf] 9[8gf] 13[12g] **1-0-13 £3,935**

Dark Dolores J R Boyle   a10
6 b/br m Inchinor - Pingin
5[10sd] **0-0-1**

Dark Empress (Ire) R M Beckett   92
3 br f Second Empire (Ire) - Good Reference (Ire)
6[7gf] **0-0-1 £450**

Dark Parade (Arg) G L Moore   21 a53
3 b c Parade Marshal (USA) - Charming Dart (Arg)
14[7gf] 5[10sd] 7[8f] 4[11sd] **0-0-4**

Dark Raider (Ire) A P Jones   69
3 br/gr f Definite Article - Lady Shikari
2[8s] 5[8f] 5[10gf] 1[9g] 10[10g] 12[9g] 11[8gs] 9[9s]
1-1-8 £5,006

Dark Shah (Ire) D M Simcock   34 a41
4 b g Night Shift (USA) - Shanjah
5[8sd] 11[7sd] 10[8f] 14[8gf] **0-0-4**

Dark Society A W Carroll   54
6 b g Imp Society (USA) - No Candles Tonight
6[8g] 4[13gs] **0-0-2**

Darko Karim D R Loder   75
2 b c Groom Dancer (USA) - Russian Rose (Ire)
4[6gf] 10[7f] 9[6gf] 11[7gf] 3[8s] 5[8s] 13[8s] **0-1-7**
£921

Darla (Ire) J W Payne   73 a71
3 b f Night Shift (USA) - Darbela (Ire)
8[7g] 5[6gf] 2[6gf] 6[6gf] 16[6gs] 11[6gf] 3[6sd] **0-2-7**
£1,716

Darling River (Fr) S Dow   a52
5 b m Double Bed (Fr) - Oh Lucky Day
10[8sd] 14[7sd] **0-0-2**

Darn Good R Hannon   76 a57
3 ch g Bien Bien (USA) - Thimbalina
9[10sd] 8[10sd] 3[12sd] 14[11gs] 6[12g] 7[14g] 1[19gf]
11[5gf] 2[16g] 10[14gf] 6[16gf] 6[16gs] 14[16g] 11[17g] 4[16g]
3-1-15 £14,378

Darsalam (Ire) A Shavuyev   116
3 ch c Desert King (Ire) - Moonsilk
2[8s] 1[9s] 1[10s] 1[12f] 1[12g] 1[14g] 6[15gf] 3[12s]
1[14g] **6-1-9 £106,134**

Darsharp Miss Gay Kelleway   39
2 b f Josr Algarhoud (Ire) - Dizzydaisy
6[6s] 19[6gs] **0-0-2**

Dart Along (USA) R Hannon   76 a65
2 b c Bahri (USA) - Promptly (Ire)
5[7gf] 5[7g] 4[6g] 4[7sd] **0-0-4 £802**

Dartanian P D Evans   56 a49
2 b g Jurado (USA) - Blackpool Mamma'S
7[5g] 5[7f] 6[6f] 3[7gf] 7[7sd] 1[7s] 7[7s] 16[7gf]
1-1-8 £3,006

Dasar M Brittain   16 a51
4 ch f Catrail (USA) - Rising Of The Moon (Ire)
6[7sd] 4[6ss] 7[7ss] 2[7sd] 3[7sd] 9[7sd] 15[7gf] 2[8sd]
0-3-8 £1,266

Dash For Cover (Ire) *R Hannon* 73
4 b g Sesaro (USA) - Raindancing (Ire)
2^10gs 11^10g 7^8g 10^8hy 5^8gf 6^8gf 9^9g 5^8gs
13^8g **0-1-9 £1,036**

Dash For Glory *J S King* 34 a29
5 ch g Bluegrass Prince (Ire) - Rekindled Flame (Ire)
9^13sd 8^12sd 8^16sd 7^11gf 3^10f 11^12g **0-0-6**
£618

Dash Of Lime *S Kirk* a60
2 b f Bold Edge - Green Supreme
4^6sd **0-0-1 £266**

Dash Of Magic *J Hetherton* 45 a51
6 b m Magic Ring (Ire) - Praglia (Ire)
1^12sd 6^12sd 2^11sd 5^12sd 1^11ss 11^10gs 6^12gf
3^11gs 1^12sd 5^14g 10^12s 7^12sw **3-2-12 £6,464**

Dash To The Top *L M Cumani* 110
2 b f Montjeu (Ire) - Millennium Dash
2^8gs 1^8gf 3^8gf **1-2-3 £29,245**

Dashiki (USA) *B W Hills* 76
3 ch f Distant View (USA) - Musicanti (USA)
3^7g **0-1-1 £900**

Datahill (Ire) *P W D'Arcy*
4 b f Danehill (USA) - Animatrice (USA)
5^12sd **0-0-1**

Daunted (Ire) *P A Blockley* a70
8 b g Priolo (USA) - Dauntess
3^12sd 1^11sd 10^12sd 8^16sd 1^11sd 1^12ss 1^12ss
1^14ss **5-1-8 £11,460**

Davala *A D Smith* 32
2 b c Lake Coniston (Ire) - Velvet Heart (Ire)
11^6gf 11^6gf 12^7gs **0-0-3**

Dave (Ire) *J R Best* 67
3 b g Danzero (Aus) - Paradise News
1^6gf 16^6gs 10^7s 15^5gf 13^9sd **1-0-5**
£3,059

David Junior (USA) *B J Meehan* 83
2 ch c Pleasant Tap (USA) - Paradise River (USA)
3^7g 1^7gf **1-1-2 £8,143**

David's Girl *D Morris* 45 a22
3 b f Royal Applause - Cheer
5^8sd 6^8gs 6^7gf 5^7g 8^7f 8^8gf 6^7s 6^7g 3^7gf
2^7gs **0-2-10 £643**

David's Symphony (Ire) *R Hannon* 39
2 ch g Almutawakel - Habemus (Fr)
11^6g 16^7gf 8^8gf 17^7gs **0-0-4**

Davids Choice *A Berry*
2 b g Wizard King - Welch's Dream (Ire)
12^7s **0-0-1**

Davids Mark *J R Jenkins* 63 a63
4 b g Polar Prince (Ire) - Star Of Flanders
10^6sd 3^6s 4^6gf 4^5sd 4^6g 1^5gf 2^5gs 10^5gf
11^5sd 3^6sd **1-5-10 £5,711**

Davorin (Jpn) *D R Loder* 80 a62
3 br c Warning - Arvola
1^7gs 6^8gf 10^7sd 6^9g 8^8s **1-0-5 £5,716**

Davy Crockett *B Smart* 69
2 b g Polar Prince (Ire) - Sing With The Band
7^5g 16^6s 5^6gf 6^6f 11^8g 1^7gf 15^6s **1-0-7**
£2,961

Dawn Air (USA) *K A Ryan* 60
3 b f Diesis - Midnight Air (USA)
3^12g 10^12gf 18^14g 15^16gs **0-1-4 £850**

Dawn Duel (Ire) *B Smart* 42
3 b f Daggers Drawn (USA) - Dawn's Folly (Ire)
9^6gs 8^7g **0-0-2**

Dawn Piper (USA) *D R Loder* 87 a93
4 b g Desert Prince (Ire) - June Moon (Ire)
1^8sd 7^7sd 2^7sd 13^7gs 2^7s 9^8gf 4^7f **1-2-7**
£7,059

Dawn Surprise (USA) *Saeed Bin Suroor* 103
3 b f Theatrical - Lignify (Arg)
2^10g 1^8f 5^7gf 1^8gf 1^8gs 2^8g **3-2-6**
£32,600

Dawton (Pol) *T R George* 49
6 br h Greinton - Da Wega (Pol)
10^11g **0-0-1**

Day Care *Mrs A J Perrett* 70
3 gr c Daylami (Ire) - Ancara
2^10g **0-1-1 £2,000**

Day Flight *J H M Gosden* 116
3 b c Sadler's Wells (USA) - Bonash
1^12s 1^10gs 4^12gs 4^11g **2-0-4 £71,000**

Day Of Reckoning *Sir Michael Stoute* 77
3 b f Daylami (Ire) - Trying For Gold (USA)
3^10gf 1^10gs **1-1-2 £4,195**

Day One *G Wragg* 75
3 c c Daylami (Ire) - Myself
3^12gf 5^14gs 2^12s **0-2-3 £2,358**

Day To Remember *E F Vaughan* 95
3 gr c Daylami (Ire) - Miss Universe (Ire)
5^7gs 1^8g 3^8gs 1^10s **2-1-4 £12,373**

Daybreaking (Ire) *R F Johnson Houghton* 56 a52
2 br c Daylami (Ire) - Mawhiba (USA)
7^7sd 5^8s **0-0-2**

Daydream Dancer *C G Cox* 57 a48
3 gr f Daylami (Ire) - Dancing Wolf (Ire)
5^7gs 12^10sd 12^10gf 10^13g 8^8gf 1^10gf
11^0f 4^12sd **2-1-9 £6,616**

Daygar *M G Quinlan* 51
2 b c Spectrum (Ire) - Milly Ha Ha
11^7gf **0-0-1**

Daytime Girl (Ire) *B W Hills* 77
3 gr f Daylami (Ire) - Snoozeandyoulose (Ire)
3^10g 5^12hy 1^10gf 6^12g **1-1-4 £6,905**

Daze *Sir Michael Stoute* 78
3 b f Daylami (Ire) - Proud Titania (Ire)
3^10gf 1^12s 7^11g 4^14gf **1-0-4 £6,812**

Dazzling Bay *T D Easterby* 107
4 b g Mind Games - Adorable Cherub (USA)
6^6s 13^6gs 3^6gf 5^6f 2^6g 24^6gf 14^6s 3^5gf
14^6gf 12^5s **0-3-10 £9,619**

De Bullions *A M Balding* 18
2 b g Mujahid (USA) - Stolen Melody
13^6g **0-0-1**

Deal In Facts *C N Kellett*
5 ch m So Factual (USA) - Timely Raise (USA)
9^7sd 16^6sd **0-0-2**

Deangate (Ire) *P T Midgley*
3 ch g Vettori (Ire) - Moonlight (Ire)
PU^11g 12^7f **0-0-2**

Dear Sir (Ire) *Mrs P N Dutfield* 28
4 ch g Among Men (USA) - Deerussa (Ire)
9^16g **0-0-1**

Debbie *B D Leavy* a45
5 b m Deploy - Elita
7^9sd 9^11sd 4^9ss **0-0-3**

Debs Broughton *W J Musson* 55
2 b f Prince Sabo - Coy Debutante (Ire)
12^5gf 15^6gf 2^6gf 7^6gs 4^7gf 5^8g **0-2-6**
£824

Decelerate *A Charlton*   a59
4 ch c Polar Falcon (USA) - Speed To Lead (Ire)
8¹⁰ˢᵈ 8¹⁰ˢᵈ **0-0-2**

Decoration *B J Meehan*   40
2 b c Mark Of Esteem (Ire) - Forever Shineing
11⁷ᵍ **0-0-1**

Dee Dee Girl (Ire) *R Hannon*   a5
3 b f Primo Dominie - Chapel Lawn
11⁸ˢᵈ **0-0-1**

Dee En Ay (Ire) *T D Easterby*   51
3 ch g Shinko Forest (Ire) - Edwina (Ire)
12⁷ᵍˢ 10⁸ᵍ 5⁸ᵍᶠ 6⁸ᵍ **0-0-4**

Dee Pee Tee Cee (Ire) *M W Easterby*   53
10 b g Tidaro (USA) - Silver Glimpse
7⁸ᵍˢ 3¹²ᵍ 11¹⁰ᵍˢ **0-1-3 £463**

Deeday Bay (Ire) *C F Wall*   80
2 b f Brave Act - Skerries Bell
1⁶ᵍ 4⁶ᵍ 2⁶ᵍˢ **1-1-3 £6,733**

Deekazz (Ire) *F Watson*   36
5 b m Definite Article - Lyric Junction (Ire)
11¹²ᵍᶠ 15¹⁰ᵍᶠ 6¹⁰ᶠ **0-0-3**

Deep Purple *M P Tregoning*   89
3 b g Halling (USA) - Seal Indigo (Ire)
1¹⁰ᵍᶠ 4¹⁰ˢ 6¹¹ᵍ **1-0-3 £6,797**

Deeper In Debt *J Akehurst*   56 a82
6 ch g Piccolo - Harold's Girl (Fr)
2⁸ˢᵈ 4⁸ˢᵈ 3⁸ˢᵈ 3⁸ˢᵈ 5⁹ˢ 10⁸ᵍᶠ 7⁸ᵍᶠ 18⁹ᵍᶠ
13⁹ᵍᶠ **0-3-9 £2,496**

Deewaar (Ire) *J C Fox*   44
4 b g Ashkalani (Ire) - Chandni (Ire)
7¹⁰ˢ 11¹⁰ᵍᶠ 18¹⁰ᵍˢ **0-0-3**

Defana *M Dods*   54 a32
3 b g Defacto (USA) - Thalya
5⁸ˢᵈ 3¹²ᵍᶠ 3¹¹ᵍ 11⁸ᵍᶠ 6¹⁴ᵍˢ 1¹⁰ᶠ 7¹⁰ᵍᶠ
8¹²ˢᵈ **1-2-8 £4,495**

Deferlant (Fr) *K Bell*   54
7 ch g Bering - Sail Storm (USA)
10¹²ᵍᶠ 15¹³ᵍᶠ 12¹²ᵍ **0-0-3**

Defining *J R Fanshawe*   111
5 b g Definite Article - Gooseberry Pie
11¹²ᵍ 3¹²ᵍᶠ 7¹⁶ˢ 4¹⁴ˢ 1¹⁴ᵍ 1¹⁶ᵍᶠ 6¹⁶ˢ
2-2-7 £82,166

Definite Guest (Ire) *R A Fahey*   89
6 gr g Definite Article - Nicea (Ire)
3⁹ᵍ 13⁹ᵍᶠ 9¹⁰ᵍˢ 15⁸ᵍ 5⁸ᵍᶠ 10⁸ᵍᶠ **0-1-6**
£6,900

Definitely Royal (Ire) *R M H Cowell*   a52
2 b f Desert Prince (Ire) - Specifically (USA)
7⁶ˢᵈ 9⁹ˢᵈ **0-0-2**

Definitely Special (Ire) *N E Berry*   13 a43
6 b m Definite Article - Legit (Ire)
8⁶ˢᵈ 7⁷ˢᵈ 9⁶ˢˢ 10⁵ˢᵈ 8⁷ˢᵈ 6⁷ˢᵈ 4⁷ᵍˢ 7⁸ᵍ
0-0-8

Degree Of Honor (Fr) *J G Given*   a2
2 ch f Highest Honor (Fr) - Sheba Dancer (Fr)
10⁷ˢ 11⁷ˢᵈ **0-0-2**

Deign To Dance (Ire) *J G Portman*   68 a68
3 b f Danetime (Ire) - Lady Montekin
5⁷ˢᵈ 19⁶ᵍ 8⁷ᵍ 5⁷ᵍᶠ 18⁸ˢᵈ 10⁸ᵍ 3⁸ᵍᶠ 2⁸ᵍᶠ
5⁹ˢ 5⁸ᵍ 3¹⁰ˢᵈ **1-3-11 £5,234**

Dejeeje (Ire) *D W Chapman*   89
3 ch c Grand Lodge (USA) - Christan (Ire)
9⁶ᶠ 7⁷ᶠ **0-0-2**

Del Mar Sunset *W J Haggas*   51 a93
5 b g Unfuwain (USA) - City Of Angels

4⁹ˢᵈ 5⁸ˢʷ 8⁸ˢᵈ 1⁸ˢˢ 12¹⁰ˢ 12⁸ᵍˢ 1⁹ˢᵈ
2-0-7 £13,976

Delaware Trail *J S Wainwright*
5 b g Catrail (USA) - Dilwara (Ire)
8⁸ˢᵈ 9⁸ʰʸ **0-0-2**

Delcienne *G G Margarson*   53 a38
3 b f Golden Heights - Delciana (Ire)
13⁸ᵍ 11⁸ˢ 3⁸ᵍᶠ 9¹⁰ᶠ 2⁸ᶠ 1⁸ᶠ 5⁸ᵍˢ 7⁸ᵍᶠ
1⁸ᵍ 8⁸ᵍˢ 9⁸ˢᵈ **2-2-11 £5,014**

Delegate *N A Callaghan*   74
11 ch g Polish Precedent (USA) - Dangora (USA)
13⁵ᵍᶠ 7⁶ᶠ 1⁶ᶠ **1-0-3 £3,347**

Delfinia *N Waggott*   40
3 b f Kingsinger (Ire) - Delvecchia
15¹⁰ᵍˢ 4¹²ᵍᶠ 6¹²ᵍᶠ **0-0-2 £279**

Delightful Gift *M Brittain*   38
4 b f Cadeaux Genereux - Delightful Chime (Ire)
6⁷ᵍᶠ 14⁸ˢᵈ 8⁷ᵍᶠ 17⁸ᶠ **0-0-4**

Delightfully *B W Hills*   68 a65
3 b f Definite Article - Kingpin Delight
7⁶ᵍˢ 2⁸ˢᵈ 4⁸ᶠ 6¹²ˢᵈ 3¹¹ᵍᶠ 1¹²ˢᵈ **1-1-6**
£4,293

Della Salute *A M Balding*   68
2 gr f Dansili - Marie Dora (Fr)
6⁶ᵍˢ 8⁷ᵍᶠ **0-0-2**

Dellagio (Ire) *C A Dwyer*   57 a56
3 b c Fasliyev (USA) - Lady Ounavarra (Ire)
8⁵ˢᵈ 19⁶ᵍˢ 15⁶ˢ 16⁷ᵍᶠ 4⁵ᵍᶠ 8⁵ᵍᶠ 8⁷ᵍᶠ 1⁶ᶠ
14⁷ᵍᶠ 10⁶ᶠ **1-0-10 £3,573**

Delphie Queen (Ire) *S Kirk*   107
3 ch f Desert Sun - Serious Delight
4⁶ᵍ 3⁶ᵍᶠ 1⁷ᵍᶠ 2⁶ᵍᶠ 1⁷ᵍˢ 6⁷ᵍᶠ 6⁶ˢ **2-2-7**
£43,638

Delsarte (USA) *Saeed Bin Suroor*   109
4 b c Theatrical - Delauncy
9¹²ᵍᶠ 2¹³ᵍ 5¹²ᵍ 6¹³ˢ 4¹²ᵍᶠ **0-1-5 £9,066**

Delta Force *P A Blockley*   58 a70
5 b g High Kicker (USA) - Maedaley
1¹⁶ˢᵈ 2¹¹ˢᵈ 1¹²ˢᵈ 4¹¹ˢᵈ 4¹⁴ˢᵈ 5¹²ˢˢ 3¹²ᵍᶠ
2¹⁷ᶠ 6¹⁴ᶠ **2-3-9 £6,594**

Delta Lady *R Bastiman*   39 a4
3 b f River Falls - Compton Lady (USA)
16⁸ˢ 8⁶ˢᵈ 9¹⁰ᵍᶠ 5⁷ᵍᶠ 14⁷ᵍ 8⁸ᵍᶠ 12⁸ˢ 9⁸ᶠ
6⁸ᶠ **0-0-9**

Delta Star *K A Ryan*   21
4 ch f Abou Zouz (USA) - Lamloum (Ire)
12⁸ʰʸ 12⁹ˢᵈ **0-0-2**

Delusion *T D Easterby*   53
3 b f Hennessy (USA) - Another Fantasy (Ire)
6⁶ᵍᶠ 3⁷ᵍᶠ 11⁸ᵍ 15⁷ᵍ 7⁷ᶠ **0-1-5 £447**

Dematraf (Ire) *Ms Deborah J Evans*   a56
2 gr f Atraf - Demolition Jo
1⁶ˢᵈ **1-0-1 £1,456**

Democratic Deficit (Ire) *J S Bolger*   110
2 b c Soviet Star (USA) - Grandiose Idea (Ire)
1⁶ᵍʸ 1⁶ᵍᶠ 2⁷ᵍᶠ 4⁷ʸ 5⁷ᵍ **2-1-5 £95,161**

Demolition Frank *M D Hammond*   32
2 b g Cayman Kai (Ire) - Something Speedy (Ire)
11⁷ᶠ 10⁷ˢ **0-0-2**

Demolition Molly *R F Marvin*   70 a71
3 b f Rudimentary - Persian Fortune
9⁵ˢᵈ 6⁵ˢᵈ 8⁵ˢᵈ 2⁵ᵍ 1⁵ˢᵈ 15⁵ˢ 19⁵ᵍ 13⁶ˢᵈ
1-1-8 £4,804

Den Perry *A Berry*   48
2 ch c Tipsy Creek (USA) - Beverley Monkey (Ire)

6⁵ᵍᶠ 10⁶ᵍᶠ 7⁶ᵍᶠ 7⁵ᵍ 8⁷ᵍᶠ 7⁶ˢ 5⁶ˢ 8⁵ᵍˢ
0-0-8 £694

Den'S-Joy *V Smith* 40
8 b m Archway (Ire) - Bonvin
19¹⁰ˢ 16¹⁰ᵍ 10¹²ᵍᶠ 11¹⁰ᶠ 8⁸ᵍᶠ **0-0-5**

Denise Best (Ire) *Miss K M George* 45 a35
6 ch m Goldmark (USA) - Titchwell Lass
11¹³ᵍ 5¹⁰ˢ 5⁸ˢᵈ **0-0-3**

Dennick *P C Haslam* 55
2 b g Nicolotte - Branston Dancer
4⁶ᵍᶠ **0-0-1 £295**

Denounce *H R A Cecil* 86
3 b c Selkirk (USA) - Didicoy (USA)
2⁸ᵍ 8⁸ᵍ **0-1-2 £2,140**

Denver (Ire) *B J Meehan* a89
3 b c Danehill (USA) - Born Beautiful (USA)
7¹⁰ˢᵈ 2⁷ˢˢ 1⁸ˢ **1-1-3 £5,325**

Deo Gratias (Pol) *M Pitman* 32
4 b c Enjoy Plan (USA) - Dea (Pol)
17¹⁷ᵍ **0-0-1**

Depressed *Andrew Reid* 63 a61
2 ch f Most Welcome - Sure Care
7⁶ˢᵈ 7⁶ᵍ 3⁶ˢᵈ 4⁵ˢᵈ 2⁵ˢᵈ 5⁶ˢᵈ **0-2-6**
£1,409

Deputy Of Wood (USA) *P F I Cole* 34
2 b/br f Deputy Minister (Can) - Wood Of Binn (USA)
8⁵ᵍˢ **0-0-1**

Deraasaat *E A L Dunlop* 84
3 ch f Nashwan (USA) - Nafhaat (USA)
8¹¹ᵍˢ 6¹⁰ᵍᶠ 12⁹ᵍᶠ **0-0-3 £450**

Derwent (USA) *J D Bethell* 69
5 b/br g Distant View (USA) - Nothing Sweeter (USA)
16¹⁰ᵍˢ 9¹²ᶠ 8¹⁰ᵍ 4¹⁰ᵍᶠ 6¹⁰ˢ 6¹⁰ᵍᶠ 9¹⁰ᵍ
3¹⁰ᵍ 13¹⁰ᵍᶠ **0-1-9 £911**

Descartes *Saeed Bin Suroor* 86
2 b c Dubai Millennium - Gold's Dance (Fr)
1⁸ʰʸ **1-0-1 £6,734**

Desert Air (Jpn) *M C Pipe* 64
5 ch g Desert King (Ire) - Greek Air (Ire)
13¹²ᵍˢ **0-0-1**

Desert Arc (Ire) *W M Brisbourne* 72
6 b g Spectrum (Ire) - Bint Albadou (Ire)
12⁷ᵍᶠ 1⁶ᶠ 1⁶ᵍᶠ 6⁶ᵍ 11⁷ᵍ 13⁶ᵍ 10⁶ᵍᶠ
2-0-7 £6,441

Desert Battle (Ire) *M Blanshard* 27 a17
3 ch g Desert Sun - Papal
15⁸ˢ 19¹²ˢ 16⁸ᵍ 7¹²ˢᵈ **0-0-4**

Desert Buzz (Ire) *J Hetherton* 60
2 b c Desert Story (Ire) - Sugar
7⁵ʰʸ 6⁵ᵍᶠ 8⁶ᶠ 5⁵ᵍ 9⁶ᵍˢ 10⁵ᵍˢ 8⁷ᵍˢ 8⁷ᵍᶠ
6⁶ᵍ **0-0-9**

Desert Chief *Saeed Bin Suroor* 79
2 b c Green Desert (USA) - Oriental Fashion (Ire)
2⁶ᵍᶠ 6⁶ˢ **0-1-2 £1,402**

Desert City *P R Webber*
5 b g Darnay - Oasis
20¹²ʰʸ **0-0-1**

Desert Classic *E A L Dunlop* 60
2 b f Green Desert (USA) - High Standard
9⁷ᵍᶠ 14⁷ᵍ **0-0-2**

Desert Commander (Ire) *Saeed Bin Suroor* 81
2 b c Green Desert (USA) - Meadow Pipit (Can)
4⁷ᵍˢ 6⁷ᵍᶠ 1⁶ᵍᶠ **1-0-3 £5,183**

Desert Coral (Ire) *P A Blockley*
3 ch f Desert Story (Ire) - Sleeping Beauty

Desert Cristal (Ire) *J R Boyle* 89
3 ch f Desert King (Ire) - Damiana (Ire)
2⁹ˢ 6⁸ˢ 3⁸ᵍ 7¹ ³⁸ᵍ 2⁷ˢ 3⁸ᵍ 9⁸ᵍ 1⁸ᵍ
3⁸ˢ **2-4-10 £18,754**

Desert Daisy (Ire) *I A Wood* 54
3 gr f Desert Prince (Ire) - Pomponette (USA)
9⁸ᵍ 13¹²ᵍ 9⁸ᵍ 12⁷ᵍᶠ 6⁶ᵍˢ 6⁶ˢ 18⁶ˢ **0-0-7**

Desert Dance (Ire) *G Wragg* a39
4 b g Desert Story (Ire) - Cindy's Star (Ire)
11⁸ˢᵈ **0-0-1**

Desert Deer *J H M Gosden* 57
6 ch h Cadeaux Genereux - Tuxford Hideaway
14⁸ᵍ **0-0-1**

Desert Demon (Ire) *B W Hills* 77
2 b c Unfuwain (USA) - Baldemosa (Fr)
5⁶ᵍ 3⁶ˢ **0-1-2 £899**

Desert Destiny *Saeed Bin Suroor* 112
4 b g Desert Prince (Ire) - High Savannah
7⁷ᵍᶠ 2⁷ᵍᶠ 5⁷ᵍ 2⁷ᵍˢ 4⁷ᵍᶠ **0-2-5 £16,992**

Desert Diplomat (Ire) *Sir Michael Stoute*
3 b g Machiavellian (USA) - Desert Beauty (Ire)
7⁸ᵍˢ 14⁸ᵍᶠ **0-0-2**

Desert Dreamer (Ire) *B W Hills* 95
3 b g Green Desert (USA) - Follow That Dream
5⁸ᵍˢ 8⁹ᵍ 6⁷ᵍ 7⁷ᵍ 11⁷ᵍᶠ 12⁷ᵍᶠ 12⁶ᵍᶠ **0-0-7**
£1,309

Desert Fern (Ire) *Ms Deborah J Evans* a39
2 b f Desert Style (Ire) - Lady Fern
4⁶ˢᵈ 14⁷ˢᵈ **0-0-2 £277**

Desert Fury *R Bastiman* 43 a44
7 b g Warning - Number One Spot
8⁸ˢᵈ 10⁶ˢᵈ 6⁸ᶠ 5⁸ᵍ 12⁶ʰʸ 8⁶ᵍ 4⁸ˢ **0-0-7**

Desert Glory (Ire) *D R Loder* 58
2 gr f Desert Prince (Ire) - True Love
11⁷ᵍ **0-0-1**

Desert Hawk *R Hannon* 73
3 b c Cape Cross (Ire) - Milling (Ire)
13⁸ᵍ 11⁸ᵍ 5⁸ᵍ 4⁹ᵍᶠ 7¹⁰ᵍᶠ 8⁹ᵍˢ 6¹⁰ᵍˢ 2⁸ᵍ
10⁸ʰʸ 2⁸ᵍ 9⁸ᵍᶠ **0-3-11 £2,757**

Desert Heat *J W Payne* 61 a68
6 b h Green Desert (USA) - Lypharitissima (Fr)
13⁹ˢᵈ 2⁹ˢˢ 1⁹ˢˢ 2⁸ˢʷ 8⁸ˢʷ 14¹⁰ˢ 4⁸ˢᵈ 2⁸ᵍ
1-3-8 £4,901

Desert Image (Ire) *C Tinkler* 77 a74
3 b c Desert King (Ire) - Identical (Ire)
1⁷ˢᵈ 2¹⁰ˢᵈ 6⁹ˢʷ 10⁹ᵍˢ 8¹¹ᵍˢ 3¹⁰ᵍ 3¹⁰ᵍᶠ
2¹²ᶠ 4¹¹ᵍᶠ 9¹¹ᵍᶠ 7¹²ᵍᶠ 7¹⁰ᵍ **1-3-12 £7,311**

Desert Imp *B W Hills* 80
2 b f Green Desert (USA) - Devil's Imp (Ire)
9⁶ᵍˢ 3⁶ᵍ 3⁶ᵍ 1⁶ᵍ **1-2-4 £6,418**

Desert Island Disc *J J Bridger* 84 a53
7 b m Turtle Island (Ire) - Distant Music
16¹⁰ᵍ 4¹⁰ᵍ 4¹²ᵍ 8¹²ᶠ 3¹²ᶠ 12⁹ᵍᶠ 6⁹ᵍᶠ 1¹²ᵍ
5¹²ᵍᶠ 11²ᵍᶠ 1¹²ᶠ 6¹⁰ˢ 3¹²ᵍ 8¹²ᵍ 11¹⁰ᵍ 3¹⁰ˢ 9¹⁶ˢ
11¹²ˢᵈ **3-2-18 £26,915**

Desert Leader (Ire) *B A McMahon* 65 a64
3 b g Green Desert (USA) - Za Aamah (USA)
8⁸ᵍᶠ 7⁸ᵍˢ 2⁶ˢᵈ 7⁸ˢ 17⁷ᵍᶠ 17⁷ˢ **0-1-6**
£1,078

Desert Light (Ire) *D Shaw* 57 a56
3 b c Desert Sun - Nacote (Ire)
1⁶ˢᵈ 3⁶ˢᵈ 7⁶ˢᵈ 7⁵ᵍ 2⁵ˢᵈ 2⁵ᵍˢ 5⁵ˢᵈ **1-3-7**

623 11^{5gs} 0-1-6
£1,675

Detroit Dancer *Ronald Thompson*   44
2 b c Makbul - First Play
15^{6f} 5^{5gs} 15^{6gs} 0-0-3

Deuxieme (Ire) *R Charlton*   74 a60
3 b f Second Empire (Ire) - Kardelle
3^{7gf} 3^{7gs} 5^{7gs} 2^{6f} 2^{6gf} 1^{6sd} 1-4-6
£6,722

Devant (NZ) *M A Jarvis*   85
4 b f Zabeel (NZ) - Frenetic (NZ)
11^{8hy} 4^{8gf} 7^{8gf} 2^{8g} 14^{8g} 3^{11hy} 5^{12gs}
0-1-7 **£3,066**

Devil's Bite *B W Hills*
3 ch g Dracula (Aus) - Niggle
PU^{7sd} PU^{9sd} 0-0-2

Devil's Island *Sir Mark Prescott*   61 a42
2 b g Green Desert (USA) - Scandalette
5^{6hy} 8^{6gf} 11^{7sd} 0-0-3

Devine Command *R Ingram*   a54
3 b g In Command (Ire) - Adriya
9^{8sd} 14^{10sd} 2^{7sd} 5^{8sd} 0-1-4 **£420**

Devine Light (Ire) *B Mactaggart*   19
4 b f Spectrum (Ire) - Siskin (Ire)
8^{10gf} 9^{9g} 6^{12gf} 11^{7f} 8^{9s} 12^{8gf} 13^{10s}
0-0-7

Devious Ayers (Ire) *J M Bradley*   47 a61
3 br g Dr Devious (Ire) - Yulara (Ire)
4^{8sd} 8^{8hy} 14^{12gf} 6^{9gs} 12^{10sd} 9^{9sd} 0-0-6
£259

Devious Paddy (Ire) *N Tinkler*   a43
4 b g Dr Devious (Ire) - Night Arcade (Ire)
12^{8sw} 7^{11ss} 0-0-2

Devise (Ire) *M S Saunders*   95
5 b g Hamas (Ire) - Soreze (Ire)
1^{6g} 6^{6g} 27^{6g} 1^{5gf} 5^{6f} 5^{5g} 4^{5gf} 7^{5g} 2^{5g}
3^{5s} 2^{5gs} 2^{5g} 8^{6gf} 2-4-13 **£28,479**

Devito (Fr) *A King*   50
3 ch g Trempolino (USA) - Snowy (Fr)
2^{12gf} 5^{12gf} 13^{16gs} 0-1-3 **£1,708**

Devon Flame *R J Hodges*   86
5 b g Whittingham (Ire) - Uaeflame (Ire)
2^{6g} 1^{5gf} 2^{6f} 2^{6gf} 4^{7g} 10^{6g} 19^{6gf} 2^{6gf}
11^{6s} 9^{5gs} 1-4-10 **£14,768**

Devote *J D Frost*   40
6 b g Pennekamp (USA) - Radiant Bride (USA)
9^{10g} 6^{12gf} 9^{18gs} 0-0-3

Dewin Coch *W M Brisbourne*   57
2 b g Wizard King - Drudwen
14^{7gs} 7^{7hy} 6^{6g} 0-0-3

Dexileos (Ire) *A D W Pinder*   48 a46
5 b g Danehill (USA) - Theano (Ire)
9^{10g} 10^{10s} 10^{8hy} 12^{8g} 7^{7f} 12^{7gf} 7^{7g}
3^{6gf} 6^{6g} 8^{6gf} 9^{7hy} 3^{7sd} 0-2-12 **£639**

Dhabyan (USA) *B Hanbury*
4 ch g Silver Hawk (USA) - Fleur De Nuit (USA)
8^{10g} 0-0-1

Dhaular Dhar (Ire) *B W Hills*   88
2 b c Indian Ridge - Pescara (Ire)
2^{7s} 1^{7g} 9^{7s} 1-1-3 **£6,777**

Dhefaaf (Ire) *B Hanbury*   44
2 b c Lujain (USA) - Paparazza (Ire)
7^{5gf} 0-0-1

Dhehdaah *Mrs P Sly*   64
3 b g Alhaarth (Ire) - Carina Clare

7^{10gf} 3^{12g} 5^{12f} 0-0-3 **£647**

Diagon Alley (Ire) *K W Hogg*   a26
4 ro g Petong - Mubadara (Ire)
8^{9sw} 6^{9sd} 0-0-2

Dial Square *P Howling*   37 a61
3 b g Bluegrass Prince (Ire) - Honey Mill
9^{7sd} 1^{8sd} 3^{7sd} 2^{7sd} 3^{8sd} 1^{8sd} 1^{8sd} 1^{10sd}
10^{7gf} 17^{8gf} 17^{12g} 10^{9sd} 9^{6sd} 4-3-13 **£7,367**

Diamond Circle *B W Hills*   60
2 br f Halling (USA) - Canadian Mill (USA)
5^{7s} 0-0-1

Diamond Dan (Ire) *John Berry*   39
2 b g Foxhound (USA) - Kawther
16^{6s} 0-0-1

Diamond Dazzler *D P Keane*
6 br g Sula Bula - Dancing Diamond (Ire)
8^{11sd} 0-0-1

Diamond George (Ire) *John Berry*   37 a52
3 b g Sri Pekan (USA) - Golden Choice
5^{6sd} 6^{7ss} 11^{7s} 0-0-3

Diamond Green (Fr) *A Fabre*   121
3 b/br c Green Desert (USA) - Diamonaka (Fr)
3^{8gs} 2^{8gf} 2^{8gf} 2^{8gs} 2^{8gs} 8^{8gf} 8^{8y} 0-4-7
£175,698

Diamond Heritage *J A Glover*   43
2 ch c Compton Place - Eccolina
12^{5gs} 10^{6hy} 5^{6hy} 0-0-3

Diamond Hombre (USA) *J W Hills*   68 a62
2 gr c Two Punch (USA) - Flowing (USA)
4^{5gf} 6^{6gf} 7^{5sd} 0-0-3 **£367**

Diamond Josh *John Berry*   69
2 ch g Primo Dominie - Exit
3^{5gf} 6^{6s} 0-1-2 **£664**

Diamond Katie (Ire) *R Guest*   76
2 b f Night Shift (USA) - Fayrooz (USA)
8^{6g} 7^{7g} 3^{6g} 0-1-3 **£8,570**

Diamond Lodge *J Noseda*   100
3 ch f Grand Lodge (USA) - Movieland (USA)
4^{8g} 1^{8gf} 2^{8gs} 1^{8gf} 1^{8g} 1^{9g} 5^{8gf} 2^{8gf}
4-2-8 **£43,637**

Diamond Max (Ire) *John Berry*   84
6 b g Nicolotte - Kawther
11^{7sd} 1^{8sd} 3^{8sd} 20^{9g} 4^{7gs} 1-1-5 **£6,179**

Diamond Orchid (Ire) *A L Forbes*   64 a54
4 gr f Victory Note (USA) - Olivia's Pride (Ire)
3^{8sd} 2^{12sd} 4^{12sw} 2^{12sd} 2^{10s} 11^{2gf} 5^{10sd}
1^{14f} 12^{14gf} 2^{16sd} 12^{16g} 4^{12sd} 2-5-12 **£9,480**

Diamond Racket *D W Chapman*   a15
4 b g Cyrano De Bergerac - Reina
15^{5sd} 6^{5sw} 11^{5sd} 9^{5sd} 0-0-4

Diamond Ribby (Ire) *P D Evans*   a21
3 br f Desert Sun - Kathleen's Dream (USA)
9^{8sd} 0-0-1

Diamond Ring *Mrs J Candlish*   53
5 b m Magic Ring (Ire) - Reticent Bride (Ire)
5^{5gs} 14^{5gf} 3^{5gs} 3^{5g} 5^{5gf} 2^{6gf} 4^{5gs}
9^{6g} 8^{5gs} 0-3-10 **£2,400**

Diamond Shannon (Ire) *D Carroll*   47 a66
3 b f Petorius - Balgren (Ire)
7^{6g} 7^{5s} 5^{6s} 1^{7sd} 2^{8sd} 14^{7sd} 19^{6gs} 8^{7sd}
6^{5sd} 1-1-9 **£4,023**

Diamond Way (USA) *D R Loder*   a69
3 ch c Boundary (USA) - Discover Silver (USA)
1^{8sd} 1-0-1 **£2,961**

Diamonds And Dust *M H Tompkins*   91

2 b c Mister Baileys - Dusty Shoes
4⁶ᵍ 3⁶ᵍ 4⁷ᵍ 1⁷ᵍᶠ 7⁷ᵍᶠ 6⁶ˢ **1-1-6 £9,884**

Diamonds Will Do (Ire) *Miss Venetia Williams*   47
7 b m Bigstone (Ire) - Clear Ability (Ire)
6¹²ᵍ **0-0-1**

Diaphanous *E A Wheeler*   47 a25
6 b m Beveled (USA) - Sharp Venita
8⁵ˢᵈ 7⁵ˢᵈ 9⁵ˢᵈ 17⁵ᵗ 14⁵ᵍˢ 7⁵ᵍᶠ 13⁵ˢᵈ
13⁸ᵍᶠ 7⁶ᵍᶠ 6⁶ᵍˢ **0-0-10**

Diatonic *D Carroll*   47 a47
2 b g Deploy - Vic Melody (Fr)
9⁵ᵍ 8⁵ˢᵈ 8⁶ᵍᶠ 2⁷ˢᵈ 7⁸ᵍ **0-1-5 £728**

Dick The Taxi *R J Smith*   71 a79
10 b g Karlinsky (USA) - Another Galaxy (Ire)
3¹²ˢᵈ 3¹²ᵍᶠ 9¹²ᵍᶠ 4¹⁰ᵍ **0-2-4 £1,597**

Dickie Deadeye *G B Balding*   76
7 b g Distant Relative - Accuracy
6¹⁰ᵍ 5¹⁰ᵍˢ 2¹⁰ˢ 2¹⁰ʰʸ 3¹⁰ᵍ 1¹²ᵍ 1¹²ᵍˢ 3¹²ᵍ
4¹⁰ᵍ 9¹²ᵍ 3¹⁰ᵍˢ 8¹²ˢ **2-5-12 £14,311**

Diction (Ire) *K R Burke*   36 a72
2 b f Diktat - Waft (USA)
7⁶ᶠ 5⁶ᵍᶠ 1⁷ˢᵈ 1⁶ˢᵈ 5⁷ᵍᶠ 2⁷ˢᵈ **2-1-6 £7,456**

Didnt Tell My Wife *C F Wall*   74 a61
5 ch g Aragon - Bee Dee Dancer
6⁷ʰʸ 6⁸ˢᵈ 9⁸ˢᵈ 4⁸ᵍ 3⁸ᵍ 1⁹ᵍˢ 3⁸ᵍˢ 15⁸ᵍᶠ
6⁸ᵍˢ 3⁸ʰʸ 8⁹ˢ **1-4-11 £6,293**

Didoe *P W Hiatt*   55
5 b m Son Pardo - My Diamond Ring
15⁸ᵍᶠ 7⁸ᵍᶠ 9¹⁰ᵍᶠ 1¹⁰ᵍᶠ 2¹⁰ᶠ 1⁸ᵍᶠ 8⁸ᵍˢ
17⁷ᵍᶠ 10⁸ᵍᶠ **2-1-9 £8,732**

Diego Cao (Ire) *G L Moore*   95 a74
3 b g Cape Cross (Ire) - Lady Moranbon (USA)
2¹⁰ˢ 1¹⁰ᵍˢ 6¹⁰ᵍ 1¹⁰ᵍ 4¹⁰ˢ 2¹⁰ᵍ 8¹²ˢᵈ **2-1-7 £15,454**

Diequest (USA) *Jamie Poulton*   57
3 ch c Diesis - Nuance (Ire)
8⁸ᵍ 8¹⁰ᵍˢ 13¹⁰ˢ **0-0-3**

Different Planet *J W Hills*   75
3 b c Inchinor - Take Heart
4⁸ᵍ 4⁸ᵍᶠ 5⁸ᵍˢ **0-0-3 £729**

Digger (Ire) *Seamus Fahey*   49 a81
5 ch g Danzig Connection (USA) - Baliana
1¹¹ˢᵈ 4¹²ˢˢ 9¹²ˢˢ 2¹²ˢˢ 5¹⁶ˢˢ 1⁷¹⁰ᵍ 12¹²ᵍˢ
1-1-7 £4,897

Digital *M R Channon*   96 a93
7 ch g Safawan - Heavenly Goddess
10⁷ˢᵈ 3⁷ˢ 4⁷ʰʸ 16⁸ᵍ 3⁸ʰʸ 6⁸ᵍˢ 8⁷ᵍ 8⁷ᵍ
5⁷ᵍᶠ 2⁷ᵍ 2⁷ˢ 2⁷ᵍ 7⁷ᵍᶠ 8⁷ᵍᶠ 8⁷ᵍ 2⁷ˢ 2⁷ᵍˢ 12⁷ᵍᶠ 4⁷ˢ **0-7-22 £28,668**

Diktatit *M R Channon*   49
2 b f Diktat - Mystique Smile
13⁵ᵍᶠ 5⁵ᵍ 7⁵ᵍᶠ **0-0-3**

Diktatorial *A M Balding*   104
2 br c Diktat - Reason To Dance
7⁷ᵍᶠ 1⁷ᵍˢ 1⁷ᵍ **2-0-3 £42,063**

Dil *Mrs N Macauley*   a19
9 b g Primo Dominie - Swellegant
7⁶ˢᵈ 7⁷ˢᵈ 12⁶ˢᵈ **0-0-3**

Diligent Lad *D W Barker*
4 b g Secret Appeal - Mohibbah (USA)
9¹²ᵍ 13¹²ᵍᶠ **0-0-2**

Diliza *G B Balding*   a41
5 b m Dilum (USA) - Little White Lies
4⁸ˢᵈ 8¹⁰ˢᵈ 6⁸ˢᵈ **0-0-3**

Dilys *W S Kittow*   a37
5 b m Efisio - Ramajana (USA)
8⁷ˢᵈ **0-0-1**

Dine 'N' Dash *A G Newcombe*   27 a4
3 ch g Komaite (USA) - Instinction
11⁷ᵍˢ 6⁶ˢ 11⁶ᶠ 9⁹ˢᵈ **0-0-4**

Dingley Lass *H Morrison*   44 a32
4 ch f Fleetwood (Ire) - Riverine
6¹⁰ˢᵈ 10¹³ᵍˢ 12¹⁶ᵍᶠ **0-0-3**

Dinner Date *Sir Michael Stoute*   54
2 ch c Groom Dancer (USA) - Misleading Lady
9⁷ˢ **0-0-1**

Disabuse *D Shaw*   56 a62
4 ch g Fleetwood (Ire) - Agony Aunt
2⁷ˢᵈ 1⁸ˢᵈ 3¹¹ˢˢ 4¹²ˢˢ 1⁰ˢ 4⁸ᵍˢ 5¹⁴ᵍ
8¹²ˢᵈ 13⁸ˢʷ 16¹²ᵍ 8⁹ˢᵈ **1-2-12 £4,485**

Disco Diva *M Blanshard*   58 a58
3 ch f Spectrum (Ire) - Compact Disc (Ire)
7⁷ˢᵈ 12⁶ᵍ 10⁷ᵍᶠ 15⁶ᵍᶠ 18⁶ᵍ 2⁷ᵍ 2⁹ˢᵈ
0-2-7 £1,638

Discomania *R Charlton*   69
2 b c Pursuit Of Love - Discomatic (USA)
12⁷ᵍᶠ 4⁷ᵍ 12⁸ˢ **0-0-4 £373**

Discuss (USA) *Sir Michael Stoute*   81
2 b f Danzig (USA) - Private Line (USA)
2⁶ᵍ **0-1-1 £2,525**

Disguise *B W Hills*   78
2 b c Pursuit Of Love - Nullarbor
5⁶ᵍˢ 2⁶ᵍ 4⁶ᵍ 2⁵ᵍᶠ **0-2-4 £3,406**

Dishdasha (Ire) *C R Dore*   45
2 b g Desert Prince (Ire) - Counterplot (Ire)
14⁶ᵍᶠ 7⁶ᵍᶠ 3⁷ᵍ 10⁷ˢᵈ 14⁷ᵍᶠ 12⁷ᶠ **0-1-6 £418**

Disparity (USA) *J R Fanshawe*   57 a57
3 b f Distant View (USA) - Eternity
14¹⁰ᵍ 10¹⁰ᵍᶠ 2¹⁰ˢᵈ 7¹²ˢᵈ 15¹²ˢᵈ 15¹²ˢᵈ
0-1-6 £1,125

Dispol Charm (Ire) *D W Chapman*   38
2 br f Charnwood Forest (Ire) - Phoenix Venture (Ire)
5⁵ᵍˢ 8⁶ᶠ **0-0-2**

Dispol Evita *Jamie Poulton*   40 a56
5 ch m Presidium - She's A Breeze
9¹²ˢᵈ 10¹²ˢᵈ 2¹²ˢᵈ 7¹²ˢᵈ 4¹⁰ˢᵈ 9¹²ᶠ 9¹²ᵍᶠ
UR¹⁰ᶠ **0-1-8 £1,587**

Dispol Foxtrot *Miss V Scott*   73
6 ch m Alhijaz - Foxtrot Pie
2⁹ᵍ 3⁸ᵍˢ **0-2-2 £2,967**

Dispol In Mind *I A Wood*   64
2 b f Mind Games - Sans Diablo (Ire)
2⁵ᵍᶠ 3⁵ᵍᶠ 1⁵ᵍᶠ **1-2-3 £4,646**

Dispol Isle (Ire) *T D Barron*   78
2 gr f Trans Island - Pictina
4⁵ᵍᶠ 4⁵ᵍ 4⁵ᵍ 3⁵ᵍ 6⁶ˢ 6⁶ˢ 3⁶ˢ **0-2-8 £6,515**

Dispol Katie *T D Barron*   85
3 ch f Komaite (USA) - Twilight Time
14⁵ᵍ 6⁶ᵍ 3⁵ᵍ 5⁵ᵍᶠ 18⁵ᵍˢ 2⁵ˢ 9⁵ᵍᶠ 11⁵ˢ
0-2-8 £5,300

Dispol Peto *Ian Emmerson*   53 a64
4 gr g Petong - Plie
11⁷ˢᵈ 5⁷ˢˢ 2⁷ˢˢ 8⁷ˢʷ 5⁷ˢᵈ 9⁷ᵍᶠ 2⁷ˢᵈ **0-2-7 £1,814**

Dispol Veleta *T D Barron*   71 a77
3 b f Makbul - Foxtrot Pie
3⁶ˢᵈ 7⁶ˢᵈ 1⁸ˢᵈ 4⁹ˢʷ 1⁸ᵍ 3⁸ᵍ 13⁸ᵍᶠ 10¹⁰ᵍᶠ

1^{8sd} 12^{8s} 9^{8gs} 11^{8sd} 2^{8gs} 3-3-13 £14,154

Dispol Verity *W M Brisbourne* 27 a11
4 b f Averti (Ire) - Fawley Mist
12^{5sd} 11^{6gf} 11^{8sd} 10^{6s} 12^{8f} 6^{8s} 0-0-6

Dissident (Ger) *D Flood* 94 a57
6 b h Polish Precedent (USA) - Diasprina (Ger)
4^{8g} UR^{8g} 1^{10sd} 8^{11gs} 2^{11gs} 2^{10gs} 1^{12g}
4^{14hy} 5^{12gf} 6^{12g} 5^{10gf} 12^{12g} 2-2-12 £15,046

Distant Connection (Ire) *A P Jarvis* 89 a103
3 b c Cadeaux Genereux - Night Owl
8^{10gs} 10^{7s} 8^{8gs} 6^{7gf} 1^{7gf} 2^{7gf} 18^{gf} 5^{7gs}
3^{7g} 2^{7gf} 10^{7gf} 1^{7sd} 3^{7sd} 3-4-13 £29,360

Distant Country (USA) *Mrs J R Ramsden* 80
5 b g Distant View (USA) - Memsahb (USA)
6^{7g} 6^{8gs} 12^{7g} 2^{8gf} 5^{6g} 2^{8f} 5^{7gf} 13^{8gf}
3^{7f} 8^{7gf} 0-3-10 £6,307

Distant Cousin *M A Buckley* 69 a50
7 b g Distant Relative - Tinaca (Ire)
7^{12sd} 5^{12gf} 3^{12gf} 15^{14gf} 8^{15g} 4^{12gf} 3^{14f}
8^{14gf} 17^{14g} 0-1-9 £2,209

Distant King *G P Kelly*
11 b g Distant Relative - Lindfield Belle (Ire)
16^{6f} 0-0-1

Distant Prospect (Ire) *A M Balding* 99
7 b g Namaqualand (USA) - Ukraine's Affair (USA)
4^{19gs} 2^{16g} 12^{16s} 12^{16g} 3^{21g} 8^{18s} 2^{12s}
0-4-7 £25,570

Distant Times *T D Easterby* 84
3 b c Orpen (USA) - Simply Times (USA)
5^{7g} 1^{6s} 3^{6gs} 13^{6gf} 11^{6gf} 5^{6s} 1^{5gf} 17^{5gs}
6^{5s} 11^{6gs} 2-1-10 £9,290

Distinction (Ire) *Sir Michael Stoute* 117
5 b g Danehill (USA) - Ivy Leaf (Ire)
14^{12g} 5^{13g} 14^{14g} 1^{12gf} 6^{16gs} 2-0-5
£75,465

Distinctive Mind *T D Easterby* 57
2 b g Mind Games - Primum Tempus
12^{6g} 8^{5gf} 9^{5gf} 0-0-3

Distinctly Game *K A Ryan* 103 a75
2 b c Mind Games - Distinctly Blu (Ire)
2^{5g} 2^{6g} 2^{6sd} 1^{5gf} 4^{5g} 2^{6g} 2^{6g} 1-5-7
£82,667

Distinctlythebest *F Watson* 7
4 b g Distinctly North (USA) - Euphyllia
9^{9gs} 8^{9f} 8^{7gf} 0-0-3

Dium Mac *N Bycroft* 38
3 b g Presidium - Efipetite
7^{7gf} 5^{8gf} 0-0-2

Diva Dancer *J Hetherton* 25 a7
4 ch f Dr Devious (Ire) - Catina
15^{8sd} 10^{11sd} 10^{10gf} 8^{16f} 11^{17g} 0-0-5

Divani (Ire) *B J Meehan*
2 b f Shinko Forest (Ire) - Supreme Crown (USA)
19^{5gf} 0-0-1

Diverted *M G Quinlan* 30 a34
3 b f Averti (Ire) - Whittle Rock
9^{8sw} 13^{7sd} 8^{10gs} 10^{7s} 12^{8f} 5^{8gf} 10^{10gf}
0-0-7

Divina *S L Keightley* 19 a42
3 b f King's Theatre (Ire) - Heuston Station (Ire)
11^{8sd} 8^{9sw} 11^{12sd} 8^{6gs} 4^{8sd} 3^{8ss} 2^{8sd}
2^{10sd} 8^{8gf} 10^{8sd} 0-2-10 £1,282

Divine Diva *R Hannon* 60
2 b f Diktat - Maid To Dance

11^{6g} 4^{6gf} 0-0-2 £275

Divine Gift *M A Jarvis* 102
3 b c Groom Dancer (USA) - Child's Play (USA)
18^{g} 4^{8gs} 4^{8s} 7^{7s} 1-0-4 £10,429

Divine Proportions (USA) *P Bary* 117
2 b f Kingmambo (USA) - Myth To Reality (Fr)
1^{5gs} 1^{5g} 1^{6g} 1^{6vs} 1^{8g} 5-0-5 £275,388

Divine Spirit *M Dods* 88
3 b g Foxhound (USA) - Vocation (Ire)
12^{5s} 12^{5gf} 17^{6gf} 3^{5f} 6^{5gf} 1^{5g} 7^{5gf} 3^{5g}
6^{5gf} 13^{5gf} 3^{5gs} 1-3-11 £11,243

Divinely Decadent (Ire) *P W Chapple-Hyam* 87
2 br f Turtle Island (Ire) - Divine Prospect (Ire)
1^{6g} 9^{7g} 1-0-2 £5,216

Diwan (Ire) *J Parkes* a20
6 b g Be My Guest (USA) - Nectarine (Ire)
11^{13gs} 9^{9sd} 0-0-2

Dixie Dancing *C A Cyzer* 62 a65
5 ch m Greensmith - Daylight Dreams
5^{7sd} 14^{8sd} 4^{8sd} 2^{7sd} 3^{6g} 0-2-5 £1,908

Dixie Queen (Ire) *M Dods* 65 a35
2 b f King Of Kings (Ire) - Dixieline City (USA)
5^{5hy} 7^{6gf} 9^{7g} 3^{7g} 10^{8g} 9^{9sd} 0-1-6 £469

Dixieanna *B W Hills* 72
2 ch f Night Shift (USA) - Dixielake (Ire)
2^{5gs} 0-1-1 £1,528

Dizzy Future *W Jarvis* 54
2 b g Fraam - Kara Sea (USA)
7^{8gf} 29^{6s} 0-0-2

Dizzy In The Head *Paul Johnson* 86
5 b g Mind Games - Giddy
19^{6s} 1^{6s} 6^{3gf} 1^{5gf} 2^{6f} 1^{6gf} 14^{5gs}
9^{5g} 12^{5gf} 1^{6s} 2^{5g} 7^{7s} 4-2-13 £24,205

Dizzy Lizzy *Nick Williams* 11
2 gr f Sendawar (Ire) - Black Velvet (Fr)
13^{7gf} 5^{5g} 9^{8s} 0-0-3

Docduckout *J W Unett*
4 b g Bluegrass Prince (Ire) - Fayre Holly (Ire)
PU^{6sd} 0-0-1

Docklands Blue (Ire) *N P Littmoden* 44 a55
3 ch f Cadeaux Genereux - Copious (Ire)
2^{5sd} 8^{6sd} 7^{5sd} 3^{6sd} 6^{7sd} 4^{7sd} 3^{7sd} 8^{7s}
8^{6gf} 0-3-9 £2,562

Docklands Dude (Ire) *M Meade* 40
2 ch g Namid - Cheeky Weeky
6^{5g} 8^{5g} 0-0-2

Docklands Grace (USA) *N P Littmoden* 60 a41
2 gr f Honour And Glory (USA) - Afarel (USA)
5^{5sd} 5^{5gf} 3^{5g} 0-0-3 £418

Doctor Dennis (Ire) *J Pearce* 61 a55
7 b g Last Tycoon - Noble Lustre (USA)
5^{6sd} 1^{6sd} 8^{7gf} 1^{6f} 14^{6gf} 6^{7gf} 14^{6g}
10^{6g} 10^{7sd} 2-0-10 £6,034

Doctor Hilary *M L W Bell* 93
2 b c Mujahid (USA) - Agony Aunt
4^{6gs} 1^{6gf} 2^{6gf} 3^{5g} 2^{6gf} 5^{6gf} 1-3-6
£9,908

Doctor John *Andrew Turnell* 53 a49
7 ch g Handsome Sailor - Bollin Sophie
4^{12sd} 2^{16sd} 1^{16sw} 6^{16s} 1^{16sd} 2^{14sf} 8^{14gf}
2^{16sd} 4^{16gs} 12^{16f} 2^{16g} 1-5-11 £6,563

Doctor's Cave *C E Brittain* 89 a89
2 b c Night Shift (USA) - Periquitum
7^{6gf} 8^{6gf} 7^{7gf} 7^{7gs} 1^{6g} 8^{6vs} 9^{6gs} 11^{6s}
10^{6sd} 1-0-9 £8,248

Doctorate *E A L Dunlop*   91 a89
3 b c Dr Fong (USA) - Aunt Tate
9^{8g} 1^{7s} 2^{7gf} 5^{8gf} 3^{7sd} 9^{8g} 1^{7gs} 8^{7g} 4^{7s}
2-2-9 £15,181

Doctored *P D Evans*   81 a76
3 ch g Dr Devious (Ire) - Polygueza (Fr)
8^{8sd} 15^{7sd} 4^{8sd} 6^{10sd} 1^{7gs} 1^{8ss} 10^{6s} 1^{8f}
1^{10g} 1^{10g} 1^{10g} 3^{10gf} 10^{10gf} 6^{10gf} 8^{10g} 4^{10sd}
7^{10gf} 10^{14g} **6-0-18 £21,955**

Doctrine *J H M Gosden*   89
3 b f Barathea (Ire) - Auspicious
4^{8gs} 8^{8gf} 5^{10g} 9^{12gf} **0-0-4 £2,750**

Doitforreel (Ire) *I A Wood*   82
2 b f Princely Heir (Ire) - Chehana
12^{6gf} 8^{5g} 3^{5f} 1^{6g} 5^{6s} 3^{5hy} **1-2-6
£5,284**

Doitnow (Ire) *R A Fahey*   97
3 b g Princely Heir (Ire) - Tony's Gift
1^{6gf} 2^{6g} 2^{6g} 6^{6g} 6^{7gs} 11^{7gf} **1-2-6
£12,705**

Dolce Piccata *B J Meehan*   85 a54
3 ch f Piccolo - Highland Rhapsody (Ire)
15^{6gs} 5^{6hy} 4^{5gf} 5^{6g} 7^{6gf} 8^{6g} 9^{5gf} 11^{5gf}
7^{5gs} 6^{5gf} 9^{6sd} **0-0-11 £793**

Dollar Law *R J Price*
8 ch g Selkirk (USA) - Western Heights
14^{8hy} **0-0-1**

Dolly Peel *G A Swinbank*
2 b f Josr Algarhoud (Ire) - Transylvania
17^{5gs} **0-0-1**

Dolly Wotnot (Ire) *N P Littmoden*   65
3 b f Desert King (Ire) - Riding School (Ire)
5^{12gs} 16^{12s} 5^{10f} 3^{11gf} **0-1-4 £627**

Dolphinelle (Ire) *Jamie Poulton*   a52
8 b g Dolphin Street (Fr) - Mamie's Joy
4^{8sd} 3^{8sd} **0-1-2 £366**

Dolzago *G L Moore*   48 a74
4 b g Pursuit Of Love - Doctor's Glory (USA)
1^{13sd} 2^{13sd} 3^{13sd} 13^{14hy} 9^{13gf} 8^{12gf} **1-2-6
£6,128**

Domart (Pol) *M Pitman*   52
4 gr g Baby Bid (USA) - Dominet (Pol)
10^{13gf} **0-0-1**

Domenico (Ire) *J R Jenkins*   69 a62
6 b g Sadler's Wells (USA) - Russian Ballet (USA)
12^{16gf} 3^{12gf} 26^{20gf} 6^{16sd} 14^{17gs} 12^{15s}
0-1-6 £515

Dominer (Ire) *J M Bradley*   35
2 b c Desert Prince (Ire) - Smart (Ire)
6^{5gf} 6^{6f} 6^{5f} 8^{6gf} **0-0-4**

Domirati *R Charlton*   88
4 b g Emarati (USA) - Julia Domna
17^{6gf} 4^{5gf} 2^{5g} 7^{5gf} 2^{5gf} 14^{5gf} 4^{5g} 5^{5g}
0-2-8 £5,245

Don Argento *Mrs A J Bowlby*   45
3 gr g Sri Pekan (USA) - Grey Galava
9^{7gs} 12^{10gf} 14^{7g} UR^{8g} 3^{10gf} 10^{10gf}
11^{10gf} **0-1-7 £435**

Don Fayruz (Ire) *B N Doran*
12 b g Fayruz - Gobolino
12^{10sd} **0-0-1**

Don Fernando *M C Pipe*   91
5 b h Zilzal (USA) - Teulada (USA)
7^{15s} 5^{16gf} 10^{20gf} 6^{22f} 2^{16gf} **0-1-5
£3,653**

Don Pasquale *D R Loder*   a66
2 br c Zafonic (USA) - Bedazzling (Ire)
5^{7sd} **0-0-1**

Don Pele (Ire) *S Kirk*   106
2 b c Monashee Mountain (USA) - Big Fandango
15^{6gf} 2^{6g} 1^{6gf} 1^{6g} 22^{6g} **2-1-5 £19,235**

Don't Matter *Mrs S M Johnson*
4 b f Petong - Cool Run
8^{12g} **0-0-1**

Don't Sioux Me (Ire) *C R Dore*   77 a57
6 b g Sadler's Wells (USA) - Commanche Belle
10^{12sd} 5^{12gf} 10^{10gf} **0-0-3**

Don't Tell Mum (Ire) *R Hannon*   91
2 b f Dansili - Zinnia
1^{5f} 6^{5gf} 2^{5g} **1-1-3 £33,739**

Don't Tell Rosey *M Blanshard*   a64
4 b g Barathea (Ire) - Patsy Western
7^{6sd} **0-0-1**

Don't Tell Trigger (Ire) *J S Moore*   71
2 b f Mujadil (USA) - Ordinate
10^{5g} 6^{6gf} 1^{6gf} 11^{6gf} 7^{7gf} 1^{7gf} 8^{6gf} 7^{8f}
2-0-8 £7,140

Donald (Pol) *M Pitman*   64
4 b g Enjoy Plan (USA) - Dahira (Pol)
3^{17f} 14^{13gf} 6^{14g} 13^{17g} **0-1-4 £420**

Donastrela (Ire) *A M Balding*   72 a42
3 b f Tagula (USA) - David's Star
6^{8sd} 11^{8gs} 11^{11gf} 1^{10f} 4^{10g} 1^{10gf} 3^{12gf}
3^{12gf} 5^{14gf} 4^{12f} 7^{12g} **2-2-11 £8,938**

Donegal Shore (Ire) *Mrs J Candlish*   42 a53
5 b h Mujadil (USA) - Distant Shore (Ire)
4^{6sd} 2^{7sd} 2^{7sd} 4^{8sw} 3^{8sd} 7^{8sd} 6^{6d} 7^{8sd}
4^{8gs} 8^{5sd} 3^{6sd} **0-5-11 £1,484**

Donna Vita *P W Chapple-Hyam*   84
3 b f Vettori (Ire) - Soolaimon (USA)
4^{11s} 8^{8gs} 9^{10g} 13^{10g} **0-0-4 £2,500**

Donna's Double *D Eddy*   61
9 ch g Weldnaas (USA) - Shadha
5^{9gs} 6^{9g} 3^{9gf} 4^{7g} 3^{12gf} 4^{9gs} 6^{8s} 2^{9gs}
16^{10gf} 2^{12gf} 8^{12gf} **0-4-11 £5,898**

Dont Call Me Babe *R Rowe*   13
2 b g Easycall - Ok Babe
13^{7s} **0-0-1**

Dont Call Me Derek *S C Williams*   84 a88
3 b g Sri Pekan (USA) - Cultural Role
5^{5sd} 6^{5sd} 8^{6sd} 7^{9gf} 7^{2gf} 8^{2hy} 1^{8sd} 3^{8s}
2^{8gf} 1^{12g} 1^{12sd} 1^{12gs} **4-3-12 £19,078**

Dont Let Go *Miss B Sanders*
3 b f Danzero (Aus) - Il Doria (Ire)
14^{8gs} 8^{7gf} **0-0-2**

Dont Tell Simon *M E Sowersby*   6
3 ch g Keen - Circumnavigate
10^{9g} 7^{10f} 11^{8gs} **0-0-3**

Dont Worry Bout Me (Ire) *T G Mills*   a21
7 b g Brief Truce (USA) - Coggle
8^{12sd} **0-0-1**

Donyana *M A Jarvis*   87
2 b f Mark Of Esteem (Ire) - Albarsha
5^{7gs} 1^{7g} 4^{8gf} **1-0-3 £11,793**

Doohulla (USA) *G A Butler*   95
3 ch f Stravinsky (USA) - Viva Zapata (USA)
5^{6gf} 7^{6g} **0-0-2**

Dooie Dancer *H R A Cecil*   60
2 b c Entrepreneur - Vayavaig
7^{8s} **0-0-1**

Dora Corbino *R Hollinshead*   47 a45
4 b f Superpower - Smartie Lee
5⁹ˢᵈ 3¹¹ˢʷ 2¹²ˢʷ 9¹²ˢˢ 6¹²ˢᵈ 3¹⁵ᵍ 2¹²ᵍ
4¹²ʰʸ 2¹⁴ˢᵈ 3¹²ᵍᶠ 4¹⁸ᵍᶠ 7¹⁴ˢᵈ **0-5-12 £2,215**

Dorchester *W J Musson*   81 a67
7 b g Primo Dominie - Penthouse Lady
6⁷ˢʷ 5⁶ᵍˢ 7⁶ᵍˢ **0-0-3**

Doringo *J L Spearing*   54
3 b c Prince Sabo - Mistral's Dancer
8⁷ᵍˢ 12¹⁰ᵍ 11¹⁰ᵍᶠ 8⁸ᵍ 2⁸ˢ **0-1-5 £962**

Doris Souter (Ire) *R Hannon*   74 a78
4 b/br f Desert Story (Ire) - Hope And Glory (USA)
2¹⁰ˢᵈ 9¹⁰ˢᵈ 5¹²ˢᵈ 9¹²ᵍ 3¹⁰ᵍᶠ 10¹⁰ᵍᶠ 3¹⁰ᵍᶠ
2¹⁰ᵍᶠ **0-3-8 £4,650**

Dorisima (Fr) *M W Easterby*   39
3 ch f Mark Of Esteem (Ire) - Suhaad
8⁶ᵍᶠ 9¹⁰ᵍ **0-0-2**

Dormy Two (Ire) *J S Wainwright*   49
4 b f Eagle Eyed (USA) - Tartan Lady (Ire)
13¹⁰ᵍˢ 3¹⁶ᵍ 6¹⁶ᵍᶠ **0-1-3 £418**

Dorn Dancer (Ire) *D W Barker*   79
2 b f Danehill Dancer (Ire) - Appledorn
9⁶ᶠ 13⁹ᵍᶠ 5⁵ᵍᶠ 8⁵ᵍ 21⁷ᵍ 6⁶ˢ 15⁷ᵍ 9⁶ˢ
1-0-8 £5,343

Dorn Hill *Mrs Mary Hambro*   32
2 b f Lujain (USA) - Benedicite
5⁵ᵍᶠ 13⁵ᵍᶠ **0-0-2**

Dorothy's Friend *R Charlton*   100
4 b g Grand Lodge (USA) - Isle Of Flame
10¹⁶ᵍ 1¹⁵ᵍᶠ 1¹⁶ᵍ 8¹⁴ᵍ 1¹¹⁶ᵍ 10¹⁴ˢ **3-0-6 £65,710**

Dorset (USA) *A M Balding*   26
3 b f Deputy Commander (USA) - Draconienne (USA)
16⁸ᵍ 14¹⁰ᵍᶠ 6¹²ᵍᶠ **0-0-3**

Dorubako (Ire) *Hideyuki Mori*   103
3 b c Danzig (USA) - Spring Pitch (USA)
2⁶ᶠ 2⁶ᶠ 1⁶ᶠ 2⁶ᶠ 2⁶ᶠ 1⁶ᶠ 4⁵ᵍ 18⁷ᵍˢ **2-0-8 £127,587**

Double Aspect (Ire) *Sir Michael Stoute*   94
3 b g Dr Fong (USA) - Spring
4¹⁰ᵍ 1¹⁰ᵍ 5¹⁰ᵍ 4¹²ᵍˢ **1-0-4 £7,618**

Double Blade *N Wilson*   36
9 b g Kris - Sesame
6¹¹ᶠ 8¹⁶ᵍᶠ **0-0-2**

Double Dagger Lady (USA) *J Noseda*   66 a62
3 b f Diesis - Darby Jane (Can)
6¹⁰ᵍᶠ 4¹⁰ᵍᶠ 5⁸ᵍᶠ 6⁷ˢ 3¹⁶ᵍᶠ **0-1-5 £877**

Double Deputy (Ire) *Saeed Bin Suroor*   88
3 b c Sadler's Wells (USA) - Janaat
1¹⁰ᵍ 1¹⁰ˢ **2-0-2 £13,795**

Double Honour (Fr) *P J Hobbs*   90
6 gr g Highest Honor (Fr) - Silver Cobra (USA)
8²²ᶠ **0-0-1**

Double Kudos (Fr) *J G Given*   75
2 gr c Highest Honor (Fr) - Black Tulip (Fr)
2⁷ᵍᶠ 7⁷ᵍ 7⁹ᶠ **0-1-3 £846**

Double M *Mrs L Richards*   74 a68
7 ch g First Trump - Girton Degree
4⁷ˢᵈ 1⁵ˢᵈ 3⁶ˢᵈ 7⁷ˢᵈ 2⁶ˢᵈ 4⁷ˢᵈ 2⁶ˢᵈ 1⁶ˢᵈ
11⁶ˢᵈ 6⁵ᵍˢ 5⁵ᵍᶠ 5⁵ᵍᶠ 3⁶ᵍ 2⁵ᵍᶠ 1⁶ᵍ 3⁵ᵍᶠ 6⁵ᵍ 6⁶ˢᵈ 7⁵ᵍ
4-8-25 £27,814

Double Obsession *Miss Venetia Williams*   108
4 b c Sadler's Wells (USA) - Obsessive (USA)
13¹²ᵍˢ 7¹²ᶠ 1¹⁶ᵍ 1²⁰ᵍᶠ 5¹⁶ᵍ 4¹⁶ᵍᶠ 2¹⁶ᵍ

4¹⁵ᵛˢ 1-1-8 £42,893

Double Ransom *Mrs L Stubbs*   72 a63
5 b g Bahamian Bounty - Secrets Of Honour
2⁸ˢᵈ 3¹⁰ˢᵈ 1⁸ˢᵈ 4⁸ᵈ 2¹⁰ʰʸ 1⁸ᵍ 6¹⁰ᵍ 2⁹ᵍˢ
1⁸ᵍ 6⁹ᵍˢ 5¹⁰ˢ **3-4-11 £14,643**

Double Spey *Miss Kate Milligan*   41
5 b g Atraf - Yankee Special
6¹¹ᵍˢ **0-0-1**

Double Turn *W M Brisbourne*   67
4 ch g Double Trigger (Ire) - Its My Turn
5¹²ᵍᶠ 10¹²ᵍˢ 6¹¹ᵍᶠ **0-0-3**

Double Vodka (Ire) *Mrs J R Ramsden*   81
3 b/br g Russian Revival (USA) - Silius
12⁸ˢ 6⁸ᵍᶠ 2⁸ᵍᶠ 4⁸ˢ 7¹¹ˢ 1⁸ˢ 1¹⁰ᵍᶠ 1⁸ᵍˢ
11¹⁰ᵍᶠ 3⁸ᵍᶠ 11¹⁰ˢ **3-1-11 £26,417**

Doughty *D J Wintle*   29
2 b g Bold Edge - Marquante (Ire)
9⁵ᵍᶠ 10⁶ᶠ 19⁶ᵍᶠ 11⁶ᵍᶠ **0-0-4**

Dove Cottage (Ire) *W S Kittow*   67
2 b c Great Commotion (USA) - Pooka
6⁵ᵍᶠ 5⁵ᵍᶠ 3⁵ᶠ 16ᵍᶠ 2⁷ˢ 5⁷ᶠ 4⁸ᵍ **1-2-7 £8,932**

Dovedale *Mrs Mary Hambro*   66 a46
4 b f Groom Dancer (USA) - Peetsie (Ire)
7⁸ʰʸ 4¹⁰ᵍˢ 5⁹ˢᵈ **0-0-3 £283**

Dovedon Hero *P J McBride*   84 a81
4 ch g Millkom - Hot Topic (Ire)
17¹²ᵍ 11¹²ᵍ 2¹²ᵍᶠ 8¹²ᵍ 4¹⁴ᵍᶠ 6¹²ᵍᶠ 12¹²ᵍˢ
2¹⁵ᵍ 7¹⁶ᵍᶠ 3¹²ᵍ 4¹⁴ᵍᶠ 2¹²ˢᵈ 4¹⁴ˢᵈ 2¹²ˢᵈ **0-5-14 £10,238**

Dovedon Lass *P J McBride*
3 b f Abou Zouz - Violette Sabo
8¹⁰ᵍᶠ **0-0-1**

Dover Street *P W D'Arcy*   62
2 ch g Zafonic (USA) - Seeker
5⁶ᶠ 8⁶ᵍᶠ 10⁶ᵍˢ 9⁸ᵍ 4¹⁰ᵍᶠ 9⁸ᵍ **0-0-6 £430**

Dowager *R Hannon*   105
3 b f Groom Dancer (USA) - Rose Noble (USA)
5⁷ˢ 4⁶ᶠ 6⁶ᵍ 3⁶ᵍ 11⁷ᵍᶠ 7⁶ᵍˢ 8⁶ᵍˢ 10⁶ᵍ
1⁶ᵍ 10⁶ˢ **1-1-10 £15,519**

Dower House *Andrew Turnell*   61 a88
9 ch g Groom Dancer (USA) - Rose Noble (USA)
4¹⁰ˢᵈ 6¹⁰ˢᵈ 5¹¹ˢˢ 10¹⁰ˢᵈ 10¹⁰ˢᵈ 5⁸ˢᵈ 16¹⁰ᵍ
12¹¹ʰʸ 10¹⁰ˢ **0-0-9 £2,039**

Down To The Woods (USA) *R D E Woodhouse*   a45
6 ch g Woodman (USA) - Riviera Wonder (USA)
9⁹ˢᵈ 14¹⁴ˢ 8¹⁰ˢᵈ **0-0-3**

Downland (Ire) *N Tinkler*   67 a81
8 b g Common Grounds - Boldabsa
8⁶ʰʸ 2⁶ˢ 1²ᵍ 6⁶ᵍᶠ 5⁷ᶠ 1⁸ˢᵈ 1⁷ˢᵈ 3⁸ˢᵈ
13⁷ᶠ 2⁷ˢᵈ 6⁷ᵍᶠ 5⁷ˢ 17⁷ᵍ **3-3-13 £12,517**

Doyen (Ire) *Saeed Bin Suroor*   131
4 b c Sadler's Wells (USA) - Moon Cactus
2¹²ᵍ 1¹²ᶠ 1¹²ᵍᶠ 7¹⁰ᵍᶠ 7¹⁰ˢ **2-1-5 £571,200**

Dr Cerullo *C Tinkler*   82 a75
3 b g Dr Fong (USA) - Precocious Miss (USA)
3¹⁰ˢᵈ 3¹⁰ˢᵈ 10¹⁰ᵍ 2¹²ᵍ 4¹²ᵍ 4¹³ᵍˢ 3¹²ᵍ
8¹⁶ˢ **0-3-8 £5,063**

Dr Cool *J Akehurst*   40
7 b g Ezzoud (Ire) - Vayavaig
14¹²ᵍᶠ 15¹²ˢ 7¹⁴ᵍˢ 9¹⁴ᶠ 20¹⁴ᵍ **0-0-5**

Dr Fox (Ire) *K A Morgan*   33 a35
3 b g Foxhound (USA) - Eleonora D'Arborea
11⁷ˢᵈ 11⁸ᵍ 7⁵ʰʸ 7⁶ᵍᶠ 16⁷ᵍ 13⁷ᵍ **0-0-6**

Dr Julian (Ire) *Michael Hourigan* 53 a35
4 b g Sesaro (USA) - Toda
12⁸ˢᵈ 5¹⁴ˢᵈ 8¹⁴ˢᵈ 9¹²ˢᵈ 6¹⁶ᵍ 4¹⁴ᵍʸ **0-0-6**
£461

Dr Raj *B A McMahon*
5 ch g In The Wings - Tawaaded (Ire)
9¹¹ˢᵈ 11⁹ˢˢ **0-0-2**

Dr Sharp (Ire) *T P Tate* 92
4 ch g Dr Devious (Ire) - Stoned Imaculate (Ire)
8¹⁶ᵍˢ 1¹⁶ʰʸ 2¹⁵ᵍ 1¹⁴ᵍ 9¹⁶ᵍ 6¹⁴ᵍ 1¹⁶ˢ 14¹⁴ᵍ
4¹⁶ˢ 2¹⁷ˢ **3-2-10 £23,676**

Dr Synn *J Akehurst* 76
3 br c Danzero (Aus) - Our Shirley
8⁷ᵍˢ 6⁶ˢ 3⁸ᵍ 6⁷ᵍᶠ 5⁶ᵍ 9⁷ᵍ 2⁶ˢ 8⁷ᵍˢ 3⁷ˢ
4⁶ᵍᶠ 18⁶ˢ 1⁶ᵍˢ 17⁷ˢ **1-4-13 £6,968**

Dr Thong *P F I Cole* 87
3 ch c Dr Fong (USA) - Always On My Mind
4⁸ᵍ 1⁷ᵍˢ 2⁷ᵍᶠ 4⁷ᵍᶠ 1⁸ᵍ 11⁷ᵍˢ 4⁷ᵍᶠ 2⁸ᵍˢ
7⁸ᵍᶠ 5⁷ᵍ **2-2-10 £20,781**

Dr Zalo *P J Makin* 79
2 ch g Dr Fong (USA) - Azola (Ire)
3⁶ᵍᶠ 5⁶ˢ **0-1-2 £852**

Dragon Flyer (Ire) *M Quinn* 103 a88
5 b m Tagula - Noble Rocket
4⁵ˢᵈ 2⁵ʸ 7⁵ᵍ 8⁵ᵍˢ 11⁵ᵍ 11⁵ᵍᶠ 3⁵ᵍ 4⁵ᵍᶠ
3⁵ᵍᶠ 11⁵ᵍᶠ 4⁵ᵍ 15ᵍᶠ 11⁵ˢ 7⁵ᵍ 3⁵ᵍ 9⁵ˢ **1-3-16**
£24,836

Dragon Prince *R C Guest* 25
4 b g Zamindar (USA) - Nawafell
10¹⁰ᵍᶠ 12⁷ᵍᶠ 14⁷ᵍᶠ **0-0-3**

Dragon Slayer (Ire) *P A Blockley* a68
2 ch c Night Shift (USA) - Arandora Star (USA)
3⁶ˢᵈ **0-1-1 £800**

Dralion *J M P Eustace* 60
2 ch c Dr Fong (USA) - Rosy Outlook (USA)
5⁶ᶠ 5⁵ᵍ 15⁶ᵍˢ **0-0-3**

Dramatic Quest *A G Juckes* 66
7 b g Zafonic (USA) - Ultra Finesse (USA)
7¹⁰ᵍᶠ 12¹²ᵍᶠ 10¹²ᵍ 11¹²ᵍ **0-0-4**

Dramatic Review (Ire) *P C Haslam* 63 a18
2 b g Indian Lodge (Ire) - Dramatic Shift (Ire)
10⁵ᵍˢ 5⁶ᵍˢ 7⁶ˢᵈ 6⁸ʰʸ 10⁸ᵍ **0-0-5**

Dramaticus *D R Loder* 103
2 b c Indian Ridge - Corinium (Ire)
3⁵ʰʸ 1⁶ʰʸ 7⁶ᵍ 8⁶ˢ **1-0-4 £4,296**

Drax *D R Loder* 73
2 b g Mark Of Esteem (Ire) - Tanasie
3⁷ᶠ 8⁷ᵍᶠ 12⁷ᵍᶠ 4⁷ᵍᶠ **0-2-4 £902**

Dream Alive *M Blanshard* 64
3 b g Unfuwain (USA) - Petite Sonnerie
8¹¹ᵍ 3⁸ᵍ 4¹⁰ˢ 14¹¹ᵍ **0-1-4 £940**

Dream Along *Mrs A J Perrett* 54
2 b c Sinndar (Ire) - Dream Quest
15⁸ᵍ UR⁸ˢ **0-0-2**

Dream Easy *P L Gilligan* 66 a64
3 b g Pyramus (USA) - Hush Baby (Ire)
8⁸ˢᵈ 5⁸ᵍᶠ 4⁷ᵍ 5⁸ᵍˢ 3⁹ᵍ 16¹⁰ᵍ 17⁸ˢ **0-1-7**
£866

Dream Falcon *R J Hodges*
4 b g Polar Falcon (USA) - Pip's Dream
16¹¹ˢ **0-0-1**

Dream Magic *M J Ryan* 85
6 b g Magic Ring (Ire) - Pip's Dream
4¹⁰ᵍ 8¹¹ˢ 5¹⁰ᵍ 13¹⁰ᵍᶠ 12¹⁰ᵍᶠ 3¹⁰ᵍ 2¹⁰ᵍ
3¹⁰ˢ 3¹⁰ᵍ 3¹⁰ᵍ 14¹¹ʰʸ 10¹⁰ᵍᶠ 9¹⁰ˢ **0-6-13**

£8,421

Dream Of Dubai (Ire) *P Mitchell* 53 a34
3 b f Vettori (Ire) - Immortelle
8⁷ˢᵈ 16⁷ᵍᶠ 8¹⁰ᵍᶠ 12⁸ᵍ 10⁷ˢᵈ 12¹⁰ˢᵈ 15⁷ʰʸ
0-0-7

Dream Scene (Ire) *J H M Gosden* 70
3 b f Sadler's Wells (USA) - Highest Accolade
3⁹ᵍᶠ **0-1-1 £546**

Dream Tonic *M R Channon* 82
2 b c Zafonic (USA) - Dream On Deya (Ire)
6⁶ᵍᶠ 9⁸ʰʸ 1⁸ᵍˢ **1-0-3 £5,486**

Dream Valley (Ire) *B W Hills* 63 a43
3 b f Sadler's Wells (USA) - Vallee Des Reves (USA)
6¹⁰ᵍˢ 6¹²ˢᵈ 5¹²ᵍᶠ **0-0-3**

Dreamer's Lass *J M Bradley* 52
2 b f Pyramus (USA) - Qualitair Dream
2⁵ᵍᶠ 9⁵ᵍᶠ 6⁶ᵍ 9⁶ᵍ 12⁶ᵍ **0-1-5 £1,263**

Dreaming Of You (Ire) *Sir Michael Stoute* 75
3 b f Spectrum (Ire) - Gay Hellene
1⁸ˢ 15⁸ᵍᶠ 7¹⁰ᵍᶠ **1-0-3 £4,127**

Dreaming Waters *R F Johnson Houghton* 54 a36
3 ch f Groom Dancer (USA) - Faraway Waters
14¹⁰ˢᵈ 12⁸ᵍᶠ 5⁶ᵍᶠ **0-0-3**

Dreams Forgotten (Ire) *P R Hedger* 57
4 b f Victory Note (USA) - Sevens Are Wild
4¹⁰ᵍᶠ 11¹⁰ᵍᶠ 17⁸ᵍ 16¹²ᵍᶠ **0-0-4 £431**

Dreams United *A G Newcombe* a1
3 br f Dancing Spree (USA) - Kaliala (Fr)
11⁸ˢᵈ **0-0-1**

Dreemon *B R Millman* 72 a53
2 ch g Tipsy Creek (USA) - Prudence
7⁶ᵍᶠ 3⁷ᵍᶠ 8⁷ᵍ 9⁷ˢᵈ 10⁸ᶠ 9⁷ᵍᶠ **0-1-6 £654**

Dress Pearl *R P Elliott* a30
3 b f Atraf - Dress Design (Ire)
7⁵ˢᵈ 3⁶ˢᵈ 2⁶ˢᵈ **0-1-3 £615**

Drizzle *Ian Williams* a34
3 ch g Hector Protector (USA) - Rainy Sky
12⁸ˢᵈ **0-0-1**

Droopys Joel *R P Elliott* 7
2 b g Primo Dominie - Zaima (Ire)
9⁵ˢᵈ 10⁵ˢ 5⁸ᵍᶠ **0-0-3**

Druid *P C Haslam* a39
3 b g Magic Ring (Ire) - Country Spirit
9⁸ˢᵈ 6⁷ˢᵈ **0-0-2**

Drum Dance (Ire) *R F Johnson Houghton* 84
2 b c Namid - Socialite (Ire)
2⁵ᵍᶠ 2⁵ᵍᶠ 4⁶ˢ 14⁶ˢ **0-2-4 £3,191**

Drury Lane (Ire) *D W Chapman* 59 a33
4 b/br g Royal Applause - Ghost Tree (Ire)
10⁷ˢᵈ 9⁶ˢˢ 11⁷ˢˢ 18⁶ˢ 15⁶ᶠ 4⁶ᵍᶠ 11⁷ᶠ
14⁶ᵍ 4⁶ᵍ 14⁶ᵍᶠ 11⁶ᵍᶠ 8⁶ᵍ 19⁶ᵍ **0-1-13 £293**

Dry Ice (Ire) *H Candy* 82
2 b g Desert Sun - Snowspin
5⁶ᵍᶠ 1⁷ᵍˢ 5⁷ᵍˢ 6⁷ᶠ 8⁷ˢ **1-0-5 £3,851**

Dry Wit (Ire) *R M Beckett* 54
3 b f Desert Prince (Ire) - Nawasib (Ire)
9⁷ᵍᶠ 6⁸ᵍˢ 11¹⁰ᵍᶠ 10¹⁰ᵍᶠ 6⁸ᶠ **0-0-5**

Du Pre *Mrs A J Perrett* 80
3 b f Singspiel (Ire) - Child Prodigy (Ire)
7⁷ᵍ 2⁸ᵍᶠ 1⁸ᵍᶠ 3¹⁰ᵍᶠ 10¹⁰ᵍ **1-2-5 £6,390**

Dual Purpose (Ire) *C Roberts* 67 a30
9 b g Rainbows For Life (Can) - Gracieuse Amie (Fr)
9¹¹ᵍᶠ 6¹⁴ᶠ 4⁷ᵍˢ 9⁸ˢ 12¹⁰ᵍ 8⁹ˢᵈ **0-0-6**
£268

Dubai Dreamer (USA) *Saeed Bin Suroor*　　a80
2 gr c Stephen Got Even (USA) - Blacktie Bid (USA)
2⁷ˢᵈ **0-1-1 £1,580**

Dubai Dreams *S R Bowring*　　45 a62
4 b g Marju (Ire) - Arndilly
4¹²ˢᵈ 2⁸ˢᵈ 5⁹ˢˢ 8¹¹ˢᵈ 7¹²ᵍᶠ 10⁸ᵍᶠ 6⁸ˢʷ
7¹⁰ᶠ 6⁷ˢᵈ 2⁷ˢᵈ **0-2-10 £1,255**

Dubai Escapade (USA) *Saeed Bin Suroor*　　54
2 b f Awesome Again (Can) - Sassy Pants (USA)
5⁵ᵍᶠ **0-0-1**

Dubai Lightning (USA) *J G M O'Shea*　　25
4 br g Seeking The Gold (USA) - Heraklia (USA)
6⁹ᵍˢ **0-0-1**

Dubai Seven Stars *M C Pipe*　　79
6 ch m Suave Dancer (USA) - Her Honour
14¹⁸ˢ **0-0-1**

Dubai Success *B W Hills*　　117
4 b c Sadler's Wells (USA) - Crystal Spray
1¹²ᵍ 4¹²ᵍ 8¹²ᵍ 2¹⁴ᵍ 2¹³ᵍ 4¹⁴ᵍ 8¹²ˢ **1-1-7**
£73,464

Dubai Surprise (Ire) *D R Loder*　　107
2 b f King's Best (USA) - Toujours Irish (USA)
3⁷ᵍ 1⁷ᵍᶠ 1⁷ᵍˢ 8⁸ᵍᶠ 2⁸ᵛˢ **2-2-5 £68,953**

Dubai Venture *Sir Michael Stoute*　　77
2 ch c Rainbow Quest (USA) - Bombazine (Ire)
6⁷ᵍᶠ **0-0-1**

Dubaian Gift *A M Balding*　　97
5 b g Bahamian Bounty - Hot Lavender (Can)
10⁵ᵍ 12⁵ᵍ 7⁵ᵍᶠ 8⁵ᵍ 19⁵ᵍᶠ **0-0-5**

Dubaian Mist *A M Balding*　　59 a38
3 b f Docksider (USA) - Robellino Miss (USA)
12⁷ˢᵈ 5⁶ᵍᶠ 2⁷ᶠ **0-1-3 £869**

Dubawi (Ire) *Saeed Bin Suroor*　　122
2 b c Dubai Millennium - Zomaradah
1⁶ᵍᶠ 1⁷ᵍˢ 1⁷ᵛ **3-0-3 £152,962**

Dubois *Saeed Bin Suroor*　　96
3 b c Sadler's Wells (USA) - Dazzle
1⁸ᵍ 10¹⁰ᵍˢ 1⁸ᵍ 12⁸ᵍ **2-0-4 £11,076**

Dubonai (Ire) *Andrew Turnell*　　53 a59
4 ch g Peintre Celebre (USA) - Web Of Intrigue
11¹²ʰʸ 8¹²ᵍᶠ 3⁸ᵍᶠ 9⁸ᶠ 9⁸ˢᵈ 1⁸ˢʷ 9⁷ᵍ 4⁹ˢᵈ
1-1-8 £3,733

Dubrovsky *J R Fanshawe*　　91
4 ch g Hector Protector (USA) - Reuval
4⁸ᵍˢ 8⁸ᵍ 6⁸ᵍᶠ 7¹⁰ᵍˢ **0-1-4 £1,085**

Duc's Dream *D Morris*　　61 a56
6 b g Bay Tern (USA) - Kala's Image
7¹²ˢᵈ 7¹⁴ᵍ 1¹¹ᶠ 8¹³ᵍᶠ 9¹²ᵍᶠ 5¹¹ᵍ 10¹²ᵍᶠ
3¹¹ᵍˢ 3¹²ᵍˢ 5¹²ᵍᶠ 10¹²ˢᵈ **1-2-11 £5,375**

Ducal Diva *J R Weymes*　　61 a46
2 b f Bahamian Bounty - Lucky Thing
7⁶ᵍˢ 2⁵ᵍᶠ 6⁵ˢᵈ 7⁵ᵍᶠ 7⁵ᵍᶠ 4⁵ˢᵈ 8⁵ˢᵈ **0-1-7**
£1,339

Duck Row (USA) *J A R Toller*　　114
9 ch g Diesis - Sunny Moment (USA)
2⁸ᵍˢ 9⁹ᵍ 5⁸ᵍᶠ 10⁷ᵍ 6¹⁰ᵍˢ 4⁸ʰʸ **0-1-6**
£8,392

Dudley Docker (Ire) *M H Tompkins*　　43
2 b g Victory Note (USA) - Nordic Abu (Ire)
15⁷ᵍᶠ **0-0-1**

Due Diligence (Ire) *John G Carr*　　2
5 ch g Entrepreneur - Kerry Project (Ire)
12⁷ᵍ 14⁷ᵍᶠ **0-0-2**

Due To Me *G L Moore*　　47 a47
4 gr f Compton Place - Always Lucky

5⁷ˢᵈ 2⁸ˢᵈ 5⁸ˢᵈ 1⁸ˢᵈ 4⁷ʰʸ 6¹⁰ˢᵈ 3⁷ᶠ 4⁷ᶠ
7⁷ᵍᶠ 8⁸ᵍˢ 7¹⁰ᵍᶠ **1-2-11 £2,225**

Duelling Banjos *J Akehurst*　　72 a47
5 ch g Most Welcome - Khadino
8⁸ˢᵈ 4⁸ᵍ 11⁸ᶠ 11⁸ᵍᶠ 7⁸ᵍᶠ 1¹⁰ᵍ 7¹⁰ᵍ **1-1-7**
£5,410

Duggan's Dilemma (Ire) *Ian Emmerson*
3 b g Lake Coniston (Ire) - Miss Ironwood
8¹¹ˢᵈ 6⁵ˢʷ **0-0-2**

Duke Of Modena *G B Balding*　　69
7 ch g Salse (USA) - Palace Street (USA)
9⁸ˢ 13⁸ˢ **0-0-2**

Duke Of Venice (USA) *Saeed Bin Suroor*　　108
3 b c Theatrical - Rihan (USA)
1⁸ᵍˢ 2¹⁰ᵍᶠ 1¹⁶ᶠ 5¹²ᵍ 10¹⁶ᵍ **2-1-5**
£51,801

Duke's View (Ire) *Mrs A J Perrett*　　67
3 b g Sadler's Wells (USA) - Igreja (Arg)
10¹³ˢ 13¹²ᵍˢ 5¹⁰ᶠ 5¹⁰ᵍ 18¹²ᵍᶠ 6¹²ᶠ 10¹⁰ˢ
6¹¹ᵍ 12¹²ᶠ **0-0-9**

Dulce De Leche *S C Williams*　　a57
3 b g Cayman Kai (Ire) - Give Us A Treat
7⁵ˢᵈ 6⁷ˢᵈ 4⁶ˢˢ 12⁷ˢᵈ 10⁶ˢˢ 7⁷ᵍˢ **0-0-6**

Dulcimer *G B Balding*　　45
3 ch f Piccolo - Superspring
13⁷ᵍ 10⁶ˢ 12⁷ᵍᶠ 11⁷ᵍᶠ **0-0-4**

Dumaran (Ire) *W J Musson*　　101 a96
6 b g Be My Chief (USA) - Pine Needle
9¹⁰ˢᵈ 14⁸ᵍ 2¹⁰ᵍˢ 3¹⁰ᵍˢ 5⁹ᵍ 9⁸ˢ 6¹⁰ᵍˢ RR⁹ᵍ
0-2-8 £13,812

Dumfries *J H M Gosden*　　82
3 ch g Selkirk (USA) - Pat Or Else
5¹²ᵍ 3¹²ᵍˢ 6¹²ᵍ 5¹⁰ᵍᶠ **0-1-4 £2,363**

Dumnoni *Julian Poulton*　　88 a76
3 b f Titus Livius (Fr) - Lamees (USA)
10⁷ˢᵈ 6⁷ᵍˢ 3⁸ᵍˢ 11⁹ᵍᶠ 4⁷ᵍᶠ 1⁷ᵍᶠ 3⁷ᵍ 2⁷ᵍᶠ
2⁸ᵍˢ 9⁷ᵍ **1-4-10 £15,776**

Dunaskin (Ire) *D Eddy*　　105
4 b g Bahhare (USA) - Mirwara (Ire)
15⁸ᵍ 8¹⁰ᵍˢ 7¹²ᵍˢ 5¹⁰ᵍᶠ 6¹²ᵍˢ 3¹²ˢ 1¹⁰ᵍ
1¹¹ᵍ 1¹⁰ˢ 11⁸ᵍ **3-1-10 £65,005**

Duncanbil (Ire) *R F Fisher*　　45 a9
3 b f Turtle Island (Ire) - Saintly Guest
11⁷ˢᵈ 15⁷ˢᵈ 2¹⁴ᵍᶠ PU¹⁶ᵍˢ **0-1-4 £826**

Dundonald *M Appleby*　　36 a55
5 ch g Magic Ring (Ire) - Cal Norma's Lady (Ire)
6⁹ˢˢ 8¹²ˢʷ 8⁸ˢʷ 3⁸ˢʷ 4⁸ˢʷ 7⁹ˢˢ 6⁸ˢˢ 5¹²ᵍˢ
8¹¹ᵍᶠ 3⁸ˢᵈ 3⁷ᵍˢ 3⁹ˢᵈ 9¹¹ˢᵈ 6⁸ᵍ **0-2-14 £829**

Dundry *G L Moore*　　81 a82
3 b g Bin Ajwaad (Ire) - China's Pearl
3¹⁰ᵍ 3¹⁰ᵍᶠ 2¹⁰ᵍˢ 2¹¹ᵍˢ 1¹²ˢᵈ 12¹²ᵍᶠ **1-4-6**
£6,828

Dune Raider (USA) *K A Ryan*　　89
3 b c Kingmambo (USA) - Glowing Honor (USA)
7¹⁰ᵍ 11¹⁰ᵍ 1¹²ᵍᶠ 6¹²ᵍ 21¹²ˢ **1-0-5**
£3,532

Dunedin Rascal *E A Wheeler*　　a42
7 b g Piccolo - Thorner Lane
15⁷ˢᵈ 8⁶ˢᵈ 10⁷ˢᵈ 11⁶ˢᵈ **0-0-4**

Dunhill Star (Ire) *B W Hills*　　106
4 b c Danehill (USA) - Sueboog (Ire)
2¹²ᵍ **0-1-1 £4,807**

Dunlea (Ire) *M J Gingell*　　25
8 b g Common Grounds - No Distractions
11¹³ᵍᶠ 16⁷ᵍ **0-0-2**

Dunlea Dancer *M Johnston* 70
3 b g Groom Dancer (USA) - Be My Lass (Ire)
3¹⁰gs 14¹²gf 2¹³g 1¹²gs 6¹⁴g **1-2-5 £5,956**

Dunlows Minstrel *Miss D Mountain* 14
2 ch c Opening Verse (USA) - Mary From Dunlow
10⁸gf **0-0-1**

Dunmaglass (USA) *P F I Cole* 67
2 ch g Cat Thief (USA) - Indian Fashion (USA)
10⁷gf 7⁷g **0-0-2**

Dunmidoe *C Drew* 20
4 b f Case Law - Rion River (Ire)
8⁸g 8⁷sd **0-0-2**

Dunn Deal (Ire) *W M Brisbourne* 69 a69
4 b g Revoque (Ire) - Buddy And Soda (Ire)
3⁵ss 10⁶sd 1⁵gs 2⁵ss 7⁵g 5⁵gf 14⁵gf 6⁵g
6⁵gs 5⁵gf **1-2-10 £5,634**

Duo Leoni *Mrs Stef Liddiard* a68
4 ch f Vettori (Ire) - La Dolce Vita
6⁷sd 1⁷ss **1-0-2 £4,036**

Duroob *E A L Dunlop* 72 a65
2 b c Bahhare (USA) - Amaniy (USA)
8⁶sd 3⁶gs 3⁷hy 1⁸gs **1-2-4 £4,224**

Dusk Dancer (Fr) *B J Meehan* a60
4 b g Groom Dancer (USA) - Nightitude
4⁷sd 12¹⁰sd 11⁸sw **0-0-3 £273**

Dusky Warbler *M L W Bell* 106
5 br g Ezzoud (Ire) - Bronzewing
2¹⁴g 2¹⁶s 8¹⁶g 12²⁰gf 5¹⁶s **0-2-5
£19,185**

Dustini (Ire) *W G M Turner* 55 a19
2 ch c Rossini (USA) - Truly Modest (Ire)
3⁵gs 5⁵gf 3⁵s 10⁶gf 7⁵sd **0-1-5 £1,331**

Dusty Carpet *M J Weeden* 31 a77
6 ch g Pivotal - Euridice (Ire)
13¹²sd 12¹²sd 7¹²sd 11¹⁶sd 18¹⁰s 12¹⁰gf
11⁸s **0-0-7**

Dusty Dane (Ire) *W G M Turner* 68 a26
2 b g Indian Danehill (Ire) - Teer On Eer (Ire)
5⁵s 5⁶gf 5⁶g 3⁷gf 9⁷sd 6⁷s 4⁸g **0-1-7
£1,379**

Dusty Dazzler (Ire) *W G M Turner* 84 a88
4 ch f Titus Livius (Fr) - Satinette
1⁶sd 6⁵sd 12⁵g 5⁶gf **1-0-4 £7,613**

Dusty Wugg (Ire) *A Dickman* 44 a42
5 b m General Monash (USA) - Welsh Berry (USA)
5⁶sd 3⁶ss 7⁶sd 5⁷g 7⁶gs **0-1-5 £186**

Dutch Gold (USA) *C E Brittain* 112 a64
4 ch c Lahib (USA) - Crimson Conquest (USA)
9⁹ft 2¹²gf 9¹²gf 10¹²g 5¹⁴gs 2⁹g 5¹⁰gs 9⁸g
0-2-8 £31,923

Dutch Key Card (Ire) *G A Butler* 65 a75
3 b g Key Of Luck (USA) - Fanny Blankers (Ire)
9¹⁰ys 5⁷f 12⁸g 5⁸gy 8⁸g 7⁷gf 5⁵sf 1⁵sd
1-0-8 £3,435

Duxford *D K Ivory* 47 a63
3 ch g Young Ern - Marsara
8⁶gf 2⁸sd **0-1-2 £1,172**

Dvinsky (USA) *G A Butler* 73 a62
3 b c Stravinsky (USA) - Festive Season (USA)
10⁵g 14⁷gf 6⁷sd 4⁵sd **0-0-4**

E Bride (USA) *J G Given* 57
2 gr/ro f Runaway Groom (Can) - Fast Selection (USA)
5⁶gf 4⁶gf 4⁷s **0-0-3 £729**

E Minor (Ire) *T Wall* a57
5 b m Blushing Flame (USA) - Watch The Clock

5¹²sd 7¹²sd 6¹²ss 6¹⁶ss 7¹²sd **0-0-5**

Eachy Peachy (Ire) *J R Best* 24
5 ch m Perugino (USA) - Miss Big John (Ire)
5¹²f **0-0-1**

Eager Angel (Ire) *R F Marvin* 54 a60
6 b m Up And At 'Em - Seanee Squaw
2⁷sd 4⁸sd 9⁷sd 1⁷ss 5⁶sd 1⁷sd 10⁸sw 3⁷sd
9⁷gs 13⁷s 9⁷sd 11⁹sd **2-2-12 £6,190**

Eagle Feathers *T D Easterby* 27
3 b f Indian Ridge - Flying Squaw
7⁹g **0-0-1**

Earl Of Links (Ire) *R Hannon* 72
2 ch c Raise A Grand (Ire) - Metroella (Ire)
3⁵gs 1⁵hy 6⁶gf 24⁵g 4⁷s 6⁵s **1-0-6
£6,484**

Earlsfield Raider *G L Moore* a62
4 ch g Double Trigger (Ire) - Harlequin Walk (Ire)
1¹²ss 7¹²sd **1-0-2 £1,435**

Earlston *Miss Gay Kelleway* a46
4 ch g Fleetwood (Ire) - Mystique Smile
4⁷sd 7⁸ss PU⁷sw **0-0-3**

Early March *Mme C Head-Maarek* 117
2 br c Dansili - Emplane (USA)
1⁷vs 1⁷g 2⁷g 6⁸vs **2-1-4 £88,387**

Easibet Dot Net *I Semple* 76 a51
4 gr g Atraf - Silvery
4¹²sw 9¹²hy 2¹²gf 3¹⁰gf 9¹²gf 5¹⁰g 3¹¹gs
11²gs 3¹²s 4¹²gf 3¹⁰g 2¹²gs **1-4-12 £10,560**

Easily Averted (Ire) *P Butler* 44 a57
3 b g Averti (Ire) - Altishaan
5⁵sd 5⁵sd 9⁶sd 15⁵s 10⁵gf 6⁷gf
15⁸gf 7⁵hy **0-0-9**

East Cape *Don Enrico Incisa* 53 a52
7 b g Bering - Reine De Danse (USA)
5¹²sd 3¹¹sd 1¹⁴ss 8¹⁴ss 11¹⁴sd 11¹⁰hy
6¹²hy 3¹⁴g 5¹²gf 2¹²gf 4¹²s 7¹⁴f 9¹⁴gs 3¹⁰s
1-4-15 £3,939

East Flares *J W Unett* a41
4 gr g Environment Friend - Ijada Bianca
10⁹sd 11¹⁰sd **0-0-2**

East Riding *Miss A Stokell* 46 a4
4 b f Gothenberg (Ire) - Bettynouche
5⁷gf 6⁷g 3⁸hy 10¹⁰f 11¹⁰gf 8¹²gf
5¹³f 5⁹g 7⁹g 10⁶gf **0-1-11 £572**

Eastborough (Ire) *B G Powell* 69 a76
5 b g Woodborough (USA) - Easter Girl
14¹²sd 3¹⁰sd 1⁹sd 7¹⁰sd 3⁸sd 4⁸sw 3¹⁰gs
4¹⁰g 6⁸g 6¹²gf 2¹⁰gf 3¹¹gf 2¹⁰g 8¹²sd **1-7-14
£7,408**

Easter Ogil (Ire) *Jane Southcombe* 100 a93
9 ch g Pips Pride - Piney Pass
5¹⁰sd 9¹²sd 3¹⁰sd 3¹²sd 2¹³sd 4⁸sd 12¹⁰sd
9¹⁰sd 12¹⁰sd 11⁸sw 8¹⁰gs 2¹⁰gs 6¹⁰gs 5¹⁰s 11¹²gs
8¹⁰gs 5⁹gs 6⁹sd **0-4-18 £3,452**

Eastern Blue (Ire) *Mrs L Stubbs* a51
5 ch m Be My Guest (USA) - Stifen
6⁶ss 5⁶sd 3⁶sd **0-1-3 £435**

Eastern Breeze (Ire) *P W D'Arcy* 110 a108
6 b g Sri Pekan (USA) - Elegant Bloom (Ire)
4¹²sd 1¹⁰sd 2¹⁰sd 7¹⁰sd 5⁹g 13¹⁰g 1¹²g
PU¹²gf **2-2-8 £28,664**

Eastern Dagger *Miss L V Davis* 53
4 b g Kris - Shehana (USA)
14⁸s 10⁷sd 7¹⁰gf 6¹⁰s 16⁷gf **0-0-5**

Eastern Hope (Ire) *Mrs L Stubbs* 69

5 b g Danehill Dancer (Ire) - Hope And Glory (USA)
12¹⁰g 7⁷s 3⁸f 11⁸gs 9⁷g 3⁸s 16⁸g 1⁸s
7⁸s **1-2-9 £4,059**

Eastern Magenta (Ire) *Mrs L Stubbs* 36
4 b g Turtle Island (Ire) - Blue Heights (Ire)
14¹⁰g **0-0-1**

Eastern Mandarin *D Eddy* 60
2 b g Tipsy Creek (USA) - Hotel Street (USA)
5⁸hy 5⁸s **0-0-2**

Eastern Pearl *Mrs L Stubbs* 50 a51
3 ch f Wolfhound (USA) - Wild Humour (Ire)
10⁵s 8⁵s 10⁵sd **0-0-3**

Eastern Scarlet (Ire) *V Smith* 47 a47
4 b g Woodborough (USA) - Cuddles (Ire)
13⁶y 5⁸gy 11⁸gs 5⁷sd 4⁹sd **0-0-5**

Eastwell Magic *J G Given* 21 a29
2 b f Polish Precedent (USA) - Kinchenjunga
13⁷sd 13⁸g **0-0-2**

Eastwell Violet *Mrs A M Thorpe*
4 b f Danzig Connection (USA) - Kinchenjunga
10¹⁴sd **0-0-1**

Easy Feeling (Ire) *R Hannon* 83
2 b f Night Shift (USA) - Talena
3⁶gf 3⁵g 4⁵g 1⁶gf 5⁶gf 12⁷g **1-1-6**
£17,132

Easy Mover (Ire) *R Guest* 76
2 ch f Bluebird (USA) - Top Brex (Fr)
5⁶g 5⁶gf 1⁷f 2⁷g 9⁷gf 12⁸g **1-0-6**
£6,629

Eau Pure (Fr) *G L Moore* a39
7 b m Epervier Bleu - Eau De Nuit
4¹³sd **0-0-1**

Ebinzayd (Ire) *L Lungo* 75
8 b g Tenby - Sharakawa (USA)
9¹⁴f 7¹⁶s 5¹⁴s 5¹⁷s **0-0-4**

Eboracum (Ire) *T D Easterby* 82 a32
3 b f Alzao (USA) - Fire Of London
8⁷gf 9⁷sd 2⁸g 2¹⁰gs 11¹²gf 4¹⁰gf 1⁹gs 1⁸gs
1⁸s **3-2-9 £20,615**

Eboracum Lady (USA) *J D Bethell* 52 a46
4 b f Lure (USA) - Konvincha (USA)
6¹¹gf 5⁸sd 10¹⁰gf **0-0-3**

Eborarry (Ire) *T D Easterby* 52
2 b g Desert Sun - Aztec Princess
4⁷gs 10⁷gf 10⁷gs **0-0-3 £355**

Ebtikaar (Ire) *J L Dunlop* 74
2 b c Darshaan - Jawlaat (USA)
8⁷gf **0-0-1**

Eccentric *Andrew Reid* 62 a93
3 ch g Most Welcome - Sure Care
4⁸sd 1⁷sd 1⁷sd 11⁶gs 4⁶sd 2⁶sd 2⁷sd 13⁷gf
2⁷sd 6⁷sd **2-3-10 £12,093**

Eccentricity (USA) *H R A Cecil* 67
2 ch f Kingmambo (USA) - Shiva (Jpn)
6⁷f **0-0-1**

Echelon *Sir Michael Stoute* 104
2 b f Danehill (USA) - Exclusive
1⁶gs 7⁸gf **1-0-2 £4,891**

Echo Of Light *Saeed Bin Suroor* 74
2 b c Dubai Millennium - Spirit Of Tara (Ire)
4⁸s **0-0-1 £551**

Echoes In Eternity (Ire) *Saeed Bin Suroor* 104
4 b f Spinning World (USA) - Magnificient Style (USA)
4⁹g 4⁸gf 5¹⁰gf 1¹⁵g 11¹³g **1-0-5**
£70,246

Ecologically Right *Mrs J R Ramsden* 77
2 b f Entrepreneur - Logic
7⁶gs 6⁷gf 1⁶gf 6⁶s **1-0-4 £4,751**

Ecomium (Ire) *J Noseda* 114
3 b c Sadler's Wells (USA) - Encens
1¹⁰gs 2¹⁰ys **1-1-2 £12,870**

Eddies Jewel *J S Wainwright* 48
4 b g Presidium - Superstream
2¹⁰gf 5⁸g 4⁷gs 5¹²gf 11¹²gs 6¹⁰gs 4⁹f
0-1-7 £949

Eden Star (Ire) *D K Ivory* 24 a31
2 b f Soviet Star (USA) - Gold Prospector (Ire)
10⁵gf 18⁶gs 11⁶sd 11⁵f **0-0-4**

Edge Fund *B R Millman* 76
2 b c Bold Edge - Truly Madly Deeply
3⁵g 3⁵gs 3⁵gf 2⁶gf 3⁶g 22⁵g 3⁶gf 9⁵gf
0-4-8 £3,976

Edge Of Blue *R Hannon* 69
2 b c Bold Edge - Blue Goddess (Ire)
6⁶gf 3⁵gf 10⁵gs 5⁶g **0-0-4 £628**

Edge Of Italy *K Bell* 60 a61
2 ch f Bold Edge - Brera (Ire)
10⁵sd 6⁶g 6⁶sd **0-0-3**

Edged In Gold *P J Makin* 36
2 ch f Bold Edge - Piccante
6⁵gs 9⁵gs **0-0-2**

Edgehill (Ire) *C R Egerton* 71
3 b g Ali-Royal (Ire) - Elfin Queen (Ire)
4⁷s 2¹⁰gf 8¹⁰gf **0-1-3 £2,098**

Edith Bankes *W G M Turner* 44
2 ch f Woodborough (USA) - Mayday Kitty
10⁸g 7⁸g **0-0-2**

Edmo Yewkay (Ire) *T D Easterby* 50
4 b/br g Sri Pekan (USA) - Mannequin (Ire)
12¹⁴g 11¹⁴s **0-0-2**

Effective *A P Jarvis* 73 a69
4 ch g Bahamian Bounty - Efficacy
10⁶sd 3⁶sd 14⁷ss 5⁷ss 9⁷sd 1⁶sd 5⁶sd 2⁶gf
8⁶gf 1⁷gf 6⁶gf **2-2-11 £8,256**

Effie Gray *P R Johnson* a41
5 b m Sri Pekan (USA) - Rose Bouquet
12¹²sd 7⁸sw 4⁸sw **0-0-3**

Efidium *N Bycroft* 82
6 b g Presidium - Efipetite
2⁷gs 9⁸gs 4⁷g 2⁸f 3⁸f 1⁷gf 5⁷gf 3⁷g 5⁷g
4⁷gs 1⁸f 2⁸gf 9⁷gf 21⁷gf **2-4-14 £25,203**

Efimac *N Bycroft* 48
4 b f Presidium - Efipetite
11⁶gs 10⁷gf 7⁵g 4⁶gf 10⁵g 7⁷f 12⁸gs 3⁸f
0-1-8 £437

Efistorm *M G Quinlan* 55
3 b c Efisio - Abundance
1⁶ho 4⁶hy 8⁵vs 11⁵gf 10⁶s **1-0-5**
£12,253

Eforetta (Ger) *D J Wintle* 43 a24
2 ch f Dr Fong (USA) - Erminora (Ger)
8⁶gs 10⁶s 12⁷sd **0-0-3**

Efrhina (Ire) *Mrs Stef Liddiard* 70 a70
4 ch f Woodman (USA) - Eshq Albahr (USA)
10¹⁰gf 7¹⁰gf 3¹⁰gf 10¹²s 2¹⁰g 8¹⁰gs 10⁸sd
3¹⁰g 4¹²sd 3¹²sd 8⁹sd 6¹²sd 4¹²sd **0-4-13**
£3,676

Ego Trip *M W Easterby* 77
3 b c Deploy - Boulevard Rouge (USA)
8⁸s 1⁸gf 3¹⁰f 9¹²gf 4¹²f 1¹²g 2¹²g 1¹⁴s

6^{12gs} **3-2-9 £12,810**

Egyptian Lady *R P Elliott* — 64
2 ch f Bold Edge - Calypso Lady (Ire)
11^{7s} 8^{5g} 5^{7f} **0-0-3**

Ehab (Ire) *G L Moore* — a48
5 b g Cadeaux Genereux - Dernier Cri
6^{8sd} **0-0-1**

Ei Ei *M C Chapman* — 25
9 b g North Briton - Branitska
7^{12gf} **0-0-1**

Eidsfoss (Ire) *T T Clement* — 49
2 b g Danehill Dancer (Ire) - Alca Egeria (Ity)
5^{5f} 9^{6g} **0-0-2**

Eight (Ire) *J M P Eustace* — 48
8 ch g Thatching - Up To You
12^{12gf} 13^{10gf} 14^{14gf} 9^{12s} 13^{8s} **0-0-5**

Eight Ellington (Ire) *Miss Gay Kelleway* — 55 a45
3 b g Ali-Royal (Ire) - Where's Charlotte
11^{6gs} 4^{6gf} 6^{5gf} 7^{6gf} 18^{6gs} 6^{6sd} **0-1-6**
£302

Eight Woods (Ire) *T D Barron* — a62
6 ch g Woods Of Windsor (USA) - Cd Super Targeting (Ire)
3^{12sd} 4^{9ss} **0-0-2 £360**

Eijaaz (Ire) *G C Bravery* — 69 a63
3 b c Green Desert (USA) - Kismah
8^{7gf} 7^{7gf} 4^{8gf} 11^{8gs} 10^{12sd} **0-0-5 £421**

Eisteddfod *P F I Cole* — 112
3 ch g Cadeaux Genereux - Ffestiniog (Ire)
1^{5s} 3^{6g} 3^{7g} 1^{6gf} 1^{7gs} 1^{6s} **5-1-7**
£59,711

Eizawina Docklands *N P Littmoden* — 68
3 b g Zilzal (USA) - Sandrella (Ire)
22^{8g} 7^{8g} 12^{8gf} 12^{8g} 8^{8gf} 7^{10g} **0-0-6**

Ejay *Julian Poulton* — 49 a50
5 b/br m Emperor Jones (USA) - Lough Erne
9^{7sd} 6^{6ss} 9^{5ss} 10^{5sd} 15^{5g} 9^{5gs} 2^{5hy}
7^{6sd} **0-2-9 £899**

Ekaterina *W Storey* — 37
2 b f Merdon Melody - Hsian
9^{6f} 14^{7g} 6^{8s} **0-0-3**

El Chaparral (Ire) *D K Ivory* — 80 a57
4 b g Bigstone (Ire) - Low Line
7^{7gs} 6^{6s} 10^{5g} 12^{7gf} 2^{8g} 11^{7gf} 2^{10gf}
10^{8gs} 1^{10g} 11^{8gs} 9^{8gs} 9^{10sd} **1-2-12 £6,264**

El Coto *B A McMahon* — 110
4 b c Forzando - Thatcherella
17^{8g} 1^{8g} 5^{7g} 5^{8gs} 9^{7gf} 13^{8gf} 4^{7gs}
20^{7gf} 4^{8gf} 8^{8s} 9^{9g} **1-2-12 £33,200**

El Giza (USA) *J M Bradley* — a27
6 ch g Cozzene (USA) - Gazayil (USA)
7^{8sd} **0-0-1**

El Hamra (Ire) *M J Haynes* — 42 a37
6 gr g Royal Abjar (USA) - Cherlinoa (Fr)
5^{7ss} 9^{10gs} 14^{16gs} **0-0-3**

El Magnifico *P D Cundell* — 43 a45
3 b g Forzando - Princess Poquito
6^{8sd} 7^{10sd} 8^{11gf} 11^{12g} 8^{12sd} **0-0-5**

El Palmar *P A Blockley* — 73 a63
3 b g Case Law - Aybeegirl
3^{5s} 3^{5hy} 17^{6gf} 1^{7gf} 2^{6sd} 9^{7g} **1-2-6**
£4,887

El Pedro *N E Berry* — 40 a50
5 b g Piccolo - Standard Rose
4^{12sw} 3^{12sd} 4^{10sd} 7^{14sf} 2^{11sd} 4^{12gf} **0-2-6**
£652

El Potro *B A McMahon* — 38
2 b c Forzando - Gaelic Air
7^{5gs} 12^{6hy} **0-0-2**

El Rey Del Mambo (USA) *G A Butler* — a67
2 b c Kingmambo (USA) - Scarab Bracelet (USA)
3^{6sd} **0-1-1 £674**

El Rey Royale *M D Hammond* — 73
2 b g Royal Applause - Spanish Serenade
1^{6gf} 6^{6s} 15^{8g} **1-0-3 £4,430**

Ela D'Argent (Ire) *Miss K Marks* — a28
5 b m Ela-Mana-Mou - Petite-D-Argent
8^{12sd} **0-0-1**

Ela Figura *A W Carroll* — 53
4 ch f The West (USA) - Chili Bouchier (USA)
6^{5gf} 12^{6s} 8^{6f} 3^{5f} 6^{5gf} 8^{5gs} 13^{5gf}
14^{5g} 5^{5s} 3^{5gs} 12^{6s} **0-2-12 £969**

Ela Jay *M G Rimell* — a42
5 b m Double Eclipse (Ire) - Papirusa (Ire)
5^{16sd} **0-0-1**

Ela Paparouna *H Candy* — 77
3 b f Vettori (Ire) - Pretty Poppy
3^{6gs} 8^{7g} 6^{7g} 3^{7g} 2^{7gf} 3^{8gf} 3^{8s} **0-5-7**
£5,572

Ela Re *C R Dore* — a51
5 ch g Sabrehill (USA) - Lucia Tarditi (Fr)
4^{12sd} 7^{14sd} 4^{12sd} 4^{12sd} 6^{9sd} **0-1-5**

Election Seeker (Ire) *G L Moore* — 62
2 b g Intikhab (USA) - Scottish Eyes (USA)
8^{7gf} 14^{7s} 9^{8gs} 7^{7s} 15^{8g} **0-0-5**

Electras Dream (Ire) *Mrs C A Dunnett* — 54 a32
3 ch f Docksider (USA) - Elli Pyrrelli (Ire)
16^{7gf} 11^{10sd} 9^{10gf} 6^{7g} **0-0-4**

Electrique (Ire) *Mrs S J Smith* — 68 a65
4 b g Elmaamul (USA) - Majmu (USA)
8^{9gs} 18^{10gf} 11^{8sd} 9^{9sd} **0-0-5**

Elegant Gracie (Ire) *R Guest* — a64
4 ch f Desert Prince (Ire) - Elegant Fragrant (Ire)
2^{12sd} 6^{12sd} 2^{11ss} 4^{11sd} **0-2-4 £1,809**

Elgin Marbles *R Hannon* — 87 a77
2 b g Lujain (USA) - Bold Gem
1^{5g} 6^{6gs} 12^{7sd} 2^{6gf} 2^{6g} 5^{6s} 5^{6sd} **1-2-7**
£8,939

Elidore *B Palling* — 76 a69
4 b f Danetime (Ire) - Beveled Edge
13^{6gs} 5^{7gf} 14^{6g} 2^{8gs} 4^{8s} 5^{8gs} 6^{10g} 14^{9s}
5^{8hy} 4^{9sd} **0-1-10 £2,572**

Elisha (Ire) *D M Simcock* — 70
2 ch f Raise A Grand (Ire) - Social Butterfly (USA)
4^{5g} 5^{5gf} 1^{5g} 10^{5g} 6^{5g} 6^{7gf} 2^{6gf} 2^{6f}
1-2-8 £8,197

Elitista (Fr) *E J O'Neill* —
3 gr f Linamix (Fr) - Elacata (Ger)
12^{8s} **0-0-1**

Elizabeth's Choice *M A Jarvis* — 40
2 b f Unfuwain (USA) - Nur (USA)
8^{7gf} 106^{gf} **0-0-2**

Elizabethan Age (Fr) *D R Loder* — 84
2 b f King's Best (USA) - Dolydille (Ire)
27^{gf} $27g$ $127g$ **0-2-3 £4,771**

Ellamyte *G F Bridgwater* — 16 a28
4 b f Elmaamul (USA) - Deanta In Eirinn
126^{sd} 79^{sd} 95^{sd} 57^{sd} 158^{gf} **0-0-5**

Elle Nino *G Wragg* — a72
2 b f Inchinor - Robellino Miss (USA)
77^{sd} **0-0-1**

Elle Royal (Ire) G L Moore   a29
5 br m Ali-Royal (Ire) - Silvretta (Ire)
1110sd 1213sd 611sf 0-0-3

Ellen Mooney Mrs G S Rees   41 a77
5 ch m Efisio - Budby
28sd 38sd 48ss 1012sd 98s 138gs 87f 0-2-7
£1,505

Ellenare (Ire) Ms Deborah J Evans
2 ch f Bahhare (USA) - Lady Ellen-M (Ire)
95hy 96sd 0-0-2

Ellens Academy (Ire) E J Alston   95 a87
9 b g Royal Academy (USA) - Lady Ellen
46sd 66sd 36sd 47sd 26g 46gf 46gf 26s 26g
36gf 56g 66gs 216s 26gf 136s 0-7-15
£35,371

Ellens Lad (Ire) W J Musson   50 a76
10 b g Polish Patriot (USA) - Lady Ellen
75sd 56sd 96sw 115s 0-0-4

Ellens Princess (Ire) R Hannon   74
2 b f Desert Prince (Ire) - Lady Ellen
57gf 47g 76g 126gs 167gs 0-0-5 £398

Ellerslie Tom O Brennan   52
2 br g Octagonal (NZ) - Tetravella (Ire)
98g 58hy 0-0-2

Elliebow T D Easterby   55
2 br f Pharly (Fr) - Primo Donna Magna
116f 156g 96gs 0-0-3

Ellina J Pearce   70 a60
3 b f Robellino (USA) - Native Flair
108gs 410s 610gf 412f 711gf 111gf 1012gf
1311g 312g 512sd 1-1-10 £5,456

Elliot's Choice (Ire) R M Stronge   68 a35
3 b g Foxhound (USA) - Indian City
45s 45s 115gf 75gs 45gf 35gs 66g 86sd
117gf 125gs 155gs 25s 46hy 145gs 56gs 147gf
85gf 67gs 117sd 0-1-19 £3,738

Elliots World (Ire) M Johnston   105
2 b c King's Best (USA) - Morning Welcome (Ire)
17gs 17g 67gf 48gf 78s 2-0-5 £26,505

Ellis Cave J J Quinn   40 a43
2 gr g Diktat - Cole Slaw
76g 126gf 47sd 76sd 106sd 0-0-5 £311

Ellovamul W M Brisbourne   58 a58
4 b f Elmaamul (USA) - Multi-Sofft
49gf 811f 412g 811g 110gf 810sd 712gs
1110gf 1010gf 1312gf 110gs 79sd 2-0-12 £5,749

Ellway Heights W M Brisbourne   61
7 b g Shirley Heights - Amina
213gf 212g 216g 513g 313gf 812s 616g 712gf
1212gf 0-3-9 £2,978

Ellway Prospect Miss I E Craig   a53
4 ch f Pivotal - Littlemisstrouble (USA)
417sd 0-0-1

Elms Schoolboy J M P Eustace   48 a23
2 ch g Komaite (USA) - Elms Schoolgirl
95g 115gf 116sd 86s 0-0-4

Elmustanser Saeed Bin Suroor   103
3 b c Machiavellian (USA) - Elfaslah (Ire)
210gs 110gf 210gf 212gf 1612s 1-3-5
£14,924

Eloquent Knight (USA) W R Muir   61
2 b/br c Aljabr (USA) - Matinee Mimic (USA)
88gf 78hy 0-0-2

Elrafa Mujahid Julian Poulton   67 a65
2 b f Mujahid (USA) - Fancier Bit

38sd 78gs 17sd 1-1-3 £2,090

Elshadi (Ire) M P Tregoning   105
3 b c Cape Cross (Ire) - Rispoto
1312g 212f 610g 210gf 0-2-4 £34,449

Elsie Hart (Ire) T D Easterby   79
2 b f Revoque (Ire) - Family At War (USA)
15hy 36gs 145gf 1-0-3 £5,408

Elsie Wagg (USA) M J Wallace   64
2 b/br f Mt. Livermore (USA) - Hoedown Honey (Can)
35g 45g 55s 66gf 76gf 0-1-5 £1,057

Elsinora A G Juckes   53 a46
3 b f Great Dane (Ire) - Deanta In Eirinn
118sd 97gf 1010gf 28g 68gf 37g 57hy 26gf
47g 27gf 17g 38gs 17gs 77sd 2-5-14 £5,538

Elsundus (USA) K A Morgan
6 b g Gone West (USA) - Aljawza (USA)
68gf 0-0-1

Eltihaab (USA) Saeed Bin Suroor   55
3 b/br f Danzig (USA) - Futuh (USA)
98g 37f 46gf 0-1-3 £1,120

Eltizaam (USA) E A L Dunlop   74 a64
2 b c Bahri (USA) - Saffaanh (USA)
67g 58sd 67g 37gs 57gf 117gs 0-1-6 £711

Elusive Dream Sir Mark Prescott   102 a75
3 b g Rainbow Quest (USA) - Dance A Dream
112sd 112gs 112gf 113gf 314s 113s 212gf
5-2-7 £45,596

Elusive Kitty (USA) G A Butler   74 a63
3 b f Elusive Quality (USA) - Al Fahda
610sd LFT7f 38gf 39gs 58s 38f 510g 610s
1212sd 0-3-9 £1,948

Elvina A G Newcombe   59
3 b f Mark Of Esteem (Ire) - Pharaoh's Joy
15gf 156g 1-0-2 £5,369

Elvina Hills (Ire) W G M Turner   60 a49
2 ch f Bluebird (USA) - Women In Love (Ire)
95s 75s 56g 67gf 107sd 0-0-5

Elvington Boy M W Easterby
7 ch g Emarati (USA) - Catherines Well
UR5gf 0-0-1

Elzees D R C Elsworth   16 a43
3 b g Magic Ring (Ire) - White Flash
98sd 810g 0-0-2

Emaradia A W Carroll   46 a64
3 ch f Emarati (USA) - Rewardia (Ire)
35sd 16sd 27ss 87sd 15sw 26ss 25ss 65ss
66f 85gf 36sd 95g 47gf 97sd 37sd 77sd 2-6-16
£9,171

Emarati's Image B Forsey   a42
6 b g Emarati (USA) - Choir's Image
1210sd 67sd 46sd 65sd 46sd 65sd 0-0-6

Embassy Lord J O'Reilly   82
3 b g Mind Games - Keen Melody (USA)
45s 86gf 95gf 0-0-3 £1,052

Embassy Sweets (USA) P F I Cole   50 a38
3 b f Affirmed (USA) - Leaveemlaughing (USA)
49s 1113f 1312sd 0-0-3 £413

Ember Days J L Spearing   73 a61
5 gr m Reprimand - Evening Falls
510sd 1711g 38s 108gf 29g 310f 110f
310gs 210g 410gf 1710gf 1-5-11 £8,997

Embossed (Ire) R Hannon   102
2 b c Mark Of Esteem (Ire) - L-Way First (Ire)
66gs 17gf 67g 27s 27g 28s 107s 1-3-7

£22,805

Emerald Bay (Ire) M Johnston 70
2 b c King's Best (USA) - Belle Etoile (Fr)
46gf 0-0-1 £420

Emerald Dancer H Morrison 23
2 b f Groom Dancer (USA) - Green Bonnet (Ire)
138gs 0-0-1

Emerald Destiny (Ire) D Carroll 51
2 b g Key Of Luck (USA) - Green Belt (Fr)
58s 1410gf 127g 0-0-3

Emerald Fire A M Balding 67 a69
5 b m Pivotal - Four-Legged Friend
66sd 107sd 116g 86gs 57s 26g 0-1-6
£1,111

Emerald Lodge J Noseda 63 a88
2 b c Grand Lodge (USA) - Emerald Peace (Ire)
35gf 55g 16sd 16sd 2-0-4 £10,423

Emerald Penang (Ire) P W Chapple-Hyam 76
2 b g Alzao (USA) - Run To Jane (Ire)
55gs 46f 17gf 77gf 108s 108g 1-0-6
£4,622

Emeraude Du Cap M L W Bell 49
2 b f Tipsy Creek (USA) - High Typha
176gf 106g 35gf 86s 0-1-4 £522

Emile Zola M P Tregoning 76
2 b c Singspiel (Ire) - Ellie Ardensky
18gf 59g 1-0-2 £6,022

Emilys Dawn D K Ivory a44
3 b f Komaite (USA) - Spice And Sugar
77sd 118sd 0-0-2

Eminence Gift K R Burke 20
2 b f Cadeaux Genereux - Germane
126gf 146f 0-0-2

Eminent Aura (USA) A Dickman
3 ch f Charismatic (USA) - Perfectly Clear (USA)
97sd 0-0-1

Emma's Venture M W Easterby 43 a28
2 b f Paris House - Emma Amour
55g 25s 65s 45gf 86f 45sw 0-1-6 £1,361

Emmervale R M H Cowell 55 a26
5 b m Emarati (USA) - Raintree Venture
56gf 96f 116f 97sd 0-0-4

Empangeni J L Dunlop 58 a62
2 b g Mtoto - Shibui
117gs 58s 108sd 0-0-3

Emperor Cat (Ire) P A Blockley 42 a53
3 b g Desert Story (Ire) - Catfoot Lane
26ss 37sd 126ss 86ss 138f 117g 67sd 66g
167hy 26sd 0-3-10 £1,622

Emperor's Well M W Easterby 72
5 ch g First Trump - Catherines Well
1210gf 310s 18gf 110gf 2-1-4 £7,799

Empire Of The Sun P J Makin a45
3 b f Second Empire (Ire) - Splicing
87sd 0-0-1

Empire's Ghodha B J Meehan 84
2 b c Mujadil (USA) - La Caprice (USA)
55g 35g 25gf 35gf 15f 55gf 35gs 45g 66gf
85gs 85gf 66s 1-3-12 £11,622

Empirical Power (Ire) Edward Lynam 99
3 b c Second Empire (Ire) - Rumuz (Ire)
58y 37gf 17f 17gf 17gf 67s 3-1-6
£50,544

Empress Eugenie (Fr) J M P Eustace 70

3 b f Second Empire (Ire) - High Finish
48gs 610hy 510gf 0-0-3 £330

Empress Josephine J R Jenkins 36 a64
4 b f Emperor Jones (USA) - Valmaranda (USA)
15ss 25ss 55sw 35ss 145gf 115g 1-2-6
£4,329

Emsam Ballou (Ire) V Smith 61 a66
3 ch f Bluebird (USA) - Persian Tapestry
37sd 38sd 36s 97s 186g 137sd 0-3-6
£2,207

Emtilaak B Hanbury 81 a77
3 b g Marju (Ire) - Just A Mirage
27sd 38g 16gf 96gf 96sd 46sd 46sd 1-2-7
£8,574

Enamoured M G Quinlan 46
2 b f Groom Dancer (USA) - Ascendancy
58s 78hy 0-0-2

Enborne Again (Ire) R A Fahey 51
2 ch c Fayruz - Sharp Ellie (Ire)
76gs 146gs 116gf 0-0-3

Encanto (Ire) J S Moore 83
2 ch f Bahhare (USA) - Born To Glamour
115gf 66g 25f 26g 26gs 16gf 46gf 56gs
36gf 1-4-9 £26,375

Enchanted N A Callaghan 99
5 b m Magic Ring (Ire) - Snugfit Annie
16g 17gf 77gf 76f 77gf 76gs 47gf 85s
156s 2-0-9 £24,462

Enchanted Ocean (USA) G B Balding 56
5 b m Royal Academy (USA) - Ocean Jewel (USA)
1310gs 1112gf 812g 712gf 1213gs 0-0-5

Enchanted Princess W J Haggas 79
4 b f Royal Applause - Hawayah (Ire)
158gs 58s 18gf 68gf 78gf 1-0-5 £7,642

Enchantment J M Bradley 109
3 b f Compton Place - Tharwa (Ire)
56s 26g 15f 15f 25gf 45g 15s 45gs 45gf
45s 3-2-10 £41,481

Encompass (Fr) H R A Cecil 68
3 b f Sadler's Wells (USA) - Totality
910g 312gf 611gf 0-1-3 £858

Encora Bay P R Chamings 61
3 b f Primo Dominie - Brave Revival
67gs 37gs 107gf 0-1-3 £660

Encore Royale J Jay 43 a43
4 b f Royal Applause - Verbena (Ire)
78sd 510s 69sd 127sd 118gf 0-0-5

Encounter J Hetherton 56
8 br g Primo Dominie - Dancing Spirit (Ire)
1110gs 79g 38s 58f 68g 88gf 88s 29gf
59gf 98g 89gs 510gs 38f 58g 28gs 148gs 38s
0-5-17 £2,984

Encouragement R Hannon 77
2 b f Royal Applause - Gentle Persuasion
85gf 36gf 105gs 45g 36gf 76g 0-2-6
£2,026

End Of An Error Mrs E Slack
5 b m Charmer - Needwood Poppy
916g 0-0-1

Endless Summer A W Carroll 93
7 b g Zafonic (USA) - Well Away (Ire)
36g 56gs 57f 106gf 45gf 66gf 95g 25s 15gs
16g 76gs 2-2-11 £18,435

Enforcer W R Muir 81
2 b c Efisio - Tarneem (USA)

46gf 56gs 26gs 87gf 17gs 107s 1-1-6
£8,815

Enford Princess R Hannon   86
3 b f Pivotal - Expectation (Ire)
46s 98g 38gs 47gs 77g 48g 68g 78gs 0-0-8
£3,513

English Fellow B A McMahon   72
2 b c Robellino (USA) - Q Factor
36gs 45f 46f 146gf 76g 177gf 168g 0-1-7
£1,148

English Rocket (Ire) D J S Ffrench Davis   33
3 b g Indian Rocket - Golden Charm (Ire)
910s 138hy 0-0-2

Enhancer Mrs L C Jewell   80
6 b g Zafonic (USA) - Ypha (USA)
710gs 711gf 311gf 516gf 612s 0-1-5 £851

Enjoy The Buzz J M Bradley   58 a51
5 b h Prince Of Birds (USA) - Abaklea (Ire)
46sd 45sd 116sd 26sd 37ss 16ss 26sw 46sw
26sw 176g 15gf 96sd 25f 15gs 76g 36gf 26gf
56gs 3-7-21 £12,327

Enna (Pol) Mrs Stef Liddiard   52 a43
5 ch m Don Corleone - Elba (Pol)
47gs 610gf 97sd 88gf 48g 127gf 410sd 28gf
98gf 68gs 77hy 411gf 38sd 110gf 1-3-14
£2,687

Enrapture (USA) Mrs A J Perrett   82
3 b f Lear Fan (USA) - Cheviot Hills (USA)
17gs 37gs 187gs 1-1-3 £6,880

Ensemble D M Simcock   53 a28
4 b g Polish Precedent (USA) - Full Orchestra
1916g 114s 917sd 1-0-3 £2,506

Entailment Mrs J R Ramsden   72
2 b g Kris - Entail (USA)
85gs 16gs 87s 1-0-3 £7,319

Entertain M L W Bell   67
2 b f Royal Applause - Darshay (Fr)
127gf 137gf 0-0-2

Entertaining H Candy   72
2 b f Halling (USA) - Quaver (USA)
66gf 57g 26gf 56g 0-1-4 £1,462

Environment Audit J R Jenkins   59 a57
5 ch g Kris - Bold And Beautiful
711sd 1011sd 712gs 1212g 1110g 711g 0-0-6

Environmentalist D A Nolan   29
5 b g Danehill (USA) - Way O'Gold (USA)
117gf 116g 137gf 89g 98gf 129gf 0-0-6

Epaminondas (USA) R Hannon   68
3 ch c Miswaki (USA) - Nora Nova (USA)
76s 177gf 127gf 210g 88g 410gf 710gs
0-1-7 £1,685

Ephesus Miss Gay Kelleway   87 a89
4 b g Efisio - Composition
38ss 77sd 78sw 912sw 98s 67g 18gf 47gf
27gf 28gf 188g 108sd 128g 38gf 68gs 310gs
1-5-16 £15,814

Epiphany E A L Dunlop   83
2 br f Zafonic (USA) - Galette
26gf 16gf 76gs 87g 1-1-4 £7,120

Epitomise R M Beckett   64
2 b f Mind Games - Yanomami (USA)
65gs 45gf 106gf 66gf 106gf 0-0-5 £320

Eqdaam (USA) J H M Gosden   82
2 b c Diesis - Awaamir

37gf 37gf 17g 1-2-3 £7,482

Equus (Ire) L A Dace   a26
3 b g Desert Style (Ire) - Iolanta (Ire)
812sd 1014sd 0-0-2

Ermine Grey D Haydn Jones   74 a84
3 gr g Wolfhound (USA) - Impulsive Decision (Ire)
810gs 78gs 38g 47sd 48g 0-1-5 £1,816

Erracht Mrs H Sweeting   72 a49
6 gr m Emarati (USA) - Port Na Blath
75ss 55sw 15gf 65gf 145gf 115gf 75g 55sd
85gf VOl5gf 165f 1-0-11 £3,474

Errol J F Coupland
5 ch g Dancing Spree (USA) - Primo Panache
916sd 0-0-1

Ersaal (USA) Evan Williams   6 a49
4 ch g Gulch (USA) - Madame Secretary (USA)
1010sd 312ss 1110sd 112sd 312sd 1012hy
1512gf 1-1-7 £1,823

Erte V Thompson   50 a54
3 ch g Vettori (Ire) - Cragreen
138gs 68g 610f 310g 212sd 1110gf 712gf
0-2-7 £1,335

Erupt R E Barr   48 a37
11 b g Beveled (USA) - Sparklingsovereign
59sd 711f 38sd 98g 88gs 48gs 38s 99f
0-2-8 £1,127

Esatto M J Attwater   59
5 b g Puissance - Stoneydale
156gf 96gf 0-0-2

Escalade W M Brisbourne   60 a27
7 b g Green Desert (USA) - Sans Escale (USA)
99sd 410g 1210f 512gf 411g 312gf 411gf
312gf 512g 612gf 810f 0-2-11 £1,697

Escayola (Ire) W J Haggas   99
4 b g Revoque (Ire) - First Fling (Ire)
814gf 214gf 1116s 1616g 216gf 116gf 518s
1-2-7 £22,101

Eshaadeh (USA) Saeed Bin Suroor   34
3 b f Storm Cat (USA) - Sarayir (USA)
57f 87g 0-0-2

Esher Common (Ire) A E Price
6 b g Common Grounds - Alsahah (Ire)
1910g 0-0-1

Eskdale (Ire) R F Fisher   65
2 b g Perugino (USA) - Gilding The Lily (Ire)
86g 95gf 37s 27gf 67s 48gf 0-2-6
£3,506

Eskimo's Nest W J Haggas   57
2 b f Polar Falcon (USA) - White House
87g 0-0-1

Espada (Ire) J A Osborne   58 a63
8 b g Mukaddamah (USA) - Folk Song (Can)
87sd 77sd 78gs 158g 47gf 48f 17g 58gf
98gf 47gf 67g 108gf 138f 107gf 1-0-14
£3,485

Esperance (Ire) J Akehurst   53 a52
4 ch g Bluebird (USA) - Dioscorea (Ire)
1110sd 1310s 58g 510gs 88gf 58gf 510sd
28f 410f 58s 0-1-10 £1,020

Esquire Saeed Bin Suroor   91
2 b c Dubai Millennium - Esperada (Arg)
68g 17g 1-0-2 £6,240

Esrar (Ire) M P Tregoning   51
2 b c Mujadil (USA) - Island Desert (Ire)
97gs 0-0-1

Essay Baby (Fr) P D Cundell   a52
4 b f Saumarez - Easter Baby
410sd 412sd 1312sd 1313sd 0-0-4

Essex Star (Ire) Miss J Feilden   45 a50
3 b f Revoque (Ire) - Touch Of White
106gf 37sd 38sd 56g 0-2-4 £886

Establishment C A Cyzer   76
7 b g Muhtarram (USA) - Uncharted Waters
1116gs 812g 816gf 1018g 1420gf 816gf 414gs
1216gf 0-0-8 £331

Esteban J J Quinn   49
4 b g Groom Dancer (USA) - Ellie Ardensky
128s 47gf 118g 0-0-3

Estepona Miss J A Camacho   67
3 ch g Polar Falcon (USA) - Kingdom Ruby (Ire)
48gs 107g 128gf 811g 1112hy 0-0-5 £322

Estihlal E A L Dunlop   79
3 b f Green Desert (USA) - Ta Rib (USA)
76s 46g 16f 26g 46g 16g 46gf 36f 56g
2-2-9 £12,838

Estilo R M Flower
4 b g Deploy - Vilcabamba (USA)
1012gf 0-0-1

Estimate John A Harris   59 a39
4 b f Mark Of Esteem (Ire) - Mistle Thrush (USA)
712sd 912sd 88sd 110gf 1210gf 79g 28gf
210gf 1110sd 410gs 810s 1-2-11 £5,534

Estimation R M H Cowell   58 a75
4 b f Mark Of Esteem (Ire) - Mohican Girl
38sd 68sd 37sd 58ss 127sd 88gf 78sd 108sd
78sd 0-0-9 £981

Estoille Mrs S Lamyman   58 a57
3 b f Paris House - Nampara Bay
76gf 125gf 85gs 77f 65sf 85gs 45sd 16s
25sd 1-1-9 £3,767

Estrella Levante R M Flower   62 a47
4 ch g Abou Zouz (USA) - Star Of Modena (Ire)
710sd 58sd 38sd 108sd 68sd 87sd 108g
1110f 1210sd 77gf 88sd 0-0-11 £209

Estuary (USA) Ms A E Embiricos   a37
9 ch g Riverman (USA) - Ocean Ballad
1113sd 1412gs 1214sd 0-0-3

Etaar E A L Dunlop   80
2 b c Zafonic (USA) - Hawayah (Ire)
47g 47gs 46gs 0-0-3 £1,303

Etching (USA) J R Fanshawe   65
4 b f Groom Dancer (USA) - Eternity
112g 916g 1614gf 514f 1817g 1-0-5
£3,748

Eternal Beauty (USA) M J Wallace
4 b f Zafonic (USA) - Strawberry Roan (Ire)
65sw 0-0-1

Eternal Bloom M Brittain   29 a49
6 b m Reprimand - Forever Roses
16sd 27sd 136sd 136ss 126sw 36sd 37sd
86sd 96gf 1-3-9 £2,197

Eternal Dancer (USA) M Johnston
3 b g Royal Academy (USA) - Tara Roma (USA)
129sw 98ss 0-0-2

Eternal Sunshine (Ire) R P Elliott   20 a23
2 b f Rossini (USA) - Sweet As A Nut (Ire)
86gf 106f 85g 35sd 105sw 0-0-5 £360

Eternally R M H Cowell   37 a51
2 ch c Timeless Times (USA) - Nice Spice (Ire)
75gf 35ss 55sd 36f 15sd 85gf 95sd 1-1-7

£3,373

Etesaal (USA) Saeed Bin Suroor   75
4 b/br c Danzig (USA) - Electric Society (Ire)
159s 0-0-1

Etlaala B W Hills   117
2 c c Selkirk (USA) - Portelet
17g 17gf 87s 2-0-3 £66,422

Etmaam M Johnston   102
3 b c Intikhab (USA) - Sudeley
17gs 58g 110gf 210gf 110g 312gf 1512g
1712g 612g 610hy 3-2-10 £27,343

Etoile Russe (Ire) P C Haslam   60
2 b g Soviet Star (USA) - To The Skies (USA)
76gf 0-0-1

Eton (Ger) D Nicholls   78
8 ch g Suave Dancer (USA) - Ermione
310g 1012gs 512g 110gf 212s 312g 510g
212g 910gs 410gf 1510gf 1-3-11 £9,586

Ettrick Water L M Cumani   109 a104
5 ch g Selkirk (USA) - Sadly Sober (Ire)
58gf 17g 17gf 107gf 17gf 67gf 47s 77sd
3-1-8 £32,974

Eugenie R Hannon   a16
3 ch f Primo Dominie - Misty Goddess (Ire)
136sd 137sd 0-0-2

Euippe J G Given   74
3 b f Air Express (Ire) - Myth
1110gf 514f 114g 416s 714gf 1-0-5
£4,032

Eukleia (USA) T D Barron   63 a34
2 ch f Devil His Due (USA) - Good Reputation (USA)
66gs 86gf 55sd 176g 0-0-4

Eunice Choice M J Haynes
3 b g College Chapel - Aquiletta
157sd 96sd 0-0-2

Eurobound (USA) D J Daly   69
3 b f Southern Halo (USA) - Eurostorm (USA)
47hy 48f 512g 512f 0-0-4 £913

Eurolink Artemis Julian Poulton   57 a49
7 b m Common Grounds - Taiga
138sd 410sd 1010sd 19sd 110gs 39sd PU12sd
119sd 2-1-8 £3,111

Eurolink Zante (Ire) A J Chamberlain   24 a42
8 b g Turtle Island (Ire) - Lady Eurolink
78sd 68sd 710sd 1111gf 0-0-4

Eva Jean H Morrison   52
3 b f Singspiel (Ire) - Go For Red (Ire)
148gf 58gf 1610s 0-0-3

Eva Peron (Ire) W G M Turner   44 a33
4 b f Alzao (USA) - High Flying Adored (Ire)
107sd 88gs 610g 810gf 78f 0-0-5

Eva Soneva So Fast (Ire) J L Dunlop   78
2 ch c In The Wings - Azyaa
107gs 57s 28gf 18gf 1-1-4 £6,958

Evaluator (Ire) T G Mills   93
3 b g Ela-Mana-Mou - Summerhill
47gs 38s 118hy 67gf 17gf 28g 28gs 88g
28gs 28gf 1-5-10 £13,872

Evanesce M R Channon   72 a66
2 b f Lujain (USA) - Search Party
25sd 25sd 45gf 25gs 26gf 16gf 25f 86g
115g 45gf 106gs 125gf 137g 1-5-13 £9,620

Evangelist (Ire) Mrs Stef Liddiard   a45
4 b f Namaqualand (USA) - Errazuriz (Ire)

37sd 96sd 16sw 76sw 66sd 147sd 1-1-6
£1,670

Evasive Quality (Fr) D R Loder   56
2 b f Highest Honor (Fr) - Exocet (USA)
106g 0-0-1

Even Easier G L Moore   60 a51
3 gr f Petong - Comme Ca
87sd 78sd 58sd 78g 610gf 47gf 48f 58g
710gf 58f 128gs 0-1-11 £560

Even Hotter D W P Arbuthnot   50
3 b f Desert Style (Ire) - Level Pegging (Ire)
125gf 56gf 116g 0-0-3

Ever Cheerful W G M Turner   59 a71
3 b g Atraf - Big Story
27sd 16sd 107sd 57sd 25sd 65ss 86sd 96gs
1-2-8 £5,441

Everest (Ire) B Ellison   93
7 ch g Indian Ridge - Reine D'Beaute
78g 1310g 1010g 910gf 148g 18g 18g 78gf
48s 319g 2-0-10 £38,271

Every Note Counts J J Quinn   58
4 b g Bluegrass Prince (Ire) - Miss Mirror
2112g 1510gs 1410f 68gf 610s 68g 0-0-6

Eviyrn (Ire) J R Jenkins   10
8 b g In The Wings - Evrana (USA)
1216gs 0-0-1

Evolving Tactics (Ire) D K Weld   109
4 b g Machiavellian (USA) - Token Gesture (Ire)
18gf 99gf 278gf 1-0-3 £32,681

Evoque H J Collingridge   59
3 b f Revoque (Ire) - Chimere (Fr)
106g 0-0-1

Ex Mill Lady John Berry   65
3 br f Bishop Of Cashel - Hickleton Lady (Ire)
45s 25gf 25gf 15gf 1-2-4 £5,397

Exalted (Ire) T A K Cuthbert   58
11 b g High Estate - Heavenward (USA)
514s 513f 813gf 613g 0-0-4

Exceed And Excel (Aus) T Martin   116
4 b c Danehill (USA) - Patrona (USA)
16g 16g 196gs 2-0-3 £315,126

Excellento (USA) Saeed Bin Suroor   103
4 ch c Rahy (USA) - Golden Opinion (USA)
178sd 98gf 0-0-2

Excelsius (Ire) J L Dunlop   102
4 ch c Dr Devious (Ire) - Folgore (USA)
98g 38s 98gf 118s 48g 28hy 58s 0-1-7
£13,693

Exclusive Danielle B W Hills   73
3 ch f Thunder Gulch (USA) - Hasta (USA)
510gs 112gf 1-0-2 £3,454

Excusez Moi (USA) C E Brittain   a74
2 b c Fusaichi Pegasus (USA) - Jiving
26sd 0-1-1 £1,568

Execute (Fr) J E Hammond   117
7 ch h Suave Dancer (USA) - She's My Lovely
210gs 111vs 1112g 610s 1-1-4 £96,747

Exit Smiling D Nicholls   70
2 ch c Dr Fong (USA) - Away To Me
25g 36gs 175g 57gf 138g 17g 107s 1-1-7
£5,216

Exit To Heaven Mrs Lucinda Featherstone   a49
4 ch f Exit To Nowhere (USA) - Shona (USA)
712sd 612sd 712sd 916sd 0-0-4

Expected Bonus (USA) Jamie Poulton   55
5 b/br g Kris S (USA) - Nidd (USA)
109g 410g 1710gf 98gf 68gf 1510gf 0-0-6
£523

Expectedtofli (Ire) T Wall
6 b m Mujadil (USA) - Zurarah
106sd 158sd 0-0-2

Expeditious (USA) Saeed Bin Suroor   41 a46
2 b/br c Forestry (USA) - Nonies Dancer Ali (USA)
227sd 67sd 0-0-2

Explicit (Ire) G C Bravery   26 a35
3 ch c Definite Article - Queen Canute (Ire)
1210sd 1010gf 98g 87sw 118sd 0-0-5

Explode Miss L C Siddall   58
7 b g Zafonic (USA) - Didicoy (USA)
48hy 98s 28g 29gs 108hy 0-2-5 £2,689

Explosive Fox (Ire) V Smith   68 a67
3 ch c Foxhound (USA) - Grise Mine (Fr)
118hy 228ys 312gy 511gy 1716gf 213f
1113sd 717s 812sd 0-2-9 £2,080

Exponential (Ire) S C Williams   80
2 b g Namid - Exponent (USA)
135gf 15g 1-0-2 £3,916

Express Lily K R Burke
5 b m Environment Friend - Jaydeeglen
1012s 0-0-1

Extemporise (Ire) T T Clement   56 a56
4 ch c Indian Ridge - No Rehearsal (Fr)
85ss 36sw 57ss 18g 17hy 67sd 157gf 29sd
2-2-8 £3,747

Exterior (USA) Mrs A J Perrett   106 a86
3 ch c Distant View (USA) - Alvernia (USA)
110sd 19gs 49gf 110hy 3-0-4 £28,414

Extinguisher T J Fitzgerald   64 a24
5 ch g Zamindar (USA) - Xaymara (USA)
186gs 96gf 96gf 87g 59g 147gf 116sw
0-0-7

Extra Cover (Ire) Ms Deborah J Evans   75 a75
3 b g Danehill Dancer (Ire) - Ballycurrane (Ire)
28sd 210gs 210s 38sd 16sd 66sd 66gf 137sd
76gf 48sd 67sd 1-4-11 £6,830

Extra Mark J R Best   73 a73
2 b g Mark Of Esteem (Ire) - No Comebacks
25gs 25sd 45g 207gf 146s 0-2-5 £2,638

Extreme Beauty (USA) C E Brittain   88
2 ch f Rahy (USA) - Mediation (Ire)
66gf 16gf 76f 36gf 107gf 1-1-5 £11,990

Extremely Rare (Ire) M S Saunders   66
3 b f Mark Of Esteem (Ire) - Colourflash (Ire)
26g 76gs 16s 107g 75s 96g 65s 66s 126g
1-1-9 £4,662

Eyes Dont Lie (Ire) D A Nolan   1
6 b g Namaqualand (USA) - Avidal Park
912gf 812s 0-0-2

Eyes Only (USA) H R A Cecil   82
3 b f Distant View (USA) - Yashmak (USA)
18gs 11-1-4 £5,616

Ezz Elkheil J R Jenkins   67 a84
5 b g Bering - Numidie (Fr)
216sd 412sd 312sd 1013sd 1212s 712gf 710gf
0-2-7 £2,902

Faayej (Ire) Sir Michael Stoute   88
4 b g Sadler's Wells (USA) - Russian Ballet (USA)
110gf 410gf 510s 313s 1-1-4 £8,340

Fabranese P Howling   a22
4 b f Dr Devious (Ire) - Babsy Babe
1212sd 0-0-1

Fabrian D W P Arbuthnot   a52
6 b g Danehill (USA) - Dockage (Can)
88sd 0-0-1

Fabuloso V Smith   44 a23
3 b f Dr Fong (USA) - Shafir (Ire)
58sd 67gf 109s 69gf 57gf 148gs 0-0-6

Face The Limelight (Ire) Jedd O'Keeffe   42
5 b g Quest For Fame - Miss Boniface
1410gs 610g 712gf 0-0-3

Fact And Fiction (Ire) M Johnston
2 b c Fasliyev (USA) - Flyleaf (Fr)
76gf 0-0-1

Factual Lad B R Millman   75 a64
6 b g So Factual (USA) - Surprise Surprise
1310g 1010f 110f 710gf 108f 910g 310gf
812sd 29sd 1-2-9 £5,813

Factual Lady T D Easterby
2 b f Factual (USA) - Shiny Kay
116f 0-0-1

Fadael (Ire) P W D'Arcy   63 a61
2 b f In The Wings - Gift Box (Ire)
75gf 67gf 38gf 37g 88f 59sd 0-1-6
£1,163

Fadeela (Ire) P W D'Arcy   72
3 ch f Desert King (Ire) - Gift Box (Ire)
58gs 87g 137g 76gf 0-0-4 £750

Failed To Hit N P Littmoden   a56
11 b g Warrshan (USA) - Missed Again
312sd 416sd 613sd 0-0-3 £376

Fair Along (Ger) W Jarvis   70
2 b g Alkalde (Ger) - Fairy Tango (Fr)
75gs 86gf 75gf 48gf 98s 98g 0-0-6 £267

Fair Compton R Hannon   64
3 b f Compton Place - Fair Eleanor
46gf 66f 55g 46g 57gf 56gf 16gs 96g 1-1-8
£4,297

Fair Options H J Cyzer   67
3 gr g Marju (Ire) - Silver Singing (USA)
176s 76gf 36gf 167f 0-1-4 £551

Fair Shake (Ire) D Eddy   75
4 b g Sheikh Albadou - Shamrock Fair (Ire)
76gs 107hy 36s 57g 156s 26g 66g 26gf
147s 86s 157g 0-3-11 £6,518

Fair Spin M D Hammond   68
4 ch g Pivotal - Frankie Fair (Ire)
76g 38g 78gf 98gs 57gs 98hy 310s 0-2-7
£1,453

Fairgame Man J S Wainwright   54 a22
6 ch g Clantime - Thalya
75g 85g 25gf 75g 55s 15gs 85gf 95gf 85gs
85gs 25gs 105sd 1-2-12 £4,103

Fairland (Ire) S Dow   54 a48
5 b g Blues Traveller (Ire) - Massive Powder
310sd 410gf 1011f 610sd 1811g 1410gf
1010gs 0-2-7 £237

Fairlie Mrs M Reveley   66
3 b f Halling (USA) - Fairy Flax (Ire)
59f 78gf 78gs 17gs 310gs 810s 1-1-6
£3,897

Fairly Glorious T H Caldwell   a42
3 b g Tina's Pet - Steamy Windows
86sd 116sd 99sw 0-0-3

Fairmile P W Harris   80
2 b c Spectrum (Ire) - Juno Marlowe (Ire)
37gs 37s 67gs 47s 0-2-4 £1,525

Fairmorning (Ire) C N Kellett   a45
5 b g Ridgewood Ben - The Bratpack (Ire)
212sd 616sd 514ss 212sd 0-2-4 £822

Fairy Monarch (Ire) P T Midgley   55
5 b g Ali-Royal (Ire) - Cookawara (Ire)
212gf 811g 212gf 1512g 810gf 612g 0-2-6
£1,814

Fairy Wind (Ger) B J Curley   25 a41
7 b h Dashing Blade - Fairy Bluebird
1213sd 912sd 316sd 812gf 0-0-4 £206

Fait Le Jojo (Fr) A G Juckes   72
7 b g Pistolet Bleu (Ire) - Pretty Davis (USA)
1214gf 1114gs 0-0-2

Faites Vos Jeux C N Kellett   39 a24
3 b f Foxhound (USA) - Desert Bloom (Fr)
137gs 156g 56g 106sd 0-0-4

Faith Healer (Ire) V Smith   52 a61
3 br f Key Of Luck (USA) - Cindy's Star (Ire)
188s 188gf 1412g 48f 610gf 18sd 107g
68f 178g 67sd 1-0-10 £3,338

Faithful Flash C A Dwyer   43
2 b f Tipsy Creek (USA) - Tudorealm (USA)
67f 87gs 46gf 67gf 56s 0-0-5

Faithful Warrior (USA) B W Hills   68
6 ch g Diesis - Dabaweyaa (Ire)
208s 0-0-1

Faithfull Girl (Ire) Miss Z C Davison   a40
2 b f Second Empire (Ire) - Cairde Nua (Ire)
95sd 95sd 86f 0-0-3

Faithisflying C A Dwyer   37
2 ch c Wolfhound (USA) - Niggle
135g 66gf 115gf 65gf 66hy 0-0-5

Falcon Goer (USA) N Tinkler   43
2 b f Zamindar (USA) - Elizabeth Eliza (USA)
86f 136gs 86g 0-0-3

Fall In Line Sir Mark Prescott   a92
4 gr g Linamix (Fr) - Shortfall
112sd 112ss 113sd 111sd 112sd 110sd 6-0-6
£20,720

Fallujah M Johnston
2 ch f Dr Fong (USA) - Brilliance
147s 0-0-1

Fame P J Hobbs   71
4 ch g Northern Amethyst - First Sapphire
612s 0-0-1

Familiar Affair T D Barron   81
3 b g Intikhab (USA) - Familiar (USA)
78g 108gs 18gs 39s 118gf 1-1-5 £6,697

Famous Grouse P Bowen   103
4 b g Selkirk (USA) - Shoot Clear
1710g 610gf 1412g 0-0-4 £1,495

Fancy Foxtrot B J Meehan   94 a88
3 b c Danehill Dancer (Ire) - Smooth Princess (Ire)
18sd 108g 149g 37g 96g 78sd 97gf 167g
67sd 1-1-9 £7,305

Fanling Lady D Nicholls   52
3 gr f Highest Honor (Fr) - Pain Perdu (Ire)
88gf 710s 1010gf 0-0-3

Fanny's Fancy C F Wall   93
4 b f Groom Dancer (USA) - Fanny's Choice (Ire)
75g 105gs 156f 36g 56g 57g 56s 0-1-7

£5,620

Fantaisiste P F I Cole   68 a79
2 b f Nashwan (USA) - Fantastic Belle (Ire)
117gf 37f 26sd 16sd 1-2-4 £7,253

Fantasia's Forest (Ire) J L Dunlop   36
2 b f Shinko Forest (Ire) - Persian Fantasia
117gf 187g 147s 0-0-3

Fantastic Love (USA) Saeed Bin Suroor   109
4 b g Peintre Celebre (USA) - Moon Flower (Ire)
810g 714s 315gf 212g 113hy 1-2-5
£79,908

Fantastic Luck (Ire) J L Dunlop   48
2 b c Josr Algarhoud (Ire) - Fantastic Fantasy (Ire)
168gf 148g 108s 0-0-3

Fantastic Night (Den) R Guest   29
2 ch f Night Shift (USA) - Gaelic's Fantasy (Ire)
167g 106s 0-0-2

Fantastic Star J G Given   22 a12
2 b f Lahib (USA) - Fervent Fan (Ire)
95gs 126f 97sd 0-0-3

Fantastic View (USA) R Hannon   109
3 ch c Distant View (USA) - Promptly (Ire)
58g 48gf 0-0-2 £2,000

Fantastico (Ire) Mrs K Walton   64
4 b f Bahhare (USA) - Minatina (Ire)
414gf 913gf 316gs 1217gs 616g 0-1-5 £863

Fantasy Believer J J Quinn   105
6 b g Sure Blade (USA) - Delicious
127hy 177gs 296g 147gf 96g 46s 16gf
107g 16g 26gf 106g 206g 26s 66gf 36g 2-4-15
£74,702

Fantasy Crusader Mrs A C Gilbert   65 a65
5 ch g Beveled (USA) - Cranfield Charger
167gf 310gs 310gf 1010f 310f 210sd 910gf
178g 310f 110f 38gf 19gf 109sd 18sd 1012sd
3-6-15 £16,574

Fantasy Defender (Ire) J J Quinn   55 a55
2 b g Fayruz - Mrs Lucky
95s 85hy 86gf 117gf 96gs 56gf 137gf 46sd
0-0-8

Fantasy Ride J Pearce   90
2 b c Bahhare (USA) - Grand Splendour
77gf 18s 58g 210gs 1-1-4 £10,203

Fantorini (USA) J H M Gosden   77
2 b c Theatrical - Beyrouth (USA)
87gf 48g 0-0-2 £528

Far For Lulu W R Muir   a12
3 ch f Farfelu - Shady Habitat
147sd 127sd 0-0-2

Far Note (USA) S R Bowring   70 a82
6 ch g Distant View (USA) - Descant (USA)
66sd 25sd 95sd 96sd 45sd 66ss 15ss 126s
15ss 46g 45gf 75gf 45gs 86g 107gs 2-2-15
£9,751

Faraway Echo James Moffatt   60 a39
3 gr f Second Empire (Ire) - Salalah
158g 67sd 38gs 88gf 58gf 112s 512sw 1-1-7
£4,281

Faraway Look (USA) D Shaw   a57
7 br g Distant View (USA) - Summer Trip (USA)
49sd 58sd 1012sd 0-0-3

Farewell Gift R Hannon   84
3 b c Cadeaux Genereux - Daring Ditty
46g 36s 27gf 36g 26gf 36g 37gf 36gf 16s
77gs 1-6-10 £14,434

Farnborough (USA) R J Price   50 a53
3 b g Lear Fan (USA) - Gretel
58sd 77sd 97g 77gf 1310gs 178gf 48gs
510hy 97sd 211sd 0-1-10 £429

Farne Isle G A Harker   65
5 ch m Midnight Legend - Biloela
412gs 312gf 78g 1312gf 0-0-4 £1,215

Farriers Charm D J Coakley   69 a63
3 b f In Command (Ire) - Carn Maire
17sd 127g 78gf 19s 58gs 1010gs 109sd
2-0-7 £7,754

Farthing (Ire) G C Bravery   75
2 b f Mujadil (USA) - Neat Shilling (Ire)
25gf 45gf 25f 35gf 0-3-4 £2,902

Fascination Street (Ire) M A Jarvis   67
3 b f Mujadil (USA) - Loon (Fr)
66gs 58hy 07s 27f 36gf 28gf 17f 68gf
1-2-8 £7,073

Fashion House (USA) Saeed Bin Suroor   73
2 b f Quiet American (USA) - Polish Style (USA)
56g 26g 0-1-2 £1,480

Fast Gate (USA) L Pantuosco   a93
5 gr h Gate Dancer (USA) - Myshiphascomin (USA)
26s 17sd 17sd 87sd 2-0-4 £12,010

Fast Heart B J Meehan   98
3 b c Fasliyev (USA) - Heart Of India (Ire)
85g 145gs 46gf 136gf 0-0-4 £1,500

Fast Lane (Ire) J S Wainwright
5 ch g Hamas (Ire) - Rainstone
137gs 178gs 0-0-2

Fasylitator (Ire) J A Osborne   76 a73
2 b c Fasliyev (USA) - Obsessed
67gf 36g 66g 107gf 46sd 67s 0-1-6
£1,241

Fatayaat (Ire) B W Hills   47
3 b f Machiavellian (USA) - Maraatib (Ire)
108f 0-0-1

Fatehalkhair (Ire) B Ellison   5
12 ch g Kris - Midway Lady (USA)
1112gs 0-0-1

Father Seamus P Butler
6 b g Bin Ajwaad (Ire) - Merry Rous
1310sd 0-0-1

Fattaan (Ire) J G M O'Shea
4 b g Danehill (USA) - Bintalshaati
1316gf 0-0-1

Favour Mrs J R Ramsden   79
4 b f Gothenberg (Ire) - Prejudice
26gf 97gf 66gf 77gs 127g 36f 115gf 76g
0-2-8 £2,810

Favourable A W Carroll   31
3 b f Mark Of Esteem (Ire) - Top Society
178gf 1110g 1610gs 0-0-3

Favourable Terms Sir Michael Stoute   116
4 b f Selkirk (USA) - Fatefully (USA)
18gf 68gf 110gf 2-0-3 £200,200

Favouring (Ire) R A Fahey   67
2 ch c Fayruz - Peace Dividend (Ire)
45gf 115hy 86f 26s 45s 76s 66gf 0-1-7
£2,267

Favourita C E Brittain   104
2 b f Diktat - Forthwith
17f 47gs 58g 27g 37s 1-2-5 £18,582

Favourite Nation (Ire) D K Weld   97

3 ch c Cadeaux Genereux - Fernanda
76gf 67gf 78gf 18g 38gf 57gf 176ys 47sh
1-0-8 £16,046

Fayr Firenze (Ire) M F Harris   50 a48
3 b g Fayruz - Shillay
97sd 47ss 66sd 26sd 57g 26sd 27g 47gf
0-3-8 £1,552

Fayr Jag (Ire) T D Easterby   118
5 g Fayruz - Lominda (Ire)
136gs 16f 136gs 105s 96s 166hy 1-0-6
£145,000

Fayrway Rhythm (Ire) Ian Emmerson
7 b g Fayruz - The Way She Moves
916sd 0-0-1

Fayrz Please (Ire) M C Chapman   24 a59
3 ch g Fayruz - Castlelue (Ire)
46sd 45sd 126ss 127g 135gf 96g 0-0-6

Feaat J H M Gosden   95
3 b f Unfuwain (USA) - Trois Heures Apres
310g 110f 612gf 612g 414gf 1-1-5 £9,306

Fearby Cross (Ire) W J Musson   71 a69
8 b g Unblest - Two Magpies
67sd 77sd 47s 57gf 87g 87gf 56gf 46gs
66gs 17s 57g 87s 1-0-12 £4,550

Fearless Spirit (USA) J H M Gosden   67
2 ch f Spinning World (USA) - Hot Princess
58gf 0-0-1

Feast Of Romance G A Huffer   55 a62
7 b g Pursuit Of Love - June Fayre
38sd 37sd 17sd 37ss 27sd 68sd 27sd 17sd
58sw 127sd 37gf 126s 67f 46f 157sd 27g 117sd
2-7-17 £9,147

Feed The Meter (Ire) T T Clement   58
4 b f Desert King (Ire) - Watch The Clock
166gf 210gf 112g 1112g 1010g 1-1-5
£5,225

Feel The Need M A Barnes
2 ch c Chocolat De Meguro (USA) - Mary Miller
95f 0-0-1

Feeling Blue B N Pollock   a12
5 b m Missed Flight - Blues Indigo
105ss 165ss 0-0-2

Felicity (Ire) J H M Gosden   102
4 b f Selkirk (USA) - Las Flores (Ire)
79g 310gf 412gf 110g 1110vs 1-1-5
£36,704

Felidae (USA) M Brittain   a29
4 ch c Storm Cat (USA) - Colcon (USA)
912sd 118sd 0-0-2

Fellbeck Fred C W Thornton   35 a22
2 gr c Paris House - Wyse Folly
85g 136gs 75g 45sd 0-0-4

Feminist (Ire) M R Channon   67
2 b f Alhaarth (Ire) - Miss Willow Bend (USA)
55s 35g 75f 96gf 0-1-4 £846

Fen Game (Ire) J H M Gosden   71
2 b c Montjeu (Ire) - Hatton Gardens
68gs 97g 0-0-2

Fen Gypsy P D Evans   77 a64
6 b g Nashwan (USA) - Didicoy (USA)
58sd 410sd 108sd 78sd 910sd 28gs 17gs 28hy
48gs 57gf 17g 28g 47gf 18gf 48gf 47s 38s
188gf 168gs 3-5-19 £17,692

Fen Shui (UAE) Saeed Bin Suroor   86
2 b f Timber Country (USA) - Crystal Gazing (USA)

17gf 87s 1-0-2 £5,265

Fender H R A Cecil   58
3 b c Rainbow Quest (USA) - Rockfest (USA)
710gf 714gs 0-0-2

Fenrir J R Weymes   83
2 ch g Loup Solitaire (USA) - Whoops
77gf 17s 57gs 38gs 88gf 710g 1-0-6
£4,531

Fenwicks Pride (Ire) R A Fahey   59
6 b g Imperial Frontier (USA) - Stunt Girl (Ire)
36s 86f 75gs 136gs 147g 115s 0-1-6
£464

Fern House (Ire) James Moffatt   45
2 b c Xaar - Certain Impression (USA)
125g 0-0-1

Fernery L M Cumani   77
4 b f Danehill (USA) - Fern
411s 710g 0-0-2 £431

Ferrara Flame (Ire) R Brotherton   59 a39
2 b f Titus Livius (Fr) - Isolette
86gf 96sw 76gf 28g 119sd 0-1-5 £1,060

Festive Affair B Smart   a53
6 b g Mujadil (USA) - Christmas Kiss
35sd 116ss 46sd 0-1-3 £367

Festive Chimes (Ire) J J Quinn   56 a34
3 b f Efisio - Delightful Chime (Ire)
76s 37gf 76sd 86gs 67f 97f 0-0-6 £531

Feu Duty (Ire) T J Etherington   68
3 b f Fayruz - Fire Reply (Ire)
65g 15f 95gs 125gf 185gf 135gf 186gf
1-0-7 £3,770

Ffifffiffer (Ire) C Tinkler   a67
6 b Definite Article - Merry Twinkle
413sd 112ss 1014sd 815s 1-0-4 £2,954

Ffizzamo Go Mrs A J Hamilton-Fairley   33
3 b g Forzando - Lady Lacey
612gf 414gf 612gs 0-0-3 £257

Fiamma Royale (Ire) M S Saunders   46 a53
6 b m Fumo Di Londra (Ire) - Ariadne
46sd 126sd 126sd 136s 65f 75gf 0-0-6

Fictional B A McMahon   90
3 b c Fraam - Manon Lescaut
15gf 66g 1-0-2 £12,570

Fiddle Me Blue H Morrison   83
3 ch f Bluebird (USA) - Fiddle-Dee-Dee (Ire)
55s 95gf 146gf 95gf 15gf 35g 65g 116s
25gs 1-1-9 £6,921

Fiddlers Creek (Ire) R Allan   60 a65
5 b g Danehill (USA) - Mythical Creek (USA)
611sd 1012sd 710s 714gf 19gs 412gs 1-0-6
£4,519

Fiddlers Ford (Ire) J Noseda   64 a79
3 b g Sadler's Wells (USA) - Old Domesday Book
310sd 210sd 210sd 610sd 412sd 712hy 410sd
1012gs 118gf 1-3-9 £8,396

Fiddles Music Miss Sheena West   49 a31
3 b f Fraam - Fiddles Delight
98sd 110gf 410f 58f 612gs 512f 710sd 18hy
610gf 710f 2-0-10 £5,572

Fiefdom (Ire) M Johnston   95
2 br c Singspiel (Ire) - Chiquita Linda (Ire)
55g 46gs 16f 26g 47gf 39g 78g 1-1-7
£7,844

Field Spark J A Glover   67 a62

4 b g Sillery (USA) - On The Top
614g 112gf 512gf 212gf 312f 1312g 212gs
1212s 811g 412gf 212sd 312sd 1-6-12 £8,846

Fiennes (USA) Mrs N Macauley   a40
6 b/br g Dayjur (USA) - Artic Strech (USA)
95sd 75sd 136sd 0-0-3

Fiery Angel (Ire) A G Newcombe   10
3 ch f Machiavellian (USA) - Flaming June (USA)
106gs 0-0-1

Fife And Drum (USA) Miss J Feilden   48 a53
7 b/br g Rahy (USA) - Fife (Ire)
78sd 1410sd 610gf 1710gf 1210f 138gf
0-0-6

Fifth Column (USA) D W Thompson   62
3 b g Allied Forces (USA) - Miff (USA)
78gf 118g 98gf 58g PU10s 0-0-5

Figaro's Quest (Ire) P F I Cole   65 a35
2 b c Singspiel (Ire) - Seren Quest
68gs 118g 89sd 0-0-3

Figgy's Brew C G Cox   57
2 ch f Ashkalani (Ire) - Marabela (Ire)
137g 0-0-1

Fight The Feeling J W Unett   41 a64
6 ch g Beveled (USA) - Alvecote Lady
412sd 212sd 212sd 812ss 1412sd 512ss 1112gf
614gf 1014g 515g 913gs 0-2-11 £1,484

Fight Your Corner Saeed Bin Suroor   107
5 b h Muhtarram (USA) - Dame Ashfield
812gs 314g 0-0-2 £1,754

Fighting Tom Cat (USA) Saeed Bin Suroor   78
2 ch c Storm Cat (USA) - Elizabeth Bay (USA)
116g 66gf 16s 1-0-3 £4,832

Figura R Ingram   45 a64
6 b m Rudimentary (USA) - Dream Baby
1410sd 310sd 512sd 610sd 610sd 610sd 510sd
1610gf 810f 88f 89gf 510sd 1410sd 0-1-13 £431

Filey Buoy R M Whitaker   38
2 b g Factual (USA) - Tugra (Fr)
136s 77gf 137gs 77g 0-0-4

Filliemou (Ire) A W Carroll   59 a40
3 gr f Goldmark (USA) - St Louis Lady
97g 1010gf 87g 58g 28gf 48f 48gf 187gf
129sd 158s 0-1-10 £1,689

Final Dividend (Ire) J M P Eustace   56
8 b g Second Set (Ire) - Prime Interest (Ire)
1112gf 511f 610gf 512gf 112f 612s 1-0-6
£3,341

Final Lap H H G Owen   a28
8 b g Batshoof - Lap Of Honour
1112sw 38sw 712sd 0-1-3 £184

Final Overture (Ire) J S Wainwright
2 b f Rossini (USA) - Two Magpies
76gf 0-0-1

Final Promise G B Balding   64
2 b c Lujain (USA) - Unerring
107s 87gs 46s 0-0-3 £460

Financial Future M Johnston   74
4 b g Barathea (Ire) - In Perpetuity
1712g 1512g 1212g 811g 712gf 712f 1412f
0-0-7

Financial Times (USA) Saeed Bin Suroor   83
2 b c Awesome Again (Can) - Investabull (USA)
26gf 0-1-1 £1,622

Finders Keepers E A L Dunlop   81 a81

3 b g Selkirk (USA) - La Nuit Rose (Fr)
27sd 37sd 17gf 86s 87gf 87f 16sd 127sd
85s 2-2-9 £14,241

Fine Frenzy (Ire) Miss S J Wilton   44 a34
4 b f Great Commotion (USA) - Fine Project (Ire)
78gs 47sd 117gf 0-0-3

Fine Lady M Johnston   69
2 ch f Machiavellian (USA) - Rua D'Oro (USA)
68s 27gf 38s 27s 0-3-4 £2,621

Fine Palette H R A Cecil   97
4 ch c Peintre Celebre (USA) - Filly Mignonne (Ire)
110s 110gf 512gf 510gs 310gf 1911g 2-1-6
£14,125

Fine Silver (Ire) P F I Cole   108
3 gr c Intikhab (USA) - Petula
47gs 108gf 18gf 48f 28g 210gf 39g 28hy
1-5-8 £54,906

Finger Of Fate M J Polglase   48 a48
4 br g Machiavellian (USA) - La Nuit Rose (Fr)
912sd 128sd 716sd 1410sd 126ss 126sd 25sf
65ss 46sd 66sd 135gf 85gs 35sd 147g 37gf
VOI5gf 106f 127gf 0-3-18 £1,198

Finished Article (Ire) W J Musson   99
7 b g Indian Ridge - Summer Fashion
138g 58g 38gf 168gf 108gs 198gf 98gs
48s 88gs 0-2-9 £4,001

Finnegans Rainbow P F I Cole   30
2 ch c Spectrum (Ire) - Fairy Story (Ire)
118g 0-0-1

Finnforest (Ire) Mrs A J Bowlby
4 ch g Eagle Eyed (USA) - Stockrose
1216sd 0-0-1

Finningley Connor Ronald Thompson   13 a9
4 b g Cosmonaut - Arroganza
107ss 168gs 117gs 0-0-3

Fiore Di Bosco (Ire) T D Barron   72
3 b f Charnwood Forest (Ire) - Carabine (USA)
56gs 106gf 47gf 46gf 66g 0-0-5 £1,385

Fire At Will A W Carroll   40
2 b c Lugana Beach - Kahyasi Moll (Ire)
75gf 75f 85gs 78g 0-0-4

Fire Dome (Ire) Andrew Reid
12 ch g Salt Dome (USA) - Penny Habit
137sd 0-0-1

Fire Dragon (Ire) Jonjo O'Neill   82
3 b g Sadler's Wells (USA) - Cattermole (USA)
411ys 112gy 512g 414gs 1-0-4 £6,353

Fire Finch M R Channon   78
3 ch f Halling (USA) - Fly For Fame
68g 610g 88f 612gf 1412gf 0-0-5 £450

Fire Up The Band D Nicholls   102 a88
5 b h Prince Sabo - Green Supreme
75sd 76g 36gs 46s 216f 15g 125gf 115s
76gf 216s 1-0-10 £19,703

Firebelly M J Wallace   55 a65
3 b f Nicolotte - Desert Delight (Ire)
58sd 77gf 106g 0-0-3 £518

Firebird H Candy   69
3 b f Soviet Star (USA) - Al Corniche (Ire)
36gf 0-1-1 £878

Firebird Rising (USA) R Brotherton   61
3 b f Stravinsky (USA) - Capable (USA)
56gf 85gf 37f 67g 96s 47f 77s 77gs 37f
147f 0-1-10 £758

Firebreak Saeed Bin Suroor   123   a120
5 b h Charnwood Forest (Ire) - Breakaway
18ft 48g 27gf 17s 2-1-4 £426,195

Firecat A P Jones   26   a6
5 ch g Beveled (USA) - Noble Soul
117sd 76sd 105gs 96s 115gf 65gf 0-0-6

Firenze J R Fanshawe   30   a77
3 ch f Efisio - Juliet Bravo
95gf 16sd 1-0-2 £3,283

Firesong S Kirk   72
2 b c Dansili - Leaping Flame (USA)
67g 0-0-1

Firewire Miss B Sanders   71
6 b g Blushing Flame (USA) - Bay Risk
18g 169gf 1-0-2 £5,447

Firework J Akehurst   69   a54
6 b g Primo Dominie - Prancing
116sd 116sd 126sd 66s 56g 96gf 16gf 96gs
126gf 46g 46gf 1-0-11 £3,596

Firozi R A Fahey   51
5 b m Forzando - Lambast
58f 0-0-1

First Candlelight J G Given   78
3 b f First Trump - No Candles Tonight
98s 177g 77gf 127gf 0-0-4

First Centurion J W Hills   84   a57
3 b c Peintre Celebre (USA) - Valley Of Hope (USA)
18hy 810gf 1112g 410gf 513gs 912sd 1-0-6
£6,352

First Charter Sir Michael Stoute   118
5 b h Polish Precedent (USA) - By Charter
913gs 112gf 212gf 116g 314g 2-2-5
£101,436

First Class Girl C B B Booth   a1
5 b m Charmer - Boulevard Girl
412sd 1010gf 0-0-2

First Class Lady P Mitchell   a31
4 ch f Lion Cavern (USA) - Tino-Ella
58sd 1212sd 0-0-2

First Counsel M A Jarvis   76
3 b g Wolfhound (USA) - Supreme Kingdom
58gf 38gs 0-1-2 £935

First Dawn M R Channon   58
3 ch f Dr Fong (USA) - Delight Of Dawn
77gf 117g 88g 168g 0-0-4

First Dynasty (USA) Miss S J Wilton   77   a80
4 b/br c Danzig (USA) - Willow Runner (USA)
19sd 78s 68gf 310g 712s 1-1-5 £4,044

First Eagle A L Forbes   38
5 b g Hector Protector (USA) - Merlin's Fancy
129sd 310f 0-1-2 £554

First Eclipse (Ire) J Balding   37
3 b f Fayruz - Naked Poser (Ire)
95gf 115gf 0-0-2

First Fought (Ire) M Johnston   11
2 b g Germany (USA) - Royal Flame (Ire)
188s 0-0-1

First Maite S R Bowring   58   a75
11 b g Komaite (USA) - Marina Plata
68sd 68sd 68ss 412sd 310gf 28gf 38sd 510gf
0-3-8 £1,969

First Of May Miss Z C Davison   a53
3 b f Halling (USA) - Finger Of Light
37sd 48sd 68sd 0-1-3 £907

First Order Sir Mark Prescott   108
3 b g Primo Dominie - Unconditional Love (Ire)
25g 225gf 65g 25g 0-2-4 £4,864

First Rhapsody (Ire) T J Etherington   26   a56
2 b f Rossini (USA) - Tinos Island (Ire)
125gf 116gf 46sd 0-0-3 £331

First Row (Ire) B J Meehan   76
2 b c Daylami (Ire) - Ballet Society (Fr)
57gf 0-0-1

First Rule C F Wall   68
2 ch c Primo Dominie - Tarsa
75hy 45gf 45g 85g 86gf 0-0-5 £650

Fisby S Kirk   61   a66
3 ch g Efisio - Trilby
58sd 58gf 146gs 108g 108f 19sd 1-0-6
£2,716

Fisher's Dream J R Norton   a29
3 b g Groom Dancer (USA) - Cremets
76sd 0-0-1

Fishlake Flyer (Ire) J G Given   64
3 b f Desert Style (Ire) - Millitrix
45s 35gf 45gf 0-1-3 £1,053

Fisio Therapy M Johnston   85
4 b g Efisio - Corn Lily
98g 411s PU10gs 0-0-3 £764

Fission Mrs Stef Liddiard   76   a73
3 ch f Efisio - Area Girl
66sd 37sd 17sd 97sd 26gf 106s 1-2-6
£4,517

Fit To Fly (Ire) Mrs J Candlish   79   a69
3 b g Lahib (USA) - Maid Of Mourne
26sw 57sd 16sd 58gf 67sd 910gs 58g 1211g
88sd 78g 1112sd 97sd 1-1-12 £4,360

Fitting Guest (Ire) G G Margarson   78
3 ch c Grand Lodge (USA) - Sarah-Clare
610gs 210gf 210gf 110gf 148f 1-2-5
£8,319

Fitz The Bill (Ire) N B King   36   a36
4 b f Mon Tresor - In The Sky (Ire)
88sd 812sd 310sd 310gf 710gf 1110g 916gf
0-1-7 £549

Fitzwarren N Bycroft   69
3 b g Presidium - Coney Hills
146gf 35s 105gs 95gf 36gf 66f 176gf 65f
186gf 127gs 0-2-10 £1,234

Five Dynasties (USA) A P O'Brien   111
3 b c Danehill (USA) - Star Begonia
311s 812gs 112f 812gf 1-0-4 £92,825

Five Gold (Ire) A C Whillans   46
3 b g Desert Prince (Ire) - Ceide Dancer (Ire)
117g 77gf 167gf 107gs 910s 0-0-5

Five Years On (Ire) W J Haggas   70   a69
3 b g Desert Sun - Snowspin
48g 48g 57sd 0-0-3 £583

Fiveoclock Express (Ire) Miss Gay Kelleway   87   a97
4 gr g Woodborough (USA) - Brooks Masquerade
47sd 27g 137s 77f 58gf 28sd 167gf 106gs
98gs 117g 119sd 0-2-11 £7,561

Fizzy Lady N E Berry   57   a65
3 b f Efisio - The Frog Lady (Ire)
48sd 46sd 17sd 77gf 118g 127g 78gs 147g
28gf 410hy 1010gf 110gf 711gs 2-1-13 £6,235

Fizzy Lizzy G A Ham   43   a34
4 b f Cool Jazz - Formidable Liz
126f 116sd 86s 16f 96sd 1-0-5 £3,220

Fizzy Pop W S Cunningham 28
5 b m Robellino (USA) - Maria Isabella (Fr)
67f 89gs 0-0-2

Flag Lieutenant Sir Michael Stoute 81
2 b c Machiavellian (USA) - Fairy Godmother
27g 0-1-1 £1,840

Flag Point (Ire) J L Dunlop 76
2 b c Indian Danehill (Ire) - Bianca Cappello (Ire)
37g 78gf 97g 118g 118s 0-1-5 £851

Flamand (USA) L M Cumani 61
2 ch f Miswaki (USA) - Sister Sorrow (USA)
56gf 0-0-1

Flambe P C Haslam a65
6 b g Whittingham (Ire) - Uaeflame (Ire)
48sd 0-0-1 £311

Flamboyant Lad B W Hills 92
3 ch c Nashwan (USA) - Cheeky Charm (USA)
310g 310gf 310gs 210gf 110f 110g 112s 3-4-7
£34,232

Flame Of Zara James Moffatt 59
5 ch m Blushing Flame (USA) - Sierra Madrona (USA)
716s 414g 715s 0-1-3

Flame Princess J R Boyle a42
4 ch f Bluegrass Prince (Ire) - Rekindled Flame (Ire)
36sd 116sd 88sd 147sd 0-0-4 £182

Flame Queen Mrs C A Dunnett 64
3 b f The West (USA) - Red Cloud (Ire)
97gf 118g 98gf 47gf 88s 410gf 1210g 78gf
88g 0-0-9 £632

Flamenco Bride D R C Elsworth 74
4 b f Hernando (Fr) - Premier Night
712gs 716gf 314gf 1114gs 0-1-4 £1,266

Flaming Spirt J S Moore 58 a46
5 b m Blushing Flame (USA) - Fair Test
410sd 412gs 210gs 1710s 0-2-4 £1,386

Flamingo Palace P J McBride
3 ch g Croco Rouge (Ire) - Chantilly (Fr)
712gf 0-0-1

Flamjica (USA) J A R Toller 71
3 ch f Real Quiet (USA) - Fiamma (Ire)
48gf 28gf 0-1-2 £2,134

Flapdoodle A W Carroll 53 a23
6 b m Superpower - My Concordia
55gf 125f 115gf 145gf 35g 116g 55gs
85sd 0-1-8 £637

Flaran E F Vaughan 65
4 b g Emarati (USA) - Fragrance
155gf VOI5gf 116gs 35g 36g 0-2-5
£1,115

Flash Ram T D Easterby 67
3 b g Mind Games - Just A Gem
65g 47f 26gf 27s 66gf 17gf 66g 37gf
198gf 1-3-9 £9,594

Flashing Blade B A McMahon 73
4 b f Inchinor - Finlaggan
156g 76gs 135g 126g 96gf 18gf 78gs 67gs
57gf 96gs 28f 1-1-11 £6,180

Flaunt N Flirt M P Tregoning 29 a59
2 b f Erhaab (USA) - Lets Fall In Love (USA)
96g 107sd 27sd 0-1-3 £1,112

Flaunting It (Ire) J A Osborne 66
2 ch f Alhaarth (Ire) - Ide Say (Ire)
57gf 87gs 46s 67gf 0-0-4 £383

Flaxby J D Bethell 62

2 b g Mister Baileys - Harryana
146s 86gf 46gf 86s 0-0-4 £1,467

Fleet Anchor J M Bradley 62
3 b c Fleetwood (Ire) - Upping The Tempo
96gf 76s 96gf 27gs 56gs 38g 58hy 108gs
118s 0-2-9 £1,529

Fleetfoot Mac P D Evans 70 a68
3 b Fleetwood (Ire) - Desert Flower
112gs 112s 814gs 1412gf 312sd 412gs 912gf
1316gs 2-1-8 £6,185

Fleeting Moon A M Balding 70 a69
4 ch f Fleetwood (Ire) - Aunt Judy
212sd 213sd 111sw 316sd 213gf 412sd 1-4-6
£5,065

Fleetwood Bay B R Millman 74
4 b g Fleetwood (Ire) - Caviar And Candy
167gs 146gs 68s 38gf 67gf 97g 28gf 68gf
78s 106gs 0-2-10 £2,251

Fletcher H Morrison 47 a45
10 b g Salse (USA) - Ballet Classique (USA)
1213sd 512gf 116sd 714gf 1212gf 1018f
414gf 1-0-7 £1,463

Flight Commander (Ire) I Semple 62
4 b g In The Wings - Lucrezia (Ire)
59gs 710g 1612hy 1115s 1212gs 0-0-5

Flight Of Esteem P W Harris a101
4 b g Mark Of Esteem (Ire) - Miss Up N Go
212sd 212sd 0-2-2 £8,698

Flighty Fellow (Ire) T D Easterby 102
4 ch g Flying Spur (Aus) - Al Theraab (USA)
158g 68s 18gf 188gf 68g 28gs 48gf 1611g
48f 38gf 108g 1-2-11 £18,812

Fling J R Fanshawe 91
3 b f Pursuit Of Love - Full Orchestra
110gs 510gf 210gf 212s 411s 514s 316gs 417s
1-2-8 £16,518

Flint River H Morrison 81 a92
6 b g Red Ransom (USA) - She's All Class (USA)
26sd 76sd 88ss 127sd 17ss 27gf 48gs 107g
97g 28f 28gs 59g 87sd 109sd 1-5-14
£18,598

Flip Flop And Fly (Ire) S Kirk 88
3 b g Woodborough (USA) - Angelus Chimes
148g 116s 17gf 77g 68gs 27gf 57gf 88gf
1-1-8 £8,952

Flipando (Ire) T D Barron 94
3 b g Sri Pekan (USA) - Magic Touch
46s 26gf 27f 16g 56gs 37gs 18g 2-4-7
£33,637

Floosie (Ire) N P Littmoden 11
2 b f Night Shift (USA) - German Lady
95gf 106g 0-0-2

Florenzar (Ire) P D Evans a21
6 b m Inzar (USA) - Nurse Tyra (USA)
109sd 910sd 0-0-2

Florian T G Mills 56 a21
6 b g Young Ern - Murmuring
128sd 88g 137gf 58f 67hy 186f 86g 0-0-7

Florida Heart A M Balding 74
3 ch f First Trump - Miami Dancer (USA)
48gf 69g 0-1-2 £547

Flossytoo J O'Reilly 69
2 b f Royal Applause - Nite-Owl Dancer
105g 15s 95gf 125gf 95g 1-0-5 £4,719

Flotta M R Channon 91 a90
5 ch g Elmaamul (USA) - Heavenly Goddess
413sd 512g 712g 414gf 414gf 312gf 714gs
112gf 612g 511g 1012gf 1012s 612s 1-0-13
£13,415

Flower Seeker C Tinkler 22
2 b f Lujain (USA) - Kingpin Delight
167gs 97hy 128gs 0-0-3

Flowerdrum (USA) W J Haggas 94
4 b f Mister Baileys - Norelands (USA)
87hy 18gf 48gf 18g 148gf 58gf 1010hy 58gf
2-0-8 £17,021

Flur Na H Alba I Semple 91 a87
5 b g Atraf - Tyrian Belle
17f 127g 37gf 46g 137s 37sd 1-1-6
£8,177

Flushing Meadows (USA) Saeed Bin Suroor 86
3 b c Grand Slam (USA) - Sheepish Grin (USA)
56g 0-0-1 £390

Fly Kicker W Storey 33
7 ch g High Kicker (USA) - Double Birthday
717g 615gf 0-0-2

Fly Me To Dunoon (Ire) K R Burke 37 a39
2 b f Rossini (USA) - Toledana (Ire)
87gf 66s 108sd 0-0-3

Fly More J M Bradley 58
7 ch g Lycius (USA) - Double River (USA)
126gs 135gs 0-0-2

Fly So High D Shaw 11 a24
3 b f Danzero (Aus) - Fly The Flag (NZ)
107sd 77sd 86g 1110g 0-0-4

Fly To Dubai (Ire) E J O'Neill 56
2 b c Fly To The Stars - Morna's Fan (Fr)
116gf 66g 137sd 0-0-3

Flying Adored J L Dunlop 87
3 b f Polar Falcon (USA) - Shining High
37s 108g 18g 18gs 58g 310s 1610s 2-2-7
£14,315

Flying Bantam (Ire) R A Fahey 88 a92
3 b g Fayruz - Natural Pearl
26g 26gf 26f 46gf 76gf 26gf 45gs 76gs 46f
16gf 36sd 16sd 26s 2-6-13 £16,965

Flying Dancer A King 67 a67
2 b f Danzero (Aus) - Alzianah
36gf 46sd 176gf 96hy 0-1-4 £1,107

Flying Edge (Ire) E J Alston 65 a58
4 b g Flying Spur (Aus) - Day Is Dawning (Ire)
126sd 27sd 77ss 56g 147f 66gf 56f 167gf
107g 87gf 46g 46s 116gs 47sd 0-2-14 £1,553

Flying Express B W Hills 93 a77
4 ch c Air Express (Ire) - Royal Loft
67gs 128gs 27gf 87gf 37gf 118gf 97sd
237g 0-2-8 £5,723

Flying Faisal (USA) J M Bradley 51 a38
6 b h Alydeed (Can) - Peaceful Silence (USA)
86sd 96sd 106sd 66sd 86sd 46sw 157sd 86sw
35sd 105ss 46sd 65gs 16gf 85g 106gf 97gf
136gf 186gf 1-1-18 £2,790

Flying Heart M R Channon 44
2 ch f Bahamian Bounty - Flying Wind
76g 86g 86s 0-0-3

Flying Highest H Candy 17
2 b f Spectrum (Ire) - Mainly Sunset
76hy 0-0-1

Flying Pass D J S Ffrench Davis 73 a69

2 b g Alzao (USA) - Complimentary Pass
85hy 36gf 86gf 27gf 27sd 57gf 66gs 48f
210gf 78s 0-4-10 £4,616

Flying Patriarch G L Moore 35
3 gr g Silver Patriarch (Ire) - Flying Wind
1310g 814g 0-0-2

Flying Red (Ire) P A Blockley
3 b f Entrepreneur - Mary Ellen Best (Ire)
811g 0-0-1

Flying Ridge (Ire) A M Balding 76
2 ch f Indian Ridge - Jarrayan
146gf 56g 56g 15g 1-0-4 £3,589

Flying Spirit (Ire) G L Moore 87
5 b g Flying Spur (Aus) - All Laughter
112gf 112f 112g 912gf 212g 3-1-5
£17,230

Flying Spud J L Spearing 54 a48
3 ch g Fraam - Lorcanjo
56ss 47sd 58s 18gs 711gf 78sd 158gf 28gs
98gs 118g 58gs 59sd 1-1-12 £3,856

Flying Tackle M Dods 58 a45
6 ch g First Trump - Frighten The Life
106sd 76gs 75g 86gf 25g 15f 155gs 95gf
175gf 116g 25f 115gf 1-3-12 £4,865

Flying Tara John A Harris
2 b f Kayf Tara - Arcady
76gf 0-0-1

Flying Treaty (USA) J L Spearing 64 a75
7 br h You And I (USA) - Cherie's Hope (USA)
116sd 87sd 98ss 612ss 87g 77gf 58sd 68g
810gf 0-0-9

Flying With Eagles J Jay 29 a21
3 ch g Most Welcome - Super Sol
136gf 146gf 137f 67sd 1716gs 0-0-5

Flyoff (Ire) K A Morgan 30
7 b g Mtoto - Flyleaf (Fr)
912sd 1012gf 0-0-2

Focus Group (USA) H R A Cecil 77
3 b c Kris S (USA) - Interim
19gf 1-0-1 £3,552

Fokine (USA) B W Hills 111 a103
3 b c Royal Academy (USA) - Polar Bird
27sd 27g 17gf 27gf 1-3-4 £59,200

Fold Walk M W Easterby 34 a46
2 ch f Paris House - Georgia
75s 45gs UR5gf 116gf 55gs 36sw 117gs
137gf 0-1-8 £633

Foley Millennium (Ire) M Quinn 81
6 ch g Tagula (Ire) - Inshirah (USA)
85s 15hy 16f 15f 15g 125g 26gf 15gf 46gf
25gs 85s 55g 55gf 155g 5-2-14 £19,943

Foley Prince Mrs Stef Liddiard 77 a65
3 b g Makbul - Princess Foley (Ire)
77sd 37sd 77ss 18s 28gf 28gf 38gf 68g
1-4-8 £7,692

Folga J G Given 71
2 b f Atraf - Desert Dawn
35gf 95gs 15g 55gf 1-0-4 £4,764

Folio (Ire) W J Musson 93
4 b g Perugino (USA) - Bayleaf
67gf 0-0-1

Follow My Lead B W Hills 55
2 b f Night Shift (USA) - Launch Time (USA)
95gf 75gf 76g 0-0-3

Follow The Game P W Harris a35
2 b c Mind Games - Play The Game
107sd 0-0-1

Following Flow (USA) W Jarvis 79 a71
2 b/br g King Of Kings (Ire) - Sign Here (USA)
97gf 37sd 17gf 27s 158gf 107gs 1-2-6
£7,376

Fong Shui P J Makin 76 a70
2 ch c Dr Fong (USA) - Manila Selection (USA)
46gf 77sd 17g 47gs 196s 1-0-5 £3,927

Fong's Thong (USA) B J Meehan 114
3 ch c Dr Fong (USA) - Bacinella (USA)
17g 18gf 57gf 78gf 2-0-4 £33,350

Fongtastic B J Meehan 85
2 ch c Dr Fong (USA) - Kelso Magic (USA)
36g 17gf 1-1-2 £4,268

Fonthill Road (Ire) R A Fahey 88
4 ch g Royal Abjar (USA) - Hannah Huxtable (Ire)
66gf 16gs 37gs 26g 26hy 16g 16gs 66s 86gs
3-3-9 £26,815

Foodbroker Founder D R C Elsworth 101
4 ch g Groom Dancer (USA) - Nemea (USA)
710gf 610f 610gs 1510g 612gs 810g 1210gf
0-0-7 £1,500

Foolish Groom R Hollinshead 72
3 ch g Groom Dancer (USA) - Scared
38s 48gf 58gs 69g 38gs 58s 98gf 28hy 38gf
PU9sd 0-4-10 £4,229

Foolish Thought (Ire) I A Wood a57
4 b g Green Desert (USA) - Trusted Partner (USA)
67sd 57sd 49sd 16sd 57sw 147sd 117sd
206g 1-0-8 £1,330

Fools Entire Mrs A C Gilbert 67 a70
3 ch g Fraam - Poly Blue (Ire)
27sd 97sd 37sd 68g 138g 147gf 186gf 77sd
96sd 36sd 47gs 58s 127gf 86s 176s 0-3-15
£2,736

Foot Fault (Ire) N A Callaghan a54
3 b f Danehill (USA) - Mockery
157sd 410sd 410sd 410sd 0-0-4

Football Crazy (Ire) P Bowen 73
5 b g Mujadil (USA) - Schonbein (Ire)
1312s 1014g 0-0-2

Footstepsinthesand A P O'Brien 112
2 b c Giant's Causeway (USA) - Glatisant
16ys 17s 2-0-2 £40,850

For Life (Ire) A P Jarvis 87
2 b c Bachir (Ire) - Zest (USA)
36g 186g 0-1-2 £1,060

For Nowt T D Easterby 34
2 b c Forzando - Angel Chimes
65g 126g 97g 106gf 137s 0-0-5

Fora Smile M D I Usher 37 a42
3 ch c Forzando - Don't Smile
76sd 107sd 107sd 78sw 116sd 57gs 710sd
0-0-7

Forbearing (Ire) F Jordan 59
7 b g Bering - For Example (USA)
312gf 210gf 612gf 0-2-3 £1,365

Force Nine (USA) J Noseda 68
2 br c Stormin Fever (USA) - Screener (USA)
58g 0-0-1

Force Of Nature (USA) H R A Cecil 76
4 b f Sadler's Wells (USA) - Yashmak (USA)
1010g 212gf 412gf 0-1-3 £1,479

Forehand (Ire) E F Vaughan 35
2 b f Lend A Hand - Set Trail (Ire)
137s 0-0-1

Foreign Affairs Sir Mark Prescott 110
6 ch h Hernando (Fr) - Entente Cordiale (USA)
112ho 316s 412g 512s 111g 112gf 212gf 212s
3-2-8 £77,373

Forest Air (Ire) Miss L A Perratt 52
4 br f Charnwood Forest (Ire) - Auriga
99g 18g 88s 79gf 58g 210g 610gf 79gf
1-1-8 £2,342

Forest Delight (Ire) C Tinkler 52
2 ch f Shinko Forest (Ire) - Laurel Delight
75gs 85gf 115s 0-0-3

Forest Heath (Ire) H J Collingridge a15
7 gr g Common Grounds - Caroline Lady (Jpn)
1010sd 1412sd 0-0-2

Forest Magic (Ire) P W D'Arcy 100
4 b c Charnwood Forest (Ire) - Adultress (Ire)
412g 912g 513gs 713g 0-0-4 £3,024

Forest Queen K W Hogg a8
7 b m Risk Me (Fr) - Grey Cree
118sw 108sd 135gf 98sd 0-0-4

Forest Rail (Ire) John A Harris 31
4 b f Catrail (USA) - Forest Heights
125gf 86g 0-0-2

Forest Tune (Ire) B Hanbury 62 a52
6 b g Charnwood Forest (Ire) - Swift Chorus
1410g 1010gs 812gf 612gf 910f 1110sd 610g
410g 510gf 310gf 0-2-10 £773

Forest Viking (Ire) J S Wainwright 55
2 b g Orpen (USA) - Berhala (Ire)
56gf 86f 116gf 226gf 196s 0-0-5 £397

Forever My Lord J R Best 44 a42
6 b g Be My Chief (USA) - In Love Again (Ire)
810sd 1012sd 913sd 613f 0-0-4

Forever Phoenix R M H Cowell 106 a99
4 b f Shareef Dancer (USA) - With Care
57sd 66sd 16sd 16sd 26sd 15sd 35gs 15s
26g LFT5g 96gf 25gf 35gf 76g 35g 65gs 15g
66g 5-6-21 £70,790

Forfeiter (USA) T D Barron 78
2 ch g Petionville (USA) - Picabo (USA)
25gf 65g 27f 27gf 37gs 197gs 0-4-6
£4,501

Forge Lane (Ire) G L Moore 59 a51
3 b g Desert Style (Ire) - March Fourteenth (USA)
97sd 98sd 97s 128g 1012sd 410gf 210gf
910f 810gf 810sd 1711gs 0-2-11 £850

Forged (Ire) L M Cumani 97
3 b c Peintre Celebre (USA) - Imitation
2010g 312gf 210g 112gf 1-2-4 £7,897

Forgery (Ire) G A Butler 76
2 ch c Dr Devious (Ire) - Memory Green (USA)
38s 0-1-1 £553

Formalise J A Geake 61
4 b g Forzando - Esilam
135gf 76gf 56gf 96gf 56g 136gf 96gf 45g
126g 145gf 0-0-10 £386

Formeric Miss L C Siddall 45 a10
8 ch g Formidable (USA) - Irish Limerick
88sd 97sd 36hy 167hy 116s 146gs 0-1-6
£611

Formidable Will (Fr) C G Cox a42
2 b g Efisio - Shewillifshewants (Ire)

116s 117sd 0-0-2

Forpetesake Ms Deborah J Evans   54
2 ch g Primo Dominie - Showcase
95g 66f 67gs 87gf 67gs 88s 1510gf 0-0-7

Forrest Gump C J Teague   51
4 ch g Zilzal (USA) - Mish Mish
108g 26gf 96gs 0-1-3 £1,252

Fort M Johnston   106
3 ch g Dr Fong (USA) - Chief's Quest (USA)
38gs 1110g 312g 212gf 1012g 510g 112gf
612g 1-2-8 £42,278

Fort Churchill (Ire) B Ellison   84
3 b g Barathea (Ire) - Brisighella (Ire)
511gf 311f 410g 212s 713gs 112s 911hy 214g
713gs 1-3-9 £7,788

Fort Dignity (USA) Sir Michael Stoute   108
3 b c Seeking The Gold (USA) - Kitza (Ire)
47g 410gs 0-0-2 £4,000

Fort McHenry (Ire) N A Callaghan   68 a41
4 b g Danehill Dancer (Ire) - Griqualand
86gs 86gf 16gf 127sd 1-0-4 £2,877

Forthright C E Brittain   96 a89
3 b g Cadeaux Genereux - Forthwith
110sd 88ft 49ft 510gs 68f 138g 710gf 98gs
67sd 98gf 68gf 1-0-11 £10,790

Fortnum R Hannon   60
2 b c Forzando - Digamist Girl (Ire)
55hy 35s 96gf 57gf 36gs 107gf 0-1-6
£1,226

Fortuna Mea W M Brisbourne
4 b f Mon Tresor - Veni Vici (Ire)
610gs 915sd 0-0-2

Fortunate Dave (USA) Ian Williams   a29
5 b g Lear Fan (USA) - Lady Ameriflora (USA)
1113sd 0-0-1

Fortunate Isle (USA) B W Hills   80
2 ch c Swain (Ire) - Isla Del Rey (USA)
27g 0-1-1 £2,655

Fortune Point (Ire) A W Carroll   64 a67
6 ch g Cadeaux Genereux - Mountains Of Mist (Ire)
410sd 108sd 28sd 110sd 312sd 210sd 1912gs
1210g 48sd 108gf 68sd 210f 910g 1-4-13
£6,768

Fortune's Princess M J Wallace   81
3 b f Desert Prince (Ire) - Golden Fortune
210gf 210gf 110gf 210g 910gf 1-3-5
£12,832

Fortunes Favourite J E Long   50 a36
4 ch f Barathea (Ire) - Golden Fortune
916sd 314sd 412sw 1214sd 110gs 712hy 1011f
1-0-7 £3,478

Forty Forte Miss S J Wilton   26 a56
8 b g Pursuit Of Love - Cominna
119sd 88sd 98sw 311sd 911s 68sd 18sd 98sd
1-1-8 £1,669

Forward Move (Ire) R Hannon   93
2 ch c Dr Fong (USA) - Kissing Gate (USA)
28g 18gf 1-1-2 £5,946

Forzeen J A Osborne   87 a93
2 ch g Forzando - Mazurkanova
35sd 45f 25gf 35sd 15g 45gf 75f 216g
15gf 85g 16sd 26sd 3-3-12 £19,747

Forzenuff J R Boyle   49 a55
3 b c Mujadil (USA) - Sada

55sd 76sd 66sd 88sd 105gf 125g 127gf
196g 0-0-8

Fossgate J D Bethell   77
3 ch g Halling (USA) - Peryllys
28g 168hy 38gf 610gf 49gf 48gs 48gs 87gs
0-2-8 £3,345

Four Amigos (USA) J G Given   87
3 b g Southern Halo (USA) - Larentia
56gs 15s 96gs 65g 36g 75g 96s 115s 45s
95g 75s 1-1-11 £11,666

Four Jays (Ire) N P Littmoden   a54
4 b g Alzao (USA) - Paparazzi (Ire)
97sd 97sd 0-0-2

Four Kings R Allan   67 a61
3 b c Forzando - High Cut
55sd 86gs 36gf 38gf 98gf 69gf 167gs 1712s
0-0-8 £1,469

Four Pence (Ire) B W Hills   71 a30
3 b c Rainbow Quest (USA) - American Queen (Fr)
413f 212gf 612sd 0-1-3 £2,093

Four Pleasure C A Dwyer   35
2 ch f King's Best (USA) - Please
166g 237g 0-0-2

Foursquare (Ire) J Mackie   93
3 b g Fayruz - Waroonga (Ire)
15s 55s 105gf 45gf 126g 35g 1-2-6
£8,683

Fourswainby (Ire) B Ellison   39
3 b g Foxhound (USA) - Arena
68g 38hy 0-0-2 £442

Fourth Dimension (Ire) D Nicholls   87
5 b g Entrepreneur - Isle Of Spice (USA)
1012gs 412gf 714g 714gf 1510g 0-0-5 £417

Fox C E Brittain   100
2 b c Diktat - Badawi (USA)
26gf 17gf 47gs 37g 67s 1-2-5 £16,616

Fox Covert (Ire) D W Barker   64
3 b g Foxhound (USA) - Serious Contender (Ire)
76g 146gs 157hy 26f 36gf 56g 86gf 46gf
145gf 106gs 35g 16g 135gf 1-3-13 £5,491

Fox Hollow (Ire) M J Haynes   27 a54
3 b c Foxhound (USA) - Soignee
78sd 96sd 37sd 28ss 67gs 29sd 311sd 912gf
1212sd 810sd 1010g 0-3-11 £2,332

Foxhaven P R Chamings   93
2 ch c Unfuwain (USA) - Dancing Mirage (Ire)
37gs 28g 28g 17g 67s 1-3-5 £10,598

Foxies Future (Ire) J R Weymes   15 a49
3 b f General Monash (USA) - Indescent Blue
36sd 166gs 0-0-2 £1,235

Foxilla (Ire) D R C Elsworth   66 a52
3 ch f Foxhound (USA) - Lilissa (Ire)
910sd 710sd 310gf 110gf 412g 310gf 210gf
1-3-7 £7,621

Foxy Gwynne A M Balding   70 a32
2 b f Entrepreneur - Nahlin
106sd 37gf 27gs 0-2-3 £1,766

Foxy Trix J W Unett
5 b/br m Mind Games - Hill Vixen
712ss 0-0-1

Fraambuoyant (Ire) C W Fairhurst   27 a2
2 b f Fraam - River Maiden (USA)
117sd 107gf 97sd 67s 0-0-4

Fraamtastic B A Pearce   44 a53

7 b m Fraam - Fading
27sd 411sd 18ss 68ss 157sd 18ss 18sd 27gs
3-2-8 £5,016

Frabrofen James Moffatt   62 a5
3 b f Mind Games - Oh My Oh My
25s 106sd 95s 0-1-3 £924

Fragrant Star C E Brittain   77
3 gr f Soviet Star (USA) - Norfolk Lavender (Can)
87g 710gf 108gf 108g 97gf 0-0-5

Fraloga (Ire) A Fabre   107
2 b f Grand Lodge (USA) - Fragrant Hill
48gs 18g 38g 1-1-3 £31,954

Frambo (Ire) J G Portman   42 a41
3 b f Fraam - Wings Awarded
911sd 711sd 510sd 1010gs 612s 412sd 412sd
412gf 316gf 312gs 616s 0-1-11 £1,101

Frambroise D R Loder   32
2 ch f Diesis - Applaud (USA)
136g 0-0-1

Francis Flute B Mactaggart   63
6 b g Polar Falcon (USA) - Darshay (Fr)
78g 27gf 48g 78g 97gf 99gf 107gs 0-1-7
£1,358

Franela D R Loder   52
2 b f Dansili - Pernilla (Ire)
107gf 87gs 0-0-2

Frangipani (Ire) P F I Cole   53
3 b f Sri Pekan (USA) - Sharkashka (Ire)
38f 1212gf 1412gf 78g 0-0-4 £533

Frank Sonata M G Quinlan   108
3 b c Opening Verse (USA) - Megdale (Ire)
68g 110gs 311g 112g 112s 915gf 712hy 212hy
3-2-8 £56,084

Frank's Quest (Ire) A B Haynes   52 a62
4 b g Mujadil (USA) - Questuary (Ire)
77sd 211sd 38ss 310sd 68sd 108gs 48sd 78hy
29sd 18sd 18sd 118sd 127gf 37sd 2-5-14
£8,435

Frankies Wings (Ire) T G Mills   54
3 b g In The Wings - River Fantasy (USA)
710gs 611gs 814f 812gs 1110g 0-0-5

Franklins Gardens M H Tompkins   115
4 b c Halling (USA) - Woodbeck
410gs 411g 713hy 612gf 612gf 216s 616hy
0-1-7 £19,700

Franksalot (Ire) Miss B Sanders   76 a81
4 ch g Desert Story (Ire) - Rosie's Guest (Ire)
167gf 17f 47gf 58g 47f 17sd 59g 39g
128gf 68sd 2-1-10 £9,618

Frankskips A Ennis   a60
5 b g Bishop Of Cashel - Kevins Lady
117sd 58sd 127sd 78sd 38sd 37sd 88sd
0-2-7 £850

Fransiscan P C Haslam   41
2 ch g Fraam - Ordained
76gs 86gf 67g 108hy 57gf 0-0-5

Frantic T D Easterby   58
2 ch f Fraam - Carn Maire
105gf 46gf 45g 0-0-3 £418

Frascati A Berry   87 a76
4 b f Emarati (USA) - Fizzy Fiona
85sd 145sd 85sd 45ss 15gf 175hy 25gs 35f
85gf 15f 15g 25gs 85g 75s 45g 35s 105g 95s
3-4-18 £28,091

Fraternity J A Pickering   a38

7 b g Grand Lodge (USA) - Catawba
69sd 711sd 912sd 0-0-3

Freak Occurence (Ire) Miss E C Lavelle   86 a84
3 b g Stravinsky (USA) - Date Mate (USA)
78g 39hy 48gs 68gf 38gs 1410g 68gs 88gs
127sd 167gs 98gs 76s 0-2-12 £3,951

Fred's First B Palling   a30
3 b g Nomination - Perecapa (Ire)
58sd 812gf 1012sd 0-0-3

Freddie Freccles J G Given   55 a64
3 ch g Komaite (USA) - Leprechaun Lady
68sd 138gf 0-0-2

Frederick James H E Haynes   23
10 b g Efisio - Rare Roberta (USA)
137s 116gf 127gf 158gs 0-0-4

Free Lift R Charlton   81
2 ch f Cadeaux Genereux - Step Aloft
16g 106g 1-0-2 £7,605

Free Option (Ire) W J Musson   a77
9 ch g Indian Ridge - Saneena
58sd 128sd 38sd 310sd 17sd 58sd 1-2-6
£2,020

Free Style (Ger) Mrs H Sweeting   56 a49
4 ch f Most Welcome - Furiella
69sd 311sd 1214sd 112sd 412sw 512sd 513sd
212gf 1212s 412gf 512gf 814f 1213g 1-2-13
£2,997

Free Trip J H M Gosden   101
3 ch c Cadeaux Genereux - Well Away (Ire)
17g 67g 138gs 27gf 57g 58f 57gf 27gf 18g
77gf 2-2-10 £26,311

Free Wheelin (Ire) W Jarvis   62 a21
4 b g Polar Falcon (USA) - Farhana
146gs 36s 136gs 116sd 75s 136gs 0-1-6
£870

Free Will R C Guest   29
7 ch g Indian Ridge - Free Guest
1612gf 0-0-1

Freedom Now (Ire) C L Tizzard   76
6 b g Sadler's Wells (USA) - Free At Last
916gs 1214gs 616gf 714f 716f 0-0-5

Freeloader (Ire) J W Hills   87
4 b g Revoque (Ire) - Indian Sand
710g 411gs 310gf 89gf 19gf 48g 58gs 410g
39g 1-3-9 £9,300

Fremen (USA) Sir Michael Stoute   99
4 ch g Rahy (USA) - Northern Trick (USA)
128g 77g 198s 0-0-3

French Gigolo C N Allen   a53
4 ch g Pursuit Of Love - French Mist
48sd 610sd 0-0-2

French Gold P F I Cole   42
2 b f Bien Bien (USA) - Shalad'Or
118gs 88s 0-0-2

French Horn M Wigham   a55
7 b g Fraam - Runcina
18sd 48sd 39ss 58sd 310sd PU8sd 1-2-6
£3,272

French Kisses Ronald Thompson   34
2 b f Paris House - Clashfern
156gf 126gs 108gs 0-0-3

French Risk (Ire) W M Brisbourne   5
4 b g Entrepreneur - Troyes
812sd 1510f 0-0-2

French School D R Loder   a59
2 b f Desert Prince (Ire) - Bint Shihama (USA)
157gf 47sd 0-0-2 £400

Frenchmans Lodge J M Bradley   46 a46
4 b g Piccolo - St Helena
117ss 137s 75g 75hy 26gf 56f 66f 65sd
0-1-8 £852

Fresh Connection G G Margarson   38 a46
3 b f Danzig Connection (USA) - Naturally Fresh
78sd 146sd 78sd 510gf 48sd 0-0-5

Friar Tuck Miss L A Perratt   63
9 ch g Inchinor - Jay Gee Ell
156hy 76g 87g 16g 46gf 67gf 46g 96gf 86g
76g 46gs 96g 76g 1-0-13 £5,592

Frida P D Cundell
2 b f Lujain (USA) - Ishona
116g 0-0-1

Friday's Takings B Smart   a46
5 ch g Beveled (USA) - Pretty Pollyanna
98sd 88sd 158gs 129sd 0-0-4

Friends Hope P A Blockley   59
3 ch f Docksider (USA) - Stygian (USA)
912g 110gs 510gf 27f 1-1-4 £4,036

Frimley's Matterry R E Barr   58 a29
4 b g Bluegrass Prince (Ire) - Lonely Street
67sd 78ss 67gf 66s 66f 56g 168s 36f 16gf
66gs 66gs 86g 1-1-12 £4,773

Frisby Ridge (Ire) T D Easterby   44
2 b f Monashee Mountain (USA) - Suave Lady (Fr)
125gs 55gs 106gf 56f 55g 45gf 97gs 36gf
0-1-8 £431

Frith (Ire) B W Hills   101
2 b c Benny The Dip (USA) - Melodist (USA)
27gf 37gf 58gf 88s 0-2-4 £5,639

Frixos (Ire) M Scudamore   50 a28
4 ch g Barathea (Ire) - Local Lass
610sd 616gf 1012gf 128gf 0-0-4

Frizzante J R Fanshawe   119
5 b m Efisio - Juliet Bravo
26g 15g 35gf 16gs 107gs 176g 2-2-6
£196,000

Frogs' Gift (Ire) G M Moore   47
2 gr f Danehill Dancer (Ire) - Warthill Whispers
146g 66g 86gf 0-0-3

From The North (Ire) A Dickman   58
3 ch f Foxhound (USA) - Best Swinger (Ire)
146g 55gf 135s 46f 107f 76g 0-0-6

Fromsong (Ire) B R Millman   105
6 b g Fayruz - Lindas Delight
25g 45g 45g 46gf 45gf 76f 85gs 65g 65gf
105s 0-1-10 £7,857

Front Stage (Ire) Sir Michael Stoute   82
2 b/br c Grand Lodge (USA) - Dreams
87g 38g 0-1-2 £794

Frontier B J Llewellyn   85
7 b g Indian Ridge - Adatiya (Ire)
210gf 110gf 210gf 312gf 1-3-4 £11,086

Fruhlingssturm M A Jarvis   114
4 b c Unfuwain (USA) - Fruhlingserwachen (USA)
512gf 110gs 710gf 310gs 410g 49s 510s 1-1-7
£20,647

Fruit Of Glory J R Jenkins   100 a98
5 b m Glory Of Dancer - Fresh Fruit Daily
97gf 58gf 47gf 46gs 35s 76g 47g 26gf 15g
46g 26g 26gs 55s 46g 76g 35s 87sd 1-6-17

£43,796

Fu Fighter C L Popham   76
3 b g Unfuwain (USA) - Runelia
810g 514gs 414g 318gf 1118gs 916gs 211g
0-2-7 £1,808

Fu Manchu D R Loder   84
2 b c Desert Style (Ire) - Robsart (Ire)
97g 17s 1-0-2 £4,338

Fubos Julian Poulton   a60
3 b g Atraf - Homebeforemidnight
57sd 68sd 177gf 0-0-3

Fuel Cell (Ire) R Hannon   77
3 b c Desert Style (Ire) - Tappen Zee
88g 118g 39gf 38f 88gf 110gf 310gf 510g
1010gf 310g 1-4-10 £6,094

Full Egalite B R Johnson   a42
8 gr g Ezzoud (Ire) - Milva
412sd 612sd 0-0-2

Full Of Zest Mrs A J Perrett   74
2 ch f Pivotal - Tangerine
27s 0-1-1 £1,090

Full Pitch W Jenks   77 a42
8 ch g Cadeaux Genereux - Tricky Note
96sd 126sw 66s 15hy 135g 126sd 85g
126gs 106sd 1-0-9 £3,262

Full Spate J M Bradley   79 a61
9 ch g Unfuwain (USA) - Double River (USA)
66g 76gs 56hy 46gs 66f 46g 66g 36gf 26gf
76g 96gf 117gf 26gf 16g 66gs 96g 86gs 126s
96sd 46g 1-5-20 £8,488

Fullandby (Ire) T J Etherington   a62
2 b c Monashee Mountain (USA) - Ivory Turner
27sd 0-1-1 £422

Fully Fledged G B Balding   9
4 b f Fraam - Alarming Motown
1012g 0-0-1

Fulvio (USA) P D Evans   36 a74
4 b g Sword Dance - One Tuff Gal (USA)
118sd 137gf 78gf 58sd 147sd 116gs 97hy
47sd 37sd 0-1-9 £210

Fun To Ride B W Hills   98
3 ch f Desert Prince (Ire) - Zafaaf
16g 26s 206gf 146g 116g 1-1-5 £9,402

Funfair Mrs A J Perrett   111
5 b g Singspiel (Ire) - Red Carnival (USA)
28f 38g 68gs 0-2-3 £12,550

Funfair Wane D Nicholls   106
5 b g Unfuwain (USA) - Ivory Bride
107gf 75s 45gf 195gf 276gf 65g 126g 16s
66s 1-0-9 £71,593

Furl Away J W Payne   61
2 b g Squared Away - Miss Pel
107g 0-0-1

Furniture Factors (Ire) Ronald Thompson
4 b g Magic Ring (Ire) - Make Hay
710hy 109sd 0-0-2

Further Outlook (USA) D K Ivory   92 a80
10 gr g Zilzal (USA) - Future Bright (USA)
15s 36sd 106gs 115gs 115gf 45g 25gf 35g
156gf 75g 105gf 66gs 55g 15s 55gs 125g 35g
55s 2-5-21 £23,124

Fusillade (Ire) A J Lockwood
4 ch g Grand Lodge (USA) - Lili Cup (Fr)
147s 1912gf 0-0-2

Fuss W Jarvis 13
3 b f Unfuwain (USA) - First Sapphire
6^{10hy} 0-0-1

Futoo (Ire) G M Moore 73
3 b g Foxhound (USA) - Nicola Wynn
6^{8hy} 5^{8gf} 1^{8g} 3^{7g} 7^{7gs} 11^{0gs} 31^{0gf} 41^{0gs}
21^{0gs} 81^{0g} 81^{0g} 2-2-11 £11,909

Future Deal C A Horgan 67 a57
3 b f First Trump - Katushka (Ire)
4^{7gs} 3^{6gf} 16^{sd} 1-1-3 £4,005

Future To Future (Ire) L A Dace 31
4 gr g Linamix (Fr) - Finir En Beaute (Fr)
1412^{s} 1416^{sd} 0-0-2

Futuristic J Pearce 18 a64
4 b g Magic Ring (Ire) - Corn Futures
28^{sd} 98^{sw} 168^{gs} 0-1-3 £844

Fyodor (Ire) W J Haggas 77
3 b g Fasliyev (USA) - Royale Figurine (Ire)
135^{gf} 66^{g} 75^{gf} 205^{gf} 76^{g} 45^{gf} 125^{s} 197^{s}
0-0-8 £556

Gabana (Ire) C F Wall 74
3 br f Polish Precedent (USA) - Out West (USA)
12^{7g} 6^{8g} 9^{8gf} 3^{8f} 2^{8g} 3^{8g} 3^{8g} 0-4-7
£3,103

Gabanna (USA) Saeed Bin Suroor 68
2 b c Kingmambo (USA) - Star Begonia
6^{8gf} 3^{10hy} 0-1-2 **£710**

Gablesea B P J Baugh
10 b g Beveled (USA) - Me Spede
16^{11s} 0-0-1

Gabor G L Moore 42
5 b g Danzig Connection (USA) - Kiomi
14^{12gf} 9^{12gf} 5^{12gf} 0-0-3

Gaelic Princess A G Newcombe 83 a80
4 b f Cois Na Tine (Ire) - Berenice (Ity)
11^{6ss} 14^{7sd} 6^{6g} 19^{6gf} 9^{6gf} 12^{6f} 15^{7gf}
5^{6gs} 0-0-8 £284

Gaelic Probe (Ire) R M H Cowell a26
10 b g Roi Danzig (USA) - Scottish Gaelic (USA)
6^{15sd} 0-0-1

Gaelic Roulette (Ire) P W Harris 70
4 b f Turtle Island (Ire) - Money Spinner (USA)
3^{12g} 8^{14gf} 10^{12gf} 0-0-3 **£1,245**

Gaff (USA) D K Weld 107
2 b c Maria's Mon (USA) - Ionlyhaveeyesforu (USA)
7^{5ft} 1^{7gy} 2^{7s} 1-1-3 **£32,338**

Gaiety Girl (USA) T D Easterby 55
3 b f Swain (Ire) - Knoosh (USA)
9^{10gf} 6^{10gf} 5^{13g} 8^{8g} 10^{7f} 20^{6g} 8^{10g} 0-0-7

Gala Sunday (USA) M W Easterby 59
4 b g Lear Fan (USA) - Sunday Bazaar (USA)
7^{8s} 19^{10g} 12^{10gs} 7^{10g} 12^{10g} 6^{9s} 7^{9gf} 6^{8f}
16^{8gf} 12^{7gf} 25^{8gf} 0-0-11

Galandora Dr J R J Naylor 58 a50
4 b f Bijou D'Inde - Jelabna
5^{12gs} 6^{12gs} 1^{16gs} 11^{16hy} 1^{16gf} 2^{14gf} 8^{14gf}
3^{16gs} 3^{17g} 7^{16gf} 7^{16gf} 5^{16sd} 7^{16sd} 2-3-13
£7,788

Galaxy Fallon M Dods 29 a39
6 b m Dancing Spree (USA) - No Comebacks
6^{11ss} 9^{7sd} 6^{10gf} 0-0-3

Galeota (Ire) R Hannon 111
2 b c Mujadil (USA) - Refined (Ire)
4^{5g} 1^{6gs} 5^{6s} 5^{6gf} 1^{6f} 1^{6gs} 3-0-6

£53,949

Galey River (USA) J J Sheehan 43 a46
5 ch g Irish River (Fr) - Carefree Kate (USA)
8^{8sd} 10^{7sd} 5^{8sd} 7^{10sd} 5^{10sd} 1^{10sd} 6^{10sd}
2^{9sd} 3^{9sd} 5^{10sd} 7^{9g} 4^{10gf} 5^{11gf} 11^{10g} 6^{10gf}
4^{10sd} 5^{10gs} 1-1-17 **£2,349**

Gallant Boy (Ire) P D Evans 74 a77
5 ch g Grand Lodge (USA) - Damerela (Ire)
8^{12sd} 13^{12sd} 4^{12sd} 9^{12sd} 13^{12sd} 5^{10gf} 7^{13f}
6^{10gf} 4^{14gf} 8^{10g} 5^{15g} 4^{10gf} 4^{12gf} 4^{12gf} 4^{12g}
13^{16g} 9^{12s} 8^{12sd} 12^{12gs} 8^{12s} 0-1-20 **£3,551**

Gallantian (Ire) G A Butler 68 a51
2 gr g Turtle Island (Ire) - Galletina (Ire)
10^{7sd} 8^{7s} 7^{7s} 0-0-3

Gallas (Ire) J S Wainwright 53
3 b c Charnwood Forest (Ire) - Nellie's Away (Ire)
15^{8hy} 9^{8gf} 8^{8g} 2^{7gs} 9^{8gf} 14^{8gf} 16^{8gs}
0-1-7 **£1,084**

Gallego S L Keightley 5 a14
2 br c Danzero (Aus) - Shafir (Ire)
12^{6g} 11^{7sd} 10^{5hy} 0-0-3

Galleon Beach B D Leavy 68
7 b g Shirley Heights - Music In My Life (Ire)
4^{16gs} 8^{16gs} 14^{21g} 0-0-3 **£300**

Gallery Breeze P A Blockley 78 a73
5 b m Zamindar (USA) - Wantage Park
1^{7g} 11^{7g} 9^{7sd} 9^{8gs} 9^{7s} 5^{8sd} 2^{7sd} 1-1-7
£4,929

Gallery God (Fr) S Dow 76
8 ch g In The Wings - El Fabulous (Fr)
15^{10gs} 9^{12g} 10^{22f} 9^{12gf} 7^{12gs} 9^{10gf} 0-0-6

Galley Law R Craggs a52
4 ch g Most Welcome - Miss Blitz
3^{12sd} 2^{12ss} 11^{1sd} 2^{8ss} 2^{12sw} 4^{12sd} 1-4-6
£2,771

Galloway Mac W A O'Gorman 63 a67
4 ch c Environment Friend - Docklands
3^{8sd} 3^{7sd} 12^{6sd} 1^{8s} 2^{7ss} 4^{10gs} 6^{10gs} 9^{8sd}
5^{8sd} 1-3-9 **£3,175**

Galvanise (USA) B W Hills 93
3 b c Run Softly (USA) - Shining Bright
6^{8g} 1^{10gf} 7^{10gf} 3^{10gs} 7^{10g} 1-1-5 **£5,503**

Gamble Of The Day (USA) Sir Michael Stoute 72
2 ch c Cozzene (USA) - Sue Warner (USA)
6^{7s} 0-0-1

Gambling Spirit H Candy 52
2 ch f Mister Baileys - Royal Roulette
11^{8gf} 0-0-1

Game Dame B W Hills 77
3 ch f Nashwan (USA) - Gentle Dame
4^{10gf} 1^{8gf} 5^{10gf} 1-0-3 **£4,176**

Game Flora M E Sowersby 55 a6
3 b f Mind Games - Breakfast Creek
1^{6hy} 4^{6g} 5^{12gf} 6^{5gf} 6^{6f} 12^{6sw} 2^{7gs}
12^{9sd} 1-2-9 **£6,708**

Game Guru P A Blockley 61 a74
5 b g First Trump - Scarlett Holly
7^{8sd} 1^{8sd} 3^{8ss} 1^{7sd} 4^{7s} 6^{8sw} 11^{1ss} 9^{11gs}
5^{11gs} 5^{11sd} 3-1-10 **£9,136**

Game Lad T D Easterby 83 a55
2 b c Mind Games - Catch Me
3^{5sd} 9^{6gs} 3^{7gf} 7^{6gf} 2^{7gs} 1^{7s} 4^{7gs}
1-3-8 **£9,035**

Gameset'N'Match W G M Turner 54 a38

3 b g Hector Protector (USA) - Tanasie
6⁹ᵍᶠ 10⁶ˢᵈ 4⁷ᵍᶠ 3⁶ᵍ **0-1-4 £1,107**

Gamut (Ire) *Sir Michael Stoute* 121
5 b h Spectrum (Ire) - Greektown
2¹²ᵍ 1¹²ᵍ 1¹²ᵍˢ 4¹²ᵍᶠ 5¹²ˢ **2-1-5**
£254,380

Ganymede *M L W Bell* 84
3 gr g Daylami (Ire) - Germane
2¹⁰ᵍˢ 3¹²ᵍˢ 2¹⁰ᵍᶠ 2¹¹ᵍᶠ 2¹⁰ᵍᶠ 8¹⁰ᵍ 4¹²ᵍᶠ
3¹²ᵍᶠ 6¹²ᵍ **0-4-9 £9,220**

Garance *R Hannon* 68
2 b f Zafonic (USA) - Arletty
11⁷ᵍᶠ 7⁷ᵍᶠ 8⁸ˢ 14⁸ᵍˢ **0-0-4**

Gardasee (Ger) *T P Tate* 45 a40
2 gr g Dashing Blade - Gladstone Street (Ire)
7⁶ˢᵈ 7⁶ˢ 6⁷ˢᵈ **0-0-3**

Garden Society (Ire) *W A O'Gorman* 65
7 ch g Caerleon (USA) - Eurobird
8⁶ᵍᶠ 7⁸ᵍᶠ 11⁸ᵍᶠ 7⁸ᵍᶠ 5¹⁰ᵍ 8¹⁰ˢ **0-0-6**

Gargoyle Girl *J S Goldie* 67 a3
7 b m Be My Chief (USA) - May Hills Legacy (Ire)
10¹²ˢᵈ 5¹⁴ᵍᶠ 1¹⁶ᵍ 10¹²ʰʸ 6¹⁴ᵍᶠ 11¹⁶ˢ 4¹⁶ᵍᶠ
6¹⁴ᵍ 6¹⁰ᵍˢ **1-0-9 £3,784**

Garhoud *E A L Dunlop* 50
2 b c Grand Lodge (USA) - Puce
9⁸ˢ **0-0-1**

Garnett (Ire) *A King* 77 a63
3 b g Desert Story (Ire) - In Behind (Ire)
4¹²ᵍᶠ 3¹²ᵍᶠ 3¹⁴ᶠ 9¹⁴ᵍᶠ 3¹²ˢᵈ 5¹⁶ᵍᶠ **0-2-6**
£2,077

Garnock Belle (Ire) *A Berry* a27
3 b f Marju (Ire) - Trojan Relation
11⁶ˢᵈ 12⁸ˢᵈ 5⁸ˢʷ 12⁸ˢˢ **0-0-4**

Garnock Venture (Ire) *A Berry* 55 a73
3 b c Mujadil (USA) - Stay Sharpe (USA)
4⁶ˢᵈ 11⁷ˢᵈ 7⁷ˢᵈ 8⁶ˢᵈ 3⁵ᵍ 7⁵ᵍˢ 7⁶ᵍᶠ
1⁶ˢᵈ 11⁶ˢ 7⁷ᵍ 5⁶ˢᵈ 5⁷ᶠ 12⁷ᵍˢ **2-1-14 £6,147**

Garrigon *N P Littmoden* a62
3 b g Hector Protector (USA) - Queen Of The Keys
5⁷ˢᵈ 7⁷ˢᵈ 4⁸ˢᵈ 15⁷ˢᵈ 4⁷ˢᵈ 6⁷ˢᵈ 2¹⁰ˢᵈ **0-1-7**
£1,094

Garryurra *Sir Michael Stoute* 66
3 gr f Daylami (Ire) - Tropical
5¹⁰ᵍ 10¹²ᵍᶠ **0-0-2**

Garston Star *J S Moore* 72 a21
3 ch g Fleetwood (Ire) - Conquista
3¹⁰ᵍᶠ 1¹¹ᵍᶠ 2¹²ᶠ 2¹²ᵍᶠ 5¹²ᶠ 1¹¹ᵍ
6¹²ˢᵈ 6¹⁶ᵍ **2-2-9 £9,487**

Gasparini (Ire) *T D Easterby* 58
3 ch c Docksider (USA) - Tarjou
12⁶ᵍˢ 10⁷ᵍˢ 12⁶ᵍᶠ 4⁹ᵍ 3⁷ᵍ 9⁷ᵍˢ 3⁷ᵍᶠ
12⁶ᵍᶠ **0-2-8 £1,692**

Gateman *M Johnston* 117
7 b g Owington - Scandalette
2⁹ᵍᶠ 6⁸ᵍᶠ 8⁹ᵍᶠ 2⁸ᵍ 1⁹ᵍ 2⁸ᵍˢ 11⁸ᵍ 3⁹ᵍ
1⁸ᵍᶠ 2⁸ᵍ 2¹⁰ᵍᶠ 2¹⁰ᵍˢ 2¹⁰ᵍ 3¹⁰ˢ **2-9-14**
£194,350

Gatwick (Ire) *M R Channon* 115
3 b c Ali-Royal (Ire) - Airport
1⁸ᵍ 3⁸ᵍ 1⁹ᵍ 1⁸ᵍᶠ 10¹²ᵍ 6¹⁰ᶠ 8¹⁰ᵍᶠ 5¹⁰ʰʸ
1¹⁰ᵍˢ 5¹⁰ᵍˢ 7⁹ᵍ 11⁹ˢ **4-1-12 £137,939**

Gaudalpin (Ire) *M J Attwater* 62 a62
2 b f Danetime (Ire) - Lila Pedigo (Ire)
3⁵ˢᵈ 4⁵ᵍ 7⁵ᵍ 4⁶ᵍ 13⁶ᵍᶠ 2⁵ᵍ 2⁶ˢᵈ
10⁵ˢᵈ **0-3-9 £2,866**

Gavioli (Ire) *J M Bradley* 60
2 b c Namid - Pamina (Ire)
5⁶ᵍᶠ 18⁶ᵍ 4⁶ᵍᶠ 2⁶ᵍᶠ 10⁶ᵍ 9⁶ᵍᶠ 3⁶ᵍᶠ 5⁶ᵍˢ
0-2-8 £2,543

Gavroche (Ire) *C A Dwyer* 95 a71
3 b c Docksider (USA) - Regal Revolution
1⁹ˢᵈ 2⁸ˢᵈ 3⁹ˢʷ 5¹²ˢˢ 2¹⁰ᵍᶠ 2⁹ʰʸ 5¹²ᵍˢ 1¹⁰ᵍᶠ
1¹⁰ᵍ 4¹⁰ᵍᶠ 1¹⁰ᵍ 9¹⁰ᵍᶠ 8¹⁰ᵍˢ 8¹⁰ᵍˢ **4-3-14**
£27,115

Gay Romance *B W Hills* 70
3 ch f Singspiel (Ire) - Gaijin
8⁷ᵍ 10⁸ᵍᶠ 6⁹ᵍᶠ 5¹⁰ᵍˢ 3⁸ᵍᶠ 10⁸ˢ **0-1-6**
£694

Gayle Storm (Ire) *C Tinkler* a46
3 b f Mujadil (USA) - Mercy Bien (Ire)
8⁷ˢᵈ 8⁸ˢᵈ 8⁸ˢᵈ 5⁸ˢᵈ **0-0-4**

Gdansk (Ire) *A Berry* 61
7 b g Pips Pride - Merry Twinkle
9⁶ˢ UR⁶ˢ 8⁶ᵍˢ **0-0-3**

Gee Bee Em *G P Enright* 70 a34
2 b f Piccolo - Cibenze
2⁶ᵍ 1⁶ᶠ 4⁶ᵍᶠ 4⁵ᵍᶠ 9⁶ᵍᶠ 11⁶ˢᵈ **1-1-6**
£5,794

Geespot *D J S Ffrench Davis* a46
5 b m Pursuit Of Love - My Discovery (Ire)
12⁶ˢᵈ 12⁷ˢᵈ 12⁷ˢᵈ 7⁸ˢᵈ 3⁸ˢᵈ 12⁷ˢᵈ
7⁷ˢᵈ **0-1-8 £189**

Geisha Lady (Ire) *R M Beckett* 68
2 b f Raise A Grand (Ire) - Mitsubishi Style
6⁵ᵍ 3⁶ᵍ 2⁶ᵍᶠ 4⁶ᵍᶠ 2⁷ᵍˢ 17⁸ᵍ **0-3-6**
£3,138

Geller *R Hannon* 68
3 b g Mind Games - Time To Tango
5¹⁰ᵍ 4¹⁰ᵍᶠ 8⁸ᵍᶠ 8⁹ᵍ 5⁷ᵍᶠ **0-0-5 £858**

Gem Bien (USA) *D W Chapman* 55
6 b g Bien Bien (USA) - Eastern Gem (USA)
17⁸ᵍ 3⁸ᵍᶠ 3⁸ᵍˢ 8⁷ˢᶠ **0-1-4 £549**

Gemi Bed (Fr) *G L Moore* 49 a55
9 b g Double Bed (Fr) - Gemia (Fr)
6¹³ˢᵈ 1¹⁶ˢᵈ 5¹⁶ˢᵈ 4¹²ᵍˢ **1-0-4 £2,975**

Gemini Girl (Ire) *M D Hammond* 46
3 b f Petardia - Miss Sabre
7⁵ᵍ 9⁵ᵍᶠ 8⁵ᵍᶠ 12⁵ˢ 7⁷ᵍ 15⁸ᵍᶠ 18⁸ᵍᶠ 8⁵ᵍᶠ
0-0-8

Gemini Lady *Mrs G S Rees* 52 a34
4 b f Emperor Fountain - Raunchy Rita
15⁸ˢ 2⁸ᵍᶠ 12⁸ᵍᶠ 13⁸ᵍ 9⁸ᶠ 4⁷ᶠ 13⁸ᵍ 8⁷ˢᵈ
0-2-8 £431

Gemma *P J Makin* a14
4 b f Petong - Gem
11¹⁰ˢᵈ 13¹³ˢᵈ **0-0-2**

Gems Bond *J S Moore* 77 a31
4 b g Magic Ring (Ire) - Jucinda
15⁸ᶠᵗ 9⁸ᶠᵗ 9⁸ᵍ 16⁸ᶠᵗ 21⁷ᵍᶠ 9⁸ᵍˢ 5⁷ᵍ
14¹⁰ᵍᶠ 11⁸ˢᵈ **0-0-9**

General *C R Dore* 77 a77
7 b g Cadeaux Genereux - Bareilly (USA)
1⁸ˢʷ 2¹²ˢˢ 7¹²ˢᵈ 5¹⁰ᵍ 2¹²ˢ 10¹²ᵍ 12¹²ᵍ
19¹²ᵍ 5¹²ᵍˢ 3⁸ˢᵈ 2⁹ʰʸ 10¹²ʰʸ 14¹⁰ᵍ 6⁹ˢ **1-4-14**
£12,653

General Feeling (Ire) *S Kirk* 83
3 b g General Monash (USA) - Kamadara (Ire)
3⁵ˢ 3⁵ᵍᶠ 11⁶ᵍᶠ 17ᵍᶠ 1⁸ᶠ 4⁸ᵍˢ 14⁷ᵍˢ
2-2-8 £12,542

General Flumpa *C F Wall* 69 a67
3 b g Vettori (Ire) - Macca Luna (Ire)

6⁷ᵍˢ 3⁹ˢᵈ 3¹²ˢ 5¹²ˢᵈ 2¹¹ᵍᶠ 6¹⁰ᵍ 3¹⁰ᵍᶠ 4¹⁰ᵍ
0-4-8 £3,625

General Haigh *J R Best*   68 a40
2 b g Mujahid (USA) - Stygian (USA)
6⁵ˢᵈ 4⁵ᵍ 4⁶ᵍˢ 9⁶ˢᵈ **0-0-4 £292**

General Jumbo *B J Meehan*   84
2 b c Dansili - Aunt Jemima
2⁸ʰʸ **0-1-1 £2,072**

General Max (Ire) *A Crook*   55
2 b c General Monash (USA) - Sawaki
3⁶ᵍᶠ 7⁷ᵍᶠ 12⁶ˢ 13⁷ᵍᶠ **0-0-4 £842**

General Nuisance (Ire) *J S Moore*   53
2 ch g General Monash (USA) - Baywood
2⁵ᵍ 6⁵ᵍ 4⁵ʰʸ 5⁵ᵍᶠ 4⁷ᶠ 3⁶ᶠ 2⁶ᵍᶠ 3⁶ᵍᶠ 7⁶ᵍᶠ
3⁶ᵍᶠ 9⁶ˢ **0-3-11 £2,698**

General Smith *G A Harker*   42
5 b g Greensmith - Second Call
13⁸ˢ 10⁷ᵍ 16⁸ᶠ 18⁶ᵍᶠ LFT5ᵍᶠ **0-0-5**

Generous Gesture (Ire) *M L W Bell*   72 a84
3 b f Fasliyev (USA) - Royal Bounty (Ire)
1⁶ˢˢ 5⁷ˢᵈ 6⁶ᵍ 1⁶ˢ 17⁷ᵍ 6⁷ᶠ 5⁷ˢᵈ 6⁶ᵍ 8⁷ᵍ
9⁶ᵍˢ 13⁶ᵍ 9⁶ˢ **2-0-12 £7,179**

Generous Measure *J M P Eustace*   16
2 b c Largesse - Stormy Heights
12⁷ˢ **0-0-1**

Generous Option *M Johnston*   87
2 ch f Cadeaux Genereux - Easy Option (Ire)
5⁶ᵍ 1⁶ᵍ 3⁶ᵍᶠ 4⁶ᵍˢ 4⁶ˢ 10⁶ˢ **1-1-6
£8,199**

Generous Share *M S Saunders*   a19
4 ch f Cadeaux Genereux - Marl
6⁷ˢᵈ **0-0-1**

Generous Spirit (Ire) *J A Osborne*   61
3 ch c Cadeaux Genereux - Miss Rossi
8⁷ᵍˢ 9⁶ᵍ 7⁵ˢ 6⁶ᵍᶠ 7⁶ᵍᶠ **0-0-5**

Genghis (Ire) *H Morrison*   88
5 br g Persian Bold - Cindys Baby
2¹²ᵍᶠ 5¹⁴ᵍ 2¹¹ᵍ 8¹²ᵍ 3¹²ᵍ 3¹⁴ᵍˢ 2¹²ᵍᶠ **0-5-7
£8,731**

Gennie Bond *R Hannon*   79
2 b f Pivotal - Miriam
4⁶ᵍᶠ 3⁶ᵍ 2⁶ᵍᶠ 11⁶ᵍᶠ 16⁷ᵍ 22⁷ᵍ **0-2-6
£2,837**

Gentle Raindrop (Ire) *S Kirk*   64
3 b f College Chapel - Dream Chaser
9⁸ᵍ 5⁷ᵍᶠ 10⁷ᵍᶠ 13⁸ᵍ 10⁸ᵍᶠ 7⁶ᵍˢ 12¹⁰ᵍˢ
10⁹ˢᵈ **0-0-8**

Gentle Response *B R Johnson*   a52
4 b f Puissance - Sweet Whisper
13⁶ˢᵈ 9⁵ˢᵈ 6⁶ˢᵈ 1⁷ˢᵈ 9⁷ˢᵈ 5⁶ˢᵈ 6⁷ˢᵈ
12⁶ᵍ **1-1-9 £1,503**

Gentle Warning *M Appleby*   18
4 b f Parthian Springs - Manx Princess
8⁸ᵍᶠ 11¹⁰ˢ 13¹⁰ᵍᶠ **0-0-3**

Gentleman George *D K Ivory*   a7
3 b g Kingsinger (Ire) - Miss Bigwig
8⁸ˢᵈ 9⁵ˢᵈ **0-0-2**

Gentleman's Deal (Ire) *E A L Dunlop*   76 a88
3 b c Danehill (USA) - Sleepytime (Ire)
4⁸ᵍ 1⁷ᵍˢ 1⁹ˢᵈ **2-0-3 £7,771**

Genuinely (Ire) *W J Musson*   45 a37
3 b f Entrepreneur - Fearless
11⁷ˢᵈ 16⁸ᵍˢ 6¹²ˢᵈ 3¹¹ᵍ 7¹⁶ᵍᶠ 3¹⁶ˢ **0-2-6
£950**

Geography (Ire) *P Butler*   18 a53

4 ch g Definite Article - Classic Ring (Ire)
PU¹⁰ˢᵈ 8⁹ˢ 6¹⁰ˢᵈ 11¹²ˢᵈ 12¹²ᵍᶠ 16¹⁰ᵍ
0-0-6

Geojimali *J S Goldie*   51
2 ch c Compton Place - Harrken Heights (Ire)
6⁶ᵍ 6⁷ᵍᶠ 5⁶ᵍᶠ **0-0-3**

Geordie Dancer (Ire) *A Berry*   55
2 b g Dansili - Awtaar (USA)
11⁵ᵍ 5⁸ᵍᶠ 7⁷ᵍᶠ **0-0-3**

George Stubbs (USA) *M J Polglase*   71 a73
6 b/br g Affirmed (USA) - Mia Duchessa (USA)
7¹⁶ˢᵈ 6¹²ˢˢ 2¹²ˢˢ 3¹⁴ˢᵈ 6¹²ˢʷ 4¹²ˢˢ 7¹⁸ᵍ
3¹⁵ˢ 1¹⁶ᵍˢ 3¹³ᵍ 5¹⁴ᵍˢ 5¹⁶ᵍᶠ 5¹³ᵍ 11¹⁶ᵍᶠ **1-3-14
£12,702**

George The Best (Ire) *M D Hammond*   73
3 b g Imperial Ballet (Ire) - En Retard (Ire)
13⁶ᵍˢ 6⁶ᵍ 4⁶ᵍˢ 14⁶ˢ 6⁶ᵍ 13⁷ᵍˢ 11⁶ˢ
20⁶ᵍˢ 5⁵ˢ 6⁵ˢ **0-0-10 £804**

Georgie Belle (USA) *C Tinkler*   61 a22
2 ch f Southern Halo (USA) - Saabikah (USA)
3⁵ᵍˢ 3⁵ᵍˢ 13⁷ˢᵈ **0-1-3 £1,033**

Georgina *M A Jarvis*   65
2 ch f Polish Precedent (USA) - Rose Bourbon (USA)
8⁷ᶠ 14⁷ᵍᶠ 7⁷ᶠ **0-0-3**

Germanicus *R Charlton*   a35
2 b c Desert King (Ire) - Simacota (Ger)
12⁹ˢᵈ **0-0-1**

Geronimo *Miss Gay Kelleway*   a66
7 b g Efisio - Apache Squaw
2⁶ˢʷ 8⁶ˢᵈ 3⁷ˢˢ 1⁸ˢʷ 9⁸ˢʷ 4⁷ˢˢ **1-2-6
£4,799**

Get Stuck In (Ire) *Miss L A Perratt*   32
8 b g Up And At 'Em - Shoka (Fr)
16⁶ᵍˢ 14⁵ᵍᶠ 12⁵ʰʸ **0-0-3**

Get To The Point *Miss J Feilden*   73
3 ch g Daggers Drawn (USA) - Penny Mint
8⁷ˢᵈ 2⁶ᵍˢ 2⁶ᵍᶠ 5⁶ᵍᶠ 9⁶ᶠ 9⁶ᵍᶠ 7⁷ᶠ 5⁵ᵍᶠ
7⁷ᵍᶠ **0-2-9 £2,150**

Ghaill Force *J G Portman*   65
2 b g Piccolo - Coir 'A' Ghaill
2⁸ᵍᶠ **0-1-1 £435**

Ghantoot *R A Fahey*   81
3 ch c Inchinor - Shall We Run
11⁸ᵍ 8⁶ˢ 7⁷ᵍᶠ 11⁸ᵍᶠ 3⁹ᵍ 1¹⁰ᵍ 3¹⁰ᵍ 13¹⁰ˢ
1-2-8 £4,969

Ghasiba (Ire) *C E Brittain*   78
2 gr f Daylami (Ire) - Night Owl
6⁶ᵍᶠ 2⁷ᵍ 7⁶ˢ 15⁷ᵍ 9⁸ᵍᶠ **0-1-5 £1,592**

Ghostzapper (USA) *R J Frankel*   a133
4 b c Awesome Again (Can) - Baby Zip (USA)
1⁷ᶠ 1⁹ˢʸ 1⁹ᶠ 1¹⁰ᶠ **4-0-4 £1,447,287**

Ghurra (USA) *E A L Dunlop*   83
2 b f War Chant (USA) - Futuh (USA)
1⁶ᵍᶠ 7⁶ᵍ 4⁶ˢ **1-0-3 £5,378**

Giant's Rock (Ire) *G A Butler*   66
2 ch g Giant's Causeway (USA) - En Garde (USA)
3⁷ᵍᶠ **0-0-1 £1,150**

Gibraltar Bay (Ire) *G G Margarson*   56
2 b f Cape Cross (Ire) - Secrets Of Honour
12⁷ᵍᶠ 4⁸ᵍᶠ 15⁸ᵍˢ **0-0-3 £268**

Gidam Gidam (Ire) *C E Brittain*   66
2 b g King's Best (USA) - Flamands (Ire)
6⁷ᵍ 6⁸ᵍ 3¹⁰ᵍ **0-1-3 £698**

Gift Horse *J R Fanshawe*   97
4 ch g Cadeaux Genereux - Careful Dancer

11^{7g} 2^{7g} 3^{7g} 8^{8g} 4^{8hy} 30^{9g} 0-2-6
£6,046

Gift Voucher (Ire) *Sir Michael Stoute*   86
3 ch c Cadeaux Genereux - Highland Gift (Ire)
11^{10g} 3^{12gf} 8^{10gf} 2^{12gf} 1^{11gf} 1-2-5
£5,949

Gifted Flame *T D Barron*   76
5 b g Revoque (Ire) - Littleladyleah (USA)
9^{10gs} 10^{8gs} 4^{8f} 7^{8g} 7^{8g} 3^{8gf} 1^{8f} 4^{9gf}
3^{7gs} 6^{8g} 8^{8g} 1^{7gf} 15^{8gf} 2-2-13 £11,137

Gifted Gamble *K A Ryan*   93
2 b c Mind Games - Its Another Gift
7^{5s} 3^{5g} 3^{5gf} 3^{5gf} 2^{5g} 2^{5gf} 1^{5gf} 5^{6gf} 9^{5gf}
2^{6s} 11^{6gf} 3^{6s} 4^{6s} 1-5-13 £28,574

Gifted Lass *J Balding*
2 b f Bold Edge - Meeson Times
14^{6g} 10^{7sd} 0-0-2

Gifted Musician *J L Dunlop*   64
2 b c Sadler's Wells (USA) - Photogenic
4^{8hy} 0-0-1 £518

Gig Harbor *P R Chamings*   84 a102
5 b g Efisio - Petonica (Ire)
1^{12sd} 11^{12sd} 1^{12sd} 5^{10sd} 6^{13sd} 11^{12gf} 4^{9gf}
13^{8g} 8^{10g} 2-1-9 £28,639

Giko *Jane Southcombe*   48 a44
10 b g Arazi (USA) - Gayane
11^{13sd} 3^{12sd} 12^{12sd} 6^{12sd} 7^{12sd} 6^{12gs} 2^{12gf}
3^{13gf} 11^{17g} 8^{14gs} 10^{12gf} 2^{8s} 16^{12g} 0-4-13
£3,552

Gildas Fortuna *P C Haslam*   70
2 b f Fort Wood (USA) - Gleaming Sky (SAF)
4^{6g} 0-0-1 £370

Gilded Cove *R Hollinshead*   a70
4 b c Polar Prince - Cloudy Reef
7^{6sd} 7^{6sd} 3^{6sd} 3^{6s} 6^{6sw} 16^{6s} 1^{5sd} 4^{6sd}
4^{6sd} 2-2-9 £6,981

Gilly's General (Ire) *J W Unett*   23 a49
4 ch g General Monash (USA) - Good Aim (Ire)
4^{7sd} 10^{7sd} 1^{7sd} 6^{7sd} 11^{7gf} 12^{7sd} 10^{7gf}
1-0-7 £1,445

Gimasha *M R Channon*   73
2 b f Cadeaux Genereux - First Waltz (Fr)
4^{6gf} 2^{6g} 12^{5s} 0-1-3 £1,989

Gin 'N' Fonic (Ire) *J D Frost*   37
4 ch g Zafonic (USA) - Crepe Ginger (Ire)
7^{7gf} 0-0-1

Ginger Cookie *B Smart*   41
2 ch f Bold Edge - Pretty Pollyanna
15^{6gf} 0-0-1

Ginger Ice *G G Margarson*   a51
4 ch g Bahamian Bounty - Sharp Top
3^{10sd} 5^{10sd} 10^{16sd} 0-0-3 £184

Gingiefly *J L Dunlop*   64
2 b c Sinndar (Ire) - Native Ring (Fr)
10^{7gf} 3^{8gf} 0-1-2 £806

Gingko *P R Webber*   70 a76
7 b g Pursuit Of Love - Arboretum (Ire)
1^{10sd} 5^{10sd} 10^{10sd} 3^{12sd} 3^{10s} 1-2-5
£4,530

Ginner Morris *J Hetherton*   a8
9 b g Emarati (USA) - Just Run (Ire)
6^{8sd} 0-0-1

Giocoso (USA) *B Palling*   88
4 b c Bahri (USA) - Wing My Chimes (USA)
6^{7gf} 9^{9gf} 9^{10gf} 18^{8gf} 4^{8gs} 5^{8gs} 4^{7s} 9^{8gf}

6^{8s} 1-0-9 £7,965

Girl Warrior (USA) *P F I Cole*   66
3 ch f Elusive Quality (USA) - Qhazeenah
6^{7gf} 4^{8f} 12^{10gf} 0-0-3 £533

Girlsweekend *Mrs L J Mongan*   a50
2 b f Benny The Dip (USA) - Snoozy
10^{6sd} 7^{7sd} 0-0-2

Gironde *Sir Michael Stoute*   93
3 b c Sadler's Wells (USA) - Sarah Georgina
4^{10gs} 3^{10g} 12^{12gf} 3^{12gs} 1^{12s} 1-2-5
£5,393

Gitche Manito (Ire) *A King*   74
2 b c Namid - Chasing Rainbows
3^{7gs} 11^{7s} 5^{7gf} 2^{7f} 0-2-4 £2,365

Giunchiglio *W M Brisbourne*   73 a68
5 ch g Millkom - Daffodil Fields
3^{10sd} 1^{10gf} 12^{9g} 3^{10g} 6^{10g} 10^{9gf} 4^{10gf}
1^{12s} 6^{10g} 13^{11s} 4^{12sd} 16^{10g} 2-1-12 £9,521

Giust In Temp (Ire) *P W Hiatt*   46 a39
5 b h Polish Precedent (USA) - Blue Stricks
4^{9sd} 2^{9sd} 9^{9sd} 6^{9sd} 9^{10gf} 4^{10gf} 8^{10gf}
10^{8gs} 0-1-8 £391

Give Him Credit (USA) *Mrs A Duffield*   52 a28
4 b g Quiet American (USA) - Meniatarra (USA)
5^{6sd} 12^{8f} 8^{7gf} 11^{6gf} 6^{7g} 0-0-5

Givemethemoonlight *Mrs Stef Liddiard*   a65
5 ch m Woodborough (USA) - Rockin' Rosie
2^{9sd} 5^{10sd} 2^{9sd} 1^{8sd} 3^{9sd} 5^{10sd} 3^{8sd} 6^{9ss}
1^{7ss} 2^{9ss} 3^{7sw} 6^{8sw} 3^{8sw} 2-7-13 £10,601

Given A Chance *Mrs S Lamyman*   51 a28
3 b g Defacto (USA) - Milly Molly Mango
4^{8sd} 5^{8sd} 8^{7sd} 5^{12s} 3^{8hy} 4^{10s} 2^{8gf} 6^{8gf}
8^{10gf} 6^{8g} 3^{8gs} 0-4-11 £1,550

Given A Choice (Ire) *J G Given*   82
2 b c Trans Island - Miss Audimar (USA)
4^{7gf} 7^{8gs} 5^{8g} 0-0-3 £372

Giverand *Miss Jacqueline S Doyle*   29
5 b/br m Royal Applause - Petersford Girl (Ire)
10^{7s} 5^{10g} 13^{5gs} 0-0-3

Gjovic *B J Meehan*   75 a79
3 br g Singspiel (Ire) - Photo Call
2^{10sd} 5^{8s} 4^{11gf} 3^{10gf} 3^{12gf} 8^{12gs}
6^{11g} 0-2-8 £3,785

Glad Big (Ger) *J A Osborne*   72
2 b c Big Shuffle (USA) - Glady Sum (Ger)
3^{6sd} 8^{6hy} 0-1-2 £459

Glads Image *D J Daly*   37
2 ch f Handsome Ridge - Secret So And So
18^{8gf} 6^{7ss} 0-0-2

Gladys Aylward *A Crook*   a28
4 b f Polar Falcon (USA) - Versami (USA)
5^{11sd} 7^{12sd} 0-0-2

Glanworth (Ire) *N A Callaghan*
3 ch c Woodman (USA) - Leo Girl (USA)
10^{11gf} 6^{12gf} 11^{8gf} 11^{8sd} 0-0-4

Glaramara *A Bailey*   103 a79
3 b g Nicolotte - Digamist Girl (Ire)
11^{7sd} 2^{10g} 3^{8gs} 8^{6gf} 13^{7gf} 4^{7g} 4^{6g}
4^{8g} 8^{8s} 17^{6s} 0-2-11 £11,267

Glasson Lodge *P D Evans*   65 a41
2 b f Primo Dominie - Petrikov (Ire)
4^{5sd} 5^{5gs} 6^{5f} 3^{6gf} 2^{5f} 2^{5f} 6^{6gf}
8^{6gf} 4^{6gf} 0-2-10 £1,815

Glebe Garden *M L W Bell*   84 a60
3 b f Soviet Star (USA) - Trounce

5^{8s} 5^{8gs} 6^{7g} 11^{8g} 8^{8gf} 1^{7gf} 2^{7s} 10^{7g}
11^{7sd} **1-1-9 £6,673**

Glen Ida *M L W Bell* 90
2 ch c Selkirk (USA) - Yanka (USA)
3^{7gs} 2^{8g} 1^{8gf} **1-2-3 £6,843**

Glen Innes (Ire) *D R Loder* 101
3 b f Selkirk (USA) - Shinko Hermes (Ire)
1^{8hy} 2^{8s} 2^{10gs} 7^{9g} PU^{10g} 4^{10s} **1-2-6**
£24,038

Glen Vale Walk (Ire) *Mrs G S Rees* 50
7 ch g Balla Cove - Winter Harvest
6^{11gf} 3^{12gf} 5^{11f} **0-1-3 £537**

Glencairn Star *J S Goldie* 12
3 b c Selkirk (USA) - Bianca Nera
11^{7gs} 11^{8s} 16^{8g} **0-0-3**

Glencalvie (Ire) *J Noseda* 79 a49
3 ch c Grand Lodge (USA) - Top Of The Form (Ire)
21^{8g} 5^{8g} 15^{8g} 4^{7gf} 1^{7gf} 16^{gf} 13^{7sd} **2-0-7**
£7,895

Glencoe Solas (Ire) *S Kirk* 81
4 ch f Night Shift (USA) - Boranwood (Ire)
6^{6s} 4^{6s} 2^{6f} 2^{6gf} 5^{6gf} 3^{6gf} 2^{6gs} 6^{6g}
12^{6g} **1-4-10 £11,763**

Glendale *D K Ivory* 55 a65
3 ch g Opening Verse (USA) - Kayartis
1^{8sd} 11^{10gs} 13^{10g} 9^{8hy} 7^{8gf} 5^{8sd} 9^{10g}
12^{10gf} 8^{7sd} 5^{9sd} **1-0-10 £1,463**

Glenviews Polly (Ire) *Ian Emmerson* a26
4 b f Poliglote - Fun Board (Fr)
6^{7sd} 8^{7sd} 11^{7sd} **0-0-3**

Glesni *S C Williams* a28
5 gr m Key Of Luck (USA) - Llwy Bren
7^{10sd} **0-0-1**

Glide *J A B Old* 75
3 ch g In The Wings - Ash Glade
3^{11gs} 12^{12gs} 3^{14g} **0-2-3 £1,195**

Gliding By *P R Chamings* 58
3 ch f Halling (USA) - Waft (USA)
9^{10gf} 13^{10gf} 7^{12f} **0-0-3**

Glimmer Of Light (Ire) *P W Harris* 74
4 b g Marju (Ire) - Church Light
6^{10gs} 13^{10gf} 7^{10gf} 9^{10gf} 16^{10g} **0-0-5**

Global Achiever *G C H Chung* 41 a74
3 b g Key Of Luck (USA) - Inflation
3^{8sd} 2^{7sd} 2^{7ss} 1^{6sw} 16^{6gs} 8^{5g} 15^{7gf} 7^{6sd}
9^{6f} 14^{6g} 12^{7sd} 1^{5sd} **2-2-12 £9,380**

Global Banker (Ire) *G C H Chung* 32 a37
2 b c Desert Prince (Ire) - Luisa Demon (Ire)
17^{6gf} 5^{5sd} **0-0-2**

Globe Beauty (Ire) *A D W Pinder* a12
6 b m Shalford (Ire) - Pen Bal Duchess
6^{10sd} 7^{7sd} **0-0-2**

Globe Trekker (USA) *James Moffatt* 73
2 gr f Aljabr (USA) - Amazonia (USA)
11^{6g} 4^{8g} 4^{8gf} 7^{8s} **0-0-4 £1,089**

Gloria Nimbus *M Mullineaux* 40
2 b f Cloudings (Ire) - Glorious Aragon
7^{5s} 9^{6gf} 6^{5gf} 9^{6g} 9^{5g} **0-0-5**

Glorious Step (USA) *J H M Gosden* 87
2 b f Diesis - Bessie's Chips (USA)
3^{7f} 1^{8gf} 8^{7hy} 1^{8f} **2-1-4 £9,814**

Glory Girl *M Brittain* 40 a34
4 ch f Factual (USA) - Glory Gold
6^{6sd} 6^{6s} **0-0-2**

Glory Quest (USA) *Miss Gay Kelleway* 81 a78

7 b g Quest For Fame - Sonseri
2^{12sd} 7^{12sd} 3^{16sd} 5^{14sd} 2^{12sw} 2^{16ss} 1^{12sd}
13^{12g} 3^{14g} 4^{12f} 1^{14gs} 20^{20gf} 3^{14g} 1^{15g} 29^{18s}
3-5-15 £23,431

Gloved Hand *J G Given* 87
2 b f Royal Applause - Fudge
1^{5gf} 14^{5gf} 10^{5gf} 6^{5gf} **1-0-4 £5,005**

Go Bananas *B J Meehan* 83 a67
3 b g Primo Dominie - Amsicora
6^{7gf} 4^{7gf} 9^{7sd} 17^{7g} **0-0-4 £1,070**

Go Between *E A L Dunlop* 92
3 b f Daggers Drawn (USA) - Pizzicato
2^{7g} 7^{7gf} 6^{6gf} 6^{7gf} 1^{7gf} 7^{7s} 13^{7g} **1-1-7**
£8,652

Go Classic *A M Hales* 31 a69
4 b f Classic Cliche (Ire) - Edraianthus
7^{16sd} 13^{14s} 14^{12gf} **0-0-3**

Go For Gold (Ire) *A P O'Brien* 115
3 br c Machiavellian (USA) - Kithanga (Ire)
3^{10gs} 2^{12g} 3^{12g} 7^{15gf} **0-1-4 £29,150**

Go Free *A M Hales* 35 a56
3 gr g Easycall - Miss Traxdata
2^{7sd} 5^{8sd} 9^{8gf} 5^{6sd} 10^{7gs} 13^{7g} **0-1-6**
£868

Go Garuda *D W P Arbuthnot* 63
3 b g Air Express (Ire) - Free As A Bird
3^{8g} 12^{8g} **0-1-2 £866**

Go Go Girl *L G Cottrell* 73
4 ch f Pivotal - Addicted To Love
1^{6s} 7^{6s} **1-0-2 £3,692**

Go Green *P D Evans* 61 a41
3 ch f Environment Friend - Sandra Mac
8^{8sd} 8^{8s} 13^{10g} 7^{10gs} 5^{8f} 7^{8gf} 2^{8g} 1^{10gf}
4^{10gf} 3^{10gs} 2^{10s} 6^{10s} 13^{10gf} 3^{12s} 2^{10gs} 13^{12g}
6^{12g} 4^{11s} **1-5-18 £6,633**

Go Mo (Ire) *S Kirk* 77 a62
2 br c Night Shift (USA) - Quiche
12^{6gf} 6^{6gs} 6^{6sd} 8^{7gf} 8^{8s} 2^{6hy} 2^{6s} **0-2-7**
£4,348

Go Padero (Ire) *M Johnston* 96
3 ch c Night Shift (USA) - Watch The Clock
1^{7s} 4^{8gs} 1^{7s} **2-0-3 £15,595**

Go Solo *B W Hills* 82
3 b c Primo Dominie - Taza
14^{7g} 3^{7gf} 3^{8gf} 5^{11g} 3^{9gf} 9^{9g} 15^{10s} 8^{8gf}
0-2-8 £3,007

Go Supersonic *Sir Michael Stoute* 73
3 b f Zafonic (USA) - Shirley Superstar
4^{8s} 4^{10g} **0-0-2 £694**

Go Tech *T D Easterby* 96
4 b g Gothenberg (Ire) - Bollin Sophie
20^{8g} 9^{7hy} 6^{7g} 8^{7f} 6^{8g} 2^{10gf} 4^{10s} 6^{10gs}
7^{8gs} 4^{10gf} 2^{10g} 1^{10f} 1^{10gf} 1^{10g} 18^{12s} **3-2-15**
£39,047

Go Yellow *P D Evans* 76 a68
3 b g Overbury (Ire) - Great Lyth Lass (Ire)
13^{7g} 11^{6s} 5^{6gf} 2^{6gf} 4^{7gf} 6^{7g} 1^{7g} 4^{6g}
10^{7gf} 2^{7g} 11^{7sd} **1-3-12 £6,542**

Goblin *D E Cantillon* 79 a76
3 b g Atraf - Forest Fantasy
4^{6gs} 1^{8sd} 5^{10g} 1^{10gf} 3^{12gf} 5^{10gf} 1^{11gf}
3^{11gf} **3-1-8 £13,693**

Godsend *R Hannon* 77
2 b f Royal Applause - Gracious Gift
2^{5gf} 1^{5gf} 2^{6gf} 3^{6gf} 8^{7g} **1-3-5 £7,658**

Gogetter Girl *J Gallagher* 68 a53
2 b f Wolfhound (USA) - Square Mile Miss (Ire)
6⁵ᵍ 2⁵ˢ 4⁵ᵍˢ 10⁵ˢ 4⁵ᵍᶠ 6⁵ᵍᶠ 11⁶ˢᵈ 9⁵ᶠ
11⁶ᵍˢ 20⁶ᵍᶠ 11⁸ˢ 6⁹ˢᵈ **0-1-12 £2,575**

Gojo (Ire) *B Palling* 73
3 b f Danetime (Ire) - Pretonic
4⁶ᵍ 2⁶ˢ 9⁶ˢ 15⁶ᵍᶠ 12⁶ᵍˢ 19⁶ˢ F⁶ˢᵈ **0-2-7**
£1,420

Golano *P R Webber* 79 a83
4 gr g Linamix (Fr) - Dimakya (USA)
2¹⁰ˢᵈ 10¹²ᵍᶠ 8¹⁰ˢ 6¹²ᵍ 13¹¹ʰʸ **0-1-5**
£1,317

Golband *L M Cumani* 44
2 b f Cadeaux Genereux - Hatheethah (Ire)
5⁶ᵍᶠ **0-0-1**

Gold Card *J R Best* 67 a42
3 b g First Trump - Fleuve D'Or (Ire)
2⁸ˢᵈ 2¹¹ᵍˢ 5¹²ᵍ 5¹²ᵍ 2¹²ᵍˢ 1¹⁰ᵍ **1-3-6**
£6,159

Gold Guest *P D Evans* 68 a72
5 ch g Vettori (Ire) - Cassilis (Ire)
1¹⁰ˢᵈ 7¹⁰ˢᵈ 7⁷ᵍᶠ 4¹¹ᵍ 5¹⁰ᵍᶠ 6¹²ᵍˢ 2¹²ᵍˢ
6¹²ˢᵈ **1-1-8 £4,190**

Gold Gun (USA) *M A Jarvis* 46
2 b c Seeking The Gold (USA) - Possessive Dancer
14⁸ᵍ 16⁸ˢ **0-0-2**

Gold History (USA) *M Johnston* 102
3 b c Seeking The Gold (USA) - Battle Hymn (USA)
2⁸ᵍ 1⁹ᵍ 3¹⁰ᵍˢ 5¹²ᶠ 16⁸ᵍ 10¹⁰ᵍᶠ 6¹⁰ˢ 5¹⁰ᵍˢ
1⁹ᵍᶠ 8¹⁰ᵍᶠ **2-1-10 £45,064**

Gold Majesty *M R Channon* 48
2 b f Josr Algarhoud (Ire) - Calcutta Queen
11⁵ᵍ 8⁶ᵍᶠ 9⁶ᵍᶠ 13⁷ˢ 8⁶ᵍ **0-0-5**

Gold Mask (USA) *J H M Gosden* 79
3 b/br c Seeking The Gold (USA) - Leo's Gypsy Dancer (USA)
6⁷ᵍˢ 2⁸ᵍ 1⁸ᵍ 15⁸ᶠ **1-1-4 £7,202**

Gold Medallist *D R C Elsworth* 113
4 ch g Zilzal (USA) - Spot Prize (USA)
6¹³ᵍ 7¹⁶ᵍˢ 4¹⁶ᵍ 1¹⁵ᵛˢ 5¹⁶ˢ 5¹⁶ˢ **1-0-6**
£49,486

Gold Quay (Ire) *N P Littmoden* 75
2 b f Docksider (USA) - Viaticum (Ire)
2⁶ᵍᶠ 4⁵ᵍᶠ 6⁵ᵍ **0-1-3 £2,543**

Gold Queen *M R Channon* 73
2 b f Grand Lodge (USA) - Silver Colours (USA)
3⁶ᵍˢ 1⁷ᵍˢ **1-1-2 £6,490**

Gold Relic (USA) *A M Balding* 51
3 b f Kingmambo (USA) - Gold Bust
12⁸ᵍᶠ 9¹⁰ᵍ **0-0-2**

Gold Ring *J A Geake* 102
4 ch g Groom Dancer (USA) - Indubitable
7¹²ᵍ 2¹²ᵍ 3¹²ᵍˢ 6¹⁴ᵍᶠ 5¹⁴ᵍᶠ 3¹²ᵍˢ 1¹¹ᵍ
6¹²ᵍᶠ 2¹⁴ˢ 4¹³ˢ 13¹²ˢ **1-4-11 £54,514**

Goldbricker *W M Brisbourne* a50
4 b g Muhtarram (USA) - Sally Slade
6⁸ˢᵈ 5⁸ˢᵈ 1⁹ˢˢ **1-0-3 £1,449**

Golden Anthem (USA) *J Pearce* 90
2 ch f Lion Cavern (USA) - Bacinella (USA)
1⁵ʰʸ 16⁶ᶠ 3⁶ᵍᶠ 6⁷ᵍᶠ 6⁶ˢ 14⁷ᵍ 7⁶ˢ **1-1-7**
£5,322

Golden Applause (Fr) *Mrs A L M King* 49
2 b f Royal Applause - Golden Circle (USA)
7⁶ᵍᶠ **0-0-1**

Golden Asha *N A Callaghan* 65
2 ch f Danehill Dancer (Ire) - Snugfit Annie

3⁵ᵍᶠ 7⁵ᵍᶠ **0-1-2 £647**

Golden Bankes (Ire) *W G M Turner* 34
3 ch f Foxhound (USA) - Semence D'Or (Fr)
12⁷ᵍᶠ 7⁶ᵍ **0-0-2**

Golden Boot *A Bailey* 69
5 ch g Unfuwain (USA) - Sports Delight
6¹²ᵍ 8¹⁴ˢ 9¹³ᵍ 1¹²ᶠ **1-0-4 £2,884**

Golden Bounty *R Hannon* 61
5 b h Bahamian Bounty - Cumbrian Melody
10⁶ᵍ 6⁶ᵍᶠ 10⁶ᵍᶠ 14⁸ᵍˢ 10⁵ᵍ **0-0-5**

Golden Chalice (Ire) *A M Balding* 99 a80
5 ch g Selkirk (USA) - Special Oasis
5⁸ˢᵈ 6⁶ˢᵈ 12⁸ᵍ 9⁷ᵍ 1⁷ˢ 19⁷ᵍˢ 17⁷ᵍˢ 12⁷ˢ
1-0-8 £12,814

Golden Chance (Ire) *M W Easterby* 55
7 b g Unfuwain (USA) - Golden Digger (USA)
8¹²ᵍᶠ 1¹¹ᶠ **1-0-2 £3,017**

Golden Dixie (USA) *C A Dwyer* 93 a82
5 ch g Dixieland Band (USA) - Beyrouth (USA)
10⁶ᵍᶠ 2⁶ᵍˢ 5⁶ᵍ 5⁶ᵍ 8⁶ᵍᶠ 24⁶ˢ 9⁶ᵍˢ 9⁷ˢᵈ
0-1-8 £2,210

Golden Drift *G Wragg* 66
3 ch f Inchinor - Carpet Of Leaves (USA)
12⁸ᵍᶠ 5⁸ᵍᶠ 7¹²ᵍˢ 2¹⁰ᵍ 5¹⁰ᵍᶠ 11¹⁰ᵍᶠ 3¹²ᵍᶠ
6¹⁴ᵍᶠ **0-2-8 £1,735**

Golden Dual *C L Tizzard* 23 a63
4 b g Danehill (USA) - Golden Digger (USA)
7¹⁰ˢᵈ 10¹⁰ˢᵈ 6¹²ˢᵈ 13¹⁴ˢᵈ 7¹²ˢᵈ 9¹²ˢᵈ 2¹³ˢᵈ
9¹²ᵍˢ 16¹⁴ᵍ 7¹²ˢᵈ **0-1-10 £846**

Golden Dynasty *R Hannon* 70
2 ch c Erhaab (USA) - Ajeebah (Ire)
8⁷ᵍ 9⁷ᵍ 6⁸ˢ 7⁸ᵍᶠ **0-0-4**

Golden Empire (USA) *E A L Dunlop* 73 a71
3 br g Red Ransom (USA) - Golden Gorse (USA)
2⁹ˢˢ 3¹²ᵍᶠ 4¹²ˢ 1¹¹ᵍ 14¹²ᵍˢ 8¹¹ᵍᶠ **1-2-6**
£9,040

Golden Feather *J H M Gosden* 77
2 ch c Dr Fong (USA) - Idolize
3⁷ˢ **0-1-1 £545**

Golden Fields (Ire) *Mrs J Candlish* 43
4 b f Definite Article - Quickstep Queen (Fr)
10¹⁶ˢ 7¹¹ᵍᶠ 8¹²ᵍᶠ 3¹⁰ˢ **0-1-4 £446**

Golden Fury *J L Dunlop* 86
2 ch c Cadeaux Genereux - Galaxie Dust (USA)
4⁶ᶠ 3⁷ᵍᶠ 4⁸ᵍ 2⁸ᵍ 3⁸ᵍᶠ **0-3-5 £4,392**

Golden Gate (Ire) *M L W Bell* 24
2 b c Giant's Causeway (USA) - Bay Queen
16⁸ˢ 13⁸ʰʸ **0-0-2**

Golden Grace *E A L Dunlop* 95
3 b c Green Desert (USA) - Chief Bee
9¹⁰ᵍ 4¹⁰ᵍˢ 4¹⁰ᵍᶠ 17¹²ᵍᶠ 12⁸ᵍ 13¹⁰ᵍ **0-0-6**
£1,864

Golden Island (Ire) *J W Hills* 94
3 ch f Selkirk (USA) - Daftiyna (Ire)
3⁹ᵍᶠ 2¹⁰ᵍ 1¹⁰ᵍ 5¹⁰ᵍ 1⁸ᵍᶠ 9⁸ᵍᶠ 3⁷ᵍ 2⁸ᵍᶠ
2-4-8 £24,315

Golden Key *J S Smith* 55
3 b g Rainbow Quest (USA) - Keyboogie (USA)
9¹⁰ᵍ 10¹⁰ᵍ **0-0-2**

Golden Legacy (Ire) *R A Fahey* 104
2 b f Rossini (USA) - Dissidentia (Ire)
2⁶ᶠ 8⁶ᶠ 16⁶ᵍᶠ 16⁶ᶠ 3⁶ᵍ 16⁵ˢ 4⁶ᵍ **3-1-7**
£44,485

Golden Legend (Ire) *K G Wingrove* a10
7 b g Last Tycoon - Adjalisa (Ire)

Golden Nun *T D Easterby* 105
7^{7sd} 7^{12sd} **0-0-2**

Golden Nun *T D Easterby* 105
4 b f Bishop Of Cashel - Amber Mill
11^{6g} 2^{7s} 3^{7s} 1^{6g} 3^{6g} 1^{6f} 7^{6gs} 5^{7gf} 7^{7gs}
5^{6s} 4^{7gf} 10^{6gf} 11^{7s} **2-3-13 £87,411**

Golden Oldie (Ire) *D Flood*
6 b g Old Vic - Misty Gold
10^{8sd} **0-0-1**

Golden Queen *M D I Usher* 39 a15
3 b f Unfuwain (USA) - Queen Linear (USA)
14^{10sd} 3^{10g} 14^{10g} **0-1-3 £376**

Golden Quest *M Johnston* 91 a82
3 ch g Rainbow Quest (USA) - Souk (Ire)
1^{12sw} 1^{12sd} 7^{12g} 1^{14gs} 5^{12gf} **3-0-5**
£14,090

Golden Sahara (Ire) *Saeed Bin Suroor* 107
3 b c Green Desert (USA) - Golden Digger (USA)
14^{8g} 3^{7gs} 1^{7gf} 3^{7gf} 14^{7g} **1-1-5**
£17,509

Golden Shell *A C Whillans*
5 ch m Hatim (USA) - Sonnenelle
10^{7s} **0-0-1**

Golden Spectrum (Ire) *D Nicholls* 65
5 ch g Spectrum (Ire) - Plessaya (USA)
3^{6g} 5^{7f} 10^{6f} 15^{8gf} 3^{7gf} 12^{6gf} 14^{7s}
12^{7g} 3^{8gf} 17^{8gf} 10^{9gs} **0-3-11 £1,980**

Golden Square *B J Meehan* 56
2 ch g Tomba - Cherish Me
9^{6hy} 6^{6g} **0-0-2**

Golden Squaw *T D Easterby* 44
2 ch f Grand Lodge - Wig Wam (Ire)
6^{7g} 11^{6gs} 14^{7gs} 9^{7gf} **0-0-4**

Goldeva *R Hollinshead* 104
5 gr m Makbul - Gold Belt (Ire)
1^{6g} 5^{6gs} 11^{6s} 5^{6gs} 4^{6gf} 1^{6gs} 5^{6g} 9^{6s}
6^{6gs} **2-0-9 £54,625**

Goldhill Prince *W G M Turner* 56 a56
2 b g Prince Sabo - Lady Mabel
8^{5g} 4^{5g} 9^{5g} 2^{5sd} 1^{6g} 1^{6f} 1^{5gf} 1^{6f} 3^{7f}
6^{6sd} 5^{7gf} 3^{6gf} 9^{6gf} **4-1-13 £14,975**

Golfagent *Miss K Marks* 22 a34
6 b g Kris - Alusha
4^{16sd} 6^{15g} **0-0-2**

Golnessa *Mrs N Macauley* 19
3 b f Pyramus (USA) - My Pretty Niece
11^{8ss} 12^{7gs} 6^{8s} **0-0-3**

Gondolin (Ire) *G Brown* 79
4 b g Marju (Ire) - Galletina (Ire)
8^{13gs} 10^{16s} **0-0-2**

Gone Fishing (Ire) *M A Jarvis* 76 a72
2 ch f Cadeaux Genereux - Dabbing (USA)
7^{6gf} 2^{7s} 3^{7gs} 7^{7sd} **0-3-4 £3,042**

Gone Loco *H S Howe* 15
3 b f Piccolo - Missed Again
9^{8gf} **0-0-1**

Gone Too Far *P Monteith* 57
6 b g Reprimand - Blue Nile (Ire)
1^{15gf} **1-0-1 £3,380**

Gone'N'Dunnett (Ire) *Mrs C A Dunnett* 66 a59
5 b g Petardia - Skerries Bell
10^{5sd} 8^{6sw} 10^{5sd} 8^{5sw} 15^{6s} 10^{6gf} 6^{6sd}
6^{6f} 1^{6f} 7^{5g} 3^{6f} 1^{5g} 8^{6g} 5^{5f} VOI^{5gf} 2^{5g}
11^{5g} 15^{5f} 11^{6gf} **2-2-19 £8,813**

Gonfilia (Ger) *Saeed Bin Suroor* 111
4 b f Big Shuffle (USA) - Gonfalon

Good Article (Ire) *A P Jones* 42
8^{8gf} 1^{9f} 2^{7s} 18^{8gf} 1^{9g} 9^{8gf} 4^{7gf} 2^{7gf} 1^{7gf}
4-2-9 £130,506

Good Article (Ire) *A P Jones* 42
3 b g Definite Article - Good News (Ire)
12^{10gs} BD^{10s} 16^{10gs} 13^{8g} **0-0-4**

Good Form (Ire) *Miss K M George* a14
4 b g Danetime (Ire) - Faapette
5^{9sd} 5^{7sd} 12^{6sd} **0-0-3**

Good Investment *P C Haslam* 69 a37
2 b g Silver Patriarch (Ire) - Bundled Up (USA)
3^{6gf} 5^{7gs} 9^{7s} 11^{7gf} **0-1-4 £652**

Good Loser (Ire) *C R Dore* 36
4 b g Mujadil (USA) - Cockney Star (Ire)
15^{8gs} 9^{10gf} **0-0-2**

Good Time Bobby *J O'Reilly* 47 a4
7 b g Primitive Rising (USA) - Goodreda
3^{8gf} 7^{15sd} 4^{7gf} 12^{5gf} 15^{6gf} 16^{5gs} 13^{8f}
13^{6sd} **0-0-8 £1,022**

Good Timing *J Hetherton* 11 a41
6 gr g Timeless Times (USA) - Fort Vally
2^{9sd} 15^{11sd} 7^{9ss} 13^{7gf} 13^{11g} **0-1-5 £421**

Good Vibrations *P F I Cole* a51
3 b f Bijou D'Inde - Showcase
3^{7sd} 5^{7ss} 6^{7sd} 7^{6sd} **0-1-4 £424**

Good Wee Girl (Ire) *P S McEntee* 71 a35
2 b f Tagula (Ire) - Auriga
7^{6f} 18^{6g} 2^{6gf} 1^{6g} 5^{6gf} 1^{7s} 8^{8s} 9^{7gf}
11^{8g} 9^{7sd} **2-1-10 £10,146**

Goodbye Ben *J H M Gosden* 49
2 b c Benny The Dip (USA) - Alifandango (Ire)
9^{7gs} **0-0-1**

Goodbye Mr Bond *E J Alston* 83 a52
4 b g Elmaamul (USA) - Fifth Emerald
5^{9sd} 6^{8sd} 3^{8sw} 4^{8hy} 3^{8gs} 4^{8s} 1^{8g} 1^{8gf} 1^{8g}
18^g 3^{8gf} 2^{9gf} 6^{8gs} 18^g 7^{9g} 6^{8s} **5-6-16**
£43,897

Goodbye Mrs Chips *Mrs L B Normile* 22
5 ch m Zilzal (USA) - Happydrome
6^{7g} **0-0-1**

Goodenough Mover *J S King* 91 a97
8 ch g Beveled (USA) - Rekindled Flame (Ire)
2^{6sd} 1^{7g} 2^{7gf} 2^{7g} 1^{7gf} 1^{7gf} 5^{7g} 2^{7gf} 7^{7gs}
15^{7g} 16^{gs} 1^{7sd} **5-4-12 £45,932**

Goodenough Star *D W Lewis* a14
4 b f Stronz (Ire) - Goodenough Girl
9^{11sd} **0-0-1**

Goodricke *D R Loder* 89
2 b c Bahamian Bounty - Star
2^{5gs} 1^{5gs} 1^{6gs} 9^{6gf} **2-1-4 £9,428**

Goodwood Finesse (Ire) *J L Dunlop* 77
3 b f Revoque (Ire) - Key To Paris (Arg)
1^{9gf} 5^{10g} 6^{14gs} 3^{11g} 6^{12s} **1-1-5 £6,867**

Goodwood Prince *S Dow* 45 a64
4 b g Emperor Jones (USA) - Scarlet Lake
5^{5sd} 12^{6sd} 17^{6gs} 16^{5gf} 12^{5gf} 10^{6f} 8^{7f}
11^{6sd} 10^{6sd} **0-0-9**

Goodwood Spirit *J L Dunlop* 80
2 b c Fraam - Rechanit (Ire)
2^{6gf} 2^{6gf} 3^{6g} 1^{7gf} 5^{7gf} **1-2-5 £9,288**

Goose Chase *M L W Bell* 66
2 b g Inchinor - Bronzewing
10^{7g} 6^{7s} 9^{7s} **0-0-3**

Goose Island (Ire) *Patrick Martin* 47 a29
3 b f Kahyasi - Sabrata (Ire)
5^{12gy} 2^{12gy} 11^{11sd} **0-1-3 £1,020**

Gordy's Joy *G A Ham*   a37
4 b f Cloudings (Ire) - Beatle Song
3¹⁵ˢᵈ 14¹⁸ᶠ 12¹⁶ᵍᶠ **0-0-3 £418**

Gortumblo *D J S Ffrench Davis*   89
2 b g Sri Pekan (USA) - Evergreen (Ire)
1⁵ᵍ 3⁶ᵍ 10⁶ᵍ 8⁶ᵍᶠ 7⁷ᵍ 9⁶ᶠ **1-1-6
£8,647**

Goslar *H Candy*   96
3 ch f In The Wings - Anna Of Brunswick
3¹⁰ᵍ 1¹²ᵍᶠ 4¹²ᵍ 4¹²ˢ 4¹⁴ˢ **1-1-5 £9,187**

Got One Too (Fr) *N J Henderson*   81
7 ch g Green Tune (USA) - Gloria Mundi (Fr)
2¹⁶ᵍᶠ 12²⁰ᵍᶠ **0-1-2 £2,561**

Got To Be Cash *W M Brisbourne*   58 a36
5 ch m Lake Coniston (Ire) - Rasayel (USA)
4⁹ˢˢ 2¹⁰ᵍˢ 1¹⁰ˢ 10¹⁰ᵍᶠ 5¹⁰ᵍᶠ 3¹⁰ᵍᶠ 11¹⁰ᵍᶠ
7¹¹ˢ 1¹⁰ᵍˢ 4¹⁰ᵍ 11⁹ʰʸ 10¹¹ᵍˢ **2-2-12 £7,754**

Gotya *J R Weymes*
4 b f Gothenberg (Ire) - Water Well
8¹²ˢˢ **0-0-1**

Government (Ire) *M C Chapman*   42
3 b g Great Dane (Ire) - Hidden Agenda (Fr)
15⁸ᵍ 4¹⁰ᵍᶠ 5⁷ᵍᶠ 7⁶ᵍ **0-0-4 £286**

Grace Darling *Miss E C Lavelle*
3 b f Botanic (USA) - Light On The Waves
5¹²ᵍˢ **0-0-1**

Graceful Air (Ire) *J R Weymes*   63 a50
3 b f Danzero (Aus) - Samsung Spirit
4⁶ˢˢ 5⁶ˢ 2⁷ᵍ 2⁸ᵍᶠ 4⁷ᵍᶠ 7⁸ᶠ 5⁷ᵍ 4⁸ᵍᶠ 4⁹ᵍᶠ
5⁷ᵍᶠ 11⁷ᵍᶠ 10⁸ᵍ 3⁸ᵍ 2⁸ᵍ 9⁹ᵍˢ 4⁸ˢᵈ **0-3-16
£5,324**

Graceful Flight *P T Midgley*   2
2 gr f Cloudings (Ire) - Fantasy Flight
16⁶ᵍˢ 10⁶ᶠ **0-0-2**

Gracia *S C Williams*   58
5 gr m Linamix (Fr) - Francia
11⁸ᵍˢ 7⁸ᵍᶠ 4⁹ˢ **0-0-3 £365**

Gracie's Gift (Ire) *P C Haslam*   46
2 b g Imperial Ballet (Ire) - Settle Petal (Ire)
4⁵ᵍᶠ 4⁵ᵍᶠ **0-0-2 £790**

Gracilis (Ire) *G A Swinbank*   46 a20
7 b g Caerleon (USA) - Grace Note (Fr)
7¹⁶ˢˢ 15¹⁹ᵍˢ 8¹⁵ˢ **0-0-3**

Gracious Air (USA) *J R Weymes*   a52
6 b m Bahri (USA) - Simply Bell (USA)
10¹⁰ˢᵈ 1⁸ˢᵈ 5⁸ˢˢ 3⁸ˢˢ 3⁹ˢʷ 10⁸ˢˢ **1-2-6
£2,064**

Grady *W M Brisbourne*   41
5 ch g Bluegrass Prince (Ire) - Lady Sabina
6⁸ᵍˢ 6¹²ᵍᶠ 12¹²ᵍᶠ 6¹¹ᵍ 12¹¹ᶠ 7¹²ᵍ 13¹²ᵍᶠ
0-0-7

Graft *Mrs P Townsley*   69
5 b g Entrepreneur - Mariakova (USA)
11¹⁰ˢ 6¹⁰ᵍˢ 2¹⁰ᵍ 14¹²ᵍᶠ 10¹²ᵍᶠ 1⁹ᵍᶠ 13⁷ᵍᶠ
1-1-7 £4,711

Graham Island *G Wragg*   87 a84
3 b g Acatenango (Ger) - Gryada
1¹¹ᵍ 6¹²ᵍˢ 6¹¹ᵍ 8¹³ᵍ 5¹²ᵍᶠ 4¹²ˢᵈ **1-0-6
£7,438**

Gralmano (Ire) *K A Ryan*   85 a72
9 b g Scenic - Llangollen (Ire)
7¹²ˢᵈ 12¹⁹ᵍˢ 6¹⁴ᵍᶠ 13²⁰ᵍᶠ **0-0-4**

Gramada (Ire) *M J Wallace*   41
2 b f Cape Cross (Ire) - Decatur
10⁶ᵍᶠ **0-0-1**

Grampian *J G Given*   109
5 b h Selkirk (USA) - Gryada
2¹²ᵍˢ 6¹²ᵍˢ 2¹⁰ᵍ 3¹²ᵍ 18¹⁴ˢ 2¹⁴ᵍ 5¹²ᵍᶠ
0-3-7 £20,208

Gran Clicquot *G P Enright*   54 a49
9 gr m Gran Alba (USA) - Tina's Beauty
8⁸ˢᵈ 8¹⁰ˢᵈ 2⁸ˢᵈ 7¹⁰ᵍᶠ 1⁹ᵍᶠ 13⁸ᵍᶠ 2⁹ᵍᶠ 7⁸ᵍᶠ
8¹⁰ᵍᶠ 12⁸ᵍ **1-2-10 £5,078**

Gran Dana (Ire) *M Johnston*   81
4 b g Grand Lodge (USA) - Olean
2¹²ᵍˢ 1¹²ᵍᶠ 10¹⁴ᵍˢ 8¹²ᵍᶠ 17¹²ᵍ 13¹⁰ᵍ
10¹⁵ˢ **1-1-8 £6,201**

Granary Girl *B Palling*   42
2 b f Kingsinger (Ire) - Highland Blue
8⁵ᵍ 8⁶ᵍ **0-0-2**

Granato (Ger) *E F Vaughan*   89
3 b c Cadeaux Genereux - Genevra (Ire)
11⁶ᵍˢ 8⁶ᵍˢ 4⁸ᵍᶠ 4⁷ᵍᶠ **0-0-4 £1,538**

Grand Apollo *J H M Gosden*   65 a72
3 ch f Grand Lodge (USA) - Narva
2⁸ᶠ 5⁸ᶠ 6⁸ˢᵈ 5⁹ˢᵈ 13¹⁰ˢᵈ **0-1-5 £2,132**

Grand But One (Ire) *B W Hills*   88 a80
3 ch c Grand Lodge (USA) - Unscathed
6⁸ᵍ 2⁸ᵍ 2⁸ᵍᶠ 3⁸ᵍᶠ 1⁸ᵍ 6⁸ᵍᶠ 1⁸ᵍᶠ 9⁹ˢᵈ
2-3-8 £14,895

Grand Central (Ire) *A P O'Brien*   91
2 b c Sadler's Wells (USA) - Rebecca Sharp
1⁷ˢ **1-0-1 £9,169**

Grand Fromage (Ire) *A King*   59
6 ch g Grand Lodge (USA) - My First Paige (Ire)
13¹⁶ᵍᶠ 9¹⁸ᵍ 3¹⁶ᵍ **0-0-3 £838**

Grand Girl *B W Duke*   49 a19
2 b f Mark Of Esteem (Ire) - Ayunli
7⁷ᵍ 11⁷ˢ 8⁷ʰʸ 5⁷ˢᵈ **0-0-4**

Grand Ideas *Julian Poulton*   a67
5 b g Grand Lodge (USA) - Afrafa (Ire)
2⁷ˢᵈ **0-1-1 £1,193**

Grand Lass (Ire) *A Sadik*   58 a53
5 b m Grand Lodge (USA) - Siskin (Ire)
3⁹ˢᵈ 4¹²ˢᵈ 1⁹ˢˢ 2⁸ˢˢ 5⁸ˢʷ 4⁹ˢˢ 3¹²ᵍˢ 13¹¹ˢ
8¹¹ᵍˢ 4¹²ˢᵈ **1-3-10 £2,732**

Grand Marque (Ire) *R Hannon*   102
2 ch c Grand Lodge (USA) - Royal Fizz (Ire)
5⁷ᵍᶠ 1⁷ᵍᶠ 1⁷ᵍ 2⁸ᵍᶠ 5⁷ᵍᶠ 7⁸ᵍᶠ **2-0-6
£19,906**

Grand Music (Ire) *J J Sheehan*   a32
4 b g Grand Lodge (USA) - Abury (Ire)
12¹²ᵍᶠ 10¹³ˢᵈ **0-0-2**

Grand Option *B W Duke*   76 a42
2 ch c Compton Place - Follow The Stars
75ˢᵈ 2⁵ˢ 2⁵ᵍˢ 3⁵ᵍ 2⁵ᵍ 50⁵ᵍ 7⁶ᵍᶠ 4⁷ᵍˢ
6⁷ᵍˢ 16⁷ᵍᶠ 1⁶ᵍ **1-3-12 £8,173**

Grand Passion (Ire) *G Wragg*   108 a110
4 b g Grand Lodge (USA) - Lovers' Parlour
2¹⁰ˢᵈ 1¹⁰ˢᵈ 9¹⁰ᵍˢ 4⁸ᵍᶠ 2¹⁰ᵍᶠ 1⁸ᵍᶠ
3⁸ᵍᶠ 6⁸ᵍ **2-2-9 £78,893**

Grand Place *R Hannon*   79
2 b g Compton Place - Comme Ca
12⁶ᵍᶠ 4⁵ᵍᶠ 2³ᵍ 1⁵ᵍ 15⁶ᵍˢ 4⁶ᵍᶠ 4⁶ᵍˢ 5⁵ᵍ
1-1-8 £6,333

Grand Prairie (Swe) *G L Moore*   a60
8 b g Prairie - Platonica (Ity)
5¹³ˢᵈ **0-0-1**

Grand Rapide *J L Spearing*   60 a24
3 ch f Grand Lodge (USA) - Vax Rapide

6[6gf] 10[7s] 9[8gf] 4[7gs] 1[8gs] 13[10gf] 12[9sd]
8[8s] **1-1-8 £3,416**

Grand Reward (USA) *A P O'Brien* 110
3 b c Storm Cat (USA) - Serena's Song (USA)
2[7g] 5[8gf] 15[7gf] 1[6gf] LFT[6gf] 3[6gf] 6[5gf] 3[6y]
15[5g] 2[6ys] **1-4-10 £44,346**

Grand Show *W R Swinburn* 73
2 b c Efisio - Christine Daae
4[6f] 5[6s] **0-0-2 £441**

Grand View *J R Weymes* 46 a43
8 ch g Grand Lodge (USA) - Hemline
6[6sd] 11[7sd] 4[6gs] 2[6g] 1[6sd] 7[6g] 7[6gf] 11[7g]
19[6g] 7[6f] **1-1-10 £1,989**

Grand Welcome (Ire) *C Tinkler* 67
2 b g Indian Lodge (Ire) - Chocolate Box
12[5g] 7[6gs] 13[7gf] 2[7hy] 2[7gf] 12[8s] **0-2-6**
£1,901

Grand Wizard *W Jarvis* 55 a74
4 b g Grand Lodge (USA) - Shouk
4[12sd] 17[14s] 10[11f] 9[12s] 6[10gs] **0-0-5 £265**

Grandalea *Sir Michael Stoute* 80 a88
3 b f Grand Lodge (USA) - Red Azalea
5[8gf] 3[8gs] 1[7sd] 6[9g] **1-1-4 £4,351**

Grande Roche (Ire) *B W Hills* 44
2 b c Grand Lodge (USA) - Arabian Lass (SAF)
14[6gs] **0-0-1**

Grande Terre (Ire) *J G Given* 49
3 b f Grand Lodge (USA) - Savage (Ire)
PU[8s] 7[11g] 14[8gf] 12[9s] 12[12g] 12[16gf] **0-0-6**

Grandma Lily (Ire) *D Carroll* 64 a81
6 b m Bigstone (Ire) - Mrs Fisher (Ire)
3[5sd] 13[5sd] 10[6sd] 8[6sd] 11[7g] 17[5g] 3[6s]
14[8g] 3[6gf] 4[7s] 4[7sd] **0-4-11 £2,392**

Grandma Ryta *John Berry* 29
2 br f Cyrano De Bergerac - Tamara
9[5gf] 9[5g] **0-0-2**

Grandma's Girl *R Guest* 67
2 b f Desert Style (Ire) - Sakura Queen (Ire)
10[6gs] 4[7f] 5[7gf] 8[8gf] 10[8s] **0-0-5 £260**

Grandos (Ire) *T D Easterby* 62
2 b c Cadeaux Genereux - No Reservations (Ire)
11[6g] 5[7s] 8[6gs] **0-0-3**

Granita *M Blanshard* 30
2 b/br f Machiavellian (USA) - Actualite
10[6gf] **0-0-1**

Granston (Ire) *J D Bethell* 84
3 gr g Revoque (Ire) - Gracious Gretclo
3[7g] 1[8g] 6[8g] 6[8gf] 7[7f] 2[7gs] 5[7gs] 3[7gf] 1[8gf]
2-3-9 £19,874

Grant (Ire) *Patrick Morris* 69 a61
4 b g Bahamian Bounty - Verify (Ire)
5[7sw] 6[5sd] 10[7y] 5[5y] 2[6y] 4[5f] 17[5s] **0-1-7**
£3,908

Granuaile O'Malley (Ire) *P W D'Arcy*
4 b f Mark Of Esteem (Ire) - Dame Laura (Ire)
13[7sd] **0-0-1**

Grasp *R M Beckett* 59
2 b c Kayf Tara - Circe
4[8s] 14[10s] **0-0-2 £349**

Grass Widow (Ire) *J J Quinn*
2 b f Mujadil (USA) - Noble Clare (Ire)
9[7s] **0-0-1**

Grasslandik *Miss A Stokell*
8 b g Ardkinglass - Sophisticated Baby

16[5sd] **0-0-1**

Gravardlax *B J Meehan* 80
3 ch g Salse (USA) - Rubbiyati
7[8gs] 4[10g] 8[11g] 10[8gf] **0-0-4 £278**

Graze On *J J Quinn* 81
2 b g Factual (USA) - Queens Check
2[5gf] 1[5gs] 2[5gs] 5[5gf] 10[6g] 11[6s] **1-2-6**
£13,947

Great As Gold (Ire) *B Ellison* 69
5 b g Goldmark (USA) - Great Land (USA)
1[22s] 2[16hy] **1-1-2 £8,305**

Great Belief (Ire) *T D McCarthy* 74
2 b c Namid - Fairy Lore (Ire)
3[5gs] 6[5gf] 4[6g] **0-1-3 £939**

Great Blasket (Ire) *E J O'Neill* 45
3 b f Petardia - Alexander Goddess (Ire)
8[8gf] 9[8hy] 8[8gs] 11[10f] **0-0-4**

Great Exhibition (USA) *Saeed Bin Suroor* 78 a78
3 b c Gone West (USA) - Touch Of Greatness (USA)
8[9f] 9[8hy] 3[7gf] 2[7gf] 2[9gs] **0-3-5 £3,162**

Great Fox (Ire) *P L Gilligan* 77
3 b c Foxhound - Good Enough (Ire)
14[6gs] 6[6s] 3[5gs] **0-1-3 £1,359**

Great General (Ire) *S L Keightley* 50
2 ch g General Monash (USA) - Racing Brenda
7[6s] 10[7gs] **0-0-2**

Great Gidding *H Morrison* 47
3 b g Classic Cliche (Ire) - Arcady
7[14gs] 3[12gf] 8[10gf] 15[14g] 5[12gf] 14[16gf] **0-1-6**
£854

Great Opinions (USA) *J H M Gosden* 79
2 b f Rahy (USA) - Gracie Lady (Ire)
9[5gf] 2[7f] 10[7gf] 11[7g] **0-1-4 £1,475**

Great Scott *M Johnston* 88
3 b g Fasliyev (USA) - Arabis
9[7g] 10[7gs] 5[10gf] 3[10gf] 4[10gf] 7[10s] 13[7g]
12[8s] 5[8gf] 7[10s] **0-1-10 £4,038**

Great View (Ire) *Mrs A L M King* 71 a56
5 b g Great Commotion (USA) - Tara View (Ire)
8[10sd] 1[13sd] 2[11s] 1[12gf] 2[12s] 4[12gf] 10[12gf]
2[13gf] 3[12gf] 7[12gf] 2[13gs] 4[11g] 9[12gf] **2-6-13**
£11,335

Greatcoat *J G Given* 46
2 ch g Erhaab (USA) - Vaula
8[7s] **0-0-1**

Greatest By Phar *J Akehurst* a44
3 b g Pharly (Fr) - Greatest Friend (Ire)
9[8sd] 12[10sd] **0-0-2**

Greek Star *K A Morgan* 45
3 b g Soviet Star (USA) - Graecia Magna (USA)
4[12gf] 15[12gf] 6[12f] **0-0-4 £427**

Green 'N' Gold *M D Hammond* 61
4 b f Cloudings (Ire) - Fishki
1[18s] 10[22s] 4[16gf] 8[14gf] 8[18gf] 8[16g] 10[17gs]
1-0-7 £4,459

Green Conversion (Ire) *G Fierro*
3 ch g Desert King (Ire) - Blue Bangor (Ire)
PU[16gf] **0-0-1**

Green Falcon *J W Hills* 57 a68
3 b c Green Desert (USA) - El Jazirah
13[7sd] 3[7sd] 3[8sd] 8[7gf] 7[10gf] 13[8gf] 11[8gf]
7[10gs] **0-2-8 £1,217**

Green Ginger *C N Kellett*
8 ch g Ardkinglass - Bella Maggio
14[8gs] **0-0-1**

Green Manalishi *D W P Arbuthnot*   96 a85
3 b c Green Desert (USA) - Silca-Cisa
4⁵ˢᵈ 2⁵ˢᵈ 2⁵ᵍ 1⁵ᵍᶠ 9⁵ᵍᶠ 3⁵ᵍᶠ 1⁵ᵍᶠ 5⁶ᵍᶠ
5⁵ᵍ 20⁵ᵍᶠ 10⁵ᵍᶠ 10⁵ᵍ 12⁵ᵍ **2-3-13 £28,978**

Green Master (Pol) *A Sadik*
4 bl g Who Knows - Green Fee (Ger)
1⁷ʰʸ 4⁸ᵍᶠ 10¹²ᵍˢ 14¹³ᵍᶠ 8¹²ˢᵈ **1-0-5 £313**

Green Ocean *J W Unett*   37
4 gr f Environment Friend - Northern Swinger
15¹⁰ᵍˢ 14¹²ᵍᶠ **0-0-2**

Green Pirate *D R Loder*   23
2 b g Bahamian Bounty - Verdura
11⁷ᵍᶠ **0-0-1**

Green Ridge *Miss A M Newton-Smith*   59 a7
3 b f Muhtarram (USA) - Top Of The Morning
2⁶ˢ 14⁵ᵍᶠ 11⁵ᵍᶠ 11⁵ᵍ 12⁸ʰʸ 11⁷ˢᵈ **0-1-6
£1,543**

Greenborough (Ire) *Mrs P Ford*   a12
6 b g Dr Devious (Ire) - Port Isaac (USA)
7¹²ˢᵈ 7⁹ˢʷ **0-0-2**

Greenslades *P J Makin*   103 a100
5 ch h Perugino (USA) - Woodfield Rose
4⁷ᵍˢ 4⁶ᵍ 2⁷ᵍᶠ 13⁶ᶠ 3⁷ᵍˢ 14⁷ᵍᶠ 6⁸ᵍ 6⁷ᵍ
10⁷ᵍᶠ 5⁷ᵍ 3⁷ˢᵈ **0-5-11 £28,319**

Greenwich Meantime *Mrs J R Ramsden*   87 a79
4 b g Royal Academy (USA) - Shirley Valentine
8¹⁶ᵍ 3¹⁶ᵍˢ 16¹⁴ᵍˢ 9¹⁴ᵍ 3¹⁴ᶠ 14¹²ᵍ 7¹⁶ᵍˢ
5¹⁶ᶠ 6¹⁶ᵍˢ 7¹⁶ᵍˢ 4¹⁶ᵍ 3¹²ᶠ 1¹²ˢᵈ **1-3-13
£6,494**

Greenwood *P G Murphy*   89 a81
6 ch g Emarati (USA) - Charnwood Queen
10⁶ˢᵈ 3⁷ˢᵈ 11⁷ˢᵈ 8⁸ˢᵈ 6⁸ˢᵈ 6⁷ᵍ 2⁷ᶠ 7⁸ˢᵈ
0-2-8 £3,180

Gregorian (Ire) *J G M O'Shea*   19
7 b g Foxhound (USA) - East River (Fr)
14¹²ᵍᶠ **0-0-1**

Grele (USA) *R Hollinshead*   50
3 gr f Loup Sauvage (USA) - Fiveblushingroses (USA)
7⁷ˢ 5⁷ᵍˢ 6⁸ᵍᶠ 4⁹ᵍ 11⁸ᶠ 12¹⁰ᵍᶠ **0-0-6**

Gretna *J L Dunlop*   77
3 ch f Groom Dancer (USA) - Llia
1¹⁰ᵍˢ 8⁹ᵍˢ 14¹⁰ᵍᶠ 8⁹ᵍ 14¹⁰ᵍ **1-0-5
£3,701**

Grey Admiral (USA) *A M Balding*   59
3 gr g Cozzene (USA) - Remarkable Style (USA)
9¹⁰ᵍ 10¹²ᵍ **0-0-2**

Grey Boy (Ger) *G C Bravery*   64
3 gr g Medaaly - Grey Perri
8⁷ˢ 5⁷ᵍᶠ **0-0-2**

Grey Clouds *T D Easterby*   87
4 gr f Cloudings (Ire) - Khalsheva
4¹⁰ᵍˢ 2¹⁰ˢ 8¹⁰ᵍ 11¹⁰ᵍᶠ 2¹⁰ᵍ 3¹⁰ᵍᶠ 2¹⁰ᵍ 2¹⁰ᵍᶠ
5⁹ˢ 10¹⁰ᵍ 8¹⁰ᶠ **1-5-11 £16,761**

Grey Cossack *N Wilson*   86
7 gr g Kasakov - Royal Rebeka
9⁷ᵍˢ 1⁶ˢ 12⁵ʰʸ 12⁶ᵍᶠ 5⁶ᵍˢ 18⁶ᵍᶠ 11⁶ᵍᶠ
11⁶ˢ 5⁶ᵍˢ 10⁶ᵍᶠ 16⁷ᵍ **1-0-11 £9,074**

Grey Fortune *M Brittain*   36 a44
5 gr m Grey Desire - Mere Melody
12⁸ᵍ 4⁷ʰʸ 7⁶ᵍᶠ 5⁷ˢᵈ **0-0-4 £267**

Grey Gurkha *P T Midgley*   35
3 gr c Kasakov - Royal Rebeka
6⁵ʰʸ 9⁶ᵍᶠ 6⁵ᵍˢ **0-0-3**

Grey Lilas (Ire) *A Fabre*   118
3 gr f Danehill (USA) - Kenmist
1⁸ᵍˢ 1⁸ᵍˢ 2⁸ᵍᶠ 3¹¹ᵍˢ 1¹⁰ᵛˢ 1⁸ᵍˢ 2¹⁰ᵍ **4-3-7
£322,448**

Grey Orchid *T J Etherington*   20
3 gr f Opening Verse (USA) - Marjorie's Orchid
14⁸ᵍ 6⁶ᵍᶠ 15⁵ᵍ 13⁷ᵍ 16¹⁰ᵍˢ **0-0-5**

Grey Pearl *Miss Gay Kelleway*   90 a94
5 gr m Ali-Royal (Ire) - River's Rising (Fr)
5⁷ˢᵈ 1⁷ˢᵈ 1⁷ˢᵈ 3⁷ˢᵈ 6⁷ˢᵈ 4⁷ˢᵈ 6⁷ᶠᵗ
4⁶ᵍᶠ 16ᵍᶠ 9⁷ᵍᶠ 11⁶ᵍ 8⁵ᵍᶠ **3-1-13 £20,917**

Grey Samurai *P T Midgley*   28
4 gr g Gothenberg (Ire) - Royal Rebeka
6¹²ᵍᶠ 12¹²ᵍˢ 8¹⁰ᵍ 12¹¹ᵍᶠ 8¹⁴ᵍᶠ **0-0-5**

Grey Swallow (Ire) *D K Weld*   126
3 gr c Daylami (Ire) - Style Of Life (USA)
1⁸ˢ 4⁸ᵍ 3⁸ᵍᶠ 1¹²ᵍᶠ 4¹⁰ᵍᶠ 18¹²ᵍ **2-1-6
£603,274**

Greyfield (Ire) *K Bishop*   58
8 b g Persian Bold - Noble Dust (USA)
5¹²ᵍᶠ 7¹⁰ᵍᶠ 6¹²ᵍᶠ 11¹²ᵍᶠ **0-0-5**

Grezie *J R Best*   42 a42
2 gr f Mark Of Esteem (Ire) - Lozzie
4⁵ᵍ 4⁵ˢᵈ 3⁵ᵍˢ 12⁷ᵍᶠ **0-0-4 £545**

Grigorovitch (Ire) *B W Hills*   41
2 b c Fasliyev (USA) - Hasty Words (Ire)
8⁶ᵍ **0-0-1**

Grist Mist (Ire) *Mrs P N Dutfield*   47
3 gr f Imperial Ballet (Ire) - Ard Dauphine (Ire)
8¹⁰ᵍˢ 14¹⁰ᵍ 17¹²ˢ 6¹¹ᵍᶠ 9¹⁰ᵍᶠ **0-0-5**

Grizebeck (Ire) *R F Fisher*   7
2 b g Trans Island - Premier Amour
8⁸ᵍ **0-0-1**

Grizedale (Ire) *J Akehurst*   99
5 ch g Lake Coniston (Ire) - Zabeta
5⁷ᵍˢ 21⁷ᵍᶠ 8⁷ᵍˢ 15⁷ᵍᶠ 13⁷ᵍ 13⁷ᵍ 6⁶ˢ
0-0-7 £324

Grooms Affection *P W Harris*   88
4 b c Groom Dancer (USA) - Love And Affection (USA)
1¹⁰ᵍᶠ 6¹²ᵍᶠ 7¹²ᵍᶠ 7¹³ᵍˢ 16⁶¹⁵ˢ **1-0-5
£10,244**

Groomsman *H Morrison*   74
2 b g Groom Dancer (USA) - Trois Heures Apres
4⁸ᵍ 11⁸ʰʸ **0-0-2 £436**

Grosvenor Square (Ire) *Saeed Bin Suroor*   90
2 b c Dubai Millennium - Embassy
6⁶ᵍ 1⁷ᵍᶠ **1-0-2 £5,681**

Ground Patrol *G L Moore*   66 a71
3 b g Ashkalani (Ire) - Good Grounds (USA)
3⁸ˢᵈ 4⁸ˢᵈ 3¹⁰ˢᵈ 6¹⁰ᵍˢ 8¹¹ᵍᶠ 7⁸ˢᵈ 4⁸ᶠ 6¹⁰ˢᵈ
4¹⁰ˢᵈ **0-2-9 £1,816**

Ground Rules (USA) *B W Hills*   81
2 b c Boundary (USA) - Gombeen (USA)
2⁷ᵍˢ 9⁷ᵍᶠ **0-1-2 £1,956**

Groundcover *Mrs A J Perrett*   61
2 b c Zafonic (USA) - Moss
10⁸ᵍᶠ 7⁸ᵍ **0-0-2**

Group Captain *S Kirk*   81
2 b c Dr Fong (USA) - Alusha
5⁶ᵍˢ 4⁷ᵍᶠ 2⁷ᵍ 2⁷ᵍᶠ 8⁷ᵍ 2⁷ᵍ 3⁸ᵍ 12⁷ˢ
0-4-8 £6,152

Grouville *C J Mann*   a74
3 b g Groom Dancer (USA) - Dance Land (Ire)
1⁸ˢᵈ 9⁸ˢᵈ 16¹⁰ᵍˢ **1-0-3 £3,339**

Growler *J L Dunlop*   73
3 ch g Foxhound (USA) - Femme Femme (USA)
15⁸ᵍˢ 3⁷ᶠ 11⁹ᵍ 2⁷ᶠ 1⁶ˢ 16⁶ᵍᶠ 7⁷ᵍᶠ **1-2-7**

£6,801

Grub Street *J Parkes* a39
8 b g Barathea (Ire) - Broadmara (Ire)
3^{7sd} 4^{8ss} 1^{8ss} 7^{11ss} **1-1-4 £3,105**

Gruff *P T Midgley* 30
5 ch g Presidium - Kagram Queen
10^{5sd} 13^{6sd} 12^{5sd} 12^{6gs} 8^{6gf} 13^{7sd} 12^{6g}
0-0-7

Grumpyintmorning *Mrs P Townsley* 44
5 b g Magic Ring (Ire) - Grecian Belle
12^{7gs} 11^{7s} PU^{8gf} 11^{11gf} **0-0-4**

Gryskirk *P W D'Arcy* 62 a67
2 b c Selkirk (USA) - Gryada
4^{5gs} 6^{5g} 3^{6gf} 7^{7gf} 8^{7gs} 7^{7gf} 3^{7sd} 10^{7sd}
5^{7gf} 10^{8g} 1^{8sd} **1-2-11 £5,510**

Guadaloup *M Brittain* 47
2 ch f Loup Sauvage (USA) - Rash
13^{6gf} **0-0-1**

Guadiaro (USA) *B W Hills* 58
2 b c El Prado (Ire) - Splendid (USA)
7^{5g} 16^{6gs} **0-0-2**

Guard *N P Littmoden* 5
4 b g Night Shift (USA) - Gaijin
11^{7f} 13^{10sd} **0-0-2**

Guardian Spirit *D Shaw* 19 a2
5 b m Hector Protector (USA) - Amongst The Stars (USA)
17^{8g} 13^{7sd} **0-0-2**

Guilded Flyer *W S Kittow* 92
5 b g Emarati (USA) - Mo Ceri
8^{10g} 1^{10gs} 9^{10g} 3^{9gf} 8^{10gf} **1-1-5**
£13,402

Guildenstern (Ire) *H Morrison* 64
2 b c Danetime (Ire) - Lyphard Abu (Ire)
9^{6gf} 4^{6s} 5^{6s} **0-0-3 £401**

Guinea A Minute (Ire) *P D Evans* 66 a57
2 ch f Raise A Grand (Ire) - Repique (USA)
9^{6gf} 3^{6gs} 6^{6gf} 6^{7gf} 5^{7sd} 3^{8s} 3^{8gs} 18^{8s}
0-2-8 £2,270

Gulchina (USA) *D R C Elsworth* 77
2 b f Gulch (USA) - Harda Arda (USA)
4^{7gs} **0-0-1 £375**

Gulf (Ire) *D R C Elsworth* 108
5 ch g Persian Bold - Broken Romance (Ire)
18^{16gs} 3^{13g} 5^{16gs} 5^{14g} **0-1-4 £4,448**

Gun Salute *G L Moore* 45 a59
4 b g Mark Of Esteem (Ire) - Affair Of State (Ire)
8^{6sd} 1^{6sd} 8^{6sd} 4^{6sd} 14^{6s} 6^{7gf} 11^{6f}
11^{6g} **1-0-9 £3,324**

Gunnerbergkamp *M D Hammond* 19
2 b g Defacto (USA) - Judys Girl (Ire)
10^{7gf} 14^{7s} **0-0-3**

Gunnhildr (Ire) *P J Makin*
4 ch f In Command (Ire) - Queen Canute (Ire)
20^{6gf} **0-0-1**

Guns Blazing *D K Ivory* 76
5 b g Puissance - Queen Of Aragon
15^{5gf} 8^{5hy} 1^{5g} 3^{5gf} 6^{5f} 10^{5f} 1^{5g} 8^{5g}
7^{5gf} 12^{5g} **2-1-10 £8,123**

Gurrun *N A Callaghan* 60
2 b c Dansili - Mashmoon (USA)
14^{7gf} 9^{7g} 11^{7s} 15^{7g} 6^{6f} **0-0-5**

Gustavo *B W Hills* 62 a62
3 b g Efisio - Washita
11^{7gs} 8^{7gs} 9^{7gs} 9^{8g} 2^{8sw} 2^{11gs} **0-2-6**
£1,902

Guyana (Ire) *S Kirk* 62 a71
2 b c Lend A Hand - Romora (Fr)
15^{7gf} 9^{7gf} 3^{6sd} 16^{7gf} 17^{6hy} **0-1-5 £546**

Gwazi *Miss D A McHale* 36 a37
4 b g Pennekamp (USA) - Made Of Pearl (USA)
11^{11sd} 3^{9ss} 14^{8gs} 6^{7sd} **0-1-4 £362**

Gwen John (USA) *H Morrison* 69
3 ch f Peintre Celebre (USA) - River Jig (USA)
5^{8gf} 3^{9gf} 11^{10g} 8^{9gf} 12^{10s} **0-1-5 £856**

Gwyneth *J L Dunlop* 68
2 b f Zafonic (USA) - Llyn Gwynant
5^{7g} 9^{7gf} **0-0-2**

Gypsy Fair *T D Barron* 31 a37
2 b f Compton Place - Marjorie's Memory (Ire)
7^{5gs} 9^{5g} 10^{6sd} **0-0-3**

Gypsy Johnny *M L W Bell* 74
2 gr c Bachir (Ire) - Gentle Gypsy
1^{7gs} 11^{8s} **1-0-2 £4,621**

Gypsy King (Ire) *A P O'Brien* 84
2 b c Sadler's Wells (USA) - Love For Ever (Ire)
1^{7sh} **1-0-1 £9,169**

Gypsy Royal (Ire) *R Ingram* 46
2 b f Desert Prince (Ire) - Menominee
11^{6gf} 9^{7gf} 11^{6g} **0-0-3**

H Harrison (Ire) *I W McInnes* 90 a75
4 b g Eagle Eyed (USA) - Penrose (Ire)
18^{7g} 8^{7gf} 5^{8gs} 4^{7f} 1^{7gf} 16^{6gf} 23^{7f}
3^{7gf} 5^{6gf} 8^{8gf} 11^{8s} 6^{7sd} 5^{8g} 8^{7gf} 3^{7g} 6^{7sd}
10^{7gs} **1-2-18 £13,445**

Haadef *J H M Gosden* 103
3 b c Sadler's Wells (USA) - Taqreem (Ire)
3^{10g} 1^{10gs} 4^{12f} 15^{12g} 14^{12g} 2^{10hy} **1-2-6**
£17,980

Haafhd *B W Hills* 129
3 ch c Alhaarth (Ire) - Al Bahathri (USA)
1^{8g} 1^{8g} 4^{8gf} 9^{8g} 1^{10s} **3-0-5 £430,874**

Haatmey *M R Channon* 87
2 b c Josr Algarhoud (Ire) - Raneen Alwatar
3^{7gf} 4^{7s} 2^{9f} 1^{10g} 4^{10g} **1-2-5 £7,056**

Habanero *R Hannon* 84 a75
3 b c Cadeaux Genereux - Queen Of Dance (Ire)
15^{10gs} 9^{0gs} 9^{8s} 3^{8gf} 18^{gf} 3^{10g} 3^{8gf} 1^{9gf}
6^{8gs} 9^{9g} 17^{8gf} 6^{10sd} **2-3-12 £16,593**

Habibti Sara *A W Carroll*
4 ch f Bijou D'Inde - Cut Velvet (USA)
12^{12sd} **0-0-1**

Habitual (Ire) *Sir Mark Prescott* 54 a56
3 b g Kahyasi - Kick The Habit
10^{7sd} 10^{8sd} 4^{16gs} 5^{11gf} 1^{16sd} 8^{16gf} 9^{12sd}
1-1-7 £1,494

Habitual Dancer *Jedd O'Keeffe* 65
3 b g Groom Dancer (USA) - Pomorie (Ire)
6^{7g} 1^{10gs} 2^{12hy} 3^{12gs} 11^{14g} 5^{17gs} 8^{16gs}
1^{15s} **2-1-8 £8,590**

Habshan (USA) *C F Wall* 77
4 ch g Swain (Ire) - Cambara
9^{8gf} 4^{8gf} 3^{8gf} 5^{8gs} 1^{8gf} 7^{8gs} 3^{8g} **1-2-7**
£7,175

Hachita (USA) *H R A Cecil* 85
2 ch f Gone West (USA) - Choice Spirit (USA)
17^{gf} 3^{7gf} 2^{8g} **1-0-3 £9,114**

Hadrian (Ire) *M Johnston* 83
2 b c King's Best (USA) - Wanton
6^{6s} 2^{7gf} 1^{7g} 12^{7gs} **1-1-4 £6,447**

Haenertsburg (Ire) *A Berry* 59

2 b f Victory Note (USA) - Olivia's Pride (Ire)
9^{6gf} 7^{6gs} 8^{7g} **0-0-3**

Hagley Park *Miss K M George*   44 a52
5 b m Petong - Gi La High
2^{5sd} 2^{5ss} 6^{5ss} 5^{5ss} 4^{5sd} 3^{5ss} 11^{5ss} 3^{5sd}
1^{5sd} 11^{5sd} 7^{5sd} 9^{5f} 9^{6sf} 5^{5gf} 14^{7sd} 5^{5sd}
1-4-16 £3,140

Haiban *G A Butler*   70
2 b c Barathea (Ire) - Aquarela
4^{8s} 2^{7s} 3^{8s} **0-1-3 £3,672**

Hail The Chief *J Akehurst*   74 a103
7 b h Be My Chief (USA) - Jade Pet
1^{8sd} 4^{8ss} 10^{10sd} 3^{8g} 14^{8gs} 6^{9gf} 8^{10g} 8^{9g}
11^{7gf} 10^{8gf} **1-1-10 £8,633**

Haithem (Ire) *D Shaw*   a47
7 b g Mtoto - Wukk (Ire)
6^{8sd} 13^{8sd} 10^{8sd} 7^{12sd} 3^{9ss} 10^{9ss} 6^{8sd}
8^{9sw} 5^{8sd} 8^{10sd} 7^{8sd} 10^{9sd} 9^{7sd}
1-1-15 £1,699

Hajeer (Ire) *P W Hiatt*   a46
6 b g Darshaan - Simouna
5^{16sd} 2^{15sd} **0-0-2 £720**

Halabaloo (Ire) *G Wragg*   75
3 b f Intikhab (USA) - Outcry
5^{7g} 11^{8s} 3^{7gf} 6^{8gs} 6^{8s} **0-1-5 £848**

Halcyon Express (Ire) *P F I Cole*   67
2 b c Mujadil (USA) - Hakkaniyah
8^{6s} 4^{7gs} **0-0-2 £324**

Halcyon Magic *M Wigham*   57
6 b g Magic Ring (Ire) - Consistent Queen
2^{6s} 9^{6s} 15^{8f} 2^{8gf} 14^{7gf} 6^{7gf} 12^{8g} 1^{7g}
5^{7hy} **1-2-9 £4,972**

Half A Handful *M J Wallace*   68 a1
3 b g Victory Note (USA) - Enaam
10^{6sd} 12^{6gs} 11^{6gs} 6^{6gf} 3^{6gf} 3^{6gf} 2^{7g}
3^{6gf} 11^{8g} **0-4-9 £2,849**

Half Inch *B I Case*   67 a50
4 b f Inchinor - Anhaar
11^{10sd} 4^{10gs} 12^{10gs} 7^{12gs} **0-0-4 £271**

Halicardia *P W Harris*   104
3 br f Halling (USA) - Pericardia
3^{8gs} 1^{10gf} 2^{10gf} **1-2-3 £27,300**

Halla San *Mrs J R Ramsden*   77
2 b g Halling (USA) - St Radegund
8^{5f} 13^{5gs} 5^{6gs} 4^{7g} 3^{8s} **0-1-5 £1,418**

Hallahoise Hydro (Ire) *B S Rothwell*   59
3 ch g Lake Coniston (Ire) - Flo Bear (Ire)
1^{5y} 11^{5y} 8^{7g} 7^{7gf} 12^{6gs} 18^{6g} **1-0-6
£6,082**

Halland *N P Littmoden*   86
6 ch g Halling (USA) - Northshiel
8^{12gf} 10^{16g} 12^{18s} **0-0-3**

Halle Bop *Saeed Bin Suroor*   86
2 b f Dubai Millennium - Napoleon's Sister (Ire)
2^{6gs} 1^{6g} **1-1-2 £6,967**

Hallhoo (Ire) *M R Channon*   90
2 gr c Indian Ridge - Nuit Chaud (USA)
3^{6gf} 1^{7g} 2^{8g} 2^{8s} 8^{8s} **1-3-5 £17,974**

Hallings Overture (USA) *C A Horgan*   73 a65
5 b g Halling (USA) - Sonata
6^{10sd} 7^{10sd} 2^{7gs} 16^{8g} **0-1-4 £1,720**

Hallowed Dream (Ire) *C E Brittain*   81
2 b f Alhaarth (Ire) - Salul
7^{8gf} 9^{7s} 8^{8gf} 2^{8gf} 6^{8s} **0-1-5 £1,937**

Hallucinate *R Hannon*   78

2 b c Spectrum (Ire) - Swift Spring (Fr)
11^{5gf} 4^{7gf} 2^{7gf} 3^{7gf} 4^{7s} 3^{8g} **0-2-6
£4,899**

Halmahera (Ire) *K A Ryan*   107
9 b g Petardia - Champagne Girl
10^{6g} 2^{6s} 6^{6g} 8^{6gf} 20^{6f} 5^{5s} 12^{5g}
6^{6gf} 9^{6s} 1^{6g} 9^{5g} 7^{6s} 9^{5gs} **1-1-14 £39,615**

Hamaasy *D Nicholls*   59
3 b g Machiavellian (USA) - Sakha
5^{6gf} 7^{5gs} 7^{5gf} 15^{5gs} **0-0-4**

Hambleden *M A Jarvis*   107
7 b g Vettori (Ire) - Dalu (Ire)
6^{10gs} 9^{12gf} 4^{12f} 4^{12g} 13^{14g} 6^{12g} 3^{13s}
0-0-7 £12,729

Hamburg Springer (Ire) *M J Polglase*   32
2 b g Charnwood Forest (Ire) - Kyra Crown (Ire)
12^{6gf} 5^{5gf} 8^{5gf} 15^{5gf} 16^{8g} **0-0-5**

Hammer Of The Gods (Ire) *Julian Poulton*   49
4 ch g Tagula (Ire) - Bhama (Fr)
3^{7gf} 3^{6hy} 11^{7g} **0-0-3 £1,196**

Hana Dee *M R Channon*   62 a49
3 b f Cadeaux Genereux - Jumairah Sun (Ire)
10^{7sd} 14^{8g} 6^{7g} 13^{8gf} 11^{7f} 4^{7g} 5^{8gf} 3^{8gf}
9^{8gf} 12^{8gs} 4^{10f} 5^{8sd} 7^{9sd} **0-1-13 £941**

Hanazakari *J A R Toller*   39 a32
3 b c Danzero (Aus) - Russian Rose (Ire)
9^{11gf} 5^{12sd} **0-0-2**

Hand Chime *W J Haggas*   76 a91
7 ch g Clantime - Warning Bell
9^{6sd} 13^{7sd} 5^{7sd} 9^{7s} 9^{7s} 2^{7gf} 7^{6gs} 10^{7hy}
6^{7g} 11^{7s} **0-1-10 £1,154**

Handsome Cross (Ire) *H Morrison*   82
3 b c Cape Cross (Ire) - Snap Crackle Pop (Ire)
5^{7s} 5^{7gf} 6^{6g} 12^{7gf} 3^{5gf} 8^{5g} 7^{5gs} **0-1-7
£1,800**

Handsome Lady *I Semple*   78
2 ch f Handsome Ridge - Il Doria (Ire)
1^{5g} 5^{5gf} 5^{5g} 6^{5g} 4^{5gf} 11^{5s} 3^{5gs}
1-0-8 £4,475

Hannah's Dream (Ire) *M Johnston*   66
2 b f King's Best (USA) - Meritxell (Ire)
6^{6gf} 2^{7gf} 3^{7g} **0-2-3 £2,331**

Hannah's Tribe (Ire) *B Smart*   50
2 b f Daggers Drawn (USA) - Cala-Holme (Ire)
9^{6f} 9^{7gs} 9^{7gs} **0-0-3**

Hanseatic League (USA) *M Johnston*   81
2 b c Red Ransom (USA) - Rhine Valley (USA)
2^{5gf} 2^{5g} 6^{5gs} 1^{6s} **1-2-4 £8,528**

Hansomelle (Ire) *B Mactaggart*   78
2 b f Titus Livius (Fr) - Handsome Anna (Ire)
4^{5gf} 1^{6gf} 2^{6g} 4^{6s} 1^{7g} 3^{7s} **2-2-6
£16,623**

Hanzano (Ire) *Are Hyldmo*   a86
6 b g Alzao (USA) - Movie Legend (USA)
7^{8ft} 5^{8ft} 5^{8g} 4^{7g} 1^{8s} 3^{6gs} 6^{8g} 7^{7g} 5^{7g}
3^{8ft} 4^{7hy} 2^{7ft} 14^{7sd} **1-1-13 £23,286**

Happy As Larry (USA) *Saeed Bin Suroor*   a87
2 b/br c Yes It's True (USA) - Don't Be Blue (USA)
1^{7sd} **1-0-1 £4,238**

Happy Banker (Ire) *M R Channon*   28
2 gr c With Approval (Can) - Tropical Paradise (USA)
14^{7gs} **0-0-1**

Happy Camper (Ire) *M R Hoad*   43 a44
4 b g Pennekamp (USA) - Happy Dancer (USA)
11^{6sd} 11^{6sd} 6^{7sd} 5^{7sd} 3^{7hy} 8^{7gf} 12^{10sd}

5^{8gs} **0-1-8 £221**

Happy Crusader (Ire) *P F I Cole*   103
3 b c Cape Cross (Ire) - Les Hurlants (Ire)
2^{8gs} 4^{11g} 8^{10f} **0-0-3 £4,747**

Happy Event *B R Millman*   84
2 b c Makbul - La Belle Vie
1^{6gf} 7^{6g} 19^{5g} 1^{6gs} 4^{7gs} **2-0-5 £7,670**

Harambee (Ire) *B S Rothwell*   36
4 b f Robellino (USA) - Hymenee (USA)
PU^{12gs} UR^{10g} 11^{10gf} 8^{12g} **0-0-4**

Harbour House *J J Bridger*   56 a51
5 b g Distant Relative - Double Flutter
7^{6sd} 2^{8sd} 8^{7sd} 6^{8sd} 3^{6sd} 1^{5g} 3^{5hy} 15^{6f}
2^{5g} 6^{5gf} 6^{6gf} 5^{7hy} 9^{6s} **1-4-13 £3,694**

Harbour Legend *J G Given*   27
2 b f Dansili - English Harbour
13^{6gf} 6^{7gf} 11^{7s} **0-0-3**

Harbour Princess *M F Harris*   22 a36
3 b f Bal Harbour - Gipsy Princess
9^{6sd} 6^{5sd} 6^{5ss} 6^{8sd} 3^{7sd} 4^{8g} 8^{10sd} **0-0-7**
£205

Harcourt (USA) *P F I Cole*   51
4 b c Cozzene (USA) - Ballinamallard (USA)
12^{10s} 14^{12g} **0-0-2**

Hard Buck (Brz) *K McPeek*   123
5 br h Spend A Buck (USA) - Social Secret
4^{9sy} 1^{11f} 2^{12gf} 2^{9y} 5^{11f} 2^{12gf} **1-2-6**
£465,658

Hard To Catch (Ire) *D K Ivory*   83 a78
6 b g Namaqualand (USA) - Brook's Dilemma
7^{6sd} 7^{6sd} 2^{7sd} 4^{7sd} 1^{6sd} 9^{6sd} 4^{6sd} 5^{7sd}
5^{6g} 16^{6gs} 10^{5gf} 1^{5f} 1^{5gf} 3^{6f} 3^{5f} 10^{6gs} 6^{6gf}
3^{6gf} **3-2-21 £15,993**

Hard Top (Ire) *Sir Michael Stoute*   71
2 b c Darshaan - Well Head (Ire)
5^{8s} **0-0-1**

Harelda *R M H Cowell*   59 a71
4 ch f Hector Protector (USA) - Hen Harrier
1^{12sd} 6^{12sd} 18^{12g} **1-0-3 £3,328**

Harford Bridge *R J Baker*
3 ch g Bandmaster (USA) - Double Or Bust
10^{8ss} **0-0-1**

Haribini *J J Bridger*   a26
4 b/br f Groom Dancer (USA) - Mory Kante (USA)
12^{10sd} 16^{10gf} **0-0-2**

Harik *G L Moore*   51 a59
10 ch g Persian Bold - Yaqut (USA)
6^{16sd} 2^{18f} 7^{16gs} **0-1-3 £1,056**

Haripur *Andrew Reid*   a59
5 b h Rainbow Quest (USA) - Jamrat Jumairah (Ire)
10^{10sd} **0-0-1**

Harlestone Linn *J L Dunlop*   53
2 ch g Erhaab (USA) - Harlestone Lake
12^{7g} 7^{8s} **0-0-2**

Harlot *John Berry*   a54
4 b f Bal Harbour - Queen Of The Quorn
12^{10sd} 10^{12sd} **0-0-2**

Haroldini (Ire) *J Balding*   65 a73
2 b g Orpen (USA) - Ciubanga (Ire)
7^{5g} 4^{6gf} 2^{5gf} 6^{6gf} 2^{6sd} 7^{7gf} 17^{6gs} 9^{6sd}
0-2-8 £2,184

Harrington Bates *R M Whitaker*   67
3 ch g Wolfhound (USA) - Fiddling
4^{5gf} 6^{6gf} 8^{7s} 5^{5gf} **0-0-4 £266**

Harrison Point (USA) *P W Chapple-Hyam*   89 a93

4 br c Nureyev (USA) - Maid's Broom (USA)
1^{7sd} 1^{8sd} 2^{8gf} 2^{7gf} 10^{8g} 1^{7sd} 13^{7gf} 6^{7g}
3-2-8 £18,242

Harrison's Flyer (Ire) *R A Fahey*   86 a81
3 b g Imperial Ballet (Ire) - Smart Pet
7^{6gf} 2^{5gs} 12^{7gs} 2^{5gf} 15^{6gf} 2^{6f} UR^{5g}
12^{5gf} 12^{5g} 1^{5s} 1^{5sd} 1^{5gs} **3-3-12 £17,203**

Harry Came Home *J C Fox*   36 a26
3 b g Wizard King - Kirby's Princess
10^{12sd} 10^{11gs} 12^{12s} 11^{8f} 16^{7gf} 11^{12sd}
11^{8gs} 14^{8y} 13^{10gf} **0-0-9**

Harry Lad *P D Evans*   a46
3 ch g Then Again - Silly Sally
5^{9sw} 5^{12sw} 6^{12gs} **0-0-3**

Harry Potter (Ger) *K R Burke*   84 a82
5 b g Platini (Ger) - Heavenly Storm (USA)
11^{9ss} 14^{7sd} 3^{8sd} 11^{8hy} 1^{8gs} 8^{7g} 6^{8gf} 9^{8g}
3^{9g} 1^{8gf} 1^{8gf} 5^{8f} 13^{8gs} 3^{9gf} 8^{8s} 14^{9g} **3-3-16**
£15,335

Harry The Hoover (Ire) *M J Gingell*   a58
4 b g Fayruz - Mitsubishi Style
12^{8sd} **0-0-1**

Harry Tu *E R Oertel*
4 b g Millkom - Risky Tu
9^{8sd} 9^{10sd} **0-0-2**

Harry Up *J G Given*   89
3 ch c Piccolo - Faraway Lass
2^{6gs} 3^{5s} 9^{5s} 3^{6g} 4^{5f} 16^{6gf} 21^{5gf} **0-1-7**
£8,401

Harry's Simmie (Ire) *R Hollinshead*   32 a29
2 ch f Spectrum (Ire) - Minstrels Folly (USA)
10^{7gf} 13^{6g} 10^{9sd} **0-0-3**

Harrycat (Ire) *V Smith*   69
3 b g Bahhare (USA) - Quiver Tree
7^{8gs} 5^{8g} 6^{8gf} 2^{12s} 3^{10s} **0-2-5 £2,646**

Harrys House *J J Quinn*   77
2 gr g Paris House - Rum Lass
4^{5gf} 7^{5gs} 4^{7s} 3^{7f} 1^{5g} 8^{6s} **1-1-6 £4,424**

Hartshead *G A Swinbank*   85
5 b g Machiavellian (USA) - Zalitzine (USA)
2^{6g} 8^{6gf} 6^{6f} 1^{6g} 1^{6g} 4^{6gf} 1^{6gf} 1^{7gf} 2^{7gf}
3^{7g} **4-3-10 £25,738**

Harvest Warrior *T D Easterby*   99
2 br g Mujahid (USA) - Lammastide
2^{5hy} 2^{5gf} 1^{6g} 5^{6gs} 2^{6hy} 12^{6gf} 2^{6s} **1-4-7**
£15,344

Hasaiyda (Ire) *Sir Michael Stoute*   91
3 b f Hector Protector (USA) - Hasainiya (Ire)
1^{9gf} 4^{10g} 1^{10gf} 8^{12g} 12^{10g} **2-0-5**
£10,772

Hasayis *J L Dunlop*   71
3 b f Danehill (USA) - Intizaa (USA)
1^{8s} 10^{7gf} 4^{7gf} 7^{8gf} **1-0-4 £4,231**

Hashid (Ire) *P C Ritchens*   69
4 b g Darshaan - Alkaffeyeh (Ire)
6^{12gs} 3^{10g} 8^{15gf} 12^{12gs} 6^{12gf} 5^{13gs} **0-1-6**
£549

Hashima (USA) *C E Brittain*   69 a59
2 b f Kingmambo (USA) - Fairy Heights (Ire)
3^{7g} 4^{7sd} **0-1-2 £1,199**

Hashimiya (USA) *Saeed Bin Suroor*   60
2 b f Gone West (USA) - Touch Of Greatness (USA)
6^{7g} **0-0-1**

Hasty Prince *Jonjo O'Neill*
6 ch g Halling (USA) - Sister Sophie (USA)

SU¹²ᵍᶠ **0-0-1**

Hat Trick Man *J Akehurst*   70
3 gr c Daylami (Ire) - Silver Kristal
6¹⁰ᵍᶠ 8¹⁰ᵍᶠ 3¹¹ˢ **0-0-3 £370**

Hatch *R M H Cowell*   93 a78
3 ch c Cadeaux Genereux - Footlight Fantasy (USA)
2⁷ˢᵈ 2⁷ˢᵈ 1⁷ˢᵈ 3⁶ᵍˢ 1⁷ᵍᶠ 3⁷ᵍ 13⁹ᵍ 4⁷ᵍᶠ
11⁸ˢᵈ 10⁶ᵍˢ **2-3-10 £14,832**

Hatch A Plan (Ire) *R Beckett*   77 a38
3 b g Vettori (Ire) - Fast Chick
9⁶ˢᵈ UR⁸ᵍˢ 7¹⁰ᵍᶠ 1¹⁰ᵍ 2¹⁰ᵍ 2¹⁰ᵍ 4¹²ᵍᶠ
10¹²ᵍˢ 11¹⁰ᵍ 5¹²ˢ **1-2-10 £6,968**

Hathlen (Ire) *M R Channon*   79
3 b c Singspiel (Ire) - Kameez (Ire)
8¹²ʰʸ 6¹²ᵍ 6¹²ʰʸ 5¹²ᵍᶠ 6¹⁴ᵍˢ 1¹⁴ᵍ 5¹⁴ᵍᶠ
6¹⁶ᵍˢ 7¹⁶ᵍ 6¹⁶ᵍᶠ **1-0-10 £3,770**

Hathrah (Ire) *J L Dunlop*   112
3 gr f Linamix (Fr) - Zivania (Ire)
1⁸ᵍˢ 3⁸ᵍ **1-1-2 £52,902**

Haulage Man *D Eddy*   68
6 ch g Komaite (USA) - Texita
10⁶ᵍᶠ 2⁶ˢ 11⁸ˢ 2⁶ᵍᶠ 9⁶ᵍ 8⁶ᶠ 12⁶ᵍˢ **0-2-7 £2,710**

Haunt The Zoo *John A Harris*   a62
9 b m Komaite (USA) - Merryhill Maid (Ire)
5⁸ᵍ 8⁸ˢᵈ 3⁸ˢᵈ 8⁸ˢᵈ 12⁸ˢᵈ **0-1-5 £581**

Haunting Memories (Ire) *M A Jarvis*   94
2 b c Barathea (Ire) - King Of All (Ire)
4⁶ᵍᶠ 1⁶ˢ 2⁷ᵍˢ 3⁸ᵍ **1-2-4 £16,652**

Havana Rose (Ire) *Timothy Cleary*   a11
4 b f Goldmark (USA) - Roses Red (Ire)
16⁸ˢ 8⁵ˢʷ **0-0-2**

Havantadoubt (Ire) *M R Bosley*   45
4 ch f Desert King (Ire) - Batiba (USA)
7¹⁰ˢ 14¹⁰ᵍᶠ 13¹⁰ᵍˢ 5¹⁰ᵍᶠ 9¹¹ᵍˢ 18¹²ᵍᵃ **0-0-6**

Have Faith (Ire) *B W Hills*   87
3 b f Machiavellian (USA) - Fatefully (USA)
3⁸ᵍᶠ 6⁸ᵍᶠ 6⁸ᵍᶠ 7¹⁰ʰʸ **0-0-4 £1,632**

Have Some Fun *P R Chamings*   33 a67
4 ch g Bering - Hilaris
3⁸ˢᵈ 2¹⁰ˢᵈ 12⁸ᵍᶠ 11⁸ᵍ 13⁷ˢᵈ 13⁷ˢᵈ **0-2-6 £1,691**

Havetoavit (USA) *J D Bethell*   71
3 b g Theatrical - Summer Crush (USA)
5¹²ᵍ 3¹²ᵍ 2¹²ᵍᶠ 4¹²ᵍᶠ 11¹¹ˢ 4¹²ᵍᶠ 1¹⁰ᵍᶠ
2¹⁰ᵍᶠ 14¹⁰ᵍ 11¹⁰ᵍ **1-3-10 £9,066**

Havoc *Ronald Thompson*
5 b g Hurricane Sky (Aus) - Padelia
9⁸ˢᵈ **0-0-1**

Hawaajes *B Hanbury*   78
3 b g Royal Applause - Aegean Blue
11⁸ᵍ 3⁷ᵍᶠ 1⁶ᵍᶠ 4⁶ᵍᶠ 12⁶ˢ **1-1-5 £6,960**

Hawadeth *V R A Dartnall*   86
9 ch g Machiavellian (USA) - Ghzaalh (USA)
5¹⁶ᵍˢ 17²⁰ᵍᶠ **0-0-2**

Hawk *P R Chamings*   a30
6 b g A P Jet (USA) - Miss Enjoleur (USA)
14⁶ˢᵈ 7⁶ˢᵈ 10⁶ˢᵈ 11⁵ˢˢ 11⁶ᶠ **0-0-5**

Hawk Arrow (Ire) *H Morrison*   60
2 ch c In The Wings - Barbizou (Fr)
7⁸ᵍ **0-0-1**

Hawkes Bay *M H Tompkins*   66
2 b c Vettori (Ire) - Nordico Princess
10⁶ᵍᶠ 3⁸ᵍ **0-1-2 £872**

Hawkit (USA) *P D Evans*   84 a67
3 b g Silver Hawk (USA) - Hey Ghaz (USA)
5⁸ˢ 2⁸ˢʷ 1⁸ˢ 7⁸ˢᵈ 1⁹ᵍ 2¹⁰ᵍᶠ 7⁸ᵍᶠ 10¹⁰ᵍ
5⁸ˢ **2-2-9 £9,421**

Hawks Tor (Ire) *M Johnston*   43
2 b c Danehill (USA) - Born Beautiful (USA)
6⁷ᵍ **0-0-1**

Hawridge King *W S Kittow*   67 a62
2 b g Erhaab (USA) - Sadaka (USA)
3⁶ᵍᶠ 5⁷ᵍᶠ 6⁸ᵍᶠ 5⁷ˢᵈ 5⁸ˢ **0-0-5 £864**

Hawridge Prince *L G Cottrell*   107
4 b g Polar Falcon (USA) - Zahwa
1¹⁰ᵍ 1¹⁰ᵍ 2¹⁰ᵍᶠ 4¹²ᵍ 2¹²ᵍˢ 16¹⁰ᵍˢ **2-2-6 £24,433**

Hawridge Sensation *L G Cottrell*   44
2 ch g Polish Precedent (USA) - Looks Sensational (USA)
7⁸ᵍᶠ **0-0-1**

Hawridge Star (Ire) *W S Kittow*   76
2 b c Alzao (USA) - Serenity
6⁷ᵍ 2⁷ˢ 12⁸ᵍˢ **0-1-3 £1,128**

Haydn (USA) *G A Huffer*   68 a87
3 b g Stravinsky (USA) - Circular (USA)
5⁶ˢᵈ 14⁶ˢ 17⁶ˢ 5⁶ᵍ 13⁶ᶠ 6¹⁰ᵍ 12¹⁰ᵍᶠ
14⁸ˢ **0-0-8 £393**

Hayraan (Ire) *G C Bravery*   56
2 b c Bluebird (USA) - Alma Latina (Ire)
7⁷ᵍ 7⁷ˢ **0-0-2**

Haystacks (Ire) *James Moffatt*   40
8 b g Contract Law (USA) - Florissa (Fr)
3¹³ᵍ 7¹⁶ᵍᶠ **0-1-2 £207**

Hazarista (Ire) *John M Oxx*   113
3 b f Barathea (Ire) - Hazaradjat (Ire)
4⁷ʸ 1⁸ᵍᶠ 1¹⁰ᵍᶠ 3¹²ᵍᶠ 3¹²ˢ 10¹⁰ᵍ **2-1-6 £103,603**

Haze Babybear *R A Fahey*   a25
4 b f Mujadil (USA) - River's Rising (Fr)
9⁶ˢᵈ 14⁶ˢᵈ 6⁵ˢᵈ **0-0-3**

Hazewind *P D Evans*   76 a78
3 gr g Daylami (Ire) - Fragrant Oasis (USA)
11⁶ˢᵈ 4⁷ˢᵈ 2⁷ˢᵈ 1⁷ˢᵈ 7⁹ᵍˢ 17⁷ˢ 7⁷ᵍᶠ 9⁷ᵍᶠ
2¹⁰ᵍᶠ 5¹⁰ᵍᶠ 1⁸ᵍ 1⁷ᵍ 6⁸ᵍ 4⁷ᵍˢ 1⁷ᵍᶠ 6⁸ˢ 4⁹ˢᵈ 4⁷ˢᵈ
3⁹ˢᵈ 3⁷ˢᵈ **4-4-20 £25,217**

Hazyview *N A Callaghan*   111
3 b c Cape Cross (Ire) - Euridice (Ire)
2¹⁰ᵍˢ 1¹⁰ᵍˢ 1¹⁰ᵍˢ 1¹⁰ᵍ 2¹¹ˢ 1¹⁰ᵍᶠ 8¹²ᵍ 3¹⁰ˢ
6¹⁰ᶠ **4-1-9 £80,140**

He Jaa (Ire) *C E Brittain*   68
3 gr f Daylami (Ire) - Calpella
7⁸ᵍ PU¹⁰ᵍ **0-0-2**

He Who Dares (Ire) *A W Carroll*   69 a65
6 b g Distinctly North (USA) - Sea Clover (Ire)
2¹⁰ˢᵈ 12⁷ˢᵈ 3¹⁰ˢᵈ 4⁸ˢᵈ 3⁸ˢ 1⁷ˢ 2¹⁰ᶠ **1-4-7 £5,329**

He's A Diamond *T G Mills*   75
2 ch g Vettori (Ire) - Azira
5⁶ᵍᶠ 1⁷ᵍᶠ 3⁷ᵍᶠ 8⁷ᵍᶠ 16⁷ᵍᶠ 15⁸ᵍ **1-1-6 £4,230**

He's A Rocket (Ire) *K R Burke*   65 a49
3 b g Indian Rocket - Dellua (Ire)
6⁶ˢᵈ 5⁶ᵍˢ 1⁵ˢ 1⁵ᵍ 3⁵ᵍˢ 6⁶ᵍᶠ 7⁵ᵍˢ 10⁵ˢ
5⁵ᵍᶠ 9⁵ᵍᶠ 2⁵ˢ 7⁵ᵍˢ 16⁵ᵍᶠ 9⁵ᵍᶠ 15⁶ᵍˢ 5⁵ˢᵈ **2-2-16 £8,299**

He's A Star *R Hannon*   61
2 ch c Mark Of Esteem (Ire) - Sahara Belle (USA)
9⁶ᵍ 4⁵ᶠ 7⁶ᵍᶠ 6⁷ᵍᶠ 6⁷ᵍᶠ 9⁸ᵍ **0-0-6**

Head Boy *S Dow* 61 a57
3 ch g Forzando - Don't Jump (Ire)
4⁷ˢᵈ 10⁸ˢᵈ 12⁸ˢᵈ 5⁶ᵍˢ 6⁸ᵍˢ 5⁷ˢ 4⁷ᵍ 2⁷ᵍᶠ
8⁸ᵍᶠ 9⁷ˢ 8⁸ᵍ 6⁷ᵍˢ 3⁷ˢᵈ **0-2-13 £2,654**

Head Of State *R M Beckett* 29 a66
3 br g Primo Dominie - Lets Be Fair
8⁵ˢᵈ 12⁵ˢᵈ 16ˢˢ 8⁶ˢᵈ 36ˢᵈ 10⁶ᵍˢ 9⁵ˢᵈ 5⁶ᵍ
1-1-8 £3,400

Head To Kerry (Ire) *D J S Ffrench Davis* 65 a51
4 b g Eagle Eyed (USA) - The Poachers Lady (Ire)
17¹⁴ᵍ 8¹⁶ᵍᶠ 9¹⁴ᵍᶠ 3¹³ᵍᶠ 5¹⁵ᵍᶠ 3¹²ᵍ 4¹²ᵍᶠ
2¹²ᵍᶠ 4¹⁴ᵍᶠ 5¹²ˢ 4¹⁰ᵍˢ 9¹⁰ᵍ 6¹²ˢᵈ **0-4-13
£3,530**

Headland (USA) *D W Chapman* 59 a67
6 b/br g Distant View (USA) - Fijar Echo (USA)
4⁷ˢᵈ 2⁸ˢᵈ 7⁶ˢᵈ 7⁷ˢᵈ 3⁷ˢᵈ 11⁶ˢˢ 3⁷ˢˢ 9⁷ˢᵈ
6⁷ˢᵈ 2⁶ᵍ 2⁶ˢᵈ 1⁷ᵍᶠ 5⁷ˢ 5⁶ˢᵈ 1⁶ˢʷ 11⁷ᵍᶠ 5⁶ᵍᶠ
17⁷ᵍˢ **2-4-18 £10,296**

Healey (Ire) *I W McInnes* 40
6 ch g Dr Devious (Ire) - Bean Siamsa
8¹⁰ᵍᶠ 12⁸ᵍᶠ 7¹⁰ˢ **0-0-3**

Heart Of Eternity (Ire) *J R Boyle* 47
2 b f Namid - Kurfuffle
14⁵ᵍ 4⁵ˢ 12⁶ᵍ **0-0-3 £324**

Heart Springs *Dr J R J Naylor* 46 a46
4 b f Parthian Springs - Metannee
7¹²ᵍᶠ 8¹⁰ᵍᶠ 10¹⁵ᵍᶠ 4¹⁶ˢᵈ 5¹⁶ˢᵈ 2¹⁸ᵍˢ 14¹⁶ᵍᶠ
9¹⁶ᵍˢ **0-1-8 £1,555**

Heart Stopping (USA) *B W Hills* 74
2 b f Chester House (USA) - Clog Dance
7⁷ᵍˢ **0-0-1**

Heart's Desire (Ire) *B W Hills* 67
3 b f Royal Applause - Touch And Love (Ire)
6⁸ᵍᶠ 2⁸ᵍ 6⁹ᵍᶠ 10⁸ᵍᶠ **0-1-4 £1,656**

Heartbeat *I A Wood* 51 a46
3 b f Pursuit Of Love - Lyrical Bid (USA)
4⁶ˢᵈ 8⁷ˢᵈ 7⁸ˢˢ 4¹⁰ᵍˢ 4⁸ᵍˢ 5¹⁰ᵍᶠ 9¹²ᵍ 7¹¹ᶠ
3⁸ᶠ **0-1-9 £661**

Heartbreaker (Ire) *M W Easterby*
4 b g In Command (Ire) - No Hard Feelings (Ire)
8¹⁴ˢᵈ **0-0-1**

Heartstead Dream *J D Bethell* 78
3 ch g Dr Fong (USA) - Robin Lane
18⁸ᵍᶠ 3¹²ᶠ 2⁸ᵍ 11¹¹ᵍᶠ 5⁸ᵍᶠ 1¹²ˢ 2¹¹ᵍᶠ 1¹²ᵍᶠ
3¹²ˢ 3¹⁶ᵍˢ 4¹²ᵍᶠ 3¹⁴ᵍ 8¹⁴ᵍˢ **3-4-13 £17,424**

Hearthstead Wings *M Johnston* 103
2 b c In The Wings - Inishdalla (Ire)
1⁶ᵍ 4⁷ᶠ 6⁷ᵍˢ 1⁸ᵍᶠ 3⁸ˢ **2-1-5 £60,275**

Heartsonfire (Ire) *P W D'Arcy* 67 a64
2 bl f Bold Fact (USA) - Jazirah
3⁵ʸ 3⁵ʸ 10⁶ᵍʸ 4⁶ᵍ 14⁵ᵍ 7⁷ᵍᶠ 4⁶ᵍᶠ 1⁶ˢᵈ
1-1-8 £5,299

Heat Of The Night *J L Dunlop* 76
2 b f Lear Fan (USA) - Hot Thong (Brz)
4⁷ᵍᶠ 9⁷ᵍᶠ 2⁷ᵍᶠ 5⁷ᵍᶠ **0-1-4 £2,212**

Heathers Girl *D Haydn Jones* 50 a58
5 ch m Superlative - Kristis Girl
11⁷ˢˢ 19ˢˢ 6⁸ˢʷ 29ˢˢ 4¹¹ᵍ 2¹¹ˢᵈ 2¹²ˢᵈ
4¹²ˢᵈ 2¹²ˢʷ 7¹²ˢᵈ 4¹²ˢᵈ **1-4-11 £6,468**

Heathwood (Ire) *J H M Gosden* a47
2 b c Green Desert (USA) - Woodsia
9⁷ˢᵈ **0-0-1**

Heathyards Joy *R Hollinshead* 39 a31
3 ch f Komaite (USA) - Heathyards Lady (USA)
7⁷ˢᵈ 12⁷ˢᵈ 4⁷ˢʷ 4⁸ˢᵈ 2⁷ᵍ 5⁷ᵍ 5⁶ʰʸ 6⁶ˢᵈ

8⁷ᵍᶠ 3⁷ᵍˢ 2⁸ᵍᶠ **0-3-11 £2,034**

Heathyards Pride *R Hollinshead* 65 a72
4 b g Polar Prince (Ire) - Heathyards Lady (USA)
1⁹ˢᵈ 19¹¹ˢ 4⁸ᶠ 5¹²ᵍ 1¹¹ᵍᶠ 1¹²ᵍᶠ 1¹²ᵍᶠ
4-0-7 £10,660

Heathyardsblessing (Ire) *R Hollinshead* a45
7 b g Unblest - Noble Nadia
8⁶ˢᵈ 6⁶ˢᵈ 5⁶ˢᵈ 12⁶ˢˢ 3⁵ˢʷ 5⁶ˢᵈ 5⁵ˢˢ **0-1-7
£188**

Heavens Walk *P J Makin* 47 a59
3 ch c Compton Place - Ghost Dancing
5⁵ᵍ 8⁶ˢ 4⁶ˢ 3⁶ˢᵈ **0-1-4 £833**

Hebenus *T A K Cuthbert* 49
5 b g Hamas (Ire) - Stinging Nettle
2⁷ᵍ 7⁶ᵍᶠ 14⁸ᶠ 4⁶ˢ **0-1-4 £464**

Hedingham Knight (Ire) *N A Callaghan* 53
2 b c Fasliyev (USA) - Exclusive Davis (USA)
6⁵ᵍᶠ 9⁶ᵍᶠ **0-0-2**

Hefin *B G Powell*
7 ch g Red Rainbow - Summer Impressions (USA)
10¹⁴ˢᵈ **0-0-1**

Heidi's Dash (Ire) *R Charlton* 59
2 b f Green Desert (USA) - Child Prodigy (Ire)
8⁵ᵍ 4⁵ᵍᶠ **0-0-2 £375**

Heir To Be *Mrs L Wadham* 74
5 b g Elmaamul (USA) - Princess Genista
5¹⁵ˢ 14¹⁶ᵍ 6¹⁶ᵍˢ **0-0-3 £223**

Heisse *D R Loder* 98
4 b c Darshaan - Hedera (USA)
5¹²ᵍ 14¹⁶ˢˢ 17¹²ˢ 8¹⁵ᵍᶠ 11¹²ᵍ **0-0-5**

Hektikos *S Dow* a28
4 ch g Hector Protector (USA) - Green Danube (USA)
11¹²ˢᵈ 11⁸ˢᵈ 5⁸ˢᵈ **0-0-3**

Helderberg (USA) *B S Rothwell* 69
4 b f Diesis - Banissa (USA)
19⁸ᵍᶠ 5⁹ᶠ 6⁸ᵍᶠ **0-0-3**

Helen House *M H Tompkins* 65
2 b f Tipsy Creek - Tiempo
7⁶ˢ 3⁶ˢ **0-1-2 £761**

Helen Sharp *M A Jarvis* 55
2 ch f Pivotal - Sunny Davis (USA)
11⁷ᵍˢ **0-0-1**

Helios Quercus (Fr) *C Diard* 112
2 br c Diableneyev (USA) - Criss Cross (Fr)
1⁵ʰᵒ 15ʰʸ 4⁵ᵍ 16ˢ 4⁵ʰᵒ 1⁷ᵛˢ 18ᵍˢ 18ᵛˢ
6-0-8 £177,569

Helixalot (Ire) *G P Enright*
3 ch g College Chapel - Last Ambition (Ire)
14¹³ˢᵈ **0-0-1**

Hellbent *A W Carroll* a43
5 b g Selkirk (USA) - Loure (USA)
8⁷ˢᵈ 12⁶ˢˢ 11⁷ˢᵈ 9⁶ˢᵈ 5⁸ˢᵈ 6¹⁰ˢᵈ 3¹²ˢᵈ
4¹⁰ᵍˢ 6⁹ˢᵈ 5¹²ˢᵈ **0-1-10 £210**

Hello It's Me *H J Collingridge* 92
3 ch g Deploy - Evening Charm (Ire)
2¹⁰ᵍ 11¹⁰ᵍˢ 2⁸ᵍ 5⁸ᵍᶠ 4¹⁰ᵍᶠ 3¹⁰ᵍˢ 5¹²ᵍᶠ
12¹⁰ᵍ **0-3-8 £13,289**

Hello Roberto *N Tinkler* 75 a80
3 b f Up And At 'Em - Hello Hobson'S (Ire)
7⁷ˢᵈ 2⁶ˢᵈ 8⁶ˢᵈ 2⁵ˢᵈ 5⁵ˢᵈ 3⁵ˢ 9⁵ˢ 1⁵ᵍ
10⁵ᵍᶠ 20⁵ᵍᶠ 10⁶ˢᵈ 4⁵ᶠ 7⁵ᵍ 7⁵ᵍ 10⁵ˢ **1-3-15
£13,239**

Hello Sid *T E Powell*
3 ch g Hello Mister - Moving Up (Ire)
9⁵ˢᵈ **0-0-1**

Hello Tiger *J A Supple*
3 gr g Terimon - Blue Peru (Ire)
8^{8sd} 19^{8gf} 10^{8sd} 5^{7g} **0-0-4**

Helm (Ire) *R Rowe* 66 a70
3 b g Alhaarth (Ire) - Pipers Pool (Ire)
10^{10gs} 4^{13sd} 6^{14gs} **0-0-3 £292**

Heneseys Leg *John Berry* 83 a68
4 b f Sure Blade (USA) - Away's Halo (USA)
1^{8s} 1^{10gf} 1^{9g} 5^{10sd} 3^{10s} 16^{12t} **3-1-6 £17,144**

Henndey (Ire) *M A Jarvis* 75
3 b g Indian Ridge - Del Deya (Ire)
2^{7gs} 2^{7s} **0-2-2 £2,290**

Henrik *M R Channon* 109
2 b c Primo Dominie - Clincher Club
1^{6gf} 2^{7gs} 3^{8s} **1-2-3 £36,571**

Henry Afrika (Ire) *G M Lyons* 88 a79
6 b g Mujadil (USA) - Floralia
7^{8sd} 12^{7sw} 1^{9g} 14^{8gf} 6^{9gf} **1-0-5 £6,082**

Henry Hall (Ire) *N Tinkler* 101
8 b h Common Grounds - Sovereign Grace (Ire)
3^{5g} 10^{5gs} 3^{5gs} 9^{5gf} 3^{5gf} 10^{5gs} 8^{5g} 15^{5g}
7^{5g} 10^{5s} 8^{5g} 12^{5s} **0-2-12 £4,696**

Henry Island (Ire) *Mrs A J Bowlby* 71
11 ch g Sharp Victor (USA) - Monterana
5^{15s} 7^{17f} 4^{16g} 7^{14gf} 10^{16gf} 2^{16gs} 10^{16g}
4^{17g} 13^{16gs} **0-2-9 £2,103**

Henry Tun *J Balding* 42 a64
6 b g Chaddleworth (Ire) - B Grade
3^{5sd} 5^{5sd} 7^{5ss} 2^{5sd} 1^{5sw} 3^{5ss} 7^{5ss} 2^{5sd}
7^{5gs} 7^{5gf} 6^{5gf} 8^{6f} 13^{5sd} **1-4-13 £3,824**

Her Own Kind (Jpn) *Saeed Bin Suroor* 82
2 b f Dubai Millennium - The Caretaker
2^{7gf} 1^{8s} **1-1-2 £5,779**

Here To Me *R Hannon* 76 a72
3 ch f Muhtarram (USA) - Away To Me
5^{7g} 3^{7gf} 4^{7g} 4^{8f} 2^{7gf} 1^{6gf} 3^{7g} 5^{6sd} 6^{7gs}
2^{8gs} 8^{7sd} **1-5-11 £9,672**

Herencia (Ire) *P A Blockley* 52
2 b c Victory Note (USA) - Originality
11^{6gs} 7^{6gf} 8^{5gs} 4^{7gs} 2^{7gf} 6^{8s} **0-1-6 £868**

Heres Harry *Miss Jacqueline S Doyle* 4
4 b c Most Welcome - Nahla
18^{6gf} 8^{5gf} **0-0-2**

Heres The Plan (Ire) *M G Quinlan* 77 a64
2 b f Revoque (Ire) - Fanciful (Ire)
1^{6gf} 7^{6gf} 6^{7gf} 10^{7gs} 4^{9sd} **1-0-5 £5,005**

Heretic *J R Fanshawe* 113
6 b g Bishop Of Cashel - Barford Lady
1^{8s} 4^{8s} 19^{7gs} 10^{7s} **1-0-4 £10,002**

Heriot *S C Burrough* 65
3 br g Hamas (Ire) - Sure Victory (Ire)
10^{8hy} 9^{8g} 8^{7gf} 7^{6gf} **0-0-4**

Hermitage Court (USA) *B J Meehan* 89
3 ch g Out Of Place (USA) - Russian Act (USA)
1^{8g} 4^{10g} 6^{9g} 12^{8gf} **1-0-4 £6,098**

Hernandita *Miss E C Lavelle* 68
6 b m Hernando (Fr) - Dara Dee
4^{17gf} 15^{20gf} 6^{15gf} **0-0-3 £536**

Hernando's Boy *K G Reveley* 63
3 b g Hernando (Fr) - Leave At Dawn
5^{10s} 9^{10gs} 7^{10s} 12^{11s} 2^{12gf} **0-1-5 £1,152**

Herne Bay (Ire) *D Burchell* 53 a66

4 b g Hernando (Fr) - Charita (Ire)
1^{16sd} 14^{14gf} 5^{16g} **1-0-3 £3,789**

Herodotus *K O Cunningham-Brown* 7 a32
6 b g Zafonic (USA) - Thalestria (Fr)
13^{12g} 12^{12gf} 13^{12gs} 7^{14g} 12^{9sd} **0-0-5**

Heron's Wing *Lady Herries* a56
3 ch g Hernando (Fr) - Celtic Wing
8^{10sd} **0-0-1**

Heversham (Ire) *J Hetherton* 75 a85
3 b c Octagonal (NZ) - Saint Ann (USA)
4^{7sd} 18^{sd} 2^{8sd} 7^{9s} 7^{8gf} 9^{8gf} 4^{7f} 2^{8f}
5^{10gf} 7^{8s} 17^{7gs} 7^{8gf} 2^{8g} 2^{8gf} 23^{8gf} 12^{8s}
1-4-17 £9,581

Hey Presto *C G Cox* 78
4 b g Piccolo - Upping The Tempo
14^{6gf} 10^{6gf} 9^{5g} 5^{6gf} 6^{6gf} 1^{7gf} 19^{7gf}
13^{7s} 18^{7gf} 9^{7g} **1-0-10 £10,351**

Heybrook Boy (USA) *M Johnston* 71
2 ch c Woodman (USA) - Liberada (USA)
8^{6s} 4^{6gf} 2^{7gf} **0-1-3 £1,366**

Heyward Place *T Keddy*
4 b f Mind Games - Ginny Binny
12^{7sd} 18^{8gf} 10^{10s} **0-0-3**

Hezaam (USA) *J L Dunlop* 89
3 b c Red Ransom - Ashraakat (USA)
12^{7g} 5^{8gf} 8^{10gf} 1^{10gs} 11^{2s} 2^{12gs} 4^{14s} 9^{12s}
2-1-8 £28,256

Hi Darl *W M Brisbourne* 39
3 ch f Wolfhound (USA) - Sugar Token
10^{8g} 13^{7gf} 13^{7gs} 8^{5f} 16^{7gf} 16^{6gs} 5^{6s}
0-0-7

Hiamovi (Ire) *R M H Cowell* 37 a57
2 b g Monashee Mountain (USA) - Dunfern
11^{5g} 5^{7sd} 2^{6sw} 12^{6gf} 10^{6sd} **0-1-5 £1,266**

Hiats *J O'Reilly* 37
2 b c Lujain (USA) - Naulakha
13^{5g} 6^{5s} 10^{5g} **0-0-3**

Hiawatha (Ire) *P A Blockley* 80 a83
5 b g Danehill (USA) - Hi Bettina
4^{11sd} 1^{9sd} 3^{10sd} 7^{10sd} 7^{8sd} 1^{10gf} 7^{10gf}
5^{10g} 7^{9s} 20^{10s} **2-1-10 £11,528**

Hibernate (Ire) *C J Teague* 45
10 ch g Lahib (USA) - Ministra (USA)
12^{12gf} 6^{12gf} 4^{12g} 10^{12gf} 13^{12gf} 5^{13gf}
0-0-6

Hiccups *D Nicholls* 89
4 b g Polar Prince (Ire) - Simmie's Special
2^{5gs} 13^{6gs} 3^{6gf} 1^{6gf} 10^{6g} 6^{6gf} 3^{6gf} 3^{6s}
9^{5gf} **1-4-9 £15,096**

Hickerthriftcastle *V Smith*
5 ch g Carlingford Castle - Sun Sprite
12^{12gf} **0-0-1**

Hidden Chance *R Hannon* 69
2 ch f Hernando (Fr) - Catch (USA)
7^{7gf} 1^{7gf} 11^{8s} 8^{7gf} 4^{10gf} 11^{8g} **1-1-6 £5,711**

Hidden Dragon (USA) *P A Blockley* 93 a108
5 b g Danzig (USA) - Summer Home (USA)
2^{7sd} 2^{7sd} 11^{7gf} 10^{7gf} 6^{6s} 4^{5gf} 7^{6s} 9^{6gf}
0-2-8 £10,644

Hidden Hope *G Wragg* 106
3 ch f Daylami (Ire) - Nuryana
2^{8gs} 1^{11gs} 5^{12gf} 4^{12g} 2^{13gs} 3^{12gf} **1-3-6 £60,338**

Hidden Jewel *B A McMahon*   87 a66
2 ch c Forzando - Manhattan Diamond
18^{5gf} 6^{6sd} 6^{7sd} 9^{7f} 2^{6s} 3^{6hy} 0-2-6
£9,886

Hidden Star *F Jordan*   68
2 br c Lujain (USA) - Inimitable
3^{6gf} 6^{6gf} 0-0-2 £551

Hiddensee (USA) *M Johnston*   30
2 b c Cozzene (USA) - Zarani Sidi Anna (USA)
13^{8g} 0-0-1

Higgys Prince *D Flood*   31
2 b g Prince Sabo - Themeda
10^{5g} 7^{5g} 0-0-2

High Accolade *M P Tregoning*   121
4 b c Mark Of Esteem (Ire) - Generous Lady
4^{12g} 2^{12f} 3^{12gf} 8^{12gf} 2^{12g} 4^{18g} 1^{12gf} 1-3-7
£113,448

High Action (USA) *Ian Williams*   96
4 ch g Theatrical - Secret Imperatrice (USA)
15^{12g} 15^{10gs} 8^{16g} 11^{5g} 1^{19gf} 8^{14g} 5^{15gf}
2-0-7 £21,454

High Cane (USA) *M D Hammond*   63
4 ch f Diesis - Aerleon Jane
12^{10sd} 3^{7gs} 17^{8gs} 20^{6s} 12^{7s} 15^{8sd} 0-1-6
£551

High Card *J M P Eustace*   77 a60
2 b g So Factual (USA) - High Cut
8^{7sd} 6^{9sd} 2^{8hy} 0-1-3 £2,072

High Chart *T G Mills*   75
2 b f Robellino - Bright Spells
1^{5g} 4^{6gs} 4^{5gf} 12^{5gf} 3^{5gf} 8^{6gf} 6^{6gs} 14^{7gf}
25^{7g} 15^{5gf} 10^{8g} 1-0-11 £4,970

High Charter *J R Fanshawe*   48
3 b g Polish Precedent (USA) - By Charter
9^{10hy} 0-0-1

High Class Pet *F P Murtagh*   21
4 b f Petong - What A Pet
12^{8g} 6^{9gs} 0-0-2

High Dawn (Ire) *R M Beckett*   45
2 b g Namid - Highbrook (USA)
6^{5gs} 0-0-1

High Diva *J R Best*   a44
5 b m Piccolo - Gifted
6^{10sd} 4^{12sd} 6^{16sd} 5^{9sw} UR^{8sd} 5^{8sd} 0-0-6

High Drama *P Bowen*   48
7 b/br g In The Wings - Maestrale
1^{18f} 2^{16gs} 4^{17gs} 1-2-3 £4,732

High Dyke *D Haydn Jones*   71
2 b c Mujahid (USA) - Gold Linnet
7^{6g} 5^{5gf} 6^{7gf} 5^{7gs} 7^{7gs} 0-0-5

High Esteem *M A Buckley*   21 a47
8 b g Common Grounds - Whittle Woods Girl
4^{6sd} 8^{6sd} 9^{6sd} 14^{5g} 0-0-4

High Finance (Ire) *J W Hills*   79 a53
4 b/br f Entrepreneur - Phylella
5^{7gf} 6^{7gf} 14^{7sd} 0-0-3 £309

High Frequency (Ire) *W R Muir*   63
3 ch g Grand Lodge - Freak Out (Fr)
10^{8g} 6^{8g} 7^{8gf} 0-0-3

High Hope (Fr) *G L Moore*   64 a79
6 ch g Lomitas - Highness Lady (Ger)
7^{12sd} 14^{9gs} 0-0-2

High Minded *K R Burke*   57
2 b g Mind Games - Pips Way (Ire)
7^{5gf} 6^{5g} 0-0-2

High Petergate (Ire) *M W Easterby*   59
2 b f Mujadil (USA) - Anamara (Ire)
5^{5gf} 4^{5gf} 10^{6gs} 16^{6gf} 0-0-4

High Point (Ire) *G P Enright*   88 a87
6 b g Ela-Mana-Mou - Top Lady (Ire)
15^{12sd} 7^{12sd} 7^{12sd} 2^{16sd} 3^{16gs} 3^{14gs} 3^{16gf}
6^{16gf} 12^{16gf} 5^{15s} 11^{6g} 3^{18s} 1-5-12 £29,073

High Policy (Ire) *R Hollinshead*   a67
8 ch g Machiavellian (USA) - Road To The Top
4^{16sd} 3^{14sd} 0-1-2 £534

High Reach *T G Mills*   101 a95
4 b g Royal Applause - Lady Of Limerick (Ire)
3^{6gs} 6^{6g} 3^{6f} 7^{6gf} 3^{6gf} 9^{5g} 10^{5g} 10^{7sd}
0-3-8 £22,051

High Reserve *J R Fanshawe*   69
3 b f Dr Fong (USA) - Hyabella
3^{8gs} 1^{8s} 1-1-2 £6,434

High Rhythm *S C Williams*   50
2 b f Piccolo - Slave To The Rythm (Ire)
6^{6g} 0-0-1

High Ridge *J M Bradley*   80
5 ch g Indian Ridge - Change For A Buck (USA)
9^{6hy} 16^{7f} 6^{6gf} 3^{6gf} 3^{6gf} 4^{6g} 16^{gf} 2^{6g}
2^{6gf} 4^{6gf} 10^{6g} 11^{6s} 14^{6gs} 3-5-14 £24,373

High School *D R Loder*   75
3 b f Sadler's Wells (USA) - High Hawk
2^{10gs} 12^{5s} 4^{10gf} 2^{10gf} 6^{12gf} 0-2-5
£2,554

High Treason (USA) *J G Given*   61
2 ch c Diesis - Fabula Dancer (USA)
12^{7gf} 8^{8g} 21^{7g} 11^{8g} 0-0-4

High View (USA) *F Jordan*   47
3 ch c Distant View (USA) - Disco Doll (USA)
7^{8hy} 16^{10g} 9^{10gf} 13^{8gs} 10^{12gs} 11^{8gs}
13^{13gs} 0-0-7

High Voltage *K R Burke*   103
3 ch g Wolfhound (USA) - Real Emotion (USA)
1^{6gs} 3^{6gf} 6^{6gf} 7^{5gf} 1^{7bg} 8^{6g} 1^{6g} 21^{6g}
12^{6s} 2-1-9 £25,847

Highbury Lass *P C Haslam*   5
2 ch f Entrepreneur - Princess Victoria
12^{5gf} 6^{7f} 10^{7s} 0-0-2

Higher Love (Ire) *M L W Bell*   73
2 b f Sadler's Wells (USA) - Dollar Bird (Ire)
6^{8gf} 2^{8s} 0-1-2 £1,715

Highest (Ire) *Saeed Bin Suroor*   109
5 b h Selkirk (USA) - Pearl Kite (USA)
7^{14gs} 7^{20gf} 0-0-2

Highest Regard *P L Gilligan*   57 a37
2 b c Mark Of Esteem (Ire) - Free As A Bird
7^{7sd} 7^{6s} 0-0-2

Highest Return (USA) *M Johnston*   67
2 b/br g Theatrical - Hasene (Fr)
4^{7gf} 11^{7gf} 0-0-2 £425

Highfluting *R M Flower*   9 a35
3 b f Piccolo - Vilcabamba (USA)
13^{10sd} 9^{10g} 16^{10gf} 7^{12gf} 0-0-4

Highland Cascade *J M P Eustace*   75
2 ch f Tipsy Creek (USA) - Highland Hannah (Ire)
16^{gf} 3^{6f} 2^{6gf} 8^{7g} 3^{6gs} 8^{6s} 1-2-6
£8,238

Highland Diva (Ire) *Sir Michael Stoute*   73
2 ch f Selkirk (USA) - Drama Class (Ire)
4^{7g} 0-0-1 £822

Highland Games (Ire) *J G Given*   95

4 b g Singspiel (Ire) - Highland Gift (Ire)
2¹⁴g 13¹⁴gs 2¹²f 4¹²gf 5¹²f 3¹²gf 3¹⁶g
13¹⁵gf PU¹⁶gf **0-4-9 £12,019**

Highland Lass *Mrs H Sweeting* 57
3 b f Nicolotte - Portvasco
8⁶gf 10⁷gf 6⁷gs 10⁶gs 13⁶g **0-0-5**

Highland Reel *D R C Elsworth* 96
7 ch g Selkirk (USA) - Taj Victory
1⁸g 11⁸gf 26⁸gf 4⁸g 9⁸g 3⁸g 4⁸gf 4⁹gs
1-1-8 £13,410

Highland Warrior *J S Goldie* 79
5 b h Makbul - Highland Rowena
3⁶gs 3⁷gf 2⁵hy 3⁵g 4⁶gs 1⁶gf 6⁵gf 7⁶g
8⁵gf 4⁶g 6⁶s 6⁶g 3⁵gf 15⁶g 2⁶s 6⁵s 4⁶gs 2⁵s
6⁵gs **1-8-19 £16,277**

Highlight Girl *A W Carroll* 38
3 ch f Forzando - Norska
14¹⁰s 9⁸gf **0-0-2**

Hilarious (Ire) *Dr J R J Naylor* 46 a46
4 b f Petorius - Heronwater (Ire)
5⁸hy 4⁷sd 5⁸gf 6⁸sd 4¹⁰gf 9¹⁰sd 6¹⁰gs 8⁷hy
12¹²gf 13¹⁰g **0-0-10 £274**

Hilbre Island *B J Meehan* 109
4 b c Halling (USA) - Faribole (Ire)
3¹⁴g 16¹²g PU¹⁶s 5¹⁶gf 9¹⁶gf **0-0-5**
£6,025

Hilites (Ire) *J S Moore* 82 a72
3 ch f Desert King (Ire) - Slayjay (Ire)
3⁶hy 11⁶g 3⁶g 10⁵gf 7⁷g 6⁷gf 3⁷gf 9⁹g
4⁹gf 9⁶gs 8⁷g 14⁶s 6⁶sd **0-1-13 £4,416**

Hill Fairy *T P Tate* 69
2 ch f Monsun (Ger) - Homing Instinct
6⁶gf 4⁸g 5⁸s **0-0-3 £377**

Hillabilla (Ire) *M Blanshard* 31
2 b f Imperial Ballet - London Rose (USA)
15⁶gs 16⁷g **0-0-2**

Hills Of Aran *A P O'Brien* 93
2 b c Sadler's Wells (USA) - Danefair
3⁷gs 1⁸g 4⁸s **1-1-3 £20,122**

Hills Of Gold *M W Easterby* 86
5 b g Danehill (USA) - Valley Of Gold (Fr)
4⁷s 1⁸gs 7⁷s 3⁸gs 2⁸gs 2¹⁰gs 1⁷g 4⁸gs 6⁸g
6⁷s 19⁹g 12⁷s **2-3-12 £16,155**

Hills Spitfire (Ire) *P W Harris* 82
3 b/br g Kahyasi - Questina (Fr)
3¹⁰gf **0-1-1 £894**

Hillside Heather (Ire) *A Berry* 70
2 ch f Tagula (Ire) - Danzig Craft (Ire)
4⁵g 3⁵gf 2⁵g 7⁵s 2⁵gf 4⁶f 5⁵g 7⁵gs 6⁵f
1⁵gf **1-2-10 £8,219**

Hilltime (Ire) *J J Quinn* 53 a46
4 b g Danetime (Ire) - Ceannanas (Ire)
9⁶g 13⁶gf 8⁵s 10⁸s 3⁸gf 15⁷f 5⁸sd **0-1-7**
£587

Hilltop Rhapsody *D J Daly* 73
3 b f Bin Ajwaad (Ire) - Saferjel
15⁸g 9¹⁰g 1⁸gf 14¹¹g 4⁸gf **1-0-5 £4,621**

Hilly Be *J R Jenkins*
3 b f Silver Patriarch (Ire) - Lolita (Fr)
8⁸s **0-0-1**

Hinchley Wood (Ire) *J R Best* a45
5 b g Fayruz - Audriano (Ire)
6⁷sd 10⁹sw 7⁷sd 10¹⁰sd 5⁷sd 5⁶sd 4⁷sd
2⁶sd 6⁶sd **0-1-9 £360**

Hinode (Ire) *J A R Toller* 59 a67

3 ch c Vettori (Ire) - Juvenilia (Ire)
14⁸g 17⁸g 3⁸sd 5¹²hy 4¹¹g 18¹⁴gs 7¹²g
0-1-7 £416

Hip Hop Harry *E A L Dunlop* 56 a89
4 b c First Trump - Rechanit (Ire)
8¹¹sd 2¹²sd 1¹⁰sd 2¹²sd 18¹²g 14¹⁰gf 5¹²gf
1-2-7 £7,802

Hirayna *W M Brisbourne* 51
5 b m Doyoun - Himaya (Ire)
3¹¹g 8⁷gf 4⁸g 4⁸gf 8¹⁰s 11¹⁰gf 16⁸g **0-0-7**
£1,357

His Majesty *N P Littmoden* 51
2 c c Case Law - Eternal Triangle (USA)
10⁵sd 4⁸gf 2⁶gf 6⁵gf **0-1-5 £1,129**

Historic Place (USA) *G B Balding* 90
4 b g Dynaformer (USA) - Captive Island
2¹²gs 4¹⁰g 8¹²g 3¹⁷s 15¹⁸s 6¹⁷s **0-2-6**
£3,373

Hit's Only Money (Ire) *P A Blockley* 86
4 br g Hamas (Ire) - Toordillon (Ire)
8⁷gs 15⁸g 9⁷gf 14⁷s 7⁶gf 7⁶g **0-0-6**

Hits Only Cash *P A Blockley* 61
2 b c Inchinor - Persian Blue
6⁵f 7⁵g 5⁶gs 7⁶hy 4⁵s 5⁵hy **0-0-6 £516**

Hobart Junction (Ire) *J A T De Giles*
9 ch g Classic Secret (USA) - Art Duo
19¹²gf **0-0-1**

Hoh Bleu Dee *S Kirk* 79
3 b g Desert Style (Ire) - Ermine (Ire)
10⁷gf 5⁸gs 15¹⁰gs 2⁸g 1⁸gf 9⁸f 4⁷s 8¹²s
1-1-8 £8,982

Hoh Hedsor *S Kirk* 48
2 ch f Singspiel (Ire) - Ghassanah
12⁷g 12⁸hy **0-0-2**

Hoh Hoh Hoh *A M Balding* 87
2 c c Piccolo - Nesting
1⁶f **1-0-1 £4,400**

Hoh My Darling *M L W Bell* 60
2 br f Dansili - Now And Forever (Ire)
7⁷s 4⁸gf 7⁸gs **0-0-3 £402**

Hoh Nelson *C J Mann* 70
3 b g Halling (USA) - Birsay
3⁸g 9¹²gf 8¹²g 6¹⁸gs 4¹⁶gs **0-1-5 £919**

Hoh's Back *Paul Johnson* 68 a43
5 b g Royal Applause - Paris Joelle (Ire)
9⁸sd 12⁸sd 2⁸sd 5⁸sd 10⁸sd 7⁸g
5⁸sd 10⁸sd 11⁸f 13⁷g 14⁸g 7⁸gf 7⁹hy 8⁸f 5⁸f
0-1-17 £1,136

Holbeck Ghyll (Ire) *A M Balding* 75
2 ch c Titus Livius (Fr) - Crimada (Ire)
3⁶g 8⁵gf 3⁵g **0-2-3 £1,440**

Hold The Line *W G M Turner* a62
3 b g Titus Livius (Fr) - Multi-Sofft
6¹⁰sd 1⁸ss 6⁸sd **1-0-3 £1,463**

Hold Up *Miss J Feilden* 56
3 ch f Daggers Drawn (USA) - Select Sale
7¹⁰gf 10¹²gf 7¹⁰gf 7⁸gf 8⁷gf 9⁸g 15⁸gs
0-0-7

Holderness Girl *M E Sowersby*
11 b m Lapierre - Isobel's Choice
6⁸gf 13⁸sd **0-0-2**

Holiday Camp (USA) *B W Hills* 71
2 b c Chester House (USA) - Arewehavingfunyet (USA)
3⁶s **0-1-1 £920**

Holiday Cocktail *S C Williams* 22

2 b g Mister Baileys - Bermuda Lily
95g 0-0-1

Hollingwood Soul *Ronald Thompson* 32
2 ch f Timeless Times (USA) - Crystal Chandelier
75gf 96f 95g 107gs 127gf 0-0-5

Hollow Jo *J R Jenkins* 69
4 b g Most Welcome - Sir Hollow (USA)
157gs 96gs 45gf 96gf 0-0-4 £424

Holly Rose *D E Cantillon* 61
5 b m Charnwood Forest (Ire) - Divina Luna
106s 210gf 410f 1310gf 411f 410gf 210gs
1610gf 1310sd 1510s 0-2-10 £1,842

Holly Springs *J H M Gosden* 84
2 b f Efisio - Anotheranniversary
26g 117g 26g 0-2-3 £3,236

Holly Walk *M Dods* 56 a53
3 ch f Dr Fong (USA) - Holly Blue
118s 212gs 514s 512gf 312sd 212sd
1312gf 312sd 0-3-9 £3,325

Hollywood Critic (USA) *P Monteith* 50
3 b g Theatrical - Lyphard's Starlite (USA)
88g 811g 58gf 311s 0-0-4 £582

Hollywood Henry (Ire) *J Akehurst* 63 a62
4 b g Bahhare (USA) - Takeshi (Ire)
18f 69gs 98gf 48sd 49sd 1-0-5 £3,822

Holy Orders (Ire) *W P Mullins* 113
7 b h Unblest - Shadowglow
414gf 422f 612gf 114gy 520g 716hy 416gs
1-0-7 £31,792

Home Affairs *Sir Michael Stoute* 83
2 b c Dansili - Orford Ness
57g 17g 97s 1-0-3 £5,255

Home By Socks (Ire) *M C Chapman* 19
5 ch m Desert King (Ire) - Propitious (Ire)
107gs 1210g 0-0-2

Home Coming *P S Felgate* a28
6 br g Primo Dominie - Carolside
66sd 87sd 0-0-2

Home Front (Ire) *Ms Deborah J Evans*
3 b g Intikhab (USA) - Felicita (Ire)
115gs 0-0-1

Homebred Star *P Bowen* 41
3 ch g Safawan - Celtic Chimes
78gs 77gs 107gf 0-0-3

Homeric Trojan *M Brittain* 37 a41
4 ch c Hector Protector (USA) - Housefull
68sd 1111ss 1216s 612sd 616sd 0-0-5

Homeward (Ire) *A M Balding* 45
3 ch f Kris - Home Truth
57gf 138gs 0-0-2

Homme Dangereux *C R Egerton* 33 a54
2 b c Royal Applause - Happy Lady (Fr)
36sd 85gf 55sd 87s 0-1-4 £590

Honest Injun *J G M O'Shea* 79 a77
3 b c Efisio - Sioux
17sd 48gs 49hy 128gf 58gs 48s 58gs 27s
28gs 58gf 1-2-10 £8,570

Honey Ryder *D R Loder* 81
2 b f Compton Place - Urania
26gf 25gf 147g 46g 0-2-4 £3,307

Honey's Gift *G G Margarson* a34
5 b m Terimon - Honeycroft
710sd 0-0-1

Honeymooning *H R A Cecil* 68
3 b f Groom Dancer (USA) - Ever Genial

710s 412gf 312gf 810gs 0-1-4 £961

Honeystreet (Ire) *J D Frost* 38
4 b f Woodborough (USA) - Ring Of Kerry (Ire)
1312gf 139gf 0-0-2

Honor Rouge (Ire) *D G Bridgwater* 69
5 ch m Highest Honor (Fr) - Ayers Rock (Ire)
612f 1312f 0-0-2

Honorine (Ire) *J W Payne* 86
4 b f Mark Of Esteem (Ire) - Blue Water (USA)
68gf 109g 58g 110gf 710s 810s 1-0-6
£12,125

Honour High *Lady Herries* 53
2 gr g Cloudings (Ire) - Meant To Be
78gf 78gs 57gs 0-0-3

Hoops And Blades *N P Littmoden* 52
3 gr c Peintre Celebre (USA) - Mare Aux Fees
168g 88gf 168g 911g 1218gs 0-0-5

Hope Sound (Ire) *B Ellison* 58
4 b g Turtle Island (Ire) - Lucky Pick
716s 416gf 0-0-2 £418

Hopelessly Devoted *P C Haslam* 55 a31
2 b f Compton Place - Alpi Dora
106g 65g 15hy 106sw 56g 45f 1-0-6
£3,377

Horizontal (USA) *N A Twiston-Davies* 59 a51
4 ch g Distant View (USA) - Proud Lou (USA)
66sd 65sd 87gs 128hy 57f 1310sd 0-0-6

Hormuz (Ire) *Paul Johnson* 33
8 b g Hamas (Ire) - Balqis (USA)
198s 117gf 118g 48g 109f 0-0-5

Horner (USA) *P F I Cole* 88
3 b c Rahy (USA) - Dynashore (Can)
118g 412gf 212gf 113f 1012g 312gf 212g
1-2-7 £9,162

Horningsheath *C F Wall* 55
2 b f Royal Applause - Pacifica
206s 107s 0-0-2

Hornpipe *Sir Michael Stoute* 79
2 b c Danehill (USA) - Dance Sequence (USA)
65gf 16gf 1-0-2 £5,300

Hors La Loi (Fr) *Ian Williams* 65
8 ch g Exit To Nowhere (USA) - Kernia (Ire)
1010gf 0-0-1

Hot Lips Page (Fr) *R Hannon* 77
3 b f Hamas (Ire) - Salt Peanuts (Ire)
57gf 18gf 48gf 88gf 108gs 1-0-5 £4,173

Houdini Bay (Ire) *R P Elliott* 30 a9
2 b f Indian Lodge (Ire) - Do The Right Thing
85s 85sd 26f 0-0-3 £720

House Martin *A M Balding* 72
2 b f Spectrum (Ire) - Guignol (Ire)
47gf 107g 0-0-2 £270

House Of Blues *Rodger Sweeney* 54 a18
3 b g Grand Lodge (USA) - Sartigila
1510g 912sd 510g 316gf 0-1-4 £409

Hout Bay *R A Fahey* 82 a64
7 ch g Komaite (USA) - Maiden Pool
15sd 36sd 66sd 25gs 45s 15s 15gs 35gs 1s
65g 75s 4-3-11 £27,155

Hov *J J Quinn* 81 a36
4 gr g Petong - Harifa
119sd 811ss 88hy 27s 66s 88s 108f 0-1-7
£1,099

How's Things *D Haydn Jones* 45 a77
4 b g Danzig Connection (USA) - Dim Ots

6^{8sw} 14^{8g} 7^{9gs} 10^{8s} 2^{7sd} **0-1-5 £1,084**

Howards Dream (Ire) *D A Nolan* 60
6 b g King's Theatre (Ire) - Keiko
10^{14gf} 4^{10g} 18^{7gf} 6^{11gf} 7^{13gf} 7^{12g} 7^{13g}
5^{12gf} 4^{11s} 8^{13s} **0-0-10 £1,500**

Howards Princess *I Semple* 69
2 gr f Lujain (USA) - Grey Princess (Ire)
5^{6g} 2^{5s} 2^{5gs} 4^{5g} 9^{5gf} **0-1-5 £3,453**

Howards Rocket *J S Goldie* 50
3 ch g Opening Verse (USA) - Houston Heiress (USA)
7^{9gs} 8^{8g} 6^{8gf} 9^{9gf} 11^{7s} **0-0-5**

Hows That *K R Burke* 60
2 ch f Vettori (Ire) - Royalty (Ire)
13^{6gf} 11^{7gf} 7^{6s} 10^{7g} 2^{6gs} 1^{6g} **1-1-6**
£3,622

Hsi Wang Mu (Ire) *R Brotherton* 50 a56
3 ch f Dr Fong (USA) - Oh Hebe (Ire)
2^{9sw} 5^{8ss} 9^{10gs} 5^{10gs} 9^{8f} 11^{10f} 13^{9sd}
0-1-7 £1,038

Huboob (Fr) *M P Tregoning* 44
2 b/br g Almutawakel - Atnab (USA)
11^{8g} **0-0-1**

Huggin Mac (Ire) *N Bycroft* 45
3 b f Spectrum (Ire) - Little Love
6^{7gs} 7^{7gf} **0-0-2**

Hugo The Boss (Ire) *J R Boyle* a45
2 ch g Trans Island - Heartland
13^{7sd} 8^{7sd} 10^{8sd} **0-0-3**

Hugs Destiny (Ire) *J G Given* 71 a70
3 b g Victory Note (USA) - Embracing
5^{8gf} 2^{10sd} **0-1-2 £852**

Hula Ballew *M Dods* 67
4 ch f Weldnaas (USA) - Ballon
9^{8hy} 5^{8gs} 13^{8g} 9^{8gf} 9^{7g} 1^{8gf}
5^{8gf} 5^{10gf} 2^{8g} 3^{8g} 11^{8gf} **1-2-13 £7,254**

Hum (Ire) *Miss D A McHale* 17
3 ch f Cadeaux Genereux - Ensorceleuse (Fr)
14^{8gf} 14^{9g} **0-0-2**

Humdinger (Ire) *D Shaw* a12
4 b f Charnwood Forest (Ire) - High Finish
11^{12sd} 10^{8ss} 8^{12sd} 12^{10g} **0-0-4**

Humid Climate *R A Fahey* 67
4 ch g Desert King (Ire) - Pontoon
8^{7s} 7^{8f} 13^{10gf} 18^{10g} **0-0-4**

Humility *C A Cyzer* 32
3 b f Polar Falcon (USA) - Rich In Love (Ire)
11^{5gf} **0-0-1**

Humourous (Ire) *Saeed Bin Suroor* 86
2 b c Darshaan - Amusing Time (Ire)
5^{7gf} 1^{8g} 9^{8g} **1-0-3 £5,161**

Hunipot *M E Sowersby* 17
2 ch f Aragon - Acinom
7^{5gs} 9^{5hy} 11^{5g} 8^{5gf} 6^{5gf} 13^{6gf} **0-0-6**

Hunter's Valley *R Hannon* 68 a53
3 b f Nicolotte - Down The Valley
8^{8gf} 2^{7gf} 4^{8f} 8^{8gf} 4^{8g} 4^{8gs} 3^{8sd} 15^{8gs}
0-3-8 £3,686

Hunting Lodge (Ire) *D R Loder* 76
3 ch c Grand Lodge (USA) - Vijaya (USA)
14^{8gs} **0-0-1**

Hunting Pink *H Morrison* a51
3 b f Foxhound (USA) - Dancing Bluebell (Ire)
2^{7sd} 3^{8sd} 4^{8sd} 7^{8sd} **0-2-4 £1,465**

Hurricane Alan (Ire) *R Hannon* 118
4 b c Mukaddamah (USA) - Bint Al Balad (Ire)

3^{9g} 1^{8gs} 5^{8g} 10^{8gf} 3^{8g} 7^{8g} 3^{8gs} 3^{8gs} 2^{8g}
3^{8g} **1-3-10 £145,495**

Hurricane Coast *D Flood* 81 a90
5 b g Hurricane Sky (Aus) - Tread Carefully
1^{6sd} 1^{6sd} 1^{6sd} 3^{6sd} 1^{5sd} 3^{5sd} 2^{6sd} 12^{7sd}
9^{6ss} 4^{5sd} 1^{6sw} 9^{6ss} 1^{7gs} 6^{6gs} 6^{8hy} 4^{7g} **6-3-16**
£24,613

Hurricane Floyd (Ire) *D Flood* 86 a40
6 ch g Pennekamp (USA) - Mood Swings (Ire)
11^{7gs} 8^{8hy} 10^{7gf} 14^{7f} 4^{8f} 2^{6g} 14^{7s}
10^{7sd} **0-1-8 £1,903**

Hursley *S Kirk* 55
2 b f Compton Place - Kilcoy (USA)
14^{8gf} 10^{7g} **0-0-2**

Husky (Pol) *R M H Cowell* 50 a50
6 b g Special Power - Hallo Bambina (Pol)
5^{12sd} 1^{10sd} 3^{10sd} 13^{10sd} 5^{10f} 4^{10f} **1-0-6**
£1,848

Huxley (Ire) *M G Quinlan* 81
5 b g Danehill Dancer (Ire) - Biddy Mulligan
12^{8s} 20^{8gf} 9^{8s} 18^{10g} 4^{8g} 8^{8gf} 1^{8g} 16^{9g}
1-1-8 £4,882

Hymn Of Victory (Ire) *T J Etherington* 66
2 b c Bluebird (USA) - Vaga Follia (Ire)
9^{5f} 5^{5g} 2^{6g} 6^{6gf} 2^{5gf} 12^{5gf} 4^{6g} **0-2-7**
£2,570

Hymns And Arias *Ronald Thompson* 30 a44
3 b f Mtoto - Ewenny
9^{8ss} 4^{11ss} 14^{10gs} 10^{10gs} 7^{8sd} 10^{7gf} **0-0-6**

Hypnotic *Sir Mark Prescott* 98 a94
2 ch c Lomitas - Hypnotize
4^{6sd} 1^{7sd} 1^{7sd} 3^{7sd} 1^{8gs} 7^{8gs} **3-1-6**
£24,095

I Got Rhythm *Mrs M Reveley* 21
6 gr m Lycius (USA) - Eurythmic
9^{16gs} 8^{14s} **0-0-2**

I Had A Dream *M A Jarvis* 96
3 b f Bering - Dirigeante (Fr)
3^{8gs} 3^{10s} 1^{10vs} 9^{8gs} 2^{10s} 7^{10s} **1-1-6**
£24,065

I See No Ships *M Mullineaux*
4 b f Danzig Connection (USA) - Killick
7^{6gf} 17^{12g} **0-0-2**

I T Consultant *Miss L A Perratt*
6 b g Rock City - Game Germaine
13^{5hy} **0-0-1**

I Wish *M Madgwick* 64 a63
6 ch m Beveled (USA) - Ballystate
9^{7sd} 3^{7sd} 4^{6s} 1^{6gf} 5^{7gf} 5^{7gf} 3^{6gf}
13^{6gf} 2^{7f} 2^{6gs} 6^{6g} 4^{7sd} **1-4-13 £7,307**

I Wish I Knew *D J Coakley* 35 a17
3 br g Petong - Hoh Dancer
6^{7sw} 11^{7s} 11^{6gf} 7^{7gf} 11^{6f} **0-0-5**

I Won't Dance (Ire) *R Hannon* 75 a61
3 b c Marju (Ire) - Carnelly (Ire)
8^{6g} 7^{7f} 7^{8gs} 4^{7gf} 8^{7sd} **0-0-5 £426**

I'Ll Do It Today *J M Jefferson* 62
3 b g Mtoto - Knayton Lass
6^{10hy} 7^{10s} **0-0-2**

I'Ll Fly *J R Fanshawe* 43
4 ch g Polar Falcon (USA) - I'Ll Try
8^{10gs} **0-0-1**

I'm A Dark Horse *K A Ryan* 39
3 b g Alzao (USA) - Romoosh

11¹²ᵍᶠ 5⁹ᶠ 7¹⁴ᵍᶠ **0-0-3**

I'm Aimee *P D Evans* 75 a71
2 ch f Timeless Times (USA) - Marfen
2⁵ˢᵈ 6⁵ˢ 3⁵ᵍˢ 7⁵ᵍˢ 4⁵ᵍᶠ 7⁵ᵍᶠ 2⁵ᵍ 2⁵ˢ 2⁵ᵍᶠ
2⁶ᵍᶠ 3⁶ʰʸ 7⁵ᵍ 4⁵ˢ 4⁵ᶠ 5⁶ᵍ **0-6-15 £11,979**

I'm Dancing *T D Easterby* 64 a34
3 b f Polish Precedent (USA) - Dancing Heights (Ire)
7⁸ˢᵈ 2¹⁰ˢ **0-1-2 £1,169**

I'm So Lucky *M Johnston* 91
2 b c Zilzal (USA) - City Of Angels
7⁶ᵍ 1⁷ᵍ 8⁹ᶠ 4⁸ˢ **1-1-4 £6,382**

Iam Foreverblowing *S C Burrough* 48
2 ch f Dr Fong (USA) - Farhana
5⁵ˢ 4⁵ˢ 5⁶ᶠ 10⁶ˢᵈ 15⁵ᵍᶠ 11⁶ᵍᶠ 9⁵ᵍ **0-0-7**
£630

Iamback *Miss Gay Kelleway* 35 a54
4 b f Perugino (USA) - Smouldering (Ire)
2⁹ˢᵈ 6⁷ˢᵈ 1⁸ˢˢ 6⁹ˢʷ 7⁸ˢʷ 4⁸ˢᵈ 3⁸ˢˢ 8⁸ᵍˢ
1⁹ˢᵈ 1⁹ˢᵈ 9¹⁰ˢᵈ 9⁹ˢᵈ 15⁷ᵍ 12⁹ˢᵈ 6⁸ˢᵈ **3-1-15**
£5,161

Ianina (Ire) *R Rohne* 101
4 b f Eagle Eyed (USA) - Ice Dream (Ger)
6⁸ᵍ 7⁸ʰʸ 7⁸ᵍᶠ 2⁸ᵍ 2⁸ᵍ 3⁸ᵍᶠ 5⁸ᶠ 8⁸ˢ **0-0-8**
£7,993

Iberus (Ger) *S Gollings* 73
6 b g Monsun (Ger) - Iberica (Ger)
25⁸ᵍ 18¹⁰ᵍˢ 7⁷ᶠ 5⁷ᵍ 4⁸ᵍᶠ 2¹¹ᵍ 7¹²ᵍᶠ
10¹⁰ᵍ 4⁸ʰʸ **0-1-9 £1,902**

Icannshift (Ire) *S Dow* 62 a58
4 b g Night Shift (USA) - Cannikin (Ire)
10⁷ˢᵈ 9¹⁰ˢᵈ 6¹⁰ˢᵈ 8¹⁰ᵍˢ 2¹⁰ˢ 1¹⁰ᵍˢ 3¹⁰ˢ
12¹⁰ᵍᶠ 3¹⁰ᵍᶠ 6⁹ᵍ 3¹⁰ᵍᶠ 11¹⁰ˢᵈ 3¹⁰ᵍˢ 10¹⁰ᵍᶠ 4¹⁰ᵍᶠ
2¹¹ᵍᶠ 6⁹ᵍᶠ 5⁸ᵍ **1-6-18 £8,547**

Icarus Dream (Ire) *P R Hedger* 73
3 ch g Intikhab (USA) - Nymphs Echo (Ire)
4⁸ᵍᶠ 6⁹ᵍʸ 2⁹ᶠ 10¹²ᶠ 2⁹ᵍ 11¹⁰ᵍᶠ 9¹¹ᵍ
10¹⁶ᵍˢ **0-1-8 £2,657**

Ice And Fire *B D Leavy* a4
5 b g Cadeaux Genereux - Tanz (Ire)
10¹¹ˢˢ **0-0-1**

Ice Dragon *M H Tompkins* 49
3 b f Polar Falcon (USA) - Qilin (Ire)
7⁷ᶠ 8⁷ˢ **0-0-2**

Ice Palace *J R Fanshawe* 102
4 ch f Polar Falcon (USA) - White Palace
3⁸ᵍᶠ 2⁸ᵍᶠ 1¹⁰ˢ 4¹⁰ʰʸ 17⁹ᵍ **1-2-5**
£28,211

Ice Planet *D Nicholls* 68
3 b c Polar Falcon (USA) - Preference
15⁷ᵍˢ 3⁵ˢ 5⁷ᵍ 14⁶ˢ 5⁶ˢ **0-1-5 £830**

Ice Ruby *D Shaw* 32 a7
2 b f Polar Prince (Ire) - Simply Style
9⁵ᵍ 9⁵ᵍ 7⁵ˢᵈ **0-0-3**

Icecap *W G M Turner* 58
4 b f Polar Falcon (USA) - Warning Light
16⁸ˢᵈ 1⁷ᶠ 13⁸ᵍᶠ 15⁷ᵍ 7⁷ᵍᶠ **1-0-5**
£5,499

Iced Diamond (Ire) *W M Brisbourne* 59 a62
5 b g Petardia - Prime Site (Ire)
1⁷ˢᵈ 9⁷ˢˢ 7⁸ᵍᶠ 7⁷ᵍᶠ 7⁸ᵍ 9⁷ᵍᶠ 4⁷ᵍᶠ 4⁸ᵍᶠ
7⁷ᵍ 2⁷ᵍ 6⁷ᵍᶠ 5⁷ˢᵈ **1-1-12 £4,961**

Iceman *J H M Gosden* 117
2 b c Polar Falcon (USA) - Virtuous
2⁵ˢ 1⁶ᵍ 1⁶ᵍᶠ 2⁷ᵍᶠ 3⁶ᵍ 4⁷ˢ **2-3-6**
£104,322

Icenaslice (Ire) *J J Quinn* 74 a52
3 b f Fayruz - Come Dancing
9⁵ᵍˢ 1⁵ᵍ 1⁵ˢ 8⁵ᵍᶠ 4⁵ᵍᶠ 9⁵ˢ 4⁵ˢ
2-1-8 £9,130

Iceni Warrior *T G Mills* a57
2 b g Lake Coniston (Ire) - Swing Job
5⁵ˢᵈ **0-0-1**

Icey Run *D G Bridgwater* 34 a42
4 b g Runnett - Polar Storm (Ire)
7¹⁴ᶠ 6¹⁶ˢᵈ **0-0-2**

Icing *W J Haggas* 64 a77
2 br f Polar Falcon (USA) - Dance Steppe
6⁶ᵍ 4⁶ˢᵈ 1⁷ˢᵈ 11⁷ᵍ **1-0-4 £5,473**

Idealistic (Ire) *L M Cumani* 83
3 b f Unfuwain (USA) - L'Ideale (USA)
10¹⁰ᵍ 2¹¹ᵍᶠ 2¹²ᵍᶠ 2¹¹ᵍᶠ 1¹²ᵍᶠ **1-3-5**
£7,713

Idle Journey (Ire) *M Scudamore* 51
3 b g Mujadil (USA) - Camassina (Ire)
18⁶ʰʸ 13⁷ᵍᶠ 1⁷ᵍᶠ 2⁸ᵍ 10⁸ʰʸ 4⁸ᵍ 8¹⁰ᵍˢ
1-1-7 £5,513

Idle Power (Ire) *J R Boyle* 89 a89
6 b g Common Grounds - Idle Fancy
8⁶ᵍˢ 10⁸ᵍˢ 1⁶ᵍ 1⁷ᶠ 14⁶ᵍ 2⁷ᵍ 3⁷ᵍ 8⁶ᵍ
9⁶ᵍᶠ 2⁷ᵍˢ 1⁷ˢᵈ 1⁷ᵍ 11⁷ˢᵈ 9⁶ˢᵈ **4-3-14**
£28,741

If By Chance *R Craggs* 76 a56
6 ch g Risk Me (Fr) - Out Of Harmony
10⁶ˢʷ 2⁶ᵍˢ 4⁶ˢ 4⁶ˢ 1⁶ᵍ 8⁵ᵍᶠ 15⁵ᵍᶠ 8⁶ˢᵈ
4⁵ˢ **1-3-9 £8,636**

If Paradise *R Hannon* 105
3 b c Compton Place - Sunley Stars
1⁵ˢ 9⁶ᵍ 6⁵ᵍ 13⁵ᵍᶠ 9⁵ᵍᶠ 9⁵ᵍᶠ 2⁵ᵍᶠ 2⁵ˢ 8⁶ˢ
1-2-9 £27,384

Iffraaj *M A Jarvis* 94
3 b c Zafonic (USA) - Pastorale
4⁷ᵍ **0-1-1 £746**

Iffy *P D Cundell* 66 a59
3 b g Orpen (USA) - Hopesay
4⁷ˢᵈ 7⁸ᵍ 4⁹ᵍ 1¹⁰ᵍᶠ 8⁹ˢᵈ **1-2-6**
£6,425

Ifit (Ire) *M R Channon* 54
2 b f Inchinor - Robin
12⁷ᵍᶠ 8⁶ᵍᶠ 9⁷ᵍ 10⁸ᵍᶠ 3⁷ᵍ **0-1-5 £508**

Ifteradh *B Hanbury* 96 a77
3 b c Bahhare (USA) - Matila (Ire)
1⁷ˢᵈ 2⁷ᵍ **1-1-2 £5,961**

Iftikhar (USA) *W M Brisbourne* 55
5 b g Storm Cat (USA) - Muhbubh (USA)
9¹¹ᵍᶠ 16⁸ᵍ 14¹¹ˢ 4¹⁰ᵍᶠ 7¹⁰ᵍᶠ 10¹⁰ᵍᶠ 14⁹ᵍˢ
12¹⁰ˢ **0-0-8 £319**

Ignition *W M Brisbourne* 58
2 ch f Rock City - Fire Sprite
5⁶ᵍᶠ 4⁷ˢ 3⁷ᵍˢ 4⁷ᶠ 10⁷ᶠ 10⁷ᵍ **0-1-6**
£1,176

Ikan (Ire) *N P Littmoden* 92 a75
4 br f Sri Pekan (USA) - Iktidar
10⁵ˢᵈ 3⁵ᵍˢ 9⁵ᵍ 16⁵ᵍˢ **0-1-4 £1,451**

Ikhtyar (Ire) *J H M Gosden* 122
4 b c Unfuwain (USA) - Sabria (USA)
3⁸ˢ 6⁸ᵍ 2¹⁰ᵍˢ 3¹⁰ᵍᶠ 6¹⁰ᵍˢ 3¹⁰ᵍᶠ **0-2-6**
£72,935

Iktibas *Saeed Bin Suroor* 89
3 b c Sadler's Wells (USA) - Bint Shadayid (USA)
1⁸ᵍ 5¹⁰ˢ **1-0-2 £4,936**

4^{12sd} 6^{12ss} 3^{12sw} 3^{12sw} **0-1-4 £1,301**

Iktitaf (Ire) *J H M Gosden* 88
3 b c Alhaarth (Ire) - Istibshar (USA)
8^{8gf} 3^{10g} 1^{10gs} 7^{10gf} 13^{10g} 3^{10s} **1-2-6**
£9,966

Il Cavaliere *K G Reveley* 52
9 b g Mtoto - Kalmia
5^{16hy} 8^{17gf} **0-0-2**

Il Colosseo (Ire) *Mrs L Stubbs* 78 a78
2 b g Spectrum (Ire) - Valley Lights (Ire)
3^{7gs} 4^{7gs} 1^{7sd} **1-1-3 £4,825**

Il Pranzo *S Kirk* 71 a68
2 b c Piccolo - St Helena
8^{5sd} 6^{5gs} 3^{5g} 5^{5gf} 7^{6g} 4^{5gs} 1^{5sd} 3^{5s}
12^{6sd} **1-2-9 £3,404**

Ile Facile (Ire) *N P Littmoden* 76 a73
3 b c Turtle Island (Ire) - Easy Pop (Ire)
2^{6sd} 4^{7sd} 2^{7sd} 4^{7sd} 1^{6sd} 9^{8sd} 2^{10gf} 7^{10g}
4^{11g} 1^{12gf} 4^{11gf} 5^{10gf} **2-3-12 £11,036**

Ile Michel *J G M O'Shea* 80 a70
7 b g Machiavellian (USA) - Circe's Isle
8^{8sw} 16^{7g} 4^{10g} 3^{10gf} 8^{8gf} 15^{8gf} 5^{7sd} 6^{7sd}
9^{7sd} **0-0-9 £1,355**

Illeana (Ger) *W R Muir* 63 a63
3 ch f Lomitas - Illyria (Ire)
4^{10gs} 7^{10g} 14^{12s} 1^{12g} 9^{11gf} 3^{12sd} 11^{16gf}
8^{16g} 6^{12sd} **1-1-9 £3,363**

Illicium (Ire) *Mrs M Reveley* 41
5 b m Fourstars Allstar (USA) - Sweet Mignonette
6^{12gf} 9^{8gs} 7^{12g} PU^{14gf} **0-0-4**

Illusionist *Mrs N Macauley* a16
6 b g Mujtahid (USA) - Merlin's Fancy
9^{7sd} 5^{9ss} 5^{12ss} **0-0-3**

Illusive (Ire) *M Wigham* 67 a67
7 b g Night Shift (USA) - Mirage
12^{6sd} 15^{6sd} 3^{6sd} 5^{7sd} 11^{6sd} 7^{6sd} 2^{7sd}
2^{7sd} 6^{2gf} 9^{6sd} 13^{5gf} 4^{6f} 14^{6gf} 5^{6sd}
0-4-15 £3,652

Illustrious Duke *M Mullineaux* a45
6 b g Dancing Spree (USA) - Killick
13^{6sd} 10^{7sd} 10^{9sw} 11^{8ss} 6^{7ss} 11^{8sd} 2^{7sd}
7^{6sd} **0-1-8 £423**

Illustrious Miss (USA) *D R Loder* 111
3 b f Kingmambo - Our Wildirish Rose (USA)
1^{7g} 1^{7s} 3^{8gf} 5^{8gf} **2-1-4 £66,047**

Iloveturtle (Ire) *M C Chapman* 52 a42
4 b g Turtle Island (Ire) - Gan Ainm (Ire)
14^{12g} 3^{14sf} 5^{12gf} UR^{12gf} 6^{12gf} 6^{16gs} **0-0-6**
£206

Iltravitore (Ire) *D R C Elsworth* 57
3 ch g Daggers Drawn (USA) - May Hinton
7^{7gf} 8^{7gf} 5^{6s} 14^{5g} 14^{6gf} 11^{6gs} **0-0-6**

Ilwadod *M R Channon* 64
3 b g Cadeaux Genereux - Wedoudah (Ire)
1^{10s} 2^{8hy} 2^{12g} 2^{14f} 2^{12gf} 7^{14g} **1-4-6**
£8,285

Im Spartacus *I A Wood* 78 a30
2 b g Namaqualand (USA) - Captivating (Ire)
8^{5sd} 2^{5g} 1^{5gf} 6^{6gs} 5^{6gf} 9^{6g} 6^{7gs} 5^{7gf}
4^{7gf} 5^{13g} 4^{7gf} 2^{8g} 5^{3s} **2-2-14 £18,188**

Impeller (Ire) *W R Muir* 101
5 ch g Polish Precedent (USA) - Almaaseh (Ire)
10^{8g} 7^{8g} 2^{8gf} 6^{9g} 9^{8gf} 5^{8g} 2^{10g} 2^{8gf}
1^{10g} 3^{10gf} 11^{9g} 2^{8gs} **1-5-12 £65,290**

Imperative (USA) *M J Gingell* a58
4 ch g Woodman (USA) - Wandesta

Imperatrice *R M H Cowell* 41
2 b f Emperor Jones (USA) - Fine Honor (Fr)
15^{5sd} 6^{6gf} 6^{5f} 17^{6gf} **0-0-4**

Imperial Dancer *M R Channon* 119
6 b h Primo Dominie - Gorgeous Dancer (Ire)
3^{12g} 6^{10g} 9^{12g} 7^{10gs} 3^{10g} 7^{10g} 3^{9g} 6^{10g}
2^{11g} 14^{12g} 5^{12s} 2^{10s} **0-4-12 £126,357**

Imperial Dragon (USA) *W A O'Gorman* 56 a44
4 b g Meadowlake (USA) - South Cove
9^{8sd} 4^{7s} 10^{7sd} **0-0-3 £275**

Imperial Dynasty (USA) *T D Barron* 60
2 b c Devil's Bag (USA) - Leasears (USA)
9^{6gs} 5^{6f} 10^{7s} 11^{7gf} **0-0-4**

Imperial Echo (USA) *T D Barron* 91
3 b g Labeeb - Regal Baby (USA)
7^{7g} 9^{6gf} 4^{6gf} 9^{6gf} 2^{6g} 2^{5g} 17^{5gf} 3^{6f} 4^{5s}
1^{6gs} 3^{6s} 4^{6s} 5^{5gs} **1-5-13 £16,915**

Imperial Miss (Ire) *B W Duke* 65
2 b f Imperial Ballet (Ire) - Miss Flite (Ire)
11^{6gf} 6^{6gf} 8^{7gf} 6^{7gf} 11^{7gf} 17^{7gf} **0-0-6**

Imperial Princess (Ire) *D K Ivory* a11
3 b f Imperial Ballet (Ire) - Rose Tint (Ire)
13^{6sd} **0-0-1**

Imperial Royale (Ire) *P L Clinton* 61 a47
3 ch g Ali-Royal (Ire) - God Speed Her
5^{12g} 9^{12g} 6^{10gs} 10^{12gf} 8^{10gf} 13^{12s} 10^{10gf}
12^{8g} 7^{9sd} **0-0-9**

Imperial Sound *T D Barron* 90
2 b c Efisio - Final Trick
1^{5gf} 2^{5gf} 10^{5g} 1^{6gf} 17^{6g} 6^{5gf} **2-1-6**
£12,245

Imperial Stride *Sir Michael Stoute* 101
3 b c Indian Ridge - Place De L'Opera
4^{8g} 7^{9s} 9^{8gs} **0-0-3 £2,500**

Imperial Wizard *M D I Usher* 39 a30
3 ch g Magic Ring (Ire) - Paula's Joy
10^{6sd} 8^{5gf} 10^{6s} 9^{6f} 14^{7gf} **0-0-5**

Imperialistic (Ire) *K R Burke* 102
3 b f Imperial Ballet (Ire) - Shefoog
4^{7g} 1^{8s} 1^{7gs} 8^{9g} 5^{8s} 5^{8gs} 3^{8hy} 7^{8s} 6^{10s}
2-2-9 £24,771

Imperioli *P A Blockley* 39
2 b c Fraam - Jussoli
13^{7gf} 6^{8s} 18^{8s} **0-0-3**

Imperium *Mrs Stef Liddiard* 76 a73
3 b g Imperial Ballet (Ire) - Partenza (USA)
4^{7sd} 7^{6sd} 2^{5sd} 11^{6s} 12^{5gs} 5^{6s} 15^{6f} 15^{6gf}
3^{5g} 12^{5gf} 7^{5gf} 10^{6sd} 2^{5g} 19^{5gf} 2^{5f} VOI^{5gf}
3^{5s} 14^{5gf} **2-3-18 £11,834**

Impersonator *J L Dunlop* 84
4 b g Zafonic (USA) - Conspiracy
10^{8gs} 4^{8s} 3^{8g} 3^{8gs} 7^{10g} 3^{10s} **0-2-6**
£3,041

Impish Jude *J Mackie* 47
6 b m Imp Society (USA) - Miss Nanna
4^{14s} **0-1-1 £293**

Impressive Flight (Ire) *T D Barron* 88
5 b m Flying Spur (Aus) - Certain Impression (USA)
8^{6gf} 12^{6s} 11^{5gf} 6^{5f} 7^{6gf} 8^{6g} **0-0-7**
£395

Improvise *C E Brittain* 78 a70
2 b f Lend A Hand - Mellow Jazz
6^{6gf} 2^{7sd} 2^{6gf} **0-2-3 £2,896**

Impulsive Bid (Ire) *Jedd O'Keeffe* 66

3 b f Orpen (USA) - Tamburello (Ire)
4^{6gs} 12^{6g} 2^{7hy} 15^{7g} 5^{7g} 9^{10gs} 11^{8gf} 9^{11g}
0-1-8 £1,597

Imshy (Ire) *R Pritchard-Gordon*   62
3 ch f Daggers Drawn (USA) - Paganina (Fr)
12^{6vs} 6^{6gs} 2^{6gs} 4^{6vs} 4^{6g} 13^{6s} 0-1-6
£7,183

Imtalkinggibberish *J R Jenkins*   82 a59
3 b g Pursuit Of Love - Royal Orchid (Ire)
7^{7gs} 5^{7gs} 8^{7gf} 2^{6gf} 11^{6s} 5^{6gf} 4^{6gs} 2^{6sd}
5^{7sd} 0-2-9 £2,771

Imtihan (Ire) *S C Burrough*   44
5 ch h Unfuwain (USA) - Azyaa
7^{11s} 11^{18g} 0-0-2

Imtiyaz (USA) *Saeed Bin Suroor*   113
5 ro h Woodman (USA) - Shadayid (USA)
2^{8gf} 2^{10gs} 4^{10gf} 0-2-3 £10,712

Imtouchingwood *P R Hedger*
3 b f Fleetwood (Ire) - Shanuke (Ire)
17^{10gf} 0-0-1

In Deep *Mrs P N Dutfield*   67
3 b f Deploy - Bobbie Dee
8^{10g} 15^{10g} 6^{12gs} 8^{10g} 2^{10g} 0-1-5 £1,780

In Dream'S (Ire) *B Gubby*   59 a53
2 b g Dr Fong (USA) - No Sugar Baby (Fr)
8^{5g} 15^{6gf} 8^{8gf} 5^{6s} 8^{7sd} 0-0-5

In Every Street (USA) *J-P Gallorini*   47 a37
3 br f Favorite Trick (USA) - Hit The Bid (USA)
7^{8sd} 6^{10gf} 0-0-2

In Excelsis (USA) *A P O'Brien*   97
2 b c Fusaichi Pegasus (USA) - Lakeway (USA)
1^{5hy} 5^{7f} 5^{7y} 1-0-3 £13,779

In Luck *B Smart*   a14
6 b m In The Wings - Lucca
7^{12sd} 0-0-1

In Rhubarb *I W McInnes*   45
2 ch g Piccolo - Versami (USA)
6^{5g} 8^{5gf} 7^{5g} 0-0-3

In Spirit (Ire) *B J Curley*
6 b g Distinctly North (USA) - June Goddess
9^{12sd} 0-0-1

In The Fan (USA) *J L Dunlop*   92
2 b g Lear Fan (USA) - Dippers (USA)
2^{7gf} 1^{7g} 3^{7gf} 2^{8g} 1-3-4 £9,201

In The Know *J H M Gosden*   48
2 b c Desert Prince (Ire) - Evocatrice
11^{6gs} 0-0-1

In The Lead (USA) *J L Dunlop*   59
2 b/br f Bahri (USA) - Air De Noblesse (USA)
7^{7g} 0-0-1

In The Pink (Ire) *M R Channon*   80
4 gr f Indian Ridge - Norfolk Lavender (Can)
8^{7hy} 17^{8gf} 1^{7gf} 2^{7g} 10^{7f} 2^{7gf} 7^{8gf} 4^{7s}
5^{7g} 3^{7gf} 1-3-10 £10,224

In The Shadows *W S Kittow*   36 a22
2 b f Lujain (USA) - Addicted To Love
7^{6gs} 12^{7gf} 13^{7sd} 0-0-3

In The Stars (Ire) *P R Webber*   a46
6 ch g Definite Article - Astronomer Lady (Ire)
8^{10sd} 0-0-1

In Tune *S C Burrough*   29 a9
4 b g Distinctly North (USA) - Lingering
14^{10g} 16^{10s} 13^{6sd} 8^{7gf} 10^{8g} 11^{10sd} 0-0-6

Inagh *M J Wallace*   62

2 b f Tipsy Creek (USA) - Compton Amber
6^{5f} 3^{6hy} 13^{9sd} 0-0-3 £549

Inca Wood (UAE) *M Johnston*   75
2 b f Timber Country (USA) - Lady Icarus
2^{8s} 2^{9g} 10^{8g} 4^{8s} 0-2-4 £3,270

Inch By Inch *P J Makin*   73 a72
5 b m Inchinor - Maid Welcome
7^{6gf} 4^{5sd} 18^{5g} 1^{5gf} 1^{5g} 1^{6gf} 1^{6sd} 4-0-7
£13,819

Inchcape Rock *L G Cottrell*   73 a30
2 ch c Inchinor - Washm (USA)
8^{5g} 9^{7sd} 12^{6gs} 2^{8s} 10^{10g} 0-1-5 £1,090

Inchconnel *V Smith*   19
3 b g Inchinor - Sharanella
11^{10g} 8^{12gs} 15^{10s} 0-0-3

Inchcoonan *K R Burke*   a52
6 b m Emperor Jones (USA) - Miss Ivory Coast (USA)
4^{8sd} 4^{7sd} 2^{6sw} 2^{7sw} 0-2-4 £1,052

Inchdura *N Tinkler*   70 a64
6 ch g Inchinor - Sunshine Coast
11^{7s} 14^{7g} 6^{7gs} 9^{8g} 12^{10g} 5^{9sd} 0-0-6

Incheni (Ire) *G Wragg*   102
3 b f Nashwan (USA) - Inchmurrin
2^{7g} 14^{8g} 3^{8gf} 1^{10gf} 4^{10g} 6^{10gf} 1-2-6
£34,875

Inching *R M H Cowell*   56 a53
4 b f Inchinor - Tshusick
4^{5sw} 4^{6sd} 9^{6sd} 8^{5ss} 14^{6gf} 17^{5gf} 2^{5gf} 6^{5gf}
7^{5f} 2^{5gf} 9^{5gf} 9^{5g} 0-2-12 £2,183

Inchinnan *James Moffatt*   58 a60
7 b m Inchinor - Westering
5^{10sd} 10^{9g} 5^{12hy} 0-0-3

Inchloss (Ire) *B A McMahon*   88
3 b g Imperial Ballet (Ire) - Earth Charter
11^{7g} 4^{8s} 1^{6s} 2^{8gs} 10^{8gf} 10^{7f} 6^{8g} 1^{8g}
2^{8gf} 2^{8g} 4^{10gs} 12^{10g} 16^{10g} 2-3-13 £20,676

Inchnadamph *T J Fitzgerald*   70
4 b g Inchinor - Pelf (USA)
6^{10hy} 2^{11gs} 2^{11g} 1^{13g} 1^{13g} 5^{12gf} 8^{14g} 2^{14s}
2-3-8 £10,908

Inchpast *M H Tompkins*   83
3 ch c Inchinor - Victor Ludorum
14^{8s} 15^{12gs} 4^{12gf} 1^{11g} 2^{12gf} 1^{12gs} 1^{14gf}
1^{14f} 4-1-8 £20,980

Incise *B J Meehan*   89
3 ch f Dr Fong (USA) - Pretty Sharp
6^{5g} 7^{5s} 10^{5g} 4^{5gf} 4^{5gf} 8^{5gf} 5^{5g} 0-0-7
£1,648

Incisor *S Kirk*   55 a78
3 b g Dracula (Aus) - Last Night's Fun (Ire)
5^{10g} 1^{10gf} 1^{10sd} 1^{8sd} 13^{10gf} 3-0-5
£8,946

Incline (Ire) *R McGlinchey*   85 a87
5 b g Danehill (USA) - Shalwar Kameez (Ire)
6^{7sd} 5^{7hy} 9^{7y} 5^{8ys} 2^{7hy} 8^{8sh} 0-1-6
£1,700

Incroyable *Sir Mark Prescott*   72
3 gr f Linamix (Fr) - Crodelle (Ire)
2^{10g} 1^{10gs} 12^{12g} 1-1-3 £5,291

Incursion *A King*   87
3 b g Inchinor - Morgannwg (Ire)
1^{10s} 1^{10gf} 3^{10gf} 7^{12gs} 7^{12gs} 1-1-5
£4,585

Indalo Grey (Ire) *Mrs Stef Liddiard*   72 a61
8 b/br g Toca Madera - Pollyfaster

6^{14gy} 4^{14gf} 5^{16f} 5^{14sd} **0-0-4 £589**

Independent Spirit *R P Elliott* 36 a12
2 ch g Wolfhound (USA) - Kigema (Ire)
9^{5g} 10^{6g} 12^{5sd} 10^{7sd} **0-0-4**

Indi Ano Star (Ire) *D Carroll* 59
3 b g Indian Rocket - Audriano (Ire)
6^{7gs} 6^{8s} 6^{8hy} 8^{8gf} 5^{7gf} 5^{9g} 9^{10s} **0-0-7**

Indian Bazaar (Ire) *N E Berry* 57
8 ch g Indian Ridge - Bazaar Promise
15^{5gf} 10^{5gf} 2^{6g} 12^{5gf} 12^{5f} 2^{5g} 16^{6gf} 6^{5g} 13^{5gf} 9^{6gf} 10^{6gs} 11^{6gf} 9^{6f} 8^{5gf} 14^{5g} **0-2-15 £2,069**

Indian Blaze *Andrew Reid* 55 a58
10 ch g Indian Ridge - Odile
6^{13sd} 2^{10sd} 1^{8sd} 2^{10sd} 10^{8sd} 3^{8sd} 6^{8sd} 7^{8sd} 6^{9gf} 10^{10sd} 15^{8g} **1-3-11 £5,027**

Indian Call *B A McMahon* 34 a25
3 ch g Classic Cliche (Ire) - Crees Sqaw
11^{10g} 18^{10gs} 11^{7gs} 12^{9sd} **0-0-4**

Indian Chase *Dr J R J Naylor* 51 a48
7 b g Terimon - Icy Gunner
2^{16sd} 6^{14gs} 12^{10gs} 9^{18gf} 8^{12gs} 4^{16gf} 8^{16sd} 1^{18gs} 2^{16sd} 10^{16sd} **1-2-10 £5,025**

Indian Dove (Ire) *G A Butler* 43 a48
2 b f Indian Danehill (Ire) - African Dance (USA)
6^{8sd} 10^{8s} **0-0-2**

Indian Edge *B Palling* 71 a53
3 ch g Indian Rocket - Beveled Edge
9^{7sd} 5^{6s} 2^{6s} 11^{7gf} 12^{6gf} 9^{6gs} 11^{8g} 8^{6sd} **0-1-8 £1,154**

Indian Haven *P W D'Arcy* 109
4 ch c Indian Ridge - Madame Dubois
5^{8gs} 9^{8g} 6^{7gs} **0-0-3 £2,500**

Indian Lily *C F Wall* 50
3 ch f Compton Place - Princess Lily
5^{6gs} 9^{7s} 6^{5s} 7^{6f} 7^{6g} 7^{6gs} 10^{7g} 15^{10gf} **0-0-8**

Indian Maiden (Ire) *M S Saunders* 73 a42
4 br f Indian Ridge - Jinsiyah (USA)
11^{6sd} 4^{6gf} 11^{6g} 11^{6g} 1^{6g} **1-0-5 £3,882**

Indian Music *A Berry* 45 a61
7 b g Indian Ridge - Dagny Juel (USA)
6^{8ss} 1^{6sd} 5^{6gs} 4^{6sd} 4^{6sf} 3^{7sd} 3^{6sd} 2^{6sd} 4^{7sd} 6^{6sd} 2^{6sd} 7^{6sd} 12^{6gf} 6^{6sd} 5^{6hy} 10^{6s} 10^{6s} **1-2-17 £3,503**

Indian Oak (Ire) *M P Muggeridge* a26
3 b f Indian Rocket - Marathon Maid
8^{5sd} 7^{5sd} 13^{7sd} 14^{7sd} **0-0-4**

Indian Pearl (Ire) *R J Hodges*
2 b f Indian Lodge (Ire) - Thatchabella (Ire)
8^{5f} **0-0-1**

Indian Pipe Dream (Ire) *J H M Gosden* 63
2 br c Indian Danehill (Ire) - Build A Dream (USA)
9^{8g} 6^{8gs} **0-0-2**

Indian Shores *M Mullineaux* 38 a40
5 b m Forzando - Cottonwood
9^{6sd} 9^{6sd} 6^{5ss} 8^{7ss} 9^{5ss} 12^{6sd} 18^{7gf} 16^{6g} 10^{6gs} 9^{12sd} **0-0-10**

Indian Smoke *J A Pickering* 33
2 b g Makbul - Indian Flower
16^{5gf} **0-0-1**

Indian Solitaire (Ire) *B P J Baugh* 80
5 b g Bigstone (Ire) - Terrama Sioux
3^{12g} 9^{12gs} 6^{10gf} 7^{10g} 9^{12s} **0-1-5 £549**

Indian Spark *J S Goldie* 96
10 ch g Indian Ridge - Annes Gift
4^{5g} 7^{6gs} 4^{6gs} 4^{5gf} 6^{6gs} 11^{6f} 11^{5s} 10^{6g} 9^{6gf} 6^{6gf} 8^{6g} 23^{6s} 7^{5gf} 9^{6s} **0-0-14 £3,103**

Indian Steppes (Fr) *Julian Poulton* 75
5 b m Indian Ridge - Ukraine Venture
6^{6g} 6^{7gf} 4^{6gf} 3^{6gf} 7^{6g} 6^{6gf} 3^{6g} **0-2-7 £2,118**

Indian Trail *D R C Elsworth* 96
4 ch g Indian Ridge - Take Heart
9^{7gf} 1^{6g} **1-0-2 £8,755**

Indian Warrior *J Jay* 44 a51
8 b g Be My Chief (USA) - Wanton
1^{7sd} 9^{7sd} 10^{7ss} 4^{6sd} 8^{6sw} 5^{6sd} 5^{7sd} 15^{7hy} 14^{8gf} 3^{6gs} **1-1-10 £1,686**

Indian Welcome *H Morrison* a68
5 ch g Most Welcome - Qualitair Ridge
8^{8sd} **0-0-1**

Indian Well (Ire) *S Kirk* 49
2 b g Indian Lodge (Ire) - Pride Of Pendle
14^{7gs} **0-0-1**

Indian's Landing (Ire) *K A Morgan* 72
3 b g Barathea (Ire) - We'Ve Just Begun (USA)
21^{5gf} 19^{8gf} 14^{10gf} 10^{10gs} 3^{10hy} 5^{10s} **0-1-6 £758**

Indiana Blues *A M Balding* 73 a68
3 ch f Indian Ridge - Blue Siren
4^{7gf} 11^{6gf} 7^{5gf} 3^{8gf} 5^{7gf} 3^{6gs} 4^{6gs} 3^{6f} 2^{7f} 1^{6gf} 3^{7sd} **1-5-11 £8,845**

Indiannie Star *M R Channon* 91
2 b f Fraam - Ajig Dancer
2^{5g} 1^{5gf} 6^{5gf} 13^{5gf} 5^{5g} 1^{5g} 3^{6g} 5^{7gf} **2-2-8 £18,228**

Indibar (Ire) *Evan Williams* 6
3 b g Indian Ridge - Barbara Frietchie (Ire)
8^{10f} **0-0-1**

Indibraun (Ire) *P C Haslam* 76 a45
2 b g Indian Rocket - The Aspecto Girl (Ire)
5^{5gs} 1^{6gf} 4^{6gf} 4^{7gf} 8^{7sd} 3^{7s} 4^{7gf} 12^{6gs} 6^{6sd} **1-1-9 £5,977**

Indiena *B J Meehan* 76 a55
2 ch f Indian Ridge - Aliena (Ire)
4^{6gs} 5^{6g} 2^{6g} 4^{6g} 2^{7g} 3^{6gf} 5^{6sd} **0-3-7 £11,777**

Individual Talents (USA) *S C Williams* 60
4 ch f Distant View (USA) - Indigenous (USA)
8^{12s} 16^{14g} 8^{12gf} **0-0-3**

Indonesia *M Johnston* 69
2 ch c Lomitas - Idraak
8^{8gs} 8^{9f} 5^{8g} **0-0-3**

Indrani *John A Harris* 46 a45
3 b f Bijou D'Inde - Tea And Scandals (USA)
13^{6sd} 6^{7sd} 4^{6ss} 8^{6sd} 7^{5sd} 4^{6sd} 7^{6sd} 2^{6hy} 8^{6sd} 5^{6g} 9^{6gf} 8^{6gf} 9^{6gs} 2^{6hy} 13^{7g} **0-2-15 £1,654**

Indrapura Star (USA) *Miss J Feilden*
4 b g Foxhound (USA) - Royal Recall (USA)
6^{8ss} 7^{10sd} **0-0-2**

Inescapable (USA) *W R Muir* 57
3 b c Cape Town (USA) - Danyross (Ire)
9^{6gf} 8^{6gf} 4^{7g} 19^{7g} 1^{7gs} 8^{8g} 14^{7g} **1-0-7 £3,389**

Infidelity (Ire) *A Bailey* 61 a58
3 b f Bluebird (USA) - Madaniyya (USA)
6^{10sd} 8^{10sd} 10^{10g} 8^{12gs} 6^{10gf} 10^{10gf} 6^{9gf} 3^{9g} 5^{12g} 16^{10gf} 4^{10g} 9^{9sd} 4^{9sd} **0-1-13 £1,246**

Ingleton *B A McMahon*   97
2 b c Komaite (USA) - Dash Cascade
7⁵ᵍ 4⁶ᵍᶠ 1⁶ᵍˢ 1⁶ᵍ 1⁶ˢ **3-0-5 £22,131**

Inglewood *C W Thornton*   a16
4 ch g Fleetwood (Ire) - Preening
7¹⁵ˢᵈ **0-0-1**

Ingrandire (Jpn) *Y Shimizu*   120
5 b h White Muzzle - Marilyn Momoko (Jpn)
2¹²ˢʸ 1¹⁶ᶠ 9²⁰ᵍᶠ **1-0-3 £790,273**

Inistrahull Island (Ire) *M H Tompkins*   1 a65
4 b g Flying Spur (Aus) - Dolcezza (Fr)
3⁶ˢᵈ 6⁷ˢᵈ 11⁸ˢᵈ 6⁶ᵍᶠ 15⁸ᵍˢ **0-1-5 £423**

Ink In Gold (Ire) *P A Blockley*   55 a48
3 b g Intikhab (USA) - Your Village (Ire)
10⁸ᵍᶠ 5⁷ʰʸ 9¹²ᵍˢ 11⁸ʰʸ 11⁷ˢˢ 4⁹ˢᵈ 3⁹ˢᵈ
0-1-7 £213

Inka Dancer (Ire) *B Palling*   69
2 ch f Intikhab (USA) - Grannys Reluctance (Ire)
3⁶ᵍ 4⁶ᵍ 3⁶ᵍ **0-2-3 £1,709**

Inmom (Ire) *S R Bowring*   63 a57
3 b f Barathea (Ire) - Zakuska
3⁸ˢ 11¹²ᵍᶠ 4⁸ˢᵈ 6¹⁰ᵍ 6¹⁰ᵍᶠ 14⁸ˢᵈ 18¹⁰ᵍˢ
6¹⁰ˢ **0-0-8 £1,042**

Inn For The Dancer *J A Glover*   a58
2 b g Groom Dancer (USA) - Lady Joyce (Fr)
8⁹ˢᵈ **0-0-1**

Innclassic (Ire) *Jane Southcombe*   66 a65
3 b f Stravinsky (USA) - Kyka (USA)
10⁶ᵍ 17⁶ᵍ 3⁶ˢᵈ 1⁶ᵍᶠ 2⁵ˢᵈ 8⁵ᵍᶠ 9⁵ᵍᶠ 15⁶ᵍ
7⁵ˢᵈ 9⁵ˢᵈ **1-2-10 £4,585**

Innocent Rebel (Ire) *E A L Dunlop*   60 a66
3 ch c Swain (Ire) - Cadeaux D'Amie (USA)
8⁸ᵍ 4¹⁰ˢᵈ 3¹⁰ᵍ 10¹⁴ᵍˢ **0-1-4 £906**

Innocent Splendour *E A L Dunlop*   79
2 b f Mtoto - Maureena (USA)
2⁷ᵍᶠ 1⁷ᵍ 7⁸ᵍ **1-1-3 £5,101**

Innpursuit *J M P Eustace*   a65
2 b c Inchinor - Quest For The Best
7⁹ˢᵈ **0-0-1**

Innstyle *J L Spearing*   67 a43
3 b f Daggers Drawn (USA) - Tarneem (USA)
6⁶ᵍᶠ 10⁵ᵍᶠ 7⁶ᵍᶠ 3⁶ᶠ 8⁶ᵍ 15⁶ᵍᶠ 1⁶ᵍˢ 9⁶ˢᵈ
10⁷ˢᵈ **1-1-9 £4,005**

Insignia (Ire) *J H M Gosden*   59 a50
2 b c Royal Applause - Amathea (Fr)
5⁵ᵍᶠ 5⁶ᵍᶠ 8⁶ˢᵈ **0-0-3**

Insignificance *John A Quinn*   51 a42
4 b g Bishop Of Cashel - Summer Pageant
7⁸ˢʷ 9⁸ˢᵈ 7⁵ʸ 2¹⁰ᵍ 5¹²ᵍᶠ 9⁷ᶠ **0-1-6**
£1,020

Insinuation (Ire) *Sir Michael Stoute*   70
2 b f Danehill (USA) - Hidden Meaning (USA)
6⁷ᵍ **0-0-1 £189**

Inspector Blue *T Keddy*   24
6 ch g Royal Academy (USA) - Blue Siren
10¹¹ᵍᶠ **0-0-1**

Instant Recall (Ire) *B J Meehan*   84 a88
3 ch c Indian Ridge - Happy Memories (Ire)
3⁷ˢᵈ 1⁷ˢᵈ 10⁷ᵍ 4⁶ˢ 5⁶ᵍ 5⁶ᵍᶠ 1⁶ˢᵈ
2⁶ᵍᶠ 4⁶ˢ 7⁶ᵍˢ 11⁷ˢᵈ **2-2-12 £13,694**

Instinct *R Hannon*   65 a52
3 b g Zafonic (USA) - Gracious Gift
5⁷ˢᵈ 7⁷ˢᵈ 3⁶ᵍˢ 9⁶ᵍˢ 10⁶ᵍ 12⁷ᵍ 3⁷ᵍᶠ 3⁸ᶠ
2⁶ᵍˢ 1⁶ᵍ 14⁶ˢ **1-3-11 £7,386**

Instructor *R Hannon*   74 a78

Insubordinate *J S Goldie*   65
3 ch g Subordination (USA) - Manila Selection (USA)
16⁸ᵍ 1⁷ʰʸ 8⁷ᵍˢ **1-0-3 £4,348**

3 ch g Groom Dancer (USA) - Doctor's Glory (USA)
2⁷ˢᵈ 1⁸ˢᵈ 16⁹ᵍ 8⁸ᵍˢ 10⁷ᵍ **1-1-5 £3,748**

Intavac Boy *C W Thornton*   69
3 ch g Emperor Fountain - Altaia (Fr)
6⁶ᵍ 6⁵ᵍᶠ 4⁵ᵍˢ 11⁶ᵍ 2⁸ᵍᶠ 2⁸ᵍ **0-2-6**
£2,492

Intellibet One *P D Evans*   65
4 b f Compton Place - Safe House
15⁶ᵍᶠ 11⁵ᵍ 15⁶ᵍ 5⁶ᵍˢ 9⁶ᵍᶠ 21⁵ᵍ
10⁵ᵍᶠ **0-2-8 £879**

Intended *A M Balding*   65
2 b f Singspiel (Ire) - Introducing
11⁷ᵍ **0-0-1**

Intensity *S B Bell*   64 a62
8 b g Bigstone (Ire) - Brillante (Fr)
3¹²ˢᵈ 9¹¹ˢˢ 16¹⁰ᵍ 2¹⁴ᵍ 11¹²ᵍᶠ **0-2-5**
£1,336

Inter Vision (USA) *A Dickman*   93
4 b g Cryptoclearance (USA) - Fateful (USA)
11⁵ᵍᶠ 14⁶ˢ 5⁶ᵍᶠ 11⁶ᵍ 7⁶ᵍˢ 4⁶ᵍᶠ 2⁶ᵍᶠ
10⁷ᶠ 7⁵ᵍᶠ 10⁶ᵍᶠ **0-1-10 £4,412**

Interceptor *J W Hills*   74
4 ch c Hector Protector (USA) - Moorish Idol
11¹⁰ᵍ **0-0-1**

Interim Payment (USA) *R Charlton*   70
2 b f Red Ransom (USA) - Interim
5⁸ᵍᶠ **0-0-1**

Internationalguest (Ire) *G G Margarson*   69 a88
5 b g Petardia - Banco Solo
11¹²ˢᵈ 2¹²ˢᵈ 14¹²ˢᵈ 8⁸ˢᵈ 7¹²ˢᵈ 2¹⁰ˢᵈ 16⁸ᵍ
10¹²ᵍˢ 5¹⁰ˢ 5¹⁰ᵍᶠ 5¹⁰ᵍˢ 14¹²ᵍˢ 8¹⁰ˢ 13¹⁰ˢᵈ 12¹⁰ᵍ
0-2-15 £4,258

Interstice *M J Gingell*   a58
7 b g Never So Bold - Mainmast
3¹¹ˢᵈ 6¹²ˢᵈ 5⁹ˢˢ **0-1-3 £413**

Interwoven (Ire) *M Johnston*   59
2 b c Woodman (USA) - Woven Silk (USA)
10⁶ᵍˢ 16⁷ᵍ **0-0-2**

Intitnice (Ire) *Miss K M George*   a19
3 b g Danehill Dancer (Ire) - Gathering Place (USA)
12⁸ˢᵈ 11⁶ˢᵈ 11⁸ᵍᶠ 17⁷ᵍˢ **0-0-4**

Into The Breeze (Ire) *J W Hills*   35
4 b g Alzao (USA) - Catalane (USA)
20⁷ᵍᶠ **0-0-1**

Into The Dark *Saeed Bin Suroor*   117
3 ch c Rainbow Quest (USA) - Land Of Dreams
1¹⁰ᵍ 1¹⁰ᵍ 1¹²ᵍ 1¹¹ˢ **4-0-4 £44,224**

Into The Shadows *K G Reveley*   78
4 ch f Safawan - Shadows Of Silver
3⁸ʰʸ 3¹²ᵍ 4⁹ᵍˢ 1¹⁰ᵍ 1¹²ˢ **2-2-5 £13,627**

Intoxicating *R F Johnson Houghton*   84
2 b c Mujahid (USA) - Salalah
1⁶ᵍ 3⁶ᵍ **1-1-2 £4,773**

Intrepid Jack *H Morrison*   35 a71
2 b c Compton Place - Maria Theresa
13⁸ʰʸ 1⁶ˢᵈ **1-0-2 £5,200**

Intricate Web (Ire) *E J Alston*   88 a91
8 b g Warning - In Anticipation (Ire)
1⁹ˢᵈ 1⁹ˢˢ 2¹¹ˢˢ 4¹²ˢʷ 6¹¹ˢ 7¹¹ˢ 1¹⁰ᵍ 3⁸ᵍᶠ
3⁸ᵍ 1²²ᵍ 1¹⁰ᵍ 10⁸ᵍ 12¹⁰ᵍᶠ 15¹¹ᵍ 5⁸ᶠ 6¹¹ʰʸ
9¹⁰ᵍ **4-3-17 £33,220**

Intrigued *Sir Mark Prescott*   106

2 gr f Darshaan - Last Second (Ire)
3⁷ᵍˢ 1⁹ᵍ 4⁸ᵍ **1-1-3 £16,352**

Intriguing (Ire) *David Wachman* 84
2 b f Fasliyev (USA) - Sea Mistress
1⁶ᵍᶠ **1-0-1 £9,169**

Intriguing Glimpse *Miss B Sanders* 82
3 b/br f Piccolo - Running Glimpse (Ire)
3⁶ˢ 2⁵ᵍᶠ 2⁵ᵍᶠ 7⁶ᵍᶠ **0-4-5 £5,303**

Introduction *R J Price* 27 a32
3 b g Opening Verse (USA) - Cartuccia (Ire)
9⁸ˢᵈ 13¹²ᵍᶠ 10¹⁶ᵍˢ 5¹²ᵍˢ 9¹²ᵍˢ **0-0-5**

Invader *C E Brittain* 68 a83
8 b g Danehill (USA) - Donya
7⁷ˢᵈ 8¹⁰ˢᵈ 6⁸ˢˢ 10⁸ˢˢ 9⁸ᵍˢ 8⁸ᵍᶠ 1⁸ˢᵈ
10¹⁰ᵍᶠ 6⁷ᵍᶠ 6⁸ᵍ 8⁹ᵍ 14⁸ᵍᶠ **1-0-12 £3,578**

Invasian (Ire) *H R A Cecil* 103
3 ch c Desert Prince (Ire) - Jarrayan
1⁸ᵍˢ 2⁸ᵍᶠ 8⁸ᵍ 15⁷ᵍᶠ 1¹⁰ᵍˢ 2¹⁰ᵍˢ 13¹⁰ˢ
2-2-7 £28,537

Inver Gold *A G Newcombe* a12
7 ch h Arazi (USA) - Mary Martin
7¹²ˢʷ **0-0-1**

Invertiel (USA) *I Semple* 74
2 br c Royal Academy (USA) - Intriguing (USA)
4⁶ᵍᶠ 2⁶ᵍᶠ 12⁷ˢ 10⁶ˢ 7⁷ᵍ 6⁷ˢ **0-1-6**
£1,642

Investment Affair (Ire) *D McCain* 35
4 b g Sesaro (USA) - Superb Investment (Ire)
10¹⁰ᵍ **0-0-1**

Invitation *A Charlton* 78
6 b g Bin Ajwaad (Ire) - On Request (Ire)
11¹²ᵍ 6¹²ᵍˢ 4¹⁴ˢ 2¹⁰ˢ 8¹⁰ᵍ 2¹⁴ᵍ 28²⁰ᵍᶠ
0-3-7 £3,866

Inviting (USA) *R Charlton* 61
3 b f Exploit (USA) - Raging Apalachee (USA)
14⁸ᵍ **0-0-1**

Invogue (Fr) *R A Fahey* 30 a17
4 b f Bin Ajwaad (Ire) - Wenda (Ire)
19⁸ˢ 13¹²ᵍ 6¹²ˢᵈ 10⁸ˢᵈ **0-0-4**

Io Callisto *R A Fahey*
3 br f Hector Protector (USA) - Queen Shirley (Ire)
9⁵ᵍˢ **0-0-1**

Ionian Spring (Ire) *C G Cox* 99
9 b g Ela-Mana-Mou - Well Head (Ire)
1¹⁰ᵍ 9¹⁰ᵍ 1¹¹ᵍˢ 9¹⁰ᵍ 18¹¹ᵍ 5¹⁰ˢ 7⁹ᵍᶠ **2-0-7**
£16,661

Iphigenia (Ire) *P W Hiatt* 77
3 b/br f Orpen (USA) - Silver Explosive
7⁸ᶠ 5⁸ᶠ 7⁷ᶠ 2⁷ᵍᶠ 4⁸ᵍ 5⁹ᵍ 3⁷ᵍᶠ 1⁷ᵍᶠ 2⁷ˢ
6⁷ᵍ 6⁷ᵍ **1-3-11 £6,522**

Ipledgeallegiance (USA) *D W Chapman* 41 a46
8 b g Alleged (USA) - Yafill (USA)
2¹²ˢᵈ 5¹¹ˢᵈ 3¹²ˢᵈ 6¹¹ˢᵈ 5¹²ˢˢ 12²ˢʷ 7¹²ˢᵈ
10¹²ˢᵈ 5¹¹ˢᵈ 5¹⁰ˢᵈ 8¹³ᵍ 5¹⁰ᵍᶠ 5¹³ᵍᶠ 2¹⁴ᵍ 11¹²ᵍᶠ
3¹⁶ᵍ 2¹⁴ˢᵈ 7¹⁵ᵍᶠ 7¹³ᵍᶠ **0-4-19 £2,767**

Ipsa Loquitur *S C Williams* 66
4 b f Unfuwain (USA) - Plaything
10¹⁰ᵍˢ 4¹⁰ᵍˢ PU¹²ᵍᶠ **0-0-3 £281**

Iqte Saab (USA) *J L Dunlop* 109
3 b c Bahri (USA) - Shuhrah (USA)
1⁷ᵍˢ 6⁷ᵍᶠ 9⁶ᵍ 5⁷ᵍᶠ 3⁷ᵍᶠ **1-1-5 £13,127**

Iranoo (Ire) *R Allan* 23
7 b g Persian Bold - Rose Of Summer (Ire)
7¹²ᵍ **0-0-1**

Ireland's Eye (Ire) *J R Norton* a38

9 b g Shareef Dancer (USA) - So Romantic (Ire)
3¹⁴ˢᵈ 4¹⁶ˢᵈ **0-0-2 £207**

Irie Rasta (Ire) *S Kirk*
5 ch g Desert King (Ire) - Seeds Of Doubt (Ire)
15¹⁰ʰʸ **0-0-1**

Irish Ballad *P W Harris* 44 a60
2 b c Singspiel (Ire) - Auenlust (Ger)
8⁸ˢ 10⁸ᵍˢ 4⁹ˢᵈ **0-0-3 £328**

Irish Blade (Ire) *H Candy* 82
3 b c Kris - Perle D'Irlande (Fr)
4¹⁰ᵍˢ 3¹²ˢ 10¹⁰ᵍᶠ 7¹²ᵍ 11¹⁰ᵍ 2¹⁶ᵍ
1¹⁴ᵍˢ 5¹⁶ᵍˢ 6¹⁶ˢ **1-3-10 £7,478**

Irish Chapel (Ire) *H E Haynes* 27
8 b g College Chapel - Heart Of Flame
8⁸ᵍᶠ 9¹¹ˢᵈ **0-0-2**

Irish Playwright (Ire) *D G Bridgwater* 35 a56
4 b g King's Theatre (Ire) - Marino Waltz
8⁷ᵍᶠ 13¹³ˢᵈ 3⁹ˢᵈ **0-1-3 £528**

Iron Temptress (Ire) *G M Moore* 48 a38
3 ch f Piccolo - River Divine (USA)
13⁷ᵍᶠ 10⁸ˢ 6¹⁴ᵍᶠ 10¹²ᵍᶠ 8¹⁴ᶠ **0-0-5**

Iron Warrior (Ire) *G M Moore*
4 b g Lear Fan (USA) - Robalana (USA)
15¹²ᵍᶠ **0-0-1**

Irony (Ire) *A M Balding* 91
5 gr g Mujadil (USA) - Cidaris (Ire)
7⁷ˢ 9⁸ᵍˢ 4⁸ᵍᶠ 13⁹ᵍ 10⁸ᵍ **0-0-5 £732**

Iroquois Princess *D Shaw* 25 a7
2 ch f Polish Precedent (USA) - Chelsea (USA)
8⁶ᵍ 9⁷ˢᵈ 9⁶ʰʸ 11⁶ˢᵈ **0-0-4**

Irreversible *J H M Gosden* a68
2 b f Diktat - Amsicora
6⁷ˢᵈ **0-0-1**

Irusan (Ire) *Jedd O'Keeffe* 62 a67
4 br g Catrail (USA) - Ostrusa (Aut)
6⁷ᵍˢ 8⁶ᵍᶠ 13⁶ᵍᶠ 4⁶ˢᵈ 7⁵ˢᵈ 6⁶ˢᵈ 8⁷ˢ 2⁹ˢᵈ
1⁷ˢᵈ **1-1-9 £4,169**

Isa'Af (Ire) *P W Hiatt* 75 a64
5 b g Darshaan - Shauna's Honey (Ire)
1¹²ˢˢ 2¹⁴ˢᵈ 1¹⁴ˢ 10¹²ᵍᶠ 2¹³ᵍᶠ 4¹²ᵍᶠ
4¹²ᵍ 1¹⁴ᵍ 6¹²ᵍ 16¹²ˢ 4¹⁶ᵍ 2¹⁶ᵍ 7¹⁴ᵍ 4¹⁸ᵍ
4-3-16 £17,035

Isaz *H Candy* 68
4 b c Elmaamul (USA) - Pretty Poppy
5⁷ᵍˢ 5⁶ˢ 5⁶ᵍᶠ 8⁶ᵍᶠ 12⁶ᵍᶠ **0-0-5**

Isidore Bonheur (Ire) *B W Hills* 98
3 b c Mtoto - Way O'Gold (USA)
4⁹ᵍ 4¹⁰ᵍ 4¹²ᵍˢ 4¹⁵ᵍᶠ 12⁸ᶠ 14¹⁰ᵍ **0-0-6**
£7,750

Isitloveyourafter (Ire) *R P Elliott* 44
2 b f Orpen (USA) - Pericolo (Ire)
9⁶ᵍˢ 5⁵ᵍ 6⁷ᵍᶠ 14⁵ᶠ 13⁶ˢᵈ **0-0-5**

Iskander *K A Ryan* 87 a41
3 b g Danzero (Aus) - Amber Mill
6⁶ᵍˢ 9²ᵍ 14⁷ᵍ 10⁶ᵍᶠ 9⁶ˢ 6⁵ᵍ 4⁸ᵍ 10⁸ᵍ
5⁹ˢ 10⁸ᵍᶠ 4⁸ᵍᶠ 13⁹ˢᵈ **0-0-12 £1,568**

Island House (Ire) *G Wragg* 107
8 ch h Grand Lodge (USA) - Fortitude (Ire)
3¹⁰ᵍˢ 7¹⁰ᵍˢ 5¹⁰ᵍᶠ 3¹²ᵍᶠ 3¹²ᵍ **0-2-5**
£8,962

Island Light (USA) *Mrs M Reveley* 47
4 ch g Woodman (USA) - Isla Del Rey (USA)
20¹²ᵍ 16¹⁰ᵍ 9¹¹ᵍˢ **0-0-4**

Island Rapture *J A R Toller* 78 a76
4 b f Royal Applause - Gersey

11^{8gs} 8^{8gf} 4^{9g} 10^{10gf} 3^{8sd} 2^{8gf} 6^{8gf}
11^{9g} 2^{8sd} 3^{9sd} 5^{8sd} **0-4-11 £4,750**

Island Sound D R C Elsworth   104
7 b f Turtle Island (Ire) - Ballet
6^{10gf} 3^{10g} 3^{9gs} **0-0-3 £4,170**

Island Spell C Grant   67
3 b f Singspiel (Ire) - Shifty Mouse
3^{7gs} 5^{7f} 3^{6s} 15^{5s} 10^{5gf} 9^{6gf} **0-0-6**
£1,840

Island Star (Ire) G P Enright   15 a39
4 b g Turtle Island (Ire) - Orthorising
8^{8sd} 10^{6sd} 14^{7sd} 4^{10sd} 6^{12g} **0-0-5**

Island Swing (Ire) J L Spearing   80
2 ch f Trans Island - Farmers Swing (Ire)
15^{5gf} 16^{gf} 16^{gf} 4^{6gf} 11^{6gs} 8^{6gs} 3^{6g} 4^{6gf}
1^{6hy} 15^{6hy} **3-0-10 £12,195**

Islands Farewell D Nicholls   56 a14
4 b g Emarati (USA) - Chief Island
7^{9gf} 17^{8s} 2^{8gf} 5^{8gf} 11^{8sw} 3^{8gs} 2^{10f} 2^{12f}
0-4-8 £4,556

Isle Dream J Balding   a6
2 ch f Forzando - La Volta
10^{5gf} 7^{6f} 13^{5sd} **0-0-3**

Isle Of Light (Ire) W R Muir   a3
2 b f Trans Island - Singled Out (Ire)
13^{6g} 8^{5sw} **0-0-2**

Isleofhopeantears (Ire) A E Jones   56
5 b g College Chapel - Fontaine Lodge (Ire)
5^{8gf} 9^{10g} 10^{10gs} **0-0-3**

Ismahaan G Wragg   65
5 ch m Unfuwain (USA) - River Divine (USA)
6^{10gf} 5^{12gs} **0-0-2**

Issy Blue J A Osborne   61
2 b f Inchinor - Mountain Bluebird (USA)
9^{7gf} 8^{6g} 11^{7gs} **0-0-3**

It Must Be Speech S L Keightley   27 a71
3 b g Advise (Fr) - Maiden Speech
5^{11sd} 2^{12sd} 5^{12sd} 16^{8gf} 15^{12g} **0-1-5 £856**

It's A Blessing N P Littmoden
3 b f Inchinor - Benedicite
12^{10sd} **0-0-1**

It's Blue Chip P W D'Arcy   68 a67
3 b g Polar Falcon (USA) - Bellateena
3^{9sd} 9^{10sd} 1^{12gs} 4^{15gs} 6^{12s} 4^{12sd} 1^{12sd}
10^{12gs} 13^{12gf} 7^{12gs} 13^{14g} 7^{12sd} **2-1-12 £8,211**

It's Definite (Ire) P Bowen   24
5 b g Definite Article - Taoveret (Ire)
25^{18s} **0-0-1**

It's Peggy Speech S L Keightley   29
2 b f Bishop Of Cashel - Marsara
17^{6gs} **0-0-1**

It's The Limit (USA) Mrs A J Perrett   98
5 b g Boundary (USA) - Beside (USA)
4^{12gf} 13^{14g} 4^{16gf} 32^{18s} **0-1-4 £1,979**

Italian Counsel (Ire) P J Hobbs   a31
7 b g Leading Counsel (USA) - Mullaghroe
12^{10sd} 4^{12sd} **0-0-2**

Italian Mist (Fr) Julian Poulton   46 a73
5 b g Forzando - Digamist Girl (Ire)
1^{6sd} 3^{6sd} 5^{6sd} 1^{6ss} 2^{7sd} 9^{7sd} 15^{5ss} 3^{5s}
1^{6sd} 7^{6s} 4^{5ss} 10^{6sd} 13^{6s} **4-3-13 £12,865**

Italian Touch (Ire) J A Glover   58
2 b g Rossini (USA) - Attached (Ire)
7^{6gf} 9^{6gs} 8^{5gf} 7^{7s} **0-0-4**

Ithaca (USA) H R A Cecil   102

3 ch f Distant View (USA) - Reams Of Verse (USA)
3^{7gs} 6^{11gs} 5^{10g} 3^{8gs} 4^{8gf} 3^{7gf} 5^{7gf} **0-2-7**
£11,662

Its A Mystery (Ire) R J Smith   22
5 b m Idris (Ire) - Blue Infanta
11^{11gf} **0-0-1**

Its Ecco Boy P Howling   57 a63
6 ch g Clantime - Laena
4^{6sd} 4^{7sd} 1^{6ss} 7^{7sw} 9^{6ss} 7^{7sd} 12^{5gf} 7^{6gf}
13^{7gf} 14^{6gf} 10^{6sd} 6^{8sd} 12^{8sd} 6^{7sd} **1-0-14**
£2,968

Its My Son L G Cottrell
3 b g Sea Raven (Ire) - Fay Eden (Ire)
9^{10gf} **0-0-1**

Itsa Monkey (Ire) M J Polglase   51 a35
2 b g Merdon Melody - Gracious Imp (USA)
9^{5sd} 6^{6f} 2^{5sd} 12^{7gf} 8^{7gf} 12^{7sd} 7^{8gs} 14^{7f}
11^{7gf} **0-1-9 £720**

Itsonlyagame R Ingram   a56
4 b c Ali-Royal (Ire) - Mena
1^{10sd} 8^{10sd} 9^{13sd} 5^{10sd} 7^{12sd} 2^{10sd} 13^{12s}
1-1-7 £1,708

Ivana Illyich (Ire) S Kirk   70
2 ch f Tipsy Creek (USA) - Tolstoya
5^{5s} 9^{5gf} 4^{6gf} 8^{6gf} 3^{6gs} 3^{7s} 7^{7gf} 10^{7gf}
0-2-8 £2,222

Ivory Coast (Ire) W R Muir   64 a63
3 b f Cape Cross (Ire) - Ivory League
4^{10sd} 11^{10sd} 2^{9f} 8^{10gf} 7^{10gf} 11^{10g} 5^{10gf}
9^{10gf} 11^{10gs} **2-1-10 £7,053**

Ivory Lace S Woodman   79 a71
3 b f Atraf - Miriam
5^{5sd} 2^{5sd} 11^{5sd} 1^{5sd} 3^{6sd} 1^{5g} 1^{5g} 4^{5gf}
1^{5g} 5^{5gs} 13^{5g} 12^{6g} 4^{6sd} **4-2-13 £15,062**

Ivory Venture I R Brown   a45
4 b f Reprimand - Julietta Mia (USA)
13^{6sd} 8^{5sd} 9^{7sd} 12^{8sd} 1^{5sd} 13^{7sd} **1-0-6**
£1,449

Ivory Wolf J L Spearing   34
2 ch g Wolfhound (USA) - Ashkernazy (Ire)
8^{5f} 7^{5gf} 10^{7gs} **0-0-3**

Ivy House Lad (Ire) I W McInnes
4 b g Presidium - Nice Spice (Ire)
5^{10sd} **0-0-1**

Ivy League Star (Ire) B W Hills   78 a75
3 b f Sadler's Wells (USA) - Ivy (USA)
5^{12gf} 10^{12sd} 1^{12hy} 5^{12sd} 5^{14gs} **1-0-5**
£3,885

Ivy Moon B J Llewellyn   52 a47
4 b f Emperor Jones (USA) - Bajan Rose
3^{8sd} 6^{7sd} 7^{8sd} 3^{6gf} 5^{7gf} 3^{7gf} 4^{8gf} 8^{7gf}
5^{8gf} 11^{8f} **0-4-10 £1,104**

Izmail (Ire) P D Evans   79 a52
5 b g Bluebird (USA) - My-Lorraine (Ire)
13^{5s} 19^{5g} 10^{5gf} 7^{5f} 10^{5g} 1^{5gf} 18^{5gf}
10^{5s} 14^{6f} 12^{5gf} 5^{5g} 18^{5g} 10^{5sd} 12^{5sd} **1-0-14**
£7,897

Izza W Storey
3 br f Wizard King - Nicholas Mistress
14^{6sd} **0-0-1**

Izzet Muzzy (Fr) D Shaw   a53
6 ch g Piccolo - Texanne (Bel)
9^{5sd} **0-0-1**

J R Stevenson (USA) M Wigham   79 a87
8 ch g Lyphard (USA) - While It Lasts (USA)
2^{8sd} 12^{10sd} 4^{8s} 6^{10g} 5^{8gs} 8^{8gf} 6^{8gs} 1^{8s}

1-2-8 £5,013

Jaamid *M A Buckley* 79
2 b c Desert Prince (Ire) - Strictly Cool (USA)
4⁷ᵍᶠ 10⁶ᵍˢ 2⁸ˢ **0-1-3 £1,718**

Jabaar (USA) *M W Easterby* 95
6 gr g Silver Hawk (USA) - Sierra Madre (Fr)
21⁸ᵍ 3¹⁰ᵍˢ 5¹⁰ᵍˢ 6¹⁰ᵍᶠ 2¹⁰ᵍ 5¹⁰ᵍ 10¹²ᵍ
8¹⁰ᵍˢ 2¹⁰ᵍˢ 18¹⁰ᵍ 11¹²ˢ 11¹²ˢ **0-3-12**
£26,061

Jabraan (USA) *Saeed Bin Suroor* 70
2 b c Aljabr (USA) - Miss Zafonic (Fr)
8⁷ᵍ **0-0-1**

Jacaranda (Ire) *Mrs A L M King* 77
4 ch g Bahhare (USA) - Near Miracle
11⁷ᵍˢ 5⁷ᵍˢ 10⁷ᵍᶠ 9⁹ᵍᶠ 2¹⁰ᵍˢ 4¹⁰ᵍˢ 1¹⁰ᵍᶠ
3¹⁰ᵍᶠ 6¹²ᵍᶠ 10¹⁰ᵍ 5¹²ᵍᶠ 10¹²ˢ **1-1-12 £6,211**

Jack Dawson (Ire) *John Berry* 82
7 b g Persian Bold - Dream Of Jenny
1¹⁴ᵍᶠ 8¹⁶ᵍᶠ **1-0-2 £13,572**

Jack Durrance (Ire) *G A Ham* 47
4 b g Polish Precedent (USA) - Atlantic Desire (Ire)
17¹⁰ᵍ 10¹⁰ᵍ 4¹²ᵍᶠ 9¹³ᵍᶠ 10¹⁷ᵍ 10¹⁴ᵍᶠ
0-0-6

Jack Of Trumps (Ire) *G Wragg* 82 a69
4 b c King's Theatre (Ire) - Queen Caroline (USA)
1¹⁰ˢᵈ 11¹⁰ˢᵈ 7¹⁰ᵍˢ 4¹²ᵍᶠ 1¹²ᵍˢ 1¹²ᵍᶠ 1¹²ᵍˢ
9¹²ᵍᶠ **4-0-8 £19,931**

Jack Sullivan (USA) *G A Butler* 99 a104
3 ch g Belong To Me (USA) - Provisions (USA)
2⁸ᶠᵗ 4⁹ᶠᵗ 4⁷ᵍ 9⁷ᶠ 5⁸ᵍᶠ **0-1-5 £86,173**

Jack The Giant (Ire) *B W Hills* 63
2 b c Giant's Causeway (USA) - State Crystal (Ire)
8⁶ᵍᶠ 9⁷ˢ **0-0-2**

Jack's Check *N Tinkler* 24
3 b f Factual (USA) - Ski Baby
14⁸ʰʸ 10⁸ᵍᶠ **0-0-2**

Jackadandy (USA) *J Howard Johnson* 66
2 b g Lear Fan (USA) - Chandra (Can)
4⁷ᵍˢ 3⁸ˢ 13⁸ᶠ **0-0-3 £1,464**

Jackie Kiely *P S McEntee* 73 a62
3 ch g Vettori (Ire) - Fudge
7⁷ˢᵈ 6¹⁰ˢᵈ 2¹⁰ˢᵈ 8¹⁰ˢᵈ 5¹²ᵍˢ 5¹³ˢ 4¹¹ᵍᶠ
2¹⁰ᶠ 1¹²ˢᵈ 14¹⁰ᶠ 1¹⁰ᵍᶠ 1¹⁰ᵍ 9¹²ᵍᶠ 10¹¹ᵍ 3¹⁰ᵍᶠ
7¹⁰ᵍ 4⁹ᵍ 10¹⁰ᵍᶠ **3-4-21**
£15,201

Jacks Delight *B D Leavy* a12
4 b g Bettergeton - Impromptu Melody (Ire)
7⁷ˢᵈ 14⁶ᵍᶠ 10⁶ˢᵈ **0-0-3**

Jacob (Ire) *P A Blockley* a38
3 b g Victory Note (USA) - Persian Mistress (Ire)
5⁶ˢˢ 4⁸ˢˢ 8⁷ˢˢ **0-0-3**

Jacobin (USA) *P J McBride* 39
3 b c Tamayaz (Can) - Simply Follow Me (USA)
10¹⁰ᵍᶠ 10¹²ᵍᶠ **0-0-2**

Jadan (Ire) *E J Alston* 82
3 b g Imperial Ballet (Ire) - Sports Post Lady (Ire)
9⁵ˢ 14⁵ˢ 3⁵ᵍ 6⁵ˢ 6⁵ˢ 1⁵ᵍˢ 5⁵ᵍᶠ 10⁵ᵍˢ
9⁶ᵍ 1⁵ˢ 6⁵ᵍˢ **2-1-11 £12,240**

Jade Star (USA) *A B Haynes* 56 a58
4 b f Jade Hunter (USA) - Danzig's Girl (USA)
4¹²ˢᵈ 1⁹ˢˢ 11¹⁰ˢᵈ 2⁹ˢˢ 6⁹ˢᵈ 4¹⁰ᵍˢ 4¹¹ᶠ
14¹⁰ᵍˢ 3¹⁰ᵍ 15⁸ˢᵈ 17¹⁰ᵍᶠ **1-2-11 £4,731**

Jadeeron *Miss D A McHale* 70 a68
5 b g Green Desert (USA) - Rain And Shine (Fr)
2¹³ˢᵈ 2¹²ˢᵈ 2¹²ˢˢ 3¹³ˢᵈ 4¹⁶ᵍ 4¹⁴ᵍᶠ 7¹⁶ᵍˢ

10¹²ᵍᶠ 6¹²ˢᵈ 6¹²ˢᵈ 3¹⁴ˢᵈ **0-5-11 £4,790**

Jagged (Ire) *J R Jenkins* 66 a72
4 b g Sesaro (USA) - Latin Mass
13⁶ˢᵈ 8⁶ʰʸ 8⁶ᵍᶠ 2⁶ˢᵈ 3⁶ᵍ 6⁶ᵍᶠ 3⁶ᵍᶠ 1⁵ˢᵈ
2⁶ˢʷ 2⁶ᶠ 4⁶ᵍ 1⁵ˢᵈ **2-5-12 £11,526**

Jagger *G A Butler* 110
4 gr c Linamix (Fr) - Sweetness Herself
13¹⁶ˢ 13¹⁴ᵍ 8¹⁴ˢ 4¹²ᵍᶠ 11¹⁴ᵍ **0-1-5**
£8,000

Jahangir *B R Johnson* a50
5 b g Zamindar (USA) - Imperial Jade
3⁸ˢᵈ 3⁷ˢᵈ 9⁶ˢᵈ 10⁶ˢᵈ 7⁸ˢᵈ **0-2-5 £421**

Jahia (NZ) *M Madgwick* 43
5 br m Jahafil - Lana (NZ)
11⁸ˢ 10⁷ˢ **0-0-4**

Jailbird *R M Beckett* 26
3 b f Nicolotte - Grace Browning
8⁶ᶠ 13⁶ᶠ **0-0-2**

Jair Ohmsford (Ire) *W J Musson* 69 a78
5 b g Hamas (Ire) - Harry's Irish Rose (USA)
1⁹ˢᵈ 4⁹ˢᵈ 1¹²ˢˢ 1¹²ᵍˢ 4¹²ᵍˢ 3¹⁰ᵍˢ **3-2-6**
£9,974

Jakarmi *B Palling* 76 a77
3 b g Merdon Melody - Lady Ploy
1⁸ˢᵈ 6⁷ˢᵈ 1⁸ˢʷ 3⁸ˢʷ 2⁸ᵍ 2⁸ˢᵈ 2¹⁰ᵍ 3⁸ˢ
2¹²ˢᵈ 1¹⁰ᵍ 1¹⁰ᵍˢ 14¹⁰ᵍ 7¹⁰ᵍ 5¹¹ᵍ 11¹²ᵍᶠ **4-6-15**
£22,151

Jake Black (Ire) *J J Quinn* 68 a52
4 b g Definite Article - Tirhala (Ire)
7¹²ˢᵈ 1⁸ˢʷ 1⁹ˢˢ 5⁸ˢᵈ 3¹⁰ʰʸ 1¹⁰ʰʸ 5¹⁰ˢ
15¹⁰ᶠ 4¹²ᵍ 4¹⁰ᵍˢ 1¹⁰ᵍᶠ 12¹⁰ᵍ 8¹⁰ᵍˢ 10¹⁰ᵍ **4-1-14**
£12,757

Jakeal (Ire) *R M Whitaker* 56 a43
5 b g Eagle Eyed (USA) - Karoi (Ire)
10⁷ˢᵈ 4⁸ᵍˢ 11⁸ᵍˢ 11⁷ᵍ 2⁷ᵍᶠ 13⁸ʰʸ **0-2-6**
£1,238

Jalamid (Ire) *J H M Gosden* 78
2 b c Danehill (USA) - Vignelaure (Ire)
1⁷ᵍᶠ 11⁷ᵍˢ **1-0-2 £4,953**

Jalissa *R Charlton* a70
2 b f Mister Baileys - Julia Domna
4⁷ˢᵈ **0-0-1 £400**

Jalons Star (Ire) *M R Channon* 38
6 b g Eagle Eyed (USA) - Regina St Cyr (Ire)
10¹⁰ᵍᶠ 7¹⁰ᵍᶠ 13¹²ᵍᶠ **0-0-3**

Jalouhar *B P J Baugh* 75 a56
4 b g Victory Note (USA) - Orient Way (Ire)
5⁶ˢᵈ 4⁶ˢᵈ 6⁷ˢᵈ 6⁸ˢᵈ 7ˢᵈ 5⁶ˢˢ 12⁵ˢˢ 2⁶ᵍᶠ
9⁶ᵍᶠ 8⁸ᵍᶠ 7⁶ᵍˢ 2⁶ᵍᶠ 10⁷ᵍᶠ 7⁶ᵍ 6⁷ᵍ 7⁶ᵍᶠ 8⁶ᵍᶠ
11⁶ᵍ **0-2-18 £2,304**

Jalousie Dream *G M Moore* 48
3 b f Easycall - Forest Maid
7¹⁰ᵍˢ 5⁹ᵍ 3¹⁰ᵍᶠ 12¹²ᵍᶠ 8¹⁴ᵍᶠ **0-1-5 £572**

Jamaaron *R Hannon* 76
2 ch c Bachir (Ire) - Kentmere (Fr)
3⁷ᵍˢ 7⁷ᵍᶠ 1⁸ᵍˢ 14⁸ᵍ **1-1-4 £5,412**

Jamaican Flight (USA) *Mrs S Lamyman* 42 a49
11 b h Sunshine Forever (USA) - Kalamona (USA)
3¹⁶ˢᵈ 4¹⁶ˢᵈ 4¹²ˢᵈ 4¹⁸ˢ 4²²ˢ 5¹⁶ˢᵈ 5¹⁸ᶠ
18¹⁶ᵍ **0-1-8 £1,960**

James Caird (Ire) *M H Tompkins* 94
4 ch g Catrail (USA) - Polish Saga
6¹⁰ᵍᶠ 2¹⁰ᵍᶠ 2⁹ᵍᶠ 2⁹⁷ᵍᶠ 7⁸ᶠ 11¹¹ᵍ 3¹⁰ᵍ 2¹⁰ᶠ
0-5-8 £25,281

Jamestown *M J Polglase* 48 a53

7 b g Merdon Melody - Thabeh
5^{8sd} 9^{11sd} 10^{8sd} 7^{8ss} 9^{8sd} 8^{11ss} 13^{7gf}
4^{9sd} 11^{8f} 4^{9f} 8^{8sd} 13^{8gs} **0-0-12 £430**

Jan Brueghel (USA) *T D Barron*   a51
5 ch g Phone Trick (USA) - Sunk (USA)
3^{7sd} 4^{7sd} 8^{7ss} **0-1-3 £371**

Jane Jubilee (Ire) *M Johnston*   92
2 b f Mister Baileys - Elsie Bamford
3^{5s} 5^{6f} 2^{6gf} 2^{7gf} 1^{7gf} 1^{7gf} 5^{7g} 10^{7gs}
11^{7g} 13^{6s} **2-2-10 £15,988**

Janes Valentine *J J Bridger*   a42
4 b f My Best Valentine - Jane Herring
4^{10sd} 8^{7sd} 4^{7sd} 15^{7sd} 8^{7sd} 17^{7hy} 6^{6sd}
0-0-7

Jango Malfoy (Ire) *B W Duke*   29 a41
3 ch g Russian Revival (USA) - Sialia (Ire)
9^{7sd} 11^{8sd} 10^{8sd} 8^{12gf} 12^{16gf} **0-0-5**

Jaolins *P G Murphy*   40 a57
3 b f Groom Dancer (USA) - On The Top
1^{6sd} 2^{7sd} 10^{7sd} 10^{6sd} 5^{7sd} 9^{7s} 7^{6s} 12^{6gf}
14^{7gf} 7^{7g} 6^{8sd} 5^{8sd} 9^{10gf} 4^{8gs} 7^{8sd} **1-1-15**
£3,417

Jarraaf *J W Unett*   a60
4 ch g Desert Story (Ire) - Bee Off (Ire)
5^{8sd} 5^{9ss} **0-0-2**

Jarvo *N P Littmoden*   66 a62
3 b g Pursuit Of Love - Pinkie Rose (Fr)
2^{10gs} 5^{8sd} 4^{7gf} 12^{8g} 10^{9g} 2^{8gf} 3^{7s} 14^{8gf}
4^{9sd} **0-3-9 £3,423**

Jasmick (Ire) *H Morrison*   74
6 ch m Definite Article - Glass Minnow (Ire)
5^{12gf} 7^{14gf} 9^{16gf} 6^{12gs} 7^{13gs} 2^{14gs} **0-1-6**
£1,568

Jasmine Hill *N Bycroft*   44
2 ch f Timeless Times (USA) - Coney Hills
10^{5s} 6^{5gf} 7^{5gs} 8^{5gf} **0-0-4**

Jasmine Pearl (Ire) *T M Jones*   52 a44
3 b f King Of Kings (Ire) - Tumbleweed Pearl
3^{7sd} 6^{6sd} 11^{7sd} 8^{6gs} 4^{6sd} 16^{6gf} 2^{6gf} 5^{6gf}
6^{6gf} 6^{7f} 13^{6g} 9^{6gf} **0-2-12 £1,255**

Jath *Julian Poulton*   84
3 b f Bishop Of Cashel - Night Trader (USA)
15^{8g} 6^{10gf} 10^{8gs} 6^{7gf} 1^{7s} 8^{8gf} 12^{7g}
10^{7s} **1-0-8 £7,184**

Java Dancer *T D Easterby*   50 a34
3 b g Danehill Dancer (USA) - Evasive Step
7^{8g} 6^{8gf} 6^{8sd} **0-0-3**

Java Dawn (Ire) *T E Powell*   43 a43
4 b f Fleetwood (Ire) - Krakatoa
10^{12s} 10^{12sd} 3^{12sd} 6^{16gs} 7^{12gf} **0-1-5**
£371

Java Gold *W G M Turner*   24 a23
3 ch f The West (USA) - Another Jade
12^{6gf} 14^{6ss} 10^{5sd} **0-0-3**

Javelin *Ian Williams*   47
8 ch g Generous (Ire) - Moss
6^{13gf} 5^{14gs} 9^{13gs} **0-0-3**

Jawwala (USA) *J R Jenkins*
5 b m Green Dancer (USA) - Fetch N Carry (USA)
RR^{17gs} 16^{16gs} **0-0-2**

Jay (Ire) *N A Callaghan*   53
2 ch f Bluebird (USA) - Welsh Dawn
9^{6gf} 9^{6gf} 2^{7f} 9^{7gf} 2^{6gf} 8^{7gf} 1^{6gf} 17^{7gf}
9^{7gf} **1-1-9 £4,064**

Jay Gee's Choice *B G Powell*   95 a98

4 b g Barathea (Ire) - Llia
6^{8g} 23^{8g} 12^{8hy} 3^{7gf} 9^{9g} 4^{8f} 11^{7g} 4^{7g}
6^{7s} 18^{f} 3^{8g} 4^{7g} 17^{sd} **2-3-13 £18,783**

Jayanjay *Miss B Sanders*   93 a86
5 b g Piccolo - Morica
13^{6sd} 4^{6sd} 3^{5f} 4^{6g} 3^{6gf} 1^{6gs} 5^{5gf} 2^{5f}
2^{6gs} 5^{5s} 8^{5g} 1^{5g} 6^{6sd} **2-5-13 £34,553**

Jaycee Star (Ire) *D Flood*
3 ch f Idris (Ire) - Shantung (Ire)
11^{6sd} 14^{6sd} 15^{7sd} **0-0-3**

Jayer Gilles *H Candy*   82
4 br g Busy Flight - Jadidh
2^{12gf} 2^{12gf} 5^{12gf} 12^{16s} **0-2-4 £2,828**

Jazil *K A Morgan*   36 a30
9 b g Nashwan (USA) - Gracious Beauty (USA)
6^{11sd} 11^{12gf} 9^{12gf} 9^{16gf} 14^{14gs} **0-0-5**

Jazrawy *L M Cumani*   64 a70
2 b c Dansili - Dalila Di Mare (Ire)
4^{6gf} 4^{8gf} 1^{9sd} **1-0-3 £4,987**

Jazz Messenger (Fr) *G A Butler*   100
4 b g Acatenango (Ger) - In The Saltmine (Fr)
6^{8gs} 15^{8gs} 9^{7g} 10^{8s} 6^{10g} **0-0-5 £722**

Jazz Princess (Ire) *Mrs John Harrington*   109
2 b/br f Bahhare (USA) - Jazz Up
1^{7s} 1^{8g} 1^{7ys} **3-0-3 £56,409**

Jazz Scene (Ire) *M R Channon*   101 a92
3 b c Danehill Dancer (Ire) - Dixie Jazz
9^{7g} 8^{8f} 2^{7g} 2^{7gs} 4^{8g} 5^{8gf} 2^{8s} 4^{8g} 2^{8s}
15^{8s} 6^{9sd} **0-4-11 £17,784**

Jazzy Millennium *B R Millman*   65 a64
7 ch g Lion Cavern (USA) - Woodcrest
8^{6gs} 3^{6f} 6^{7f} 3^{5g} 3^{7gf} 7^{5gf} 4^{6gf} 1^{6gf} 2^{7hy}
2^{7gf} 12^{6gf} 5^{7sd} **1-6-12 £7,258**

Je Suis Belle *Miss Gay Kelleway*   72
2 ch f Efisio - Blossom
7^{6gf} 3^{5gs} 2^{6s} 1^{6s} 13^{7g} **1-2-5 £9,950**

Jedburgh *J L Dunlop*   105
3 b c Selkirk (USA) - Conspiracy
9^{8g} 3^{8g} 3^{7gf} 2^{7gs} 8^{7gf} 2^{8g} 5^{7gf} 13^{7g}
0-4-8 £14,508

Jedeydd *M Dods*   62
7 b g Shareef Dancer (USA) - Bilad (USA)
10^{7gf} 4^{7gf} 4^{7g} 7^{7gf} 4^{8g} 10^{7gf} 7^{7gf}
10^{7gf} 1^{6g} 9^{6g} **1-0-11 £3,361**

Jeepstar *T D Easterby*   85
4 b g Muhtarram (USA) - Jungle Rose
16^{12s} 10^{12gs} 6^{12gf} 2^{10gf} 2^{10gf} 11^{2gs} 8^{14gf}
1^{12gf} 2^{15s} 4^{12s} **2-4-10 £29,743**

Jeffslottery *J R Weymes*   55
2 b g Rock City - Thieves Welcome
11^{7gs} 6^{8s} 7^{7gs} 2^{8s} **0-1-4 £414**

Jelani (Ire) *Andrew Turnell*   108
5 b h Darshaan - No Rehearsal (Fr)
15^{12g} 6^{12g} 3^{14gs} **0-1-3 £16,900**

Jelly Baby *W J Haggas*   14 a63
3 b f Marju (Ire) - Daisy May
14^{10gs} 1^{12sd} 1^{12sd} 9^{12g} **2-0-4 £5,806**

Jem's Law *J R Jenkins*
5 b m Contract Law (USA) - Alnasr Jewel (USA)
10^{8s} 13^{10gf} **0-0-2**

Jenavive *N J Hawke*   a38
4 b f Danzig Connection (USA) - Promise Fulfilled (USA)
9^{13sd} **0-0-1**

Jenna Stannis *R M Beckett*   66
2 ch f Wolfhound (USA) - Darling Splodge

11^{7gs} 8^{7g} 10^{8gf} **0-0-3**

Jennverse *D K Ivory* — 47
2 b f Opening Verse (USA) - Jennelle
6^{5s} **0-0-1**

Jerome *T D Easterby* — 61
3 b g Nicolotte - Mim
8^{8hy} **0-0-1**

Jerry's Girl (Ire) *Miss L A Perratt* — 68
2 ch f Danehill Dancer (Ire) - Lurgoe Lady (Ire)
3^{5f} 6^{6gf} 4^{6gf} 1^{5gf} 8^{6f} **1-1-5 £5,216**

Jesse Samuel *J R Jenkins* — 41
3 ch g First Trump - Miss Kellybell
14^{7s} 4^{7g} 8^{7s} **0-0-3**

Jessiaume *H Candy* — 68
2 gr f Mister Baileys - Jucinda
4^{6s} **0-0-1 £365**

Jessica's Style (Ire) *J G Given* — 32 a33
2 b f Desert Style (Ire) - Mugello
13^{6f} 7^{5sd} 9^{6gs} **0-0-3**

Jessie *Don Enrico Incisa* — 46 a44
5 ch m Pivotal - Bold Gem
5^{7sd} 6^{7sd} 5^{8sd} 2^{8ss} 2^{7sd} 2^{7sw} 4^{7ss} 7^{7s}
5^{7sd} 4^{7g} 3^{8g} 12^{8f} **0-5-12 £3,207**

Jessinca *A P Jones* — 45 a26
8 b m Minshaanshu Amad (USA) - Noble Soul
8^{9sd} 10^{7sd} 6^{8ss} 10^{7sd} 3^{10gf} 2^{10gf} 9^{10gs}
5^{10gf} 11^{10s} **0-2-9 £1,408**

Jeune Loup *P C Haslam* — 69
2 b g Loup Sauvage (USA) - Secret Waters
8^{6g} 4^{7g} 7^{6s} **0-0-3**

Jewel In The Sand (Ire) *R Hannon* — 104
2 b f Bluebird (USA) - Dancing Drop
1^{5gf} 1^{6f} 1^{6gf} 11^{7gf} 7^{6g} **3-0-5 £68,675**

Jewel Of India *Mrs A L M King* — 66 a84
5 ch g Bijou D'Inde - Low Hill
7^{8sd} 11^{10sd} 6^{8gs} **0-0-3**

Jezadil (Ire) *Mrs L Stubbs* — 25 a15
6 b m Mujadil (USA) - Tender Time
13^{12sd} 13^{13sd} 3^{10gs} 9^{13g} 6^{12g} **0-0-5 £210**

Jidiya (Ire) *S Gollings* — 73
5 b g Lahib (USA) - Yaqatha (Ire)
8^{12gf} 9^{8gf} 2^{10gf} 8^{12g} 3^{11g} 3^{10f} 14^{12g}
0-2-7 £2,771

Jilly Why (Ire) *Ms Deborah J Evans* — 80 a72
3 b f Mujadil (USA) - Ruwy
8^{6sw} 4^{6gs} 1^{6f} 1^{5g} 7^{6f} 9^{6s} 2^{5s} 4^{6sd} 11^{5g}
5^{6sd} 6^{5sd} **2-1-11 £12,422**

Jim Lad *Dr J R J Naylor*
4 b g Young Ern - Anne's Bank (Ire)
5^{10gs} **0-0-1**

Jimmy Byrne (Ire) *B Ellison* — 84
4 ch g Red Sunset - Persian Sally (Ire)
15^{7gs} 4^{10s} 1^{10s} 7^{10f} 5^{10gf} 6^{12gf} 1^{11g}
11^{11gs} 3^{11s} 6^{10gs} 13^{10s} **3-1-11 £17,177**

Jimmy Hay *J C Fox*
3 b g Bluegrass Prince (Ire) - Priory Bay
14^{7gf} 12^{10sd} 15^{10gf} 12^{13gs} **0-0-4**

Jimmy Ryan (Ire) *T D McCarthy* — 101
3 b c Orpen (USA) - Kaysama (Fr)
7^{6g} 7^{6gf} 1^{5gf} 2^{5g} 1^{5gf} **2-1-5 £18,966**

Jinksonthehouse *M D I Usher* — 58
3 b f Whittingham (Ire) - Aldwick Colonnade
4^{6s} 16^{6g} 1^{5f} 7^{6gf} 4^{6f} 11^{5g} 1^{5g} 4^{5gf}
2^{5gf} 4^{5gf} 11^{5gs} **2-1-11 £7,494**

Joans Jewel *G G Margarson* — 41 a50

3 ch f Wolfhound (USA) - Chatter's Princess
5^{6sd} 5^{5sd} 6^{7sd} 15^{6gf} 7^{6gf} 14^{6g} 13^{7gf}
11^{7gs} **0-0-8**

Joe Charlie *K A Ryan* — a2
3 ch g Daggers Drawn (USA) - La Ballerine
10^{6ss} **0-0-1**

Joe Jo Star *P A Blockley* — 62
2 b c Piccolo - Zagreb Flyer
6^{5g} 6^{5hy} 9^{5g} 16^{6gs} **0-0-4**

Joe Ninety (Ire) *J S Moore* — 43 a57
2 ch g Daggers Drawn (USA) - Sea Idol (Ire)
5^{5sd} 6^{5sd} 7^{5s} 10^{6g} 3^{7f} 8^{6gf} 11^{7gf} 4^{6s}
11^{6gf} **0-0-9 £946**

Joely Green *N P Littmoden* — 53 a60
7 b g Binary Star (USA) - Comedy Lady
5^{16sd} 10^{13sd} 6^{12sd} 6^{13sd} 6^{16sd} 10^{12gf} 2^{16gf}
12^{17gf} 8^{18f} 11^{19gf} 15^{16gs} 4^{12f} 10^{16sd} **0-1-13**
£1,089

Joey Perhaps *J R Best* — 60 a51
3 b g Danzig Connection (USA) - Realms Of Gold (USA)
17^{8s} 12^{6f} 12^{10f} 6^{8gs} 3^{10gs} 2^{9gf} 3^{8f}
6^{10sd} **0-3-8 £3,019**

Joey The Schnoze *Miss D A McHale* — a2
6 ch g Zilzal (USA) - Linda's Design
7^{13sd} 8^{12gf} **0-0-2**

Johannian *J M Bradley* — 78
6 b g Hernando (Fr) - Photo Call
13^{8s} 13^{8gf} 3^{8gf} 5^{8gf} 9^{10gf} 2^{8gs} 9^{9gf} 4^{8gf}
6^{8gs} 3^{8gs} 2^{8s} 1^{8gf} 2^{8g} 11^{8hy} **1-5-14**
£11,059

John Forbes *B Ellison* — 87
2 b c High Estate - Mavourneen (USA)
9^{7f} 1^{6s} 10^{7gs} 8^{7gf} 9^{8s} 11^{6g} 12^{8s} 7^{6s}
5^{7gs} **1-0-9 £6,825**

John O'Groats (Ire) *B Mactaggart* — 67 a32
6 b g Distinctly North (USA) - Bannons Dream (Ire)
7^{5gs} 11^{5gf} 14^{8gf} 9^{7gf} 10^{5gf} 11^{6f}
16^{5gf} 18^{5gs} 12^{5sd} 12^{5f} 13^{5gs} 11^{6s} **1-0-13**
£1,477

John Robie (USA) *G A Butler* — 83 a75
2 ch c Rahy (USA) - Diamond Flower (USA)
6^{5gf} 3^{6gf} 4^{6sd} **0-1-3 £1,962**

John's Champ (Ire) *R E Barr*
4 b g Mujadil (USA) - Big Buyer (USA)
8^{10s} **0-0-1**

Johnny Alljays (Ire) *J S Moore* — 43
3 b g Victory Note (USA) - It's Academic
11^{8s} 9^{8gf} 10^{7gf} 8^{6f} 8^{8f} 4^{8f} 4^{7f} 10^{8gf}
0-0-8

Johnny Chi (Ire) *P W D'Arcy*
2 ch c Indian Lodge (Ire) - Bring Me Home (Ire)
19^{7gs} **0-0-1**

Johnny Jumpup (Ire) *R M Beckett* — 98
2 ch c Pivotal - Clarice Orsini
1^{5s} 1^{6g} 7^{7s} 1^{8g} 2^{7s} **3-1-5 £24,643**

Johnny Parkes *Mrs J R Ramsden* — 88
3 b g Wolfhound (USA) - Lucky Parkes
1^{5g} 11^{5s} 3^{5gf} 7^{5f} **1-1-4 £5,031**

Johnny Rook (Ire) *E A L Dunlop* — a55
3 ch g Woodman (USA) - Tani (USA)
7^{10sd} **0-0-1**

Johnston's Diamond (Ire) *E J Alston* — 96 a84
6 b g Tagula (Ire) - Toshair Flyer
8^{6sd} 12^{6sd} 16^{sw} 7^{6s} 4^{5gs} 25^{6gf} 8^{6gf}
22^{6f} 9^{6gf} 18^{6g} 14^{5g} 12^{5g} 3^{6s} 6^{5s} 3^{6s} 8^{7g}
3^{6s} **1-4-18 £16,056**

Joint Aspiration *M R Channon* — 104
2 ch f Pivotal - Welcome Home
1⁷ᵍˢ 1⁷ᵍ 6⁸ᵍᶠ **2-0-3 £13,896**

Joint Destiny (Ire) *E J O'Neill* — 52 a51
3 b f Desert Prince (Ire) - Brogan's Well (Ire)
5⁹ˢᵈ 8⁷ˢᵈ 2⁸ˢᵈ 1¹⁰ˢᵈ 7¹¹ᶠ 4⁹ᵍᶠ 8¹⁰ᵍᶠ 6⁹ᵍᶠ
1-1-8 £2,045

Jolie (Ire) *R Dickin* — 23
2 b f Orpen (USA) - Arabian Dream (Ire)
9⁶ᵍᶠ **0-0-1**

Jolizero *P W Chapple-Hyam* — 68 a56
3 br g Danzero (Aus) - Jolis Absent
4⁸ᵍᶠ 9¹⁰ᵍ 3¹²ᵍᶠ 2¹²ᵍˢ 5¹⁴ˢ 9¹¹ˢ 6¹²ˢᵈ 1¹⁰ʰʸ
1-2-8 £7,498

Jomacomi *M Johnston* — 84 a66
3 b c Hector Protector (USA) - Stylish Rose (Ire)
1¹²ˢʷ 3¹²ᵍ 6¹²ᵍˢ 7¹²ᵍ 6¹²ᵍ **1-1-5 £4,162**

Jomus *L Montague Hall* — 59 a72
3 b g Soviet Star (USA) - Oatey
5⁷ˢᵈ 2⁸ˢᵈ 1⁸ˢᵈ 2⁸ˢˢ 9⁷ᵍᶠ 10⁸ᵍᶠ 10⁸ᵍᶠ 4⁸ᵍᶠ
7⁹ᵍᶠ 3⁸ᵍ 5¹⁰ᵍˢ 10¹⁰ˢᵈ 6⁹ˢᵈ **1-3-13 £5,998**

Jonanaud *H J Manners* — 63 a65
5 b g Ballet Royal (USA) - Margaret Modes
6¹³ˢᵈ 7¹⁰ᵍˢ **0-0-2**

Jonny Ebeneezer *D Flood* — 106 a64
5 b g Hurricane Sky (Aus) - Leap Of Faith (Ire)
7⁷ˢˢ 13⁶ᵍˢ 18⁶ˢ 2⁷ᵍˢ 9⁷ʰʸ 2⁷ᵍᶠ 1⁷ᵍᶠ 9⁷ᶠ
3⁷ˢᵈ 1⁶ˢᵈ 7⁶ᵍ 2⁷ᵍˢ 2⁷ᵍᶠ 1⁵ᵍᶠ 1⁶ᵍᶠ 4⁶ˢᵈ 1⁶ᵍᶠ
1⁶ᵍˢ 6⁶ˢ **8-6-25**
£91,566

Jonny Fox'S (Ire) *J Gallagher* — 33 a49
2 ch g Foxhound (USA) - Lala Salama (Ire)
6⁵ˢᵈ 8⁵ᵍ 6⁵ᵍ 13⁵ᵍˢ 8⁵ᶠ **0-0-5**

Jonnyem *G A Swinbank* — 54
3 b g Emarati (USA) - Deerlet
13⁹ᵍ 4⁸ᵍ 9⁷ᶠ 18¹²ᵍ **0-0-4 £322**

Jonquil (Ire) *J H M Gosden* — 92
2 b c Machiavellian (USA) - Jumilla (USA)
4⁷ᵍᶠ 1⁷ᵍᶠ 8⁷ᵍᶠ **1-0-3 £11,140**

Jools *D K Ivory* — 87 a57
6 b g Cadeaux Genereux - Madame Crecy (USA)
7⁸ˢᵈ 11⁸ˢᵈ 1⁸ᵍˢ 5⁸ᵍˢ 3⁸ˢ 8¹⁰ᵍᶠ 14¹⁰ᵍᶠ
4⁸ᵍᶠ 4⁸ᵍᶠ 6⁹ᵍᶠ 5⁷ᵍ 9⁸ᵍᶠ UR⁸ᵍᶠ 6⁸ᶠ 7⁸ᵍˢ 10⁹ᵍ
1-0-16 £8,681

Jordans Elect *I Semple* — 82
4 ch g Fleetwood (Ire) - Cal Norma's Lady (Ire)
5⁹ᵍ 1⁸ᵍˢ 12⁸ᶠ 1⁹ᵍᶠ 8⁸ᶠ 4⁸ᵍˢ 3⁹ᵍᶠ
2-1-8 £10,195

Jordans Spark *I Semple* — 63 a53
3 ch g Opening Verse (USA) - Ribot's Pearl
5¹¹ᵍ 7¹⁰ᵍᶠ 12¹¹ᵍ 6¹¹ˢ 1⁹ᵍˢ 6¹⁰ᵍ 14⁸ᵍ 6⁹ˢᵈ
1-0-8 £3,493

Jorobaden (Fr) *C F Wall* — 98 a52
4 gr g Poliglote - Mercalle (Fr)
2¹⁰ˢᵈ 1¹⁰ᵍˢ 6¹²ᵍ 1⁸¹⁴ᵍˢ 6¹⁶ᵍ 18¹⁶ˢ
15¹⁴ᵍ **2-1-8 £11,771**

Josear *S C Williams* — 52
2 b c Josr Algarhoud (Ire) - Real Popcorn (Ire)
4⁵ˢ 8⁵ᵍ 10⁵ᵍᶠ **0-0-3 £265**

Joseph Henry *M Johnston* — 99
2 b c Mujadil (USA) - Iris May
1⁵ᵍᶠ 1⁵ˢ 4⁶ᵍ 4⁵ˢ 3⁶ˢ 5⁶ˢ **2-1-6**
£13,632

Josephus (Ire) *R Charlton* — 79
3 ch c King Of Kings (Ire) - Khulasah (USA)

11⁸ᵍˢ **0-0-1**

Josh *M A Jarvis* — 106
2 b c Josr Algarhoud (Ire) - Charlie Girl
1⁶ˢ 3⁶ᵍᶠ 7⁶ᵍ 1⁶ᵍ 6⁶ᵍ 3⁷ᵛˢ **2-1-6**
£29,423

Joshar *M W Easterby* — 42 a30
2 b f Paris House - Penny Hasset
8⁵ˢ 3⁵ˢ 8⁵ᵍ 3⁶ˢᵈ 3⁶ᵍᶠ 4⁶ᶠ 13⁶ᵍᶠ **0-1-7**
£1,505

Joshua's Gold (Ire) *D Carroll* — 62 a59
3 b g Sesaro (USA) - Lady Of The Night (Ire)
2⁷ˢᵈ 3⁷ᵍ 6⁸ᵍᶠ 13⁸ᵍᶠ 9⁷ᵍᶠ 8⁷ᵍᶠ 1⁸ᵍᶠ 4⁷ᵍᶠ
2⁷ᵍᶠ 3⁷ᵍ 13⁷ᵍᶠ 5⁸ᵍᶠ 7⁸ᵍᶠ 15⁸ᵍᶠ **1-5-14**
£6,895

Joshuas Boy (Ire) *K A Ryan* — 41
4 ch g Bahhare (USA) - Broadway Rosie
3⁶ᵍ 8⁷ᵍᶠ 9⁶ᵍᶠ **0-1-3 £232**

Jostle *D R Loder* — 36
2 b g Josr Algarhoud (Ire) - Russell Creek
10⁷ᵍᶠ **0-0-1**

Joy And Pain *G L Moore* — 69 a59
3 b g Pursuit Of Love - Ice Chocolate (USA)
14⁷ˢᵈ 8¹⁰ˢᵈ 6⁸ᵍᶠ 7⁷ˢᵈ 1⁷ˢᵈ 6⁶ᵍˢ 2⁷ᵍ 3⁷ᵍᶠ
8⁸ᶠ 17⁶ᵍ 16⁷ˢ **1-2-11 £4,978**

Joyce's Choice *J S Wainwright* — 58 a52
5 b g Mind Games - Madrina
2⁵ᵍ 9⁶ᵍ LFT⁵ᵍˢ 5⁵ᵍ 4⁵ᵍᶠ 10⁵ˢ 12⁵ᵍˢ
10⁵ᵍˢ 2⁵ᵍᶠ 6⁵ᵍᶠ 1⁵ᵍˢ 4⁵ˢᵈ **1-2-12 £4,105**

Joyeaux *S L Keightley* — 66 a65
2 b f Mark Of Esteem (Ire) - Divine Secret
8⁷ˢᵈ 6⁶ʰʸ 4⁶ˢᵈ **0-0-3**

Juantorena *M L W Bell* — 93
2 ch c Miswaki (USA) - Millyant
2⁶ᵍᶠ 2⁵ᵍ 4⁵ᵍᶠ 3⁶ᵍᶠ 4⁵ᵍˢ 2⁵ᵍ 1⁵ᵍᶠ **1-3-7**
£11,414

Jubilee Coin *G B Balding* — 23
2 ch f Fumo Di Londra (Ire) - Money Supply
10⁶ᵍ 10⁶ᵍ **0-0-2**

Jubilee Street (Ire) *Mrs A Duffield* — 68 a38
5 b g Dr Devious (Ire) - My Firebird
9⁷ˢᵈ 4⁶ᵍˢ 3⁷ᵍᶠ 1⁷ᵍᶠ 10⁷ᵍᶠ 7⁸ᵍᶠ 6⁷ᵍᶠ 1⁷ᵍᶠ
2⁷ᵍˢ 1⁷ᵍᶠ 8⁷ᵍᶠ 7⁷ˢ 16⁷ˢ **3-2-13 £15,873**

Jubilee Treat (USA) *G Wragg* — 73
4 b f Seeking The Gold (USA) - Dance Treat (USA)
13⁸ᵍᶠ 7¹⁰ᵍᶠ 6¹⁰ˢ **0-0-3 £450**

Judda *R F Marvin* — 28
3 b g Makbul - Pepeke
15⁶ᵍᶠ 11⁷ᵍᶠ 12⁷ˢᵈ 11¹⁰ʰʸ **0-0-4**

Judge Damuss (Ire) *A Crook*
2 ch c Tagula (Ire) - Acicula (Ire)
18⁶ˢ 12⁸ᵍˢ **0-0-2**

Jules Lee *W G M Turner* — 5
2 ch g Bluegrass Prince (Ire) - Jade's Girl
13⁷ᵍᶠ 13⁸ᵍ **0-0-2**

Jumbo's Flyer *F P Murtagh* — 5
7 ch g Jumbo Hirt (USA) - Fragrant Princess
10⁶ᶠ **0-0-1**

Jumeirah Scarer *M R Channon* — a71
3 b g Tagula (Ire) - Mountain Harvest (Fr)
2⁸ˢᵈ 2⁸ˢᵈ **0-2-2 £2,220**

Jun Fan (USA) *B Ellison* — 62
2 br c Artax (USA) - Ringside Lady (NZ)
5⁵ᵍᶠ 6⁶ᶠ **0-0-2**

Jungle Lion *John A Harris* — 47 a57
6 ch g Lion Cavern (USA) - Star Ridge (USA)

6^{8sd} 2^{11sd} 10^{14sd} 1^{12sw} 13^{12sd} 1^{14sd} 6^{12sd}
8^{14g} 6^{16sd} **2-1-9 £5,358**

Juniper Banks *Miss A Stokell*   48 a64
3 ch g Night Shift (USA) - Beryl
6^{5g} 6^{6gf} 10^{5s} 12^{6gs} 3^{5sd} 12^{5sd} 6^{5sd}
0-1-7 £427

Just A Fluke (Ire) *M Johnston*   79
3 b c Darshaan - Star Profile (Ire)
4^{10gs} 7^{10hy} 2^{9f} 3^{10s} 13^{10g} 5^{9gf} 2^{9gs} 1^{8g}
4^{8s} **1-3-9 £9,354**

Just A Glimmer *L G Cottrell*   88 a93
4 b f Bishop Of Cashel - Rockin' Rosie
3^{7sd} 7^{7sd} 1^{7ss} 2^{7ss} 7^{7gs} 1^{7s} 13^{7g} 15^{7g}
12^{7sd} **2-2-9 £11,779**

Just A Try (USA) *R Hannon*   65
2 ch c Lure (USA) - Boubasis (USA)
8^{7g} 6^{7gs} 7^{8g} **0-0-3**

Just Beware *Miss Z C Davison*   a34
2 b f Makbul - Bewails (Ire)
13^{6gf} 8^{7g} 10^{7sd} **0-0-3**

Just Bonnie *J M Bradley*   19
2 b c Lujain (USA) - Fairy Flight (Ire)
6^{6gf} 9^{5gf} 17^{6g} 15^{6gs} **0-0-4**

Just Cliff *W R Muir*   61 a54
2 b c Handsome Ridge - Justfortherecord
11^{6sd} 4^{7gs} 4^{7sd} **0-0-3**

Just Dance Me (Fr) *R Charlton*   67
3 gr f Linamix (Fr) - Reine De La Ciel (USA)
2^{9g} 6^{8g} **0-0-2 £1,720**

Just Dashing *J E Long*   16
5 b g Arrasas (USA) - Smitten
12^{10g} 9^{6gf} 16^{10s} **0-0-3**

Just Do It (UAE) *M R Channon*   71 a55
2 b c Timber Country (USA) - Poised (USA)
6^{8sd} 2^{8gs} 5^{8s} 14^{7f} 9^{8s} **0-1-5 £1,870**

Just Elizabeth *M E Sowersby*   15
2 b f Aragon - Collison Lane
13^{6hy} 8^{7s} 21^{6gs} **0-0-3**

Just Fly *S Kirk*   84 a94
4 b g Efisio - Chrysalis
2^{6sd} 2^{7sd} 2^{7sd} $1^{7.8s}$ 3^{7g} 12^{7g} 13^{7g} 8^{7g}
12^{7s} 13^{7g} 2^{8gf} 2^{8gf} 5^{6sd} **0-6-13 £12,492**

Just James *J Noseda*   99
5 b g Spectrum (Ire) - Fairy Flight (Ire)
15^{6gs} 13^{8gf} 11^{7g} **0-0-3**

Just One Look *M Blanshard*   68 a76
3 b f Barathea (Ire) - Western Sal
7^{7sd} 8^{6g} 7^{6g} 15^{7g} 8^{8sd} 6^{8g} 10^{8gs} 5^{7g}
7^{8s} 3^{9sd} 3^{9sd} **0-2-11 £807**

Just One Smile (Ire) *T D Easterby*   66
4 b f Desert Prince (Ire) - Smile Awhile (USA)
16^{6hy} 3^{7s} 6^{6g} 10^{7gf} 7^{6g} 10^{6gf} 11^{6gf}
0-1-7 £1,078

Just Red *R Hollinshead*   a9
6 ch g Meqdaam (USA) - Orchard Bay
10^{12sd} **0-0-1**

Just Tim (Ire) *R Hannon*   83 a76
3 ch c Inchinor - Simply Sooty
4^{10sd} 1^{8g} 4^{8gs} 12^{8gf} 1^{8gf} 5^{8gf} 7^{8gf} 14^{8g}
2-0-8 £10,913

Just Waz (USA) *R M Whitaker*   68
2 ch g Woodman (USA) - Just Tops (USA)
8^{7gs} 1^{7s} 5^{8gf} 10^{8s} **1-0-4 £4,527**

Just Wiz *N P Littmoden*   a72
8 b g Efisio - Jade Pet

6^{12sd} 3^{12ss} 10^{10sd} 2^{8sw} 3^{9ss} 11^{8gs} 2^{12sd}
5^{8sd} **0-1-8 £2,279**

Justalord *J Balding*   89 a96
6 b g King's Signet (USA) - Just Lady
8^{5sd} 2^{5sd} 1^{5sd} 2^{5sd} 3^{5sd} 13^{5s} 6^{5f} 1^{5gf}
7^{5gf} 1^{5gf} **3-3-10 £32,219**

Justaquestion *I A Wood*   92
2 b f Pursuit Of Love - Queenbird
7^{5g} 1^{5gs} 1^{6gs} 12^{6f} 3^{7g} 2^{7gf} 1^{7g} 5^{7gs} 9^{7g}
6^{7s} 4^{8gs} **3-2-11 £47,816**

Juste Pour L'Amour *P L Gilligan*   82
4 ch g Pharly (Fr) - Fontaine Lady
8^{8gf} 4^{7gf} 7^{10gf} 9^{7g} 10^{8g} 4^{7gf} 7^{6gf} 7^{6gf}
1^{8gf} 5^{8gs} 2^{9g} 6^{7g} 4^{8gf} **1-1-13 £8,280**

Justenjoy Yourself *C A Dwyer*   41 a29
2 b f Tipsy Creek (USA) - Habibi
6^{5gs} 8^{5gf} 6^{5sd} 4^{5g} 8^{6s} 3^{6s} 15^{7gf} **0-1-7**
£368

Justice Jones *J L Spearing*   42
3 b g Emperor Jones (USA) - Rally For Justice
9^{8ss} 10^{7gs} 17^{10g} 16^{10s} 10^{10f} 10^{7f} 16^{6g}
0-0-7

Juwwi *J M Bradley*   55 a75
10 ch g Mujtahid (USA) - Nouvelle Star (Aus)
10^{6sd} 4^{5sd} 11^{6sd} 9^{5sd} 4^{6ss} 4^{5ss} 14^{6gs}
6^{5sd} 2^{6f} 6^{6g} 6^{6s} 14^{5sd} 11^{5g} 17^{5gs} **0-1-14**
£736

Kabeer *P S McEntee*   71 a63
6 ch g Unfuwain (USA) - Ta Rib (USA)
4^{7f} 3^{7gf} 11^{7gf} 8^{8gf} 5^{7sd} 6^{8gf} 12^{10g} 6^{7sd}
0-1-8 £852

Kabis Amigos *H R A Cecil*   60
2 ch c Nashwan (USA) - River Saint (USA)
9^{8g} 9^{8hy} **0-0-2**

Kabis Booie (Ire) *H R A Cecil*   66
3 ch c Night Shift (USA) - Perfect Welcome
3^{10gf} 9^{11gs} **0-1-2 £670**

Kabreet *E A L Dunlop*   67 a86
3 b c Night Shift (USA) - Red Rabbit
3^{7sd} 1^{6sd} 9^{6g} 15^{6gf} 8^{6s} 8^{5gs} **1-0-6**
£6,387

Kafil (USA) *J J Bridger*   a23
10 b/br g Housebuster (USA) - Alchaasibiyeh (USA)
13^{6sd} 7^{7sd} 7^{6sd} **0-0-3**

Kaggamagic *J R Norton*   63 a46
2 ch g Abou Zouz (USA) - Meadmore Magic
5^{6f} 4^{6s} 7^{12g} 8^{8sd} 6^{6sd} **0-0-6**

Kagoshima (Ire) *J R Norton*   a47
9 b g Shirley Heights - Kashteh (Ire)
2^{16sd} 2^{14sd} 3^{14sd} 3^{16sd} 6^{16sw} **0-4-5**
£1,330

Kahira (Ire) *M L W Bell*   75
2 ch f King's Best (USA) - Sine Labe (USA)
8^{8g} 2^{7g} **0-1-2 £1,756**

Kahyasi Princess (Ire) *M Johnston*   61
4 b f Kahyasi - Dungeon Princess (Ire)
5^{14g} **0-0-1**

Kaid (Ire) *R Lee*
9 b g Alzao (USA) - Very Charming (USA)
7^{12ss} **0-0-1**

Kaieteur (USA) *B J Meehan*   109
5 b h Marlin (USA) - Strong Embrace (USA)
6^{10gs} 8^{10gf} 5^{10g} 4^{10gf} **0-0-4 £2,500**

Kajul *C A Horgan*   36 a28
3 b f Emperor Jones (USA) - Andbell

10[7gs] 10[8sd] **0-0-2**

Kalaman (Ire) *Sir Michael Stoute* 123
4 b c Desert Prince (Ire) - Kalamba (Ire)
2[9g] 1[8gf] 3[10gs] 1[10gf] 6[10g] **2-2-5**
£138,740

Kalamansi (Ire) *N A Callaghan* 45
3 b f Sadler's Wells (USA) - Musk Lime (USA)
6[9g] 16[10gf] 12[7gf] 8[9gf] 8[11gf] **0-0-5**

Kalani Star (Ire) *I Semple* 75 a61
4 b c Ashkalani (Ire) - Bellissi (Ire)
6[8g] 7[7gv] 3[7gf] 7[8f] 4[7gf] 5[7sd] 7[7sd] **0-1-7**
£1,320

Kalanisha (Ire) *John Berry* 45 a30
4 ch g Ashkalani (Ire) - Camisha (Ire)
7[10gs] 6[12hy] 11[12sd] 3[14sd] 5[10sd] **0-1-5 £425**

Kali *R Charlton* 80 a83
3 gr f Linamix (Fr) - Alkarida (Fr)
3[10gs] 3[8gf] 2[7g] 1[7gf] 6[7gs] 4[7sd] 6[7s] 2[9sd]
1-4-8 £8,017

Kalika (Ire) *Ms Deborah J Evans* 20 a18
2 b f Bachir (Ire) - Ruwy
6[6sd] 12[6gf] 8[7sd] 13[7gf] **0-0-4**

Kalimenta (USA) *S Kirk* 55
3 ch f Rahy (USA) - Toujours Elle (USA)
4[8vs] 2[8g] 6[10ho] 6[10g] 7[10gf] 11[9s] 15[10g]
0-0-7 £1,831

Kalishka (Ire) *Andrew Turnell* 63
3 b c Fasliyev (USA) - Andromaque (USA)
6[8gs] 5[8gf] 14[8gf] 11[10gf] 8[8gf] 13[10g] **0-0-6**

Kallista's Pride *J R Best* 66 a48
4 b f Puissance - Clan Scotia
9[7gf] 2[5gf] 9[5g] 1[6g] 12[6gf] 6[5gf] 11[5s] 5[5g]
12[5g] 13[6gf] 7[6sd] **1-1-11 £4,699**

Kalmini (USA) *M R Channon* 75
2 b/br f Rahy (USA) - Kilma (USA)
7[7g] 2[7gf] 1[7g] 5[8s] 4[7g] 12[8g] **1-1-6**
£8,360

Kalou (Ger) *B J Curley* 54 a54
6 br g Law Society (USA) - Kompetenz (Ire)
3[10sd] 7[10g] 3[10gf] 9[12gs] 7[11gs] **0-2-5 £945**

Kaluana Court *R J Price* 8
8 b m Batshoof - Fairfields Cone
13[17g] 19[14g] 33[18s] 7[12s] **0-0-4**

Kalush *Ronald Thompson* 3
3 b g Makbul - The Lady Vanishes
17[8g] 9[10gs] 6[10f] 8[8gf] **0-0-4**

Kama's Wheel *John A Harris* 33
5 ch m Magic Ring (Ire) - Tea And Scandals (USA)
8[8g] 7[8g] 6[8f] 7[8gs] **0-0-4**

Kamakiri (Ire) *R Hannon* 98
2 b c Trans Island - Alpine Flair (Ire)
7[7gs] 1[7gf] 1[7gf] **2-0-3 £13,437**

Kamala *R Brotherton*
5 b m Priolo (USA) - Fleeting Vision (Ire)
6[12sd] **0-0-1**

Kamanda Laugh *B W Hills* 90 a76
3 ch g Most Welcome - Kamada (USA)
1[6sd] 2[7s] 1[7gf] 1[8g] 1[8s] 5[8gs] **4-1-6**
£31,825

Kamenka *R A Fahey* 73 a24
3 ch f Wolfhound (USA) - Aliuska (Ire)
4[6s] 4[5gf] 4[5gs] 17[6gs] 11[6s] 3[6g] 3[6gs] 6[6sd]
0-2-8 £2,048

Kames Park (Ire) *I Semple* 80

Kanad *B Hanbury* 74
2 b g Bold Edge - Multi-Sofft
3[6gf] 2[5gf] 7[6f] 2[6gf] 5[6gf] 1[7gs] **1-3-6**
£4,785

Kandidate *C E Brittain* 99 a68
2 b c Kabool - Valleyrose (Ire)
15[7gf] 3[7g] 7[7g] 6[8gf] 2[8sd] **0-2-5 £4,207**

Kangarilla Road *Mrs J R Ramsden* 75
5 b g Magic Ring (Ire) - Kangra Valley
18[5g] 7[5gf] 2[5gf] 13[5gf] 14[5gf] 14[5gf] **0-1-6**
£1,124

Kangrina *Sir Mark Prescott* a79
2 b f Acatenango (Ger) - Kirona
5[8sd] 4[9sd] 1[9sd] **1-0-3 £3,412**

Kanz Wood (USA) *A W Carroll* 27 a50
8 ch g Woodman (USA) - Kanz (USA)
15[7sd] 5[8sd] 9[8sd] 5[8gs] 5[7hy] 3[8sd] 4[8sd] 3[7sd]
6[8sd] 10[7sd] **0-1-10 £643**

Kapaje *P D Evans* 67
2 b f Lake Coniston (Ire) - Reina
18[6gf] 5[6gf] 3[7g] 8[8gf] **0-1-4 £549**

Kaparolo (USA) *Mrs A J Perrett* 43
5 ch g El Prado (Ire) - Parliament House (USA)
7[16hy] 14[16gs] **0-0-2**

Karakum *A J Chamberlain* 40
5 b g Mtoto - Magongo
4[13gf] 10[12g] 9[12f] **0-0-3 £272**

Karamea (Swi) *J L Dunlop* 76
3 gr f Rainbow Quest (USA) - Karapucha (Ire)
3[10g] 1[12g] 5[12g] 11[12gs] 8[12g] **1-1-5 £6,389**

Karaoke (Ire) *S Kirk* 75 a76
4 b g Mujadil (USA) - Kayoko (Ire)
14[10sd] 7[10sd] 1[10sd] 15[10g] 11[10g] 5[8gs] 5[10s]
4[10gf] 2[10f] 2[10gf] 8[10gf] 8[10gs] 9[9gf] 3[10gf] 1[10gf]
7[10gf] 5[12f] **2-4-17 £12,915**

Karaoke King *J E Long* a51
6 ch h King's Signet (USA) - Brampton Grace
6[7sd] 15[7sd] 11[6sd] 9[7sd] PU[7s] **0-0-5**

Karashinko (Ire) *R Guest*
3 b g Shinko Forest (Ire) - Kayoko (Ire)
13[8gf] 14[5gf] **0-0-2**

Karathaena (Ire) *M E Sowersby* 55 a41
4 b f Barathea (Ire) - Dabtara (Ire)
8[7sd] 12[8sd] 8[8gs] 14[10gs] 10[8s] 8[12hy] 10[12gf]
0-0-7

Kareeb (Fr) *W J Musson* 80 a84
7 b g Green Desert (USA) - Braari (USA)
6[8sd] 14[7gs] 19[6s] 4[7gf] 21[7f] 6[7g] 14[7gf]
6[7s] 4[7gf] 11[7g] **0-2-10 £929**

Karelian *K A Ryan* 73
3 gr g Linamix (Fr) - Kalikala
7[11gs] 0[11ho] 4[11vs] 1[11g] 2[12g] 3[10s] 6[16gs]
1-1-7 £9,783

Karen's Caper (USA) *J H M Gosden* a85
2 b f War Chant (USA) - Miss Caerleona (Fr)
2[7sd] 1[8sd] **1-1-2 £5,633**

Karita *M L W Bell*
2 ch f Inchinor - Ebba
9[5s] **0-0-1**

Karlu (Ger) *J L Dunlop* 73
2 ch c Big Shuffle (Ger) - Krim (Ger)
9[7g] 17[hy] **1-0-2 £3,059**

Karma Chamelian (USA) *J W Hills* 43

3 b f Diesis - Wild Rumour (Ire)
12⁸ᵍᶠ 5⁷ᵍᶠ 7⁶ᵍᶠ **0-0-3**

Karminskey Park *T J Etherington*　　71 a50
5 b m Sabrehill (USA) - Housefull
6⁵ʰʸ 2⁵ʰʸ 6⁵ʰʸ 5⁵ᵍᶠ 3⁵ᵍᶠ 2⁵ᵍᶠ 1⁵ᵍ 7⁵ᵍˢ
7⁵ᵍ 7⁵ᵍᶠ 9⁵ᵍᶠ 8⁵ᵍˢ 5⁶ᵍˢ 10⁶ᵍ 6⁶ˢᵈ **1-3-15**
£10,684

Karyon (Ire) *Miss Kate Milligan*　　43
4 b f Presidium - Stealthy
5¹²ᵍᶠ 9¹⁴ˢᵈ 10¹⁴ᵍᶠ **0-0-3**

Kashimo (Ger) *G L Moore*　　60 a60
5 b h Lomitas - Kardia
5¹²ˢᵈ 3¹²ˢᵈ 4¹¹ᵍᶠ **0-1-3 £713**

Kashmar Flight *T D Easterby*　　56
2 b f Fraam - Evasive Step
8⁵ˢ 7⁶ᶠ 6⁷ᶠ 5⁷ᵍᶠ 11⁸ᶠ **0-0-5**

Kashtanka (Ire) *J J Quinn*　　47
2 ch c Ashkalani (Ire) - Spark (Ire)
17⁶ᵍˢ 6⁷ᵍˢ 6⁷ᶠ **0-0-3**

Kaska (Ire) *B W Hills*　　68
3 b f King Of Kings (Ire) - Antiguan Jane
7⁸ᵍ 6¹⁰ᵍ **0-0-2**

Kasthari (Ire) *J Howard Johnson*　　117
5 gr g Vettori (Ire) - Karliyka (Ire)
1¹⁸ᵍ 11¹⁶ˢ **1-0-2 £41,500**

Katali *A Bailey*
7 ch m Clantime - Portvally
11⁶ˢᵈ **0-0-1**

Katana *I A Wood*　　62 a58
2 b f Spectrum (Ire) - Karlaska
14⁸ᵍˢ 12⁸ᵍˢ 5⁸ˢᵈ 5⁸ᵍ **0-0-4**

Katavi (USA) *J Noseda*　　a58
3 b f Stravinsky (USA) - Halholah (USA)
5⁷ˢᵈ 7⁷ˢᵈ **0-1-2 £542**

Katayeb (Ire) *M P Tregoning*　　14
3 b f Machiavellian (USA) - Fair Of The Furze
8¹⁰ᵍ **0-0-1**

Kathology (Ire) *D R C Elsworth*　　85
7 b g College Chapel - Wicken Wonder (Ire)
17⁵ᵍᶠ 6⁵ᶠ 7⁵ᵍ 8⁵ᵍˢ 3⁵ᵍᶠ 5⁵ᵍᶠ 7⁵ᵍˢ **0-1-7**
£1,082

Kathryn Janeway (Ire) *W R Muir*　　58
2 b f In The Wings - Freak Out (Fr)
12⁷ᵍ 6⁸ˢ **0-0-2**

Kathys Job *A D Smith*　　52
2 b f Silver Wizard (USA) - Kathy Fair (Ire)
9⁵ᵍ **0-0-1**

Katie Boo (Ire) *A Berry*　　85
2 br f Namid - Misty Peak (Ire)
3⁵ᵍᶠ 2⁵ᵍᶠ 1⁵ᶠ 3⁶ᵍ 5⁵ᵍ 2⁵ᵍᶠ 2⁵ᶠ 1⁶ᵍ **2-4-8**
£22,052

Katie Kai *Miss S E Forster*　　5
3 b f Cayman Kai (Ire) - Yemaail (Ire)
5⁸ˢ **0-0-1 £258**

Katie Killane *M Wellings*　　39
2 ch f Komaite (USA) - Efficacy
7⁵ᵍ 12⁶ᵍ 13⁵ᵍᶠ 12⁵ˢᵈ **0-0-4**

Katie Mernagh (Ire) *P S McEntee*　　23
4 b f Danetime (Ire) - White Jasmin
5¹⁴ˢ **0-0-1**

Katie's Bath Time *Ian Emmerson*
3 b f Lugana Beach - Eucharis
11⁶ˢˢ 12⁵ᵍ **0-0-2**

Katie's Biscuit *Ian Emmerson*　　53
2 b f Cayman Kai (Ire) - Peppers (Ire)

6⁶ᶠ 10⁷ᵍᶠ 6⁷ˢ **0-0-3**

Katie's Role *Ian Emmerson*　　29 a48
3 b f Tragic Role (USA) - Mirkan Honey
3⁷ˢᵈ 4⁷ˢᵈ 4⁷ˢᵈ 3⁸ˢˢ 7¹⁰ᵍ 13¹⁰ᵍˢ **0-1-6**
£897

Katiypour (Ire) *Miss B Sanders*　　83 a83
7 ch g Be My Guest (USA) - Katiyfa
7¹⁰ˢᵈ 3¹⁰ˢᵈ 1⁸ˢᵈ 2⁸ˢᵈ 8⁹ˢ 1⁸ᵍᶠ 4⁸ᵍᶠ 12¹⁰ᵍ
3¹⁰ᵍᶠ 4⁸ᶠ 5⁹ᵍˢ 7¹⁰ᵍ 7¹⁰ᵍᶠ 3¹⁰ˢᵈ **2-4-14**
£12,635

Katy Jem *D M Simcock*　　17
2 b f Night Shift (USA) - Top Jem
15⁷ᵍˢ **0-0-1**

Katy O'Hara *Miss S E Hall*　　37 a48
5 b m Komaite (USA) - Amy Leigh (Ire)
9⁶ˢˢ 2⁶ˢˢ 6⁶ˢʷ 10⁷ᶠ **0-1-4 £470**

Katz Pyjamas (Ire) *G F H Charles-Jones*
3 b f Fasliyev (USA) - Allepolina (USA)
19⁶ᵍˢ 13⁸ᶠ **0-0-2**

Kauri Forest (USA) *J R Fanshawe*　　86 a66
3 ch g Woodman (USA) - Kentucky Fall (Fr)
3⁷ᵍˢ 2⁸ᵍ 2⁷ᵍᶠ 3⁸ˢᵈ 4⁷ˢᵈ **0-4-5 £5,174**

Kavi (Ire) *Simon Earle*　　a62
4 ch g Perugino (USA) - Premier Leap (Ire)
7¹⁰ˢᵈ 8¹⁰ˢᵈ 11¹²ˢᵈ **0-0-3**

Kay Two (Ire) *Ms F M Crowley*　　103
2 ch c Monashee Mountain (USA) - Tricky
2⁵ʰʸ 2⁵ᵍᶠ 4⁶ᵍᶠ 1⁵ᵍᶠ 5⁶ᵍ 1⁵ˢ 1⁵ʰʸ 3⁵ˢ 8⁶ᵛˢ
3-2-9 £61,550

Kayf Aramis *I A Wood*
2 b c Kayf Tara - Ara
12⁷ᵍᶠ **0-0-1**

Kaymich Perfecto *R M Whitaker*　　47
4 b g Sheikh Albadou - Manhattan Diamond
7¹⁰ᵍ 1⁸ˢᵈ 3⁸ᵍ 2⁹ˢᵈ 2⁸ˢᵈ 13⁸ˢᵈ 14⁸ᵍᶠ
13¹⁰ᵍ **1-0-8 £4,542**

Kedross (Ire) *J Jay*　　33 a38
3 ch f King Of Kings (Ire) - Nom De Plume (USA)
7⁷ˢᵈ 7⁶ˢᵈ 14⁸ˢᵈ 5¹²ᵍᶠ 7⁷ˢᵈ 15⁷ᵍᶠ **0-0-6**

Keelung (USA) *M A Jarvis*　　96 a78
3 b g Lear Fan (USA) - Miss Universal (Ire)
4⁸ˢᵈ 2⁸ˢᵈ 2¹⁰ᵍ 1¹⁰ʰʸ 3¹⁰ˢ 2¹⁰ᵍˢ 16¹²ᵍᶠ
7¹²ᵍ 14¹⁰ˢᵈ 17¹⁰ᵍ **1-4-10 £11,895**

Keep Bacckinhit (Ire) *G L Moore*　　81
2 b f Raise A Grand (Ire) - Taispeain (Ire)
3⁶ᵍᶠ 10⁶ᵍ 3⁶ᵍᶠ 1⁷ᵍᶠ 5⁷ˢ 17⁷ᵍ 4⁶ᵍᶠ 6⁷ᵍˢ
1-1-8 £12,937

Keep Me Warm *W G M Turner*　　64 a71
2 ch g Atraf - Little Greenbird
4⁵ˢ 2⁶ˢᵈ **0-1-2 £1,392**

Keep On Movin' (Ire) *T G Mills*　　78
3 b f Danehill Dancer (Ire) - Tormented (USA)
5¹⁰ᵍˢ 8¹²ᵍˢ 2¹²ᵍ 7¹²ᵍ 4¹²ᵍᶠ 13¹⁴ᵍᶠ **0-1-6**
£3,058

Keep The Peace (Ire) *K G Wingrove*　　10
6 br g Petardia - Eiras Mood
17¹²ᵍᶠ **0-0-1**

Keepasharplookout (Ire) *Mrs L Stubbs*　　56
2 b g Rossini (USA) - Zoyce
4⁵ˢ 4⁵ᵍ 10⁶ʰʸ 4⁵ᵍ **0-0-4 £902**

Keeper's Lodge (Ire) *B A McMahon*　　78
3 ch f Grand Lodge (USA) - Gembira (USA)
4⁷ᵍˢ 16⁸ᵍᶠ 7⁸ᶠ 1⁸ᵍ 8⁶ˢ 3⁸ᵍᶠ 5¹⁰ˢ 2¹⁰ˢ
15¹¹ᵍ **1-1-9 £9,306**

Keepers Knight (Ire) *P F I Cole*　　66 a67

3 b c Sri Pekan (USA) - Keepers Dawn (Ire)
1¹⁰ˢᵈ 3¹⁰ˢᵈ 5¹⁰ˢᵈ 7¹²ˢˢ 15¹¹ᵍˢ 9⁸ᵍᶠ 3¹⁰ᵍᶠ
5¹⁰ᵍˢ 4¹¹ᵍˢ 5¹⁰ˢ 8¹⁰ʰʸ **1-1-11 £5,270**

Kehaar M A Magnusson 107
3 ch c Cadeaux Genereux - Lighthouse
1⁷ᵍᶠ 1⁸ᵍˢ 11⁷ᵍᶠ 1⁷ᵍᶠ **3-0-4 £60,444**

Kelbrook A Bailey 64
5 b g Unfuwain (USA) - Pidona
5⁸ᵍ 8¹²ᵍᶠ 4¹⁰ᵍ **0-0-3 £417**

Kelseas Kolby (Ire) P Butler 63 a61
4 b g Perugino (USA) - Notre Dame
13⁷ᵍˢ 13⁷ᵍ 1⁷ᵍᶠ 4⁸ᵍᶠ 3⁸ᶠ 4⁸ᵍˢ 4⁸ᶠ 2⁷ᵍᶠ
2⁸ᵍᶠ 5⁸ˢᵈ 3⁸ᵍᶠ 18¹⁰ᵍˢ **1-5-12 £6,589**

Keltic Flute Mrs Lucinda Featherstone a34
5 b g Piccolo - Nanny Doon
11⁸ˢᵈ 4⁷ˢᵈ 10⁸ˢˢ 6⁷ˢˢ 7⁷ˢᵈ 6⁶ˢᵈ 7⁷ˢᵈ
0-0-7

Keltic Rainbow (Ire) D Haydn Jones 42 a38
3 b f Spectrum (Ire) - Secrets Of Honour
4⁹ˢʷ 6¹⁰ᵍˢ 9⁸ˢᵈ 9¹²ᵍᶠ 4¹²ᵍˢ 5⁸ʰʸ 9¹²ᵍ
12¹⁰ᵍ **0-0-8**

Keltos (Fr) C Laffon-Parias 117
6 gr h Kendor (Fr) - Loxandra
1⁷ˢ 2⁸ˢ 2⁸ʰʸ 3⁷ᵍˢ 5⁸ᵍ 2⁷ˢ 3⁸ᵛˢ **1-4-7
£63,672**

Kelucia (Ire) J S Goldie 95
3 ch f Grand Lodge (USA) - Karachi (Spa)
5⁸ᵍ 11⁸ᵍ 5⁸ᵍᶠ 6⁸ᶠ 6⁸ᵍˢ 6¹⁰ᵍᶠ 6⁸ᵍᶠ 7⁸ᵍ
16⁸ᵍ **0-0-9 £7,203**

Kempsey J J Bridger 64 a71
2 ch c Wolfhound (USA) - Mockingbird
10⁵ᵍᶠ 6⁵ᵍᶠ 4⁵ˢᵈ 4⁵ᵍ 4⁵ˢ 6⁵ᵍᶠ 13⁵ᵍᶠ 8⁶ˢ
6⁸ˢᵈ **0-0-9 £900**

Ken's Dream Ms A E Embiricos 87
5 b g Bin Ajwaad (Ire) - Shoag (USA)
10¹⁰ᵍ 3¹⁰ᵍᶠ 4¹⁰ᵍᶠ 11⁰ᵍᶠ 4¹¹ᵍ 6¹⁰ᵍᶠ **1-1-6
£6,582**

Kenmore B W Hills 90
2 b c Compton Place - Watheeqah (USA)
4⁶ᵍᶠ 2⁶ˢ **0-1-2 £2,500**

Kennington Mrs C A Dunnett 58 a61
4 ch g Compton Place - Mim
1⁷ˢᵈ 13⁷ˢᵈ 4⁵ˢˢ 9⁷ˢˢ 3⁶ᵍˢ 4⁶ˢᵈ 9⁶ˢᵈ 7⁷ᵍᶠ
2⁶ᶠ 7⁶ˢᵈ 7⁶ᵍᶠ 4⁵ᵍˢ 12⁵ᵍᶠ 2⁵ˢᵈ 4⁵ˢ 5⁶ᵍ **1-4-16
£6,276**

Kenny The Truth (Ire) Mrs J Candlish 48 a53
5 b g Robellino (USA) - Just Blink (Ire)
3⁸ˢᵈ 2⁸ˢᵈ 3⁸ˢᵈ 3⁸ˢᵈ 4⁸ˢʷ 5⁹ˢʷ 1⁸ˢˢ 4⁸ˢᵈ
3⁸ᵍˢ 3⁸ˢᵈ 9⁸ᶠ PU¹²ˢᵈ 6⁸ˢᵈ 5⁸ˢᵈ 12¹¹ˢ **1-6-15
£3,542**

Kensington (Ire) R Guest 68 a59
3 b g Cape Cross (Ire) - March Star (Ire)
6⁷ˢ 3⁶ˢ 2⁶ᵍᶠ 6⁶ᵍᶠ 1⁶ᵍᶠ 6⁶ˢᵈ 5⁶ˢᵈ **1-2-7
£5,750**

Kentmere (Ire) P R Webber 62 a72
3 b g Efisio - Addaya (Ire)
6⁸ᵍᶠ 10⁸ˢᵈ **1-0-2 £2,982**

Kentucky Bankes W G M Turner 21
2 b c Bluegrass Prince (Ire) - Countess Bankes
11⁵ˢᵈ 6⁸ᵍᶠ 8⁶ᵍᶠ **0-0-3**

Kentucky Blue (Ire) T D Easterby 89
4 b g Revoque (Ire) - Delta Town (USA)
3¹¹ˢ 12¹²ᵍˢ 13¹⁰ᵍˢ **0-1-3 £1,529**

Kentucky Bullet (USA) A G Newcombe a59
8 b g Housebuster (USA) - Exactly So
3¹¹ˢᵈ 7¹²ˢᵈ 6¹²ˢᵈ 3¹²ˢˢ 6¹²ˢᵈ 9¹²ˢᵈ 5¹²ˢᵈ

5¹²ˢᵈ **0-2-8 £834**

Kentucky Express T D Easterby 72
3 b c Air Express (Ire) - Hotel California (Ire)
7⁷ᶠ 2⁶ᵍᶠ 3⁶ᵍᶠ **0-2-3 £2,490**

Kentucky King (USA) P W Hiatt 89 a89
4 b g Tale Of The Cat (USA) - Anna's Honor (USA)
6⁶ˢᵈ 6⁸ˢʷ 8¹⁰ˢᵈ 1⁸ˢᵈ 7⁸ˢᵈ 3⁸ᵍˢ 12¹⁰ᵍ 12⁸ˢ
11⁸ᵍᶠ 3¹⁰ᵍ 5⁷ˢᵈ 2⁸ᵍˢ RR¹²ᵍᶠ 4⁸ᵍˢ RR¹⁰ᵍˢ **1-4-15
£7,143**

Kenwyn M Blanshard 42
2 b g Efisio - Vilany
9⁵ᵍ 15⁶ᵍˢ **0-0-2**

Keon (Ire) R Hollinshead 68
2 b c Rossini (USA) - Lonely Brook (USA)
7⁷ˢ **0-0-1**

Kerashan (Ire) Sir Michael Stoute 80
2 b c Sinndar (Ire) - Kerataka (Ire)
4⁷ᵍᶠ 2⁸ᵍᶠ 15⁸ˢ **0-1-3 £2,260**

Keresforth I A Wood 54
2 b g Mind Games - Bullion
10⁵ˢˢ 7⁵ᵍ 2⁵ᵍᶠ 1⁵ᵍᶠ 9⁵ᵍ 2⁵ᵍᶠ 8⁶ᵍᶠ **1-1-7
£4,369**

Kergolay (Ire) W R Muir a54
2 b c King's Theatre (Ire) - Trim Star
6⁹ˢᵈ 10⁸ˢᵈ **0-0-2**

Kernel Dowery (Ire) W R Swinburn 70 a65
4 b g Sri Pekan (USA) - Lady Dowery (USA)
8¹⁰ᵍ 8¹⁰ᵍˢ 2¹⁰ᵍᶠ 1¹⁰ᶠ 1¹⁰ᶠ 7¹⁰ᶠ 7¹⁰ᶠ 4¹⁰ʰʸ
5¹⁰ᵍᶠ 13¹⁰ᵍˢ 4¹²ˢᵈ 14¹²ˢᵈ **2-1-12 £7,567**

Kerny (Ire) J J Quinn 52
2 b c Rossini (USA) - Queen Of Sweden (Ire)
9⁵ˢᵈ 6⁵ᶠ 11⁵ᵍ 10⁵ᵍᶠ **0-0-4**

Kerristina D J S Ffrench Davis 51 a27
3 b f So Factual (USA) - Arch Angel (Ire)
13⁸ˢ 11⁸ᶠ 10⁸ᶠ 7¹²ˢᵈ 12¹⁰ᵍᶠ 10¹⁰ᵍᶠ **0-0-6**

Kerry's Blade (Ire) P C Haslam 71 a58
2 ch g Daggers Drawn (USA) - Treasure (Ire)
11⁶ᵍᶠ 5⁶ᵍ 6⁶ᵍˢ 2⁸ᵍ 6⁸ᵍ 8⁹ˢᵈ **0-1-6
£2,136**

Keshya D J Coakley 67 a67
3 b f Mtoto - Liberatrice (Fr)
3⁸ᵍ 4¹⁰ᵍ 2⁸ˢᵈ 4⁸ᵍ **0-2-4 £2,280**

Kew The Music M R Channon 61 a66
4 b g Botanic (USA) - Harmonia
7⁶ᵍˢ 10⁶ᵍˢ 10⁷ᵍ 11⁷ᵍᶠ 16⁸ᵍ VOI⁵ᵍᶠ
15⁸ʰʸ 8⁶ᵍ 1⁶ᵍ 10⁵ᵍᶠ 9⁶ᵍ 8⁶ˢᵈ **1-0-12 £3,369**

Key Factor M W Easterby 56 a2
3 b f Defacto (USA) - Onemoretime
4⁶ᵍᶠ 10⁷ᵍ 11⁷ᶠ 14⁶ˢʷ 12⁷ˢᵈ **0-0-5 £267**

Key In B W Hills 48 a63
3 ch f Unfuwain (USA) - Fleet Key
12⁸ᵍ 6¹⁰ᵍ 3¹³ˢᵈ 6¹⁴ˢ **0-1-4 £587**

Key Of Gold (Ire) D Carroll 59 a61
3 b g Key Of Luck (USA) - Damaslin
8⁷ˢᵈ 11⁶ᵍ 4⁶ᵍᶠ 16⁷ᵍ 11⁶ᵍˢ **0-0-5 £314**

Key Of Solomon (Ire) H Morrison 78
2 ch c Machiavellian (USA) - Minerva (Ire)
6⁸ᵍˢ 3⁸ˢ 3⁶ᵍᶠ **0-2-3 £2,384**

Key Partners (Ire) P A Blockley 86
3 b g Key Of Luck (USA) - Teacher Preacher (Ire)
1⁷ᵍˢ 7¹⁰ᵍᶠ 2⁷ᵍˢ 8⁷ᵍᶠ 11⁸ᵍ **1-1-5 £9,688**

Key Secret M L W Bell 90 a53
2 ch f Whittingham (Ire) - Foxkey
1⁵ˢᵈ 1⁵ᵍᶠ 1⁵ᵍ 4⁵ᵍˢ 1⁵ᵍˢ 6⁶ᵍ 7⁵ˢ 3⁵ʰᵒ

4-0-9 £24,656

Keyaki (Ire) *C F Wall* — 84
3 b f Shinko Forest (Ire) - Woodie Dancer (USA)
6⁷ˢ 6⁷ˢ 1⁷ᶠ 1⁷ᵍ 4⁸ᵍᶠ 4⁷ˢ 9⁷ᵍˢ 8⁷ˢ **2-0-8**
£9,990

Keyalzao (Ire) *A Crook* — 30
2 b f Alzao (USA) - Key Partner
15⁶ˢ 8⁶ᵍᶠ 9⁷ᵍ 1²⁷ᵍᶠ **0-0-4**

Keynes (Jpn) *J H M Gosden* — 69 a51
2 ch c Gold Fever (USA) - Eternal Reve (USA)
3⁷ˢᵈ 11⁷ˢᵈ 2⁸ᵍᶠ **0-2-3 £1,787**

Khabfair *Mrs A J Perrett* — 106 a110
3 b c Intikhab (USA) - Ruby Affair (Ire)
4⁶ᵍᶠ 1⁶ᵍᶠ 3⁶ᵍ 6⁶ᵍˢ 8⁶ᵍˢ 1⁷ᵍᶠ 2⁷ˢᵈ **2-2-7**
£33,461

Khafayif (USA) *B Hanbury* — 67
3 b f Swain (Ire) - Copper Play (USA)
15⁷ᵍ 3⁷ᵍᶠ 10⁷ᵍ 5⁷ᵍ **0-1-4 £640**

Khalidia (USA) *M A Magnusson* — 81
3 b g Boundary (USA) - Maniches Slew (USA)
1⁶ᶠ 2⁶ᵍᶠ **1-1-2 £5,305**

Khanjar (USA) *K R Burke* — 87 a87
4 ch c Kris S (USA) - Alyssum (USA)
2⁹ᵍᶠ 4⁸ᵍ 13¹⁰ᵍᶠ 1⁷ˢᶠ 2⁸ᵍˢ 8⁷ˢ 2⁹ᵍ **1-3-7**
£10,639

Kharish (Ire) *J Noseda* — 87
2 b c Desert Prince (Ire) - Moy Water (Ire)
4⁷ᵍ 3⁷ᵍ 2⁸ᵍˢ 1⁸ᵍ 4⁸ᵍᶠ **1-3-5 £9,437**

Kheleyf (USA) *Saeed Bin Suroor* — 113
3 b/br c Green Desert (USA) - Society Lady (USA)
1⁷ᵍᶠ 14⁶ᵍˢ 3⁷ᵍ 6⁸ˢ 5⁷ᵍ **1-1-5 £49,950**

Khuzdar (Ire) *Mrs A Malzard* — a54
5 ch g Definite Article - Mariyda (Ire)
7¹⁶ˢᵈ 3¹⁶ˢᵈ 2¹²ˢᵈ 11¹²ˢᵈ 5¹³ˢᵈ 1¹²ᵍˢ **1-2-6**
£2,376

Kiama *H Morrison* — 58
2 b f Dansili - Catriona
8⁸ᵍᶠ 6⁸ʰʸ **0-0-2**

Kibryaa (USA) *M A Jarvis* — 86
3 ch c Silver Hawk (USA) - Fleur De Nuit (USA)
6⁸ᵍᶠ 2⁸ˢ 2⁷ᵍˢ 4⁸ᵍᶠ 5⁸ᵍ 7⁸ᵍˢ **0-2-6**
£7,153

Kid'Z'Play (Ire) *J S Goldie* — 72
8 b g Rudimentary (USA) - Saka Saka
16¹²ᵍ 3¹²ᵍ 4¹⁰ʰʸ 2¹¹ᵍᶠ 1¹⁰ᵍ 5¹⁰ˢ 3¹⁰ᵍ 4¹²ˢ
5¹³ᵍˢ 6¹¹ˢ 8¹⁶ᵍˢ **1-3-11 £9,325**

Kikis Girls (Ire) *M Wigham* —
3 b f Spectrum (Ire) - Jane Heller (USA)
7¹⁰ᵍᶠ 15⁸ᵍˢ **0-0-2**

Kilcullen Lass (Ire) *W A Murphy* — 35 a38
3 ch f Fayruz - Foretell
10⁸ˢᵈ 10⁸ᵍ 11⁹ᵍʸ **0-0-3**

Kildare Chiller (Ire) *P R Hedger* — 34
10 ch g Shahrastani (USA) - Ballycuirke
6¹²ᵍˢ **0-0-1**

Kilindini *Miss E C Lavelle* — 70
3 gr g Silver Patriarch (Ire) - Newlands Corner
6¹⁰ˢ UR¹⁰ᵍᶠ 5¹⁰ᵍᶠ 4¹⁰ᵍˢ 9¹³ᶠ **0-0-5 £415**

Kilkenny Kitten (Ire) *N Tinkler* — 39 a34
2 b f Blue Ocean (USA) - El Tina
6⁵ᵍˢ 7⁵ˢᵈ 13⁵ᵍᶠ **0-0-3**

Killala (Ire) *R N Bevis* — 71
4 b g Among Men (USA) - Hat And Gloves
3⁷ᵍᶠ 5⁷ᵍᶠ 5⁷ᵍ 2⁷ᵍ 8⁸ᵍᶠ 4⁷ᵍᶠ 16¹⁰ᵍ 13⁹ˢᵈ
0-3-8 £2,496

Killena Boy (Ire) *W Jarvis* — 64 a37
2 b g Imperial Ballet (Ire) - Habaza (Ire)
8⁶ˢᵈ 8⁶ᵍ 4⁷ᵍᶠ 26⁶ˢ **0-0-4 £278**

Killerby Nicko *T D Easterby* — 52 a45
3 ch g Pivotal - Bit Of A Tart
6⁶ˢˢ 7⁵ᵍ 6⁶ᶠ 9⁶ᵍᶠ 5⁸ˢᵈ UR⁶ˢ 3⁷ᵍ 9⁷ᵍᶠ 5⁶ˢ
0-1-9 £421

Killing Joke *J J Lambe* — 62
4 b c Double Trigger (Ire) - Fleeting Vision (Ire)
11¹⁸ˢ 15¹⁶ᵍˢ **0-0-2**

Killing Me Softly *J Gallagher* — 55 a47
3 b g Kingsinger (Ire) - Slims Lady
2⁸ˢᵈ 8¹¹ˢᵈ 4¹¹ᵍˢ 12¹²ᵍ 10⁹ˢᵈ **0-2-5 £720**

Killington (Ire) *G A Butler* — 72 a39
2 ch g Kris - Miss Pickpocket (Ire)
2⁵ᵍᶠ 9⁶ˢᵈ 19⁶ᵍᶠ **0-1-3 £1,257**

Killmorey *S C Williams* — 76
3 ch g Nashwan (USA) - Zarma (Fr)
16⁸ᵍ 10⁸ᵍᶠ 2⁸ᵍᶠ 6¹⁰ᵍ 1¹²ˢ **1-1-5 £5,212**

Killoch Place (Ire) *W Storey* — 43
3 b g Compton Place - Hibernica (Ire)
12¹⁰ᵍˢ 17¹¹ᵍˢ 7⁸ˢ 10⁷ᶠ 3⁶ᵍᶠ 4⁷ᵍ 8⁸ᵍˢ 9⁷ᵍ
0-1-8 £464

Kilmeena Lad *J C Fox* — a75
8 b g Minshaanshu Amad (USA) - Kilmeena Glen
2⁷ˢᵈ 5⁶ˢᵈ **0-1-2 £990**

Kilmeena Star *J C Fox* — 17 a57
6 b g So Factual (USA) - Kilmeena Glen
10⁶ˢᵈ 9⁷ˢˢ 12⁷ˢᵈ 4⁷ˢᵈ 1⁶ˢᵈ 2⁶ˢᵈ 8⁵ʰʸ 7⁶ˢᵈ
10⁶ᶠ **1-1-9 £3,666**

Kilminchy Lady (Ire) *W R Muir* — 41
3 b f Cape Cross (Ire) - Lace Flower
5¹⁰ᶠ 13⁸ᵍᶠ 10⁸ᵍᶠ **0-0-3**

Kilmovee *N Tinkler* — 64
2 gr f Inchinor - Christmas Rose
5⁶ᵍ 9⁶ᶠ 5⁵ᵍ 5⁵ᵍᶠ 11⁶ᵍ 11⁵ᶠ 8⁶ʰʸ **0-0-7**

Kimberley Hall *J A Glover* — 32
2 ch f Bachir (Ire) - Sedna (Fr)
7⁵ᵍˢ 10⁵ᵍˢ 13⁶ᵍ 11⁶ᵍᶠ **0-0-4**

Kimoe Warrior *M Mullineaux* — a30
6 ch g Royal Abjar (USA) - Thewaari (USA)
5¹²ˢᵈ 13⁸ˢᵈ **0-0-2**

Kinbrace *M P Tregoning* — 62 a25
3 b f Kirkwall - Cache
6⁷ᵍᶠ 5⁸ᵍᶠ 5⁸ᵍ 9⁸ˢᵈ **0-0-4**

Kind (Ire) *R Charlton* — 92
3 b f Danehill (USA) - Rainbow Lake
3⁷ᵍ 1⁷ᵍᶠ 1⁶ᵍ 1⁶ᵍ 1⁵ˢ **5-1-6**
£46,209

Kind Emperor *P L Gilligan* — 70
7 b g Emperor Jones (USA) - Kind Lady
9⁷ᵍᶠ 4¹⁰ᵍᶠ 7¹⁰ˢ 2¹¹ᵍ 6¹⁰ᵍᶠ 6¹⁰ˢ **0-1-6**
£1,857

Kindlelight Debut *D K Ivory* — 80 a73
4 b f Groom Dancer (USA) - Dancing Debut
13⁸ᵍᶠ 17⁷ᵍ 3⁷ᵍᶠ 9⁸ᵍᶠ 7⁸ᵍ 16⁷ᵍᶠ 21⁷ᵍ
3⁸ˢᵈ 10⁷ᵍᶠ 6⁸ˢᵈ 11⁷ˢᵈ **0-2-11 £1,719**

Kindlelight Dream (Ire) *D K Ivory* — a52
2 b f Tagula (Ire) - Dioscorea (Ire)
8⁵ˢ 6⁷ˢᵈ LFT⁷ˢᵈ **0-0-3**

Kindling *M Johnston* — 80
2 br f Dr Fong (USA) - Isle Of Flame
5⁶ᶠ 4⁷ᵍᶠ 1⁹ᵍˢ **1-0-3 £5,813**

Kindness *A D W Pinder* — 57 a51
4 ch f Indian Ridge - Kissing Gate (USA)

6⁸ˢᵈ 7⁸ʰʸ 9⁸ᶠ 2⁸ᵍᶠ 2¹⁰ᵍᶠ 8¹⁰ᵍᶠ 2⁹ᵍᶠ 11⁸ᵍᶠ
14¹⁰ᵍᶠ 7⁸ᵍ 6⁸ᵍ 4⁹ˢᵈ **0-3-12 £4,852**

Kinfayre Boy *K W Hogg*
2 b g Grey Eagle - Amber Gambler (Ity)
8⁷ᵍ **0-0-1**

King After *J R Best*   76 a68
2 b g Bahamian Bounty - Child Star (Fr)
1⁵ˢᵈ 6⁵ᵍˢ 6⁵ᵍˢ 5⁶ᵍᶠ 5⁷ˢ 8⁶ᵍˢ 12⁶ᵍᶠ 14⁵ᵍᶠ
1-0-8 £3,891

King At Last *K Bell*   a56
5 b g Zamindar (USA) - Louis' Queen (Ire)
8⁸ˢᵈ 7⁷ˢᵈ **0-0-2**

King Carnival (USA) *R Hannon*   97
3 ch c King Of Kings (Ire) - Miss Waki Club (USA)
12⁷ᵍᶠ 7⁸ᵍᶠ 7⁷ᵍᶠ 15⁷ᵍ **0-0-4**

King Egbert (Fr) *A W Carroll*   62 a55
3 b g Fasliyev (USA) - Exocet (USA)
4⁵ᵍᶠ 7⁵ᵍ 3⁵ᵍᶠ 8⁵ᵍ 6⁵ˢᵈ 5⁶ˢ **0-1-6 £833**

King Eider *B Ellison*   85
5 b/br g Mtoto - Hen Harrier
13¹⁶ᵍ 9¹²ᵍ 24¹⁸ˢ **0-0-3**

King Flyer (Ire) *Miss J Feilden*   87 a69
8 b g Ezzoud (Ire) - Al Guswa
8¹⁶ˢᵈ 2¹⁶ᵍ 3¹⁶ᵍ 11¹⁴ᵍᶠ 2¹⁸ᵍ 19²⁰ᵍᶠ 9¹⁶ᵍᶠ
7¹⁵ᵍ 5¹⁶ᵍ 3¹²ˢᵈ 6¹²ˢᵈ **0-4-11 £5,974**

King Forever *J Noseda*   71
2 b c King's Best (USA) - Elude
6⁷ᵍᶠ **0-0-1**

King Gabriel (Ire) *D J S Ffrench Davis*   69
2 b g Desert King (Ire) - Broken Spirit (Ire)
11⁷ᵍ 6⁸ˢ **0-0-2**

King Halling *R Ford*   59 a46
5 b h Halling (USA) - Flower Fairy (Fr)
8¹²ᵍᶠ 6¹⁶ᵍ 14¹²ᵍᶠ 4¹¹ᵍ 5¹²ˢᵈ **0-0-5 £266**

King Harson *J D Bethell*   90
5 b g Greensmith - Safari Park
10⁷ᵍ 2⁷ᶠ 11⁷ᵍᶠ 26⁷ᶠ 6⁷ᵍᶠ 11⁷ᵍ 1⁷ˢ 5⁷ᵍˢ
18⁷ˢ 17⁷ᵍ 2⁷ˢ **1-2-11 £16,073**

King Henrik (USA) *A Crook*   57
2 b g King Of Kings (Ire) - Ma Biche (USA)
4⁷ᶠ 6⁷ᵍᶠ 7⁷ᵍᶠ 18⁷ᶠ **0-0-4 £284**

King Jock (USA) *D K Weld*   97
3 b c Ghazi (USA) - Glen Kate
1⁸ᵍᶠ 16⁸ᶠ 10⁶ᵍᶠ 5⁷ᵍᶠ 5⁷ᵍᶠ 1⁵ᶠ **2-0-6
£19,247**

King Marju (Ire) *P W Chapple-Hyam*   92
2 b c Marju (Ire) - Katoushka (Ire)
6⁷ᵍᶠ 2⁶ᵍᶠ 1⁶ᵍᶠ 2⁷ᵍˢ 3⁷ˢ **1-3-5 £11,865**

King Nicholas (USA) *J Parkes*   57 a65
5 b g Nicholas (USA) - Lifetime Honour (USA)
7⁸ˢˢ 1¹⁶ˢˢ 10⁷ᵍ 4⁶ʰʸ 9⁶ᵍ 6⁶ᵍ 8⁶ˢᵈ
6⁷ᵍˢ 19ˢᵈ 4⁹ˢᵈ **3-1-11 £7,891**

King Of Blues (Ire) *M A Magnusson*   78 a65
2 ch c Bluebird (USA) - Highly Respected (Ire)
10⁶ᶠ 8⁷ᵍᶠ 4⁷ˢᵈ 1⁷ᵍᶠ 7⁷ˢ 3⁸ᵍᶠ **1-1-6
£8,230**

King Of Cashel (Ire) *R Hannon*   89
3 b c King Of Kings (Ire) - Jaya (USA)
3⁷ᵍᶠ 9⁷ᵍˢ **0-0-2 £1,464**

King Of Diamonds *J R Best*   83 a86
3 b c Mtoto - Capricious Lass
2⁶ˢᵈ 6⁷ˢᵈ 2⁶ˢᵈ 12⁸ᵍᶠ 7⁸ᵍᶠ 1⁸ᵍˢ 10⁷ᵍˢ 4⁹ᵍ
11⁸ᵍ 2¹²ˢᵈ 2¹⁰ˢᵈ **1-4-11 £11,278**

King Of Dreams (Ire) *M Johnston*   103
3 b c Sadler's Wells (USA) - Koniya (Ire)

1¹⁰ᵍ 11¹⁰ᵍ 1¹⁰ᵍ 5¹¹ᵍ F¹²ᵍ **2-0-5
£19,616**

King Of Fire *Miss B Sanders*   46
2 b g Magic Ring (Ire) - Alaskan Princess (Ire)
9⁶ᵍᶠ **0-0-1**

King Of Knight (Ire) *G Prodromou*   69 a64
3 gr g Orpen (USA) - Peace Melody (Ire)
4⁸ᵍᶠ 5⁸ᵍˢ 9⁷ᵍᶠ 7¹²ᵍᶠ 9¹⁰ᵍᶠ 4⁸ˢ 2¹²ˢᵈ 4¹²ˢᵈ
0-1-8 £1,898

King Of Love *M Johnston*   66
2 b c King's Best (USA) - Fadaki Hawaki (USA)
1⁶ᵍ **1-0-1 £5,772**

King Of Meze (Ire) *G Prodromou*   34 a38
3 b g Croco Rouge (Ire) - Cossack Princess (Ire)
8⁸ˢᵈ 6⁶ˢᵈ 11⁶ˢˢ 9¹²ˢᵈ 9⁸ᵍˢ **0-0-5**

King Of Music (USA) *G Prodromou*   59 a59
3 ch g Jade Hunter (USA) - Hail Roberta (USA)
8⁷ᶠ 7⁷ᵍᶠ 6⁸ˢ 2⁸ˢᵈ **0-1-4 £830**

King Priam (Ire) *M J Polglase*   a49
9 b g Priolo (USA) - Barinia
8¹²ˢᵈ 4¹²ˢᵈ 1¹²ˢᵈ 4⁸ˢᵈ 5¹¹ˢᵈ 9¹⁶ˢᵈ 6¹²ˢᵈ
6¹²ˢᵈ 4¹⁴ˢᵈ 5¹²ˢᵈ 6¹⁴ˢˢ 5¹¹ˢˢ 4¹⁴ˢˢ 20¹²ᵍ 7¹²ˢᵈ
6¹⁴ˢᶠ 6¹²ˢᵈ **1-0-17 £1,270**

King Revo (Ire) *P C Haslam*   88
4 b g Revoque (Ire) - Tycoon Aly (Ire)
1¹²ᵍ 15¹²ᵍˢ **1-0-2 £10,387**

King Spinner (Ire) *Mrs A J Bowlby*
7 b g Mujadil (USA) - Money Spinner (USA)
12¹⁴ᵍ **0-0-1**

King Summerland *B Mactaggart*   57
7 b g Minshaanshu Amad (USA) - Alaskan Princess (Ire)
5⁸ˢ 4⁹ᵍˢ **0-0-2 £327**

King Top *T D Easterby*   22
3 b g Inchinor - Panorama
4¹¹ᵍ **0-0-1 £270**

King Zafeen (Ire) *M W Easterby*   72
2 b c Lend A Hand - Groom Dancing
13⁷ᵍᶠ 4⁸ᶠ 9⁸ᵍ 16⁸ˢ **0-0-4 £439**

King's Account (USA) *M Johnston*   87
2 ch c King Of Kings (Ire) - Fighting Countess (USA)
2⁷ᵍˢ 2⁷ˢ 2⁸ᵍ 1⁷ᵍᶠ 1⁸ᵍˢ **2-3-5 £12,597**

King's Ballet (USA) *P R Chamings*   46 a53
6 b g Imperial Ballet (Ire) - Multimara (USA)
8⁶ˢᵈ 2⁵ˢˢ 9⁵ˢˢ 4⁵ˢˢ 11⁵ᵍˢ 11⁵ˢ
13⁵ʰʸ 16⁶ᵍᶠ **0-1-9 £830**

King's Caprice *G B Balding*   97
3 ch g Pursuit Of Love - Palace Street (USA)
7⁶ˢ 3⁶ᵍᶠ 4⁶ᵍᶠ 7⁷ᵍˢ 4⁶ᵍᶠ 4⁶ᵍ 1⁷ˢ 5⁷ᵍˢ
16⁶ˢ 2⁷ˢ 7⁶ˢ **2-1-12 £19,903**

King's County (Ire) *L M Cumani*   104
6 b g Fairy King (USA) - Kardelle
3⁸ᵍ 11⁸ᵍˢ 3⁷ᵍᶠ 29⁸ᵍᶠ 14⁸ᵍ 2⁹ᵍᶠ 12⁹ᵍ
0-3-7 £10,790

King's Envoy (USA) *Mrs J C McGregor*   67
5 b g Royal Academy (USA) - Island Of Silver (USA)
4⁹ᵍᶠ 3⁹ᵍ 5¹²ᵍᶠ 9¹⁰ᵍ 10⁹ʰʸ 15¹¹ˢ **0-0-6
£1,089**

King's Gait *T D Easterby*   79
2 b g Mujahid (USA) - Miller's Gait
6⁵ᵍ 1⁵ʰʸ 4⁶ᵍˢ **1-0-3 £5,818**

King's Kama *Sir Michael Stoute*   77 a77
2 b c Giant's Causeway (USA) - Maid For The Hills
4⁶ᵍᶠ 4⁷ᵍᶠ 3⁷ˢᵈ **0-1-3 £1,506**

King's Majesty (Ire) *Sir Michael Stoute*   52 a84
2 b c King's Best (USA) - Tiavanita (USA)

7⁷ᵍᶠ 2⁷ˢᵈ 1⁷ˢᵈ **1-1-3 £6,439**

King's Minstrel (Ire) *R Rowe* 41
3 b g Cape Cross (Ire) - Muwasim (USA)
14⁸ᵍ 7⁸ᵍᶠ 10¹⁰ᵍ 7⁸ᵍ **0-0-4**

King's Mountain (USA) *C J Gray* 20
4 b g King Of Kings (Ire) - Statistic (USA)
18¹¹ᵍˢ 10¹⁴ᵍ **0-0-2**

King's Thought *S Gollings* 105
5 b h King's Theatre (Ire) - Lora's Guest
6¹²ᵍ 8¹⁰ᵍˢ 4¹⁰ˢ 6¹⁰ᵍ 4¹⁰ᵍˢ 4¹⁰ᵍ 3⁸ᵍᶠ **0-2-7**
£6,614

King's Welcome *C W Fairhurst* 31
6 b g Most Welcome - Reine De Thebes (Fr)
6¹²ᵍˢ 10¹⁰ˢ **0-0-2**

Kingdom Of Dreams (Ire) *Sir Michael Stoute* 56
2 b c Sadler's Wells (USA) - Regal Portrait (Ire)
7⁷ˢ **0-0-1**

Kingham *Mrs Mary Hambro* a50
4 ch g Desert Prince (Ire) - Marie De Flandre (Fr)
11⁸ˢᵈ 7⁶ˢᵈ **0-0-2**

Kingkohler (Ire) *K A Morgan* a75
5 b g King's Theatre (Ire) - Legit (Ire)
6¹²ˢᵈ **0-0-1**

Kings College Boy *R A Fahey* 76
4 b g College Chapel - The Kings Daughter
17⁶ᵍ 8⁶ᵍᶠ 3⁵ᵍᶠ 2⁵ᵍᶠ 3⁵ᵍˢ 8⁵ᵍˢ 3⁶ᵍᶠ 7⁵ᵍ
3⁵ᵍᶠ 9⁵ᵍˢ 1⁵ˢ 9⁵ᵍˢ 2⁵ᵍ 4⁵ᵍˢ 12⁵ˢ 4⁵ᵍ 8⁵ˢ
1-8-17 £15,427

Kings Empire *D Carroll* 84
3 b g Second Empire (Ire) - Dancing Feather
4¹⁰ᵍᶠ 4¹⁰ᵍ 19¹¹ʰʸ 14¹⁰ˢ **0-0-4 £875**

Kings Point (Ire) *R Hannon* 108 a97
3 b c Fasliyev (USA) - Rahika Rose
5⁸ˢᵈ 10⁷ᵍ 5⁸ᵍᶠ 3⁶ᶠ 11⁷ᶠ 4⁷ᵍᶠ 13⁷ᵍˢ 3⁸ᵍᶠ
7⁷ᵍᶠ 8⁷ᵍ 7⁷ᵍ **0-2-11 £10,325**

Kings Quay *R Hannon* 101
2 b c Montjeu (Ire) - Glen Rosie (Ire)
1⁵ᵍ 12⁶ᵍᶠ 2⁶ᵍᶠ 1⁷ᵍˢ 6⁷ᵍ **2-0-5 £21,296**

Kings Rock *Mrs Lucinda Featherstone* 66 a61
3 ch g Kris - Both Sides Now (USA)
2⁸ˢᵈ 6⁹ˢʷ 9¹⁰ˢᵈ 7⁸ᵍ 6⁷ʰʸ 3⁸ᵍ 10⁸ᵍ 1⁸ᵍᶠ
2⁸ᵍᶠ 1⁷ᵍˢ 18⁷ᵍᶠ 12⁷ˢ 14⁸ᵍᶠ **2-3-13 £8,789**

Kings Square *M W Easterby* 15
4 b g Bal Harbour - Prime Property (Ire)
12¹²ᵍ **0-0-1**

Kings Topic (USA) *P Burgoyne* 53 a55
4 ch g Kingmambo - Topicount (USA)
2¹⁰ˢᵈ 11⁰ˢᵈ 11⁰ˢᵈ 7¹⁰ᵍᶠ **2-1-4 £3,720**

Kingscross *M Blanshard* 90
6 ch g King's Signet (USA) - Calamanco
4⁶ᵍˢ 2⁶ᵍˢ 1⁶ᵍˢ 15⁶ᵍᶠ 19⁶ˢ 2⁶ˢ 2⁶ᵍ
6⁶ᵍ 4⁶ᵍˢ 4⁷ᵍ 20⁷ᵍˢ **1-5-12 £19,825**

Kingsdon (Ire) *T J Fitzgerald* 69 a62
7 b g Brief Truce (USA) - Richly Deserved (Ire)
10¹²ˢᵈ 11⁰ˢᵈ 9¹⁰ˢᵈ 4¹⁰ˢᵈ 4¹⁰ʰʸ 11⁰ᵍ 11⁰ˢᵈ
11⁰ˢᵈ 11⁰ˢ 3¹⁰ᵍˢ **5-1-10 £11,436**

Kingsgate Bay (Ire) *J R Best* 74 a59
2 b g Desert Sun - Selkirk Flyer
7⁶ᵍᶠ 5⁵ˢᵈ 5⁵ᵍᶠ 1⁶ᵍ **1-0-4 £5,505**

Kingsholm *A M Balding* 73
2 ch c Selkirk (USA) - Putuna
6⁷ᵍᶠ 3⁸ᵍˢ 7⁸ᶠ **0-1-3 £848**

Kingsmaite *S R Bowring* 73 a90
3 b g Komaite (USA) - Antonias Melody
11⁷ᵍ 4⁷ᵍˢ 9⁷ᵍᶠ 5⁶ᵍᶠ 1⁶ᵍ 3⁷ˢᶠ 16⁶ᵍᶠ 5⁸ᵍᶠ

14⁷ᵍ 2⁶ˢᵈ **1-2-10 £7,945**

Kingston Town (USA) *M C Pipe* 56 a69
4 ch g King Of Kings (Ire) - Lady Ferial (Fr)
9¹⁰ˢᵈ 7⁹ˢᵈ 4⁸ˢᵈ 7¹¹ˢˢ 6¹⁰ᵍᶠ 7¹⁰ᵍᶠ 2⁸ˢᵈ 5⁸ˢ
10¹⁰ˢᵈ **0-1-9 £746**

Kingsword (USA) *Sir Michael Stoute* 102
3 bl c Dynaformer (USA) - Western Curtsey (USA)
5¹⁰ᵍ 2¹⁰ᵍ 14¹⁰ᵍᶠ **0-1-3 £3,799**

Kiniska *B Palling* 49
3 b f Merdon Melody - Young Whip
9⁸ᵍᶠ 11⁸ˢᵈ **0-0-2**

Kinkozan *N P Littmoden* 51
3 ch c Peintre Celebre (USA) - Classic Design
6⁸ᵍ 12¹⁰ˢᵈ **0-0-2**

Kinnaird (Ire) *P C Haslam* 110
3 ch f Dr Devious (Ire) - Ribot's Guest (Ire)
4⁸ᵍᶠ 5⁸ᶠ 2¹⁰ᵍ 2¹⁰ᵍˢ 2¹⁰ᵍ **0-3-5 £53,999**

Kinrande (Ire) *P J Makin* 68 a78
2 b c Sri Pekan (USA) - Pipers Pool (Ire)
3⁸ᵍᶠ 3⁸ˢᵈ **0-2-2 £1,470**

Kinsman (Ire) *T D McCarthy* 50 a63
7 b g Distant Relative - Besito
2⁷ˢᵈ 1⁷ˢᵈ 5⁸ˢᵈ 4⁷ˢᵈ 6⁷ᶠ 10⁷ᵍ 11⁷ᶠ 11⁸ᵍᶠ
5⁷ˢᵈ **1-1-9 £3,859**

Kintore *J S Goldie* 34
3 ch c Inchinor - Souadah (USA)
6⁹ᵍˢ 4⁹ᵍ 10⁹ᵍ **0-0-3 £267**

Kipsigis (Ire) *Lady Herries* 65 a68
3 b g Octagonal (NZ) - Kisumu
7¹⁰ᵍˢ 4¹⁰ᵍ 4¹³ˢᵈ **0-0-3 £721**

Kirat *G L Moore* a50
6 b g Darshaan - Kafsa (Ire)
11¹²ˢᵈ 4¹²ˢᵈ **0-0-2 £317**

Kirkby's Treasure *A Berry* 82
6 ro g Mind Games - Gem Of Gold
1⁷ᵍᶠ 2⁷ᵍᶠ 1⁸ᵍᶠ 9⁸ᵍ 1⁷ᵍ 2⁷ᵍ 13⁷ᵍ 2⁷ᵍᶠ
2⁶ᵍˢ 6⁸ˢ 17⁶ˢ 3⁷ᵍᶠ 5⁷ˢ 3⁷ˢ 2⁷ᵍˢ **3-8-16**
£33,556

Kirkham Abbey *M A Jarvis* 76
4 b g Selkirk (USA) - Totham
7¹⁰ᵍᶠ 3¹⁰ᵍ 2¹⁰ᶠ 6¹⁰ᵍ 5⁹ᵍᶠ 1¹⁰ᶠ 11¹⁰ᵍᶠ
11⁰ᵍᶠ **2-2-8 £11,092**

Kirkhammerton (Ire) *J A Osborne* 36
2 ch g Grand Lodge (USA) - Nawara
14⁶ᵍˢ 8⁶ᵍ 7⁶ᵍᶠ 14⁶ᵍˢ **0-0-4**

Kirov King (Ire) *B G Powell* 59
4 b c Desert King (Ire) - Nymphs Echo (Ire)
9¹²ᵍˢ 7¹⁴ʰʸ 7¹²ᵍᶠ 15¹⁰ᵍᶠ 6¹²ᵍᶠ 10¹⁰ᵍˢ **0-0-6**

Kiss Again *L M Cumani* a18
3 b f Halling (USA) - Kissogram
10⁷ˢᵈ **0-0-1**

Kiss The Rain *P A Blockley* 38 a42
4 b f Forzando - Devils Dirge
6⁶ˢᵈ 12⁶ˢᵈ 16⁷ᵍᶠ 8⁶ᵍ **0-0-4**

Kisses For Me (Ire) *A P O'Brien* 101
3 b f Sadler's Wells (USA) - Fanny Cerrito (USA)
5¹⁰ᵍ 10⁸ᵍᶠ 7¹²ᵍ 3⁹ᵍᶠ 3¹²ᵍᶠ 8¹²ˢ 3⁹ᵍˢ
13⁸ʸˢ **0-2-9 £14,732**

Kissing A Fool *W G M Turner* 45 a21
2 b g Tipsy Creek (USA) - Amathus Glory
5⁵ᵍˢ 1⁵ˢ 11⁵ᵍ 5⁶ˢᵈ **1-0-4 £3,010**

Kissing Lights (Ire) *M L W Bell* 98
2 b f Machiavellian (USA) - Nasaieb (Ire)
5⁶ᵍᶠ 1⁵ᶠ 6⁶ᵍᶠ 3⁶ᵍᶠ 8⁶ˢ 3⁵ᶠ **1-1-6**

£18,844

Kiswahili *Sir Mark Prescott*   86
2 ch f Selkirk (USA) - Kiliniski
2⁷ᵍ 1⁸ˢ **1-1-2 £5,765**

Kitchen Sink (Ire) *P J Makin*   46
2 ch g Bold Fact (USA) - Voodoo Rocket
10⁶ᵍ 10⁵ˢ **0-0-2**

Kitley *B G Powell*   58 a40
3 b c Muhtarram (USA) - Salsita
13¹⁰ᵍˢ 16⁸ˢ 6⁷ᵍᶠ 14⁸ᶠ 10¹⁰ˢᵈ **0-0-5**

Kitty O'Shea *A P O'Brien*   85
2 b f Sadler's Wells (USA) - Eva Luna (USA)
1⁸ˢ **1-0-1 £8,759**

Kittylee *J S Wainwright*   a1
5 b m Bal Harbour - Courtesy Call
12¹²ˢᵈ 6¹⁴ˢᵈ **0-0-2**

Knead The Dough *D E Cantillon*   54 a58
3 b g Wolfhound (USA) - Ridgewood Ruby (Ire)
2⁶ˢᵈ 6⁶ᶠ 7⁷ᵍˢ 2⁶ᵍ 19⁶ᵍ 5⁶ˢᵈ **0-2-6**
£1,197

Knickyknackienoo *A G Newcombe*   66 a63
3 b g Bin Ajwaad (Ire) - Ring Fence
4⁷ˢᵈ 2⁷ˢ 2⁷ˢ 12⁹ᵍᶠ 3⁷ᵍᶠ 18ᵍ 78ᵍᶠ 2⁸ᵍᶠ
5⁸ᵍ 3⁸ˢᵈ 11⁸ᵍᶠ **1-5-11 £8,247**

Knight Of Hearts (Ire) *P A Blockley*   39 a47
3 gr g Idris (Ire) - Heart To Heart (Ire)
5¹²ˢˢ 5⁹ˢᵈ 11⁸ᵍᶠ 11⁸ˢᵈ 4¹¹ˢ 8¹⁶ˢ 2⁹ˢᵈ
0-1-7 £712

Knight Of Silver *J D Frost*   45
7 gr g Presidium - Misty Rocket
8¹⁷ᵍ **0-0-1**

Knight Onthe Tiles (Ire) *J R Best*   31 a46
3 ch g Primo Dominie - Blissful Night
11⁷ˢᵈ 9⁷ˢᵈ 9⁶ᵍᶠ 14⁷ᵍˢ 8⁷ᵍᶠ 12⁶ᵍᶠ **0-0-6**

Knight To Remember (Ire) *R E Barr*   44 a50
3 ch g Fayruz - Cheerful Knight
3⁷ˢᵈ 4⁷ˢᵈ 9⁸ˢˢ 9⁵ʰʸ 9⁷ᵍᶠ 9⁷ᵍᶠ 5⁶ˢᵈ 7⁸ᵍ
13⁸ᵍᶠ **0-1-9 £370**

Knightsbridge Hill (Ire) *A King*   74
2 b c Raise A Grand (Ire) - Desert Gem
5⁷ᵍᶠ 6⁸ᵍˢ 4⁷ᵍᶠ 17⁸ᵍ **0-0-4 £278**

Knock Bridge (Ire) *P D Evans*   72
2 b f Rossini (USA) - Touraneena
4⁶ᶠ 2⁵ᵍᶠ 8⁵ᵍᶠ 3⁵ʰʸ 15⁵ᵍˢ 1⁷ᵍˢ 12⁷ᵍˢ **1-2-7**
£9,890

Knockdoo (Ire) *J S Goldie*   a6
11 ch g Be My Native (USA) - Ashken
10¹²ˢᵈ 3¹⁶ˢᵈ **0-1-2 £362**

Knocktopher Abbey *A G Newcombe*   45 a10
7 ch g Pursuit Of Love - Kukri
12¹³ˢᵈ 7⁹ᵍˢ 11¹²ᵍ **0-0-3**

Knot In Doubt (Ire) *J A Glover*   36
3 b g Woodborough (USA) - In The Mind (Ire)
9⁷ᵍᶠ 12⁷ᵍᶠ **0-0-2**

Knot In Wood (Ire) *R A Fahey*   66
2 b c Shinko Forest (Ire) - Notley Park
10⁶ᵍᶠ 6⁶ᶠ 3⁶ᵍ **0-1-3 £844**

Known Maneuver (USA) *M C Chapman*   a41
6 b g Known Fact (USA) - Northernmaneuver (USA)
4¹²ˢᵈ 4¹²ˢᵈ 9¹⁴ˢˢ **0-0-3**

Kodiac *J L Dunlop*   83
3 b c Danehill (USA) - Rafha
1⁷ᵍᶠ 7⁸ᵍᶠ 1⁷⁷ᵍˢ **1-0-3 £4,033**

Kolyma (Ire) *J L Dunlop*   61
2 ch f Grand Lodge (USA) - Koniya (Ire)

8⁶ᵍᶠ 5⁷ᵍ 12⁸ᵍᶠ **0-0-3**

Komac *B A McMahon*   71 a65
2 b c Komaite (USA) - Star Of Flanders
6⁵ᵍˢ 2⁵ᵍᶠ 4⁵ᵍ 6⁵ᵍ 1⁵ˢᵈ 7⁵ᵍᶠ PU⁶ᵍᶠ **1-1-7**
£5,780

Komati River *J Akehurst*   17 a17
5 b g Wesaam (USA) - Christening (Ire)
8¹²ˢᵈ 16¹²ˢ 12¹²ᵍᶠ **0-0-3**

Komena *J W Payne*   48 a37
6 b m Komaite (USA) - Mena
5⁶ˢᵈ 9⁶ˢᵈ 8⁶ˢᵈ 8⁶ᶠ 10⁶ᵍᶠ 5⁶ᵍ 16⁷ᵍᶠ 8⁶ᵍˢ
14⁷ᵍᶠ **0-0-9**

Komoto *G A Butler*   56 a70
3 b g Mtoto - Imperial Scholar (Ire)
1⁸ˢᵈ 9⁸ᵍ 10¹²ᵍᶠ 4¹²ʰʸ 17¹⁷ᵍ **1-0-5**
£3,212

Komreyev Star *R A Fahey*   45
2 b c Komaite (USA) - L'Ancressaan
9⁶ᵍ 13⁶ᵍᶠ 8⁶ʰʸ **0-0-3**

Kong (Ire) *J L Dunlop*   78
2 b c Sadler's Wells (USA) - Hill Of Snow
4⁸ˢ 3⁸ᵍ **0-1-2 £1,312**

Konker *J R Cornwall*   53
9 ch g Selkirk (USA) - Helens Dreamgirl
3¹⁰ˢ **0-0-1 £571**

Koodoo *K A Ryan*   56
3 gr g Fasliyev (USA) - Karsiyaka (Ire)
8⁸ᵍ 6⁷ᶠ 8¹⁰ᶠ 8⁹ᵍ 13⁸ᵍᶠ 5⁹ᵍˢ 8¹⁰ˢ **0-0-7**

Kool (Ire) *P F I Cole*   98
5 b g Danehill Dancer (Ire) - New Rochelle (Ire)
3⁷ᵍˢ 5⁷ˢ 5⁷ᵍᶠ 3⁷ᵍ 5⁷ᵍᶠ 4⁷ᵍᶠ 9⁷ᵍᶠ 2⁷ᵍ
3⁷ᵍˢ 6⁷ᵍᶠ 2⁷ᵍᶠ **0-5-12 £28,341**

Kool Acclaim *S C Williams*   76
3 b f Royal Applause - Carrie Kool
2⁶ᵍᶠ 1⁶ᵍᶠ 12⁵ᵍᶠ **1-1-3 £4,467**

Kool Ovation *A Dickman*   71
2 b g Royal Applause - Carrie Kool
9⁶ᵍᶠ 3⁵ᵍ 3⁶ᵍᶠ **0-2-3 £1,455**

Kostar *C G Cox*   79 a83
3 ch g Komaite (USA) - Black And Amber
4⁶ᵍᶠ 1⁶ᵍᶠ 11⁶ᵍˢ 4⁶ᵍᶠ 2⁵ˢᵈ **1-1-5 £7,742**

Krasivi's Boy (USA) *G L Moore*   70 a67
2 b/br c Swain (Ire) - Krasivi (USA)
9⁸ˢᵈ 2⁸ᵍˢ 4⁸ˢᵈ 12⁸ᵍ **0-1-4 £1,794**

Krataios (Fr) *C Laffon-Parias*   111
4 b c Sabrehill (USA) - Loxandra
1⁷ᵍ 4⁸ᵛˢ 12⁸ᵍ **1-0-3 £15,387**

Kristal's Dream (Ire) *J L Dunlop*   80
3 b f Night Shift (USA) - Kristal's Paradise (Ire)
3¹⁰ᵍᶠ 5¹⁰ᵍᶠ 7¹⁰ᵍᶠ 2¹²ᵍ 5¹²ᵍᶠ 12¹²ᵍᶠ **0-2-6**
£1,798

Kristalchen *J G Given*   60
2 b f Singspiel (Ire) - Crystal Flite (Ire)
7⁷ᵍᶠ 9⁸ˢ 78ᵍᶠ 4¹⁰ʰʸ **0-0-4 £355**

Kristensen *D Eddy*   89 a83
5 ch g Kris S (USA) - Papaha (Fr)
5¹⁶ᵍˢ 9¹⁹ᵍˢ 6¹⁶ᵍᶠ 2¹⁴ᵍᶠ 5¹⁶ˢ 10¹⁶ᵍ 7²¹ᵍ
3¹²ᵍ 8¹⁷ˢ 2¹⁶ᵍᶠ 10¹⁸ˢ 3¹⁶ᵍˢ 4¹⁷ˢᵈ **0-4-13**
£15,433

Kristiansand *P Monteith*   71
4 b g Halling (USA) - Zonda
8⁹ᵍ 6⁹ᵍᶠ 4⁹ᵍᶠ 10⁹ᵍˢ **0-0-4 £377**

Kristikhab (Ire) *A Berry*   62
2 ch g Intikhab (USA) - Alajyal (Ire)
7⁵ᵍˢ 5⁵ᵍˢ 4⁶ᵍᶠ 2⁵ᵍᶠ 10⁶ˢᵈ 12⁶ᵍ 7⁵ᵍᶠ 5⁶ᵍᶠ

8^{hy} 19^{6g} 8^{6s} 15^{5hy} **0-1-12 £1,616**

Kristineau *Mrs E Slack* 48
6 ch m Cadeaux Genereux - Kantikoy
5^{14gf} 7^{17gf} 6^{13gf} 9^{17g} 18^{10gf} **0-0-5**

Kristinor (Fr) *J R Fanshawe* 72
2 ch g Inchinor - Kristina
6^{7gf} 9^{8gs} **0-0-2**

Kristoffersen *R M Stronge* a70
4 ch g Kris - Towaahi (Ire)
9^{12sd} 8^{12sd} **0-0-2**

Krugerrand (USA) *W J Musson* 94 a79
5 ch g Gulch (USA) - Nasers Pride (USA)
9^{10sd} 13^{8g} 10^{8gs} 13^{8s} 1^{9gf} 3^{8gf} 6^{10gf}
11^{10g} 5^{10gf} 1^{8gs} 5^{9gf} 27^{9g} 13^{8gs} **2-0-13**
£25,570

Krullind (Ire) *P W Chapple-Hyam* 64
2 b g Rossini (USA) - Jemima Yorke
21^{6s} 6^{7gs} 6^{6s} **0-0-3**

Krumpet *G G Margarson* 64
2 b f Mujahid (USA) - Dame Jude
7^{7gf} 9^{7g} **0-0-2**

Krynica (USA) *Sir Michael Stoute* 76
2 br f Danzig (USA) - Bionic
1^{6gf} 4^{6gs} 14^{7gf} **1-0-3 £5,814**

Kryssa *G L Moore* 81 a71
3 ch f Kris - Alessandra
4^{6sd} 1^{5sd} 3^{7sd} 3^{5g} 5^{6g} 1^{7g} 3^{7gf} 1^{8g} 3^{9gf}
1^{8gf} 11^{8g} 6^{10sd} **4-3-12 £21,440**

Kschessinka (USA) *W J Haggas* 85
3 br f Nureyev (USA) - Gran Dama (USA)
1^{6gf} 3^{6gf} 6^{6gf} **1-0-3 £7,347**

Kudbeme *N Bycroft* 43
2 b f Forzando - Umbrian Gold (Ire)
12^{5gf} 6^{7g} **0-0-2**

Kumakawa *D K Ivory* 24 a57
6 ch g Dancing Spree (USA) - Maria Cappuccini
13^{7sd} 5^{8ss} 8^{8sd} 3^{8sd} 7^{10sd} 8^{10sd} 2^{8ss} 6^{8sd}
7^{8sd} 9^{8gs} 8^{8g} 5^{8g} 10^{9sd} 9^{8sd} **0-2-14 £1,050**

Kumala Ocean (Ire) *P A Blockley* 56 a48
2 ch f Blue Ocean (USA) - Kumala (Ire)
2^{7sd} 5^{7gf} 9^{7g} 2^{7f} 8^{7f} 5^{6sd} **0-2-6**
£1,192

Kumari (Ire) *W M Brisbourne* a20
3 b f Desert Story (Ire) - Glow Tina (Ire)
11^{6sd} **0-0-1**

Kunda (Ire) *R Hannon* 99
3 b f Intikhab (USA) - Ustka
6^{7g} 2^{9g} 3^{7gf} 7^{8gs} 7^{8gf} 10^{8gf} **0-2-6**
£14,300

Kuringai *B W Duke* 72 a65
3 b g Royal Applause - Talighta (USA)
10^{6sd} 4^{6sd} 3^{5g} 8^{6gs} 17^{6g} 10^{6f} 10^{6gf}
10^{5gf} **0-1-8 £849**

Kussharro *Bruce Hellier* 23
3 ch c Case Law - Risking
5^{7g} 9^{6gf} **0-0-2**

Kuster *L M Cumani* 95
8 b g Indian Ridge - Ustka
14^{12gs} 6^{12gf} 1^{10g} 6^{14g} **1-0-4 £7,398**

Kustom Kit For Her *S R Bowring* a45
4 b f Overbury (Ire) - Antonias Melody
6^{7sd} 8^{6sd} 10^{6ss} 13^{12sd} 2^{12ss} 3^{9ss} 2^{8ss}
2^{11sw} 4^{10sd} 8^{8ss} 8^{10sd} **0-4-12 £1,441**

Kwaheri *Mrs P N Dutfield*
6 b m Efisio - Fleeting Affair

9^{14gs} **0-0-1**

Kwai Baby (USA) *J J Bridger* 2
3 gr f Charnwood Forest (Ire) - Roses In The Snow (Ire)
7^{10gf} 9^{10g} 9^{8g} 8^{17s} **0-0-4**

Kwame *Miss E C Lavelle* 79 a63
2 b f Kingsinger (Ire) - Admire
2^{5gf} 1^{5g} 2^{5g} 13^{5g} 2^{5s} 5^{6gs} 3^{6gf} 9^{6gs}
5^{6sd} **1-4-9 £9,305**

Kyalami (Ire) *P Delaney* a40
5 b g Kylian (USA) - Nikkicola (USA)
3^{16sd} 14^{14sd} **0-1-2 £235**

Kyber *R F Fisher* 58
3 ch g First Trump - Mahbob Dancer (Fr)
5^{14gf} 4^{8gf} 3^{9gs} 3^{12s} 10^{16gf} 6^{10gs} 4^{12s}
5^{14s} **0-1-8 £1,850**

Kyle Of Lochalsh *J S Goldie* 45 a62
4 gr g Vettori (Ire) - Shaieef (Ire)
3^{8sd} 11^{10sd} 10^{10g} 12^{10gf} 5^{9g} 5^{10g} 12^{10gf}
6^{10s} **0-1-8 £213**

Kylkenny *H Morrison* 78 a84
9 b g Kylian (USA) - Fashion Flow
3^{12s} 11^{12gs} 13^{10g} 6^{10gf} 5^{12gf} 3^{10gf} 4^{12gs}
4^{10gf} 4^{10gf} 14^{12g} 10^{12gf} 8^{10g} **0-2-12 £2,739**

Kythia (Ire) *H Morrison* 77
3 b f Kahyasi - Another Rainbow (Ire)
4^{10gf} 3^{12g} 7^{12gf} 6^{13gs} 9^{12gf} 14^{10gs}
0-2-7 £2,005

L'Escapade (Ire) *A M Balding* 79
2 b c Grand Lodge (USA) - Brief Escapade (Ire)
3^{7gf} 5^{8g} 4^{7gf} 3^{8gf} **0-2-4 £2,562**

L'Etang Bleu (Fr) *P Butler* a10
6 gr g Graveron (Fr) - Strawberry Jam (Fr)
8^{13sd} **0-0-1**

La Bella Grande (Ire) *R Charlton* 48
2 ch f Giant's Causeway (USA) - La Belle Otero (USA)
12^{7gs} **0-0-1**

La Bella Rosa (Ire) *J S Wainwright* 48
2 b f Revoque (Ire) - Tempesta Rossa (Ire)
10^{5hy} 8^{6g} 17^{6f} **0-0-3**

La Calera (Ger) *G C H Chung* 47 a43
3 ch f Big Shuffle (USA) - La Luce
3^{8sd} 1^{8sd} 8^{7hy} 8^{8s} 5^{7gf} 3^{7f} 3^{8hy} 12^{6gf}
9^{7gs} 5^{10gf} 11^{8gs} 4^{7gs} 4^{7sd} **1-2-13 £3,915**

La Concha (Ire) *Mrs L C Jewell* 57 a45
3 b g Kahyasi - Trojan Crown (Ire)
8^{8sd} 9^{12sd} 11^{10sd} 8^{10gs} 8^{14s} 8^{11f} **0-0-6**

La Coruna *R Charlton* 57
3 b f Deploy - Valencia
4^{6hy} **0-0-1 £722**

La Cucaracha *B W Hills* 103
3 b f Piccolo - Peggy Spencer
2^{5g} 6^{6g} 3^{6gf} **0-2-3 £10,350**

La Cygne Blanche (Ire) *Mrs N Macauley* 25 a45
2 gr f Saddlers' Hall (USA) - Ivory's Promise
11^{6gf} 14^{7sd} 6^{6sd} **0-0-3**

La Danseuse *G C Bravery* a50
3 b f Groom Dancer (USA) - Alik (Fr)
5^{10sd} **0-0-1**

La Fonteyne *C B B Booth* 53 a42
3 b f Imperial Ballet (Ire) - Baliana
5^{6s} 17^{8g} 2^{6sd} 12^{7g} 5^{6sd} 16^{6g} 3^{7hy} 19^{7gs}
4^{7s} **0-2-9 £1,468**

La Hermana *A Wohler* 94
3 ch f Hernando (Fr) - La Candela (Ger)
5^{8g} 5^{8s} 4^{11g} 4^{10ho} 7^{10gf} 2^{10s} **0-1-6**

£23,155
La Landonne *P M Phelan* 71 a66
3 b f Fraam - Le Pin
4⁶ˢ 3⁸ᵍᶠ 6⁶ᵍ 6⁷ˢᵈ 11⁷ᵍᶠ 13⁸ˢ 2⁹ˢᵈ **0-2-7**
£1,747
La Mago *F P Murtagh*
4 b f Wizard King - Dancing Dancer
14⁹ᵍ **0-0-1**
La Muette (Ire) *M Appleby* 57
4 b f Charnwood Forest (Ire) - Elton Grove (Ire)
7¹⁶ˢᵈ 10¹²ʰʸ 8⁸ᵍˢ 16¹¹ᵍˢ **0-0-4**
La Musique *P J McBride* a13
2 b c Merdon Melody - Daleside Ladybird
18⁸ᵍᶠ 12⁸ˢᵈ **0-0-2**
La Peregrina *Sir Mark Prescott* a58
3 b/br f Zafonic (USA) - Flawless
2⁷ˢᵈ 5⁸ˢᵈ **0-1-2 £1,266**
La Persiana *W Jarvis* 105
3 gr f Daylami (Ire) - La Papagena
5⁸ᵍᶠ 2⁸ᵍᶠ 1¹⁰ᶠ 1¹⁰ᵍᶠ 1¹⁰ᵍᶠ 2¹⁰ʰʸ 3¹⁰ᵍ **3-3-7**
£38,242
La Petite Chinoise *R Guest* 79 a63
3 ch f Dr Fong (USA) - Susi Wong (Ire)
6⁷ˢᵈ 8⁷ˢᵈ 4⁹ᵍᶠ 2¹¹ᵍᶠ 2¹¹ᵍᶠ 5¹²ᵍᶠ 1¹¹ᶠ **1-2-7**
£6,669
La Professoressa (Ire) *Mrs P N Dutfield* 61
3 b f Cadeaux Genereux - Fellwah (Ire)
6⁸ᶠ 12⁷ᵍᶠ 11¹⁰ᵍᶠ 5¹⁰ᵍᶠ 3⁹ˢ 13¹⁰ᵍ **0-1-6**
£664
La Providence *D W Chapman*
2 b f Takhlid (USA) - Petite Danseuse
9⁵ˢʷ 14⁷ᵍᶠ 11⁷ˢᵈ **0-0-3**
La Puce *M J Attwater* 67 a77
3 b f Danzero (Aus) - Verbena (Ire)
4⁸ˢᵈ 8¹⁰ˢᵈ 18ˢˢ 18ˢʷ 4⁸ˢˢ 6⁸ᶠ 8⁷ᵍᶠ 7⁷ᵍᶠ
8⁷ᵍᶠ 2⁷ˢᵈ 18ˢ **3-1-11 £11,423**
La Rose *J W Unett* a20
4 b f Among Men (USA) - Marie La Rose (Fr)
6¹²ˢʷ **0-0-1**
La Sylphide *G M Moore* 95
7 ch m Rudimentary (USA) - Primitive Gift
2¹¹ˢ 5¹²ᵍˢ 6¹¹ᵍˢ 10¹⁰ᵍᶠ 2¹⁰ᵍˢ 1¹¹ˢ 3¹⁰ˢ
4¹²ˢ **1-3-8 £31,249**
La Vie Est Belle *B R Millman* 69 a68
3 b f Makbul - La Belle Vie
6⁵ˢᵈ 10⁶ˢ 4⁶ᵍᶠ 9⁶ᵍ 11⁸ᵍᶠ 6⁶ᵍˢ 1⁵ˢ 8⁵ᵍᶠ
4⁶ᵍˢ 5⁶ˢᵈ 2⁶ᵍˢ **1-2-11 £6,993**
La Vigna (Ire) *Mrs Lucinda Featherstone* a30
3 ch g Woodborough (USA) - Bona Fide
8⁷ˢᵈ 10⁵ˢˢ 7⁶ˢᵈ **0-0-3**
La Viola *K R Burke* 60
2 b f Fraam - Arasong
6⁶ᵍ 5⁷ᵍˢ **0-0-2**
Laabbij (USA) *M P Tregoning* 74
3 ch c Shuailaan (USA) - United Kingdom (USA)
6⁸ᵍ 10¹⁰ˢ 5¹⁰ᵍᶠ 3¹⁰ᵍᶠ 2¹²ᵍˢ **0-2-5**
£1,490
Laawaris (USA) *J A Osborne* 66
3 b g Souvenir Copy (USA) - Seattle Kat (USA)
8¹⁰ᵍˢ 12⁹ʰʸ 9¹¹ᵍᶠ **0-0-3**
Labelled With Love *J R Boyle* 53 a52
4 ch g Zilzal (USA) - Dream Baby
2¹⁰ᵍᶠ 5¹⁰ᶠ 6⁸ᵍᶠ 9⁸ˢᵈ 5⁷ˢᵈ 2⁸ᵍ 2⁹ˢᵈ **0-3-7**
£1,699
Labrett *Miss Gay Kelleway* a90

7 b g Tragic Role (USA) - Play The Game
3⁸ˢᵈ 9¹⁰ˢᵈ 5⁸ˢᵈ 2⁸ˢᵈ 3⁷ˢˢ 7⁸ˢᵈ **0-3-6**
£3,261
Laconia (Ire) *J S Moore* 72 a52
3 b f Orpen (USA) - Mislead (Ire)
4⁵ˢᵈ 5⁵ᵍ 2⁵ᵍ 6⁵ˢ 2⁵ᵍᶠ 2⁵ᵍᶠ 7⁵ᵍᶠ 8⁵ᵍᶠ
11⁵ˢᵈ **0-3-10 £3,657**
Laconicos (Ire) *J A Osborne* 79 a67
2 ch c Foxhound (USA) - Thermopylae
2⁵ᵍˢ 3⁵ᵍᶠ 2⁷ᵍᶠ 10⁷ᵍᶠ 8⁶ˢᵈ **0-3-5 £2,042**
Ladeena (Ire) *J L Dunlop* 83
2 b/br f Dubai Millennium - Aqaarid (USA)
2⁷ᵍˢ **0-1-1 £1,502**
Ladies Knight *D Shaw* a63
4 b g Among Men (USA) - Lady Silk
6⁵ˢᵈ 3⁵ˢᵈ 2⁶ˢᵈ 5⁵ˢˢ 8⁶ˢᵈ 6⁶ˢᵈ 3⁵ˢˢ 7⁶ˢᵈ
5⁵ˢᵈ 8⁶ˢᵈ **0-3-10 £1,731**
Ladruca *G G Margarson* 54
2 b/br f Dracula (Aus) - Promissory
8⁶ᵍᶠ 7⁶ᵍ 5⁷ᵍᶠ 17⁹ᶠ 19⁷ᵍᶠ **1-0-5 £3,562**
Lady Alruna (Ire) *P T Midgley* a10
5 ch m Alhaarth (Ire) - In Tranquility (Ire)
8⁷ˢᵈ **0-0-1**
Lady Ann Summers (USA) *B J Meehan* 78 a41
2 ch f Two Punch (USA) - Why Walk (USA)
10⁵ᵍᶠ 3⁵ᵍᶠ 4⁶ᵍ 10⁵ᵍˢ 14⁷ˢᵈ **0-1-5**
£1,164
Lady Arnica *A W Carroll*
5 b m Ezzoud (Ire) - Brand
7¹⁴ˢᵈ 8¹⁶ˢᵈ **0-0-2**
Lady At Leisure (Ire) *M J Ryan* a40
4 ch f Dolphin Street (Fr) - In A Hurry (Fr)
6¹⁰ˢᵈ 11⁸ˢᵈ 10¹⁰ˢᵈ 1¹⁰ˢᵈ 10¹⁰ʰʸ **1-0-5**
£1,260
Lady Bahia (Ire) *R P Elliott* a64
3 b f Orpen (USA) - Do The Right Thing
7⁹ˢʷ 6¹⁰ˢᵈ 16⁶ˢ 7⁵ˢᵈ 11⁵ˢ **2-0-5 £5,803**
Lady Blade (Ire) *B Hanbury* 62 a53
3 b f Daggers Drawn (USA) - Singhana (Ire)
7⁸ᶠ 4¹⁰ˢᵈ 8¹²ᵍᶠ 5¹⁰ᵍᶠ 9⁹ˢ 9⁸ˢᵈ 13⁹ˢᵈ **0-0-7**

Lady Chef *B R Millman* 77
2 ch f Double Trigger (Ire) - Dundeelin
8⁵ᵍ 5⁶ᵍ 1⁷ᵍᶠ 3⁷ᵍᶠ 8⁸ᶠ 11⁸ˢ **1-1-6**
£5,230
Lady Dan (Ire) *M W Easterby* 74
2 b f Danzero (Aus) - Dubai Lady
4⁵ʰʸ 3⁵ᵍᶠ 2⁵ᵍᶠ 9⁷ᵍ 6⁵ᵍ 7⁶ᶠ 3⁵ᵍ PU⁵ᵍᶠ
0-3-8 £2,802
Lady Doris Watts *M R Channon* 65
2 b f Emarati (USA) - Wrong Bride
8⁶ᵍ 2⁷ᵍˢ 7⁶ᵍ 6⁶ˢ **0-1-4 £439**
Lady Double U *T D Easterby* 37 a41
4 b f Sheikh Albadou - Bollin Victoria
11⁷ˢᵈ 7⁷ˢˢ 9⁶ʰʸ 15⁵ᵍᶠ 7⁶ᶠ **0-0-5**
Lady Dulcet *D Burchell*
4 b f Thowra (Fr) - Freedom Weekend (USA)
10⁸ᵍˢ **0-0-1**
Lady Edge (Ire) *M W Easterby* 1
2 ch f Bold Edge - Lady Sheriff
11⁵ᵍ **0-0-1**
Lady Ellendune *D J S Ffrench Davis*
3 b f Piccolo - Eileen's Lady
13⁶ˢᵈ **0-0-1**
Lady Erica *K R Burke* 54 a52

2 b f Komaite (USA) - Zamarra
2⁵sd 5⁵gs 4⁵sd 3⁵sd 9⁵hy 10⁵g **0-2-6**
£1,180

Lady Filly *W G M Turner* 87
2 ch f Atraf - Just Lady
1⁵s 1⁵gs 1¹s 7⁵gf 5⁵gs 5⁶s **3-0-6**
£18,651

Lady Franpalm (Ire) *M J Haynes* 39
4 b f Danehill Dancer (Ire) - Be Nimble
15⁷gs 7⁷s 9⁷gf 13⁶sd 10⁶gs **0-0-5**

Lady Georgina *J R Fanshawe* 89
3 gr f Linamix (Fr) - Georgia Venture
3⁸gs 6⁸g 1⁷gf 2⁷gf 1⁷g 5⁷f **2-2-6**
£12,487

Lady Heccles *M R Hoad*
5 b m Sayaarr (USA) - Rae Un Soleil
10⁸sd **0-0-1**

Lady Hen *M J Wallace* 61
2 b f Efisio - Royale Rose (Fr)
8⁶gs 6⁶g 8⁶gf **0-0-3**

Lady Hopeful (Ire) *R P Elliott* 60 a60
2 b f Lend A Hand - Treble Term
5⁵g 4⁵gf 2⁷sd 2⁷g 7⁵g 5⁶gf 5⁵gf 14⁷g 4⁶g
14⁵hy **0-2-10 £2,399**

Lady Indiana (Ire) *J S Wainwright*
2 b f King's Theatre (Ire) - Najeyba
9⁶g 16⁶f 7⁷g 11⁸gs **0-0-4**

Lady Jeannie *M J Haynes* 36 a32
7 b m Emarati (USA) - Cottonwood
7⁸gf 10¹⁰gf 11¹⁰gs 8¹⁶sd **0-0-4**

Lady Justice *W Jarvis* 53 a44
4 b f Compton Place - Zinzi
13⁶s 4⁵gf 14⁶gf 8⁵sd 6⁵gf **0-0-5 £277**

Lady Karr *M Johnston* 69
3 b f Mark Of Esteem (Ire) - Percy's Lass
7⁹gf 3¹⁰g 11¹²s **1-1-3 £4,088**

Lady Korrianda *Lady Herries* 37 a39
3 ch f Dr Fong (USA) - Prima Verde
9⁶gs 9⁷sd **0-0-2**

Lady Lakota (Ire) *A P Jarvis* 31
2 b f Indian Lodge (Ire) - Milady Lillie (Ire)
14⁶g **0-0-1**

Lady Lakshmi *M Madgwick* a44
4 ch f Bahhare - Polish Honour (USA)
3¹²sd 2¹³sd 3¹⁰sd **0-3-3 £839**

Lady Le Quesne (Ire) *A M Balding* 81
2 ch f Alhaarth (Ire) - Lady Moranbon (USA)
6⁶gf 2⁵gf 1⁶gs 1⁵gf 13⁷g 7⁷g **2-1-6**
£10,102

Lady Lexie *R Guest* 39
3 b f Cape Cross (Ire) - Lady Of The Land
6⁸gf **0-0-1**

Lady Liesel *J L Spearing* 32 a42
4 b f Bin Ajwaad (Ire) - Griddle Cake (Ire)
10⁸sd 14⁶sd 3⁸sd 7⁸sd 11⁷sd 7⁸sd
12¹⁰gf 9¹⁰sd 12⁸g **0-1-10 £209**

Lady Londra *D K Ivory* 68
2 b f Fumo Di Londra (Ire) - Lady Phyl
7⁶gf 9⁶gs **0-0-2**

Lady Lucinda *John A Harris*
3 b f Muhtarram (USA) - Lady Phyl
10¹⁰s 12¹⁰gf **0-0-2**

Lady Luisa (Ire) *J S Moore* 63
2 b f Lujain (USA) - Lady Of Dreams (Ire)
11⁷g 5⁷gf 8⁷gs 11⁸g 14⁷gf **0-0-5 £268**

Lady McNair *P D Cundell* 80
4 b f Sheikh Albadou - Bonita Bee
4¹²gs 11¹⁰g 2¹⁰gf 4¹⁰gf **0-2-4 £2,553**

Lady Misha *Jedd O'Keeffe* 75
2 b f Mister Baileys - Hakone (Ire)
5⁵gs 5⁶gs 10⁶f 3⁷g 1⁷gs 2⁸s 5⁸gs 11⁸s
1-2-8 £7,582

Lady Mo *G G Margarson* 71 a75
3 b f Young Ern - Just Run (Ire)
5⁶sd 3⁸sd 5⁸sd 1⁸ss 1⁷sd 12⁷sd 1⁷sd 2⁸sd
3⁷g 13⁷g 8⁷g 1⁷g 2⁸gf 2⁷gf 3⁷f 5⁷s 5⁷gf
4-6-17 £17,378

Lady Mytton *A Bailey* 69
4 ch f Lake Coniston (Ire) - The In-Laws (Ire)
5⁸s 16⁷s **0-0-2 £366**

Lady Natilda *D Haydn Jones* a53
4 ch f First Trump - Ramajana (USA)
4⁶sw 3⁶sd 11⁶ss 6⁷sd **0-1-4 £684**

Lady Netbetsports *B S Rothwell* 67
5 b m In The Wings - Auntie Maureen (Ire)
7¹⁰gf 3¹³g 7¹⁵g 2¹⁶gs 8¹⁴gs 10¹⁶s **0-1-6**
£1,812

Lady Of The Links (Ire) *N Tinkler* 36 a7
3 b f Desert Style (Ire) - Itkan (Ire)
4⁵s 8⁶s 5⁸hy 16⁶gf 8⁷s 11⁶sd **0-0-6**

Lady Oriande *A M Balding* 19 a22
3 b f Makbul - Lady Roxanne
6⁶sd 8⁶gs **0-0-2**

Lady Peaches *D Mullarkey* 72
3 ch f Bien Bien (USA) - Upper Club (Ire)
7¹⁰g 3¹⁰s 8¹⁰gf 4¹¹gf 5¹²gf **0-1-5 £829**

Lady Pekan *P S McEntee* 67 a71
5 b m Sri Pekan (USA) - Cloudberry
6⁶sw 3⁵sd 5⁵sd 6⁵sw 7⁵sd 7⁵ss 5²gf 2⁵s
9⁵gf 9⁵s 3⁵gf 5⁵f 3⁵gf 9⁵gf 8⁵s 13⁵f 17⁵g
8⁵sd **0-5-18 £6,297**

Lady Pilot *C E Brittain* 82
2 b f Dansili - Mighty Flyer (Ire)
9⁷gf 12⁶g 6⁶g 7⁷gf **0-0-4**

Lady Piste (Ire) *G G Margarson* 57 a57
3 b f Ali-Royal (Ire) - Alpine Lady (Ire)
12⁷sd 4⁶sd 2⁵sd 5⁶sd 3⁷sd 1⁷sd 7⁷sd 1⁷gf
4⁸gf **2-2-9 £7,835**

Lady Predominant *G F Bridgwater* 26 a45
3 b f Primo Dominie - Enlisted (Ire)
4¹⁰sd 4⁸sd 11⁸sd 6⁷sd 11⁷sd 1⁸sd 12⁸g
5⁸sd 13⁸f 14⁸gs 16⁶gf 10⁹sd **1-0-12 £1,424**

Lady Protector *J Balding* 59 a58
5 b m Sri Pekan (USA) - Scared
4⁵sd 1⁵sd 7⁵ss 3⁵sd 9⁵ss 10⁵ss 7⁵g 1⁵gf
1⁵gf 3⁵f 3⁵g 3⁵gf 8⁵gs 7⁵gf **3-4-14 £12,270**

Lady Redera (Ire) *H S Howe* 36
3 b f Inzar (USA) - Era
16⁸g 13⁸f 11¹⁰gf **0-0-3**

Lady Stratagem *E W Tuer* 46
5 gr m Mark Of Esteem (Ire) - Grey Angel
7¹⁴g 10¹⁰gf 3¹²gf 9¹⁴gf 14¹²g 13⁹f **0-1-6**
£592

Lady Stripes *A J Martin* 40 a52
3 gr f Alzao (USA) - Shamaya (Ire)
8⁷sd 6¹⁰sd 7⁶ss 7¹⁰sd 4⁸gf 3¹²gf 10⁹y
0-1-7 £1,034

Lady Suesanne (Ire) *C A Dwyer* 44 a2
2 b f Cape Cross (Ire) - Lady At War
8⁶gf 12⁷sd 11⁷f 12⁶g **0-0-4**

Lady Sunset (Ire) *K A Ryan*   42
3 b f Entrepreneur - Sunset Reigns (Ire)
10⁵ᵍ 8⁵ˢ 17⁸ᵍᶠ 11⁶ᶠ **0-0-4**

Lady Taverner *H J Cyzer*   57
3 b f Marju (Ire) - Prompting
15⁸ᵍᶠ 10¹⁰ᵍᶠ 5⁸ᵍᶠ 9⁹ᵍᶠ 8⁸ᶠ **0-0-5**

Lady Tilly *D A Nolan*
7 b m Puissance - Lady Of Itatiba (Bel)
9⁷ˢ **0-0-1**

Lady Vee (Ire) *P D Niven*   52
2 b f Rossini (USA) - Dama De Noche
8⁶ᵍˢ 5⁶ᵍᶠ 10⁸ᵍᶠ 16⁶ᵍ **0-0-4**

Lady West *Dr J R J Naylor*
4 b f The West (USA) - Just Run (Ire)
14⁸ᵍ **0-0-1**

Lady Xanthia *I A Wood*   a30
3 ch f Bien Bien (USA) - Carmosa (USA)
8⁷ˢˢ 4¹⁰ˢᵈ 8¹³ˢᵈ **0-0-3**

Lady's View (USA) *D J Daly*   87
3 b f Distant View (USA) - Karasavina (Ire)
3⁷ᶠ 7⁷ᵍᶠ 11¹⁰ᵍ 6⁸ᵍˢ **0-0-4 £1,666**

Ladystgeorge *M Mullineaux*
5 b m Mind Games - Indiahra
11⁶ˢᵈ **0-0-1**

Ladywell Blaise (Ire) *J J Bridger*   a49
7 b m Turtle Island (Ire) - Duly Elected
7⁸ˢᵈ 3⁸ˢᵈ 6⁸ˢᵈ **0-1-3 £234**

Laffah (USA) *G L Moore*
9 b g Silver Hawk (USA) - Sakiyah (USA)
12¹⁸ᵍ **0-0-1**

Lafi (Ire) *D Nicholls*   106
5 ch g Indian Ridge - Petal Girl
7⁶ᵍᶠ 3⁶ᵍ 1⁶ᶠ **1-1-3 £50,800**

Laggan Bay (Ire) *J S Moore*   79 a78
4 b g Alzao (USA) - Green Lucia
7¹⁴ˢ 6¹²ᵍ 7¹²ᵍ 7¹⁵ˢ 19¹⁸ˢ 2¹⁶ˢ 5¹⁷ˢᵈ **0-1-7 £2,755**

Laggan Minstrel (Ire) *B J Llewellyn*
6 b g Mark Of Esteem (Ire) - Next Episode (USA)
12⁸ˢᵈ 12⁷ᵍᶠ **0-0-2**

Lago D'Orta (Ire) *C G Cox*   109
4 ch g Bahhare (USA) - Maelalong (Ire)
6⁸ᵍ 4⁹ᵍ 7¹⁰ᵍˢ 8¹⁰ᵍᶠ 6⁸ᵍ 12⁸ᵍˢ 11⁷ᵍ 22⁸ˢ **0-0-9 £4,600**

Lago Di Como *Mrs P Townsley*   a63
7 b g Piccolo - Farmer's Pet
1¹¹ˢᵈ 9¹²ˢᵈ **1-0-2 £1,459**

Lagosta (SAF) *G M Moore*
4 ch g Fort Wood (USA) - Rose Wine
13¹²ᵍᶠ **0-0-1**

Lahob *N B King*   53 a52
4 ch c First Trump - Mystical Song
8¹²ᵍᶠ 6¹⁵ᵍ 7¹²ᵍᶠ 10¹⁴ᵍᶠ 7¹³ᵍˢ 3⁹ˢᵈ **0-1-6 £212**

Laird Dara Mac *N Bycroft*
4 b c Presidium - Nishara
7¹²ˢʷ **0-0-1**

Lakaam *G P Enright*   49 a49
3 b f Danzero (Aus) - Langtry Lady
14¹⁰ˢᵈ 8¹²ˢᵈ 3¹²ᵍˢ **0-1-3 £733**

Lake 'O' Gold *D W Thompson*   35
5 ch m Karinga Bay - Ginka
8¹⁶ᵍ **0-0-1**

Lake Carezza (USA) *J Noseda*   62
2 b c Stravinsky (USA) - May Wedding (USA)

5⁶ᵍ 9⁶ˢ **0-0-2**

Lake Charlotte (USA) *D R Loder*   73
3 b f Danzig (USA) - Quinpool (USA)
3⁷ᵍ 2⁷ᵍ 3⁶ᵍᶠ 1⁵ᵍˢ 6⁶ᶠ **1-3-5 £5,964**

Lake Chini (Ire) *M A Jarvis*   80 a52
2 b c Raise A Grand (Ire) - Where's The Money
11⁷ˢᵈ 7⁷ᵍ 2⁶ˢ **0-1-3 £1,463**

Lake Diva *J G Given*   55 a71
3 ch f Docksider (USA) - Cutpurse Moll
3⁸ᵍ 4⁹ˢ 10⁸ᵍ 1⁹ˢᵈ **1-1-4 £3,626**

Lake Eyre (Ire) *J Balding*   a49
5 b m Bluebird (USA) - Pooh Wee
5⁶ˢᵈ 9⁶ˢᵈ 8⁶ˢᵈ 5⁶ˢᵈ 5⁶ˢᵈ **0-0-5**

Lake Garda *B A McMahon*   96
3 b c Komaite (USA) - Malcesine (Ire)
5⁵ˢ 3⁵ˢ 1⁶ˢ 1⁶ᵍ 22⁶ᵍ **2-1-5 £28,480**

Lake Of Dreams *Dr J R J Naylor*   40 a24
5 b g Polish Precedent (USA) - Rainbow Lake
11¹⁰ᵍˢ 12¹⁰ᵍᶠ 5¹⁴ˢᵈ **0-0-3**

Lake Verdi (Ire) *Miss Gay Kelleway*   57 a61
5 ch g Lake Coniston (Ire) - Shore Lark (USA)
14⁶ᵍᶠ 4⁶ˢᵈ 3⁵ᵍˢ 9⁵ᵍᶠ 7⁶ᵍᶠ 2⁶ᵍᶠ 6⁶ᵍˢ 10⁶ᵍᶠ **0-1-8 £1,352**

Lake Wakatipu *M Mullineaux*   56
2 b f Lake Coniston (Ire) - Lady Broker
7⁶ᵍ 4⁶ᵍˢ 3⁷ᵍ 6⁸ˢ 6⁷ᵍˢ **0-0-5 £1,114**

Lakelands Lady (Ire) *J Balding*   43 a55
4 ch f Woodborough (USA) - Beautyofthepeace (Ire)
13⁶ˢᵈ 7⁵ˢᵈ 11⁵ˢ 17⁶ᵍᶠ 9⁵ᵍˢ 14⁵ᵍˢ 4⁶ᵍˢ 4⁷ˢᵈ **0-0-8**

Lakesdale (Ire) *Miss D Mountain*   57 a62
2 b f Desert Style (Ire) - Option (Ire)
11⁵ᵍ 2⁶ᵍᶠ 2⁷ᶠ 9⁶ᵍ 4⁷ᵍᶠ 9⁷ᵍᶠ 2⁷ᵍᶠ 3⁷ˢ 6⁶ˢᵈ 1⁶ᵍᶠ 10⁷ᵍᶠ 13⁸ᵍ 8⁶ᵍ **1-4-13 £6,302**

Lakeside Guy (Ire) *P S McEntee*   63 a56
3 b g Revoque (Ire) - Glen Of Imaal (Ire)
15⁷ˢᵈ 8⁶ˢᵈ 4⁵ˢᵈ 8⁵ˢᵈ 3⁵ᵍᶠ 5⁵ᵍᶠ 6⁵ᵍᶠ 2⁵ᵍᶠ 11⁶ᵍ 3⁶ˢᵈ 4⁵ˢᵈ **0-2-11 £2,597**

Lakota Brave *Mrs Stef Liddiard*   69 a95
10 ch g Anshan - Pushkinia (Fr)
2⁸ˢᵈ 4¹⁰ˢᵈ 7⁸ˢˢ 13¹⁰ˢᵈ 10⁸ˢʷ 6⁷ˢˢ 4⁸ˢ 10⁸ᵍˢ 2⁸ˢ **0-2-9 £5,280**

Lama Albarq (USA) *E A L Dunlop*   50 a50
2 ch c Nureyev (USA) - Nuts In May (USA)
14⁶ᵍᶠ 6⁶ᵍᶠ 10⁷ˢᵈ **0-0-3**

Lambriggan Lad *Miss Victoria Roberts*   17 a35
2 b g Mazurek - Alfs Classic (Fr)
9⁸ᵍ 9⁷ˢᵈ 8¹⁰ʰʸ **0-0-3**

Lamh Eile (Ire) *T D Barron*   87
2 b f Lend A Hand - Mothers Footprints (Ire)
1⁶ᵍ 1⁷ᵍᶠ 3⁷ᵍ 13⁷ᵍ **2-1-4 £11,167**

Lampos (USA) *Miss J A Camacho*   53 a58
4 b/br g Southern Halo (USA) - Gone Private (USA)
3¹²ˢᵈ 1¹⁴ˢᵈ 2¹⁶ˢᵈ 5¹⁶ˢᵈ 7¹⁴ˢᵈ 7¹⁶ᵍˢ 11¹⁴ˢ 8¹²ˢᵈ **1-2-9 £2,536**

Lanas Turn *T D Easterby*   44 a25
2 b f Mister Baileys - Lana Turrel (USA)
14⁵ᵍᶠ 5⁷ˢᵈ 8⁷ᵍ 16⁶ᵍ 4⁷ᵍᶠ 6⁷ᵍˢ 9⁷ᵍᶠ **0-0-7 £282**

Land 'n Stars *Jamie Poulton*   91
4 b g Mtoto - Uncharted Waters
9¹⁴ʰʸ 1¹⁶ᵍᶠ 5²⁰ᵍᶠ 4¹⁶ᵍᶠ 1¹⁶ᵍᶠ 3¹⁶ᵍ 6¹⁸ˢ 5¹⁶ˢ **2-1-8 £21,005**

Land Army (Ire) *Miss J Feilden*   38
3 b f Desert Style (Ire) - Family At War (USA)

13⁸ᵍᶠ **0-0-1**

Land Of Fantasy *Lady Herries*   a66
5 ch g Hernando (Fr) - Height Of Folly
1¹⁶ˢᵈ 2¹⁶ˢᵈ 3¹⁶ˢᵈ **1-2-3 £4,757**

Land Of Nod (Ire) *G Brown*   55
3 b f Barathea (Ire) - Rafif (USA)
4⁸ˢ 7¹⁰ᵍ 14¹²ᵍᶠ 5⁷ˢ 6⁸ᵍ 16⁸ᵍ **0-0-6**
£281

Landescent (Ire) *Miss K M George*   40 a55
4 b g Grand Lodge (USA) - Traumerei (Ger)
7¹³ˢᵈ 4¹⁵ˢᵈ 5¹³ˢᵈ 1¹⁰ˢᵈ 1¹⁰ˢᵈ 5⁹ˢˢ 6¹⁰ᶠ
2-0-7 £3,321

Landing Strip (Ire) *J M P Eustace*   50 a35
4 b g Dolphin Street (Fr) - Funny Cut (Ire)
20⁶ᵍˢ 20⁶ᵍˢ 5⁶ᶠ 11⁵ᵍ 25⁶ᵍᶠ 11⁵ᵍ 7⁶ˢᵈ
0-0-7

Landinium (Ity) *V Valiani*   99
5 b m Lando (Ger) - Hollywood Girl
4¹⁰ᵍˢ 4¹⁰ᵍˢ 1¹²ᵍᶠ 3¹²ᵍ 6¹¹ᵍᶠ 5¹⁰ᵍˢ **1-1-6**
£22,275

Landofheartsdesire (Ire) *J S Wainwright*   15 a20
5 b m Up And At 'Em - Ahonita
6⁷ˢᵈ 7⁷ˢᵈ 16⁸ᵍᶠ **0-0-3**

Landucci *J W Hills*   72 a71
3 b c Averti (Ire) - Divina Luna
2⁸ˢᵈ 7⁸ˢ 6⁸ᵍᶠ 1⁷ˢ 3⁷ᵍ 4⁶ᵍᶠ 10⁷ᵍ 2⁷ˢᵈ
1-4-8 £6,953

Lane Marshal *J O'Reilly*   44 a21
2 gr g Danzig Connection (USA) - Evening Falls
6⁵ʰʸ 5⁵ʰʸ 15⁶ᵍ 7⁵ᵍᶠ 7⁷ᵍˢ 6⁵ᵍᶠ 5⁷ˢ 11⁶ˢʷ
5⁶ᵍˢ **0-0-9**

Lange Bleu (Fr) *Mrs S C Bradburne*   2
5 ch g Beyssac (Fr) - Dear Blue (Fr)
8¹²ᵍ 11⁹ᵍᶠ **0-0-2**

Langford *M H Tompkins*   93
4 ch g Compton Place - Sharpening
2⁸ᵍᶠ 1⁸ᵍᶠ 12⁸ᵍᶠ 15⁸ᵍ 1⁸ᵍᶠ 4⁸ᵍ 11⁹ᵍᶠ
11¹⁰ᵍˢ 5⁸ᵍᶠ 19⁹ᵍ **2-1-10 £17,932**

Langston Boy *M L W Bell*   63 a72
2 b g Namid - Blinding Mission (Ire)
4⁵ᵍˢ 2⁵ᵍˢ 3⁵ʰʸ 9⁷ᵍˢ 2⁷ˢᵈ 4⁷ᵍ 8⁸ˢ **0-3-7**
£3,512

Lanos (Pol) *P Wegmann*   62 a65
6 ch g Special Power - Lubeka (Pol)
5¹²ˢᵈ 5¹²ˢᵈ 5¹⁴ˢ **0-0-3**

Lapadar (Ire) *J R Weymes*   a25
5 b/br m Woodborough (USA) - Indescent Blue
6¹⁶ˢᵈ 4¹²ˢᵈ **0-0-2**

Lapdancing *Miss L A Perratt*   21
3 ch f Pursuit Of Love - Petrikov (Ire)
9⁹ᵍᶠ 8⁹ᵍ **0-0-2**

Lara Bay *A M Balding*   53 a42
4 b f Polish Precedent (USA) - Way O'Gold (USA)
11¹⁰ᶠ 12¹²ˢᵈ 9¹⁰ᵍᶠ **0-0-3**

Lara Falana *Miss B Sanders*   72 a67
6 b m Tagula (Ire) - Victoria Mill
7⁷ˢᵈ 2¹⁰ˢᵈ 5¹⁰ˢᵈ 4¹⁰ᵍᶠ 2¹⁰ᶠ 6¹⁰ˢᵈ 4¹⁰ᵍᶠ
1¹⁰ˢᵈ 8⁹ᵍ **1-2-9 £10,078**

Lara's Girl *I A Wood*   47
2 b f Tipsy Creek (USA) - Joe's Dancer
9⁶ᵍᶠ 4⁷ᶠ 8⁶ᵍᶠ 10⁷ᵍᶠ 3⁷ᵍᶠ 3⁷ᵍˢ 11⁸ᵍ **0-2-7**
£1,013

Larad (Ire) *J S Moore*   52 a53
3 br g Desert Sun - Glenstal Priory
3⁸ˢᵈ 5¹⁰ˢᵈ 9⁸ˢᵈ 7⁸ˢᵈ 5⁸ˢᵈ 5⁸ˢᵈ 1¹⁰ˢᵈ 3⁸ˢᵈ

3⁹ˢᵈ 4⁸ˢ 6⁷ˢ 1¹⁰ᵍᶠ 7¹¹ᵍˢ 6¹⁰ᶠ 7¹⁰ᶠ 6¹⁰ᵍˢ 5¹⁰ᶠ
9¹⁰ᵍᶠ 4¹⁰ᵍˢ 1⁹ˢᵈ **3-1-20 £5,451**

Largo (Ire) *J L Dunlop*   88
4 ch f Selkirk (USA) - Lady Of The Lake
10¹²ᵍ 5¹²ᵍ **0-0-2 £365**

Largs *J Balding*   32 a60
4 ch f Sheikh Albadou - Madam Zando
8⁷ˢᵈ 3⁶ˢᵈ 3⁷ˢˢ 2⁶ˢᵈ 6⁶ˢ 3⁶ˢᵈ 2⁷ˢᵈ **0-5-7**
£2,617

Lark In The Park (Ire) *W M Brisbourne*   38 a9
4 ch f Grand Lodge (USA) - Jarrayan
12⁸ˢᵈ 11⁸ˢ 9⁸ᵍᶠ 5⁸ᶠ 10⁸ᵍᶠ 11⁹ᶠ **0-0-6**

Larking About (USA) *W J Musson*   55
4 ch f Silver Hawk (USA) - Milly Ha Ha
11¹⁰ʰʸ 9¹⁰ᶠ 13¹²ᵍᶠ 6¹⁴ᵍᶠ 7¹⁴ᵍᶠ 2¹⁶ʰʸ
13¹⁴ᵍᶠ **0-1-7 £1,257**

Larkwing (Ire) *G Wragg*   96
3 b c Ela-Mana-Mou - The Dawn Trader (USA)
2¹⁰ᵍˢ 3¹⁰ᵍˢ 1¹²ᵍᶠ 2¹²ᵍ 5¹²ᵍ SU¹²ᵍᶠ 7¹²ᵍ
1-3-7 £27,218

Larky's Lob *J O'Reilly*   55 a70
5 b g Lugana Beach - Eucharis
2⁶ˢᵈ 1⁷ˢᵈ 4⁷ˢᵈ 5⁷ˢᵈ 3⁷ᵍ 2⁶ˢˢ 4⁷ˢᵈ 6⁷ˢʷ
3⁶ˢʷ 1⁶ˢᶠ 2⁶ˢᵈ 2⁶ˢᵈ 1⁵ˢᵈ 6⁶ˢᵈ 2⁵ᵍˢ 3⁵ᵍˢ 6⁶ˢᵈ
9⁵ˢ 8⁵ˢᵈ **3-8-19 £10,552**

Las Ramblas (Ire) *D A Nolan*   37
7 b g Thatching - Raise A Warning
13⁵ᶠ 19⁵ˢ 8⁶ˢ 9⁶ˢ **0-0-4**

Lasanga *Lady Herries*   68 a61
5 ch g Zamindar (USA) - Shall We Run
14⁸ᵍˢ 17¹⁰ᵍᶠ 2⁸ᵍ 6⁷ˢᵈ **0-1-4 £1,272**

Laska (Ire) *H R A Cecil*   57
3 br f Fasliyev (USA) - Dacian (USA)
4⁶ᵍᶠ 4⁶ᵍᶠ 11⁷ᵍᶠ **0-0-3 £866**

Lasser Light (Ire) *D G Bridgwater*   56 a36
4 b/br g Inchinor - Light Ray
10¹⁰ᵍ 7⁸ˢ 5¹¹ᵍˢ 11¹²ᶠ 12⁹ˢᵈ **0-0-5**

Last Appointment (USA) *J M P Eustace*   82 a84
4 b c Elusive Quality (USA) - Motion In Limine (USA)
5⁷ᵍ 7⁷ᵍᶠ 3⁷ˢᵈ 13⁷ˢᵈ **0-1-4 £882**

Last Chapter (Ire) *John Berry*   18
2 b g Desert Story (Ire) - Dutosky
16⁷ᵍˢ **0-0-1**

Last Pioneer (Ire) *T P Tate*   64
2 b g New Frontier (Ire) - Toordillon (Ire)
9⁶ᵍ 9⁷ᵍˢ 4⁸ˢ 4⁸ᵍˢ **0-0-4 £760**

Last Rebel (Ire) *R T Phillips*   a35
5 b g Danehill (USA) - La Curamalal (Ire)
6⁷ˢᵈ 15¹²ᵍᶠ **0-0-2**

Lasting Delight *Sir Mark Prescott*   a49
3 b f Robellino (USA) - Last Result
10¹⁰ˢᵈ **0-0-1**

Lasting Image *S C Williams*   27
2 br f Zilzal (USA) - Minsden's Image
15⁶ᵍ **0-0-1**

Lastofthewhalleys *K W Hogg*
6 b m Noble Patriarch - Pride Of Whalley (Ire)
9⁷ˢ **0-0-1**

Latalomne (USA) *N Wilson*   83
10 ch g Zilzal (USA) - Sanctuary
1¹²ᵍᶠ 4¹³ᵍ 11¹²ᵍᶠ 12¹⁴ᵍᶠ **1-0-4 £4,164**

Late Arrival *M D Hammond*   46 a40
7 b g Emperor Jones (USA) - Try Vickers (USA)
17⁸ᵍˢ 7⁸ᶠ 10⁸ᶠ 2⁸ᵈ 6⁸ˢᵈ 7¹⁰ᵍᶠ 4¹²ˢ
9¹⁰ᶠ **0-2-9 £742**

Late Opposition *E A L Dunlop*　　77
3 b c Unfuwain (USA) - Hawa (USA)
4^{10gs} 2^{12gs} 2^{12g} 2^{12s} 11^{10gf} 9^{10g} 3^{10g}
1^{11s} 2^{14s} 2^{17s} 11^{14g} **1-7-11 £12,383**

Lateen Sails *Saeed Bin Suroor*　　106
4 ch c Elmaamul (USA) - Felucca
7^{10gs} 15^{8gf} 5^{11g} **0-0-3 £1,625**

Lateral Thinker (Ire) *P D Evans*　　68 a68
2 b f Desert Sun - Miss Margate (Ire)
2^{5sd} 2^{5g} 3^{5g} 4^{5sd} 1^{6gf} 16^{5g} 5^{6gf} 2^{7sd}
6^{7sd} 8^{7gf} 6^{6gf} 4^{8g} 1^{7sd} **2-4-13 £9,943**

Latice (Ire) *J-M Beguigne*　　121
3 ch f Inchinor - Laramie (USA)
1^{9vs} 1^{11gs} 8^{12s} 7^{12g} **2-0-4 £226,901**

Latif (USA) *J H M Gosden*　　74
3 b c Red Ransom (USA) - Awaamir
16^{8g} 4^{7gf} **0-0-2 £525**

Latin Express (Ire) *W R Muir*　　49
2 b c Marju (Ire) - Sea Port
9^{6g} 14^{6s} **0-0-2**

Latin Queen (Ire) *J D Frost*　　51
4 b/br f Desert Prince (Ire) - Atlantic Dream (USA)
5^{12f} 8^{11gf} 5^{10gf} 5^{12gf} 9^{10gs} **0-0-5**

Latin Review (Ire) *A P Jarvis*　　47
3 ch f Titus Livius (Fr) - Law Review (Ire)
19^{6gf} **0-0-1**

Laugh 'n Cry *C A Cyzer*　　59
3 b f In The Wings - The Kings Daughter
10^{10g} 5^{9gf} **0-0-2**

Laura Lea *Ronald Thompson*　　39
4 b g Bishop Of Cashel - Kirriemuir
PU^{9ss} 12^{7gs} **0-0-2**

Laurel Dawn *I W McInnes*　　73 a63
6 gr g Paris House - Madrina
7^{5sd} 11^{6sd} 10^{5g} 7^{5gf} 1^{5g} 5^{5gf} 2^{5g} 5^{6g}
8^{5gf} 6^{5gf} 7^{6gf} 14^{5gs} 8^{6gs} 8^{5s} 8^{5gs} 3^{6g} 3^{6g}
1-3-17 £5,748

Lauren Louise *N Tinkler*　　16 a14
2 b f Tagula (Ire) - Movie Star (Ire)
11^{6gs} 9^{7sd} 11^{8g} **0-0-3**

Laurens Girl (Ire) *M G Quinlan*　　56 a19
3 b f Imperial Ballet (Ire) - Tresor Vert (USA)
9^{8sd} 6^{10gf} 4^{10g} **0-0-3 £316**

Lauro *Miss J A Camacho*　　81 a79
4 b f Mukaddamah (USA) - Lapu-Lapu
3^{8sd} 2^{8gs} 4^{10g} 4^{8g} 8^{8g} 1^{9s} 12^{10s} 5^{9sd}
1-2-8 £13,489

Laurollie *Dr J R J Naylor*　　39
2 b f Makbul - Madonna Da Rossi
10^{7gf} 12^{7g} 10^{8g} 9^{6s} **0-0-4**

Lavish Times *A Berry*　　49 a51
3 ch c Timeless Times (USA) - Lavernock Lady
7^{5sd} 5^{5ss} 3^{5sw} 11^{5g} 6^{5sd} 3^{5g} 6^{5g} 8^{5gs}
6^{5f} 5^{5g} 7^{5sd} 11^{6f} **0-1-12 £937**

Law Breaker (Ire) *J A Gilbert*　　97 a95
6 ch g Case Law - Revelette
5^{6sd} 5^{5sd} 2^{6g} 9^{6g} 16^{6g} 12^{6gs} 8^{5gs} 16^{6gs}
11^{6sd} **0-1-9 £3,678**

Law Maker *M A Buckley*　　53 a45
4 b g Case Law - Bo' Babbity
11^{6sd} 9^{5sd} 10^{6sd} 13^{6sd} 6^{6sd} 9^{6sd} 4^{6sd}
2^{5sd} 5^{5gf} 7^{5gf} 4^{5gf} 3^{5gf} 6^{5gf} 2^{5f} 10^{5gf} 15^{5gf}
0-4-16 £2,954

Lawaaheb (Ire) *B R Johnson*　　60 a57
3 b g Alhaarth (Ire) - Ajayib (USA)

8^{12g} 14^{10g} 13^{10sd} 7^{10g} **0-0-4**

Lawgiver (Ire) *T J Fitzgerald*　　6
3 b c Definite Article - Marylou Whitney (USA)
8^{10gs} 15^{10gf} **0-0-2**

Lawood (Ire) *K A Ryan*　　80 a64
4 gr g Charnwood Forest (Ire) - La Susiane
4^{8sd} 8^{7ss} 1^{10g} 2^{12s} 4^{11gf} 12^{10gf} 9^{12gf}
1-1-7 £5,227

Lawrence Of Arabia (Ire) *Sir Mark Prescott*　　65
4 b g Desert King (Ire) - Cumbres (Fr)
8^{9gf} 6^{12gf} 6^{14gf} 9^{16hy} 8^{14f} 14^{12g} **0-0-6**

Lay Down Sally (Ire) *J White*　　a40
6 ch m General Monash (USA) - Sally Fay (Ire)
6^{6sd} 7^{6sd} **0-0-2**

Layed Back Rocky *M Mullineaux*　　52 a51
2 ch c Lake Coniston (Ire) - Madam Taylor
6^{6g} 9^{7s} 2^{7g} 6^{8s} 6^{6hy} 7^{6sd} **0-1-6 £1,564**

Layman (USA) *A Fabre*　　117
2 ch c Sunday Silence (USA) - Laiyl (Ire)
1^{7s} 1^{6g} 2^{6vs} 3^{7g} **2-1-4 £100,461**

Lazzaz *P W Hiatt*　　59 a69
6 b g Muhtarram (USA) - Astern (USA)
4^{11sd} 3^{12sd} 5^{12sd} 3^{12sd} 3^{13sd} 3^{14sd} 7^{12ss}
2^{12sd} 8^{12gf} 5^{12gf} 6^{12gf} 4^{12gf} 3^{10gf} 4^{12g} 2^{12gf}
6^{10gf} 5^{14gf} 5^{10s} **2-9-24 £10,901**

Le Chiffre (Ire) *D R Loder*　　62
2 br c Celtic Swing - Implicit View
3^{7g} **0-1-1 £545**

Le Corvee (Ire) *A King*　　91 a87
2 b c Rossini (USA) - Elupa (Ire)
1^{7gf} 3^{8g} 4^{7g} 2^{9sd} **1-1-4 £7,327**

Le Meridien (Ire) *J S Wainwright*　　59
6 ch m Magical Wonder (USA) - Dutch Queen
5^{5f} 17^{5g} 7^{5s} 7^{6g} 6^{5gs} 5^{5gs} 1^{6gf} 8^{5gf}
3^{6gf} 10^{6gs} **1-1-10 £6,035**

Le Tiss (Ire) *M R Channon*　　98
3 b g Croco Rouge (Ire) - Manarah
4^{9s} 9^{11g} 2^{12g} 1^{14f} 4^{12gf} 12^{12g} 13^{14s}
1-2-7 £13,853

Le Vie Dei Colori *L M Cumani*　　121
4 b c Efisio - Mystic Tempo (USA)
1^{9g} 1^{8hy} 4^{10gs} 3^{8g} 8^{8gs} 3^{7s} **2-1-6
£114,768**

League Of Nations (Ire) *P F I Cole*　　70 a26
2 b c Indian Danehill (Ire) - Athens Belle (Ire)
8^{6g} 5^{6sd} 2^{7f} **0-1-3 £1,185**

Leaping Brave (Ire) *B R Millman*　　78
3 b g Indian Rocket - Island Heather (Ire)
4^{7s} 2^{8gf} 4^{7gf} 9^{8g} 8^{7gf} 9^{8gf} **0-2-6
£2,725**

Learn The Lingo *Mrs H Dalton*
8 b g Teenoso (USA) - Charlotte Gray
11^{9ss} **0-0-1**

Learned Lad (Fr) *Jamie Poulton*　　41 a73
6 ch g Royal Academy (USA) - Blushing Storm (USA)
2^{10sd} 5^{10sd} 10^{10sd} 11^{8sd} 12^{10gf} 12^{9gf}
15^{9gf} 15^{9gf} 18^{8g} 14^{8g} **0-1-10 £954**

Lebenstanz *L M Cumani*　　63 a63
4 b/br f Singspiel (Ire) - Reamur
6^{8sd} 6^{10g} 6^{10gf} 6^{12gf} 9^{16gs} 8^{14gf} **0-0-6**

Leg Spinner (Ire) *M R Channon*　　86
3 b g Intikhab (USA) - Road Harbour (USA)
3^{8gf} 3^{9f} 12^{7f} 7^{14gf} 1^{12gf} 1^{14gf} **3-1-6
£17,183**

Legacy (Jpn) *T T Clement*　　88 a33

4 b g Carnegie (Ire) - Idraak
7⁹ᵍᶠ 11⁸ᶠᵗ 15⁸ᵍᶠ 7⁸ʰʸ **0-0-4**

Legal Approach *M Johnston* 97
5 b h Zafonic (USA) - Legaya
4¹²ᵍˢ 10¹²ᵍˢ **0-0-2 £833**

Legal Belle *J L Spearing* 59
2 ch f Superpower - Legal Sound
4⁶ˢ **0-0-1 £380**

Legal Set (Ire) *Miss A Stokell* 69 a65
8 gr g Second Set (Ire) - Tiffany's Case (Ire)
4⁶ˢᵈ 10⁷ˢᵈ 5⁶ˢᵈ 12⁶ˢᵈ 2⁷ˢᵈ 12⁶ᵍ 15⁷ᵍᶠ
9⁷ᶠ 10⁶ᵍ 9⁵ᵍᶠ 4⁶ᵍᶠ 2⁶ᵍ 1⁶ᵍ 4⁶ᵍ 7⁶ᵍ 2⁶ᵍᶠ 4⁶ᵍ
10⁶ᵍᶠ 8⁷ˢᵈ **1-7-34**
£19,196

Legalis (USA) *K A Ryan* a59
6 ch g Gone West (USA) - Loyalize (USA)
3⁶ˢᵈ 2⁶ˢᵈ 13⁶ˢᵈ 3⁶ˢᵈ 1⁷ˢᵈ 3⁷ˢʷ 6⁷ˢʷ 4⁶ˢˢ
2⁷ˢˢ **1-4-9 £5,043**

Legality *Julian Poulton* 46 a33
4 b f Polar Falcon (USA) - Lady Barrister
14¹⁰ˢᵈ 6¹⁰ᵍᶠ 8¹⁰ᵍ 10¹¹ˢᵈ **0-0-4**

Legally Fast (USA) *P F I Cole* 48
2 b c Deputy Minister (Can) - Earthly Angel (USA)
10⁸ˢ 9⁸ᵍˢ **0-0-2**

Legend Of Dance *B J Meehan* 54 a40
2 b f Dansili - Hard Task
12⁷ᵍ 13⁸ᵍᶠ 8⁸ˢᵈ **0-0-3**

Legion Of Honour (Ire) *Miss S J Wilton* 43
5 b h Danehill (USA) - Total Chic (USA)
11⁸ᶠ 14¹²ˢᵈ 13¹¹ᵍᶠ **0-0-3**

Leicester Square (Ire) *Saeed Bin Suroor* 109
3 ch c Gone West (USA) - Stage Manner
2⁸ᵍᶠ 7¹⁰ᶠ **0-1-2 £6,600**

Leighton (Ire) *R M Stronge* 83
4 b g Desert Story - Lady Fern
9¹¹ˢ 5¹⁰ᵍ 4¹⁰ᵍᶠ 7¹⁰ˢ 2⁹ᵍᶠ 8¹⁰ᵍᶠ 3¹²ᵍᶠ
11¹³ᵍˢ 9¹²ᵍ **0-1-9 £2,974**

Leighton Buzzard *P W Chapple-Hyam* 56 a47
2 b g Cyrano De Bergerac - Winsome Wooster
7⁶ᵍˢ 10⁵ᵍᶠ 9⁶ˢᵈ **0-0-3**

Leitrim House *B J Meehan* 116 a106
3 ch c Cadeaux Genereux - Lonely Heart
1⁸ˢᵈ 1⁷ᵍ 4⁸ᵍᶠ 7⁷ᵍᶠ **2-0-4 £76,556**

Leitrim Rock (Ire) *A G Newcombe* 39
4 b g Barathea (Ire) - Kilshanny
15¹¹ᵍˢ 8⁸ᶠ 4¹⁰ᶠ 6⁸ᵍ 8⁸ᵍᶠ **0-0-5**

Lekka Ding (Ire) *C F Wall* 65 a46
2 b/br f Raise A Grand (Ire) - Non Dimenticar Me (Ire)
9⁷ˢᵈ 8⁷ˢ **0-0-2**

Lemarate (USA) *D W Chapman* a40
7 b g Gulch (USA) - Sayyedati
3⁷ˢᵈ 3⁶ˢᵈ 8⁸ˢᵈ 12⁷ˢˢ 5⁸ˢᵈ **0-2-5 £392**

Lennel *A Bailey* 78
6 b g Presidium - Ladykirk
5¹¹ᵍˢ 7¹²ˢ 4⁹ᵍ 11¹⁰ᵍ 7¹²ᵍᶠ 12¹²ᵍᶠ 13¹⁰ᵍ
6¹¹ᵍˢ 4¹¹ˢ 1¹⁰ᵍᶠ 3¹²ᵍᶠ 2¹²ᶠ 3¹¹ᵍ 3¹²ˢ 7¹²ᵍ 5¹⁰ˢ
6¹³ˢ 2¹²ᵍ **1-6-18 £13,430**

Lenwade *G G Margarson* 50 a42
3 gr f Environment Friend - Branitska
11¹¹⁰ᵍˢ 10¹⁰ᵍ 3¹⁰ˢᵈ 7¹⁰ˢᵈ 15⁸ᵍˢ 7⁸ᵍᶠ 4⁸ᵍᶠ
5¹⁰ᵍᶠ 2¹⁰ᵍᶠ 2¹⁰ᵍᶠ 1¹⁰ᵍ 3¹⁰ᶠ 2¹⁰ᵍ 2¹⁰ᵍˢ **1-5-14**
£5,343

Leo's Lucky Star (USA) *M Johnston* 101
2 b c Forestry (USA) - Leo's Lucky Lady (USA)
16⁶ᵍᶠ 16⁶ᵍᶠ 8⁷ˢ 10⁷ᵍᶠ **2-0-4 £12,711**

Leoballero *D J Daly* 96
4 ch g Lion Cavern (USA) - Ball Gown
5⁸ᵍᶠ 3⁷ᵍᶠ 5⁷ᵍᶠ 4⁸ᵍˢ 15¹⁰ᵍᶠ 2⁷ᵍ 21⁸ˢ **0-2-7**
£6,730

Leonalto (Ire) *B J Meehan* 58
2 ch g Raise A Grand (Ire) - Chrismas Carol (Ire)
7⁵ᵍˢ 5⁵ᵍˢ 3⁵ᵍᶠ 6⁵ᵍ 5⁵ᵍᶠ 8⁵ᵍᶠ **0-0-6 £775**

Leonora Truce (Ire) *R P Elliott* a31
5 b m Brief Truce (USA) - Eleonora D'Arborea
8⁸ˢᵈ 11⁶ˢᵈ 8⁷ˢˢ **0-0-3**

Leopard Creek *Mrs J R Ramsden* 60 a43
3 ch f Weldnaas (USA) - Indigo
9⁶ᵍ 12⁶ˢ 2⁵ᶠ 10⁶ᶠ 2⁵ᵍ 8⁵ᵍ 16⁵ᵍˢ 15⁷ᵍ
7⁶ᶠ 5⁵ˢᵈ **0-2-10 £2,400**

Leopard Spot (Ire) *Miss Lucinda V Russell* 45
6 b g Sadler's Wells (USA) - Savoureuse Lady
7¹⁴ᵍ 8¹⁷ᵍˢ 7¹³ᵍˢ **0-0-3**

Leophin Dancer (USA) *P W Hiatt* 37 a44
6 b g Green Dancer (USA) - Happy Gal (Fr)
6¹²ˢᵈ 7¹²ˢᵈ 1¹²ˢᵈ 2¹²ˢᵈ 2¹²ˢᵈ 3¹³ˢᵈ 4¹²ᵍ
1-3-7 £2,408

Leporello (Ire) *P W Harris* 116
4 b c Danehill (USA) - Why So Silent
3¹⁰ᵍˢ 7⁹ᵍ **0-1-2 £3,850**

Lerida *T D Barron* 18
2 ch g Groom Dancer (USA) - Catalonia (Ire)
6⁵ᵍ **0-0-1**

Les Arcs (USA) *R C Guest* 82
4 br g Arch (USA) - La Sarto (USA)
10⁸ˢ 12¹⁰ᵍˢ 2¹⁰ᵍ 18ᵍˢ 3⁸ᵍᶠ 6¹⁰ᵍᶠ 16¹²ᵍ
6⁸ᶠ 10⁸ˢ 3⁷ˢ **1-3-10 £7,991**

Leslingtaylor (Ire) *J J Quinn* 74
2 b g Orpen (USA) - Rite Of Spring
5⁵ᵍˢ 3⁶ᵍˢ 1⁶ᶠ 5⁷ᵍˢ 11⁷ᵍˢ **1-1-5 £4,737**

Let It Be *K G Reveley* 56
3 ch f Entrepreneur - Noble Dane (Ire)
2¹⁰ᵍˢ 5¹⁰ˢ 7¹²ᵍᶠ 5¹⁰ᶠ 1¹²ᵍᶠ 1¹²ᵍᶠ 5¹²ᵍᶠ
2¹⁴ᵍˢ 10¹²ᵍ 5¹⁶ᵍᶠ **2-2-10 £8,578**

Let Me Try Again (Ire) *T G Mills* 101
4 b g Sadler's Wells (USA) - Dathiyna (Ire)
8¹²ᵍ 4¹⁶ˢ **0-0-2 £2,500**

Let Slip *W Jarvis* 57
2 b f Second Empire (Ire) - Loose Talk
12⁷ᵍˢ **0-0-1**

Let The Lion Roar *J L Dunlop* 121
3 b c Sadler's Wells (USA) - Ballerina (Ire)
1¹⁰ᵍ 3¹⁰ᵍˢ 3¹²ᵍ 5¹²ᵍᶠ 2¹²ᵍ 8¹⁵ᵍᶠ **1-3-6**
£225,024

Let's Party (Ire) *P L Clinton* 2
4 b f Victory Note (USA) - Mashoura
11⁸ᵍˢ 11⁸ʰʸ 7⁸ᵍ **0-0-3**

Let's Pretend *B W Hills* 65
3 b f Rainbow Quest (USA) - Imaginary (Ire)
4¹²ᶠ **0-0-1 £281**

Lets Get It On (Ire) *J J Quinn* 80
3 b f Perugino (USA) - Lets Clic Together (Ire)
15⁷ᵍ 8⁵ˢ 5⁶ᵍˢ 2⁶ᵍˢ 7⁶ᵍᶠ 8⁶ᵍᶠ 5⁶ᵍ 3⁶ᵍ
15⁵ᵍˢ 6⁵ˢ **0-1-10 £4,855**

Lets Roll *C W Thornton* 91
3 b g Tamure (Ire) - Miss Petronella
2⁸ᵍ 6¹⁰ᵍˢ 2⁸ᵍᶠ 2⁹ᵍᶠ 3⁸ˢ 1¹¹ˢ 1¹²ˢ 5¹⁴ˢ
2¹³ˢ **4-2-5-10 £44,238**

Levantine (Ire) *Miss J Feilden* 53 a54
7 b g Sadler's Wells (USA) - Spain Lane (USA)
3⁷ˢˢ 5⁶ˢʷ 6⁸ˢᵈ 1⁸ˢᵈ 2⁸ᵍ 4⁸ᵍ 7⁹ˢᵈ **1-2-7**

£2,181

Levelled *D W Chapman* 47 a49
10 b g Beveled (USA) - Baino Charm (USA)
8^{5ss} 9^{5ss} 7^{6sw} 10^{6sd} 4^{5sd} 5^{5sd} 5^{5sd} 7^{5sd}
2^{5sd} 3^{5sf} 3^{6sd} 1^{5sd} 11^{6sd} 6^{5s} 5^{6sd} 14^{5gs} 6^{5gs}
4^{6gf} 14^{5sd} 15^{5gs} **1-3-20 £2,577**

Levitator *Sir Michael Stoute* 80
3 b c Sadler's Wells (USA) - Cantilever
9^{10g} 2^{13f} 2^{14gf} 7^{14gf} 1^{14gs} 4^{14s} **1-2-6**
£11,023

Lewis Island (Ire) *B Ellison* 61 a75
5 b g Turtle Island (Ire) - Phyllode
14^{10s} 13^{10g} 4^{12sd} **0-1-3 £270**

Lexicon *Miss Lucinda V Russell*
4 ch f Weldnaas (USA) - Swift Move
17^{9gs} **0-0-1**

Leyaaly *B A Pearce* a42
5 ch m Night Shift (USA) - Lower The Tone (Ire)
6^{12sd} 9^{12sd} 7^{10gs} 1^{9sd} 2^{7sd} 4^{8sd} 20^{9gf}
1-1-7 £2,343

Liability (Ire) *N Tinkler* 43
2 b f Bluebird (USA) - Madaniyya (USA)
11^{7gs} 6^{8g} 6^{7gf} **0-0-3**

Liakoura (Ger) *Mrs A J Perrett* 96
2 b g Royal Academy (USA) - Lady Member (Fr)
1^{7gs} 8^{7gf} 1^{8g} **2-0-3 £13,123**

Liameliss *M A Allen* 48
2 ch f Dr Fong (USA) - Ivory Palm (USA)
6^{6gf} 15^{7gf} 10^{7gf} 13^{6gf} **0-0-4**

Libera *M G Quinlan* 49
3 b f Turtle Island (Ire) - Princess Louise
9^{7g} **0-0-1**

Liberty Flag (USA) *J H M Gosden* 72
3 b f Kingmambo (USA) - Banner Dancer (USA)
2^{8gf} 1^{8gf} **1-1-2 £6,848**

Liberty Royal *P J Makin* 70 a75
5 b g Ali-Royal (Ire) - Hope Chest
6^{8sd} 10^{8gs} 6^{9s} 3^{9gf} 8^{9gf} 3^{8f} 4^{8gf} 1^{8g}
9^{8gs} 9^{8sd} **1-2-10 £4,953**

Liberty Run (Ire) *N A Callaghan* 43 a76
2 ch c Grand Lodge (USA) - Bathe In Light (USA)
17^{8s} 3^{7sd} **0-1-2 £792**

Liberty Seeker (Fr) *P Monteith* 62
5 ch g Machiavellian (USA) - Samara (Ire)
8^{10s} 8^{12gf} 2^{15gf} **0-1-3 £1,040**

Libre *F Jordan* 65 a21
4 b g Bahamian Bounty - Premier Blues (Fr)
9^{10g} 5^{10s} 4^{10hy} 10^{11gf} 7^{7gf} 9^{8sd} 1^{7g} 9^{9gs}
12^{7gf} 15^{7gs} **1-0-10 £5,033**

Librettist (USA) *Saeed Bin Suroor* 115
2 b c Danzig (USA) - Mysterial (USA)
1^{7g} 1^{7g} 5^{7s} **2-0-3 £18,047**

Lieuday *Mrs K Harvey* 54 a22
5 b g Atraf - Figment
5^{7sd} 14^{8g} 3^{7gf} 10^{7gf} 3^{8g} **0-1-5 £752**

Life Is Beautiful (Ire) *W H Tinning* 61
5 b m Septieme Ciel (USA) - Palombella (Fr)
6^{10gs} 1^{12gf} 5^{10gf} 1^{12g} 6^{12gf} 2^{14gf} 4^{12g}
2^{10gf} **2-3-8 £7,030**

Lifted Way *P R Chamings* 87 a83
5 b h In The Wings - Stack Rock
9^{8sd} 18^{gs} 1^{8sd} 14^{8gf} 6^{7g} 5^{8gf} 4^{7gs} 10^{8gs}
14^{7g} **2-0-9 £11,357**

Light Brigade *J M P Eustace* 3 a46
5 b g Kris - Mafatin (Ire)

6^{14sd} 7^{12sd} 10^{12sd} 5^{12sd} 16^{8gf} **0-0-5**

Light Of Dubai (USA) *Saeed Bin Suroor* 81
2 b f Gone West (USA) - A. P. Assay (USA)
4^{7g} **0-0-1 £630**

Light Of Morn *R Guest* 99
3 gr f Daylami (Ire) - My Emma
2^{12s} 3^{12gf} 1^{11gf} 4^{12gf} 6^{15g} 4^{12g} **1-1-6**
£8,275

Light The Dawn (Ire) *W M Brisbourne* 50
4 ch f Indian Ridge - Flaming June (USA)
14^{8s} 7^{6gf} 11^{8gf} 5^{7g} 11^{7sd} **0-0-5**

Light Wind *Mrs A J Perrett* 90
3 ch f Unfuwain (USA) - River Spey
5^{12s} 1^{12gf} 1^{12gf} 5^{12gf} 6^{11s} 3^{12gs} 6^{14s}
2-0-7 £13,747

Lighted Way *A M Balding* 71
2 b f Kris - Natchez Trace
12^{6gf} 6^{6gs} 6^{5gs} 2^{6g} 2^{5hy} **0-2-5 £2,384**

Lightening Fire (Ire) *T J Etherington* 56
2 b g Woodborough (USA) - Glowlamp (Ire)
9^{6gf} 7^{7gf} 12^{8f} 11^{8g} **0-0-4**

Lighthorne Lad *J R Jenkins* 26
2 ch c Hornbeam - Give Me A Day
9^{5gf} 11^{5gf} 13^{6g} **0-0-3**

Lightning Prospect *P C Haslam* 17
2 ch f Zaha (Can) - Lightning Blaze
12^{5gs} **0-0-1**

Lightning Star (USA) *G L Moore* 39
9 b g El Gran Senor (USA) - Cuz's Star (USA)
7^{12gf} **0-0-1**

Ligne D'Eau *P D Evans* 65
3 ch c Cadeaux Genereux - Miss Waterline
7^{6hy} 5^{6gf} 3^{6gf} 6^{6s} 6^{7gf} 11^{6gs} 6^{8hy} 1^{6gs}
1-1-8 £4,387

Lilian *Miss Gay Kelleway* 35 a4
4 b f First Trump - Lillibella
6^{9sd} 5^{8sd} 6^{9ss} 9^{10sd} 8^{12gf} 11^{14gf} 6^{8gf}
0-0-7

Lill's Star Lad *P R Wood*
6 ch g Kasakov - Lady Khadija
10^{7sd} 13^{10gf} **0-0-2**

Lillas Forest *P C Haslam* 55
2 b g Forestry (USA) - Lines Of Beauty (USA)
11^{7g} 8^{8g} **0-0-2**

Lillebror (Ger) *B J Curley* 59
6 b g Top Waltz (Fr) - Lady Soliciti (Ger)
12^{14s} 7^{16g} 3^{14gf} 11^{16gf} **0-1-4 £1,055**

Lilli Marlane *N A Callaghan* 78 a78
4 b f Sri Pekan (USA) - Fivefive (Ire)
2^{8s} 6^{8gs} 9^{10gf} 9^{10gf} 1^{10gf} 7^{10gs} 14^{10g}
5^{10gf} 11^{8sd} 4^{8sd} 8^{8sd} **1-1-11 £5,780**

Lillianna (Ire) *H R A Cecil* 64
3 ch f Barathea (Ire) - Machikane Akaiito (Ire)
4^{8s} 10^{8gf} 3^{8g} 10^{10g} 7^{10gs} 7^{11g} **0-1-6**
£1,162

Lilting Prose (Ire) *R Hannon* 63
2 ch f Indian Ridge - Kirkwood
5^{6gf} 11^{6g} **0-0-2**

Lily Lenat *J R Boyle* 67 a69
2 b f Josr Algarhoud (Ire) - Rushing River (USA)
10^{5g} 4^{5g} 3^{5g} 9^{6g} 13^{7gf} 5^{6sd} **0-1-6 £738**

Lily Of The Guild (Ire) *W S Kittow* 58 a62
5 ch m Lycius (USA) - Secreto Bold
10^{7sd} 10^{7sd} 2^{7sd} 4^{7sd} 4^{6f} 5^{7g} 8^{6g} 13^{7gf}
13^{6gf} 2^{7sd} **0-2-10 £1,643**

Limerick Boy (Ger) *Miss Venetia Williams* 89
6 b g Alwuhush (USA) - Limoges (Ger)
6¹³gs **0-0-1 £1,125**

Limit (Ire) *M R Channon* 67 a69
2 b f Barathea (Ire) - Orlena (USA)
3⁸s 9⁸s 2⁸sd 6⁷sd **0-2-4 £2,141**

Limit Down (Ire) *M J Wallace* a50
3 b g Desert Story (Ire) - Princess Raisa
6⁹sw 5⁶sd 3⁶sd 6⁶sd **0-1-4 £367**

Limited Magician *C Smith*
3 b f Wizard King - Pretty Scarce
13⁶sd 9⁶sd **0-0-2**

Limonia (Ger) *D K Ivory* 56
2 b f Perugino (USA) - Limoges (Ger)
5⁵hy 6⁵gf 7⁵gf 6⁵gs 7⁵hy **0-0-5**

Lin In Gold (Ire) *P A Blockley* 65
3 b g Second Empire (Ire) - Wasmette (Ire)
5⁸gf **0-0-1**

Linby Lad (Ire) *J A Glover* a60
4 ch g Dolphin Street (Fr) - Classic Look (Ire)
14¹⁰sd 13¹⁰sd **0-0-2**

Lincoln Dancer (Ire) *R A Fahey* 87 a64
7 b g Turtle Island (Ire) - Double Grange (Ire)
10⁷sd 10⁷sd 4⁷g 3⁶s 4⁶s 1⁶g 12⁶gs **1-2-7
£8,067**

Lincolneurocruiser *J O'Reilly* 82
2 b c Spectrum (Ire) - Rush Hour (Ire)
5⁵g 2⁵hy 3⁶gs 1⁶f 2⁶g 12⁶gf **1-2-6
£7,561**

Linda Green *P A Blockley* 60
3 b f Victory Note (USA) - Edge Of Darkness
1⁵g 4⁵g **1-0-2 £3,258**

Linda's Colin (Ire) *P W D'Arcy* 21 a77
2 b c Xaar - Capable Kate (Ire)
12⁷gf 2⁹sd 2⁹sd **0-2-3 £1,892**

Linden's Lady *J R Weymes* 60 a25
4 b f Compton Place - Jubilee Place (Ire)
10⁶g 6⁶gf 11⁶gf 5⁸f 6⁷g 5⁶gf 12⁵g 5⁷gf
4⁷g 3⁷g 8⁷f 11⁶sd **0-1-12 £433**

Line Ahead (Ire) *Sir Michael Stoute* 33
2 b f Sadler's Wells (USA) - Alignment (Ire)
16⁸gs **0-0-1**

Line Drawing *B W Hills* 82
3 b c Unfuwain (USA) - Fine Detail (Ire)
2¹⁰gs 4¹⁰gf 3¹¹f 3¹⁰gs 2¹²gs **0-3-5
£5,375**

Linens Flame *B G Powell* 82
5 ch g Blushing Flame (USA) - Atlantic Air
1¹⁴s 1¹⁵s 2¹⁴hy 10¹⁶gf 8¹⁴g 16¹²g 4¹⁶s
10¹⁶s **2-1-8 £9,268**

Linnet (Ger) *Mrs A J Perrett* 74
2 b f Dr Fong (USA) - Lauderdale (Ger)
6⁷gs **0-0-1**

Linngari (Ire) *Sir Michael Stoute* 92 a90
2 ch c Indian Ridge - Lidakiya (Ire)
3⁷gf 1⁷sd 1⁷g **2-0-3 £14,267**

Linning Wine (Ire) *P A Blockley* 87 a103
8 b g Scenic - Zallaka (Ire)
13¹⁰sd 2⁸sd 4⁸g 8¹⁰gs 6⁸gf 4⁸gf 5⁸gs 5⁸gs
5⁹gs 8⁷sd 1⁷sd **1-2-11 £8,166**

Linzis Lad *K A Ryan* 50
2 ch c Magic Ring (Ire) - Come On Katie
10⁷f 8⁷gs **0-0-2**

Lion Hunter (USA) *Miss E C Lavelle* 94 a91
5 b g Quest For Fame - Prodigious (Fr)

13¹⁰sd 6¹⁰sd 10¹⁰gs 3¹⁰g 8¹²g **0-1-5 £867**

Lion's Domane *A Berry* 41 a43
7 b g Lion Cavern (USA) - Vilany
9⁶sd 5⁷ss 6⁶sw 8⁷sw PU⁷g 8⁷sd 11⁷g 10⁸g
8⁸g 14⁷gf 8⁷gf **0-0-11**

Liquid Form (Ire) *B Hanbury* 81
4 br g Bahhare (USA) - Brogan's Well (Ire)
10⁷s 7¹¹gs 7¹⁰gf 6¹⁰gf 8¹⁰gf 5¹⁰g 12¹⁰gf
0-0-7

Liquid Lover (Ire) *R Hannon* 56
2 b c Night Shift (USA) - New Tycoon (Ire)
10⁶gf 11⁷gf 13⁷g 12⁷gf **0-0-4**

Liquidate *H Morrison* 71
3 b g Hector Protector (USA) - Cut And Run
1¹²g 10¹²g 10¹⁴gs **1-0-3 £3,445**

Lirage *M Mullineaux* 18
2 b f Wizard King - Diamond Rouge
12⁶hy **0-0-1**

Lisa Mona Lisa (Ire) *V Smith* 70 a55
2 b f Desert Style (Ire) - Amneris (Ire)
1⁵g 4⁵gs 1⁷f 10⁷gs 4⁶sd 1⁷gf 8⁷s 6⁸g
3-0-8 £11,734

Liseberg *I A Wood* 82
2 b c Gothenberg (Ire) - Read And Approved (Ire)
14⁷gs **0-0-1**

Lissahanelodge *P R Hedger* 45 a49
5 br g Grand Lodge (USA) - Lissahane Lass
1¹²sd 2¹³sd 7¹²gf 6¹²gf 6¹³gf 6¹⁴f **1-1-6
£1,899**

Listen To Me *D Haydn Jones* 43
2 gr g Petong - Time Clash
5⁵gs 12⁵s 5⁷gf 14⁶gf **0-0-4**

Listen To Reason (Ire) *J G Given* 67
3 b g Mukaddamah (USA) - Tenalist (Ire)
1⁷gf 11⁸gf 8⁷gf 12⁷gf **1-0-4 £3,454**

Literatim *L M Cumani* 93
4 b c Polish Precedent (USA) - Annie Albright (USA)
4⁷gs 1⁷gf 2⁸gs 8¹⁰g 3⁸g **1-2-5 £13,522**

Literature (USA) *Saeed Bin Suroor* 75
2 b f Notebook (USA) - Deputy's Mistress (USA)
1⁷gf **1-0-1 £5,954**

Lithos *J A Osborne* 80
2 ch c Inchinor - Leisure (Fr)
2⁸gf 6⁸gs 5⁸g 1⁸gf **1-1-4 £4,485**

Little Biscuit (Ire) *K R Burke* 59 a49
2 br f Indian Lodge (Ire) - Arjan (Ire)
1⁵ss 1⁵s 2⁵g 5⁵gf 4⁵gf 5⁵g 6⁵g 4⁵s
12⁵gs 8⁵hy **2-2-10 £8,602**

Little Bob *J D Bethell* 73
3 ch g Zilzal (USA) - Hunters Of Brora (Ire)
4⁸g 4²gf 3¹⁰g 7⁹s 1⁹gs 12⁸g 7¹⁰s
9¹⁰s **1-2-9 £6,186**

Little Dalham *P W Chapple-Hyam* 80
2 b c Diktat - Almost Amber (USA)
4⁷gf 2⁶g 16⁷gf 8⁷gs 4⁶hy **1-2-5 £10,591**

Little Edward *B G Powell* 98 a97
6 gr g King's Signet (USA) - Cedar Lady
5⁵sd 8⁵g 5⁵gf 8⁵gf 16⁶g 5⁶f 11⁵gs 23⁵gf
13⁵gf 5⁶gs 6⁵gf 6⁵g 4⁵gf **0-1-14 £3,232**

Little Englander *H Candy* 65
4 b g Piccolo - Anna Karietta
5¹⁰hy 9¹²gf 8¹³gf 1⁸gs 7⁸gf 10⁸gf 4⁸gf
4⁷g **1-2-10 £4,720**

Little Eye (Ire) *J R Best* 68 a68
3 b g Groom Dancer (USA) - Beaming

4^{10sd} 9^{10sd} 3^{7sd} 9^{7f} 6^{8sd} 4^{8gf} 7^{9g} 2^{10gf}
1^{10gf} **1-2-9 £6,818**

Little Flute *T Keddy*   51 a51
3 b c Piccolo - Nordic Victory (USA)
4^{5sd} 7^{5sd} 7^{6ss} 7^{6sd} 10^{7sd} 1^{6sd} 6^{6f} 6^{6gf}
4^{5gs} 5^{6gs} **1-0-10 £1,431**

Little Fox (Ire) *J J Bridger*   35
9 br m Persian Bold - Dance Land (Ire)
6^{12gf} 7^{12f} 11^{16sd} **0-0-3**

Little Gannet *S Dow*   41 a29
3 ro f Bien Bien (USA) - Lady Kalliste
13^{10sd} 14^{11gf} **0-0-2**

Little Good Bay *J H M Gosden*   a96
4 b c Danehill (USA) - Brave Kris (Ire)
11^{7sd} **0-0-1**

Little Indy *R Brotherton*   57 a33
2 ch c Forzando - Indian Nectar
11^{5gs} 11^{7g} 10^{7gf} 6^{7hy} 9^{6sd} **0-0-5**

Little Jimbob *R A Fahey*   82 a67
3 b g Desert Story (Ire) - Artistic Licence
1^{9f} 2^{8g} 4^{8gs} 3^{8gf} 5^{7g} 2^{8gf} 4^{10g} 8^{10sd}
1-4-8 £14,193

Little London *J L Dunlop*
3 b g Bahhare (USA) - North Kildare (USA)
PU^{8gs} **0-0-1**

Little Miss Gracie *A B Haynes*   87
2 gr f Efisio - Circled (USA)
3^{7g} 3^{7s} 2^{8gf} 4^{8hy} 1^{8f} 4^{8g} **1-3-6**
£18,497

Little Miss Lili *G G Margarson*
3 b f Danzig Connection (USA) - Little Miss Rocker
8^{8f} 13^{10gf} **0-0-2**

Little Miss Tricky *P Mitchell*
5 br m Magic Ring (Ire) - Mistook (USA)
8^{10sd} **0-0-1**

Little Richard (Ire) *M Wellings*   8 a49
5 b g Alhaarth (Ire) - Intricacy
8^{12sd} 9^{14sd} 4^{13sd} 3^{12ss} 1^{16sd} 4^{12sd} 8^{12sd}
2^{12sd} 3^{13sd} 5^{16sd} 4^{15sd} 10^{14gs} **1-3-12 £2,278**

Little Ridge (Ire) *H Morrison*   83 a76
3 b g Charnwood Forest (Ire) - Princess Natalie
10^{6g} 10^{9g} 12^{7sd} 1^{5s} 3^{5sd} **1-1-5 £7,743**

Little Sky *D Mullarkey*   24 a12
7 gr m Terimon - Brown Coast
7^{12sd} 17^{12gf} 9^{14f} **0-0-3**

Little Task *J S Wainwright*   44 a41
6 b g Environment Friend - Lucky Thing
3^{8gf} 1^{10gf} 4^{12gf} 1^{12gf} 14^{12gf} 4^{12gf} 6^{11gf}
11^{12gf} 9^{9sd} **2-1-9 £5,280**

Little Tobias (Ire) *Andrew Turnell*   61
5 ch g Millkom - Barbara Frietchie (Ire)
6^{16gs} 13^{14s} 1^{14gf} 3^{16g} 3^{16f} 14^{17gf} 4^{15s}
1-1-7 £4,527

Little Venice (Ire) *C F Wall*   91
4 b f Fumo Di Londra (Ire) - Petrine (Ire)
16^{6gs} 5^{7g} 3^{7gf} 1^{8gf} 11^{8g} 9^{8gf} 7^{8gs} 1^{8g}
2-1-8 £18,180

Little Waltham *K A Morgan*
2 ch f Tomba - Post Impressionist (Ire)
14^{6g} 10^{8sd} 8^{6s} **0-0-3**

Little Warning *R M Beckett*   62
2 b f Piccolo - Iltimas (Ire)
7^{5gf} 7^{5f} 5^{5gf} 17^{6s} **0-0-4**

Little Wizzy *P D Evans*   58
2 b f Wizard King - Little Unknown

3^{5g} 7^{5g} 1^{5s} 3^{5s} 6^{5gf} 19^{5gs} 18^{6hy} **1-1-7**
£5,944

Littlestar (Fr) *A Dickman*   59
3 b g Robellino (USA) - Green Charter
14^{10gs} 10^{12gs} 13^{12s} 12^{11gf} 2^{10g} 11^{10gf}
0-1-6 £1,160

Littleton Liberty *Andrew Reid*
3 b f Royal Applause - Lammastide
8^{7sd} 7^{5sd} **0-0-2**

Littleton Telchar (USA) *M J Ryan*   72
4 ch c Atticus (USA) - Miss Waikiki (USA)
5^{9f} 1^{10gf} 7^{10gf} 10^{10gf} 9^{12gs} **1-0-5**
£4,407

Littleton Valar (Ire) *J R Weymes*   43 a31
4 ch g Definite Article - Fresh Look (Ire)
8^{9sd} 4^{10gs} 4^{11sd} 7^{10gf} **0-0-4**

Littleton Zephir (USA) *Mrs P Townsley*   46 a53
5 b m Sandpit (Brz) - Miss Gorgeous (Ire)
7^{7sd} 2^{9sd} 8^{8sd} 12^{9sw} 1^{8sd} 5^{7sd} 7^{8sd} 8^{10gs}
11^{10gf} **1-1-9 £2,183**

Litzinsky *C B B Booth*   33 a54
6 b g Muhtarram (USA) - Boulevard Girl
7^{16sd} 9^{16g} **0-0-2**

Live In Hope *Jedd O'Keeffe*   24
2 b f High Estate - Movieland (USA)
13^{6f} 10^{6gf} 14^{6gf} **0-0-3**

Live Wire Lucy (USA) *C Tinkler*   69
3 b/br f King Of The Heap (USA) - Approach The Bench (USA)
10^{9f} 3^{9f} 8^{6f} 11^{7gs} 9^{10gf} 9^{10g} 12^{10g}
14^{8g} **0-0-8 £2,089**

Lively Felix *D G Bridgwater*   a40
7 b g Presidium - Full Of Life
4^{6sd} 10^{7ss} 6^{7ss} 7^{7ss} 10^{7sd} **0-0-5**

Livia (Ire) *J G Portman*   50 a53
3 b f Titus Livius (Fr) - Passing Beauty
10^{7sd} 6^{10sd} 10^{8sd} 4^{7sd} 12^{6gs} 6^{7s} 9^{7s}
12^{7g} 7^{8f} 14^{10gf} 2^{8gs} 4^{9sd} 11^{9sd} **0-1-13 £435**

Livvies Lady (Ire) *D K Ivory*   a15
2 b f Opening Verse (USA) - Indian Wardance (Ity)
11^{7sd} 14^{7sd} **0-0-2**

Liwa's Lake (USA) *Saeed Bin Suroor*   69
2 ch f Greenwood Lake (USA) - Champagne Sweep (USA)
3^{5gf} 7^{5g} 11^{5gs} **0-0-3 £750**

Lizarazu (Ger) *F Jordan*   65
5 b h Second Set (Ire) - Lilly (Ger)
9^{8g} 8^{8gf} 11^{8gf} 12^{8gs} 10^{7s} **0-0-5**

Lizhar (Ire) *J J Quinn*   33 a63
3 b f Danetime (Ire) - Amelesa (Ire)
4^{6sd} 6^{5sd} 4^{5sd} 7^{6sd} 4^{5sd} 2^{5sw} 8^{5ss} 4^{6sd}
6^{6sd} 5^{6g} 14^{6g} **0-1-11 £720**

Llamadas *Mrs Stef Liddiard*   65 a56
2 b g Josr Algarhoud (Ire) - Primulette
3^{5g} 9^{5gf} 3^{6g} 4^{7sd} 10^{7g} 3^{5gf} 6^{5g} 6^{5g}
15^{7f} 2^{5sd} 7^{6sd} **0-4-11 £3,216**

Loaded Gun *W M Brisbourne*   60 a54
4 ch g Highest Honor (Fr) - Woodwardia (USA)
12^{8sd} 2^{10s} 4^{12g} 7^{11s} 3^{10gs} 4^{9s} 13^{9sd}
0-3-7 £2,667

Loaderfun (Ire) *H Candy*   90
2 br g Danehill Dancer (Ire) - Sideloader Special
4^{5gf} 2^{6gs} 1^{6s} 2^{6gf} **1-1-4 £10,324**

Lobengula (Ire) *H Alexander*   61
2 b g Spectrum (Ire) - Playwaki (USA)
10^{6g} 5^{7s} **0-0-2**

Local Poet *B A McMahon*   90

3 b c Robellino (USA) - Laugharne
1⁶g 5⁷gs 8⁵s 5⁶gf 17⁶gf 18⁶g 14⁵g **1-0-7**
£6,566

Locator (Ire) *J M P Eustace* 44
3 b g Mujadil (USA) - Lifeboat (Ire)
10⁸g 17⁸g **0-0-2**

Loch Inch *J M Bradley* 60
7 ch g Inchinor - Carrie Kool
12⁵gf 9⁵f 12⁵gf 4⁵f 9⁵g 4⁵gs 2⁵gf 3⁶gf
3⁵gf PU⁵.₁₀ **0-4-10 £3,185**

Loch Laird *M Madgwick* 52 a53
9 b g Beveled (USA) - Daisy Loch
7⁶sd 8⁶sd 1⁷sd 9⁷sd 5⁶s 10⁷f 13⁷g 5⁷gf
4⁸gs 13⁷hy 10⁷g 7⁷sd **1-1-12 £3,791**

Loch Quest (Ire) *Mrs A J Perrett* 73
2 ch g Giant's Causeway (USA) - Taibhseach (USA)
5⁸gf 8⁸g 8⁸gs **0-0-3**

Lochbuie (Ire) *G Wragg* 106
3 b c Definite Article - Uncertain Affair (Ire)
4¹⁰g 1¹²g 1¹²gs 1¹²g 1¹⁴gf 14⁴s 4¹⁴g 3¹⁴g
3-2-8 £37,250

Lochridge *A M Balding* 108
5 ch m Indian Ridge - Lochsong
2⁵gf 14⁵gf 13⁶f 3⁶gs 2⁶gf 4⁶gs 14⁶g
0-3-7 £17,874

Lockstock (Ire) *M S Saunders* 77 a57
6 b g Inchinor - Risalah
7⁸sd 13¹⁰sd 1⁸s 8⁸gf 7⁷gf 9⁷g 5⁸gf 4⁸gs
1-1-8 £4,819

Locombe Hill (Ire) *N Wilson* 75 a67
8 b g Barathea (Ire) - Roberts Pride
11⁷sd 2⁸sd 10⁸s 9⁷gf 5⁶gf 15⁷g 4⁶g 4⁶gs
11⁷gf 1⁷s 5⁷gs 3⁷gf 1⁷s 2⁶s 2⁷gs 9⁸hy **2-3-16**
£16,003

Lodger (Fr) *J Noseda* 95
4 ch c Grand Lodge (USA) - Light River (USA)
12¹²gs 6¹²gf 4¹²gf 9¹⁴g 10¹⁶gf **0-0-5**
£1,007

Lodgician (Ire) *J J Quinn* 67
2 b c Grand Lodge (USA) - Dundel (Ire)
4⁶s 3⁷gs 9⁷gf 4⁸g 11⁷f 13⁶gf **0-1-6**
£1,867

Logger Rhythm (USA) *R Dickin* 63
4 b g Woodman (USA) - Formidable Dancer (USA)
7⁸g 12¹⁰gs 4¹²g 13¹²gf 15⁸s **0-0-5 £425**

Logistical *A D W Pinder* 57 a32
4 b c Grand Lodge (USA) - Magic Milly
13⁷hy 10⁷gf 5⁷gf 11⁷gf 15⁷gf 9⁷g 14⁷gf
9⁷sd **0-0-8**

Loitokitok *P D Cundell* 62 a29
2 b g Piccolo - Bonita Bee
8⁸sd 10⁸g 8⁸gf **0-0-3**

Lojo *C A Dwyer* 53
2 ch f Pivotal - Myhat
7⁶gf 3⁶gf 2⁶f 1⁷f **1-2-4 £4,395**

Lola Lola (Ire) *J L Dunlop* a29
3 b f Piccolo - French Gift
10⁸g 8⁸sd 18⁷gs **0-0-3**

Lola Sapola (Ire) *N A Callaghan* 73
2 b f Benny The Dip (USA) - Cutpurse Moll
7⁶g 9⁷gs 9⁷s 1⁷f 4⁸g 7⁸s **1-1-6 £5,204**

Lola's Destiny *P A Blockley* a45
3 b f Mark Of Esteem (Ire) - Kristiana
5⁹sd 6⁸sd 8⁸ss **0-0-3**

Lomapamar *Mrs A J Perrett* 73

3 b f Nashwan (USA) - Morina (USA)
3¹¹gs 12¹¹g 13¹³sd 1¹⁰hy **1-0-4 £5,554**

Lommel (UAE) *D R Loder* 20
3 b c Lomitas - Idrica
15⁸g 8⁷g **0-0-2**

Londoner (USA) *S Dow* 68 a70
6 ch g Sky Classic (Can) - Love And Affection (USA)
7¹⁰sd 10⁸sd 8¹⁰sd 1¹¹²sd 3⁸sd 2⁷gf 2⁷f
1⁷f 7⁸f 5⁸gf 3⁷f 5⁸gf 2⁸f 1⁸f 7⁸gs 1⁸sd
6⁸sd **2-5-17 £10,917**

Lone Piper *J M Bradley* 34 a41
9 b g Warning - Shamisen
12⁵sd 8⁵sd 9⁵ss 6⁵s 4⁵sw 3⁵sw 6⁵sd 6⁵ss
11⁵gs 6⁶gf 14⁶gf **0-1-11 £195**

Loner *R A Fahey* 60
6 b g Magic Ring (Ire) - Jolis Absent
15⁸s 2⁸gf 9⁷gf **0-1-3 £856**

Long Road (USA) *J Noseda* 84
3 b g Diesis - Tuviah (USA)
2⁸g 2⁸gf 2⁸s 1¹⁰gf **1-2-4 £13,950**

Long Weekend (Ire) *D Shaw* 45 a57
6 b g Flying Spur (Aus) - Friday Night (USA)
7⁶sd 6⁶sd 6⁷ss 2⁶sd 1⁶sd 1⁵sd 4⁶sd 6⁶sd
11⁶s 6⁶gf 9⁶g 12⁶gf 9⁶g 21⁶gf 4⁶sd 3⁷sd
2-2-16 £3,989

Look Again *Mrs A J Perrett* 91
3 ch g Zilzal (USA) - Last Look
1¹⁰gs 4¹⁰g **1-0-2 £4,273**

Look At The Stars (Ire) *C G Cox* 84
2 b g Bachir (Ire) - Pizzazz
9⁶gs 1⁶g **1-0-3 £3,588**

Look Here's Carol (Ire) *B A McMahon* 98
4 ch f Safawan - Where's Carol
3⁶gs 3⁶g 6⁶g 3⁷gf 1⁷g 7⁷gf 5⁷s 2⁷g 7⁷gf
10⁷gf **1-4-10 £24,131**

Looking Down *John Allen* 3
4 ch f Compton Place - High Stepping (Ire)
13⁷s 12⁷gf **0-0-2**

Looking Great (USA) *R F Johnson Houghton* 59
2 b g Gulch (USA) - Shoofha (USA)
7⁵gf 14⁶gs 9⁸gf 13⁸gs **0-0-4**

Lookouthereicome *T T Clement* 47 a46
3 b f Rudimentary (USA) - Sylvatica
8⁸sd 12⁸sd 9¹²gf 10¹⁰gf 8⁸gf **0-0-5**

Looks Could Kill (USA) *G A Butler* 90
2 b/br g Red Ransom (USA) - Mingling Glances (USA)
2⁷gf 1⁸s 4⁸g 3⁸s 2⁷s **1-3-5 £15,508**

Looks The Business (Ire) *W G M Turner* 56 a72
3 b g Marju (Ire) - Business Centre (Ire)
2¹⁰sd 4⁹sw 5¹⁰sd 9¹⁰gs 14⁷gs 8¹⁰gf **0-1-6**
£1,443

Lord Arthur *M W Easterby* 43 a50
3 b g Mind Games - Flower O'Cannie (Ire)
11⁶sd 4⁶sd 9⁶sd 9⁶hy 15⁸g **0-0-5 £257**

Lord Baskerville *W Storey* 62 a41
3 br g Wolfhound (USA) - My Dear Watson
13⁷sd 12⁶sd 6⁵g 12⁶hy 3⁵g 7⁶f 8⁵s 13⁵s
13⁵gf 2⁶gf 2⁶gf 4⁶s 8⁸gf 4⁷gs 4⁶g 16⁸gf 13⁸gf
12⁸g **0-5-18 £3,648**

Lord Chalfont (Ire) *M J Polglase* 22 a13
2 ch g Daggers Drawn (USA) - Byproxy (Ire)
12⁵g 9⁵ss 7⁶sd 9⁷sd 9⁷gf 9⁸gf 9⁸gs 16⁸g
0-0-8

Lord Chamberlain *J M Bradley* 65 a65
11 b g Be My Chief (USA) - Metaphysique (Fr)

2^{8sd} 1^{7sd} 4^{8sd} 4^{8sd} 11^{7sd} 2^{7sw} 2^{8sw} 9^{8ss}
3^{8f} 4^{8f} 4^{7gf} 8^{7g} 3^{7gf} 11^{8gs} 2^{8gf} 7^{8g} 1^{8gf}
4^{8gf} 9^{7g} **2-8-22 £11,077**

Lord Conyers (Ire) *B Ellison*   42
5 b m Inzar (USA) - Primelta
7^{12gs} 12^{10hy} 4^{8hy} 4^{8gf} **0-0-4 £557**

Lord Dundee (Ire) *R C Guest*   46
6 ch g Polish Precedent (USA) - Easy To Copy (USA)
9^{13g} 9^{12g} 4^{12gf} **0-0-3**

Lord Elrond *P W Chapple-Hyam*   54
2 b c Magic Ring (Ire) - Cactus Road (Fr)
8^{5gf} **0-0-1**

Lord Eurolink (Ire) *M H Tompkins*   42
10 b g Danehill (USA) - Lady Eurolink
16^{10g} 19^{10g} **0-0-2**

Lord Gizzmo *P W Hiatt*   a24
7 ch g Democratic (USA) - Figrant (USA)
11^{12sd} 6^{12sd} 10^{12ss} **0-0-3**

Lord Greystoke (Ire) *C P Morlock*   34 a1
3 b g Petardia - Jungle Story (Ire)
9^{10sd} 17^{8s} 13^{8g} 12^{13gs} 11^{10gf} **0-0-5**

Lord John *M W Easterby*   59 a27
2 b c Piccolo - Mahbob Dancer (Fr)
8^{5g} 4^{5gs} 7^{5gf} 4^{6gf} 9^{6sd} 7^{5gs} 4^{6s} 10^{6g}
2^{5gf} 3^{5f} **0-2-10 £2,822**

Lord Kintyre *B R Millman*   64
9 b g Makbul - Highland Rowena
8^{5gs} **0-0-1**

Lord Lahar *M A Buckley*   55 a58
5 b g Fraam - Brigadiers Bird (Ire)
6^{10gf} 8^{12gf} 12^{16gf} 5^{8gs} 7^{10s} 4^{13f}
17^{16f} 2^{12sd} 6^{14gs} 1^{12sd} 10^{12sd} **1-1-12 £4,112**

Lord Lamb *Mrs M Reveley*   56
12 gr g Dunbeath (USA) - Caroline Lamb
3^{16f} 4^{12s} 8^{16s} 5^{12gf} 3^{16gf} **0-2-5 £889**

Lord Links (Ire) *R Hannon*   86
3 ch g Daggers Drawn (USA) - Lady From Limerick (Ire)
4^{7gf} 9^{8f} 7^{8g} 17^{7gf} 7^{8g} 4^{7g} 8^{7gs} 3^{9g} 1^{8gs}
1-1-9 £10,077

Lord Mayfair (USA) *T D Barron*   81
2 b g Silic (Fr) - Spring Wedding (USA)
2^{6gs} 5^{7g} 6^{6hy} **0-1-3 £1,330**

Lord Mayor *Sir Michael Stoute*   103
3 b g Machiavellian (USA) - Misleading Lady
3^{10gs} 1^{10g} 5^{10f} 5^{12s} 6^{10hy} **1-1-5**
£47,685

Lord Melbourne (Ire) *A G Juckes*   a56
5 b g Lycius (USA) - Adana (Ire)
2^{6sd} 1^{7sd} 4^{6sd} 3^{7sd} 13^{7sd} 5^{7sd} 1^{6sw} 6^{8sw}
8^{7sd} **2-2-9 £4,050**

Lord Nellsson *J S King*   64
8 b g Arctic Lord - Miss Petronella
4^{12f} 7^{12gf} 10^{11gf} 5^{18gs} 8^{13f} 7^{17g} **0-0-6**
£269

Lord Normacote *C A Dwyer*   60
2 b g Loup Sauvage (USA) - Blessed Event
7^{6gf} 8^{7gf} 4^{7gf} 13^{8s} 16^{7gf} 7^{8g} **0-0-6**

Lord Of Adventure (Ire) *Jamie Poulton*   48
2 b c Inzar (USA) - Highly Fashionable (Ire)
8^{6gf} **0-0-1**

Lord Of Dreams (Ire) *D W P Arbuthnot*   67 a71
2 ch c Barathea (Ire) - The Multiyorker (Ire)
11^{6gf} 5^{8gs} 13^{6gf} 3^{8sd} 4^{8s} 2^{8g} **0-2-6**
£2,139

Lord Of Methley *R M Whitaker*   53

5 gr g Zilzal (USA) - Paradise Waters
11^{8gs} 8^{8hy} 7^{12gf} 1^{8gs} **1-0-4 £3,607**

Lord Of The East *D Nicholls*   85
5 b g Emarati (USA) - Fairy Free
10^{7gs} 3^{7gs} 2^{6gs} 14^{6gf} 1^{7f} 3^{6g} 2^{6gf} 3^{6gs}
2^{7g} 1^{6gf} 10^{6gf} 17^{6gf} 20^{7gf} **2-6-13 £16,764**

Lord Of The Fens *C N Kellett*   18
4 b g Danzig Connection (USA) - Zizi (Ire)
17^{6gf} 17^{8gf} 6^{6gf} **0-0-3**

Lord Of The Sea (Ire) *Jamie Poulton*   69 a74
3 b g Perugino (USA) - Sea Mistress
3^{8sd} 3^{10sd} 8^{8sd} 10^{10sd} 7^{11gf} 9^{10gf} 4^{8g}
13^{7gf} 6^{8gs} 12^{8gf} 7^{8sd} 8^{7sd} **0-2-12 £2,307**

Lord Wishingwell (Ire) *J S Wainwright*   42
3 b g Lake Coniston (Ire) - Spirito Libro (Ire)
8^{10gs} 3^{6hy} 3^{6f} 10^{6s} 4^{7gf} 6^{5gf} 7^{6g} 14^{8f}
8^{7g} 17^{6gs} **0-2-10 £1,019**

Lord Zinc *D W P Arbuthnot*
3 b g Forzando - Zolica
17^{5gf} **0-0-1**

Lorien Hill (Ire) *B W Hills*   78
3 b f Danehill (USA) - Lothlorien (USA)
6^{8gs} 5^{8gf} 7^{7gf} 2^{7g} 8^{7g} 3^{7gf} 7^{7gs} 5^{8gf}
1-2-9 £7,522

Lorna Dune *J G M O'Shea*   62 a51
2 b f Desert Story (Ire) - Autumn Affair
3^{6hy} 6^{6gf} 8^{5g} 6^{5gf} 7^{7sd} 3^{7gf} 1^{8g} 12^{10gf}
5^{8g} **1-2-9 £3,609**

Los Organos (Ire) *P W Chapple-Hyam*   87
2 br f Turtle Island (Ire) - Spicebird (Ire)
3^{8hy} 8^{8gs} **0-1-2 £1,036**

Lost Soldier Three (Ire) *L M Cumani*   107
3 b g Barathea (Ire) - Donya
6^{8g} 1^{10g} 5^{10gf} 4^{10g} 2^{13gs} 1^{14s} 1^{15gf} 4^{14g}
3-1-8 £45,469

Lost Spirit *P W Hiatt*
8 b g Strolling Along (USA) - Shoag (USA)
14^{10sd} 11^{12gf} **0-0-2**

Lottie *Miss V Haigh*   38
3 b f Robellino (USA) - Montserrat
7^{7g} 5^{7g} 4^{7gf} 17^{6g} 14^{7gs} **0-0-5 £814**

Lottie Dundass *W R Swinburn*   73
2 ch f Polar Falcon (USA) - Sand Grouse (USA)
5^{6gf} 2^{7gs} 7^{7gf} 4^{8f} **0-1-4 £1,317**

Loughlorien (Ire) *R E Barr*   58
5 b g Lake Coniston (Ire) - Fey Lady (Ire)
8^{5gf} 8^{6gf} 11^{5gf} 9^{5g} 9^{6g} 3^{6gf} 3^{5gf} 4^{5gf}
7^{6gf} 1^{5f} 2^{6g} 3^{5s} **1-5-12 £3,990**

Louis Georgio *M R Hoad*   34 a12
5 b g Royal Applause - Swellegant
12^{5gf} 12^{6sd} 12^{6gf} **0-0-3**

Louis Prima *Miss L A Perratt*   24
3 gr g Paris House - Chanson D'Amour (Ire)
8^{5gf} 8^{6f} 11^{5g} 15^{6s} **0-0-4**

Louise Paris (Ire) *P Butler*
2 b f Soviet Star (USA) - Avantage Service (Ire)
11^{8sd} **0-0-1**

Louise Rayner *M L W Bell*   67 a35
2 b f Vettori (Ire) - Showery
5^{7f} 4^{7g} 9^{7gf} 9^{7sd} 1^{10hy} **1-0-5 £4,909**

Louisiade (Ire) *T D Easterby*   65
3 b g Tagula (Ire) - Titchwell Lass
11^{5s} 3^{6gs} 8^{10g} 3^{8gf} 3^{8g} 7^{8s} 10^{8gf}
0-3-8 £3,544

Louphole *P J Makin*   85 a92

2 ch g Loup Sauvage (USA) - Goodwood Lass (Ire)
3⁵ᵍ 4⁶ᵍᶠ 1⁵ᵍᶠ 7⁵ᵍ 7⁶ᵍᶠ 3⁵ᵍᶠ 1⁵ᵍ 10⁶ˢ
16ˢᵈ **3-1-9 £24,693**

Love Affair (Ire) *R Hannon* 75
2 b f Tagula (Ire) - Changing Partners
2⁷ᵍᶠ 7⁷ˢ 8⁶ᵍᶠ 2⁷ᵍ **0-2-4 £10,190**

Love Always *Mrs A J Perrett* 76
2 b f Piccolo - Lady Isabell
4⁷ᵍ 2⁷ᵍᶠ **0-1-2 £2,445**

Love And Honour *Julian Poulton*
2 b f Silver Patriarch (Ire) - Fox Star (Ire)
20⁸ˢ **0-0-1**

Love And Laughter (Ire) *T D Easterby* 72
2 b f Theatrical - Hoh Dear (Ire)
6⁶ˢ 1⁷ᵍᶠ 14⁷ᶠ **1-0-3 £4,841**

Love Angel (USA) *M Johnston* 80
2 b/br c Woodman (USA) - Omnia (USA)
4⁶ᵍᶠ 3⁶ᵍᶠ **0-0-2 £1,230**

Love Attack (Ire) *D Carroll* 35 a34
2 b f Sri Pekan (USA) - Bradwell (Ire)
6⁷ˢᵈ 6⁷ˢᵈ 18⁶ᵍˢ **0-0-3**

Love Beauty (USA) *M Johnston* 78
2 b/br c Seeking The Gold (USA) - Heavenly Rhythm (USA)
4⁶ᵍᶠ 11⁷ᵍᶠ 2⁸ˢ 5⁸ᵍˢ **0-1-4 £2,185**

Love From Russia *A Berry* 32
2 b g Xaar - Heart
15⁶ᵍˢ 11⁸ᵍ 7⁶ᶠ 11⁶ᵍ **0-0-4**

Love In Seattle (Ire) *M Johnston* 86
4 b c Seattle Slew (USA) - Tamise (USA)
13¹⁰ˢ 1⁸ᵍ 12⁸ᵍᶠ 7⁸ᵍᶠ 10⁸ᵍᶠ 14¹⁰ᵍ **1-0-6**
£5,382

Love In The Mist (USA) *E A L Dunlop* a42
3 b f Silver Hawk (USA) - Fast Nellie (USA)
10⁷ˢᵈ **0-0-1**

Love Me Tender *H R A Cecil* 70
2 b f Green Desert (USA) - Easy To Love (USA)
7⁷ᵍᶠ 5⁷ˢ 8⁶ˢ **0-0-3**

Love Of Life *Julian Poulton* 49
3 b f Spectrum (Ire) - Night Over Day
10¹⁰ᵍˢ 14⁷ᵍˢ 6⁸ᶠ 7⁷ᵍ 2⁷ᶠ 11⁸ᵍ LFT⁷ˢᵈ
0-1-7 £904

Love Palace (Ire) *M Johnston* 95
2 b c King's Best (USA) - Vijaya (USA)
2⁷ᵍˢ 2⁸ˢ 4⁷ᵍ 1⁸ˢ 5⁸ˢ **1-1-5 £10,194**

Love Thirty *M R Channon* 92
2 b f Mister Baileys - Polished Up
6⁶ᵍᶠ 2⁶ˢ 5²ᵍ 1⁶ᵍ **1-1-4 £12,044**

Love Triangle (Ire) *D R C Elsworth* 82 a69
3 ch g Titus Livius (Fr) - Kirsova
3⁷ᵍᶠ 7⁶ᵍ 11⁷ᵍˢ 9⁸ᵍˢ 4⁸ᵍᶠ 5¹⁰ᵍᶠ 7¹⁰ˢᵈ **0-1-7**
£1,577

Love You Always (USA) *Miss J Feilden* 85
4 ch g Woodman (USA) - Encorenous (USA)
8¹⁰ˢ 6¹⁰ᵍᶠ 8¹⁰ˢ **0-0-3 £300**

Love's Design (Ire) *Miss S J Wilton* 52 a49
7 b/br g Pursuit Of Love - Cephista
8¹²ˢʷ 6⁸ˢᵈ 8⁹ˢᵈ 10⁷ˢˢ 5⁹ˢˢ 5⁸ˢ 4⁷ˢᶠ **0-0-7**

Loveisdangerous *Don Enrico Incisa* 40 a44
3 b f Pursuit Of Love - Brookhead Lady
5⁵ˢᵈ 10⁵ᵍˢ 8⁶ᵍᶠ **0-0-3**

Lovelorn *M W Easterby* 51 a50
2 b g Mind Games - Love Letters
3⁶ˢᵈ 10⁶ᶠ 13⁵ᵍ **0-1-3 £554**

Lovers Walk (USA) *W J Haggas* a52

3 b f Diesis - Starlight Way (USA)
6⁷ˢᵈ **0-0-1**

Loves Travelling (Ire) *L M Cumani* 99
4 b g Blues Traveller (Ire) - Fast Love (Ire)
2¹²ᵍ 1¹²ᵍ 2¹²ᵍˢ 10¹⁴ᵍ 14¹²ᵍᶠ **1-2-5**
£24,340

Loveyoulongtime *A M Balding* 38
3 gr f Compton Place - Sky Red
8⁶ᵍᶠ 8⁵ᵍᶠ 4⁵ᵍᶠ **0-0-3**

Low Cloud *J J Quinn* 83
4 b g Danehill (USA) - Raincloud
6¹⁰ᵍˢ 11¹⁰ᵍ 3⁷ᵍᶠ 5⁸ᶠ 1⁸ᵍᶠ 4⁷ᵍ 5⁹ᵍˢ 4¹⁰ᵍ
12⁹ᵍᶠ 10⁸ˢ 17¹⁰ˢ **1-1-11 £6,232**

Lowestoft Playboy *Mrs C A Dunnett* 69 a65
2 ch g Pivotal - Red Typhoon
8⁵ᵍᶠ 6⁵ᵍᶠ 5⁵ᵍᶠ 7⁵ᵍᶠ 21⁶ᵍᶠ 4⁶ˢᵈ 5⁵ˢᵈ 20⁸ˢ
0-0-8 £421

Loyal Love (USA) *Saeed Bin Suroor* 88
2 b/br f Danzig (USA) - Always Loyal (USA)
6⁶ᵍ 1⁶ᵍ **1-0-2 £8,206**

Loyal Tycoon (Ire) *D K Ivory* 97
6 br g Royal Abjar (USA) - Rosy Lydgate
17⁶ᵍ 7⁶ᵍ 5⁶ᵍᶠ 8⁶ᶠ 1⁶ᵍᶠ 8⁷ᵍ
5⁶ᵍᶠ 5⁶ᵍᶠ 22⁶ᵍᶠ 2⁶ᵍ **1-2-12 £14,517**

Loyalty Lodge (Ire) *J D Bethell* 55
2 ch g Grand Lodge (USA) - Gaily Grecian (Ire)
10⁶ᵍˢ 6⁶ᵍᶠ 10⁷ˢ 14⁷ᵍᶠ **0-0-4**

Lualua *T D Barron* 82
3 ch g Presidium - Tawny
4⁶ᵍ 2⁵ᵍᶠ 3⁶ᵍᶠ 14⁵ᵍᶠ 4⁵ᵍ 3⁵ᵍˢ 14⁵ᵍᶠ 13⁵ᵍˢ
6⁵ᵍᶠ **0-3-9 £5,955**

Luas Line (Ire) *David Wachman* 96
2 b f Danehill (USA) - Streetcar (Ire)
7⁶ᵍ 1⁶ᶠ 2⁷ᵍᶠ 7⁷ᵍˢ **1-1-4 £26,563**

Lubeck *D R Loder* 79
2 b g Lujain (USA) - Milling (USA)
5⁶ᵍ 1⁶ᵍ 9⁶ᵍ **1-0-3 £4,192**

Lubinas (Ire) *F Jordan* 41 a45
5 b g Grand Lodge (USA) - Liebesgirl
7¹⁴ˢ 5¹⁵ˢᵈ **0-0-2**

Lucayan Belle *M L W Bell*
3 b f Cadeaux Genereux - Floppie (Fr)
7¹⁰ᵍˢ **0-0-1**

Lucayan Dancer *D Nicholls* 68
4 b g Zieten (USA) - Tittle Tattle (Ire)
6⁷ˢ 5⁸ˢ 5¹⁰ᵍˢ 16⁸ᵍ 1¹⁰ˢ 4¹¹ˢ 1¹⁰ᶠ 2¹⁰ᵍ
3¹⁰ˢ 4¹⁰ˢ **2-4-10 £10,282**

Lucayan Legend (Ire) *R Hannon* 100
3 b c Docksider (USA) - Capo Di Monte
6⁸ʰʸ 3⁸ᵍ 1⁸ᵍᶠ 2⁸ᶠ 15¹⁰ᵍᶠ **1-2-5 £16,739**

Lucayan Monarch *P S McEntee* a67
6 ch g Cadeaux Genereux - Flight Soundly (Ire)
2⁷ˢᵈ 1⁷ˢᵈ 1⁷ˢᵈ 2⁷ˢᵈ 5⁷ˢˢ 13⁸ˢᵈ 8⁷ˢᵈ 2⁸ˢᵈ
3⁷ˢᵈ 2⁸ˢᵈ 3⁸ˢᵈ 6⁷ˢᵈ 5⁷ˢᵈ 2⁷ˢᵈ **2-6-14 £8,116**

Luceball (Ire) *Patrick Morris* 50 a44
4 b f Bluebird (USA) - Mysterious Plans (Ire)
9⁶ˢᵈ 11⁶ˢᵈ 15⁵ᶠ 9⁶ᵍ 1⁵ᵍ 15⁵ᵍ **1-0-6**
£4,379

Lucefer (Ire) *G C H Chung* 57 a49
6 b g Lycius (USA) - Maharani (USA)
9⁸ˢᵈ 8⁷ᵍᶠ 3¹⁰ˢ 4¹⁰ᵍᶠ 4⁸ᵍᶠ 8⁹ᵍ 3⁸ᵍᶠ 1⁸ᵍˢ
8⁸ˢ 5⁷ᵍ 9⁸ᵍ 12⁸ᵍˢ 9⁵ˢᵈ **1-2-13 £6,385**

Luchi *A Charlton* a46
3 ch f Mark Of Esteem (Ire) - Penmayne
6⁶ˢᵈ 10⁶ˢᵈ **0-0-2**

Lucid Dreams (Ire) *M Wigham* a62
5 b g Sri Pekan (USA) - Scenaria (Ire)
5⁷ˢᵈ 7⁷ˢᵈ 4⁷ˢᵈ 1⁸ˢᵈ 2⁸ˢᵈ 3⁸ˢᵈ 1⁸ˢᵈ 5⁸ˢᵈ
2-3-8 £7,206

Luciferous (USA) *Jane Southcombe* 64
2 ch f Devil's Bag (USA) - Vital Laser (USA)
5⁶ᵍᶠ 6⁶ᵍˢ **0-0-2**

Lucius Verrus (USA) *D Shaw* 35 a56
4 b g Danzig (USA) - Magic Of Life (USA)
3⁵ˢʷ 14⁷ˢᵈ 1⁵ˢᵈ 16⁵ʰʸ 5⁶ˢᵈ 2⁵ˢᵈ 9⁶ˢᵈ 5⁶ˢᵈ
6⁶ˢᵈ 15⁶ᵍ 3⁶ˢʷ **1-2-11 £4,621**

Lucky Again (Ire) *J K Price* 48
3 br g Be My Guest (USA) - Persian Fantasia
17⁸ᵍ 4¹⁰ˢ 7¹⁰ᵍᶠ 5¹²ᶠ **0-0-4**

Lucky Archer *Ian Williams* 43 a14
11 b g North Briton - Preobrajenska
7¹⁰ᵍ 11⁸ᵍᶠ 11⁸ᵍᶠ 7¹⁰ᵍᶠ 6¹⁰ᶠ 12¹¹ˢᵈ **0-0-6**

Lucky Arthur (Ire) *J G M O'Shea* 61
3 ch f Grand Lodge (USA) - Soltura (Ire)
8¹⁰ˢ 5¹⁰ᵍᶠ 8¹⁰ᵍᶠ 3¹¹ᵍᶠ 2¹²ᶠ 3¹²ᵍ 15¹²ᵍᶠ
8¹²ᵍ 10¹²ᵍˢ **0-2-9 £2,202**

Lucky Emerald (Ire) *B Palling* 69 a44
2 b f Lend A Hand - Anita's Love (Ire)
2⁵ᵍ 7⁵ᵍˢ 1⁵ᵍᶠ 14⁶ᵍᶠ 5⁵ᵍˢ 9⁶ˢᵈ **1-1-6**
£4,483

Lucky Judge *G A Swinbank* 78 a50
7 b g Saddlers' Hall (Ire) - Lady Lydia
4¹²ʰʸ 12¹²ᵍ 1¹⁶ᵍ 5¹⁴ˢᵈ 1¹⁶ˢ 6¹⁶ˢ
5¹⁶ᵍˢ **3-0-8 £20,014**

Lucky Largo (Ire) *Miss L A Perratt* 62
4 b/br g Key Of Luck (USA) - Lingering Melody (Ire)
10¹⁰ˢ 5⁸ᵍˢ 14⁹ᵍ 8⁸ᵍ 4⁸ᵍᶠ 7⁸ᵍ 2⁹ᵍ 6¹²ᵍ
7¹¹ᵍ 10¹⁰ᵍᶠ 8⁸ᵍᶠ 14⁹ᵍˢ 8¹⁰ˢ 8⁸ᶠ 11¹¹ˢ **0-1-15**
£2,053

Lucky Leo *Ian Williams* 81
4 b g Muhtarram (USA) - Wrong Bride
9¹⁰ᵍˢ 1¹²ᵍᶠ 1¹¹ᵍᶠ 9¹²ᵍˢ **2-0-4 £9,246**

Lucky Pipit *B W Hills* 104
3 b f Key Of Luck (USA) - Meadow Pipit (Can)
5⁷ᵍ 2⁷ᵍᶠ 1⁷ᵍ 8⁷ᵍᶠ 14⁷ᵍᶠ 4⁷ᵍᶠ 8⁷ᵍᶠ **1-1-7**
£18,560

Lucky Piscean *C W Fairhurst* 55
3 b g River Falls - Celestine
5⁷ᵍˢ 8⁸ᵍˢ 19⁷ᵍˢ 15¹⁰ᵍˢ 11¹⁶ᵍᶠ **0-0-5**

Lucky Red Pepper *P W Chapple-Hyam* 73
2 b c Barathea (Ire) - Mutige
1⁷ᵍᶠ **1-0-1 £4,475**

Lucky Romance *B J Meehan* a34
5 b m Key Of Luck (USA) - In Love Again (Ire)
5⁹ˢᵈ 9⁸ˢᵈ **0-0-2**

Lucky Spin *R Hannon* 106
3 b f Pivotal - Perioscope
2⁷ᵍ 1⁷ˢ 1⁷ᵍ 1⁷ᵍᶠ 12⁷ᵍᶠ 3⁷ᵍ **3-2-6**
£35,236

Lucky Story (USA) *M Johnston* 127
3 b c Kris S (USA) - Spring Flight (USA)
2⁸ᵍˢ 7⁸ᵍˢ 2⁸ᵍᶠ 9¹⁰ˢ **0-2-4 £68,200**

Lucky Valentine *G L Moore* 55 a56
4 b f My Best Valentine - Vera's First (Ire)
2⁵ᶠ 4⁵ᶠ 3⁵ᶠ 3⁵ˢᵈ 6⁶ᶠ **0-3-5 £1,619**

Lucretius *D K Ivory* 39 a46
5 b g Mind Games - Eastern Ember
9⁸ˢᵈ 13⁶ˢᵈ 14⁷ˢᵈ 4⁸ˢᵈ 4⁶ᵍ **0-0-5**

Lucy Parkes *E J Alston* 50

2 ch f Piccolo - Janette Parkes
8⁵ᵍˢ 4⁵ᵍ 11⁵ᵍˢ 10⁵ᵍᶠ 14⁵ᵍᶠ **0-0-5 £377**

Lugana Point *J Balding* 32 a25
2 b c Lugana Beach - Raisa Point
7⁵ᵍᶠ 9⁶ˢᵈ **0-0-2**

Luis Melendez (USA) *P F I Cole* 82
2 ch c Horse Chestnut (SAF) - Egoli (USA)
4⁸ᵍ 3⁸ᵍ 1⁸ᵍ **1-1-3 £7,122**

Lujain Rose *H Morrison* 58
2 b f Lujain - Rose Chime (Ire)
9⁸ᵍᶠ **0-0-1**

Luke After Me (Ire) *G A Swinbank* 61 a37
4 b g Victory Note (USA) - Summit Talk
7⁸ˢᵈ 2⁷ᵍ 3⁷ᵍᶠ 10⁷ᵍ 2⁷ᵍ 12⁷ᵍᶠ 4⁷ᶠ 3⁷ᵍᶠ
10⁷ᶠ 9⁷ᵍᶠ 9⁷ᵍᶠ **0-4-11 £2,826**

Luke Sharp *K A Ryan* 24
3 gr g Muhtarram (USA) - Heaven-Liegh-Grey
15⁶ᵍᶠ 8⁷ᵍ 8⁶ˢᵈ **0-0-3**

Lumback (Ire) *N Wilson* 2
5 b g Desert Style (Ire) - Bellingham Jester
9⁷ᵍᶠ **0-0-1**

Luna Blu (Ire) *Miss M E Rowland* 18
2 b f Mujahid (USA) - Blu Tamantara (USA)
14⁷ᵍ **0-0-1**

Lunar Exit (Ire) *Lady Herries* 90
3 gr g Exit To Nowhere (USA) - Moon Magic
6¹⁰ᵍᶠ 11¹⁰ᵍᶠ 6¹²ᵍᶠ 16¹²ᵍᵒ **0-0-4 £636**

Lunar Leader (Ire) *M J Gingell* 57
4 b f Mujadil (USA) - Moon River (Fr)
10¹⁰ᵍ 12¹¹ᵍˢ 19¹²ˢ 12⁸ᵍ 10¹²ᵍᶠ 17⁸ᵍᶠ
UR¹⁰ᵍˢ **0-0-7**

Lunar Lord *D Burchell* 55
8 b g Elmaamul (USA) - Cache
7¹⁰ᵍ 8¹⁰ᵍ 7¹⁴ᵍᶠ 8¹⁰ᵍᶠ 4¹²ᵍᶠ 2¹⁴ᵍ 2¹⁴ᵍᶠ
8¹²ᵍᶠ 6¹³ᵍˢ 12¹²ᵍ **0-2-10 £2,380**

Lunar Sky (USA) *C E Brittain* 70
2 b f Lemon Drop Kid (USA) - Celestial Bliss (USA)
7⁷ᶠ 6⁷ᵍˢ 4⁹ᶠ 14¹⁰ᵍᶠ **0-0-4 £302**

Lunar Sovereign (USA) *Saeed Bin Suroor* 108
5 br h Cobra King (USA) - January Moon (USA)
3¹²ᵍᶠ 11¹²ᵍᶠ 10¹⁰ᵍᶠ 11¹²ᵍᶠ **0-1-4**
£11,173

Lundy's Lane (Ire) *C E Brittain* 98 a95
4 b g Darshaan - Lunda (Ire)
4⁸ˢᵈ 8⁸ᵍ 27⁸ᵍ 21¹⁰ᵍ 7⁸ᶠ 10⁹ᵍ **0-0-6**
£619

Lupine Howl *B A McMahon* 44
3 b c Wolfhound (USA) - Classic Fan (USA)
9⁶ᵍ 12⁷ᵍᶠ 9⁶ᶠ 13⁷ᶠ 6¹⁰ᵍ 10⁷ᵍ **0-0-6**

Luteur Des Pictons (Fr) *B G Powell* a24
5 ch g Ragmar (Fr) - Ezera (Fr)
12¹²ˢᵈ **0-0-1**

Luxi River (USA) *Michael McElhone* 34 a54
4 b g Diesis - Mariella (USA)
5¹²ˢᵈ 5¹²ˢᵈ 4¹¹ˢᵈ 4¹²ˢᵈ 7¹⁶ᵍ **0-0-5 £256**

Luxor *Mrs G S Rees* 56
7 ch g Grand Lodge (USA) - Escrime (USA)
11¹¹ᵍᶠ 8⁹ᵍ 7¹⁰ᵍ 11¹⁰ᵍᶠ 10¹⁰ᵍ 8¹¹ᵍ 15¹⁰ᵍ
0-0-7

Lyca Ballerina *Andrew Slattery* 76
3 b f Marju (Ire) - Lovely Lyca
5⁷ᵍ 3⁸ˢ 4⁷ᵍ 1⁷ᵍ 10⁸ˢ 3⁷ᵍ 11⁸ᵍᶠ 6⁷ᵍᶠ
15⁷ˢ 8⁷ᵍˢ 9⁷ʰʸ **1-3-11 £7,494**

Lydgate (USA) *Saeed Bin Suroor* 108
4 b c Pulpit (USA) - Mariuka (USA)

2^{7f} 4^{8f} 4^{7f} 2^{7f} 1^{5g} 9^{5gf} 4^{6gf} 8^{5s} **1-0-8**
£66,848

Lydia's Look (Ire) *T J Etherington*   54 a48
7 b m Distant View (USA) - Mrs Croesus (USA)
12^{6sd} 5^{5sd} 5^{6sd} 4^{6sd} 5^{5gf} 1^{5g} 6^{5g} 13^{5gs}
9^{5gs} **1-0-9 £4,030**

Lyes Green *R M Beckett*   48 a57
3 gr g Bien Bien (USA) - Dissolve
4^{12gs} 12^{13sd} **0-0-2**

Lyford Lass *I Semple*   69
3 b f Bahamian Bounty - Ladykirk
2^{8hy} 1^{8hy} 8^{8gs} 14^{10s} 12^{10s} **1-1-5**
£4,268

Lygeton Lad *Miss Gay Kelleway*   71 a108
6 b g Shaamit (Ire) - Smartie Lee
5^{10sd} 5^{12sd} 6^{10sd} 5^{7sd} 1^{7sd} 7^{9s} 8^{7s} 7^{8gf}
8^{7gf} 4^{7gf} 6^{7gf} 5^{7sd} **1-0-12 £12,100**

Lyns Resolution *D Burchell*   60
4 b g Awesome - Our Resolution
14^{8gf} 4^{8gf} **0-0-2 £383**

Lyonels Glory *U Suter*   108
3 b c Green Desert (USA) - La Virginia (Ger)
2^{10hy} 3^{10vs} 3^{12gs} 6^{12g} 1^{10g} 3^{10gs} **1-1-6**
£51,947

Lyric Dances (Fr) *J Jay*   29
2 ch f Sendawar (Ire) - Romanche (Fr)
11^{6gs} **0-0-1**

Lyrical Girl (USA) *H J Manners*   48 a56
3 b f Orpen (USA) - Lyric Theatre (USA)
1^{10sd} 5^{10sd} 10^{10gf} 6^{7g} 14^{8gf} 12^{12g} **1-0-6**
£2,905

Lyrical Lady *Mrs A J Bowlby*   20
3 b f Merdon Melody - Gracious Imp (USA)
15^{5gf} 10^{6gf} 19^{6gf} 8^{8g} **0-0-5**

Lyrical Way *P R Chamings*   62 a67
5 b g Vettori (Ire) - Fortunate
4^{10sd} 12^{10sd} 5^{10sd} 7^{10gf} 6^{10g} 4^{12f} **0-0-6**
£257

Lysander's Quest (Ire) *R Ingram*   51 a53
6 br g King's Theatre (Ire) - Haramayda (Fr)
15^{10gf} 8^{14f} 5^{12sd} 1^{12gf} 9^{12g} **1-0-5**
£1,718

Lysandra (Ire) *Sir Michael Stoute*   79
2 b f Danehill (USA) - Oriane
2^{7gf} 4^{7gs} **0-1-2 £2,207**

Lytham (Ire) *M J Wallace*   70 a72
3 b g Spectrum (Ire) - Nousairya (Ire)
14^{8g} 4^{10gy} 10^{9g} 9^{9gy} 8^{10gf} 3^{8s} 2^{9sd} **0-2-7**
£2,182

M For Magic *C W Fairhurst*   48
5 ch g First Trump - Celestine
5^{6gf} 2^{6hy} 4^{7f} 5^{6gf} 14^{6gs} **0-1-5 £1,175**

Ma Yahab *L M Cumani*   79 a85
3 ch c Dr Fong (USA) - Bay Shade (USA)
3^{10gf} 3^{10g} 7^{12gf} 4^{11g} 4^{9gf} 2^{10sd} **0-3-6**
£4,039

Ma'Am (USA) *I A Wood*   a63
2 ch f Royal Anthem (USA) - Hide The Bride (USA)
8^{8sd} **0-0-1**

Mabel Riley (Ire) *M A Buckley*   10 a47
4 b f Revoque (Ire) - Mystic Dispute (Ire)
5^{8sd} 7^{8sd} 9^{7gs} **0-0-3**

Mabella (Ire) *B R Millman*   65
2 b f Brave Act - Wee Merkin (Ire)
8^{6gf} 5^{5g} 7^{6gf} 4^{6gf} 10^{6gs} 12^{7gf} **0-0-6**
£275

Mac *M P Tregoning*   72
4 ch g Fleetwood (Ire) - Midnight Break
15^{16gf} 17^{12s} **0-0-2**

Mac Cois Na Tine *K A Ryan*   66
2 b g Cois Na Tine (Ire) - Berenice (Ity)
7^{5gs} 2^{6gf} 3^{7gf} 7^{7gs} **0-2-4 £1,692**

Mac Love *J Akehurst*   117
3 b g Cape Cross (Ire) - My Lass
5^{6gs} 4^{6s} 2^{6g} 2^{6f} 6^{6g} 6^{6g} 1^{6gf} 13^{6g} 1^{7gf}
9^{6gf} 1^{7g} **3-2-11 £75,081**

Mac Regal (Ire) *M G Quinlan*   86
3 b c King's Theatre (Ire) - Shine Silently (Ire)
3^{10g} 2^{10gs} 14^{12g} **0-0-3 £8,206**

Mac The Knife (Ire) *A W Carroll*   49
3 b g Daggers Drawn (USA) - Icefern
17^{6gs} 10^{6s} 8^{7gf} 8^{7gf} 8^{6f} 13^{7gs} **0-0-6**

Mac's Elan *A B Coogan*   57 a55
4 b g Darshaan - Elabella
16^{7gs} 5^{7gs} 7^{10sd} 6^{10s} 2^{8g} 2^{12s} **0-2-6**
£2,357

Mac's Talisman (Ire) *V Smith*   55 a75
4 ch c Hector Protector (USA) - Inherent Magic (Ire)
17^{6gf} 10^{6sd} 12^{7sd} 3^{8g} 15^{8g} 11^{6gs}
1^{7sd} 1^{9sd} **2-2-9 £7,402**

Macabre *Saeed Bin Suroor*   81
2 b c Machiavellian (USA) - Lady In Waiting
2^{7gf} **0-1-1 £2,300**

Macaroni Gold (Ire) *W Jarvis*   67 a72
4 b g Rock Hopper - Strike It Rich (Fr)
9^{16sd} 14^{4sd} 4^{16sd} 5^{16s} 7^{16gf} 3^{14s} 3^{16sd}
6^{16g} 6^{14gs} **0-2-9 £1,480**

Macaulay (Ire) *R Charlton*   a79
2 ch c Zafonic (USA) - Wigging
3^{7sd} **0-1-1 £790**

Macchiato *I W McInnes*   51 a26
3 br f Inchinor - Tereyna
7^{12gs} 5^{11gf} 13^{10g} 9^{10sd} 9^{11gf} 8^{14sd} 9^{12gf}
0-0-7

Machinist (Ire) *D Nicholls*   92
4 b g Machiavellian (USA) - Athene (Ire)
7^{6f} 17^{7f} 9^{8g} 1^{6gf} 2^{6gf} 4^{6s} 5^{6s} 7^{6s}
1-2-8 £20,355

Maclean *Sir Michael Stoute*   85
3 b g Machiavellian (USA) - Celtic Cross
2^{8g} 1^{9g} 3^{8gf} 6^{10s} 5^{8g} 6^{8gf} 1^{10s} 11^{10g}
2-2-8 £20,158

Macpursie *T G McCourt*   52 a36
3 br f Botanic (USA) - Jeethgaya (USA)
5^{7sd} 4^{8ss} 3^{10f} 6^{12g} 11^{12g} **0-1-5 £800**

Mad *Andrew Reid*   a55
3 br f Pursuit Of Love - Emily-Mou (Ire)
8^{12sd} 10^{8s} 8^{9sd} 6^{7sd} **0-0-4**

Mad Carew (USA) *G L Moore*   79 a82
5 ch g Rahy (USA) - Poppy Carew (Ire)
5^{12sd} 1^{10sd} 13^{10sd} 4^{12sd} 11^{10s} 5^{8gf} 5^{10gf}
4^{8gf} 10^{9gf} 5^{12g} 4^{10s} **1-0-11 £4,151**

Mad Marty Wildcard *R Brotherton*   24
2 ch c Komaite (USA) - Done And Dusted (Ire)
13^{6g} 13^{6s} **0-0-2**

Mad Maurice *B J Curley*   32
3 ch g Grand Lodge (USA) - Amarella (Fr)
17^{7gs} 12^{7s} 10^{11gf} 13^{11gf} 13^{12gf} **0-0-5**

Madaar (USA) *R Bastiman*   30 a11
5 b g Spinning World (USA) - Mur Taasha (USA)
12^{8sd} 8^{10gf} **0-0-2**

Madaeh (USA) *J L Dunlop* 85
3 b/br f Swain (Ire) - Tamgeed (USA)
4¹⁰ᵍᶠ 14⁸ᵍᶠ **0-0-2 £1,500**

Madalyar (Ire) *Jonjo O'Neill*
5 b g Darshaan - Madaniyya (USA)
12⁸ˢʷ **0-0-1**

Madam Caversfield *R Hannon* 70
2 b f Pursuit of Love - Madam Alison
5⁵ᶠ 7⁶ᵍᶠ 3⁷ᵍᶠ 4⁷ᵍᶠ 4⁷ᵍᶠ 6⁷ᶠ 2⁸ˢ 9⁸ˢ **0-2-8
£2,560**

Madame Fatale (Ire) *Jedd O'Keeffe* 28 a40
2 br f Daggers Drawn (USA) - Taajreh (Ire)
15⁸ᵍ 10⁹ˢᵈ **0-0-2**

Madame Guillotine *J Balding* 14
2 b f Sure Blade (USA) - Delicious
13⁶ᵍ 13⁶ˢᵈ **0-0-2**

Madame Marie (Ire) *S Dow* 58 a55
4 b f Desert King (Ire) - Les Trois Lamas (Ire)
11¹⁰ᵍˢ 7⁷ˢ 2⁸ᵍ 15⁸ᶠ 6⁹ᵍᶠ 7¹⁰ᵍˢ 7¹⁰ˢᵈ
8¹²ˢᵈ 8¹⁶ˢᵈ 4¹²ᶠ **0-1-10 £816**

Madame Roux *C Drew* a8
6 b m Rudimentary (USA) - Foreign Mistress
6⁶ˢᵈ 5⁶ˢᵈ **0-0-2**

Madame Topflight *Mrs G S Rees* 91
2 b f Komaite (USA) - Jamarj
8⁵ᵍᶠ 2⁵ᵍˢ 1⁶ᵍᶠ 5⁶ᵍᶠ 2⁵ʰʸ 8⁶ˢ 9⁶ᵍ **1-2-7
£10,453**

Madamoiselle Jones *H S Howe* 81
4 b f Emperor Jones (USA) - Tiriana
10¹⁰ᵍˢ 4⁸ᵍ 5⁷ᵍᶠ 18⁸ᵍᶠ 6⁸ᵍᶠ 4⁹ᵍˢ 6⁸ᵍ 11⁸ᵍˢ
10⁹ᵍ **1-0-9 £8,478**

Maddie's A Jem *J R Jenkins* 84
4 b f Emperor Jones (USA) - Royal Orchid (Ire)
1⁶ᵍˢ 1⁵ˢ 3⁶ᵍˢ 5⁶ᵍᶠ 6⁶ᵍᶠ 4⁶ᵍᶠ 2⁶ᵍ 1⁵ᵍˢ 6⁵ˢ
2⁶ᶠ **3-3-10 £17,924**

Madge *J H M Gosden* 64
2 b f Marju (Ire) - Aymara
6⁷ᵍᶠ **0-0-1**

Madhahir (Ire) *Mervyn Torrens* 67 a61
4 b g Barathea (Ire) - Gharam (USA)
8¹⁶ˢᵈ 11¹⁶ˢᵈ 1¹²ᵍˢ 3¹¹ᵍᶠ 10¹⁴ˢ 8¹⁶ʰʸ
10¹²ᵍᶠ 6¹²ᵍ 8⁹ᵍʸ 18⁹ˢ 15¹¹ˢ **1-1-11 £3,470**

Madhavi *R Hannon* 76
2 gr f Diktat - Grey Galava
7⁶ᵍˢ 3⁶ᵍ 5⁶ᵍ 9⁶ᵍˢ 20⁷ᵍ 17⁶ˢ **0-1-6
£1,170**

Madiba *P Howling* 62 a70
5 b g Emperor Jones (USA) - Priluki
1¹¹ˢᵈ 6¹²ˢᵈ 11¹³ˢᵈ 2¹⁴ˢᵈ 2¹⁶ˢʷ 2¹⁶ˢʷ 12¹⁶ᵍ
2¹⁶ᵍ 2¹⁶ˢᵈ 9¹⁶ᵍᶠ 11¹⁴ᵍᶠ 8¹⁶ᵍᶠ PU¹⁶ᵍ 5¹⁶ʰʸ 2¹⁶ᵍ
6¹⁶ᵍ 2¹⁶ˢ 6¹²ˢᵈ **1-7-18 £9,081**

Madid (Ire) *J H M Gosden* 111
3 br c Cape Cross - Waffle On
1⁸ᵍ 1⁷ᵍ 9⁸ᵍᶠ **2-0-3 £23,302**

Madra Rua (Ire) *Miss L A Perratt* 32
3 b g Foxhound (USA) - Fun Fashion (Ire)
9⁶ᵍˢ 7⁵ᶠ 11⁵ˢ **0-0-3**

Madrasee *L Montague Hall* 73 a75
6 b m Beveled (USA) - Pendona
2⁵ˢᵈ 12⁶ˢᵈ 9⁵ˢᵈ 4⁶ˢᵈ 5⁶ˢᵈ 7⁵ˢ 5⁵ˢ 13⁶ᵍᶠ
8⁶ᵍᶠ 18⁵ᵍ 6⁶ᵍ 7⁶ˢ 6⁵ᵍ 2⁵ˢ **0-2-14 £2,595**

Maeveen (Ire) *V Smith* 25 a32
4 b f Flying Spur (Aus) - Cool Gales
10¹²ᵍᶠ 10¹²ᶠ 4¹⁰ˢᵈ **0-0-3**

Mafaheem *M Johnston* 84

**2 b c Mujahid (USA) - Legend Of Aragon
1⁶ᵍ 1-0-1 £5,489**

Mafruz *R A Fahey*
5 ch g Hamas (Ire) - Braari (USA)
9¹⁰ˢ 11⁸ᵍ **0-0-2**

Maganda (Ire) *M A Jarvis* 80
3 b f Sadler's Wells (USA) - Minnie Habit
1¹⁰ᵍˢ 6¹¹ᵍ 13⁸ᵍᶠ 18⁹ᵍ **1-0-4 £4,442**

Magari *J G Given* 54 a11
3 b f Royal Applause - Thatcher's Era (Ire)
4⁷ᶠ 8⁸ˢ 12⁸ˢʷ 5⁷ᶠ 3⁸ᵍ 4⁸ᵍˢ **0-1-6 £812**

Magdelaine *P M Phelan* a20
2 b f Sinndar (Ire) - Crystal Drop
18⁸ᵍˢ 12⁹ˢᵈ 12⁷ˢᵈ **0-0-3**

Magenta Rising (Ire) *D W Thompson*
4 ch f College Chapel - Fashion Queen
9¹²ˢᵈ 17⁸ᵍˢ **0-0-2**

Maggie Jordan (USA) *B J Meehan* 82
2 b f Fusaichi Pegasus (USA) - Pharapache (USA)
1⁶ˢ **1-0-1 £4,745**

Maggie Maquette *W S Kittow* a49
4 ch f Atraf - Bronze Maquette (Ire)
5⁶ˢᵈ 6⁵ˢᵈ 12⁵ˢᵈ **0-0-3**

Maggie Tulliver (Ire) *P W Harris* 67 a67
2 b f Spectrum (Ire) - Eliza Acton
12⁶ᵍᶠ 7⁷ᵍ 15⁷ᵍ 1⁹ˢᵈ **1-0-4 £3,620**

Maggie's Pet *K Bell* a56
7 b m Minshaanshu Amad (USA) - Run Fast For Gold
2⁸ˢᵈ 5⁹ˢᵈ 2⁸ˢᵈ 2⁹ˢᵈ 4⁸ˢᵈ 5⁸ˢʷ 1⁸ˢᵈ 6⁷ˢᵈ
1-3-8 £4,868

Maghanim *J L Dunlop* 106
4 b c Nashwan (USA) - Azdihaar (USA)
5⁷ᵍ 3⁸ᵍᶠ 2⁷ᶠ 10⁷ᵍˢ 9⁷ᵍᶠ 10⁹ᵍᶠ **0-1-6
£11,496**

Magic Amigo *J R Jenkins* 79 a69
3 ch g Zilzal (USA) - Emaline (Fr)
2⁷ˢᵈ 1¹⁰ˢ 13¹⁰ᵍᶠ 2¹⁰ᵍᶠ 3¹⁰ᶠ 8¹²ˢᵈ 4¹⁰ᵍˢ
3¹⁰ᵍ 6¹⁰ᵍᶠ 2¹⁰ᵍˢ 6¹⁰ˢ 14¹⁰ˢᵈ **1-4-12 £8,278**

Magic Amour *Ian Williams* 66
6 ch g Sanglamore (USA) - Rakli
2⁷ᵍᶠ 6⁸ᵍᶠ 7⁸ᶠ 4⁷ᵍᶠ 18⁷ᵍᶠ 16⁷ᶠ 16ᵍˢ 15⁷ᵍᶠ
7⁶ᵍᶠ **1-1-9 £6,448**

Magic Box *A M Crow* a11
6 b g Magic Ring (Ire) - Princess Poquito
15⁸ˢᵈ **0-0-1**

Magic Charm *Jedd O'Keeffe* 45 a26
6 b m Magic Ring (Ire) - Loch Clair (Ire)
10¹²ˢᵈ 10¹³ˢᵈ 8¹²ˢˢ 4¹³ᶠ 15¹²ᵍᶠ 6¹²ᵍᶠ
13¹²ᵍᶠ 8¹²ᵍ 6¹⁴ᵍᶠ **0-0-9 £273**

Magic Combination (Ire) *L Lungo* 89
11 b g Scenic - Etage
2¹⁶ˢ 5¹⁴ᶠ 2¹⁸ᵍᶠ 2¹⁶ˢ 1¹⁴ᵍˢ 1¹⁴ᵍ 11¹⁴ᵍᶠ
2-3-7 £15,598

Magic Eagle *P T Midgley* 32 a32
7 b g Magic Ring (Ire) - Shadow Bird
5⁶ˢᵈ 7⁶ˢᵈ 10⁶ˢʷ 8⁵ˢᵈ 12⁷ᵍ 7⁷ˢᵈ **0-0-6**

Magic Flo *G C Bravery* 58 a48
2 ch f Magic Ring (Ire) - Moore Stylish
9⁶ᵍ 6⁷ˢᵈ 10⁷ᵍˢ **0-0-3**

Magic Genie (Ire) *M W Easterby* 41
2 b f Lujain (USA) - Haut Volee
5⁶ᵍᶠ 8⁶ᵍ 7⁵ᵍˢ **0-0-3**

Magic Glade *R Brotherton* 96 a93
5 b g Magic Ring (Ire) - Ash Glade
8⁶ˢᵈ 2⁵ˢᵈ 2⁵ˢᵈ 1⁵ᵍᶠ 3⁵ᵍᶠ 15⁵ᵍᶠ 13⁵ᵍᶠ 3⁵ᵍᶠ

2-3-8 £26,263

Magic Mamma's Too *J R Weymes* 48 a63
4 b g Magic Ring (Ire) - Valona Valley (Ire)
2⁸ˢᵈ 5⁷ˢᵈ 3⁸ˢᵈ 4⁸ˢˢ 9⁷ᵍ 5⁸ᵍˢ 16⁸ᶠ **0-2-7**
£1,463

Magic Merlin *P W Harris* 81
3 b g Magic Ring (Ire) - St James's Antigua (Ire)
3⁸ᶠ 1⁸ᵍᶠ 4⁸ᵍ **1-1-3 £4,845**

Magic Music (Ire) *W M Brisbourne* 63
5 b m Magic Ring (Ire) - Chiming Melody
9⁶ᵍˢ 10⁶ᵍᶠ 13⁶ᵍᶠ **0-0-3**

Magic Red *M J Ryan* a64
4 ch g Magic Ring (Ire) - Jacquelina (USA)
1¹⁴ˢᵈ 1¹⁴ˢᵈ 4¹⁶ˢᵈ 2¹⁴ˢᵈ **2-1-4 £6,764**

Magic Spin *R F Johnson Houghton* 63 a49
4 b f Magic Ring (Ire) - Moon Spin
6⁶ᵍˢ 5⁷ᵍˢ 6⁸ˢᵈ **0-0-3**

Magic Sting *M L W Bell* 80 a43
3 ch g Magic Ring (Ire) - Ground Game
5¹⁰ᵍˢ 5⁸ˢᵈ 6¹²ᵍ 1¹⁰ˢ 1¹¹ᵍᶠ 12¹⁰ᵍ 3¹⁰ᵍ
3¹⁰ᵍˢ 2¹⁰ᵍ 1¹⁰ᵍ 2⁹ˢ 5¹⁰ˢ **3-3-12 £16,350**

Magic Stone *A Charlton* a43
4 br g Magic Ring (Ire) - Ridgewood Ruby (Ire)
14⁷ˢᵈ 4⁸ˢᵈ **0-0-2**

Magic Tree (UAE) *M R Channon* 55
2 ch f Timber Country (USA) - Moyesii (USA)
13⁷ᵍᶠ **0-0-1**

Magic Verse *R Guest* 62 a56
3 ch f Opening Verse (USA) - Festival Sister
18⁸ᵍ 15¹⁰ᵍᶠ 4⁸ˢᵈ 4⁸ˢᵈ 4⁸ˢᵈ 5¹⁰ᶠ 4⁸ʰʸ 1⁸ᵍ
8⁸ˢ 10⁸ˢ **1-1-10 £1,938**

Magic Warrior *J C Fox* 41 a62
4 b g Magic Ring (Ire) - Clarista (USA)
3⁸ˢᵈ 4¹⁰ˢᵈ 6¹⁰ˢᵈ 9¹⁰ˢᵈ 13⁸ᵍᶠ 10⁸ᵍ **0-1-6**
£213

Magical Mimi *Jedd O'Keeffe* 74
3 b f Magic Ring (Ire) - Naval Dispatch
11⁸ᵍ 17⁸ᵍ 8⁸ᵍᶠ 4⁸ᵍᶠ 5⁹ᵍᶠ 13¹⁰ᵍᶠ 5⁸ᵍᶠ
15⁸ᵍ **0-0-8 £316**

Magical Quest *Mrs A J Perrett* 89
4 b c Rainbow Quest (USA) - Apogee
8¹¹ᵍᶠ 1¹⁴ᶠ 11¹⁶ᵍᶠ **1-0-3 £3,591**

Magical Romance (Ire) *B J Meehan* 107
2 b f Barathea (Ire) - Shouk
4⁵ᵍ 1⁶ᵍᶠ 6⁶ᵍᶠ 1⁶ᵍˢ 1⁶ᵍ **3-0-5 £121,586**

Magico *A B Haynes* 54 a38
3 ch g Magic Ring (Ire) - Silken Dalliance
7⁸ˢᵈ 7⁶ˢᵈ 14⁷ˢᵈ 3⁸ᶠ 2⁸ᵍᶠ 9⁸ᶠ 15⁷ᵍ **0-2-7**
£1,206

Magistretti (USA) *P L Biancone* 120
4 b c Diesis - Ms Strike Zone (USA)
6¹²ᵍ 4¹²ᵍᶠ 4¹⁰ᵍ 2¹⁰ᶠ 1¹¹ʸ 2¹²ʸ 4¹²ʸ **1-2-7**
£437,426

Magnetic Pole *Sir Michael Stoute* 88
3 b c Machiavellian (USA) - Clear Attraction (USA)
2¹⁰ᵍ 3⁹ᵍ 8¹²ˢ 2¹²ᵍᶠ 2¹⁰ᶠ 1¹²ˢ **1-4-6**
£10,152

Maharaat (USA) *Sir Michael Stoute* 77
3 b c Bahri (USA) - Siyadah (USA)
5⁸ᵍ 5¹⁰ˢ 2¹⁰ᵍᶠ **0-1-3 £1,108**

Mahlstick (Ire) *D W P Arbuthnot* 8 a38
6 b g Tagula (Ire) - Guv's Joy (Ire)
6⁸ˢᵈ 3⁷ˢᵈ 4⁷ˢᵈ 4⁶ˢᵈ 20⁶ᵍᶠ 9⁸ᵍ **0-1-6**
£181

Mahmjra *M R Channon* 55 a40

Mahmoom *M R Channon* 100
3 ch c Dr Fong (USA) - Rohita (Ire)
17⁷ᵍ 14⁸ᵍ 6⁶ᵍ 8⁶ᵍᶠ 16ᵍᶠ 2⁶ᵍ 6⁷ᵍᶠ 2⁶ᵍˢ
1-2-8 £25,984

Maid For Life (Ire) *M J Wallace* 33
4 b f Entrepreneur - Arandora Star (USA)
6¹⁰ᶠ 6¹⁰ˢ 16⁸ᵍ **0-0-3**

Maid The Cut *A D Smith* 40 a51
3 ch f Silver Wizard (USA) - Third Dam
4⁸ˢᵈ 8⁷ˢˢ 12⁷ᵍˢ 5⁸ᵍˢ 6¹⁰ᵍᶠ 5¹³ᵍˢ **0-0-6**
£260

Maid To Treasure (Ire) *J L Dunlop* 73
3 b f Rainbow Quest (USA) - Maid For The Hills
4¹⁰ᵍˢ 6¹⁰ᵍ 3¹⁰ʰʸ 12¹²ˢ **0-1-4 £1,319**

Maidanni (USA) *Saeed Bin Suroor* 82
2 b/br c Private Terms (USA) - Carley's Birthday (USA)
4⁸ᵍᶠ 1⁸ᵍ 8⁸ˢ **1-0-3 £5,681**

Maids Causeway (Ire) *B W Hills* 111
2 ch f Giant's Causeway - Vallee Des Reves (USA)
2⁶ᵍᶠ 1⁷ᵍ 2⁷ᵍᶠ 1⁷ᵍᶠ 3⁸ᵍ 2⁸ᵍᶠ 1⁷ˢ **3-4-7**
£129,225

Maidstone Midas (Ire) *W S Kittow* 53 a60
3 b c Nashwan (USA) - Be Mine
15¹⁰ᵍ 4¹¹ˢ 5¹⁰ˢᵈ 6¹¹ᵍᶠ **0-0-4 £3,000**

Majestic Desert *M R Channon* 113
3 b f Fraam - Calcutta Queen
1⁷ᵍ 9⁸ᵍ 7⁸ᵍᶠ 2⁸ᶠ 2⁷ᵍʸ 2⁸ᵍ 4⁸ˢ 4⁸ᵍ 2⁸ᵍ
1-4-9 £223,303

Majestic Missile (Ire) *W J Haggas* 111
3 b c Royal Applause - Tshusick
5⁵ᵍᶠ 8⁵ᵍᶠ 6⁵ᵍ **0-0-3 £4,250**

Majestic Movement (USA) *J H M Gosden* 70
2 ch c Diesis - Zarara (USA)
5⁸ᵍˢ 10⁷ˢ 3¹⁰ᵍᶠ 5⁸ˢ **0-1-4 £860**

Majestic Star *M J Ryan*
3 b f Fraam - Fun While It Lasts
7¹⁰ʰʸ **0-0-1**

Majestic Vision *W R Swinburn* 73
3 ch g Desert King (Ire) - Triste Oeil (USA)
9¹⁰ᵍˢ 6¹⁴ᵍ 2¹⁴ᵍᶠ 5¹⁶ᵍ 3¹⁴ᵍˢ 10¹⁴ᵍˢ **0-2-6**
£1,935

Majestical (Ire) *W R Muir* 60 a54
2 b g Fayruz - Haraabah (USA)
3⁵ˢᵈ 4⁵ᵍᶠ 12⁵ᵍᶠ 10⁵ᵍ 4⁶ᶠ 2⁵ᵍᶠ 4⁶ᵍ 7⁵ᵍᶠ
6⁵ᵍˢ **0-1-9 £1,894**

Majhool *I W McInnes* 54 a59
5 b g Mark Of Esteem (Ire) - Be Peace (USA)
8⁵ˢᵈ 4⁷ˢᵈ 5⁷ˢᵈ 1⁷ᵍᶠ 11⁷ᵍᶠ 18⁷ᵍᶠ **1-0-6**
£2,606

Majik *D J S Ffrench Davis* 63 a75
5 ch g Pivotal - Revoke (USA)
7⁶ˢᵈ 3⁷ˢᵈ 4⁷ˢᵈ 15⁶ˢ 4⁶ᵍˢ 10⁶ˢ 4⁷ˢ 5⁶ᵍ
3⁶ˢ **0-0-9 £2,281**

Majlis (Ire) *B J Llewellyn* 57 a75
7 b g Caerleon (USA) - Ploy
9¹²ˢᵈ 12¹²ˢᵈ 5¹³ˢᵈ 9¹⁴ᵍᶠ 10¹²ᵍᶠ **0-0-5**
£533

Major Blade (Ger) *Mrs H Dalton* 44
6 b g Dashing Blade - Misniniski
14¹⁰ᵍ 15¹⁰ᵍᶠ 10¹⁰ᵍᶠ **0-0-3**

Major Effort (USA) *Sir Michael Stoute* 81
3 b c Rahy (USA) - Tethkar
4⁸ᵍᶠ 12⁸ᵍˢ **0-0-2 £429**

Mahmoom *M R Channon*
2 b c Josr Algarhoud (Ire) - Jamrat Samya (Ire)
10⁸ᵍ 8⁸ˢ 11⁸ˢᵈ **0-0-3**

Major Faux Pas (Ire) *J A Osborne*   a84
2 b g Barathea (Ire) - Edwina (Ire)
1⁷ˢᵈ **1-0-1 £3,101**

Major Project (Ire) *P C Haslam*
3 ch g General Monash (USA) - Mini Project (Ire)
9⁸ˢᵈ 12⁸ᵍᶠ **0-0-2**

Majorca *J H M Gosden*   93
3 b c Green Desert (USA) - Majmu (USA)
3⁶ᵍ 2⁶ᵍᶠ 4⁶ᵍᶠ 1⁷ᶠ 1⁸ˢ 15⁸ᵍˢ **2-2-6**
£20,447

Majors Cast (Ire) *J Noseda*   97 a102
3 b c Victory Note (USA) - Ziffany
3⁷ᵍᶠ 1⁷ᵍ 3⁷ˢ 1⁷ˢᵈ 3⁷ᵍᶠ **2-2-5 £16,025**

Makarim (Ire) *M R Bosley*   46 a64
8 ch g Generous (Ire) - Emmaline (USA)
10¹³ˢᵈ 11¹⁶ˢᵈ 3¹⁶ˢʷ 5¹⁶ˢʷ 8¹³ˢᵈ 4¹⁵ᵍᶠ
14¹⁷ᵍ 5¹⁴ᵍᶠ **0-1-8 £775**

Make It Happen Now *S C Burrough*   31 a6
2 b/br f Octagonal (NZ) - Whittle Woods Girl
7⁵ˢ 4⁵ᵍᶠ 17⁵ᵍᶠ 9⁶ᵍᶠ 13⁵ˢᵈ 11⁸ᶠ **0-0-6**
£315

Make It Snappy *P W Harris*   58 a60
2 b f Mujadil (USA) - Snap Crackle Pop (Ire)
8⁷ˢ 17⁷ᵍ 3⁷ˢᵈ **0-1-3 £810**

Make My Hay *J Gallagher*   55 a49
5 b g Bluegrass Prince (Ire) - Shashi (Ire)
3¹¹ˢᵈ 6¹³ˢᵈ 1¹²ʰʸ 2¹²ᵍᶠ 5¹²ᵍᶠ 5¹³ᵍ 5¹²ᵍ
6¹²ᵍ 2¹²ᵍ 4¹²ˢ **1-2-10 £3,455**

Make Us Flush *A Berry*   73 a22
2 b f Mind Games - Pearls
4⁵ˢ 7⁶ᵍᶠ 4⁶ᵍᶠ 9⁶ᵍᶠ 1⁶ᵍ 1⁵ˢ 7⁶ᵍᶠ 2⁵ᵍ 1⁶ʰʸ
7⁶ᵍˢ 12⁶ˢ 6⁶ʰʸ 11⁶ˢᵈ **3-1-13 £12,158**

Makepeace (Ire) *M R Channon*   62
2 b c Xaar - Marillette (USA)
11⁶ᵍᶠ 4⁷ᵍ 7⁷ˢ 18⁷ᵍᶠ **0-0-4 £321**

Makes Perfect (Ire) *S Kirk*   48
2 b f Orpen (USA) - Practice (USA)
8⁶ᵍᶠ 6⁶ᶠ **0-0-2**

Makfool (Fr) *M R Channon*   103 a76
3 b c Spectrum (Ire) - Abeyr
12⁷ˢᵈ 3⁸ᵍ 4⁷ᵍˢ 9⁸ᵍˢ 2⁸ᵍᶠ 1⁷ᵍ 21⁸ᶠ 8⁷ᵍˢ
12⁷ᵍᶠ **1-1-9 £45,328**

Makhlab (USA) *B W Hills*   108
4 b c Dixieland Band (USA) - Avasand (USA)
5⁸ᵍ 5⁷ᵍˢ 4⁷ᵍ 2⁷ᵍᶠ 2⁷ᵍ 13⁷ᵍ **0-2-6**
£13,547

Maksad (Ire) *J E Hammond*   87
4 b c Machiavellian (USA) - Balaabel (USA)
2⁸ˢ 15⁷ᵍᶠ 3⁶ᵍˢ 2⁸ˢᵈ **0-2-4 £9,824**

Maktavish *I Semple*   93 a89
5 b g Makbul - La Belle Vie
1¹ˢᵈ 1⁵ᵍ 2⁵ᵍˢ 1⁵ᵍˢ 3⁵ᵍˢ 14⁵ᵍᶠ 14⁵ᵍᶠ 8⁵ᵍ
4⁵ᵍ 6⁵ᵍ 12⁵ᵍᶠ 9⁵ᵍ 14⁵ˢ **3-2-13 £31,747**

Maktu *P F I Cole*   70
2 ch g Bien Bien (USA) - Shalateeno
5⁸ᵍᶠ 3⁸ˢ 4⁸ᵍᶠ **0-1-3 £545**

Maktub (Ity) *M A Jarvis*   118
5 b h Love The Groom (USA) - Carmen The Best (Ire)
8¹⁶ˢ 6¹⁴ᵍˢ 2¹²ᵍ 11¹⁰ᵍˢ 2¹²ᵍ 2¹²ᶠ 7¹²ʸ
0-3-7 £134,242

Makulu (Ire) *C J Mann*   75
4 b g Alzao (USA) - Karinski (USA)
15¹²ᵍˢ 18¹⁶ᵍ 2¹⁰ᵍᶠ 7¹⁰ᵍ **0-1-4 £1,872**

Malaah (Ire) *Julian Poulton*   a38
8 gr g Pips Pride - Lingdale Lass

8⁸ˢᵈ 14⁶ˢᵈ 4⁷ˢᵈ 8⁶ˢᵈ 10⁷ˢᵈ **0-0-5**

Malahide Express (Ire) *E J Alston*   63 a71
4 gr g Compton Place - Gracious Gretclo
4⁵ˢᵈ 5⁶ˢᵈ 9⁵ᵍˢ 2⁵ˢˢ 8⁷ᵍᶠ 5⁵ʰʸ 5⁵ᵍ 4⁵ᵍᶠ
15⁷ᵍᶠ 9⁵ᵍᶠ 9⁵ᵍ 3⁵ᵍᶠ 13⁵ˢᵈ **1-2-13 £7,782**

Malaika *R Hollinshead*   64
2 b f Polar Prince (Ire) - Gold Belt (Ire)
5⁵ᵍˢ 4⁵ᵍᶠ 3⁵ˢ **0-1-3 £1,424**

Malak Al Moulouk (USA) *J M P Eustace*   71
4 ch g King Of Kings (Ire) - Honor To Her (USA)
4¹⁰ᵍ 2¹⁰ᵍᶠ 11¹²ᵍˢ 11⁸ᵍ **0-1-4 £1,377**

Malapropism *M R Channon*   98 a77
4 ch g Compton Place - Mrs Malaprop
6⁵ᵍᶠ 15⁵ᵍᶠ 12⁶ᵍ 7⁵ᵍˢ 6⁵ᵍ 12⁵ᵍᶠ 4⁵ᵍᶠ 9⁵ᵍ
6⁵ᵍ 6⁵ᵍˢ 15⁷ᵍᶠ 7⁵ᵍ 6⁵ᵍ 1⁵ᵍˢ 15⁵ˢ 10⁵ˢ 10⁶ˢᵈ
3-0-17 £34,327

Malarkey *Mrs Stef Liddiard*   83 a35
7 b g Mukaddamah (USA) - Malwiya (USA)
5¹²ˢᵈ 1¹⁶ᵍ 2¹⁵ˢ 1¹⁶ᵍ 5¹⁶ᵍᶠ 3¹⁸ᵍ 25²⁰ᵍᶠ
2-2-7 £18,244

Malcheek (Ire) *T D Easterby*   68
2 br c Lend A Hand - Russland (Ger)
4⁶ᵍᶠ **0-0-1 £444**

Malibu (Ire) *S Dow*   83
3 b g Second Empire (Ire) - Tootle
4⁹ᵍˢ 6¹⁰ᵍ 5¹⁰ᵍᶠ 11¹⁰ᵍˢ 18ᵍᶠ 5⁹ᵍᶠ 7⁹ᵍˢ
12⁷ᵍ 15⁸ᵍᶠ **1-0-9 £6,914**

Malinsa Blue (Ire) *J A Glover*   83
2 b f Desert Style (Ire) - Talina's Law (Ire)
6⁶ᵍˢ 2⁶ᵍᶠ 2⁶ᵍ 6⁶ᵍᶠ 2⁷ᶠ 1⁷ᶠ 12⁷ᵍ **1-3-7**
£12,747

Mallard (Ire) *J G Given*   72 a82
6 b g Tagula (Ire) - Frill
3⁸ᵍ 12⁷ᵍ 2⁸ˢᵈ 6⁸ᵍ 8⁸ᵍ 7⁷ᵍˢ 11⁷ˢᵈ 4⁷ˢᵈ
3⁷ˢᵈ **0-3-9 £2,746**

Mallia *T D Barron*   41 a53
11 b g Statoblest - Pronetta (USA)
4⁶ˢ 1⁶ˢᵈ 6⁷ˢᵈ 3⁶ˢᵈ 2⁶ˢᵈ 4⁶ˢᵈ 8⁶ᵍ 12⁶ᵍˢ
1-2-8 £3,923

Malmand (USA) *R Brotherton*   a41
5 ch g Distant View (USA) - Bidski (USA)
8⁹ˢᵈ 19ˢᵈ 10¹⁰ˢᵈ 4⁹ˢˢ 7⁹ˢʷ **1-0-5 £1,473**

Maluti *R Guest*   61 a51
3 ch g Piccolo - Persian Blue
8⁵ᵍ 6⁶ᵍᶠ 3⁶ᶠ 1⁵ᶠ 4⁵ˢ 2⁵ᵍᶠ VOI⁵ᵍᶠ 7⁵ᵍᶠ
5⁵ˢᵈ **1-2-9 £4,956**

Malvern Light *W J Haggas*   101
3 b f Zieten (USA) - Michelle Hicks
4⁷ᵍ 8⁷ˢ 8⁶ᵍ 3⁷ᵍᶠ **0-1-4 £4,791**

Mambazo *S C Williams*   52 a74
2 b c Dansili - Kalindi
8⁶ᵍ 17⁶ᵍˢ 12⁷ᵍ 9⁸ᵍᶠ 2⁶ˢᵈ **0-1-5 £956**

Mambina (USA) *M R Channon*   74 a56
3 ch f Kingmambo (USA) - Sonata
8⁸ˢᵈ 4¹¹ᵍˢ 4¹⁰ʰʸ 5¹²ˢ 8¹⁰ᶠ 4¹⁰ᵍᶠ 8¹¹ᵍ 2¹⁰ᵍˢ
2¹¹ˢ 3¹⁰ᵍ 2¹⁰ᵍˢ 4¹⁰ᶠ 1¹⁰ᵍ 11¹⁰ᵍ 6¹⁰ᵍ 6¹⁰ˢ 3¹⁰ʰʸ
2-5-17 £16,121

Mambo's Melody *P W Chapple-Hyam*   32
2 b f Kingmambo (USA) - Key Academy
14⁷ᵍ **0-0-1**

Mamcazma *D Morris*   93 a91
6 gr g Terimon - Merryhill Maid (Ire)
7¹²ᵍᶠ 12¹⁶ˢ 4¹⁴ᵍ 11¹⁴ᵍ 11¹⁶ᵍᶠ 11¹⁵ˢ
10¹⁴ᵍˢ 2¹⁶ᵍᶠ 11¹⁶ˢ 1¹⁷ˢᵈ **1-1-10 £12,489**

Mamool (Ire) *Saeed Bin Suroor*   119

5 b h In The Wings - Genovefa (USA)
3¹⁰ʰᵒ 1¹²ᵍᶠ 15¹²ᵍ 7¹⁶ᵍˢ **1-0-4 £76,526**

Mamore Gap (Ire) *R Hannon*   71 a69
6 b h General Monash (USA) - Ravensdale Rose (Ire)
8⁸ˢᵈ 13¹⁰ˢᵈ 9¹⁰ᵍ 5⁸ᵍ 8¹⁰ᵍᶠ 5¹⁰ᵍˢ 5⁸ˢ
11⁸ᵍᶠ **0-0-8**

Man At Arms (Ire) *R Hannon*   85
3 b c Daggers Drawn (USA) - Punta Gorda (Ire)
4¹⁰ᵍᶠ 1¹²ᶠ 4¹²ᵍᶠ 8¹²ᵍ 12¹²ᵍˢ 4¹⁴ᵍᶠ 6¹⁴ᵍᶠ
10¹⁴ᵍᶠ 9¹²ᵍ 7¹⁴ᵍ **1-0-10 £4,976**

Man Crazy (Ire) *C A Dwyer*   58 a59
3 b f Foxhound (USA) - Schonbein (Ire)
8⁶ˢᵈ 6⁷ˢᵈ 17⁶ᵍ 14⁷ᵍ 7⁶ᵍ 4⁶ᵍ 10⁶ᵍ 7⁶ᵍᶠ
4⁵ᵍ 9⁷ᵍ 11⁶ˢ 4⁶ˢ **0-1-12 £705**

Man Of Letters (UAE) *G G Margarson*   82
3 b c Belong To Me (USA) - Personal Business (USA)
4⁸ᵍ 3⁸ˢ 2⁷ᵍˢ 2⁷ᵍ 1⁷ᵍ 2¹⁰ᵍᶠ 5¹⁰ᵍˢ 3⁸ᵍˢ
9¹⁰ᵍ **1-5-9 £14,142**

Man The Gate *P D Cundell*   65
5 b g Elmaamul (USA) - Girl At The Gate
2¹²ᵍˢ 5¹⁰ᵍˢ 11¹⁴ˢ 3¹²ᵍᶠ 6¹²ᵍᶠ 2¹¹ᵍᶠ 1¹²ᵍˢ
5¹²ᵍ 8¹²ᵍˢ 8¹¹ᵍ 7¹²ᵍ **1-3-11 £6,539**

Mana D'Argent (Ire) *M Johnston*   94
7 b g Ela-Mana-Mou - Petite-D-Argent
11¹⁶ᵍˢ 5¹⁹ᵍˢ 11¹⁴ᵍˢ 18²⁰ᵍᶠ 11¹⁶ᵍ 1¹⁶ᵍᶠ
5²¹ᵍ 7¹⁶ᵍᶠ 30¹⁸ˢ 5¹⁷ˢ **1-0-10 £13,532**

Manaar (Ire) *J Noseda*   91
4 b g Titus Livius (Fr) - Zurarah
8⁷ᵍˢ 5⁷ᵍᶠ 7⁷ᶠ 2⁷ᵍ BD⁷ᵍᶠ 2⁷ᵍ 18⁷ᵍ **0-2-7**
£7,568

Manashin *R P Elliott*
4 b f Whittingham (Ire) - Montagne
7⁸ˢᵈ 4¹²ˢʷ **0-0-2**

Mandahar (Ire) *A W Carroll*   9 a51
5 b g Bluebird (USA) - Madiriya
9⁸ˢᵈ 15⁷ˢᵈ 7⁶ˢ 16⁷ᵍˢ 12¹⁰ˢᵈ 10¹¹ˢᵈ **0-0-6**

Mandarin Spirit (Ire) *G C H Chung*   71 a71
4 b g Primo Dominie - Lithe Spirit (Ire)
11⁶ᵍᶠ 5⁷ᶠ 5⁷ᵍᶠ 10⁶ᵍˢ 5⁷ᵍᶠ 1⁷ᵍᶠ 4⁶ˢᵈ 3⁷ˢ
1-1-8 £6,820

Mandatum *L M Cumani*   82
3 b g Mtoto - Reamur
2¹²ᵍᶠ 2¹⁰ᵍᶠ 1¹²ᵍᶠ 4¹⁵ˢ **1-1-4 £9,913**

Mandinka *J F Coupland*   32
4 b g Distinctly North (USA) - Primo Panache
13⁸ᵍ 4¹⁰ᵍˢ 8¹¹ᵍᶠ 10¹⁰ᶠ **0-1-4**

Mandobi (Ire) *E F Vaughan*   108
3 ch c Mark Of Esteem (Ire) - Miss Queen (USA)
4⁶ᵍ 2⁷ᵍ 1⁸ᶠ 2⁸ᵍᶠ **1-2-4 £46,562**

Mandoob *B R Johnson*   56 a70
7 b g Zafonic (USA) - Thaidah (Can)
4¹²ˢᵈ 1¹²ˢˢ 1¹²ˢˢ 10¹²ˢʷ 12¹⁴ˢ 2¹²ˢᵈ
12¹²ᵍᶠ 4¹²ˢᵈ 4¹²ˢᵈ 6¹⁶ˢᵈ **2-1-10 £6,665**

Mandy's Collection *A G Newcombe*   a20
5 ch m Forzando - Instinction
15⁵ˢᵈ UR⁶ˢᵈ 5⁶ˢᵈ 9⁵ˢᵈ **0-0-4**

Maneki Neko (Ire) *M H Tompkins*   73
2 b c Rudimentary (USA) - Ardbess
4⁶ᵍ 2⁶ᵍᶠ 2⁸ᵍᶠ 15⁷ᵍˢ **0-2-4 £2,214**

Mango Mischief (Ire) *J L Dunlop*   97
3 ch f Desert King (Ire) - Eurolink Mischief
1¹⁰ᵍᶠ 2¹⁰ᵍᶠ 4¹⁰ᵍᶠ 2¹⁰ᵍ 10¹⁰ᵍᶠ 1¹⁰ˢ **2-2-6**
£39,924

Mangrove Cay (Ire) *J Hetherton*   63 a66

2 b c Danetime (Ire) - Art Duo
8⁷ᵍ 4⁷ᵍ 5⁶ˢᵈ 5⁶ˢᵈ **0-0-4 £313**

Mangus *K O Cunningham-Brown*   39 a42
10 b g Mac's Imp (USA) - Holly Bird
3⁵ˢᵈ 7⁵ˢᵈ 6⁵ˢʷ 8⁵ˢˢ 7⁵ˢᵈ 5⁵ᵍ **0-1-6 £234**

Manhattan Jack *G A Swinbank*   71
3 ch g Forzando - Manhattan Diamond
8⁹ᵍ 5¹⁰ᵍᶠ 2¹¹ᵍᶠ 9¹¹ˢ **0-1-4 £1,255**

Maniatis *Andrew Reid*   75 a76
7 b g Slip Anchor - Tamassos
6¹²ˢˢ 1¹²ˢᵈ 10¹²ᵍˢ 2¹¹ˢᵈ 1¹²ˢᵈ 3¹⁰ᵍ
3-1-7 £10,702

Manic *Andrew Reid*   58 a66
2 br f Polar Falcon (USA) - Gentle Irony
8⁵ᵍᶠ 1⁶ˢᵈ 3⁶ʰʸ **1-1-4 £4,773**

Manikato (USA) *K G Wingrove*   35 a23
10 b g Clever Trick (USA) - Pasampsi (USA)
7⁷ˢᵈ 7⁹ˢᵈ 9⁸ˢʷ 11¹¹ᶠ 9¹⁰ᵍᶠ **0-0-5**

Mannora *P Howling*   58 a34
4 b f Prince Sabo - Miss Bussell
4⁶ᵍᶠ 12⁶ᶠ 13⁶ᵍ 9⁶ᵍᶠ 11⁶ᵍ 9⁵ˢᵈ **0-1-6**

Manny *Miss A Stokell*
4 b g Emarati (USA) - Needwood Nymph
8¹²ˢᵈ 12¹⁴ˢ 5⁹ˢᵈ **0-0-3**

Mannyman (Ire) *W Jarvis*   53
3 b/br f Dr Devious (Ire) - Lithe Spirit (Ire)
8⁷ᵍˢ 7⁷ᵍ 13⁷ˢᵈ **0-0-3**

Manorshield Minx *S Kirk*   53
2 b f Pursuit Of Love - Polly's Teahouse
9⁶ᵍᶠ 9⁸ᵍᶠ 10⁷ˢ 12⁸ᵍᶠ **0-0-4**

Manorson (Ire) *M A Magnusson*   96
5 ch g Desert King (Ire) - Familiar (USA)
10¹²ᵍ 11¹²ᵍ 2¹²ᵍ 4¹²ˢ **0-2-4 £5,746**

Manrique (USA) *M Johnston*   15
2 ch c Rahy (USA) - Dance Trick (USA)
20⁶ᵍˢ **0-0-1**

Mansfield Park *Saeed Bin Suroor*   105
3 b f Green Desert (USA) - Park Appeal
3⁸ᵍᶠ 3⁸ᵍᶠ 1⁸ᵍ **1-2-3 £11,045**

Mansiya *C E Brittain*   63
2 ch f Vettori (Ire) - Bay Shade (USA)
2⁷ᵍᶠ 6⁸ᵍᶠ **0-1-2 £1,006**

Mantel Mini *B A Pearce*   9 a25
5 b m Reprimand - Foretell
9⁸ˢᵈ 6¹⁰ᵍˢ 12⁸ˢᵈ 10⁶ᵍᶠ **0-0-4 £231**

Mantilla *Ian Williams*   a36
7 b m Son Pardo - Well Tried (Ire)
7¹³ˢᵈ **0-0-1**

Mantles Pride *Dr P Pritchard*
9 br g Petong - State Romance
9⁸ᵍˢ **0-0-1**

Mantles Prince *A G Juckes*
10 ch g Emarati (USA) - Miami Mouse
6¹⁶ˢʷ **0-0-1**

Many Thanks *B S Rothwell*   a19
4 b f Octagonal (NZ) - Answered Prayer
5¹²ˢˢ 6¹²ˢᵈ **0-0-2**

Manyana (Ire) *M P Tregoning*   108
3 b c Alzao (USA) - Sometime (Ire)
5¹⁰ᵍ 1¹¹ᵍ 11¹²ᵍˢ 8¹²ᵍ **1-0-4 £17,765**

Maple Syrple (Can) *Saeed Bin Suroor*   86 a90
3 br f American Chance (USA) - Sweet And Lowdown (USA)
8⁷ᵍᶠ 4⁶ʰ **0-0-2**

Maraahel (Ire) *Sir Michael Stoute*   119

3 b c Alzao (USA) - Nasanice (Ire)
2^{11g} 2^{12gf} 1^{12g} 4^{15gf} **1-2-4 £66,375**

Maraakeb (Fr) *J H M Gosden*　　　　　91
3 br c Linamix (Fr) - Raheefa (USA)
6^{10g} 1^{10g} **1-0-2 £5,564**

Marabar *D W Chapman*　　　　　64 a58
6 b m Sri Pekan (USA) - Erbaya (Ire)
11^{7sd} 6^{7sd} 5^{7sd} 7^{6sd} 10^{5ss} 1^{6gs} 7^{7gs}
17^{5hy} 3^{5hy} 1^{7sd} 2^{6sd} 2^{7sd} 6^{7sd} 6^{8f} 11^{6gf} 4^{5gs}
14^{6g} 8^{7sd} **2-3-18 £8,316**

Marajuana *A M Balding*　　　　　78
2 b f Robellino (USA) - Mara River
1^{5gf} **1-0-1 £4,316**

Marakash (Ire) *V Thompson*　　　　　a53
5 b g Ashkalani (Ire) - Marilaya (Ire)
2^{8sd} 8^{8sd} 6^{8sd} **0-1-3 £732**

Maraud *L R James*　　　　　a37
10 ch g Midyan (USA) - Peak Squaw (USA)
5^{16sd} 3^{16sd} **0-0-2 £194**

Maravedi (Ire) *W M Brisbourne*　　　　　a29
4 ch f Hector Protector (USA) - Manuetti (Ire)
12^{9sd} 8^{8sd} 8^{14sd} 9^{13s} **0-0-4**

Marble Arch *H Morrison*　　　　　30
8 b g Rock Hopper - Mayfair Minx
10^{16gs} **0-0-1**

Marburyanna *M Mullineaux*
4 ch f Classic Cliche (Ire) - Lake Mistassiu
17^{8hy} 11^{7sd} **0-0-2**

Marbush (Ire) *M A Jarvis*　　　　　89
3 ro c Linamix (Fr) - Fig Tree Drive (USA)
8^{8g} 2^{9g} 1^{8gf} 5^{8g} 3^{10gs} **1-3-5 £8,137**

Marbye (Ire) *B Grizzetti*　　　　　112
4 b f Marju (Ire) - Hambye
1^{9g} 4^{8hy} 1^{8gf} 5^{8gf} 1^{8g} 6^{8g} 13^{10gs} **3-0-7 £149,727**

Marcela Zabala *J G Given*　　　　　55 a10
2 b f Zaha (Can) - Bay Bianca (Ire)
7^{5sd} 1^{5gf} 8^{6sd} 1^{6s} 10^{6gs} 21^{6s} **2-0-6 £5,474**

Marchetta *P W Harris*　　　　　72
2 b f Mujadil (USA) - My Lewicia (Ire)
6^{7g} 5^{7g} 3^{7gs} **0-1-3 £1,006**

Marching Song *R Hannon*　　　　　93
2 b c Royal Applause - Marl
5^{5g} 3^{5gf} 2^{5gf} 4^{7gs} 2^{6gf} 1^{6gf} 2^{6gs} 5^{6gs}
1-4-8 £13,676

Marcus Eile (Ire) *K R Burke*　　　　　22 a70
3 b g Daggers Drawn (USA) - Sherannda (USA)
4^{10sd} 4^{8sd} 8^{8ss} 19^{7gs} **0-0-4 £641**

Mardonicdeclare *P S Felgate*
3 b g Perpendicular - Daisy Girl
9^{8gf} **0-0-1**

Maren (USA) *E F Vaughan*　　　　　86
3 b g Gulch (USA) - Fatina
7^{7g} 18^{8gf} 12^{9g} **0-0-3**

Marengo *M J Polglase*　　　　　31 a28
10 b g Never So Bold - Born To Dance
11^{12sd} 7^{14sd} 6^{11sd} 7^{11ss} 7^{9sw} 6^{10hy} 4^{8g}
7^{8sd} 13^{10g} 9^{8sd} 11^{6g} **0-0-11**

Margalita (Ire) *P Mitchell*　　　　　65 a73
4 b f Sesaro (USA) - Mamma Luigi (Ire)
6^{6sd} 17^{6gs} 20^{8gf} 6^{5g} 10^{6gf} 9^{7gf} 16^{5gf}
11^{5g} 10^{7sd} 8^{6sd} **0-0-10**

Margaret's Dream (Ire) *Ms Caroline Hutchinson* 56
3 b f Muhtarram (USA) - Acidanthera

16^{10gf} 13^{9gy} 7^{7gf} 15^{8f} 4^{5s} 3^{6s} **0-2-6 £737**

Margarets Wish *T Wall*　　　　　43 a37
4 gr f Cloudings (Ire) - Gentle Gain
11^{8sd} 4^{10sd} 7^{10sd} 12^{8sw} 1^{10gs} 8^{10hy} 10^{11gs}
10^{10gf} 15^{8g} 6^{10gf} 8^{10gs} **1-0-11 £1,477**

Margery Daw (Ire) *P S McEntee*　　　　　55 a59
4 b f Sri Pekan (USA) - Suyayeb (USA)
5^{8sd} 8^{10gs} 8^{10sd} 11^{12gf} 6^{12gf} 3^{12f} 16^{12gf}
7^{10f} 5^{8f} 19^{10s} 10^{10gf} 8^{10sd} 15^{10g} **0-0-13 £412**

Margold (Ire) *R Hollinshead*　　　　　54 a1
4 ch f Goldmark (USA) - Arcevia (Ire)
7^{8sd} 11^{14sd} 3^{12gf} 18^{12gf} 17^{12gf} **0-1-5 £468**

Marhaba Million (Ire) *M R Channon*　　　　　46
2 gr c Linamix (Fr) - Modelliste
8^{8gs} **0-0-1**

Marhoon (USA) *E F Vaughan*　　　　　73 a85
2 ch c Lion Cavern (USA) - United Kingdom (USA)
4^{6s} 2^{7s} 18^{sd} **1-1-3 £6,164**

Maria Bonita (Ire) *Mrs Stef Liddiard*　　　　　71 a62
3 b f Octagonal (NZ) - Nightitude
4^{10gs} 12^{10gf} 4^{10f} 8^{10gf} 4^{10sd} 3^{11g} 3^{11gs}
3^{12sd} **0-3-8 £2,532**

Maria Delfina (Ire) *J H M Gosden*　　　　　a67
2 ch f Giant's Causeway (USA) - Photographie (USA)
3^{8sd} **0-1-1 £664**

Maria Maria (Ire) *Mrs N Macauley*　　　　　47
3 ch f Among Men (USA) - Yiayia's Girl
11^{9sd} 7^{8sd} 4^{8s} 10^{11f} 11^{8sd} **0-0-5 £383**

Marian's Gift *M W Easterby*　　　　　12
2 ch f Bold Edge - Thimbalina
11^{5gf} **0-0-1**

Marianis *J G Portman*　　　　　56
2 b f Lujain (USA) - Without Warning (Ire)
4^{6gf} 10^{6gf} 5^{7gs} **0-0-3 £369**

Marians Maid (Ire) *J S Moore*　　　　　47
2 b f Monashee Mountain (USA) - Speedy Action
13^{6gf} 6^{6gf} 13^{7gf} **0-0-3**

Marias Magic *M Johnston*　　　　　73
3 b f Mtoto - Majoune (Fr)
6^{7gf} 1^{10gs} 9^{10s} **1-0-3 £3,688**

Mariday *Lady Herries*　　　　　30 a55
3 br g Trifolio - Classic Hand
6^{10gf} 9^{13sd} 6^{12s} **0-0-3**

Marinaite *S R Bowring*　　　　　77 a79
3 b f Komaite (USA) - Marina's Song
2^{8sd} 1^{7sd} 5^{7gs} 2^{6g} 2^{6ss} 14^{5g} 3^{8gf} 12^{7gf}
3^{8g} 14^{7s} 13^{6s} **1-5-11 £8,760**

Marine City (Jpn) *M A Jarvis*　　　　　77
3 b f Carnegie (Ire) - Marienbad (Fr)
1^{12s} 6^{12gs} 6^{11gf} 3^{12s} 4^{16g} 3^{16gf} 5^{16s} **1-0-7 £6,697**

Marinnette (Ire) *M P Sunderland*　　　　　95
3 ch f Be My Guest (USA) - Al Cairo (Fr)
5^{9hy} 7^{10gf} 4^{10g} 5^{12gf} 1^{12hy} 6^{12gy} 14^{10s}
1-1-7 £13,796

Marino Mou (Ire) *Miss D Mountain*　　　　　46
4 b c Darshaan - Lia's Dance
7^{9ss} 7^{9sd} 6^{12sd} 3^{15s} 10^{16g} 9^{16gf} **0-1-6 £540**

Marita *J G Given*　　　　　a33
3 ch f Dancing Spree (USA) - Maria Cappuccini
5^{8sd} 7^{8sd} **0-0-2**

Maritima *Sir Michael Stoute*   68
2 b f Darshaan - Armeria (USA)
UR⁷ᵍ **0-0-1**

Maritime Blues *J G Given*   69 a54
4 b g Fleetwood (Ire) - Dixie D'Oats
11¹⁰ᵍ 7¹⁰ᵍˢ 7¹⁰ᵍˢ 1¹²ᵍᶠ 6¹²ᶠ 3¹²ᵍˢ
12¹²ᵍᶠ 11¹⁰ᵍᶠ 1¹⁰ˢ 7¹⁰ᵍˢ 5¹⁰ᵍ 8¹¹ˢ 8¹²ˢᵈ 2¹⁰ˢ
2-2-15 £9,730

Mark Your Card *T D Easterby*   42
2 ch f Mark Of Esteem (Ire) - Charollas
8⁶ˢ 13⁷ᵍˢ 12⁸ᵍ 11⁶ᵍ **0-0-4**

Mark Your Way *P R Chamings*   33
4 b g Spectrum (Ire) - Titania's Way
11¹⁰ᵍᶠ 13¹⁰ˢ 10¹¹ᵍᶠ **0-0-3**

Marker *G B Balding*   89
4 ch g Pivotal - Palace Street (USA)
6⁷ˢ 8⁶ᵍˢ 13⁶ᵍ 4⁷ˢ 9⁶ᵍᶠ 4⁷ᵍ 10⁷ᵍᶠ 10⁷ᵍ
4⁶ʰʸ 1⁶ˢ 10⁶ˢ **1-0-11 £21,524**

Market Avenue *R A Fahey*   69 a67
5 b m Factual (USA) - The Lady Vanishes
6¹⁰ᶠ 7¹⁰ᵍᶠ 5⁹ᵍ 7⁸ᵍᶠ 5⁹ᵍᶠ 1¹⁰ᵍ 11¹⁰ᵍ 9¹⁰ᵍᶠ
6¹⁰ᵍ 6⁹ˢᵈ **1-0-10 £3,836**

Market Leader *Mrs A J Perrett*   69
3 b f Marju (Ire) - I Will Lead (USA)
3¹²ᵍᶠ 3¹⁴ᵍˢ 3¹²ᵍᶠ 3¹⁴ᵍˢ **0-1-4 £2,597**

Market Trend *M Johnston*   81
2 b f Selkirk (USA) - Equity Princess
2⁶ᵍ 1⁷ˢ 7⁷ᵍ 10⁸ˢ **1-1-4 £7,200**

Marko Jadeo (Ire) *K A Morgan*   96
6 b g Eagle Eyed (USA) - Fleeting Quest
3⁶ᵍᶠ 7⁵ᵍᶠ 14⁶ᵍᶠ 3⁶ᵍʸ 3⁶ᵍᶠ 1⁷ˢᵈ 10⁸ᵍ **1-3-7 £8,306**

Marksgold (Ire) *P F I Cole*   57 a58
3 b g Goldmark (USA) - Lady Of Shalott
3⁷ᵍˢ 6⁷ˢᵈ 6⁶ˢ 10⁷ᵍ 5¹²ˢᵈ 9⁷ᵍ **0-1-6 £570**

Marlenes Girl (Ire) *A Berry*   48
2 b f Foxhound (USA) - Premier Place (USA)
15⁵ᵍˢ 6⁵ᵍ 16⁵ᵍˢ **0-0-3**

Marmaduke (Ire) *M Pitman*   a72
8 ch g Perugino (USA) - Sympathy
2¹⁶ˢᵈ 5¹⁶ˢᵈ 4¹²ˢᵈ **0-1-3 £834**

Marne (Ire) *J M P Eustace*
2 b g Mtoto - Perfect Poppy
4⁵ˢˢ **0-0-1**

Marnie *J Akehurst*   59 a58
7 ch m First Trump - Miss Aboyne
9⁸ˢᵈ 1⁸ˢᵈ 3⁸ˢᵈ 9⁸ᵍ 2⁸ᶠ 2⁸ᶠ 5⁸ᶠ 5⁸ᵍ 5⁹ᵍᶠ
8⁸ᵍᶠ 6⁸ᵍ **1-3-11 £6,292**

Maromito (Ire) *R Bastiman*   68 a56
7 b g Up And At 'Em - Amtico
11⁵ˢᵈ 10⁶ˢˢ 3⁷ˢˢ 1⁵ˢᶠ 1⁵ˢᵈ 10⁵ᵍᶠ 9⁵ˢᵈ
3⁵ᵍᶠ 8⁵ᵍᶠ 1⁵ᵍ 4⁵ᵍᶠ 9⁵ᵍ **3-1-12 £9,854**

Maron *F Jordan*   a36
7 b g Puissance - Will Be Bold
5⁶ˢᵈ 2⁵ˢʷ 4⁶ˢᵈ **0-1-3 £391**

Marrel *D Burchell*   50
6 b g Shareef Dancer (USA) - Upper Caen
5¹⁶ᵍ 6¹²ᵍᶠ **0-0-2**

Marsad (Ire) *J Akehurst*   95
10 ch g Fayruz - Broad Haven (Ire)
18⁶ᵍ 3⁶ᵍˢ 8⁶ᵍᶠ 2⁶ᵍᶠ 11⁶ᵍᶠ 20⁶ᵍᶠ 8⁶ᵍˢ
2⁶ᵍˢ 8⁶ᵍᶠ 14⁶ᵍ 4⁶ˢ **0-3-11 £13,074**

Marsh Orchid *W Jarvis*   74
3 b g Lahib - Majalis
5⁷ᵍˢ 2⁸ᵍᶠ 2⁹ᶠ 9¹⁰ˢ **0-2-4 £2,059**

Marshal Bond *B Smart*   a4
6 b g Celtic Swing - Arminda
9⁹ˢᵈ **0-0-1**

Marshallspark (Ire) *R A Fahey*   79
5 b g Fayruz - Lindas Delight
7⁷ᵍˢ 15⁶ᵍᶠ 9⁶ᵍᶠ 5⁶ᵍ 16⁶ᶠ 8⁶ᵍᶠ 16⁶ᶠ 6⁵ᵍᶠ
2⁶ᵍ **2-1-9 £13,538**

Marshman (Ire) *M H Tompkins*   98 a94
5 ch g College Chapel - Gold Fly (Ire)
17⁸ᵍ 3⁷ᵍˢ 7⁷ˢ 8⁷ᵍᶠ 12⁷ᵍᶠ 10⁷ᵍ 3⁷ˢ
3⁷ˢ 5⁷ˢ 1⁷ᵍ 5⁷ˢ 6⁷ˢᵈ **1-3-13 £18,127**

Martaline *A Fabre*   115
5 gr h Linamix (Fr) - Coraline
12¹²ᵍᶠ 5¹²ᵍ 1¹³ᵍˢ 2¹³ʰʸ 7¹⁰ᵍ 6¹²ʰʸ **1-1-6 £38,486**

Martha Reilly (Ire) *Mrs Barbara Waring*   a32
8 ch m Rainbows For Life (Can) - Debach Delight
6¹⁶ˢᵈ 9¹⁶ˢᵈ **0-0-2**

Martillo (Ger) *R Suerland*   118
4 b c Anabaa (USA) - Maltage (USA)
5⁹ᵍᶠ 1⁸ᵛˢ 9⁸ᵍᶠ 1⁸ᵍ 9⁸ˢ 2⁸ˢ **2-1-6 £146,501**

Martin House (Ire) *Mrs K Walton*   40
5 b g Mujadil (USA) - Dolcezza (Fr)
18⁷ᵍᶠ 9¹¹ˢ **0-0-2**

Marton Mere *A J Lockwood*   23
8 ch g Cadeaux Genereux - Hyatti
8¹²ᵍᶠ 14¹²ᵍᶠ **0-0-2**

Mary Carleton *R M H Cowell*   31
3 ch f Halling (USA) - Anne Bonny
13⁷ᵍᶠ 6⁷ᶠ 13⁷ˢ 10¹⁰ᵍᶠ 10¹²ˢᵈ **0-0-5**

Mary Gray *M Johnston*   66
2 gr f Mujahid (USA) - Ancestry
5⁶ᵍᶠ 11⁷ᵍᶠ 12⁷ᵍ 9⁸ˢ **0-0-4**

Mary Read *B Smart*   100
2 ch f Bahamian Bounty - Hill Welcome
3⁵ˢ 1⁵ᵍ 3⁵ᵍᶠ 1⁵ᵍᶠ 2⁵ᵍ 9⁵ᵍ 2⁵ˢ 7⁶ˢ **2-4-8 £37,904**

Marysienka *J Balding*   72 a27
3 b f Primo Dominie - Polish Romance (USA)
11⁶ˢ 5⁶ᵍᶠ 9⁵ᵍˢ 3⁵ᵍ 4⁵ᵍ 11⁵ᵍ 12⁶ˢᵈ **0-1-7 £1,113**

Mas O Menos (Ire) *Ms Deborah J Evans*   54
2 b g King's Theatre (Ire) - Promising Lady
2⁵ˢ 11⁶ˢᵈ 20⁶ᵍ 2⁶ᶠ 13⁵ᵍᶠ 17⁶ᵍ **0-1-6 £2,134**

Masa (USA) *Saeed Bin Suroor*   82
2 gr f Dixie Union (USA) - My Yellow Diamond (USA)
1⁶ᵍᶠ 9⁶ᶠ 6⁶ᵍᶠ **1-0-3 £6,851**

Masafi (Ire) *Sir Mark Prescott*   97 a80
3 b c Desert King (Ire) - Mrs Fisher (Ire)
2⁸ˢᵈ 1⁸ˢᵈ 1⁹ᵍᶠ 1¹⁰ᵍᶠ 1¹⁰ᵍᶠ 1⁸ˢᵈ 1⁹ᵍᶠ
5⁸ᶠ 7¹⁰ᶠ **7-1-10 £29,668**

Masjoor *N A Graham*   26 a65
4 ch g Unfuwain (USA) - Mihnah (Ire)
7¹²ˢᵈ 2¹²ˢᵈ 11¹⁴ˢ **0-1-3 £1,139**

Masked (Ire) *J W Hills*   85
3 b g Soviet Star (USA) - Moon Masquerade (Ire)
8¹⁰ᵍ 7¹⁰ˢ 4⁸ᵍᶠ 1¹¹ᵍᶠ 5¹²ᵍ 2¹²ᵍ 2¹⁴ᵍᶠ
11¹⁴ᵍᶠ 9¹⁴ᵍ **1-2-9 £7,673**

Masquerader (USA) *Saeed Bin Suroor*   48
2 ch c Unbridled (USA) - Guise (USA)
7⁷ᵍˢ **0-0-1**

Massey *T D Barron*   55 a102
8 br g Machiavellian (USA) - Massaraat (USA)

1⁶sd 12⁶sd 1⁶sd 7⁶g 12⁶gf 15⁷gf 12⁷s
7⁵f 13⁷sd 2-0-9 £19,309

Massif Centrale *D R C Elsworth* 106
3 ch c Selkirk (USA) - Madame Dubois
7¹²s 2¹⁰g 11¹²g 1¹²gf 7¹²g 5¹⁴g 1¹²g 6¹²hy
2-1-8 £23,186

Master Cobbler (Ire) *G A Butler* 81
2 b c Alhaarth (Ire) - Lady Joshua (Ire)
4⁵gf 2⁶gf 2¹⁰g 4⁹gs 0-2-4 £3,339

Master Joseph *M R Channon* 62
2-b c Komaite (USA) - Petit Peu (Ire)
4⁶f 7⁶gf 8⁷gf 11⁷gs 2⁸s 5⁷gf 0-1-6
£2,960

Master Mahogany *R J Hodges* 66 a30
3 b g Bandmaster (USA) - Impropriety
9⁶sd 4⁸s 9¹⁰g 8¹⁰gf 6⁹gf 5¹²gf 4¹⁰g 6¹⁰g
10⁸gf 3⁸gf 10⁸g 1⁸g 6⁸g 1-2-13 £5,251

Master Marvel (Ire) *M Johnston* 96
3 ch c Selkirk (USA) - Insijaam (USA)
2⁸g 1⁹gf 1⁸g 8¹⁰g 19⁸f 6⁸g 9¹⁰g 2-1-7
£20,731

Master Nimbus *J J Quinn* 23
4 b g Cloudings (Ire) - Miss Charlie
10⁸f 0-0-1

Master Of The Race *Sir Michael Stoute* 93
2 ch c Selkirk (USA) - Dust Dancer
2⁷gs 0-1-1 £1,538

Master Rat *R J Hodges* 16
3 b g Thowra (Fr) - Race Against Time
13⁷gs 12⁵g 17⁶gs 0-0-3

Master Rattle *Jane Southcombe* 38 a52
5 b g Sabrehill (USA) - Miss Primula
10⁷sd 11⁶sd 11⁷sd 5⁶sd 2⁷sd 11⁷sd 8⁷sd
9⁷sd 1⁵gs 2⁶gf 1-2-10 £2,559

Master Robbie *M R Channon* 99
5 b g Piccolo - Victoria's Secret (Ire)
12⁷s 19⁷gs 24⁶g 8⁷gf 1⁷gf 6⁷gf 19⁷f
9⁷gs 12⁷gf 8⁷gf 15⁷gf 14⁷g 8⁷gf 7⁷g 4⁷g 15⁷g
1-0-16 £15,063

Master Role (Ire) *M A Jarvis* a65
4 ch c Master Willie - Calaloo Sioux (USA)
2⁹sd 6¹²sw 0-1-2 £1,020

Master T (USA) *G L Moore* a43
5 b g Trempolino (USA) - Our Little C (USA)
12¹⁰sd 7¹³sd 0-0-2

Master Theo (USA) *H J Collingridge* 79 a78
3 b g Southern Halo (USA) - Lilian Bayliss (Ire)
7⁸g 3⁸gf 3⁷g 3⁸s 3⁸g 8⁷gf 3⁸gs 4⁸sd 2⁸gs
0-5-9 £6,768

Master Wells (Ire) *J D Bethell* 85
3 b g Sadler's Wells (USA) - Eljazzi
1¹⁰hy 8¹²gs 8¹²g 2¹²g 7¹²g 11¹⁴gf 2¹⁶s
1¹⁶gs 4¹⁷s 8¹³gs 7¹⁷s 2-2-11 £15,579

Masterman Ready *P W Harris* 74
3 b g Unfuwain (USA) - Maria Isabella (Fr)
8¹⁰g 7¹⁰g 6¹²gs 8¹⁴gf 1¹⁴gf 3¹⁴s 6¹⁴f 1¹⁶g
2-1-8 £7,865

Mastman (Ire) *B J Meehan* 90
2 ch c Intikhab (USA) - Spanker
2⁷gf 5⁷g 4⁷gf 1⁸g 3⁸g 1-1-5 £10,150

Match Ball (USA) *Saeed Bin Suroor*
2 b/br f Grand Slam (USA) - Glitters (USA)
11⁵s 0-0-1

Material Witness (Ire) *W R Muir* 110
7 b g Barathea (Ire) - Dial Dream

13⁶gs 11⁷s 2⁷g 8⁶gf 1⁷gf 1⁷gf 1⁷gs 2⁷gf
9⁶gf 4⁷s 1⁷gs 6⁷gf 7⁷g 15⁷gf 4-2-14
£84,920

Mathmagician *R F Marvin* 32 a39
5 ch g Hector Protector (USA) - Inherent Magic (Ire)
4⁸sd 5⁸gw 4⁸ws 8⁸ss 4¹¹ss 6¹¹sd 6¹⁶sd
10¹¹gs 3⁸sf 5⁸sd 0-1-10 £206

Matouraka (Fr) *P W Chapple-Hyam*
3 b/br f Great Palm (USA) - Madragoa (Fr)
8⁹g 11²sd 8¹²s 1¹²sd 16⁹s 2-0-5
£11,268

Matriarchal *Don Enrico Incisa* 20 a6
4 ch f Presidium - Mayor
13⁷gf 5⁶gf 8⁷sd 11⁵gf 9⁶g 0-0-5

Matrimony *E A L Dunlop*
3 b c Groom Dancer (USA) - Zonda
PU¹⁰gf 0-0-1

Matsunosuke *A B Coogan* 59
2 b c Magic Ring (Ire) - Lon Isa
F⁶f 10⁶s 0-0-2

Matty Tun *J Balding* 102
5 b g Lugana Beach - B Grade
9⁵gs 5⁵g 5⁵gs 7⁵gf 2⁹gf 10⁵s 5⁵gs 10⁵g
10⁵gf 10⁵g 1⁵s 1-0-11 £13,351

Maunby Raver *P C Haslam* 60 a49
3 ch g Pivotal - Colleen Liath
7⁷sd 4⁶gf 13⁶gf 0-0-3

Maunby Rocker *P C Haslam* a37
4 ch g Sheikh Albadou - Bullion
14¹⁰sd 9⁸ss 6⁷ss 5¹²sw 0-0-4

Maureen Ann *T J Fitzgerald* 54
4 b f Elmaamul (USA) - Running Glimpse (Ire)
9⁷g 10⁷gf 10⁸g 14⁷g 7⁷f 0-0-5

Maureen's Lough (Ire) *J Hetherton* 58
2 b f Bachir (Ire) - Tadjnama (USA)
3⁵s 6⁵g 1⁷f 5⁷g 4⁷gs 4⁷gf 1⁷gf 9⁷gf 5⁷gs
16⁶g 15⁷gf 2⁷gf 6⁸gf 2-2-13 £8,068

Mauro (Ire) *P M Phelan* 57
2 b f Danehill Dancer (Ire) - Stop The Traffic (Ire)
4⁵gs 2⁵s 4⁵gf 6⁶gs 11⁵g 0-1-5 £1,572

Mawhoob (USA) *Mrs N Macauley*
6 gr g Dayjur (USA) - Asl (USA)
9¹²sd 0-0-1

Maxamillion (Ire) *S Kirk* 80
2 b c Mujadil (USA) - Manazil (Ire)
5⁷hy 4⁸s 1⁷s 6⁵g 1-0-4 £5,030

Maxi's Princess (Ire) *P J Makin* 49
3 b f Revoque (Ire) - Harmer (Ire)
6⁵g 9⁵gf 11⁵gf 0-0-3

Maxilla (Ire) *L M Cumani* 80
4 b/br f Lahib (USA) - Lacinia
4¹⁰s 8¹⁰s 5¹⁰g 6¹⁰gs 2¹²g 4¹⁴gf 0-1-6
£3,604

Maximinus *M Madgwick* 61 a55
4 b g The West (USA) - Candarela
4¹⁰s 9¹²sd 6¹²gf 13¹²gf 8¹⁶sd 0-0-5

May Morning (Ire) *B W Hills* 76
2 b f Danehill (USA) - Golden Digger (USA)
4⁵gs 2⁶f 0-1-2 £1,528

Mayadeen (Ire) *M P Tregoning* 79
2 b c King's Best (USA) - Inaaq
3⁷g 1⁸gs 1-1-2 £4,949

Maybe Someday *J Balding* 25 a66
3 ch g Dr Fong (USA) - Shicklah (USA)
3¹⁰sd 4⁹sd 6⁷sd 3¹⁰sd 3⁸sd 10¹⁰sd 2⁷sd

15⁸ᵍ 9⁷ˢᵈ 7⁷ᶠ 14⁷ᵍ **0-3-11 £3,162**

Mayfair Maundy *W G M Turner*
4 ch f The West (USA) - Mayfair Ballerina
4⁷ᵍ 10⁵ʰʸ **0-0-2**

Maynooth Prince (Ire) *H Alexander* 36
2 b g Spectrum (Ire) - Muffle
7⁷ᵍᶠ 11⁸ᵍˢ **0-0-2**

Mays Dream *D Nicholls* 25
2 b f Josr Algarhoud (Ire) - Amber Mill
8⁷ˢ **0-0-1**

Maystock *G A Butler* 80 a85
4 ch f Magic Ring (Ire) - Stockline
1¹³ˢᵈ 10¹²ˢᵈ 3¹⁰ˢᵈ 8¹²ᵍ 10¹²ᵍ 3¹⁰ᵍᶠ 11¹²ᵍ
7¹⁰ᵍ 11¹²ˢ **1-2-9 £6,455**

Mayzin (Ire) *R M Flower* 52 a75
4 b g Fayruz - Peep Of Day (Ire)
3⁷ˢᵈ 2⁷ˢᵈ 4⁶ˢᵈ 1⁷ˢᵈ 2⁷ˢᵈ 3⁷ˢᵈ 3⁶ˢᵈ 1⁶ˢᵈ
4⁶ˢᵈ 10⁶ᵍᶠ 8⁷ᵍᶠ 7⁵ᵍ 14⁶ᵍ 14⁶ᵍᶠ 7⁶ᵍᶠ 10⁸ᵍᶠ
3⁵ˢ 5⁶ᵍᶠ **2-6-18 £12,126**

Mazepa (Ire) *N A Callaghan* 102
4 b c Indian Ridge - Please Believe Me
6⁶ᵍˢ 3⁶ᵍ 8⁶ᵍˢ 5⁶ᵍᶠ 15⁷ᵍ 12⁶ˢ **0-1-6**
£2,503

Mazram *I W McInnes* 24
5 b m Muhtarram (USA) - Royal Mazi
15⁸ᵍˢ 8⁷ᶠ 13⁷ᵍ **0-0-3**

Mazuna (Ire) *C E Brittain* 107
3 b f Cape Cross (Ire) - Keswa
1¹¹ᵍᶠ 2¹⁰ᵍ 3¹²ᵍᶠ 2¹⁰ᵍ 2¹⁵ᵍ 1¹²ᵍᶠ 6¹⁰ᵍˢ
2-3-7 £60,189

Mbosi (USA) *M Johnston* 91
3 b g Kingmambo (USA) - April Starlight (USA)
3⁸ᵍᶠ 3⁹ᵍˢ 8⁸ᵍˢ 2¹⁰ᵍ 14¹⁰ᵍᶠ 3¹⁰ᵍᶠ 13⁸ᵍˢ
13⁹ᵍ **0-1-8 £5,419**

Mccracken (Ire) *R Ford* 32
8 b g Scenic - Sakanda (Ire)
6²²ˢ **0-0-1**

Mceldowney *M Johnston* 82
2 b c Zafonic (USA) - Ayodhya (Ire)
3⁶ᵍᶠ 2⁷ᵍᶠ 2⁷ᵍᶠ 2⁶ᵍᶠ 3⁶ᵍ 10⁷ᵍ 7⁷ᶠ 2⁷ᵍ 5⁶ˢ
1⁷ˢ **1-5-10 £11,236**

Mcqueen (Ire) *Mrs H Dalton* 84 a69
4 ch g Barathea (Ire) - Bibliotheque (USA)
15¹²ˢᵈ 6¹⁰ˢ 8¹⁰ᵍ 12¹²ᵍᶠ 8⁸ˢᵈ 9¹²ˢᵈ 2¹⁰ᵍ
1⁸ᵍˢ 1¹⁰ˢ 8¹⁰ᵍ 5¹¹ʰʸ 1⁹ˢ 1¹⁰ˢ 2¹⁰ʰʸ **4-2-14**
£19,064

Meadaaf (Ire) *E F Vaughan* 89
3 b c Swain (USA) - Virgin Hawk (USA)
1¹⁰ᵍᶠ 2¹²ᵍ 3¹⁰ᵍᶠ 6¹¹ˢ 3¹³ᵍˢ **1-3-5 £7,982**

Meadow Hawk (USA) *Ian Williams* 4
4 ch g Spinning World (USA) - Sophonisbe
10¹⁴ᵍˢ **0-0-1**

Measured Leap *Patrick Martin* 39 a15
3 br f Inchinor - Lochspring (Ire)
20¹⁰ᵍ 8¹⁰ᵍ 15¹⁰ʸ 5⁷ᶠ 3⁵ˢ 10⁶ˢᵈ **0-1-6**
£500

Meath (Ire) *A P O'Brien* 106
3 b c Sadler's Wells (USA) - Twyla
2⁸ˢ 2⁸ᵍʸ 1¹⁰ᵍᶠ 14¹²ᵍ **1-2-4 £50,126**

Mecca's Mate *D W Barker* 64
3 gr f Paris House - Clancassie
5⁵ᵍˢ 6⁷ᵍ 5⁶ᵍˢ 1⁵ᵍˢ 3⁶ˢ **1-1-5 £4,413**

Medalla (Fr) *M Brittain* 76
4 gr c Medaaly - Sharp Cracker (Ire)
3⁸ᵍˢ 5¹⁰ˢ 7⁸ᵍ 7¹⁰ᵍ **0-1-4 £1,372**

Medallist *Evan Williams* 65
5 b g Danehill (USA) - Obsessive (USA)
6⁸ᵍˢ 6¹⁰ʰʸ **0-0-2**

Medica Boba *H Morrison* 59 a31
3 b f Dr Fong (USA) - Silly View (Ire)
7⁸ᶠ 8⁸ᵍᶠ 13⁸ᵍᶠ 11⁸ᵍˢ 11¹⁰ᵍᶠ 3¹⁶ᵍ 13¹⁶ˢᵈ
0-1-7 £500

Meditation *I A Wood* 38 a65
2 ch f Inchinor - Trojan Desert
9⁷ᶠ 7⁷ˢᵈ 7⁷ˢᵈ 1⁷ˢᵈ 20⁷ᵍˢ **1-0-5 £4,238**

Medusa *D Morris* 47
4 b f Emperor Jones (USA) - Diebiedale
9⁶ˢ 10⁷ᵍᶠ 10⁷ᶠ **0-0-3**

Meelup (Ire) *Jane Southcombe* 64 a64
4 ch g Night Shift (USA) - Centella (Ire)
11⁷ˢᵈ 2⁷ˢᵈ 2⁸ˢᵈ 1⁸ˢᵈ 7¹⁰ˢᵈ 12⁸ˢᵈ 13⁸ᵍ
2⁸ᵍˢ 2⁸ᵍˢ 10⁸ᵍˢ 16⁷ᵍᶠ 12⁸ᵍ 8⁷ᵍ 15⁸ᵍ 11⁹ˢᵈ
1-3-15 £6,728

Megabond *C A Dwyer* 63 a62
3 b g Danehill Dancer (Ire) - Apple Peeler (Ire)
5⁶ˢᵈ 10⁷ˢᵈ 4⁶ˢᵈ 11⁶ᵍᶠ 10⁶ᵍ 1⁷ᶠ 11⁸ᶠ
5⁷ˢᵈ 9⁷ˢᵈ **1-0-9 £1,809**

Megan's Magic *M E Sowersby* 76
4 b f Blue Ocean (USA) - Hot Sunday Sport
6⁸ʰʸ 1¹⁰ᵍˢ 2⁸ᵍˢ 7⁸ᵍˢ 7¹⁰ᵍᶠ 3¹⁰ᵍᶠ 6¹⁰ˢ 4¹⁰ᵍᶠ
4¹⁰ˢ 9¹⁰ᵍ 5⁸ᵍ **1-2-11 £6,327**

Megell (Ire) *M G Quinlan* 63
2 ch f Entrepreneur - Shalwell (Ire)
6⁵ˢ 2⁶ᵍᶠ 11⁵ᵍ 5⁷ᵍᶠ 16ᵍᶠ 14⁶ᵍˢ **1-1-6**
£3,762

Mehmaas *R E Barr* 62
8 b g Distant Relative - Guest List
10⁸ᵍ 18⁸ˢ 18⁸ᶠ 16⁷ᵍᶠ 4⁸ᵍ 13⁸ˢ 8⁸ˢᵈ 1⁷ᵍ
13⁷ᵍˢ 11⁷ᶠ 5⁸ᵍˢ 7⁸ˢ **1-0-12 £2,958**

Meissen *E F Vaughan* 75 a75
3 ch f Amfortas (Ire) - Musetta (Ire)
2¹⁰ᵍᶠ 2¹²ᵍᶠ 1¹³ˢᵈ **1-2-3 £7,255**

Mekuria (Jpn) *M Johnston* 78
3 b f Carnegie (Ire) - Noble Air (Ire)
9¹²ᵍ 18¹²ᵍ 4¹⁰ᵍˢ **0-0-3 £452**

Mel's Moment (USA) *Mrs A J Perrett* 79 a71
2 b c Storm Creek (USA) - One Moment In Time (USA)
14⁷ˢ 6⁸ᵍ 4⁷ˢᵈ 6⁸ˢᵈ **0-0-5**

Melaina *M S Saunders* 64 a54
3 b f Whittingham (Ire) - Oh I Say
2⁶ˢᵈ 7⁶ˢˢ 6⁶ˢˢ 1⁶ˢᵈ 1⁶ˢ 9⁶ᵍ 5⁶ᵍᶠ 15⁶ᵍ
2-1-8 £7,492

Melalchrist *J J Quinn* 91
2 b g Almaty (Ire) - Lawless Bridget
1⁵ʰʸ 2⁵ᵍᶠ 2⁵ᵍᶠ 1⁵ᵍᶠ 3⁶ᵍᶠ 10⁶ᵍ 10⁶ˢ **2-2-7**
£13,384

Melandre *M Brittain* 71
2 b f Lujain (USA) - Talighta (USA)
6⁵ᵍ 9⁵ᵍˢ 4⁵ᵍᶠ 5⁵ᵍᶠ 1⁵ᵍᶠ 2⁵ᵍᶠ 9⁵ᵍ **1-1-7**
£6,712

Melford Red (Ire) *R F Marvin*
4 b g Sri Pekan (USA) - Sunflower (Ire)
15⁸ˢᵈ **0-0-1**

Melinda's Girl *A P Jarvis* 30
3 b f Intikhab (USA) - Polish Honour (USA)
9⁸ˢ 6¹⁰ᶠ 9⁸ˢ **0-0-3**

Melodian *M Brittain* 72 a44
9 b h Grey Desire - Mere Melody
5¹¹ˢᵈ 4¹⁰ˢ 5¹⁰ᵍˢ 1¹⁰ˢ 2¹⁰ʰʸ 3¹⁰ʰʸ 2¹⁰ᵍˢ
1¹¹ᵍ 6⁹ʰʸ 9¹²ˢ 10¹⁰ᵍ 15¹²ᵍ 10¹⁰ˢ **2-3-13**

£10,826

Melody King *P D Evans*　　　70
3 b g Merdon Melody - Retaliator
15^{6gs} 3^{6f} 2^{5g} 5^{5gf} 4^{6f} 3^{5gf} 6^{5g} 5^{5gf}
UR^{5gf} 8^{6gf} 6^{6g} 9^{5gf} 4^{7gs} 12^{6gs} 10^{6s} **0-3-15**
£2,866

Melody Que (Ire) *J Howard Johnson*　　57
2 b f Sadler's Wells (USA) - Bex (USA)
6^{7gs} **0-0-1**

Melograno (Ire) *Mark Campion*　　37 a51
4 ch g Hector Protector (USA) - Just A Treat (Ire)
2^{11sd} 8^{12sd} 12^{11g} 12^{10gf} 1^{12sd} **1-1-5**
£1,876

Melrose Avenue (USA) *M Johnston*　　96
2 b c USA (USA) - Sham Street (USA)
5^{7gf} 1^{7gs} 5^{7gf} 4^{8gs} **1-0-4 £8,603**

Melvino *T D Barron*　　70
2 b g Josr Algarhoud (Ire) - Safe Secret
4^{6gs} 7^{5gf} 3^{6gf} 4^{6gf} 10^{6gs} 18^{6gf} **0-0-6**
£1,413

Membership (USA) *C E Brittain*　　109 a40
4 ch c Belong To Me (USA) - Shamisen
11^{6ft} 5^{8gf} 5^{9gf} 2^{8f} 8^{7s} **0-1-5 £16,759**

Memory Man *W R Muir*　　65 a66
3 b g Primo Dominie - Surrealist (Ity)
11^{6gf} 4^{7gf} 3^{8sd} 7^{7gf} 9^{7f} **0-1-5 £780**

Menai Straights *R F Fisher*　　65 a59
3 ch g Alhaarth (Ire) - Kind Of Light
6^{9ss} 15^{7gs} 6^{8gf} 3^{8gf} 5^{7f} 1^{7g} 3^{7g} 9^{7gf}
6^{7gf} 6^{7g} 7^{7gs} 2^{7sd} **1-1-12 £5,826**

Meneef (USA) *M P Tregoning*　　79
3 b c Kingmambo - Black Penny (USA)
3^{7g} 2^{8gs} 3^{8gf} **0-2-3 £2,911**

Menelaus *D R Loder*　　51
3 b c Machiavellian (USA) - Mezzogiorno
6^{11gf} **0-0-1**

Menhoubah (USA) *C E Brittain*　　102 a105
3 b f Dixieland Band (USA) - Private Seductress (USA)
2^{8ft} 3^{9ft} 7^{9ft} 2^{11gs} 1^{11g} 13^{11gs} 6^{10gf}
8^{12s} 8^{10g} **1-3-9 £307,026**

Menna *R Hollinshead*　　56
2 b f Mark Of Esteem (Ire) - Pouneta
5^{5gf} 7^{6g} **0-0-2**

Menokee (USA) *Sir Michael Stoute*　　108
3 b c Cherokee Run (USA) - Meniatarra (USA)
2^{10s} **0-1-1 £6,600**

Mephisto (Ire) *L M Cumani*　　110
5 b g Machiavellian (USA) - Cunning
10^{12g} 5^{12g} 1^{12gf} 1^{12gs} 1^{14g} 1^{14s} **4-0-6**
£184,528

Mercari *G M Moore*　　60
2 ch f Bahamian Bounty - Aonach Mor
9^{6gf} 12^{6g} 8^{6f} 6^{5gf} 4^{6g} **0-1-5**

Merchant (Ire) *M L W Bell*　　102
2 ch c Tagula (Ire) - Easy Pop (Ire)
5^{7gs} 3^{6gs} 2^{6f} 1^{6gs} 1^{7s} 1^{8s} 1^{8g} 4^{8s} 7^{8vs}
4-2-9 £56,398

Mercurious (Ire) *J Mackie*　　53 a55
4 ch f Grand Lodge (USA) - Rousinette
4^{13sd} 1^{16sd} 5^{15g} 4^{16sd} 2^{14sd} 1^{16sd} 2^{16gs}
5^{14sd} 1^{16g} **3-2-9 £9,304**

Merdiff *W M Brisbourne*　　68 a73
5 b g Machiavellian (USA) - Balwa (USA)
12^{7gs} 7^{9f} 10^{8sd} 2^{7sd} 18^{g} 7^{5sd} 10^{8gf} 4^{7sd}
2^{7g} 15^{7s} 16^{8gf} 1^{6sd} **2-3-12 £11,415**

Merger (USA) *D K Weld*　　105
2 gr c Mr Greeley (USA) - Toledo Queen (Ire)
1^{8gy} 2^{8ys} **1-1-2 £22,260**

Merlin's City *Miss L C Siddall*
4 b f Merdon Melody - Sharp Ego (USA)
19^{6gs} 10^{10s} **0-0-2**

Merlin's Dancer *D Nicholls*　　96
4 b g Magic Ring (Ire) - La Piaf (Fr)
10^{6gs} 5^{6gs} 1^{6gf} 8^{5gf} 11^{5gf} 7^{5gf} 4^{5g} 1^{6gf}
13^{6g} **2-1-9 £18,009**

Merlins Profit *M Todhunter*　　48
4 b g Wizard King - Quick Profit
5^{7g} 4^{11f} 2^{10gf} 7^{11g} UR^{8gs} 4^{9gs} 3^{9f} 6^{10g}
8^{9gs} **0-2-9 £917**

Mermaid's Cry *R Brotherton*　　45
2 b f Danzero (Aus) - Little Tramp
2^{6f} 7^{5g} 11^{6sd} 9^{5g} **0-1-4 £1,100**

Merrymadcap (Ire) *M Blanshard*　　63
2 b g Lujain - Carina Clare
13^{6gf} 5^{7g} 6^{7gs} 6^{7gf} 8^{8s} 6^{7s} 15^{7gf} 11^{6gf}
0-0-8

Merrymaker *W M Brisbourne*　　78 a84
4 b g Machiavellian (USA) - Wild Pavane
4^{12gf} 6^{12gf} 4^{11f} PU^{12f} 1^{13g} 2^{12g} 1^{12g}
11^{12gf} 8^{12g} 3^{12s} 5^{12gf} 5^{13s} 1^{12sd} 5^{12s} **3-3-14**
£15,305

Mersey Sound (Ire) *S Kirk*　　58
6 b g Ela-Mana-Mou - Coral Sound (Ire)
17^{16g} 13^{14s} **0-0-2**

Merwaha (Ire) *M P Tregoning*　　72
3 b f Green Desert (USA) - Samheh (USA)
4^{8gf} 3^{8gf} 4^{8gf} **0-0-3 £1,693**

Mesayan (Ire) *A C Stewart*　　60
3 ch c Grand Lodge (USA) - Missish
9^{8gf} 4^{8g} **0-0-2 £433**

Meshaheer (USA) *Saeed Bin Suroor*　　107
5 b h Nureyev (USA) - Race The Wild Wind (USA)
9^{7g} 2^{7s} 1^{7s} **1-1-3 £14,123**

Mesmerised *Miss A Stokell*　　a19
4 b f Merdon Melody - Gracious Imp (USA)
13^{5sd} 9^{6sd} 14^{6sd} 13^{6sd} 6^{5sd} 7^{7sd} 10^{5f}
12^{10gf} **0-0-8**

Messe De Minuit (Ire) *R Charlton*　　78
3 ch c Grand Lodge (USA) - Scrimshaw
9^{12g} 3^{10gs} 6^{12gf} **0-0-3 £594**

Meteorite Sun (USA) *G Lellouche*　　73
6 b g Miesque's Son (USA) - Myth To Reality (Fr)
8^{10s} 3^{10s} 0^{13hy} 10^{11gs} 9^{10gs} 0^{12sd} 9^{10gs}
0^{12g} 0^{11s} 6^{10vs} 0^{12vs} **0-1-11 £1,208**

Methodical *I A Wood*　　61
2 b f Lujain (USA) - Simple Logic
4^{6gs} 9^{6gs} 5^{6g} 19^{6hy} **0-0-4 £284**

Meticulous *M C Chapman*　　17 a17
6 gr g Eagle Eyed (USA) - Careful (Ire)
7^{7sd} 7^{8sd} 9^{12sd} 10^{12sd} 12^{7sd} 8^{8sd} 8^{5sd}
8^{7gs} 13^{6gs} 6^{7sd} **0-0-10**

Metolica *C Smith*　　16
2 b f Diktat - South Sea Bubble (Ire)
11^{5ss} 11^{6g} 11^{7gs} **0-0-3**

Mexican (USA) *M D Hammond*　　18 a44
5 b g Pine Bluff (USA) - Cuando Quiere (USA)
19^{10gs} 7^{7g} 3^{8sd} 5^{12sd} 2^{8sd} 7^{8s} **0-2-6**
£1,069

Mexican Pete *P W Hiatt*　　85
4 b g Atraf - Eskimo Nel (Ire)

15^{12s} 3^{12gs} 8^{14g} 2^{12gf} 7^{12g} 4^{12g} 4^{12g}
3^{12gf} 2^{12gf} 6^{12gf} 9^{12f} **0-3-11 £8,883**

Mezereon *D Carroll* a55
4 b f Alzao (USA) - Blown-Over
7^{10sd} 7^{9sd} **0-0-2**

Mezuzah *M W Easterby* 75
4 b g Barathea (Ire) - Mezzogiorno
8^{8s} 5^{8g} 9^{8s} 16^{10g} 10^{7s} 13^{10s} **0-0-6**

Mi Odds *Mrs N Macauley* 62 a101
8 b g Sure Blade (USA) - Vado Via
1^{8ss} 5^{8ss} 14^{10sd} 10^{10g} 8^{11gf} 10^{11gs} 11^{11g}
1-0-7 £8,061

Michabo (Ire) *D R C Elsworth* 85
3 b g Robellino (USA) - Mole Creek
4^{9gf} 3^{10gf} 2^{10g} 6^{10gf} 2^{10gf} 1^{10gs} 3^{12gs}
11^{11g} **1-4-8 £10,554**

Michaels Dream (Ire) *J Hetherton* 49 a31
5 b g Spectrum (Ire) - Stormswept (USA)
6^{14sd} 3^{10f} 3^{12gf} 11^{12gf} 4^{12gf} 12^{12gf} 10^{12s}
0-3-7 £1,393

Michaels Pride (Ire) *M Johnston* 31
2 b f Distant View (USA) - Ruacana Falls (USA)
10^{8hy} **0-0-1**

Michelle Ma Belle (Ire) *S Kirk* 82 a83
4 b f Shareef Dancer (USA) - April Magic
8^{7sd} 2^{7sd} 2^{7gs} 8^{7g} 14^{8gf} 7^{7g} 1^{6gf} 13^{6gs}
12^{6s} 16^{6g} **1-2-10 £5,760**

Mickehaha *I A Wood* 34
2 b c Lake Coniston (Ire) - Minnehaha
8^{7g} **0-0-1**

Mickey Boggitt *A Berry*
2 b g Mind Games - Valldemosa
11^{5gf} 7^{7f} **0-0-2**

Mickey Pearce (Ire) *J G M O'Shea* 39
2 b c Rossini (USA) - Lucky Coin
16^{6gf} 10^{6gf} 13^{7gs} 8^{7s} **0-0-4**

Mickledo *A Bailey* 47
2 b c Perryston View - Ever So Lonely
11^{6s} 9^{5gs} **0-0-2**

Mickledor (Fr) *M Dods* 60
4 ch f Lake Coniston (Ire) - Shamasiya (Fr)
8^{6gf} 13^{6f} 3^{5g} 8^{7gf} 1^{6g} 1^{6g} 13^{6gf} 8^{6gf}
3^{6hy} 6^{6g} 5^{7f} 6^{6s} **2-2-12 £7,903**

Micklegate *J D Bethell* 58
3 b f Dracula (Aus) - Primulette
4^{7f} 4^{7g} 12^{7gs} PU^{7f} **0-0-4 £551**

Midas Way *P R Chamings* 100
4 ch g Halling (USA) - Arietta's Way (Ire)
2^{13s} 7^{15gf} 3^{16gf} 23^{18s} **0-2-4 £10,900**

Midcap (Ire) *B W Hills* 72
2 b f Entrepreneur - Tis Juliet (USA)
12^{6g} 6^{7gf} 8^{7g} 3^{7gf} 6^{7gf} **0-1-5 £916**

Middle Earth (USA) *A M Balding* 74 a77
2 ch c Dixieland Band (USA) - Lite Twilight (USA)
2^{5gf} 8^{6s} 2^{6sd} **0-2-3 £3,273**

Middle Eastern *P A Blockley* 65
2 b c Mujahid (USA) - Swissmatic
5^{6s} 4^{6g} 10^{5g} 9^{6s} **0-0-4 £277**

Middleham Park (Ire) *P C Haslam* 43 a56
4 b g Revoque (Ire) - Snap Crackle Pop (Ire)
2^{8sd} 7^{7gf} 9^{8g} 10^{12gf} 4^{9sd} **0-1-5 £830**

Middleham Rose *P C Haslam* a34
3 b f Dr Fong (USA) - Shallop
6^{9sd} 6^{8sd} 2^{12sd} 14^{10f} 5^{12sd} **0-1-5 £408**

Middlemarch (Ire) *J S Goldie* 106

---

4 ch c Grand Lodge (USA) - Blanche Dubois
7^{8g} 4^{10gf} 13^{10gs} 5^{9gf} 8^{8gf} **0-0-5 £1,901**

Middlemiss (Ire) *J W Mullins* 33 a24
4 b f Midhish - Teresa Deevey
7^{10gs} 10^{8sd} 2^{7g} **0-0-3 £368**

Middlethorpe *M W Easterby* 73
7 b g Noble Patriarch - Prime Property (Ire)
1^{12g} 5^{14g} 6^{14s} 7^{12g} 10^{12s} **1-0-5 £3,571**

Middleton Grey *A G Newcombe* 74 a95
6 gr g Ashkalani (Ire) - Petula
7^{9sd} 3^{6sw} 2^{7ss} 12^{7gs} 3^{7g} 5^{7gf} 2^{7gs} 1^{6gs}
14^{7gs} **1-4-9 £14,326**

Midges Pride *Mrs A Duffield*
4 b g Puissance - It's All Academic (Ire)
10^{8sd} **0-0-1**

Midmaar (Ire) *M Wigham* a25
3 b c Cape Cross (Ire) - Khazinat El Dar (USA)
10^{12sd} 12^{10sd} 10^{8sw} **0-0-4**

Midnight Arrow *A Berry* 39
6 b m Robellino (USA) - Princess Oberon (Ire)
15^{8g} 8^{7f} **0-0-2**

Midnight Ballard (USA) *R F Johnson Houghton* 81
a62
3 b/br g Mister Baileys - Shadow Music (USA)
6^{6g} 4^{6g} 2^{7gf} 15^{7gf} 1^{7gf} 8^{7gf} 19^{6gf} 9^{7sd}
11^{6sd} **1-1-9 £5,189**

Midnight In Moscow (Ire) *P C Haslam* 38
2 b g Soviet Star (USA) - Solar Display (USA)
6^{6gf} 14^{6s} 9^{6s} **0-0-3 £238**

Midnight Lace *R Hannon* 65
2 ch f Tomba - Royal Passion
9^{5g} 9^{6g} 8^{6gf} 12^{6hy} **0-1-4 £731**

Midnight Mambo (USA) *R Guest* 49 a46
4 b f Kingmambo (USA) - Witching Hour (Fr)
5^{7ss} 5^{10sd} 7^{9ss} 12^{8gf} 14^{10s} 2^{10gf} **0-1-6**
£489

Midnight Parkes *E J Alston* 78
5 br g Polar Falcon (USA) - Summerhill Spruce
20^{6g} 4^{6gf} 8^{5gf} 3^{6g} 5^{6gf} 9^{6g} 3^{6gf} 1^{5gf}
12^{5gf} 9^{6gf} 3^{5gf} 13^{5gf} 7^{5f} 3^{6gs} **1-4-14**
£15,898

Midnight Prince *M W Easterby* 49
3 b g Dracula (Aus) - Phylian
6^{7gf} 5^{8gf} 8^{10gs} **0-0-3**

Midnight Promise *J A Glover* a25
3 b g Aragon - Uninvited
7^{7sd} 13^{7sd} **0-0-2**

Midnight Tycoon *B Smart* 86
2 b c Marju (Ire) - Midnight Allure
1^{5gs} 3^{5gf} 4^{6g} 9^{5s} **1-0-4 £6,744**

Midshipman *A W Carroll* 63 a69
6 b h Executive Man - Midler
7^{8sd} 16^{12sd} 9^{12s} 7^{12gs} 17^{16gs} 3^{10hy} 10^{10g}
9^{11f} 2^{8sd} 2^{8sd} 2^{12sd} 4^{8sd} 10^{10s} 6^{8g} 5^{12sd} 1^{9sd}
1-4-16 £7,035

Midshipman Easy (USA) *P W Harris* 74
3 ch g Irish River (Fr) - Winger
3^{10gs} 2^{10s} 11^{10gs} 7^{12g} 6^{12gs} 14^{10gf} 10^{12s}
0-2-7 £1,771

Mighty Empire (Ire) *M H Tompkins* 79
2 b c Second Empire (Ire) - Barnabas (Ity)
7^{6gf} 14^{5gs} 4^{7gf} 1^{7gf} 2^{8gf} 7^{8gf} **1-1-6**
£10,699

Mighty Max *G A Ham*
6 b g Well Beloved - Jokers High (USA)

10^{16sd} 0-0-1

Mighty Pip (Ire) *M R Bosley* 42
8 b g Pips Pride - Hard To Stop
12^{11gs} 5^{10g} 0-0-2

Migration *Mrs S Lamyman* 44
8 b g Rainbow Quest (USA) - Armeria (USA)
9^{14s} 10^{16sd} 10^{13g} 17^{10g} 0-0-4

Mijdaaf (Fr) *A C Stewart* 84
3 b c Mtoto - Zobaida (Ire)
6^{10gf} 2^{10gf} 0-1-2 £1,788

Mikado *A P O'Brien* 118
3 b c Sadler's Wells (USA) - Free At Last
4^{14g} 4^{12g} 3^{14s} 5^{15gf} 1^{10ys} 1-1-5
£49,404

Mikao (Ire) *M H Tompkins* 76 a55
3 b g Tagula (Ire) - Oumaladia (Ire)
5^{8g} 3^{8gf} 2^{10gf} 4^{11g} 2^{12sd} 1^{10s} 1-3-6
£9,657

Mikasa (Ire) *R F Fisher* 37 a31
4 b g Victory Note (USA) - Resiusa (Ity)
10^{7sd} 7^{12sd} 8^{12gs} 3^{12g} 8^{11f} 10^{8sd} 5^{11g}
10^{17g} 11^{12gf} 9^{15gf} 6^{16gf} 0-1-11 £412

Mikes Mate *C J Teague*
3 b g Komaite (USA) - Pitcairn Princess
14^{7g} 12^{9g} 13^{12gs} 0-0-3

Military Two Step (Ire) *K R Burke* 44
3 b g General Monash (USA) - Con Dancer
14^{8g} 13^{8s} 9^{7hv} 9^{7gf} 11^{7g} 14^{7gs} 0-0-6

Milk And Sultana *G A Ham* 67 a72
4 b f Millkom - Premier Princess
13^{8s} 6^{10gf} 9^{13f} 8^{12g} 2^{12g} 11^{12gf} 2^{12gf}
4^{12s} 11^{1g} 1^{10g} 4^{10gs} 15^{10gs} 3^{12sd} 7^{12gs} 8^{14sd}
2-3-15 £12,715

Milk It Mick *J A Osborne* 112 a106
3 b c Millkom - Lunar Music
2^{8sd} 5^{7g} 8^{8g} 3^{6gf} 3^{8g} 2^{8gf} 0-3-6
£16,464

Mill By The Stream *A P Jarvis* 51
2 b g Lujain (USA) - Lonesome
14^{6gf} 10^{5gf} 12^{6gf} 6^{8gf} 18^{6gf} 9^{6g} 0-0-6

Mill Emerald *R Ford*
7 b m Old Vic - Milinetta
12^{14sd} 0-0-1

Mill End Chateau *M W Easterby* 41
2 ch g Paris House - Mill End Quest
9^{5gf} 12^{6gf} 0-0-2

Mill End Teaser *M W Easterby* a7
3 b f Mind Games - Mill End Quest
10^{5ss} 0-0-1

Millafonic *L M Cumani* 100
4 b c Zafonic (USA) - Milligram
6^{10gf} 8^{10f} 8^{10gs} 12^{10hy} 0-0-4

Millagros (Ire) *I Semple* 80 a70
4 b f Pennekamp (USA) - Grey Galava
11^{8gs} 4^{10gf} 4^{8gf} 6^{9g} 3^{9gf} 3^{9gf} 1^{8s} 3^{8f}
3^{8gf} 4^{10s} 9^{9sd} 1-3-11 £8,731

Millbag (Ire) *M R Channon* 107
3 b c Cape Cross (Ire) - Play With Fire (Fr)
1^{6s} 7^{6gf} 5^{5gf} 1-0-3 £17,400

Millenary *J L Dunlop* 121
7 b h Rainbow Quest (USA) - Ballerina (Ire)
3^{16s} 1^{14gs} 3^{16g} 1^{18g} 1^{16s} 3-2-5
£174,000

Millenio (Ger) *D Flood* a68

4 ch c Big Shuffle (USA) - Molto In Forma (Ger)
3^{8g} 3^{6g} 3^{6g} 6^{7s} 2^{8sd} 15^{8sd} 0-1-6
£3,196

Millennium Force *M R Channon* 111
6 b g Bin Ajwaad (Ire) - Jumairah Sun (Ire)
8^{7g} 16^{8gs} 4^{7gf} 2^{7gs} 3^{7g} 3^{7gf} 8^{7g} 8^{8g}
4^{7gs} 9^{7gf} 5^{7hv} 2^{7s} 2^{6gs} 0-4-13 £33,195

Millennium Hall *P Monteith* 69
5 b g Saddlers' Hall (Ire) - Millazure (USA)
13^{9g} 6^{8g} 3^{12hy} 3^{13gf} 1^{12gf} 1^{13gf} 12^{12g}
6^{12g} 6^{13g} 13^{9gs} 6^{13gs} 7^{14gf} 6^{16gf} 2-2-13
£13,159

Miller Hill *J Naouri* a38
2 b g Prince Sabo - Atlantic Heiress
12^{5hy} 2^{6sd} 8^{5gf} 6^{7gs} 0-1-4 £718

Millfields Dreams *R Brotherton* 65
5 b g Dreams End - Millfields Lady
1^{6gf} 11^{6g} 12^{7g} 11^{6g} 7^{6gf} 6^{6gf} 10^{6g} 8^{8gf}
7^{5gf} 5^{7gs} 1-0-10 £3,926

Millietom (Ire) *K A Ryan* 66
3 b g General Monash (USA) - June Lady
9^{5sd} 0-0-1

Millinsky (USA) *R Guest* 66
3 ch f Stravinsky (USA) - Millyant
6^{5gf} 3^{5gf} 2^{5gf} 3^{5g} 2^{6gf} 0-4-5 £4,561

Million Percent *K R Burke* 88
5 b g Ashkalani (Ire) - Royal Jade
11^{6gs} 6^{6gf} 2^{6gf} 2^{6gf} 6^{6gf} 6^{6gs} 9^{6s} 0-2-7
£4,529

Millkom Elegance *G A Ham* 46
5 b m Millkom - Premier Princess
8^{12gf} 3^{8gs} 11^{8f} 0-1-3 £464

Millquista D'Or *G A Ham* a45
2 b f Millkom - Gild The Lily
17^{8gf} 7^{9sd} 0-0-2

Millstreet *Saeed Bin Suroor* 113
5 ch g Polish Precedent (USA) - Mill Path
8^{12gf} 5^{10g} 8^{10gf} 0-0-3 £11,500

Millville *M A Jarvis* 93 a90
4 ch g Millkom - Miss Topville (Fr)
1^{10sd} 9^{7sd} 7^{12sd} 1^{13sd} 8^{12g} 5^{12gf} 4^{12g} 5^{14g}
13^{12g} 2^{12s} 10^{12s} 3-2-11 £25,934

Milly Golightly *M Dods* 38
3 b f Mind Games - Milliscent
11^{8g} 6^{10gf} 8^{7f} 0-0-3

Milly Waters *W M Brisbourne* 58 a86
3 b f Danzero (Aus) - Chilly Waters
5^{8g} 5^{8sd} 12^{9sd} 0-0-3 £1,012

Milly's Lass *J M Bradley* a27
6 b m Mind Games - Millie's Lady (Ire)
7^{5sd} 0-0-1

Millybaa (USA) *R Guest* 102
4 b f Anabaa (USA) - Millyant
2^{6y} 4^{6g} 7^{5gs} 12^{6gs} 4^{6gs} 8^{6y} 8^{5g} 9^{6ys}
10^{6gs} 0-1-9 £11,570

Mimas Girl *S R Bowring* a40
5 b m Samim (USA) - Cocked Hat Girl
5^{6sd} 9^{6sd} 5^{8ss} 3^{6sd} 7^{8sd} 9^{8ss} 13^{7sd} 3^{7sd}
6^{7sd} 0-2-9 £401

Mimi Mouse *T D Easterby* 86
2 br f Diktat - Shifty Mouse
6^{5gs} 4^{6gf} 3^{5gf} 1^{5gf} 1^{5gf} 14^{6g} 8^{5s} 2-1-7
£16,272

Mimic *R Guest* 76 a76
4 b f Royal Applause - Stripanoora

13^{6g} 8^{6f} 10^{6gf} 9^{6gf} 1^{6gs} 5^{5gs} 11^{6f} 11^{6g} 3^{6sd} **1-1-9 £4,217**

Mina Alsalaam *M R Channon*   22
2 b f Lujain (USA) - Rain And Shine (Fr)
15^{6g} 13^{6gf} **0-0-2**

Mind Alert *Miss J A Camacho*   70 a66
3 b g Mind Games - Bombay Sapphire
11^{6gf} 2^{6gf} 15^{6g} 8^{7gf} 9^{6s} 9^{5gf} 5^{7gs} 17^{sd}
5^{9sd} **1-1-9 £4,714**

Mind Play *M E Sowersby*   a27
3 b f Mind Games - Diplomatist
6^{8ss} 9^{11sd} **0-0-2**

Mind The Time *J Hetherton*   a32
3 b g Mind Games - Rare Indigo
9^{6sd} 6^{6ss} 4^{5sd} 9^{5gf} **0-0-4**

Mindful *M J Polglase*   35 a33
2 b c Mind Games - Blushing Victoria
11^{5g} 6^{5sd} 10^{6sd} 13^{5gs} **0-0-4**

Mindset (Ire) *C Laffon-Parias*   52
3 b f Vettori (Ire) - Eden (Ire)
8^{7gs} 10^{8vs} **0-0-2**

Mine (Ire) *J D Bethell*   116
6 b h Primo Dominie - Ellebanna
2^{8s} 3^{8gs} 1^{7gf} 1^{8gf} 5^{8gs} 7^{7s} 5^{8f} 3^{7gf}
2-4-9 £117,315

Mine Behind *J R Best*   96
4 b g Sheikh Albadou - Arapi (Ire)
1^{6gs} 6^{6g} 2^{6gf} 2^{6gf} 8^{5gf} 7^{6g} 12^{6gf} 1^{6g}
12^{6gf} 16^{6gs} 7^{6gf} 1^{5g} 4^{5gs} 12^{6g} 4^{5g} **3-4-15**
£26,443

Mineko *E F Vaughan*   73
2 b f Nashwan (USA) - Musetta (Ire)
8^{7gs} **0-0-1**

Mineral Star (Ire) *M H Tompkins*   75
2 b c Monashee Mountain (USA) - Summit Talk
9^{7gf} 3^{8g} **0-1-2 £819**

Ming The Merciless *J G Given*   a44
4 b g Hector Protector (USA) - Sundae Girl (USA)
5^{8sd} 6^{11sd} **0-0-2**

Ming Vase *D Carroll*   58 a54
2 b c Vettori (Ire) - Minstrel's Dance (Can)
6^{5hy} 2^{7sd} 5^{7sd} 6^{6hy} 8^{8s} 5^{6gf} 3^{6g} **0-2-7**
£1,775

Mingun (USA) *A P O'Brien*   112
4 b/br c A.P. Indy (USA) - Miesque (USA)
3^{10ys} 8^{10s} **0-1-2 £3,524**

Minimum Bid *Miss B Sanders*   56 a62
3 b f First Trump - La Noisette
9^{5gf} 13^{5gf} 2^{5gf} 9^{6g} 2^{5sd} 10^{6gf} 10^{7gf}
0-2-7 £2,098

Minirina *C Smith*   9 a25
4 b f Mistertopogigo (Ire) - Fabulous Rina (Fr)
8^{5ss} 4^{5sd} 4^{5sd} 7^{5sd} 8^{5gf} **0-0-5**

Minivet *R Allan*   63 a16
9 b g Midyan (USA) - Bronzewing
7^{16sd} 5^{12gf} 4^{13gs} 1^{14g} 9^{12gs} **1-0-5**
£7,446

Mink Mitten *D J Daly*   51
2 b f Polish Precedent (USA) - Trefoil (Fr)
10^{7gf} 8^{7g} **0-0-2**

Minnesinger *R M Beckett*   29
2 b f Fraam - Rose Alto
7^{8s} **0-0-1**

Minnesota (USA) *H Candy*   83
2 ch c Silver Hawk (USA) - Coco (USA)

2^{6f} 1^{7g} 3^{8gf} 3^{7g} **1-1-4 £10,439**

Minority Report *L M Cumani*   81
4 b g Rainbow Quest (USA) - Queen Sceptre (Ire)
3^{8gf} 8^{8gf} 2^{8gf} 12^{12gf} **0-2-4 £2,300**

Minstrel Hall *P Monteith*   58
5 b m Saddlers' Hall (Ire) - Mindomica
4^{12g} 5^{10g} 7^{10gf} **0-0-3**

Minstrel's Double *F P Murtagh*   29
3 ch g Jumbo Hirt (USA) - Hand On Heart (Ire)
5^{7gf} 10^{12gs} **0-0-2**

Mintlaw *I Semple*   76
2 b f Mujahid (USA) - Rynavey
2^{6gf} 6^{8s} 1^{7gs} **1-1-3 £5,901**

Miracle Baby *G B Balding*   46
2 b f Atraf - Musica
7^{6hy} **0-0-1**

Mirage Prince (Ire) *W M Brisbourne*   71
2 ch g Desert Prince (Ire) - Belle Bijou
6^{5gs} 10^{6gf} 6^{7gf} 5^{7gf} 4^{8g} 13^{7gs} **0-0-6**
£423

Mirasol Princess *D K Ivory*   79 a79
3 ch f Ali-Royal (Ire) - Yanomami (USA)
8^{6g} 7^{5gf} 4^{5f} 6^{5gf} 6^{6sd} 4^{5gf} 15^{5gf}
1^{5gf} 7^{5s} 3^{5g} 9^{5gf} **1-1-12 £5,944**

Mirjan (Ire) *L Lungo*   99
8 b g Tenby - Mirana (Ire)
3^{16gf} 1^{16s} 7^{18s} **1-1-3 £105,432**

Mis Chicaf (Ire) *J S Wainwright*   94
3 b f Prince Sabo - Champagne Season (USA)
2^{6g} 1^{6gf} 1^{6gf} 18^{6gf} **2-1-4 £10,751**

Misaro (Ger) *P A Blockley*   80
3 b g Acambaro (Ger) - Misniniski
8^{5hy} 5^{7gf} 6^{7g} 2^{9gs} 4^{6gs} 13^{5s} **0-2-6**
£1,857

Misbehaviour *P Butler*   a34
5 b g Tragic Role (USA) - Exotic Forest
13^{7sd} 7^{8sd} 8^{10sd} **0-0-3**

Mischief *K Bell*
8 ch g Generous (Ire) - Knight's Baroness
14^{12gf} PU^{14gf} **0-0-2**

Mishap *W Jarvis*
2 b f Mark Of Esteem (Ire) - Classic Colleen (Ire)
14^{8gs} **0-0-1**

Miskina *W M Brisbourne*   32 a64
3 b f Mark Of Esteem (Ire) - Najmat Alshemaal (Ire)
13^{8g} 3^{8sd} 7^{9gs} 1^{7sd} 5^{8s} 15^{8g} 4^{7sd} **1-1-7**
£3,990

Miss Adelaide (Ire) *B W Hills*   66 a66
3 b f Alzao (USA) - Sweet Adelaide (USA)
4^{8sd} 4^{8hy} 2^{10gf} 7^{8gf} 2^{7sd} **0-2-5 £3,467**

Miss Bear (Ire) *B Smart*   43
2 b f Orpen (USA) - The Poachers Lady (Ire)
10^{7f} 9^{8g} **0-0-2**

Miss Cassia *R Hannon*   74
2 b f Compton Place - Miller's Melody
3^{5g} 2^{5g} SU^{6g} 3^{5gf} 1^{5s} 17^{7g} 6^{5gf} **1-2-7**
£6,895

Miss Celerity *M J Haynes*   a39
4 b f Compton Place - Film Buff
11^{8sd} 10^{6sd} 4^{8sd} 10^{8sd} 13^{8gs} 10^{7sd}
11^{8sd} **0-0-7**

Miss Ceylon *S P Griffiths*   41
4 b f Brief Truce (USA) - Five Islands
10^{6sd} 11^{5gs} 19^{5gs} 7^{5gf} 16^{5gs} 13^{5gf} 11^{5s}
0-0-7

Miss Champers (Ire) *P A Blockley*   a75
4 b/br f Grand Lodge (USA) - Katherine Gorge (USA)
9⁸ˢᵈ 18ˢˢ 18ˢˢ 4⁹ˢˢ 9⁷ˢᵈ **2-0-5 £6,181**

Miss Chancelot *S P Griffiths*   a6
3 b f Forzando - Suedoro
12⁶ᵍᶠ 8⁷ᶠ 8⁶ᵍ 11⁶ˢᵈ **0-0-4**

Miss Childrey (Ire) *D J S Ffrench Davis*   98
3 ch f Dr Fong (USA) - Blazing Glory (Ire)
5⁷ʸˢ 3⁷ᵍʸ 13⁸ᵍᶠ 9⁶ᶠ 8⁹ᵍˢ 7⁸ᵍᶠ 12⁷ᵍᶠ **0-1-7**
£5,447

Miss Cotswold Lady *A W Carroll*   67 a13
2 b f Averti (Ire) - Celtic Bay (USA)
5⁵ᵍ 4⁵ᶠ 2⁶ᵍᶠ 8⁵ᵍ 8⁶ᵍᶠ 20⁷ᵍᶠ 11⁵ˢᵈ **0-1-7**
£1,880

Miss Cuisina *P D Evans*   31
2 b f Vettori (Ire) - Rewardia (Ire)
16⁷ᵍᶠ 8⁷ˢᵈ 9⁷ˢ **0-0-3**

Miss Danbys *J M Jefferson*   a5
9 b m Charmer - Dohty Baby
6¹¹ˢᵈ **0-0-1**

Miss Dangerous *M Quinn*   a7
9 b m Komaite (USA) - Khadine
11⁵ˢˢ **0-0-1**

Miss De Bois *W M Brisbourne*   15
7 ch m Elmaamul (USA) - Petite Melusine (Ire)
12¹²ᵍᶠ 8¹⁰ᵍˢ 17⁸ᵍᶠ **0-0-3**

Miss Defying *R Curtis*
2 b f Shambo - Dugy
11⁸ᵍˢ **0-0-1**

Miss Dinamite *M J Attwater*
2 b f Polar Prince (Ire) - Over The Moon
18⁸ᵍᶠ **0-0-1**

Miss Eloise *T D Easterby*   65
3 b f Efisio - Zaima (Ire)
6⁸ʰʸ 2⁸ᵍ 6⁸ᵍᶠ 9⁸ˢ 11⁰ᵍᶠ 8¹⁰ᵍ 11¹⁰ᵍˢ 9¹⁰ᵍˢ
13¹¹ᵍ **1-1-9 £4,986**

Miss Faye *J M Bradley*   24
4 b/br f Puissance - Bingo Bongo
7⁷ᵍˢ 3⁷ᵍ 10⁶ᵍᶠ **0-0-3 £184**

Miss Fleurie *R Craggs*   36 a36
4 b f Alzao (USA) - Miss Sancerre
9⁶ˢᵈ 12⁷ᵍˢ 7⁸ˢᵈ 2¹²ˢᵈ 6¹²ᵍ 7¹²ᵍᶠ 18¹²ᵍᶠ
2¹⁰ˢ **0-2-8 £1,303**

Miss George *D K Ivory*   89 a93
6 b m Pivotal - Brightside (Ire)
1⁷ˢᵈ 9⁶ᵍ 7⁷ˢᵈ 3⁶ᵍ 9⁷ˢ 6⁶ᵍᶠ 8⁶ᵍᶠ 12⁵ᵍᶠ
36⁶ᶠ 11⁶ᵍˢ 3⁵ᶠ 10⁵ᵈ 15⁶ᵍᶠ 3⁷ˢᵈ 2⁷ˢᵈ 1⁸ˢᵈ
7⁹ˢᵈ **2-5-17 £28,495**

Miss Glory Be *E R Oertel*   47 a67
6 b m Glory Of Dancer - Miss Blondie (USA)
11¹⁰ˢᵈ 3⁸ˢᵈ 5⁸ˢˢ 2⁸ˢᵈ 3¹⁰ˢᵈ 3¹⁰ˢᵈ 7⁸ˢʷ
6¹⁰ᵍᶠ 3¹⁰ᵍˢ **0-5-9 £2,404**

Miss Good Time *J G Given*   51
2 gr f Timeless Times - Fort Vally
9⁵ᵍᶠ 6⁵ᵍ 9⁶ᵍˢ 6⁶ᵍ 6⁶ˢ 5⁶ᵍᶠ 6⁷ᵍᶠ **0-0-7**

Miss Grace *J J Sheehan*   57 a76
4 ch f Atticus (USA) - Jetbeeah (Ire)
9⁸ᵍ 4¹⁰ˢᵈ 11⁸ᵍᶠ 3⁹ᵍ **0-1-4 £822**

Miss Hermione *Mrs C A Dunnett*   58
2 ch f Bahamian Bounty - Try Vickers (USA)
12⁶ˢᵈ 10⁸ᵍˢ 5⁶ˢ **0-0-3**

Miss Hoofbeats *Miss J Feilden*   15
3 b f Unfuwain (USA) - Oiselina (Fr)
14¹⁰ᵍ 8¹²ˢᵈ 15¹²ˢᵈ 10¹⁰ᵍᶠ **0-0-4**

Miss Inkha *R Guest*   66

---

3 b f Intikhab (USA) - Santi Sana
16⁷ᵍ 12⁸ᵍ 6⁸ᵍ 6⁸ᵍ 2¹⁰ʰʸ 11¹¹ᵍ 3¹²ʰʸ
5¹²ᵍˢ **0-2-8 £1,677**

Miss Issy (Ire) *J Gallagher*   a63
4 b f Victory Note (USA) - Shane's Girl (Ire)
3⁷ˢᵈ **0-1-1 £429**

Miss Ivanhoe (Ire) *G Wragg*   102
4 b f Selkirk (USA) - Robellino Miss (USA)
9⁷ᵍˢ 6⁷ˢ 15⁸ᵍ **0-0-3 £750**

Miss Jellybean (Ire) *N Tinkler*   35
2 b f Namid - Elfin Queen (Ire)
9⁵ᵍᶠ 7⁵ᵍᶠ 7⁵ᵍˢ **0-0-3**

Miss Judged *A P Jones*   a46
3 b f Case Law - Marie's Crusader (Ire)
13⁷ˢᵈ 7⁸ˢᵈ 6⁶ˢᵈ 9⁶ˢˢ 9⁵ˢᵈ **0-0-5**

Miss Judgement (Ire) *W R Muir*   72 a55
3 b f Revoque (Ire) - Mugello
5⁶ˢᵈ 3⁶ᵍᶠ 2⁶ᶠ 1⁶ᵍᶠ 3⁶ᵍ 8⁶ˢᵈ 10⁷ᵍᶠ 1⁶ᵍᶠ
17⁶ᵍᶠ 13⁶ᶠ 18⁶ᵍˢ 7⁶ᵍˢ **2-3-12 £9,461**

Miss Koen (Ire) *D L Williams*   60 a56
5 b m Barathea (Ire) - Fanny Blankers (Ire)
6⁸ˢˢ 3¹³ˢᵈ 1¹²ˢᵈ 8¹⁰ˢᵈ 3¹²ᵍˢ 8¹²ᵍˢ 11¹⁴ᵍ
10¹³ᵍᶠ **1-2-8 £3,479**

Miss L'Augeval *G Wragg*   81
2 b f Zilzal (USA) - Miss Sancerre
4⁶ᵍ 1⁷ᵍᶠ 11⁷ʸˢ 10⁷ᵍ 2⁸ʰʸ **1-1-5**
£12,464

Miss Ladybird (USA) *J G Given*   48
3 b/br f Labeeb - Bird Dance (USA)
8⁸ʰʸ **0-0-1**

Miss Langkawi *G Wragg*   76
3 gr f Daylami (Ire) - Miss Amanpuri
10⁹ᵍˢ 9¹²ᵍ 3¹²ˢ 12¹⁰ˢ **0-0-4 £1,589**

Miss Lehman *K G Reveley*   26
6 ch m Beveled (USA) - Lehmans Lot
6⁸ᵍᶠ **0-0-1**

Miss Librate *J M Bradley*   33
6 b m Librate - Hayley's Lass
8⁸ᵍ 8⁸ˢᵈ **0-0-2**

Miss Lyvennet *M Todhunter*   9
3 ch f Then Again - Precious Girl
17⁷ᵍ **0-0-1**

Miss Madame (Ire) *R Guest*   76 a58
3 b f Cape Cross (Ire) - Cosmic Countess (Ire)
3⁷ˢᵈ 3⁵ᵍᶠ 6⁵ᵍ 1⁸ᵍᶠ 2⁸ᶠ 1⁷ᵍᶠ 6⁸ᶠ 16⁸ᵍᶠ
2-2-8 £11,034

Miss Malone (Ire) *R Hannon*   76
2 b f Daggers Drawn (USA) - Queen Molly
7⁶ᵍᶠ 7⁶ᵍ 2⁶ᵍᶠ 4⁶ᵍᶠ 9⁷ᵍᶠ 14⁷ʸˢ 5⁵ʰʸ 7⁶ᵍᶠ
0-1-8 £1,732

Miss Mambo (USA) *D K Weld*   108
3 b f Kingmambo (USA) - Troika (USA)
1⁸ᵍˢ 1⁸ᵍ 3⁸ᵍᶠ 2⁸ᵍˢ 2⁸ᵍ 5⁸ᵍ 1⁸ʸˢ **3-3-7**
£110,236

Miss Meggy *T D Easterby*   95
2 b f Pivotal - Selkirk Rose (Ire)
1⁵ᵍᶠ 1⁵ᵍᶠ 9⁵ᵍᶠ 6⁶ᵍᶠ 5⁵ᵍˢ 6⁷ᵍ 4⁶ˢ **2-0-7**
£23,127

Miss Merenda *D E Cantillon*   54 a48
3 b f Sir Harry Lewis (USA) - Cool Merenda (Ire)
15⁸ᵍ 7¹¹ᵍᶠ 9¹⁰ᵍᶠ 4⁹ˢᵈ **0-0-4 £264**

Miss Millietant *L Montague Hall*   a33
3 b f Up And At 'Em - Annie Hall
13¹⁰ˢᵈ 6⁷ˢᵈ 8⁷ˢᵈ **0-0-3**

Miss Monica (Ire) *H R A Cecil*   70

3 ch f Grand Lodge (USA) - Bea's Ruby (Ire)
6^{8s} 4^{9gf} 3^{10f} 14^{8g} 11^{10g} **0-0-5 £954**

Miss Monza *B R Millman*   69
3 b f Hazaaf (USA) - Monstrosa
8^{6gf} 10^{7gs} 3^{6gs} 12^{6f} 8^{6gf} **0-1-5 £857**

Miss Mytton (USA) *A Bailey*
3 ch f Mt. Livermore (USA) - Sisterella (USA)
15^{7g} **0-0-1**

Miss Noteriety *C J Teague*
4 b f Victory Note (USA) - Mystic Maid (Ire)
11^{7sd} 7^{6gf} 10^{5sd} **0-0-3**

Miss Ocean Monarch *D W Chapman*   42 a16
4 ch f Blue Ocean (USA) - Faraway Grey
11^{7sd} 7^{8sf} 8^{9sd} 9^{8sd} 2^{8gf} 9^{8f} 8^{10gf} 7^{12g}
13^{12gf} **0-1-9 £420**

Miss Particular (Ire) *B W Hills*   60
2 b f Sadler's Wells (USA) - Viz (USA)
11^{7g} **0-0-1**

Miss Patricia *J G Portman*   76
2 b f Mister Baileys - Zoena
7^{6g} 7^{6gf} 4^{6gs} 3^{7gf} **0-1-4 £1,320**

Miss Peaches *G G Margarson*   47 a54
6 b m Emperor Jones (USA) - Dear Person
2^{8sd} 8^{9sd} 3^{8sd} 4^{8sd} 6^{7gf} 5^{8f}
10^{10gf} **1-2-9 £2,523**

Miss Pebbles (Ire) *S C Williams*   78
4 ch f Lake Coniston (Ire) - Sea Of Stone (USA)
1^{10gs} 4^{10s} 7^{10s} 7^{8gf} 5^{8gf} 1^{10gf} 2^{10g} 5^{10s}
13^{10s} 13^{12gs} **2-1-10 £10,281**

Miss Polaris *P W Harris*   79 a81
3 b f Polar Falcon (USA) - Sarabah (Ire)
6^{8gs} 1^{8gf} 2^{9sd} **1-1-3 £6,803**

Miss Poppets *D R C Elsworth*   a58
4 ch f Polar Falcon (USA) - Alifandango (Ire)
9^{6sd} 11^{7sd} **0-0-2**

Miss Porcia *P W Chapple-Hyam*   57
3 ch f Inchinor - Krista
1^{7gf} 2^{7g} 7^{8g} **1-1-3 £3,932**

Miss Prim *G P Kelly*   15 a23
3 ch f Case Law - Calamanco
8^{6g} 8^{6sd} **0-0-2**

Miss Procurer (Ire) *P F I Cole*   57
3 b f Entrepreneur - Kariyh (USA)
5^{7g} 11^{8gf} 4^{7g} 5^{8g} 3^{10gs} **0-0-5 £632**

Miss Rosie *T D Easterby*   67
2 b f Xaar - Disallowed (Ire)
4^{6gf} 4^{7gf} 7^{7gs} **0-0-3 £748**

Miss Shangri La *G Wragg*   44
3 b f Rainbow Quest (USA) - Miss Rinjani
11^{7g} 9^{10gf} 6^{10f} 10^{10f} **0-0-4**

Miss Sharapova (Ire) *G A Butler*   74
2 b f Almutawakel - Dolcezza (Fr)
4^{7gf} **0-0-1 £805**

Miss St Albans *M Wigham*   26
3 b f Robellino (USA) - Alieria (Ire)
12^{10g} 7^{10s} 15^{7gf} 10^{10gf} 20^{7gs} **0-0-5**

Miss Sudbrook (Ire) *D Haydn Jones*   61 a5
2 ch f Daggers Drawn (USA) - Missed Opportunity (Ire)
11^{6gf} 4^{7hy} 10^{6sd} **0-0-3**

Miss The Boat *J L Dunlop*   79
2 b f Mtoto - Missed Again
2^{7g} **0-1-1 £3,300**

Miss Tilly *G B Balding*   34
3 b f Nicolotte - Little White Lies

14^{6s} 17^{7gf} **0-0-2**

Miss Tolerance (USA) *P W D'Arcy*   71 a61
2 ch f Mt. Livermore (USA) - Acquiesce
12^{7gf} 3^{6g} 7^{6sd} **0-1-3 £812**

Miss Trendsetter (Ire) *K A Ryan*   17
2 b f Desert Style (Ire) - Chummy's Friend (Ire)
18^{6g} 8^{7gf} 15^{7s} **0-0-3**

Miss Trial *M A Jarvis*   74
2 b f Zafonic (USA) - Perfect Alibi
6^{6s} 3^{6gf} 3^{7f} 3^{6g} **0-2-4 £2,003**

Miss Trinity *C N Allen*   21 a34
4 b f Catrail (USA) - Rosy Sunset (Ire)
14^{7sd} 10^{5ss} 9^{6sd} 19^{7gf} **0-0-4**

Miss Truant *M L W Bell*   64
2 b f Zaha (Can) - Miss Runaway
6^{5gf} 6^{5g} **0-0-2**

Miss Wizz *W Storey*   52 a34
4 b f Wizard King - Fyas
9^{8sd} 4^{7sd} 1^{6sd} 4^{5gf} 4^{5g} 5^{5g} 1^{6s} 8^{7gf}
11^{6gf} 13^{6sw} 11^{7f} 8^{6s} **2-0-13 £4,683**

Miss Wong One (Ire) *F J Bowles*   59
4 b f Eagle Eyed (USA) - Fakhira
10^{6sd} 2^{5y} 23^{5y} **0-1-3 £1,133**

Miss Woodpigeon *J D Frost*   43
8 b m Landyap (USA) - Pigeon Loft (Ire)
3^{12gf} 7^{10gf} **0-1-2 £528**

Missatacama (Ire) *D J Daly*   a71
2 b f Desert Style (Ire) - Delta Town (USA)
4^{7sd} 5^{8sd} **0-0-2 £326**

Missed A Beat *M Blanshard*   72
2 b f Mister Baileys - Lonely Heart
8^{6gf} 4^{8gf} 14^{7gf} 1^{6gf} 5^{6hy} 20^{6hy} **1-0-6
£3,500**

Missed Turn *J M P Eustace*   42 a29
2 b f Mind Games - Miss Beverley
5^{5ss} 4^{5g} 4^{6sd} 5^{6gf} 9^{6gf} 12^{7g} **0-0-6 £278**

Missella (Ire) *M Johnston*   49
2 gr f Danehill (USA) - Delage
16^{7g} 4^{8s} **0-0-2 £336**

Missie *G A Swinbank*   31
4 ch f Compton Place - About Face
9^{7f} 12^{5gf} **0-0-2**

Missie Baileys *D R C Elsworth*   67 a66
2 ch f Mister Baileys - Jilly Woo
6^{6gs} 5^{7sd} 8^{7gf} 1^{8g} **1-0-4 £3,445**

Missin Margot *Ms Deborah J Evans*   35 a38
2 b f Fraam - Abstone Queen
5^{6f} 7^{6sd} 6^{5g} **0-0-3**

Mission Affirmed (USA) *T P Tate*   67 a76
3 ch g Stravinsky (USA) - Affirmed Legacy (USA)
9^{6sd} 1^{7ss} 5^{8s} 18^{sd} 12^{8hy} 4^{8sd} 10^{8gs} 5^{9gf}
2^{8sd} 3^{7gf} 8^{8gf} **2-2-11 £9,979**

Mission Man *R Hannon*   85
3 b c Revoque (Ire) - Opopmil (Ire)
4^{7g} 2^{7gs} 1^{6s} 4^{7gf} 7^{6gf} 4^{8g} 5^{8gf} 7^{8gs}
11^{7gs} **1-1-9 £6,733**

Mission To Mars *P R Hedger*   a105
5 b g Muhtarram (USA) - Ideal Candidate
1^{12sd} 1^{12sd} 3^{12sw} **2-1-3 £11,983**

Missperon (Ire) *K A Ryan*   79
2 b f Orpen (USA) - Secret Hideaway (USA)
5^{6f} 3^{6f} 1^{6gf} 3^{5g} 4^{6gf} 12^{6gf} 2^{6s} **1-3-7
£9,925**

Missus Links (USA) *R Hannon*   74
3 b f Lure (USA) - Cozisaidso (USA)

5⁶ᵍ 2⁶ᵍ 5⁷ᵍᶠ 13⁶ᵍᶠ 6⁶ᵍ 4⁶ˢ 8⁶ᵍ **0-2-7**
£2,184

Missy Cinofaz *I A Wood*   27 a53
2 ch f Zafonic (USA) - Dancing Wolf (Ire)
13⁷ᵍ 4⁷ˢᵈ **0-0-2 £326**

Mist Opportunity (Ire) *P C Haslam*   43
2 b g Danetime (Ire) - Lady Of The Mist (Ire)
10⁵ᵍᶠ 11⁷ᶠ 8⁷ᵍ 12⁷ᵍˢ **0-0-4**

Mistblack *A Senior*
4 b f Wizard King - Dear Heart
8⁵ˢᵈ **0-0-1**

Mister Arjay (USA) *B Ellison*   64 a62
4 b c Mister Baileys - Crystal Stepper (USA)
9⁸ᵍ 6¹⁰ᵍ 11¹²ˢᵈ 11¹⁰ˢ **0-0-4 £158**

Mister Aziz (Ire) *J M P Eustace*   61 a40
2 b c Mister Baileys - Aziz Presenting (Ire)
10⁶ᵍᶠ 8⁷ˢᵈ 5⁵ᵍᶠ 11⁶ᵍᶠ **0-0-4**

Mister Bell *J G M O'Shea*   42
2 gr c Lujain (USA) - Zaragossa
3⁵ᵍˢ 6⁵ᶠ 12⁶ᵍᶠ 8⁶ᵍ 14⁵ᵍˢ **0-0-5 £640**

Mister Benji *B P J Baugh*   a61
5 b g Catrail (USA) - Katy-Q (Ire)
9⁸ˢᵈ 5⁷ˢᵈ 7⁹ˢᵈ **0-0-3**

Mister Buzz *M D Hammond*   61
2 b c Mind Games - Compact Disc (Ire)
11⁶ᶠ 11⁶ˢ 8⁶ᵍ 4⁶ᵍᶠ 4⁶ᵍˢ 13⁶ᵍ 10⁸ˢ **0-0-7**
£296

Mister Chalk *T Keddy*
3 gr c Silver Patriarch (Ire) - B B Glen
18¹⁰ˢ **0-0-1**

Mister Clinton (Ire) *D K Ivory*   68 a54
7 ch g Lion Cavern (USA) - Thewaari (USA)
11⁷ˢᵈ 10⁸ˢᵈ 11¹⁰ˢᵈ 11⁸ˢᵈ 6⁷ˢᵈ 3⁷ᶠ 4⁷ᶠ
8¹⁰ᵍᶠ 1⁸ᵍ 2⁷ᵍᶠ 10⁸ᵍᶠ 1⁸ᶠ 6⁷ˢ 8⁷ᵍᶠ 9⁸ᵍᶠ 9⁸ᵍᶠ
2-2-16 £9,385

Mister Completely (Ire) *J R Best*   51 a59
3 b g Princely Heir (Ire) - Blue Goose
2⁶ˢᵈ 6⁷ˢᵈ 5⁷ˢᵈ 7⁶ᵍˢ 10⁶ᵍᶠ 9¹⁰ˢᵈ 11⁷ᵍ
7¹²ˢᵈ 1⁸ᶠ 6⁸ˢᵈ 10¹⁶ᵍᶠ 1¹⁰ˢᵈ 14¹⁰ˢ 5¹⁰ᵍᶠ 3¹⁰ᵍᶠ
3¹⁴ˢ **2-2-16 £7,652**

Mister Elegant *J L Spearing*   64
2 b c Fraam - Risky Valentine
18⁶ᵍᶠ 4⁸ᵍˢ 6⁸ᵍˢ **0-0-3 £446**

Mister Genepi *W R Muir*   103
2 b c Mister Baileys - Ring Queen (USA)
5⁷ᵍˢ 2⁷ᵍᶠ 2⁷ˢ 3⁷ᵍ 7⁷ᵍᶠ 3⁷ᵍ 1⁸ᵍ **1-4-7**
£15,666

Mister Graham *K F Clutterbuck*   26 a43
9 b g Rock Hopper - Celestial Air
9¹²ᵍˢ 4¹⁶ˢᵈ 6¹⁰ˢᵈ **0-0-3**

Mister Links (Ire) *Saeed Bin Suroor*   107
4 b c Flying Spur (Aus) - Lady Anna Livia
3⁶ᵍ 1⁷ᵍᶠ **1-0-2 £8,208**

Mister Mal (Ire) *B Ellison*   64 a65
8 b g Scenic - Fashion Parade
10⁷ˢʷ 6⁷ᵍ 16ʰʸ 9⁶ᵍᶠ 7⁶ᵍᶠ 3⁵ᵍˢ 1⁶ˢᵈ 2⁵ᵍˢ
7⁵ᵍˢ **2-2-9 £9,935**

Mister Marmaduke *I Semple*   86 a14
3 b g Marju (Ire) - Lalique (Ire)
13⁵ᵍ 4⁷ᵍᶠ 3⁶ᵍ 5⁵ᵍᶠ 8⁸ᵍ 9⁷ᵍᶠ 13⁶ˢᵈ **0-1-7**
£2,671

Mister Merlin (Ire) *D Carroll*   12
3 ch g Titus Livius (Fr) - Official Secret
19¹²ᵍ 20¹²ᵍ **0-0-2**

Mister Minty (Ire) *D Carroll*   12

2 b c Fasliyev (USA) - Sorb Apple (Ire)
13⁶ᵍ **0-0-1**

Mister Monet (Ire) *M Johnston*   124
3 b c Peintre Celebre (USA) - Breyani
2⁸ᵍˢ 1⁹ᵍᶠ 1¹⁰ᵍᶠ 1¹¹ᵍ 1¹⁰ʰʸ PU¹⁰ˢ **4-1-6**
£111,102

Mister Muja (Ire) *W R Swinburn*   59 a69
3 gr g Mujadil (USA) - Remiss (Ire)
7⁷ᵍˢ 6⁷ᵍˢ 1⁷ˢᵈ **1-0-3 £3,877**

Mister Putt (USA) *Mrs N Smith*   64
6 b/br g Mister Baileys - Theresita (Ger)
2¹⁵ˢ 15¹⁶ᵍˢ **0-1-2 £1,081**

Mister Regent *K A Ryan*   62
3 b g Mind Games - River Of Fortune (Ire)
3⁶ᵍˢ 8⁶ᵍ 12⁷ᶠ 10⁷ᵍᶠ 14⁷ᵍᶠ 8⁷ᵍᶠ **0-1-6**
£566

Mister Right (Ire) *K Bell*   59
3 ch g Barathea (Ire) - Broken Spirit (Ire)
3⁸ᵍ 10¹⁰ˢ **0-1-2 £636**

Mister Rushby *Miss V Haigh*   a16
4 b g Hamas (Ire) - Final Rush
12⁶ˢᵈ 9¹²ˢᵈ 9⁸ˢᶠ **0-0-3**

Mister Saif (USA) *R Hannon*   92
3 ch g Miswaki (USA) - Shawgatny (Ire)
7⁷ᵍ UR⁸ᵍ 5⁷ᵍˢ 9⁸ˢ 4⁷ᵍ 2⁷ᵍᶠ 11⁷ᵍ 12⁷ᵍᶠ
0-2-8 £4,928

Mister Sweets *D Carroll*   81 a61
5 ch g Nashwan (USA) - Keyboogie (USA)
6⁶ᵍ 10⁶ᵍᶠ 1⁷ᵍᶠ 5⁷ᵍ 14⁶ᵍᶠ 12⁶ᵍ 6⁷ˢᶠ
19⁶ᵍᶠ 22⁸ᵍᶠ 9⁷ᵍ 20⁷ˢ **1-0-11 £3,484**

Mister Trickster (Ire) *R Dickin*   68
3 b c Woodborough (USA) - Tinos Island (Ire)
6¹⁰ᵍˢ 13¹¹ᵍˢ 11¹²ˢ 1⁷ᵍ 11⁷ᵍᶠ 8⁸ᵍ 13⁸ᵍˢ
3⁸ᶠ **1-1-8 £4,256**

Mister Troubridge *G B Balding*   45
2 ch c Mister Baileys - So True
13⁷ˢ 9⁷ᵍˢ 9⁷ˢ **0-0-3**

Misternando *M R Channon*   109
4 b c Hernando (Fr) - Mistinguett (Ire)
9¹⁶ˢ 9¹²ᵍˢ 6¹⁶ᵍᶠ 8²⁰ᵍᶠ 3¹⁶ᵍˢ 3¹⁶ᵍᶠ **0-3-6**
£42,335

Misters Sister *J G Given*   41
2 b f Robellino (USA) - Baileys On Line
14⁸ᵍ 7¹⁰ʰʸ 13¹⁰ˢ **0-0-3**

Mistral Sky *Mrs Stef Liddiard*   82 a82
5 b g Hurricane Sky (Aus) - Dusk In Daytona
2⁷ˢᵈ 11⁷ˢᵈ 13⁶ˢʷ 2⁷ᵍˢ 11⁷ᵍ 4⁷ᵍᶠ 3⁷ᵍᶠ
3⁷ᵍᶠ 5⁸ᵍᶠ 4⁷ᵍ 7⁷ᵍᶠ 2⁶ᵍᶠ 2⁶ᵍᶠ 1⁶ᵍˢ 2⁶ˢᵈ
12⁶ˢᵈ **2-7-17 £19,240**

Mistress Hollie (Ire) *Mrs P N Dutfield*   a33
3 b f Titus Livius (Fr) - Soden (Ire)
8⁸ˢᵈ **0-0-1**

Mistress Twister *T D Barron*   78
3 b f Pivotal - Foreign Mistress
3⁷ᶠ 3⁸ᵍᶠ 3⁷ᶠ 11⁸ᵍˢ 1⁸ᵍᶠ **1-3-6**
£10,324

Misty Bay *J Balding*
2 b f Namaqualand (USA) - Paris Mist
9⁵ᵍ **0-0-1**

Misty Man (USA) *Miss J Feilden*   26 a46
6 ch g El Gran Senor - Miasma (USA)
3¹²ˢᵈ 5⁹ˢᵈ 1¹²ˢᵈ 4¹¹ˢᵈ 5¹⁰ʰʸ 5¹¹ˢᵈ 8⁹ˢᵈ
1-1-7 £2,816

Misty Miller *T D Easterby*   57
2 b c Mind Games - Antonia's Folly

5^{5s} 8^{5g} 6^{6gf} **0-0-3**

Misty Princess *M J Polglase* 48 a54
2 gr f Paris House - Miss Whittingham (Ire)
11^{5g} 5^{5g} 8^{5g} 14^{5gf} 9^{6sd} 13^{6g} 8^{5sd} **0-0-7**

Mitcham (Ire) *T G Mills* 72
8 br g Hamas (Ire) - Arab Scimetar (Ire)
18^{6gs} **0-0-1**

Mitchelland *James Moffatt* 74 a68
2 b f Namaqualand (USA) - Precious Girl
4^{5g} 1^{5hy} 9^{5gs} 6^{5gf} 6^{6g} 3^{5s} 5^{7gs} 5^{6s} 5^{6s}
13^{6hy} 5^{5sd} 2^{7sd} **1-2-12 £6,985**

Mith Hill *E A L Dunlop* 78 a81
3 b c Daylami (Ire) - Delirious Moment (Ire)
7^{11g} 1^{10gs} 1^{12sd} 1^{12sd} 17^{12s} **3-0-5**
£11,588

Mitraillette (USA) *Sir Michael Stoute* 79
2 ch f Miswaki (USA) - Crockadore (USA)
6^{6g} 5^{6gf} 4^{7g} 1^{7gf} **1-0-4 £4,154**

Mitrash *D McCain* 25
4 b g Darshaan - L'Ideale (USA)
8^{12gs} **0-0-1**

Mitsuki *J D Bethell* 65
5 b m Puissance - Surrealist (Ity)
9^{6g} 5^{6gf} 8^{6gf} 9^{5gs} **0-0-4**

Mitzi Caspar *P L Gilligan* 4 a52
3 ch f Kirkwall - Petrovna (Ire)
7^{8ss} 15^{8g} 15^{8g} 24^{8g} 3^{6sd} 2^{7sd} 1^{7sd} 9^{8sd}
13^{6gf} 14^{8sw} 12^{7g} **1-2-11 £3,656**

Mix It Up *R M Beckett* 18
3 gr f Linamix (Fr) - Hawayah (Ire)
10^{8g} **0-0-1**

Mizhar (USA) *J J Quinn* a63
8 b/br g Dayjur (USA) - Futuh (USA)
11^{7sd} 5^{6sd} 2^{7ss} 5^{7sd} 8^{6ss} 11^{6gs} 1^{7sd} 3^{7sd}
2^{8sd} PU^{6gf} **1-3-10 £4,059**

Mizz Tee (Ire) *T D Easterby* 82
2 b f Orpen (USA) - D D's Jakette (USA)
2^{5gs} 1^{5gf} 5^{5gf} **1-1-3 £7,715**

Mkuzi *John M Oxx* 113
5 ch h Halling (USA) - African Peace (USA)
6^{10gf} 6^{12gf} 8^{12gf} 5^{10y} 1^{12f} 1^{14g} 3^{12gf}
2^{14gf} 8^{16s} **2-1-9 £66,654**

Moaning Myrtle *J R Fanshawe* a58
3 br f Desert King (Ire) - Grinning (Ire)
4^{12sd} 11^{13sd} **0-0-2**

Moayed *N P Littmoden* 94 a100
5 b g Selkirk (USA) - Song Of Years (Ire)
1^{8sd} 2^{10sd} 6^{10sd} 3^{7sd} 3^{7hy} 1^{6g} 10^{5gf} 4^{7gf}
14^{7s} 16^{sd} **3-3-10 £50,771**

Mobane Flyer *R A Fahey* 73
4 b g Groom Dancer (USA) - Enchant
12^{7g} 10^{7g} 6^{8gs} 3^{9hy} 3^{10gf} 1^{8gf} 3^{8gf} 2^{8hy}
2^{10s} 6^{10hy} **1-5-10 £8,894**

Mobarhen (USA) *Sir Michael Stoute* 77
2 br/br c Red Ransom (USA) - Fit For A Queen (USA)
5^{7gf} 5^{8gs} 2^{8f} 3^{8g} 9^{8s} **0-2-5 £2,378**

Mobo-Baco *R J Hodges* 63 a61
7 ch g Bandmaster (USA) - Darakah
4^{10g} 4^{8s} 9^{8gf} 9^{8f} 7^{8gf} 5^{8g} 9^{7gf}
6^{8gf} 9^{8s} 3^{8gf} 2^{8g} 2^{9sd} **1-4-15 £5,818**

Mocca (Ire) *D J Coakley* 93
3 b f Sri Pekan (USA) - Ewan (Ire)
4^{10g} 5^{11g} 1^{10gf} 6^{12gf} 2^{10g} 6^{10gf} 3^{10s} 5^{10s}
1-2-8 £12,034

Mochaccino (Ire) *D Shaw* 32 a12
2 b f Tagula (Ire) - Cafe Solo
14^{5sd} 8^{5gs} 12^{6gf} 11^{5sd} **0-0-4**

Model Figure (USA) *B W Hills* 52
3 b f Distant View (USA) - Sylph (USA)
10^{7gf} **0-0-1**

Modem (Ire) *D Shaw* a23
7 b g Midhish - Holy Water
10^{12sd} BD^{10sd} **0-0-2**

Modesta (Ire) *H R A Cecil* 101
3 b f Sadler's Wells (USA) - Modena (USA)
4^{10g} 1^{11gf} 2^{12g} 8^{12gf} 6^{14s} 5^{15g} 1^{14s} **2-1-7**
£26,398

Modesty Blaise (Swe) *C A Horgan* a69
4 br f Mango Express - Singoalla (Ire)
1^{7sd} 7^{8sd} 5^{7ss} 12^{12sd} **1-0-4 £1,463**

Modraj *J L Dunlop* 75
2 b f Machiavellian (USA) - Saleela (USA)
9^{6g} 3^{6gs} **0-1-2 £864**

Modulor (Fr) *L R James* 75
12 gr g Less Ice - Chaumontaise (Fr)
10^{12gf} 10^{12gs} **0-0-2**

Mokabra (Ire) *M R Channon* 105
3 b c Cape Cross (Ire) - Pacific Grove
6^{7g} 3^{7g} 8^{8g} 17^{8f} **0-0-4 £6,217**

Mokaraba *J L Dunlop* 86
2 ch f Unfuwain (USA) - Muhaba (USA)
4^{7gf} 8^{8gs} 2^{8f} 2^{8s} **0-2-4 £5,178**

Molcon (Ire) *N A Callaghan* 90
3 b g Danetime (Ire) - Wicken Wonder (Ire)
5^{6gs} 1^{6s} 5^{6s} 3^{6gf} 4^{7f} 4^{7gf} 10^{7g} 1^{7gf}
8^{7gf} 7^{7s} 17^{8gf} 10^{7s} **2-1-12 £18,582**

Molehill *J G Given* 63
3 b f Salse (USA) - Mountain Lodge
7^{12gs} 5^{12gf} 4^{12gf} 7^{17gs} 8^{16gs} **0-0-5 £429**

Molem *Sir Michael Stoute* 71
2 br g Green Desert (USA) - Injaad
6^{7gf} 4^{8hy} **0-0-2 £542**

Molinia *Mrs Stef Liddiard* 59 a62
3 b f Nicolotte - Themeda
11^{8s} PU^{8gf} 4^{7gf} 11^{8gf} 4^{7g} 7^{7gf} 3^{7gf}
14^{7g} 1^{7sd} **1-2-9 £2,860**

Molly Dancer *M R Channon* 63
2 b f Emarati (USA) - Perfect Partner
9^{6gf} 9^{6gf} 3^{6gf} 5^{5s} 6^{5gf} **0-1-5 £421**

Molly Marie (Ire) *T D Easterby* 78
2 b f Fasliyev (USA) - Snoozeandyoulose (Ire)
2^{5g} 4^{6g} 6^{5s} 2^{6g} 7^{7s} 10^{7g} 9^{6gf} 2^{6hy} **0-3-8**
£4,328

Molly Moon (Ire) *M Blanshard* 69
3 gr f Primo Dominie - Snowing
14^{5gf} 8^{5gf} 7^{6g} **0-0-3**

Molly's Secret *C G Cox* 53 a56
6 b m Minshaanshu Amad (USA) - Secret Miss
1^{12sd} 8^{12sd} 9^{12sd} 3^{10gf} 7^{12gf} 3^{12gf}
6^{10s} 3^{11gf} **1-3-9 £4,492**

Mollzam (Ire) *M P Tregoning* 46
2 b c Danehill (USA) - Matilda Bay (Ire)
9^{7g} 12^{7gs} **0-0-2**

Molotov *I W McInnes* 63 a43
4 b g Efisio - Mindomica
1^{5gf} 10^{5sd} 17^{6gf} 4^{5gf} 1^{5g} 3^{6gf} 3^{5f} 4^{6g}
1^{5s} **3-4-9 £8,647**

Mombassa (Ire) *Edward Lynam* 105
4 b g Mujadil (USA) - Twilight Tango

4^{7gf} 6^{6gf} 18^{5g} 11^{7gf} 10^{7gf} 5^{7g} 4^{8y} 1^{8ys}
8^{8s} 2^{7sh} **1-1-10 £21,635**

Moments I Treasure (USA) *E A L Dunlop*   45 a45
3 ch f Mt. Livermore (USA) - Munnaya (USA)
6^{8sd} 9^{12gs} **0-0-2**

Moments Of Joy *R Guest*   93
4 b f Darshaan - My Emma
7^{12g} **0-0-1**

Mommkin *M R Channon*   78
3 b f Royal Academy (USA) - Walimu (Ire)
5^{11gf} 5^{10gf} 5^{10g} 4^{10gf} 9^{12gf} **0-0-5 £423**

Momtic (Ire) *W Jarvis*   90
3 ch c Shinko Forest (Ire) - Uffizi (Ire)
3^{9gs} 3^{8gs} 9^{9g} 4^{10gs} 4^{8gf} 1^{9gf} 2^{8g} 5^{10gs}
1-3-8 £16,158

Mon Plaisir *C F Wall*   34 a7
2 br f Singspiel (Ire) - Mademoiselle Chloe
12^{7sd} 10^{7s} **0-0-2**

Mon Secret (Ire) *B Smart*   61 a62
6 b g General Monash (USA) - Ron's Secret
4^{8sd} 7^{7ss} 12^{7g} 6^{7gf} 14^{7g} 6^{8gf} 1^{7g} 11^{8gf}
9^{9sd} 6^{9sd} **1-0-10 £3,295**

Mona Lisa *A P O'Brien*   112 a81
2 ch f Giant's Causeway (USA) - Colorsnap
4^{7g} 2^{7gf} 4^{8gf} 11^{9ft} **0-1-4 £13,126**

Monad (Ire) *Mrs P N Dutfield*   54 a52
2 b f General Monash (USA) - Moon River (Fr)
10^{7gs} 11^{7gs} 8^{7s} 8^{8sd} **0-0-4**

Monash Girl (Ire) *B R Johnson*   44
3 b f General Monash (USA) - Maricica
6^{8f} 11^{8gf} 11^{8s} **0-0-3**

Monash Lad (Ire) *M H Tompkins*   73
2 ch g General Monash (USA) - Story Time (Ire)
12^{5gf} 5^{6gf} 3^{6gf} 3^{6gf} 4^{6gf} 3^{6s} **0-2-6**
£2,943

Monashee Miss *J A Pickering*   27 a27
2 ch f Monashee Mountain (USA) - Most Uppitty
4^{5s} 8^{6sd} 3^{7sd} 10^{7sd} PU^{7sd} **0-0-5 £631**

Monashee Prince (Ire) *J R Best*   83
2 ch g Monashee Mountain (USA) - Lodema (Ire)
2^{5gf} 1^{5g} 5^{5gs} 3^{5gf} 4^{5gf} 12^{5gs} 13^{6gs} 9^{6s}
1-2-8 £5,884

Monashee Rose (Ire) *J S Moore*   77
2 br f Monashee Mountain (USA) - Thorn Tree
7^{5gf} 1^{5f} 1^{5gf} 2^{6g} 10^{5gf} 10^{5gf} 6^{5hy} **2-1-7**
£11,255

Monduru *G L Moore*   a53
7 b g Lion Cavern (USA) - Bint Albadou (Ire)
8^{10sd} 1^{8ss} 2^{10sd} 2^{10sd} 3^{10sd} 2^{9sd} 1^{10sd}
2-3-7 £4,467

Monica's Revenge (Ire) *R M Beckett*   48 a36
2 b f Josr Algarhoud (Ire) - Unimpeachable (Ire)
9^{6gf} 8^{7hy} 8^{9sd} **0-0-3**

Monkey Madge *B Smart*   68
2 br f Cape Cross (Ire) - Runelia
2^{6g} 7^{6g} **0-1-2 £935**

Monkey Or Me (Ire) *P T Midgley*   36 a36
3 b g Sri Pekan (USA) - Ecco Mi (Ire)
8^{7sd} 2^{8ss} 4^{7sd} 2^{8sd} 3^{7g} 3^{7sd} 4^{8gf} 12^{10gs}
15^{8f} **0-2-9 £827**

Monolith *L Lungo*   85
6 b g Bigstone (Ire) - Ancara
3^{13g} 16^{18s} **0-1-2 £1,484**

Monsal Dale (Ire) *Mrs L C Jewell*   32 a32
5 ch g Desert King (Ire) - Zanella (Ire)

8^{12ss} 7^{16sd} 14^{14g} 6^{16sd} **0-0-4**

Monsieur Bond (Ire) *B Smart*   119
4 ch c Danehill Dancer (Ire) - Musical Essence
5^{6g} 1^{7ys} 16^{6g} 12^{6f} 6^{6gs} 9^{7gs} 5^{6g} 4^{7s}
2-0-8 £107,508

Monsieur Mirasol *K A Ryan*   76
2 b g Mind Games - Nom Francais
3^{5gf} 3^{5g} 5^{5f} 1^{6s} 8^{6gf} 2^{6hy} 4^{5gs} 7^{7gf} 5^{6gf}
15^{6gf} 14^{6hy} **1-2-11 £6,672**

Monsoon Rain (USA) *Saeed Bin Suroor*   84
2 b c Old Trieste (USA) - Smokey Mirage (USA)
2^{7gf} 1^{8g} **1-1-2 £8,555**

Mont Saint Michel (Ire) *G Wragg*   65
2 b c Montjeu (Ire) - Band Of Angels (Ire)
14^{7g} 6^{8g} **0-0-2**

Montana *J L Spearing*   59
4 b c Puissance - Mistral's Dancer
10^{5gs} 4^{6gf} 18^{6g} **0-0-3 £259**

Montara (Ire) *Lindsay Woods*   50 a55
5 b h Perugino (USA) - Tatra
6^{9f} 3^{10g} 2^{10g} 9^{12gy} 1^{9sd} 5^{9sd} **1-2-6**
£3,007

Monte Major (Ire) *M A Jarvis*   75 a74
3 b g Docksider (USA) - Danalia (Ire)
3^{7sd} 4^{7sd} 2^{8ss} 1^{7sd} 2^{6gs} 9^{6g} **1-3-6**
£8,048

Monte Mayor Lad (Ire) *D Haydn Jones*   56 a51
4 b g Sesaro (USA) - Alcalali (USA)
14^{6gs} 7^{6gf} 10^{8sd} **0-0-3**

Montecito *R Hannon*   78
2 b f Montjeu (Ire) - Dancing Fire (USA)
8^{6gs} 8^{7g} 3^{6gs} 12^{6s} **0-0-4 £1,864**

Montecristo *R Guest*   75
11 br g Warning - Sutosky
9^{12g} 15^{12g} 7^{12s} 4^{12s} 4^{14s} **0-0-5 £812**

Montgomery *A G Newcombe*   48
3 b g In Command (Ire) - Lightening Reef
6^{12gf} 6^{9gs} 5^{10gf} 8^{10gf} **0-0-4**

Montgomery's Arch (USA) *P W Chapple-Hyam*   118
2 b/br c Arch (USA) - Inny River (USA)
1^{7gs} 16^{gf} 4^{7g} 3^{7s} **2-1-4 £86,749**

Montjeu Baby (Ire) *R Hannon*   56
2 b f Montjeu (Ire) - Catch The Lights
11^{6g} 14^{7g} 12^{7gf} 8^{8gs} **0-0-4**

Montmartre (Ire) *J Howard Johnson*   63
4 br f Grand Lodge (USA) - French Quarter
13^{14g} 8^{8f} **0-0-2**

Montosari *P Mitchell*   41 a62
5 ch g Persian Bold - Sartigila
1^{13sd} 6^{10sd} 3^{12sd} 1^{12sd} 2^{10sd} 13^{12gf} 3^{16sd}
10^{12g} 12^{16sd} **2-3-9 £4,208**

Monturani (Ire) *G Wragg*   111
5 b m Indian Ridge - Mezzogiorno
3^{8gs} 6^{11gs} 2^{8gf} 4^{8gf} 4^{8g} 5^{10vs} 1^{10g} 11^{10gs}
1-2-8 £114,237

Moon Bird *C A Cyzer*   12
2 b f Primo Dominie - Time For Tea (Ire)
13^{6gf} **0-0-1**

Moon Dazzle (USA) *W J Haggas*   105
3 b f Kingmambo (USA) - June Moon (Ire)
1^{8gf} 4^{8f} 5^{8gs} 5^{8gf} 2^{8gf} 6^{8gf} **1-1-6**
£26,232

Moon Emperor *J R Jenkins*   82 a91
7 b g Emperor Jones (USA) - Sir Hollow (USA)
11^{12sd} 6^{12sd} 9^{16ss} 4^{14gs} 6^{14g} 6^{14gf} 8^{16g}

13^{16g} 7^{16gs} **0-1-9 £1,125**

Moon Forest (Ire) *P W Chapple-Hyam* 81
2 br c Woodborough (USA) - Ma Bella Luna
2^{7gs} 4^{6gs} 1^{7gs} 1^{7s} **2-1-4 £8,423**

Moon Legend (USA) *W Jarvis* 71 a61
3 ch f Gulch (USA) - Highland Legend (USA)
7^{7gf} 3^{7f} 9^{7gf} 1^{7f} 9^{6gf} 6^{7sd} **1-1-6 £6,448**

Moon Mischief (Ire) *N P Littmoden* 53 a65
2 b f Desert Sun - Moonlight Path (Ire)
7^{6gf} 3^{5sd} 8^{5g} 9^{6gf} **0-0-4 £518**

Moon Royale *Mrs N Macauley* 26 a14
6 ch m Royal Abjar (USA) - Ragged Moon
8^{6sd} 8^{7sd} 8^{11ss} 14^{8gs} **0-0-4**

Moon Shot *A G Juckes* 12 a75
8 gr g Pistolet Bleu (Ire) - La Luna (USA)
1^{12sw} 2^{12sd} 4^{12sd} 15^{10s} **1-1-4 £4,717**

Moon Spinner *Andrew Reid* 44 a34
7 b m Elmaamul (USA) - Lunabelle
10^{12f} 8^{8gf} 9^{7sd} 12^{14s} **0-0-4**

Moonfleet (Ire) *M F Harris* 59
2 b f Entrepreneur - Lunasa (Ire)
8^{7gs} 3^{6g} 8^{8g} 19^{8s} **0-0-4 £207**

Moonglade (USA) *Miss J Feilden* 36 a9
4 ch f Carson City (USA) - Moonshine Girl (USA)
10^{6sd} 13^{6sd} 8^{6g} 5^{6gf} 15^{7g} 6^{5f} 12^{6gf} **0-0-7**

Moonlight Appeal (Ire) *J S Wainwright*
2 ch f Bahamian Bounty - Divine Appeal
13^{6g} **0-0-1**

Moonlight Man *R Hannon* 105
3 ch c Night Shift (USA) - Fleeting Rainbow
2^{7g} 2^{6s} 7^{7gf} 15^{6g} 2^{7g} 4^{7gf} 2^{7gf} 6^{8gf} 9^{7gf} **0-4-9 £24,143**

Moonlight Song (Ire) *John A Harris* 45 a18
7 b m Mujadil (USA) - Model Show (Ire)
3^{7g} 10^{7s} 8^{8sd} 15^{7sd} 14^{7g} 13^{7gf} 13^{7sd} **0-1-7 £232**

Moonlight Tango (USA) *J H M Gosden* 78
3 br f Benny The Dip (USA) - Summer Dance
5^{10g} 5^{10g} 4^{12gf} **0-0-3 £520**

Moonmaiden *M R Channon* 70
2 ch f Selkirk (USA) - Top Table
10^{7gs} 5^{8s} 5^{8gs} 7^{7gf} **0-0-4**

Moonshaft (USA) *E A L Dunlop* 66 a70
3 br c Capote (USA) - Moonshine Girl (USA)
17^{10gs} 7^{10gs} 4^{10hy} 8^{12gf} 4^{9gs} 5^{9sd} 13^{7sd} **0-0-7 £857**

Moonshine Beach *P W Hiatt* 84
6 b g Lugana Beach - Monongelia
4^{15s} 7^{22s} 6^{14g} 3^{16gf} 6^{18g} 4^{19gf} PU^{15gf} 1^{16g} 1^{17g} 13^{16gf} 3^{16f} 1^{16gs} 1^{16gs} 13^{16gf} 3^{17g} 1^{17gf} 1^{18g} **6-3-18 £28,013**

Moonshine Bill *P W Hiatt* 60
5 ch g Master Willie - Monongelia
3^{11s} 7^{10s} **0-1-2 £500**

Moonside *J A Geake* 32
2 gr f Docksider (USA) - Moon Magic
12^{6g} 15^{7g} 14^{7gs} **0-0-3**

Moonstruck *J M P Eustace* a49
2 ch c Fraam - Easter Moon (Fr)
7^{8sd} **0-0-1**

Moors Myth *B W Hills* 77 a60
3 b g Anabaa (USA) - West Devon (USA)
3^{7gs} 6^{7g} 5^{7gf} 6^{8g} 1^{7f} 7^{7sd} **1-1-6**

£4,339

Moose Malloy *M J Ryan* a3
7 ch g Formidable (USA) - Jolimo
5^{8sd} **0-0-1**

Morag *I A Wood* 66 a15
3 b f Aragon - Minnehaha
4^{8gs} 10^{10gf} 8^{8gf} 11^{7f} 6^{8gs} 6^{8g} 2^{7gf} 7^{7s} 7^{7gf} 11^{9gf} 15^{7g} 10^{7sd} **0-2-12 £1,488**

Morahib *W J Musson* 61
6 ch h Nashwan (USA) - Irish Valley (USA)
2^{10gf} 10^{10gs} **0-1-2 £838**

Morgan Lewis (Ire) *G B Balding* 79
3 b g Orpen (USA) - Party Piece
7^{5gf} 1^{6g} 3^{6gs} 2^{5s} 3^{5s} **1-3-5 £7,517**

Moritat (Ire) *P D Evans* 58 a16
4 b g Night Shift (USA) - Aunty Eileen
13^{6sd} 6^{5gf} 3^{5gf} 5^{6gf} 6^{6gs} 3^{6g} 14^{5gf} 10^{6g} **0-2-8 £1,453**

Mornin Reserves *I Semple* 86
5 b g Atraf - Pusey Street Girl
13^{5g} 15^{5gf} 11^{5gs} **0-0-3**

Morning After *J R Fanshawe* 70 a71
4 b f Emperor Jones (USA) - Onefortheditch (USA)
8^{8gf} 6^{8sd} 6^{7g} 4^{8sd} **0-0-4 £270**

Morning Hawk (USA) *J S Moore* 43 a43
3 b f Silver Hawk (USA) - Dawn Aurora (USA)
7^{8sd} 4^{11sd} 5^{9ss} 6^{10sd} 9^{16gs} 4^{16gf} 9^{14gf} 4^{16s} 11^{10g} **0-0-9**

Morning Major (USA) *T D Barron* 44
2 b g Parade Ground (USA) - North Of Seattle (USA)
10^{6s} 8^{7g} 10^{7gs} **0-0-3**

Morning Sun *K O Cunningham-Brown*
4 b f Starborough - Malham Tarn
9^{9sd} **0-0-1**

Morning World *J R Weymes* 24
2 b c Bahamian Bounty - Snap Cracker
10^{5g} 10^{5g} 6^{5gf} **0-0-3**

Morozov (USA) *C N Allen*
5 b h Sadler's Wells (USA) - High Hawk
PU^{16s} PU^{14gs} **0-0-2**

Morris Dancing (USA) *B P J Baugh* 5 a44
5 b g Rahy (USA) - Summer Dance
9^{11sd} 7^{9sd} 9^{12ss} 14^{8ss} 5^{10sd} 11^{12sd} 8^{8sf} 7^{9sd} 13^{11sd} 5^{12sd} 10^{13gf} **0-1-11 £206**

Morse (Ire) *J A Osborne* 92 a90
3 b c Shinko Forest (Ire) - Auriga
16^{7g} 2^{6gs} 2^{6g} 3^{6g} 1^{6s} 2^{6g} 8^{6gf} 11^{6sd} 6^{7g} 16^{6g} 13^{6g} 15^{8g} 1^{7gs} 8^{6s} 2^{7sd} 5^{7s} **2-5-16 £48,390**

Morson Boy (USA) *M Johnston* 94
4 b g Lear Fan (USA) - Esprit D'Escalier (USA)
12^{12gs} 12^{16g} 7^{14g} 15^{14g} 7^{16g} **0-0-5**

Morvern (Ire) *J G Given* 42 a44
4 ch g Titus Livius (Fr) - Scotia Rose
4^{12sd} 14^{14sd} 5^{14gf} 6^{13g} **0-0-4**

Moscow Ballet (Ire) *A P O'Brien* 109
3 b c Sadler's Wells (USA) - Fire The Groom (USA)
6^{10gs} 6^{9gs} 1^{10f} 7^{12gf} 3^{10f} **1-0-5 £50,608**

Moscow Blue *J H M Gosden* 56
3 ch g Soviet Star (USA) - Aquamarine
6^{9s} 7^{8gf} **0-0-2**

Moscow Mary *A G Newcombe* 33 a24
3 b f Imperial Ballet (Ire) - Baileys Firecat
8^{5sd} 10^{6sd} 12^{6f} 10^{7f} 7^{6gf} 13^{8gs} **0-0-6**

Moscow Music *M G Quinlan*   100
2 ch c Piccolo - Anna Karietta
2^{5g} 1^{5s} 2^{5gf} 6^{6gf} 2^{5s} 3^{6g} 5^{7g} **1-4-7**
£53,694

Moscow Times *D R C Elsworth*   76 a73
3 b g Soviet Star (USA) - Bargouzine
6^{6g} 5^{7gf} 7^{8g} 1^{8gf} 3^{8gf} 11^{8g} 5^{7sd} **1-1-7**
£4,313

Moshkil (Ire) *M P Tregoning*   63
2 b c In The Wings - Brentsville (USA)
10^{7gf} 11^{8gs} 6^{8g} **0-0-3**

Moss Vale (Ire) *B W Hills*   117
3 b c Shinko Forest (Ire) - Wolf Cleugh (Ire)
4^{6gs} 1^{5s} 1^{6gf} 1^{6f} 20^{6gs} 9^{5s} 2^{6y} 2^{6s}
3-3-8 £73,161

Mossmann Gorge *G A Swinbank*   63
2 b g Lujain (USA) - North Pine
11^{5f} 6^{6g} 5^{6gf} 2^{7s} **0-1-4 £2,128**

Most Definitely (Ire) *T D Easterby*   85
4 b g Definite Article - Unbidden Melody (USA)
2^{14f} 12^{16s} 6^{16s} 2^{16f} 3^{14g} 2^{14f} 2^{14gf} 1^{14gs}
2^{16gs} **1-6-9 £18,031**

Most-Saucy *I A Wood*   65 a62
8 br m Most Welcome - So Saucy
6^{11gs} 6^{12g} 5^{12gf} 7^{12gf} 3^{12gf} 4^{12gf} 5^{13f}
7^{13gf} 4^{12g} 3^{16sd} 3^{12gf} 10^{12f} 1^{16sd} 9^{17g} 9^{16sd}
1-1-15 £5,423

Mostanad *E A L Dunlop*   47
2 b g Alhaarth (Ire) - Jeed (Ire)
10^{6g} **0-0-1**

Mostarsil (USA) *G L Moore*   77
6 ch g Kingmambo (USA) - Naazeq
12^{16gs} 6^{14s} 3^{16gf} 4^{14g} 1^{14gf} 6^{12g} 7^{14gf}
6^{12f} **1-1-8 £7,435**

Mostashaar (Fr) *Sir Michael Stoute*   77
2 b c Intikhab (USA) - Nasanice (Ire)
7^{7gf} 5^{7g} **0-0-2**

Motarassed *J L Dunlop*   86
2 b c Green Desert (USA) - Sayedati Eljamilah (USA)
3^{6f} 1^{6gf} 5^{7g} **1-0-3 £6,842**

Moth Ball *J A Osborne*   111
2 b c Royal Applause - Chrysalis
2^{6gf} 3^{6gs} 1^{6g} 7^{6gs} 3^{5gf} 1^{6f} 4^{6gf} 1^{6g}
3-3-8 £40,603

Mothecombe Dream (Ire) *B J Meehan*   52
2 b c Foxhound (USA) - Another Shadow (Ire)
12^{7gf} 10^{8gf} 7^{8s} **0-0-3**

Motivator *M L W Bell*   118
2 b c Montjeu (Ire) - Out West (USA)
1^{8s} 1^{8s} **2-0-2 £124,803**

Motive (Fr) *Sir Michael Stoute*   97
3 ch c Machiavellian - Mistle Song
5^{8hy} 1^{10gf} 2^{10gf} 8^{10gf} 8^{10g} 9^{12g} **1-1-6**
£9,179

Motorway (Ire) *R Charlton*   84
3 b c Night Shift (USA) - Tadkiyra (Ire)
6^{10g} 1^{10gf} 5^{10gf} **1-0-3 £4,368**

Motu (Ire) *J L Dunlop*   74
3 b g Desert Style (Ire) - Pink Cashmere (Ire)
7^{6gs} 11^{6s} 8^{8gf} 7^{7gf} 7^{8g} 9^{7gs} 3^{8gs} 6^{8g}
0-1-8 £598

Mouftari (USA) *B W Hills*   76 a73
3 b c Miswaki (USA) - Nature's Magic (USA)
5^{8g} 4^{10gs} 5^{11gf} 2^{10f} 3^{12sd} 5^{10gf} **0-2-6**
£2,285

Mount Arafat *M Salaman*   17
2 b/br g Erhaab (USA) - Cache
9^{8s} 8^{8g} 11^{10g} **0-0-3**

Mount Benger *R M Beckett*   69
4 ch g Selkirk (USA) - Vice Vixen (Can)
6^{10g} 11^{10gf} 4^{10gs} 1^{11s} 9^{12s} 3^{10gs} 10^{11s}
2^{12gs} **1-2-8 £6,287**

Mount Butler (Ire) *J G Given*   46
2 b g Celtic Swing - Baylands Sunshine (Ire)
7^{6gf} 13^{8g} 6^{10hy} **0-0-3**

Mount Cottage *J G Given*   43
3 b f Cape Cross (Ire) - Brecon Beacons (Ire)
6^{8gf} 4^{8hy} 6^{10s} 14^{10gs} **0-0-4 £435**

Mount Ephram (Ire) *R F Fisher*   64
2 b g Entrepreneur - Happy Dancer (USA)
4^{5hy} 5^{6hy} 6^{6gf} 4^{7g} 1^{7g} 4^{7gf} 2^{7gf} 7^{8gf} 8^{7s}
17^{8s} **1-1-10 £4,760**

Mount Hillaby (Ire) *M W Easterby*   71 a71
4 b f Mujadil (USA) - Tetradonna (Ire)
1^{7sd} 9^{8sd} 7^{8g} 2^{8gs} 9^{9hy} 1^{8gf} 10^{7gf} 5^{7g}
1^{9sd} **3-1-9 £15,964**

Mount Kellet (Ire) *J G Given*   a38
2 ch g Bluebird (USA) - Antinnaz (Ire)
16^{6gs} 7^{5sd} 7^{7sd} **0-0-3**

Mount Logan *R Curtis*   a24
9 b h Shareef Dancer (USA) - Double Entendre
11^{10sd} **0-0-1**

Mount Pekan (Ire) *J S Goldie*   52
4 b g Sri Pekan (USA) - The Highlands (Fr)
17^{10gs} 3^{8gs} 7^{9gf} 6^{8g} 17^{8g} 5^{7gf} 8^{7g} 8^{7gs}
7^{8gs} **0-1-9 £672**

Mount Royale (Ire) *N Tinkler*   60 a69
6 ch g Wolfhound (USA) - Mahabba (USA)
8^{8sd} 7^{8sd} 6^{6sd} 3^{7sd} 1^{7sd} 1^{7sw} 8^{7sw} 7^{7ss}
6^{6s} 2^{7sd} 2^{7sd} 2^{7g} 3^{7g} 12^{6sd} **2-5-14**
£10,436

Mount Superior (USA) *P W D'Arcy*   a45
8 b g Conquistador Cielo (USA) - Zum Solitair (USA)
1^{6sd} 5^{6ss} 10^{8sd} 7^{6sd} **1-0-4 £1,277**

Mount Vettore *Mrs J R Ramsden*   85 a73
3 br g Vettori (Ire) - Honeyspike (Ire)
1^{6sd} 2^{7g} 8^{8s} 11^{8g} 8^{8gf} 9^{10gf} 9^{8gs} 6^{7g}
6^{8gf} 3^{7gf} 2^{8gf} **1-3-11 £8,305**

Mountain Breeze *D Shaw*   9 a32
2 b f Monashee Mountain (USA) - Breezy Louise
12^{7gs} 10^{9sd} 9^{6g} **0-0-3**

Mountain Meadow *Mrs A J Perrett*   74
3 ch g Deploy - Woodwardia (USA)
2^{10g} 1^{12gf} **1-1-2 £4,444**

Mountcharge (Ire) *G A Huffer*   66
3 b g Intikhab (USA) - Zorilla
19^{8g} 10^{7gf} 5^{8f} 10^{10g} 13^{8gs} **0-0-5**

Mouseman *C N Kellett*   40
3 b g Young Ern - Scottish Royal (Ire)
5^{5gf} 9^{6gf} 12^{5gf} **0-0-3**

Movie King (Ire) *S Gollings*   70
5 ch g Catrail (USA) - Marilyn (Ire)
7^{12gs} 15^{10g} 2^{10g} 13^{10gf} 13^{10g} 6^{10gf} 3^{10gf}
13^{8g} **0-1-8 £2,045**

Moyne Pleasure (Ire) *Paul Johnson*   47 a47
6 b g Exit To Nowhere (USA) - Ilanga (Ire)
8^{16sd} 8^{12sd} 11^{8ss} 6^{12sw} 8^{11ss} 8^{16s} 2^{11sf}
7^{12g} 2^{9sd} 3^{12sd} 1^{9sd} 4^{8gf} 6^{10g} 7^{12sd} 8^{8sd} 7^{12gf}
LFT^{10s} 10^{10g} **1-2-18 £2,474**

Mozafin *M R Channon*   87

2 b c Zafonic (USA) - Bedara
6^{5g} 2^{6f} 4^{6s} 3^{7gf} 2^{7s} 8^{7s} 2^{7g} 1^{8s} **1-3-8** £11,479

Mpenzi *J L Dunlop*   65
2 b f Groom Dancer (USA) - Muschana
7^{7g} 14^{8hy} **0-0-2**

Mr Aitch (Ire) *J A Osborne*   69 a78
2 b c Soviet Star (USA) - Welsh Mist
2^{8gf} 4^{8sd} **0-1-2** £1,945

Mr Belvedere *A J Lidderdale*   58 a51
3 b g Royal Applause - Alarming Motown
11^{8g} 9^{7gf} 10^{8g} 3^{7gf} 2^{8f} 10^{8g} 4^{10sd} 8^{10f} 15^{5g} **0-2-9** £1,284

Mr Bountiful (Ire) *M Dods*   62 a68
6 b g Mukaddamah (USA) - Nawadder
8^{7sd} 9^{7g} 4^{7gf} 8^{7f} 10^{7gf} 6^{6gf} 4^{6f} 13^{7gf} 4^{6sd} **0-1-9**

Mr Dinglawi (Ire) *D B Feek*   a62
3 b g Danehill Dancer (Ire) - Princess Leona (Ire)
12^{7sd} 10^{8sd} 5^{12sd} 7^{12s} **0-0-4**

Mr Dinos (Ire) *P F I Cole*   119
5 b h Desert King (Ire) - Spear Dance
4^{14gs} 2^{16gf} 6^{20gf} **0-1-3** £34,598

Mr Dip *A W Carroll*   55 a27
4 b g Reprimand - Scottish Lady
7^{8sd} 6^{8ss} 10^{8s} 7^{10gf} 5^{11gf} 2^{12g} 6^{11s} 15^{12gf} **0-1-8** £1,038

Mr Ed (Ire) *P Bowen*   89
6 ch g In The Wings - Center Moriches (Ire)
2^{14gf} 2^{14gs} 1^{14gf} 2^{14gs} 2^{18s} **1-4-5** £45,219

Mr Fleming *Dr J D Scargill*   a39
5 b/br g Bin Ajwaad (Ire) - Fabulous Night (Fr)
3^{10sd} 11^{10sd} 15^{10g} **0-1-3** £205

Mr Fortywinks (Ire) *B Ellison*   51
10 ch g Fool's Holme (USA) - Dream On
12^{16gs} 5^{16g} 8^{14gf} 6^{16g} 3^{16gf} **0-1-5** £519

Mr Hullabalou (Ire) *R Ingram*   75 a46
3 b g Princely Heir (Ire) - Lomalou (Ire)
10^{6sd} 15^{6gs} 4^{6s} 5^{7gf} 7^{6g} 9^{8gf} 8^{6g} 7^{7g} 1^{6gf} **1-0-9** £3,982

Mr Independent (Ire) *E A L Dunlop*   56
3 b g Cadeaux Genereux - Iris May
9^{8s} 8^{10gf} 13^{9gf} **0-0-3**

Mr Jack Daniells (Ire) *W R Muir*   83
3 b g Mujadil (USA) - Neat Shilling (Ire)
3^{7s} 6^{8gf} 3^{8gf} 8^{8g} 4^{8gf} 1^{8gf} 4^{10gf} 13^{10g} 3^{8g} 25^{7gs} **1-3-10** £11,716

Mr Kalandi (Ire) *P W D'Arcy*   63
2 gr c Grand Lodge (USA) - Singhana (Ire)
3^{6gf} 7^{6gf} 14^{7gf} 6^{6gf} 8^{7gs} **0-1-5** £552

Mr Lambros *A M Balding*   90 a91
3 ch c Pivotal - Magical Veil
1^{7sd} 2^{7sd} 7^{7gf} 7^{7g} 11^{6s} **1-1-5** £4,808

Mr Lear (USA) *R A Fahey*   59
5 b g Lear Fan (USA) - Majestic Mae (USA)
9^{12gs} 8^{12gf} 9^{10hy} **0-0-3**

Mr Lehman *Mrs M Reveley*   a21
7 ch g Presidium - Lehmans Lot
10^{8sd} 7^{11sd} **0-0-2**

Mr Lewin *R A Fahey*   44 a52
3 ch g Primo Dominie - Fighting Run
7^{7g} 9^{8hy} 5^{9sd} 10^{8s} 8^{7sd} **0-0-5**

Mr Loverman (Ire) *Miss V Haigh*   a16
4 ch g Spectrum (Ire) - Soviet Artic (Fr)
12^{8sd} 8^{8sd} 12^{7sd} **0-0-3**

Mr Malarkey (Ire) *Mrs C A Dunnett*   88
4 b g Pivotal - Girl Next Door
4^{6gs} 10^{6g} 4^{6gf} 6^{6gf} 3^{6gf} 3^{6gf} 8^{5gf} 6^{6g} 16^{6f} 7^{5s} 6^{6gf} 12^{5g} **1-3-12** £8,961

Mr Marucci (USA) *B Ellison*   59 a60
2 b c Miner's Mark (USA) - Appealing Style (USA)
5^{7js} 9^{7f} 5^{9sd} **0-0-3**

Mr Maxim *R M Whitaker*   54
2 ch g Lake Coniston (Ire) - White Hare
9^{6f} 5^{6g} 8^{7s} 9^{7gf} 4^{7gf} 7^{10gf} **0-1-6**

Mr Mayfair (Ire) *J A Osborne*   58 a63
2 ch g Entrepreneur - French Gift
7^{7s} 7^{8sd} **0-0-2**

Mr Midasman (Ire) *R Hollinshead*   65 a55
3 b c Entrepreneur - Sifaara (Ire)
6^{10g} 9^{7gs} 11^{8s} 13^{8hy} 10^{7gf} 4^{8gf} 6^{8sd} 3^{11g} 3^{10g} 3^{9sd} **0-3-10** £2,429

Mr Midaz *D W Whillans*   50
5 ch g Danzig Connection (USA) - Marmy
5^{11s} 5^{14gf} 5^{12g} **0-0-3**

Mr Mischief *P C Haslam*   54 a99
4 b g Millkom - Snow Huntress
3^{12sd} 12^{12sd} 1^{12sw} 12^{12s} **1-1-4** £9,781

Mr Mistral *G Wragg*   81
5 b g Zilzal (USA) - Miss Sancerre
2^{7f} 1^{8s} 25^{7gf} **1-1-3** £7,758

Mr Moon *J Parkes*   29 a11
3 b g Pursuit Of Love - Sound Of Sleat
6^{7sd} 6^{8gf} 12^{8f} 10^{10f} 7^{13g} 6^{8gf} 10^{7f} 5^{10gs} 9^{10f} 15^{10g} **0-0-10**

Mr Perry (Ire) *V Y Gethin*   a35
8 br g Perugino (USA) - Elegant Tune (USA)
9^{12sw} 5^{8sw} 10^{8sd} **0-0-3**

Mr Pertemps *J J Quinn*   50 a67
6 b g Primo Dominie - Amber Mill
3^{6sw} 1^{6sd} 2^{6sd} 5^{5sd} 14^{6g} 8^{6sd} 6^{5s} **1-2-7** £4,427

Mr Smithers Jones *S C Williams*   a63
4 br g Emperor Jones (USA) - Phylian
2^{11sd} 1^{14sd} 3^{12sd} 3^{14ss} **1-2-4** £2,625

Mr Spliffy (Ire) *M C Chapman*   49 a53
5 b g Fayruz - Johns Conquerer (Ire)
7^{7sd} 5^{5sd} 1^{5sd} 12^{6sd} 7^{5sd} 5^{5sw} 18^{6gs} 11^{5gf} 11^{5gf} 11^{5g} 10^{5gf} 11^{5gf} 8^{5gf} 10^{6gf} 2^{5gf} **1-1-15** £2,657

Mr Strowger *A Charlton*   43
3 b c Dancing Spree (USA) - Matoaka
6^{8s} 3^{11gf} 15^{8s} 11^{10hy} **0-1-4** £521

Mr Stylish *J S Moore*   a36
8 b g Mazilier (USA) - Moore Stylish
6^{7sd} 6^{7ss} **0-0-2**

Mr Tambourine Man (Ire) *P F I Cole*   91
3 b c Rainbow Quest (USA) - Girl From Ipanema
6^{10g} 7^{10s} 7^{10gs} 1^{10gf} 3^{10g} 1^{10gf} 4^{12g} 2^{12gf} 7^{11g} 10^{12gf} **2-1-10** £16,085

Mr Uppity *Julian Poulton*   44 a47
5 b g Shareef Dancer (USA) - Queenfisher
13^{5ss} 7^{5sd} 2^{6sd} 4^{7sd} 3^{6sd} 5^{6gf} 5^{6f} 4^{6sd} 2^{6gf} 8^{7gf} 5^{6gf} 4^{6sd} **0-4-13** £1,473

Mr Velocity (Ire) *E F Vaughan*   86
4 b g Tagula (Ire) - Miss Rusty (Ire)
3^{8gs} 2^{8g} 1^{7g} 11^{7g} 8^{8gf} 3^{9g} 1^{9g} 1^{8gf} 2^{8hy} 6^{7gs} **3-4-10** £26,134

Mr Whizz *A P Jones*   49 a44

7 ch g Manhal - Panienka (Pol)
9¹⁰sd 1⁸sd 4⁸sd 4⁸sw 3⁸sd 2¹⁰gs 2¹⁰hy
11¹⁰f 5¹⁶gs 1¹²f 11¹⁷gs 4¹²g 7¹⁰g **2-2-13**
£5,859

Mr Wolf D W Barker   82
3 b g Wolfhound (USA) - Madam Millie
2⁵g 2⁵s 1⁵s 1⁶g 6⁵gf 6⁶gf 13⁶g 9⁵g 13⁶g
5⁵s 2⁵s 6⁵s **2-3-12 £11,081**

Mrs Boz A W Carroll   a17
4 b f Superpower - Bar None
4⁶sd 9⁷gf 12⁷f **0-0-3**

Mrs Brown Sir Mark Prescott   41 a55
3 b f Royal Applause - Shifting Mist
3⁷sd 5⁸sd 6⁷ss 10¹²gf 5¹⁰sd 8¹⁰sd 4⁹sd 5⁸s
14⁸s **0-0-9 £531**

Mrs Cee (Ire) M G Quinlan
3 b f Orpen (USA) - Cutleaf
7⁷sd **0-0-1**

Mrs Chippy (Ire) M H Tompkins   10
2 ch f Docksider (USA) - Pile (USA)
16⁷gs **0-0-1**

Mrs Cube P Howling   43 a50
5 ch m Missed Flight - Norska
1⁹sw 1⁸sw 3⁸ss 3⁹ss 4¹⁰sd 10¹⁰gf 14¹⁰f
2-1-7 £3,123

Mrs Kepple M Johnston   35
2 b f King's Best - Sabayik (Ire)
4⁵gs 8⁵gf 7⁷g **0-0-3 £320**

Mrs Moh (Ire) T D Easterby   91
3 b f Orpen (USA) - My Gray (Fr)
11⁶gs 14⁷gs 5⁷f 1⁷g 18⁹g 2⁸g 2⁸s
UR⁸g 4⁷s **2-3-10 £30,746**

Mrs Pankhurst B W Hills   71 a51
3 b f Selkirk (USA) - Melodist (USA)
5¹⁰g 9¹⁰hy 5¹⁰gf 6⁸gf 8⁸g 4⁸gs 5¹⁰g 12¹⁰sd
0-0-8 £518

Mrs Philip P J Hobbs   55
5 b m Puissance - Lightning Legacy (USA)
7¹²f 8¹⁰g 11¹⁰s 9¹⁰gs **0-0-4**

Mrs Shilling J R Fanshawe   72 a72
3 b f Dr Fong (USA) - Papaha (Fr)
3⁷gs 4⁷gf 2⁷gf 4⁸gf 3⁹sd **0-3-5 £3,728**

Mrs Spence M W Easterby   45
3 b f Mind Games - Maid O'Cannie
13⁵s 6⁵s 14⁷s 19⁶gf 15⁵s **0-0-5**

Mrs St George (Ire) J G Burns   89
3 b f Orpen (USA) - Tamarzana (Ire)
4⁵y 2⁶y 7⁶f 1⁶g 1⁶gf 2⁵f 8⁶g 13⁵y 5⁶ys
2-2-9 £17,744

Mrs Willy Nilly J M Bradley   20
2 ch f Timeless Times (USA) - Laena
15⁵g 12⁵s 16⁶g **0-0-3**

Ms Polly Garter J M Bradley   46
2 b f Petong - Utopia
4⁵s 12⁵gf 6⁵f 11⁵g 8⁵gs 18⁵gs **0-0-6**
£352

Ms Three R Ford   56 a43
2 b f Josr Algarhoud (Ire) - Swing Along
12⁶g 6⁵sw 5⁵gf 6⁵gf 10⁶g 12⁵sd 7⁶sd
0-0-7

Mt Desert J H M Gosden   67
2 b c Rainbow Quest (USA) - Chief Bee
6⁸gs 6⁸g **0-0-2**

Mtilly M Johnston   50
3 br f Mtoto - Corn Lily

8⁸gf 10¹⁰hy **0-0-2**

Mubtaker (USA) M P Tregoning   121
7 ch h Silver Hawk (USA) - Gazayil (USA)
1¹³g 7¹²s 4¹²g **1-0-3 £107,299**

Mudawin (Ire) M P Tregoning   101
3 b g Intikhab (USA) - Fida (Ire)
12⁸g 1⁸g 13⁸g 1¹⁰gf 14¹²gf **2-0-5**
£16,090

Muddy (Ire) G A Huffer   59 a49
2 ch g Monashee Mountain (USA) - Schonbein (Ire)
5⁶s 8⁶gf 11⁷g 8⁶hy 7⁶sd **0-0-5**

Muestra (Ire) Mrs P N Dutfield   35 a44
2 ch f Raise A Grand (Ire) - Iva's Flyer (Ire)
11⁵g 10⁵s 8⁵hy 7⁵f 5⁶gf 3⁷sd 9⁷gf 10⁷g
0-1-8 £374

Mufreh (USA) A G Newcombe   62 a94
6 br g Dayjur (USA) - Mathkurh (USA)
1⁷sd 5⁷sd 2⁶ss 4⁷gs 12⁷gs **1-2-5**
£11,704

Mugeba Miss Gay Kelleway   64 a57
3 b f Primo Dominie - Ella Lamees
5⁷sd 5⁸sd 1⁷f 2⁶gf 2⁷gf 7⁶gf 6⁷s **1-2-7**
£4,647

Muhareb (USA) C E Brittain   100
5 ch g Thunder Gulch (USA) - Queen Of Spirit (USA)
5¹²gf 9¹²g 11¹⁰g 5¹⁰gf 17¹²g 19¹²s **0-0-6**
£1,118

Muhaymin (USA) J L Dunlop   86
3 ch c A.P. Indy (USA) - Shadayid (USA)
8¹⁰g 9⁸gf 4¹⁰g 7⁸g **0-0-4 £521**

Mujagem (Ire) M W Easterby
8 br m Mujadil (USA) - Lili Bengam
8⁷sd **0-0-1**

Mujalina (Ire) M C Pipe   19
6 b g Mujadil (USA) - Talina's Law (Ire)
27¹⁸s **0-0-1**

Mujawer (USA) M P Tregoning   65
3 b g Gulch (USA) - Good Cents (USA)
5⁷g 12⁹gf 11⁷gs **0-0-3**

Mujazaf M R Channon   74
2 b c Grand Lodge (USA) - Decision Maid (USA)
3⁸f **0-1-1 £858**

Mujkari (Ire) J M Bradley   a25
8 ch g Mujtahid (USA) - Hot Curry (USA)
12⁹sd **0-0-1**

Mukafeh (USA) J L Dunlop   107
3 b c Danzig (USA) - Bint Salsabil (USA)
7⁷g 2⁸gf 5⁷gf **0-1-3 £4,810**

Mulan Princess (Ire) S C Burrough   a31
4 b f Mukaddamah (USA) - Notley Park
13⁶sd **0-0-1**

Mulberry Lad (Ire) W R Muir   69 a64
2 b c Entrepreneur - Taisho (Ire)
5⁵g 2⁵f 4⁵gf 2⁶f 7⁶f 6⁶sd 6⁶sd **0-2-7**
2,405

Mulberry Wine M Blanshard   71
2 b f Benny The Dip (USA) - Top Berry
6⁷g 4⁷gs 5⁷gf 8⁶gs 12⁷gf 16⁸g **0-0-6**

Mulsanne P A Pritchard   12
6 b g Clantime - Prim Lass
12¹¹gf **0-0-1**

Multahab P S McEntee   52 a66
5 b/br g Zafonic (USA) - Alumisiyah (USA)
2⁵sd 4⁵sd 2⁵sd 4⁵sd 12⁵g 10⁵gf 10⁶f 8⁶gf
VOI⁵gf 9⁵s 6⁵g 9⁵sd 10⁶sd **0-2-13 £2,660**

Multicolour *R Hannon*
4 ch f Rainbow Quest (USA) - Raymouna (Ire)
15¹⁰ˢ **0-0-1**

Multiple Choice (Ire) *N P Littmoden*　　　51 a70
3 ch g Woodborough (USA) - Cosmona
7⁵ˢᵈ 16⁶ᵍˢ 9⁵ˢ 10⁵ᵍ 2⁸ˢᵈ 4⁸ˢᵈ 6⁷ᶠ 4⁸ˢᵈ
13⁶ᵍ 7⁶ˢᵈ 10⁷ˢᵈ **0-1-11 £1,160**

Mumbling (Ire) *B G Powell*　　　41
6 ch g Dr Devious (Ire) - Valley Lights (Ire)
15¹²ᵍ **0-0-1**

Munaahej (Ire) *K A Morgan*
3 b c Soviet Star (USA) - Azyaa
15⁷ᵍˢ **0-0-1**

Munaawashat (Ire) *K R Burke*　　　86
3 b f Marju (Ire) - Simaat (USA)
3¹⁰ᶠ 18ᵍᶠ 2⁸ᵍˢ 8¹⁰ᵍ 1⁸ᵍ 1⁸ᵍˢ 8⁸ᶠ 6⁸ˢ
3-2-8 £19,947

Munaawesh (USA) *D W Chapman*　　　70 a43
3 b c Bahri (USA) - Istikbal (USA)
9⁸ˢᵈ 3⁶ᵍˢ 9⁸ˢᵈ 14⁷ᵍˢ 9⁸ʰʸ 13⁸ᵍᶠ 9⁸ˢᵈ
13¹⁰ᵍ 7¹²ˢᵈ 4¹¹ˢ 2⁹ᵍ 8¹⁰ᵍˢ 4⁹ᵍᶠ 2¹⁰ᵍᶠ 2¹⁴ᵍᶠ 9¹⁰ᵍᶠ
4¹⁴ᵍᶠ 5¹²ᵍ 10¹⁶ᵍ 8¹¹ˢᵈ **0-3-20 £6,147**

Munaddam (USA) *Saeed Bin Suroor*　　　94
2 ch c Aljabr (USA) - Etizaaz (USA)
2⁶ᵍᶠ 2⁶ᵍ 1⁶ᵍ **1-2-3 £7,654**

Munfarid (Ire) *P G Murphy*　　　54 a64
4 ch g Alhaarth (Ire) - Meursault (USA)
3¹²ˢᵈ 7¹³ˢᵈ 4¹³ˢᵈ 11¹²ˢᵈ 9¹⁴ˢ 11¹⁵ˢ 11¹⁴ˢᵈ
0-1-7 £527

Mungo Jerry (Ger) *J G Given*　　　75
3 b g Tannenkonig (Ire) - Mostly Sure (Ire)
3¹¹ᵍ 6¹¹ᵍᶠ 3¹²ᵍ **0-2-3 £1,533**

Munsef *J L Dunlop*　　　70
2 b c Zafonic (USA) - Mazaya (USA)
12⁶ˢ 3⁷ˢ **0-1-2 £645**

Muqarrar (Ire) *T J Fitzgerald*　　　51 a51
5 ch h Alhaarth (Ire) - Narjis (USA)
6⁷ˢᵈ 6⁸ˢᵈ 16⁸ˢᵈ 16⁸ᵍˢ 1⁸ˢ **1-0-5 £1,470**

Muqbil (USA) *J L Dunlop*　　　119
4 ch c Swain (Ire) - Istiqlal (USA)
8¹⁰ᵍˢ 1¹⁰ᵍ 1¹⁰ᵍ 2¹¹ᵍ 4¹⁰ᵍᶠ 5¹²ᵍᶠ **2-1-6
£44,170**

Muqtadi (Ire) *M Quinn*　　　50 a54
6 b g Marju (Ire) - Kadwah (USA)
8⁸ˢᵈ 3⁶ˢᵈ 9⁷ˢᵈ 6⁶ˢᵈ 10⁷ˢᵈ 4⁸ˢᵈ 1⁸ˢᵈ 5¹⁰ˢᵈ
8⁸ˢᵈ 10⁷ˢˢ 4¹⁰ˢᵈ 5⁸ᵍˢ 4⁵ ⁹⁷ʰʸ 6⁸ᶠ 9⁸ᶠ 10⁸ᵍᶠ
13⁸ᵍ **1-1-18 £3,039**

Muraabet *J L Dunlop*　　　81
2 b c Dubai Millennium - Mahasin (USA)
3⁸ˢ 6⁷ˢ **0-1-2 £1,102**

Muraqeb *Mrs Barbara Waring*　　　43 a45
4 ch g Grand Lodge (USA) - Oh So Well (Ire)
13¹⁰ˢᵈ 13¹⁰ˢᵈ 10¹²ˢᵈ 5¹⁴ˢˢ 11¹⁶ᵍ 11¹⁶ᵍˢ
10⁸ᵍˢ 6¹⁰ˢ **0-0-8**

Murashah (USA) *Saeed Bin Suroor*
4 ch c Storm Cat (USA) - Shadayid (USA)
13⁸ᵍ **0-0-1**

Murbaat (Ire) *E F Vaughan*　　　80
3 b c Deploy - Ozette
3⁸ᵍᶠ 2¹⁰ˢᵈ **0-2-2 £1,896**

Murdinga *A M Hales*　　　a63
5 br g Emperor Jones (USA) - Tintinara
12¹⁰ˢᵈ **0-0-1**

Murzim *J Gallagher*　　　a18
5 b g Salse (USA) - Guilty Secret (Ire)

12¹³ˢᵈ **0-0-1**

Musahim (USA) *B W Hills*　　　75
2 b/br c Dixieland Band (USA) - Tabheej (Ire)
7⁶ᵍˢ 3⁶ᵍ **0-1-2 £740**

Musanid (USA) *Sir Michael Stoute*　　　111
4 ch c Swain (Ire) - Siyadah (USA)
3¹⁰ᵍ 6¹²ᶠ 3¹⁰ᵍ 3¹²ᵍˢ **0-1-4 £9,998**

Musardiere *Mrs J R Ramsden*　　　56
2 b f Montjeu (Ire) - Majestic Image
7⁶ᶠ 5⁶ᵍᶠ 11⁷ᵍᶠ **0-0-3**

Museeb (USA) *J L Dunlop*　　　87
2 b c Danzig (USA) - Elle Seule (USA)
4⁶ᵍ 2⁷ᵍ **0-1-2 £2,360**

Mushajer *M P Tregoning*　　　86
2 gr g Linamix (Fr) - Luxurious (USA)
3⁶ᵍ 4⁷ᵍ **0-1-2 £1,220**

Music Maid (Ire) *H S Howe*　　　81
6 b m Inzar (USA) - Richardstown Lass (Ire)
13⁸ᵍᶠ 17ᵍᶠ 10⁷ᵍ 7⁷ᵍᶠ 8⁷ᵍ 11⁷ˢ 11⁸ᵍᶠ
1-0-7 £6,279

Music Mix (Ire) *E A L Dunlop*　　　58 a70
3 gr c Linamix (Fr) - Baldemara (Fr)
12⁸ˢ 11¹⁰ᵍ 4¹²ᵍˢ 4¹⁰ᵍˢ 8¹⁰ᵍˢ 9¹²ᵍ
1-0-7 £3,024

Music Teacher *H Morrison*　　　32
2 ch f Piccolo - Duena
12⁶ᵍ **0-0-1**

Musical Day *B J Meehan*　　　81 a74
2 ch f Singspiel (Ire) - Dayville (USA)
11⁷ᵍ 7⁷ᵍᶠ 10⁷ᵍ 2⁷ᵍˢ 12⁷ᵍ 4⁷ᵍ 3⁹ˢᵈ 1⁸ˢᵈ
1-3-8 £8,267

Musical Fair *J A Glover*　　　86 a79
4 b f Piccolo - Guarded Expression
21⁶ᵍ 14⁶ᵍˢ 8⁶ᵍᶠ 2⁵ᵍᶠ 1⁵ᶠ 5⁵ᵍᶠ 6⁵ᵍᶠ 10⁵ᵍ
11⁵ᵍˢ 12⁵ᵍᶠ 3⁵ᵍ 5⁶ˢᵈ 12⁵ˢᵈ **1-3-14
£10,044**

Musical Gift *G A Huffer*　　　36 a76
4 ch g Cadeaux Genereux - Kazoo
1⁹ˢˢ 4⁷ˢᵈ 4⁸ˢʷ 5⁸ˢᵈ 7⁸ᵍˢ 7⁷ˢᵈ **1-0-6
£3,657**

Musical Lyrics (USA) *M Johnston*　　　27
3 b f Quiet American (USA) - Foreign Courier (USA)
8⁹ᵍˢ **0-0-1**

Musical Top (USA) *H Morrison*　　　59 a55
4 ch f Mt. Livermore (USA) - Brief Escapade (Ire)
9⁶ʸˢ 13⁶ᵍᶠ 3⁷ᶠ 9⁷ʰʸ 16⁶ᶠ 4⁸ᵍ 5⁹ˢᵈ **0-2-7
£450**

Musicanna *J R Fanshawe*　　　76
3 b f Cape Cross (Ire) - Upend
2⁸ᵍᶠ 1⁸ʰʸ **1-1-2 £5,415**

Musico (Ire) *B R Millman*　　　74
2 ch c Bold Fact (USA) - Scherzo Impromptu
4⁶ᵍ 6⁶ᵍᶠ 4⁶ᵍᶠ 2⁷ᵍᶠ 3⁶ᵍˢ 16⁶ᵍᶠ 12⁸ˢ **0-1-7
£3,175**

Musiotal *J S Goldie*　　　57
3 ch c Pivotal - Bemuse
13⁷ᵍᶠ 5⁵ᵍ 5⁵ᵍˢ 10⁶ᵍᶠ 2⁶ˢ 1⁷ᵍ 8⁶ᵍ 4⁸ˢ
8⁵ˢ 14⁷ᵍˢ **1-1-10 £5,014**

Muskatsturm (Ger) *B J Curley*　　　72
5 b g Lecroix (Ger) - Myrthe (Ger)
8¹⁵ˢ 10¹²ˢ 7¹⁵ᵍ 10¹⁴ˢ **0-0-4**

Muslin *J R Fanshawe*　　　60 a54
3 ch f Bien Bien (USA) - Moidart
11¹⁰ᵍ 3¹⁰ˢ 8¹²ˢᵈ 13¹⁴ᵍ 2¹¹ᵍ 5¹⁴ᵍᶠ 6¹²ᵍ
11¹⁶ˢᵈ **0-2-8 £1,396**

Must Be Magic *H J Collingridge* 52 a64
7 b g Magic Ring (Ire) - Sequin Lady
4¹⁰ˢᵈ 5¹⁰ˢᵈ 10¹⁰ˢᵈ 9⁸ᵍᶠ 14⁹ᵍ 13⁹ᵍᶠ 16¹²ˢ
16¹¹ᵍˢ **0-0-8**

Must Be So *J J Bridger* 36 a42
3 b f So Factual (USA) - Ovideo
5⁷ˢᵈ 8⁸ˢᵈ 13⁷ˢᵈ 11⁶ˢᵈ 6⁶ˢᵈ 8⁶ʰʸ 4⁵ᶠ 10⁵ᶠ
13⁷ᵍᶠ 5⁶ᶠ 12⁵ᵍᶠ **0-0-11**

Mustajed *M P Tregoning* 91
3 b g Alhaarth (Ire) - Jasarah (Ire)
6⁷ᵍ 8⁸ᵍᶠ **0-0-2 £218**

Mustakhlas (USA) *J L Dunlop* 53
3 ch g Diesis - Katiba (USA)
11⁸ᵍ **0-0-1**

Mustang Ali (Ire) *S Kirk* 70
3 ch g Ali-Royal (Ire) - Classic Queen (Ire)
6¹⁰ᵍ 7¹²ᵍᶠ 3¹²ᵍ 5¹⁴ᵍ 5¹⁰ᵍ 3¹²ᶠ 5¹¹ᵍᶠ 6¹¹ᶠ
6¹⁰ᵍᶠ 13¹²ᵍˢ 8¹²ˢ **0-2-11 £1,436**

Mutabari (USA) *J L Spearing* 25 a25
10 ch g Seeking The Gold (USA) - Cagey Exuberance (USA)
7⁸ˢᵈ 9⁸ˢᵈ 10⁹ˢᵈ 10⁷ᵍᶠ 14⁷ᶠ 9⁷ᵍᶠ 8⁷ᵍᶠ
PU⁸ᵍˢ **0-0-8**

Mutafanen *E A L Dunlop* 112
3 gr c Linamix (Fr) - Doomna (Ire)
1¹⁰ᵍ 3¹⁰ˢ 3⁹ᵍ 3¹⁰ᶠ 20¹⁰ᵍ 4¹⁰ᵍᶠ 4¹¹ᵍ
10¹⁰ᵍˢ 6¹⁴ᵍ **1-4-9 £28,501**

Mutahayya (Ire) *J L Dunlop* 107
3 b c Peintre Celebre (USA) - Winsa (USA)
2⁸ᵍˢ 5¹¹ᵍ 12¹⁰ᶠ 14⁹ˢ **0-1-4 £7,350**

Mutajammel (Fr) *Sir Michael Stoute* 86
2 b c Kingmambo (USA) - Irtifa
4⁷ˢ 1⁸ᵍ **1-0-2 £7,296**

Mutamaasek (USA) *J L Dunlop* 77
2 b/br c Swain (USA) - Tamgeed (USA)
5⁷ᵍ 7⁸ˢ 4⁸ᵍˢ 5¹⁰ᵍᶠ **0-0-4 £485**

Mutamared (USA) *M P Tregoning* 90
4 ch c Nureyev (USA) - Alydariel (USA)
1⁷ᶠ 3⁷ᵍ 8⁷ᵍˢ **1-1-3 £6,729**

Mutanabi (USA) *Saeed Bin Suroor* a73
2 b c Wild Rush (USA) - Freudenau (USA)
2⁶ˢᵈ 3⁷ˢᵈ **0-2-2 £1,746**

Mutarafaa (USA) *D Shaw* a60
5 b g Red Ransom (USA) - Mashaarif (USA)
4⁸ˢʷ 3⁸ˢᵈ 2⁸ˢᵈ 4⁸ˢᵈ 7¹⁰ˢᵈ 7⁸ˢᵈ 8⁸ˢᵈ 2⁸ˢᵈ
13⁷ˢᵈ 9⁸ˢᵈ 16⁸ʰʸ **0-3-11 £2,077**

Mutared (Ire) *N P Littmoden* 38 a33
6 b g Marju (Ire) - Shahaada (USA)
12⁹ˢᵈ 14⁹ᵍᶠ 11⁸ˢᵈ 16¹⁰ᵍᶠ 10⁸ᶠ 19⁸ᵍᶠ
0-0-6

Mutasallil (USA) *Saeed Bin Suroor* 110
4 b c Gone West (USA) - Min Alhawa (USA)
1¹⁰ᵍᶠ 1¹⁰ᵍᶠ 2¹⁰ᵍᶠ 7¹¹ᵍ 1¹²ᵍᶠ **3-1-5
£32,124**

Mutassem (Fr) *T Keddy* 64 a60
3 b c Fasliyev (USA) - Fee Eria (Fr)
8⁸ˢᵈ 7⁷ˢ 13⁷ᵍᶠ 11⁸ᵍˢ 9⁷ᵍˢ 13⁶ᵍᶠ 2⁶ᵍ
8⁹ˢᵈ 7⁷ˢᵈ 8⁶ˢ **0-1-10 £962**

Mutawaffer *B W Hills* 101
3 b c Marju (Ire) - Absaar (USA)
7¹⁰ᵍˢ 4⁷ˢ **0-0-2 £648**

Mutawaqed (Ire) *M A Magnusson* 96
6 ch g Zafonic (USA) - Waqood (USA)
11⁶ᵍˢ 4⁶ᵍᶠ 2⁶ᵍ 8⁶ˢ 1⁶ᵍᶠ 16⁶ᵍᶠ 2⁵ˢ 9⁶ᵍ
4⁶ˢ 19⁶ᵍ **1-4-10 £54,243**

Mutawassel (USA) *B W Hills* 98

3 b c Kingmambo (USA) - Danzig Darling (Can)
4¹⁰ᵍˢ 3¹⁰ᵍˢ 16¹⁰ᵍᶠ **0-0-3 £10,200**

Mutayam *D A Nolan* 52
4 b g Compton Place - Final Shot
6⁶ᵍ 8⁵ᵍˢ 6⁵ᵍˢ 14⁵ᵍᶠ 1⁵ᵍ 21⁵ᵍˢ 7⁶ˢ **1-0-7
£3,454**

Muy Bien *J R Jenkins* 82 a79
3 ch c Daggers Drawn (USA) - Primula Bairn
2⁶ˢᵈ 2⁶ˢᵈ 10⁶ˢᵈ 3⁵ˢˢ 1⁶ᵍˢ 2⁶ˢ 3⁶ˢ 9⁷ˢ
1-5-8 £9,390

Muyassir (Ire) *Miss B Sanders* 55 a61
9 b g Brief Truce (USA) - Twine
8¹⁰ˢᵈ 1⁸ˢᵈ 12⁸ᵍᶠ 8⁸ᵍᶠ 8⁸ᵍᶠ 10⁸ᵍ 9⁸ˢᵈ 7⁹ˢᵈ
1-0-8 £2,982

Muzio Scevola (Ire) *M R Channon* 59 a67
3 ch g Titus Livius (Fr) - Dancing Sunset (Ire)
2¹²ˢᵈ 5¹²ᵍˢ 5¹¹ᵍ 6¹⁵ᵍˢ 3¹⁶ᵍ 11¹⁷ᵍᶠ **0-1-6
£1,896**

My Ace *James Moffatt* 36
6 b m Definite Article - Miss Springtime
6⁹ᵍᶠ **0-0-1**

My Bayard *J Balding* 70 a77
5 ch g Efisio - Bay Bay
6⁸ˢ 2⁷ˢ 5⁸ˢʷ 19¹²ᵍ 1⁷ˢᵈ 15⁷ᶠ 4⁶ᵍ 3⁶ᵍ
7⁵ᵍᶠ 3⁶ᵍˢ **1-2-10 £5,419**

My Country Club *A G Juckes* 47 a24
7 b h Alzao (USA) - Merry Rous
6⁷ᵍˢ 6⁷ᵍᶠ 7⁸ˢᵈ 18⁶ᵍ 6¹⁰ᵍᶠ **0-0-5**

My Dream (Ire) *R Hannon* 27
2 b f King's Theatre (Ire) - Dream Chaser
4⁵ᶠ **0-0-1 £309**

My Dubai (Ire) *Saeed Bin Suroor* 79
2 ch f Dubai Millennium - Pastorale
3⁷ᵍˢ **0-1-1 £751**

My Gacho (Ire) *Mrs P N Dutfield* 80 a76
2 b c Shinko Forest (Ire) - Floralia
17⁶ᵍˢ 3⁷ᵍˢ 3⁶ᵍᶠ 12⁶ˢ 3⁶ˢᵈ **0-3-5 £6,816**

My Galliano (Ire) *B G Powell* 71
8 b g Muharib (USA) - Hogan Stand
13¹⁰ˢ 3¹⁰ᵍ 6¹⁰ᵍˢ 5¹⁰ᵍᶠ **0-0-4 £869**

My Girl Pearl (Ire) *M S Saunders* 55 a43
4 b f Sri Pekan (USA) - Desert Bloom (Fr)
12⁷ˢᵈ 2⁷ˢᵈ 4⁷ˢᵈ 2⁷ᵍᶠ 9⁶ᵍᶠ 6⁶ᵍ 4⁷ᵍᶠ 16ᵍᶠ
7⁶ᵍᶠ 3⁶ᵍˢ 6⁶ᵍ 1⁷ᵍᶠ 4⁷ᵍ 8⁷ʰʸ **2-5-14 £8,057**

My Hope (Ire) *R Charlton* 65
3 b f Danehill (USA) - Lady Elgar (Ire)
10⁸ʰʸ 8⁹ᵍ 9⁸ᵍᶠ 8⁸ᵍ 3¹⁰ᵍᶠ 10⁸ᵍᶠ **0-1-6
£572**

My Last Bean (Ire) *B Smart* 51
7 gr g Soviet Lad (USA) - Meanz Beanz
6¹¹ᵍˢ 18¹²ᵍᶠ **0-0-2**

My Legal Eagle (Ire) *R J Price* 66 a54
10 b g Law Society (USA) - Majestic Nurse
1¹⁵ˢᵈ 4¹⁵ˢᵈ 2¹⁶ˢᵈ 1¹⁴ᵍᶠ 1¹⁴ᵍᶠ 1¹³ᵍᶠ 2¹⁴ᵍ
4-2-7 £15,129

My Lilli (Ire) *P Mitchell* 47 a61
4 b f Marju (Ire) - Tamburello (Ire)
3¹⁰ˢᵈ 4¹⁰ˢᵈ 7¹²ˢᵈ 6¹²ˢᵈ 4⁸ˢᵈ 1⁸ˢᵈ 3¹⁰ˢᵈ 8⁸ᶠ
14¹⁰ˢᵈ **1-2-9 £4,023**

My Line *K G Reveley* 7 b g Perpendicular - My Desire
10¹⁸ˢ **0-0-1**

My Little Sophia *M Mullineaux* 37 a18
4 b f Wizard King - David James' Girl
5⁷ˢʷ 11⁸ˢ 7¹²ᵍᶠ 15⁷ˢᵈ **0-0-4**

My Maite (Ire) *R Ingram* 52 a64
5 b g Komaite (USA) - Mena
2¹⁰ˢᵈ 4¹⁰ˢᵈ 10¹⁰ˢᵈ 9¹⁰ˢᵈ 18⁹ᶠ 6¹⁰ᶠ 11⁸ᵍ
4⁹ᵍᶠ 5⁸ᵍᶠ 11¹⁰ᵍᶠ 3¹⁰ᶠ 3¹⁰ᵍᶠ 3¹⁰ᵍᶠ 4⁹ˢᵈ **1-5-14**
£3,613

My Michelle *B Palling* 59 a38
3 b f Ali-Royal (Ire) - April Magic
14⁶ᵍˢ 8⁸ᶠ 4⁸ᵍᶠ 5¹⁰ᵍˢ 4⁸ᵍᶠ 6¹⁰ᵍᶠ 11⁹ˢᵈ
0-0-7

My Paris *K A Ryan* 99 a66
3 b g Paris House - My Desire
3⁷ˢᵈ 2⁷ˢᵈ 2⁷ᵍ 2⁹ᵍ 5⁸ᵍᶠ 2¹⁰ᶠ 2¹⁰ᵍᶠ 1⁹ˢ
1⁷ᵍᶠ 1⁷ᵍˢ **3-6-10 £38,130**

My Pension (Ire) *P Howling* 66 a76
3 b g Orpen (USA) - Woodenitbenice (USA)
7⁸ʰʸ 4⁷ˢ 3⁷ᶠ 11⁸ᵍ 11⁸ˢ 6¹⁰ᵍ 3⁹ˢᵈ 1⁸ˢᵈ
2⁹ˢᵈ **1-2-9 £4,853**

My Portfolio (Ire) *R Charlton* 69
2 b g Montjeu (Ire) - Elaine's Honor (USA)
4⁸ᵍˢ 7⁸ᵍ 11⁸ᵍ **0-0-3 £467**

My Princess (Ire) *N A Callaghan* 81
2 b f Danehill Dancer (Ire) - Shanoora (Ire)
3⁶ᵍᶠ 5⁸ᵍ 3⁶ᶠ 1⁷ᶠ 7⁶ᵍ 5⁸ˢ 5⁸ᵍᶠ 2⁷ᵍ
14⁷ᵍˢ **1-2-9 £6,935**

My Putra (USA) *P F I Cole* 81
2 b/br c Silver Hawk (USA) - Petite Triomphe (USA)
3⁶ˢ 2⁸ᵍᶠ **0-2-2 £2,998**

My Rascal (Ire) *M J Wallace* 60 a54
2 b g Imperial Ballet (Ire) - Derena (Fr)
7⁷ᵍᶠ 10⁷ᵍˢ 9⁷ᵍᶠ 7⁷ˢᵈ **0-0-4**

My Renee (USA) *M J Grassick* 107
4 b/br f Kris S (USA) - Mayenne (USA)
3¹⁴ᵍᶠ 1¹²ᵍᶠ 2¹²ᵍᶠ **1-1-3 £46,295**

My Sharp Grey *J Gallagher* a36
5 gr m Tragic Role (USA) - Sharp Anne
8¹⁰ˢᵈ **0-0-1**

My Sunshine (Ire) *B W Hills* 59 a43
3 b f Alzao (USA) - Sunlit Ride
10¹⁰ᵍˢ 7⁸ᵍᶠ 8⁸ᵍᶠ 8⁸ˢᵈ 11⁸ᵍ 14⁸ᵍ **0-0-6**

My True Love (Ire) *R J Baker* 58
5 b g Beneficial - Elfi (Ire)
5¹⁸ᵍᶠ 9¹²ᵍ 4¹⁴ᶠ 10¹⁶ᵍᶠ **0-0-4 £276**

My Wild Rover *K A Morgan* a15
4 b g Puissance - June Fayre
8⁶ˢᵈ 7⁵ˢᵈ 10⁵ʰʸ 16⁶ᵍᶠ **0-0-4**

Myannabanana (Ire) *J R Weymes* 44 a60
3 ch g Woodborough - Raging Storm
5¹⁰ˢᵈ 3⁹ˢᵈ 4¹¹ˢᵈ 4⁸ˢˢ 7⁸ˢˢ 5¹⁰ᵍˢ 12⁸ˢ 8¹⁰ᵍ
7⁹ᵍᶠ 9¹⁰ᵍˢ 7¹⁰ᶠ 9¹⁴ᶠ 7¹⁰ᵍᶠ 11¹⁰ˢ **0-1-14 £773**

Mynd *R M Whitaker* 72 a71
4 b g Atraf - Prim Lass
1⁵ˢʷ 1⁵ˢˢ 2⁵ˢʷ 11⁶ˢᵈ 2⁵ᵍˢ 1⁵ᵍ 9⁵ᵍ 9⁵ʰʸ
6⁵ᵍᶠ 4⁵ˢ 14⁵ᵍ 5⁵ᵍˢ 12⁵ᵍˢ 17⁶ᵍᶠ 9⁵ˢ **3-2-15**
£12,826

Myrtus *J R Weymes* a33
5 ch g Double Eclipse (Ire) - My Desire
3¹²ˢᵈ 7¹⁶ˢᵈ 5¹⁶ˢᵈ **0-0-3 £360**

Mysterinch *Jedd O'Keeffe* 97
4 b g Inchinor - Hakone (Ire)
3⁸ˢ 7¹⁰ᵍ 8⁹ᵍ 2⁷ᵍᶠ 7⁸ᵍ 3⁹ᵍˢ 17⁷ᵍᶠ 4⁸ᵍˢ
0-1-8 £6,143

Mysterium *N P Littmoden* a48
10 gr g Mystiko (USA) - Way To Go
3¹⁵ˢᵈ 4¹⁶ˢᵈ 11⁶ˢʷ 5¹⁶ˢᵈ 6¹⁶ˢᵈ **1-0-5**
£1,980

Mysterlover (Ire) *N P Littmoden* a55
4 b g Night Shift (USA) - Jacaranda City (Ire)
12¹⁰ˢᵈ 7¹²ˢᵈ 7¹³ˢᵈ 12¹⁶ˢᵈ **0-0-4**

Mystery Lot (Ire) *A King* 75 a58
2 b f Revoque (Ire) - Mystery Bid
6⁷ˢᵈ 2⁷ᵍˢ 2⁷ʰʸ 3⁸ᵍ **0-3-4 £3,095**

Mystery Maid (Ire) *H S Howe* 46
2 b f King's Theatre (Ire) - Duly Elected
11⁵ᵍ 6⁶ᵍᶠ 12⁶ᵍᶠ 13⁶ᵍᶠ 14⁷ᵍᶠ **0-0-5**

Mystery Mountain *Mrs J R Ramsden* a36
4 b g Mistertopogigo (Ire) - Don't Jump (Ire)
9⁶ˢᵈ 5⁷ˢᵈ 4⁶ˢʷ **0-0-3**

Mystery Pips *N Tinkler* 48 a13
4 b f Bin Ajwaad (Ire) - Le Shuttle
11⁵ᵍ 10⁵ᵍᶠ 7⁵ᶠ 11⁵ᵍ 4⁵ᵍᶠ 15⁵ᵍ 4⁵ᵍᶠ
3⁵ᵍᶠ 14⁵ᵍˢ 12⁵ᵍˢ 12⁵ˢᵈ **0-1-12 £1,319**

Mystery Solved (USA) *P A Blockley* 28
4 b f Royal Academy (USA) - Golden Rhyme
11¹²ᵍˢ 15⁸ˢᵈ **0-0-2**

Mystic Lad *Jamie Poulton* 24 a66
3 gr g Magic Ring (Ire) - Jilly Woo
2⁸ˢᵈ 19⁸ᵍ **0-1-2 £1,266**

Mystic Man (Fr) *K A Ryan* 97 a54
6 b g Cadeaux Genereux - Shawanni
9⁷ˢᵈ 11⁸ˢˢ 15⁸ᵍ 13⁸ᵍ 18⁸ᶠ 38ᵍᶠ 10⁷ᶠ 4⁷ˢ
3⁶ᵍˢ 7⁶ᵍᶠ 12⁶ˢ 9⁸ᵍ **1-3-12 £11,324**

Mystic Moon *J R Jenkins* 54 a44
3 br f First Trump - Misty Moon
9⁷ˢᵈ 9⁷ˢᵈ 6¹⁰ᵍˢ 8⁸ᵍ 4¹⁰ᵍˢ 14¹⁰ˢ 11¹⁰ˢᵈ
4¹⁰ᵍ 9¹⁰ᵍᶠ 8¹⁰ᵍˢ 8⁸ʰʸ 8¹⁰ᵍ **0-0-12**

Mystic Promise (Ire) *Mrs N Macauley* a31
3 gr g Among Men (USA) - Ivory's Promise
11⁶ˢᵈ 9⁶ˢˢ 8⁸ˢᵈ 5⁸ˢˢ 9¹⁰ˢᵈ 3⁸ˢᵈ 4⁵⁷ˢᶠ
6⁹ˢᵈ 10⁸ˢᵈ **0-0-10 £205**

Mystical Girl (USA) *M Johnston* 101
3 ch f Rahy (USA) - Miss Twinkletoes (Ire)
3⁸ᵍ 3⁸ʰʸ 1⁸ᵍᶠ 2¹¹ᵍᶠ 1⁸ᵍˢ 3¹⁰ᵍ 12⁸ᵍᶠ 6¹⁰ᵍᶠ
8⁸ᵍᶠ 5¹⁰ʰʸ 1⁸ᵍᶠ **3-4-11 £36,169**

Mystical Land (Ire) *J H M Gosden* 108
2 b c Xaar - Samsung Spirit
2⁵ˢ 1⁵ᵍˢ 2⁵ᵍᶠ 3⁶ᵍᶠ 2⁶ᵍᶠ 5⁶ᵛˢ 2⁶ᵍˢ **1-4-7**
£61,330

Mythical Charm *J J Bridger* 62 a55
5 b m Charnwood Forest (Ire) - Triple Tricks (Ire)
6⁹ˢᵈ 13¹⁰ˢᵈ 7⁸ˢᵈ 9¹⁰ˢᵈ 6¹⁰ˢᵈ 3¹⁰ˢᵈ 3⁸ˢᵈ
7⁸ᵍᶠ 11⁹ᵍ 7⁸ᵍ 5⁷ᵍᶠ 15⁸ᵍ 7⁶ᵍ 2⁸ᵍˢ 2⁸ᵍᶠ
9⁸ᵍ 12⁹ˢ **0-3-18 £3,181**

Mythical King (Ire) *R Lee* 55 a16
7 b g Fairy King (USA) - Whatcombe (USA)
8¹²ʰʸ 6¹⁰ᵍ 11¹²ˢᵈ **0-0-3**

Mytori *D Shaw* 21
2 ch f Vettori (Ire) - Markievicz (Ire)
15⁷ᵍᶠ 6⁸ᵍ 6⁶ʰʸ **0-0-3**

Mytton's Bell (Ire) *A Bailey* 72 a66
2 b f Bold Edge - Ionian Secret
2⁶ᵍᶠ 3⁶ˢᵈ 10⁶ˢ 3⁶ᵍᶠ 7⁶ᵍ 5⁷ᵍᶠ 15⁶ᵍˢ 3⁷ˢ
1⁷ˢ 10⁵ʰʸ **1-4-10 £7,002**

Mytton's Dream *A Bailey* 53
2 br f Diktat - Courtisane
6⁶ˢ 6⁵ˢ 1⁵ᵍᶠ 9⁵ᵍ 4⁶ᵍᶠ 12⁷ᵍˢ 12⁷ᵍᶠ **1-0-7**
£3,953

Naaddey *M R Channon* 92
3 b c Seeking The Gold (USA) - Bahr
7⁹ᵍ 6⁸ᵍᶠ 4⁸ᵍᶠ **0-0-3 £1,045**

Naahy *M R Channon* 112

4 ch c Bahamian Bounty - Daffodil Fields
1^{7g} 1^{7gf} 7^{7gf} 4^{7gf} 4^{7g} 6^{7g} 7^{8gs} 7^{7f} 5^{7gf}
2-0-9 £48,927

Nabtat Saif *R Hannon* 55 a81
3 b f Compton Place - Bahawir Pour (USA)
7^{8h} 4^{8h} 7^{9ft} 11^{10gf} 10^{7g} 14^{10gf} **0-0-6**
£558

Nadeszhda *Sir Mark Prescott* a80
4 ch f Nashwan (USA) - Ninotchka (USA)
1^{12sd} 10^{11s} **1-0-2 £3,454**

Nadir *P Howling* 60
3 b c Pivotal - Amid The Stars
9^{8gs} 6^{8g} 10^{10s} **0-0-3**

Nafferton Girl (Ire) *J A Osborne* 43 a41
3 b f Orpen (USA) - Petomi
4^{6gs} 7^{9sd} 8^{10sd} 10^{10f} **0-0-4**

Nafferton Heights (Ire) *M W Easterby* 47
3 b c Peintre Celebre (USA) - Gold Mist
10^{7gs} 5^{10gs} 8^{12gf} 9^{14f} 18^{16gs} 6^{12gf} 12^{8gf}
0-0-7

Naheef (Ire) *Saeed Bin Suroor* 109 a110
5 b h Marju (Ire) - Golden Digger (USA)
3^{10ft} 5^{11gf} 8^{12gf} 1^{12gs} 5^{10g} 10^{10s} **1-0-6**
£36,740

Naivety *C E Brittain* 77
2 ch f Machiavellian (USA) - Innocence
2^{7s} 7^{7gf} **0-1-2 £1,692**

Najaaba (USA) *Miss J Feilden* 84 a85
4 b f Bahhare (USA) - Ashbilya (USA)
1^{8sd} 1^{8sd} 1^{9sd} 1^{8sd} 10^{8ss} 5^{8gs} 6^{9g}
5^{8gs} 10^{8g} 7^{8sd} **5-0-11 £17,755**

Najeebon (Fr) *M R Channon* 89
5 ch g Cadeaux Genereux - Jumairah Sun (Ire)
11^{6g} 15^{6gf} 6^{6gf} 6^{6gf} 3^{6gf} 7^{7g}
12^{6g} 9^{6gs} 2^{6gf} 3^{6g} 10^{6gs} **0-4-12 £6,697**

Nakwa (Ire) *E J Alston* 74 a64
6 b g Namaqualand (USA) - Cajo (Ire)
1^{12sd} 2^{12sd} 2^{12sd} 5^{14sd} 3^{12hy} 2^{14s} 2^{13g}
1^{14gf} 2^{14gs} 6^{14g} 10^{16gf} 10^{13gf} 16^{11s} 22^{18s}
2-5-14 £13,469

Namat (Ire) *M P Tregoning* 74
3 b f Daylami (Ire) - Masharik (Ire)
2^{9gf} 1^{10g} **1-1-2 £4,645**

Named At Dinner *Mrs A Duffield* 45
3 ch g Halling (USA) - Salanka (Ire)
11^{10gs} 16^{8gf} 19^{6gf} 20^{8gs} 15^{7gf} 7^{7f}
10^{7gs} 8^{10gf} **0-0-8**

Namking *C W Thornton* 52 a40
2 b g Namid - Kingdom Queen (Ire)
7^{5g} 8^{5gf} 6^{6sd} **0-0-3**

Namroc (Ire) *E F Vaughan* 93
3 b c Indian Ridge - Hesperia
1^{8gf} 4^{8gs} 2^{8f} 4^{10g} 7^{10hy} **1-2-5 £9,265**

Namroud (USA) *R A Fahey* 84
5 b g Irish River (Fr) - Top Line (Fr)
20^{6g} 6^{7hy} 10^{8gf} 25^{7f} 7^{7g} 7^{8g} 4^{8s} 9^{7s}
6^{7s} 9^{7s} **0-0-10 £1,110**

Nan Jan *R Ingram* 76 a78
2 b f Komaite (USA) - Dam Certain (Ire)
8^{6g} 7^{6g} 2^{6gf} 4^{6sd} **0-1-4 £1,988**

Nanabanana (Ire) *Mme C Head-Maarek* 102
2 b f Anabaa (USA) - Tanabata (Fr)
4^{6g} 2^{7hy} 1^{7s} 2^{7vs} 2^{7gs} 2^{6s} **1-3-6**
£32,302

Nanna (Ire) *R Hollinshead* 74 a58

3 b f Danetime (Ire) - Pre Catelan
5^{7sd} 2^{6sd} 9^{6ss} 3^{6sw} 7^{5sd} 2^{5sd} 1^{5gf} 6^{6f}
2^{5sd} 1^{5s} 1^{5gf} 6^{5gf} 7^{5gs} 3^{5gf} 8^{5sd} **3-5-15**
£15,425

Nanton (USA) *P F I Cole* 49 a75
2 gr/ro c Spinning World (USA) - Grab The Green (USA)
7^{5g} 6^{8sd} **0-0-2**

Nantucket Sound (USA) *M C Pipe* 76
3 b g Quiet American (USA) - Anna
9^{8gs} 4^{8s} 1^{10f} 8^{10gf} 8^{12gs} **1-1-5 £3,925**

Napapijri (Fr) *D P Keane* 58
2 gr f Highest Honor (Fr) - Les Marettes (Fr)
5^{7s} 7^{8s} 4^{8gs} **0-0-3 £305**

Narciso (Ger) *M W Easterby* 52 a22
4 ch g Acatenango (Ger) - Notturna
10^{8gs} 8^{7g} 9^{6sd} 10^{7gf} 6^{14gf} 13^{10gf} 6^{16f}
0-0-7

Narrative (Ire) *D R Loder* 101
6 b h Sadler's Wells (USA) - Barger (USA)
8^{13gs} 4^{8gf} 6^{8gf} 18^{10g} **0-0-4 £1,372**

Nashaab (USA) *P D Evans* 100 a85
7 b g Zafonic (USA) - Tajannub (USA)
12^{10sd} 7^{8sd} 7^{6g} 9^{6gs} 28^{g} 3^{8g} 1^{8gf} 5^{7s}
7^{7gf} 8^{8gf} 14^{9g} 1^{8g} 14^{8s} 39^{sd} **2-3-14**
£30,908

Nassau Street *D J S Ffrench Davis* 38 a40
4 gr g Bahamian Bounty - Milva
3^{9sw} 8^{12ss} 11^{10gs} 3^{7gf} **0-2-4 £396**

Nasseem Dubai (USA) *Mrs A Duffield* 77 a73
2 ch c Silver Hawk (USA) - Fleur De Nuit (USA)
7^{6f} 6^{7s} 2^{7gs} 5^{8f} 3^{7s} 7^{6sd} 7^{6s} **0-2-7**
£1,972

Nassiria *C E Brittain* 69 a76
3 b f Singspiel (Ire) - Naskhi
6^{8g} 6^{10gs} 11^{10gf} 12^{12gf} 7^{10gf} 3^{10f} 3^{12sd}
0-2-7 £2,032

Natalie Jane (Ire) *G A Butler* 82
2 ch f Giant's Causeway - Kirk
7^{8gf} 3^{8gs} 1^{10hy} 3^{10gs} **1-2-4 £7,954**

Nataliya *J L Dunlop* 105
3 b f Green Desert (USA) - Ninotchka (USA)
3^{7g} 7^{8g} 9^{8gs} 4^{8gf} 11^{6gs} PU^{7gf} **0-1-6**
£7,000

Nathan Brittles (USA) *T D Barron* 83
4 ch g Cat's Career (USA) - Doc's Answer (USA)
1^{7g} **1-0-1 £5,687**

Nathan Detroit *P J Makin* 45
4 b g Entrepreneur - Mainly Sunset
15^{6gf} 13^{6gf} **0-0-2**

National Trust *Sir Michael Stoute* 46
2 b c Sadler's Wells (USA) - National Treasure
11^{7gs} **0-0-1**

Native Title *D Nicholls* 97
6 b g Pivotal - Bermuda Lily
4^{5gs} 8^{6gf} 1^{6g} 18^{6f} 16^{5s} 3^{6g} 19^{6gf} 10^{6s}
8^{5s} **1-1-9 £26,178**

Native Turk (USA) *J A R Toller* 57 a69
3 b c Miswaki (USA) - Churn Dat Butter (USA)
14^{8gf} 11^{7gs} 2^{8sd} 5^{9gf} **0-1-4 £1,034**

Natmsky (Ire) *G A Harker* 13
5 b g Shadeed (USA) - Cockney Lass
19^{12gf} 9^{12gf} 15^{8f} **0-0-3**

Naughty Girl (Ire) *P D Evans* 54 a51
4 b f Dr Devious (Ire) - Mary Magdalene
11^{7sd} 8^{6sd} 8^{8ss} 15^{6s} 15^{6gf} 9^{5gf} 9^{6f} 5^{8f}

4^{8gs} 4^{7gf} 12^{8g} 2^{8gf} 12^{8gf} 1^{8f} 10^{8f} 8^{7g}
1-1-16 £4,531

Nautical *A W Carroll*   62 a75
6 gr g Lion Cavern (USA) - Russian Royal (USA)
14^{11gs} 9^{10s} 4^{10sd} 6^{10gf} 4^{8g} 3^{8gf} 11^{8gf}
2^{8gf} 7^{6gs} 1^{7g} 19^{sd} 8^{8sd} 2^{7sd} **2-2-13 £9,510**

Nautical Star *A C Whillans*   36
9 b g Slip Anchor - Comic Talent
5^{13g} **0-0-1**

Naval Attache *N P Littmoden*   48
2 b g Slip Anchor - Cayla
10^{8g} 17^{8s} **0-0-2**

Naval Force *H Morrison*   74 a71
2 b c Forzando - Barsham
9^{6gf} 4^{7sd} 3^{6f} 16^{6gs} 13^{7s} **0-1-5 £860**

Navigation (Ire) *T J Etherington*   59 a65
2 ch c Bahamian Bounty - Bridge Pool
11^{6gf} 6^{6gf} 7^{5sd} **0-0-3**

Nawaaem (USA) *B W Hills*   76
2 b/br f Swain (Ire) - Alattrah (USA)
5^{7gs} **0-0-1**

Nawamees (Ire) *G L Moore*   93 a90
6 b g Darshaan - Truly Generous (Ire)
4^{16sd} 2^{12sd} 2^{12gf} 10^{14g} 12^{12gf} **0-2-5
£8,432**

Nawow *P D Cundell*   82 a76
4 b g Blushing Flame (USA) - Fair Test
15^{12sd} 3^{16g} 5^{16g} 6^{14gs} 10^{11g} 2^{12g} 7^{14gs}
4^{12s} **0-2-8 £3,359**

Nayyir *G A Butler*   126
6 ch g Indian Ridge - Pearl Kite (USA)
3^{9gf} 16^{6gs} 2^{8g} 2^{8gs} 4^{8gf} 6^{7s} **0-3-6
£212,231**

Nazaaha (USA) *J L Dunlop*   71
2 gr f Elnadim (USA) - Taatof (Ire)
4^{6gf} **0-0-1 £476**

Nazzwah *M R Channon*   58
3 ch f Rahy (USA) - Baaderah (Ire)
6^{7gf} 6^{9gf} 9^{8gf} **0-0-3**

Ndola *B J Curley*   a48
5 b g Emperor Jones (USA) - Lykoa
1^{9sd} 12^{11sd} 12^{10sd} 3^{10sd} **1-1-4 £1,670**

Ne Oublie *J Mackie*   65
2 b c Makbul - Parkside Prospect
6^{5g} 4^{5gf} 3^{5gs} 10^{5gf} **0-1-4 £645**

Neap Tide *J H M Gosden*   29
3 br g Zafonic (USA) - Love The Rain
13^{10g} 19^{7gf} **0-0-2**

Nearly A Fool *G G Margarson*   76 a76
6 b g Komaite (USA) - Greenway Lady
1^{7sd} 1^{6sd} 12^{7sd} 2^{7sd} 17^{ss} 8^{7sd} 1^{7gs} 3^{8gf}
4^{8gf} 8^{7sd} 5^{7g} 11^{7gf} 5^{8gs} 1^{7sd} 2^{7sd} **5-3-15
£19,250**

Neath *Mrs A J Perrett*   73
3 b f Rainbow Quest (USA) - Welsh Autumn
5^{10gs} 3^{10g} 7^{10s} **0-1-3 £856**

Nebraska City *B Gubby*   55 a33
3 b g Piccolo - Scarlet Veil
10^{6sd} 6^{6f} 13^{8gf} 4^{6gf} 6^{7gf} 13^{6gf} 13^{6gs}
0-0-7

Nebraska Tornado (USA) *A Fabre*   119 a97
4 b/br f Storm Cat (USA) - Media Nox
5^{9g} 4^{8gf} 3^{8g} 3^{8g} 8^{9ft} **0-1-5 £54,627**

Neckar Valley (Ire) *R A Fahey*   49
5 b g Desert King (Ire) - Solar Attraction (Ire)

12^{10s} **0-0-1**

Necklace *A P O'Brien*   115
3 b f Darshaan - Spinning The Yarn
12^{8g} 6^{8gf} 4^{12g} 3^{10f} 4^{9g} **0-1-5 £68,647**

Nee Lemon Left *A Berry*   60
2 b f Puissance - Via Dolorosa
2^{5gf} 6^{5g} 3^{5gf} 7^{5gf} 6^{5gs} 4^{5gs} 12^{5gf} **0-1-7
£2,397**

Needles And Pins (Ire) *M L W Bell*   92
3 b f Fasliyev (USA) - Fairy Contessa (Ire)
4^{6g} 7^{6g} 5^{6g} 7^{5gf} 12^{5s} **0-0-5 £2,250**

Needwood Bucolic (Ire) *R Allan*   41 a12
6 br g Charnwood Forest (Ire) - Greek Icon
10^{5g} 9^{7gf} 7^{5gf} 13^{6sd} 9^{6g} 13^{7gf} 7^{7gf}
0-0-7

Needwood Mystic *Mrs A J Perrett*   68
9 b m Rolfe (USA) - Enchanting Kate
2^{12f} **0-1-1 £1,030**

Needwood Spirit *Mrs A M Naughton*   7
9 b g Rolfe (USA) - Needwood Nymph
15^{12g} 16^{16f} **0-0-2**

Neferura *W J Haggas*   54
2 b f Mister Baileys - Boadicea's Chariot
11^{6g} 9^{7gf} 13^{8s} **0-0-3**

Negas (Ire) *J Howard Johnson*   42
2 b g Titus Livius (Fr) - Alzeam (Ire)
17^{5gf} 10^{5gf} 11^{7g} 17^{6s} **0-0-4**

Negwa (Ire) *M R Channon*   40
3 b f Bering - Ballet
5^{10g} 8^{10gf} 10^{8gs} **0-0-3**

Nella Fantasia (Ire) *G C Bravery*   67
2 ch f Giant's Causeway (USA) - Paper Moon (Ire)
6^{5gf} 6^{6g} **0-0-2**

Nellie Gwyn *J G Given*   30
2 b f King's Best (USA) - On Tiptoes
15^{6gs} **0-0-1**

Nelson's Luck *E A Wheeler*   10
3 b g Young Ern - A Little Hot
15^{7gf} **0-0-1**

Nemo Fugat (Ire) *D Nicholls*   115
5 b g Danehill Dancer (Ire) - Do The Right Thing
17^{6gs} 13^{6gf} 5^{8g} 6^{8gf} 7^{9g} 2^{6gf} 5^{6gf} 2^{7f}
15^{7s} 15^{7s} 3^{8gf} 8^{8gf} **0-3-12 £3,046**

Neon Blue *R M Whitaker*   76
3 b/br g Atraf - Desert Lynx (Ire)
5^{6g} 16^{6gf} 7^{7gf} 3^{6gf} 3^{6g} 3^{6s} 1^{7gf} 6^{7g} 7^{7gf}
8^{8s} 11^{7gs} **2-3-11 £18,810**

Nepal (Ire) *T D Barron*   63
2 ch f Monashee Mountain (USA) - Zetonic
6^{6f} 2^{7gf} 4^{7g} **0-1-3 £1,116**

Nephetriti Way (Ire) *P R Chamings*   80
3 b f Docksider (USA) - Velvet Appeal (Ire)
7^{8s} 5^{7g} 5^{7gf} 5^{8gf} **0-0-4 £368**

Neptune *J C Fox*   41 a48
8 b g Dolphin Street (Fr) - Seal Indigo (Ire)
5^{16sd} 11^{12sd} 9^{12sd} 2^{12sd} 4^{12sd} 5^{12hy} 3^{12sd}
5^{12sd} 3^{12g} **0-3-9 £1,321**

Neqaawi *B Hanbury*   71
3 br f Alhaarth (Ire) - Jinsiyah (USA)
5^{7gf} 1^{7f} 11^{7g} **1-0-3 £3,493**

Nero's Return (Ire) *M Johnston*   97
3 b g Mujadil (USA) - Snappy Dresser
6^{8gs} 3^{7gf} 6^{6gf} 15^{6gf} 7^{10gs} 5^{6gf} 7^{6g} **0-0-7
£1,263**

Nesnaas (USA) *M G Rimell*   37

3 ch g Gulch (USA) - Sedrah (USA)
11^{7gf} 15^{7gf} **0-0-2**

Nessen Dorma (Ire) *J G Given*   85 a74
3 b g Entrepreneur - Goldilocks (Ire)
4^{10sd} 5^{10sd} 5^{12g} 2^{12gs} 1^{15gs} 3^{12gs} 3^{14gs}
8^{16f} 9^{16gs} 7^{13s} **1-3-10 £10,822**

Neutral Night (Ire) *R Brotherton*   a49
4 b f Night Shift (USA) - Neutrality (Ire)
3^{6sd} 10^{8sd} 7^{6sd} 5^{7ss} 3^{7sw} 2^{7ss} 4^{8ss} 3^{6sd}
3^{7sd} 1^{7sd} 2^{6sd} 2^{7sd} 8^{7sd} **1-6-13 £3,537**

Neutrino *L M Cumani*   72 a60
2 b c Mtoto - Fair Seas
12^{7g} 4^{7s} 4^{7sd} **0-0-3 £550**

Nevada Desert (Ire) *R M Whitaker*   79
4 b g Desert King (Ire) - Kayanga
4^{10gs} 5^{8gf} 2^{10s} 7^{12gf} 1^{8gs} 8^{8gs} 18^{10s} 8^{8s}
6^{7s} **1-2-9 £13,090**

Never Away *N A Callaghan*   59
2 b f Royal Applause - Waypoint
9^{6gs} 10^{6g} 13^{7gs} 11^{6g} 11^{7gf} **0-0-5**

Never Cried Wolf *T R Greathead*   a52
3 b g Wolfhound (USA) - Bold Difference
6^{8sd} 10^{8sd} 7^{7sd} 6^{8sd} 12^{8sd} **0-0-5**

Never Forget Bowie *R Allan*   38
8 b g Superpower - Heldigvis
8^{9gs} 11^{6gs} 5^{7s} **0-0-3**

Never Promise (Fr) *C Roberts*   33
6 b m Cadeaux Genereux - Yazeanhaa (USA)
6^{9f} 8^{8s} **0-0-2**

Never Will *M Johnston*   84
3 b c Cadeaux Genereux - Answered Prayer
2^{7gf} 2^{8g} 1^{9gs} 12^{9g} 23^{8f} **1-2-5 £9,904**

Never Without Me *J F Coupland*   76 a75
4 ch g Mark Of Esteem (Ire) - Festival Sister
6^{6sw} 4^{6ss} 5^{5ss} 2^{5ss} 1^{5sd} 8^{5g} 3^{6sd} 4^{6hy}
1^{6sd} 1^{6sd} 2^{6gf} 4^{6gf} 2^{5gf} 2^{5s} 5^{5gs} 12^{6gf} **3-4-16**
£17,466

Neverletme Go (Ire) *G Wragg*   73
2 b f Green Desert (USA) - Cassandra Go (Ire)
4^{5gf} 5^{6g} **0-0-2 £435**

Nevinstown (Ire) *Niall Moran*   a39
4 b c Lahib (USA) - Moon Tango (Ire)
8^{8sd} **0-0-1**

New Day Dawning *C Smith*   52
3 ch f First Trump - Tintinara
13^{6s} 6^{5gf} 16^{5g} 20^{6gf} **0-0-4**

New Mexican *Mrs J R Ramsden*   99
3 ch g Dr Fong (USA) - Apache Star
4^{8g} 5^{9g} **0-0-2 £1,475**

New Morning (Ire) *M A Jarvis*   109
3 b f Sadler's Wells (USA) - Hellenic
2^{11gf} 1^{12gf} 4^{12gf} 5^{12g} 1^{10gf} 6^{10g} **2-1-6**
£41,738

New Options *W J Musson*   28 a66
7 b g Formidable (USA) - No Comebacks
5^{6sw} 4^{6sd} 8^{6sd} 5^{6ss} 10^{6sd} 3^{6sd} 9^{6gs} 3^{7sd}
17^{6s} 14^{10g} 7^{7sd} 5^{6sd} **0-2-12 £708**

New Order *B W Hills*   83
3 b f Singspiel (Ire) - Eternal
3^{7gs} 1^{8g} 1^{7gs} 6^{8gf} 17^{10s} **2-1-5 £13,424**

New Prospective *D Nicholls*
6 b g Cadeaux Genereux - Amazing Bay
12^{7sd} **0-0-1**

New Realm (USA) *E F Vaughan*   37
2 b c Red Ransom (USA) - Mystery Rays (USA)

14^{7gs} **0-0-1**

New Seeker *C G Cox*   107
4 b g Green Desert (USA) - Ahbab (Ire)
2^{8s} 4^{7f} 8^{8g} 6^{7gf} 10^{6gf} **0-1-5 £10,850**

New South Wales *Saeed Bin Suroor*   112
4 b c In The Wings - Temora (Ire)
3^{16gf} 10^{20gf} **0-1-2 £11,990**

New Wish (Ire) *M W Easterby*   63
4 b g Ali-Royal (Ire) - False Spring (Ire)
5^{8gf} 9^{7f} 12^{7gf} 11^{8g} **0-0-4**

New York (Ire) *W J Haggas*   59
3 b f Danzero (Aus) - Council Rock
13^{7gf} 10^{7gf} 3^{7gf} 5^{8f} 8^{6gs} **0-1-5 £417**

New York City (Ire) *L M Cumani*   26
3 b c Alzao (USA) - Eurolinka (Ire)
8^{10gs} **0-0-1**

Newclose *N Tinkler*   23 a44
4 b g Barathea (Ire) - Wedgewood (USA)
3^{8sd} 3^{7sd} 3^{11sd} 4^{12sd} 7^{8g} **0-3-5 £715**

Newcorp Lad *Mrs G S Rees*   76
4 b g Komaite (USA) - Gleam Of Gold
15^{8gs} 4^{10s} 9^{8f} 8^{10gf} 7^{9gs} 4^{9g} 4^{8gf} 2^{8gf}
4^{8g} 14^{8gs} 3^{8gf} 1^{8gf} 4^{8gf} 7^{8g} **1-5-14 £7,360**

Newcorr (Ire) *J J Bridger*   36 a37
5 b g Magical Wonder (USA) - Avionne
10^{8sd} 14^{12sd} 6^{8sd} 3^{8sd} 2^{8g} 4^{7sd} 7^{7gf}
7^{10gs} **0-1-8 £549**

Newnham (Ire) *L M Cumani*   76
3 ch g Theatrical - Brief Escapade (Ire)
2^{8gs} 4^{10gs} 2^{12gf} 3^{12s} **0-3-4 £3,412**

News Sky (USA) *B W Hills*   83
3 b c Gone West (USA) - Dubian
15^{8g} 2^{8g} 2^{10gf} 3^{10gf} 3^{10g} 8^{10gs} **0-2-6**
£4,588

Newsround *M A Jarvis*   92
2 ch c Cadeaux Genereux - Ring The Relatives
2^{6gs} 1^{6g} 7^{6g} **1-1-3 £8,151**

Newton (Ire) *A P O'Brien*   106
3 b c Danehill (USA) - Elite Guest (Ire)
1^{7ys} 4^{7g} 6^{8gf} 6^{8gf} 11^{8gf} 10^{6y} 8^{7hy} **1-0-7**
£28,549

Newtonian (USA) *J Parkes*   35 a73
5 ch g Distant View - Polly Adler (USA)
3^{12sd} 8^{12sd} 4^{12gs} **0-0-3 £412**

Newtown Chief *J G Cromwell*   16 a18
3 b g So Factual (USA) - Polish Descent (Ire)
15^{7gf} 13^{12gf} 11^{10sd} 11^{8gf} **0-0-4**

Next Flight (Ire) *R E Barr*   60 a55
5 b g Woodborough - Sans Ceriph (Ire)
6^{11sd} 2^{14sd} 3^{11ss} 2^{14ss} 3^{12gf} 1^{14s} 4^{12hy}
3^{14gf} 2^{14sd} 3^{16s} 4^{16g} 6^{14sd} 8^{14gf} **1-7-13**
£8,071

Next Time (Ire) *M J Polglase*   59
2 b f Danetime (Ire) - Muckross Park
4^{5g} 5^{5gf} 10^{5gs} 7^{6g} 4^{5gf} 4^{5gf} 8^{5g} 11^{5gf}
0-0-8 £929

Next Time Around (Ire) *Mrs L Stubbs*   92
2 b c Namid - In Due Course (USA)
1^{5g} 3^{5gs} 5^{5gf} 12^{5gf} 4^{5s} 11^{6g} **1-1-6**
£10,886

Niagara (Ire) *M H Tompkins*   62
7 b g Rainbows For Life (Can) - Highbrook (USA)
12^{12gs} 6^{10f} 16^{10g} **0-0-3**

Nibbles (Ire) *R P Elliott*
2 b g Soviet Star (USA) - Tumbleweed Pearl

13^{6sw} 0-0-1

Nice Tune *C E Brittain* — 90
2 b f Diktat - Military Tune (Ire)
3^{7g} 4^{8gf} 7^{7g} 5^{7hy} 0-1-4 £3,525

Nicholas Nickelby *M J Polglase* — 66 a53
4 gr g Fayruz - Alasib
7^{7hy} 6^{7f} 2^{8gf} 10^{12gf} 13^{8gs} 4^{7sd} 3^{6g} 4^{6gs}
4^{5gs} 2^{7f} 5^{6gf} 11^{8g} 0-3-12 £2,983

Niciara (Ire) *M C Chapman* — a12
7 b g Soviet Lad (USA) - Verusa (Ire)
8^{16sd} 9^{16sd} 0-0-2

Nick The Silver *G B Balding* — 57
3 gr c Nicolotte - Brillante (Fr)
14^{10gs} 6^{12gf} 10^{13gf} UR^{12gs} 11^{14gf} 12^{12gf}
0-0-6

Nickel Sungirl (Ire) *R Hollinshead*
4 b f Petorius - Sharp Hint
11^{8sd} 0-0-1

Nietzsche (Ire) *J Noseda* — 82
3 b c Sadler's Wells (USA) - Wannabe
9^{10gs} 2^{10g} 5^{10gf} 2^{10hy} 0-2-4 £3,074

Nifty Roy *K W Hogg* — 20 a8
4 b g Royal Applause - Nifty Fifty (Ire)
16^{10f} 13^{8f} 13^{6sd} 11^{6g} 0-0-4

Night Air (Ire) *D R Loder* — 83
3 b g Night Shift (USA) - Pippas Song
1^{7g} 5^{7gf} 2^{7gf} 2^{7gs} 1-2-4 £10,269

Night Cap (Ire) *T D McCarthy* — 49 a54
5 ch g Night Shift (USA) - Classic Design
6^{6sd} 7^{5sd} 11^{6sd} 2^{6sd} 7^{6sd} 3^{6g} 17^{6gf} 4^{6gf}
8^{6g} 0-2-9 £919

Night Club Queen (Ire) *J W Hills* — 33
2 ch f Night Shift (USA) - Play The Queen (Ire)
13^{6gf} 9^{6gs} 14^{6g} 0-0-3

Night Dance *M Wigham* — 5
12 ch g Weldnaas (USA) - Shift Over (USA)
18^{8g} 0-0-1

Night Driver (Ire) *G L Moore* — 45
5 b g Night Shift (USA) - Highshaan
13^{8s} 14^{8gf} 12^{8gs} 11^{10gf} 13^{10gf} 10^{12sd}
0-0-6

Night Frolic *J W Hills* — 68
3 b f Night Shift (USA) - Miss D'Ouilly (Fr)
1^{8hy} 3^{9f} 7^{10gf} 6^{8g} 6^{9gf} 9^{8s} 4^{8hy} 2^{8g} 5^{8s}
1-1-9 £7,575

Night Guest (Ire) *R Hannon* — 64
2 b c Danehill Dancer - Meadow Grass (Ire)
8^{7gs} 12^{8g} 15^{8gs} 0-0-3

Night Hour (Ire) *M P Tregoning* — 87
2 b c Entrepreneur - Witching Hour (Ire)
4^{8g} 1^{8s} 7^{8s} 1-0-3 £6,182

Night Kiss (Fr) *R Hannon* — 55
4 ch f Night Shift (USA) - Roxy
13^{8hy} 9^{7g} 10^{8gf} 0-0-3

Night Mail *M W Easterby* — 23 a42
4 b g Shaamit (Ire) - Penlanfeigan
6^{11sd} 8^{9f} 0-0-2

Night Market *N Wilson* — 59 a8
6 ch g Inchinor - Night Transaction
11^{8sd} 18^{9f} 9^{10gf} 18^{7f} 18^{10s} 6^{8f} 1-0-6
£3,188

Night Of Joy (Ire) *M A Jarvis* — 89
2 b f King's Best (USA) - Gilah (Ire)
4^{6gf} 4^{7f} 1^{8s} 9^{8g} 7^{8s} 2-0-6
£16,205

Night Out (Fr) *G C Bravery* — 57
2 b f Night Shift (USA) - My Lucky Day (Fr)
9^{5s} 6^{6gf} 10^{5gf} 0-0-3

Night Prospector *J W Payne* — 106
4 b c Night Shift (USA) - Pride Of My Heart
11^{5gs} 1^{5g} 10^{5gs} 12^{5s} 8^{5gf} 1-0-5
£63,800

Night Sight (USA) *Mrs S Lamyman* — 77
7 b g Eagle Eyed (USA) - El Hamo (USA)
9^{12gf} 2^{12gf} 3^{12g} 4^{15g} 4^{12gs} 1^{10gf} 5^{12g} 1^{12f}
4^{12gf} 5^{10gf} 2^{12g} 2-3-11 £17,313

Night Spot *R Charlton* — 88
3 ch g Night Shift (USA) - Rash Gift
6^{10gs} 3^{10gf} 2^{10gf} 1^{10g} 6^{12gs} 11^{12g} 1-1-6
£10,932

Night Storm *S Dow* — a70
3 b f Night Shift (USA) - Monte Calvo
5^{10sd} 3^{8sd} 3^{8sd} 3^{7sd} 6^{8sd} 15^{7s} 1^{7sd} 1-3-7
£5,161

Night Warrior (Ire) *D Flood* — a73
4 b g Alhaarth (Ire) - Miniver (Ire)
10^{10sd} 4^{12sd} 4^{12sd} 2^{12ss} 7^{12sd} 0-2-5
£1,273

Night Wolf (Ire) *M R Channon* — 70 a74
4 gr g Indian Ridge - Nicer (Ire)
6^{8sd} 15^{8hy} 8^{8gf} 3^{7gf} 8^{8g} 13^{7gf} 16^{7gf}
8^{6gf} 5^{6gf} 14^{7g} 11^{8f} 0-1-11 £1,036

Night Worker *R Hannon* — 51
3 b c Dracula (Aus) - Crystal Magic
6^{6gs} 10^{6s} 9^{8s} 10^{6gf} 6^{7gf} 5^{5gf} 14^{6gf}
10^{7gs} 9^{8s} 7^{7hy} 0-0-11

Nightfall (USA) *Saeed Bin Suroor* — 82 a60
2 b c Rahy (USA) - Quality Gift
1^{6gf} 6^{6gf} 11^{7sd} 1-0-3 £6,734

Nights Cross (Ire) *M R Channon* — 108
3 b g Cape Cross (Ire) - Cathy Garcia (Ire)
4^{5s} 3^{6g} 16^{7g} 7^{5gf} 3^{6gf} 3^{6gf}
3^{6gs} 8^{5s} 10^{6hy} 1^{5g} 14^{6ys} 1-3-13 £33,553

Nikiforos *J W Hills* — 64 a64
3 b c Inchinor - Putout
8^{7gf} 8^{8gf} 8^{8g} 4^{7sd} 4^{7gf} 7^{6gs} 12^{6gf} 0-0-7
£536

Nimbus Twothousand *P R Wood* — a44
4 b f Cloudings (Ire) - Blueberry Parkes
5^{8sd} 0-0-1

Nimello (USA) *A G Newcombe* — 86 a95
8 b g Kingmambo (USA) - Zakota (Ire)
9^{10sd} 9^{8ss} 18^{sd} 8^{8s} 1^{9gs} 13^{8gs} 13^{8hy}
2-0-7 £11,651

Nina Fontenail (Fr) *B R Millman* — 43 a42
3 gr f Kaldounevees (Fr) - Ninon Fontenail (Fr)
9^{11gs} 12^{14gf} 5^{12gf} 4^{12gf} 2^{10sd} 5^{8gs}
0-1-7 £1,163

Ninah *J M Bradley* — 45 a32
3 b f First Trump - Alwal
16^{7s} 11^{6gf} 10^{8gf} 17^{6f} 10^{8g} 15^{6s} 8^{9sd}
0-0-7

Ninah's Intuition *J M Bradley* — 58
2 b c Piccolo - Gina Of Hithermoor
4^{5g} 4^{5hy} 8^{5gf} 0-0-3 £386

Nine Red *J M Bradley* — 55 a63
3 b f Royal Applause - Sarcita
10^{7g} 9^{7gf} 9^{8f} 2^{7sd} 15^{7s} 9^{7gs} 0-1-6
£1,660

Ninja Storm (Ire) *G L Moore* — 71 a63
2 b c Namid - Swan Lake (Ire)

4⁵ᵍˢ 5⁵ᵍᶠ 6⁵ˢᵈ 7⁵ˢ **0-0-4 £266**

Niobe's Way P R Chamings 75
3 b f Singspiel (Ire) - Arietta's Way (Ire)
7¹⁰ᵍᶠ 4⁸ᵍᶠ 3¹⁰ᵍˢ 2¹⁴ᵍˢ 6¹⁷ˢ **0-1-5 £2,319**

Nip Nip (Ire) A D Smith 39
2 b f Royal Applause - Rustic Bliss
9⁷ᵍˢ 8⁶ᵍˢ **0-0-2**

Nippy Nipper Miss J Feilden 2 a47
3 b f Fraam - Elite Hope (USA)
18⁷ᵍˢ 10⁹ˢᵈ 14⁸ˢ **0-0-3**

Nisr J W Payne 82
7 b g Grand Lodge (USA) - Tharwa (Ire)
2⁶ᵍˢ **0-1-1 £1,788**

Nistaki (USA) T D Easterby 74
3 ch c Miswaki (USA) - Brandywine Belle (USA)
4⁷ˢ 6⁸ᵍᶠ 4⁸ᵍ 2⁶ᶠ **0-1-4 £2,896**

Nite-Owl Fizz J O'Reilly a54
6 b g Efisio - Nite-Owl Dancer
4⁸ˢᵈ 2⁸ˢᵈ 7⁸ˢᵈ 4⁸ˢˢ **0-1-4 £426**

Niteowl Dream J O'Reilly 40 a22
4 ch f Colonel Collins (USA) - Nite-Owl Dancer
4⁷ᵍᶠ 13⁷ˢᵈ 13⁸ᵍᶠ 12⁵ˢᵈ **0-0-4**

Niteowl Express (Ire) J O'Reilly 16 a38
3 b f Royal Applause - Nordan Raider
8⁶ˢˢ 6⁶ˢˢ 5⁸ˢᵈ 4⁶ˢᵈ 10⁶ᵍ 9⁷ᵍ **0-0-6**

Niteowl Lad (Ire) J O'Reilly 66
2 ch g Tagula (Ire) - Mareha (Ire)
7⁵ʰʸ 19⁶ˢ 2⁵ᵍᶠ 5⁵ᵍᶠ **0-1-4 £1,110**

Nivernais H Candy 83
5 b g Forzando - Funny Wave
13⁶ᵍˢ 7⁶ᵍ 9⁵ᵍ 8⁵ᶠ 6⁶ᵍᶠ 7⁷ᵍ 6⁵ᵍᶠ 3⁶ᵍˢ
1⁶ᵍˢ 5⁶ᵍᶠ **1-1-10 £5,698**

No Chance To Dance (Ire) H J Collingridge 55
4 b g Revoque (Ire) - Song Of The Glens
14¹⁰ᵍ 10⁸ᶠ 4⁸ᵍᶠ 3⁹ᵍˢ 6⁸ᵍ 6¹⁰ᵍᶠ 7⁹ᵍˢ 9¹⁰ᵍˢ
0-1-8 £948

No Commission (Ire) R F Fisher 73 a49
2 b g General Monash (USA) - Price Of Passion
9⁵ᵍˢ 5⁵ᵍ 4⁶ᵍᶠ 7⁶ᵍˢ 5⁶ˢᵈ 4⁶ᵍˢ 8⁵ᵍ 2⁶ᵍ 1⁶ᵍᶠ
11⁷ᵍᶠ 5⁷ˢ 9⁶ᵍ 13⁶ˢ **1-1-13 £9,156**

No Dilemma (USA) E A L Dunlop
3 ch g Rahy (USA) - Cascassi (USA)
13¹⁰ᵍˢ **0-0-1**

No Grouse R A Fahey 75 a72
4 b g Pursuit Of Love - Lady Joyce (Fr)
11⁷ˢᵈ 5⁸ˢˢ 9⁷ˢˢ 7⁷ᵍ 3⁷ᵍᶠ 12⁷ᵍᶠ 15⁶ᵍᶠ
12⁸ᵍ 7⁷ᵍᶠ 7⁷ᵍᶠ 8⁸ᵍᶠ 14⁷ᶠ 5⁷ᵍᶠ 4⁷ᵍᶠ 2⁷ᵍ 5⁷ˢ
0-1-16 £2,882

No Refuge (Ire) J Howard Johnson 109
4 ch g Hernando (Fr) - Shamarra (Fr)
3¹⁴ˢ 11⁵ˢ 18¹⁸ˢ **1-0-3 £11,620**

No Time (Ire) M J Polglase 84 a106
4 b c Danetime (Ire) - Muckross Park
6⁶ˢᵈ 6⁶ˢᵈ 2⁵ˢᵈ 1⁵ˢᵈ 1⁵ˢᵈ 11⁵ᵍ 10⁵ᵍᶠ
19⁶ᵍᶠ 12⁵ᵍ **2-1-10 £29,239**

Nobbler J W Hills 62
2 br c Classic Cliche (Ire) - Nicely (Ire)
7⁸ᵍᶠ 11⁸ᵍ 6¹⁰ˢ **0-0-3**

Noble Calling (Fr) R J Hodges 61 a48
7 b h Caller I.D. (USA) - Specificity (USA)
10¹⁰ˢᵈ 3¹⁷ᶠ 7¹⁰ᵍᶠ 3¹⁸ᶠ 2¹⁵ᵍᶠ **0-3-5
£2,370**

Noble Cyrano Jedd O'Keeffe a28
9 ch g Generous (Ire) - Miss Bergerac
6¹¹ˢᵈ 7¹¹ˢᵈ **0-0-2**

Noble Desert (Fr) R Guest 41 a24
3 b f Green Desert (USA) - Sporades (USA)
7⁷ᵍˢ 5⁶ᵍᶠ 10⁶ˢʷ 12⁸ᶠ 7⁸ᵍ 12⁸ᵍˢ **0-0-6**

Noble Duty (USA) Saeed Bin Suroor 87
2 b c Dubai Millennium - Nijinsky's Lover (USA)
2⁸ᵍ 3⁸ᵍ **0-2-2 £4,853**

Noble Locks (Ire) J W Unett a67
6 ch g Night Shift (USA) - Imperial Graf (USA)
8⁶ˢʷ 14⁶ˢᵈ 11⁷ˢʷ 12⁶ˢᵈ 4⁶ˢᵈ 13⁶ˢᵈ **0-0-6
£264**

Noble Mind P G Murphy 69 a49
3 b g Mind Games - Lady Annabel
2⁸ᵍˢ 7⁷ᵍᶠ 9¹⁰ᵍᶠ 3⁸ˢᵈ 11⁹ˢᵈ **0-2-5 £1,889**

Noble Mount A B Haynes 49 a56
3 b g Muhtarram (USA) - Our Poppet (Ire)
5⁶ˢᵈ 7⁶ˢᵈ 11⁵ˢ 3⁵ᵍᶠ 7⁶ˢᵈ 12⁷ˢᵈ **0-1-6
£442**

Noble Penny Mrs K Walton 54
5 b m Pennekamp (USA) - Noble Form
10⁸ˢ 6⁸ᵍ 2⁷ᵍᶠ 10⁷ᵍᶠ 4⁸ᵍ 6⁸ᵍ 5⁷ᵍˢ **0-1-7
£1,105**

Noble Philosopher K Bell
4 ch g Faustus (USA) - Princess Lucy
7¹¹ˢᵈ **0-0-1**

Noble Pursuit R E Barr 55 a64
7 b g Pursuit Of Love - Noble Peregrine
2⁸ˢˢ 2⁸ˢᵈ 7⁷ˢᵈ 7⁹ˢʷ 3⁸ˢʷ 5¹²ˢᵈ 5⁸ˢᵈ 7⁸ˢᵈ
12⁷ᶠ 2⁸ᵍˢ 4⁷ᵍᶠ 13¹⁰ᵍᶠ 3⁷ᵍ 12⁸ᶠ 9⁸ᵍˢ 8⁸ˢ
0-6-16 £3,167

Nobratinetta (Fr) Mrs M Reveley 75
5 b m Celtic Swing - Bustinetta
13¹⁴ˢ 4¹⁶ᵍ 15¹⁴ᵍ **0-0-3 £425**

Nocatee (Ire) P C Haslam 58 a48
3 b g Vettori (Fr) - Rosy Sunset (Ire)
3⁹ˢᵈ 3¹¹ˢᵈ 4¹¹ˢᵈ 3¹⁴ˢ 1¹⁴ᶠ **1-3-5 £4,162**

Nod 'N' A Wink C A Dwyer
6 b g Factual (USA) - Singing Reply (USA)
11⁸ˢᵈ **0-0-1**

Nod's Nephew D E Cantillon 63 a56
7 b g Efisio - Nordan Raider
2⁸ˢˢ 7⁸ˢᵈ 2⁸ᵍˢ 2¹¹ᵍ **0-3-4 £2,036**

Nod's Star Miss J A Camacho 47 a29
3 ch f Starborough - Barsham
5⁸ʰʸ 9⁷ᵍˢ 9⁸ᵍᶠ 7¹²ˢᵈ 7¹⁰ᵍᶠ 3¹⁴ᵍˢ 7¹⁶ᵍ **0-1-7
£592**

Nodina S C Williams 63
2 br c Primo Dominie - Princess Tara
12⁶ᵍᶠ 5⁵ᵍᶠ 10⁶ᵍ **0-0-3**

Nofa's Magic (Ire) J L Dunlop 73
4 b f Rainbow Quest - Garah
3¹²ʰʸ 8¹⁰ᵍ **0-1-2 £575**

Noodles T D Easterby 62
2 b c Mind Games - Salacious
8⁶ᵍˢ 2⁶ᵍ 8⁶ᵍᶠ 10⁵ᶠ 16⁶ˢ **0-1-5 £1,776**

Noora (Ire) M P Tregoning 82 a66
3 ch f Bahhare (USA) - Esteraad (Ire)
2⁷ᵍˢ 10⁷ᵍᶠ 2⁷ᵍ 4⁷ᵍˢ 3⁸ˢ 1⁸ˢᵈ **1-3-6
£9,353**

Noorain M R Channon 75
2 ch f Kabool - Abeyr
3⁵ᵍ 4⁶ᵍ 2⁷ᵍᶠ 7⁷ᵍᶠ **0-2-4 £2,279**

Nopekan (Ire) Miss K Marks 98
4 b g Sri Pekan (USA) - Giadamar (Ire)
5¹²ᵍʸ 6¹⁰ᵍᶠ 13¹²ᶠ 7¹¹ᵍ 8¹²ᵍᶠ 7¹⁰ᵍ **0-0-6**

Nopleazinu Mrs N Macauley 42 a39

4 ch f Sure Blade (USA) - Vado Via
5^{6g} 10^{8gf} 6^{9sd} 0-0-3

Norcroft *P S McEntee*   79 a66
2 b g Fasliyev (USA) - Norcroft Joy
2^{5gs} 1^{5g} 6^{5s} 7^{6gs} 8^{6g} 7^{6gf} 4^{7s} 11^{6gf}
12^{8gf} 3^{7sd} 9^{10gs} 1-1-11 £6,067

Nordhock (USA) *N A Callaghan*   59
2 gr f Luhuk - Starlight Dreams (USA)
6^{6gf} 1^{6f} 6^{7gf} 3^{7gf} 1-0-4 £3,272

Nordwind (Ire) *P W Harris*   94 a78
3 b c Acatenango (Ger) - Narola (Ger)
3^{8gf} 4^{8gs} 1^{8sd} 1^{10gf} 2^{10gf} 1^{12g} 1^{11g} 12^{12g}
4-2-8 £34,169

Norma Speakman (Ire) *E W Tuer*   35
4 ch f Among Men (USA) - Bride Bank (Ire)
11^{12gf} 6^{10gf} 20^{12gf} 10^{12gf} 0-0-4

Norse Dancer (Ire) *D R C Elsworth*   125
4 b c Halling (USA) - River Patrol
4^{8gs} 3^{8g} 14^{8gf} 4^{10gs} 4^{8g} 1^{8gs} 2^{10g} 2^{10gf}
10^{8gf} 4^{10s} 1-3-10 £350,088

North Landing (Ire) *R C Guest*   9 a7
4 b g Storm Bird (Can) - Tirol Hope (Ire)
7^{7sd} 9^{10gs} 0-0-2

North Light (Ire) *Sir Michael Stoute*   125
3 b c Danehill (USA) - Sought Out (Ire)
1^{10gs} 1^{12g} 2^{12gf} 5^{12g} 2-1-4 £1,081,375

North Point (Ire) *R Curtis*   53
6 b g Definite Article - Friendly Song
13^{12gf} 8^{17f} 4^{12f} 0-0-3 £259

North Sea (Ire) *M R Channon*   59
3 b f Selkirk (USA) - Sea Spray (Ire)
7^{10gs} 7^{8gf} 0-0-2

North Shore (Ire) *R Hannon*   73
2 b c Soviet Star (USA) - Escape Path
6^{7gf} 5^{8g} 9^{6s} 0-0-3

Northanger Abbey (Ire) *J H M Gosden*   66
2 ch c In The Wings - Glenstal Priory
16^{7gs} 13^{7gf} 5^{10g} 12^{10gf} 0-0-4

Northern Desert (Ire) *P W Hiatt*   58
5 b g Desert Style (Ire) - Rosie's Guest (Ire)
10^{8hy} 18^{8s} 12^{7gs} 0-0-3

Northern Games *K A Ryan*   85
5 b g Mind Games - Northern Sal
13^{8f} 13^{7f} 1^{6gf} 4^{7f} 2^{6gs} 4^{7gf} 2^{7s} 1^{6gs}
1^{7s} 15^{6s} 3-3-10 £15,226

Northern Nymph *R Hollinshead*   75 a86
5 b g Makbul - Needwood Sprite
2^{16ss} 3^{16ss} 10^{18g} 8^{14s} 5^{14s} 6^{16hy} 2^{14gf}
3^{14gs} 4^{14g} 7^{14gs} 5^{16g} 5^{17g} 2^{14g} 0-4-13 £6,103

Northern Revoque (Ire) *A Berry*   37
2 b f Revoque (Ire) - Delia (Ire)
5^{5gs} 13^{6g} 13^{6f} 5^{5sd} 7^{6s} 7^{7gf} 4^{7s} 7^{7s}
16^{7g} 7^{8s} 0-0-10

Northern Secret *A M Balding*   70
2 b f Sinndar (Ire) - Northern Goddess
7^{7gf} 3^{7g} 7^{7gs} 15^{7gf} 0-1-4 £796

Northern Spirit *C W Moore*   54
3 b g Kadeed (Ire) - Elegant Spirit
9^{10g} 6^{14s} 9^{12g} 3^{14f} 11^{16gs} 1^{12gf} 1-1-6 £3,840

Northern Splendour (USA) *Saeed Bin Suroor*   98
2 ch c Giant's Causeway (USA) - Ribbonwood (USA)
3^{6gf} 1^{7s} 1^{8g} 2-1-3 £10,137

Northern Summit (Ire) *J R Norton*   a11
3 b g Danehill Dancer (Ire) - Book Choice

12^{12g} 6^{12sd} 6^{12sd} 0-0-3

Northern Svengali (Ire) *D A Nolan*   49
8 b g Distinctly North (USA) - Trilby's Dream (Ire)
16^{5gf} 13^{5gf} 8^{5gf} 5^{5gs} 5^{5gs} 6^{6g} 0-0-6

Northside Lodge (Ire) *W R Swinburn*   85 a97
6 b g Grand Lodge (USA) - Alongside
2^{10sd} 2^{10sd} 2^{10sd} 3^{10sd} 14^{10s} 10^{10gs}
3^{10gf} 5^{10gf} 2^{12gf} 11^{12s} 7^{12s} 11^{12f} 5^{12f} 9^{10g}
0-5-14 £12,388

Norton (Ire) *T G Mills*   101
7 ch g Barathea (Ire) - Primrose Valley
21^{8s} 5^{8g} 7^{10s} 4^{8hy} 7^{8gf} 8^{8g} 3^{7gs} 1^{8gs}
14^{8gf} 11^{8gs} 1-1-10 £16,379

Norton Rose *T J Fitzgerald*
2 ch f Dr Fong (USA) - Bonica
18^{6s} 0-0-1

Norwegian *D R Loder*   32 a69
3 b c Halling (USA) - Chicarica (USA)
5^{8sd} 1^{8s} 4^{10sd} 3^{8gf} 1-1-5 £3,729

Nossenko (USA) *J Noseda*   a50
3 b f Stravinsky (USA) - Humble Fifteen (USA)
2^{6sd} 0-1-1 £1,163

Nostradamus (USA) *K J Burke*   67
5 b/br h Gone West (USA) - Madam North (Can)
10^{16g} 0-0-1

Not Amused (UAE) *Ian Williams*
4 ch g Indian Ridge - Amusing Time (Ire)
13^{12s} 0-0-1

Nota Bene *D R C Elsworth*   95
2 b c Zafonic (USA) - Dodo (Ire)
2^{6gf} 1^{6g} 1^{6s} 2-1-3 £19,204

Notability (Ire) *M A Jarvis*   80
2 b c King's Best (USA) - Noble Rose (Ire)
8^{8s} 2^{7g} 1^{8gs} 1-1-3 £5,572

Notable Guest (USA) *Sir Michael Stoute*   95
3 b c Kingmambo - Yenda
5^{10gs} 3^{10g} 1^{9gf} 1-1-3 £7,805

Nothing Daunted *T A K Cuthbert*   11
7 ch g Selkirk (USA) - Khubza
12^{6s} 0-0-1

Nothing Matters *P R Chamings*   a31
3 b f Foxhound (USA) - Dawn Alarm
6^{8sd} 9^{8sd} 10^{7sd} 0-0-3

Notjustaprettyface (USA) *H Morrison*   95
2 b/br f Red Ransom (USA) - Maudie May (USA)
1^{5gf} 4^{5g} 4^{6s} 10^{5s} 1-0-4 £10,722

Notnowcato *Sir Michael Stoute*   81
2 ch c Inchinor - Rambling Rose
2^{7gf} 3^{7gs} 0-2-2 £2,840

Noul (USA) *K A Ryan*   63 a72
5 ch g Miswaki (USA) - Water Course (USA)
9^{9sd} 2^{9sd} 5^{12sd} 5^{10g} 5^{12hy} 15^{9g} 0-1-6
£828

Nounou *D J Daly*   75 a59
3 b c Starborough - Watheeqah (USA)
7^{7gs} 5^{7sd} 7^{10gf} 8^{7g} 1^{10gs} 5^{12g} 1^{12g} 5^{12s}
2-0-8 £11,066

Nouveau Riche (Ire) *H Morrison*   83
3 ch f Entrepreneur - Dime Bag
2^{8gf} 3^{8f} 1^{8gf} 2^{8g} 5^{11s} 1-4-6
£10,398

Nova Tor (Ire) *N P Littmoden*   91 a52
2 b f Trans Island - Nordic Living (Ire)
1^{5sd} 1^{5g} 11^{5gf} 4^{5g} 1^{5g} 5^{6gf} 4^{5gf} 8^{6gf}
15^{5gs} 3^{5s} 11^{5gf} 6^{6y} 10^{6g} 4-0-13 £23,957

Novelina (Ire) *W J Haggas* a56
2 b f Fusaichi Pegasus (USA) - Novelette
3^{9sd} **0-1-1 £557**

Now And Again *I W McInnes* a50
5 b g Shaamit (Ire) - Sweet Allegiance
3^{8sd} 4^{7sd} 3^{9ss} 3^{7sd} **0-1-4 £1,248**

Now Look Away (Ire) *B A McMahon* 30
3 b g Dushyantor (USA) - Where's Carol
8^{11g} **0-0-1**

Nowaday (Ger) *T P Tate* 62
2 b g Dashing Blade - Notre Dame (Ger)
7^{6s} 6^{7gs} 6^{7gs} 8^{7gs} **0-0-4**

Nowell House *M W Easterby* 85 a50
8 ch g Polar Falcon (USA) - Langtry Lady
6^{12sd} 6^{12gs} **0-0-2**

Nufoos *M Johnston* 102
2 b f Zafonic (USA) - Desert Lynx (Ire)
3^{5gs} 1^{6gf} 11^{6f} 8^{6gf} 1^{5gs} 2^{6s} 2^{6g} **2-3-7**
£30,923

Nuit Sombre (Ire) *N J Henderson* 78
4 b g Night Shift (USA) - Belair Princess (USA)
13^{8gs} 5^{8s} 4^{8g} 6^{8f} **0-0-4 £770**

Nukhbah (USA) *A G Newcombe* 72
3 b f Bahri (USA) - El Nafis (USA)
3^{8gs} 4^{8s} 5^{9gf} 13^{10gf} 14^{8g} **0-1-5 £977**

Numero Due *G M Moore* 63
2 b c Sinndar (Ire) - Kindle
6^{10gf} 3^{8hy} **0-0-2 £707**

Numitas (Ger) *P J Hobbs* 93
4 b c Lomitas - Narola (Ger)
8^{19gs} 23^{20gf} **0-0-2**

Numpty (Ire) *N Tinkler* 17 a33
3 b g Intikhab (USA) - Atsuko (Ire)
5^{6sd} 5^{6ss} 11^{10sd} 12^{10g} 10^{8s} 6^{7sd} **0-0-6**

Nunki (USA) *H R A Cecil* 91
3 ch g Kingmambo (USA) - Aqua Galinte (USA)
3^{10gs} 1^{11gf} 7^{10gf} 9^{10g} 4^{10gf} 3^{10hy} **1-2-6**
£9,646

Nuts For You (Ire) *R Charlton* 73 a53
3 b f Sri Pekan (USA) - Moon Festival
1^{10gf} 11^{12sd} **1-0-2 £3,935**

Nutty Times *W G M Turner* 47 a45
2 ch f Timeless Times (USA) - Nuthatch (Ire)
2^{5ss} 3^{5sd} 3^{5g} 13^{5g} 7^{6sd} 8^{5f} **0-1-6**
£1,563

Nuzooa (USA) *M P Tregoning* 100
3 b/br f A.P. Indy (USA) - Min Alhawa (USA)
1^{10gf} 5^{12g} 7^{10g} 1^{12ss} **2-0-4 £19,814**

Nuzzle *M Quinn* 52 a46
4 b f Salse (USA) - Lena (USA)
7^{8sd} 12^{9sd} 10^{10sd} 5^{12g} 11^{10sd} 2^{11gf} 6^{10f}
10^{10gf} 3^{8f} 7^{8f} 3^{8gf} 11^{10g} 9^{10g} 9^{10gf} 5^{9sd}
0-2-15 £2,950

Nyramba *J H M Gosden* 107
3 b f Night Shift (USA) - Maramba
2^{7g} 5^{8gf} 5^{8gs} 2^{7gf} 5^{6gs} 5^{7gf} **0-2-6**
£32,887

Nysaean (Ire) *R Hannon* 117
5 b h Sadler's Wells (USA) - Irish Arms (Fr)
5^{10gs} 4^{10gs} 5^{10gs} 2^{10gs} 1^{10gf} 3^{11gf} 4^{10gs}
5^{10gs} 3^{12s} 6^{11g} **1-1-10 £89,806**

O'So Neet *P Burgoyne* a32
6 b/br g Teenoso (USA) - Unveiled
7^{7sd} 9^{10hy} **0-0-2**

O'l Lucy Broon *J S Goldie* 49 a49

3 b f Royal Applause - Jay Gee Ell
9^{5g} 14^{6g} 15^{5f} 7^{5s} 5^{6sd} **0-0-5**

Oakley Absolute *R Hannon* 53
2 ch c Bluegrass Prince (Ire) - Susie Oakley Vii
11^{7hy} 7^{8gs} 10^{8hy} **0-0-3**

Oakley Rambo *R Hannon* 88
5 br g Muhtarram (USA) - Westminster Waltz
5^{7gs} 14^{8gs} 6^{8s} 2^{7s} 14^{7g} 6^{8gf} 7^{7g} 7^{8gs}
8^{7s} 12^{7sd} **0-1-10 £4,672**

Oases *D Shaw* 63 a65
5 ch g Zilzal (USA) - Markievicz (Ire)
8^{7ss} 2^{6gs} 8^{6g} 6^{6hy} 7^{6s} 18^{7f} 13^{6g} 3^{7gf}
5^{7gf} 6^{7gf} 10^{7s} 4^{7gs} 9^{7g} 5^{7sd} **0-2-14 £2,687**

Oasis Star (Ire) *P W Harris* 98
3 b f Desert King (Ire) - Sound Tap (USA)
1^{7g} 1^{8gs} 5^{8gf} 1^{7gf} 2^{7gf} 7^{8gf} 5^{7g} 5^{7gf} 9^{7s}
3-1-9 £43,941

Oasis Way (Gr) *P R Chamings* 68
2 b f Wadood (USA) - Northern Moon
5^{7g} 5^{8gf} 16^{7g} 6^{8s} 7^{7s} **0-0-5**

Oatcake *G A Butler* 61
2 ch f Selkirk (USA) - Humble Pie
3^{6gs} **0-1-1 £688**

Obay *E A L Dunlop* 92
3 ch g Kingmambo (USA) - Parade Queen (USA)
4^{10gs} 1^{12gs} 4^{11gf} 2^{12gf} 3^{12gf} 2^{12s} 13^{14gs}
1-1-7 £11,080

Obe Bold (Ire) *A Berry* 71 a68
3 b f Orpen (USA) - Capable Kate (Ire)
4^{5sd} 3^{6ss} 11^{5gf} 2^{6gf} 8^{6g} 8^{5gs} 1^{6sd} 5^{5g}
11^{5s} 4^{6g} 3^{5gf} 8^{6f} 1^{6g} 14^{6gs} 4^{6f} 12^{6s}
8^{6sd} **2-3-18 £13,698**

Obe Gold *M R Channon* 103
2 b c Namaqualand (USA) - Gagajulu
3^{5hy} 1^{5g} 4^{6g} 2^{6gf} 4^{7g} UR^{6gf} 3^{6s} 3^{6f} 1^{6g}
1^{6gf} 2^{6s} 5^{6vs} **3-3-12 £200,422**

Obe One *A Berry* 77 a62
4 b g Puissance - Plum Bold
9^{5gf} 16^{6g} 11^{6gf} 6^{6gf} 4^{5gf} 8^{5gf} 2^{5gf} 3^{5gf}
8^{6g} 6^{5gs} 7^{5g} 4^{5gf} 18^{6gf} 4^{5gf} 4^{6gf} 5^{5gf} 11^{6s}
5^{5f} 7^{6sd} **0-5-19 £7,196**

Obezyana (USA) *G A Huffer* a79
2 ch c Rahy (USA) - Polish Treaty (USA)
21^{8s} 2^{8sd} **0-1-2 £1,332**

Oblique (Ire) *Sir Mark Prescott* 48 a63
2 b f Giant's Causeway (USA) - On Call
12^{7sd} 11^{7sd} 4^{6hy} **0-0-3 £475**

Oboe *T Keddy* a28
3 ch f Piccolo - Bombay
9^{6sd} 8^{6sd} 6^{8sd} **0-0-3**

Obrigado (USA) *W J Haggas* 92 a89
4 b g Bahri (USA) - Glorious Diamond (USA)
10^{8gf} 2^{7gf} 27^{7ft} 7^{7gf} 9^{8gf} 2^{7sd} 10^{7sd}
1-2-7 £11,713

Observation *Mrs J Candlish* 18
3 ch f Polish Precedent (USA) - Search Party
8^{10gs} 12^{8gs} 15^{10g} 10^{13gs} **0-0-4**

Observer (Ire) *D R Loder* 81
2 b c Distant View (USA) - Virgin Stanza (USA)
1^{5gs} 3^{6gf} 7^{6g} **1-0-3 £4,610**

Ocean Avenue (Ire) *C A Horgan* 91
5 b g Dolphin Street (Fr) - Trinity Hall
1^{12gf} 8^{12f} 6^{14gf} 1^{12g} 7^{12gf} **2-0-5**
£17,269

Ocean Gift *D R C Elsworth* 87

2 b g Cadeaux Genereux - Sea Drift (Fr)
6^6g 4^7g 8^6gs 8^8s **0-0-4 £494**

Ocean Of Storms (Ire) *Christian Wroe*   84
9 b/br h Arazi (USA) - Moon Cactus
2^8ft 1^10ft 10^9g 12^12f 4^10gf 5^11g 2^9gf
7^10g **1-2-8 £9,125**

Ocean Rock *C A Horgan*   39 a59
3 b c Perugino (USA) - Polistatic
7^12sd 15^10g 13^10gs 14^12gf 11^13gs **0-0-5**

Ocean Tide *R Ford*   82 a63
7 b g Deploy - Dancing Tide
3^16ss 3^18g 4^16gf 8^18g 3^18gf 5^16gf
2^16gs 5^16s **0-4-9 £5,755**

Oceancookie (Ire) *A M Balding*   66 a59
2 b f Dashing Blade - Sankaty Light (USA)
5^6gf 5^7sd 6^6s **0-0-3 £1,117**

Oceanico Dot Com (Ire) *A Berry*   74 a44
2 br f Hernando (Fr) - Karen Blixen
7^5gf 12^6g 2^5gs 1^5gs 3^5gf 1^5gf 6^5gf 8^6g
13^6sd **2-2-9 £19,633**

Ochil Hills Dancer (Ire) *A Crook*   67
2 b f Bluebird (USA) - Classic Dilemma
7^5gf 5^6gf 7^5g 4^5gs 5^6gf 6^5gf 14^5gf 11^6s
0-0-8 £364

Ocotillo *Mrs L B Normile*
4 b g Mark Of Esteem (Ire) - Boojum
12^10gs **0-0-1**

Octennial *C Smith*   27
5 gr g Octagonal (NZ) - Laune (Aus)
11^6g 13^6g **0-0-2**

October Mist (Ire) *Mrs M Reveley*   74
10 gr g Roselier (Fr) - Bonny Joe
1^12hy **1-0-1 £3,740**

Odabella (Ire) *John Berry*   72
4 b f Selkirk (USA) - Circe's Isle
3^8gf 3^8gs 8^10gf 4^13g **0-1-4 £1,115**

Oddsmaker (Ire) *P D Evans*   95
3 b g Barathea (Ire) - Archipova (Ire)
3^8s 2^10hy 5^12gs 1^8gs 20^8f 1^8g 5^8g 3^8g
7^7gf 13^10gf 10^10g **2-3-12 £25,750**

Odiham *H Morrison*   95
3 b g Deploy - Hug Me
1^10gs 9^12gf 4^12g 10^12g 5^12g 4^12s **1-1-6
£15,344**

Oeuf A La Neige *G C H Chung*   78
4 b g Danehill (USA) - Reine De Neige
5^6g 8^7f 6^6gf 1^6gf 5^7f 7^6gs 1^6g 1^6s 5^5g
8^6g 10^6s **3-0-11 £13,340**

Ofaraby *M A Jarvis*   96 a88
4 b g Sheikh Albadou - Maristax
3^10sd 1^10s 6^12s 4^10gs 2^11g 5^10gf 13^11g
3^10gs 1^10s **2-3-9 £20,804**

Off Beat (USA) *T D Barron*   61 a78
3 ch g Mister Baileys - Off Off (USA)
6^7sd 3^7sd 13^6gs 7^6f 18^7gf 12^8g
8^10gf 6^8f 7^10sd 8^12gs **0-1-11 £764**

Off Colour *Mrs A J Perrett*   62
2 b c Rainbow Quest (USA) - Air Of Distinction (Ire)
4^7gs 10^7gf 6^8g **0-0-3 £489**

Off Hire *C Smith*   47 a51
8 b g Clantime - Lady Pennington
2^5ss 3^5ss 4^5ss 8^5sd 9^6f 5^5g 11^5gs **0-2-7
£1,250**

Officer's Pink *P F I Cole*   60
4 ch f Grand Lodge (USA) - Arethusa

10^6gf 8^6gf 10^6gf **0-0-3**

Ogilvy (USA) *J H M Gosden*   74
3 ch c Distant View (USA) - Shoogle (USA)
14^8g 8^10gf 2^9gf **0-1-3 £1,848**

Oh Boy (Ire) *R Hannon*   79
4 b c Tagula (Ire) - Pretty Sally (Ire)
17^8gs 14^7g 5^8gs 18^8f 18^8f 17^8g 16^7g
10^7s 15^8g 7^8s **2-0-10 £8,963**

Oh Dara (USA) *P A Blockley*   81
2 b f Aljabr (USA) - Sabaah Elfull
15^gf 3^5g 7^5g 5^5gf **1-1-4 £6,113**

Oh Golly Gosh *N P Littmoden*   79 a67
3 ch g Exit To Nowhere (USA) - Guerre De Troie
2^8s 2^8hy 9^8g 4^8gf 2^7f 18^10g 5^8gf 3^9f
1^7sw 9^7gf 10^7sd **1-4-11 £6,796**

Oh So Hardy *M A Allen*   53
3 b/br f Fleetwood (Ire) - Miss Hardy
14^10g 4^12gf 3^12gf **0-1-3 £850**

Oh So Rosie (Ire) *J S Moore*   65 a61
4 b f Danehill Dancer (Ire) - Shinkoh Rose (Fr)
4^7gs 3^8gs 3^8s 9^7s 3^8gf 2^8f 5^8f 11^9gf
13^8gf 1^8g 9^8f 12^8gf 4^8gf 2^8gs 5^8gf 2^8sd 7^7s
9^9sd **1-8-18 £9,859**

Ok Pal *T G Mills*   91 a93
4 b g Primo Dominie - Sheila's Secret (Ire)
UR^5sd 3^6ss 13^5gs 7^6g 6^5s 12^5g 6^5gs 1^5g
2^5gs 3^6gs 1^5g **2-3-11 £18,388**

Oktis Morilious (Ire) *C R Dore*   65 a53
3 b g Octagonal (NZ) - Nottash (Ire)
8^7sd 9^9ss 4^8sd 1^10sd 2^10sd 3^12gs 4^10sd
2^11gf 12^10f 2^10f 1^11g 9^10gf 4^12gf 11^10gs
1^12gs 8^10g 4^16gf 6^17gf **3-3-19 £10,414**

Old Bailey (USA) *T D Barron*   52 a63
4 gr g Lit De Justice (USA) - Olden Lek (USA)
6^6hy 9^6s 5^7g 9^7gf 1^7sd 9^6f 9^7sd 11^7sd 9^7sd
5^6g 5^5g 13^6f 3^8sd 1^6hy **2-1-13 £6,582**

Old Harry *P C Ritchens*   36
4 b g Case Law - Supreme Thought
15^7gf 15^10gf 13^6gf 8^6gf **0-0-4**

Oldenway *R A Fahey*   84 a67
5 b g Most Welcome - Sickle Moon
10^10sd 9^10sd 2^10g 2^10g 4^12gf 2^10gf 1^10g
4^10g 7^12g 1^9gf **2-3-10 £18,654**

Oldstead Flyer (Ire) *D Carroll*   a31
2 b/br c Foxhound (USA) - Princess Tycoon (Ire)
10^5gf 6^6sd 14^7gf 9^7sd **0-0-4**

Oligarch (Ire) *N A Callaghan*   84
2 b c Monashee Mountain (USA) - Courtier
2^6g 10^6g 3^8g 1^8s 7^7gs **1-2-5 £15,184**

Olimp (Pol) *Miss A M Newton-Smith*
8 ch g Saphir (Ger) - Olgierda (Pol)
8^16sd **0-0-1**

Olivander *R M Beckett*   77
3 b g Danzero (Aus) - Mystic Goddess (USA)
8^7gs 3^7f 9^9gf 2^8f **0-2-4 £1,911**

Olivia Rose (Ire) *J Pearce*   89
5 b m Mujadil (USA) - Santana Lady (Ire)
7^10gs 1^10s 3^10s 1^10f 2^10gf 3^10g 1^10gf 4^10gf
1^10s 3^10g 9^10gf 9^10g 11^10gf **4-2-13 £25,680**

Olivia Twist *W G M Turner*   35
2 ch f Fraam - Tricata
9^7gs **0-0-1**

Ollijay *Mrs H Dalton*   48 a17
3 b g Wolfhound (USA) - Anthem Flight (USA)
6^7gf 6^7gs 10^7gs 12^7g 7^9sd **0-0-5**

Olympias (Ire) *H Morrison* 60
3 b f Kahyasi - Premier Amour
5¹⁰ᵍˢ 8¹²ˢ 7⁹ᵍᶠ 6¹⁴ᵍ 4¹²ᵍᶠ 14¹⁸ᵍˢ 3¹³ᶠ
16¹⁷ᵍ **0-1-8 £991**

Omaha City (Ire) *B Gubby* 80 a79
10 b g Night Shift (USA) - Be Discreet
10⁸ˢᵈ 10⁸ᵍ 2⁸ˢᵈ 1⁸ᵍᶠ 12⁸ᵍ 10⁸ᵍ 13⁸ᵍᶠ
10⁷ᵍ 10⁷ᵍ 18ᵍᶠ 2⁸ˢᵈ 1⁸ˢᵈ **3-2-12 £14,572**

Oman Gulf (USA) *J G Given* 73
3 b g Diesis - Dabaweyaa (Ire)
10¹⁰ᵍˢ 4⁸ᵍᶠ 18⁸ˢ 37ᵍˢ **0-0-4 £719**

Oman Sea (USA) *B W Hills* 43
3 b f Rahy (USA) - Ras Shaikh (USA)
5⁸ᵍ **0-0-1 £517**

Omasheriff (Ire) *Bruce Hellier* 101
2 ch c Shinko Forest (Ire) - Lady Of Leisure (USA)
1⁵ᵍ 1⁶ˢ 2⁷ᵍ 4⁶ᵍ **2-0-4 £44,101**

On Action (USA) *Mrs A Duffield* 54
2 b c Miswaki (USA) - Dancing Action (USA)
3⁶ᶠ 5⁶ᶠ **0-1-2 £648**

On Cloud Nine *J G M O'Shea* 68 a29
3 ro f Cloudings (Ire) - Princess Moodyshoe
2¹⁰ᵍˢ 6¹²ᵍᶠ 7¹⁰ᵍ 12¹⁰ᵍˢ 4¹²ᵍᶠ 3¹²ᵍˢ 1¹²ᵍ
5¹²ᵍᶠ 9¹²ˢᵈ **1-3-9 £4,508**

On Every Street *R Bastiman* 81
3 b g Singspiel (Ire) - Nekhbet
4¹⁰ᵍᶠ 3¹¹ᵍᶠ 1¹¹ᶠ 4¹⁰ᵍᶠ 6⁹ᵍᶠ 7⁹ˢ 19¹⁰ˢ
15¹⁰ˢ **1-1-8 £5,505**

On Guard *P G Murphy* 20 a47
6 b g Sabrehill (USA) - With Care
3¹⁰ˢᵈ 6¹²ˢᵈ 18¹¹ˢ 10¹⁰ˢ 4⁹ˢᵈ 15¹²ᵍᶠ **0-1-6
£236**

On The Bright Side *D Nicholls* 66
2 b f Cyrano De Bergerac - Jade Pet
3⁵ᵍ **0-1-1 £545**

On The Level *Mrs N Macauley* a22
5 ch m Beveled (USA) - Join The Clan
9⁵ˢᵈ 10⁵ˢᵈ 12⁶ᶠ **0-0-3**

On The Trail *D W Chapman* 63 a65
7 ch g Catrail (USA) - From The Rooftops (Ire)
8⁶ˢˢ 11⁶ˢᵈ 11⁵ˢˢ 10⁶ˢʷ 1⁶ˢʷ 36ˢᵈ 1⁶ˢᵈ
2⁶ˢᵈ 1⁶ˢᵈ 36ˢᵈ 47ˢᵈ 35ᵍˢ 36ˢᵈ 1⁵ᵍᶠ 1⁵ᵍˢ 45ᵍˢ
5⁶ᵍ 2⁶ᶠ 47ˢᵈ 36ˢᵈ **6-9-23
£26,202**

On The Waterfront *J W Hills* 69 a66
3 ch c Docksider (USA) - Film Buff
5⁸ˢᵈ 5¹⁰ˢᵈ 47ˢᵈ 2⁸ᵍᶠ 10⁸ᵍᶠ 4⁸ᵍ 2⁸ᵍᶠ 5⁸ᵍ
0-3-8 £3,499

On The Waterline (Ire) *P D Evans* 78 a59
2 b f Compton Place - Miss Waterline
2⁵ᵍ 35ᵍˢ 4⁵ᵍˢ 2⁵ᵍ 11⁶ᵍˢ 20⁷ᵍ 1⁶ˢ
6⁶ˢᵈ 7⁶ˢ **1-2-10 £9,623**

On The Wing *A P Jarvis* 21
3 b f Pivotal - Come Fly With Me
12⁸ᵍᶠ **0-0-1**

Once (Fr) *J A Osborne* 76 a72
4 gr g Hector Protector (USA) - Moon Magic
3¹⁴ᵍᶠ 22²⁰ᵍᶠ 10¹⁶ᵍᶠ 7¹¹ᵍ 10¹³ᶠ 12¹⁰ᵍᶠ
7¹⁴ˢᵈ **1-1-8 £5,682**

Once Around (Ire) *T G Mills* 33 a53
3 b/br g Grand Lodge (USA) - Lady Lucre (Ire)
7¹⁰ˢᵈ 12⁸ˢᵈ 11¹²ˢ 7¹²ˢᵈ **0-0-4**

One 'N' Only (Ire) *Miss L A Perratt* 54
3 b f Desert Story (Ire) - Alpina (USA)
47ᵍᶠ 55ᵍ 4⁹ᵍ 3⁸ᵍᶠ **0-1-4 £1,525**

One Alone *Jean-Rene Auvray* 40 a40
3 b f Atraf - Songsheet
8⁹ˢʷ 12⁷ᵍᶠ 11⁷ᵍ 10⁸ᵍ 4¹⁰ˢᵈ 3¹²ˢᵈ **0-1-6
£367**

One Cool Cat (USA) *A P O'Brien* 121
3 b c Storm Cat (USA) - Tacha (USA)
13⁸ᵍ 5⁸ᵍ 16ᵍᶠ 3⁵ˢ 6⁶ᵍ **1-1-5 £59,705**

One For Me *Jean-Rene Auvray* 44
6 br m Tragic Role (USA) - Chantallee's Pride
17²¹ᵍ **0-0-1**

One Good Thing (USA) *Saeed Bin Suroor* 64
2 b c Touch Gold (USA) - Once To Often (USA)
10⁶ᵍˢ 5⁸ᵍ 12⁸ˢ **0-0-3**

One Great Idea (Ire) *T D Barron* 75
2 b g Night Shift (USA) - Scenaria (Ire)
2⁵ᵍ 5⁶ᵍ 2⁵ᵍᶠ **0-2-3 £2,803**

One Last Time *R Bastiman* 67
4 b g Primo Dominie - Leap Of Faith (Ire)
147ᵍˢ 19⁸ᵍˢ 9⁸ᵍ 2⁶ᶠ 14⁵ᶠ 13⁵ᵍᶠ **0-1-6
£1,126**

One Of Distinction *E A L Dunlop* 22
3 b f Nashwan (USA) - Air Of Distinction (Ire)
8¹⁰ᵍᶠ **0-0-1**

One Of Each (Ire) *D Carroll* 49 a15
2 ch f Indian Lodge (Ire) - Indian City
5⁵ᵍᶠ 5⁵ᵍˢ 11⁵ˢᵈ **0-0-3**

One Of Them *Mrs G Harvey* 3 a35
5 ch g Pharly (Fr) - Hicklam Millie
16¹⁰ˢ 11¹²ˢᵈ **0-0-2**

One Off *Sir Mark Prescott* 94
4 b g Barathea (Ire) - On Call
7¹⁴ᵍᶠ 4¹⁸ᶠ **0-0-2 £774**

One Putra (Ire) *M A Jarvis* 93
2 b c Indian Ridge - Triomphale (USA)
5⁶ᵍ 16ᵍˢ 3⁶ˢ 6⁶ᵍˢ **1-0-4 £8,122**

One So Marvellous *L M Cumani* 84
3 ch f Nashwan (USA) - Someone Special
9⁸ᵍ 9¹⁰ᵍˢ 1¹⁰ᵍᶠ 2¹⁰ᵍᶠ **1-1-4 £8,089**

One To Win (Ire) *J Noseda* a75
2 b f Cape Cross (Ire) - Safe Exit (Fr)
2⁷ˢᵈ **0-1-1 £1,600**

One Upmanship *J G Portman* 69 a64
3 ch g Bahamian Bounty - Magnolia
11⁶ᵍ 8⁶ᶠ 11⁷ᵍᶠ 6⁷ᵍᶠ 3⁶ᵍᶠ 2⁷ᵍᶠ 6⁸ᵍᶠ 1⁸ᵍ
2¹⁰ˢᵈ 3⁹ᵍˢ 7¹⁰ˢᵈ 13⁹ˢᵈ **1-4-12 £6,767**

One Way Ticket *J M Bradley* 78 a39
4 ch c Pursuit Of Love - Prima Cominna
16⁸ᵍ 12⁷ʰʸ 13⁷ᶠ 3⁶ᵍᶠ 2⁶ᵍᶠ 9⁶ᵍᶠ 3⁶ᶠ 1⁶ᵍᶠ
8⁶ˢᵈ 7⁶ᵍ 8⁶ᵍᶠ 4⁵ᵍᶠ VOI⁵ᵍᶠ 5⁵ᵍ 11⁵ᵍ 2⁵ᵍ
1-3-16 £12,071

Onefortheboys (Ire) *D Flood* 9 a45
5 b g Distinctly North (USA) - Joyful Prospect
7⁸ˢᵈ 9⁸ˢᵈ 6⁸ˢᵈ 2⁵ˢᵈ 4⁶ˢᵈ 8⁶ˢᵈ 9⁶ˢᵈ 36ˢᵈ
7⁷ˢᵈ 6⁵ˢᵈ 36ˢᵈ 17⁶ᵍᶠ 15⁶ᵍ **0-2-13 £829**

Oneiro Way (Ire) *P R Chamings* 59
2 b g King's Best (USA) - Koumiss
9⁷ᵍˢ 10⁸ᵍˢ **0-0-2**

Oneshottwolions (Ire) *E A L Dunlop* 53
2 b c Giant's Causeway (USA) - Fernanda
12⁷ᵍ **0-0-1**

Oniz Tiptoes (Ire) *J S Wainwright* 41
3 ch g Russian Revival (USA) - Edionda (Ire)
14⁶ᶠ 6¹²ᵍᶠ 4¹⁰ᵍ 2¹²ᵍᶠ 10¹²ᵍˢ **0-1-5
£1,051**

Online Investor *D Nicholls* 79

5 b g Puissance - Anytime Baby
12⁶ˢ 13⁷ᵍ 5⁶ᵍˢ 2⁵ᵍᶠ 11⁷ᶠ 5⁵ᵍᶠ 5⁵ᵍᶠ
12⁵ᵍᶠ 14⁵ˢ 17⁵ᵍᶠ 11⁵ᵍ 10⁶ᵍᶠ 2⁵ᵍˢ 4⁵ᵍ 4⁵ᵍᶠ 8⁵ᶠ
6⁶ᵍˢ **0-3-17 £3,219**

Only For Gold *Dr P Pritchard* a29
9 b g Presidium - Calvanne Miss
5⁵ˢʷ 7⁷ˢᵈ **0-0-2**

Only For Sue *W S Kittow* 62 a34
5 ch g Pivotal - Barbary Court
8¹²ˢᵈ 9¹²ˢᵈ 3¹⁴ᵍ 1¹²ˢ 8¹⁴ᵍᶠ **1-1-5 £3,520**

Only If I Laugh *P A Blockley* 65 a76
3 ch g Piccolo - Agony Aunt
3⁵ˢᵈ 4⁵ˢᵈ 8⁵ˢ 2⁵ᶠ 3⁶ˢᵈ 9⁵ᵍ 5⁵ᵍ 3⁵ᵍ 12⁵ᵍᶠ
4⁵ˢᵈ **0-3-10 £3,110**

Only One Legend (Ire) *K A Ryan* 58 a71
6 b g Eagle Eyed (USA) - Afifah
9⁶ˢᵈ 12⁵ˢᵈ 11⁶ˢᵈ 10⁶ˢᵈ 7⁶ˢᵈ 3⁶ᵍˢ 9⁶ᵍ
3⁶ᵍᶠ 1⁷ˢᵈ 5⁷ˢᵈ 13⁷ˢᵈ 8⁶ᵍᶠ 18⁷ᵍᶠ **1-2-13
£3,657**

Only Words (USA) *A J Lockwood* 25
7 ch g Shuailaan (USA) - Conversation Piece (USA)
6¹⁶ᵍˢ **0-0-1**

Onlytime Will Tell *D Nicholls* 102 a76
6 ch g Efisio - Prejudice
8⁸ˢᵈ 20⁸ᵍ 5⁶ᵍˢ 4⁷ᵍᶠ 2⁶ᵍᶠ 7⁸ᶠ 1⁶ᵍ 4⁶ᵍˢ
6⁶ˢ 1⁶ˢ 8⁶ᵍˢ **2-1-11 £25,468**

Ontos (Ger) *Miss V Scott*
8 b/br g Super Abound (USA) - Onestep (Ger)
12¹⁸ˢ **0-0-1**

Onward To Glory (USA) *J L Dunlop* 70
4 b c Zabeel (NZ) - Landaria (Fr)
9¹²ᵍˢ 11¹⁴ᵍᶠ 4¹¹ᵍᶠ 6¹²ʰʸ 10¹²ᵍˢ 1¹⁴ˢ **1-0-6
£3,811**

Onya *J W Hills* a29
4 ch f Unfuwain (USA) - Reel Foyle (USA)
10⁷ˢᵈ **0-0-1**

Onyergo (Ire) *J R Weymes* 70
2 b c Polish Precedent (USA) - Trick (Ire)
3⁷ˢ 3⁷ᵍˢ 3⁸ᵍˢ **0-3-3 £2,402**

Onyx *W De Best-Turner* 34 a44
3 b g Bijou D'Inde - Prime Surprise
6⁶ᵍ 8⁶ˢ 7⁶ˢᵈ **0-0-3**

Oops (Ire) *J F Coupland* 57
5 b g In The Wings - Atsuko (Ire)
8¹⁴ᵍ 1¹⁶ᵍˢ 6¹⁶ˢ 2¹⁶ᵍᶠ 3¹⁶ᵍˢ 2¹⁶ᵍˢ 4¹⁶ᵍᶠ
4¹⁶ᶠ 9¹⁶ᵍ **1-4-9 £6,540**

Oos And Ahs *C W Fairhurst*
4 b f Silver Wizard (USA) - Hot Feet
8¹²ˢᵈ **0-0-1**

Open Book *H Morrison* 54 a49
3 br f Mark Of Esteem (Ire) - Sweetness Herself
10¹²ˢ 11¹⁰ᵍᶠ 10¹⁰ᵍᶠ 8¹¹ᵍᶠ 3¹²ᵍᶠ 7¹⁶ˢᵈ 3¹²ᵍ
0-2-7 £470

Open Handed (Ire) *B Ellison* 64 a38
4 b g Cadeaux Genereux - Peralta (Ire)
6⁷ˢᵈ 10⁸ˢʷ 11⁷ᵍ 1⁸ᵍˢ 13⁸ᵍˢ 5⁷ᵍᶠ 5⁷ᵍᶠ
7⁸ᵍˢ 8⁸ᵍˢ 10⁹ᵍˢ **1-0-10 £2,625**

Open Mind *E J Alston* 52
3 b f Mind Games - Primum Tempus
4⁵ᵍ 3⁶ᶠ 7⁵ᵍᶠ 6⁶ᶠ 13⁶ᵍˢ 16⁶ᵍ **0-1-6 £762**

Open Verdict (Ire) *A P Jarvis* 56
2 b g Mujadil (USA) - Law Review (Ire)
16⁵ᵍᶠ 4⁵ᵍ 14⁶ᵍ **0-0-3 £259**

Opening Ceremony (USA) *R A Fahey* 80 a66
5 br m Quest For Fame - Gleam Of Light (Ire)

6¹⁰ᵍ 2¹⁰ᵍ 4¹⁰ˢ 2⁹ˢ 1¹⁰ᵍ 5¹¹ᵍˢ 1¹⁰ᵍᶠ 5¹⁰ᵍᶠ
2¹⁰ˢ 4¹⁰ˢ 8¹⁰ˢᵈ **2-4-11 £33,302**

Opera Babe (Ire) *H S Howe* 24
3 b f Kahyasi - Fairybird (Fr)
7¹⁵ᵍˢ 11¹²ᵍᶠ **0-0-2**

Opera Comique (Fr) *Saeed Bin Suroor* 87
3 b f Singspiel (Ire) - Grace Note (Fr)
6¹⁰ᵍ 8¹⁵ᵍ 10¹⁴ˢ **0-0-3 £450**

Opera Star (Ire) *B W Hills* 60 a53
3 b f Sadler's Wells (USA) - Adjalisa (Ire)
5⁸ˢᵈ 10¹⁰ᵍ 3¹²ᶠ 6¹⁸ᵍᶠ 8¹²ˢʷ **0-0-5 £538**

Operashaan (Ire) *G L Moore* a51
4 b g Darshaan - Comic Opera (Ire)
8¹⁰ˢᵈ **0-0-1**

Ophistrolie (Ire) *S Kirk*
2 b c Foxhound (USA) - Thoughtful Kate
10⁸ʰʸ **0-0-1**

Optimaite *B R Millman* a67
7 b g Komaite (USA) - Leprechaun Lady
6¹²ˢᵈ **0-0-1**

Optimal (Ire) *Sir Mark Prescott* 67
3 gr f Green Desert (USA) - On Call
10¹⁰ᵍ 6¹¹ᵍᶠ 1¹⁰ᶠ 14¹⁰ᵍᶠ **1-0-4 £4,056**

Optimum (Ire) *D R Loder* 64 a43
2 br g King's Best (USA) - Colour Dance
14⁷ᵍᶠ 5⁸ᶠ 10⁷ˢᵈ **0-0-3**

Optimum Night *P D Niven* 28 a22
5 b g Superlative - Black Bess
10⁹ᵍᶠ 3¹⁰ᵍ 8⁹ˢᵈ 4⁷ˢᵈ 5⁸ᵍᶠ 9¹¹ᵍ **0-0-6
£207**

Optimus (USA) *G A Butler* a78
2 ch c Elnadim (USA) - Ajfan (USA)
5⁶ˢᵈ 2⁷ˢᵈ 4⁷ˢᵈ **0-1-3 £1,703**

Orange Touch (Ger) *Mrs A J Perrett* 117
4 b c Lando (Ger) - Orange Bowl
6¹⁰ᵍ 1¹²ᵍˢ 1¹⁴ᵍˢ 8¹⁴ᵍ **2-0-4 £31,392**

Orangino *J S Haldane* 50
6 b g Primo Dominie - Sweet Jaffa
10⁶ᵍˢ 2⁶ᶠ 7⁸ᵍ 2⁶ᵍ 8⁶ᵍᶠ 15⁶ᵍˢ 21⁸ᵍᶠ **0-2-7
£2,008**

Oranmore Castle (Ire) *B W Hills* 85
2 b c Giant's Causeway (USA) - Twice The Ease
2⁶ᵍ 6⁶ˢ **0-1-2 £2,045**

Oration *Sir Michael Stoute*
3 b c Singspiel (Ire) - Blush Rambler (Ire)
13¹⁰ᵍᶠ **0-0-1**

Oratorio (Ire) *A P O'Brien* 119
2 b c Danehill (USA) - Mahrah (USA)
1⁶ᵍᶠ 7⁶ᵍᶠ 1⁶ᵍ 2⁶ᵍᶠ 1⁷ᵍᶠ 1⁷ᵍ 2⁷ˢ **4-2-7
£339,662**

Orcadian *J M P Eustace* 108
3 b g Kirkwall - Rosy Outlook (USA)
3⁸ᵍᶠ 7⁷ᵍ 6⁷ᵍᶠ 5⁹ˢ 1¹²ʰʸ **1-1-5 £33,950**

Orchestration (Ire) *J W Unett* 48 a52
3 ch g Stravinsky (USA) - Mora (Ire)
4⁶ˢᵈ 4⁶ˢˢ 12⁷ᵍᶠ 9⁵ᵍᶠ 17⁶ᵍ 6⁹ˢᵈ 7⁹ˢᵈ **0-0-7
£573**

Oriental Moon (Ire) *M J Gingell* a38
5 ch m Spectrum (Ire) - La Grande Cascade (USA)
8¹²ˢᵈ **0-0-1**

Oriental Warrior *M P Tregoning* 105
3 b c Alhaarth (Ire) - Oriental Fashion (Ire)
5⁸ᵍᶠ **0-0-1 £375**

Orientor *J S Goldie* 118
6 b h Inchinor - Orient

2^{6g} 4^{7ys} 5^{6s} 9^{6gs} 5^{6gf} 3^{5gf} 1^{5gs} 5^{5s} 7^{6g}
6^{5g} **1-1-10 £48,247**

Original Sin (Ire) I R Brown   a41
4 b g Bluebird (USA) - Majakerta (Ire)
10^{10sd} 12^{7sd} 11^{8sd} **0-0-3**

Orinocovsky (Ire) N P Littmoden   39 a65
5 ch g Grand Lodge (USA) - Brillantina (Fr)
11^{1sd} 7^{12sd} 3^{12sd} 10^{16sd} 2^{12ss} 3^{12sd} 2^{14ss}
17^{11s} 11^{12sd} 3^{12sd} 12^{12f} **2-3-11 £7,849**

Orion Express M W Easterby   65 a45
3 b c Bahhare (USA) - Kaprisky (Ire)
6^{6g} 6^{7gs} 7^{8hy} 10^{10gf} 4^{7f} 6^{8g} 4^{8gs} 6^{10gs}
6^{10gs} 13^{8gs} 10^{9sd} **0-0-11 £737**

Orion's Belt P A Fahy   65 a51
4 ch g Compton Place - Follow The Stars
14^{7sd} 3^{6sd} 7^{7sd} 3^{10g} 8^{8g} 2^{8hy} 10^{10ys} 9^{9y}
16^{8sh} **0-3-9 £2,910**

Orlar (Ire) J A Osborne   69 a69
2 b f Green Desert (USA) - Soviet Maid (Ire)
5^{7gf} 8^{8s} 3^{7sd} **0-1-3 £810**

Oro Street (Ire) G F Bridgwater   a46
8 b g Dolphin Street (Fr) - Love Unlimited
5^{12sd} 3^{12ss} **0-0-2 £181**

Oro Verde R Hannon   91
3 ch c Compton Place - Kastaway
9^{6s} 6^{6s} 3^{5gf} 8^{5gf} 16^{7s} **0-0-5 £2,616**

Orpen Annie (Ire) Miss J Feilden   58 a34
2 b f Orpen (USA) - Nisibis
18^{5gf} 3^{6gf} 6^{7gs} 8^{6sd} 4^{7gf} 8^{7gf} 2^{8g} **0-2-7**
£1,898

Orpen Wide (Ire) M C Chapman   69
2 b c Orpen (USA) - Melba (Ire)
18^{6gs} 3^{6g} 3^{7gs} 10^{8g} 8^{6s} 2^{6hy} 5^{6s} **0-2-7**
£2,227

Orpenberry (Ire) E J Alston   44
3 b f Orpen (USA) - Forest Berries (Ire)
13^{6gf} 11^{6gf} 8^{8gf} 14^{7gf} 12^{7gs} **0-0-5**

Orpendonna (Ire) K A Ryan   74 a70
2 b f Orpen (USA) - Tetradonna (Ire)
11^{6gs} 3^{8gf} 6^{8g} 6^{6sd} **0-1-4 £980**

Orphan (Ire) K R Burke   63
2 b g Orpen (USA) - Ballinlee (Ire)
10^{6g} 5^{6s} 4^{5gf} 4^{5g} **0-0-4 £578**

Oscar Pepper (USA) T D Barron   77
7 b g Brunswick (USA) - Princess Baja (USA)
5^{8g} 10^{8f} 6^{9f} 3^{9gf} 4^{10gf} 5^{10g} 2^{8s} 4^{9gf}
1^{10gf} 4^{10gf} 3^{8f} 12^{8gf} **1-3-12 £7,436**

Osla R Brotherton   34
3 ch f Komaite (USA) - Orlaith
8^{6gf} 10^{7sd} 8^{7g} 10^{10g} 6^{11g} 14^{8gf} **0-0-6**

Otago (Ire) J R Best   71 a65
3 b g Desert Sun - Martino
3^{6gf} 12^{7f} 4^{5gf} 5^{6g} 11^{7gf} 4^{8gf} 2^{8gs} 1^{8g}
13^{8gf} 1^{8f} 12^{8g} 5^{9sd} **2-1-12 £10,604**

Otylia R M H Cowell   33 a45
4 ch f Wolfhound (USA) - Soba
5^{6sd} 4^{6sw} 8^{6sw} 15^{6gf} 7^{6g} 14^{6s} 8^{5sd} **0-0-7**
£258

Oude (USA) Saeed Bin Suroor   106
2 b/br c Dubai Millennium - Chosen Lady (USA)
1^{7g} 2^{7g} 3^{7gf} **1-2-3 £21,388**

Ouija Board E A L Dunlop   124
3 b f Cape Cross (Ire) - Selection Board
1^{10g} 1^{12g} 1^{12gf} 3^{12g} 11^{11y} **4-1-5**
£925,840

Oulton Broad F Jordan   a42
8 b g Midyan (USA) - Lady Quachita (USA)
7^{12sd} 5^{16sd} 6^{16sd} **0-0-4**

Ouninpohja (Ire) G A Swinbank   78
3 b g Imperial Ballet (Ire) - Daziyra (Ire)
4^{10g} 3^{8g} 2^{7gf} 5^{10gf} 1^{10gs} **1-2-5 £8,912**

Our Chelsea Blue (USA) I A Wood   a50
6 ch m Distant View (USA) - Eastern Connection (USA)
7^{6sw} 3^{5ss} 6^{5ss} 13^{6sd} 9^{5sd} 8^{6sd} **0-1-6**
£417

Our Choice (Ire) N P Littmoden   58 a56
2 b c Indian Danehill (Ire) - Spring Daffodil
8^{5gs} 4^{5g} 7^{6gf} 6^{7sd} 7^{8s} 6^{8gs} **0-0-6 £266**

Our Destiny A W Carroll   63 a67
6 b g Mujadil (USA) - Superspring
3^{8sd} 2^{9sd} 4^{12sd} 7^{9ss} 1^{8sd} 1^{8ss} 6^{8sd} 3^{8gs}
1^{8sd} 2^{10g} 4^{10s} 3^{12gf} 1^{10gf} 9^{10f} 4^{10f} 1^{10gf} 7^{13g}
5^{10gf} 3^{9sd} **5-6-25**
£16,144

Our Emmy Lou Sir Mark Prescott   66 a49
3 ch f Mark Of Esteem (Ire) - Regent's Folly (Ire)
2^{12gf} 4^{12gf} 5^{12gs} 6^{12sw} 1^{11g} 5^{10f} 9^{12sd}
1-1-7 £4,574

Our Fred T G Mills   35 a69
7 ch g Prince Sabo - Sheila's Secret (Ire)
6^{5sd} 7^{5sd} 13^{5g} **0-0-3**

Our Fugitive (Ire) A W Carroll   93
2 gr c Titus Livius (Fr) - Mystical Jumbo
4^{5s} 8^{5gf} 3^{5gf} 2^{5gf} 1^{5s} 2^{6s} **1-3-6**
£9,201

Our Gamble (Ire) R Hannon   59
3 b f Entrepreneur - Manilia (Fr)
6^{6hy} 11^{7gf} 9^{6g} 10^{6g} 5^{7f} 8^{5g} **0-0-6 £216**

Our Glenard S L Keightley   44 a53
5 b g Royal Applause - Loucoum (Fr)
2^{11sd} 2^{10sd} 11^{12sd} 5^{11ss} 6^{13sd} 4^{10sd} 10^{10hy}
7^{10sd} 4^{10gf} **0-2-9 £1,301**

Our Imperial Bay (USA) Mrs J Candlish   46 a68
5 b g Smart Strike (Can) - Heat Lightning (USA)
10^{16sd} 10^{14s} 11^{1sd} 8^{12sd} 3^{16sd} 12^{8gf} 3^{12sd}
6^{14sd} 3^{14sd} 7^{16gf} 8^{12g} 5^{12gf} **1-2-12 £2,495**

Our Jaffa (Ire) D J Daly   86 a85
3 br f Bin Ajwaad (Ire) - Griddle Cake (Ire)
4^{10g} 1^{8f} 1^{8gf} 2^{8gf} 5^{7sd} 7^{8g} 6^{8g} **2-1-7**
£12,658

Our Kes (Ire) P Howling   58 a39
2 gr f Revoque (Ire) - Gracious Gretclo
8^{5gf} 8^{8g} 11^{8gf} 4^{8gf} 13^{8g} 9^{8sd} **0-0-6**
£403

Our Kid T G McCourt   49
3 ch g Pursuit Of Love - Flower Princess
7^{10gs} 11^{12g} 6^{12sd} 14^{7gf} 16^{7s} 8^{7sh} **0-0-6**

Our Little Rosie M Blanshard   a62
3 b f Piccolo - Villella
7^{8sd} 8^{8sd} 5^{10sd} 1^{12ss} 19^{11g} PU^{12sd} 14^{11g}
15^{12sd} 8^{12sd} **1-0-9 £3,487**

Our Little Secret (Ire) A Berry   38 a57
2 ch f Rossini (USA) - Sports Post Lady (Ire)
5^{5gf} 3^{5sd} 3^{5sd} **0-2-3 £582**

Our Louis J S Wainwright   51
2 b f Abou Zouz (USA) - Ninfa Of Cisterna
6^{5s} 8^{5gs} 5^{5gf} 4^{5gf} 1^{5gf} 5^{5gf} 7^{5gf} 8^{5f}
10^{5gs} 7^{5gf} 7^{5f} **1-0-11 £3,161**

Our Nigel (Ire) Mrs P N Dutfield   33
2 gr g Namid - Mystical

8^{5g} 7^{5f} 7^{5gs} 15^{6g} **0-0-4**

Our Old Boy (Ire) *J A Gilbert* a23
4 br g Petorius - Minzal Legend (Ire)
8^{5sd} 8^{5sd} 12^{7ss} **0-0-3**

Our Place (Ire) *B N Doran*
5 b g Distinctly North (USA) - Simplyhectic (Ire)
10^{16sw} **0-0-1**

Our Sion *R Brotherton* 21
4 b g Dreams End - Millfields Lady
9^{6s} 14^{6gf} 15^{6gf} **0-0-3**

Our Teddy (Ire) *A M Balding* 94 a100
4 ch g Grand Lodge (USA) - Lady Windley
4^{8sd} 24^{8g} 17^{8g} 5^{8gf} 4^{9gf} 4^{10gf} 14^{8gs} 9^{8gf} **0-0-8 £3,475**

Our Wildest Dreams *C W Fairhurst* 30
2 b f Benny The Dip (USA) - Imperial Scholar (Ire)
10^{8gf} **0-0-1**

Out After Dark *C G Cox* 91
3 b g Cadeaux Genereux - Midnight Shift (Ire)
5^{6s} 1^{6gf} 1^{5s} 3^{6g} 2^{5g} 6^{7gf} **2-2-6 £15,318**

Out For A Stroll *S C Williams* 72
5 b g Zamindar (USA) - The Jotter
16^{8s} 10^{7s} 7^{7g} 10^{8gs} 7^{7g} **0-0-5**

Out Of My Way *T M Jones* a24
3 ch f Fraam - Ming Blue
14^{7sd} 14^{7sd} 8^{8sd} 4^{10sd} 11^{11gf} **0-0-5**

Out Of Tune *Mrs L B Normile* a25
4 ch g Elmaamul (USA) - Strawberry Song
9^{7sd} 9^{5gf} **0-0-2**

Outeast (Ire) *G A Harker* 43
4 b f Mujadil (USA) - Stifen
4^{5s} **0-0-1**

Outer Hebrides *D R Loder* 86 a86
3 b g Efisio - Reuval
14^{7g} 15^{8g} 4^{7gf} 2^{7sd} 2^{7s} **0-2-5 £3,950**

Outrageous Flirt (Ire) *A Dickman* 59
2 b f Indian Lodge (Ire) - Sofia Aurora (USA)
7^{5gf} 12^{5g} 7^{5g} 3^{6gs} 3^{7gf} 2^{7s} **0-3-6 £1,752**

Outside Investor (Ire) *N J Gifford* 31 a26
4 b/br g Cadeaux Genereux - Desert Ease (Ire)
12^{8sd} 16^{10gf} 12^{12g} **0-0-3**

Outward (USA) *R Bastiman* 31
4 b g Gone West (USA) - Seebe (USA)
13^{8g} 17^{8f} 15^{12gf} 15^{10gf} 10^{16gf} **0-0-5**

Ovambo (Ire) *P J Makin* 104
6 b g Namaqualand (USA) - Razana (Ire)
4^{12gs} 6^{12gf} 4^{12g} **0-1-3 £3,460**

Over Rating *K A Ryan* a51
4 ch f Desert King (Ire) - Well Beyond (Ire)
7^{9sd} 10^{12sd} 6^{10sd} **0-0-3**

Over The Limit (Ire) *Mrs A J Perrett* 48
2 b f Diktat - Premiere Cuvee
9^{6gs} **0-0-1**

Over The Rainbow (Ire) *B W Hills* 86 a80
3 b c Rainbow Quest (USA) - Dimakya (USA)
1^{10sd} 10^{10g} 15^{12gf} 10^{10gs} 6^{10g} 7^{10s} 10^{12s} **1-0-7 £6,938**

Over The Years (USA) *T P Tate* 35
3 b g Silver Hawk (USA) - Sporting Green (USA)
5^{12gs} 4^{14s} 16^{16gs} 11^{14gs} **0-0-4 £281**

Over Tipsy *R Hannon* 46
2 b c Tipsy Creek (USA) - Over Keen
9^{6gs} 10^{6gf} 13^{7g} 9^{8s} **0-0-4**

Over To You Bert *R J Hodges* 51 a49
5 b g Overbury (Ire) - Silvers Era
8^{8sd} 6^{6sd} 5^{8sw} 1^{8sd} 4^{8gs} 7^{8gs} 13^{8gf} 14^{7gf} 3^{8gf} 3^{8g} 1^{8g} 8^{7gf} 4^{10f} 7^{10gs} 6^{8gf} **2-2-15 £7,063**

Overdrawn (Ire) *J A Osborne* 94 a65
3 b g Daggers Drawn (USA) - In Denial (Ire)
7^{8gs} 9^{8g} 10^{8gf} 13^{7g} 8^{7f} 17^{7gf} 16^{8gf} 11^{8gs} 5^{7sd} **0-0-9**

Overjoy Way *P R Chamings* 58 a60
2 b f Cadeaux Genereux - May Light
7^{7gf} 8^{8gf} 5^{7sd} **0-0-3**

Override (Ire) *J M P Eustace* 70 a76
4 b c Peintre Celebre (USA) - Catalonda
1^{7sd} 5^{7g} **1-0-2 £2,975**

Overstrand (Ire) *Mrs M Reveley* 79
5 b g In The Wings - Vaison La Romaine
5^{16gf} **0-0-1**

Overtop Way (Gr) *P R Chamings* 49 a61
2 b c Denebola Way (Gr) - Dada (Gr)
15^{7gs} 7^{9sd} **0-0-2**

Ovigo (Ger) *P A Blockley* a78
5 b g Monsagem (USA) - Ouvea (Ger)
1^{8sw} 4^{7sd} 6^{8sd} 3^{9sd} PU^{8ss} **1-2-5 £3,604**

Owed *Mrs G S Rees* 60
2 b c Lujain (USA) - Nightingale
10^{6gs} 10^{6g} 4^{6g} **0-0-3**

Own Line *J Hetherton* 19
5 b g Classic Cliche (Ire) - Cold Line
13^{16g} **0-0-1**

Oxford Street Pete (Ire) *A Bailey* 68
2 b g Rossini (USA) - Thabeh
3^{7gf} 13^{7s} 7^{7g} **0-1-3 £744**

Paarl Rock *S T Lewis*
9 ch g Common Grounds - Markievicz (Ire)
8^{16sw} 10^{12ss} 7^{16sd} **0-0-3**

Pablo *Patrick O Brady* 88
5 b h Efisio - Winnebago
19^{8g} 1^{7gs} 10^{8gs} 9^{8gs} 13^{8gs} 14^{8ys} 14^{10s} 16^{8sh} **1-0-8 £10,115**

Pacific Ocean (Arg) *Mrs Stef Liddiard* 61 a63
5 b h Fitzcarraldo (Arg) - Play Hard (Arg)
2^{9ss} 3^{9sd} 3^{12ss} 6^{8g} 8^{10s} 4^{8f} 3^{11gf} 6^{10gf} 7^{10f} 13^{10gf} 3^{8sw} **0-5-11 £2,977**

Pacific Pirate (Ire) *M G Quinlan* 65
2 b c Mujadil (USA) - Jay And-A (Ire)
10^{6gs} 6^{6gf} 9^{7g} **0-0-3**

Pacific Run (USA) *B J Meehan* 30
3 b c Gone West (USA) - Miss Union Avenue (USA)
12^{10s} 8^{12s} **0-0-2**

Pacific Star (Ire) *E A L Dunlop* 64
2 b g Tagula (Ire) - Acidanthera
10^{6gf} 6^{7gf} 5^{7gf} 6^{7gf} **0-0-4**

Packin Em In *J R Boyle* a49
6 b h Young Ern - Wendy's Way
3^{7sd} 2^{6sd} 9^{6sd} 1^{7sd} 12^{6sd} 11^{7hy} 9^{6g} **1-2-7 £2,053**

Paddy Boy (Ire) *J R Boyle* 30 a48
3 br g Overbury (Ire) - Arts Project (Ire)
3^{8ss} 7^{10sd} 11^{10g} 8^{12gf} 7^{12sd} **0-0-5 £207**

Paddy Mul *W Storey* 55 a47
7 ch h Democratic (USA) - My Pretty Niece
2^{12sd} 1^{14sd} 4^{16sd} 3^{14ss} 4^{14ss} 5^{16s} 3^{12s} 3^{12gf} 1^{16g} 4^{14sd} 4^{13gf} PU^{16f} **2-2-12 £6,734**

Paddy Oliver (Ire) *B Palling* 25

2 b g Petorius - Creggan Vale Lass
11⁷ᵍˢ **0-0-1**

Paddys Tern N M Babbage   19
2 b c Fraam - Great Tern
12⁶ᵍᶠ **0-0-1**

Paddywack (Ire) D W Chapman   79
7 b g Bigstone (Ire) - Millie's Return (Ire)
15⁶ˢ 4⁵ʰʸ 16⁶ᵍᶠ 3⁶ᵍᶠ 5⁶ᵍᶠ 3⁵ᵍᶠ 13⁶ᵍ 1⁵ᵍˢ
1⁵ᵍˢ 7⁶ᵍ 3⁵ᵍᶠ 6⁶ᵍᶠ 3⁵ᵍˢ 3⁵ᵍˢ 8⁵ᵍᶠ 4⁵ˢ 5⁵ᵍˢ 5⁵ˢ
2-6-18 £26,126

Padrao (Ire) D R Loder   60
2 b c Cape Cross (Ire) - Dazilyn Lady (USA)
11⁶ᵍˢ **0-0-1**

Pagan Ceremony (USA) Mrs A J Perrett   36 a46
3 ch g Rahy (USA) - Delightful Linda (USA)
11¹²ᵍˢ 10¹²ˢ 14¹³ˢᵈ **0-0-3**

Pagan Dance (Ire) Mrs A J Perrett   102 a96
5 b g Revoque (Ire) - Ballade D'Ainhoa (Fr)
3¹²ˢᵈ 4¹²ˢ 2¹²ᵍ 2¹²ᶠ 6¹⁶ˢ 13¹⁶ᵍ 11¹⁴ˢ
2¹²ᵍᶠ 4¹²ᵍᶠ **0-4-9 £26,946**

Pagan Magic (USA) J A R Toller   81 a81
3 b c Diesis - Great Lady Slew (USA)
3¹⁰ˢ 11⁹ᵍ 11²ᵍ 13¹⁰ᵍˢ 5¹²ᵍˢ 4¹²ᵍ 7¹²ᵍ
3¹²ˢᵈ 9¹⁷ˢᵈ **1-2-9 £8,115**

Pagan Prince J A R Toller   85
7 br g Primo Dominie - Mory Kante (USA)
8⁸ᵍˢ 1⁸ᵍˢ 4⁸ᵍ 6⁸ᵍᶠ 4⁹ᵍ 5⁸ˢ **1-1-6**
£6,973

Pagan Quest J A R Toller   59
2 b c Lujain (USA) - Rohita (Ire)
7⁶ᵍ 18⁶ˢ **0-0-2**

Pagan Sky (Ire) J A R Toller   94
5 ch g Inchinor - Rosy Sunset (Ire)
14¹⁰ᵍ 15¹⁰ᵍᶠ 6¹⁰ᵍᶠ 4¹⁰ᵍˢ 5¹²ᵍ 3¹⁰ʰʸ 9¹²ˢ
0-2-7 £8,318

Pagan Storm (USA) Mrs L Stubbs   67 a53
4 ch g Tabasco Cat (USA) - Melodeon (USA)
15⁷ˢᵈ 11⁷ˢᵈ 7⁷ᵍᶠ 8⁶ᵍ 5⁶ᵍ 10⁶ᶠ 10⁷ᶠ
14⁶ᵍᶠ 3⁷ᵍᶠ 8⁷ᵍᶠ 15⁸ᵍᶠ 11⁷ᵍᶠ 9⁸ᵍ 6⁷ˢᵈ **0-1-14**
£536

Pagan Sword Mrs A J Perrett   51
2 ch c Selkirk (USA) - Vanessa Bell (Ire)
8⁷ᵍˢ **0-0-1**

Pageant J M Bradley   a36
7 br m Inchinor - Positive Attitude
10⁸ˢᵈ 6⁷ˢᵈ 5⁸ˢᵈ 4⁸ˢᵈ 11⁸ˢᵈ 9⁸ˢˢ 5⁷ˢˢ 7⁸ˢˢ
0-0-8

Paint The Lily (Ire) F Watson   57
3 b f Barathea (Ire) - Chocolate Box
12¹⁰ᵍ 11¹⁰ᵍ 4¹⁰ᵍ 10¹²ᵍᶠ 13¹⁶ᶠ **0-0-5**
£419

Paintbox Mrs A J Perrett   67 a53
3 b f Peintre Celebre (USA) - Photogenic
6⁸ᵍᶠ 3⁸ᵍˢ 2⁹ᵍᶠ 6¹⁰ᵍ 12¹⁰ˢᵈ **0-2-5 £2,294**

Paintbrush (Ire) Mrs L Stubbs   a39
4 b f Groom Dancer (USA) - Bristle
5¹⁰ˢᵈ 4¹⁰ˢᵈ **0-0-2**

Painted Moon (USA) C E Brittain   57
3 ch f Gone West (USA) - Crimson Conquest (USA)
9⁷ᵍ **0-0-1**

Pairing (Ire) G L Moore   a54
6 ch g Rudimentary (USA) - Splicing
14⁷ˢᵈ **0-0-1**

Paita Mario Hofer   109
2 b f Intikhab (USA) - Prada (Ger)

1¹⁰ᵛˢ **1-0-1 £80,479**

Palabelle (Ire) P W Harris   61
3 b f Desert Prince (Ire) - Moviegoer
9⁸ᵍᶠ 7⁸ᶠ 7⁸ᵍᶠ 5⁸ᵍ 9¹⁰ᵍ **0-0-5**

Palace Theatre (Ire) T D Barron   78
3 b g Imperial Ballet (Ire) - Luminary
8⁶ˢ 3⁶ᵍ **0-1-2 £888**

Palace Walk (Fr) A M Balding   57
2 b c Sinndar (Ire) - Page Bleue
9⁸ᵍˢ 6⁸ᵍ 15⁸ʰʸ **0-0-3**

Palanzo (Ire) N Wilson   74
6 b g Green Desert (USA) - Karpacka (Ire)
5⁵ᵍ 7⁶ᵍ 10⁶ᵍᶠ **0-0-3**

Palatinate (Fr) H Candy   81
2 br c Desert Prince (Ire) - Dead Certain
4⁶ᵍᶠ 3⁷ˢ 1⁷ˢ 4⁷ᵍˢ **1-1-4 £5,399**

Palawan A M Balding   76 a81
8 br g Polar Falcon (USA) - Krameria
11⁵ˢᵈ 7⁵ˢᵈ 6⁵ˢᵈ 10⁵ˢ 13⁵ᵍˢ 15⁵ᵍᶠ 20⁵ᵍᶠ
11⁵ᵍˢ 18⁵ᵍᶠ 12⁵ᵍᶠ **0-0-10 £231**

Palvic Moon C Smith   56 a30
3 ch f Cotation - Palvic Grey
5⁶ʰʸ 3⁶ˢ 6⁶ˢᵈ 12⁶ˢ 17⁵ᵍˢ 17⁷ᵍ **0-1-6**
£557

Pamir (Ire) L M Cumani   71 a75
2 b g Namid - Mijouter (Ire)
9⁶ᵍᶠ 3⁶ˢ 16ˢᵈ **1-1-3 £4,266**

Pancake Role A W Carroll   32
4 b g Tragic Role (USA) - My Foxy Lady
6¹³ᵍᶠ 14¹⁰ᵍᶠ 11¹¹ᵍ 11¹⁰ᵍˢ **0-0-4**

Pancakehill D K Ivory   a57
5 ch m Sabrehill (USA) - Sawlah
7⁷ˢᵈ 11⁸ˢᵈ 9⁸ˢᵈ 10⁸ˢᵈ 6⁸ˢᵈ 7⁶ˢᵈ 14¹⁰ˢᵈ
10⁸ˢᵈ **0-0-8**

Panfield Belle (Ire) H J Collingridge   12
3 b f Danetime (Ire) - Make Hay
6⁵ᵍᶠ **0-0-1**

Pangloss (Ire) G L Moore   72
3 ch g Croco Rouge (Ire) - Kafayef (USA)
3¹²ᵍˢ 7¹⁰ᵍᶠ 5¹²ᵍ 9¹²ᵍᶠ 4¹²ᵍˢ 5¹⁶ᵍˢ 6¹²ˢ
6¹¹ᵍˢ **0-1-8 £1,789**

Pango H Morrison   93
5 ch g Bluegrass Prince (Ire) - Riverine
2⁸ᵍᶠ 2⁸ᵍᶠ 1⁷ᵍᶠ 1⁷ᵍ 1⁸ᵍ 2⁸ˢ 4⁷ᵍᶠ 10⁸ᵍᶠ
8⁸ᵍ **3-4-9 £40,710**

Panjandrum N E Berry   58 a73
6 b g Polar Falcon (USA) - Rengaine (Fr)
8⁵ˢᵈ 3⁵ˢᵈ 5⁶ˢᵈ 1⁶ˢᵈ 7⁶ˢʷ 6⁵ˢᵈ 8⁵ˢˢ 12⁶ˢᵈ
4⁵ᵍᶠ 15⁵ʰʸ 8⁵ᵍᶠ 1⁵ˢᵈ **2-1-12 £6,681**

Panshir (Fr) C F Wall   86
3 ch g Unfuwain (USA) - Jalcamin (Ire)
5⁸ᵍ 7⁸ᵍ 3⁷ᵍˢ 11⁸ᵍᶠ 1⁷ᵍᶠ 6⁸ᵍ 2⁷ᵍ 6⁷ᵍᶠ
1-2-8 £7,451

Pants Andrew Reid   a57
5 b m Pivotal - Queenbird
8⁷ˢᵈ 7⁷ˢᵈ 14⁷ˢᵈ **0-0-3**

Panzer (Ger) R Charlton   57
3 b g Vettori (Ire) - Prompt
6¹⁰ᵍˢ **0-0-1**

Papality W Jarvis   70
2 b f Giant's Causeway (USA) - Papabile (USA)
5⁶ᵍˢ 8⁷ᵍᶠ **0-0-2**

Paparaazi (Ire) R A Fahey   57 a60
2 b c Victory Note (USA) - Raazi
5⁷ᵍᶠ 9⁷ᵍᶠ 3⁷ˢᵈ **0-1-3 £211**

Papeete (Ger) *Miss B Sanders*   59 a59
3 b f Alzao (USA) - Prairie Vela
4^{8g} 4^{8f} 7^{11gf} 13^{10gf} 1^{12gs} 11^{16g} 2^{12sd}
1-1-7 £4,433

Paper Talk (USA) *B W Hills*   86
2 br c Unbridled's Song (USA) - Journalist (Ire)
3^{6gf} 2^{7g} **0-1-2 £2,966**

Papineau *Saeed Bin Suroor*   121
4 ch c Singspiel (Ire) - Early Rising (USA)
1^{12gf} 1^{16gf} 1^{20gf} **3-0-3 £212,999**

Pappy (Ire) *A W Carroll*   46 a5
3 b f Petardia - Impressive Lady
4^{8sd} 11^{8gf} 3^{7gs} 18^{6g} 11^{7gf} 8^{8gs} **0-1-6**
£480

Par Indiana (Ire) *I Semple*   64
3 b f Indian Rocket - Paryiana (Ire)
3^{9gf} 3^{11gs} 6^{11gf} 6^{9s} **0-1-4 £1,251**

Par Jeu *D J Daly*   59
2 b f Montjeu (Ire) - Musical Twist (USA)
10^{7gf} **0-0-1**

Parachute *J A B Old*   27
5 ch g Hector Protector (USA) - Shortfall
12^{12s} **0-0-1**

Paradise Breeze *C A Horgan*   35
3 b f Perugino (USA) - Paradise Forum
11^{6gf} 9^{7gs} 5^{6gf} **0-0-3**

Paradise Garden (USA) *P L Clinton*   37 a34
7 b g Septieme Ciel (USA) - Water Course (USA)
9^{11gs} 5^{11sf} 4^{8sd} 3^{10gf} 8^{11gs} **0-1-5 £211**

Paradise Isle *C F Wall*   108
3 b f Bahamian Bounty - Merry Rous
10^{5gf} 4^{5gf} 2^{5g} 1^{6g} 7^{6g} 1^{6g} 3^{6s} **2-2-7**
£42,657

Paradise Mill (USA) *J H M Gosden*   80
2 b f Horse Chestnut (SAF) - Eaton Place (Ire)
2^{7s} **0-1-1 £2,900**

Paradise Valley *Mrs Stef Liddiard*   57 a57
4 b g Groom Dancer (USA) - Rose De Reve (Ire)
1^{12sw} 6^{12sw} 8^{12sd} 5^{10sd} 7^{16ss} 2^{10sd} 14^{11s}
5^{12s} 4^{12gf} 3^{14gf} 1^{12gf} **2-2-11 £6,872**

Paragon Of Virtue *P Mitchell*   a87
7 ch g Cadeaux Genereux - Madame Dubois
3^{10sd} 4^{10sd} 7^{10sd} 3^{8sd} 6^{10sd} 5^{8sd} **0-2-6**
£2,788

Parallel Lines (Ire) *P D Evans*   35 a47
3 ch g Polish Precedent (USA) - Phone Booth (USA)
9^{8sd} 8^{6ss} 12^{6sd} 4^{8sd} 8^{5sd} 10^{7s} 3^{6sd} 6^{5f}
9^{6gf} 8^{5gf} **0-0-10 £229**

Parasol (Ire) *D R Loder*   114
5 br g Halling (USA) - Bunting
2^{10gs} 9^{12gf} 10^{9g} 4^{9gs} 9^{18gf} **0-1-4 £8,452**

Parchment (Ire) *J Howard Johnson*   30
2 ch c Singspiel (Ire) - Hannalou (Fr)
4^{5hy} **0-0-1 £262**

Pardishar (Ire) *G L Moore*   71
6 b g Kahyasi - Parapa (Ire)
11^{10g} **0-0-1**

Pardon Moi *Mrs C A Dunnett*   52 a44
3 ch f First Trump - Mystical Song
3^{7sd} 4^{6sd} 4^{6sd} 7^{6sd} 7^{5s} 4^{6sd} 16^{hy} 13^{6gf}
4^{6gf} 7^{6f} 18^{6g} 6^{6gf} 9^{6gf} 10^{6g} 14^{6gf} 18^{7gs}
1-1-16 £1,863

Paris Bell *T D Easterby*   82
2 b/br c Paris House - Warning Bell
3^{5s} 5^{5hy} 8^{5f} 7^{7gf} 4^{6hy} 8^{5f} 1^{6s} 1^{6hy} 1^{6s}

Paris Dreamer *M W Easterby*   a28
3 b f Paris House - Stoproveritate
8^{6sd} 7^{9ss} 8^{11sd} **0-0-3**

Paris Heights *R M Whitaker*   63
2 gr g Paris House - Petra Nova
10^{7f} 6^{7s} 4^{7gs} 17^{7f} 17^{6gf} 8^{8gs} **0-0-6**
£390

Paris Latino (Fr) *C L Tizzard*   a29
5 b g Nikos - Tarbelissima (Fr)
10^{5sd} 12^{8sd} **0-0-2**

Paris Tapis *P S McEntee*   55 a55
2 gr f Paris House - Time Of Night (USA)
7^{6f} 4^{7sd} 2^{6gf} 2^{5hy} 1^{5sw} 7^{5sd} 6^{5s} **1-2-7**
£4,275

Parisi Princess *G P Kelly*   43
3 ch f Shaddad (USA) - Crambella (Ire)
9^{10s} 7^{14f} 9^{10gf} **0-0-3**

Parisian Playboy *Jedd O'Keeffe*   59 a13
4 gr g Paris House - Exordium
9^{7ss} 17^{7gf} 7^{8hy} 7^{8gf} 1^{8s} 2^{8gf} 1^{7gs} 14^{8g}
11^{8gs} 11^{7gs} **2-1-10 £9,372**

Park Approach (Ire) *J Noseda*   75
2 gr f Indian Ridge - Abyat (USA)
4^{6gs} 3^{5gs} 2^{5g} **0-2-3 £2,902**

Park Ave Princess (Ire) *M J Polglase*   44 a63
3 b f Titus Livius (Fr) - Satinette
2^{7sd} 2^{5sd} 3^{7sd} 2^{7sd} 9^{5sf} 18^{8gs} 12^{6f}
0-4-8 £3,189

Park Law (Ire) *J H M Gosden*   89
2 b f Fasliyev (USA) - Blanche Dubois
2^{7g} 1^{7gf} 5^{7gf} 6^{8gf} **1-1-4 £7,699**

Park Romance (Ire) *B J Meehan*   96
2 b f Dr Fong (USA) - Park Charger
2^{6gf} 1^{6gf} 5^{6f} 3^{7gf} **1-2-4 £11,611**

Park Star *D Shaw*   59 a61
4 b f Gothenberg (Ire) - Miriam
6^{5sd} 3^{6sd} 2^{6sd} 10^{6sd} 10^{5g} UR^{6gs} 4^{6s} 4^{7s}
17^{7g} 9^{6sd} **0-3-10 £2,146**

Parker *B Palling*   35 a69
7 b g Magic Ring (Ire) - Miss Loving
4^{7sd} 3^{7ss} 6^{7ss} 11^{7sd} 6^{7sd} 12^{8s} 5^{6sd} 10^{7g}
16^{7gf} 16^{7gf} **0-2-10 £633**

Parkside Pursuit *J M Bradley*   83 a63
6 b g Pursuit Of Love - Ivory Bride
9^{5g} 1^{5gf} 1^{5gf} 9^{5gf} 4^{6gf} 1^{6f} 3^{6f} 1^{5f}
15^{6gf} 14^{gf} 11^{5gs} 7^{5g} 8^{5s} 11^{6sd} 5^{5sd} **4-1-15**
£17,675

Parkview Love (USA) *D Shaw*   100 a91
3 b/br c Mister Baileys - Jerre Jo Glanville (USA)
8^{8sd} 3^{7g} 12^{7gs} 12^{8gf} 8^{7g} 18^{8f} 16^{7gf}
4^{10g} 5^{8g} 3^{10f} 11^{10g} 11^{7s} **0-2-12 £7,012**

Parliament Act (Ire) *B A McMahon*   43
3 b g Mujadil (USA) - Law Student
13^{6gf} 8^{5gf} 8^{6gf} **0-0-3**

Parliament Square (Ire) *D R Loder*   87 a68
3 b c Sadler's Wells (USA) - Groom Order
3^{10gs} 5^{10g} 2^{13sd} **0-2-3 £2,017**

Parnassian *G B Balding*   81
4 ch g Sabrehill (USA) - Delphic Way
7^{8s} 8^{8g} 3^{8s} 3^{7s} 1^{8g} 3^{8gf} 8^{9gf} 5^{8gf} 1^{8g}
1^{8gs} 5^{9gf} 4^{8gf} 3^{8gs} 7^{9g} 3^{8s} 1^{8gs} 8^{8hy} **4-4-17**
£23,039

Parsley's Return *N A Callaghan*   17
2 b g Danzero (Aus) - The Frog Queen

7^{6f} 5^{6f} 107^{7gf} **0-0-3**

Part Time Love *M R Channon* 52
2 b c Royal Applause - Keen Melody (USA)
6^{6gf} 1^{6f} **1-0-2 £2,541**

Partners In Jazz (USA) *T D Barron* 94
3 gr c Jambalaya Jazz (USA) - Just About Enough (USA)
5^{6gf} 10^{6g} 13^{6s} 5^{5s} 1^{6gs} 4^{6s} 10^{6g} **1-0-7**
£14,364

Party Boss *C E Brittain* 43
2 gr c Silver Patriarch (Ire) - Third Party
8^{7gf} **0-0-1**

Party Ploy *K R Burke* 78 a68
6 b g Deploy - Party Treat (Ire)
18^{14s} 7^{14g} 2^{14gf} 1^{13gf} 1^{12f} 7^{12g} 1^{11g} 2^{12s}
1^{12gf} 7^{12f} 4^{10s} 4^{12f} 5^{12sd} **4-3-13 £25,937**

Party Princess (Ire) *J A Glover* 68 a68
3 b f Orpen (USA) - Summer Queen
12^{6gs} 7^{7hy} 1^{6gf} 4^{6gf} 10^{5gf} 13^{6g} 12^{6gf}
19^{6gs} 17^{6gs} 1^{6sd} **2-1-10 £7,613**

Pas De Surprise *P D Evans* 60 a60
6 b g Dancing Spree (USA) - Supreme Rose
3^{8sd} 12^{8sd} 5^{8sd} 5^{8sd} 8^{8sd} 10^{8sd} 10^{7gf}
5^{9g} 4^{9gf} 4^{8g} 5^{9gf} 4^{8gf} 13^{8g} 7^{8gf} 12^{8gf} 10^{9gs}
6^{9sd} 11^{9sd} **0-2-18 £1,349**

Pascali *H Morrison* 52
4 b f Compton Place - Pass The Rose (Ire)
7^{6gf} **0-0-1**

Paso Doble *B R Millman* 62 a70
6 b g Dancing Spree (USA) - Delta Tempo (Ire)
5^{11sd} 8^{9sd} 2^{8sd} 6^{8sw} 2^{9sw} 13^{12sd} 5^{9gf} 4^{7gf}
2^{8sd} 14^{9gf} 9^{10gf} 10^{12gf} **0-3-12 £2,641**

Pass Go *J J Lambe* 38
3 b g Kris - Celt Song (Ire)
8^{7gf} 13^{5s} 7^{5g} 10^{6f} 14^{10sd} **0-0-5**

Pass The Port *J R Fanshawe* 73 a72
3 ch g Docksider (USA) - One Of The Family
5^{8hy} 1^{8sd} 6^{8g} 9^{8s} **1-0-4 £3,454**

Passando *A M Balding* a34
4 b f Kris - Iota
11^{10sd} **0-0-1**

Passing Glance *A M Balding* 120
5 br h Polar Falcon (USA) - Spurned (USA)
1^{9g} 10^{8g} 4^{8gs} 5^{8gs} **1-0-4 £49,000**

Passion Fruit *C W Fairhurst* 57
3 b f Pursuit Of Love - Reine De Thebes (Fr)
17^{8gs} 12^{7f} 7^{8gf} 6^{8s} 1^{7s} **1-0-5 £1,473**

Passionately Royal *R A Fahey* 36
2 b c Royal Applause - Passionelle
8^{5g} 10^{6hy} **0-0-2**

Pastoral Pursuits *H Morrison* 118
3 b c Bahamian Bounty - Star
2^{7g} 1^{6g} 1^{7gf} 5^{7s} **2-1-4 £88,028**

Pat's Miracle (Ire) *John Berry*
4 ch f College Chapel - Exemplaire (Fr)
8^{12sd} **0-0-1**

Pat's Nemesis (Ire) *B R Johnson* 11
3 b f Sri Pekan (USA) - Exemplaire (Fr)
13^{6gs} 12^{7s} 14^{7sd} **0-0-3**

Patandon Girl (Ire) *A Bailey* a45
4 b f Night Shift (USA) - Petite Jameel (Ire)
9^{6sd} 11^{6sd} **0-0-2**

Patau *M J Wallace* 35
2 ch c Inchinor - Haste
14^{7gf} **0-0-1**

Patavellian (Ire) *R Charlton* 121

6 b/br g Machiavellian (USA) - Alessia
3^{5gf} 10^{6gs} 3^{6g} 7^{5g} 3^{6vs} **0-3-5 £40,172**

Patrician Dealer *M S Saunders* 34 a13
2 br g Millkom - Double Fault (Ire)
9^{7hy} 11^{9sd} **0-0-2**

Patrixprial *M H Tompkins* 81
3 gr c Linamix (Fr) - Magnificent Star (USA)
5^{10gs} 5^{12gf} 1^{14s} 8^{16g} 4^{13gs} 6^{16s} **1-0-6**
£5,392

Patrixtoo (Fr) *M H Tompkins* 65
3 gr c Linamix (Fr) - Maradadi (USA)
7^{10gs} 5^{10gs} 11^{7gf} 2^{10gf} 4^{11g} 8^{12gf} 5^{12s}
0-2-7 £1,292

Patronage *M L W Bell* 80
2 b c Royal Applause - Passionate Pursuit
5^{7s} 5^{7g} 3^{8gf} **0-1-3 £670**

Patronofconfucius (Ire) *J R Boyle* 41
2 b g Imperial Ballet (Ire) - Shefoog
9^{7g} 12^{7s} **0-0-2**

Patterdale *W J Haggas* 78
3 b g Octagonal (NZ) - Baize
2^{7gs} 1^{6gf} 7^{7g} 2^{8gf} 6^{10g} 6^{8hy} **1-2-6**
£6,865

Pattern Man *J R Norton* 40
3 b c Wizard King - Quick Profit
8^{14gs} PU^{16gs} 16^{14sd} **0-0-3**

Patternmaker (USA) *W Jarvis* 60
2 b/br g Elnadim (USA) - Attasliyah (Ire)
6^{6s} **0-0-1**

Patterson (Ire) *M Madgwick* 21 a32
3 br f Turtle Island (Ire) - Richmond Lillie
8^{10gf} 12^{12sd} 6^{12gf} **0-0-3**

Patxaran (Ire) *P C Haslam* 63
2 b f Revoque (Ire) - Stargard
8^{6gf} 5^{6gf} 4^{7gf} 6^{8s} 3^{8f} 6^{10gf} 18^{8s} **0-1-7**
£1,196

Paula *M Dods* 50
4 b f Compton Place - Be My Bird
11^{8hy} 6^{12g} 6^{10gf} 15^{9f} **0-0-4**

Paula Jo *J S Wainwright* 46
2 b f Factual (USA) - Superstream
6^{5gf} 8^{5gf} 11^{6g} 14^{5gs} 13^{5f} **0-0-5**

Paula Lane *R Curtis* 25 a48
4 b f Factual (USA) - Colfax Classic
8^{12sd} 5^{16sd} 12^{11s} 6^{15s} **0-0-4**

Pauline's Prince *R Hollinshead* 62 a65
2 b c Polar Prince (Ire) - Etma Rose (Ire)
6^{5gf} 1^{7sd} 4^{7sd} 9^{6gf} 3^{8s} **1-0-5 £4,340**

Pavilion *B J Meehan*
2 b f Robellino (USA) - Chiltern Court (USA)
14^{7gf} **0-0-1**

Pawan (Ire) *Miss A Stokell* 74 a49
4 ch g Cadeaux Genereux - Born To Glamour
5^{6gs} 2^{6sd} 2^{6s} 8^{6sd} 3^{5hy} 5^{6s} 3^{7f} 11^{6gf}
2^{7gf} 10^{7gf} 1^{7f} 6^{8f} 6^{8g} 3^{7g} 11^{7gf} 1^{9s} 9^{8gs}
5^{10g}
2-6-24 £17,187

Pawn Broker *D R C Elsworth* 110 a100
7 ch g Selkirk (USA) - Dime Bag
10^{10sd} 18^{8f} 4^{10gs} 6^{10gf} 26^{9g} 8^{9s} **1-0-6**
£22,290

Pawn In Life (Ire) *T D Barron* a68
6 b g Midhish - Lady-Mumtaz
9^{7sd} 10^{7sd} 9^{7sd} 2^{7sw} 7^{7sw} 8^{6ss} **0-1-6**
£836

Pax *D Nicholls*   92
7 ch g Brief Truce (USA) - Child's Play (USA)
6^{5g} 6^{5gs} 8^{5g} 1^{6gf} 8^{6g} 9^{6gf} 8^{6gf} 10^{5gf}
16^{6gf} 7^{6g} 8^{5s} 13^{5gs} **1-0-12 £6,435**

Pay Attention *T D Easterby*   70
3 b f Revoque (Ire) - Catch Me
4^{8s} 8^{10gs} 2^{10s} 7^{9f} 2^{10gs} 1^{10gs} 4^{12gs} 5^{10s}
1-3-8 £5,350

Pay The Silver *I A Wood*   76 a63
6 gr g Petong - Marjorie's Memory (Ire)
11^{11gs} 4^{8s} 11^{8gf} 2^{12sd} 10^{9gf} 3^{12f} 3^{12g}
9^{16sd} PU^{12f} **0-2-9 £2,448**

Pay Time *R E Barr*   39
5 ch m Timeless Times (USA) - Payvashooz
6^{6s} 20^{5gf} 9^{5gf} 5^{7f} 6^{6gf} 15^{6gs} 8^{5s} **0-0-7**

Payola (USA) *C E Brittain*   82
3 b f Red Ransom (USA) - Bevel (USA)
1^{10gf} 6^{12s} 5^{12g} 6^{10s} **1-0-4 £4,461**

Pays D'Amour (Ire) *Miss L A Perratt*   73 a69
7 b g Pursuit Of Love - Lady Of The Land
9^{5ss} 11^{7gs} 1^{6gs} 12^{6f} 3^{7sd} 7^{6sd} 5^{6s} 13^{7gf}
3^{6gf} 8^{6gf} 2^{6g} 10^{5gs} 7^{6s} 9^{6s} 8^{6gs} **1-2-15**
£5,795

Peace Lily *R F Johnson Houghton*   65
2 b f Dansili - Shall We Run
5^{6g} 9^{7gs} **0-0-2**

Peace Treaty (Ire) *S R Bowring*   30 a21
3 b f Turtle Island (Ire) - Beautyofthepeace (Ire)
10^{8sd} 8^{8sd} 8^{9ss} 7^{8sd} 11^{8gf} 6^{5gf} 10^{7g}
0-0-7

Peaceful Frontier *C Smith*   6
2 b f Monashee Mountain (USA) - Edge Of Darkness
13^{5gs} BD^{5gf} 14^{6gf} **0-0-3**

Peak Of Perfection (Ire) *M A Jarvis*   100 a73
3 b g Deploy - Nsx
5^{10g} 3^{8sd} 5^{12g} 1^{12sd} 1^{12g} 1^{14gf} 2^{14s} 8^{16gf}
6^{15s} **3-1-9 £21,457**

Peak Park (USA) *J A R Toller*   55 a54
4 br g Dynaformer (USA) - Play Po (USA)
7^{16gf} 7^{18gf} 2^{14f} 10^{16gs} 3^{16hy} 2^{16sd} 2^{16sd}
3^{17sd} **0-5-8 £3,662**

Peak To Creek *J Noseda*   116
3 b c Royal Applause - Rivers Rhapsody
3^{8g} 2^{7gf} 3^{7g} **0-1-3 £15,400**

Pearl Farm *C A Horgan*   9 a61
3 b f Foxhound (USA) - Trinity Hall
9^{6s} 3^{7sd} **0-1-2 £596**

Pearl Grey *Saeed Bin Suroor*   99
3 gr f Gone West (USA) - Zelanda (Ire)
3^{6g} 2^{7gf} 14^{6s} **0-2-3 £10,450**

Pearl Island (USA) *D J Wintle*   11
3 b c Kingmambo (USA) - Mother Of Pearl (Ire)
13^{7gs} 16^{8hy} **0-0-2**

Pearl Of Love (Ire) *M Johnston*   101
3 b c Peintre Celebre (USA) - Aunt Pearl (USA)
7^{9gs} 10^{8gf} **0-0-2**

Pearl Of York (Den) *R Guest*   66 a49
3 b f Richard Of York - Laser Show (USA)
10^{10g} 13^{10gf} 2^{10f} 5^{12sd} 1^{9g} 3^{9gf} 5^{10gs}
1-1-7 £5,062

Pearl Pride (USA) *M Johnston*   53
3 ch f Theatrical - Spotlight Dance (USA)
10^{10s} 12^{10gf} 8^{7gs} 10^{12gs} **0-0-4**

Pearl's A Singer (Ire) *M L W Bell*   70

---

2 ch f Spectrum (Ire) - Cultured Pearl (Ire)
11^{8gf} 5^{8s} 5^{7gf} 13^{8g} **0-0-4**

Pearnickity *A W Carroll*   36
3 b f Bob's Return (Ire) - The Robe
13^{10gf} 8^{12gf} 9^{10gf} 8^{12gs} **0-0-4**

Pearson Glen (Ire) *G A Swinbank*   32
5 ch g Dolphin Street (Fr) - Glendora
16^{8gf} **0-0-1**

Peartree House (Ire) *D W Chapman*   41 a24
10 b g Simply Majestic (USA) - Fashion Front
11^{8sd} 8^{8sd} 7^{7sd} 5^{8hy} 6^{7sd} 6^{8gf} 19^{8f}
11^{7sd} 8^{8gf} 16^{8f} **0-0-11**

Pebble Mill (Ire) *M Johnston*   44
2 b c Cape Cross (Ire) - Mill Path
10^{6gf} 12^{8g} **0-0-2**

Pedlar Of Dreams (Ire) *T D Barron*   67
2 b f Fayruz - Beautyofthepeace (Ire)
3^{5s} 5^{5g} 9^{6gf} **0-1-3 £830**

Pedler's Profiles *Miss K M George*   a32
4 br g Topanoora - La Vie En Primrose
8^{10sd} 9^{8sd} 12^{7sd} **0-0-3**

Pedrillo *Sir Mark Prescott*   108
3 b g Singspiel (Ire) - Patria (USA)
3^{8gf} 1^{8s} 22^{9g} **1-1-3 £12,469**

Pedro Jack (Ire) *M A Buckley*   58 a64
7 b g Mujadil (USA) - Festival Of Light
11^{6gs} 1^{6sd} 9^{6gs} 9^{6gf} 12^{6gf} 3^{6gf} 12^{6sd}
1-0-7 £1,856

Pee Jay's Dream *M W Easterby*   52 a39
2 ch g Vettori (Ire) - Langtry Lady
6^{5sd} 10^{6gs} 7^{6g} 12^{6gf} **0-0-4**

Peeptoe (Ire) *J L Dunlop*   81
2 ch f Machiavellian (USA) - Alfaguara (USA)
3^{5g} 2^{6g} 5^{6g} 4^{6gf} 7^{5gf} **0-2-5 £3,072**

Peeress *Sir Michael Stoute*   105 a89
3 ch f Pivotal - Noble One
1^{8f} 1^{8f} 1^{7gf} 3^{7gf} 4^{8sd} **3-1-5 £34,833**

Pella *M Blanshard*   71 a67
3 ch f Hector Protector (USA) - Norpella
7^{10gs} 8^{11gs} 6^{10s} 2^{8gf} 5^{8gf} 3^{8g} 2^{9gf} 3^{10gf}
8^{8gf} 1^{8s} 7^{8g} 1^{8gf} 4^{8g} 5^{10sd} **2-4-14 £12,859**

Penalty Clause (Ire) *K A Morgan*   a35
4 b g Namaqualand (USA) - Lady Be Lucky (Ire)
5^{14sd} **0-0-1**

Penalty Kick (Ire) *N A Callaghan*   75
2 b c Montjeu (Ire) - Dafrah (USA)
11^{7g} 6^{7gs} 8^{8g} 1^{10gf} 5^{8s} **1-0-5 £3,948**

Penang Sapphire *G A Butler*   61 a60
2 b g Spectrum (Ire) - Penang Pearl (Fr)
6^{6sd} 16^{6gs} 15^{6gf} 1^{5hy} **1-0-4 £4,192**

Pending (Ire) *J R Fanshawe*   72
3 b g Pennekamp (USA) - Dolcezza (Fr)
3^{8gf} 8^{8g} 6^{8gf} 8^{8gs} 3^{10hy} 15^{11g} **0-1-6**
£1,162

Penel (Ire) *B R Millman*   57 a36
3 b g Orpen - Jayess Elle
6^{7sd} 8^{8s} 2^{7gs} 5^{6gf} 13^{9sd} **0-1-5 £1,155**

Peninsular (Fr) *J H M Gosden*   59
2 ch c Giant's Causeway (USA) - Blue Note (Fr)
7^{5g} **0-0-1**

Penkenna Princess (Ire) *R M Beckett*   106
2 b f Pivotal - Tiriana
8^{6g} 1^{6g} 3^{6gf} 1^{7g} 2^{7s} **2-2-5 £35,997**

Pennestamp (Ire) *Mrs P N Dutfield*   63
2 b c Pennekamp (USA) - Sopran Marida (Ire)

12^{5g} 6^{6gf} 6^{6g} 4^{5gf} 4^{6gf} 3^{5gs} 9^{6gs} 5^{6gf}
8^{8g} **0-0-9 £1,187**

Penny Cross *J G Given* — 83
4 b f Efisio - Addaya (Ire)
11^{7s} 14^{8g} 11^{8g} 7^{7gf} 3^{9g} **0-0-5 £1,085**

Penny Island (Ire) *A King* — 71
2 b c Trans Island - Sparklingsovereign
7^{7gf} 6^{7gf} 3^{8gs} 5^{8gf} 10^{7gs} **0-1-5 £764**

Penny Pictures (Ire) *M C Pipe* — 94
5 b g Theatrical - Copper Creek
3^{20gf} 5^{16g} 20^{18s} **0-1-3 £6,880**

Penny Pie (Ire) *P W Harris* — a45
4 b f Spectrum (Ire) - Island Lover (Ire)
13^{10sd} **0-0-1**

Penny Stall *J L Dunlop* — 69
3 b f Silver Patriarch (Ire) - Madiyla
9^{10gf} 4^{14g} 2^{16s} 6^{17gs} 4^{14gs} **0-3-5 £1,702**

Penny Valentine *J R Best* — a19
4 ch f My Best Valentine - Precision Finish
9^{8sd} 6^{10sd} 15^{12sd} **0-0-3**

Penny Wedding (Ire) *J R Fanshawe* — 53
2 b f Pennekamp (USA) - Eilean Shona
9^{8gf} 6^{8g} **0-0-2**

Penrith (Fr) *M Johnston* — 93
3 b c Singspiel (Ire) - Queen Mat (Ire)
1^{8gf} 3^{10gf} 11^{9gf} 3^{8gf} 5^{8gf} 20^{11g} 2^{8gs} 3^{8g}
4^{8g} 13^{8s} **1-4-10 £21,822**

Pension Fund *M W Easterby* — 55
10 b g Emperor Fountain - Navarino Bay
5^{10hy} 5^{11gs} 6^{8gf} 4^{10gf} **0-1-4 £389**

Pentecost *A M Balding* — 114
5 ch g Tagula (Ire) - Boughtbyphone
10^{8g} 6^{8gs} 25^{8gf} 1^{8s} 4^{8g} 9^{8gf} 1^{8g} 9^{8gs}
9^{8f} 1^{9gs} 8^{8g} **3-0-11 £92,698**

Penwell Hill (USA) *T D Barron* — 58 a80
5 b g Distant View (USA) - Avie's Jill (USA)
1^{8sd} 7^{9ss} 2^{8sd} 2^{8ss} 16^{8gs} 6^{10gf} 14^{10gf}
11^{8gf} 3^{8gf} 1^{8f} 11^{9gs} **2-3-11 £8,223**

Penzance *J R Fanshawe* — 88
3 ch g Pennekamp (USA) - Kalinka (Ire)
6^{9hy} 4^{10gf} 1^{10gf} 10^{12g} 13^{10gf} 14^{11g} **1-0-6**
£6,371

Peopleton Brook *D W P Arbuthnot* — 60 a56
2 b c Compton Place - Merch Rhyd-Y-Grug
5^{5f} 6^{5sd} 18^{5g} 15^{6gs} 17^{7gf} 10^{6g} **0-0-6**

Pepe (Ire) *R Hollinshead* — 57 a57
3 b f Bahhare (USA) - Orange And Blue
6^{9sd} 6^{11sd} 3^{12sd} 12^{11gs} 1^{12sd} 4^{12sd} 11^{12sd}
8^{12sd} 1^{14f} **2-0-9 £6,439**

Pepper Road *R Bastiman* — 61 a60
5 ch g Elmaamul (USA) - Floral Spark
20^{8gs} 14^{7g} 1^{8f} 2^{7gf} 2^{8f} 2^{7gf} 10^{8gf} 6^{8sd}
9^{7sd} **1-3-9 £6,996**

Peppermint Tea (Ire) *M L W Bell* — 80
2 b f Intikhab (USA) - Karayb (USA)
10^{6gf} 11^{6g} 2^{6g} **0-1-3 £1,605**

Pequenita *G L Moore* — 61
4 b f Rudimentary (USA) - Sierra Madrona (USA)
6^{10s} 5^{9s} **0-0-2**

Percheron (Ire) *P A Blockley* — 66
2 ch g Perugino (USA) - Silvery Halo (USA)
9^{6gs} 9^{7gs} 3^{5g} **0-1-3 £630**

Percussionist (Ire) *J H M Gosden* — 121
3 b c Sadler's Wells (USA) - Magnificent Style (USA)
1^{12gs} 1^{11s} 4^{12g} 10^{12gf} 2^{11s} 3^{15g} 6^{12s}

5^{16hy} **2-1-8 £131,746**

Percy Douglas *Miss A Stokell* — 60 a20
4 b c Elmaamul (USA) - Qualitair Dream
11^{5ss} 10^{5ss} 9^{6gs} 11^{5hy} 13^{5gf} 8^{8g} 6^{10gf}
11^{8g} 18^{5g} 7^{5gs} 5^{5gf} 11^{5gf} 19^{6gf} 6^{6s} 7^{5g} 9^{6gs}
0-0-16 £233

Percy-Verance (Ire) *J J Quinn* — 41
6 ch g Dolphin Street (Fr) - Sinology
5^{11f} 4^{17g} **0-0-2**

Peregian (Ire) *Andrew Reid* — 22 a55
6 b g Eagle Eyed (USA) - Mo Pheata
5^{8ss} 3^{7sd} 11^{7s} 15^{7gf} **0-1-4 £184**

Perelandra (USA) *M J Wallace* — 77
4 ch f Cadeaux Genereux - Larentia
1^{11g} 10^{12f} 4^{13s} 4^{12gf} **1-0-4 £3,985**

Pererin *N B King* — 51
3 b g Whittingham (Ire) - Antithesis (Ire)
13^{6gs} 1^{7g} 9^{7gf} 8^{7f} 8^{7g} 3^{8gf} 8^{8f} 6^{8g}
11^{8gs} 8^{7gs} 3^{8s} **1-2-11 £2,277**

Perestroika (Ire) *B Ellison* — 58
6 ch g Ashkalani (Ire) - Licentious
10^{16ss} 12^{12g} 4^{12gf} 8^{14gf} 4^{14gs} 10^{14gf}
0-0-6 £703

Perez (Ire) *R Hannon* — 73
2 b c Mujadil (USA) - Kahla
10^{6g} 13^{6gs} 6^{7gf} 8^{6g} **0-0-4**

Perfect Balance (Ire) *N Tinkler* — 63
3 b/br g Shinko Forest (Ire) - Tumble
17^{8g} 1^{8s} 6^{10g} 5^{9gs} 4^{10s} 11^{12sd} 7^{9g} 17^{14g}
1-0-8 £3,766

Perfect Choice (Ire) *B J Meehan* — 90
2 gr c Daylami (Ire) - Fairy Contessa (Ire)
7^{6g} 1^{6gf} 8^{7f} 6^{7gf} **1-0-4 £5,459**

Perfect Hindsight (Ire) *C J Gray* — 55
3 b g Spectrum (Ire) - Vinicky (USA)
7^{6gs} 15^{7gf} 8^{6gf} 16^{6gf} **0-0-4**

Perfect Love *E J Alston* — 62
4 b f Pursuit Of Love - Free Spirit (Ire)
12^{7f} 12^{7g} 13^{7gf} 15^{7gf} 14^{5gf} **0-0-5**

Perfect Portrait *Mrs A Malzard* — 77
4 ch g Selkirk (USA) - Flawless Image (USA)
3^{7gs} 7^{7gs} 7^{7g} 4^{7f} 1^{5g} **1-0-5 £2,045**

Perfect Punch *C F Wall* — 73
5 b g Reprimand - Aliuska (USA)
2^{10g} 7^{10gf} 7^{12g} 7^{11g} 2^{14gs} 16^{14g} **0-2-6**
£2,381

Perfect Setting *P J Makin* — 64
4 b g Polish Precedent (USA) - Diamond Park (Ire)
6^{5gf} 10^{5g} 9^{5g} **0-0-3 £126**

Perfect Solution (Ire) *J A R Toller* — 49 a58
2 ch f Entrepreneur - Pearl Barley (Ire)
11^{6gf} 8^{6sd} **0-0-2**

Perfect Storm *M Blanshard* — 101
5 b h Vettori (Ire) - Gorgeous Dancer (Ire)
7^{12g} 17^{12g} 5^{12g} 4^{12gs} 7^{12gf} 14^{12s} 10^{10hy}
7^{8s} **0-0-8 £2,119**

Perfect Tone (USA) *M A Magnusson* — 64
2 ch f Silver Hawk (USA) - Copper Cachet (USA)
5^{8g} **0-0-1**

Perfectperformance (USA) *Saeed Bin Suroor* — 112
2 ch c Rahy (USA) - Balistroika (USA)
1^{7g} 2^{7gf} 18^{8f} 18^{9f} 7^{7s} **3-1-5 £86,390**

Perfidious (USA) *J R Boyle* — 28 a79
6 b g Lear Fan (USA) - Perfolia (USA)
3^{10sd} 2^{12sd} 5^{12sd} 10^{10sd} 15^{10g} **0-3-5**

£4,358

Performing Art *P W Chapple-Hyam* 31
2 b c Sadler's Wells (USA) - Charming Life (NZ)
10⁸ᵍ **0-0-1**

Perianth (Ire) *B J Meehan* 61 a51
2 ch c Bluebird (USA) - Meandering Rose (USA)
4⁵ˢ 9⁵ᵍᶠ 10⁶ᵍᶠ 10⁷ˢᵈ 3⁶ᵍ 8⁶ᵍᶠ 10⁶ᵍᶠ
0-1-7 £760

Perida (Ire) *D Carroll* 43
4 b f Perugino (USA) - Razida (Ire)
5¹²ᵍˢ 9¹²ᵍᶠ 19¹⁷ᵍ 9¹¹ᵍ **0-0-4**

Perle D'Or (Ire) *W J Haggas* 87
3 b f Entrepreneur - Rose Society
1⁷ᶠ 1⁸ᶠ 1⁸ᵍᶠ 5⁸ᶠ **3-0-4 £12,966**

Perrywinkle *James Moffatt*
2 b f Perryston View - Crab 'n Lobster (Ire)
18⁶ᵍˢ **0-0-1**

Perrywinkle Boy *M D Hammond* 52
3 b g Piccolo - Flower Arrangement
4⁸ᵍᶠ 8⁸ᵍˢ 10⁷ʰʸ PU¹⁰ᵍˢ 7⁷ˢ **0-0-5 £415**

Persario *J R Fanshawe* 97
5 b m Bishop Of Cashel - Barford Lady
1⁶ᵍˢ 17⁶ᵍ **1-0-2 £9,759**

Persian Carpet *I A Wood* 66
2 b f Desert Style (Ire) - Kuwah (Ire)
7⁷ᵍᶠ 4⁷ᵍᶠ 2⁶ᵍᶠ 2⁶ᵍ 6⁶ᵍᶠ 23⁷ᵍ 20⁶ˢ **0-2-7 £2,709**

Persian Dagger (Ire) *J L Dunlop* 69
3 b g Daylami (Ire) - Persian Fantasy
12¹⁰ᵍˢ 7¹⁰ᵍˢ 10⁶ˢ 5¹²ᶠ 3¹⁵ᵍᶠ **0-1-5 £711**

Persian Genie (Ire) *G B Balding* 62
3 br f Grand Lodge (USA) - Persia (Ire)
8¹⁰ᵍ 8¹⁰ᵍᶠ 7¹⁰ᵍᶠ 8¹⁰ᵍᶠ 11¹²ˢ 2¹²ˢ 6¹²ᵍᶠ
0-1-7 £1,076

Persian Khanoom (Ire) *J A Osborne* a62
2 b f Royal Applause - Kshessinskaya
6⁸ˢᵈ **0-0-1**

Persian King (Ire) *J A B Old* 69
7 ch g Persian Bold - Queen's Share
12¹²ᵍˢ 14¹²ˢ 9¹²ᵍᶠ 7¹⁴ᵍ 6¹³ᵍᶠ 3¹²ᵍᶠ 4¹¹ᶠ
0-1-7 £1,066

Persian Lightning (Ire) *J L Dunlop* 113
5 b g Sri Pekan (USA) - Persian Fantasy
4¹⁰ᵍ 4¹²ᵍᶠ 1¹⁰ᵍ 4¹⁰ᶠ 6¹²ᵍᶠ **1-0-5 £27,559**

Persian Majesty (Ire) *P W Harris* 116
4 b c Grand Lodge (USA) - Spa
6¹⁰ᵍˢ 3¹²ᵍᶠ 3¹²ᶠ 5¹²ᵍᶠ 4¹²ᵍᶠ 9¹²ᵍᶠ **0-1-6 £22,024**

Persian Punch (Ire) *D R C Elsworth*
11 ch g Persian Heights - Rum Cay (USA)
PU¹⁶ˢ **0-0-1**

Persian Rock (Ire) *J A Osborne* 83
2 b c Namid - Cairo Lady (Ire)
2⁵ᵍ 16⁶ᵍᶠ 16ᵍˢ 12⁶ᵍ 8⁷ᵍᶠ **2-1-5 £10,943**

Personify *Saeed Bin Suroor* 80
2 ch c Zafonic (USA) - Dignify (Ire)
1⁶ᶠ 4⁸ᵍ 9⁶ˢ **1-0-3 £5,359**

Pertemps Bianca *A D Smith* a18
4 b f Dancing Spree (USA) - Bay Bianca (Ire)
6⁸ˢᵈ 12¹²ˢᵈ 7⁷ˢᵈ **0-0-3**

Pertemps Magus *R A Fahey* 71 a59
4 b f Silver Wizard (USA) - Brilliant Future
3⁷ᵍ 1⁷ˢ 6⁷ˢ 3⁷ˢ 6⁷ˢ 6⁷ˢᵈ 4⁷ˢᵈ **1-2-7 £5,294**

Pertemps Red *A D Smith*
3 ch c Dancing Spree (USA) - Lady Lullaby (Ire)
13¹²ˢᵈ 12⁷ᵍˢ **0-0-2**

Pertemps Sia *A D Smith* 41
4 b c Distinctly North (USA) - Shamrock Dancer (Ire)
13¹⁸ᶠ 5¹⁷ᵍ 3¹⁴ᵍᶠ **0-1-3 £395**

Pertemps Wizard *A D Smith*
4 br g Silver Wizard (USA) - Peristyle
9⁸ˢᵈ **0-0-1**

Pertino *J M Jefferson* 35
8 b g Terimon - Persian Fountain (Ire)
9¹²ᶠ **0-0-1**

Peruvia (Ire) *R M Beckett* 58 a52
4 b f Perugino (USA) - Dane's Lane (Ire)
7¹⁰ˢ 5¹¹ˢᵈ 11⁹ᵍˢ **0-0-3**

Peruvian Breeze (Ire) *Evan Williams* 61 a66
3 b g Foxhound (USA) - Quietly Impressive (Ire)
5⁹ᵍˢ 6¹¹ᵍ 1¹²ˢᵈ 7¹²ᶠ 9¹²ˢᵈ 2¹²ᵍᶠ **1-1-6 £3,619**

Peruvian Chief (Ire) *N P Littmoden* 103 a95
7 b g Foxhound (USA) - John's Ballad (Ire)
9⁶ᶠᵗ 6⁵ᶠᵗ 7⁷ᵍᶠ 10⁶ᶠᵗ 8⁵ˢᵈ 2⁵ᵍ 9⁵ᵍ 9⁵ᵍᶠ
7⁵ᵍᶠ UR⁶ᵍᶠ 12⁵ᵍ 10⁶ᵍ 3⁶ᵍᶠ 12⁶ᵍᶠ **0-2-14 £7,489**

Peruvian Prince (USA) *J A R Toller* 85
2 b c Silver Hawk (USA) - Inca Dove (USA)
2⁷ᵍᶠ **0-1-1 £2,765**

Peruvian Style (Ire) *N P Littmoden* 79 a88
3 b g Desert Style (Ire) - Lady's Vision (Ire)
1⁵ˢᵈ 1⁵ˢᵈ 10⁶ᵍˢ 5⁶ᵍ 10⁶ᵍ 7⁵ᵍˢ 6⁵ᵍᶠ 5⁶ᵍᶠ
2⁶ᶠ 7⁵ᵍᶠ 1⁷ᵍ 18⁶ᵍ **3-1-12 £21,507**

Pesquera *J Noseda* 67
2 b f Green Desert (USA) - Rose Des Andes (Ire)
10⁶ᵍ 3⁶ˢ **0-1-2 £802**

Petana *M Dods* 53 a39
4 gr f Petong - Duxyana (Ire)
5⁶ᵍ 12⁵ᵍᶠ 4⁵ᵍᶠ 8⁵ᵍ 1⁵ᵍᶠ 7⁵ˢᵈ 10⁵ᵍᶠ 10⁵ᶠ
1-0-8 £4,026

Petardias Magic (Ire) *C A Dwyer* 91 a74
3 ch c Petardia - Alexander Confranc (Ire)
4⁸ˢᵈ 16⁹ˢ 3⁹ᵍˢ 7⁶ᵍˢ 2⁶ˢ 4⁶ᵍ 14⁶ˢ 11⁵ˢ
1-2-8 £22,774

Peter Paul Rubens (USA) *P F I Cole* 114
3 ch c Belong To Me (USA) - Skybox (USA)
9⁸ʰʸ 4⁷ᵍˢ 1⁷ᵍᶠ 5⁷ᶠ 1⁷ᵍᶠ 1⁷ᵍᶠ 1⁸ᵍ 2⁷ᵍᶠ
4-1-8 £64,669

Peter Roughley (Ire) *A Berry* 59 a57
2 b g Indian Lodge (Ire) - Dahabiah
7⁸ˢ 4⁷ᵍˢ 2⁷ˢ 6⁶ˢᵈ **0-1-4 £834**

Peter's Imp (Ire) *A Berry* 52
9 b g Imp Society (USA) - Catherine Clare
1¹²ᵍᶠ 5¹⁶ᵍᶠ 3¹²ᵍᶠ 4¹⁶ᶠ 8¹⁶ᶠ 3¹²ᵍˢ **1-2-6 £4,733**

Peters Choice *I Semple* 75
3 ch g Wolfhound (USA) - Dance Of The Swans (Ire)
13⁵ᵍᶠ 12⁵ˢ 5⁵ᵍ 12⁵ᵍᶠ 7⁵ᵍ 2⁵ᵍᶠ 8⁵ᵍᶠ **0-1-7 £2,430**

Peters Delite *R A Fahey* 70
2 b c Makbul - Steadfast Elite (Ire)
9⁶ᵍ 3⁵ᶠ 3⁵ʰʸ 9⁶ᵍᶠ **0-1-4 £1,481**

Peters Ploy *T Keddy* 2
4 ch g Deploy - Alpi Dora
12⁶ˢᵈ 10¹⁰ᵍᶠ 14¹²ˢᵈ 8¹²ˢᵈ **0-0-4**

Petite Colleen (Ire) *D Haydn Jones* 67 a67
3 b f Desert Sun - Nishiki (USA)

16^{11gs} 4^{10gf} 15^{10g} 6^{12gs} 12^{12gf} 5^{8gs} 11^{10g} 4^{9sd} **0-0-8 £342**

Petite Elle *P J McBride* — 51 a32
2 b f Wolfhound (USA) - Start Again (Ire)
3^{5ss} 4^{6f} 4^{7sd} 3^{6f} **0-1-4 £721**

Petite Girl *J L Spearing* — 17
2 gr f Daylami (Ire) - Pagoda (Fr)
10^{6gf} **0-0-1**

Petite Mac *N Bycroft* — 38
4 b f Timeless Times (USA) - Petite Elite
15^{5gs} 7^{5gs} **0-0-2**

Petite Noire *J G Portman* — a25
2 b f Lujain (USA) - Coffee Cream
9^{5g} 6^{7sd} 5^{6sd} **0-0-3**

Petite Rose (Ire) *J H M Gosden* — 96
3 b f Turtle Island (Ire) - Double Grange (Ire)
1^{6gs} 2^{6g} 8^{6g} **1-1-3 £9,568**

Petite Spectre *R Hannon* — 32 a75
2 ch f Spectrum (Ire) - Petite Epaulette
17^{6s} 8^{7sd} 1^{6sd} **1-0-3 £5,187**

Petongski *B Ellison* — 40
6 b g Petong - Madam Petoski
19^{5g} 8^{5hy} 7^{6s} **0-0-3**

Petrion *R Guest* — 37 a41
3 b f Petong - Rion River (Ire)
12^{6gf} 9^{7gf} 3^{7sd} 6^{8gf} 16^{7gs} **0-1-5 £434**

Petrolero (Arg) *James Moffatt* — 25
5 gr g Perfect Parade (USA) - Louise (Arg)
9^{11g} **0-0-1**

Petrolina (Ire) *H Morrison* — 24 a53
3 b f Petardia - Arbitration (Ire)
11^{6s} 13^{12sd} 4^{8sd} 8^{8sd} 9^{7s} **0-0-5**

Petrosa (Ire) *D R C Elsworth* — 75
4 ch f Grand Lodge (USA) - Top Brex (Fr)
4^{9g} 5^{10gf} 8^{11g} 3^{8gf} 5^{10s} **0-1-5 £1,356**

Petrula *K A Ryan* — 85
5 ch g Tagula (Ire) - Bouffant
2^{10gs} 6^{10g} 14^{12f} 16^{10s} 7^{10g} **0-1-5 £4,526**

Petticoat Hill (UAE) *J H M Gosden* — a37
2 b f Timber Country (USA) - Crinolette (Ire)
13^{7sd} **0-0-1**

Pevensey (Ire) *J H M Gosden* — 89
2 b g Danehill (USA) - Champaka (Ire)
6^{6gs} 11^{6gf} 1^{8g} 3^{10g} **1-0-4 £9,651**

Phantom Flame (USA) *M Johnston* — a42
4 b g Mt. Livermore (USA) - Phantom Creek
5^{7sd} 2^{9ss} 11^{7ss} 8^{8sd} **0-1-4 £466**

Phantom Song (Ire) *D Carroll* — 21
2 gr c Shinko Forest (Ire) - Natural Pearl
14^{6g} 15^{5gs} **0-0-2**

Phantom Stock *W Jarvis* — 72 a72
4 b g Alzao (USA) - Strike Alight (USA)
2^{16sd} 1^{16sd} 4^{13sd} 2^{16sd} 1^{16sd} 7^{16ss} 4^{18g} **2-2-7 £8,268**

Phantom Wind (USA) *J H M Gosden* — 111
3 b f Storm Cat (USA) - Ryafan (USA)
6^{7g} 5^{6g} 1^{7gf} 3^{8gf} 4^{9g} **1-0-5 £60,944**

Pharaoh Hatshepsut (Ire) *W G Young* — 36
6 b m Definite Article - Maid Of Mourne
10^{7ss} 10^{16gf} 11^{9g} 11^{7s} 10^{9g} 10^{7gf} 9^{7f} 6^{6gf} 10^{5s} **0-0-10**

Pharly Reef *D Burchell* — 24
12 b g Pharly (Fr) - Hay Reef
4^{10gs} **0-0-1**

Pharoah's Gold (Ire) *D Shaw* — 59 a71
6 b g Namaqualand (USA) - Queen Nefertiti (Ire)
2^{8sd} 10^{8sd} 5^{7ss} 7^{7gs} 3^{8sd} 7^{8sd} 1^{9g} 8^{8hy}
7^{8gs} 9^{10sd} 4^{9g} 16^{7gf} 11^{7s} 17^{9gs} 8^{8gs} 13^{8g}
10^{7hy} 11^{9sd} **1-2-18 £5,776**

Pheckless *J M Bradley* — 61 a74
5 ch g Be My Guest (USA) - Phlirty
15^{7sd} 3^{7sd} 4^{6sd} 10^{5sd} 9^{8sd} 8^{6sd} 3^{6gs}
12^{6gf} 13^{7g} 11^{7sd} **0-2-10 £1,283**

Phi (USA) *Sir Michael Stoute* — 77
2 b/br c Rahy (USA) - Salchow (USA)
7^{7g} 2^{8gf} 5^{8g} **0-1-3 £1,608**

Phi Phi (Ire) *W J Haggas* — 55
2 b f Fasliyev (USA) - Council Rock
7^{5gf} **0-0-1**

Philharmonic *R A Fahey* — 104
3 b g Victory Note (USA) - Lambast
4^{5s} 10^{6g} 20^{6s} 5^{6s} 16^{6g} **0-0-5 £2,024**

Philly Dee *N E Berry* — 34 a33
3 b f Bishop Of Cashel - Marbella Beach (Ire)
3^{5sd} 10^{6sd} 10^{5sd} 9^{6ss} 8^{5sd} 10^{5gf} 7^{6sd}
7^{6gf} **0-1-8 £183**

Philosophic *Mrs L C Jewell* — a21
10 b g Be My Chief (USA) - Metaphysique (Fr)
7^{16sd} 14^{13sd} 13^{13sd} **0-0-3**

Phlaunt *R F Johnson Houghton* — 63 a30
2 b f Faustus (USA) - Phlirty
4^{6g} 9^{5gf} 3^{6g} 3^{7hy} 8^{7sd} **0-1-5 £1,446**

Phluke *R F Johnson Houghton* — 73 a69
3 b g Most Welcome - Phlirty
5^{7sd} 3^{7sd} 7^{7sd} 5^{6gs} 1^{7gs} 2^{8gs} 7^{7s} 4^{9gf}
8^{8g} 6^{8g} 13^{7gf} 10^{8gf} **1-1-12 £5,853**

Phoebe Woodstock (Ire) *P W Harris* — 68
2 ch f Grand Lodge (USA) - Why So Silent
3^{7gf} **0-1-1 £810**

Phoenix Eye *M Mullineaux* — 50 a25
3 b c Tragic Role (USA) - Eye Sight
8^{10gs} 8^{11gf} 9^{7g} 12^{7sd} **0-0-4**

Phoenix Nights (Ire) *A Berry* — 52 a33
4 b g General Monash (USA) - Beauty Appeal (USA)
10^{9sd} 5^{9sd} 10^{8ss} 12^{5sw} 6^{10g} 4^{12gs} 4^{9gf}
6^{8gs} 9^{9gf} 6^{8s} **0-0-10 £1,680**

Phoenix Reach (Ire) *A M Balding* — 116
4 b c Alhaarth (Ire) - Carroll's Canyon (Ire)
6^{10gf} 6^{12gs} 10^{12gf} **0-0-3 £5,250**

Phone Tapping *M H Tompkins* — 56
3 b g Robellino (USA) - Miss Party Line (USA)
10^{8gf} 6^{8g} 6^{8g} 10^{11g} 7^{10s} **0-0-5**

Photofit *J L Dunlop* — 66
4 b g Polish Precedent (USA) - Photogenic
6^{7gs} 14^{8s} **0-0-2**

Phred *I A Wood* — 67 a21
4 ch g Safawan - Phlirty
6^{8gs} 4^{8g} 6^{7s} 5^{8gf} 4^{7g} 2^{8gf} 9^{8gf} 10^{9gf}
5^{9gs} 19^{8g} 9^{9gf} 9^{9sd} **0-1-12 £1,925**

Phrenologist *Andrew Reid* — a71
4 gr g Mind Games - Leading Princess (Ire)
13^{7sd} 9^{7gf} 11^{6sd} 12^{6sd} **0-0-4**

Physical (Ire) *Mrs A J Perrett* — 56
2 b c Efisio - St Clair
9^{6s} 8^{6s} **0-0-2**

Piano Star *Sir Michael Stoute* — 94
4 b g Darshaan - De Stael (USA)
8^{10gs} 10^{10gs} **0-0-2**

Pianoforte (USA) *D R Loder* — 83

2 b g Grand Slam (USA) - Far Too Loud (Can)
6^{6g} 2^{7gf} 4^{8s} **0-1-3 £2,078**

Pic Up Sticks *M R Channon* 106
5 gr g Piccolo - Between The Sticks
3^{7gf} 1^{7gf} 6^{7f} 3^{5g} 6^{6f} 8^{5gf} 17^{6gf} 16^{6g}
1^{6gf} 9^{6g} 7^{5s} 5^{6s} **2-2-12 £57,631**

Piccled *E J Alston* 90 a82
6 b g Piccolo - Creme De Menthe (Ire)
8^{6ss} 3^{5g} 16^{5gf} 19^{5hy} 10^{5gf} 15^{gf} 15^{5s}
5^{5gf} 24^{5gf} LFT^{5g} 16^{5gf} 3^{5s} **1-2-12 £13,581**

Piccleyes *R Hannon* 65
3 b g Piccolo - Dark Eyed Lady (Ire)
8^{7gf} 12^{7gf} 8^{6gf} 16^{gf} 11^{6gf} 9^{7g} 3^{5gf} 6^{5gf}
8^{6g} 3^{6gf} 2^{6gf} **1-3-11 £6,221**

Piccolo Prince *E J Alston* 71 a71
3 ch g Piccolo - Aegean Flame
8^{6sd} 1^{5sd} 2^{5sd} 1^{6ss} 2^{6sd} 1^{6gs} 2^{5s} 9^{6s}
2^{6gf} 12^{6gf} 14^{6g} 5^{5gf} 8^{6gs} 5^{6s} **3-4-14**
£14,593

Piccolomini *M Johnston* 69
2 b c Diktat - La Dama Bonita (USA)
3^{7gs} **0-1-1 £649**

Pick A Berry *G Wragg* 53 a22
3 b f Piccolo - Bonne De Berry
15^{7sd} 9^{6s} 6^{6gf} 9^{8gf} 7^{6gf} **0-0-5**

Pick Of The Crop *J R Jenkins* 60 a72
3 ch g Fraam - Fresh Fruit Daily
1^{6sd} 2^{7ss} 8^{7sd} 11^{9gs} 22^{7gs} 18^{7g} **1-1-6**
£2,715

Pickapeppa *R F Johnson Houghton* 69
2 ch f Piccolo - Cajole (Ire)
9^{6gf} 5^{7gf} **0-0-2**

Pickle *S C Williams* 85 a48
3 b f Piccolo - Crackle
3^{6sd} 7^{6sd} 4^{6s} 1^{7s} 7^{7g} 3^{7gf} 6^{8gf} 1^{7g}
1^{7gf} 1^{8gf} 2^{9gf} 12^{8g} 4^{9g} **4-4-14 £28,727**

Pico Alto *B Palling*
3 b f Lugana Beach - Noble Canonire
16^{8gf} 12^{7gs} 11^{8sd} 11^{9sd} **0-0-4**

Picot De Say *John Berry* 63
2 b g Largesse - Facsimile
11^{6gf} 7^{6gf} 11^{8g} 3^{8g} 2^{8s} 5^{8s} **0-2-6**
£2,100

Piddies Pride (Ire) *P S McEntee* 75 a65
2 b f Indian Lodge (Ire) - Fairybird (Fr)
5^{5g} 6^{6gf} 6^{6g} 4^{6g} 16^{gf} 15^{gf} 3^{6gf} 2^{6gf}
11^{7gf} 4^{6g} 12^{6gf} 5^{6gf} 9^{6sd} 7^{6s} 2^{5s} **2-3-16**
£14,376

Pie Corner *M Madgwick* 35
2 ch c Fumo Di Londra (Ire) - Ballystate
11^{5s} 10^{5g} 13^{7gf} 13^{6gf} **0-0-4**

Pieter Brueghel (USA) *D Nicholls* 94
5 b g Citidancer (USA) - Smart Tally (USA)
8^{7gf} 4^{6gf} 9^{6s} 10^{6gf} 1^{6g} 3^{6gf} 3^{6g} 2^{6s}
16^{6s} 11^{6gf} **1-3-10 £27,734**

Pike Bishop (Ire) *R Charlton* 99
2 b c Namid - Pink Cashmere (Ire)
1^{5gf} 1^{5gf} **2-0-2 £8,814**

Pilca (Fr) *I W McInnes* 31
4 ch g Pistolet Bleu (Ire) - Caricoe
11^{10gf} **0-0-1**

Pilgrim Princess (Ire) *E J Alston* 43 a50
6 b m Flying Spur (Aus) - Hasaid Lady (Ire)
3^{6sd} 5^{6sd} 4^{7sd} 6^{6sd} 10^{7sw} 9^{7ss} 7^{6hy} 4^{6sd}
5^{6f} **0-1-9 £469**

Pilgrims Progress (Ire) *D W Thompson* 78
4 b g Entrepreneur - Rose Bonbon (Fr)
4^{14g} 8^{13gs} 5^{16gf} 8^{15s} 8^{14s} **0-0-5 £434**

Pillars Of Wisdom *J L Dunlop* 72
2 ch c Desert Prince (Ire) - Eurolink Mischief
7^{7gf} 3^{7gf} **0-1-2 £874**

Pinafore *H Morrison* 62 a63
2 ch f Fleetwood (Ire) - Shi Shi
3^{6gs} 2^{7sd} 2^{6g} 4^{5sd} **0-3-4 £1,426**

Pinchbeck *M A Jarvis* 97
5 b g Petong - Veuve Hoornaert (Ire)
16^{6gs} 4^{6gf} 16^{7gf} 17^{6gs} 4^{6g} 6^{6g} 10^{6gs}
2-1-8 £14,102

Pinching (Ire) *H R A Cecil* 75
3 ch f Inchinor - Input
4^{7g} 3^{8s} 2^{8gf} 3^{9s} 13^{8g} 2^{8gf} **0-2-6**
£4,656

Pine Bay *B Gubby* 64 a22
3 b f Sure Blade (USA) - Opuntia
6^{7gf} 7^{8gf} 14^{10sd} 23^{7gs} 16^{gf} **1-0-5**
£4,160

Pink Bay *W S Kittow* 57 a61
2 b f Forzando - Singer On The Roof
4^{6gf} 2^{6sd} **0-1-2 £1,326**

Pink Sapphire (Ire) *D R C Elsworth* 78
3 ch f Bluebird (USA) - Highbrook (USA)
15^{6gs} 2^{8gf} 4^{7gf} 6^{10g} 4^{7gf} 12^{6g} **0-1-6**
£3,168

Pink Supreme *I A Wood* 60
3 ch f Night Shift (USA) - Bright Spells
13^{7g} 11^{6gf} 10^{6gf} 7^{7g} 11^{6g} 6^{7gs} 10^{6gf}
4^{6gs} 9^{6g} 16^{6gf} **0-0-10**

Pins 'n Needles (Ire) *C A Cyzer* 10 a53
3 gr f Mark Of Esteem (Ire) - Khalisiyn
10^{7sd} 6^{10sd} 13^{10g} 10^{12sd} **0-0-4**

Pintle *J L Spearing* 83
4 b f Pivotal - Boozy
4^{6f} 1^{7f} 1^{7gf} 6^{8g} 4^{7g} 1^{7gf} **3-0-6**
£19,381

Piper *D W Barker* 22
4 ch g Atraf - Lady-H
14^{7gs} **0-0-1**

Piper General (Ire) *J S Moore* 41
2 br g General Monash (USA) - Pipewell (Ire)
7^{7gs} **0-0-1**

Piper Lily *M Blanshard* 77
2 b f Piccolo - Polly Golightly
5^{5s} 1^{5g} 6^{5gf} 8^{5g} 12^{6g} 8^{5s} **1-0-6**
£5,496

Piper's Ash (USA) *R Charlton* 95
2 b f Royal Academy (USA) - Merida
6^{6gf} 1^{5gf} **1-0-2 £4,085**

Pips Pearl (Ire) *Mrs P N Dutfield* 44
2 b f Lil's Boy (USA) - Penka (Ire)
18^{6gf} 18^{6gf} 8^{6g} 10^{8gf} 5^{6gf} 17^{7g} **0-0-6**

Pips Song (Ire) *P W Hiatt* a58
9 ch g Pips Pride - Friendly Song
7^{6sd} 8^{6sd} 1^{6sd} 9^{6sd} 9^{7sd} 3^{6sd} 10^{6sd} 5^{6sd}
11^{6sd} **1-1-10 £2,968**

Pipssalio (Spa) *Jamie Poulton* 51 a46
7 b g Pips Pride - Tesalia (Spa)
6^{16sd} 2^{12sw} 6^{14s} 2^{12hy} 13^{12sd} 11^{16gs} **0-2-6**
£910

Piquet *J J Bridger* 44 a54
6 br m Mind Games - Petonellajill

3^{10sd} 1^{8sd} 6^{7sd} 6^{8sd} 9^{10sd} 7^{8sd} 14^{10gf}
6^{12f} 3^{10sd} 12^{10gf} 1^{10sd} 8^{10f} 7^{10sd} 13^{10gf} 8^{10gf}
2-2-15 £5,211

Piran (Ire) *B J Meehan* 63
2 b g Orpen (USA) - Dancing At Lunasa (Ire)
8^{7gf} 9^{7g} 5^{8gf} 12^{8s} **0-0-4**

Piri Piri (Ire) *P J McBride* 73
4 b/br f Priolo (USA) - Hot Curry (USA)
6^{10gf} 2^{11f} 3^{12gf} 8^{10gf} 3^{12gf} 2^{10gf} 7^{10gf}
9^{11g} 10^{10gf} **0-3-9 £4,997**

Pirlie Hill *Miss L A Perratt* 61 a9
4 b f Sea Raven (Ire) - Panayr
3^{6g} 4^{6g} 9^{6sd} 2^{6f} 5^{5gf} 8^{6g} 1^{5gf} 6^{5gf} 7^{5gf}
4^{5g} 4^{5gs} 11^{5gf} 6^{5g} 5^{5gf} 13^{6g} 16^{6gs} 9^{5f}
1-2-17 £5,803

Piroetta *J A Osborne* 47
2 b f Averti (Ire) - Bint Albadou (Ire)
10^{7gf} **0-0-1**

Pirouettes (Ire) *E R Oertel* 43 a57
4 b f Royal Applause - Dance Serenade (Ire)
9^{7sd} 20^{8g} 11^{6gf} 9^{10sd} 4^{7sd} 9^{8gs} **0-0-6**

Piste Bleu (Fr) *R Ford* 61
4 b f Pistolet Bleu (Ire) - Thamissia (Fr)
15^{12sd} 13^{12gs} 9^{12gf} 1^{12gf} 6^{12gf} 4^{12g} 13^{12g}
16^{10gf} **1-0-8 £3,535**

Pitcairn Island *M Johnston* 42
2 ch f Indian Ridge - Girl From Ipanema
10^{7s} 12^{6gs} **0-0-2**

Pitch Up (Ire) *T G Mills* 88 a95
2 b c Cape Cross (Ire) - Uhud (Ire)
7^{5g} 3^{5gf} 6^{5gf} 1^{5gf} 1^{5sd} 5^{5gs} 7^{5f} 9^{6s}
11^{5s} **2-0-9 £11,181**

Pitton Mill *W G M Turner* 2 a37
4 b g Millkom - Sea Song
11^{12sd} 15^{12gf} **0-0-2**

Pittsburgh *A M Balding* 83
2 ch c Nashwan (USA) - Oatey
4^{8g} 7^{8gs} **0-0-2 £913**

Pivotal Flame *B A McMahon* 98
2 b c Pivotal - Reddening
1^{6gs} 5^{7gs} 4^{7s} 1^{7gs} 6^{6gf} 1^{6s} **3-0-6**
£39,213

Pivotal Point *P J Makin* 119
4 b g Pivotal - True Precision
10^{6gs} 10^{6gf} 1^{5g} 2^{5gf} 1^{6gf} 1^{5gs} 5^{5g} 1^{6gf}
4-1-8 £168,999

Pivotal's Princess (Ire) *B A McMahon* 76
2 ch f Pivotal - Art Princess (Ire)
3^{5gs} 3^{5gf} 2^{6g} **0-2-3 £3,048**

Pizazz *B J Meehan* 97
3 ch c Pivotal - Clare Celeste
5^{6g} 2^{8hy} 5^{8g} 2^{7gf} 2^{7gf} 24^{8f} 3^{7gf} 1^{7gf}
16^{7gf} 13^{7g} **1-4-10 £13,462**

Place Cowboy (Ire) *J A Osborne* 83
3 b c Compton Place - Paris Joelle (Ire)
1^{6g} 5^{6f} 2^{7gf} 4^{7gs} 6^{7g} **1-1-5 £6,596**

Plain Chant *C Roberts* 33
7 b g Doyoun - Sing Softly
8^{19gf} **0-0-1**

Planet (Ire) *Sir Michael Stoute* 37 a66
2 b c Soviet Star (USA) - Laurentia (USA)
14^{7g} 8^{7sd} 2^{9sd} **0-1-3 £1,314**

Planet Tomato (Ire) *P F I Cole* 86
2 b c Soviet Star (USA) - Via Splendida (Ire)
3^{5g} 2^{5hy} **0-2-2 £2,534**

Planters Punch (Ire) *R Hannon* 79
3 b c Cape Cross (Ire) - Jamaican Punch (Ire)
9^{7gs} 16^{10g} 7^{10gf} 1^{10g} 9^{12gs} 7^{10g} 9^{10g} 3^{10g}
2^{10gf} 2^{10g} 2^{10g} **1-4-11 £9,044**

Plateau *D Nicholls* 92
5 b g Zamindar (USA) - Painted Desert
6^{6g} 28^{6g} 2^{5gf} 21^{5gf} 20^{6gf} 3^{5g} 9^{5s} **0-2-7**
£20,900

Platinum Boy (Ire) *M Wellings* 13 a37
4 b g Goldmark (USA) - Brown Foam
10^{12sd} 9^{12sd} 10^{12sw} 11^{10sd} 3^{10sd} 7^{8sd}
7^{10sd} 5^{10sd} 11^{10gf} **0-1-9 £209**

Platinum Charmer (Ire) *K R Burke* 61 a67
4 b g Kahyasi - Mystic Charm
2^{12sd} 1^{12sd} 10^{12sd} 2^{16ss} 1^{12g} 4^{11sd} 2^{11f}
4^{12f} 8^{12g} 3^{12gf} 2^{11f} 5^{12gf} 1^{12gf} 7^{12s} 6^{15s} 5^{14s}
7^{11sd} **3-5-17 £11,306**

Platinum Chief *A Berry* 14 a46
3 b g Puissance - Miss Beverley
6^{8sd} 6^{8sd} 5^{7sd} 9^{8sw} 5^{9sd} 3^{7sf} 4^{8sd} 4^{9sd}
10^{8gf} **0-0-9 £205**

Platinum Pirate *K R Burke* 67 a67
3 b g Merdon Melody - Woodland Steps
2^{10sd} 9^{10sd} 2^{10sd} 1^{10s} 3^{10gs} 6^{10gs} 5^{10s}
4^{11gf} 7^{10sd} 1^{10sd} 1^{10gs} 3^{10s} 10^{10hy} **3-4-13**
£17,430

Plattocrat *R P Elliott* 31 a26
4 b g Dancing Spree (USA) - No Comebacks
5^{8sd} 7^{6sd} 7^{8g} 12^{6sd} 7^{7gf} **0-0-5**

Plausabelle *A W Carroll* 57
3 b f Royal Applause - Sipsi Fach
7^{8s} 2^{8hy} 9^{12hy} 12^{12gf} 3^{10gs} 2^{10f} **0-3-6**
£2,650

Play Bouzouki *L M Cumani* 67 a68
3 b f Halling (USA) - Balalaika
3^{8gf} 4^{8gs} 7^{10g} 6^{9sd} **0-1-4 £904**

Play Master (Ire) *D Haydn Jones* 76 a76
3 b g Second Empire (Ire) - Madam Waajib (Ire)
2^{7sd} 1^{8sd} 2^{8ss} 9^{10g} 1^{8gs} 11^{8gs} 3^{8sd} 24^{7gf}
5^{8g} **2-3-9 £11,776**

Play That Tune *H R A Cecil* 96
4 ch f Zilzal (USA) - Military Tune (Ire)
7^{8gs} 5^{9g} 4^{8g} 3^{8gs} 3^{7gs} 9^{7s} **0-1-6**
£4,841

Play The Melody (Ire) *C Tinkler* 66
3 b/br g Revoque (Ire) - Dumayla
3^{10s} 1^{10g} **1-1-2 £4,318**

Play Up Pompey *J J Bridger* 57 a55
2 b g Dansili - Search For Love (Fr)
10^{7gf} 8^{6gf} 9^{7sd} 13^{7g} 10^{8gs} 8^{6s} **0-0-6**

Playful Act (Ire) *J H M Gosden* 113
2 b f Sadler's Wells (USA) - Magnificent Style (USA)
2^{7gs} 1^{7s} 1^{8g} 1^{8gf} **3-1-4 £165,255**

Playful Dane (Ire) *W S Cunningham* 89
7 b g Dolphin Street (Fr) - Omicida (Ire)
1^{6f} 5^{6gf} 9^{6g} 1^{5gf} 3^{6gf} 1^{5gf} 2^{5gf} 1^{5g}
4-2-8 £20,781

Playful Spirit *J Balding* 45 a55
5 b m Mind Games - Kalimat
7^{6sd} 6^{8sd} 3^{6ss} 7^{6sd} 7^{6sd} 3^{5sd} 7^{6gf}
8^{5gf} 11^{6gf} 15^{6sd} 9^{5gs} 13^{6gs} **0-3-13 £1,263**

Playtime Blue *Mrs H Sweeting* 68 a77
4 b g Komaite (USA) - Miss Calculate
2^{6sw} 9^{6sd} 1^{5ss} 2^{6sw} 1^{5sw} 4^{5s} 3^{5gs}
10^{5hy} 6^{5gf} 7^{5gf} 5^{5f} 3^{5gs} 3^{5gf} 9^{5g} 7^{5gf} 10^{6gf}
9^{6sd} 9^{5sd} **2-7-19 £11,721**

Plea Bargain *J H M Gosden*   90
2 b c Machiavellian (USA) - Time Saved
3⁸ᵍˢ 1⁷ˢ **1-1-2 £5,085**

Pleasant *L G Cottrell*   74
3 b f Topanoora - Devon Peasant
4¹⁰ᵍᶠ 2¹⁰ᵍˢ 12¹⁰ᵍ 8¹⁰ˢ **0-1-4 £1,414**

Pleasantly Perfect (USA) *Richard E Mandella*   a128
6 b h Pleasant Colony (USA) - Regal State (USA)
1⁹ᶠᵗ 1¹⁰ᶠᵗ 2⁹ᶠᵗ 1¹⁰ᶠᵗ 3¹⁰ᶠᵗ **3-1-5**
£2,703,911

Pleasure Seeker *M D I Usher*   54
3 b f First Trump - Purse
7⁶ˢ 9⁸ᶠ 9⁸ᶠ 10⁷ˢ 6¹⁰ʰʸ **0-0-5**

Pleasure Time *C Smith*   17 a47
11 ch g Clantime - First Experience
5⁵ˢˢ 7⁵ˢˢ 10⁶ˢᵈ 1⁵ˢᵈ 6⁵ˢᵈ 16⁶ᶠ 7⁵ˢᵈ **1-0-7**
£1,435

Plenty Cried Wolf *R A Fahey*   70 a63
2 b g Wolfhound (USA) - Plentitude (Fr)
17⁶ᵍˢ 14⁶ᵍˢ 4⁷ᶠ 7⁷ᶠ 3⁷ᵍᶠ 6⁹ˢᵈ 3⁷ˢ **0-2-7**
£1,109

Plovers Lane (Ire) *M P Tregoning*   49
3 b g Dushyantor (USA) - Sweet Alma
14¹⁰ᵍ 8¹²ᵍᶠ **0-0-2**

Plum *E F Vaughan*   77
4 br f Pivotal - Rose Chime (Ire)
1⁷ʰʸ 7⁷ˢ **1-0-2 £3,523**

Plummet (USA) *J H M Gosden*   82
3 b f Silver Hawk (USA) - Fairy Heights (Ire)
4¹⁰ᵍᶠ 2¹⁰ᵍᶠ 3¹⁰ᵍᶠ **0-2-3 £2,756**

Plumpie Mac (Ire) *N Bycroft*   44
3 b f Key Of Luck (USA) - Petrine (Ire)
6⁷ˢ 11⁷ᵍˢ 16⁸ᵍᶠ **0-0-3**

Plungington Tavern (Ire) *P A Blockley*   20
2 b c Josr Algarhoud (Ire) - Hever Golf Lady
9⁷ˢ **0-0-1**

Plutocrat *L Lungo*   79
8 b g Polar Falcon (USA) - Choire Mhor
2¹⁶ᵍᶠ 10¹²ᵍᶠ **0-1-2 £2,064**

Poacher's Paradise *M W Easterby*   31 a22
3 ch g Inchinor - Transylvania
12⁶ˢᵈ 8⁶ˢˢ 6¹⁰ˢˢ 10⁸ˢ **0-0-4**

Pocketwood *Jean-Rene Auvray*   49
2 b g Fleetwood (Ire) - Pocket Venus (Ire)
11⁷ᵍᶠ **0-0-1**

Poetical (Ire) *M J Grassick*   101
3 ch f Croco Rouge (USA) - Abyat (USA)
3⁸ᵍᶠ 1⁸ᵍᶠ 12⁷ᵍᶠ 3⁷ʰʸ 15⁸ʸˢ **1-2-5**
£14,192

Poetry 'n Passion *C A Cyzer*   46 a33
3 b f Polish Precedent (USA) - Ghassanah
7⁸ˢ 7⁶ᵍˢ 10⁷ˢᵈ 5¹¹ˢ **0-0-4**

Point Calimere (Ire) *Liam McAteer*   73 a65
3 b g Fasliyev (USA) - Mountain Ash
7⁵ˢᵈ 4⁶ᵍˢ 5⁵ˢ 16⁷ᵍ 15⁶ˢ 14⁶ᵍᶠ 16⁷ʸ
16⁵ʸˢ 2⁷ˢ **1-1-10 £4,908**

Point Man (Ire) *J W Payne*   31 a21
4 b g Pivotal - Pursuit Of Truth (USA)
8⁶ˢᵈ 3⁸ᵍ 4⁷ˢᵈ **0-0-3 £185**

Point Of Dispute *P J Makin*   88 a86
9 b g Cyrano De Bergerac - Opuntia
5⁷ᵍᶠ 2⁷ᵍ 8⁷ᵍˢ 4⁷ˢᵈ 9⁷ˢᵈ 3⁷ˢᵈ **0-2-6**
£3,038

Pointed (Ire) *Mrs J Candlish*   42
3 br f Selkirk (USA) - Tragic Point (Ire)

15⁷ᵍˢ 10¹⁰ᵍᶠ 3¹⁰ᶠ 13¹⁴ˢᵈ **0-1-4 £546**

Poise (Ire) *Sir Michael Stoute*   87
3 b f Rainbow Quest (USA) - Crepe Ginger (Ire)
1¹⁰ᵍᶠ **1-0-1 £4,290**

Poker *Mrs J Candlish*   6 a51
3 ch g Hector Protector (USA) - Clunie
1⁸ˢᵈ 14⁸ˢ 18⁷ᵍ 13⁹ˢᵈ **1-0-4 £2,933**

Poker Player (Ire) *B J Meehan*   76
2 ch g Raise A Grand (Ire) - Look Nonchalant (Ire)
5⁶ˢ **0-0-1**

Polanski Mill *C A Horgan*   55 a15
5 b g Polish Precedent (USA) - Mill On The Floss
PU¹⁴ˢ 11¹³ᵍᶠ 9¹⁷ᵍ 10¹⁶ᵍᶠ 10¹⁶ˢᵈ **0-0-5**

Polar Bear *W J Haggas*   116
4 ch g Polar Falcon (USA) - Aim For The Top (USA)
3⁷ˢ 24⁸ᵍᶠ 1⁷ˢ 1⁷ˢ 7⁸ᵍ 3⁷ˢ **2-2-6**
£50,236

Polar Ben *J R Fanshawe*   116
5 b g Polar Falcon (USA) - Woodbeck
2⁷ᵍˢ 2⁷ᵍᶠ 1⁸ᵍ 9⁷ˢ **1-2-5 £42,200**

Polar Dancer *Mrs A J Perrett*   63
3 b f Polar Falcon (USA) - Petonica (Ire)
18¹²ˢ 3¹⁰ᵍ 11¹²ᵍᶠ 11¹²ᵍˢ 3¹⁰ᵍᶠ 3¹⁰ᵍ 8¹¹ᵍˢ
0-2-7 £2,504

Polar Dawn *B R Millman*   72
2 b f Polar Falcon (USA) - Leave At Dawn
2⁶ᵍᶠ 6⁶ᵍᶠ 4⁷ᵍˢ 1⁷ᵍˢ 10⁶ˢ **1-1-5 £8,254**

Polar Force *Miss K B Boutflower*   45 a68
4 ch g Polar Falcon (USA) - Irish Light (USA)
4⁶ˢᵈ 9⁶ˢᵈ 7⁶ˢᵈ 3⁶ˢᵈ 16⁵ᵍ 3⁶ᵍᶠ 10⁶ᶠ **0-1-7**
£894

Polar Galaxy *C W Fairhurst*   47 a20
3 br f Polar Falcon (USA) - June Brilly (Ire)
9⁷ᵍᶠ 5⁸ᵍᶠ 12⁸ᵍᶠ 4⁶ᵍ 10⁶ˢᵈ **0-0-5**

Polar Haze *J Pearce*   50 a66
7 ch g Polar Falcon (USA) - Sky Music
4⁶ˢᵈ 2⁶ˢᵈ 6⁶ˢˢ 1⁶ˢᵈ 5⁶ˢᵈ 7⁶ˢˢ 4⁶ˢˢ 5⁶ˢᵈ
5⁶ˢᵈ 8⁷ᵍᶠ 4⁶ᵍᶠ 13⁶ᶠ 2⁶ᵍˢ **1-2-13 £3,790**

Polar Impact *G L Moore*   81
5 br h Polar Falcon (USA) - Boozy
1⁷ˢᵈ 12⁷ˢ 5⁶ᵍ 16⁶ᶠ 4⁵ᵍᶠ 5⁶ᵍˢ 9⁶ˢ **2-1-7**
£14,607

Polar Jem *G G Margarson*   101
4 b f Polar Falcon (USA) - Top Jem
3¹⁰ˢ 4¹⁰ˢ 1¹⁰ᵍᶠ 1¹⁰ᵍᶠ 1⁹ᵍ 1¹⁰ᵍᶠ 6¹⁰ᵍ 3¹⁰ᵍ
2¹²ᵍᶠ 1¹⁰ᵍ 6¹²ᵍᶠ **5-2-11 £60,808**

Polar Kingdom *T D Barron*   82 a90
6 b g Pivotal - Scarlet Lake
3⁶ˢᵈ 1⁶ˢᵈ 1⁷ˢᵈ 10⁶ˢˢ 12⁶ᵍˢ 3⁶ᵍ 12⁶ˢ
2-2-7 £17,654

Polar Magic *J R Fanshawe*   81 a88
3 ch c Polar Falcon (USA) - Enchant
1⁷ˢ 2⁷ᵍˢ 1⁷ˢᵈ **2-1-3 £14,280**

Polar Passion *R Hollinshead*   36
2 b f Polar Prince (Ire) - Priorite (Ire)
5⁷ᵍ 11⁶ʰʸ **0-0-2**

Polar Sun *J R Fanshawe*   67
3 b g Polar Falcon (USA) - Barford Lady
6⁷ᵍᶠ 3⁷ᵍ 6⁶ˢ **0-1-3 £836**

Polar Tryst *Lady Herries*   75
5 ch m Polar Falcon (USA) - Lovers Tryst
1¹³ᶠ 12¹²ᵍᶠ **1-0-2 £3,672**

Polar Way *Mrs A J Perrett*   121
5 ch g Polar Falcon (USA) - Fetish
14⁶ᶠ 3⁷ᵍ 2⁷ᵍᶠ 9⁷ᵍ 1⁷ᵍˢ 3⁷ᵍ 4⁷ˢ **1-3-7**

£55,926

Pole Star *J R Fanshawe*   80
6 b/br g Polar Falcon (USA) - Ellie Ardensky
10^{16s} **0-0-1**

Polesworth *C N Kellett*   44 a27
2 b f Wizard King - Nicholas Mistress
5^{7sd} 10^{7s} 10^{7gf} **0-0-3**

Polish Baron (Ire) *J R Cornwall*
7 b g Barathea (Ire) - Polish Mission
6^{12sd} **0-0-1**

Polish Eagle *E A L Dunlop*   78
2 b c Polish Precedent (USA) - Tinashaan (Ire)
11^{8s} 2^{7s} **0-1-2 £1,290**

Polish Emperor (USA) *W R Swinburn*   88 a84
4 ch g Polish Precedent (USA) - Empress Jackie (USA)
4^{6sd} 2^{5sd} 2^{5sd} 5^{5s} 16^{6g} 3^{5gf} 13^{6g}
8^{5gf} 10^{5g} 6^{5s} 10^{5g} 1^{5gf} 7^{5sd} **2-3-14**
£16,349

Polish Index *J R Jenkins*   1
2 b c Polish Precedent (USA) - Glossary
17^{8gf} **0-0-1**

Polish Rhapsody (Ire) *J A Supple*   a38
3 b f Charnwood Forest (Ire) - Polish Rhythm (Ire)
11^{8sd} 11^{7sd} 6^{10s} 9^{10sd} **0-0-4**

Polish Rose *E F Vaughan*   57
3 ch f Polish Precedent (USA) - Messila Rose
8^{7gf} 5^{8f} 8^{10hy} **0-0-3**

Polish Spirit *B R Millman*   70
9 b g Emarati (USA) - Gentle Star
14^{9gf} 7^{8gf} 6^{10gf} 1^{10gs} 19^{12gs} **1-0-5**
£4,358

Polka Princess *M Wellings*   a40
4 b f Makbul - Liberatrice (Fr)
12^{9sd} 13^{11sd} 7^{13sd} 3^{16sd} 13^{12sd} 10^{12sd}
9^{12sd} 12^{12sd} 5^{15sd} **0-1-9 £209**

Pollito (Ire) *B J Meehan*   75 a73
2 b g Rossini (USA) - Bezee
5^{6gf} 6^{6gf} 4^{7g} 3^{8sd} **0-1-4 £967**

Polly Alexander (Ire) *M J Wallace*   88
2 ch f Foxhound (USA) - Fiveofive (Ire)
5^{5s} 1^{5s} 1^{5gs} 3^{5g} 2^{6g} 1^{6g} 9^{6gf} 7^{6g} 14^{6s}
3-1-9 £33,249

Polly Perkins (Ire) *N P Littmoden*   101
2 b f Pivotal - Prospering
1^{5gf} 1^{5gf} 11^{5gf} 8^{6gf} 1^{5gs} **3-0-5**
£32,755

Polonius *H Candy*   78
3 b g Great Dane (Ire) - Bridge Pool
6^{7gs} **0-0-1 £386**

Polygonal (Fr) *Mrs J R Ramsden*   104
4 b g Octagonal (NZ) - Sectarine (Fr)
1^{10s} 3^{10g} 6^{9gf} 19^{10g} 5^{10gf} 1^{10gf} 8^{10gf}
2-1-7 £22,092

Pomfret Lad *D Nicholls*   92
6 b g Cyrano De Bergerac - Lucky Flinders
19^{5g} 14^{6gs} 12^{6gs} 14^{bg} 22^{6s} 12^{7g} 17^{6g}
18^{5g} **0-0-8**

Pompey Blue *P J McBride*   54 a63
3 b f Abou Zouz (USA) - Habla Me (Ire)
5^{6sd} 5^{6sd} 7^{5sd} 7^{6g} 9^{5gf} 12^{5gf} 8^{5gs} **0-0-7**

Pompey Chimes *G B Balding*   42
4 b g Forzando - Silver Purse
4^{6s} 13^{7gs} 15^{6gf} **0-0-3 £418**

Pon My Soul (Ire) *M G Quinlan*   62

2 b g Imperial Ballet (Ire) - Erin Anam Cara (Ire)
17^{gs} 6^{7gf} 8^{8g} 6^{8g} **1-0-4 £3,160**

Ponderon *R F Johnson Houghton*   92
4 ch g Hector Protector (USA) - Blush Rambler (USA)
8^{16gs} 6^{19gs} 11^{16g} **0-0-3 £1,800**

Ponente *B W Hills*   59
2 b f Robellino (USA) - Polmara (Ire)
6^{6gs} 9^{7gf} 3^{7s} **0-1-3 £425**

Pongee *L M Cumani*   109
4 b f Barathea (Ire) - Puce
3^{12g} 1^{12gf} 1^{12g} 2^{14gf} 2^{12s} **2-3-5**
£148,807

Pont Allaire (Ire) *H Candy*   79
3 b f Rahy (USA) - Leonila (Ire)
1^{8s} 7^{10g} 5^{8gf} **1-0-3 £3,738**

Pont Neuf (Ire) *P D Evans*   74 a58
4 b f Revoque (Ire) - Petite Maxine
13^{10sd} 8^{12sd} 4^{12sw} 2^{12gf} 5^{12g} 1^{12gs} 1^{12gf}
7^{12gf} 2^{12gs} 3^{12s} 9^{12g} 15^{14g} 9^{12sd} 11^{12sd} **2-3-14**
£9,921

Pooka's Daughter (Ire) *J M Bradley*   a35
4 b f Eagle Eyed (USA) - Gaelic's Fantasy (Ire)
5^{8sd} 7^{7sd} 10^{8sd} 7^{6sd} 8^{8ss} 2^{7ss} 14^{7sd}
12^{7sd} **0-1-8 £366**

Pop Up Again *G A Swinbank*   72
4 ch f Bahamian Bounty - Bellair
8^{7f} 9^{8gf} 12^{7s} 15^{6gf} 12^{7gs} **0-0-5**

Pope's Hill (Ire) *L M Cumani*   77
3 b c Sadler's Wells (USA) - Ghost Tree (Ire)
4^{12gf} 4^{12gf} 6^{12gf} 3^{11gf} 4^{16gf} 4^{16gs} 6^{16gf}
0-1-7 £2,238

Poppyfields *M Blanshard*   27
2 b f Danzero (Aus) - Shalverton (Ire)
17^{7gs} **0-0-1**

Poppyline *W R Muir*   57 a54
4 b f Averti (Ire) - Shalverton (Ire)
9^{7sd} 11^{8gf} UR^{8f} 3^{8f} 6^{8gf} 3^{8g} 10^{7gf} 7^{8f}
6^{6gs} 5^{6gf} 4^{6gf} **0-2-11 £1,078**

Poppys Footprint (Ire) *K A Ryan*   83
3 ch f Titus Livius (Fr) - Mica Male (Ity)
21^{7g} 11^{7g} 10^{6gs} 5^{8gs} 3^{7gf} 4^{7gf} 9^{7f} PU^{8g}
1^{8f} 10^{8s} **1-1-10 £8,375**

Porlezza (Fr) *Y De Nicolay*   117
5 ch m Sicyos (USA) - Pupsi (Fr)
1^{5g} 2^{5gs} 8^{6gs} 14^{7gs} **1-1-4 £32,113**

Port 'n Starboard *C A Cyzer*   67 a58
3 ch g Polar Falcon (USA) - Sally Slade
4^{11gf} 5^{10gf} 4^{10gs} 4^{11gs} 12^{12sd} 11^{10sd} **0-0-6**
£739

Port D'Argent (Ire) *M Johnston*   54
2 b f Docksider (USA) - Petite-D-Argent
10^{7gs} **0-0-1**

Port Moreno (Ire) *J G M O'Shea*   22 a33
4 b g Turtle Island (Ire) - Infra Blue (Ire)
5^{16sd} 9^{12sw} 18^{17g} **0-0-3**

Port Natal (Ire) *Patrick Morris*   47 a47
6 b g Selkirk (USA) - Play Around (Ire)
7^{7sd} 2^{6sd} UR^{8sw} 7^{6sw} 1^{8y} 6^{8hy} 13^{6gf} 12^{6y}
13^{8sh} **1-1-9 £4,851**

Port Sodrick *C L Tizzard*   61 a58
3 b/br g Young Ern - Keepsake (Ire)
6^{8sd} 6^{8gf} 4^{10sd} 5^{10g} 9^{10gf} 7^{13gs} 2^{17s} **0-1-7**
£1,052

Port St Charles (Ire) *P R Chamings*   67 a78
7 b/br g Night Shift (USA) - Safe Haven

5^6sd 11^6sd 9^6sd 12^6sw 4^8ss 4^6g 15^6gs
8^6gf 4^5f 3^5g 7^5gf 7^5f 14^5g 4^6gf 7^5gf 6^5f
12^5gs 2^6sd 7^6gs **0-2-19 £2,297**

Porthcawl *Mrs A J Perrett*   84
3 b f Singspiel (Ire) - Dodo (Ire)
1^8s 1^8g 10^8gf **2-0-3 £13,820**

Portichol Princess *R M Stronge*
4 b f Bluegrass Prince (Ire) - Barbrallen
6^10sd **0-0-1**

Portmanteau *Sir Michael Stoute*   93
3 b f Barathea (Ire) - Dayanata
13^8gs 1^10gf 8^9gf 1^10gf 2^10gf **2-1-5**
£13,618

Portmeirion *E F Vaughan*   57
3 b f Polish Precedent (USA) - India Atlanta
10^8gs **0-0-1**

Portrait Of A Lady (Ire) *H R A Cecil*   99
3 ch f Peintre Celebre (USA) - Starlight Smile (USA)
3^12s 1^12gf 3^12gf 1^12gf 1^12g 3^12g 6^14gf
3-3-7 £25,126

Posh Nosh (Ire) *Patrick Martin*   54
3 b f Alzao (USA) - Frenzy
12^10g 7^10g 13^8v 19^10gf 14^8sd **0-0-5**

Posh Sheelagh *J G Given*   a18
3 b f Danzero (Aus) - Button Hole Flower (Ire)
9^7sd **0-0-1**

Posteritas (USA) *H R A Cecil*   93
3 b f Lear Fan (USA) - Imroz (USA)
3^8gf 2^8f 1^10gf 5^10g 1^10hy 6^10g 11^12gf
2-2-7 £26,040

Postgraduate (Ire) *H Morrison*   a79
2 b c Almutawakel - Institutrice (Ire)
5^7sd 1^6sd **1-0-2 £5,096**

Potent Heir (USA) *Saeed Bin Suroor*   86
2 b c Forest Wildcat (USA) - Penniless Heiress (USA)
1^6g **1-0-1 £4,813**

Potsdam *Niall Moran*   54 a50
6 ch g Rainbow Quest (USA) - Danilova (USA)
7^8sd 2^7ss 7^8hy 4^7f 1^8gf PU^7f **1-2-6**
£5,111

Pouilly Fume *D J S Ffrench Davis*   2
3 b f Polish Precedent (USA) - Feather Bride (Ire)
18^10s **0-0-1**

Poule De Luxe (Ire) *J L Dunlop*   69
3 b f Cadeaux Genereux - Likely Story (Ire)
1^7gs 13^7s **1-0-2 £5,590**

Power And Demand *K G Wingrove*   a9
7 b g Formidable (USA) - Mazurkanova
4^8sd 8^7sd **0-0-2**

Power Bird (Ire) *R Flint*   45 a58
4 b f Bluebird (USA) - Polynesian Goddess (Ire)
2^7sd 11^7sd 9^8sd 13^7gf 8^7sd 5^6gf 12^8gf
0-1-7 £852

Power Nap *N Tinkler*   33
3 b f Acatenango (Ger) - Dreams Are Free (Ire)
6^10g 9^7g 13^12gf 9^10gf 16^7gs **0-0-5**

Power To Burn *K Bell*   22 a53
3 b g Superpower - Into The Fire
3^6sd 5^6ss 9^6gs 17^6gs **0-1-4 £421**

Powerful Parrish (USA) *P F I Cole*   74
3 b f Quiet American (USA) - Parish Business (USA)
11^8gf 2^8gf 4^10f 12^10g 7^10gf 8^12f **0-1-6**
£1,420

Powerscourt *A P O'Brien*   124
4 b c Sadler's Wells (USA) - Rainbow Lake

11^11gf 2^10gf 5^10gs 2^10g 4^10f 3^10gf 3^12y
1-4-7 £439,612

Prague *J R Boyle*   a8
6 b g Cyrano De Bergerac - Basenite
14^10sd **0-0-1**

Prairie Falcon (Ire) *B W Hills*   89
10 b g Alzao (USA) - Sea Harrier
3^12g 7^12gf 9^16g PU^15gf **0-1-4 £1,487**

Prairie Law (Ger) *Ian Williams*   46
4 b g Law Society (USA) - Prairie Charm (Ire)
1^12sd 8^10sd 7^12sd 6^10g 4^10gf 3^10gs 9^16gf
13^12g **1-1-8 £1,965**

Prairie Oyster *D R C Elsworth*   8
3 b f Emperor Jones (USA) - Soba Up
11^9gf **0-0-1**

Prairie Sun (Ger) *Mrs A Duffield*   58 a45
3 b f Law Society (USA) - Prairie Flame (Ire)
4^12sd 4^12gs 5^15gs 1^12gf 7^12g 10^12sd 10^10gf
6^12gf 10^12gf 6^14gf 3^14gf **1-1-11 £4,873**

Prairie Wolf *M L W Bell*   82
8 ch g Wolfhound (USA) - Bay Queen
15^10s 14^10gs 9^10gf 10^10gf 5^10g 1^10gs 9^10g
9^10g 13^10gf 7^10s **1-0-10 £3,861**

Prakara (Ire) *L M Cumani*   17
2 ch f Indian Ridge - Prima Volta
15^7gs **0-0-1**

Pralin Star (Ire) *Mrs H Sweeting*   52
2 ch g Daggers Drawn - Polaregina (Fr)
15^7g 4^7hy 12^8gf **0-0-3 £263**

Prayerful *R H Alner*   45
5 b m Syrtos - Pure Formality
5^11g **0-0-1**

Pre Eminance (Ire) *C R Egerton*   70
3 b c Peintre Celebre (USA) - Sorb Apple (Ire)
6^8gf **0-0-1**

Precious Freedom *J Balding*   a12
4 b g Ashkalani (Ire) - Prayers'n Promises (USA)
10^6sd 15^6sd 7^5sd **0-0-3**

Precious Mystery (Ire) *A King*   70 a55
4 ch f Titus Livius (Fr) - Ascoli
4^12gf 2^12gs 12^12sd 1^12s 6^14s **1-1-5**
£6,151

Precious Sammi *Julian Poulton*   42 a53
2 b g Mark Of Esteem (Ire) - Night Over Day
8^7gs 5^7sd 11^8gs 9^7sd **0-0-4**

Pregnant Pause (Ire) *S Kirk*   58 a51
3 b g General Monash (USA) - Dissidentia (Ire)
4^5sd 10^7sd 4^8f 5^8f 4^8f **0-0-5 £549**

Prelude *W M Brisbourne*   63
3 b f Danzero (Aus) - Dancing Debut
5^7gs 8^8gf 8^10g 6^12gf 6^11gf 1^10gs 5^12gf
10^12g **1-0-9 £3,863**

Premier Dream (USA) *J G M O'Shea*   73
3 ch c Woodman (USA) - Marina Duff
6^8s 6^8g 3^8gs 1^8hy 14^8gf 4^8g 11^8gs 14^10gf
1-1-8 £5,178

Premier Fantasy *T D Barron*   90
2 b c Pivotal - Hemaca
6^6gs 1^5g **1-0-2 £4,979**

Premier Rouge *E F Vaughan*   75
3 b g Croco Rouge (Ire) - Petit Point (Ire)
4^7g 4^8g 3^10gs 2^8s 3^8hy 8^8gs **0-2-6**
£3,184

Premier Times *M D Hammond*   52
2 ch g Timeless Times (USA) - Lady Magician

5⁵ᵍˢ 1⁶ˢ 6⁷ᵍᶠ 7⁶ᵍᶠ 8⁷ˢ **1-0-5 £3,250**

Prenup (Ire) *L M Cumani* 82
3 ch f Diesis - Mutual Consent (Ire)
4¹²ˢ 1¹⁰ᶠ 1¹²ᵍ 2¹²ᵍᶠ 2¹¹ˢ 8¹²ᵍᶠ 6¹²ᶠ **2-3-7**
£13,756

Present 'n Correct *J M Bradley* a4
11 ch g Cadeaux Genereux - Emerald Eagle
9⁷ˢᵈ 8⁷ˢᵈ 10⁶ˢᵈ **0-0-3**

Present Oriented (USA) *H R A Cecil* 76
3 ch c Southern Halo (USA) - Shy Beauty (Can)
5¹⁰ᵍ 8¹⁰ᵍ **0-0-2**

Preskani *Mrs N Macauley* 24 a25
2 b g Sri Pekan (USA) - Lamarita
16⁷ᵍᶠ 12⁵ˢᵈ 13⁶ᵍˢ 9⁶ˢᵈ **0-0-4**

Press Express (Ire) *M R Channon* 78
2 ch c Entrepreneur - Nawaji (USA)
7⁷ˢ 6⁷ˢ 1⁷ᵍᶠ 8⁸ᵍ 13⁶ˢ 7⁷ˢ **1-0-6**
£3,620

Presto Shinko (Ire) *R Hannon* 89 a70
3 b g Shinko Forest (Ire) - Swift Chorus
1⁶ˢᵈ 6⁶ˢ 3⁶ˢ 2⁶ᵍᶠ 1⁶ᵍ 3⁶ᵍᶠ 4⁶ᵍˢ 12⁶ᵍˢ
2-2-8 £19,659

Presto Vento *R Hannon* 79
4 b f Air Express (Ire) - Placement
7⁶ᵍ 11⁷ˢ **0-0-2**

Preston Hall *Mrs L C Jewell* 44 a55
3 b g Accordion - Little Preston (Ire)
7¹⁰ˢᵈ 8¹⁰ˢᵈ 6⁷ᵍˢ 5¹⁰ᵍᶠ 12¹²ᵍˢ **0-0-5**

Presumptive (Ire) *R Charlton* 89
4 b g Danehill (USA) - Demure
5⁷ˢ 3⁸ᵍ 13⁸ᵍ 1⁷ᵍˢ 17⁷ˢ 10⁷ᵍ **1-1-6**
£12,384

Pretty Kool *S C Williams* 57 a53
4 b f Inchinor - Carrie Kool
10⁸ᵍᶠ 5⁶ᵍᶠ 3⁷ˢᵈ 1⁶ᵍˢ 7⁷ᵍ 13⁶ᵍ **1-1-6**
£3,446

Pretty Star (Ger) *M Johnston* 98
4 b c Lando (Ger) - Pretty Ballerina
8¹²ᵍ 12¹²ᵍˢ 15¹²ᵍ **0-1-3 £3,555**

Pretty Woman (Ire) *S C Williams* 26
2 ch f Night Shift (USA) - Kind Of Cute
11⁵ᵍᶠ 10⁵ᵍᶠ **0-0-2**

Pride Of Kinloch *J Hetherton* 64 a43
4 ch f Dr Devious (Ire) - Stormswept (USA)
7⁶ˢᵈ 6⁷ˢᵈ 9⁷ᵍˢ 4⁸ᵍˢ 13⁸ʰʸ 3⁷ᶠ 7⁷ᵍᶠ 9⁶ᵍᶠ
17⁶ᵍ 3⁶ˢ 2⁶ᵍᶠ 6⁶ᵍᶠ 15⁶ᶠ 15⁸ʰʸ **0-4-14**
£3,129

Pride Of London (Ire) *I A Wood* 54
2 b f Danetime (Ire) - Kavana (Ire)
17⁶ᵍ 8⁷ᵍᶠ 12⁷ᵍˢ **0-0-3**

Pride Of Poona (Ire) *R M H Cowell* a35
2 b f Indian Ridge - Scandalous
8⁶ˢᵈ 8⁷ˢᵈ **0-0-2**

Pridewood Dove *R J Price*
5 b m Alderbrook - Flighty Dove
11¹⁰ᵍ PU¹⁸ᵍᶠ **0-0-2**

Prideyev (USA) *B J Llewellyn*
4 ch g Nureyev (USA) - Pride Of Baino (USA)
9¹⁶ˢʷ **0-0-1**

Prima Stella *J A R Toller* 42 a79
5 gr m Primo Dominie - Raffelina (USA)
4⁶ˢᵈ 1⁶ˢᵈ 10⁷ˢᵈ 2⁷ˢᵈ 6⁶ˢʷ 6⁷ˢᵈ 12⁶ˢᵈ 7⁶ᵍᶠ
8⁶ᵍᶠ **1-1-9 £6,584**

Primarily *A Berry* 61 a55
2 b c Mind Games - Prim N Proper

11⁵ᵍᶠ 5⁶ʰʸ 2⁶ᵍ 3⁷ˢ 6⁶ˢᵈ **0-2-5 £1,477**

Primatech (Ire) *K A Morgan* 49
3 b f Priolo (USA) - Ida Lupino (Ire)
19⁵ᵍᶠ 7⁷ᵍ 8¹²ᵍᶠ 11⁷ᶠ 14⁹ᵍ 8⁷ᵍˢ 4⁸ᶠ 9⁸ᵍˢ
3⁷ᵍˢ **0-1-9 £214**

Prime Contender *B W Hills* 65
2 b c Efisio - Gecko Rouge
7⁶ˢ 5⁶ᵍˢ **0-0-2**

Prime Offer *J Jay* 73 a69
8 b g Primo Dominie - Single Bid
13⁷ˢˢ 2⁸ˢᵈ 4⁸ˢᵈ 1⁸ᶠ 2⁷ᶠ 18⁹ᶠ 5⁸ˢ 4⁸ᶠ 2⁷ˢ
18⁸ᵍᶠ **2-3-10 £9,877**

Prime Powered (Ire) *G L Moore* 92
3 b g Barathea (Ire) - Caribbean Quest
5¹⁰ᵍ 5¹⁰ᵍ 8¹²ᵍ 2¹⁰ᵍ 8¹⁰ᵍ 4¹¹ᵍ 14¹⁰ʰʸ **0-1-7**
£5,554

Prime Recreation *P S Felgate* 77 a72
7 b g Primo Dominie - Night Transaction
6⁵ˢᵈ 16⁵ˢᵈ 6⁵ˢᵈ 8⁵ˢʷ 9⁵ˢ 15⁵ᵍˢ 3⁵ᵍ 9⁵ᵍᶠ
12⁵ᵍ 4⁵ᵍ 11⁵ᵍᶠ 12⁵ˢ 15⁵ 8⁵ᵍ 3⁵ˢ **1-2-15**
£9,383

Primed Up (Ire) *G L Moore*
2 b g Rainbow Quest (USA) - Cape Mist (USA)
12⁷ᵍᶠ **0-0-1**

Primeshade Promise *D Burchell* 50
3 ch f Opening Verse (USA) - Bonnie Lassie
13⁸ᵍᶠ 11¹⁰ᵍᶠ 3⁷ᵍᶠ 8⁸ʰʸ 7⁸ᵍ **0-1-5 £534**

Primo Way *B W Hills* 93 a84
3 b c Primo Dominie - Waypoint
1⁶ᵍˢ 3⁶ᵍ 6⁶ᵍᶠ 3⁷ᶠ 11⁷ᵍᶠ 3⁷ᵍˢ 14⁷ᵍ 7⁷ˢᵈ
1-3-8 £7,142

Primus Inter Pares (Ire) *D Nicholls* 104
3 b g Sadler's Wells (USA) - Life At The Top
1⁸ᵍ 16⁸ᵍˢ **1-0-2 £8,856**

Prince Aaron (Ire) *C N Allen* 99 a91
4 b g Marju (Ire) - Spirito Libro (USA)
1⁶ˢᵈ 1⁶ˢᵈ 6⁶ˢᵈ 2⁶ˢᵈ 16⁶ˢᵈ 3⁶ᵍᶠ 16⁶ᵍᶠ 5⁶ᵍ
1⁷ᵍ 1⁶ᵍˢ 24⁶ˢ **6-2-11 £52,362**

Prince Albert *J R Jenkins* 31
6 ch g Rock City - Russell Creek
8⁸ᵍˢ 11¹⁰ˢ 3¹⁰ʰʸ **0-1-3 £215**

Prince Charming *J H M Gosden* 105
2 b c Royal Applause - Miss Primula
1⁵ᵍˢ 1⁵ˢ 8⁵ᵍᶠ 6⁵ʰʸ 1⁵ˢ 8⁶ᵍ 5⁵ˢ 4⁶ᵛˢ **3-0-8**
£39,953

Prince Cyrano *W J Musson* 79
5 b g Cyrano De Bergerac - Odilese
22⁶ᵍ 15⁶ᵍˢ 14⁶ᵍ 6⁷ˢ 11⁷ᵍᶠ 3⁶ᵍᶠ 5⁶ᵍᶠ 2⁵ˢ
9⁵ˢ 13⁵ᵍˢ 8⁵ᵍ **0-2-11 £3,505**

Prince Dayjur (USA) *D Nicholls* 85
5 b/br g Dayjur (USA) - Distinct Beauty (USA)
18⁶ᵍᶠ 16⁶ᶠ 11⁵ᵍᶠ 7⁶ᵍᶠ **1-0-4 £5,499**

Prince Du Soleil (Fr) *J R Jenkins* 24 a40
8 b g Cardoun (Fr) - Revelry (Fr)
6⁸ˢᵈ 6⁸ˢᵈ 8¹⁰ˢᵈ 8⁷ᶠ **0-0-4**

Prince Hector *W J Haggas* 86
5 ch g Hector Protector (USA) - Ceanothus (Ire)
10⁶ᵍˢ 2⁶ᵍᶠ 6⁷ᵍᶠ 2⁸ᵍᶠ 4⁷ᵍ **0-2-5 £3,838**

Prince Holing *M Todhunter* 69
4 ch g Halling (USA) - Ella Mon Amour
5¹⁰ˢ 7¹³ᵍ 8¹²ᵍ 8¹²ᵍˢ 7¹⁴ᵍᶠ **0-0-5 £397**

Prince Ivor *M J Gingell* a37
4 b g Polar Falcon (USA) - Mistook (USA)
9¹⁰ˢᵈ 7¹⁰ˢᵈ 8¹⁰ˢᵈ 19¹⁰ᵍ **0-0-4**

Prince Kirk (Fr) *E Borromeo* 121

4 b c Selkirk (USA) - Princess Manila (Can)
1^{10g} 3^{10hy} 1^{9g} **2-0-3 £122,045**

Prince Minata (Ire) *P W Hiatt*   40 a39
9 b g Machiavellian (USA) - Aminata
8^{12sd} 13^{10sd} 3^{8sd} 10^{8sd} 4^{12gs} 11^{8sd} 6^{8sd}
0-1-7 £208

Prince Namid *Mrs A Duffield*   71
2 b c Namid - Fen Princess (Ire)
4^{5g} 3^{5hy} 1^{5s} **1-1-3 £4,187**

Prince Nasseem (Ger) *A G Juckes*
7 b h Neshad (USA) - Penola (Ger)
7^{16sw} **0-0-1**

Prince Nureyev (Ire) *B R Millman*   96
4 b g Desert King (Ire) - Annaletta
9^{10gs} 9^{10gs} 9^{12f} 2^{10gs} **0-1-4 £6,600**

Prince Of Aragon *Miss Suzy Smith*   a33
8 b g Aragon - Queens Welcome
7^{7sd} 13^{8sd} **0-0-2**

Prince Of Blues (Ire) *M Mullineaux*   70 a73
6 b g Prince Of Birds (USA) - Reshift
9^{6sw} 2^{5sd} 10^{5sd} 13^{6sw} 10^{5sw} 4^{5sd} 10^{5gs}
4^{5s} 5^{6g} 13^{5gs} 8^{5gf} 3^{6gs} 3^{5gf} 5^{6g} 7^{5g} 7^{10g}
3^{6g} 23^{6gf} 10^{5g} 12^{5gs} **0-3-23**
£7,544

Prince Of Gold *R Hollinshead*   74 a73
4 b c Polar Prince (Ire) - Gold Belt (Ire)
8^{10g} 5^{8sd} 7^{8gs} 7^{8g} 6^{7gf} 7^{8g} 1^{7g} 10^{8f}
10^{8g} 14^{10g} 8^{8gf} 10^{8gf} 13^{7gs} 5^{7gf} 3^{6gf} 2^{5g} 9^{7s}
1^{6sd} 2^{6sd} **2-3-19 £11,000**

Prince Of Perles *D Shaw*   a38
3 b g Mind Games - Pearls
10^{8sd} 14^{7sd} 3^{6ss} 9^{7sd} **0-1-4 £426**

Prince Of The Wood (Ire) *A Bailey*   54 a56
4 ch g Woodborough (USA) - Ard Dauphine (Ire)
2^{16sd} 1^{16sd} 4^{14gf} 7^{18g} 5^{17gf} 9^{16s} 4^{15gf}
1-1-7 £2,123

Prince Of Thebes (Ire) *A M Balding*   97
3 b g Desert Prince (Ire) - Persian Walk (Fr)
1^{8gf} 3^{10gs} **1-1-2 £11,336**

Prince Prospect *Mrs L Stubbs*   27 a55
8 b g Lycius (USA) - Princess Dechtra (Ire)
7^{9sd} 1^{9ss} 2^{9ss} 2^{12sw} 9^{12gs} 8^{9sd} 7^{9gs} **1-2-7**
£2,773

Prince Pyramus *C Grant*   36
6 b g Pyramus (USA) - Rekindled Flame (Ire)
10^{5hy} 18^{5gf} **0-0-2**

Prince Renesis *I W McInnes*   45 a45
3 b g Mind Games - Stoneydale
8^{6s} 10^{7f} 9^{6gf} 6^{10gs} 16^{10gf} 5^{9sd} **0-0-6**

Prince Samos (Ire) *R Hannon*   78 a78
2 b c Mujadil (USA) - Sabaniya (Fr)
4^{6gf} 7^{6gs} 5^{6s} 3^{6sd} 3^{6s} **0-2-5 £2,317**

Prince Slayer *T P McGovern*   a35
8 b g Batshoof - Top Sovereign
9^{10sd} **0-0-1**

Prince Tum Tum (USA) *J L Dunlop*   100
4 b c Capote (USA) - La Grande Epoque (USA)
10^{8gs} 6^{7gf} 4^{7g} 3^{7gs} **0-0-4 £3,714**

Prince Valentine *D B Feek*   62 a38
3 b g My Best Valentine - Affaire De Coeur
10^{10sd} 7^{7sd} 3^{8s} 8^{8hy} 4^{10f} 7^{10f} 4^{10gf} 9^{10sd}
16^{10s} 14^{8g} **0-1-10 £905**

Prince Vector *A King*   71
2 b c Vettori (Ire) - The In-Laws (Ire)
11^{7g} **0-0-1**

Prince Vettori *D J Coakley*   55 a62
2 b c Vettori (Ire) - Bombalarina (Ire)
9^{7g} 8^{8g} 6^{8sd} **0-0-3**

Princeable Lady (Ire) *T D Easterby*   58
2 b f Desert Prince (Ire) - Saucy Maid (Ire)
7^{6gf} 10^{6g} 12^{6gf} 9^{5g} **0-0-4**

Princelet (Ire) *M A Jarvis*   64
2 b c Desert Prince (Ire) - Soeur Ti (Fr)
4^{8s} **0-0-1 £276**

Princely Vale (Ire) *W G M Turner*   70
2 b c Princely Heir (Ire) - Lomalou (Ire)
7^{5g} 4^{8gf} 1^{6f} 1^{7g} 1^{6f} 3^{6gf} 4^{7gf} 5^{6hy} 2^{5s}
3-2-9 £12,337

Princelywallywogan *I A Wood*   63
2 b c Princely Heir (Ire) - Dublivia
6^{7g} **0-0-1**

Princess Alina (Ire) *A M Balding*   a60
3 b f Sadler's Wells (USA) - Eilanden (Ire)
8^{10sd} 8^{10sd} **0-0-2**

Princess Bankes *Miss Gay Kelleway*   39 a26
3 b f Vettori (Ire) - Lady Bankes (Ire)
11^{8sd} 6^{8sd} 11^{6gf} 10^{7sd} 7^{7gf} 4^{10gf} 3^{12f}
15^{10gs} 7^{10gs} **0-1-9 £369**

Princess Erica *J Balding*   49 a18
4 b f Perpendicular - Birichino
15^{6s} 12^{6gs} 11^{6sd} 4^{6gf} 10^{6gf} 9^{6f} **0-0-6**
£441

Princess Galadriel *J R Best*   71 a60
3 b f Magic Ring (Ire) - Prim Lass
2^{6s} 1^{6gf} 3^{6gf} 2^{8f} 7^{10gf} 1^{6gf} 1^{7gf} 6^{7gs}
1^{7s} 3^{8gf} 10^{8hy} 2^{8s} 12^{9sd} **2-6-13 £14,932**

Princess Ismene *M Appleby*   51 a55
3 b f Sri Pekan (USA) - Be Practical
1^{8sd} 5^{8sd} 2^{7sd} 2^{7sd} 4^{7sd} 3^{10sd} 3^{10gf} 4^{8sd}
13^{10g} 5^{8gs} 4^{11gf} 6^{11f} RR^{7gf} 9^{10s} LFT^{8gf} PU^{9sd}
1-3-16 £5,026

Princess Kai (Ire) *R Ingram*   58 a56
3 b f Cayman Kai (Ire) - City Princess
1^{5sd} 9^{5sd} 8^{6sd} 3^{5sd} 4^{5g} 2^{5g} 2^{5gf} 6^{5gf}
13^{6gf} **1-3-9 £6,709**

Princess Kiotto *T D Easterby*   75 a55
3 b f Desert King (Ire) - Ferghana Ma
5^{8g} 2^{12sd} 3^{14g} 1^{16gs} 1^{16gf} 2^{18g} **2-3-6**
£9,297

Princess Links *R Hannon*
2 b f Bahamian Bounty - Miss Prism
15^{8hy} **0-0-1**

Princess Magdalena *L G Cottrell*   42
4 ch f Pennekamp (USA) - Reason To Dance
11^{8s} 7^{12gf} 9^{10gf} 7^{12gs} **0-0-0**

Principal Witness (Ire) *W R Muir*   83 a57
3 b g Definite Article - Double Eight (Ire)
13^{8g} 4^{8gf} 2^{8gf} 26^{8f} 5^{10sd} 13^{8gs} **0-1-6**
£1,565

Principessa *B Palling*   74
3 b f Machiavellian (USA) - Party Doll
5^{8gs} 11^{10g} 9^{10gf} 10^{10gf} 2^{10g} 9^{10gf} 9^{10g}
2^{12gf} 4^{12s} 3^{10g} 2^{10g} 10^{10g} 10^{12sd} **0-5-13**
£6,604

Prins Willem (Ire) *J R Fanshawe*   97
5 b g Alzao (USA) - American Gardens (USA)
2^{12g} 3^{12g} 4^{16g} 5^{14g} 9^{12g} 12^{12g} 3^{12s} **0-3-7**
£7,469

Printsmith (Ire) *J R Norton*   48 a51
7 br m Petardia - Black And Blaze
1^{8sd} 4^{8sd} 4^{7ss} 3^{8sw} 2^{8ss} 1^{8sd} 12^{8sd} 5^{8s}

11^{8s} 9^{8sd} 4^{8g} **2-2-11 £3,626**

Priors Dale *K Bell*   71 a70
4 b g Lahib (USA) - Mathaayl (USA)
2^{10sd} 6^{8sd} 6^{8sd} 4^{8gf} 14^{8g} 14^{8gs} **0-2-6 £1,625**

Prithee *J H M Gosden*   70
2 b f Barathea (Ire) - Bina Ridge
7^{7gs} **0-0-1**

Private Benjamin *Jamie Poulton*   58 a65
4 gr g Ridgewood Ben - Jilly Woo
9^{13sd} 1^{12sd} 7^{12sd} 6^{12sd} 3^{12gf} 9^{10gf} 1^{12gf} 9^{12gf} 5^{12f} 10^{12gs} 12^{12gs} 5^{11g} 3^{16sd} **2-2-13 £8,650**

Private Charter *B W Hills*   109 a86
4 b c Singspiel (Ire) - By Charter
13^{10sd} 2^{10g} 10^{12gf} 6^{11gf} 7^{12gf} 1^{12g} **1-1-6 £22,053**

Private Jessica *J R Fanshawe*   52
3 ch f Cadeaux Genereux - Rose Bay
10^{7g} 9^{6s} 4^{7g} 15^{8sw} 17^{8g} **0-0-5 £259**

Private Seal *Julian Poulton*   50 a49
9 b g King's Signet (USA) - Slender
6^{10sd} 3^{10sd} 2^{12sd} 2^{10sd} 9^{12sd} 12^{12sd} 5^{10sd} 11^{10gf} 8^{10gf} 9^{11f} 3^{10f} 2^{10sd} 6^{10gf} 3^{10gf} 4^{10s} 9^{10gf} **0-7-17 £3,361**

Privy Seal (Ire) *J H M Gosden*   112
3 b g Cape Cross (Ire) - Lady Joshua (Ire)
1^{8gs} 2^{10gs} 2^{12gs} 3^{12g} 9^{10f} 4^{10gs} 2^{10g} **1-4-7 £199,843**

Prize Fighter (Ire) *P W Chapple-Hyam*   75 a85
2 b g Desert Sun - Papal
2^{7gf} 1^{7sd} 2^{7sd} **1-2-3 £5,719**

Prize Ring *G M Moore*   57
5 ch g Bering - Spot Prize (USA)
6^{12gf} 2^{14gs} 6^{14gf} 9^{14g} **0-1-4 £1,720**

Prizeman (USA) *G B Balding*   100
6 b g Prized (USA) - Shuttle (USA)
24^{8g} 2^{8g} **0-1-2 £3,080**

Pro Tempore *Mrs J R Ramsden*   66
2 b f Fraam - Record Time
4^{5gf} 1^{5gf} 6^{5f} 6^{5g} 3^{6g} 9^{7f} 8^{6gf} 6^{7g} **1-1-8 £4,822**

Proclamation (Ire) *J Noseda*   90
2 gr c King's Best (USA) - Shamarra (Fr)
1^{8s} **1-0-1 £7,163**

Procrastinate (Ire) *R F Fisher*   62
2 ch g Rossini - May Hinton
3^{5hy} 7^{5gf} 6^{6hy} 5^{6gf} 3^{5gf} 5^{6f} 2^{5gs} 11^{7gf} 3^{5gf} 10^{5gf} **0-2-11 £2,833**

Procreate (Ire) *Miss L A Perratt*   42
4 b g Among Men (USA) - Woodbury Princess
17^{7gf} 8^{10f} 12^{10gy} 8^{7gf} 7^{7y} 6^{6s} **0-0-6**

Profit's Reality (Ire) *P A Blockley*   88
2 br c Key Of Luck (USA) - Teacher Preacher (Ire)
7^{6hy} 5^{6gf} 5^{6gs} 4^{6s} 3^{6gs} 1^{7g} 3^{6s} 8^{8g} **1-2-8 £7,458**

Promenade *M L W Bell*   70
3 b f Primo Dominie - Hamsah (Ire)
5^{6g} 10^{5f} 9^{5gf} **0-0-3**

Promote *Ms A E Embiricos*   48
8 gr g Linamix (Fr) - Rive (USA)
14^{10sd} 6^{14gf} 6^{19gf} 10^{16g} 11^{16gf} **0-0-5**

Promoted Deputy (USA) *Saeed Bin Suroor*   a76
2 b f Deputy Minister (Can) - Shouldnt Say Never (USA)
1^{7sd} **1-0-1 £5,200**

Promoter *J Noseda*   98
4 ch g Selkirk (USA) - Poplina (USA)
10^{16g} 9^{14gs} 2^{10gf} 9^{16s} 4^{16g} 18^{21g} 2^{15s} **0-3-7 £15,054**

Promotion *Sir Michael Stoute*   110
4 b g Sadler's Wells (USA) - Tempting Prospect
1^{10g} 2^{10f} 2^{10g} **1-2-3 £49,159**

Propellor (Ire) *A Dickman*   85
2 ch c Pivotal - Clunie
3^{6s} 1^{6gf} 3^{6gf} 4^{6s} 4^{6s} **1-1-5 £7,184**

Prophet's Calling (Ire) *Miss D A McHale*   44 a41
2 b g Brave Act - Arbitration (Ire)
14^{7gf} 10^{8g} 8^{6sd} **0-0-3**

Propinquity *P W Harris*   101
2 b c Primo Dominie - Lydia Maria
1^{7g} 3^{7g} 3^{7s} 5^{8g} **1-2-4 £11,318**

Proprioception (Ire) *M R Channon*   39
2 ch f Danehill Dancer (Ire) - Pepper And Salt (Ire)
11^{8gs} **0-0-1**

Proprius *B Smart*   a32
4 b g Perpendicular - Pretty Pollyanna
5^{7sd} 16^{8sd} **0-0-2**

Prospect Court *J D Bethell*   75
2 ch c Pivotal - Scierpan (USA)
8^{5gs} 3^{5g} 13^{5gf} 1^{6gf} 9^{6gf} 12^{6gs} 7^{6gf} 13^{6g} **1-1-8 £7,798**

Prospect Park *C Laffon-Parias*   118
3 b c Sadler's Wells (USA) - Brooklyn's Dance (Fr)
11^{1gs} 11^{1gs} 2^{12vs} 2^{12gs} 1^{12gs} 2^{12s} 16^{12g} **3-3-7 £260,043**

Prospect Point *C A Dwyer*   a32
2 ch f Cayman Kai (Ire) - Sassy Lady (Ire)
4^{7sd} 8^{6sd} **0-0-2**

Protecting Heights (Ire) *J L Dunlop*   67
3 br g Hector Protector (USA) - Height Of Fantasy (Ire)
17^{8g} 6^{10g} **0-0-2**

Protective *J G Given*   92
3 ch c Hector Protector (USA) - You Make Me Real (USA)
4^{9g} 7^{11gf} 11^{2gs} 16^{12g} 9^{12gs} 3^{13s} 9^{12gs} 16^{12s} **1-0-9 £10,244**

Protocol (Ire) *Mrs S Lamyman*   32 a8
10 b g Taufan (USA) - Ukraine's Affair (USA)
7^{12gs} 9^{22s} 7^{12sd} **0-0-3**

Proud Boast *D Nicholls*   98
6 b m Komaite (USA) - Red Rosein
7^{5g} 1^{5gs} 8^{5g} 9^{6gs} 14^{5s} 2^{5g} 3^{5gf} 18^{5gf} 11^{6gf} 6^{6g} 5^{6gf} 11^{5g} **1-2-12 £21,786**

Proud Native (Ire) *D Nicholls*   78
10 b g Imp Society (USA) - Karamana
19^{5gs} 17^{6gf} 8^{5g} 3^{5gf} 10^{5gs} **0-1-5 £562**

Proud Scholar (USA) *Mrs A J Perrett*   82
2 br f Royal Academy - Proud Fact (USA)
2^{7g} 6^{7g} **0-1-2 £2,330**

Proud Tradition (USA) *J H M Gosden*   70
3 b f Seeking The Gold (USA) - Family Tradition (Ire)
9^{11gs} 6^{10gf} **0-0-2 £450**

Proud Victor (Ire) *D Shaw*   a48
4 b g Victory Note (USA) - Alberjas (Ire)
4^{8sd} 5^{8sd} 6^{8sd} 6^{12sd} 5^{8sd} **0-0-5**

Proud Western (USA) *B Ellison*   43
6 b/br g Gone West (USA) - Proud Lou (USA)
9^{5hy} 12^{5s} 16^{5gf} 13^{7gf} 5^{8g} **0-0-5**

Psychiatrist *R Hannon*   102
3 ch g Dr Devious (Ire) - Zahwa
3^{8gs} 2^{9g} 4^{8gf} 10^{7gf} 6^{7g} 13^{8gf} **0-1-6**

£10,961

Ptarmigan Ridge *Miss L A Perratt* 93
8 b h Sea Raven (Ire) - Panayr
10^{5g} 8^{5gf} 1^{5gs} 12^{5gf} 19^{5gf} 6^{5s} 5^{5gs} 1^{5g}
19^{5g} 3^{5g} 3^{6g} 7^{5s} 11^{5s} **2-2-13 £35,812**

Public Forum *Sir Michael Stoute* 76
2 b c Rainbow Quest (USA) - Valentine Girl
1^{8hy} **1-0-1 £4,595**

Pugin (Ire) *D R Loder* 107 a106
6 b h Darshaan - Gothic Dream (Ire)
5^{10sd} 5^{12g} 8^{12gf} 9^{22f} **0-0-4 £3,125**

Pukka (Ire) *L M Cumani* 109
3 b c Sadler's Wells (USA) - Puce
1^{11g} 9^{12g} 2^{12s} 5^{12g} **1-1-4 £21,511**

Pulse *J M Bradley* 70 a50
6 b g Salse (USA) - French Gift
14^{5gs} 9^{6sd} 2^{5gf} 3^{5hy} 6^{5g} 6^{5gf} 4^{5gf} 5^{5f}
3^{5g} 7^{5g} 11^{5gs} 5^{5gf} 5^{6gf} 4^{5s} 7^{5g} 10^{5g} 6^{6f}
9^{5gf} 7^{6sd} **0-5-22 £4,297**

Punctilious *Saeed Bin Suroor* 114
3 b f Danehill (USA) - Robertet (USA)
1^{10gs} 3^{12gf} 1^{12gf} 2^{12gf} 4^{12s} 2^{10g} **2-2-6**
£277,601

Pup's Pride *Mrs N Macauley* a17
7 b g Efisio - Moogie
6^{9sd} 7^{8ss} 13^{8sd} **0-0-3**

Purdey *H Morrison* 52
4 ch f Double Trigger (Ire) - Euphorie (Ger)
9^{12s} 5^{14gf} 4^{18f} 5^{17g} **0-0-4 £264**

Pure Emotion *W R Muir* a48
3 b f Primo Dominie - Yasalam (Ire)
5^{7sd} 8^{6sd} 7^{7sd} 7^{8ss} **0-0-4**

Pure Folly (Ire) *Sir Mark Prescott* 9 a61
3 b f Machiavellian (USA) - Spirit Willing (Ire)
3^{5sd} 4^{5sd} 4^{6sd} 8^{7f} 7^{5sf} **0-1-5 £1,212**

Pure Imagination (Ire) *J M Bradley* 71
3 ch g Royal Academy (USA) - Ivory Bride
6^{7gf} 3^{7gf} 12^{7gf} 6^{6s} 20^{6gf} 4^{6gs} 8^{6gf} 13^{6g}
1^{6s} 8^{5s} **1-2-10 £6,425**

Pure Mischief (Ire) *C R Dore* 79 a77
5 b g Alhaarth (Ire) - Bellissi (Ire)
3^{9ss} 1^{10hy} 1^{10s} 5^{10hy} 1^{11sd} 3^{10s} 2^{11s} 4^{11hy}
6^{10g} 5^{10s} 5^{8sd} 7^{8hy} 3^{8sd} **3-4-13 £15,625**

Pure Speculation *M L W Bell* 60 a66
4 b f Salse (USA) - Just Speculation (Ire)
8^{12sd} 10^{10sd} 6^{10gs} 4^{8s} 8^{8hy} **0-0-5 £333**

Pure Vintage (Ire) *R A Fahey* 57
3 b g Fasliyev (USA) - Tootling (Ire)
8^{7f} 6^{8gs} 8^{7gf} 8^{10gs} 6^{7gf} **0-0-5**

Puri *J G Given* 48 a50
5 b g Mujadil (USA) - Prosperous Lady
4^{8sd} 7^{7ss} 10^{7sd} PU^{11gf} 4^{7gf} 18^{8gf} **0-0-6**
£536

Purple Door *R M Beckett* 55
2 b f Daggers Drawn (USA) - Carreamia
6^{6gf} 10^{7gf} 6^{6gf} 23^{6s} **0-0-4**

Purple Rain (Ire) *M L W Bell* 57 a37
3 b f Celtic Swing - Calypso Grant (Ire)
7^{8s} 10^{8g} 6^{8s} 5^{8sd} 10^{8g} **0-0-5**

Purr *M Wigham* 49
3 b g Pursuit Of Love - Catawba
12^{10g} 6^{11gf} 13^{10f} 15^{11gs} 8^{10g} 9^{10gs}
14^{12gf} 14^{14s} **0-0-8**

Pushkin (Ire) *M Johnston* 96
6 b h Caerleon (USA) - Palmeraie (USA)

3^{10ft} 20^{14g} 2^{18f} 5^{13s} 34^{18s} **0-1-5**
£4,459

Pussy Cat *K O Cunningham-Brown* 49
2 b f Josr Algarhoud (Ire) - Swan Lake (Fr)
8^{6gf} 6^{6gs} 13^{7g} 5^{7f} 10^{8s} **0-0-5**

Putra Kuantan *M A Jarvis* 109
4 b c Grand Lodge (USA) - Fade
6^{10gs} 3^{10g} 1^{8gf} 15^{8gf} 6^{8gs} 11^{8gf} 13^{9g}
12^{8s} **1-1-8 £18,689**

Putra Pekan *M A Jarvis* 115
6 b h Grand Lodge (USA) - Mazarine Blue
1^{8s} 1^{8gs} 7^{8g} 2^{8s} 3^{9s} 8^{8gs} **2-2-7**
£53,240

Putra Sandhurst (Ire) *M A Jarvis* 107
6 b h Royal Academy (USA) - Kharimata (Ire)
1^{12gs} 9^{10g} 7^{12g} 7^{12g} 8^{10gf} **1-0-5**
£10,332

Putra Sas (Ire) *P F I Cole* 103
3 b c Sri Pekan (USA) - Puteri Wentworth
2^{8gs} 2^{10gs} 6^{12g} **0-0-3 £18,568**

Puya *H Candy* 76
2 b f Kris - Pervenche
2^{6s} 2^{6s} **0-2-2 £3,064**

Pyrrhic *R M Flower* a57
5 b g Salse (USA) - Bint Lariaaf (USA)
3^{10sd} 7^{10sd} 2^{10sd} 10^{12sd} 6^{10sd} 5^{10sd} 13^{12sd}
6^{10sd} 8^{10sd} 6^{10sd} **0-2-11 £1,221**

Qabas (USA) *P Bowen* 75
4 b g Swain (Ire) - Classical Dance (Can)
5^{10gf} 8^{10f} 6^{10gf} **0-0-3**

Qadar (Ire) *M P Tregoning* 84 a75
2 b c Xaar - Iktidar
2^{6gf} 3^{6gf} 1^{7sd} **1-1-3 £6,449**

Qasirah (Ire) *M A Jarvis* 97
3 b f Machiavellian (USA) - Altaweelah (USA)
10^{7g} 5^{11gs} 3^{9g} 6^{8gf} 11^{8gs} 10^{8gf} **0-1-6**
£7,500

Qawaafil (USA) *E A L Dunlop* 68
2 b/br f Intidab (USA) - Indihash (USA)
5^{6gf} 8^{6g} 7^{6gf} 1^{7s} 15^{7gs} **1-0-5 £2,976**

Qobtaan (USA) *M R Bosley* 10 a64
5 b g Capote (USA) - Queen's Gallery (USA)
6^{9sd} 1^{8sd} 18^{7sd} 9^{8sd} 9^{8sd} 7^{8sd} 17^{8g}
4^{9sd} 1^{9sd} **3-0-10 £7,252**

Qualitair Wings *J Hetherton* 81
5 b g Colonel Collins (USA) - Semperflorens
3^{7g} 11^{8gf} 17^{8g} 8^{7gf} 2^{9gs} 9^{7gs} 2^{8gf} 8^{8gf}
8^{8gs} 3^{8gs} 8^{10s} 5^{8s} 8^{7s} **0-4-13 £7,410**

Quantica (Ire) *T D Barron* 60
5 b g Sri Pekan (USA) - Touche-A-Tout (Ire)
6^{6s} 15^{6g} 15^{6gf} 15^{6g} 16^{6g} 6^{6g}
0-0-7

Quantum Leap *S Dow* 79 a70
7 b g Efisio - Prejudice
11^{10sd} 6^{10sd} 3^{8sd} 3^{7sd} 8^{8gf} 3^{8gf} 1^{7gf}
6^{7g} 6^{7g} 4^{8gf} 2^{7gf} 4^{6gs} 22^{7gf} 20^{7g} **1-4-16**
£9,814

Quarry Island (Ire) *M Todhunter* 51 a45
3 b f Turtle Island (Ire) - Last Quarry
5^{10sd} 2^{8s} 9^{8sd} 7^{7sd} 7^{10sd} 2^{12gs} 8^{10s} 1^{12f}
1-2-8 £4,134

Quarrymount *Sir Mark Prescott* 88 a69
3 b g Polar Falcon (USA) - Quilt
12^{6gf} 2^{9g} 1^{10sd} 2^{11gf} 1^{12hy} 2^{12s} 2^{12gf}
1^{14g} 2^{12s} 5^{15s} **3-4-10 £22,300**

Quarter To *W De Best-Turner*
5 gr m Chocolat De Meguro (USA) - Miss Lakeland
15^{7sd} 0-0-1

Quartino *J H M Gosden*   76
3 b c Dynaformer (USA) - Qirmazi (USA)
10^{10gf} 9^{12gs} 8^{11g} 7^{16gf} 2^{10s} 0-1-5
£1,287

Quatre Saisons *J M Bradley*   39
2 ch c Bering - Inseparable
7^{6s} 0-0-1

Quay Walloper *J R Norton*   40
3 b g In Command (Ire) - Myrrh
7^{9g} 12^{14f} 8^{12sd} 14^{14g} 12^{12gf} 17^{10gs} 0-0-6

Qudraat (Ire) *E F Vaughan*   93
3 b c In The Wings - Urgent Liaison (Ire)
5^{10g} 8^{12gf} 1^{12gs} 2^{11g} 7^{12g} 12^{12s} 1-1-6
£6,269

Qudrah (Ire) *E J O'Neill*   91 a91
4 b f Darshaan - Alwiyda (USA)
7^{10sd} 8^{12ss} 5^{10sd} 4^{14g} 8^{12g} 5^{12gf} 12^{10hy}
16^{14gs} 0-0-8 £1,500

Quedex *R J Price*   88 a55
8 b g Deploy - Alwal
1^{16gf} 5^{18g} 2^{16s} 1^{14gs} 1^{16s} 9^{21g} 10^{12sd}
4^{18s} 3-2-8 £28,485

Queen Charlotte (Ire) *Mrs K Walton*   73
5 ch m Tagula (Ire) - Tisima (Fr)
2^{8gf} 11^{7f} 9^{8gf} 7^{8gf} 5^{8gf} 6^{8g} 11^{7g} 0-1-7
£1,660

Queen Excalibur *A G Juckes*   48 a38
5 ch m Sabrehill (USA) - Blue Room
8^{7sd} 9^{8sd} 7^{8sd} 9^{8sd} 7^{12g} 6^{11gs} 3^{11g} 5^{12sd}
0-0-8 £226

Queen Louisa *F Watson*
4 b f Piccolo - Queen Of Scotland (Ire)
10^{6sw} 11^{10s} 0-0-2

Queen Lucia (Ire) *J G Given*   62 a43
3 b f Pursuit Of Love - Inquirendo (USA)
4^{8g} 4^{9g} 4^{7f} 5^{10gf} 4^{10gf} 7^{10sd} 2^{9s} 3^{8gs}
7^{9sd} 0-2-9 £2,779

Queen Nefitari *M W Easterby*   58
2 b f Celtic Swing - Opalette
10^{8g} 0-0-1

Queen Of Bulgaria (Ire) *J Pearce*   38 a35
3 b f Imperial Ballet (Ire) - Sofia Aurora (USA)
9^{5sw} 7^{9gs} 10^{6s} 13^{6gf} 9^{6f} 11^{6gf} 13^{6g}
19^{6gs} 0-0-8

Queen Of Iceni *J L Dunlop*   74
2 b f Erhaab (USA) - Princess Genista
19^{7g} 2^{7g} 10^{7gs} 0-1-3 £1,752

Queen Of Night *D W Chapman*   61 a83
4 b f Piccolo - Cardinal Press
7^{6sd} 4^{6sd} 18^{5hy} 4^{7sd} LFT^{6gf} 10^{6s} 1^{5sd}
1^{5sd} 2^{5gf} 12^{5gf} 5^{5gf} 6^{5gs} 6^{5gs} 2-1-13
£6,043

Queen Of Poland *D R Loder*   108
2 b f Halling (USA) - Polska (USA)
1^{7f} 1^{7gf} 2^{8g} 6^{8g} 2-1-4 £38,293

Queen Tomyra (Ire) *L M Cumani*   48 a70
2 b f Montjeu (Ire) - Kama Tashoof
13^{8gf} 11^{7g} 3^{7sd} 0-1-3 £443

Queen's Dancer *M R Channon*   65
2 b f Groom Dancer (USA) - Special Beat
15^{8gf} 5^{8hy} 2^{8hy} 0-1-3 £1,966

Queen's Echo *M Dods*   57 a41
3 b f Wizard King - Sunday News'N'Echo (USA)
2^{7hy} 5^{8g} 8^{10gs} 9^{9sd} 0-1-4 £1,069

Queen's Fantasy *D Haydn Jones*   63 a68
3 ch f Grand Lodge (USA) - Alcalali (USA)
10^{9sd} 4^{12gs} 16^{10g} 2^{10gf} 1^{12sd} 6^{14sd} 6^{10gf}
1-1-7 £4,964

Queen's Glory (Ire) *W R Muir*   63 a23
2 b f Mujadil (USA) - Karenaragon
6^{5hy} 2^{6gf} 6^{5f} 5^{5f} 5^{6gf} 7^{6gf} 11^{6sd} 6^{6sd}
6^{6gs} 3^{5f} 0-2-10 £1,511

Queens Hand (Ire) *G A Swinbank*   26 a37
2 b f Lend A Hand - Winchester Queen (Ire)
11^{7g} 7^{6sd} 0-0-2

Queens Rhapsody *A Bailey*   86 a94
4 b/br g Baryshnikov (Aus) - Digamist Girl (Ire)
2^{6sd} 9^{7sd} 2^{6ss} 4^{7s} 7^{7sd} 4^{7gs} 10^{8g} 9^{8gs}
7^{7gf} 5^{6s} 3^{7gs} 3^{7gs} 0-4-12 £10,287

Queens Square *N Tinkler*   37 a7
3 b f Forzando - Queens Check
9^{5s} 7^{6ss} 7^{8gf} 17^{6f} 0-0-4

Queensberry *Mrs L J Mongan*
5 b g Up And At 'Em - Princess Poquito
13^{16sd} 10^{12sd} 0-0-2

Queenslander (Ire) *G A Swinbank*   18
3 b f Inchinor - Royal Subject (USA)
11^{9gf} 0-0-1

Queenstown (Ire) *B J Meehan*   58 a71
3 b g Desert Style (Ire) - Fanciful (Ire)
10^{8g} 3^{8sd} 5^{8gf} 7^{8gf} 11^{7gf} 4^{7gs} 0-1-6
£717

Querido (USA) *Saeed Bin Suroor*   82
2 b c Spectrum (Ire) - Polent
4^{6g} 1^{7gf} 1-0-2 £4,051

Quest On Air *J R Jenkins*   39 a38
5 b g Star Quest - Stormy Heights
2^{12sd} 11^{14gf} 6^{11f} 0-1-3 £462

Queue Up *J G Given*   78
2 b g Royal Applause - Faraway Lass
3^{6f} 12^{6gf} 11^{6gs} 0-1-3 £561

Quick *M C Pipe*   53
4 b g Kahyasi - Prompt
PU^{19gf} 9^{15gf} 0-0-2

Quick Grand (Ire) *Miss L A Perratt*   44
2 br f Raise A Grand (Ire) - Rose 'n Reason (Ire)
6^{6gf} 6^{5gf} 6^{6gf} 0-0-3

Quickfire *Sir Michael Stoute*   79
2 b f Dubai Millennium - Daring Miss
2^{6g} 1^{7gf} 1-1-2 £7,605

Quicks The Word *C W Thornton*   66
4 b g Sri Pekan (USA) - Fast Tempo (Ire)
8^{6gs} 12^{6s} 4^{5hy} 9^{5gf} 12^{6f} 7^{8gs} 2^{8g} 2^{8g}
6^{8g} 2^{7s} 0-3-10 £3,303

Quickstyx *M R Channon*   73 a68
3 b f Night Shift (USA) - Red Bouquet
1^{8sd} 4^{8g} 5^{7gs} 4^{10gs} 4^{10gf} 6^{12gf} 7^{16gf} 6^{12g}
6^{12gs} 1-1-9 £5,076

Quiet Reading (USA) *M R Bosley*   a76
7 b g Northern Flagship (USA) - Forlis Key (USA)
3^{8sd} 4^{8sd} 6^{8sd} 3^{8sw} 2^{8sd} 8^{8hy} 11^{8sd}
4^{8sd} 9^{8sd} 0-4-10 £3,902

Quiet Storm (Ire) *G Wragg*   100
4 b f Desert Prince - Hertford Castle
7^{10g} 16^{8g} 3^{8gf} 6^{7gf} 0-0-4 £4,168

Quiet Times (Ire) *K A Ryan*   66 a99

5 ch g Dolphin Street (Fr) - Super Times
1⁶ˢᵈ 4⁵ˢᵈ 9⁶ˢᵈ 4⁶ˢᵈ 1⁶ˢˢ 5⁶ˢ 5⁶ʰʸ 8⁶ᵍˢ
18⁶ᵍ 2⁶ˢᵈ **2-2-10 £17,864**

Quiff *Sir Michael Stoute* 122
3 b f Sadler's Wells (USA) - Wince
1¹⁰ᵍ 3¹²ᵍᶠ 1¹²ˢ 2¹⁵ᵍᶠ **2-2-4 £256,851**

Quincannon (USA) *T D Barron* a54
3 b g Kayrawan (USA) - Sulalat
6⁶ˢᵈ **0-0-1**

Quinn *C W Fairhurst* 20
4 ch g First Trump - Celestine
10¹⁶ˢᵈ 10¹²ᵍᶠ **0-0-2**

Quintillion *T J Etherington* 29 a15
3 gr g Petong - Lady Quinta (Ire)
8⁶ˢᵈ 12⁶ᵍᶠ 7⁸ᵈ 10⁶ᵍ **0-0-4**

Quintoto *R A Fahey* 61 a45
4 b g Mtoto - Ballet
6⁹ᵍᶠ 14¹⁰ᵍᶠ 9¹⁰ᵍᶠ 15⁸ᵍˢ 12⁹ˢᵈ 13⁹ˢᵈ **0-0-6**

Quito (Ire) *D W Chapman* 117 a114
7 b r Machiavellian (USA) - Qirmazi (USA)
1⁶ˢˢ 10⁸ˢˢ 6⁷ˢᵈ 2⁸ᵍ 5⁷ˢᵈ 5⁷ᵍˢ 6⁷ᵍ 1⁶ᵍˢ
10⁸ᵍ 6⁷ᵍᶠ 5⁶ˢ 1⁶ᵍ 6⁷ᵍ 5⁶ˢ 3⁶ˢ 3⁷ˢ 5⁸ᵍˢ 1⁶ᵍˢ
4-3-18 £86,224

Quizzene (USA) *M Johnston* 71
2 gr c Cozzene (USA) - Company Binness (USA)
5⁸ˢ 1¹⁰ˢ **1-0-2 £3,464**

Raakaan *A C Stewart* 76
3 b c Halling (USA) - Glimpse
3⁸ᵍˢ 1¹⁰ᵍᶠ **1-1-2 £4,238**

Rabbit *Mrs A L M King* 48
3 b f Muhtarram (USA) - Ninia (USA)
12⁸ᵍˢ 9⁸ᵍᶠ 5⁶ᵍˢ **0-0-3**

Rabitatit (Ire) *J G M O'Shea* 69
3 b f Robellino (USA) - Coupled
2⁸ᵍ 4⁹ᶠ 9⁸ᵍᶠ 2⁹ᵍᶠ 5⁸ᵍ 5¹⁰ᵍˢ 6⁸ᵍᶠ 2¹⁰ᵍˢ
7¹⁰ᵍᶠ 4⁹ˢ 12¹⁰ᶠ **0-2-11 £5,737**

Raccoon (Ire) *T D Barron* 100
4 b g Raphane (USA) - Kunucu (Ire)
4⁵ᵍᶠ 1⁵ᵍᶠ 1⁵ᵍᶠ 16⁵ᵍᶠ 8⁶ᵍᶠ 7⁵ᵍ 19⁶ᵍ 11⁶ˢ
2-1-8 £43,534

Race The Ace *J L Dunlop* 101
3 b g First Trump - Princess Genista
4¹⁰ᵍˢ 5¹⁰ᵍᶠ 2¹²ᵍᶠ 3¹⁴ᵍ 3¹⁶ᵍᶠ 1¹⁶ᵍˢ 2¹⁶ᵍᶠ
1¹⁶ˢ **2-4-8 £16,787**

Rachel's Verdict *J R Fanshawe* 75
3 b f Royal Applause - Shady Street (USA)
4⁶ᵍᶠ 5⁶ᵍᶠ 1⁶ᵍˢ **1-0-3 £5,862**

Racing Night (USA) *J R Best* 61 a59
4 b g Lear Fan (USA) - Broom Dance (USA)
11⁸ˢᵈ 9⁸ᵍˢ **0-0-2**

Radiant Bride *K R Burke* a53
4 ch f Groom Dancer (USA) - Radiancy (Ire)
11¹³ˢᵈ 2¹⁶ˢᵈ 6¹³ˢᵈ 1¹⁶ˢᵈ 2¹²ˢˢ 8¹³ˢᵈ 1¹³ˢᵈ
4¹⁶ˢʷ **2-2-8 £3,991**

Radish (Ire) *E F Vaughan* 65
3 b f Alhaarth (Ire) - Nichodoula
12⁸ᵍ 1¹⁰ˢ **1-0-2 £3,562**

Radlett Lady *D K Ivory* 37 a48
3 ch f Wolfhound (USA) - Royal Dream
8⁶ˢᵈ 10⁵ˢ 14⁶ᵍᶠ 9⁶ᵍᶠ 11⁵ᵍˢ 16ˢᵈ **1-0-6**
£1,473

Radmore Spirit *J W Unett* 35 a5
4 b f Whittingham (Ire) - Ruda (Fr)
8⁹ˢˢ 10⁵ᵍᶠ 10⁵ˢᵈ **0-0-3**

Raetihi *A Senior* 29 a13
3 b f Wizard King - Foreno
11⁶ᵍᶠ 4⁵ˢ 10⁵ᵍ 9⁶ˢᵈ **0-0-4 £364**

Rafferty (Ire) *T D Barron* 88
5 ch g Lion Cavern (USA) - Badawi (USA)
7⁸ᵍ 5⁷ᵍ 3⁸ᵍᶠ 4⁸ᵍˢ 7⁸ᵍ 9⁸ᵍᶠ **0-1-6**
£1,267

Raffish *J M P Eustace* 79 a71
2 ch g Atraf - Valadon
8⁷ᵍᶠ 4⁷ᵍˢ 1⁸ˢᵈ 28⁶ˢ **1-0-4 £3,763**

Rafters Music (Ire) *Julian Poulton* 65 a75
9 b g Thatching - Princess Dixieland
3⁶ˢʷ 8⁶ˢʷ 2⁶ˢˢ 16⁷ᵍˢ 5⁶ᵍˢ 5⁵ᵍ 4⁶ˢᵈ **0-2-7**
£1,355

Ragamuffin *T D Easterby* 73
6 ch g Prince Sabo - Valldemosa
7⁶ᵍˢ 13⁶ᵍᶠ 5⁶ᵍᶠ 11⁶ᵍ **0-0-4**

Ragasah *E R Oertel* a36
6 b m Glory Of Dancer - Slight Risk
7¹⁰ˢᵈ 4⁸ˢᵈ **0-0-2**

Ragazzi (Ire) *T D Barron* 36 a66
3 ch g Raphane (USA) - Zalotti (Ire)
10⁶ʲˢ 9⁶ᶠ 17⁷ᵍˢ 3⁶ˢᵈ 5⁸ˢᵈ 11⁷ᶠ **0-1-6**
£469

Ragged Glory (Ire) *R Hannon* 72 a74
2 br c Foxhound (USA) - Resurgence
4⁵ᵍ 5⁶ᵍ 2⁷ᵍ 13⁸ᵍˢ 2⁸ˢᵈ 6⁹ˢᵈ **0-2-6**
£2,804

Ragged Jack (Ire) *G A Butler* 72 a69
3 b g Cape Cross (Ire) - Isticanna (USA)
2⁶ᵍᶠ 3⁶ᵍᶠ 1⁵ᵍ 5⁷ˢᵈ 6⁶ˢᵈ 6¹⁰ᵍ 12⁷ˢ **1-2-7**
£5,642

Raheed (Ire) *Mrs C A Dunnett* 56 a55
3 b g Daggers Drawn (USA) - In Due Course (USA)
6⁸ˢᵈ 10¹⁰ᵍˢ 15¹⁰ᶠ 8⁷ᵍᶠ 4⁶ᵍ **0-0-5 £315**

Raheel (Ire) *P Mitchell* 48 a66
4 ch g Barathea (Ire) - Tajawuz
5¹³ˢᵈ 4¹⁰ˢᵈ 7⁸ˢᵈ 6¹²ˢᵈ 1¹⁰ˢᵈ 4¹⁰ˢᵈ 3¹⁰ˢᵈ
7⁸ˢᵈ 8⁸ᵍᶠ 12¹⁰ᵍˢ 7⁸ˢᵈ 11¹²ˢᵈ 11¹²ˢᵈ 12¹⁰ᵍˢ
1-1-14 £3,667

Rahjel Sultan *B A McMahon* 57 a38
6 b g Puissance - Dalby Dancer
3¹²ˢˢ 6⁸ˢˢ 1⁸ᵍ 6⁸ˢ 26⁸ᵍᶠ **1-0-5 £3,760**

Rahwaan (Ire) *C W Fairhurst* 92
5 b g Darshaan - Fawaakeh (USA)
11⁸ᵍ 17¹⁹ᵍˢ **1-0-2 £9,755**

Rain Stops Play (Ire) *M R Channon* 81
2 b c Desert Prince (Ire) - Pinta (Ire)
3⁷ᵍᶠ 8⁷ᵍ 2⁸ᵍˢ 1⁸ˢ **1-2-4 £7,123**

Rainbow Colours (Ire) *J R Fanshawe* 50
3 gr f Linamix (Fr) - Mill Rainbow (Fr)
7¹⁰ᵍᶠ 9⁸ᶠ **0-0-2**

Rainbow Iris *B Smart* 70 a44
2 b/br f Mister Baileys - Kastaway
4⁵ᵍᶠ 5⁶ᵍˢ 2⁸ᵍˢ 14⁶ᵍᶠ 6⁶ˢ 5⁶ᵍ 8⁶ˢᵈ 4⁶ˢ
0-1-8 £3,351

Rainbow Queen *Sir Michael Stoute* 96
4 b f Rainbow Quest (USA) - Dazzle
3¹⁰ᵍᶠ 11¹⁰ˢ 11¹⁰ᵍ **0-0-3 £1,582**

Rainbow Rising (Ire) *J Howard Johnson* 91
2 b/br c Desert King (Ire) - Fantastic Bid (USA)
4⁶ᶠ 2⁵ˢ 9⁶ᵍ **0-1-3 £11,737**

Rainbow Sky *B W Hills* 37
2 b f Rainbow Quest (USA) - Safayn (USA)
20⁷ᵍ **0-0-1**

Rainbow Treasure (Ire) *J S Goldie* 57
2 ch f Rainbow Quest (USA) - Gaily Royal (Ire)
7⁷ᵍ 6⁷ˢ 12⁶ᵍ **0-0-3**

Rainbow World (Ire) *Andrew Reid* 64 a68
4 b c Rainbow Quest (USA) - Far Fetched (Ire)
11⁸ˢʷ 3¹²ˢᵈ 8¹²ˢᵈ 18¹²ᵍˢ 3¹²ᵍᶠ 10¹²ᵍᶠ
3¹⁰ᵍᶠ 7⁹ᵍᶠ 7¹⁰ᵍᶠ 9¹⁰ᵍᶠ **0-3-10 £1,690**

Rainsborough Hill *A King* 35
3 b g Groom Dancer (USA) - Ellebanna
8¹⁰ˢ 17¹²ᵍᶠ **0-0-2**

Rainstorm *W M Brisbourne* 47 a39
9 b g Rainbow Quest (USA) - Katsina (USA)
6⁸ˢᵈ 5¹⁰ᶠ 6⁹ᵍᶠ 7¹²ᵍᶠ 7⁹ᵍᶠ 11¹⁰ᵍᶠ 23⁷ᵍᶠ
2¹⁰ᵍᶠ 8⁸ᶠ 5⁸ᵍᶠ **0-1-10 £1,228**

Raise A Tune (Ire) *J A Osborne* 51 a74
2 ch c Raise A Grand (Ire) - Magic Melody
9⁸ᵍᶠ 1⁸ˢᵈ **1-0-2 £3,454**

Raison Detre *J Pearce* 45
2 b c Mtoto - Kelimutu
12⁷ᵍˢ **0-0-1**

Rajam *D Nicholls* 82
6 b g Sadler's Wells (USA) - Rafif (USA)
8¹²ᵍ 6¹⁴ᵍ 7¹⁸ˢ 1¹²ᵍᶠ 3¹³ᶠ 7¹⁴ᵍᶠ 6¹²ᵍᶠ 5¹²ᵍ
2¹²ᵍ 2¹²ᵍᶠ 4¹²ᵍᶠ 8¹²ᵍᶠ 9¹⁶ˢ 9¹²ᵍ **1-3-14
£10,212**

Rajayoga *M H Tompkins* 58 a24
3 ch g Kris - Optimistic
11⁸ˢᵈ 7⁸ᵍᶠ 4¹⁰ᵍ 7¹⁰ᵍᶠ 7¹⁰ˢ **0-0-5**

Rajwa (USA) *Saeed Bin Suroor* 94
2 ch c Dubai Millennium - Zelanda (Ire)
2⁶ᵍ 2⁶ˢ 2⁶ᶠ **0-2-3 £8,198**

Rakti *M A Jarvis* 129
5 b h Polish Precedent (USA) - Ragera (Ire)
1¹⁰ᵍᶠ 8¹⁰ᵍˢ 5¹⁰ᵍᶠ **2-0-4 £361,380**

Rambo Blue *A W Carroll* 64 a52
4 b g Elmaamul (USA) - Copper Trader
12¹⁰ᵍᶠ 6¹⁰ᵍˢ 10⁹ˢᵈ **0-0-3**

Rampage *W J Haggas* 73
3 ch f Pivotal - Noor El Houdah (Ire)
1⁶ˢ **1-0-1 £3,750**

Ramsgill (USA) *J A R Toller* a59
2 b c Prized (USA) - Crazee Mental
8⁹ˢᵈ **0-0-1**

Rancho Cucamonga (Ire) *T D Barron* 71
2 ch f Raphane (USA) - Kunucu (Ire)
7⁵ᵍᶠ 7⁵ᵍ 1⁶ᵍ 8⁶ᵍᶠ 7⁶ᵍᶠ 5⁵ᵍ 5⁵ᵍᶠ 18⁶ᵍˢ
2⁶ˢᶠ **1-1-9 £5,421**

Randalls Touch *B D Leavy*
2 b c Mind Games - L A Touch
11⁵ᵍ 12⁶ˢᵈ 8⁷ˢᵈ **0-0-3**

Random Quest *B J Llewellyn* 95
6 b g Rainbow Quest (USA) - Anne Bonny
7¹⁶ᵍ 7¹⁹ᵍˢ 8¹⁶ᵍ 2¹⁶ᵍ 9¹⁶ᵍᶠ **0-1-5
£14,300**

Rangoon (USA) *Mrs A J Perrett* 75
3 ch c Distant View (USA) - Rustic (Ire)
2⁶ˢ 2⁷ᵍˢ 5⁷ˢ 2⁷ᵍ 1⁸ᵍᶠ **1-3-5 £7,398**

Rani Two *W R Muir* 77
5 b m Wolfhound (USA) - Donya
11¹⁰ᵍᶠ 9¹⁰ᵍᶠ 6¹⁰ᵍᶠ 5¹⁰ᵍ 4¹⁰ᵍᶠ 4¹⁰ˢ 10¹⁰ᵍ
2¹⁰ᵍᶠ 2¹⁰ᵍˢ 11¹⁰ᵍ **0-2-10 £4,099**

Ranny *Dr J D Scargill* 55 a56
4 b f Emperor Jones (USA) - Defined Feature (Ire)
4⁸ˢᵈ 2⁷ˢᵈ 2⁷ˢᵈ 15⁷ᵍᶠ 6⁶ᵍᶠ 4⁷ᵍᶠ 4⁸ᵍ 5⁷ˢᵈ
6⁸ᵍᶠ **0-3-9 £2,776**

Ransacker *C E Brittain* 63
2 b g Bahamian Bounty - Hazy Heights
5⁶ᶠ 3⁶ᵍᶠ **0-1-2 £554**

Ranville *M A Jarvis* 92
6 ch g Deploy - Kibitka (Fr)
9¹²ᵍᶠ 10¹⁴ᵍ 5¹²ᵍˢ 8¹⁵ˢ **0-0-4 £404**

Raphael (Ire) *T D Easterby* 87
5 b m Perugino - Danny's Miracle
11⁷ᵍ 1⁷ᵍ 11⁸ᵍˢ 3⁸ᶠ 15⁷ˢ 4⁷ᵍᶠ 8⁷ᵍ 2⁷ᵍˢ
2⁷ᵍ 2⁸ᶠ 16⁸ᵍᶠ **1-5-11 £22,215**

Rapid Flow *Mrs A J Perrett* 67
2 b c Fasliyev (USA) - Fleet River (USA)
8⁷ᵍ 8⁶ᵍˢ **0-0-2**

Rapid River *Mrs L Stubbs* 61
2 b f Lahib (USA) - Cast A Spell
8⁶ᵍᶠ **0-0-1**

Rapid Romance (USA) *E A L Dunlop* 61
2 b f Theatrical - Fast Nellie (USA)
5⁶ᵍ 6⁶ᵍᶠ 4⁶ʰʸ **0-0-3 £274**

Rare Coincidence *R F Fisher* 68 a76
3 ch g Atraf - Green Seed (Ire)
1⁸ˢᵈ 1⁸ˢᵈ 3⁸ˢˢ 6⁸ˢ 8⁸ˢᵈ 4⁹ᵍˢ 4⁸ᵍᶠ 4⁹ᵍᶠ
11⁸ˢᵈ 9⁹ᵍ 3⁸ʰʸ 4⁷ᵍᶠ 10⁷ˢ **2-1-14 £7,983**

Rare Presence (Ire) *C P Morlock* 8
5 b g Sadler's Wells (USA) - Celebrity Style (USA)
11¹²ᵍᶠ **0-0-1**

Rarefied (Ire) *T D Easterby* 83
3 b g Danehill (USA) - Tenuous
8¹⁰ᵍˢ 1¹²ᵍ 7¹²ᵍˢ 7¹²ᵍ 8⁸ᵍˢ 7⁸ᵍˢ 9⁸ᵍᶠ 4¹⁰ᵍᶠ
10¹⁰ᵍ **1-0-9 £6,240**

Rasa Sayang (USA) *T D Barron* 67
2 b/br c Salt Lake (USA) - Annie Ruth (USA)
9⁵ᵍ 2⁵ᵍᶠ 2⁶ᵍᶠ 6⁶ᶠ **0-2-4 £2,626**

Rashida *J Noseda* 67
2 b f King's Best (USA) - Nimble Lady (Aus)
3⁶ᵍ 8⁷ᵍᶠ **0-0-2 £772**

Rasid (USA) *C A Dwyer* 83 a78
6 b g Bahri (USA) - Makadir (USA)
1¹⁰ˢᵈ 16¹²ˢᵈ 2¹²ˢᵈ 3¹²ˢ 1¹⁰ˢ 13¹²ᵍ 13¹⁰ᵍᶠ
5¹⁰ˢᵈ 3¹⁰ᵍᶠ 1¹⁰ᵍˢ 12¹⁰ᵍˢ 11¹¹ᵍ 20¹⁰ᵍ 12¹²ˢᵈ
11¹⁰ʰʸ **3-2-15 £14,026**

Rasseem (Ire) *Saeed Bin Suroor* 76
2 b f Fasliyev (USA) - Yorba Linda (Ire)
2⁵ᵍᶠ 7⁵ᵍˢ 3⁶ᶠ 6⁶ᵍᶠ **0-1-4 £2,344**

Rathmullan *E A Wheeler* 40 a44
5 ch g Bluegrass Prince (Ire) - National Time (USA)
12⁶ˢᵈ 8²ᵍᵈ 3⁶ˢᵈ 4⁶ᵍᶠ 3⁷ˢᵈ 1⁶ˢᵈ 3⁷ˢᵈ 5⁸ˢᵈ
9⁷ᵍᶠ 13⁶ˢᵈ 10⁷ᵍᶠ 4⁶ᶠ 10⁸ˢᵈ 3⁸ᵍ 5⁶ˢᵈ **1-2-15
£2,432**

Ratio *J E Hammond* 114
6 ch g Pivotal - Owdbetts (Ire)
1⁵ᵍˢ 10⁶ᵍ 11⁶ᵍᶠ 12⁵ᵍ 7⁶ᵛˢ **1-0-5
£15,845**

Ratukidul (Fr) *D Sepulchre* 80
2 b f Danehill (USA) - Whakilyric (USA)
1⁷ᵍ 5⁸ᶠ 9⁷ᵍˢ **1-0-3 £5,174**

Rave Reviews (Ire) *J L Dunlop* 105
3 b f Sadler's Wells (USA) - Pieds De Plume (Fr)
3¹⁰ᵍ 1¹⁰ᵍ 9¹²ᵍᶠ 9¹³ᵍˢ **1-1-4 £20,700**

Ravel (Ire) *M R Bosley* 39
3 b g Fasliyev (USA) - Lili Cup (Fr)
12⁷ᵍ 13⁶ᵍᶠ 11¹⁰ᶠ **0-0-3**

Raven (Ire) *M E Sowersby* 59
2 b f Alzao (USA) - Eman's Joy
9⁸ᵍ 6⁶ᵍˢ **0-0-2**

Ravenglass (USA) *J G M O'Shea* 86
5 b h Miswaki (USA) - Urus (USA)
8^{12g} 6^{16g} 5^{12gf} PU^{18g} **0-0-4**

Rawaabet (Ire) *M P Tregoning* 59
2 b c Bahhare (USA) - Haddeyah (USA)
8^{7g} 11^{7gf} **0-0-2**

Rawalpindi *J A R Toller* 55 a68
3 ch g Intikhab (USA) - Just A Treat (Ire)
8^{7s} 10^{7gf} 9^{8gf} 2^{12sd} 5^{13f} 9^{17gf} **0-1-6**
£854

Rawdon (Ire) *J H M Gosden* 76
3 b c Singspiel (Ire) - Rebecca Sharp
9^{8g} 5^{10gf} **0-0-2**

Rawyaan *J H M Gosden* 111
5 b h Machiavellian (USA) - Raheefa (USA)
1^{12gf} 6^{12gf} 8^{12gf} 7^{13gs} 13^{12gf} **1-0-5**
£36,312

Raybers Magic *J R Weymes* 7
3 b f Magic Ring (Ire) - Kirkadian
8^{10gf} 8^{8g} 13^{7gs} 7^{9gf} **0-0-4**

Raymond's Pride *K A Ryan* 89 a38
4 b g Mind Games - Northern Sal
9^{6sd} 11^{5sd} 5^{6gs} 1^{5hy} 1^{6s} 4^{5g} 5^{5hy} 13^{6gf}
9^{7s} **2-1-9 £10,934**

Rayshan (Ire) *J Howard Johnson* 85
4 b g Darshaan - Rayseka (Ire)
14^{19gs} 7^{12gf} 16^{16s} 19^{14s} **0-0-4**

Raysoot (Ire) *E F Vaughan* 68 a68
3 b c Cape Cross (Ire) - Mashkorah (USA)
8^{6gs} 2^{8sd} 5^{8gf} 9^{7g} 18^{gf} **1-1-5 £5,362**

Rayware Boy (Ire) *D Shaw*
8 b g Scenic - Amata (Ire)
9^{13sd} **0-0-1**

Raza Cab (Ire) *G A Huffer* 87 a93
2 b g Intikhab (USA) - Laraissa
3^{7gf} 1^{7sd} 6^{7g} 2^{7sd} 9^{8gf} **1-2-5 £5,340**

Raze *Sir Michael Stoute* 53
2 ch f Halling (USA) - Rive (USA)
8^{7s} **0-0-1**

Razkalla (USA) *Saeed Bin Suroor* 115
6 b g Caerleon (USA) - Larrocha (Ire)
1^{10gf} 4^{12gf} 4^{12gf} 5^{12g} 9^{16gs} **1-0-5**
£136,330

Reaching Out (Ire) *H J Collingridge* 60
2 b g Desert Prince (Ire) - Alwiyda (USA)
10^{7sd} 15^{7g} **0-0-2**

Read Federica *Sir Michael Stoute* 82
2 ch f Fusaichi Pegasus (USA) - Reading Habit (USA)
1^{7gs} **1-0-1 £4,881**

Ready Teddy Go *D K Ivory* a31
2 b g Danzig Connection (USA) - Mariette
7^{7sd} **0-0-1**

Real Cool Cat (USA) *M Johnston* 60
2 gr f Storm Cat (USA) - Hail Kris (USA)
4^{6g} 10^{7s} **0-0-2 £422**

Real Estate *J S King* 44
10 b g High Estate - Haitienne (Fr)
10^{12gf} 7^{15gf} 8^{16gs} 12^{17g} **0-0-4**

Real Quality (USA) *I Semple* 86
2 br g Elusive Quality (USA) - Pleasant Prize (USA)
2^{6gs} 1^{7g} **1-1-2 £4,606**

Real Ting *Ms Deborah J Evans*
8 br g Forzando - St Helena
9^{6sd} **0-0-1**

Realism (Fr) *P W Hiatt* 87 a73

Reap *J Pearce* 69 a50
6 b g Emperor Jones (USA) - Corn Futures
7^{10sd} 3^{8hy} 8^{8g} 6^{8f} 17^{10g} 4^{10s} **0-1-6**
£1,583

Rebate *R Hannon* 67 a76
4 b g Pursuit Of Love - Aigua Blava (USA)
8^{10sd} 5^{10sd} 12^{10gs} 12^{8gs} 12^{8gf} 3^{8sd} 3^{10f}
6^{10gf} 3^{10f} 5^{10gf} 9^{8g} 5^{10gf} 6^{11g} 5^{10sd} 7^{10gs}
0-1-15 £1,641

Rebel Leader *W R Muir* 79
7 br g Ezzoud (Ire) - Haitienne (Fr)
12^{8g} **0-0-1**

Rebel Raider (Ire) *B N Pollock* a64
5 b g Mujadil (USA) - Emily's Pride
1^{9sd} 9^{9sd} 2^{12sd} **1-1-3 £3,761**

Rebel Rebel (Ire) *N A Callaghan* 94
2 b c Revoque (Ire) - French Quarter
7^{6g} 3^{7g} 5^{8s} 4^{7gf} 1^{8g} 1^{7gf} 2^{7gf} **2-2-7**
£12,495

Rebel Rouser *W R Muir* 34 a31
3 b g Kris - Nanouche
5^{8s} 5^{9sd} 7^{12sd} **0-0-3**

Rebuttal (USA) *B J Meehan* 119
2 b c Mr Greeley (USA) - Reboot (USA)
2^{6gs} 1^{6s} 3^{6gs} 2^{6g} **1-3-4 £56,257**

Reckless Fred *Miss K M George* a41
5 ch g So Factual (USA) - Winnie Reckless
7^{6sd} 10^{8sd} 10^{10sd} **0-0-3**

Reckless Moment *Jane Southcombe*
3 b f Victory Note (USA) - Blue Indigo (Fr)
16^{8gs} **0-0-1**

Recognise (Ire) *M Johnston* 71
3 ch g Groom Dancer (USA) - Broken Romance (Ire)
2^{12s} 4^{11gs} 2^{12gf} 2^{18gf} **0-3-4 £3,827**

Recount (Fr) *J R Best* 83 a52
4 b g Sillery (USA) - Dear Countess (Fr)
9^{10s} 11^{14gf} 6^{7gf} 5^{8gf} 12^{8sd} 11^{9gf} 2^{10gf}
3^{10gf} 4^{12gf} 3^{10s} 9^{10g} **0-3-11 £3,125**

Rectangle (Ire) *D Nicholls* 75
4 ch g Fayruz - Moona (USA)
20^{5g} 8^{5gs} 11^{5gf} 13^{5gs} 2^{6gf} 11^{5gf} 7^{5gf}
11^{5g} 18^{5gs} **0-1-9 £1,516**

Red Acer (Ire) *P D Evans*
3 ch g Shinko Forest (Ire) - Another Baileys
9^{10sd} 9^{9sw} 14^{12gf} **0-0-3**

Red Admiral (USA) *Saeed Bin Suroor* 89
2 b c Red Ransom (USA) - Ausherra (USA)
14^{7gs} 1^{8g} **1-0-2 £5,099**

Red Affleck (USA) *P W Chapple-Hyam* 83
2 b g Nicholas (USA) - Lucie Mon Amour (USA)
3^{5gf} 2^{7s} 1^{7gs} 7^{8s} 4^{7s} 8^{7gs} **1-2-6**
£7,718

Red Apache (Ire) *H J Collingridge* 45
2 b c Namid - Special Dissident
13^{7gf} 13^{6s} **0-0-2**

Red Birr (Ire) *A M Balding* 82
3 b g Bahhare (USA) - Cappella (Ire)
9^{7g} 4^{10gf} 1^{10g} 7^{10gs} 8^{14gf} **1-0-5 £6,070**

Red Bloom *Sir Michael Stoute* 118
3 b f Selkirk (USA) - Red Camellia
4^{8g} 3^{8f} 1^{9g} 4^{10g} **1-1-4 £76,402**

Red Chairman *D R Loder*   78
2 br g Red Ransom (USA) - Chine
9^{7gf} 5^{7gf} 4^{6gf} 6^{6gf} **0-0-4 £359**

Red Contact (USA) *Julian Poulton*   39
3 b g Sahm (USA) - Basma (USA)
14^{7gf} **0-0-1**

Red Crystal *C R Wilson*
6 b m Presidium - Crystallography
6^{11sd} **0-0-1**

Red Damson (Ire) *Sir Mark Prescott*   92 a83
3 b g Croco Rouge (Ire) - Damascene (Ire)
2^{14f} 1^{12sd} 2^{14gf} **1-2-3 £6,856**

Red Delirium *P A Blockley*   22 a53
8 b g Robellino (USA) - Made Of Pearl (USA)
6^{8sd} 4^{11sd} 5^{11sd} 2^{8sw} 5^{8ss} 5^{8sd} 2^{11sd} 5^{12sd}
12^{9g} **0-2-9 £846**

Red Duchess *Sir Michael Stoute*   65
2 ch f Halling (USA) - Red Empress
9^{7g} 9^{8gf} **0-0-2**

Red Feather (Ire) *Edward Lynam*   109
3 b f Marju (Ire) - Galyph (USA)
2^{7gf} 1^{7f} 3^{7gv} 1^{8g} 4^{8gf} 9^{8g} **2-1-6**
£61,161

Red Finesse *M A Jarvis*   57
2 b f Soviet Star (USA) - Jouet
8^{6gf} 9^{6s} **0-0-2**

Red Flyer (Ire) *P C Haslam*   a49
5 br g Catrail (USA) - Marostica (Ity)
1^{7sd} **1-0-1 £1,480**

Red Forest (Ire) *J Mackie*   76 a65
5 b g Charnwood Forest (Ire) - High Atlas
3^{12sd} 1^{12sd} 6^{12s} 1^{12gf} 1^{12gf} 5^{10gf} 9^{12g}
3^{12sd} 3^{13gf} 3^{14gf} 1^{14gf} 6^{12s} 1^{14gf} 7^{15s} **5-4-14**
£22,471

Red Fort (Ire) *M A Jarvis*   118
4 b g Green Desert (USA) - Red Bouquet
1^{11s} 3^{12g} 1^{10f} 4^{10g} 2^{10gf} **2-3-5 £47,838**

Red Galaxy (Ire) *D W P Arbuthnot*   58 a15
4 b f Tagula (Ire) - Dancing Season
15^{7gs} PU^{8s} 17^{6g} 13^{9sd} **0-0-4**

Red Hot Ruby *P T Midgley*   37
3 ch f Komaite (USA) - Gleam Of Gold
14^{6gf} 3^{5gs} 3^{5g} 11^{6g} **0-1-4 £1,111**

Red Lancer *R J Price*   111 a89
3 ch g Deploy - Miss Bussell
6^{8sd} 1^{11sd} 1^{9sw} 2^{12ss} 2^{9s} 2^{8s} 2^{8g} 2^{10gs}
1^{12gs} 3^{11g} 6^{16f} 14^{16s} 6^{12s} 7^{12g} 6^{12g} **3-5-15**
£64,211

Red Lantern *R M H Cowell*   a22
3 ch g Young Ern - Croft Sally
11^{7sd} 11^{7sd} **0-0-2**

Red Leicester *J A Glover*   62 a48
4 b f Magic Ring (Ire) - Tonic Chord
3^{6gs} 12^{6gf} 5^{6gf} 15^{6sd} 6^{5sd} 10^{5gf} 5^{6g}
16^{5gs} 10^{5gs} 6^{5gs} 3^{5sd} **1-2-11 £4,368**

Red Marteeney *J G Given*   56
2 ch c Indian Lodge (Ire) - Miss Rossi
11^{6g} 6^{6gf} 13^{6gf} **0-0-3**

Red Melodica (USA) *W P Browne*   42 a31
4 b f Red Ransom (USA) - Melodica
19^{10gf} 8^{7sd} 16^{7sd} 16^{7gf} 9^{8s} 15^{8sh} **0-0-6**

Red Monarch (Ire) *P A Blockley*   71 a30
3 ch g Woodborough (USA) - Sans Ceriph (Ire)
9^{6ss} 10^{6g} 7^{5gf} 6^{8gf} 2^{6f} 1^{6s} 1^{5gs} 10^{6gs}

2-1-8 £8,119

Red Moor (Ire) *R Hollinshead*   a53
4 gr g Eagle Eyed (USA) - Faakirah
2^{11ss} 6^{9ss} 1^{12sd} 2^{12sd} 3^{15sd} 10^{12sd} **1-3-6**
£4,248

Red Mountain *D W Barker*   34
3 b c Unfuwain (USA) - Red Cascade (Ire)
9^{11g} 7^{9gs} 11^{12s} **0-0-3**

Red Opera *Sir Mark Prescott*   53 a41
2 ch g Nashwan (USA) - La Papagena
7^{8f} 9^{8gf} 12^{7sd} 8^{7sd} **0-0-4**

Red Peony *Sir Mark Prescott*   94
2 b f Montjeu (Ire) - Red Azalea
1^{7gf} 3^{7gs} 6^{8g} 2^{7g} **1-1-4 £13,573**

Red Racketeer (USA) *E A L Dunlop*   78
2 b c Red Ransom (USA) - Furajet (USA)
4^{7s} **0-0-1 £322**

Red Rackham (Ire) *J Nicol*   a64
4 b g Groom Dancer (USA) - Manarah
7^{13sd} 16^{12sd} **0-0-2**

Red Riot (USA) *D R Loder*   67
2 b c Red Ransom (USA) - Musical Treat (Ire)
5^{7gs} 3^{9g} 9^{10g} **0-0-3 £836**

Red River Rebel *J R Norton*   66
6 b g Inchinor - Bidweaya (USA)
12^{12gf} 4^{12gf} 8^{13f} 2^{12gf} 2^{13g} 4^{12gf} **0-2-6**
£3,062

Red River Rock (Ire) *C Tinkler*   79 a79
2 b c Spectrum (Ire) - Ann's Annie (Ire)
3^{7g} 9^{8gs} 9^{8gs} 4^{9sd} **0-1-4 £812**

Red Rocky *R Hollinshead*   49 a35
3 b f Danzero (Aus) - Post Mistress (Ire)
7^{6sd} 10^{6f} 5^{8g} 8^{6f} 2^{7g} 16^{6g} 3^{8gf} 5^{7g}
3^{7gs} 3^{10g} 8^{9sd} **0-4-11 £2,155**

Red Romeo *G A Swinbank*   97
3 ch c Case Law - Enchanting Eve
2^{6gs} 4^{6gf} 4^{6g} 1^{6gf} 1^{6g} 1^{6gf} 2^{6s} 3^{6gs}
3-3-8 £26,236

Red Rudy *R M Beckett*   71
2 ch g Pivotal - Piroshka
6^{6gf} 3^{7gs} 7^{7gf} 7^{6hy} **0-1-4 £562**

Red Sahara (Ire) *W J Haggas*   89
3 ch f Desert Sun - Red Reema (Ire)
1^{7g} 6^{8gf} 6^{7gf} 2^{8gs} 4^{8gs} 11^{8gs} 8^{8g} 10^{7gf}
1-1-8 £8,561

Red Sail *J R Fanshawe*   74
3 ch f Dr Fong (USA) - Manhattan Sunset (USA)
3^{8gf} 3^{9gf} 9^{10g} 5^{10g} **0-2-4 £1,792**

Red Scorpion (USA) *W M Brisbourne*   73 a81
5 ch g Nureyev (USA) - Pricket (USA)
1^{16sd} 6^{16sd} 5^{16sd} 8^{16g} 2^{16f} 3^{15gf} 8^{14g}
6^{16gf} 5^{16f} 12^{16g} **1-2-10 £4,663**

Red Silk *Mrs A J Perrett*
3 b f Polish Precedent (USA) - Red Tulle (USA)
14^{10sd} 14^{10gs} **0-0-2**

Red Skelton (Ire) *Ms Deborah J Evans*   55 a71
3 ch g Croco Rouge (Ire) - Newala
10^{10hy} 8^{10g} 10^{12g} 10^{10g} 3^{10sd} 8^{12f} 12^{12hy}
11^{16g} 16^{12sd} 11^{12sd} **0-1-10 £880**

Red Sovereign *I A Wood*   89 a44
3 b f Danzig Connection (USA) - Ruby Princess (Ire)
12^{6s} 15^{6g} 15^{6gf} 7^{5g} 5^{5g} 8^{6gs} 7^{5sd} **1-0-7**
£4,864

Red Spell (Ire) *R Hannon*   88
3 ch c Soviet Star (USA) - A-To-Z (Ire)

12^{8gs} 5^{8g} 1^{8gf} 2^{8gf} 6^{8g} 3^{8gf} **1-2-6**
£14,359

Red Storm *J R Boyle* a55
5 ch m Dancing Spree (USA) - Dam Certain (Ire)
13^{9sd} 6^{12sd} 1^{9sd} 5^{9ss} 14^{10sd} 6^{9ss} **1-0-6**
£1,634

Red Sun *J Mackie* 67
7 b g Foxhound (USA) - Superetta
1^{16gf} 2^{16gf} 6^{17gf} 10^{16s} 6^{14gs} 3^{16g} 12^{17g}
1-2-7 £6,578

Red Top (Ire) *P Gallagher* 91
3 b f Fasliyev (USA) - Petite Epaulette
2^{7g} 3^{8s} 2^{7gf} 7^{8gf} 2^{7g} 1^{8g} 7^{9f} **1-4-7**
£14,220

Red Wine *J A Osborne* 90 a88
5 b g Hamas (Ire) - Red Bouquet
5^{12sw} 7^{16gs} **0-0-2**

Redbank (Ire) *S Dow* a53
3 b g Night Shift (USA) - Bush Rose
2^{8sd} 9^{7sd} 8^{7sd} 7^{8sd} **0-1-4 £728**

Redi (Ity) *L M Cumani* 74 a78
3 b c Danehill Dancer (Ire) - Rossella
7^{8sd} 4^{10gf} 6^{8f} 3^{12gf} 1^{12gs} 9^{14gs} 2^{12sd}
1-2-7 £4,909

Redmarley (Ire) *J G Given* 33
3 b g Croco Rouge (Ire) - Dazzling Fire (Ire)
6^{9g} 7^{12gf} **0-0-2**

Redoubtable (USA) *D W Chapman* 57 a49
13 b h Grey Dawn Ii - Seattle Rockette (USA)
6^{6sd} 1^{6sd} 4^{6sd} 1^{7sd} 13^{7sd} 9^{6hy} 1^{6g} 7^{6s}
11^{7gf} 2^{6gf} 1^{7gf} 6^{8g} 8^{7gf} 4^{6f} 11^{7gf} 11^{6gs} 4^{6hy}
13^{6g} 9^{7gs} 12^{7sd} **4-2-20 £9,263**

Redspin (Ire) *J S Moore* 74 a63
4 ch g Spectrum (Ire) - Trendy Indian (Ire)
3^{16sd} 12^{10g} 15^{16g} 2^{20gf} 4^{14g} 4^{14gs} 12^{16gf}
12^{21g} 8^{14gf} 3^{14gf} 8^{16g} 10^{16gs} **0-3-12 £4,112**

Redswan *A E Jones* 67
9 ch g Risk Me (Fr) - Bocas Rose
2^{8g} **0-1-1 £1,076**

Redwood Rocks (Ire) *B Smart* 85
3 b g Blush Rambler (USA) - Crisp And Cool (USA)
20^{7g} 1^{7g} 13^{7gs} 6^{8g} 11^{7gf} **1-0-5**
£11,895

Redwood Star *P L Gilligan* 62
4 b f Piccolo - Thewaari (USA)
4^{5gf} 12^{5gf} 10^{6gf} 3^{5f} 17^{5g} 4^{5f} VOI^{5gf}
3^{5g} 2^{5gf} **0-4-9 £2,934**

Reedsman (Ire) *R C Guest* 15 a51
3 ch g Fayruz - The Way She Moves
2^{6sd} 13^{8s} 12^{8gf} 15^{6f} 11^{12gf} **0-1-5 £734**

Reem One (Ire) *M A Jarvis* 80
3 b f Rainbow Quest (USA) - Felona
1^{9s} 2^{10s} 2^{12s} **1-2-3 £10,890**

Reem Two *D McCain* 47
3 b f Mtoto - Jamrat Samya (Ire)
6^{8g} 3^{9gf} 2^{12s} 7^{9g} **0-2-4 £2,591**

Reference (Ire) *R Hannon* 31
2 b c Almutawakel - Uffizi (Ire)
18^{7gf} 16^{6gs} 12^{8gs} **0-0-3**

Reflex Blue *R J Price* a48
7 b g Ezzoud (Ire) - Briggsmaid
1^{16sd} 4^{16sd} **1-0-2 £2,534**

Refuse To Bend (Ire) *Saeed Bin Suroor* 126
4 b c Sadler's Wells (USA) - Market Slide (USA)
8^{9gf} 8^{8g} 1^{8gf} 10^{9gs} 11^{8g} 3^{8gf} 5^{10s} **2-1-7**

£418,990

Regal Ali (Ire) *Mrs A Malzard*
5 ch g Ali-Royal (Ire) - Depeche (Fr)
12^{9ss} **0-0-1**

Regal Attire (USA) *A M Balding* 63
2 ch c Kingmambo (USA) - Style Setter (USA)
6^{7gf} **0-0-1**

Regal Dream (Ire) *J W Hills* 78
2 b c Namid - Lovely Me (Ire)
7^{5gf} 3^{6g} 3^{6g} **0-1-3 £1,526**

Regal Fantasy (Ire) *P A Blockley* 38
4 b f King's Theatre (Ire) - Threesome (USA)
12^{11f} 10^{12gf} 1^{16gf} 5^{16gs} **1-0-4 £3,373**

Regal Flight (Ire) *J M Bradley* 52
3 b g King's Theatre (Ire) - Green Belt (Fr)
6^{7gf} 14^{10gf} 6^{8gf} 9^{7gf} 16^{6g} **0-0-5**

Regal Gallery (Ire) *C A Horgan* a78
6 b m Royal Academy (USA) - Polistatic
1^{10sd} 1^{12sd} 3^{10sd} 2^{12sd} 4^{12sd} 6^{14sd}
13^{12sd} **2-2-8 £8,290**

Regal Lustre *J R Weymes* 54
2 b f Averti (Ire) - Noble Lustre (USA)
3^{5gf} 5^{6g} 2^{5g} 6^{7gf} 6^{6gf} **0-1-5 £1,384**

Regal Performer (Ire) *S Kirk* 59
3 b g Ali-Royal (Ire) - Khatiynza
10^{10gs} 19^{10g} 2^{11gf} 2^{11gf} 3^{12f} 4^{12gs} 5^{12gf}
6^{12f} 6^{12gs} **0-2-9 £3,030**

Regal Repose *A J Chamberlain* a15
4 b f Classic Cliche (Ire) - Ideal Candidate
7^{16sd} 7^{11sd} 6^{15sd} 14^{16gf} **0-0-4**

Regal Setting (Ire) *Sir Mark Prescott* 93
3 br g King's Theatre (Ire) - Cartier Bijoux
6^{12g} 1^{14gs} 1^{14s} **2-0-3 £27,396**

Regal Song (Ire) *T J Etherington* 44 a66
8 b g Anita's Prince - Song Beam
13^{6sd} 10^{7ss} 8^{5gs} 19^{5gs} 20^{5gs} 13^{5s}
1^{6sd} **1-0-8 £1,494**

Regal Vintage (USA) *C Grant* 40
4 ch g Kingmambo (USA) - Grapevine (Ire)
8^{12hy} 5^{22s} **0-0-2**

Regency Malaya *M F Harris* a48
3 b f Sri Pekan (USA) - Paola (Fr)
8^{8sd} 5^{11sd} 2^{8sd} 7^{8ss} 7^{8sd} 3^{10sd} 2^{8sd} 5^{9sd}
6^{10sd} **0-3-9 £1,066**

Regency Red (Ire) *W M Brisbourne* 56 a56
6 ch g Dolphin Street (Fr) - Future Romance
4^{14gf} 11^{16g} 1^{12gf} 15^{12g} 12^{16g} 4^{14gs} 7^{12sd}
1-0-7 £3,503

Regent's Secret (USA) *J S Goldie* 69 a69
4 br g Cryptoclearance (USA) - Misty Regent (Can)
4^{8gf} 7^{7g} 7^{7f} 2^{8g} 4^{9sd} 11^{8gf} 3^{7gf} 3^{8g}
12^{9ss} 6^{8gf} 11^{8gf} 3^{8gf} 3^{8g} 1^{9sd} **1-5-14 £7,957**

Regina *Sir Michael Stoute* 89
2 b f Green Desert (USA) - Dazzle
3^{5gf} 1^{5gf} 6^{6g} 1^{5gs} **2-0-4 £8,500**

Regis Flight *R Hollinshead* 67
2 b c Piccolo - Anthem Flight (USA)
8^{6gs} 6^{6g} **0-0-2**

Registrar *Mrs A J Perrett* 70 a71
2 ch c Machiavellian (USA) - Confidante (USA)
5^{7gf} 2^{8g} 7^{8sd} **0-1-3 £1,744**

Regulated (Ire) *D B Feek* 60 a69
3 b g Alzao (USA) - Royal Hostess (Ire)
2^{7sd} 11^{9sw} 1^{10sd} 5^{8sd} 5^{10gf} 1^{10gf} 6^{12gf}
9^{10f} 5^{10sd} 12^{12sd} 7^{12gs} 10^{9gf} 11^{10gf} **2-1-13**

£6,692

Rehearsal *C G Cox*   94
3 b g Singspiel (Ire) - Daralaka (Ire)
2^{8g} 1^{8g} 5^{10gf} 6^{8gs} 8^{12g} **1-1-5 £9,716**

Rehia *J W Hills*   57 a48
3 b f Desert Style (Ire) - Goes A Treat (Ire)
7^{5sd} 4^{6sd} 5^{5sd} 4^{6sd} 4^{5sw} 11^{5g} 3^{5gf} 5^{5f}
10^{5f} 3^{5gf} 1^{5gf} 17^{5gf} 10^{6sd} **1-1-13 £4,450**

Reidies Choice *J G Given*   81
3 b g Royal Applause - Fairy Ring (Ire)
12^{6gs} 2^{7gf} 7^{8gf} 4^{7g} 2^{7gf} 9^{7gf} 3^{7gf} 5^{7gs}
2^{7gf} **0-4-9 £5,944**

Reign Of Fire (Ire) *J W Hills*   38 a25
3 b f Perugino (USA) - White Heat
14^{8gs} 13^{10gf} 11^{8sd} 12^{10f} 13^{10gf} **0-0-5**

Rejoyce (Ire) *J Jay*
3 ch f Dancing Spree (USA) - Zoyce
8^{8sd} **0-0-1**

Relative Hero (Ire) *Miss S J Wilton*   51
4 ch g Entrepreneur - Aunty (Fr)
9^{8gf} 8^{10gf} 2^{12gf} 3^{10gf} 6^{12gs} 4^{12gs} **0-2-6**
£1,633

Relaxed (USA) *Sir Michael Stoute*   90
3 b f Royal Academy (USA) - Sleep Easy (USA)
1^{7g} 8^{8f} **1-0-2 £5,486**

Released (USA) *J H M Gosden*   51
2 b f Red Ransom (USA) - Ispirata (Ire)
11^{8gf} **0-0-1**

Rellim *J Balding*   a59
5 b m Rudimentary (USA) - Tycoon Girl (Ire)
5^{5sd} 8^{5sd} 11^{5ss} 16^{5gs} 13^{5gf} **0-0-5**

Remaadd (USA) *M P Tregoning*   111
3 gr/ro c Daylami (Ire) - Bint Albaadiya (USA)
1^{10g} 3^{12gs} 2^{12gs} **1-1-3 £16,283**

Remembrance *M J Gingell*   a13
4 b g Sabrehill (USA) - Perfect Poppy
12^{10sd} **0-0-1**

Reminiscent (Ire) *R F Johnson Houghton*   68 a71
5 b g Kahyasi - Eliza Orzeszkowa (Ire)
4^{16sd} 2^{12gf} 4^{12sd} 5^{12gf} 8^{13gf} 14^{12g} **0-1-6**
£1,402

Remonstrate (Ire) *T D Easterby*   59
3 b g Alhaarth (Ire) - Truffa (Ire)
6^{7gf} 9^{8gs} **0-0-2**

Ren's Magic *J R Jenkins*
6 gr g Petong - Bath
12^{14gs} **0-0-1**

Rendezvous Point (USA) *J H M Gosden*   69
3 ch f Kingmambo (USA) - Reggie V (USA)
8^{10g} 8^{10gf} **0-0-2**

Rene Barbier (Ire) *J A Glover*   64
3 b g Desert Style (Ire) - Sweet Decision (Ire)
10^{6s} 4^{6s} 1^{5gf} 5^{6gf} 6^{5g} 8^{6g} 12^{7gf} 9^{6gf}
9^{7gs} **1-0-9 £5,862**

Reno's Magic *W G M Turner*   38
3 b f Hello Mister - Mountain Magic
8^{5s} **0-0-1**

Repeat (Ire) *J W Unett*   47 a63
4 ch g Night Shift (USA) - Identical (Ire)
1^{7sd} 2^{7sw} 10^{7sd} 4^{8ss} 4^{8sd} 8^{8sw} 7^{7sw} 10^{5g}
6^{8gf} 14^{6g} 11^{7gf} 7^{6sd} **1-0-12 £2,061**

Repent At Leisure *Julian Poulton*   41
4 b g Bishop Of Cashel - Sutosky
8^{11gf} 8^{14s} 11^{12gf} **0-0-3**

Repertory *M S Saunders*   105

11 b g Anshan - Susie's Baby
9^{5g} 11^{5g} 10^{5gf} 7^{5g} 6^{6f} 9^{5gs} **0-0-6 £525**

Repetoire (Fr) *K O Cunningham-Brown*
4 ch f Zafonic (USA) - Lady Kate (USA)
10^{9sd} 6^{16sd} **0-0-2**

Repulse Bay (Ire) *J S Goldie*   60
6 b g Barathea (Ire) - Bourbon Topsy
6^{8gf} 8^{13g} 3^{16gf} 7^{14gf} 5^{12g} 14^{11g} 9^{12g}
12^{10gf} 7^{16gf} 7^{10s} 8^{14gf} 17^{11s} **0-1-12 £416**

Reqqa *M Johnston*   96
2 b c Royal Applause - Kangra Valley
6^{6g} 1^{6gf} 4^{6gs} 4^{6f} **1-0-4 £7,486**

Rescind (Ire) *Jedd O'Keeffe*   a36
4 b f Revoque (Ire) - Sunlit Ride
10^{9sd} **0-0-1**

Reservoir (Ire) *W J Haggas*   85
3 b g Green Desert (USA) - Spout
2^{9gs} 1^{11gf} 7^{10gf} 5^{12s} 11^{14s} 2^{12g} **1-2-6**
£9,610

Residential *Mrs A J Perrett*   66
3 ch g Zilzal (USA) - House Hunting
4^{7gf} 6^{8gs} 4^{10s} **0-0-3 £345**

Resistance Heroine *E A L Dunlop*   71
2 b f Dr Fong (USA) - Odette
7^{6g} 12^{7gf} 3^{7gf} 7^{8s} 4^{7gf} **0-1-5 £668**

Resonance *N A Twiston-Davies*   71 a60
3 b f Slip Anchor - Music In My Life (USA)
2^{12sd} 8^{10sd} 3^{12gs} 7^{14gs} **0-2-4 £1,794**

Resonate (Ire) *A G Newcombe*   86 a71
6 b h Erin's Isle - Petronelli (USA)
4^{7g} 10^{9gf} 1^{10gf} 2^{12sd} **1-2-4 £11,462**

Resplendent Cee (Ire) *P W Harris*   68
5 ch h Polar Falcon (USA) - Western Friend (USA)
18^{6s} **0-0-1**

Resplendent King (USA) *T G Mills*   73 a72
3 b g King Of Kings (Ire) - Sister Fromseattle (USA)
3^{7sd} 3^{8sd} 5^{8sd} 5^{7sd} 3^{9s} 2^{9gf} 3^{12f} 3^{10g}
13^{9g} **0-5-9 £4,108**

Resplendent One (Ire) *T G Mills*   104
3 b c Marju (Ire) - Licentious
6^{8gf} 27^{8f} 4^{8gs} 4^{8gf} 8^{8hy} **0-1-5 £3,268**

Resplendent Prince *T G Mills*   a68
2 ch c Primo Dominie - Last Result
8^{7sd} **0-0-1**

Ressource (Fr) *G L Moore*   a41
5 b g Broadway Flyer (USA) - Rayonne
5^{13sd} **0-0-1**

Restart (Ire) *P C Haslam*   67
3 b g Revoque (Ire) - Stargard
10^{8gf} 8^{14g} 1^{14gs} 8^{14gf} 2^{16gf} 12^{17gf} **1-1-6**
£4,918

Restoration (Fr) *J H M Gosden*   68
2 gr c Zafonic (USA) - Restless Mixa (Ire)
2^{7s} **0-1-1 £1,455**

Retail Therapy (Ire) *M A Buckley*   35 a55
4 b f Bahhare (USA) - Elect (USA)
2^{12sd} 6^{12sd} 12^{14g} 15^{12gf} **0-1-4 £1,054**

Retirement *M H Tompkins*   91
5 b g Zilzal (USA) - Adeptation (USA)
1^{8s} 3^{8gs} 10^{8g} 10^{8gs} 7^{8gs} 11^{8gs} 11^{7gs}
1-1-7 £7,597

Reveillez *J R Fanshawe*   97
5 gr g First Trump - Amalancher (USA)
6^{16gs} 5^{14gf} **0-0-2 £554**

Revelino (Ire) *Miss S J Wilton*   68

5 b g Revoque (Ire) - Forelino (USA)
6¹²ˢ **0-0-1**

Revenir (Ire) *E F Vaughan*   78 a76
3 ch g Spectrum (Ire) - Petite Liqueurelle (Ire)
7⁷ᵍᶠ 2⁸ᵍ 2⁸ˢᵈ 2⁷ᵍᶠ 4¹⁰ᵍ 1¹⁰ˢᵈ 10¹⁰ˢ **1-3-7**
£7,355

Reversionary *M W Easterby*   52 a54
3 b g Poyle George - Harold's Girl (Fr)
8⁵ᵍ 10⁸ᵍ 5⁷ʰʸ 10⁶ᵍᶠ 15⁶ᵍᶠ 7⁶ˢ 1⁸ᵍ 9⁸ᵍˢ
3⁸ˢᵈ 2⁹ᵍˢ 2¹⁰ˢ 1⁸ˢᵈ **2-3-12 £6,799**

Revien (Ire) *G A Huffer*   54 a72
2 b c Rossini (USA) - Kazimiera (Ire)
3⁵ᵍ 3⁶ˢᵈ **0-2-2 £1,003**

Reviewer (Ire) *M Meade*   67 a19
6 b g Sadler's Wells (USA) - Clandestina (USA)
15¹²ˢᵈ 7¹²ᵍᶠ 12¹³ᵍᶠ 5¹²ᵍ 5¹²ᵍˢ **0-0-5**

Revivalist *M L W Bell*   31
2 b f Benny The Dip (USA) - Brave Revival
9⁷ᵍᶠ **0-0-1**

Rewayaat *B Hanbury*   49
3 b f Bahhare (USA) - Alumisiyah (USA)
9⁵ᶠ **0-0-1**

Rex Romelio (Ire) *K R Burke*   a51
5 ch g Priolo (USA) - Romelia (USA)
10⁸ˢᵈ 2¹¹ˢᵈ 12¹⁰ˢᵈ **0-1-3 £744**

Rhapsody In Silver (Fr) *J Jay*   43
2 gr c Medaaly - Concert
9⁷ᵍˢ **0-0-1**

Rhetoric (Ire) *I R Brown*   a42
5 b g Desert King (Ire) - Squaw Talk (USA)
8¹⁶ˢᵈ 4¹²ˢᵈ 1¹¹ˢᶠ 12¹⁰ʰʸ 6¹⁴ˢᵈ **1-0-5**
£1,456

Rhetorical *P Butler*   45
3 b g Unfuwain (USA) - Miswaki Belle (USA)
5¹⁰ᵍᶠ 12¹⁰ᵍ 6¹⁴ᵍ 10¹⁶ᶠ 11¹²ᵍ **0-0-5**

Rhinefield Boy *J S Goldie*
3 ch g Wolfhound (USA) - Rhinefield Beauty (Ire)
8⁵ᵍᶠ 11⁵ᵍᶠ **0-0-2**

Rhoslan (Ire) *C A Dwyer*   57
2 b c Trans Island - Flimmering
10⁷ᵍ 13⁸ᵍᶠ 10⁷ᵍ **0-0-3**

Rhum *I Semple*   47
4 ch g Bahamian Bounty - Rynavey
PU⁸ᵍˢ 5¹⁰ˢ 10¹⁰ᵍˢ **0-0-3**

Ribbons And Bows (Ire) *C A Cyzer*   72 a64
4 gr f Dr Devious (Ire) - Nichodoula
13¹²ᵍˢ 6¹²ᵍ 8¹²ˢᵈ 4¹²ᶠ 13¹²ᵍᶠ 9¹⁶ˢᵈ 4¹⁰ˢ
5¹¹ᵍˢ 5¹⁴ᵍˢ 1⁹ˢᵈ 8⁹ˢᵈ **1-0-11 £3,383**

Ribbons Of Gold *J A Osborne*   44
2 b f Primo Dominie - In Love Again (Ire)
6⁵ˢ 10⁶ᵍᶠ **0-0-2**

Rich Albi *T D Easterby*   69
2 b g Mind Games - Bollin Sophie
6⁵ᵍᶠ 14⁵ᵍᶠ 4⁶ᵍˢ 12⁶ᵍ 18⁸ᵍ **0-0-5 £284**

Rich Chic (Ire) *M D Hammond*   39
3 b/br f Sri Pekan (USA) - Ring Side (Ire)
12⁸ᵍˢ 4⁸ˢ 8⁸ᵍ **0-0-3 £516**

Richemaur (Ire) *M H Tompkins*   81
4 b f Alhaarth (Ire) - Lady President (Ire)
4⁸ᵍᶠ 16⁸ᵍˢ 12⁸ᵍˢ 4¹²ᵍ 11¹²ᵍᶠ 9¹¹ᵍᶠ **0-0-6**
£970

Richie Boy *P A Blockley*   71 a53
3 b c Dr Fong (USA) - Alathezal (USA)
9⁷ᵍᶠ 8⁸ᵍᶠ 10¹⁰ˢᵈ 12⁸ˢ 1¹³ᵍˢ 8¹⁰ᵍ 1⁸ʰʸ
1¹⁰ˢ **3-0-8 £8,575**

Richmond Lodge (Ire) *M Madgwick*   18
4 br g Sesaro (USA) - Richmond Lillie
14¹⁰ᵍᶠ 5¹⁰ʰʸ **0-0-2**

Richtee (Ire) *R A Fahey*   78
3 ch f Desert Sun - Santarene (Ire)
1¹⁰ᶠ 2⁹ᵍ 5¹¹ˢ 1¹²ᵍᶠ 3¹¹ᵍᶠ 1¹²ˢ 4¹²ˢ 6¹⁶ᵍᶠ
3-1-8 £16,121

Ricky Martan *G C Bravery*   44 a49
3 ch c Foxhound (USA) - Cyrillic
10⁸ˢᵈ 9⁸ˢᵈ 8⁶ˢᵈ 9⁷ˢᵈ 10⁶ˢ 6⁷ᶠ 11⁸ᵍᶠ
6¹⁰ˢᵈ 13¹²ᵍ 9¹²ˢᵈ **0-0-10**

Ridapour (Ire) *D J Wintle*   13
5 b g Kahyasi - Ridiyara (Ire)
12¹⁸ᵍ **0-0-1**

Ridder *D J Coakley*   95
2 b c Dr Fong (USA) - Frond
4⁶ᵍᶠ 5⁶ᶠ 7⁶ᵍ 2⁶ᵍᶠ 2⁶ᵍˢ 1⁶ᵍᶠ 3⁷ᵍʸ **1-2-7**
£16,123

Ride Safari *P Winkworth*   66
2 b g Fraam - Vocation (Ire)
6⁵ᵍᶠ 3⁵ᶠ 4⁷ᵍᶠ **0-0-3 £413**

Ridge Boy (Ire) *R Hannon*   81
3 b c Indian Ridge - Bold Tina (USA)
5⁸ᵍ 6⁸ᵍᶠ 7⁶ᵍᶠ 1⁸ᵍᶠ 12⁹ᵍᶠ 3¹⁰ᵍ 2⁸ᵍ 1⁹ᵍ
10⁸ʰʸ **2-2-9 £14,755**

Ridgeback *I Semple*   60
4 ch g Indian Ridge - Valbra
16⁶ᵍ **0-0-1**

Ridicule *J G Portman*   57 a29
5 b g Piccolo - Mockingbird
10⁶ˢᵈ 8⁶ᵍ 12⁸ᵍˢ 7⁶ʰʸ 11⁶ᵍᶠ 7⁵ᵍᶠ 17⁶ᵍ
11⁶ᵍᶠ **0-0-8**

Rifleman (Ire) *P Bowen*   63
4 ch g Starborough - En Garde (USA)
15⁷ᵍ 17¹⁰ᵍ 8⁹ᵍᶠ 7⁹ˢ **0-0-4**

Right Answer *A P Jarvis*   95
2 b f Lujain (USA) - Quiz Show
4⁵ᵍ 1⁵ᵍ 2⁵ᵍᶠ 2⁵ᵍ 5⁶ᵍᶠ 3⁵ᵍ 20⁶ᵍ 10⁵ˢ
1-3-8 £16,192

Right To Roam (Ire) *J A R Toller*   56 a51
2 b c Namid - Lloc
4⁶ᶠ 7⁶ᵍᶠ 5⁶ˢᵈ **0-0-3 £256**

Rightful Ruler *B W Hills*   77
2 b c Montjoy (USA) - Lady Of The Realm
4⁸ᵍ 4⁸ᵍˢ 14⁸ˢ **0-0-3 £586**

Rightprice Premier (Ire) *K A Ryan*   64 a74
2 b f Cape Cross (Ire) - Machudi
3⁵ᵍᶠ 2⁵ˢ 1⁵ˢᵈ 5⁵ᶠ **1-2-4 £5,412**

Righty Ho *W H Tinning*   50
10 b g Reprimand - Challanging
1¹³ᵍ 3¹¹ᶠ 3¹⁰ᵍᶠ 7¹²ᵍᶠ 6¹²ᵍᶠ 1¹⁴ᵍᶠ 10¹⁴ᵍᶠ
3¹²ᵍᶠ **2-3-8 £5,967**

Rigonza *T D Easterby*   68
3 ch g Vettori (Ire) - Desert Nomad
11⁷ᵍˢ 8¹⁰ʰʸ 5⁹ᵍ 13¹¹ˢ 3⁹ˢ 4⁹ᵍˢ 2¹²ˢ **0-1-7**
£1,971

Riley Boys (Ire) *J G Given*   85 a53
3 ch g Most Welcome - Scarlett Holly
1⁷ˢˢ 12⁷ᵍˢ 1⁷ᵍᶠ 2⁷ᵍᶠ 2⁸ᵍᶠ 2⁸ᵍˢ
2⁸ᵍ 6⁸ᵍˢ **3-6-10 £19,385**

Rileys Dream *B J Llewellyn*   53
5 b m Rudimentary (USA) - Dorazine
8⁶ᵍˢ 5⁷ᵍˢ 10⁶ˢ 9⁶ᵍᶠ 1⁸ᵍᶠ 13⁷ᵍᶠ 12⁶ᵍ 5⁷ᵍᶠ
1⁶ᶠ 2⁷ʰʸ 17⁶ᵍ **2-1-11 £6,643**

Rileys Rocket *R Hollinshead*   17

5 b m Makbul - Star Of Flanders
11⁹ˢʷ 10¹⁰ᵍᶠ 11¹¹⁰ᵍ 12⁷ˢᵈ **0-0-4**

Rill J H M Gosden · 70
2 ch f Unfuwain (USA) - River Cara (USA)
4⁸ᵍᶠ **0-0-1 £490**

Ring Of Destiny P W Harris · 89
5 b g Magic Ring (Ire) - Canna
14¹²ᵍ 11¹²ᵍˢ 8¹²ᵍ **0-0-3**

Ringarooma M H Tompkins · 68
2 b f Erhaab (USA) - Tatouma (USA)
5⁶ᵍˢ 9⁷ᵍᶠ 4⁷ᵍ 2⁶ᵍᶠ 13⁶ᵍˢ **0-1-5 £1,116**

Ringmoor Down D W P Arbuthnot · 112
5 b m Pivotal - Floppie (Fr)
6⁵ᵍ 1⁵ᵍ 3⁶ᵍᶠ 4⁵ᵍᶠ 2⁵ᵍˢ 4⁶ᵍˢ 1⁵ᵍᶠ 1⁵ᵍᶠ
7⁶ᵍᶠ 8⁵ᵍ 2⁶ˢ **3-3-11 £114,314**

Ringside Jack C W Fairhurst · 53
8 b g Batshoof - Celestine
3¹⁸ˢ 7¹⁴ˢ 9¹⁶ʰʸ **0-1-3 £637**

Ringsider (Ire) G A Butler · 93
3 ch g Docksider (USA) - Red Comes Up (USA)
11⁸ᵍˢ 17¹⁰ᵍ 2⁸ᵍ 19⁹ᶠ 9¹⁰ᵍˢ 1¹²ᵍᶠ **2-1-6**
£20,427

Rinjani (USA) Saeed Bin Suroor · 89
3 b c Gone West (USA) - Ringshaan (Fr)
9¹⁰ᵍᶠ 7¹⁰ᵍˢ **0-0-2**

Rinneen (Ire) T Hogan · 53
3 b f Bien Bien (USA) - Sparky's Song
9¹⁰ᵍ 9¹²ˢ 5¹¹ᵍᶠ 3¹²ᵍˢ 4¹²ᵍᶠ 5¹⁶ˢ 9¹⁰ˢ **0-1-7**
£664

Rio Branco B W Hills · a68
3 b f Efisio - Los Alamos
1⁷ˢᵈ **1-0-1 £3,454**

Rio De Janeiro (Ire) A P O'Brien · 89
3 b c Sadler's Wells (USA) - Alleged Devotion (USA)
12¹⁰ᵍᶠ 21⁰ᵍ 11⁰ᶠ 7¹²ᵍ **1-1-4 £8,310**

Rio De Jumeirah C E Brittain · 91
3 b f Seeking The Gold (USA) - Tegwen (USA)
3¹¹ˢ 6¹⁰ᵍᶠ 11¹⁰ᵍˢ 5⁸ᵍ 1¹⁰ᵍˢ 2¹⁰ᵍᶠ **1-1-6**
£13,125

Rio Riva Miss J A Camacho · 84 a79
2 b c Pivotal - Dixie Favor (USA)
2⁶ʰʸ 2⁶ˢᵈ **0-2-2 £2,680**

Ripcord (Ire) B R Johnson · 32 a26
6 b g Diesis - Native Twine
5¹²ˢᵈ 6¹²ˢᵈ 8¹²ᵍᶠ **0-0-3**

Ripple Effect C A Dwyer · 58 a85
4 ch f Elmaamul (USA) - Sharp Chief
2⁶ˢᵈ 1⁷ˢᵈ 2⁷ˢᵈ 10⁶ˢᵈ 1⁷ˢᵈ 5⁶ˢᵈ 6⁷ˢˢ
7⁶ᵍˢ **2-2-9 £9,189**

Riquewihr P Howling · 66
4 ch f Compton Place - Juvenilia (Ire)
4⁶ᵍˢ 3⁶ᵍˢ 4⁶ᵍ **0-2-3 £1,191**

Rise Andrew Reid · 75 a50
3 b f Polar Falcon (USA) - Splice
9⁶ˢᵈ 16⁶ᵍˢ 6⁶ˢ 7⁷ᵍᶠ 1⁶ᵍ 2⁶ᵍ 7⁶ˢ
1⁶ᵍᶠ 2⁶ᵍᶠ 8⁶ᵍ **2-2-11 £11,084**

Rising Shadow (Ire) R A Fahey · 86
3 b g Efisio - Jouet
6⁶ᵍᶠ 2⁶ˢ 4⁷ᵍᶠ 6⁷ᵍᶠ 10⁶ᵍ 15⁶ˢ **0-1-6**
£3,127

Risk Free P D Evans · 57 a79
7 ch g Risk Me (Fr) - Princess Lily
10⁸ᵍ 6⁵ᵍᶠ 7⁷ᵍᶠ 13⁷ˢ 13⁷ᵍ 8⁷ˢᵈ **0-0-6**

Risk Seeker E Lellouche · 121
4 b c Elmaamul (USA) - Robertet (USA)

2¹⁶ˢ 1¹⁶ˢ 4¹⁶ᵍᶠ 4¹⁵ᵍ **1-1-4 £45,964**

Riska King R A Fahey · 77 a75
4 b g Forzando - Artistic Licence
7⁸ˢᵈ 7⁷ˢˢ 12⁸ᵍˢ 19⁷ᶠ 8⁷ᵍᶠ 4⁸ᵍᶠ 3⁸ᵍˢ 3⁷ᵍ
6⁷ᵍˢ 1⁷ᵍˢ 5⁸ᵍ 4⁸ᵍˢ 1⁹ˢᵈ 7⁸ˢᵈ **2-1-14 £11,572**

Risky Way B S Rothwell
8 b g Risk Me (Fr) - Hot Sunday Sport
8¹²ˢʷ **0-0-1**

Riva Royale I A Wood · 88
4 b f Royal Applause - Regatta
8⁷ᵍˢ 10⁷ˢ 14⁶ᵍ 4⁷ᵍᶠ 6⁷ᵍᶠ 9⁷ᵍ **0-0-6**
£483

Rival (Ire) S T Lewis
5 b g Desert Style (Ire) - Arab Scimetar (Ire)
10¹²ˢʷ 9⁸ˢʷ **0-0-2**

Rivelli (Ire) B R Foster
5 b m Lure (USA) - Kama Tashoof
11⁸ˢʷ **0-0-1**

Rivendell M Wigham · a25
8 b m Saddlers' Hall (Ire) - Fairy Kingdom
6⁶ˢᵈ 9⁷ˢᵈ 8⁸ˢˢ **0-0-3**

River Alhaarth (Ire) P W Chapple-Hyam · 72
2 b c Alhaarth (Ire) - Sudden Interest (Fr)
5⁷ᵍᶠ 1⁸ᵍ **1-0-2 £5,668**

River Biscuit (USA) R Hannon · 69
2 ch c Diesis - Elle Est Revenue (Ire)
8⁷ᵍᶠ 5⁷ᵍᶠ 14⁸ᵍˢ 5⁷ᵍˢ **0-0-4**

River Canyon (Ire) W Storey
8 b g College Chapel - Na-Ammah (Ire)
9⁷ˢᵈ **0-0-1**

River Card M H Tompkins · 58
2 ch f Zaha (Can) - Light Hand
7⁸ᵍ 10⁷ˢ **0-0-2**

River Days (Ire) Miss Gay Kelleway · a52
6 b m Tagula - Straw Boater
9⁶ˢᵈ 2⁵ˢˢ 10⁵ˢʷ 6⁵ˢʷ 5⁶ˢᵈ 2⁵ˢˢ 4⁵ˢᵈ **0-2-7**
£1,879

River Falcon J S Goldie · 96
4 b g Pivotal - Pearly River
5⁵ᵍ 7⁵ᵍᶠ 1⁵ᵍˢ 11⁵ᵍᶠ 7⁶ᵍᶠ 3⁶ˢ 11⁶ᵍᶠ 1⁶ᵍ
11⁵ᵍ 18⁶ˢ 4⁵ˢ 5⁶ᵍ 10⁵ˢ 14⁶ˢ **2-1-14**
£29,218

River Gypsy D R C Elsworth · 73
3 b c In The Wings - River Erne (USA)
2¹²ˢ **0-1-1 £1,744**

River Lark (USA) M A Buckley · 46 a53
5 b m Miswaki (USA) - Gold Blossom (USA)
6⁶ˢᵈ 4⁵ˢᵈ 4⁵ˢˢ 6⁵ˢᵈ 8⁵ᵍˢ 6⁶ᵍˢ 5⁵ʰʸ 13⁵ᵍ
3⁵ˢᵈ 17⁶ᵍ **0-1-10 £688**

River Liffey M L W Bell · 83
2 b c Forzando - Rion River (Ire)
8⁶ᵍˢ 2⁷ˢ 2⁸ᵍˢ **0-2-3 £2,888**

River Line (USA) C W Fairhurst · 45
3 b g Keos (USA) - Portio (USA)
4¹⁰ᶠ 7⁹ᵍ 12¹⁰ᵍˢ 10¹⁶ᵍˢ 9¹⁴ᵍᶠ **0-0-5 £273**

River Nurey (Ire) B W Hills · 72
3 gr c Fasliyev (USA) - Dundel (Ire)
3⁷ᶠ 2⁷ᵍᶠ 5⁸ᵍᶠ 2⁸ᵍᶠ 2⁸ʰʸ 4⁸ᵍ **0-4-6**
£5,444

River Of Babylon M L W Bell · 86 a77
3 b f Marju (Ire) - Isle Of Flame
2⁷ᵍˢ 6⁷ᵍᶠ 5⁸ˢ 1⁷ᵍᶠ 1⁸ˢᵈ 7⁷ʰᵒ **2-1-6**
£7,573

River Of Diamonds R Guest · 63
3 b g Muhtarram (USA) - City Gambler

8[8gs] 7[10s] 2[12s] 1[11s] **1-1-4 £4,283**

River Of Fire *C N Kellett*   46 a36
6 ch g Dilum (USA) - Bracey Brook
7[15g] 3[15sd] 9[16sd] 4[10gf] 8[11f] 9[18f] 11[12gf]
1[16gs] 5[15gf] 6[16gf] **1-0-10 £3,199**

River Royale *P W Chapple-Hyam*   88
2 b c Royal Applause - Trundley Wood
3[6gs] 3[6s] 3[7gs] **0-3-3 £2,609**

River Treat (Fr) *G Wragg*   86
3 ch g Irish River (Fr) - Dance Treat (USA)
1[7gs] 6[7g] 5[6gf] 9[6g] 4[7gf] 2[10g] 9[10gf] **1-1-7**
£7,952

Riverweld *G M Moore*   55
2 ch g Weldnaas (USA) - Riverain
6[6g] 4[7f] 2[7g] 5[7gs] 12[7gf] 12[7g] **0-1-6 £836**

Riviera Red (Ire) *L Montague Hall*   a56
4 b g Rainbow Quest (USA) - Banquise (Ire)
11[12gf] 8[13sd] **0-0-2**

Riyadh *M Johnston*   74
6 ch g Caerleon (USA) - Ausherra (USA)
9[18g] 8[16gf] 9[16g] 10[16gs] 3[16g] 9[14gf] 3[17gf]
7[20gf] 7[16gs] 2[16gf] 16[21g] 2[16gs] 6[16hy] 7[16g] 4[16gf]
6[17g] 4[17gf] 3[18g] **0-5-18 £7,510**

Riyma (Ire) *Sir Michael Stoute*   54
2 b f Dr Fong (USA) - Riyafa (Ire)
10[7f] 9[7gs] **0-0-2**

Ro Eridani *Miss S E Forster*   a32
4 b f Binary Star (USA) - Hat Hill
7[8sd] 11[10sd] 12[10sd] **0-0-3**

Road Rage (Ire) *E A L Dunlop*   75
2 b f Giant's Causeway (USA) - Endorsement
3[7g] 1[7gf] 8[8g] **1-1-3 £5,587**

Road To Heaven (USA) *E A L Dunlop*   62
2 ch c Southern Halo (USA) - Glory Way (USA)
3[7gs] 8[7gf] 11[7gf] 13[8g] **0-0-4 £978**

Roaming Vagabond (Ire) *N A Callaghan*   29
3 ch g Spectrum (Ire) - Fiveofive (Ire)
6[11gs] 18[12gf] 7[8f] **0-0-3**

Roan Raider (USA) *Miss V Haigh*   61 a34
4 gr/ro g El Prado (Ire) - Flirtacious Wonder (USA)
11[7sd] 11[6sd] 18[7gf] 3[5g] 4[5gf] 10[6gf] 5[6gf]
3[5gf] 5[6f] 12[6gf] 2[5gs] 12[5gs] 2[5gs] 5[6f] 9[5f] 8[5gf]
7[6g] **0-4-17 £3,487**

Rob Roy (USA) *Sir Michael Stoute*   86
2 b/br c Lear Fan - Camanoe (USA)
1[7g] **1-0-1 £8,628**

Robbie Can Can *A W Carroll*   73 a67
5 b g Robellino (USA) - Can Can Lady
1[12sd] 3[12ss] 1[12sd] 2[12g] **2-2-4 £7,137**

Robbo *K G Reveley*   59
10 b g Robellino (USA) - Basha (USA)
8[18g] **0-0-1**

Robeson *D M Simcock*   72
2 br g Primo Dominie - Montserrat
9[7gf] 5[8gf] **0-0-2**

Robin Sharp *J Akehurst*   a50
6 ch h First Trump - Mo Stopher
2[8sd] 6[8sd] 11[7sd] 5[7sd] 12[7ss] 7[7sd] 4[8sd]
12[7hy] 2[8sd] **0-2-9 £1,244**

Robinzal *T D Easterby*   69
2 b g Zilzal (USA) - Sulitelma (USA)
9[7gf] 3[7gs] 2[7gs] 6[7f] 7[8gs] **0-2-5 £1,701**

Robmantra *B J Llewellyn*   69
2 b c Prince Sabo - Eliza Jane
6[7f] 5[6gf] 3[5g] 6[5gs] 15[7gf] 4[5hy] 8[5gs] 7[5hy]

0-0-8 **£1,187**

Robury *E J Alston*   19
2 b g Robellino (USA) - Youdontsay
7[5hy] 9[6gf] 11[5g] **0-0-3**

Robwillcall *A Berry*   59
4 b f Timeless Times (USA) - Lavernock Lady
14[5g] 5[5gf] 1[5gf] 5[5gf] 5[5gf] 10[5gs] 5[5f] 5[5gs]
13[6gs] 7[5s] 2[5s] **1-1-11 £4,357**

Rocamadour *M R Channon*   86
2 b c Celtic Swing - Watch Me (Ire)
5[7gs] 1[8gs] 2[8gs] 2[9g] **1-1-4 £10,232**

Rocinante (Ire) *J J Quinn*   62 a57
4 b g Desert Story (Ire) - Antapoura (Ire)
9[9ss] 8[8sd] 8[8sd] 3[7ss] 11[11s] 18[hy] 1[8s] 8[9sd]
14[8gf] 6[8sd] 13[9gs] 9[8hy] 8[7sd] **2-1-13 £7,152**

Rock Chick *J H M Gosden*   49
2 ch f Halling (USA) - Band (USA)
9[6gf] **0-0-1**

Rock Concert *I W McInnes*   a72
6 b m Bishop Of Cashel - Summer Pageant
1[9sd] 2[8sw] 3[9sd] 8[9sd] **1-2-4 £4,037**

Rock Dove (Ire) *Sir Mark Prescott*   75
2 b f Danehill (USA) - Littlefeather (Ire)
1[5gf] **1-0-1 £5,973**

Rock Fever (Ire) *M J Wallace*   58
2 ch f Desert Sun - Icefern
8[6gf] 10[6g] 7[7s] 14[6s] **0-0-4**

Rock Haven (Ire) *P W Harris*   30
2 b c Danehill Dancer (Ire) - Mahabba (USA)
10[6gf] **0-0-1**

Rock Lobster *J G Given*   70 a73
3 b g Desert Sun - Distant Music
7[10s] 5[12gs] 6[10s] 3[12sd] 6[12sd] 1[10gf] 4[10gs]
6[10g] **1-1-8 £4,740**

Rockburst *K R Burke*   93
2 b f Xaar - Topwinder (USA)
5[5s] 2[6gf] 1[6gf] 3[6g] 8[7s] 1[6gf] 15[6s] **2-1-7**
£9,589

Rockerfella Lad (Ire) *M Todhunter*   48
4 b g Danetime (Ire) - Soucaro
10[10gs] 18[9gs] **0-0-2**

Rocket (Ire) *H J Manners*   57 a47
3 ch g Cadeaux Genereux - Prends Ca (Ire)
9[7gs] 4[7sd] 3[5s] 11[7g] 3[6g] **0-2-5 £1,288**

Rocket Force (USA) *E A L Dunlop*   83
4 ch g Spinning World (USA) - Pat Us (USA)
11[10gs] 10[10g] 11[10g] **0-0-3**

Rockets 'n Rollers (Ire) *R Hannon*   109 a94
4 b c Victory Note (USA) - Holly Bird
3[7ss] 3[8g] 3[7ys] 2[7gs] 3[7gs] 1[7g] 4[8s] 5[7gs] 4[7gf]
8[7s] 7[8f] 10[7g] **1-4-12 £38,918**

Rockley Bay (Ire) *P J Makin*   61 a27
3 b g Mujadil (USA) - Kilkee Bay (Ire)
8[6s] 15[7gf] 7[6gf] 9[8g] 2[6g] 19[6g] 7[8sd] **0-1-7**
£872

Rockpiler *J Howard Johnson*   72
2 b g Halling (USA) - Emma Peel
4[6gf] 14[8f] **0-0-2 £414**

Rocky Rambo *R D E Woodhouse*   70
3 b g Sayaarr (USA) - Kingston Girl
8[12g] 12[8sd] **0-0-2**

Rocky Reppin *J Balding*   57 a48
4 b g Rock City - Tino Reppin
13[10g] 13[8gs] 15[8g] 17[7gf] 3[7sd] 4[8sd] 10[8sd]
8[8gs] 11[8gs] **0-2-9 £434**

Rockys Girl *M J Ryan* 35 a46
2 b f Piccolo - Lady Rockstar
11⁶ᵍᶠ 7⁷ˢᵈ 15⁷ᵍᶠ 13⁷ˢ 15⁶ˢ **0-0-5**

Rodiak *P R Hedger*
5 b g Distant Relative - Misty Silks
10¹⁴ˢᵈ 13¹⁰ˢᵈ **0-0-2**

Roehampton *Sir Michael Stoute* 103
3 b c Machiavellian (USA) - Come On Rosi
6⁹ᵍ 5¹²ᵍˢ 3¹⁰ᵍᶠ 13¹²ᵍᶠ 8¹⁰ʰʸ **0-1-5**
£5,375

Rojabaa *W G M Turner* 53
5 b g Anabaa (USA) - Slava (USA)
6¹⁰ᶠ 5¹⁰ᵍ 5¹⁰ᶠ 5¹⁰ᵍᶠ 11¹⁰ᵍᶠ **0-0-5**

Roko *D Shaw* 54 a51
2 b g Komaite (USA) - Robert's Daughter
7⁵ˢᵈ 9⁶ᵍᶠ 11⁶ᵍ 4⁵ᵍˢ 3⁵ᵍˢ 3⁵ʰʸ 1⁶ˢʷ 12⁷ᵍᶠ
8⁵ʰʸ 13⁵ʰʸ **1-1-10 £5,341**

Rolex Free (Arg) *D Flood* 57 a64
6 ch g Friul (Arg) - Karolera (Arg)
12¹²ˢᵈ 6¹⁶ˢˢ 8¹⁰ᵍᶠ 8¹⁰ˢᵈ 3¹⁰ᵍᶠ 1¹²ˢᵈ 4¹²ᶠ
1¹²ˢᵈ 11¹⁶ˢ 4¹¹ᵍ 3¹²ᵍ 20¹⁷ᵍ **2-2-12 £6,659**

Rollerbird *A M Balding* a73
2 b f Sinndar (Ire) - Speedybird (Ire)
2⁸ˢᵈ **0-1-1 £1,328**

Rollswood (USA) *P R Hedger* 64 a64
4 ch g Diesis - Spit Curl (USA)
5¹⁰ˢᵈ 6¹¹ᵍ 6¹²ˢᵈ 8¹⁰ᵍˢ 7¹²ˢᵈ **0-0-5**

Roma Valley (Fr) *R Guest* 28
2 gr f Sagamix (Fr) - Lois (Ire)
13⁷ᵍᶠ 19⁷ᵍ **0-0-2**

Roman Army (Ire) *A M Balding* 58
2 b c Trans Island - Contravene (Ire)
5⁸ʰʸ **0-0-1**

Roman Empire *K A Ryan* 60 a64
4 b g Efisio - Gena Ivor (USA)
7⁸ˢᵈ 4⁶ˢᵈ 1⁶ˢᵈ 3⁷ˢᵈ 3⁶ˢᵈ 5⁷ˢᵈ 4⁷ˢ 10⁶ᵍˢ
1⁶ᵍ 8⁶ˢᵈ **2-2-10 £7,125**

Roman Forum *H R A Cecil* 70
3 b c Selkirk (USA) - Flit (USA)
6¹⁰ᵍᶠ 5¹²ᵍᶠ **0-0-2**

Roman King (Ire) *B D Leavy* 25
9 b g Sadler's Wells (USA) - Romantic Feeling
10¹²ᵍˢ **0-0-1**

Roman Love (Ire) *J R Fanshawe* a38
3 ch f Perugino (USA) - Bordighera (USA)
4⁷ˢʷ **0-0-1**

Roman Maze *W M Brisbourne* 73 a77
4 ch g Lycius (USA) - Maze Garden (USA)
12⁷ᵍᶠ 5⁷ᵍᶠ 7⁸ᵍᶠ 7⁷ᵍ 7⁷ᵍᶠ 4⁷ᵍᶠ 2⁸ᵍᶠ 4⁷ˢ
2⁷ᵍᶠ 12⁷ˢ 3⁶ˢᵈ **0-3-11 £5,735**

Roman Mistress (Ire) *T D Easterby* 76
4 ch f Titus Livius (Fr) - Repique (USA)
11⁶ᵍ 4⁵ᵍᶠ 6⁵ᶠ 3⁶ᵍᶠ 8⁵ᵍˢ 5⁵ᵍ 7⁶ᵍᶠ 4⁵ᵍᶠ
1⁵ᵍˢ 10⁵ᵍˢ 22⁵ᵍˢ 9⁵ᵍ **1-1-12 £5,432**

Roman Quintet (Ire) *D W P Arbuthnot* 71 a73
4 ch g Titus Livius (Fr) - Quintellina
9⁵ˢᵈ 10⁶ˢᵈ 14⁵ˢ 3⁵ᵍ 2⁶ᵍ 2⁶ˢ 2⁶ᵍ 2⁷ˢᵈ
0-5-8 £6,183

Roman The Park (Ire) *T D Easterby* 45 a42
3 b f Titus Livius (Fr) - Missfortuna
3⁸ˢᵈ 1⁸ˢᵈ 2⁷ˢᶠ 3⁸ˢᵈ 1⁸ᵍᶠ 3⁸ᵍᶠ 4⁹ᵍ 3⁸ᵍᶠ
2⁸ᶠ 10⁸ᵍˢ **2-3-10 £5,322**

Romanova (Ire) *D R Loder* 69
2 b f Grand Lodge (USA) - Millitrix
8⁶ᵍˢ 4⁷ᵍᶠ 13⁷ᵍ **0-0-3 £458**

Romantic Drama (Ire) *Mrs A L M King*
3 b f Primo Dominie - Antonia's Choice
13⁶ᵍˢ 13⁸ᵍ 13⁷ᵍˢ **0-0-3**

Romantic Gift *J M P Eustace* 64
2 b f Cadeaux Genereux - Last Romance (Ire)
10⁵ᵍᶠ 8⁶ᵍᶠ 8⁷ᵍᶠ 12⁷ᵍˢ 13⁶ˢ **0-0-5**

Romany Nights (Ire) *Miss Gay Kelleway* 88 a78
4 b g Night Shift (USA) - Gipsy Moth
5⁶ˢʷ 11⁶ˢʷ 4⁷ˢˢ 3⁶ᵍˢ 4⁶ᵍᶠ 2⁶ᵍᶠ 2⁶ᵍˢ 2⁵ᵍᶠ
4⁵ᵍ 6⁵ᵍ 16⁶ᵍᶠ 2⁶ᵍ 7⁵ᵍᶠ 5⁶ᵍᶠ 3⁶ᵍᶠ 12⁶ᵍˢ
0-6-16 £12,780

Romany Prince *D R C Elsworth* 110
5 b g Robellino (USA) - Vicki Romara
3¹⁴ᵍᶠ 3²²ᶠ 2¹⁶ᵍˢ 5¹⁶ᵍᶠ 5¹⁶ᵍ 7¹⁸ᵍ **0-3-6**
£17,887

Romaric (USA) *J R Norton* 87
3 b g Red Ransom (USA) - Eternal Reve (USA)
4⁷ᵍˢ 10⁸ᵍᶠ 15⁷ᵍˢ **0-0-3 £836**

Rome (Ire) *G P Enright* 71 a62
5 br g Singspiel (Ire) - Ela Romara
3¹²ˢᵈ 12¹⁴ʰʸ 3¹⁴ᵍ 5¹⁴ᵍᶠ 5¹²ᵍᶠ 4¹⁴ᵍᶠ 14¹⁶ᵍ
11¹²ᵍᶠ **0-2-8 £2,002**

Romeo's Day *M R Channon* 51 a61
3 ch g Pursuit Of Love - Daarat Alayaam (Ire)
11¹⁰ˢ 2¹⁰ᵍᶠ 4¹²ᵍ 3¹¹ᵍᶠ 11¹⁴ᶠ 7¹⁶ᵍˢ 8¹⁶ᵍᶠ
8¹²ᵍˢ 5¹²ᵍˢ 4¹⁰ᵍ 10¹⁰ᵍᶠ 1¹⁰ᵍ 1¹²ˢᵈ **2-2-13**
£5,738

Romil Star (Ger) *K R Burke* 58 a75
7 b g Chief's Crown (USA) - Romelia (USA)
7¹⁴ᵍ 8¹⁶ᵍˢ 2¹⁶ᵍ 1¹¹ˢᵈ 4¹²ᶠ 1¹⁵ˢᵈ 1¹²ˢᵈ
3¹¹ˢᵈ 5¹²ˢ 2¹²ˢᵈ 1¹²ˢ 11¹⁴ᵍᶠ 6¹²ᵍ **4-3-13**
£12,039

Rondelet (Ire) *R M Beckett* 87
3 b g Bering - Triomphale (USA)
2⁸ᵍˢ 9⁸ᵍˢ 2⁸ᵍᶠ 3⁹ᵍᶠ 2¹⁰ᵍ 1¹⁰ᵍ 7¹⁰ᵍᶠ 4¹⁰ᵍ
5¹⁰ᵍ 5⁹ᵍ **1-4-10 £13,891**

Ronnie From Donny (Ire) *B Ellison* 73 a64
4 b g Eagle Eyed (USA) - New Rochelle (Ire)
4⁷ˢᵈ 11⁶ˢᵈ 7⁸ˢʷ URᶦ⁶ᵍˢ 5⁷ᵍ 5⁷ˢ 11⁶ʰʸ
11⁶ᶠ 5⁷ᵍᶠ 5⁷ᵍ 5⁷ᵍᶠ 17⁶ᵍᶠ 10⁶ᵍᶠ 14⁶ᵍᶠ 12⁶ˢᵈ
10⁷ˢᵈ **0-0-16 £313**

Ronnies Lad *Andrew Reid* 53 a34
2 b g Lake Coniston (Ire) - Lycius Touch
5⁵ˢᵈ 8⁵ˢˢ 1⁶ᵍᶠ 2⁶ᶠ 2⁶ᶠ 8⁷ᵍᶠ 4⁶ᶠ **1-2-7**
£5,100

Rood Boy (Ire) *J S King* 61 a58
3 b c Great Commotion (USA) - Cnocma (Ire)
4⁷ˢˢ 5⁸ᵍ 5⁸ᵍˢ 12⁸ᵍᶠ 5⁸ᵍ 10⁹ˢ **0-0-6**
£314

Roodeye *R F Johnson Houghton* 94
2 b f Inchinor - Roo
2⁵ᶠ 1⁵ᵍ 5⁵ᵍ 6⁵ᵍ 3⁶ᵍ 4⁶ᵍ 13⁶ᵍᶠ **1-2-7**
£9,777

Rooftop Protest (Ire) *T Hogan* 77
7 b g Thatching - Seattle Siren (USA)
4¹²ᵍʸ 3¹⁶ᶠ 3¹⁶ʸ 1¹⁶ᵍᶠ 6¹⁶ᵍᶠ 1¹⁶ᶠ 1¹⁶ᵍ
8¹⁶ᵍ 5¹⁴ʸˢ **4-2-10 £27,351**

Rooks Bridge (Ire) *G A Ham* 26 a36
2 ch g General Monash (USA) - Lisa's Pride (USA)
14⁶ᵍᶠ 13⁷ˢᵈ 7⁷ˢᵈ **0-0-4**

Roppongi Dancer *Mrs N Macauley* 30 a27
5 b m Mtoto - Ice Chocolate (USA)
5¹⁵ˢᵈ 3¹²ˢᵈ 8¹⁶ˢᵈ 5¹⁶ˢᵈ 7¹¹ᶠ **0-1-5 £181**

Rosablanca (Ire) *J G Given* a39
2 b f Sinndar (Ire) - Elegant Bloom (Ire)
14⁷ˢᵈ **0-0-1**

Rosacara *D J Daly*   71
3 b f Green Desert (USA) - Rambling Rose
2⁷ᵍ 2⁸ᵍᶠ 15⁹ᵍ 7⁷ᶠ **0-2-4 £2,174**

Rosapenna (Ire) *C F Wall*   58 a58
2 b f Spectrum (Ire) - Blaine (USA)
5⁶ᵍᶠ 14⁶ᵍ 5⁶ˢᵈ 6⁷ᵍᶠ 11⁸ˢ **0-0-5**

Rose Bien *P J McBride*   36
2 b/br f Bien Bien (USA) - Madame Bovary
9⁸ᵍˢ **0-0-1**

Rose Of York (Ire) *T D Walford*   52
4 b f Emarati (USA) - True Ring
4⁶ᵍᶠ 10⁶ᵍˢ **0-0-2** £312

Rose Tea (Ire) *Miss E C Lavelle*   5
5 ro m Alhaarth (Ire) - Shakamiyn
8¹⁵ᵍ **0-0-1**

Roseanna (Fr) *Mme C Head-Maarek*   100
3 b f Anabaa (USA) - Dancing Rose (Fr)
3⁷ᵍ 10⁸ʰʸ 8⁷ˢ **0-1-3 £5,500**

Rosecliff *A M Balding*   68
2 b c Montjeu (Ire) - Dance Clear (Ire)
4⁸ˢ 4¹⁰ˢ **0-0-2 £636**

Rosein *Mrs G S Rees*   73 a71
2 b f Komaite (USA) - Red Rosein
1⁵ˢᵈ 7⁵ᵍᶠ 6⁶ᵍˢ **1-0-3 £3,393**

Rosencrans (USA) *Saeed Bin Suroor*   37 a106
3 b c Forest Wildcat (USA) - General's Mistress (USA)
3⁸ᶠᵗ 1⁸ᶠᵗ 1⁷ˢᵈ 4⁸ˢᵈ 6⁷ᵍ **2-1-5 £68,994**

Roses Of Spring *R M H Cowell*   86
6 gr m Shareef Dancer (USA) - Couleur De Rose
7⁵ˢ 3⁵ᵍᶠ 17⁵ᵍᶠ 10⁵ᶠ 10⁵ᵍ 6⁵ᵍ 7⁵ᶠ 11⁶ᵍ
0-1-8 £2,293

Rosie Mac *N Bycroft*   58
3 ch f First Trump - Carol Again
6⁷ᶠ 3⁷ˢ 4⁷ᵍ 6⁷ᵍᶠ 6¹⁰ᵍᶠ 10⁸ᵍˢ 4¹⁰ᵍ **0-1-7**
£1,563

Rosie Maloney (Ire) *N P Littmoden*
3 b f Docksider (USA) - Magic Lady (Ire)
11⁷ᵍˢ **0-0-1**

Rosie Muir *Mrs A L M King*   45 a16
2 br f Mind Games - Step On Degas
10⁶ᵍ 7⁶ᵍ 10⁶ˢᵈ **0-0-3**

Rosie's Result *M Todhunter*   54
4 ch g Case Law - Precious Girl
10⁵ʰʸ 10⁵ᵍᶠ 10⁵ᵍˢ 15ᵍˢ 9⁵ᵍᶠ 11⁵ᵍᶠ 6⁵ᵍˢ
13⁶ʰʸ 11⁵ᶠ **1-0-9 £3,708**

Rosiella *M Blanshard*   70
2 b f Tagula (Ire) - Queen Of Silk (Ire)
12⁶ᵍᶠ 5⁶ᵍᶠ 1⁶ᵍᶠ 3⁶ᵍˢ 4⁵ᵍᶠ 6⁶ᵍˢ 16⁵ᵍᶠ
1-1-7 £4,423

Rosings *P W Harris*   48
3 ch f Grand Lodge (USA) - Hajat
14⁸ᵍᶠ 9⁹ᵍᶠ **0-0-2**

Roskilde (Ire) *M R Channon*   76
4 b g Danehill (USA) - Melisendra (Fr)
8⁸ᵍᶠ 14⁸ᶠ **0-0-2**

Ross Is Boss *C J Teague*
2 gr g Paris House - Billie Grey
10⁶ᵍ 23⁶ᵍᶠ **0-0-2**

Ross Moor *Mrs A J Perrett*   36
2 b c Dansili - Snipe Hall
14⁸ᵍᶠ **0-0-1**

Rossall Point *J L Dunlop*   69
3 b g Fleetwood (Ire) - Loch Clair (Ire)
4¹⁰ᵍ 5¹²ᵍᶠ 8¹⁰ᵍᶠ 4¹⁴ᵍᶠ 12¹⁶ᵍˢ 3¹⁶ᵍˢ 3¹⁷ˢ
0-2-7 £1,641

Rossbeigh (Ire) *D R Loder*   61
2 b c Alhaarth (Ire) - Ring Of Kerry (Ire)
10⁷ˢ **0-0-1**

Rosselli (USA) *A Berry*   67
8 b g Puissance - Miss Rossi
13⁶ᵍ 75ʰʸ 11⁶ᵍˢ 10⁸ᵍ 8⁷ᵍᶠ 8⁶ᵍ F7ᵍᶠ **0-0-7**

Rossin Gold (Ire) *P A Blockley*   a43
2 b g Rossini (USA) - Sacred Heart (Ire)
6⁶ˢᵈ **0-0-1**

Rosti *P C Haslam*   13 a53
4 b g Whittingham (Ire) - Uaeflame (Ire)
1⁷ˢᵈ 1⁸ˢᵈ 3⁸ˢᵈ 8⁸ˢᵈ 6⁸ˢʷ 3⁷ᵍ **2-1-6**
£3,546

Rotuma (Ire) *M Dods*   82
5 b g Tagula (Ire) - Cross Question (USA)
9¹⁰ˢ 5¹⁰ˢ 8⁸ᵍ 3¹¹ᵍᶠ 1¹⁰ᵍ 6¹⁰ᵍᶠ 1¹⁰ᵍ 2¹⁰ᵍˢ
5¹⁰ˢ 1¹⁰ᵍᶠ 9¹⁰ᵍˢ 9¹⁰ˢ 7¹⁰ˢ 8¹⁰ˢ **3-2-14**
£20,073

Rouge Blanc (USA) *G A Harker*   5
4 b f King Of Kings (Ire) - Style N' Elegance (USA)
9¹⁶ᵍ 7¹⁶ᵍᶠ 13¹⁴ᵍᶠ **0-0-3**

Rouge Et Noir *K G Reveley*   56
6 b g Hernando (Fr) - Bayrouge (Ire)
14⁸ᵍ 7⁸ᵍᶠ 4¹⁰ᵍᶠ 3¹⁴ᵍᶠ 9¹⁶ᶠ **0-1-5 £769**

Rousing Thunder *W Storey*   a3
7 b g Theatrical - Moss (USA)
10¹⁶ˢᵈ 16¹¹ˢᵈ **0-0-2**

Route Sixty Six (Ire) *Jedd O'Keeffe*   55 a26
8 b m Brief Truce (USA) - Lyphards Goddess (Ire)
8⁹ˢᵈ 6⁸ʰʸ 2⁹ᵍ 16⁷ᵍ 8⁸ᵍ 6¹⁰ˢ **0-1-6**
£2,170

Rovella *Mrs H Dalton*   37 a19
3 b f Robellino (USA) - Spring Flyer (Ire)
7¹²ˢ 12¹⁰ˢ 7⁸ˢᵈ 8¹²ᵍᶠ **0-0-4**

Roving Vixen (Ire) *J L Spearing*   43 a43
3 b f Foxhound (USA) - Rend Rover (Fr)
13⁷ˢᵈ 8⁷ᵍˢ 4⁷ˢᵈ 13¹⁰ʰʸ 3⁸ˢᵈ 3⁸ˢᵈ 4⁸ᶠ 7⁸ᶠ
9⁸ᵍᶠ 5⁷ᵍˢ 8⁹ᵍᶠ 5⁷ᵍˢ **0-2-12 £579**

Rowan Lodge (Ire) *M H Tompkins*   83
2 ch c Indian Lodge (Ire) - Tirol Hope (Ire)
14⁶ᵍᶠ 3⁶ᵍˢ 1⁶ᵍᶠ 2⁷ᵍᶠ 1⁶ˢ 9⁶ᵍˢ 2⁷ᵍ 9⁶ᵍᶠ
4⁶ᵍ **2-3-9 £13,722**

Rowan Pursuit *J Akehurst*   40 a74
3 b f Pursuit Of Love - Golden Seattle (Ire)
1⁷ˢᵈ 7⁷ˢᵈ 5⁷ˢᵈ 7⁸ˢᵈ 11⁸ᵍᶠ 16⁷ˢ **1-1-6**
£3,643

Rowan Tree *A P O'Brien*   97
2 b c Singspiel (Ire) - Dashing Water
1⁶ᵍ 8⁷ᵍˢ 7⁷ᵍ 7⁷ʸ **1-0-4 £9,450**

Rowan Warning *W J Haggas*   31
2 b c Diktat - Golden Seattle (Ire)
5⁶ᵍᶠ **0-0-1**

Roxanne Mill *P A Blockley*   84
6 b m Cyrano De Bergerac - It Must Be Millie
3⁵ˢ 2⁵ˢ 6⁵ᵍˢ 3⁵ᵍᶠ 2⁵ᶠ 3⁵ᵍᶠ 5⁵ᵍ 6⁵ᵍ 1⁵ᵍᶠ
2⁵ᵍᶠ 9⁵ˢ 2⁵ᵍ 16⁵ᵍᶠ **1-7-13 £13,350**

Roy McAvoy (Ire) *M A Barnes*   8 a44
6 b g Danehill (USA) - Decadence
10⁸ˢʷ 14⁶ˢᵈ 10⁸ˢᵈ 4¹⁰ˢᵈ 10⁷ᵍᶠ **0-0-5**

Royal Abigail (Ire) *E A L Dunlop*   45
2 b f Inchinor - Lady Abigail (Ire)
15⁶ᵍ 13⁷ᵍᶠ **0-0-2**

Royal Accolade *B Hanbury*   42
2 b f Royal Applause - Zafaaf

9⁵ˢ 16⁵ᵍᶠ 7⁵ᵍ **0-0-3**

Royal Advocate *J W Hills* 46 a65
4 b g Royal Applause - Kept Waiting
4⁸ˢᵈ 5⁸ˢᵈ 6⁶ᵍᶠ **0-0-3 £270**

Royal Alchemist *M D I Usher* 92
2 b f Kingsinger (Ire) - Pure Gold
16ᵍˢ 2⁶ᵍᶠ 7⁷ᵍᶠ 8⁷ᵍˢ 5⁶ᵍˢ 13⁷ᵍ **1-1-6**
£10,965

Royal Approach *M Blanshard* 61
3 b f Royal Applause - Passionelle
5¹¹ᵍ 11¹²ˢᵈ 9¹⁰ᵍˢ **0-0-3**

Royal Atalza (Fr) *G A Huffer* a68
7 gr g Saint Preuil (Fr) - Crystalza (Fr)
1¹²ˢˢ 8¹⁶ˢˢ **1-0-2 £3,308**

Royal Awakening (Ire) *R E Barr* 50 a31
3 b g Ali-Royal (Ire) - Morning Surprise
8⁶ˢᵈ 11⁵ˢ 4⁷ᵍᶠ 5⁶ᶠ 7⁶ᶠ 4⁷ᵍᶠ **0-0-6 £265**

Royal Axminster *Mrs P N Dutfield* 50 a35
9 b g Alzao (USA) - Number One Spot
7¹¹ˢᵈ 5¹²ˢᵈ 2¹²ᵍᶠ 7¹²ᵍᶠ UR¹¹ᵍᶠ 1¹²ᵍᶠ **1-1-6**
£4,253

Royal Bathwick (Ire) *B R Millman* 82
4 b f King's Theatre (Ire) - Ring Of Light
3¹⁰ᵍ 3¹²ᵍᶠ 4¹²ᵍˢ 6¹²ˢ 8¹²ˢ **0-2-5 £2,748**

Royal Castle (Ire) *Mrs K Walton* 42
10 b g Caerleon (USA) - Sun Princess
6¹⁶ᵍᶠ 6¹⁶ᶠ **0-0-2**

Royal Cavalier *R Hollinshead* 107 a73
7 b g Prince Of Birds (USA) - Gold Belt (Ire)
12¹²ˢᵈ 1¹²ᵍ 4¹³ᵍˢ 5¹²ᵍ 9¹⁴ᵍ 17¹⁴ˢ **1-0-6**
£18,040

Royal Challenge *G A Butler* 89
3 b c Royal Applause - Anotheranniversary
2⁵ᵍᶠ 1⁵ᵍˢ 1⁵ᵍᶠ 6⁵ᵍᶠ 3⁵ᵍˢ 2⁵ᵍ 8⁶ᵍᶠ **2-3-7**
£15,343

Royal Cozyfire (Ire) *B Palling* 57
2 b g Revoque (Ire) - Mystic Thoughts (Ire)
5⁶ᵍᶠ 1⁵ᵍᶠ **1-0-2 £2,562**

Royal Dignitary (USA) *D R Loder* 90 a90
4 b/br g Saint Ballado (Can) - Star Actress (USA)
3⁷ᶠᵗ 6⁸ᶠᵗ 5⁸ᵍᶠ 15⁷ˢᵈ **0-1-4 £5,027**

Royal Distant (USA) *M W Easterby* 70
3 ch f Distant View (USA) - Encorenous (USA)
6⁸ˢ 7⁷ᵍˢ 7¹²ᵍˢ 9¹⁰ᵍᶠ 8¹⁰ᵍᶠ 9⁹ᵍ 8¹⁰ᵍᶠ 2¹⁰ᵍᶠ
7¹²ᵍᶠ 14⁸ᵍˢ 7¹²ᵍᶠ 9¹⁴ᵍ 9¹⁰ˢ **0-1-13 £2,100**

Royal Exposure (Ire) *H Alexander* a10
7 b g Emperor Jones (USA) - Blue Garter
4⁹ˢᵈ **0-0-1**

Royal Fashion (Ire) *I W McInnes* a49
4 b f Ali-Royal (Ire) - Fun Fashion (Ire)
6¹⁰ˢᵈ 9⁸ˢᵈ **0-0-2**

Royal Flight *P W Harris* 52
3 b c Royal Applause - Duende
13⁷ᵍˢ 14⁸ᵍˢ 13⁸ᵍ **0-0-3**

Royal Flynn *M Dods* 59
2 b g Royal Applause - Shamriyna (Ire)
6⁶ᵍᶠ 4⁷ᵍᶠ 10⁶ᵍᶠ 6⁷ᵍᶠ 5⁸ᵍ **0-0-5 £282**

Royal Game *D R Loder* a42
2 b g Vettori (Ire) - Ground Game
10⁸ˢᵈ **0-0-1**

Royal Grand *T D Barron* 51 a72
4 ch c Prince Sabo - Hemline
3⁶ˢᵈ 11⁶ˢᵈ 8⁷ˢˢ 13⁷ᵍ **0-1-4 £622**

Royal Indulgence *W M Brisbourne* 55
4 b g Royal Applause - Silent Indulgence (USA)

1⁹ᵍᶠ 4¹⁰ᵍᶠ 4¹⁰ᶠ **1-0-3 £3,922**

Royal Island (Ire) *M Johnston* 101
2 b c Trans Island - Royal House (Fr)
1⁵ʰʸ 1⁵ᵍᶠ 2⁶ᵍ 9⁵ᵍᶠ 11⁵ᵍ 10⁶ˢ **2-1-6**
£15,708

Royal Jelly *J H M Gosden* 67 a74
2 b f King's Best (USA) - Baked Alaska
11⁷ᵍᶠ 8⁷ᵍ 1⁷ˢᵈ **1-0-3 £5,265**

Royal Jet *M R Channon* 80
2 b g Royal Applause - Red Bouquet
3⁸ᵍᶠ 6⁸ᵍᶠ 2¹⁰ᵍᶠ 5¹⁰ʰʸ **0-2-4 £2,586**

Royal Logic *M R Channon* 35
3 b f Royal Applause - Lucie Edward
10⁶ᵍᶠ 7⁹ᵍᶠ 6⁸ᵗ 14⁷ᵍ **0-0-4**

Royal Lustre *J H M Gosden* 72
3 b c Deputy Minister (Can) - Snow Bride (USA)
11⁸ᵍ 3⁸ᵍᶠ 9¹⁰ᵍˢ 2¹⁰ᵍᶠ 5¹⁰ᵍ **0-1-5 £2,970**

Royal Melbourne (Ire) *Miss J A Camacho* 61
4 ch g Among Men (USA) - Calachuchi
1¹²ʰʸ 6¹²ᵍᶠ 10¹¹ᵍ 9¹²ᵍᶠ **1-0-4 £3,409**

Royal Millennium (Ire) *M R Channon* 121
6 b g Royal Academy (USA) - Galatrix
1⁶ˢ 12⁷ᵍˢ 4⁶ᵍ 1⁶ʸ 3⁵ᵍ 1⁶ˢ **3-1-6**
£119,679

Royal Mougins *G Wragg* 69
2 br c Daylami (Ire) - Miss Riviera Golf
12⁶ᵍ 5⁷ᵍˢ 5⁸ᵍˢ 3⁸ᵍ 5⁷ˢ **0-1-5 £664**

Royal Nite Owl *J Balding* 45 a45
3 b g Royal Applause - Nite-Owl Dancer
8⁸ˢˢ 11⁸ˢ 4⁷ˢᶠ 4⁶ᶠ 3⁶ᶠ 11⁶ᵍˢ **0-2-6**
£462

Royal Orissa *D Haydn Jones* 84
2 b c Royal Applause - Ling Lane
4⁶ᵍᶠ 5⁷ᵍ 3⁶ᵍˢ 8⁶ᵍᶠ 2⁶ᵍᶠ 5⁶ᵍ 2⁷ᵍˢ **0-3-7**
£14,249

Royal Ovation *N P Littmoden*
5 b g Royal Applause - Thevetia
10⁸ˢᵈ **0-0-1**

Royal Pardon *M L W Bell* 56
2 b f Royal Applause - Miss Mercy (Ire)
7⁶ᶠ 8⁶ᵍ 4⁶ᵍᶠ 4⁶ᵍ 5⁷ᵍᶠ **0-1-5 £744**

Royal Pavillion (Ire) *W J Musson* 57 a65
3 b g Cape Cross (Ire) - Regal Scintilla
3⁶ˢᵈ 16ˢˢ 4⁶ᵍˢ 10⁶ᵍˢ **1-1-4 £4,195**

Royal Prince *J R Fanshawe* 103
3 gr c Royal Applause - Onefortheditch (USA)
4⁷ᵍˢ 1⁷ᶠ 1⁷ᵍᶠ 3⁷ᵍᶠ 3⁸ᵍ 4⁸ᵍᶠ 1⁸ᵍ **3-0-7**
£28,721

Royal Prodigy (USA) *R J Hodges* a69
5 ch g Royal Academy (USA) - Prospector's Queen (USA)
9¹³ˢᵈ 4¹³ˢᵈ 2¹²ˢˢ 19¹⁷ᵍ **0-1-4 £822**

Royal Racer (Fr) *J R Best* 56
6 b g Danehill (USA) - Green Rosy (USA)
1¹⁰ᵍˢ 3¹⁰ˢ 6¹⁰ˢ 7⁷ᵍ 9⁸ᵍ 1¹⁰ᵍᶠ 6¹⁰ᵍᶠ 15⁹ᵍˢ
2-1-8 £7,196

Royal Rebel *M Johnston* 111
8 b g Robellino (USA) - Greenvera (USA)
5¹⁶ˢ 7¹⁶ᵍᶠ 4²⁰ᵍᶠ 4¹⁶ᵍˢ 2¹⁶ᵍᶠ 7¹⁶ᵍ **0-1-6**
£36,810

Royal Sailor (Ire) *J M P Eustace* 66 a56
2 b g Bahhare (USA) - Old Tradition (Ire)
11⁸ᵍᶠ 7⁸ᵍ 7⁷ˢᵈ 11⁸ʰʸ **0-0-4**

Royal Sapphire (USA) *M Johnston* 65
2 b c Kingmambo (USA) - Amethyst (Ire)
9⁷ˢ **0-0-1**

Royal Shepley *J Balding*
3 b f Royal Applause - Dekelsmary
13⁶ˢᵈ 15⁶ˢˢ 10⁶ˢˢ **0-0-3**

Royal Starlet *Mrs A J Perrett*   58
3 b f Royal Applause - Legend
8⁸ᵍ 8¹²ᶠ 4¹¹ᵍᶠ 5¹²ᵍˢ 9¹⁰ᵍᶠ 12¹⁶ᵍˢ 8¹¹ᵍ
0-0-7

Royal Storm (Ire) *Mrs A J Perrett*   108
5 b h Royal Applause - Wakayi
15⁷ᵍˢ 1⁶ᵍ 4⁶ᶠ 6⁷ᵍˢ 9⁷ᵍᶠ 14⁶ᵍᶠ 2⁷ᵍᶠ 8⁷ᵍᶠ
9⁷ᵍᶠ 1⁷ᵍ 14⁷ᵍᶠ 9⁷ᵍ 4⁶ᵍˢ **2-2-13 £40,964**

Royal Supremacy (Ire) *J M Bradley*   12
3 ch f Desert Prince (Ire) - Saucy Maid (Ire)
16⁶ˢ 18⁶ᵍᶠ 11⁵ᵍᶠ **0-0-3**

Royal Tigress (USA) *A P O'Brien*   101
3 b f Storm Cat (USA) - Warm Mood (USA)
3⁸ʰʸ 1⁷ˢ 13⁸ᵍᶠ 7⁸ᶠ 5⁷ᵍʸ 7¹²ᵍᶠ 7¹²ˢ **1-1-7**
£28,573

Royal Trigger *Ian Williams*   48
4 b g Double Trigger (Ire) - Jeronime (USA)
20¹²ᵍˢ 19¹⁰ᵍ 11¹³ᵍᶠ 15¹⁷ᵍ 16¹²ᵍᶠ 14¹³ᵍˢ
0-0-6

Royal Upstart *W M Brisbourne*   30 a42
3 b g Up And At 'Em - Tycoon Tina
12¹⁰ᵍˢ 3⁹ˢᵈ 4⁹ᵍˢ 6¹⁴ᶠ 5¹¹ᶠ 7¹²ᵍᶠ 8¹²ᵍᶠ
0-1-7 £610

Royal Warrant *A M Balding*   102 a86
3 b c Royal Applause - Brand
3⁸ˢᵈ 6⁷ˢᵈ 1⁸ˢᵈ 3⁸ˢᵈ 4⁹ᵍ 2¹⁰ᵍ 2¹⁰ᵍᶠ 2¹⁰ᵍᶠ
6¹⁰ᵍᶠ **1-5-9 £44,925**

Royal Wedding *D R Loder*   64
2 b g King's Best (USA) - Liaison (USA)
7⁶ᵍᶠ 8⁶ˢ 8⁷ᵍ **0-0-3**

Royal Windmill (Ire) *M D Hammond*   56 a53
5 b g Ali-Royal (Ire) - Salarya (Fr)
8⁷ᵍ 13⁸ᵍˢ 5⁸ᵍ 2⁸ᵍ 7⁷ᵍᶠ 6⁸ᵍˢ 6⁸ᵍ 3⁶ᵍᶠ
14⁵ᶠ 2⁷ˢᵈ **0-3-10 £1,906**

Royal Zephyr (USA) *Sir Mark Prescott*   44
3 b f Royal Academy (USA) - Cassation (USA)
10⁸ᵍ **0-0-1**

Royale Pearl *R Ingram*   47 a47
4 gr f Cloudings (Ire) - Ivy Edith
10⁸ˢᵈ 13¹⁰ˢᵈ 4¹²ˢᵈ 1¹³ˢᵈ 4¹⁴ᵍᶠ 5¹²ˢᵈ 5¹⁶ᵍᶠ
13¹⁶ˢᵈ **1-0-8 £1,477**

Royaltea *Ms Deborah J Evans*   36 a45
3 ch f Desert King (Ire) - Come To Tea (Ire)
6⁷ˢᵈ 6⁷ˢᵈ 4⁸ˢᵈ 7⁸ˢˢ 7⁹ˢᵈ 8⁹ᵍ 10⁷ᵍᶠ **0-0-7**
£260

Rozanee *J W Payne*   32 a64
4 ch f Nashwan (USA) - Belle Genius (USA)
6¹²ˢᵈ 13¹¹ᵍˢ 12¹⁰ᵍˢ **0-0-3**

Rubaiyat (Ire) *G Wragg*   68 a68
3 b g Desert Story (Ire) - Lovers' Parlour
12⁸ʰʸ 17⁸ᶠ 4¹²ˢᵈ 2¹⁰ˢᵈ 5¹⁰ˢᵈ 3⁸ᵍᶠ
3⁹ˢᵈ 2⁸ˢᵈ **0-5-9 £3,376**

Rubies *R F Johnson Houghton*   74
2 ch f Inchinor - Fur Will Fly
2⁵ᵍˢ 6⁵ᵍ 2⁶ᵍ 4⁷ᵍ **0-2-4 £3,083**

Ruby Muja *Miss E C Lavelle*   58
2 b f Mujahid (USA) - Ruby Julie
10⁵ᵍ 8⁵ᵍˢ 3⁵ᵍᶠ 1⁵ᵍˢ 15⁶ᵍᶠ **1-1-5 £3,740**

Ruby Murray *B J Meehan*   61
2 b f Zafonic (USA) - Poppadam
13⁶ᵍˢ 9⁶ᵍ 13⁶ᵍ 10⁷ᵍ **0-0-4**

Ruby Rebel *P T Midgley*

Royal Shepley 2 ch f Tomba - Miss Chiquita (Ire)
15⁵ᵍˢ 10⁵ᵍᶠ 10⁶ᶠ 9⁶ᶠ **0-0-4**

Ruby Rocket (Ire) *H Morrison*   110
3 b f Indian Rocket - Geht Schnell
5⁷ᵍ 2⁶ᵍ 3⁶ˢ 2⁶ᵍᶠ 2⁶ᵍᶠ 7⁶ʸ 1⁶ˢ 3⁶ᵍˢ
1-6-9 £58,735

Ruby Wine *J M P Eustace*   73
2 b f Kayf Tara - Cribella (USA)
2⁶ᵍˢ **0-1-1 £1,736**

Ruby's Dream *J M Bradley*   67 a11
2 b f Tipsy Creek (USA) - Sure Flyer (Ire)
4⁵ˢ 2⁵ʰʸ 3⁵ᵍᶠ 4⁵ᵍᶠ 3⁵ᶠ 5⁶ᵍ 4⁵ˢ 8⁶ᵍ 12⁵ᵍᶠ
13⁵ᵍˢ 12⁶ˢᵈ **0-3-11 £2,437**

Rubyanne (Ire) *M J Wallace*   84
2 b f Fasliyev (USA) - Phyliel (USA)
6⁵ᵍᶠ 1⁵ᵍ 8⁵ᵍ **1-0-3 £3,354**

Rudaki *M G Quinlan*   60
2 ch g Opening Verse (USA) - Persian Fountain (Ire)
13⁷ᵍᶠ 4⁶ˢ 3⁷ᵍᶠ 24⁶ˢ **0-1-4 £793**

Rudood (USA) *Lady Herries*   37 a82
4 b g Theatrical - Kardashina (Fr)
5⁸ˢᵈ 9⁸ᶠ **0-0-2**

Rue De Paris *John A Harris*   41 a35
4 br g Paris House - Innocent Abroad (Den)
11⁶ˢ 5⁷ᵍᶠ 7⁶ˢᵈ 15⁷ᵍᶠ **0-0-4**

Ruggtah *M R Channon*   65 a62
3 gr f Daylami (Ire) - Raneen Alwatar
10⁹ᵍᶠ 3¹²ᶠ 5¹³ˢᵈ 10¹⁴ᵍˢ **0-1-4 £563**

Rule Of Law (USA) *Saeed Bin Suroor*   122
3 b c Kingmambo (USA) - Crystal Crossing (Ire)
2¹⁰ᵍˢ 2¹²ᵍ 4¹²ᵍᶠ 1¹²ᵍ 1¹⁵ᵍᶠ **2-2-5**
£679,532

Rules For Jokers (Ire) *J A Osborne*   a17
3 b g Mujadil (USA) - Exciting
22⁷ʰʸ 6⁷ˢᵈ **0-0-2**

Rum Creek *S Kirk*   65
2 ch c Tipsy Creek (USA) - Carnbrea Belle (Ire)
15⁷ᵍˢ 8⁶ᵍᶠ 11⁷ˢ 16⁶ᵍ **0-0-4**

Rum Destiny (Ire) *J S Wainwright*   32 a37
5 b g Mujadil (USA) - Ruby River
12⁶ᵍᶠ 18⁵ᵍ 20⁵ᵍˢ 13⁵ᵍᶠ 13⁵ᵍᶠ 8⁶ˢᵈ **0-0-6**

Rum Shot *H Candy*   113
3 b c Efisio - Glass
4⁶ᵍ 9⁶ᵍᶠ 1⁶ᵍᶠ 3⁷ᵍ 6⁶ʰʸ 14⁷ᵍ **1-1-6**
£24,850

Ruman (Ire) *M J Attwater*   53
2 b g Fayruz - Starway To Heaven (Ity)
11⁶ʰʸ 7⁶ᵍ **0-0-2**

Rumbalara *J H M Gosden*   82
2 b f Intikhab (USA) - Bint Zamayem (Ire)
7⁷ᵍᶠ 2⁷ᵍ 1⁸ᵍ **1-1-3 £5,406**

Rumbling Bridge *J L Dunlop*   56
3 ch g Air Express (Ire) - Rushing River (USA)
9⁸ᵍᶠ 9¹⁰ᵍᶠ 2¹²ʰʸ 3¹²ˢ **0-2-4 £1,918**

Rumour *J R Fanshawe*   a75
4 b f Lion Cavern (USA) - Thea (USA)
1⁸ˢᵈ **1-0-1 £2,919**

Rumour Mill (Ire) *N E Berry*   42 a37
3 b c Entrepreneur - Pursuit Of Truth (USA)
5⁹ˢʷ 15¹⁰ᵍ 10¹⁰ᵍᶠ 11⁸ˢᵈ 17¹²ᵍᶠ 8⁸ᵍᶠ 8¹⁰ᵍᶠ
10⁸ᵍˢ 12¹⁰ᵍᶠ 12⁸ᶠ 15⁸ᵍᶠ **0-0-11**

Run On *D G Bridgwater*   49 a22
6 b h Runnett - Polar Storm (Ire)
15⁶ˢ 12⁶ᵍᶠ 13⁶ᶠ 16⁶ᵍ 5⁵ᵍ 5⁵ᶠ 15⁶ᵍ
10⁵ˢᵈ **0-0-8**

Rusky Dusky (USA) *R Hannon* 77
2 b c Stravinsky (USA) - Celtic Shade
11⁶ᵍ 3⁶ᶠ 2⁶ᵍᶠ 5⁶ᵍᶠ 5⁵ˢ 6⁶ᵍᶠ 6⁶ᵍ 4⁵ᵍᶠ
0-2-8 £3,901

Russalka *Julian Poulton* 55 a42
3 b f Opening Verse (USA) - Philarmonique (Fr)
10¹⁰ˢᵈ 15⁸ᵍ 5⁸ˢᵈ 8¹³ˢ 2¹⁰ᶠ 6¹⁰ᵍᶠ 7¹⁰ᵍᶠ
6¹⁰ᵍᶠ 13¹⁰ᵍˢ 10¹⁰ᶠ 5⁷ᵍˢ 11⁸ᵍ **0-1-12 £1,045**

Russian Applause *P R Chamings* 65
4 b g Royal Applause - Zeffirella
9⁸ᵍˢ 11¹⁰ᵍ 4⁷ᵍˢ 5⁸ᵍ **0-0-4 £330**

Russian Blue (Ire) *A P O'Brien* 113
2 b c Danehill (USA) - Soviet Artic (Fr)
1⁵ʰʸ 1⁵ᵍ 1⁵ᵍᶠ 2⁶ᵍᶠ 3⁶ᵍᶠ 3⁶ᵛˢ 3⁷ʸ 5⁶ᵍ
3-2-8 £130,529

Russian Cafe (Ire) *M A Magnusson* 64
3 b f Stravinsky (USA) - Bistro (USA)
3⁶ᵍˢ 2⁶ᵍˢ **0-2-2 £1,701**

Russian Comrade (Ire) *J C Tuck*
8 b g Polish Patriot (USA) - Tikarna (Fr)
PU⁸ᵍˢ **0-0-1**

Russian Consort (Ire) *A King* 68 a94
2 ch c Groom Dancer (USA) - Ukraine Venture
2⁷ˢᵈ 1⁸ˢᵈ 11⁷ˢ **1-1-3 £4,977**

Russian Dance (USA) *Sir Michael Stoute* 22
3 br f Nureyev (USA) - Population
8⁸ᵍᶠ **0-0-1**

Russian General (Ire) *P F I Cole* 51
2 b c Soviet Star (USA) - Azra (Ire)
1⁵ᵍᶠ **1-0-1 £4,104**

Russian Icon *L A Dace*
3 b f Wace (USA) - Lady Millennium (Ire)
12¹⁰ˢᵈ 10¹⁴ᶠ **0-0-2**

Russian Revolution *Saeed Bin Suroor* 80
2 b c Dubai Millennium - Russian Snows (Ire)
3⁸ᵍᶠ 1⁸ˢ **1-1-2 £6,322**

Russian Rhythm (USA) *Sir Michael Stoute* 118
4 ch f Kingmambo (USA) - Balistroika (USA)
1⁸ᵍ **1-0-1 £116,000**

Russian Rio (Ire) *P C Haslam* 66 a31
2 b g Imperial Ballet (Ire) - L'Harmonie (USA)
9⁵ˢᵈ 5⁵ᵍ 5⁵ᵍᶠ **0-0-3**

Russian Rocket (Ire) *Mrs C A Dunnett* 81 a77
2 b g Indian Rocket - Soviet Girl (Ire)
7⁵ʰʸ 5⁵ᵍᶠ 2⁵ᶠ 1⁵ˢᵈ 2⁵ᵍ 5⁵ˢᵈ 17⁶ᵍᶠ 1⁵ˢ
9⁶ˢᵈ **2-2-9 £12,016**

Russian Ruby (Fr) *N A Callaghan* 79
3 b f Vettori (USA) - Pink Sovietstaia (Fr)
5⁸ᵍᶠ **0-0-1**

Russian Servana (Ire) *J Pearce* 47
2 b f Rossini (USA) - Ring Of Light
9⁶ᶠ 2⁵ᵍ 5⁵ᵍᶠ 5⁶ᵍᶠ **0-1-4 £832**

Russian Symphony (USA) *C R Egerton* 70 a74
3 ch g Stravinsky (USA) - Backwoods Teacher (USA)
10⁷ᵍˢ 6⁷ˢ 7⁶ᵍᶠ 8⁶ᵍᶠ 2⁷ˢᵈ 1⁷ˢᵈ **1-1-6**
£4,929

Russian Valour (Ire) *M Johnston* 83
3 b c Fasliyev (USA) - Vert Val (USA)
10⁷ᵍ 6⁶ˢ 7⁵ᵍᶠ 7⁶ᵍ **0-0-4 £450**

Russiannightingale *J O'Reilly*
2 b g Fraam - Nightingale Song
12⁶ᵍ 9⁷ˢ **0-0-2**

Rust En Vrede *D Carroll* a67
5 b g Royal Applause - Souveniers
1⁸ˢʷ 1⁸ˢᵈ **2-0-2 £4,469**

Rustic Charm (Ire) *Miss K Marks*

4 b f Charnwood Forest (Ire) - Kabayil
PU¹⁰ᵍˢ **0-0-1**

Rustler *R Charlton* a57
2 b c Green Desert (USA) - Borgia
7⁹ˢᵈ **0-0-1**

Rusty Boy *A Crook* 28
3 b g Defacto (USA) - Berl's Gift
7⁷ᵍᶠ 7¹²ᵍᶠ 9⁵ᵍᶠ **0-0-3**

Rutland Chantry (USA) *S Gollings* 44
10 b g Dixieland Band (USA) - Christchurch (Fr)
5¹¹ˢ 10¹⁴ᵍ **0-0-2**

Rutters Rebel (Ire) *N Tinkler* 77
3 b g Entrepreneur - No Quest (Ire)
5¹²ˢ 9¹²ᵍˢ 4¹¹ᵍᶠ 7¹²ᵍᶠ 2¹²ᵍ 4¹²ᵍ 9¹²ˢ 1¹¹ᵍᶠ
11¹²ᶠ 6¹²ᵍᶠ 9¹²ᵍᶠ **1-1-11 £5,854**

Ryan's Bliss (Ire) *T D McCarthy* 48 a62
4 b f Danetime (Ire) - Raja Moulana
8⁸ˢᵈ 8⁸ˢᵈ 2¹⁰ˢᵈ 5¹⁰ˢᵈ 3¹⁰ˢᵈ 2¹⁰ˢᵈ 8¹¹ᶠ
9¹¹ᵍᶠ 10¹⁰ˢᵈ 5¹⁰ᶠ 6¹⁰ᵍ 1¹⁰ˢᵈ 3⁸ˢᵈ **1-4-13**
£3,031

Ryan's Future (Ire) *J Akehurst* 87 a87
4 b c Danetime (Ire) - Era
5¹⁰ˢᵈ 8¹⁰ˢᵈ 9¹⁰ᵍ 5⁸ᵍᶠ 2⁹ᵍˢ 7¹⁰ˢ 4¹⁰ᵍᶠ 5¹⁰ᵍᶠ
8¹⁰ᵍ 1¹⁰ʰʸ **1-1-10 £7,377**

Ryan's Quest (Ire) *T D McCarthy* 48 a41
5 b m Mukaddamah (USA) - Preponderance (Ire)
8⁵ˢᵈ 15⁵ᵍᶠ 8⁵ᶠ 3⁵ᵍᶠ **0-1-4 £826**

Ryans Lil Ol Gal *A B Coogan* 8
2 b f Namaqualand (USA) - Kirby's Princess
14⁵ᵍ 12⁵ˢˢ 11⁶ᵍ **0-0-3**

Rydal (USA) *G A Butler* 91 a72
3 ch g Gilded Time (USA) - Tennis Partner (USA)
13⁷ˢᵈ 4⁷ᵍ 11⁵ᵍᶠ 2⁵ᵍˢ 4⁶ˢ 7⁵ᵍᶠ 1⁵ᵍˢ
4⁵ˢ 5⁵ʸ 8⁷ᵍᶠ 8⁵ˢ **1-1-12 £10,845**

Rye (Ire) *J A Osborne* 63 a64
3 b f Charnwood Forest (Ire) - Silver Hut (USA)
1⁸ˢᵈ 6¹²ˢᵈ 7¹²ᵍˢ 4¹²ᵍˢ **1-0-4 £1,463**

Ryedane (Ire) *T D Easterby* 63
2 b c Danetime (Ire) - Miss Valediction (Ire)
9⁶ʰʸ 9⁵ᵍᶠ 9⁵ᵍ 5⁶ᵍᶠ 3⁵ᵍᶠ 7⁵ᵍ 12⁶ᵍ **0-1-7**
£1,167

Rymer's Rascal *E J Alston* 56
12 b g Rymer - City Sound
3⁸ʰʸ 2⁸ᶠ 8⁸ᶠ 8⁸ᵍˢ 2⁸ᵍ 15⁸ᵍ 6⁸ᵍˢ 1⁸ᶠ 2⁸ᶠ
3⁹ᵍˢ **1-5-10 £7,765**

Saadigg (Ire) *M A Jarvis* 88 a65
2 b c Indian Danehill (Ire) - White Cap'S
3⁷ˢᵈ 4⁸ˢᵈ 1⁸ᵍ 6¹⁰ᵍ **1-1-4 £4,608**

Saameq (Ire) *I Semple* 53
3 b g Bahhare (USA) - Tajawuz
6¹⁰ᵍ 7¹⁰ˢ 7⁹ᵍ 3¹²ᵍ 4¹¹ᵍᶠ 4¹¹ᵍᶠ **0-1-6**
£1,025

Sabalara (Ire) *P W Harris* 54
4 b f Mujadil (USA) - Sabaniya (Fr)
8⁷ᵍˢ 7⁸ˢ 15⁷ˢ 13⁸ᶠ **0-0-4**

Sabana (Ire) *J M Bradley* 58 a59
6 b g Sri Pekan (USA) - Atyaaf (USA)
4⁶ˢᵈ 3⁶ˢᵈ 5⁶ˢᵈ 9⁷ˢˢ 1⁶ˢˢ 3⁶ˢʷ 11⁶ˢᵈ 6⁶ˢᵈ
13⁶ˢ 8⁶ˢ 11⁶ᵍᶠ 14⁶ᵍ 1⁶ᵍ 6⁶ᵍ 9⁶ᶠ **2-2-15**
£5,963

Sabander Bay (USA) *J H M Gosden* 55
3 b f Lear Fan (USA) - Sambac (USA)
8⁶ᵍˢ 8⁸ˢ **0-0-2**

Sabbaag (USA) *D R Loder* a75
3 ch c Mark Of Esteem (USA) - Saabga (USA)
2⁷ˢᵈ 1⁸ˢᵈ 10¹⁰ˢᵈ **1-1-3 £4,537**

Sabbeeh (USA) *Saeed Bin Suroor* 101

3 b c Red Ransom (USA) - Capistrano Day (USA)
9^{7g} 1^{8s} **1-0-2** £5,997

Sabbiosa (Ire) *J L Dunlop* — 63
2 b f Desert Prince (Ire) - Alla Marcia (Ire)
7^{6gf} 10^{7gf} 8^{7g} 7^{8gs} **0-0-4**

Sable 'n Silk *D Haydn Jones* — a3
3 b f Prince Sabo - Sibilant
7^{7ss} 6^{7ss} **0-0-2**

Sabo Prince *J M Bradley* — 24
2 ch g Atraf - Moving Princess
7^{6g} 5^{6gf} 9^{5f} 8^{5gf} **0-0-4**

Sabreline *B R Foster*
5 ch m Sabrehill (USA) - Story Line
9^{9ss} **0-0-1**

Sabrina Brown *G B Balding* — 77
3 br f Polar Falcon (USA) - So True
2^{6g} 2^{8g} 14^{7g} 6^{8hy} 1^{6gs} 2^{7gs} 14^{7g} **1-3-7**
£10,223

Saccharine *M J Polglase* — 47 a19
3 b f Whittingham (Ire) - Sweet And Lucky
10^{8gf} 3^{5gf} 6^{6gf} 7^{7sw} **0-0-4** £515

Sachin *J R Boyle* — 70 a59
3 b g Bijou D'Inde - Dark Kristal (Ire)
7^{6sd} 6^{7sd} 9^{7gf} 4^{9gf} 1^{8g} 3^{8g} 8^{8s} 7^{9sd}
1-1-8 £4,467

Sachsenwalzer (Ger) *C Grant* — 36
6 ch g Top Waltz (Fr) - Stairway To Heaven (Ger)
9^{10g} **0-0-1**

Sacranun *L M Cumani* — 80
2 ch c Pivotal - Spanish Craft (Ire)
2^{6g} 3^{6s} 7^{6g} 4^{6hy} **0-1-4** £4,187

Sacred Nuts (Ire) *M L W Bell* — 100
2 b c Sri Pekan (USA) - Sagrada (Ger)
5^{6gf} 1^{6gf} 1^{6g} 3^{7gf} 5^{6gf} 4^{6s} **2-1-6**
£17,553

Sacsayhuaman *D W Thompson*
5 b m Halling (USA) - La Dolce Vita
7^{12ss} **0-0-1**

Saddler's Quest *B P J Baugh* — 45
7 b g Saddlers' Hall (Ire) - Seren Quest
13^{11s} 9^{12gf} 8^{12s} 13^{12g} **0-0-4**

Sadie Thompson (Ire) *M R Channon* — 77
2 b f King's Best (USA) - Femme Fatale
8^{7g} 17^{9f} **1-0-2** £5,954

Sadie's Star (Ire) *M Dods* — 47 a20
2 b f Indian Lodge (Ire) - Nishiki (USA)
8^{7f} 5^{7gf} 12^{9sd} **0-0-3**

Sadler's Pride (Ire) *Andrew Turnell* — 73
4 b g Sadler's Wells (USA) - Gentle Thoughts
2^{11g} 2^{14gs} 4^{14gs} 12^{12gf} 15^{18gs} 8^{12g} 5^{12f}
0-2-7 £3,604

Sadler's Rock (Ire) *G L Moore* — 65 a58
6 b g Sadler's Wells (USA) - Triple Couronne (USA)
9^{12sd} 7^{12gs} **0-0-2**

Sadlers Swing (USA) *J J Sheehan* — 16 a45
8 b g Red Ransom (USA) - Noblissima (Ire)
2^{8sw} 4^{9sw} 9^{8g} **0-1-3** £414

Safa Park *Saeed Bin Suroor* — 65
3 ch g Machiavellian (USA) - Ozone Friendly (USA)
8^{9gf} 9^{10gf} **0-0-2**

Safari Sunset (Ire) *P Winkworth* — 94
2 b f Fayruz - Umlani (Ire)
1^{5gf} 3^{5gf} 4^{5g} 3^{5g} 8^{6gf} 9^{5f} **1-2-6**
£13,388

Safendonseabiscuit *S Kirk* — 81
2 b c Danzig Connection (USA) - The Fugative

5^{6gf} 3^{6gf} 3^{7gf} 4^{7gf} 2^{6gf} 10^{6gf} 12^{6gs} 3^{6f}
1^{6gf} 18^{6s} **1-4-10** £8,244

Saffa Garden (Ire) *C E Brittain* — 58
2 b f King's Best (USA) - Allegheny River (USA)
8^{5gf} 10^{6gs} 11^{6g} **0-0-3**

Saffron Fox *J G Portman* — 85
3 ch f Safawan - Fox Oa (Fr)
4^{8s} 7^{10gs} 4^{8gs} 2^{8g} 10^{10gf} 7^{10s} 5^{8gf} 18^{10s}
0-1-8 £3,309

Saffron River *R Hollinshead* — a38
3 b c Polar Prince (Ire) - Cloudy Reef
5^{6sd} **0-0-1**

Safirah *M A Jarvis* — 70
3 b f Singspiel (Ire) - Princess Haifa (USA)
3^{10gf} 5^{10gf} 5^{10gf} 10^{11hy} 2^{10gs} 1^{10s} **1-1-6**
£5,257

Safranine (Ire) *Miss A Stokell* — 63 a35
7 b m Dolphin Street (Fr) - Webbiana
11^{6sd} 10^{5ss} 12^{5ss} 9^{6g} 9^{7f} 10^{6gf} 9^{5f}
16^{6g} 8^{5f} 6^{8g} 9^{6gf} 17^{5gf} 14^{6gf} 6^{6gf} **0-0-14**
£499

Safsoof (USA) *Saeed Bin Suroor* — 88 a83
2 c Gilded Time (USA) - Halcyon Bird (Ire)
2^{5g} 10^{5gf} 1^{5sd} 3^{5gf} **1-1-4** £6,071

Sahaat *C R Dore* — 75 a82
6 b/br g Machiavellian (USA) - Tawaaded (Ire)
7^{8ss} 22^{8g} 14^{12gs} 14^{14g} 5^{10gf} 10^{8gs} 2^{8sd}
5^{12gs} 8^{8gs} 4^{10gs} 6^{12g} 7^{10gf} 4^{10g} 1^{10g} **1-2-14**
£5,951

Sahara Mist (Ire) *D Shaw* — 41 a34
2 b f Desert Style (Ire) - Tereed Elhawa
14^{5g} 5^{5s} 5^{5s} 12^{5g} 10^{8f} **0-0-5**

Sahara Prince (Ire) *Michael Cunningham* — 89
4 b g Desert King (Ire) - Chehana
8^{7s} 8^{8gf} 5^{7g} 3^{7gf} 7^{7g} 2^{7gf} 1^{6hy} 2^{6gy}
8^{8gf} 5^{7sh} **1-5-11** £18,441

Sahara Scirocco (Ire) *I A Wood*
3 b g Spectrum (Ire) - St Bride's Bay
14^{7sd} 11^{9sd} **0-0-2**

Sahara Silk (Ire) *D Shaw* — 51 a74
3 b f Desert Style (Ire) - Buddy And Soda (Ire)
10^{5sd} 14^{6ss} 1^{5sd} 3^{5sd} 4^{5sd} 1^{6sd} 2^{5sd}
8^{6ss} 3^{5sd} 12^{5g} 9^{5gf} 7^{6gf} **2-2-13** £8,830

Sahara Storm (Ire) *L M Cumani* — 62 a65
3 b f Desert Prince (Ire) - Deluge
10^{7sd} 10^{7g} **0-0-2**

Saharan Song (Ire) *B W Hills* — 58
3 ch f Singspiel (Ire) - Sahara Baladee (USA)
12^{8g} 9^{9g} 9^{10gf} 12^{10gs} 12^{9sd} **0-0-5**

Sahem (Ire) *C J Teague* — 89
7 b g Sadler's Wells (USA) - Sumava (Ire)
5^{18g} 7^{12g} 4^{13g} 7^{14gs} 1^{14f} 2^{13g} 17^{16g} 3^{12gf}
3^{12gs} 1^{13gs} 12^{14g} 3^{12gf} 6^{13s} **2-3-13** £22,710

Sahool *M P Tregoning* — 109
3 b f Unfuwain (USA) - Mathaayl (USA)
2^{10g} 2^{10g} 12^{12gf} 2^{12g} 1^{12gf} 5^{12s} **1-4-6**
£87,450

Saida Lenasera (Fr) *Mrs P Sly* — 68 a63
3 b f Fasliyev (USA) - Lanasara
9^{12gs} 6^{10gf} 6^{12gf} 10^{10gs} 5^{10gf} 5^{12g} 7^{12sd}
0-0-7

Saif Sareea *A L Forbes* — 53
4 b g Atraf - Slipperose
11^{6gf} 8^{6g} 14^{8s} **0-0-3**

Sailing Through *R Dickin* — 81
4 b g Bahhare (USA) - Hopesay
13^{10gf} **0-0-1**

Sailmaker (Ire) *R Charlton*   78
3 ch g Peintre Celebre (USA) - Princess Amalie (USA)
2⁸ᵍ 3⁸ʰʸ 7¹⁰ᵍᶠ 3¹⁰ᵍ 4¹⁰ᵍ **0-3-5 £3,439**

Sailorman *G A Butler*   a52
3 b g Alzao (USA) - Sweet Pea
9¹⁰ˢᵈ **0-0-1**

Saint Clements (USA) *M Johnston*   40
2 b g Lemon Drop Kid (USA) - Sophisticated Lynn (USA)
9⁶ᵍᶠ 10⁶ᵍᶠ 4⁸ʰʸ **0-0-3**

Saint Etienne (Ire) *A M Balding*   86 a55
3 b f Robellino (USA) - Stop Out
1⁷ˢᵈ 5⁷ᵍᶠ 10⁷ᵍᶠ **1-0-3 £4,854**

Saint Lazare (Ire) *J G Given*
3 b c Peintre Celebre (USA) - Height Of Passion
16¹⁰ᵍˢ **0-0-1**

Saint Zita (Ire) *B J Meehan*   a51
3 b f Desert Sun - Chatelsong (USA)
7⁸ˢᵈ 10¹⁰ˢᵈ 7¹¹ᵍ **0-0-3**

Saintly Place *C Smith*   57 a26
3 ch g Compton Place - Always On A Sunday
12⁶ᵍ 13⁶ᵍˢ 15⁶ᵍˢ 5⁸ᶠ 2⁷ᵍ 8⁷ᵍˢ 9⁷ˢᵈ **0-1-7
£778**

Saintly Scholar (USA) *E A L Dunlop*   a58
3 b f Danzig (USA) - Tres Facile (USA)
10⁷ˢᵈ 9⁷ˢᵈ 5⁷ˢᵈ **0-0-3**

Saintly Thoughts (USA) *R J Hodges*
9 b/br g St Jovite (USA) - Free Thinker (USA)
15¹⁴ˢ **0-0-1**

Sake (Ire) *N Tinkler*   41
2 b g Shinko Forest (Ire) - Drosera (Ire)
12⁸ᵍᶠ 12⁸ᵍ **0-0-2**

Salagama (Ire) *P F I Cole*   87
4 br f Alzao (USA) - Waffle On
4⁸ᵍˢ 3⁹ᵍ 9⁸ᵍᶠ 20⁸ᵍ **0-0-4 £2,273**

Salamanca *S Kirk*   95
2 ch f Pivotal - Salanka (Ire)
1⁶ᵍˢ 1⁷ᵍ 6⁷ᵍ **2-0-3 £152,141**

Salamba *M H Tompkins*   69
3 ch g Indian Ridge - Towaahi (Ire)
5⁹ᵍ 10¹⁴ᵍᶠ 8¹⁴ᵍ 5¹⁴ᵍ 7¹⁴ᵍˢ 7¹⁸ᵍ **0-0-6**

Saleen (Ire) *P D Cundell*   a18
4 b f Kahyasi - Sabrata (Ire)
10⁸ˢᵈ **0-0-1**

Salerno *Miss Gay Kelleway*   a19
5 ch g Mark Of Esteem (Ire) - Shamwari (USA)
8⁵ˢᵈ 9⁵ˢᵈ **0-0-2**

Salford City (Ire) *D R C Elsworth*   118
3 b c Desert Sun - Summer Fashion
1⁷ᵍ 6⁸ᵍ 5¹²ᵍ 9¹⁰ᵍˢ **1-0-4 £67,475**

Salford Flyer *Jane Southcombe*   50 a44
8 b g Pharly (Fr) - Edge Of Darkness
12¹³ˢᵈ 6¹²ˢᵈ 7¹⁰ᵍ 3¹⁰ᵍ 3¹²ˢ 16¹²ᵍᶠ **0-2-6
£813**

Salford Rocket *W J Musson*   21 a13
4 b g Slip Anchor - Mysterious Maid (USA)
8⁹ˢᵈ 9¹⁰ˢ 6¹²ᵍᶠ 9¹³ᵍᶠ 6¹⁴ˢᵈ 9¹⁴ˢ **0-0-6**

Salinja (USA) *Mrs A J Perrett*   89
2 b c Boundary (USA) - Lasha (USA)
3⁶ᵍ 3⁷ˢ 2⁸ᵍ **0-3-3 £3,824**

Salinor *E F Vaughan*   89
4 ch g Inchinor - Salanka (Ire)
1⁸ᵍ 1⁸ᵍᶠ 16⁸ᵍ 6⁸ᵍ 12⁸ᵍ **2-0-5 £7,439**

Salisbury Plain *D R Loder*   52
3 b c Mark Of Esteem (Ire) - Wild Pavane
10⁹ʰʸ 18⁹ᵍ **0-0-2**

Sally Traffic *R M Whitaker*   a19
5 b m River Falls - Yankeedoodledancer
7⁶ˢᵈ **0-0-1**

Salon Prive *C A Cyzer*   60 a70
4 b g Green Desert (USA) - Shot At Love (Ire)
9⁶ˢᵈ 15⁸ᵍᶠ 2⁶ˢᵈ 6⁶ᵍᶠ 2⁶ᵍ 11⁶ᵍ **0-2-6
£1,846**

Salonika Sky *C W Thornton*   14 a15
3 ch f Pursuit Of Love - Willisa
12⁶ˢᵈ 6⁵ˢᵈ 12⁶ˢᵈ 9⁵ᵍ 14⁶ᵍᶠ **0-0-5**

Salsa Brava (Ire) *N P Littmoden*   103
2 b f Almutawakel - Ridotto
1⁵ᵍᶠ 3⁶ᶠ 2⁶ᵍᶠ 2⁶ˢ 4⁶ᵍˢ **1-3-5 £48,180**

Salsalino *A King*   104
4 ch g Salse (USA) - Alicedale (USA)
6¹²ᵍ 8¹⁴ᵍˢ 12¹²ᵍᶠ 15¹⁴ˢ 15¹⁵ᵍᶠ **0-0-5
£750**

Salselon *L M Cumani*   120
5 b h Salse (USA) - Heady
9⁸ᵍˢ 2⁸ᵍ 3⁸ᵍᶠ 7⁸ᵍ 5⁸ˢ 2⁹ᵍ 3¹⁰ᵍᶠ 2⁸ᵍ 6¹⁰ˢ
3⁸ˢ **0-4-10 £130,467**

Saltango (Ger) *A M Hales*   79 a66
5 b g Acatenango (Ger) - Salde (Ger)
8¹⁰ˢᵈ 3¹²ᵍ 5¹⁴ᵍᶠ **0-1-3 £2,655**

Salut Saint Cloud *G L Moore*   72 a67
3 b g Primo Dominie - Tiriana
6⁸ˢ 8⁷ᵍᶠ 5⁷ˢᵈ 1¹⁰ᵍ 3¹²ᶠ 3¹²ˢᵈ 3¹²ᶠ 1¹⁴ˢᵈ
4¹²ˢᵈ 1¹⁶ˢ 8¹⁶ᵍᶠ **3-1-11 £10,679**

Salviati (USA) *J M Bradley*   90
7 b g Lahib (USA) - Mother Courage
20⁵ᵍˢ 12⁵ᵍᶠ 16⁵ᵍᶠ 23⁶ᶠ 12⁵ˢ 15⁵ᵍᶠ 8⁶ᵍ
12⁵ᵍᶠ 4⁵ᵍᶠ 5⁵ᵍ 1⁵ᵍᶠ 18⁵ᵍ 10⁵ᵍ 10⁵ᵍˢ 9⁵ᵍ
1-0-15 £10,271

Sam The Sorcerer *J R Norton*   43 a43
3 b g Wizard King - Awham (USA)
9⁶ˢ 1⁶ˢᵈ 9⁷ˢᵈ 3⁶ˢ 11⁶ʰʸ 16⁶ˢ **1-1-6
£1,913**

Sam's Secret *J A Glover*   85
2 b f Josr Algarhoud (Ire) - Twilight Time
2⁶ᵍᶠ 3⁵ᶠ 2⁶ᵍᶠ 12⁷ˢ **0-2-4 £4,918**

Samalan *J Parkes*   17
2 b g Grey Desire - Shalari (Ire)
9⁶ᵍᶠ 11⁵ᵍᶠ **0-0-2**

Samar Qand *Julian Poulton*   a41
5 b m Selkirk (USA) - Sit Alkul (USA)
5⁹ˢᵈ 3¹¹ˢᵈ 3¹¹ˢˢ 4¹¹ˢᵈ 13¹²ᵍˢ **0-2-5 £386**

Samara Sound *A G Newcombe*   34 a54
3 b c Savahra Sound - Hosting
10⁶ˢˢ 6⁶ˢᵈ 13⁵ᵍ **0-0-3**

Samaria (Ger) *C F Wall*   73 a69
3 b/br f Acatenango (Ger) - Suanita (Ger)
13¹²ᵍᶠ 4¹⁰ᵍᶠ 2¹¹ᵍᶠ 4¹²ᵍˢ 3¹³ˢᵈ 7¹⁴ˢ **0-2-6
£2,280**

Samba Beat *R F Marvin*
5 ch m Efisio - Special Beat
11⁸ˢʷ 9⁸ˢ 9¹¹ˢᵈ 8⁷ˢᵈ **0-0-4**

Sambarina (Ire) *C G Cox*   66
2 b f Victory Note (USA) - Brazalia
3⁶ᵍ 5⁶ᵍ **0-1-2 £586**

Sammagefromtenesse (Ire) *A E Jones*   32 a38
7 b g Petardia - Canoora
6¹¹ᵍʸ 5⁸ʸˢ 2¹⁰ˢᵈ **0-1-3 £366**

Sammy's Shuffle *Jamie Poulton*   49 a54
9 b g Touch Of Grey - Cabinet Shuffle
9¹⁰ˢᵈ 4¹⁰ˢᵈ 7¹⁰ˢᵈ 9¹²ᵍᶠ 11¹⁰ᵍᶠ 4¹⁰ᶠ 8¹⁰ˢᵈ
5¹⁰ᶠ **0-1-8**

Samson Quest *A M Balding*   51 a64
2 b c Cyrano De Bergerac - Zenita (Ire)
5^{7sd} 9^{7s} **0-0-2**

Samuel Charles *W M Brisbourne*   80 a83
6 b g Green Desert (USA) - Hejraan (USA)
1^{8sd} 2^{8sd} 3^{8gf} 1^{8f} 2^{7f} 2^{7f} 3^{7g} 3^{8g} 4^{7g}
2^{7g} 1^{17g} 1^{7f} 6^{7gf} 10^{7gf} 1^{7sd} 4^{7sd} 3^{7sd}
4-6-17 £22,747

San Antonio *Mrs P Sly*   60
4 b g Efisio - Winnebago
8^{7s} 6^{10gf} 12^{8gf} **0-0-3**

San Deng *W R Muir*   61 a44
2 gr c Averti (Ire) - Miss Mirror
8^{6gf} 3^{6g} 13^{6gs} 14^{6gf} 8^{6sd} **0-0-5 £642**

San Dimas (USA) *R Allan*   16
7 gr g Distant View (USA) - Chrystophard (USA)
9^{16gf} **0-0-1**

San Hernando *D R C Elsworth*   79
4 b g Hernando (Fr) - Sandrella (Ire)
6^{14s} 4^{16g} 10^{14s} 7^{16gf} 4^{13gf} 9^{14g} 4^{16g}
2^{14gf} 8^{16g} 8^{16g} 19^{14gs} 1^{16gs} 3^{16s} **1-3-13**
£7,237

San Lorenzo (UAE) *M R Channon*   66
3 ch f Machiavellian (USA) - Sanchez
8^{7gf} 3^{6gf} 2^{6gf} **0-2-3 £2,265**

San Marco (Ire) *M Sheppard*   a23
6 b g Brief Truce (USA) - Nuit Des Temps
11^{14sd} 7^{12sw} **0-0-2**

Sanbonah (USA) *N A Callaghan*   16
3 b f King Of Kings (Ire) - Oh Nellie (USA)
14^{8gf} **0-0-1**

Sanchi (Ire) *J H M Gosden*   84
2 b c Darshaan - Samara (Ire)
3^{8g} **0-1-1 £1,087**

Sand And Stars (Ire) *M H Tompkins*   87
3 ch f Dr Devious (Ire) - Charm The Stars
3^{11gf} 5^{10gf} 2^{12gs} 1^{12g} 2^{12gf} 8^{14s} 3^{12g}
2^{12gs} **1-4-8 £16,131**

Sand Iron (Ire) *S L Keightley*   67 a62
2 b f Desert Style (Ire) - Mettlesome
6^{7sd} 4^{6hy} 8^{7sd} **0-0-3 £283**

Sand N Sea (Ire) *T Hogan*   94
3 b f Desert Story (Ire) - Poscimur (Ire)
10^{7hy} 9^{8gy} 1^{10gf} 3^{9gf} 16^{8gf} 11^{12gf} 7^{8gf}
7^{10gf} 8^{8hy} 12^{9gs} **1-1-10 £15,947**

Sand Repeal (Ire) *Miss J Feilden*   70
2 b g Revoque (Ire) - Columbian Sand (Ire)
7^{7g} 3^{8s} 2^{10hy} **0-2-3 £2,009**

Sandgate Cygnet *I Semple*   a75
4 ch f Fleetwood (Ire) - Dance Of The Swans (Ire)
1^{6sd} **1-0-1 £3,283**

Sandokan (Ger) *B J Curley*   59
3 b g Tiger Hill (Ire) - Suivez (Fr)
7^{10g} 11^{8g} 7^{10hy} 8^{12s} **0-0-4**

Sandorra *M Brittain*   49 a53
6 b m Emperor Jones (USA) - Oribi
3^{7sd} 1^{7sd} 6^{8sd} 11^{8sd} 10^{8sw} 1^{7sd} 6^{7s}
12^{7sd} 8^{7sd} 5^{7s} 8^{7sd} **2-1-11 £3,356**

Sandy Bay (Ire) *A R Dicken*   43
5 b g Spectrum (Ire) - Karinski (USA)
12^{12ss} 8^{9gf} 8^{7gf} 11^{12gf} 4^{9s} 12^{10g} 3^{12gf}
5^{12s} **0-0-8 £1,153**

Sandy's Legend (USA) *J H M Gosden*   48 a62
2 ch c Tale Of The Cat (USA) - Avasand (USA)
11^{8g} 5^{9sd} 2^{9sd} **0-1-3 £1,114**

Sangiovese *H Morrison*   84 a85

5 b g Piccolo - Kaprisky (Ire)
10^{10sd} 3^{7sd} 3^{8sw} 5^{7s} 2^{8g} 3^{8gf} 1^{10gf} 1^{12g}
7^{12gs} 5^{12gf} 14^{10gf} 5^{10g} 1^{8hy} **3-4-13 £21,509**

Sant Jordi *B J Meehan*   95 a71
2 b c Cape Cross (Ire) - Foresta Verde (USA)
3^{6sd} 1^{6g} 2^{7gs} 3^{8ys} **1-1-4 £15,884**

Santa Catalina (Ire) *R J Price*   a46
5 br m Tagula (Ire) - Bui-Doi (Ire)
7^{8sd} 10^{8sd} 5^{8ss} 4^{8ss} 10^{12ss} 13^{10sd} **0-0-6**

Santa Caterina (Ire) *J L Dunlop*   73
3 b f Daylami (Ire) - Samara (Ire)
4^{10g} 5^{12g} 2^{10g} 11^{11g} 7^{11g} 3^{8hy} 2^{10s} 7^{10hy}
0-3-8 £3,379

Santa Fe (Ire) *Sir Michael Stoute*   102
2 b c Green Desert (USA) - Shimna
5^{6gf} 4^{7g} **1-0-3 £8,811**

Santando *C E Brittain*   99 a103
4 b g Hernando (Fr) - Santarem (USA)
5^{12sd} 3^{10sd} 10^{10ft} 5^{12gf} 14^{12g} 8^{14g} 4^{14g}
9^{16g} 12^{14s} 10^{15gf} 8^{12s} **0-1-11 £5,334**

Santiburi Lad (Ire) *N Wilson*   75
7 b g Namaqualand (USA) - Suggia
3^{10hy} 2^{12gf} 1^{11gs} 1^{10gs} 2^{11gs} 17^{10gf} 8^{8gf}
7^{11hy} 14^{10g} **2-3-9 £10,132**

Saorsie *J C Fox*   a19
6 b g Emperor Jones (USA) - Exclusive Lottery
7^{16sd} **0-0-1**

Saposcat (Ire) *W G M Turner*   19
4 b g Groom Dancer (USA) - Dance Of Joy
8^{10gf} **0-0-1**

Sapphire Dream *A Bailey*   81
2 b f Mind Games - Bombay Sapphire
2^{5s} 2^{5gs} 1^{6gf} 6^{5gf} 17^{6f} 4^{6g} 5^{10g} 11^{6gf}
1-2-8 £13,009

Sapphire Princess *I A Wood*   43 a54
2 b f Namaqualand (USA) - Breakfast Creek
4^{5gf} 5^{5gf} 5^{5f} 6^{6gf} 1^{6sd} 5^{5gf} 7^{6gf} 19^{7gf}
1-0-8 £2,940

Sapphire Sky *D K Ivory*
3 b/br f Compton Place - Jewel (Ire)
12^{6sd} 12^{5s} 15^{5gf} **0-0-3**

Sarah Brown (Ire) *I A Wood*   48
2 b f Benny The Dip - Lalique (Ire)
7^{6f} 10^{7gf} 10^{8ss} 10^{8s} **0-0-4**

Saratoga Splendour (USA) *Jedd O'Keeffe*   38
3 b f Diesis - Saratoga One (USA)
6^{8hy} 11^{6gf} 9^{9g} **0-0-3**

Sarem (USA) *M P Tregoning*   77
2 b/br c Kingmambo (USA) - Storm Beauty (USA)
7^{7g} 4^{7g} **0-0-2 £663**

Sarenne *M Johnston*   45
3 b f Desert Sun - Fabulous Pet
6^{9gs} 6^{9g} 5^{12s} **0-0-3**

Sargents Dream *J A Gilbert*
4 b f Regal Embers (Ire) - Dance Lady
10^{6sd} **0-0-1**

Sariba *A Charlton*   46 a41
5 b m Persian Bold - En Vacances (Ire)
7^{16sw} 6^{13sd} 1^{16sd} 5^{17f} 6^{18t} **1-0-5 £1,456**

Saristar *P F I Cole*   97
3 b f Starborough - Sari
1^{6gs} 18^{6gf} 7^{7gf} 5^{7gs} 1^{6f} 13^{7gf} 6^{6g} 9^{6s}
2-0-8 £16,770

Sarn *M Mullineaux*   51 a27
5 b g Atraf - Covent Garden Girl

9^{8ss} 4^{8sf} 15^{7g} 7^{14gf} 4^{11gs} 8^{12gf} 3^{12gf}
2^{13g} 7^{14g} 4^{16g} 7^{12gf} 4^{16gf} **0-2-12 £2,497**

Saros (Ire) *B Smart* — 68 a63
3 b/br c Desert Sun - Fight Right (Fr)
15^{8s} 1^{7sf} 1^{8sd} 6^{8sd} 14^{7sd} 2^{7g} 7^{7gf} 3^{7gf}
7^{7f} 1^{7gf} 9^{7gf} 11^{7sd} 3^{9sd} **3-3-13 £9,053**

Sarraaf (Ire) *I Semple* — 78 a69
8 ch g Perugino (USA) - Blue Vista (Ire)
4^{7ss} 2^{7g} 3^{8gf} 2^{7gf} 5^{8gs} 7^{8g} 5^{8gs} 3^{7gf} 3^{8f}
3^{7g} 5^{7s} 9^{8gf} 5^{8gf} 2^{7gf} 9^{9gs} 3^{9gf} 4^{8gf} 6^{9gf} 9^{9sd} 6^{9sd}
0-9-23 £11,876

Sartaena (Ire) *R M Beckett* — 35
2 b f Imperial Ballet (Ire) - Joza
8^{5gf} 7^{5gs} 7^{5f} **0-0-3**

Sashay *R Hollinshead* — 51 a63
6 b m Bishop Of Cashel - St James's Antigua (Ire)
5^{16sw} 2^{16sd} 10^{16gs} 3^{13gf} 6^{17f} 11^{16gs} **0-2-6**
£1,420

Saspys Lad *W M Brisbourne* — 59
7 b g Faustus (USA) - Legendary Lady
6^{12s} 5^{11gf} 15^{12gs} **0-0-3**

Sastre (Ire) *P M Phelan* — 61
2 b f Bluebird (USA) - No Rehearsal (Fr)
17^{5gf} 4^{6gs} 12^{7sd} 9^{6gs} **0-0-4 £312**

Satan's Sister *A W Carroll*
3 ch f Tout Ensemble - Winter Greeting
10^{8gf} **0-0-1**

Satchem (Ire) *C E Brittain* — 110
2 br c Inchinor - Mohican Princess
2^{6gf} 1^{6f} 1^{7gs} 1^{6gf} 4^{6g} **3-1-5 £48,028**

Satin Finish (Ire) *M R Channon* — 93
2 b f Kingmambo (USA) - Shimaal
4^{6gs} 1^{5s} 4^{6gf} 10^{5g} 6^{6gs} **1-0-5 £8,675**

Satin Kiss (USA) *Saeed Bin Suroor* — 93
2 b f Seeking The Gold (USA) - Satin Flower (USA)
1^{6gf} 10^{6gf} 1^{6g} 4^{6g} **2-0-4 £12,259**

Satin Rose *T D Easterby* — 53 a31
2 b f Lujain - Shamwari (USA)
5^{6gf} 6^{7sd} 13^{7gs} 6^{7gf} 15^{6g} **0-0-5**

Satsu (Ire) *J G Given* — 51 a7
3 ch f Shinko Forest (Ire) - Cap And Gown (Ire)
9^{8g} 8^{10s} 6^{8s} 12^{7sd} **0-0-4**

Sattam *M P Tregoning* — 86
5 b g Danehill (USA) - Mayaasa (USA)
2^{7g} 3^{8gf} 8^{8g} **0-2-3 £4,265**

Saturday's Child (Fr) *M S Saunders*
2 ch f Hamas (Ire) - Pleasant Whisper (Fr)
11^{6g} **0-0-1**

Saucepot *M D I Usher* — 64
2 ch f Bold Edge - Apple Sauce
9^{5g} 6^{5g} 2^{5gf} 11^{5g} 3^{5gf} 6^{5f} 9^{6g} **0-2-7**
£1,420

Saucy *B J Meehan* — 48 a48
3 b f Muhtarram (USA) - So Saucy
6^{10gs} 6^{8s} 9^{11gf} 5^{10sd} 3^{10f} 5^{9g} 13^{10gs}
0-1-7 £505

Saucy Pickle *Miss Z C Davison* — a28
3 b f Makbul - Bewails (Ire)
10^{8sd} 10^{7sd} **0-0-2**

Savannah Bay *P J Hobbs* — 104
5 ch g In The Wings - High Savannah
7^{16s} 4^{13g} 8^{16gf} 7^{22f} **0-0-4 £1,500**

Savannah River (Ire) *Miss Kate Milligan* — 48
3 b f Desert King (Ire) - Hayward
8^{6s} 3^{10g} 2^{13s} 5^{14f} 4^{12g} 3^{12gf} 6^{16gs} 16^{12gf}
4^{14gs} 10^{10gs} **0-3-10 £3,121**

Savannah Sue *J R Norton* — 19 a9
3 b f Emarati (USA) - Bidweaya (USA)
7^{6s} 9^{7sd} 10^{6sd} 14^{5s} **0-0-4**

Savernake Brave (Ire) *Mrs H Sweeting* — 54 a48
3 b g Charnwood Forest (Ire) - Jordinda (Ire)
5^{7sd} 2^{6gf} 8^{5gf} 4^{6sd} 14^{7sd} 7^{5sd} 1^{7gf}
12^{7gf} 4^{7sd} 13^{7sd} **1-1-11 £2,165**

Savile's Delight (Ire) *R Brotherton* — 86 a73
5 b g Cadeaux Genereux - Across The Ice (USA)
3^{6sd} 2^{6sd} 16^{5g} 1^{6hy} 2^{5g} 7^{6gf} 1^{6g}
1^{7gs} 4^{7gf} 3^{7gs} 13^{6gf} 4^{5sd} **3-4-13 £20,595**

Saviours Spirit *T G Mills* — 71 a77
3 ch g Komaite (USA) - Greenway Lady
2^{6sd} 2^{6sd} 16^{5d} 9^{7g} 10^{7gs} 2^{6sd} 5^{6sd} **1-3-7**
£7,572

Savoie *H R A Cecil* — 54
2 ch f Grand Lodge (USA) - Spry
13^{7gs} **0-0-1**

Savoy Chapel *J A Osborne* — 53 a48
2 br c Xaar - Royal Gift
9^{6sd} 12^{7gf} 13^{7gs} 8^{8gf} **0-0-4**

Sawah *D Shaw* — a26
4 gr g Linamix (Fr) - Tarhhib
5^{6sd} 10^{7sd} **0-0-2**

Sawwaah (Ire) *D Nicholls* — 91
7 b g Marju (Ire) - Just A Mirage
24^{8g} 8^{8g} 1^{7f} 3^{7f} 4^{9g} 16^{7f} 13^{7s} 8^{7gf}
3^{7gf} 15^{8gf} 2^{8g} 1^{7g} 13^{8s} 4^{7gf} 10^{7g} **2-4-15**
£23,960

Saxe-Coburg (Ire) *G A Ham* — 66 a56
7 b g Warning - Saxon Maid
5^{8sd} 1^{10s} 9^{10g} 3^{10f} 3^{14gf} 10^{12gf} 3^{13gf}
5^{13gf} 3^{14gf} 4^{12g} 9^{12gs} 4^{12s} 6^{13gs} 13^{14gs} PU^{12sd}
1-3-15 £6,984

Saxon Lil (Ire) *J L Spearing* — 25
2 b f Second Empire (Ire) - Salva
13^{7gs} **0-0-1**

Say What You See (Ire) *M C Pipe* — 80 a81
4 b c Charnwood Forest (Ire) - Aster Aweke (Ire)
9^{9ss} 4^{10sd} 2^{10sd} 1^{10sd} 5^{10g} 4^{10gf} 2^{10gf}
2^{10gf} 9^{10g} 4^{10gf} 8^{9gf} **1-3-11 £9,579**

Sayadaw (Fr) *H R A Cecil* — 111
4 b c Darshaan - Vingt Et Une (Fr)
4^{12g} **0-0-1 £2,500**

Sayrianna *T J Fitzgerald* — 51
3 b f Sayaarr (USA) - Arianna Aldini
13^{8gs} 11^{10gf} 4^{12gs} **0-0-4**

Saywaan (USA) *Saeed Bin Suroor* — 83
2 ch f Fusaichi Pegasus (USA) - Sharp Cat (USA)
1^{7g} **1-0-1 £5,694**

Scale The Heights (Ire) *B W Hills* — 66
2 b g Spectrum (Ire) - Decrescendo (Ire)
9^{7gf} 8^{7g} 7^{8s} 13^{8gf} **0-0-4**

Scalloway (Ire) *D J Wintle* — 20 a51
4 b g Marju (Ire) - Zany
16^{8gs} 14^{12sd} **0-0-2**

Scandinavia (USA) *A P O'Brien* — 109 a87
2 b c Fusaichi Pegasus (USA) - Party Cited (USA)
2^{7f} 2^{7g} 1^{8gf} 2^{8gf} 8^{9ft} **1-3-5 £36,932**

Scarborough Flyer *J Balding* — a7
2 b c Almaty (Ire) - Calamanco
12^{6g} 10^{6sd} **0-0-2**

Scarlet Empress *R Hannon* — 50
3 b f Second Empire (Ire) - Daltak
15^{6gs} 9^{6f} **0-0-2**

Scarlet Invader (Ire) *J L Dunlop* — 78

2 b g Indian Ridge - Scarlet Plume
4⁶ᵍ 8⁷ᵍᶠ 2⁷ᵍˢ 6⁸ˢ 12⁸ˢ **0-1-5 £1,429**

Scarlett Breeze *J W Hills* 51 a29
3 b f Shinko Forest (Ire) - La Suquet
17⁶ᵍᶠ 13⁶ᵍᶠ 12⁶ᶠ 5⁵ᵍᶠ 8⁵ᵍᶠ 4⁵ᵍᶠ 11⁵ˢᵈ
4⁶ᵍ 7⁶ᶠ 14⁶ᵍ 15⁶ᵍˢ **0-0-11 £413**

Scarlett Rose *Dr J D Scargill* 69 a49
3 b f Royal Applause - Billie Blue
6⁶ᵍˢ 10⁷ᵍᶠ 3⁷ᵍᶠ 3⁷ᵍᶠ 7⁷ᵍˢ 15⁷ᵍᶠ 13⁷ˢᵈ
0-2-7 £2,169

Scarp (USA) *J Noseda* 64
2 b/br c Gulch (USA) - Rhetorical Lass (USA)
9⁷ˢ 11⁷ˢ 7⁸ᵍᶠ **0-0-3**

Scarpia *J S Moore* 46 a37
4 ch g Rudimentary (USA) - Floria Tosca
9⁷ᵍᶠ 17⁷ᵍᶠ 5¹⁰ˢᵈ **0-0-3**

Scarrabus (Ire) *B G Powell* 68 a55
3 b g Charnwood Forest (Ire) - Errazuriz (Ire)
4¹¹ᵍˢ 10¹²ᵍˢ 6¹⁰ᵍᶠ 3¹⁰ᵍᶠ 4¹²ᵍᶠ 3¹²ˢᵈ 5¹²ˢᵈ
7¹⁶ᵍ **0-2-8 £1,695**

Scarrottoo *S C Williams* 65 a57
6 ch g Zilzal (USA) - Bold And Beautiful
8⁷ˢᵈ 3⁶ˢᵈ 5⁷ˢᵈ 16⁷ˢᵈ 11⁷ˢᵈ 5⁷ˢᵈ 5⁶ᵍˢ 1⁷ᵍᶠ
4⁷ᵍ 12⁷ᶠ 3⁷ᵍ 1⁷ᵍᶠ 5⁸ᵍᶠ 14⁸ᵍᶠ 3⁷ᵍᶠ 16⁷ᵍ 9³ˢᵈ
5⁷ˢᵈ **2-3-18 £9,844**

Scary Night (Ire) *J Balding* 21 a62
4 b g Night Shift (USA) - Private Bucks (USA)
12⁶ˢᵈ 11⁶ˢᵈ 1⁵ˢˢ 6⁵ˢˢ 7⁶ˢᵈ 10⁶ˢᵈ 6⁶ˢᵈ
13⁵ˢᵈ 2⁵ˢᵈ 18⁵ᵍˢ 10⁵ˢᵈ 9⁶ˢᵈ **1-1-12 £3,670**

Scenic Flight *Mrs A J Bowlby* 24 a18
3 b f Distant View (USA) - Bird Of Time (Ire)
13⁷ˢ 8⁷ˢᵈ 9⁶ʰʸ **0-0-3**

Scenic Lady (Ire) *L A Dace* 57
8 b m Scenic - Tu Tu Maori (Ire)
5¹⁰ᵍᶠ 7¹²ᵍᶠ **0-0-2**

Scent *J L Dunlop* 62
2 b f Groom Dancer (USA) - Sweet Pea
5⁶ᵍˢ 12⁷ᵍ 3⁷ʰʸ 5⁸ᵍ **0-1-4 £438**

Schapiro (USA) *Jonjo O'Neill* 80
3 b g Nureyev (USA) - Konvincha (USA)
11⁹ʰʸ 3¹²ᵍᶠ 4¹²ᵍ 1¹²ᵍᶠ **1-1-4 £6,839**

Schinken Otto (Ire) *J M Jefferson* 45
3 ch c Shinko Forest (Ire) - Athassel Rose (Ire)
14⁸ᵍ 6⁷ᵍ 7⁸ᵍˢ 5⁹ᵍ 12⁶ᵍ **0-0-5**

Scholarship (Ire) *C F Wall* 10 a69
3 b g College Chapel - Royal Bracelet (Ire)
20⁷ᵍᶠ 3⁸ˢᵈ 2¹⁰ᵍᶠ **0-1-2 £417**

Science Academy (USA) *P F I Cole* 70 a65
3 ch f Silver Hawk (USA) - Dance Design (Ire)
10¹²ˢ 5¹²ᵍᶠ 6¹²ᶠ 2¹²ᵍᶠ 1¹¹ᵍᶠ 11²ᵍˢ 6¹²ᵍˢ
7¹⁰ˢᵈ **2-1-8 £6,928**

Scientist *D Burchell* 77
3 ch g Dr Fong (USA) - Green Bonnet (Ire)
10⁷ᵍˢ 13⁶ᵍ 3⁷ᵍᶠ 9⁸ᵍᶠ 6⁹ᵍᶠ 12⁸ᵍᶠ 1⁷ᵍˢ
8⁸ʰʸ **1-1-8 £5,911**

Scissors (Ire) *Miss J Feilden* 56
2 ch f Desert King (Ire) - Clipping
10⁶ᵍᶠ 8⁷ᵍˢ **0-0-2**

Scooby Dooby Do *R M Whitaker* 51
3 b f Atraf - Redgrave Design
5⁵ˢ 6⁶ˢ 15⁶ˢ 6⁵ᵍᶠ 18⁶ᵍˢ 17⁷ᵍˢ **0-0-6**

Scorch *V Smith* 51 a35
3 b g Mark Of Esteem (Ire) - Red Hot Dancer (USA)
4⁷ˢᵈ 9⁸ᵍᶠ 2¹⁰ᵍᶠ **0-1-3 £985**

Scorchio (Ire) *M F Harris* 46 a47
3 b g Desert Sun - White-Wash

6⁹ˢᵈ 2¹⁰ˢᵈ 5¹²ˢᵈ 4¹¹ᵍᶠ 6¹²ᵍᶠ **0-0-5 £739**

Scorpio Sally (Ire) *M D Hammond* 58
2 b f Mujadil (USA) - Clear Procedure (USA)
14⁶ᵍᶠ 5⁶ᵍˢ 6⁷ᵍ 5⁷ᵍˢ 5⁷ᵍ 16¹⁰ᵍᶠ **0-0-6**

Scotland The Brave *J D Bethell* 76
4 ch f Zilzal (USA) - Hunters Of Brora (Ire)
14⁸ᵍˢ 3⁷ᵍᶠ 8⁸ᶠ 4⁷ᵍᶠ 1⁷ᵍˢ 4⁸ᵍᶠ 2⁸ˢ
9⁷ˢ 7⁷ᵍˢ **1-2-10 £13,238**

Scott *J Jay* 69 a69
3 gr g Polar Falcon (USA) - Circled (USA)
7⁷ᵍ 10⁸ᵍ 6¹²ᵍᶠ 12¹²ᵍᶠ 1¹²ˢᵈ 1¹²ˢᵈ 4¹²ˢᵈ
1¹²ᵍ 2¹²ˢ 3¹⁴ˢ **2-3-10 £10,508**

Scott's View *M Johnston* 118
5 b g Selkirk (USA) - Milly Of The Vally
4¹⁰ᵍᶠ 1¹²ᵍᶠ 11¹²ᵍᶠ 1¹²ᶠ 3¹²ᵍᶠ 1¹⁰ᵍˢ 3¹⁰ᵍᶠ
3¹¹ᵍ 7¹²ᵍ 5¹⁰ᵍᶠ 5¹⁰ᵍᶠ 4¹⁰ᵍ **3-3-12 £360,181**

Scottish Exile (Ire) *K R Burke* 74 a61
3 b f Ashkalani (Ire) - Royal Jade
6⁶ˢᵈ 4⁵ˢᵈ 4⁵ᵍ 3⁵ˢᵈ 1⁵ᵍ 10⁵ᵍᶠ 8⁵ᵍ 2⁵ᵍᶠ
1⁵ᵍᶠ 11⁵ᵍᶠ 3⁵ᵍᶠ 4⁵ᶠ 7⁶ᵍˢ 10⁵ᵍᶠ **2-2-14
£10,779**

Scottish River (USA) *M D I Usher* 88 a78
5 b g Thunder Gulch (USA) - Overbrook
3⁹ˢᵈ 10¹⁰ˢᵈ 1⁹ˢᵈ 5¹⁰ˢᵈ 1⁸ˢʷ 1⁹ˢʷ 7⁸ˢʷ 5⁸ˢˢ
6¹⁰ˢ 1¹⁰ˢ 4⁸ᵍᶠ 6¹⁰ᵍ 8⁸ᵍᶠ 1¹⁰ᵍˢ 2¹⁰ᵍ 4¹⁰ᵍ 17¹¹ᵍ
4¹²ᵍ 10¹⁰ᵍᶠ 6¹²ᵍᶠ **5-2-20 £22,079**

Scotty's Future (Ire) *D Nicholls* 78 a86
6 b g Namaqualand (USA) - Persian Empress (Ire)
7¹⁰ˢᵈ 11⁰ˢᵈ 8¹⁰ˢᵈ 8¹⁰ˢᵈ 6¹⁰ᵍˢ 5⁹ᵍᶠ
4⁹ᵍᶠ 8⁹ᵍˢ **2-0-9 £4,634**

Scramble (USA) *B Ellison* 52
6 ch g Gulch (USA) - Syzygy (Arg)
6⁷ᵍ 14⁸ᶠ 11⁸ᵍᶠ 6⁸ᵍᶠ **0-0-4**

Screenplay *Miss Sheena West* 49
3 ch g In The Wings - Erudite
10¹⁰ᵍ **0-0-1**

Screwdriver *R Hannon* 99
2 b c Entrepreneur - Lust
2⁶ᵍ 1⁶ᵍ **1-1-2 £21,889**

Scripted *Sir Mark Prescott* 67 a66
2 b g Diktat - Krameria
4⁶ˢᵈ 4⁷ᵍ **0-0-2 £609**

Scriptorium *L M Cumani* 69 a59
3 b g Singspiel (Ire) - Annie Albright (USA)
6¹⁰ˢᵈ 10¹⁰ᵍˢ 2⁹ᶠ 4¹⁰ᶠ 2¹⁰ᵍᶠ 8¹⁰ᵍᶠ 10⁸ᵍ
7⁷ᵍ **0-2-8 £2,379**

Scriptwriter (Ire) *Saeed Bin Suroor* 77
2 b c Sadler's Wells (USA) - Dayanata
5⁷ᵍˢ 2⁸ˢ **0-1-2 £1,106**

Scrooby Baby *J A Osborne* 69 a73
2 b f Mind Games - Lunar Music
2⁶ᵍ 7⁶ᵍ 2⁶ˢᵈ 4⁶ᵍᶠ 12⁷ˣᵈ 15⁶ᵍᶠ **0-2-6
£2,052**

Scrunch *B J Meehan* 70 a52
3 b f Royal Applause - Antonia's Folly
6⁶ˢ 9⁷ᵍᶠ 4⁷ᵍ 3⁶ˢᵈ **0-0-4 £951**

Scurra *A C Whillans* 69
5 b g Spectrum (Ire) - Tamnia
6¹²ʰʸ 13¹⁰ʰʸ 3⁸ᵍ 11¹ᵍ 2¹⁰ˢ 4¹³ᵍ 6¹¹ᵍ 5¹⁰ˢ
2¹²ᵍ 4¹⁴ˢ 7¹²ᵍˢ **1-3-11 £5,921**

Sea Cove *J M Jefferson* 45 a50
4 b f Terimon - Regal Pursuit (Ire)
4¹²ˢᵈ 5¹⁶ᵍᶠ 5¹²ˢᵈ 5¹²ˢ 4¹⁴ˢᵈ **0-0-5**

Sea Fern *D Eddy* 43
3 b g Petong - Duxyana (Ire)
5⁵ˢ 11⁵ᵍᶠ 7⁵ᵍᶠ 10⁵ᵍᶠ 6⁶ᵍ 10⁶ᵍᶠ **0-0-6**

Sea Hunter *M R Channon* 90
2 b c Lend A Hand - Ocean Grove (Ire)
7⁵ᵍ 1⁵ᵍ 4⁵ᵍᶠ 2⁷ᵍˢ 3⁷ᵍᶠ 5⁷ˢ 10⁸ᵍᶠ 4⁸ˢ
1-2-8 £10,306

Sea Jade (Ire) *J W Payne* 44 a40
5 b m Mujadil (USA) - Mirabiliary (USA)
4⁸ᵍ 2⁸ᵍ 2⁷ˢᵈ 8⁶ᶠ **0-1-4 £822**

Sea Lark *W J Haggas* a36
2 b g Green Horizon - Fiora (Ire)
9⁷ˢᵈ **0-0-1**

Sea Map *S Kirk* 53
2 ch c Fraam - Shehana (USA)
9⁷ᵍᶠ 10⁷ᵍᶠ UR⁸ᵍᶠ 10⁸ᵍˢ 6⁸ʰʸ **0-0-5**

Sea Mark *B Ellison* 64
8 ro g Warning - Mettlesome
3⁷ᵍˢ 5⁷ᵍᶠ 11⁸ᵍᶠ **0-1-3 £646**

Sea Nymph (Ire) *Sir Michael Stoute* 83
3 b f Spectrum (Ire) - Sea Picture (Ire)
5⁸ᵍ 2⁸ᵍᶠ 1⁸ᵍˢ 2⁸ᵍˢ 13⁸ᵍ **1-2-5 £7,348**

Sea Of Gold *H J Cyzer* 73 a62
3 b f Docksider (USA) - Shadow Bird
14⁷ᵍ 6⁸ᵍᶠ 2¹⁰ᶠ 6⁸ᵍᶠ 4¹⁰ˢᵈ 15⁸ᵍ 11⁸ˢᵈ
0-1-7 £1,503

Sea Of Happiness *C Grant* 16
4 b g Pivotal - Ella Lamees
13¹²ᵍᶠ 9¹⁶ᶠ 15¹²ᵍᶠ **0-0-3**

Sea Plume *Lady Herries* 72
5 b m Slip Anchor - Fine Quill
5¹²ˢ 10¹⁴ᵍᶠ 8¹⁴ᵍ 9¹⁴ᵍᶠ **0-0-4**

Sea Storm (Ire) *D R MacLeod* 87 a87
6 b g Dolphin Street (Fr) - Prime Interest (Ire)
16⁷ᵍ 5⁷ᵍ 8⁸ᵍ 3⁷ᶠ 7⁷ᵍᶠ 1⁸ᵍᶠ 10⁹ᵍᶠ 7⁸ᵍᶠ
6⁸ᵍᶠ 5⁷ᵍ 6⁸ᶠ 4⁷ᶠ 3⁸ˢ 19⁷ᵍᶠ 2⁷ˢ 17ᵍᶠ 8⁷ˢ 5⁹ˢᵈ
2-4-18 £21,146

Sea Tern *D G Bridgwater* 1
4 b f Emarati (USA) - Great Tern
9⁷ˢᵈ 14¹⁰ᵍᶠ **0-0-2**

Sea The World (Ire) *D Shaw* 3 a69
4 b g Inzar (USA) - Annie's Travels (Ire)
5⁵ˢᵈ 1⁵ˢᵈ 3⁵ˢᵈ 2⁵ˢˢ 6⁵ˢᵈ 9⁵ˢˢ 11⁶ˢ **1-2-7**
£4,569

Sea Ya Maite *S R Bowring* 25 a43
10 b g Komaite (USA) - Marina Plata
14¹²ˢᵈ 5¹²ˢᵈ 2⁸ᵈ 3¹¹ˢᵈ 5⁹ˢˢ 4¹¹ˢᵈ 5¹⁴ˢᵈ
10¹¹ˢˢ 2⁸ˢᵈ 4⁸ˢᵈ 7⁸ᵍᶠ 8⁸ˢᵈ 7⁸ˢᵈ **0-3-13 £1,182**

Seafield Towers *Miss L A Perratt* 81
4 ch g Compton Place - Midnight Spell
15⁵ᵍᶠ 10⁶ᵍᶠ 3⁵ᵍᶠ 14⁵ᵍᶠ 12⁵ᵍᶠ 12⁶ᵍ 9⁵ᵍ
7⁶ᵍᶠ 8⁶ᵍᶠ 13⁶ᵍᶠ **0-1-10 £2,168**

Seagold *A E Jones* 42 a2
3 b f Shahrastani (USA) - Raeleen
16¹⁰ᵍ 10⁸ᶠ 14¹²ˢᵈ 14¹⁰ˢᵈ **0-0-4**

Seal Of Office *A M Hales*
5 ch g Mark Of Esteem (Ire) - Minskip (USA)
17⁸ᵍᵈ PU¹⁰ᵍᶠ **0-0-2**

Seamless *W J Haggas* 64 a69
2 b c Gold Away (Ire) - Fallara (Fr)
5⁶ᵍ 5⁶ˢᵈ 2⁶ˢᵈ **0-1-3 £1,600**

Seamus Shindig *H Candy* 87
2 b g Aragon - Sheesha (USA)
1⁵ᶠ 4⁶ˢ **1-0-2 £6,358**

Sean's Memory (USA) *Mrs C A Dunnett* a55
4 b g Theatrical - Memories (USA)
8¹²ˢᵈ 2¹²ˢᵈ 6¹⁶ˢᵈ PU¹⁴ˢᵈ **0-1-4 £1,024**

Search Mission (USA) *Mrs A J Perrett* 86
3 b f Red Ransom (USA) - Skimble (USA)

2⁷ᶠ 9⁷ᵍᶠ **0-1-2 £1,716**

Season Ticket (Ger) *W J Haggas* 46
2 b f Kornado - Second Game (Ger)
15⁵ᵍ 8⁶ᵍˢ 17⁶ᵍᶠ 10⁷ᵍᶠ **0-0-4**

Seasons Estates *B R Millman* 67
2 b f Mark Of Esteem (Ire) - La Fazenda
4⁵ˢ 10⁵ᵍ 4⁷ᵍˢ 37ᵍᶠ 1⁷ᵍᶠ **1-1-5 £4,966**

Seattle Art (USA) *Dr P Pritchard*
10 b g Seattle Slew (USA) - Artiste
12¹⁰ᵍᶠ **0-0-1**

Seattle Prince (USA) *S Gollings*
6 gr g Cozzene (USA) - Chicken Slew (USA)
8¹⁶ʰʸ 17¹⁶ᵍ **0-0-2**

Seattle Robber *S Kirk* 62 a64
2 b g Robellino (USA) - Seattle Ribbon (USA)
14⁷ᵍ 4⁶ˢᵈ **0-0-2 £399**

Secam (Pol) *Mrs P Townsley* 44 a47
5 gr g Alywar (USA) - Scytia (Pol)
13¹²ˢᵈ 3⁸ˢᵈ 9⁶ᵍ 11⁸ᵍᶠ 11⁸ˢᵈ **0-1-5 £422**

Secluded *E F Vaughan* 73
4 b g Compton Place - Secret Dance
5¹⁰ᵍᶠ 8¹⁰ᵍ 14⁸ᵍ 1¹⁰ʰʸ 5¹⁰ᵍ 15¹⁰ᵍ **1-0-6**
£3,507

Second Generation (Ire) *R J Hodges* a36
7 ch g Cadeaux Genereux - Title Roll (Ire)
5⁵ˢᵈ 5⁵ˢᵈ 3⁶ˢᵈ 4⁶ˢᵈ 5⁹ˢᵈ **0-0-5 £179**

Second Minister *D Flood* 1 a61
5 ch g Lion Cavern (USA) - Crime Of Passion
3⁵ˢᵈ 8⁶ˢᵈ 6⁶ˢˢ 18⁶ᵍ 10⁶ᵍ 11⁶ˢᵈ 13⁶ˢᵈ
0-1-7 £624

Second Of May *P R Chamings* 51
4 ch f Lion Cavern (USA) - Giant Nipper
8¹⁰ᶠ **0-0-1**

Second Paige (Ire) *Mrs L Wadham* a38
7 b g Nicolotte - My First Paige (Ire)
4¹⁶ˢᵈ **0-0-1**

Second Reef *R A Fahey* 43 a57
2 b c Second Empire (Ire) - Vax Lady
3⁵ˢᵈ 19⁶ᵍᶠ **0-1-2 £595**

Second User *J R Jenkins* 1 a8
3 b g Zilzal (USA) - Glossary
11⁸ˢᵈ 13¹⁰ˢᵈ 20¹⁰ˢ 18¹⁰ᵍᶠ **0-0-4**

Second Venture (Ire) *P Howling* a41
6 b g Petardia - Hilton Gateway
8⁸ˢᵈ 3⁸ˢᵈ 8⁷ˢˢ **0-1-3 £211**

Second Warning *D J Daly* 59 a52
3 ch c Piccolo - St Helena
5⁹ˢ 8⁸ˢᵈ 5⁸ᵍˢ 6¹⁰ᵍˢ **0-0-4**

Second Wind *D A Nolan*
9 ch g Kris - Rimosa's Pet
9⁶ˢ 12⁸ˢ **0-0-2**

Secret Affair *A King* 71 a52
2 b c Piccolo - Secret Circle
8⁶ˢᵈ 8⁷ᵍᶠ 10⁸ˢ **0-0-3**

Secret Bloom *J R Norton* a48
3 b g My Best Valentine - Rose Elegance
4⁷ˢᵈ 4⁸ˢᵈ 11⁷ˢᵈ 5¹¹ˢᵈ 4⁸ˢˢ 2⁸ˢᵈ 4⁸ˢᵈ 1⁹ˢᵈ
3⁹ˢᵈ 7⁹ˢᵈ 6¹¹ˢᵈ **1-1-11 £2,031**

Secret Cavern (USA) *J A Osborne* 78
2 b c Lion Cavern (USA) - River Dyna (USA)
6⁶ᵍ 7⁷ᶠ 4⁷ˢ **0-0-3 £361**

Secret Charm (Ire) *B W Hills* 108
3 b f Green Desert (USA) - Viz (USA)
5⁸ᵍ 5⁸ᵍᶠ 11⁸ᶠ 1⁸ᵍᶠ 5⁸ᵍ **1-0-5 £24,497**

Secret Connection *M Wigham*

4 b f Danzig Connection (USA) - Red Secret (Ire)
7^9ss **0-0-1**

Secret Diva (Ire) *Mrs P N Dutfield* 31 a17
2 ch f Dr Devious (Ire) - Deerussa (Ire)
9^5g 12^6gf 10^5gf 7^7gf 9^6gf 11^8sd **0-0-6**

Secret Flame *W J Haggas* 79 a71
3 b f Machiavellian (USA) - Secret Obsession (USA)
3^8g 3^10gf 1^9g 9^8gf 6^10g 5^10sd **1-2-6**
£7,388

Secret Formula *S Kirk* 70
4 b f So Factual (USA) - Ancient Secret
20^7gs 18^7g **0-0-2**

Secret History (USA) *M Johnston* 79
2 b f Bahri (USA) - Ravnina (USA)
2^6gf 3^6gs 5^6gf 1^7gs 7^7f 2^8s 3^7s **1-3-7**
£8,004

Secret Jewel (Fr) *Lady Herries* 62
4 b f Hernando (Fr) - Opalette
6^10gs 8^12gf 5^12gs 17^12s 12^10gs 2^12g 2^14s
0-2-7 £1,806

Secret Of Secrets *L R James*
3 b g Timeless Times (USA) - Sophisticated Baby
13^5g 10^6gf **0-0-2**

Secret Pact (Ire) *M Johnston* 89
2 br c Lend A Hand - Schust Madame (Ire)
4^5g 2^6hy 3^7g 7^6s 1^7f 1^7f 2^8g 3^8s **2-4-8**
£14,540

Secret Place *E A L Dunlop* 96 a88
3 ch g Compton Place - Secret Circle
1^7sd 1^7sd 3^8sd 9^7g 1^7gf 16^7g 13^7g **3-0-7**
£18,960

Secretary General (Ire) *P F I Cole* 99
3 b c Fasliyev (USA) - Katie McLain (USA)
7^8g 2^8gs 8^8gf 5^8gf 9^8gs 1^8gf 2^10gs 2^12g
8^12gf 11^12g **1-3-10 £20,583**

Sedge (USA) *P T Midgley* 62
4 b g Lure (USA) - First Flyer (USA)
1^7gf 12^8s 16^8gf 7^8gf 7^8gf 4^9gs **1-0-6**
£3,293

Seejay *J Pearce* 38 a55
4 b f Bahamian Bounty - Grand Splendour
3^8sd 17^10s 8^8gf 9^10gf 11^8sd **0-1-5 £421**

Seeking A Way (USA) *J H M Gosden* 67 a74
3 b f Seeking The Gold (USA) - Seattle Way (USA)
2^12f 3^10gf 7^14gs 6^13f 2^13sd 3^12s **0-3-6**
£3,861

Seeking An Alibi (USA) *Saeed Bin Suroor* 56 a68
2 ch c Storm Cat (USA) - Seeking Regina (USA)
10^8g 8^8sd **0-0-2**

Seeking The Dia (USA) *Hideyuki Mori* 106
3 b c Storm Cat (USA) - Seeking The Pearl (USA)
1^7f 1^8f 1^8^7g 8^8g 12^6gs 15^7gs **3-0-6**
£599,547

Seel Of Approval *R Charlton* 112
5 b g Polar Falcon (USA) - Petit Point (Ire)
2^6g **0-1-1 £4,576**

Seeyaaj *Jonjo O'Neill* 81
4 b g Darshaan - Subya
5^12gf 9^11g 10^16s **0-0-3**

Seguidilla (Ire) *G C Bravery* 23
3 b f Mujadil (USA) - Alzeam (Ire)
14^6gs 6^5s **0-0-2**

Sekwana (Pol) *Miss A M Newton-Smith* 12 a27
5 b m Duke Valentino - Surmia (Pol)
13^10sd 10^13sd 11^7f **0-0-3**

Selebela *L M Cumani* 101

3 ch f Grand Lodge (USA) - Risarshana (Fr)
7^8s 1^12gf 1^12g 1^12f 2^12g 2^12g 3^12gf 2^12s
10^15s **3-4-9 £38,095**

Selective *E F Vaughan* 92 a97
5 b g Selkirk (USA) - Portelet
4^8s 13^7gf 24^7t 4^8sd 10^8g 4^7gs 6^10f 5^8g
5^8s **0-0-9 £3,475**

Self Belief *M C Chapman* 55
3 b f Easycall - Princess Of Spain
11^5gf 12^5g 15^5gf **0-0-3**

Self Defense *P R Chamings* 114
7 b g Warning - Dansara
8^16s 6^16g 5^14g 5^14s 2^12gf 3^12hy **0-2-6**
£18,725

Self Respect (USA) *J Noseda* 60
2 b c Lear Fan (USA) - Cap Of Dignity
7^10s **0-0-1**

Selika (Ire) *M H Tompkins* 73
2 ch g Daggers Drawn (USA) - Hint-Of-Romance (Ire)
12^6gs 9^7g 4^8g 8^8g **0-0-4 £411**

Selkirk Grace *K A Morgan* 68
4 b g Selkirk (USA) - Polina
5^10gs 4^12s **0-0-2 £270**

Selkirk Storm (Ire) *M W Easterby* 81
2 b c Trans Island - Force Divine (Fr)
1^6hy 2^5gf 15^6g 7^10g 14^7gf 10^6hy 3^6s
14^6s **1-2-9 £5,801**

Semelle De Vent (USA) *J H M Gosden* 58 a61
3 b f Sadler's Wells (USA) - Heeremandi (Ire)
3^12ss 3^12gs 20^12s 9^12sd 2^10sd 7^10gf 3^9sd
1^9sd **1-3-8 £4,962**

Semenovskii *R Bastiman* 80 a71
4 b g Fraam - Country Spirit
3^6sd 6^5gf 11^6gf 1^6gf 15^6g 16^6gf 15^6g
13^7s 5^7s **1-1-9 £6,087**

Semper Paratus (USA) *V Smith* 59 a59
5 b g Foxhound (USA) - Bletcha Lass (Aus)
4^6sd 8^7sd 12^8gs 2^6s 12^8sd 3^6sd 14^6gf
11^7g 12^6g 1^7hy **1-2-10 £4,456**

Sendeed (USA) *Saeed Bin Suroor* 55
2 b/br c Gulch (USA) - Aghsaan (USA)
14^7gf 16^7s **0-0-2**

Sendintank *S C Williams* 104 a78
4 ch g Halling (USA) - Colleville
1^12sd 1^12sd 1^12sd 1^12sd 3^12gs 1^16hy 1^15s
1^14s 1^12g 3^14g 1^16gs 1^17s **10-2-12 £69,724**

Seneschal *M R Channon* 90
3 b g Polar Falcon - Broughton Singer (Ire)
10^8g 8^10s 12^10gf 10^10s 9^7gs 14^7g 7^7gs
1^7g 6^7gs 2^7gs 6^7s 1^7s **2-1-12 £13,869**

Senior Minister *P W Hiatt* 65
6 b g Lion Cavern - Crime Ofthecentury
8^10f 1^8f 10^7g 8^8g 12^10gf 12^8gf 15^8g
19^7gf 12^9sd **1-0-9 £2,541**

Senior Whim *P R Webber* 3
2 b c Lahib (USA) - Euphorie (Ger)
8^10hy **0-0-1**

Senna (Ire) *P D Cundell* a1
4 b g Petardia - Saborinie
12^8sd **0-0-1**

Sennen Cove *R Bastiman* 52 a32
5 ch g Bering - Dame Laura (Ire)
10^6sd 7^7sd 6^7sd 3^10sd 6^8sd 6^8g 1^8gf 1^7gf
9^8gf 7^8f **2-0-10 £4,688**

Senor Bond (USA) *B Smart* 67 a61
3 ch g Hennessy (USA) - Troppa Freska (USA)
6^8ss 3^6s 12^7gs 6^6gf 10^7sd 10^6sd **0-0-6**

£562

Senor Eduardo *S Gollings* 63
7 gr g Terimon - Jasmin Path
9^{7gs} 11^{7gf} 3^{8gs} 5^{8gf} 1^{10g} 6^{10gf} 2^{9gs} 3^{12g}
15^{8gf} 3^{10gf} 7^{12gf} 12^{9gs} 1-4-12 £5,553

Senor Miro *J Akehurst*
6 b g Be My Guest (USA) - Classic Moonlight (Ire)
PU^{7sw} 0-0-1

Senor Set (Ger) *P A Blockley* a60
3 b g Second Set (Ire) - Shine Share (Ire)
2^{8sd} 0-1-1 £1,063

Senor Toran (USA) *P Burgoyne* 35 a50
4 b g Barathea (Ire) - Applaud (USA)
3^{10sd} 4^{10sd} 3^{10sd} 16^{10gs} 2^{10sd} 5^{12gf} 0-3-6
£942

Sentiero Rosso (USA) *B Ellison* 98
2 b c Intidab (USA) - Kheyrah (USA)
4^{5g} 2^{5gs} 1^{5hy} 3^{6gs} 9^{5s} 9^{6gf} 8^{6g} 13^{7s}
1-1-8 £9,409

Sentry (Ire) *J H M Gosden* 93
4 b g In Command (Ire) - Keep Bobbin Up (Ire)
1^{12g} 4^{12g} 3^{14s} 3^{16g} 21^{20gf} 7^{16g} 1-2-6
£14,425

Senza Scrupoli *M D Hammond* 49
4 ch g Inchinor - Gravette
3^{10gs} 0-1-1 £463

Seraph *John A Harris* 38 a46
4 ch g Vettori (Ire) - Dahlawise (Ire)
3^{9sd} 1^{11sd} 8^{12sd} 3^{12sw} 3^{12sd} 2^{12sd} 1^{12sd}
9^{13sd} 3^{14sd} 9^{12gf} 11^{12sd} 2-5-11 £4,382

Serbelloni *P W Harris* 61
4 b g Spectrum (Ire) - Rose Vibert
5^{10g} 0-0-1

Serene Pearl (Ire) *G M Moore* 52 a44
2 b f Night Shift (USA) - Shanjah
11^{5g} 8^{5gf} 6^{5f} 6^{5gf} 4^{5sd} 13^{7sd} 10^{5g} 0-0-7
£320

Serengeti Sky (USA) *John A Quinn* 13
3 br c Southern Halo (USA) - Genovefa (USA)
8^{10s} 4^{12gs} 6^{10s} 0-0-3 £271

Sergeant Cecil *B R Millman* 102
5 ch g King's Signet (USA) - Jadidh
20^{12s} 3^{12gf} 5^{14gs} 1^{12g} 2^{14g} 2^{14g} 2^{15gf}
3^{12gf} 1-5-8 £53,245

Sergeant Lewis *J A Osborne* 21
2 gr c Mind Games - Silver Blessings
6^{7f} 18^{6gf} 0-0-2

Sergeant Shinko (Ire) *M Dods* a33
2 ch g Shinko Forest (Ire) - Sea Modena (Ire)
11^{7gf} 11^{9sd} 9^{10hy} 0-0-3

Sergeant Slipper *C Smith* 48 a58
7 ch g Never So Bold - Pretty Scarce
13^{6ss} 3^{5ss} 10^{6ss} 3^{5ss} 5^{6sw} 7^{7ss} 1^{6sd}
5^{6s} 14^{6f} 14^{6gf} 2-3-11 £5,621

Sergeant Small (Ire) *John Berry* 17
2 b g Dr Devious (Ire) - Yavarro
17^{6gs} 20^{6gf} 0-0-2

Sergeant's Inn *T T Clement*
7 b g Sabrehill (USA) - Pink Brief (Ire)
7^{14ss} 0-0-1

Serieux *Mrs A J Perrett* 100 a87
5 b g Cadeaux Genereux - Seranda (Ire)
10^{8sd} 11^{8g} 14^{10gs} 2^{8g} 18^{8g} 21^{8gf} 8^{8gf}
12^{8gs} 9^{7gf} 4^{7g} 2^{8gf} 5^{8g} 0-2-12 £9,708

Serramanna *H R A Cecil* 75
3 ch f Grand Lodge (USA) - Spry

6^{10g} 5^{10gs} 3^{10g} 3^{12gs} 8^{14gs} 0-2-5 £1,520

Serraval (Fr) *G B Balding* 66
6 ch m Sanglamore (USA) - Saone (USA)
2^{10gf} 3^{11g} 5^{12gs} 3^{10gs} 0-3-4 £2,086

Serre Chevalier (Ire) *P W Harris* 81
3 b g Marju (Ire) - Ski Lodge (Ire)
2^{8gf} 18^{8gf} 8^{7g} 15^{7gs} 1-1-4 £7,337

Ses Seline *John A Harris* 37
3 b f Salse (USA) - Absentee
4^{8gs} 5^{8s} 8^{12gf} 13^{14gs} 16^{10g} 0-0-5 £738

Sessay *D Nicholls* 74
3 b g Cyrano De Bergerac - Green Supreme
4^{7g} 3^{6s} 5^{7f} 18^{5gf} 6^{6gs} 8^{7gf} 6^{5gs} 1^{6g} 9^{5s}
1-1-9 £4,336

Set Alight *Mrs C A Dunnett* 52 a42
3 b f Forzando - Me Spede
9^{7g} 4^{7f} 3^{7gf} 8^{6sd} 8^{7s} 0-1-5 £690

Settlement Craic (Ire) *T G Mills* 95 a69
3 b c Ela-Mana-Mou - Medway (Ire)
1^{12sd} 4^{12g} 3^{10gs} 11^{12gf} 1^{12gs} 13^{12g} 15^{12g}
2-1-7 £11,796

Seven Magicians (USA) *Sir Michael Stoute* 70
2 b/br f Silver Hawk (USA) - Mambo Jambo (USA)
4^{7gf} 0-0-1 £405

Seven No Trumps *J M Bradley* 83
7 ch g Pips Pride - Classic Ring (Ire)
2^{5s} 5^{6gs} 12^{6gs} 11^{5g} 11^{5s} 3^{5gf} 6^{6gf}
10^{5gf} 4^{5f} 8^{5g} 8^{5g} 2^{5gs} 8^{5gf} 10^{5gs} 4^{5g} 7^{5gs}
PU^{5sd} 0-3-17 £7,190

Seven Shirt *E G Bevan* 49
3 b g Great Dane (Ire) - Bride's Answer
8^{8gs} 14^{8s} 7^{9gf} 6^{7hy} 17^{8gs} 0-0-5

Seven Year Itch (Ire) *M P Tregoning* 81
4 b g Danehill (USA) - Itching (Ire)
2^{10s} 2^{10gf} 0-2-2 £2,852

Severely (Fr) *B W Hills* 55
2 b f Cape Cross (Ire) - Sevres (USA)
7^{6gf} 0-0-1

Sevillano *P D Cundell* 109
3 b g Nicolotte - Nashville Blues (Ire)
1^{6gs} 1^{5g} 7^{6g} 2-0-3 £16,022

Sew'N'So Character (Ire) *M Blanshard* 99
3 b c Imperial Ballet (Ire) - Hope And Glory (USA)
4^{8gs} 10^{9g} 3^{10gf} 4^{8g} 4^{8g} 7^{7gf} 4^{10gs} 6^{10gs}
7^{8g} 2^{11hy} 4^{10hy} 0-2-11 £11,926

Sewmore Character *M Blanshard* 36 a79
4 b c Hector Protector (USA) - Kyle Rhea
4^{8sd} 6^{10sd} 2^{8sd} 5^{8sd} 15^{8gs} 14^{7gs} 2^{10sd}
9^{12sd} 15^{12sd} 0-2-9 £3,297

Sewmuch Character *M Blanshard* 73 a73
5 b g Magic Ring (Ire) - Diplomatist
4^{6s} 15^{6gs} 6^{7gf} 4^{6gf} 2^{6gf} 7^{6gf} 1^{6gs} 17^{6gs}
6^{9g} 3^{6sd} 10^{7sd} 1-2-11 £5,856

Seyaadi *E A L Dunlop* 77 a69
2 b g Intikhab (USA) - Sioux Chef
5^{7gf} 2^{7gs} 5^{7sd} 0-1-3 £1,617

Seyed (Ire) *V Smith* 51
4 b g Desert Prince (Ire) - Royal Bounty (Ire)
3^{7gf} 0-1-1 £215

Sforzando *J A R Toller* 74
3 b f Robellino (USA) - Mory Kante (USA)
1^{7gf} 5^{7gf} 7^{7gf} 7^{8gs} 1-0-4 £3,630

Sgt Pepper (Ire) *R Hannon* 94
3 b c Fasliyev (USA) - Amandine (Ire)
8^{7gf} 11^{7gf} 4^{7gs} 6^{8gf} 5^{9gs} 15^{10g} 0-0-6
£1,977

Shaaban (Ire) *Miss J Feilden* 69
3 b g Woodman (USA) - Ashbilya (USA)
13⁸ᵍ 7⁸ᵍᶠ 7⁸ᵍᶠ 5¹⁰ᵍ 9⁸ᵍˢ **0-0-5**

Shaamit's All Over *B A Pearce* 35 a32
5 br m Shaamit (Ire) - First Time Over
7¹²ˢᵈ 14¹⁰ˢᵈ 3⁸ˢᵈ 6⁷ᵍ 8⁸ᵍ **0-0-5 £205**

Shades Of Green *N A Callaghan* 44 a52
2 b f Loup Sauvage (USA) - Green Light (Fr)
10⁸ᵍᶠ 6⁷ˢᵈ **0-0-2**

Shadowfax *Miss Gay Kelleway* a59
4 b g Anabaa (USA) - Prends Ca (Ire)
4⁶ˢᵈ 11⁶ˢᵈ 8⁶ˢᵈ 7⁸ˢʷ 2⁶ˢᵈ 8⁷ˢᵈ **0-1-6
£1,287**

Shady Deal *J M Bradley* 54
8 b g No Big Deal - Taskalady
11⁵ˢʷ 9⁵ˢʷ 13⁵ᵍˢ 8⁶ˢ 3⁶ˢ 14⁶ᵍᶠ 7⁶ᵍᶠ 3⁶ᵍ
15⁵ᶠ 8⁶ᵍ **0-2-10 £843**

Shady Reflection (USA) *J H M Gosden* 91
3 b f Sultry Song (USA) - Woodland Melody (USA)
1⁸ˢ 5¹⁰ᵍᶠ **1-0-2 £18,150**

Shahama (Ire) *M P Tregoning* 57
2 gr c Daylami (Ire) - Albertville (USA)
12⁷ᵍᶠ 12⁸ᵍˢ **0-0-2**

Shaheer (Ire) *B J Meehan* 75
2 b g Shahrastani (USA) - Atmospheric Blues (Ire)
6⁶ᵍ 2⁶ᵍᶠ 12⁶ᵍ 6⁷ᵍᶠ 13¹⁰ᵍ **0-1-5 £1,096**

Shahm (Ire) *B J Curley* a48
5 b g Marju (Ire) - Istibshar (USA)
8⁶ˢˢ 7⁸ˢᵈ **0-0-2**

Shahzan House (Ire) *M A Jarvis* 106
5 b h Sri Pekan (USA) - Nsx
3¹⁰ˢ 2¹⁰ˢ 3¹⁰ᵍ 3¹⁰ᵍˢ 3¹¹ᵍ 3¹⁰ˢ 6¹⁰ʰʸ **0-6-7
£27,142**

Shalati Princess *J C Fox* 47 a49
3 b f Bluegrass Prince (Ire) - Shalati (Fr)
7⁸ˢᵈ 11⁸ˢᵈ 6⁸ˢᵈ 7⁷ˢᵈ 4¹⁰ˢᵈ 9¹²ˢ 3¹⁰ˢᵈ
7¹²ˢᵈ 5¹⁰ˢᵈ **0-1-9 £205**

Shalaya (Ire) *Sir Michael Stoute* 89
3 b f Marju (Ire) - Shalama (Ire)
5¹⁰ᵍᶠ 11⁹ᵍᶠ **0-0-2**

Shalbeblue (Ire) *B Ellison* 43
7 b g Shalford (Ire) - Alberjas (Ire)
11¹²ᵍᶠ 9¹²ᵍᶠ 8¹²ᵍᶠ 8¹⁰ᵍᶠ 11¹²ˢ **0-0-5**

Shaman *G L Moore* 42 a49
7 b g Fraam - Magic Maggie
5¹⁰ˢᵈ 12¹²ˢᵈ 4¹⁰ˢ **0-0-3**

Shamara (Ire) *C F Wall* 97
4 b f Spectrum (Ire) - Hamara (Fr)
2¹⁰ᵍ 2⁹ᵍ 4¹⁰ˢ 7¹⁰ᵍ 2¹⁰ᵍ 6¹⁰ˢ **0-3-6
£13,363**

Shamardal (USA) *M Johnston* 125
2 b c Giant's Causeway (USA) - Helsinki
1⁶ᵍ 1⁷ᵍ 1⁷ˢ **3-0-3 £198,819**

Shambar (Ire) *P R Chamings* 98
5 gr g Linamix (Fr) - Shamawna (Ire)
3¹⁰ᵍˢ 5¹⁰ᵍᶠ 3¹⁰ᵍˢ **0-1-3 £2,582**

Shamdian (Ire) *N J Henderson* 80 a47
4 b g Indian Ridge - Shamadara (Ire)
9¹⁰ᵍ 9⁷ˢᵈ **0-0-2**

Shameless *H Alexander* 15 a2
7 ch g Prince Daniel (USA) - Level Edge
9¹²ˢᵈ 8¹⁰ˢ 9¹²ᵍᶠ 9¹²ᵍˢ **0-0-4**

Shamrock Bay *J G Given* 63
2 b f Celtic Swing - Kabayil
9⁶ᵍᶠ 4⁷ᵍᶠ 8⁷ᵍ **0-0-3 £446**

Shamrock City (Ire) *P Howling* 79

7 b g Rock City - Actualite
6¹⁰ᵍ 31⁸ᵍᶠ 12⁹ᵍᶠ **0-0-3 £225**

Shamrock Tea *R A Fahey* 62
3 b g Imperial Ballet (Ire) - Yellow Ribbon (Ire)
12⁶ᵍᶠ 5⁵ᵍᶠ 1⁶ˢ 4⁶ᵍ 13⁶ᵍ 14⁶ᵍᶠ 20⁷ᵍ
1-0-7 £4,124

Shamwari Fire (Ire) *I W McInnes* 56 a40
4 ch g Idris (Ire) - Bobby's Dream
4⁹ˢᵈ 6⁷ˢᵈ 13⁷ˢᵈ 7⁸ᵍ 1⁷ᵍᶠ 6⁷ᵍ 8⁸ᶠ 10⁸ᵍᶠ
3⁷ᵍᶠ 3⁸ᵍᶠ 8⁸ᵍᶠ 13⁸ᵍˢ 1¹⁰ᵍᶠ 3⁸ᶠ 6¹⁰ᵍ 9¹⁰ᵍᶠ 3⁸ᵍ
2-4-17 £4,831

Shanghai Lily (Ire) *Sir Michael Stoute* 100
2 b f King's Best (USA) - Marlene-D
1⁶ᵍˢ 1⁷ᵍ **2-0-2 £17,028**

Shanghai Surprise *J Balding* 45
3 b g Komaite (USA) - Shanghai Lil
5⁸ˢ 8⁸ᵍˢ 8⁵ᵍᶠ 7⁵ᵍᶠ 9⁵ˢᵈ **0-0-5**

Shankly Bond (Ire) *B Smart* 61
2 ch g Danehill Dancer (Ire) - Fanellan
8⁷ᵍˢ 9⁶ᵍ 6⁷ᵍ **0-0-3**

Shannkara's Quest (USA) *C N Kellett* a12
3 b/br c Coronado's Quest (USA) - Shannkara (Ire)
12⁸ˢᵈ 11⁸ˢᵈ 12⁶ˢ **0-0-3**

Shannon Springs (Ire) *B W Hills* 96
2 b c Darshaan - Our Queen Of Kings
2⁷ᵍ 3⁷ᵍ 2⁸ᵍ 7⁸ˢ **0-2-4 £6,178**

Shannon's Dream *P W Hiatt* 30
8 gr m Anshan - Jenny's Call
7¹²ᵍᶠ 4¹²ᵍᶠ **0-0-2**

Shanty Star (Ire) *M Johnston* 108
4 gr g Hector Protector (USA) - Shawanni
9¹⁴ᵍˢ PU¹⁶ᵍᶠ 3¹²ᵍ 9¹⁶ˢ **0-0-4 £3,300**

Shape Up (Ire) *R Craggs* 66 a37
4 b g Octagonal (NZ) - Bint Kaldoun (Ire)
3¹²ˢᵈ 2¹⁰ˢ 4¹²ᵍᶠ 1¹²ᵍᶠ 1¹²ᵍᶠ 1¹²ᵍˢ **3-3-6
£11,930**

Sharaab (USA) *B Hanbury* 75
3 b/br c Erhaab (USA) - Ghashtah (USA)
6¹⁰ᵍˢ 8¹⁰ᵍᶠ 5⁷ᵍᶠ 2⁸ᵍᶠ 9¹⁰ᵍᶠ 7¹⁰ᵍᶠ 16⁸ᵍ
0-1-7 £1,998

Sharabad (Fr) *Mrs L B Normile* 46
6 b g Ela-Mana-Mou - Sharbada (Fr)
5¹⁰ᵍᶠ 9¹⁰ᵍᶠ 7¹⁰ᵍᶠ 10⁸ᵍᶠ 10¹²ᵍ **0-0-5**

Sharaby (Ire) *E A L Dunlop* 81
2 b f Cadeaux Genereux - Shawanni
3⁷ᵍᶠ 12⁷ᵍᶠ 11⁷ᵍˢ 2⁷ᵍˢ **0-2-4 £2,262**

Sharadi (Ire) *V Smith* 82
3 b g Desert Sun - Sharadiya (Ire)
7¹¹ᵍᶠ 10¹¹ˢ 8¹²ᵍᶠ 2¹⁴ᵍˢ 2¹⁶ᵍˢ 2¹⁴ᵍ 1¹⁶ᵍᶠ
3¹⁴ᵍ 1¹⁷ˢ **2-4-9 £13,490**

Sharaiji Blossom (USA) *Saeed Bin Suroor* 78
2 b f Saint Ballado (Can) - Lilac Garden (USA)
3⁷ᵍᶠ 1⁸ᵍᶠ **1-1-2 £7,263**

Shardda *F Watson* 66 a2
4 b f Barathea (Ire) - Kronengold (USA)
3⁸ʰʸ 15⁸ˢ 12⁹ʰʸ 11⁸ᵍ 10⁸ᵍ 5¹⁰ˢ 13⁸ˢᵈ
0-1-7 £590

Shareb (USA) *B W Hills* 57
2 b c El Prado (Ire) - My Hansel (USA)
11⁶ˢ **0-0-1**

Shared Dreams *L M Cumani* 80
2 b f Seeking The Gold (USA) - Coretta (Ire)
3⁷ᵍˢ **0-1-1 £751**

Shares (Ire) *P Monteith* 66
4 b g Turtle Island (Ire) - Glendora
2¹⁰ˢ 4¹⁰ᵍˢ **0-1-2 £2,210**

Sharmy (Ire) *Ian Williams* 90
8 b g Caerleon (USA) - Petticoat Lane
11^{10gf} 11^{12s} **0-0-2**

Sharoura *R A Fahey* 74 a63
8 ch m Inchinor - Kinkajoo
5^{5f} 8^{6gf} 1^{6gf} 13^{6gf} 3^{6g} 4^{6gf} 2^{6gf} 4^{7f}
8^{7g} 12^{6gf} 3^{7s} 11^{6g} 12^{7sd} **1-3-13 £14,698**

Sharp As A Tack (Ire) *B J Meehan* 88
2 b f Zafonic (USA) - Pretty Sharp
8^{6gf} 2^{6gf} 1^{7gs} 12^{7gs} 2^{7g} 6^{7hy} **1-1-6**
£9,538

Sharp Diversion (USA) *J G Given* 47
2 ch f Diesis - Jamie De Vil (USA)
6^{5gf} **0-0-1**

Sharp Hat *D W Chapman* 68 a73
10 b g Shavian - Madam Trilby
5^{5sd} 2^{6sd} 13^{6sd} 7^{6sd} 5^{6ss} 5^{5ss} 8^{5ss} 12^{6sd}
7^{5hy} 7^{6gf} 7^{6s} 3^{5gf} 7^{5g} 2^{5gf} 4^{5gs} 5^{5gs} 16^{6gf}
14^{5g} 9^{6gs} 4^{5sd} **0-3-20 £3,091**

Sharp N Frosty *W M Brisbourne* 67
2 b g Somayda (Ire) - Wily Miss
4^{5g} 7^{5s} 4^{7f} 4^{7gf} UR^{5s} 9^{8g} 5^{10hy} **0-0-7**
£959

Sharp Needle *J Noseda* 75 a84
3 b f Mark Of Esteem (Ire) - Blushing Sunrise (USA)
9^{7g} 2^{9g} 5^{8gf} 1^{9gf} 1^{8f} 4^{8f} 18^{sd} **3-1-7**
£12,983

Sharp Reply (USA) *Sir Michael Stoute* 76
2 b c Diesis - Questonia
4^{7s} **0-0-1 £272**

Sharp Rigging (Ire) *A M Hales* 45
4 b g Son Of Sharp Shot (Ire) - In The Rigging (USA)
16^{10g} **0-0-1**

Sharp Secret (Ire) *J A R Toller* 63 a28
6 b m College Chapel - State Treasure (USA)
5^{8gf} 18^{gf} 8^{8gf} 7^{8f} 7^{9sd} **1-0-5 £4,114**

Sharp Spice *D L Williams* a39
8 b m Lugana Beach - Ewar Empress (Ire)
6^{12sd} **0-0-1**

Sharpinch *P R Chamings*
6 b g Beveled (USA) - Giant Nipper
16^{7sd} **0-0-1**

Sharplaw Destiny (Ire) *W J Haggas* 33 a43
3 b f Petardia - Coolrain Lady (Ire)
5^{7sd} 10^{10sd} 12^{7gf} 9^{8f} **0-0-4**

Sharplaw Star *W J Haggas* 95 a73
2 b f Xaar - Hamsah (Ire)
1^{5g} 3^{5gf} 1^{5gf} 3^{5sd} **2-1-4 £19,726**

Sharplaw Venture *W J Haggas* 82 a76
4 b f Polar Falcon (USA) - Breakaway
3^{8g} 8^{8sd} 7^{8gf} **0-0-3 £2,024**

Sharvie *C J Hemsley* a15
7 b g Rock Hopper - Heresheis
7^{16sd} 5^{16sw} **0-0-2**

Shastye (Ire) *J H M Gosden* 69 a73
3 b f Danehill (USA) - Saganeca (USA)
7^{10gf} 3^{12gf} 4^{10gf} 1^{13sd} 9^{14s} **1-0-5**
£5,278

Shatin Leader *Miss L A Perratt* 60
2 b f Atraf - Star Dancer
PU^{5gf} 6^{5gf} 3^{5gf} 4^{5f} 11^{5gf} 18^{6gs} 18^{6g}
0-1-7 £822

Shatin Special *G C H Chung* 40 a50
4 ch f Titus Livius (Fr) - Lawn Order
5^{11sd} 2^{12sd} F^{11sd} 4^{12ss} 1^{12sw} 6^{11ss} 6^{12sw}
6^{10gf} 9^{12gf} 8^{12gf} 3^{12sd} 8^{12sd} **1-2-12 £2,441**

Shatin Star *G C H Chung* 20
2 b/br c Killer Instinct - Anetta
13^{7gf} **0-0-1**

Shayadi (Ire) *B Ellison* 77
7 b g Kahyasi - Shayrdia (Ire)
5^{10gs} **0-0-1 £514**

Shaymee's Girl *Ms Deborah J Evans* 45 a61
3 b f Wizard King - Mouchez Le Nez (Ire)
5^{6ss} 3^{6ss} 3^{6ss} 8^{5g} 3^{6g} 10^{5sd} 2^{5sd} **0-3-7**
£2,522

Shazana *B W Hills* 61 a52
3 gr f Key Of Luck (USA) - Shawanni
6^{7g} 7^{10g} 6^{10sd} **0-0-3**

She's A Diamond *T T Clement*
7 b m Mystiko (USA) - Fairy Kingdom
14^{8sd} **0-0-1**

She's A Fox *A W Carroll* 44
3 b f Wizard King - Foxie Lady
7^{8s} 11^{8gf} **0-0-2**

She's My Dream (Ire) *J S Moore* 20 a34
2 ch f General Monash (USA) - She's My Love
10^{5sd} 8^{5gf} 10^{5sd} 7^{6gf} **0-0-4**

She's My Outsider *I A Wood* 77
2 b f Docksider (USA) - Solar Flare (Ire)
11^{7gf} 3^{7gf} 18^{gf} 7^{7s} **1-1-4 £4,434**

She's Our Lass (Ire) *D Carroll* 85 a82
3 b f Orpen (USA) - Sharadja (Ire)
12^{7sd} 10^{7g} 1^{7s} 3^{8g} 1^{7f} 1^{7g} 18^{g} 18^{s} 2^{8s}
7^{8s} **5-2-10 £22,609**

Sheapys Lass *A Crook* a30
3 b f Perugino (USA) - Nilu (Ire)
11^{5sd} 11^{6sd} 12^{8sd} 14^{5ss} **0-0-4**

Shebaan *P S McEntee* 34
3 b f Compton Place - Chairmans Daughter
17^{7g} 13^{8gf} 8^{6gf} 11^{7gf} 11^{7s} 17^{7gs} **0-0-6**

Sheboygan (Ire) *J G Given* 82
2 ch f Grand Lodge (USA) - White Satin (Ire)
3^{6g} 1^{7gf} 3^{7hy} **1-1-3 £8,106**

Sheer Focus (Ire) *I W McInnes* 21 a14
6 b g Eagle Eyed (USA) - Persian Danser (Ire)
18^{10gf} 13^{8g} 12^{9sd} **0-0-3**

Sheer Tenby (Ire) *Paul A Roche* 99
7 b h Tenby - Take My Pledge (Ire)
16^{gf} 4^{9gf} 19^{6f} 11^{6gf} 7^{7gf} **1-0-5**
£12,552

Shekan Star *K G Reveley* 50
2 b f Sri Pekan (USA) - Celestial Welcome
15^{6gs} 12^{6gs} 16^{6gs} **0-0-4**

Sherbourne *M G Quinlan* 44 a27
2 b f Tipsy Creek (USA) - Margarets First
10^{5hy} 10^{5gf} 6^{5gf} 12^{7gf} 10^{7s} 15^{7gf} 14^{8g}
7^{9sd} **0-0-8**

Sheriff's Deputy *J W Unett* 72
4 b g Atraf - Forest Fantasy
8^{8gf} 8^{8gs} 3^{8g} 15^{11s} 9^{8gf} **0-1-5 £689**

Sherwood Forest *Miss L A Perratt* 51
4 ch g Fleetwood (Ire) - Jay Gee Ell
8^{8g} 3^{9g} 6^{11g} 8^{11gf} 5^{10gf} 2^{16gf} 6^{14gf} 13^{12g}
8^{12g} **0-2-9 £1,459**

Sherzabad (Ire) *Miss I E Craig* 10
7 b/br g Doyoun - Sheriya (USA)
10^{12gf} **0-0-1**

Sheshalan (Ire) *Sir Michael Stoute* 35
3 ch c Indian Ridge - Sheshara (Ire)
4^{10hy} **0-0-1 £437**

Shibumi *H Morrison* 57
3 ch f Cigar - Hurricane Rose
5⁵ᵍᶠ 5⁶ᵍᶠ 4⁷ᵍᶠ 4⁸ᵍᶠ **0-2-4**

Shielaligh *Miss Gay Kelleway* 70 a64
3 ch f Aragon - Sheesha (USA)
8⁵ˢᵈ 7⁶ᵍˢ 3⁵ᶠ 10⁶ᵍᶠ 6⁶ᵍᶠ 6⁵ 5⁵ᵍˢ 5⁶ᵍˢ
0-1-8 £1,022

Shifty *D Carroll* 57 a52
5 b g Night Shift (USA) - Crodelle (Ire)
5¹²ˢᵈ 12¹⁰ˢᵈ 13⁸ʰʸ 9⁸ˢ 4⁷ᵍ 8⁷ᵍ 5⁸ˢ 2⁸ᶠ
4⁷ˢᵈ 4⁷ᵍ 9⁷ᵍ 9⁸ᵍ 13⁸ᵍᶠ **0-2-13 £1,251**

Shifty Night (Ire) *Mrs C A Dunnett* 46 a54
3 b f Night Shift (USA) - Bean Island (USA)
15⁶ᵍᶠ 9⁵ᵍᶠ 4⁶ˢᵈ 1⁶ˢᵈ 10⁷ᵍᶠ 7⁶ᵍᶠ 10⁶ᵍᶠ
9⁷ᵍᶠ 4⁶ˢᵈ 12⁶ˢ 4⁷ˢᵈ **1-1-11 £3,722**

Shingle Street (Ire) *M H Tompkins* 70
2 b g Bahhare (USA) - Sandystones
7⁶ᵍᶠ 9⁶ᵍᶠ 8⁸ᵍ 2⁸ˢ 5⁷ˢ **0-1-5 £1,311**

Shinko Femme (Ire) *N Tinkler* 59
3 b f Shinko Forest (Ire) - Kilshanny
10⁷ᵍˢ 13⁸ᶠ 13⁶ᵍᶠ 5⁸ᵍ 1⁷ᵍ 9⁷ᵍᶠ 9⁷ᵍ 1⁷ᵍᶠ
3⁷ᵍˢ 8⁷ᵍ **2-1-10 £6,461**

Shiny Thing (USA) *A King* 60
2 br f Lear Fan (USA) - Juliet's Jewel (USA)
5⁷ᵍᶠ 8⁸ᵍˢ **0-0-2**

Shirley Not *D Nicholls* 8
8 gr g Paris House - Hollia
20⁵ᵍ 12⁷ᵍˢ **0-0-2**

Shirley Oaks (Ire) *Miss Z C Davison* 58 a51
6 b m Sri Pekan (USA) - Duly Elected
12⁷ˢᵈ 5⁶ˢᵈ 10⁷ˢᵈ 2⁶ˢᵈ 3⁷ˢᵈ 1⁶ˢᵈ 6⁷ʰʸ 3⁷ˢᵈ
1⁷ᵍᶠ 2⁷ᵍ 9⁸ᵍᶠ 11⁷ᵍᶠ 6⁷ᵍᶠ 7⁸ᵍᶠ **2-3-14 £7,155**

Shish (Ire) *J A Osborne* 32 a45
2 b f Rossini (USA) - Kebabs (Ire)
6⁵ˢᵈ 6⁶ˢᵈ 4⁵ˢᵈ 3⁵ᵍᶠ 7⁶ᵍᶠ **0-0-5 £358**

Shivaree *M R Channon* 87
2 ch f Rahy (USA) - Shmoose (Ire)
3⁶ᵍᶠ 1⁶ᵍˢ 4⁶ᵍᶠ 7⁷ᵍᶠ 3⁶ˢ 10⁸ᵍᶠ 13⁷ᵍˢ **1-0-7
£10,388**

Shohrah (Ire) *M P Tregoning* 105
2 ch f Giant's Causeway (USA) - Taqreem (Ire)
1⁶ᵍᶠ 5⁸ᵍᶠ **1-0-2 £10,395**

Sholay (Ire) *P Mitchell* 39 a42
5 b g Bluebird (USA) - Splicing
8¹³ˢᵈ 7⁸ˢᵈ 9¹²ˢᵈ 12¹⁰ᵍᶠ 4¹²ᵍ 10¹¹ᵍ **0-0-6
£259**

Sholto *J O'Reilly* 65 a36
6 b g Tragic Role (USA) - Rose Mill
7⁵ʰʸ 2⁵ᵍᶠ 15⁵ᶠ 11⁶ˢᵈ **0-1-4 £1,272**

Shongweni (Ire) *P J McBride* 75 a69
3 gr g Desert King (Ire) - Spend A Rubble (USA)
4¹¹ᵍᶠ 3¹²ˢᵈ 3¹²ᵍᶠ 8¹⁴ᵍᶠ 5¹⁶ᵍˢ **0-2-5
£1,351**

Shooting Lodge (Ire) *Sir Michael Stoute* 66
3 b f Grand Lodge (USA) - Sidama (Fr)
5¹⁰ᵍˢ **0-0-1**

Short Change (Ire) *A W Carroll* 54
5 b g Revoque (Ire) - Maafi Esm
8¹²ᵍᶠ 4¹²ˢ 5¹⁰ᶠ 1¹¹ᶠ **1-1-4 £3,066**

Short Chorus *J Balding* 62 a28
3 ch f Inchinor - Strawberry Song
8⁵ᵍ 4⁵ˢ 9⁶ˢᵈ 1⁵ᵍˢ 2⁵ˢ 4⁵ᵍᶠ 2⁵ᵍᶠ 4⁵ᵍˢ
13⁵ᵍᶠ 3⁵ˢ **1-3-10 £6,879**

Shortbread *J L Dunlop* 63
2 ch c Selkirk (USA) - Breadcrumb
13⁷ᵍ 8⁸ʰʸ **0-0-2**

Shosolosa (Ire) *B J Meehan* 73
2 br f Dansili - Hajat
11⁶ᵍᶠ 2⁶ᵍ 2⁶ᵍ 3⁶ᵍᶠ 10⁷ᵍ 5⁷ᵍ 16⁷ᵍˢ **0-3-7
£10,569**

Shot To Fame (USA) *P W Harris* 114
5 b g Quest For Fame - Exocet (USA)
5⁸ˢ 1⁸ʰʸ 1⁸ᵍᶠ 2⁸ᵍ 1⁸ᵍ 5⁸ˢ 5⁸ᵍ
12⁸ᵍ **3-1-9 £63,093**

Shotley Dancer *N Bycroft* 53 a40
5 ch m Danehill Dancer (Ire) - Hayhurst
4⁸ˢᵈ 10⁷ˢʷ 12⁷ˢᵈ 4⁷ˢᵈ 3⁸ᵍ 5⁸ˢᵈ 3¹²ᵍᶠ
1¹²ᵍᶠ 4¹²ᵍᶠ 2¹⁶ᵍˢ 1¹⁰ˢ 11¹⁶ᶠ **2-4-12 £10,940**

Show Me Heaven *T T Clement* a7
7 b m Rock City - Tufty Lady
12¹⁰ˢᵈ **0-0-1**

Show No Fear *G M Moore* 74
3 b c Groom Dancer (USA) - La Piaf (Fr)
1⁹ᵍˢ 8⁹ʰʸ 11⁸ᵍᶠ 1⁰ᵍᶠ **1-0-4 £5,681**

Showtime Annie *A Bailey* 71 a62
3 b f Wizard King - Rebel County (Ire)
6⁸ˢʷ 1⁶ˢˢ 16⁶ᵍ 4⁷ˢᵈ 1⁸ᵍᶠ 5⁷ᵍ 8⁷ᵍᶠ 9⁷ᵍᶠ
2⁸ˢ 12⁸ᵍᶠ 16⁷ᵍˢ **2-1-11 £9,085**

Showtime Faye *A Bailey* 21 a3
2 b f Overbury (Ire) - Rebel County (Ire)
9⁷ᵍᶠ 8⁷ᵍˢ 8⁷ˢᵈ **0-0-3**

Shredded (USA) *J H M Gosden* 84
4 b c Diesis - Shiitake (USA)
9¹⁰ˢ 2¹⁰ᵍ 1¹⁴ᵍ 8¹²ᵍᶠ 6¹³ᵍˢ 3¹³ᵍˢ 14¹²ˢ
1-2-7 £8,679

Shrine Mountain (USA) *C E Brittain* 83
2 b c Distorted Humor (USA) - Fancy Ruler (USA)
9⁶ᵍ 2⁷ᵍᶠ 7⁷ᵍ 16⁸ᵍᶠ **0-0-4 £1,026**

Shrink *M L W Bell* 69 a69
3 b f Mind Games - Miss Mercy (Ire)
2⁵ˢᵈ 1⁵ˢᵈ 4⁶ᵍ 4⁶ᶠ 16⁶ᵍᶠ 9⁵ᵍᶠ 3⁶ᵍᶠ **1-2-7
£6,048**

Shuchbaa *K A Ryan* 38
2 b f Zaha (Can) - Little Miss Rocker
3⁶ᶠ 11⁶ᵍᶠ 12⁷ᵍˢ 7⁶ᵍˢ **0-1-4 £550**

Shuheb *C E Brittain* 96
3 ch f Nashwan (USA) - Shimna
5⁹ᵍᶠ 4¹⁰ᵍᶠ **0-0-2 £1,500**

Shujune Al Hawaa (Ire) *M R Channon* 67
2 ch f Grand Lodge (USA) - Bank On Her (USA)
5⁵ᵍ 6⁵ᵍᶠ 9⁷ᵍᶠ 11⁷ˢ 18⁷ᵍᶠ 6⁸ᵍ 10⁸ᵍˢ
0-0-8 £850

Shush *C E Brittain* 45
6 b g Shambo - Abuzz
15¹⁴ᵍˢ 7¹²ˢ **0-0-2**

Shyshiyra (Ire) *K A Ryan* 16
3 b f Kahyasi - Shiyra
10¹⁰ᵍᶠ **0-0-1**

Si Si Amiga (Ire) *B W Hills* 95
3 b f Desert Style (Ire) - No Hard Feelings (Ire)
4¹¹ᵍˢ 4¹⁰ᵍᶠ 5¹⁰ᵍᶠ 8¹²ᵍ 12¹⁴ˢ **0-0-5
£4,750**

Si Si Si *J G Given* 39
2 b f Lomitas - Notturna
7⁷ᵍᶠ **0-0-1**

Sian Thomas *M P Tregoning* 62
3 ch f Magic Ring (Ire) - Midnight Break
3⁹ᵍᶠ 12⁸ᵍˢ 5¹⁰ᵍ **0-0-3 £820**

Sideshow *D R Loder* 58
2 ch f In The Wings - Sheer Harmony (USA)
11⁸ᵍˢ 4⁸ˢ **0-0-2 £428**

Siegfrieds Night (Ire) *M C Chapman* 68 a68

3 ch g Night Shift (USA) - Shelbiana (USA)
1^{6sd} 4^{5sd} 3^{6ss} 2^{11sd} 3^{12ss} 3^{10g} 3^{12g} 6^{12gs}
2^{15gs} 1^{12g} 3^{12g} 3^{14f} 5^{12gf} 5^{12sd} 3^{12g} 7^{12gf} 7^{12gf}
2^{14gf} 5^{14gf} 9^{16gf} 2-10-20 £17,472

Siena Gold *B J Meehan* 93
2 b/br f Key Of Luck (USA) - Corn Futures
1^{5g} 1^{5g} 8^{5gf} 1^{5g} 8^{5g} 4^{5hy} 7^{6g} 3^{6s} 3-1-8
£96,991

Siena Star (Ire) *P Bowen* a83
6 b g Brief Truce (USA) - Gooseberry Pie
2^{10sd} 0-1-1 £1,039

Sienna Sunset (Ire) *W M Brisbourne* 64 a56
5 ch m Spectrum (Ire) - Wasabi (Ire)
10^{8s} 6^{10s} 6^{10gf} 2^{10gf} 4^{10f} 1^{10s} 3^{10s}
12^{10gf} 7^{10gs} 11^{9s} 3^{9sd} 1-3-11 £12,672

Siera Spirit (Ire) *M G Quinlan* 62 a52
3 b f Desert Sun - Jay And-A (Ire)
4^{6sd} 3^{6sd} 8^{7sd} 2^{6gs} 3^{7s} 0-3-5 £2,443

Sierra *C E Brittain* 60
3 ch f Dr Fong (USA) - Warning Belle
5^{10gf} 6^{10gf} 6^{8gf} 5^{8gs} 12^{10gf} 0-0-5

Sierra Vista *D W Barker* 89
4 ch f Atraf - Park Vista
14^{5g} 3^{5gf} 10^{5g} 9^{5gs} 5^{6g} 1^{6s} 6^{6g} 9^{7g}
15^{6s} 5^{6g} 8^{6s} 9^{5gs} 1-1-12 £21,626

Sights On Gold (Ire) *Saeed Bin Suroor* 118
5 ch h Indian Ridge - Summer Trysting (USA)
1^{10g} 1^{11g} 7^{10g} 2^{9s} 2-1-4 £54,322

Sign Of Luck (Ire) *C E Brittain* 57 a68
2 ch f Daylami (Ire) - Ascot Cyclone (USA)
9^{7gf} 4^{7sd} 0-0-2 £405

Sign Of Promise *S C Williams*
2 b f Groom Dancer (USA) - Happy Omen
12^{8gs} 0-0-1

Sign Writer (USA) *J Noseda* 83 a54
2 b c Quiet American (USA) - Mata Cara
6^{6gf} 2^{6g} 4^{5sd} 3^{6s} 8^{8g} 0-2-5 £2,571

Signor Panettiere *R Hannon* 75
3 b c Night Shift (USA) - Christmas Kiss
8^{6g} 2^{6f} 6^{5gf} 7^{5gf} 2^{5gf} 0-2-5 £2,213

Signora Panettiera (Fr) *M R Channon* 54 a25
3 ch f Lord Of Men - Karaferya (USA)
6^{12gs} 8^{12s} 6^{12sd} 11^{11f} 9^{12f} 7^{12s} 4^{14f} 6^{14s}
0-0-8

Silber Mond *M L W Bell* 51
2 gr c Monsun (Ger) - Salinova (Fr)
11^{8s} 10^{10s} 0-0-2

Silca's Gift *M R Channon* 106
3 b f Cadeaux Genereux - Odette
1^{7g} 8^{8g} 5^{6g} 9^{7gf} 9^{6gs} 1-0-5 £30,000

Silence Is Golden *B J Meehan* 115
5 ch m Danehill Dancer (Ire) - Silent Girl
1^{10gs} 2^{9g} 9^{11gs} 2^{10gs} 2^{10gf} 1-3-5
£84,800

Silencio (Ire) *A King* 65
3 b g Sillery - Flabbergasted (Ire)
7^{10g} 13^{10s} 14^{10gf} 7^{10g} 5^{13gf} 7^{12f} 0-0-6

Silent Angel *Mrs Lucinda Featherstone*
4 b f Petong - Valls D'Andorra
11^{5sd} 10^{5sw} 0-0-2

Silent Hawk (Ire) *Saeed Bin Suroor* 89
3 b c Halling (USA) - Nightbird (Ire)
4^{8g} 1^{10gf} 12^{10g} 4^{10gf} 10^{10s} 11^{10g} 5^{10s}
1-0-7 £8,554

Silent Jo (Jpn) *Saeed Bin Suroor* 87
2 b c Sunday Silence (USA) - Jo Knows (USA)

3^{7gf} 2^{7gf} 3^{7g} 0-2-3 £4,599

Silent Spring (USA) *B W Hills* 60
2 b f Honour And Glory (USA) - Polar Bird
8^{6gs} 0-0-1

Silent Storm *H J Cyzer* 69 a78
4 ch c Zafonic (USA) - Nanda
3^{6sd} 3^{8gf} 13^{8g} 10^{7sd} 2^{6sd} 3^{6sd} 1^{6sd} 1-3-7
£6,468

Silistra *Mrs L C Jewell* 43 a36
5 gr g Sadler's Wells (USA) - Dundel (Ire)
8^{12sd} 14^{10sd} 11^{12gf} 14^{7gf} 5^{10gf} 7^{8gf} 6^{7gf}
0-0-7

Silk Cravat (Ire) *G Wragg* 48
3 ch g Dr Devious (Ire) - Dances With Dreams
8^{8gf} 0-0-1

Silk Fan (Ire) *P W Harris* 101
3 b f Unfuwain (USA) - Alikhlas
1^{7gs} 6^{7gf} 4^{8s} 4^{7g} 4^{10g} 4^{8g} 1-0-6
£18,117

Silken Brief (Ire) *D J Daly* a81
5 gr m Ali-Royal (Ire) - Tiffany's Case (Ire)
6^{10sd} 11^{8sd} 0-0-2

Silken John (Ire) *J G Portman* 50
3 ch g Grand Lodge (USA) - Lady Ela (Ire)
13^{10gf} 5^{12s} 11^{14gs} 0-0-3

Silloth Spirit *Mrs A M Naughton* 11
4 b g Atraf - Gaelic Air
12^{8g} 4^{10f} 13^{8gf} 0-0-3 £433

Silsong (USA) *B R Millman* 61
2 ch f Stephen Got Even (USA) - Silver Trainor (USA)
5^{7gs} 15^{7gs} 8^{8gs} 11^{10gf} 0-0-4

Silvaline *T Keddy* 88 a73
5 gr g Linamix (Fr) - Upend
6^{10sd} 11^{10sd} 4^{10gs} 5^{10s} 14^{10g} 6^{10gf}
8^{8g} 11^{10sd} 11^{10gs} 8^{12g} 3^{10gf} 10^{11g} 2^{10s} 6^{10gs}
10^{10sd} 2-2-16 £29,981

Silver Bark *E A L Dunlop* 56
2 b f Royal Applause - Argent Du Bois (USA)
8^{6gf} 5^{6g} 0-0-2

Silver Cache (USA) *J Noseda* 55 a55
3 b f Silver Hawk (USA) - Nina Ashley (USA)
10^{8sd} 9^{9sd} 5^{8sd} 4^{10gf} 0-0-4

Silver Chime *D M Simcock* 76 a64
4 gr f Robellino (USA) - Silver Charm
9^{6sd} 11^{6s} 4^{6f} 1^{6gf} 5^{6gf} 6^{6gf} 11^{6gf}
9^{6gs} 11^{6gf} 14^{7gf} 10^{6gs} 12^{6sd} 1-1-13 £7,119

Silver City *Mrs A J Perrett* 83
4 ro g Unfuwain (USA) - Madiyla
2^{10gf} 7^{11g} 10^{10g} 12^{10gf} 10^{12g} 4^{12g} 0-1-6
£1,912

Silver Court *R J Price*
2 b c Silver Patriarch (Ire) - Double Stake (USA)
6^{7gs} 14^{8gs} 9^{10hy} 0-0-3

Silver Creek *I A Wood* 46 a18
2 gr c Tipsy Creek (USA) - Silver Wedding
11^{5gf} 12^{7g} 16^{7gs} 10^{7sd} 0-0-4

Silver Crystal (Ire) *Mrs N Macauley* a4
4 b f Among Men (USA) - Silver Moon
9^{11sd} 8^{8sd} 8^{10sd} 0-0-3

Silver Dreamer (Ire) *H S Howe* 39
2 b f Brave Act - Heads We Called (Ire)
11^{8s} 11^{7gf} 0-0-2

Silver Emperor (Ire) *P A Blockley* a36
3 gr g Lil's Boy (USA) - Just Possible
7^{7sd} 7^{8sd} 0-0-2

Silver Gilt *J H M Gosden* 110

4 b g Silver Hawk (USA) - Memory's Gold (USA)
3^{12gs} 3^{10g} 1^{16gs} 6^{16gf} 9^{16g} 8^{18g} **1-1-6**
£22,387

Silver Highlight (Can) *A M Balding*   84
2 gr/ro f Silver Charm (USA) - Rare Opportunity (USA)
9^{7g} 2^{8gf} 2^{8g} **0-2-3 £2,175**

Silver Island *R M H Cowell*   41 a33
3 ch g Silver Patriarch (Ire) - Island Maid
7^{8sd} 7^{6sd} 12^{10gs} 6^{7gf} 15^{7gs} **0-0-5**

Silver Louie (Ire) *G B Balding*   a22
4 gr f Titus Livius (Fr) - Shakamiyn
12^{10sd} 11^{8sd} RR^{9g} **0-0-3**

Silver Mascot *I Semple*   64 a59
5 gr g Mukaddamah (USA) - Always Lucky
4^{6sd} 7^{6sd} 2^{7ss} 2^{7sd} 5^{7sw} 1^{7sw} 4^{7ss} 2^{6sd}
3^{7gs} 10^{7gf} 11^{6gf} 1^{6f} 2^{6g} 12^{7sd} 10^{5gf} 12^{6gs}
26^{5gs} **2-5-17 £8,722**

Silver Mistress *B N Doran*
5 gr m Syrtos - Galava (Can)
7^{12hy} **0-0-1**

Silver Phantom (Ire) *D R Loder*
2 b g Spectrum (Ire) - Beat It (USA)
11^{5gs} **0-0-1**

Silver Prelude *D K Ivory*   91
3 gr g Prince Sabo - Silver Blessings
7^{6g} 8^{5f} 11^{5gf} 3^{5gf} 1^{5gf} 8^{5gs} 16^{5gf} 9^{5g}
17^{5gf} 10^{5g} 14^{5g} **1-1-11 £11,085**

Silver Prophet (Ire) *M R Bosley*   76 a67
5 gr g Idris (Ire) - Silver Heart
18^{10g} 5^{10s} 5^{12gf} 5^{13gf} 7^{14g} 16^{12gf} 1^{12s}
5^{13gs} 6^{14gs} 3^{12s} 3^{12sd} **1-2-11 £6,137**

Silver Reign *G B Balding*   40
3 gr g Prince Sabo - Primo Donna Magna
5^{6s} 6^{6gs} 9^{6s} 18^{6s} **0-0-4**

Silver Rhythm *K R Burke*   51 a13
3 ch f Silver Patriarch (Ire) - Party Treat (Ire)
3^{10hy} 5^{11gs} 7^{11gf} 8^{12gf} 7^{12sd} 5^{12gs} **0-0-6**
£535

Silver Sash (Ger) *M L W Bell*   89
3 gr f Mark Of Esteem (Ire) - Salinova (Fr)
6^{10gf} 3^{10g} 1^{14gf} 5^{12s} 8^{14gf} 11^{12s} **1-1-6**
£3,759

Silver Seeker (USA) *A R Dicken*   61 a83
4 gr g Seeking The Gold (USA) - Zelanda (Ire)
5^{7ss} 13^{7hy} 10^{7f} 2^{7gf} 6^{7gf} 9^{7gf} 7^{6gs}
15^{6g} 11^{8gf} **0-1-10 £1,171**

Silver Song *J L Dunlop*   50
2 gr c Silver Patriarch (Ire) - Singing The Blues
12^{8g} 11^{8gs} 11^{10s} **0-0-3**

Silver Swing *W J Haggas*   32 a32
2 gr c Celtic Swing - Poetry In Motion (Ire)
9^{6sd} 10^{6s} 6^{6g} **0-0-3**

Silver Visage (Ire) *Miss J Feilden*   59 a64
2 b g Lujain (USA) - About Face
5^{5gf} 5^{6gf} 5^{7gf} 16^{8g} 5^{8sd} **0-0-5**

Silver Wraith (Ire) *N A Callaghan*   102
2 b c Danehill Dancer (Ire) - Alpine Lady (Ire)
4^{6gf} 2^{6f} 1^{5f} 3^{7gs} 1^{7gf} 3^{6gf} 5^{7s} **3-3-8**
£23,569

Silverhay *T D Barron*   75
3 b g Inchinor - Moon Spin
4^{8hy} 2^{11gf} 4^{11gf} 1^{8gs} 1^{8gf} 4^{8gs} 3^{8s} **2-3-7**
£14,329

Silverleaf *M R Channon*   72
2 b c Lujain (USA) - Lovely Millie (Ire)
6^{7gf} 5^{7gf} 5^{7gs} 7^{8g} 20^{8g} **0-0-5**

Silverstein (USA) *J H M Gosden*   78
3 b/br c Seeking The Gold (USA) - Salchow (USA)
3^{8g} **0-1-1 £904**

Silvertown *L Lungo*   72
9 b g Danehill (USA) - Docklands (USA)
12^{10s} 7^{10g} 16^{12g} 17^{10g} 4^{14gs} **0-0-5 £599**

Simianna *A Berry*   101
5 b m Bluegrass Prince (Ire) - Lowrianna (Ire)
5^{5gs} 5^{5g} 2^{5gs} 8^{6g} 6^{5gf} 7^{6g} 2^{6f} 7^{6f} 7^{6s}
4^{6gf} 6^{6gf} 5^{6gf} 7^{6gf} 3^{6gs} 2^{5gs} 1^{6g} 5^{5s} 8^{6gf}
7^{7gf} **1-4-19 £55,406**

Simlet *E W Tuer*   44
9 b g Forzando - Besito
5^{16g} **0-0-1**

Simon's Seat (USA) *P Howling*   67 a63
5 ch g Woodman (USA) - Spire (USA)
6^{16g} 6^{15gf} 6^{12gf} 10^{16hy} 8^{13sd} 6^{17sd} **0-0-6**

Simonda *Mrs A J Perrett*   79
3 ch f Singspiel (Ire) - Jetbeeah (Ire)
2^{8g} 1^{12f} **1-1-2 £4,954**

Simonovski (USA) *S C Burrough*   64 a49
3 b c Miswaki (USA) - Earthra (USA)
7^{7sd} 8^{10g} 3^{10g} 2^{16gf} 15^{16g} 17^{14gs} **0-2-6**
£1,479

Simple Exchange (Ire) *D K Weld*   110
3 b c Danehill (USA) - Summer Trysting (USA)
4^{10f} 1^{10f} 4^{10f} 6^{10g} **1-0-4 £96,972**

Simple Ideals (USA) *Don Enrico Incisa*   48 a3
10 b/br g Woodman (USA) - Comfort And Style
5^{16s} 4^{16s} 8^{14sd} 6^{16gs} 7^{16gs} 5^{16gs} **0-0-6**
£290

Simplify *D R Loder*   79
2 b c Fasliyev (USA) - Simplicity
4^{5g} 5^{6f} 3^{7f} 2^{6gf} 5^{6gf} 7^{7gf} 1^{6gs} 8^{6gf}
13^{7gs} **1-1-9 £6,280**

Simply Honest (Ire) *A J Martin*   56
9 ch g Simply Great (Fr) - Susans Glory
4^{16gf} 11^{16gf} 5^{16g} 4^{16g} 11^{12g} 8^{14gf} **0-0-6**
£577

Simply Red *R Brotherton*   38
3 ch g Vettori (Ire) - Amidst
9^{7g} 8^{8s} 7^{6sd} 12^{6gf} **0-0-4**

Simply St Lucia *J R Weymes*   70 a64
2 b f Charnwood Forest (Ire) - Mubadara (Ire)
1^{7sd} 3^{8g} **1-0-4 £5,138**

Simply The Guest (Ire) *Don Enrico Incisa*   34 a67
5 b g Mujadil (USA) - Ned's Contessa (Ire)
2^{8sd} 2^{8sd} 18^{sd} 4^{7ss} 11^{8sd} 13^{6f} 16^{7g}
2-2-8 £7,105

Simpsons Mount (Ire) *R M Flower*   70 a75
3 ch g Tagula (Ire) - Brunswick
6^{5sd} 6^{5sd} 3^{5sd} 7^{6g} 5^{10g} 10^{6g} 16^{6gf} 5^{5gf}
16^{5gf} 10^{6gf} 1^{6sd} **2-1-11 £12,376**

Sinamay (USA) *J J Quinn*
3 b f Saint Ballado (Can) - Chenille (Ire)
10^{8gs} **0-0-1**

Singhalese *J A Osborne*   88
2 ch f Singspiel (Ire) - Baize
4^{7gf} 3^{8gs} 3^{7s} 18^{gf} **1-2-4 £20,212**

Singhalongtasveer *W Storey*   54
2 b g Namaqualand (USA) - Felinwen
10^{6g} 5^{7f} 3^{6s} 7^{7gf} 9^{7gs} 5^{7f} 9^{6g} 9^{7g} **0-0-8**
£500

Singitta *B Palling*   41
3 b f Singspiel (Ire) - Ferber's Follies (USA)

11^{10gs} 7^{12gf} 9^{10s} **0-0-3**

Single Track Mind *J R Boyle*   48 a50
6 b g Mind Games - Compact Disc (Ire)
10^{7sd} 2^{7sd} 5^{8sd} 4^{7sd} 7^{7sd} 9^{7sd} 2^{8sd} 3^{7sd}
5^{8sd} 8^{7hy} 7^{7f} 6^{7g} 4^{8gf} 7^{10gf} 7^{9gf} 13^{9sd} **0-3-16**
£1,315

Singlet *D J Daly*   65
3 ch c Singspiel (Ire) - Ball Gown
7^{10g} 8^{10gf} **0-0-2**

Singularity *K F Clutterbuck*   a26
4 b g Rudimentary - Lyrical Bid (USA)
11^{12ss} 11^{8sd} 11^{8sd} LFT^{8sd} **0-0-4**

Sinistra *H R A Cecil*   38
3 br f Dracula (Aus) - Sardegna
10^{10g} **0-0-1**

Sinjaree *Mrs S Lamyman*   53 a53
6 b g Mark Of Esteem (Ire) - Forthwith
10^{8sd} 5^{9sw} 1^{9sw} 7^{9ss} 6^{10s} 12^{10g} 7^{11g}
14^{8gs} 7^{8gs} 4^{9sd} 6^{8s} **1-0-11 £1,463**

Sink Or Swim (Ire) *J J Bridger*   a30
6 b m Big Sink Hope (USA) - Cragreagh VII
10^{12sd} 11^{8sd} 5^{10sd} 8^{12hy} **0-0-4**

Sion Hill (Ire) *J O'Reilly*   64 a57
3 b g Desert Prince (Ire) - Mobilia
13^{5gf} 10^{5gf} 11^{7gf} 10^{8gf} 9^{8g} 7^{7sd} **0-0-6**

Sir Alfred *A King*   59 a48
5 b g Royal Academy (USA) - Magnificent Star (USA)
8^{12g} 4^{14gf} 10^{12gs} 11^{9sd} **0-0-4 £279**

Sir Anthony (Ire) *B Smart*   88
2 b c Danehill Dancer (Ire) - Brief Fairy (Ire)
1^{6gs} 3^{6gs} 2^{7gs} 6^{7s} 2^{7gs} 3^{8gf} **1-3-6**
£9,997

Sir Bluebird (Ire) *R Hannon*   64 a30
2 ch c Bluebird (USA) - Persian Tapestry
11^{5gs} 9^{6gs} 6^{6g} 10^{6sd} **0-0-4**

Sir Bond (Ire) *B Smart*   33
3 ch g Desert Sun - In Tranquility (Ire)
9^{10g} 4^{12gs} 5^{10g} **0-0-3 £416**

Sir Desmond *R Guest*   87 a83
6 gr g Petong - I'm Your Lady
3^{6sd} 8^{6sd} 18^{6s} 3^{5g} 5^{5g} 6^{6gs} 4^{6s} 20^{6s}
4^{5gs} 1^{6s} **1-2-10 £16,232**

Sir Don (Ire) *D Nicholls*   73
5 b g Lake Coniston (Ire) - New Sensitive
9^{7g} 10^{7gs} 17^{6gs} 20^{6gf} 16^{9f} 16^{9g} 37^{9f}
5^{6gf} 8^{6gf} 24^{6gf} 14^{6gs} 14^{7s} 9^{5g} 16^{7s} **1-1-14**
£6,887

Sir Edward Burrow (Ire) *W Storey*   43
6 b g Distinctly North (USA) - Alalja (Ire)
8^{14s} 2^{13s} **0-1-2 £419**

Sir Edwin Landseer (USA) *Christian Wroe*   69
4 gr c Lit De Justice (USA) - Wildcat Blue (USA)
16^{8ft} 20^{7f} 13^{6g} 20^{5g} 11^{5gf} 7^{5g} **0-0-6**

Sir Ernest (Ire) *M J Polglase*   79
3 b g Daggers Drawn (USA) - Kyra Crown (Ire)
7^{5g} 6^{5s} 11^{5f} 2^{5gs} 11^{5g} 2^{5gf} 17^{5gf}
14^{5s} 14^{5g} 6^{5g} **0-2-11 £4,351**

Sir Francis (Ire) *J Noseda*   54 a73
6 b g Common Grounds - Red Note
9^{8sd} 10^{7sd} 8^{7sd} 10^{5hy} **0-0-5**

Sir Frank Gibson *Mrs Jane Galpin*   40 a44
3 b g Primo Dominie - Serotina (Ire)
7^{8sd} 4^{8sd} 2^{11sd} 3^{11sd} 8^{12ss} 5^{10sd} 5^{12sd}
5^{12g} 9^{10sd} **0-2-9 £1,246**

Sir Galahad *T D Easterby*   56 a40

3 ch g Hector Protector (USA) - Sharpening
7^{6ss} 7^{6sd} 5^{10s} 3^{8s} 4^{8hy} **0-1-5 £417**

Sir George Turner *M Johnston*   101
5 ch g Nashwan (USA) - Ingozi
10^{10gs} 10^{14gs} 8^{10gf} 10^{10g} 13^{10f} 7^{10g} 8^{12g}
11^{7gf} 3^{8s} **0-1-9 £2,326**

Sir Haydn *J R Jenkins*   74
4 ch g Definite Article - Snowscape
3^{10g} 6^{10gs} 10^{10s} 6^{12gf} 7^{12gf} 5^{10gs} 3^{10gf}
11^{12gf} 11^{10s} 7^{10gf} 8^{10gf} **0-2-11 £1,095**

Sir Jasper (Ire) *M F Harris*   a62
3 b g Sri Pekan (USA) - Ashover Amber
1^{7sd} 9^{6sd} 3^{8sd} 4^{7ss} 10^{7ss} **1-0-5 £3,861**

Sir Laughalot *Miss E C Lavelle*   77 a80
4 b g Alzao (USA) - Funny Hilarious (USA)
2^{7sd} 7^{7sd} 3^{7sd} 2^{8sd} 3^{8sd} 2^{8gs} 15^{11g} **0-5-7**
£5,365

Sir Loin *N Tinkler*   67
3 ch g Compton Place - Charnwood Queen
10^{5gs} 7^{5s} 5^{5s} 2^{5gf} 6^{6gf} 8^{5gs} 2^{5gs} 2^{5gf}
2^{5s} **0-4-9 £4,498**

Sir Monty (USA) *Mrs A J Perrett*   68
2 ch g Cat's Career (USA) - Lady Of Meadowlane (USA)
5^{8gf} 6^{7gs} 4^{8gs} 9^{8s} **0-0-4 £382**

Sir Night (Ire) *Jedd O'Keeffe*   54
4 b g Night Shift (USA) - Highly Respected (Ire)
4^{10f} 7^{11gf} 8^{12f} **0-1-3 £283**

Sir Ninja (Ire) *S Kirk*   65
7 b g Turtle Island (Ire) - The Poachers Lady (Ire)
2^{12gs} 4^{11gs} 7^{10g} **0-1-3 £844**

Sir Sandrovitch (Ire) *R A Fahey*   48
8 b g Polish Patriot (USA) - Old Downie
14^{5hy} 14^{5gf} 6^{5gf} 7^{5g} **0-0-4**

Siraj *P S McEntee*   57 a72
5 b g Piccolo - Masuri Kabisa (USA)
8^{7sd} 1^{6sd} 10^{5s} 9^{6s} 7^{7sd} 4^{6sd} 9^{7sd} **1-0-7**
£2,618

Sirce (Ire) *D J Coakley*   49
2 b f Josr Algarhoud (Ire) - Trading Aces
17^{6gf} 6^{6gf} 8^{6g} 12^{8f} 4^{8gs} **0-0-5**

Sister Gee (Ire) *R Hollinshead*   40 a54
2 b f Desert Story (Ire) - My Gloria (Ire)
4^{7sd} 3^{6sd} 2^{5sd} 13^{6gs} 2^{6sd} **0-3-5 £2,221**

Sister Moonshine (Fr) *R Pritchard-Gordon*   99
3 ch f Piccolo - Cootamundra (Fr)
3^{6gs} 15^{6gs} 5^{5gs} 10^{5gs} 6^{5gs} 10^{5s} **1-1-6**
£15,987

Sister Sophia (USA) *W J Musson*   70 a55
4 b/br f Deputy Commander (USA) - Sophiaschoice (USA)
14^{8gf} 1^{7sd} 7^{7s} 17^{8gs} 7^{8sd}
0-1-7 £607

Six Pack (Ire) *Andrew Turnell*   a48
6 ch g Royal Abjar (USA) - Regal Entrance
2^{8ss} 2^{10sd} 4^{9sd} 10^{10sd} **0-2-4 £888**

Six Perfections (Fr) *P Bary*   119
4 b f Celtic Swing - Yogya (USA)
2^{9g} 5^{8gf} 2^{8s} 3^{8y} **0-3-4 £227,729**

Sixtilsix (Ire) *H Alexander*   27 a42
3 ch g Night Shift (USA) - Assafiyah (Ire)
8^{7gs} 12^{10gf} 3^{10sd} 11^{10f} 6^{9sd} **0-1-5 £438**

Skater Boy *Miss Sheena West*   8
3 b g Wizard King - Makalu
8^{10f} **0-0-1**

Skelligs Rock (Ire) *B W Duke*   70
4 b c Key Of Luck (USA) - Drew (Ire)
5^{12gs} 8^{14hy} **0-0-2**

Skelthwaite *Miss D A McHale*   30
3 b g Desert Story (Ire) - Skip To Somerfield
9^{7gs} 9^{7sw} 3^{10gf} 11^{11g} UR^{10sd} **0-1-5 £215**

Ski Jump (USA) *R A Fahey*   89
4 gr g El Prado (Ire) - Skiable (Ire)
1^{10g} 6^{12g} 9^{11g} 6^{12g} 7^{14g} 7^{12gf} 12^{14gs} 4^{10g}
4^{16ss} **1-1-9 £6,943**

Skibereen (Ire) *Mrs A M Thorpe*   76 a49
4 b g Ashkalani (Ire) - Your Village (Ire)
5^{10sd} 6^{12sd} 4^{10g} 5^{9gf} 3^{8g} 5^{8f} 10^{10gf}
12^{8gs} 17^{8gf} 2^{10g} 2^{10gf} 8^{12g} **0-3-13 £3,160**

Skiddaw Jones *Miss L A Perratt*   56
4 b g Emperor Jones (USA) - Woodrising
11^{8g} 5^{10gf} 8^{10g} 6^{9gf} 2^{9gf} 6^{10s} 14^{8f} **0-1-7**
£1,121

Skiddaw Wolf *B Smart*   62
2 ch f Wolfhound (USA) - Stealthy
8^{5gf} 3^{6g} 6^{5g} 5^{5gf} 4^{5gf} 2^{6g} 9^{5hy} **0-2-7**
£2,743

Skidmark *D R C Elsworth*   103 a103
3 b c Pennekamp (USA) - Flourishing (Ire)
2^{8sd} 1^{10sd} 1^{10sd} 3^{8sd} 4^{10s} 10^{9gs} 6^{10g} **2-2-7**
£19,216

Skidrow *M L W Bell*   85
2 b c Bachir (Ire) - Flourishing (Ire)
7^{7gf} 1^{7g} 2^{8g} 2^{8hy} 3^{8s} **1-2-5 £7,529**

Skip Of Colour *P A Blockley*   73 a73
4 b g Rainbow Quest (USA) - Minskip (USA)
4^{8sd} 5^{9ss} 1^{6sd} 2^{6ss} 10^{6sd} 6^{6g} 5^{5g} 22^{6s}
1-1-8 £4,585

Skippit John *Ronald Thompson*   59 a49
2 b g Abou Zouz (USA) - Lady Quinta (Ire)
2^{5hy} 6^{5gf} 6^{6f} 8^{7gs} 9^{6s} 7^{6sw} **0-1-6**
£1,376

Sky Cove *M W Easterby*
3 b g Spectrum (Ire) - Aurora Bay (Ire)
13^{8sd} **0-0-1**

Sky Crusader *R Ingram*   83 a77
2 b c Mujahid (USA) - Red Cloud (Ire)
1^{7gf} 6^{7g} 5^{7sd} 3^{7gf} **1-1-4 £5,422**

Sky Dome (Ire) *M H Tompkins*   55
11 ch g Bluebird (USA) - God Speed Her
5^{7gf} **0-0-1**

Sky Galaxy (USA) *E A L Dunlop*   69
3 ch f Sky Classic (Can) - Fly To The Moon (USA)
7^{7gf} 10^{8gf} 6^{8gf} **0-0-3**

Sky Quest (Ire) *W R Swinburn*   97
6 b g Spectrum (Ire) - Rose Vibert
1^{10gf} 1^{10g} 12^{10gs} **2-0-3 £20,384**

Skye's Folly (USA) *J G Given*   78 a82
4 b g Kris S (USA) - Bittersweet Hour (USA)
7^{16g} 14^{16gf} 13^{16g} 3^{15g} 3^{16f} 3^{14gf} 4^{14gs}
4^{14g} 2^{14sd} 3^{17sd} **0-5-10 £7,552**

Skyharbor *A M Balding*   81 a59
3 b g Cyrano De Bergerac - Pea Green
15^{8gs} 5^{6gf} 11^{6g} 5^{5gf} 2^{5g} 3^{5s} 4^{5g} 13^{6gf}
9^{6g} 7^{5sd} **0-1-10 £3,800**

Skylark *Don Enrico Incisa*   51 a30
7 ch m Polar Falcon (USA) - Boozy
7^{7sd} 12^{7gf} 14^{8sd} **0-0-3**

Skylarker (USA) *W S Kittow*   86 a86
6 b g Sky Classic (Can) - O My Darling (USA)
2^{9sd} 3^{9ss} 3^{8ss} 12^{10sd} 13^{8gs} 14^{10s} 4^{10f}
4^{10gf} 1^{13gf} 5^{12gf} 5^{12g} 1^{12gf} 2^{12s} **2-4-13**
£16,336

Skyscape *Mrs A J Perrett*   59
2 b f Zafonic (USA) - Aquarelle

3^{8gs} **0-1-1 £610**

Skywards *Saeed Bin Suroor*   101
2 b c Machiavellian (USA) - Nawaiet (USA)
5^{5gs} 1^{5gf} 3^{5gf} 7^{5g} 10^{5f} **1-1-5 £11,374**

Slalom (Ire) *Julian Poulton*   74 a77
4 b g Royal Applause - Skisette
1^{9ss} $1^{9^{10g}}$ 7^{8sd} 5^{8g} 8^{8g} 5^{11hy} 13^{10g} 2^{8sd}
1-1-8 £4,478

Slate Grey *K R Burke*   51
2 gr g Paris House - Slipperose
13^{6gf} 11^{6f} 8^{5gf} 8^{5g} 12^{9gs} 20^{6s} **0-0-6**

Slavonic (USA) *K A Ryan*   72
3 ch g Royal Academy (USA) - Cyrillic (USA)
5^{9s} 4^{8g} 4^{10gf} 6^{10gf} 4^{10gf} 7^{8gf} 9^{10s} 11^{12gs}
0-0-8 £973

Sleeping Indian *J H M Gosden*   112
3 b c Indian Ridge - Las Flores (Ire)
1^{8g} 1^{8gs} **2-0-2 £21,534**

Slip Catch (Ire) *W Jarvis*   58
2 b f Intikhab - Buckle (Ire)
14^{6gs} 6^{7gf} **0-0-2**

Slip Dance (Ire) *Eamon Tyrrell*   103
2 br f Celtic Swing - Hawala (Ire)
3^{6y} 1^{6gs} 4^{6gf} 1^{6gf} 6^{6g} 2^{7gf} 6^{7gf} 1^{6y} 5^{6g}
3-2-9 £114,821

Slite *Miss D Mountain*   52
2 gr f Mind Games - Sapphire Mill
12^{6gf} 2^{7gf} 5^{5gs} 5^{7gf} 5^{8gs} **0-1-5 £1,096**

Small Stakes (Ire) *P J Makin*   62 a70
2 b c Pennekamp (USA) - Poker Chip
7^{5g} 5^{6sd} **0-0-2**

Small Time Blues (Ire) *M J Polglase*
2 b f Danetime (Ire) - Barinia
10^{6gf} **0-0-1**

Smart Boy Prince (Ire) *C Smith*   59 a62
3 b g Princely Heir (Ire) - Miss Mulaz (Fr)
1^{7sd} 1^{8sd} 7^{8sd} 5^{7sd} 9^{11gs} 3^{8sd} 8^{8f} 11^{10gs}
6^{11g} 13^{8g} 2^{10gf} 2^{10g} **2-3-12 £7,172**

Smart Danny *J J Quinn*   44 a38
3 gr g Danzero (Aus) - She's Smart
13^{6ss} 5^{5g} 5^{6sd} 7^{5gf} 8^{6s} 8^{5s} 5^{6gf} 12^{6g}
0-0-8

Smart Dawn *C Tinkler*   48
2 ch f Cadeaux Genereux - Blugem (Fr)
19^{6gf} 13^{7gf} 14^{8s} **0-0-3**

Smart Hostess *J J Quinn*   100
5 gr m Most Welcome - She's Smart
15^{5g} 9^{6gs} 9^{5s} 3^{6gf} 18^{6g} 13^{5s} **0-1-6**
£2,324

Smart John *W M Brisbourne*   78
4 b g Bin Ajwaad (Ire) - Katy-Q (Ire)
4^{10s} 1^{11gf} 4^{10gf} 2^{10gf} 1^{12g} 3^{14gs} 5^{12g} 4^{12s}
1^{13gs} 3^{12f} 9^{12gf} 6^{12g} **3-3-12 £16,018**

Smart Minister *J J Quinn*   63 a27
4 gr g Muhtarram (USA) - She's Smart
12^{8sd} 13^{8s} 7^{7gf} 1^{6gf} 15^{7gf} 6^{6gf} **1-0-6**
£3,809

Smart Scot *B P J Baugh*   a57
5 ch g Selkirk (USA) - Amazing Bay
1^{8sd} 1^{7sd} 1^{7sw} 1^{7ss} 2^{8sd} 14^{8sd} 5^{9sd} 11^{7sd}
4-1-8 £6,049

Smart Starprincess (Ire) *M J Attwater*   55 a68
3 b f Soviet Star (USA) - Takeshi (Ire)
1^{5sd} 1^{5sd} 3^{5sd} 5^{9gf} 7^{19g} 12^{6gf}
10^{5gf} 4^{5s} 12^{5s} **2-2-10 £7,190**

Smarter Charter *Mrs L Stubbs*   47 a42

11 br g Master Willie - Irene's Charter
5^{12sd} 7^{12sd} 2^{10g} 7^{10hy} 6^{14gf} 5^{12gf} 1^{11g}
4^{12gf} 5^{14f} 6^{12gs} 4^{13gf} 3^{10sd} 7^{14gs} 5^{13s} **0-2-14**
£597

Smarty Jones (USA) John C Servis   a131
3 ch c Elusive Quality (USA) - I'Ll Get Along (USA)
1^{8ft} 1^{8ft} 1^{9ft} 1^{9my} 1^{10sy} 1^{10ft} 2^{12th} **6-1-7**
£1,448,901

Smeorach James Moffatt   36
3 ch f My Generation - Mohican
7^{8g} 8^{11gf} 7^{16gf} **0-0-3**

Smiddy Hill R Bastiman   86
2 b f Factual (USA) - Hello Hobson'S (Ire)
3^{5g} 2^{5g} 4^{5gs} 1^{5gf} 4^{5gf} 5^{5g} 1^{5gf} 9^{5gf} 2^{5gf}
3^{5g} 6^{5gs} **2-4-11 £14,751**

Smiling Starduster (Ire) D Carroll   20 a20
2 b c Danehill Dancer (Ire) - Evriza (Ire)
13^{7gs} 12^{6sw} 7^{7g} **0-0-3**

Smirfys Dance Hall (Ire) W M Brisbourne   52 a11
4 b f Halling (USA) - Bigger Dances (USA)
4^{8gf} 9^{12f} 11^{9sd} **0-0-3 £432**

Smirfys Night D Nicholls   55
5 b g Tina's Pet - Nightmare Lady
17^{5g} 11^{5gf} 19^{5gs} 5^{6g} 4^{5gs} 12^{5gf} **0-1-6**
£338

Smirfys Party D Nicholls   56
6 ch g Clantime - Party Scenes
14^{6g} 13^{6gf} 8^{6g} 3^{6g} 5^{5gs} 9^{6gs} 8^{5gf} **0-1-7**
£586

Smirfys Systems W M Brisbourne   82 a70
5 b g Safawan - Saint Systems
7^{6s} 17^{8gs} 5^{6gf} 8^{6gs} 9^{6gf} 2^{6gf} 10^{7s} 8^{6sd}
0-1-8 £1,720

Smith N Allan Oils M Dods   68 a70
5 b g Bahamian Bounty - Grand Splendour
1^{7sd} 10^{7sd} 9^{7g} 7^{7gf} 8^{8f} 10^{7g} 11^{8f} 7^{7f}
5^{7g} 2^{7gf} 2^{7gf} 4^{7gf} 6^{7gf} 7^{7gf} 5^{7sd} **1-2-15**
£6,591

Smokin Beau N P Littmoden   116
7 b g Cigar - Beau Dada (Ire)
6^{6g} 2^{6gs} 7^{5g} 10^{5gs} 17^{5gf} 4^{6gf} 14^{5gf}
15^{6gf} 1^{5g} 1^{6s} 1^{5s} **3-2-11 £67,841**

Smokin Joe J R Best   44 a70
3 b g Cigar - Beau Dada (Ire)
4^{6sd} 10^{5sd} 5^{6sd} 14^{6s} 18^{10g} 12^{6gf} 8^{6sd}
14^{6gf} 16^{5gf} 5^{7sd} **0-1-11 £783**

Smokincanon W G M Turner   62 a62
2 ch c Fumo Di Londra (Ire) - Secret Miss
3^{5gs} 1^{5sd} 6^{5g} 5^{5sd} **1-0-4 £1,698**

Smoothie (Ire) Ian Williams   66 a65
6 gr g Definite Article - Limpopo
7^{12gf} 6^{12g} 13^{12g} 1^{10gf} 9^{10gs} 3^{12sd} 1^{12sd}
2-1-7 £9,928

Smoothly Does It Mrs A J Bowlby   73
3 b g Efisio - Exotic Forest
11^{10g} 2^{8s} 9^{9gf} 6^{10gf} 9^{8g} 4^{8gf} 8^{8gf} 1^{8s}
2^{8hy} 6^{10s} 9^{8gs} **1-2-11 £6,744**

Snap M Johnston   85
3 ch g Dr Fong (USA) - Reactress (USA)
2^{6s} 1^{6g} 3^{7gf} 1^{7s} 3^{7g} **2-3-5 £13,383**

Sninfia (Ire) G A Ham   54
4 b f Hector Protector (USA) - Christmas Kiss
10^{10g} 7^{12g} 7^{8s} 4^{14gf} 7^{11g} 9^{14gf} 8^{14gf}
14^{14sd} 10^{12gs} **0-1-9 £288**

Snookered Again M W Easterby   55 a69
2 b g Lujain (USA) - Highest Bid (Fr)
5^{5g} 1^{6sd} 7^{6gf} 3^{7sd} 10^{7s} 8^{7gf} **1-1-6**

£4,188

Snow Bunting Jedd O'Keeffe   70
6 ch g Polar Falcon (USA) - Marl
8^{7gs} 14^{7gf} 3^{6gf} 15^{5gf} 2^{6g} 8^{7gf} 5^{6g} 3^{6g}
36^{6gf} 4^{6gf} 7^{6gf} 6^{6f} 1^{7g} **1-4-13 £10,320**

Snow Chance (Ire) W M Brisbourne   a23
3 ch f Compton Place - Snowscape
13^{10f} 8^{8sd} 13^{16gf} **0-0-3**

Snow Goose J L Dunlop   106
3 b f Polar Falcon (USA) - Bronzewing
11^{7g} 4^{7gf} 28^{gs} 38^{gf} 3^{10gf} 28^{s} 18^{s} 48^{s}
1-3-8 £68,658

Snow Joke (Ire) Mrs P N Dutfield   57
3 b f Desert Sun - Snowcap (Ire)
7^{7gs} 4^{7gf} 28^{gs} 14^{10gf} 11^{8g} 10^{8gf} 5^{7gs}
17^{7g} **0-0-8 £434**

Snow Lynx (USA) Saeed Bin Suroor   15
2 ch f Lemon Drop Kid (USA) - Snow Forest (USA)
16^{7gs} **0-0-1**

Snow Ridge (Ire) Saeed Bin Suroor   123
3 b c Indian Ridge - Snow Princess (Ire)
28^{g} 7^{12g} **0-1-2 £66,000**

Snow Tempest (USA) T G Mills   62
2 b g Theatrical - January's Storm (USA)
7^{7g} 9^{7gs} 14^{7g} 6^{8g} **0-0-4**

Snow Wolf J M Bradley   85 a45
3 ch g Wolfhound (USA) - Christmas Rose
7^{5gf} 1^{6gf} 2^{6gf} 9^{6gf} 9^{6gf} 4^{5g} 14^{5g} 14^{5gs}
9^{5sd} **1-1-9 £6,460**

Snow's Ride W R Muir   67
4 gr g Hernando (Fr) - Crodelle (Ire)
14^{18g} 16^{16gs} 15^{14gs} 9^{16gf} 7^{14gf} 6^{16gf}
4^{16gs} 14^{14gs} 4^{16gs} 2^{14s} **0-2-10 £1,700**

Snowdrift D J Daly   a41
2 b f Desert Prince (Ire) - Snowing
13^{6gf} 5^{5sd} **0-0-2 £210**

Snowed Under J D Bethell   65
3 gr g Most Welcome - Snowy Mantle
5^{8gs} 5^{9g} 5^{12g} 12^{10g} 7^{10gf} 1^{10gs} 6^{10gf} 3^{10f}
9^{10s} **1-1-9 £4,059**

Snuki G L Moore   a53
5 b g Pivotal - Kennedys Prima
9^{10sd} 10^{10sd} 9^{10sd} **0-0-3**

So Determined (Ire) G A Butler   57 a53
3 b g Soviet Star (USA) - Memory Green (USA)
12^{7gf} 2^{10f} 11^{12sd} **0-0-3 £1,236**

So Elegant (Ire) J Jay   29 a35
2 b f Bahhare (USA) - Soignee
10^{7gs} 5^{7sd} **0-0-2**

So Independent C R Wilson   33
2 b f Tipsy Creek (USA) - So Bold
8^{6gf} 11^{6f} **0-0-2**

So Sober (Ire) D Shaw   48 a54
6 b g Common Grounds - Femme Savante
1^{5sd} 5^{5ss} 4^{5ss} 8^{6sd} 8^{5sw} 4^{5ss} 3^{5g} 8^{5gf}
12^{5gs} 9^{5gf} 5^{5s} 6^{5sd} **1-1-12 £1,872**

So Sure (Ire) J G M O'Shea   31 a48
4 b g Definite Article - Zorilla
4^{11ss} 6^{10sd} 9^{10g} **0-0-3**

So Vital J Pearce   58 a79
4 b c Pivotal - Sumoto
1^{12sd} 7^{14sd} 3^{12sd} 14^{12g} 11^{12gf} 13^{17gf}
1-1-6 £4,044

So Will I M P Tregoning   110
3 ch c Inchinor - Fur Will Fly
3^{7g} 1^{6g} 8^{6s} 4^{6g} 7^{7g} 5^{7g} 3^{6gf} 4^{7g} **1-1-8**

£31,450

Soaked *D W Chapman* — 71 a55
11 b g Dowsing (USA) - Water Well
2^{5sd} 6^{5sd} 7^{6sd} 9^{5ss} 4^{5ss} 7^{6sw} 2^{5ss} 3^{5ss}
4^{5sd} 15^{5hy} 4^{5gf} 1^{5g} 2^{5gf} 1^{1s} 5^{5gf} 2^{5gf} 3^{5gf}
14^{5gf} **2-9-21 £12,619**

Soar *J R Fanshawe* — 110
2 b f Danzero (Aus) - Splice
1^{5g} 2^{5gf} 1^{6gf} 1^{6s} 6^{6g} **3-1-5 £98,815**

Soba Jones *J Balding* — 79 a85
7 b g Emperor Jones (USA) - Soba
1^{6sw} 2^{6sd} 4^{5sd} 3^{6sd} 2^{6sd} 5^{6ss} 6^{6gs} 5^{6g}
4^{6g} 2^{5gf} 5^{6gf} 9^{5gs} 5^{5gs} **1-4-13 £13,464**

Social Contract *S Dow* — 49 a49
7 b g Emarati (USA) - Just Buy Baileys
13^{7sd} 7^{7sd} 7^{7sd} 6^{8sd} 8^{7sd} 6^{7sd} 2^{7sd} 10^{7sd}
12^{7sd} 7^{7ss} 8^{6gs} 8^{7gf} 8^{7g} 8^{7hy} 6^{6g} **0-1-15 £476**

Society Music (Ire) *M Dods* — 79
2 b f Almutawakel - Society Fair (Fr)
1^{5s} 3^{6gf} 1^{7gf} 3^{7gf} 6^{7gs} 7^{6gs} 5^{7gf} 8^{7gf}
9^{6s} **2-0-9 £11,713**

Society Pet *D G Bridgwater* — 40
5 b m Runnett - Polar Storm (Ire)
9^{6gs} 19^{6gf} **0-0-2**

Society Times (USA) *D A Nolan* — 36
11 b g Imp Society (USA) - Mauna Loa (USA)
7^{8gf} 10^{9gf} 7^{9gs} 8^{9gf} 5^{11s} **0-0-5 £750**

Sofistication (Ire) *T G Mills* — a71
3 b f Dayjur (USA) - Cieladeed (USA)
9^{7sd} 1^{7sd} **1-0-2 £3,838**

Soft Focus (Ire) *J A Osborne* — 12 a53
2 b f Spectrum (Ire) - Creme Caramel (USA)
7^{8sd} 7^{9sd} 11^{8sd} 12^{6hy} **0-0-4**

Soft Mist (Ire) *J J Quinn* — 36 a45
4 gr f Up And At 'Em - Morgiana
6^{8sd} 11^{9sd} 14^{8gs} 8^{10hy} 11^{8f} 17^{8f} **0-0-6**

Sokoke *R M Beckett* — 68 a22
3 ch g Compton Place - Sally Green (Ire)
2^{5gf} 3^{5gf} 8^{6s} 8^{6f} 7^{6sd} **0-2-5 £1,348**

Sol Rojo *J A Osborne* — 42 a74
2 b g Efisio - Shining Cloud
12^{6g} 9^{7sd} 7^{8sd} 5^{9sd} **0-0-4**

Solanich *R Hannon* — a3
2 ch g Inchinor - Gussy Marlowe
11^{6sd} **0-0-1**

Solar Falcon *A G Newcombe* — 23
2 ch f Polar Falcon (USA) - Beryl
10^{8gf} 15^{8gs} **0-0-2**

Solar Power (Ire) *J R Fanshawe* — 101
3 b f Marju (Ire) - Next Round (Ire)
2^{8gf} 4^{8s} 4^{8gf} 4^{7gf} 3^{7s} 1^{6g} 2^{6s} 2^{6g} **1-4-8**
£26,550

Solar Prince (Ire) *H Alexander* — 12
3 b g Desert Prince (Ire) - Quiche
17^{5gf} 17^{8hy} 14^{6s} **0-0-3**

Solarias Quest *A King* — 77
2 b g Pursuit Of Love - Persuasion
3^{8gf} 3^{8s} 2^{10hy} **0-2-3 £2,858**

Soldera (USA) *J R Fanshawe* — 106
4 b f Polish Numbers (USA) - La Pepite (USA)
3^{8gf} 4^{10g} 9^{10vs} 4^{8gf} 12^{9s} **0-1-5**
£22,392

Soldier's Tale (USA) *J Noseda* — 102
3 ch c Stravinsky (USA) - Myrtle
2^{6g} 1^{7gs} **1-1-2 £6,589**

Sole Agent (Ire) *G L Moore* — 63
2 b g Trans Island - Seattle Siren (USA)
11^{8gf} 3^{8s} 10^{7s} **0-1-3 £655**

Soleil D'Hiver *P C Haslam* — 29 a26
3 b f Bahamian Bounty - Catriona
7^{9sd} 5^{8sd} 9^{7gf} **0-0-3**

Solent (Ire) *R Hannon* — 93
2 b c Montjeu (Ire) - Stylish
1^{7gf} 9^{7g} 3^{8g} **1-0-3 £5,858**

Soliniki *J A Osborne* — 54 a49
3 b g Danzero (Aus) - Pride Of My Heart
17^{7gs} 7^{6s} 24^{7gs} 8^{6sd} **0-0-4**

Solipsist (Ire) *N I M Rossiter* — 53
3 ch c Grand Lodge (USA) - Mijouter (Ire)
14^{8g} 10^{7gf} **0-0-2**

Soller Bay *K R Burke* — 79
7 b g Contract Law (USA) - Bichette
2^{8gs} 16^{8gs} 8^{8g} 4^{8s} 12^{8gs} 11^{9gs} 11^{12s}
0-1-7 £1,610

Solmorin *R J Baker* — a32
6 b m Fraam - Reclusive
5^{10sd} **0-0-1**

Solo Flight *H Morrison* — 95
7 gr g Mtoto - Silver Singer
2^{10gf} 6^{12g} 15^{10gf} 2^{10gs} 9^{10gs} 1^{11g} 3^{12g}
7^{12s} **1-3-8 £12,905**

Solo Sole (Ity) *L M Cumani* — 47
3 b g Grand Lodge (USA) - Storm Flash
14^{10g} 13^{8s} 10^{8gf} **0-0-3**

Solor *D J Coakley* — 81 a67
3 b c Spectrum (Ire) - Bayadere (USA)
4^{8sd} 1^{10g} 11^{10hy} **1-0-3 £3,620**

Solskjaer (Ire) *A P O'Brien* — 109
4 b c Danehill (USA) - Lyndonville (Ire)
1^{7gf} 2^{8gf} 2^{10gf} 1^{10gf} 8^{10g} **2-2-5**
£88,290

Solved (USA) *P A Blockley* — 38
3 b f Hennessy (USA) - Claradane (Ire)
8^{5f} **0-0-1**

Somayda (Ire) *Miss Jacqueline S Doyle* — 45
9 b g Last Tycoon - Flame Of Tara
11^{9gf} 11^{10gf} 15^{9gf} 3^{6g} 15^{12gf} 6^{12gf} 5^{8gs}
0-1-7 £550

Some Night (Ire) *J H M Gosden* — 54
2 b f Night Shift (USA) - Some Merit
5^{6gf} 11^{5gs} 10^{6g} **0-0-3**

Someone's Angel (USA) *E A L Dunlop*
3 gr f Runaway Groom (Can) - Yazeanhaa (USA)
10^{6hy} **0-0-1**

Somerset West (Ire) *J R Best* — 78 a51
4 b g Catrail (USA) - Pizzazz
6^{5sd} 8^{6sd} 13^{6sd} 1^{7sd} 1^{7s} 9^{7f} 7^{6g} 1^{5g} 7^{6g}
9^{6g} **3-0-10 £7,262**

Something (Ire) *T G Mills* — 85
2 b c Trans Island - Persian Polly
2^{6g} 6^{6gs} **0-1-2 £1,866**

Something Exciting *D R C Elsworth* — 106
2 ch f Halling (USA) - Faraway Waters
4^{7g} 10^{7gf} 13^{7g} 1^{8s} 1^{8g} 1^{8s} 2^{8gs} **3-1-7**
£25,372

Somethingabouther *P W Hiatt* — 50 a42
4 b f Whittingham (Ire) - Paula's Joy
4^{6sd} 5^{5sw} 8^{5ss} 3^{5sd} 7^{6sd} 5^{5sd} 13^{5gf} 2^{5gf}
9^{5f} 19^{5g} 14^{5f} **0-2-11 £1,091**

Somewhere My Love *T G Mills* — 32 a67
3 br f Pursuit Of Love - Grand Coronet

1^{8sd} 11^{7sd} 10^{8sd} 3^{8sd} 16^{6g} **1-0-5 £4,715**

Somewin (Ire) *Miss K Marks*   26
4 b f Goldmark (USA) - Janet Oliphant
11^{16gf} **0-0-1**

Somnus *T D Easterby*   124
4 b g Pivotal - Midnight's Reward
7^{6gs} 2^{6s} 5^{6gs} 1^{7gs} 2^{6g} 1^{7s} **2-2-6 £227,708**

Son And Heir (Ire) *N J Hawke*   a9
3 b c Princely Heir (Ire) - Margarets Memory (Ire)
12^{8sd} **0-0-1**

Son Of Rembrandt (Ire) *D K Ivory*   30 a50
3 b g Titus Livius (Fr) - Avidal Park
9^{6sd} 13^{5sd} 5^{5sd} 3^{7sd} 6^{6gs} 3^{7sd} 11^{6gf}
12^{8sd} 18^{7gf} **0-2-9 £733**

Son Of Thunder (Ire) *M Dods*   70 a44
3 ch g Dr Fong (USA) - Sakura Queen (Ire)
6^{7g} 18^{9f} 6^{9g} 2^{8gf} 8^{8g} 18^{9f} 9^{7gf} 10^{9sd}
2-1-8 £6,791

Sonderborg *Miss A M Newton-Smith*   58 a57
3 b f Great Dane (Ire) - Nordico Princess
6^{7sd} 4^{8sd} 5^{7sd} 3^{8sd} 2^{7sw} 2^{7sd} 2^{7sd} 10^{7sd}
11^{10gs} 2^{8gf} 6^{7gf} 14^{8sd} 16^{10gf} 9^{8gf} 6^{9s} 6^{10sd}
6^{12sd} 3^{8g} 13^{8gs} **0-6-19 £3,586**

Sonearsofar (Ire) *J Parkes*   38
4 b g General Monash (USA) - Not Too Near (Ire)
11^{7g} 6^{7gf} 7^{8gs} 13^{10gs} 11^{7sd} **0-0-5**

Song Koi *J G Given*   43 a44
3 b f Sri Pekan (USA) - Eastern Lyric
10^{6g} 2^{5g} 18^{5gf} 4^{6sd} 7^{5sd} **0-1-5 £1,063**

Song Of The Sea *J W Hills*   60 a23
3 ch f Bering - Calypso Run
8^{10gs} 9^{10g} 4^{12gf} 12^{16gf} 13^{18gs} 7^{12sd} **0-0-6 £450**

Song Of Vala *R Charlton*   82 a61
3 ch g Peintre Celebre (USA) - Yanka (USA)
9^{9s} 5^{12gf} 7^{10gf} 6^{8gf} 3^{8gs} 4^{8sd} **0-1-6 £1,246**

Song Sparrow *G A Butler*   a43
2 b f Vettori (Ire) - Fanfare
12^{7sd} 6^{7sd} 9^{6sd} **0-0-3**

Song Thrush (USA) *P F I Cole*   89
2 gr/ro f Unbridled's Song (USA) - Virgin Michael (USA)
1^{7gs} **1-0-1 £4,881**

Songerie *Sir Mark Prescott*   102
2 b f Hernando (Fr) - Summer Night
1^{7hy} 9^{7ys} 1^{8s} **2-0-3 £28,770**

Songgaria *J G M O'Shea*   52
2 b f Kingsinger (Ire) - Paula's Joy
2^{5gf} 3^{6gf} 7^{5gf} 2^{7gs} **0-3-4 £2,031**

Songlark *Saeed Bin Suroor*   111
4 br c Singspiel (Ire) - Negligent
5^{10g} 2^{12gf} 4^{12f} **0-1-3 £11,277**

Sonic Anthem (USA) *D Nicholls*
2 b g Royal Anthem (USA) - Whisperifyoudare (USA)
17^{6gs} **0-0-1**

Sonntag Blue (Ire) *J A Osborne*   57 a58
2 b g Bluebird (USA) - Laura Margaret
11^{6gf} 10^{6g} 9^{6sd} 10^{6gs} **0-0-4**

Sono *P D Niven*   69
7 b g Robellino (USA) - Sweet Holland (USA)
9^{16gf} 5^{16g} 4^{16gf} **0-0-3 £417**

Sonoma (Ire) *M L W Bell*   74
4 ch f Dr Devious (Ire) - Mazarine Blue (USA)
5^{16g} 8^{16g} 6^{14hy} 9^{14g} 12^{14gf} 11^{6gf} 4^{14g}

4^{16f} 4^{16hy} 3^{16gf} **1-0-10 £4,630**

Sooyou Sir (Ire) *Mrs A Duffield*   29
2 b/br g Orpen (USA) - Naivement (Ire)
10^{7g} 13^{10gf} 8^{7s} **0-0-3**

Sophomore *John A Harris*   a34
10 b g Sanglamore (USA) - Livry (USA)
9^{8sd} 6^{11sd} 3^{9sw} 14^{11ss} **0-1-4 £198**

Sophrano (Ire) *P A Blockley*   59
4 b g Spectrum (Ire) - Sophrana (Ire)
5^{8gf} 3^{7f} 9^{6g} 3^{6s} 3^{8gs} 7^{7s} 4^{7f} 12^{7gs}
0-2-8 £2,771

Sorbiesharry (Ire) *Mrs N Macauley*   a58
5 gr g Sorbie Tower (Ire) - Silver Moon
5^{9sd} 2^{8sd} 3^{8sd} 5^{9sd} 1^{8sd} 5^{11ss} 10^{8ss} 1^{9ss}
4^{8sd} 11^{9sd} 5^{8sd} 8^{8sw} 11^{9sd} 3^{11sd} **2-3-14 £7,346**

Sorceress *J Gallagher*   37
2 b f Wizard King - Aonia
9^{6f} 11^{6g} **0-0-2**

Sorrento King *C N Kellett*   a8
7 ch g First Trump - Star Face
7^{14sd} **0-0-1**

Sotonian (Hol) *P S Felgate*   39 a45
11 br g Statoblest - Visage
5^{5sd} 3^{5ss} 3^{6sw} 7^{5sw} 5^{6sd} 3^{5sd} 4^{6sd}
5^{5sd} 16^{6f} 11^{6sd} 18^{6gf} 20^{6gs} **1-3-13 £2,521**

Soul Dance *P J Makin*   63
3 b f Imperial Ballet (Ire) - Piccante
2^{6gf} **0-1-1 £1,280**

Soul Provider (Ire) *M J Attwater*   52 a53
3 ch f Danehill Dancer (Ire) - Wing And A Prayer (Ire)
5^{6sd} 3^{6ss} 4^{6ss} 3^{8sd} 2^{6gs} 4^{7gs} 9^{8f} 5^{7f}
8^{7gs} 12^{7sd} 7^{7s} 12^{7sd} **0-2-12 £2,284**

Soulacroix *Mrs A J Perrett*   98
3 b c Kylian (USA) - California Dreamin
2^{12gf} 1^{13gs} 7^{14s} 3^{12s} 10^{12s} **1-2-5 £14,081**

Soumillon *Ms Deborah J Evans*   a35
2 br f Benny The Dip (USA) - Kembla
12^{9sd} 9^{6sd} **0-0-2**

Sound And Vision (Ire) *M Dods*   58
2 b g Fayruz - Lyrical Vision (Ire)
5^{6gf} 6^{6gf} 5^{7gf} 6^{6s} 5^{6g} 14^{6gf} **0-0-6**

Sound Blaster (Ire) *Liam McAteer*   73
3 ch g Zafonic (USA) - Blasted Heath
5^{10gf} 9^{8gf} **0-0-2**

Sound Breeze *M Johnston*   67
2 ch c Giant's Causeway (USA) - Madame Est Sortie (Fr)
4^{6s} **0-0-1 £365**

Sound Of Fleet (USA) *P F I Cole*   91
3 ch c Cozzene (USA) - Tempo (USA)
4^{10g} 6^{8g} 11^{10gf} 5^{10gf} 8^{10g} 2^{13gf} 10^{14s}
12^{14gf} 15^{14gs} **1-1-9 £10,051**

Sound That Alarm *G A Butler*   74
2 b g Groom Dancer (USA) - Warning Star
2^{5g} **0-0-1-2 £1,039**

Sound The Drum (USA) *J H M Gosden*   80
2 b c Stravinsky (USA) - Uhavethebeat (USA)
3^{6gf} 2^{6gs} **0-2-2 £2,858**

Sounds Lucky *Andrew Reid*   14 a61
8 b g Savahra Sound - Sweet Lucky
10^{6sd} 5^{6sd} 12^{6sd} 1^{5sd} 2^{6sd} 6^{6sd} 8^{6sd} 4^{6sd}
12^{5ss} 16^{6sd} 15^{6g} 13^{6sd} **1-1-12 £3,626**

South Face *R M Beckett*   77
3 ch g Hector Protector (USA) - Crystal Cavern (USA)
2^{7g} **0-1-1 £1,729**

South O'The Border *T G Mills*   56
2 b g Wolfhound (USA) - Abbey's Gal
9^{7gf} 11^{7gf} 10^{7gs} 13^{8gs} **0-0-4**

Southampton Joe (USA) *J G M O'Shea*   31
4 ch g Just A Cat (USA) - Maple Hill Jill (USA)
12^{8g} 6^{10gf} **0-0-2**

Southburgh (Ire) *Mrs C A Dunnett*   8
3 b g Spectrum (Ire) - College Night (Ire)
20^{8g} **0-0-1**

Southern Africa (USA) *G A Butler*   89
2 b/br c Cape Town (USA) - Al Fahda
1^{5gf} 2^{5gs} 1^{7gf} **2-1-3 £18,810**

Southern Bazaar (USA) *C A Dwyer*   86
3 ch c Southern Halo (USA) - Sunday Bazaar (USA)
2^{8f} 1^{8f} **1-0-2 £4,579**

Southern Star (Ger) *R C Guest*   52
4 gr g Sternkoenig (Ire) - Sun Mate (Ire)
4^{12hy} **0-0-1 £287**

Southern Tide (USA) *J J Sheehan*   58
2 b c Southern Halo (USA) - My Own Lovely Lee (USA)
17^{7gf} 11^{6gs} 10^{7hy} 13^{8gf} **0-0-4**

Sovereign Dreamer (USA) *P F I Cole*   77
4 b c Kingmambo (USA) - Spend A Dream (USA)
18^{12gs} 6^{12f} 11^{12g} 7^{15gf} 7^{11f} 11^{12f} 11^{14g}
0-0-7

Sovereign Girl *B N Doran*   16
3 b f Sovereign Water (Fr) - The Quaker
15^{10gf} 6^{12gf} **0-0-2**

Sovereign Spirit (Ire) *P W Harris*   59
2 b g Desert Prince (Ire) - Sheer Spirit (Ire)
11^{7gs} 7^{7gf} 6^{8f} **0-0-3**

Sovereign State (Ire) *D W Thompson*   55
7 b g Soviet Lad (USA) - Portree
1^{12gf} 4^{13g} 5^{12gf} 2^{13gf} 8^{16gs} 2^{14gf} 8^{12g}
1-2-7 £4,773

Sovereignty (Jpn) *D R Loder*   79
2 b g King's Best (USA) - Calando (USA)
2^{6f} 4^{6gs} **0-1-2 £1,871**

Soviet Sceptre (Ire) *Miss D Mountain*   69 a41
3 ch c Soviet Star (USA) - Princess Sceptre
3^{6s} 10^{6gf} 4^{8g} 6^{7gf} 8^{7s} 9^{10g} 1^{10gf} 5^{11gs}
12^{9sd} **1-1-9 £4,109**

Soviet Song (Ire) *J R Fanshawe*   124
4 b f Marju (Ire) - Kalinka (Ire)
2^{8gs} 3^{8gs} 1^{8gf} 2^{8gf} 1^{8g} 1^{8gf} 6^{8gf}
4-3-8 £542,124

Soviet Spirit *C A Dwyer*   60
3 ch f Soviet Star (USA) - Kristina
5^{8s} 19^{10s} 5^{7g} 3^{8f} 5^{8gf} 13^{7g} 4^{10gf} 7^{8hy}
7^{10g} 10^{8sd} **0-1-10 £421**

Soviet Treat (Ire) *J S Bolger*   89
3 b f Ashkalani (Ire) - Mystery Treat
5^{8gf} 6^{8hy} 3^{7gf} 13^{5ys} **0-1-4 £5,126**

Sovietta (Ire) *R M Beckett*   66
3 b f Soviet Star (USA) - La Riveraine (USA)
4^{10gf} 3^{12gf} 9^{12f} 11^{12g} **1-0-4 £4,503**

Sowerby *M Brittain*   60
2 b c Grey Desire - Brief Star (Ire)
9^{6gs} 6^{6gf} 4^{5gf} 10^{5g} 9^{5gs} **0-0-5 £360**

Soyuz (Ire) *K A Ryan*   96 a89
4 ch g Cadeaux Genereux - Welsh Mist
2^{8gs} 3^{8gs} 1^{8s} 5^{7g} 9^{7s} 19^{7g} 7^{5sd} 1^{7gs}
2-2-9 £16,819

Space Cowboy (Ire) *G L Moore*   54
4 b c Anabaa (USA) - Lady Moranbon (USA)
14^{10g} **0-0-1**

Space Maker *M L W Bell*   85
2 b c Almutawakel - Into Orbit
4^{6gf} 8^{5g} 15^{gf} **1-0-3 £4,483**

Space Shuttle *T D Easterby*   100
2 b c Makbul - Sky Music
3^{5gs} 2^{5gf} 1^{5gf} 3^{5gf} 3^{6f} 1^{6g} 1^{6gs}
12^{6s} **3-3-9 £37,299**

Spaced (Ire) *R Hannon*   85
2 b c Indian Rocket - Tolomena
12^{6gf} 6^{7gf} 1^{7gs} 3^{7s} 18^{g} **2-1-5 £20,412**

Spainkris *M Todhunter*   a7
5 b g Kris - Pennycairn
9^{12sd} **0-0-1**

Spanish Ace *A M Balding*   99 a58
3 b g First Trump - Spanish Heart
14^{7sd} 8^{7g} 18^{8gf} 10^{7g} 5^{6g} 5^{6g} 15^{5gf} 4^{5s}
1^{5gs} 18^{6g} **1-0-10 £8,214**

Spanish Don *D R C Elsworth*   109
6 b g Zafonic (USA) - Spanish Wells (Ire)
14^{8g} 13^{8g} 9^{8gf} 1^{9gf} 1^{10gf} 5^{10g} 9^{10gs} 1^{9g}
11^{10s} **4-0-9 £113,342**

Spanish Gold *A M Balding*   a2
4 b f Vettori (Ire) - Spanish Heart
12^{9sd} **0-0-1**

Spanish Law *M Dods*   36
2 b g Zaha (Can) - Misty Moon
7^{7g} **0-0-1**

Spanish Ridge (Ire) *J L Dunlop*   74
2 b c Indian Ridge - Spanish Lady (Ire)
5^{7g} 4^{7gf} 18^{7g} **0-0-3 £437**

Spanish Star *Mrs N Macauley*   a56
7 b g Hernando (Fr) - Desert Girl
4^{11sd} 6^{12sd} 1^{12sd} 3^{11sd} 3^{12ss} 8^{12sd} 11^{12sd}
7^{12sd} 10^{12sd} 4^{12sd} **1-1-10 £3,477**

Spark Up *J W Unett*   62 a66
4 b f Lahib (USA) - Catch The Flame (USA)
7^{7sd} 7^{8sd} 6^{7ss} 3^{8ss} 4^{8ss} 4^{8sd} 1^{8sd} 8^{10s}
6^{8gf} 16^{7gf} 7^{7g} 6^{8gf} **1-1-12 £4,911**

Sparkford (USA) *J H M Gosden*   48
2 b c Red Ransom (USA) - Arsaan (USA)
12^{8g} **0-0-1**

Sparkling Clear *R M H Cowell*   17 a14
3 b f Efisio - Shoot Clear
9^{6sd} 10^{6gs} 6^{6sd} 7^{7g} **0-0-4**

Sparkling Jewel *R Hannon*   74
4 b f Bijou D'Inde - Jobiska
8^{6gf} 6^{6gf} 2^{6f} 8^{6gf} **0-1-4 £1,257**

Sparkling Water (USA) *D L Williams*   56
5 b h Woodman (USA) - Shirley Valentine
11^{16g} **0-0-1**

Sparkwell *B W Hills*   80
2 b c Dansili - West Devon (USA)
5^{7g} **0-0-1**

Spartan Odyssey *A Senior*   3 b g Overbury (Ire) - Spartan Native
7^{7ss} **0-0-1**

Spartan Principle *R Guest*   a21
4 b f Spartan Monarch - Altar Point
8^{9ss} **0-0-1**

Spartan Spear *J Balding*   26
3 b g Sure Blade (USA) - Confection
11^{6s} 11^{7f} 9^{8s} **0-0-3**

Speagle (Ire) *E J O'Neill*   58
2 ch c Desert Sun - Pohutakawa (Fr)
12^{6f} 5^{7g} 6^{7g} 12^{8g} **0-0-4**

Spear (Ire) *D R Loder*   80

2 b c Almutawakel - Les Hurlants (Ire)
2^{7gf} 3^{7s} 1^{9f} **1-2-3 £5,577**

Spear Thistle *J H M Gosden*   85
2 ch g Selkirk (USA) - Ardisia (USA)
4^{8g} 4^{8g} 1^{8hy} **1-0-3 £7,704**

Spearious (Ire) *B R Millman*   59
3 b g Tagula (Ire) - Gloria Crown (Ire)
4^{5gf} **0-0-1**

Special Branch *Jedd O'Keeffe*
4 ch g Woodborough (USA) - Sixslip (USA)
16^{17gs} 16^{12g} **0-0-2**

Special Delivery (Ire) *E Lellouche*   102
4 b f Danehill (USA) - Seconde Bleue
1^{11gs} 4^{10gs} 3^{9g} **1-1-3 £18,880**

Special Gold *T D Easterby*   68
2 b c Josr Algarhoud (Ire) - Inya Lake
5^{5s} 4^{5g} **0-0-2 £421**

Specialise *D W Barker*   28
2 b f Atraf - Summerhill Special (Ire)
11^{7gf} PU^{7gf} 10^{7f} **0-0-3**

Spectacular Hope *J W Mullins*
4 b f Marju (Ire) - Distant Music
8^{16sw} **0-0-1**

Spectait *Sir Mark Prescott*   72 a62
2 b g Spectrum (Ire) - Shanghai Girl
2^{7hy} 11^{6sd} 3^{9sd} **0-2-3 £1,531**

Spectested (Ire) *A W Carroll*   58 a47
3 ch g Spectrum (Ire) - Nisibis
7^{11gs} 9^{14s} 2^{12sd} 5^{11gf} 9^{12gs} 4^{10g} 2^{16s}
0-2-7 £2,201

Spector (Ire) *J J Sheehan*   52
4 gr g Spectrum (Ire) - Safkana (Ire)
7^{8gf} 13^{7s} 16^{8gf} **0-0-3**

Spectrometer *R C Guest*   57
7 ch g Rainbow Quest (USA) - Selection Board
14^{12g} 19^{16s} 19^{12g} **0-0-3**

Spectrum Of Light *C W Fairhurst*   51
2 b f Spectrum (Ire) - Empress Of Light
12^{6f} 5^{9gf} **0-0-2**

Spectrum Star *F P Murtagh*   19
4 b g Spectrum (Ire) - Persia (Ire)
9^{10gs} 7^{13s} **0-0-2**

Speed Cop *A M Balding*   100 a94
4 ch f Cadeaux Genereux - Blue Siren
2^{5sd} 3^{5g} 9^{5g} 18^{5gf} 4^{6g} 6^{5s} 9^{5g} 8^{5gf}
0-2-8 £13,114

Speed Dial Harry (Ire) *K R Burke*   75 a69
2 b g General Monash (USA) - Jacobina
5^{5sd} 2^{5s} 3^{5g} 1^{6sd} 3^{6f} 2^{5g} 1^{5g} 7^{6gf} 4^{6gf}
7^{6sd} **2-2-10 £9,244**

Speed Of Sound *A M Balding*   59
2 ch f Zafonic (USA) - Blue Siren
3^{5s} 3^{5gf} 4^{5gf} **0-0-3 £4,075**

Speed On *H Candy*   38 a29
11 b g Sharpo - Pretty Poppy
8^{6s} 7^{5sd} **0-0-2**

Speed Racer *Don Enrico Incisa*   54 a21
3 b f Zieten (USA) - Sharenara (USA)
14^{7f} 5^{6s} 14^{6gf} 3^{8gf} 6^{7hy} 3^{7f} 7^{8gf} 7^{8gs}
9^{7sd} **0-1-9 £1,378**

Speedbird (USA) *G Wragg*   76
3 ch f Sky Classic (Can) - Egoli (USA)
12^{7g} 2^{7gf} 7^{8gf} **0-1-3 £1,117**

Speedfit Free (Ire) *Miss A Stokell*   52 a58
7 b g Night Shift (USA) - Dedicated Lady (Ire)
2^{6sd} 5^{6sd} 6^{6ss} 2^{6ss} 4^{6gs} 9^{7g} 10^{6gs} 3^{6sd}

7^{5ss} 14^{8g} 4^{6sd} 9^{7f} 9^{7gf} 6^{6gf} 10^{6gs} 7^{6f} 20^{6gf}
11^{7gf} 14^{6sd} **0-2-22 £947**

Speedie Rossini (Ire) *S C Williams*   46
2 b g Rossini (USA) - Skatt
12^{8gs} 9^{7gf} 14^{7g} 12^{8gf} **0-0-4**

Speedy James (Ire) *D Nicholls*   59 a28
8 ch g Fayruz - Haraabah (USA)
8^{6sd} 14^{6ss} 2^{6gs} 16^{6gs} **0-1-4 £874**

Speedy Spirit *M Salaman*   35
2 ch f Wolfhound (USA) - Ansellady
9^{6g} 16^{8gs} 11^{6s} **0-0-3**

Speightstown *P F I Cole*   77
2 gr c Grand Lodge (USA) - Farfala (Fr)
7^{7gs} 3^{8gs} 1^{8gf} 7^{8g} **1-1-3 £6,210**

Spence Appeal (Ire) *K A Ryan*   59
2 b g Nicolotte - It's All Academic (Ire)
9^{6g} 8^{8gf} 11^{7s} **0-0-3**

Sperrin Valley (Ire) *J S Moore*
2 ch f Rossini (USA) - Astra (Ire)
12^{7sd} **0-0-1**

Spes Bona (USA) *W J Haggas*   51 a36
3 b c Rakeen (USA) - Novelette
10^{8gf} 4^{8g} 13^{8gs} 15^{8gf} 7^{12sd} **0-0-5 £371**

Spiders Web *T Keddy*   a33
4 gr g Linamix (Fr) - Cattermole (USA)
14^{7sd} 12^{8sd} 9^{12sd} 10^{10sd} BD^{10sd} 2^{8sw}
3^{11sd} 11^{8sd} 7^{10sd} 10^{8f} 11^{10gf} **0-2-11 £576**

Spill A Little *M R Channon*   76
2 b c Zafonic (USA) - Lypharitissima (Fr)
6^{7gs} 5^{8g} 9^{8g} **0-0-3**

Spin King (Ire) *M L W Bell*   84
3 b g Intikhab (USA) - Special Dissident
7^{10g} 4^{8g} 11^{7gf} 3^{7gf} 4^{8g} 7^{7g} 6^{7gf} 13^{7s}
0-2-8 £2,755

Spindor (USA) *M A Magnusson*   70 a68
5 ch g Spinning World (USA) - Doree (USA)
2^{7sd} 5^{7sd} 3^{7sd} 4^{7sw} 2^{6sd} 1^{7sd} 7^{6sd} 3^{7sd}
3^{8g} 6^{8gf} 12^{8gf} 9^{8sd} 4^{7sd} **1-5-13 £6,844**

Spinetail Rufous (Ire) *D Flood*   60 a29
6 b g Prince Of Birds (USA) - Miss Kinabalu
11^{7sd} 16^{9f} 16^{9g} 7^{7s} 7^{6s} **2-0-5 £3,006**

Spinnakers Girl *J R Weymes*   66 a53
2 b f Bluegrass Prince (Ire) - Brac Princess (Ire)
9^{6gf} 3^{7gf} 2^{7g} 4^{7ss} 8^{7sd} 11^{7s} 4^{8s} 8^{7s}
0-1-8 £1,845

Spinning Coin *J G Portman*   65
2 b f Mujahid (USA) - Cointosser (Ire)
19^{6gf} 6^{7gf} 7^{7gf} 8^{8gs} 9^{8f} **0-0-5**

Spinning Dove *N A Graham*   a70
4 ch f Vettori (USA) - Northern Bird
3^{7sd} 2^{8sd} LFT^{8sd} 5^{8sd} LFT^{7gf} **0-2-5**
£1,787

Spinning Jenni *J M Bradley*
4 b f Mind Games - Giddy
13^{6sd} **0-0-1**

Spirit Of Chester (Ire) *Mrs P N Dutfield*   98
2 b f Lend A Hand - It Takes Two (Ire)
4^{5g} 2^{6f} 9^{6g} 3^{6s} **0-2-4 £19,223**

Spirit Of France (Ire) *M Johnston*   93
2 b c Anabaa (USA) - Les Planches
2^{5hy} 2^{5g} 1^{6gf} 2^{6gf} 5^{7g} 6^{8gf} **1-3-6**
£12,842

Spirit's Awakening *J Akehurst*   69
5 b g Danzig Connection (USA) - Mo Stopher
10^{8g} 6^{8gf} 3^{8gs} 2^{8gf} 4^{7gf} 2^{7gs} 8^{8gs} 9^{8gf}
18^{8gf} 8^{8hy} 14^{7s} **1-4-11 £11,173**

Spitfire Bob (USA) *M E Sowersby*   43 a49
5 b g Mister Baileys - Gulf Cyclone (USA)
10⁹ˢᵈ 12¹²ᶠ **0-0-2**

Spitting Image (Ire) *K G Reveley*   68
4 ch f Spectrum (Ire) - Decrescendo (Ire)
8¹⁴ᵍ 3¹⁴ᵍᶠ 7¹³ᵍ 2¹²ᶠ 4¹⁴ᵍᶠ 1¹⁶ᶠ 2¹⁶ᵍᶠ 3¹⁶ˢ
1¹⁶ᶠ 6¹⁶ᵍˢ 7¹⁴ᵍᶠ **2-3-11 £10,139**

Splendid Touch *J R Jenkins*   a7
4 b f Distinctly North (USA) - Soft Touch (Ger)
10¹¹ˢᵈ 8¹¹ᵍ **0-0-2**

Spliff *H Candy*   95
3 b c Royal Applause - Snipe Hall
1⁶ˢ 7⁶ᵍᶠ 12⁶ᵍ 11⁵ᵍ 11⁶ᵍˢ 5⁶ᵍᶠ 11⁶ˢ
1-0-7 £12,897

Splodger Mac (Ire) *N Bycroft*   61
5 b g Lahib (USA) - Little Love
14⁷ᵍᶠ 10⁸ᵍ 18ᵍᶠ 2⁷ᶠ 6⁸ᵍˢ 10⁸ᵍˢ 2⁸ᶠ 4⁸ᵍᶠ
19⁸ᵍᶠ **1-2-9 £10,330**

Sporting Gesture *M W Easterby*   82
7 ch g Safawan - Polly Packer
8¹²ᵍˢ 5¹²ᶠ 4¹²ᵍᶠ 4¹²ᵍ 4¹²ˢ 3¹²ᵍᶠ 6¹²ᵍᶠ
UR¹²ᵍ 2¹²ᶠ 5¹⁴ᵍˢ **0-3-10 £6,265**

Sportsman (Ire) *M W Easterby*   30 a33
5 b g Sri Pekan (USA) - Ardent Range (Ire)
4¹⁶ˢʷ 4¹⁶ˢᵈ 11¹²ᵍᶠ **0-0-3 £291**

Spot In Time *I W McInnes*   62
4 b f Mtoto - Kelimutu
7¹²ˢʷ 8¹⁰ᵍ 8¹⁰ᵍ 7⁷ᵍᶠ 8¹²ᵍˢ **0-0-5**

Spotlight *Christophe Clement*   106
3 ch f Dr Fong (USA) - Dust Dancer
4⁷ᵍ 16⁸ᵍ 2¹⁰ᵍᶠ 1⁹ᵍ 2⁹ᶠ **1-1-5 £81,725**

Spree (Ire) *R Hannon*   93
2 gr f Dansili - Ibiza (Ger)
6⁵ˢ 15ᵍᶠ 9⁵ᵍᶠ 12⁵ˢ 7⁶ᵍᶠ **1-0-5 £4,947**

Spree Vision *P Monteith*   59
8 b g Suave Dancer (USA) - Regent's Folly (Ire)
6¹⁰ʰʸ 8¹²ᵍ 4¹²ᵍ 2¹¹ᵍ 2¹²ᵍᶠ 4¹²ᵍᶠ 5¹²ˢ 6⁹ᵍˢ
4¹⁰ˢ **0-2-9 £2,567**

Spring Adieu *Mrs A J Perrett*   59
3 b f Green Desert (USA) - Nanda
4⁹ᵍᶠ 9¹⁰ᵍᶠ 11¹⁰ᵍᶠ 4¹²ᵍˢ 7¹³ᶠ **0-0-5 £690**

Spring Breeze *M Dods*   63
3 ch g Dr Fong (USA) - Trading Aces
6¹⁰ˢ 9¹²ᵍᶠ 2¹⁴ᶠ 3¹⁶ᵍˢ 2¹⁶ᵍᶠ 5¹⁴ᵍˢ 2¹⁶ᵍᶠ
1¹⁶ᶠ 6¹⁶ᵍᶠ 3¹⁵ˢ **1-5-10 £6,901**

Spring Dancer *T J Fitzgerald*   53 a45
3 b f Imperial Ballet (Ire) - Roxy Music (Ire)
13⁷ˢᵈ 8⁶ᵍˢ 13⁷ᵍ 5¹¹ᵍᶠ 3⁸ˢᵈ 6⁷ᶠ 12⁸ᵍˢ 6⁷ᶠ
7⁷ˢᵈ **0-1-9 £432**

Spring Gift *D W Thompson*
7 b m Slip Anchor - Belmez Melody
8¹¹ˢᵈ **0-0-1**

Spring Goddess (Ire) *A P Jarvis*   87
3 b f Daggers Drawn (USA) - Easter Girl
3¹⁰ᵍᶠ 9¹⁰ᵍ 4¹⁰ᵍᶠ 3¹⁰ᵍ 3⁹ᵍ **0-2-5 £5,779**

Spring Jim *J R Fanshawe*   85
3 b g First Trump - Spring Sixpence
4⁷ᵍᶠ 1⁸ᵍᶠ 2⁹ᵍᶠ 4¹⁰ᵍᶠ 2¹⁰ᵍ **1-2-5 £9,889**

Spring Pursuit *E G Bevan*   52
8 b g Rudimentary - Pursuit Of Truth (USA)
4¹³ᵍˢ **0-0-1 £321**

Spring Surprise *B W Hills*   62
3 b f Hector Protector (USA) - Tender Moment (Ire)
6⁸ᵍˢ **0-0-1 £450**

Spring Time Girl *B Ellison*   22
2 b f Timeless Times (USA) - Daira

10⁵ᵍᶠ **0-0-1**

Spring Whisper (Ire) *C A Dwyer*   8 a43
3 b f Halling (USA) - Light Fresh Air (USA)
7¹⁰ˢᵈ 13⁷ˢᵈ 17¹²ᵍ 18¹⁰ᵍ **0-0-4**

Springalong (USA) *P D Evans*   58 a72
4 ch g Gone West (USA) - Seven Springs (USA)
7¹⁰ˢᵈ 4¹⁰ˢᵈ 5¹⁰ˢᵈ 13¹⁰ᵍ 10⁸ᵍ 7¹⁰ᶠ 8¹²ˢᵈ
6¹⁰ᵍ **0-0-8 £290**

Springtime Romance (USA) *E A L Dunlop*   81
3 br f Kris S (USA) - Khamsin (USA)
3¹⁰ᵍˢ 6¹²ᵍˢ 1⁹ᵍᶠ 6¹⁰ᵍ 4⁹ᵍ 8⁸ᵍˢ **1-1-6
£6,562**

Spuradich (Ire) *L M Cumani*   102
4 b c Barathea (Ire) - Svanzega (USA)
10⁸ᵍᶠ 3¹⁰ᵍᶠ 6¹⁰ᵍᶠ 1¹⁰ᵍˢ **1-0-4 £60,161**

Spy Gun (USA) *T Wall*   53 a67
4 ch g Mt. Livermore (USA) - Takeover Target (USA)
3⁸ˢʷ 5⁸ˢᵈ 8⁸ᵍᶠ 8⁷ˢˢ 5⁸ˢʷ 7⁸ˢˢ 4⁷ˢˢ 15¹¹ˢ
6⁷ᵍˢ 2⁸ˢᵈ 13⁷ᵍᶠ 13⁸ᵍᶠ **0-1-12 £1,534**

Spy King (USA) *M Johnston*   91
2 ch c Distant View (USA) - Regal Princess (USA)
2⁶ᵍᶠ 1⁶ᵍˢ 1⁶ˢ 3⁶ᵍˢ **2-2-4 £12,233**

Spy Master *J Parkes*   20 a34
6 b g Green Desert (USA) - Obsessive (USA)
3⁵ˢᵈ 2⁶ˢʷ 5⁶ˢʷ 7⁶ˢˢ 6⁵ˢᵈ 5⁶ˢᵈ 10⁶ˢᵈ 11⁶ᵍ
8⁶ˢᵈ 23⁵ᵍˢ **0-2-10 £569**

Square Dancer *D A Nolan*   8
8 b g Then Again - Cubist (Ire)
8⁶ᵍ 12⁶ᵍˢ 16⁷ᵍᶠ **0-0-3**

Squaw Dance *W J Haggas*   102
2 ch f Indian Ridge - Likely Story (Ire)
6⁶ᵍ 3⁶ʰʸ 2⁸ˢ 8⁶ᵍˢ **1-2-4 £16,749**

Squeaky *Miss K M George*   a42
7 ch m Infantry - Steady Saunter Vii
13⁷ˢᵈ **0-0-1**

Squirtle Turtle *P F I Cole*   63 a77
4 ch g Peintre Celebre (USA) - Hatton Gardens
11¹¹ˢᵈ 9¹²ˢᵈ 13¹²ᵍᶠ 4¹²ᵍᶠ 5¹²ᶠ 4¹⁶ᵍᶠ **1-0-6
£3,141**

Sri Diamond *S Kirk*   82
4 b g Sri Pekan (USA) - Hana Marie
10⁸ʰʸ 8⁸ᵍ 6⁸ᵍˢ 2⁸ᵍᶠ **0-1-4 £1,360**

Sri Lipis *P F I Cole*   75
2 ch c Cadeaux Genereux - Katrina (Ire)
4⁷ᵍᶠ 4⁷ᵍᶠ **0-0-2 £1,015**

St Andrews (Ire) *M A Jarvis*   111
4 b c Celtic Swing - Viola Royale (Ire)
2⁷ᵍᶠ 6⁷ᶠ 2⁸ᵍˢ 7⁷ᵍ 7⁸ᵍ 1⁸ʰʸ 18⁹ᵍ 1⁸ʰʸ
2-1-8 £59,502

St Andrews Storm (USA) *R Hannon*   99
2 b c Storm Creek (USA) - L'Amour Toujours (USA)
1⁶ᵍᶠ 4⁶ᵍᶠ 4⁶ᵍ 8⁷ˢ **1-0-4 £7,858**

St Austell *J A R Toller*   64 a60
4 b c Compton Place - Paris Joelle (Ire)
8⁶ᵍˢ 11⁵ˢ 11⁶ᶠ 16⁶ᵍᶠ **0-0-4**

St Barchan (Ire) *J G M O'Shea*   72
3 ch g Grand Lodge (USA) - Moon Tango (Ire)
4¹⁰ᵍᶠ 2⁹ᵍˢ 3¹⁰ˢ 1¹¹ᵍˢ **1-2-4 £8,785**

St Francis Wood (USA) *J Noseda*   82 a71
3 ch f Irish River (Fr) - Francisco Road (USA)
13⁷ᵍ 2¹⁰ˢᵈ 1⁸ᶠ 18⁸ᵍᶠ **1-1-4 £4,693**

St George's Girl *J R Jenkins*   20
3 b f Muthabb (Ire) - Nickelodeon
17⁸ᵍˢ 7⁶ʰʸ 8⁶ˢᵈ 11⁷ᶠ **0-0-4**

St Ivian *Mrs N Macauley*   53 a75
4 b g Inchinor - Lamarita

4^{6sw} 6^{5sd} 11^{6sd} 2^{6sd} 7^{5sd} 7^{6ss} 2^{7ss} 9^{7gs}
19^{5gs} 9^{6sd} 14^{7f} 8^{5g} 7^{7sd} 7^{6sd} 10^{6gf} 3^{5sd}
0-3-16 £2,874

St Jerome N P Littmoden
4 ch g Danzig Connection (USA) - Indigo Dawn
17^{14s} 15^{12gf} 17^{14gf} **0-0-3**

St Jude J Balding   35
4 b c Deploy - Little Nutmeg
7^{8gf} 7^{10s} 12^{8gs} **0-0-3**

St Pancras (Ire) D W Chapman   91
4 b c Danehill Dancer (Ire) - Lauretta Blue (Ire)
14^{7gs} 8^{10g} 8^{10gs} 2^{8gf} 8^{10g} 1^{8f} 5^{8g} 3^{7gf}
2^{7gs} 8^{10gs} 7^{7gs} **1-3-11 £11,409**

St Petersburg M H Tompkins   106
4 ch g Polar Falcon (USA) - First Law
2^{8g} 1^{8s} 21^{8g} 2^{8hy} 1^{8gs} 3^{8s} 6^{8g} **2-3-7**
£34,621

St Savarin (Fr) J R Best   81 a78
3 ch g Highest Honor (Fr) - Sacara (Ger)
2^{7sd} 5^{8sd} 3^{6sd} 1^{7sd} 7^{8gs} 13^{7gf} 3^{7gs} 3^{7gs}
1^{7gf} 10^{7sd} 11^{7sd} 11^{7g} 5^{8gs} 2^{10gf} 5^{9sd} **2-5-15**
£19,320

St Tropez (Ire) Mrs A J Hamilton-Fairley   49
3 b f Revoque (Ire) - Kaziranga (USA)
9^{8gs} 15^{10s} 9^{7g} 18^{8g} **0-0-4**

Staff Nurse (Ire) Don Enrico Incisa   40 a42
4 b f Night Shift (USA) - Akebia (USA)
12^{12hy} 9^{12sd} 14^{14sd} 8^{14sd} 5^{12gf} 3^{14sd} 3^{12sw}
2^{12gf} 4^{13s} **0-3-9 £2,020**

Stafford King (Ire) J G M O'Shea   36
7 b h Nicolotte - Opening Day
14^{12gf} 9^{10gs} 10^{18gs} **0-0-3**

Stagbury Hill (USA) J W Hills   99
2 ch c Woodman (USA) - Shalabia
1^{6gf} 6^{7g} 3^{8g} 6^{6gf} **1-0-4 £5,604**

Stage Direction (USA) J D Frost
7 b g Theatrical - Carya (USA)
12^{12g} **0-0-1**

Stage Left H R A Cecil   72
3 ch f Nashwan (USA) - Interval
2^{10hy} **0-1-1 £1,516**

Stage Right D R C Elsworth   93 a55
3 b c In The Wings - Spot Prize (USA)
4^{7sd} 6^{8gs} 11^{2gf} 5^{12g} 4^{13gs} 6^{12gs} 3^{14gs}
1-0-7 £12,053

Stage School (USA) M Johnston   65
2 b/br f Sunday Silence (USA) - Danseur Fabuleux (USA)
2^{6s} **0-1-1 £1,523**

Stage Secret (Ire) Miss E C Lavelle   60
3 ch c Zilzal (USA) - Tuxford Hideaway
7^{10gf} **0-0-1**

Stage Two (Ire) M Johnston   52 a17
3 b g Sadler's Wells (USA) - Meteor Stage (USA)
12^{12sd} 6^{12ss} 4^{12gf} 7^{13s} 9^{12hy} 2^{12gf} 8^{14f}
0-1-7 £790

Stagecoach Ruby G L Moore   42 a41
3 b f Bijou D'Inde - Forum Girl (USA)
10^{10sd} 9^{8sd} 5^{10sd} 4^{8sd} 3^{8sd} 3^{7g} 7^{7f} 7^{6f}
5^{7gf} 1^{10sd} 8^{7gf} **1-0-11 £1,720**

Stagnite Mrs H Sweeting   65 a40
4 ch g Compton Place - Superspring
17^{6gf} 6^{6f} 2^{6g} 15^{8gf} 8^{5g} 8^{5f} 6^{5g} 5^{6f} 11^{6g}
11^{5f} 11^{6sd} **1-1-11 £4,763**

Stakhanov W J Haggas   47
2 b g Dr Fong (USA) - Russian Grace (Ire)
15^{7s} **0-0-1**

Stakhanovite (Ire) James Leavy   61
4 b c Darshaan - Homage
9^{8g} 8^{10gf} **0-0-2**

Stallone N Wilson   79
7 ch g Brief Truce (USA) - Bering Honneur (USA)
13^{10gs} 3^{10g} 4^{10gf} 3^{12gf} 6^{12s} 8^{12gf} 8^{12f}
6^{12f} 6^{10gf} 3^{12g} 5^{12gs} **0-3-11 £3,714**

Stamford Blue J S Moore   69 a57
3 b g Bluegrass Prince (Ire) - Fayre Holly (Ire)
2^{6sd} 4^{5sd} 6^{6sd} 2^{6sd} 8^{7sd} 6^{5sd} 11^{7sd} 1^{6gs}
2^{6gs} 9^{6sd} **1-3-10 £5,257**

Stan's Girl I A Wood   55
2 b f Fraam - Gigetta (Ire)
8^{5gs} 3^{5s} 2^{6g} 12^{6s} 9^{6hy} **0-2-5 £1,926**

Stanbury (USA) M R Channon   78
2 ch c Zamindar (USA) - Staffin
2^{5gs} **0-1-1 £1,342**

Stance G L Moore   85
5 b g Salse (USA) - De Stael (USA)
9^{20gf} 2^{21g} 14^{16gf} 26^{18s} **0-1-4 £8,800**

Stancomb Wills (Ire) M H Tompkins   80
2 b c Trans Island - First Nadia
13^{7s} 7^{7s} 2^{7gf} 2^{8gs} **0-2-4 £2,842**

Stanhope Forbes (Ire) N P Littmoden   a40
3 b c Danehill Dancer (Ire) - Hinari Disk Deck
3^{6sd} 5^{6sd} **0-1-2 £412**

Stanley Arthur D Nicholls   18
2 b g Mind Games - Midnight Orchid (Ire)
13^{6gs} 13^{7g} **0-0-2**

Stanley Crane (USA) B Hanbury   57 a53
3 br g Bahri (USA) - Grey Starling
12^{10gf} 5^{7f} 4^{9f} 5^{8sd} 4^{8g} 3^{10gf} 10^{10gs}
0-1-7 £1,731

Star Applause J S Goldie   42 a19
4 b f Royal Applause - Cominna
11^{5sd} 10^{6sd} 6^{5gf} 16^{5g} 13^{5gf} 15^{5gf} 4^{6gf}
0-0-7 £424

Star Fern R M H Cowell   31 a60
3 br g Young Ern - Christening (Ire)
5^{8sd} 5^{7sd} 13^{7sd} 11^{7s} 15^{7gf} 12^{6g} 4^{6sd}
10^{7sd} **0-0-8**

Star Lad (Ire) R Brotherton   36 a57
4 ch g Lake Coniston (Ire) - Simply Special (Ire)
3^{7sd} 1^{7sw} 9^{7sd} 7^{6ss} 1^{6sw} 4^{6sw} 5^{5sd} 10^{6s}
3^{5sd} 15^{6g} 8^{6sd} **2-2-11 £4,719**

Star Magnitude (USA) J H M Gosden   77
3 ch c Distant View (USA) - Stellaria (USA)
11^{8gf} 2^{7gs} 2^{7gf} 5^{10gs} **0-2-4 £3,233**

Star Member (Ire) A P Jarvis   102
5 b g Hernando (Fr) - Constellation (Ire)
5^{14hy} 1^{14gs} 4^{16gf} 11^{4gf} 2^{14g} 6^{14s} 6^{15gf}
15^{12s} **2-1-8 £28,861**

Star Of Kildare (Ire) N Tinkler   36 a9
2 b f Raphane (USA) - Lady Fleetsin (Ire)
15^{5gf} 10^{5gf} 8^{5gf} 12^{5gs} 7^{5sw} **0-0-5**

Star Of Light B J Meehan   81
3 b g Mtoto - Star Entry
3^{7g} 4^{10g} **0-1-2 £1,591**

Star Of Normandie (USA) G G Margarson   89 a84
5 b m Gulch (USA) - Depaze (USA)
8^{10sd} 12^{10sd} 9^{10gf} 9^{10s} 8^{8sd} 2^{10s} **0-1-6**
£6,000

Star Ovation (Ire) H Alexander   35
7 ch g Fourstars Allstar (USA) - Standing Ovation
14^{7gf} **0-0-1**

Star Pupil A M Balding   84

Star 3 ch g Selkirk (USA) - Lochangel
4⁷ᵍˢ 2⁶ˢ 7⁶ˢ 14⁸ᵍᶠ 5⁸ᵍᶠ 5⁷ᵍˢ 5⁷ˢ 4⁷ᵍˢ
1⁷ᵍ **1-2-9 £9,648**

Star Sensation (Ire) *P W Harris* 89
4 b/br f Sri Pekan (USA) - Dancing Sensation (USA)
6⁸ᵍ 5⁸ᵍᶠ 6⁸ᵍᶠ 13⁸ᵍ 10⁷ᵍ 4⁸ᵍˢ 9⁸ᵍ 11⁷ᵍ
0-0-8 £1,391

Star Seventeen *Mrs N S Sharpe* a34
6 ch m Rock City - Westminster Waltz
5¹²ˢˢ 9¹²ˢᵈ 15¹⁴ˢᵈ **0-0-3**

Star Side (Ire) *C Tinkler* 63
2 b c Ashkalani (Ire) - Rachel Pringle (Ire)
6⁷ᵍ **0-0-1**

Star Welcome *W J Musson* a50
3 ch f Most Welcome - My Greatest Star
7⁷ˢᵈ 3⁸ˢᵈ **0-1-2 £209**

Star Wonder *B N Doran* a6
4 b f Syrtos - Galava (Can)
9⁷ˢˢ **0-0-1**

Starbeck (Ire) *P Howling* 89 a67
6 b m Spectrum (Ire) - Tide Of Fortune
9⁷ᵍˢ 7⁷ˢ 5⁸ᵍᶠ 4⁷ᵍᶠ 10⁸ᵍᶠ 12⁸ᵍ 5⁷ᵍ 4⁷ᵍˢ
8⁶ᵍᶠ 11⁷ᵍᶠ 4⁷ˢ 13⁷ᵍᶠ 8⁸ˢᵈ 9⁷ᵍᶠ 8⁷ˢ **0-0-15**
£3,638

Starbright *Miss S E Hall*
3 b g Polar Falcon (USA) - Treasure Hunt
12⁹ᵍ **0-0-1**

Starchy *M Johnston* 79
2 b f Cadeaux Genereux - Sahara Star
1⁶ʰʸ **1-0-1 £6,175**

Starcross Venture *R A Fahey* a42
3 b f Orpen (USA) - Maculatus (USA)
8⁶ˢᵈ 8⁶ˢᵈ **0-0-2**

Starduster *B R Millman* 70
2 gr f Paris House - To The Stars (Ire)
9⁵ᵍᶠ 2⁵ᵍ 10⁵ᶠ 2⁵ᵍᶠ 2⁵ᵍ 2⁵ᵍˢ **0-4-6**
£7,681

Stargem *J Pearce* 66 a66
3 b f Compton Place - Holy Smoke
2⁶ᵍᶠ 2⁶ˢᵈ 9⁶ᵍᶠ 2⁶ˢ 2⁶ᵍ **0-4-5 £5,182**

Starjestic *M S Saunders*
3 b f Bijou D'Inde - Risalah
13¹⁰ˢ **0-0-1**

Starlight River (Ire) *J Parkes* 63 a43
2 b f Spectrum (Ire) - Prosaic Star (Ire)
8⁵ᵍ 7⁶ᵍ 3⁵ᵍˢ 9⁵ᵍᶠ 4⁷ᵍᶠ 8⁸ˢᵈ **0-2-6 £709**

Starmix *P F I Cole* 67 a42
3 br g Linamix (Fr) - Danlu (USA)
9¹²ˢᵈ 9¹⁰ˢ 4⁸ᵍ 11¹²ᵍˢ 7⁸ᵍᶠ 8¹⁰ᵍᶠ **0-0-6**
£429

Starry Lodge (Ire) *L M Cumani* 105
4 b c Grand Lodge (USA) - Stara
1¹²ᵍ 3¹²ᵍ 5¹²ᵍ 5¹²ᵍᶠ **1-1-4 £39,680**

Starry Mary *R J Price* 63
6 b m Deploy - Darling Splodge
2¹²ᵍˢ 2¹⁶ᵍˢ 16¹⁴ˢ 5¹⁶ᵍᶠ 10¹⁰ᵍ **0-2-5**
£1,911

Stars At Midnight *J M Bradley* 38 a8
4 b f Magic Ring (Ire) - Boughtbyphone
16¹⁰ᶠ 14⁸ᵍˢ 6⁷ᵍ 11⁷ˢᵈ **0-0-4**

Start Of Authority *J Gallagher* 48
3 ch g Muhtarram (USA) - Heiden's Delight (USA)
15¹⁰ᵍᶠ 5⁸ʰʸ 9⁸ᵍᶠ **0-0-3**

Startled *J Jay*
5 ch m Zilzal (USA) - Zelda (USA)
11⁷ˢᵈ **0-0-1**

State City (USA) *Saeed Bin Suroor* 100 a87
5 ch h Carson City (USA) - Wajna (USA)
7⁶ᶠᵗ 4⁷ᵍ **0-0-2 £728**

State Dilemma (Ire) *B W Hills* 97
3 b c Green Desert (USA) - Nuriva (USA)
5⁸ᵍ 1⁷ᵍˢ 12⁸ᶠ 8⁸ᵍˢ 14⁸ˢ 4⁸ᵍᶠ 7⁸ᵍ **1-0-7**
£20,547

State Of Balance *K Bell* a67
6 ch m Mizoram (USA) - Equilibrium
8¹⁰ˢᵈ 4⁹ˢᵈ 1¹⁰ˢᵈ 6⁸ˢᵈ 8¹²ˢᵈ **1-0-5 £3,740**

Stateroom (USA) *J A R Toller* 76 a76
6 ch g Affirmed (USA) - Sleet (USA)
5¹⁰ˢᵈ 3¹⁰ᵍᶠ 11⁹ᵍᶠ **0-0-3 £1,282**

Statoyork *D Shaw* a38
11 b g Statoblest - Ultimate Dream
4⁵ˢˢ 11⁶ˢˢ **0-0-2**

Stavros (Ire) *J S Wainwright* 40
4 b g General Monash (USA) - Rivers Rainbow
9⁶ᵍˢ 13⁵ᵍ 5⁵ʰʸ 19⁵ᵍᶠ **0-0-4**

Steal The Thunder *A Berry* 50
2 br g Timeless Times (USA) - Lavernock Lady
8⁵ᵍᶠ 5⁵ᵍ 5⁶ᵍ 8⁵ᵍᶠ 12⁵ᵍ 7⁵ᵍˢ 5⁵ᵍˢ 6⁷ˢ
0-0-8 £518

Stealing Beauty (Ire) *L M Cumani* 79
4 b f Sadler's Wells (USA) - Imitation
4¹²ᵍᶠ 7¹²ᵍᶠ 5¹²ᵍ **0-0-3 £724**

Stedfast McStaunch (Ire) *B J Meehan* 76
2 gr g Desert Style (Ire) - Aneydia (Ire)
4⁵ʰʸ 2⁶ˢ 3⁶ᶠ 1⁷ᶠ **1-2-4 £6,124**

Steel Blue *R M Whitaker* 99
4 b g Atraf - Something Blue
1⁶ᵍ 1⁷⁶ᵍˢ 25⁶ᵍ 1⁶ᵍᶠ 2⁶ᵍˢ 5⁶ᵍᶠ 3⁵ˢ **2-2-7**
£26,239

Steely Dan *J R Best* 71 a89
5 b g Danzig Connection (USA) - No Comebacks
9⁶ˢᵈ 9⁷ˢᵈ 12⁷ˢᵈ 2⁸ˢᵈ 2¹⁰ˢᵈ 1⁷ˢᵈ 3⁸ˢᵈ 1¹⁰ˢᵈ
1¹⁰ˢᵈ 2¹²ˢᵈ 1¹²ˢᵈ 1⁸ˢᵈ 6¹¹ᵍᶠ 10⁸ᵍˢ 4⁸ᶠ 10⁸ᵍᶠ
9⁷ᵍᶠ **5-4-17 £19,702**

Steenberg (Ire) *M H Tompkins* 117
5 ch g Flying Spur (Aus) - Kip's Sister
2⁷ʸˢ 1⁶ᵍ 2⁶ᵍˢ 9⁶ᶠ 18⁶ᵍˢ 12⁶ᵍᶠ **1-2-6**
£40,095

Stella Marais (Ire) *P R Chamings* 34
3 b f Second Empire (Ire) - Karakapa (Fr)
6⁸ᶠ **0-0-1**

Stellite *J S Goldie* 51
4 ch g Pivotal - Donation
7¹⁰ʰʸ 1⁷ᵍ 7⁸ˢ 10⁷ᵍˢ 7⁷ˢ 2⁶ˢ **1-1-6**
£2,046

Stepastray *R E Barr* 48
7 gr g Alhijaz - Wandering Stranger
5¹⁰ᶠ 13⁹ᶠ 9¹²ᵍᶠ 7¹⁰ᵍᶠ 5⁹ᵍᶠ 9¹²ᵍᶠ 11⁸ᵍˢ
5⁹ᵍ 7⁹ᶠ **0-0-9**

Stephanie's Mind *G A Huffer* 78
2 b f Mind Games - Adorable Cherub (USA)
8⁵ᵍᶠ 3⁶ᵍᶠ 4⁶ᵍᶠ 4⁵ᵍᶠ 8⁵ᵍˢ **0-1-5 £1,542**

Stephano *B W Hills* 79
3 ch g Efisio - Polo
7⁷ᵍ 5⁸ᵍ 10⁸ʰʸ 1¹⁰ᵍᶠ 1¹¹ᵍ 2¹⁰ᵍᶠ 13¹⁰ᵍ
2-1-7 £10,952

Steppenwolf *W De Best-Turner* 34 a48
3 gr g Sesaro (USA) - Lozzie
6⁸ˢᵈ 7¹⁰ˢᵈ 7¹⁰ˢᵈ 13¹²ᵍᶠ 7¹⁰ˢ 12¹⁰ᵍᶠ 8¹⁰ˢᵈ
9⁸ᵍ 5¹⁴ᵍᶠ 6¹⁶ᶠ **0-0-10**

Sterling Guarantee (USA) *N Wilson* a59
6 b g Silver Hawk (USA) - Sterling Pound (USA)

2[10sd] 4[12sd] 7[12sd] 4[12sd] **0-1-4 £754**

Sterling Supporter *D W Thompson*
2 b f Josr Algarhoud (Ire) - Riyoom (USA)
12[6f] **0-0-1**

Stetchworth Prince *D R Loder*   98
2 b c Cadeaux Genereux - Elfin Laughter
16[gf] 4[6gf] 6[6s] **1-0-3 £12,359**

Steve's Champ (Chi) *Rune Haugen*   110
4 br c Foxhound (USA) - Emigracion (Chi)
10[6ft] 6[6g] 2[6g] 16[gs] 8[5g] 6[7g] 6[6g] 1[5s] 16[gf]
2[5g] **3-1-10 £56,505**

Stevedore (Ire) *B R Millman*   80 a65
3 ch c Docksider (USA) - La Belle Katherine (USA)
14[8gf] 7[8gs] 7[7gf] 4[8sd] 7[7g] 5[8gf] 1[7gs] 5[8gs]
13[7gs] 5[7g] 6[7sd] **2-0-11 £9,233**

Stevmarie Star *J A Glover*   42
2 b f Muhtarram (USA) - Cabaret Artiste
9[6hy] 6[7gs] 12[6sd] **0-0-3**

Stiletto Lady (Ire) *C N Kellett*   24 a61
3 b f Daggers Drawn (USA) - Nordic Pride
4[8sd] 14[8gf] 12[8g] 11[9g] **0-0-4 £261**

Sting Like A Bee (Ire) *J S Goldie*   59 a64
5 b g Ali-Royal (Ire) - Hidden Agenda (Fr)
1[9sd] 7[8sd] 2[11ss] 4[8sw] 4[10g] 6[9g] 6[10gf] 1[9g]
5[11g] **2-2-9 £9,178**

Stocking Island *B Hanbury*   76
3 ch f Desert King (Ire) - Rawya (USA)
13[7g] 2[10gs] 3[12gf] 8[10gf] 7[14g] 3[12s] PU[12sd]
0-2-7 £2,967

Stoic Leader (Ire) *R F Fisher*   88 a74
4 b g Danehill Dancer (Ire) - Starlust
4[5sw] 8[7ss] 1[7s] 1[7sd] 4[6gs] 13[7gs] 1[8g] 1[7g]
1[6gs] 9[7g] 18[8gf] 2[8g] 4[8g] 2[7g] 6[7g] 5[10g] 2[8g] 5[8gf] **5-5-
24 £30,531**

Stokesies Wish *J L Spearing*   70
4 ch f Fumo Di Londra (Ire) - Jess Rebec
12[5gs] 11[6gs] 15[6g] 2[6g] 12[6g] 5[6gf] 4[6gf]
8[6gf] 6[6gf] 3[6gf] 3[6gs] 11[7s] 7[5gf] 1[6gs] 5[6s] **1-2-15
£6,786**

Stolen *W R Muir*   52 a36
2 b c Groom Dancer (USA) - Jezyah (USA)
12[7gs] 12[8gf] 9[9sd] 8[8s] **0-0-4**

Stolen Hours (USA) *J Akehurst*   74
4 b/br c Silver Deputy (Can) - Fasta (USA)
18[12s] 16[14s] 8[12gf] 9[10gf] 2[13gf] 2[12gf] 3[12gs]
1[12gf] 3[12s] 7[10g] **1-3-10 £10,357**

Stolen Song *M J Ryan*   62 a65
4 b g Sheikh Albadou - Sparky's Song
4[10sd] 1[16sd] 6[12ss] 16[16g] 11[14g] 6[10gf] 3[12gf]
2[12gf] 6[12gs] **1-2-9 £4,605**

Stone Crest (Ire) *T H Caldwell*   15
6 b m Bigstone (Ire) - Hillcrest (Ire)
11[7gf] 12[8sd] 14[8gs] **0-0-3**

Stoneacre *D Nicholls*
4 ch f Gothenberg (Ire) - Musical Star
11[6g] **0-0-1**

Stonor Lady (USA) *P W D'Arcy*   11 a48
3 b/br f French Deputy (USA) - Blush With Love (USA)
10[8sd] 11[7sd] 10[7sd] 18[ss] 8[10gs] 9[8gf] **1-0-6
£2,583**

Stoop To Conquer *J L Dunlop*   84
4 b g Polar Falcon (USA) - Princess Genista
8[14s] 10[16gf] 11[7gf] 4[18gf] 1[14gs] 9[16gf] 1[16s]
3-0-7 £19,361

Stop The Nonsense (Ire) *E J O'Neill*   37 a64
3 b g Orpen (USA) - Skip The Nonsense (Ire)
5[8sd] 14[10g] 18[8g] 8[7gf] **0-0-4**

Stopwatch (Ire) *Mrs L C Jewell*   a31
9 b g Lead On Time (USA) - Rose Bonbon (Fr)
11[10sd] 9[12sd] 5[16sd] 13[16gs] **0-0-4**

Storm Chase (USA) *A P Jarvis*   34 a21
2 b/br g Awad (USA) - Night Duja (USA)
12[6sd] 7[5gf] **0-0-2**

Storm Clear (Ire) *D J Wintle*   a45
5 b h Mujadil (USA) - Escape Path
10[10sd] **0-0-1**

Storm Clouds *T D Easterby*   35
3 gr g Cloudings (Ire) - Khalsheva
9[7g] 13[10gf] **0-0-2**

Storm Fury (USA) *P W Chapple-Hyam*   65
2 b g Storm Creek (USA) - Danseuse Du Nord (Ire)
13[7gs] 3[6g] 7[7g] 9[6gs] 10[6gf] 11[7gf] **0-0-6
£838**

Storm Shower (Ire) *Mrs N Macauley*   a44
6 b g Catrail (USA) - Crimson Shower
4[7sd] **0-0-1**

Storm Silk (Can) *Saeed Bin Suroor*   97
2 b/br c Stormin Fever (USA) - Carpenter's Lace (USA)
4[6g] 1[7gf] **1-0-2 £7,606**

Stormont (Ire) *H J Collingridge*   99 a81
4 gr c Marju (Ire) - Legal Steps (Ire)
4[6ft] 10[7f] 7[6gf] 12[5gf] 7[5gs] 8[7g] 26[6gf]
0-0-7 £2,793

Stormville (Ire) *M Brittain*   61
7 b g Catrail (USA) - Haut Volee
13[6gs] 11[7g] 2[7gs] 9[7s] 13[7g] **0-1-5 £1,248**

Stormy Day *Mrs A J Perrett*   56 a75
4 b f Rainbow Quest (USA) - Broken Peace (USA)
6[12f] 1[12sd] 5[12sd] **1-0-3 £3,571**

Stormy Nature (Ire) *W R Swinburn*   79 a82
3 b/br f Mujadil (USA) - Ossana (USA)
3[6gs] 9[6s] 10[6gf] 8[6gs] 11[6gs] 1[7sd] 2[7sd] **1-2-7
£6,494**

Story Of One (Ire) *N P Littmoden*   59 a59
2 b g Desert Story (Ire) - One O One (Ire)
2[5gs] 9[5hy] 1[5sd] 3[6f] 5[6f] 5[5g] **1-1-6
£3,767**

Storyville *D R Loder*   43
2 br g Lujain (USA) - Slow Jazz (USA)
13[6gf] **0-0-1**

Straffan (Ire) *D Nicholls*   60 a50
2 b/br f Shinko Forest (Ire) - Katherine Gorge (USA)
6[5gs] 3[5gs] 3[5sd] 2[6gf] 5[5gf] 4[6f] 1[5f] 2[5gf]
2[5gf] 12[5g] **1-5-10 £6,554**

Strangely Brown (Ire) *S C Williams*   82 a32
3 b g Second Empire (Ire) - Damerela (Ire)
7[9sw] 8[6g] 3[10s] 9[10gf] 14[12sd] 2[16gs] 1[16gf]
1[16gf] 1[17s] 3[16gf] 5[14g] 4[17s] **3-2-12 £18,332**

Strategy *P R Webber*   82
4 br f Machiavellian (USA) - Island Story
12[8gf] 6[10gf] 8[10gf] **0-0-3**

Strathclyde (Ire) *A M Hales*   59 a19
5 b g Petong - It's Academic
10[5sd] 17[5gf] 12[6gf] 7[5gs] **0-0-4**

Strathspey *P J McBride*   61 a74
5 ch m Dancing Spree (USA) - Diebiedale
5[12sd] 5[10s] 4[8s] **0-0-3**

Strathtay *A Berry*   66
2 ch f Pivotal - Cressida
3[5gf] 8[6gf] 5[6gf] 6[6s] 8[7gf] 13[7f] 2[6g] 1[7s] 4[8s]
1-3-9 £8,936

Stravmour *R Hollinshead*   a57
8 ch h Seymour Hicks (Fr) - La Stravaganza

7¹²sd 5¹²ss 3¹²sw 3¹⁶sw 1¹⁴ss 1¹⁶sd 1¹²sd
3-1-7 £4,997

Stravonian *D A Nolan*   44
4 b g Luso - In The Evening (Ire)
7¹²gf 7⁹gs 5¹⁰gs 6¹²s **0-0-4**

Straw Bear (USA) *Sir Mark Prescott*   106
3 ch c Diesis - Highland Ceilidh (Ire)
2⁸gf 3⁹gs 5⁸gs 1¹⁰s 1¹¹hy 3¹⁰gf **2-3-6**
£23,087

Strawberry Dale (Ire) *J D Bethell*   90
2 b f Bering - Manchaca (Fr)
1⁵g 1⁷gf 9⁷gf 9⁷g **2-0-4 £9,223**

Strawberry Fair *Saeed Bin Suroor*   71
3 b f Kingmambo (USA) - Storm Song (USA)
4⁸gf 7⁸gf 10⁸gf 6⁷f **0-0-4 £287**

Strawberry Patch (Ire) *Miss L A Perratt*   65
5 b g Woodborough (USA) - Okino (USA)
11⁶g 10⁵gs 5⁵g 11⁵gf 2⁶gf 1⁵g 7⁵s 6⁶gf
2⁵gs 13⁵f 17⁶gs **1-2-11 £10,386**

Stream Of Gold (Ire) *Sir Michael Stoute*   106
3 b c Rainbow Quest (USA) - River Dancer
5¹⁰gf 1⁸gs 4⁸g 1⁷s **2-0-4 £22,454**

Street Ballad (Ire) *Mrs J R Ramsden*   62
2 b f Fasliyev (USA) - Nancy Maloney (Ire)
4⁶gf 7⁷gs 3⁶gf 7⁸f 11⁷g 7⁷s **0-1-6 £852**

Street Cred *A M Balding*   79
2 ch g Bold Edge - Trump Street
1⁶gf 8⁶g 9⁷g 12⁶gs **1-0-4 £5,421**

Street Dancer (Ire) *J J Quinn*   52
2 b g Imperial Ballet (Ire) - Life On The Street
15⁶s 11⁷f 8⁶g 5⁶hy **0-0-4**

Street Games *D G Bridgwater*   20 a30
5 b g Mind Games - Pusey Street
5¹⁰gs 6¹⁰sd **0-0-2**

Street Life (Ire) *W J Musson*   83 a76
6 ch g Dolphin Street (Fr) - Wolf Cleugh (Ire)
2¹¹sd 5⁹sd 2¹⁰g 3¹⁰gs 3¹⁰s 4¹⁰gf 3¹⁰gf
5¹⁰gf 4¹²gs 4¹⁰gf 4¹⁰g 1¹⁰s **1-7-12 £13,397**

Strensall *R E Barr*   86
7 b g Beveled (USA) - Payvashooz
17⁵gf 2⁵gf 7⁵gf 7⁵gf 3⁵gs 4⁵gs 7⁵gs 5⁵gf
11⁵g 5⁵g 5⁵s 2⁵gf 8⁵g 9⁵gf 11⁵s 10⁵gs **0-3-16**
£8,130

Stretford End (Ire) *B Smart*   86
2 b g Zieten - Creese (USA)
F⁶g 2⁶gs 4⁶gs **0-1-3 £1,435**

Stretton (Ire) *J D Bethell*   89
6 br g Doyoun - Awayil (USA)
7¹⁰gs 6⁸gf 9¹⁰gf 9⁹gf 3¹⁰g 4¹⁰gs 4¹⁰gf
8¹⁰gf 1¹⁰gs 7¹⁰g 3¹⁰s **1-2-11 £15,689**

Strider *Sir Michael Stoute*   84 a80
3 ch c Pivotal - Sahara Belle (USA)
2⁹sd 4¹⁰gf 4¹⁰s 1⁹gs 14¹⁰gs **1-1-5**
£8,804

Strides Of Fire (Ire) *John A Codd*   18
3 b c General Monash (USA) - Lagrion (USA)
16⁶s 10⁶s **0-0-2**

Strike *J H M Gosden*   88
3 b c Silver Hawk (USA) - Shemozzle (Ire)
2¹¹g 6¹²s 1¹²gf 5¹⁶f **1-1-4 £8,856**

Strike Gold *S Kirk*   74
2 b c Mujahid (USA) - Gracious Beauty (USA)
13⁷gs 3⁷gf 7⁷hy **0-1-3 £557**

Strike Lucky *P J Makin*   50 a56
4 ch g Millkom - Lucky Flinders
1⁶sd 15⁶sd 8⁶g 12⁶sd **1-0-4 £1,438**

Striking Ambition *R Charlton*   115 a94
4 b c Makbul - Lady Roxanne
9⁵sd 13⁶g 3⁶hy 1⁶ys 2⁶vs **1-2-5 £43,207**

Striking Endeavour *N P Littmoden*   79
2 b c Makbul - Nineteenth Of May
1⁵s 6⁶f 20⁶gf 14⁶s **1-0-4 £3,454**

Strong Hand *M W Easterby*   81 a89
4 b f First Trump - Better Still (Ire)
6⁸g 3⁸s 9⁷gs 9⁸s 12⁸gs 6¹⁰s 2⁸s 4⁷s 4⁹sd
0-3-9 £5,035

Stunning Magic *Mrs Barbara Waring*   a31
4 b g Magic Ring (Ire) - Absolutelystunning
8¹⁰sd 9¹²sd **0-0-2**

Stunning Spark *T D McCarthy*   18
2 b f Fraam - Lady Jo
9⁸gf 12⁸g **0-0-2**

Stylish Dancer *M Blanshard*   48 a38
3 b f Muhtarram (USA) - Iltimas (USA)
11¹⁰gf 5¹¹gf 7¹²gf 6¹⁰sd 15¹²sd 9¹⁰hy **0-0-6**

Stylish Prince *J G M O'Shea*
4 b g Polar Prince (Ire) - Simply Style
8¹¹sd **0-0-1**

Stylish Sunrise (Ire) *I A Wood*   51 a52
3 b g Desert Style (Ire) - Anita At Dawn (Ire)
8⁸sd 4¹⁰gf 5¹¹gf 7¹³gf 3¹⁰sd 14¹⁰gs
5¹⁶sd **0-2-8 £798**

Sualda (Ire) *R A Fahey*   85
5 b g Idris (Ire) - Winning Heart
5¹²gf 2¹²gf 1¹²gf 2¹³g 3¹¹gf 1¹²gf 4¹⁶gf
1¹²g 10¹⁴gf **3-3-9 £34,129**

Suave Quartet (USA) *G A Butler*   12
3 b g Slew City Slew (USA) - Leallah M (USA)
5⁸f **0-0-1**

Subadar Major *D McCain*
7 b g Komaite (USA) - Rather Gorgeous
9¹⁶gs 15¹⁶g 18¹⁶f **0-0-3**

Sublimity (Fr) *Sir Michael Stoute*   115
4 b g Selkirk (USA) - Fig Tree Drive (USA)
1⁸g 7⁸gs 4¹⁰gf 11⁹g 3⁸gf 11⁸gs **1-0-6**
£24,520

Submissive *B W Hills*   70 a70
3 ch c Young Em - Sublime
8⁷gs 1⁸sd 10⁸gs **1-0-3 £3,367**

Subpoena *M A Jarvis*   91
2 b c Diktat - Trefoil
1⁷g 7⁷g **1-0-2 £5,209**

Subtle Affair (Ire) *M G Quinlan*   65
2 b f Barathea (Ire) - Uncertain Affair (Ire)
7⁸g 3¹⁰s **0-1-2 £533**

Subtle Breeze (USA) *J H M Gosden*   69 a52
3 ch f Storm Cat (USA) - Morning Devotion (USA)
3⁷gf 7⁸gs 6⁸sd **0-1-3 £620**

Subtle Move (USA) *D Shaw*   a2
4 b f Known Fact (USA) - Substance (USA)
14⁵sd **0-0-1**

Subyan Dreams *P W Chapple-Hyam*   94
2 b f Spectrum (Ire) - Subya
5⁶g 3⁶g 3⁷gs 9⁷gs 5⁸gs **0-1-5 £3,398**

Succession *Sir Mark Prescott*   86
2 ch f Groom Dancer (USA) - Pitcroy
9⁶g 10⁶gs 10⁷s 6⁸gs 1⁸g 17⁹f 1⁸gf 3⁸g
3-1-8 £19,015

Successor *M D I Usher*   62
4 ch g Entrepreneur - Petralona (USA)
11⁸gs 6⁸gf **0-0-2**

Suchwot (Ire) *F Jordan* 62
3 b g Intikhab (USA) - Fairy Water
10⁸ᵍ 6¹¹ᵍˢ 2⁸ʰʸ 9⁸ʰʸ 19¹²ᵍ **0-1-5**
£1,295

Sudden *J J Bridger*
9 ch g Positive Statement (USA) - Tala 'a Ranee
6¹⁰ˢᵈ **0-0-1**

Sudden Dismissal (Ire) *G A Butler* 93
2 b c Inchinor - Suddenly
4⁶ᵍˢ 1⁶ᵍˢ 7⁶ᵍᶠ 1⁷ᵍˢ 7⁷ˢ **2-0-5 £9,884**

Sudden Flight (Ire) *P D Evans* 76 a79
7 b g In The Wings - Ma Petite Cherie (USA)
9¹²ˢᵈ 13¹²ˢᵈ 8¹²ˢᵈ 3¹²ˢᵈ 11¹²ᵍˢ 11¹⁰ˢ
4¹⁶ᵍᶠ 3¹⁴ᵍ 1¹⁶ᵍ 6¹⁶ᵍ 5¹²ᵍᶠ 8¹⁴ᵍᶠ 3¹²ˢ 9¹²ʰʸ
1-2-14 £8,017

Sudden Impulse *A Charlton* 64 a43
3 b f Silver Patriarch (Ire) - Sanshang (Fr)
6⁸ᶠ 7¹⁰ˢᵈ **0-0-2**

Sudra *D J Daly* a63
7 b g Indian Ridge - Bunting
3⁸ˢᵈ 3⁸ˢᵈ 4⁷ˢᵈ 4⁷ˢˢ 3⁷ˢᵈ 1⁷ˢᵈ 4⁸ˢˢ 3⁸ˢᵈ
9⁸ˢʷ **1-4-9 £2,899**

Suerte *R M H Cowell* 38 a44
4 b f Halling (USA) - Play With Me (Ire)
10⁹ˢᵈ 13⁸ᵍ 12⁹ˢᵈ 8¹⁰ᵍᶠ 13⁸ˢᵈ **0-0-5**

Suez *M A Jarvis* 106
2 b f Green Desert (USA) - Repeat Warning
1⁶ᵍ 1⁶ᵍ 2⁶ᵍ **2-1-3 £71,236**

Sugar Cube Treat *M Mullineaux* 44 a10
8 b m Lugana Beach - Fair Eleanor
10⁶ˢᵈ 13⁶ˢʷ 14⁶ᵍˢ 5⁶ˢ 8⁶ˢ 9⁵ᵍᶠ 6⁵ᵍ
12⁸ᵍᶠ UR⁶ᵍ **0-0-9**

Sugar Snap *C Drew*
4 b f Sesaro (USA) - Cuddle Bunny (Ire)
11¹²ˢᵈ 14⁶ˢᵈ **0-0-2**

Suggestive *W J Haggas* 115
6 b g Reprimand - Pleasuring
4⁸ᵍ 5⁶ᵍ 2⁷ᵍ 1⁷ᵍᶠ 4⁷ᵍˢ 10⁸ᵍ 2⁷ᵍ 2⁷ᵍ 6⁷ᵍᶠ
6⁷ᵍ 8⁷ᵍ **1-3-11 £61,444**

Sugitani (USA) *Saeed Bin Suroor* 50
2 b c Kingmambo (USA) - Lady Reiko (Ire)
8⁷ᵍ 16⁷ᵍ **0-0-2**

Suitcase Murphy (Ire) *Ms Deborah J Evans* 47 a21
3 b g Petardia - Noble Rocket
10⁶ˢᵈ 6⁵ᶠ 3⁶ᵍ 10⁶ᵍᶠ 15⁸ᵍˢ **0-1-5 £440**

Suivez Moi (Ire) *P W Chapple-Hyam* 45
2 ch c Daggers Drawn (USA) - Pamiers
12⁶ˢ **0-0-1**

Sujosise *J J Quinn* 32
3 b c Prince Sabo - Statuette
12⁶ᵍ 9⁵ᵍ 11⁶ᵍᶠ 13⁶ˢ **0-0-4**

Sukuma (Ire) *A M Balding* 46 a22
2 ch f Highest Honor (Fr) - Selva (Ire)
8⁶ᵍᶠ 7⁷ˢᵈ 11⁶ᵍᶠ **0-0-3**

Sulamani (Ire) *Saeed Bin Suroor* 127
5 b h Hernando (Fr) - Soul Dream (USA)
4¹⁰ᵍᶠ 2¹²ᵍᶠ 3¹²ᵍᶠ 1¹⁰ᵍ 1¹²ᵍ **2-2-5**
£778,410

Summer Bounty *F Jordan* 84
8 b g Lugana Beach - Tender Moment (Ire)
12¹¹ᵍˢ 1⁸ʰʸ 1¹⁰ᵍ 11¹⁰ᵍᶠ 3¹⁰ᵍᶠ 2¹⁰ˢ 10¹⁰ᵍ
5¹⁰ᵍ **2-2-8 £10,060**

Summer Charm *W Jarvis* 48 a9
2 b f Dansili - Regent's Folly (Ire)
11⁶ᵍˢ 12⁷ᵍˢ 11⁶ᵍᶠ 11⁷ˢᵈ **0-0-4**

Summer Cherry (USA) *Jamie Poulton* 47

Summer Squall (USA) - Cherryrob (USA)
7 b g Summer Squall (USA) - Cherryrob (USA)
15¹²ᵍᶠ 2¹²ᵍᶠ 5¹²ᵍᶠ 7¹²ᵍᶠ 7¹²ᶠ 13¹⁰ᵍᶠ **0-1-6**
£872

Summer Joy *D K Ivory*
3 b f Myfontaine - Marycee (Ire)
9⁸ˢ 14⁷ᵍᶠ **0-0-2**

Summer Recluse (USA) *J M Bradley* a84
5 gr g Cozzene (USA) - Summer Retreat (USA)
8⁸ˢᵈ 7⁷ˢᵈ 5⁸ˢᵈ 4⁸ˢᵈ **0-0-4 £398**

Summer Serenade *L M Cumani* 77
3 b f Sadler's Wells (USA) - Summer Sonnet
2¹⁰ᵍᶠ 3¹⁰ᵍᶠ **0-2-2 £2,216**

Summer Shades *W M Brisbourne* 79 a60
6 b m Green Desert (USA) - Sally Slade
6⁸ˢᵈ 5⁸ᵍᶠ 2⁸ᵍᶠ 4⁸ᶠ 4⁸ᶠ 3⁸ᵍᶠ 5⁹ˢ 6⁸ᵍᶠ 1⁸ᵍᶠ
2⁸ᵍᶠ 5⁸ᵍ 2⁸ᵍᶠ 11⁹ˢᵈ 11⁹ˢᵈ **1-4-14 £12,994**

Summer Silks *R A Fahey* 57
2 ch f Bahamian Bounty - Sadler's Song
8⁵ᵍˢ 4⁷ᵍ 12⁷ᵍˢ 15⁷ᵍᶠ 17⁷ᵍ **0-0-5**

Summer Special *D W Barker* 54
4 b g Mind Games - Summerhill Special (Ire)
5⁶ᵍˢ 5¹⁰ʰʸ 3⁹ᵍ 12¹²ʰʸ 5¹²ᵍᶠ 11¹²ᵍᶠ 3⁸ᵍ
3⁸ᵍ 7⁸ᵍ 13⁷ᵍ 7⁸ᵍˢ 4⁸ˢ 13⁸ᶠ **0-3-13 £1,514**

Summer Stock (USA) *J A Supple* a46
6 b g Theatrical - Lake Placid (Ire)
11¹⁰ˢᵈ 7⁹ˢᵈ **0-0-2**

Summer Sunset (Ire) *D K Weld* 94
3 ch f Grand Lodge (USA) - Elegant Bloom (Ire)
5⁷ᵍʸ 5⁷ᵍᶠ 1⁸ᵍᶠ 10⁷ᵍ 7⁷ᵍʸ 9⁷ˢ **0-0-6**

Summer Wine *C F Wall* 38
5 b m Desert King (Ire) - Generous Lady
9¹⁰ˢ **0-0-1**

Summerise *C N Allen* 51 a48
3 b f Atraf - Summerhill Special (Ire)
7⁸ˢᵈ 6¹⁰ᵍˢ 3⁸ˢ 8¹⁰ˢ 6⁸ᵍ **0-1-5 £631**

Summitville *J G Given* 104
4 b f Grand Lodge (USA) - Tina Heights
3¹⁰ᵍˢ 2¹²ᵍᶠ 6¹²ᵍ 3¹⁴ᵍᶠ 6¹¹ᵍ 4¹²ᵍᶠ **0-1-6**
£27,042

Sumora (Ire) *G A Butler* 102 a82
2 b f Danehill (USA) - Rain Flower (Ire)
1⁵ˢᵈ 1⁵ᵍ 6⁵ᶠ 8⁵ˢ **2-0-4 £18,712**

Sun And Showers (Ire) *J H M Gosden* 54
2 b c Rainbow Quest (USA) - Las Flores (Ire)
9⁸ˢ **0-0-1**

Sun Bird (Ire) *R Allan* 94
6 ch g Prince Of Birds (USA) - Summer Fashion
5¹²ᵍˢ **0-0-1 £875**

Sun Hill *M Blanshard* 76 a86
4 b g Robellino (USA) - Manhattan Sunset (USA)
1¹⁴ˢᵈ 1¹⁶ˢʷ 1¹⁶ˢˢ 13¹⁸ᵍ 10¹⁵ˢ 5¹⁴ˢ 12¹⁴ᵍ
14¹²ʰʸ 12¹⁶ᵍˢ 13¹⁶ˢ 8¹⁷ˢᵈ **3-0-11 £11,387**

Sun Kissed (Jpn) *Saeed Bin Suroor* 94
2 ch c Sunday Silence (USA) - Flying Kiss (Ire)
1⁶ᵍᶠ 2⁸ᵍ 9⁸ˢ **1-1-3 £6,913**

Sun On The Sea (Ire) *B J Meehan* 63
4 ch f Bering - Shimmer (Fr)
6¹⁰ᵍˢ **0-0-1 £750**

Suncliff *Mrs A Duffield*
2 b g Most Welcome - Marjorie's Orchid
13⁹ˢᵈ **0-0-1**

Sundance (Ire) *H J Collingridge* 95 a90
2 ch c Namid - Titchwell Lass
1⁵ᵍˢ 2⁵ˢᵈ 1⁵ᵍˢ 6⁵ˢ 10⁶ᵍ **2-1-5 £12,235**

Sunday City (Jpn) *D R Loder* 77
3 ch c Sunday Silence (USA) - Diamond City (USA)

3¹²ᵍᶠ 3¹²ᵍᶠ 5¹⁰ᶠ 5¹⁴ᵍᶠ 2¹³ᶠ 13¹⁶ᵍᶠ **0-3-6**
£2,856

Sunday Symphony *Saeed Bin Suroor*　　89
2 br c Sunday Silence (USA) - Darrery
2⁸ˢ 1⁸ᶠ 1¹⁰ᵍ 5¹⁰ᵍˢ **2-1-4 £13,888**

Sundried Tomato *P W Hiatt*　　68 a81
5 b g Lugana Beach - Little Scarlett
10⁶ˢᵈ 6⁷ˢᵈ 4⁶ˢᵈ 6⁶ˢˢ 10⁶ˢʷ 9⁶ᵍ 8⁷ˢ
5⁶ˢ 10⁶ˢ 10⁶ᵍ **0-0-11 £628**

Sundrop (Jpn) *Saeed Bin Suroor*　　114
3 b f Sunday Silence (USA) - Oenothera (Ire)
2⁸ᵍ 6¹²ᵍ 1¹⁰ˢ **1-1-3 £93,655**

Sungio *B G Powell*　　40 a59
6 b g Halling (USA) - Time Or Never (Fr)
1¹⁶ˢᵈ 3¹³ˢᵈ 1¹²ˢʷ 2¹³ˢᵈ 3¹³ˢᵈ 5¹⁶ˢᵈ
8¹⁶ᵍˢ 1¹⁷ˢᵈ **3-3-9 £9,619**

Sunisa (Ire) *B W Hills*　　86 a73
3 b f Daggers Drawn (USA) - Winged Victory (Ire)
2⁸ˢᵈ 1⁸ˢᵈ 3¹⁰ᵍᶠ 8⁹ᵍᶠ 2⁹ᵍ 19¹⁰ᵍᶠ 5¹⁰ˢ **1-3-7**
£6,831

Sunley Sense *M R Channon*　　81
8 b g Komaite (USA) - Brown Velvet
3⁵ᵍᶠ 9⁵ᵍᶠ 10⁵ᵍ 12⁵ᵍˢ 6⁵ᵍᶠ **0-1-5 £1,075**

Sunny Glenn *Simon Earle*　　101
6 ch h Rock Hopper - La Ballerine
11¹²ᵍ 6¹²ᵍᶠ 7¹²ᵍᶠ 16¹¹ʰʸ **0-0-4**

Sunny Lady (Fr) *E A L Dunlop*　　82 a76
3 ch f Nashwan (USA) - Like The Sun (USA)
2¹¹ᵍˢ 2¹²ᵍᶠ 2¹²ᵍᶠ 2¹⁴ᵍ 1¹²ᶠ 4¹²ᵍ 4¹²ᵍᶠ
6¹²ˢᵈ **1-4-8 £9,972**

Sunny Nature *J H M Gosden*
2 b f Sadler's Wells (USA) - Bright Spells (USA)
19⁷ᵍˢ **0-0-1**

Sunny Times (Ire) *J W Payne*　　59
2 b f Raise A Grand (Ire) - Dragon Star
5⁶ᵍᶠ 7⁵ᵍᶠ 10⁶ᵍᶠ 5⁸ᵍᶠ 2⁸ᵍˢ 8⁸ˢ **0-1-6**
£428

Sunnyside Royale (Ire) *R Bastiman*　　29 a52
5 b g Ali-Royal (Ire) - Kuwah (Ire)
13¹⁴ᵍ 1¹⁴ˢᶠ 3¹¹ˢᵈ 8¹⁶ˢᵈ **1-0-4 £1,650**

Sunridge Fairy (Ire) *A J Lockwood*　　26 a16
5 b m Definite Article - Foxy Fairy (Ire)
14⁸ˢᵈ 6¹⁰ᵍᶠ **0-0-2**

Sunset Blues (Fr) *K O Cunningham-Brown*　　a41
4 ch g Green Tune (USA) - Sunset Reef
5⁸ˢʷ 10⁸ˢᵈ 10⁹ˢˢ 3⁸ˢᵈ 8⁸ˢᵈ **0-1-5 £207**

Sunset Dreamer (USA) *P Mitchell*　　38 a51
3 ch f Boundary (USA) - Quaff (USA)
6⁸ˢᵈ 11⁷ˢᵈ 11⁷ᵍˢ 14¹⁰ˢᵈ 13¹⁰ᵍᶠ 18⁸ᵍˢ
0-0-6

Sunset King (USA) *J C Fox*　　a21
4 b c King Of Kings (Ire) - Sunset River (USA)
12⁸ˢᵈ **0-0-1**

Sunset Mirage (USA) *E A L Dunlop*　　73
3 br f Swain (Ire) - Yafill (USA)
2¹⁰ᵍˢ 6¹¹ᵍᶠ 1⁹ᶠ 11⁸ᵍᶠ 8⁹ᵍᶠ 4¹⁰ᵍᶠ
2¹⁰ᶠ 3¹⁰ᵍˢ 2⁹ᵍˢ **1-3-10 £8,974**

Sunset Strip *M R Channon*　　75
2 b c Josr Algarhoud (Ire) - Shady Street (USA)
2⁶ᵍᶠ 2⁷ᵍˢ 3⁶ᵍᶠ 6⁶ʸˢ **0-3-4 £3,469**

Sunshine On Me *C F Wall*　　56 a58
3 ch f Kris - Degannwy
9⁹ᵍᶠ 5¹²ˢᵈ 9¹³ˢᵈ 12¹²ˢᵈ **0-0-4**

Sunstrach (Ire) *L M Cumani*　　112
6 b h Polar Falcon (USA) - Lorne Lady
3¹⁰ᵍˢ 4⁹ᵍ 3¹⁰ᵍˢ 3¹⁰ᵍˢ **0-2-4 £22,342**

Supamach (Ire) *P F I Cole*　　69 a66
3 b f Machiavellian (USA) - Supamova (USA)
3¹⁰ˢᵈ 4⁸ᵍᶠ 10⁸ᵍᶠ 16¹¹ᵍ 9⁸ˢ 9⁹ˢᵈ
0-1-7 £1,448

Super Boston *Miss L C Siddall*　　38
4 b g Saddlers' Hall (Ire) - Nasowas (Ire)
12⁸ᵍ 6¹⁰ˢ **0-0-2**

Super Canyon *J Pearce*　　28 a66
6 ch g Gulch (USA) - Marina Park
4⁶ˢʷ 2⁷ˢˢ 14⁷ˢᵈ 13⁷ᵍᶠ 19⁶ᵍᶠ 9⁷ˢᵈ **0-1-6**
£1,559

Super Dominion *R Hollinshead*　　51 a51
7 ch g Superpower - Smartie Lee
5⁹ˢᵈ 1⁸ᵍ 4⁹ˢᵈ 9⁷ˢᵈ 10⁸ˢᵈ 12⁸ˢᵈ 8⁸ᵍˢ
5⁸ˢᵈ 4⁸ᶠ 8⁸ˢᵈ **2-1-11 £4,746**

Super Fellow (Ire) *C N Kellett*　　56
10 b g Shy Groom (USA) - Killough
3¹⁶ᵍᶠ 11⁶ᵍˢ 1¹⁷ᵍˢ 5¹⁶ᶠ 5¹⁷ᵍᶠ **2-1-5**
£9,727

Super King *N Bycroft*　　67 a48
3 b g Kingsinger (Ire) - Super Sisters (Aus)
9⁸ᵍᶠ 12⁸ᵍᶠ 7⁸ˢᵈ 8⁷ᵍˢ 5¹⁰ᵍˢ 2¹⁰ᵍˢ 3¹⁰ˢ
19¹²ʰʸ 9¹⁰ᵍ **0-1-9 £1,709**

Super Song *P D Evans*　　60 a27
4 b g Desert Prince (Ire) - Highland Rhapsody (Ire)
12⁸ˢᵈ 9⁸ˢ 10⁸ˢˢ 10⁶ᵍᶠ 16⁶ᵍᶠ 13⁶ᵍᶠ 6⁷ᵍᶠ
22⁵ᵍ 19⁷ᵍᶠ 13⁷ʰʸ **0-0-10**

Superchief *Miss B Sanders*　　13 a73
9 b g Precocious - Rome Express
14⁷ˢᵈ 6⁷ˢᵈ 4⁶ˢᵈ 3⁷ˢᵈ 5⁷ˢ 5⁶ˢᵈ 2⁷ˢᵈ 5⁸ˢᵈ
10⁸ˢᵈ 11⁶ᵍᶠ 12⁷ˢᵈ 10⁷ˢᵈ **0-2-12 £1,493**

Superclean *A W Carroll*　　20 a38
4 ch f Environment Friend - Star Mover
9⁸ˢᵈ 10¹²ˢᵈ 6¹⁰ᵍˢ 9¹²ˢᵈ **0-0-4**

Superfling *R Hannon*　　56 a34
3 ch g Superpower - Jobiska
9⁷ᵍˢ 4⁶ᶠ 9⁶ᵍᶠ 12⁷ˢᵈ **0-0-4 £276**

Superpridetwo *P D Niven*　　a11
4 b g Superpower - Lindrake's Pride
9⁷ˢᵈ **0-0-1**

Superstitious (Ire) *B A McMahon*　　67
2 b c Bluebird (USA) - Stellar Empress (USA)
7⁶ᵍ 10⁶ᵍ 6⁷ᵍ 21⁶ᵍᶠ 18⁷ᵍˢ **0-0-5**

Supremacy *Sir Michael Stoute*　　109
5 ch g Vettori (Ire) - High Tern
10¹⁶ˢ 4¹²ᵍ 7¹⁶ᵍᶠ 4¹⁴ᵍˢ 9¹⁵ᵍᶠ 3¹⁶ᵍᶠ **0-0-6**
£5,533

Supreme Salutation *D K Ivory*　　90 a80
8 ch g Most Welcome - Cardinal Press
12⁷ˢᵈ 1⁸ˢᵈ 1⁸ʰʸ 1⁸ʸˢ 1⁸ˢᵈ 1¹⁰ᵍ
11⁸ᵍˢ 4⁸ᵍˢ 15¹⁰ᵍ 14⁸ᵍᶠ **4-0-11 £14,051**

Surdoue *P Howling*　　a70
4 b g Bishop Of Cashel - Chatter's Princess
8¹²ˢᵈ 2¹¹ˢᵈ 4¹²ˢᵈ 2¹²ˢᵈ 9⁹ˢʷ 11⁸ˢ 18⁸ᵍ
13¹²ˢᵈ 10⁹ˢᵈ **0-2-9 £1,653**

Sure Future *R M Stronge*　　33
8 b g Kylian (USA) - Lady Ever-So-Sure
3¹²ʰʸ **0-1-1 £219**

Surf The Net *R Hannon*　　88
3 b f Cape Cross (Ire) - On The Tide
3⁷ᵍ 15⁸ᵍᶠ 10⁷ᵍˢ 3⁷ᵍ 4⁸ᵍ 9⁸ᵍᶠ 19⁷ᵍˢ
11⁷ᵍˢ **0-0-8 £4,053**

Surface To Air *Mrs P N Dutfield*　　51 a56
3 b g Samraan (USA) - Travelling Lady
12¹⁰ˢᵈ 7¹⁰ᵍᶠ 10¹⁰ᶠ 7¹⁰ᵍᶠ 5¹⁶ˢᵈ **0-0-5**

Surreptitious *D R Loder*　　67
3 ch f Machiavellian (USA) - Nadma (USA)

1⁷ᵍ 3⁸ᵍˢ 8⁷ᵍˢ **1-1-3 £6,086**

Surrey Downs Girl *Mrs L Stubbs*
2 ch f Lake Coniston (Ire) - Kingston Girl
7⁵ˢᵈ **0-0-1**

Surwaki (USA) *C G Cox*   84
2 b c Miswaki (USA) - Quinella
3⁷ᵍᶠ 2⁷ᵍˢ 9⁷ᵍᶠ **0-2-3 £3,051**

Susiedil (Ire) *P W Harris*   51
3 b f Mujadil (USA) - Don't Take Me (Ire)
10⁸ᵍˢ 10⁸ˢ 6⁸ᵍᶠ 6⁸ᶠ 13⁷ᵍᶠ 15⁷ᶠ 7⁸ᵍ 12⁹ˢᵈ **0-0-8**

Suspicious Minds *J W Mullins*   50 a57
3 b f Anabaa (USA) - Paloma Bay (Ire)
7⁸ˢᵈ 14⁸ᵍ 11⁸ᵍᶠ 13¹⁰ᵍ **0-0-4**

Sussex Style (Ire) *R M Flower*   44 a52
3 b g Desert Style (Ire) - Anita's Love (Ire)
10⁶ˢᵈ 9⁸ˢᵈ 6⁶ˢᵈ 7⁶ˢᵈ 6⁵ᵍᶠ 15⁶ᵍᶠ 8⁶ᵍᶠ 5⁶ᶠ
0-0-8

Sustainable Style (Fr) *L A Dace*   31
3 gr f Formal Gold (Can) - Spectacular Face (USA)
8⁸ˢ 10¹⁰ˢ 8⁸ᵍ 16⁸ˢ **0-0-4**

Suturia *Noel T Chance*   a48
2 b f Cadeaux Genereux - Cream Tease
12⁷ˢᵈ **0-0-1**

Suvari *G C Bravery*   34 a48
3 b f Indian Ridge - Falconera (Ire)
6⁷ˢᵈ 13⁸ᵍᶠ **0-0-2**

Svenson *J S Wainwright*   43 a14
3 ch c Dancing Spree (USA) - Bella Bambola (Ire)
12⁶ˢᵈ 10⁷ˢᵈ 11¹⁰ᵍᶠ 11⁸ᵍᶠ 9⁸ᵍ 13⁸ᶠ 6⁶ᵍ
13⁶ᵍˢ **0-0-8**

Swagger Stick (USA) *J L Dunlop*   98
3 gr c Cozzene (USA) - Royal State (USA)
1¹⁰ᵍˢ 1¹²ᵍˢ 6¹²ᵍᶠ 8¹²ᵍ 10¹⁰ᵍ 6¹⁰ˢ 9¹⁰ᵍ
7¹⁰ᵍˢ 5¹²ˢ **2-0-9 £14,791**

Swahili Dancer (USA) *L M Cumani*   39
3 b c Swain (Ire) - Bella Ballerina
5¹⁰ᶠ **0-0-1**

Swain Davis *D J S Ffrench Davis*
4 b f Swain (Ire) - Exclusive Davis (USA)
13¹⁴ˢᵈ **0-0-1**

Swainson (USA) *P Mitchell*   86 a77
3 br c Swain (Ire) - Lyphard's Delta (USA)
3¹⁰ˢᵈ 4¹⁰ˢ 1¹⁰ˢᵈ 2¹⁰ᵍ 16¹⁰ᵍˢ 5¹²ᵍᶠ 14¹²ᵍ
1-2-7 £7,214

Swainsworld (USA) *T D Easterby*   75
3 b/br g Swain (Ire) - Highest Dream (Ire)
4⁷ᶠ 4⁷ᶠ 1⁸ᵍ 8⁸ᵍˢ **1-0-4 £6,531**

Swallow Falls (Ire) *D McCain*   62
2 b f Lake Coniston (Ire) - Common Cause
8⁵ᵍ 5⁷ᵍ 10⁶ʰʸ **0-0-3**

Swallow Senora (Ire) *P W Chapple-Hyam*   63
2 b f Entrepreneur - Sangra (USA)
11⁷ᵍˢ **0-0-1**

Swan Nebula (USA) *Saeed Bin Suroor*   89
2 b/br f Seeking The Gold (USA) - Bright Tiara (USA)
3⁶ᵍ 5⁷ᵍ 16⁶ᶠ 1⁷ᵍ 7⁶ˢ **2-1-5 £32,933**

Sweeney Todd (Ire) *J G Portman*   48
2 ch g Raise A Grand (Ire) - Optional
6⁷ᶠ 8⁷ᵍᶠ **0-0-2**

Sweep The Board (Ire) *A P Jarvis*   59
3 b g Fasliyev (USA) - Fun Board (Fr)
13⁹ᵍᶠ 6⁸ᵍˢ 11¹²ᵍᶠ **0-0-3**

Sweet At Heart (Ire) *P A Blockley*   31
3 b f Catrail (USA) - Lost Shadow
9⁸ˢᵈ 7¹²ᵍˢ 5¹²ᵍᶠ **0-0-3**

Sweet Az *S C Burrough*   39
4 b f Averti (Ire) - Yen Haven (USA)
13⁸ᵍᶠ 13⁶ᵍᶠ 8¹⁰ᵍ **0-0-3**

Sweet Cando (Ire) *Miss L A Perratt*   69
3 b/br f Royal Applause - Fizzygig
6⁶ᵍˢ 9⁷ᶠ 2⁵ᵍ 7⁵ᵍ 5⁵ˢ 8⁶ᵍᶠ 11⁵ᵍ 3⁵ˢ
10⁵ᵍˢ 8⁶ˢ 6⁵ˢ **0-2-11 £3,389**

Sweet Coincidence *I A Wood*   66
2 b f Mujahid (USA) - Sibilant
3⁶ᵍ 8⁶ᵍ **1-1-3 £4,311**

Sweet Coral (Fr) *B S Rothwell*   a41
4 b f Pennekamp (USA) - Sweet Contralto
7⁷ˢᵈ 4⁸ˢᵈ 8⁸ˢˢ 8⁶ˢʷ 7⁷ˢʷ **0-0-5**

Sweet Indulgence (Ire) *Dr J D Scargill*   87
3 ch c Inchinor - Silent Indulgence (USA)
7⁸ᵍᶠ 10⁸ᵍˢ 5⁸ᵍ 3⁸ᵍᶠ 4⁸ᵍˢ 7¹⁰ᵍˢ **0-0-6**
£2,230

Sweet Lorraine *T G Mills*   69
2 b f Dashing Blade - Royal Future (Ire)
2⁷ᵍᶠ 7⁷ᵍ **0-1-2 £1,664**

Sweet Marguerite *T D Easterby*   59
2 b f Diktat - Margaret's Gift
5⁶ᵍᶠ 4⁶ᵍᶠ 4⁵ᵍ 6⁶ᵍ 18⁷ᵍᶠ 8⁶ᵍˢ 7⁵ᵍᶠ 7⁶ᵍ
0-0-8 £587

Sweet Namibia (Ire) *J W Hills*   a62
2 ch f Namid - Almond Flower (Ire)
3⁶ˢᵈ 3⁶ˢᵈ **0-2-2 £1,010**

Sweet Pickle *D J Coakley*   72
3 b f Piccolo - Sweet Wilhelmina
2⁶ᶠ 4⁶ᶠ 6⁶ᵍᶠ 20⁶ᵍᶠ 8⁷ᵍˢ 6⁶ᵍᶠ **0-1-6**
£1,319

Sweet Potato (Ire) *T D Barron*   57
2 b f Monashee Mountain (USA) - Villafranca (Ire)
5⁶ᵍˢ 8⁷ᵍᶠ 8⁷ᵍ **0-0-3**

Sweet Reflection (Ire) *W J Musson*   9 a38
4 b f Victory Note (USA) - Shining Creek (Can)
9¹⁰ˢᵈ 9¹⁰ˢᵈ 5¹²ˢᵈ 13⁹ᵍᶠ **0-0-4**

Sweet Reply *I A Wood*   84 a49
3 ch f Opening Verse (USA) - Sweet Revival
16⁷ᵍ 5⁸ᵍᶠ 1⁷ᶠ 9⁷ᵍᶠ 10⁷ᵍˢ 5⁷ᵍˢ 13⁷ᵍ
10⁷ᵍˢ 11¹⁰ˢᵈ **1-0-9 £5,395**

Sweet Repose (USA) *E A L Dunlop*   46
3 b f Gulch (USA) - Bint Baladee
7⁸ᵍ 8¹⁰ᵍᶠ **0-0-2**

Sweet Royale *Miss L A Perratt*   75
2 b f Royal Applause - Sorara
2⁵ᵍᶠ 1⁵ᵍ 5⁵ᵍ 11⁵ᵍ **1-1-4 £4,387**

Sweet Sioux *P W Harris*   a14
2 ch f Halling (USA) - Mohican Girl
10⁷ˢᵈ **0-0-1**

Sweet Stream (Ity) *J E Hammond*   112
4 b f Shantou (USA) - Snug Dinner (Ire)
11¹⁰ˢ 3¹³ᵍˢ 1¹²ˢ 3¹²ˢ **1-2-4 £156,426**

Sweet Talking Girl *J M Bradley*   18
4 b f Bin Ajwaad (Ire) - Arabellajill
9⁶ᵍ 16⁶ˢ 18⁶ᵍᶠ 12⁶ᵍˢ 12⁵ᵍ **0-0-5**

Sweetest Revenge (Ire) *M D I Usher*   67 a74
3 ch f Daggers Drawn (USA) - Joza
11⁶ᵍᶠ 6⁶ˢᵈ 9⁵ᵍᶠ 7⁷ˢᵈ 3⁶ˢᵈ 7⁶ᵍᶠ **0-2-6**
£1,647

Sweetwater (Ger) *Mrs Stef Liddiard*   32 a68
4 b f Goofalik (USA) - Safrane (Ger)
3¹¹ˢ 7¹⁰ʰᵒ 6¹⁵ᵍˢ 6¹³ʰʸ 2¹²ᵍˢ 6¹²ˢᵈ 7¹²ˢ
8¹⁷ˢᵈ **0-2-8 £8,169**

Swell Lad *P F I Cole*   70
2 b g Sadler's Wells (USA) - Lydara (USA)

11^{7f} 15^{7gf} 6^{7g} 2^{8f} 9^{8gf} 13^{8s} **0-1-6**
£1,852

Swellmova *J R Boyle*   70
5 b g Sadler's Wells (USA) - Supamova (USA)
2^{10gf} 1^{12gf} 6^{12gs} **1-1-3 £4,568**

Swift Alchemist *Mrs H Sweeting*   61 a44
4 b f Fleetwood (Ire) - Pure Gold
8^{8gs} 10^{8g} 3^{7hy} 10^{8sd} 12^{7gf} 11^{10gf} 7^{12gs}
7^{12s} 1^{10gs} 18^{10gf} 14^{12gs} **1-1-11 £5,948**

Swift Dame (Ire) *R Hannon*   46 a54
2 b f Montjeu (Ire) - Velvet Appeal (Ire)
15^{7g} 5^{7sd} 12^{6gf} 7^{5s} **0-0-4**

Swift Oscar *J W Hills*   65 a65
2 b c Mark Of Esteem (Ire) - Surf Bird
6^{6gf} 7^{7g} 4^{6sd} **0-0-3 £400**

Swift Sailing (USA) *B W Hills*   73
3 b c Storm Cat (USA) - Saytarra (USA)
13^{8gs} 11^{7gf} 10^{7gf} 2^{10gf} 4^{10f} **0-1-5**
£2,093

Swift Sailor *M Johnston*   75
3 gr c Slip Anchor - New Wind (Ger)
3^{10gs} 1^{12s} **1-1-2 £5,416**

Swift Tango (Ire) *E A L Dunlop*   114 a93
4 b g Desert Prince (Ire) - Ballet Society (Fr)
1^{10sd} 11^{10ft} 2^{10gf} 3^{8g} 4^{10s} 1^{12g} 2^{12g} 3^{12f}
6^{12g} 4^{10gf} 3^{12g} 1^{13s} 2^{14gs} 3^{12gf} 2^{16gf} **3-7-15**
£95,337

Swinbrook (USA) *J A R Toller*   85
3 ch g Stravinsky (USA) - Dance Diane (USA)
9^{6g} 12^{6gf} 2^{6g} 1^{5gf} 14^{6g} 15^{6gs} **1-1-6**
£5,470

Swing West (USA) *A E Jones*   a19
10 b g Gone West (USA) - Danlu (USA)
4^{16ss} 9^{14sd} **0-0-2**

Swing Wing *P F I Cole*   115
5 b g In The Wings - Swift Spring (Fr)
5^{16gs} 16^{19gs} 1^{15g} 2^{16s} 4^{16g} 4^{13hy} **1-1-6**
£78,226

Swinton *M Brittain*   34
3 gr c Grey Desire - Portite Sophie
7^{7hy} 8^{8g} **0-0-2**

Swords *D J Daly*   72
2 b c Vettori (Ire) - Pomorie (Ire)
13^{8gf} 8^{8g} 5^{10g} 15^{8s} **0-0-4 £262**

Swords At Dawn (Ire) *J Barclay*
3 ch f Daggers Drawn (USA) - Caraway
10^{9gs} **0-0-1**

Sworn To Secrecy *S Kirk*   63 a40
3 ch f Prince Sabo - Polly's Teahouse
8^{6sd} 9^{6g} 7^{8sd} 10^{8gf} 11^{7gf} 6^{6gf} 11^{5gf}
11^{7g} 7^{7gf} **0-0-9**

Swynford Pleasure *J Hetherton*   56
8 b m Reprimand - Pleasuring
2^{12gf} 5^{12gf} 4^{12gf} 3^{12g} **0-2-4 £2,236**

Sybill *J W Unett*
4 b f Danzig Connection (USA) - Stock Pile
5^{7ss} 7^{7sd} **0-0-2**

Sydney Star *B W Hills*   86
3 b f Machiavellian (USA) - Sena Desert
1^{7gs} 9^{8gf} 7^{7gs} **1-0-3 £8,209**

Sydneyroughdiamond *M Mullineaux*   68
2 b g Whittingham (Ire) - November Song
9^{6s} 5^{7s} 8^{6g} 8^{6hy} 10^{6s} **0-0-5**

Sylva Royal (Ire) *C E Brittain*   42 a64
3 gr f Royal Applause - Trim Star
4^{7sd} 4^{6gf} 6^{6gf} 6^{6sw} 1^{7sd} 4^{8s} 3^{8sd} **1-1-7**

£2,676

Sylvan Twister *P Mitchell*   a39
5 br g First Trump - Storm Party (Ire)
5^{10sd} 5^{10sd} 5^{13sd} 3^{12sd} **0-1-4 £183**

Sylvaticus (Ire) *R Hannon*
3 b c Shinko Forest (Ire) - Calamity Kate (Ire)
8^{7gf} 17^{8sd} **0-0-2**

Systematic *M Johnston*   118
5 b h Rainbow Quest (USA) - Sensation
3^{12g} 2^{12g} 1^{13gs} 10^{12g} 5^{12f} 6^{12gf} **1-2-6**
£72,903

Szeroki Bor (Pol) *M Pitman*   a17
5 b g In Camera (Ire) - Szuana (Pol)
8^{16ss} **0-0-1**

T K O Gym *D Nicholls*   a38
5 b g Atraf - Pearl Pet
7^{7sd} 5^{8sw} **0-0-2**

Taakeed *M A Jarvis*   44
2 b c Mark Of Esteem (Ire) - Walimu (Ire)
13^{7gs} **0-0-1**

Taaqaah *M P Tregoning*   88
3 ch g Grand Lodge (USA) - Belle Ile (USA)
2^{7f} 2^{8gf} 10^{6gf} 2^{7gf} **0-3-4 £4,637**

Tabarka (Ger) *P A Blockley*   a32
3 b f Big Shuffle (USA) - Tirana (Ger)
5^{5ss} 11^{6ss} **0-0-2**

Tableau (USA) *B W Hills*   89
3 ch c Marquetry (USA) - Model Bride (USA)
3^{7g} 1^{8gf} 1^{8g} 9^{10s} 7^{8gs} **2-1-5 £13,680**

Taboor (Ire) *J W Payne*   65 a66
6 b g Mujadil (USA) - Christoph's Girl
9^{5sd} 8^{6sd} 8^{5sd} 5^{5sd} 11^{5sw} 7^{5gs} 5^{5gf} 12^{5hy}
2^{5g} 9^{5f} 6^{5g} 11^{5gf} 1^{5f} VOI^{5gf} 2^{5s} 9^{6g} 5^{5s}
2^{6sd} **1-3-18 £11,338**

Taca D'Oli (Fr) *E J O'Neill*
5 br m Octagonal (NZ) - Marie De Fontenoy (Fr)
13^{10sd} **0-0-1**

Tadawul (USA) *E F Vaughan*   70
3 b f Diesis - Barakat
10^{8g} 1^{9gf} 6^{8gs} 8^{10s} **1-0-4 £5,330**

Tafaahum (USA) *M Johnston*   21
3 b g Erhaab (USA) - Makadir (USA)
18^{8g} 6^{8gf} **0-0-2 £222**

Taffrail *D Burchell*   90
6 b g Slip Anchor - Tizona
5^{14g} 7^{12gf} **0-0-2 £750**

Tag Team (Ire) *A M Balding*   81 a83
3 ch g Tagula (Ire) - Okay Baby (Ire)
1^{5sd} 5^{3sd} 14^{6gs} 5^{5gf} 1^{6f} 3^{6gf} 2^{6sd}
12^{5gs} **3-3-9 £15,198**

Tagula Bay (Ire) *T D Easterby*   63
2 b f Tagula (Ire) - Nezool Almatar (Ire)
2^{5hy} 3^{6f} 5^{5gf} **0-2-3 £1,896**

Tagula Blue (Ire) *J A Glover*   76
4 b g Tagula (Ire) - Palace Blue (Ire)
UR^{8hy} 9^{7s} LFT^{8gf} 3^{11g} 6^{8gf} 5^{8gf} 4^{9hy}
13^{8gf} 1^{8gs} 3^{8gs} 5^{10hy} **1-2-11 £6,103**

Tagula Sunrise (Ire) *R A Fahey*   83
2 ch f Tagula (Ire) - Lady From Limerick (Ire)
2^{5f} 2^{5gf} 5^{5gf} 15^{5g} 3^{6gs} 2^{5gf} 1^{6gf} 1^{6hy}
2-5-8 £47,306

Tahirah *R Guest*   94 a90
4 b f Green Desert (USA) - Kismah
11^{6gf} 7^{7gf} 8^{7gf} 8^{8gf} 8^{7gf} 3^{7gf}
12^{7s} 28^{5d} **0-2-9 £9,900**

Tahlal (Ire) *Mrs A Duffield*   60 a22

2 b c Dr Fong (USA) - Chatterberry
5⁵ᵍᶠ 11⁶ᵍˢ 8⁷ᵍˢ 4⁷ᵍᶠ 11⁸ˢᵈ **0-0-5**

Tahreeb (Fr) *M P Tregoning*   115
3 ch c Indian Ridge - Native Twine
4⁷ᵍ 2¹⁰ᵍ 1⁸ᵍᶠ 1⁹ᵍ 4⁸ᵍˢ 3⁸ᵍ **2-2-6**
£56,286

Tahrir (Ire) *B W Hills*   86
2 gr f Linamix (Fr) - Miss Sacha (Ire)
2⁷ᵍ 3⁷ᵍ **0-1-2 £4,792**

Tahtheeb (Ire) *M P Tregoning*   106
3 b f Muhtarram (USA) - Mimnah (Ire)
1⁹ᵍᶠ 2¹⁰ᵍᶠ 4¹⁰ˢ **1-1-3 £17,406**

Taili *D A Nolan*
3 b f Taipan (Ire) - Doubtfire
7⁸ᵍᶠ 6¹²ᵍᶠ 9¹²ˢ **0-0-3**

Taipan Tommy (Ire) *S Dow*   59
2 ch g Shinko Forest (Ire) - Adieu Cherie (Ire)
6⁵ˢ 6⁶ᵍᶠ 8⁶ᵍ 6⁵ᵍᶠ 6⁶ᵍᶠ **0-0-5**

Taiyo *J W Payne*   52 a56
4 b f Tagula (Ire) - Tharwa (Ire)
6⁷ˢᵈ 5⁸ˢᵈ 4⁹ˢᵈ 4⁹ˢˢ 9⁸ˢʷ 11⁸ˢᵈ PU⁸ᵍᶠ
18⁸ᶠ 1⁸ᵍᶠ 5⁸ᵍᶠ 6⁷ᵍ 8⁷ˢᵈ **1-0-12 £2,908**

Taj India (USA) *M Johnston*   70
2 b/br c Gone West (USA) - Circle Of Gold (Ire)
5⁶ᵍᶠ 8⁷ᵍᶠ **0-0-2**

Tajaathub (USA) *E F Vaughan*   74
2 ch f Aljabr (USA) - Tajannub (USA)
4⁷ᵍ **0-0-1 £439**

Tak's Girl *P T Midgley*   13
2 ch f Takhlid (USA) - Sans Rivale
13⁵ᵍ 7⁵ᵍ 19⁶ᵍ 9⁷ᵍᶠ **0-0-4**

Take A Bow *P R Chamings*   111
3 b c Royal Applause - Giant Nipper
1⁸ᵍˢ 1⁸ᵍˢ 4⁷ᵍᶠ 1⁷ᵍᶠ 2⁸ˢ 2⁸ᵍ 2⁹ᵍ 3⁸ᵍˢ
3-5-8 £66,705

Take Good Time (Ire) *Thomas Cooper*   39
4 ch g Among Men (USA) - Bold Motion
4⁵ʰʸ 12⁶ᵍᶠ **0-0-2**

Take It There *R Hannon*   63
2 ch f Cadeaux Genereux - Feel Free (Ire)
9⁷ᵍᶠ 10⁷ᵍ **0-0-2**

Takemetoyourheart *I A Wood*   a18
2 ch f Zaha (Can) - Mother Molly (USA)
12⁶ˢᵈ 11⁸ᵍᶠ **0-0-2**

Takes Tutu (USA) *K R Burke*   84 a80
5 b g Afternoon Deelites (USA) - Lady Affirmed (Ind)
9⁷ᵍˢ 15⁸ᵍ 7¹⁰ᵍ 2⁹ᵍᶠ 2⁹ᵍᶠ 5⁸ᵍᶠ 5⁸ᵍ 17⁷ᵍᶠ
2⁷ᵍᶠ 20⁷ᵍᶠ 20⁸ᵍᶠ 2⁸ᶠ 5⁹ᵍᶠ 7⁹ᵍ 4⁷ˢᵈ **0-4-15**
£8,759

Takhleed (USA) *M P Tregoning*   77 a71
2 b c Stravinsky (USA) - Bold Threat (Can)
5⁷ˢᵈ 5⁸ᵍ **0-0-2 £456**

Takhmin (Ire) *M Johnston*   81
2 b c Almutawakel - Magdalene (Fr)
9⁶ᶠ 2⁶ᵍˢ 3⁷ᵍᶠ 6⁸ˢ **0-1-4 £2,311**

Talbot Avenue *M Mullineaux*   108
6 b g Puissance - Dancing Daughter
8⁵ᵍˢ 5⁵ᵍᶠ 5⁶ᵍᶠ 8⁵ᵍᶠ 2⁵ᵍˢ 2⁵ᵍ 7⁶ᵍᶠ 2⁶ᵍᶠ
8⁵ˢ 2⁵ᵍᶠ 2⁵ᵍᶠ 7⁵ᵍ 2⁶ᵍ **0-6-13 £29,508**

Talcen Gwyn (Ire) *M F Harris*   79
2 b g Fayruz - Cheerful Knight (Ire)
4⁵ᶠ 1⁵ᶠ 4⁵ᵍ 7⁵ᵍ 4⁶ᵍᶠ 5⁵ˢ 9⁶ᵍᶠ 4⁵ᵍᶠ 1⁵ᵍᶠ
10⁵ᵍ 4⁵ᵍˢ 7⁵ˢ **2-0-12 £16,515**

Tale Of Dubai (USA) *Saeed Bin Suroor*   31
2 ch f Tale Of The Cat (USA) - Jamaican Me Smile (USA)
14⁸ᵍᶠ **0-0-1**

Tale Of The Tiger *Julian Poulton*
3 ch g Bijou D'Inde - La Belle Dominique
12⁶ˢᵈ 5⁸ˢˢ **0-0-2**

Talk To Mojo *J H M Gosden*   15
7 ch g Deploy - Balnaha
18¹²ᵍ **0-0-1**

Talldark'N'Andsome *N P Littmoden*   65
5 b g Efisio - Fleur Du Val
12¹⁰ᵍ 15¹²ˢ **0-0-2**

Tally (Ire) *M J Polglase*   72 a69
4 ch g Tagula (Ire) - Sally Chase
8⁷ˢᵈ 13⁶ˢᵈ 12⁶ˢᵈ 12¹⁰ᵍ 6⁸ʰʸ 11⁷ᵍᶠ 3⁵ᵍᶠ
1⁶ᵍ 2⁶ᵍᶠ 19⁶ᵍᶠ 12⁵ᵍᶠ 2⁵ᵍˢ 4⁵ᵍ 4⁵ᵍˢ 3⁵ᵍˢ
16⁵ᵍᶠ 7⁶ᵍ 1⁶ˢᵈ
10⁶ˢᵈ 17⁵ᵍ **2-4-26 £16,333**

Talwandi (Ire) *Sir Michael Stoute*   84
3 b c Alhaarth (Ire) - Talwara (USA)
6¹⁰ᵍˢ 3¹¹ᵍᶠ 1¹²ᵍᶠ **1-1-3 £4,333**

Tamalain (USA) *Mrs A J Perrett*   77
2 b f Royal Academy (USA) - Woodland Orchid (Ire)
5⁷ᵍ 4⁸ᵍᶠ **0-0-2 £426**

Tamarella (Ire) *G G Margarson*   51 a50
4 b f Tamarisk (Ire) - Miss Siham (Ire)
9⁶ˢᵈ 7⁶ˢᵈ 8⁵ˢᵈ 5⁵ᵍᶠ 12⁵ᵍᶠ 7⁵ᵍᶠ 11⁶ᵍᶠ 8⁶ᵍᶠ
5⁵ᶠ 9⁵ᶠ 14⁶ᵍᶠ 17⁶ᵍˢ 11⁵ˢᵈ **0-0-13**

Tamarillo *M L W Bell*   95 a105
3 gr f Daylami (Ire) - Up And About
5⁸ᶠ 2⁹ʰ 1⁹ʰ 6⁹ᶠᵗ 5¹¹ᵍ 9¹⁶ᶠ 10¹⁰ᵍ **1-1-7**
£115,921

Tamarina (Ire) *N E Berry*   28 a33
3 ch f Foxhound (USA) - Tamasriya (Ire)
7⁹ˢᵈ 15⁷ˢᵈ 14¹²ˢᵈ 10¹⁰ᵍᶠ 12⁸ᵍᶠ 5¹⁰ᵍᶠ
5¹⁰ᵍˢ 11⁸ᵍᶠ **0-0-8**

Tamatave (Ire) *Saeed Bin Suroor*   88
2 b c Darshaan - Manuetti (Ire)
6⁸ˢ 4⁸ᵍᶠ 2⁸ᵍᶠ 4⁸ˢ **0-1-4 £2,201**

Taminoula (Ire) *Mrs A J Perrett*   78 a73
3 b f Tagula (Ire) - Taormina (Ire)
7⁹ᵍ 7⁸ᵍˢ 6⁸ᵍ 13⁸ᵍᶠ 12¹⁰ᵍ 8⁹ˢᵈ **0-0-6**

Tamora *A P Jarvis*   58 a64
2 ch f Dr Fong (USA) - Tahara (Ire)
6⁶ᵍ 14⁶ᵍᶠ 8⁷ᵍᶠ 3⁹ˢᵈ 14⁸ᵍ **0-1-5 £420**

Tanaffus *D W Chapman*   3 a19
4 ch g Cadeaux Genereux - El Rabab (USA)
12⁶ˢᵈ 10⁸ˢᵈ 12⁷ˢ 13⁶ᵍˢ 17⁶ˢ **0-0-5**

Tanaji *P R Webber*   a55
5 b m Marju (Ire) - Hamsaat (Ire)
14¹⁰ˢᵈ **0-0-1**

Tancred Arms *D W Barker*   45
8 b m Clantime - Mischievous Miss
13⁷ᵍ 4⁷ᵍ 9⁷ᵍ 12⁷ᵍ 4⁷ᵍˢ 8⁸ᶠ **0-1-6 £312**

Tancred Imp *D W Barker*   44
3 b f Atraf - Tancred Mischief
8⁸ˢ 5³ˢ 3⁹ᵍ 12¹²ᵍ 10¹²ᵍᶠ 3¹⁰ᵍˢ 9¹¹ᵍᶠ
0-2-7 £1,169

Tancred Miss *D W Barker*   32 a43
5 b m Presidium - Mischievous Miss
1⁷ˢᵈ 8⁷ᵍ 3⁸ˢᵈ 11⁷ᵍˢ 9⁸ˢ **1-1-5 £3,409**

Tancred Times *C F Wall*   71 a31
9 ch m Clantime - Mischievous Miss
11⁵ˢᵈ 4⁶ᵍ 4⁶ᵍ 8⁷ᵍ 3⁶ᵍᶠ 3⁵ᵍ 16ᵍᶠ 4⁶ᵍᶠ
16ᵍᶠ 3⁶ᵍᶠ 2⁶ᵍˢ 8⁶ᵍˢ **2-3-12 £14,036**

Tandava (Ire) *Mrs S C Bradburne*   78
6 ch g Indian Ridge - Kashka (USA)
11⁴ᵍᶠ 10¹³ᵍ 5¹⁴ᵍᶠ 4¹³ᵍᶠ 9¹⁶ˢ 5¹³ᵍᶠ **1-0-6**
£4,364

Tangible *Sir Mark Prescott* 50 a64
2 b f Hernando (Fr) - Trinity Reef
7⁸ˢ 5⁷ˢᵈ 10⁹ˢᵈ **0-0-3**

Tania Di Sceptre (Ity) *Ms Caroline Hutchinson* 42
4 b f King's Theatre (Ire) - Timarete (Ity)
12¹⁴ᵍ 13⁹ᵍˢ 4¹⁶ʰʸ 11¹⁴ᵍʸ 13¹⁷ˢᵈ **0-1-5**
£360

Tank (Ire) *Miss Sheena West* 23
3 ch g Woodborough (USA) - Fiddes (Ire)
7¹⁰ᵍ **0-0-1**

Tanmeya *A C Stewart* 42
3 gr f Linamix (Fr) - Ta Awun (USA)
12¹⁰ᵍ **0-0-1**

Tanne Blixen *P S Felgate* 14 a30
3 b f Great Dane (Ire) - Night Transaction
9⁶ˢᵈ 12⁷ᵍˢ 11⁶ᵍᶠ 9⁶ˢᵈ **0-0-4**

Tanning *H Morrison* 62
2 b f Atraf - Gerundive (USA)
6⁵ᵍᶠ 2⁵ᵍᶠ 3⁶ᵍᶠ 14⁷ᵍᵈ **0-2-4 £1,153**

Tannoor (USA) *M A Jarvis* 79
3 b c Miswaki (USA) - Iolani
3¹¹ᵍˢ 1¹⁰ᵍᶠ 5¹⁰ᵍᶠ 10⁹ᵍᶠ 6¹⁰ᵍᶠ 4⁸ᵍˢ **1-1-6**
£6,674

Tante Rose (Ire) *R Charlton* 121
4 b f Barathea (Ire) - My Branch
1⁶ᵍ 1⁶ᵍˢ 1⁶ᵍ **3-0-3 £176,900**

Tantien *John A Harris* 64
2 b f Diktat - Tahilla
5⁵ˢ 4⁶ʰʸ 9⁵ᵍᶠ 5⁶ᵍᶠ 20⁷ᵍᶠ 13⁷ᵍᶠ **0-0-6**
£590

Tantric *J O'Reilly* 66 a41
5 br g Greensmith - Petunia (Ger)
9⁷ˢʷ 10⁷ˢˢ 3⁷ᵍᶠ 8⁷ᵍ 9⁷ᵍᶠ 3⁶ᵍᶠ 3⁵ᵍᶠ 4⁵ᵍˢ
3⁵ᵍˢ **0-4-9 £2,926**

Tanzani (USA) *C E Brittain* 81
2 b c Giant's Causeway (USA) - Aunt Pearl (USA)
4⁶ᶠ 7⁶ᵍ **0-0-2 £364**

Tanzanite (Ire) *D W P Arbuthnot* 72
2 b f Revoque (Ire) - Resume (Ire)
11⁶ᵍˢ 6⁶ᵍᶠ 3⁸ʰʸ **0-1-3 £1,036**

Tap *Ian Emmerson* 65
7 b g Emarati (USA) - Pubby
1⁷ᵍ 1⁷ᵍ 5⁷ᵍᶠ 11⁷ᵍˢ **2-0-4 £6,076**

Tap Dancer (Ire) *B G Powell* 16 a29
6 b g Sadler's Wells (USA) - Watch Out (USA)
9⁸ˢᵈ 9¹⁰ᵍ **0-0-2**

Tapa *A M Balding* 55
2 b f Tagula (Ire) - Tweed Mill
6⁶ᵍ 21⁶ˢ **0-0-2**

Tapau (Ire) *J M Bradley* 61
6 b m Nicolotte - Urtica (Ire)
5⁵ˢ 9⁶ᵍᶠ 10⁶ᵍᶠ 14⁶ᵍᶠ 13⁷ᵍ 8⁷ᶠ 20⁷ᵍ
0-0-7

Tapleon *C J Teague* 27
3 br f Danzig Connection (USA) - Reem El Fala (Fr)
6⁵ˢ 9⁶ᵍ 10⁷ˢᵈ **0-0-3**

Tappit (Ire) *N E Berry* 55 a48
5 b g Mujadil (USA) - Green Life
15⁶ᵍˢ 15⁶ᵍ 11⁵ᵍᶠ 11⁷ʰʸ 3⁶ᵍᶠ 9⁵ᵍ 5⁶ᶠ
16⁵ᶠ 12⁶ᵍᶠ 15⁶ᵍᶠ 6⁶ᵍˢ 13⁵ᵍᶠ 5⁶ᵍ 1⁶ᵍˢ 5⁶ˢ 6⁶ˢᵈ
1-1-16 £1,938

Tara Tara (Ire) *J J Quinn* 81
2 b f Fayruz - Gobolino
1⁵ᵍˢ 8⁵ᵍˢ 15⁵ᵍᶠ 10⁵ᵍ **1-0-4 £4,361**

Tarabut *E A L Dunlop* 56
2 b f Green Desert (USA) - Nabadhaat (USA)

8⁷ᵍᶠ 7⁷ᵍ **0-0-2**

Taragan *J J Quinn* 44
2 b f Kayf Tara - Morgannwg (Ire)
7⁶ʰʸ 9⁷ˢ **0-0-2**

Tarakala (Ire) *John M Oxx* 105
3 ch f Dr Fong (USA) - Tarakana (USA)
7⁷ʰʸ 1⁹ʸ 1¹²ᵍᶠ 3¹²ᶠ 3¹²ᵍᶠ 2¹²ᵍᶠ 1¹²ˢ 4¹⁵ᵍ
3¹²ᵍʸ **3-2-9 £73,746**

Taranai (Ire) *B W Duke* 42 a51
3 ch f Russian Revival (USA) - Miss Flite (USA)
4⁷ˢᵈ 11¹⁰ˢᵈ 12⁷ˢᵈ 7⁸ˢᵈ 12⁷ˢ 4⁷ᵍ 6⁶ʰʸ
0-0-7

Taranaki *P D Cundell* 94 a78
6 b h Delta Dancer - Miss Ticklepenny
8⁶ˢᵈ 4⁷ˢ 1⁷ᵍˢ 4⁶ᵍˢ 8⁷ˢ 1⁷ᵍ 5⁷ᵍᶠ 8⁷ᵍ
15⁷ᵍᶠ 12⁷ˢᵈ 3⁷ᵍ 6⁷ᵍˢ 5⁷ˢᵈ 19⁶ᵍˢ 4⁷ᵍ 10⁷ˢ
2-3-16 £19,585

Tarandot (Ire) *G G Margarson* 81
3 b f Singspiel (Ire) - Rifada
2¹⁰ᵍᶠ 1¹²ᵍᶠ 7¹⁶ᶠ 9¹⁰ᵍᶠ **1-1-4 £4,894**

Taras Treasure (Ire) *J J Quinn* 71
2 b f Desert King (Ire) - Oklahoma
2⁶ᶠ 6⁶ᶠ 4⁶ᵍᶠ 3⁷ᵍᶠ 5⁶ᶠ 1⁶ᵍ 5⁷ˢ **1-2-7**
£5,385

Tarawan *A M Balding* 12
8 ch g Nashwan (USA) - Soluce
14¹¹ˢ 17¹⁰ᵍˢ **0-0-2**

Tardis *M L W Bell* 39
3 ch f Vettori (Ire) - Time Lapse
7¹⁰ᶠ 8⁸ᶠ 8¹⁰ᵍ 11⁸ᵍ 6⁸ᵍᶠ 10⁷ᵍ 7⁷ᵍˢ **0-0-7**

Tarfah (USA) *G A Butler* 102
3 b f Kingmambo (USA) - Fickle
1⁸ᵍᶠ 1⁸ᵍˢ 2¹⁰ˢ 1⁸ᵍᶠ **3-1-4 £33,086**

Tarjman *E F Vaughan* 102
4 b c Cadeaux Genereux - Dodo (Ire)
7⁸ˢᵈ 5⁸ᵍᶠ **0-0-2 £800**

Tarkeez (USA) *R M H Cowell* 75 a27
3 b g Lear Fan (USA) - Mt Morna (USA)
3⁷ʸ 9¹⁰ʸ 12⁹ᵍ 3¹⁰ᵍᶠ 9⁸ᵍ 8⁸ˢᵈ **0-2-6**
£1,425

Tarkwa *R M H Cowell* 38 a49
5 gr m Doyoun - Shining Fire
6⁶ˢᵈ 13¹⁰ˢᵈ 1⁸ˢᵈ 7¹⁰ᵍᶠ 7⁹ᵍᶠ 5⁸ᶠ **1-0-6**
£1,435

Tarot Card *B W Hills* 65
3 b f Fasliyev (USA) - Well Beyond (Ire)
9⁸ᵍᶠ **0-0-1**

Tarraman (USA) *M Johnston* 80
2 b c Fusaichi Pegasus (USA) - Gerri N Jo Go (USA)
2⁸ᵍ **0-1-1 £1,666**

Tartan Special *K R Burke* 62
2 b c Fasliyev (USA) - Colchica
4⁶ᵍ 6⁶ˢ 5⁶ᵍᶠ **0-0-3 £419**

Tartatartufata *D Shaw* 55 a57
2 b f Tagula (Ire) - It's So Easy
13⁵ᵍˢ 4⁵ʰʸ 9⁵ˢᵈ 8⁵ᵍ 2⁵ˢᵈ 8⁵ᵍˢ 18⁶ˢ **0-1-7**
£1,609

Tartiruga (Ire) *L G Cottrell* 58
3 b g Turtle Island (Ire) - Palio Flyer
13⁷ᵍᶠ 13¹⁰ᵍ 11¹²ᵍ 8⁸ᵍᶠ 5⁷ᵍˢ 6⁸ᵍᶠ 2¹⁰ʰʸ
4¹⁰ᵍ **0-1-8 £956**

Tartouche *Lady Herries* 99
3 b f Pursuit Of Love - Megan's Flight
1¹⁰ᵍ 1¹⁰ᵍ 1¹⁰ᵍ 2¹¹ˢ **3-1-4 £35,188**

Taruskin (Ire) *N A Callaghan* 91

3 b g Danehill Dancer (Ire) - Jungle Jezebel
3^{7g} 18^{gf} 3^{6s} 11^{7g} 12^{8gs} 11^{8g} **1-2-6**
£9,313

Tasdeed *E F Vaughan* 85
2 ch c Cadeaux Genereux - Miss Universe (Ire)
1^{7s} **1-0-1 £3,542**

Tashkil (Ire) *J H M Gosden* 88
3 b g Royal Applause - Surprise Visitor (Ire)
14^{7gf} 5^{6gf} 7^{7s} **0-0-3 £372**

Tashreefat (Ire) *E F Vaughan* 69
3 b f Danehill (USA) - Aigue
3^{10gf} 4^{10gf} 2^{12f} 4^{14gs} **0-1-4 £2,687**

Tashyra (Ire) *A M Balding* 60
2 b f Tagula (Ire) - Shiyra
4^{6gf} 4^{5gs} 11^{6g} 11^{6g} **0-0-4**

Task's Muppet (Ire) *J A Osborne* 57
2 ch f Raise A Grand (Ire) - Highland Crumpet
5^{6gf} 5^{5gs} 5^{6gf} 10^{6g} 4^{5hy} **0-1-5 £322**

Tasneef (USA) *T D McCarthy* 63
5 b g Gulch (USA) - Min Alhawa (USA)
8^{12gf} 6^{13f} 6^{11gf} 8^{12gf} 4^{13gs} 4^{12g} 5^{10gs}
0-0-7

Tass Heel (Ire) *W Jarvis* 24
5 b g Danehill (USA) - Mamouna (USA)
13^{12g} **0-0-1**

Tata Naka *Mrs C A Dunnett* 73 a36
4 ch f Nashwan (USA) - Overcast (Ire)
9^{10sd} 18^{7gs} 5^{7gf} 11^{6gf} 10^{8sd} 2^{10g} 2^{11gf}
3^{12gs} 4^{12gf} 1^{10g} 7^{10f} 10^{10s} 8^{10s} **1-3-13**
£12,686

Tatweer (Ire) *D Shaw* 58 a48
4 b g Among Men (USA) - Sandystones
5^{6s} 1^{5hy} 12^{5gf} 9^{5s} 10^{8gs} 8^{8gf} 18^{12gf}
2^{8gs} 5^{8sw} **1-1-9 £4,358**

Tavalu (USA) *Saeed Bin Suroor* 40
2 b c Kingmambo (USA) - Larrocha (Ire)
6^{7g} 11^{8gs} **0-0-2**

Tawny Way *W Jarvis* 98
4 b f Polar Falcon (USA) - Ma Petite Anglaise
5^{11s} 1^{10g} 2^{12g} 6^{13g} 7^{12g} 1^{12gf} 1^{12s} 11^{12gf}
9^{12s} **3-1-9 £27,988**

Tawoos (Fr) *A Lund* 17
5 b m Rainbow Quest (USA) - Queen Of Dance (Ire)
0^{9g} 3^{9g} 2^{8g} 1^{8gs} 3^{9g} 9^{12s} 2^{10gf} 1^{9hy} 1^{8g}
13^{10s} **3-0-10 £42,009**

Tawqeet (USA) *J L Dunlop* 72
2 ch c Kingmambo (USA) - Caerless (Ire)
14^{8s} 1^{8hy} **1-0-2 £6,389**

Taxman (Ire) *C E Brittain* 46 a61
2 ch c Singspiel (Ire) - Love Of Silver (USA)
12^{7s} 4^{9sd} **0-0-2 £278**

Tayif *Andrew Reid* 74 a74
8 gr g Taufan (USA) - Rich Lass
2^{6sd} 1^{6sd} 1^{6sd} 2^{6sd} 6^{6sd} 7^{7sd} 2^{6sd} 14^{6sd}
5^{6gs} 3^{6s} 1^{6gf} 7^{6sd} **3-4-12 £13,377**

Tbm Can *W M Brisbourne* 67
5 b g Rock City - Fire Sprite
6^{14gf} 5^{13g} 6^{12gf} **0-0-3**

Tcherina (Ire) *T D Easterby* 76
2 b f Danehill Dancer (Ire) - Forget Paris (Ire)
7^{6gf} 7^{6g} 2^{7gf} 3^{8gs} 11^{8gf} 1^{8s} **1-2-6**
£7,567

Te Anau *W J Musson* a30
7 b m Reprimand - Neenah
7^{8sd} 6^{8sd} 6^{10sd} 8^{11sd} **0-0-4**

Te Quiero *Miss Gay Kelleway* 76 a108

6 gr g Bering - Ma Lumiere (Fr)
9^{7sd} 8^{12sd} 11^{10sd} 2^{8sw} 2^{8ss} 7^{8gs} 7^{9ft}
7^{10gf} 7^{8gf} 12^{7g} 11^{6gs} 12^{7sd} **0-2-12 £10,320**

Tea For Texas *I W McInnes*
7 ch m Weldnaas (USA) - Polly's Teahouse
11^{6sd} **0-0-1**

Team Player *F Poulsen* 63
3 b c Mark Of Esteem (Ire) - Colorspin (Fr)
8^{8gf} 8^{10gs} **0-0-2**

Team Tactics (Ire) *L A Dace* 31 a31
3 b f Son Of Sharp Shot (Ire) - Sportin' Notion (USA)
10^{11gf} 11^{7sd} **0-0-2**

Team-Mate (Ire) *Miss J Feilden* 76 a74
6 b g Nashwan (USA) - Ustka
8^{12sd} 5^{12gf} 5^{12gs} **0-0-3 £209**

Technician (Ire) *Miss K M George* a19
9 ch g Archway (Ire) - How It Works
5^{6sd} **0-0-1**

Tedburrow *E J Alston* 95
12 b g Dowsing (USA) - Gwiffina
5^{5hy} 3^{6gs} 4^{6gf} **0-1-3 £2,942**

Tedsdale Mac *N Bycroft* 68
5 ch g Presidium - Stilvella
8^{7gf} 4^{6f} 2^{7g} 5^{8gf} 2^{8gs} 3^{10s} 2^{8gf} 2^{10gf}
5^{12s} 2^{8gf} 10^{12f} 11^{8gf} 1^{8g} 8^{10g} 4^{10s} **1-7-15**
£19,818

Tedstale (USA) *T D Easterby* 90
6 ch g Irish River (Fr) - Carefree Kate (USA)
16^{7gs} 12^{8g} 5^{8gf} 15^{9gf} 3^{8g} 6^{8gf} 4^{8gf} 5^{8gf}
3^{8gf} 9^{8gs} 4^{10gs} 8^{9gf} 12^{9g} **0-2-13 £6,762**

Tedzar (Ire) *B R Johnson* a29
4 b g Inzar (USA) - Chesham Lady (Ire)
8^{8sd} **0-0-1**

Tee Jay Kassidy *Julian Poulton* 44 a41
4 b g Petong - Priceless Fantasy
1^{7sd} 2^{8sd} 5^{7gs} 2^{7sd} 13^{7hy} 4^{8sd} 2^{7f} 5^{7f}
7^{7f} **1-3-9 £3,358**

Teeba (USA) *J L Dunlop* 84
2 ch f Seeking The Gold (USA) - Shadayid (USA)
4^{6s} **0-0-1 £544**

Teehee *B Palling* 37 a76
6 b g Anita's Prince - Regal Charmer
4^{7ss} 6^{7sd} 11^{6sd} 7^{8sd} 2^{7sd} 3^{7sd} 4^{7sd} 12^{8g}
0-2-8 £1,529

Tefi *J Balding* a41
6 ch g Efisio - Masuri Kabisa (USA)
9^{7sd} 3^{7sw} 5^{7sd} **0-0-3 £371**

Telefonica (USA) *Sir Michael Stoute* 59 a65
3 b f Distant View (USA) - Call Account (USA)
4^{8gf} 11^{7gf} 2^{8sd} **0-1-3 £1,267**

Telegram Sam (Ire) *R A Fahey* 49
2 b c Soviet Star (USA) - She's The Tops
9^{6g} 11^{7s} **0-0-2**

Telemachus *J G Given* 96
4 b g Bishop Of Cashel - Indian Imp
6^{11s} 11^{10gs} 10^{10gf} 10^{10g} 8^{10g} 8^{12gs} 14^{10g}
14^{11g} 1^{10s} 5^{10gs} 8^{10gs} **2-0-11 £23,319**

Telepathic (Ire) *A Berry* 90 a46
4 b g Mind Games - Madrina
10^{6sw} 7^{5sw} 7^{5sd} 6^{6g} 7^{6gs} 10^{5gf} 9^{6gs} 4^{7f}
6^{8g} 9^{7gf} 5^{7g} 6^{8g} 5^{8gf} 4^{7gf} 11^{6gf} 7^{6gf} 8^{6g}
5^{6s} 13^{5gs} 8^{5s} **0-0-20 £1,376**

Tell The Trees *M C Pipe* 58
3 br f Tamure (Ire) - Bluebell Copse
7^{9gf} 5^{10f} 5^{16gs} 1^{16gf} **1-0-4 £2,863**

Temper Tantrum *J R Best* 64 a70

6 b g Pursuit Of Love - Queenbird
5⁷ˢᵈ 5⁷ˢᵈ 2⁶ˢᵈ 13⁷ˢᵈ 4⁷ᵍᶠ 12⁷ᵍ 5⁷ᵍᶠ 4⁸ᵍᶠ
6⁷ʰʸ 5⁷ᵍᶠ 8⁷ᵍ 3⁹ˢᵈ 1⁹ˢᵈ 3⁹ˢᵈ **1-3-14 £5,557**

Tempestad (Ire) *H R A Cecil* 89
2 b f Giant's Causeway (USA) - Arutua (USA)
3⁷ᵍ 5⁸ᵍˢ **0-1-2 £1,503**

Temple Belle Xpres *S R Bowring* 34
2 b f Overbury (Ire) - Kustom Kit Xpres
12⁶ᵍˢ 10⁶ᵍᶠ **0-0-2**

Temple Place (Ire) *M L W Bell* 99
3 b c Sadler's Wells (USA) - Puzzled Look (USA)
3⁹ᵍ 3¹²ᵍˢ **0-0-2 £10,450**

Templet (USA) *I Semple* 73 a81
4 b g Souvenir Copy (USA) - Two Step Trudy (USA)
2¹²ʰʸ 3¹¹ᵍ 4¹¹ᵍᶠ 5¹⁰ᵍ 3¹¹ᵍ 13¹⁰ᵍᶠ 10¹²ᵍ
2⁹ˢ 1⁹ᵍˢ 4⁸ᵍ 11¹¹ʰʸ 4⁷ˢᵈ **1-3-12 £10,464**

Tempsford (USA) *Sir Mark Prescott* 96 a63
4 b c Bering - Nadra (Ire)
5¹²ˢˢ 17¹⁴ᵍˢ 5¹⁶ᵍᶠ 31¹⁸ˢ 1¹²ˢ 13¹²ˢ **1-0-6**
£14,099

Temptation Island (Ire) *John A Quinn* 49 a17
5 b m Spectrum (Ire) - Kiya (USA)
10⁸ˢʷ 13⁸ˢʷ 17¹²ʰʸ 8⁵ʸ 21⁶ᵍᶠ 10⁵ᵍᶠ 11⁷ᶠ
16¹⁰ᵍ 8¹⁰ᶠ DSQ¹⁰ᶠ 16⁵ˢ **0-0-11**

Ten Carat *Mrs A J Perrett* 100
4 ch g Grand Lodge (USA) - Emerald (USA)
3¹⁶ᵍᶠ 13²¹ᵍ 9¹⁵ˢ **0-1-3 £1,564**

Ten Past Six *R C Guest*
12 ch g Kris - Tashinsky (USA)
13¹²ᵍᵈ **0-0-1**

Ten-Cents *C A Cyzer* 72
2 b f Dansili - Daylight Dreams
4⁶ᵍˢ 4⁶ᵍ 4⁶ᵍ **0-0-3 £1,209**

Tender (Ire) *Mrs Stef Liddiard* 73 a57
4 b f Zieten (USA) - Jayess Elle
3⁵ᵍᶠ 5⁶ᵍᶠ 7⁷ᵍᶠ 8⁵ᶠ 5⁶ᶠ 8⁶ᵍ 15⁶ᵍᶠ
4⁶ᵍ 1⁵ˢᵈ 13⁵ᵍᶠ 7⁵ᵍᶠ 3⁵ᵍˢ 6⁵ᵍ 6⁵ᵍ **1-1-15**
£4,425

Tender Falcon *R J Hodges* 89
4 br g Polar Falcon (USA) - Tendresse (Ire)
5¹⁰ᵍᶠ 11²ᵍ 9¹²ᵍ 2¹²ᵍᶠ 1¹²ᵍ 1¹²ᵍ 3¹²ᵍᶠ 8¹²ˢ
3-2-8 £35,828

Tenny's Gold (Ire) *B W Hills* 70 a68
3 b f Marju (Ire) - Itatinga (USA)
4⁸ᵍᶠ 3⁸ᵍ 5¹⁰ᵍ 4⁸ʰʸ 3⁷ᵍ 1⁷ˢᵈ 7⁹ˢᵈ **1-2-7**
£5,519

Tentative (USA) *R Charlton* 75
3 ch f Distant View (USA) - Danzante (USA)
11⁵ᵍ 6⁶ᵍᶠ **0-0-2 £214**

Teorban (Pol) *D J S Ffrench Davis* 65 a37
5 b g Don Corleone - Tabaka (Pol)
6¹⁶ˢˢ 14ᵍᶠ 7¹⁶ᵍᶠ 7¹⁶ᵍˢ 9¹⁶ᵍ 2¹⁷ᵍ **1-1-6**
£4,061

Tequila Sheila (Ire) *K R Burke* 81
2 ch f Raise A Grand (Ire) - Hever Rosina
7⁶ᵍᶠ 1⁶ᵍ 6⁶ᵍᶠ 1⁶ᵍˢ 6⁶ᵍ 7⁶ˢ 4⁷ᵍ **2-1-7**
£9,909

Terdad (USA) *J G Given* a12
11 ch g Lomond (USA) - Istiska (Fr)
10¹⁶ˢᵈ **0-0-1**

Terenure Girl *P S Felgate* 21 a11
3 br f Averti (Ire) - Royal Fontaine (Ire)
6⁶ᵍ 10⁶ᵍᶠ 14⁷ˢᵈ **0-0-3**

Teresa *J L Dunlop* 85
4 b f Darshaan - Morina (USA)
2¹⁶ᵍˢ 6¹⁵ˢ 6²⁰ᵍᶠ 7¹⁶ᵍᶠ 11²¹ᵍ 7¹⁶ˢ 17¹⁴ᵍˢ
2¹⁶ˢ 9¹⁶ˢ **0-2-9 £5,964**

Terminate (Ger) *N A Callaghan* 63 a44
2 ch g Acatenango (Ger) - Taghareed (USA)
11⁷ᵍᶠ 7⁸ˢᵈ 5⁸ˢ 14⁸ᵍ **0-0-4**

Termonfeckin *P W Hiatt* 28
6 b g Runnett - Crimson Sol
10¹⁶ᵍ 15¹⁴ᵍ 7¹¹ᵍ **0-0-3**

Tern Intern (Ire) *Miss J Feilden* a28
5 b/br g Dr Devious (Ire) - Arctic Bird (USA)
10⁸ˢʷ 11⁷ˢᵈ 11⁸ˢᵈ 15⁸ˢᵈ **0-0-4**

Terraquin (Ire) *J J Bridger* 76 a81
4 b g Turtle Island (Ire) - Play The Queen (Ire) †
10⁸ˢᵈ 4³ᵍᵈ 13⁷ˢ 19⁶ˢ 5⁸⁷ᵍ 5⁷ᵍ 5⁷ᵍ
7⁷ᵍᶠ 7⁹ᵍᶠ 19⁸ᵍ 9⁸ˢ 3⁷ᵍ 6⁸ᵍ 14⁷ˢ **0-1-15**
£977

Tesary *E A L Dunlop* 76
2 b f Danehill (USA) - Baldemara (Fr)
6⁶ᵍˢ 2¹⁵ᵍ 4⁶ᵍᶠ 3⁵ᵍ 3⁶ᵍˢ 13⁶ᵍᶠ 2⁶ᵍˢ
1-4-8 £8,740

Tetchy *J G Given* 35
4 b f Robellino (USA) - Putout
12⁸ˢ 14⁸ᵍˢ **0-0-2**

Tetcott (Ire) *A G Newcombe* 69 a55
3 ch f Definite Article - Charlene Lacy (Ire)
5⁷ᵍ 3⁷ᵍˢ 4⁶ᵍˢ 3⁷ᵍˢ 10¹⁰ˢᵈ **0-2-5 £1,898**

Tetou (Ire) *B J Meehan* 59 a57
4 ch f Peintre Celebre (USA) - Place Of Honour
9¹⁰ˢᵈ 11¹⁰ᵍᶠ **0-0-2**

Tetra Sing (Ire) *P C Haslam* 57
2 b f Sinndar (Ire) - Tetralogy (USA)
7⁷ˢ 9⁷ᵍᶠ 11⁸ᵍᶠ **0-0-3**

Tewitfield Lass *A Berry* 32
2 b f Bluegrass Prince (Ire) - Madam Marash (Ire)
13⁷ˢ 5⁷ᵍᶠ 9⁷ᵍᶠ 11⁷ˢ **0-0-4**

Texas Gold *W R Muir* 108
6 ch g Cadeaux Genereux - Star Tulip
2⁵ᵍᶠ 4⁵ᵍᶠ 26⁶ᶠ 6⁵ᵍ 6⁵ᵍ 12⁶ᵍᶠ 2⁵ᵍ 2⁶ᵍ
16ᵍᶠ 4⁵ᵍ 4⁵ᵍ 11⁶ᵍˢ **1-4-12 £46,712**

Text *Mrs Stef Liddiard* 68 a48
3 b g Atraf - Idle Chat (USA)
7⁸ᵍ 2⁷ᵍᶠ 3⁷ᵍ 5⁶ˢ 6⁷ᵍᶠ 9⁸ᵍ 10⁹ˢᵈ **0-1-7**
£1,491

Teyaar *M Wellings* 6 a61
8 b g Polar Falcon (USA) - Music In My Life (Ire)
14⁶ˢᵈ 6⁶ˢᵈ 7⁶ˢᵈ 13⁶ˢˢ 5⁶ˢᵈ 12⁶ᵍˢ
2⁵ˢᵈ 4⁶ˢᵈ **0-1-9 £822**

Thadea (Ire) *J G Given* 45
3 b/br f Grand Lodge (USA) - Kama Tashoof
12⁸ᵍ 13⁷ˢ PU⁷ᵍᶠ **0-0-3**

Thajja (Ire) *J L Dunlop* 105
3 b c Daylami (Ire) - Jawlaat (USA)
1⁸ᵍˢ 8⁸ᵍᶠ 2⁸ᵍᶠ 17⁸ˢ **1-1-4 £13,780**

Thakafaat (Ire) *J L Dunlop* 84
2 b f Unfuwain (USA) - Frappe (Ire)
5⁷ᵍᶠ 1⁷ˢ 6⁸ˢ **1-0-3 £5,499**

Thaminah (USA) *M P Tregoning* 89
3 b f Danzig (USA) - Bashayer (USA)
5⁷ᵍᶠ 12⁶ˢ **0-0-2 £750**

Thara'A (Ire) *E A L Dunlop* 69 a39
3 b f Desert Prince (Ire) - Tycoon's Drama (Ire)
2⁸ᵍ 5⁷ᵍ 9⁷ˢᵈ **0-1-4 £1,243**

Tharua (Ire) *E A L Dunlop* 74
2 b f Indian Danehill (Ire) - Peig Sayers (Ire)
3⁷ᵍ 3⁸ᵍˢ **0-2-2 £1,541**

That's Racing *J Hetherton* 39 a40
4 ch g Classic Cliche (Ire) - All On
2¹¹ˢᵈ 6¹²ᵍˢ 12²²ˢ 9¹⁴ˢᵈ 9¹⁰ᵍˢ **0-1-5 £414**

Thats All Jazz *C R Dore* a43
6 b m Prince Sabo - Gate Of Heaven
8^{7sd} 10^{7sd} 10^{10sd} BD^{10sd} 10^{10sd} 0-0-5

The Abbess *H Candy* 80
2 gr f Bishop Of Cashel - Nisha
1^{6gs} 1-0-1 £6,337

The Baroness (Ire) *E R Oertel* 14 a45
4 b f Blues Traveller (Ire) - Wicken Wonder (Ire)
8^{6sd} 9^{5sd} 19^{5gf} 0-0-3

The Beduth Navi *D G Bridgwater* 50 a56
4 b g Forzando - Sweets (Ire)
2^{12sd} 2^{16sd} 1^{12sw} 2^{11ss} 3^{14sd} 4^{16gs} 8^{15sd}
1-4-7 £3,005

The Best Yet *A G Newcombe* 40 a81
6 ch h King's Signet (USA) - Miss Klew
4^{7sd} 8^{8sd} 12^{6gf} 0-0-3 £628

The Block Monster (Ire) *P A Blockley* a1
5 b m Petorius - Balgren (Ire)
9^{6sd} 10^{8ss} 12^{8ss} 0-0-3

The Bonus King *J Jay* 90 a87
4 b g Royal Applause - Selvi
4^{8sw} 5^{7sd} 2^{8s} 8^{11s} 13^{10g} 11^{8s} 7^{8gf} 2^{7gf}
4^{8gf} 10^{7g} 11^{7gf} 7^{8gs} 6^{9sd} 0-2-14
£6,357

The Butterfly Boy *P F I Cole* 26 a40
3 ch c Inchinor - Crime Of Passion
10^{7gs} 3^{5sd} 14^{6gf} 12^{5gf} 0-0-4 £409

The Cat's Whiskers (NZ) *P W Chapple-Hyam* 88
4 b f Tale Of The Cat (USA) - Good Faith (NZ)
3^{8f} 1^{8f} 9^{8gs} 2^{8f} 1^{7f} 7^{8f} 2^{7gs} 9^{7gf} 6^{5g}
2-0-9 £5,561

The Chequered Lady *T D McCarthy* 32
2 b f Benny The Dip (USA) - Hymne D'Amour (USA)
12^{7g} 0-0-1

The Coires (Ire) *R Hannon* 87
2 b c Green Desert (USA) - Purple Heather (USA)
8^{7g} 7^{7gf} 1^{7s} 6^{8gf} 11^{7gf} 1-0-5 £5,499

The Composer *M Blanshard* 81
2 b c Royal Applause - Superspring
4^{8gf} 1^{8gs} 1-0-2 £6,212

The Copt *Mrs S Lamyman*
5 b g Charmer - Coptic Dancer
14^{8sd} 15^{6sd} 0-0-2

The Count (Fr) *F P Murtagh* 15
5 b g Sillery (USA) - Dear Countess (Fr)
5^{8s} 0-0-1

The Crooked Ring *P D Evans* 97
2 b g Magic Ring (Ire) - My Bonus
5^{5g} 2^{5g} 3^{5s} 2^{6gs} 5^{6gf} 4^{5g} 1^{6gf} 1^{6gf}
2^{6gf} 3^{6g} 6^{6g} 5^{6s} 3-4-13 £25,080

The Duke Of Dixie (USA) *P F I Cole* 79
2 b c Dixieland Band - Money Madam (USA)
3^{6gf} 3^{7s} 6^{10g} 0-2-3 £1,734

The Fairy Flag (Ire) *A Bailey* 62
6 ch m Inchinor - Good Reference (Ire)
4^{10hy} 11^{10g} 12^{11s} 7^{14s} 0-0-4 £289

The Fisio *S Gollings* 81 a82
4 b g Efisio - Misellina (Fr)
1^{5sd} 1^{5sd} 5^{5sd} 6^{5sd} 3^{5sd} 8^{6sd} 7^{5s} 2^{6g}
14^{5g} 4^{5s} 1^{5gs} 8^{5g} 2^{6gf} 14^{5gf} 9^{5gf} 9^{5s} 16^{5gs}
3-3-17 £12,892

The Footballresult *Mrs G Harvey* 35 a19
3 b f The West (USA) - Bunny Gee
11^{7sd} 10^{8sd} 5^{7g} 11^{7gf} 9^{10f} 0-0-5

The Fox's Head (Ire) *B Mactaggart* 40
3 b f Imperial Ballet (Ire) - Lovely Leitrim (Ire)

5^{9g} 7^{11gf} 0-0-2

The Fun Merchant *J Pearce* 74 a69
3 b g Mind Games - Sinking
7^{7gs} 1^{8g} 1^{8gf} 2^{8gf} 7^{8g} 5^{8g} 9^{10sd} 7^{9sd} 3^{8s}
2-2-9 £8,730

The Gaikwar (Ire) *N E Berry* 66 a73
5 b h Indian Ridge - Broadmara (Ire)
6^{7sd} 4^{7sd} 2^{8sd} 5^{7sd} 8^{10sd} 1^{8sd} 2^{9s} UR^{8hy}
11^{8gf} 17^{9gf} 17^{7g} 4^{7gf} 3^{8gf} 2^{8gf} 3^{8gs} 6^{8gs}
1-6-16 £9,689

The Gambler *Paul Johnson* 56 a43
4 ch g First Trump - Future Options
9^{7gf} 14^{10hy} 11^{6s} 2^{7g} 8^{6sd} 16^{8gf} 12^{7gf}
12^{6f} 6^{6hy} 5^{8f} 0-1-10 £1,272

The Gay Fox *B G Powell* a52
10 gr g Never So Bold - School Concert
2^{7sd} 4^{6ss} 2^{6sd} 3^{6sd} 8^{7sd} 9^{7sd} 3^{7sw} 11^{7sd}
8^{7sd} 6^{7sd} 0-4-10 £1,334

The Geezer *D R C Elsworth* a71
2 ch c Halling (USA) - Polygueza (Fr)
4^{8sd} 0-0-1 £332

The Great Gatsby (Ire) *J H M Gosden* 112
4 b c Sadler's Wells (USA) - Ionian Sea
3^{12g} 7^{12gf} 4^{13g} 8^{15vs} 0-0-4 £56,901

The Job *A D Smith* 58 a61
3 ch c Dancing Spree (USA) - Bay Bianca (Ire)
6^{7sd} 2^{7sd} 5^{8g} 15^{8s} 5^{7sd} 0-1-5 £1,075

The Jobber (Ire) *M Blanshard* 85 a85
3 b g Foxhound (USA) - Clairification (Ire)
4^{6g} 10^{5gf} 6^{6gf} 2^{6sd} 2^{6gs} 14^{6g} 5^{6gf} 0-2-7
£4,337

The Keep *R Hannon* 56 a22
2 ch h Shinko Forest (Ire) - Poyle Amber
7^{6sd} 10^{6gf} 9^{7g} 4^{6gf} 11^{6gs} 8^{9sd} 0-0-6

The Kelt (Ire) *Eoin Doyle* 48
7 b g Leading Counsel (USA) - Casheral
3^{16y} 1^{17g} PU^{14sd} 1-1-3 £3,531

The Khamsin (Den) *Ms C Erichsen* 108
5 b h Kateb (Ire) - Medinova
3^{11g} 2^{12g} 0^{11gs} 3^{13g} 5^{12g} 7^{8s} 2^{9f} 7^{12gf}
0-0-8 £12,854

The Kiddykid (Ire) *P D Evans* 114
4 b g Danetime (Ire) - Mezzanine
3^{6g} 7^{6g} 1^{6gf} 4^{6s} 6^{5gs} 8^{6g} 2^{6gf} 7^{6hy} 1-2-8
£52,904

The King Of Rock *A G Newcombe* 61 a53
3 b c Nicolotte - Lv Girl (Ire)
8^{6sd} 5^{11gs} 4^{10gs} 8^{12g} 2^{12sd} 4^{12f} 6^{12gf}
5^{10gs} 0-1-8 £1,578

The King's Bishop *S C Williams* 74 a62
3 b g Bishop Of Cashel - Kennedys Prima
4^{8sd} 13^{7sd} 3^{7gs} 0-1-3 £915

The Lady Would (Ire) *D G Bridgwater* a30
5 ch m Woodborough (USA) - Kealbra Lady
10^{5sd} 8^{6sd} 7^{6sd} 0-0-3

The Last Cast *H Morrison* 83
5 ch g Prince Of Birds (USA) - Atan's Gem (USA)
1^{14s} 11^{11s} 1-0-2 £9,628

The Last Mohican *P Howling* a43
5 b g Common Grounds - Arndilly
4^{15sd} 2^{16sd} 3^{13sd} 2^{16sd} 4^{23sd} 4^{13sd} 7^{12sd}
8^{13sd} 3^{12sd} 2^{15sd} 1^{12sd} 10^{12sd} 8^{12sd} 7^{14sd} 1-4-14
£3,347

The Laverton Lad *C W Thornton*
3 ch g Keen - Wyse Folly
11^{9sd} 0-0-1

The Leather Wedge (Ire) *A Berry*   40 a54
5 b h Hamas (Ire) - Wallflower
6^{5sd} 11^{4ss} 14^{5ss} 10^{5sw} 5^{5ss} 2^{5ss} 5^{5ss} 5^{5sd}
9^{5gf} 3^{5sd} 9^{5sd} 4^{5s} **0-2-12 £1,160**

The Loose Screw (Ire) *G M Moore*   53
6 b g Bigstone (Ire) - Princess Of Dance (Ire)
10^{11s} 9^{10hy} 13^{10f} 12^{14gf} 12^{8g} 5^{9gs} 5^{8hy}
6^{8gs} 2^{7s} **0-1-9 £421**

The Lord *W G M Turner*   86
4 b g Averti (Ire) - Lady Longmead
3^{6gf} 7^{5gf} 6^{6hy} 13^{5g} 6^{5s} **0-0-5 £1,600**

The Mog *Miss M E Rowland*
5 b g Atraf - Safe Secret
7^{8ss} **0-0-1**

The Nibbler *G C H Chung*   49 a36
3 b g General Monash (USA) - Spoilt Again
4^{8f} 6^{8sd} 7^{10sd} 6^{8g} 12^{8s} **0-0-5**

The Number *I Semple*   70 a54
3 gr g Silver Wizard (USA) - Elite Number (USA)
3^{8gf} 3^{8s} 5^{7gf} 2^{8g} 6^{8gf} 7^{9sd} **0-2-6**
£2,958

The Old Soldier *A Dickman*   60 a58
6 b g Magic Ring (Ire) - Grecian Belle
7^{6gs} 13^{6hy} 2^{7gf} 12^{6g} 2^{7gs} 5^{5s} 2^{7sd} **0-3-7**
£1,739

The Palletman *M F Harris*   a16
4 ch g Lion Cavern (USA) - Aquarela
9^{8sd} **0-0-1**

The Pen *P C Haslam*   64
2 ch f Lake Coniston (Ire) - Come To The Point
7^{6gf} 1^{6gf} 2^{7gf} 1^{8s} **2-1-4 £9,451**

The Persuader (Ire) *M Johnston*   46
4 b g Sadler's Wells (USA) - Sister Dot (USA)
13^{14g} 19^{12g} 10^{16hy} 13^{13gf} **0-0-4**

The Pheasant Flyer *B J Meehan*   92
2 ch g Prince Sabo - Don't Jump (Ire)
3^{6g} 1^{6gf} 1^{6gf} 12^{7s} **2-1-4 £9,909**

The Plainsman *P W Hiatt*   23
2 b g Atraf - Mylania
6^{6gf} **0-0-1 £187**

The Player *A M Balding*   66
5 b g Octagonal (NZ) - Patria (USA)
12^{9g} **0-0-1**

The Prince *Ian Williams*   97
10 b g Machiavellian (USA) - Mohican Girl
1^{8f} 1^{9s} 2^{8sd} 1^{9gs} 1^{9gf} 1^{9g} 3^{8gs}
6-2-8 £44,423

The Quiet Woman (Ire) *Francis Ennis*   77
2 b f Barathea - Tajawuz
3^{5hy} 2^{5y} 5^{6gy} 4^{6g} 14^{5g} 6^{7s} **0-2-6**
£7,633

The Recruiter *J G M O'Shea*   a15
4 gr g Danzig Connection (USA) - Tabeeba
8^{11sd} **0-0-1**

The Ring (Ire) *K G Reveley*   79
4 b g Definite Article - Renata's Ring (Ire)
7^{16g} 2^{16gs} 3^{16hy} 13^{16s} 5^{16gf} 9^{13gf} 5^{15g}
5^{14g} **0-2-8 £3,994**

The Rip *T D Easterby*   56
3 ch g Definite Article - Polgwynne
7^{9f} 3^{8g} 12^{12g} **0-1-3 £644**

The Roundsills *M Mullineaux*   15
10 ch g Handsome Sailor - Eye Sight
11^{11s} 6^{12gf} **0-0-2 £240**

The Spook *Miss L A Perratt*   41
4 b g Bin Ajwaad (Ire) - Rose Mill

10^{9g} 15^{8f} 9^{7gf} 5^{9gs} 7^{10s} **0-0-5**

The Stick *M R Channon*   47 a59
3 b f Singspiel (Ire) - Fatah Flare (USA)
7^{7sd} 10^{12g} 11^{8hy} 7^{8gf} 12^{10f} 9^{9g} **0-0-6**

The Tatling (Ire) *J M Bradley*   119
7 b/br g Perugino (USA) - Aunty Eileen
2^{5gf} 3^{5gf} 4^{5gs} 1^{5gf} 9^{5gs} 3^{5gf} 2^{5s} 2^{5gs}
1^{5g} 3^{6gf} 2^{5g} **2-7-11 £231,937**

The Terminator (Ire) *A Berry*   49
2 b g Night Shift (Ire) - Surmise (USA)
7^{5s} 10^{6gs} 20^{6s} 7^{6gf} 9^{5gs} 4^{7g} 7^{9gs} **0-0-7**
£391

The Trader (Ire) *M Blanshard*   118
6 ch g Selkirk (USA) - Snowing
1^{5gf} 3^{5gs} 10^{5gf} 1^{6s} 5^{7gs} 19^{6g} 14^{5g} **2-1-7**
£63,200

The Varlet *D Burchell*   77
4 b g Groom Dancer (USA) - Valagalore
10^{14g} 3^{12gf} 6^{12gf} 1^{14gf} 10^{16gf} 13^{13gs}
16^{16g} **1-1-7 £4,157**

The Violin Player (USA) *H J Collingridge*   75 a77
3 b g King Of Kings (Ire) - Silk Masque (USA)
9^{8s} 8^{8gf} 8^{8gf} 7^{10gs} 5^{11f} 7^{12g} 2^{10sd} 1^{10sd}
1-1-8 £4,616

The Warley Warrior *M W Easterby*   42
3 b g Primo Dominie - Brief Glimpse (Ire)
6^{6hy} 11^{6g} 13^{6gf} **0-0-3**

The Way We Were *T G Mills*   74
3 ch g Vettori (Ire) - Pandrop
6^{8gs} 5^{9gf} 12^{8gf} 3^{8gf} 13^{8g} **0-1-5 £566**

The Whistling Teal *G Wragg*   116
8 b g Rudimentary (USA) - Lonely Shore
7^{12g} 2^{13gs} 1^{13g} 5^{14g} 4^{12hy} **1-1-5**
£37,526

The Wizard Mul *W Storey*   53
4 br g Wizard King - Longden Pride
14^{6gs} 10^{8gs} 12^{7gs} 8^{6gs} 8^{7g} 14^{6g} 3^{9gs}
5^{10s} **0-1-8 £609**

Theas Dance *D R Loder*   71
2 b f Danzig (USA) - Teggiano (Ire)
5^{7f} 8^{6g} 3^{6s} 9^{7gf} **0-0-4 £766**

Theatre (USA) *Jamie Poulton*   91
5 b g Theatrical - Fasta (USA)
15^{14s} SU^{14gf} 2^{16gf} 2^{15gf} 3^{14gs} 15^{16g}
13^{15s} 7^{16gf} 12^{16gf} 13^{18s} **0-2-10 £4,868**

Theatre Belle *T D Easterby*   52
3 b f King's Theatre (Ire) - Cumbrian Rhapsody
8^{8g} 13^{7g} 13^{12sd} 6^{12gs} 5^{12gf} 11^{14gf} 7^{16f}
0-0-7

Theatre Lady (Ire) *P D Evans*   57 a48
6 b m King's Theatre (Ire) - Littlepace
1^{10sd} 2^{8sd} 8^{8sd} 3^{8sd} 6^{10sd} 3^{10sd} 8^{8sd} 4^{11s}
3^{8sd} 5^{10gf} 6^{8f} 6^{11f} 11^{11f} 11^{11g} 5^{10gf} 1^{12gf}
10^{10gf} 6^{14gf} 1^{12g} **4-5-19 £10,637**

Theatre Of Dreams *D Nicholls*   83
2 b g Averti (Ire) - Loch Fyne
5^{5g} 4^{5s} 1^{5gf} 10^{5g} 6^{5gs} 12^{5s} **1-0-6**
£7,556

Theatre Time (USA) *Ian Williams*   68
4 b g Theatrical - Kyka (USA)
6^{10gf} 7^{12g} **0-0-2**

Theatre Tinka (Ire) *R Hollinshead*   65 a64
5 b g King's Theatre (Ire) - Orange Grouse (Ire)
5^{11sd} 5^{12sd} 5^{12sd} 2^{12sd} 11^{11gs} 11^{11gs} 5^{12sd}
2^{13f} 8^{15gf} 4^{14gf} 3^{12g} 16^{12gs} **0-3-12 £3,319**

Theflyingscottie *J D Frost*   33
2 gr g Paris House - Miss Flossa (Fr)

10^6gf 12^5gf **0-0-2**
Theme Park *S C Burrough*   a20
4 b g Classic Cliche (Ire) - Arcady
7^14sd 7^12sd **0-0-2**
Theme Song (Ire) *Anthony Mullins*   94
5 b h Singspiel (Ire) - Glatisant
13^12gf 3^13gf 1^12gf 11^14g **1-1-4 £41,482**
Themesofgreen *M R Channon*   52
3 ch g Botanic (USA) - Harmonia
9^5gf 7^6gf 8^6gf 5^7g **0-0-4**
Thevenis *J S King*
3 ch c Dr Fong (USA) - Pigeon Hole
9^12ss **0-0-1**
Thewhirlingdervish (Ire) *T D Easterby*   92
6 ch g Definite Article - Nomadic Dancer (Ire)
3^14s 4^16gs 10^16g 3^14gf 1^18gf 3^16g 2^19gf
6^16gf 9^16g 11^16gf **1-3-10 £21,586**
Thihn (Ire) *J L Spearing*   101
9 ch g Machiavellian (USA) - Hasana (USA)
10^8g 1^7gs 11^8g 28^9g **0-1-4 £12,441**
Thingmebob *M H Tompkins*   88
4 b f Bob Back (USA) - Kip's Sister
5^10gs 5^12gf **0-0-2 £2,250**
Think It Over (Ire) *A P Jones*   a15
5 ch m Bijou D'Inde - Good News (Ire)
13^7sd 9^8sd 12^8sd **0-0-3**
Think Quick (Ire) *R Hollinshead*   41 a43
4 b f Goldmark (USA) - Crimson Ring
14^11sd 5^12sd 6^9ss 6^12sw 3^12sw 4^12ss 7^12sw
3^12sw 12^11ss 7^11sd 6^11sd 2^12sd 7^14gf 4^12gf 12^14sd
0-2-15 £1,670
Third Empire *C Grant*   68
3 b g Second Empire (Ire) - Tahnee
3^10s 9^10s 5^8s 2^9gf 4^10gf 8^9hy **0-2-6**
£2,848
Thirteen Tricks (USA) *Mrs A J Perrett*   78
3 b f Grand Slam (USA) - Talltalelady (USA)
13^9hy 3^9g 4^10g 1^10f 11^10g **1-1-5 £5,323**
This Is My Song *Mrs A J Perrett*   73
2 b f Polish Precedent (USA) - Narva
7^6gs 3^7s **0-1-2 £846**
This Way That Way *G C Bravery*   a19
3 b g Dr Devious (Ire) - Ellway Dancer (Ire)
10^8sd **0-0-1**
Thistle *J H M Gosden*   76
3 ch c Selkirk (USA) - Ardisia (USA)
9^8gs 2^8gs 2^8g 2^8gf 1^8g **1-3-5 £8,493**
Thomas Lawrence (USA) *P F I Cole*   68
3 ch g Horse Chestnut (SAF) - Olatha (USA)
6^6gf 3^6s 7^6f **0-1-3 £844**
Thornaby Green *T D Barron*   67
3 b g Whittingham (Ire) - Dona Filipa
4^5f 4^6gf 1^6gf 11^7gf 5^6g 4^6gs 7^7gf 2^6s
18^6gs **1-2-9 £6,924**
Thornber Court (Ire) *A Berry*   64
2 b f Desert Sun - Goldfinch
7^6gf 4^6gs 8^5g 2^5gf 3^5g 5^5gs **0-2-6**
£1,789
Thorntoun Piccolo *J S Goldie*   66
2 ch f Groom Dancer (USA) - Massorah (Fr)
8^7s 5^7s **0-0-2**
Thorny Mandate *R F Johnson Houghton*   49
2 b c Diktat - Rosa Canina
11^7gs 12^7s **0-0-2**
Threat *J M Bradley*   51 a36
8 br g Zafonic (USA) - Prophecy (Ire)

9^6sd 4^6sd 7^5sd 10^7sd 3^6sd 4^5gs 4^5g 6^5hy
7^6gf 5^7gf 4^6gf **0-1-11 £183**
Three Aces (Ire) *R M Beckett*   56
2 ch f Raise A Grand (Ire) - Fallacy
9^5g 5^5g 6^5gf 19^7gf 7^7gf 11^8gs 7^8s **0-0-7**
Three Boars *W Jarvis*   51
2 ch g Most Welcome - Precious Poppy
7^6gf 10^8gf 9^10gf **0-0-3**
Three Degrees (Ire) *R M Beckett*   77
2 gr f Singspiel (Ire) - Miss University (USA)
3^6gs 2^7g **0-2-2 £2,065**
Three Deuces (USA) *B J Meehan*   61 a65
2 gr/ro f Two Punch (USA) - Too Fast To Catch (USA)
5^5gs 4^7sd 6^6sd **0-0-3 £326**
Three Eagles (USA) *M Scudamore*   21
7 ch g Eagle Eyed (USA) - Tertiary (USA)
6^16g **0-0-1**
Three Graces (Ger) *Saeed Bin Suroor*   110
4 ch g Peintre Celebre (USA) - Trefoil
18^gf 7^7f 3^7gf **1-1-3 £39,612**
Three Pennies *M Dods*   69 a63
2 b f Pennekamp (USA) - Triple Zee (USA)
10^6f 1^7g 3^7gs 11^7gf 12^7f 10^6gs 5^9sd
1-0-7 £4,533
Three Secrets (Ire) *P W Chapple-Hyam*   97
3 b f Danehill (USA) - Castilian Queen (USA)
7^6g 1^7gf 2^7g 3^8s 11^8gf **1-1-5 £11,424**
Three Ships *Miss J Feilden*   65 a56
3 ch g Dr Fong (USA) - River Lullaby (USA)
10^8g 5^7f 9^7sd **0-0-3**
Three Strikes (Ire) *S C Williams*   54
2 b f Selkirk (USA) - Special Oasis
10^5gf 5^5s **0-0-2**
Three Valleys (USA) *R Charlton*   110
3 ch c Diesis - Skiable (Ire)
2^8g 11^8g **0-1-2 £11,000**
Three Welshmen *D Burchell*   59
3 b g Muhtarram (USA) - Merch Rhyd-Y-Grug
14^7sd 8^8ss 5^8g 1^8s 3^7s 13^12g 7^8f 8^10g
2^8g **1-2-9 £4,967**
Three Wrens (Ire) *D J Daly*   58
2 b f Second Empire (Ire) - Three Terns (USA)
3^8gs 1^8s **1-1-2 £1,923**
Threezedzz *P D Evans*   90 a59
6 ch g Emarati (USA) - Exotic Forest
12^7g 7^7g 9^6g 17^gf 11^6gf 1^7gf 7^7sd 1^8gs
3^8gs 3^8gs 1^7s 14^7gf 20^9g 15^10g 13^8s **4-2-15**
£23,038
Through The Slips (USA) *J G Given*   39 a47
3 ch f Boundary (USA) - Fast Selection (USA)
7^10gf 8^8gf 3^7sw 16^7f **0-1-4 £417**
Throw The Dice *K A Ryan*   84
2 b c Lujain (USA) - Euridice (Ire)
2^6s 1^6g 4^6hy **1-1-3 £6,071**
Throwmeupsomething (Ire) *A Berry*   58
3 b g Cape Cross (Ire) - Hawksbill Special (Ire)
10^12s **0-0-1**
Thumamah (Ire) *B P J Baugh*   33 a36
5 b m Charnwood Forest (Ire) - Anam
9^8sd 11^8sd 14^8s 6^8gf 11^7sd 15^8gs **0-0-6**
Thunder Calling (USA) *P F I Cole*   67
2 b f Thunder Gulch (USA) - Glorious Calling (USA)
4^6gf **0-0-1 £365**
Thunderclap *J J Quinn*   43 a63

5 b/br g Royal Applause - Gloriana
1^{8ss} 2^{8sw} 8^{8sd} 10^{8sd} 16^{8s} 9^{7s} **1-1-6**
£3,849

Thundering Surf *J R Jenkins*   67
7 b g Lugana Beach - Thunder Bug (USA)
13^{12g} 9^{12gf} **0-0-2**

Thunderwing (Ire) *K R Burke*   93
2 b/br c Indian Danehill (Ire) - Scandisk (Ire)
3^{7gf} 1^{7gs} 1^{8hy} 5^{8s} 5^{8s} **3-0-5 £14,550**

Thurlestone Rock *B J Meehan*   84
4 ch g Sheikh Albadou - Don't Smile
11^{6gf} 5^{6gf} 17^{6gf} 1^{6gf} 11^{6g} **1-0-5**
£7,490

Thwaab *F Watson*   39
12 b g Dominion - Velvet Habit
9^{8g} 13^{8f} 8^{8f} 10^{8g} **0-0-4**

Thyolo (Ire) *C G Cox*   105
3 ch g Bering - Topline (Ger)
2^{8g} 10^{10gs} 3^{8f} 11^{8gs} 7^{8gf} 15^{10gs} 8^{12g}
0-2-7 £9,796

Ti Adora (Ire) *P W Chapple-Hyam*   54
2 b f Montjeu (Ire) - Wavy Up (Ire)
9^{7gf} 14^{7g} 8^{10s} **0-0-3**

Tiamo *M H Tompkins*   67
2 ch c Vettori (Ire) - Speed To Lead (Ire)
12^{7s} 6^{8gf} 7^{8g} **0-0-3**

Tiber Tiger (Ire) *N P Littmoden*   86
4 b g Titus Livius (Fr) - Genetta
4^{8gs} 1^{8gf} 7^{8gf} 2^{8f} 13^{8g} 19^{8g} 5^{8gf} 5^{8gf}
5^{7f} 6^{8gs} 13^{9g} 10^{8g} 13^{8gf} 11^{10s} **1-2-14**
£7,889

Ticero *C E Brittain*   66 a44
3 ch g First Trump - Lucky Flinders
13^{8g} 14^{6s} 8^{7gf} 11^{6sd} 4^{7gf} 12^{8g} 12^{8sd}
0-1-7 £295

Ticki Tori (Ire) *Julian Poulton*   80
2 b f Vettori (Ire) - Lamees (USA)
3^{8g} 3^{7s} **0-2-2 £1,467**

Tickle *P J Makin*   44 a53
6 b m Primo Dominie - Funny Choice (Ire)
4^{5sd} 8^{6sd} 3^{6sd} 6^{6gs} 6^{5s} 13^{6gf} 10^{5sd} **0-1-7**
£216

Ticklepenny Lock (Ire) *C Smith*   a22
3 b c Mujadil (USA) - Barncogue
12^{7sd} 9^{8sd} 10^{11sd} **0-0-3**

Tictactoe *D J Daly*   36 a41
3 b f Komaite (USA) - White Valley (Ire)
6^{7sd} 6^{5s} 9^{7f} 7^{7gs} **0-0-4**

Tidal *A W Carroll*   93
5 br m Bin Ajwaad (Ire) - So Saucy
6^{10s} 1^{12gf} 1^{10gf} 7^{12gf} 3^{10g} 4^{10g} 7^{12gf}
1^{10gf} 10^{10g} **3-1-9 £26,738**

Tidal Fury (Ire) *J Jay*   66
2 b c Night Shift (USA) - Tidal Reach (USA)
12^{6gf} 4^{7gs} **0-0-2 £281**

Tides *W J Musson*   43
3 b f Bahamian Bounty - Petriece
8^{7g} 6^{6gf} 8^{6gf} **0-0-3**

Tidy (Ire) *M D Hammond*   85 a56
4 b c Mujadil (USA) - Neat Shilling (Ire)
11^{6sw} 1^{7hy} 5^{6s} UR^{6sd} 8^{7g} 3^{7s} 7^{7g} 15^{7g}
4^{7g} 4^{8hy} 5^{7gs} 16^{7gs} **1-1-12 £19,039**

Tiegs (Ire) *Mrs A L M King*
2 ch f Desert Prince (Ire) - Helianthus
12^{7gf} **0-0-1**

Tiffin Brown *P C Haslam*   52

2 br g Erhaab (USA) - Cockatrice
10^{6g} **0-0-1**

Tiffin Deano (Ire) *P C Haslam*   53
2 b g Mujadil (USA) - Xania
5^{5gs} 8^{5g} 10^{6g} 13^{7f} 4^{5g} **0-0-5 £262**

Tiger Bond *B Smart*   53
2 br g Diktat - Blackpool Belle
10^{5gs} 5^{5gf} **0-0-2**

Tiger Dance (USA) *A P O'Brien*   90
2 b c Storm Cat (USA) - Mariah's Storm (USA)
1^{7gf} **1-0-1 £11,461**

Tiger Dawn (Ire) *W J Haggas*   27 a64
2 b g Anabaa (USA) - Armorique (Ire)
13^{8gs} 1^{7sd} **1-0-2 £2,660**

Tiger Frog (USA) *J Mackie*   69
5 b g French Deputy (USA) - Woodyoubelieveit (USA)
1^{11gf} 5^{12gf} 3^{12gf} **1-1-3 £4,801**

Tiger Hunter *P Howling*   34 a43
2 b g Lake Coniston (Ire) - Daynabee
8^{6f} 10^{6gf} 15^{8gf} 37^{5d} **0-1-4 £380**

Tiger Tiger (Fr) *Jamie Poulton*   99 a75
3 b c Tiger Hill (Ire) - Adorable Emilie (Fr)
18^{8d} 3^{8sd} 1^{9s} 2^{10s} 7^{9g} 7^{10g} 4^{12g} 2^{8g}
1^{10hy} 4^{10s} **3-3-10 £28,586**

Tiger Tops *J A Supple*   a67
5 ch g Sabrehill (USA) - Rose Chime (Ire)
5^{7sd} 9^{8sd} **0-0-2**

Tiggers Touch *B R Millman*   66
2 b f Fraam - Beacon Silver
4^{6gf} 9^{7g} 6^{7s} 7^{8g} **0-0-4 £454**

Tight Circle *Mrs G Harvey*   71
2 b f Danzero (Aus) - Tight Spin
7^{5g} 5^{5g} 6^{5g} 1^{6gf} **1-0-4 £3,164**

Tight Squeeze *P W Hiatt*   80 a89
7 br m Petoski - Snowline
6^{12sd} 5^{12sd} 3^{12sd} 7^{10sd} 8^{10sd} 1^{10sd} 8^{13sd}
1^{10sd} 7^{12g} 8^{10gf} 6^{10gf} 3^{10g} **2-1-12 £12,511**

Tigress (Ire) *J W Unett*   a64
5 b m Desert Style (Ire) - Ervedya (Ire)
6^{6sd} 5^{6sd} 2^{5ss} 6^{5ss} 2^{5sw} 7^{5ss} 9^{5ss} **0-2-7**
£1,760

Tikitano (Ire) *D K Ivory*   9
3 b f Dr Fong (USA) - Asterita
18^{6gf} 14^{7gf} 13^{5gf} 10^{5sd} **0-0-4**

Till There Was You *W G M Turner*   30 a3
3 b f Vettori (Ire) - Fleur Rouge
12^{8sd} 10^{7gs} 11^{5gf} 12^{7g} **0-0-4**

Tilla *H Morrison*   78
4 b f Bin Ajwaad (Ire) - Tosca
5^{14g} 6^{18gf} 10^{14gf} 2^{14g} 2^{14gs} 6^{15s} 5^{14gf}
9^{14gs} **0-2-8 £3,496**

Tillerman *Mrs A J Perrett*   116
8 b h In The Wings - Autumn Tint (USA)
5^{8gf} 6^{8g} 8^{7gf} **0-0-3 £10,750**

Tillingborn Dancer (Ire) *M D Hammond*   49
2 b g Imperial Ballet (Ire) - Exhibit Air (Ire)
10^{5f} 11^{6g} 9^{7gf} 10^{7g} 9^{6s} **0-0-5**

Tilt *J R Fanshawe*   61
2 b g Daylami (Ire) - Tromond
8^{8g} **0-0-1**

Timber Ice (USA) *H R A Cecil*   61
4 b/br f Woodman (USA) - Salchow (USA)
10^{12gf} 5^{11gf} 5^{10gf} **0-0-3**

Timber Scorpion (UAE) *M Johnston*   66
2 b c Timber Country (USA) - Aqraba
5^{9f} 7^{10g} **0-0-2**

Timbuktu C W Thornton   47 a3
3 b g Efisio - Sirene Bleu Marine (USA)
7⁹ˢᵈ 9¹⁰ᵍˢ 7¹⁰ᵍ 2¹³ᵍ 8¹²ᵍ 12¹⁴ᵍ **0-1-6**
£414

Time Flyer W De Best-Turner   36 a45
4 b g My Best Valentine - Sally's Trust (Ire)
7⁷ˢᵈ 10⁸ˢᵈ 10¹²ˢᵈ 12¹⁰ˢᵈ 16⁸ᵍᶠ 6⁶ᵍ **0-0-6**

Time For Mee R A Fahey   19
2 ch f Timeless Times (USA) - Heemee
9⁵ᵍᶠ 11⁶ᵍ **0-0-2**

Time For You J M Bradley   64 a47
2 b f Vettori (Ire) - La Fija (USA)
10⁶ᵍᶠ 4⁷ᵍᶠ 16ᵍᶠ 11⁷ᵍᶠ 4⁶ᵍˢ 8⁷ˢᵈ 27⁶ˢ
1-0-7 £4,053

Time Marches On K G Reveley   48 a33
6 b g Timeless Times (USA) - Tees Gazette Girl
4⁹ˢʷ 9¹²ˢʷ 1¹⁰ᶠ 8¹⁰ᶠ **1-0-4 £3,604**

Time N Time Again E J Alston   77 a89
6 b g Timeless Times (USA) - Primum Tempus
5⁶ˢʷ 15ˢᵈ 8⁵ˢᵈ 16ˢᵈ 35ˢᵈ 36ˢʷ 16ˢʷ
5⁶ˢˢ 16⁶ᵍ 78ᵍˢ 6⁶ᵍˢ 36ᵍᶠ 75ᵍ 35ᵍ 26ᵍ 26ᵍ
36ᵍˢ 6⁶ᵍᶠ **3-8-19 £20,390**

Time To Regret J S Wainwright   64 a50
4 b g Presidium - Scoffera
6⁹ˢᵈ 2⁷ᵍᶠ 4⁷ᵍᶠ 13⁸ᶠ 18ᵍᶠ 7⁷ᵍˢ 10⁸ᵍᶠ 12⁸ᵍ
28ᵍᶠ 5¹⁰ᵍᶠ 19ᵍˢ 6⁹ˢᵈ 4⁸ʰʸ **2-3-13 £9,904**

Time To Relax (Ire) J J Quinn   69 a58
3 b f Orpen (USA) - Lassalia
2⁶ˢˢ 4⁶ˢᵈ 18ᵍ 8¹⁰ᵍˢ 29ᵍˢ 38ᵍᶠ **1-3-6
£6,896**

Time To Remember (Ire) R A Fahey   60 a49
6 b g Pennekamp (USA) - Bequeath (USA)
14⁷ᵍ 14⁶ᵍ 16⁵ᵍᶠ 6⁷ᶠ 17⁶ᵍᶠ 14⁶ᵍ 7⁷ᵍᶠ
25ᵍ 15⁶ᵍᶠ 12⁷ᵍᶠ 108ᵍ 12⁶ᵍ 6⁹ˢᵈ **0-1-13
£3,380**

Time To Succeed J S Wainwright   13
2 b g Pennekamp (USA) - Ivory League
12⁸ᵍˢ 19⁶ᵍᶠ **0-0-2**

Time Traveller T M Jones
2 b g Timeless Times (USA) - Belltina
10⁶ˢᵈ 17⁶ᵍᶠ **0-0-2**

Time's The Master (Ire) M F Harris
3 b g Danetime (Ire) - Travel Tricks (Ire)
13⁶ˢˢ **0-0-1**

Timely Twist S Kirk   a16
3 b f Kirkwall - Timely Raise (USA)
7¹⁰ˢᵈ **0-0-1**

Times Review (USA) T D Easterby   86
3 b c Crafty Prospector (USA) - Previewed (USA)
2⁶ᵍ 5⁷ᵍᶠ 16ᵍ 14⁶ᵍᶠ 8⁶ᵍ 7⁶ᵍᶠ 11⁶ᵍ **1-1-7
£7,391**

Timmy M E Sowersby   36
2 b c Timeless Times (USA) - Ohnonotagain
8⁵ʰʸ 12⁶ᵍ 10⁵ᵍ 11⁷ᵍˢ 5⁶ˢ 15⁶ᵍᶠ 14⁶ˢʷ
0-0-7

Tinian K R Burke   59 a57
6 b g Mtoto - Housefull
5⁸ˢᵈ 3⁸ˢᵈ 10⁸ˢᵈ 3⁸ˢᵈ 12⁸ˢʷ 4⁷ᵍ 9⁸ᵍˢ 4⁸ᵍ
5⁷ˢᵈ 4⁸ˢᵈ 3⁸ᵍᶠ 2¹⁰ᶠ 4⁸ᵍ 8¹⁰ˢ 3¹²ˢᵈ **0-3-15
£2,786**

Tinker's First W G M Turner   16 a6
2 b f First Trump - Tinker Osmaston
9⁵ᵍᶠ 15⁶ᵍᶠ 10⁷ˢᵈ **0-0-3**

Tinta P A Blockley
4 b f Robellino (USA) - Albahaca (USA)
12¹⁶ˢᵈ **0-0-1**

Tintawn Gold (Ire) S Woodman   57 a39
4 b f Rudimentary (USA) - Clear Ahead
11¹⁰ˢᵈ 9⁹ᵍᶠ 4¹²ᵍᶠ 2¹¹ᵍᶠ 10¹⁰ᵍᶠ 2¹²ᵍᶠ 19¹²ᵍ
0-3-7 £1,479

Tiny Tim (Ire) A M Balding   43 a44
6 b g Brief Truce (USA) - Nonnita
4⁶ˢᵈ 4⁸ˢᵈ 2⁷ˢᵈ 3⁸ˢᵈ 5⁷ˢᵈ 2⁸ˢᵈ 26ˢᵈ 17ᵍ
5⁶ˢᵈ 26ˢᵈ 27ˢᵈ 11⁷ᵍᶠ **1-6-12 £3,409**

Tioga Gold (Ire) L R James   a25
5 b g Goldmark (USA) - Coffee Bean
5¹¹ˢᵈ 9¹⁴ᵍᶠ 10¹⁴ˢᵈ 11¹⁴ˢ **0-0-4**

Tip The Dip (USA) J H M Gosden   92
4 ch c Benny The Dip (USA) - Senora Tippy (USA)
2¹¹ᵍ 10¹²ᵍ 3¹⁰ˢ 23¹²ˢ **0-2-4 £3,269**

Tip Toes (Ire) M R Channon   43
2 b f Bianconi (USA) - Tip Tap Toe (USA)
10⁵ᵍᶠ 6⁵ᶠ 7⁶ᵍᶠ 4⁶ˢ 5⁶ᵍᶠ 12⁷ᵍᶠ 6⁷ˢ 4⁸ᵍ
8⁸ᵍˢ **0-1-9 £250**

Tipsy Lady D R C Elsworth   61
3 b f Intikhab (USA) - Creme De Menthe (Ire)
15⁶ˢ 7⁷ᵍᶠ 9⁸ᶠ 8⁹ᵍᶠ 5⁸ᵍᶠ 5⁸ˢ 15⁷ˢ **0-0-7**

Tipsy Lillie Julian Poulton   56 a21
2 ch f Tipsy Creek (USA) - Belle De Nuit (Ire)
5⁵ʰʸ 7⁶ᶠ 11⁶ᵍᶠ 8⁶ˢᵈ 15ᵍ 4⁵ᵍᶠ 16ᵍᶠ 4⁶ᵍᶠ
4⁶ʰʸ **2-0-9 £5,453**

Tit For Tat J G Given   57
2 b f Diktat - Wenda (Ire)
14⁵ᵍᶠ 5⁷ᶠ 4⁷ᵍˢ 19⁸ᵍ 12⁶ᵍ **0-0-5 £281**

Titian Flame (Ire) Mrs P N Dutfield   28 a30
4 ch f Titus Livius (Fr) - Golden Choice
19⁹ᵍᶠ 9⁸ˢᵈ **0-0-2**

Titian Lass C E Brittain   19 a54
5 ch m Bijou D'Inde - Liebsidelass (Ire)
4⁹ˢᵈ 1⁸ˢᵈ 5⁷ˢᵈ 2⁸ˢᵈ 5⁸ˢᵈ 16⁸ᶠ **1-1-6
£2,479**

Titian Time (USA) J H M Gosden   107
2 b f Red Ransom (USA) - Timely
2⁷ᵍ 3⁷ᵍ 2⁸ᵍ 28ᵍ **1-2-4 £49,138**

Tito Gofirst J Pearce   37
2 b c Gone West (USA) - Torgau (Ire)
9⁶ˢ **0-0-1**

Titus Rock (Ire) D McCain
2 b f Titus Livius (Fr) - Cossack Princess (Ire)
12⁵ᵍ **0-0-1**

Titus Salt (USA) T D Barron   56 a81
3 ch g Gentlemen (Arg) - Farewell Partner (USA)
3⁷ˢˢ 13⁷ᵍ **0-1-2 £628**

Tiviski (Ire) E J Alston   74
2 b f Desert Style (Ire) - Mummys Best
3⁵ᵍ 4⁵ᵍᶠ 1⁵ˢ 8⁵ᵍᶠ 4⁶ᵍᶠ 5⁵ᵍ 9⁶ᵍᶠ 9⁶ᵍᶠ 9⁷ᵍˢ
14⁶ʰʸ **1-1-10 £10,759**

Tiyoun (Ire) Jedd O'Keeffe   88
6 b g Kahyasi - Taysala (Ire)
2¹⁴ᵍ 6¹³ᵍ 1¹⁶ᵍᶠ 7¹⁴ᵍᶠ 2¹⁶ᵍᶠ 10²¹ᵍ **1-2-6
£8,791**

Tiz Molly (Ire) M R Channon
3 ch f Definite Article - Almadaniyah
PU¹⁰ᵍᶠ **0-0-1**

Tiz Wiz W Storey   39
3 b f Wizard King - Dannistar
9⁸ˢ 26ᵍ 10⁶ᶠ 10⁷ᵍˢ 13⁸ˢ **0-1-5 £465**

Tizdubai (USA) Saeed Bin Suroor   89
3 b f Cee's Tizzy (USA) - Cee's Song (USA)
6⁹ᵍ 7⁸ᵍᶠ **0-0-2 £750**

Tizi Ouzou (Ire) M C Pipe   52

3 ch f Desert Prince (Ire) - Tresor (USA)
6^{10g} 2^{10gf} **0-1-2 £1,087**

Tizzy May (Fr) *R Hannon* 105
4 ch c Highest Honor (Fr) - Forentia
13^{10gs} 2^{10g} 5^{12gf} 10^{12g} 4^{12gf} 8^{16gs} 7^{12gf}
5^{10gf} 5^{12gs} 9^{12gf} 9^{10hy} **0-1-11 £7,726**

Tizzy's Law *M A Buckley* 69
3 b f Case Law - Bo' Babbity
1^{5s} 6^{6g} 4^{6gf} 5^{5gs} 8^{5gf} 11^{5gs} 1^{5g} 5^{5s}
5^{5gf} **2-0-9 £9,868**

To Wit To Woo *B W Hills* 37 a65
4 b g Efisio - Sioux
2^{9ss} 8^{9ss} 9^{10ss} 5^{8hy} **0-1-4 £1,254**

Toberoe Commotion (Ire) *B J Llewellyn* a7
6 b g Great Commotion (USA) - Fionn Varragh (Ire)
11^{12sd} 14^{8f} **0-0-2**

Toby's Dream (Ire) *M Johnston* 77
2 b c Mujadil (USA) - Islandagore (Ire)
10^{6g} 1^{6f} 8^{6g} 6^{6f} 11^{6g} **1-0-5 £3,835**

Toccata Aria *J M Bradley* 59
6 b m Unfuwain (USA) - Distant Music
11^{11gf} 1^{10gs} 9^{12gf} 7^{8gf} **2-0-4 £6,961**

Toddeano *G Fierro*
8 b g Perpendicular - Phisus
9^{7ss} 13^{7gf} **0-0-2**

Todlea (Ire) *J A Osborne* 82 a64
4 b g Desert Prince (Ire) - Imelda (USA)
6^{10sd} 4^{8gs} 4^{10g} 3^{10gf} 6^{10gf} 2^{9gf} 2^{10f} 3^{9gf}
1^{8gf} 13^{8f} 3^{8gs} 3^{9gf} 13^{8gf} **1-6-13 £11,517**

Toffee Vodka (Ire) *J W Hills* 72 a69
2 b f Danehill Dancer (Ire) - Vieux Carre
6^{6gf} 3^{6g} 1^{6sd} 7^{6gf} 9^{7g} **1-1-5 £5,108**

Tohama *J L Dunlop* 72
2 b f In The Wings - Tanouma (USA)
6^{7gf} 8^{7gs} 5^{7s} 10^{8g} **0-0-4**

Toile *J G Given*
3 ch f Zafonic (USA) - Princess Sadie
6^{14g} **0-0-1 £239**

Tojoneski *I W McInnes* 59 a46
5 b g Emperor Jones (USA) - Sampower Lady
10^{12sd} 7^{8sd} 7^{7sd} 4^{8sd} 2^{9sd} 2^{8g} 2^{7hy} 3^{8gf}
3^{8f} 4^{7gf} 2^{9gf} 7^{8g} 3^{8gf} 9^{8gf} 7^{7hy} **0-8-15**
£4,058

Tokewanna *W M Brisbourne* 54 a61
4 b f Danehill (USA) - High Atlas
11^{7sd} 18^{7g} 3^{8g} 7^{7gf} 4^{7sd} 5^{8gf} 4^{8f} 3^{7f}
5^{8g} 10^{8gs} 1^{7sd} 1^{9sd} 10^{9sd} **2-1-13 £4,258**

Tolaga Bay *T J Fitzgerald*
6 ch m Dr Devious (Ire) - Swordlestown Miss (USA)
4^{12sd} **0-0-1**

Toldo (Ire) *G M Moore* 72
2 gr g Tagula (Ire) - Mystic Belle (Ire)
7^{5g} 9^{6g} 9^{5g} 4^{5g} 12^{6f} 2^{7s} 1^{7gf} 8^{hy} 1^{8g}
11^{7s} **3-1-10 £14,977**

Toledo Sun *V Smith* 50 a59
4 b g Zamindar (USA) - Shafir (Ire)
3^{11ss} 5^{11gf} 11^{15sd} 2^{14gf} **1-2-4 £4,077**

Tom Bell (Ire) *J G M O'Shea* 59
4 b g King's Theatre (Ire) - Nordic Display (Ire)
2^{12gs} 9^{14g} 4^{12gf} 4^{13gf} 2^{17g} 4^{16gs} 12^{12gf}
1^{12f} **1-2-8 £5,030**

Tom Forest *J R Fanshawe* 78
2 b c Forest Wildcat (USA) - Silk Masque (USA)
6^{6gf} 2^{6gf} 2^{6gf} 5^{7gf} 11^{7s} 11^{7s} **0-2-6**
£4,449

Tom From Bounty *W De Best-Turner* 33

4 ch g Opera Ghost - Tempus Fugit
10^{6gs} **0-0-1**

Tom Tun *J Balding* 106
9 b g Bold Arrangement - B Grade
7^{6g} 3^{6gs} 8^{6gs} 4^{6g} 2^{6gf} 16^{6s} 3^{6g} 5^{6gs}
10^{6s} 8^{6g} 3^{5s} 7^{6gs} **0-4-12 £17,317**

Tomasino *K G Reveley* 76
6 br g Celtic Swing - Bustinetta
4^{10gf} 6^{12s} 7^{10g} 7^{12gf} 9^{12gf} 3^{16gs} 8^{13s}
1-0-7 £4,384

Tombola (Fr) *J L Dunlop* 68
2 b g Trempolino (USA) - Green Charter
4^{7g} 12^{7gf} 13^{7gf} **0-0-3 £424**

Tomina *Miss E C Lavelle* 82
4 b g Deploy - Cavina
2^{16g} 11^{16s} **0-1-2 £3,064**

Tommy Carson *Jamie Poulton* 51 a46
9 b g Last Tycoon - Ivory Palm (USA)
3^{16sd} 10^{11f} 11^{6sd} 6^{16gs} **1-1-4 £3,419**

Tommy Smith *J S Wainwright* 72
6 ch g Timeless Times (USA) - Superstream
9^{5gs} 20^{5g} 8^{5gf} 11^{5gf} 1^{9gf} 8^{5gf} 16^{5gf}
8^{5gf} 15^{5gs} 14^{5gf} **1-0-10 £4,134**

Tomobel *M H Tompkins* 64
2 b f Josr Algarhoud (Ire) - Eileen's Lady
10^{5gf} 9^{7g} 15^{6gf} **0-1-4 £1,244**

Tomokim (Ire) *M Quinn*
3 b c Mujadil (USA) - Snowtop
11^{8sd} **0-0-1**

Tomoohat (USA) *Sir Michael Stoute* 89
2 b f Danzig (USA) - Crystal Downs (USA)
1^{6s} **1-0-1 £7,072**

Tomsk (Ire) *Miss K M George* 22 a36
4 b g Definite Article - Merry Twinkle
6^{8sd} 3^{10gs} 10^{10sd} **0-1-3 £387**

Tomthevic *J M Bradley* 53 a12
6 ch g Emarati (USA) - Madame Bovary
14^{5gf} 11^{5gf} 8^{5gf} 7^{5f} 4^{5gf} 11^{5gs} 5^{5g}
11^{5gf} 16^{6g} 10^{5s} 11^{5sd} **0-0-11**

Ton-Chee *K W Hogg* 17
5 b g Vettori (Ire) - Najariya
6^{16sw} 7^{16sd} 6^{17g} 10^{16g} **0-0-4**

Tong Ice *B A Pearce* a22
5 gr g Petong - Efficacious (Ire)
8^{8sd} 6^{6sd} 5^{6sd} **0-0-3**

Toni Alcala *R F Fisher* 80 a66
5 b g Ezzoud (Ire) - Etourdie (USA)
3^{12sw} 5^{16ss} 4^{16s} 7^{12hy} 2^{14gf} 3^{22s} 1^{14g} 6^{16g}
1^{13f} 3^{14gf} 5^{13gf} 2^{17gf} 4^{14f} 5^{18gf} 1^{16g} 1^{16gs}
5^{16f} 5^{16s} 13^{17gf} 10^{18g} **4-4-23**
£25,112

Tonight (Ire) *W M Brisbourne* 51
2 b g Imperial Ballet (Ire) - No Tomorrow (Ire)
3^{6f} 4^{6gf} 3^{7f} 6^{7gf} 7^{8hy} 10^{7gf} 8^{8g} **0-0-7**
£721

Tonto (Fr) *Miss D Mountain* a63
3 gr g Second Empire (Ire) - Malabarista (Fr)
7^{6sd} 4^{7sd} 3^{8sd} 7^{8sd} 6^{8sd} 10^{10sd} 8^{8g} **0-1-7**
£832

Tony James (Ire) *C E Brittain* 107
2 b c Xaar - Sunset Ridge (Fr)
1^{6gf} 4^{6gf} 5^{6gf} 1^{6s} 6^{7g} 9^{6vs} **2-0-6**
£89,460

Tony The Tap *N A Callaghan* 89 a65
3 b g Most Welcome - Laleston
1^{5sd} 2^{5gf} 2^{5gf} 2^{5gf} 5^{7g} 2^{6gf} 1^{5gf} 9^{6gf}
7^{6g} 5^{6gs} 2^{5g} 12^{7gf} **2-5-12 £29,200**

Tony Tie *J S Goldie* 88
8 b g Ardkinglass - Queen Of The Quorn
6^{10s} 2^{10gs} 2^{8g} 5^{10gf} 15^{10gf} 2^{8gf} 1^{8g} 6^{7s}
1^{8g} 11^{8gf} 6^{9s} 9^{8gs} 5^{8s} 7^{8s} 17^{9g} 10^{7s} **2-3-16**
£17,503

Too Keen *J M Jefferson* a19
3 ch f Keen - Janie-O
5^{7sd} 11^{7s} 8^{8sd} **0-0-3**

Top Achiever (Ire) *C W Moore* 62
3 ch g Intikhab (USA) - Nancy Maloney (Ire)
7^{8s} 7^{8gs} 11^{8g} 8^{8g} 2^{12gs} **0-1-5 £860**

Top Dirham *M W Easterby* 81
6 ch g Night Shift (USA) - Miller's Melody
2^{8hy} 3^{8gs} 2^{8g} 11^{9gf} 8^{8g} 1^{8gf} 6^{7g} 6^{8gf}
1-3-8 £14,238

Top Form (Ire) *E A L Dunlop* 80
2 b f Almutawakel - Top Of The Form (Ire)
8^{6gf} 5^{6gf} 16^{gf} 5^{6gf} 21^{7g} 11^{5g} **1-0-6**
£6,253

Top Gear *D R C Elsworth* 84
2 b c Robellino (USA) - Bundle
2^{8gs} **0-1-1 £1,780**

Top Line Dancer (Ire) *M D Hammond* 64
3 b c Fasliyev (USA) - Twafeaj (USA)
4^{6g} 12^{7s} 8^{7f} 9^{8g} **0-0-4 £259**

Top Mark *H Morrison*
2 b c Mark Of Esteem (Ire) - Red White And Blue
11^{8hy} **0-0-1**

Top Of The Class (Ire) *P D Evans* 63 a52
7 b m Rudimentary (USA) - School Mum
10^{9sd} 6^{9sd} 3^{12sd} 3^{9ss} 4^{12sd} 8^{12sd} 7^{10sd}
14^{12sd} 3^{10sd} 5^{12sd} 7^{12ss} 4^{11gs} 7^{11gs} 7^{10f} 7^{12sd}
8^{12gf} **0-4-16 £1,409**

Top Place *B A Pearce* 38 a38
3 b f Compton Place - Double Top (Ire)
7^{5sd} 8^{6sd} 9^{6sd} 5^{6sd} 5^{6g} 10^{5g} 6^{7gf} 8^{6gs}
0-0-8

Top Pursuit *J L Spearing* 48
2 b g Pursuit Of Love - Top Of The Parkes
7^{7gf} **0-0-1**

Top Romance (Ire) *Sir Michael Stoute* 95
3 ch f Entrepreneur - Heart's Harmony
8^{7g} 4^{9g} 8^{10gf} **0-0-3 £2,500**

Top Seed (Ire) *M R Channon* 112
3 b c Cadeaux Genereux - Midnight Heights
2^{10g} 4^{10gs} 13^{12gs} 3^{16f} 2^{15gf} 16^{14s} 8^{12gf}
PU^{12hy} PU^{12s} **0-2-9 £23,662**

Top Spec (Ire) *R Hannon* 88
3 b g Spectrum (Ire) - Pearl Marine (Ire)
8^{10gs} 11^{10gf} 5^{10g} 12^{10gs} 2^{8gf} 7^{10g} 1^{10gs}
2^{10gf} 1^{10g} 9^{10gf} 4^{12s} 7^{10s} **2-2-12 £21,434**

Top Style (Ire) *J Howard Johnson* 52 a40
6 ch g Topanoora - Kept In Style
7^{11sd} 2^{7sd} 2^{10sd} 1^{10s} **1-2-4 £2,230**

Top Tenor (Ire) *V Thompson* a56
4 b g Sadler's Wells (USA) - Posta Vecchia (USA)
12^{16sd} 11^{12sd} 6^{12sd} 3^{12sd} **0-1-4 £181**

Top The Charts *R Hannon* 88
2 b c Singspiel (Ire) - On The Tide
4^{7s} 4^{7g} 3^{8gs} 2^{7s} **0-2-4 £6,238**

Top Trees *W S Kittow* 56
6 b g Charnwood Forest (Ire) - Low Line
9^{12gf} 6^{17g} 1^{14gf} 5^{16gf} 8^{13gs} 5^{13gs} **1-0-6**
£6,857

Toparudi *M H Tompkins* 75
3 b g Rudimentary (USA) - Topatori (Ire)

9^{8g} 1^{8gs} 11^{8gf} 3^{8g} **1-1-4 £5,419**

Topatoo *M H Tompkins* 67
2 ch f Bahamian Bounty - Topatori (Ire)
3^{6s} **0-1-1 £730**

Topkamp *M L W Bell* 101
4 b f Pennekamp (USA) - Victoria Regia (Ire)
2^{6g} 3^{6f} 3^{6gf} 6^{6gs} **0-2-4 £17,956**

Topkat (Ire) *D R C Elsworth* 84
3 b g Simply Great (Fr) - Kitty's Sister
8^{10g} 2^{10gf} 5^{9gf} 1^{12gs} 7^{14gf} **1-1-5 £8,334**

Topple *H Candy* 30
3 b f Master Willie - Top Cover
9^{9gf} **0-0-1**

Toppling *J M Bradley* 55 a39
6 b g Cadeaux Genereux - Topicality (USA)
12^{6sd} 8^{6gf} 8^{6gf} 8^{6g} 4^{6gf} 13^{6g} 11^{6gf} 9^{7gf}
14^{8gf} 11^{7g} **0-1-10**

Topton (Ire) *P Howling* 83 a81
10 b g Royal Academy (USA) - Circo
4^{10sd} 3^{8sd} 1^{8sd} 13^{8gs} 15^{8s} 9^{8gf} 4^{8gf} 6^{8g}
2^{8f} 6^{8g} 5^{8gs} 4^{8gf} 7^{8gf} 5^{8gs} 13^{7s} **1-2-15**
£6,772

Toque *H Morrison* 53 a67
2 ch f King's Best (USA) - Barboukh
9^{7g} 9^{8sd} **0-0-2**

Torcello (Ire) *G Wragg* 93
6 b g Royal Academy (USA) - Vanya
5^{10f} 4^{10hy} **0-0-2 £1,664**

Torchlight (USA) *J H M Gosden* 44
4 b/br f Seeking The Gold (USA) - Cap Beino (USA)
11^{8gf} 13^{8gf} **0-0-2**

Torinmoor (USA) *Mrs A J Perrett* 98
3 ch g Intikhab (USA) - Tochar Ban (USA)
5^{10s} 3^{10gf} 3^{10gf} 5^{12g} 4^{10gs} **0-2-5 £9,633**

Tornado Bay (Ire) *I A Wood* 22
3 b f Desert Style (Ire) - Dromoland
11^{9g} 7^{12sd} **0-0-2**

Toro Bravo (Ire) *R M Beckett* a53
4 b g Alhaarth (Ire) - Set Trail (Ire)
5^{8sd} 3^{9sd} **0-0-2 £414**

Toronto Heights (USA) *P W Chapple-Hyam* 58 a81
3 ch g King Of Kings (Ire) - Revoltosa (Ire)
2^{6sd} 16^{sd} 16^{7sd} 19^{7g} 7^{6sd} 12^{6gs} **2-1-7**
£9,148

Torquemada (Ire) *W Jarvis* 71 a69
3 ch c Desert Sun - Gaelic's Fantasy (Ire)
3^{6sd} 11^{6gs} 16^{6s} 8^{7gf} 3^{6sd} 7^{6sd} 9^{6gs} 1^{7gf}
5^{6gf} 3^{7sd} **1-3-10 £5,824**

Torrens (Ire) *S P Griffiths* 74
2 b c Royal Anthem (USA) - Azure Lake (USA)
4^{7gs} 1^{8s} 7^{8s} 10^{8g} 3^{8s} 14^{7gs} **1-1-6**
£4,886

Torrent *D W Chapman* 61 a55
9 ch g Prince Sabo - Maiden Pool
2^{5sd} 6^{6sd} 3^{6ss} 1^{5ss} 5^{5ss} 3^{5ss} 8^{6sw} 7^{5ss}
1^{5ss} 9^{5ss} 9^{5g} 9^{5g} 15^{gf} 2^{5g} 7^{5gs} 8^{6f} 7^{5gf} 2^{5gf} **3-5-21**
£12,038

Torrestrella (Ire) *Christophe Clement* 115
3 b f Orpen (USA) - Sea Ring (Fr)
1^{8s} 1^{9gs} 1^{8gf} 11^{11gs} 6^{9g} 5^{8f} **3-0-6**
£168,530

Torrid Kentavr (USA) *B Ellison* 75
7 b g Trempolino (USA) - Torrid Tango (USA)
7^{8hy} 1^{8s} 2^{8gf} **1-1-3 £6,468**

Tortuette *Jean-Rene Auvray* a15
3 b f Turtle Island (Ire) - Allmosa

9^{9sw} 10^{8sd} 9^{8ss} **0-0-3**

Torzal *Miss M E Rowland*
4 br g Hector Protector (USA) - Alathezal (USA)
15^{12g} **0-0-1**

Toshi (USA) *M Johnston* — 56
2 b c Kingmambo (USA) - Majestic Role (Fr)
7^{6g} 8^{7s} **0-0-2**

Toss The Caber (Ire) *M R Channon* — 40
2 ch g Dr Devious (Ire) - Celtic Fling
7^{6gf} 8^{6gf} **0-0-2**

Total Force (Ire) *R Hannon* — 54
3 b c Night Shift (USA) - Capegulch (USA)
11^{8gf} 16^{7gf} **0-0-2**

Total Turtle (Ire) *P F I Cole* — 94
5 b g Turtle Island (Ire) - Chagrin D'Amour (Ire)
6^{12gf} 5^{16gf} **0-0-2 £750**

Totally Scottish *K G Reveley* — 52
8 b g Mtoto - Glenfinlass
3^{16gs} 3^{16g} **0-2-2 £866**

Totally Yours (Ire) *W R Muir* — 88
3 b f Desert Sun - Total Aloof
9^{7g} 4^{7g} 17^{8gf} 5^{7gs} 11^{9g} 8^{6g} 9^{6gf} 2^{6gs}
10^{6s} 9^{6s} **0-1-10 £4,345**

Touch Of Ebony (Ire) *C Roberts* — 53
5 b g Darshaan - Cormorant Wood
15^{8f} 10^{12g} 2^{14gs} 3^{13s} **0-2-4 £639**

Touch Of Silk (Ire) *B W Hills* — 77
2 ch f Night Shift (USA) - Blew Her Top (USA)
5^{5gf} 2^{5gf} 15^{6f} 11^{6g} **0-1-4 £1,500**

Touch Of Spice *J R Jenkins* — a26
2 ch g Lake Coniston (Ire) - Soft Touch (Ger)
16^{6g} 9^{7sd} 16^{8gf} **0-0-3**

Touch Of Spirit *J R Jenkins*
5 b m Dancing Spree (USA) - Soft Touch (Ger)
9^{8sd} **0-0-1**

Tough Love *T D Easterby* — 91
5 ch g Pursuit Of Love - Food Of Love
22^{8g} 7^{7hy} 7^{7gs} 16^{8g} 10^{8gf} 5^{8g} 10^{8s}
15^{7gf} **0-0-8**

Tournedos (Ire) *M R Channon* — 105
2 b c Rossini (USA) - Don't Care (Ire)
1^{5g} 2^{5gf} 2^{5gf} 8^{5g} 1^{5g} 7^{6vs} 3^{6g} 2^{5f} 5^{6y}
2^{5hy} 6^{5s} **2-5-11 £78,297**

Tout Les Sous *Jean-Rene Auvray* — 10
3 ch g Tout Ensemble - Suzie Sue (Ire)
7^{12gf} 9^{12gf} **0-0-2**

Tout Seul (Ire) *R F Johnson Houghton* — 109
4 b c Ali-Royal (Ire) - Total Aloof
1^{7gs} 15^{8g} 11^{7gf} 10^{8gs} 4^{8g} 4^{8gs}
1-0-7 **£21,400**

Town End Tom *D M Simcock* — 56
2 b g Entrepreneur - Prima Silk
5^{5gf} 6^{6gf} 6^{5gf} 16^{7gf} 16^{5gs} **0-0-5**

Town House *B P J Baugh* — 72 a5
2 gr f Paris House - Avondale Girl (Ire)
5^{5g} 5^{5gs} 2^{5s} 7^{5gf} 7^{5g} 7^{5s} 9^{5f} 10^{5sd}
1-1-8 **£4,205**

Trackattack *J A Osborne* — 68 a57
2 ch g Atraf - Verbena (Ire)
3^{6gf} 5^{6sd} 7^{6gf} 10^{7gf} 12^{6gf} **0-1-5 £528**

Tractor Boy *W J Haggas* — 80
2 b c Mind Games - Day Star
12^{5gs} 1^{6g} **1-0-2 £5,278**

Trade Fair *R Charlton* — 116
4 b c Zafonic (USA) - Danefair
14^{6gs} 3^{7gf} 1^{7gf} 6^{7g} 3^{6g} **1-1-4 £43,619**

Trafalgar Square *R Guest* — 43
2 b c King's Best (USA) - Pat Or Else
8^{7gf} **0-0-1**

Tragedian (USA) *J H M Gosden* — 80
2 ch c Theatrical - Foreign Courier (USA)
3^{7g} **0-1-1 £920**

Tragic Dancer *D J Wintle* — 35
8 b g Tragic Role (USA) - Chantallee's Pride
8^{12gs} **0-0-1**

Traianos (USA) *P F I Cole* — 73
2 b/br c Mt. Livermore (USA) - Shiitake (USA)
5^{6gf} 6^{7g} 5^{7gf} 7^{8g} **0-0-4**

Trance (Ire) *T D Barron* — 93
4 ch g Bahhare (USA) - Lady Of Dreams (Ire)
9^{10f} 4^{10g} 1^{12g} 13^{9g} 1^{14g} 11^{14g} 7^{14gs} 3^{14s}
9^{18s} 5^{17s} **2-0-10 £19,915**

Tranquil Sky *N A Callaghan* — 90
3 b f Intikhab (USA) - Tranquillity
18^{7g} 16^{8g} 5^{9g} 2^{8gf} 7^{8gf} 4^{8g} 7^{8gf} 5^{7gf}
5^{8gs} **0-1-9 £5,958**

Tranquilizer *D J Coakley* — 62 a69
2 b f Dr Fong (USA) - Tranquillity
6^{8gf} UR^{8gs} 7^{8gf} 2^{8gs} 3^{9sd} **0-2-5 £1,745**

Transaction (Ire) *J M P Eustace* — 91 a71
2 ch g Trans Island - Meranie Girl (Ire)
3^{5sd} 2^{6g} 1^{6g} 1^{6gf} 6^{6g} 8^{6g} 15^{6hy} **2-2-7**
£31,137

Transcendantale (Fr) *Mrs S Lamyman* — 71
6 b/br m Apple Tree (Fr) - Kataba (Fr)
2^{11gf} 3^{10gs} 5^{10s} 6^{12gf} 9^{10gf} 7^{8gf} 4^{10gf}
8^{8gf} 4^{12g} 5^{8gs} 9^{12g} 7^{8f} 15^{8f} **0-2-13 £3,020**

Transgress (Ire) *R Hannon* — 77
2 b c Trans Island - Ned's Contessa (Ire)
3^{7gf} 8^{7gs} 6^{6g} 5^{7gf} **0-1-4 £896**

Transit *B Ellison* — 48
5 b g Lion Cavern (USA) - Black Fighter (USA)
5^{12hy} **0-0-1**

Transkei *Mrs L Stubbs* — 20
3 b f Sesaro (USA) - In The Sky (Ire)
13^{8g} 4^{12s} 10^{9g} 12^{7s} **0-0-4 £264**

Transvestite (Ire) *J W Hills* — 77 a71
2 b c Trans Island - Christoph's Girl
5^{5g} 4^{6gf} 3^{5g} 6^{7g} 11^{7gf} 3^{6sd} **0-2-6**
£1,629

Trappeto (Ire) *W R Muir* — 59
2 b c Barathea (Ire) - Campiglia (Ire)
11^{7gs} **0-0-1**

Travel Tardia (Ire) *P A Blockley* — 24 a57
6 br h Petardia - Annie's Travels (Ire)
13^{10sd} 8^{8sd} 4^{7sw} 1^{7ss} 7^{11sd} 15^{7g} **1-0-6**
£1,459

Travel Tip (USA) *J H M Gosden* — 69
2 ch c Gone West (USA) - Cap Beino (USA)
4^{8f} PU^{8g} **0-0-2 £429**

Traveller's Tale *P G Murphy* — 69 a70
5 b g Selkirk (USA) - Chere Amie (USA)
13^{10sd} 7^{10g} 6^{10g} 12^{10g} 7^{12g} 7^{10f}
6^{12gf} 2^{11g} 2^{12s} 11^{13gs} 3^{12sd} 4^{12sd} 9^{12sd} **0-3-14**
£2,803

Travellers Joy *R J Hodges* — 35 a27
4 b f The West (USA) - Persian Fortune
9^{6sd} 8^{5gs} 3^{5sd} 8^{5sd} 6^{9gf} 6^{5g} 8^{6g}
0-0-8 £204

Travelling Band (Ire) *A M Balding* — 74 a68
6 b g Blues Traveller (Ire) - Kind Of Cute
13^{10sd} 13^{8g} 6^{10g} 9^{10s} 2^{9gs} 12^{9gs} 13^{8gs}

0-1-7 £1,728

Travelling Times *J S Wainwright*   47 a54
5 b g Timeless Times (USA) - Bollin Sophie
5⁶ˢᵈ 6⁶ˢᵈ 11⁶ᵍ 15⁶ᶠ 4⁵ᵍ 12⁶ᵍ 2⁶ˢᵈ 6⁶ˢʷ
6⁵ˢᵈ **0-2-9 £1,158**

Traytonic *J R Fanshawe*   108
3 b c Botanic (USA) - Lady Parker (Ire)
5⁵ᵍᶠ 14⁶ᵍᶠ 1⁶ᵍˢ 3⁶ᵍᶠ 8⁶ᵍ 7⁶ᵍˢ 4⁷ᵍᶠ 6⁷ˢ
1-1-8 £21,176

Tre Colline *N Tinkler*   70 a82
5 b g Efisio - Triple Joy
12⁶ᵍˢ 11⁷ˢ 16⁶ˢ 9⁷ᶠ 15⁷ᵍᶠ 1⁸ˢᵈ 5⁷ˢᵈ
1⁸ˢᵈ 4⁸ˢᵈ 6⁸ᵍ 1⁸ˢᵈ 7⁷ᵍ 6⁷ˢᵈ 8⁷ˢᵈ 4⁷ˢᵈ **3-0-15**
£10,901

Treason Trial *Mrs Stef Liddiard*   69
3 b g Peintre Celebre (USA) - Pampabella (Ire)
11⁸ᵍ 6⁹ᵍ 4⁸ᵍᶠ 3⁸ᵍ 1¹⁰ᵍᶠ 3¹⁰ᵍˢ 3¹²ʰʸ 4¹⁶ᵍ
1¹⁴ᵍ **2-2-9 £10,650**

Treasure Cay *P W D'Arcy*   87 a72
3 ch c Bahamian Bounty - Madame Sisu
5⁵ˢᵈ 3⁶ᵍ 5⁶ᵍᶠ 3⁵ᵍᶠ 1⁵ᵍˢ 9⁵ᵍˢ 3⁵ᵍᶠ 2⁵ᵍᶠ
6⁵ᵍˢ **1-4-9 £13,372**

Treasure House (Ire) *J Jay*   77 a92
3 b g Grand Lodge (USA) - Royal Wolff
8⁷ˢᵈ 12⁸ᵍ 5⁶ˢ 8⁷ᵍᶠ 14⁶ᵍᶠ 14⁵ᵍˢ 13⁵ᵍ
0-0-7 £750

Treasure The Lady (Ire) *John M Oxx*   95
3 b f Indian Ridge - Kasora (Ire)
4⁷ˢ 5⁹ᵍᶠ 4⁹ᵍˢ 9⁸ᵍᶠ 6⁸ʸˢ **0-0-5 £2,728**

Treasure Trail *S Kirk*   76 a49
5 b g Millkom - Forever Shineing
5¹⁶ˢᵈ 10¹⁴ʰʸ 11¹⁴ᵍ 1¹⁷ᶠ 6¹⁶ᵍᶠ **1-0-5**
£3,643

Treasury (Ire) *C E Brittain*   35
2 b f King's Best (USA) - Copious (Ire)
17⁸ᵍᶠ **0-0-1**

Treat Me Wild (Ire) *R Hannon*   69
2 ch f Loup Sauvage (USA) - Goes A Treat (Ire)
1⁵ᵍ 6⁷ᵍ 5⁷ᵍᶠ 1⁶ᵍᶠ 4⁶ᵍˢ 9⁷ᶠ 16⁶ˢ **2-0-7**
£7,518

Trebello *M Johnston*   32
3 b c Robellino (USA) - Trempkate (USA)
8⁹ˢ **0-0-1**

Treble Seven (USA) *C E Brittain*   59
2 b/br f Fusaichi Pegasus (USA) - Nemea (USA)
6⁷ᵍ 12⁶ᵍ **0-0-2**

Tree Chopper (USA) *M P Tregoning*
3 ch f Woodman (USA) - Gazayil (USA)
7¹⁰ᵍ **0-0-1**

Tree Roofer *N P Littmoden*   a53
5 b g King's Signet (USA) - Armaiti
12⁷ˢᵈ 9⁵ˢᵈ 8⁶ˢᵈ 2⁶ˢᵈ **0-1-4 £836**

Tree Tops *J H M Gosden*   76
3 b f Grand Lodge (USA) - The Faraway Tree
5⁷ᵍ 2⁸ˢ 3¹⁰ᵍᶠ 3¹⁰ᵍ 6¹²ᵍᶠ 11¹⁰ᵍ 15¹⁰ˢ
11¹⁰ˢ **0-3-8 £2,728**

Treetops Hotel (Ire) *B R Johnson*   64 a64
5 ch g Grand Lodge (USA) - Rousinette
2¹⁰ˢᵈ 9⁸ᵍᶠ 11⁷ᵍᶠ 9⁷ᵍ 2⁸ᶠ 4¹²ᵍᶠ 2⁷ᵍᶠ 11¹¹ᵍ
12⁶ᵍˢ 4⁸ˢᵈ **0-3-10 £5,406**

Tregarron *R Hannon*   77
3 br c Efisio - Language Of Love
1⁵ᵍᶠ 4⁵ᵍᶠ 2⁶ᵍᶠ 7⁵ˢ 3⁶ᵍˢ 1⁵ᵍ 10⁶ᵍᶠ 16⁷ᵍˢ
1-2-8 £9,574

Tregenna *R M H Cowell*   43
3 b f Forzando - Nineteenth Of May
4⁷ᵍ 5⁷ᵍᶠ 14⁸ᵍˢ 18¹⁰ᵍᶠ **0-0-4 £774**

Tremar *T G Mills*   108 a85
2 b c Royal Applause - Sabina
4⁵ˢ 3⁵ᵍˢ 2⁶ˢ 1⁶ˢᵈ 4⁶ᵍᶠ 1⁶ᵍ 6⁷ˢ **2-2-7**
£37,618

Trempjane *R Hannon*   75
2 b f Lujain (USA) - Trempkate (USA)
1⁶ᵍ 5⁵ᵍᶠ 5⁶ᵍᶠ 8⁷ᵍᶠ 8⁶ᵍᶠ **1-0-5 £5,188**

Trench Coat (USA) *A M Balding*   59 a68
3 ch c Gulch (USA) - Glamor Queen (USA)
2⁷ˢᵈ 7⁷ᵍ 10⁷ᵍᶠ 13⁸ˢᵈ **0-1-4 £1,175**

Tresor Secret (Fr) *P Butler*   76 a53
4 b g Green Desert (USA) - Tresor (USA)
16¹⁰ᵍ 5¹⁰ᵍᶠ 7⁸ᵍᶠ 2¹²ˢᵈ 2¹²ˢᵈ **0-2-5**
£1,490

Trevian *S C Williams*   65 a71
3 ch g Atraf - Ascend (Ire)
14⁷ˢᵈ 1⁸ˢᵈ 6¹⁰ˢᵈ 6⁸ˢᵈ 5⁸ˢᵈ 8⁸ᵍᶠ **1-0-6**
£3,262

Trew Class *M H Tompkins*   80
3 ch f Inchinor - Inimitable
7⁸ˢ 17¹⁰ˢ 1¹⁰ᵍᶠ 1¹⁰ᵍᶠ 3¹⁰ᵍˢ 8¹⁰ᵍ 6¹²ᵍᶠ
2-0-7 £11,926

Trew Flight (USA) *M H Tompkins*   48
2 b c Rahy (USA) - Magdala (Ire)
19⁸ˢ 5⁷ˢ **0-0-2**

Trew Style *M H Tompkins*   76
2 ch c Desert King (Ire) - Southern Psychic (USA)
15⁸ˢ 4⁷ᵍˢ **0-0-2 £384**

Triage (Ire) *M R Channon*
3 b f Mujadil (USA) - Trebles (Ire)
8⁶ˢ **0-0-1**

Tribute (Ire) *K A Ryan*   78
3 b g Green Desert (USA) - Zooming (Ire)
10⁵ˢ 7⁵ᵍᶠ 5⁶ᵍᶠ 5⁵ᵍᶠ 5⁶ᵍ 24⁷ᵍ 11⁵ˢᵈ **0-0-7**

Trick Cyclist *M W Easterby*   81 a86
3 b g Mind Games - Sabonis (USA)
2⁵ˢᵈ 4⁵ˢᵈ 7⁶ᵍˢ 6⁵ᶠ 7⁶ᵍ 2⁵ᵍᶠ 1⁵ᶠ 3⁶ᵍᶠ 5⁵ˢ
15⁵ᵍᶠ 4⁶ᵍˢ 8⁵ᵍˢ **1-3-12 £7,632**

Trickshot *T D Easterby*   59
2 ch f Mister Baileys - Zizi (Ire)
2⁶ᵍˢ 16⁶ᵍᶠ 7⁷ᵍ **0-1-3 £1,190**

Trickstep *I Semple*   65 a49
3 b g Imperial Ballet (Ire) - Trick Of Ace (USA)
17⁷ˢ 25⁸ˢ 12¹²ᵍʸ 13⁹ᶠ 2¹³ᵍ 6¹²ᵍ 1¹⁰ˢ
5¹²ˢᵈ **1-1-8 £6,588**

Tricky Venture *P W Hiatt*   69
4 gr g Linamix (Fr) - Ukraine Venture
2¹⁰ˢ 4¹⁰ᵍˢ **0-1-2 £1,505**

Trifti *C A Cyzer*   56 a62
3 b g Vettori (Ire) - Time For Tea (Ire)
4⁸ˢᵈ 11¹⁰ᵍˢ 10⁶ᵍᶠ 8⁶ˢᵈ 4⁸ˢᵈ 2⁷ᵍᶠ 9⁸ᵍ
12⁸ᶠ **0-1-8 £1,078**

Trigger Mead *Mrs Stef Liddiard*
4 b f Double Trigger (Ire) - Normead Lass
11¹⁰ˢᵈ **0-0-1**

Triggers Double *K Bell*
3 ch c Double Trigger (Ire) - Princess Alaska
15¹²ˢᵈ **0-0-1**

Trigony (Ire) *T D Easterby*   60
2 b g Brave Act - Lulu Island
12⁷ᵍ 12⁷ᵍˢ 6⁹ᶠ **0-0-3**

Trilemma *Sir Mark Prescott*   91
3 b f Slip Anchor - Thracian
9¹⁰ʰʸ 11¹⁰ᵍ 6¹²ᵍᶠ 1¹⁶ᵍˢ 1¹⁶ᵍ 1¹⁶ᵍᶠ 7¹⁶ˢ
3-0-7 £18,034

Trim Image *H Alexander* 69
2 br f Averti (Ire) - Altizaf
2^{5y} 3^{5gf} 3^{5g} 3^{5gs} 1^{5gs} 12^{5gf} **1-1-6**
£6,997

Trinaree (Ire) *S Gollings* 23
3 b g Revoque (Ire) - Ball Cat (Fr)
11^{5gf} 12^{6f} 15^{7g} 16^{8gf} **0-0-4**

Trinculo (Ire) *D Nicholls* 97 a87
7 b g Anita's Prince - Fandangerina (USA)
7^{6sd} 10^{5sd} 8^{5sd} UR^{5sd} 2^{5g} 5^{5g} 11^{5gs}
11^{5g} 6^{6g} 15^{5gs} 9^{5s} 10^{5g} 1^{5s} 1^{5s} **1-1-14**
£7,609

Trinity (Ire) *M Brittain* 50
8 b h College Chapel - Kaskazi
8^{6s} 10^{7g} 10^{5g} 19^{6g} **0-0-4**

Trinity Fair *J G Given* 45
3 b f Polish Precedent (USA) - Chita Rivera
11^{8gf} 13^{10gf} 10^{8gf} 10^{11gf} **0-0-4**

Triphenia (Ire) *M L W Bell* 41
6 b g Ashkalani (Ire) - Atsuko (Ire)
9^{12gf} **0-0-1**

Triple Jump *T D Easterby* 80
3 ch g Inchinor - Meteoric
2^{8g} 1^{8gf} 3^{10s} 15^{11hy} **1-2-4 £9,470**

Triple Zero (Ire) *A P Jarvis* 65
2 b f Raise A Grand (Ire) - Locorotondo (Ire)
8^{6g} 14^{7gf} 1^{8gf} **1-0-3 £3,786**

Tripti (Ire) *J J Bridger* 47 a51
4 b f Sesaro (USA) - Chatelsong (USA)
2^{6sd} 10^{6sd} 10^{6sd} 8^{6sd} 10^{6sd}
13^{5gf} 12^{5gf} 4^{5g} 5^{6g} **0-2-11 £1,922**

Trishay *A P Jarvis* a28
3 gr f Petong - Marjorie's Memory (Ire)
10^{7sd} 10^{8gf} **0-0-2**

Tritonville Lodge (Ire) *Miss E C Lavelle* 54
2 b g Grand Lodge (USA) - Olean
7^{8hy} **0-0-1**

Trivial Pursuit *W Jarvis* 19
3 b c Mind Games - Chushan Venture
9^{7f} **0-0-1**

Trofana Falcon *H J Collingridge* 37
4 b g Polar Falcon (USA) - Silk St James
11^{12gs} 16^{10g} **0-0-2**

Trois Etoiles (Ire) *J W Hills* 62 a51
3 ch f Grand Lodge (USA) - Stardance (USA)
5^{6gf} 9^{7gf} 5^{8g} 5^{10g} 3^{8gf} 6^{8g} 10^{9sd} 6^{9sd}
0-1-8 £610

Trojan Flight *Mrs J R Ramsden* 81
3 ch g Hector Protector (USA) - Fairywings
4^{6gs} 5^{8hy} 4^{7hy} 6^{7gf} 8^{8gf} 6^{9gf} 4^{8g} 3^{6g}
2^{5gs} 1^{5gs} 2^{6gs} 1^{6gf} 9^{5gs} 4^{6s} 2^{5f} 4^{5s} 7^{6gs}
2-5-17 £19,833

Trojan Wolf *P Howling* a43
9 ch g Wolfhound (USA) - Trojan Lady (USA)
7^{11sd} 4^{14ss} 16^{11ss} 5^{11sd} **0-0-4**

Tromp *D J Coakley* 53 a66
3 ch c Zilzal (USA) - Sulitelma (USA)
5^{7gf} 6^{7gf} 2^{9sd} **0-1-3 £1,056**

Trompe L'Oeil (Ire) *Andrew Reid* 43 a54
3 b f Distant View (USA) - Milly Ha Ha
8^{10sd} 7^{10sd} 6^{10sd} 9^{7sd} 8^{8g} 13^{8s} **0-0-6**

Troodos Jet *A Berry* 64 a64
3 b g Atraf - Costa Verde
4^{6gf} 14^{6gf} 4^{6sd} 1^{5s} 12^{6gs} 13^{6s} 14^{5s} **1-0-7**
£5,424

Tropical Coral (Ire) *C Tinkler* a68
4 ch f Pennekamp (USA) - Tropical Dance (USA)
6^{9sd} **0-0-1**

Tropical Son *D Shaw* a53
5 b g Distant Relative - Douce Maison (Ire)
2^{9sd} 5^{8sd} 1^{10sd} 9^{9sd} 2^{13sd} 5^{12s} 7^{10sd}
5^{12sd} 9^{12sd} **1-2-9 £2,914**

Tropical Storm (Ire) *J Noseda* 77
3 ch g Alhaarth (Ire) - Rainstone
3^{7gf} 9^{7s} 4^{6gf} 2^{6gs} 1^{7hy} **1-2-5 £5,794**

Trotters Bottom *Andrew Reid* 67 a60
3 b g Mind Games - Fleeting Affair
7^{5sd} 5^{6g} **0-0-2**

Troubadour (Ire) *A P O'Brien* 111
3 b c Danehill (USA) - Taking Liberties (Ire)
1^{8f} 2^{8g} 18^{7g} 11^{8g} **2-1-4 £44,233**

Trouble Mountain (USA) *M W Easterby* 83 a79
7 br g Mt. Livermore (USA) - Trouble Free (USA)
3^{11sd} 3^{10gs} 3^{11gs} 5^{12gs} 2^{10f} 4^{12gf} 4^{10gf}
7^{10gf} 2^{11hy} 11^{11hy} 4^{8gs} 2^{10s} 3^{11hy} 5^{10s} **1-7-14**
£15,272

Trouble Next Door (Ire) *N P Littmoden* a44
6 b g Persian Bold - Adjacent (Ire)
3^{12sd} 2^{12sd} **0-2-2 £828**

Troubleinparadise (Ire) *J G Given* a9
3 b f Pursuit Of Love - Sweet Holland (USA)
17^{10s} 18^{11gs} 13^{12sd} **0-0-3**

Troublesome Gerri *S C Burrough* 39
2 b f Thowra (Fr) - Sid's Pretence
6^{5s} 3^{5gf} 5^{6gf} **0-0-3 £631**

Trousers *Andrew Reid* 69 a68
5 b g Pivotal - Palo Blanco
7^{8sd} 1^{8hy} 3^{8gs} 4^{8gs} **1-1-4 £9,368**

Trouville (Ire) *Gerard O'Leary* 58 a61
5 b m Mukaddamah (USA) - Trouville Lass (Ire)
12^{7s} 9^{8y} 9^{7f} 5^{7f} 7^{7g} 6^{8g} 12^{10gf} 8^{12g}
1^{13g} 9^{13gy} 5^{12sd} **1-0-11 £4,379**

Truckle *M Johnston* 69
2 b c Vettori (Ire) - Proud Titania (Ire)
8^{6gs} 6^{8f} 4^{8g} **0-0-3 £409**

True (Ire) *Mrs S Lamyman* 67
3 ch f Barathea (Ire) - Bibliotheque (USA)
7^{8gs} 11^{7y} 2^{7gf} 12^{7g} 3^{7gf} 4^{7gs} 12^{7gf} 6^{8gs}
8^{7gs} 2^{8g} 14^{8gf} 5^{8gf} 9^{8s} **0-3-13 £3,246**

True Companion *N P Littmoden* 78 a73
5 b g Brief Truce (USA) - Comanche Companion
8^{10sd} 1^{10sd} 3^{10sd} 8^{8sd} 3^{10sd} 1^{11gs} 4^{12gs}
2^{10gf} 13^{10sd} **2-3-9 £10,830**

True Holly *S Kirk* a38
4 b f Bishop Of Cashel - Polly's Teahouse
9^{6sd} 7^{6sd} 5^{7ss} **0-0-3**

True Lover (Ger) *J W Mullins* 110
7 b g Winged Love (Ire) - Truneba (Ger)
3^{16s} **0-1-1 £6,600**

True Magic *J D Bethell* 79
3 b f Magic Ring (Ire) - True Precision
5^{5s} 6^{5gf} 2^{5f} 2^{5g} 1^{5gf} 1^{5gs} 8^{5gf} 13^{5gf}
7^{5g} **2-2-9 £14,410**

True Night *D Nicholls* 93
7 b g Night Shift (USA) - Dead Certain
13^{7gf} 14^{6gs} 10^{7y} 12^{6gf} 4^{7f} 2^{6gf} 3^{7gf}
3^{7f} 11^{8g} 3^{8g} 1^{7g} 11^{7g} 3^{8gf} 12^{8gf} 12^{8s} 2^{9gf}
12^{7s} 8^{7g} **2-6-18 £43,285**

True Patriot *D R Gandolfo*
3 b g Rainbow Quest (USA) - High Standard
17^{10g} 8^{11gf} **0-0-2**

True To Yourself (USA) *J G Given* 40 a49

3 b g Royal Academy (USA) - Romilly
10⁸ˢ 2⁹ˢᵈ 1¹²ˢᵈ 8¹²ᵍ 6¹²ˢᵈ **1-1-5 £1,834**

Trueno (Ire) *L M Cumani* 89
5 b g Desert King (Ire) - Stitching (Ire)
11¹⁰ᵍᶠ 2¹⁰ᵍ 11¹⁰ᵍ 5¹⁰ᵍˢ 5¹⁰ᵍˢ 7¹²ᵍ 6¹⁰ᵍ
1-1-7 £7,084

Trullitti (Ire) *J L Dunlop* 78
3 b f Bahri (USA) - Penza
3¹⁰ᵍˢ 5¹⁰ᵍˢ PU¹²ᵍ 1¹¹ᵍˢ 3¹²ˢ 11¹⁴ˢ **1-2-6 £6,121**

Truman *J A R Toller* 72 a72
3 b c Entrepreneur - Sabria (USA)
7⁶ᵍᶠ 3⁶ᵍᶠ 5⁷ᵍᶠ 11⁷ᵍˢ 2⁹ˢᵈ **0-2-5 £2,056**

Trust Rule *B W Hills* 104
4 b c Selkirk (USA) - Hagwah (USA)
12¹⁰ᵍˢ 6¹²ᵍ 5¹²ᵍ 10¹²ᶠ 11¹²ᵍ 14¹⁴ˢ 16¹⁴ᵍ
4¹⁵ᵍᶠ 7¹²ᵍᶠ **0-0-9 £3,221**

Trusted Instinct (Ire) *C A Dwyer* 10 a39
4 b c Polish Precedent (USA) - Trust In Luck (Ire)
14¹²ˢᵈ 10⁸ˢᵈ 16⁸ˢ 18¹²ᵍᶠ 9⁸ᶠ 5⁶ʰʸ 17⁸ᶠ
0-0-7

Trusted Mole (Ire) *W M Brisbourne* 65 a44
6 b g Eagle Eyed (USA) - Orient Air
5¹²ᵍᶠ 1¹²ᵍᶠ 6¹³ᵍᶠ 2¹¹ᶠ 1¹³ᵍᶠ 8¹³ᵍᶠ 10¹²ᵍᶠ
7¹²ᶠ 7¹²ˢᵈ **2-1-9 £7,491**

Try The Air (Ire) *C Tinkler* a16
3 ch f Foxhound (USA) - Try To Catch Me (USA)
11⁸ˢᵈ **0-0-1**

Trylko (USA) *J G Given* 67
2 ch f Diesis - Gossamer (USA)
2⁶ᵍ **0-1-1 £1,490**

Trysting Grove (Ire) *E G Bevan* 51 a56
3 b f Cape Cross (Ire) - Elton Grove (Ire)
9⁸ᵍ 8⁷ᵍ 9⁷ᶠ 5⁷ᵍˢ 15⁸ᵍᶠ 1¹²ᵍˢ 1¹¹ˢᵈ **2-0-7 £4,042**

Tsarbuck *R M H Cowell* 48 a64
3 b g Perugino (USA) - Form At Last
15⁸ᵍᶠ 7⁹ˢ 8⁸ʰʸ 1⁷ˢᵈ 5⁸ᵍᶠ 2⁷ˢᵈ 5⁷ˢ 2⁶ˢᵈ
3⁷ˢᵈ 3⁶ˢᵈ 12⁶ᵍ 9⁶ᵍ 6⁷ᵍˢ 4⁶ˢᵈ 10⁷ˢᵈ **1-4-15 £4,471**

Tsaroxy (Ire) *J Howard Johnson* 77
2 b c Xaar - Belsay
3⁶ˢ 3⁶ᵍ 16ᵍˢ 5⁶ˢ 10⁶ˢ **1-0-5 £5,567**

Tshukudu *M Blanshard* 43 a33
3 ch f Fleetwood (Ire) - Pab's Choice
7⁷ˢᵈ 12¹²ˢᵈ 9⁸ˢᵈ 10⁸ᵍᶠ 3¹⁰ᵍᶠ 11¹⁰ˢᵈ 2¹⁰ᵍˢ
7¹⁰ᵍᶠ 11¹⁰ˢᵈ 14¹⁰ᵍ **0-2-10 £1,131**

Tucker *D R C Elsworth* 85
2 b c Inchinor - Tender Moment (Ire)
8⁶ˢ **1-0-2 £4,754**

Tudor Bell (Ire) *J G M O'Shea* 85
3 b c Definite Article - Late Night Lady (Ire)
8⁸ᵍ 2¹⁰ˢ 3¹⁰ᵍ 1¹¹ᵍˢ 1¹²ᵍᶠ 6¹²ᵍᶠ 2¹⁴ᶠ 1¹⁴ᵍ
3¹⁶ᶠ 11¹⁶ᵍ 4¹⁶ᵍᶠ 5¹⁶ᵍˢ **3-3-12 £22,576**

Tumbaga (USA) *R Charlton* 71
3 b c Seeking The Gold (USA) - Didina
13⁸ᵍ 13¹⁰ᵍ 5⁸ᵍᶠ **0-0-3**

Tumblebrutus (USA) *A P O'Brien* 87
3 br c Storm Cat (USA) - Mariah's Storm (USA)
9⁸ᵍ 3⁷ᵍ **0-1-2 £1,441**

Tumbleweed Galore (Ire) *B J Meehan* 74 a74
2 b g Bluebird (USA) - Mary Hinge
7⁷ˢ 3⁷ᵍᶠ 3⁷ᵍᶠ 3⁸ˢ 6⁸ˢ 2⁷ᵍᶠ 3⁹ˢᵈ 5⁷ˢ
0-5-8 £3,669

Tungsten Strike (USA) *Mrs A J Perrett* 110
3 ch g Smart Strike (Can) - Bathilde (Ire)
11¹²ᵍˢ 1¹⁴ᵍᶠ 1¹⁶ᵍ 3¹⁴ᵍᶠ 2¹⁶ᵍᶠ 1¹⁴ᵍ 28¹⁸ˢ

3-2-7 £35,774

Tuning Fork *J Akehurst* 101
4 b g Alzao (USA) - Tuning
12¹⁰ᵍˢ 7¹²ᵍᶠ 10¹¹ᵍ 14¹⁰ᶠ 15⁸ᵍˢ 3⁸ᵍᶠ 12⁷ᵍ
8¹⁰ᵍˢ 9⁹ᵍᶠ 11⁸ᵍᶠ **0-1-10 £11,000**

Turbo (Ire) *J A Geake* 100 a84
5 b g Piccolo - By Arrangement (Ire)
14¹⁰ˢᵈ 10¹⁰ᵍˢ 4¹²ᵍ 1³¹²ᵍ 12¹²ᵍ 7¹²ᵍᶠ
13¹⁰ᵍˢ 2¹⁰ʰʸ 12¹²ˢ **0-2-9 £6,546**

Turf Princess *Ian Emmerson* 59 a56
3 b f Wizard King - Turf Moor (Ire)
1⁷ˢᵈ 2⁷ˢᵈ 4⁷ˢˢ 5⁷ˢᵈ 3⁷ʰʸ 7⁷ᵍᶠ 4⁷ᵍˢ 9⁸ˢᵈ
14⁶ʰʸ 17⁶ᵍ **1-2-10 £4,655**

Turftanzer (Ger) *Don Enrico Incisa* 45 a46
5 b g Lomitas - Tower Bridge (Ger)
5¹²ˢᵈ 7¹⁴ˢᵈ 4¹¹ˢˢ 6⁸ˢˢ 16¹²ᵍˢ 8¹⁰ʰʸ 9¹¹ᶠ
12¹²ᵍᶠ 4¹⁰ᵍ 5¹²ᵍ 7¹²ᵍᶠ 10⁸ˢ 5¹⁰ᶠ 9¹⁰ᶠ 6¹⁰ˢ
0-0-15

Turibius *T E Powell* 77 a86
5 b g Puissance - Compact Disc (Ire)
6⁵ˢᵈ 1⁵ˢᵈ 3⁵ˢᵈ 8⁵ᵍᶠ 18⁶ᵍᶠ 9⁵ᵍᶠ 12⁵ᵍᶠ
26⁵ᵍᶠ 10⁵ᵍˢ 4⁶ᵍ **1-1-10 £5,735**

Turkana Girl *G Wragg* 52
2 ch f Hernando (Fr) - Miss Penton
6⁶ᵍᶠ **0-0-1**

Turkish Delight *J Balding* 60 a38
3 b f Prince Sabo - Delicious
5⁶ˢˢ 6⁶ᵍᶠ 12⁶ᵍᶠ 8⁶ᵍ 3⁶ᵍᶠ 10⁶ᵍ 14⁶ᵍᶠ
15⁶ᵍᶠ 13⁶ᵍ 15⁵ᵍᶠ **0-1-10 £682**

Turks And Caicos (Ire) *P C Haslam* 52 a56
3 b/br g Turtle Island (Ire) - Need You Badly
2⁸ˢᵈ 2⁸ˢˢ 1¹¹ˢᵈ 7¹¹ᵍᶠ 6⁹ˢᵈ 6¹²ˢᵈ **1-2-6 £3,762**

Turks Wood (Ire) *M H Tompkins* 75
2 b g Charnwood Forest (Ire) - Nairasha (Ire)
4⁵ᵍᶠ 5⁶ᵍ 5⁶ᵍᶠ 10⁸ᵍ 8⁸ˢ 8⁶ᵍ **0-0-6**

Turn 'n Burn *C A Cyzer* 75 a64
3 b g Unfuwain (USA) - Seasonal Splendour (Ire)
7¹²ᵍˢ 3¹⁰ᵍᶠ 2¹²ᵍᶠ 4¹²ˢᵈ **0-2-4 £2,562**

Turn Around *P A Blockley* a72
4 b g Pivotal - Bemuse
7⁶ˢʷ 14⁸ᵍˢ 2⁸ˢᵈ 1⁷ˢᵈ 5⁷ˢᵈ 1⁷ˢᵈ 14⁶ˢᵈ
2-1-7 £6,008

Turn Of Phrase (Ire) *R A Fahey* 70 a41
5 b g Cadeaux Genereux - Token Gesture (Ire)
8¹⁶ˢᵈ 8¹²ᵍᶠ 2¹⁴ᵍᶠ 1¹²ᵍ 4¹⁴ᵍ **1-1-5 £4,810**

Turn On The Style *R P Elliott* 69
2 ch g Pivotal - Elegant Rose
9⁶ᵍ 7⁶ᵍᶠ 2⁵ᵍᶠ 1⁵ᵍ **1-1-4 £4,675**

Turnaround (Ger) *Mrs J R Ramsden* 84
2 gr g Highest Honor (Fr) - Tamacana
3⁵ᵍ 2⁶ˢ 1⁵ᶠ 13⁶ᵍ 2⁷ᶠ 8⁶ᵍ **1-3-6 £11,351**

Turnberry (Ire) *J W Hills* 60 a57
3 b c Petardia - Sunrise (Ire)
4⁷ˢᵈ 3⁷ˢˢ 6⁸ˢᵈ 2⁸ˢ 2⁷ᵍᶠ 5⁷ᶠ **0-3-6 £3,335**

Turner *W M Brisbourne* 69
3 gr g El Prado (Ire) - Gaily Royal (Ire)
6¹²ᵍᶠ 3¹⁰ᵍᶠ 3¹⁰ᵍ 8¹⁰ᵍᶠ 10¹⁰ᵍᶠ 17¹¹ᵍ **0-1-6 £1,672**

Turnkey *M R Channon* 101
2 br c Pivotal - Persian Air
2⁵ᵍ 1⁵ʰʸ 5⁶ᵍᶠ 4⁶ᵍ 7⁶ˢ **1-1-5 £10,243**

Turnover *J W Wallace* 49
2 ch f Gold Away (Ire) - Turn To Vodka (Fr)
5⁷ʰʸ 13⁸ᵍ **0-0-2**

Turnstile *R Hannon* 80
3 gr c Linamix (Fr) - Kissing Gate (USA)
4¹¹g 2¹²gf 9¹⁴gs 3¹²gs 2¹²gf 8¹²gs 6¹⁴gf
1¹⁴gs **1-3-8 £7,838**

Turtle Bay *A P Jarvis* a45
2 ch f Dr Fong (USA) - My Valentina
8⁷ˢᵈ **0-0-1**

Turtle Dancer (Ire) *B Ellison* 73
6 b g Turtle Island (Ire) - Love Me Please (Ire)
2¹⁰ʰʸ 11¹⁴ˢᵈ **0-1-2 £1,152**

Turtle Magic (Ire) *W G M Turner* 67 a32
2 b f Turtle Island (Ire) - Theda
8⁵ˢᵈ 2⁵gs 3⁵g 6⁵g 6⁵ˢᵈ 4⁶gf 9⁶g 3⁵gf 4⁶ˢᵈ
6⁵gf 4⁵gs 11⁶gf **0-2-12 £2,035**

Turtle Patriarch (Ire) *Mrs A J Perrett* 67 a42
3 b c Turtle Island (Ire) - La Doyenne (Ire)
10⁶gs 16⁹g 8⁸gf 4¹⁰gs 2¹²g 6¹¹g 12¹²ˢᵈ
2¹⁰s **0-2-8 £2,809**

Turtle Valley (Ire) *S Dow* 80 a62
8 b g Turtle Island (Ire) - Primrose Valley
5¹³ˢᵈ 9¹⁶ˢᵈ 3¹⁴s 1¹⁵s 9¹⁴s 12¹⁴s **1-1-6
£6,348**

Tuscan Dream *A Berry* a41
9 b g Clantime - Excavator Lady
11⁵ˢᵈ 9⁵ˢˢ 7⁵ˢˢ 7⁵ˢʷ 2⁵ˢᵈ 2⁵ˢᵈ 5⁵ˢᵈ 1⁵ˢᵈ
5⁵ˢᶠ 5⁵ˢᵈ 11⁵ˢᵈ **1-2-11 £2,249**

Tuscan Flyer *R Bastiman* 70
6 b g Clantime - Excavator Lady
9⁶gs 13⁶f 3⁷f 12⁶gf 4⁵g 11⁵gs 4⁵gf 7⁶gf
7⁵s 11⁵gf 3⁵f **0-4-11 £2,011**

Tuscan Treaty *T T Clement* 49 a29
4 b f Brief Truce (USA) - Fiorenz (USA)
14⁷ˢᵈ 8⁸s 4⁷gf 7⁶f 6⁶gf 13⁶gf 13⁸g 4⁶g
0-0-8

Tuscarora (Ire) *A W Carroll* 67
5 b m Revoque (Ire) - Fresh Look (Ire)
7⁶s 9⁸gf 5⁸f 2⁸g 6⁷g 1⁸gs 9⁷g 5⁹g 1⁸gf
3⁷g 3⁸gs 4⁸g 8⁶gf **2-4-13 £13,269**

Tuvalu (Ger) *A M Balding* 69
2 ch c Dashing Blade - Tepana (Ger)
8⁷gf 5⁷gf 6⁷gs 4⁸g **0-0-4 £555**

Tweed *C Roberts* 6
7 ch g Barathea (Ire) - In Perpetuity
10¹²g **0-0-1**

Twelve Bar Blues *E Lellouche* 62
3 ch f Nashwan (USA) - Throw Away Line (USA)
11¹⁰g 7¹⁰g 5¹²gf 10¹⁰gf **0-0-4**

Twentytwosilver (Ire) *N J Hawke* a28
4 gr/ro g Emarati (USA) - St Louis Lady
10¹⁰ˢᵈ **0-0-1**

Twice Nightly *J D Bethell* 64
2 b g Wolfhound (USA) - Dusty's Darling
3⁵g 3⁶g 6⁵g 5⁷gf 9⁷gs 7⁷gf 8⁶gs **0-1-7
£1,642**

Twice Upon A Time *B Smart* 76
5 ch m Primo Dominie - Opuntia
4⁵gs 4⁵g 14⁵gf 15⁶g 8⁶gf 4⁵g 14⁵gf 8⁵gf
6⁵gf 7⁵gf **0-0-10 £2,055**

Twilight Blues (Ire) *J Noseda* 106
5 ch h Bluebird (USA) - Pretty Sharp
5⁶gf 11⁶f 5⁵ss 2⁷gf 8⁶s **0-1-5 £8,600**

Twilight Years *T D Easterby* 44
3 b g Silver Patriarch (Ire) - Adjusting (Ire)
9¹¹gf 7¹²gf 4¹⁴gf 6¹⁶gf 10¹⁴gs **0-0-5**

Two Miles West (Ire) *A P O'Brien* 114
3 b c Sadler's Wells (USA) - User Friendly

1¹²gf 2¹⁶f 2¹⁴gy 4¹²gf 6¹⁴g **1-2-5
£31,338**

Two Of A Kind (Ire) *J W Hills* a47
4 ch g Ashkalani (Ire) - Dulcinea
1¹²ˢᵈ **1-0-1 £3,265**

Two Of Clubs *Miss S J Wilton* 34 a73
3 b g First Trump - Sulaka
3⁷ˢᵈ 3⁸ˢᵈ 1⁷ˢʷ 5⁷g 1⁷ˢᵈ **2-1-5 £4,702**

Two Step Kid (USA) *J Noseda* 106
3 ch c Gone West (USA) - Marsha's Dancer (USA)
6⁷gs 4⁵gf 1⁶gf 3⁶g 4⁶gf 4⁶gf 4⁶gf **1-2-7
£72,499**

Two Steps To Go (USA) *E A Elliott* a43
5 b g Rhythm (USA) - Lyonushka (Can)
4¹²ˢᵈ 4¹¹ˢᵈ 5⁹ˢᵈ **0-0-3**

Twofan (USA) *M Johnston* 84
3 b c Lear Fan (USA) - Double Wedge (USA)
2¹⁰ʰʸ 2¹¹g 1¹⁴gs 6¹⁴gs 4¹⁵g 5¹⁴gf **1-2-6
£7,970**

Twyla Tharp (Ire) *J H M Gosden* 66
2 b f Sadler's Wells (USA) - Sumoto
10⁸gs 2⁸s **0-1-2 £1,347**

Tybalt *P W Harris* 63
2 b c Polar Falcon (USA) - Once Removed
2⁶gf 5⁶gs 8⁶gf 12⁷gf 3⁷gf 17⁸s **0-2-6
£1,538**

Tycheros *S C Williams* 43
2 b g Polar Falcon (USA) - Marie De Flandre (Fr)
11⁶g **0-0-1**

Tychy *S C Williams* 103
5 ch m Suave Dancer (USA) - Touch Of White
5⁶g 3⁵gf 2⁷⁶f 11⁵gf 5⁵gf 1⁶g 8⁶gs 4⁵g
15⁶g 9⁶g 7⁶s **1-1-11 £35,300**

Tycoon *A P O'Brien* 122
3 b c Sadler's Wells (USA) - Fleeting Glimpse
3¹²gf 6¹²gf 9¹⁰g 3¹⁵gf 3¹²y **0-2-5
£184,430**

Tycoon Hall (Ire) *Mrs John Harrington* 33
4 ch h Halling (USA) - Tycooness (Ire)
16¹⁰gs **0-0-1**

Tyne *T D Barron* 78
3 b g Komaite (USA) - High Typha
7⁵s 6⁵f 4⁶g 9⁵gs **0-0-4 £433**

Tyneham *W G M Turner* 28 a61
4 b c Robellino (USA) - Diamond Wedding (USA)
1⁹ˢᵈ 11⁸s **1-0-2 £1,487**

Type One (Ire) *J J Quinn* 72 a84
6 b g Bigstone (Ire) - Isca
11⁶ˢᵈ 1⁵ˢᵈ 13⁶ˢˢ 7⁵ˢᵈ 18⁶g 17⁶s 2⁶gs
14⁶f 7⁶gs 4⁶s **1-1-10 £4,068**

Typhoon Ginger (Ire) *G Woodward* 18
9 ch m Archway (Ire) - Pallas Viking
9⁷s **0-0-1**

Typhoon Tilly *C R Egerton* 78 a83
7 b g Hernando (Fr) - Meavy
6¹²ˢᵈ 14¹⁶ˢᵈ 3¹⁶ˢᵈ 6¹²gf 10¹⁶gs 3¹⁴gs
2¹³gs 1¹⁶g 6¹⁶g 7¹⁶gs 6¹⁷ˢᵈ **1-3-12 £7,005**

Tyrone Sam *K A Ryan* 49
2 b g Mind Games - Crystal Sand (Ger)
7⁵gf 9⁵gf 14⁷gs **0-0-3**

Tyrrellspass (Ire) *J D Frost* 21 a6
7 b g Alzao (USA) - Alpine Chime (Ire)
10⁷ˢˢ 5¹⁰gs **0-0-2**

Tyson Returns *P A Blockley* 43 a23
2 b g Mujahid (USA) - Mabrookah
11⁶gs 9⁶ˢᵈ **0-0-2**

Tytheknot *Jedd O'Keeffe* 77
3 b g Pursuit Of Love - Bundled Up (USA)
2⁸ˢ 3¹⁰ʰʸ 6⁸ˢ 4¹⁰ᵍˢ 3¹⁰ᵍᶠ 1¹⁰ˢ 5⁸ˢ 13¹⁰ˢ
15¹⁰ˢ **1-2-9 £8,899**

Tytherley *J R Boyle*
3 b f Man Among Men (Ire) - Sharp Thistle
PU⁸ᵍᶠ **0-0-1**

Tyup Pompey (Ire) *D R C Elsworth* 51
3 ch g Docksider (USA) - Cindys Baby
4¹⁰ᵍᶠ 14¹⁰ᵍˢ 5¹⁰ʰʸ **0-0-3 £535**

Tyzack (Ire) *J Balding* 56
3 b g Fasliyev (USA) - Rabea (USA)
5⁶ˢ 7⁷ᶠ 8⁸ˢ 10⁷ᵍᶠ 8¹⁰ᶠ **0-0-5**

Ugly Sister (USA) *G C Bravery* 41 a18
2 gr f Aljabr (USA) - Cinderella Ball (USA)
9⁶ᵍᶠ 7⁷ˢᵈ 6⁷ʰʸ 20⁷ᵍᶠ **0-0-4**

Uhoomagoo *K A Ryan* 101 a88
6 b g Namaqualand (USA) - Point Of Law
1⁷ˢˢ 7⁸ᵍ 7⁸ᵍ 7⁸ᵍᶠ 1⁷ᵍᶠ 1⁹ᵍ 11⁸ᵍᶠ 13⁷ᶠ
3⁷ᵍᶠ 7⁸ᵍᶠ 14⁷ᵍᶠ 12⁷ᵍᶠ 9⁷ˢᵈ **3-1-13 £52,885**

Uhuru Peak *M W Easterby* 62 a42
3 ch c Bal Harbour - Catherines Well
3⁵ˢˢ 10⁶ˢᵈ 5⁶ᵍ 11⁶ᵍᶠ 7⁷ᶠ 3⁶ᵍᶠ 2⁶ˢ 13⁶ᵍᶠ
6⁸ˢ 8⁶ᵍ 3⁷ᵍˢ **0-4-11 £3,162**

Uig *H S Howe* 78
3 ch f Bien Bien (USA) - Madam Zando
8¹⁰ᵍ 8¹⁰ᵍ 3¹⁰ᵍᶠ 2¹⁰ᵍᶠ 9¹²ˢ 4⁸ᵍˢ 2¹⁰ᵍ 7¹¹ˢ
2¹⁰ᵍ **0-4-9 £5,186**

Ulshaw *B J Llewellyn* 49
7 ch g Salse (USA) - Kintail
11²²ˢ 10¹⁹ᵍᶠ 16¹⁷ᵍ 10¹⁶ᵍᶠ **0-0-4**

Ultimata *J R Fanshawe* 88
4 ch f Unfuwain (USA) - Last Look
9¹⁰ᵍᶠ 2⁸ᵍᶠ 2⁸ᵍ 9¹⁰ʰʸ 15⁹ᵍ 1¹⁰ˢ 6¹⁰ˢ **1-2-7
£4,967**

Ultra Marine (Ire) *J S Wainwright* 33
4 b c Blues Traveller (Ire) - The Aspecto Girl (Ire)
7¹⁰ᵍ 17¹²ᵍᶠ 13¹³ᵍ **0-0-3**

Ulundi *P R Webber* 95 a101
9 b g Rainbow Quest (USA) - Flit (USA)
10¹⁰ˢᵈ 11¹²ᵍᶠ 12¹⁰ᵍᶠ 12¹⁰ᶠ **0-0-4**

Ulysees (Ire) *I Semple* 79
5 b g Turtle Island (Ire) - Tamasriya (Ire)
1⁶ᵍ 7⁶ᵍ 3⁶ᵍ 1⁶ᵍ 8⁷ˢ 5⁶ᵍ 14⁶ᵍ 7⁶ˢ 4⁶ˢ
7⁷ˢ 11⁶ˢ 5⁶ᵍˢ 8⁷ˢ **2-1-13 £10,767**

Umniya (Ire) *M R Channon* 102
2 b f Bluebird (USA) - Sparky's Song
3⁵ˢ 2⁶ᵍˢ 1⁶ᶠ 3⁶ᵍᶠ 3⁶ᵍᶠ 4⁶ᶠ 5⁶ᵍᶠ 6⁶ˢ 6⁷ᵍˢ
4⁷ᵍᶠ 3⁷ᵍ 5⁷ᵍ 3⁸ᵍ 6⁸ˢ 8⁸ᵛˢ **1-4-15 £68,261**

Un Autre Espere *M Wellings* 41 a26
5 b g Golden Heights - Drummer's Dream (Ire)
12⁹ˢʷ 6⁸ˢʷ 10⁸ˢˢ 9⁹ˢˢ 8⁷ˢᵈ 5⁷ˢᵈ 1⁷ᵍˢ 5⁸ˢᶠ
14¹²ˢ **1-0-9 £1,477**

Unbridled's Dream (USA) *H J Cyzer* 44
3 gr/ro c Unbridled's Song (USA) - Diamond Dream (Fr)
19⁸ᵍ **0-0-1**

Uncle Batty *G J Smith* 47
4 b g Bob Back (USA) - Aunt Sadie
4¹⁰ᵍᶠ 5¹²ᵍᶠ **0-0-2**

Uncle Bulgaria (Ire) *G C Bravery* 62 a51
2 b c Alhaarth (Ire) - Istibshar (USA)
3⁷ˢᵈ 7⁷ᵍ 10⁸ᵍ 5⁸ᵍ 6⁸ˢ **0-1-5 £531**

Uncle John *S Kirk* 64 a67
3 b g Atraf - Bit O' May
7⁹ᵍᶠ 7¹⁰ᵍ 4¹⁰ᵍ 2¹²ᵍᶠ 4¹²ᵍᶠ 9¹⁰ᵍ 9¹⁰ᵍᶠ
12¹⁰ʰʸ 3¹²ˢᵈ 2¹²ˢᵈ 3¹²ˢᵈ **0-4-11 £3,873**

Under My Skin (Ire) *T G Mills* 47
3 ch f Mark Of Esteem (Ire) - Convenience (Ire)
12¹⁰ᵍᶠ 7⁷ᵍˢ **0-0-2**

Under My Spell *P D Evans* 82
3 b f Wizard King - Gagajulu
17⁷ᵍ 10⁶ᵍ 2⁶ᵍˢ 2⁶ᵍᶠ 5⁶ᵍᶠ 1⁶ᵍᶠ 10⁶ᵍ 9⁶ᵍᶠ
8⁶ᵍᶠ 10⁸ᵍˢ **1-2-10 £6,601**

Undergraduate (Ire) *Sir Michael Stoute* 70
2 b g Unfuwain (USA) - Starlet
5⁸ˢ **0-0-1**

Underthemistletoe (Ire) *B Smart* 49
2 b f Lujain (USA) - Christmas Kiss
6⁶ᶠ 3⁵ᵍ 10⁶ᵍᶠ 6⁵ᵍ **0-0-4 £420**

Undeterred *T D Barron* 81
8 ch g Zafonic (USA) - Mint Crisp (Ire)
11⁶ˢ 5⁶ᵍᶠ 7⁶ᵍᶠ 10⁶ᵍ 4⁶ᵍᶠ 4⁶ᵍ 4⁶ᵍᶠ 1⁶ᵍᶠ
12⁶ᵍᶠ 13⁶ᵍ **1-3-10 £12,106**

Unfurled (Ire) *J L Dunlop* 83
2 ch c Unfuwain (USA) - Peony
6⁸ᵍᶠ 2⁸ˢ **0-1-2 £2,204**

Unicorn Reward (Ire) *M D Hammond* 66
4 b c Turtle Island (Ire) - Kingdom Pearl
23⁸ᵍ 4³ˢ 12⁸ᵍᶠ **0-0-3 £814**

Unintentional *R Brotherton* 44 a28
3 b f Dr Devious (Ire) - Tamnia
6⁸ˢᵈ 8⁸ˢᵈ 6¹⁰ˢ 14¹¹ᵍᶠ PU¹²ᵍˢ 10¹⁰ʰʸ 10⁷ˢᵈ
0-0-7

Union Jack Jackson (Ire) *J G Given* 66 a62
2 b c Daggers Drawn (USA) - Beechwood Quest (Ire)
4⁶ᵍ 7⁶ᵍ 7⁶ᵍˢ 6⁷ˢᵈ 4⁸ᵍ 4⁸ˢ **0-2-6 £945**

United Nations *D R Loder* 94
3 ch c Halling (USA) - Congress (Ire)
1⁸ᵍ 3⁸ᵍˢ 4⁸ᵍ 8⁸ᵍ **1-0-4 £9,841**

United Spirit (Ire) *M A Magnusson* 69 a72
3 b f Fasliyev (USA) - Atlantic Desire (Ire)
7⁷ᵍ 6⁷ᵍ 3⁷ᵍᶠ 1⁶ᵍᶠ 1⁷ˢᵈ 4⁷ᵍˢ 5⁶ᵍᶠ 14⁶ᵍˢ
2-1-8 £6,993

United Union (Ire) *D Haydn Jones* 43
3 b/br g Imperial Ballet (Ire) - Madagascar
4⁶ᵍˢ 9⁵ᵍ **0-0-2**

Unleaded *J Akehurst* 34 a48
4 ch f Danzig Connection (USA) - Mo Stopher
2¹⁵ˢᵈ 1¹⁶ˢᵈ 2¹⁶ˢᵈ 5¹⁶ˢᵈ 8¹⁴ˢ 4¹⁶ˢᵈ 5¹⁶ˢᵈ
1-2-7 £2,186

Unlimited *Mrs A Duffield* 70 a69
2 b g Bold Edge - Cabcharge Blue
2⁵ˢᵈ 1⁵ˢˢ 2⁵ᵍᶠ 5⁵ᵍᶠ 7⁷ˢᵈ 3⁶ᵍᶠ 5⁶ᵍˢ 10⁶ˢ
1-1-8 £5,704

Uno Mente *Don Enrico Incisa* 59
5 b m Mind Games - One Half Silver (Can)
10¹⁰ᵍˢ 8¹⁰ᶠ 6⁸ᶠ 3⁸ᵍᶠ 7⁸ᵍᶠ 9⁸ᵍᶠ
9¹⁰ᵍᶠ 11⁸ᵍˢ 19¹⁰ᵍᶠ **0-1-10 £633**

Unprecedented (Ire) *T T Clement* 51 a8
3 br g Primo Dominie - Misellina (Fr)
11⁸ˢᵈ 12⁷ᵍˢ 4⁹ᵍ 7⁸ᵍᶠ 7⁸ᵍ 11⁸ᵍ **0-0-6
£368**

Unreal *B W Hills* 82
2 b f Dansili - Illusory
6⁵ᵍ 2⁶ᵍˢ 6⁶ᵍ 2⁶ᵍˢ 1⁵ᵍ **1-2-5 £9,446**

Unscrupulous *J R Fanshawe* 103
5 ch g Machiavellian (USA) - Footlight Fantasy (USA)
3⁸ᵍᶠ 1⁷ᶠ **1-0-2 £24,238**

Unshakable (Ire) *Bob Jones* 102
5 b g Eagle Eyed (USA) - Pepper And Salt (Ire)
8⁸ᵍ 11¹⁰ᵍˢ 18ᵍˢ 3⁸ᵍˢ 10⁸ᵍᶠ 5⁸ᵍ 4⁸ˢ 5⁹ᵍ
7⁸ˢ 12⁸ᵍˢ **1-1-10 £30,591**

Unshaken *D A Nolan*
10 b h Environment Friend - Reel Foyle (USA)
13[6gf] 12[8g] **0-0-2**

Unshooda *B W Hills* 95
3 ch f Machiavellian (USA) - Rawaabe (USA)
7[7g] 9[6g] **0-0-2**

Unsuited *J E Long* 75 a44
5 b m Revoque (Ire) - Nagnagnag (Ire)
10[10sd] 3[9sd] 2[9sw] 6[9sw] 4[8gs] 10[10hy] 1[9g] 1[9g]
3[11g] 8[10g] 16[10gs] **3-3-11 £12,137**

Untidy Daughter *B Ellison* 57
5 b m Sabrehill (USA) - Branitska
5[10gs] 7[12gf] 3[10gf] 7[10s] **0-1-4 £862**

Up Tempo (Ire) *K A Ryan* 82 a88
6 b g Flying Spur (Aus) - Musical Essence
2[7sd] 1[6sd] 3[7sw] 1[6ss] 1[6gs] 1[7s] 4[7gs] 2[6s]
10[7f] 11[7gf] 5[7gf] 8[6gf] 1[7sd] **5-3-13 £20,965**

Up The Aisle *M Mullineaux*
7 b g Rambo Dancer (Can) - Mardessa
11[10gf] 5[10f] **0-0-2**

Up The Order *P J McBride*
2 b f Forzando - Art Deco Lady
12[6sd] **0-0-1**

Upthedale (Ire) *J R Weymes* 41 a31
3 b g General Monash (USA) - Pimpinella (Ire)
7[7s] 4[9sd] 3[9gs] UR[10] 5[12gf] 10[14f] 6[12gf]
0-1-7 £667

Urabande *Julian Poulton* 28 a56
2 b f Tipsy Creek (USA) - La Belle Mystere
12[5g] 2[5ss] 10[5sd] 6[5g] 4[6f] 7[6f] **0-1-6**
£1,116

Urban Calm *J W Unett* 63
3 b f Cadeaux Genereux - Silver Sun
4[5s] 2[5s] 2[5gf] 9[6g] 4[5gs] **0-2-5 £3,546**

Urban Rose *R M H Cowell* 66
3 b f Piccolo - Blue Lamp (USA)
7[6g] 14[7s] 3[6gf] 8[6gf] 4[6gf] 9[6g] 4[5gf] 13[5g]
0-2-8 £1,213

Uredale (Ire) *Mrs A Duffield* 62 a35
2 b c Bahhare (USA) - Baileys First (Ire)
5[5hy] 8[5sd] 6[5gf] 5[7gf] 1[7gf] 13[7gs] 14[8g] **1-0-7**
£2,618

Urowells (Ire) *E A L Dunlop* 90
4 b g Sadler's Wells (USA) - Highest Accolade
8[12gf] 9[12gs] 7[12gs] 11[10s] 9[8s] **0-0-5**

Ursa Major *T Keddy* 48
10 b g Warning - Double Entendre
12[10gf] 7[10f] 6[14gf] 8[10g] 7[10gf] **0-0-5**

Ushindi (Ire) *M L W Bell* 71
2 b f Montjeu (Ire) - Fern
13[7g] 12[8gs] 4[7gf] 3[7g] **0-1-4 £1,575**

Ustad (Ire) *J L Dunlop* 62
2 br c Giant's Causeway (USA) - Winsa (USA)
8[7s] 7[8g] **0-0-2**

Utah Flats (Ire) *Mrs J R Ramsden* a32
3 ch g Bluebird (USA) - Desert Rose
7[7sd] 10[6sd] **0-0-2**

Vademecum *B Smart* 67 a34
3 br g Shinko Forest (Ire) - Sunshine Coast
6[7gs] 10[6gs] 10[7gf] 10[7gf] 10[6s] 13[7g] 11[7sd]
0-0-7

Vague Star (Ity) *R Ingram* 72 a73
2 b c Soviet Star (USA) - Simova (USA)
13[6gf] 3[5gf] 3[6sd] 8[7sd] **0-2-4 £1,761**

Val D'Isere *B J Meehan* a24
2 ch c Tomba - Dancing Diana

12[6sd] **0-0-1**

Val De Fleurie (Ger) *J G M O'Shea* 56
9 b m Mondrian (Ger) - Valbonne
6[12gs] **0-0-1**

Val De Maal (Ire) *G C H Chung* 73 a70
4 ch g Eagle Eyed (USA) - Miss Bojangles
3[6sd] 14[7s] 4[6gf] 7[7gf] 4[6gs] 6[6s] 11[6gf] 9[6sd]
6[6sd] **0-2-9 £1,217**

Valance (Ire) *C R Egerton* 88
4 br g Bahhare (USA) - Glowlamp (Ire)
3[12gf] 5[14g] 1[16gf] 4[6gf] 8[21g] 2[14gf] 13[16gf]
1-2-7 £17,347

Valazar (USA) *D W Chapman* 51 a49
5 b g Nicholas (USA) - Valor's Minion (USA)
10[5sd] 9[5sw] 7[5ss] 2[5sd] 3[6sf] 2[6gf] 3[5g] 4[5sd]
16[5gf] **0-3-9 £1,603**

Valdasho *Miss K M George*
5 b m Classic Cliche (Ire) - Ma Rivale
9[10sd] **0-0-1**

Valdesco (Ire) *Mrs S J Smith* 66
6 ch g Bluebird (USA) - Allegheny River (USA)
11[12g] 7[11gs] 13[17gs] **0-0-3**

Vale De Lobo *A W Carroll* 71 a65
2 b f Loup Sauvage (USA) - Frog
5[6sd] 1[7sd] 3[8s] **1-1-3 £3,929**

Valentia (Ire) *M H Tompkins* a40
3 b f Perugino (USA) - Teide
8[5sd] **0-0-1**

Valentin (Ire) *R Hannon* 99
2 ch f King Of Kings (Ire) - Slip Ashore (Ire)
1[6g] 2[6gf] 8[7gf] 8[6g] **1-1-4 £15,438**

Valet *J G M O'Shea* 17
2 b c Kayf Tara - Val De Fleurie (Ger)
19[7g] 9[8gs] **0-0-2**

Valeureux *J Hetherton* 64
6 ch g Cadeaux Genereux - La Strada
3[10gf] 2[10gf] 4[12gs] 8[12gf] **0-2-4 £2,507**

Valiant Act (Ire) *D M Simcock* 65
2 b f Brave Act - Jungle Story (Ire)
6[7hy] 3[7gs] **0-1-2 £219**

Valiant Air (Ire) *J R Weymes* 49 a41
3 b g Spectrum (Ire) - Shining Desert (Ire)
4[12ss] 5[12gf] 2[12s] 4[12sd] 10[14s] 7[14f] 4[12gf]
5[10gf] 11[10g] 7[12gs] 3[12sd] **0-2-11 £1,878**

Valiant Effort *M Meade* 32
5 b/br g In The Wings - Viz (USA)
16[12g] **0-0-1**

Valiant Romeo *R Bastiman* 61 a35
4 b g Primo Dominie - Desert Lynx (Ire)
5[5g] 2[5g] 2[5gf] 4[5gf] 11[5gf] 5[5gs] 2[5gf] 15[5gf]
3[5s] 3[5gf] 3[5s] 12[6sd] **0-7-12 £6,695**

Valios (Ire) *C Laffon-Parias* 51
2 b c Royal Applause - Swing And Brave (Ire)
11[6gs] 7[6gf] 0[9hy] 0[7s] **0-0-4**

Valixir (Ire) *A Fabre* 118
3 b c Trempolino (USA) - Vadlamixa (Fr)
1[9ho] 3[11gf] 3[12gs] 1[10s] 1[12s] 10[12g] **3-1-6**
£206,789

Valjarv (Ire) *N P Littmoden* 96 a79
3 b f Bluebird (USA) - Iktidar
9[7sd] 7[7g] 13[8g] 10[6gf] 7[7gf] 4[6gf] 4[6g] 2[6g]
9[6g] 9[6gs] 5[6g] 13[6g] 4[6s] 4[6s] 12[8sd] **0-2-15**
£10,239

Vallee Enchantee (Ire) *E Lellouche* 121
4 b f Peintre Celebre (USA) - Verveine (USA)
4[11vs] 3[12g] 5[12gf] 6[12g] **0-1-4 £54,292**

Valuable Gift *R C Guest*   26 a27
7 ch g Cadeaux Genereux - Valbra
8^{6sd} 3^{8sd} 8^{6sd} 13^{6gs} 8^{6f} **0-0-5**

Value Plus (Ire) *Joseph Quinn*   72
2 b f Mujadil (USA) - Brittas Blues (Ire)
2^{5g} 2^{6gy} 2^{6f} 2^{6gs} **BD**^{6g} **0-4-5 £11,285**

Vamose (Ire) *Miss Gay Kelleway*   62 a59
3 ro g Victory Note (USA) - Narrow Band (Ire)
4^{8gf} 8^{11gf} 4^{9s} 4^{7sd} **0-0-4 £1,019**

Vamp *R M Beckett*   80
3 b f Dracula (Aus) - Circe
7^{7g} 2^{8f} 3^{10gf} 1^{10f} 5^{10gf} 11^{10gf} 4^{10g} 3^{12gf}
2^{10s} **1-3-9 £6,976**

Vampire Queen (Ire) *R P Elliott*   a56
3 b f General Monash (USA) - Taniokey
1^{6sd} 4^{6ss} 7^{6ss} 8^{7sd} **1-0-4 £2,947**

Vanbrugh (Fr) *Miss D A McHale*   51 a78
4 ch g Starborough - Renovate
1^{16sd} 9^{16sd} 6^{14sd} 11^{16g} 13^{14g} 10^{14gf}
13^{14gf} 9^{17gf} 7^{18f} 9^{14sd} 8^{16gf} 7^{6hy} 7^{14s} 6^{16gf}
11^{14gs} 12^{14sd} 11^{17sd} **1-0-17 £2,905**

Vancouver Gold (Ire) *K R Burke*   69
2 b f Monashee Mountain (USA) - Forest Berries (Ire)
3^{7f} 5^{7gf} **0-1-2 £537**

Vandenberghe *J A Osborne*   58 a65
5 b g Millkom - Child Star (Fr)
1^{9sd} 5^{10gf} 3^{9sd} 4^{12gf} 3^{11f} 5^{10gf} 6^{12g} 3^{12gf}
3^{14gf} 3^{16sd} 4^{16sd} 7^{12gf} 7^{12g} 1^{16sd} **2-5-14**
£8,068

Vanderlin *A M Balding*   112 a112
5 ch g Halling (USA) - Massorah (Fr)
3^{7sd} 3^{8gf} 5^{9g} 3^{8gf} 1^{7g} 8^{7g} 3^{7s} 3^{7gf} 2^{7g}
7^{7s} **1-5-10 £40,529**

Vanilla Moon *J R Jenkins*   52 a50
4 b f Emperor Jones (USA) - Daarat Alayaam (Ire)
5^{12sd} 2^{10sd} 4^{13sd} 3^{12gf} 6^{12g} 4^{11g} 6^{11gf}
4^{16sd} **0-2-8 £816**

Vanished (Ire) *M J Polglase*   a32
4 b f Fayruz - Where's The Money
12^{5sd} 8^{5sd} 9^{5ss} **0-0-3**

Vantage (Ire) *N P Littmoden*   82 a84
3 b g Marju (Ire) - Anna Comnena (Ire)
2^{10sd} 2^{10sd} 3^{12gs} 1^{12gs} 4^{12gs} 5^{12gf} 13^{10g}
4^{9gs} 5^{10g} 7^{12gf} **1-3-10 £8,843**

Var (USA) *C E Brittain*   121
5 b/br h Forest Wildcat (USA) - Loma Preata (USA)
1^{5f} 1^{6gf} 2^{5g} 1^{5g} **3-1-4 £117,929**

Varenka (Ire) *Sir Mark Prescott*   91
2 b f Fasliyev (USA) - Castara Beach (Ire)
5^{7gf} 1^{7gs} 2^{8g} **1-1-3 £16,422**

Variety Club *A M Balding*   5
3 b g Royal Applause - Starfida
16^{7gf} 14^{8g} 10^{8gf} **0-0-3**

Varnay *D R Loder*   69
3 b f Machiavellian (USA) - Valleria
11^{7gs} **0-0-1**

Varuni (Ire) *J G Portman*   64 a61
3 b f Ali-Royal (Ire) - Sauvignon (Ire)
1^{10sd} 7^{10sd} 2^{12gs} 15^{12s} 9^{10gf} 5^{12gs} 4^{12s}
1-1-7 £5,503

Vas Y Carla (USA) *D R Loder*   69
3 ch f Gone West (USA) - Lady Carla
12^{8gf} 2^{7gf} 10^{8gf} **0-1-3 £1,280**

Vaudevire *R P Elliott*   42 a19
3 b g Dancing Spree (USA) - Approved Quality (Ire)
6^{7ss} 9^{8sd} 3^{5sd} 7^{6sd} 4^{6g} 4^{5g} 7^{5gf} **0-0-7**

£464

Vaughan *Mrs A J Perrett*   94
3 b c Machiavellian (USA) - Labibeh (USA)
8^{9gf} 4^{12gf} 8^{12g} **0-0-3 £1,057**

Velocitas *H J Collingridge*   63 a63
3 b g Magic Ring (Ire) - Folly Finnesse
4^{6g} 10^{6gs} 12^{7gf} 9^{8g} 5^{8gf} 2^{9sd} 2^{9sd} **0-2-7**
£2,000

Velocitys Image (Ire) *E J Alston*   a13
4 b f Tagula (Ire) - Pike Creek (USA)
7^{5sw} 7^{7sd} **0-0-2**

Velvet Heights (Ire) *J L Dunlop*   81
2 b c Barathea (Ire) - Height Of Fantasy (Ire)
10^{7gf} 7^{7gf} 1^{8gs} 7^{8s} 11^{8gf} **1-0-5 £5,512**

Velvet Jones *G F H Charles-Jones*
11 gr g Sharrood (USA) - Cradle Of Love (USA)
7^{7gs} **0-0-1**

Velvet Rhythm *K R Burke*   a15
4 b f Forzando - Bold Gayle
8^{7sd} 8^{7sd} 12^{11sd} **0-0-3**

Velvet Touch *J R Jenkins*   55 a56
3 b f Danzig Connection (USA) - Soft Touch (Ger)
2^{6sd} 5^{6gs} 6^{6gs} 5^{5s} 11^{5sd} 8^{6sd} 12^{6sd}
14^{6s} **0-1-9 £842**

Velvet Waters *R F Johnson Houghton*   77
3 b f Unfuwain (USA) - Gleaming Water
3^{10gf} 6^{10f} 4^{14f} 1^{12f} 2^{11gf} 2^{12gf} 1^{12gf}
3^{12gs} 3^{14gf} 9^{12g} **2-5-10 £12,795**

Velveteen Rabbit *J H M Gosden*   70
2 b f Singspiel (Ire) - Velvet Lady
9^{6gs} 3^{7gf} 2^{7g} 7^{7gf} 8^{8gs} **0-2-5 £2,420**

Venables (USA) *R Hannon*   15 a100
3 ch c Stravinsky (USA) - Hope For A Breeze (Can)
5^{7sd} 11^{7g} 11^{6g} **0-0-3 £1,875**

Vendors Mistake (Ire) *Andrew Reid*   53 a41
3 b f Danehill (USA) - Sunspangled (Ire)
8^{7sd} 6^{6sd} 3^{6gf} 3^{5gf} 6^{5f} 6^{6s} **0-2-6 £800**

Veneer (Ire) *R Hannon*   53
2 b g Woodborough (USA) - Sweet Lass
4^{5gs} 8^{5s} 15^{6g} 5^{7s} **0-0-4**

Venerdi Tredici (Ire) *P A Blockley*   26
3 b f Desert Style (Ire) - Stifen
11^{9g} 12^{7g} 7^{10gs} **0-0-3**

Venetian King (USA) *J Howard Johnson*   72
2 b g King Of Kings (Ire) - Vena (Ire)
5^{6gf} 2^{7gf} **0-1-2 £1,700**

Venetian Romance (Ire) *A P Jones*   41 a20
3 ch f Desert Story (Ire) - Cipriani
5^{7sd} 10^{8s} 18^{10gf} 10^{8f} 7^{8g} 7^{12gf} 3^{12gs}
12^{14gs} 9^{10g} 8^{14gs} **0-1-10 £430**

Veneziana *P F I Cole*   24
3 ch f Vettori (Ire) - Fairy Story (Ire)
15^{12gf} 8^{8g} **0-0-2**

Vengeance *Mrs A J Perrett*   105
4 b g Fleetwood (Ire) - Lady Isabell
7^{10gs} 3^{12s} 1^{12gf} 5^{12gs} 5^{10gf} **1-1-5**
£21,300

Vengerov *M L W Bell*   68 a72
3 b g Piccolo - Shining Cloud
1^{8sd} 6^{8ss} 3^{12f} 10^{10gs} **1-0-4 £4,040**

Verasi *G L Moore*   60 a60
3 b g Kahyasi - Fair Verona (USA)
4^{8hy} 10^{12g} 7^{11gf} 7^{13sd} 9^{14gs} **0-0-5 £432**

Verbier (USA) *N A Callaghan*   75
2 b/br f Fusaichi Pegasus (USA) - Oh Nellie (USA)
6^{6g} 1^{7gf} 5^{8g} **1-0-3 £5,804**

Veritable *S Kirk*   66
2 br f So Factual (USA) - Madam Trilby
4^{5g} 11^{6gf} 10^{6g} **0-0-3 £357**

Verkhotina *R Charlton*   85
3 b f Barathea (Ire) - Alusha
6^{7gs} 1^{6gf} 9^{6gf} 3^{7g} 8^{8g} **1-1-5 £5,086**

Vermilion Creek *R Hollinshead*   60 a41
5 b m Makbul - Cloudy Reef
5^{7sd} 8^{11sd} 6^{12sd} 6^{9sw} 6^{8gs} 2^{8s} 9^{8gf} 6^{8gs}
11^{8g} 1^{8f} **1-1-10 £4,776**

Vermilliann (Ire) *R Hannon*   72
3 b f Mujadil (USA) - Refined (Ire)
10^{5g} 9^{6g} 16^{5gf} **0-0-3**

Verstone (Ire) *R F Fisher*   7 a3
2 b f Brave Act - Golden Charm (Ire)
8^{5gs} 8^{5sd} 8^{5s} **0-0-3**

Vertedanz (Ire) *Miss I E Craig*   18
4 b f Sesaro (USA) - Blade Of Grass
18^{7gf} 20^{8gf} 12^{7gf} **0-0-3**

Very Wise *W J Haggas*   77
2 b c Pursuit Of Love - With Care
1^{8s} **1-0-1 £3,594**

Vespone (Ire) *Saeed Bin Suroor*   119
4 ch c Llandaff (USA) - Vanishing Prairie (USA)
2^{9gf} 2^{11vs} 2^{10gs} 8^{9g} 2^{10g} 12^{10f} 5^{10gf}
0-4-7 £167,851

Vesta Flame *P T Midgley*   a37
3 b f Vettori (Ire) - Ciel De Feu (USA)
3^{9sd} 3^{8ss} 11^{12g} **0-2-3 £380**

Vettorious *J G Given*   40
2 ch c Vettori (Ire) - Sleepless
12^{7s} **0-0-1**

Viable *Mrs P Sly*   41
2 b g Vettori (Ire) - Danseuse Davis (Fr)
9^{7gs} **0-0-1**

Viagrah (Ire) *M J Polglase*
3 b g Danetime (Ire) - Classic Choice
10^{9sw} **0-0-1**

Vibe *M Johnston*   69
3 gr g Danzero (Aus) - Courting
UR^{8g} 7^{8hy} 13^{7gs} 4^{7gf} 11^{10gf} 6^{10g} **0-0-6**
£327

Vicario *M L W Bell*   65
3 gr g Vettori (Ire) - Arantxa
5^{10s} 1^{11gf} 3^{12gf} 3^{12gf} 12^{12gs} 6^{12gf} 5^{14gs}
4^{16gs} 3^{16gf} **1-3-9 £6,600**

Vicars Destiny *Mrs S Lamyman*   73
6 b m Sir Harry Lewis (USA) - Church Leap
2^{18g} 2^{18s} 13^{16gs} 8^{14gf} 10^{17gf} 6^{16gf} 4^{16gs}
3^{16gs} 3^{17gs} 2^{16gs} 3^{18f} 3^{17gf} 9^{18g} **0-5-13**
£10,304

Vicat Cole *Mrs L J Mongan*   68 a68
3 ch g Hector Protector (USA) - Dancing Spirit (Ire)
23^{8g} 5^{12sd} 7^{12gf} 8^{10gf} **0-0-4**

Vicious Knight *D Nicholls*   94
6 b g Night Shift (USA) - Myth
14^{9gf} 21^{8gf} 12^{7gs} 13^{7gf} 10^{7gf} 5^{8s} 3^{8gs}
13^{8g} 7^{8hy} **0-0-9 £2,262**

Vicious Prince (Ire) *R M Whitaker*   73
5 b g Sadler's Wells (USA) - Sunny Flower (Fr)
4^{12s} 8^{11gs} 8^{12g} 5^{16s} **0-0-4 £273**

Vicious Warrior *R M Whitaker*   94
5 b g Elmaamul (USA) - Ling Lane
2^{8g} 3^{8gf} 5^{10gf} 3^{9gf} 7^{10g} 2^{8gf} 2^{8gf} 3^{8gs}
15^{9g} 6^{8g} **0-5-10 £16,939**

Victimised (Ire) *A B Haynes*   45

2 b g Victory Note (USA) - Eurolink Virago
9^{5gs} 14^{7gf} 5^{6gf} **0-0-3**

Victor Buckwell *B Ellison*   41
2 br c Pivotal - Lonely Shore
11^{7s} 9^{7g} 8^{8hy} **0-0-3**

Victoria Peek (Ire) *D Nicholls*   63
2 b f Cape Cross (Ire) - Night Spirit (Ire)
4^{5s} 8^{6g} 7^{5g} **0-0-3 £637**

Victorian Dancer (Ire) *K A Ryan*
3 b f Groom Dancer (USA) - Victoria Regia (Ire)
10^{7hy} **0-0-1**

Victoriana *H J Collingridge*   56
3 b f Wolfhound (USA) - Silk St James
6^{6s} 4^{6s} 5^{5gs} 15^{6gf} **0-0-5 £422**

Victory Design (Ire) *J Noseda*   69
2 b c Danehill (USA) - Sun Silk (USA)
6^{6gs} **0-0-1**

Victory Flip (Ire) *R Hollinshead*   a42
4 b f Victory Note (USA) - Two Magpies
13^{6sd} 6^{8sd} 7^{5sd} 3^{8ss} **0-1-4 £417**

Victory Hymn (Ire) *M R Channon*   47
2 b f Victory Note (USA) - Nordic Union (Ire)
7^{6g} 5^{7g} 13^{7gf} **0-0-3**

Victory Lap (Ger) *M R Channon*   65
3 ch f Grand Lodge (USA) - Vicenca (USA)
8^{12s} 6^{12gf} 5^{12gf} 7^{18gf} **0-0-4**

Victory Quest (Ire) *Mrs S Lamyman*   a91
4 b g Victory Note (USA) - Marade (USA)
16^{12sd} 7^{12ss} 1^{14sd} 1^{16ss} 4^{16ss} **2-0-5**
£8,462

Victory Vee *M Blanshard*   a32
4 ch g Vettori (Ire) - Aldevonie
9^{7sw} 6^{8sw} 11^{12ss} 10^{7sd} **0-0-4**

Victory Venture (Ire) *Ian Williams*   47
4 b g Victory Note (USA) - Shirley Venture
14^{10gf} 9^{11g} 13^{10gf} 16^{12gs} **0-0-4**

Vienna's Boy (Ire) *W J Musson*   87
3 b c Victory Note (USA) - Shinkoh Rose (Fr)
4^{6gs} 4^{6s} 6^{6gf} 4^{6g} 6^{5gf} 13^{5gf} 5^{6g} 2^{6g}
5^{6gf} 4^{8gf} 4^{7gs} 1^{7s} 19^{7gs} **1-1-13 £11,620**

View The Facts *P L Gilligan*   a12
5 br m So Factual (USA) - Scenic View (Ire)
8^{5ss} 10^{10sd} **0-0-2**

Viewforth *J S Goldie*   82
6 b g Emarati (USA) - Miriam
4^{5gf} 4^{5hy} 12^{6g} 9^{6gf} 7^{6gf} 14^{6gf} 12^{5s} 4^{5g}
3^{5gs} 8^{5g} 15^{5gf} 8^{5g} 12^{6g} 8^{6gs} 24^{5gs} 3^{6s}
0-4-16 £3,514

Vigorous (Ire) *M Todhunter*   75
4 b f Danetime (Ire) - Merrily
15^{6gs} 5^{5gs} 8^{5f} 16^{5gf} 6^{5gf} 2^{6gf} 5^{5gf} **0-1-7**
£1,568

Vijay (Ire) *I Semple*   60 a60
5 ch g Eagle Eyed (USA) - Foolish Fun
10^{5ss} 3^{5sw} 10^{6sw} 6^{5g} 15^{6g} 2^{5gf} 9^{5gf} 7^{5gf}
6^{5gf} 14^{6g} 8^{6gf} 6^{7gf} **0-3-13 £2,221**

Viking Spirit *P W Harris*   94
2 b c Mind Games - Dane Dancing (Ire)
8^{6gs} 2^{6gf} 2^{6gs} 1^{6gf} 1^{6gs} 7^{6g} **2-2-6**
£14,155

Villa Chigi (Ire) *B Smart*   32
2 ch g Pistolet Bleu (Ire) - Musical Refrain (Ire)
10^{7g} **0-0-1**

Villarosi (Ire) *P W Chapple-Hyam*   74
2 b f Rossini (USA) - Trinida
5^{7gs} **0-0-1**

Villarrica (USA) *Sir Michael Stoute* 75
2 ch f Selkirk (USA) - Melikah (Ire)
4⁷ˢ 3⁷ᵍᶠ **0-1-2 £982**

Vin Du Pays *M Blanshard* 19 a62
4 b g Alzao (USA) - Royale Rose (Fr)
9¹⁵ˢ 11¹¹ᵍ 10¹⁴ᵍˢ 10¹²ᵍ 14¹⁶ᵍˢ 10¹²ˢᵈ
11¹⁴ˢᵈ **0-0-7**

Vinando *C R Egerton* 105
3 ch c Hernando (Fr) - Sirena (Ger)
1¹⁰ᵍˢ 7¹¹ᵍ 1¹²ᵍᶠ 5¹²ᵍᶠ 1¹²ᵍ **3-0-5**
£22,553

Vincent *John A Harris* a56
9 b g Anshan - Top-Anna (Ire)
4¹⁶ˢᵈ 3¹⁶ˢᵈ 1¹⁵ˢᵈ 6¹⁶ˢᵈ 3¹⁶ˢᵈ **1-2-5**
£3,354

Vindication *R M H Cowell* 97 a75
4 ch g Compton Place - Prince's Feather (Ire)
12⁷ᵍᶠ 6⁷ᵍᶠ 6⁷ᵍᶠ 7⁷ᵍᶠ 10⁷ᵍᶠ 9⁷ᵍ 9⁷ˢᵈ
20⁷ᵍˢ **0-0-8 £224**

Vinnie Roe (Ire) *D K Weld* 126
6 b/br h Definite Article - Kayu
2¹⁴ᵍᶠ 2¹²ᵍ 1¹⁴ᵍ 2¹⁶ᵍˢ **1-3-4 £438,906**

Vino Venus *Miss Sheena West* 43
2 b f Tipsy Creek (USA) - Galaxy Glow
8⁶ᵍᶠ 5⁶ᵍ **0-0-2**

Vintage Premium *R A Fahey* 112 a102
7 b g Forzando - Julia Domna
7¹⁰ˢᵈ 6⁸ˢˢ 8¹⁰ˢᵈ 1¹⁰ᵍˢ 2¹²ᵍˢ **1-1-5**
£21,472

Vintage Style *J R Weymes* 22
5 ch g Piccolo - Gibaltarik (Ire)
15⁶ᵍᶠ 19⁶ᵍ **0-0-2**

Viola Da Braccio (Ire) *D J Daly* 57 a44
3 ch f Vettori (Ire) - Push A Button
10⁸ˢ 5⁸ᵍᶠ 5¹¹ᵍᶠ 6⁸ˢᵈ **0-0-4**

Violet Avenue *J G Given* 59
3 ch f Muhtarram (USA) - Ivoronica
10⁸ᵍᶠ 6⁸ᵍᶠ 4⁸ᵍ 7⁸ᵍᶠ 5⁷ᵍᶠ 7⁸ˢ 13¹¹ᵍˢ **0-0-7**
£457

Violet Park *B J Meehan* 78
3 b f Pivotal - Petonellajill
2⁷ᵍˢ 2⁷ᵍ 3⁸ᵍᶠ 1⁷ᵍᶠ 1⁷ˢ 12⁷ᵍˢ **2-3-6**
£15,465

Vip *Saeed Bin Suroor* 67
2 ch c Dubai Millennium - Danish (Ire)
4⁷ˢ **0-0-1 £322**

Virgin's Tears *P W Chapple-Hyam* 48
2 b f Bishop Of Cashel - Lola Mora
7⁸ᵍ 10⁶ˢ **0-0-2**

Vision Victory (Ger) *T P Tate* 53
2 b g Dashing Blade - Val D'Isere (Ger)
4⁵ʰʸ 10⁵ʰʸ 10⁶ᶠ 11⁷ᶠ 13⁸ˢ **0-0-5 £334**

Visionist (Ire) *J A Osborne* 101
2 b c Orpen (USA) - Lady Taufan (Ire)
1⁶ᵍ 4⁷ᵍᶠ 3⁶ᵍᶠ 3⁶ᵍᶠ **1-2-4 £36,229**

Vita Spericolata (Ire) *J S Wainwright* 98
7 b m Prince Sabo - Ahonita
8⁵ᵍˢ 9⁵ᵍˢ 3⁵ʰʸ 5⁵ᵍᶠ 17⁶ᵍ 12⁵ᵍˢ 8⁶ᵍˢ 5⁵ᵍᶠ
5⁶ᵍᶠ 6⁶ᵍˢ 9⁵ᵍˢ **0-1-1 £5,400**

Vitelucy *Miss S J Wilton* a41
5 b m Vettori (Ire) - Classic Line
5¹²ˢʷ 5¹²ˢˢ 3¹⁶ˢᵈ 5¹²ˢᵈ 5¹²ˢᵈ **0-1-5 £206**

Vittorioso (Ire) *Miss Gay Kelleway* 52 a56
3 b g Victory Note (USA) - Miss Anita (Ire)
5⁷ˢᵈ 3⁵ˢᵈ 3⁵ˢᵈ 2⁵ˢˢ 7⁵ˢᵈ 8⁵ᵍᶠ 5⁵ᵍᶠ 10⁶ᵍ
7⁷ᵍˢ 6¹⁰ᵍᶠ 5¹⁰ᵍ **0-3-11 £2,065**

Viva Atlas Espana *Miss B Sanders*
4 b f Piccolo - Bay Risk
16⁷ˢᵈ 8¹⁰ˢ **0-0-2**

Vivre Sa Vie *Sir Mark Prescott* 2 a63
3 ch f Nashwan (USA) - La Strada
4⁹ˢᵈ 3⁸ˢˢ 2¹²ˢˢ 5¹²ˢʷ 7¹⁴ˢ **0-1-5 £1,741**

Vizulize *A W Carroll* 54 a54
5 b m Robellino (USA) - Euridice (Ire)
12⁷ˢᵈ 6⁸ˢᵈ 5⁷ˢᵈ 9⁷ˢᵈ 9⁸ˢᵈ 4⁷ˢᵈ 10⁸ˢᵈ
11⁸ᵍ 3⁸ᵍˢ **0-1-9 £215**

Vlasta Weiner *J M Bradley* 22 a45
4 b g Magic Ring (Ire) - Armaiti
7⁶ˢᵈ 2⁷ˢᵈ 5⁸ˢᵈ 10⁸ˢᵈ 4⁷ˢˢ 6⁸ˢᵈ 4⁸ˢᵈ 6⁸ˢᵈ
12⁶ˢᵈ 16⁶ᵍᶠ **0-1-10 £420**

Vocative (Ger) *P C Haslam* 60
2 gr f Acatenango (Ger) - Vadinaxa (Fr)
7⁸ᵍᶠ **0-0-1**

Voice Mail *A M Balding* 86 a68
5 b g So Factual (USA) - Wizardry
7¹⁰ᵍˢ 9⁹ˢ 1⁸ᵍᶠ 1¹⁰ᶠ 3¹⁰ᶠ 11⁹ᵍ 2⁸ᶠ 7⁹ᵍᶠ
3¹⁰ᵍ 4⁸ᵍᶠ 8⁸ᶠ 3¹²ᵍᶠ 12¹⁰ᵍᶠ 8⁸ˢᵈ **2-4-14**
£13,868

Voice Of An Angel (Ire) *A Berry* 35 a46
2 b f Desert Style (Ire) - Madame Curie
5⁵ˢᵈ 8⁵ᵍ 5⁵ˢᵈ 12⁵ᵍᶠ 5⁵ᵍᶠ **0-0-5**

Voile (Ire) *R Hannon* 86 a81
3 b f Barathea (Ire) - Samriah (Ire)
7⁷ᵍᶠ 8⁶ˢ 9⁸ˢᵈ **0-0-3**

Voir Dire *Mrs P N Dutfield* 63
2 b c Vettori (Ire) - Bobbie Dee
13⁷ᵍᶠ 7⁷ᵍ 8⁸ᵍˢ 8⁸ᵍˢ 3¹⁰ʰᵛ **0-1-5 £707**

Voix Du Nord (Fr) *D Smaga* 115
3 b c Valanour (Fr) - Dame Edith (Fr)
1¹¹ᵍˢ 1¹¹ᵍᶠ **2-0-2 £122,627**

Volaticus (Ire) *D Nicholls* 65
3 b c Desert Story (Ire) - Haysel (Ire)
2⁶ᵍ 14⁶ᵍˢ 4⁸ᵍᶠ 4⁵ˢ 12⁶ᵍᶠ **0-2-5 £2,373**

Volitio *S Kirk* 53
2 b c Mind Games - Millie's Lady (Ire)
16⁷ᵍˢ 13⁷ᵍ 11⁸ᵍᶠ 7⁸ᵍˢ 10⁸ˢ **0-0-5**

Von Wessex *W G M Turner* 58 a21
2 b g Wizard King - Gay Da Cheen (Ire)
6⁵ᵍ 5⁵ˢᵈ 1⁵ᵍᶠ 6⁵ᵍˢ 3⁵ᵍ 3⁵ᵍᶠ 1⁵ᵍ 4⁵ᵍˢ 6⁵ʰʸ
6⁵ᵍˢ 2⁵ᶠ **2-2-11 £8,133**

Vonadaisy *W J Haggas* 67 a73
3 b f Averti (Ire) - Vavona
1⁷ᵍˢ 2¹⁷ᵍˢ 5⁸ˢᵈ 9⁹ˢᵈ 4⁷ˢᵈ **1-0-5 £4,290**

Vondova *R Hannon* 86
2 b f Efisio - Well Proud (Ire)
3⁵ᶠ 7⁷ᵍ 1⁶ᵍˢ 8⁷ᵍᶠ 2⁶ᵍ 9⁶ᵍ **1-1-6**
£12,804

Voom *M R Channon* 47
2 b f Fraam - Natalie Jay
8⁶ᶠ 4⁶ᶠ 3⁵ᶠ **0-1-3 £361**

Vortex *Miss Gay Kelleway* 113 a104
5 b g Danehill (USA) - Roupala (USA)
1⁸ˢᵈ 1⁸ˢʷ 1⁸ˢˢ 12¹⁰ˢᵈ 17⁸ᵍ 1⁹ᶠᵗ
3⁷ᵍᶠ 10⁸ᵍᶠ 2⁸ᵍ 4⁷ᵍᶠ 2⁸ᵍ 1⁸ᶠᵗ 4⁷ᵍᶠ **7-4-15**
£127,279

Vrisaki (Ire) *Miss D Mountain* 51 a55
3 b g Docksider (USA) - Kingdom Queen (Ire)
2⁷ˢᵈ 8⁷ˢˢ 4⁷ˢ 9⁸ᵍᶠ 7¹¹ᵍᶠ 3¹¹ᶠ 6¹⁰ᶠ 3¹¹ᶠ
11¹²ᵍᶠ 17¹²ᵍᶠ 14¹¹ᵍᶠ **0-3-11 £1,967**

Vrubel (Ire) *V Smith* a52
5 ch g Entrepreneur - Renzola
2⁹ˢᵈ 9¹¹ˢᵈ **0-1-2 £425**

Waaedah (USA) *D J Barry*   44
3 ch f Halling (USA) - Agama (USA)
19⁷ᵍ 16⁸ᶠ 12⁷ˢ **0-0-3**

Waatheb (Ire) *R Hannon*   75 a64
2 b c Barathea (Ire) - Bally Souza (Ire)
11⁶ᵍᶠ 7⁶ˢ 8⁸ˢᵈ **0-0-3**

Wafani *W J Musson*
5 b g Mtoto - Wafa (Ire)
11¹⁰ᵍᶠ **0-0-1**

Waggledance (Ire) *J S Wainwright*   64
2 b g Mujadil (USA) - Assertive Lass (USA)
5⁵ᵍᶠ 9⁵ᵍˢ 8⁵ᵍᶠ 7⁵ᵍ 2⁵ᵍᶠ 9⁵ᵍᶠ **0-1-6**
£1,798

Wahchi (Ire) *G P Kelly*   60
5 ch g Nashwan (USA) - Nafhaat (USA)
7¹⁰ˢ 19¹²ᵍ 16¹²ᵍˢ 10¹⁰ᵍ 6¹⁰ᵍ **0-0-5**

Wahoo Sam (USA) *T D Barron*   80
4 ch g Sandpit (Brz) - Good Reputation (USA)
12⁷ᵍˢ 8⁸ᵍ 3⁸ᶠ 1⁹ᵍˢ 1⁹ᵍ 8¹⁰ᵍᶠ 1⁹ᵍᶠ 2⁹ˢ
11⁹ᵍˢ **3-2-9 £18,225**

Wainwright (Ire) *P A Blockley*   53 a71
4 b g Victory Note (USA) - Double Opus (Ire)
1⁶ˢʷ 9⁶ˢᵈ 9⁶ᵍˢ 11⁵ᵍ 11⁶ᵍᶠ 6⁷ᵍᶠ **1-0-6**
£3,386

Wait For Spring (USA) *J H M Gosden*   73
3 b f Seeking The Gold (USA) - Polish Spring (Ire)
5¹⁰ᵍᶠ 2¹⁰ᵍˢ 16⁸ᵍˢ 9¹⁰ᵍ **0-1-4 £1,660**

Wait For The Will (USA) *G L Moore*   96
8 ch g Seeking The Gold (USA) - You'd Be Surprised (USA)
16¹²ᵍ 10¹⁴ᵍᶠ 1¹²ᵍᶠ 1¹²ᵍᶠ 2¹²ᵍᶠ 5¹⁴ᵍˢ
10¹²ᵍᶠ **2-1-8 £15,419**

Wake (USA) *M L W Bell*   89 a97
4 b c Storm Cat (USA) - Ladies Cruise (USA)
1⁸ˢᵈ 6⁹ᵍ 10¹⁰ᵍᶠ 6⁸ˢ 2⁹ˢᵈ **1-1-5 £9,489**

Wake Up Henry *R Charlton*   59
3 ch g Nashwan (USA) - River Saint (USA)
8⁸ʰʸ 3¹⁰ᵍᶠ 4¹²ᶠ 13¹⁰ᶠ **0-1-4 £1,150**

Walker Bay (Ire) *J S Moore*   a42
6 ch m Efisio - Lalandria (Fr)
5¹⁰ˢᵈ 9¹³ˢᵈ **0-0-2**

Walkonthewildside *D R Loder*   78
2 b c Giant's Causeway (USA) - Wannabe Grand (Ire)
5⁶ᵍᶠ 4⁷ᵍᶠ 1⁷ᵍᶠ 9⁷ᵍ **1-0-4 £6,842**

Wall Street Runner *C A Dwyer*   23 a64
3 ch f Kirkwall - Running Tycoon (Ire)
20⁶ᵍˢ 8⁷ˢᵈ 7⁹ˢᵈ 10⁷ˢᵈ 8⁷ˢᵈ **0-0-5**

Waltzing Beau *B G Powell*   53 a57
3 ch g Dancing Spree (USA) - Blushing Belle
2⁹ˢᵈ 9¹⁰ˢᵈ 12¹²ᵍ 9¹⁴ᵍ 8¹⁰ᶠ 2¹¹ᵍ 3¹⁰ᵍᶠ
6¹⁰ᵍᶠ 6¹⁶ˢᵈ 8¹²ᶠ **0-3-10 £2,359**

Waltzing Wizard *A Berry*   61 a60
5 b g Magic Ring (Ire) - Legendary Dancer
3⁷ˢᵈ 5⁸ˢᵈ 4⁷ˢᵈ 5⁷ˢʷ 5⁷ᵍ 7⁷ᵍ 5⁷ᵍᶠ 4⁷ᵍᶠ
9⁸ᶠ 6⁷ᵍᶠ 3⁷ᵍᶠ 4⁷ᵍ 13⁷ᵍᶠ 6⁷ᶠ 11⁷ᵍ 5⁷ˢᵈ **0-2-17**
£2,142

Wanchai Lad *D Nicholls*   89
3 b c Danzero (Aus) - Frisson
3⁵ˢ 7⁶ᵍᶠ 5⁵ᵍᶠ 9⁵ᵍ 11⁵ᵍᶠ 15⁵ˢ 11⁷ˢ **0-1-7**
£2,105

Wandering Act (Ire) *M J Wallace*   47
2 b c Brave Act - Cwm Deri (Ire)
7⁷ᶠ 7⁸ˢ **0-0-2**

Wanna Shout *R Dickin*   53 a66
6 b m Missed Flight - Lulu
2⁸ˢᵈ 1⁸ˢᵈ 2¹⁰ˢᵈ 1⁸ˢᵈ 7¹⁰ˢᵈ 5¹⁰ᶠ 8⁸ᵍᶠ
6¹²ˢᵈ 3¹⁰ˢᵈ 6⁷ˢᵈ **2-3-11 £7,188**

Wansdyke Lass *M R Channon*   64
2 b f Josr Algarhoud (Ire) - Silankka
5⁷ᵍᶠ **0-0-1**

Want (USA) *J H M Gosden*   65
3 ch c Miswaki (USA) - Substance (USA)
10⁸ᵍ 10⁸ᵍ **0-0-2**

War At Sea (Ire) *M P Tregoning*   72
2 b c Bering - Naval Affair (Ire)
5⁷ˢ **0-0-1**

War Owl (USA) *Ian Williams*   79 a69
7 gr g Linamix (Fr) - Ganasheba (USA)
2⁸ˢᵈ 8¹⁰ˢᵈ 1¹⁰ˢᵈ 1¹⁰ᵍ 3¹¹ᵍˢ 5¹¹ˢ 12¹⁰ˢ
1¹⁰ᵍᶠ 9¹⁰ᵍ 8¹⁰ᵍᶠ 4⁹ˢ 14¹⁰ᵍ **3-2-12 £15,381**

War Pennant *M R Channon*   48 a28
2 b g Selkirk (USA) - Bunting
6⁸ᵍᶠ 9⁹ˢᵈ **0-0-2**

Waraqa (USA) *T M Jones*   a12
5 b m Red Ransom (USA) - Jafn
14⁶ˢᵈ **0-0-1**

Warbreck *C R Egerton*   54 a56
3 ch g Selkirk (USA) - Wigging
15⁷ᵍ 7⁸ᵍ 8⁵ʰʸ 5⁸ˢᵈ **0-0-4**

Warden Complex *J R Fanshawe*   96 a93
3 b g Compton Place - Miss Rimex (Ire)
3⁷ˢᵈ 2⁶ᵍˢ 1⁷ᵍᶠ 1⁷ᶠ 7⁷ᵍ 5⁷ᵍᶠ 2⁷ˢᵈ **2-3-7**
£18,974

Warden Warren *Mrs C A Dunnett*   81 a83
6 b g Petong - Silver Spell
3⁷ˢᵈ 4⁷ˢᵈ 6⁷ˢᵈ 7⁵ʷ 7⁷ˢˢ 9⁷ˢˢ 1⁷ˢᵈ 18⁸ᵍˢ
12⁶ᵍᶠ 4⁷ᵍᶠ 1⁷ᶠ 9⁷ᵍᶠ 9⁷ᵍᶠ 2⁷ᵍᶠ 12⁷ˢ 18⁷ᵍˢ
3-3-16 £14,590

Wares Home (Ire) *K R Burke*   65 a58
3 b g Indian Rocket - Pepilin
7⁷ˢᵈ 6⁸ˢᵈ 8⁸ᵍˢ 3⁶ᵍᶠ 4⁷ᵍ 3⁶ᵍ 3⁷ᶠ 2⁶ᵍᶠ
3⁷ᵍᶠ 11⁸ᵍᶠ 3⁶ᵍᶠ 7⁶ʰʸ 7⁷ˢᵈ **0-3-13 £3,151**

Warif (USA) *M E Sowersby*   35 a23
3 ch c Diesis - Alshoowg (USA)
5¹⁰ʰʸ 7¹⁰ᵍᶠ 8¹²ˢᵈ 11⁹ˢᵈ **0-0-4**

Warlingham (Ire) *P Howling*   65 a67
6 b g Catrail (USA) - Tadjnama (USA)
10⁶ˢᵈ 8⁷ˢᵈ 1⁷ˢˢ 1⁷ˢᵈ 5⁷ˢˢ 7⁷ˢʷ 1⁷ᵍᶠ 10⁷ᵍᶠ
5⁷ᶠ 7⁶ᵍᶠ 5⁷ᶠ 8⁶ᶠ 8⁷ᵍᶠ 9⁶ᵍᶠ 17⁶ᵍ 12⁷ˢᵈ 7⁶ˢᵈ
7⁷ˢᵈ **3-0-18 £8,477**

Warningcamp (Ger) *Lady Herries*   76
3 b g Lando (Ger) - Wilette (Ger)
4¹⁰ᵍ 6¹⁰ᵍ 3¹⁰ᵍᶠ 16⁸ᵍˢ **0-1-4 £989**

Warrad (USA) *G A Butler*   97 a96
3 b c Kingmambo (USA) - Shalimar Garden (Ire)
4⁸ᵍˢ 3⁸ˢᵈ 5¹⁰ᵍᶠ 3⁹ᵍˢ **0-1-4 £5,846**

Warren Place *J Hetherton*   35 a20
4 ch g Presidium - Coney Hills
13⁸ˢᵈ 18⁶ᵍᶠ 8⁵ᵍˢ 9⁵ᵍ **0-0-4**

Warrsan (Ire) *C E Brittain*   126
6 b h Caerleon (USA) - Lucayan Princess
5¹²ᵍᶠ 3¹²ᵍ 1¹²ᵍ 2¹⁰ᵍˢ 9¹²ᵍᶠ 1¹²ˢ 9¹²ᵍ **2-1-7**
£631,612

Wasalat (USA) *M R Channon*   76
2 b f Bahri (USA) - Saabga (USA)
4⁶ᵍᶠ 2⁶ᵍˢ 3⁶ᵍᶠ 2⁷ᵍᶠ 9⁷ᵍᶠ 6⁷ˢ **0-3-6**
£4,124

Washbrook *Andrew Turnell*   60
3 b g Royal Applause - Alacrity
16⁸ˢ 11⁸ᵍᶠ 3⁷ᶠ 8⁷ᵍᶠ 17⁸ᵍᶠ 15⁷ᵍˢ **0-1-6**
£605

Washington Pink (Ire) *C Grant*   42
5 b g Tagula (Ire) - Little Red Rose

15^{12gs} 13^{10gs} 4^{14s} 8^{12g} 10^{14gf} 11^{16g}
0-0-6

Wasted Talent (Ire) *J G Portman*   81
4 b f Sesaro (USA) - Miss Garuda
1^{12g} 2^{12gf} 11^{20gf} 10^{12g} 4^{12g} **1-1-5**
£6,357

Watamu (Ire) *P J Makin*   94
3 b c Groom Dancer (USA) - Miss Golden Sands
13^{8g} 9^{9hy} 1^{11gf} 2^{12gf} 6^{12g} 3^{10gf} 5^{10g}
1-2-7 £17,123

Watchful Witness *Dr J R J Naylor*   57 a33
4 ch c In The Wings - Eternal
3^{14gs} 4^{12gf} 16^{12gf} 11^{16sd} **0-1-4 £921**

Watching *R A Fahey*   92
7 ch g Indian Ridge - Sweeping
3^{7g} 22^{6g} 2^{5gs} 5^{5gf} 5^{5gf} 7^{6gf} 10^{5gs} 11^{5gs}
13^{7gf} 2^{6g} 3^{6s} 3^{7s} 11^{7g} **0-5-13 £16,959**

Watchmyeyes (Ire) *N P Littmoden*   78 a82
2 ch g Bold Fact (USA) - Shadow Smile (Ire)
6^{6gf} 4^{7gf} 4^{6gs} 2^{7gf} 2^{8sd} 1^{9sd} 1^{9sd} **2-2-7**
£8,918

Water Of Life (Ire) *J R Boyle*   a44
5 b m Dr Devious (Ire) - Simulcast
7^{10sd} 12^{10sd} **0-0-2**

Water Pistol *Mrs A J Perrett*   69
2 b g Double Trigger (Ire) - Water Flower
8^{7g} 9^{8g} 6^{8g} 9^{7s} **0-0-4**

Water Taxi *R Charlton*   73
3 ch c Zafonic (USA) - Trellis Bay
4^{12s} 3^{12gf} 3^{13f} **0-0-3 £1,857**

Waterfront Dancer *J R Best*   34 a8
2 b g Groom Dancer (USA) - Azula
15^{5gf} 9^{5gf} 11^{5sd} 13^{6g} **0-0-4**

Waterline Blue (Ire) *P D Evans*   51 a35
3 b g Mujadil (USA) - Blues Queen
5^{7gf} 11^{6sd} **0-0-2**

Waterline Dancer (Ire) *P D Evans*   a36
4 b/br f Danehill Dancer (Ire) - Thrill Seeker (Ire)
8^{10sd} 8^{8sd} 9^{7sd} 7^{8sw} 4^{7ss} 14^{7hy} **0-0-6**

Waterline Lover *P D Evans*   54
2 ch f Efisio - Food Of Love
6^{5g} 10^{5g} 11^{5s} 4^{6gf} 7^{6gs} 6^{6gf} 4^{5gs} 17^{5gs}
0-0-8 £645

Waterline Spirit *P D Evans*
4 b g Piccolo - Gina Of Hithermoor
16^{12g} 11^{16gf} **0-0-2**

Waterloo Corner *R Craggs*
2 b g Cayman Kai (Ire) - Rasin Luck
9^{7gs} **0-0-1**

Waterpark *R Craggs*   65 a4
6 b m Namaqualand (USA) - Willisa
13^{6s} 1^{7s} 13^{8sd} 2^{8f} **1-1-4 £9,891**

Watership Crystal (Ire) *J H M Gosden*   50
3 b f Sadler's Wells (USA) - Crystal Spray
10^{10gf} **0-0-1**

Watership Down (Ire) *B G Powell*   40
7 b g Dolphin Street (Fr) - Persian Myth
9^{14gf} 16^{12gf} **0-0-2**

Waterside (Ire) *G L Moore*   92 a72
5 ch g Lake Coniston (Ire) - Classic Ring (Ire)
10^{6gs} 12^{6g} 3^{6hy} 11^{6gs} 3^{6sd} 1^{7gf} 1^{7gf} 2^{7g}
4^{6gf} 6^{8gf} 16^{7gf} 3^{7gs} 1^{7gs} 12^{7g} 13^{7g} **3-3-15**
£27,443

Waverley Road *M Madgwick*   a34
7 ch g Pelder (Ire) - Lillicara (Fr)
13^{12sd} 4^{16sd} **0-0-2**

Wavertree Girl (Ire) *N P Littmoden*   68 a63
3 b f Marju (Ire) - Lust
3^{7sd} 8^{8sd} 5^{7gs} 7^{7g} 4^{6f} 3^{6g} 10^{7sd} 11^{6gf}
0-2-8 £1,407

Wavertree Spirit *N P Littmoden*   39
3 ch g Hector Protector (USA) - Miss Clarinet
6^{10gf} **0-0-1**

Wavertree Warrior (Ire) *N P Littmoden*   78
2 br c Indian Lodge (Ire) - Karamana
9^{6gf} 3^{6g} 2^{6gf} 10^{6y} 3^{7gs} 9^{8s} **0-3-6**
£4,802

Wavet *J Pearce*   a51
4 b f Pursuit Of Love - Ballerina Bay
7^{10sd} 2^{8sd} **0-1-2 £868**

Way Out *B P J Baugh*   5
3 b f Robellino (USA) - Exit
11^{8gf} 10^{8g} **0-0-2**

Wayward Melody *G L Moore*   a26
4 b f Merdon Melody - Dubitable
4^{12sd} **0-0-1**

Wayward Shot (Ire) *M W Easterby*   62
2 b g Desert Prince - Style Parade (USA)
5^{5gf} 7^{5f} 12^{5gs} 5^{7f} 4^{7gs} **0-0-5 £552**

Wazir (USA) *J H M Gosden*   81 a86
2 b/br c Pulpit (USA) - Top Order (USA)
2^{6sd} 1^{6gf} **1-1-2 £6,862**

Waziri (Ire) *H Morrison*   76
3 b g Mtoto - Euphorie (Ger)
1^{10gf} 7^{10g} 9^{14gf} 3^{9gs} 10^{10g} 7^{8hy} 15^{10g}
1-1-7 £6,290

We'Re Stonybroke (Ire) *Thomas Cooper*   63
5 b g College Chapel - Mokaite
11^{7s} 8^{6f} 19^{8g} 13^{8hy} 12^{7g} 6^{ys} 5^{6s} 9^{7hy}
0-1-8 £630

We'll Meet Again *M W Easterby*   61
4 ch g Bin Ajwaad (Ire) - Tantalizing Song (Can)
3^{8f} 12^{7g} 48^{gf} 5^{10gf} **0-2-4 £444**

Weakest Link *E J Alston*   44 a59
3 b g Mind Games - Sky Music
2^{7sd} 3^{6sd} 3^{7sd} 7^{7sd} 15^{6g} 14^{8gf} 4^{6g} **0-2-7**
£838

Weaver Of Dreams (Ire) *G A Swinbank*
4 b g Victory Note (USA) - Daziyra (Ire)
11^{12hy} **0-0-1**

Weaver Spell *J R Norton*   35 a14
3 b g Wizard King - Impy Fox (Ire)
5^{6sd} 6^{7sf} 4^{8gs} 9^{12gf} 10^{14f} 17^{10g} **0-0-6**

Web Racer (Ire) *J R Weymes*   35 a17
2 b f Bold Fact (USA) - Sky Lover
5^{6gf} 9^{7f} 8^{7sd} **0-0-3**

Webbington Lass (Ire) *Dr J R J Naylor*   14
3 b f Petardia - Richardstown Lass (Ire)
8^{10sd} 11^{7gs} 14^{6gs} **0-0-3**

Webbswood Lad (Ire) *Mrs Stef Liddiard*   a68
3 b g Robellino (USA) - Poleaxe
3^{8sd} 2^{8sd} **0-2-2 £1,923**

Wedding Cake (Ire) *Sir Michael Stoute*   70 a73
3 ch f Groom Dancer (USA) - Greektown
8^{8gs} 3^{10f} 4^{11gf} 1^{12sd} 10^{11g} **1-0-5**
£4,608

Wedding Party *Mrs A J Perrett*   86 a83
2 ch f Groom Dancer (USA) - Ceanothus (Ire)
3^{6gf} 1^{6sd} 4^{7sd} 1^{7g} 2^{7hy} **2-2-5 £35,253**

Wedlock *T D Easterby*   61
2 b c Pursuit Of Love - Promise Fulfilled (USA)
4^{6gs} 8^{6gf} 12^{6gs} **0-0-3 £450**

Wedowannagiveuthat (Ire) *T D Easterby* 56 a10
3 b f Desert Prince (Ire) - Mimansa (USA)
7⁸ᵍ 14⁷ᵍˢ 6⁷ᵍᶠ 12¹⁰ᵍᶠ 12⁸ˢᵈ 12⁸ᵍᶠ **0-0-6**

Wee Dinns (Ire) *S Kirk* 94
3 b f Marju (Ire) - Tir-An-Oir (Ire)
7¹⁰ᵍ 5⁸ˢ 2¹⁰ᶠ 2¹⁰ᵍᶠ 1¹⁰ᵍ 2⁹ᵍ 6¹⁰ᵍ 6¹⁰ʰʸ
1-3-8 £12,366

Weecandoo (Ire) *C N Allen* 95
6 b m Turtle Island (Ire) - Romantic Air
7¹⁰ᵍˢ 9¹⁰ᵍᶠ 5¹⁰ᵍᶠ 7¹⁰ᵍ 6⁹ᵍ 6¹⁰ˢ
0-0-7 £1,200

Weet A Head (Ire) *R Hollinshead* 83 a65
3 b c Foxhound (USA) - Morale
5⁹ˢʷ 3¹¹ˢ 5¹⁰ʰʸ 6¹⁰ᵍˢ 3⁸ᵍᶠ 4⁸ᵍᶠ 6¹⁰ᵍᶠ 8⁸ᵍ
8⁸ᵍˢ 3¹²ᶠᵍ **0-3-10 £3,675**

Weet An Haul *P A Blockley* 52 a26
3 b g Danzero (Aus) - Island Ruler
7⁶ᵍᶠ 8⁸ˢᵈ 3⁸ᵍᶠ 12⁹ˢᵈ **0-1-4 £535**

Weet An Store (Ire) *R Hollinshead*
3 gr c Spectrum (Ire) - Karmisymixa (Fr)
8¹²ᵍᶠ **0-0-1**

Weet For Me *R Hollinshead* 78
8 b g Warning - Naswara (USA)
18¹⁴ᵍˢ 9¹⁶ᵍᶠ 2¹⁶ᵍ 6¹⁵ᵍ 5¹⁴ᵍ 6¹⁴ᵍᶠ 14¹⁴ᵍˢ
12¹⁴ᵍˢ **0-1-8 £2,016**

Weet N Measures *R Hollinshead* 54 a50
2 b c Weet-A-Minute (Ire) - Weet Ees Girl (Ire)
5⁵ʰʸ 5⁶ˢʷ 8⁶ˢᵈ **0-0-3**

Weet Watchers *P A Blockley* 68 a68
4 b g Polar Prince (Ire) - Weet Ees Girl (Ire)
1⁷ˢᵈ 6⁷ˢᵈ 4⁷ˢˢ 3⁸ᵍˢ 16⁷ᶠ 5⁷ᵍᶠ 16ᵍᶠ PU⁷ᵍ
13⁷ᵍᶠ 13⁶ˢᵈ **2-1-10 £6,213**

Weet Yer Tern *P A Blockley* 65 a52
2 b c Brave Act - Maxime (Ire)
4⁵ᵍ 2⁵ᵍᶠ 4⁶ˢᵈ **0-1-3 £2,167**

Weir's Annie *H Candy* 32
3 b f Puissance - Hyde Princess
7⁶ˢ 16⁵ᵍᶠ 13⁵ᵍᶠ **0-0-3**

Wekiwa Springs (Fr) *R McGlinchey* a9
7 gr g Kendor (Fr) - Ti Mamaille (Fr)
6⁸ˢᵈ **0-0-1**

Welcome Archie *J S Haldane* 31
4 ch g Most Welcome - Indefinite Article (Ire)
9⁸ᵍ 9⁸ᵍˢ 10⁷ᵍᶠ 12⁸ᵍ **0-0-4**

Welcome Back *K A Ryan* a34
7 ch g Most Welcome - Villavina
3¹⁵ˢᵈ **0-1-1 £179**

Welcome Dream *Mrs A Duffield* 37
2 ch f Most Welcome - Sweet Dreams
7⁵ᵍˢ 11⁷ˢᵈ **0-0-2**

Welcome Signal *J R Fanshawe* 78 a56
4 ch g Most Welcome - Glenfinlass
12¹⁰ˢᵈ 5⁸ᵍᶠ 5¹⁰ᵍ 8¹⁰ᵍᶠ 3⁷ˢ 2⁷ᵍᶠ 2⁸ᵍˢ **0-3-7**
£3,073

Welcome Stranger *J M P Eustace* 103
4 b g Most Welcome - Just Julia
8⁸ᵍˢ 9⁸ᵍ 9¹⁰ᵍᶠ 2⁸ᵍᶠ 1⁸ᶠ 2¹⁰ᵍᶠ 18⁸ᵍᶠ 2⁸ᵍᶠ
8⁸ᶠ 1⁸ᵍᶠ 14⁸ᵍˢ **3-3-11 £33,328**

Welkino's Boy *J Mackie* 69
3 ch g Most Welcome - Khadino
13¹⁰ᵍ 5¹²ᵍᶠ 6¹⁰ᵍᶠ 3¹⁴ᵍᶠ 3¹⁴ˢ 12¹⁴ᵍ **0-1-6**
£1,423

Well Connected (Ire) *P D Niven* 18
4 b g Among Men (USA) - Wire To Wire
11⁹ᵍ 11⁸ᶠ **0-0-2**

Well Established (Ire) *M A Jarvis* 70
2 b c Sadler's Wells (USA) - Riveryev (USA)
6⁸ˢ **0-0-1**

Well Knit *P W D'Arcy* 51 a56
3 b f Robellino (USA) - Wydah
7⁸ˢᵈ 15⁷ˢᵈ 7⁸ʸ 13¹⁰ˢ 13¹¹ᵍᶠ **0-0-6**

Well Known *R Charlton* 80
3 b f Sadler's Wells (USA) - Danefair
1¹⁰ᵍ 8¹²ᵍᶠ 9¹⁰ᵍᶠ **1-0-3 £5,551**

Wellington Hall (Ger) *P W Chapple-Hyam* 72
6 b g Halling (USA) - Wells Whisper (Fr)
11¹¹ᵍᶠ 9¹²ᵍᶠ 11⁰ᵍᶠ 3¹³ᵍˢ 5¹¹ᵍ 1¹⁰ˢ **3-1-6**
£15,839

Welsh And Wylde (Ire) *B Palling* a22
4 b g Anita's Prince - Waikiki (Ger)
10¹²ˢᵈ 6¹⁶ˢᵈ **0-0-2**

Welsh Dream *Miss S E Forster* 42
7 b g Mtoto - Morgannwg (Ire)
6¹⁶ᵍ 6¹⁶ᵍᶠ **0-0-2**

Welsh Emperor (Ire) *T P Tate* 111
5 b g Emperor Jones (USA) - Simply Times (USA)
1⁶ˢ 4⁶ᵍˢ 6⁶ˢ 5⁶ʰʸ 2⁷ˢ 8⁶ᵍ 1⁶ˢ 8⁶ᵛˢ **2-1-8**
£34,048

Welsh Empress *P L Gilligan* 52
3 b f Bahamian Bounty - Azola (Ire)
7⁸ᵍ 3⁸ᵍᶠ 10⁸ᶠ 10⁸ᵍˢ 12⁷ᵍ 15⁷ᵍᶠ **0-1-6**
£421

Welsh Galaxy (Ire) *P L Gilligan* 48 a10
2 b f Pennekamp (USA) - Jamaiel (Ire)
10⁷ˢᵈ 17⁸ᵍˢ 13⁸ᵍ 10⁸ᵍᶠ 10⁶ᵍᶠ **0-0-5**

Welsh Main *F Jordan* 66
7 br g Zafonic (USA) - Welsh Daylight
9¹⁴ᵍ **0-0-1**

Welsh Whisper *S A Brookshaw* 26 a45
5 b m Overbury (USA) - Grugiar
7⁸ˢᵈ 7⁸ˢᵈ 4⁸ˢˢ 8⁹ˢʷ 7⁸ˢʷ 5⁷ˢˢ 6⁶ˢᵈ 6⁷ˢᵈ
1⁶ˢᵈ 3⁷ˢᵈ 9⁶ᵍᶠ **1-1-12 £1,643**

Welsh Wind (Ire) *M Wigham* 53 a65
8 b g Tenby - Bavaria
3¹⁰ˢᵈ 2¹⁰ˢᵈ 12⁸ˢᵈ 3¹⁰ˢᵈ 1⁸ˢᵈ 9¹²ˢᵈ 4¹⁰ˢᵈ
9¹⁰ᵍ **1-3-8 £4,719**

Wembury Point (Ire) *B G Powell* 54 a58
2 gr c Monashee Mountain (USA) - Lady Celina (Fr)
9⁶ᵍ 10⁷ᵍ 11⁷ᵍᶠ 6⁷ᶠ 13⁷ᵍᶠ 9⁸ˢ 5⁸ˢᵈ **0-0-7**

Wendy's Girl (Ire) *R P Elliott* 64 a63
3 b f Ashkalani (Ire) - Mrs Evans (Ire)
7⁵ˢˢ 8⁷ˢᵈ 5⁶ᵍˢ 2⁷ˢᵈ PU⁶ˢᵈ 4⁵ᵍˢ 7⁵ᵍᶠ 1⁶ᶠ
12⁶ˢ 1⁶ᵍᶠ 6⁵ᵍᶠ 5⁵ᵍᶠ 5⁵ᵍˢ 3⁵ˢᶠ 3⁵ʰʸ **2-2-15**
£8,525

Wessex (USA) *James Moffatt* 79
4 ch g Gone West (USA) - Satin Velvet (USA)
15⁷ᵍ 6⁷ᶠ 8⁸ᵍᶠ 7⁷ᵍ 5⁸ᵍᶠ 9¹⁰ᵍᶠ 11⁸ᵍ 8⁶ᵍᶠ
0-0-8

West Country (UAE) *Doug Watson* 59 a81
3 br c Gone West (USA) - Crystal Gazing (USA)
4⁸ᶠᵗ 3⁸ᶠᵗ 18⁷ᵍ 8⁶ᵍ 4¹²ᶠ 14⁶ᶠᵗ **0-0-6**
£2,002

West End Wonder (Ire) *M J Wallace* 43
5 b g Idris (Ire) - Miss Plum
15¹⁰ᵍ 4¹⁰ᶠ 7¹¹ᵍᶠ **0-0-3 £309**

West Highland Way (Ire) *I Semple* 80 a71
3 b g Foxhound - Gilding The Lily (Ire)
1⁷ᶠ 5⁸ᵍᶠ 9⁸ˢ 5⁷ˢᵈ **1-0-4 £3,409**

Westborough (Ire) *N Tinkler* 68 a38
3 ch g Woodborough (USA) - Filey Brigg

2^{5hy} 5^{5f} 8^{7sd} 5^{6s} 2^{5g} 7^{5gf} 8^{5sf} 6^{5gs} 7^{5g} 2^{6g} 9^{6gf} 1^{6g} 1^{5s} 2-2-13 £9,291

Westbrook Blue *W G M Turner* 78 a71
2 b c Kingsinger (Ire) - Gold And Blue (Ire)
3^{5g} 1^{5sd} 3^{5gf} 4^{5sd} 6^{5g} 1-1-5 £5,255

Westcourt Dream *M W Easterby* 57
4 ch f Bal Harbour - Katie's Kitty
3^{8f} 1^{10gf} 8^{12gs} 6^{10gf} 14^{12g} 8^{9gs} 1-1-6 £4,246

Wester Lodge (Ire) *J M P Eustace* 75
2 ch c Fraam - Reamzafonic
9^{7gf} 2^{7g} 8^{7s} 0-1-3 £1,090

Western (Ire) *J Akehurst* 58 a81
4 ch g Gone West - Madame Est Sortie (Fr)
2^{16sd} 14^{12gs} 9^{16ss} 11^{12gs} 11^{14gf} 12^{12s} 12^{14gs} 18^{12gs} 10^{12sd} 0-1-9 £826

Western Bluebird (Ire) *Miss Kate Milligan* 46
6 b g Bluebird (USA) - Arrastra
6^{16g} 4^{16gf} 11^{14gf} 2^{16g} 7^{16g} 0-1-5 £1,236

Western Command (Ger) *Mrs N Macauley* a51
8 b g Saddlers' Hall (Ire) - Western Friend (USA)
10^{8sd} 8^{11sd} 4^{8sd} 5^{12sd} 6^{9sd} 6^{12ss} 8^{11sd} 5^{9sw} 11^{11ss} 9^{12sd} 5^{16sd} 5^{14sd} 3^{12sd} 3^{12sd} 5^{12sd} 9^{9sd} 5^{14sd} 2^{12sd} 6^{12sd} 0-2-22 £1,145

Western Ridge (Fr) *B J Llewellyn* 36
7 b g Darshaan - Helvellyn (USA)
8^{12s} PU^{15gf} 0-0-2

Western Roots *K A Morgan* 81 a85
3 ch g Dr Fong (USA) - Chrysalis
2^{7sd} 4^{8sd} 8^{10sd} 7^{8s} 6^{7gf} 1^{8g} 5^{8g} 5^{8gf} 9^{8gf} 11^{10sd} 12^{9sd} 2^{7sd} 16^{8s} 1-2-13 £5,965

Westerner *E Lellouche* 121
5 b h Danehill (USA) - Walensee
1^{16gs} 2^{16g} 2^{20gf} 9^{12gs} 1^{16s} 1^{20g} 1^{16hy} 4-2-7 £281,698

Westernmost *M Todhunter* 20
6 b g Most Welcome - Dakota Girl
12^{17g} 0-0-1

Westfield Boy *N P Littmoden* 46
2 b c Unfuwain (USA) - Pick Of The Pops
20^{8s} 12^{10s} 0-0-2

Westlake Bond (Ire) *B Smart* 63
2 b f Josr Algarhoud (Ire) - Rania
5^{6g} 2^{6gs} 0-1-2 £1,376

Westland (USA) *Mrs A J Perrett* 79
2 gr c Cozzene (USA) - Cherie Yvonne (USA)
2^{6s} 1^{6s} 1-1-2 £6,789

Westmead Etoile *J R Jenkins* a39
4 b f Unfuwain (USA) - Glossary
9^{8sd} 3^{8ss} 10^{8sd} 7^{7sd} 10^{7hy} 3^{7sd} 0-2-6 £669

Westmead Tango *J R Jenkins* a34
4 b f Pursuit Of Love - Tango Teaser
6^{6sd} 6^{5sd} 11^{6sd} 7^{6sd} 0-0-4

Westmoreland Road (USA) *Mrs A J Perrett* 112
4 b g Diesis - Tia Gigi (USA)
2^{12gf} 2^{12g} 4^{14g} 7^{11g} 0-2-4 £10,622

Wet Lips (Aus) *R C Guest* 58
6 ch g Grand Lodge (USA) - Kissing (Aus)
13^{12g} 0-0-1

Wethaab (USA) *Miss A Stokell* a9
7 b g Pleasant Colony (USA) - Binntastic (USA)
8^{11sd} 8^{11sd} 5^{9sd} 6^{12sd} 9^{15g} 0-0-5

Whaleef *B J Llewellyn* 83

6 br g Darshaan - Wilayif (USA)
2^{10gs} 0-1-1 £1,740

What's Up Doc (Ire) *J S Bolger* 85
3 b c Dr Massini (Ire) - Surprise Treat (Ire)
1^{10gf} 6^{12g} 9^{8s} 1-0-3 £3,526

What-A-Dancer (Ire) *G A Swinbank* 83 a94
7 b g Dancing Dissident (USA) - Cool Gales
4^{7sd} 3^{7sd} 1^{7sd} 4^{7gf} 8^{7f} 4^{7gf} 4^{7g} 9^{7gf} 6^{7gf} 5^{8g} 4^{7gf} 6^{7f} 1-2-12 £19,165

Whatatodo *M L W Bell* 70
2 b f Compton Place - Emerald Dream (Ire)
7^{6gf} 3^{6gf} 8^{6g} 1^{7gf} 2^{7gf} 14^{6gs} 4^{7gf} 12^{6s} 1-2-8 £6,028

Whatsheworth *P S McEntee*
2 b g Pyramus (USA) - Princess Aurora
10^{5gf} 6^{5gf} 0-0-2

Whazzat *B W Hills* 103
2 b f Daylami (USA) - Wosaita
1^{6gf} 1^{7f} 2-0-2 £27,961

Whenwillitwin *J S Moore* 53
3 b g Bluegrass Prince (Ire) - Madam Marash (Ire)
6^{10f} 6^{12gs} 7^{10g} 0-0-3

Where With All (Ire) *Saeed Bin Suroor* 94
2 b c Montjeu (Ire) - Zelding (Ire)
1^{6gs} 7^{7f} 1^{7gs} 2-0-3 £10,809

Whinhill House *D W Barker* 51 a56
4 ch g Paris House - Darussalam
16^{6f} 19^{5gf} 18^{5gs} 3^{5gs} 12^{6gs} 3^{5sd} 0-2-6 £425

Whiplash (Ire) *K O Cunningham-Brown* 58 a50
3 b g Orpen (USA) - La Colombari (Ity)
12^{8gs} 4^{7gs} 18^{8s} 1^{7g} 18^{7gf} 6^{8sd} 10^{10sd} 12^{8f} 6^{7gs} 13^{8gs} 9^{7g} 1-0-11 £3,536

Whippasnapper *J R Best* 73 a75
4 b g Cayman Kai (Ire) - Give Us A Treat
10^{7sd} 16^{8d} 2^{5sd} 16^{5d} 3^{7sd} 9^{7sd} 2^{6gs} 1^{6gs} 8^{5gf} 3^{6gs} 2^{7f} 2^{7f} 7^{7gf} 10^{7gf} 11^{7sd} 4^{7g} 13^{7gf} 13^{6s} 6^{6sd} 3-7-19 £18,541

Whipper (USA) *Robert Collet* 124
3 b c Miesque's Son (USA) - Myth To Reality (Fr)
1^{7ho} 5^{8g} 2^{7gs} 1^{8s} 5^{8gs} 10^{8y} 2-1-6 £282,901

Whirling *J G Given* 36 a56
2 ch f Groom Dancer (USA) - Supersonic
8^{8s} 11^{9sd} 0-0-2

Whirly Bird *Mrs A J Perrett* 53 a76
3 b f Nashwan (USA) - Inchyre
3^{10s} 1^{9sd} 1-1-2 £3,980

Whispered Promises (USA) *M Johnston* 87
3 b g Real Quiet (USA) - Anna's Honor (USA)
12^{10gs} 3^{12g} 8^{12gs} 5^{10gf} 0-0-4 £820

Whispering Death *W J Haggas* 37
2 br c Pivotal - Lucky Arrow
23^{6s} 11^{7s} 11^{7s} 0-0-3

Whispering Valley *Mrs A J Perrett* 51
4 ch f The West (USA) - Taciturn (USA)
12^{11gf} 9^{14f} 9^{10g} 15^{11gs} 15^{8g} 0-0-5

Whist Drive *Mrs N Smith* 60
4 ch g First Trump - Fine Quill
6^{15s} 0-0-1

Whistful (Ire) *C F Wall* 73
3 b f First Trump - Atmospheric Blues (Ire)
3^{6g} 9^{6s} 3^{8gf} 5^{6gf} 11^{6g} 4^{6gs} 8^{6gf} 4^{6g} 0-2-8 £1,494

Whistler *J M Bradley* 97
7 ch g Selkirk (USA) - French Gift

12⁵ˢ 17⁵ᵍ 9⁵ᵍᶠ 3⁵ᵍᶠ 7⁵ᵍᶠ 1⁵ᵍ 7⁵ᵍᶠ 3⁵ᶠ
1⁵ᵍ 7⁶ᵍᶠ 1⁵ᵍˢ 4⁵ᵍ 15⁵ᵍᶠ 3⁵ᵍᶠ 4⁵ᵍ 15⁵ᵍ 4⁶ᵍ
2⁵ˢ 6⁵ˢ 5⁵ˢ **3-6-20 £37,160**

Whistling Along *J M Bradley* 36
2 b c Atraf - Forest Song
8⁵ᵍˢ 6⁵ˢ 10⁶ᵍ 8⁵ᵍᶠ **0-0-4**

Whitbarrow (Ire) *J M Bradley* 103
5 b g Royal Abjar (USA) - Danccini (Ire)
5⁵ᵍ 12⁵ᵍˢ 12⁵ᵍˢ 1⁵ᵍᶠ 7⁵ᵍᶠ 7⁵ᵍᶠ 14⁶ᶠ 9⁵ˢ
8⁵ᵍ 9⁵ᵍᶠ 21⁶ᵍᶠ 13⁵ᵍ 7⁵ᵍ 5⁶ᵍ 4⁶ᵍ 9⁵ˢ 9⁵ᵍ 3⁵ˢ
2⁵ˢ **1-2-19 £20,275**

White Hawk *D R Loder* 80
3 b c Silver Hawk (USA) - Polska (USA)
4¹⁰ᵍ 12⁸ᵍˢ 16⁸ᵍᶠ **0-0-3 £730**

White Ledger (Ire) *R A Fahey* 63 a71
5 ch g Ali-Royal (Ire) - Boranwood (Ire)
12⁶ˢᵈ 11⁷ˢᵈ 3⁶ᵍ 1⁵ˢ 1⁵ˢ 8⁵ˢ 6⁵ˢ 2⁵ˢᵈ
2-2-8 £9,960

White O' Morn *J W Unett* 44 a37
5 gr m Petong - I'm Your Lady
11⁷ˢᵈ 4⁵ˢˢ 2⁵ˢᵈ 4⁵ˢˢ 1⁵ˢʷ 9⁵ˢˢ 2⁵ˢᵈ 12⁵ˢᵈ
4⁵ᵍᶠ 10⁵ᵍ 7⁵ᵍˢ **1-2-11 £2,396**

White Park Bay (Ire) *Miss Suzy Smith* 44 a22
4 b f Blues Traveller (Ire) - Valiant Friend (USA)
5¹¹ˢᵈ 2¹²ᵍˢ 12¹²ˢᵈ 6¹¹ᵍ **0-1-4 £1,057**

White Sail *H R A Cecil* 32
3 b f Polar Falcon (USA) - Felucca
11⁷ᶠ **0-0-1**

White Star Magic *J R Weymes* 63 a55
2 ch c Bluegrass Prince (Ire) - Bless
7⁷ˢ 9⁸ʰʸ 6⁶ᵍ 4⁷ˢᵈ **0-0-4**

Whitgift Rock *S Dow* 76 a78
3 b c Piccolo - Fly South
1⁸ˢᵈ 2⁸ˢᵈ 13⁷ᵍˢ 7⁷ᵍᶠ 7⁸ᵍᶠ 3⁸ᵍ 2¹⁰ᵍˢ 10¹⁰ᵍ
7⁷ˢᵈ 12⁹ᵍ 12¹⁰ˢᵈ **1-3-11 £7,825**

Whitkirk Star (Ire) *S P Griffiths*
3 b g Alhaarth (Ire) - Three Stars
6⁸ʰʸ 8¹⁰ˢ **0-0-2**

Whitland *Mrs P N Dutfield* 55
2 b g Namaqualand (USA) - Whittle Rock
14⁷ᵍˢ 8⁷ˢ 9⁸ᵍᶠ **0-0-3**

Whitsbury Cross *D R C Elsworth* 90
3 b c Cape Cross (Ire) - Vallauris
5⁸ᵍ 5⁸ᵍ 1¹⁰ᵍᶠ 11¹⁰ᶠ 4¹⁰ᵍˢ 3¹⁰ᵍᶠ 5¹⁰ᵍ **1-1-7**
£6,261

Whittinghamvillage *A Berry* a21
3 b f Whittingham (Ire) - Shaa Spin
6⁷ˢᵈ **0-0-1**

Whittle Warrior *C W Fairhurst* 34
4 b g Averti (Ire) - Polish Descent (Ire)
14⁶ᶠ **0-0-1**

Who Cares Wins *J R Jenkins* 13
8 ch g Kris - Anne Bonny
9¹⁴ᵍˢ **0-0-1**

Who's Winning (Ire) *B G Powell* 88 a91
3 ch g Docksider (USA) - Quintellina
18⁶ᵍˢ 8⁵ᵍᶠ 6⁶ᵍᶠ 8⁷ᵍᶠ 2⁶ᵍᶠ 1⁶ᶠ 2⁵ᵍ 15ᵍᶠ
16ᵍᶠ 7⁶ˢᵈ **3-2-10 £21,178**

Whole Grain *Sir Michael Stoute* 72
3 b f Polish Precedent (USA) - Mill Line
4¹⁰ᵍ **0-0-1 £434**

Whoopsie *J A Glover* 37
2 b f Unfuwain (USA) - Oops Pettie
9⁸ᵍ 16⁸ᵍᶠ 11⁸ˢ **0-0-3**

Why Dubai (USA) *R Hannon* 89
3 br f Kris S (USA) - Highest Goal (USA)

8⁸ᵍˢ 6⁹ᵍ 6⁸ᵍᶠ 10⁷ᵍᶠ **0-0-4 £689**

Why Harry *J J Quinn* 58 a65
2 b g Cyrano De Bergerac - Golden Ciel (USA)
3⁵ˢᵈ 7⁵ᵍ 1⁵ᵍˢ 6⁵ᵍ 6⁵ᵍᶠ **1-1-5 £3,462**

Wicked Uncle *S Gollings* 87
5 b g Distant Relative - The Kings Daughter
10⁵ᵍ 9⁵ᵍᶠ 1⁵ᵍᶠ **1-0-3 £3,542**

Wiggy Smith *H Candy* 91
5 ch g Master Willie - Monsoon
5¹⁰ᵍ 17¹²ᵍ 1¹⁰ᵍ 2¹⁰ˢ **1-1-4 £12,522**

Wigmo Princess *S C Burrough* a6
5 ch m Factual (USA) - Queen Of Shannon (Ire)
11¹²ˢˢ **0-0-1**

Wigwam Willie (Ire) *M J Wallace* 75
2 b g Indian Rocket - Sweet Nature (Ire)
4⁶ᵍᶠ 5⁵ᵍ 2⁶ˢ 19⁶ᵍᶠ **0-1-4 £1,714**

Wild Pitch *P Mitchell* 66 a57
3 ch g Piccolo - Western Horizon (USA)
7¹⁰ˢᵈ 1¹⁰ˢ 3⁹ᵍᶠ 12¹²ᵍˢ 6¹⁰ᵍ **0-1-5 £874**

Wild Power (Ger) *J G M O'Shea* 65
6 b g Turtle Island (Ire) - White On Red (Ger)
4¹⁰ᵍ 2¹²ᵍ 4¹⁰ᵍᶠ **0-3-3 £1,482**

Wild Tide *D W Thompson* 33
5 b m Runnett - Polly Two
16⁸ᵍ 9⁷ᶠ 7⁶ᵍ 9⁸ˢ 10⁸ᶠ **0-0-5**

Wild Wild Wes *R Ingram*
4 ch g The West (USA) - Dam Certain (Ire)
15¹²ˢᵈ 13¹⁰ˢᵈ **0-0-2**

Wilford Maverick (Ire) *M J Attwater* 60 a32
2 b c Fasliyev (USA) - Lioness
7⁶ᵍᶠ 9⁶ˢᵈ 13⁶ᵍˢ 10⁵ˢᵈ **0-0-4**

Wilfred (Ire) *Jonjo O'Neill* 58
3 b g Desert King (Ire) - Kharaliya (Fr)
7¹²ᵍˢ 8¹²ᵍᶠ **0-0-2**

Wilheheckaslike *W Storey* a4
3 b g Wizard King - La Ciotat (USA)
8⁸ˢˢ 8⁶ᵍˢ 9⁵ˢᶠ 6⁶ᵍᶠ 17⁶ᶠ 6¹⁴ᵍᶠ **0-0-6**

Wilko (USA) *J Noseda* 112 a120
2 ch c Awesome Again (Can) - Native Roots (USA)
3⁵ʰʸ 7⁶ᵍˢ 1⁶ᶠ 3⁷ᶠ 3⁷ᵍˢ 2⁷ᵍ 1⁷ᵍᶠ 2⁷ᵍˢ 4⁷ᵍᶠ
3⁸ᵍᶠ 1⁹ᶠᵗ **3-6-11 £490,901**

Will He Wish *S Gollings* 103 a87
8 b g Winning Gallery - More To Life
12⁶ᵍ 8⁷ˢᵈ 5⁶ᵍˢ 6⁷ᵍˢ 7⁷ᵍ 18⁷ᵍᶠ 10⁶ᵍᶠ
12⁷ᶠ 13⁷ᵍ 1⁷ᵍ 3⁸ᵍᶠ 6⁷ᵍˢ 2⁸ᵍˢ 11⁸ᶠ 3⁸ʰʸ **1-2-15**
£12,974

Will The Till *J M Bradley* 52
2 b g Fraam - Prim Ajwaad
11⁵ᵍᶠ 9⁶ᵍ 17⁷ᵍ **0-0-3**

Willheconquertoo *Andrew Reid* 78 a83
4 ch g Primo Dominie - Sure Care
8⁸ˢᵈ 15⁷ᶠ 3⁶ᵍ 5⁶ᵍᶠ 16⁶ᶠ 9⁵ᵍˢ 14⁶ᵍˢ 5⁶ᵍ
4⁶ᶠ 4⁶ˢᵈ 13⁶ˢᵈ 4⁶ˢᵈ 25ˢᵈ **1-3-13 £6,014**

Willhego *J R Best* 67 a64
3 ch g Pivotal - Woodrising
9⁵ˢ 8⁸ᶠ 2¹⁰ˢᵈ 3¹⁰ˢᵈ 1¹⁰ᵍ 5¹²ˢᵈ 13⁸ᵍ 8¹²ˢᵈ
1-2-8 £4,905

Willhewiz *R M Stronge* 87 a79
4 b c Wizard King - Leave It To Lib
13⁵ᵍ 5⁵ᵍˢ 6⁶ᵍᶠ 7⁶ᵍᶠ 15ᵍᶠ 16⁶ᵍᶠ 8⁶ᵍᶠ
16⁵ᵍ 13⁷ᵍ 4⁵ᵍˢ 17⁶ᵍᶠ 10⁵ᵍ 2⁶ˢᵈ 9⁶ˢᵈ **2-1-15**
£11,945

William James *M J Wallace* 50 a39
2 b g Mujahid (USA) - Pain Perdu (Ire)
5⁵ᵍᶠ 11⁷ᵍ 6⁵ˢᵈ **0-0-3**

William Tell (Ire) *M R Channon* 79

2 b c Rossini (USA) - Livry (USA)
6⁷ʰ 4⁸ᵍˢ 5⁸ᵍ 2⁸ˢ 2⁸ᵍ 2⁸ᵍˢ **0-3-6 £4,765**

William's Well *M W Easterby* 65
10 ch g Superpower - Catherines Well
10⁶ʰʸ 12⁶ᵍ 9⁶ᵍ 5⁶ᵍ 13⁶ᵍ 6⁶ᵍ 3⁶ᵍˢ 3⁶ᵍ
16⁵ᵍˢ 5⁶ᵍ **0-2-10 £920**

Willjojo *R A Fahey* 62 a43
3 b f Mind Games - Millie's Lady (Ire)
3⁵ᵍ 5⁶ᶠ 4⁶ˢᵈ 1⁷ᵍ 1⁷ᵍᶠ 5⁷ᵍ **2-1-6 £6,998**

Willofcourse *H Candy* 50
3 b g Aragon - Willyet
9⁶ᵍᶠ **0-0-1**

Willyever *F J Bowles* 61
10 b g Merdon Melody - Stonebroker
9⁷ˢᵈ 17⁶ᵍᶠ 12⁷ᶠ 6⁶ᶠ 3⁷ᵍʸ 7⁸ᵍ 11⁸ʸˢ 11⁶ᵍ
10⁷ˢ 9⁷ˢᵈ **0-1-10 £500**

Wilom (Ger) *M R Hoad* a51
6 ch g Lomitas - Whispering Willows
2⁸ˢᵈ 5⁸ˢᵈ 4⁸ˢᵈ 5⁸ˢᵈ 8¹⁰ˢᵈ 9¹⁰ˢᵈ 12⁸ˢᵈ 6⁸ᵍ
0-1-8 £754

Wilson Bluebottle (Ire) *M W Easterby* 30 a53
5 ch g Priolo (USA) - Mauras Pride (Ire)
6⁸ˢᵈ 1⁹ˢʷ 8⁸ˢʷ 2⁹ˢˢ 2⁸ˢᵈ 10⁹ˢᵈ 8⁸ˢᵈ 12⁹ᶠ
9¹⁰ᵍᶠ 6⁶ˢᵈ 6⁸ˢᵈ **1-2-11 £2,711**

Wiltshire (Ire) *M R Channon* 58
2 br g Spectrum (Ire) - Mary Magdalene
12⁷ᵍˢ 13⁷ᵍᶠ 10⁸ᶠ 8⁸ᵍ 1⁵ᶠ 14⁸ᵍᶠ 3⁶ᵍ
1-1-7 £2,967

Win Alot *M C Chapman*
6 b g Aragon - Having Fun
10¹⁴ˢ **0-0-1**

Wind Chime (Ire) *A G Newcombe* 72 a55
7 ch h Arazi (USA) - Shamisen
7¹⁰ˢᵈ 2⁸ˢᵈ 11⁸ˢᵈ 18ᶠ 3⁷ᵍᶠ 11⁹ᵍᶠ 7⁹ᵍᶠ 7⁹ˢᵈ
1-2-8 £7,351

Windermere (Ire) *T M Walsh* 113
5 b h Lear Fan (USA) - Madame L'Enjoleur (USA)
1¹⁴ᵍᶠ 12²²ᶠ **1-0-2 £22,922**

Windermere Island *M L W Bell* 66
2 b f Cadeaux Genereux - Corndavon (USA)
4⁶ᵍᶠ **0-0-1 £365**

Winds Of March (Ire) *J H M Gosden* 95
3 b f Sadler's Wells (USA) - Alidiva
1¹⁰ᵍ 4¹⁰ᵍ **1-0-2 £7,116**

Winds Of Time (Ire) *Mrs A J Perrett* 81
2 b f Danehill (USA) - Windmill
1⁶ᵍˢ **1-0-1 £8,092**

Windscreamer *J W Hills* 90
2 b f Josr Algarhoud - St James's Antigua (Ire)
1⁷ᵍ 6⁷ᵍᶠ 7⁸ᵍ **1-0-3 £8,172**

Windsor Beauty (Ire) *R Rowe*
6 b/br g Woods Of Windsor (USA) - Tumble Dale
7¹⁵ˢ **0-0-1**

Windsor Knot (Ire) *J H M Gosden* 108
2 ch c Pivotal - Triple Tie (USA)
4⁷ᵍᶠ 1⁷ᵍᶠ 1⁷ˢ **2-0-3 £31,350**

Windwood (Ire) *J W Hills* 58 a53
2 b g Piccolo - Presently
8⁵ᵍ 7⁶ᵍ 5⁶ˢᵈ **0-0-3**

Windy Britain *V Valiani* 98
5 b m Mark Of Esteem (Ire) - For My Love
12¹⁰ᵍᶠ 4¹⁰ᵍᶠ 2¹⁰ᵍ 6¹⁰ᵍ 8¹¹ᵍ 7¹⁰ʰʸ 1¹⁰ˢ
7¹⁰ᵍˢ **1-1-8 £16,688**

Windy Prospect *P A Blockley* 99 a89
2 ch c Intikhab (USA) - Yellow Ribbon (Ire)
3⁵ˢᵈ 5⁵ᵍ 2⁵ᵍ 1⁶ˢᵈ 7⁵ᵍᶠ 3⁷ᵍᶠ 2⁶ᵍᶠ 2⁶ᶠ 1⁷ˢᵈ

1⁶ˢ **3-4-10 £29,727**

Wing Collar *T D Easterby* 81
3 b g In The Wings - Riyoom (USA)
11¹²ᵍ 3¹⁰ˢ 3¹⁰ᵍᶠ 2¹²ᵍ 8¹¹ˢ 4¹⁶ᵍˢ 3¹⁰ᵍᶠ
1¹²ᵍᶠ 2¹⁴ᵍˢ **1-5-9 £11,537**

Wing Commander *R A Fahey* 102
5 b g Royal Applause - Southern Psychic (USA)
4⁸ᵍ 3¹⁰ˢ 9⁷ᵍᶠ 14⁸ᵍᶠ 8¹⁰ᵍ 1⁸ᵍᶠ 16⁸ᵍᶠ 3⁸ᵍ
7¹⁰ˢ 5¹⁰ᵍ 7⁸ˢ 21⁹ᵍ **1-3-12 £23,086**

Winged D'Argent (Ire) *M Johnston* 102
3 b c In The Wings - Petite-D-Argent
1¹⁰ˢ 5¹⁰ᵍˢ 1¹³ᵍˢ 1¹¹ˢ 2¹⁶ᵍˢ **3-1-5
£28,613**

Wingman (Ire) *J W Hills* 92
2 b c In The Wings - Precedence (Ire)
10⁷ᵍᶠ 5⁷ᵍ 1⁸ᵍ 3⁹ʰʸ **1-0-4 £13,262**

Wings Of Morning (Ire) *D Carroll* 69 a74
3 ch g Fumo Di Londra (Ire) - Hay Knot
1⁷ˢᵈ 5⁷ˢˢ 5⁷ˢˢ 3¹¹ˢ 11⁸ᵍᶠ 7⁷ˢᵈ 3⁹ˢ 4⁶ˢᵈ
11⁷ᵍ 12⁷ˢᵈ **1-1-10 £4,208**

Wingspeed (Ire) *Mrs A J Perrett* 77
2 b g Bluebird (USA) - Aneeda
5⁷ᵍ 2⁷ᵍᶠ 4⁷ᶠ **0-1-3 £2,086**

Winners Delight *A P Jarvis* 86 a88
3 ch g First Trump - Real Popcorn (Ire)
8⁹ˢ 9⁹ᵍˢ 5⁸ᵍˢ 5¹²ᵍᶠ 3¹⁰ᵍ 7¹⁰ᵍ 8¹⁰ᵍ 3¹⁰ᵍ
6¹⁴ᵍ 1¹²ˢᵈ **1-2-10 £10,664**

Winning Pleasure (Ire) *J Balding* a66
6 b g Ashkalani (Ire) - Karamana
6⁶ˢᵈ **0-0-1**

Winning Venture *A W Carroll* 93 a72
7 b g Owington - Push A Button
6⁶ᵍˢ 21⁶ᵍ 3⁸ᵍ 2⁷ᵍᶠ 7⁸ᵍ 7⁸ˢ 2⁷ˢ 8⁷ᵍ
10⁷ˢᵈ 18⁷ᵍˢ **0-3-10 £4,300**

Winslow Boy (USA) *P Monteith* 65
3 b/br g Expelled (USA) - Acusteal (USA)
8¹⁰ᵍ 4¹²ᵍᶠ 6¹¹ᵍᶠ 1¹¹ᶠ 1¹⁴ᵍ 6¹⁴ᵍᶠ 3¹⁴ᵍˢ 6¹⁴ˢ
6¹²ᵍᶠ 2¹⁵ˢ **1-3-10 £6,904**

Winslow Homer (Fr) *J H M Gosden* 14
3 b c Peintre Celebre (USA) - Armorique (Ire)
10¹⁰ᵍˢ **0-0-1**

Winter Mist *N P Littmoden* 9 a14
2 gr f Tomba - Misty Goddess (Ire)
17⁶ᵍ 9⁶ˢᵈ 11⁷ᵍᶠ 15¹⁰ˢ **0-0-4**

Winter Moon *B R Millman* 46
2 b f Mujadil (USA) - Crofters Ceilidh
9⁶ᵍᶠ **0-0-1**

Winthorpe (Ire) *J J Quinn* 78 a62
4 b g Tagula - Zazu
10⁶ˢᵈ 10⁶ˢᵈ 12⁶ᵍ 10⁶ˢ 16⁶ᵍˢ 4⁶ᵍᶠ 17⁶ᵍᶠ
3⁵ˢ 2⁵ᵍˢ 16⁵ᵍᶠ 5⁵ᵍᶠ 4⁵ᵍ 4⁵ᵍᶠ 3⁶ᶠ 15⁶ᵍᶠ 6⁵ᵍ
0-4-16 £7,251

Wise Dennis *A P Jarvis* 96 a77
2 b g Polar Falcon (USA) - Bowden Rose
7⁶ᵍᶠ 10⁷ᵍᶠ 3⁶ᵍᶠ 3⁷ˢᵈ 3⁸ᵍ 1⁷ᵍᶠ 2⁸ᵍ **1-3-7
£24,563**

Wise Owl *M Johnston* 82
2 b c Danehill (USA) - Mistle Thrush (USA)
2⁶ᵍᶠ 4⁶ᵍˢ 1⁶ᶠ 14⁶ᵍ **1-1-4 £7,885**

Wise Wager (Ire) *R A Fahey* 81 a72
2 b f Titus Livius (Fr) - Londubh
2⁵ˢᵈ 3⁵ᶠ 3⁵ᵍ 3⁵ᵍᶠ 1⁵ᶠ 2⁵ᵍˢ 2⁵ᵍ 7⁵ᵍᶠ **1-4-8
£18,185**

Wistman (UAE) *D R Loder* 82
3 br g Woodman (USA) - Saik (USA)
1⁷ᵍˢ 3⁷ᵍˢ **1-0-2 £5,307**

Witches Broom *C A Cyzer* 59 a14
3 b f Fraam - Carte Blanche
8⁸ˢᵈ 3⁷ᵍᶠ 6⁸ᵍᶠ 16⁶ᵍᶠ **0-1-4 £429**

Witching *D J Daly* 22
3 b f Hector Protector (USA) - Charming Life
6¹⁰ᵍᶠ **0-0-1**

Witchry *M A Jarvis* 84
2 b g Green Desert (USA) - Indian Skimmer (USA)
4⁶ᵍ 3⁵ᵍᶠ 1⁵ᵍᶠ 7⁵ᵍˢ **1-1-4 £6,708**

Witchy Vibes *M Appleby*
2 ch f Tomba - Risk The Witch
14⁶ʰʸ 13⁷ᵍˢ **0-0-2**

With Honours *T J Fitzgerald* 8
2 b f Bien Bien (USA) - Fair Test
7⁷ˢ **0-0-1**

With Reason (USA) *Saeed Bin Suroor* 111
6 ch g Nashwan (USA) - Just Cause
13⁸ᵍ 1⁸ᵍ **1-0-2 £23,200**

Withering Lady (Ire) *Mrs P N Dutfield* 77
2 b f Tagula (Ire) - Princess Oberon (Ire)
3⁵ᵍˢ 4⁵ᵍ 6⁵ᵍ 2⁵ᵍ 7⁵ᵍ 1⁵ᵍᶠ 8⁶ᵍˢ 5⁶ᵍˢ 4⁵ᵍᶠ
1-3-9 £5,983

Withorwithoutyou (Ire) *B A McMahon* 78
3 b f Danehill (USA) - Morningsurprice (USA)
6⁵ᵍ 5⁶ᵍ 14⁵ᵍ 10⁷ᵍᶠ 8⁷ᵍᶠ **0-0-5 £750**

Wittily *A Berry* a10
4 ch f Whittingham (Ire) - Lucky Dip
13⁵ˢᵈ **0-0-1**

Witty Girl *M J Polglase* 46
2 b f Whittingham (Ire) - Zando's Charm
3⁵ᵍᶠ 4⁶ᶠ 11⁶ᵍᶠ **0-1-3 £366**

Witwatersrand (Ire) *B W Hills* 69
2 b f Unfuwain (USA) - Valley Of Gold (Fr)
4⁷ᵍᶠ **0-0-1 £405**

Wiz In *T Keddy* a44
2 gr g Wizard King - Great Intent
8⁶ˢᵈ 11⁸ˢᵈ **0-0-2**

Wizard Looking *R Hannon* 72 a41
3 b g Wizard King - High Stepping (Ire)
6⁸ᵍᶠ 10⁷ᵍᶠ 16⁷ᵍᶠ 6⁸ᵍᶠ 7⁸ˢᵈ 7⁸ᵍᶠ **0-0-6**

Wizard Of Edge *R J Hodges* 65 a56
4 b g Wizard King - Forever Shineing
6¹⁰ˢᵈ 8¹²ᵍᶠ 4⁹ᵍˢ **0-0-3 £317**

Wizard Of Noz *J Noseda* 107
4 b g Inchinor - Winning Girl
2⁸ᵍᶠ 6⁸ᵍᶠ 22⁸ᵍᶠ 5⁸ᵍˢ 5⁷ᵍᶠ 5⁷ᵍᶠ 5⁸ᵍˢ 1⁷ᵍ
11⁷ˢ **1-1-9 £23,786**

Wizard Of The West *D P Keane* 47
4 b g Wizard King - Rose Burton
9¹²ᵍᶠ 13¹²ᵍᶠ 9¹⁶ᵍˢ **0-0-3**

Wizard Of Us *M Mullineaux* 67 a43
4 b g Wizard King - Sian's Girl
1⁷ᵍˢ 13⁹ˢᵈ 2⁸ʰʸ **1-1-3 £4,624**

Wizardmicktee (Ire) *A Bailey* 73
2 b c Monashee Mountain (USA) - Epsilon
8⁶ˢ 2⁷ᵍᶠ 2⁶ˢ 4⁶ˢ 8⁵ᵍᶠ 16⁵ʰʸ **0-2-6
£3,821**

Wizards Princess *D W Thompson* 25
4 b f Wizard King - Chalice
5¹²ˢ 8⁹ᵍᶠ **0-0-2**

Wizzskilad *Mrs P N Dutfield* 60 a39
2 b c Wizard King - Sure Babe
7⁵ˢᵈ 4⁵ᵍˢ 6⁵ᵍ 3⁵ʰʸ 8⁵ᵍᶠ 4⁵ᵍᶠ 10⁵ᵍ 3⁵ᵍˢ
0-2-8 £1,002

Wodhill Be *D Morris* 49 a49
4 b f Danzig Connection (USA) - Muarij

5⁷ˢᵈ 6⁷ˢᵈ 5⁸ˢᵈ 9⁷ᵍᶠ 10⁸ʰʸ 3⁷ᵍᶠ 11⁷ᶠ 13⁸ᵍ
8⁷ᵍᶠ 7⁸ᵍᶠ 7⁸ᵍᶠ 2⁷ᵍ 8⁶ᵍˢ **0-2-13 £865**

Wodhill Folly *D Morris* a52
7 ch m Faustus (USA) - Muarij
4⁹ˢᵈ 6⁹ˢ 8⁹ˢˢ **0-0-3**

Wodhill Gold *D Morris* 40 a46
3 ch g Dancing Spree (USA) - Golden Filigree
15⁸ʸ 9⁷ˢᵈ **0-0-2**

Wodhill Hope *D Morris* 50
4 b f Distinctly North (USA) - Golden Filigree
4¹⁴ᵍˢ 3¹¹ᶠ 8¹²ᵍᶠ 11¹⁴ᵍᶠ 10¹³ᵍˢ 9¹²ᵍ **0-0-6
£687**

Wolds Dancer *T D Easterby* 61
2 b f Fraam - Dancing Em
6⁶ᵍ 7⁶ᶠ 7⁷ᵍᶠ **0-0-3**

Wolf Cub *Miss Gay Kelleway*
3 ch g Wolfhound (USA) - Ansellady
16⁷ˢ **0-0-1**

Wolf Hammer (USA) *J Howard Johnson* 75
2 ch g Diesis - Polly's Link (USA)
7⁷ˢ 2⁶ᵍᶠ 2⁵ʰʸ **0-0-3 £2,708**

Woman In White (Fr) *J H M Gosden* 72
3 gr f Daylami (Ire) - Nicer (Ire)
8⁷ᵍ 2⁹ᵍᶠ 6¹⁰ᵍᶠ 3¹¹ᵍᶠ 6¹²ᵍᶠ **0-2-5 £2,261**

Won Of A Few *M Wigham* a40
4 b g Danzig Connection (USA) - Wonderful Day
9⁹ˢᵈ 7⁵ˢᵈ **0-0-2**

Wonder Wolf *R A Fahey* 36
3 b f Wolfhound (USA) - Wrangbrook
7⁶ᶠ 5⁹ᶠ 9⁸ᶠ **0-0-3**

Wonderful Mind *T D Easterby* 73
2 b c Mind Games - Signs And Wonders
8⁵ᵍ 5⁵ᵍ 2⁵ᵍ 1⁵ᵍᶠ 5⁵ᵍ 6⁵ᵍᶠ 3⁵ᵍ 2⁵ᵍᶠ 13⁵ᵍᶠ
5⁵ᵍᶠ 7⁵ᵍ **1-3-11 £8,912**

Wonky Donkey *S C Williams* 10 a54
3 b g Piccolo - Salinas
3⁸ˢʷ 4⁸ˢˢ 3⁶ˢᵈ 12⁶ᵍᶠ 5⁵ˢᵈ 16⁷ᵍᶠ **0-2-6
£1,153**

Wood Dalling (USA) *I Semple* 63
6 b g Woodman (USA) - Cloelia (USA)
7⁷ᶠ 7⁸ᶠ 6⁹ᵍˢ 1⁷ᵍᶠ 8⁹ᵍᶠ 6⁹ᵍᶠ 10⁷ˢ 6⁷ᵍ
13⁸ᵍᶠ **1-0-9 £3,851**

Wood Fern (UAE) *M R Channon* 54 a44
4 b g Green Desert (USA) - Woodsia
13⁷ˢᵈ 10⁷ˢ 12⁹ᵍˢ 11⁸ʰʸ 5⁷ᵍᶠ 11⁸ᵍᶠ 9⁸ᵍ
15⁷ᵍ 13⁸ᵍᶠ 6⁸ᵍˢ 1⁷ʰʸ 20⁷ᵍ 13⁷ᵍ 4⁷ʰʸ 8⁸ᵍ 10⁸ᵍ
3⁸ᵍˢ **1-1-17 £2,808**

Wood Spirit (Ire) *Mrs P N Dutfield* 58
2 b f Woodborough (USA) - Windomen (Ire)
6⁵ᵍ 6⁶ˢ 4⁸ᵍˢ **0-0-3**

Wood Sprite *J G Given* 22
2 b f Mister Baileys - Woodbeck
9⁸ˢ **0-0-1**

Wood Street (Ire) *R J Baker* 32
5 b g Eagle Eyed (USA) - San-Catrinia (Ire)
9¹⁰ᶠ **0-0-1**

Woodbury *Mrs H Sweeting* 67 a66
5 b m Woodborough (USA) - Jeewan
7⁶ˢᵈ 4⁶ˢᵈ 1⁶ˢᵈ 16⁶ᵍᶠ 4⁶ᵍ 1⁶ᶠ 7⁶ᵍ 6⁶ᵍˢ
2⁶ˢᵈ **2-1-10 £11,272**

Woodbury Lane (USA) *Saeed Bin Suroor* 55
2 br f Wild Wonder (USA) - Maximum Blue (USA)
5⁸ᵍˢ **0-0-1**

Woodcote (Ire) *C G Cox* 100
2 b c Monashee Mountain (USA) - Tootle
1⁵ᵍˢ 3⁶ᵍ **1-1-2 £7,466**

Woodcracker *M L W Bell*   104
3 ch g Docksider (USA) - Hen Harrier
1¹⁰ᵍ 2¹⁰ᵍˢ 13¹²ᵍᶠ 1¹⁰ᵍᶠ **2-1-4 £37,048**

Woodford Consult *M W Easterby*   45 a45
2 b f Benny The Dip (USA) - Chicodove
8⁸ᵍ 10⁷ˢᵈ 3⁸ˢ **0-1-3 £207**

Woodford Wonder (Ire) *M W Easterby*   27
2 b f Xaar - Unscathed
18⁶ᵍᶠ 14⁵ᵍᶠ 10⁷ᵍ **0-0-3**

Woodland Glade *R Hannon*   76
3 b f Mark Of Esteem (Ire) - Incendio
2⁷ᵍˢ 2⁸ˢ 5⁷ᵍ **0-2-3 £3,546**

Woodsley House (Ire) *Mrs P N Dutfield*   86
2 b c Orpen (USA) - Flame And Shadow (Ire)
2⁷ᵍˢ 2⁷ᵍᶠ 2⁸ᵍ 5⁷ˢ **0-3-4 £7,438**

Woodstock Express *P Bowen*   19
4 b g Alflora (Ire) - Young Tess
11¹⁸ᶠ **0-0-1**

Woodwind Down *M Todhunter*   52
7 b m Piccolo - Bint El Oumara
1¹²ᵍ 8¹⁵ᵍᶠ 18¹²ᵍ **1-0-3 £3,354**

Woody Valentine (USA) *M Johnston*   89
3 ch g Woodman (USA) - Mudslinger (USA)
4¹²ᵍ 2¹⁰ˢ 1¹⁰ʰʸ 6⁹ᵍ 6⁹ᵍᶠ 1¹⁰ᵍᶠ 2⁸ᵍᶠ 7¹⁰ᵍᶠ
7⁸ᵍᶠ 5¹⁰ᵍᶠ 2⁸ᵍ 4¹⁰ˢ **2-4-12 £22,770**

Woolfall Joanna *G G Margarson*   30
2 gr f Petong - Real Princess
19⁶ˢ 14⁷ᵍˢ **0-0-2**

Woolly Back (Ire) *R Hollinshead*   78
3 b g Alzao (USA) - Hopping Higgins (Ire)
2¹²ˢ 2¹²ᵍᶠ 6¹²ᵍˢ 10¹²ˢ **0-1-4 £3,404**

Woolsack (USA) *H Morrison*   74
2 ch c Spinning World (USA) - Rich And Famous (Fr)
5⁷ˢ 6⁷ᵍˢ **0-0-2**

Woolstone Boy (USA) *J Jay*   68
3 ch g Will's Way (USA) - My Pleasure (USA)
13¹⁰ᵍˢ 5¹⁰ʰʸ **0-0-2**

Wor Kid *R P Elliott*   35
2 br f Charnwood Forest (Ire) - Patience Please
8⁶ᵍ 9⁷ˢ **0-0-2**

Worcester Lodge *R Charlton*   78
3 ch g Grand Lodge (USA) - Borgia
1¹²ᵍᶠ 13¹²ˢ **1-0-2 £3,549**

Word Perfect *M W Easterby*   91
2 b f Diktat - Better Still (Ire)
3⁵ᵍˢ 1⁵ᵍ 1⁵ᵍˢ 5⁶ˢ 8⁶ᵍˢ 5⁶ˢ 7⁶ᵍᶠ 3⁶ᵍ 2⁶ˢ
2-3-9 £17,198

Worlaby Dale *Mrs S Lamyman*   a44
8 b g Terimon - Restandbethankful
4¹⁶ˢᵈ 4¹⁴ˢᵈ 7¹⁶ˢᵈ 6¹⁶ˢᵈ **0-0-4**

World At My Feet *N Bycroft*   82
2 b f Wolfhound (USA) - Rehaab
2⁵ᵍˢ 1⁵ᵍ 3⁵ᵍᶠ 9⁵ᵍ 4⁵ᵍˢ 9⁶ˢ 14⁶ᵍᶠ 4⁵ᵍˢ
16⁶ˢ **1-2-9 £8,910**

World Music (USA) *Saeed Bin Suroor*   67 a45
2 b f Dixieland Band (USA) - Headline
3⁵ᵍˢ 6⁶ˢᵈ **0-1-2 £640**

World Report (USA) *R Hannon*   80
2 b/br c Spinning World (USA) - Miss Woodchuck (USA)
4⁶ˢ 6⁷ᵍᶠ 4⁷ᵍ 5⁶ˢ **0-0-4 £1,288**

Worth A Gamble *H E Haynes*   a26
6 ch g So Factual (USA) - The Strid (Ire)
8¹¹ˢᵈ **0-0-1**

Worth A Grand (Ire) *J J Bridger*   66 a42
2 br g Raise A Grand (Ire) - Ballykett Pride (Ire)
7⁷ᵍ 5⁶ᵍ 5⁶ᶠ 11⁸ˢ 6⁵ʰʸ 5⁷ˢᵈ **0-0-6**

Worth Abbey *R Hannon*   66
2 b g Mujadil (USA) - Housefull
8⁷ᵍᶠ 10⁶ᵍᶠ 14⁶ᵍ 8⁶ᵍ **0-0-4**

Wotchalike (Ire) *R J Price*   80
2 ch c Spectrum (Ire) - Juno Madonna (Ire)
5⁷ᵍᶠ 8⁶ᵍᶠ 2⁷ˢ 2⁸ᵍˢ 1⁸ˢ 6¹⁰ᵍˢ **1-2-6**
£7,826

Wou Oodd *M R Channon*   78
3 ch f Barathea (Ire) - Abyaan (Ire)
4¹⁰ᵍ 3¹⁰ᵍᶠ 5¹⁰ᵍ 4¹²ᵍ 13¹⁰ᵍ **0-1-5 £1,597**

Wrenlane *R A Fahey*   70 a71
3 ch g Fraam - Hi Hoh (Ire)
2⁶ᵍᶠ 6⁶ᵍ 5⁷ᵍˢ 9⁸ᵍᶠ 4⁸ˢ 8⁸ᵍˢ 3¹⁰ᵍˢ 4⁸ᵍ 1⁸ᵍ
3⁹ˢᵈ 1⁹ˢᵈ **2-3-11 £10,391**

Wub Cub *A Dickman*   a28
4 b f Averti (Ire) - Ray Of Hope
6⁶ˢʷ 10⁶ˢᵈ 10⁵ˢᶠ **0-0-3**

Wujood *H Morrison*   74
2 b c Alzao (USA) - Rahayeb
7⁷ᵍ 10⁷ᵍᶠ 7⁷ᵍᶠ 2⁸ˢ **0-1-4 £1,396**

Wunderbra (Ire) *M L W Bell*   80 a68
3 b f Second Empire (Ire) - Supportive (Ire)
3⁶ᵍˢ 4⁷ˢᵈ 5⁶ˢᵈ 1⁶ᵍᶠ 3⁵ᵍᶠ 1⁵ᵍ 1⁵ˢᶠ 1⁵ʰʸ
2⁵ˢ 5⁵ˢ **4-3-10 £21,774**

Wunderwood (USA) *Lady Herries*   111
5 b g Faltaat (USA) - Jasoorah (Ire)
9¹²ᵍ 9¹²ᵍ 1¹²ᵍᶠ 1¹²ᶠ 1¹⁰ᵍᶠ 3¹²ᵍᶠ 8¹⁰ˢ **3-1-7**
£52,036

Wuxi Venture *R A Fahey*   67
9 b g Wolfhound (USA) - Push A Button
7¹⁰ʰʸ 6⁸ᵍˢ 9⁸ᵍᶠ 18¹⁰ᵍᶠ 12¹⁰ᵍᶠ **0-0-5**

Wyatt Earp (Ire) *J A R Toller*   84 a84
3 b g Piccolo - Tribal Lady
12⁶ᵍˢ 1⁶ᵍ 10⁶ᵍ 7⁶ᵍˢ 9⁶ᵍᶠ 2⁶ᵍᶠ 3⁷ˢᵈ **1-2-7**
£9,862

Wychbury (USA) *M J Wallace*   78
3 ch g Swain (Ire) - Garden Rose (Ire)
5⁶ᵍᶠ 2⁷ᶠ 2⁷ᶠ 8⁸ᵍᶠ 1⁷ᵍᶠ 5⁷ᵍᶠ 8¹⁰ᵍ 9⁹ᵍ
1-2-8 £8,920

Wyoming *J A R Toller*   62
3 ch f Inchinor - Shoshone
3⁷ˢ 8¹⁰ᵍᶠ 8¹⁰ᵍ 7¹²ᵍˢ 3¹²ᵍ 7¹⁶ᵍˢ 3¹²ᵍᶠ **0-3-7**
£1,910

Wyvern (Ger) *W J Haggas*   46
3 b c Unfuwain (USA) - Wladinova (Ger)
8¹⁰ᵍᶠ **0-0-1**

Xaara Doon (Ire) *M J Attwater*   a46
2 b f Xaar - Hill Of Doon (Ire)
9⁷ˢᵈ **0-0-1**

Xaarist (Ire) *T P Tate*   30
2 b c Xaar - Can Can Lady
12⁶ˢ 11⁷ᵍ **0-0-2**

Xaloc Bay (Ire) *B P J Baugh*   47 a66
6 br g Charnwood Forest (Ire) - Royal Jade
2⁷ˢᵈ 8⁷ˢᵈ 12⁶ˢˢ 1⁸ˢᵈ 1⁸ˢᵈ 2⁸ˢᵈ 3⁸ˢᵈ 6⁷ˢˢ
7⁷ᵍ 3⁸ˢᵈ 7⁸ˢᵈ 6⁸ˢᵈ 12⁶ᵍˢ **2-3-13 £6,352**

Xanadu *Miss L A Perratt*   61
8 ch g Casteddu - Bellatrix
13⁷ᵍ 2⁶ᵍ 13⁷ᵍᶠ 9⁶ᶠ 10⁵ᵍᶠ 6⁶ᵍᶠ 2⁶ᶠ
15⁵ᵍᶠ 10⁶ᵍ 6⁵ᵍᶠ 7⁶ᵍ **0-2-12 £2,560**

Xebec (Ire) *P F I Cole*   53
2 b c Xaar - Via Camp
8⁶ᵍ 11⁸ˢ **0-0-2**

Xeeran *M A Jarvis*   60
2 b f Xaar - Cyclone Flyer
5⁵ᵍᶠ 5⁵ᶠ 4⁶ᵍˢ 3⁶ᵍᶠ 13⁶ʰʸ **0-1-6**

£1,122

Xeight Express (Ire) *M A Buckley* 26
2 b f Ashkalani (Ire) - Believing
8^{6f} 13^{6g} 9^{5g} 10^{7gs} **0-0-4**

Xellance (Ire) *P J Hobbs*
7 b g Be My Guest (USA) - Excellent Alibi (USA)
29^{20gf} **0-0-1**

Xixita *Dr J D Scargill* a39
4 ch f Fleetwood (Ire) - Conquista
6^{12sd} 4^{14sd} 8^{16sd} **0-0-3**

Xpres Digital *S R Bowring* 74 a75
3 b c Komaite (USA) - Kustom Kit Xpres
13^{7gs} 4^{6gs} 8^{7s} 8^{6sd} 11^{6g} 11^{6sd} **0-1-6**
£1,317

Xpressions *R A Fahey* 45
3 b g Turtle Island (Ire) - Make Ready
6^{12gf} 6^{12gf} **0-0-2**

Xsynna *Miss M E Rowland* 46 a48
8 b g Cyrano De Bergerac - Rose Ciel (Ire)
3^{6sd} 14^{7sd} 6^{6sd} 7^{7ss} 3^{6g} 10^{5f} 7^{6g} **0-2-7**
£640

Xtra Torrential (USA) *D M Simcock* 87
2 b c Torrential (USA) - Offering (USA)
1^{8g} 4^{8s} **1-0-2 £10,319**

Yaahomm *D R Loder* 80
3 ch c Unfuwain (USA) - Walesiana (Ger)
3^{11g} 1^{9g} 8^{10gf} 7^{10gf} **1-0-4 £5,639**

Yaheska (Ire) *N E Berry*
7 b m Prince Of Birds (USA) - How Ya Been (Ire)
13^{14qs} **0-0-1**

Yajbill (Ire) *M R Channon* 99
2 b c Royal Applause - Tee Cee
2^{6g} 3^{6gf} 2^{6gf} 2^{6g} 1^{6g} 1^{6gf} 1^{6gs} 5^{6g} **3-3-8**
£28,781

Yakimov (USA) *D J Wintle* 77 a86
5 ch g Affirmed (USA) - Ballet Troupe (USA)
11^{7sd} 26^{8g} 14^{8hy} 10^{7g} **0-0-4**

Yallambie *K A Morgan* 33
5 b m Revoque (Ire) - Tahnee
6^{11g} 6^{8sd} **0-0-2**

Yamato Pink *Mrs H Sweeting* 55 a51
3 ch f Bijou D'Inde - Time Or Never (Fr)
15^{7sd} 1^{6sd} 2^{6gf} 5^{7gf} 3^{6f} 11^{6g} 4^{6g} 6^{6g}
1-3-8 £2,946

Yankeedoodledandy (Ire) *P C Haslam* 86 a81
3 b g Orpen (USA) - Laura Margaret
1^{9sw} 2^{8sd} 1^{8sd} 2^{11sd} 1^{12ss} 2^{12g} 3^{12g} 2^{10gf}
3^{14g} 2^{12s} 2^{13gs} **3-7-11 £20,710**

Yankey *C E Brittain* 10
2 b c Amfortas (Ire) - Key
14^{8gs} 5^{9g} 10^{7gf} 13^{8gs} **0-0-4**

Yardstick *S Kirk* 60 a57
2 ch c Inchinor - Fair Verona (USA)
7^{7g} 6^{8gf} 9^{8sd} 11^{10gf} 19^{8s} **0-0-5**

Yashin (Ire) *P A Blockley* 69 a72
3 b g Soviet Star (USA) - My Mariam
13^{7gf} 10^{6sd} 3^{8gf} 2^{7g} 10^{7gf} 4^{7gf} 14^{7s}
3^{7g} 1^{10g} 4^{12sd} 2^{7sd} **1-4-11 £7,775**

Yawmi *B W Hills* 66
4 ch c Zafonic (USA) - Reine Wells (USA)
11^{10gs} 8^{13g} **0-0-2**

Ydravlis *D J S Ffrench Davis*
6 ch m Alflora (Ire) - Levantine Rose
11^{12sd} **0-0-1**

Yeats (Ire) *A P O'Brien* 117
3 b c Sadler's Wells (USA) - Lyndonville (Ire)

1^{10s} 1^{10gy} 2-0-2 £94,626

Yehudi (Ire) *A P O'Brien* 111
2 b c Sadler's Wells (USA) - Bella Vitessa (Ire)
1^{8s} 1^{9sh} 2^{10vs} **2-1-3 £63,392**

Yeldham Lady *J Pearce* 61 a48
2 b f Mujahid (USA) - Future Options
7^{6gs} 13^{7gf} 2^{6sd} 7^{6s} 7^{6gf} 3^{8g} **0-2-6**
£1,214

Yellow River (Ire) *R Williams* a56
4 b g Sesaro (USA) - Amtico
4^{9sd} 10^{9ss} 8^{7sw} 12^{7s} 14^{6gf} **0-0-5**

Yenaled *N Wilson* 79 a78
7 gr g Rambo Dancer (Can) - Fancy Flight (Fr)
3^{8sd} 8^{7sd} 5^{7sd} 9^{9sw} 11^{10g} 4^{8sd} 5^{8g} 1^{10hy}
1^{8sd} 2^{12gf} 2^{10g} 4^{10gf} 2^{9gs} 1^{9gf} 7^{9gf} 4^{9gs} 1^{12gf}
1^{12gs} **5-5-18 £28,153**

Yeoman Lad *M J Gingell* 77 a11
4 b g Groom Dancer (USA) - First Amendment (Ire)
15^{7g} 11^{10gf} 4^{8gf} 5^{10g} 8^{10sd} **0-0-5 £275**

Ylang Ylang (Ire) *W Jarvis* a64
3 ch f Hennessy (USA) - Princess Alydar (USA)
4^{8sd} 1^{9sw} 6^{12ss} **1-0-3 £3,640**

Ynys *B Palling*
3 b g Turtle Island (Ire) - Kiss Me Goodknight
12^{8sd} 11^{9sw} **0-0-2**

Yomalo (Ire) *R Guest* 81
4 ch f Woodborough (USA) - Alkariyh (USA)
11^{5g} 8^{6s} 5^{6f} 6^{6gf} 2^{6f} 5^{6g} 6^{6gf} 2^{6gs} 1^{6g}
1-2-9 £6,777

York Cliff *W M Brisbourne* 70 a80
6 b g Marju (Ire) - Azm
12^{7sd} 5^{10sd} 4^{12ss} 5^{12sd} 7^{9gs} 8^{10s} 12^{8hy}
0-0-7 £960

Yorke's Folly (USA) *C W Fairhurst* 50
3 b f Stravinsky (USA) - Tommelise (USA)
7^{6gf} 8^{7g} 10^{6gf} 12^{6f} 3^{6f} 5^{6g} 16^{6gs} **0-1-7**
£633

Yorker (USA) *Ms Deborah J Evans* 69 a78
6 b g Boundary (USA) - Shallows (USA)
2^{7sd} 5^{8sd} 3^{7sd} 4^{8ss} 2^{7sw} 2^{7sw} 8^{7sw} 10^{7ss}
7^{8g} 3^{8sd} 6^{7sd} 12^{7gs} 1^{6s} 3^{7g} 10^{7sd} 11^{9sd}
14^{8hy} **1-6-17 £9,455**

Yorkie *P A Blockley* 63 a59
5 b g Aragon - Light The Way
1^{6sd} 10^{5ss} 11^{6sd} 7^{5gf} 2^{5f} 2^{5f} 7^{5gf} 4^{6gf}
VOI^{5gf} 8^{5g} **1-2-10 £5,496**

Yorkies Boy *N E Berry* 61
9 gr g Clantime - Slipperose
5^{5gf} 4^{5gf} 7^{6g} 9^{5f} 12^{6g} 8^{5gf} 4^{5gf} 10^{6gf}
3^{6gs} 1^{6g} 7^{6gf} 12^{7gf} 10^{6g} 5^{5gf} 6^{6g} 10^{6s}
2-2-16 £6,570

Yorkshire Blue *J S Goldie* 67
5 b g Atraf - Something Blue
7^{7g} 7^{7gf} 1^{7gf} 9^{7gf} 7^{7g} 1^{7f} 5^{7g} 1^{7f} 10^{7gf}
13^{7s} **3-0-9 £18,456**

Yorkshire Lad (Ire) *J A Osborne* 63
2 b c Second Empire (Ire) - Villaminta (Ire)
8^{5g} 6^{6gf} 5^{6s} **0-0-3**

Yorkshire Spirit *N Tinkler*
3 b g Imperial Ballet (Ire) - Barnacla (Ire)
9^{8hy} **0-0-1**

Yoshka *M Johnston* 100
3 ch c Grand Lodge (USA) - Greenvera (USA)
3^{12gs} 1^{12gf} 1^{16gf} 2^{14gf} 11^{15gf} **2-1-5**
£16,035

You Found Me *C Tinkler* 65
2 b f Robellino (USA) - Hana Marie

8⁶ᵍᶠ 6⁷ᵍᶠ 3⁸ˢ 9¹⁰ᵍᶠ 6⁸ᵍ **0-1-5 £549**

Young Alex (Ire) *N M Babbage*   72
6 ch g Midhish - Snipe Hunt (Ire)
5⁸ᵍ 2⁷ˢ 19⁷ᵍ **0-1-3 £1,182**

Young Boldric *K Bell*   37
2 b g Faustus (USA) - Bold Byzantium
13⁶ᵍˢ 9⁶ᵍ 10⁷ʰʸ **0-0-3**

Young Dynasty *E A Wheeler*   38 a53
4 ch g Young Ern - Miss Michelle
7⁸ˢᵈ 5⁸ˢᵈ 5¹⁰ˢᵈ 10⁷ˢ 5⁷ˢᵈ 16⁹ᵍᶠ 17⁸ᵍ **0-0-7**

Young Kate *J R Best*   55 a26
3 b f Desert King (Ire) - Stardyn
6⁶ᵍˢ 12⁷ˢᵈ 8⁵ˢᵈ **0-0-3**

Young Love *A B Haynes*   54 a35
3 ch f Pursuit Of Love - Polar Fair
8¹⁰ˢ 6⁹ᵍᶠ 4⁸ᵍᶠ 14⁷ᵍᶠ 6⁸ᵍᶠ 4⁷ʰʸ 4⁸ᶠ 4¹⁰ˢᵈ
0-0-8 £299

Young Mick *G G Margarson*   69
2 br g King's Theatre (Ire) - Just Warning
13⁷ᵍᶠ 3⁸ᵍᶠ 4⁸ᵍˢ 13⁸ᵍ **0-1-4 £927**

Young Mr Grace (Ire) *T D Easterby*   91
4 b c Danetime (Ire) - Maid Of Mourne
15⁶ᵍ 3⁷ˢ 4⁷ᵍ 2⁸ᵍᶠ 5⁸ᵍᶠ 1⁷ᵍ 6⁸ᵍˢ 2⁷ᵍˢ 1⁸ᵍ
3⁸ᵍˢ 9⁸ᵍˢ 1⁸ˢ 5⁸ʰʸ 16⁷ᵍ 5⁷ˢ **3-5-15 £37,421**

Young Owen *A G Juckes*   a28
6 b g Balnibarbi - Polly Potter
5¹²ˢʷ 9¹²ˢᵈ **0-0-2**

Young Patriarch *C J Mann*   54
3 b g Silver Patriarch (Ire) - Mortify
10¹⁰ᵍˢ 16¹²ᵍᶠ 13⁸ᵍ **0-0-3**

Young Rooney *M Mullineaux*   77
4 b g Danzig Connection (USA) - Lady Broker
4¹⁰ᵍ 11¹²ᵍ 3¹⁰ˢ 2⁹ᵍ 2¹⁰ᵍ 6⁸ʰʸ 3¹⁰ᵍᶠ 2¹⁰ᵍˢ
6¹⁰ˢ 3¹²ˢ **0-5-10 £10,382**

Young Thomas (Ire) *M L W Bell*   68
2 ch g Inchinor - Splicing
13⁶ᵍᶠ 4⁷ᵍ 4⁷ᵍ 3⁷ˢ 3⁸ˢ 5⁸ˢ 19⁸ᵍ **0-2-7**
£3,974

Young Valentino *A W Carroll*   20
2 ch g Komaite (USA) - Caprice
12⁶ˢ **0-0-1**

Young Warrior (Ire) *D Nicholls*   53
3 b g Desert Style (Ire) - Arctic Splendour (USA)
16⁷ᵍˢ 5⁸ᵍᶠ 6⁹ᶠ **0-0-3**

Youngs Forth *A W Carroll*   a36
4 b f Most Welcome - Pegs
10⁷ˢᵈ 8⁶ˢᵈ 5⁷ˢᵈ 5⁸ˢ PU⁸ˢᵈ **0-0-5**

Your Just Lovely (Ire) *A M Balding*   a34
3 b f Second Empire (Ire) - Nawaji (USA)
14⁷ˢᵈ 9⁶ᵍˢ **0-0-2**

Yours Sincerely (Ire) *P A Blockley*   37
2 ch c Mark Of Esteem (Ire) - Evrobi (Ire)
46ᵍᶠ **0-0-1 £432**

Zabadani *Mrs A J Perrett*   a62
2 ch f Zafonic (USA) - Blou Dan (USA)
9⁸ˢᵈ **0-0-1**

Zabadou *F Kirby*   30 a30
3 b g Abou Zouz (USA) - Strapped
9⁸ˢ 10⁹ᵍˢ 7⁶ˢᵈ **0-0-3**

Zabeel Palace *D R Loder*   71
2 b c Grand Lodge (USA) - Applecross
7⁷ᵍ 5⁷ᵍᶠ 4⁷ᵍᶠ **0-0-3 £256**

Zachy Boy *J S Moore*   55 a38
2 b g Inchinor - Ellway Dancer (Ire)
6⁵ˢᵈ 7⁵ᵍᶠ 5⁵ᵍ 11⁵ʰʸ 17⁶ᵍ 6⁶ᵍᶠ 6⁵ᵍᶠ 5⁶ᶠ

4⁵ᶠ 6⁵ᵍᶠ **0-0-10**

Zadalrakib *Sir Michael Stoute*   72
2 ch c Machiavellian (USA) - Party Doll
5⁷ᵍˢ **0-0-1**

Zafarshah (Ire) *P D Evans*   70 a68
5 b g Danehill (USA) - Zafarana (Fr)
1⁷ˢᵈ 4⁷ˢᵈ 1⁷ˢᵈ 4⁷ˢᵈ 6⁷ˢᵈ 2⁸ᵍᶠ 8⁸ˢᵈ 3⁷ᵍᶠ
8⁸ᶠ 11⁷ᵍ 4⁸ᵍᶠ 10⁸ᵍᶠ 1⁸ᵍ 5⁸ᵍᶠ **3-1-14**
£12,461

Zaffeu *N P Littmoden*   74 a67
3 ch g Zafonic (USA) - Leaping Flame (USA)
10¹⁰ˢᵈ 6¹⁰ˢᵈ 6¹²ˢᵈ 2¹¹ᵍˢ 4¹²ʰʸ 5¹⁰ᵍᶠ 1¹²ᶠ
8¹²ᵍ 6¹⁰ᵍᶠ 11¹²ᵍᶠ 12¹¹ᵍ 9¹¹ᵍ 11¹²ᵍˢ 2¹¹ˢ
1-2-14 £6,631

Zagala *S L Keightley*   a69
4 b f Polar Falcon (USA) - Whittle Woods Girl
2⁶ˢᵈ 9⁶ˢᵈ 2⁶ˢᵈ 7⁷ˢᵈ 8⁷ˢᵈ 9⁶ˢᵈ 6⁶ˢᵈ **0-2-7**
£2,063

Zagreus (Ger) *M W Easterby*   70
2 gr g Fasliyev (USA) - Zephyrine (Ire)
3⁷ᵍᶠ **0-1-1 £557**

Zahunda (Ire) *W M Brisbourne*   47 a49
5 b m Spectrum (Ire) - Gift Of Glory (Fr)
6⁸ˢᵈ 7⁷ˢˢ 2⁸ˢᵈ 7⁹ˢˢ 4⁸ˢʷ 6⁸ˢʷ 3⁸ˢˢ 3⁸ˢˢ
6⁸ᵍ 4⁸ˢ 9⁸ᵍ 2⁷ᵍᶠ 4⁷ᵍᶠ 5⁷ᵍᶠ 14⁷ˢ 10⁸ˢ **0-3-16**
£3,385

Zak Attack *D J Daly*   45
3 ch g Young Ern - Premiere Moon
19⁸ᵍ **0-0-1**

Zak Facta (Ire) *Miss D A McHale*   37 a57
4 b g Danetime (Ire) - Alexander Goddess (Ire)
5⁶ˢᵈ 5⁷ˢᵈ 2⁶ˢᵈ 8⁶ˢᵈ 11⁶ˢ 11⁷ᵍ
7⁷ᵍᶠ 11⁹ˢᵈ 11⁶ˢᵈ **0-1-11 £1,036**

Zakfree (Ire) *N P Littmoden*   67 a62
3 b g Danetime (Ire) - Clipper Queen
2¹⁰ˢᵈ 2¹⁰ˢ 2¹⁰ˢ **0-3-4 £3,774**

Zalaal (USA) *Saeed Bin Suroor*   67 a76
2 b c A.P. Indy (USA) - Scoot Yer Boots (USA)
6⁷ᵍ 2⁸ˢᵈ 9⁸ˢ **0-1-3 £1,199**

Zalam (Ire) *P A Blockley*   51
4 b g Alzao (USA) - Zarlana (Ire)
7¹⁰ᵍ 15¹⁰ᵍᶠ **0-0-2**

Zalda *R Charlton*   73
3 ch f Zilzal (USA) - Gold Luck (USA)
1¹²ᵍᶠ 6¹²ᵍᶠ 5¹⁴ᵍ 13¹⁴ᵍᶠ 1¹⁴ᵍˢ **2-0-5**
£7,819

Zalebe *J Pearce*   53
3 b f Bahamian Bounty - Alo Ez
12⁸ᵍᶠ 7⁷ᵍˢ 1⁷ᵍ 11⁷ᵍ **1-0-4 £2,723**

Zalkani (Ire) *B G Powell*   51 a68
4 ch g Cadeaux Genereux - Zallaka (Ire)
3¹⁰ˢᵈ 3¹⁰ˢᵈ 12⁸ˢᵈ 13¹⁰ᵍˢ 9⁸ᵍ 5¹⁰ᶠ 10¹¹ᵍᶠ
11⁸ᵍ 4¹⁰ᵍˢ 11¹⁰ˢᵈ 8¹⁰ˢ 2¹⁰ˢᵈ **0-3-12 £1,589**

Zalongo *Sir Michael Stoute*   86
2 ch c Zafonic (USA) - Tamassos
1⁷ˢ **1-0-1 £4,192**

Zambezi River *J M Bradley*   43 a26
5 ch g Zamindar (USA) - Double River (USA)
11⁸ᵍ 7⁸ˢᵈ 17⁷ˢ 6⁶ᵍᶠ 12⁶ᵍᶠ 8⁷ᵍˢ 15⁵ᵍᶠ
11⁶ˢᵈ **0-0-8**

Zamboozle (Ire) *D R C Elsworth*   72
2 ch c Halling (USA) - Blue Sirocco
4⁷ᵍᶠ 7⁸ᵍˢ **0-0-2 £822**

Zameel (Ire) *Jedd O'Keeffe*   35
3 b g Marju (Ire) - Impatiente (USA)
12¹²ᵍᶠ **0-0-1**

Zameyla (Ire) *M A Jarvis* 86
3 b f Cape Cross (Ire) - Angelic Sounds (Ire)
8⁶ᵍᶠ 2⁷ᵍᶠ 2⁷ᶠ 1⁸ˢ 1⁸ᵍˢ 11⁸ˢ 10⁸ˢ **2-2-7**
£15,755

Zamir *W Storey*
5 ch g Zamindar (USA) - Fairy Flax (Ire)
11¹²ᵍˢ **0-0-1**

Zamyatina (Ire) *P L Clinton* 46
5 br m Danehill Dancer (Ire) - Miss Pickpocket (Ire)
11⁷ᵍˢ 12⁷ᵍ 7⁸ᵍᶠ 13⁸ᶠ 5⁷ᵍ 9⁸ᵍ 10⁶ᶠ 12⁸ᶠ
0-0-8

Zan Lo (Ire) *B S Rothwell* 55
4 ch f Grand Lodge (USA) - Zanella (Ire)
7¹²ˢ 8¹⁰ʰʸ 6¹⁰ᵍᶠ 10¹²ᵍᶠ 7¹²ᵍˢ 7¹²ᵍᶠ 9¹²ᵍᶠ
4¹⁴ᵍᶠ 1¹⁴ᵍᶠ 15¹⁶ᶠ 11¹²ᵍᶠ 14¹⁴ᵍ 11¹⁴ᵍˢ **1-0-13**
£3,244

Zandeed (Ire) *Miss L A Perratt* 66
6 b g Inchinor - Persian Song
11⁹ᵍᶠ 3⁷ˢ 1⁸ᵍˢ 4¹⁰ᵍ 12⁸ᵍᶠ 5¹¹ˢ 7¹⁰ˢ **1-1-7**
£12,108

Zanderido *B S Rothwell* 52
2 b g Forzando - Triple Concerto
4⁵ᵍᶠ 12⁶ᵍ 6⁶ᵍᶠ 16⁷ᵍᶠ **0-0-4 £337**

Zando *P C Haslam* 56 a61
2 b g Forzando - Rockin' Rosie
8⁶ˢᵈ 11⁵ᵍᶠ 6⁷ᵍ 10⁷ᵍᶠ **0-0-4**

Zangeal *C F Wall* 79 a70
3 ch c Selkirk (USA) - Generous Lady
4¹⁰ˢᵈ 3¹⁰ᵍ 4¹²ᵍᶠ 4¹⁰ᵍᶠ 4⁸ᵍ **0-1-5 £2,469**

Zanjeer *N Wilson* 77 a23
4 b g Averti (Ire) - Cloudslea (USA)
8⁷ˢᵈ 1⁸ᵍ 6⁸ˢ 3⁷ᵍᶠ 1⁷ᵍˢ 7⁸ᵍᶠ 5⁸ˢ 12⁷ˢᵈ
2-1-8 £10,082

Zantero *R P Elliott* 64 a40
2 b c Danzero (Aus) - Cruinn A Bhord
4⁶ˢᵈ 6⁷ᵍᶠ 4⁵ˢᵈ 6⁶ᵍ 8⁸ᵍ 6⁷ᶠ 5⁷ᵍˢ **0-0-7**
£608

Zap Attack *J Parkes* 61
4 b g Zafonic (USA) - Rappa Tap Tap (Fr)
16⁶ᶠ 7⁷ᵍᶠ 4⁸ᶠ 16⁷ᵍᶠ 17⁶ᵍᶠ **0-0-5 £281**

Zaqrah (USA) *J L Dunlop* 71
3 b f Silver Hawk (USA) - Istiqlal (USA)
10⁷ᵍ **0-0-1**

Zara Louise *R P Elliott* a29
4 b f Mistertopogigo (Ire) - Petonica (Ire)
4⁶ˢᵈ 10⁷ˢᵈ 8⁶ˢᵈ **0-0-3**

Zargus *A M Balding* 53 a62
5 b g Zamindar (USA) - My First Romance
5⁵ˢᵈ 10⁶ᵍ 10⁵ᵍᶠ 11⁵ᵍ 13⁵ᵍ **0-0-5 £207**

Zariano *R M Stronge* 60 a76
4 b g Emperor Jones (USA) - Douce Maison (Ire)
2⁸ˢᵈ 8⁷ˢᵈ 9¹⁰ᵍ 8⁸ᵍ 12⁸ᵍᶠ 9⁷ˢᵈ **0-1-6**
£858

Zarin (Ire) *D W Chapman* 55 a67
6 b g Inzar (USA) - Non Dimenticar Me (Ire)
9⁸ˢᵈ 3⁷ˢˢ 13⁸ˢᵈ 9⁸ᵍˢ 7⁷ᵍˢ 18⁸ˢᵈ
5⁸ᵍˢ 8⁸ᵍ 20⁸ᵍᶠ 8⁹ˢᵈ **1-2-12 £4,000**

Zarneeta *W De Best-Turner* 47 a14
3 b f Tragic Role (USA) - Compton Amber
8⁷ᵍ 12¹⁰ᵍ 7¹⁰ᵍᶠ 7¹²ᵍ 7¹⁰ᵍ 8¹⁰ᵍ 3¹⁰ˢ
15¹⁰ᵍˢ 6⁹ˢᵈ **0-1-9 £690**

Zarova (Ire) *M W Easterby* 53
2 gr c Zafonic (USA) - Estarova (Fr)
11⁶ᵍᶠ 6⁵ᵍᶠ 15⁶ᵍᶠ 14⁶ᵍ **0-0-4**

Zarzu *C R Dore* 88 a95
5 b g Magic Ring (Ire) - Rivers Rhapsody

3⁶ˢᵈ 5⁵ˢᵈ 4⁵ˢᵈ 3⁵ˢᵈ 4⁵ᵍ 3⁶ᵍ 12⁶ᵍᶠ 9⁵ᵍᶠ
13⁵ˢ 1⁵ᵍˢ 6⁵ᵍᶠ 5⁵ᵍ 12⁵ᵍ 8⁵ˢ 5⁵ᵍᶠ 19⁶ᵍ 13⁵ᵍ
1-4-17 £12,554

Zathonia *R Charlton* 72
3 b f Zafonic (USA) - Danthonia (USA)
2⁸ᵍᶠ 3⁸ᵍᶠ 2⁸ᵍᶠ **0-3-3 £3,573**

Zaville *M A Jarvis* 51
2 gr f Zafonic (USA) - Colleville
10⁷ᵍᶠ 10⁸ᵍ **0-0-2**

Zawrak (Ire) *I W McInnes* 69 a62
5 ch g Zafonic (USA) - Gharam (USA)
6¹³ˢᵈ 3¹⁰ˢᵈ 11¹⁰ˢᵈ 1⁸ᶠ 15⁸ᵍ 5¹⁰ᵍ 2⁸ᵍᶠ
8⁹ᵍᶠ 16¹¹ᵍ 13⁷ᵍᶠ 4⁹ˢᵈ 7⁹ˢᵈ **1-2-12 £4,886**

Zayn Zen *M A Jarvis* 75
2 ch f Singspiel (Ire) - Roshani (Ire)
6⁷ˢ 4⁸ᵍᶠ 2⁸ᵍᶠ 5⁸ˢ **0-1-4 £2,397**

Zazous *A King* 60
3 b c Zafonic (USA) - Confidentiality (USA)
6⁶ᵍᶠ 3⁷ᵍᶠ 9⁷ᵍᶠ 11⁸ᵍ 11¹¹²ᵍ **0-0-5 £855**

Zeena *M P Tregoning* 60
2 b f Unfuwain (USA) - Forest Fire (Swe)
5⁶ˢ 4⁷ˢ 5⁸ᵍᶠ **0-0-3 £282**

Zeis (Ire) *Andrew Reid* 67 a66
4 ch g Bahhare (USA) - Zoom Lens (Ire)
9⁸ˢᵈ 10⁸ˢᵈ 12¹⁰ᵍ 1¹⁰ᶠ 11²ᵍᶠ 7¹⁰ᵍ 10¹¹ᵍ
9¹²ˢᵈ 7¹²ˢᵈ 9¹⁴ˢᵈ **2-0-10 £6,973**

Zeitgeist (Ire) *L M Cumani* 98
3 b c Singspiel (Ire) - Diamond Quest
4¹²ᵍ 1¹¹ᵍᶠ 2¹²ᵍᶠ 5¹²ᵍ 9¹²ᵍ 1¹³ˢ 2¹²ᵍ 8¹⁴ʰʸ
2-2-8 £26,152

Zeitlos *R M Flower*
5 b g Timeless Times (USA) - Petitesse
12⁶ˢᵈ **0-0-1**

Zelea (Ire) *J Parkes* a36
5 br m Be My Guest (USA) - Ebony And Ivory (Ire)
5¹²ˢᵈ 4¹¹ˢᶠ 4¹²ˢᵈ **0-0-3**

Zeloso *M F Harris* a47
6 b g Alzao (USA) - Silk Petal
6¹⁰ˢᵈ 2¹⁰ˢᵈ **0-1-2 £864**

Zendaro *W M Brisbourne* 54 a41
2 b g Danzero (Aus) - Countess Maud
4⁵ˢˢ 6⁶ᵍᶠ 9⁶ᵍ 18⁶ᵍ 6⁶ᵍ **0-0-5**

Zerlina (USA) *W J Musson* 87 a87
3 b f Singspiel (Ire) - Tass
7⁸ᵍˢ 7⁸ᵍˢ 8⁷ˢ 4⁷ˢᵈ 2⁸ᵍ 1⁸ᵍᶠ 11⁸ˢᵈ **1-1-7**
£12,784

Zero Tolerance (Ire) *T D Barron* 104
4 ch g Nashwan (USA) - Place De L'Opera
1¹¹ˢ 4¹⁰ᵍᶠ 17⁸ᵍᶠ 12¹⁰ᵍ 7¹⁰ᵍ 2¹⁰ˢ 2¹⁰ᵍˢ
1⁸ᵍˢ **2-2-8 £36,405**

Zhitomir *M Dods* 67 a60
6 ch g Lion Cavern (USA) - Treasure Trove (USA)
1⁷ᵍ 6⁵ᵍ 7⁵ˢᵈ 4⁷ˢ 4⁷ˢ 10⁷ᵍ 2⁷ʰʸ 1⁷ᵍˢ
6⁷ˢᵈ 2⁷ˢᵈ **3-2-11 £9,577**

Zibeline (Ire) *B Ellison* 98
7 b g Cadeaux Genereux - Zia (USA)
3¹²ᵍ 10¹⁶ˢ 14¹⁵ᵍᶠ **0-1-3 £4,400**

Ziet D'Alsace (Fr) *A W Carroll* 64 a64
4 b f Zieten (USA) - Providenc Mill (Fr)
14⁸ᵍᶠ 2⁷ᵍᶠ 12⁸ᶠ 12⁸ᶠ 2⁷ᶠ 10⁷ᵍᶠ 17ᵍᶠ 8ᵍ
4⁷ᶠ 6⁷ᶠ 7⁶ᵍᶠ 2⁹ˢᵈ 11⁸ˢᵈ 5⁹ˢᵈ 3⁹ˢᵈ **1-4-15**
£6,495

Zietory *P F I Cole* 98 a92
4 b f Zieten (USA) - Fairy Story (Ire)
5⁹ᵍ 8⁸ᵍᶠ 3⁸ᵍᶠ 1⁸ˢ 11⁷ᵍ 3⁸ˢᵈ **1-2-6**
£25,700

Zietzig (Ire) *D Nicholls*   55 a17
7 b g Zieten (USA) - Missing You
14⁶ᵍˢ 8⁷ᵍ 11⁷ˢᵈ 13⁵ᵍ 8⁶ᵍ 5⁶ᵍ 6⁶ᵍᶠ 1⁶ᶠ
10⁶ᵍᶠ **1-0-9 £4,241**

Ziggy Dan *R H Buckler*
4 b g Slip Anchor - Nikatino
5¹²ˢʷ **0-0-1**

Zilch *M L W Bell*   104
6 ch g Zilzal (USA) - Bunty Boo
1⁷ˢ 2⁷ʰʸ 2⁶ᵍˢ 1⁶ˢ 4⁶ᵍ 10⁷ˢ 16⁶ᶠ 11⁷ᵍˢ
7⁶ᵍˢ 8⁶ˢ 20⁶ᵍ **3-2-11 £56,421**

Zilmy (Ire) *P W Harris*   58
3 ch g Zilzal (USA) - My Lewicia (Ire)
7⁸ᵍ **0-0-1**

Zimbali *J M Bradley*   64
2 ch f Lahib (USA) - Dawn
5⁵ᵍ 4⁵ᵍˢ 1⁵ᵍ 3⁵ˢ 4⁶ᵍᶠ 2⁶ᶠ 2⁶ᶠ **1-2-7**
£4,142

Zinging *J J Bridger*   43 a56
5 b g Fraam - Hi Hoh (Ire)
5⁶ˢᵈ 7¹⁰ˢᵈ 6⁷ˢᵈ 4⁸ˢᵈ 7⁸ˢᵈ 7⁷ˢᵈ 6⁷ᵍˢ 5⁸ᵍ
5⁷ᵍᶠ 6⁷ᶠ 9⁷ᶠ 10⁸ˢᵈ 4⁷ʰʸ 7⁷ᵍᶠ 6⁶ᵍᶠ 4⁸ᵍ **0-0-16**
£271

Zohar (USA) *B J Meehan*   82
2 b c Aljabr (USA) - Dafnah (USA)
1⁶ᵍ 13⁷ˢ **1-0-2 £5,720**

Zolash (Ire) *J S Moore*   67 a43
2 b c General Monash (USA) - Zolba (Ire)
5⁵ᵍᶠ 9⁶ᵍᶠ 6⁶ᵍᶠ 7⁷ᵍᶠ 4⁸ᵍᶠ 4⁷ᵍᶠ 3⁷ᵍᶠ 6⁸ᶠ
9⁸ᵍ 9⁹ˢᵈ **0-1-10 £1,598**

Zoltano (Ger) *M Todhunter*   76
6 b g In The Wings - Zarella (Ger)
3¹⁶ˢ 1¹⁶ᵍᶠ 17¹⁶ᵍˢ **1-1-3 £7,264**

Zolushka (Ire) *B W Duke*   a36
3 ch f Russian Revival (USA) - Persian Myth
3⁸ˢᵈ 10⁸ˢᵈ 12⁷ˢᵈ 10⁷ˢᵈ **0-1-4 £364**

Zomerlust *J J Quinn*   85
2 b g Josr Algarhoud (Ire) - Passiflora
3⁵ᵍᶠ 1⁶ˢ 2⁶ᵍˢ 4⁷ᶠ 4⁶ᵍ 2⁶ˢ 3⁷ᵍˢ **1-4-7**
£11,830

Zonergem *Lady Herries*   101 a91
6 ch g Zafonic (USA) - Anasazi (Ire)
7¹⁰ˢᵈ 6¹²ˢᵈ 3⁸ᵍᶠ 3¹⁰ᵍ 25⁹ᵍ **0-2-5**
£14,301

Zonic *Sir Michael Stoute*   56 a62
2 b f Zafonic (USA) - Ferber's Follies (USA)
7⁶ᵍᶠ 7⁷ˢᵈ 3⁶ᶠ **0-1-3 £882**

Zonic Boom (Fr) *J R Fanshawe*   71 a61
4 b/br g Zafonic (USA) - Rosi Zambotti (Ire)
5⁸ᵍ 3⁸ᵍ 8⁸ᵍˢ 3¹⁰ᵍ 9¹⁰ᵍ 6¹²ˢᵈ **0-2-6**
£1,340

Zonnebeke *Mrs C A Dunnett*   53 a43
3 b f Orpen (USA) - Canlubang
4⁷ˢᵈ 5⁷ˢᵈ 2⁸ˢᵈ 7⁸ˢˢ 3⁷ˢᵈ 14⁷ˢᵈ 10⁶ᶠ 3⁷ᵍ
4⁷ᶠ 1⁸ᵍᶠ 2⁸ᵍᶠ 10⁸ᵍᶠ 6⁸ʰʸ 12⁷ᵍ 10⁷ᵍˢ 15⁶ˢ
6⁶ˢᵈ **1-4-17 £5,641**

Zonus *B W Hills*   107
3 b c Pivotal - Jade Mistress
1⁷ᵍ 4⁸ᵍ 2⁸ᵍˢ 3⁸ᵍᶠ 11⁸ᶠ 3⁷ᵍˢ 7⁸ᵍ 1⁸ˢ
10⁷ᵍ **2-3-9 £39,461**

Zoom Zoom *Mrs L Stubbs*   80 a79
4 b c Abou Zouz (USA) - Iltimas (USA)
1⁶ˢ 10⁶ᵍᶠ 5⁵ᵍ 13⁶ˢ 4⁷ᵍᶠ 14⁶ᵍˢ 1⁷ˢᵈ **2-0-7**
£9,605

Zoomiezando *Mrs Lucinda Featherstone*   53
3 b g Forzando - Zarah
7⁸ᵍᶠ 7⁹ᶠ 14⁷ᵍˢ **0-0-3**

Zoripp (Ire) *J G Given*   49
2 b g Spectrum (Ire) - Allspice
6⁷ᵍˢ 10⁷ᵍᶠ 12⁷ᵍˢ **0-0-3**

Zorn *P Howling*   9
5 br h Dilum - Very Good
17¹⁰ˢ 10⁸ᵍ **0-0-2**

Zosima (USA) *Saeed Bin Suroor*   116
3 b/br f Capote (USA) - Grafin (USA)
3⁸ᵍᶠ 4¹⁰ᵍᶠ 11⁷ᵍᶠ **0-1-3 £15,500**

Zouave (Ire) *C J Mann*   84
3 b g Spectrum (Ire) - Lady Windley
7¹¹ᵍ 12¹²ᵍ 5¹⁴ᶠ 10¹⁶ᶠ **0-0-4 £386**

Zouche *W M Brisbourne*   36
4 b g Zamindar (USA) - Al Corniche (Ire)
11⁸ᶠ 10⁸ᵍˢ 13¹¹ᵍᶠ **0-0-3**

Zucchero *D W P Arbuthnot*   78
8 br g Dilum - Legal Sound
12⁸ᵍ 3⁸ᵍ 10⁸ᵍ **0-1-3 £587**

Zuhair *D Nicholls*   70
11 ch g Mujtahid (USA) - Ghzaalh (USA)
13⁵ᵍ 10⁶ᵍ 7⁶ᶠ 11⁶ᵍᶠ 15⁵ᵍᶠ 9⁶ᵍˢ **0-0-6**

Zuleta *B D Leavy*   51
3 ch f Vettori (Ire) - Victoria
8¹⁰ᵍᶠ 9¹⁰ᶠ 6¹²ᵍˢ 2¹²ᵍˢ 2¹²ᵍˢ 2¹⁴ᶠ 4¹⁰ᵍᶠ
2¹³ᵍˢ **0-5-8 £2,737**

Zuloago (USA) *A G Newcombe*   a57
3 b f Stravinsky (USA) - Attitre (Fr)
5⁷ˢᵈ 3⁹ˢʷ 2⁸ˢ 12⁸ˢᵈ 11⁸ˢᵈ **0-2-6**
£1,557

Zuma (Ire) *R Hannon*   78 a53
3 b c Grand Lodge (Ire) - Paradise Waters
7⁸ᵍ 3⁸ᵍᶠ 7¹⁰ᵍᶠ 5¹⁰ᵍ 5¹⁰ᵍ 4¹²ᵍᶠ 4¹²ˢᵈ 2¹¹ᵍˢ
6¹²ˢ **0-2-9 £3,699**

Zuri (Ire) *L M Cumani*   63 a40
3 b f Kris S (USA) - Amizette (USA)
6⁸ᵍᶠ 4¹⁰ᵍᶠ 9⁸ᶠ 9¹²ᵍᶠ 7¹⁰ᵍᶠ 9⁸ᵍ 8⁸ˢᵈ **0-0-7**
£427

Zwadi (Ire) *J A Osborne*   74
3 b f Docksider (USA) - Local Custom (Ire)
4⁸ᵍᶠ 8⁸ᶠ 5⁷ᵍ 7⁶ᵍᶠ 3⁷ᵍᶠ 2⁶ᵍˢ 4⁶ᶠ 3⁷ᶠ 4⁸ᵍ
0-3-9 £3,908

Zweibrucken (Ire) *S Kirk*   86
3 b f Alhaarth (Ire) - Solar Attraction (Ire)
17⁹ᵍ 10⁹ᵍᶠ 1⁸ᵍˢ 11⁸ᵍ 11⁸ᵍᶠ 7⁸ˢ **1-0-6**
£7,124